Delightful DOUGHCRAFTS

Delightful DOUGHCRAFTS

Elisabeth Bang

WARD LOCK

Dedicated to
Brenda Willoughby
and Cameron Scott

With thanks to Daler Rowney UK
for supplying the paints and varnish
for the models in the book.

A WARD LOCK BOOK

First published in the UK in
by Ward Lock
Wellington House
125 Strand
London WC2R 0BB

A Cassell Imprint

Text and illustrations copyright © Elisabeth Bang 1997
Photographs and volume copyright © Ward Lock 1997

Photography by Paul Bricknell

Distributed in the United States
by Sterling Publishing Co., Inc.
387 Park Avenue South, New York, NY 10016–8810

A British Library Cataloguing in Publication Data block for
this book may be obtained from the British Library

ISBN 0-7063-7558-0

Printed and bound in Hong Kong
by Colorcraft Ltd

CONTENTS

INTRODUCTION

Throughout history, flour, salt and water have been an essential part of our diet. From biblical times through to the modern day, these ingredients have also had enormous religious significance. Today, most of us are familiar with the beautiful sculptured corn sheaths and other symbolic decorations seen at harvest festival. Across Europe and the Americas, there are exquisite examples of decorations and gifts crafted from dough, each country demonstrating its own unique interpretations. These may be glazed with egg, simulating the beautiful characteristics of baked bread, or painted and varnished, highlighting the qualities of bright colours. The combination of these three ingredients is the basis of our salt dough modelling medium. It is so cheap that it makes it an inexpensive hobby from which all the family can take pleasure.

I began this charming craft as a challenge when booking my first stall at a national craft fair. The fair manager was right in saying, 'You'll become hooked!' Six years on with my first book *Christmas Doughcrafts* published, my ovens have been brimming over with ideas for this book. The popularity of doughcraft has led me to teaching it to Guide groups and the handicapped.

Once you get your hands on the dough it will remind you of the fun you had with plasticine as a child, since dough has similar therapeutic and tactile qualities – with the bonus that you can harden it in the oven to produce lasting models. The possibilities of this medium are endless, its versatility giving ample scope to both the complete beginner and the skilled doughcrafter. Whether you are wanting to make a few decorations for your child's nursery or a gift for a new mother in hospital, you will find this book packed with over 150 enchanting ideas. These range from the very simple flat plaque shapes to more complicated ones such as free-standing models. It is important to read the first four chapters before following the step-by-step instructions, as this will enable you to reproduce closely the ideas from the beautiful colour photographs and clear illustrations. In no time you will soon master the craft and be able to develop your own delightful samples.

The models in the book have been given a star rating from one star for simple designs to three stars for more complicated ones. Keep your ideas simple at first, experimenting with biscuit cutters on rolled dough to get the feel of the dough. The teddy bear swag (see page 49) is an example of something a beginner can easily make. As your confidence begins to grow, try your hand at three-dimensional shapes and move on to more adventurous and exciting designs.

The following are just a few ways you can work dough. Try rolling the dough with a roller or the palms of your hand, moulding it into figures, plaiting it into garlands, or forcing it through an icing nozzle or garlic press to achieve different textures and dimensions. Many unusual patterns can be imprinted on your dough. Experiment with items from your tool or work box such as wire mesh, buttons and suchlike. You can even use leaves to make impressions as you would when making chocolate leaves. Finish off your work with an egg glaze for a rustic look or use poster paints and varnish to enhance the colours.

I am confident that you will have great fun with this craft and your skills will develop with practice. You will not only amaze yourself at the results you can achieve, but also family and friends are bound to be thrilled with the originality of their gifts.

Take note, though. You are sure to become addicted to this charming craft, to such an extent that your ovens will be brimming over with ideas, as mine is. Many a time my husband has come home expecting a delicious dinner only to find the oven full of my dough samples!

With careful planning, why not make some extra samples for the school bazaar or local church fête. Above all else, have fun. Good luck with your projects.

GETTING STARTED

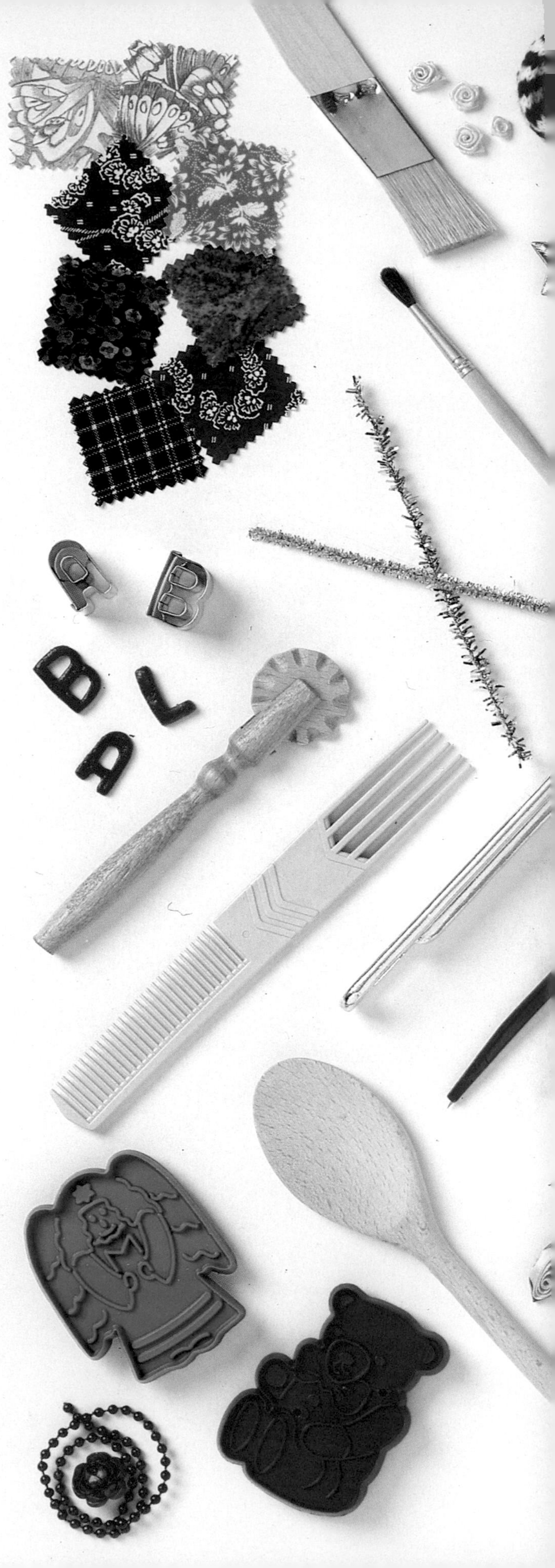

INSPIRATION

Many sources of inspiration lend themselves to doughcraft for the nursery. Look in baby magazines, books, baby shop catalogues, at greetings cards, wrapping paper and suchlike. Another excellent source of ideas is nursery and fairy tale books, which you can often pick up at your local charity shop. When you are out shopping, keep a notebook handy to jot down ideas that you see; you will be amazed what flashes of inspiration will come to you. Go to local craft fairs to see other doughcrafters' work, and pick up a few tips from them!

EQUIPMENT

'Be prepared', the Guide's motto wisely states! You must have all the ingredients, tools and baking equipment to hand before you get your hands covered in dough. There is nothing worse than having to delve into a drawer with flour-covered hands. Keep a damp cloth handy to wipe them, just in case.

   You will probably already have most of the basic items you need in your kitchen cupboards and drawers to get you off to a good start. The utensils listed below, with their uses in doughcrafting, will give you some idea of what can be achieved using just a few household items.

◆ *Baking parchment:* use to line trays to prevent your models from sticking.

◆ *Baking sheet:* for baking your work on in the oven.

◆ *Bamboo skewers or cocktail sticks:* for making simple indents such as eyes, dots, holes and so on, for supporting pieces of dough, or attaching one piece to another, such as in the flat-figure method on pages 24–26.

◆ *Biscuit cutters:* for cutting basic flat shapes such as circles, stars and scallops. Cook shops sell a wide range of pre-shaped cutters such as angels, trees, teddies, animals and suchlike, which are ideal for your decorations and mobiles.

◆ *Bowls:* a large one for mixing the dough, and smaller ones for using to shape the dough over.

◆ *Coffee mill:* this is optional, but very useful to grind salt finely so it is like icing sugar in texture, which is ideal for smooth or fine models.

◆ *Decorations:* experiment with seeds such as poppy, and cloves, coarse salt and peppercorns. Other decorations such as ribbons, bows, pom-poms, dried flowers, beads or sequins are usually glued on once the model has been hardened and varnished.

◆ *Eggs:* yolk and white are whisked together for glazing the hardened dough, giving it a rustic baked bread quality.

◆ *Flour:* for the basic dough use plain flour, but experiment with rye or wholemeal for a darker-coloured dough.

◆ *Flan rings:* use as large plaque cutters.

◆ *Foil:* aluminium cooking foil can be used as a padding in models to reduce the weight of the finished piece. It is also ideal for propping models up whilst baking and protecting them from burning when glazed with egg yolk.

◆ *Forks:* for imprinting the dough with dots or rows of dots and decorative edging.

◆ *Garlic press:* the hole sizes in these vary from manufacturer to manufacturer. Have at least one fine-holed and one thick-holed press. These are ideal for making strands of hair or beards on figures, thatched-roof effects, wool coats on animals, and grass.

◆ *Glue:* strong adhesive or glue from a glue gun can be useful for fixing decorations to finished dough pieces.

◆ *Graters:* have at least two thicknesses: a coarse one for larger print impressions and a fine one, such as a nutmeg grater, for fine impressions, giving a mesh-textured effect to the dough, or to give the impression of seeds on fruit.

◆ *Greaseproof paper:* ideal for laying over dough figures to trace the outline for the dough clothes.

◆ *Icing nozzles:* small size for imprinting patterns on the dough; large-sized biscuit nozzles for modelling the centre of flowers such as the daffodil featured in the flower modelling section on pages 22–23.

◆ *Kitchen knife and craft knife:* a pointed knife for cutting and shaping the dough. A craft knife is useful for cutting card and fine areas of dough that need removing, such as a small circle from the middle of a piece of dough.

◆ *Mug:* straight-sided for measuring salt, flour and water.

◆ *Paints:* poster or water colour paints.

◆ *Pair of compasses:* for drawing perfect circles on card or greaseproof paper.

◆ *Pastry brush:* use to brush the dough with egg glaze before browning, and for brushing the dough with water when joining soft pieces.

◆ *Rolling pins:* a large one is essential for rolling dough to an even, flat surface, and a smaller one useful for rolling small amounts of dough.

◆ *Scissors:* larger kitchen scissors are useful for cutting greaseproof paper, parchment and foil. Small ones are best for snipping the dough into points to make a feather or spiny effect, or for leaves on trees.

◆ *Sieves and strainers:* these are both useful for pushing dough through or making an impression on the dough.

◆ *Spatula or fish slice:* to ease models off the baking sheet.

◆ *Spoons:* a tablespoon to measure out your cooking oil and wallpaper paste and a teaspoon for modelling.

◆ *Varnish:* for poster or water colour paints.

◆ *Other helpful items:* cooking trays, racks, string, wire and cutters, assorted-sized paint brushes, food colours, methylated spirit for cleaning varnish brushes, ruler, plastic bags, fine rubber gloves, card, pencil.

◆ *Useful decorations and trims:* ribbon, ribbon trims, beads, bead trim, paper clips, household glue, dried flowers and foliage, fluffy pom-poms, scraps of fabric and felt, buttons, transfers, Christmas tree trims, and a variety of purchased bases such as the sun hat on page 75 or Santa's sack on page 112.

These are simple projects, and with the help of biscuit cutters or a flan ring you can achieve excellent results at your first attempt. The clown (see page 59) needs a little practice, but it is easily achievable once you have experimented with the basic figure shape.

CHOOSING A PROJECT

All the projects have been given one*, two** or three*** stars to indicate the level of difficulty. Newcomers to the craft should choose an item marked with one star to begin with. Projects that will get you accustomed to working with the dough and the rolling method are the cut-out farm animals (see page 91), name plaques (see page 47) or tempting mince pies (see page 84)!

Ideally, your room and hands should not be too hot when making salt dough. Lighting situated under cabinets over work tops is best left off if possible, as warm conditions – whether from lights, heating or your own body heat – can dry the dough out too quickly and make it more difficult to work. Have all your equipment at hand, and keep any dough which is not in use in a polythene bag or sealable container to prevent it from drying out.

It is advisable to remove any rings or bracelets and keep the cuffs on your sleeves out of the way. After working with the dough, treat your hands to some hand cream to prevent them drying out from the salt in the dough.

If you have sensitive skin, wear fine surgical gloves when mixing dough.

11

DOUGH RECIPES

The more experienced you become at doughcraft, the more likely it is that you will have established a preference for a particular dough recipe and quantities, so jot down your preferences in your notebook as you work. In this book we use three easy recipes: the basic recipe, ideal for general modelling; the fine recipe, excellent for delicate pieces such as the doll's house models (see pages 76–80) and the mini babies (see page 41); and the strong extensible recipe made with wallpaper paste, suitable for rolling into the large flat sheets required for plaques. The resulting qualities you will get by using the different recipes can be seen by looking at the items featured in the book, as each sample stipulates the recipe used and the quantities of dough required. The specific amounts of dough may vary slightly according to individual modelling techniques.

Wherever you are using coloured and plain dough in a single project, it is best to make up at least two quantities of dough to save you running short and not being able to match your colours in a new batch of dough.

Have your dough ingredients ready before you start

Basic dough ingredients

Use a straight-sided mug for measuring out the quantities to ensure accuracy at all times. This recipe is ideal for all basic projects, and perfect for children as it does not contain fungicide.

+ = 2 mugs of plain white flour

= 1 heaped mug of salt

= 1 mug of tepid water

Fine dough ingredients

For precision work or miniature models such as the featured doll's house items (see pages 76–80), it is best to use the fine dough recipe, which is smoother and more malleable than the basic dough. Add a tablespoon of cooking oil to the water before mixing it into the dry ingredients. An extra-smooth dough can be made by grinding the salt in a coffee mill to the consistency of icing sugar.

Strong extensible dough ingredients

To achieve a strong dough with extending qualities that is ideal for making larger plaques, add a tablespoon of wallpaper paste flakes to the basic dry ingredients before adding the water.

Wallpaper adhesives usually contain fungicides. Do not allow young children to use dough containing fungicides in case they put sticky fingers in their mouths. Also keep a special rolling pin to use with this dough as wooden rolling pins may absorb the fungicide.

PREPARING THE DOUGH

The mixing methods are the same for all three dough recipes used in this book.

1. Use a straight-sided mug to measure the dry ingredients into a large mixing bowl. Make a well in the centre.

2. Add the vegetable oil, if using, to the tepid water, then pour the liquid into the well of the dry ingredients.

3. Mix together thoroughly with a spoon, then use your fingertips to integrate all the dough ingredients fully.

4. Hold the mixture in one hand and let it drop into the bowl. The dough mixture should drop slowly from your hand when it is of the correct consistency. If it is too wet it will drop quickly, so gradually work in a little more flour. If it is too dry, add a little more water.

5. Dust a work surface with flour. Turn the dough out on to the prepared work surface and knead it thoroughly. To do this, pull the dough towards you with your fingers then push it back down with your knuckles.

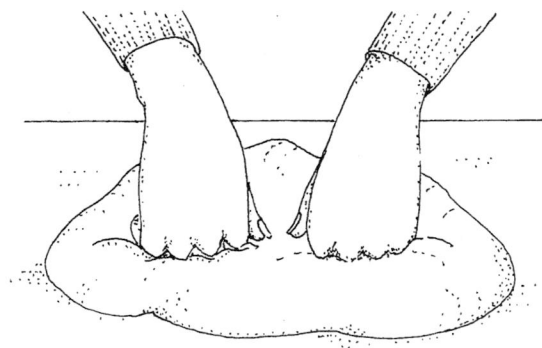

Kneading the dough

6. Return the dough to the bowl and cover with a polythene bag to keep it airtight. Allow the dough to relax for ten minutes; the dough is then ready for modelling.

Remember to keep dough not in use in an airtight container to prevent it from drying out. Dough lasts for several days kept sealed in the refrigerator. If it is a bit sticky after keeping, gradually add extra flour until it returns to a firm consistency.

You can mix the ingredients in a food processor; this saves time if you require large amounts of dough for a major project.

DOUGH PASTE

Dough paste is used for gluing pieces of hardened dough to each other, or for repairing hair-line cracks in cooked dough.

1. Put a ball of dough measuring about 2 in (5 cm) in diameter in a cup, add 2 tablespoons of cold water and stir into a creamy paste the thickness of double cream.

2. Use a pastry brush coated with the paste to paint the pieces that need joining together.

COLOURING DOUGH

There are a variety of ways to colour your dough, so experiment with the following methods to see what suits your requirements.

◆ Try different coloured flours for a rustic-coloured dough.

◆ Add about a teaspoon of poster colour paint to a fist-sized ball of dough for matt-coloured dough.

◆ Coffee powder, cocoa powder and turmeric powder all give the dough pleasant hues.

◆ Painting with poster paints is another method of colouring your dough after you have prepared your model. There is more detail on painting on page 38.

Using food colouring

Using food colouring is one of the most effective methods of colouring dough and saves time as you do not have to paint your projects.

1. Use a piece of dough about the size of a clenched fist. Make a well in the middle of the piece of dough and shake in four to five drops of your chosen food colour, then wrap the dough around the colour. You can intensify the colour or make it paler by regulating the number of drops of colour added.

2. Place the dough in a polythene bag, then knead it until all the food colour is evenly mixed. Keep your coloured dough in separate bags or sealed containers to prevent them drying out.

To achieve a marbled pattern effect in your dough, knead or twist different coloured pieces of dough together. Segment the dough with a knife to reveal the unusual patterns. The cut pieces can be turned into pretty beads by making a hole through the middle of each one with a cocktail stick and threading them on to fine elastic after they have been hardened.

CHAPTER TWO

MODELLING TECHNIQUES

MODELLING BASICS

It is best to carry out the major part of your modelling on a work top dusted with flour. You can work on a piece of baking parchment, but remember that if you do this the back of your model may have a few wrinkles when dry as the moisture from the dough causes the paper to contract into fine ripples. You can also work directly on a baking sheet, although this does limit the size of your model. It is best to do this only for delicate samples that may otherwise become dislodged when moved from the work surface to the baking sheet for baking. The baking sheet method ensures you have a smooth surface on the back of the piece, which is important to have on such items as plaques and clock faces.

CUT SHAPES

This method is ideal when you want quick results or are working with children. There are many end uses for cut shapes, such as the wild animals (see page 90), the delightful teddy bear swag (see page 49), Christmas decorations, gift tags and suchlike. Look through the book at the variety of models you can make using this simple method.

Use the basic dough recipe on pages 12–13 for making cut shapes.

You can either use one of your favourite biscuit cutters to cut out shapes, or make a template from one of the patterns in the book – or from any other source. To make a template, first choose your design, copy it on to tracing paper, then cut it out in card to make the template. To alter the size of the original, use a photocopier, or draw a grid of even squares over the design, then a grid of larger squares on to your tracing paper. Copy the design to the larger size, using the grid to help you enlarge the shapes. For a more permanent template, cut one from patchwork plastic; it not only has a grid to help trace the design but can also be washed after use and used repeatedly without disintegrating.

There are many ways you can decorate your samples – test your imagination! Sticking on transfers, painting, adding seeds or ribbons are a few ideas for you to try.

1. Roll half the quantity of basic dough into a flat sheet about ¼ in (6 mm) thick. Check there are no cracks and, if there are, moisten them with a wet fingertip and press them together again.

2. If you are using a biscuit cutter, press your chosen cutter firmly on to the dough, then lift it up to release the shape.

Lift cut-out shapes with a spatula or fish slice

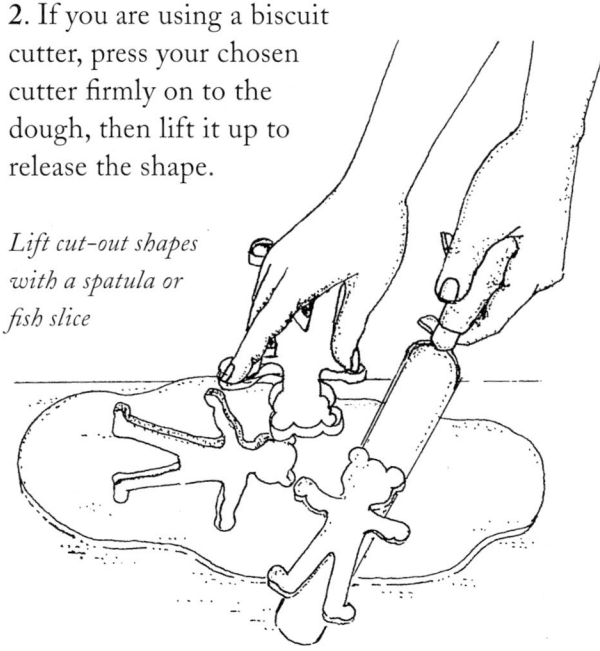

3. If you are using a template, lay the template on the dough, then cut round it with the point of a craft knife.

4. To add more dough to your work, moisten the edge of the additional piece with water and bond to the foundation piece by pressing the two gently together.

5. If your completed model is to be hung, make a hole in the top with a cocktail stick for inserting a loop of string or ribbon, or to hang from a nail. Insert half a paper clip to keep the hole open. See the section on hanging techniques on page 39 for details of this method.

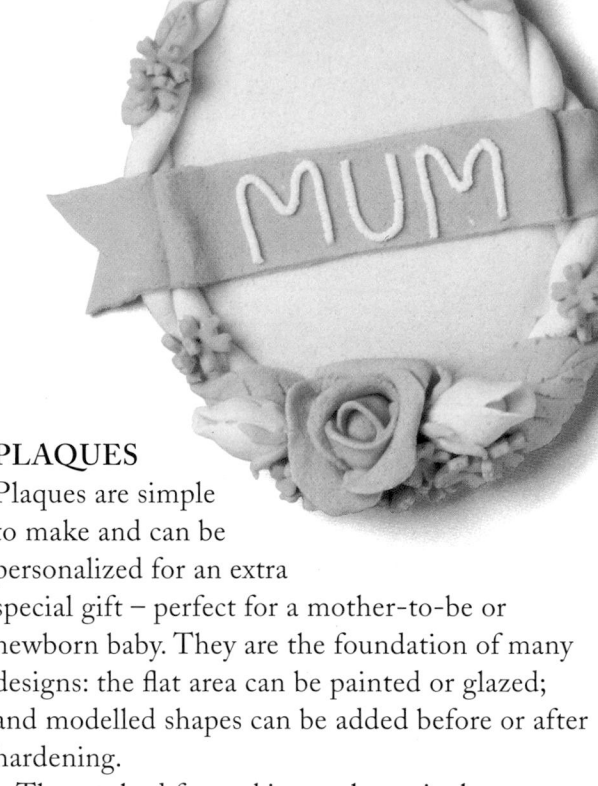

PLAQUES

Plaques are simple to make and can be personalized for an extra special gift – perfect for a mother-to-be or newborn baby. They are the foundation of many designs: the flat area can be painted or glazed; and modelled shapes can be added before or after hardening.

The method for making a plaque is the same as for cut shapes, but the surface area of a plaque tends to be greater than for cut shapes, so use the strong extensible dough to ensure a more elastic and tougher dough. Look in your cupboards for shapes to cut around: saucepans, flan rings and suchlike all make ideal templates.

1. Roll out the dough into a flat sheet about ½ in (12 mm) thick and smooth out any cracks with a moistened fingertip.

2. Cut round your chosen shape using a pointed knife, going gently so you do not stretch or tear the dough.

3. To add more dough to your work, moisten the edge of the additional piece with water and bond to the foundation piece by pressing the two gently together.

4. Remember that your completed plaque will need a hanging loop. See page 39 for details of the various methods.

BAS-RELIEF

These models are formed over a flat base such as a plaque or any other pre-hardened surface which supports the soft dough. Whatever you are attaching the dough over, remember to moisten the surfaces that touch, if you are using soft dough, or join them with dough paste if you are joining hardened dough. Dough adheres quite well to a wooden base, but if it does come unstuck it can easily be repaired with glue from a glue gun. Use the strong extensible dough for bas-relief projects.

ROLLED DOUGH

Rolling dough into long tubular shapes is one of the easiest techniques for children to master – after all, they are familiar with the technique from using plasticine or play dough. Use the basic dough (see page 12) for rolled dough modelling.

There are many end uses for dough tubes. They form the foundation of plaits, twists, circles, hanging loops, garlands, coils, and can be scored with a knife to give a sculpted effect.

1. Squeeze a ball of dough into a flat tube shape. Place your fingertips on the top of the dough and gently roll the dough backwards and forwards, splaying your fingers out as you roll. Continue rolling with an even pressure, moving your hands from the centre to the edges, until the tube is round and of equal diameter along its length.

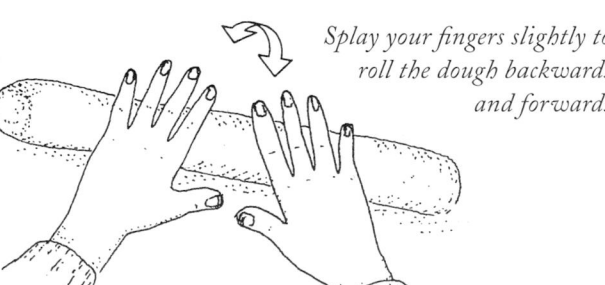

Splay your fingers slightly to roll the dough backwards and forwards

Uneven rolling will cause your tube to taper and split. A 2 in (5 cm) diameter ball of dough makes a tube about 6 in (15 cm) long and ¾ in (2 cm) in diameter.

2. To join the ends of a tube together, cut each end at an angle with a sharp knife, then moisten the ends with water and press them together. Conceal the join by moistening with water and gently smoothing it out with your fingertips.

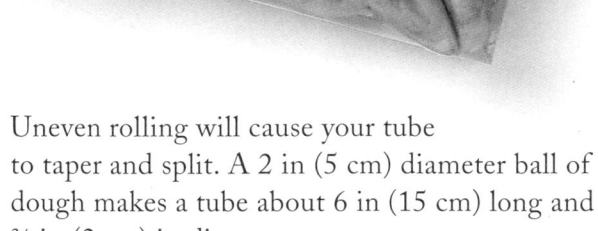

Cut dough tube ends at an angle and join together with water

3. Attach dough decorations to the rolled dough with water and remember to fix a hanging loop (see page 39) if necessary.

TWISTS

Dough twists make excellent garlands, as you can see from the sweetie garland above (and see page 64) – a novel idea that is easy for you to copy. Use the basic dough, and follow the instructions for making rolled dough (see page 17).

The diameter of the tubes determines the overall circumference of your garland; the narrower the tube the more refined the end result. Tubes measuring ¾ in (2 cm) in diameter by 16 in (40 cm) long, make a garland measuring about 6 in (15 cm) in diameter.

1. Roll two tubes of equal length and diameter, following the method for the single rolled tube on page 17. Hold the two left ends of the tubes between your left thumb and index finger and do the same with the two right ends. Gently twist each end in opposite directions, bonding the two tubes into one long twist.

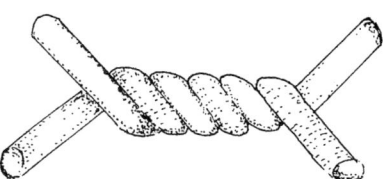

Dough twist

2. To join the ends of a twist together, cut each end at an angle with a sharp knife, then moisten the ends with water and press them together.

Conceal the join by moistening with water and gently smoothing it out with your fingertips.

3. Make a self-hanging loop if the twisted garland is to be a wall hanging (see page 39) and fix it to the back.

BRAIDED DOUGH

You can plait three dough tubes of equal diameter and length together to make a braid which is ideal for garlands and decorations. Use the basic dough and follow the instructions for making the rolled dough (see page 17).

1. Lay one tube on a work surface, then cross a second tube over it from left to right. Lay the third tube right to left over the previous one.

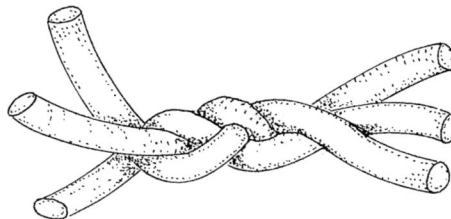

Braided dough

2. Continue plaiting down the lengths of the tubes for the length you require. Moisten the ends to seal the dough together or, if you want to create a circle, cut and moisten the ends (see page 17) to fix them together.

3. There are several imaginative ways in which to decorate your finished samples, and the equipment and finishing techniques on pages 8–11 and pages 35–39 will give you further decorative information. If you are adding dough decorations to a piece before baking, use water to moisten the joins and seal the dough together. Join hardened dough pieces with dough paste.

Any addition to your piece that may be affected by the oven heat, such as plastic or glue, should be added after you have hardened the piece.

Vegetables *

A selection of vegetables and fruit would make delightful decorations on a dough garland to celebrate harvest festival, or to give to a new mother to hang in her kitchen. Have a look at the displays in the greengrocer's shop – there's so much choice of traditional and exotic vegetables to choose from. Use the basic dough (see page 12) to make your vegetables to scale with one another, then harden them and paint them in realistic colours. Use varnish where you want a shiny finish.

Pea pod

Roll a piece of dough to 2½ in (6.5 cm) long by ½ in (12 mm) in diameter for the pea pod. Hollow the centre of the dough into a boat shape using the handle of a teaspoon. Pinch the ends into points for the stalk and the tip of the pod. Roll some graded-sized balls of dough to imitate peas and fill the pod with them.

Carrot or parsnip

Roll a piece of dough to a tube 3¾ in (9.5 cm) long by 1 in (2.5 cm) in diameter, then pinch at one end to form the root tip. Cut a small piece of dough with scissors to simulate the cut leaves and attach them to the top with water.

Garlic

Model six to eight curved tubes of dough about 1¼ in (3 cm) long and ½ in (12 mm) wide for each garlic segment. Form the inner stem of the bulb from a piece of dough about 1½ in (4 cm) long and slightly wider at the base. Fix the segments around the stem with water, leaving the stem protruding above the segments for about ½ in (12 mm).

New potato

Form a piece of dough into an irregular oval shape 2 in (5 cm) long by 1¼ in (3 cm) in diameter to resemble a new potato. Randomly indent the surface of the dough with the point of a kitchen knife to form the eyes of the potato.

Radish

Roll a ball of dough to 1 in (2.5 cm) in diameter, then pinch one end into a point to form the root tip. Cut a small piece of dough with scissors to simulate the cut leaves at the top end and attach them to the top of the radish with water.

Cherry tomato

Roll a ball of dough to 1½ in (4 cm) in diameter. Pinch a scrap of dough into a star shape about 1¼ in (3 cm) in diameter, wet the base and press it on the top of the ball, forming the calyx. Fix a ¾ in (2 cm) long stem in the middle of the calyx with water.

Fruit *

The fruit in your fruit bowl and from the greengrocer should give you plenty of inspiration and an idea of the detail required for your models. The following can all be made from the basic dough. The quantities required will depend how many fruits you intend to make. Half the quantity of basic dough will be sufficient to make a small bowl of fruit. Make sure you mould them in scale to one another. After hardening, paint the fruits in realistic colours and varnish those that need a glossy surface.

Apple

Roll the dough into a ball 2 in (5 cm) in diameter. Press a clove in at the top and bottom for the stalk and flower tip.

Banana

Roll a piece of dough into a tube 4 in (10 cm) long by 1 in (2.5 cm) wide. Pinch in one end for about ½ in (12 mm) to form the stem. Curve the tube into a banana shape and lightly score down the length four times and about ¼ in (6 mm) apart for the ridges of the banana.

Blackcurrants or redcurrants

Form small balls of dough ¼ in (6 mm) to ½ in (12 mm) in diameter. Roll tiny balls of dough the diameter of a bamboo skewer and attach one with water to the top of each of the larger balls, indenting them with a cocktail stick to simulate the flower tip on the fruit.

Cherries

Roll two balls of dough for the cherries to ¾ in (2 cm) in diameter and indent the top of each ball with a cocktail stick. Bend a 4 in (10 cm) length of florists' wire in half and insert one end in the top of each cherry for the stalk. If the wire becomes loose after hardening, squeeze a drop of strong adhesive into the indented hole and secure in position.

Grapes

Make about twenty balls of dough, ten ½ in (12 mm) and ten ¾ in (2 cm) in diameter. Beginning the bunch at the top, attach several large balls together and on top of each other with water, gradually working down to the smaller balls at the base. The overall shape of the bunch of grapes is triangular. Shape some vines leaves as described on page 23. Attach the vine leaves at the top of the bunch with a little water.

Orange

Roll a ball of dough to 2½ in (6 cm) in diameter and then roll it over a nutmeg grater to give the appearance of orange peel. Finish off by pressing a clove into the base for the flower tip.

Pear

Roll a piece of dough to 3 in (8 cm) long by 2 in (5 cm) wide and pinch in about 1¼ in (3 cm) from the top to form the waist of the pear.

Raspberries, loganberries or mulberries

These fruits are all made from tiny balls of dough stuck on to a larger ball which acts as a support. Roll a ball of dough to about ¾ in (2 cm) in diameter. Attach tiny balls of dough around it, wetting each ball as you work to ensure they stick to the main ball. Make a calyx from five tiny tubes of dough pinched in at the base of each ball to form the pointed tip.

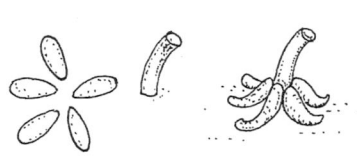

Making a fruit calyx

Strawberries

Roll the dough into balls varying from ½ in (12 mm) to 1 in (2.5 cm) in diameter, then pinch in at the base of each ball to form the pointed tip of the strawberries. The calyx for each fruit is made from five tiny tubes of dough pinched into a star shape and curled at one end. Indent the surface of the strawberries with a nutmeg grater to resemble the seeds.

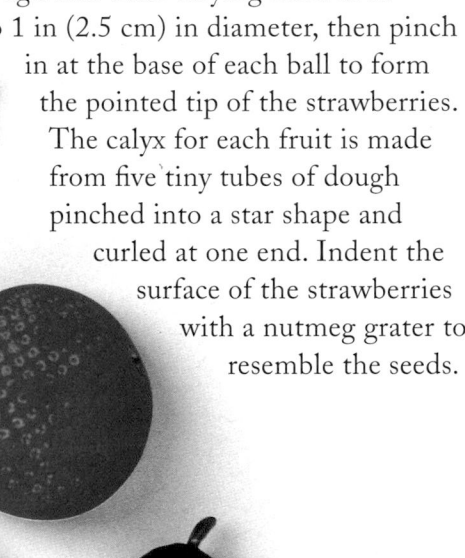

Flowers *

Use fine dough for making flowers. Look at flowers themselves to help in your modelling. To model fine petals, roll the dough balls between the two layers of a polythene bag. The dough can be rolled very thinly and will peel away cleanly from the polythene, enabling you to make some of the finest specimens. Once hardened, paint them carefully in delicate colours to match your favourite blooms.

Daffodil

Model a 2 in (5 cm) in diameter ball of dough for the trumpet over the end of a large metal biscuit-making nozzle. Frill the end of the trumpet by pulling the dough out at the edge with a cocktail stick, then pressing the dough in with the stick next to where you pulled it out; continue this sequence all around the edge.

Dry the trumpet in the oven. Before it is completely hardened, slip it off the support and make a hole in the end for gluing in the stamens.

Model six petals in dough about 1½ in (4 cm) long by 1 in (2.5 cm) wide. Curve one end of each petal to look like the rounded tip of a daffodil petal, leaving the other end flat. Arrange the petals in a circle around a saucer or tart tin. Slightly overlap the flat ends and press them together where they meet to ensure the petals harden with curled tips.

Stand the trumpet in the middle of the petals, securing with some dough paste, and harden. Make stamens from pipe cleaners or use purchased ones and glue in the middle of the trumpet section.

Modelling a flower over an icing nozzle

Daisy

Roll out the dough into a circle 1¼ in (3 cm) in diameter and cut out a circle using a matching-sized lid as a cutter. Roll a small, flat ball of dough for the middle of the flower and press it on to the centre of the dough circle with water. Indent the centre of the flower with a cocktail stick to reproduce the tiny stamens. For the petal divisions, snip around the circle with scissors. Pinch the cut pieces into daisy-shaped petals.

Freesia

Flatten five balls of dough between two polythene sheets, then shape into tapered petals 1½ in (4 cm) long. Pinch the narrow ends of the petals together to form the neck of the flower. Glue a stamen in the centre when hardened.

Jasmine

Model a five-pointed star around the end of a cocktail stick to 1 in (2.5 cm) in diameter. Ease it off the stick and harden it over an upturned lid with the neck end uppermost, using the lid as a support for the petals.

Pansy

Flatten five balls of dough about ½ in (12 mm) in diameter into petal shapes between polythene sheets. Place one petal at the base with two petals each side and slightly overlapping. Press the remaining two petals over the lower ones to form the top of the flower. Indent the centre of the flower with a cocktail stick to allow the stamen to be glued in position when hard.

Simple rose

Roll six balls of dough to about ½ in (12 mm) in diameter and flatten five into heart-shaped petals between two sheets of polythene. To form the centre of the rose, flatten the remaining ball into a petal shape and roll one edge inwards, then continue rolling until the petal is rolled up. Attach the heart-shaped petals around the centre with water to secure them.

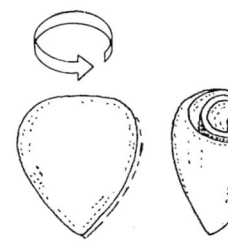

Rolling flower petals

Cabbage rose

Roll a ¾ in (2 cm) in diameter dough ball. Make five or six petals of about 1 in (2.5 cm) wide in the same way as the simple rose and attach to the ball of dough with water. Curl the petals out with a cocktail stick.

Making the cabbage rose

Leaves *

Use the basic dough or the fine dough (see page 12) for making leaves.

Cut leaves

You can use leaf-shape cutters to cut leaves; these are available from cake-making suppliers. Alternatively you can make paper or card templates from the outlines shown here or from your own patterns. Roll out the dough to a thickness of no more than ¼ in (6 mm), then cut round the templates using a sharp knife. The above versions require the veins marked on them with the point of a sharp knife. Alternatively, you can make leaves by impressing a real one in the thinly rolled dough. Cut out the outlined shape with a craft knife. The veins will already be imprinted in the dough for you.

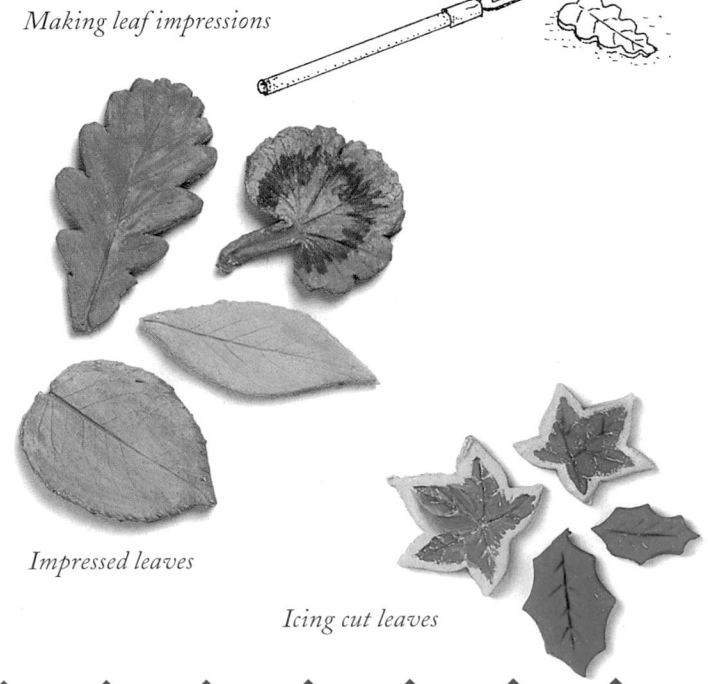

Making leaf impressions

Impressed leaves

Icing cut leaves

CHAPTER THREE

MAKING FIGURES

PERSONALISING FIGURES

Figure-making is very simple and one of my favourite areas of doughcraft. It has such wide appeal as you can personalize the models with a few minor details by adding the most obvious characteristics of the person your gift is for: glasses, freckles and suchlike. The features and clothes section on pages 30–34 will help you in this. Once you have made your first figure, experiment with the many positions in which they can be modelled. Whether adult, baby or animal, use the following method as a base for constructing your figures. The flat-figure method gives the technique for the facial features; these are the same for the different types of figure modelling, so are only explained once on pages 24–25.

Figures with a flat base *

- *Measure 9 in (23 cm)*
- *1 quantity of the basic dough or fine dough (see page 12)*

Flat figures are added to a plaque, over a frame, or can be used on their own with an attached hanging loop.

1. Begin with the head as this determines the proportions for the rest of the figure. To make the head for a figure measuring 9 in (23 cm) high, you will need a ball of dough 1½ in (4 cm) in diameter.

2. Roll the dough ball in the palm of your hand, using the fingers of the other hand to roll it in a circular motion.

3. Flatten the ball into a disc grading from ¼ in (6 mm) at the edges to ¾ in (2 cm) at the centre. Insert a cocktail stick for ¾ in (2 cm) at the base to secure the head to the body. Press the dough gently around the stick to secure in position.

4. Tiny balls of dough attached with water on the face make three-dimensional noses, ears, eyes and lips. See the illustrated features on pages 30–31 for more ideas. Glass beads can also be used for eyes; see the baby featured on page 51 for an example of this method. The ball of dough for the mouth can be indented or pulled down with a cocktail stick to look open, singing or crying. A simple mouth can be made by horizontally slitting the dough below the nose with a knife. Enlarge the slit with the knife point and insert a small piece of moistened dough for the tongue. Press the dough pieces together gently.

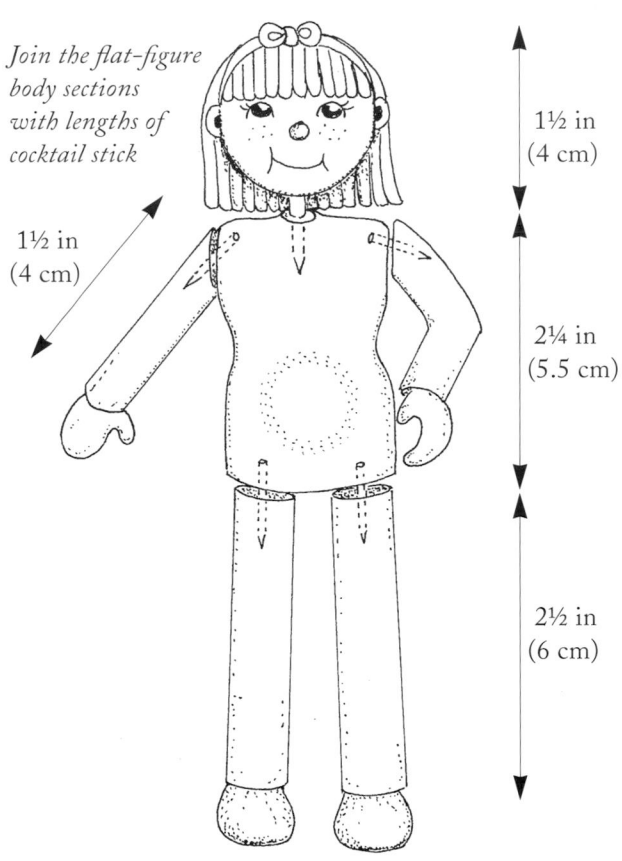

Join the flat-figure body sections with lengths of cocktail stick

1½ in (4 cm)

1½ in (4 cm)

2¼ in (5.5 cm)

2½ in (6 cm)

5. You may wish to paint features on the face after hardening the dough. See the painting section on page 38 for details of this.

6. Model the body from an oblong tube of dough 2¼ in (5.5 cm) long by 1½ in (4 cm) wide and ¾ in (2 cm) thick. Squeeze the dough at the top in the centre to form the neck, moisten and insert the cocktail stick with the head attached over the neck, gently pressing the two sections together. Be careful not to pierce the surface of the dough with the stick.

7. Additional body features such as breasts or a large tummy can be added at this stage. The pieces of dough for these are shaped and fixed with water in the appropriate areas. Pinch the body in at the waist to give it further definition for waisted clothes such as dresses and trousers.

8. Roll two tubes of dough for the legs 2½ in (6 cm) long by ¾ in (2 cm) in diameter. Attach the legs by moistening the areas of contact and applying pressure or, for a very secure model, by inserting cocktail sticks as you did to attach the head. The former method is adequate if the figure is going to be supported on a base.

9. Model two tubes of dough for the arms measuring 1½ in (4 cm) long by ½ in (12 mm) in diameter. Angle the ends at the top by cutting them with a knife before moistening the top and pressing them on to the shoulders. For a more secure model, you can attach them with cocktail sticks, as for the head and legs.

10. Hands and feet are made from balls of dough that are shaped and then moistened and pressed on to the appropriate arm or leg. The hands are about ¾ in (2 cm) in diameter and the feet about 1 in (2.5 cm) in diameter. The ideas illustrated on pages 30−31 give you a variety of hand and feet shapes. Indent the dough with a pointed knife to create the fingers and use the knife to round off the fingertips.

11. Make shoes from flattened balls of dough with the top section cut away into a U shape. Press this shape over the foot and use your fingers to mould it into your chosen shoe style. Fine detail such as tongues and eyelets are added at this stage. The tip of a cocktail stick is used for making the holes for laces.

12. Hairstyles vary and are best added after you have made the clothes, as this allows you to drape long hair over the clothes without interfering with the neckline details. The easiest method for making hair is by pressing a ball of dough through a garlic press. The hole size will determine the thickness of the strands. Moisten the head before draping the hair over it. Make fringes from short lengths of dough strands.

13. Another technique is to cut the hair out from a thin sheet of dough. Cut the fringe first and attach it to the face before fixing the sides. Joseph and Mary on pages 110–111 are examples of hair-making methods. The illustrations show how to cut the fringe and sides with scissors. Embroidery cotton that is stranded and cut into short lengths makes perfect hair for very small figures such as the miniature jack-in-the-box on page 78, but this must always be glued on after hardening.

Cutting dough hair with scissors

Your figures may be dressed with dough clothes or fabric ones. The method for each version is explained on pages 32–34.

Animals are modelled using the same technique as for a human figure. The bear illustration is a guide from which to work.

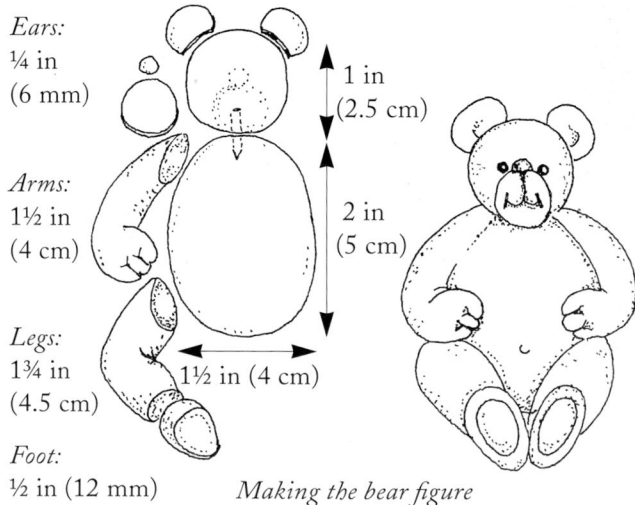

Ears: ¼ in (6 mm)

Arms: 1½ in (4 cm)

Legs: 1¾ in (4.5 cm)

Foot: ½ in (12 mm)

1 in (2.5 cm)

2 in (5 cm)

1½ in (4 cm)

Making the bear figure

All-in-one torso **

- ◆ *Measures 9 in (23 cm)*
- ◆ *1 quantity of the basic dough or fine dough (see page 12)*

This method is slightly more complicated as it is sculpted, so care is needed when you model the neck, arms and legs as they require extra shaping for a realistic figure shape. This method is ideal for dainty figures and animals. It is also a good method for figures that you want to look as though they are in action, such as the ballerina.

1. Roll a ball of dough for the head about 1½ in (4 cm) in diameter and secure it on to half a cocktail stick.

2. Roll a ball of dough into a tube about 8 in (20 cm) long by 2 in (6 cm) in diameter. Cut the dough into four sections for the arms and the legs as in the illustration. Mould the limbs between your index finger and thumb, squeezing the dough along its length and in at the wrists and ankles. Shape the feet and hands in the same way. Add extra dough for a raised effect.

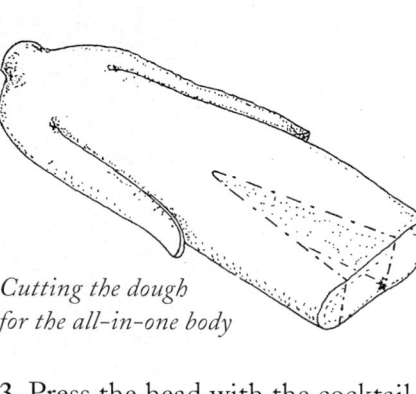

Cutting the dough for the all-in-one body

3. Press the head with the cocktail stick attached down on to the neck section. Moisten the join with water and smooth over.

Tubby figures *

- *Measure 4 in (10 cm)*
- *1 quantity of the basic dough (see page 12)*

Very rounded figures are made in this way with the legs as part of the body. The head, arms, feet and hands are added to the body.

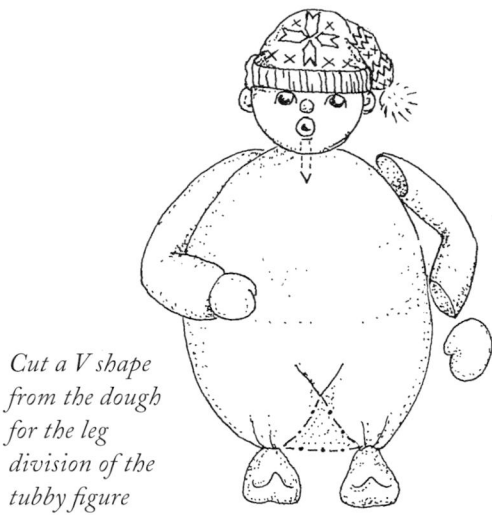

Cut a V shape from the dough for the leg division of the tubby figure

1. Roll a ball of dough for the head 1¼ in (3 cm) in diameter and insert half a cocktail stick at the base to fix it to the body.

2. Roll a large ball of dough to about 2½ in (6 cm) in diameter and gently flatten it into a dome-shaped disc for the body. Cut a V shape from the base of the disc for the leg division.

3. Model two tubes about 1¼ in (3 cm) long by ½ in (12 cm) in diameter for the arms; two balls each ¾ in (2 cm) in diameter for the hands, and two balls measuring 1 in (2.5 cm) in diameter for the shoes and attach to the body parts with water. Press the cocktail stick with the head attached down into the top of the figure. Moisten and gently seal the join.

4. The figure is dressed with dough clothes or has clothes painted on to it after hardening.

SUPPORTED FIGURES

Supported figures make excellent foundations for dressing with fabric, or where you require the figure to be free standing. These may be modelled on a hollow cone-shaped base or a pre-dried dough base.

Hollow cone base **

- *Measure 9 in (23 cm) high*
- *1 quantity of the basic dough (see page 12)*

Flexible card is used as the support vehicle for this method. An old cereal box is ideal for this purpose. Rose Red is an example of a hollow-based figure dressed in fabric.

1. Cut the card into a circle 8 in (20 cm) in diameter. Snip up to the centre of the circle with scissors, roll the card into a cone and fasten it together with staples. Level the base to stand the cone up firmly and cut the pointed tip off the top of the cone.

2. Roll out the dough to a circle about ½ in (12 mm) larger than the card and ¼ in (6 mm) thick. Form the dough into a cone shape in the same way as for the card one, then press the edges together with water. Sit the dough cone over the card cone and press the dough around the card and into shape with your fingers.

For a supported figure, model the dough over a card cone base

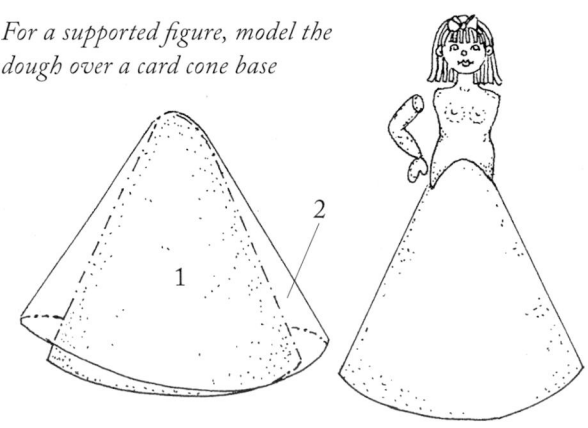

◆ ◆ ◆ ◆ ◆ ◆ ◆ ◆ ◆ ◆ ◆ ◆ ◆ ◆ ◆

Pre-hardened base **

- ◆ *Body measures 3 in (7.5 cm) long*
- ◆ *1 quantity of the basic dough (see page 12)*

This version is easy for a beginner to master. Joseph is an example of this method. Figures with a solid base are excellent when you want to add dough clothes as the hard base supports them. Dough moulded around scrunched up silver foil gives you a firm support that is lighter in weight.

1. Roll the dough into a tube about 1 in (2.5 cm) in diameter by 3 in (7.5 cm) long, level one end and pinch the other end in for the neck. Insert half a cocktail stick for attaching the head.

2. Make a ball of dough about 1 in (2.5 cm) in diameter and press it on to the cocktail stick attached to the body section. Harden the figure.

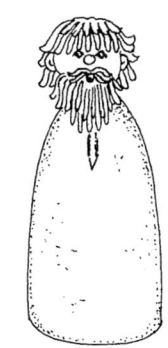

3. Dress the figure with dough clothes after hardening. Add arms and hands over the clothing, fixing them in position with dough paste.

For a figure with a pre-hardened base, secure the dough head to the base and harden before adding clothes

3. Make the head from a ball of dough measuring about 1¼ in (3 cm) in diameter. Moisten the top of the base, then attach the head, pressing gently down on top of the cone-shaped dough.

4. Harden the figure at this stage, without the arms, to give a firm foundation to work on, then the figure can be dressed with fabric or dough clothes before adding the arms. Use dough paste to attach the arms and hands after hardening; these will need propping in position over the clothes until they have set. Fabric clothes should be protected with greaseproof paper to prevent the paste staining them.

Make extra body supports and heads on sticks with leftover scraps of dough. They will come in useful if you need to make a speedy gift for someone and save wasting any dough.

◆ ◆ ◆ ◆ ◆ ◆ ◆ ◆ ◆ ◆

POSED FIGURES

These figures take a little practice. For perfect results make them in stages, as shown in the illustrations, hardening each stage as you progress. The dough may need propping up in the oven with a support until the model has hardened. The following examples are two of the most common poses you will require; you can base other positions on the same principle.

Sitting position **

- ◆ *Figure measures 9 in (23 cm) long*
- ◆ *1 quantity of the basic dough or fine dough (see page 12)*

1. Use the flat figure on pages 24–26 for the proportions and modelling method for your figure. Begin modelling the legs from one tube with feet attached to the ends. Experiment with the position in which you want the legs to be on the finished model. For crossed legs, lie one leg over the other and harden. If your figure is to be seated on an object, sit the U part of the tube on the support with the legs hanging down. The larger the figure, the heavier the dough will be. Support the feet during the drying process with a solid ovenproof object.

To model a seated figure, support the leg on an ovenproof object, then add the body and head to the hardened leg section

2. Next work the body section over the U part of the legs, attaching it with dough paste. Insert half a cocktail stick with about ½ in (12 mm) protruding at the top for the head to be attached. Larger figures need propping up behind the body section until fully hardened in the oven; use a scrunched up foil, wood or metal object for this.

3. Roll the dough into a ball for the head and sit it on the cocktail stick protruding from the body section; secure the head with dough paste. Make the arms and hands as for the flat-figure method and attach to the body with paste. These can be positioned in any way that you require, but again they may need propping until hard.

4. Remember, clothing is added over the body section of the figure before you add the arms and hands. This allows for the addition of minute details such as collars and belts and the arms to be positioned as you wish. Fix additional features to the hardened dough with dough paste.

Reclining position *

- *Measures 3 in (7.5 cm)*
- *1 quantity of the basic dough or fine dough (see page 12)*

This is a useful pose for tiny babies, such as the one shown here and those on page 41.

This figure does not have to be hardened at each stage. The definition for the reclining part of the body is in curved back and leg areas. Use the following measurements: the head from a ¾ in (2 cm) diameter ball of dough; the body from a tube about 1¼ in (3 cm) long by 1 in (2.5 cm) in diameter; two tubes about 1 in (2.5 cm) long by ¼ in (6 mm) in diameter for the arms; two tubes about 1¼ in (3 cm) long by ½ in (12 mm) for the legs.

1. Model the body section and the head using the flat-figure method on pages 24–26. The body is shaped with the tummy facing upwards. Press the head on to the body with water.

2. Model the arms, hands, legs and feet and attach them to the relevant areas of the body with water. Bend the arms and legs at the appropriate joints in the position you want them to be.

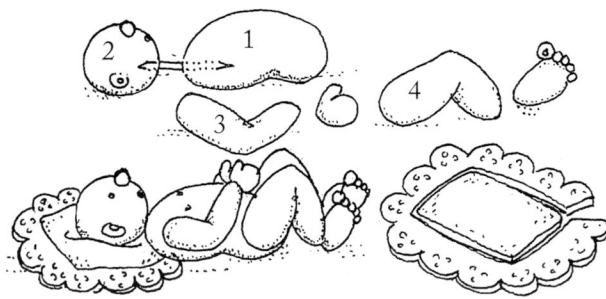

Model the pieces separately for a reclining figure, joining the head and body with a length of cocktail stick

3. If dressing the figure, make the trousers first. The top is made over the body section before the sleeves. The arms and the legs may be repositioned once the figure is clothed.

FEATURES – FACES, HANDS AND FEET

The variety of different features available contribute towards the charm of doughcraft; it is the minute detailing that authenticates your work. Use a combination of the features illustrated to personalize your samples, which can be painted or modelled. See the flat-figure method on pages 24–25 for in-depth modelling detail.

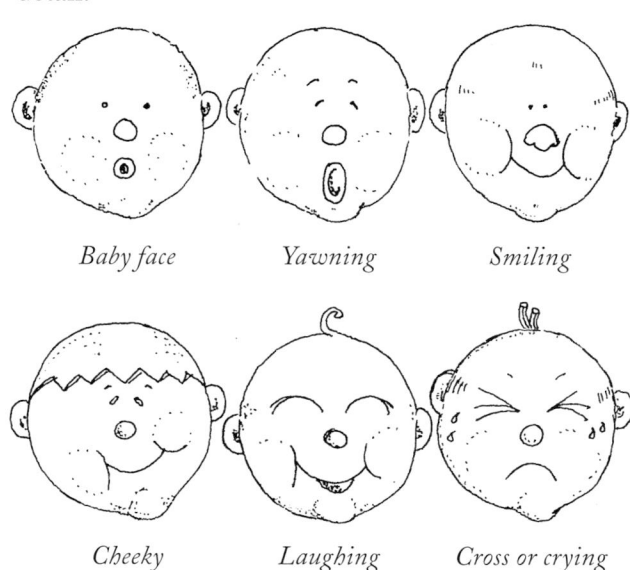

Baby face   *Yawning*   *Smiling*

Cheeky   *Laughing*   *Cross or crying*

Make sure the feet and hands are right for your chosen figure. Small details make all the difference. Watch babies' feet in particular to see how they curl their toes. This will help you in your modelling.

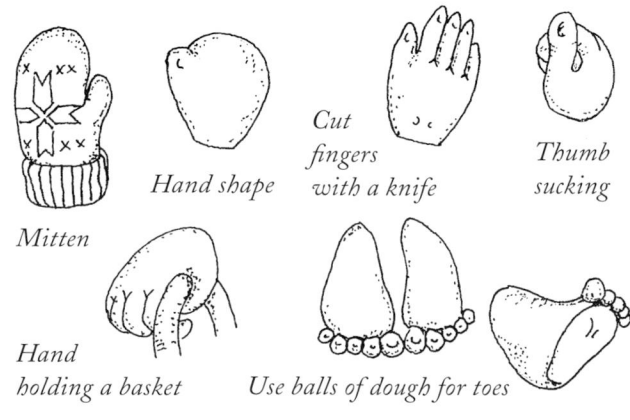

Mitten   *Hand shape*   *Cut fingers with a knife*   *Thumb sucking*

Hand holding a basket   *Use balls of dough for toes*

Baby

Cut hair

Plaits

Curls

Stranded hair

Santa

Headscarf

Clowns

Old man

Scarecrow
with button eyes

Soldier

Spectacles are
made from a
length of wire
or an opened
paper clip.
Bend the wire
into a spectacle
shape with pliers.

Animals can be personalized in the
same way as humans – just look at
your pets for ideas.

Squirrel

Rabbits

Fox

Elephant

Panda

Pig

Cow

CLOTHES

Make your model's clothes in dough or fabric. Before you begin making the clothes, there are a few considerations to take into account depending on the final look of your figure. Do you want the undergarments to show? Is the figure to be positioned or is the model free standing? Whatever your model, you will need to work in layers, from the base or undergarments to the top outer garments.

Dough clothes *

This shows you how to make a T-shirt, waistcoat and shorts for a flat-modelled figure. The principles are the same for making all dough clothes, and you can use them as a guide to making patterns for the clothes used in other projects featured in the book.

◆ *1 quantity of the basic dough (see page 12)*

1. Lay a piece of greaseproof paper over the chest section of the body and mark the relevant details such as neck, arm to shoulder position and waistline. On the tracing, draw a curved neck and mark the length of the T-shirt to fit the body, taking note of the marked features. Make a pattern for the shorts in the same way.

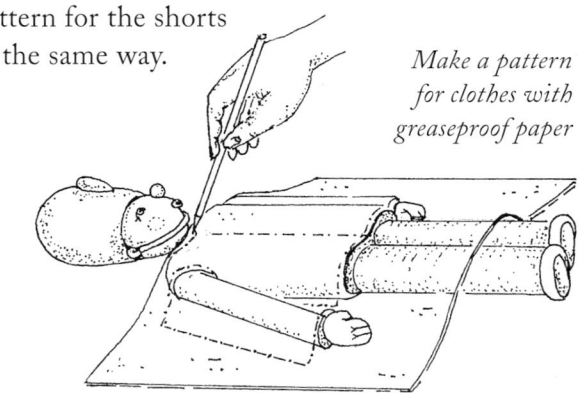

Make a pattern for clothes with greaseproof paper

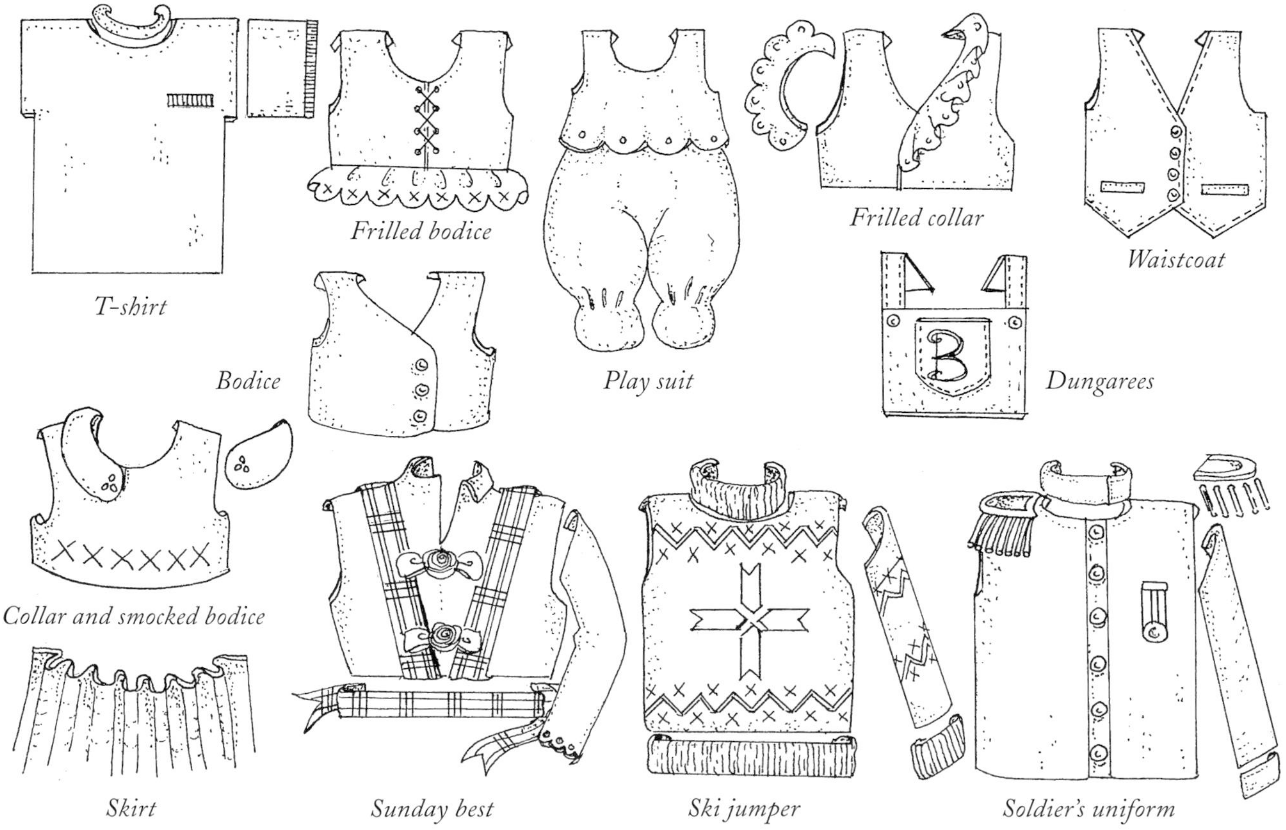

T-shirt

Frilled bodice

Play suit

Frilled collar

Waistcoat

Bodice

Dungarees

Collar and smocked bodice

Skirt

Sunday best

Ski jumper

Soldier's uniform

2. Roll out the dough to about ½ in (6 mm) thick, place the patterns on top and cut them out with a craft knife.

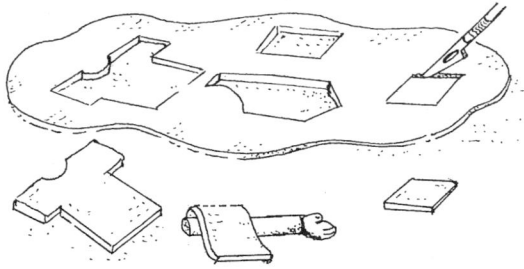

Cut out the dough using the paper templates

3. Moisten the figure with water, or with dough paste if already hardened. Place the dough shorts over the pelvic section of the figure and press the dough down gently. Next lay the T-shirt over the chest area and on top of the waistline of the shorts. The sleeves on the T-shirt are made from oblong pieces of dough attached over each arm with water or paste.

4. Use the greaseproof paper pattern to make the waistcoat; draw the V neck and armhole positions on it. Cut the waistcoat shape from thinly rolled dough, remembering to allow a small overlap where one front edge overlaps the other for the buttons. Moisten the T-shirt with water before laying the waistcoat on top of it. Press the two layers of clothing gently on to the body and around the sides. Refer to the gingerbread boy on page 100 for these items of his clothing.

If your figure is free standing you will need to make a back to your clothes. These are made in the same way as the front, but take note of back detailing such as necklines, they are usually higher than the front, except where you are making an item of clothing such as a sun dress. The sides of the dough clothes are secured together with water or dough paste.

Skirts are made from an oblong of dough rolled to the length required and twice the width of the figure. This piece of dough is laid over the body and pinched in at the waist to form the gathers.

Fabric clothes ***
Fabric clothes can be very simple or more complicated depending on the base figure and how much detail you want to include. You can make clothes to sew by taking paper patterns in the same way as the dough clothes. These require backs if they are to be on free-standing figures. Seam the pieces of fabric together with small tacking stitches on the wrong side. Hems need not be sewn as they can be held up by glue or disguised with braid trim. Felt is ideal for fabric clothing as it does not fray.

Draping fabric **
This method is uncomplicated as you do not need to make patterns; you simply drape fabric around the figure and cut away with scissors relevant features such as the necklines. Skirts are made from oblong strips of fabric gathered with a needle and thread and drawn in around the waist of the model. Bodices may be made from scalloped lace as it makes excellent bra-cups, and they can be glued on to the body. Capes are made in the same way as skirts.

Additional features such as dress straps or frill collars are all made from scraps of ribbon and lace. Keep odds and ends in a little tin so that you can choose suitable items.

HATS

There are several ways to make these, either in dough, fabric, felt, knitted tubing or from a baby's sock. See the diagrams for outlines of dough shapes required for each hat style.

Butcher's boater

Bowler

Sailor's cap

Bonnet

American footballer

Flower fairy

Clown

Chef

Police officer

Mob caps are made from circles of fabric cut with pinking shears and gathered about ¼ in (6 mm) from the edge with a needle and thread.

Lace can be glued in gathers around a face to make a frilled hat suitable for a baby. You can see this effect on the baby label on page 51 where the head has been surrounded by a frilled cap.

A length of knitted tubing is gathered in at one end with small stitches to make the top of a pull-on ski-type hat. Sew a pom-pom over the stitches and turn the other end up into a cuff.

A hat suitable for Father Christmas or an elf is made from a circle of felt slit up to the centre with the slit edges overlapped and glued down forming the 'dunce hat' shape. A pom-pom can be glued to the pointed end.

Cut the heel and toe section off a baby's sock, sew the raw edge together and stitch a pom-pom over it. The baby boy and girl on pages 56–57 have hats made with this method, but it is also an ideal way to make hats for larger models.

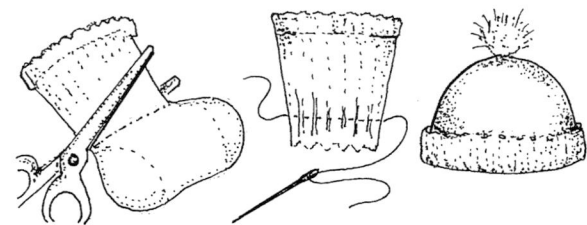

Making a hat from a baby's sock

SHOES

The easiest way to show a shoe is by painting details such as laces or bows on to the ball of dough at the end of the leg.

Modelled shoes are formed over the dough foot. Roll a piece of dough out to about ¼ in (6 mm) thick and cut a U shape from it that is large enough to cover three-quarters of the foot. Moisten the foot and press the shoe piece over it. The opening detail is shaped with a knife. A tongue may be inserted at this stage if the shoe is a lace-up. A court shoe or ballerina pump has to have the front piece of dough cut away to give it shape.

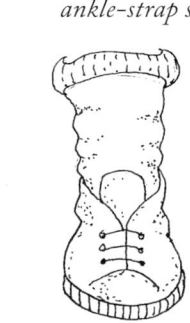

Making a child's ankle-strap shoe

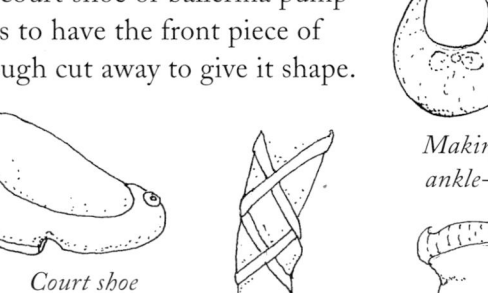

Court shoe

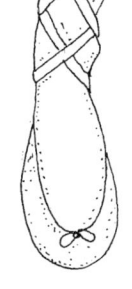

Boot

Ballet shoe

Lace-up shoe

CHAPTER FOUR

FINISHING TECHNIQUES

TEXTURES AND EFFECTS

There are many useful techniques you can adopt to decorate your dough model. Look around for inspiration and practise on scraps of dough to test the results.

Impressions

To create a textured surface, try forcing dough through a garlic press or sieve, or pressing carved buttons or the rough side of a nutmeg grater into the dough. The photographs and textures used in the book will give you further inspiration.

High-relief

This can be achieved in several ways, such as using the garlic press to make stranded dough that is ideal for hair, straw or fur. You can achieve this effect by adding layers of dough, giving a bas-relief, or adding modelled shapes such as fruit or flowers to the surface. For examples showing the different methods you can use, see Chapter 8 on making garlands (pages 61–65) and Chapter 13 on fairy tales (pages 92–103).

Tiles and scalloped edging

A scalloped-edge icing cutter is used to make these. For tiles, cut several strips of dough with the cutter, then overlap one strip horizontally over the other, ensuring the scallop comes between the two above and below. Score each side of the scallop vertically with a knife for the tile effect. The gingerbread house on pages 98–99 demonstrates this method.

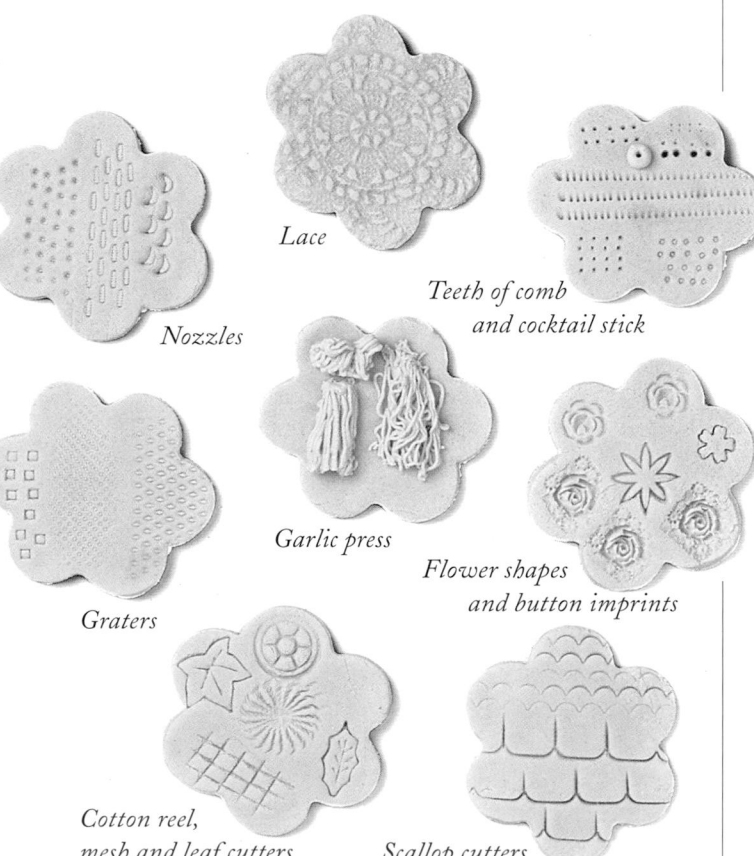

Nozzles

Lace

Teeth of comb and cocktail stick

Graters

Garlic press

Flower shapes and button imprints

Cotton reel, mesh and leaf cutters

Scallop cutters

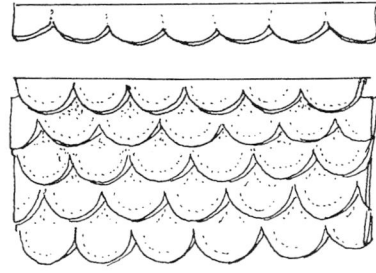

Overlapping scalloped tiles

A ¼ in (6 mm) deep scalloped edging can be made by using an icing cutter designed for the purpose. Tiny scalloped edging is made by slitting the strip at regular intervals of about ¼ in (6 mm), then rounding each of the edges of the slit with the point of a knife into a scallop.

Woven textures

A basket-weave effect is achieved by laying one strip of dough alternately over or under another. The method is used to make delightful baskets such as the

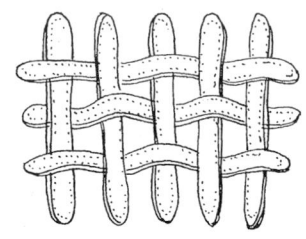

Creating a woven texture

egg basket in the photograph. Lay the base strips of dough horizontally on the work surface. Start weaving a vertical strip over and under the horizontal bars. Work in rows until you achieve the required depth of basket. Trim the excess dough from the edges of the woven texture with a sharp knife, curving the edges and the sides into an attractive basket shape.

Spines, feathers and foliage

These are made by snipping into the dough with a pair of pointed scissors. Cut the dough and lift it with the scissors to make the snipped piece prominent. The method is excellent for the spines of a hedgehog, for feathers or fir trees.

Snip spines with sharp scissors

HARDENING THE DOUGH

There are several methods you can adopt to achieve a firm base and the ones listed below are a selection of the best to ensure good results.

Air drying

The simplest and cheapest method of drying is air drying the dough. Leave your model in a warm spot such as on a wire rack over a radiator to dry. The length of time needed for drying may vary from days to a couple of weeks – the thicker the piece the longer it will take. Your dough work can be dried in the garden on a sunny day, beginning in a shady spot and then moving into the sun as it dries out. Watch out for hungry squirrels, who will have a nibble if you are not careful, and for kittens, who are apt to play football with your best specimen! Bring your samples indoors before the night mists can moisten them.

To speed up the air drying process, you can complete the hardening by finishing off in a cool oven at about 110°C/225°F/gas mark ¼.

Air drying tends to make the edges retract or curl, so regularly turn flat samples over to prevent this from happening to them.

Oven drying

Oven temperatures vary according to the method by which they are heated: electric fan ovens and gas ovens tend to be fiercer than ordinary electric ovens. Also, the age of the oven will influence the temperature as it will be affected by how airtight the seal on the door is. Solid-fuel stoves or Agas are fine for drying, using the coolest oven. You will need to experiment carefully with your own oven, and prop the oven door open if it gets too hot. Whatever type of oven you have, you will need to experiment with different thicknesses of dough and oven placements to ensure your models dry evenly without cracking.

As a rule for all oven types, allow 30 minutes per ¼ in (6 mm) thickness of dough. Regularly turn your work in the oven to ensure it dries evenly.

Place your samples flat on a baking sheet before baking. You can line it with baking parchment, if you wish, to stop it sticking. Use a fish slice or spatula to transfer your models to and from the sheet. You may need to support heavy sections of dough before they set in position; use scrunched up foil or an ovenproof utensil for this purpose. Your samples can be covered with aluminium foil to prevent them from burning.

For the most economical usage of your oven, dry your work on several tiers of racking. Extra shelving can be made from cake racks propped up on wooden or brick supports.

Dough can be dried with additions such as fabric, seed pods, dried flowers and so on, but keep an eye on them to prevent them from burning.

Remember to wear oven gloves when removing the hardened samples from the oven and lay them on a wire rack until cool. It is advisable to weight the edges of thin pieces of dough to prevent them from curling up or becoming warped as they cool off.

◆ *Slow drying:* oven temperatures of 75°C/150°F/ bottom of the oven at gas mark ¼ for 8–12 hours. Slow drying is suitable for thick or solid pieces of dough such as in free-standing figures.

◆ *Quick drying:* to speed up the drying process of thin models such as plaques, the above temperatures can be increased after the first hour up to 150°C/300°F/gas mark 2 for about 3 hours.

Whichever method you use, keep a constant eye on your work. At the first signs of bubbling, reduce the oven temperature immediately and move the tray into the lower, cooler part of the oven. You can prick the bubble with a pin to

release the air and gently press the dough flat. Prevent the edges on plaques from curling during oven drying by weighting them down with ovenproof objects.

To test if the piece is hard, wear oven gloves to lift it off the tray, as the dough will be very hot. Tap the piece gently on the back – it has a hollow ring to it when ready.

Microwave drying
This is possible but not a method I would recommend. You have to be very careful that your work does not split or bubble in a microwave. To avoid disappointing results and seeing your fine work ruined, experiment with scraps of dough rolled to different thicknesses to gauge the best achievable results.

Remember to use microwave proof utensils and padding for your models when using the microwave to avoid explosions in the oven!

Drying coloured dough
A slow drying process is best for dough that is pre-coloured as this will help it to retain the true colour. Oven temperatures should be 100°C/200°F/gas mark ¼.

BAKED BREAD FINISH
Browning and glazing hardened dough gives it an attractive rustic look, imitating the scrumptious appearance that newly baked bread conjures up in the imagination, and looking good enough to eat! Turn the oven to 200°C/400°F/gas mark 6. Paint the hardened piece

to be browned with a solution of a tablespoon of salt in half a cup of water and dry in the hot oven for 10 minutes. When the dough is dry it will look white. You can now glaze it with a wash of whisked egg. Brown the egg-coated piece in the oven for a few minutes, keeping a close eye on it to prevent it from bubbling; cover the piece with foil if you see this happening. Specific areas of your model may be browned under the grill, which allows you to regulate the depth of colour.

PAINTING DOUGH

It is possible to paint soft dough or to do it after hardening. Poster colour paints are best for this as they are non toxic and do not require spirit-based cleaners, therefore are not harmful for children to use. Water colours can be used too, and they have a beautiful translucent quality on dough. For more solid colours, give your work a base coat of white poster paint before painting.

Use assorted sized brushes to paint your work; finer ones for minute detail and thicker ones for covering large surface areas with paint. See the features illustrated on pages 30–31 to give you inspiration for characterizing your figures. You must let your work dry completely before varnishing.

VARNISHING

Work can be left unvarnished but it will not be so long lasting as moisture from the atmosphere encourages the salt in the dough to crystallize.

There are a variety of varnishes on the market. Check with your craft shop that the varnish and paint you intend to use are compatible with each other. The best varnish to use is a water/poster colour paint varnish, as it allows the true colour to shine through. Clear polyurethane varnishes, such as those used for boats, can be used, but they have a slight yellowing effect when applied. They are ideal for rustic-looking or egg-glazed models. Varnish comes in matt or gloss and you can experiment to see the finish that best suits your requirements.

Make sure you allow the paint 24 hours to dry thoroughly, then give your model at least two coats of varnish to ensure they are long lasting, leaving the varnish to dry thoroughly between coats. Make sure that the varnish coats all the dough layers. For example, it must seep through the layers on stranded hair to protect the model.

Adults should varnish work for children, and it is best carried out in an airy room as the varnish may give off strong vapours that could be an irritant if inhaled. Ensure that varnishes are kept away from naked flames as they are flammable.

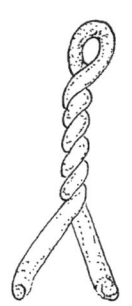

HANGING MODELS

There are several methods of making a hanging device for your models. Some need to be carried out whilst the dough is still soft, others will depend on the weight of your model.

Cocktail stick method

Press the pointed end of the stick into the dough, gently ease the dough and push the stick through to the back. When hard, thread string or ribbon through the hole to hang the model from a hook.

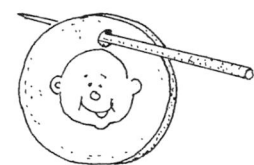

Paper clip

Cut the paper clip in half using wire cutters. Embed half the clip in the top edge of your sample, as in the illustration. This method is fine for light models up to 4 oz (100 g).

String loops

Cut a piece of string to a 4 in (10 cm) in length, fold it in half and secure at the back of the model with two balls of dough. If you are attaching it to a hardened sample you will need dough paste to ensure proper adhesion. This method is suitable for heavier pieces such as the tulip in a plant pot plaque on page 107 or a weight up to about 1¼ lb (550 g).

Linen loops

These can be purchased from picture framers and are ideal for lightweight models. Simply wet the glue on the back of the loop and press on to the back of your hardened model.

Self-hanging loops

A self-hanging loop is made by bending a thin tube of dough in half and twisting the ends together several times, leaving a loop at the top. Fix to the back of the dough with water, or with dough paste if the pieces are hardened.

BACKING MODELS

Models can be neatened on the back with felt, which prevents the rough surface from scratching varnished table tops. Lay the model on the felt and trace around it with a felt pen. Cut the shape to fit the base of the model and glue in position. You can also buy felt discs for this purpose from most hardware shops.

STORAGE

Your work will last for years if you take note of a few tips. Moisture is one of the major reasons for it to become dull, soften and for crystals to form on the surface. It is best that you display your work in even temperatures; over direct heat may cause it to warp and crack. Models are not suited to being out of doors, though can be kept in a porch for a considerable time. Do not leave varnished samples in the direct sunlight as this will fade the colours. If samples do deteriorate, what a good excuse to make some more!

Occasionally wipe the piece with a duster to remove dust and restore the brightness of the colours and varnish. Delicate detailing such as hair needs to be handled with caution, and a hair dryer on a low setting is ideal for blowing the dust away, or use a soft paint brush.

PROBLEM SOLVING

There are very few problems with this craft, and none that is insurmountable. Your models may crack in the oven when drying or through general wear and tear but can easily be restored.

Cracks

◆ If these are caused when rolling out the dough, your dough is too dry. Moisten the dough, knead it and re-roll.

◆ Cracks appearing in the oven implies the heat is too fierce, so reduce it.

◆ Cracks forming after your dough has been hardened are usually due to it not being completely dried out. Ensure the samples are cooled on a wire rack before you paint them.

◆ Cracks may appear in your model after hardening when you add a soft piece of dough to a hardened base. This usually is a sign that the base was not thick enough to tolerate the drying process. See the photograph.

Cracks in your models can be repaired with dough paste and small pieces of dough. Gently sand the area to be repaired before you moisten the crack and fill it with dough. The dough has to be air-dried if the sample is varnished. Re-paint the area and give the whole model a new coat of varnish to freshen up.

A crack or a piece breaking off hardened dough can be repaired as described. If joining in a new section it will need propping up until hard.

Air bubbles

If bubbles appear while the piece is drying, prick the bubble with a pin and gently press the air out of it, then move the piece to a cooler part of the oven to finish off the drying process.

Air bubbles may happen if you have your piece too high under the grill. Use aluminium foil to protect any high spots.

Crystals appearing

Gently sand the area and allow the piece to dry in the air before giving it a fresh coat of varnish. Check where the piece was displayed, as it must have been in a moist environment.

Dough collapsing

If your dough is too moist your models may collapse in the oven or before you get to that stage! Add more flour to your mixture and re-knead it.

Your figure may need supporting in the oven or padding with foil. The dough is quite heavy even when hard.

Cracks can be repaired with dough paste or pieces of dough so your finished sample will look perfect

CHAPTER FIVE

MOTHER AND BABY

Babies on blankets **

- *Assorted sizes from 2 in (5 cm) to 3 in (7.5 cm) long*
- *1 quantity of the fine dough (see page 12)*

These cute little babies make fun decorations and can be glued on a gift-wrapped parcel or greetings card. They are modelled using the reclining figure method on page 30. Sit or lie the figure on a dough or felt blanket.

Mini babies **

- *Measure about 2½ in (6 cm) long*
- *1 quantity of the fine dough (see page 12)*

These appealing little babies are simple once you have made the basic figure shape. Follow the step-by-step instructions for figures on page 30, reducing the scale. Study a baby or look at a baby catalogue to see the funny things they do with their feet and hands. All these add to the charm of the final model. Sit the baby on a dough blanket or wrap one around it; lie the baby on its back or front. Make a girl or a boy, adding the appropriate appendage! Bend the arms and legs into typical baby poses.

Decorated gift basket with frill *

- ◆ *Double-lidded basket measures about 48 in (122 cm) in circumference by 8¾ in (22 cm) deep*
- ◆ *Printed fabric for frill needs to be double the circumference of the basket by 8 in (20 cm) deep*
- ◆ *1 quantity of the fine dough (see page 12)*

1. Remove the lids from the basket by untying the threads attaching them to the basket.

2. Model three large roses about 2 in (4 cm) in diameter, five rosebuds about 1 in (2.5 cm) long and three leaves about 1½ in (4 cm) long to decorate each basket lid. Use the modelling method for roses and leaves on page 23.

3. Moisten the middle of the lids with water, then press the modelled pieces gently on to the wicker, ensuring they stay in position as they harden. Harden the decorated lids in the oven.

4. Make the frill using the method below before securing the lids back on to the basket.

Frill

1. Halve the strips of fabric and hem all the way around with a ½ in (12 mm) hem. Run a line of machine gathering stitches down the middle of each strip and draw up into gathers to fit half the circumference of the basket.

2. Lay the gathered strip over the edge of the basket and sew in position with small tacking stitches. It is best to use a long needle such as a beading needle, enabling you to sew stitches through the wicker from front to back.

3. Where the strips meet at the sides, catch the edges together with small hand sewn stitches. To complete, sew a ribbon bow each side of the basket handle.

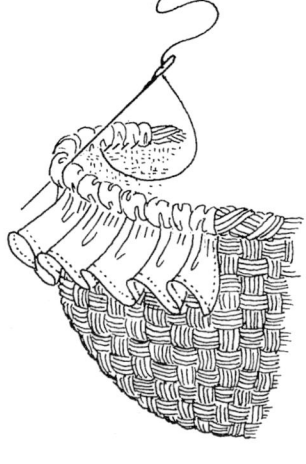

Use a long beading needle to sew the frill to the basket

Strawberry-decorated basket with fabric cover **

- *Basket measures 13 x 9¼ x 4 in (32.5 x 23.5 x 10 cm)*
- *1 quantity of the fine dough (see page 12)*

1. Model three strawberries 1 in (2.5 cm) long, two flowers ¾ in (2 cm) in diameter and six leaves 1¼ in (3 cm) long on the basket using the methods on pages 22–23. Moisten the basket before pressing the decorations on to it. Harden in the oven.

2. Paint and varnish the flowers and fruit before attaching the fabric cover.

Cover
1. Cut a strip of fabric 10 in (25.5 cm) wide and 44 in (110 cm) long. Seam the two short ends together by machine on the wrong side of the fabric. Make a ½ in (12 mm) hem on one long edge, leaving an opening for inserting the ribbon.

2. Sew the raw edge of the fabric to the inside edge of the basket. A long beading needle is best for sewing through the gaps in the basket.

3. Insert a 36 in (1 m) length of ribbon in the channel at the top of the fabric and draw it up to close the opening.

Strawberries in a basket plaque *

- *Straw base measures 10 in (25 cm) in diameter*
- *1 quantity of the basic dough (see page 12)*

1. Pad the inside of the basket with kitchen paper to fill the excess space.

2. Model the strawberries on the basket and the base using the method for making strawberries on page 21 and making different-sized fruits to add authenticity. Harden the fruit in stages so the ones on top have a firm foundation to support them as they harden.

3. Make some leaves and add a few flowers (see pages 22–23) to give colour contrast. You will need about fifteen large strawberries, five small and ten flowers for a basket of the above measurements.

4. Harden the final arrangement before painting and varnishing. A colour co-ordinated ribbon bow can be added to complete the effect.

Potty training **

- *Measures 4 in (10 cm) high*
- *1 quantity of the basic dough (see page 12)*

1. Shape the potty base from a 2 in (5 cm) diameter ball of dough. Press your index fingers into the middle of the ball and use them to hollow it slightly. Cut a circular piece of dough for the rim, large enough to fit the potty base and just under a ¼ in (6 mm) thick. Make a hole in the middle of the rim using an icing nozzle to cut out the dough. Mosten the rim and fix it on the base, then harden it in the oven.

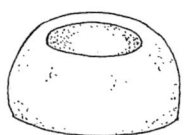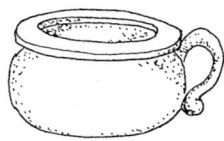

Shape the potty with your fingers

2. Model the back view of the figure on the hardened pot, using dough paste to secure it in position. See figure section on pages 25–26 for the modelling technique. For greater authenticity, remember to add baby's dimples!

3. After hardening, paint and varnish the model.

4. Make the bath hat from a 2 in (5 cm) circular piece of fabric cut out with pinking shears, then gathered with small running stitches to fit the baby's head. Glue the hat on to the head.

Make a mini-pot using the same method as for the potty

You have to be careful with these cards, as the more fragile ones may not stand up to the rigours of the postal service. Most will be fine if wrapped in a padded envelope or bubble-wrap.

Model and harden the pieces, then paint and varnish them before gluing them on to stiff coloured card. Use a variety of decorations such as ribbons and bows to complete the models.

Bonnet *

- *Measures 2 in (5 cm) long by 1½ in (4 cm) wide*
- *¼ quantity of the fine dough (see page 12)*

1. Make a half circle to the above measurements using the pattern on page 115 as a guide, then use a nutmeg grater to reproduce the knitted texture of a baby's bonnet.

2. Form a scalloped-edged strip using an appropriate icing cutter. Attach the strip on to the long edge of the bonnet with water.

3. After hardening, paint and varnish the bonnet before gluing the ribbon trim along the edge.

Socks *

- *Measure 2½ in (6 cm) square*
- *¼ quantity of the fine dough (see page 12)*

1. Roll out the dough to ¼ in (6 mm) thick. Cut out two sock shapes the dough, using the pattern on page 115 as a guide.

2. Cut two strips of dough for the rolled cuff and attach them over the top straight edge of each sock, rolling forwards on to itself. Mark the cuffs with lines, imitating the ribbing on a knitted sock. Lay one sock over the other, bonding with water, then harden them.

3. Paint and varnish the socks before gluing the decorative bow on to the topmost sock.

Baby rompers *

♦ *Measure 2 in (5 cm)*
♦ *¼ quantity of the fine dough (see page 12)*

1. Cut the rompers from a sheet of dough, using the illustration from the clothes section on pages 32–34 as a guide. Mark the detailing with a pointed knife.

2. After the dough has hardened, paint and varnish the rompers.

3. Stick them to the card over a large nappy pin.

Washing line of clothes *

♦ *Dungarees measure 2½ in (6 cm) long*
♦ *¼ quantity of the fine dough (see page 12)*

1. Cut each item of clothing from a sheet of dough, using the illustrations from the clothes section on pages 32–34 as a guide. Mark the detailing with a pointed knife.

2. After hardening, paint and varnish the clothes.

3. Glue a length of crochet cotton on to the card for the washing line. Glue the clothing along the line, attaching purchased pegs before the glue dries. These are found in stationers or doll's house suppliers.

Baby pram *

♦ *Measures 2½ in (6 cm)*
♦ *¼ quantity of the fine dough (see page 12)*

1. Cut out the pram shapes from a sheet of dough, using the pattern on page 115 as a guide.

2. Assemble the pieces, moistening them with water, and mark the patterns with a knife.

3. After hardening, paint and varnish the model.

Christening robe *

♦ *Measures 2½ in (6 cm) long*
♦ *¼ quantity of the fine dough (see page 12)*

1. Model a dress to the above length, using the illustrations in the clothes section on pages 32–34 as a guide. Use the point of a knife to shape and mark detail such as the smocking.

2. After hardening, paint and varnish the model. Add a fabric bow at the top of the card.

Mum plaque *

- *Measures 9 x 6 in (23 x 15 cm)*
- *1 quantity of the basic dough for the plaque (see page 12)*
- *1 quantity of the fine dough for the flowers (see page 12)*

1. Roll a piece of dough to a thickness of about ½ in (12 mm) and large enough to cut the oval shape of the above measurements from it for the plaque base. Add a dough twist around the edge. Make a hole at the top for hanging (see page 39).

2. Cut the ribbon strip from thinly rolled dough, angling the ends as photographed, and lay in the middle section on the oval. Pleat the strip each side of the plaque.

3. Model the flowers following the methods in the flower section on pages 22–23.

4. Make strands of dough by pressing a piece of dough through a garlic press. Shape single strands of dough into letters.

Baby sleeping door knob indicator **

- *Measures 10 x 7 in (25.5 x 18 cm)*
- *1 quantity of the basic dough (see page 12)*

1. Roll the dough into a flat sheet ½ in (12 mm) thick. Cut out an oblong shape to the above measurements. Curve the dough as shown with a craft knife. Ensure the hook shape fits over the door knob from which it is to hang.

2. Use the outline on page 114 as a guide for the sleeping baby and cloud. Make the pillow from an oblong piece of dough about 1½ in (4 cm) long and 1¼ in (3 cm) deep. Attach a dough or fabric frill around its edge. Position the pillow on the dough base and secure with water. (If attaching a fabric frill, glue the frill on after varnishing.)

3. Model the profile of the baby's head over the pillow from a ball of dough about 1 in (2.5 cm) in diameter. Cut a cloud shape from a flat piece of dough and lay to the left of the head, working the rest of the baby's body over it. See the section on figure-making on pages 24–26 for a more detailed method for making the body section.

4. Harden the plaque before painting and varnishing. Add adhesive stars and write a message to warn that baby is asleep such as: Shh! Quiet! or Baby sleeping! These can be written in felt pen or painted.

Name plaques *

◆ *Measure about 6 in (15 cm) square*
◆ *1 quantity of the basic dough or strong extensible dough (see page 12)*

Name plaques make excellent gifts as you can personalize them for the recipients. For a newborn baby, put the baby's name, date of birth and weight on your plaque. An older baby or child can have relevant features and added hair colour.

1. Roll the dough to a flat sheet between ¼ in (6 mm) and ½ in (12 mm) thick.

2. Cut out the size and outline of your choice with a craft knife, taking care not to stretch or tear the dough. A flan ring makes an ideal cutter for cutting out a scalloped-edged plaque.

3. Make a hanging loop on the back or a hole at the top of the plaque for a ribbon or hook (see page 39). The plaque with the ribbon inserts can have a colour co-ordinated ribbon for a boy or girl inserted after painting and varnishing. Make the eyelet holes with the blunt end of a bamboo or metal skewer.

4. Next model the plaque details on to the base, and bond the dough pieces with water. The featured ideas should give you inspiration for your own original designs.

5. Harden, then paint the plaque. For a rustic finish, give the plaque an egg glaze.

6. Add fabric trims to make the plaque more realistic, such as the gathered frill collars on the twins' plaque. Use adhesive lettering for adding the names or dates to the plaque. Add a hanging ribbon.

◆ ◆ ◆ ◆ ◆ ◆ ◆ ◆ ◆ ◆ ◆ ◆ ◆

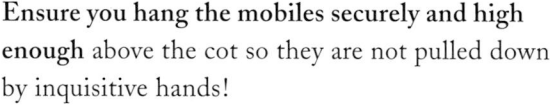

Mobiles *

- ◆ *Assorted sizes*
- ◆ *1 quantity of the basic dough (see page 12)*

These are not the portable telephones popular today, but the hanging variety that will amuse babies for hours as they lie in their cots! There are many ways to make them. The simplest are made from dough shapes cut out with biscuit cutters; the more colourful they are, the more eye-catching they will be to a baby. Experiment with a variety of decorations. The contents of your sewing basket is likely to have a range of suitable items such as beads, sequins or transfers that are ideal glued on to the flat base.

Mobile frame
1. Cut the pointed ends off three bamboo skewers. Cut two bars to three-quarters of the length of the other bar. The longer one forms the main bar with the two shorter ones hanging from it.

2. Glue wooden beads at each end of the three bars. Sew a ribbon hanging loop over the centre of the long bar, and knot crochet cotton threads of equal length to the ends of this bar.

3. Attach the short bars to each side of the long bar by knotting the free ends of the crochet threads over their centre points.

Ensure you hang the mobiles securely and high enough above the cot so they are not pulled down by inquisitive hands!

Tie threads of equal length to the ends of the short bars to suspend your mobile shapes.

Mobile shapes
Cut four shapes from thinly rolled dough about ¼ in (6 mm) thick. Keep the four models to the same size and weight so the mobiles are balanced when they swing. Harden and paint each shape on both sides before you attach it to the threads and knot them on the mobile.

◆ ◆ ◆ ◆ ◆ ◆ ◆ ◆ ◆ ◆ ◆ ◆ ◆

Teddy bear swag *

◆ *Teddy measures 6 in (15 cm) high*
◆ *1 quantity of the basic dough (see page 12)*

This charming swag comes to life with the pretty patterns painted to give it the look of printed cotton fabrics. Base your patterns on a selection of mini prints; mail order fabric suppliers have an excellent stock of samples that you can obtain cheaply that will give you something to copy. Why not make a swag to adorn a fireplace for Christmas? Bears painted in a tartan design would look striking.

1. Make a template of the bear shape in card using the outline from the pattern section on page 113.

2. Cut as many bear shapes as you require from a sheet of dough rolled to a thickness of about ¼ in (6 mm) to fill the width of the area you wish to hang your swag, such as across a fireplace.

Cut out the hearts with a heart-shaped biscuit cutter. Make a hole in the front paws and each side of the hearts with a cocktail stick so that you can thread all the bears and hearts on to the hanging ribbon to join them up into the swag.

3. Each bear has a raised snout made from a flattened disc of dough of about ½ in (12 mm) in diameter. Mark a horizontal slit below the nose with a knife for the mouth and mark the eyes with a bamboo skewer.

4. Harden, then paint the models.

5. Thread the ribbon through the holes to join the pieces up into the swag. Knot the ends of the ribbons into loops to hang up the swag.

Decorated sweet basket **

- *Basket measures 7 in (18 cm) wide by 5 in (13 cm) deep*
- *Figure measures about 2 in (5 cm) long*
- *1 quantity of the basic dough (see page 12)*

This is easy if you have already made a flat figure. If not, follow the method for figure-making on pages 24–26.

1. Wet the inside edge of the basket to ensure the arm section bonds to it. Model the U shape for the arms with the hands attached and press it on to the wet section of the wicker work. Insert a 1 in (2.5 cm) long piece of cocktail stick at the top for attaching the head.

Model the arms as if the figure is climbing out of the basket

2. Roll a piece of dough about 1¼ in (3 cm) in diameter to a ball for the head and sit it on the cocktail stick, moistening the two surfaces with water for better adhesion.

3. Harden the basket in the oven. You will need to put an ovenproof weight in the bottom of the basket to stop it tipping up.

4. Paint and varnish the hardened figure. Fill the basket with a selection of sweets, or chocolate eggs at Easter.

For an alternative version, model an elf figure using the figure method on page 30 around the handle of the basket.

Decorative dummy *

- *Measures 3½ in (9 cm) long*
- *¼ quantity of the basic dough (see page 12)*

1. Roll out a sheet of dough about ¼ in (6 mm) thick and cut out a disc 2 in (5 cm) in diameter. Harden it in the oven.

2. Model the teat section from a length of dough about 2 in (5 cm) long and 1 in (2.5 cm) in diameter and secure it to the hardened disc with dough paste. Attach a hanging loop made from a tube of dough measuring 4 in (10 cm) long and ½ in (12 mm) in diameter to the top of the disc. Harden the model.

3. Paint and varnish the dummy when cool.

4. Tie a hanging ribbon to the loop for hanging on a Champagne bottle; this would make an original decorative gift to take to a new mother in hospital. This is not for baby!

Gift wrapping ideas **

- *Assorted sizes*
- *1 quantity of the basic dough or fine dough (see page 12)*

You can model small baby figures on dough blankets using the figure method from page 30, or the head of the child to whom the gift is to be given. Glue the finished model on to the wrapped parcel or a luggage label or gift tag. Make your own labels from coloured card with ribbon ties. See the hat-making section on page 34 for ideas on making mob caps and bonnets.

You can personalise your gift tags and decorations for Christmas or other presents

CHAPTER SIX

ALPHABET AND NUMBERS

ROLLED DOUGH IDEAS

These are made using the rolled dough method.
You can make them any size, and embellish
them in all kinds of interesting ways.
Use them to decorate plaques, to make
initial badges, fridge magnets or
brooches – and that's just a few
ideas to start you off.

Letters of the alphabet **

- ◆ *Measure 4½ in (11. 5 cm) high*
- ◆ *2–3 quantities of the basic dough for the full alphabet (see page 12)*

The letters of the alphabet are easily made using the twisted dough method on page 18. You can also make them from a simple tube of dough and paint it with pretty mini prints to resemble padded tubes of fabric. Give your letters an egg glaze for a rustic finish, then decorate them with dough flowers, animals or whatever sparks your imagination – there are endless possibilities. Experiment with the ones featured to get you off to a good start. Make up your child's name in dough letters and glue the letters on to a hardboard base with a wooden frame surround. Initials can have individual hanging hooks enabling them to be hung on a bedroom door (see page 39).

Numbers **

- ◆ *Measure 4 in (10 cm) high*
- ◆ *1 quantity of the basic dough or fine dough (see page 12)*

The foundation for the numbers are simply made from tubes of dough and the decorations are miniature animals. The above alphabet ideas can be used to decorate your numbers. Glue the numbers on to coloured card for a birthday, or stick a brooch pin on the reverse to make them into brooches.

Decorated letters for name plaques *

- ◆ *Assorted sizes*
- ◆ *1 quantity of the basic dough (see page 12)*

These are great for personalized gifts. You can make the letters in a two-tone effect, one colour with a glaze finish, or paint patterns on them to resemble padded fabric tubes.

1. The letters are made from single tubes of dough or dough twists (see pages 17–18).

2. Arrange the letters according to your child's name. If adding the bear decoration, use it to fill the open spaces between the letters.

3. The completed letters can be glued on to a painted hardboard base with tile adhesive, or in an appropriately sized picture frame.

CHAPTER SEVEN

PLAQUES

Mrs Bear with pram **

- *Measures 8 in (20 cm) high by 9 in (23 cm) wide*
- *1 quantity of the basic dough (see page 12)*

1. Model Mrs Bear in profile, using the flat-figure method on pages 24–26, and the outline on page 115. Shape her paws to appear as though holding the pram handle.

2. Make the pram from two semi-circles of dough. The base is about 4 in (10 cm) across the straight edge and the hood is about 2 in (5 cm) along the straight edge. Indent these with the rough side of a nutmeg grater to resemble the basket weave and fabric textures. Add the wheels and the quilt.

3. Roll a piece of dough to a thickness of ½ in (12 mm) and shape it into an oval for the 'grass base' to fit Mrs Bear and the pram. It measures about 7 in (18 cm) wide x 4 in (10 cm) deep. Moisten the dough base and lay Mrs Bear and the pram over it, pressing them gently down to adhere. Add the flower and grass details.

4. Harden the completed model in the oven, then paint and varnish it.

The plaque is delicate so it needs to be glued on to a firm base such as a cork notice board. If you do not want to do this, you will need to make a dough base, harden, paint and varnish it, then fix it behind the figure and pram for support.

Baby girl **

- *Measures 10 in (25 cm) high*
- *2 quantities of the basic dough (see page 12)*

Time permitting, make these plaques in stages to ensure all the layers of dough are dry before the next one is added. Use dough paste to attach each new layer or piece of dough.

1. Model the figure using the basic figure method on pages 24–26 to the length above. Pad the stomach area with dough, giving the figure a chubby appearance.

2. Roll out two triangles of dough for the sleeves, which are large enough to cover the arms. Allow enough fullness in the dough to be gathered. Moisten the arms, lay the sleeves on top and pinch the dough down the lengths to form it into soft gathers.

3. Roll a piece of dough to a large flat sheet of about ¼ in (6 mm) thick. Cut out the play suit shape, allowing enough dough to cover the body and the feet, and be tucked under all the way around the edges, including the feet.

4. Snip up the middle of the dough to make a division for the legs. Moisten the body and lay the dough suit over it. Press it down around the edges and pinch it into gathers at the ankles.
   Bond the dough neatly at the armhole seams with a little water.

Add gathered lace frills to the dough play suit

Pinch dough into gathers at the ankles

Tuck dough under at edge for a rounded effect

5. Attach a string hanging loop at the back of the model (see page 39).

6. Harden the figure in the oven, then paint and varnish when it is cold.

7. Glue broderie anglaise frills at the neck and on the cuffs. These are made by gathering three 6 in (15 cm) lengths of scalloped broderie anglaise with small running stitches. Draw the thread up to form gathered strips to fit the wrists and neckline of the model (see illustration opposite).

8. The hat is made from the top half of a baby's sock (see page 34). Glue a purchased milk bottle in the baby's hand to complete the effect.

Baby boy **

- ◆ *Measures 10 in (25 cm) high*
- ◆ *2 quantities of the basic dough (see page 12)*

This chubby little boy has chocolate food colouring added to the basic recipe to darken his skin tone. Experiment with coffee, cocoa powder or turmeric to achieve a variety of skin colours.

1. Model the figure to the above length using the method from the technique section on pages 24–26. Make the teddy bear to match the scale of the boy figure.

2. The jumper is modelled over the arms and body section before the dungarees. See the clothes section on pages 32–34 for more detail. If you are hardening the figure in stages, remember the right arm is clutching the teddy bear. This will have to be added after the dungarees so the bear lies over them.

Personalise the dungarees with your child's initial if you wish

3. Finish off the figure as given for the baby girl. Make the hat from a baby's sock, but do not cut off the toe and heel section as they are knotted to form little ears.

Make the dungarees in sections, joining the dough with water

Drummer boy **

- ◆ *Measures 9 in (23 cm) high*
- ◆ *1 quantity of the basic dough (see page 12)*

1. Model the figure using the figure-making method on pages 24–26. Fashion the arms and hands to appear as though they are beating the drum with the sticks. The hands will need propping in position during the hardening process with foil.

Drummer boy's face

Ballerina **

- ◆ *Measures 9 in (23 cm) high*
- ◆ *1 quantity of the basic dough (see page 12)*

The method for making the ballerina is given in the figure-making section on page 26. Fix a hanging loop to the back (see page 39). Paint and varnish the figure before adding the clothes.

Clothes

1. For the skirt you will need a strip of lace 12 in (30 cm) long and 6 in (15 cm) deep. To gather it up, sew a line of running stitches about 4 in (10 cm) down from the top edge. Draw the thread up into gathers, then fold the top edge of the lace down to form the tier effect of the skirt. Tie the thread around the waist of the ballerina.

2. The bodice and bra-cups are made from a piece of scalloped lace 2 in (5 cm) long and 1 in (2.5 cm) deep that is glued on to the body and over the breasts.

2. Make the drum sticks from halved pieces of cocktail stick and beads stuck on to the ends. You can use a purchased Christmas tree decoration for the drum. Impress the drum on the body to indent the dough, which allows it to be glued in position after hardening. Fix a hanging loop to the back (see page 39).

3. Harden the figure, then paint and varnish. Use lampshade braid for the shoulder straps, gluing them to the body and the drum.

Juggling clown **

◆ *Measures 10 in (25 cm) high*
◆ *2 quantities of the basic dough (see page 12)*

This cheerful chap is a riot of colour and would look great on a nursery wall. Model the figure first, using the figure method on pages 24–26. Note the hands have holes in them to hold the wire that supports the paper balls.

Clown's face

1. Make the clown's suit in the same way as for the baby girl (see page 56). Remember to moisten the figure before adding each new layer of dough. The frilled collar and cuffs are made from dough cut out with a scalloped-shaped biscuit cutter. See the clothes section on pages 32–34 for an explanation of this method. The feet are made from long, flattened tubes of dough curled up at the ends.

2. Harden the figure. Fix a hanging loop to the back (see page 39). Thread the cotton balls on to the wire and glue them at evenly spaced intervals along the wire. Curve the wire into a U shape, then glue the ends of the wire securely in the holes on the hands. Paint the clown in bright colours, then varnish to complete the figure.

Babies in the bath **

- ◆ *Measures 10 in (25 cm) square*
- ◆ *2 quantities of the basic dough (see page 12)*

1. Use the outline on page 114 as a modelling guide. Make the bath from an oblong piece of dough measuring 7 in (18 cm) wide, 3¼ in (8 cm) deep and ½ in (12 mm) thick and curve each side of the lower edge. Fashion the rim of the bath from a thin tube of dough and model the legs and the feet as featured.

2. Model the babies over the top edge of the bath. They need padding behind their backs with dough so they stand away from the work surface.

Tiny balls of dough are used to form the bubbles around the figures. Harden the figures.

3. Roll a piece of dough to a large sheet measuring ½ in (12 mm) thick and cut a 10 in (25 cm) square piece of dough from it for the wall behind the bath. Secure the bath on to the base with dough paste. Shape the window and curtains around the babies in the bath. Make a hole in the plaque for hanging (see page 39) and then harden the model.

4. Paint and varnish the completed plaque before adding the mob caps; the method is explained under hats in the clothes section on page 34.

CHAPTER EIGHT

GARLANDS

BRAIDS AND TWISTS

Most of the garlands use the rolled dough technique on page 17, using a braided or twisted shape decorated with a variety of features. You can also use purchased cane or straw garlands and add your own decorations. All the garlands need a hanging loop, and you will find full details of these on page 39.

Baby asleep in a garland **

- *Measures 7 in (18 cm) in diameter*
- *1 quantity of the fine dough (see page 12)*

1. Roll two tubes of dough 14 in (35 cm) long and ¾ in (2 cm) in diameter, then twist them together. Cut the ends of the tubes at an angle, then moisten the ends and press one over the other to seal.

2. Model the baby in a play suit using the figure method on page 30. Secure the baby figure firmly on the inner curved edge of the garland with a little water.

3. Use a small petal-shaped icing cutter to cut out forget-me-not flowers from pre-coloured blue dough. Roll tiny balls of yellow dough about the diameter of a bamboo skewer, put one in the middle of each flower and indent it with a cocktail stick for the centre.

4. Add a hanging loop (see page 39). Harden the garland before painting and varnishing. Tie a ribbon bow at the top to complete the sample.

Heart-shaped garland decorated with flowers *

- *Measures 9 in (23 cm) long*
- *2 quantities of the basic dough (see page 12)*

1. Roll two tubes of dough 20 in (50 cm) long and 1¼ in (3 cm) in diameter, then twist them together to form the heart base. Cut the ends at an angle, then moisten the ends and press them firmly together. Form the circle into a heart shape by denting at the top and pinching in at the base.

2. Use pre-coloured dough to model groups of flowers and leaves around the topmost edge of the heart. For the flower and leaf methods see pages 22–23.

3. Add a hanging loop (see page 39). Harden the garland and tie a ribbon bow to complete the model.

Rustic garland **

- *Measures 10 in (25.5 cm) in diameter*
- *2 quantities of the basic dough (see page 12)*

1. Roll three tubes each measuring 24 in (60 cm) long and ¾ in (2 cm) in diameter, then plait them together. Cut the ends at an angle, moisten the ends and join the tubes into a ring.

2. Make the roses and leaves using the methods on pages 22–23. Indent the surface of the leaves with the teeth of a comb to achieve the ridged effect. Fashion a heart to imitate one made in lace as featured. Use a cocktail stick to make the eyelets on the lace.

3. Model the babies using the reclining figure method on page 30.

4. Add a hanging loop (see page 39). Harden the model in the oven, then give it a salt water and egg glaze and brown in the oven for a rustic look (see pages 37–38).

5. Complete the garland with a brown ribbon bow tied at the top. Write the baby's name in felt pen or use transfer lettering on the heart.

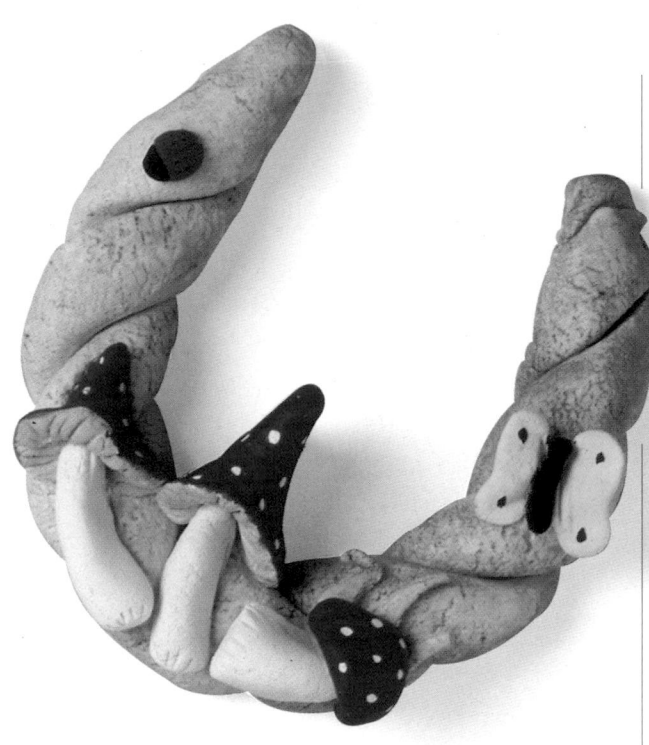

Horseshoe-shaped garland*

- *Measures 7 in (18 cm) in diameter*
- *1 quantity of the basic dough (see page 12)*

1. Roll a tube of dough 14 in (35 cm) long and ¾ in (2 cm) in diameter. Twist the tubes together and fashion the U shape from the twisted dough. Pinch the ends together and make a hole in each end for inserting a ribbon hanging loop.

2. Make the mushrooms, ladybird and butterfly as featured in the photograph, moisten and fix to the garland.

3. Harden the garland in the oven and give the U shape section an egg-glaze finish (see pages 37–38).

4. To complete the effect, you can thread a ribbon through the holes at the top and tie in a bow for a hanging garland.

Doily garland*

- *Measures 8 in (20 cm) in diameter*
- *1 quantity of the basic dough (see page 12)*
- *1 quantity of the fine dough (see page 12)*

1. Roll two tubes of basic dough to 18 in (46 cm) long and ¾ in (2 cm) in diameter, then twist them together. Cut, moisten and seal the ends into a circle.

2. Add a hanging loop (see page 39). Harden the garland, then give it an egg glaze.

3. Model ten to fifteen flowers from pre-coloured fine dough over a flattened disc of dough that measures the diameter of the inner part of the doily collar. Make a few loose flowers to glue around the collar's inner edge.

4. Glue the decorated doily collar on to the dough base. Twist the ribbon round the garland. Finish with a bow at the top.

Plaited dough garland*

- ◆ *Measures 9 in (23 cm) in diameter*
- ◆ *1 quantity of the basic dough (see page 12)*

1. Roll out three tubes of dough each measuring 14 in (50 cm) long and ¾ in (2 cm) in diameter, then plait them together. Cut the ends at an angle, moisten the ends and join the dough up into a ring.

2. Add a hanging loop (see page 39), then harden the garland.

3. Paint the dough tubes with a selection of mini printed fabric designs. Add a matching ribbon bow to finish.

Sweetie garland*

- ◆ *Measures 6 in (15 cm) in diameter*
- ◆ *1 quantity of the basic dough (see page 12)*

1. Roll two tubes of dough 14 in (35 cm) long and ¾ in (2 cm) in diameter, then twist them together. Cut, moisten and seal the ends of the tubes into a circle.

2. Model the centre of the sweet shapes from ¾ in (2 cm) long by ½ in (12 mm) wide oblongs of dough. The twists at each end of the sweets are made from strips of dough with one scalloped edge. When you attach the frills to the middle section, pinch the straight edge into gathers and press one frill at each side with water.

3. Add a hanging loop (see page 39), then harden, paint and varnish the garland. Add a ribbon bow to complete.

Winter garland **

- *Measures 10 in (5.5 cm) in diameter*
- *1 quantity of the basic dough (see page 12)*

1. Use a plaited straw ring from a craft shop as a base. Using the figure method on pages 24–26, model two figures each side of the ring as featured. The arms and legs are worked over the straw to resemble a clinging figure. Moisten and fix to the ring.

2. Harden the dough-decorated ring in the oven.

3. Paint the figures and varnish before gluing on the felt hats and knitted scarves. See page 34 for hat method.

4. Glue or wire a bunch of acorns or similar greenery in the middle of the lower edge. Tie a ribbon bow at the top and fix a hanging loop at the back (see page 39).

PICTURE FRAMES

DOUGH OR WOODEN FRAMES

Frames can be made in dough, or you can decorate purchased wooden frames with dough. Our selection will inspire you to come up with your own ideas.

Rabbits-decorated frame **

◆ *Measures 12 x 10 in (30 x 25.5 cm)*
◆ *1 quantity of the basic dough (see page 12)*

The frame support is made from four lengths of wooden door frame surround. The ends of each piece have been mitred to form the rectangle, and to achieve this you will need a mitre box and saw. Follow the manufacturer's instructions on the mitre box for making cut angles in the wood. The four corners are tacked together with panel pins on the reverse. Alternatively, use a purchased frame which has a deep border surround.

1. Model the figures as though in a sitting position over the moistened frame to ensure they adhere. See figure-making on pages 24–26 for the modelling technique. Make the ladybird to sit at the top of the frame. Harden the figures before painting and varnishing.

2. Use masking tape to secure the photo at the back of the frame. Cut a piece of felt to the same size and glue it on the back to neaten. Screw a hanging loop at the top of the frame on the reverse.

Teddy-decorated frame *

- *Measures 8 x 6 in (20 x 15 cm)*
- *1 quantity of the basic dough (see page 12)*

1. This is made in the same way as the rabbits-decorated frame. You can make a wooden frame yourself, or use a purchased frame as the base. Make a dough twist to fit the border of the frame before making the bear. See technique section on

page 18 for dough twist and page 26 for the bear shape. Moisten the wood to ensure the twist adheres to it.

2. Harden the decorated frame before giving it an egg-glaze finish (see pages 37–38).

3. Screw a hanging loop at the top of the frame on the reverse.

Patchwork frame *

◆ *Measures about 7 in (18 cm) square*
◆ *1 quantity of the basic dough (see page 12)*

1. Roll a piece of dough to 7 in (18 cm) square and about ¾ in (2 cm) thick. Cut the middle out of the square with a heart-shaped biscuit cutter for the photo.

2. Mark a diamond pattern in the dough with the point of a kitchen knife.

3. Harden the frame in the oven before painting it with mini prints to simulate a patchwork effect. Varnish or leave matt.

4. Secure the photo at the back of the frame with masking tape. Neaten the reverse of the frame with a piece of felt cut to size and glued in position. Glue a linen hanging loop at the back (see page 39).

Basket frame **

- *Measures 5 in (13 cm) square*
- *1 quantity of the fine dough (see page 12)*

1. Model the basket from a half circle of dough about 4½ in (11.5 cm) wide and 3½ in (9 cm) deep and mark the surface with a basket weave design with the point of a kitchen knife. Make a twisted dough handle using the twisted dough method on page 18 and attach it as featured.

2. Use floral icing cutters to cut out small flower shapes and attach them to the basket with water.

3. Secure the photo at the back of the dough frame with masking tape. Neaten the reverse of the frame with a piece of felt cut to size and glued in position. Glue a linen hanging loop at the back (see page 39).

Heart-shaped frames *

- *Assorted sizes*
- *1 quantity of the basic dough (see page 12)*

Use an assortment of heart-shaped biscuit cutters to make these frames. The modelling and finishing methods are the same as for the other dough frames featured.

Chapter Ten

Room Decorations

Teddy bear clock **

- *Measures 12 in (30 cm) high*
- *Clock face measures 7½ in (19 cm) in diameter*
- *1 quantity of the basic dough (see page 12)*
- *1 quantity of the strong extensible dough (see page 12)*

1. Roll out the extensible dough to ¼ in (6 mm) thick and 7½ in (19 cm) in diameter. Make a circular card template to the correct diameter from the outline on page 119, then cut round it with a craft knife to make the clock face. Make a hole in the centre to insert the clock movement, then harden the dough.

2. Make a deep circular dough rim ¾ in (2 cm) wide and ¼ in (6 mm) deep and bond it with dough paste to the outer edge of the clock face.

3. Use the outline from the pattern section on page 119 for modelling the bear. Pad the mouth section from underneath the snout with scraps of dough to give a rounded, chubby appearance. Attach a string loop on the back of the bear's head for hanging the clock (see page 39).

4. Mark the features on the face and paws with the point of a kitchen knife.

5. Harden the model before painting and varnishing.

6. When the model has completely dried, glue on the toy eyes, a ribbon bow and adhesive transfer numbers. Attach a purchased clock movement at the back, following the manufacturer's instructions for fitting.

Decorated coat hangers *

- *Heads measure 2 in (5 cm) deep*
- *1 quantity of the basic dough (see page 12)*

1. Model an animal head using the ideas on page 31 or your child's head, in the middle of the bar of the coat hanger below the metal hook. Fix to the hanger with water.

2. Harden the shape on the hanger. Paint and varnish the model when it is dry. You can personalize the hanger by painting a name on the bar in enamel paint or with a felt pen.

Clown book ends *

- ◆ *Seated figure measures 6 in (15 cm) high*
- ◆ *1 quantity of the basic dough (see page 12)*

The clowns show the finishing methods of a painted figure and an egg-glazed figure, each with its own individual charm. You can make wooden book ends or buy them from a mail order craft supplier, many of which are listed in the directory at the back of wood craft magazines.

1. Model two heads measuring 2 in (5 cm) in diameter, press a cocktail stick half way into the heads, then harden them.

2. Fashion the bodies in a lying down position, using the figure method on page 30. Dress them in play suits using the same technique as for the juggling clown on page 59. Insert the cocktail stick protruding from the heads at the top of the body sections and bond firmly to the bodies with a little dough paste.

3. Moisten the inside section of the book ends with water and sit one clown on each. Position the legs with the knees up and place the hands over the knees holding the wooden ball. Harden the figures in the oven.

4. Paint or egg glaze (see pages 37–38) the figures. The book end supporting the painted clown has been given a coat of enamel paint.

Rabbit-decorated money box ***

- *Bottle measures 10 in (25.5 cm) high*
- *1 quantity of the basic dough (see page 12)*

Not just a money box, this charming item has an open holder attached which can be used for keeping a bottle, pencils or other bits and pieces.

1. You will require two empty tins as formers, one 17 fl oz (500 ml) sized lager tin as a former for the baby's bottle and one 14 oz (400 g) sized tin for the bottle holder.

2. Roll a piece of dough to a flat sheet ¼ in (6 mm) thick, and long and wide enough to wrap around the lager tin. Trim the excess dough away. Oil or cover the tin with baking parchment, wrap the dough around the tin and neaten the join with water, smoothing it flat with your fingers.

3. Make a second tube as the above but to half its depth over the tin former. Harden both tubes in the oven. Ease the tins from out of the dough tubes once cooled.

4. Model a teat shape in dough and sit it on a circle of dough that is the same diameter as the lager tin. See the details for the dummy on page 51 for more detail of making this section of the bottle. Make a cut in the circular base of the teat to be able to insert coins. Harden.

5. Attach the teat section over the top edge of the larger tube with dough paste. Make two circular bases: one for the bottle that holds the coins and one for the smaller tube. Cut out a circular hole in the middle of the larger base for the plastic stopper to keep the

money inside. (Stoppers can be made from the plastic ends found in cardboard postal tubes.) Attach each base to their matching tubes with dough paste and harden.

6. Join the two tubes together down one side with dough paste and harden. Model the rabbits and the carrots using the modelling techniques on pages 19 and 24–26. Paint and varnish the hardened model.

Balloon lampshade **

- ◆ *Shade measures 16 in (40 cm) in diameter*
- ◆ *Basket measures 4 in (10 cm) deep by 3½ in (9 cm) wide*
- ◆ *1 quantity of the fine dough (see page 12)*

1. You will need two pieces of cord 12 in (30 cm) long and ¼ in (6 mm) wide. Glue one end of each of the lengths of cord to the base of the paper lantern at opposite sides around the inside edge.

2. Wad half of the wicker basket with kitchen paper before modelling the figures over it. See the figure-making section on pages 24–26 for techniques of modelling the doll and bear figures. Make the top half of two bears and two girl dolls to fill the basket. Moisten the rim of the basket with water to ensure the paws and hands adhere properly when you sit the figures in it. Prop the figures from behind their backs with foil during the hardening process.

3. Paint and varnish the hardened model. Glue ribbon bows on to the doll's hair. Knot the free ends of the cords around the handles of the basket, so the basket hangs from the balloon shade. Glue cord and tassels on to the basket.

Rose-decorated straw hat *

♦ *Hat measures 7 in (17.5 cm) in diameter*
♦ *1 quantity of the basic dough (see page 12)*

1. Tie a piece of 1 in (2.5 cm) wide ribbon around the crown of a doll's straw hat and form it into a bow. Cut the ends of the bow into points.

2. Model the flowers and leaves from pre-coloured dough, following the instructions on pages 22–23. Fix to the ribbon with water, then harden. Or you can harden the flowers, then glue them on to the ribbon.

Ribbon bow *

♦ *Measures 4 in (10 cm) at the widest point*
♦ *1 quantity of the basic dough (see page 12)*

1. Roll and cut out a strip of dough measuring 6 x 2 x ¼ in (15 x 5 cm x 6 mm). Cut the ends into the V shape of a ribbon that has been cut with scissors.

2. Make a second strip of dough of the same size and fold the ends back under to the middle. Moisten the first strip in the middle and press the second over it. For a full bow effect, pad the inside of the folded pieces with dough.

Making the ribbon bow

3. For the knot in the middle of the bow, make a strip of dough 1¼ in (3 cm) x ¼ in (6 mm) and long enough to wrap around the middle section and reach to the back. Indent the dough with a cocktail stick to resemble folds that appear when a ribbon has been knotted in a bow shape. Moisten and fix with water.

4. Attach a string hanging loop at the back of the bow (see page 39).

Doll's house items for display box **

♦ *1 quantity of the fine dough (see page 12)*

Make sure you make your models the right size to fit your own display box. As a guide, the teapot measures 1½ in (4 cm) in diameter; most models are about 1¾ in (4.5 cm) high.

Harden your models before painting and varnishing, or simply harden pre-coloured dough.

Wash jug and basin *

Model the jug shape from a piece of dough, copying the illustration. Pinch the dough jug at the waist and indent at the top for the jug lip. Use a tart tin as a former to model the basin shape.

Cup, saucer and teapot *

Make a pre-hardened former from a ball-shaped piece of dough covered in foil. Model the cup over the former. Make the teapot from a 1½ in (4 cm) ball of dough pinched in at the top to form the waist section. The handle is made from a small tube of dough and attached with water.

Fruit on plate *

Model a boat-shaped plate to 1¼ in (3 cm) wide and fill it with tiny modelled fruit shapes such as pears, apples and bananas (see pages 20–21).

Egg basket *

Make a shallow bowl base shape from a small piece of dough about 1¾ in (4.5 cm) in diameter. Twist two thin tubes of dough together to form a mini garland and sit it on the top edge of the bowl for the basket. Roll ten to fifteen tiny dough egg shapes and fill the basket with them. Harden the filled basket before attaching a dough twist handle with dough paste.

The display box would make an excellent advent calendar for Christmas. Mark the frame of the boxes on to some red card and prick a door outline in each segment with a darning needle so that it is easy to open. Put your toy figures on the shelves before gluing the card over them. Number the doors from one to twenty-four. Your child will love pulling open the boxes to find their hidden toy in the run up to Christmas day.

Garland *

Model a ring of tiny flowers from pre-coloured dough, with a tube of dough for a hanging loop and a few leaves. Fix together with water.

Plant *

Shape a plant pot and fill with a ball of dough. Make a second ball of dough about the same size and join with a cocktail stick. Decorate the surface of the plant with leaf and flower shapes.

Gingerbread house *

The base of the house is made from one piece of dough that is hardened before adding the scalloped roof tiles; this is necessary to prevent it sagging. Add the decorations with dough paste when the house is almost hard.

Cricket bat and ball *

Form a tube of dough to 3½ in (9 cm) making one end narrower for the bat handle. Roll a small piece of dough into a ball and sit it on the base of the bat. Once hardened, painted and varnished, wrap a length of black stranded cotton around the handle of the bat for a touch of authenticity.

Clock *

Roll an oblong of dough to 1¼ in (4.5cm) high and 1 in (2.5 cm) across. Mark it as featured with a cocktail stick. Use an icing nozzle to cut a small circular piece of dough for the clock face. Moisten and fix in position. Form tiny balls of dough for the feet of the clock. Draw the hands and numbers on to the clock face boldly with a black felt pen.

Jack-in-the-box **

Make six ½ in (12 mm) rectangles and harden them in the oven. Cement the five cooled rectangles together with dough paste to form the box. Fix the remaining rectangle on the back of the box as a lid and prop it up as it dries in the oven. Model the top half of the clown figure in the opened box. The hair under the hat is made from short lengths of stranded cotton glued on to the head.

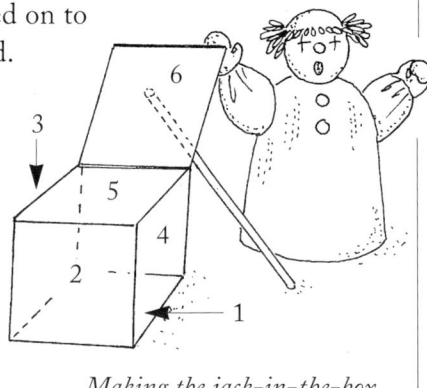

Making the jack-in-the-box

Toy soldier **

Model a miniature toy soldier using the figure method on pages 24–26, or the drummer boy on page 58.

Skating boots **

Make a pair of skating boots from a ¼ in (6 mm) thick piece of dough, adding tubes of dough for the blades and using a cocktail stick to make the eyelet holes for the laces.

Honey jar *

Model a 1 in (2.5 cm) piece of dough into an earthenware jar shape and harden. Roll a thin rectangular piece of dough to form the label and secure with dough paste. Roll a circular piece of dough for the frilled cover, and frill the edge of the cover following the method for scallops on page 35. Sit the frill on the jar, then tie a piece of stranded string around it to look gathered.

Radio *

Model a shape with a rounded top, like an old-fashioned radio. Impress the shapes for the speaker and add small balls of dough for the control knobs.

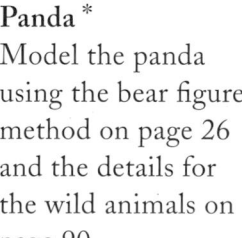

Panda *

Model the panda using the bear figure method on page 26 and the details for the wild animals on page 90.

Birthday cake *

Form a piece of dough into a cake shape with a diameter of 1¾ in (4.5cm). Make a plate from a scrap of dough and fix the cake on it with a little water. Roll a strip of dough about 1 in (2.5 cm) wide and long enough to wrap around the cake for a frill. Fringe the top edge with scissors and secure it around the side of the cake with water. Model a tiny piece of dough with a tapered end around a strand of string for the candle. Glue the hardened candle and bead trim on the cake after hardening, painting and varnishing.

Plum pudding *

Make a bowl shape and fill it with a ball of dough. Moisten the edge and fix on a rolled-dough rim. Roll out a piece of dough, impress it with a linen pattern and wrap it around the ball, pinching together at the top. Mark the pleats to resemble gathered fabric with the point of a kitchen knife.

Drum and sticks *

Flatten a ball of dough into a circular drum shape with a diameter of 1¼ in (3 cm). Make two strips of dough long enough to encompass the top and bottom edges of the drum, forming the lipped edges. Secure them with a little water. The drum sticks are made from two halves of a cocktail stick with a bead glued on at one end.

Christmas tree *

Form a piece of dough into a cone shape and sit it over a miniature terracotta pot. Starting at the top of the cone, snip into the dough with scissors to make the fir tree points, then harden the tree shape. When the tree is almost hard you can, if you wish, attach small balls of dough for tree decorations with dough paste and complete the drying. (This is done at this stage to prevent the cut dough from sagging under the weight of the dough balls.)

Christmas garland *

Use pre-coloured dough to make a tiny twisted garland. Decorate with balls and a bow at the top.

Christmas pudding *

Roll a piece of dough into a ball with a diameter of 1¼ in (3 cm) and fix it to a circular base of dough for the plate. Trim with dough holly leaves and berries.

Blancmange *

Oil a canapé shell mould. Press a piece of dough into it and up to the edge, then harden the dough. Ease the dough out of the mould, then paint and varnish it. Glue a red bead on the top of the blancmange shape for the cherry.

Tap dough out of the mould

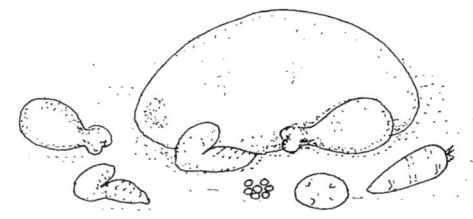

Turkey and vegetables on a plate *

Model the turkey as in the illustration and fix it to an oval-shaped dough plate. Make carrots, peas and potatoes in dough and arrange them around the turkey, securing with a little water.

Model the legs and wings of the turkey separately, then fix them to the body with water

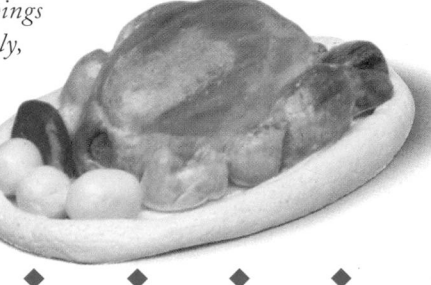

Decorated pots **

- *Assorted pots measure 2–5 in (5–13 cm)*
- *1 quantity of the basic dough (see page 12)*

1. Model the top half of a dough figure using the modelling method for human and animal figures on page 26, inside a painted plant pot. Remember to wet the inside of the pot before attaching the dough.

2. The teddy bear pot has a hardened bear figure glued on to the outside of a painted pot. To achieve the correct shape, model the bear on an unpainted pot that has a piece of parchment between the pot and the dough so you can easily remove it when it is hard.

3. Harden the figures, then paint and varnish them to match your room.

The teddy bear could be painted in a tartan pattern on a red pot and filled with sweets to give as an appealing Christmas gift.

Tooth fairy pot **

- *Measures 4 in (10 cm) high*
- *1 quantity of the fine dough (see page 12)*

1. First you will need to make a pot with a lid. To do this, press your thumb in a 2½ in (6 cm) ball of dough, with your index finger, then turn the ball around, forming an edge between your thumb and index finger as you turn. As it widens, use both fingers and thumbs.

2. Form two dough circles, one for the pot lid and one for the pot lip, each large enough to cover the top of the pot base. Cut the middle out of one circle to form the lip on the pot. Harden all the pieces of the model.

3. Model the fairy figure on the hard pot using the figure method on page 26 and the clothes details on pages 32–33.

4. Write your child's name or 'Tooth Fairy' on the side of the pot in felt pen.

5. Harden the model, then paint and varnish it.

Toy cupboard plaque ***

- *Measures 12 in (30 cm) high by 10 in (25 cm) wide*
- *1 quantity of the strong extensible dough (see page 12)*
- *1 quantity of the fine dough (see page 12)*

Model the plaque in stages, hardening each section as you progress, to provide you with a firm base to model over.

1. First make the foundation wall from the strong extensible dough. Roll the dough out to a ¼ in (6 mm) thick sheet of the above dimensions.

2. Harden the sheet of dough, remembering to weight the edges to prevent them from curling.

3. Model the box frame of the toy cupboard and the shelves on the back wall and use dough paste to secure each length. Make the doors as featured and fix to the cupboard with dough paste. They will need supporting from underneath as they harden; a flat strip of wood or thick card is ideal for this.

4. The toys, hats and accessories are modelled in fine dough. Use the ideas and methods from the figure section (see pages 24–34) and the doll's house items (see pages 76–80) as inspiration for the contents of the toy cupboard. Remember to make items appropriate for a boy or girl, and in suitable colours. Harden and fix to the base with dough paste.

5. Paint and varnish the model before gluing on lace and ribbon trims. Use stranded embroidery cotton for Jack's hair.

Toy chest **

- ◆ *Chest measures 6 in (15 cm) wide by 4 in (10 cm) high by 3 in (7.5 cm) deep*
- ◆ *1 quantity of the fine dough (see page 12)*

1. Fill up to three-quarters of the chest with scrunched up paper towel. Model some toys by using the figure method on pages 24–26 and some items from the doll's house section on pages 76–80 to model toys for filling the top portion of the toy chest.

2. Fashion a tube of dough into a trumpet shape. Add balls of dough for the keys.

3. Harden the filled chest and trumpet in the oven, before painting and varnishing.

Fruit tarts and mince pies *

- *Tarts measure 2½ in (6 cm) in diameter*
- *1 quantity of the basic dough (see page 12)*

1. Roll out the dough to ¼ in (6 mm) thick, then use circular biscuit cutters to cut out the bases of the tarts and pies. Lay these in a sectioned baking sheet, pressing them around the curved edge. Harden the bases in the oven.

2. Fill each of the tart bases with a selection of the ideas featured in the photograph. These range from flattened dough imitating strawberry jam, to blackcurrants and strawberries that look like the real thing! See the section on fruit modelling on pages 20–21 for a detailed method of modelling the different fruits shown.

3. Press soft dough through an icing nozzle to simulate the piped cream effect around the edge of the tarts. Fix the filling and decorations to the hardened bases with dough paste.

4. The mince pie is made from two tart bases, one upturned over another that has been padded in the centre with dough.

5. Harden the models, then paint and varnish them.

Sweets *

Make a selection of these and display in a glass dish. Look at the real thing to guide your own modelling methods. Keep them away from young children!

Sweets in wrappers *
◆ *Measure 1½ in (4 cm) long*
◆ *1 quantity of the basic dough (see page 12)*

1. Roll a small piece of dough into a ball about ½ in (2 cm) in diameter. Cut two lengths of dough with a scalloped edge, each measuring 3 in (7.5 cm) long and ¼ in (6 mm) thick and roll each piece up.

2. Fix the rolls at each end of the dough ball, pinching in the join to splay out the scalloped edges.

3. Paint the hardened sweets with coloured patterns, such as stars or stripes.

Truffles *
◆ *Measure 1 in (2.5 cm) in diameter*
◆ *1 quantity of the basic dough (see page 12)*

1. Roll dough balls to the above diameter. Press a walnut-sized piece of dough through a sieve and shave lengths of about ¼ in (6 mm) from it to simulate chocolate vermicelli. Moisten the dough balls, then roll them in the mock vermicelli.

2. Harden the truffles, then paint and varnish them and display them in paper cases.

Sunday best figurine ***

- *Measures 8 in (20 cm) high*
- *1 quantity of the basic dough (see page 12)*

Model the figure in stages over a purchased cane chair to prevent the figure collapsing under the weight of the dough clothes. (Florists sell cane chairs for dried flower arrangements.)

1. Form a tube of dough 12 in (30 cm) long and 1 in (2.5 cm) in diameter into the U shape for the legs. Fashion shoes and socks on the ends of the tube, as shown in the clothes section on page 33. Bend the tube in half, moisten the seat of the chair and press the U part of the tube down on to it. Cross one leg over the other and support in this position until set. Form two narrow scalloped-edged strips in dough, moisten and attach to the leg to make the frill on the top edge of the socks. Press a cocktail stick into the middle part of the U bend. Harden the legs before the next stage of modelling.

2. Make a tubby body section about 3½ in (9 cm) long and 2½ in (6 cm) wide from dough and press it down on to the cocktail stick, allowing the stick to protrude at the top for about ½ in (12 mm).

3. Model two pillows with scalloped edges and use to support the body section. Harden the body before proceeding.

Follow the seated figure instructions in the numbered order for making Sunday best

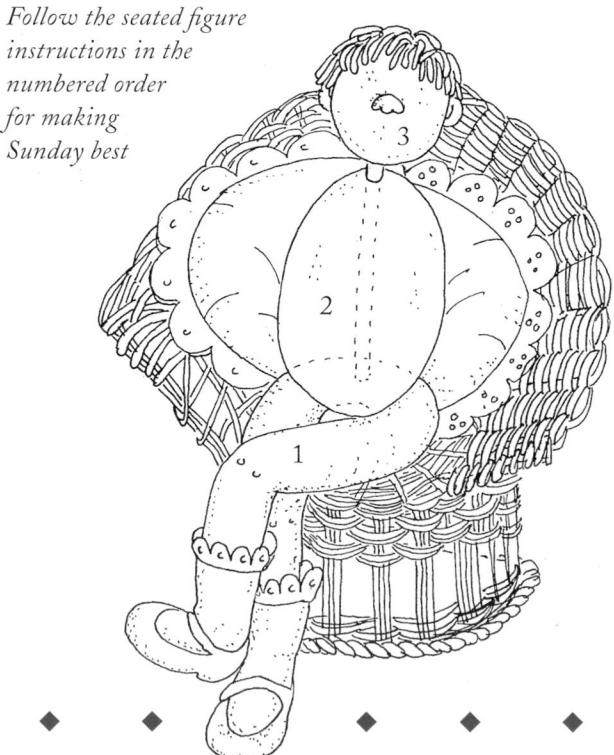

4. Make the skirt from a rectangular piece of dough measuring 10 in (25 cm) long, 4 in (10 cm) wide and ¼ in (6 mm) thick. Scallop the lower edge and gather the straight edge around the waist, draping it over the legs and securing with a little dough paste. Turn the edge of the skirt back over the crossed leg. Harden the piece.

5. Attach two tubes of dough about 2½ in (6 cm) long and ¾ in (2 cm) in diameter with dough paste each side of the shoulders. Model the hands using the method from the figure section on page 30 and attach them to the ends of the tubes with a little water.

6. Make the head from a ball of dough about 2 in (5 cm) in diameter and sit it on the protruding end of the cocktail stick, securing in position with dough paste. Harden the model.

Model the features to match those of the recipient

7. Complete the figure by adding hair, a hat and a false yoke on the bodice front. Fix these with dough paste. Make the hat in dough using the same technique as the fabric mob cap and bonnet in the clothes section on page 34.

8. Model a cat sitting at the side of the chair, rubbing its head against the chair. The chair supports the cat's head. Fix with dough paste.

9. Harden the completed figure, then paint and varnish it.

CHAPTER ELEVEN

TOY TOWN CHARACTERS

Inhabitants of Toy Town **

- *Measure about 5 in (12.5 cm) high*
- *1 quantity of the fine dough (see page 12) for each figure*

The figures use the flat-figure modelling method which is given in detail on pages 24–26. Outlines are provided on page 116 as a modelling guide, and these are numbered to show the modelling order you need to follow.

1. Shape the head, inserting half a cocktail stick, then model the features.

2. Shape the body and attach to the head. Roll out and attach the legs and arms, then the hands and feet.

3. Add the dough clothes, remembering to start with the undergarments and work outwards.

4. Harden, then paint and varnish the models. Add a hanging loop (see page 39) if you wish.

Nurse   *Policeman*   *Butcher*

Rocking horse *

◆ *Measures about 3 in (2.5 cm) high*

◆ *¼ quantity of the basic dough (see page 12)*

The rocking horse is a simple cut-shape model.

1. Make a template from the pattern on page 117 and use it to cut out the shape from dough rolled out to a ¼ in (6 mm) thick sheet.

2. Harden the rocking horse, then paint and varnish it. Add a magnet, a brooch back or hanging loop (see page 39), depending on how you want to use your model.

You can use the same principle to make other toy town animals such as a teddy bear or a cat. Look

at other ideas in the book or make your own templates – children's books are an excellent source of simple illustrations for inspiration.

Baker

Farmer's wife

Nutcracker

CHAPTER TWELVE

WILD ANIMALS AND FARMYARD CHARACTERS

Wild animals *

- *Animals measure about 3 in (7.5 cm) high*
- *¼ quantity of the basic dough (see page 12) for each figure*

You could glue magnets on the backs of these charming animals and use them to pin notices on a refrigerator. Or make them into a wall hanging by gluing them on to a large notice board with tile adhesive. Add individual hanging loops for small wall decorations, or make tiny versions into badges.

1. The hedgehog is made from two small balls of dough, shaped and joined together. Snip the spines with scissors and add the features. The squirrel, snake and ladybirds are made from small balls of dough. The bird, parrot and monkey are made from simple cut shapes.

2. Use the illustrations on page 117 to make card templates for the lion, panda, elephant and zebra. Roll out the dough to ¼ in (6 mm) thick. Cut round the template shapes with a craft knife.

3. Shape the pieces together, moistening with water to join sections, and add the features.

4. Harden the animals, then paint and varnish them.

Farmyard animals *

- ◆ *Horse, cow and sheep measure about 3 in (7.5 cm) high*
- ◆ *¼ quantity of the basic dough (see page 12) for each figure*

The farmyard animals are made in the same way as the wild animals. The sheep, cat and duck are simple shapes to copy. Use a garlic press to shred the dough for the sheep's wool, then moisten the base shape and gently press the dough in place. Use the outlines on page 118 for the cow and horse. When completed, tie a ribbon round the duck's neck, and a tiny bell around the cow's neck.

Farmyard figures **

- ◆ *Measure 5 in (12.5 cm) high*
- ◆ *1 quantity of the basic dough or the fine dough (see page 12) for each figure*

1. Model the figures using the flat-figure method on pages 24–26. See the outlines on page 118 for the modelling details.

2. When modelling the scarecrow's arms, use a cocktail stick to make a hole in the end of each arm. When the model is complete, glue two or three 1 in (2.5 cm) lengths of raffia into the holes for hands. Make a dough smock following the clothes instructions on pages 32–33.

3. Similarly, make a hole in the farmer's hand so that you can insert a piece of twig as his walking stick when the model is complete. Make his dog separately, then fix it to the farmer's leg with a little dough paste. Use a purchased basket to hang over the farmer's arm.

$\mathcal{F}$AIRY $\mathcal{T}$ALES

Goldilocks and the three bears ***

- *Notice board measures 16 in (40 cm) square*
- *2 quantities of the basic dough (see page 12)*

Curtain and pelmet

1. Cut a pelmet front from a ½ in (12 mm) thick piece of wood measuring 15½ x 2½ in (39 x 6 cm). Cut the curtain rail from dowelling 14½ in (37 cm) long by ½ in (12 mm) in diameter. Cut two pieces of wood each 2½ in (6 cm) long by ½ in (12 mm) thick for the pelmet sides.

2. From a 20 x 36 in (50 x 90 cm) piece of check fabric cut a strip 18½ in (47 cm) long by 3 in (7.5 cm) deep.

3. Snip the remaining check fabric in half to make a pair of curtains, hem the long edges on each one by machine or hand sew. On one curtain, fold under a ¼ in (6 mm) then over ½ in (12 mm) hem, and machine or hand sew in position to form a channel for the dowelling. Repeat for the other curtain.

4. Measure the curtains against the length of the board and turn a hem under on each one, finishing the hem with machine or hand stitching. Fit the curtain rod through the channel at the top of each curtain. Secure the rod ends with wood glue between the pelmet sides, in the centre of each one.

Fixing the pelmet

5. Glue the pelmet sides on to the board flush with the top and side edges of the board. Weigh down with a heavy object until dry. Glue the front of the pelmet over the side pieces. Cut a strip of cardboard to fit the gap at the top of the pelmet and glue in position.

6. Cover the box pelmet with the prepared fabric strip, using spray mount to fix it in position. The front edge of the fabric pelmet can be scalloped on a sewing machine. A pinked edge is just as effective if you cannot sew this type of edging on your machine.

Goldilocks and the bears

See the pattern section on page 120 for the outline of the model.

1. Model the mattress and pillow first over a flat baking sheet covered with baking parchment, choosing the scale to fit within the frame of the notice board. Scallop a length of dough long enough to gather around the edge of the pillow. Prick holes in each half circle with a cocktail stick to imitate broderie anglaise. Moisten the pieces with water to join.

2. Model Goldilock's head on top of the pillow and the top half of her body as an oblong tube on top of the mattress. Use a fine-holed garlic press to create her beautiful golden tresses and drape them around her head over the pillow. Curl the ends of her hair with a cocktail stick.

3. Make a frilled valance from a gathered strip of scalloped-edged dough that is long enough to fit along the edge of the mattress. Fashion the quilt from dough and make a turned down scalloped-

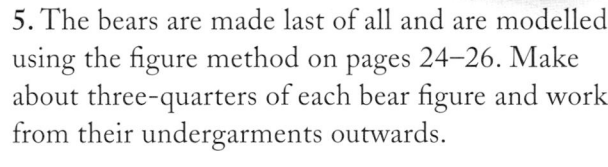

edge oblong piece of dough to form the sheet. Prick the edges with a cocktail stick to match the pillow edging.

4. Model the bed head and foot end as illustrated and gently lift the model over each piece with a spatula, securing in place with water.

Goldilock's bed ends

5. The bears are made last of all and are modelled using the figure method on pages 24–26. Make about three-quarters of each bear figure and work from their undergarments outwards.

6. Harden the model, then paint it. You can use your own ideas for the patterns on the quilt.

7. Varnish the model, then glue it to the centre of the hessian board. Draw the curtains up and tie a cord tassel in the middle of each one. Fix hanging loops and string on the back to hang up the decoration.

Snow White
and the seven dwarfs **

- Snow White measures 12 in (30 cm) high
- Dwarfs heights vary from 6 in (15 cm) to 8 in (20 cm) high
- The hessian-covered notice board is 24 x 38 in (60 x 96 cm)
- 2-3 quantities of the basic dough recipe (see page 12)

See the outline on pages 121–124 for the modelling details.

Because of the number of figures and the size involved, make a wall hanging of this theme, allowing you to include all the characters in the woodland scene.

1. Begin modelling Snow White so that you can then gauge the heights of the dwarfs around her. She is modelled on the basic flat-figure method (see pages 24–26) and is 12 in (30 cm) high. Form the blouse and skirt before adding the waistcoat and apron. Finally add her hair, draping the strands from the garlic press over her head and shoulders. Place the figure on a prepared baking sheet, secure a basket in one hand and harden the completed figure.

2. Make Dozy reclining against the toadstool. Model the toadstool as a prop for the reclining figure. Use a pointed knife to mark the underside of it. Model Dozy's head and lay it in the middle of the mushroom stem.

3. Form the body from a curved tube of dough with a big bulge for the tummy, following the instructions on modelling detail on page 25. Make the arms and legs but do not attach them yet. Cut the jacket from dough using the clothes method on pages 32–34. Moisten the tops of the arms and attach the right arm first. Lay the jacket over the body and then lay the bent arm on top. The left arm is tucked under the figure and brought around to the front over the jacket. Model the hands at this stage.

4. Dress the legs with knickerbockers and tuck the right one under the bottom edge of the jacket flaps. Insert the left leg under the right, then position both legs as in the photo. Model boots from balls of dough over the legs and pinch the ends into points. Snip V shapes out of a narrow strip of dough to make pointed cuffs on the top of the boots.

5. Cut a 2½ in (6 cm) length by 1¼ in (3 cm) wide piece of striped tubular knitting. Pick up the stitches at one end with a threaded needle, draw them together tightly and knot the thread to secure. Sew a pom-pom over the gathered end. Roll up about 1¼ in (3 cm) at the other end to form the hat cuff. Bend the pom-pom end down towards the cuff and catch it in position by sewing a few tacking stitches on the underside. Position the hat on Dozy's head as in the photograph opposite. Place the figure on the baking sheet and harden.

6. Work the remaining six dwarfs and other woodland features to fit around Snow White and Dozy, using the outlines from the pattern section for modelling ideas. Lay cut out tracings of the models on the notice board to ensure they fit within the frame of the board. Remember to model the clothes in layers, such as a shirt before a jacket.

7. Harden all the dough pieces in the oven. Paint the finished models in appropriate colours. Allow the paint twenty-four hours to dry before coating with varnish.

8. Glue the models on to the notice board in their correct places with tile adhesive. Make grass and the tree from pieces of felt cut to shape with scissors and glue to the board. Screw hanging loops into the back of the wood frame and tie string between them for hanging.

Thumbelina **

◆ *Nut shell measures 3 in (7.5 cm) wide by 1¾ in (4.5 cm) deep*
◆ *1 quantity of the fine dough (see page 12)*

This charming model would make a lovely ornament for a little girl's bedroom. The life-size dough thimble demonstrates the scale of the tiny figure sleeping in the nut-shell bed.

1. Roll a piece of dough into a ball about 2½ in (6 cm) in diameter for the walnut shell. Press the dough in the middle to form a hollow boat shape and pinch the front to a rounded point. Slightly flatten the base of the shell to prevent it from rolling over. Mark the lines on the shell with a sharp knife, copying a real walnut shell.

2. Form the head and top half of Thumbelina's body from a tiny ball and tube of dough no more than 1 in (2.5 cm) long.

3. Make three violet-shaped petals and drape over the edge of the shell for the pillow. Lie the half figure over them. Cover Thumbelina with a large rose petal quilt made in dough, fixing in position with a little water.

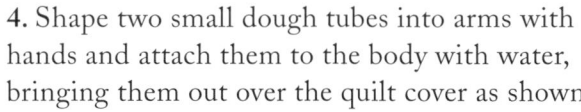
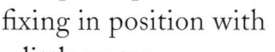

4. Shape two small dough tubes into arms with hands and attach them to the body with water, bringing them out over the quilt cover as shown.

5. Press a 1 in (2.5 cm) dough ball through a fine mesh sieve for her delicate hair. Drape the hair over the head and the petals.

6. Roll a ball of dough to about 1¾ in (4.5 cm) in diameter, then flatten it into a pyramid and form a thimble shape from it with a rounded top edge. Roll out a thin strip of dough about ¾ in (2 cm) wide and long enough to wrap around the base of the thimble to form the band. Press the strip on to the base of the thimble with water. Indent the thimble with an icing nozzle to simulate the markings on a real thimble.

7. Harden both models, then paint and varnish them in delicate colours.

The princess and the pea ***

◆ *Measures 12 in (30 cm) high*
◆ *2 quantities of the basic dough (see page 12)*

You will find this plaque great fun to make. The richly patterned mattresses make the plaque lifelike. They are easily made from layers of flattened dough tubes. See the outline on page 125 for the modelling details.

1. Begin by modelling the mattress at the top from an oblong of dough, then make the pillow. Model half the figure of the princess and lay her head on the pillow. Make the quilt from a thin sheet of dough and lay this over the figure with her hand out over the top, securing with a little water. Use a fine-holed garlic press to make up the strands of her hair.

2. Model 18 flattened tubes for the mattresses and lay underneath the top one; the overall height needs to be about 5½ in (14 cm).

3. Next make the four-poster bed. The drawer base and top canopy must equal the width of the bed. Dough balls about ½ in (12 mm) in diameter joined up into a length form the wooden carved bed posts. Finally lay the feet of the bed over a thin oblong of dough to form the rug, sealing with a little water.

4. Harden the model. Paint and varnish before gluing on lampshade edging for the carpet fringe.

Gingerbread cottage ***

- *Measures 8 in (20 cm) high by 10 in (25 cm) wide by 8 in (20 cm) deep*
- *2–3 quantities of the basic dough (see page 12)*

1. Scale the dimensions given in the illustrations for the sides, ends and roof of the cottage on to baking parchment and use this as a guideline for modelling over. The sides and ends are made from ½ in (12 mm) tubes that are bonded together with water in layers. Make the door and window openings by cutting the dough away with a craft knife. The thatched roof over the window has been padded to make it stand out. Harden all four walls before assembling.

2. The method for making roof tiles is explained on page 35 in the tile modelling section. These are hardened before attaching over the apex section of the cottage walls with dough paste.

Making the gingerbread house

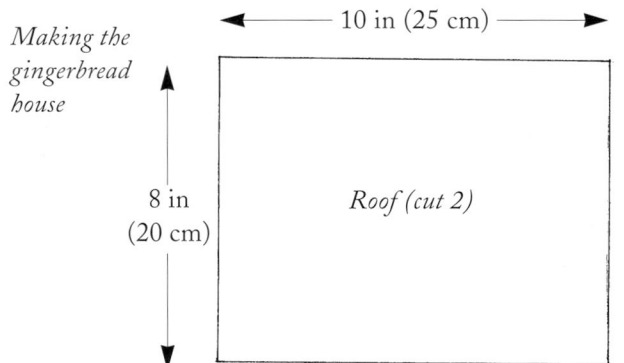

← 10 in (25 cm) →

8 in (20 cm)

Roof (cut 2)

3. To join the walls, secure one end wall to one side wall on the inside with a tube of dough pressed down the right angle that is formed by the two edges and sealed with dough paste. Repeat for the other side, then join the remaining edges in the same way so you have joined the four foundation walls of the cottage. Support the walls while they harden.

Joining the sides with dough tubes

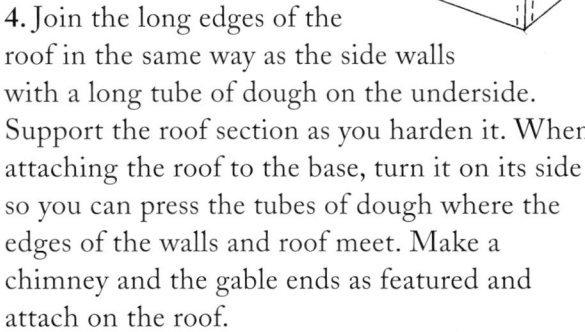

4. Join the long edges of the roof in the same way as the side walls with a long tube of dough on the underside. Support the roof section as you harden it. When attaching the roof to the base, turn it on its side so you can press the tubes of dough where the edges of the walls and roof meet. Make a chimney and the gable ends as featured and attach on the roof.

5. Use tiny figure cutters to cut out the gingerbread children from leftover dough. Bond them to the house with dough paste. Harden the completed cottage. Why not make a fence and toadstools from leftover dough?

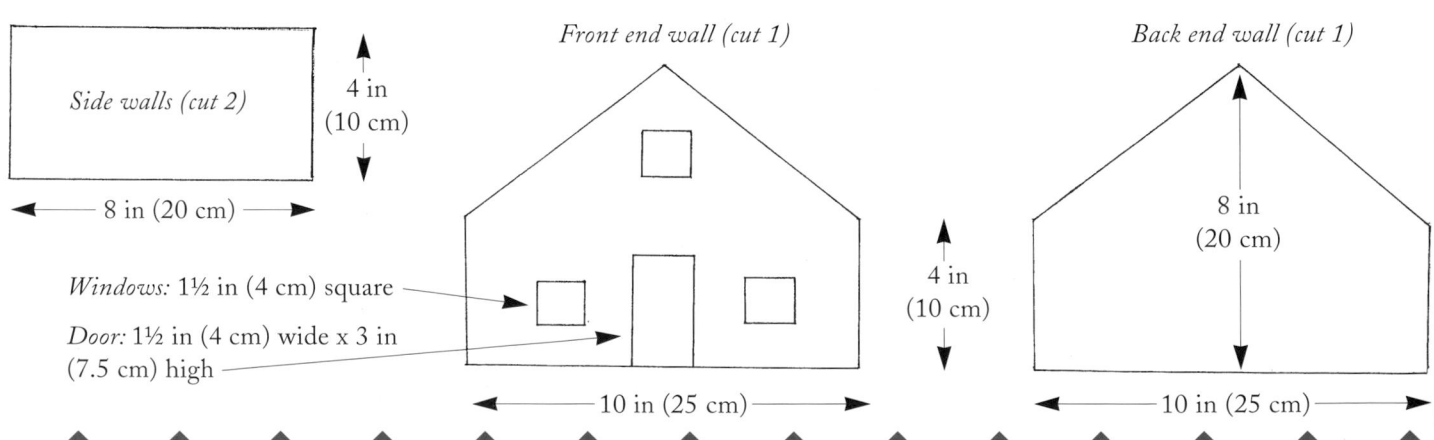

Side walls (cut 2)

4 in (10 cm)

← 8 in (20 cm) →

Windows: 1½ in (4 cm) square

Door: 1½ in (4 cm) wide x 3 in (7.5 cm) high

Front end wall (cut 1)

← 10 in (25 cm) →

4 in (10 cm)

Back end wall (cut 1)

8 in (20 cm)

← 10 in (25 cm) →

6. It is possible to use a glue gun to fix the sections of the cottage together, but if you do this remember the cottage cannot go back in the oven. All the decorations will have to be hardened before gluing. Paint and varnish the cottage as depicted. Curtains can be made from small pieces of check fabric glued on to the inside of the windows.

7. You may like to model a witch following the instructions on page 109 so she can fly above the cottage with her cat perched on her twiggy broomstick.

Gingerbread boy *

- *Measures 9 in (23 cm) high*
- *1 quantity of the basic dough (see page 12)*

See the outline on page 113 for modelling details.

This cheeky gingerbread boy really looks as though he is up to mischief, with his socks falling about his ankles, he is off to discover life!

1. Make a card template of the figure from the pattern provided. Roll half the quantity of dough to a flat sheet about H in (12 mm) thick and large enough to fit the tracing. Slightly press the card into the dough to mark the shape and use a pointed knife tip to cut out the figure. Remove the excess dough. Bend the left arm to appear as though it is waving.

2. Make the clothes for the figure following the method for the T-shirt, waistcoat and shorts explained in the clothes section on pages 32–33.

3. Attach a string hanging loop at the back of the head (see page 39).

4. Harden the model, then paint the face, arms and any uncovered flesh brown to look like gingerbread. Paint the clothes according to the details on the sample.

Rapunzel **

- *Measures 12 in (30 cm) high*
- *2–3 quantities of the basic dough (see page 12)*

See the outline on page 121 for modelling details.

1. Begin by making the tower foundation. Roll an entire quantity of a basic recipe to an oblong measuring 4 in (10 cm) at the top and increasing to 6 in (15 cm) at the base by 1½ in (4 cm) thick, trimming away any excess dough. Attach a string hanging loop at the back of the tower (see page 39). Harden the base before the next stage of modelling the figures.

2. Roll half a quantity of dough to a flat sheet ½ in (12 mm) thick and large enough to cover the tower base. Moisten the base with dough paste and lay the dough sheet over it. Smooth the dough around the edges and trim any overlapping pieces. Make the arched opening for the window by cutting the shape out of the dough with a sharp knife. The window measures 2¾ in (7 cm) long and 1¾ in (4.5 cm) wide.

3. Carve the stonework in the top layer of dough with the pointed end of a knife. Round all the corners of each cut section softly to imitate large stone boulders.

4. Model the prince and the top half of the Rapunzel figure for the window space. Make a long thin dough plait for her hair (see page 18). This needs to be long enough to reach the base of the tower. Lie the hair gently on the surface of the tower to enable you to lift it up to position the Prince's leg underneath it. Fix the pieces with dough paste.

5. Remember to make the mouse, the blackbird and the grass around the base of the tower and attach with dough paste; the small details add to the charm of the plaque. Harden your finished model in the oven.

6. When painting the stonework, blend several colours to achieve natural colours for the stones and moss; the effect is very good and shows the beauty of natural stone. Varnish the painted model before gluing on the decorations, such as the bead necklace and ribbon bow.

7. The plaque could be glued on to a hessian notice board and given a background made from scraps of felt as Snow White and the seven dwarfs (see page 94).

Snow White and Rose Red **

♦ *Measure 5 in (13 cm) high*
♦ *1 quantity of the basic dough (see page 12)*

These charming figurines make delightful gifts for little girls. Why not paint the models' hair to match that of the recipient?

1. Make a hard base for the figures by modelling the dough into two pyramid shapes, each about 4½ in (11.5 cm) high. Use the hollow base method for these (see pages 27–28). Harden the base shapes in the oven.

2. Model the head and body of the two figures over the hardened formers using dough paste to secure. Harden the figures in the oven.

3. Cut two strips of fabric long and wide enough to be gathered around the figures. They need to be about 16 in (40 cm) long and 6 in (15 cm) wide. Tack a length of narrow broderie ribbon to one long edge of each white fabric piece. Seam the narrow edges of each white fabric strip to form two skirts. Run a gathering thread around the top of each skirt, gather up the skirts and fit them on to the model; fasten the thread with a knot.

4. Model the arms for each model, and secure on to the body at the shoulders with dough paste. Sit a piece of baking parchment under the arms so they do not stick to the skirts during the drying process. The hands will need supporting during baking; to do this rest them over an ovenproof prop (a pottery mug is about the correct height for

this). Make hair for each model using a fine-holed garlic press. The bun shape is made by wrapping stranded dough around a small ball of dough. Harden the figures in the oven.

5. Paint and varnish the figures when they have cooled. Slip a piece of baking parchment under the arms to prevent any varnish from dripping on to the fabric skirts.

6. Round the corners on the narrow edges of the two oblong check fabric strips measuring 10 in (25 cm) x 4 in (10 cm). Sew a 1 in (2.5 cm) wide broderie ribbon around all the edges of the blue fabric as featured, and around the lower edge and the sides on the red fabric. Run a gathering thread along the top edge of the red fabric and 2 in (5 cm) down from top edge on the blue. Gather the red fabric up by the thread and knot it to fit the waist measurement. Do the same on the blue fabric to fit the neck of the corresponding model.

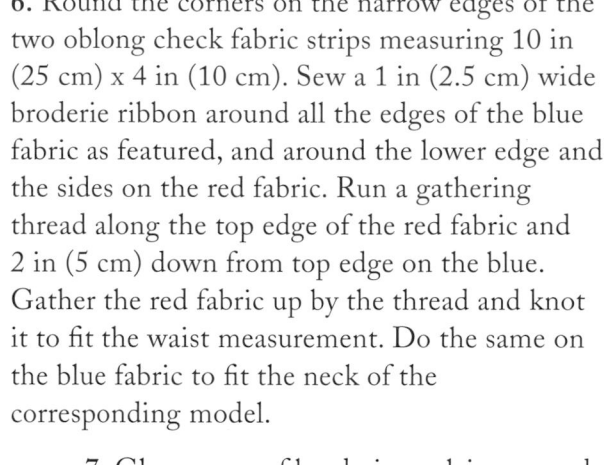

7. Glue scraps of broderie anglaise around Snow White's body for her bodice. Glue the scalloped lace over the shoulders and breasts on Rose Red, forming her sleeves and bodice. Dress Snow White in a blue cape and Rose Red in a red overskirt. To ensure the skirts and capes stay puffed out, you can pad them from underneath with polyester wadding.

8. Complete each model by gluing on relevant coloured trims as featured. For the bouquet frill, run a gathering thread around a 4 in (10 cm) length of broderie anglaise trim, draw it up into a tight circle and knot the ends of the thread to secure it. Glue a large ribbon rosebud in the centre of it, then glue the bouquet in position on the model. Make one bouquet for each figure.

CHAPTER FOURTEEN

CELEBRATIONS

BIRTHDAYS

Age badges **

- ◆ *Measure about 3 in (8 cm) long*
- ◆ *1 quantity of the basic dough (see page 12)*

1. Model the heads of each brooch, then press a cocktail stick half way into the head at the neck and harden the models. Make each body shape following the illustration, press into the end of the cocktail stick, and join together with dough paste.

2. After hardening again, paint and varnish your model before gluing a brooch pin on the back of the age badge.

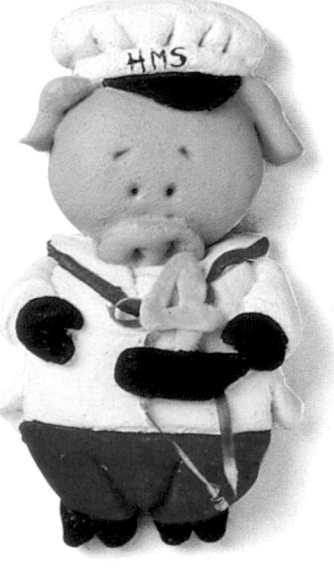

EASTER

Easter chicks *

- Measure 2¼ in (6 cm)
- ½ quantity of the basic dough (see page 12)

1. Model each chick from two balls of dough, one for the head and one larger one for the body. Moisten each ball and sit the head on the body. Indent the eyes with a cocktail stick and insert two glass beads in the spaces. Make the top and bottom beak from two tiny triangles of dough.

2. Harden the model, then paint and varnish it.

Decorated egg cups *

- Measures 3½ in (9 cm) high
- ½ quantity of the basic dough (see page 12)

Use one of the many ideas featured in the book to decorate the base of your egg cups. Some of the ones featured are simple – such as the heads of animals and the Toy Town characters – or you could model your own child's head. The wood must be moistened before attaching the dough decoration and hardening. Use felt cut to shape for the detail on the chick.

Easter hanging garland *

- *Measures 10 in (25.5 cm) in diameter*
- *1 quantity of the basic dough (see page 12)*

This novel garland is modelled over a twisted willow cane ring that can be purchased from garden centres.

1. Wind a 36 in (1 m) length of ribbon in a spiral around the ring and secure the ends together with glue. Tie or glue a ¼ in (6 mm) wide ribbon to a chocolate, plastic or real blown egg, then tie the free end to the ring so it hangs down. Repeat so you have four hanging eggs. Tie three ribbons to the top edge of the ring to hang.

2. Model the four daffodil flowers following the instructions on flower making on pages 22–23, and harden them. Glue the flowers at evenly spaced intervals on the top of the ring with a glue gun.

The daffodils make original candle holders. They can be displayed on their own with a yellow candle in the trumpet. (Not for use in the nursery though!)

To blow an egg, leave it in a warm room for a few hours. Prick the narrow end with a darning needle and make a slightly larger hole in the other end. Place your fingers over both holes and shake the egg hard. Hold the egg over a bowl, seal your lips against the shell and blow through the small hole until all the egg has come out the larger hole. Leave the shell to drain and dry out. Use the egg for scrambled egg.

Tulips in a plant pot *

- ◆ *Measures 10 in (25.5 cm) high*
- ◆ *1 quantity of the basic dough (see page 12)*

1. Make the plant pot from dough measuring about 4 in (10 cm) deep and 6 in (15 cm) at the widest. Attach a ledge of dough behind the top edge of the pot to support the flowers and leaves; this needs to be the width of the pot and about 2 in (5 cm) deep.

2. Model the flowers and leaves over the pot and the ledge (see pages 22–23). The flowers are padded underneath with dough to give them their rounded shape. Add a hanging loop (see page 39).

3. Harden the model, then paint and varnish it. Stencil the pot with a gold star motif.

Easter eggs in a basket *

- ◆ *Measures 12 in (30 cm) high*
- ◆ *1 quantity of the basic dough (see page 12)*

1. Model a basket shape to a width of about 9 in (23 cm) and 7 in (18 cm) deep, using the method for weaving on page 36. Make a narrow ledge about 1¼ in (3 cm) deep at the back of he rim of the basket to support the eggs. Add the eggs by overlapping one oval shape on another and bonding to the ledge support with water.

2. Model the flowers and leaves (see pages 22–23) and attach to the front of the basket with water. Add a hanging loop (see page 39).

3. Harden the basket, then paint and varnish it.

HALLOWEEN

Witch *

- ◆ *Measures 4 in (10 cm) high*
- ◆ *1 quantity of the basic dough (see page 12)*

See the outline on page 126 for modelling details.

1. Make the figure to the above height, using the outline as a guide, and modelling it on to a moistened bamboo skewer. Add a hanging loop (see page 39).

2. Harden the model, then paint and varnish it.

3. Make the broom from a few bristles cut from your household broom or from twigs glued on to the end of the stick.

Bat *

- ◆ *Measures 6 in (15 cm) wide*
- ◆ *½ quantity of the basic dough (see page 12)*

1. Make a card template from the outline on page 126. Roll out to the dough to about ½ in (12 mm) thick. Cut out the shape round the template with a craft knife. Make the head three-dimensional by adding a nose and mouth opening. Make a hole for a hanging loop.

2. Harden the model, then paint and varnish it.

3. Hang the finished model from an elastic thread so that it bounces up and down.

Spider *

- ◆ *Body measures 2½ in (6 cm) in diameter*
- ◆ *½ quantity of the basic dough (see page 12)*

1. Flatten a ball of dough slightly to the above measurement, forming it into a dome-shaped body by pressing between thumb and fingers.

2. Mark a smiling mouth at the front using the pointed tip of a kitchen knife.

3. Indent and make four holes each side of the mouth for the eight legs and a hole through the middle for threading a piece of elastic.

4. Harden the model, then paint and varnish it.

5. Glue on two goggle eyes and chenille-covered wires for the legs. Hang the spider from an elastic thread.

Pumpkin *

◆ *Measures 5 in (12.5 cm) wide*
◆ *½ quantity of the basic dough (see page 12)*

The pumpkin could be lit from behind by a torch or night light (but never have a naked flame near a child).

1. Make a card template using the outline on page 126. Roll out the dough to ¼ in (6 mm) thick, then cut out the shape round the template with a craft knife. Cut the eyes and teeth out with a pointed craft knife.

2. Make the calyx and stalk for the top of the pumpkin and fix on with water. Add a hanging loop (see page 39).

3. Harden the model, then paint and varnish it.

Flying witch **

◆ *Figure measures 12 in (30 cm) long*
◆ *1 quantity of the basic dough (see page 12)*

1. Model the witch using the flat-figure method on pages 24–26, to the above length.

2. Make a hole in the hands and feet with a cocktail stick.

3. Model a tiny cat to sit on the stick.

4. Harden the models, then carefully paint and varnish them.

5. Glue in a twig at the front and tiny twigs at the back for the witch's broom. Glue the cat on the front of the broomstick.

6. Make the moon from yellow card and glue to the back of the cat.

CHRISTMAS

Angel on raffia bow *

- ◆ *Figure measures 6 in (15 cm) long*
- ◆ *1 quantity of the basic dough (see page 12)*

1. Use a purchased raffia bow as the base. These can be bought from most garden centres, florists or craft shops.

2. Model an angel using the flat-figure method on pages 24–26 to the above length.

3. Harden the figure in the oven, paint and varnish before gluing on star-shaped sequins.

Why not model this angel (below left) from scraps of dough? Use the figure method on pages 24–26 for the head. Cut the wings from dough with a pointed knife. Glue on gathered lace for the collar.

The nativity scene *

- ◆ *Figures measure 4 in (10 cm) high*
- ◆ *1 quantity of the basic dough (see page 12)*

1. Use the pre-hardened base method given on page 28 for modelling Mary, Joseph and baby Jesus. Make the straw by pushing a piece of dough through a garlic press.

2. The twig backdrop can be purchased from garden centres or florists. A wooden wine crate could be lined with straw as an alternative idea.

Santa's sack *

◆ *Sack measures 6 in x 5 in (15 x 13 cm)*
◆ *½ quantity of the basic dough (see page 12)*

1. The sack can be bought from a garden centre or make your own from hessian fabric or felt.

2. Model Santa's face, then harden, paint and varnish it. Make a hat (see page 34) and glue it on to the head before gluing the head on the sack. For an extra special personalized gift, model your child's name in dough letters and glue in position.

Elves in a basket *

◆ *Basket measures 5 in (13 cm) in diameter*
◆ *1 quantity of the basic dough (see page 12)*

The technique is the same as the method of the decorated sweet basket on page 50. You need to model the top half of two figures and give them felt hats.

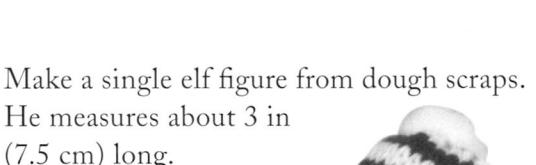

Make a single elf figure from dough scraps. He measures about 3 in (7.5 cm) long.

TEMPLATES AND OUTLINES

The templates and outlines on the following pages are either drawn three-quarters of the actual size of the models or actual size. The simplest way to enlarge those at three-quarter size is to photocopy them at 133 per cent. If you cannot do this, draw a grid of ¾ in (2 cm) squares over the templates, then copy the design on to 1 in (2.5 cm) squares. The outlines show the finer details on the models. The red numbers show the sequence of working the samples.

Teddy bear swag (see page 49)
(three-quarter size)

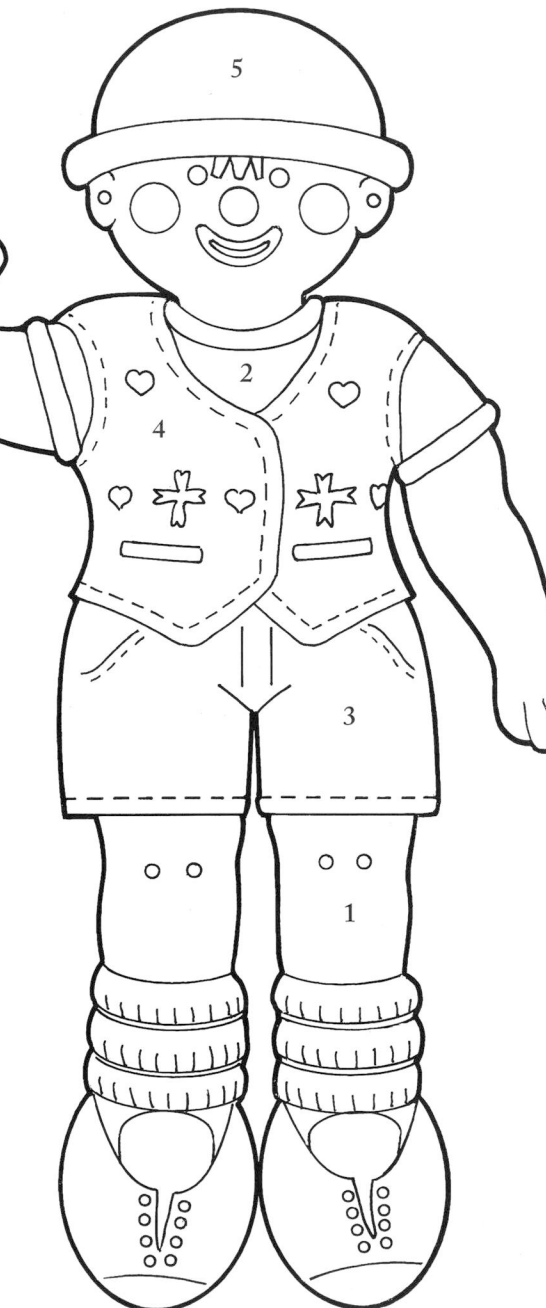

Gingerbread boy (see page 100)
(three-quarter size)

Baby sleeping door knob indicator
(see page 46)
(three-quarter size)

Babies in the bath (see page 60)
(three-quarter size)

Bonnet (see page 45)
(three-quarter size)

Pram (see page 45)
(three-quarter size)

Socks (see page 45)
(three-quarter size)

Mrs Bear with pram (see page 55)
(three-quarter size)

Toy Town characters
(see pages 88–89)
(three-quarter size)

Wild animals (see page 90)
(actual size)

Rocking horse (see page 89)
(actual size)

Farmyard characters
(see page 91)
(actual size)

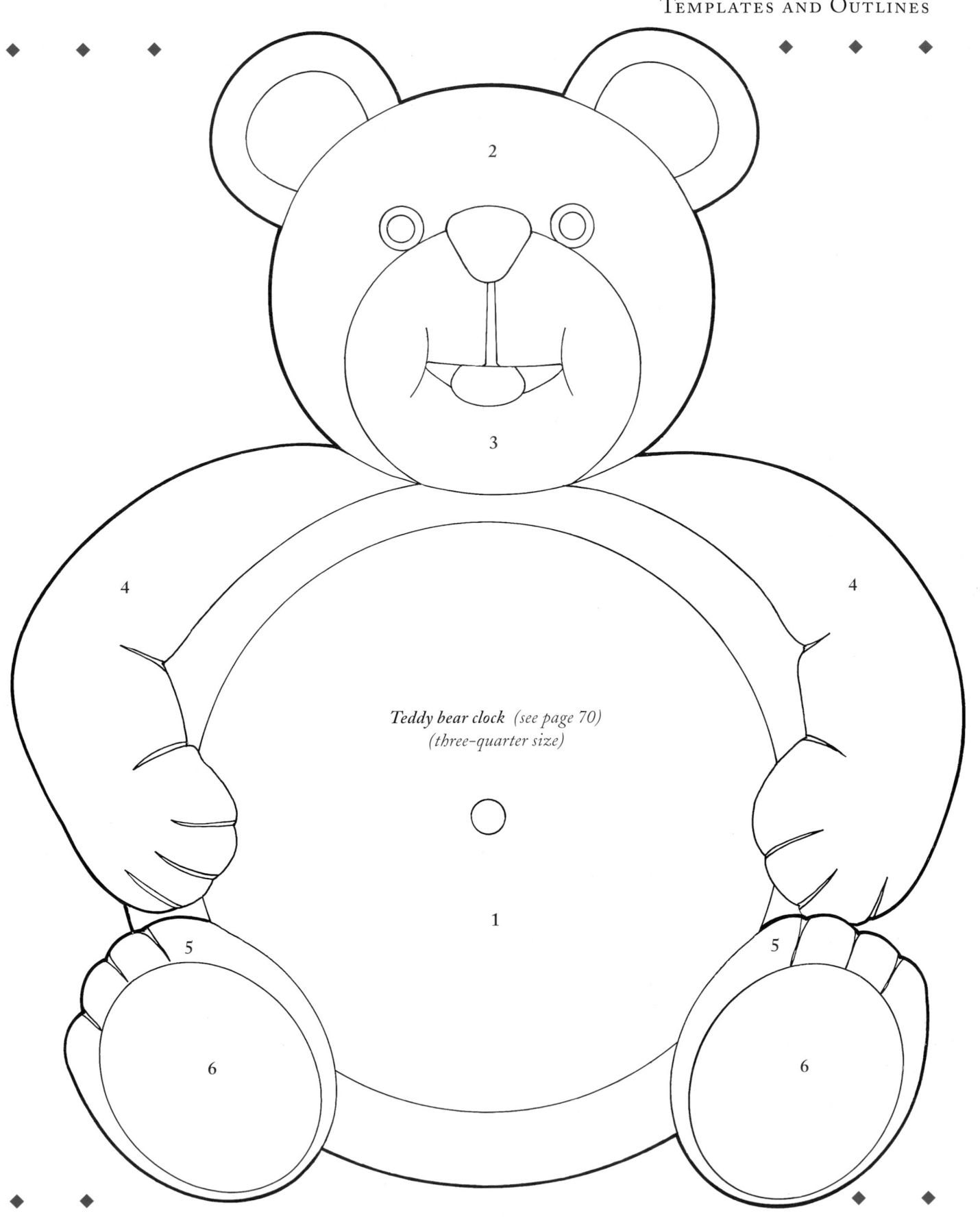

Teddy bear clock (see page 70)
(three-quarter size)

Goldilocks and the three bears (see pages 92–93)
(three-quarter size)

Dwarf (see page 94)
(three-quarter size)

Rapunzel (see page 101)
(three-quarter size)

Snow White and the seven dwarfs (see pages 94–95)
(three-quarter size)

The princess and the pea (see pages 96–97)
(three-quarter size)

Witch (see page 108)
(actual size)

Bat (see page 108)
(actual size)

Pumpkin (see page 109)
(three-quarter size)

INDEX

DAVIDSON'S
Principles
and Practice of
MEDICINE

The Editors

Christopher Haslett BSc (Hons) FRCP(Ed) FRCP FRSE
Professor of Respiratory Medicine, University of Edinburgh
Head of the Division of Clinical Sciences and Community Health,
University of Edinburgh
Honorary Consultant Physician, Royal Infirmary of Edinburgh

Edwin R. Chilvers BMedSci PhD FRCP(Ed) FRCP
Professor of Respiratory Medicine, University of Cambridge
Honorary Consultant Physician,
Addenbrooke's and Papworth Hospitals, Cambridge

Nicholas A. Boon MA MD FRCP(Ed) FESC
Consultant Cardiologist, Royal Infirmary of Edinburgh
Honorary Senior Lecturer, Department of Medicine,
University of Edinburgh

Nicki R. Colledge BSc (Hons) FRCP(Ed)
Consultant Geriatrician, Liberton Hospital, Edinburgh
and Royal Infirmary of Edinburgh;
Honorary Senior Lecturer, Department of Medicine,
University of Edinburgh

International Editor

John A.A. Hunter OBE BA MD FRCP(Ed)
Professor Emeritus of Dermatology, University of Edinburgh

Illustrated by

Robert Britton

CHURCHILL
LIVINGSTONE

EDINBURGH LONDON NEW YORK PHILADELPHIA
ST LOUIS SYDNEY TORONTO 2002

DAVIDSON'S

Principles and Practice of

MEDICINE

19TH EDITION

CHURCHILL LIVINGSTONE
An imprint of Elsevier Science Limited

First edition 1952   Eleventh edition 1974
Second edition 1954   Twelfth edition 1977
Third edition 1956   Thirteenth edition 1981
Fourth edition 1958   Fourteenth edition 1984
Fifth edition 1960   Fifteenth edition 1987
Sixth edition 1962   Sixteenth edition 1991
Seventh edition 1964   Seventeenth edition 1995
Eighth edition 1966   Eighteenth edition 1999
Ninth edition 1968   Nineteenth edition 2002
Tenth edition 1971

ISBN 0-443-07035-0

International edition 0-443-07036-9

Hardback edition 0-443-07111-X

British Library Cataloguing in Publication Data
A catalogue record for this book is available from the British
Library

Library of Congress Cataloging in Publication Data
A catalog record for this book is available from the Library of
Congress

Note
Medical knowledge is constantly changing. As new information
becomes available, changes in treatment, procedures, equipment
and the use of drugs become necessary. The editors and publishers
have taken care to ensure that the information given in this text is
accurate and up to date. However, readers are strongly advised to
confirm that the information, especially with regard to drug usage,
complies with the latest legislation and standards of practice.

ELSEVIER
SCIENCE
your source for books,
journals and multimedia
in the health sciences
www.elsevierhealth.com

The
publisher's
policy is to use
paper manufactured
from sustainable forests

Printed in India

Commissioning Editor: Laurence Hunter
Project Development Manager: Wendy Lee
Project Manager: Nancy Arnott
Designer: Erik Bigland
Illustration Manager: Bruce Hogarth
Medical Illustrator: Robert Britton
Charts: Hard Lines Agency
Page Layout: Jim Hope, Kate Walshaw

Preface

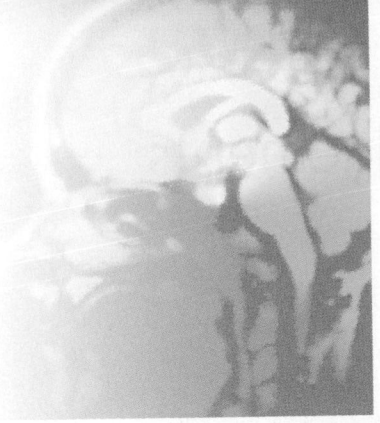

This 19th edition of *Davidson's Principles and Practice of Medicine* is published in the 50th anniversary year of the book. The first edition, essentially a heavily edited compilation of the lecture notes that Sir Stanley Davidson and his senior lecturers distributed to their medical students, was published in Edinburgh in July 1952 and was an immediate success. Since then the book has acquired a large following of medical students, doctors and other health professionals all around the world; during the course of the last 50 years, the text has been translated into many languages and more than two million copies have been sold. In common with all successful textbooks *Davidson* has only endured because it has evolved to meet the changing needs of its many readers; the golden jubilee edition therefore contains a wealth of new material and features. The editors believe that, like its illustrious predecessors, it will continue to provide an easily read, concise and up-to-date account of clinical medicine that will meet the needs of both medical students and its wider audience.

The preface to the first edition of *Davidson* emphasised that the book would concentrate on common disorders and everyday problems illustrated by an account of the applied anatomy and physiology of the relevant system. Subsequent editions have stuck to these important principles yet, while each edition has introduced new material and novel presentation techniques, the size of the book has changed very little. Nevertheless, its content and appearance are now very different from those early days; for example, the first edition contained just four photographs and 56 black-and-white drawings, whereas the present edition contains almost 350 colour photographs, over 200 radiographs and scans, and more than 500 colour line drawings, as well as over 1000 information boxes. The invaluable comments and feedback received from our readers have a major impact on how the book is revised at each edition.

Professor John Hunter, one of the editors of the 18th edition, has become the book's first international editor. He has recruited an International Advisory Board of outstanding and committed clinical teachers from Australia, northern Europe, India, Pakistan, the Middle East, South Africa, Hong Kong, Singapore, Malaysia and Canada (see p. x). The Board has provided enthusiastic support and invaluable advice that will help to ensure that *Davidson* maintains its international perspective and world-wide reputation.

A multidisciplinary approach is likely to produce the most favourable outcome in many diseases and physicians now find themselves increasingly involved in the management of patients who would previously have been treated in isolation by surgeons (and vice versa). The editors are therefore delighted that four surgeons have joined the writing team. Moreover, while there were just 14 contributors to the first edition of *Davidson*, that number has now risen to a total of 54, reflecting the increasing complexity of clinical medicine. The editors have, however, tried to maintain a uniform approach throughout by developing vertical themes; the structure of the system-based chapters, for example, follows an identical format beginning with a brief overview of the clinical examination. Dr Nicki Colledge, a specialist in medicine of the elderly, has joined the editorial team and has taken responsibility for many of these vertical themes, including new panels focusing on 'Issues in older people'.

The recognition that patients present with a problem and not a disease has encouraged the growth of problem-based learning and was anticipated by the introduction of sections on 'Major manifestations of disease' in the 17th edition. These have proved to be a very popular feature and have been enhanced and expanded in this golden jubilee edition. Chapter 1, 'Infection and immune failure', for example, has been completely rewritten to adopt a problem-based approach and overall the book now details over 120 different major manifestations of disease.

The new discipline of evidence-based medicine could transform the practice of clinical medicine and provides a useful vehicle for the development of guidelines and teaching materials. The principles of evidence-based medicine are explained in Chapter 2, 'Drug therapy', and throughout the book panels have been used to illustrate the sections on management. As such evidence is constantly changing, references to key websites have been included to allow the reader to keep up to date by using the resources afforded by the World Wide Web.

The publication of the golden jubilee edition is a major milestone in the history of this book. The current editors have striven to refresh and modernise the presentation of the text and figures whilst retaining the book's traditional clarity. They would like to acknowledge the enormous contribution of Sir Stanley Davidson and all the previous editors and authors, whose work laid the foundations of what remains one of the world's leading undergraduate textbooks of medicine.

Edinburgh and Cambridge 2002

C.H., E.R.C., N.A.B.
N.R.C., J.A.A.H.

Acknowledgements

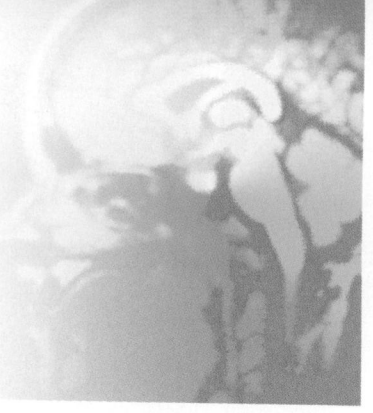

Since the last edition of *Davidson's Principles and Practice of Medicine* Dr Nicki Colledge has joined the Editorial Board and a total of 29 new authors have contributed new chapter material. These changes have increased the breadth and depth of expertise necessary in any major revision. We remain indebted to those authors who have stepped down from this edition. They include Dr Peter L. Chiodini, Dr Graham K. Crompton, Professor Alex M. Davison, Professor Christopher R.W. Edwards, Dr Niall D.C. Finlayson, Professor George E. Griffin, Professor Roland Jung, Professor Jonathan R. Lamb, Professor Anne de Looy, Dr Raashid Luqmani, Dr Michael J. Mackie, Dr David M. Mitchell, Professor George Nuki, Dr Alex T. Proudfoot, Professor James Shepherd, Dr Claire L. Shovlin, Professor J.G. Patrick Sissons, Dr Charles P. Swainson and Professor A. Stewart Truswell.

We would like to extend special thanks to Dr Simon Walker, Department of Clinical Biochemistry, University of Edinburgh, for his careful revision of the Appendix, Dr Tariq Sethi for his help with Chapter 5, 'Oncology', and Dr Paul Flynn for his assistance with the hyperlipidaemia section of Chapter 10, 'Nutritional, metabolic and environmental disease'.

Detailed chapter reviews were commissioned to help us establish the changes required to the book and for these we are extremely grateful to Dr N. Bateman, Dr J. Compston, Dr K. Davies, Dr J. Duffield, Dr I.S. Farooqi, Dr S. Forbes, Dr N. Grubb, Dr C. Hutchison, Dr G. Kavenagh, Dr P. Leslie, Dr D. McKeown, Dr C. Mumford, Dr A. Patrick, Dr J. Plevris, Dr S. Pringle, Dr J. Satsangi, Dr A. Stewart, Dr J. White, Dr C. Whitworth and Dr A. Zeman.

We gratefully acknowledge the assistance of Dr Michael J. Ford and Dr Andrew T. Elder, who compiled the on-line multiple choice questions which accompany this edition; we are sure these will be of great help to our readers.

The publishers are particularly grateful for the advice of the following clinical teachers, which was of great value in shaping new developments in this edition: Dr H. Bourne, Dr H. Chapel, Dr M. Field, Professor R.G. Finch, Professor C.D. Forbes, Dr H. Galley, Dr R.D. Griffiths, Professor J.R. Hampton, Dr M. Hasan, Professor C.J. Hawkey, Professor P.W. Macfarlane, Professor M. Marber, Dr M.A. Mir, Dr M.Y. Morgan, Professor P.A. O'Neill, Dr A. Owens, Dr H. Parfrey, Dr J. Potokar, Dr A.C. Rankin, Dr N. Sheron and Dr P. Sivasothy.

As part of the publishers' review, medical students from eight medical schools in the UK supplied many innovative ideas on how to enhance the book. We are indebted to the following for their enthusiastic support: Michal Ajzensztejn, Hannah Baynes, Andrew Birnie, Victoria Buchan, B. Canton Smith, Sandy Dalgety, Anish Dhital, Catriona Finlayson, Bibek Gooptu, Alice Gwyn, William Harris, Dom Hurford, Jessica Jebaratnam, Fionna Keenan, Jacqueline Kelly, Emily Laithwaite, Anna Lecras, Jez Leftley, Alan Macfarlane, David Macfarlane, Andrew Mackay, Philip Murray, Jessica Redgrave, Jonathan Rohrer, Jamie Rylance, Paul Stimpson, Clare Verrill, Emma Wall, Andrew Wilkinson, Penelope Wong and Veronica Yu.

Once again we have had to beg, borrow and steal many of the new illustrations that appear in this edition from our colleagues and we are grateful to them for their patience and support. They are acknowledged on pages 1223–1224.

We are especially grateful to all those working for Churchill Livingstone, in particular Laurence Hunter, Wendy Lee and Robert Britton, for their expertise in the shaping, collation and illustration of this edition. We would also like to thank Anne McCarthy for her labours in compiling the extensive index and Lynda Carey for her expert proofreading.

Edinburgh and Cambridge
2002

C.H., E.R.C., N.A.B.
N.R.C., J.A.A.H.

Sir Stanley Davidson
(1894–1981)

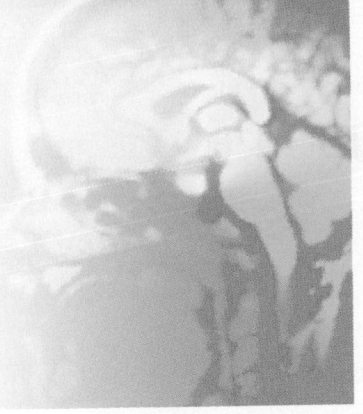

This famous textbook, now celebrating its 50th year, was inspired by one of the great Professors of Medicine of the present century. Stanley, as he was known by all, began his medical undergraduate training at Trinity College, Cambridge, but this was interrupted by World War I and later resumed in Edinburgh. He served in the Gordon Highlanders until he was seriously wounded in Belgium. That this period had a profound effect on his subsequent attitudes and values was clear from his emotional recollection, in later years, of the carnage and shocking waste of young life.

In the 1920s he favoured appointments in bacteriology, and this is reflected in his early interests. However, he soon decided to dedicate his life to clinical medicine and clinical research. Exciting contemporary discoveries led to an affection for haematology which he always retained and which was transmitted to many of his disciples.

In 1930 Stanley was appointed Professor of Medicine at the University of Aberdeen. This was one of the first full-time Chairs of Medicine anywhere, and the first in Scotland. The period in Aberdeen was marked by several developing qualities of academic leadership: toughness, fairness and integrity which quickly earned respect; finding and attracting young talent; recognition of the need for decent facilities and accommodation for teaching and research; and a research emphasis on the needs of the community.

Appointment to the Chair of Medicine at his Alma Mater, Edinburgh, came in 1938 and he was to remain in this post until retirement in 1959. World War II was to inhibit and delay Stanley's aspirations for the Edinburgh Medical School, but those of us who were privileged to be undergraduate students at the time have much to remember. He was a splendid educator and a particularly gifted bedside teacher where everything had to be questioned and explained. He seemed to be totally at ease with everyone, and would stop and talk with students, nurses, domestic staff and frequently with a complete stranger. He had endless time to listen to and communicate with his patients, who quickly seemed at ease with him. His main thesis was that if you could take a good history and do a careful physical examination, the rest might not be too difficult or expensive. He gave most of the systematic lectures in Medicine himself, the substance of which was made available in typewritten notes; these were marked by an emphasis on essentials and far surpassed any textbook available at the time.

When the war ended Stanley's priority was to develop the old municipal hospitals in the north of Edinburgh, to extend the teaching capacity of the Medical School and to recognise and establish units for the specialist branches of medicine that were beginning to emerge. These units were to be headed by the best physicians and teachers that could be found and were to retain a commitment to general internal medicine. Within a few years Stanley's far-sightedness became a reality.

But Stanley will be best remembered for this textbook, *The Principles and Practice of Medicine*. He conceived the idea in the late 1940s. It was to be of modest size and price and yet sufficiently comprehensive and up to date to provide the good student with the main elements of sound medical practice. The origins of the book were Stanley's lecture notes. Each of the senior members of Stanley's now extended departmental family was given a chapter to write. In the early days there was occasional annoyance when a carefully drafted manuscript was massacred by Stanley's editorial pencil; but no offence was taken because none was intended. The book was to be readable without ambiguity, uncertainty or wordiness. The result, a masterpiece of clarity and uniformity of style, is the basis from which this 19th edition has evolved. Although the format and presentation have seen many changes, Stanley's original vision and objectives remain. Half a century after its first publication, his book continues to inform and educate students, doctors and health professionals all over the world. It is an honour to salute the memory of a great physician and teacher and, for a fortunate few, a great mentor and friend.

Edinburgh
2002

Professor John Richmond

Contributors

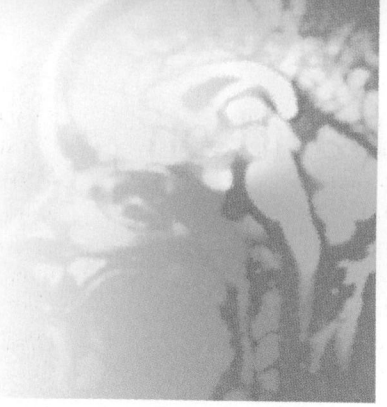

C.M.C. Allen MA MD FRCP
Consultant Neurologist, Addenbrooke's Hospital,
Cambridge

Jeffrey K. Aronson MA DPhil FRCP
Reader in Clinical Pharmacology, University of Oxford;
Honorary Consultant in Clinical Pharmacology and
Honorary Consultant Physician, Oxford Radcliffe
Hospitals Trust

Peter Bloomfield MD FRCP FACC
Consultant Cardiologist and Honorary Senior Lecturer,
Department of Cardiology, Royal Infirmary of Edinburgh

Nicholas A. Boon MA MD FRCP(Ed) FESC
Consultant Cardiologist, Royal Infirmary of Edinburgh;
Honorary Senior Lecturer, Department of Medicine,
Royal Infirmary of Edinburgh

Andrew W. Bradbury BSc MD FRCS(Ed)
Professor of Vascular Surgery, University of Birmingham;
Consultant Vascular Surgeon, Heartlands and Solihull
NHS Trust (Teaching), Birmingham

David A. Cameron MA MSc MD FRCP(Ed)
Senior Lecturer in Medical Oncology, University of
Edinburgh

Peter B. Carey FRCP
Clinical Director and Consultant Physician, Department of
Genitourinary Medicine, Royal Liverpool and Broadgreen
University Hospitals NHS Trust

Edwin R. Chilvers BMedSci PhD FRCP(Ed) FRCP
Professor of Respiratory Medicine, University of
Cambridge; Honorary Consultant Physician,
Addenbrooke's and Papworth Hospitals, Cambridge

Nicki R. Colledge BSc (Hons) FRCP(Ed)
Consultant Geriatrician, Liberton Hospital, Edinburgh and
Royal Infirmary of Edinburgh; Honorary Senior Lecturer,
University of Edinburgh

Paul A. Corris FRCP
Professor of Thoracic Medicine and Honorary Consultant
Physician, University of Newcastle upon Tyne and
Freeman Hospital

Jenny I.O. Craig MD FRCP(Ed) FRCPath
Consultant Haematologist, Addenbrooke's Hospital,
Cambridge

Allan D. Cumming MD FRCP(Ed)
Senior Lecturer and Associate Dean (Teaching),
Faculty of Medicine, University of Edinburgh;
Honorary Consultant Physician, Lothian University
Hospitals NHS Trust

Michael Doherty MA MD FRCP ILTM
Professor of Rheumatology, University of Nottingham;
Honorary Consultant Rheumatologist, City Hospital,
Nottingham

Marie T. Fallon MD FRCP(Glasg) MRCGP
Senior Lecturer in Palliative Medicine, University of
Edinburgh

Miles Fisher MD FRCP(Glasg) FRCP(Ed)
Consultant Physician, Glasgow Royal Infirmary;
Honorary Clinical Senior Lecturer, University of
Glasgow

Keith Alexander Arthur Fox BSc (Hons) FRCP FESC
Duke of Edinburgh Professor of Cardiology, University of
Edinburgh; Consultant Cardiologist, Royal Infirmary of
Edinburgh

Brian M. Frier BSc (Hons) MD FRCP(Ed) FRCP(Glasg)
Consultant Physician, Department of Diabetes, Royal
Infirmary of Edinburgh; Honorary Professor of Diabetes,
University of Edinburgh

O. James Garden BSc MD FRCS(Glasg) FRCS(Ed)
Regius Professor of Clinical Surgery and Honorary
Consultant Surgeon, Royal Infirmary of Edinburgh

Ian S. Grant FRCP(Ed) FRCP(Glasg) FFARCSI
Consultant in Intensive Care Medicine and Anaesthesia,
Western General Hospital, Edinburgh

Christopher Haslett BSc (Hons) FRCP(Ed) FRCP FRSE
Professor of Respiratory Medicine, University of
Edinburgh; Head of the Division of Clinical Sciences and
Community Health, University of Edinburgh; Honorary
Consultant Physician, Royal Infirmary of Edinburgh

Peter Clive Hayes BMSc MD PhD FRCP(Ed)
Professor of Hepatology and Honorary Consultant
Physician, Royal Infirmary of Edinburgh

Andrew Haynes MRCP FRCPath DM
Leukaemia Research Fund Senior Lecturer in
Haematological Oncology, City Hospital, Nottingham

Alison L. Jones BSc (Hons) MD FRCP(Ed) FiBiol FRCP
Consultant Physician and Clinical Toxicologist,
Head of Medicine, National Poisons Information Service,
Guy's and St Thomas NHS Trust, London

Peter C. Lanyon DM MRCP MRCGP DRCOG
Consultant Rheumatologist, University Hospital NHS
Trust, Queen's Medical Centre, Nottingham

Geoffrey G. Lloyd MD MPhil FRCP(Ed) FRCP FRCPsych
Consultant Liaison Psychiatrist, Royal Free Hampstead
NHS Trust, London

Diana Nancy Johanna Lockwood BSc MD FRCP
Consultant Physician and Leprologist, Hospital for
Tropical Diseases, London; Senior Lecturer, London
School of Hygiene and Tropical Medicine

Christopher A. Ludlam PhD FRCP(Ed) FRCPath
Professor of Haematology and Coagulation Medicine,
University of Edinburgh; Director, Haemophilia and
Thrombosis Centre, Royal Infirmary of Edinburgh

Christian J. Lueck PhD FRCP(Ed)
Consultant Neurologist and Part-time Senior Lecturer,
Department of Clinical Neuroscience, Western General
Hospital, Edinburgh

David Brian Lorimer McClelland MD(Leiden) FRCP(Ed) FRCPath
Strategy Director, Scottish National Blood Transfusion
Service, Ellen's Glen Road, Edinburgh

Fred Nye MD FRCP
Consultant Physician, Tropical and Infectious Diseases
Unit, Royal Liverpool University Hospital

Kelvin R. Palmer MD FRCP(Ed) FRCP
Consultant Gastroenterologist, Western General Hospital,
Edinburgh

Simon Paterson-Brown MS MPhil FRCS
Consultant General and Gastrointestinal Surgeon,
Royal Infirmary of Edinburgh

Ian D. Penman MD FRCP(Ed)
Consultant Gastroenterologist, Western General Hospital,
Edinburgh

William D. Plant BSc MRCPI FRCP(Ed)
Consultant Renal Physician, Department of Renal
Medicine, Cork University Hospital and Department of
Medicine, University College Cork, Ireland

Ian Power MD FRCA FFPMANZCA FANZCA
Professor of Anaesthesia, Critical Care and Pain Medicine,
University of Edinburgh

Stuart H. Ralston MD FRCP FMedSci
Professor of Medicine and Bone Metabolism, University
of Aberdeen; Honorary Consultant Physician, Aberdeen
Royal Infirmary

Jonathan L. Rees BMedSci FRCP FRCP(Ed) FMedSci
Grant Chair of Dermatology, University of Edinburgh

Richard N. Sandford PhD FRCP
Wellcome Trust Senior Fellow in Clinical Research and
Honorary Consultant in Medical Genetics, Addenbrooke's
Hospital, Cambridge

Lance N. Sandle BSc FRCPath
Consultant Chemical Pathologist, Trafford General
Hospital, Manchester

John Savill BA PhD FRCP FRCP(Ed) FMedSci
Professor of Medicine, University of Edinburgh; Director
of the Medical Research Council/University of Edinburgh
Centre for Inflammation Research

Olivia M.V. Schofield FRCP(Ed)
Consultant Dermatologist, Royal Infirmary of Edinburgh

Michael Sharpe MA MD MRCP MRCPsych
Reader in Psychological Medicine, University of
Edinburgh; Honorary Consultant to the Edinburgh
Hospitals

Prakash Shetty MD PhD
Professor of Human Nutrition, London School of Hygiene
and Tropical Medicine; Chief, Nutrition Planning,
Assessment and Evaluation, Food and Nutrition Division,
Food and Agriculture Organisation of the UN, Rome, Italy

Kenneth J. Simpson MD PhD FRCP(Ed)
Senior Lecturer, University of Edinburgh; Consultant
Physician, Scottish Liver Transplantation Unit, Royal
Infirmary of Edinburgh

John F. Smyth MD MSc FRCP FRCP(Ed) FRCS(Ed) FRCR FRSE
Professor of Medical Oncology, University of Edinburgh;
Honorary Consultant Physician, Lothian University
Hospitals NHS Trust

Laurence H. Stewart MD FRCS(Ed) FRCS(Urol)(Ed)
Consultant Urological Surgeon, Department of Urology,
Western General Hospital, Edinburgh

Christopher B. Summerton MA MD FRCP FRCP(Ed)
Consultant in Gastroenterology and General Medicine,
Trafford Healthcare NHS Trust, Manchester

W.T. Andrew Todd BSc FRCP(Ed) FRCP(Glasg)
Consultant Physician, Lanarkshire Area Infectious
Diseases Unit, Monklands Hospital, Airdrie; Honorary
Senior Lecturer, Glasgow University

Anthony Toft CBE MD FRCP
Consultant Physician, Royal Infirmary of Edinburgh

David F. Treacher MA FRCP
Consultant Physician in Intensive Care,
St Thomas's Hospital, London

A. Neil Turner PhD FRCP
Professor of Nephrology, Renal Medicine, Royal Infirmary
of Edinburgh

Brian R. Walker BSc MD FRCP(Ed)
British Heart Foundation Senior Research Fellow and
Professor of Endocrinology, University of Edinburgh,
Western General Hospital, Edinburgh

Stephen J. Watt BSc AFOM FRCP(Ed)
Senior Lecturer, Department of Environmental and
Occupational Medicine, University of Aberdeen

Edmund Wilkins FRCP FRCPath
Consultant Physician in Infectious Diseases,
North Manchester General Hospital

International Advisory Board

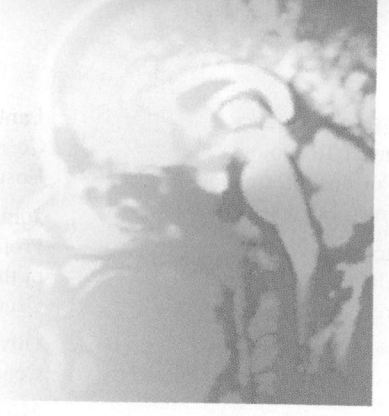

INTERNATIONAL EDITOR'S PREFACE

It is very encouraging for the authors and editors of *Davidson* to know that they are contributing to a book which is popular world-wide and which, in many countries, remains the cornerstone of the clinical phase of the medical curriculum. It is also reassuring that the clear, precise and no-nonsense approach, a legacy of Sir Stanley's influence, continues to be highly rated by both students and their teachers in countries as far apart as Canada, India, Pakistan, South Africa and Australia.

To ensure that those contributing to the book remain fully aware of their readers' diverse needs, the editorial team felt that an International Advisory Board could provide much helpful advice, especially on the relevance of the content in an international setting. The Board comprises nearly 30 practising doctors from 12 countries. All have established a reputation in their own specialty and have a keen interest in student education. Draft manuscripts of nearly every chapter have been vetted by at least two appropriate members of the Board. Their advice has been welcomed by the editors and is reflected in the current text. I am personally most grateful to members of the Board for their patience and prompt advice.

The publishers and editors also felt that they needed more first-hand feedback on the book from a country where *Davidson* is a (medical) household name. India was the obvious choice; the majority of its half million doctors have read at least one edition of *Davidson* from cover to cover! It was a great pleasure to be able to spend time visiting medical schools and colleges in several cities and to hear how the busy doctors and students thought we could improve our textbook. These intensive meetings contributed many ideas for changes and modifications that we have endeavoured to put into practice. I am grateful to all those who took time out to assist us. We intend to continue these discussions in other countries in the future.

We hope that our readers all over the world will appreciate the increased international flavour of this anniversary edition.

Edinburgh
2002

J.A.A.H.

MEMBERS OF THE INTERNATIONAL ADVISORY BOARD

Dr S. Aaron
Associate Professor and Clinical Skills Coordinator,
Faculty of Medicine, University of Alberta, Edmonton,
Canada

Dr S.K. Agarwal
Director—Professor and Head of Department of Medicine,
Maulana Azad Medical College, New Delhi, India

Dr Samar Banerjee
Professor, Department of Medicine, NRS Medical College
Kolkata, India

Dr Wilma Beswick
Clinical Dean, St Vincent's Hospital and Geelong Hospital
Clinical School, University of Melbourne, Australia

Professor Jan D. Bos
Professor and Chairman, Department of Dermatology,
Academic Medical Centre, University of Amsterdam,
Netherlands

Professor Y.-C. Chee
Chairman, Medical Board and Head of General Medicine,
Tan Tock Seng Hospital, Singapore

Dr Tapas Das
Professor of Medicine, Department of Medicine,
Medical College, Kolkata, India

Professor V. Diehl
Professor of Medicine and Director of Clinic for Internal
Medicine, Universitätsklinikum, Cologne, Germany

Professor M.J. Field
Professor of Medicine and Associate Dean,
Northern Clinical School/Royal North Shore Hospital,
University of Sydney, Australia

Dr S.M. Wasim Jafri
Kamruddin Mohammad Jassani Professor of Medicine,
Chair Medicine and Chief of Gastroenterology,
Aga Khan University, Karachi, Pakistan

Dr G. John
Professor of Medicine, Christian Medical College,
Vellore, Tamil Nadu, India

Professor K.V. Johny
Chairman of Department of Medicine, Chairman of
Faculty of Internal Medicine and Head of Nephrology
Division, Kuwait University, Kuwait

Professor J.A. Ker
Professor of Medicine, Department of Medicine,
University of Pretoria, South Africa

Professor Dato' Khalid B.A.K.
Professor of Medicine and Consultant Endocrinologist,
Department of Medicine, University Kebangsaan,
Kuala Lumpur, Malaysia

Professor C.-L. Lai
Chief of Division of Gastroenterology and Hepatology,
Department of Medicine, Queen Mary Hospital,
Hong Kong

Professor K. Mattson
Senior Staff Member, Department of Medicine,
Division of Respiratory Diseases, Helsinki University
Central Hospital, Finland

Professor W.F. Mollentze
Head of Internal Medicine, University of the Free State,
Bloemfontein, South Africa

Dr Prem Pais
Professor and Head of Medicine, Department of Medicine,
St John's Medical College, Bangalore, India

Dr J.N. Pande
Professor and Head of Department of Medicine,
All India Institute of Medical Sciences, New Delhi, India

Dr S.K. Rajan
Professor and Head of Department of Medicine,
Stanley Medical College, Chennai, India

Dr P.S. Shankar
Director, Professor of Medicine, K.J. Somaiya Medical
College and Research Centre, Mumbai, India

Dr Raymond A. Smego, Jr
Ibne-e-Sina Professor and Chair, Department of Medicine,
Aga Khan University, Karachi, Pakistan

Professor Dato' Tahir Azhar
Dean and Professor of Medicine, Faculty of Medicine,
International Islamic University Malaysia, Malaysia

Professor C.F. Van der Merwe
Professor and Head of Department of Gastroenterology,
Medical University of Southern Africa, Medunsa,
South Africa

Dr S. Varma
Professor and Head of Department of Internal Medicine,
Postgraduate Institute of Medical Education and Research,
Chandigarh, India

Dr G. Wittert
Associate Professor of Medicine and Senior Consultant
Endocrinologist, Department of Medicine,
Royal Adelaide Hospital, Australia

Dr M.E. Yeolekar
Vice Dean, Indian College of Physicians, Professor and
Head of Department of Internal Medicine, Lokmanya
Tilak Municipal Medical College and General Hospital,
Mumbai, India

An introduction to Davidson's Principles and Practice of Medicine

The first section of this book, 'Principles of medical practice', covers aspects of clinical practice, such as infection, drug therapy, critical care and pain relief, that are relevant to all medical specialties, while the second section, 'System-based diseases', is devoted to individual medical specialties such as cardiology and neurology. Although each chapter has been written by a team of experts in the field, a uniform approach has been adopted and great care has been taken to avoid unnecessary duplication. The system-based chapters in the second section therefore follow a standard format, beginning with an overview of the clinical examination, followed by an account of functional anatomy, physiology and investigations, then a discussion of the common presentations or major manifestations of disease, and finishing with a description of the individual diseases of that system. The clinical examination sections, boxes and special features such as 'Major manifestations', 'Issues in older people' and 'Evidence-based medicine' panels have been produced in a uniform style that is described below.

CLINICAL EXAMINATION OVERVIEWS

The skills that are required to obtain a clear history and elicit important physical signs are a prerequisite to best medical practice. A detailed account of history-taking and clinical examination has always been beyond the scope of this book but can be found in our sister title *Macleod's Clinical Examination*. Nevertheless, the editors of this edition of *Davidson* have tried to emphasise the value of good clinical skills by introducing a two-page overview of the important elements of the clinical examination at the beginning of each system-based chapter.

The left-hand page of each of these sections uses a manikin to illustrate the key steps in the examination of the relevant system, beginning with simple observations and progressing in a logical sequence around the body. The right-hand page has been used to expand on selected themes and includes useful tips on examination technique and the interpretation of physical signs. In Chapter 20, 'Musculoskeletal disorders', this is followed by an illustrated account of a validated screening examination for disease of the locomotor system known as 'GALS' (gait, arms, legs, spine). These overviews are intended to act as an aide-mémoire and not as a replacement for a detailed text on clinical examination.

MAJOR MANIFESTATIONS OF DISEASE

Medical students, and indeed junior doctors, are not only expected to learn a bewildering mix of facts about various disorders, but must also develop an analytical, problem-based approach to help them formulate a differential diagnosis and a logical plan of investigations for patients who present with particular symptoms or signs of disease. Few, if any, textbooks of medicine effectively combine a practical, problem-orientated diagnostic guide with structured, discussion-related facts. We have tried to achieve this goal by incorporating a 'Major manifestations' section into all system-based chapters. These were a popular feature of the last two editions, and have now been expanded to include over 120 major manifestations. Many patients present with non-specific symptoms such as weight loss, dizziness or breathlessness and these major manifestations of disease are spread across several chapters with appropriate cross-references.

CLASSIFICATION OF BOXES AND TABLES

Boxes and tables are a popular and efficient way of presenting information, and are particularly useful for revision. In the present edition boxes and tables are classified by the type of information they contain using the following symbols:

Causes

Clinical features/complications

Investigations

Treatment/adverse effects

Other information

ISSUES IN OLDER PEOPLE

In most developed countries older people comprise 20% of the population and are the chief users of health care. Older people contract the same diseases as those who are younger but there are often important differences in the way they present and how they are best managed.

Chapter 7, 'Frail older people', concentrates on the principles of managing the most impaired group who suffer from multiple pathology and disability, and who tend to present with non-specific problems such as falls. Many of those aged over 65 years are still relatively robust, however, and may suffer from specific single-organ pathology that will be managed by appropriate specialists.

Therefore, in this edition of *Davidson*, we have integrated organ-specific issues in older people into the system-based chapters, by incorporating bullet point panels wherever these are relevant (see example below). Their content includes common presentations, implications of physiological changes of ageing, effects of age on investigations, problems in treatment in old age, and the benefits and risks of intervention in older people. This provides a 'real-life' insight into the care of older people wherever they may present.

ISSUES IN OLDER PEOPLE
OBSTRUCTIVE PULMONARY DISEASE

- Both COPD and asthma are common in old age and are not mutually exclusive. A bias towards misdiagnosis of COPD rather than asthma is well recognised in elderly men and those of lower socio-economic class.
- Older people perceive acute bronchoconstriction less well than younger patients, so their description of symptoms is not a reliable indicator of severity, and 'on demand' bronchodilators may not be appropriate as a first step in treatment.
- The beneficial effects of stopping smoking on the rate of loss of lung function decline with age but remain valuable up to the age of 80.
- Most older people cannot use metered dose inhalers because of difficulty coordinating and triggering the device. Even mild cognitive impairment virtually precludes their use. Spacer devices are much preferred by patients. Frequent demonstration and reinstruction in the use of all devices are required.
- Mortality rates for acute asthma are higher in old age, partly because patients under-estimate the severity of bronchoconstriction and develop less tachycardia and pulsus paradoxus for the same degree of bronchoconstriction.

EVIDENCE-BASED MEDICINE

Students and clinicians alike are under increasing pressure to base their practice on the best available evidence. This needs to be up to date, relevant, authoritative and easily accessible. In this 19th edition of *Davidson* we have incorporated over 175 evidence-based medicine (EBM) panels

that summarise the results of the most recent systematic reviews (SRs) or randomised controlled trials (RCTs) in key therapeutic areas. An example and guide to the use of those boxes is given below. These panels also provide details of the landmark trials in each area and, when available, a web address which gives the reader access to additional references and, in particular, more detailed management guidelines. In areas not covered by EBM panels the reader is referred to www.cochrane.co.uk.

The EBM panels only contain recommendations that are supported by evidence obtained from meta-analysis of several RCTs or one (or more) high-quality RCT that address the specific question being asked. All recommendations therefore conform to 'Grade A' criteria as described and used by the Scottish Intercollegiate Guidelines Network (SIGN).

Certain EBM panels incorporate data on the numbers needed to treat (NNT); 'NNT' defines the number of people you would need to treat for a given period of time to prevent one additional adverse outcome or to achieve one additional beneficial outcome. Likewise, the absolute risk reduction (ARR) values quoted refer to the difference in risk between the experimental and control groups in the trial. A detailed account of evidence-based medicine in drug therapy, including details relating to the calculation of NNT, risk ratios and odds ratios, can be found in Chapter 2, 'Drug therapy' (see pp. 147–163). Further guidance on applying research evidence to clinical practice is available at www.clinicalevidence.org.

TERMINOLOGY

A recent European Community Directive requires member states to use Recommended International Non-proprietary Names (rINNs) for drugs. This terminology, with the exception of adrenaline and noradrenaline, is therefore used throughout the book; however, the British Approved Name (BAN) has been placed in parentheses in cases that may cause confusion. A more detailed account of drug nomenclature and a list of drug names whose rINN and BAN differ significantly can be found in Chapter 2, 'Drug therapy'. British English spellings have been retained for drug classes and groups (e.g. amphetamines not amfetamines).

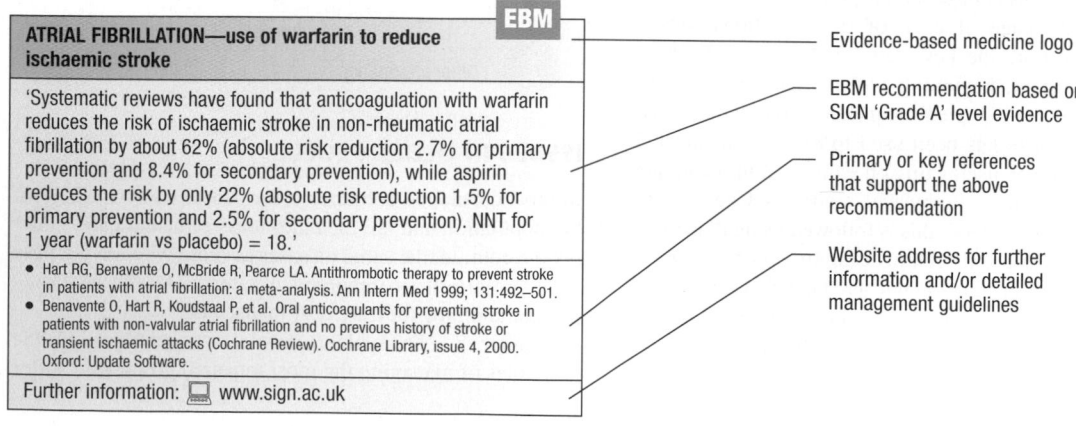

The International System of Units (SI units) has been used throughout. The reference ranges used in Edinburgh's laboratories are quoted in the Appendix but it is important to appreciate that these may vary from those used in other laboratories. In this edition the Appendix gives the equivalent values in traditional units as well as SI units.

FINDING WHAT YOU ARE LOOKING FOR

Detailed contents pages precede Part 1 of this book and list the main headings within each chapter, including 'Major manifestations of disease'. In addition, the first page of each chapter gives a breakdown of that chapter's content. The book contains numerous cross-references to help readers find their way around, and in the index the entries for EBM panels are indicated with a symbol. A list of up-to-date reviews and useful websites with links to management guidelines appears at the end of each chapter.

ON-LINE MULTIPLE CHOICE QUESTIONS

Multiple choice questions are widely used for examination purposes as a reliable and discriminatory test of factual knowledge. Lack of familiarity with the MCQ format may result in unexpected failure, although more usually failure is attributable to a lack of adequate reading and understanding of clinical medicine and the basic sciences.

To help students acquire the factual knowledge necessary for good medical practice 500 five-part multiple choice questions which are linked to the content of this edition of *Davidson* are provided with detailed answers free on-line at:

www.fleshandbones.com/medicine/davidson

FEEDBACK

We hope that you will find this edition of *Davidson* informative and easy to use. The editors would be delighted to hear from you if you have any comments or suggestions to make. Please e-mail us at:

Davidson.feedback@Elsevier.com

Contents

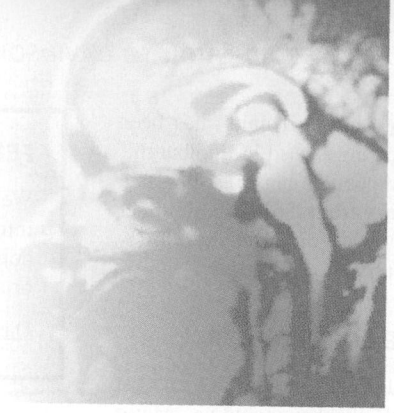

Part 1
PRINCIPLES OF MEDICAL PRACTICE

Part 2
SYSTEM-BASED DISEASES

Contents in detail

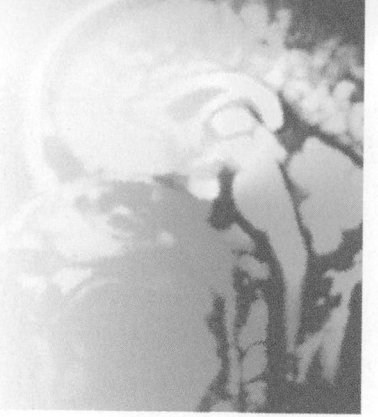

Part 1
PRINCIPLES OF MEDICAL PRACTICE

Infection and immune failure

W.T.A. TODD • D.N.J. LOCKWOOD • F.J. NYE • E.G.L. WILKINS • P.B. CAREY

Fifty years ago, when the first edition of Davidson's textbook was published, infectious disease was a major killer in both the developed and the developing world. Although vaccination was well established, antimicrobial therapy was in its infancy and infection management involved the isolation of infections in fever hospitals away from most centres of urban life. Over the last half-century the management of infection has moved into district and central hospitals and become integrated into the activity of most departments. In this edition for the first time a real attempt has been made to include the most up-to-date information on infection management in the relevant systems sections of the textbook. There nevertheless remain a number of generalised infections and symptom complexes that do not 'fit' this systems-based approach. This chapter covers these and includes important sections on international/imported infections and the new epidemic of human immunodeficiency virus (HIV) disease.

In this chapter an introduction is given to the body's response to infection, the common presentation of infection as fever, rashes or gastrointestinal upset, and the specific problems of infection in the immunocompromised state and in an international setting. An overview of the management of infection with antimicrobial agents is included.

Infection differs from other diseases in a number of aspects:

- Most importantly, it is caused by living microorganisms that can usually be identified, thus establishing the aetiology early in the illness. Many such organisms are sensitive to antimicrobial agents and most infections are potentially curable, unlike many non-infectious degenerative and chronic diseases.
- Communicability is another factor which differentiates infections from non-infectious diseases. Transmission of pathogenic organisms to other people, directly or indirectly, may lead to an outbreak requiring specific expertise in its management.
- Many infections are preventable by hygienic measures, by vaccines or by the judicious use of drugs (chemoprophylaxis).

PATTERNS OF INFECTION

PATTERNS OF INFECTION IN DEVELOPED COUNTRIES

During the 20th century the incidence of communicable diseases in developed countries has fallen dramatically. This is due to immunisation, antimicrobial chemotherapy, improved nutrition, and better sanitation and housing. Infections such as diphtheria, poliomyelitis and tetanus have decreased and in some locations almost disappeared. Smallpox, a lethal virus infection, has been eradicated from the world while another lethal infection, HIV, has emerged in pandemic proportions.

The pattern of infection in developed countries during the past two decades has been influenced by a number of factors (see Box 1.1). These include the development of microbial resistance, immunosuppression, foreign travel, altered sexual

1.1 INFLUENCES ON PATTERNS OF INFECTION IN DEVELOPED COUNTRIES
Vaccines
• Improved uptake of vaccines • New vaccines, e.g. *Haemophilus influenzae* type B and hepatitis A
Animal husbandry and preparation of food
• *Salmonella* and *Campylobacter* infections originating in poultry and eggs • *Escherichia coli* type O157 causing haemorrhagic colitis, associated with beef • *Listeria* infections from soft cheeses
Microbial resistance
• Increased resistance in common bacterial pathogens including *Staphylococcus aureus* (methicillin-resistant, MRSA), Gram-negative bacilli, *Streptococcus pneumoniae*, vancomycin-resistant enterococci (VRE) and *Mycobacterium tuberculosis*
Sexual behaviour
• Increase in HIV infection and other sexually transmitted diseases
International travel
• Importation of malaria (in 1996 there were 2500 cases in the UK, 2117 cases in continental France and 1021 cases in Germany) • Legionnaires' disease from holiday hotels • HIV infection
Immunosuppression
• Advances in the treatment of malignant disease and in organ transplantation leading to infections with opportunistic organisms
Resurgence of infections
• Tuberculosis—world-wide, especially in association with HIV infection • Poliomyelitis in the Netherlands (in a religious sect refusing vaccines) • Streptococcal infections in the USA (including rheumatic fever) • Measles in the USA (mainly in immigrants in inner cities) • Diphtheria in the former Soviet Union • Hepatitis A and typhoid fever in the former Yugoslavia
Intravenous drug addiction

behaviour, intravenous drug use, changes in animal husbandry and food production, and the availability and uptake of vaccines. Infections which had declined or been controlled are now resurgent, e.g. tuberculosis in a multi-resistant form. In addition, the identification of microorganisms as causative agents in conditions previously unrecognised as having an infectious aetiology has opened up new therapeutic avenues; for example, the aetiological role of *Helicobacter pylori* in peptic ulceration has revolutionised treatment of that condition.

PATTERNS OF INFECTION IN TROPICAL COUNTRIES

In less developed countries, especially in the tropics, infection continues to be one of the most common causes of disease and death, particularly in children, determining the strength of the working man, the health of the mother and the pattern of systemic disease, including neoplasia, in the community (see Box 1.2). Multiple disease is common and the clinical

1.2 PATTERNS OF INFECTION IN TROPICAL COUNTRIES

Killers of children, preventable but variably prevalent

- Measles
- Diphtheria
- Pertussis
- Poliomyelitis
- Tetanus
- Hepatitis B
- Gastroenteritis
- Malaria
- Meningococcal disease
- Acute diarrhoeal illness

Chronic disabling infections, widely prevalent

- Leprosy
- Tuberculosis
- Trachoma
- Malaria
- Trypanosomiasis cruzi
- Amoebiasis
- Intestinal helminths
- Schistosomiasis
- Filarial infection

Epidemic diseases, actual (marked *) and potential

- Louse-borne typhus and relapsing fever
- Cholera*
- Malaria
- Visceral leishmaniasis*
- HIV infection*
- Tuberculosis*, in association with HIV epidemic
- Influenza
- Enteric fevers

Infections liable to focal outbreaks (zoonotic or vector-borne)

- Dengue fever, e.g. Thailand
- Plague, e.g. Vietnam
- Cutaneous leishmaniasis, e.g. Sudan
- Yellow fever, e.g. Kenya, Nigeria
- African trypanosomiasis, e.g. Zambia
- Anthrax, e.g. USA (bioterrorism)

patterns of illness differ from those in temperate zones. The complex interaction between chronic parasitism, respiratory and diarrhoeal diseases, tuberculosis, malnutrition and its immunosuppressive effects, and HIV infection has a particularly deleterious effect on the health of children. Up to 40% of children may die before they reach 5 years of age in these situations. Chronic infections can damage important organs: liver and kidneys in schistosomiasis, the heart in trypanosomiasis cruzi, lungs, bones and lymph nodes in tuberculosis, bone marrow reserves in malaria and hookworm infections, the gut in tropical sprue and nerves in leprosy. These organs may then fail under increased demands of work, growth, pregnancy or additional disease. Chronic ill health is thereby imposed on millions of children and adults in the tropics.

Disease control by vaccination (yellow fever), vector control (malaria and sleeping sickness) and general improvement in living standards (plague and relapsing fever) has had a significant impact, but control is imperfect and the diseases reappear. Other epidemic diseases, such as cholera in Asia and meningococcal meningitis in Africa, remain largely uncontrolled and kill hundreds of thousands of people annually. Efficient vaccines exist for many diseases such as poliomyelitis, measles, rubella, meningitis, tetanus and hepatitis A and B, but in many countries they have made little impact because of cost and the practical difficulties of delivery. Development, especially in the form of dams and irrigation, has often encouraged the spread of vector-borne diseases such as malaria and schistosomiasis, while the exploitation of the Amazonian forests has resulted in mutilating outbreaks of mucocutaneous leishmaniasis. Migration to urban slums increases the risk of gastrointestinal disease, tuberculosis and 'Western' diseases such as hypertension, and has contributed

materially to the acquired immunodeficiency syndrome (AIDS) epidemic which is wreaking havoc in developing countries, especially Africa, the Indian subcontinent and South-east Asia. Lack of material resources has severely limited the availability of therapeutic agents, particularly in the management of HIV disease in the developing world.

Finally, in developing countries infectious diseases are often associated with natural disasters such as drought, flooding and earthquakes as well as with war and political strife.

MICROORGANISM–HOST INTERACTIONS

EFFECTS OF INFECTION ON THE BODY

Infection has many effects on the body, summarised in Box 1.3. They may be acute, chronic, allergic or toxigenic.

1.3 CLINICAL EFFECTS OF INFECTION ON THE BODY

Acute

- Fever; anorexia, protein catabolism, negative nitrogen balance, acute-phase protein response, hypoalbuminaemia, low serum iron, sequestration of iron, anaemia, neutrophilia
- Inflammation; pain, dysfunction, tissue damage
- Convulsions; especially in children
- Confusion; especially in the elderly
- Shock; sustained fall in circulating blood volume associated with lowered systemic vascular resistance
- Haemorrhage; haemolytic anaemia, intravascular coagulation
- Organ failure; kidneys, liver, lung, heart, brain, necrosis of skin

Chronic

- Weight loss and muscle-wasting
- Malnutrition; especially associated with diarrhoea
- Retardation of growth and intellect in children
- Anaemia; iron sequestration, maturation arrest in marrow, folate deficiency
- Tissue destruction; e.g. lung in pneumonia or tuberculosis, nerves in leprosy, liver in hepatitis B
- Post-infective syndromes; e.g. lactose intolerance, malabsorption, irritable colon, depression, post-viral fatigue syndrome

'Allergic' (immune-mediated)

- Rash; e.g. urticaria with helminths, maculo-papular in typhoid and endocarditis, erythema nodosum in tuberculosis
- Arthritis; e.g. in rheumatic fever, Reiter's syndrome
- Pericarditis; e.g. in meningococcal infection
- Encephalitis; e.g. in measles or following vaccines
- Peripheral neuropathy; e.g. in post-infective polyneuritis
- Haemolytic anaemia; e.g. in infectious mononucleosis
- Nephritis; e.g. in streptococcal infection

'Toxic' (toxin-mediated)

- Erythematous rash in streptococcal infection
- Multisystem disturbance in staphylococcal toxic shock syndrome
- Diarrhoea; e.g. staphylococcal enterotoxin, *Bacillus carvus*
- Organ disturbance; e.g. diphtheria
- Neurological; e.g. tetanus, botulinum, diphtheria

Chronic effects are seen especially in children in tropical countries.

PATHOLOGY OF INFECTION

Disease due to infection is the result of interaction between a microorganism and the defence mechanisms of the body. The outcome of this interaction can range from no demonstrable effect to death, and will depend on the number and virulence of the organisms, the physiological and anatomical effects that they induce, and the effectiveness of the body's natural defences. It is now demonstrated that there are strong genetic influences which determine the response to infection. Clear examples of this are the genetic polymorphisms in expression of cytokine release (e.g. tumour necrosis factor-α, TNF-α) and cytokine receptor expression (e.g. interferon-γ).

Organisms act directly and/or through their toxins. Many of these effects are generalised, but some act at specific anatomical sites—for example, poliomyelitis virus in anterior horn cells, hepatitis virus in hepatocytes, pneumococcus in the lung alveoli, and tetanus and diphtheria toxins at nerve terminals.

Shock is an especial problem in severe infections (see p. 195). Its aetiology is complex and results from reduced systemic vascular resistance brought about by dilated small vessels and leaky capillaries under the influence of several mediators, which include kinins, complement components, histamine, cytokines and endogenous opiates. Endotoxin from Gram-negative bacteria is well known to mediate release of these agents. However, Gram-positive shock caused by other cell wall components and lipoteichoic acid is clinically indistinguishable from Gram-negative shock. The cycle of shock, tissue anoxia and organ failure is difficult to break and may kill the patient within hours.

SOURCE AND SPREAD OF INFECTION

Infection may originate from the patient (endogenous), usually from skin, nasopharynx or bowel, or from outside sources (exogenous), often another person who may be either suffering from an infection or carrying a pathogenic microorganism. Carriers are usually healthy and may harbour the organism in the throat (for example, diphtheria or meningococci), bowel (salmonella) or blood (hepatitis B or HIV). Non-human sources of infection include water (cholera), milk (tuberculosis), food (botulism), animals (rabies), birds (psittacosis) and also the soil (legionnaires' disease).

Microorganisms may be transmitted by several routes. Endogenous infection may develop as a result of local spread, e.g. from bowel to peritoneum, or be spread via the blood stream. An example of the latter type is endocarditis caused by *Strep. sanguis* originating in the patient's mouth and entering the blood during dental procedures. Exogenous infection may be acquired directly or indirectly by one of the routes shown in Box 1.4.

1.4 SOURCE AND SPREAD OF INFECTION

Source/route of transmission	Method of spread	Examples of infection
Contact Person-to-person	Skin or mucous membrane contact	Staphylococci/streptococci (impetigo), scabies, wound infection, infectious mononucleosis Sexually transmitted diseases (including HIV and hepatitis B)
Soil	Via wounds and abrasions	Tetanus, Buruli ulcer, hookworm, mycetoma
Water	Penetration of skin	Schistosomiasis, leptospirosis
Air-borne spread	Respiratory droplets or dust	Measles, rubella, chickenpox, whooping cough, scarlet fever, mumps, meningococcal infection, tuberculosis Upper respiratory tract infection, influenza
	Water aerosols	Legionellosis, small, round, structured viruses
Faecal-oral spread	Faecal contamination of food or drink	Salmonella infection, bacillary and amoebic dysentery, enteroviral infections, cholera, giardiasis, hepatitis A, *Campylobacter* infection, E. coli, toxoplasmosis, dracunculiasis
Transplacental	Maternal blood	Rubella, cytomegalovirus (CMV) infection, toxoplasmosis, syphilis, malaria HIV infection
Medical and nursing procedures	Needles, ventilators, infusion fluid	Hepatitis B, staphylococcal infection, *Pseudomonas* infection, tuberculosis
Zoonoses (animal to humans)	Beef or pork	Tapeworms, toxoplasmosis, *Trichinella* infection
	Poultry or eggs	Salmonellosis, *Campylobacter*, E. coli
	Milk	Tuberculosis, *Campylobacter* infection, brucellosis
	Cheese	Listeriosis, brucellosis
	Rats' or dogs' urine	Leptospirosis, Lassa fever
	Dogs' faeces	*Toxocara* infection, hydatid disease, toxoplasmosis
	Dog bite	Rabies
	Birds	Psittacosis
	Fish	Tapeworms, mycobacterial infections
Arthropods (see Box 1.44, p. 63)		

The incubation period is the period between the invasion of the tissues by pathogens and the appearance of clinical features of infection. The period of infectivity is the time that the patient is infectious to others. Incubation periods of major infections and periods of infectivity in childhood infectious diseases are shown in the Appendix.

VACCINE DEVELOPMENT

The potential to prevent disease by inducing immunity through vaccination remains an important area of clinical medicine. There is a need both to generate vaccines for those diseases where at present none exists, such as HIV infection, and to improve the efficacy of other vaccines that are currently in use, e.g. for influenza.

Of the different features required for an ideal vaccine (see Box 1.5), safety and protection are perhaps the most important.

1.5 CHARACTERISTICS OF EFFECTIVE VACCINES

Safety
- No disease must be caused by the vaccine itself

Protection
- Protection must be at the population level and prevent disease when the infectious agent is encountered

Long-lasting effects
- Protection must be long-lasting, i.e. induce T and B cell memory

Cost
- Inexpensive to produce and deliver

Administration
- Easy to deliver with no side-effects

1.6 APPROACHES TO VACCINE DESIGN

Intact pathogen
- Heat-killed or chemically denatured
- Attenuated by growth conditions or genetic manipulation

Subunit vaccines
- Recombinant proteins
- Synthetic peptides

Vaccine vehicles
- Live vectors: viral (e.g. adenovirus) and bacteria (e.g. mycobacteria)

Adjuvants
- Conjugated to lipid or protein carrier molecules
- Microencapsulated in lipids

DNA immunisation
- Injection of plasmid DNA

The design of potential vaccines is greatly influenced by the qualitative nature of the immune response (cell-mediated or humoral immunity) required to mediate protection. To meet these specific needs, different approaches have been adopted (see Box 1.6). Older polysaccharide vaccines, such as pneumococcal polyvalent vaccine, produce an antibody response that is short-lived and without long-lasting memory (lack of T-cell activation). However, conjugation of the polysaccharide moiety to a protein, as in haemophilus B conjugate vaccine or meningococcal C vaccine, provides an immunological memory and sustained response. New vaccines of this type are becoming available for *Salmonella typhi* and *Strep. pneumoniae* infections. Furthermore, the route of administration may also be important and, where down-regulation of the immune response is required, delivery via the mucosal surfaces of the gastrointestinal and respiratory tracts is an effective way of inducing immunological tolerance. The World Health Organisation (WHO) has provided guidelines for the immunisation of children in developing countries (see Appendix). General guidelines for immunisation are shown in Boxes 1.7 and 1.8.

Vaccination has been a very successful means of controlling infection throughout the world. The world-wide eradication of smallpox (declared by WHO in 1980) is the best example of this. Vaccination becomes successful once the 'herd immunity' of the population reaches the required level to prevent ongoing spread of the wild-type virus. For example, measles, being very infectious, requires over 90% vaccination in susceptibles before this can be achieved. Significant reductions in notifications of both measles and mumps have followed the introduction of effective vaccination schedules (see Figs 1.31 and 1.36, pp. 34 and 36). From the mid-1990s in the UK public concern about possible reported links of measles, mumps and rubella (MMR) vaccine to autism and inflammatory bowel disease (IBD) has significantly reduced vaccine uptake to levels that may allow reappearance of wild virus activity. In the UK the Medical Research Council set up an expert group that has concluded that there is no scientific evidence to link MMR to autism or IBD. The UK Committee on the Safety of Medicines working party concluded similarly. Following discussion with all major health organisations the Chief Medical Officers of England,

1.7 GUIDELINES FOR IMMUNISATION AGAINST INFECTIOUS DISEASE

- The principal contraindication to inactivated vaccines is a significant reaction to a previous dose
- Live vaccines should not be given to pregnant women or to the immunosuppressed, or in the presence of an acute infection
- If two live vaccines are required, they should be given either simultaneously in opposite arms or 3 weeks apart
- Live vaccines should not be given for 3 months after an injection of human normal immunoglobulin (HNI)
- HNI should not be given for 2 weeks after a live vaccine
- Hay fever, asthma, eczema, sickle-cell disease, topical steroid therapy, antibiotic therapy, prematurity and chronic heart and lung diseases, including tuberculosis, are *not* contraindications to immunisation

1.8 VACCINES AND TOXOIDS

Live attenuated vaccines	Inactivated/ conjugated vaccines	Toxoid (inactivated toxin)
Childhood immunisation		
Measles	Pertussis	Diphtheria
Mumps	*H. influenzae*	Tetanus
Rubella	type B (HIB)	
Poliomyelitis*	Meningococcal	
BCG (tuberculosis)	A and C	
MMR		
Travel		
Yellow fever	Typhoid	
Typhoid*	Cholera	
	Rabies	
	Japanese	
	encephalitis	
	Hepatitis A	
Special risk groups		
Influenza*	Pneumococcal	
Varicella	Hepatitis B	
	Influenza	
	Meningococcal	
	(types A	
	and C only)	
	Plague	
	Poliomyelitis*	

* Both live and inactivated vaccines available. Vaccinated groups are not exclusive.

Scotland and Wales have advised that the MMR vaccine is safe, is the best way to protect children against these diseases, and should be given at the appropriate times in the UK vaccination schedule (see Appendix).

THE FEBRILE PATIENT

THERMOREGULATION

Human metabolic processes are critically temperature-dependent, and an individual's body temperature rarely varies by more than 1°C from baseline. The central thermostat is situated in the hypothalamus. Heat- and cold-sensitive neurons are located in the anterior hypothalamus and pre-optic area. The posterior hypothalamus integrates signals from the anterior hypothalamus with temperature information from peripheral receptors and then modulates the body's heat production, conservation and loss. The latter are controlled by neuronal mechanisms involving the limbic system, lower brain stem, spinal cord and autonomic nerves. Temperature in healthy adults is tightly controlled at a mean of 36.8°C; there is, however, a physiological diurnal variation of approximately 0.5°C, with the maximum occurring between 1600 and 2000 hrs and the minimum between 0200 and 0600 hrs. 'Fever' can be defined as a regulated elevation in body temperature above the customary set point of the hypothalamic thermostat.

THE FEBRILE RESPONSE

The initiation of fever begins when exogenous or endogenous stimuli, including pyrogens, are presented to specialised host cells, principally monocytes and macrophages. This process stimulates the synthesis and release of various pyrogenic cytokines including interleukin-1, tissue necrosis factor-α, interleukin-6 and interferon-γ. After release into the circulation these polypeptides can be found in virtually all body fluids. Cytokine/receptor interactions in the pre-optic region of the anterior hypothalamus activate phospholipase A. This enzyme liberates plasma membrane arachidonic acid as substrate for the cyclo-oxygenase pathway. The resulting mediator, prostaglandin E_2, then modifies the responsiveness of thermosensitive neurons in the thermoregulatory centre.

The role of exogenous pyrogens

Exogenous pyrogens are molecules which interact with host cells to induce the secretion of pyrogenic cytokines. Most act directly on monocytes or macrophages.

The best-characterised exogenous pyrogens are found in bacterial cell walls. 'Endotoxin' is a hydrophobic lipopolysaccharide which is a component of the cell walls of Gram-negative bacteria. Biological activity lies in the lipid A moiety, and the most important fatty acid producing fever has been identified as β-hydroxymyritic acid. As well as provoking the febrile response, endotoxin also plays a major role in the induction of septic shock. The molecule is widely distributed in Gram-negative bacteria and is found in non-virulent and weakly virulent species as well as in major pathogens such as salmonellae.

Muramyl dipeptide (MDP) is an exogenous pyrogen found in all bacteria with cell walls (and is therefore absent from mycoplasmas). A constituent of peptidoglycan, MDP is relatively more important in Gram-positive than Gram-negative organisms, as the latter possess only a thin peptidoglycan layer. On a weight-to-weight basis, however, MDP is $10–10^3$ times less active than endotoxins. MDP induces fever by interacting with specific receptors on monocytes and polymorphs.

The role of viruses as pyrogens is complex. Viruses which invade macrophages stimulate cytokine production by a mechanism which probably involves double-stranded RNA. Interferon production by infected non-phagocytic cells also contributes to fever, as does necrosis of tissue brought about by virus invasion.

Fever as a defensive adaptation?

There is suggestive evidence that, for some microorganisms at least, a febrile host response may assist in curtailing infection and speeding recovery. Experimental data support the notion that raised body temperature interferes with the growth and/or virulence factors of a selection of bacterial and viral pathogens. Conversely, suppression of fever by antipyretics may increase viral shedding and the incidence of complications in infections caused by influenza, measles and rhinoviruses. Nevertheless, the role of the febrile response as a defence mechanism requires further study.

FEVER IN GENERAL PRACTICE

Presentation

(See Fig. 1.1 and Box 1.9)

- *'Feeling hot'*. It is wise to obtain objective evidence of raised body temperature. Patients who complain of feeling hot do not necessarily have fever.
- *Rigors*. Shivering (followed by excessive heat or sweating) implies a rapid rise in body temperature but rarely gives a clue to aetiology.
- *Excessive sweating*. Night sweats are characteristic of tuberculosis, but sweating from any cause is usually worse at night. Non-infective causes of sweating include alcohol misuse, anxiety, thyrotoxicosis and diabetes mellitus.
- *Headache*. Fever from any cause may provoke headache. Severe headache and photophobia, though characteristic of meningitis, may also accompany pyelonephritis, pneumonia and bacterial enteritis.
- *Delirium*. Mental confusion during fever is relatively more common in young children and the frail elderly.
- *Muscle pain*. Myalgia is characteristic of virus infections such as influenza and enterovirus infection, but may also accompany septicaemic illness including meningococcal disease.
- *Recurrent fever*. There is a long list of disorders causing recurrent fever, but the source is often a focus of bacterial infection somewhere below the diaphragm:

1.9 FEVER IN GENERAL PRACTICE*
Rash ❶
• A purpuric or petechial rash suggests meningococcal disease *but* some patients with this infection have an erythematous (blanching) rash, or no rash at all; differential diagnosis includes petechiae induced by vomiting (superior vena cava distribution), Henoch–Schönlein purpura, vasculitic drug reactions and thrombocytopenia • Vesicular rashes may be caused by chickenpox, Coxsackie A virus infection (hand, foot and mouth disease) and erythema multiforme • Parvovirus B19 infection produces an erythematous or lace-like rash and a characteristic 'slapped cheek' appearance • Measles is now uncommon in the UK
Oral temperature ❷
• The equilibrium time with a mercury in glass thermometer is a minimum of 90 seconds
Mouth and oropharynx ❸
• Palatal petechiae or a cheesy grey-white tonsillar exudate suggests infectious mononucleosis
Neck stiffness ❼
• Stiffness on forward flexion implies meningeal irritation; stiffness in all directions suggests local disease of the spine or soft tissues
Cervical lymph nodes ❽
• Enlargement of anterior and tonsillar nodes is usually associated with tonsillitis or pharyngitis; posterior lymphadenopathy may suggest a glandular fever syndrome or HIV infection
Renal angle tenderness ❿
• True renal tenderness is difficult to distinguish from lumbar myalgia which occurs in many systemic viral and bacterial infections
* Numbers refer to Figure 1.1.

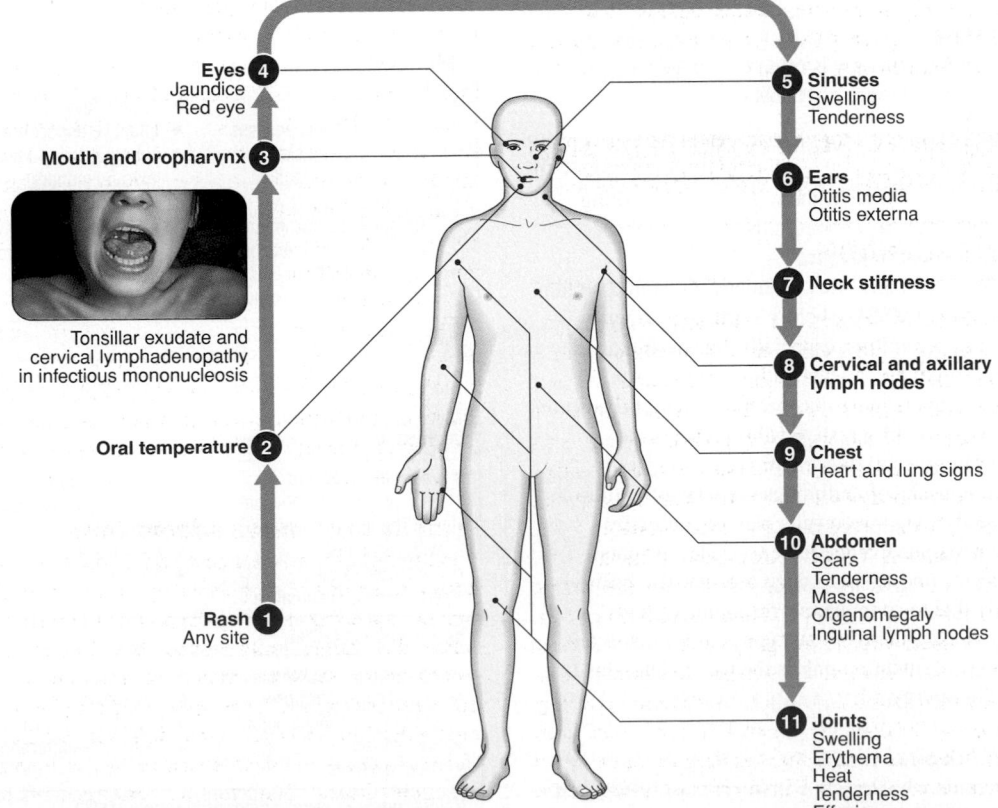

Tonsillar exudate and cervical lymphadenopathy in infectious mononucleosis

Eyes ④ Jaundice Red eye

Mouth and oropharynx ③

Oral temperature ②

Rash ① Any site

⑤ Sinuses Swelling Tenderness

⑥ Ears Otitis media Otitis externa

⑦ Neck stiffness

⑧ Cervical and axillary lymph nodes

⑨ Chest Heart and lung signs

⑩ Abdomen Scars Tenderness Masses Organomegaly Inguinal lymph nodes

⑪ Joints Swelling Erythema Heat Tenderness Effusion

Fig. 1.1 Fever in general practice: clinical examination.

cholecystitis or cholangitis, intra-abdominal, retroperitoneal or psoas abscess, or urinary tract infection (often associated with obstruction or calculi).

History-taking

- *Symptoms of common infections*. Enquire about sore throat, nasal discharge, sneezing and sinus pain. Elicit symptoms of lower respiratory tract infection (cough, sputum, wheeze or breathlessness).
- *Genitourinary symptoms*. Ask specifically about frequency of micturition, dysuria, loin pain, and vaginal or urethral discharge (urinary tract infection, pelvic inflammatory disease and sexually transmitted disease).
- *Abdominal symptoms*. Ask about diarrhoea, weight loss and abdominal pain (gastroenteritis, intra-abdominal sepsis, inflammatory bowel disease, malignancy).
- *Joint symptoms*. Is there anything to suggest active arthritis: joint pain, swelling, or limitation of movement?
- *Rash*. Enquire about appearance.
- *Travel history*. Always ask about foreign travel. If the patient has been in an endemic area, malaria *must* be excluded whatever the presenting symptoms.
- *Drug history*. Drug fever is uncommon and therefore easily missed. The culprits include penicillins and cephalosporins, sulphonamides, antituberculous agents, anticonvulsants (particularly phenytoin), methyldopa and quinidine.
- *Alcohol consumption*. Alcoholic hepatitis, cirrhosis and hepatocellular carcinoma are all recognised causes of fever.

Management

Empirical antibiotic therapy is often used in general practice. The guiding principles are as follows:

- Do not give antibiotics for virus infections such as colds and minor sore throats.
- Avoid giving antibiotics if there is a risk of masking serious sepsis such as endocarditis, e.g. in a febrile patient with a heart murmur.
- If possible, take diagnostic specimens, e.g. a mid-stream sample of urine (MSSU), before starting treatment.
- Avoid giving penicillins, especially amoxicillin or ampicillin, to young patients with sore throats unless infectious mononucleosis has been excluded, because of the higher risk of drug rash. Erythromycin is the treatment of choice in this situation.
- 'Therapeutic trials' of antibiotics are very difficult to interpret. False negative results may be caused by antibiotic resistance, inadequate tissue levels, poor compliance or undiagnosed deep sepsis. False positives are usually due to spontaneous resolution of fever.
- Always give parenteral benzylpenicillin for suspected meningococcal infection unless the patient has a history of penicillin allergy.

Referral to hospital

Very sick patients who present with fever must be referred to hospital immediately. In this context severe sepsis is easily

overlooked; mental confusion, a drop in blood pressure, body pain and general 'toxicity' are useful pointers to diagnosis. Non-specific diarrhoea often accompanies septicaemic illness, particularly in pneumococcal infection. Although a haemorrhagic rash is characteristic of meningococcal disease, skin changes may be atypical or absent. Other categories of patient who might be considered for referral to hospital include:

- immunocompromised or immunosuppressed patients
- those with in-dwelling prosthetic devices or grafts
- intravenous drug users
- patients with valvular heart disease
- patients with imported fever.

FEVER IN THE RETURNING TRAVELLER

See page 50.

PYREXIA OF UNKNOWN ORIGIN INVESTIGATED IN HOSPITAL

Pyrexia of unknown origin (PUO) may be defined as a consistently elevated body temperature of more than

1.10 AETIOLOGY OF PUO	
Infections (30%)	
• Sepsis Intra-abdominal abscess: cholecystitis/cholangitis Urinary tract infection: prostatitis Dental and sinus infections Bone and joint infections • Imported infections, e.g. malaria, dengue, brucellosis	• Enteric fevers • Infective endocarditis • Tuberculosis (particularly extrapulmonary) • Viral infections (CMV, Epstein–Barr virus (EBV), HIV) and toxoplasmosis • Fungal infections
Malignancy (20%)	
• Lymphoma and myeloma • Leukaemia	• Solid tumours (renal, liver, colon, stomach, pancreas)
Connective tissue disorders (15%)	
• Vasculitic disorders (incl. polyarteritis nodosa and rheumatoid disease with vasculitis) • Temporal arteritis/ polymyalgia rheumatica	• Systemic lupus erythematosus (SLE) • Still's disease • Polymyositis • Rheumatic fever
Miscellaneous (20%)	
• Inflammatory bowel disease • Liver disease: cirrhosis and granulomatous hepatitis • Sarcoidosis • Drug reactions	• Atrial myxoma • Thyrotoxicosis • Hypothalamic lesions • Familial Mediterranean fever
No diagnosis or resolves spontaneously (15%)	

1.11 FEVER INVESTIGATED IN HOSPITAL: THE INTERPRETATION OF PHYSICAL SIGNS*

Rash or skin nodules ❷

- Vasculitic lesions: think of cutaneous or systemic vasculitic disorders, granulomatous disease, lymphoma, acute endocarditis and drug reactions
- Nodular skin lesions: think of disseminated fungal infection and malignancy. Cancers of the colon, bladder and ovary often metastasise to the abdominal wall; nodules on the scalp or chest wall suggest a breast or bronchial primary. Leukaemia and lymphoma may produce papules, nodules or plaques

Eyes ❸

- Red eye: conjunctivitis, scleritis or uveitis. Consider immune complex disorders, connective tissue disease, Reiter's syndrome, reactive arthritis etc.
- Conjunctival petechiae: consider endocarditis
- Proptosis: may suggest thyroid eye disease. If unilateral, consider orbital infiltration by malignancy or granulomatous disease

Optic fundi ❹

- Look for haemorrhages and exudates (vasculitis), Roth's spots (endocarditis), choroidal tubercles and disseminated fungal lesions

Upper airways ❺

- Examine for nasal obstruction or bleeding, and for sinus pain or swelling (granulomatous disease, malignancy)

Rectal examination ❸

- Perianal disease (suggests inflammatory bowel disease)
- Local sepsis or abscess
- Rectal carcinoma
- Prostatic malignancy or prostatitis

* Numbers refer to Figure 1.2.

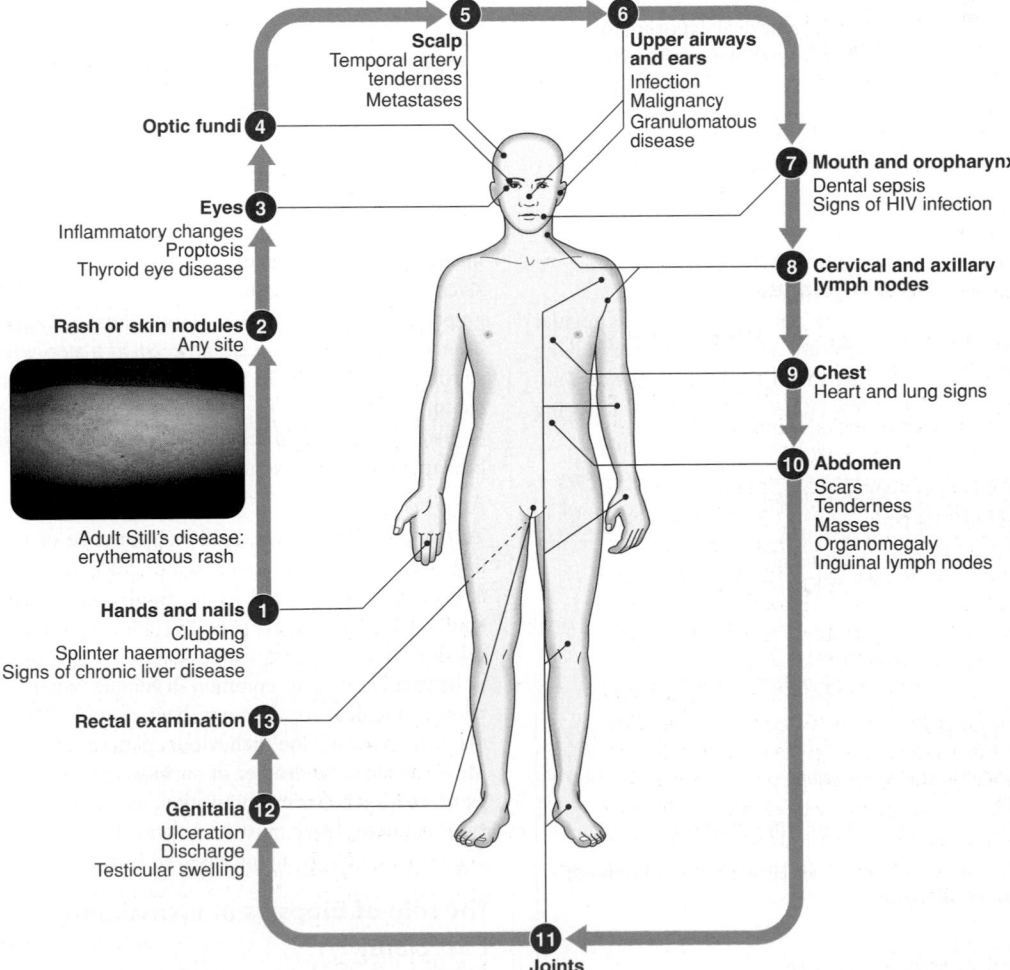

Fig. 1.2   Fever investigated in hospital: clinical examination.

37.5°C persisting for more than 2 weeks with no diagnosis after initial investigation (e.g. after a week's appraisal in hospital).

The following account applies to immunocompetent individuals with PUO admitted from the community.

Aetiology

See Box 1.10.

History-taking

- Travel abroad and countries of origin. Take a careful history of which countries the patient has visited or lived in. Important areas include sub-Saharan Africa, the Indian subcontinent, the Far East, the Middle East, Oceania, Latin America and the Caribbean. Malaria, respiratory infections, viral hepatitis and dengue are the most common causes of imported fever. For other causes see pages 50–69.
- Personal and social history. Take a sexual history. Ask about possible recent exposure to sexually transmitted diseases, and assess the lifetime risk of sexually acquired HIV infection. Enquire about illicit drug usage, particularly by injection (HIV, hepatitis B and C, infective endocarditis).
- Check on occupational or recreational exposure to birds (psittacosis) or animals (toxoplasmosis, Q fever, brucellosis, leptospirosis) and on consumption of unpasteurised milk or milk products (brucellosis and Q fever).

Clinical features

See Figure 1.2 and Box 1.11.

Investigations and management

It is essential to reassess the patient clinically at regular intervals while investigations are under way. History-taking should be repeated and expanded, and physical examination performed every few days to pick up emerging

---

1.12 TESTS USED IN THE FIRST WEEK OF INVESTIGATING PUO
- Full blood count (FBC) and differential - Erythrocyte sedimentation rate (ESR) and C-reactive protein (CRP) - Serum ferritin - Urea, creatinine and electrolytes - Liver function tests and gamma-glutamyl transferase - Blood glucose - Bone biochemistry - Creatine phosphokinase - Malaria blood films (if travel history) - Urinalysis - Midstream urine (MSU) for microscopy and culture - Faeces culture - Sputum for routine microscopy and culture, and microscopy and culture for mycobacteria - Blood cultures × 3 - Chest radiograph - Ultrasound examination of abdomen - Electrocardiogram (ECG)

1.13 SEROLOGICAL INVESTIGATIONS IN THE MANAGEMENT OF PUO	
Viral	
- CMV - EBV - HIV	- Hepatitis A, B and C - Parvovirus
If travel history: - Arbovirus	
Bacterial	
- Chlamydia - Q fever - Brucellosis - Mycoplasma - Syphilis	- Leptospirosis - Lyme disease - Yersinia - Antistreptolysin O (ASO) titre
If travel history: - Rickettsia - Melioidosis	- Relapsing fever - *Bartonella*
Fungal	
- Cryptococcus (antigen detection)	
If travel history: - Histoplasmosis	- Coccidioidomycosis
Protozoan and parasitic	
- Toxoplasmosis	
If travel history: - Schistosomiasis - Amoebiasis	- Leishmaniasis - Trypanosomiasis

---

physical signs, such as the appearance of enlarged lymph nodes, a heart murmur or missing pulses (embolisation, vasculitis).

The best strategy for investigating PUO is to carry out investigations in order of increasing complexity and invasiveness. The differential diagnosis will depend on geographical location and HIV status. Pursue diagnostic clues immediately, but otherwise proceed in a step-wise manner, starting with blood tests and progressing through imaging techniques to more invasive procedures such as 'blind' biopsies. A suggested scheme of investigation based on this principle is summarised in Boxes 1.12–1.14.

Factitious fever

This is defined as fever, or the appearance of fever, which is engineered by the patient (see p. 268). The desired effect is usually accomplished by manipulating the thermometer and/or temperature chart, or by inducing infection by the self-injection of contaminated materials. This practice tends to be relatively more common in female patients and those with a medical or nursing background. The condition may be part of the behaviour pattern characteristic of Münchausen's syndrome; in an individual case 'secondary gain', i.e. psychological motivation, may or may not be apparent. Factitious fever must be excluded as soon as possible; diagnostic clues are summarised in Box 1.15.

The role of biopsies in investigation

Liver biopsy

Blind liver biopsy is a low-yield investigation which carries an estimated mortality of approximately 0.01%. The procedure

1.14 FURTHER NON-INVASIVE INVESTIGATIONS IN THE MANAGEMENT OF PUO

Nucleic acid detection (polymerase chain reaction, PCR)
- Increasingly used, e.g. for TB, herpes simplex virus (HSV), CMV, HIV, parvovirus, dengue, *Toxoplasma*, Whipple's disease

Immunology
- Autoantibody screen, including anti-double-stranded DNA, anti-neutrophil cytoplasmic antibody (ANCA)
- Immunoglobulins
- Complement (C3 and C4) levels
- Cryoglobulins

Tuberculosis screening tests
- Tuberculin (Mantoux) test
- Early morning specimen of urine (EMSU) × 3 for mycobacterial microscopy and culture

Imaging techniques

Ultrasound of abdomen
- Liver tumour or metastases, liver abscess
- Dilated intrahepatic bile ducts
- Renal tumour, abscess or hydronephrosis
- Ascites

Echocardiogram
- Vegetations
- Atrial myxoma
- Intracardiac thrombus

CT/MRI of thorax and abdomen
- Enlarged lymph nodes
- Organomegaly
- Lung and liver metastases/primary tumours
- Tumours and abscesses

Limited skeletal survey
- Multiple myeloma
- Bone metastases

Isotope bone scan
- Malignancy
- Osteomyelitis/septic arthritis

Labelled white cell scan
- Abscesses/local sepsis
- Inflammatory bowel disease

1.15 CLUES TO THE DIAGNOSIS OF FACTITIOUS FEVER
- A patient who looks well
- Bizarre temperature chart with absence of diurnal variation and/or temperature-related changes in pulse rate
- Temperature > 41°C
- Absence of sweating during defervescence
- Normal ESR and CRP despite high fever
- Evidence of self-injection or self-harm
- Useful methods for the detection of factitious fever include supervised (observed) temperature measurement, and measuring the temperature of freshly voided urine

may occasionally lead to a diagnosis of tuberculosis, lymphoma, or granulomatous disease including sarcoidosis. Biopsy material should ideally be sent for culture, including tuberculosis culture. Liver biopsy is unlikely to be helpful in

patients who have normal liver function tests and normal-looking liver parenchyma on imaging.

Many cases of PUO affecting the liver may be elucidated without biopsy. Raised transaminases should prompt serological screening for viral hepatitis, while elevations of gamma-glutamyl transferase (GT) and liver alkaline phosphatase may point to metastases or biliary disease (infection or obstruction). Glandular fever syndromes, Q fever and syphilis may involve the liver as part of a wider systemic process, and are usually best diagnosed serologically.

Bone marrow biopsy
Overall, the diagnostic yield of a bone marrow biopsy is about 15%, a figure which is likely to be lower if there are no abnormalities in the peripheral blood. A biopsy is most useful in revealing haematological malignancy, myelodysplasia and tuberculosis. It may also lead to a diagnosis of brucellosis, enteric fever or visceral leishmaniasis. Bone marrow should always be sent for culture as well as microscopy.

Temporal artery biopsy
Temporal artery biopsy should be considered in patients over the age of 50, even if the erythrocyte sedimentation rate (ESR) is not significantly elevated. Since arteritis is patchy, diagnostic yield is increased if a 5 cm section of artery is removed for examination.

Prognosis in PUO
The overall mortality of PUO is 30–40% (age under 55 years: 5%; age over 55 years: 30%). Older patients are more likely to have a malignancy. If no cause is found on exhaustive investigation, the long-term mortality is low. On long-term follow-up of these patients no single disease features strongly and in most cases the fever settles spontaneously.

FEVER IN THE INJECTING DRUG USER

History-taking
It is important to know the duration of injecting drug usage as the risk of blood-borne virus infections (hepatitis B and C, and HIV) increases with each year of injecting behaviour. The site of drug injection is also important. Femoral vein injecting may be associated with vascular complications such as deep vein thrombosis (50% of which are septic), accidental arterial injection, false aneurysm formation and the compartment syndrome. Septic complications include local or iliopsoas abscess, and septic arthritis of the hip joint or sacroiliac joint. In the UK subcutaneous and intramuscular injection has been associated with infection by *Clostridium novyi*. This organism causes a local septic lesion with much toxin production. The resulting toxaemia produces shock and multi-organ failure, often associated with a leukaemoid neutrophil response in the peripheral blood. There is a high mortality.

It is useful to know the technical details of injecting drug usage. Sharing of needles and other injecting paraphernalia (including spoons and filters) greatly increases the risk of blood-borne virus infection (see Fig. 1.3). Some users lubricate their needles by licking them prior to injection, thus introducing anaerobic mouth organisms such as anaerobic

streptococci and Bacteroides species. Contamination of commercially available lemon juice (used to dissolve heroin before injection) has been associated with blood-stream infection with Candida species.

Clinical features
See Figure 1.4 and Box 1.16.

Diagnosis and management
Acute viral hepatitis (see p. 860) may present with fever and immunologically mediated manifestations such as reactive arthritis. Jaundice may be delayed for a few days, or occasionally may be so mild as to be overlooked. Serological tests may reveal evidence of recent infection with hepatitis A or B; in acute hepatitis C antibody is not usually detectable until several weeks after onset of illness. Other causes of jaundice in this situation include bacteraemia, acute bacterial endocarditis and acute drug toxicity, e.g. from oral 'ecstasy' usage (see p. 842).

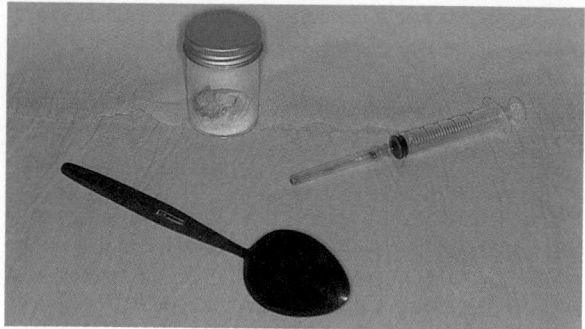

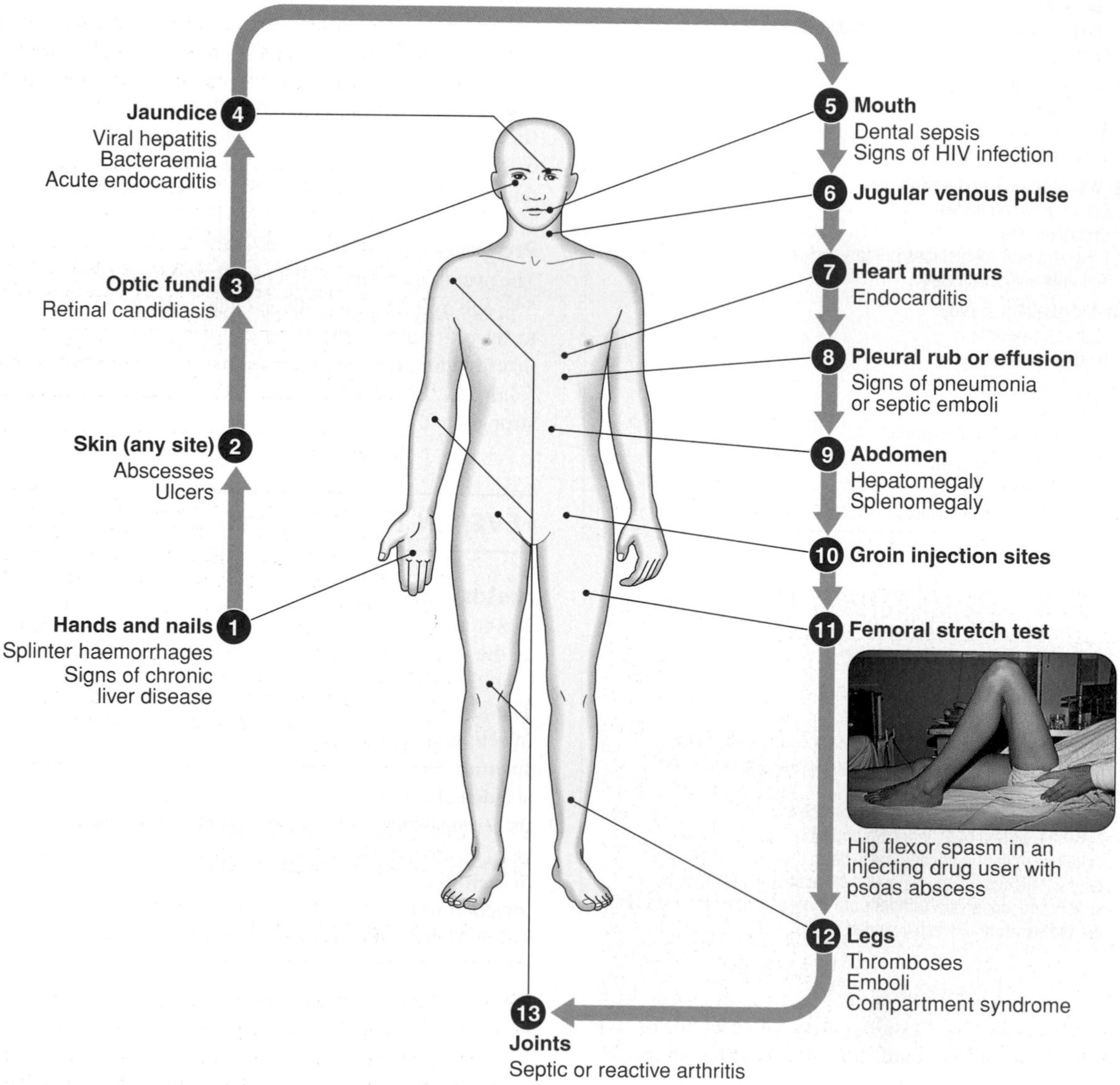

Fig. 1.3 Sharing any injecting equipment may transmit blood-borne viruses.

4 Jaundice
Viral hepatitis
Bacteraemia
Acute endocarditis

3 Optic fundi
Retinal candidiasis

2 Skin (any site)
Abscesses
Ulcers

1 Hands and nails
Splinter haemorrhages
Signs of chronic liver disease

5 Mouth
Dental sepsis
Signs of HIV infection

6 Jugular venous pulse

7 Heart murmurs
Endocarditis

8 Pleural rub or effusion
Signs of pneumonia or septic emboli

9 Abdomen
Hepatomegaly
Splenomegaly

10 Groin injection sites

11 Femoral stretch test

Hip flexor spasm in an injecting drug user with psoas abscess

12 Legs
Thromboses
Emboli
Compartment syndrome

13 Joints
Septic or reactive arthritis

14 Fig. 1.4 Fever in the injecting drug user: clinical examination.

1.16 FEVER IN THE INJECTING DRUG USER: CLINICAL EXAMINATION*

Mouth ❺

- Many injecting drug users have very poor dental hygiene as a result of self-neglect, poor diet and the use of oral methadone syrup. Dental sepsis may be the cause of fever. Look for signs of HIV infection, such as oropharyngeal candidiasis or oral hairy leucoplakia. Kaposi's sarcoma is rare in heterosexual drug users

Jugular venous pulse ❻

- Systolic 'V' waves may occur in tricuspid endocarditis

Pleural rub or effusion ❽

- Pulmonary infarction as a result of deep venous thrombosis (DVT) and pulmonary embolus
- Septic pulmonary emboli from infected DVT
- Small septic emboli from right-sided endocarditis
- Pneumonia causing pleurisy

Groin injection sites ❿

- Sinuses
- Abscesses
- Haematomas
- False aneurysm

Femoral stretch test ⓫

- Passive extension of the hip joint causes pain and reflex muscle spasm (iliopsoas abscess)

Legs ⓬

- Signs of DVT
- Vasculitic or ischaemic lesions from arterial spasm, emboli or endocarditis
- Compartment syndrome with associated neurological deficit or ischaemia

* Numbers refer to Figure 1.4.

Chest signs and radiological lung abnormalities may be caused by pneumonia, or by septic pulmonary emboli from peripheral thromboses or right-sided endocarditis (see Fig. 1.5). Blood-borne bacterial infection should be suspected if lung abscesses or pneumatoceles are detected radiologically.

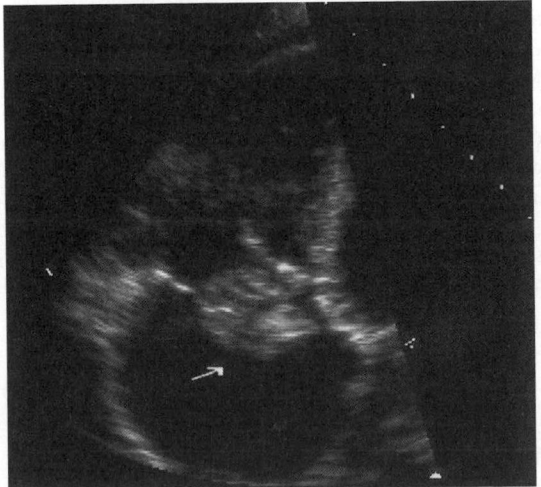

Fig. 1.5   Endocarditis in an injecting drug user. Large vegetation on the tricuspid valve (arrow).

An acute compartment syndrome is an occasional complication of groin injection. Rapid rise in pressure within fascial compartments leads to acute ischaemia and muscle necrosis. The syndrome may follow massive DVT or inadvertent arterial injection; characteristic signs include leg pain and swelling and neurological deficit, e.g. sensory loss in the leg or foot. Disappearance of peripheral arterial pulses occurs late in the natural history. Clinical diagnosis is supported by the finding of myoglobinuria and/or raised serum creatine kinase levels. Once diagnosed, urgent surgical decompression by fasciotomy is essential to preserve function and avoid the need for amputation.

Diagnosis and treatment of endocarditis are discussed on page 463. In drug users right-sided endocarditis caused by *Staph. aureus* is customarily treated with high-dose intravenous flucloxacillin. Additional gentamicin is probably unnecessary. A 28-day course of oral ciprofloxacin and rifampicin gives results comparable to intravenous therapy and is a useful alternative in this group of patients (see EBM panel).

Local sepsis in drug users is usually caused by skin organisms (staphylococci and streptococci) and occasionally by anaerobes. Clindamycin and co-amoxiclav are therefore appropriate antibiotics for oral therapy.

EBM

STAPHYLOCOCCAL ENDOCARDITIS IN INJECTING DRUG USERS—oral antibiotic therapy for patients in whom i.v. administration is difficult or impractical

'For selected patients with right-sided staphylococcal endocarditis, oral ciprofloxacin plus rifampicin is effective and is associated with less drug toxicity than intravenous therapy.'

- Heldman AW, Hartert TV, Ray SC, et al. Oral antibiotic treatment of right-sided staphylococcal endocarditis in injection drug users: prospective randomised comparison with parenteral therapy. Am J Med 1996; 101:68–76.

ISSUES IN OLDER PEOPLE
FEVER

- Fever may be missed because oral temperatures are unreliable in older people. Rectal measurements may be needed but core temperature is increasingly measured using eardrum reflectance.
- Fever frequently causes acute confusion, especially in those with underlying cerebrovascular disease or other causes of dementia.
- Prominent causes of PUO in older people include endocarditis, tuberculosis and intra-abdominal sepsis. Non-infective causes include polymyalgia rheumatica and temporal arteritis.
- In the very frail, e.g. nursing home residents, the most common infective causes of fever are pneumonia, urinary infection, soft tissue infection and gastroenteritis.

GENERALISED INFECTIONS

GLANDULAR FEVER SYNDROMES

These include infectious mononucleosis, acute cytomegalovirus (CMV) infection and acquired toxoplasmosis.

When these infections occur in immunocompetent subjects, they have a number of clinical and epidemiological features in common:

- Case-to-case spread of clinical illness seldom occurs.
- Most acquired infections are subclinical.
- Chronic latent infection becomes established.
- Activation of latent infection may occur.
- Infection is occasionally acquired from blood or leucocyte transfusion.
- Transformed atypical lymphocytes appear in the peripheral blood during the acute infection.
- CMV and *Toxoplasma* (but not Epstein–Barr virus) can cause intrauterine infection and congenital disease.

INFECTIOUS MONONUCLEOSIS

Virology and epidemiology

The disease is caused by the Epstein–Barr virus (EBV), a gamma herpes virus. In developing countries and poorer communities in Western societies subclinical infection in childhood is virtually universal. In richer communities, particularly among upper socio-economic groups, primary infection may be delayed until adolescence or early adult life. Under these circumstances about 50% of infections result in typical infectious mononucleosis (IM). Virus is usually acquired from asymptomatic excreters. Productive cycles of infection occur in the mouth, pharynx and urogenital tract. Saliva is the main means of spread, either by droplet infection or environmental contamination in childhood, or by kissing among adolescents and adults. There is a good correlation between sexual maturity and IM, and the age/sex distribution of the disease resembles that of gonorrhoea. IM is not highly contagious, isolation is unnecessary, and documented outbreaks seldom occur.

Clinical features

To make a presumptive diagnosis of IM, clinical features must include one or more of the following:

- lymphadenopathy, especially posterior cervical
- pharyngeal inflammation or exudate
- fever
- splenomegaly
- palatal petechiae
- periorbital oedema
- clinical or biochemical evidence of hepatitis
- non-specific skin rash.

It is difficult to diagnose IM outside the usual age range. In children under 10 years the illness is mild and short-lived, but in adults over 30 years of age it can be severe and prolonged. In both groups pharyngeal symptoms are often absent. Diagnostic problems may also occur when IM presents with jaundice, as a PUO or with an unusual complication (see Box 1.17).

Laboratory investigations

To establish the diagnosis, 20% or more of the peripheral lymphocytes must have an atypical morphology (see Fig. 1.6) and the serum must contain the characteristic heterophil antibody. This antibody, which is present during the acute illness and during convalescence, agglutinates erythrocytes of other species, e.g. sheep and horse. The

1.17 COMPLICATIONS OF INFECTIOUS MONONUCLEOSIS	
Common	
• Severe pharyngeal oedema	• Chronic fatigue syndrome (10%)
• Antibiotic-induced rash	
Uncommon	
Neurological	
• Cranial nerve palsies	• Transverse myelitis
• Polyneuritis	• Meningoencephalitis
Haematological	
• Haemolytic anaemia	• Thrombocytopenia
Renal	
• Glomerulonephritis	• Interstitial nephritis
Cardiac	
• Myocarditis	• Pericarditis
Pulmonary	
• Interstitial pneumonitis	
Rare	
• Ruptured spleen	• Agranulocytosis
• Respiratory obstruction	• Agammaglobulinaemia
• Arthritis	

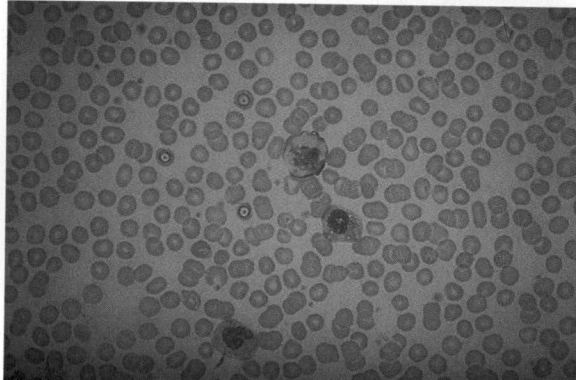

Fig. 1.6   Infectious mononucleosis: atypical lymphocytes in peripheral blood.

antibody, which has a specific absorption pattern, is detected by the classical Paul–Bunnell titration or by a more convenient slide test such as the 'Monospot'. Sometimes antibody production is delayed and an initially negative test should be repeated. However, many children and 10% of adolescents with IM do not produce heterophil antibody at any stage.

Specific EBV serology (immunofluorescence) can be used to confirm the diagnosis if necessary. Acute infection is characterised by:

- antiviral capsid (VCA) antibodies in the IgM class
- antibodies to EBV early antigen (EA)
- absent antibodies to EBV nuclear antigen (anti-EBNA).

Management

Treatment is largely symptomatic: for example, aspirin gargles to relieve a sore throat. If a throat culture yields a β-haemolytic streptococcus, a course of erythromycin should

Fig. 1.7 Skin reactions to ampicillin and amoxicillin are common in infectious mononucleosis.

be prescribed. Amoxicillin and similar semi-synthetic penicillins should be avoided because they commonly induce a maculo-papular rash in patients with IM (see Fig. 1.7).

When pharyngeal oedema is severe a short course of steroids, e.g. prednisolone 30 mg daily for 5 days, may help to relieve the swelling.

Return to work or school is governed by the patient's physical fitness rather than laboratory tests. However, contact sports should be avoided until splenomegaly has completely resolved because of the danger of splenic rupture. Unfortunately, about 10% of patients with IM eventually suffer from a chronic fatigue syndrome (see p. 265).

ACQUIRED CYTOMEGALOVIRUS INFECTION

Virology and epidemiology

Cytomegalovirus (CMV) is a β-herpes virus. Like EBV it circulates readily among children, especially in crowded communities. Although most primary infections are asymptomatic, many children continue to excrete virus for months or years.

A second peak in virus acquisition occurs among teenagers and young adults. CMV infection is persistent, and is characterised by subclinical cycles of active virus replication and by persistent low-level virus shedding. Most post-childhood infections are therefore acquired from asymptomatic excreters who shed virus in saliva, urine, semen and genital secretions. Sexual transmission and oral spread are common among adults, but infection may also be acquired by women caring for children with asymptomatic infections. Most post-childhood CMV infections are subclinical, although some young adults develop a mononucleosis-like syndrome, which accounts for 20–50% of heterophil antibody-negative IM. The peak incidence occurs between the ages of 25 and 35, rather later than with EBV-related mononucleosis. Many patients have a prolonged influenza-like illness lasting 2 weeks or more.

Clinical features

Physical signs such as a palpable liver and spleen resemble those of IM, but in CMV mononucleosis hepatomegaly is relatively more common, while lymphadenopathy, pharyngitis

and tonsillitis are found less often. Jaundice is uncommon and usually mild. Unusual complications include:

- neurological involvement
- autoimmune haemolytic anaemia
- pericarditis
- pneumonitis
- arthropathy.

Laboratory investigations

Atypical lymphocytosis is not as prominent as in IM and heterophil antibody tests are negative. Liver function tests are often abnormal, with an alkaline phosphatase level raised out of proportion to transaminases. Serological diagnosis depends on the detection of CMV-specific IgM antibody.

Management

Only symptomatic treatment is available. Amoxicillin and similar antibiotics should not be prescribed because of the risk of a skin reaction. Since CMV infection in immunocompetent subjects is self-limiting, the use of potentially toxic antiviral agents is usually inappropriate.

Gestational CMV infection

Most CMV infections in pregnancy are subclinical. However, heterophil antibody-negative 'glandular fever' in pregnancy requires full investigation as CMV can cause congenital infection and disease at any stage of gestation. The risk of spread to the fetus is around 40%, and 10% of infected infants will have long-term central nervous system sequelae.

ACQUIRED TOXOPLASMOSIS

Parasitology and epidemiology

Toxoplasma gondii is a coccidian intracellular parasite found in all species of warm-blooded animals. The sexual phase of the parasite's life cycle (see Fig. 1.8) occurs in the small intestinal epithelium of the domestic cat. Oöcysts are shed in cat faeces and are spread to intermediate hosts, including humans, through widespread contamination of soil. Oöcysts may survive in moist conditions for weeks or months. Once they are ingested by the secondary host, the parasite undergoes a cycle of asexual multiplication and then forms microscopic tissue cysts which persist for the lifetime of the host. Cats become infected or reinfected by ingesting tissue cysts in prey such as rodents and birds.

Human acquisition of infection occurs via oöcyst-contaminated soil, salads and vegetables, or by the ingestion or tasting of raw or undercooked meats containing tissue cysts. Sheep, pigs and rabbits are the most important food sources. In Western cultures toxoplasmosis is the most common protozoal infection; around 22% of adults in the UK are seropositive. Most primary infections are subclinical; however, toxoplasmosis is thought to account for about 15% of heterophil antibody-negative glandular fever.

Clinical features

The peak incidence of clinical illness is in adults aged 25–35 years. The most common presenting feature is painless

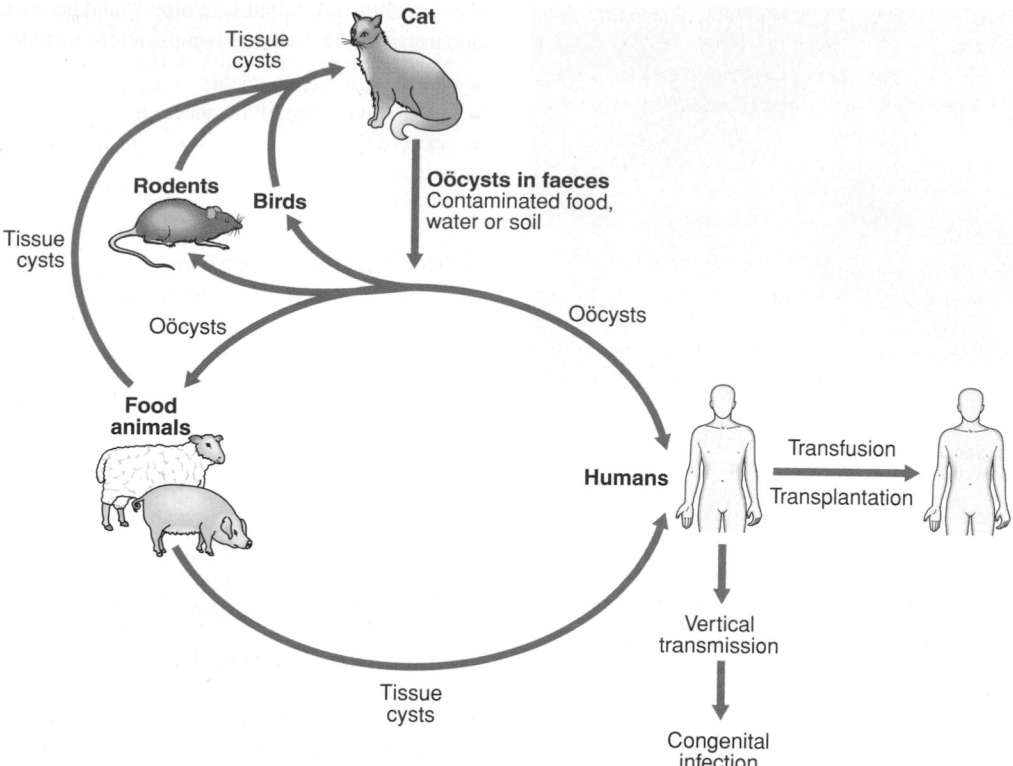

Fig. 1.8 Life cycle of *Toxoplasma gondii*.

enlargement of lymph nodes. In particular, the cervical nodes are involved, but lymphadenopathy can be local or generalised and may involve the mediastinal, mesenteric or retroperitoneal groups. The spleen is seldom palpable. Most patients have no systemic symptoms, but some complain of malaise, fever, fatigue, muscle pain, sore throat and headache. Complete resolution usually occurs within a few months, though symptoms and lymphadenopathy tend to fluctuate unpredictably and some patients do not recover completely for a year or more. Sites other than lymph nodes are seldom involved clinically, but in some patients other organs such as brain, meninges, heart, lung, liver or skeletal muscle are involved. Retinochoroiditis (see Fig. 1.9) is nearly always the result of remote or congenital infection but has also been reported to arise de novo in the acquired form of the disease. Generalised toxoplasmosis has been described after accidental laboratory infection with highly virulent strains.

Laboratory investigations

The heterophil antibody test is negative, and atypical lymphocytes may be scanty or absent. A number of antibody tests are available for serological diagnosis. The Sabin–Feldman dye test detects IgG antibody. Recent infection is indicated by a fourfold or greater increase in titre when paired sera are tested in parallel. Peak titres of 1/1000 or more are reached within 1–2 months of the onset of infection. The dye test then becomes an unreliable indicator of recent infection. The detection of significant levels of *Toxoplasma*-specific IgM antibody using indirect immunofluorescence

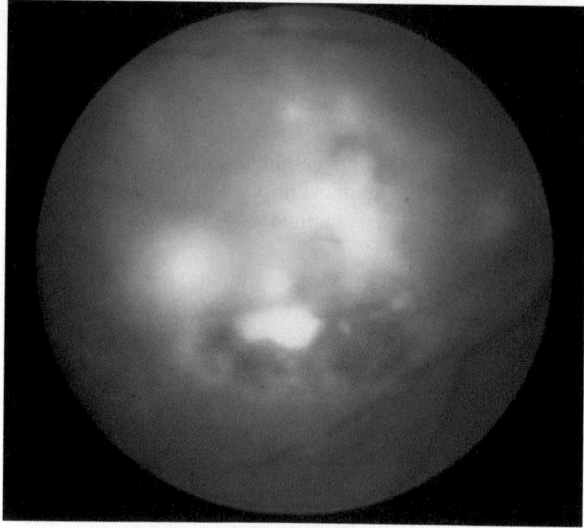

Fig. 1.9 Retinochoroiditis due to toxoplasmosis.

or enzyme-linked immunosorbent assay (ELISA) is useful in confirming acute infection.

If necessary, the presence of *Toxoplasma* organisms in a lymph node biopsy can be sought by staining sections histochemically with *Toxoplasma gondii* antiserum, or by the use of PCR to detect *Toxoplasma*-specific DNA.

Management

In immunocompetent subjects uncomplicated toxoplasmosis is self-limiting, and responds poorly to antimicrobial therapy.

Treatment with pyrimethamine and sulfadiazine is therefore usually reserved for rare cases of severe or progressive disease, and for infection in immunocompromised patients. A few individuals develop the chronic fatigue syndrome after acute toxoplasmosis, but there is no evidence that their immune response is other than normal, and antimicrobial therapy is unnecessary.

Congenital toxoplasmosis
Acute toxoplasmosis, mostly subclinical, affects 0.3–1% of pregnancies, with a 60% transmission rate to the fetus. The overall incidence of congenital disease (40% of infected fetuses) is greatest in the first trimester, but extends into the third trimester of pregnancy. Many fetal infections are subclinical at birth, but long-term sequelae occur in almost all cases. The main features are retinochoroiditis, microcephaly and hydrocephalus. The cost benefits of routine *Toxoplasma* screening and treatment (see EBM panel) in pregnancy are being debated in many countries.

TOXOPLASMOSIS IN PREGNANCY—do spiramycin and other antiparasitic drugs reduce the incidence of spontaneous abortion, fetal infection or overt neonatal disease?

'There is insufficient evidence to determine the effects on mother or baby of current antiparasitic treatment for women who seroconvert in pregnancy.'

• Olliaro P. Congenital toxoplasmosis. Clinical Evidence 2000; 3:316–319.
• Wallon M, Liou C, Garner P, et al. Congenital toxoplasmosis: systematic review of evidence of efficacy of treatment in pregnancy. BMJ 1999; 318:1511–1514.
• Peyron F, Wallon M, Liou C, Garner P. Treatments for toxoplasmosis in pregnancy (Cochrane Review). Cochrane Library, issue 1, 2000. Oxford: Update Software.

Further information: www.clinicalevidence.org
www.cochrane.co.uk

BRUCELLOSIS

Microbiology and epidemiology

Brucellosis is an enzootic infection (i.e. endemic in animals). Although six species of *Brucella* are known, only four are important to humans: *B. melitensis* (goats, sheep and camels), *B. abortus* (cattle), *B. suis* (pigs) and *B. canis* (dogs).

B. melitensis is enzootic in the Middle East, Africa, India, Central Asia and South America. *B. abortus* is found in Africa, Asia and South America, and *B. suis* in South Asia. *B. melitensis* causes the most severe disease; *B. suis* is often associated with abscess formation.

Infected animals may excrete brucellae in their milk for long periods of time and human infection is acquired by ingesting contaminated milk, cheese, yoghurt and butter. Uncooked meat and offal may also spread infection. Animal urine, faeces, vaginal discharge and uterine products may act as sources of infection through abraded skin or via splashes and aerosols to the respiratory tract and conjunctiva.

Clinical features

Brucellae are intracellular organisms that can survive for long periods within the reticulo-endothelial system. This

1.18 FOCAL MANIFESTATIONS OF BRUCELLOSIS

Musculoskeletal
- Suppurative arthritis; synovitis, bursitis
- Osteomyelitis
- Spinal spondylitis
- Paravertebral or psoas abscess

CNS
- Meningitis
- Cranial nerve palsies
- Stroke
- Intracranial or subarachnoid haemorrhage
- Myelopathy
- Radiculopathy

Ocular
- Uveitis
- Retinal thrombophlebitis

Cardiac
- Myocarditis
- Endocarditis

explains many of the features of clinical brucellosis including the chronicity of the disease, and the tendency to relapse even after adequate antimicrobial therapy.

Acute illness is characterised by a high swinging temperature, rigors, sweating, lethargy, headache, and joint and muscle pains. Occasionally, there is delirium, abdominal pain and constipation. Physical signs are non-specific, e.g. a palpable spleen or enlarged lymph nodes. Enlargement of the spleen may lead to hypersplenism and thrombocytopenia.

Localisation of infection, which occurs in about 30% of patients, is more likely if diagnosis and treatment are delayed. Focal manifestations of infection are summarised in Box 1.18.

Diagnosis

Definitive diagnosis of brucellosis depends on the isolation of the organism. Blood cultures are positive in 75–80% of infections caused by *B. melitensis* and 50% of those caused by *B. abortus*. The non-radiometric 'Bactec' system gives a good isolation rate, but if brucellosis is suspected prolonged incubation and blind subcultures are recommended. Bone marrow culture should not be used routinely but may increase the diagnostic yield, particularly if antibiotics have been given before specimens are taken. Cerebrospinal fluid (CSF) culture in neurobrucellosis is positive in about 30% of cases.

World-wide the serum agglutination test is the serological technique most commonly employed to detect brucellosis. The test has many pitfalls and good quality control is essential. Agglutination should be carried out to a high dilution (at least 1/640) to avoid the prozone phenomenon whereby non-agglutinating IgG and IgA molecules completely block the agglutinating reaction. Significant agglutination titres may persist for months or years after recovery and in endemic areas a single titre of 1/320 or a fourfold rise in titre is needed to support a diagnosis of acute infection. The test usually takes several weeks to become positive but should eventually detect 95% of acute infections. The pre-treatment of serum with 2-mercaptoethanol helps to distinguish between IgG and IgM responses. The new ELISA test also identifies IgM and IgG antibodies; IgM decreases rapidly within the first few months of illness.

Specialist laboratory techniques including the use of the anti-human globulin (Coombs) test may be necessary to distinguish chronic disease from past inactive infection.

Management

Aminoglycosides show synergistic activity with tetracyclines when used against brucellae. Standard therapy therefore consists of doxycycline 100 mg 12-hourly for 6 weeks, with streptomycin 1 g i.m. daily for the first 2 weeks. The relapse rate with this treatment is about 5%. An alternative oral regimen consists of doxycycline 100 mg 12-hourly plus rifampicin 900 mg (15 mg/kg) daily for 6 weeks, but failure and relapse rates are higher, particularly with spondylitis. Rifampicin may antagonise doxycycline activity by reducing serum levels through enzyme induction.

Chronic illness should be treated for a minimum of 3 months and many authorities would extend this to 6 months, depending upon the condition of the patient and the result of sequential serological tests. The optimum therapy for neuro-brucellosis is unknown, and there is no current agreement on the combination or number of drugs to use. Treatment should continue for at least 3 months, and longer if CSF pleocytosis persists.

LEPTOSPIROSIS

Microbiology and epidemiology

Leptospires are tightly coiled, thread-like organisms about 5–7 microns in length; each end is bent into a hook. *Leptospira interrogans* is pathogenic for humans. The genus can be separated into more than 200 serovars belonging to 23 serogroups.

Leptospirosis appears to be ubiquitous in wildlife and in many domestic animals. The most frequent hosts are rodents, especially the common rat *(Rattus norvegicus)*. In this and other reservoir species the organisms persist indefinitely in the convoluted tubules of the kidney without causing apparent disease, and are shed into the urine in massive numbers. Particular leptospiral serogroups are associated with characteristic animal hosts; *L. icterohaemorrhagiae* is the classical parasite of rats, *L. canicola* of dogs, *L. hebdomadis* of cattle, and *L. pomona* of pigs. There is nevertheless considerable overlap in host–serogroup associations.

Leptospires can enter their human hosts through intact skin or mucous membranes, but entry is facilitated by cuts and abrasions. Prolonged immersion in water will also favour invasion. After a relatively brief bacteraemia, invading leptospires are distributed throughout the body; in humans the main organs affected are the kidneys, liver, meninges and brain. The mechanism of tissue damage is uncertain since it is often associated with the lysis of the organisms rather than their multiplication. Leptospirosis is common in the tropics and also in water sports enthusiasts.

Clinical features

The incubation period averages 1–2 weeks. Four main clinical syndromes can be discerned.

Bacteraemic leptospirosis

This can occur with any serogroup. It produces a non-specific illness in which there is high fever accompanied by weakness, muscle pain and tenderness, and sometimes diarrhoea and vomiting. Conjunctival congestion is the only notable physical sign. The illness comes to an end after about a week, or else merges into one of the other forms of infection.

Aseptic meningitis

Classically associated with *L. canicola* infection, this illness is very difficult to distinguish from viral meningitis. The conjunctivae may be congested but there are no other differentiating signs. Laboratory clues to the correct diagnosis include a neutrophil leucocytosis, abnormal liver function tests, and the occasional presence of albumin and casts in the urine.

Icteric leptospirosis (Weil's disease)

Less than 10% of symptomatic infections result in severe icteric illness. Weil's disease is a dramatic life-threatening event, characterised by fever, haemorrhages, jaundice and renal impairment. Conjunctival hyperaemia is a frequent feature. The patient may have a transient macular erythematous rash, but the characteristic skin changes are those of purpura, with large areas of bruising. In severe cases there may be epistaxis, haematemesis and melaena, or bleeding into the pleural, pericardial or subarachnoid spaces. Thrombocytopenia, probably related to activation of endothelial cells with platelet adhesion and aggregation, is present in 50% of cases. Jaundice is deep and the liver is enlarged, but there is usually little evidence of hepatic failure or encephalopathy. Renal failure, primarily caused by impaired renal perfusion and acute tubular necrosis, becomes manifest as oliguria or anuria, with the presence of albumin, blood and casts in the urine.

Weil's disease may also be associated with myocarditis, encephalitis and aseptic meningitis. Uveitis and iritis may appear months after apparent clinical recovery.

Pulmonary syndrome

A pulmonary syndrome has long been recognised in the Far East, and has recently been described during an outbreak of leptospirosis in Nicaragua. This syndrome is characterised by haemoptysis, patchy lung infiltrates on chest radiograph, and respiratory failure. Total bilateral lung consolidation and the acute respiratory distress syndrome (ARDS—see p. 198) develop in fatal cases.

Diagnosis

Results of routine laboratory tests are non-specific but may nevertheless be helpful. The characteristic change in the peripheral blood is a polymorphonuclear leucocytosis. Severe infections are often accompanied by thrombocytopenia and elevated blood levels of creatine phosphokinase. In jaundiced patients liver function tests are mildly hepatitic in pattern with moderately raised transaminases; the prothrombin time may be a little prolonged. The CSF in leptospiral meningitis shows a variable cellular response, a moderately elevated protein level and a normal glucose content.

In the tropics dengue, malaria, typhoid fever, scrub typhus and hantavirus infection are important differential diagnoses.

Definitive diagnosis of leptospirosis depends upon the isolation of the organism, serological tests or the detection of specific DNA:

- Blood cultures are most likely to be positive if taken before the 10th day of illness. Special media are required and cultures may have to be incubated for several weeks.
- Leptospires appear in the urine during the second week of illness and in untreated patients may be recovered on culture for several months.
- At present the serological investigation of choice is the microscopic agglutination test. Less cumbersome assays including ELISA and immunofluorescent techniques are under rapid development.
- PCR shows great promise as a rapid and specific means of diagnosis. The technique can detect leptospiral DNA in blood in early symptomatic disease, and is positive in urine from the eighth day and for many months afterwards. Currently, the major disadvantage with this test is that it is genus-specific only.

Management and prevention

Therapy with either doxycycline or intravenous penicillin has been reported to be effective (see EBM panel) but may not prevent the development of renal failure. Doxycycline is given in doses of 100 mg orally 12-hourly for 1 week. Intravenous benzylpenicillin is administered as 1.5 mega-units 6-hourly for 1 week. A Jarisch–Herxheimer reaction (see p. 100) may occur during treatment but is usually mild. Uveitis is treated with a combination of systemic antibiotics and local corticosteroids.

The general care of the patient is critically important. Blood should be taken early for grouping and cross-matching and haemorrhage treated by prompt blood transfusion. Renal failure demands very careful management since it is the usual cause of death. The renal damage is, however, essentially reversible, and peritoneal dialysis or haemodialysis may be life-saving.

Trials in military personnel have shown that infection with *L. interrogans* can be prevented by taking prophylactic doxycycline, 200 mg weekly.

EBM

ANTIBIOTICS FOR TREATING LEPTOSPIROSIS—are they clinically effective, and which regimen is safest and most efficient?

'Antibiotic regimens for the treatment of leptospirosis are a form of care for which the evidence is insufficient to provide clear guidelines for practice. However, the evidence suggests that penicillin may cause more good than harm.'

- Guidugli F, Castro AA, Atallah AN. Antibiotics for treating leptospirosis (Cochrane Review). Cochrane Library, issue 1, 2001. Oxford: Update Software.
- Watt G, Padre LP, Tuazon L, et al. Placebo-controlled trial of intravenous penicillin for severe and late leptospirosis. Lancet 1980; 1:433–435.

Further information: www.cochrane.co.uk

LYME BORRELIOSIS

Microbiology and epidemiology

The causative agent of Lyme disease (named after the town of Old Lyme in Connecticut, USA) is a flagellated spirochaetal bacterium of the genus *Borrelia*. *B. burgdorferi* is the type species found in the northern hemisphere. In Europe two additional genospecies are also encountered, *B. afzelii* and *B. garinii*. The reservoir of infection is maintained in ixodid (hard) ticks which feed on a variety of large mammals, particularly deer. Birds may spread ticks over a wide area. The organism is transmitted to humans, who are incidental hosts, via the bite of infected ticks; larval, nymphal and adult forms are all capable of spreading infection.

Lyme disease is found in the USA, Europe, Russia, China, Japan and Australia. Incidence parallels the burden of infection among tick vectors and peaks in the summer.

Clinical features

Clinical features can be classified into three stages: early localised, early disseminated and late disease. Progression may be arrested at any stage.

Early localised disease

The characteristic feature is a skin reaction around the site of the tick bite, known as erythema migrans. This is a red macule or papule which appears 2–30 days after the bite. It then enlarges peripherally with central clearing, and may persist for months. Atypical forms of erythema migrans are fairly common. Other acute manifestations such as fever, headache and regional lymphadenopathy may develop with or without the rash.

Early disseminated disease

During this stage the organism seeds to other organs via the blood stream and lymphatics. There may be a pronounced systemic reaction with malaise, arthralgia, and occasionally metastatic areas of erythema migrans. Neurological involvement may follow weeks or months after infection. Common features include lymphocytic meningitis, cranial nerve palsies (especially unilateral or bilateral facial palsy) and peripheral neuropathy. Radiculopathy, often painful, may present a year or more after initial infection. Carditis sometimes accompanied by atrioventricular conduction defects is not uncommon in the USA but appears to be rare in Europe.

Late disease

Late manifestations include arthritis, polyneuritis and encephalopathy. Prolonged arthritis particularly affecting large joints is a well-described feature but is rare in the UK. Brain parenchymal involvement causing neuropsychiatric abnormalities may also be encountered, but is again very rare in the UK. Acrodermatitis chronica atrophicans is an uncommon late complication seen more frequently in Europe than North America. Doughy, patchy discoloration occurs on the peripheries, eventually leading to shiny atrophic skin. The lesions are easily mistaken for those of peripheral vascular disease.

Diagnosis

The diagnosis of Lyme borreliosis is primarily clinical. Culture from biopsy material is not generally available, has a low yield, and may take longer than 6 weeks. Antibody detection is therefore the best means of confirming the diagnosis but unfortunately lacks specificity. Immunofluorescence ELISA assays can give false positive reactions in a number of conditions including other spirochaetal infections, infectious mononucleosis, rheumatoid arthritis and SLE. Immunoblot (Western blot) techniques are more specific but are technically demanding. Antibody responses may not become detectable until several weeks after the onset of infection, and may be suppressed by antibiotic therapy. True positive results may reflect past rather than active infection. DNA detection by PCR is being developed and has been applied to blood, urine, and biopsies of skin and synovium. PCR positivity in CSF is useful in confirming the diagnosis of neuroborreliosis but has low sensitivity.

Management

It is questionable whether asymptomatic patients with positive antibody tests should be treated. However, erythema migrans always requires therapy because of the risk of progressive disease; in untreated patients organisms can be recovered from skin biopsies long after the skin eruption has resolved. Standard therapy consists of a 14-day course of doxycycline (200 mg daily) or amoxicillin (500 mg 8-hourly). Some 15% of patients with early disease will develop a mild Jarisch–Herxheimer reaction during the first 24 hours of therapy.

Disseminated disease and arthritis require prolonged therapy; a minimum of 30 days' treatment with either doxycycline or amoxicillin plus probenecid is required. Arthritis may respond poorly, and prolonged or repeated courses may be necessary. Neuroborreliosis is treated with parenteral β-lactam antibiotics for 3–4 weeks. Ceftriaxone (2 g daily), cefotaxime (2 g 8-hourly) or benzylpenicillin (3 g 6-hourly) have all been used successfully. The cephalosporins may be superior to penicillin in this situation.

Prevention

Protective clothing and insect repellents should be used in tick-infested areas. Since the risk of borrelial transmission is lower in the first few hours of a blood feed, prompt removal of ticks is advisable. Unfortunately, larval and nymphal ticks are tiny and may not be noticed. The value of prophylactic antibiotics is difficult to evaluate. Where risk of transmission is high, a single 200 mg dose of doxycycline, given within 72 hours of exposure, has been shown to prevent erythema migrans. A recombinant subunit vaccine has proved effective in preventing clinical disease during recent controlled trials in the USA.

Q FEVER

Microbiology and epidemiology

Coxiella burnetii is a Gram-negative pleomorphic coccobacillus, first identified in 1937 as the cause of Q (or query) fever. It is an intracellular organism which survives within phagolysosomes. The formation of spores allows the organism to survive cold and drying. *C. burnetii* can exist in two serologically distinct forms: phase I on initial isolation and phase II after serial passage in culture.

Infection is enzootic in a wide range of animals and birds world-wide. The main sources for human infections are cattle, sheep and goats. Farmers, veterinarians and abattoir workers are at particular risk. Transmission may occur via urine, faeces, milk and uterine products, and after exposure to contaminated straw, manure and dust. Inhalation of small particulate aerosols is the usual mode of transmission and a single organism may constitute an infective dose.

Clinical features

Atypical pneumonia (see p. 526)

Fever and headache are characteristic features of Q fever pneumonia; cough is relatively less common. Moderately raised transaminase levels are found in most cases. Radiographic appearances are variable and therefore unhelpful in diagnosis. Some infections progress rapidly with extensive pulmonary consolidation.

Endocarditis (see p. 463)

The prime manifestation of chronic infection is culture-negative endocarditis. Previously abnormal or prosthetic valves are usually involved.

Hepatitis

Q fever hepatitis may present with illness resembling acute viral hepatitis, or as a PUO. In the latter situation, characteristic granulomata are seen on liver biopsy.

Neurological involvement

Meningoencephalitis accompanied by severe headache may complicate either acute or chronic Q fever. CSF examination reveals a mononuclear cell response with an elevated protein content but a normal glucose level.

Diagnosis

The complement fixation test is the technique most commonly used for diagnosis; a fourfold rise in titre is diagnostic of acute infection. Microagglutination, microimmunofluorescence and ELISA tests are also available. In chronic infection including endocarditis the characteristic finding is that of an elevated antibody level against phase I antigens.

Management

Q fever pneumonia and granulomatous hepatitis are treated with a 2-week course of tetracycline. Erythromycin, the usual drug of choice for the treatment of atypical pneumonia, is less effective when *Coxiella burnetii* is the cause. Prolonged therapy is required for Q fever endocarditis. Most authorities advise 2–3 years' therapy, but treatment may have to be continued indefinitely. Combination therapy is usually recommended, e.g. doxycycline plus rifampicin. Treatment is continued until inflammatory markers improve significantly and antibody titres fall. Patients should be followed up clinically and serologically for 2 years after completing therapy. Medical treatment has a high failure rate and valve replacement is often required.

RASHES AND INFECTION

Many infective processes produce skin manifestations as part of the disease, either as a direct result of infection or toxin or as part of an immune reaction. The presentation of rashes due to infection is shown in Box 1.19.

1.19 PATTERNS OF RASH ASSOCIATED WITH INFECTION

Macular or maculo-papular

- Measles*
- Rubella
- Enteroviral infections
- Herpes virus type 6 infections
- Infectious mononucleosis
- Toxoplasmosis
- Drug rashes
- CMV infections
- HIV seroconversion illness
- Typhoid and paratyphoid fevers
- Rickettsial infections
- Dengue fever
- Secondary syphilis

Haemorrhagic

- Meningococcal infection
- Viral haemorrhagic fevers
- Leptospirosis
- Septicaemia with disseminated intravascular coagulation
- Rickettsial infections
- Trypanosomiasis

Urticarial

- Toxocariasis
- Hydatidosis
- Fascioliasis
- Strongyloidiasis
- Schistosomiasis

Vesicular/pustular

- Chickenpox*
- Shingles
- Herpes simplex infections*
- Hand, foot and mouth disease
- Herpangina (mouth)
- Poxviruses (monkeypox)

Nodular

- Erythema nodosum (primary TB and leprosy, streptococcal infection, mycoplasma)

Erythematous

- Scarlet fever*
- Toxic shock syndrome*
- Parvovirus B19 infection*
- Lyme disease
- Drug rashes
- Dengue fever

Chancres (ulcerating nodules)

- Syphilis*
- Trypanosomiasis
- Typhus (tick and mite)
- Anthrax
- Rat-bite fever

* Rash is illustrated later in this chapter.

DIRECT SKIN AND SOFT TISSUE INFECTIONS

IMPETIGO

This superficial infection of the skin occurs most commonly in young children with poor hygiene and affects moistened or damaged skin, often at mucocutaneous borders. Insect bites, ear piercing or paronychia may precede it. Around 80% of cases are caused by group A streptococci but recently *Staph. aureus* has increased in incidence as a cause.

Small papules develop into vesicles that progress to pustulation, rupturing to produce a honey-coloured crusting.

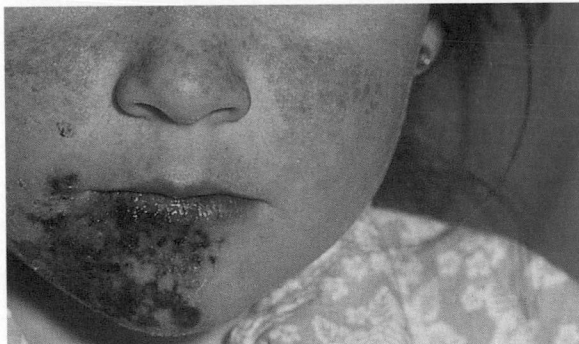

Fig. 1.10 Impetigo. Note the classical honey-coloured crusting.

Multiple viable bacteria are present in the lesions, spreading by close contact (see Fig. 1.10). Despite its alarming appearance, the red, blistering underlying skin usually heals without scarring.

Careful hygiene and infection control are necessary to prevent spread amongst nursery children, playgroups and so on. *Strep. pyogenes* (group A) remains sensitive to natural penicillins and these should be used. Sodium fusidate or mupirocin is also useful when applied topically.

BULLOUS IMPETIGO

This form of impetigo occurs if infecting staphylococci produce exfoliatoxin A or B. Often occurring on the face and limbs of young children, the blistering lesions contain profuse numbers of staphylococci. It may become quite extensive in the immunocompromised (e.g. HIV-infected).

Appropriate isolation of affected children and a combination of appropriate topical antimicrobials, e.g. sodium fusidate cream plus systemic antistaphylococcal antibiotics such as flucloxacillin, are effective.

ECTHYMA

This skin infection often occurs around areas of damaged skin. Commonly caused by streptococci or staphylococci, it progresses to form deep, punched-out ulcers typically with a violaceous border (see Fig. 1.11).

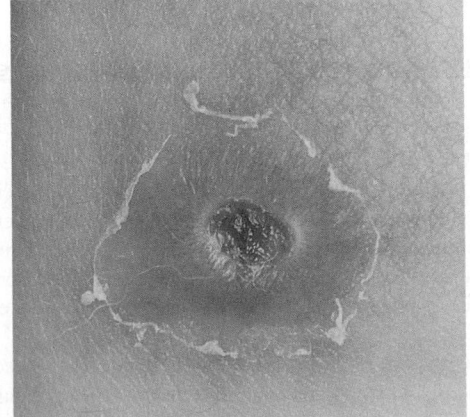

Fig. 1.11 Ecthyma. Note the 'punched-out' appearance.

These lesions heal with marked scarring and require aggressive treatment with penicillin and antistaphylococcal antibiotics such as flucloxacillin.

FOLLICULITIS, FURUNCLES AND CARBUNCLES

These lesions are invariably caused by *Staph. aureus*. Folliculitis is a pustular swelling in hair follicles. A furuncle occurs when a deep inflammatory nodule develops in established folliculitis. Furuncles eventually become fluctuant and discharge pustular material or progress to carbuncles (see Fig. 1.12). Here, more extensive involvement of the subcutaneous fat occurs, producing multiple abscesses separated by fibrous septa. Eventually, discharge along hair follicles occurs.

The best treatment for these is application of a warm moist poultice to encourage the discharge of pus. Any evidence of surrounding cellulitis or occurrence in the mid-facial region indicates the need for urgent antistaphylococcal antibiotics such as flucloxacillin to prevent secondary sepsis.

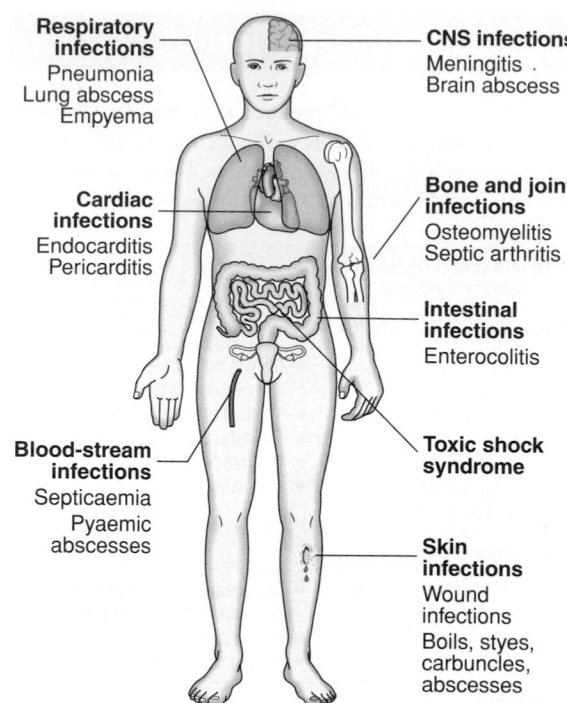

Respiratory infections
Pneumonia
Lung abscess
Empyema

Cardiac infections
Endocarditis
Pericarditis

Blood-stream infections
Septicaemia
Pyaemic abscesses

CNS infections
Meningitis
Brain abscess

Bone and joint infections
Osteomyelitis
Septic arthritis

Intestinal infections
Enterocolitis

Toxic shock syndrome

Skin infections
Wound infections
Boils, styes, carbuncles, abscesses

Fig. 1.13   Infections caused by *Staphylococcus aureus*.

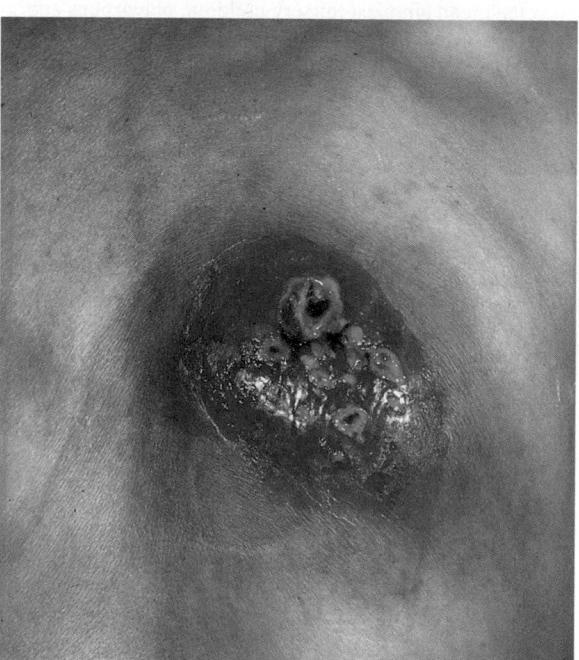

Fig. 1.12   Staphylococcal carbuncle.

OTHER STAPHYLOCOCCAL SKIN INFECTIONS AND DISEASES (see Fig. 1.13)

Wound infections

Many wound infections are caused by staphylococci and may significantly prolong hospital stays in otherwise uncomplicated surgery (see Fig. 1.14). Infection control and aseptic surgical technique are the best means of prevention. Antibiotic prophylaxis in clean surgery is also well established as a method to reduce wound infection.

Treatment is by drainage of any abscesses plus adequate dosage of antistaphylococcal antibiotics. These should be instituted early in the course of any post-operative wound infection, particularly where implants have been inserted.

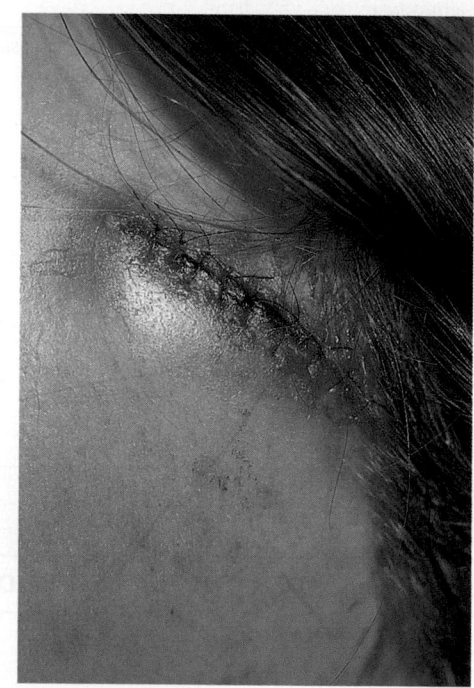

Fig. 1.14   Typical staphylococcal wound infection.

Cannula-related infection

Skin staphylococci, e.g. *Staph. epidermidis* associated with cannula sepsis and thrombophlebitis, are an important and unfortunately extremely common reason for morbidity

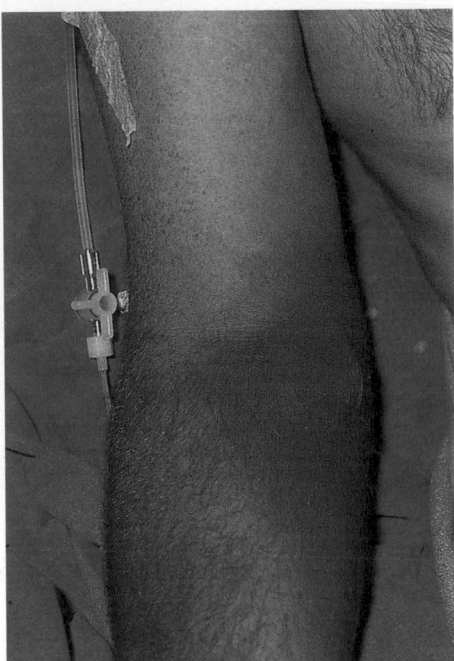

Fig. 1.15   Cannula-related infection.

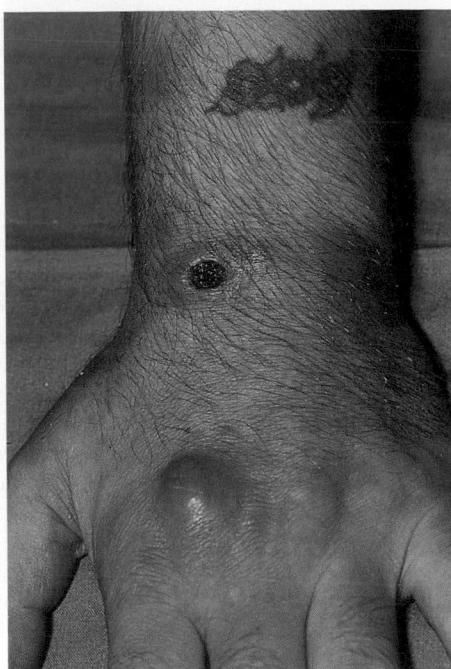

Fig. 1.16   Skin abscesses in an intravenous drug user.

following hospital admission (see Fig. 1.15). Local poultice application usually relieves symptoms.

Antibiotic treatment with benzylpenicillin and flucloxacillin may be necessary if spreading infection is present.

Methicillin-resistant *Staph. aureus*

Staph. aureus has, perhaps more than any other organism, shown the ability to develop resistance to antibiotic therapy. In the 1960s the so-called 'hospital staphylococcus', resistant to penicillin, caused severe problems in 'clean' orthopaedic and other prosthetic surgery. The introduction of methicillin and flucloxacillin re-established effective treatment for these infections. Resistance to methicillin due to the production of an additional penicillin-binding protein has been recognised in *Staph. aureus* for more than 30 years. Hospitals world-wide now experience methicillin-resistant *Staph. aureus* as a major nosocomial pathogen, and the recent recognition of variable resistance to vancomycin/teicoplanin (glycopeptides) in glycopeptide intermediate *Staph. aureus* (GISA) strains threatens our ability to manage serious infections produced by such organisms. Clinicians must be aware of the potential danger of these infections and prepared to take whatever appropriate infection control measures are locally advised.

Injection site infection in intravenous drug users

Poor hygiene and injection techniques in intravenous drug users, plus sharing unsterile equipment, often lead to skin and subcutaneous tissue sepsis. Mixed infections including staphylococci are involved in such cases (see Fig. 1.16). A diagnostic aspiration of skin lesions with appropriate microbiological investigation should be undertaken.

Broad-spectrum antibiotics should be started and modified by microbiological results.

Secondary spread

In all cases of superficial staphylococcal skin infection, the potential for haematogenous spread to distant body sites is present. In any patient with superficial staphylococcal infections, especially intravenous drug users, the possibility of endocarditis must always be considered (see p. 463).

ERYSIPELAS

This distinctive superficial cellulitis, common at the extremes of age, usually affects the face or limbs. It is caused most frequently by group A streptococci. The erythematous indurated lesion has a sharply demarcated edge and is painful and swollen (see Fig. 1.17). Local drainage lymph nodes are inflamed. Around 5% of cases have systemic involvement

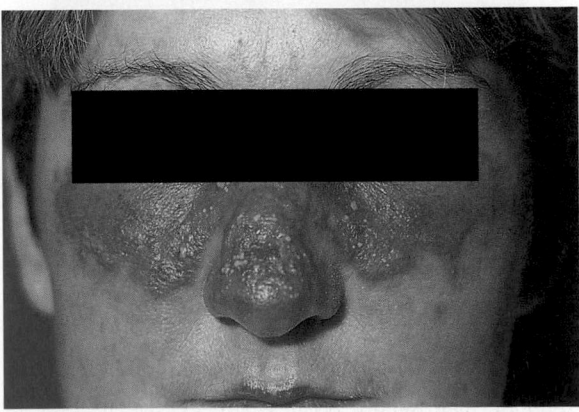

Fig. 1.17   Erysipelas. Note the blistering and crusted rash with raised erythematous edge.

and evidence of bacteraemia. A streptococcal throat infection is present in 20% of cases and group A streptococci may be isolated by aspiration of the lesion in up to 30% of cases. Aggressive treatment with penicillins or other anti-Gram-positive antibiotics is the most effective means of therapy. The lesions heal with local desquamation.

CELLULITIS

This is an acute spreading infection of deep subcutaneous tissues, commonly due to both group A streptococci and *Staph. aureus* (see Fig. 1.18). Diabetics and the immuno-suppressed often have anaerobes or Gram-negative organisms present. The lesion is not elevated and often develops following relatively minor skin trauma. Marked regional lymphadenopathy is present and a moderately severe systemic illness can ensue. Deep venous thrombosis and thrombo-embolism may complicate involvement in the lower limbs. Cellulitis implies predisposition to future infection at the same site.

Aggressive intravenous anti-Gram-positive antibiotics (a natural penicillin plus an antistaphylococcal penicillin, clindamycin or vancomycin) should be considered in severe infections. In diabetics and the immunosuppressed, appro-priate Gram-negative/anaerobic cover should be included. Intravenous therapy is continued for 5–7 days, followed by a switch to appropriate oral therapy. Leg elevation is universally helpful and anticoagulation may be required.

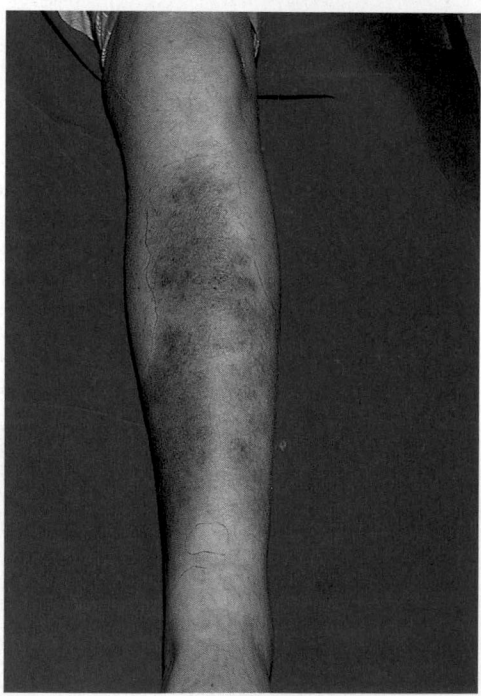

Fig. 1.18   Acute cellulitis of the leg.

SEVERE NECROTISING SOFT TISSUE INFECTIONS

Cellulitis may rapidly progress to extensive necrosis of subcutaneous tissue and overlying skin. Several different clinical presentations are recognised, depending upon the

> **1.20 SEVERE NECROTISING SOFT TISSUE INFECTIONS**
>
> - Necrotising fasciitis
>   Type 1 (polymicrobial): Fournier's gangrene, synergistic necrotising cellulitis
>   Type 2 (monomicrobial): *Strep. pyogenes* group A
> - Clostridial anaerobic cellulitis (confined to skin and subcutaneous tissue)
> - Non-clostridial anaerobic cellulitis
> - Progressive bacterial synergistic gangrene (*Staph. aureus* + microaerophilic streptococcus)
> - Pyomyositis (discrete abscesses within individual muscle groups)
> - Clostridial myonecrosis (gas gangrene)
> - Anaerobic streptococcal myonecrosis (non-clostridial infection mimicking gas gangrene)
> - Group A streptococcal necrotising myositis (streptococcal myositis without abscess formation)

causative organism, the structure and anatomical level involved, and the predisposing conditions in the patient (see Box 1.20).

Aggressive intravenous antibiotic therapy against anaero-bic, Gram-negative and Gram-positive organisms is required. Urgent surgical débridement should be considered if the lesion is not rapidly controlled.

Necrotising fasciitis

There are two major categories of necrotising fasciitis:

- Type 1 is a polymicrobial infection with Enterobacteriaceae and anaerobic organisms. It often occurs following surgery or in diabetic or immunocompromised patients.
- Type 2 (sometimes known as streptococcal gangrene) is caused by pure growth of *Strep. pyogenes* Lancefield group A.

Both types produce a severe, rapidly progressive and destructive inflammation of the dermis, subcutaneous tis-sues, subcutaneous fat and tissue planes including the deep fascia. Necrotising fasciitis is associated with profound tox-aemia and multisystem failure. The whole process is hyper-acute, often arising from an apparently minor breach in skin integrity. The affected area is erythematous, hot, shiny and exquisitely tender.

The skin rapidly changes and frank, full-thickness gangrene resembling a thermal burn ensues. The central area of skin involvement becomes anaesthetic due to cutaneous nerve damage. Central anaesthesia surrounded by exquisitely ten-der erythematous skin is pathognomonic of necrotising fasci-itis. Systemic toxicity develops with high fever, marked leucocytosis and often hypocalcaemia due to subcutaneous fat necrosis. Subcutaneous gas may be present in type 1 necrotising fasciitis. Recently, a form of this condition has been recognised which occurs in tropical regions due to *Vibrio fulnificus* and is associated with liver disease and contact with shellfish.

Management

Necrotising fasciitis requires urgent and extensive surgical débridement (see Fig. 1.19) and appropriate antibiotic therapy

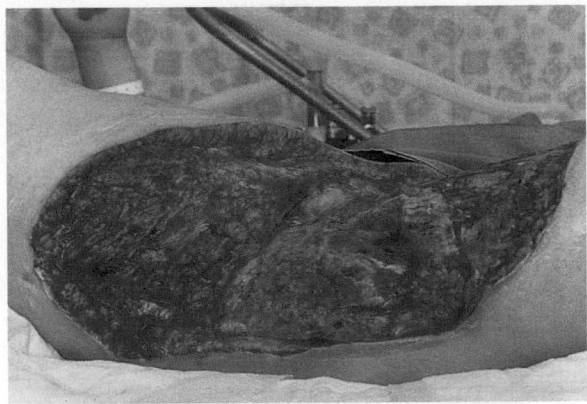

Fig. 1.19   Excision following necrotising fasciitis in an intravenous drug user.

against Gram-positive, anaerobic and Gram-negative organisms. Usually intravenous benzylpenicillin, a quinolone plus either clindamycin or metronidazole are used. Despite this, mortality is between 30 and 80% and up to 50% may require amputation of affected limbs and/or plastic surgical management. Culture of débrided tissue plus Gram's staining of exudate from lesions help to delineate and confirm the infecting organism. Empirical antibiotic therapy should be started prior to microbiological confirmation.

CLOSTRIDIAL SOFT TISSUE INFECTIONS

Although *Clostridia* may colonise or contaminate wounds, no action is required unless evidence of spreading infection is present. In anaerobic cellulitis, usually due to *Cl. perfringens* or other strains infecting devitalised tissue following a wound, gas forms locally and extends along tissue planes, but bacteraemia and invasion of healthy tissue are not found. Prompt surgical débridement of devitalised tissue with penicillin or clindamycin therapy usually results in an excellent outcome.

Gas gangrene or myonecrosis is defined as acute invasion of healthy living muscle undamaged by previous trauma. It usually develops (70% of cases) following deep penetrating injury sufficient to create an anaerobic (ischaemic) environment and allow clostridial introduction and proliferation. *Cl. perfringens* accounts for the majority of these infections. Severe pain at the site of the injury progresses rapidly over 18–24 hours. Skin colour changes from pallor to bronze/purple discoloration and the skin is tense and exquisitely tender. Gas in tissues may be obvious with crepitus on clinical examination or visible on radiograph, CT or ultrasound. Signs of systemic toxicity develop rapidly with high leucocytosis, multi-organ dysfunction, raised creatine kinase and evidence of disseminated intravascular haemolysis. Antibiotic therapy with high-dose intravenous penicillin, clindamycin, cephalosporins and metronidazole is very effective, and should be coupled with aggressive surgical débridement of the affected tissues. Use of hyperbaric oxygen is controversial.

BACTEROIDES INFECTION

Bacteria of the *Bacteroides fragilis* group are commonly found in the gastrointestinal tract and cause both skin and soft tissue infections and bacteraemia. They are often associated with mixed infections in compromised hosts such as diabetics and are frequently linked to rectal or colonic pathology, surgery or pelvic disease. Antimicrobial resistance is widespread in this group which are nevertheless usually sensitive to β-lactam–β-lactamase inhibitor combinations, metronidazole or carbapenems.

ANTHRAX

There are three recognised forms of infection with *Bacillus anthracis*:

- cutaneous anthrax
- gastrointestinal anthrax
- inhalational (pulmonary) anthrax.

Cutaneous anthrax

This skin lesion is associated with occupational exposure to anthrax spores during processing of hides and bone products or with bioterrorism. It accounts for the vast majority of clinical cases. Animal infection is a serious problem in Africa, India, Pakistan and the Middle East.

Spores are inoculated into exposed skin. A single lesion develops as an irritable papule on an oedematous haemorrhagic base. This progresses to a depressed black eschar. Despite extensive oedema, pain is infrequent.

Gastrointestinal anthrax

This is associated with the ingestion of meat products that have been contaminated or incompletely cooked. The caecum is the seat of the infection, which produces nausea, vomiting, anorexia and fever, followed in 2–3 days by severe abdominal pain and bloody diarrhoea. Toxaemia and death can develop rapidly thereafter.

Inhalational anthrax

This form of the disease is extremely rare unless associated with bioterrorism. Without rapid and aggressive therapy at the onset of symptoms the mortality rate is greater than 90%. Fever, dyspnoea, cough, headache and symptoms of septicaemia develop 3–14 days following exposure. Typically, there is little on the chest radiograph other than widening of the mediastinum and pleural effusions.

Management

B. anthracis can be cultured from lesional skin swabs. Skin lesions are readily curable with early antibiotic therapy. Treat with ciprofloxacin 500 mg daily until penicillin susceptibility is confirmed; treatment can then be changed to penicillin G 600 000 units i.m. 6-hourly or penicillin V 500 mg 6-hourly. Aggressive fluid resuscitation and the addition of an aminoglycoside may improve the outlook. Ventilatory assistance will be required in inhalational disease. Prophylaxis with ciprofloxacin (500 mg 12-hourly) is recommended for anyone at high risk of exposure to biological warfare.

TOXIC ERYTHEMATOUS RASHES

A generalised toxic erythema can be a manifestation of:

- drug reactions
- radiation
- immune-mediated reactions
- infective processes.

Streptococci and staphylococci frequently cause this type of rash through the production of one or other of the pyrogenic (erythrogenic) exotoxins.

STREPTOCOCCAL SCARLET FEVER

Group A and occasionally group C and G streptococci are implicated. A diffuse erythematous rash blanching on pressure occurs (see Fig. 1.20), classically with circumoral pallor. The tongue, initially coated, becomes red and swollen ('strawberry tongue'—see Fig. 1.21). The source is often a relatively uncomplicated streptococcal pharyngitis or tonsillitis. Common in school-age children, it can occur in young adults who have contact with young children. The disease lasts about 7 days, the rash disappearing in 7–10 days followed by a fine desquamation. Residual petechial lesions in the antecubital fossa may be seen ('Pastia's sign'—see Fig. 1.22).

Treatment involves active therapy for the underlying infection (benzylpenicillin or orally available penicillin) plus symptomatic measures.

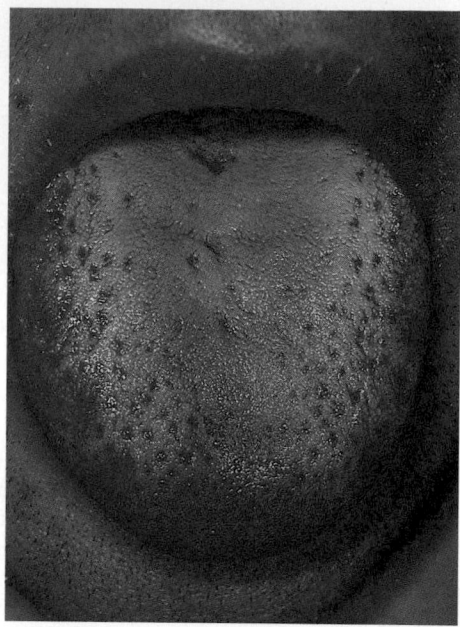

Fig. 1.21   The 'strawberry tongue' of acute streptococcal disease.

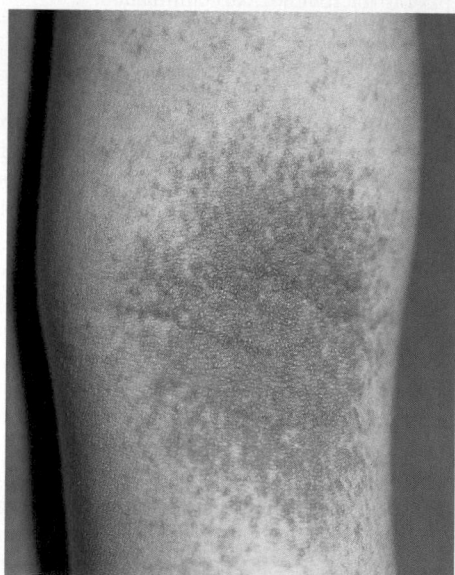

Fig. 1.22   Pastia's sign. Petechial rash in the cubital fossa.

STREPTOCOCCAL TOXIC SHOCK SYNDROME

This is associated with severe group A streptococcal skin infections producing pyogenic exotoxin A. Initially, an influenza-like illness with, in 50% of cases, signs of necrotising fasciitis occurs. A faint erythematous rash, mainly on the chest, rapidly progresses to a toxic multisystem shock-like state. Without aggressive management, multi-organ failure will develop.

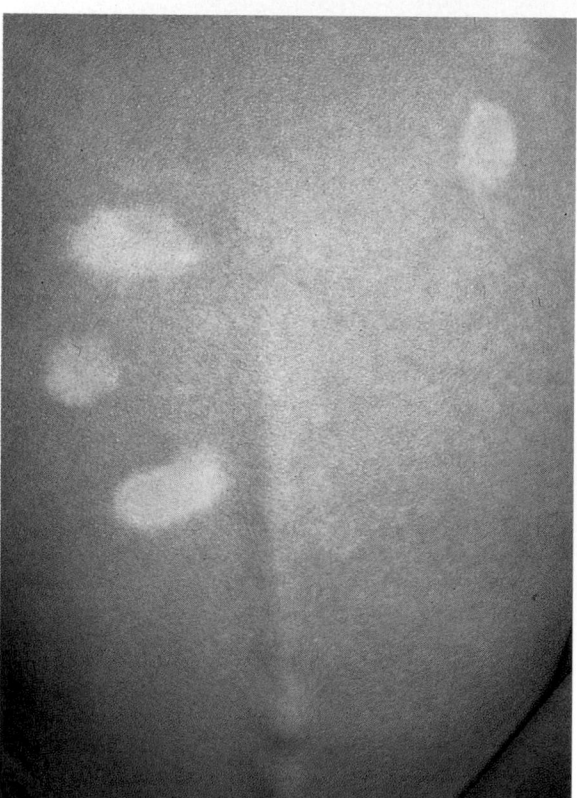

Fig. 1.20   Scarlet fever. Note blanching on pressure.

If necrotising fasciitis is present, it should be treated as described on page 26. Fluid resuscitation must be undertaken linked to parenteral antistreptococcal antibiotic therapy, usually with benzylpenicillin plus or minus clindamycin.

Other streptococcal infections are shown in Box 1.21.

1.21 STREPTOCOCCAL AND RELATED INFECTIONS	
Strep. pyogenes	
• Skin and soft tissue infection (including erysipelas, impetigo, necrotising fasciitis) • Bone and joint infection • Tonsillitis	• Puerperal sepsis • Scarlet fever • Glomerulonephritis • Rheumatic fever
Alpha-haemolytic streptococci (Strep. mitis, sanguis, mutans, salivarius)	
• Endocarditis	• Septicaemia in immunosuppressed
Group B streptococci	
• Neonatal infections including meningitis	• Female pelvic infections
Enterococcus faecalis	
• Endocarditis	• Urinary tract infection
Anaerobic streptococci (examples)	
• Peritonitis • Dental infections	• Liver abscess • Pelvic inflammatory disease
N.B. All streptococci can cause septicaemia.	

STAPHYLOCOCCAL SCALDED SKIN SYNDROME

When staphylococcal exfoliatoxin A or B is absorbed into the blood stream from a localised infection, intraepidermal desquamation occurs at remote or generalised areas of the body. Most commonly affecting neonates or children less than 5 years old, this is most frequently seen on the face, axillae or groins, subsequently spreading to the whole body. This is the most severe form of exfoliatoxin-related staphylococcal disease (see Fig. 1.23).

Cases require isolation and aggressive treatment with parenteral antistaphylococcal antibiotics, e.g. flucloxacillin or vancomycin. The skin lesions should be managed as superficial burns. Most will heal without scarring.

STAPHYLOCOCCAL TOXIC SHOCK SYNDROME (TSS)

This serious and life-threatening disease is associated with infection by *Staph. aureus* producing toxic shock syndrome toxin 1 (TSST1). It is most commonly seen in young women during, or immediately after, menstruation and is associated with the use of highly absorbent intravaginal tampons. *Staph. aureus* has been shown to grow in and around the tampon with the liberation of TSST1. TSS has also been described in both sexes in any age group associated with toxin-producing staphylococcal infections. The toxin acts as

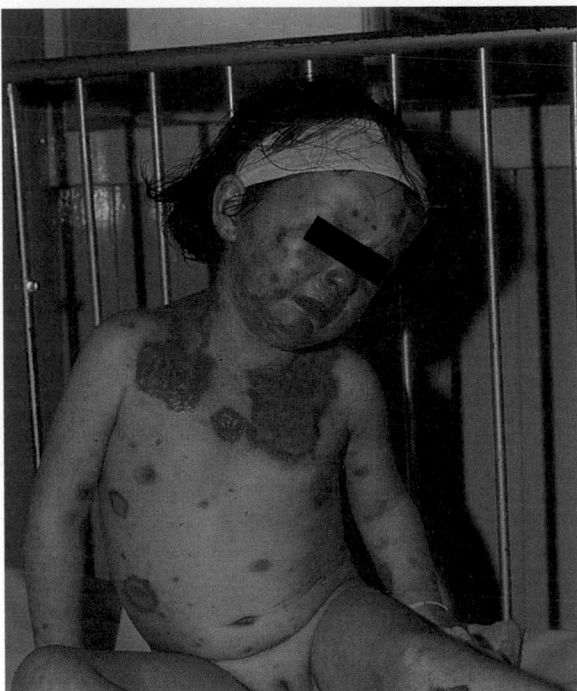

Fig. 1.23   Staphylococcal scalded skin syndrome following superinfection of chickenpox lesions.

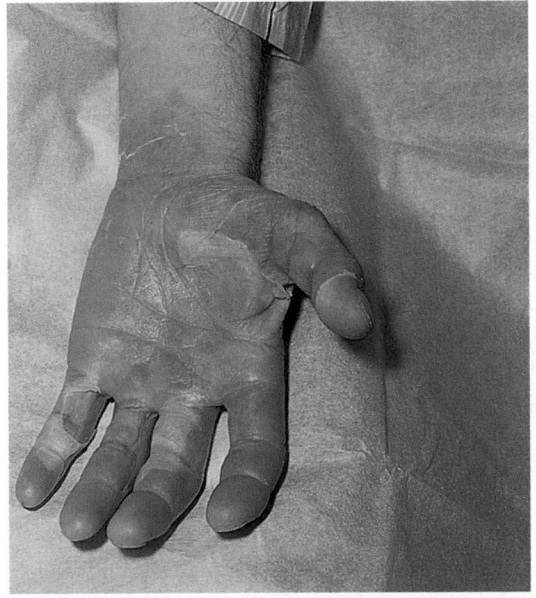

Fig. 1.24   Full-thickness desquamation after toxic shock syndrome.

a 'super-antigen', triggering significant T helper cell activation and very high peripheral polymorphonuclear leucocyte numbers.

TSS has an abrupt onset with high fever, generalised systemic upset (myalgia, headache, sore throat and vomiting), a generalised erythematous blanching rash resembling scarlet fever, and hypotension. It rapidly progresses over a matter of hours to multisystem involvement with cardiac, renal and hepatic compromise, leading to death in 10–20%. Recovery is accompanied at 7–10 days by desquamation at the lower dermal level (see Fig. 1.24).

Diagnosis

The diagnosis is clinical (fever, rash, hypotension plus systemic upset in any person with distant staphylococcal infection). It may be confirmed in menstrual cases by vaginal examination, the finding of a retained tampon and microbiological examination by Gram stain demonstrating typical staphylococci. Subsequent culture and demonstration of toxin production are confirmatory.

Management

Immediate and aggressive fluid resuscitation with an intravenous antistaphylococcal antibiotic (flucloxacillin or vancomycin) is required. The rapid progression of symptoms and signs may require intensive care involvement. Women who recover should be advised not to use tampons for at least 1 year and should also be warned that due to an inadequate antibody response to TSST1 the condition can recur.

RASHES WITH HAEMORRHAGE

See yellow fever (p. 60), viral haemorrhagic fevers (p. 61), spotted fever group (p. 63) and meningococcal meningitis (p. 1193).

ERYTHEMATOUS AND VESICULOPUSTULAR ERUPTIONS

The herpes virus group consists of at least eight organisms (see Box 1.22), all with particular tropism for specific body tissues and the potential for latency after primary infection. Recurrent disease occurs due to changes in immune surveillance or immune deficiency.

HERPES SIMPLEX VIRUS (HSV)

Types 1 and 2 of this common virus affect humans. Type 1 HSV produces mucocutaneous lesions, predominantly of the head and neck (see Fig. 1.25), whilst type 2 disease is a sexually transmitted anogenital infection (see pp. 103 and 115). By puberty 30–100% of UK adults will have antibodies to HSV, depending on social class. The source of infection is a case of primary or active recurrent disease. Primary infection normally occurs as a gingivostomatitis in infancy and may be subclinical or mistaken for 'teething'. It may present as a keratitis (dendritic ulcer), viral paronychia ('whitlow'—see Fig. 1.26), vulvovaginitis, cervicitis (often unrecognised), balanitis or rarely as encephalitis.

Recurrent disease involving reactivation of HSV from latency in the dorsal root ganglion produces the classical 'cold sore' or 'herpes labialis'. Prodromal hyperaesthesia is followed by rapid vesiculation, pustulation and crusting. Recurrences can be precipitated by disturbance of local skin

1.22 HERPES VIRUS INFECTIONS	
Virus	**Infection**
Herpesvirus hominis (herpes simplex) Type 1	Herpes labialis ('cold sores') Keratoconjunctivitis Finger infections ('whitlows') Encephalitis Primary stomatitis Genital infections
Type 2	Genital infections Neonatal infection (acquired during vaginal delivery)
Cytomegalovirus (CMV) (see p. 17)	Congenital infection Disease in immunocompromised patients Pneumonitis Retinitis Enteritis Generalised infection
Epstein–Barr virus (EBV) (see p. 16)	Infectious mononucleosis Burkitt's lymphoma Nasopharyngeal carcinoma Oral hairy leucoplakia (AIDS patients)
Varicella zoster virus (VZV)	Chickenpox Shingles (herpes zoster)
Human herpes virus 6 (HHV-6) and 7 (HHV-7)	Exanthem subitum ? Disease in immunocompromised patients
Human herpes virus 8 (HHV-8)	Associated with Kaposi's sarcoma

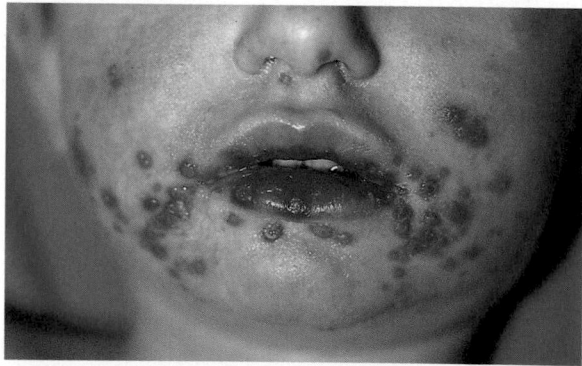

Fig. 1.25 Acute herpes simplex (HSV-1). There were also vesicles in the mouth—herpetic stomatitis.

integrity by ultraviolet light or systemic upset from menstruation or fever of any cause. Type 2 (genital) disease is a common cause of recurrent painful genital ulceration (see p. 103).

Complications

Neonatal HSV disease contracted from the birth canal may be disseminated and potentially fatal. Active HSV in a preterm mother is an indication for either elective caesarean section or antiviral therapy. Active antiviral therapy should also be administered in the immunocompromised (lymphoma, leukaemia or HIV/AIDS)—see Box 1.23.

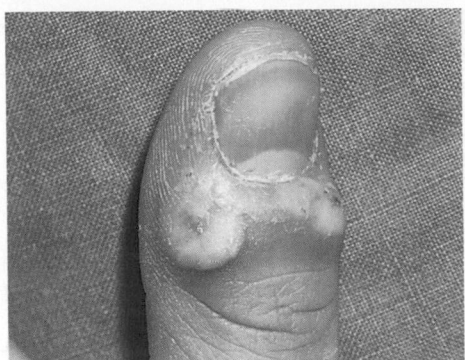

Fig. 1.26   Herpetic whitlow.

1.23 THERAPY FOR HERPES SIMPLEX VIRUS INFECTION	
Disease state	**Treatment**
Primary HSV	Famciclovir 250 mg 8-hourly
	Valaciclovir 500 mg 8-hourly
	Aciclovir 200 mg 5 times daily
Severe and preventing oral intake	Aciclovir 5 mg/kg 8-hourly i.v.
Recurrent HSV-1 or 2	Aciclovir ointment 3–5 times daily
	Oral aciclovir 200–400 mg 6-hourly
	Famciclovir 125 mg 12-hourly
	Valaciclovir 500 mg 12-hourly
In immunocompromised	Aciclovir 400 mg 6-hourly
	Famciclovir 500 mg 12-hourly
	Valaciclovir 1 g 12-hourly
Severe complications	Aciclovir i.v. 10 mg/kg 8-hourly (up to 20 mg/kg in severe encephalitis)
Disease suppression	Aciclovir 400 mg 12-hourly
	Famciclovir 250 mg 12-hourly
	Valaciclovir 500 mg daily

HSV infection in patients with eczema can result in a spreading and potentially serious infection, eczema herpeticum (see Fig. 1.27). Dendritic ulcers may produce corneal scarring and permanently damage eyesight. These require aggressive antiviral therapy.

Encephalitis, the most serious complication of HSV disease, may occur following either primary or secondary disease. A haemorrhagic necrotising temporal lobe cerebritis produces temporal lobe epilepsy and decreasing conscious level/coma. Without treatment, mortality is 80%. Any suggestion of HSV encephalitis is an indication for immediate empirical systemic antiviral therapy.

Diagnosis

Differentiation from other vesicular eruptions requires demonstration of virus by PCR, electron microscopy or culture from vesicular fluid. CSF PCR is very useful in HSV encephalitis. Serology is of limited value, only confirming primary infection.

Management

The acyclic antivirals are the treatment of choice for HSV infection. Therapy must commence in the first 48 hours

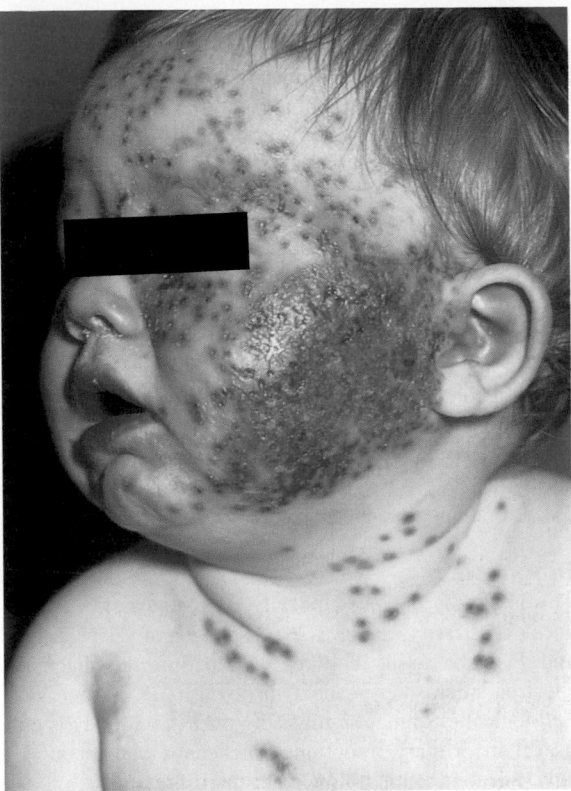

Fig. 1.27   Eczema herpeticum. HSV-1 infection spreads rapidly in eczematous skin.

of clinical disease (primary or recurrent), since after that stage it is unlikely to influence clinical outcome or modify the disease process. Severe manifestations should be treated regardless of the time of presentation (see Box 1.23).

HUMAN HERPES VIRUS 6 AND 7 (HHV 6 AND 7)

These viruses were only identified in the 1990s. They are associated with a benign febrile illness of children with a maculo-papular erythematous rash, 'roseola infantum'/ 'exanthem subitum'. In the immunocompromised they cause lymphadenopathy.

HUMAN HERPES VIRUS 8 (HHV8)

This virus has been linked to Kaposi's sarcoma (KS) tumour cells in both AIDS-related and endemic non-AIDS-related forms. There is some sero-epidemiological evidence that the infection may be transmitted via the sexual route, explaining the increased incidence of KS among homosexual HIV sufferers. Contradictory evidence in children from endemic areas has thrown some doubt on this theory.

CHICKENPOX

Varicella zoster virus (VZV) is dermo- and neurotropic. Spread by the aerosol route, it is highly infectious to susceptible individuals. Disease in children is usually well tolerated. It is more severe in adults, pregnant women and the immunocompromised. Pneumonitis can be fatal and is more likely in smokers, pregnancy and the immunocompromised. The incubation period is 14–21 days, after which a vesicular eruption begins (see Fig. 1.28), often first on mucosal surfaces, followed by rapid dissemination in a centripetal distribution (most dense on trunk and sparse on limbs). New lesions occur every 2–4 days, each crop associated with fever. The rash progresses from small pink macules to vesicles and pustules within 24 hours. These then crust. Infectivity lasts until crusts separate. Due to intense itch secondary bacterial infection from scratching is the most common complication of primary chickenpox. Self-limiting cerebellar ataxia may rarely occur 7–10 days after recovery from the rash. Maternal infection in early pregnancy carries a 3% risk of neonatal damage but disease within 5 days of delivery can lead to severe neonatal varicella.

Diagnosis

This is usually obvious clinically from the classical appearance of the rash (see Fig. 1.28). Aspiration of vesicular fluid and PCR or tissue culture will confirm the diagnosis. Electron microscopy cannot distinguish HSV from VZV. Serological examination for rising titres of antibody is only useful in primary infection. Chickenpox can recur as a subclinical infection following primary disease.

Management

Aciclovir, valaciclovir and famciclovir, although effective if commenced within 48 hours of rash appearance, do not have a licence in the UK for uncomplicated primary VZV infection. They are required in the management of the immunocompromised or any case of pneumonitis (see EBM panel).

Human varicella zoster immunoglobulin may be used to attenuate infection in highly susceptible contacts of chickenpox such as:

- bone marrow recipients
- patients with debilitating disease
- HIV-positive contacts without VZV immunity
- pregnant women with no known VZV antibody (screen for antibody if in doubt)

EBM

CHICKENPOX/SHINGLES—effectiveness of antiviral therapy

'A meta-analysis of RCTs of aciclovir therapy for chickenpox demonstrated that this treatment shortened symptoms by an average of 1 day. There was no effect on the transmission of varicella or the development of complications. Aciclovir therapy for uncomplicated chickenpox was deemed not to be cost-effective.'

'Aciclovir therapy for herpes zoster (shingles) reduced the mean duration of pain by 10 days and the incidence of post-herpetic neuralgia by 8% (range 2–32%), the effect being most marked in the over-65-year age group. Aciclovir therapy was deemed to be cost-effective in the management of herpes zoster (shingles).'

'An RCT of the newer antiviral agents (valaciclovir and famciclovir) in the management of shingles has shown them to be comparable in effect but not cost.'

- Nathwani D, Macdonald T, Davey P. Cost effectiveness of acyclovir for varicella infections in immunocompromised patients: a British perspective. Infect Dis Clin Prac 1995; 4:138–145.
- Tyring SK, Beutner KR, Tucker BA, et al. Randomised, controlled clinical trial of valacyclovir and famciclovir in immunocompetent patients 50 years and older. Arch Fam Med; 9:863–869.

- immunosuppressed contacts who have received high-dose steroids in the previous 3 months
- neonates whose mothers develop chickenpox between 1 week before and 4 weeks after delivery
- neonates in contact with chickenpox/shingles whose mothers have no history of chickenpox or any demonstrable antibody
- premature infant (less than 30 weeks' gestation) contacts of chickenpox or shingles or premature infants weighing less than 1 kg at birth.

VZV vaccine, now in use in the USA, offers effective protection.

SHINGLES (HERPES ZOSTER)

This is produced by reactivation of latent VZV from the dorsal root ganglion of sensory nerves. Commonly seen in the elderly, it may present in younger patients with immune deficiency or after intrauterine infection.

Although thoracic dermatomes are most commonly involved (see Fig. 1.29), the ophthalmic division of the trigeminal nerve is frequently implicated, when vesicles may appear on the cornea and lead to ulceration. Geniculate ganglion involvement causes the Ramsay Hunt syndrome of

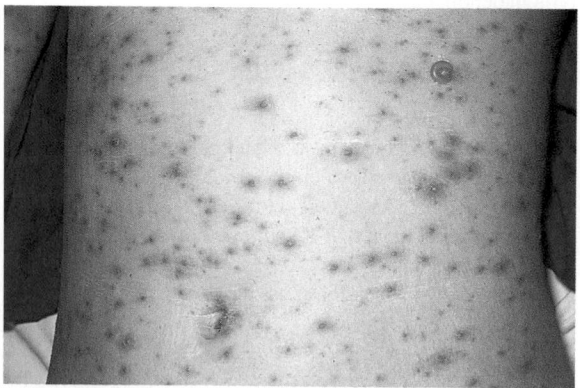

Fig. 1.28   Chickenpox.

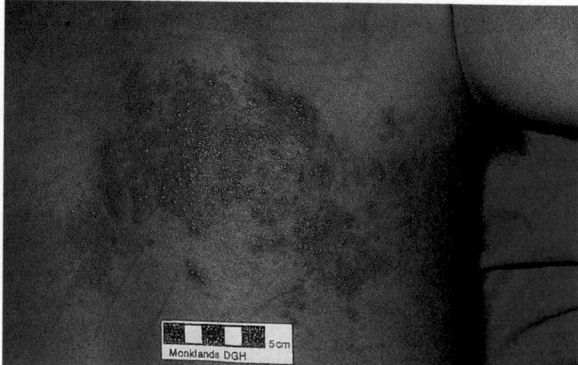

Fig. 1.29   Typical 'shingles' varicella zoster virus infection reactivating in a thoracic dermatome: 'a band of roses from Hell'.

facial palsy, ipsilateral loss of taste and buccal ulceration, plus rash in the external auditory canal. This may be mistaken for Bell's palsy (see p. 1183). Bowel and bladder dysfunction occurs with sacral nerve root involvement. The virus occasionally causes myelitis or encephalitis.

Clinical features

Burning discomfort in the affected dermatome progresses to frank neuralgia. Discrete vesicles appear in the dermatome 3–4 days later and often coalesce. This is associated with a brief viraemia and influenza-like features and potentially produces distant satellite 'chickenpox' lesions elsewhere.

Severe disease, multiple dermatomal involvement or recurrence suggests underlying immunodeficiency. Chickenpox may be contracted from a case of shingles but not the reverse.

Complications

The most common and most troublesome complication is post-herpetic neuralgia, which is persistence of pain for 1–6 months or more following healing of the rash.

Management

Early therapy with aciclovir 800 mg 5 times daily or valaciclovir 1 g 8-hourly, or in severe infection and in the immunocompromised aciclovir 10 mg/kg 8-hourly intravenously has been shown, especially in patients over 65, to reduce both early- and late-onset pain (see EBM panel). Post-herpetic neuralgia requires aggressive analgesia plus the use of transcutaneous nerve stimulation ('TENS' machine) and neurotransmitter modification with agents such as amitriptyline 25–100 mg daily or gabapentin (commencing at 300 mg daily and building slowly to 300 mg 12-hourly or more) (see p. 1120).

HAND, FOOT AND MOUTH DISEASE

This systemic infection is usually caused by Coxsackie virus A16. Mostly affecting children and occasionally adults, it often causes local or household outbreaks. A relatively mild illness of fever and lymphadenopathy develops after an incubation period of approximately 10 days; 2–3 days later a vesicular rash appears on palmoplantar surfaces of hands and feet, with associated mouth lesions that ulcerate rapidly. A papular erythematous rash may appear on buttocks and thighs.

The disease is self-limiting, lasting a maximum of 2 weeks, but the lesions are painful and may require analgesia.

HERPANGINA

This infection by Coxsackie viruses (A1–10, 16 and 22, B1–5) primarily affects children and teenagers. It is characterised by discrete vesicles at the soft/hard palate junction, often associated with high fever, an extremely sore throat and headache.

The lesions are short-lived, rupturing after 2–3 days and rarely persisting for more than a week. Treatment is symptomatic. Culture or PCR of the lesions differentiates herpangina from HSV.

ERYTHEMA MULTIFORME AND STEVENS–JOHNSON SYNDROME

These conditions form a spectrum ranging from relatively mild, maculo-papular erythematous lesions through a bullous form of erythema multiforme to the potentially life-threatening Stevens–Johnson syndrome (see Fig. 1.30 and p. 1098). These rashes can be produced by an immune reaction to recent infection with organisms such as *Mycoplasma pneumoniae*, Coxsackie, herpes simplex and adenovirus infections, and occasional streptococcal infections. They are frequently associated with recent drug ingestion (see p. 1099) or autoimmune disease.

An infectious aetiology should be carefully sought with serological or other investigations and appropriately treated. The dermatological management of the condition is dealt with elsewhere (see p. 1098).

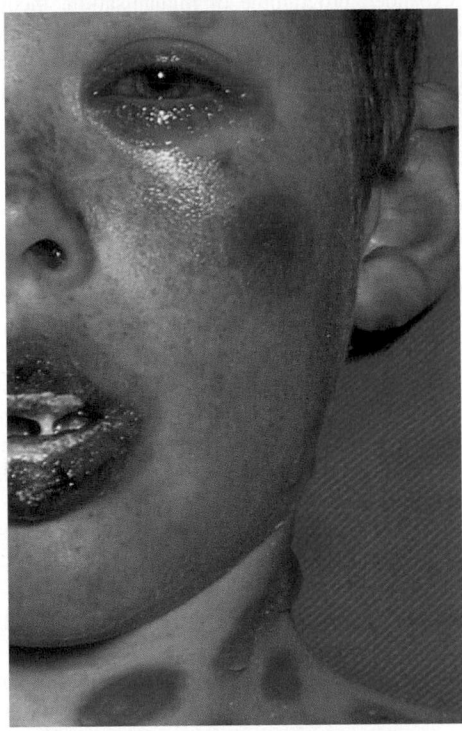

Fig. 1.30   Stevens–Johnson syndrome. Note the widespread bullous lesions of erythema multiforme plus mucocutaneous involvement.

VIRAL EXANTHEMATA

MEASLES

This paramyxovirus infection is endemic world-wide. It is probably the most infectious of all microbial agents. Before immunisation campaigns, it occurred in almost 100% of children. Maternal antibody gives protection for the first 6 months of life. In temperate areas there is a natural epidemic cycle every 2–3 years, less obvious in the tropics. With live attenuated vaccine, the condition is potentially completely controllable by immunisation (see Fig. 1.31). WHO has set the objective of eradicating measles by the year 2010 as part

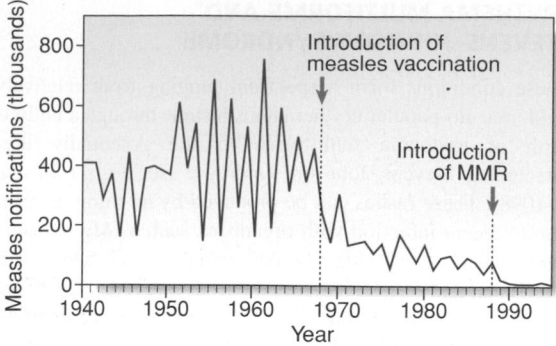

Fig. 1.31 Effectiveness of measles vaccination in England and Wales. (MMR = measles, mumps, rubella vaccine)

of its expanded programme of immunisation. Incomplete vaccination of only 70–80% of the population may lead to outbreaks in older children and adults in whom complications are more frequent. This necessitates repeat mass immunisation campaigns or second dosing of vaccine in an older age group. Natural illness produces life-long immunity.

Clinical features

Infection is by droplet spread with an incubation period of 14 days to onset of rash. A prodromal illness 1–3 days pre-rash heralds the most infectious, 'catarrhal' stage with upper respiratory symptoms and the presence of Koplik's spots on the internal buccal mucosa (see Fig. 1.32). These small white spots surrounded by erythema are pathognomonic of measles. At this stage the patient is miserable and irritable, corresponding to the peak of a second viraemia. As natural antibody develops the rash appears (see Fig. 1.33), lasting 5–6 days and gradually fading with 'staining' in the pale-skinned. Generalised lymphadenopathy and diarrhoea are common, with bacterial pneumonia in approximately 4% of cases. Convulsions occur in approximately 1% and long-term damage can occur in the form of the rare subacute sclerosing panencephalitis (SSPE), occurring up to 7 years after infection. The typical rash may be missing in the immunocompromised and persistent infection with a giant

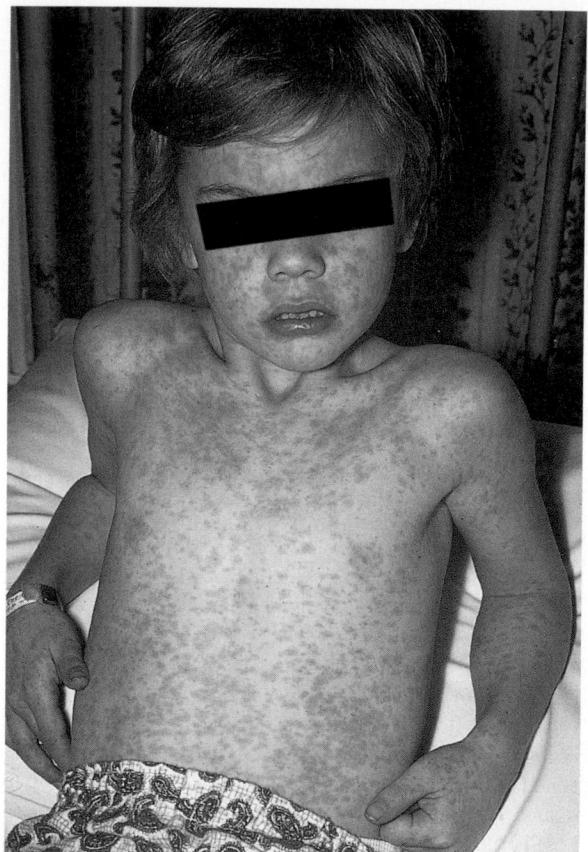

Fig. 1.33 Typical measles rash.

cell pneumonitis or rapidly progressive encephalitis may occur. As with many childhood exanthemata, disease is more severe and prolonged in adults.

Measles is a serious disease in the malnourished, vitamin-deficient or immunocompromised. Mortality clustering at the extremes of age is 1:1000 in the developed world, compared to up to 25% in developing countries. Death usually results from bacterial superinfection such as pneumonia, diarrhoeal disease or cancrum oris.

Management

Normal immunoglobulin attenuates disease in the immuno-compromised or in non-immune pregnant women. Vaccination can be used in outbreaks and vitamin A may improve outlook in uncomplicated disease. Antibiotic therapy is only effective where signs of superinfection already exist and should not be used empirically (see EBM panel).

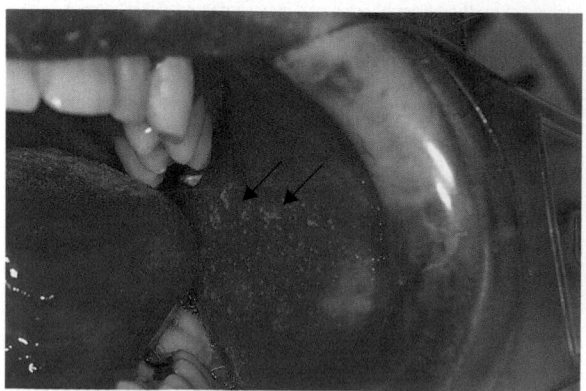

Fig. 1.32 Koplik's spots (arrows) seen on buccal mucosa in the early stages of clinical measles.

EBM

PREVENTION OF PNEUMONIA AFTER MEASLES—role of antibiotics

'Analysis of six RCTs (five unblinded) assessing the role of antibiotics in preventing pneumonia in children with measles suggests that antibiotics should be given only if a child has clinical signs of pneumonia or other evidence of sepsis.'

• Shann F, D'Souza RM, D'Souza R. Antibiotics for preventing pneumonia in children with measles (Cochrane Review). Cochrane Library, issue 4, 2000. Oxford: Update Software.

Further information: 💻 www.update-software.com

RUBELLA (GERMAN MEASLES)

Rubella is endemic in countries without universal vaccination policies. Outbreaks occur in spring and early summer, with epidemics every 7–10 years. The virus is transmitted by aerosol with infectivity from up to a week before and after the onset of the rash. In non-immunised communities 80–85% of young adults have evidence of past infection. In childhood most cases are subclinical. In 1941 Sir Norman Gregg recognised the association between rubella infection in early pregnancy and significant congenital abnormalities. Initial infection via the upper respiratory tract and local lymph nodes is followed by viraemia to target organs such as skin, joints and placenta. If placental infection takes place in the first trimester, persistence of the virus is likely and has the potential for severe congenital disease (see Box 1.24). Adenopathy lasting several weeks occurs with post-auricular, post-cervical and sub-occipital nodes usually involved and occasional splenomegaly. A maculo-papular non-confluent rash starts simultaneously on the face and moves to the trunk. Petechial lesions ('Forchheimer spots') appear on the soft palate, associated with a mild coryza/conjunctivitis. Fever only occurs on the first day of the rash.

Other than congenital infection, complications are rare and are more common in adult females. An immune-mediated arthritis/arthralgia affects 30% of women and involves the fingers, wrists and knees; it takes 1–2 months to resolve. Encephalitis occurs in approximately 1 in every 5000 cases, with a 20–50% mortality. Recovery is complete in survivors. A mild hepatitis is frequently seen and haemorrhagic manifestations occur in 1:3000 cases.

1.24 RUBELLA INFECTION: RISK OF CONGENITAL MALFORMATION	
Stage of gestation	**Likelihood of malformations**
1–2 months	65–85% chance of illness, multiple defects/spontaneous abortion
3 months	30–35% chance of illness, usually a single defect, deafness or congenital heart disease
4 months	10% risk of congenital defects, most commonly deafness
> 20 weeks	Occasional deafness

Diagnosis

Laboratory confirmation of the diagnosis of rubella is required, particularly if there has been contact with a pregnant woman. Detection of rubella-specific IgG with absent IgM indicates previous infection. Specific IgM or rising IgM is indicative of recent infection. However, this may persist for 1–3 months and occur as a reaction in other common rashes such as parvovirus B19 and Epstein–Barr virus infections. The most important investigation in early pregnancy is the detection of maternal rubella-specific IgG which indicates established immunity and allows the patient to be reassured that there is no serious congenital disease.

Prevention

Rubella vaccine should be given to all children at the age of 12–15 months and again at about 4 years.

PARVOVIRUS B19 (SLAPPED CHEEK SYNDROME, FIFTH DISEASE, ERYTHEMA INFECTIOSUM)

This virus produces a mild or subclinical infection in normal hosts. A biphasic illness occurs with symptoms during viraemia and at a later immune complex stage of the disease. Transmission is air-borne although blood-borne infection has been described in haemophiliacs. A week after infection non-specific symptoms occur and a few days later the immune response commences, accompanied by bone marrow depression. Reduction of erythroid precursors progresses to thrombocytopenia, lymphopenia and neutropenia. This is transient and rarely clinically significant. The disease is relevant in individuals with short red cell life, such as sickle-cell disease or spherocytosis where significant anaemia may progress to life-threatening levels. Haematopoiesis usually recovers spontaneously after 10–14 days. Two to three weeks after infection, the immune-mediated classic red 'slapped cheek' rash with circumoral pallor (see Fig. 1.34) and arthralgia appears. A second-stage erythematous maculo-papular rash may occur on the trunk and limbs. Apart from rare cases in the immunocompromised, there is spontaneous recovery. Infection during the first two trimesters of pregnancy can result in intrauterine infection and impact on fetal bone marrow; it causes 10–15% of non-immune (non-rhesus-related) hydrops fetalis. This is rare, occurring in only 1:30 000 infected pregnancies.

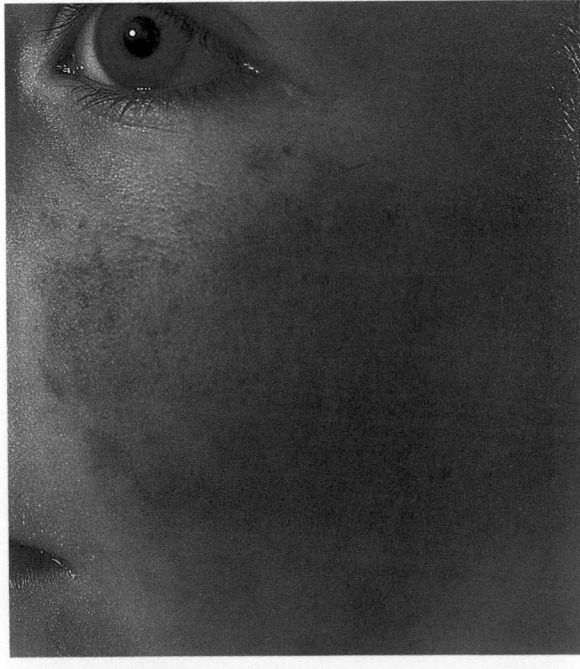

Fig. 1.34 Slapped cheek syndrome. The typical facial rash of human parvovirus B19 infection.

Diagnosis

Parvovirus B19 DNA may be detected in the serum and a PCR test will remain positive from then until some 4 months after infection. IgM responses, although commonly used for diagnostic purposes, may persist for months. During the early stages of erythropoietic disturbance, haemophagocytosis may be demonstrable in the bone marrow and occasionally in peripheral blood.

Management

In the normal individual, this infection is self-limiting and symptomatic relief for arthritic symptoms should be given. Passive prophylaxis with normal immunoglobulin has been suggested for non-immune pregnant women exposed to infection. The pregnancy should be closely monitored by ultrasound scanning and any suggestion of hydrops should result in consideration of fetal transfusion.

MUMPS

This paramyxovirus is endemic world-wide. In non-vaccinated populations, it occurs in epidemics every 2–3 years, primarily infecting 5–9-year-old children. If vaccination has been employed without complete eradication of the disease, there is increased susceptibility in older teenagers. Infection is by droplets or direct salivary spread and initial infection is through the upper respiratory tract. A primary viraemia seeds the virus to target organs: parotid glands, other exocrine glands, meninges and sites of gametogenesis. The incubation period of 16–18 days ends with 2–3 days of infectivity and a second viraemia. Infectivity lasts for 5–7 days.

Classical tender parotid enlargement, which is bilateral in 75%, follows a prodrome of pyrexia and malaise (see Fig. 1.35). Other salivary glands are involved in approximately 10% of cases.

Complications commonly occur. Oophoritis and orchitis only occur post-pubertally. Oophoritis causing abdominal pain is present in 5% of post-pubertal mumps in women, and 35% of post-pubertal males with mumps develop orchitis,

33% bilaterally. Some degree of testicular atrophy does result but sterility is most unlikely. Meningitis occurs in approximately 50% of cases. In non-vaccinated communities mumps is the most common cause of sporadic viral meningitis. The CSF pleocytosis is lymphocytic, often 200–400 cells/mm³. A raised protein and reduced glucose level mimicking early bacterial meningitis may be present. Mumps meningitis is three times more common in males than females. Encephalitis is found in two forms: acute and post-infectious. It occurs in 1:6000 cases and has a mortality of 1.4%.

Transient hearing loss and labyrinthitis are recognised but uncommon. However, 1:20 000 cases will have persisting measurable deafness.

There appears to be no apparent added danger to the immunocompromised and natural infection results in life-long immunity. Abortion may occur if infection takes place in the first trimester of pregnancy but in the later trimesters infection appears to carry no added risk.

Management

Symptomatic relief is important. Prednisolone up to 40 mg orally for 4 days may be used to relieve the discomfort of orchitis.

Prevention

Mumps vaccine, usually as part of the measles, mumps and rubella combined vaccine (MMR), is given after the first birthday and at a pre-school visit. If used widely, this will markedly reduce the incidence of natural infection and abolish the epidemic pattern of disease (see Fig. 1.36).

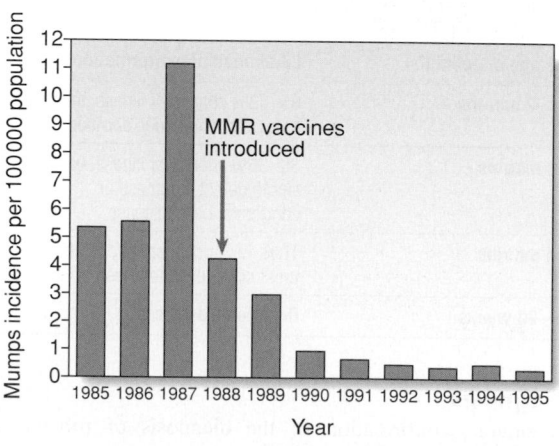

Fig. 1.36   Effect of mumps vaccination on incidence of disease.

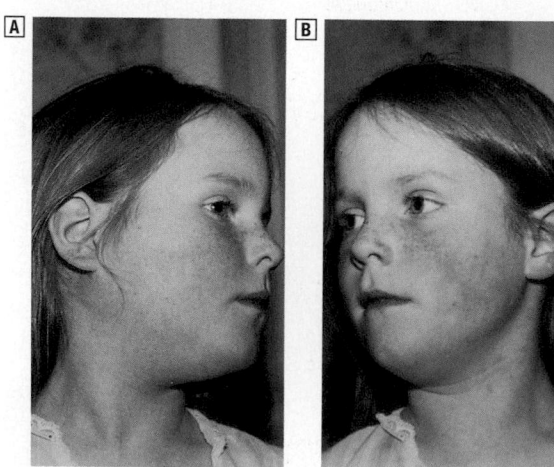

Fig. 1.35   **Typical unilateral mumps.** A Note the loss of angle of the jaw on the affected (right) side. B Comparison showing normal (left) side.

FOOD POISONING AND GASTROENTERITIS

Acute gastroenteritis is a major cause of morbidity and mortality. Infants and young children are particularly at risk. WHO estimates that there are more than 1000 million cases of acute diarrhoea annually in developing countries, with 3–4 million deaths. Even in developed countries diarrhoea remains an important problem with 38 million cases annually in the US. Although other causes are important (see Box 1.25), the majority of episodes may be directly linked to infection or infectious agents spread by the faecal-oral route and either transmitted on fomites, on contaminated hands, or in food or water. Measures such as the provision of clean potable water, appropriate disposal of human and animal sewage with separation from water supplies, and simple principles of food hygiene are all very effective means of halting the spread of these infections. Oral fluid replacement is vital in the management of these cases.

PRINCIPLES OF FOOD HYGIENE

An understanding of the temperatures at which spoilage and pathogenic bacteria are inhibited and destroyed (see Fig. 1.37) underpins the essentials of food hygiene. Following high-profile outbreaks such as the Central Scotland *E. coli* O157 outbreak of 1996, UK butchers' premises and food preparation establishments have had to be licensed and registered respectively; all proprietors are now required to have gained certification in food hygiene. An essential element of this is an understanding of hazard analysis of critical control points (HACCP) in the process of food preparation (see Fig. 1.38). National systems of surveillance, based on compulsory notification of food poisoning and recommendations for the setting up of outbreak control teams, allow for the rapid recognition of outbreaks and their speedy control.

The clinical features of food-borne disease all involve gastrointestinal upset but the pattern of symptomatology is dependent on the pathogenic mechanisms involved. Some organisms (*Bacillus cereus*, *Staph. aureus* and *Vibrio cholerae*) elute exotoxins which exert their major effects on the stomach and small bowel, where they cause mucosal inflammation. They frequently produce vomiting and/or a so-called 'secretory' diarrhoea. This is watery without blood and faecal leucocytosis. In general, the 'incubation period', i.e. the time from ingestion to the onset of symptoms, of these intoxications is short and, other than dehydration, little systemic upset occurs. Other organisms, such as *Shigella*, *Salmonella*, *Campylobacter* and enterohaemorrhagic *E. coli*, may directly invade the mucosa of the small bowel or produce cytotoxins that damage and ulcerate the mucosa with inflammation, typically affecting the terminal small bowel and colon. Here the incubation period is longer and more systemic upset occurs with prolonged diarrhoea. If the colon is inflamed, blood may be present in the stool and faecal leucocytes present.

1.25 CAUSES OF ACUTE DIARRHOEA

Infectious

Toxin-mediated
- *Bacillus cereus* (see p. 39)
- Staphylococcal enterotoxin (see p. 38)
- Clostridial sp. enterotoxin (see p. 39)
- Scombrotoxic (see p. 41)
- Ciguatera fish poisoning (see p. 41)
- Dinoflagellates (see p. 40)
- Plant toxins (see p. 40)
- Heavy metals (see p. 41)

Infective food poisoning
- Rotavirus gastroenteritis
- *Campylobacter* (see p. 41)
- *Salmonella* (see p. 42)
- Verocytotoxigenic *E. coli* (see p. 43)
- Other *E. coli*, e.g. travellers' diarrhoea (see p. 47)
- Shigella (see p. 45)
- *Clostridium difficile* (see p. 43)
- Norwalk-like agents (see p. 41)

Protozoal
- Giardiasis (see p. 46)
- Amoebic dysentery (see p. 45)
- Cryptosporidium (see pp. 47 and 118)
- Isosporiasis (see p. 118)
- Microsporidiosis (see p. 118)

Non-infectious

Gastrointestinal
- Acute diverticulitis (see p. 772)
- Inflammatory bowel disease (see p. 808)
  Ulcerative colitis
  Crohn's disease
- Bowel malignancy (see p. 820)
- Pelvic inflammatory disease (see p. 101)
- Overflow from constipation (see p. 826)

Metabolic upset
- Ketosis (e.g. diabetic decompensation)
- Vasoactive intestinal peptide release (see p. 755)
- Carcinoid syndrome (see p. 801)
- Uraemia (see p. 600)

Generalised illness
- Sepsis (+ sepsis syndrome)
- Meningococcal sepsis (see p. 199)
- Pneumonia (esp. 'atypical disease'; see p. 526)
- Malaria (see p. 51)

Drugs
- NSAIDS
- Cytotoxic agents
- Antibiotics

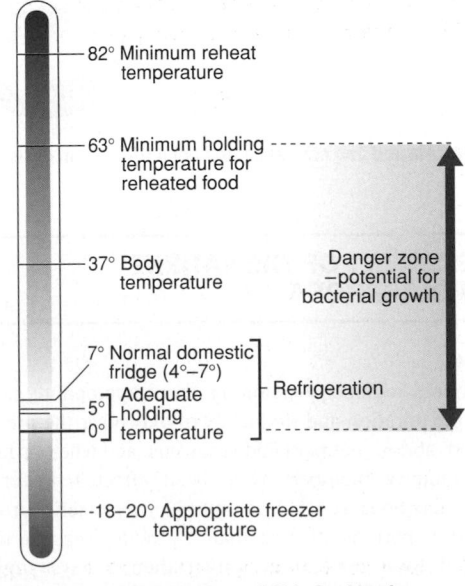

Fig. 1.37 Important temperatures (°C) in food hygiene.

- 82° Minimum reheat temperature
- 63° Minimum holding temperature for reheated food
- 37° Body temperature
- 7° Normal domestic fridge (4°–7°)
- 5° Adequate holding temperature
- 0°
- Danger zone – potential for bacterial growth
- Refrigeration
- -18–20° Appropriate freezer temperature

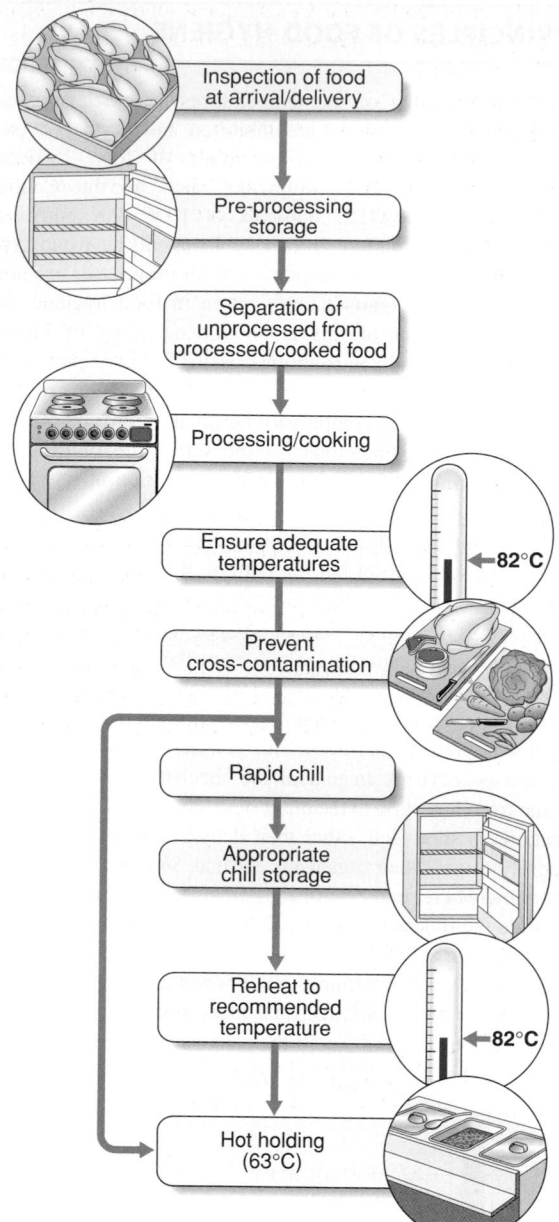

Fig. 1.38 Hazard and critical control point (HACCP) analysis.

ASSESSMENT OF THE PATIENT WITH DIARRHOEA

History

This should include questioning about appropriate suspect foods, the duration and frequency of diarrhoea, the presence of blood, abdominal pain and tenesmus, and whether family or community members have been affected. Fever and bloody diarrhoea suggest an invasive, dysenteric process. Incubation periods of less than 18 hours suggest toxin-mediated food poisoning; longer than 5 days suggests diarrhoea caused by protozoa or helminths.

Examination

The degree of dehydration can be assessed by skin turgor and blood pressure measurement. The urine output and ongoing stool losses should be measured carefully.

Investigations

These should include stool inspection for blood and microscopy for leucocytes. Stool culture should be performed where possible but often the results will come too late to influence immediate management. A full blood count and serum electrolytes will also indicate the degree of inflammation and dehydration. In a malarious area a blood film for malaria parasites should be obtained.

ACUTE FOOD POISONING WITH PREDOMINANT VOMITING

STAPHYLOCOCCAL FOOD POISONING

Staph. aureus is a common commensal in the anterior nares. With poor hygiene, transmission takes place via the hands of

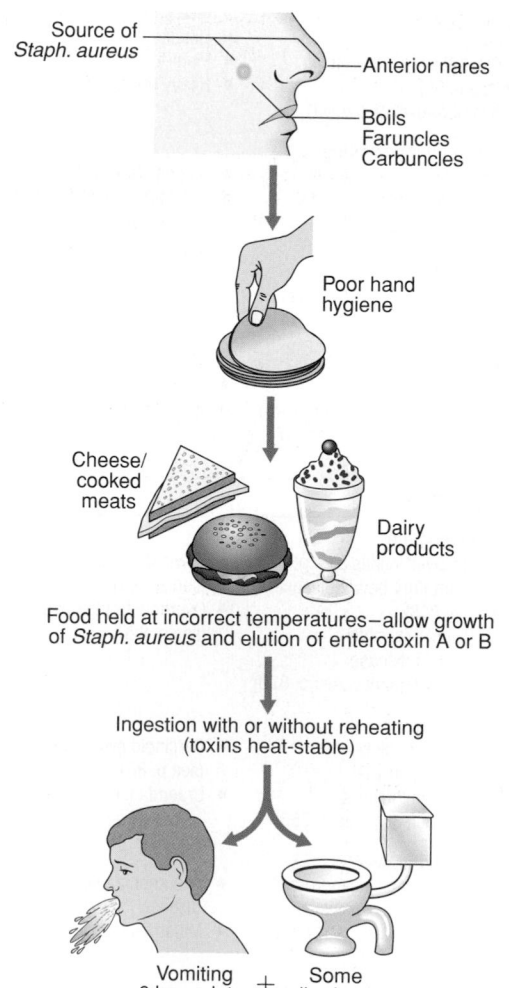

Fig. 1.39 Staphylococcal food poisoning.

food handlers to foodstuffs such as dairy products, cheese and cooked meats. Inappropriate storage of these foods allows growth of the organism and production of one or more heat-stable enterotoxins (see Fig. 1.39).

Clinical features

Following ingestion, symptoms of nausea and profuse vomiting develop within 1–6 hours. Diarrhoea may not be marked. These toxins act as super-antigens, stimulating a non-specific T-cell activation and a significant neutrophil leucocytosis. This may be clinically misleading. Most cases settle rapidly but severe dehydration and rare fatalities have occurred due to acute fluid loss and shock.

Management

Antiemetics and appropriate fluid replacement are the mainstays of treatment. Suspect food should be cultured for staphylococci and demonstration of toxin production. The public health authorities should be notified if food vending is involved.

BACILLUS CEREUS

The 'Chinese restaurant syndrome' (rapid onset of vomiting within hours of food consumption) is caused by the ingestion of the pre-formed toxins of *B. cereus*. Fried rice or freshly made vanilla sauces are frequent sources. The organism grows and produces enterotoxin during storage; 1–4 hours after ingestion, brisk vomiting and some diarrhoea occur, with rapid resolution within 24 hours.

A longer incubation form occurs if viable bacteria are ingested and toxin formation takes place within the gut lumen. The incubation period is 12–24 hours and watery diarrhoea and cramps are the predominant symptoms. The disease is self-limiting but can be quite severe (see Fig. 1.40).

Management

Rapid and judicious fluid replacement and appropriate notification of the public health authorities are all that is required.

CLOSTRIDIUM PERFRINGENS

Spores of *Cl. perfringens* are widespread in the guts of large animals and in soil. If contaminated meat products are incompletely cooked and stored in anaerobic conditions, *Cl. perfringens* spores germinate and viable organisms multiply to large numbers. Subsequent reheating of the food causes heat-shock sporulation of the organisms during which they elute an enterotoxin. Symptoms (diarrhoea and cramps) occur some 6–12 hours following ingestion (see Fig. 1.41).

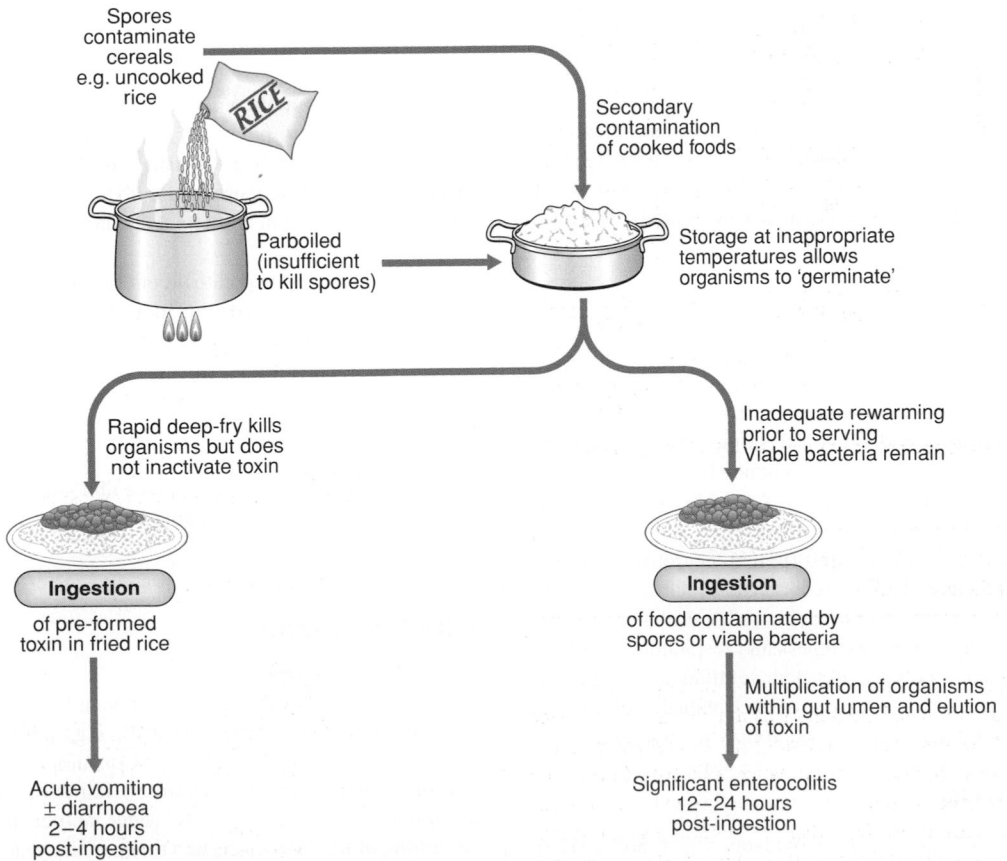

Fig. 1.40 *Bacillus cereus* food poisoning.

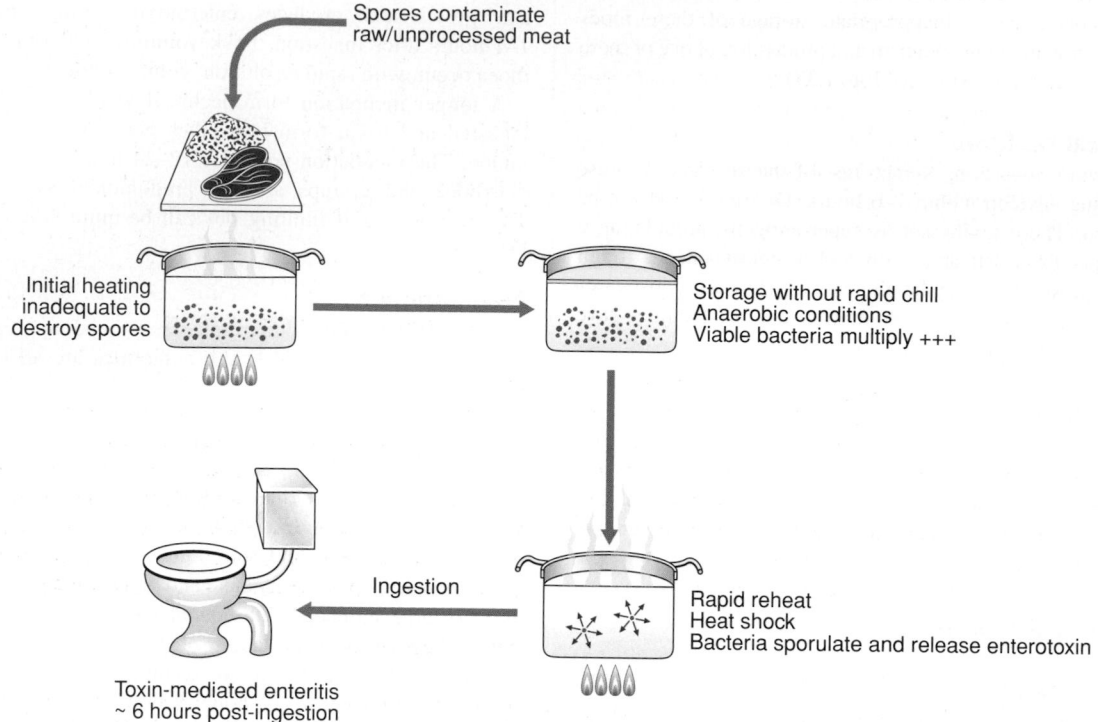

Fig. 1.41 *Clostridium perfringens* **food poisoning.**

'Point source' outbreaks, in which a number of cases all become symptomatic following ingestion, classically occur after school or canteen lunches where meat stews are served. Clostridial enterotoxins are potent and most people who ingest them will be symptomatic. The illness is usually self-limiting.

CLOSTRIDIUM BOTULINUM

Botulism is a syndrome of paralysis and neurological dysfunction produced by the neurotoxins of *Cl. botulinum*. This organism may contaminate many different foodstuffs from canned meat and salmon to home-produced and preserved vegetables. Contaminated honey has been implicated in outbreaks involving neonates. Anaerobic conditions are necessary for the organism's growth.

Ingestion of this extremely potent neurotoxin in even picogram amounts causes predominately bulbar and ocular palsies (difficulty in swallowing, blurred or double vision, ptosis) progressing to limb weakness and respiratory paralysis.

Management includes assisted ventilation and general supportive measures until the toxin eventually dissociates from nerve endings at 6–8 weeks following ingestion.

PLANT TOXINS

Legumes and beans produce oxidants which are toxic to persons with glucose-6-phosphate dehydrogenase (G6PD) deficiency. Consumption produces headache, nausea and fever progressing to potentially severe haemolysis, haemoglobinuria and jaundice (favism). Red kidney beans, if incompletely cooked, cause acute abdominal pain and diarrhoea from their lectin content. Adequate cooking abolishes this.

Alkaloids develop in potato tubers exposed to light causing green discoloration. Ingestion induces acute vomiting and anticholinesterase-like activity.

Fungi and mushrooms of the *Psilocybe* spp. produce hallucinogens. Many fungal species induce a combination of gastroenteritis and cholinergic symptoms of blurred vision, salivation, sweating and diarrhoea. *Amanita phalloides* (death head mushroom) causes acute abdominal cramps and diarrhoea followed by inexorable hepatorenal failure, often fatal.

CHEMICAL TOXINS

Paralytic shellfish toxin

Saxitoxin from dinoflagellates responsible for 'red tides' is concentrated in bivalve molluscs, e.g. mussels, clams, oysters, cockles and scallops. Consumption produces gastrointestinal symptoms within 30 minutes, followed by respiratory paralysis. The UK water authorities ban the harvesting of molluscs at certain times of the year associated with excessive dinoflagellate numbers.

Ciguatera fish poisoning

Warm-water coral reef fish derive ciguatoxin from dino-flagellates in their food chain. Consumption produces gastrointestinal symptoms 1–6 hours later with associated paraesthesiae of the lips and extremities, distorted temperature sensation, myalgia and progressive flaccid paralysis. In the South Pacific and Caribbean there are 50 000 cases per year with a case fatality of 0.1%. Exotic fish imports are a major source in the UK. The gastrointestinal symptoms resolve rapidly but the neuropathic features may persist for months.

Scombrotoxic fish poisoning

Histidine in scombroid fish—tuna, mackerel, bonito, skipjack and the canned dark meat of sardines—may under poor storage conditions be converted by bacteria to histamine and other chemicals. Consumption produces symptoms within minutes with flushing, burning, sweating, urticaria, pruritus, headache, colic, nausea and vomiting, diarrhoea, bronchospasm and hypotension. Management is with salbutamol and antihistamines. Occasionally, intravenous fluid replacement is required.

Heavy metals

Thallium and cadmium can cause acute vomiting and diarrhoea resembling staphylococcal enterotoxin poisoning.

NORWALK-LIKE AGENTS (SMALL ROUND STRUCTURED VIRUSES)

These have been identified both in outbreaks related to infected food handlers and in endemic person-to-person gastroenteritis. Seroprevalence surveys suggest that many adults are susceptible to this infection.

These viruses spread by faeco-oral transmission, or by aerosol spread if susceptible individuals are in the vicinity of a sufferer actively vomiting.

After a 48-hour incubation period there is a brisk 2–3-day illness with marked nausea, predominant vomiting and little diarrhoea. Illness transmitting step-wise through nurseries and families remains very common.

CALICIVIRUS

This organism may produce seasonal symptoms and seroprevalence surveys suggest that the infection is more common than its rate of identification in cases of gastroenteritis would suggest.

ACUTE WATERY DIARRHOEA

This is the predominant symptom in acute infective gastroenteritis. A frequent accompaniment of the diarrhoea is the presence of blood per rectum; a number of aetiologies are commonly associated with this (see Box 1.27).

ROTAVIRUS

Rotaviruses are the major cause of diarrhoeal illness in young children, accounting for 30–50% of cases admitted to hospital in developed countries, and 10–20% of deaths due to gastroenteritis in developing countries. Infection is endemic in developing countries and there are winter epidemics in developed countries. These viruses transmit easily and resist alcohol denaturation; person-to-person spread, especially by health-care workers in hospitals, is well documented. The virus infects enterocytes to cause decreased surface absorption and loss of enzymes on the brush border. The incubation period is 48 hours and patients present with watery diarrhoea, vomiting, fever and abdominal pain. Diagnosis is aided by commercially available enzyme immunoassay kits which simply require fresh or refrigerated stool for effective demonstration of the pathogens.

The disease is self-limiting but dehydration needs appropriate management. Immunity develops to natural infection. Rotavirus vaccines have been developed and gave good protection to children in Venezuela but were associated with intussusception; this has hampered vaccine uptake.

ASTROVIRUSES

Astroviruses are less frequently identified as a cause of infection/diarrhoea than rotaviruses (accounting for some 10% of the incidence of the latter). Seroprevalence in the community mimics rotavirus and they are therefore probably under-diagnosed.

OTHER VIRUSES

Adenoviruses are frequently identified from stool culture and implicated as a cause of diarrhoea. Two serotypes (40 and 41) appear to be more commonly found in association with diarrhoea rather than the more frequent upper respiratory types 1–7.

CAMPYLOBACTER JEJUNI

This infection is essentially a zoonosis, the organisms originating in the gut of cattle and poultry. The most common source of the infection is meat, such as chicken, or contaminated milk products. There has been an association with pet puppies. *Campylobacter* infection accounts for some 100 000 cases per annum in the UK, most of which are sporadic.

The incubation period is 2–5 days. Colicky abdominal pain, which may be quite severe and mimic surgical pathology, plus nausea, vomiting and quite significant diarrhoea ensue, the latter frequently becoming blood-stained. The majority of *Campylobacter* infections affect fit young adults and are self-limiting after 5–7 days. About 10–20% will have prolonged symptomatology, occasionally meriting treatment with antibiotics such as ciprofloxacin or a macrolide. Approximately 1% of cases will develop bacteraemia and possible distant foci of infection. *Campylobacter* species have been clearly linked to Guillain–Barré syndrome and post-infectious reactive arthritis (see pp. 1180 and 1010).

SALMONELLA SPECIES

These Gram-negative organisms produce two distinct clinical entities:

- The serotypes *S. typhi* and *S. paratyphi* A, B, C have a purely human reservoir and produce the septicaemic illness 'enteric fever' (typhoid or paratyphoid fever—see p. 57).
- All other *Salmonella* serotypes, of which there are more than 2000, are subdivided into five distinct subgroups which produce gastroenteritis. They are widely distributed throughout the animal kingdom. Some strains have a clear relationship to particular animal species, e.g. *S. arizonae* and pet reptiles. Transmission is by contaminated water or food, particularly poultry, egg products and related fast foods, direct person-to-person spread or the handling of exotic pets such as salamanders, lizards or turtles. The incidence of *Salmonella* enteritis is falling in the UK due to an aggressive culling policy in broiler chicken stocks coupled with vaccination. Two serotypes remain important in the UK: *S. enteritidis* phage type 4 and *S. typhimurium* dt.104. The latter may be significantly resistant to commonly used antibiotics such as ciprofloxacin.

The incubation period of *Salmonella* gastroenteritis is 12–72 hours and the predominant feature is diarrhoea. Vomiting may be present at the outset and blood is quite frequently noted in the stool. Approximately 5% of cases will be bacteraemic. Reactive (post-infective) arthritis occurs in approximately 2% of cases. Evidence of bacteraemia is a clear indication for antibiotic therapy as salmonellae are notorious for persistent infection and often colonise endothelial surfaces: for example, an atherosclerotic aorta or a major blood vessel. Antibiotics are not indicated for uncomplicated *Salmonella* gastroenteritis (see EBM panel).

EBM

SALMONELLA GASTROENTERITIS—use of antibiotics

'In 12 randomised or semi-randomised trials comparing antibiotic therapy with placebo or no therapy there was no evidence of a clinical benefit of antibiotic therapy in otherwise healthy adults or children with non-severe *Salmonella* diarrhoea. Antibiotics appeared to increase side-effects and to prolong *Salmonella* detection.'

- Sirinavin S, Garner P. Antibiotics for treating salmonella gut infections (Cochrane Review). Cochrane Library, issue 1, 2001. Oxford: Update Software.

LISTERIOSIS

Listeria monocytogenes is an environmental bacterium which can contaminate food, including poultry and cheese. Outbreaks have been associated with soft cheeses and pâtés. It does not usually cause intestinal symptoms but is a cause of bacteraemia, focal infection and meningitis, especially in pregnancy, the neonate, the immunosuppressed, diabetics and alcoholics. It merits active treatment and is susceptible to amoxicillin; gentamicin should be added in the presence of immunocompromise.

ESCHERICHIA COLI

Epidemiology

Many serotypes of this major member of the Enterobacteriaceae may be present in the human gut at any given time. Production of disease depends on either colonisation with a new or previously unrecognised strain, or the acquisition by current colonising bacteria of a particular pathogenicity factor for mucosal attachment or toxin production. Travel to unfamiliar areas of the world assumes contact with previously unknown strains of endemic *E. coli* and the development of travellers' diarrhoea. Enteropathogenic strains may be found in the gut of healthy individuals and if these persons move to a new environment close contacts may develop symptoms.

The genus *Escherichia* can cause five different clinicopathological features, all associated with diarrhoea.

Enterotoxigenic E. coli (ETEC)

These cause most cases of travellers' diarrhoea in developing countries although other causes are possible (see Box 1.26). The organisms produce either a heat-labile or a heat-stable enterotoxin, causing marked secretory diarrhoea and vomiting after 1–2 days' incubation. The illness is usually mild and self-limiting after 3–4 days. Antibiotics have been used to limit the duration of symptoms and prophylaxis may help to prevent this disease (see EBM panel).

1.26 MOST COMMON CAUSES OF TRAVELLERS' DIARRHOEA

- ETEC
- *Shigella* spp.
- *Campylobacter jejuni*
- *Salmonella* spp.
- *Pleisomonas shigelloides*
- Non-cholera *Vibrio* spp.
- *Aeromonas* spp.

EBM

TRAVELLERS' DIARRHOEA—role of antibiotic therapy

'Analysis of 20 trials (12 placebo-controlled) of randomly allocated antibiotic treatment for acute non-bloody diarrhoea in patients over 5 years old demonstrates a shorter duration of diarrhoea in those receiving antibiotics. In the five trials where data were available, the incidence of side-effects was higher in the antibiotic group.'

- De Bruyn G, Hahn S, Borwick A. Antibiotic treatment for traveller's diarrhoea (Cochrane Review). Cochrane Library, issue 4, 2000. Oxford: Update Software.

Further information: www.update-software.com

Entero-invasive E. coli (EIEC)

This illness is very similar to *Shigella* dysentery (see p. 45) and is caused by invasion and destruction of colonic mucosal cells. No enterotoxin is produced. Acute watery diarrhoea, abdominal cramps and some scanty blood-staining of the stool are common. The symptoms are rarely severe and are usually self-limiting.

Enteropathogenic E. coli (EPEC)

These are very important in infant diarrhoea. Ability to attach to the gut mucosa inducing a specific 'attachment and effacement' lesion is the basis of their pathogenicity. This causes destruction of microvilli and disruption of normal absorptive capacity. The symptoms vary from mild non-bloody diarrhoea to quite severe illness. Bacteraemia/septicaemia is virtually unheard of.

Entero-aggregative E. coli (EAEC)

These strains have the genetic codes for adherence to the mucosa but also produce a locally active enterotoxin and demonstrate a particular 'stacked brick' aggregation in the small bowel. They have been associated with prolonged diarrhoea in children in South America, South-east Asia and India.

Enterohaemorrhagic E. coli (EHEC)

A number of distinct 'O' serotypes of *E. coli* possess both the genetic codes for attachment and effacement (see EPEC above) and plasmids encoding for two distinct enterotoxins (verocytotoxin) which are identical to toxins produced by *Shigella* ('shiga-toxins 1 and 2'). *E. coli* O157:H7 is perhaps the best known of these verocytotoxigenic *E. coli* (VTEC), but others, including types O126 and O11, are also implicated. Although the incidence is considerably lower than *Campylobacter* and *Salmonella*, it is increasing in the developing world.

The reservoir of infection is in the gut of herbivores. Contaminated meat products, such as hamburgers, have long been recognised as a source of this infection. The organism has an extremely low infecting dose (10–100 organisms), and run off water from pasture lands where cattle have grazed which is used to irrigate vegetable crops, contaminated milk, lettuce, radish shoots and apple juice have all been implicated as sources (see Fig. 1.42).

The incubation period is between 1 and 7 days. Initial watery diarrhoea becomes frankly and uniformly blood-stained in 70% of cases and is associated with a severe and often constant abdominal pain. There is little systemic upset, vomiting or fever. Enterotoxins, if produced, have both a local effect on the bowel and a distant effect on particular body tissues such as glomerular apparatus, heart and brain. The potentially life-threatening haemolytic uraemic syndrome (HUS—see p. 610) occurs in 10–15% of sufferers from this infection, arising 5–7 days after the onset of symptoms. It is most likely at the extremes of age, is heralded by a high peripheral leucocyte count and may be induced, particularly in children, by antibiotic therapy.

Management

HUS is treated by dialysis if necessary and may be averted by active intervention with processes such as plasma exchange.

ANTIBIOTIC-ASSOCIATED DIARRHOEA (*CL. DIFFICILE* INFECTION)

A history of any antibiotic therapy in the 6 weeks prior to the onset of diarrhoea can be related to the finding of *Cl. difficile* or its toxins in the stool. This is a potent cause of diarrhoea and can produce life-threatening pseudomembranous colitis. This diagnosis (see p. 827) should be actively considered in the elderly and treated with metronidazole 400 mg 8-hourly for 10 days. If there is no response, then vancomycin orally may be used 125 mg 6-hourly for 1 week.

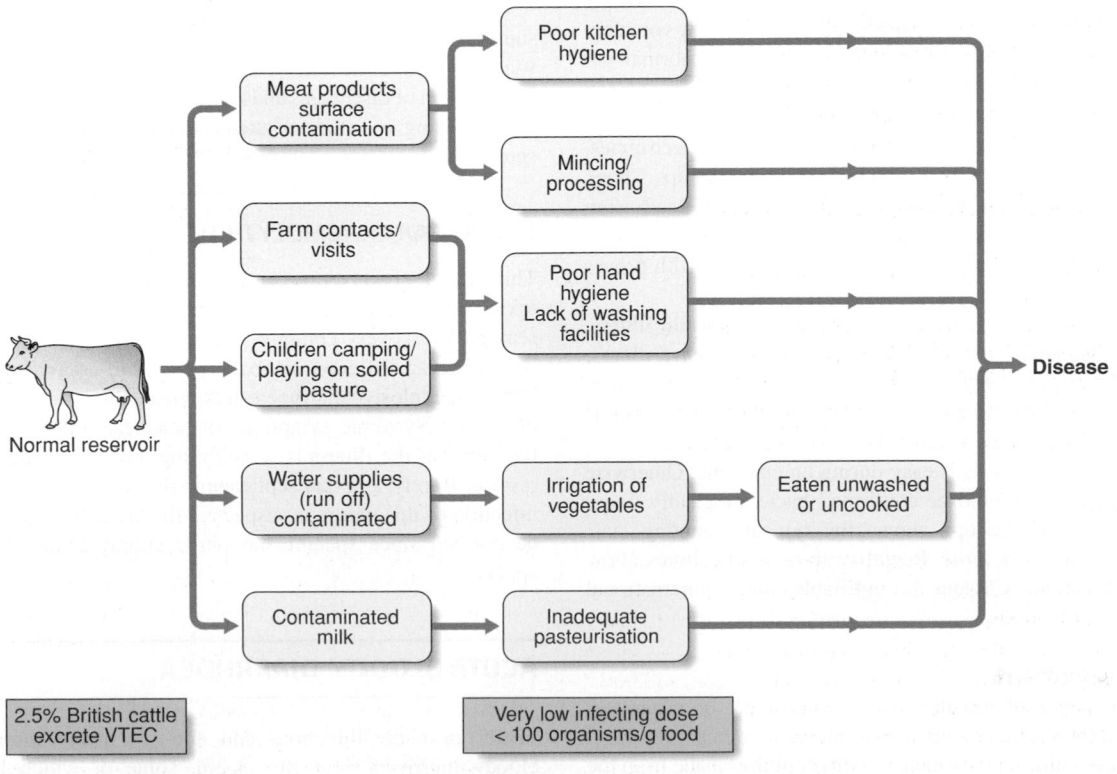

Fig. 1.42 VTEC infections.

YERSINIA ENTEROCOLITICA

This organism, commonly found in pork, causes mild to moderate gastroenteritis and can produce significant mesenteric adenitis after an incubation period of 3–7 days. It predominantly causes disease in children but adults may also be affected. The illness resolves slowly with 10–30% of cases complicated by persistent arthritis or Reiter's syndrome (see p. 1010).

CHOLERA

Cholera, caused by *Vibrio cholerae* serotype 01, originated in the Ganges valley. Devastating epidemics have occurred, often following large religious festivals, and pandemics have spread world-wide. The seventh pandemic, due to the El tor biotype, began in 1961 and spread via the Middle East to become endemic in Africa. In 1990 it reached Peru and spread throughout South and Central America. Since August 2000 there has been a massive outbreak in South Africa. El tor is more resistant than classical *Vibrio*, and causes carriage in 5% of infections. A new classical toxigenic strain, serotype 0139, established itself in Bangladesh in 1992 and started a new pandemic.

Infection spreads via the stools or vomit of symptomatic patients or of the much larger number of subclinical cases. It survives for up to 2 weeks in fresh water and 8 weeks in salt water. Transmission is normally through infected drinking water, shellfish, and food contaminated by flies or on the hands of carriers.

Clinical features

Severe diarrhoea without pain or colic, succeeded by vomiting, begins suddenly. Following the evacuation of normal gut faecal contents, typical 'rice-water' material is passed consisting of clear fluid with flecks of mucus. Classical cholera produces enormous loss of fluid and electrolytes, leading to intense dehydration with muscular cramps. Shock and oliguria develop but mental clarity remains. Death from acute circulatory failure may occur rapidly unless fluid and electrolytes are replaced. Improvement is rapid with proper treatment.

The majority of infections, however, cause mild illness, with slight diarrhoea. Occasionally, a very intense illness, 'cholera sicca', occurs, with loss of fluid into dilated bowel, killing the patient before typical gastrointestinal symptoms appear. The disease is more dangerous in children.

Clinical diagnosis is easy during an epidemic. Otherwise the diagnosis should be confirmed bacteriologically. Stool dark-field microscopy shows the typical 'shooting star' motility of *V. cholerae*. Rectal swab or stool cultures allow identification. Cholera is notifiable under international health regulations.

Management

Maintenance of circulation by replacement of water and electrolytes is paramount. Early intervention improves prognosis. A clinical assessment of dehydration is made from the appearance of the patient. Oral rehydration solution (ORS) is effective and safe for all but the most severely dehydrated patients. The addition of resistant starch to ORS reduces faecal fluid loss and shortens the duration of diarrhoea in adolescents and adults with cholera. The effect is caused by enhanced sodium absorption in the colon due to short-chain fatty acids produced in the colon from non-absorbed carbohydrates. Ringer-Lactate is the best fluid for intravenous replacement. Vomiting usually stops once the patient is rehydrated, and fluid should then be given orally up to 500 ml hourly. The fluid required is calculated every 8 hours from the urine volume, stool and vomit output, and estimated insensible loss (as much as 5 litres/24 hours in a hot humid climate). Total fluid requirements may exceed 50 litres over a period of 2–5 days. Accurate records are greatly facilitated by the use of a 'cholera cot' which has a reinforced hole under the patient's buttocks beneath which a graded bucket is placed.

Children require careful attention to fluid balance and are prone to hypoglycaemia.

Three days' treatment with tetracycline 250 mg 6-hourly, a single dose of doxycycline 300 mg or ciprofloxacin 1 g in adults all reduce the duration of excretion of *Vibrio* and the total volume of fluid needed for replacement.

Prevention

Strict personal hygiene is vital and drinking water should come from a clean piped supply or be boiled. Flies must be denied access to food. Parenteral vaccination with a killed suspension of *V. cholerae* may provide limited protection. Oral vaccines containing killed *V. cholerae* and the B subunit of cholera toxin are available but of limited efficacy.

In epidemics public education, and control of water sources and population movement are vital. Mass single-dose vaccination and treatment with tetracycline are valuable. Disinfection of discharges and soiled clothing, and scrupulous hand-washing by medical attendants reduce the danger of spread.

VIBRIO PARAHAEMOLYTICUS

This marine organism produces a disease similar to enterotoxigenic *E. coli* (see above). It is acquired from raw seafood and is very common where ingestion of such food is widespread. After an incubation period of approximately 20 hours, explosive diarrhoea, abdominal cramps and vomiting occur. Systemic symptoms of headache and fever are frequent but the illness is self-limiting, taking 4–7 days to resolve. Rarely, a severe septicaemic illness arises. If *Vibrio* infection of this nature is suspected, the laboratory ought to be notified since specific halophilic culture requirements apply.

ACUTE BLOODY DIARRHOEA

There are many infectious and non-infectious causes of bloody diarrhoea (see Box 1.27), some of which have already been described. Dysentery is an acute inflammation

1.27 CAUSES OF BLOODY DIARRHOEA

Infectious

- *Campylobacter* spp. (see p. 41)
- *Shigella* dysentery (see below)
- Non-typhoidal salmonellae (see p. 42)
- Entero-invasive *E. coli* (EIEC; see p. 42)
- Enterohaemorrhagic *E. coli* (EHEC or VTEC; see p. 43)
- *Clostridium difficile* (see p. 43)
- *Vibrio parahaemolyticus* (see p. 44)
- *Entamoeba histolytica* (amoebic dysentery; see below)

Non-infectious

- Diverticular disease
- Rectal or colonic malignancy (see p. 820)
- Inflammatory bowel disease
- Bleeding haemorrhoids (see p. 829)
- Anal fissure (see p. 830)
- Ischaemic colitis (see p. 820)
- Intussusception

of the large intestine characterised by diarrhoea with blood and mucus in the stools. Its causes are bacillary or amoebic infection.

BACILLARY DYSENTERY (SHIGELLOSIS)

Shigellae are Gram-negative rods, closely related to *E. coli*, that invade the colonic mucosa. There are four main groups: *dysenteriae*, *flexneri*, *boydii* and *sonnei*. In the tropics bacillary dysentery is usually caused by *Sh. flexneri*, whilst in Britain most cases are caused by *Sh. sonnei*. Shigellae are often multi-resistant to antibiotics, especially in tropical countries. Such organisms have been responsible for epidemics of bacillary dysentery in Bangladesh and other tropical countries. The organism only infects humans and its spread is facilitated by its low infecting dose of around 10 organisms.

Epidemiology

Spread may occur by contaminated food or by flies, but transmission by unwashed hands after defaecation is by far the most important factor. Outbreaks occur in mental hospitals, residential schools and other closed institutions, and dysentery is a constant accompaniment of wars and natural catastrophes which bring crowding and poor sanitation in their wake.

Clinical features

Disease severity varies from mild *Sh. sonnei* infections that may escape detection to more severe *Sh. flexneri* infections, while those due to *Sh. dysenteriae* may be fulminating and cause death within 48 hours.

In a moderately severe illness, the patient complains of diarrhoea, colicky abdominal pain and tenesmus. Stools are small, and after a few evacuations contain blood and purulent exudate with little faecal material. Fever, dehydration and weakness with tenderness over the colon occur. Arthritis or iritis may occasionally complicate bacillary dysentery

(Reiter's syndrome, see p. 1010), and may be associated with HLA-B27. Shigella infection may spread rapidly amongst promiscuous homosexuals.

Management

Oral rehydration therapy or, if diarrhoea is severe, intravenous replacement of water and electrolyte loss will be necessary. Antibiotic therapy with ciprofloxacin 500 mg 12-hourly for 3 days is effective in known shigellosis and appropriate in epidemics. The use of antidiarrhoeal medication should be avoided in all but the mildest cases.

Prevention

The prevention of faecal contamination of food and milk and the isolation of cases may be difficult except in limited outbreaks. Hand-washing is very important.

AMOEBIASIS

Amoebiasis is caused by *Entamoeba histolytica*, which is spread between humans by its cysts. It is common throughout the tropics and occasionally acquired in Britain. The parasite is now known to consist of two separate species: *E. dispar* (non-pathogenic) and *E. histolytica*, which is pathogenic. Cysts of these two species are morphologically identical, distinguishable only by molecular techniques, isoenzyme studies or monoclonal antibody typing. Only *E. histolytica* can give rise to amoebic dysentery or extraintestinal amoebiasis, e.g. amoebic liver abscess (see p. 879).

Pathology

Cysts of *E. histolytica* are ingested in water or uncooked food contaminated by human faeces. Lettuce is a common vehicle of infection. In the colon vegetative trophozoite forms emerge from the cysts (see Fig. 1.43). The parasite may invade the mucous membrane of the large bowel producing lesions, maximal in the caecum but found as far down as the anal canal. These are flask-shaped ulcers varying greatly in size and surrounded by healthy mucosa. A localised granuloma (amoeboma), presenting as a palpable mass in the rectum or a filling defect in the colon on radiography, is a rare complication. This responds well to anti-amoebic treatment so should be differentiated from colonic carcinoma.

Amoebic ulcers may cause severe haemorrhage but rarely perforate the bowel wall. Cutaneous amoebiasis causes progressive genital, perianal or peri-abdominal surgical wound ulceration.

Clinical features

Intestinal amoebiasis or amoebic dysentery

The incubation period of amoebiasis ranges from 2 weeks to many years, followed by a chronic course with grumbling abdominal pains and two or more unformed stools a day. Diarrhoea alternating with constipation is common, as is mucus, sometimes with streaks of blood; the stools often have an offensive odour. There may be tenderness along the line of the colon, especially over the caecum (which may simulate acute appendicitis) and pelvic colon.

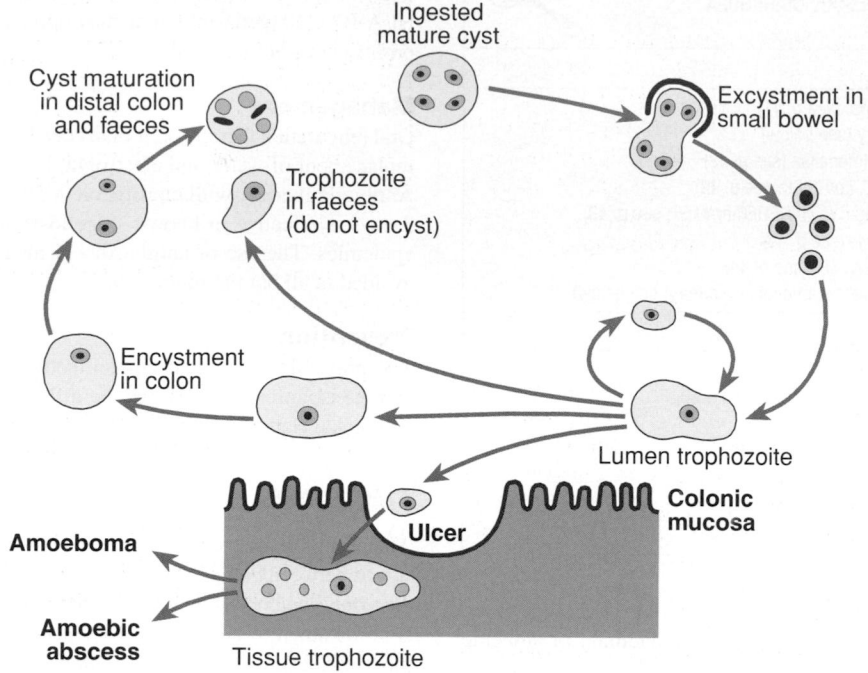

Fig. 1.43 Amoebiasis. The life cycle of *Entamoeba histolytica*.

Acute bowel symptoms, with very frequent motions and the passage of much blood and mucus, simulating bacillary dysentery or ulcerative colitis, occur particularly in the aged, in the puerperium and with superadded pyogenic infection of the ulcers.

Any exudate should be examined at once under the microscope for motile trophozoites containing red blood cells. Movements cease rapidly as the stool preparation cools. Sigmoidoscopy may reveal typical flask-shaped ulcers, which should be scraped and examined immediately for *E. histolytica*. Several stools may need to be examined in chronic amoebiasis before cysts are found. In endemic areas one-third of the population are symptomless passers of amoebic cysts.

Antibodies are detectable by immunofluorescence in over 95% of patients with hepatic amoebiasis and intestinal amoeboma but in only about 60% of dysenteric amoebiasis.

Management
Intestinal amoebiasis responds quickly to oral metronidazole (800 mg 8-hourly for 5 days) or tinidazole (single doses of 2 g daily for 3 days). Diloxanide furoate 500 mg should be given orally 8-hourly for 10 days after treatment to eliminate luminal cysts. Hepatic amoebiasis is dealt with on page 879.

Prevention
Personal precautions against contracting amoebiasis consist of not eating fresh uncooked vegetables or drinking unboiled water.

PARASITIC CAUSES OF ACUTE DIARRHOEA

GIARDIASIS

Infection with *Giardia intestinalis*, known also as *G. lamblia*, is world-wide and common in the tropics. It particularly affects children, tourists and immunosuppressed individuals. It is the parasite most commonly imported into Britain. The cysts remain viable in water for up to 3 months and infection usually occurs by ingesting contaminated water. The parasites attach to the duodenal and jejunal mucosa, causing inflammation.

Clinical features
After an incubation period of 1–3 weeks, there is diarrhoea, abdominal pain, weakness, anorexia, nausea and vomiting. On examination there may be abdominal distension and tenderness.

Stools obtained at 2–3-day intervals should be examined for cysts. Duodenal or jejunal fluid gives a higher diagnostic yield. Thus if endoscopy is being performed, giardiasis should be considered and juice aspirated for microscopic examination. On jejunal biopsy fresh mucus examination may show *Giardia* on the epithelial surface.

Management
Treatment is with a single dose of tinidazole 2 g, or metronidazole 2 g once daily for 3 days or 400 mg 8-hourly for 10 days.

CRYPTOSPORIDIOSIS

Cryptosporidium parvum is a coccidian protozoan of humans and domestic animals. Infection is acquired by the faecal-oral route through contaminated water supplies. The incubation period is approximately 7–10 days, followed by watery diarrhoea and abdominal cramps. The illness is usually self-limiting, but in immunocompromised patients, especially those with AIDS, the illness can be devastating, with persistent severe diarrhoea and substantial weight loss (see p. 118).

CYCLOSPORIASIS

Cyclospora cayetanensis is a newly recognised coccidian protozoan parasite of humans. It has been reported from Nepal, the Indian subcontinent and South America. Infection is acquired by ingestion of contaminated water. The incubation period is approximately 2–11 days followed by acute onset of diarrhoea with abdominal cramps. The disease can remit and relapse. Although usually self-limiting, the illness may last as long as 6 weeks with significant associated weight loss and malabsorption. The disease is more severe in immunocompromised individuals. Diagnosis is by detection of oöcysts on faecal microscopy. Treatment may be necessary in a few cases, and the agent of choice is co-trimoxazole 960 mg 12-hourly for 7 days.

TRAVELLERS' DIARRHOEA

Diarrhoea is the most common illness amongst travellers, affecting 20–50%. The risk of diarrhoea varies with destination (highest in Africa, Asia and Latin America), age and mode of travel. A wide range of organisms can cause this syndrome.

Stool microscopy is important to establish the presence of faecal leucocytes or parasites. Stool culture should be performed to investigate bloody or persistent diarrhoea.

Management
Most travellers' diarrhoea is self-limiting and only requires oral fluid and salt replacement. If it is bloody, then care should be taken to assess whether the use of antibiotics would be appropriate. Ciprofloxacin may be useful in shortening the duration of illness (see EBM panel, p. 42).

CHRONIC DIARRHOEA

This is defined as diarrhoea persisting for more than 14 days. The differential diagnosis can be wide, and parasitic and bacterial causes, tropical malabsorption, inflammatory bowel disease and neoplasia should all be considered. Box 1.28 gives causes of chronic diarrhoea in the tropics; most are considered later in this chapter. Tropical sprue is defined as clinical malabsorption with no defined aetiology. It was typically associated with a long residence in the tropics or overland travel but is now rarely seen. *Giardia* infection

1.28 CAUSES OF CHRONIC DIARRHOEA IN THE TROPICS	
• *Giardia intestinalis* • Strongyloidiasis • Hypolactasia (primary and secondary) • Enteropathic *E. coli*	• Tropical malabsorption • Chronic calcific pancreatitis • HIV enteropathy • Intestinal flukes • Chronic intestinal schistosomiasis

may progress to a malabsorption syndrome that mimics tropical sprue (see p. 767).

Clinical features
The key signs and symptoms are diarrhoea with pale, bulky stools, abdominal symptoms with distension and flatulence, nutritional deficiencies and general ill health.

Investigations
Malabsorption should be investigated systematically (see p. 768). Appropriate tests should be carried out to establish the parasitic causes of chronic diarrhoea.

Management
Specific causes of chronic diarrhoea should be treated appropriately. If no cause is found, empirical treatment for *Giardia lamblia* infection is often helpful.

THE MANAGEMENT OF ACUTE DIARRHOEA

All patients with acute, potentially infective diarrhoea should be appropriately isolated to minimise person-to-person spread of infection.

There are three elements to the management of acute diarrhoea in individual cases:

• fluid replacement
• antibiotics/antimicrobial therapy
• adjunctive antidiarrhoeal therapy.

FLUID REPLACEMENT

By far the most important and, occasionally, the life-saving aspect of the management of acute gastroenteritis is replacement of fluid losses. Most clinicians significantly underestimate the potential for serious dehydration produced by relatively mild gastroenteritis, particularly in a tropical/subtropical setting.

Although normal daily intake in an adult is 1–2 litres, the actual volumes traversing the gastrointestinal tract are in excess of 50 litres (see Fig. 1.44). Infective and toxic processes in the gut disturb or reverse the resorptive power of the colon/small intestine, resulting in marked dehydration. Cholera is the archetype of this process, where 10–20 litres of fluid may be lost in 24 hours.

The fluid lost in diarrhoea is isotonic so a source of electrolytes, either in continued food intake or replacement fluid, is required. The absorption of electrolytes from the gut

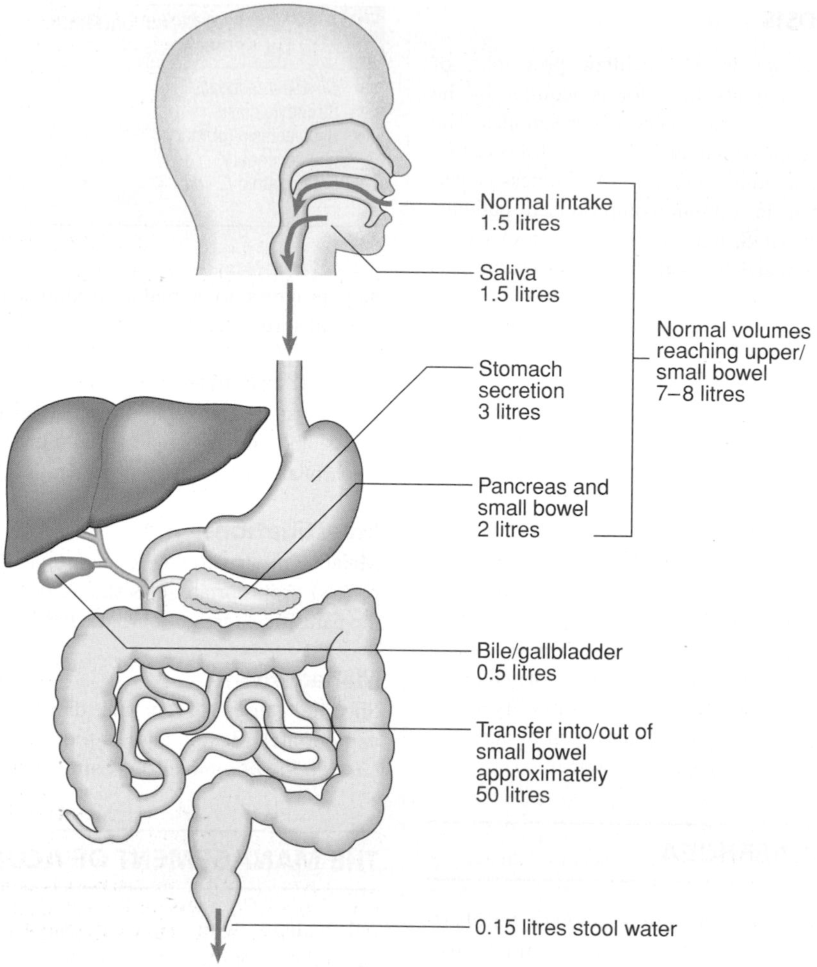
Normal intake
1.5 litres
Saliva
1.5 litres
Normal volumes
reaching upper/
small bowel
7–8 litres
Stomach
secretion
3 litres
Pancreas and
small bowel
2 litres
Bile/gallbladder
0.5 litres
Transfer into/out of
small bowel
approximately
50 litres
0.15 litres stool water

Fig. 1.44 Fluid exchange (daily) in the adult gastrointestinal system.

is an active process requiring energy. Infected mucosa is capable of very rapid fluid and electrolyte transport if an energy source is available. During gastroenteritis a source of carbohydrate, either starch or sugar, is required; otherwise, fluids, even with electrolyte content, will not be absorbed. This is the basis of oral rehydration solution (ORS). Many commercial equivalents are available. Those in the developed world often have relatively high sucrose levels (for supposed palatability) and reduced sodium levels (see Box 1.29).

ORS can be just as effective as intravenous replacement fluid even in the management of cholera. If intravenous fluid is used, it adds cost and potential danger from infection if hygiene is suboptimal.

Regardless of the type of fluid replacement used, there are three elements to the calculations of appropriate volumes:

- replacement of established losses
- replacement of ongoing losses
- replacement of normal daily requirement.

Replacement of established losses

The average adult with 48 hours of moderate diarrhoea (6–10 stools per 24 hours) will be 1–2 litres depleted from diarrhoea alone. Any associated vomiting will compound this. Adults with this symptomatology should therefore be given rapid replacement of 1–1.5 litres, either orally (ORS) or by intravenous infusion (normal saline) within the first 2–4 hours of their presentation. Children require careful calculation of fluid requirements.

Longer symptomatology or more persistent/severe diarrhoea rapidly produces fluid losses comparable to diabetic ketoacidosis and is a metabolic emergency requiring active intervention.

1.29 COMPOSITION OF ORS AND OTHER REPLACEMENT FLUIDS (mmol/l)

Fluid	Na	K	Cl	Calories
WHO	90	20	80	160
Dioralyte	30	20	30	200
Pepsi	6.5	0.8	–	480
7-up	7.5	0.2	–	320
Apple juice	0.4	26	–	480
Orange juice	0.2	49	–	440
Breast milk	22	36	28	670

Replacement of ongoing losses

The average adult's diarrhoeal stool accounts for a loss of 200 ml of isotonic fluid. Stool losses should be carefully charted and an estimate of ongoing replacement fluid calculated. Currently, commercially available rehydration sachets are conveniently produced to provide 200 ml of ORS. One sachet per diarrhoea stool is an appropriate and effective means of ongoing rehydration.

Replacement of normal daily requirement

The average adult has a minimal daily requirement of 1–1.5 litres of fluid in addition to the calculations above. In mild to moderate gastroenteritis adults should be encouraged to drink normally, and infants should continue to breast-feed, with allowance for ongoing and established losses including insensible losses being given as supplements. Wherever possible, continue normal dietary intake.

The most common mistake in the management of gastroenteritis of any cause is inadequate fluid replacement.

ANTIMICROBIAL AGENTS

Antibiotics in non-specific gastroenteritis have been shown to shorten symptoms by only 1 day in an illness usually lasting 1–3 days. The benefit of this, when related to the potential for the development of antimicrobial resistance (10–30% of *Salmonella* and *Campylobacter* are now resistant to ciprofloxacin), does not support this treatment.

Antimicrobials in *Salmonella* illness increase the stool carriage time (see EBM panel, p. 42). Recent evidence has suggested that in EHEC (VTEC) infections the use of antibiotics may make the complication of HUS more likely due to increased toxin release from organisms. Antibiotics should therefore not be used routinely in bloody diarrhoea in childhood.

Dysentery produced by *Sh. dysenteriae* is a clear indication for antibiotic therapy, and the use of antimicrobials may be advantageous in cholera epidemics by reducing infectivity and controlling the spread of infection. Generally, in mild to moderate cases of gastroenteritis there should be a very high threshold for antibiotic use. However, severe disease or certain clinical conditions will lower this threshold (see Box 1.30) such that a decision to administer antimicrobials is appropriate.

ANTIDIARRHOEAL, ANTIMOTILITY AND ANTISECRETORY AGENTS

In general these agents are not recommended and may be contraindicated in the management of infective or potentially infective gastroenteritis.

Although widely used, antimotility agents such as loperamide, diphenoxylate or opiates are potentially dangerous in dysentery in childhood. Their use should be avoided in any case with bloody stool.

Antisecretory agents such as bismuth and chlorpromazine may be effective but can cause significant sedation. They do not reduce stool fluid losses although the stools may appear more bulky. Adsorbents such as kaolin or charcoal have little effect.

ISSUES IN OLDER PEOPLE
INFECTIOUS DIARRHOEA

- The overall incidence of diarrhoeal illnesses in older people is not increased, but the impact of these illnesses is greater.
- The majority of deaths due to gastroenteritis in the developed world are in adults aged over 70 years.
- Most deaths in older people are presumed to be due to dehydration leading to organ infarction and failure.
- There is an increased risk of infection due to age-associated achlorhydria, diminished intestinal motility and frequent antibiotic use.
- Age is associated with the development of *Cl. difficile* diarrhoea in community, hospital and nursing home settings, partly due to antibiotic exposure.

TROPICAL AND INTERNATIONAL HEALTH

Tropical diseases are important to us all. This section will illustrate the huge burden of mortality and morbidity that they produce. This burden is not confined to the residents of endemic countries but affects people all over the world in many ways. Malaria kills 1 million children in Africa each year; leprosy has left 4 million people with disabilities. Tropical disease also spreads beyond the tropics and may present to doctors unfamiliar with its signs and symptoms. Tourists, travellers, business people and refugees can all present with acute and chronic tropical illnesses and good physicians will ask about their patient's travel history.

Controlling tropical diseases has proved difficult. War can undermine good control programmes as in central Africa where trypanosomiasis is resurgent, and these programmes can be difficult to maintain. Drug resistance can emerge rapidly, as happened with malaria. Altering the environment can cause diseases such as the arboviruses Ebola and Hanta to emerge from rural habitats. Tropical disease can travel;

1.30 SEVERITY MARKERS IN ACUTE GASTROENTERITIS

Chronic conditions

- Age > 65
- Diabetes mellitus
- Rheumatoid or other autoimmune disease
- Chronic renal disease
- Valvular heart disease (esp. with valve replacements)
- Acquired or secondary immunodeficiency
- Any internal prostheses

Current drug therapy

- Diuretic therapy
- Angiotensin-converting enzyme (ACE) inhibitor therapy
- Steroid therapy
- Cytotoxic therapy
- Proton pump or H_2-receptor blockers

Current illness

- Number of stools per 24 hours
- Presence of blood per rectum
- Abdominal pain
- Associated systemic toxicity

cholera skipped continents to South America. Treatment of tropical diseases is often difficult; few new drugs have been developed and for many diseases our current treatments, such as the use of antimony for leishmaniasis, would have been familiar to physicians 50 years ago.

Diagnosing tropical infections requires a good grasp of geography and a regular updating of disease patterns so that a patient's tropical residence can be matched against the diseases which might have been encountered. This section is organised according to the major ways in which tropical diseases present: fever, eosinophilia and skin problems. Diarrhoea is covered on pages 38–49. Running through each section is the imperative of asking your patients where they have been and what they did; this approach can make detecting tropical infections both easier and interesting.

FEVER IN/FROM THE TROPICS

Presentation of illness as fever is common both in patients returning from the tropics and in tropical residents. Here the presentation and management of infections that could be acquired in the tropics or during a tropical residence will be considered. Non-tropical infection may also present after tropical travel and it is important to enquire about all systems, as discussed in the investigation of a pyrexia of unknown origin (see p. 10). The common final diagnoses in febrile patients returning from the tropics are malaria, typhoid fever, viral hepatitis and dengue fever.

In this section fevers will be considered first by their duration, acute being less than 14 days. They will then be considered by their presentation: fever without localising signs, fever and rash, fever and haemorrhage, and fever following tick bites. These categories are not mutually exclusive and diseases may have features of several categories. Disease may also have different stages of evolution; patients with leptospirosis may present with few localising signs and only develop a haemorrhagic rash later in their illness. It is only by regular re-examination of patients with fever that these evolving signs can be detected.

History
Vital questions to ask anyone returning from the tropics are listed in Box 1.31.

1.31 KEY QUESTIONS FOR DIAGNOSING A FEVER IN THE TROPICS
• Where have you been?
• What have you done?
• How long were you there?
• Did you have insect bites or contact with animals?

Geography and exposures
It is important to establish which countries were visited and the arrival and departure dates. Most tropical infections are transmitted more easily in rural than urban centres.

The potential infections acquired by an aid worker who has been working in an African rural community are different from those of a business traveller who has stayed in five-star

1.32 SPECIFIC EXPOSURES THAT ASSIST IN DIAGNOSIS OF FEVER FROM THE TROPICS	
Exposure	**Infection or disease**
Mosquito bite	Malaria, dengue fever, filariasis
Tsetse fly bite	African trypanosomiasis
Tick bite	Typhus, Lyme disease, Crimean–Congo haemorrhagic fever, babesiosis, Kyasanur forest disease
Louse bite	Typhus
Flea bite	Plague, tularaemia
Sandfly bite	Visceral leishmaniasis, arboviruses
Infected person contact	Viral haemorrhagic fevers (Lassa, Ebola, Marburg, Crimean–Congo), viral hepatitis, typhoid fever, meningococcal disease
Animal contact	Q fever, brucellosis, anthrax, viral haemorrhagic fevers, histoplasmosis, rabies, plague
Raw or uncooked foods	Enteric bacterial infections, viral hepatitis
Untreated water	Enteric bacterial infections, viral hepatitis
Unpasteurised milk	Brucellosis, salmonellosis, abdominal tuberculosis
Fresh-water swimming	Schistosomiasis, leptospirosis
Promiscuous sexual contact	HIV infection, viral hepatitis B, syphilis, gonococcal bacteraemia

hotels. A detailed living history should be taken, covering living and sleeping conditions, whether bed nets were used, what type of food and water was consumed, and whether there was any contact with animals, hospitals or fresh water. Sometimes there are unique exposures that point to a specific diagnosis, e.g. unprotected intercourse with a commercial sex worker. Box 1.32 lists exposures aiding diagnosis.

Vaccinations and prophylaxis
Ask about vaccinations and their validity; vaccinations against yellow fever, and hepatitis A and B virtually rule out these infections. Oral and injectable typhoid vaccinations are 70–90% effective. Enquire about malaria prophylaxis and establish precisely which tablets, if any, were being taken. A sexual history should always be taken. It is also useful to ask about local remedies which patients may have used, either conventional modern medicine or traditional medical preparations. Remember that locally manufactured medications may have low amounts of bio-available drugs.

Examination
A careful examination is vital. This must be repeated regularly. Pay particular attention to the skin, throat, eyes, nail beds, lymph nodes, abdomen and heart. Patients may be unaware of tick bites or eschars (see Fig. 1.45). The temperature should be measured at least twice daily.

Investigations
Initial investigations in all settings should start with thick and thin blood films for malaria parasites, full blood count,

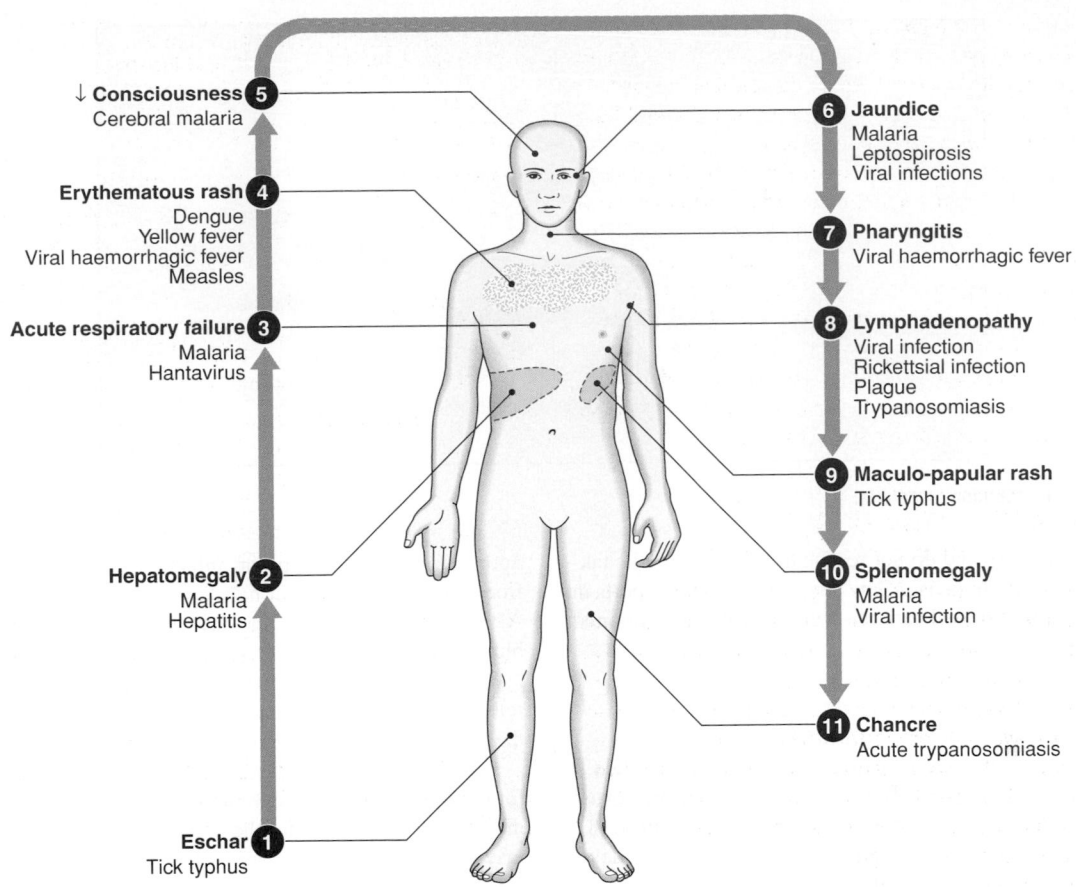

↓ **Consciousness** ⑤
Cerebral malaria

Erythematous rash ④
Dengue
Yellow fever
Viral haemorrhagic fever
Measles

Acute respiratory failure ③
Malaria
Hantavirus

Hepatomegaly ②
Malaria
Hepatitis

Eschar ①
Tick typhus

⑥ **Jaundice**
Malaria
Leptospirosis
Viral infections

⑦ **Pharyngitis**
Viral haemorrhagic fever

⑧ **Lymphadenopathy**
Viral infection
Rickettsial infection
Plague
Trypanosomiasis

⑨ **Maculo-papular rash**
Tick typhus

⑩ **Splenomegaly**
Malaria
Viral infection

⑪ **Chancre**
Acute trypanosomiasis

Fig. 1.45 Acute fever in/from the tropics: clinical examination.

WCC differential	Potential diagnoses	Further investigations
1.33 DIFFERENTIAL WHITE CELL COUNTS (WCC): ACUTE FEVER IN THE ABSENCE OF LOCALISING SIGNS		
Neutrophil leucocytosis	Bacterial sepsis *Leptospira* and *Borrelia* infections	Blood culture
	Leptospirosis	Culture of blood and urine, serology
	Tick-borne relapsing fever	Blood films
	Louse-borne relapsing fever	Blood film
	Amoebic liver abscess	Ultrasound
Normal WCC and differential	Typhoid fever	Blood, stool and urine culture
	Typhus	Serology
	Arboviral infection	Serology (PCR and viral culture)
Lymphocytosis	Viral fevers	Serology
	Infectious mononucleosis	Monospot test
	Rickettsial fevers	Serology

urinalysis and chest radiograph if indicated. Box 1.33 gives the diagnoses that should be considered in acute fever with no localising signs.

FEVER WITHOUT LOCALISING SIGNS

In the absence of localising signs malaria is the most important diagnosis to consider. Thick and thin blood films should be taken, together with total and differential white counts and blood cultures.

MALARIA

Malaria is caused by *Plasmodium falciparum*, *P. vivax*, *P. ovale* and *P. malariae*. It is transmitted by the bite of female anopheline mosquitoes and occurs throughout the tropics and subtropics at altitudes below 1500 m (see Fig. 1.46). There are up to 250 million clinical cases per year and over 1 million die, mainly children. Following WHO-sponsored campaigns of prevention and effective treatment, the incidence of malaria was greatly reduced in 1950–60 but since 1970 there has been a resurgence. Furthermore, *P. falciparum* has now become resistant to chloroquine, notably in Asia and Africa. Due to increased travel and neglect of chemoprophylaxis, over 2000 cases are imported annually into Britain. Most are due to *P. falciparum*, usually from Africa, and of these 1% die because of late diagnosis. Immigrants returning home after a long residence in the UK are particularly at risk. They have lost their

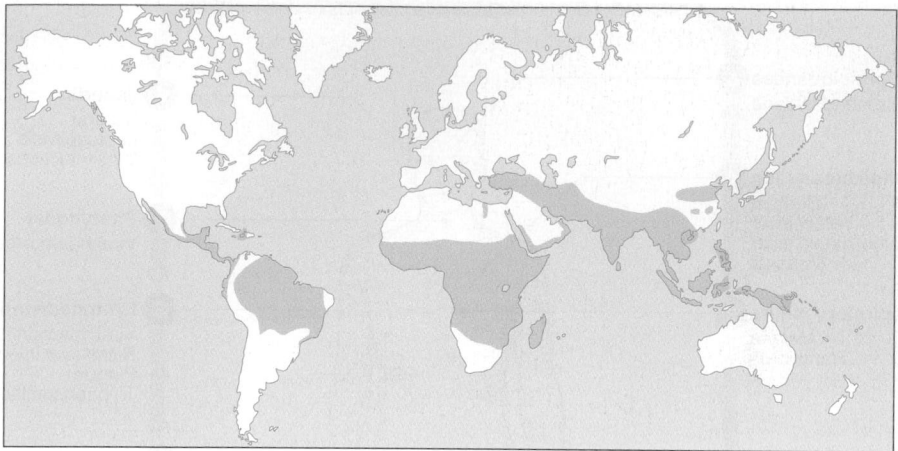

Fig. 1.46   Distribution of malaria.

partial immunity and do not realise that they should be taking malaria prophylaxis. A few people living near airports in Europe have acquired malaria from accidentally imported mosquitoes.

Pathogenesis

Life cycle of the malarial parasite

The female anopheline mosquito becomes infected when it feeds on human blood containing gametocytes, the sexual forms of the malarial parasite (see Figs 1.47 and 1.48). Development in the mosquito takes from 7–20 days.

Sporozoites inoculated by an infected mosquito disappear from human blood within half an hour and enter the liver. After some days merozoites leave the liver and invade red blood cells, where further asexual cycles of multiplication take place, producing schizonts. Rupture of the schizont releases more merozoites into the blood and causes fever, the periodicity of which depends on the species of parasite.

P. vivax and *P. ovale* may persist in liver cells as dormant forms, hypnozoites, capable of developing into merozoites months or years later. Thus the first attack of clinical malaria may occur long after the patient has left the endemic area,

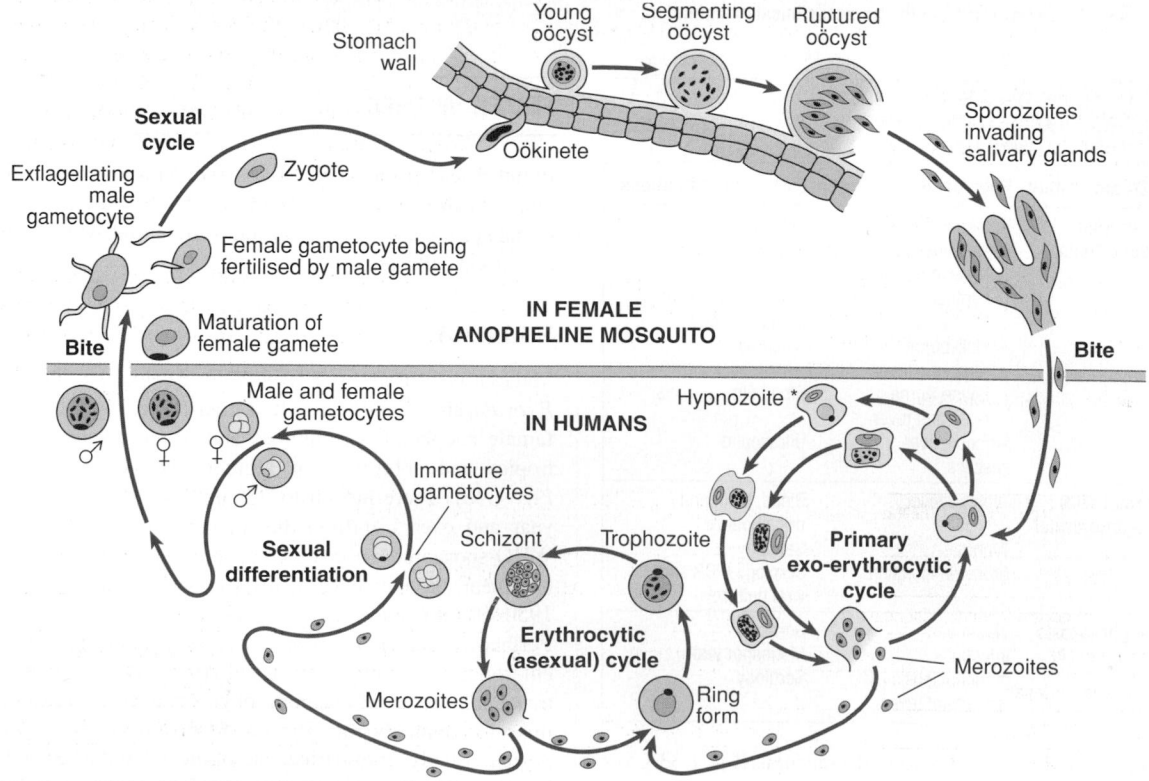

Fig. 1.47   Malarial parasites. Life cycle. Hypnozoites(*) are present only in *P. vivax* and *P. ovale* infections.

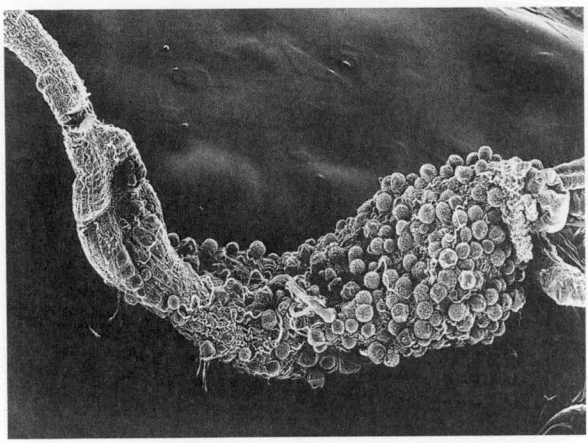

Fig. 1.48 Scanning electron micrograph of *P. falciparum* oöcysts lining the anopheline mosquito's stomach.

and the disease may relapse after treatment with drugs that kill only the erythrocytic stage of the parasite.

P. falciparum and *P. malariae* have no persistent exo-erythrocytic phase but recrudescences of fever may result from multiplication in the red cells of parasites which have not been eliminated by treatment and immune processes (see Box 1.34).

Pathology

The pathology in malaria is due to haemolysis of infected red cells and adherence of infected red blood cells to capillaries. Malaria is always accompanied by haemolysis and in a severe or prolonged attack anaemia may be profound. Anaemia is worsened by dyserythropoiesis, splenomegaly and depletion of folate stores. Haemolysis is most severe with *P. falciparum*, which invades red cells of all ages but especially young cells. *P. vivax* and *P. ovale* invade reticulocytes, and *P. malariae* normoblasts, so that infections remain lighter.

Effects on red blood cells and capillaries

In *P. falciparum* malaria, red cells containing schizonts adhere to capillary endothelium in brain, kidney, liver, lungs and gut. The vessels become congested and the organs anoxic. Rupture of schizonts liberates toxic and antigenic substances which may cause further damage. Thus the main effects of malaria are haemolytic anaemia and, with *P. falciparum*, widespread organ damage (see Box 1.35 and Fig. 1.49). *P. falciparum* does not grow well in red cells that contain haemoglobin F, C or especially S. Haemoglobin S heterozygotes (AS) are protected against the lethal complications of malaria. *P. vivax* cannot enter red cells that lack the Duffy blood group. West African and American black people are protected.

Clinical features

P. falciparum infection

This is the most dangerous of the malarias. The onset is often insidious, with malaise, headache and vomiting, and is often mistaken for influenza. Cough and mild diarrhoea are also common. The fever has no particular pattern. Jaundice is common due to haemolysis and hepatic dysfunction. The liver and spleen enlarge and become tender. Anaemia develops rapidly.

A patient with *falciparum* malaria, apparently not seriously ill, may develop serious complications (see Box 1.35). Cerebral malaria is the most serious complication and is manifested by either confusion or coma, usually without localising signs. Children die rapidly without any special symptoms other than fever. Immunity is impaired in pregnancy, and abortion from parasitisation of the maternal side of the placenta is frequent. Splenectomy increases the risk of severe malaria.

P. vivax and P. ovale infection

In many cases the illness starts with a period of several days of continued fever before the development of classical bouts of fever on alternate days. Fever starts with a rigor. The patient feels cold and the temperature rises to about 40°C. After half an hour to an hour the hot or flush phase begins. It lasts several hours and gives way to profuse perspiration and a gradual fall in temperature. The cycle is repeated 48 hours later. Gradually the spleen and liver enlarge and may become tender. Anaemia develops slowly. Herpes simplex is common. Relapses are common in the first 2 years of leaving the malarious area.

P. malariae infection

This is usually associated with mild symptoms and bouts of fever every third day. Parasitaemia may persist for many years with the occasional recrudescence of fever, or without producing any symptoms. *P. malariae* causes glomerulo-nephritis and the nephrotic syndrome in children.

1.34 RELATIONSHIPS BETWEEN LIFE CYCLE OF PARASITE AND CLINICAL FEATURES OF MALARIA			
Cycle/feature	*P. vivax, P. ovale*	*P. malariae*	*P. falciparum*
Pre-patent period (minimum incubation)	8–25 days	15–30 days	8–25 days
Asexual cycle	48 hrs synchronous	72 hrs synchronous	< 48 hrs asynchronous
Periodicity of fever	'Tertian'	'Quartan'	Aperiodic
Exo-erythrocytic cycle	Persistent as hypnozoites	Pre-erythrocytic only	Pre-erythrocytic only
Delayed onset	Common	Rare	Rare
Relapses	Common up to 2 years	Recrudescence many years later	Recrudescence up to 1 year

1.35 SEVERE MANIFESTATIONS AND COMPLICATIONS OF *FALCIPARUM* MALARIA AND THEIR IMMEDIATE MANAGEMENT

Manifestation/complication	Immediate management
Coma (cerebral malaria)	Maintain airway Nurse on side Exclude other treatable causes of coma (e.g. hypoglycaemia, bacterial meningitis) Avoid harmful ancillary treatments such as corticosteroids, heparin and adrenaline (epinephrine) Intubate if necessary
Hyperpyrexia	Tepid sponging, fanning, cooling blanket Antipyretic drug
Convulsions	Maintain airway Treat promptly with diazepam or paraldehyde injection
Hypoglycaemia	Measure blood glucose Give 50% dextrose injection followed by 10% dextrose infusion (glucagon may be ineffective)
Severe anaemia (packed cell volume < 15%)	Transfuse fresh whole blood or packed cells if pathogen screening is available
Acute pulmonary oedema	Prop up at 45°, give oxygen, venesect 250 ml of blood into donor bag, give diuretic, stop intravenous fluids Intubate and add PEEP/CPAP (see p. 203) in life-threatening hypoxaemia Haemofilter
Acute renal failure	Exclude pre-renal causes Check fluid balance, urinary sodium If urine output inadequate despite fluid replacement, give diuretic/dopamine Peritoneal dialysis (haemofiltration or haemodialysis if available)
Spontaneous bleeding and coagulopathy	Transfuse screened fresh whole blood (cryoprecipitate/fresh frozen plasma and platelets if available) Vitamin K injection
Metabolic acidosis	Exclude or treat hypoglycaemia, hypovolaemia and Gram-negative septicaemia Give oxygen
Shock ('algid malaria')	Suspect Gram-negative septicaemia Make blood cultures Give parenteral antimicrobials Correct haemodynamic disturbances
Aspiration pneumonia	Give parenteral antimicrobial drugs Change position Physiotherapy Give oxygen
Hyperparasitaemia (e.g. > 10% of circulating erythrocytes parasitised in non-immune patient with severe disease)	Consider exchange or partial exchange transfusion, manual or haemophoresis

Diagnosis

Thick and thin blood films should be taken whenever malaria is suspected. In the thick film erythrocytes are lysed, releasing all blood stages of the parasite. This, as well as the fact that more blood is used in thick films, facilitates the diagnosis of low-level parasitaemias. A thin film is essential to confirm the diagnosis, to identify the species of parasite and, in *P. falciparum* infections, to quantify the parasite load (by counting the percentage of infected erythrocytes). *P. falciparum* parasites may be very scanty, especially in patients who have been partially treated. With *P. falciparum*, only ring forms are normally seen in the early stages. With the other species all stages of the erythrocytic cycle may be found. Gametocytes appear after about 2 weeks. They persist after treatment and are harmless, but are the source for infecting mosquitoes. Immunochromatographic 'dipstick' tests for *P. falciparum* antigen are now marketed and provide a useful non-microscopic means of diagnosing this infection. They should be used in parallel with blood film examination but are about 100 times less sensitive than a carefully examined blood film.

Management

Chemotherapy of mild P. falciparum malaria

P. falciparum is now resistant to chloroquine almost worldwide, so quinine is the drug of choice as quinine dihydrochloride or sulphate 600 mg *salt* (10 mg/kg) 8-hourly by mouth until clinically better and the blood is free of parasites (usually 3–5 days). Reduce the dose to 12-hourly if quinine toxicity develops. This regimen should be followed by a single dose of sulfadoxine 1.5 g combined with pyrimethamine 75 mg, i.e. 3 tablets of Fansidar. In pregnancy a 7-day course of quinine alone should be given. If sulphonamide sensitivity is suspected, quinine may be followed by doxycycline 100 mg daily for 7 days. Decreased efficacy of quinine has been reported in some areas, notably the Thailand/Myanmar

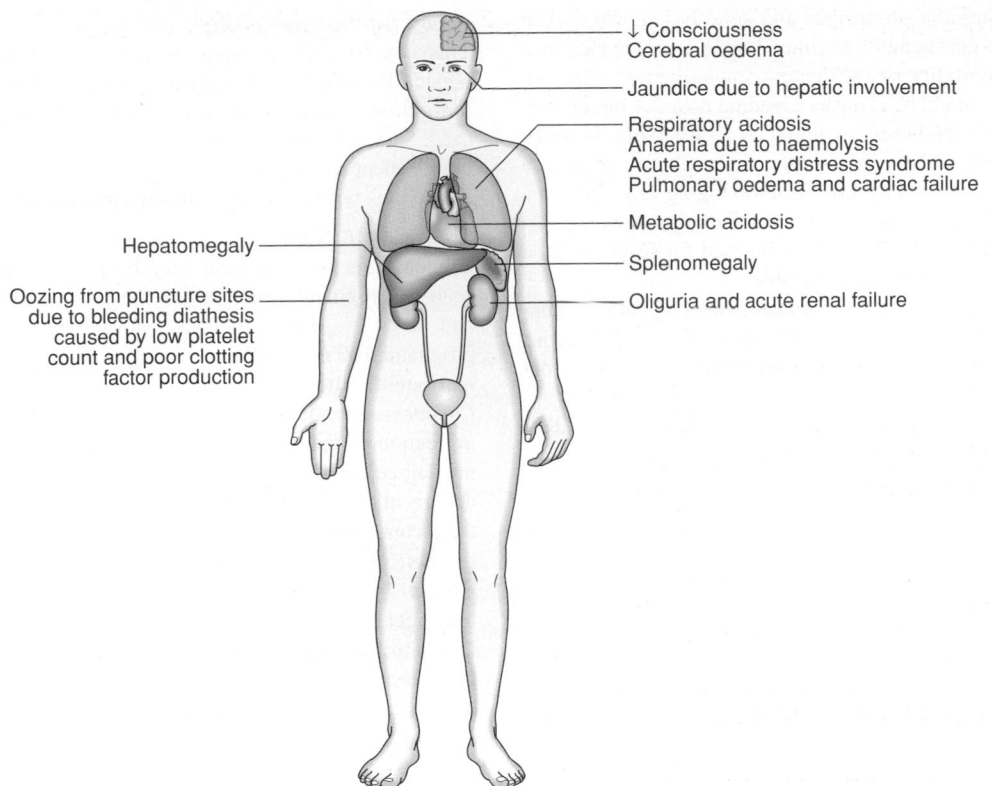

↓ Consciousness
Cerebral oedema

Jaundice due to hepatic involvement

Respiratory acidosis
Anaemia due to haemolysis
Acute respiratory distress syndrome
Pulmonary oedema and cardiac failure

Metabolic acidosis

Splenomegaly

Oliguria and acute renal failure

Hepatomegaly

Oozing from puncture sites
due to bleeding diathesis
caused by low platelet
count and poor clotting
factor production

Fig. 1.49 Organ involvement in severe malaria.

border. Alternatives to quinine plus Fansidar are atovaquone 250 mg plus proguanil 100 mg (Malarone) 4 tablets once daily for 3 days, or artemether 200 mg/day orally for 5 days then mefloquine 500 mg 2 doses 2 hours apart. Mefloquine may occasionally cause alarming neuropsychiatric side-effects which can persist for several days due to its plasma half-life of 14 days.

Management of complicated P. falciparum malaria

Severe malaria is a medical emergency and cerebral malaria is the most common presentation and cause of death in adults with malaria. Cerebral malaria is assumed when asexual parasites are present in the blood film and the patient has impaired consciousness and other encephalopathies have been excluded, particularly bacterial meningitis and locally occurring viral encephalitides. Complications of severe malaria include hypoglycaemia, severe anaemia, renal failure and metabolic acidosis (see Box 1.35). Severe malaria should be considered in any non-immune patient with a parasite count greater than 2%.

The management of severe malaria should include early appropriate antimalarial chemotherapy, active treatment of complications, correction of fluid, electrolyte and acid–base balance, and avoidance of harmful ancillary treatments (see Box 1.36).

Quinine is indicated if a chloroquine-resistant infection is at all likely. Although quinine resistance has increased in South-east Asia and South America, there is still no high-grade resistance that precludes its use in severe malaria. Quinine is given as an intravenous infusion over 4 hours.

1.36 INEFFECTIVENESS OF ANCILLARY TREATMENTS IN MALARIA

- Corticosteroids (dexamethasone)
- Other anti-inflammatory agents
- Other anti-cerebral oedema agents (urea, mannitol, invert sugar)
- Low molecular weight dextran
- Adrenaline (epinephrine)
- Heparin
- Epoprostenol
- Pentoxifylline (oxpentifylline)
- Hyperbaric oxygen
- Ciclosporin A
- Hyperimmune serum
- Iron-chelating agents (desferrioxamine B)
- Anti-tumour necrosis factor antibodies

Treatment should be started with a loading dose infusion of 20 mg/kg quinine *salt*. Up to a maximum of 1.4 g quinine can be given over 4 hours, then after 8–12 hours maintenance dosage at 10 mg/kg quinine *salt* up to a maximum of 700 mg. The dose should be repeated at intervals of 8–12 hours until the patient can take drugs orally. The loading dose should *not* be given if the patient has received quinine, quinidine or mefloquine during the previous 24 hours. Quinine may instead be given intramuscularly but may cause muscle necrosis; the hydrochloride is less irritant than the dihydrochloride. Those with cardiac disease should be monitored by ECG, with special attention to QRS duration and QTc. Artemesinin derivatives may also be used as antimalarial chemotherapy. Four recently published randomised controlled trials have compared parenteral quinine and intramuscular artemether and none has shown a clear and unequivocal benefit for either drug in outcome measures as either mortality or incidence of neurological sequelae. Artesunate should be given as a loading dose 2.4 mg/kg then 1.2 mg/kg i.v. 12-hourly to a total dose of 600 mg. It can be given intramuscularly in children. Artemether is given as a loading dose 3.2 mg/kg i.m. then 1.6 mg/kg i.m. daily to a total of 640 mg. Change to an oral formulation as soon as possible. Mefloquine should not be used for severe malaria since no parenteral form is available.

The management of severe malaria involves careful attention to all the major organ systems (see Box 1.35). Numerous ancillary treatments have been tested but none has proven beneficial (see Box 1.36).

Exchange transfusion has not been tested in randomised controlled trials but may be beneficial for non-immune patients with persisting high parasitaemias (> 10% circulating erythrocytes).

Cheap and affordable drugs are urgently needed for the treatment of severe malaria. A combination of chlorproguanil and dapsone (Lapdap) is in third-stage research trials in uncomplicated malaria in sub-Saharan African children.

P. vivax, *P. ovale* and *P. malariae* infections should be treated with chloroquine; 600 mg chloroquine *base* followed by 300 mg *base* in 6 hours then 150 mg *base* 12-hourly for 2 more days.

Radical cure of malaria due to P. vivax and P. ovale

Relapses can be prevented by taking one of the antimalarial drugs in suppressive doses. Radical cure is achieved in most patients by a course of primaquine (15 mg daily for 14 days), which destroys the hypnozoite phase in the liver. Haemolysis may develop in those who are glucose-6-phosphate dehydrogenase (G6PD)-deficient. Cyanosis due to the formation of methaemoglobin in the red cells is more common but not dangerous.

Prevention

Every person going to a malarious area should receive anti-malaria advice. This comprises avoiding bites and taking appropriate chemoprophylaxis.

Avoiding mosquito bites

This can be done by wearing long sleeves and trousers outside the house, especially at night when the anopheline mosquitoes bite. Repellent creams and sprays can be used. Screened windows, the use of a mosquito net and burning repellent coils or tablets also reduce the risk. Impregnation of bed nets with permethrin also reduces mosquito biting.

Chemoprophylaxis

Clinical attacks of malaria may be preventable by drugs such as proguanil which attack the pre-erythrocytic form, and also by drugs such as atovaquone 250 mg plus proguanil 100 mg (Malarone), doxycycline, chloroquine or mefloquine after the parasite has entered the erythrocyte ('suppression'). Box 1.37 gives the recommended doses for protection of the non-immune. It is important to determine the degree of risk of malaria in the area to be visited and the degree of chloroquine resistance. These factors will guide the recommendations for prophylaxis and are summarised in the *British National Formulary* (BNF) in the UK. Expert advice is required for individuals unable to tolerate the first-line agents listed, or in whom they are contraindicated. Doses for children vary, depending on age and body weight. Reference should be made to standard dosage recommendations (BNF). Chemoprophylaxis is begun 1 week before entering the malarious area and is continued for 4 weeks after leaving it. Resistance to the cheap and well-tolerated drug proguanil is increasing, and frequently coincides with the much more serious spread of chloroquine resistance. Chloroquine should not be taken continuously as prophylactic for over 5 years without regular ophthalmic examination, as it may cause irreversible retinopathy. Pregnant and lactating women may take proguanil or chloroquine safely. Mefloquine is contraindicated in the first trimester of pregnancy. Fansidar should not be used for chemoprophylaxis, as deaths have occurred from agranulocytosis or Stevens–Johnson syndrome (see p. 33 and 1098). Mefloquine is useful in areas of multiple drug resistance, such as East and Central Africa and Papua New Guinea. Experience shows it to be safe for at least 2 years. There are several contraindications to its use (see Box 1.37).

1.37 CHEMOPROPHYLAXIS OF MALARIA			
Area	**Antimalarial tablets**	**Adult prophylactic dose**	**Regimen**
Chloroquine resistance high[1]	Mefloquine[2] *or* Doxycycline *or* Malarone	250 mg 100 mg 1 tablet from 1–2 days before travelling to 1 week after return	One tablet weekly Daily Daily
Chloroquine resistance moderate	Chloroquine[3] *plus* Proguanil	150 mg base 100 mg	Two tablets weekly Two tablets daily
Chloroquine resistance absent	Chloroquine *or* Proguanil	150 mg base 100 mg	Two tablets weekly One or two tablets daily

[1] Choice of regimen is determined by area to be visited, length of stay, level of malaria transmission, level of drug resistance, presence of underlying disease in the traveller and concomitant medication taken.
[2] Contraindicated in the first trimester of pregnancy, lactation, cardiac conduction disorders, epilepsy, psychiatric disorders; may cause neuropsychiatric disorders.
[3] British preparations of chloroquine usually contain 150 mg base, French preparations 100 mg base and American preparations 300 mg base.

Malaria control in endemic areas

There are major initiatives under way to reduce malaria in endemic areas. The provision of permethrin-impregnated bed nets has been shown to reduce mortality in African children. WHO now has a 'Roll back malaria' programme. New combination drugs such as artemether-lumefatrine and pyronaridine are being assessed in trials. In developing new drugs known targets can be better exploited by new 4-aminoquinolones, and new targets can be identified such as the phospholipid biosynthesis inhibitors that are at an early stage of development. Trial vaccines are being evaluated in Thailand and Africa.

FEVER WITH RASH

The combination of fever and rash in someone in or from the tropics raises a distinctive set of diagnostic possibilities (see Box 1.38). It is important to ask about and examine carefully for a rash that may be transient and minimal or may have characteristic features that aid in diagnosis, e.g. the blanching of the dengue rash.

1.38 DIAGNOSTIC POSSIBILITIES FOR FEVER AND RASH IN OR FROM THE TROPICS	
• Typhoid and paratyphoid fevers • Dengue and arboviral infections • Leptospirosis • Meningococcal infections • Measles • Rickettsial infections	• African trypanosomiasis • Viral infection—EBV, CMV etc. • HIV seroconversion • Secondary syphilis • Connective tissue diseases • Cat scratch disease

TYPHOID AND PARATYPHOID (ENTERIC) FEVERS

In developing countries typhoid and paratyphoid fevers, which are transmitted by the faecal-oral route, are important causes of fever. Elsewhere they are relatively rare.

Aetiology

The enteric fevers are caused by infection with *Salmonella typhi* and *S. paratyphi* A and B. High levels of transmission continue in India, sub-Saharan Africa and Latin America. The bacilli may live in the gallbladder of carriers for months or years after clinical recovery and pass intermittently in the stool and less commonly in the urine. The incubation period of typhoid fever is about 10–14 days; that of paratyphoid is somewhat shorter.

Pathology

After a few days of bacteraemia, the bacilli localise mainly in the lymphoid tissue of the small intestine. The typical lesion is in the Peyer's patches and follicles. These swell at first, then ulcerate and ultimately heal, but during this sequence they may perforate or bleed.

Clinical features

Typhoid fever

Clinical features are outlined in Box 1.39. The onset may be insidious. The temperature rises in a stepladder fashion for 4 or 5 days. There is malaise, with increasing headache, drowsiness and aching in the limbs. Constipation may be present, although in children diarrhoea and vomiting may be prominent early in the illness. The pulse is often slower than would be expected from the height of the temperature, i.e. a relative bradycardia.

At the end of the first week a rash may appear on the upper abdomen and on the back as sparse, slightly raised, rose-red spots, which fade on pressure. It is usually visible only on white skin. Cough and epistaxis occur. Around the seventh to tenth day the spleen becomes palpable. Constipation is then succeeded by diarrhoea and abdominal distension with tenderness. Severe diarrhoea has been described in HIV patients with typhoid. Bronchitis and delirium may develop. By the end of the second week the patient may be profoundly ill unless the disease is modified by antibiotic treatment. In the third week toxaemia increases and the patient may pass into coma and die. Such extreme cases are rare in countries with developed health services.

Following recovery, up to 5% of patients become chronic carriers of *S. typhi* and classically such patients have gallbladder disease.

1.39 CLINICAL FEATURES OF TYPHOID FEVER	
First week	
• Fever • Headache • Myalgia	• Relative bradycardia • Constipation • Diarrhoea and vomiting in children
End of first week	
• Rose spots on trunk • Splenomegaly • Cough	• Abdominal distension • Diarrhoea
End of second week	
• Delirium, complications, then coma and death (if untreated)	

Paratyphoid fever

The course tends to be shorter and milder than that of typhoid fever and the onset is often more abrupt with acute enteritis. The rash may be more abundant and the intestinal complications less frequent.

Complications

These are given in Box 1.40. Haemorrhage from, or a perforation of, the ulcerated Peyer's patches may occur at the end of the second week or during the third week of the illness. A drop in temperature to normal or subnormal levels may occur in those with intestinal haemorrhage. This can be falsely reassuring as it occurs even before there is clinical evidence of bleeding such as melaena. Additional complications may involve almost any viscus or system because of the septicaemia present during the first week; these include

1.40 COMPLICATIONS OF TYPHOID FEVER	
Bowel	
• Perforation	• Haemorrhage
Septicaemic foci	
• Bone and joint infection • Meningitis	• Cholecystitis
Toxic phenomena	
• Myocarditis	• Nephritis

cholecystitis, pneumonia, myocarditis, arthritis, osteo-myelitis and meningitis. Bone and joint infection is seen, especially in children with sickle-cell disease.

Investigations

In the first week the diagnosis may be difficult because in this invasive stage with bacteraemia the symptoms are those of a generalised infection without localising features. A white blood count may be helpful as there is typically a leucopenia. Blood culture is the most important diagnostic method in a suspected case. The faeces will contain the organism more frequently during the second and third weeks. The Widal reaction detects antibodies to the causative organisms. However, it is not a reliable diagnostic test and should be interpreted with caution, particularly in typhoid-vaccinated patients.

Management

Several antibiotics are effective in enteric fever. Cipro-floxacin in a dose of 500 mg 12-hourly is the drug of choice. Alternatives include co-trimoxazole (two tablets or intravenous equivalent 12-hourly), amoxicillin (750 mg 6-hourly) and chloramphenicol (500 mg 6-hourly). However, an increasing number of salmonellae, including *S. typhi*, are now resistant to many antibiotics and some are only sensitive to ciprofloxacin. The third generation cephalosporins, ceftri-axone and cefotaxime, are useful when the organism is resistant to ciprofloxacin. Treatment should be continued for 14 days. Pyrexia may persist for up to 5 days after the start of specific therapy. Even with effective chemotherapy there is still a danger of complications, recrudescence of the disease and the development of a carrier state. The chronic carrier should be treated for 4 weeks with ciprofloxacin; chole-cystectomy may be necessary in some cases.

Prevention

Improved sanitation and living conditions reduce the incidence of typhoid. Travellers to countries where enteric infections are endemic should be inoculated with one of the three available typhoid vaccines (two inactivated injectable and one oral live attenuated).

DENGUE

The dengue flavivirus is a common cause of fever in and from the tropics. It is endemic in South-east Asia and India and is also seen in Africa; there have been recent large epidemics in the Caribbean and Americas (see Fig. 1.50). The principal vector is *Aedes aegypti*, which breeds in standing water; collections of water in containers and tyre dumps are a particular risk in large cities. *Aedes albopictus* is a vector in some South-east Asian countries. There are four serotypes of dengue virus, all producing a similar clinical syndrome; homotypic immunity is life-long but heterotypic immunity between serotypes lasts only a few months. The incubation period from being bitten by an infected mosquito is usually 2–7 days.

Clinical features

The disease varies in severity. The clinical features are listed in Box 1.41. Subclinical infections are common. The morbilliform rash characteristically blanches under pressure.

Dengue haemorrhagic fever or dengue shock syndrome

This occurs mainly in children in South-east Asia (see Fig. 1.50). In mild forms there is thrombocytopenia and haemoconcentration. In the most severe form, after 3–4 days

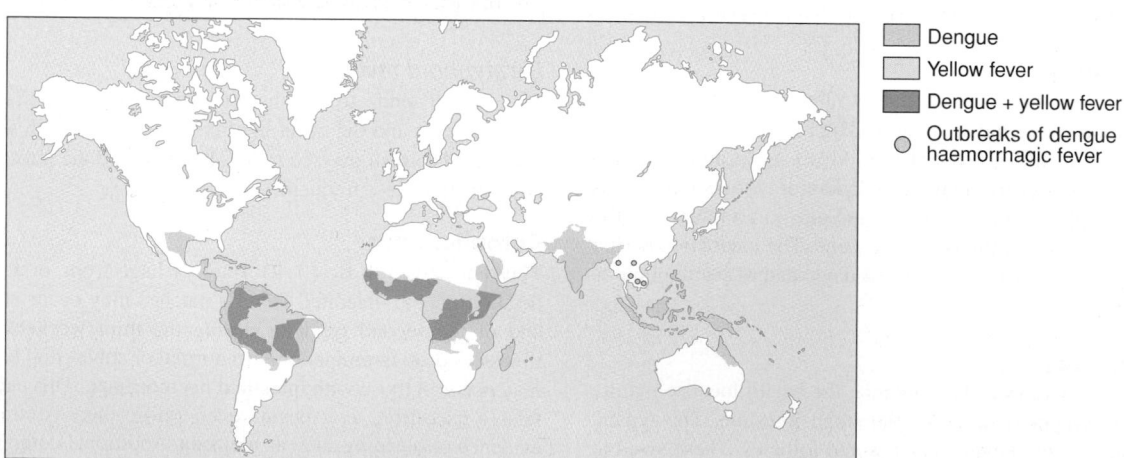

▓	Dengue
░	Yellow fever
▓	Dengue + yellow fever
○	Outbreaks of dengue haemorrhagic fever

Fig. 1.50 Endemic zones of yellow fever and dengue.

1.41 CLINICAL FEATURES OF DENGUE FEVER

Prodrome

- 2 days of malaise and headache

Acute onset

- Fever, backache, arthralgias, headache, generalised pains ('breakbone fever'), pain on eye movement, lacrimation, anorexia, nausea, vomiting, relative bradycardia, prostration, depression, lymphadenopathy, scleral injection

Fever

- Continuous or 'saddle-back', with break on fourth or fifth day; usually lasts 7–8 days

Rash

- Transient macular in first 1–2 days. Maculo-papular, scarlet morbilliform from days 3–5 on trunk, spreading centrifugally and sparing palms and soles. May desquamate on resolution

Convalescence

- Slow

of fever, hypotension and circulatory failure develop with features of a capillary leak syndrome. Minor (petechiae, ecchymoses, epistaxis) or major (gastrointestinal bleeding) haemorrhagic signs may occur. The pathogenesis is unclear but pre-existing immunity to a dengue virus serotype heterotypic to the one causing the current infection predisposes to the syndrome. In vitro such heterotypic antibody causes enhanced virus entry and replication in monocytes; it is believed that enhancing antibody from previous dengue infection with a different serotype, or from acquired maternal antibody in infants, facilitates development of a very heavy viral load. Disseminated intravascular coagulation, complement activation and release of vasoactive mediators may contribute to the pathogenesis of the syndrome, possibly triggered by immunopathological mechanisms. Cytokine release is thought to be the cause of vascular damage at the site of post-capillary endothelial junctions. Even with good treatment the case fatality may be up to 10%. Adults rarely have classical dengue shock syndrome but may have a stormy and fatal course characterised by elevated liver enzymes, haemostatic abnormalities and gastrointestinal bleeding.

Investigations

Diagnosis of dengue is usually easy in an endemic area when a patient has the characteristic symptoms and signs. However, mild cases may resemble other viral disease. Leucopenia is usual and thrombocytopenia common. The virus can be recovered from the blood and there are tests for viral antigen. Antibody titres rise but serological tests may detect cross-reacting antibodies from other flaviviruses, including yellow fever vaccine.

Management and prevention

There is no specific treatment. The severe pains can be relieved by paracetamol, but occasionally opiates are required. Aspirin should be avoided. Volume replacement,

blood transfusions and management of shock are indicated in the capillary leak syndrome. Corticosteroids have not been shown to help. No existing antivirals are effective.

Breeding places of *Aedes* mosquitoes should be abolished and the adults destroyed by insecticides. There is as yet no vaccine but a tetravalent live attenuated version is at an advanced stage of development.

AFRICAN TRYPANOSOMIASIS (SLEEPING SICKNESS)

African sleeping sickness is caused by trypanosomes (see Fig. 1.51) conveyed to humans by the bites of infected tsetse flies. Two trypanosomes affect humans: *Trypanosoma brucei gambiense* and *T. rhodesiense*. *Gambiense* trypanosomiasis has a wide distribution in West and Central Africa reaching to Uganda and Kenya; *rhodesiense* trypanosomiasis is found in parts of East and Central Africa, where it is currently on the increase. In West Africa transmission is mainly at the riverside, where the fly rests in the shade of trees. Animal reservoirs of *T. gambiense* have not been identified. *T. rhodesiense* has a large reservoir in numerous wild animals and transmission takes place in the shade of woods bordering grasslands.

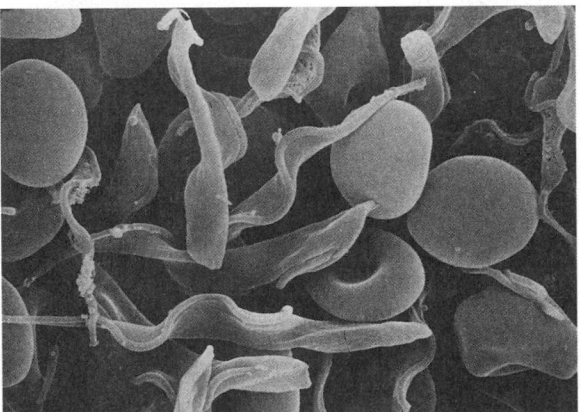

Fig. 1.51 Trypanosomiasis. Scanning electron micrograph showing trypanosomes swimming among erythrocytes.

Clinical features

A bite by a tsetse fly is painful and commonly becomes inflamed, but if trypanosomes are introduced, the site may again become painful and swollen about 10 days later ('trypanosomal chancre') and the regional lymph nodes enlarge ('Winterbottom's sign'). Within 2–3 weeks of infection the trypanosomes invade the blood stream.

Rhodesiense infections

In these infections the disease is more acute and severe than in *gambiense* infections, so that within days or a few weeks the patient is usually severely ill and may have developed pleural effusions and signs of myocarditis or hepatitis. There may be a petechial rash. The patient may die before there are signs of involvement of the central nervous system. If the illness is less acute, drowsiness, tremors and coma develop.

Gambiense infections

In these infections the disease usually runs a slow course over months or years, with irregular bouts of fever and enlargement of lymph nodes. These are characteristically firm, discrete, rubbery and painless, and are particularly prominent in the posterior triangle of the neck. The spleen and liver may become palpable. After some months, in the absence of treatment, the central nervous system is invaded. This is shown clinically by headache and changed behaviour, insomnia by night and sleepiness by day, mental confusion and eventually tremors, pareses, wasting, coma and death.

Investigations

Trypanosomiasis should be considered in any febrile patient from an endemic area. In *rhodesiense* infections thick and thin blood films, stained as for the detection of malaria, will reveal trypanosomes. The trypanosomes may be seen in the blood or from puncture of the primary lesion in the earliest stages of *gambiense* infections, but it is usually easier to demonstrate them by puncture of a lymph node. Concentration methods include buffy coat microscopy and miniature anion exchange chromatography. Serological tests are useful in the diagnosis of chronic infection and are employed in fieldwork. If the central nervous system is affected, the cell count and protein content of the CSF are increased and the glucose is diminished. Very high levels of serum IgM or the presence of IgM in the CSF are suggestive of trypanosomiasis.

Management

The prognosis is good if treatment is begun early before the brain has been invaded. At this stage suramin or pentamidine may be used, the latter being employed only for *gambiense* infections. Once the nervous system is affected an arsenical or difluoromethyl ornithine will be required.

Prevention

In endemic *gambiense* areas various measures may be taken against tsetse flies and field teams detect and treat early human infection. In *rhodesiense* areas control is difficult.

AMERICAN TRYPANOSOMIASIS (CHAGAS DISEASE)

Chagas disease occurs widely in South and Central America. The cause is *Trypanosoma cruzi*, transmitted to humans from the faeces of a reduviid bug in which the trypanosomes have a cycle of development before becoming infective to humans. Bugs live in the mud and wattle walls and thatch roofs of simple rural houses, and emerge at night to feed on the sleeping occupants. While feeding they defaecate. Infected faeces are rubbed in through the conjunctiva, mucosa of mouth or nose or abrasions of the skin. Over 100 species of mammals, domestic, peridomestic and wild, may serve as reservoirs of infection. In some areas blood transfusion accounts for about 5% of cases. Congenital transmission occurs occasionally.

Pathology

The trypanosomes migrate via the blood stream and develop into amastigote forms in the tissues. These multiply in many sites, especially in the myocardium causing pseudocysts, in smooth muscle fibres, and also in the ganglion cells of the autonomic nervous system.

Clinical features

The entrance of *T. cruzi* through an abrasion produces a dusky-red firm swelling and enlargement of regional lymph nodes. A conjunctival lesion, though less common, is more characteristic; the unilateral firm reddish swelling of the lids may close the eye and constitutes 'Romaña's sign'. Young children are most commonly affected. In a few patients an acute generalised infection soon appears, with a transient morbilliform or urticarial rash, fever, lymphadenopathy and enlargement of the spleen and liver. Neurological features include personality changes and signs of meningoencephalitis. The acute infection may be fatal to infants. In many patients the early infection is silent.

After a latent period of several years features of the chronic infection appear, notably damage to Auerbach's plexus with resulting dilatation of various parts of the alimentary canal, especially the colon and oesophagus, so-called 'mega' disease. Dilatation of the bile ducts and bronchi are also recognised sequelae. Chronic low-grade myocarditis and damage to conducting fibres cause a cardiomyopathy characterised by cardiac dilatation, arrhythmias, partial or complete heart block and sudden death. Autoimmune processes may be responsible for much of the damage. There are geographical variations of the basic pattern of disease.

Investigations

T. cruzi may be seen in a blood film in the acute illness. In chronic disease it may be recovered in up to 50% of cases by xenodiagnosis in which infection-free, laboratory-bred reduviid bugs are fed on the patient; subsequently the hind gut or faeces of the bug are examined for parasites. Complement fixation, direct agglutination and fluorescent antibody tests are positive in 95% of cases.

Management

Nifurtimox is given orally. The dose, which has to be carefully supervised to minimise toxicity while preserving parasiticidal activity, is 10 mg/kg divided into three equal doses, daily by mouth for 60–90 days. The paediatric dose is 15 mg/kg daily. Cure rates of 80% in acute disease are obtained. Benznidazole is an alternative drug at a dose of 5–10 mg/kg daily by mouth, in two divided doses for 60 days; children receive 10 mg/kg daily. Both nifurtimox and benznidazole are toxic, with adverse reaction rates of 30–55%. Specific drug treatment of chronic Chagas disease is not usually undertaken and does not reverse established tissue damage. Surgery may be needed for 'mega' disease.

Prevention

Preventative measures include improving housing and destruction of reduviid bugs by spraying of houses with insecticides. Blood donors should be screened.

FEVER WITH HAEMORRHAGE

The major causes of fever and haemorrhage are yellow fever and the viral haemorrhagic fevers (VHF). These fevers all occur in well-recognised geographical areas and have a non-specific presentation with fever and myalgia. Diagnosis rests on being aware that the patient has travelled to a yellow fever or VHF area, together with excluding other causes of fever, principally malaria.

YELLOW FEVER

Yellow fever, caused by a flavivirus, is normally a zoonosis of monkeys that inhabit tropical rainforests in West and Central Africa and South and Central America, among whom it may cause devastating epidemics (see Fig. 1.50). It is transmitted by mosquitoes living in tree-tops. *Aedes africanus* in Africa and the *Haemagogus* species in America are the vectors. The infection is brought down to humans either by infected mosquitoes when trees are felled, or by monkeys raiding human settlements. In towns yellow fever may be transmitted between humans by *Aedes aegypti*, which breeds efficiently in small collections of water. The distribution of this mosquito is far wider than that of yellow fever and poses a continual risk of spread. It is surprising that there is no yellow fever in Asia; this may be because there are strain differences between the Asian and African *Aedes* mosquitoes or there may be unrecognised demographic obstacles to transmission.

Humans are infectious during the viraemic phase, which starts 3–6 days after the bite of the infected mosquito and lasts for 4–5 days. The incubation period is 3–6 days.

Pathology

In the liver, acute mid-zonal necrosis leads to deposits of hyalin called Councilman bodies, and intranuclear eosinophilic inclusions called Torres bodies. Another characteristic feature is the absence of inflammatory infiltrate. The kidneys show tubular degeneration, which may partly be due to reduced blood flow. Widespread petechial haemorrhages are most marked in the stomach and duodenum. Haemorrhage is due to liver damage and disseminated intravascular coagulation.

Clinical features

Yellow fever is often a mild febrile illness lasting less than a week. However, the classical disease starts suddenly with rigors and high fever. Backache, headache and bone pains are severe. Nausea and vomiting then develop. The face is flushed and the conjunctivae are injected. Bradycardia and leucopenia are characteristic of this phase of the illness, which lasts 3 days and is followed by a remission lasting a few hours or days. The fever then returns with acute hepatic and renal failure. There is jaundice and a haemorrhagic diathesis with petechiae, haemorrhages into the mucosa and gastrointestinal bleeding plus oliguria. Patients commonly die in the third stage, often after a period of coma.

1.42 DIAGNOSIS OF YELLOW FEVER
• Clinical features in endemic area
• Virus isolation from blood in first 4 days
• Fourfold rise in antibody titre
• Post-mortem liver biopsy
• Differentiate from malaria, typhoid, viral hepatitis, leptospirosis, haemorrhagic fevers, aflatoxin poisoning

Investigations

Diagnostic procedures are listed in Box 1.42.

Management

Treatment is supportive, with meticulous attention to fluid and electrolyte balance, urine output and blood pressure. Blood transfusions, plasma expanders and peritoneal dialysis may be necessary. Patients should be isolated as their blood and body products may contain viral particles.

Prevention

A single vaccination with the 17D non-pathogenic strain of virus gives full protection for at least 10 years. The vaccine does not produce appreciable side-effects, unless there is allergy to egg protein. Vaccination is not recommended in people who are immunosuppressed, whether it be the result of immunosuppressive therapy or of underlying disease.

VIRAL HAEMORRHAGIC FEVERS

The viral haemorrhagic fevers are zoonoses caused by several different viruses (see Box 1.43). They are endemic worldwide, each virus having its own niche. They are mainly rural and transmission is associated with poverty and poor medical facilities. Dengue has already been described (see p. 58). Serological surveys have shown that Lassa fever is widespread in West Africa where it accounts for 15% of adult hospital admissions and 50% of adults have antibodies. Ebola and Marburg viruses cause small epidemics but with high fatality rates. The most recent Ebola outbreak was in Uganda in 2000–2001. Lassa fever remains very rare in Britain, with about 1 case arriving in the country every 2 years. Patients returning from rural Africa with a fever should be put into isolation until a diagnosis is made. It is vital to exclude malaria in these patients. Ask about contact with potential animal vectors, hospitals and attendance at ritual funerals. Kyasanur forest disease is a tick-borne viral haemorrhagic fever currently confined to a small focus in Karnataka, India and causing about 500 cases annually. Monkeys are the principal hosts but with forest felling there are fears that this disease will increase.

Pathogenesis

The virus causes endothelial dysfunction with the development of leaky capillary syndrome. Hypovolaemic shock and acute respiratory distress syndrome develop (see p. 198).

Clinical features

All the haemorrhagic fevers start with high fever and severe body pains. Sore throat is another feature. In Lassa fever

1.43 COMMON VIRAL HAEMORRHAGIC FEVERS

Disease	Reservoir	Transmission	Geography	Case mortality	Clinical features[1]
Lassa fever	Multimammate rat (*Mastomys natalensis*) Patient	Urine Body fluids	West Africa	Up to 50% (responds to ribavirin)	Encephalopathy ARDS
Marburg/ Ebola virus disease	? Patient	Via monkeys' body fluids	Central Africa	25–90%	Thrombocytopenia Blood oozing
Yellow fever	Monkeys	Mosquitoes	Tropical Africa, South and Central America	10–60%	Hepatic failure Blood oozing
Dengue	Humans	*Aedes aegypti* et al.	Tropical and subtropical coasts	Nil–10%[2]	Joint and bone pain Petechiae
Crimean–Congo	*Ixodes* tick	*Ixodes* tick	Africa, Asia, Eastern Europe	15–70%	Thrombocytopenia Blood oozing Petechiae
Bolivian and Argentinian	Rodents (*Calomys* spp.)	Urine	South America	?	Thrombocytopenia Petechiae
Haemorrhagic fever with renal syndrome (Hantan fever)	Rodents	Faeces	Northern Asia, northern Europe	30%	Petechiae Renal failure ARDS

[1] All have circulatory failure.
[2] Mortality of uncomplicated and haemorrhagic dengue fever, respectively.

retrosternal pain, pharyngitis and proteinuria had a positive predictive value of 80% in West Africa. Joint and abdominal pain are prominent in Lassa fever. A macular blanching rash may be present, but bleeding is unusual, occurring in only 20% of hospitalised patients. Bradycardia and ECG abnormalities are common. Encephalopathy may develop. Deafness affects 30% of survivors.

Investigations
There is leucopenia, thrombocytopenia and proteinuria. In Lassa fever an aspartate amino transferase (AST) > 150 i.u./l is associated with a 50% mortality.

Diagnosis
The causative virus may be isolated, or antigen-detected, in maximum security laboratories from serum, pharynx, pleural exudate and urine. The diagnosis should be considered in the UK and other non-endemic areas in patients presenting with fever within 21 days of leaving West Africa, particularly if they have organ failure or haemorrhagic features (although most patients initially suspected of having viral haemorrhagic fevers in the UK turn out to have malaria).

Management
Strict isolation and general supportive measures, preferably in a special unit, are required. Ribavirin is given intravenously (100 mg/kg, then 25 mg/kg daily for 3 days and 12.5 mg/kg daily for 4 days). Isolation and good infection control practices will prevent further transmission.

Prevention
Ribavirin has been used as prophylaxis in close contacts of Lassa fever patients but there are no formal trials of its efficacy.

FEVER FOLLOWING ARTHROPOD BITES

There is a group of acute febrile illnesses transmitted by arthropods exemplified by rickettsial fevers, Lyme disease, plague and babesiosis. It is important to ask about exposures that would put patients at risk of bites or contact with ticks, lice or fleas.

RICKETTSIAL FEVERS
The rickettsial fevers are the most common of the tick-borne infections and present acutely with headache, skin rash and sometimes neurological disturbance. There are three main groups of rickettsial fevers, as described below; these are compared in Box 1.44.

Pathogenesis
The rickettsia are intracellular Gram-negative organisms which parasitise the intestinal canal of arthropods. Infection is usually conveyed to humans through the skin from the excreta of arthropods but the saliva of some biting vectors is infected. The organisms multiply in capillary endothelial cells, producing lesions in the skin, central nervous system, heart, lungs, kidneys and skeletal muscles. Endothelial proliferation, associated with a perivascular reaction, may cause thromboses and small haemorrhages. In epidemic typhus the brain is the target organ; in scrub typhus the cardiovascular system and lungs are particularly attacked. An eschar is often found in tick- and mite-borne typhus. An eschar is a necrotic sore, often scabbed, at the site of the bite and is due to vasculitis following immunological recognition of the inoculated organism. Regional lymph nodes often enlarge.

1.44 ESSENTIAL FEATURES OF RICKETTSIAL INFECTIONS

Disease	Reservoir	Vector	Primary complex[1]	Rash	Gangrene	Target organs	Mortality
Rocky Mountain spotted fever	Rodents, dogs, ticks	*Ixodes* tick	Often	Morbilliform Haemorrhagic	Often	Bronchi, myocardium, brain, skin	2–12%[2]
Other tick-borne typhus	Rodents, dogs, ticks	*Ixodes* tick	Usual	Maculo-papular	–	Skin, meninges	Rare[3]
Scrub typhus	Rodents, mites	*Trombicula* mite	Often	Maculo-papular	Unusual	Bronchi, myocardium, brain, skin	Rare[3]
Epidemic typhus	Humans	Louse	–	Morbilliform Haemorrhagic	Often	Brain, skin, bronchi, myocardium	Up to 40%
Endemic typhus	Rats	Flea	–	Slight	–	–	Rare[3]

[1] Eschar at bite site and local lymphadenopathy.
[2] Highest in adult males.
[3] Except in infants, elderly and debilitated.

Spotted fever group

Rocky Mountain spotted fever. Rickettsia rickettsii is transmitted by tick bites. It is widely distributed and increasing in western and south-eastern states of the USA and also in South America. The incubation period is about 7 days. The rash appears on about the third or fourth day, and is at first like measles, but in a few hours the typical maculo-papular eruption develops. The rash first appears on the wrists, forearms and ankles, and spreads in 24–48 hours to the back, limbs and chest and lastly to the abdomen where it is least pronounced. Larger cutaneous and subcutaneous haemorrhages may appear in severe cases. The liver and spleen become palpable. At the extremes of life the mortality is 5–10%.

Tick-borne South African typhus. R. conorii causes Mediterranean and African tick typhus, which also occurs in the Indian subcontinent. Infected ticks may be picked up by walking on grasslands or dogs may bring ticks into the house. A careful search is needed to find the tell-tale eschar, and a maculo-papular rash on the trunk, limbs, palms and soles. There may be delirium and meningeal signs in severe infections but recovery is the rule.

Typhus group

Scrub typhus fever. Scrub typhus is caused by R. tsutsugamushi, transmitted by mites. It occurs in the Far East, Myanmar, Pakistan, Bangladesh, India, Indonesia, the South Pacific islands and Queensland, particularly where patches of forest cleared for plantations have attracted rats and mites.

In many patients one eschar or more develops, surrounded by an area of cellulitis and enlargement of regional lymph nodes. The incubation period is about 9 days.

Mild or subclinical cases are common. The onset of symptoms is usually sudden with headache, often retro-orbital, fever, malaise, weakness and cough. In severe illness the general symptoms increase, with apathy and prostration. An erythematous maculo-papular rash often appears on about the fifth to the seventh day and spreads to the trunk, face and limbs including the palms and soles, with generalised painless lymphadenopathy. The rash fades by the 14th day. The temperature rises rapidly and continues as a remittent fever with sweating until it falls by lysis on about the 12th–18th day. In severe infection the patient is prostrate with cough, pneumonia, confusion and deafness. Cardiac failure, renal failure and haemorrhage may develop. Convalescence is often slow and tachycardia may persist for some weeks.

Epidemic (louse-borne) typhus. Epidemic typhus is caused by R. prowazekii and is transmitted by infected faeces of the human body louse usually through scratching the skin. Patients suffering from epidemic typhus infect the lice, which leave when the patient is febrile. In conditions of overcrowding the disease spreads rapidly. It is prevalent in parts of Africa, especially Ethiopia and Rwanda, and in the South American Andes and Afghanistan. Large epidemics have occurred in Europe, usually as a sequel to war. The incubation period is usually 12–14 days.

There may be a few days of malaise but the onset is more often sudden with rigors, fever, frontal headaches, pains in the back and limbs, constipation and bronchitis. The face is flushed and cyanotic, the eyes are congested and the patient soon becomes dull and confused.

The rash appears on the fourth to the sixth day and often resembles measles. In its early stages it disappears on pressure but soon becomes petechial with subcutaneous mottling. It appears first on the anterior folds of the axillae, sides of the abdomen or backs of hands, then on the trunk and forearms. The neck and face are seldom affected.

During the second week symptoms increase in severity. Sores develop on the lips. The tongue becomes dry, brown, shrunken and tremulous. The spleen is palpable, the pulse feeble and the patient stuporous and delirious. The temperature falls rapidly at the end of the second week and the patient recovers gradually. In fatal cases the patient usually dies in the second week from toxaemia, cardiac or renal failure, or pneumonia.

Endemic (flea-borne) typhus. Flea-borne or 'endemic' typhus caused by *R. mooseri* is endemic world-wide. Humans are infected when the faeces or contents of a crushed flea which has fed on an infected rat are introduced into the skin. The incubation period is 8–14 days. The symptoms resemble those of a mild louse-borne typhus. The rash may be scanty and transient.

Investigations

Routine blood investigations are unhelpful. Diagnosis is made on clinical grounds and response to treatment. Differential diagnoses include malaria, typhoid, meningococcal sepsis and leptospirosis.

The Weil–Felix reaction is the non-specific agglutination of the somatic antigens of non-motile *Proteus* species by the patient's serum. A fourfold rise in titre is diagnostic.

Species-specific antibodies may be detected by complement fixation, microagglutination and fluorescence in specialised laboratories.

Management of the rickettsial diseases

The different rickettsial fevers vary greatly in severity but all respond to tetracycline or chloramphenicol. Tetracycline is given 500 mg 6-hourly for 7 days, chloramphenicol 500 mg 6-hourly for 7 days. Louse-borne typhus and scrub typhus can be treated with a single dose of 200 mg doxycycline, repeated for 2–3 days to prevent relapse. Chloramphenicol- and doxycycline-resistant strains of *R. tsutsugamushi* have been reported from Thailand and patients here may need treatment with rifampicin.

Nursing care is important, especially in epidemic typhus. Sedation may be required for delirium and blood transfusion for haemorrhage. Relapsing fever and typhoid are common intercurrent infections in epidemic typhus, and pneumonia in scrub typhus. They must be sought and treated. Convalescence is usually protracted, especially in older people.

Prevention of rickettsial infections

Vector and reservoir control

Lice, fleas, ticks and mites need to be controlled with insecticides.

LYME DISEASE

See page 21.

LOUSE-BORNE RELAPSING FEVER

The human body louse, *Pediculus humanus*, causes itching. Borreliae *(B. recurrentis)* are liberated from the infected lice when they are crushed during scratching, which also inoculates the borreliae into the skin.

Pathology

The borreliae multiply in the blood, where they are abundant in the febrile phases, and invade most tissues, especially the liver, spleen and meninges. Hepatitis causing jaundice is frequent in severe infections and there may be petechial haemorrhages in the skin, mucous membranes and serous surfaces of internal organs. Thrombocytopenia is marked.

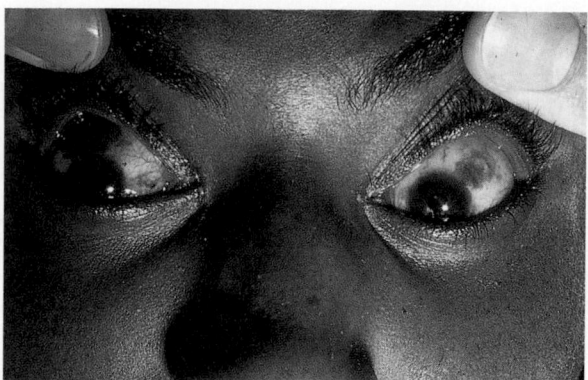

Fig. 1.52 Louse-borne relapsing fever. Injected conjunctivae.

Clinical features

Onset is sudden with fever. The temperature rises to 39.5–40.5°C and is accompanied by a rapid pulse, headache, generalised aching, injected conjunctivae (see Fig. 1.52) and frequently a petechial rash, epistaxis and herpes labialis. As the disease progresses, the liver and spleen frequently become tender and palpable and jaundice is common. There may be severe serosal and intestinal haemorrhage. Mental confusion and meningism may occur. The fever ends by crisis between the fourth and tenth days, often associated with profuse sweating, hypotension, circulatory and cardiac failure. There may be no further fever but in a proportion of patients, after an afebrile period of about 7 days, there may be one or more relapses which are usually milder and less prolonged. In the absence of specific treatment the mortality rate may be as high as 40%, especially among the elderly and malnourished.

Investigations

The organisms are demonstrated in the blood during fever either by dark ground illumination of a wet film or by staining thick and thin films.

Management

The problems of treatment are to eradicate the organism, to minimise the severe Jarisch–Herxheimer reaction (JHR—see p. 100) which inevitably follows successful chemotherapy, and to prevent relapses. The safest treatment is procaine benzylpenicillin (procaine penicillin) 300 mg intramuscularly, followed the next day by 0.5 g tetracycline. Tetracycline alone is effective and prevents relapse, but may give rise to a worse reaction. Doxycycline, 200 mg once by mouth as an alternative to tetracycline, has the advantage of also being curative for typhus, which often accompanies epidemics of relapsing fever. JHR is best managed in a high-dependency unit with expert nursing and medical care.

Prevention

The patient, clothing and all contacts must be freed from lice as in epidemic typhus.

PLAGUE

Epidemics of plague, such as the 'Black Death', have attacked humans since ancient times. The disease continues to have a rat reservoir. Plague foci are widely distributed throughout the world and human cases are reported from about 10 countries per year. There was an outbreak of plague in India in 1994 centred around Surat (see Fig. 1.53). The causative organism, *Yersinia pestis*, is a small Gram-negative bacillus. It is spread between rodents by their fleas. If domestic rats become infected, infected fleas may bite humans. In the late stages of human plague, *Y. pestis* may be expectorated and spread between humans by droplets. 'Pneumonic plague' may follow. Hunters and trappers can contract plague from handling rodents.

Pathology

Organisms inoculated through the skin are taken rapidly to the draining lymph nodes where they elicit a severe inflammatory response that may be haemorrhagic. If the infection is not contained, septicaemia ensues and necrotic, purulent or haemorrhagic lesions develop in many organs. Oliguria and shock follow, and disseminated intravascular coagulation may result in widespread haemorrhage. Inhalation of *Y. pestis* causes alveolitis. The incubation period is 3–6 days, but less in pneumonic plague.

Bubonic plague

In this, the most common form of the disease, the onset is usually sudden with a rigor, high fever, dry skin and severe headache. Soon, aching and swelling at the site of the affected lymph nodes begin. The groin is the most common site of the bubo, made up of the swollen lymph nodes and surrounding tissue. Some infections are relatively mild but in the majority of patients toxaemia quickly increases with a rapid pulse, hypotension and mental confusion. The spleen is usually palpable.

Septicaemic plague

Those not exhibiting a bubo usually deteriorate rapidly. Meningitis, pneumonia and expectoration of blood-stained sputum containing *Y. pestis* may complicate bubonic or septicaemic plague.

Pneumonic plague

The onset is very sudden with cough and dyspnoea. The patient soon expectorates copious blood-stained, frothy, highly infective sputum, becomes cyanosed and dies. Radiographs of the lung show a lobar opacity.

Investigations

Early diagnosis is urgent and requires a high index of clinical suspicion. Delayed diagnosis is associated with a high case fatality rate. An aspirate from a bubo, sputum or the buffy coat (leucocyte fraction) of blood is used to show the characteristic organism by staining with methylene blue or by immunofluorescence. Blood, sputum and aspirate should be cultured. Plague is notifiable under the international health regulations.

Management

If the diagnosis is suspected on clinical and epidemiological grounds, treatment must be started as soon as, or even before, samples have been collected for laboratory diagnosis. Streptomycin (1 g 12-hourly) or gentamicin (1 mg/kg 8-hourly) are the drugs of choice. Tetracycline (500 mg 6-hourly) and chloramphenicol (12.5 mg/kg 6-hourly) are alternatives. Treatment may also be needed for acute circulatory failure, disseminated intravascular coagulation or hypoxia.

Prevention

Rats and fleas should be controlled. In endemic areas people should avoid handling and skinning wild animals.

A formalin-killed vaccine is available for those at occupational risk. Patients are isolated and attendants must wear gowns, masks and gloves. Contacts should be protected by tetracycline 2 g daily, or co-trimoxazole one tablet daily for a week.

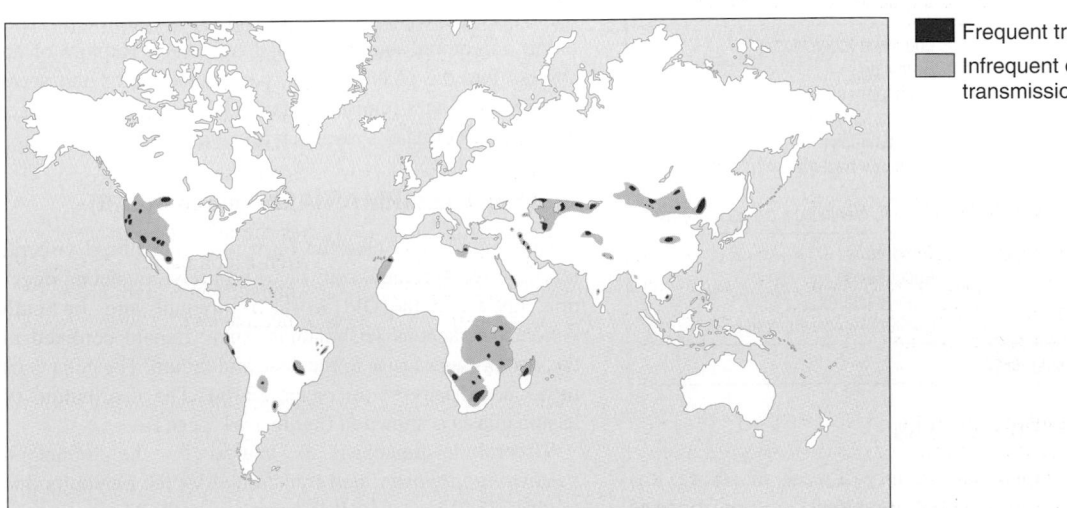

Frequent transmission

Infrequent or suspected transmission

Fig. 1.53   Foci of the transmission of plague.

BABESIOSIS

This is caused by a tick-borne intra-erythrocytic protozoan parasite. Patients present with fever 1–4 weeks after a tick bite. Severe illness is seen in splenectomised patients. The diagnosis is made by blood film examination. Treatment is with quinine and clindamycin.

CHRONIC FEVER

Chronic fever can be defined as a fever lasting more than 14 days. When this is in a patient in or returned from the tropics it is imperative to take and retake a careful history looking for risk factors, and to carry out repeated examinations to detect new signs. The principal infectious causes of chronic fever are listed in Box 1.45. It is especially important to consider tuberculosis and HIV infection (see Box 1.46, p. 121 and p. 532).

1.45 INFECTIOUS CAUSES OF CHRONIC FEVER	
• Typhoid	• Brucellosis
• Tuberculosis	• Melioidosis
• HIV	• Q fever
• Amoebic liver abscess	• African trypanosomiasis
• Visceral leishmaniasis	

1.46 DIFFERENTIAL WHITE CELL COUNTS (WCC) IN CHRONIC FEVER	
WCC differential	**Potential diagnoses**
Neutrophil leucocytosis	Deep sepsis/abscess* Amoebic liver abscess Cholangitis
Eosinophilia	Invasive schistosomiasis Other invasive parasitic infections
Leucopenia	Malaria Disseminated tuberculosis Visceral leishmaniasis Brucellosis
Normal WCC	Localised tuberculosis Brucellosis Secondary syphilis Trypanosomiasis Toxoplasmosis Subacute bacterial endocarditis SLE Chronic meningococcal septicaemia
Variable WCC	Tumours Reticuloses Drug reactions Connective tissue disease
* May show spiking fever.	

AMOEBIC LIVER ABSCESS

This often occurs without a history of recent diarrhoea. It is common in the tropics and an important cause of imported fever in Britain. The life cycle of the amoeba is shown in Figure 1.43, page 46.

Pathogenesis

Amoebic trophozoites emerge from the vegetative cyst form in the colon and may invade the bowel mucosa. They may enter a portal venous radicle and be carried to the liver where they multiply rapidly and destroy the parenchyma, causing an amoebic abscess. The liquid contents at first have a characteristic pinkish colour which may later change to chocolate brown.

Clinical features

The abscess is usually found in the right hepatic lobe. Early symptoms may be local discomfort only and malaise; later, a swinging temperature and sweating may develop. An enlarged, tender liver, cough, and pain in the right shoulder are characteristic, but symptoms may remain vague and signs minimal. The absence of toxicity in the presence of a high swinging fever is noticeable. The less common abscess in the left lobe is difficult to diagnose. There is usually neutrophil leucocytosis and a raised diaphragm, with diminished movement on the right side. A large abscess may penetrate the diaphragm and rupture into the lung, from where its contents may be coughed up. Rupture into the pleural cavity, the peritoneal cavity or pericardial sac is less common but more serious.

Investigations

An amoebic abscess of the liver is suspected from the clinical and radiographic appearances and confirmed by ultrasonic scanning. Aspirated pus from an amoebic abscess has the characteristic appearance described above but only rarely contains free amoebae.

Antibodies are detectable by immunofluorescence in over 95% of patients with hepatic amoebiasis.

Management

Early hepatic amoebiasis responds promptly to treatment with metronidazole (800 mg 8-hourly for 5 days) or tinidazole (2 g daily for 3 days) as above. The luminal amoebicide diloxanide furoate (500 mg 8-hourly for 10 days) is given to eliminate the intestinal infection. If the abscess is large or threatens to burst, or if the response to chemotherapy is not prompt, aspiration is required and repeated if necessary. Rupture of an abscess into the pleural cavity, pericardial sac or peritoneal cavity necessitates immediate aspiration or surgical drainage. Small serous effusions resolve without drainage.

VISCERAL LEISHMANIASIS (KALA-AZAR)

Leishmaniasis may take the form of a generalised visceral febrile infection, kala-azar, or of a purely cutaneous infection, known in the Old World as oriental sore. In South America cutaneous leishmaniasis may remain confined to the skin or metastasise to the nose and mouth. The cutaneous forms are discussed on pages 83–84. The distribution of leishmaniasis is shown in Figure 1.64, page 83.

Visceral leishmaniasis is caused by the protozoon *Leishmania donovani* and transmitted by the phlebotomine sandfly (see Fig. 1.54). It is prevalent in the Mediterranean and Red Sea littorals, Sudan, parts of East Africa, Asia Minor, mountainous regions of southern Arabia, eastern

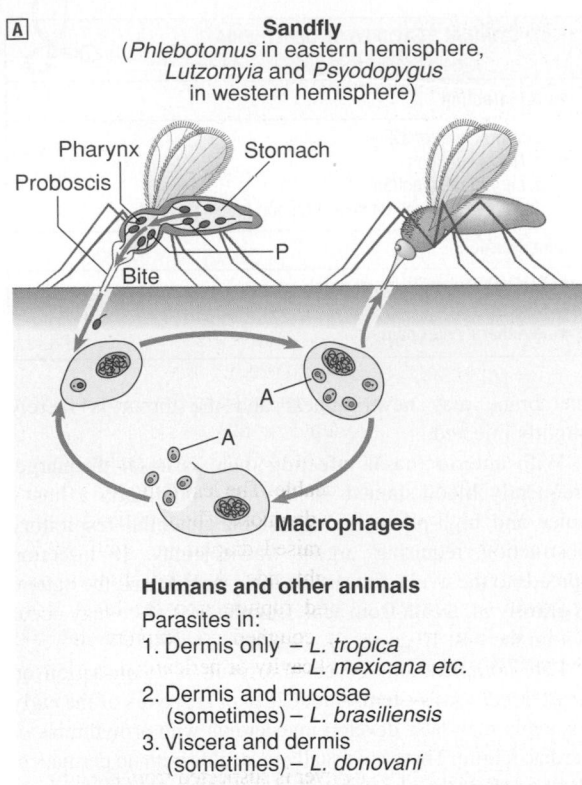

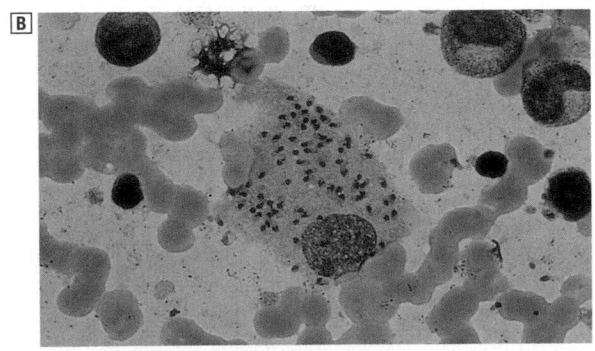

Fig. 1.54 Leishmaniasis. A Life cycle of leishmania. (A = amastigote (Leishman–Donovan body); P = promastigote) B Bone marrow smear showing numerous intracellular, and a few extracellular, amastigotes.

parts of India, China and South America. In India there is currently a massive epidemic centred around Bihar; here humans are the chief hosts. In most other areas, including the Mediterranean, dogs and foxes are the main reservoirs of infection. In these regions the disease is endemic and occurs chiefly in young children or tourists. In Africa various wild rodents provide the reservoir, and the disease is rural, occurring in older children and visiting hunters and soldiers. Transmission has also been reported to follow blood transfusion in northern Europe. The disease has presented unexpectedly in immunosuppressed patients—for example, after renal transplantation and in AIDS.

Pathology

Multiplication of leishmaniae takes place in macrophages, especially in the liver and spleen, the bone marrow and lymphoid tissue. The disease is accompanied by malnutrition and immunosuppression. Acute intercurrent pneumococcal infection or tuberculosis is a common complication. Granulocytopenia and thrombocytopenia occur. Anaemia is due to haemolysis, hypersplenism and ineffective erythropoiesis. Serum albumin is low and globulin, mainly IgG, high. Hepatocellular damage and bleeding are late complications.

Clinical features

The incubation period is usually about 1 or 2 months but may be up to 10 years. The onset is usually insidious with a low-grade fever, the patient remaining ambulant, or it may be abrupt with sweating and high intermittent fever, sometimes showing a double rise of temperature in 24 hours. The spleen soon becomes enlarged, often massively; hepatomegaly is less marked. If not treated, the patient will become anaemic and wasted, frequently with increased pigmentation, especially on the face. Cough and diarrhoea develop. In Africa lymphadenopathy is common, and is rarely the only clinical finding.

After recovery post-kala-azar dermal leishmaniasis sometimes develops. It may present first as hypopigmented or erythematous macules on any part of the body or as a nodular eruption especially on the face.

Investigations

Diagnosis is established by demonstrating the parasite in stained smears of aspirates of bone marrow, lymph node, spleen or liver, or by culture of these aspirates. PCR is also useful in confirming speciation. Amastigotes are scanty in skin biopsies from post-kala-azar dermal leishmaniasis. Antibody is detected by immunofluorescence or the direct agglutination test early in the disease. The leishmanin skin test is negative; it is performed and read in the same way as the tuberculin test, using a suspension of killed promastigotes as antigen.

Management

The response to treatment varies with the geographic area in which the disease has been acquired. In Europe the disease is readily cured. Resistance to antimonials has become a problem in India and Sudan. Where resources permit, liposomal amphotericin B is the drug of choice for visceral leishmaniasis. The dosage regimen is 2–3 mg/kg per dose, equivalent to 21–24 mg/kg total dose for the course, given in seven doses over 10 days. However, pentavalent antimonials remain the drugs of choice in many areas when cost, availability, efficacy and familiarity are considered. Sodium stibogluconate contains 100 mg Sb/ml; the Indian preparation meglumine antimoniate contains 85 mg Sb/ml. The dose is 20 mg Sb/kg i.v. or i.m. daily for 20–30 days. It may be reduced progressively by 2 mg Sb/kg if not well tolerated. The principal side-effects of sodium stibogluconate are myalgia, cardiac toxicity and pancreatitis. A new oral preparation, miltefosine, has undergone trials in India where a

28-day course gave 100% cure. There was little associated toxicity but anxieties about potential teratogenicity have not yet been resolved.

Intercurrent infection is sought and treated. Rarely, blood transfusion is needed for anaemia or bleeding. Measurement of spleen size, haemoglobin and serum albumin are useful in assessing progress. A small proportion of patients relapse, and should be retreated for 2 months with a full 20 mg Sb/kg daily. Patients with HIV and visceral leishmaniasis are particularly difficult to treat. They have a reduced response rate to therapy and invariably relapse.

Prevention

Infected or stray dogs should be destroyed in an endemic area, where they are the reservoir. Sandflies should be combated. They are extremely sensitive to insecticides. Mosquito nets treated with permethrin will keep out the tiny sandfly. Insect repellent creams may be helpful.

Early diagnosis and treatment of human infections reduce the reservoir and control epidemic kala-azar in India. Serology is useful for case detection in the field. There is no vaccine currently available.

DIPHTHERIA

In many parts of the developing world diphtheria remains an important cause of illness, having been eradicated from much of the developed world by mass vaccination in the mid-20th century. Recent outbreaks have occurred in the former Soviet Union and continue to occur in South-east Asia. The disease is notifiable in all countries of Europe and North America and international guidelines have been produced by WHO for the management of infection.

Infection with *Corynebacterium diphtheriae* occurs most commonly in the upper respiratory tract, and sore throat is frequently the presenting feature. The disease is usually spread by droplet infection from cases or carriers. The organisms remain localised at the site of infection and serious consequences result from the absorption of a soluble exotoxin which damages the heart muscle and the nervous system. Infection may occur rarely on the conjunctiva or in the genital tract, or may complicate wounds, abrasions or diseases of the skin, especially in chronic lesions and alcoholics.

The average incubation period is 2–4 days. Cases must be isolated until cultures from three daily nose and throat swabs are negative.

Clinical features (see Box 1.47)

The disease begins insidiously. Fever is seldom significant although tachycardia is usually marked. The diagnostic feature is the 'wash-leather' elevated greyish-green membrane on the tonsils. It has a well-defined edge, is firm and adherent, and is surrounded by a zone of inflammation. There may be swelling of the neck ('bull-neck') and tender enlargement of the lymph nodes. In the mildest infections, especially in the presence of a high degree of immunity, a

1.47 CLINICAL FEATURES OF DIPHTHERIA
Acute infection
• Membranous tonsillitis
• *or* Nasal infection
• *or* Laryngeal infection
• *or* Skin/wound/conjunctival infection (rare)
Complications
• Laryngeal obstruction or paralysis
• Myocarditis
• Peripheral neuropathy

membrane may never appear and the throat is merely slightly injected.

With anterior nasal infection there is nasal discharge, frequently blood-stained. In laryngeal diphtheria a husky voice and high-pitched cough signal potential respiratory obstruction requiring urgent tracheostomy. If infection spreads to the uvula, fauces and the nasopharynx, the patient is gravely ill. Death from acute circulatory failure may occur within the first 10 days.

Late complications occur as a result of toxin action on heart or nervous system. About 25% of survivors of the early toxaemia may later develop myocarditis with arrhythmias or cardiac failure. These are usually reversible with no permanent damage other than heart block in survivors.

Neurological involvement occurs in 75% of cases. After tonsillar or pharyngeal diphtheria it usually commences after 10 days with palatal palsy. Paralysis of accommodation often follows, manifest by difficulty in reading small print. Generalised polyneuritis with weakness and paraesthesia may follow in the next 10–14 days. Recovery from such neuritis is always ultimately complete.

Management

A clinical diagnosis of diphtheria must be notified to the public health authorities and sent urgently to a hospital for infectious diseases. Treatment should begin once appropriate swabs have been taken before waiting for microbiological confirmation. Three main areas of management are:

● administration of diphtheria antitoxin
● administration of antibiotics
● strict isolation procedures.

Antitoxin has no neutralising effect on toxin already fixed to tissues so must be injected intramuscularly without awaiting the result of a throat swab. However, since the antitoxin is hyperimmune horse serum, undesirable reactions to this foreign protein may occur. A potentially lethal immediate anaphylactic reaction with dyspnoea, pallor and collapse is recognised. 'Serum sickness' with fever, urticaria and joint pains may occur 7–12 days after injection. A careful history of previous horse serum injections or allergic reactions should alert the physician. A small test injection of serum should be given half an hour before the full dose in every patient. Adrenaline (epinephrine) solution must be available to deal with any immediate type of reaction (0.5–1.0 ml of 1/1000 solution i.m.). An antihistamine is also given.

In a severely ill patient the risk of anaphylactic shock is outweighed by the mortal danger of diphtheritic toxaemia and up to 100 000 units of antitoxin are injected intravenously if the test dose has not given rise to symptoms. For disease of moderate severity, 16 000–40 000 units i.m. will suffice, and for mild cases 4000–8000 units.

Penicillin 1200 mg 6-hourly i.v. or amoxicillin 500 mg 8-hourly should be administered for 2 weeks to eliminate *C. diphtheriae*. Patients allergic to penicillin can be given erythromycin. Due to poor immunogenicity all sufferers should be immunised with diphtheria toxoid following recovery. Patients must be managed in strict isolation attended by staff with a clearly documented immunisation history until three swabs 24 hours apart are culture-negative.

Prevention

Active immunisation should be given to all children (see Appendix). If diphtheria occurs in a closed community, contacts should be given erythromycin, which is more effective than penicillin in eradicating the organism in carriers. All contacts should also be immunised or given a booster dose of toxoid. Adults should be given a dilute preparation of vaccine to avoid severe reactions.

EOSINOPHILIA AND TROPICAL INFECTIONS

Eosinophilia is associated with parasite infections, particularly those with a tissue migration phase during their life cycle. Eosinophils have an important role in mediating antibody-dependent damage to helminths, phagocytosing immune complexes and modulating type 1 hypersensitivity reactions. Anybody with an eosinophil count of $> 0.4 \times 10^9$ should be investigated for both parasitic and non-parasitic causes of eosinophilia. Box 1.48 gives the main causes of eosinophilia, Box 1.49 the main parasitic causes and Box 1.50 the tropical diseases that are not associated with eosinophilia.

This section covers the major parasite infestations associated with eosinophilia, the soil-transmitted helminths, the filariases and schistosomiasis. A few non-eosinophil-associated worms will also be considered here. The response to parasite infections is often different when travellers and residents of endemic areas are compared. Travellers will often have recent and light infections associated with eosinophilia. Residents have often been infected for a long time, have evidence of chronic pathology and no longer have an eosinophilia.

1.48 CAUSES OF EOSINOPHILIA

- Metazoan parasite infections
- Atopy and allergic drug reactions
- Skin diseases
- Pulmonary eosinophilia
- HIV, human T-cell lymphotropic virus 1 (HTLV 1)
- Lymphomas
- Leukaemias
- Polyarteritis nodosa
- Sarcoidosis
- Hypereosinophilic syndrome

1.49 PARASITE INFECTIONS THAT CAUSE EOSINOPHILIA

Infestation	Pathogen	Clinical syndrome associated with eosinophilia
Strongyloidiasis	Strongyloides stercoralis	
Soil-transmitted helminthiases		
Hookworm	Necator americanus Ancylostoma duodenale	
Ascariasis	Ascaris lumbricoides	Loeffler's syndrome
Toxocariasis	Toxocara canis	Visceral larva migrans
Schistosomiasis	Schistosoma haematobium S. mansoni S. japonicum	
Filariases		
Loiasis	Loa loa	
Wuchereria bancrofti	W. bancrofti	
Brugia malayi	B. malayi	
Mansonella perstans	M. perstans	
Onchocerciasis	Onchocerca volvulus	
Cysticercosis	Taenia saginata T. solium	Migratory phase
Hydatid disease	Echinococcus granulosus	Leakage from cyst
Liver flukes	Fasciola hepatica Clonorchis sinensis Opisthorchis felineus	Migratory phase

1.50 TROPICAL INFECTIONS NOT ASSOCIATED WITH EOSINOPHILIA

- Amoebiasis
- Arboviral infections
- Brucellosis
- Enteric fever
- Giardiasis
- Leishmaniasis
- Leprosy
- Malaria
- Trypanosomiasis
- Tuberculosis
- Tapeworms

History

A careful geographical history and an awareness of the overlap between where the patient has travelled to and the known endemic areas for diseases such as schistosomiasis, onchocerciasis and the filariases will indicate possible causes for the eosinophilia. Establish how long patients spent in endemic areas and ask about any occupational and behavioural risks (see Box 1.32, p. 50). Contact with fresh water in sub-Saharan Africa and particularly swimming in Lake Malawi are important risk factors for schistosomiasis. Walking barefoot is a risk factor for acquiring any of the soil-transmitted helminthiases.

Clinical features

Symptoms that would suggest a parasitic cause for eosinophilia include transient rashes (schistosomiasis, strongyloidiasis), fever (Katayama syndrome—see p. 78), itching (onchocerciasis), haematuria, haematospermia (schistosomiasis) or migrating subcutaneous swellings (loiasis, gnathostomiasis) (see Box 1.51).

1.51   EOSINOPHILIC SYNDROMES ASSOCIATED WITH HELMINTIC INFECTIONS
Urticarial rashes
• Strongyloidiasis, onchocerciasis, fascioliasis, hydatid disease, trichinosis
Cutaneous larva migrans
• *Ancylostoma braziliense*
Dermatitis
• Onchocerciasis
Migratory subcutaneous swellings
• Loiasis, gnathostomiasis
Lymphangitis, orchitis
• Lymphatic filariasis
Myositis
• Trichinosis, cysticercosis
Febrile hepatosplenomegaly
• Schistosomiasis, toxocariasis
Pneumonitis
• Migratory stage of larval helminths (Loeffler's syndrome), lymphatic filariasis (tropical pulmonary eosinophilia), systemic strongyloidiasis
Enteritis and colitis
• Strongyloidiasis, capillariasis, trichinosis, rarely other intestinal worms
Meningitis
• Angiostrongyliasis, strongyloidiasis

Investigations

To establish a parasitic infestation direct visualisation of adult worms, larvae or ova is the best evidence. Serological evidence may be helpful but a serological response may not distinguish between an active and an old infection. Radiological investigations may also provide circumstantial evidence of parasite infestation. Box 1.52 gives the initial investigations for eosinophilia.

1.52 INITIAL INVESTIGATION OF EOSINOPHILIA	
Investigation	**Pathogens sought**
Stool microscopy	Ova, cysts and parasites
Terminal urine	Ova of *Schistosoma haematobium*
Duodenal aspirate	Filaria of *Strongyloides*, liver fluke ova
Day bloods	Microfilariae *Wuchereria bancrofti*, *Loa loa*
Night bloods	Microfilariae *Brugia malayi*
Skin snips	*Onchocerca volvulus*
Serology	Schistosomiasis, filariasis, strongyloidiasis, hydatid, trichinosis etc.

PARASITIC CAUSES OF EOSINOPHILIA

SOIL-TRANSMITTED HELMINTHIASES

Soil-transmitted helminthiases are of two types: the hook worms which have a soil stage developing into larvae which then penetrate the host, and a group of nematodes which survive in the soil merely as eggs that have to be ingested for the cycle to continue. The geographical distribution of hook worms is limited by the larval requirement for warmth and humidity.

ANCYLOSTOMIASIS (HOOKWORM)

Ancylostomiasis is caused by parasitisation of the small intestine with *Ancylostoma duodenale* or *Necator americanus*. It is one of the main causes of anaemia in the tropics. In the early stages of infection eosinophilia is common. The adult hookworm is 1 cm long and lives in the duodenum and upper jejunum. Eggs are passed in the faeces. In warm, moist, shady soil the larvae develop into the filariform infective stage; they then penetrate human skin and are carried to the lungs (see Fig. 1.55). After entering the alveoli they ascend the bronchi, are swallowed and mature in the small intestine, reaching maturity 4–7 weeks after infection.

Hookworm infection is widespread in the tropics and subtropics. *A. duodenale* is endemic in the Far East and Mediterranean coastal regions and is also present in Africa, while *N. americanus* is endemic in West, East and Central Africa and Central and South America as well as in the Far East.

Pathology

The larvae may cause allergic inflammation at the site of entry through the skin. When infection is heavy, the passage through the lungs may cause pulmonary eosinophilia. The worms attach themselves to the mucosa of the small intestine by their buccal capsule (see Fig. 1.56) and withdraw blood. The mean daily loss of blood from one *A. duodenale* is 0.15 ml and for *N. americanus* 0.03 ml. The degree of iron and protein deficiency which develops depends not only on the load of worms but also on the nutrition of the patient and especially on the iron stores. In a light infection there may be no anaemia.

Clinical features

Dermatitis usually on the feet (ground itch) may be experienced at the time of infection. The passage of the larvae through the lungs in a heavy infection causes a paroxysmal cough with blood-stained sputum, associated with patchy pulmonary consolidation. When the worms have reached the small intestine, vomiting and epigastric pain resembling peptic ulcer disease may occur. Sometimes frequent loose stools are passed. Iron deficiency anaemia, protein-losing enteropathy and hypoproteinaemia may develop in the undernourished. High-output cardiac failure may result from the chronic iron deficiency anaemia. The mental and physical

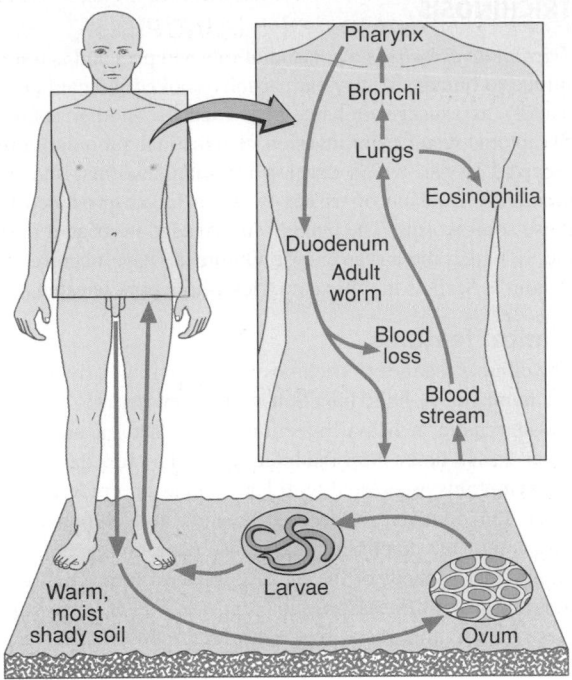

Fig. 1.55   Ancylostomiasis. Life cycle of *Ancylostoma*.

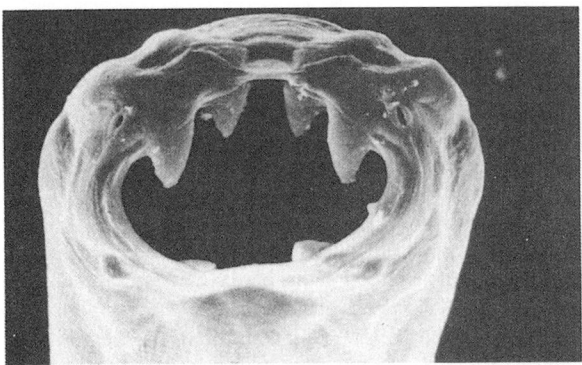

Fig. 1.56   *Ancylostoma duodenale.* Electron micrograph showing the ventral teeth.

development of children may be retarded. A well-nourished person with a light infection may be asymptomatic.

Investigations

The characteristic ovum can be recognised in the stool. If hookworms are present in numbers sufficient to cause anaemia, tests of the stool for occult blood will be positive and ova will be present in large numbers.

Management

Mebendazole 100 mg 12-hourly for 3 days is preferred, but for single-dose treatment albendazole (400 mg) is the best choice. Anaemia associated with hookworm infection responds well to oral iron. The management of anaemic heart disease is best accomplished by treatment with anthelmintics and iron. Blood transfusion should only be used with great care in very severely anaemic patients (< 4 g/dl).

STRONGYLOIDIASIS

Strongyloides stercoralis is a very small nematode (2 mm × 0.4 mm) which parasitises the mucosa of the upper part of the small intestine, often in large numbers causing persistent eosinophilia. The eggs hatch in the bowel but only larvae are passed in the faeces. In moist soil they moult and become the infective filariform larvae. After penetrating human skin they undergo a development cycle similar to that of hookworms but the female worms burrow into the intestinal mucosa and submucosa. Some larvae in the intestine may develop into filariform larvae which may then penetrate the mucosa or the perianal skin and lead to autoinfection and persistent infection. Patients with *Strongyloides* infection persisting for more than 35 years have been described. Strongyloidiasis occurs in the tropics and subtropics and is especially prevalent in the Far East.

Pathology

In the intestine female worms burrow into the mucosa and induce an inflammatory reaction; with heavy infections the mucosa may be severely damaged, leading to malabsorption. Granulomatous changes, necrosis, and even perforation and peritonitis may occur. Eosinophilia commonly persists. Actively motile larvae are passed in the faeces. Immunosuppression may cause fatal systemic strongyloidiasis.

Clinical features

These are shown in Box 1.53. The classic triad of symptoms consists of abdominal pain, diarrhoea and urticaria. Cutaneous manifestations are characteristic and occur in 66% of patients, either urticaria or larva currens. Systemic strongyloidiasis (the *Strongyloides* hyperinfestation syndrome) with dissemination of larvae throughout the body occurs in association with immune suppression (intercurrent disease, HTLV1 infection, corticosteroid treatment). Patients present with severe, generalised abdominal pain, abdominal distension and shock. Massive larval invasion of the lungs causes cough, wheeze and dyspnoea; cerebral involvement has manifestations ranging from subtle neurological signs to coma. Gram-negative sepsis frequently complicates the picture.

1.53   CLINICAL FEATURES OF STRONGYLOIDIASIS
Penetration of skin by infective larvae
• Itchy rash
Presence of worms in gut
• Abdominal pain, diarrhoea, steatorrhoea, weight loss
Allergic phenomena
• Urticarial plaques and papules, wheezing, arthralgia
Autoinfection
• Transient itchy linear urticarial weals across abdomen and buttocks (larva currens)
Systemic (super)infection
• Diarrhoea, pneumonia, meningoencephalitis, death

Investigations

The faeces should be examined microscopically for motile larvae. Excretion is intermittent so repeated examinations may be necessary. Larvae can also be found in jejunal aspirate or detected using the string test. Serology (ELISA) is helpful, but definitive diagnosis depends upon finding the larvae. Larvae may also be cultured from faeces.

Management

Ivermectin 200 mg/kg as a single dose, or two doses of 200 mg/kg on successive days, is effective. Albendazole is given orally in a dose of 15 mg/kg body weight 12-hourly for 3 days. A second course may be required. For the *Strongyloides* hyperinfestation syndrome, ivermectin is given at 200 mg/kg on days 1, 2, 15 and 16.

ASCARIS LUMBRICOIDES (ROUNDWORM)

This pale yellow worm is 20–35 cm long. Humans are infected by eating food contaminated with mature ova. *Ascaris* larvae hatch in the duodenum, migrate through the lungs, ascend the bronchial tree, are swallowed and mature in the small intestine. This tissue migration can provoke both local and general hypersensitivity reactions with pneumonitis, eosinophilic granulomata, bronchial asthma and urticaria.

Clinical features

Intestinal ascariasis causes symptoms ranging from occasional vague abdominal pain through to malnutrition. The large size of the adult worm and its tendency to aggregate and migrate can result in severe obstructive complications. In endemic areas ascariasis causes up to 35% of all intestinal obstructions, most commonly in the terminal ileum. Obstruction can be complicated further by intussusception, volvulus, haemorrhagic infarction and perforation. Other complications include blockage of the bile or pancreatic duct and obstruction of the appendix by adult worms.

Investigations

The diagnosis is made microscopically by finding ova in the faeces. Adult worms are frequently expelled rectally or orally. Occasionally, the worms are demonstrated radiographically by a barium examination.

Management

Mebendazole 100 mg 12-hourly for 3 days, albendazole 400 mg or piperazine 4 g as a single dose, is effective for intestinal ascariasis. Patients should be warned that they may expel numerous whole, large worms. Obstruction due to ascariasis should be treated with nasogastric suction, piperazine and intravenous fluids.

Prevention

Community chemotherapy programmes have been used to reduce *Ascaris* infection. The whole community can be treated every 3 months and over several years. Alternatively, schoolchildren can be targeted; treating them lowers the prevalence of ascariasis in the whole community.

TRICHINOSIS

Trichinella spiralis is a parasite of rats and pigs and is transmitted to humans if they eat partially cooked infected pork, usually as sausage or ham. Bear meat is another source. Symptoms result from invasion of intestinal submucosa by ingested larvae, which develop into adult worms, and the secondary invasion of tissues by fresh larvae produced by these adult worms. The main tissue invaded is striated muscle, in which the larvae encyst. Outbreaks have occurred in Britain as well as in other countries where pork is eaten.

Clinical features

The clinical features of trichinosis are determined by the larval numbers. A light infection with a few worms may be asymptomatic; a heavy infection causes nausea and diarrhoea 24–48 hours after the infected meal. A few days later, the symptoms associated with larval invasion predominate: fever and oedema of the face, eyelids and conjunctivae. Invasion of the diaphragm may cause pain, cough and dyspnoea; involvement of the muscles of the limbs, chest and mouth causes stiffness, pain and tenderness in affected muscles. Larval migration may cause acute myocarditis and encephalitis. An eosinophilia is usually found after the second week. An intense infection may prove fatal but those who survive recover completely.

Investigations

Commonly, a group of people who have eaten infected pork from a common source develop symptoms at about the same time. Biopsy from the deltoid or gastrocnemius after the third week of symptoms in suspected cases may reveal encysted larvae. Serological tests are also helpful.

Management

Treatment is with albendazole 20 mg/kg daily for 7 days. Given early in the infection this may kill newly formed adult worms in the submucosa and thus reduce the number of larvae reaching the muscles. Corticosteroids are necessary to control the serious effects of acute inflammation.

HELMINTHS NOT ASSOCIATED WITH EOSINOPHILIA

ENTEROBIUS VERMICULARIS (THREADWORM)

This helminth is common throughout the world. It affects children especially. The male worm is 2–5 mm long and the female 8–13 mm. After the ova are swallowed, development takes place in the small intestine, but the adult worms are found chiefly in the colon.

Clinical features

The gravid female worm lays ova around the anus and causes intense itching, especially at night. The ova are often carried to the mouth on the fingers and so reinfection takes place (see Fig. 1.57). In females the genitalia may be involved. The adult worms may be seen moving on the buttocks or in the stool.

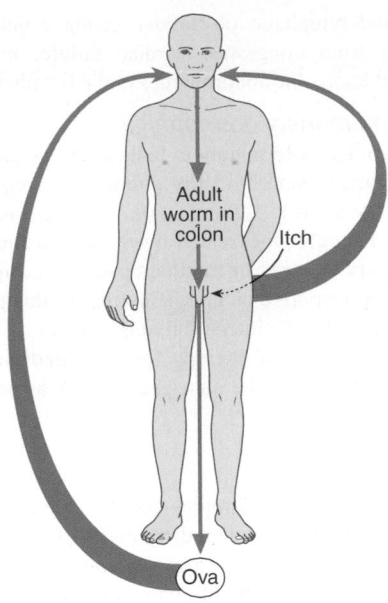

Fig. 1.57   Threadworm. Life cycle of *Enterobius vermicularis*.

Investigations

Ova are detected by applying the adhesive surface of Cellophane tape to the perianal skin in the morning. This is then examined on a glass slide under the microscope. A perianal swab, moistened with saline, is an alternative method for diagnosis.

Management

A single dose of mebendazole 100 mg, albendazole 400 mg or piperazine 4 g is given and may be repeated after 2 weeks to control auto-reinfection. Where infection constantly recurs in a family, each member should be treated as above. During this period all nightclothes and bed linen are laundered. Fingernails must be kept short and hands washed carefully before meals. Subsequent therapy is reserved for those family members who develop recurrent infection.

TRICHURIS TRICHIURA (WHIPWORM)

Infections with whipworm are common all over the world under unhygienic conditions. Infection takes place by the ingestion of earth or food contaminated with ova which have become infective after lying for 3 weeks or more in moist soil. The adult worm is 3–5 cm long and has a coiled anterior end resembling a whip. Whipworms inhabit the caecum, lower ileum, appendix, colon and anal canal. There are usually no symptoms, but intense infections in children may cause persistent diarrhoea or rectal prolapse, and stunting. The diagnosis is readily made by identifying ova in faeces. Treatment is with mebendazole in doses of 100 mg 12-hourly for 3–5 days or a single dose of albendazole 400 mg.

PREVENTION OF HELMINTHIASES

This is achieved by preventing contact with faecally contaminated soil; the provision of adequate sewerage disposal could eliminate hookworm infestation. The use of footwear also reduces hookworm infection. Transmission of intestinal nematodes is through contaminated soil or unwashed hands. Safe disposal of faeces, the provision of clean drinking water and strict personal hygiene form the basis of control.

FILARIASES

Filarial infections cause the highest eosinophilia of all helmintic infections. The larval stages are inoculated by biting mosquitoes or flies, each specific to a particular filarial species. The larvae develop into adult worms (2–50 cm long) which, after mating, produce millions of microfilariae (170–320 microns long) that migrate in blood or skin. The life cycle is completed when the vector takes up microfilariae while feeding on humans, normally the only host.

Disease is due to the host's immune response to the worms, particularly dying worms, and its pattern and severity vary with the site and stage of each species (see Box 1.54). The worms are long-lived; microfilariae survive 2–3 years and adult worms 10–15 years. The infections are chronic and worst in individuals constantly exposed to reinfection.

1.54 PATHOGENICITY OF FILARIAL INFECTIONS DEPENDING ON SITE AND STAGE OF WORMS		
Worm species	**Adult worm**	**Microfilariae**
Wuchereria bancrofti and *Brugia malayi*	Lymphatic vessels[+++]	Blood[−] Pulmonary capillaries[++]
Loa loa	Subcutaneous[+]	Blood[+]
Onchocerca volvulus	Subcutaneous[+]	Skin[+++] Eye[+++]
Mansonella perstans	Retroperitoneal[−]	Blood[−]
Mansonella streptocerca	Skin[+]	Skin[++]
(+++ = severe; ++ = moderate; + = mild; − = rarely pathogenic)		

LYMPHATIC FILARIASIS

Infection with the filarial worms *Wuchereria bancrofti* and *Brugia malayi* is associated with a range of clinical outcomes ranging from subclinical infection to hydrocele and elephantiasis. *W. bancrofti* is transmitted by night-biting *Culex quinquefasciatus* mosquitoes. The adult worms, 4–10 cm in length, live in the lymphatics, and the females produce microfilariae which at night circulate in large numbers in the peripheral blood. In the mosquito, ingested microfilariae develop into infective larvae. The infection is widespread in tropical Africa, the North African coast, coastal areas of Asia, Indonesia and northern Australia, the South Pacific islands, the West Indies and also in North and South America. *B. malayi* is similar to *W. bancrofti* and is found in Indonesia, Borneo, Malaysia, Vietnam, South China, South India and Sri Lanka.

Pathology

Four factors are central to the pathogenesis of lymphatic filariasis: the living adult worm, the inflammatory response caused by the death of the worm, microfilariae and secondary infections. Toxins released by the adult worm cause lymphangiectasia. Dilatation of the lymphatic vessel leads to lymphatic dysfunction and the chronic clinical manifestations of lymphatic filariasis, lymphoedema and hydrocele. Death of the adult worm results in acute filarial lymphangitis. Lymphatic obstruction persists after death of the adult worm. Secondary bacterial infections cause tissue destruction. Microfilariae are central to the pathogenesis of tropical pulmonary eosinophilia (see Fig. 1.58).

Clinical features

Acute filarial lymphangitis presents with fever, pain, tenderness and erythema along the course of inflamed lymphatic vessels. Inflammation of the spermatic cord, epididymitis and orchitis are common. The whole episode lasts a few days but may recur several times a year. Temporary oedema becomes more persistent and regional lymph nodes enlarge. Progressive enlargement, coarsening, corrugation and fissuring of the skin and subcutaneous tissue develop gradually, causing irreversible 'elephantiasis'. The scrotum may reach an enormous size. Chyluria and chylous effusions are milky and opalescent; on standing, fat globules rise to the top. Elephantiasis develops only in association with repeated skin sepsis.

The acute lymphatic manifestations of filariasis must be differentiated from thrombophlebitis and infection. The

oedema and lymphatic obstructive changes must be distinguished from congestive cardiac failure, malignancy, trauma and idiopathic abnormalities of the lymphatic system.

Tropical pulmonary eosinophilia

This condition is seen mainly in India and is likely to be due to microfilariae trapped in the pulmonary capillaries and destroyed by allergic inflammation. Patients present with paroxysmal cough, wheeze and fever. The chest radiograph shows miliary changes or mottled opacities. Lung function tests show a restrictive picture. If untreated, this progresses to debilitating chronic interstitial lung disease.

There is no specific therapy for this condition but the lymphatic damage can be managed actively as outlined for filarial elephantiasis.

Investigations

In the earliest stages of lymphangitis the diagnosis is made on clinical grounds, supported by eosinophilia and sometimes by positive filarial serology. Microfilariae are found in the peripheral blood at night and can be seen moving in a wet blood film or by microfiltration of a sample of lysed blood. They are usually present in hydrocele fluid which may occasionally yield an adult filaria. By the time elephantiasis develops, microfilariae become difficult to find. Calcified filariae may sometimes be demonstrable by radiography. Movement of adult worms can be seen on scrotal ultrasound. Indirect fluorescence and ELISA detect antibodies in over 95% of active cases and 70% of established elephantiasis. The test becomes negative 1–2 years after cure. Serological tests cannot distinguish the different filarial infections. In tropical pulmonary eosinophilia, serology is strongly positive and IgE levels are massively elevated but circulating microfilariae are not found.

Management

Treatment of the individual is aimed at reversing and halting disease progression. Diethylcarbamazine (DEC) kills microfilariae and adult worms. The dose is 6 mg/kg daily orally in three divided doses for 12 days. The full dose must be reached slowly, starting with 50 mg and doubling daily unless serious allergic reactions ensue. Most adverse effects seen with DEC treatment are due to the host response to dying microfilariae, and the reaction intensity is directly proportional to the microfilarial load. The main symptoms are fever, headache, nausea, vomiting, arthralgia and prostration. These usually occur within 24–36 hours of the first dose of DEC. Antihistamines or corticosteroids may be required to control these allergic phenomena. Both the 12-day course and a single dose of DEC reduce microfilaria levels by about 90% 6–12 months after treatment. No carefully controlled trials have evaluated the effects of DEC treatment alone on the chronic manifestations of lymphatic filariasis. Ivermectin may also be used.

Chronic lymphatic pathology

Experience in India and Brazil shows that active management of chronic lymphatic pathology can alleviate symptoms. Patients should be taught meticulous local care of their lymphoedematous limbs with assiduous skin care to prevent

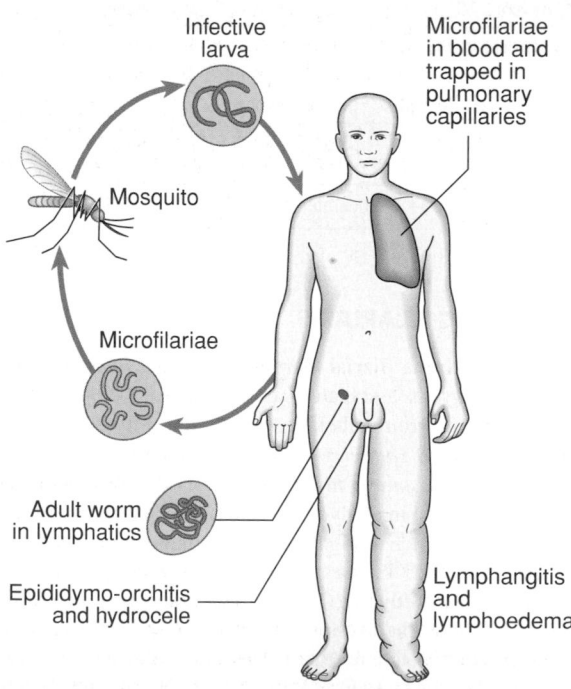

Fig. 1.58 *Wuchereria bancrofti* and *Brugia malayi.* Life cycle of organisms and pathogenesis of lymphatic filariasis.

Infective larva

Microfilariae in blood and trapped in pulmonary capillaries

Mosquito

Microfilariae

Adult worm in lymphatics

Epididymo-orchitis and hydrocele

Lymphangitis and lymphoedema

secondary bacterial and fungal infections. Tight bandaging, massage and bed rest with elevation of the affected limb may help to control the lymphoedema. Prompt diagnosis and antibiotic therapy of bacterial cellulitis are important in preventing further lymphatic damage and worsening of existing elephantiasis. Patient education is a critical feature of lymphoedema treatment, both to alter fatalistic beliefs about inevitable progression of disease and to foster motivation. Plastic surgery may be indicated in established elephantiasis. Great relief can be obtained by removal of excess tissue but recurrences are probable unless new lymphatic drainage is established. Hydroceles can be repaired surgically; chyluria can also be corrected surgically.

Prevention

Treatment of the whole population in endemic areas with annual single-dose DEC, 100 mg for adults (50 mg for children), has reduced but not eliminated the infection. Ivermectin, alone or in combination with albendazole, is under evaluation as an alternative to DEC. This mass treatment should be combined with mosquito control programmes.

NON-FILARIAL ELEPHANTIASIS

This occurs in certain filaria-free geographical areas and affects one or both legs. It is due to lymphatic damage by silicates absorbed from volcanic soil. There is no specific therapy for this condition but the lymphatic damage can be managed actively as outlined above for filarial elephantiasis.

LOIASIS

Loiasis is caused by infection with the filaria *Loa loa*. The adults, 3–7 cm × 4 mm, parasitise chiefly the subcutaneous tissue of humans. The larval microfilariae circulate harmlessly in the peripheral blood in the daytime. The vector is *Chrysops*, a forest-dwelling, day-biting fly.

Pathology

The adult worms move harmlessly about in the subcutaneous tissues and other interstitial planes. From time to time a short-lived, inflammatory, oedematous swelling (a Calabar swelling) is produced around an adult worm. Heavy infections, especially when treated, may cause encephalitis. The incubation period is commonly over a year but may be just 3 months.

Clinical features

The infection is often symptomless. The first sign is usually a Calabar swelling, an irritating, tense, localised swelling that may be painful, especially if it is near a joint. The swelling is generally on a limb; it measures a few centimetres in diameter but sometimes is more diffuse and extensive. It usually disappears after a few days but may persist for 2 or 3 weeks. A succession of such swellings may appear at irregular intervals, often in adjacent sites. Sometimes there is urticaria and pruritus elsewhere. Occasionally, a worm may be seen wriggling under the skin, especially of an eyelid, and may cross the eye under the conjunctiva, taking many minutes to do so.

Investigations

Diagnosis is by demonstrating microfilariae in blood taken during the day, but they may not always be found in patients with Calabar swellings. Antifilarial antibodies are positive in 95% of patients; there is massive eosinophilia. Occasionally, a calcified worm may be seen on a radiograph.

Management

DEC (see above) is curative, gradually increased to a dose of 9–12 mg/kg daily which is continued for 21 days. Treatment may precipitate a severe reaction in patients with a heavy microfilaraemia characterised by fever, joint and muscle pain, and encephalitis; microfilaraemic patients should be given steroid cover.

Prevention

Protection is afforded by building houses away from trees and by having dwellings wire-screened. Protective clothing and repellents are also useful. DEC in a dose of 5 mg/kg daily for 3 days each month is partially protective.

ONCHOCERCIASIS (RIVER BLINDNESS)

Onchocerciasis is the result of infection by *Onchocerca volvulus*. Only about 0.3 mm in diameter, the adult female may be as long as 50 cm; the male is 13 cm. The infection is conveyed by flies of the genus *Simulium* which inflict a painful bite. In West Africa the vector is *S. damnosum*, in northern Nigeria also *S. bovis*, and in East Africa and Zaire *S. neavei*. The flies breed in rapidly flowing, well-aerated water, the larvae being attached to submerged vegetation, rocks or crabs. Adult flies bite during the day both inside and outside houses. Humans are the only known definitive hosts.

Onchocerciasis is endemic in well-defined areas throughout tropical Africa, in southern Arabia and Yemen, and also in South Mexico, Guatemala, Colombia, Venezuela and Brazil. It is estimated that over 20 million people are infected. In parts of West and Central Africa it affects the whole adult population and blindness rates of 10% are common, reaching 35% in some parts of Ghana. Due to onchocerciasis huge tracts of fertile land lie virtually untilled, and individuals and communities are impoverished.

Pathology

Infective larvae of *O. volvulus* are introduced into the skin by the bite of an infected *Simulium* fly (see Fig. 1.59). The worms mature in 2–4 months and live for up to 17 years in small colonies in subcutaneous and connective tissues. At sites of trauma, over bony prominences and around joints, fibrosis may form nodules around adult worms which otherwise cause no direct damage. Innumerable microfilariae, discharged by the female *O. volvulus*, move actively in these nodules and in the adjacent tissues, are widely distributed in the skin, and may invade the eye. Live microfilariae elicit little tissue reaction, but dead ones may cause severe allergic inflammation leading to hyaline necrosis and loss of collagen and elastin. Death of microfilariae in the eye causes conjunctivitis, sclerosing keratitis with pannus formation, uveitis which may lead to glaucoma and cataract and, less commonly, choroidoretinitis and optic neuritis.

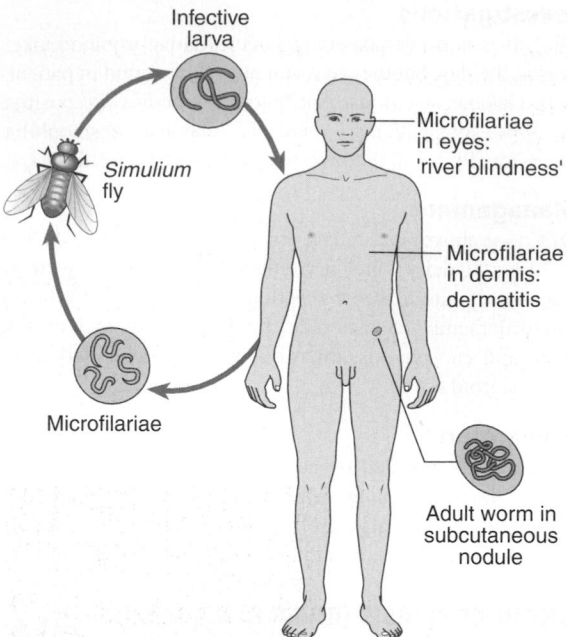

Fig. 1.59 *Onchocerca volvulus.* Life cycle of organism and pathogenesis of onchocerciasis.

Clinical features

The infection may remain symptomless for months or years. The first symptom is usually itching, localised to one quadrant of the body and later becoming generalised and involving the eyes. Evanescent oedema of part or all of a limb in Europeans is an early sign, followed by papular urticaria spreading gradually from the site of infection. This is difficult to see on dark skins, in which the most common signs are papules excoriated by scratching, spotty hyperpigmentation from resolving inflammation, and more chronic changes of a rough, thickened or inelastic, wrinkled skin. Superficial lymph nodes enlarge and may hang down in folds of loose skin at the groins. Hydrocele, femoral hernias and scrotal elephantiasis occur. Firm subcutaneous nodules occur in chronic infection (onchocercomas), which are palpable and 1 cm or more in diameter.

Eye disease is most common in highly endemic areas and is associated with chronic heavy infections and nodules on the head. Early manifestations include itching, lacrimation, conjunctival injection and evidence of the features listed under 'Pathology'. Classically, 'snowflake' deposits are seen in the edges of the cornea.

Investigations

The finding of nodules or characteristic lesions of the skin or eyes in a patient from an endemic area, associated with eosinophilia, is suggestive. Skin snips or shavings, taken with a corneoscleral punch or scalpel blade from calf, buttock and shoulder, are placed in saline under a cover slip on a microscope slide and examined after 4 hours. Microfilariae are seen wriggling free in all but the lightest infections. If negative, a test dose of DEC is given to see if it aggravates the rash. Slit-lamp examination of the eye may reveal

microfilariae moving in the anterior chamber of the eye, or trapped in the cornea. A nodule may be removed and incised, showing the coiled, thread-like adult worm. Filarial antibodies may be detected in up to 95% of patients, but antibody positivity can be much lower in lightly infected expatriates.

Management

Ivermectin, in a single dose of 100–200 mg/kg, kills microfilariae and prevents their return for 9 months. It is nontoxic and does not trigger severe reactions, in contrast to DEC which is no longer used for this infection. In the rare event of a severe reaction causing oedema or postural hypotension, prednisolone 20–30 mg may be given daily for 2 or 3 days. Retreatment with ivermectin may be necessary.

Prevention

Mass treatment with ivermectin is in use. It reduces morbidity in the community and prevents eye disease from getting worse. *Simulium* can be destroyed in its larval stage by the application of insecticide to streams. Dimethyl phthalate applied to skin or clothing will repel the fly for several hours. Long trousers, skirts and sleeves discourage the fly from biting.

OTHER FILARIASES

Mansonella perstans

This filarial worm is transmitted by the midges *Culicoides austeni* and *C. grahami*. It is common throughout equatorial Africa as far south as Zambia, and also in Trinidad and parts of northern and eastern South America.

M. perstans has never been shown to cause disease but it may be responsible for a persistent eosinophilia and occasional allergic manifestations. *M. perstans* is resistant to ivermectin and DEC and the infection may persist for many years.

Dirofilaria immitis

This dog heart worm infects humans with skin and lung lesions. It is not uncommon in the US, Japan and Australia.

SCHISTOSOMIASIS

Schistosomiasis (bilharziasis) is one of the most important causes of morbidity in the tropics and is being spread by irrigation schemes. Schistosome eggs have been found in Egyptian mummies dated 1250 BC. Recent travellers, especially those overlanding through Africa, may present with eosinophilia; residents of schistosomiasis-endemic areas are more likely to present with chronic urinary tract pathology or portal hypertension.

There are three species of the genus *Schistosoma* which commonly cause disease in humans: *S. haematobium*, *S. mansoni* and *S. japonicum*. *S. haematobium* was discovered by Theodor Bilharz in Cairo in 1861 and the genus is sometimes called *Bilharzia* and the disease bilharziasis. The ovum is passed in the urine or faeces of infected individuals and gains access to fresh water where the ciliated miracidium inside it is liberated and enters its intermediate host, a species of freshwater snail, in which it multiplies. Large numbers of fork-tailed cercariae are then liberated into the water, where they may survive for 2–3 days. Cercariae can penetrate the skin or the mucous membrane of the mouth of their definitive host, humans. They transform into schistosomulae and moult as they pass through the lungs and are carried by the blood stream to the liver and so to the portal vein where they mature (see Fig. 1.60). The male worm is up to 20 mm in length and the more slender cylindrical female, usually enfolded longitudinally by the male, is rather longer. Within 4–6 weeks of infection they migrate to the venules draining the pelvic viscera, where the females deposit ova.

Pathology

The pathological changes and symptoms depend on species and stage of infection (see Box 1.55). Most of the disease is due to the passage of eggs through mucosa and to the granulomatous reaction to eggs deposited in tissues. The eggs of *S. haematobium* pass mainly through the wall of the bladder, but may also involve rectum, seminal vesicles, vagina, cervix and uterine tubes. *S. mansoni* and *S. japonicum* eggs pass mainly through the wall of the lower bowel or are carried to the liver. The most serious, though rare, consequences of the ectopic deposition of eggs are transverse myelitis and paraplegia. Granulomas are composed of macrophages, eosinophils, epithelioid and giant cells around an ovum. Later there is fibrosis and eggs calcify, often in sufficient numbers to become radiologically visible. Eggs of

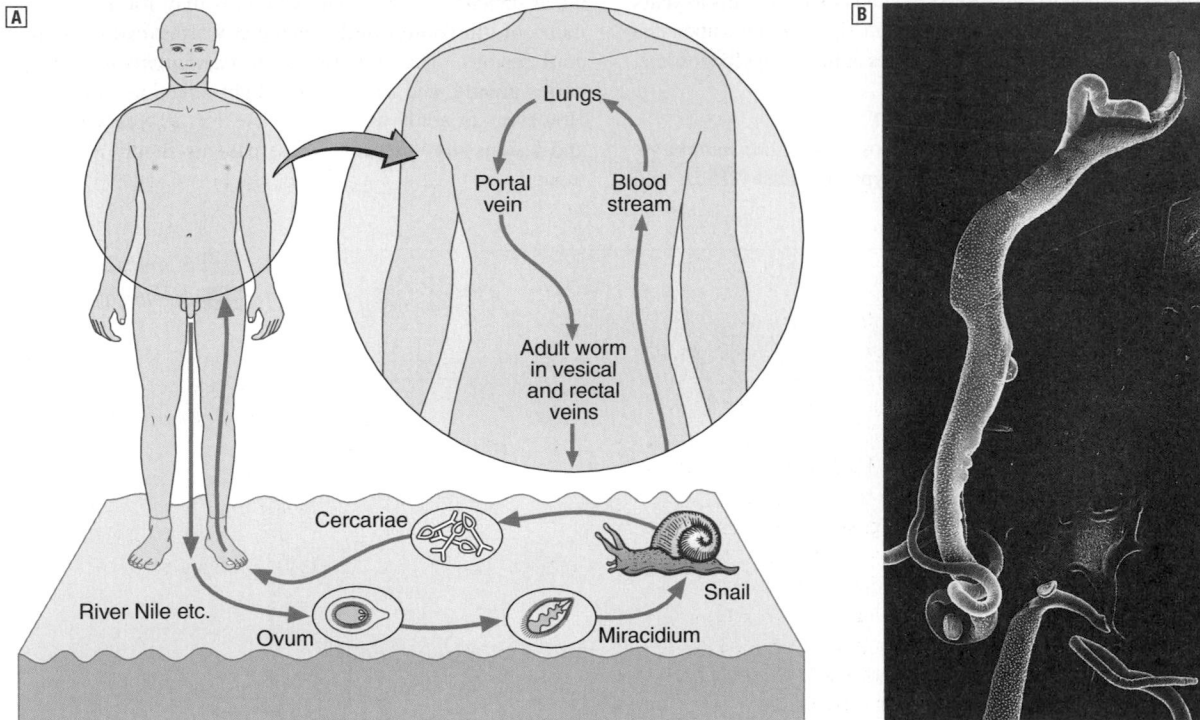

Fig. 1.60 *Schistosoma.* A Life cycle. B Scanning electron micrograph of adult schistosome worms showing the larger male worm embracing the thinner female.

1.55 PATHOGENESIS OF SCHISTOSOMIASIS			
Stage	**Time**	***S. haematobium***	***S. mansoni* and *S. japonicum***
Cercarial penetration	Days	Papular dermatitis at site of penetration	As for *S. haematobium*
Larval migration and maturation	Weeks	Pneumonitis, myositis, hepatitis, fever, 'serum sickness', eosinophilia, seroconversion	As for *S. haematobium*
Early egg deposition	Months	Cystitis, haematuria	Colitis, granulomatous hepatitis, acute portal hypertension
		Ectopic granulomatous lesions: skin, CNS etc. Immune complex glomerulonephritis	As for *S. haematobium*
Late egg deposition	Years	Fibrosis and calcification of ureters, bladder; bacterial infection, calculi, hydronephrosis, carcinoma Pulmonary granulomas and pulmonary hypertension	Colonic polyposis and strictures, periportal fibrosis, portal hypertension As for *S. haematobium*

S. *haematobium*, and of the other two species after the development of portal hypertension, may reach the lungs.

Clinical features

During the early stages of infection there may be itching lasting 1–2 days at the site of cercarial penetration. After a symptom-free period of 3–5 weeks acute schistosomiasis (Katayama syndrome) may present with allergic manifestations such as urticaria, fever, muscle aches, abdominal pain, headaches, cough and sweating. On examination hepatomegaly, splenomegaly, lymphadenopathy and pneumonia may be present. There is eosinophilia and schistosomiasis serology may be positive. These allergic phenomena (Katayama syndrome) may be severe in infections with *S. mansoni* and *S. japonicum* but are rare with *S. haematobium*. The features subside after 1–2 weeks. Chronic schistosomiasis is due to egg deposition and occurs months to years after infection. The symptoms and signs depend upon the intensity of infection and the species of infecting schistosome.

Schistosomiasis haematobium

Humans are the only natural hosts of *S. haematobium*, which is highly endemic in Egypt and East Africa, and occurs throughout most of Africa and the Middle East. There is also a solitary focus in Maharashtra, India (see Fig. 1.61).

Painless terminal haematuria is usually the first and most common symptom. Frequency of micturition follows, due to bladder neck obstruction. Later the disease may be complicated by frequent urinary tract infections, bladder or ureteric stone formation, hydronephrosis, renal functional abnormalities and ultimately renal failure with a contracted calcified bladder. Pain is often felt in the iliac fossa or in the loin and radiates to the groin. In several endemic areas there is a strong epidemiological association of *S. haematobium* infection with squamous cell carcinoma of the bladder. Disease of the seminal vesicles may lead to haemospermia. Females may develop schistosomal papillomata of the vulva, and schistosomal lesions of the cervix may be mistaken for cancer. Intestinal symptoms may follow involvement of the bowel wall. Ectopic worms cause skin or cord lesions. The severity of *S. haematobium* infection varies greatly, and many with a light infection suffer little. However, as adult worms can live for 20 years or more and lesions may progress, these patients should always be treated.

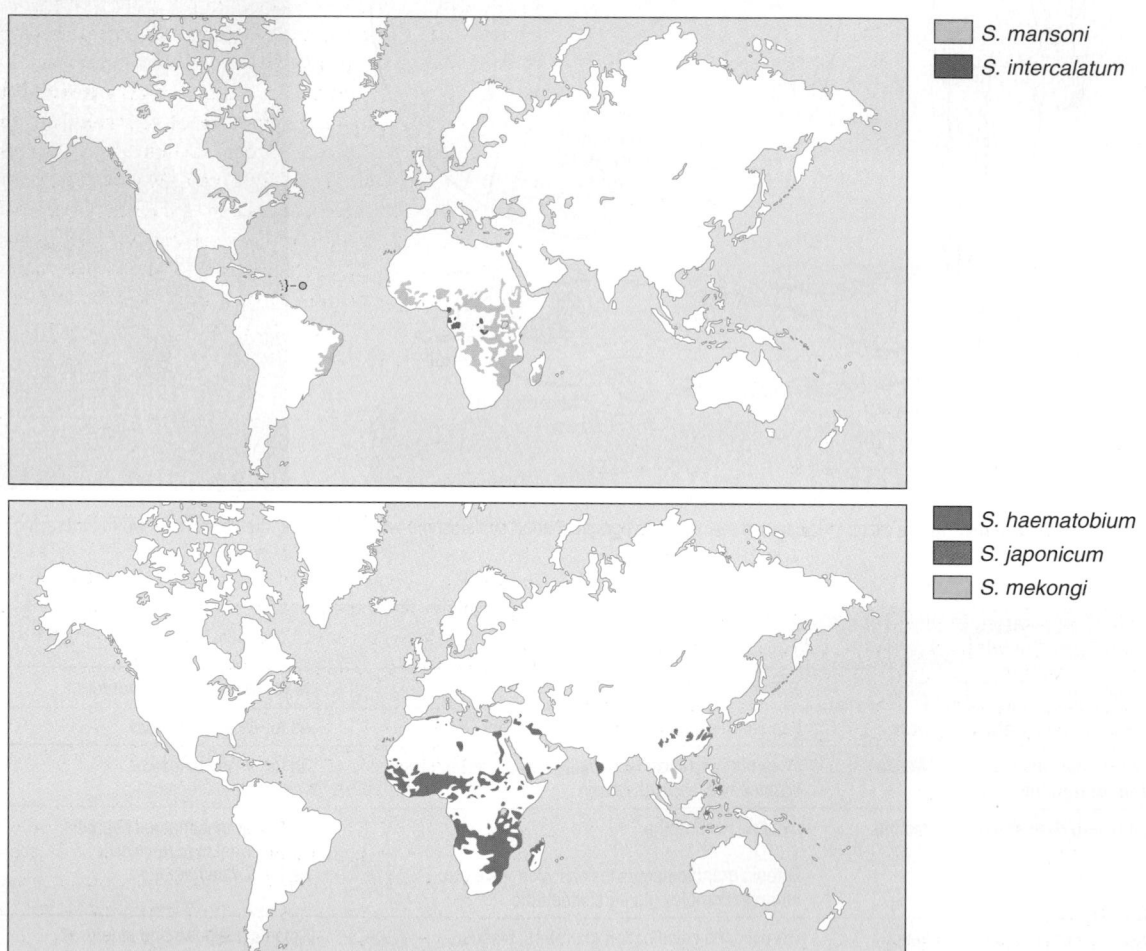

□ *S. mansoni*
■ *S. intercalatum*

■ *S. haematobium*
■ *S. japonicum*
□ *S. mekongi*

Fig. 1.61 Geographical distribution of schistosomiasis.

Schistosomiasis mansoni

S. mansoni is endemic throughout Africa, the Middle East, Venezuela, Brazil and the Caribbean (see Fig. 1.61).

Characteristic symptoms begin 2 months or more after infection. They may be slight, no more than malaise, or consist of abdominal pain and frequent stools which contain blood-stained mucus. With severe advanced disease increased discomfort from rectal polypi may be experienced. The early hepatomegaly is reversible but portal hypertension may cause massive splenomegaly, fatal haematemesis from oesophageal varices, or progressive ascites. Liver function is initially preserved because the pathology is fibrotic rather than cirrhotic. *S. mansoni* infections predispose to the carriage of *Salmonella*.

Schistosomiasis japonicum

In addition to humans the adult worm infects the dog, rat, fieldmouse, water buffalo, ox, cat, pig, horse and sheep. *S. japonicum* is prevalent in the Yellow River and Yangtze-Jiang basins in China, where the infection is a major public health problem. It also has a focal distribution in the Philippines, Indonesia and Thailand. There is now no human transmission of this parasite in Japan. A related parasite, *S. mekongi*, occurs in Laos, Thailand and Myanmar. The pathology of *S. japonicum* is similar to that of *S. mansoni*, but as this worm produces more eggs, the lesions tend to be more extensive and widespread. The clinical features resemble those of severe infection with *S. mansoni*, with added neurological features. The small bowel as well as the large may be affected, and hepatic fibrosis with splenic enlargement is usual. Deposition of eggs or worms in the central nervous system, especially in the brain, causes symptoms in about 5% of infections, notably epilepsy, hemiplegia, blindness and paraplegia.

Investigations

A history of residence in an endemic area, with characteristic symptoms, will indicate the need for investigation. Diagnosis depends on demonstrating eggs or serological evidence. In *S. haematobium* infection, dipstick urine testing shows blood and albumin. The terminal spined eggs can usually be found by microscopic examination of the centrifuged deposit of terminal stream urine. Ultrasound is useful for assessing the urinary tract and can be performed easily in the field. Bladder wall thickening, hydronephrosis and bladder calcification can be detected. Cystoscopy reveals 'sandy' patches, bleeding mucosa and later distortion.

In a heavy infection with *S. mansoni* or *S. japonicum* the characteristic egg with its lateral spine can usually be found in the stool. When the infection is light, or of long duration, a rectal biopsy can be examined. Sigmoidoscopy may show inflammation or bleeding. Biopsies should be examined for ova. Serological tests (ELISA) are useful as screening tests but remain positive after chemotherapeutic cure.

Management

The object of specific treatment is to kill the adult schistosomes and so stop egg-laying. It may not be possible or desirable to kill all adult worms by mass treatment campaigns in communities where reinfection is likely, but a reduction in egg output of around 90% is often achieved which significantly reduces morbidity, and possibly transmission, without impairing what little acquired immunity there may be. Praziquantel is the drug of choice for all forms of schistosomiasis. The drug is effective in producing parasitological cure in 80% of treated individuals and achieves over 90% reduction in egg counts in the remaining individuals. Side-effects are uncommon but include nausea and abdominal pain in individuals with heavy egg burdens. Praziquantel therapy in early infection will reverse pathologies such as hepatomegaly and bladder wall thickening.

Surgery may be required to deal with residual lesions but large vesical granulomas usually respond well to chemotherapy. Ureteric stricture and the small fibrotic urinary bladder may require plastic procedures. Removal of rectal papillomas by diathermy or by other means may provide relief. Granulomatous masses in the brain or spinal cord may require neurosurgery if the manifestations do not respond to chemotherapy and corticosteroids.

Prevention

This presents great difficulties and so far no satisfactory single means of controlling schistosomiasis has been established. The life cycle is terminated if the ova in urine or faeces are not allowed to contaminate fresh water containing the snail host. The provision of latrines and of a safe water supply, however, remains a major problem in rural areas throughout the tropics. In the case of *S. japonicum*, moreover, there are so many hosts besides humans that the proper use of latrines would be of little avail. Mass treatment of the population helps against *S. haematobium* and *S. mansoni* but this method has so far had little success with *S. japonicum*. Attack on the intermediate host, the snail, presents many difficulties and has not on its own proved successful on any scale. For personal protection, contact with infected water must be avoided.

LIVER FLUKES

Liver flukes infect at least 20 million people and remain an important public health problem in many endemic areas. They are associated with abdominal pain, hepatomegaly and relapsing cholangitis. *Clonorchis sinensis* is a major aetiological agent of bile duct cancer. The three major flukes have similar life cycles and pathologies, as outlined in Box 1.56.

CYSTICERCOSIS AND HYDATID DISEASE

Cestodes are ribbon-shaped worms which inhabit the intestinal tract. They have no alimentary system and absorb nutrients through the tegumental surface. The anterior end, or scolex, has suckers for attaching to the host. From the scolex arises a series of progressively developing segments, the proglottides, which when shed may continue to show active movements. Cross-fertilisation takes place between segments.

1.56 DISEASES CAUSED BY FLUKES IN THE BILE DUCT			
	Clonorchiasis	**Opisthorchiasis**	**Fascioliasis**
Parasite	*Clonorchis sinensis*	*Opisthorchis felineus*	*Fasciola hepatica*
Other mammalian hosts	Dogs, cats, pigs	Dogs, cats, foxes, pigs	Sheep, cattle
Mode of spread	Ova in faeces, water	As for *C. sinensis*	Ova in faeces on to wet pasture
1st intermediate host	Snails	Snails	Snails
2nd intermediate host	Fresh-water fish	Fresh-water fish	Encysts on vegetation
Geographical distribution	Far East, especially South China	Far East, especially North-east Thailand	Cosmopolitan, including UK
Pathology	*E. coli* cholangitis, abscesses, biliary carcinoma	As for *C. sinensis*	Toxaemia, cholangitis, eosinophilia
Symptoms	Often symptom-free, recurrent jaundice	As for *C. sinensis*	Obscure fever, tender liver, may be ectopic, e.g. subcutaneous fluke
Diagnosis	Ova in stool or duodenal aspirate	As for *C. sinensis*	As for *C. sinensis*, also serology
Prevention	Cook fish	Cook fish	Avoid contaminated watercress
Treatment	Praziquantel 25 mg/kg 8-hourly for 2 days	As for *C. sinensis* but for 1 day only	Triclabendazole 10 mg/kg single dose; repeat treatment may be required*
* In UK available from the Hospital for Tropical Diseases, London.			

Ova, present in large numbers in mature proglottides, remain viable for weeks and during this period they may be consumed by the intermediate host. Larvae liberated from the ingested ova pass into the tissues.

Humans acquire tapeworm by eating undercooked beef infected with *Cysticercus bovis*, the larval stage of *Taenia saginata* (beef tapeworm), undercooked pork containing *C. cellulosae*, the larval stage of *T. solium* (pork tapeworm), or undercooked freshwater fish containing larvae of *Diphyllobothrium latum* (fish tapeworm). Usually only one adult tapeworm is present in the gut but up to 10 have been reported. The life cycles of *Spirometra mansoni* and *Dipylidium caninum* involve cats and dogs; *Hymenolepis nana* has no intermediate host. *Echinococcus granulosus* is a dog tapeworm.

TAENIA SAGINATA

Infection with *T. saginata* occurs in all parts of the world. The adult worm may be several metres long and produces little or no intestinal upset in human beings, but knowledge of its presence, by noting segments in the faeces or on underclothing, may distress the patient. Ova may be found in the stool. The ova of *T. saginata* and *T. solium* are indistinguishable microscopically.

Praziquantel is the drug of choice, and prevention depends on efficient meat inspection and the thorough cooking of beef. Niclosamide is an alternative (see below).

TAENIA SOLIUM AND CYSTICERCOSIS

T. solium, the pork tapeworm, is common in central Europe, South Africa, South America and parts of Asia. It is not as large as *T. saginata*. The adult worm is found only in humans following the eating of undercooked pork containing cysticerci.

Human cysticercosis is acquired by ingesting tapeworm ova, either by ingesting ova from contaminated fingers or by eating contaminated food (see Fig. 1.62). The larvae are liberated from eggs in the stomach, penetrate the intestinal

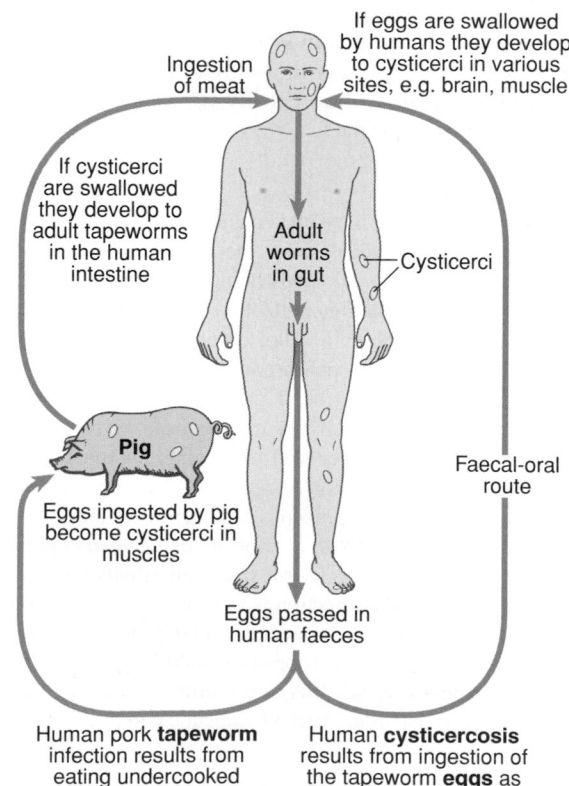

Fig. 1.62 Cysticercosis. Life cycle of *Taenia solium*.

mucosa and are carried to many parts of the body where they develop and form cysticerci, 0.5–1 cm cysts that contain the head of a young worm. They do not grow further or migrate. Common locations are the subcutaneous tissue, skeletal muscles and brain.

Clinical features

When superficially placed, cysts can be palpated under the skin or mucosa as pea-like ovoid bodies. Here they cause few or no symptoms, and will eventually die and become calcified.

Heavy brain infections, especially in children, may cause features of encephalitis. More commonly, however, cerebral signs do not occur until the larvae die, 5–20 years later. Epilepsy, personality changes, staggering gait or signs of internal hydrocephalus are the most common features.

Investigations

Calcified cysts in muscles can be recognised radiologically. In the brain, however, less calcification takes place and larvae are only occasionally demonstrated radiologically; usually CT or MRI will show them. Epileptic fits starting in adult life should suggest the possibility of cysticercosis if the patient has lived or travelled in an endemic area. The subcutaneous tissue should be palpated and any nodule excised for histology. Radiological examination of the skeletal muscles may be helpful. Antibody detection by fluorescent antibody test, ELISA or immunoblotting is available for serodiagnosis.

Management and prevention

Niclosamide, followed by a mild laxative (after 1–2 hours) to prevent retrograde intestinal autoinfection, is useful only for the intestinal infection. Praziquantel improves the prognosis of cerebral cysticercosis; the dose is 50 mg/kg in three divided doses daily for 10 days. Albendazole, 15 mg/kg daily for a minimum of 8 days, has now become the drug of choice for parenchymal neurocysticercosis. Prednisolone, 10 mg 8-hourly, is also given for 14 days, starting 1 day before the albendazole or praziquantel. In addition, anti-epileptic drugs should be given until the reaction in the brain has subsided. Operative intervention is indicated for hydrocephalus. Studies from India and Peru suggest that most small solitary cerebral cysts will resolve without treatment.

Cooking pork well will prevent infection with *T. solium*. Cysticercosis is avoided if food is not contaminated by ova or segments. Great care must be taken by nurses and other adults while attending a patient harbouring an adult worm.

ECHINOCOCCUS GRANULOSUS (TAENIA ECHINOCOCCUS) AND HYDATID DISEASE

Dogs are the definitive hosts of the tiny tapeworm *E. granulosus*. The larval stage, a hydatid cyst, normally occurs in sheep, cattle, camels and other animals that are infected from contaminated pastures or water. By handling a dog or drinking contaminated water, humans may ingest eggs (see Fig. 1.63). The embryo is liberated from the ovum in the small intestine and gains access to the blood stream and thus

[A]

Sheep etc.
Hydatid cysts in liver, lung etc.

Faeces
Ova

Dog etc.
Worms in gut

Human
Hydatid cysts in liver, lung etc.

[B]

[C]
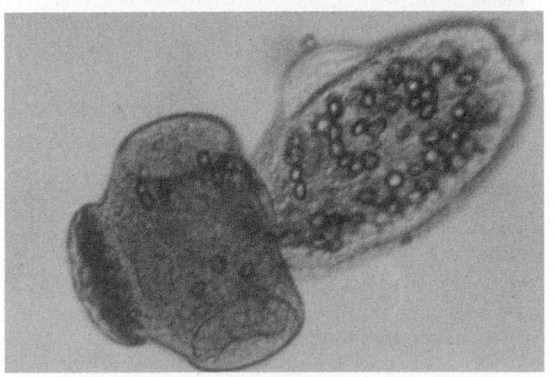

Fig. 1.63   Hydatid disease. [A] Life cycle of *Echinococcus granulosus*. [B] Daughter cysts removed at surgery. [C] Within the daughter cysts are the protoscolices.

to the liver. The resultant cyst grows very slowly, sometimes intermittently, and may outlive the patient. It may calcify or rupture, giving rise to multiple cysts. The disease is common in the Middle East, North and East Africa, Australia and Argentina. Foci of infection persist in rural Wales and Scotland. *E. multilocularis*, which has a cycle between foxes and voles, causes a similar but more severe infection, 'alveolar hydatid disease', which invades the liver like cancer.

Clinical features

A hydatid cyst is typically acquired in childhood and it may, after growing for some years, cause pressure symptoms. These vary, depending on the organ or tissue involved. In nearly 75% of patients with hydatid disease the right lobe of the liver is invaded and contains a single cyst. In others a cyst may be found in lung, bone, brain or elsewhere.

Investigations

The diagnosis depends on the clinical, radiological and ultrasound findings in a patient who has lived in close contact with dogs in an endemic area. Complement fixation and ELISA are positive in 70–90% of patients.

Management and prevention

Hydatid cysts should be excised wherever possible. Great care is taken to avoid spillage and cavities are sterilised with

0.5% silver nitrate or 2.7% sodium chloride. Albendazole (400 mg 12-hourly for 3 months) is used for inoperable disease, and to reduce the infectivity of cysts pre-operatively. Praziquantel 20 mg/kg 12-hourly for 14 days kills protoscolices perioperatively.

Prevention is difficult in situations where there is a close association with dogs and sheep. Personal hygiene, satisfactory disposal of carcasses, meat inspection and deworming of dogs can greatly reduce the prevalence of disease.

OTHER TAPEWORMS

There are many other cestodes whose adult or larval stages may infect humans. Sparganosis is a condition in which an immature worm develops in humans, usually subcutaneously, as a result of eating or applying to the skin the secondary or tertiary intermediate host.

SKIN CONDITIONS IN THE TROPICS

Community-based studies in the tropics consistently show that scabies, skin infections (bacterial and fungal) and eczema are the most common skin problems in the tropics. Bacterial skin infections are discussed on pages 23–27. The

1.57 COMMON CAUSES OF SKIN LESIONS IN THE TROPICS

Lesion type	Aetiology	Clinical features
Papules		
Scabies (see p. 1085)	*Sarcoptes scabiei*	Raised linear burrows
Insect bites	Mosquito	Pruritic weal, flare or papule
	Flea	Discrete pruritic papule with central haemorrhagic punctum
	Tick	Painful swelling with central necrosis and erythematous margin
	Bedbug	Pruritic papules in a linear configuration
Prickly heat	Heat with humidity	Erythematous, papular and vesicular eruption around sweat glands
Ringworm (see p. 1083)	*Tinea corporis*	Circular, raised, sharply marginated
Onchocerciasis (see p. 75)	*Onchocerca volvulus*	Pruritic, papular rash
Linear lesions		
Cutaneous larva migrans	*Ancylostoma caninum*	Severely pruritic serpiginous track
Larva currens	*Strongyloides stercoralis*	Pruritic, fast-moving erythematous band
Ulcers		
Ecthyma (see p. 23)	*Staphylococcus aureus*, β-haemolytic streptococcus	Vesicle or crusted pustule
Oriental sore, Delhi boil, chiclero ulcer etc.	*Leishmania*	Indolent, slow-healing ulcer
Anthrax (see p. 27)	*Bacillus anthracis*	Single black, oedematous, painless lesion
Rickettsial eschar	*Rickettsia conorii* and *R. tsutsugamushi*	Small ulcer with black centre, systemic illness
Buruli ulcer	*Mycobacterium ulcerans*	Nodule and ulceration
Tropical ulcer	*Fusobacterium ulcerans* and *Treponema vincenti*	Sharply defined painful ulcer, usually on lower leg
Vesicles		
Insect bites	Spanish fly *(Lytta vesicatoria)* Rove beetle	Blister produced from contact with insect toxins
Subcutaneous swellings		
Myiasis	*Dermatobia hominis* larva, *Cordylobia anthropophaga* larva	Larva protruding from subcutaneous cavity
Tungiasis (jiggers)	*Tunga penetrans*	Small black dot, developing into an inflammatory nodule
Fungal infections	*Sporothrix schenckii*	Hard, non-tender subcutaneous nodules, later ulcerate
Dracunculiasis	*Dracunculus medinensis*	Erythema, ulceration and induration; worm may protrude

other conditions are dealt with in Chapter 21. Cutaneous leishmaniasis, onchocerciasis and deep fungal infections are rare and have defined geographical distributions. In travellers secondarily infected insect bites, pyoderma, cutaneous larva migrans and non-specific dermatitis are the most common skin lesions. Enquire about habitation, work and travel when investigating these lesions. Box 1.57 lists the common lesions, their aetiology and clinical features.

CUTANEOUS LARVA MIGRANS

Cutaneous larva migrans (CLM) is the most common linear lesion seen in travellers. Intensely pruritic, linear serpiginous lesions result from the larval migration of the dog hookworm *(Ancylostoma caninum)*. The track moves across the skin at a rate of 2–3 cm/day. This contrasts with the rash of *Strongyloides* (see p. 71), which is fast-moving and evanescent. Dog hookworms rarely establish infection in humans. The most common site for CLM is the foot but elbows, breasts and buttocks may be affected. Most patients with CLM have recently visited a beach where the affected part

was exposed. The diagnosis is clinical. Treatment may be local with 12-hourly application of 15% tiabendazole cream or systemic with albendazole 400 mg daily for 3 days or a single dose of ivermectin.

CUTANEOUS LEISHMANIASIS

Cutaneous leishmaniasis (CL) is caused by the protozoon *Leishmania*. The geographical origin of the parasite is critical (see Fig. 1.64); in the Old World cutaneous disease is mild, while in the Americas the disease may involve the nose and mouth. The disease is commonly imported into Britain. CL should be considered in the differential diagnosis of an ulcerating skin lesion, especially in travellers who have visited forests in Central and South America.

Old World cutaneous leishmaniasis (oriental sore)

Cutaneous leishmaniasis is found around the Mediterranean basin, throughout the Middle East and Central Asia as far as

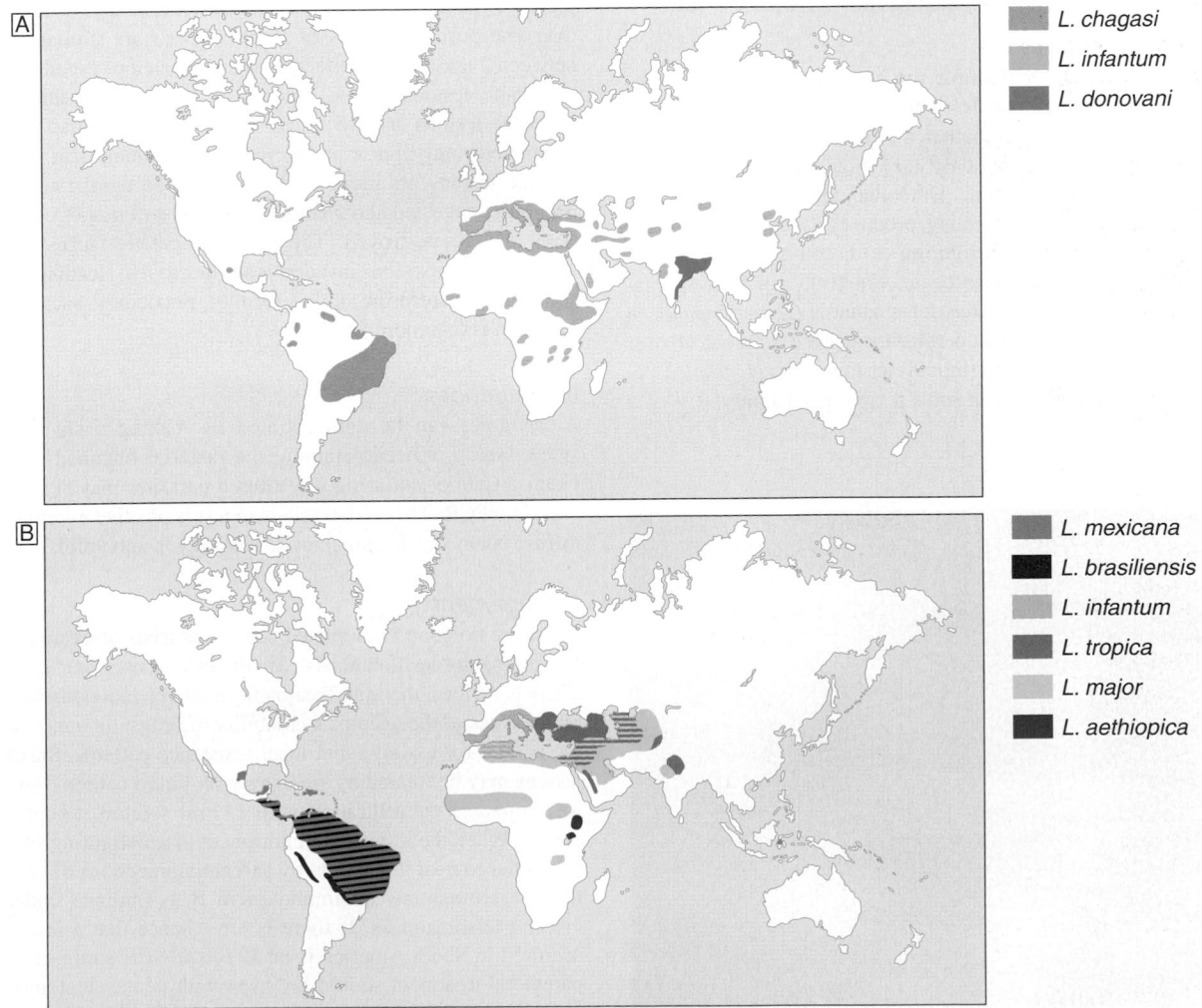

Fig. 1.64 World distribution of human leishmaniasis. Ⓐ Visceral leishmaniasis. Ⓑ Cutaneous leishmaniasis.

1.58 TYPES OF OLD WORLD *LEISHMANIA*		
Leishmania species	**Host**	**Clinical features**
L. tropica	Dogs	Slow evolution, less severe
L. major	Gerbils, desert rodents	Rapid necrosis, wet sores
L. aethiopica	Hyraxes	Solitary facial lesions with satellites

Pakistan, and in sub-Saharan West Africa and Sudan (see Fig. 1.64). The parasites *L. tropica*, *L. major* and *L. aethiopica* are the main species (see Box 1.58).

Pathogenesis

Inoculated parasites are taken up by dermal macrophages where they multiply and form a focus for lymphocytes, epithelioid cells and plasma cells. Self-healing may occur with necrosis of infected macrophages, or the lesion may become chronic with ulceration of the overlying epidermis. The incubation period is 2–3 months (range 2 weeks–5 years).

Clinical features

Lesions, single or multiple, on exposed parts of the body, start as small red papules which increase gradually in size, reaching 2–10 cm in diameter. A crust forms, overlying an ulcer with a granular base (see Fig. 1.65). Tiny satellite papules are characteristic. Untreated, the lesions heal slowly over many months. Healing produces a depressed mottled scar which may be disfiguring or disabling. Two forms of cutaneous leishmaniasis occur which do not heal spontaneously: diffuse cutaneous leishmaniasis (*L. aethiopica*), in which an immune defect permits the disease to spread all over the skin, and recidivans (lupoid) leishmaniasis (*L. tropica*), in which apparently healed sores relapse persistently.

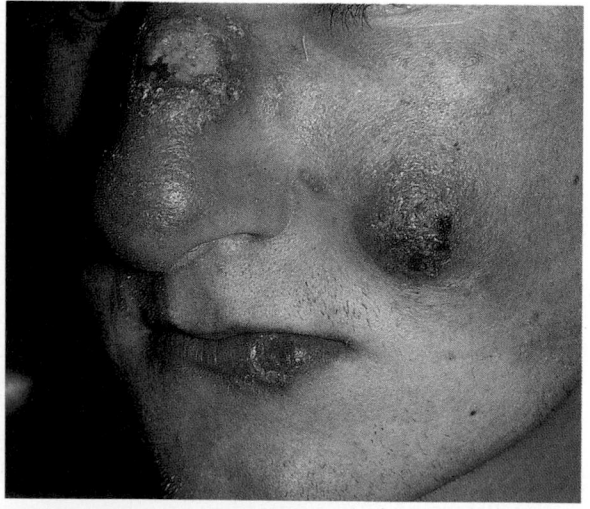

Fig. 1.65   Cutaneous leishmaniasis.

New World cutaneous and mucosal leishmaniasis

In South and Central America, cutaneous leishmaniasis is endemic in hot, moist forest regions but spread is now occurring into urban areas (see Fig. 1.64). The two main parasite groups are *L. mexicana* and the *Vianna* subgenus which includes *L. brasiliensis*, *L. panamensis* and *L. peruviana*. The *Vianna* subgenus extends widely from the Amazon basin as far as Paraguay and Costa Rica and is responsible for deep sores and mucosal leishmaniasis. *L. mexicana* is responsible for chiclero ulcers, the self-healing sores of Mexico.

Pathogenesis

Microscopically, the appearances are similar to Old World cutaneous leishmaniasis. Mucosal lesions begin as a perivascular infiltration; later endarteritis may cause destruction of the surrounding tissues.

Clinical features

Clinically, lesions of *L. mexicana* and *L. peruviana* closely resemble those seen in the Old World, but lesions on the pinna of the ear are common and are chronic and destructive. The primary lesions of *L. brasiliensis* are similar but between 2 and 40% of infected persons develop 'espundia', metastatic lesions in the mucosa of the nose or mouth. Mucosal lesions usually occur 1–2 years after the skin lesions but may appear many years later. Young men with chronic lesions are particularly at risk. The nasal mucosa becomes congested and ulcerates; later, all soft tissues of the nose may be destroyed. The lips, soft palate, fauces and larynx may also be invaded and destroyed, leading to considerable suffering and deformity. Secondary bacterial infection is common.

Investigations

Amastigotes can be demonstrated by making a slit skin smear (see p. 90) and staining the material obtained with Giemsa stain or culturing it. Cultured parasites may be speciated by PCR. The leishmanin skin test is positive except in diffuse cutaneous leishmaniasis. Serology is unhelpful.

Management

There are no good randomised controlled trials of treatment for cutaneous leishmaniasis. Small lesions may self-heal. There is no ideal therapy. Treatment should be individualised on the basis of the lesions, availability of drugs, tolerance of the patient for toxicity, and local resistance patterns. Small lesions may be treated by freezing with liquid carbon dioxide, curettage or infiltration with 1–2 ml sodium stibogluconate. When the lesions are multiple or in a disfiguring site, it is better to treat the patient by parenteral injections of pentavalent antimonials or amphotericin B as outlined under visceral leishmaniasis. If there is any chance that a lesion acquired in South America is an *L. brasiliensis* strain, then parenteral treatment should be given with pentavalent antimony (20 mg/kg for 20 days) to prevent the development of mucosal disease.

Prevention
Personal protection against sandfly bites is important. No effective vaccine is yet available.

TROPICAL ULCER

Tropical ulcer is due to a synergistic bacterial infection between a fusobacterium *(F. ulcerans)*, an anaerobe and *Treponema vincenti*. It is common in hot humid regions.

Clinical features
The ulcer is most common on the lower legs and develops as a papule that rapidly breaks down to a sharply defined, painful ulcer. The base of the ulcer has a foul slough.

Management
Penicillin and metronidazole are useful in the early stages but rest, elevation and dressings are the mainstays of treatment.

BURULI ULCER

This ulcer is caused by *Mycobacterium ulcerans* and occurs world-wide in tropical rainforests. In 1999 a survey in Ghana found 6500 cases; there are an estimated 10 000 cases in West Africa.

Pathogenesis
The ulcer starts with acute necrosis. Clumps of acid-fast bacilli are present on the ulcer floor. Later, healing occurs with granuloma formation.

Clinical features
The initial lesion is a small subcutaneous nodule on the arm or leg. This breaks down to form a shallow, necrotic ulcer with deeply undermined edges which extends rapidly. Healing may occur after 6 months but the accompanying fibrosis causes contractures and deformity.

Management
Antibiotics are not clinically useful. Infected tissue should be removed surgically.

Prevention
Health campaigns in Ghana have successfully focused on early removal of the small, pre-ulcerative nodules.

YAWS

Yaws is a granulomatous disease mainly involving the skin and bones which is caused by *Treponema pertenue*, morphologically indistinguishable from the causative organisms of syphilis and pinta. The three infections induce similar serological changes and possibly some degree of cross-immunity. Organisms are transmitted by bodily contact from a patient with infectious yaws through minor abrasions of the skin of another patient, usually a child. The mass WHO campaigns between 1950 and 1960 treated over 60 million people and eradicated yaws from many areas, but the disease has persisted patchily throughout the tropics; there was a resurgence in the 1980s and 1990s in West and Central Africa and the South Pacific.

Pathology
A proliferative granuloma containing numerous treponemes develops at the site of the inoculation. This primary lesion is followed by secondary eruptions. In addition, there may be hypertrophic periosteal lesions of many bones, with underlying cortical rarefaction. Lesions of late yaws are characterised by destructive changes which closely resemble the osteitis and gummas of tertiary syphilis and which heal with much scarring and deformity. The incubation period is 3–4 weeks.

Clinical features

Early yaws
The primary lesion or 'mother yaw' is usually on the leg or buttocks. The secondary eruption usually follows a few weeks or months later, as crops of papillomas covered with a whitish-yellow exudate, especially in the flexures and around the mouth. Sometimes a lesion erupts through the palm or sole, and walking becomes painful ('wet crab yaws'). Phalanges, nasal bones and tibiae swell and become distorted. Most of the lesions of early yaws will eventually subside, even if untreated.

Latent yaws
Following the spontaneous resolution of 'early yaws', serological changes may persist, to be followed by further manifestations of 'early yaws' or, after an interval of as much as 5–10 years, by the tertiary lesions or 'late yaws'.

Late yaws
Solitary or multiple lesions appear as nodules or ulcers in the skin, hyperkeratotic lesions of palms or soles ('dry crab yaws') and gummatous lesions of bone. They heal with scarring. Lesions of the facial and palatal bones cause terrible disfigurement (gangosa).

Investigations and management
See Box 1.59.

Prevention
The disease disappears with improved housing and cleanliness. In few fields of medicine have chemotherapy and improved hygiene achieved such dramatic success as in the control of yaws.

1.59 DIAGNOSIS AND TREATMENT OF YAWS, PINTA AND BEJEL
Diagnosis of early stages
• Detection of spirochaetes in exudate of lesions by dark ground microscopy
Diagnosis of latent and early stages
• Positive serological tests, as for syphilis (see p. 99)
Treatment of all stages
• Single intramuscular injection of 1.2 g long-acting (e.g. benzathine) penicillin G

PINTA AND BEJEL

These two treponemal infections occur in poor rural populations with low standards of domestic hygiene, but in separate parts of the world. They have features in common, notably that they are transmitted by contact, usually within the family and not sexually, and in the case of bejel, through common eating and drinking utensils. Their diagnosis and management are as for yaws (see Box 1.59).

Pinta

Pinta is probably the oldest of the human treponemal infections and *T. carateum* the parent of the organism that came to Europe with the return of Christopher Columbus's sailors in 1493, starting the epidemic of venereal syphilis known as the 'Great Pox'. It is found only in South and Central America, where its incidence is declining. The early lesions are scaly papules or dyschromic patches on the skin. The late lesions are often depigmented and disfiguring. The infection is confined to the skin.

Bejel

Bejel is the Middle Eastern name for non-venereal syphilis, which has a patchy distribution across sub-Saharan Africa, the Middle East, Central Asia and Australia. It has been eradicated from Eastern Europe. Transmission is most commonly from the mouth of the mother or child and the primary mucosal lesion is seldom seen. The early and late lesions resemble those of secondary and tertiary syphilis (see pp. 96–100) but cardiovascular and neurological disease is rare.

SUBCUTANEOUS SWELLINGS

These may be due to direct invasion of the skin (as in myiasis), due to parasite emergence through the skin (dracunculiasis) or a manifestation of immune reactivity to parasite antigens in the skin (Calabar swellings, see p. 75).

JIGGERS (TUNGIASIS)

This is widespread in tropical America and Africa and is caused by the sand flea *Tunga penetrans*. The pregnant flea burrows into the skin around toes and produces large numbers of eggs. The burrows are intensely irritating and the whole inflammatory nodule should be removed with a sterile needle. Secondary infection of tunga lesions is common.

MYIASIS

Myiasis is due to skin infestation with larvae of the South American botfly, *Dermatobia hominis*, and the African Tumbu fly, *Cordylobia anthropophaga*. The larvae develop in a subcutaneous space with a central sinus. This orifice is the air source for the larvae, and periodically the larval respiratory spiracles protrude through the sinus. Patients with myiasis feel movement within the larval burrow and experience intermittent sharp, lancinating pains. Myiasis is

diagnosed clinically and should be suspected in any furuncular lesion accompanied by pain and a crawling sensation in the skin. The larva may be extruded by squeezing gently on the burrow and catching it with tweezers. Alternatively, the larva may be suffocated by blocking the respiratory orifice with petroleum jelly. Secondary infection of myiasis is remarkably infrequent and rapid healing follows removal of intact larvae.

DRACUNCULIASIS (GUINEA WORM)

Guinea worm (*Dracunculus medinensis*) infestation manifests when the female worm, over a metre long, emerges from the skin. Humans are infected by ingesting a small crustacean, *Cyclops*, which inhabits wells and ponds and contains the infective larval stage of the worm. The worm was widely distributed across Africa and the Middle East. It has now nearly been eradicated from Pakistan and India and numbers have decreased spectacularly elsewhere.

Pathology

Ingested larvae mature, penetrate the intestinal wall and migrate through the host connective tissues. After 9–18 months the mature female surfaces under the skin, usually on the leg, where a vesicle is raised, ruptures and discharges worm larvae. The worm is attracted to the surface by cooling; hence the larvae are likely to be expelled into water, where they complete the life cycle.

The disease can be extremely disabling. It is especially liable to affect those who collect water at water-holes, or farmers at the beginning of the rains, and thus seriously interferes with planting.

Clinical features

The adult worm may sometimes be felt beneath the skin. Some hours before the head of the worm emerges from the skin there is painful, hot, local vesicular inflammation. The larvae are discharged over 3–4 weeks; during this time the ulcer persists and there is pain and cellulitis. A marked allergic inflammation occurs if the worm dies or is broken during extraction. Secondary infection is common with cellulitis and arthritis, especially if the worm is close to an ankle or knee. Tetanus is a well-recognised complication.

Diagnosis

This is clinical. Discharge fluid may contain larvae. A radiograph may show calcified worms.

Management

Traditionally, the protruding worm is extracted by winding it out gently over several days on a matchstick. The worm must never be broken. Metronidazole or tiabendazole may reduce inflammation and aid the extraction of the worm. Antibiotics for secondary infection and prophylaxis of tetanus are also required.

Prevention

The global elimination campaign is based on the provision of clean drinking water and eradication of water fleas from drinking water. The latter is being achieved by simple filtration of water through a plastic mesh filter and chemical treatment of water supplies.

MYCETOMA (MADURA FOOT)

Mycetoma, in this restricted sense, is a chronic fungal infection of the deep soft tissues and bones, most commonly of the limbs but also of the abdominal or chest wall or head. It is produced by the fungal groups *Eumycetes* and *Actinomycetes*. Both groups produce characteristically coloured grains.

Pathology

The histology is that of a chronic granuloma with a fibrous stroma and cyst-like spaces in which lie the characteristic grains.

Clinical features

The fungus is usually introduced by a thorn and the infection is most common in the foot. The mycetoma begins as a painless swelling at the site of implantation, which grows and spreads steadily within the soft tissues, causing further swelling, and eventually penetrates bones. Nodules develop under the epidermis and these rupture revealing sinuses through which grains are discharged. Some sinuses may heal with scarring while fresh sinuses appear elsewhere.

There is little pain and usually no fever or lymphadenopathy, but there is progressive disability. When the lesion is in the scalp, the skull may be affected but the dura mater appears to be an effective barrier. *Nocardia brasiliensis* often affects the skin of the back. It is seldom localised and may spread widely.

Investigations

Diagnosis is confirmed by demonstration of fungal grains in pus or tissue biopsy. Culture is usually necessary for species identification. Serology may be helpful.

Management

Localised lesions that can be excised without residual disability are best so treated. Medical treatment of fungal mycetomas is unsatisfactory.

Among the fungal causes of mycetoma *Madurella mycetomatis* is the most sensitive to therapy, responding to ketoconazole in about 60% of cases. For the other cases treatment with griseofulvin or itraconazole may slow the progress of infection. Amputation should be considered carefully as in many countries it may deprive patients of their livelihood.

Actinomycetes may be susceptible to treatment with combinations of rifampicin and dapsone for 3 months or cotrimoxazole for 4–24 months. *Nocardia* infection may respond to dapsone alone.

LEPROSY

Leprosy (Hansen's disease) is a chronic granulomatous disease affecting skin and nerve; it is caused by *Mycobacterium leprae*. The clinical form of the disease is determined by the degree of cell-mediated immunity (CMI) expressed by that individual towards *M. leprae* (see Fig. 1.66). High levels of CMI with elimination of leprosy bacilli produce tuberculoid leprosy, whereas absent CMI results in lepromatous leprosy. The medical complications of leprosy are due to nerve damage, immunological reactions and bacillary infiltration. Nerve damage accompanying leprosy is a serious complication causing considerable morbidity. Leprosy patients are frequently stigmatised and using the word 'leper' is inappropriate.

Organism

M. leprae still cannot be grown in vitro but does grow in the nude mouse footpad and nine-banded armadillos. It grows at 30–33°C, has a doubling time of 12 days and is a stable, hardy organism which withstands drying for up to 5 months. It possesses a complex cell wall and synthesises a species-specific phenolic glycolipid (PGL). The genome of *M. leprae* has undergone massive gene decay and differs from *M. tuberculosis* by only 29 functional genes. Analysis of these proteins will be critical for understanding the survival and pathogenesis of *M. leprae*.

Epidemiology

Some 4 million people have or are disabled by leprosy. World-wide active transmission continues with 800 000 new cases annually and high rates of childhood cases. About 70% of the world's leprosy patients live in India with Brazil, Indonesia, Myanmar, Madagascar and Nepal being the next most endemic countries. Intensive week-long leprosy elimination campaigns in 1999 detected many new cases; in Nepal 11 696 new cases were found, doubling the national caseload. All new cases seen in the UK have acquired their infection abroad. Age, sex and household contact are important determinants of leprosy risk; leprosy incidence reaches a peak at 10–14 years, and an excess of male cases has been regularly found. HIV infection is not a risk factor for leprosy. HIV/leprosy coinfected patients have typical skin lesions and typical leprosy histology and granuloma formation even with low circulating CD4 counts.

Transmission

Untreated lepromatous patients discharge bacilli from the nose. Infection occurs through the nose followed by haematogenous spread to skin and nerve. The incubation period is 2–5 years for tuberculoid cases and 8–12 years for lepromatous cases.

Pathogenesis

M. leprae has a predilection for Schwann cells and skin macrophages and the host response is critical in determining the outcome of infection. There are three important aspects of leprosy pathogenesis: the spectrum of immune responses, nerve damage and immune-mediated reactions. Figure 1.66 shows the Ridley–Jopling spectrum of response. At the tuberculoid pole, well-expressed CMI and delayed hypersensitivity control bacillary multiplication; organised epithelioid granulomata are seen in tissue biopsies. In the lepromatous form, there is cellular anergy towards *M. leprae*,

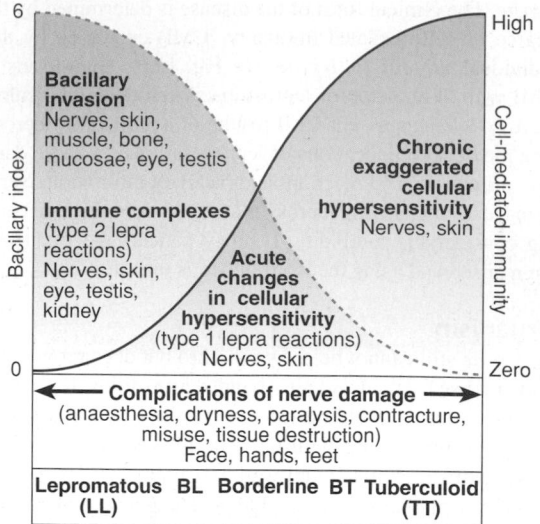

Fig. 1.66 **Leprosy: mechanisms of damage and tissue affected.**
Mechanisms under the broken line are characteristic of disease near the lepromatous end of the spectrum and those under the solid line of the tuberculoid end. They overlap in the centre where, in addition, instability predisposes to type 1 lepra reactions. At the peak in the centre neither bacillary growth nor cell-mediated immunity has the upper hand. (BL = borderline lepromatous; BT = borderline tuberculoid)

resulting in abundant bacillary multiplication. Between these two poles is a continuum, varying from patients with moderate CMI (borderline tuberculoid) to patients with little cellular response (borderline lepromatous). The polar groups are stable but the central groups are immunologically unstable.

Both T cells and macrophages are important in the response to *M. leprae* antigens. Tuberculoid patients have a Th1-type response to *M. leprae*, producing interleukin-2 (IL-2) and interferon-γ (IFN-γ), and positive lepromin (a soluble *M. leprae* preparation) skin test responses. This strong cell-mediated response clears antigen, but with local tissue destruction. Lepromatous patients have a specific cell-mediated T cell and macrophage anergy to *M. leprae* and poor lymphocyte responses to *M. leprae* antigens in vitro. They are negative on lepromin skin testing. They produce Th2-type cytokines.

Nerve damage occurs across the spectrum in skin lesions and peripheral nerves. In tuberculoid disease epithelioid granulomata are found. In lepromatous leprosy bacilli are found in Schwann cells and the perineurium. Immune-mediated events are responsible for leprosy reactions (see below).

Clinical features

Patients commonly present with skin lesions or the effects of a peripheral nerve lesion, weakness or an ulcer in an anaesthetic hand or foot. Borderline patients may present as a reaction to nerve pain, sudden palsy, multiple new skin lesions. Box 1.60 gives the cardinal signs of leprosy.

Skin. The most common skin lesions are macules or plaques. In lepromatous leprosy, papules, nodules or diffuse infiltration of the skin occurs. Tuberculoid patients have few, hypopigmented lesions whilst lepromatous patients have numerous, sometimes confluent lesions.

Anaesthesia. Anaesthesia occurs in skin lesions when dermal nerves are involved or in the distribution of a large peripheral nerve. In skin lesions the small dermal sensory and autonomic nerve fibres are damaged causing local sensory loss and loss of sweating within that area.

Peripheral neuropathy. Peripheral nerve trunks are affected at 'sites of predilection'. These are the ulnar (at the elbow), median (at the wrist), radial in the radial groove of the humerus causing wrist drop, radial cutaneous (at the wrist), common peroneal (at the knee), posterior tibial and sural nerves at the ankle, facial nerve as it crosses the zygomatic arch, and great auricular in the posterior triangle of the neck. Damage to peripheral nerve trunks produces characteristic signs with regional sensory loss and dysfunction of muscles supplied by that peripheral nerve. All these nerves should be examined for enlargement and tenderness and tested for motor and sensory function. The central nervous system is not affected.

Eye involvement. Blindness due to leprosy is a devastating complication for a patient with anaesthetic hands and feet. Eyelid closure is impaired when the facial nerve is affected. Damage to the trigeminal (5th) nerve causes anaesthesia of the cornea and conjunctiva. The cornea is then susceptible to trauma and ulceration.

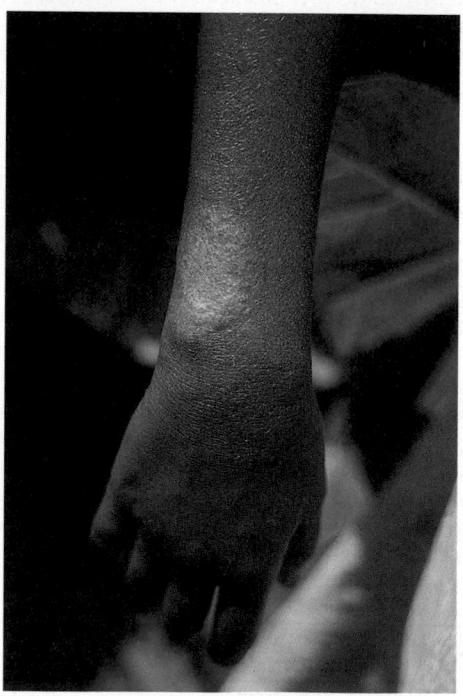

Fig. 1.67 **Tuberculoid leprosy.** Single lesion with a well-defined active edge and anaesthesia within the lesion.

1.60 CARDINAL FEATURES OF LEPROSY	

- Skin lesions, typically anaesthetic at tuberculoid end of spectrum
- Thickened peripheral nerves
- Acid-fast bacilli on skin smears or biopsy

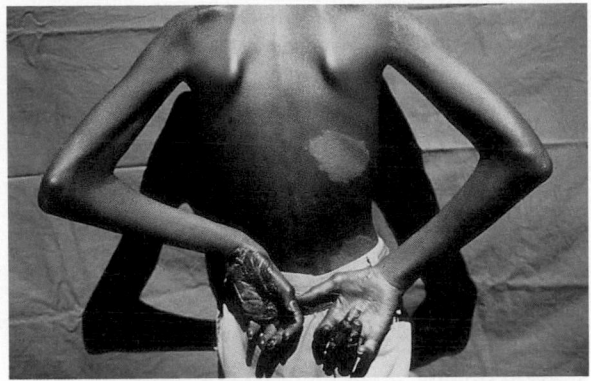

Fig. 1.68 Borderline tuberculoid leprosy with severe nerve damage. This boy has several well-defined, hypopigmented, macular, anaesthetic lesions. He has severe nerve damage affecting both ulnar and median nerves bilaterally and has sustained severe burns to his hands.

Tuberculoid leprosy

Tuberculoid leprosy (see Fig. 1.67) has a good prognosis; it may self-heal and peripheral nerve damage is limited.

Borderline tuberculoid

The skin lesions (see Fig. 1.68) are similar to those in tuberculoid leprosy but are more numerous. Damage to peripheral nerves may be widespread and severe. These patients are prone to type 1 reactions with consequent nerve damage.

Borderline leprosy

Borderline leprosy is unstable and patients have numerous skin lesions varying in size, shape and distribution. Annular lesions with a broad, irregular edge and a sharply defined, punched-out centre are characteristic. Nerve damage is variable.

Borderline lepromatous leprosy

Borderline lepromatous leprosy is characterised by widespread small macules. They may experience both type 1 and type 2 reactions. Peripheral nerve involvement is widespread.

Lepromatous leprosy

The earliest lesions are ill defined; gradually, the skin becomes infiltrated and thickened. Facial skin thickening leads to the characteristic leonine facies (see Fig. 1.69). Dermal nerves are destroyed, sweating is lost, and a 'glove and stocking' neuropathy is common. Nerve damage to large peripheral nerves occurs late in the disease. Nasal collapse occurs secondary to bacillary destruction of the bony nasal spine. Testicular atrophy is caused by diffuse infiltration and

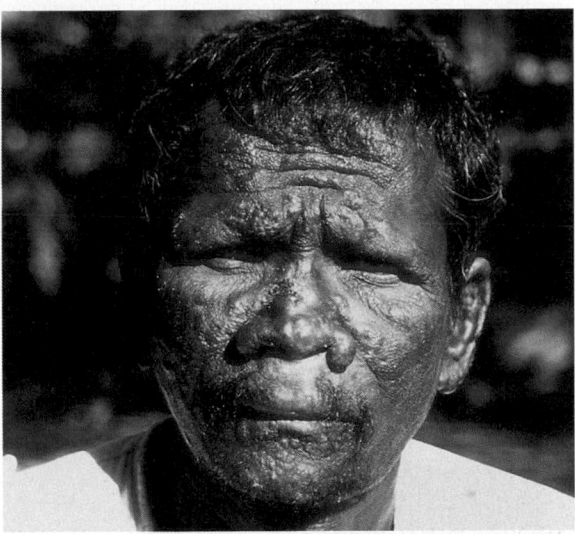

Fig. 1.69 Lepromatous leprosy. Widespread nodules and infiltration with loss of the eyebrows. This man also has early collapse of the nose.

1.61 CLINICAL CHARACTERISTICS OF THE POLAR FORMS OF LEPROSY

Clinical and tissue-specific features	Lepromatous	Tuberculoid
Skin and nerves Number and distribution	Widely disseminated	One or a few sites, asymmetrical
Skin lesions Definition		
Clarity of margin	Poor	Good
Elevation of margin	Never	Common
Colour		
Dark skin	Slight hypopigmentation	Marked hypopigmentation
Light skin	Slight erythema	Coppery or red
Surface	Smooth, shiny	Dry, scaly
Central healing	None	Common
Sweat and hair growth	Impaired late	Impaired early
Loss of sensation	Late	Early and marked
Nerve enlargement and damage	Late	Early and marked
Bacilli (bacterial index)	Many (5 or 6+)	Absent (0)
Natural outcome	Progression	Healing
Other tissues	Upper respiratory mucosa, eye, testes, bones, muscle	None
Reactions	Immune complexes	Cell-mediated

the acute orchitis that occurs with type 2 reactions. This results in azoospermia and gynaecomastia (see Box 1.61).

Pure neural leprosy

This occurs principally in India and accounts for 10% of patients. There is asymmetrical involvement of peripheral nerve trunks and no visible skin lesions. On nerve biopsy all types of leprosy have been found.

Leprosy reactions

Leprosy reactions (see Box 1.62) are events superimposed on the cardinal features shown in Box 1.60).

Type 1 (reversal) reactions

These occur in 30% of borderline patients (BT, BB, BL) and are delayed hypersensitivity reactions caused by increased recognition of *M. leprae* antigens in skin and nerve sites. Skin lesions become erythematous (see Fig. 1.70); peripheral nerves become tender and painful. Loss of nerve function can be sudden, with foot drop occurring overnight. Reversal reactions may occur spontaneously, after starting treatment and also after completion of multidrug therapy.

Type 2 (erythema nodosum leprosum—ENL) reactions

These are partly due to immune complex deposition and occur in BL and LL patients who produce antibodies and have a high antigen load. They manifest with malaise, fever and crops of small pink nodules on the face and limbs. Iritis and episcleritis are common. Other signs are acute neuritis,

Fig. 1.70 Reversal reactions. Erythematous, oedematous lesions.

lymphadenitis, orchitis, bone pain, dactylitis, arthritis and proteinuria. ENL may continue intermittently for several years.

Investigations

The diagnosis is clinical by finding a cardinal sign of leprosy, and is supported by finding acid-fast bacilli in slit skin smears or typical histology in a skin biopsy. Skin lesions should be tested for anaesthesia. The peripheral nerves should be palpated for thickening and tenderness. Neither serology nor PCR testing for *M. leprae* DNA is sensitive or specific enough for diagnosis.

Slit skin smears

The bacterial load is assessed by scraping dermal material on to a glass slide. The smears are then stained and acid-fast bacilli are scored on a logarithmic scale, the bacterial index (BI). Smears are useful for confirming the diagnosis and monitoring response to treatment.

Differential diagnosis

Skin

The anaesthesia of tuberculoid and borderline tuberculoid lesions differentiates them from fungal infections, vitiligo, psoriasis and eczema. The presence of acid-fast bacilli in smears differentiates lepromatous nodules from onchocerciasis, Kaposi's sarcoma and post-kala-azar dermal leishmaniasis.

Nerves

Leprosy is the most common cause of peripheral nerve thickening. Uncommon conditions such as Charcot–Marie–Tooth disease and amyloid are differentiated from leprosy by the absence of skin lesions and acid-fast bacilli. Always compare with nerves on the other side. The causes of other polyneuropathies such as HIV, diabetes, alcoholism, vasculitides and heavy metal poisoning should all be considered where appropriate.

Outside leprosy-endemic areas doctors often fail to diagnose leprosy. Of new patients seen between 1995 and 1999 at the Hospital for Tropical Diseases, London, diagnosis had been delayed in over 80% of cases. Patients had been misdiagnosed by dermatologists, neurologists, orthopaedic

1.62 REACTIONS IN LEPROSY		
	Lepra reaction type 1 (reversal)	**Lepra reaction type 2 (erythema nodosum leprosum)**
Mechanism	Cell-mediated hypersensitivity Arthus phenomenon	Immune complexes
Clinical features	Painful tender nerves, loss of function Swollen skin lesions New skin lesions Rarely, fever	Tender papules and nodules, may ulcerate Painful tender nerves, loss of function Iritis, orchitis, myositis, lymphadenitis Fever, oedema
Management	Mild: aspirin 600 mg 6-hourly Severe[1]: prednisolone 40–80 mg, reducing over 3–9 months	Mild: aspirin 600 mg 6-hourly Severe[1]: thalidomide[2] or prednisolone 20–40 mg, reducing over 1–6 months; local if eye involved[3]

[1] Includes any threat to nerve or eye function.
[2] See text for details.
[3] 1% hydrocortisone drops or ointment and 1% atropine drops.

surgeons and rheumatologists. These delays had serious consequences for patients, with over half of them having nerve damage and disability. Always consider leprosy as a possible cause of peripheral neuropathy or neuropathic ulcers in patients of Indian or African origin.

Management

Effective treatment (see Box 1.63) can only be achieved with the patient's cooperation and confidence. All leprosy patients should be given an appropriate multidrug combination. Patients can be classified into paucibacillary (skin smear negative tuberculoid and BT) and multibacillary (skin smear positive BT, all BB, BL and LL). The first-line anti-leprosy drugs are rifampicin, clofazimine and dapsone. Box 1.64 gives the drug combinations, doses and duration of treatment. Studies from India have shown that multibacillary patients with an initial BI > 4 need longer treatment and should be treated to smear negativity.

Rifampicin is a potent bactericidal for *M. leprae*. Four days after a single 600 mg dose bacilli from a previously untreated multibacillary patient were no longer viable in a mouse footpad test. As *M. leprae* can develop resistance to rifampicin as a single-step mutation, rifampicin should always be given in combination with other anti-leprotics.

Dapsone is bacteriostatic. It commonly causes mild haemolysis but rarely anaemia. The 'dapsone syndrome', only occasionally seen in leprosy, starts 6 weeks after commencing dapsone and manifests as exfoliative dermatitis associated with lymphadenopathy, hepatosplenomegaly, fever and hepatitis. Clofazimine is a red, fat-soluble crystalline dye, weakly bactericidal for *M. leprae*. Skin discoloration (red to purple-black) and ichthyosis are troublesome side-effects, particularly on pale skins. New drugs bactericidal for *M. leprae* have been identified, notably the fluoroquinolones pefloxacin and ofloxacin, minocycline and clarithromycin. These agents are now established second-line drugs. Minocycline causes a black pigmentation of skin lesions and so may not be an appropriate substitute for clofazimine if pigmentation is to be avoided.

More than 10 million patients have been treated successfully with multidrug treatment (MDT). Clinical improvement has been rapid and toxicity rare. The treatment duration has been shortened. Monthly supervision of the rifampicin component has been crucial to success. At the end of 6 months' treatment for borderline disease there may still be signs of inflammation which should not be mistaken for active infection. The distinction between relapse and reaction may be difficult. WHO studies have reported a cumulative relapse rate of 1.07% for paucibacillary leprosy and 0.77% for multibacillary leprosy at 9 years after completion of MDT. *M. leprae* is such a slow-growing organism that relapse only occurs after many years. A single-dose triple drug combination (rifampicin, ofloxacin and minocycline) has been tested in India for patients with single skin lesions. Although single-dose treatment is clinically less effective than the conventional 6-month treatment for paucibacillary leprosy, it is an operationally attractive field regimen and has been recommended for use by WHO.

Treatment of reactions

The principles of treating immune-mediated reactions are:

- Control the acute inflammation and ease the pain.
- Treat the neuritis.
- Halt eye damage.

Type 1 reactions should be treated with oral prednisolone starting at 40 mg/day, and reduced by 5 mg/day each month. ENL is difficult to treat and requires high-dose steroids (80 mg daily, tapered down rapidly) or thalidomide. The chronicity of ENL reactions makes corticosteroid dependency a problem in these patients. Thalidomide is effective at controlling ENL but its teratogenic side-effects in early pregnancy limit its use in women of childbearing age. Chloroquine can also be used.

Patient education

Educating leprosy patients about their disease is vital for successful management. Reassure patients that after 3 days

---

1.63 PRINCIPLES OF LEPROSY TREATMENT

- Stop the infection with chemotherapy
- Treat reactions
- Educate the patient about leprosy
- Prevent disability
- Support the patient socially and psychologically

1.64 MODIFIED WHO-RECOMMENDED MULTIDRUG THERAPY REGIMENS IN LEPROSY

Type of leprosy*	Monthly supervised drug treatment	Daily self-administered drug treatment	Duration of treatment
Paucibacillary	Rifampicin 600 mg	Dapsone 100 mg	6 months
Multibacillary	Rifampicin 600 mg Clofazimine 300 mg	Clofazimine 50 mg Dapsone 100 mg	12 months
Paucibacillary single-lesion	Ofloxacin 400 mg Rifampicin 600 mg Minocycline 100 mg		Single dose

* WHO classification for field use when slit skin smears are not available:
- paucibacillary single-lesion leprosy (one skin lesion)
- paucibacillary (2–5 skin lesions)
- multibacillary (more than 5 skin lesions).
In this field classification WHO recommends treatment of multibacillary patients for 12 months only.

of chemotherapy they are not infectious and can lead a normal social life. Emphasise that gross deformities are not inevitable, and that care of anaesthetic limbs is as important as chemotherapy.

Prevention of disability

The morbidity and disability associated with leprosy are secondary to nerve damage. Nerve damage produces anaesthesia, dryness and muscle weakness. These three factors lead to misuse of the affected limb, with resultant ulceration, infection and, ultimately, severe deformity. Monitoring sensation and muscle power in hands, feet and eyes should be part of the routine follow-up so that new nerve damage is detected early. The patient with an anaesthetic hand or foot needs to develop daily self-care and protection when performing dangerous tasks. Soaking dry hands and feet followed by rubbing with oil keeps the skin moist and supple. Physiotherapy can prevent contractures, muscle atrophy and over-stretching of paralysed muscles.

Anaesthetic feet need protective footwear. For anaesthesia alone, a well-fitting 'trainer' with firm soles and shock-absorbing inners provides adequate protection. Once there is deformity, then special footwear is needed to protect pressure points and ensure even weight distribution.

Teach patients to work out the causation of any injury so that recurrence can be avoided. Plantar ulceration occurs secondary to increased pressure over bony prominences. Ulceration is treated by rest. Unlike ulcers in diabetic feet, ulcers in leprosy heal if they are protected from weight-bearing. No weight-bearing is permitted until the ulcer has healed. Appropriate footwear should be provided to prevent recurrence.

Social, psychological and economic rehabilitation

The social and cultural background of the patient determines many of the problems that may be encountered. The patient may have difficulty in coming to terms with leprosy. The community may reject the patient. Education, employment, confidence in family, friends and doctor, and plastic surgery to correct stigmatising deformity all have a role to play.

Leprosy in women

Women with leprosy are in double jeopardy; not only may they develop post-partum nerve damage but they are also at particular risk of social ostracisation with rejection by spouse and family.

Prognosis

The majority of patients, especially those who have no nerve damage at the time of diagnosis, do well on MDT, with resolution of skin lesions. Borderline patients are at risk of developing type 1 reactions which may result in devastating nerve damage.

Prevention and control

The current strategy of leprosy control in endemic countries has been very successful. Vertical programmes provide case detection, treatment with WHO MDT and contact examination, and are supported by case-finding campaigns, especially in schools. Effective treatment is not merely restricted to chemotherapy but also involves good case management with effective monitoring and supervision. An important secondary role of leprosy control programmes is the prevention of disabilities. BCG vaccination has been shown to give good but variable protection against leprosy. Combining *M. leprae* with BCG does not enhance the protection from BCG.

SPLENOMEGALY IN/FROM THE TROPICS

Splenomegaly (see p. 906) is occasionally the presenting feature of a tropically acquired infection. If it is acute and accompanied by a fever, then the causes listed in Box 1.65 should be considered. If it is moderate or massive, then endocarditis, splenic abscess, visceral leishmaniasis and hyper-reactive malarious splenomegaly should be considered.

Investigations

These will be guided by the context of the splenomegaly, particularly the travel and exposure history. Every patient should have several thick and thin blood films, blood cultures, a full blood count and film examination. Serologies where appropriate can help diagnose a viral infection. Imaging can detect a splenic abscess and indicate whether portal hypertension is present. The diagnosis of visceral leishmaniasis will require a bone marrow or splenic aspirate.

1.65 CAUSES OF TROPICAL SPLENOMEGALY	
Mild	
Parasite infection	
• Malaria	• Toxoplasmosis
• Katayama fever	• Trypanosomiasis
Viral	
• EBV	• CMV
• Hepatitis	• HIV
• Dengue	
Bacterial	
• Typhoid	• Brucellosis
Spirochaetal	
• Leptospirosis	
Fungal	
• Histoplasmosis	
Moderate	
• Subacute bacterial endocarditis	• Portal hypertension due to schistosomiasis
• Splenic abscess	• Disseminated tuberculosis
Massive	
• Visceral leishmaniasis	• Hyper-reactive malarial splenomegaly

HYPER-REACTIVE MALARIAL SPLENOMEGALY (TROPICAL SPLENOMEGALY SYNDROME)

In some hyper-endemic areas gross splenomegaly is associated with an exaggerated immune response to malaria and is seen, unexpectedly, in adults who have high antibody titres to malaria and low parasitaemias. The condition, which is more common in females and in certain racial and family groups, is characterised by enormous over-production of IgM, levels reaching 3–20 times the local mean value. Much of the IgM is aggregated with other immunoglobulin or complement and precipitates in the cold, in vitro. IgM aggregates are phagocytosed by reticulo-endothelial cells in the spleen and liver, and the demonstration of this by immunofluorescence in a liver biopsy section is diagnostic. Light microscopy of the liver usually shows sinusoidal lymphocytosis. Anaemia and lymphocytosis can be confused with leukaemia. Portal hypertension may develop.

Management

Splenomegaly and anaemia usually resolve over a period of months of continuous treatment with proguanil 100 mg daily, which should be continued for life to prevent relapse. Complicating folate deficiency is treated with folic acid 5 mg daily.

OTHER SYSTEMIC INFECTIONS

JAPANESE B ENCEPHALITIS

This flavivirus is an important cause of encephalitis in Japan, China, South-east Asia and India. These regions are endemic for Japanese B encephalitis and epidemics also occur. In China, despite 70 million children being immunised, there are still 10 000 cases annually. Swine and birds are the virus reservoirs; transmission is by mosquitoes.

Clinical features

There is an initial systemic illness with fever, malaise and anorexia, followed by photophobia, vomiting, headache and changes in brain-stem function. Most children die from respiratory failure and frequently have evidence of cardiac and respiratory instability, reflecting viraemic spread via the vertebral vessels and infection of brain-stem nuclei. Other patients have evidence of multifocal CNS disease that involves the basal ganglia, thalamus and lower cortex, and develop tremors, dystonia and parkinsonian symptoms. Asymptomatic infection is common; of symptomatic infections there is a case fatality rate of 25% and 50% of survivors are left with neurological sequelae.

Diagnosis

Other infectious causes of encephalitis should be excluded (see p. 1197). Serological testing can be carried out. There is a CSF antigen test.

Management

Treatment should be supportive, anticipating and treating complications.

NIPAH VIRUS ENCEPHALITIS

In 1999 a newly discovered paramyxovirus, the Nipah virus, caused an epidemic of encephalitis amongst Malaysian pig farmers. Infection is through direct contact with pig secretions. Mortality is in the region of 30%. Antibodies to the Hendra virus are present in 76% of the cases.

MELIOIDOSIS

Melioidosis is caused by *Burkholderia (Pseudomonas) pseudomallei*, which is a saprophyte found in soil and water (paddy fields). Infection is by inoculation and inhalation. Diabetics and patients with severe burns are particularly susceptible. The disease is most common in the Far East, India, South-east Asia and Australia.

Pathology

A bacteraemia is followed by the formation of abscesses in the lungs, liver and spleen.

Clinical features

There is high fever, prostration and sometimes diarrhoea, with signs of pneumonia and enlargement of the liver and spleen. A chest radiograph resembles that of acute caseous tuberculosis. In more chronic forms multiple abscesses recur in subcutaneous tissue and bone.

Investigations

Culture of blood, sputum or pus may yield *B. pseudomallei*. Except in fulminating infections, antibodies may be detected by indirect haemagglutination, direct agglutination, and complement-fixation tests.

Management

In acute illness prompt treatment, without waiting for confirmation by culture, may be life-saving. Ceftazidime 120 mg/kg plus tetracycline 3 g daily are given in divided doses for about 2–3 weeks, followed by doxycycline 200 mg daily for 2–3 months, until pulmonary cavities have healed. Abscesses should be drained surgically. In chronic cases profound wasting is a major clinical problem.

SYSTEMIC FUNGAL INFECTIONS

HISTOPLASMOSIS

Histoplasmosis is caused by *Histoplasma capsulatum*; this is a yeast in its parasitic phase but is a filamentous fungus of soil at other times. A variant, *H. duboisii*, is found in parts of tropical Africa.

H. capsulatum multiplies in soil enriched by the droppings of birds and bats, and the spores remain viable for years. Natural infections are found in several species of small mammal, including bats. Infection is by inhalation of infected dust. The infection is an especial hazard for explorers of caves and people who clear out bird (including chicken) roosts.

H. capsulatum is found in all parts of the USA, especially in the east central states, and less commonly in Latin America from Mexico to Argentina, Europe, North, South and East Africa, Nigeria, Malaysia, Indonesia and Australia. Disseminated histoplasmosis is also seen in immunocompromised patients, e.g. those with AIDS (see p. 115).

Pathology

The parasite in its yeast phase multiplies mainly in monocytes and macrophages, and produces areas of necrosis in which the parasites may abound. From these foci the blood stream may be invaded, producing metastatic lesions in the liver, spleen and lymph nodes. Pulmonary histoplasmosis may cause pathological changes similar to those of tuberculosis, including the production of a primary complex with enlarged regional lymph nodes, multiple small discrete lesions and occasionally cavitation. Healed lesions may calcify.

Investigations

In an area where the disease occurs, histoplasmosis should be suspected in every obscure infection in which there are pulmonary signs or where there are enlarged lymph nodes or hepatosplenomegaly. Tissue is obtained by biopsy for an impression smear, histology and culture. Radiological examination in long-standing cases may show calcified lesions in the lungs, spleen or other organs. In the more acute phases of the disease single or multiple soft pulmonary shadows with enlarged tracheobronchial nodes are seen.

Delayed hypersensitivity to the intradermal injection of histoplasmin develops in patients with either active or healed infections but is usually negative in acute disseminated disease. Complement-fixing antibodies are detected within 3 weeks of the onset of an acute primary infection and increase in titre as the disease progresses. Precipitating antibodies may also be detected.

Management

Specific treatment with amphotericin B is indicated only in severe infections; the dosage (0.5 mg/kg in 500 ml of 5% glucose) is given intravenously over a 6-hour period, gradually increasing to a maximum of 1.0 mg/kg. Treatment is given on alternate days to a total adult dose of 2 g. If badly tolerated, the dose may have to be reduced. Side-effects are anorexia, nausea, fever, headache, and venous thrombosis which may be controlled by the addition of 10 mg prednisolone to the intravenous solution. Plasma urea rises and haemoglobin falls during treatment but later they return to normal. Amphotericin may have to be continued for up to 3 months or longer, depending on the clinical response. Severe dyspnoea in histoplasmosis should be treated with prednisolone 20–40 mg daily for a few days. Itraconazole 200–400 mg daily can be used in chronic pulmonary histoplasmosis and chronic disseminated histoplasmosis.

HISTOPLASMA DUBOISII

H. duboisii, the fungus of African histoplasmosis, is larger than the classical *H. capsulatum*. It is found throughout East, Central and West Africa.

The disease differs in several ways from *H. capsulatum* infection. The bones, skin, lymph nodes and liver develop granulomatous lesions or cold abscesses resembling tuberculosis, but the lungs are seldom involved. The visceral form with liver and splenic invasion is often fatal, while ulcerative skin lesions and bone abscesses follow a more benign course.

Radiological examination may show rounded foci of bone destruction, sometimes associated with abscess formation. Multiple lesions of the ribs are common and the bones of the limbs may be involved. Systemic disease is treated in the same way as *H. capsulatum* infections. A solitary lesion in bone may require only local surgical treatment.

ASPERGILLOSIS

This is the most common respiratory mycosis in Britain and is discussed on page 540.

COCCIDIOIDOMYCOSIS

This is caused by *Coccidioides immitis* and is found in the southern USA, and Central and South America. The disease is acquired by inhalation. The infection behaves like tuberculosis or histoplasmosis. In 60% of cases it is asymptomatic, but in 40% of cases it affects the lungs, lymph nodes and skin. Rarely, it may be carried by the blood stream to the bones, adrenals, meninges and other organs. Pulmonary coccidioidomycosis has two forms: primary and progressive. Primary coccidioidomycosis behaves like primary tuberculosis or histoplasmosis and is often asymptomatic. The progressive form of the disease is associated with marked systemic upset and features of lobar pneumonia. In more chronic cases it may resemble chronic tuberculosis. Infections, including subclinical attacks, are followed by immunity.

The fungi grow readily on culture media but as they are highly infective, diagnostic investigations are usually limited to intradermal, complement fixation and precipitin tests.

Amphotericin B (as for histoplasmosis), itraconazole, ketoconazole or fluconazole may be helpful but relapse is common. Some localised pulmonary lesions can be treated by surgery.

PARACOCCIDIOIDOMYCOSIS

This is caused by *Paracoccidioides brasiliensis* and occurs in South America. Mucocutaneous lesions occur early. Involvement of lymphatic nodes and the lungs is prominent and the gastrointestinal tract may also be attacked. Most patients respond to ketoconazole 200 mg/day for at least 6 months; itraconazole 100–200 mg daily is an alternative. Liver function must be monitored for either agent. For those who do not respond, amphotericin B (as for histoplasmosis) may be used.

BLASTOMYCOSIS

North American blastomycosis is caused by *Blastomyces dermatitidis*. It also occurs in Africa. Systemic infection begins in the lungs and mediastinal lymph nodes and resembles pulmonary tuberculosis. Bones, skin and the genitourinary tract may also be affected. Treatment is with itraconazole 200–400 mg daily, ketoconazole 200–400 mg daily or amphotericin B (see above).

CRYPTOCOCCOSIS

This is caused by *Cryptococcus neoformans*. Its distribution is world-wide. It causes local gumma-like tumours and granulomatous lesions of the lung, bones, brain and meninges. The CSF often contains the fungus when the nervous system is affected. Immunocompromised individuals are at special risk, including those with HIV infection (see p. 124).

The diagnosis is made by culture or recognition of spores in the CSF, biopsy and serological detection of antigen.

Amphotericin B should be given intravenously (see above) and flucytosine orally (see p. 143). Surgical removal of local pulmonary lesions may be necessary. Recovery may be monitored by the fall in antigen titre. Cryptococcal meningitis is particularly important in HIV infection.

CANDIDIASIS

Candida albicans is a cause of systemic fungal infection in the immunosuppressed (see p. 116).

TRAVEL MEDICINE

In 1999 49 million overseas visits were made by UK residents; these included almost 1 million to Africa and half a million to the Indian subcontinent. Malaria remains a major risk to travellers but the principal causes of death whilst travelling are road traffic accidents, drowning and exacerbation of chronic disease. Good travel insurance is imperative. The key principles of travel medicine are assessing the risks that the traveller will be exposed to, advising on malaria prophylaxis, and ensuring that the traveller is aware of the role of personal protection in preventing disease. Information on local disease patterns can be obtained from the WHO and CDC websites; advice on available vaccines can be obtained from the UK Department of Health book *Health information for overseas travel* (see p. 146).

Assessing the risks
Risks of encountering local disease need to be assessed so that balanced advice about vaccinations and other protection can be given. Ask about:

● Type of travel—holiday or business.
● Accommodation—five-star or adventurous.
● Urban or rural travel. Rural travel often poses greater risks.
● Itinerary. Malaria may be confined to certain areas. In

Thailand the coastal areas are malaria-free but the jungle highlands have multidrug-resistant parasites.
● Activities—jungle trekking, water sports.
● Length of trip.

Effective vaccines are available for many diseases, including yellow fever, rabies, typhoid and hepatitis. However, some vaccines, such as Japanese B encephalitis vaccine, have adverse effects and the degree of protection needed should be balanced against potential side-effects.

Malaria prophylaxis
The risk of malaria is often difficult to gauge but a proxy is the entomological inoculation rate (EIR)—the number of infective *Plasmodium falciparum* bites received per person per year. The EIR in Tanzania is 667, which implies a risk of two infective bites per night. All travellers to malarious areas should be encouraged to take chemoprophylaxis, especially young children (see p. 56). Advice on the best combinations can be obtained from the WHO and CDC websites. Personal protection is also important in avoiding malaria. Travellers should be advised to:

● sleep under bed nets
● wear long-sleeved shirts and trousers, especially after dusk
● use insect repellents.

Travellers should also be made aware of the importance of seeking prompt medical advice when they develop a fever so that malaria can be excluded.

Personal protection
Travellers can be advised on ways of reducing the risk of travellers' diarrhoea such as:

● drinking bottled water wherever possible, ensuring that the seal on the bottle is intact
● avoiding food exposed to flies
● avoiding salads and unpeeled fruit.

Skin protection with sunscreen will reduce sunburn.
Unplanned sexual activity often occurs when travelling. The risk of sexually transmitted diseases can be reduced for both partners by using condoms.

SEXUALLY TRANSMITTED INFECTIONS

Sexually transmitted infections (STIs) are a group of contagious conditions whose principal mode of transmission is by intimate sexual activity involving the moist mucous membranes of the penis, vulva, vagina, cervix, anus, rectum, mouth, pharynx and their adjacent skin surfaces. A wide range of infections may be sexually transmitted, including syphilis, gonorrhoea, HIV infection, genital herpes, genital warts, chlamydial infection and trichomoniasis. Genital candidiasis may be sexually transmitted but many cases occur spontaneously. Bacterial vaginosis is not regarded as an STI although it is a common cause of vaginal discharge in sexually active women. Chancroid, lymphogranuloma venereum and granuloma inguinale are usually seen in tropical countries. Hepatitis viruses A, B, C and D (see p. 860) may also be acquired sexually, as well as by other routes.

Whilst fluctuations in incidence occur, many STIs are presently increasing in most countries throughout the world.

THE APPROACH TO A PATIENT WITH A SUSPECTED STI

Patients concerned about the possible acquisition of an STI are often anxious and so staff must be friendly, sympathetic and reassuring. They should have the ability to put patients at ease and emphasise that clinic attendance is confidential. The history focuses on genital symptoms, with reference to genital ulceration, rash, irritation, pain, swelling and urinary symptoms, especially dysuria. In males, the clinician should ask about urethral discharge, and in females, vaginal discharge, pelvic pain or dyspareunia. Enquiry about general health should include menstrual and obstetric history, cervical cytology, recent medication, especially with antimicrobial or antiviral agents, previous STI and allergy. Immunisation status for hepatitis A and B should be noted, as should information about smoking and recreational drug use. Sexual partners, whether male or female, casual or regular, should be recorded. Sexual practices—insertive or receptive vaginal, anal, orogenital or oroanal—should be noted. Choice of contraception should be recorded for women together with condom use for both sexes. Examination should include external genitalia, inguinal and perianal areas, mouth and throat. In females the passage of a bivalve speculum allows inspection of the vaginal walls and cervix. Proctoscopic examination of the anus and rectum is required for those who have had receptive anal sex. The history will indicate other systems to examine. Ideally, all patients should have a complete examination, particularly when considering syphilis or HIV infection.

Several STIs may be present at the same time and so all patients should be fully investigated (see below) at their first visit. Tests of cure should follow treatment.

The presence of an STI in a child may be indicative of sexual abuse or, very uncommonly, of accidental infection. Vertical transmission is possible for some infections. In an older child, STI may be the result of voluntary sexual activity. As in adults, STIs in children should be fully investigated.

SPREAD AND CONTROL OF STI

Spread
Implicit in the transmission of STI is the acquisition of an infection from one person and its transmission to another. The rate of spread of infection depends on the infectivity of the STI, the rate of partner change of infected individuals and the susceptibility to infection of non-infected partners. People with many sexual partners (core groups) are at particular risk, contributing significantly to STI rates in a community (see below). Social, educational, economic or religious factors may influence patterns of sexual activity.

Unlike condoms and to a lesser extent the diaphragm, oral contraceptives and the intrauterine contraceptive device

---

1.66 THOSE AT PARTICULAR RISK FROM STIs*

- Sex workers, male and female
- Clients of sex workers
- Men who have sex with men
- Injecting drug users (sex for money or drugs) and their partners
- Frequent travellers

* Adapted from WHO/UNAIDS, 1997.

---

provide no barrier to infection. People from all socioeconomic groups may acquire STIs. Those at particular risk are listed in Box 1.66.

Control
Good control of STIs is based on a number of important principles:

- accurate diagnosis (see Box 1.67)
- effective treatment
- investigations to establish cure before resumption of sexual activity
- counselling around safer sexual practices
- partner notification
- the exhibition of a confidential, friendly, well-advertised and easily accessible environment for patient care
- the availability of STI screening for all people who have unprotected sex
- serological tests for blood, organ/tissue and semen donors (syphilis, hepatitis B and C, HIV); semen donors should be screened for other STIs
- serological tests for pregnant women (syphilis, HIV; hepatitis B and C if appropriate).

Best practice dictates that patients found to have syphilis (or other treponemal infection), HIV or hepatitis A, B or C should not donate blood, organs/tissue or semen, and that those with other STIs should not donate semen. Certain STIs such as syphilis, chancroid and genital herpes require modified treatment in people with HIV infection (see Further information, p. 146, for websites), and recurrent vulvovaginal candidiasis may present more frequently in women with HIV infection (see p. 116).

Rates for STIs are higher in younger people but it should not be forgotten that older people have sexual relationships and that STIs are no respecters of age.

SEXUALLY TRANSMITTED BACTERIAL INFECTIONS

SYPHILIS

Syphilis is caused by infection with the spirochaete *Treponema pallidum*. In adults this is usually sexually acquired with entry of treponemes through abrasions in skin or mucous membranes. Transmission by kissing, blood transfusion and percutaneous injury has been reported. Infection is systemic from the outset but in some patients clinical signs may be minimal or absent. Transplacental

1.67 INVESTIGATIONS FOR SEXUALLY TRANSMITTED INFECTIONS

Patients and focus	Investigation
FEMALES	
Urethral meatus	Gram stain smear and culture for gonococci Swab for *Chlamydia* (PCR or ligase chain reaction, LCR)
Vagina	Wet (saline) mount and Gram stain for *Candida*, *Trichomonas* and bacterial vaginosis (clue cells pH and amine test for bacterial vaginosis) Culture for *Candida* and *Trichomonas* Culture for aerobic/anaerobic bacteria if indicated
Cervical os	Gram stain and culture for gonococci Swab for *Chlamydia* (PCR or LCR) Cervical cytology
Rectum (if anal sex, or gonococci found at other site)	Gram stain smear and culture for gonococci Swab for *Chlamydia*
Throat (if oral sex)	Culture for gonococci Swab for Chlamydia
MALES	
Urethra	Gram stain smear and culture for gonococci Swab for *Chlamydia*
Rectum (if anal sex)	Gram stain smear and culture for gonococci Swab for *Chlamydia*
Throat (if oral sex)	Culture for gonococci Swab for Chlamydia
ALL PATIENTS	
Eyes (if gonococcal or chlamydial conjunctivitis suspected)	Gram stain smear and culture for gonococci Swab for *Chlamydia*
Contacts of gonorrhoea	Genital and rectal tests (if indicated), as above Throat swab for culture for gonococci Genital swabs for *Chlamydia* and from rectum/throat if indicated
Genital ulcers	Serum for dark-field microscopy for *Treponema pallidum* Swab for herpes simplex virus culture Swab for bacterial culture if secondary infection If indicated, tests for lymphogranuloma venereum, chancroid or granuloma inguinale; see Box 1.78, page 104 Blood for syphilis and HIV serology Urinalysis (dipstick) for blood, protein, glucose and bilirubin
THOSE AT INCREASED RISK (injecting drug users, men who have sex with men and people with multiple sexual partners)	Blood for hepatitis B and C serology (and HAV serology for men who have sex with men)

1.68 CLASSIFICATION OF SYPHILIS

Stage	Acquired	Congenital
Early	Primary Secondary Latent	Clinical and latent
Late	Latent Benign tertiary Cardiovascular Neurosyphilis	Clinical and latent Stigmata

in Box 1.68. All infected patients must be treated (see Box 1.73, p. 100).

Acquired syphilis

Early syphilis

Primary syphilis. The incubation period is usually between 14 and 28 days with a range of 9–90 days. Non-specific (anticardiolipin) and specific antitreponemal antibodies are produced in response to infection. The primary lesion or chancre (see Fig. 1.71) develops at the site of infection, usually in the genital area. A dull red macule develops, becomes papular and then erodes to form an indurated ulcer (the chancre). The inguinal lymph nodes are moderately enlarged, mobile, discrete and rubbery. Both chancre and lymph nodes are painless and non-tender, unless associated with concurrent or secondary infection. Without treatment, the chancre will resolve within 2–6 weeks to leave a thin atrophic scar. Chancres may also develop on the vaginal wall and on the cervix. Extragenital chancres may be found in about 10% of patients, affecting sites such as the finger, lip, tongue, tonsil, nipple, anus or rectum. Chancre must be included in the differential diagnosis of all genital ulcers (see Box 1.69).

Secondary syphilis. This usually starts 6–8 weeks after the development of the chancre due to dissemination of treponemes to produce a multisystem disease. Constitutional features such as mild fever, malaise and headache may be present whilst over 75% of patients present with rash.

Initially, the rash may be macular on the trunk and limbs, with evolution to maculo-papular or papular forms, which are generalised, symmetrical and non-irritable with involvement of the palms and soles. Scales may form on the papules

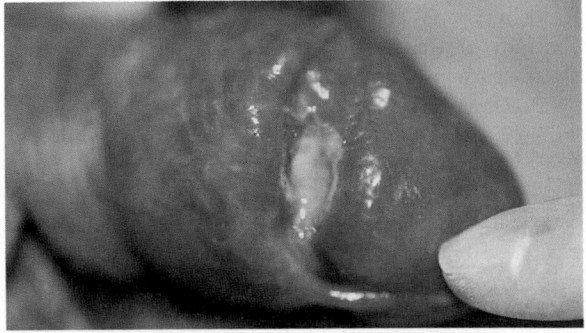

Fig. 1.71 Primary syphilis. A painless ulcer (chancre) is shown in the coronal sulcus of the penis. This is usually associated with inguinal lymphadenopathy.

infection of the fetus can occur. Penicillin remains the drug of choice for all stages of infection.

The natural history of untreated syphilis is variable and may be latent throughout, though clinical features may develop at any time. The classification of syphilis is shown

1.69 DIFFERENTIAL DIAGNOSIS OF GENITAL ULCERATION	
Associated with infection	
• Primary syphilis (chancre) • Secondary syphilis • Gumma • Herpes simplex virus (see pp. 103–104) • Varicella zoster virus (see pp. 31–33) • Erosive balanitis • Trauma with secondary infection • Chancroid • Lymphogranuloma venereum • Granuloma inguinale • Scabies (see p. 1085)	
Other	
• Circinate balanitis (see p. 1010 for Reiter's syndrome) • Stevens–Johnson syndrome (see pp. 33 and 1098) • Behçet's syndrome (see p. 1044) • Erythroplasia of Queyrat (intraepidermal carcinoma) • Squamous cell carcinoma • Fixed drug eruption	

1.70 DIFFERENTIAL DIAGNOSIS OF SECONDARY SYPHILIS	
Macular rash	
• Drug eruption • Rubella • Measles	• Pityriasis rosea • Infectious mononucleosis • Primary HIV infection (see p. 113)
Papular rash	
• Drug eruption • Scabies • Varicella zoster virus (chickenpox)	• Acne vulgaris • Psoriasis • Lichen planus
Oral lesions	
• Herpes simplex virus • Aphthous ulcers • Ulcerative stomatitis • Agranulocytosis • Infectious mononucleosis	• Primary HIV infection • Behçet's syndrome • Reiter's syndrome • Stevens–Johnson syndrome
Genital lesions	
• Fixed drug eruption • Herpes simplex virus • Varicella zoster virus (shingles) • Circinate balanitis (Reiter's syndrome)	• Lichen planus • Psoriasis • Erythroplasia of Queyrat
Condylomata lata	
• Genital warts (see pp. 105 and 1084)	
Lymphadenopathy	
• Infectious mononucleosis • HIV infection	• Lymphoma

later. Untreated, the rash may last for up to 12 weeks. Condylomata lata (papules coalescing to plaques) may develop in warm, moist sites such as the vulva or perianal area. Generalised lymphadenopathy may be present in over 50% of patients. Lymph nodes are similar to those of primary syphilis. Mucosal lesions, known as mucous patches, may affect the genitalia, mouth, pharynx or larynx. They are modified papules, which become eroded. Rarely, confluence produces the characteristic 'snail track ulcers' in the mouth.

Other features such as meningitis, cranial nerve palsies, anterior or posterior uveitis, hepatitis, gastritis, glomerulonephritis or periostitis are sometimes seen. Clinical features resolve without treatment though relapse may occur, usually within the first year of infection. Thereafter, the disease enters the phase of latency.

The differential diagnosis of secondary syphilis is summarised in Box 1.70. Syphilis must be distinguished clinically from yaws, endemic (non-venereal) syphilis (bejel) and pinta (see pp. 85–86) in countries where these other treponemal infections occur. These diseases are caused by treponemes morphologically indistinguishable from *T. pallidum* and cannot be differentiated by serological tests; in adults, however, a Venereal Diseases Research Laboratory/rapid plasma reagin (VDRL/RPR) test > 1:8 is generally associated with syphilis as adults with late yaws usually have low titres.

Latent syphilis. This stage is divided into early latency, within 2 years of infection, during which time syphilis may be transmitted sexually, and late latency (not sexually infectious) thereafter. Transmission of syphilis from a pregnant woman to her fetus, and rarely by blood transfusion, is possible for several years following infection. Latency implies positive syphilis serology in the absence of clinical disease or CSF abnormalities of neurosyphilis in an untreated patient.

Late syphilis

Late latent syphilis may persist for many years or for life. Without treatment, over 60% of patients might be expected to suffer little or no ill health.

Tertiary syphilis. Benign tertiary syphilis may develop between 3 and 10 years after infection but is now rarely seen in the UK. Skin, mucous membranes, bone, muscle or viscera can be involved. The characteristic feature is a chronic granulomatous lesion called a gumma, which may be single or multiple. Healing with scar formation may impair the function of the structure affected. Skin lesions may take the form of nodules or ulcers whilst subcutaneous lesions may ulcerate with a gummy discharge. Healing occurs slowly with the formation of the characteristic tissue paper scars. Mucosal lesions may occur in the mouth, pharynx, larynx or nasal septum, appearing as punched-out ulcers. Of particular importance is gummatous involvement of the tongue, healing of which may lead to leucoplakia with the attendant risk of malignant change. Gummas of tibia, skull, clavicle and sternum have been described in the past, as has involvement of the brain, spinal cord, liver, testis and, rarely, other organs. Resolution of active disease should follow treatment though some tissue damage may be permanent. Paroxysmal cold haemoglobinuria may be seen at this stage.

Cardiovascular syphilis may present many years after initial infection. Aortitis is the key feature. Aortic valve, coronary ostia or aorta may be affected. Clinical features include aortic incompetence, angina or aortic aneurysm. Signs and symptoms do not differ from other causes (see p. 447). Syphilitic aortic aneurysm is more commonly found in the ascending aorta. Aneurysm of the aortic arch is also seen, whilst aneurysm of the descending aorta is rare.

Treatment with penicillin will not correct anatomical damage and surgical intervention may be required in the management of the consequences of aortitis.

Neurosyphilis may also take years to develop. Asymptomatic infection is associated with CSF abnormalities in the absence of clinical signs. Meningovascular disease, tabes dorsalis or general paralysis of the insane characterises the symptomatic forms (see p. 1201). Neurosyphilis and cardiovascular syphilis may coexist and are sometimes referred to as quaternary syphilis.

Congenital syphilis

The division between early infectious and late non-infectious congenital syphilis is 2 years.

Treponemal infection may give rise to a variety of outcomes after 4 months of gestation when the fetus becomes immunocompetent:

- miscarriage or stillbirth, premature or at term
- birth of a syphilitic baby (a very sick baby with hepatosplenomegaly, bullous rash and perhaps pneumonia)
- birth of a baby who develops signs of early congenital syphilis during the first few weeks of life
- birth of a baby with latent infection who either remains well or develops late congenital syphilis/stigmata later in life.

The stigmata are the result of treponemal infection causing permanent tissue damage to the fetus in utero or to the baby after birth, in either the early or the late stage (see Box 1.71).

Congenital syphilis is rare where antenatal serological screening is practised. Antisyphilitic treatment in pregnancy treats the fetus, if infected, as well as the patient.

Investigations

T. pallidum may be found in serum collected from chancres, or from moist or eroded lesions in secondary or early congenital syphilis using the dark-field microscope (see Box 1.67). The direct fluorescent antibody test or PCR is also used diagnostically in some centres. Serological tests for syphilis are listed in Box 1.72.

Non-treponemal tests are positive from about the fourth week in primary syphilis and at birth in congenital syphilis (test baby's blood not cord blood), unless infection has occurred late in pregnancy. Many centres use treponemal enzyme immunoassays (EIAs) for syphilis screening. In primary syphilis, EIA for antitreponemal IgM becomes positive before the non-treponemal tests, and in early congenital syphilis is consistent with a positive diagnosis. All positive results must be confirmed by repeat tests. Passively transferred maternal antibodies from an adequately treated mother may give rise to positive serological tests in her baby. In this situation, non-treponemal tests should become negative within 3–6 months of birth.

Biological false positive reactions occur occasionally, most often to VDRL or RPR tests (when treponemal tests will be negative), acute for up to 6 months and chronic thereafter. Acute reactions may be associated with infections such as infectious mononucleosis, chickenpox and malaria, and may also occur in pregnancy. Chronic reactions may be

associated with autoimmune diseases, amongst others. False negative results for non-treponemal tests may be found in secondary syphilis due to the prozone phenomenon from using undiluted serum.

In benign tertiary and in cardiovascular syphilis, examination of CSF should be considered, as asymptomatic neurological disease may coexist. CSF should be examined in patients with clinical signs of neurosyphilis (see p. 1202) and also in congenital syphilis (early and late). Chest radiograph, ECG and echocardiogram are useful in the investigation of cardiovascular syphilis. Biopsy may be required in the diagnosis of gumma.

1.71 CLINICAL FEATURES OF CONGENITAL SYPHILIS
Early congenital syphilis
• Maculo-papular rash • Condylomata lata • Mucous patches • Fissures around mouth, nose and anus • Rhinitis with nasal discharge (snuffles) • Hepatosplenomegaly • Osteochondritis/periostitis • Generalised lymphadenopathy • Choroiditis • Meningitis • Anaemia/thrombocytopenia
Late congenital syphilis
• Benign tertiary syphilis • Periostitis • Paroxysmal cold haemoglobinuria • Neurosyphilis • 8th nerve deafness • Interstitial keratitis • Clutton's joints (painless effusion into knee joints)
Stigmata
• Hutchinson's incisors (anterior-posterior thickening with notch on narrowed cutting edge) • Mulberry molars (imperfectly formed cusps/deficient dental enamel) • High arched palate • Maxillary hypoplasia • Saddle nose (following snuffles) • Rhagades (radiating scars around mouth, nose and anus following rash) • Salt and pepper scars on retina (from choroiditis) • Corneal scars (from interstitial keratitis) • Sabre tibia (from periostitis) • Bossing of frontal and parietal bones (healed periosteal nodes)

1.72 SEROLOGICAL TESTS FOR SYPHILIS
Non-treponemal (non-specific) tests
• Venereal Diseases Research Laboratory (VDRL) test • Rapid plasma reagin (RPR) test
Treponemal (specific) antibody tests
• Treponemal antigen-based enzyme immunoassay (EIA) for IgG and IgM • *T. pallidum* haemagglutination assay (TPHA) • Fluorescent treponemal antibody-absorbed (FTA-ABS) test

Management

Antimicrobial treatment for syphilis is summarised in Box 1.73. Doxycycline is indicated for patients allergic to penicillin, except in pregnancy when erythromycin stearate is given. Erythromycin crosses the placenta poorly so the newborn baby must be treated with a course of penicillin and consideration given to retreating the mother. Some specialists recommend penicillin desensitisation for pregnant mothers, allowing for a course of penicillin to be given during temporary tolerance. Babies should be treated in hospital with the help of a pediatrician. All patients must be followed up to ensure cure and partner notification is of particular importance. Resolution of clinical signs in early syphilis with declining titres for non-treponemal tests, usually to undetectable levels within 6 months for primary syphilis and 12–18 months for secondary syphilis, are indicators of successful treatment. Specific treponemal antibody tests may remain positive for life. In patients who have syphilis of many years' duration, there may be little serological response following treatment. A diagnosis of congenital syphilis requires that mother, partner and siblings are investigated.

Treatment reactions

- *Anaphylaxis.* Penicillin is a common cause; on-site facilities should be available for management (see p. 201).
- *Jarisch–Herxheimer reaction.* This is an acute febrile reaction following initiation of treatment, characterised by headache, malaise and myalgia and resolving within 24 hours. It is common in early syphilis and may cause worsening of neurological or ophthalmic disease (uveitis, optic neuritis). Fetal distress or premature labour may be consequences in pregnancy. Admission to hospital for initiation of treatment is recommended. It is rare in late syphilis but possible life-threatening events may be associated with local reactions in the coronary ostia (coronary occlusion), central nervous system (cerebral artery occlusion) or laryngeal stenosis (gumma). Prednisolone 10–20 mg orally 8-hourly for 3 days is recommended for patients with cardiovascular, neurological or ophthalmic disease or for laryngeal gumma, to prevent the reaction, though efficacy awaits proof. Antisyphilitic treatment is started after 24 hours. Inpatient management is advised.
- *Procaine reaction.* Fear of impending death occurs immediately after the accidental intravenous injection of procaine penicillin and may be associated with hallucinations or fits. Although the symptoms are short-lived, verbal assurance and sometimes physical restraint are required. The reaction can be prevented by aspiration before injection to ensure that the needle is not in a blood vessel.

GONORRHOEA

Gonorrhoea is caused by infection with *Neisseria gonorrhoeae* which may involve columnar epithelium in the lower genital tract, rectum, pharynx and eyes. Transmission is usually the result of vaginal, anal or oral sex. Gonococcal conjunctivitis may be the result of accidental infection from contaminated fingers. Untreated mothers may infect their babies during delivery, resulting in ophthalmia neonatorum.

Clinical features

In males the anterior urethra is commonly infected, causing urethral discharge and dysuria. The incubation period is about 2–10 days. Examination will usually show a muco-purulent or purulent urethral discharge. Symptoms may be absent in about 10%. Rectal infection in men who have sex

1.73 MANAGEMENT OF SYPHILIS

Medication	Regimen
Early syphilis (primary, secondary and early latent)	
Procaine benzylpenicillin G[1]	600 000 U i.m. daily for 10 days (17 days if neurological involvement)
Benzathine penicillin G	2.4 million U i.m. once a week for two doses
Penicillin allergy	
Doxycycline hyclate[2]	100 mg orally 12-hourly for 14 days *or*
Erythromycin	500 mg orally 6-hourly for 14 days
Late latent syphilis	
Procaine benzylpenicillin G[1]	600 000 U i.m. daily for 17 days
Benzathine penicillin G	2.4 million U i.m. weekly for three doses
Penicillin allergy	
Doxycycline hyclate[2]	200 mg orally 12-hourly for 28 days
Benign tertiary syphilis	As for late latent syphilis
Cardiovascular syphilis	As for late latent syphilis
Neurosyphilis	
Procaine benzylpenicillin G[1]	1.8–2.4 million U i.m. daily *plus* probenecid 500 mg orally 6-hourly, for 17 days *or*
Benzylpenicillin	3–4 million U i.v. 4-hourly for 17 days
Penicillin allergy	
Doxycycline hyclate[2]	200 mg orally 12-hourly for 28 days
Pregnancy	
Penicillin regimen depends on stage of syphilis	
Penicillin allergy	
Erythromycin	500 mg orally 6-hourly for 14 days (early syphilis) Investigate and treat baby at birth and consider treating mother after delivery with doxycycline hyclate[2] Penicillin desensitisation might be considered, followed by treatment with penicillin (see above)
Early congenital syphilis	
Benzylpenicillin	50 000 U/kg i.v. 12-hourly for the first 7 days of life *then* 50 000 U/kg i.v. 8-hourly for 3 days *or*
Procaine benzylpenicillin G[1]	50 000 U/kg i.m. daily for 10 days
Late congenital syphilis	Dose depends on weight and age of child Adult regimen from age 15

[1] Jenacillin A (one vial contains procaine penicillin G 1.5 million U and benzylpenicillin 0.5 million U) is the preparation used in the UK and is imported from Germany. See guidelines at www.agum.org.uk for Jenacillin A reconstitution and doses.
[2] Doxycycline hyclate should be avoided in pregnancy, breastfeeding and children under 12 years.

with men is usually asymptomatic but may present with anal discomfort, discharge or rectal bleeding. Proctoscopy may reveal no abnormality, or clinical evidence of proctitis such as inflamed rectal mucosa and mucopus.

In females, urethra, paraurethral glands/ducts, Bartholin's glands/ducts or endocervical canal may be infected. The rectum may also be involved either due to contamination from a urogenital site or as a result of anal sex. Occasionally, the rectum is the only site infected. About 50% of women who have gonorrhoea are asymptomatic. There may be vaginal discharge or dysuria but these symptoms may be associated with other infections such as *Chlamydia* (see p. 102), trichomoniasis or candidiasis (see p. 107), making full investigation essential (see Box 1.67, p. 97). Lower abdominal pain, dyspareunia and intermenstrual bleeding may be indicative of pelvic inflammatory disease (PID). Clinical examination may show no abnormality or pus may be expressed from urethra, paraurethral ducts or Bartholin's ducts. The cervix may be inflamed, with mucopurulent discharge and contact bleeding. PID may be associated with lower abdominal tenderness; adnexal and cervical motion tenderness on bimanual examination and fever may be present. Rectal infection is described above.

Pharyngeal gonorrhoea is usually the result of receptive orogenital sex and is often symptomless. When present, signs or symptoms are similar to other causes of sore throat.

Gonococcal conjunctivitis is an uncommon complication, presenting with purulent discharge from the eye(s), severe inflammation of the conjunctivae and oedema of the eyelids, associated with pain and photophobia. Gonococcal ophthalmia neonatorum presents similarly with purulent conjunctivitis and oedema of the eyelids. Both should be treated urgently to prevent corneal damage.

Differential diagnosis of uncomplicated gonorrhoea is given in Box 1.74. Concurrent chlamydial infection may be present.

Investigations

Gram-negative intracellular diplococci may be seen on microscopy (see Fig. 1.72) of smears from infected sites (except pharynx, where the presence of other diplococci might cause diagnostic difficulty) and must be confirmed by culture (see Box 1.67, p. 97).

Management of adults

Uncomplicated gonorrhoea responds to a single adequate dose of a suitable antimicrobial (see Box 1.75). Cure rates should exceed 95%. Longer courses of antibiotics are required for complicated infection. PID should be treated with antimicrobials effective against gonococci, *Chlamydia* and anaerobes, and appropriate analgesia given. Hospital admission is required for women with severe symptoms. Partner(s) of patients with gonorrhoea should be seen as soon as possible.

Prognosis

Symptoms gradually resolve without treatment but patients remain infectious for several months. Delay in treatment could lead to complications, which include:

- acute prostatitis
- epididymo-orchitis

1.74 DIFFERENTIAL DIAGNOSIS OF UNCOMPLICATED GONORRHOEA	
Males	
• Non-gonococcal urethritis	
Females	
• Urinary tract infection	• Candidiasis
• Trichomoniasis	• Bacterial vaginosis
Both sexes	
• Proctitis	• Pharyngitis

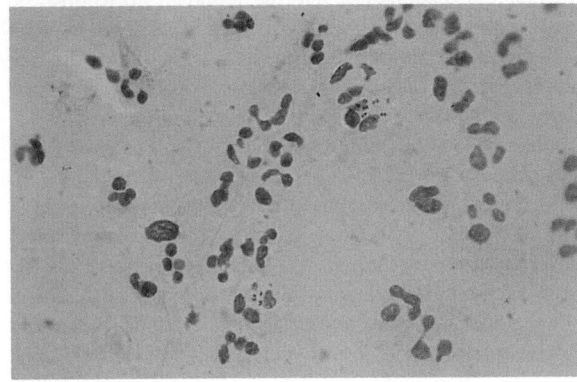

Fig. 1.72 A Gram-stained urethral smear from a man with gonococcal urethritis. Gram-negative diplococci are seen with polymorphonuclear leucocytes.

1.75 TREATMENT OF UNCOMPLICATED ANOGENITAL GONORRHOEA
Uncomplicated infection
• Ciprofloxacin 500 mg orally stat[1,2] *or*
• Ofloxacin 400 mg orally stat[1,2] *or*
• Ampicillin 2 g or 3 g *plus* probenecid 1 g orally stat[3]
Quinolone resistance
• Ceftriaxone 250 mg i.m. stat *or*
• Spectinomycin 2 g i.m. stat
Pregnancy and breastfeeding
• Ceftriaxone 250 mg i.m. stat *or*
• Ampicillin 2 g or 3 g *plus* probenecid 1 g orally stat[3] *or*
• Spectinomycin 2 g i.m. stat
Pharyngeal gonorrhoea
• Ceftriaxone 250 mg i.m. stat *or*
• Ciprofloxacin 500 mg[1,2] orally stat *or*
• Ofloxacin 400 mg[1,2] orally stat
[1] Contraindicated in pregnancy and breastfeeding.
[2] If prevalence of quinolone resistance for *N. gonorrhoeae* < 5%.
[3] If prevalence of penicillin resistance for *N. gonorrhoeae* < 5%.

- Bartholin's gland abscess
- PID and potential sequelae; infertility or ectopic pregnancy
- perihepatitis characterised by right hypochondrial pain and tenderness
- disseminated gonococcal infection
- purulent conjunctivitis in adults or in neonates (ophthalmia neonatorum).

NON-GONOCOCCAL URETHRITIS (NGU) AND CHLAMYDIAL INFECTION IN MALES

NGU (sometimes called non-specific urethritis or NSU) is usually sexually acquired and has a complex aetiology. Patients may complain of urethral discharge and/or dysuria or may be asymptomatic. Urethral discharge, if present, may be noticeable only after urethral massage. Diagnosis is made microscopically by finding five or more polymorphonuclear leucocytes (PMNL) in at least five high-power fields (× 1000) in a Gram-stained urethral smear. Gonococcal infection is excluded on smear and culture. *Chlamydia trachomatis* (chlamydia) may be found in up to 50% on urethral swab (see Boxes 1.67, p. 97, and 1.76) but in about 30% no cause is found. Complications, including epididymo-orchitis, sexually acquired reactive arthropathy (SARA) and Reiter's syndrome (see p. 1010), are seen infrequently.

Chlamydia is transmitted in a similar way to gonorrhoea and similar sites are infected (see p. 100). Urethral symptoms are usually milder and may be absent in up to 50%. The incubation period varies from a few weeks to a few months. Without treatment, symptoms may resolve but the patient remains infectious for several months. The treatment of uncomplicated NGU and chlamydia is similar, and should cure over 80% and 95% of cases respectively (see Box 1.77).

1.76 CAUSES OF NON-GONOCOCCAL URETHRITIS (NGU) IN MALES	
Most frequently isolated organisms	
• *Chlamydia trachomatis* • *Mycoplasma genitalium*	• *Ureaplasma urealyticum*
Less common	
• *Trichomonas vaginalis* • *Candida albicans* • *Neisseria meningitidis* • Herpes simplex virus	• Urinary tract infection • Urethral stricture • Foreign body • Associated with Reiter's disease
No cause	
• About 30%	

1.77 TREATMENT OF CHLAMYDIAL INFECTION AND NGU
Standard regimens
• Doxycycline 100 mg 12-hourly orally for 7 days[1] *or*   • Azithromycin 1 g orally as a single dose[2]
Alternative regimens
• Erythromycin 500 mg 6-hourly orally for 7 days *or* 500 mg 12-hourly for 2 weeks *or*   • Ofloxacin 200 mg 12-hourly orally for 7 days[1]
Persistent or recurrent NGU
• Erythromycin 500 mg orally 6-hourly for 14 days *plus* metronidazole 400 mg[3] orally 12-hourly for 5 days
[1] Contraindicated in pregnancy and breastfeeding.   [2] Safety in pregnancy and breastfeeding has not been fully assessed.   [3] Avoid alcoholic drinks during and for 48 hours after therapy.

Complications of chlamydial infection are shown below. Conjunctivitis is milder than in gonorrhoea and pharyngitis has no specific presentation. It should be noted that in men aged less than 35 years, epididymo-orchitis is most often caused by sexually transmitted pathogens, such as *Chlamydia* or gonococci, though other bacteria such as Gram-negative enteric organisms may be implicated.

Patients should be followed up to ensure cure. Partner(s) of men with NGU (including chlamydia) should be investigated and treated as for chlamydial infection, even if the *Chlamydia* swab is negative.

CHLAMYDIAL INFECTION IN FEMALES

The cervix and urethra are commonly involved. Infection may be asymptomatic in about 80% of patients or associated with vaginal discharge and/or dysuria. These symptoms may also be found in gonorrhoea (see p. 100), trichomoniasis or candidiasis (see pp. 106–107). Full investigation is essential (see Box 1.67, p. 97). Post-coital or intermenstrual bleeding may also be presenting features. Lower abdominal pain, dyspareunia and intermenstrual bleeding may suggest PID. Examination may reveal mucopurulent cervicitis, contact bleeding from cervix, evidence of PID or no obvious clinical signs. Treatment regimens for females with uncomplicated chlamydial infection are similar to those for males (see Box 1.77). Without treatment, some infections may clear spontaneously whilst others persist. Eventually, complications such as PID may develop, with the risk of tubal damage and subsequent infertility or ectopic pregnancy. The patient's male partner(s) should be investigated and treated, even in the absence of chlamydial infection.

Other complications include:

- perihepatitis
- chronic pelvic pain
- perinatal transmission to neonate: ophthalmia neonatorum, pneumonia
- conjunctivitis in adults
- Reiter's syndrome or SARA.

OTHER CHLAMYDIAL INFECTIONS

Chlamydia trachomatis also causes trachoma (see below) and lymphogranuloma venereum (see p. 104).

Chlamydia psittaci causes psittacosis (see p. 527).

Chlamydia pneumoniae is a cause of atypical pneumonia (see p. 526).

Trachoma

Trachoma is a specific communicable keratoconjunctivitis caused by *Chlamydia trachomatis*, and is the most common cause of avoidable blindness in the world. Transmission is usually by contact or from fomites in unhygienic surroundings. Some infections occur during birth from infected genital passages.

Vast numbers of people suffer from trachoma in the hot, dry, dusty areas of the subtropics and tropics, but it is also present in southern Europe and among immigrants in Britain.

The disease varies markedly in incidence and in severity in different geographical regions. In endemic areas the disease is most common in children.

Pathology

The infection lasts for years, may be latent over long periods and may recrudesce. The conjunctiva of the upper lid is first affected with vascularisation and cellular infiltration. Scarring causes inversion of the lids (entropion) so that the lashes rub against the cornea (trichiasis). The cornea becomes vascularised and opaque.

Clinical features

The onset is usually insidious and infection may not be apparent to the patient. Early symptoms include conjunctival irritation and blepharospasm, but the problem may not be detected until vision begins to fail. Trachoma may also present as an acute ophthalmia neonatorum.

The early follicles of trachoma are characteristic (see Fig. 1.73), but clinical differentiation from conjunctivitis due to other viruses may be difficult.

Investigations

Intracellular inclusions may be demonstrated in conjunctival scrapings by staining with iodine or immunofluorescence. Chlamydia may be isolated in chick embryo or cell culture.

Management

Ophthalmic ointment or oily drops of 1–3% tetracycline should be applied 12-hourly for 3 months. In mass therapy in endemic areas topical application 12-hourly for 3–6 consecutive days each month for 6 months has given good results. Oral tetracycline (15 mg/kg daily), doxycycline (15 mg/kg daily) or sulphonamide (30 mg/kg daily) given for 2 weeks is just as effective. Deformity and scarring of the lids, corneal opacities, ulceration and scarring require surgical treatment after control of local infection.

Prevention

Personal and family cleanliness should be improved. Proper care of the eyes of newborn and young children is essential. Family contacts should be examined. Population surveys lead to the discovery and treatment of asymptomatic infections. Trachoma clinics are required in areas of high endemicity.

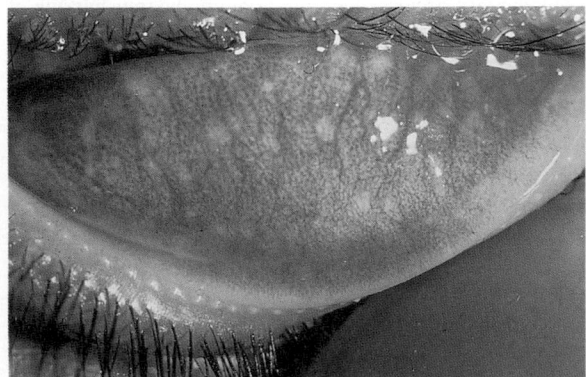

Fig. 1.73 Trachoma. Trachoma is characterised by hyperaemia and numerous pale follicles.

OTHER SEXUALLY TRANSMITTED BACTERIAL INFECTIONS

Chancroid, granuloma inguinale and lymphogranuloma venereum are described in Box 1.78.

SEXUALLY TRANSMITTED VIRAL INFECTIONS

GENITAL HERPES SIMPLEX

Infection with herpes simplex virus type 1 (HSV-1) or type 2 (HSV-2) produces a wide spectrum of clinical problems (see p. 30). Transmission is usually sexual—either vaginal, anal, orogenital or oroanal, but perinatal infection of the neonate may also occur. Primary infection at the site of HSV entry, which may be symptomatic or asymptomatic, establishes latency in local sensory ganglia. Recurrences, either symptomatic or asymptomatic viral shedding, are a consequence of HSV reactivation. The first symptomatic episode, either due to HSV-1 or HSV-2, is usually more severe in patients lacking serological evidence of previous HSV infection. Classically, HSV-1 has been associated with orolabial herpes and HSV-2 with anogenital herpes. HSV-1 now accounts for about 50% of anogenital infections in the UK.

Clinical features

The first symptomatic episode presents with irritable vesicles that soon rupture to form small, tender ulcers on the external genitalia (see Fig. 1.74). Lesions at other sites such as the urethra, vagina, cervix, perianal area, anus or rectum may be

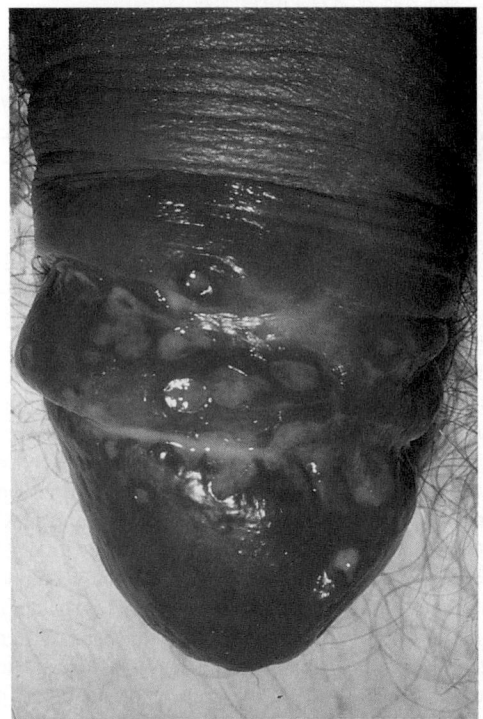

Fig. 1.74 Penile herpes simplex (HSV-2) infection.

1.78 SALIENT FEATURES OF LYMPHOGRANULOMA VENEREUM, CHANCROID AND GRANULOMA INGUINALE (DONOVANOSIS)

Infection and distribution	Organism	Incubation period	Genital lesion	Lymph nodes	Diagnosis	Management
Lymphogranuloma venereum (LGV) East/West Africa, India, South-east Asia, South America, Caribbean	*Chlamydia trachomatis* types L1, 2, 3	3–30 days	Small, transient, painless ulcer, vesicle, papule; often unnoticed	Tender, usually unilateral, matted, adherent, multilocular, suppurative bubo; inguinal/femoral nodes involved; there may be late sequelae[1]	Serological tests for L1–3 serotypes; swab from ulcer or bubo pus for *Chlamydia*	Doxycycline hyclate[2] 12-hourly orally for 21 days *or* Erythromycin 500 mg 6-hourly orally for 21 days
Chancroid Africa, Asia, Central and South America	*Haemophilus ducreyi*: short Gram-negative bacillus	3–10 days	Single or multiple painful ulcers with ragged undermined edges	As above but unilocular, suppurative bubo; inguinal nodes involved in ~50%	Microscopy and culture of scrapings from ulcer or pus from bubo	Azithromycin[3] 1 g orally once *or* Ceftriaxone 250 mg i.m. once *or* Ciprofloxacin[2] 500 mg 12-hourly orally for 3 days *or* Erythromycin 500 mg 6-hourly orally for 7 days
Granuloma inguinale Australia, Caribbean, India, South Africa, South America, Papua New Guinea	*Klebsiella granulomatis* (Donovan bodies)	3–40 days	Ulcers or hypertrophic granulomatous lesions; usually painless[4]	Initial swelling of inguinal nodes, then spread of infection to form abscess or ulceration through adjacent skin	Microscopy of cellular material for intracellular bipolar staining Donovan bodies	Azithromycin[3] 1 g weekly orally *or* 500 mg daily orally *or* Doxycycline hyclate[2] 100 mg 12-hourly orally *or* Ceftriaxone 1 g i.m. daily *or* Erythromycin 500 mg 6-hourly orally Treatment for at least 3 weeks and until lesions have healed

[1] The genito-ano-rectal syndrome is a late manifestation of LGV.
[2] Doxycycline hyclate and ciprofloxacin are contraindicated in pregnancy and breastfeeding.
[3] The safety of azithromycin in pregnancy and breastfeeding has not been fully assessed.
[4] Mother-to-baby transmission of granuloma inguinale may rarely occur.

Partners of patients with LGV, chancroid and granuloma inguinale should be investigated and treated, even if asymptomatic.

associated with dysuria, urethral or vaginal discharge, or anal, perianal or rectal pain. Constitutional symptoms such as fever, headache and malaise are frequent. Inguinal lymph nodes become enlarged and tender, and there may be nerve root pains in the 2nd and 3rd sacral dermatomes. Complications such as urinary retention due to autonomic neuropathy, and aseptic meningitis are occasionally seen. Extragenital lesions may develop at other sites such as buttock, finger or eye due to autoinoculation. Oropharyngeal infection may result from orogenital sex. First episodes usually heal within 2–4 weeks in the absence of treatment.

Recurrent symptomatic episodes are usually milder and of shorter duration than first episodes. They occur more often in HSV-2 infection. Their frequency tends to decrease with time. Prodromal symptoms such as irritation or burning at the subsequent site of recurrence, or neuralgic pains affecting buttocks, legs or hips, are commonly seen. It should be noted that a first symptomatic episode might be a recurrence in a patient who has had a previous asymptomatic primary infection. Recurrent episodes of asymptomatic viral shedding also occur and are important in the transmission of HSV.

Diagnosis
Swabs are taken from vesicular fluid or ulcers for tissue culture and typing. Electron microscopy of such material will only give a presumptive diagnosis, as herpes group viruses appear similar. Type-specific antibody tests are available but not yet in general use.

Management
First episode
The following 5-day oral regimens are all recommended and should be started within 5 days of the beginning of the episode, or whilst lesions are still forming. Treatment may be continued for longer than 5 days if new lesions develop.

Intravenous therapy should be given if oral therapy cannot be tolerated or if aseptic meningitis is associated:

- aciclovir 200 mg five times daily
- famciclovir 250 mg 8-hourly
- valaciclovir 500 mg 12-hourly.

Analgesia may be required and saline bathing can be soothing. Topical applications of petroleum jelly will help to prevent the development of adhesions between ulcerated surfaces.

Hospital admission will be required for severe symptoms and complications such as aseptic meningitis or urinary retention associated with autonomic neuropathy. Catheterisation via the suprapubic route is preferable for urinary retention to prevent the possible introduction of HSV into the bladder.

Recurrent genital herpes

Symptomatic recurrences are usually mild and may require no specific treatment other than saline bathing. For more severe episodes patient-initiated treatment at onset, with one of the following 5-day oral regimens, should reduce the duration of the recurrence:

- aciclovir 200 mg five times daily
- valaciclovir 500 mg 12-hourly
- famciclovir 125 mg 12-hourly.

In addition, treatment started when prodromal symptoms develop may abort recurrence.

Suppressive therapy may be required for patients with frequent recurrences. Treatment should be given for a maximum of 1 year before stopping to assess recurrence rate. About 20% of patients will experience reduced attack rates but for those where recurrences remain unchanged, resumption of suppressive therapy is justified. Recommended oral regimens are:

- aciclovir 400 mg 12-hourly
- aciclovir 200 mg 6-hourly
- famciclovir 250 mg 12-hourly
- valaciclovir 500 mg daily.

Management in pregnancy

Genital herpes acquired during the first or second trimester of pregnancy is treated with aciclovir as clinically indicated. Although aciclovir is not licensed for use in pregnancy, there is considerable clinical evidence to support its safety. Vaginal delivery is advised unless there is a recurrence at the beginning of labour, when delivery by caesarean section (CS) is recommended in the UK to prevent neonatal herpes. Aciclovir during the last 4 weeks of pregnancy has been shown to reduce the chance of a clinical recurrence at term and thus the need for CS in women who have acquired genital herpes during the first and second trimesters. Third-trimester acquisition should be treated with aciclovir as clinically indicated and CS recommended, particularly after 34 weeks, as the risk for viral shedding is very high in labour. CS is also recommended if there is recurrence at the onset of labour in women who have acquired genital herpes prior to pregnancy. CS may not completely prevent neonatal herpes and there are no randomised controlled trials to show efficacy.

Pregnant women with no previous anogenital herpes should be advised about the risk of acquiring infection as a result of orogenital sex. Partners of men with anogenital herpes should be strongly advised to refrain from sex during recurrences. Consistent condom use during pregnancy may reduce transmission of herpes simplex virus but this has yet to be proved.

ANOGENITAL WARTS

Human papillomavirus (HPV) DNA typing has demonstrated over 90 genotypes (see p. 1084). Most anogenital warts are benign and associated with HPV-6 and 11 infections. Some genotypes are associated with dysplastic conditions and cancers in the genital tract and anus. Anogenital warts are usually acquired as the result of sexual transmission of HPV. The frequency of non-sexual acquisition, such as from digital warts, is unknown. Perinatal transmission may also occur.

The disease spectrum encompasses:

- subclinical infection in the genital tract
- clinically obvious warts affecting penis, vulva, vagina, cervix, perineum or anus
- HPV-related cellular changes (koilocytes) on cervical cytology
- penile, vulval, vaginal, cervical or anal intraepithelial neoplasia or cancer
- oral warts
- juvenile laryngeal papillomas
- Buschke–Lowenstein tumour (giant condyloma).

Anogenital warts usually develop after an incubation period of up to 6 months. They may be single or multiple, exophytic, papular or flat. Perianal warts, whilst being more commonly found in men who have sex with men, are also found in heterosexual males and in females. Rarely, a giant condyloma develops with local tissue destruction. Atypical warts should be biopsied. In pregnancy warts may dramatically increase in size and number, making treatment difficult. Rarely, they are large enough to obstruct labour when delivery by CS will be required. Perinatal transmission of HPV may lead to anogenital warts or subclinical infection in the infant, or possibly laryngeal papillomas, which may present early or later in life.

A variety of treatments are available. Some are shown below:

- 0.5% podophyllotoxin solution (contraindicated in pregnancy) applied 12-hourly for 3 days, followed by 4 days' rest, for up to 4 weeks; suitable for external warts and home treatment
- topical 90% trichloroacetic acid each week: caution—very caustic to skin and mucous membranes; suitable for external and internal warts. Protect surrounding areas with petroleum jelly. Sodium bicarbonate should be available to neutralise accidental spills. For use in specialist centres only
- imiquimod cream applied 3 times weekly (wash off after 6–10 hours) for up to 16 weeks; suitable for external warts and home treatment. Contraindicated in pregnancy

- cryotherapy; suitable for external and internal warts
- hyfrecation; suitable for external and internal warts. (Hyfrecation results in smoke plume which contains HPVDNA and the potential to cause respiratory infection in the operator/patient. Masks should be worn during the procedure and adequate extraction provided)
- surgical removal.

Partners with genital warts should be treated. Females with abnormal cervical cytology should be referred for colposcopy, biopsy and treatment when necessary to prevent the potential development of cervical cancer. Colposcopy is also recommended for women with cervical warts before treatment. Patients and partners tend to use condoms whilst warts are present. The use of condoms to prevent the transmission of HPV to non-infected partners should be encouraged. However, HPV may affect parts of the genital area not protected by condoms. HPV vaccines are under development.

MOLLUSCUM CONTAGIOSUM

Infection by molluscum contagiosum virus, both sexual and non-sexual, produces flesh-coloured umbilicated hemispherical papules usually up to 5 mm in diameter after an incubation period of 3–12 weeks. Larger lesions may be seen in HIV infection (see p. 116). Lesions are often multiple and, once established in an individual, may spread by autoinoculation. They may be found on the genitalia, lower abdomen and upper thighs when sexually acquired. Diagnosis is made on clinical grounds and by expression of the central core, in which the typical pox-like viral particles can be seen on electron microscopy, differentiating molluscum contagiosum from genital warts. On average, lesions may be present for 2 years before spontaneous resolution occurs. Treatment regimens are therefore cosmetic and include cryotherapy, hyfrecation, topical applications of 0.5% podophyllotoxin cream (contraindicated in pregnancy), or expression of the central core.

HEPATITIS

The hepatitis viruses A–D (see pp. 862–866) may be sexually transmitted:

- *Hepatitis A (HAV)*. Insertive oroanal sex, insertive digital sex, insertive anal sex and multiple sexual partners have been linked with HAV transmission in men who have sex with men. HAV transmission in heterosexual men and women is also possible through oroanal sex.
- *Hepatitis B (HBV)*. Insertive oroanal sex, anal sex and multiple sexual partners are linked with HBV infection in men who have sex with men. Heterosexual transmission of HBV is well documented and commercial sex workers are at particular risk. Hepatitis D (HDV) may also be sexually transmitted.
- *Hepatitis C*. Sexual transmission of HCV is well documented both in men who have sex with men and in heterosexuals. Commercial sex workers are at greatest risk. Sexual transmission is less efficient than for HBV.

The sexual partner(s) of patients with HAV and HBV should be seen as soon as possible and offered immunisation (see pp. 862 and 864), if susceptible to these viruses and where appropriate. Patients with HAV should abstain from all forms of unprotected sex until non-infectious. Those with HBV should likewise abstain from unprotected sex until they are non-infectious or until their partners have been vaccinated successfully. No active or passive immunisation is available for protection against HCV but the consistent use of condoms is likely to protect susceptible partners. Sexual partners of patients with HAV, HBV and HCV should be screened for STIs. Active immunisation against HAV and HBV should be offered to susceptible people at risk of infection. Many STI clinics offer HAV immunisation to at-risk men who have sex with men, along with routine HBV immunisation. A combined HAV and HBV vaccine is available. The vertical transmission of HBV from mother to baby can be reduced dramatically by passive and active immunisation of the baby as soon as possible after birth.

OTHER GENITAL CONDITIONS

BALANITIS AND BALANOPOSTHITIS

Balanitis refers to inflammation of the glans penis, often extending to the undersurface of the prepuce when it is called balanoposthitis. Tight prepuce and poor hygiene may be aggravating factors. Aetiology is multifactorial. A variety of infections, skin conditions or other causes may be found (see Box 1.79). Candidiasis is sometimes associated with immune deficiency, diabetes mellitus, and the use of broad-spectrum antimicrobials, corticosteroids or antimitotic drugs.

Clinical features

Patients may complain of a penile rash, irritation, discomfort or discharge from under the prepuce, or difficulty in retracting it. Presentation will depend on cause. *Candida* can produce erythema and white adherent plaques whilst

1.79 CAUSES OF BALANITIS, BALANOPOSTHITIS, VULVOVAGINAL AND OTHER GENITAL CONDITIONS	
Infection	
• *Candida albicans*	• *Staph. aureus*
• *Trichomonas vaginalis*	• Herpes simplex virus
• Bacterial vaginosis	• Human papillomavirus
• Anaerobes	• Mycobacteria
• Group A and B streptococci	• Syphilis
Skin disorders	
• Circinate balanitis/vulvitis	• Eczema
• Zoon's balanitis	• Pemphigus
• Lichen sclerosus	• Penile intraepithelial neoplasia
• Lichen planus	• Kaposi's sarcoma
• Psoriasis	• Vulval pain syndromes
• Seborrhoeic dermatitis	• Atrophic vaginitis
Other	
• Fordyce's spots	• Fixed drug eruption
• Pearly penile papules	• Contact dermatitis
• Poor hygiene	• Stevens–Johnson syndrome

herpes simplex virus may cause ulcers. Erosive balanitis with foul-smelling discharge may be associated with anaerobic infection. Circinate balanitis occurs in Reiter's syndrome (see p. 1010) or sometimes alone. Painless erosions with raised edges develop on the glans, which may coalesce to produce a geographical appearance. Genital dermatoses may be diagnosed by clinical appearance and biopsy. Infections are investigated as in Box 1.67, page 97. Swabs from glans and undersurface of prepuce should be taken for the diagnosis of infection, and urine should be tested for glucose.

Management

Treatment should be given for specific infections (see Box 1.80). Local saline bathing is usually helpful, especially when no cause is found. Circinate balanitis should be treated with 1% hydrocortisone cream. The patient's partner(s) should be seen when a sexually transmissible cause is found for balanitis.

VULVOVAGINAL CONDITIONS

Vulval irritation, vaginal discharge and dysuria are troublesome complaints in women, particularly during their reproductive years. It is important to remember that vaginal discharge may be physiological. The vulva and/or vagina may be affected by a variety of infections or other conditions (see Box 1.80). Women with vulvovaginal candidiasis usually present with vulval irritation and vaginal discharge. External dysuria (discomfort when urine comes into contact with inflamed vulva) may also be noted. Vulval erythema, sometimes with oedema and fissures, is seen, usually with a curd-like vaginal discharge.

T. vaginalis infection (trichomoniasis) produces symptoms similar to genital candidiasis with vulval irritation/discomfort and offensive vaginal discharge, prominent features and dysuria sometimes present. Some patients have no symptoms. Vulvovaginitis is associated with vaginal discharge, which varies from thin and scanty to thick and profuse. Cervicitis is present in about 2%. Occasionally, clinical signs are absent. In pregnancy trichomoniasis may be associated with pre-term birth and low birth weight. Metronidazole is the treatment of choice for trichomoniasis. There have been concerns about its safety in pregnancy but published data do not support an association with increased teratogenicity. If patients are concerned about its use during the first trimester of pregnancy, clotrimazole pessaries may be prescribed for symptomatic patients, followed by metronidazole to eradicate infection after the first trimester (see Box 1.80).

1.80 TREATMENT OF BALANITIS AND VULVOVAGINAL INFECTIONS		
Cause	**Vulvovaginal condition**	**Balanitis**
Candidiasis	Clotrimazole[1] 500 mg pessary once at night and clotrimazole cream 12-hourly *or* Econazole[1] pessary 150 mg for 3 nights and econazole cream 12-hourly (topical creams for 7 days) *or* Fluconazole[2] 150 mg orally stat	Clotrimazole cream[1] 12-hourly until symptom-free, or alternative Fluconazole 150 mg orally stat for severe symptoms
Trichomoniasis	Metronidazole[3] 400–500 mg 12-hourly orally for 5–7 days *or* Metronidazole[3] 2 g orally as a single dose *Pregnancy* Metronidazole[3] 400–500 mg 12-hourly orally for 5–7 days *or if preferred by patient* Clotrimazole[1] pessaries 100 mg each night for 7 nights, for symptomatic infection in first trimester of pregnancy; metronidazole,[3] as above, thereafter	Metronidazole[3] 400–500 mg orally for 5–7 days *or* Metronidazole[3] 2 g as a single dose
Bacterial vaginosis	Metronidazole[3] 400–500 mg 12-hourly orally for 5–7 days, *or alternatives*: Metronidazole[3] vaginal gel 0.75% daily for 5 days Clindamycin[1,4] vaginal cream 2% daily for 7 days *Pregnancy* Metronidazole[3] oral regimen as above for symptomatic women Metronidazole[3] 400 mg 12-hourly orally for 7 days for asymptomatic women with history of second trimester miscarriage or idiopathic pre-term birth	
Anaerobic infection	Metronidazole[3] 400 mg 12-hourly orally for 7 days	Metronidazole[3] 400 mg 12-hourly orally for 7 days
Streptococcal/ staphylococcal infection	Choice of antibiotic depends on sensitivity tests	

[1] Clotrimazole, econazole and clindamycin damage latex condoms and diaphragms.
[2] Avoid in pregnancy and breastfeeding.
[3] Avoid alcoholic drinks until 48 hours after finishing treatment. Avoid high-dose regimens in pregnancy or breastfeeding.
[4] Pseudomembranous colitis has been reported with the use of clindamycin cream.

Bacterial vaginosis (BV) presents with offensive vaginal discharge in about 50% of patients. A mixture of *Gardnerella vaginalis*, *Mycoplasma hominis*, *Mobiluncus* and *Prevotella* species replaces vaginal lactobacilli. The aetiology is unknown. Thin white discharge coats the vagina and vestibule. BV has been linked with endometritis and PID following termination of pregnancy and a variety of adverse pregnancy outcomes, and these must be considered in management. BV can be seen in both sexually active and non-sexually active women and spontaneous recovery can occur. Diagnosis is made based on the presence of three of the following four criteria:

- thin, white, homogenous vaginal discharge
- vaginal fluid pH > 4.5
- clue cells seen on microscopy
- fishy odour on adding 10% potassium hydroxide to vaginal fluid on microscope slide.

(See Box 1.67, p. 97, for investigation of these infections and Box 1.80 for their treatment.) Partner notification is required if a sexually transmissible cause is found for vulvovaginitis but partners of women with candidiasis are usually not seen unless symptomatic. The partner(s) of women with trichomoniasis should be treated with metronidazole whether infection is found or not.

Genital dermatoses can be diagnosed on clinical appearance and biopsy. Many other conditions may present on the vulva or in the vagina (see Box 1.80). Patients with pubic lice (*Phthirus pubis* infestation) or who have sexually acquired scabies (see p. 1085) must be screened for other STIs.

HUMAN IMMUNODEFICIENCY VIRUS INFECTION AND THE HUMAN ACQUIRED IMMUNODEFICIENCY SYNDROME

EPIDEMIOLOGY AND BIOLOGY OF HIV

The acquired immunodeficiency syndrome (AIDS) was first recognised in 1981 and is caused by the human immunodeficiency virus (HIV-1). HIV-2 causes a similar illness to HIV-1 but is less aggressive and restricted mainly to Western Africa. The viruses almost certainly originated from closely related African primate viruses, simian immunodeficiency viruses (SIVs). Sequence analysis has led to the estimate that HIV-1 was introduced into humans in the early 1930s. Since 1981 AIDS has grown to be the second leading cause of disease burden world-wide and the leading cause of death in Africa (accounting for over 20% of deaths). It is now recognised that the immune deficiency is a consequence of continuous high-level HIV replication leading to virus and immune-mediated destruction of the key immune effector cell, the CD4 lymphocyte. The developing global epidemic has led to an unprecedented biomedical research programme on its pathogenesis and methods of control.

GLOBAL EPIDEMIC AND REGIONAL PATTERNS

In 2000, WHO estimated that there were over 36 million people living with HIV/AIDS, 5.3 million new infections and 3 million deaths. The cumulative death toll since the epidemic began was estimated at 21.8 million with 95% of cases occurring in sub-Saharan Africa; 13.2 million children have been orphaned. In Botswana, South Africa and Zimbabwe, 25–40% of adults are infected, with rates of up to 20% in most other sub-Saharan African countries. Spread of infection continues to rise alarmingly in other heavily populated parts of the world including some Eastern European (e.g. the Ukraine, Latvia and Russia) and South-east Asian (e.g. Thailand, Cambodia and Myanmar) countries. In India it is estimated that 4 million persons are infected.

Many different cultural, social and behavioural aspects determine the regional characteristics of HIV disease. In the USA and northern Europe, the epidemic has predominantly been in homosexual men, whereas in southern and Eastern Europe, Vietnam, Malaysia, North-east India and China the incidence has been greatest in injection drug users. In Africa, South America and much of South-east Asia the dominant route of transmission is heterosexual and from mother to child (vertical). The economic and demographic impact of HIV infection in developing countries is profound as it affects the most economically productive and fertile ages.

The epidemic in industrialised nations is changing. Heterosexual transmission has become the dominant route, causing 25–30% of new cases in Europe and the USA with racial and ethnic minorities representing an increasing fraction. In 1999 in the UK, 71% of patients with heterosexually acquired infection were recent arrivals from a country with a high prevalence of HIV, mainly sub-Saharan Africa. High-risk sexual behaviour is also increasing, with rates of rectal gonorrhoea and primary syphilis rising in the UK, USA and the Netherlands. Some of this relates to a misperception that HIV is 'treatable'.

MODES OF TRANSMISSION

HIV is present in blood, semen and other body fluids such as breast milk and saliva. Exposure to infected fluid leads to a risk of contracting infection, which is dependent on the integrity of the exposed site, the type and volume of body fluid, and the viral load. HIV can enter either as free virus or within cells. The major modes of spread are sexual, parenteral (blood or blood product recipients, injection drug users and those experiencing occupational injury) and vertical. The transmission risk after exposure is > 90% for blood or blood products, 15–40% for vertical, 0.5–1.0% for injection drug use, 0.2–0.5% for genital mucous membrane and < 0.1% for non-genital mucous membrane. Important factors increasing the risk of acquisition and measures available to reduce it are outlined in Boxes 1.81 and 1.82.

World-wide, the major route of transmission (> 70%) is heterosexual. About 5–10% of new HIV infections are in children and more than 90% of these are infected during pregnancy, birth or breastfeeding. The rate of mother-to-child

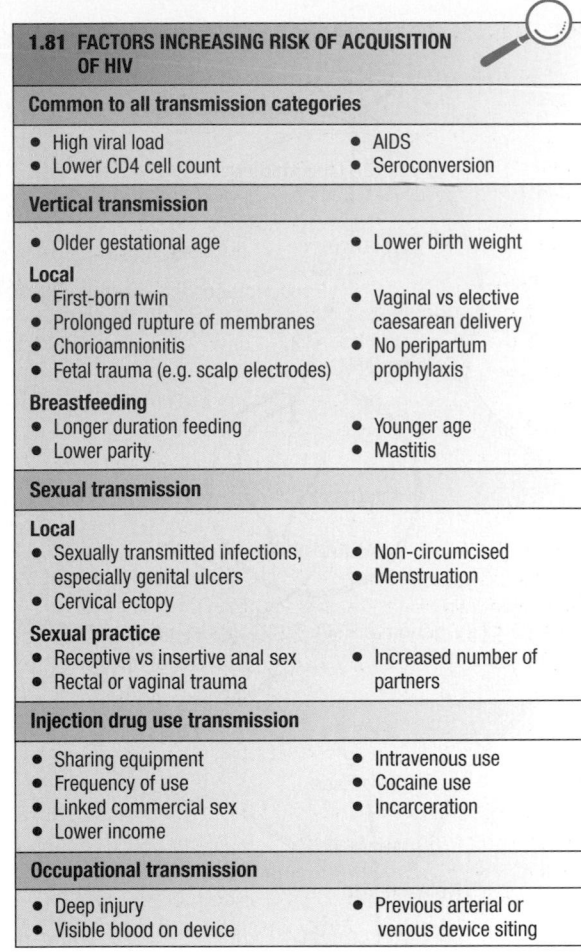

1.81 FACTORS INCREASING RISK OF ACQUISITION OF HIV	
Common to all transmission categories	
• High viral load	• AIDS
• Lower CD4 cell count	• Seroconversion
Vertical transmission	
• Older gestational age	• Lower birth weight
Local	
• First-born twin	• Vaginal vs elective
• Prolonged rupture of membranes	caesarean delivery
• Chorioamnionitis	• No peripartum
• Fetal trauma (e.g. scalp electrodes)	prophylaxis
Breastfeeding	
• Longer duration feeding	• Younger age
• Lower parity	• Mastitis
Sexual transmission	
Local	
• Sexually transmitted infections, especially genital ulcers	• Non-circumcised
	• Menstruation
• Cervical ectopy	
Sexual practice	
• Receptive vs insertive anal sex	• Increased number of
• Rectal or vaginal trauma	partners
Injection drug use transmission	
• Sharing equipment	• Intravenous use
• Frequency of use	• Cocaine use
• Linked commercial sex	• Incarceration
• Lower income	
Occupational transmission	
• Deep injury	• Previous arterial or
• Visible blood on device	venous device siting

1.82 PREVENTION MEASURES FOR HIV TRANSMISSION
Sexual
• Comprehensive school sex education programmes
• Public awareness campaigns for HIV
• Easily accessible/discreet testing centres
• Safe sex practices
Avoidance of penetrative intercourse
Correct/consistent condom use
Reduction of sexual partners/high-risk practices
• Targeting safe sex methods to high-risk groups
• Control of sexually transmitted diseases
Condom usage/education/early treatment
Parenteral
• Blood product transmission
Donor questionnaire
Routine screening of donated blood
Use of blood substitutes
• Injection drug use
Education (safe practice/support services/unprotected sex)
Needle/syringe exchange
Avoidance of high-risk situations ('shooting galleries', institutions)
Support for detoxification/drug rehabilitation services
Perinatal
• Routine antenatal HIV antibody testing
• Counselling about risks of pregnancy if HIV-seropositive
• Measures to reduce vertical transmission
Highly active antiretroviral therapy (HAART) treatment during pregnancy
Perinatal antiretroviral prophylaxis
Caesarean section
Zidovudine (ZDV) to neonate
Avoidance of breastfeeding
Occupational
• Education/training
Universal precautions
Needlestick avoidance
• Post-exposure prophylaxis

transmission is higher in developing countries (25–44%) than in industrialised nations (13–25%), although postnatal transmission via breast milk may account for some of this increased risk. Of those infected vertically, 80% are infected close to the time of delivery and 20% in utero. Around 70% of patients with haemophilia A and 30% of those with haemophilia B had been infected through contaminated blood products by the time HIV antibody screening was adopted in the USA and Europe. The risk of HIV transmission with a single blood unit is now 1 in 10^6 and represents blood donors in the seroconverting phase of infection. There have been approximately 100 definite and 200 possible cases of HIV acquired occupationally in health-care workers. Confirmation requires the demonstration of seroconversion in the context of exposure.

EBM

PREVENTION MEASURES FOR HIV TRANSMISSION

'Two SRs and one case-controlled study have shown that interventions can be successful in preventing the transmission of HIV.'

• Brocklehurst P. Interventions aimed at decreasing the risk of mother to child transmission of HIV infection. Cochrane Library, issue 1, 2001. Oxford: Update Software.
• Cardo DM, Culver DH, Ciesielski CA. A case control study of HIV seroconversion in health care workers after percutaneous exposure. N Engl J Med 1997; 337:1485–1490.
• Hurley SF, Jolley DJ, Kaldor JM. Effectiveness of needle exchange programmes for prevention of HIV infection. Lancet 1997; 349:1797–1800.

Further information: www.cochrane.co.uk
www.clinicalevidence.org

VIROLOGY AND IMMUNOLOGY

A glossary of terms and abbreviations is given in Box 1.83.

HIV is a single-stranded RNA retrovirus from the Lentivirus family. Following mucosal exposure, HIV is transported to the lymph nodes via dendritic, CD4 or Langerhans cells, where infection becomes established. Free or cell-associated virus is then disseminated widely through the blood with seeding of 'sanctuaries' (CNS, spleen, testes, intestinal mucosal lymphoid tissue) and latent CD4 cell reservoirs. With time, there is gradual attrition of the CD4 cell population, resulting in increasing impairment of cell-mediated immunity with consequent susceptibility to opportunistic infections. This underlies the pathogenesis of the clinical disease.

Each mature virion is spherical in shape; it has a lipid membrane lined by a matrix protein and studded with glycoprotein (gp) 120 and gp 41 spikes surrounding a cone-shaped protein core. This core houses two copies of the ssRNA genome and viral enzymes. The virus infects the CD4 cell in a complicated sequence of events involving initial attachment and receptor engagement through the

1.83 GLOSSARY AND EXPLANATION

• CD4 cells	Strictly, refers to all cells bearing the CD4 receptor (including Langerhans cells and dendritic cells). In the context of this chapter, refers to CD4 lymphocytes
• Class	Type of drug defined by mode of action (e.g. NRTI)
• HAART	Highly active antiretroviral therapy (combination treatment)
• Immune therapy	Drugs designed to improve CD4 or CD8 responses
• NNRTI	Non-nucleoside reverse transcriptase inhibitor
• NRTI	Nucleoside reverse transcriptase inhibitor
• PEP	Post-exposure prophylaxis
• PI	Protease inhibitor
• Resistance test	In vitro assessment of drug susceptibility
• Salvage therapy	Drugs used for multiresistant virus
• Seroconversion	Clinical illness following recent HIV infection
• STI	Structured treatment interruption
• TDM	Therapeutic drug monitoring
• Undetectable VL	Plasma VL below detection (< 50 copies/ml)
• Viral load (VL)	Quantitative level of plasma RNA virus
• Virological failure	Detectable VL despite treatment

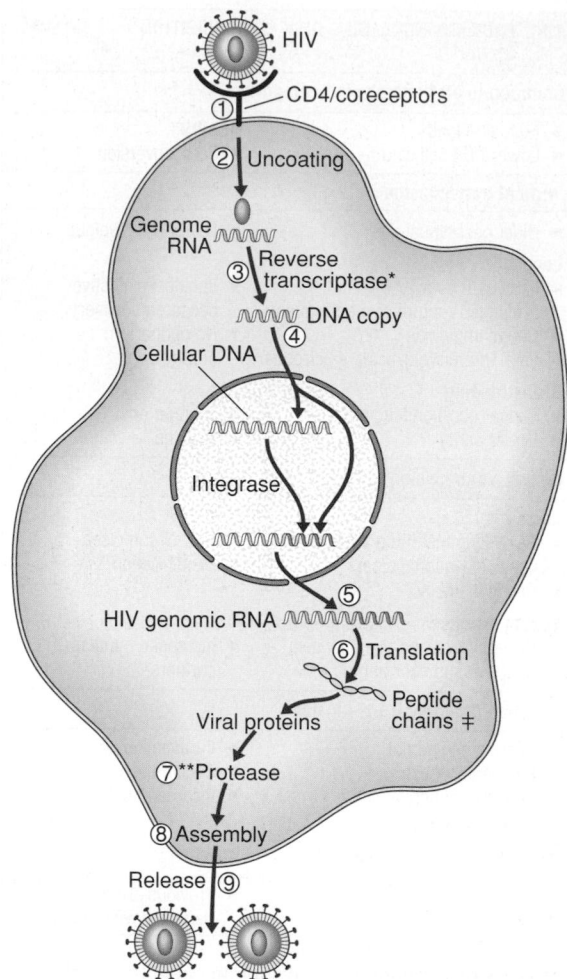

Fig. 1.75 **Schematic representation of HIV entry, disassembly, replication and release from susceptible cell (lymphocyte or macrophage).** (1) HIV binds to cell surface via receptors (CD4 molecule and coreceptors). (2) Viral uncoating in cytoplasm. (3) RNA viral genome transcribed to DNA copy–reverse transcriptase (RT) enzyme.* (4) DNA copy integrates into host cell genome in cell nucleus via integrase enzyme. (5) Following cell activation viral DNA is translated to RNA copies in cytoplasm. (6) Viral peptide chains translated from cytoplasmic viral RNA. (7) HIV protease cleaves functional viral proteins from polypeptides.** (8) Virion assembly. (9) Viral release from cell surface—cell lysis.

* RT inhibitors act here.

** Protease inhibitors act here.

viral gp 120 and the CD4 cell receptor (see Fig. 1.75). Other cells expressing the CD4 cell receptor and permissive to infection are monocyte-macrophages, follicular dendritic cells and microglial cells in the central nervous system. HIV can also infect astrocytes through CD4 cell receptor-independent attachment and fusion involving the chemokine receptor CXCR4.

Having penetrated the cell, a DNA copy is transcribed from the RNA genome by the reverse transcriptase (RT) enzyme that is carried by the infecting virion. Reverse transcription is an error-prone process, and multiple mutations arise with ongoing replication (hence the rapid generation of viral resistance to drugs). This DNA may persist in the cytoplasm as unintegrated non-productive circles (2-LTRs) or else be transported into the nucleus and integrated randomly within the host cell genome. Integrated virus is known as proviral DNA. On host-cell activation, this DNA copy is used as a template to transcribe new RNA copies, following which translation results in the production of viral proteins. The precursor polyproteins are then cleaved by the viral protease enzyme to form new viral structural proteins and viral enzymes such as the reverse transcriptase and protease. These then migrate to the cell surface and are assembled using the host cellular apparatus to produce infectious viral particles. These bud from the cell surface incorporating the host cell membrane as their own lipid bilayer coat and cell lysis occurs (see Fig. 1.76). The new infectious virus (virion) is then available to infect uninfected cells and repeat the process. It has been calculated that each day more than 10^{10} virions are produced and 10^{9} CD4 cells destroyed. This represents a turnover of 30% of the total viral burden and 6–7% of the total body CD4 cells daily. A small percentage of T cells (< 0.01%) enter a post-integration latent phase and represent the main reservoir of HIV (see Fig. 1.77). Within these cells there is ongoing low-level replication even when plasma levels of HIV are below the levels of detection as a result of antiretroviral treatment. They are important as sanctuary sites from antiviral therapy, continuing sources of virus (including the generation of drug-resistant strains) and as eventual targets for eradication strategies. The half-life of the virus is 1–2 hours in plasma, 1.5 days in productively infected CD4 cells and > 12 months in latently infected CD4 cells.

On the basis of DNA sequencing, HIV-1 can be subdivided into group M ('major', world-wide distribution), group O ('outlier', restricted to West Africa and divergent from group M) and group N (rare and highly divergent). Groups M and

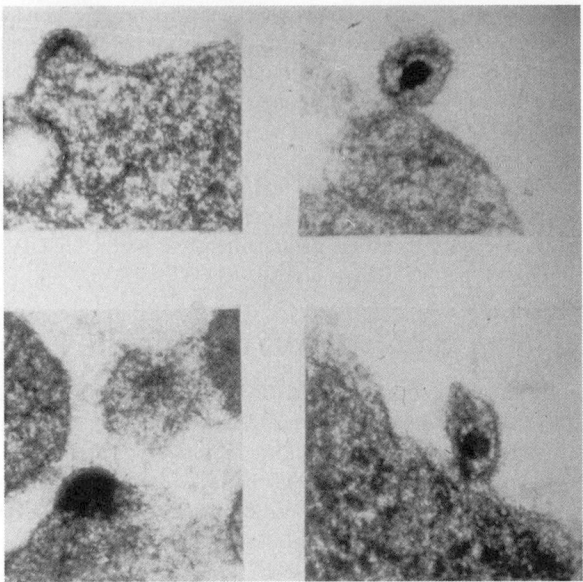

Fig. 1.76 Human immunodeficiency virus. Transmission electron micrograph of the virus budding from the surface of an infected CD4 lymphocyte.

O can be subdivided further into subtypes or clades. There are 10 subtypes for group M, lettered A–K. Subtype B predominates in North America, Australia and Europe, subtype A in Africa, subtype C in South Africa and India, and subtype E in Thailand. Although it would appear that the clinical disease produced by each one is identical, certain subtypes are suited to transmission in certain categories. Many countries host several group M subtypes (e.g. in Africa) and genetic recombinants have been identified (e.g. A/E), especially in sub-Saharan Africa. HIV-2 is an important but separate retrovirus occurring in West Africa or countries with ties to this region and has at least five subtypes. The virus differs from HIV-1 in that patients have lower viral loads, slower CD4 decline, lower rates of vertical transmission, and slower progression to AIDS (12-fold lower).

As CD4 cells are pivotal in orchestrating the immune response, any depletion in numbers renders the body susceptible to opportunistic infections and oncogenic virus-related tumours. The predominant opportunist infections seen in HIV disease are intracellular parasites (e.g. *Mycobacterium tuberculosis*) or pathogens susceptible to cell-mediated rather than antibody-mediated immune responses. The reduction in the number of CD4 cells circulating in peripheral blood is tightly correlated with the amount of plasma viral load. (The exact mechanisms underlying the decline are not well understood.) Both are monitored closely in patients and are used as measures of disease progression. Virus-specific CD8 cytotoxic T-cell lymphocytes develop rapidly after infection and are the most important mechanism in recognising, binding and lysing infected CD4 cells. They play a crucial role in controlling HIV replication after infection and determine the viral 'set-point' and subsequent rate of disease progression.

DIAGNOSIS

LABORATORY CONFIRMATION

Confirmation of HIV infection is by ELISA antibody testing. This is based on using immunodominant proteins (e.g. gp 160, gp 120, p24, p17/18) that are recombinant, synthetic or produced from infected cell lysates, which then react with antibodies in the person's serum. False positive reactions are exceedingly rare but it is important that any positive result is confirmed using a different commercial assay and by

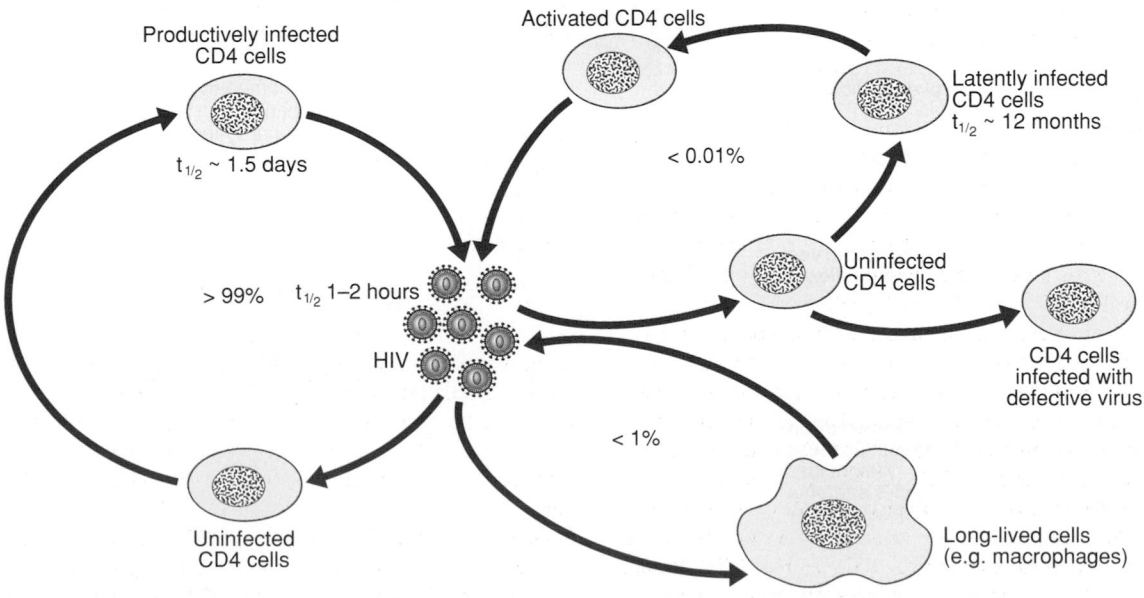

Fig. 1.77 Viral dynamics.

a different immunoassay (e.g. competitive ELISA or immunoblot). False negative results are also rare but may occur with HIV-2 infections and have been reported with the earlier assays for non-B subtypes and type O strains. For seroconversion (HIV antibody-negative) and vertical transmission (HIV antibody-positive), serology is unhelpful and HIV-RNA must be measured. This is based on nucleic acid amplification using reverse transcriptase (PCR), branched chain (bDNA) or sequence-based (NASBA) techniques that all have similar sensitivity and specificity.

PRE- AND POST-TEST COUNSELLING

Prior to HIV antibody testing, the patient must see a counsellor. Pre-test counselling involves an assessment of the risk of exposure and explores a person's knowledge about HIV infection (differences between HIV and AIDS, advantages and disadvantages of being tested, modes of transmission, safer sex etc.). It also allows the counsellor to assess how the person will cope with a positive result and to help him or her plan for this possibility (e.g. whom to tell). The counsellor must explain the test procedure and how the result is given, and obtain informed consent. Where the test result returns positive, it is vital to provide emotional support, review coping strategies and organise continued contact and medical follow-up. Many of the implications of a positive result are the same the world over (fear of disclosure, discrimination) but there is a real risk of violence and social rejection in some developing nation societies. Imparting knowledge on HIV takes time, but it is important that an assessment of the need for any behavioural change is made and individuals persuaded of its importance (e.g. safer sex, needle exchange); written information should also be supplied. Counselling is also important for those uninfected but at risk (to modify behaviour patterns), for HIV-infected patients (to help cope with decisions on treatment etc.), and for HIV-uninfected partners and families.

CLINICAL DIAGNOSIS AND INVESTIGATION

Following a positive diagnosis of HIV, it is imperative that a full medical history is taken and examination performed. Close attention should be paid to features indicating early symptomatic (e.g. lymphadenopathy, fevers and night sweats, unexplained weight loss, diarrhoea, skin rashes) or advanced disease (e.g. breathlessness, pain on swallowing, visual symptoms). Evidence of previous negative tests and/or a history consistent with seroconversion may allow an estimate as to when the individual was infected. Other important features are the patient's birthplace, residence and travel history; remote or recent TB contact; sexual risk behaviour and history of sexually transmitted infections; immunisations (hepatitis A/B, BCG, influenza); contact with animals; cardiac risk factors; and occupation, hobbies

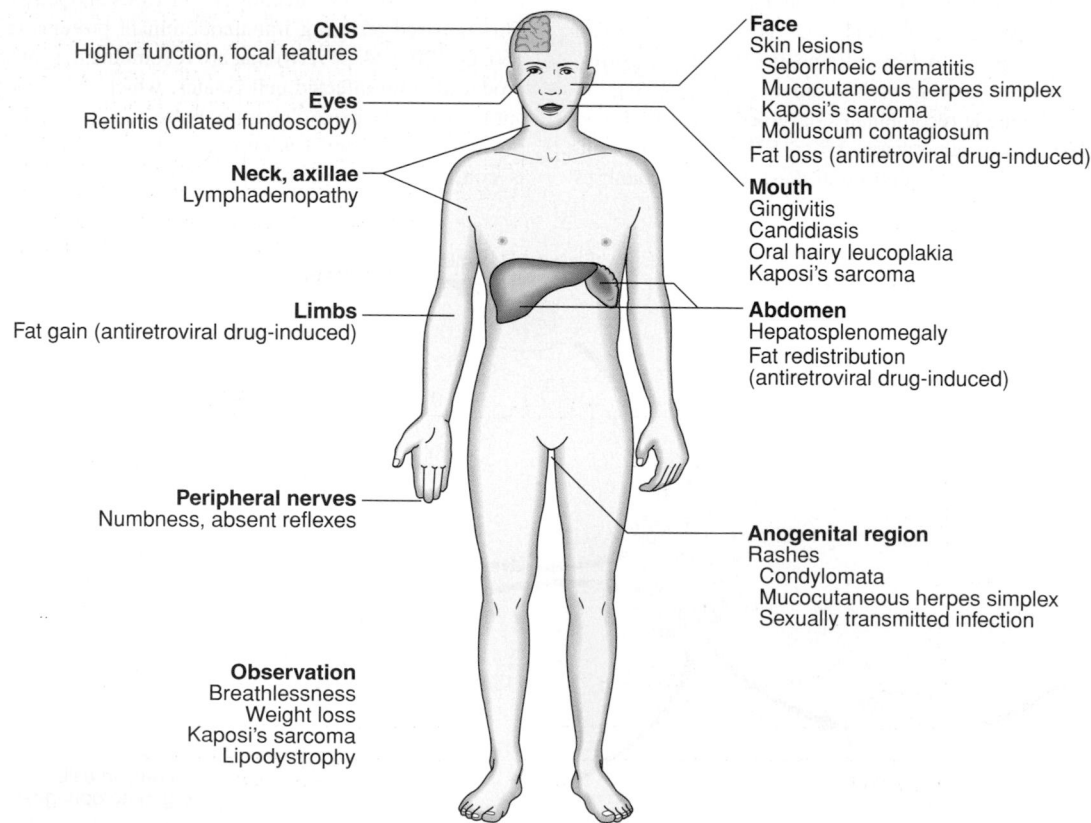

Fig. 1.78 HIV: clinical examination.

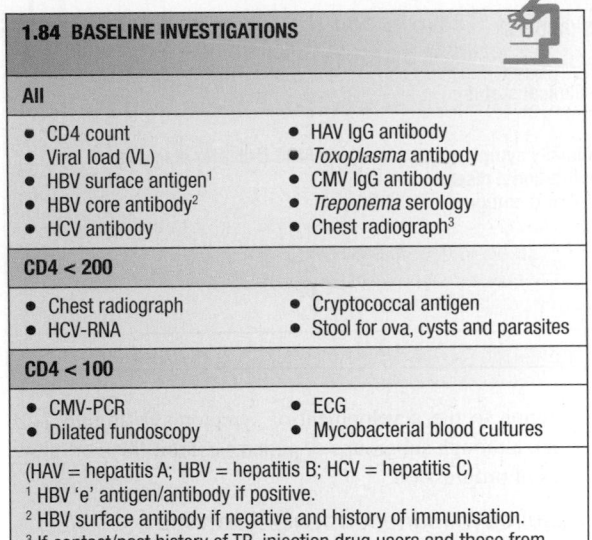

1.84 BASELINE INVESTIGATIONS

All

- CD4 count
- Viral load (VL)
- HBV surface antigen[1]
- HBV core antibody[2]
- HCV antibody
- HAV IgG antibody
- *Toxoplasma* antibody
- CMV IgG antibody
- *Treponema* serology
- Chest radiograph[3]

CD4 < 200

- Chest radiograph
- HCV-RNA
- Cryptococcal antigen
- Stool for ova, cysts and parasites

CD4 < 100

- CMV-PCR
- Dilated fundoscopy
- ECG
- Mycobacterial blood cultures

(HAV = hepatitis A; HBV = hepatitis B; HCV = hepatitis C)
[1] HBV 'e' antigen/antibody if positive.
[2] HBV surface antibody if negative and history of immunisation.
[3] If contact/past history of TB, injection drug users and those from TB-endemic areas.

and recreational drug use. The patient should be encouraged to inform the GP, and those who know the diagnosis or can be contacted if needed (e.g. partner, family GP) should be documented. Particular features on examination are detailed in Figure 1.78. Baseline investigations are given in Box 1.84. A genitourinary infection screen should be performed on every patient soon after diagnosis. This needs to include a baseline pelvic examination and cervical smear on women and proctoscopy/anoscopy on men. Repeat *Toxoplasma*, CMV, hepatitis and treponemal serology needs to be performed every 18–24 months in patients initially found to be negative and cervical cytology should be performed annually in women. Patients should be assessed for their need for hepatitis A and hepatitis B vaccines and immunised if there is no evidence of naturally acquired infection. HBV surface antibody levels should be monitored and boosters given when

< 100 IU/ml. Response to all immunisations is less when the CD4 count is < 200 cells/mm³ although some protection is afforded.

NATURAL HISTORY AND CLASSIFICATION OF HIV

Primary infection

Primary infection is symptomatic in 70–80% of cases and usually occurs 2–4 weeks after exposure. The major clinical manifestations are fever (80%), an erythematous maculo-papular rash mainly over the trunk (60%), fatigue (80%), pharyngitis with cervical lymphadenitis (50%), myalgia and arthralgia (50%), headache with retro-orbital pain (40%), and mucosal ulceration (mouth 20%, genital 10%). Rarely, presentation may be neurological (aseptic meningitis, encephalitis, myelitis, polyneuritis). This coincides with a surge in plasma HIV RNA levels to > 1 million copies/ml (peak between 4 and 8 weeks), and a fall in the CD4 count to 300–400 cells/mm³ but occasionally to below 200 when opportunistic infections (e.g. oropharyngeal candidiasis, *Pneumocystis carinii* pneumonia) may rarely occur (see Fig. 1.79). Symptomatic recovery occurs after 1–2 weeks but occasionally may take up to 10 weeks and parallels the return of the CD4 count and fall in the viral load. In many patients the illness is mild and only identified by retrospective enquiry at later presentation. However, the CD4 count rarely recovers to its previous value. Diagnosis is made by detecting HIV-RNA in the serum or by immunoblot assay (which shows antibodies developing to early proteins). The appearance of specific anti-HIV antibodies in serum (seroconversion) takes place later at 3–12 weeks (median 8 weeks), although very rarely seroconversion may take place after 3 months. Factors likely to indicate a faster progression of HIV are the presence and duration of symptoms, evidence of candidiasis, and neurological involvement. The level of the viral

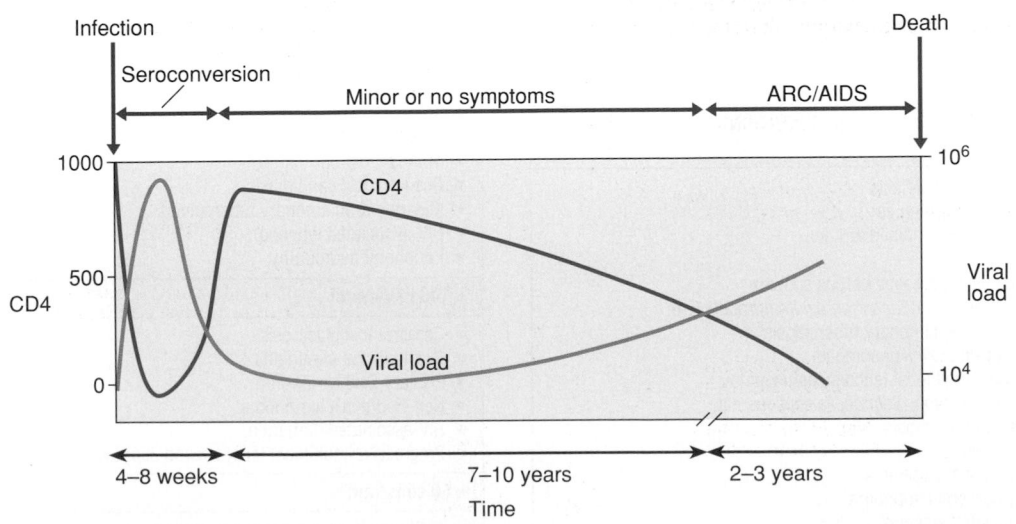

Fig. 1.79 Virological and immunological progression of HIV infection.

1.85 CDC 1993-REVISED CLASSIFICATION FOR HIV INFECTION AND AIDS (ADULTS)

CD4 count	Clinical status		
	A Asymptomatic disease Acute seroconversion Persistent generalised lymphadenopathy	**B** Minimally symptomatic constitutional disease Not A or C category	**C** AIDS indicator diseases
> 500/mm³	A1	B1	C1*
200–499/mm³	A2	B2	C2*
< 200/mm³	A3*	B3*	C3*

Fulfils criteria for 'AIDS' definition (A3 and B3 in the USA only).

load post-seroconversion strongly correlates with the spread of subsequent progression of disease. The differential diagnosis of primary HIV includes acute EBV, CMV, streptococcal pharyngitis, toxoplasmosis and secondary syphilis.

Asymptomatic infection

Asymptomatic infection (category A disease) follows for a variable period, during which the infected individual remains well with no evidence of disease except for the possible presence of persistent generalised lymphadenopathy (PGL; defined as enlarged glands at ≥ 2 extra-inguinal sites) (see Box 1.85). At this stage the bulk of virus replication takes place within lymphoid tissue (e.g. follicular dendritic cells). There is sustained viraemia with a decline in CD4 count dependent on the height of the viral load but usually between 50 and 150 cells/year (see Fig. 1.79).

Mildly symptomatic disease

Mildly symptomatic disease (category B disease) then develops in the majority, indicating some impairment of the cellular immune system. These diseases correspond to AIDS-related complex conditions but by definition are not AIDS-defining. Included in this category are chronic weight loss, fever or diarrhoea (but not fulfilling criteria for AIDS), oral or vaginal candidiasis, oral hairy leucoplakia, recurrent herpes zoster infections, severe pelvic inflammatory disease, bacillary angiomatosis, cervical dysplasia and idiopathic thrombocytopenic purpura. The median interval from

infection to the development of symptoms is around 7–10 years, although subgroups of patients exhibit 'fast' or 'slow' rates of progression.

Acquired immunodeficiency syndrome

Acquired immunodeficiency syndrome (category C disease) is defined by the development of specified opportunistic infections, tumours etc. (see Box 1.86). The correlation between CD4 count and HIV-related diseases is presented in Box 1.87.

1.87 CORRELATIONS BETWEEN CD4 COUNT AND HIV-ASSOCIATED DISEASES

> 500 cells/mm³

- Acute primary infection
- Progressive generalised lymphadenopathy
- Recurrent vaginal candidiasis

200–500 cells/mm³

- Pulmonary tuberculosis
- Herpes zoster
- Oropharyngeal candidiasis
- Oral hairy leucoplakia
- Salmonellosis
- Kaposi's sarcoma
- HIV-associated idiopathic thrombocytopenic purpura
- Cervical intraepithelial neoplasia II–III
- Lymphoid interstitial pneumonitis

< 200 cells/mm³

- *Pneumocystis carinii* pneumonia
- Mucocutaneous herpes simplex
- *Cryptosporidium*
- *Microsporidium*
- Oesophageal candidiasis
- Miliary/extrapulmonary tuberculosis
- HIV-associated wasting
- Peripheral neuropathy

< 100 cells/mm³

- Cerebral toxoplasmosis
- Cryptococcal meningitis
- Primary CNS lymphoma
- Non-Hodgkin's lymphoma
- HIV-associated dementia
- Progressive multifocal leucoencephalopathy

< 50 cells/mm³

- CMV retinitis/gastrointestinal disease
- Disseminated *Mycobacterium avium intracellulare*

1.86 COMMON AIDS-DEFINING CONDITIONS

- Oesophageal candidiasis
- Cryptococcal meningitis
- Chronic cryptosporidial diarrhoea
- CMV retinitis
- Chronic mucocutaneous herpes simplex
- Disseminated *Mycobacterium avium intracellulare*
- Miliary or extrapulmonary tuberculosis
- *Pneumocystis carinii* pneumonia
- Progressive multifocal leucoencephalopathy
- Recurrent non-typhi *Salmonella* septicaemia
- Cerebral toxoplasmosis
- Kaposi's sarcoma
- Non-Hodgkin's lymphoma
- Primary cerebral lymphoma
- HIV-associated wasting
- HIV-associated dementia

CLINICAL SYNDROMES AND SPECIFIC CONDITIONS

HIV disease is unique for the range of unusual organisms and malignancies that occur. Most of these have a predilection for one site but in the face of profound CD4 cell loss (< 50 cells/mm³), a disseminated presentation is more likely. The following sections are organ-based, with reference where necessary to other areas where a particular pathogen or neoplasm is discussed in more detail.

MUCOCUTANEOUS DISEASE

Presentation and differential diagnosis

Mucocutaneous manifestations are common in HIV and range from the trivial to being a marker of significant systemic infection (see Boxes 1.88 and 1.89). Most patients are affected at some time and for many it is a major problem. Dermatological problems may present atypically, coexist with other pathologies and be harder to manage than in an HIV-negative person. Type and severity of rash are often dependent upon the level of CD4 count. The presence of either oropharyngeal candidiasis or oral hairy leucoplakia in a young person is an indicator for HIV.

Specific skin conditions

Fungal infections

Early HIV-associated skin diseases include xerosis with pruritus, seborrhoeic dermatitis, and an itchy folliculitic rash which may be fungal *(Malassezia furfur)*, staphylococcal or eosinophilic in aetiology. Dermatophyte infection affecting skin (feet, body, face) and nails is also common, and may be extensive and difficult to treat. Seborrhoeic dermatitis is very common in HIV and severity increases as the CD4 count falls, being present in up to 80% of patients with AIDS. It presents as dry scaly red patches on the face (typically on the cheeks, in the nasolabial folds, around the eyebrows, behind the ears and on the scalp). If severe, it may affect other hairy areas such as chest, axillae and groin. The cause is multifactorial but *Malassezia furfur* is important.

Viral infections

The major viral infections affecting the skin are herpes simplex, varicella zoster, human papillomavirus (HPV) and molluscum contagiosum.

Herpes simplex (type 1 or 2) may affect lips, mouth, skin or anogenital area and is seen in 20% of cases. In later-stage HIV, the lesions are usually chronic, extensive, harder to treat and recurrent (see Fig. 1.80). Persistent and severe anogenital ulceration is usually herpetic and a marker for underlying HIV.

Varicella zoster usually presents with a dermatomal vesicular rash on an erythematous base and may be the first clue to a diagnosis of HIV infection. It can occur at any stage but is more frequent with failing immunity. In patients with a low CD4 count (< 100 cells/mm³) the rash may be more severe, multidermatomal, persistent or recurrent, or may become disseminated. Involvement of the trigeminal nerve, scarring on recovery and associated motor defects are

1.88 DIFFERENTIAL DIAGNOSIS OF HIV-RELATED SKIN DISEASE

Early HIV

Infection
- Herpes simplex
- Varicella zoster
- HPV
- Impetigo
- Dermatophytosis
- Scabies
- Syphilis

Other
- Xeroderma
- Pruritus
- Seborrhoeic dermatitis
- Itchy folliculitis
- Psoriasis
- Acne

Late HIV

Common
- Kaposi's sarcoma
- Molluscum contagiosum
- Chronic mucocutaneous herpes simplex

Rare
- Bacillary angiomatosis
- CMV
- Non-Hodgkin's lymphoma
- Cryptococcus
- Histoplasmosis
- Mycobacterial (TB/atypical)

1.89 DIFFERENTIAL DIAGNOSIS OF HIV-RELATED ORAL DISEASE

Early HIV
- Oral hairy leucoplakia
- Herpes simplex
- Oropharyngeal candidiasis
- Aphthous ulcers
- Periodontitis
- Syphilis
- HPV
- Herpes zoster

Late HIV
- Kaposi's sarcoma
- Drug reaction (e.g. ddC)
- Lymphoma
- CMV

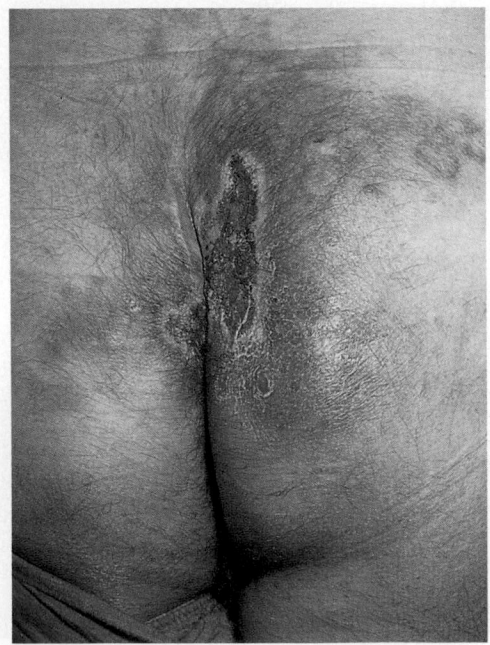

Fig. 1.80 Severe mucocutaneous herpes simplex. Perianal or perioral infection is not uncommon in later-stage HIV infection.

probably also more common. Diagnosis of herpetic infection can be confirmed on culture, smear preparations showing characteristic inclusion bodies, electron microscopy or biopsy. Oral aciclovir should be given for all cases of active disease, irrespective of the time since onset of rash (a higher dose is used in herpes zoster). In patients with severe mucocutaneous herpes simplex or herpes zoster which is disseminated, multidermatomal, ophthalmic or very dense, or when the CD4 count is < 350 cells/mm³, parenteral aciclovir must be used.

Human papillomavirus infection is frequent amongst HIV patients and is usually anogenital (see p. 105), where disease may be extensive and very difficult to manage. Lesions on the hands and feet (especially periungual) are also common and may attain considerable size requiring surgery. Occasionally, myriads of flat-topped papules occur over the body and face. Both oncogenic (16, 18, 31, 33) and non-oncogenic genotypes (6, 11) are found. There is often improvement on HAART.

Molluscum contagiosum is an epidermal poxvirus infection, which in non-HIV-infected persons is a self-limiting infection of children with a propensity to involve the trunk. It is found in approximately 10% of AIDS patients (see Fig. 1.81). The lesions are usually 2–5 mm diameter papules with a central umbilicus and most frequently affect the face, neck, scalp and genital region. Lesions may become widespread and attain a large size (giant mollusca). With improvement in CD4 counts, lesions often disappear.

Bacterial and parasitic infections

Bacterial infections include *Staph. aureus* (folliculitis, cellulitis and abscesses), bacillary angiomatosis, and syphilis (primary and secondary—see pp. 96–100). Bacillary angiomatosis is a bacterial infection due to the cat-scratch bacillus, *Bartonella henselae*. Skin lesions range from solitary superficial reddish-purple lesions resembling Kaposi's sarcoma or pyogenic granuloma, to multiple subcutaneous nodules or even hyperpigmented plaques. Lesions are painful and may bleed or ulcerate. The infection may become disseminated with fevers, lymphadenopathy and hepatosplenomegaly. Diagnosis is made by Warthin–Starry silver staining which reveals aggregates of bacilli.

In HIV, scabies (due to the mite *Sarcoptes scabiei*—see p. 1085) may cause intensely pruritic, encrusted papules affecting most areas. Classically, the interdigital web spaces, wrists, periumbilical area, buttock and sides of the feet are involved. Commonly in HIV the infestation may be heavy, the rash hyperkeratotic (Norwegian scabies) and the patient highly infectious. Uniquely, the face and neck are often affected. Rarely, cutaneous disease may be a manifestation of mycobacterial infection (tuberculosis or an atypical mycobacterium) or disseminated fungal infection.

Specific oral conditions

Candidiasis

Candida infection in HIV is almost exclusively mucosal, affects nearly all patients with CD4 counts that drop below 200 cells/mm³, and is nearly always caused by *Candida albicans* in early disease (see Fig. 1.82). Pseudomembranous candidiasis describes white patches on the buccal mucosa that can be scraped off to reveal a red raw surface. The tongue, palate and pharynx may also be involved. Less common is erythematous candidiasis when patients present with a sore mouth with reddened mucosa and a smooth shiny tongue. Hypertrophic candidiasis (leucoplakia-like lesions

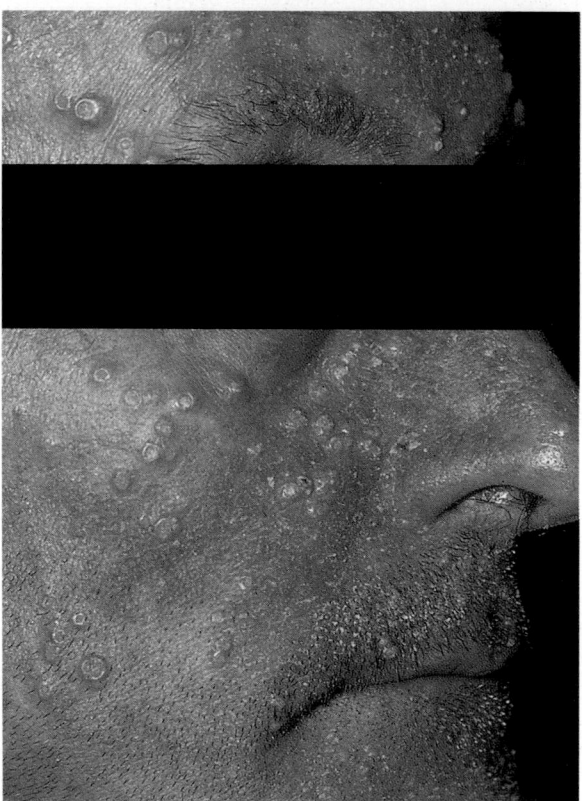

Fig. 1.81 Molluscum contagiosum. Extensive and disfiguring involvement of the face may occur.

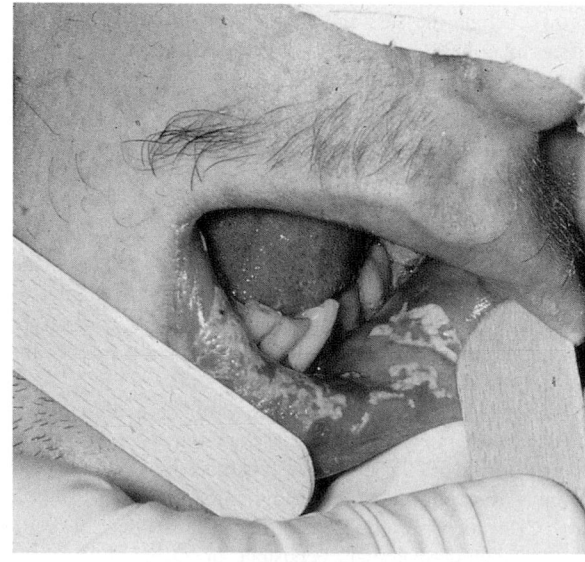

Fig. 1.82 Oral candidiasis. A careful examination of the mouth is important as plaques may initially be quite small.

which do not scrape off but which respond to antifungal treatment) and angular cheilitis may also be present. Diagnosis is clinical but it is important to perform a mouth swill for culture, speciation and sensitivities in patients unresponsive to fluconazole or other azole drugs. The cause is mostly *Candida albicans* although occasionally non-*albicans Candida* may be responsible (e.g. *C. glabrata*, *C. krusei*), in which case azole resistance is more likely. Prophylaxis is not recommended and therapeutic courses of azoles should be given with each attack.

Oesophageal infection may coexist although in up to 30% there is no oropharyngeal candidiasis visible. Up to 80% of patients presenting with pain on swallowing have *Candida* oesophagitis (see p. 778 for differential diagnosis) with pseudomembranous plaques visible on barium swallow (as linear defects) and endoscopy (see Fig. 1.83). The pain is usually associated with dysphagia and, when untreated, leads to weight loss. Treatment is with an oral azole drug.

Oral hairy leucoplakia

Oral hairy leucoplakia has the appearance of corrugated white plaques running vertically on the side of the tongue and is virtually pathognomonic of HIV disease (see Fig. 1.84). It is usually asymptomatic and does not require treatment. The aetiology is closely associated with EBV. High-dose aciclovir is sometimes effective in eradicating the infection but relapse often follows cessation of treatment.

Kaposi's sarcoma is discussed in more detail on page 126.

Investigations and management

Diagnosis of mucocutaneous conditions in HIV is clinical, including Kaposi's sarcoma. Rarely, bacterial, viral or fungal cultures are necessary. In any person with an unusual rash, especially if persistent and unresponsive to topical antifungal/steroid combinations, or in the presence of severe immune compromise (CD4 < 50 cells/mm³), a skin biopsy for histology and culture should be performed. First-line treatment is outlined in Box 1.90.

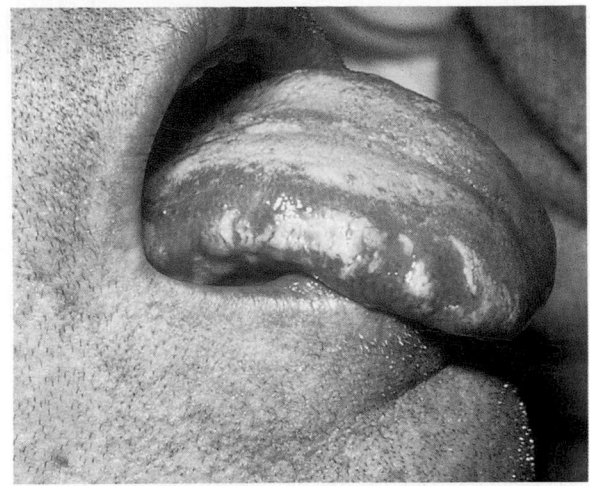

Fig. 1.84 Oral hairy leucoplakia. This tends to occur along the edge of the tongue.

1.90 FIRST-LINE TREATMENTS IN HIV-RELATED MUCOCUTANEOUS DISEASE	
Condition	**Treatment**
Seborrhoeic dermatitis	Topical antifungal/hydrocortisone cream Ketoconazole shampoo
Herpes infections	Aciclovir
Bacillary angiomatosis	Doxycycline or azithromycin
Molluscum contagiosum	Curettage or cryotherapy
Oral candidiasis	Fluconazole or another azole compound
Oral hairy leucoplakia	Aciclovir
Anogenital HPV	Podophyllin, imiquimod or cryotherapy
Scabies	Permethrin, malathion or benzyl benzoate
Kaposi's sarcoma	Liposomal doxorubicin or vincristine and bleomycin

GASTROINTESTINAL DISEASE

Presentation and differential diagnosis

Pain on swallowing, weight loss and chronic diarrhoea are common presenting features of later-stage HIV (see Box 1.91) and indicate disease at different sites in the gastrointestinal tract. A range of opportunistic organisms and HIV-related tumours may be responsible (see Box 1.92).

Specific conditions

Cytomegalovirus (CMV)

Gastrointestinal CMV occurs in up to one-third of patients with AIDS and is only seen if the CD4 count is < 100 cells/mm³ (usually < 50). It may cause disease through the entire gastrointestinal tract, including the liver and biliary tree, but most commonly disease occurs in the oesophagus and colon. It accounts for 10–20% of oesophageal disease. Oesophageal CMV presents with gradual onset of localised pain on swallowing, retrosternal pain, dysphagia, fever and

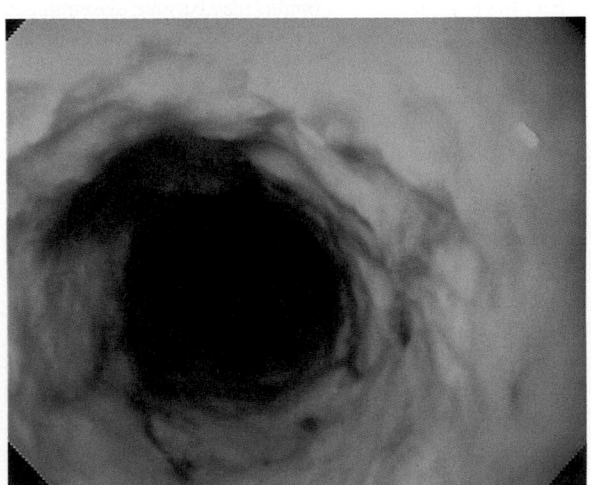

Fig. 1.83 Oesophageal candidiasis. Endoscopy may show pseudomembranous plaques of extensive confluent infection.

1.91 PRESENTATION OF HIV-RELATED GASTROINTESTINAL DISEASE

Disease site	Major symptoms
All	Weight loss, appetite loss
Mouth	Pain, ulcers, loose teeth, swelling
Oesophagus	Pain on swallowing, retrosternal chest pain, dysphagia
Small bowel	High-volume watery diarrhoea, pain, malabsorption
Large bowel	Small-volume bloody diarrhoea, pain

1.92 DIFFERENTIAL DIAGNOSIS OF HIV-RELATED GASTROINTESTINAL DISEASE

Site	Major causes
Oesophagus	*Candida*, herpes simplex, CMV, Kaposi's sarcoma, aphthous ulcers
Small bowel	*Cryptosporidium*, *Microsporidium*, *Giardia*, MAI, CMV
Large bowel	*Salmonella*, CMV, *Cryptosporidium*, *Clostridium difficile*, *Campylobacter*
Biliary tract	*Cryptosporidium*, CMV, *Microsporidium*
Liver	Hepatitis B, hepatitis C, CMV, drug toxicity, *M. tuberculosis*

(MAI = disseminated *M. avium intracellulare*)

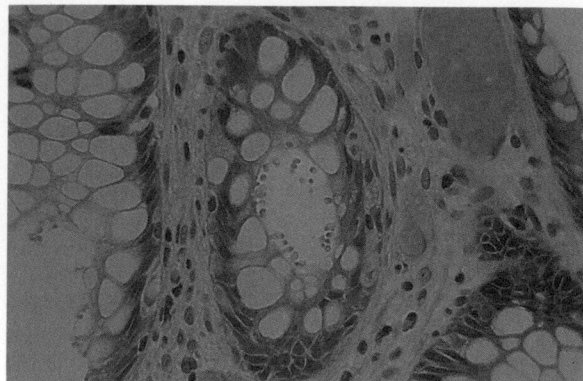

Fig. 1.85 Cryptosporidial infection. Duodenal biopsy may be necessary to confirm cryptosporidiosis or microsporidiosis.

weight loss. The diagnosis is suspected when there is failure to respond to an empirical course of fluconazole (oesophageal candidiasis accounts for up to 80% of patients with pain on swallowing), distal focal disease on barium swallow, or inflammation with erosions/ulcers on endoscopy. Confirmation is on biopsy showing classical intracellular 'owl's-eye' inclusion bodies on immunofluorescence. Rarely, strictures may complicate long-standing disease. CMV colitis may occur in up to 5% of patients. Presentation is usually with watery diarrhoea often with blood, colicky abdominal pain, weight loss and fever. It should be suspected in a patient with pathogen-negative diarrhoea or with thickened and dilated large bowel on abdominal radiograph. Endoscopy may show a range of abnormalities from generalised hyperaemia to segmental or confluent shallow or deep ulcers. Again diagnosis is on biopsy. As up to 20% of cases have disease proximal to the splenic flexure, colonoscopy should be performed where possible. Toxic megacolon (see p. 811), haemorrhage and perforation may complicate infection.

Cryptosporidium

Cryptosporidium is a highly contagious zoonotic protozoal enteric pathogen that infects a wide range of animals. In HIV-negative persons, it normally causes a self-limiting diarrhoeal illness. In HIV patients, it accounts for 15–20% of the causes of diarrhoea, characteristically producing large-volume watery stools and abdominal pain. If the CD4 count is over 200 cells/mm³, infection is usually self-limiting and

the organism eradicated. Below this level, the infection becomes chronic with persistent, often severe, watery diarrhoea, malabsorption and significant weight loss. Prior to the advent of HAART, the majority of these patients would die from their infection. Diagnosis is confirmed on stool microscopy in 90% using acid-fast or immunofluorescence stains. Cryptosporidia are also readily identifiable on duodenal biopsy, which may be necessary as stainable oöcysts are intermittently or never seen in the stool of some patients (10%) (see Fig. 1.85). Treatment is rarely successful unless the CD4 count can be increased above 100 cells/mm³ with HAART. Patients with CD4 counts below this figure should be advised to boil drinking water and minimise contact with animals (especially young). Cryptosporidium can rarely cause acalculous cholecystitis (see p. 884), sclerosing cholangitis (see p. 874) and pneumonitis.

Microsporidium

Microsporidia are a distinct group of intracellular protozoa carried by a wide range of animals, birds and fish. Three main species infect humans: *Enterocytozoon bieneusi*, *Encephalocytozoon hellem* and *Encephalocytozoon intestinalis*. *E. bieneusi* is restricted to the small bowel and hepatobiliary tract, whereas *E. intestinalis* may become disseminated through macrophage infection with disease in the conjunctiva, respiratory tract or kidneys. Like cryptosporidia they account for 10–20% of the causes of diarrhoea in HIV patients, complete their life cycle in the single host, cause chronic diarrhoea with weight loss and malabsorption (although not as rapid or severe), and only cause persistent disease when there is significant immune compromise (CD4 < 100 cells/mm³). Also, although *E. intestinalis* can be treated with albendazole, reconstitution of the immune system with HAART offers the only chance of cure for patients infected with *E. bieneusi*. Diagnosis is on stool microscopy and duodenal biopsy. Occasionally, electron microscopy is necessary to confirm the presence of infection and is the only way to speciate the microsporidia.

Other infections

Isospora (Africa and Latin America) and *Cyclospora* (Asia) are common to their localities and cause watery diarrhoea, weight loss and malabsorption akin to *Cryptosporidium*, overall accounting for 2–4% of cases in the UK. Diagnosis is on stool microscopy and treatment for both is co-trimoxazole. *Giardia*, *Entamoeba histolytica*, adenovirus and bacterial overgrowth also occur more frequently in HIV patients. HIV enteropathy is a term given to a complex of chronic diarrhoea and partial villous atrophy for which no other cause can be found (10–20%). Of the standard enteric pathogens, *Salmonella* is important because of the increased probability of bacteraemia and recurrent disease, and *Cl. difficile* toxin-associated colitis because of the frequent use of antimicrobials.

Hepatitis B and hepatitis C

With the rapid decline of traditional opportunistic infections and the increasing life expectancy of HIV-infected persons treated with HAART, the contribution of hepatitis B and C coinfection is becoming increasingly recognised. The majority of persons with HIV have evidence of HBV exposure. Carriage rate depends on the mode of acquisition (highest for injection drug users), place of birth and ethnic group (reflecting vertical transmission), immunisation history (although response rates are lower in HIV patients) and the likelihood of immune clearance after infection. This is determined by whether infection preceded HIV infection (carriage rate 5–10%) or came after (rate increased and dependent on CD4 count when infected). For HCV, only 15–20% of patients ever clear their infection and the major determinant of coinfection rate is the mode of acquisition (> 80% for haemophiliacs, 70–80% for injection drug users, 10–15% for homosexuals, and 3–5% for heterosexuals). For HBV coinfection, DNA levels are higher although the immunosuppression seen in more advanced disease affords some protection, as hepatic damage is immune-mediated. Both α-interferon and lamivudine therapy work and should be contemplated in coinfected patients. Patients with HCV coinfection have a higher HCV viral load, accelerated natural progression to cirrhosis (5–8 years after infection) and an increased risk of complications. However, their response to combination therapy with α-interferon and ribavirin is little different from that of HIV-uninfected persons and treatment should be considered for patients with stable HIV disease. For both, therapy may be associated with a flare of hepatitis because of improved immune responsiveness. When the CD4 count is < 200 cells/mm^3, HCV-RNA should be assessed because HCV antibody may be absent. All patients with HIV should receive HBV and HAV immunisation. Hepatitis is described on pages 860–866.

Mycobacterium avium intracellulare (MAI)

With the advent of HIV and until the introduction of HAART and primary prophylaxis, disseminated MAI occurred in up to 35% of all patients with a median CD4 count of 13 cells/mm^3 at presentation. Like other opportunistic infections, the incidence has now fallen by 90% but it remains a problem in late-stage AIDS, especially those cases that are newly diagnosed. The organism is an environmental *Mycobacterium* commonly found in water and food. Acquisition of infection is probably from the respiratory and gastrointestinal tracts where colonisation precedes disseminated infection in two-thirds of patients. All organs are affected with heavy infiltration of organisms and little inflammatory response; the reticulo-endothelial system bears the major burden of infection. Presentation is with fever and sweats, weight loss, chronic diarrhoea, vomiting and abdominal pain; hepatosplenomegaly and lymphadenopathy are usually detectable on examination. Anaemia and a raised alkaline phosphatase are commonly found. CT usually reveals intra-abdominal and mediastinal lymphadenopathy. Mycobacterial disease is confirmed by identifying acid-fast bacilli on Ziehl–Neelsen staining of induced sputum, bone marrow, liver or duodenal biopsy. MAI is confirmed following positive mycobacterial growth from these sites or from blood (positive in 91% of patients and the usual source) or stool, and speciation using DNA probes or conventional tests. Therapy must consist of multiple agents, and a combination of ethambutol, azithromycin, rifabutin and ciprofloxacin is effective. With an effective response to HAART (CD4 count > 100 cells/mm^3), therapy can probably be halted and replaced with azithromycin prophylaxis. In patients who respond to HAART with immune reconstitution, focal disease (e.g. joint, lymph node) has been described. Rarely, other non-tuberculous mycobacteria have been described in HIV-infected patients, including *M. kansasii*, *M. haemophilum* and *M. genavensae*; presentation is similar.

Investigations and management

Investigation of chronic diarrhoea revolves around stool microscopy (specific stains are often necessary) and culture, specific imaging, and endoscopy with biopsy. Additional tests include blood culture (bacterial, mycobacterial), CMV-PCR and cryptococcal antigen. Initial first-line treatments are detailed in Box 1.93.

1.93 FIRST-LINE TREATMENTS IN HIV-RELATED GASTROINTESTINAL DISORDERS	
Condition	**Treatment**
Candida	Fluconazole or another azole compound
Herpes simplex	Aciclovir
CMV	Ganciclovir, foscarnet or cidofovir
Cryptosporidium	Paramomycin and azithromycin
Microsporidium	Albendazole*
MAI	Rifabutin, ethambutol, azithromycin, ciprofloxacin
Isospora and *Cyclospora*	Co-trimoxazole
Hepatitis B	3TC or α-interferon
Hepatitis C	α-interferon and ribavirin
Kaposi's sarcoma	Liposomal doxorubicin or vincristine and bleomycin
Non-Hodgkin's lymphoma	Chemotherapy
* *Enterocytozoon intestinalis* only.	

RESPIRATORY DISEASE

Presentation and differential diagnosis

More than half of the patients with AIDS will develop pulmonary disease at some time. Several factors influence the likely cause including CD4 count, ethnicity, age and risk group, prophylactic history, and geographical location. The history is also vital in discriminating acute bacterial pneumonia (rapid onset, pleuritic chest pain, rigors) from *Pneumocystis carinii* pneumonia (subacute onset, breathlessness, dry cough), a common differential in later-stage disease. The chest radiograph is important in distinguishing presenting syndromes (see Box 1.94).

1.94 DIFFERENTIAL DIAGNOSIS OF HIV-RELATED PULMONARY DISEASE	
Appearance	**Major causes**
Diffuse infiltrate	PCP, tuberculosis, KS, NHL, atypical bacterial pneumonia, LIP
Nodules/focal consolidation	KS, tuberculosis, NHL, *Cryptococcus*, pyogenic bacterial pneumonia
Hilar lymphadenopathy	Tuberculosis, KS, NHL, *Cryptococcus*, *Histoplasma*
Pleural effusion	KS, tuberculosis, pyogenic bacterial pneumonia, cavity-based lymphoma

(KS = Kaposi's sarcoma; NHL = non-Hodgkin's lymphoma; LIP = lymphoid interstitial pneumonitis)

Specific conditions

Pneumocystis carinii

Pneumocystis carinii pneumonia (PCP) was the first major indicator disease for HIV at the beginning of the epidemic and is still the most common AIDS-defining illness. The organism is a fungus on genetic analysis but with a life cycle (cyst, sporozoite and trophozoite), morphology and drug susceptibility pattern characteristic of a protozoan. It cannot be cultured, but the cyst and trophozoite are easily stained (Giemsa, methenamine-silver or immunofluorescence). PCP represents reactivation of latent infection in the majority of patients but reinfection probably also occurs. Transmission is likely to be air-borne and the source other infected humans; however, environmental reservoirs have not been excluded.

The risk of developing PCP is inversely correlated with the CD4 count. Cases rarely occur when the CD4 count is > 200 cells/mm³ whereas 40% of patients with a CD4 count of < 100 cells/mm³ and not taking primary prophylaxis will develop the disease annually. In those taking prophylaxis, PCP may still occur but at a lower CD4 count and with a better prognosis. However, disease is rare when daily co-trimoxazole (the drug of choice) is the prophylactic agent; dapsone, atovaquone, or aerosolised pentamidine inhaled every 2–4 weeks is an effective alternative. Co-trimoxazole provides systemic cover (rarely, *Pneumocystis* can affect other sites) and also prophylaxis for *Toxoplasma gondii*. Side-effects (typically a rash but occasionally Stevens–Johnson syndrome (see p. 1098), leucopenia, thrombocytopenia and hepatitis) occur in approximately 20–25% of patients. The incidence of PCP has fallen 72% in the last 5 years as a result of instituting primary prophylaxis when the CD4 count falls below 200 cells/mm³ and increasing or maintaining CD4 counts above 200 cells/mm³ with HAART.

Clinical presentation is with a subacute history of dry cough, fever, disproportionate breathlessness (especially on exercise), and failure to respond to standard antibiotics. The chest is often clear on auscultation although with severe disease, 'wet' crackles are usual; there may also be other markers of HIV (e.g. oropharyngeal candidiasis or mucocutaneous herpes simplex). Non-specific diagnostic tests include chest radiograph, raised lactate dehydrogenase (from lung damage), exercise-induced O_2 desaturation (below 90% is indicative of impaired gas exchange), hypoxaemia on arterial blood gases and impaired CO transfer factor. The chest radiograph appearances may be normal in early disease (15–20%) but classically demonstrate perihilar ground-glass changes (see Fig. 1.86); later, an ARDS picture is common. Atypical appearances (20%) include unilateral infiltration, upper lobe disease (often when on inhaled pentamidine prophylaxis), focal consolidation, cavitation or nodular shadows. Complications include pneumothorax, bacterial superinfection, respiratory failure, steroid-induced candidiasis and extrapulmonary disease. The differential diagnosis includes *M. tuberculosis* (see p. 532), lymphoma, unusual fungi (*Histoplasma*, *Penicillium*, *Cryptococcus*, *Coccidioides*), pulmonary Kaposi's sarcoma, atypical pneumonia (*Mycoplasma* etc.) and *Nocardia* (see Box 1.94). Specific diagnostic tests are cytology of nebulised hypertonic saline-induced sputum (30–80% sensitivity), bronchoscopy with lavage (90%) or together with transbronchial biopsy (95%). PCR of induced sputum and saliva is also under evaluation.

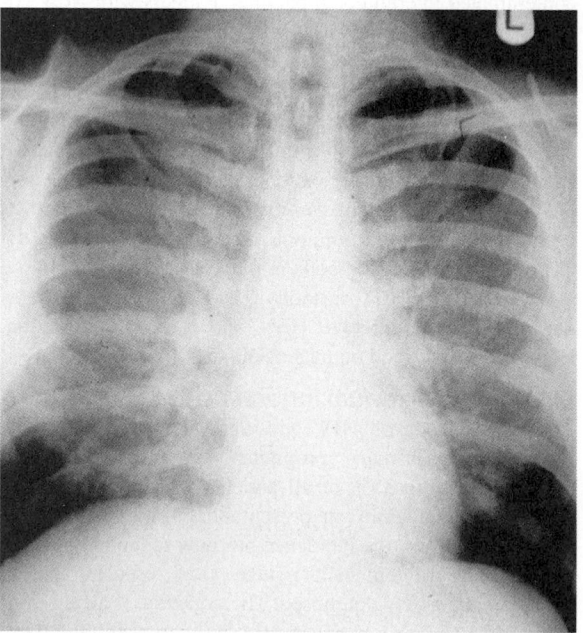

Fig. 1.86 *Pneumocystis* **pneumonia.** Typical chest radiograph appearance. Note the sparing at the apex and base of both lungs.

Treatment is outlined in Box 1.95. Poor prognostic factors include delayed diagnosis, not being on prophylaxis, low CD4 count, extensive chest radiograph changes, low hypoxaemia ratio, high lactate dehydrogenase, hypoalbuminaemia and additional pulmonary infection. Continuous positive airways pressure (CPAP) or mechanical ventilation may be necessary in the context of respiratory failure.

Mycobacterium tuberculosis

Approximately one-third of the 36 million HIV-infected persons in the world are coinfected with *M. tuberculosis*; 75% of these people reside in sub-Saharan Africa. Patients with HIV are at greater risk of reactivating latent infection (7–10% annual risk compared to 5–10% lifetime risk in an HIV-uninfected individual), of acquiring TB from an open contact (10–20% compared to 5–10%), of developing progressive primary disease (30–40% compared to 5–10%), and of developing disseminated, miliary or extrapulmonary disease (> 60% compared to < 25%). Patients are also at risk of developing second episodes of TB from exogenous infection as demonstrated by isolate typing. Escalating TB case rates in sub-Saharan Africa are largely attributable to the explosive HIV epidemic. The present estimated annual new case (8 million) and death (2 million) rates are expected to continue to rise inexorably. The risk of active TB occurring depends on the overlapping prevalence of each condition in the region involved. In addition to the devastating effect of HIV on TB, *M. tuberculosis* affects HIV adversely with enhanced replication and acceleration of the disease process. In the UK there has been an overall rise of 34% in TB notifications since 1987 although the impact of HIV on this increase is low and noticeable only in London.

The clinical presentation depends mainly on immune function. When the CD4 count is > 200 cells/mm³, disease is more likely to be reactivated upper-lobe open cavitatory disease; as immunosuppression increases, miliary, atypical pulmonary and extrapulmonary (especially pericardial, abdominal and meningeal) TB become progressively more common, as does mycobacteraemia (see Fig. 1.87). Constitutional symptoms of fever and night sweats are usually present. Approximately 5% of patients with smear-positive pulmonary TB have normal chest radiographs. Confirmation of the clinical diagnosis when the immune system is relatively preserved is by sputum microscopy (Ziehl–Neelsen and auramine stains) and radiometric culture. Rapid diagnostic tests involving nucleic acid amplification are being employed more frequently for sputum analysis in smear-negative pulmonary cases, in culture speciation and for rifampicin resistance testing. In patients with late-stage HIV and low CD4 counts, diagnosis is usually made by mycobacterial culture of blood, bone marrow or tissue. Response to quadruple anti-TB combination therapy is good although mortality is increased because of other disseminated bacterial infections (e.g. *Salmonella* and pneumococcal). Also, because of rifampicin-induced P450 CYP3A4 activity and lowered concentrations of protease inhibitors (and NNRTIs but to a lesser extent), antiretroviral therapy must be carefully selected and dosed to minimise the possibility of subtherapeutic levels and the selection of drug-resistant HIV. Drug reactions are more common in HIV-infected persons and may be life-threatening with thiacetazone and streptomycin. Where compliance is likely to be a problem, thrice-weekly directly observed therapy (DOT) should be considered.

In the early 1990s, nosocomially acquired multidrug-resistant TB (MDRTB) presented a serious public health problem initially in the USA, soon followed by southern European countries. By definition resistance is present to rifampicin and isoniazid but also usually to the remaining

1.95 FIRST-LINE TREATMENTS IN HIV-RELATED PULMONARY DISEASE	
Condition	**Treatment**
Pneumocystis carinii (moderate to severe)	Co-trimoxazole, pentamidine, or clindamycin and primaquine; adjunctive steroid therapy reduces mortality
Pneumocystis carinii (mild)	Co-trimoxazole,[1] atovaquone, pentamidine[2]
Mycobacterium tuberculosis	Rifampicin, isoniazid, ethambutol, pyrazinamide
Mycobacterium avium intracellulare	Rifabutin, ethambutol, azithromycin, ciprofloxacin
Pulmonary Kaposi's sarcoma	Liposomal doxorubicin, or vincristine and bleomycin
Community-acquired pneumonia	Cefotaxime and clarithromycin
Cryptococcus neoformans	Amphotericin B or fluconazole
[1] Oral. [2] Inhaled.	

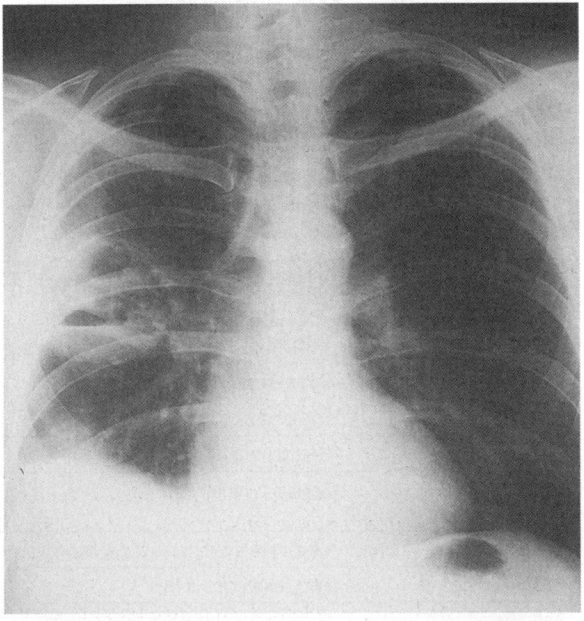

Fig. 1.87 Chest radiograph of pulmonary tuberculosis in HIV infection. Appearances are often atypical but in this case there is a typical large cavity accompanied by a pleural effusion.

first-line and often many of the second-line agents; treatment often entails six to seven drug combinations. Case fatality rates were initially > 80%. Strengthened infection control procedures have meant that such outbreaks are now infrequent in the West. Prophylaxis with isoniazid (with or without rifampicin) or rifampicin and pyrazinamide reduces the risk of TB by 70% in patients with positive tuberculin skin tests (and no history of BCG). However, this protection is lost on discontinuing the drugs. Its place in prophylaxis for TB in HIV infection is uncertain.

Bacterial infections

Bacterial pneumonia (see p. 526) is a common cause of morbidity and mortality in HIV. The incidence, severity, likelihood of bacteraemia and mortality rate are all increased compared to HIV-uninfected persons. Susceptibility to particular respiratory pathogens is influenced by risk group, the level of immune depletion, age and the presence of neutropenia. *Strep. pneumoniae* (150-fold greater risk), *Haemophilus influenzae* and *Staph. aureus* can occur at any CD4 count whereas *Pseudomonas* and *Nocardia* infections are more likely in later-stage disease. Chest radiograph appearances may be atypical. The infection usually responds to standard antibiotic therapy.

Kaposi's sarcoma and non-Hodgkin's lymphoma are discussed in more detail on pages 126–127.

Investigations and management

Important investigations for evaluating chest disease in HIV are a search for the pathogen (Gram and Ziehl–Neelsen stains) and culture from an appropriate specimen (blood, sputum, induced sputum and bronchial alveolar lavage fluid); assessment of gas exchange (exercise oximetry, arterial gases); and radiology. First-line treatment is given in Box 1.95.

NERVOUS SYSTEM AND EYE DISEASE

Presentation and differential diagnosis

Disease of the central and peripheral nervous system is common in HIV. It may be a direct consequence of HIV infection or an indirect result of CD4 cell depletion. Presentation may be as a space-occupying lesion, encephalitis, meningitis, myelitis, spinal root disease or neuropathy (see Box 1.96).

Specific conditions

Toxoplasma gondii

Toxoplasma infection results in a mild/subclinical illness in immunocompetent individuals with the formation of latent tissue cysts that persist for life and have a predilection for brain tissue. The prevalence of latent infection varies between regions and increases with age. The seroconversion rate is 0.5–1% per year. In the presence of advanced HIV-induced immunosuppression, there is a > 30% chance that a seropositive patient will reactivate these dormant cysts and develop clinical cerebral toxoplasmosis (see Fig. 1.88). Patients usually present with a short history of headache,

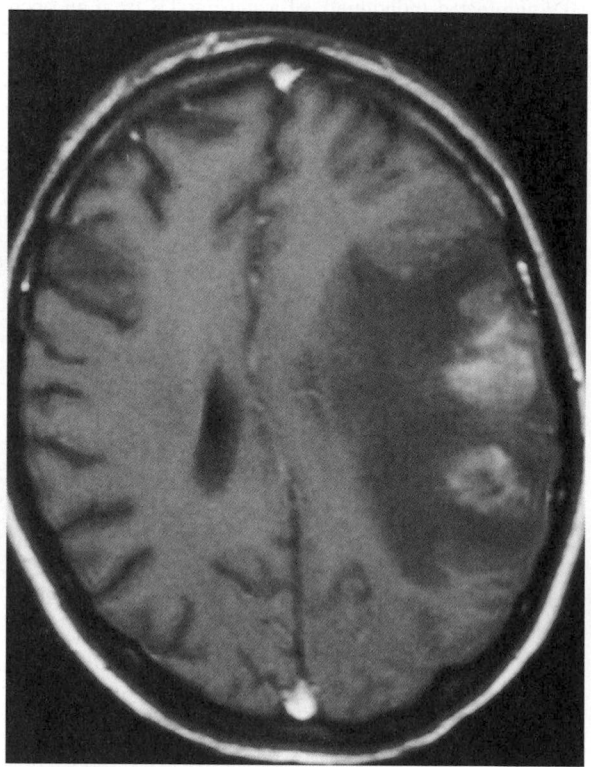

Fig. 1.88   Cerebral toxoplasmosis. Multiple cortical ring-enhancing lesions with surrounding oedema are characteristic.

1.96 PRESENTATION AND DIFFERENTIAL DIAGNOSIS OF HIV-RELATED DISORDERS OF THE NERVOUS SYSTEM		
Site of disease	**Presentation**	**Main causes**
Brain	Space-occupying lesion	*Toxoplasma*, PCNSL, PMFL, tuberculosis
	Encephalopathy	HIV, CMV, varicella zoster virus, herpes simplex, syphilis
Meninges	Headache, meningitis	HIV*, *Cryptococcus*, tuberculosis, syphilis
Spinal cord	Spastic paraparesis	HIV-vacuolar myelopathy, transverse myelitis (varicella zoster virus, herpes simplex, human T-cell lymphotropic virus 1)
Nerve root	Weakness/numbness in legs, incontinence	CMV, non-Hodgkin's lymphoma
Peripheral nerves	Pain, numbness in legs	HIV, drugs (ddC, d4T, ddI)
Retinitis	Floaters, flashing lights, field defects	CMV, HIV, toxoplasmosis, retinal necrosis
* Primary infection. (PCNSL = primary CNS lymphoma; PMFL = progressive multifocal leucoencephalopathy)		

fever and drowsiness, which is soon followed by confusion, seizures and focal signs. The localising neurology reflects the tendency for lesions to occur in the cortex, basal ganglia and brain stem. Imaging using contrast-enhanced CT or MRI typically shows multiple ring-enhancing lesions with marked surrounding oedema and mass effect. CSF examination rarely adds anything and is often contraindicated because of raised intracranial pressure. However, positive CSF-PCR reactions for JC virus (progressive multifocal leucoencephalopathy) and EBV (primary CNS lymphoma—see below) have high predictive value for these conditions that often mimic cerebral toxoplasmosis and may therefore avoid the need for a brain biopsy. Despite the characteristic imaging, it is often impossible to distinguish *Toxoplasma* encephalitis from PCNSL with confidence. If *Toxoplasma* serology is completely negative, the diagnosis is unlikely to be toxoplasmosis. However, the response to a trial of anti-*Toxoplasma* therapy (see Box 1.97) is usually diagnostic with clinical improvement occurring in patients within the first week and significant reduction in the size of their lesions in the second week. Despite the excellent response, there remains a significant neurological morbidity (up to 15%) and occasional mortality. Dexamethasone should be given if there is significant mass effect.

Primary CNS lymphoma (PCNSL)

PCNSL usually complicates late-stage HIV (CD4 < 50 cells/mm³), occurring in approximately 5% of AIDS patients and accounting for 20% of all focal CNS lesions. Tumours are nearly always high-grade, diffuse, B-cell neoplasms and are closely associated with EBV (found in over 90%). The time course of the disease is weeks to months with features of raised intracranial pressure developing early and focal signs later; seizures occur in 15%. Characteristically, imaging demonstrates a large, single, homogeneously enhancing periventricular lesion with mild to moderate surrounding oedema and mass effect (see Fig. 1.89). Ring enhancement may be present if central necrosis develops. Multiple lesions are noted in half of patients but rarely number more than two to three. CSF abnormalities are detectable in the majority but cytology is only positive in 25%. However, lumbar puncture

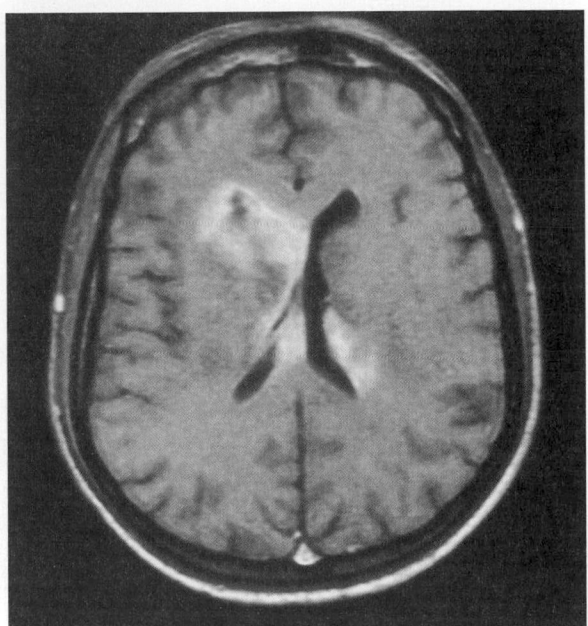

Fig. 1.89 Primary CNS lymphoma. A single enhancing periventricular lesion with moderate oedema is typical.

is often contraindicated because of raised intracranial pressure. The presence of EBV-DNA in CSF has a high sensitivity and specificity for PCNSL. Functional neuroimaging studies such as positron emission tomography (PET) may distinguish lymphoma (which results in a 'hot spot') from other mass lesions. Biopsy is the definitive method of diagnosis but carries a significant risk of morbidity, may be non-diagnostic in up to one-third, and may be misleading because of the presence of dual pathology. Distinction from cerebral toxoplasmosis may be impossible although, in the absence of *Toxoplasma* antibodies, this diagnosis is extremely unlikely. However, a trial of anti-*Toxoplasma* therapy should always be given; failure to improve clinically or on scanning is consistent with PCNSL. Treatment is usually palliative with dexamethasone and symptomatic relief. Whole brain irradiation may provide temporary respite. Life expectancy is measured in months.

Progressive multifocal leucoencephalopathy (PMFL)

PMFL is a fatal demyelinating disease caused by the JC papovavirus that was first described in non-HIV immunocompromising states. It occurs in approximately 2–3% of AIDS patients at very low CD4 counts. Seroprevalence studies demonstrate that up to 90% of young adults have been exposed to JC virus, most infections occurring in childhood. It is assumed that with advancing HIV-induced immune depletion, reactivation of latent JC virus occurs, resulting in a rapidly progressive demyelinating disease. Patients usually present with slow-onset visual field defects, ataxia or hemiparesis; seizures are uncommon. MRI is the investigation of choice and shows high-intensity occipitoparietal white matter signals on T2-weighted images (see Fig. 1.90). There is never any mass effect and contrast enhancement is seen in < 10%. Diagnosis is usually based on MRI. The

1.97 FIRST-LINE TREATMENT FOR HIV-RELATED DISORDERS OF THE NERVOUS SYSTEM	
Diagnosis	**Treatment**
Cerebral toxoplasmosis	Pyrimethamine* and sulfadiazine or clindamycin
PMFL	Cidofovir and HAART
Primary CNS lymphoma	Radiotherapy, HAART
HIV dementia	HAART
CMV encephalitis/radiculitis/retinitis	Ganciclovir, foscarnet or cidofovir
Cryptococcal meningitis	Amphotericin B and 5-flucytosine, or fluconazole
* Folinic acid should be given with pyrimethamine.	

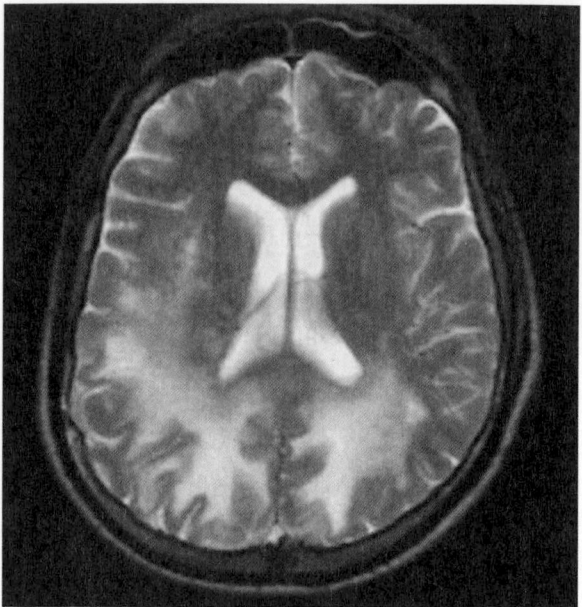

Fig. 1.90 Progressive multifocal leucoencephalopathy. Non-enhancing white matter lesions without surrounding oedema are seen.

presence of JC-DNA in CSF is diagnostic. Recently, HAART has improved the prognosis significantly, with some patients entering prolonged clinical remission with resolution of the MRI changes. However, prognosis is poor and many patients progress to death over a few months.

Less frequent causes of intracranial mass lesions include CMV, which presents with headache, neck stiffness, confusion, a lymphocytic CSF and periventricular changes on MRI. Retinitis may also be present. CMV-DNA can usually be detected in CSF. *M. tuberculosis*, *C. neoformans* and *T. pallidum* predominantly affect the meninges but can produce mass lesions with focal neurology.

HIV-associated dementia

HIV is a neurotropic virus and infects the CNS early during infection. It may present as aseptic meningitis at seroconversion, and minor cognitive defects such as mental slowness and poor memory as the disease progresses, through to dementia in later-stage disease. This is characterised by global deterioration of cognitive function, severe psychomotor retardation, paraparesis, ataxia, and urinary and faecal incontinence. Changes in affect are common and depression or psychosis may be the predominant feature. The incidence has fallen dramatically as a result of HAART. Higher plasma and CSF viral load, lower CD4 count and age are predictors for HIV-associated dementia. Investigations show diffuse cerebral atrophy with widened sulci and enlarged ventricles on imaging and a raised protein in the CSF. An EEG may show features consistent with encephalopathy. Combination therapy using agents providing optimal CNS penetration improves minor cognitive defects in early disease and may slow or even reverse the progression of HIV-associated dementia. Appropriate psychotropic medication may also be necessary.

Cryptococcosis

Cryptococcus neoformans is a budding encapsulated yeast; it is the most common cause of meningitis associated with late-stage HIV (CD4 < 50 cells/mm³). Rarely, non-meningeal disease (lung, prostate or skin) and disseminated disease may occur. Patients usually present with a 2–3-week history of headache (75%), fever (65%), vomiting and mild confusion; neck stiffness is often absent (< 25%). Less common are seizures, photophobia and blurred vision; papilloedema is found in 10%, but focal features are rare. Around 10% of patients are asymptomatic. Protein, cell counts and glucose may be normal in the CSF although numerous organisms are present on India ink stain (60–80%), cultures are usually positive (> 95%), and the CSF and serum cryptococcal antigen are strongly positive (95%). Although clinically disseminated infection is rare, the organism may be cultured from blood, urine, gut or bone marrow. The antigen titre, the number of organisms, the CSF white cell count and opening pressure, and the admission level of consciousness, as well as the delay before commencing treatment are all prognostically significant. Deafness and blindness are the most common complications and result from prolonged raised intracranial pressure, arachnoiditis and direct cryptococcal nerve infiltration. Between 10 and 20% of patients require treatment for raised intracranial pressure with repeated lumbar punctures, acetazolamide or shunting. Around 5–10% of patients die within the first 2 weeks of therapy, mainly related to raised intracranial pressure.

Spinal cord, nerve root and peripheral nerve disease

A variety of neuropathies occur in HIV infection. At seroconversion, Guillain–Barré syndrome, transverse myelitis, facial palsy, brachial neuritis, polyradiculitis and peripheral neuropathy have all rarely been described. Vacuolar myelopathy is a slowly progressive myelitis resulting in paraparesis with variable sensory loss. Ataxia and incontinence occur in advanced cases. CSF may show a raised protein but is frequently normal. MRI of the spine is normal. Therapy is aimed at reducing spasticity with antispasmodics, and increasing stability with physiotherapy. A predominantly distal HIV-related sensory neuropathy of the lower limbs affects up to 30% of patients. It is associated with lower CD4 (usually < 200 cells/mm³), higher viral load, older age and wasting. It results from axonal degeneration with unmyelinated nerve fibres bearing the brunt. Hyperaesthesia (85%), pain in the soles of the feet (67%) and paraesthesia (38%) are common. Diminished pin-prick, light touch and vibration sensation accompanied by loss of ankle reflexes (75%) is typical. The NRTI drugs, especially ddC, d4T and ddI, and hydroxyurea (hydroxycarbamide) can produce an identical picture but with remission if the offending agent is withdrawn early on. Treatment is often difficult although amitriptyline, lamotrigine and recombinant nerve growth factor are beneficial. Treatment is supportive. Polyradiculitis occurs in late-stage HIV (CD4 count < 50 cells/mm³) and is nearly always a result of CMV. It causes rapidly progressive flaccid paraparesis, saddle anaesthesia, loss of lower limb reflexes and sphincter dysfunction.

Pain in the legs and back is an early symptom. A neutrophil CSF pleocytosis, nerve root involvement on nerve conduction studies, and the presence of CMV-DNA by PCR confirm the diagnosis. Despite treatment, functional recovery may not occur. Lastly, proximal myopathy can result from HIV (when it may occur at any stage) or ZDV (< 1% of patients). Presentation is with pain and slowly progressive weakness involving the major muscle groups; neurology is normal. Muscles may be tender and the creatine kinase is usually elevated. Distinction can be made by muscle biopsy when typical 'red-ragged' fibres are seen with ZDV.

CMV is discussed in more detail on page 17.

Psychiatric disease
Significant psychiatric morbidity is often associated with HIV and may occur from before testing (fear of being infected, knowledge of friends who have died), during the process of being tested, on receiving a positive result (e.g. concerns over the response of others, confidentiality, stigmatisation, discrimination), through the asymptomatic phase (e.g. worry about life expectancy, coping with medication side-effects) to late-stage disease (e.g. facing up to death, living wills, funeral arrangements). Mild cognitive dysfunction is a common occurrence in later-stage disease and usually improves with HAART. It is also an early feature of HIV-related dementia. Disorders of mental state may also result from drugs directly (e.g. efavirenz) or indirectly (sexual dysfunction). Psychiatric morbidity is a major risk factor for poor compliance to drugs, which is a critical component of HAART management. Psychiatric disease is described in Chapter 8.

Retinitis
CMV coinfection is very common in HIV-infected adults, with over 95% of male homosexuals and 50% of other risk groups being seropositive. Prior to HAART, approximately one-quarter of patients with CD4 counts < 100/mm³ would proceed to develop active CMV retinitis within 24 months (through either reactivation or reinfection). Since HAART, there has been a 90% fall in the incidence of CMV infections. Patients present with floaters, flashing lights, field defects or, rarely, diminished central visual acuity; a few asymptomatic patients are diagnosed on routine dilated fundoscopy. This usually reveals haemorrhagic exudates along the retinal vessels or a well-demarcated peripheral V-shaped area of disease. Macular disease is rare but is the most sight-threatening. If left untreated, the leading edge will progressively advance. Around 30% of patients have bilateral disease at presentation. No recovery of vision occurs in affected areas and there is always a risk of retinal detachment because of necrosis. Differential diagnosis includes *Toxoplasma*, acute retinal necrosis (due to VZV), HIV-related cotton wool spots, progressive outer retinal necrosis (PORN), syphilis and *Pneumocystis*. High-dose (induction) treatment must commence immediately, followed by a reduced maintenance dose. Patients who respond to HAART with an increase in the CD4 count to > 200 cells/mm³ with HIV and CMV viral suppression and inactive retinal disease can probably discontinue maintenance therapy safely but must be monitored closely for relapse (CMV-PCR and

dilated fundoscopy). If the CD4 count falls, maintenance treatment should be reintroduced. Occasionally, an immune vitritis may occur on HAART, often after stopping maintenance therapy.

Toxoplasmosis is discussed on page 17 and syphilis on page 96.

Investigations and management
Imaging is pivotal in evaluating patients. CSF for standard and PCR analysis (herpes simplex, varicella zoster, JC virus, CMV, enterovirus, EBV) should be taken if lumbar puncture is not contraindicated. Additional investigations include *Toxoplasma* and *Treponema* serology, cryptococcal antigen, dilated fundoscopy (CMV, toxoplasmosis) and chest radiograph. First-line treatments are outlined in Box 1.97.

MISCELLANEOUS CONDITIONS
Haematology
Disorders of all three major cell lines may occur in HIV, being most frequent in later-stage disease (anaemia 70%, leucopenia 50% and thrombocytopenia 40%), when pancytopenia may also be seen. Numerous causes for anaemia exist, including marrow infiltration with opportunistic infections (e.g. MAI, tuberculosis, CMV) or neoplasms (non-Hodgkin's lymphoma, Kaposi's sarcoma); bone marrow suppression from drugs (ZDV and, less frequently, other NRTIs) or as a direct effect of HIV; and chronic blood loss (especially Kaposi's sarcoma) or malabsorption (chronic protozoal infections) in gastrointestinal tract disease. Haemolytic anaemia is uncommon but is seen with lymphoma. Leucopenia is usually seen in the context of marrow replacement as above or drug toxicity (e.g. ZDV and other NRTIs, co-trimoxazole, ganciclovir, chemotherapy agents). Lymphopenia (< 1000 cells/dl) is a good marker of HIV. Thrombocytopenia may appear early (5–10%) when it may be the first indicator of HIV, or in later-stage disease. The disease is very similar to idiopathic thrombocytopenic purpura, with detectable platelet antibodies and short-lived response to intravenous immunoglobulin. However, the treatment of choice is HAART.

Renal, cardiac and endocrine conditions
HIV-associated nephropathy (HIVAN) is the most important renal condition. Several drugs used in HIV management also cause renal disease, including indinavir (renal stones), pentamidine, cidofovir and co-trimoxazole. It usually presents with nephrotic syndrome, chronic renal disease or a combination of both. HAART may have some effect in slowing progression of renal disease. Doses of NRTIs must be adjusted according to creatinine clearance.

With increasing life expectancy and drug-related toxicity, cardiac disease will become an increasingly important issue. HIV-related dilated cardiomyopathy can be detected in 25–40% of AIDS patients but symptomatic heart disease is rare (3–6%). Cardiomyopathy may very rarely be a result of ZDV toxicity through drug-induced mitochondrial dysfunction. Patients with HIV have an increased incidence of cardiac risk factors. In these patients, protease inhibitor (PI)-related hyperlipidaemia may present an additional risk.

Hypoadrenalism may be seen in up to one-quarter of AIDS patients and should be screened for in patients complaining of fatigue (see p. 719). Postural hypotension and characteristic biochemistry (hyperkalaemia, hyponatraemia) may be absent. Hypopituitarism has also been described (see p. 736).

NEOPLASMS

Kaposi's sarcoma (1000-fold higher rate than in HIV-uninfected) and non-Hodgkin's lymphoma (60-fold) are the most common opportunistic malignancies associated with HIV and are considered AIDS-defining diagnoses. Increased incidence rates are also seen with Hodgkin's lymphoma (5-fold) and anogenital cancers (5-fold).

Specific conditions

Kaposi's sarcoma (KS)

Prior to the HIV epidemic, KS was a rare tumour restricted to elderly males of Mediterranean or Jewish descent, immunosuppressed transplant recipients, and children and young adults in sub-Saharan Africa. Together with *Pneumocystis carinii* pneumonia, it has become a hallmark of AIDS where it is particularly seen in homosexuals, bisexuals and patients from sub-Saharan Africa; haemophiliacs, injection drug users and heterosexuals rarely develop KS. Epidemiologically, the disease was strongly suspected of being a sexually transmissible agent and the identification of a novel herpes virus (HHV-8) confirmed this link. In HHV-8 coinfected male homosexuals, there is a 10-year cumulative risk of 30–50% for developing KS with a median time to development of 3–5 years. Although HHV-8 represents a predominantly sexually transmitted infection in the West (exposure of the virus to rectal mucosa presenting the greatest risk), non-sexual and non-parenteral horizontal routes of transmission (possible salivary) are more important in sub-Saharan Africa. The virus can also be transmitted vertically. The exact role of HHV-8 in KS pathogenesis is not fully understood. Histologically, the tumour consists of spindle cells, endothelial cells, fibroblasts and inflammatory cells. Clinically, cutaneous KS lesions (see Fig. 1.91) are discrete, pink to purple, raised papules and nodules that are often symmetrically arranged and develop on crease lines. Significant oedema from lymphatic involvement can occur. They may be hyperkeratotic, coalescing plaques, which may be painful (especially if on the soles of the feet) and bleed or ulcerate. Favoured sites include the nose, genitals and lower limbs. As the disease progresses, the lesions become more numerous and larger. Disease may be very indolent or fulminant with rapid visceral involvement and clinical deterioration. This is more likely with lower CD4 counts. Oral KS (see Fig. 1.92) is the most common oral cancer and typically involves the palate, gum margins and fauces; it is a strong predictor of gastrointestinal (frequently asymptomatic) and pulmonary disease (always symptomatic). Hepatosplenomegaly usually indicates disease of these organs. Pulmonary KS occurs in 10–15% of patients and presents with breathlessness, cough, haemoptysis, chest pain and

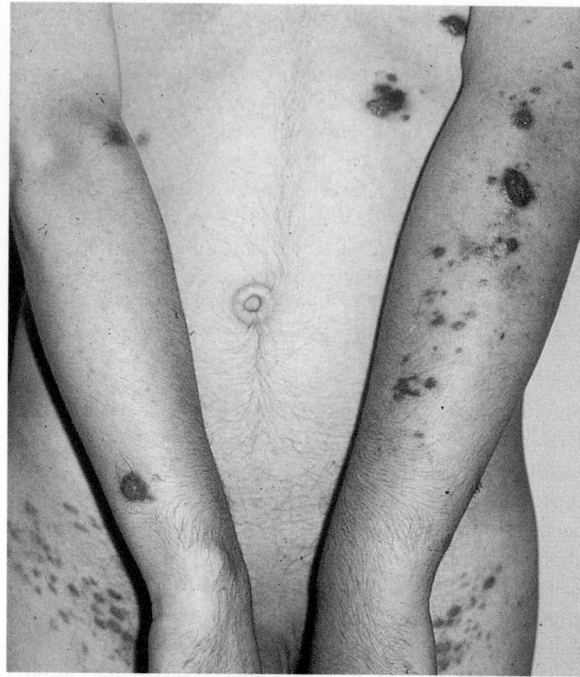

Fig. 1.91 Widespread cutaneous Kaposi's sarcoma. Lesions tend to be pleomorphic and slightly raised.

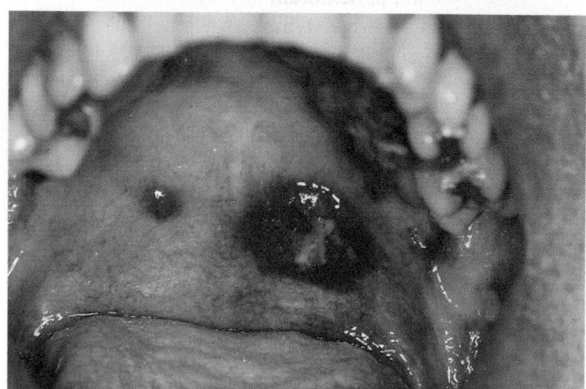

Fig. 1.92 Oral Kaposi's sarcoma. A full examination is important to detect disease that may affect the palate, gums, fauces or tongue.

fever. Typically, disease affects middle and lower zones with patchy coarse reticulonodular shadowing; a pleural effusion is present in approximately 25%. About 20% develop ocular lesions that resemble subconjunctival haemorrhages.

Prognosis from KS depends upon the CD4 count and the extent of disease. For limited and localised disease, therapeutic options include surgical excision, intralesional chemotherapy, liquid nitrogen or laser therapy, radiation or retinoic acid gel. For widespread mucocutaneous or visceral KS, chemotherapy should be used. First-line agents are cyclical liposomal doxorubicin (response rate 60%) or a combination of vincristine and bleomycin (30–50%). For refractory or relapsed disease, paclitaxel is the best drug. With the widespread use of HAART, there has been a 68% fall in the incidence of KS. It is also apparent that combination therapy alone can result in regression of mucocutaneous lesions and even visceral disease, as well as maintaining remission. It is therefore a vital component of management.

HIV-associated lymphoma

In the majority of patients, lymphoma (see p. 938) represents a late manifestation of HIV, with risk increasing as immuno-compromise worsens (median CD4 count at diagnosis is 50 cells/mm^3). It is the initial AIDS-defining illness in 2–3% of patients. The risk over non-HIV is 60-fold for non-Hodgkin's lymphoma (NHL) and 5-fold for Hodgkin's disease, with a lifetime risk of developing NHL of 5–10%. It is seen in all groups at risk for HIV. HAART has reduced the incidence of NHL by 40% with an effect dependent on the histological type (most noticeable with PCNSL—see p. 123—whereas no effect with Burkitt's lymphoma), the time on combination treatment and the CD4 count (greatest effect where < 50 cells/mm^3). However, this is a modest effect compared to the decreases seen in opportunistic infections. Histological subtypes have distinct associations with herpes viruses and underlying genetic mutations. Over 95% of AIDS-associated lymphomas are of B-cell lineage and comprise several histological types: diffuse large cell (30%); small-cleaved cell, Burkitt's and non-Burkitt's (30%); and large-cell immunoblastic (25%). The EBV genome is present in approximately 50% of non-Hodgkin's and nearly all Hodgkin's lymphomas (see Fig. 1.93). HHV-8 is found in body cavity (pleura, pericardium or peritoneum) lymphoma and is a high-grade B-cell lymphoma which accounts for < 2% of NHL. After diagnosis of NHL or HD, a staging evaluation is required (Ann Arbor classification—see p. 939). This requires CT of the thorax, abdomen and pelvis, bone marrow aspirate and biopsy, and lumbar puncture for cytology. Most HIV-associated disease is stage IVB (60–90%) at presentation, reflecting widely disseminated disease with prominent symptoms of weight loss, fever and night sweats. Lymphadenopathy occurs in 75% of cases and extranodal sites are affected in up to 60% (bone marrow, gastrointestinal tract, CNS and liver—up to 30%; oral cavity, skin and lungs—up to 5%). About 20% of patients with lep-tomeningeal CNS NHL are asymptomatic. Poor prognostic factors associated with shorter survival are CD4 < 100 cells/mm^3, previous AIDS diagnosis, disseminated disease,

poor general health at presentation, raised LDH, age > 35 years, not being on HAART, and intravenous drug user risk group. HAART therapy is associated with significant improvement in predicting response to chemotherapy, event-free remission and overall survival. Management includes chemotherapy, support of bone marrow reserves, prevention of infection and control of HIV. Multi-agent chemotherapy is used (e.g. CHOP or VAPEC-B—see p. 942) although lower doses are often employed because there appears to be no advantage in higher-dose regimens and HIV patients are more susceptible to side-effects. Intrathecal chemotherapy should be used for patients with meningeal involvement. The remission rate in persons with less than two poor prognosis risk factors is approximately 50%, with prolonged remission over 24 months seen in 20–30%. Use of HAART with chemotherapy is safe although certain agents, in particular ZDV (marrow suppression) and d4T/ddC/ddI (peripheral neuropathy), may aggravate the side-effects of chemotherapy agents. Where possible, its introduction should not be delayed. For primary CNS lymphoma, see page 123.

Genital cancer

HIV-infected persons have a fivefold greater risk of developing anogenital (vulval/vaginal, anal, penile) and in situ cervical (cervical intraepithelial neoplasia III) cancer. This is closely associated with HPV coinfection, which is more frequently observed in HIV (60% of females; 90% of males), including the most oncogenic genotypes (HPV-16, 18, 31, 33, 35). Patients are more likely to have multiple genotypes, which persist with time, and to demonstrate a more rapid progression from dysplasia to in situ cancer. Both a higher viral load and a lower CD4 count are associated with higher coinfection rates. Invasive cervical cancer is an AIDS-defining diagnosis although there has not been any increase in HIV-infected women. However, disease tends to present late and is more aggressive. Annual cervical smears should be taken from all HIV-infected women and regular anal smears considered for homosexual men.

MANAGEMENT OF HIV

Management of HIV involves both treatment of the virus and prevention of opportunistic infections. The aims of HIV treatment are to reduce the viral load to an undetectable level for as long as possible; improve the CD4 count (above 200 cells/mm^3 significant HIV-related events rarely occur); increase the quantity and improve quality of life without unacceptable drug-related side-effects or lifestyle alteration; and reduce transmission (mother-to-child and post-exposure) (see Boxes 1.98 and 1.99).

DRUGS

Nucleoside reverse transcriptase inhibitors (NRTIs)

The first drug to enter clinical practice was zidovudine (ZDV, AZT) in 1987 following demonstration that it significantly reduced AIDS-associated diagnoses and deaths over 6 months. Further drugs in this class are didanosine (ddI), zalcitabine

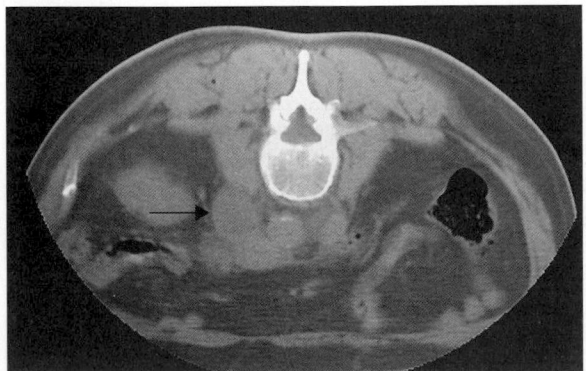

Fig. 1.93 Non-Hodgkin's lymphoma. CT image showing para-aortic lymph node (arrow). Scanning is often necessary to identify nodal or visceral disease in the abdomen.

HIV INFECTION—role of combination therapy   EBM

'In antiretroviral-naïve patients, two large RCTs have shown that PI-based HAART halves the risk of a new AIDS-defining diagnosis or death occurring. One large open-label study has shown that NNRTI-based HAART is equivalent to a PI-based HAART regimen as measured by viral load and CD4 count responses.'

- Hammer SM, Squires KE, Hughes MD, et al. A controlled trial of two nucleoside analogues plus indinavir in persons with HIV infection and CD4 counts of 200/mm³ or less. N Engl J Med 1997; 337:725–783.
- Staszewski S, Morales-Ramirez J, Tashima KT, et al. Efavirenz plus zidovudine and lamivudine, efavirenz plus indinavir, and indinavir plus zidovudine and lamivudine in the treatment of HIV-1 infection in adults. N Engl J Med 1999; 341:1865–1873.

Further information: www.aidsmap.com
www.clinicalevidence.org

(ddC), lamivudine (3TC), stavudine (d4T) and abacavir, which have appeared sequentially. The NRTIs act through intracellular phosphorylation to the triphosphate form and incorporation into the DNA where they inhibit further lengthening of the complementary strand to the viral RNA template. Each drug specifically competes with a natural nucleoside (e.g. ZDV and d4T with thymidine, 3TC and ddC with cytidine). CNS penetration is good with all NRTIs and ZDV has been demonstrated to be of benefit in AIDS dementia. The inclusion of two NRTIs remains the cornerstone of highly active antiretroviral therapy (HAART) combination therapy with no clinical or virological difference being identified between the various permutations in the initial regimen.

1.98 ANTIRETROVIRAL DRUGS

	Nucleoside reverse transcriptase inhibitors) (NRTIs)	Non-nucleoside reverse transcriptase inhibitors (NNRTIs)	Protease inhibitors (PIs)	Others
Licensed	ddC (zalcitabine) ddI (didanosine) 3TC (lamivudine) ZDV (zidovudine) d4T (stavudine) Abacavir	Nevirapine Efavirenz	Indinavir Saquinavir (soft gel) Ritonavir Nelfinavir Lopinavir/ ritonavir	Hydroxyurea (hydroxycarbamide) Tenofovir
Restricted use		Delavirdine[1]	Amprenavir[2] Saquinavir (hard gel)[3] Atazanavir[1]	T-20[1]
Clinical trials	DAPD FTC	DPC-083 Capravirine TMC-120	Tipranavir	Fusion inhibitors Chemokine receptor inhibitors

[1] Expanded access only.
[2] Licensed for virological failure.
[3] Only to be given with ritonavir.

1.99 ANTIRETROVIRAL DRUG SIDE-EFFECTS

Drug class	Class-specific	Drug-association strongest	Individual drug	Individual side-effects
NRTIs	Peripheral neuropathy Pancreatitis Hepatic steatosis/lactic acidosis Anaemia/neutropenia Myopathy/cardiomyopathy Extremity fat loss	d4T, ddC ddI ddI, d4T ZDV ZDV d4T	ddC ZDV Abacavir	Mouth/oesophageal ulcers Nail pigmentation Hypersensitivity
PIs	Gastrointestinal intolerance Fat redistribution Hyperlipidaemia Insulin resistance/hyperglycaemia Bleeding in haemophilia Liver enzyme derangement	Nelfinavir, ritonavir Ritonavir, indinavir Ritonavir-based	Indinavir Ritonavir Amprenavir	Renal stones, crystalluria, hyperbilirubinaemia, ↑BP, skin, hair, nail defects Perioral/extremity paraesthesia, taste perversion Rash, perioral/extremity paraesthesia, taste perversion
NNRTIs	Rash Stevens–Johnson syndrome	Nevirapine Nevirapine	Efavirenz Nevirapine	Vivid dreams, dizziness, insomnia, hyperlipidaemia Hepatitis
HAART	Bone demineralisation			

Resistance occurs to all NRTIs unless they are part of a maximally suppressive HAART regimen. To 3TC this is rapid and to high level, for ZDV intermediate, and for ddI, d4T, ddC and abacavir it appears more gradually and to a lesser degree. Due to varying degrees of cross-resistance (e.g. between the thymidine analogues, d4T and ZDV), NRTIs used in the second combination are not as effective as the same combination in first-line HAART. With mounting individual NRTI exposure, multidrug resistance to all NRTIs is now being recognised. Many of the major and longer-term side-effects may have a common pathway through inhibition of mitochondrial DNA synthesis although displaying some organ specificity (see Box 1.99). Once-daily administration (ddI, 3TC, FTC) and NRTI combinations (ZDV/3TC and ZDV/3TC/abacavir) improve adherence. Hypersensitivity to abacavir occurs in 3% (rash, fever, influenza-like illness) in the first 6 weeks and can be life-threatening if not recognised early or if the patient is rechallenged with the drug.

Protease inhibitors (PIs)

The first PI to enter clinical practice was saquinavir (hard gel formulation) in 1995 followed by indinavir, ritonavir, nelfinavir, saquinavir (soft gel), amprenavir and lopinavir/ritonavir. In several early clinical endpoint studies, significant reductions in AIDS diagnoses and deaths for patients receiving a PI were demonstrated. The subsequent dramatic fall in morbidity and mortality can be directly linked to the introduction of these drugs and their use in HAART. Protease inhibitors prevent post-translational cleavage of polypeptides into functional virus proteins. Given with two NRTIs the combination controls viral replication in plasma and tissues, and allows reconstitution of the immune system.

Short- and long-term side-effects are not infrequent. Fat redistribution occurs in 20–30% of patients on PIs by 2 years (see Fig. 1.94). The syndrome is characterised by peripheral fat-wasting (cheeks, limbs, buttocks), localised collections (buffalo hump, peripheral lipomatosis, breast enlargement in women) and central adiposity. One-quarter of patients have a pattern of predominant peripheral fat loss, one-quarter central fat gain, and half a mixed pattern. The underlying pathogenesis is not understood. PI use is also associated with insulin resistance (60%), abnormal glucose tolerance (35%) and frank diabetes (8%). Increases in total cholesterol, low-density lipoprotein (LDL) ratio and/or triglycerides, and decreases in HDL occur in 30–50% of patients. Coronary artery disease appears to be more common in HIV. This is partly a result of the metabolic risk factors and partly the greater frequency of other recognised risk factors in those with HIV such as smoking. Although the frequency of these clinical and metabolic complications may vary between different PIs, all have been implicated.

PIs inhibit the p450 cytochrome system (mainly the CYP3A4 isoenzyme), giving rise to the potential for multiple drug interactions. Common drugs that interact with PIs (in particular ritonavir) are rifampicin, midazolam, simvastatin and certain antihistamines. The potent enzyme inhibition produced by ritonavir can be used to raise the trough level of

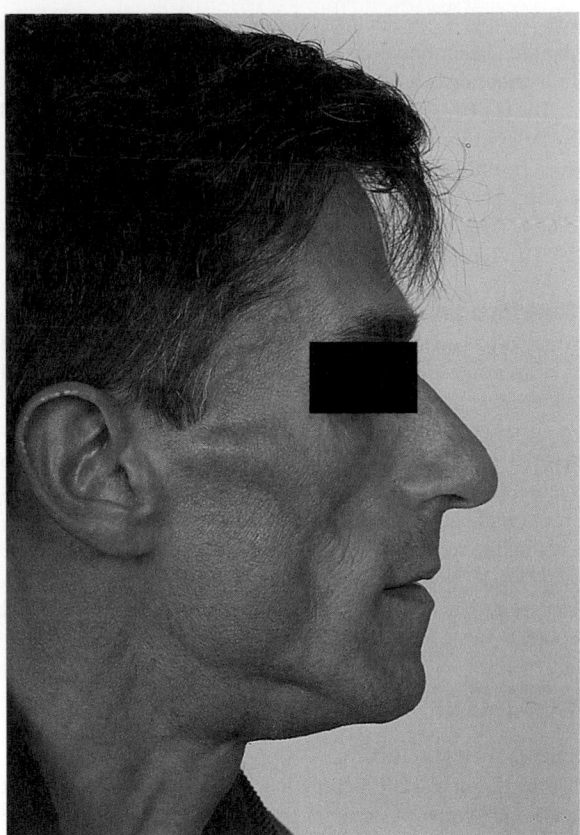

Fig. 1.94 Lipodystrophy. Facial and extremity fat atrophy is an important feature.

coadministered PIs such as saquinavir, indinavir and lopinavir (where the combination has been formulated as a single tablet). This allows the number of pills and frequency of administration to be reduced as well as dietary restrictions relaxed. Adequate plasma levels are necessary for, and predictive of, successful treatment. Monitoring the levels (therapeutic drug monitoring) and adjusting the dose accordingly may be necessary to optimise the antiviral effect and reduce toxicity.

Non-nucleoside reverse transcriptase inhibitors (NNRTIs)

There are three main NNRTIs, nevirapine, delavirdine and efavirenz. Activity is through inhibiting reverse transcriptase by binding near to the active enzyme site. They do not require intracellular activation and are not active against HIV-2. Efavirenz and nevirapine have equal potency to PIs when combined with two NRTIs, a half-life over 24 hours allowing for once- or twice-daily dosing, good bioavailability, low tablet number, and apparent freedom from long-term side-effects. The major disadvantage is the potential for development of cross-resistance to all current drugs in this class through a single mutational change.

Rash is the major class-specific side-effect (see Box 1.99). CNS side-effects including dizziness, vivid dreams, insomnia, depression and poor concentration are described in half the patients treated with efavirenz. They usually resolve by 4 weeks and are only sufficiently severe to require discontinuation in 2–5%. No association with fat redistribution has been identified for the NNRTIs.

The CYP3A4 isoenzyme is induced by nevirapine, inhibited by delavirdine, and both inhibited and induced by efavirenz. As a result, both efavirenz and nevirapine induce the metabolism of certain PIs requiring dose increases if given concurrently. They also reduce methadone levels by approximately 50% and may precipitate opiate withdrawal.

New drugs

Many drugs presently in trial or earlier stages of development are improvements on currently available compounds and either have increased potency, activity against resistant virus or easier compliance, or are likely to reduce short- and long-term complications (see Box 1.99). More exciting is the recognition of agents acting with potent activity at novel sites in the replication cycle: for example, the fusion (e.g. T-20), chemokine receptor (e.g. SCH-C, AMD-3100) and integrase (e.g. S-1360) inhibitors. For many patients, these new drugs represent their only realistic chance of obtaining virological control.

TREATMENT

The naïve patient

The decision to start therapy is a major one. It is dependent upon the symptom status of the patient, the CD4 count, the viral load (VL) and the wishes of the patient. Exactly when this should be and with what combination are not clear. Arguments for earlier treatment include possible reduction of antigenically distinct primary drug-resistant viral variants, greater potential for immune reconstitution, lower incidence of certain side-effects and reduction of viral transmission. On the other hand, starting therapy early will allow the potential development of drug resistance and thereby reduce drug options for the future, exposes the patient to short- and long-term drug toxicity, and may increase the transmission of drug-resistant virus. Currently, there is a clear move to delay therapy until there are clinical or immunological indications to commence and not just on the basis of a high VL (see Box 1.100). Nevertheless, the risk of HIV-related opportunistic infection increases and treatment is less effective when the CD4 count is < 200 cells/mm³. Also, the higher the VL, the faster the CD4 count falls. A potent combination (HAART) should always be used (see Box 1.101). The advantages and disadvantages of each regimen are presented in Box 1.102. When starting treatment certain factors need to be considered (see Box 1.103). Commencing antiretroviral therapy is not a medical emergency and there is always time to decide on the optimum regimen for a particular patient.

Despite careful and appropriate choice of HAART, the chances of a VL of < 50 copies/mm³ at 24 weeks are only approximately 75%. The factors that reduce the probability of achieving prolonged viral suppression are suboptimal potency of the regimen, a high baseline VL and a CD4 count of < 200/mm³, a slow VL fall or failure to achieve an undetectable level, poor adherence, prior exposure to antiretroviral drugs and resistant virus.

1.100 INDICATIONS TO START HAART

CD4 count (cells/mm³)	Decision
Seroconversion	Consider
> 350	Monitor 2-monthly
200–350	Monitor/recommend based on VL*
< 200	Recommend

* Symptomatic patients should commence treatment. The higher the VL, the earlier treatment should be recommended.

1.101 COMBINATION TREATMENTS FOR THE NAÏVE PATIENT

Standard

2 NRTIs
- d4T + 3TC
- d4T + ddI
- ZDV + 3TC
- ZDV + ddI

PI or NNRTI
- Indinavir
- Saquinavir (soft gel)
- Ritonavir
- Nelfinavir
- Lopinavir/ritonavir
- Efavirenz
- Nevirapine

Alternative

2 NRTIs
- ZDV + ddC
- ddI + 3TC
- Abacavir + another RTI

PI or NNRTI
- Ritonavir + saquinavir
- Ritonavir + indinavir
- Nelfinavir + saquinavir

Other regimens

Equal potency
- ZDV + 3TC + abacavir
- NNRTI + PI + NRTI
- 2PI + 2NRTI

Uncertain potency
- NNRTI + PI
- 2NNRTI + 2NRTI

Suboptimal potency
- d4T + ddI + hydroxyurea (hydroxycarbamide)
- d4T + ddI + 3TC
- Saquinavir (hard gel) + 2NRTI
- Amprenavir + ZDV + 3TC

The 'treatment-experienced' patient

A change in antiretroviral therapy may be necessary because of drug side-effects (early or late), difficulties in adherence, or virological failure. In a patient with a previously undetectable VL, virus rebound is usually the first evidence of treatment failure.

With increasing time on a failing regimen, the VL rises towards baseline levels, resistance mounts, the CD4 count falls and clinical progression occurs. The causes of virological failure are listed in Box 1.104. In essence, most early failures are related to adherence difficulties and most late failures are a result of virological resistance. A resistance test should be obtained while on the failing regimen and any change should also take into account prior drug exposure. Therapeutic drug monitoring will confirm that virological failure is not related to inadequate PI levels. Any decision made without the benefit of a resistance test should usually

1.102 HAART OPTIONS

Regimen	Advantages	Disadvantages
PI + 2 NRTIs	Durable and effective Clinical endpoint data Active in late-stage disease and high viral loads Resistance to other PIs rare after early failure* Preserves NNRTI option	Short-term side-effects frequent Fat redistribution, glucose intolerance, hyperlipidaemia Challenging adherence Potential drug interactions Poor CNS entry Resistance to other PIs common after late failure*
NNRTI + 2 NRTIs	Durable and effective Active in late-stage disease and high viral loads Easy adherence Few long-term side-effects Good CNS penetration Preserves PI option	No clinical endpoint data NNRTI cross-resistance early and common after initial failure* Short-term side-effects common
Abacavir + 3TC + ZDV	Easy adherence Few long-term side-effects No significant drug interactions Good CNS penetration Preserves PI and NNRTI options No lipid abnormalities	No clinical endpoint data Limited surrogate marker data in late-stage disease Potential for multi-NRTI resistance May be less effective at high viral loads Reduced future NRTI choice Hypersensitivity reaction with abacavir

* Within HAART combination.

1.103 FACTORS TO CONSIDER WHEN CHOOSING HAART

- Ease of compliance
- Fit of the drug regimen around the patient's lifestyle
- Wishes of the patient
- Stage of disease
- Coexisting/past medical history
- Possibility of additive side-effects (e.g. d4T/ddC and neuropathy)
- Potential for drug interactions with non-HIV medications
- Antagonistic NRTI combinations (ZDV/d4T and ddC/3TC)
- CNS penetration
- Possibility of acquisition of resistance virus

1.104 CAUSES OF VIROLOGICAL FAILURE

Causes	Influences
Insufficient drug activity	Suboptimal potency High baseline VL
Insufficient plasma drug levels	Poor adherence Poor absorption Drug toxicity Drug interactions
Insufficient intracellular active drug	Drug competition
Viral resistance	Primary acquisition Insufficient drug activity Insufficient plasma drug levels

involve switching all three agents. General rules for managing patients with significant past drug exposure and virological rebound differ in that the patient is often late-stage with a low CD4 count and a multiple class-resistant virus. Again, a resistance test will assist in deciding which drugs are unlikely to be of benefit. As a rule, as many new agents as possible should be used including expanded drugs. Occasionally, HAART must be stopped because of life-threatening drug toxicity or because of overriding medical problems where predicted drug interactions will occur. It is also necessary when the patient requests it and in terminal care.

Enhancing the immune system

In the knowledge that HAART alone will not cure a patient of HIV because of the long-lived cellular latency of the virus, focus has turned towards the possibility of bolstering the immune system with the hope that virological control without drugs may be achievable. This can be achieved by allowing wild virus stimulation of the immune system through interrupting therapy in a controlled and safe setting (structured therapeutic interruption, STI) or by direct anti-HIV cytotoxic T-cell stimulation through immunisation with viral proteins. Whether either approach will prove to be beneficial in the long term is unknown. Interleukin-2 is a cytokine that mobilises CD4 cells and increases production, leading to a significant rise in circulating CD4 cell numbers. It is the subject of large-scale trials to define its value and place in treatment.

SPECIAL SITUATIONS

Seroconversion

Seroconversion (primary infection) occurs 2–6 weeks after exposure and manifests as an influenza-like or glandular fever-like syndrome. Very little published data exist as to the merits or potential dangers of antiretroviral treatment at this time (see Box 1.105). Nevertheless, there is a body of opinion that seroconversion may represent a therapeutic window of opportunity associated with long-term benefit.

Children

The general principles for the drug management of HIV in children are the same as that for adults although much of the information underpinning these has been extrapolated from adult trials. Knowledge is also scarce about the pharmacokinetic handling of drugs and long-term side-effects, both of which may differ significantly from adults. Children should be treated if they are symptomatic, or have a low CD4 count or a high VL. As the CD4 count is higher in infants and children up to 6 years of age, the CD4 percentage is a better marker of immunological health and the need to initiate HAART. Several factors make it harder for an undetectable VL to be achieved with HAART treatment in children. Viral loads are higher and persist for prolonged periods before reaching a 'set-point', adherence is more difficult, and not all antiretroviral drugs are available in a suitable formulation for children (suspension, powder, crushable tablet, or a capsule that can be opened). Coordinated, comprehensive family-centred systems of care are necessary to support the child and parents to optimise compliance to medications. As in adults, PI-based or NNRTI-based HAART should be used. Nelfinavir (powder or crushed tablets) is the most convenient PI to use (ritonavir, amprenavir and lopinavir/ritonavir are also available) and nevirapine the most convenient NNRTI; any of the NRTIs can be used. Virological failure occurs in 50% at 1 year and a change of treatment is decided on the same basis as it is for adults.

Perinatal transmission

There is now clear evidence that reduction in perinatal transmission of HIV can be achieved with short-course perinatal prophylaxis using single-drug regimens of ZDV or nevirapine. The likelihood of transmission is decreased to the order of 8.3–18% for ZDV alone, 2.6–10.2% for ZDV and 3TC, 8.2% for nevirapine and 0.8–1.8% for ZDV and caesarean section. Higher rates of reduction are observed in industrialised countries, when drugs are started at 16 weeks, when they are continued in the neonate for 6 weeks, and when HAART is used. The risk of transmission is < 1% when the maternal VL is < 1000 copies/mm³. All patients should be treated in an effort to prevent transmission. For perinatal prophylaxis, nevirapine should be given as a single dose to the mother at the onset of labour and to the newborn within 48 hours. ZDV should be commenced as an intra-venous infusion at the onset of labour and the neonate should be treated for 6 weeks.

Post-exposure prophylaxis

Combination therapy is now recommended for occupational post-exposure prophylaxis (PEP) where the risk is deemed to be significant, although there is no evidence for this practice. The first dose should be given as soon as possible. However, protection is not absolute and health-care workers have been reported to seroconvert despite taking a full course of three drugs started within hours of exposure. PEP is also being used for non-occupational settings such as condom breakage in HIV-serodiscordant partners, victims of rape, relapses in injecting drug users, and sharps-related home exposures in families of HIV patients. As for occupational PEP, a careful risk assessment should be made. Benefits will be greatest in those presenting early, where the risk of transmission is high and where adherence is likely. Approximately 77% of persons receiving PEP experience side-effects and only 40% complete therapy. Recommended PEP is ZDV, 3TC and indinavir or nelfinavir for 28 days.

PREVENTION OF INFECTION

Patients should be assessed for their need for hepatitis A and hepatitis B vaccines and immunised if there is no evidence of naturally acquired infection. HBV surface antibody levels need to be monitored and boosters given when < 100 IU/ml. Pneumococcal vaccine (every 5 years) and influenza vaccine (every year) should be given to all patients. Response to all immunisations is less when the CD4 count is < 200 cells/mm³ although some protection is afforded. Live attenuated vaccines (e.g. BCG, oral polio, yellow fever) should be avoided in symptomatic children and in those where the risk of infection is less than the risk of vaccine-associated complication. Nevertheless, MMR vaccine is safe and should be given. Prophylaxis against infection is another vital aspect of management. Primary prophylaxis is to prevent the initial disease occurring and secondary prophylaxis is to prevent recurrence of infection. Primary prophylaxis is introduced at certain CD4 count levels when there is a risk of infection occurring (see Box 1.106). Secondary prophylaxis is started after successful treatment of the opportunistic infection, usually with the same drugs used to treat the infection but at lower doses. There is now firm evidence with primary prophylaxis for *Pneumocystis carinii* pneumonia and *Toxoplasma* that, where HAART has been successful, the drugs can be stopped when the CD4 threshold at which they were introduced is reached. Vaccine development is slow. An effective, safe and cheap vaccine would radically alter the future global epidemic of HIV. Subunit and synthetic peptide vaccines (e.g. gp120 with an adjuvant) are safe but elicit inadequate cell-mediated immunity. Construct vaccines with a live viral vector (e.g. canarypox or adenovirus) with HIV genes inserted stimulate good CD8 responses and are on trial. However, the massive viral turnover and the frequent generation of antigenically distinct variants provide a significant challenge.

1.106 PROPHYLAXIS OF OPPORTUNISTIC INFECTIONS

Organism/infection	Indication	First-line	Alternatives
Pneumocystis	CD4 < 200 cells/mm³	Co-trimoxazole	Dapsone, atovaquone or inhaled pentamidine
Toxoplasmosis	CD4 < 100 cells/mm³	Co-trimoxazole	Pyrimethamine and dapsone or atovaquone
CMV*	CD4 < 50 cells/mm³	Ganciclovir	
Tuberculosis*	Positive tuberculin skin test	Rifampicin and isoniazid	Isoniazid or rifampicin and pyrazinamide
MAI	CD4 < 50 cells/mm³	Azithromycin	Clarithromycin or rifabutin

* Place in primary prophylaxis uncertain.

EBM

PRIMARY PROPHYLAXIS IN HIV

'Large RCTs have shown reductions in the incidence of PCP and cerebral toxoplasmosis with co-trimoxazole; MAI with azithromycin or clarithromycin; and tuberculosis with isoniazid alone or in combination with other drugs.'

- Bucher HC, Griffith L, Guyatt GL, Opravil M. Meta-analysis of prophylactic treatments against *Pneumocystis carinii* pneumonia and toxoplasma encephalitis in HIV-infected patients. J Acquir Immune Defic Syndr Hum Retrovirol 1997; 15:104–114.
- Wilkinson D. Drugs for preventing tuberculosis in HIV-infected persons (Cochrane Review). Cochrane Library, issue 4, 1999. Oxford: Update Software.
- Oldfield EC, Fessel WJ, Dunne MW, et al. Once weekly azithromycin therapy for prevention of *Mycobacterium avium* complex infection in patients with AIDS: a randomised, double-blind, placebo-controlled multicenter trial. Clin Infect Dis 1998; 26:611–619.

Further information: www.clinicalevidence.org
www.cochrane.co.uk

EBM

DISCONTINUING PROPHYLAXIS IN HIV

'Three RCTs have shown that discontinuing primary prophylaxis is safe in persons with CD4 counts of > 200 cells/mm³ on HAART.'

- Mussini C, Pezzotti P, Govoni A, et al. Discontinuation of primary prophylaxis for *Pneumocystis carinii* pneumonia and toxoplasma encephalitis in human immunodeficiency virus type-1 infected patients: the changes in opportunistic prophylaxis study. J Infect Dis 2000; 181:1635–1642.
- El-Sadr WM, Burman WJ, Grant LB, et al. Discontinuation of prophylaxis for *Mycobacterium avium* complex disease in HIV-infected patients who have a response to antiretroviral therapy. N Engl J Med 2000; 342:1085–1092.

Further information: www.clinicalevidence.org
www.cochrane.co.uk

HUMAN T-CELL LYMPHOTROPIC VIRUS (HTLV) INFECTIONS

There are two other retroviruses, HTLV 1 and HTLV 2, associated with disease in humans.

HTLV 1 is endemic in Japan, the Caribbean and certain areas of West Africa. It is transmitted by blood transfusion, by drug users sharing needles and from mother to child, principally through breastfeeding. It can also be transmitted by sexual intercourse, especially from male to female. HTLV 1 is associated with adult T-cell leukaemia/lymphoma and with a degenerative neurological disease characterised by demyelination of the long motor neurons in the spinal cord, known as tropical spastic paraparesis in the Caribbean and HTLV 1-associated myelopathy in Japan. These diseases also occur in Europe and in North America in immigrants from areas of the world where HTLV 1 infection is endemic.

HTLV 2, a much more rarely isolated virus than HTLV 1, has been isolated from Native Americans and in Africa, and also from intravenous drug users in the USA. Its role in human disease is uncertain; although it was first isolated from a case of hairy cell leukaemia, it is infrequently associated with this disease.

THE MANAGEMENT OF INFECTION

The production of disease by microorganisms is a dynamic process between an infecting organism and the various defences of the human immune system. Not all infection requires antibiotic therapy (see EBM panels).

Public health measures control spread of infection and vaccination may improve 'herd immunity' in communities. Individual case management combines non-specific measures to combat the symptoms of the body's reaction to invasion by microorganisms, e.g. fever, headache and myalgia, with the treatment of complications of infection such as shock, organ failure and haemorrhage and with specific antimicrobial therapy to kill or inhibit the growth of causative microorganisms.

EBM

ANTIBIOTICS AND THE COMMON COLD

'Analysis of seven RCTs comparing antibiotic therapy with placebo in acute upper respiratory infections indicates that there is not enough evidence of important benefits to support such treatment. Moreover, there is a significant increase in adverse effects associated with antibiotic use.'

- Arrol B, Kenealy T. Antibiotics for the common cold (Cochrane Review). Cochrane Library, issue 4, 2000. Oxford: Update Software.

Further information: www.update-software.com

EBM

PHARYNGITIS, 'SORE THROAT'—role of antibiotics

'In an analysis of 25 studies comprising 11 452 cases of sore throat, antibiotics shortened the duration of symptoms by a mean of 1 day half-way through the illness and by 16 hours overall. They are most effective if a throat swab is positive for *Streptococcus*. By 7 days 90% of treated and untreated cases were symptom-free. Suppurative complications were reduced by antibiotics: otitis media OR = 0.22, acute sinusitis OR = 0.46, quinsy OR = 0.46.'

- Del Mar CB, Kenealy PP, Spinks AB. Antibiotics for sore throat (Cochrane Review). Cochrane Library, issue 4, 2000. Oxford: Update Software.

Further information: www.update-software.com

PRINCIPLES OF ANTIMICROBIAL THERAPY

Antimicrobial drugs constitute one of the most important and successful groups of therapeutic agents. The science of effective antimicrobial use requires an understanding of a number of principles:

- *Minimal inhibitory concentration (MIC)*, expressed as a percentage (MIC_{90}), is defined as the lowest concentration of antibiotic required to inhibit 90% of the colonies of a particular organism. The lower the MIC, the more sensitive the organism to that agent and vice versa. As an in vitro measurement the MIC does not always accurately predict clinical outcome. Roxithromycin has in vitro MICs much lower than those in vivo due to a marked inhibitory effect of serum.
- Co-administration of certain antimicrobials, e.g. aminoglycosides and β-lactams, produces a *synergistic effect* greater than their combined MICs. This can be harnessed clinically in the management of difficult infections such as bacterial endocarditis (see p. 463).
- *Drug absorption* is very important, e.g. phenoxy-methylpenicillin is erratically absorbed orally, and antacids or iron compounds in the stomach reduce the absorption of quinolones and tetracyclines.

- *Protein binding* determines the availability of the drug and may produce side-effects due to the competition with other drugs, e.g. warfarin.
- *Lipophilic drugs*, e.g. quinolones, cross cell membranes well whilst *hydrophilic drugs*, e.g. aminoglycosides, remain in the ECF space.
- The *plasma half-life* (T½) of the drug allows recommendations on the timing of dosing schedules.
- Certain classes of antimicrobial, e.g. aminoglycosides and macrolides, exhibit a clinically useful 'post-antibiotic effect' (PAE) with inhibition of microbial multiplication beyond the time when the MIC is reached in plasma. This allows reduction in dosing schedules.
- Some antibiotics have efficacy reduced by the 'inoculum effect', where the presence of large numbers of organisms inhibits the antibiotic despite apparent (MIC-based) sensitivity.

Details of individual compounds should be available in the manufacturer's data sheet or publications such as the *British National Formulary*.

ANTIMICROBIAL RESISTANCE

Although effective antimicrobial therapy is potentially available for all infections, the use of antimicrobials has produced

1.107 MECHANISMS OF ACTION AND RESISTANCE OF COMMON CLASSES OF ANTIMICROBIAL

Class of antimicrobial	Mechanisms of action	Mechanisms of resistance
Beta-lactams	Inhibit cell wall synthesis Competitively block transpeptidases, penicillin-binding proteins and peptidoglycan synthesis Periplasmic space in Gram-positive organisms Intracellular in Gram-negative Only act on dividing bacteria	Altered porin channels Gram-negative Modification of penicillin-binding proteins (MRSA) Production of hydrolysing β-lactamase enzymes (chromosomal or plasmid-mediated)
Glycopeptides	Inhibit late stages of cell wall peptidoglycan synthesis at two stages	Large molecules; cannot penetrate Gram-negative porins so Gram-negative intrinsically resistant chemical substitution to prevent binding to transpeptidase
Aminoglycosides	Bind to 30S subunit of bacterial ribosomes (Require specific transport mechanism across Gram-negative outer/inner membranes) Disrupt bacterial protein synthesis	Membrane impermeability Enzyme inactivation of active sites (Multiple enzymes now involved, specific for different aminoglycosides)
Macrolides, lincosamides and streptogramins	Reversibly bind to 50S subunit of bacterial ribosomes, block peptide bond formation and disrupt protein synthesis	Modification of bacterial target (cross-resistance to all macrolides/lincosamides/streptogramins)
Tetracyclines	Inhibit protein synthesis by preventing tRNA binding to ribosomes and modify ribosomal subunits pH-dependent accumulation in cells	Active efflux of antibiotic from cells
Chloramphenicol	Competitively inhibits transfer of tRNA-binding to 50S ribosomal subunit	Specific enzyme (acyltransferase) that inactivates the antibiotic often plasmid-mediated Reduced entry of drug through modified porins
Quinolones	Inhibit topoisomerases (DNA gyrase) and topoisomerase IV to prevent supercoiling or uncoiling of DNA, so effectively preventing DNA replication and causing cell death	Mutation of topoisomerases Porin impermeability Active efflux
Imidazoles	Under aerobic conditions form superoxide-damaging proteins, nuclear acids and lipids	
Sulphonamides	Inhibit dihydrofolate and tetrahydrofolate reductase, so inhibit folic acid synthesis from para-aminobenzoic acid (PABA)	Hyperproduction of PABA enzyme mutation

high levels of resistance in some species. Some organisms are becoming resistant to all known antimicrobials. Methicillin-resistant *Staph. aureus* (MRSA) and now glycopeptide-resistant *Staph. aureus* and enterococci (GRSA, GRSE) are examples. Multidrug-resistant *M. tuberculosis* (MDR-TB; see p. 532) is a similar serious threat. Inappropriate antibiotic use, e.g. for viral upper respiratory infections, inadequate dosage or treatment length, and widespread availability 'across the counter', coupled with poor compliance in patients, has caused this unfortunate predicament.

Mechanisms of action and resistance of antimicrobials

The mechanisms of action and of microbial resistance for the major classes of antimicrobial are shown in Box 1.107. The ability of bacteria to exchange genetic material via transposons, bacteriophages and plasmids has resulted in commensal organisms acquiring multidrug resistance and potentially passing this to transient pathogens in the gut lumen.

SELECTION OF APPROPRIATE ANTIBIOTIC THERAPY

The selection of antibiotic therapy for an infection requires a knowledge of:

- the infecting organism including the most likely pathogen to be present in given clinical or geographical circumstances
- the local patterns of antimicrobial resistance in common pathogens
- an understanding of the pharmacokinetics of the antimicrobials selected
- the physiology of the patient, metabolic upset, renal or hepatic dysfunction, age and available routes of administration.

The human body is in contact with many potentially infectious agents: bacteria, viruses, fungi or protozoa. Most

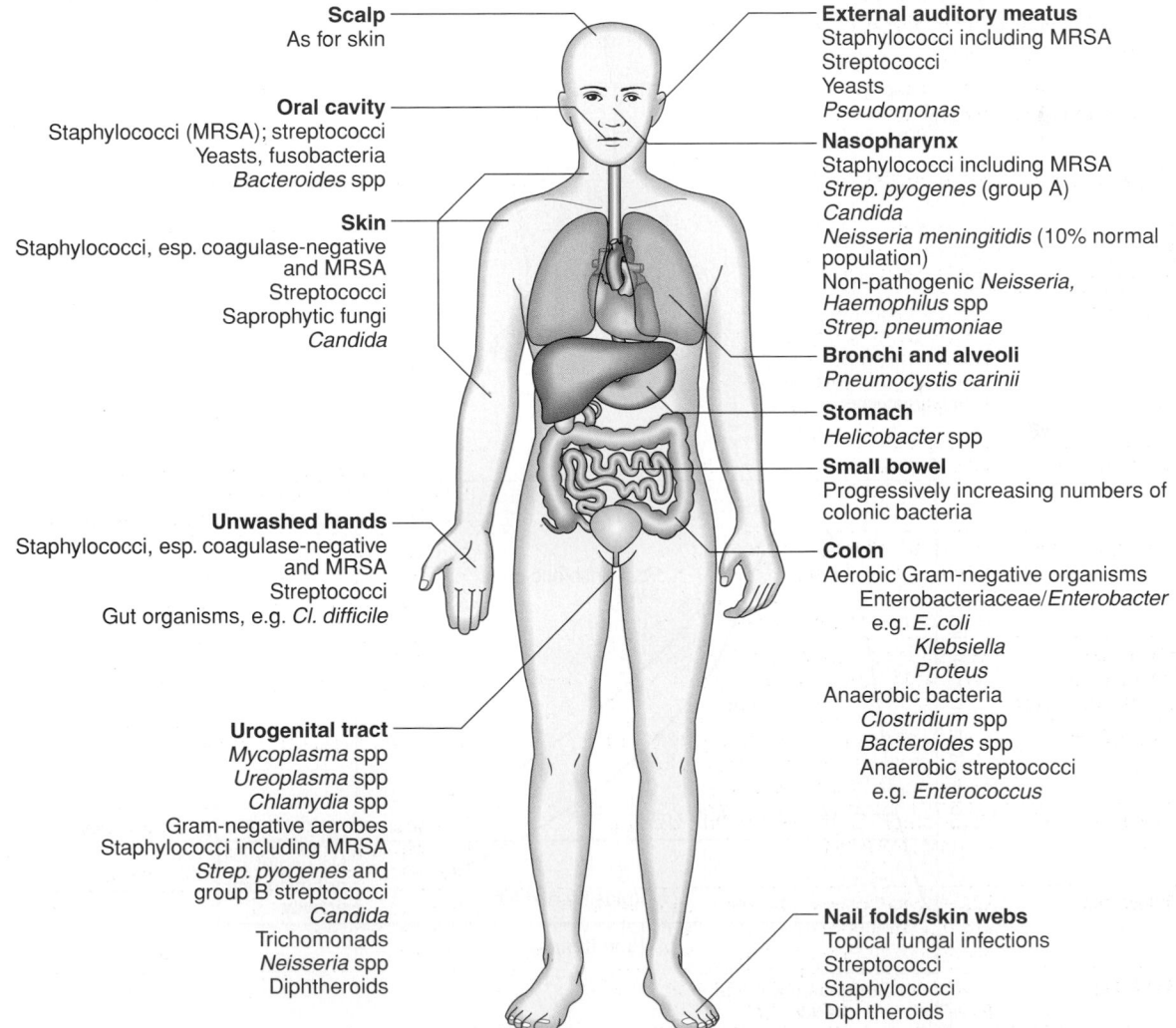

Scalp
As for skin

Oral cavity
Staphylococci (MRSA); streptococci
Yeasts, fusobacteria
Bacteroides spp

Skin
Staphylococci, esp. coagulase-negative
and MRSA
Streptococci
Saprophytic fungi
Candida

Unwashed hands
Staphylococci, esp. coagulase-negative
and MRSA
Streptococci
Gut organisms, e.g. *Cl. difficile*

Urogenital tract
Mycoplasma spp
Ureoplasma spp
Chlamydia spp
Gram-negative aerobes
Staphylococci including MRSA
Strep. pyogenes and
group B streptococci
Candida
Trichomonads
Neisseria spp
Diphtheroids

External auditory meatus
Staphylococci including MRSA
Streptococci
Yeasts
Pseudomonas

Nasopharynx
Staphylococci including MRSA
Strep. pyogenes (group A)
Candida
Neisseria meningitidis (10% normal population)
Non-pathogenic *Neisseria,*
Haemophilus spp
Strep. pneumoniae

Bronchi and alveoli
Pneumocystis carinii

Stomach
Helicobacter spp

Small bowel
Progressively increasing numbers of colonic bacteria

Colon
Aerobic Gram-negative organisms
Enterobacteriaceae/*Enterobacter*
e.g. *E. coli*
Klebsiella
Proteus
Anaerobic bacteria
Clostridium spp
Bacteroides spp
Anaerobic streptococci
e.g. *Enterococcus*

Nail folds/skin webs
Topical fungal infections
Streptococci
Staphylococci
Diphtheroids

Fig. 1.95   Endogenous infection: reservoirs of infection in adults.

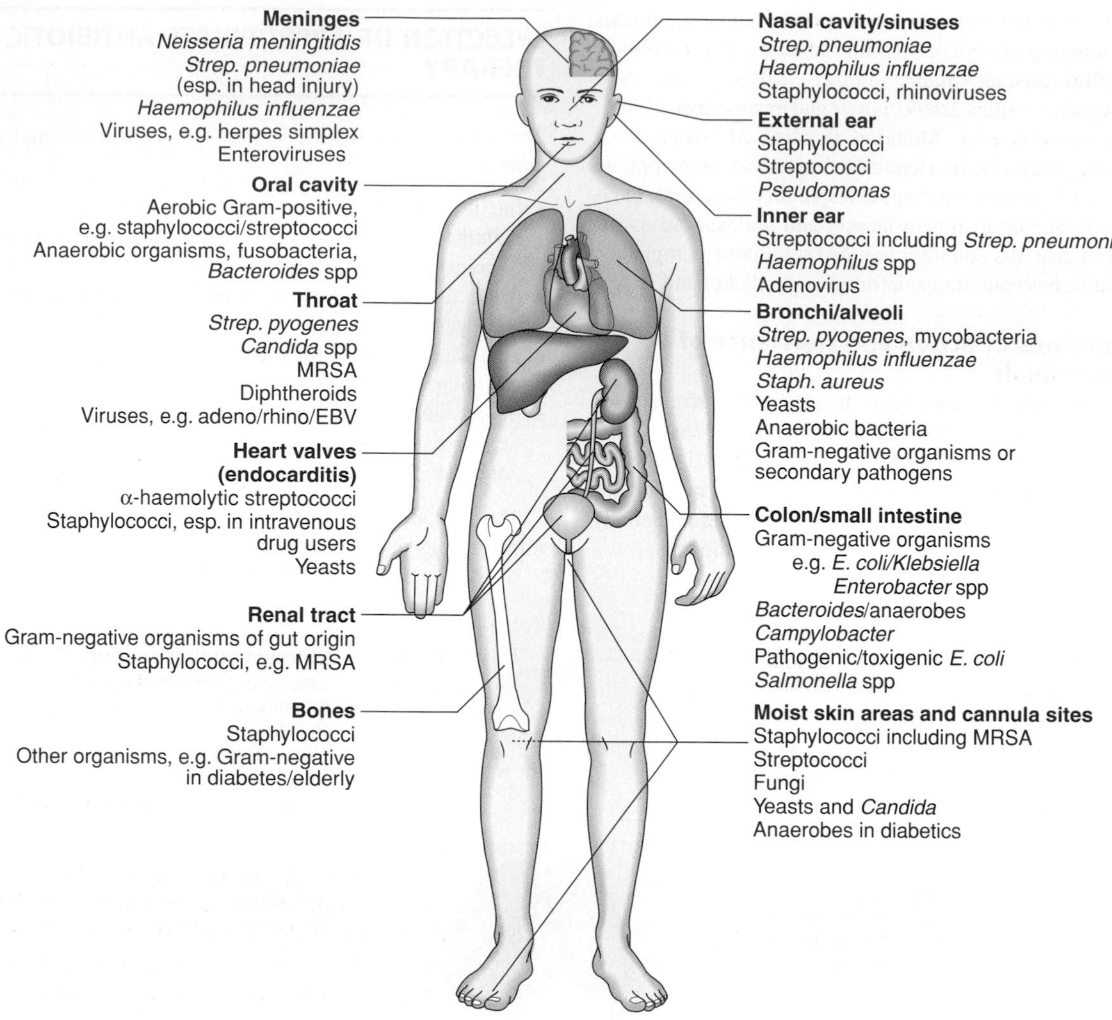

Meninges
Neisseria meningitidis
Strep. pneumoniae
(esp. in head injury)
Haemophilus influenzae
Viruses, e.g. herpes simplex
Enteroviruses
Oral cavity
Aerobic Gram-positive, e.g. staphylococci/streptococci
Anaerobic organisms, fusobacteria, *Bacteroides* spp
Throat
Strep. pyogenes
Candida spp
MRSA
Diphtheroids
Viruses, e.g. adeno/rhino/EBV
Heart valves (endocarditis)
α-haemolytic streptococci
Staphylococci, esp. in intravenous drug users
Yeasts
Renal tract
Gram-negative organisms of gut origin
Staphylococci, e.g. MRSA
Bones
Staphylococci
Other organisms, e.g. Gram-negative in diabetes/elderly
Nasal cavity/sinuses
Strep. pneumoniae
Haemophilus influenzae
Staphylococci, rhinoviruses
External ear
Staphylococci
Streptococci
Pseudomonas
Inner ear
Streptococci including *Strep. pneumoniae*
Haemophilus spp
Adenovirus
Bronchi/alveoli
Strep. pyogenes, mycobacteria
Haemophilus influenzae
Staph. aureus
Yeasts
Anaerobic bacteria
Gram-negative organisms or secondary pathogens
Colon/small intestine
Gram-negative organisms
e.g. *E. coli/Klebsiella*
Enterobacter spp
Bacteroides/anaerobes
Campylobacter
Pathogenic/toxigenic *E. coli*
Salmonella spp
Moist skin areas and cannula sites
Staphylococci including MRSA
Streptococci
Fungi
Yeasts and *Candida*
Anaerobes in diabetics

Fig. 1.96 Common infecting organisms.

C(max)
Post-antibiotic effect (PAE)
Concentration of antibiotic
Area under curve
Time above MIC
Antimicrobial activity
MIC
No useful antimicrobial activity
t½ (plasma half-life)
0
Time (hours)
24
Initial dose
Suggested dosage frequency

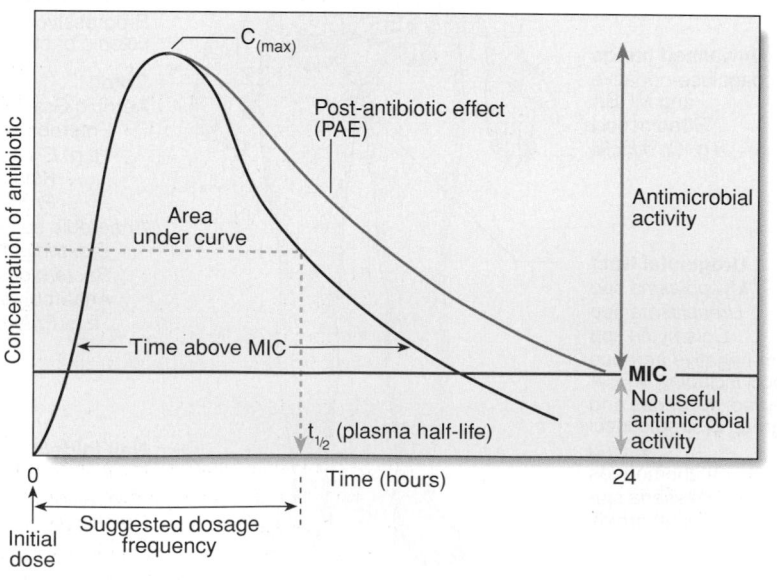

Fig. 1.97 Antimicrobial pharmacokinetics.

are harmless colonisers causing no clinical upset but forming a natural reservoir of potential infection in the human host (see Fig. 1.95).

The clinical history should determine the systems of the body most likely to be involved in disease. Figure 1.96 shows common pathogens found in different systems.

Once likely pathogens have been identified and appropriate laboratory specimens sent to confirm their presence, the most appropriate antibiotic should be selected. In many hospitals, policies or 'sepsis protocols' have been devised using local sensitivity patterns to guide in initial antimicrobial therapy. This prevents inappropriate therapy, and attempts to limit resistance development and maximise effectiveness. Appropriate dosage should maintain the antibiotic concentration above the MIC in the given body compartment (see Fig. 1.97).

An algorithm for the selection of antibiotics is given in Figure 1.98.

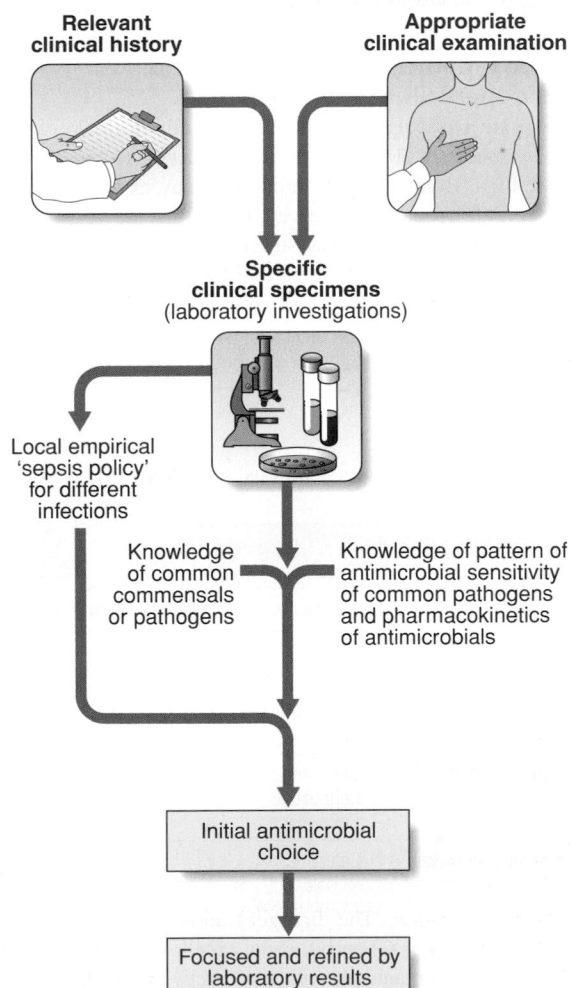

Fig. 1.98   Selection of appropriate antimicrobial agents.

ANTIMICROBIAL AGENTS

BETA-LACTAM ANTIBIOTICS

These antibiotics have a β-lactam ring structure and exert a bactericidal action on rapidly dividing organisms. Generally, they achieve good levels in lung, kidney, bone, muscle and liver, and in pleural, synovial, pericardial and peritoneal fluids. They are classified into eight groups:

- natural penicillins: benzylpenicillin, phenoxymethylpenicillin
- penicillinase-resistant penicillins: methicillin, flucloxacillin
- aminopenicillins: ampicillin, amoxicillin
- carboxy- and ureidopenicillins: ticarcillin, piperacillin
- cephalosporins: first–fourth-generation compounds
- monobactams: aztreonam
- carbapenems: imipenem, meropenem
- β-lactamase inhibitors, e.g. clavulanic acid.

Pharmacokinetics: key points
- Not inhibited by abscess environment (low pH, low O_2, high protein and polymorphonuclear cells).
- Poor penetration to monocytes, low CSF levels except in the presence of inflammation.
- Inoculum effect reduces activity.
- Generally safe in pregnancy (except imipenem/cilastatin).

Adverse reactions
Generalised allergy to penicillin occurs in 0.7–10% of cases and anaphylaxis in 0.004–0.015%. Over 90% of patients with infectious mononucleosis develop a rash if given aminopenicillins; this does not imply lasting allergy. Established penicillin allergy does not imply allergy to other classes, particularly the cephalosporins. The second- and third-generation cephalosporins have a low incidence of allergy and an almost negligible rate of anaphylaxis even in the presence of established penicillin allergy.

Adverse effects
Gastrointestinal upset and diarrhoea are common side-effects, and a mild reversible hepatitis is well recognised with many of the drugs in this class. Leucopenia, thrombocytopenia and coagulation deficiencies can occur. Interstitial nephritis and increased renal damage in combination with aminoglycosides are also well recognised (see p. 617). Seizures and encephalopathy have been reported, particularly with high doses in the presence of renal insufficiency. Direct intrathecal injection of a β-lactam is contraindicated. Thrombophlebitis occurs in up to 5% of patients receiving parenteral therapy with these agents.

Drug interactions
Synergism occurs in combination with aminoglycosides. Simultaneous dual β-lactam administration is unpredictable, either synergy or antagonism resulting. Ampicillin decreases the biological effect of oral contraceptives and the whole class is significantly affected by concurrent administration of probenecid, producing a 2–4-fold increase in the peak serum concentration.

Natural penicillins (benzylpenicillin, phenoxymethylpenicillin)

(Dose: benzylpenicillin 1.2–2.4 g i.v. 6-hourly, phenoxy-methylpenicillin 250–500 mg oral 6-hourly) Natural penicillins are primarily effective against Gram-positive organisms (except staphylococci) and anaerobic organisms. *Strep. pyogenes* has remained sensitive to natural penicillins world-wide (see Fig. 1.99).

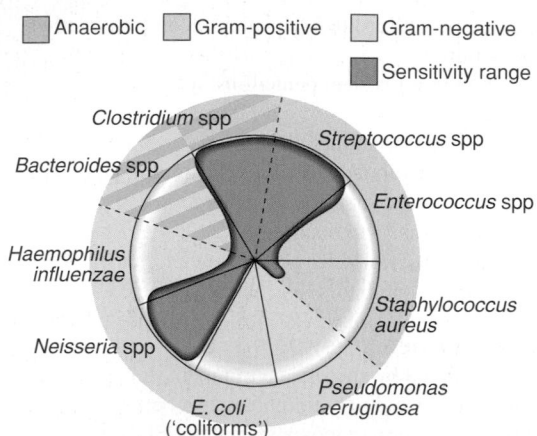

Fig. 1.99   Penicillin: spectrum of activity.

Methicillin/flucloxacillin

(Dose: flucloxacillin 500 mg 6-hourly oral or i.v.) These are the mainstay of treatment for staphylococcal infections and other Gram-positive organisms, being resistant to staphylococcal penicillinase (see Fig. 1.100).

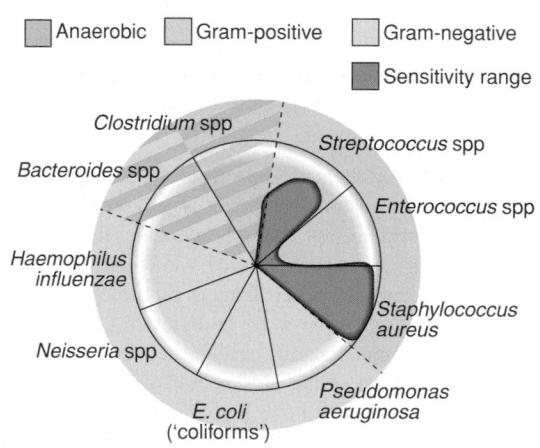

Fig. 1.100   Flucloxacillin: spectrum of activity.

The aminopenicillins

(Dose: ampicillin 500 mg 6-hourly, amoxicillin 500 mg 8-hourly oral or i.v.) Ampicillin and amoxicillin have the same spectrum of activity as the natural penicillins with additional Gram-negative cover against Enterobacteriaceae. Amoxicillin has much better oral absorption than ampicillin.

Many organisms are resistant due to β-lactamase production but the addition of β-lactam inhibitors (e.g. clavulanic acid, producing co-amoxiclav) to aminopenicillins has improved clinical usefulness (see Fig. 1.101).

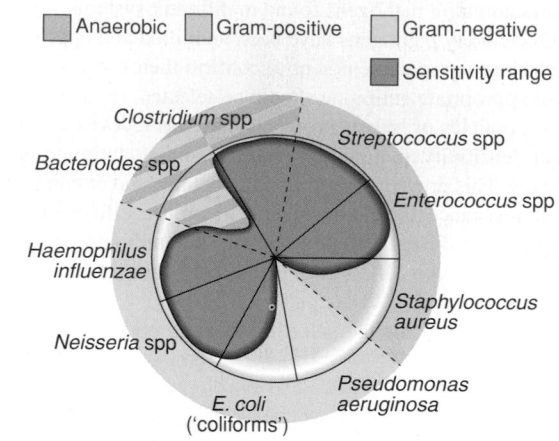

Fig. 1.101   Amoxicillin: spectrum of activity.

Carboxypenicillins (ticarcillin) and ureidopenicillins (piperacillin)

These are particularly active against Gram-negative organisms, especially *Pseudomonas* spp, resistant to the aminopenicillins. Beta-lactamase inhibitors may also be used to extend their spectrum of activity. Penicillins are very cheap, well-tolerated, safe and easy-to-use antibiotics. The potential for synergy with aminoglycosides can be put to therapeutic advantage. Oral absorption is, however, poor or unreliable, major adverse/allergic reactions can occur, and resistance is increasing. Broad-spectrum drugs are only available intravenously.

Cephalosporins

These are arranged in 'generations' (see Box 1.108).

1.108 CEPHALOSPORINS		
Class	**Examples**	**Route of administration**
First generation	Cefalexin Cefazolin	Oral I.v.
Second generation	Cefuroxime Cefoxitin	Oral/i.v.
Third generation	Cefixime Ceftriaxone Ceftazidime	Oral I.v. I.v.
Fourth generation	Cefepime	I.v.

First generation. The first-generation compounds, e.g. cefalexin (250 mg 6-hourly), show excellent activity against Gram-positive organisms, with some activity against Gram-negative organisms. Many of them are potentially nephrotoxic.

Second generation. Second-generation cephalosporins retain Gram-positive activity but have extended Gram-negative activity and some anti-anaerobic activity.

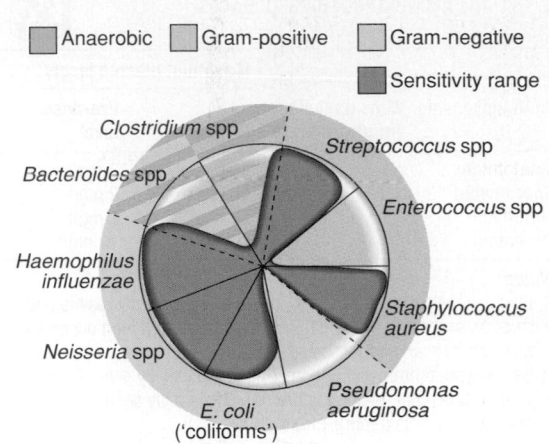

Fig. 1.102   Cefuroxime: spectrum of activity.

Cefuroxime, usually given i.v. 750 mg–1.5 g 8-hourly, is the best-known example (see Fig. 1.102).

Third generation. Third-generation cephalosporins further improve anti-Gram-negative cover but some, such as ceftazidime, have particularly good antipseudomonal activity whilst losing some of their Gram-positive effectiveness. Ceftriaxone has excellent Gram-negative activity and retains good activity against *Strep. pyogenes* and haemolytic

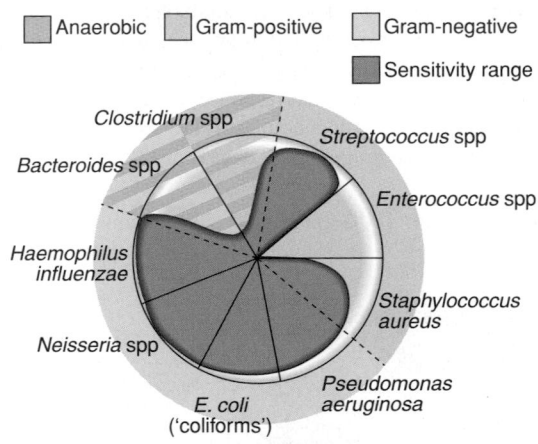

Fig. 1.103   Ceftazidime: spectrum of activity.

streptococci. They are only available intravenously and, although effective (see Fig. 1.103), are very expensive.

Fourth generation. Fourth-generation cephalosporins retain excellent broad-spectrum activity.

Cephalosporins are safe and reliable antibiotics, have a broad spectrum of activity and show some synergy with aminoglycosides. The more active compounds are only available in intravenous form. They are associated with *Cl. difficile* enteritis (see p. 828). The group shows little anti-anaerobic activity and none against *Enterococcus* spp. Oral formulations of the third- and fourth-generation compounds are expensive and poorly absorbed.

Monobactams

Aztreonam (dose 1–2 g 12-hourly) is the only agent available in this class. It has excellent anti-Gram-negative antibiotic activity but no useful activity against Gram-positive organisms or anaerobes. It is only available as a parenteral preparation.

Carbapenems

These have the broadest antibiotic activity of the β-lactam antibiotics and include activity against anaerobes (see Fig. 1.104). They are very expensive and only available in intravenous formulation. Meropenem is used in doses of 500 mg infusion 8-hourly.

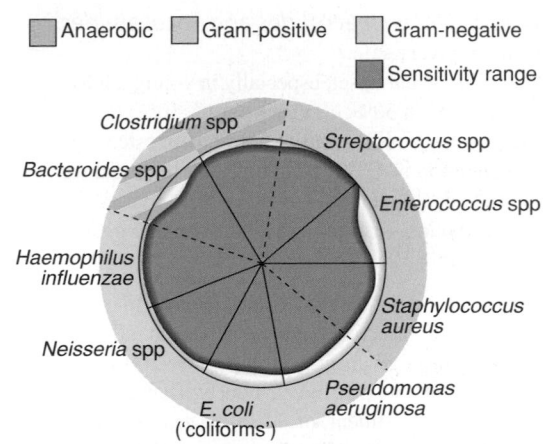

Fig. 1.104   Imipenem: spectrum of activity.

MACROLIDE AND LINCOSAMIDE ANTIBIOTICS

Erythromycin. First launched in 1952, it remains the 'reference' macrolide antibiotic (see Fig. 1.105).

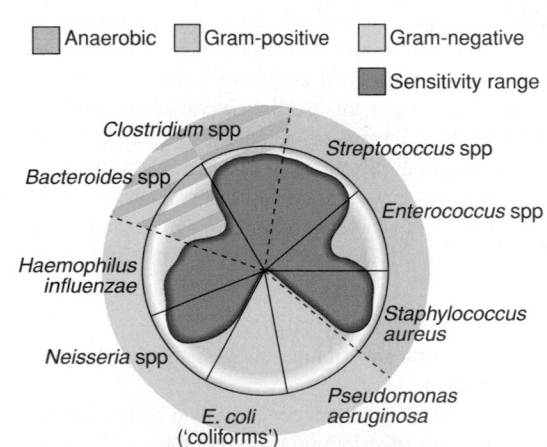

Fig. 1.105   Erythromycin: spectrum of activity.

Lincosamides (lincomycin, clindamycin). Although chemically unrelated, the lincosamides possess closely related properties, modes of action and resistance patterns. Both classes bind to the same element of the ribosome so are potentially competitive and should not be administered together.

Macrolide pharmacokinetics: key points

- Poorly absorbed orally.
- Short half-life (except azithromycin).
- High protein binding.
- Excellent intracellular accumulation, good CSF penetration.

Lincosamide (e.g. clindamycin) pharmacokinetics: key points

- Good bioavailability.
- Food has no effect on absorption.
- Limited CSF penetration.

Adverse effects (macrolides and lincosamides)

- Generally very safe.
- Gastrointestinal upset, especially in young adults (erythromycin 30%, clindamycin 10–30%).
- Cholestatic jaundice with erythromycin esteolate.
- Prolongation of QT interval on ECG, potential for torsades de pointes.
- Clindamycin—diarrhoea in 2–30% linked to *Cl. difficile*. See Figure 1.105.

The macrolides are used in the clinical management of Gram-positive infections where penicillin allergy occurs. Erythromycin is given in a dose of 250–500 mg 6-hourly, clarithromycin 250–500 mg 12-hourly. They are particularly useful in the treatment of *Mycoplasma*, *Chlamydia* and rickettsial infections. The long intracellular half-life of azithromycin allows single-dose/short-course therapy (500 mg daily for 3 days) for genitourinary infections caused by these organisms.

AMINOGLYCOSIDES

Aminoglycosides are very effective anti-Gram-negative antibiotics. Due to their marked oto- and nephrotoxicity, it was thought they would become obsolete. Careful monitoring of renal function and drug levels, plus short treatment regimens, minimises this. Aminoglycosides are particularly useful where β-lactam or quinolone resistance occurs in hospital-acquired infections. They are not subject to an inoculum effect (reduced activity in the presence of a high concentration of bacteria) and they all exhibit a post-antibiotic effect (PAE) and synergism with β-lactam antibiotics.

Pharmacokinetics: key points

- Negligible oral absorption (unless significant renal impairment).
- Hydrophilic so excellent penetration to body cavities and serosal fluids (distribution matches ECF).
- Very poor intracellular penetration (except hair cells in cochlea and renal cortical cells.
- Negligible CSF and corneal penetration.
- Peak plasma levels 30 minutes after infusion.
- Post-antibiotic effect allows once-daily administration (except in endocarditis, pregnancy, chronic renal disease and ascites).
- Monitoring of therapeutic levels required (see Box 1.109).

1.109 THE AMINOGLYCOSIDES: DOSAGES

Aminoglycoside	Max. daily dose (mg/kg/24 hrs)	Maximum plasma levels	
		Peak level	Pre-dose level
Gentamicin	5	10 mg/l	2 mg/l
Tobramycin	5	10 mg/l	2 mg/l
Netilmicin	6	12 mg/l	2 mg/l
Amikacin	15	30 mg/l	10 mg/l

Notes
1. Plasma levels should be monitored in all patients if possible and *must* be measured in the elderly, in infants, and if high doses are given or *if renal function is impaired*.
2. Gentamicin, tobramycin and netilmicin are usually given 8- or 12-hourly if renal function is normal. Single daily dosage is also effective and less nephro-ototoxic.
3. 60–80 mg 12-hourly of gentamicin is recommended for synergistic activity with β-lactams.

Adverse reactions

- Renal toxicity (usually reversible), worse with concomitant vancomycin, cisplatin, amphotericin B, contrast media.
- Cochlear toxicity (permanent) more likely in elderly.
- Neuromuscular blockade after rapid intravenous infusion (increased with calcium channel blockers, myasthenia gravis and hypomagnesaemia).

Aminoglycosides are very effective in Gram-negative sepsis and body fluid infection, exerting synergism with β-lactam antibiotics. The post-antibiotic effect can be utilised to reduce toxicity and allow once-daily dosing (see Fig. 1.106). They cause very little local irritation at injection sites and negligible allergic responses. Intravenous therapy and close monitoring of blood levels are required. As a rule courses should be limited to 10 days or less.

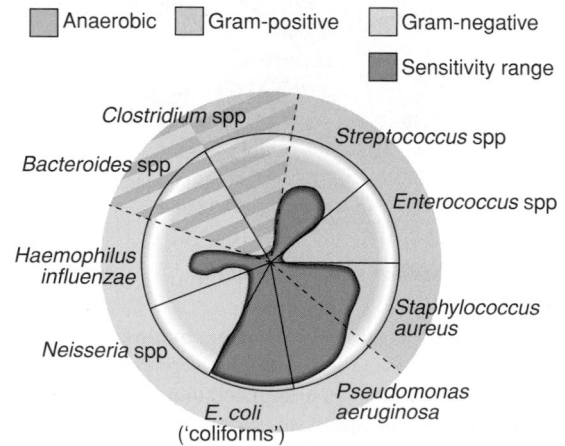

Fig. 1.106 **Gentamicin: spectrum of activity.**

QUINOLONES

Of these synthetic agents (see Box 1.110), the early quinolones had purely anti-Gram-negative activity, fluoroquinolones (e.g. ciprofloxacin) have 10–100 times greater activity against Gram-negative organisms (see Fig. 1.107),

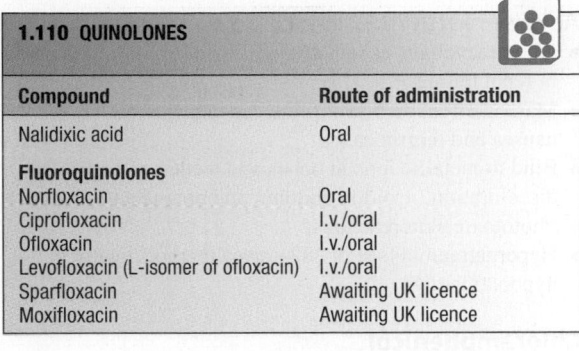

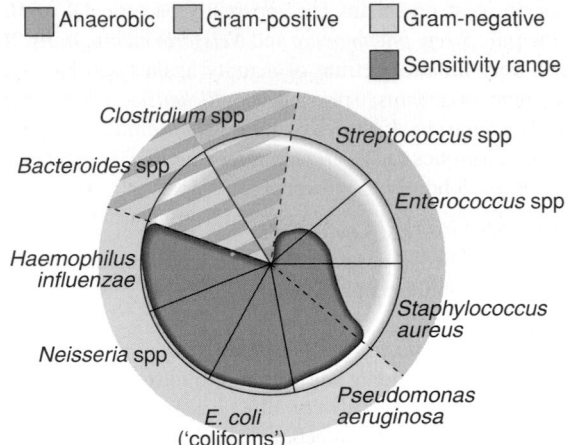

Fig. 1.107   Ciprofloxacin: spectrum of activity.

and newer drugs, currently in late phases of development, have improved anti-Gram-positive and anti-anaerobic capability. Resistance has emerged since the early 1990s. Recently in Spain, other European countries and the USA, resistance to ciprofloxacin of up to 10–20% in *E. coli* has been demonstrated.

Pharmacokinetics: key points
- Well absorbed after oral administration but delayed by food, antacids, ferrous sulphate and multivitamins.
- Wide volume of distribution.
- Good intracellular penetration concentrating in phagocytes with high bioavailability.
- Tissue concentration twice that of serum.

Adverse reactions
- Very few side-effects.
- Rare skin reactions (phototoxicity).
- Gastrointestinal side-effects in 1–5%, tremor, dizziness and occasional seizures in 5–12%.
- Coadministration with xanthines and theophyllines reduces clearance of these drugs so may produce insomnia and increases seizure potential.
- Bone and joint disease in animal studies limits use in children.

The quinolones allow excellent anti-Gram-negative activity from oral dosing and have useful activity against atypical or intracellular organisms, e.g. *Mycoplasma* and *Chlamydia*.

Other than recent additions to the class, they have poor Gram-positive activity and little action against anaerobic infections (see Fig. 1.108). (Normal dose: ciprofloxacin 250–750 mg 12-hourly orally or 200–400 mg 12-hourly i.v.; levofloxacin 250–500 mg daily orally or 500 mg daily/12-hourly i.v.)

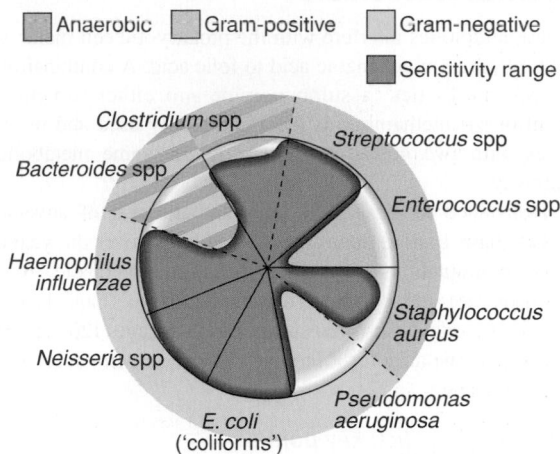

Fig. 1.108   The newer quinolones (moxifloxacin): spectrum of activity.

GLYCOPEPTIDES (VANCOMYCIN AND TEICOPLANIN)

Vancomycin is effective against Gram-positive organisms and, with teicoplanin, remains useful against MRSA and resistant enterococci. Some coagulase-negative staphylococci, enterococci and MRSA demonstrate levels of intermediate sensitivity or resistance to it. The inappropriate use of vancomycin should be limited, particularly in the management of *Cl. difficile* infections, to prevent further resistance development. Gram-negative organisms are not sensitive to glycopeptides. (Dose: vancomycin 500 mg–1 g i.v. 12-hourly, 125 mg 6-hourly orally for *Cl. difficile*). Teicoplanin has greater in vitro activity than vancomycin against Gram-positive organisms (200–400 mg daily i.v.). It is not approved by the Federal Drug Administration for use in the USA. Neither drug has any activity against Gram-negative organisms or achieves any useful oral absorption.

Pharmacokinetics of vancomycin: key points
- Must be given by slow intravenous infusion with good tissue distribution and has a short half-life.
- Only enters CSF in the presence of inflammation.

Pharmacokinetics of teicoplanin: key points
- Long half-life allows once-daily dosing.
- More lipophilic than vancomycin, with good tissue penetration.

Adverse effects of vancomycin
- Histamine release due to rapid infusion produces the 'red-man' anaphylactoid reaction.
- Nephrotoxicity enhanced by concomitant aminoglycosides.
- Requires therapeutic monitoring.

Adverse effects of teicoplanin
- Rash, bronchospasm, eosinophilia and anaphylaxis.
- Markedly less toxic than vancomycin; only requires monitoring in renal impairment.

FOLATE ANTAGONISTS

These antibiotics interfere with the prokaryotic cell metabolism of para-aminobenzoic acid to folic acid. A combination of two antibiotics (a sulphonamide and either trimethoprim or pyrimethamine) is most commonly used and interferes with two consecutive steps in the same metabolic pathway.

Resistance to these antibiotics and the risk of adverse effects have limited their clinical usefulness over the years. Two combinations—trimethoprim/sulfamethoxazole (co-trimoxazole) and pyrimethamine/sulfadoxine (Fansidar)—remain important. Co-trimoxazole in high dosage (120 mg/kg) is the first-line drug for *Pneumocystis pneumoniae* infection in HIV disease.

Pharmacokinetics: key points
- Well absorbed orally with good bioavailability.
- Displace bilirubin from albumin so predispose to kernicterus in infants.
- Sulphonamides are hydrophilic, distributing well to the ECF.
- Trimethoprim is lipophilic with high tissue concentrations.

Adverse reactions
- Most are dose- and time-related (urinary tract infection therapy should be no more than 3 days).
- Fatal marrow dysplasia and haemolysis in G6PD more common in the elderly.
- Skin and mucocutaneous reactions especially common and related to sulphonamide component.
- All reactions more common in high-dose therapy in HIV disease.

TETRACYCLINES AND CHLORAMPHENICOL

Tetracyclines

Of this mainly bacteriostatic class, the newer drugs doxycycline and minocycline show better absorption and distribution than older ones. Most streptococci, *Haemophilus*, *Moraxella*, *E. coli* and *Proteus* species are now resistant and tetracyclines are mostly used against *Mycoplasma*, *Chlamydia* and *Rickettsia*, plus *Borrelia* and other spirochaetes.

They have been used widely in veterinary practice therapeutically and as growth promoters. This practice, now banned in the European Union, is still prevalent in the USA and may account for much enterobacterial resistance.

Pharmacokinetics of tetracyclines: key points
- Best oral absorption in the fasting state (doxycycline 100% absorbed unless gastric pH rises).
- CSF levels increased in chronic inflammation (useful in Lyme disease).

Adverse reactions
- All tetracyclines except doxycycline are contraindicated in renal failure.
- Marked effect on bowel flora, causing side-effects of nausea and diarrhoea.
- Bind to metallic ions in bones and teeth, causing discoloration (avoid in children and pregnancy).
- Phototoxic skin reactions.
- Hypernatraemia (see p. 282—used therapeutically in hyponatraemia).

Chloramphenicol

This widely used but potentially toxic antibiotic is bacteriostatic to most organisms but apparently bactericidal to *H. influenzae*, *Strep. pneumoniae* and *Neisseria meningitidis*. It has a very broad spectrum of activity against aerobic and anaerobic organisms, spirochaetes, *Rickettsia*, *Chlamydia* and *Mycoplasma*. It also has quite useful clinical activity against anaerobes such as *Bacteroides fragilis*. (Dose 50 mg/kg, divided 6-hourly.)

Pharmacokinetics: key points
- Well absorbed after i.v. or oral dose (not i.m.). Good tissue distribution and levels.
- Good CSF levels.
- Crosses placenta and reaches breast milk.
- Competes for binding site with macrolides and lincosamides.

Adverse reactions
- Dose-dependent 'grey baby' syndrome in infants (cyanosis and circulatory collapse due to inability to conjugate drug and excrete active form in urine).
- Reversible dose-dependent bone marrow depression (adults) if > 4 g per day administered or cumulative dose > 25 g.
- Severe idiopathic aplastic anaemia in 1:25 000–40 000 treatment regimens (unrelated to dose, duration of therapy or route of administration).

Chloramphenicol remains a potent and cheap antibiotic, widely used throughout the world. Its use, however, is increasingly reserved for severe and life-threatening infections where other antibiotics are either unavailable or impractical. In the developed world its use is now confined to bacterial meningitis from *N. meningitidis* or *H. influenzae* (B) and to enteric fever or other life-threatening conditions without alternative therapy.

NITROIMIDAZOLES (METRONIDAZOLE, TINIDAZOLE)

The main clinical use of nitroimidazoles is in anaerobic infections, being highly active against strictly anaerobic bacteria, especially *Bacteroides fragilis*, *Cl. difficile* and other *Clostridia* species (metronidazole 400 mg 8-hourly). They retain significant antiprotozoal activity used against amoebae and *Giardia*. They can be used as radiosensitising agents in some solid tumours.

Pharmacokinetics: key points
- Almost completely absorbed after oral administration (60% after rectal administration).
- Well distributed, especially brain and CSF.
- Safe in pregnancy.

Adverse effects
- Metallic taste (dose-dependent).
- Severe vomiting if taken with alcohol—'antabuse effect'.

OTHER ANTIMICROBIALS

Oxazolidinones

These are organically synthesised antibiotics and show excellent oral absorption with activity similar to vancomycin against Gram-positive organisms such as streptococci, staphylococci and MRSA. They are competitively inhibited by coadministration of chloramphenicol and vancomycin/clindamycin.

Linezolid. This is the only oxazolidinone currently available for clinical use. It is rapidly absorbed, is approximately 30% protein-bound and appears very safe. Some 60% of patients taking this drug complain of some mild gastrointestinal side-effects and tongue discoloration.

Streptogramins

These recently introduced antibiotics are active against highly resistant *Strep. faecium* or resistant MRSA infections. They are only available in intravenous formulations and show good tissue penetration but do not cross the blood–brain barrier or the placenta. Significant phlebitis occurs at injection sites and a raised creatinine and eosinophilia are recognised. They should be reserved for these resistant organisms.

Fusidic acid

This antibiotic, active against Gram-positive bacteria including Gram-positive anaerobes, is available in intravenous, oral or topical formulations. It is lipid-soluble and efficiently distributed to peripheral compartments, including brain tissue. It demonstrates unpredictable antibacterial activity when combined with other antibiotics, so reducing its usefulness. It can be combined with clindamycin and rifampicin in the treatment of MRSA. It interacts with coumarin derivatives and oral contraceptives.

Nitrofurantoin

This drug has very rapid renal elimination and is active against aerobic Gram-negative and Gram-positive bacteria including enterococci. It is used only as a urinary tract antibiotic, being safe in pregnancy and childhood. It can produce eosinophilic lung infiltrates, fever, pulmonary fibrosis, nerve disease, hepatitis and haemolytic anaemia.

Spectinomycin

Chemically similar to the aminoglycosides and given intramuscularly, spectinomycin is rapidly and completely absorbed. It was developed to treat strains of *N. gonorrhoeae* resistant to β-lactam antibiotics. Unfortunately, resistance to spectinomycin is very common and its only indication is the treatment of gonococcal urethritis in pregnancy or when the patient is allergic to β-lactam antibiotics.

ANTIFUNGAL AGENTS (see Box 1.111)

Polyenes (amphotericin B)

Amphotericin B is the most important antifungal agent available and has been so since 1960. It is useful in the treatment of severe candidiasis, aspergillosis, cryptococcosis and the endemic mycoses of the Americas. It is also frequently used as empirical therapy in patients with neutropenic fever (see p. 905) where fungal infections are common.

Pharmacokinetics of amphotericin B: key points
- Parent compound extremely lipophilic, insoluble in water.
- Very poor oral absorption.
- Long half-life in serum allows once-daily administration.
- Poor penetration to CSF (but still useful in the management of fungal meningitis).
- Lozenge form for mucocutaneous infections.

Adverse reactions
- Danger of insoluble emboli during therapy (in-line filter should always be used).
- Immediate rare anaphylaxis on infusion; test dose should always be given.
- Infusion-related problems in 50% of cases.
- Renal toxicity occurs rapidly in 80% of those treated (reversible and ameliorated by concomitant fluid infusion).

1.111 ANTIFUNGAL DRUGS	
Drug	**Dose**
For topical application	
Nystatin	
Clotrimazole	
Econazole	
Amphotericin B	
For oral administration	
Miconazole	250 mg 6-hourly
Ketoconazole	200 mg daily
Fluconazole	50–200 mg daily (max. 14 days)*
Itraconazole	100–200 mg daily
Voriconazole	Awaiting licence
Flucytosine	200 mg/kg daily
Griseofulvin	500 mg daily
Terbinafine	250 mg daily
For intravenous infusion	
Amphotericin B (also a liposomal preparation)	Initially 1 mg/kg/day (consult expert)
Miconazole	600 mg 8-hourly
Flucytosine	200 mg/kg daily
Fluconazole	200–400 mg daily

* Up to 400 mg daily for several weeks may be necessary in severely immunocompromised patients with invasive fungal infections. Invasive fungal infections requiring high doses and prolonged therapy should be treated by physicians with experience of these diseases. In an immunocompromised host (HIV) chronic antifungal secondary prophylaxis may be required.

Lipid formulations of amphotericin B

Lipid formulations of amphotericin B have been developed to maximise the antifungal spectrum but reduce the toxicity of the parent compound. These are either a mixture of amphotericin B complexed with two phospholipids or an encapsulated formulation in unilamellar liposomes.

The drug becomes active when it dissociates from its lipid component following administration. It is only available intravenously. Adverse reactions are similar to but considerably less frequent than with amphotericin B.

Flucytosine

This drug has particular activity against yeasts (*Candida* spp and *Cryptococcus*). Although it is effective alone, the target organisms develop resistance fairly rapidly. Flucytosine should always be administered in combination with another antifungal agent.

The oral dose provides 90% of the predicted intravenous levels and is so effective that in the USA the intravenous formulation of this drug is no longer available.

Adverse reactions

These include neutropenia, anaemia, thrombocytopenia or profound pancytopenia; there may be slow recovery on withdrawal of the drug and asymptomatic disturbance of liver transaminases.

Azole antifungals

These include miconazole, clotrimazole, ketoconazole, fluconazole and itraconazole. New agents voriconazole, posaconazole and ravuconazole have an extended spectrum of activity and are awaiting release. Miconazole and clotrimazole are used solely for cutaneous and mucosal infections. Ketoconazole has a broad spectrum as the first oral antifungal agent with reasonable activity against *Candida* and *Aspergillus* spp. It is relatively cheap and cost-effective but has significant hepatic side-effects.

Fluconazole. This has ease of administration, an excellent safety profile and wide efficacy in *Candida* syndromes. The drug is highly water-soluble and distributes widely to all body sites and tissues, including CSF, where 89% of plasma levels can be recorded. It is well absorbed orally and has a long half-life of 30 hours, but lacks activity against *Aspergillus* spp.

Itraconazole. This is the only oral antifungal agent active against *Aspergillus*. It is similar to fluconazole except for poor absorption orally, requiring a low gastric pH. It is lipophilic and distributes extensively, particularly to toe and fingernails; CSF penetration is poor.

Other antifungal agents

Nystatin

Nystatin has a broad antifungal spectrum. Due to renal toxicity it is only available in topical formulation. It is particularly useful against mucosal candidiasis. The azole antifungals have gradually replaced nystatin but remain considerably more expensive. It may find a resurgence of use in azole-resistant candidiasis in HIV/AIDS.

Griseofulvin

For many years the standard therapy in the treatment of tinea unguium, griseofulvin has been largely superseded by other agents. It remains a cheap and effective agent; 50% is absorbed in fasting patients with virtually 100% bioavailability. Absorption is maximised by a fatty meal. It is deposited in keratin precursor cells, which then become virtually impervious to fungal invasion. The duration of treatment depends on the response and is 2–4 weeks for tinea corporis or capitis, 4–8 weeks for tinea pedis and 4–6 months for tinea unguium.

Terbinafine

This has largely replaced griseofulvin as the major agent available against dermatophytes, yeasts, moulds and dimorphic fungi. It is well absorbed orally with minimal improvement with food. It can be given once daily and distributes with high concentration to sebum and skin with a long half-life of greater than 1 week. It is used for nail and skin infections and topical therapy is reserved for the tinea infections. The major adverse reaction is hepatic toxicity. Terbinafine is not recommended for breastfeeding mothers and should not be applied vaginally.

ANTIVIRAL AGENTS (see Box 1.112)

These drugs are used against the herpes viruses.

Aciclovir, valaciclovir, famciclovir, ganciclovir and foscarnet

These drugs are predominantly acyclic analogues of guanosine. They are phosphorylated by virus-derived thymidine kinase (TK) enzymes and disrupt viral DNA metabolism. Aciclovir and its prodrug valaciclovir, and penciclovir and its prodrug famciclovir all have activity against herpes simplex and varicella zoster virus but very little or no activity against cytomegalovirus. Aciclovir is slowly and incompletely absorbed by oral dosing; much better levels are achieved intravenously or by use of the prodrug valaciclovir.

These drugs are extremely well tolerated with very few side-effects. Renal dysfunction may occur after rapid infusion of very large doses. CNS disturbance (agitation, hallucination, disorientation, tremors and mild clonus) have also been described. Famciclovir has good bioavailability orally and very rare adverse effects.

These drugs are extremely useful in the treatment of oral or genital herpes simplex infections and in larger dose against either acute chickenpox or herpes zoster infections (see Box 1.23, p. 31). In varicella zoster pneumonitis the intravenous formulation of aciclovir should be used.

Ganciclovir

By chemical modification of the aciclovir molecule, enhanced activity against cytomegalovirus is produced at the expense of increased toxicity. Although ganciclovir has the same activity as aciclovir against HSV-1 and 2 and varicella zoster virus, its toxicity limits its use. Despite very poor oral absorption, an oral formulation is available allowing maintenance therapy following intravenous medication for cytomegalovirus infection in HIV disease.

1.112 ANTIVIRAL DRUGS

Drug	Routes of administration	Indications	Side-effects
Aciclovir Valaciclovir	Topical Oral Intravenous	Herpes zoster Chickenpox (esp. in immunosuppressed) Herpes simplex infection: encephalitis, genital tract, eye	Rash, headache, gastrointestinal toxicity, neurotoxicity (i.v. only) Increase in urea and creatinine
Famciclovir Penciclovir	Oral Topical or systemic	Herpes zoster and genital herpes simplex infection Herpes zoster	Rash, headache Local irritation Herpes simplex keratitis
Amantadine	Oral	Prophylaxis of influenza A	CNS symptoms, nausea
Ribavirin	Oral	Lassa fever Respiratory syncytial virus infection in infants (inhalation) Chronic hepatitis C infection (with interferons)	Reticulocytosis Respiratory depression
Ganciclovir	Intravenous/oral	Cytomegalovirus infection in immunosuppressed	Leucopenia, thrombocytopenia
HAART (see p. 130)	Oral	HIV infection (including AIDS)	CNS symptoms, anaemia Lipodystrophy

Adverse effects

- Bone marrow suppression (thrombocytopenia, neutropenia).
- Azoospermia.
- Mutually antagonistic antiviral with zidovudine (ZDV).
- Nephrotoxicity with ciclosporin or amphotericin B.

Cidofovir

This is a newly formulated agent with potent activity against cytomegalovirus. It retains its activity against most CMV clinical isolates that are resistant to ganciclovir and has some in vitro activity against herpes simplex virus, varicella zoster virus (including the TK-deficient aciclovir-resistant strains) and some other viruses.

Adverse effects

- Nephrotoxicity ameliorated by intravenous hydration.
- Anterior uveitis after intravenous infusion.

Foscarnet

This analogue of inorganic pyrophosphate acts as a non-competitive inhibitor of herpes virus DNA polymerase. It is particularly useful in TK-deficient or mutated invasive HSV isolates resistant to aciclovir. It should only be administered by the intravenous route. It is equally effective against cytomegalovirus. It has very variable CSF penetration.

Adverse effects

- Significant nephrotoxicity (at least 15–20% of cases receiving this treatment). Intravenous fluids ameliorate.
- Hypocalcaemia, hypomagnesaemia and hypokalaemia may induce cardiac arrhythmias.

Other antiviral agents

Ribavirin

This has in vitro activity against influenza virus, respiratory syncytial virus (RSV), arenaviruses (including Lassa), bunyaviruses, herpes viruses, adenoviruses, poxviruses and retroviruses. Recent clinical studies have shown therapeutic benefit when ribavirin is combined with interferon-α (IFN-α) for the treatment of hepatitis C (see p. 865). The drug is well absorbed after oral administration. Ribavirin is administered as an inhaled aerosol in the treatment of RSV pneumonitis or bronchiolitis (see p. 526) and orally (in combination with INF-α) for the treatment of chronic hepatitis C. Inhaled ribavirin is generally well tolerated although bronchospasm, rash and ocular irritation can occur. Parenteral administration produces a mild haemolytic anaemia which is reversible but may require discontinuation of therapy.

Interferon

The interferons are naturally occurring cytokines produced as an early response to viral infection, induce an antiviral state in exposed cells and modulate other immune functions. Currently, interferon-α preparations are used in the treatment of chronic hepatitis B and in combination with ribavirin for the treatment of hepatitis C infections. The drug is only available by injection.

Adverse effects.
- Influenza-like syndrome after every dose (modified by premedication with paracetamol).
- Dose-limiting leucopenia, thrombocytopenia and depression.

Conjugation of interferon with polyethylene glycol (pegylated interferon or peginterferon) improves the pharmacokinetics and bioavailability and may be used in therapy of hepatitis C infection.

Amantadine, rimantadine

Amantadine and rimantadine are antiviral agents with some activity against influenza A (but not influenza B). A dose of 200 mg daily of either preparation will prevent 70–80% of symptomatic influenza during susceptible epidemics. They are most commonly used either with vaccination to provide short-term prophylaxis, during outbreaks, or to treat early presentation of disease. Treatment must be started within

48 hours of the onset of symptoms and will reduce severity of disease by 1–2 days. Resistance develops very rapidly and both drugs are embryotoxic and teratogenic.

Zanamivir, oseltamivir

Zanamivir and oseltamivir are new agents indicated for the treatment of both influenza A and B (see p. 526). They must be used within 48 hours of the onset of influenza symptoms and have been shown to reduce the duration of fever and illness by 1–2½ days. Use of amantadine or rimantadine is appropriate if influenza virus A is known to be the predominant agent in a particular year or location. For optimal use of antiviral agents, patients must present early, and accurate and rapid diagnosis is required.

3TC (lamivudine)

This drug, currently approved for the treatment of HIV infection (see p. 128), has been shown to have excellent activity in animal models against hepatitis B. It is being incorporated into treatment regimens with interferon-α. The drug has significant bone marrow toxicity. The common mode of transmission of both HIV and hepatitis B needs to be recognised. The potential for induction of HIV resistance must be borne in mind should 3TC be selected for hepatitis B therapy.

ISSUES IN OLDER PEOPLE
PROBLEMS WITH ANTIBIOTIC THERAPY

- Hypersensitivity reactions generally increase in incidence due to previous exposure.
- Renal function may be significantly impaired in old age despite 'normal' creatinine levels (see p. 582):
  —Nephrotoxicity is more likely, e.g. first-generation cephalosporins, aminoglycosides.
  —Beta-lactam antibiotics may accumulate and result in myoclonus, seizures or coma.
- Gastric acid production is reduced in old age so gastric pH is increased:
  —Penicillin absorption is increased and ketoconazole absorption reduced.
- Hepatic metabolism is reduced in old age:
  —There is an increased risk of isoniazid-related hepatotoxicity.

FURTHER INFORMATION

FEVER
Armstrong D, Cohen J. Infectious diseases. London: Mosby; 1999.
Corbel MJ. Recent advances in brucellosis. J Med Microbiol 1997; 46:101–103.
Hirschmann JV. Fever of unknown origin in adults. Clin Infect Dis 1997; 24:291–302.
Mackowiak PA, Bartlett JG, Borden EC, et al. Concepts of fever: recent advances and lingering dogma. Clin Infect Dis 1997; 25:119–138.
Mandell GL, Bennett JE, Dolin R. Principles and practice of infectious diseases. Edinburgh: Churchill Livingstone; 2000.
O'Connell S. Lyme borreliosis. Curr Opin Infect Dis 1997; 10:91–95.
Vinetz JM. Leptospirosis. Curr Opin Infect Dis 1997; 10:357–361.

TROPICAL AND INTERNATIONAL HEALTH
Bern C, Martines J, de Zoysa I, et al. The magnitude of the global problem of diarrhoeal disease: a 10-year update. Bull WHO 1992; 70:705–714.
Crook LD, Tempest B. Plague: a clinical review of 27 cases. Arch Intern Med 1992; 152:1253–1256.
Dance DAB. Melioidosis: the tip of the iceberg. Clin Microbiol Rev 1991; 4:52–60.
Department of Health, UK. Health information for overseas travel. UK Stationery Office; 2001.
Gonzalez-Ruiz A, Hague R, Aguirra WT, et al. Value of microscopy in the diagnosis of dysentery associated with invasive Entamoeba histolytica. J Clin Pathol 1994; 47:236–239.
Gonzalez-Ruiz A, Wright SG. Disparate amoebae. Lancet 1998; 351:1672–1673.
Herwaldt BL. Leishmaniasis. Lancet 1999; 354:1191–1199.
Jacobson RR, Krahenbuhl JL. Leprosy. Lancet 1999; 353:655–660.
Lockwood DNJ. Leprosy—a view for the new millennium. J Clin Microbiol 2000; 49:301–303.
McGinnis MR. Mycetoma. Dermatol Clin 1996; 14:97–104.
Pepin J, Milord F. The treatment of human African trypanosomiasis. Adv Parasitol 1994; 33:1–47.
Rex JH, Walsh TJ, Anaissie EJ. Fungal infections in iatrogenically compromised hosts. Adv Intern Med 1998; 43:321–371.
Rinaldi MG. Controversies in medical mycology. Dermatology 1997; 194(suppl 1):45–47.
Sanchez JL, Taylor DN. Cholera. Lancet 1997; 349:1825–1830.
Shirtcliffe P, Cameron E, Nicholson KG, Wiselka M. Don't forget dengue! Clinical features of dengue in returning travellers. J Roy Coll Phys Lond 1998; 32:235–237.
Srinivasan H. Management of disabilities in patients with leprosy: a practical guide. Geneva: WHO; 1993.
Watt G, Chowiyagune C, Ruangweerayud R, et al. Scrub typhus infections poorly responsive to antibiotics in northern Thailand. Lancet 1996; 348:86–89.
White NJ. Variation in virulence of dengue virus. Lancet 1999; 354:1401.
WHO. Severe falciparum malaria. In: Severe and complicated malaria. 3rd edn. Trans R Soc Trop Med Hyg 2000; 94(suppl 1):S1/41.
WHO Expert Committee on Leprosy. Seventh report (WHO Tech Rep Series 874). Geneva: WHO; 1998.
Winstanley PA. Chemotherapy for falciparum malaria: the armoury, the problems and the prospects. Parasitol Today 2000; 16:146–153.

www.cdc.gov/travel
www.who.int/home/map#ht.html

SEXUALLY TRANSMITTED INFECTIONS
Arya OP, Hart CA. Sexually transmitted infections and AIDS in the Tropics. Oxford/New York: CABI; 1998.
Clinical Effectiveness Group, Association for Genitourinary Medicine and the Medical Society for the Study of Venereal Disease. Clinical Effectiveness Guidelines; 2001. Website: www.mssvd.org.uk.
HMSO. Immunisation against infectious diseases. London: HMSO; 1996.
Holmes KK, March P-A, Sparling PF, Wiesner PJ. Sexually transmitted diseases. 3rd edn. New York: McGraw–Hill; 1999.
UK national guidelines on sexually transmitted infections and closely related conditions. Sex Transm Infect 1999; 75(suppl 1).

www.agum.org.uk

HIV AND AIDS
Bartlett JG. Medical management of HIV infection. Updated regularly on the Web at www.hopkins-aids.edu.
Gazzard B, ed. AIDS care handbook. 2nd edn. London: Mediscript; 2002.

www.medscape.com

MANAGEMENT OF INFECTION
Kucers A. The use of antibiotics. London: Butterworth–Heinemann; 1997.

Drug therapy

J.K. ARONSON

The purpose of drug therapy is to cure or ameliorate disease or to alleviate symptoms. However, all drugs have adverse effects to a greater or lesser extent. Before prescribing, the potential benefit of therapy should be weighed against the potential harm (the benefit to harm ratio, often called the benefit to risk ratio).

BENEFIT AND HARM IN DRUG THERAPY

The benefit to harm ratio of drug therapy can be assessed by considering various factors (see Box 2.1).

The benefit to harm ratio will be high if the disease is life-threatening, the drug highly effective and the only one available, and the risk of serious adverse effects negligible. For example, N-acetylcysteine is highly effective in preventing liver damage after paracetamol overdose (see p. 170), its adverse effects are uncommon and usually mild, and there are no other agents that are as effective.

The benefit to harm ratio will be low if the disease is trivial, the drug poorly effective with more effective and safer competitors, and the risk of serious adverse effects high. For example, amidopyrine, used in some countries to treat headache, can cause severe bone marrow depression, and there are much safer and equally effective alternatives.

Most cases lie somewhere between these two extremes.

When assessing the benefit to harm ratio, remember that some drugs are more likely to cause adverse effects when given in dosages that are within or only a little above the usual therapeutic range; these drugs are said to have a low therapeutic index (see Box 2.2). Assessment of the benefit to harm ratio is best made by using the tenets that are collectively known as evidence-based medicine.

2.1 FACTORS THAT DETERMINE THE BENEFIT TO HARM RATIO IN DRUG THERAPY		
	Benefit to harm ratio	
Factor	**High**	**Low**
Seriousness of the problem	Life-threatening	Trivial
Efficacy of the drug	High	Low
Seriousness of adverse effects	Trivial	Serious
Frequency of adverse effects	Rare	Frequent
Efficacy of therapeutic alternatives	Poor	Good
Safety of therapeutic alternatives	Poor	Good

2.2 SOME DRUGS WITH A LOW THERAPEUTIC INDEX

- Aminoglycoside antibiotics
- Anticoagulants
- Anticonvulsants
- Antihypertensive drugs
- Cardiac glycosides
- Cytotoxic and immunosuppressant drugs
- Oral contraceptives
- Drugs that act on the central nervous system

EVIDENCE-BASED MEDICINE IN DRUG THERAPY

For many years doctors have tried to use the available evidence when making decisions about the use of drugs or other therapeutic measures; this started happening as long ago as the 18th century and perhaps before. However, in the early 1990s it was pointed out that the ways in which they did so were somewhat haphazard. For example, treatment strategies would often be formulated in unsystematic reviews of the published data, using selected pieces of evidence that experts in the field judged to be the most valuable or relevant. Inevitably, bias crept in when such judgements were made. The discipline of evidence-based medicine was therefore invented in order to introduce a more systematic approach to the use of evidence in making therapeutic and other decisions.

This was made possible by:

- the development of statistical techniques for the systematic analysis of data
- the realisation that it was important to analyse all the available data, both published and unpublished
- the development of computerised databases of relevant information, linked to methods by which that information could be traced.

The tenets of evidence-based medicine are that well-formulated questions about medical management, including diagnosis and therapy, can be answered by:

- carrying out high-quality, randomised, controlled clinical trials
- tracing all the available evidence
- analysing the evidence systematically
- determining how valid and useful the evidence is
- applying the evidence to the management of the individual patient.

It needs to be appreciated that although there are well-established methods for carrying out the first four of these procedures (yielding what is known as 'best evidence'), it is the last that is the most important and the most difficult. This is because the evidence on which decisions are made is usually derived from large populations, which may not have included patients like those you want to treat; even if the trials were representative of your patients, there is so much interindividual variability that mean values taken from studies of populations may not be applicable to individuals. Methods for dealing with this are available, but are not as well developed or easily applied as the methods for obtaining the best evidence. In addition, there are many therapeutic problems for which adequate evidence is not available at all; in such cases one uses what evidence there is, indifferent though it may be.

In this chapter the ways in which evidence-based medicine can inform drug therapy are described. However, the principles apply equally well to other forms of patient care, including examination, investigation and other forms of treatment.

BENEFICIAL EFFECTS AND THE NUMBER NEEDED TO TREAT (NNT)

Benefit in drug therapy is often expressed as the so-called number needed to treat (NNT), which is the number of patients that you would need to treat in order to prevent one clinical event (for example, a stroke or a pregnancy). A simple example illustrates how this is calculated. Of 239 patients with the acute pain of third molar extraction, 122 were given placebo, of whom 9 (7.4%) had at least 50% pain relief by 6 hours, compared with 65 (55.6%) of the 117 patients who were given ibuprofen; the difference was therefore 55.6 − 7.4 = 48.2%, or an effect size of 0.482. This is known as the absolute risk reduction, and the NNT is the inverse of this: 1/0.482 = 2.1. In other words, 1 out of every 2 people who take a single dose of ibuprofen will have better than 50% pain relief in the 6 hours after the dose. The 95% confidence interval of this estimate (the calculation of which is more complicated) was 1.7–2.6; in other words, the mean estimate of the NNT was 2.1 and there was a 95% chance that the true value lay between 1.7 and 2.6.

When a drug is given repeatedly, rather than as a single dose, the duration of therapy also has to be stated. For example, in a systematic analysis of the use of warfarin to prevent strokes in patients with atrial fibrillation there were 53 strokes in 1450 patients who took warfarin (3.66%) and 133 in 1450 patients who took placebo (9.17%). The effect size was thus 9.17 − 3.66 = 5.51% (0.0551) and the NNT was 18 (1/0.0551). The confidence interval was 14–27. So, on the basis of these results, if you treat 18 patients with warfarin for 1 year, you will prevent one stroke (see EBM panel, p. 402). Note that these numbers cannot be multiplied up to longer durations of treatment. In other words, this analysis does not imply that if you treat 18 patients for 2 years you will prevent two strokes; a longer trial would be needed to find out what the actual value was.

For a further perspective on the meaning of the NNT, consider oral contraception. On average a woman who has unprotected sex for 1 year has a 40% chance of falling pregnant, while a woman who takes some form of oral contraception has a 3% chance; this 37% difference translates into an NNT of 2.7 (1/0.37). Now because oral contraception is so effective you might expect the NNT to be very close to 1, but that is not so, since the NNT takes into account the rate that occurs without treatment. In other words, if you treat 100 women for a year with an oral contraceptive, you will prevent 100/2.7 (i.e. 37) pregnancies. But 97 of the women taking the treatment do not fall pregnant; that is because the other 60 women would not have fallen pregnant anyway, even without treatment. Of course, that means that they have taken the treatment without benefit and may have had adverse effects as well; however, it would not have been possible to identify these women, either in advance or even retrospectively.

ADVERSE EFFECTS AND THE NUMBER NEEDED TO HARM (NNH)

The other side of the coin, the number needed to harm (NNH), can be similarly calculated from data on adverse effects of drugs. For example, in a meta-analysis of 13 trials of the effect of thiazide diuretics in essential hypertension, 205 out of 3275 patients taking a thiazide had erectile impotence, compared with 67 out of 5295 patients taking placebo; the NNH for this effect is 20 (see Box 2.3).

2.3 CALCULATION OF NNH, RISK RATIO AND ODDS RATIO

(A) A THEORETICAL CASE

Group	Number with adverse event	Number without adverse event	Total
Active treatment	a	b	a+b
Placebo	c	d	c+d
Total	a+c	b+d	a+b+c+d

1. **Calculation of number needed to harm (NNH)**
   Rate of event in treated group = a/(a+b)
   Rate of event in placebo group = c/(c+d)
   Difference (absolute harm increase) = a/(a+b) − c/(c+d)
   NNH = 1/[a/(a+b) − c/(c+d)]

2. **Calculation of risk ratio (RR)**
   Rate of event in treated group = a/(a+b)
   Rate of event in placebo group = c/(c+d)
   Risk ratio = [a/(a+b)]/[c/(c+d)]

3. **Calculation of odds ratio (OR)**
   Odds of event in treated group = a/b
   Odds of event in placebo group = c/d
   Odds ratio = (a/b)/(c/d)

(B) A REAL CASE*

Group	Number with adverse event	Number without adverse event	Total
Drug	205	3070	3275
Placebo	67	5228	5295
Total	272	8298	8570

1. **Calculation of number needed to harm (NNH)**
   Rate of event in treated group = 205/3275
   Rate of event in placebo group = 67/5295
   Difference (absolute harm increase) = 205/3275 − 67/5295 = 0.0499
   NNH = 20

2. **Calculation of risk ratio (RR)**
   Rate of event in treated group = 205/3275
   Rate of event in placebo group = 67/5295
   Relative risk = [205/3275]/[67/5295] = 5.0 (i.e. a fivefold risk)

3. **Calculation of odds ratio (OR)**
   Odds of event in treated group = 205/3070
   Odds of event in placebo group = 67/5228
   Odds ratio = [205/3070]/[67/5228] = 5.2 (i.e. relative odds of about 5 to 1 on)

* Erectile impotence with thiazide diuretics in hypertension over a mean of 4 years, a meta-analysis of 13 RCTs (Hypertension 1999; 34:710).

THE BENEFIT TO HARM RATIO ASSESSED FROM THE NNT AND NNH

Although you might expect to be able to express the benefit to harm ratio as the simple ratio of the NNT to the NNH, the comparison is not straightforward, since the quality of the benefit and the severity of the harm also need to be considered. How, for example, do you compare the benefit of long-term oral anticoagulation in patients with atrial fibrillation (the prevention of embolic stroke) with the harm that anticoagulation can cause (gastrointestinal haemorrhage)?

However, knowing the numbers can help. Consider, for instance, tamoxifen, which prolongs survival in breast cancer (by an anti-oestrogenic action) and reduces the risk of myocardial infarction (by an oestrogenic effect on blood lipids), but can cause endometrial cancer and venous thromboembolism:

- NNT to prevent one death = 17
- NNT to prevent one myocardial infarction = 29
- NNH for one case of endometrial cancer = 143
- NNH for one venous thromboembolism = 130.

These figures suggest that if you treat 1000 women with breast cancer for 2–5 years you will prevent about 60 deaths (1000/17) and 34 myocardial infarctions, at the cost of 7 cases of endometrial cancer and 7 cases of venous thromboembolism, clearly a favourable benefit to harm ratio. Of course, calculations of this sort yield probabilities that relate to the patients that have been studied in clinical trials. They do not necessarily apply to the whole population and they certainly do not tell you what the outcome will be in the individual case.

There are other ways of expressing results of this kind. For example, you can calculate the risk ratio (RR) or odds ratio (OR), each with its confidence interval (see Box 2.3). The larger the effect, the higher the odds ratio is relative to the risk ratio; at incidences of up to about 15% the risk ratio and odds ratio are very similar, but at higher incidences the odds ratio starts to over-estimate the risk ratio considerably. Note that two treatments may have exactly the same risk ratio but different values of NNH. For example, a treatment that increased the risk of an adverse event from 1% to 2% would have a risk ratio of 2 but an NNH of 100 (1/0.01), while a treatment that increased the risk of an adverse event from 25% to 50% would also have a risk ratio of 2 but an NNH of 4 (1/0.25), a much more important effect. When it was reported that third-generation progestogens approximately doubled the risk of deep venous thrombosis compared with older progestogens, the announcement caused some women to panic; what they did not appreciate was that the baseline risk was very low and the NNH therefore very high.

OBTAINING THE BEST EVIDENCE

Although the well-designed, large, randomised clinical trial (RCT), preferably placebo-controlled, is the gold standard for obtaining the best evidence, there are other ways. Some of these are listed in Box 2.4, roughly in the order of the

---

2.4 SOME METHODS OF OBTAINING EVIDENCE IN DRUG THERAPY

- Prospective, randomised, double-blind, placebo-controlled trial*
- Prospective, randomised, double-blind, comparative trial (drug vs drug)*
- Systematic review (meta-analysis)*
- Systematic review (other types of analysis)*
- Cohort study*
- Case-control study*
- Point prevalence study*
- Subgroup analysis of a large trial (generates hypotheses for further trials)
- N-of-one trial
- Other trials (e.g. non-randomised, non-controlled, historical controls, retrospective analysis)
- Non-systematic review
- Case report

* All assumed to be the same size.

---

quality of evidence they yield. A well-designed RCT is more reliable than a meta-analysis of the same size; however, a very large meta-analysis (i.e. one that is much bigger than the largest RCT) may provide better evidence. Furthermore, depending on the quality of the design and conduct, the evidence that any of these forms of study provides can vary; for instance, a well-conducted cohort study may provide better evidence than a poorly designed RCT.

One of these methods is worthy of further mention, the N-of-one (or controlled single-patient) trial. As mentioned above, it may be difficult to extrapolate from the results of large randomised clinical trials to the practical application of drug therapy in the individual patient. In some cases, evidence from large RCTs may not even be available (if, for example, the disease is rare). In such cases an N-of-one trial may help. Here the patient is given either the active drug or a matching placebo at different times and double-blind, and the response to each is noted; thus, in N-of-one trials patients act as their own controls. This type of trial is useful only in the symptomatic treatment of chronic stable conditions, if the course of the disease is predictable, if the treatment has a rapid and easily measured therapeutic effect, and if the effect of a single dose of the drug is not long-lasting.

PRACTICAL PRESCRIBING

WHEN TO PRESCRIBE A DRUG

Drug therapy is not always necessary. For example, a mild tremor in Parkinson's disease may not be unduly troublesome; even though drug treatment may alleviate the tremor, it may also cause unwanted effects, outweighing the benefit. Do not be tempted to prescribe a drug simply to end a consultation. If a patient expects drug therapy, discuss the pros and cons. Try to estimate the benefit to harm ratio and prescribe only if you think it is favourable.

2.5 EXAMPLES OF CHOOSING A THERAPEUTIC CLASS OF DRUG

Indication	Therapeutic class
Acute attack of asthma	Bronchodilators
Diabetes mellitus	Oral hypoglycaemic drugs Insulin
Congestive cardiac failure	Diuretics Angiotensin-converting enzyme (ACE) inhibitors Vasodilators
Hypertension	Diuretics ACE inhibitors Beta-adrenoceptor antagonists (β-blockers) Calcium antagonists

2.6 EXAMPLES OF CHOOSING A GROUP OF DRUGS FROM WITHIN A CLASS

Therapeutic class	Therapeutic group
Anticoagulants	Coumarins/warfarin Heparins
Diuretics	Thiazides Loop diuretics Potassium-sparing diuretics
Antibiotics	Penicillins Cephalosporins Tetracyclines Aminoglycosides Macrolides Quinolones

2.7 EXAMPLES OF CONTRAINDICATIONS TO ANTIBIOTICS

Antibiotic	Example of contraindication
Cephalosporins	Allergy
Penicillins	Allergy
Quinolones	Pregnancy and children (teratogenic in animals)
Sulphonamides	Late pregnancy (risk of kernicterus in neonate)
Tetracyclines	Children (affects growing bones and teeth) Renal impairment (e.g. elderly people)

HOW TO CHOOSE A DRUG TO PRESCRIBE

If you decide to prescribe a drug, the first step will be to choose the therapeutic class. Sometimes the choice is restricted, sometimes wide, as a few examples illustrate (see Box 2.5).

Having chosen the class of drug, the next step is to choose the group of drugs within that class. Again the choice may be restricted or wide (see Box 2.6). The choice of an anticoagulant depends on whether short-term or long-term treatment is indicated. The choice of a diuretic in the treatment of cardiac failure depends on the severity of the problem, whether acute or chronic therapy is indicated, the convenience of the timing of the diuresis, and potassium balance. The choice of an antibiotic depends on the sensitivities of the infecting organism, the site of infection and contraindications, as some examples show (see Box 2.7).

Drug interactions can also affect therapy, as in the case of antibiotics (see Box 2.8).

The last step is to choose a particular drug from within the group. In some cases the choice is unimportant. For example, all thiazide diuretics have equal efficacy and adverse effects. In contrast, the choice of a specific penicillin is important and will depend on the type of organism (see Box 2.9).

2.9 EXAMPLES OF CHOOSING A PARTICULAR DRUG FROM WITHIN A GROUP

Therapeutic group	Drug
Thiazide diuretics	Bendroflumethiazide (bendrofluazide) Cyclopenthiazide Hydrochlorothiazide Hydroflumethiazide Polythiazide
Penicillins	Benzylpenicillin Penicillin V (phenoxymethylpenicillin) Amoxicillin Co-amoxiclav (amoxicillin + clavulanic acid) Ampicillin Flucloxacillin Ticarcillin

2.8 EXAMPLES OF DRUG INTERACTIONS WITH ANTIBIOTICS

Antibiotic	Interacting drug	Mechanism	Effect
Gentamicin	Furosemide (frusemide)	Additive	Ototoxicity
Chloramphenicol	Warfarin	Inhibition of metabolism	Potentiation of anticoagulation
Metronidazole	Alcohol	Inhibition of aldehyde dehydrogenase	'Disulfiram reaction'
Metronidazole	Warfarin	Inhibition of metabolism	Potentiation of anticoagulation
Rifampicin	Oestrogens (oral contraceptives)	Induction of metabolism	Reduced contraceptive effect
Rifampicin	Warfarin	Induction of metabolism	Reduced effect of warfarin
Tetracycline	Antacids	Chelation	Reduced effect of tetracycline
Tetracycline	Warfarin	Altered clotting factor activity	Potentiation of anticoagulation

How to make a rational choice

Many factors dictate the choice of a particular drug:

- *Absorption*. Bumetanide is better absorbed than furosemide (frusemide). Oral bumetanide may be effective in congestive cardiac failure if oral furosemide has failed; alternatively, use intravenous furosemide.
- *Distribution*. Some antibiotics are well distributed to a particular tissue; for example, tetracyclines are concentrated in the bile, and lincomycin and clindamycin in bones.
- *Metabolism*. In severe liver disease (for example, hepatic cirrhosis) it is advisable to avoid drugs that are extensively metabolised: for example, opiate analgesics. Genetic factors may influence the extent of metabolism of a drug. Although many examples of such variability have been described, these factors do not have a large impact on drug prescribing; however, some important examples are listed in Box 2.10.
- *Excretion*. In renal insufficiency it is advisable to avoid drugs that are extensively excreted; for example, avoid the aminoglycoside antibiotics if alternative antibiotics are suitable.
- *Efficacy*. Insulin is more efficacious at lowering the blood sugar than the oral hypoglycaemic drugs.
- *Features of the disease*. Choose an antibiotic to match the known or suspected sensitivity of the infective organism: for example, amoxicillin for a patient with a community-acquired bronchopneumonia, because the likely organism will be the pneumococcus (*Streptococcus pneumoniae*). Sputum culture, with identification of the organism and its sensitivity to different antibiotics, will help.
- *Severity of disease*. Mild pain will generally respond to aspirin or paracetamol; more severe pain may require more potent analgesics, such as codeine phosphate or even morphine. Moderate hypertension often responds to a single drug, such as a thiazide diuretic or a β-adrenoceptor antagonist (β-blocker); more severe hypertension may require a combination of drugs.
- *Coexisting diseases*. In hypertension coexisting left ventricular failure would prompt the use of a diuretic combined with an ACE inhibitor; coexisting angina pectoris without heart failure would prompt the use of a β-blocker.
- *Avoiding adverse effects*. In asthma avoid β-blockers. In penicillin hypersensitivity choose an alternative drug (for example, a cephalosporin in bronchopneumonia). Genetic factors may increase the risk of an adverse drug reaction; some important examples are listed in Box 2.10.
- *Avoiding adverse drug interactions*. Avoid aspirin and other non-steroidal anti-inflammatory drugs (NSAIDs), which can cause gastrointestinal bleeding, in patients taking warfarin. Avoid tetracyclines, sulphonamides, chloramphenicol and the antifungal imidazoles (e.g. ketoconazole) in patients taking warfarin because they inhibit its metabolism.
- *Patient concordance*. Atenolol, which can be taken once daily, is often prescribed instead of short-acting β-blockers, in the hope that minimising the frequency of drug administration will improve patient concordance (compliance).
- *Cost*. If two drugs are of equal efficacy and safety, one would generally choose the cheaper. However, pharmacoeconomics is a complicated subject beyond the scope of this text, and the true costs of drug therapy cannot always be calculated merely on the basis of the relative costs of two drugs.

CHOOSING THE ROUTE OF ADMINISTRATION

There are several reasons for choosing a particular route of administration, as some examples illustrate (see Box 2.11).

CHOOSING A FORMULATION

Oral formulations include tablets, capsules, granules, elixirs and suspensions. Drugs for injection come as lyophilised powders for reconstitution before injection or as solutions ready for injection; solutions come in single-dose ampoules, single-dose or multiple-dose vials, and half-litre or litre bottles for infusion.

2.10 SOME EXAMPLES OF GENETIC FACTORS THAT CAUSE VARIABILITY IN DRUG RESPONSE		
Process	**Example of drug affected**	**Clinical outcome**
Acetylation	Isoniazid	Better response and increased risk of some adverse effects (e.g. peripheral neuropathy) in slow acetylators
Oxidation (CYP2D6)	Nortriptyline	Increased risk of toxicity in poor metabolisers
Oxidation (CYP2C18)	Proguanil (active metabolite cycloguanil)	Reduced efficacy in poor metabolisers
Sulphoxidation	Penicillamine	Increased risk of toxicity in poor metabolisers
Pseudocholinesterase activity	Suxamethonium	Prolonged duration of effect in pseudocholinesterase deficiency
Glucose-6-phosphate dehydrogenase (G6PD) activity	Many antimalarial drugs (e.g. chloroquine, quinine)	Risk of haemolysis in G6PD deficiency
Porphyria	Enzyme-inducing drugs (e.g. carbamazepine, rifampicin)	Increased risk of an acute attack

2.11 REASONS FOR CHOOSING A PARTICULAR ROUTE OF ADMINISTRATION

Reason	Example
Only one route possible	Dopamine (intravenous) Glibenclamide (oral)
Patient concordance	Intramuscular depot injections of phenothiazines and thioxanthenes in schizophrenia
Poor absorption	Intravenous furosemide (frusemide) in heart failure
Vomiting	Phenothiazines (rectal) Sumatriptan (sublingual)
Avoiding first-pass metabolism	Glyceryl trinitrate (sublingual)
Rapid action	Glyceryl trinitrate (sublingual) Sumatriptan (sublingual)
Direct access to the site of action	Inhaled bronchodilators in asthma Rectal corticosteroids in ulcerative colitis Local application to skin, eyes etc.
Ease of access	Benzodiazepines in status epilepticus (e.g. rectal diazepam if intravenous access is difficult) Subcutaneous fluids (hypodermoclysis)
Controlled release	Insulin (subcutaneous)

Some examples show how the choice of formulation can be important.

Potassium salts are available as modified-release formulations, as effervescent tablets that dissolve in water for drinking, or as elixirs immediately ready to drink. Patient preference may dictate the choice, but it would be logical to choose a soluble formulation in a patient with gastrointestinal hurry, in whom the modified-release formulation might pass through the gut unabsorbed.

Lithium salts and theophylline come in several different ordinary and modified-release formulations, each with different absorption characteristics. A formulation that produces adequate plasma lithium or theophylline concentrations in one patient may not be suitable for another, and it is sometimes worth changing the formulation if plasma concentrations are suboptimal. These are examples of drugs that should be prescribed by specific brand name rather than the non-proprietary name.

Iron salts are available as tablets for twice- or thrice-daily administration or as modified-release formulations for once-daily administration. Adverse effects are fewer with the modified-release formulations but the iron is more erratically absorbed. It is usual to start with an ordinary formulation of iron and change to a modified-release formulation if adverse effects are intolerable.

CHOOSING A DOSAGE REGIMEN

The dose of the drug and the frequency and timing of its administration constitute the dosage regimen. Each prescription should be treated as an experiment in which you try to find the regimen that produces the best therapeutic effect with minimal adverse effects, according to some simple principles:

- Generally, start with a dosage at the lower end of the recommended dosage range. Exceptions to this rule include corticosteroids and carbimazole, which are begun in high dosages and then reduced to maintenance dosages. Some drugs are given in a loading dose (for example, digoxin, warfarin and amiodarone), followed by a maintenance dose.
- Increase the dosage slowly, monitoring the therapeutic effect at regular intervals and looking for adverse effects.
- If adverse effects occur, reduce the dosage or try another drug; in some cases lower dosages may be possible by combining drugs (for example, azathioprine reduces corticosteroid dosage requirements in immunosuppression).
- Think of drug interactions and avoid potentially dangerous combinations.
- Remember that pharmacokinetic and pharmacodynamic variability can alter dosage requirements (see below).
- Take particular care with drugs that have a low therapeutic index.

Pharmacokinetic variability

Because absorption, distribution and elimination of drugs vary from patient to patient, flexibility in dosages is necessary. The examples in Box 2.12 show how to respond to differences or changes in pharmacokinetics.

2.12 THERAPEUTIC APPROACHES TO PHARMACOKINETIC PROBLEMS

Pharmacokinetic problem	Therapeutic approach
Poor absorption	Increase the dose Choose another route of administration Use another drug
Altered tissue distribution	One-off doses may have to be altered Usually does not affect chronic therapy, unless distribution to the target tissue is altered
Altered protein binding	Usually does not affect long-term doses (but does alter steady-state total plasma drug concentration)
Reduced renal elimination (see Box 2.14)	Reduce dosage (use creatinine clearance as a guide)
Reduced hepatic elimination (see Box 2.15)	Low-clearance drugs: reduce oral and intravenous doses High-clearance drugs: reduce oral (but not intravenous) doses

Pharmacodynamic variability

Pharmacological responses are usually governed by the dose-response curve. An example is seen in Figure 2.1, which shows the effect of two loop diuretics, bumetanide and furosemide (frusemide), on urinary sodium excretion.

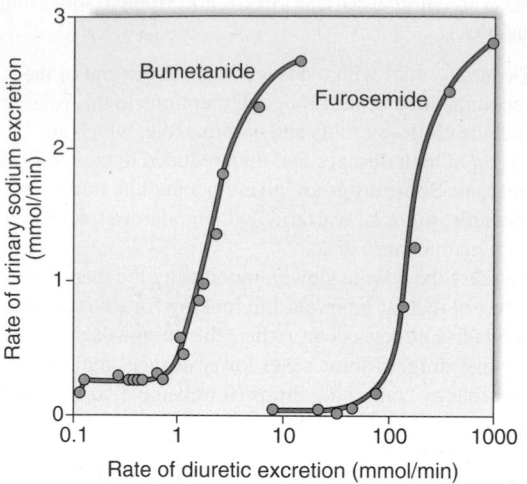

Fig. 2.1 Dose-response curves for bumetanide and furosemide (frusemide). The two drugs have different potencies but the same efficacy. The rate of diuretic excretion reflects the luminal concentration of diuretic.

The two diuretics have different potencies, which can be dealt with by using different dosages; however, they both have the same efficacy, so that comparable dosages should produce the same diuretic effect.

Variability in dose-responsiveness dictates flexibility in prescribing. If a therapeutic effect does not occur with the first dosage chosen, an effect may be produced by making small increases within the therapeutic dosage range. Of course, increasing the dosage will also increase the risk of dose-related adverse effects. Certain diseases can alter a dose-response curve (for example, there is resistance to digoxin in hyperthyroidism) and the pharmacodynamics of one drug can be affected by another drug.

CHOOSING THE FREQUENCY OF DRUG ADMINISTRATION

It is thought that patient concordance with therapy is improved if drugs are given only once or twice daily, rather than three or four times, although the evidence that this is true is scanty. However, it makes sense to simplify the therapeutic regimen, and in general, therefore, try to choose drugs that can be given no more than twice daily. A modified-release formulation may be useful in this respect. In some special cases the frequency of drug administration is an important consideration in therapy (see Box 2.13).

CHOOSING THE TIME OF DRUG ADMINISTRATION

For many drugs the time of administration is unimportant, but there are occasionally pharmacokinetic or therapeutic reasons for giving drugs at particular times (see Box 2.13). Meal times do not usually affect drug administration, since although food may reduce the speed of absorption of a drug it generally does not reduce the extent of absorption. Tetracyclines are an exception; their absorption is greatly reduced by divalent and trivalent cations, and they should not be taken with food or antacids. Food may sometimes help reduce adverse gastrointestinal effects; for example, the effects of aspirin on the stomach may be reduced by taking it with food.

ALTERING DRUG DOSAGES IN SPECIAL CIRCUMSTANCES

Altering dosages in renal insufficiency

If a drug is more than 50% eliminated unchanged by the kidneys or has active metabolites that are eliminated by the kidneys, the maintenance dosage must be altered in renal insufficiency; it is not usually necessary to alter a one-off

2.13 SOME SPECIAL EXAMPLES OF FREQUENCY AND TIMING OF DRUG ADMINISTRATION		
Drug	**Recommended frequency or timing**	**Reasons**
Furosemide (frusemide)	Once in the morning	Kidney refractory to a second dose within 6 hrs; night-time diuresis undesirable
Corticosteroids	Once in the morning	Minimises inhibitory effects on adrenal function
Salmeterol	Once at night	Prevents early morning symptoms
Antidepressants	Once at night	Allows adverse effects to occur during sleep
Digoxin	Once at night	Allows blood samples for plasma concentration measurement to be taken 12 hrs later
Long-acting nitrates	Nitrate-free period of 12 hrs in each 24 hrs	To avoid tolerance
Tetracyclines	2 hrs before or after food	Divalent and trivalent cations chelate tetracyclines
Opiates	In anticipation of pain	Better relief in chronic pain
Glyceryl trinitrate	When required	According to symptoms
Levodopa	Adjusted according to response (usually several times a day)	Dictated by the duration of action (often wears off quickly during long-term therapy)

dose. Creatinine clearance can be used as a guide to reducing maintenance dosages; the serum creatinine concentration can also be used, but it is a less reliable indicator of renal function and does not rise above the reference range until renal function is impaired by at least 50%.

In some cases dosages should be reduced because the pharmacological effects interact with renal impairment (for example, ACE inhibitors worsen potassium retention). Some drugs should be avoided entirely in renal insufficiency, for either pharmacokinetic or pharmacodynamic reasons (see Box 2.14).

Diuretics are relatively ineffective in severe renal insufficiency, partly because they cannot gain access to their site of action, the luminal epithelium. Thiazide diuretics should therefore not be used and high dosages of loop diuretics may be required for efficacy. Potassium-sparing diuretics should not be used because of the increased risk of hyperkalaemia.

2.14 SOME DRUGS WHOSE DOSAGES ARE AFFECTED BY RENAL INSUFFICIENCY*
Mild renal insufficiency (creatinine clearance 20–50 ml/min or serum creatinine 150–300 µmol/l)
<ul><li>ACE inhibitors (monitor carefully; increase dosage if renal function does not worsen with low doses)</li><li>Aminoglycosides</li><li>Chlorpropamide</li><li>Digoxin</li><li>Fibrates</li><li>Lithium</li><li>Zidovudine</li></ul>
Moderate renal insufficiency (creatinine clearance 10–20 ml/min or serum creatinine 300–700 µmol/l)
<ul><li>Some β-blockers (e.g. atenolol, sotalol)</li><li>Opioid analgesics</li></ul>
Severe renal insufficiency (creatinine clearance < 10 ml/min or serum creatinine > 700 µmol/l; many of these patients receive renal replacement therapy, which may affect drug pharmacokinetics)
<ul><li>Azathioprine</li><li>Cephalosporins</li><li>Cimetidine</li><li>Isoniazid</li><li>Penicillins</li><li>Sulphonylurea hypoglycaemic drugs (gliclazide, glipizide, gliquidone)</li></ul>
Drugs to avoid in severe renal insufficiency
<ul><li>Chloramphenicol</li><li>Chloroquine</li><li>Fibrates</li><li>Lithium—even in moderate renal insufficiency</li><li>Mesalazine—even in mild renal insufficiency</li><li>Metformin—even in mild renal insufficiency</li><li>Methotrexate—even in moderate renal insufficiency</li><li>NSAIDs—even in mild renal insufficiency</li><li>Sulphonylurea hypoglycaemic drugs (chlorpropamide, glibenclamide)</li><li>Tetracyclines (except doxycycline and minocycline)—even in mild renal insufficiency</li></ul>
* These guidelines are based on those recommended in the *British National Formulary*.

Altering dosages in hepatic failure

The liver has a large functional capacity, and chronic hepatic insufficiency usually has to be considerable before it affects drug dosages. However, hepatic drug clearance may be reduced in acute hepatitis, in hepatic congestion due to cardiac failure, and if there is intrahepatic arteriovenous shunting (for example, in hepatic cirrhosis). In chronic liver disease, jaundice, ascites, a prolonged prothrombin time, hypoalbuminaemia, malnutrition and encephalopathy all make clinically important impairment of drug metabolism more likely.

In contrast to renal insufficiency there is no easy way of calculating changes in dosage in patients with impaired hepatic function, because there are no good tests of hepatic drug-metabolising capacity or of biliary excretion. Dosages of drugs that are metabolised by the liver should therefore be altered according to the therapeutic response, and with careful clinical monitoring for signs of adverse effects.

If a drug has a high rate of hepatic clearance (see Box 2.15), it will be mostly cleared during its first passage through the liver (the so-called 'first-pass' effect). In such cases hepatic impairment increases the amount of drug that escapes metabolism in the liver after oral administration, reducing oral dosage requirements but not altering intravenous dosage requirements. For example, clomethiazole is normally extensively metabolised pre-systemically by the liver, and this is reduced by chronic liver disease such as alcoholic cirrhosis. When using oral clomethiazole in a patient with cirrhosis, take care to ensure that overdosage, with the risk of respiratory depression, does not occur.

The pharmacological effects of some drugs are altered in liver disease, with increased risk of adverse effects (see Box 2.16).

2.15 SOME DRUGS OF LOW AND HIGH HEPATIC CLEARANCE RATES	
Low	
<ul><li>Aspirin</li><li>Codeine</li><li>Diazepam</li><li>Isoniazid</li><li>Nortriptyline</li><li>Paracetamol</li></ul>	<ul><li>Phenobarbital</li><li>Phenytoin</li><li>Procainamide</li><li>Quinidine</li><li>Theophylline</li><li>Warfarin</li></ul>
High	
<ul><li>Clomethiazole</li><li>Glyceryl trinitrate</li><li>Labetalol</li><li>Lidocaine (lignocaine)</li></ul>	<ul><li>Morphine</li><li>Pethidine</li><li>Propranolol</li><li>Simvastatin</li></ul>

2.16 SOME DRUGS WHOSE ACTIONS ARE INCREASED IN LIVER DISEASE	
Drug	**Adverse effect**
Oral anticoagulants	Increased anticoagulation (reduced clotting factor synthesis)
Metformin	Lactic acidosis
Chloramphenicol	Bone marrow suppression
NSAIDs	Gastrointestinal bleeding
Sulphonylureas	Hypoglycaemia

ISSUES IN OLDER PEOPLE
ALTERING DRUG DOSAGES

- Drug handling and the response to drugs change as you get older, and there is much more variability in drug response in elderly people than in younger people, because people age at different rates. This means that responses to drugs are much less predictable, and so dosage regimens of some drugs are different. Adverse drug reactions are more likely in old people; frail old people are particularly at risk, partly because they tend to have poorer renal function and smaller livers and partly because they are less able to maintain their homeostatic control mechanisms than younger people or fit old people.

- Polypharmacy is common in old people and the scope for drug interactions is large; the error rate in taking drugs is about 60% in patients over 60 years of age, and the rate of error increases markedly if more than three drugs are prescribed.

- Choice of formulation is very important. Many old people find it difficult to swallow tablets, and the more frail and the more ill they are, the more difficult it becomes. For example, many potassium tablets are large and can be difficult to swallow. Tablets or capsules can adhere to the oesophageal mucosa, and to avoid hold-up tablets should be swilled down with at least 60 ml of water. Elixirs may be preferable, but not all drugs are available as elixirs and they may have their own problems. For example, the taste of a potassium elixir may not be acceptable.

- Drug distribution may be altered in old people. Dosages should be adjusted for body weight, particularly for drugs with a low therapeutic index. Old people have an increased proportion of body fat, and lipid-soluble drugs tend to accumulate to a greater extent than in younger patients.

- Drug metabolism may be reduced in old people—for example, clomethiazole, lidocaine (lignocaine), nifedipine, phenobarbital, propranolol and theophylline. Dosages of these drugs should therefore be reduced. Renal function falls with age, and drugs that are mainly excreted in the urine, or that have active metabolites that are excreted, may require dosage reductions (see above). Some drugs are best avoided in old people. For example, tetracyclines accumulate when renal function is poor, causing nausea and vomiting, which in turn cause dehydration and further deterioration in renal function.

- Drug sensitivity may be altered (usually increased) in old age. Old people are more sensitive to the effects of digoxin, probably because of increased sensitivity of their sodium/potassium pump. This, combined with reduced renal function and an increased susceptibility to potassium loss due to diuretics, makes them more liable to digoxin toxicity. In contrast, there is reduced sensitivity of β-adrenoceptors in old people, and this may reduce some of the pharmacological effects of β-adrenoceptor agonists and antagonists. Altered sensitivity to drugs in old people may be due to altered physiological responses. For example, reduced baroreceptor function can lead to increased hypotension after the administration of antihypertensive drugs. Other examples include increased sensitivity to the anticoagulant effects of warfarin and increased responsiveness of the brain to centrally active drugs— for example, antidepressants, hypnotics, neuroleptic drugs, sedatives and tranquillisers. Some of these principles are illustrated in Figure 2.2, which shows the difference in nifedipine pharmacokinetics and pharmacodynamic responses between young and old men. After an intravenous dose of nifedipine (2.5 mg) the old men had higher plasma nifedipine concentrations and a fall in blood pressure; the difference in blood pressure response was partly due to the difference in plasma concentration but mostly due to a difference in baroreceptor reflexes, as shown by the difference in heart rate response.

- In general, when prescribing drugs for old people, try to use as few drugs as possible, start with low dosages, and increase the dosages carefully only if required. Choose easily swallowed formulations and keep therapy as simple as possible (for example, with once-daily drugs and formulations). Take greater care in frail old people than in fit old people.

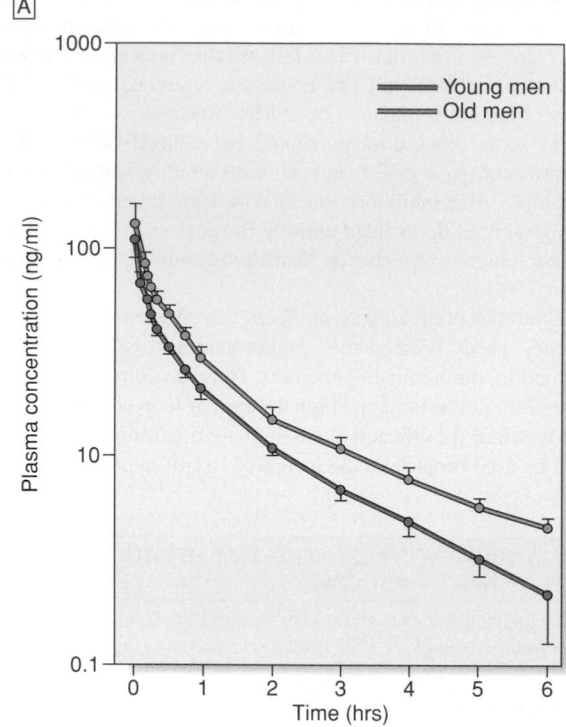

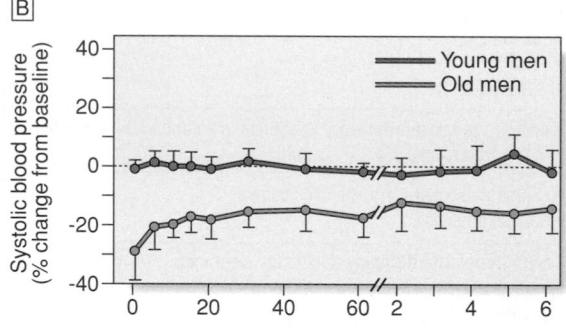

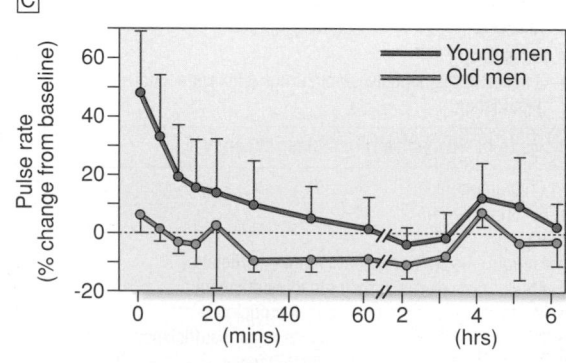

Fig. 2.2 Differences between young men and old men given an intravenous dose of nifedipine. A Old men have higher plasma concentrations than young men. B and C Old men have a greater fall in blood pressure and a smaller rise in heart rate than young men.

WHEN TO STOP DRUG TREATMENT

A single dose of aspirin may be enough to treat a headache, or a single dose of diamorphine may be sufficient to treat the pain of myocardial infarction. In contrast, life-long therapy is usually required for the treatment of diabetes mellitus, essential hypertension, hypothyroidism and pernicious anaemia.

However, there may be difficulty with treatments of intermediate duration. For example, it is still not clear for how long treatment with warfarin should be continued in the treatment of deep venous thrombosis and pulmonary embolism (see p. 565). The duration of treatment of infections with antibiotics varies from infection to infection, and depends on the infecting organism, the site of infection and the response to treatment. For example, uncomplicated urinary tract infection with cystitis usually requires treatment for only a few days, pyelonephritis requires treatment for 1–2 weeks, and acute prostatitis for 4–6 weeks. When you start a drug treatment it is wise to plan the likely duration of therapy. You should also review long-term treatment at regular intervals to assess whether continued treatment is required. A hospital admission is often an opportunity for revising drug therapy, and it is not uncommon for drugs to be withdrawn in the interim or even permanently following an acute severe illness.

ADVERSE DRUG REACTIONS

An adverse drug effect may be due to either a toxic effect or a side-effect. A toxic effect is an adverse effect that arises through an exaggeration of the same pharmacological effect that is responsible for the therapeutic effect of the drug—for example, hypokalaemia due to diuretic therapy—and is therefore dose-related. A side-effect is an adverse effect that arises through some pharmacological action other than that which produces the therapeutic effect; such effects may be dose-related (for example, anticholinergic effects of tricyclic antidepressants) or not dose-related (for example, a rash associated with an antibiotic). The term 'adverse effects' covers all types of unwanted effects. A classification and examples of important adverse drug effects are given in Box 2.17.

2.17 EXAMPLES OF ADVERSE EFFECTS CLASSIFIED BY CAUSE

Mechanism	Example
1. Dose-related effects	
Pharmaceutical variation	Changing modified-release formulations (e.g. lithium)
Pharmacokinetic variation	
Pharmacogenetic variation	Suxamethonium apnoea
Hepatic disease	Sedation due to clomethiazole
Renal disease	Digoxin toxicity
Wrong route of administration	Intrathecal vincristine
Pharmacodynamic variation	
Pharmacogenetic variation	Porphyria
Hepatic disease	Encephalopathy due to opioid analgesics
Altered fluid and electrolyte balance	Digoxin toxicity due to hypokalaemia
2. Non-dose-related effects	
Acute hypersensitivity reactions	Anaphylaxis (e.g. penicillin)
Anaphylactoid (non-allergic) reactions	Polyethoxylated castor oil (used as a solvent for some i.v. drugs)
Immediate pseudoallergic reactions	Aspirin-induced asthma
Pharmacogenetic variation	Haemolysis in G6PD deficiency
3. Dose-related and time-related effects	
Long-term adaptive changes	Tardive dyskinesia (e.g. phenothiazines)
Pharmacogenetic variation	Acute porphyria (enzyme inducers)
Effects related to over-rapid infusion	Red man syndrome (vancomycin)
4. Time-related (not dose-related) effects	
Delayed hypersensitivity reactions (Gell and Coombs types II, III and IV)	Thrombocytopenia (e.g. quinine; type II)
	Interstitial nephritis (e.g. penicillin; type III)
	Contact dermatitis (e.g. antihistamines; type IV)
Delayed pseudoallergic reactions	Ampicillin rash
5. Withdrawal effects	
Following down-regulation of receptors	Opiate withdrawal syndrome
Following up-regulation of receptors	β-blocker withdrawal syndrome (myocardial ischaemia, tachycardia)
6. Failure of therapy	
Pharmaceutical	Inadequate formulations
	Chemical instability (e.g. glyceryl trinitrate)
Pharmacokinetic	Drug interactions (e.g. oral contraceptives and rifampicin)
Pharmacodynamic	Pharmacological tolerance (non-receptor-mediated) (e.g. nitrates)
7. Genetic/genomic mechanisms	
Gametic	Azoospermia due to sulfasalazine
Teratogenic	Vaginal adenocarcinoma with diethylstilbestrol
Carcinogenic	Lymphoma with ciclosporin

Dose-related toxic effects can be avoided by using dosages at the lower end of the recommended range and increasing cautiously, monitoring carefully for therapeutic and adverse effects. Dose-related side-effects may not be avoidable; if they occur despite careful dosage adjustment, it may be necessary to use a different drug. Adverse effects that are due to long-term therapy cannot necessarily be avoided; careful monitoring will help to minimise their impact. Delayed effects can be minimised by reducing the length of exposure to a drug or avoided by not using drugs that are known to have delayed effects.

DRUG INTERACTIONS

A drug interaction occurs when the effects of one drug (the object drug) are altered (increased or decreased) by the effects of another drug (the precipitant drug). Although a drug interaction usually results in an adverse effect, in some cases it may prove beneficial—for example, the pharmaco-dynamic synergy between diuretics and ACE inhibitors in the treatment of hypertension. The classification of drug interactions by mechanism is shown in Box 2.18.

PHARMACEUTICAL INTERACTIONS

Pharmaceutical interactions are physico-chemical inter-actions, either of a drug with an intravenous infusion solution or of two drugs in the same solution, resulting in the loss of activity of the drugs involved. Pharmaceutical interactions are too numerous to remember in detail, but they can be simply avoided:

- by giving intravenous drugs by bolus injection, if possible, or via an infusion burette
- by using only dextrose or saline for drug infusion

- by not mixing drugs in the same infusion solution, unless the mixture is known to be safe (e.g. potassium chloride can be given with insulin).

PHARMACOKINETIC INTERACTIONS

Pharmacokinetic interactions occur when the absorption, distribution or elimination (metabolism or excretion) of the object drug is altered by the precipitant drug.

Absorption interactions

Absorption interactions are usually not important. Exceptions include impaired absorption of tetracyclines by chelation with divalent and trivalent cations. Metoclopramide increases the rate of gastric emptying and this hastens the absorption of analgesics in the treatment of an acute attack of migraine, a beneficial effect.

Distribution interactions: protein-binding displacement

Protein-binding displacement causes an increase in the circulating concentration of unbound drug. However, this is only important if the object drug is highly protein-bound (greater than 90%) and is not widely distributed to body tissues. In practice, this limits important interactions of this type to warfarin and phenytoin. When these drugs are dis-placed their clearance rate increases in proportion to the degree of displacement and so at steady state the total con-centration of drug in the plasma falls to a new equilibrium value, and the unbound concentration is the same as it was before the precipitant drug was introduced, in spite of an increase in the unbound fraction. This means that, provided the patient can 'weather' the increase, if any, in unbound concentration of the object drug for as long as it takes to reach the new steady state, such an interaction will not be clinically important.

2.18 CLASSIFICATION OF DRUG INTERACTIONS BY MECHANISM

Mechanism	Example		
	Object drug	Precipitant drug	Result
Pharmaceutical	Sodium bicarbonate	Calcium gluconate	Precipitation of calcium carbonate
Pharmacokinetic			
Reduced absorption	Tetracyclines	Calcium, aluminium, magnesium salts	Reduced tetracycline absorption
Reduced protein binding	Phenytoin	Aspirin	Reduced phenytoin plasma concentration with same therapeutic effect
Reduced metabolism (CYP3A4)	Terfenadine	Grapefruit juice	Cardiac arrhythmias
Reduced metabolism (CYP2C19)	Phenytoin	Ticlopidine	Phenytoin toxicity
Reduced metabolism (CYP2D6)	Clozapine	Paroxetine	Clozapine toxicity
Reduced metabolism (other enzymes)	Azathioprine	Allopurinol	Azathioprine toxicity
Increased metabolism	Ciclosporin	St John's wort	Loss of immunosuppression
Reduced renal elimination	Lithium	Diuretics	Lithium toxicity
Pharmacodynamic			
Direct antagonism	Opiates	Naloxone	Reversal of opiate effects
Direct potentiation	Alcohol	Antidepressants	Increased sedation
Indirect potentiation	Anti-arrhythmic drugs	Diuretics	Cardiac arrhythmias (hypokalaemia)

Metabolism interactions

Drug interactions involving metabolism are important interactions. They occur when the metabolism of an object drug is either inhibited or increased by a precipitant drug. There are two phases of drug metabolism. Phase I metabolic reactions (for example, dealkylation, deamination, hydroxylation, sulphoxidation) are carried out by isoenzymes of the mixed-function oxidase system and are subject to interactions. Phase II reactions are conjugations (for example, acetylation, methylation, glucuronidation, sulphatation), which are not affected by interactions.

Induction of drug metabolism

Induction of the metabolism of a drug reduces the amount of drug in the body and therefore reduces its effects. This can result, for example, in pregnancy despite what would otherwise have been adequate oral contraception.

Inhibition of drug metabolism

Inhibition of drug metabolism occurs through inhibition of either the mixed-function oxidase reactions or other specific metabolic pathways.

Examples of the former include the inhibition of warfarin metabolism by chloramphenicol, cimetidine, ketoconazole, metronidazole and quinolones, inhibition of phenytoin metabolism by isoniazid, and inhibition of theophylline metabolism by quinolone and macrolide antibiotics (for example, erythromycin).

Examples of the latter include the inhibition by allopurinol of the metabolism of azathioprine and 6-mercaptopurine by xanthine oxidase and of dietary amines by monoamine oxidase inhibitors.

Excretion interactions

Competition for renal tubular secretion reduces drug excretion. For example, probenecid inhibits the tubular secretion of penicillin, increasing the blood concentration of penicillin and prolonging its therapeutic effects, a beneficial interaction. Amiodarone, quinidine and verapamil inhibit the tubular secretion of digoxin by inhibiting the transport protein P glycoprotein, increasing plasma digoxin concentrations and causing toxicity. Salicylates inhibit the active secretion of methotrexate. Diuretics inhibit the renal excretion of lithium.

PHARMACODYNAMIC INTERACTIONS

In pharmacodynamic interactions the effect of a drug is altered at its site of action. Such interactions are either direct or indirect.

Direct pharmacodynamic interactions

Direct pharmacodynamic interactions occur when two drugs either act on the same site (antagonism or synergism) or act on two different sites with a similar end result. For example, naloxone reverses the effects of opiates and vitamin K reverses the effects of warfarin (beneficial antagonistic interactions). The anticoagulant effects of warfarin are increased in direct synergistic interactions with anabolic steroids and tetracyclines. Any drug that has a depressant action on central nervous function can potentiate the effect of another such drug, whether or not the two drugs have effects on the same receptors; for example, alcohol potentiates the action of any other centrally acting drug.

Indirect pharmacodynamic interactions

In indirect pharmacodynamic interactions a pharmacological, therapeutic or toxic effect of the precipitant drug in some way alters the therapeutic or toxic effect of the object drug, but the two effects are not themselves related and do not themselves interact.

The effects of anticoagulants can be increased by three indirect effects: reduced platelet aggregation (for example, by salicylates, dipyridamole, ticlopidine and NSAIDs) or thrombocytopenia; gastrointestinal ulceration (for example, NSAIDs); and increased fibrinolysis (for example, metformin).

Alterations in fluid and electrolyte balance by diuretics increase the effects of cardiac glycosides and class I anti-arrhythmic drugs (for example, lidocaine (lignocaine), quinidine, procainamide and phenytoin).

AVOIDING ADVERSE DRUG INTERACTIONS

The simple way of avoiding adverse drug interactions is to avoid combinations that are known to be dangerous. If that is not possible, the dosage of the object drug should be reduced in advance of starting the precipitant drug and the precipitant drug should be introduced slowly. When a theoretical interaction is anticipated on the basis of the known properties of two drugs, even if it has not been previously described, careful monitoring will help recognise adverse effects early.

WRITING A DRUG PRESCRIPTION

A prescription should be a precise, accurate, clear and readable set of instructions, sufficient for a nurse to administer a drug accurately in hospital, or for a pharmacist to provide a patient with both the correct drug and the instructions on how to take it (see Fig. 2.3). The information that should be written on a prescription is given in Box 2.19.

2.19 INFORMATION TO BE GIVEN ON A PRESCRIPTION OUTSIDE HOSPITAL

- The date
- The patient's name, initials and address
- The age of a child if under 12
- The name of the drug, preferably in capitals (use generic names when possible)
- The formulation to be prescribed
- The strength of the formulation
- The dose
- The frequency of administration
- The route of administration
- The doctor's name, address and signature

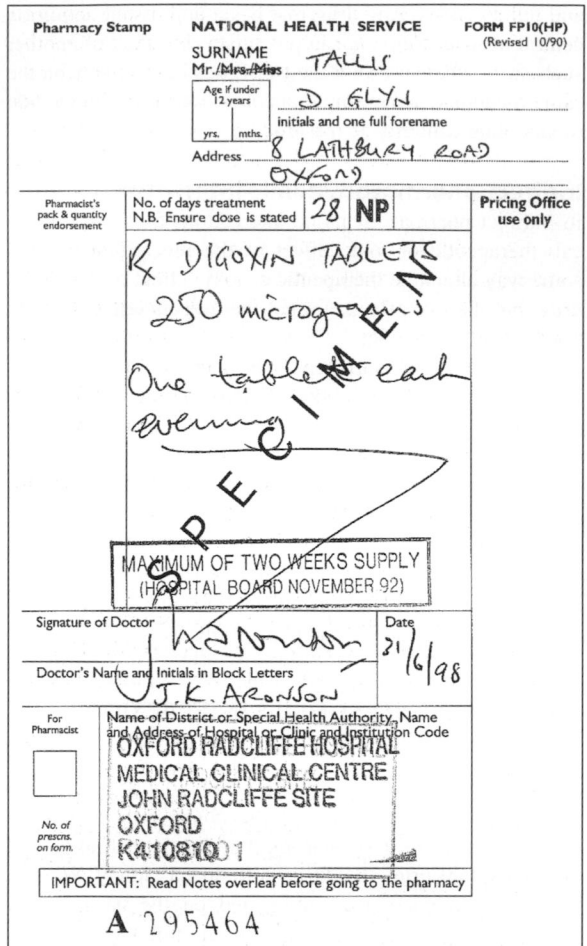

Fig. 2.3 An example of a prescription for a prescription-only medicine (digoxin).

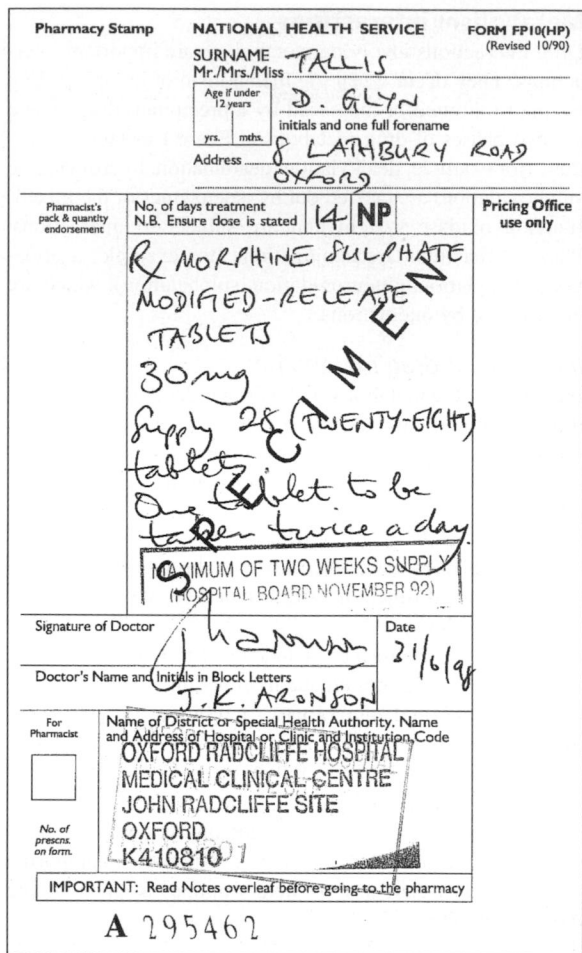

Fig. 2.4 An example of a prescription for a controlled drug (morphine).

WRITING DRUG DOSES

- Quantities of 1 gram or more should be written in grams. For example, write 2 g.
- Quantities of less than 1 gram but more than 1 milligram should be written in milligrams. For example, write 100 mg, not 0.1 g.
- Quantities of less than 1 milligram should be written in micrograms or nanograms as appropriate. Do not abbreviate micrograms or nanograms. For example, write 100 micrograms, not 0.1 mg, 100 µg, 100 mcg or 100 ug.
- If a decimal point cannot be avoided for values less than 1, write a zero before it. For example, write 0.5 ml, not .5 ml.
- For liquid medicines given orally the dose should be stated as the number of milligrams in either 5 ml or 10 ml of solution. For example, write paracetamol oral suspension 250 mg in 5 ml.

PRESCRIBING CONTROLLED DRUGS

Because of the problems of drug addiction and misuse of drugs, in the United Kingdom problem drugs are the subject of the Misuse of Drugs Act 1971, the Misuse of

2.20 REQUIREMENTS FOR PRESCRIPTIONS FOR CONTROLLED DRUGS

- Written completely in the prescriber's handwriting in ink
- Signed and dated by the prescriber
- The prescriber's address specified
- The name and address of the patient specified
- The form and strength (if appropriate) of the drug stated
- The total quantity of the drug or the number of dose units to be dispensed stated in both words and figures
- The exact size of each dose stated in both words and figures

Drugs (Notification of and Supply to Addicts) Regulations 1973 and the Misuse of Drugs Regulations 1985. The requirements for the prescription of controlled drugs are listed in Box 2.20 and a sample prescription for a controlled drug is shown in Figure 2.4. Doctors in other countries should make themselves familiar with local regulations.

ABBREVIATIONS

Some abbreviations that are used in prescribing are listed in Box 2.21. Other abbreviations should be avoided and instructions should be written in plain English.

2.21 ACCEPTABLE ABBREVIATIONS IN PRESCRIPTIONS

Abbreviation	Latin meaning	English translation
b.d. or b.i.d.	Bis in die	Twice a day
gutt.	Guttae	Drops
i.m.	–	Intramuscular(ly)
i.v.	–	Intravenous(ly)
o.d.	Omni die	(Once) every day
o.m.	Omni mane[1]	(Once) every morning
o.n.	Omni nocte[1]	(Once) every night
p.o.	Per os	By mouth
PR	Per rectum	By the anal route
p.r.n.	Pro re nata	Whenever required
PV	Per vaginam	By the vaginal route
q.d.s.	Quater die sumendum[2]	Four times a day
s.c.	–	Subcutaneous(ly)
stat.	Statim	Immediately
t.d.s.	Ter die sumendum[2]	Three times a day

[1] Sometimes written simply as mane or nocte.
[2] The abbreviations t.i.d. or q.i.d. (ter or quater in die) are sometimes used instead.

DRUG NOMENCLATURE

Drugs have different kinds of name:

- the chemical name, whose form generally follows the rules issued by the International Union of Pure and Applied Chemistry (IUPAC)
- the approved (official or generic) name, which is usually the International Non-proprietary Name (INN), recommended or proposed by the World Health Organisation, but may be some locally approved name (for example, the British Approved Name (BAN) or United States Adopted Name (USAN))
- the proprietary name (brand name or trade name), given to it by a pharmaceutical manufacturer.

For example:

- chemical name:
  (R)-1-(3,4-dihydroxyphenyl)-2-methylaminoethanol
- International Non-proprietary Name: epinephrine; British Approved Name: adrenaline
- proprietary names: EpiPen® for intramuscular injection and Eppy® or Simplene® eye drops.

Since the chemical name is generally, as in this case, unsuitable for routine prescribing, either the approved name or proprietary name is used. Which should one choose? For some drugs the question is trivial, since only one proprietary formulation exists; for example, donepezil is currently available in the UK only as Aricept®.

However, several proprietary formulations of the same chemical entity may become available when the patent expires on a drug with a previously unique proprietary name. For instance, amoxicillin was first marketed as Amoxil®. When the patent expired the number of proprietary brands

multiplied. This can cause prescribing and dispensing problems. For example, in the UK, whether the prescriber writes 'donepezil BP' or 'Aricept', the patient will receive Aricept®. However, if the prescriber writes 'amoxicillin BP', the pharmacist may dispense any proprietary formulation, provided that it conforms to the description laid out in the BP *(British Pharmacopoeia)*, and will generally dispense the cheapest available.

By writing the proprietary name the prescriber can ensure that a particular formulation of a drug is prescribed. However, in some hospitals (in the UK, for example) the hospital pharmacy may stock only one formulation, and even if the hospital doctor writes 'Amoxil' on an inpatient prescription chart the pharmacist may dispense some other approved formulation for which the hospital will have negotiated an economic deal with the supplier.

There are advantages and disadvantages to the prescribing of drugs by their generic (non-proprietary) as opposed to their proprietary names. The advantages relate to:

- *Awareness of the prescription*. The name of the compound often indicates to what class it belongs, usually by virtue of its suffix: e.g. -statin (HMG CoA reductase inhibitors), -olol (β-blockers, although beware stanozolol), -floxacin (quinolone antibiotics).
- *Drug stocks*. If, say, 'Almodan' rather than 'amoxicillin' is prescribed and an outside pharmacy stocks only Amoxil®, the pharmacist cannot legally dispense the prescription without first consulting the doctor; clearly this can cause inconvenience to all concerned and might result in delayed treatment.
- *Expense*. It is generally cheaper to prescribe by the approved name, since the pharmacist will dispense the cheapest variant held in stock.

The disadvantages of prescribing by non-proprietary name relate to:

- *Remembering names*. Proprietary names are chosen by pharmaceutical companies because they are catchy, usually easier to remember than the corresponding generic name, and shorter and easier to spell (compare, for example, 'Librium' with 'chlordiazepoxide'). Furthermore, a single proprietary name will do when the formulation may in fact contain two or more drugs (compare, for example, 'Fefol' with 'ferrous sulphate plus folic acid'). However, in recent years there has been a move in the UK to counteract this problem by giving single approved names to some common combinations of drugs; for example, the combination of dihydrocodeine with paracetamol (acetaminophen) is known as co-dydramol.
- *Quality of product*. For a few drugs a change in tablet excipients (the non-therapeutic components) has significant effects on the absorption of the drug from the formulation; important examples include lithium salts, nifedipine and theophylline, which should always be prescribed by brand name.
- *Continuity of treatment*. Patients not infrequently become confused if the drug they are being given

changes its form with every prescription; continuity can be achieved by prescribing the same proprietary formulation every time.

In hospital it is usually better to prescribe by approved name, since the pharmacy will dispense whatever formulation is held in stock. The proprietary name can be used when a combination product is prescribed for which no single approved name exists (for example, 'Fefol'). In general practice it is also usually best to prescribe by approved name. Many practitioners prefer to prescribe by proprietary name and in some cases (for example, lithium salts, nifedipine and theophylline) should do so. However, doctors who make the effort to prescribe when possible by approved name will generally find it just as easy as prescribing by proprietary name.

There is currently some difficulty in countries of the European Union over certain drug names, following the issue of directives from Brussels (particularly directive 92/27/EEC), requiring member states to use the International Non-proprietary Names rather than locally approved names such as the British Approved Names. In the UK this has little or no effect in most cases, since most of the International Non-proprietary Names are identical or very similar to the corresponding British Approved Names. However, in a few cases (see Box 2.22) the names are

2.22 SOME DRUG NAMES WHOSE BANs AND INNs ARE CONSIDERED TO BE SIGNIFICANTLY DIFFERENT

British Approved Name (BAN)	International Non-proprietary Name (INN)
Acrosoxacin	Rosoxacin
Adrenaline	Epinephrine
Amethocaine	Tetracaine
Bendrofluazide	Bendroflumethiazide
Benzhexol	Trihexyphenidyl
Chlorpheniramine	Chlorphenamine
Dicyclomine	Dicycloverine
Dothiepin	Dosulepin
Eformoterol	Formoterol
Flurandrenolone	Fludroxycortide
Frusemide	Furosemide
Hydroxyurea	Hydroxycarbamide
Lignocaine	Lidocaine
Methotrimeprazine	Levomepromazine
Methylene blue	Methylthioninium chloride
Mitozantrone	Mitoxantrone
Mustine	Chlormethine
Nicoumalone	Acenocoumarol
Noradrenaline	Norepinephrine
Oxpentifylline	Pentoxifylline
Procaine penicillin	Procaine benzylpenicillin
Salcatonin	Calcitonin (salmon)
Thymoxamine	Moxisylyte
Thyroxine sodium	Levothyroxine sodium
Trimeprazine	Alimemazine

2.23 USUAL THERAPEUTIC AND TOXIC PLASMA CONCENTRATIONS OF COMMONLY MEASURED DRUGS

Drug	Optimal sampling time	Concentration below which a therapeutic effect is unlikely		Concentration above which a toxic effect is more likely	
		Mass units	Molar units	Mass units	Molar units
Aspirin (salicylate)					
Analgesic	Just before next dose	20 mg/l	0.15 mmol/l	300 mg/l	2.2 µmol/l
Anti-inflammatory	Just before next dose	150 mg/l	1.1 mmol/l	300 mg/l	2.2 µmol/l
Carbamazepine	Just before next dose	4 mg/l	17 mmol/l	10 mg/l	42 µmol/l
Cardiac glycosides					
Digitoxin	Just before next dose	15 µg/l	20 nmol/l	30 µg/l	39 nmol/l
Digoxin	11 hrs after last dose	0.8 µg/l	1.0 nmol/l	2 µg/l	2.6 nmol/l
Ciclosporin*	Just before next dose	125 µg/l	104 nmol/l	200 µg/l	166 nmol/l
Lithium	12 hrs after last dose	–	0.4 mmol/l	–	1.0 mmol/l
Phenytoin	Just before next dose	10 mg/l	40 mmol/l	20 mg/l	80 µmol/l
Theophylline	Just before next dose	10 mg/l	55 mmol/l	20 mg/l	110 µmol/l

* Measured in whole blood by specific radioimmunoassay or high-performance liquid chromatography (HPLC).

Notes
1. Care should be taken in comparing results between different laboratories (particularly with ciclosporin).
2. The concentration below which a therapeutic effect is unlikely and the concentration above which a toxic effect is more likely together constitute a target range within which satisfactory therapy is likely to be achieved; however, dosages should be adjusted according to the clinical response, not the concentration, which should only be used as a guide.
3. Note the units used when interpreting results. Laboratories may report in mass units or molar units or both; µg/l = ng/ml; mg/l = µg/ml.
4. Remember that pharmacokinetics differ from individual to individual; for within-patient comparisons always use the same time after the last dose.
5. Remember that pharmacodynamics differ from individual to individual and that different individuals respond differently to the same concentration of drug; other factors that can alter the individual response should be considered.
6. For paracetamol see Figure 3.3, page 171.
7. For aminoglycosides consult your laboratory.

considered to be different enough to warrant extra care. In this textbook we have used the International Non-proprietary Names (with the British Approved Names in parentheses in cases that might cause confusion). The only exceptions are adrenaline and noradrenaline, for which we have used the British Approved Names, the corresponding International Non-proprietary Names being epinephrine and norepinephrine; this is because it is thought that in these cases changing to the International Names could be dangerous for patients.

MONITORING DRUG THERAPY

There is no space here for a detailed discussion of how to monitor drug therapy, which can be done using clinical, pharmacodynamic or pharmacokinetic methods. For some drugs whose effects can be monitored by measuring plasma concentrations, target concentrations are given in Box 2.23.

FURTHER INFORMATION

Aronson JK. Where name and image meet: the argument for 'adrenaline'. BMJ 2000; 320:506–509.

Association of the British Pharmaceutical Industry. Medicines compendium (formerly Compendium of data sheets and summaries of product characteristics). London: Datapharm Communications. *New edition each year.*

British National Formulary. London: British Medical Association and Pharmaceutical Society of Great Britain. *Guide to currently available formulations, with notes on dosages, uses, adverse effects and interactions; chapters on prescribing, especially in renal failure, in liver disease, in pregnancy and during breastfeeding, and appendices on drug interactions and intravenous additives.*

Grahame-Smith DG, Aronson JK. Oxford textbook of clinical pharmacology and drug therapy. 3rd edn. Oxford: Oxford University Press; 2002. *Contains a more detailed account of the principles outlined here.*

Sackett DL, Richardson WS, Rosenberg W, et al. Evidence-based medicine: how to practise and teach EBM. Edinburgh: Churchill Livingstone; 2000. *A useful introduction to evidence-based medicine.*

www.bnf.org *British National Formulary.*

www.cebm.utoronto.ca *Evidence-based medicine.*

www.clinicalevidence.org *A compendium of best evidence, published by the British Medical Journal.*

www.cochrane.co.uk *The Cochrane collaboration.*

Poisoning

A.L. JONES

Acute poisoning remains one of the most common medical emergencies in the UK, accounting for 10–20% of all acute medical admissions. At least 50% involve more than one drug, with alcohol being the most frequent second agent.

Substances involved in poisoning vary widely between different countries (see Box 3.1). In the UK, poisoning with paracetamol accounts for 48% of all overdoses. By contrast, in the USA only 7% of all cases of poisoning are due to paracetamol, and in Nepal it is very rare. Poisoning with tri-cyclic antidepressants, selective serotonin (5-hydroxytryp-tamine, 5-HT) re-uptake inhibitors and drugs of misuse is very common in the UK and USA. Australia has a similar range of ingested toxins to the UK but envenomation with snakes, spiders and marine creatures is also very common. In South and South-east Asia, pesticide ingestion is endemic, and is the most common cause of death by poisoning. The toxicity of available poisons and the paucity of medical facilities in the developing world mean that the mortality rate for self-poisoning is high at 10–20%. This compares with a mortality rate of 0.5–1% in most industrialised countries. Reducing deaths from self-harm requires interventions both to reduce the incidence of harmful behaviour and to improve the medical management of acute poisoning. Clinical features of poisoning with specific agents and their management are discussed later in this chapter.

3.1 SUBSTANCES FREQUENTLY INVOLVED IN POISONING
In the United Kingdom
• Analgesic drugs, including paracetamol and non-steroidal anti-inflammatory drugs
• Cardiovascular toxic drugs, especially tricyclic antidepressants
• Drugs of misuse
• Carbon monoxide*
• Alcohol
In South and South-east Asia
• Organophosphorus* and carbamate insecticides
• Aluminium and zinc phosphide
• Snake bites
• Antimalarial drugs such as chloroquine
• Antidiabetic medication
* Indicates the most common cause of death by poisoning.

GENERAL APPROACH TO THE POISONED PATIENT

TAKING A HISTORY

In most cases, the diagnosis of poisoning is apparent on the basis of the history given by the patient. However, such information may not always be forthcoming, either because patients do not know what has been taken or because they may have been under the influence of alcohol or the drug itself at the time of ingestion. A few patients deliberately mislead doctors but in our experience this is very rare, with the exception of drug misusers.

Full details of the amount and type of substance that has been taken must be recorded, as well as the timing of inges-tion or exposure. Whether the drugs belonged to the patient, or to a friend or relative, and the source of the drug (i.e. over the counter, prescription, street) are important in the preven-tion of future poisoning. The nature of any drug taken should be corroborated or identified from descriptions of the tablets or remaining pills (or their packets or bottles) by the use of drug identification software (e.g. TICTAC®), which can be accessed by many pharmacies and poisons informa-tion centres.

Ask the patient why the overdose was taken and take time to listen to the explanation. Reasons often include relationship difficulties, work- or school-related difficulties, drug addic-tion, psychiatric illness or bereavement. Whilst 'accidental overdose' can occur, in general all patients presenting with poisoning should undergo psychiatric evaluation (see p. 252).

Details of the past medical history should be recorded. In particular, a history of asthma, jaundice, drug misuse (and by which routes), head injury, epilepsy, cardiovascular prob-lems, previous psychiatric illness and self-harm should be taken. It is important to ask about allergies and alcohol his-tory. Identifying family problems and taking a good social history are also very important.

CLINICAL FEATURES OF POISONING

First ensure that:

- the Airway is clear
- the patient is Breathing adequately
- the Circulation is not compromised.

If the patient is alert and has a stable circulation, proceed to an examination. The only exception is where immediate eye or skin decontamination is required (see Fig. 3.2, p. 169). A standard clinical examination should be carried out on every poisoned patient. Particular care should be taken to look for needle marks or previous evidence of self-harm, e.g. razor marks on forearms. Examination find-ings such as pupil size, respiratory rate and heart rate may support the diagnosis in an unconscious patient but on their own may merely help to narrow down the potential list of toxins. Clinical signs that can help identify which toxin has been taken are shown in Figure 3.1. The weight of the patient is also important as it is often critical in determining whether (given the dose ingested) toxicity is likely to occur, and allows the dose of any antidote to be calculated (e.g. N-acetylcysteine in paracetamol poisoning).

The Glasgow Coma Scale (GCS, see p. 1143) is the method most frequently used to assess the degree of impaired consciousness, though remarkably it has never been validated for use in poisoned patients. When patients are unconscious and no history is available, the diagnosis of poisoning depends on the exclusion of other causes of coma (especially meningitis, intracerebral bleeds, hypoglycaemia, diabetic ketoacidosis, uraemia and encephalopathy—see p. 1143) and consideration of circumstantial evidence.

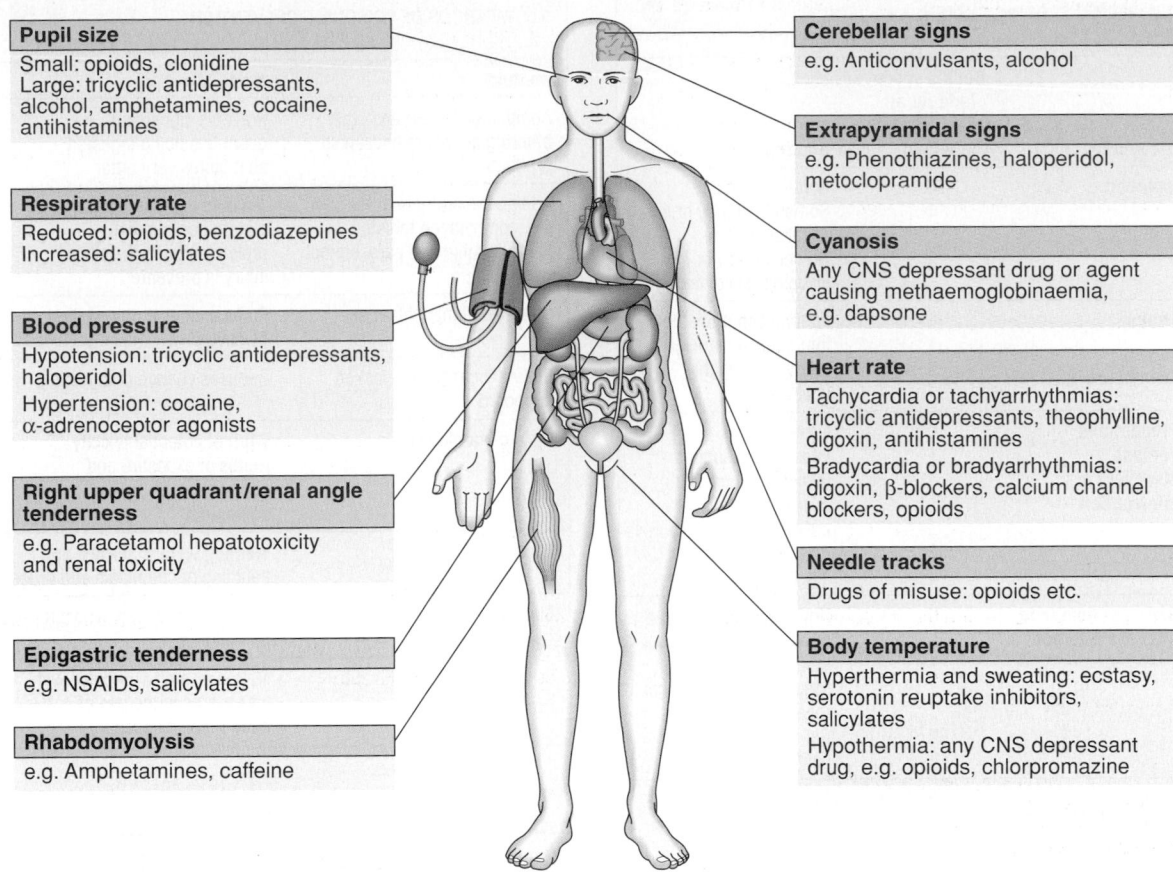

Pupil size
Small: opioids, clonidine
Large: tricyclic antidepressants, alcohol, amphetamines, cocaine, antihistamines

Respiratory rate
Reduced: opioids, benzodiazepines
Increased: salicylates

Blood pressure
Hypotension: tricyclic antidepressants, haloperidol
Hypertension: cocaine, α-adrenoceptor agonists

Right upper quadrant/renal angle tenderness
e.g. Paracetamol hepatotoxicity and renal toxicity

Epigastric tenderness
e.g. NSAIDs, salicylates

Rhabdomyolysis
e.g. Amphetamines, caffeine

Cerebellar signs
e.g. Anticonvulsants, alcohol

Extrapyramidal signs
e.g. Phenothiazines, haloperidol, metoclopramide

Cyanosis
Any CNS depressant drug or agent causing methaemoglobinaemia, e.g. dapsone

Heart rate
Tachycardia or tachyarrhythmias: tricyclic antidepressants, theophylline, digoxin, antihistamines
Bradycardia or bradyarrhythmias: digoxin, β-blockers, calcium channel blockers, opioids

Needle tracks
Drugs of misuse: opioids etc.

Body temperature
Hyperthermia and sweating: ecstasy, serotonin reuptake inhibitors, salicylates
Hypothermia: any CNS depressant drug, e.g. opioids, chlorpromazine

Fig. 3.1   Clinical signs of poisoning by pharmaceutical agents or drugs of misuse.

ROLE OF THE TOXICOLOGY LABORATORY

In most patients the diagnosis of poisoning is made on the history and clinical signs alone. In some cases, such as poisoning with paracetamol (see p. 170), aspirin (see p. 171) or iron (see Box 3.7, p. 174), subsequent management of the patient depends on measurement of the amount of toxin in the blood.

In unconscious patients, a qualitative screen of the urine (e.g. urine immunofluorescence drugs of misuse screening test) is an effective way to confirm recent use of drugs such as benzodiazepines, cocaine, ecstasy, opioids and cannabis. Routine screens may not, however, detect fentanyl derivatives, tramadol and other synthetic opioids. Occasionally, measuring drugs of misuse and their metabolites in blood by gas chromatography-mass spectroscopy (GC-MS) is required for medico-legal purposes, particularly where there is a fatality, and in such cases urine and serum should be saved for later analysis.

PSYCHIATRIC ASSESSMENT OF THE POISONED PATIENT

In order to decide on the most appropriate placement and staffing ratios for a self-poisoned patient, an initial assessment of suicidal intent must be made. Use of the Beck's depression scale or similar may be valuable for this (see Box 3.2). If the sum of all the scores for each parameter is greater than 4 (e.g. suicide note left and no one likely to find patient after overdose), this indicates significant suicidal intent and means that the patient is at risk of further self-harm and should have a nurse with him or her at all times whilst an inpatient.

Suicide attempts were once much more common in women than in men but now the ratios are more equal. There is a higher incidence in lower socio-economic groups, those who lost a parent at an early age, those with alcohol or drug misuse, recipients of child abuse, the unemployed and those with recent broken relationships. A thorough psychiatric and social assessment should be carried out in all patients once sufficient time has elapsed to allow the toxic effects of any drugs to wear off. This can be performed by nurses, physicians or psychiatrists. The interviewer needs to assess the severity of any current symptoms of psychiatric illness and to determine what personal or social supports need to be provided. Most patients have depressive and anxiety symptoms which are reactive to an acute life crisis superimposed on a background of chronic social and personal difficulties. They need neither psychotropic medication nor specialised psychiatric treatment but do need support, e.g. from social workers. Admission to a psychiatric ward is necessary for

3.2 BECK'S SCORING SYSTEM ⓘ

Parameter	Beck's score (add up all those relevant below)	Scoring
Isolation	0	Someone present
	1	Someone nearby or in vocal contact
	2	No one nearby or in visual/vocal contact
Timing	0	Intervention probable
	1	Intervention not likely
	2	Intervention highly unlikely
Precautions against discovery or interruption	0	None
	1	Passive precautions (avoiding others but doing nothing to prevent intervention)
	2	Active precautions, e.g. locking door
Acting to gain help after the attempt	0	Notified potential helper regarding the attempt
	1	Contacted but did not specifically notify helper regarding the attempt
	2	Did not contact or notify helper
Final acts in anticipation of death	0	None
	1	Thought about or made some arrangement
	2	Definite plans made, e.g. changing will
Active preparation for attempt	0	None
	1	Minimal
	2	Extensive
Suicide note	0	None
	1	Note written but torn up or note thought about
	2	Note present
Overt communication of intent before attempt	0	None
	1	Equivocal communication
	2	Unequivocal attempt

3.3 METHODS OF POISONING PREVENTION ⓘ

Method	Mode of action
Addition of 'Bitrex' and other bittering agents to household products	Prevents significant quantities being ingested as it tastes very bitter
Adding the antidote to the toxin, e.g. combination tablets of methionine and paracetamol	Antidote is present so glutathione remains replete and hepatocellular injury is prevented
Child-resistant containers	Reduce chance of ingestion by children
Secure location, e.g. locked cupboard	Reduces chance of ingestion
Hazard warning labels	Warn of potential toxicity, routes of exposure and appropriate protective equipment
Education	Warning on safe storage and handling of chemicals and drugs
Supervision	The key to reduced exposure for children
Legislation, e.g. Health and Safety regulations	Makes a safer workplace with safeguards in the use of dangerous chemicals

GENERAL MANAGEMENT OF THE POISONED PATIENT

The majority of patients who present after poisoning have taken an overdose. Some present with eye or skin contamination and these are treated with appropriate washing methods (see Fig. 3.2). Only patients who have ingested significant overdoses need further measures such as gastric decontamination and methods to increase elimination. In the seriously poisoned patient, meticulous supportive care, including the treatment of seizures, coma and cardiovascular complications, is critical to good outcome. Seizures are seen most commonly in poisoning by theophyllines, non-steroidal anti-inflammatory drugs (NSAIDs), anticonvulsants and tricyclic antidepressants, and are best treated by airway management and i.v. diazepam (10 mg for an adult, repeated as necessary; see p. 1127). Cardiovascular support measures are discussed on page 201. Ventilatory support may be required until consciousness returns, and complications such as aspiration pneumonia should be treated promptly. It is important that patients are observed closely for signs of deterioration whilst the effects of the toxin they have taken wear off. This often approximates to five half-lives of the drug concerned.

Activated charcoal is the most common method used to prevent drug absorption and is given orally as a black slurry; owing to its large surface area and porous structure, this is highly effective in adsorbing most toxins (see EBM panel).

patients with major psychiatric illness (see p. 252) who remain intent on suicide. In our unit, about 20% of patients make a repeat suicide attempt during the following 12 months and 1% actually kill themselves. Factors associated with an increased risk of suicide include male sex, age over 45, living alone, unemployment, recent bereavement, divorce or separation, chronic ill health, drug or alcohol misuse, violent method used, suicide note written and a history of previous attempts.

Preventing poisoning is much better than curing it, and a number of important measures have been taken to achieve this (see Box 3.3).

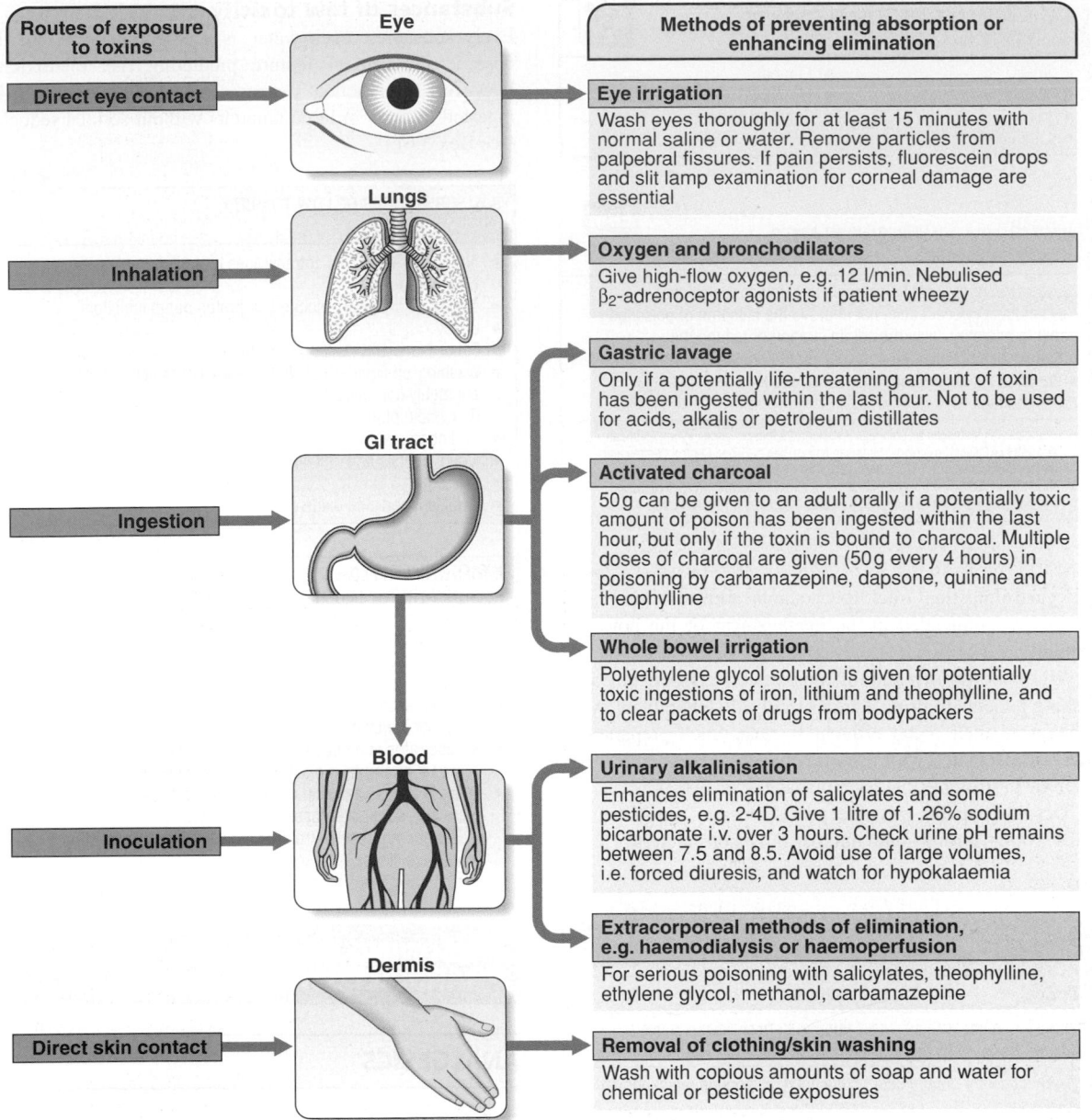

Fig. 3.2 Routes of exposure to toxins and methods of preventing absorption or enhancing elimination.

SINGLE-DOSE ACTIVATED CHARCOAL AFTER POISON INGESTION

EBM

'A position statement based on available RCT data recommends that activated charcoal should be given to all patients who present within 1 hour of ingestion of a potentially toxic amount of poison which binds to charcoal.'

• Chyka PA, Seger D. Position Statement: single-dose activated charcoal. American Academy of Clinical Toxicology; European Association of Poison Centres and Clinical Toxicologists. J Toxicol Clin Toxicol 1997; 35:721–741.

There are, however, a few agents that do not bind to activated charcoal (see Box 3.4). It should not be mixed with ice-cream or flavouring agents as these reduce its adsorptive capacity. In patients who cannot swallow or who have a reduced level of consciousness the activated charcoal should be given via a nasogastric tube. In all cases the airway must be adequately protected to avoid aspiration pneumonitis. Poisoning with certain drugs is best treated with multiple doses of activated charcoal (see Fig. 3.2), and in such circumstances it is important that a laxative is given to avoid obstruction due to charcoal 'briquette' formation in

3.4 SUBSTANCES WHICH DO NOT BIND TO ACTIVATED CHARCOAL

- Acids
- Alkalis
- Iron
- Lithium
- Ethanol
- Methanol
- Ethylene glycol

IPECACUANHA ADMINISTRATION AFTER POISON INGESTION `EBM`

'Systematic review of clinical trials has demonstrated that ipecacuanha (ipecac) does not improve the outcome of poisoned patients and may delay the administration or reduce the effectiveness of activated charcoal, oral antidotes and whole bowel irrigation. Ipecacuanha-induced emesis is therefore no longer recommended.'

- Krenzelok EP, McGuigan M, Lheureux P. Position Statement: ipecac syrup. American Academy of Clinical Toxicology; European Association of Poison Control Centres and Clinical Toxicologists. J Toxicol Clin Toxicol 1997; 35:699–709.
- Pond SM, Lewis-Driver DJ, Williams GM, et al. Gastric emptying in acute overdose: a prospective randomised controlled trial. Med J Aust 1995; 163:345–349.

the gastrointestinal tract. Ipecacuanha administration is no longer recommended in the management of the poisoned patient.

Whole bowel irrigation is most effectively performed by asking patients to drink 1 litre of polyethylene glycol every hour until their rectal effluent is clear. Such preparations are not associated with osmotic changes. Contraindications include gastrointestinal haemorrhage or obstruction.

Despite popular misconceptions, specific antidotes are only available for a small number of poisons (see Box 3.5).

3.5 ANTIDOTES AVAILABLE FOR THE TREATMENT OF SPECIFIC POISONINGS

Poison	Antidote
Anticoagulants (e.g. warfarin, rodenticides)	Vitamin K, fresh frozen plasma
β-adrenoceptor antagonists (β-blockers)	Glucagon, adrenaline (epinephrine)
Calcium channel blockers	Calcium gluconate
Cyanide	Oxygen, dicobalt edetate, nitrites, sodium thiosulphate, hydroxocobalamin
Ethylene glycol/methanol	Ethanol, 4-methylpyrazole
Lead	DMSA (2,3-dimercaptosuccinic acid), disodium calcium edetate
Mercury	DMPS (2,3-dimercapto-1-propane sulphonate)
Iron salts	Desferrioxamine
Opioids	Naloxone
Organophosphorus insecticides, nerve agents	Atropine, pralidoxime (P2S)
Paracetamol	N-acetylcysteine, methionine
Cardiac glycosides	Digoxin-specific antibody fragments (F(ab))

Substances of low toxicity

Every substance, even water, is a potential toxin, but the dose is the critical feature predicting risk of toxicity. However, for practical purposes, some substances can be ingested by man in large amounts without serious sequelae (see Box 3.6).

3.6 SUBSTANCES OF LOW TOXICITY

- Antibiotics—but NOT tetracyclines or antituberculous drugs, which are toxic
- Anti-ulcer drugs: H_2-blockers or proton pump inhibitors
- Chalk
- Paper glues and wallpaper paste
- Washing-up liquid—but NOT dishwasher tablets, which are highly corrosive
- Household plants
- Oral contraceptive pills
- 'Lead' pencils and 'felt-tip' pens
- Silica gel
- Emollient and zinc oxide creams

ISSUES IN OLDER PEOPLE
POISONING IN THE ELDERLY

- Drugs that are renally cleared accumulate more rapidly and to higher levels in elderly patients due to reduced glomerular filtration rate.
- CNS depressant drugs have a greater sedative action in the elderly and may precipitate confusion.
- Suicide rates in most countries are highest in older people, and in the UK attempts in old age are usually by overdose.
- There is a close association between depression and self-harm in old age, so all overdoses should be taken seriously in older people and aggressive treatment given for any underlying depressive illness.

POISONING BY SPECIFIC PHARMACEUTICAL AGENTS

ANALGESICS

PARACETAMOL

Paracetamol causes hepatic damage in overdose. More rarely, it can also cause renal failure. The management of a patient with paracetamol overdose is summarised in Figure 3.3. If a patient presents within 1 hour of the paracetamol overdose, activated charcoal can be given in addition to the management shown in the figure. The antidote of choice is intravenous N-acetylcysteine, which provides complete protection against toxicity if given within 10 hours of the overdose; its efficacy declines thereafter. For this reason, if a patient presents more than 8 hours after ingestion, N-acetylcysteine administration should not be delayed to await a paracetamol blood concentration result but should be stopped if the paracetamol concentration is subsequently shown to be below the treatment line. Methionine 12 g orally 4-hourly, to a total of four doses, is a suitable alternative antidote for paracetamol poisoning when

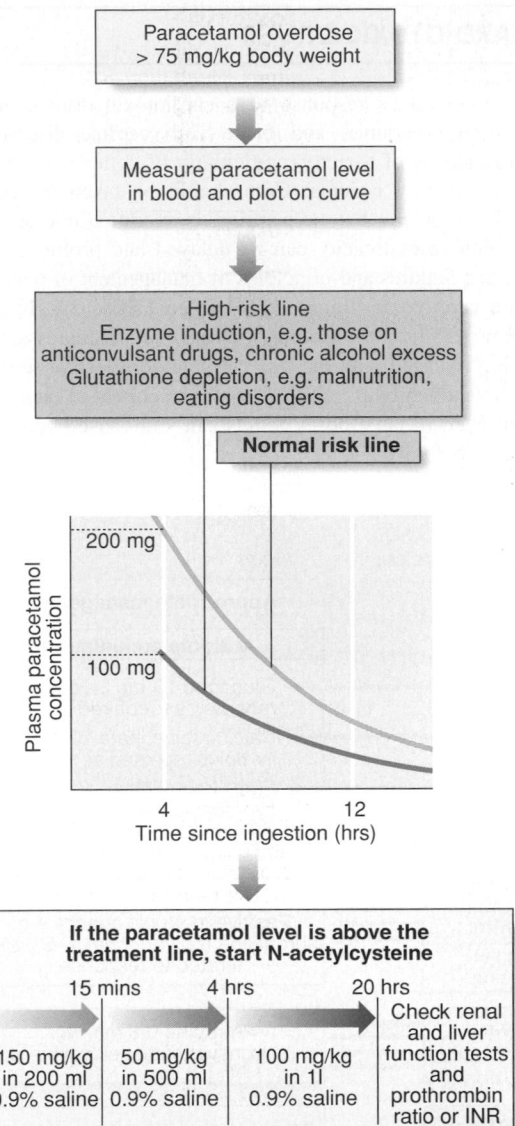

Fig. 3.3 The management of a paracetamol overdose patient.
Do not check a paracetamol concentration before 4 hours have elapsed; it is uninterpretable. If more than 8 hours have elapsed since ingestion, start the N-acetylcysteine immediately and only stop it if the concentration is below the treatment line. (INR = international normalised ratio)

N-acetylcysteine is not available. If a patient presents more than 15 hours after ingestion, liver function tests, prothrombin ratio (or international normalised ratio—INR) and renal function tests should be carried out, the antidote started, and a poisons information centre or local liver unit contacted for advice. In some cases an arterial blood gas sample will need to be taken. Liver transplantation should be considered in individuals who develop acute liver failure due to paracetamol (see p. 845).

If multiple ingestions of paracetamol have taken place over several hours or days (i.e. a staggered overdose), there is no merit in measuring the plasma paracetamol concentration as it will be uninterpretable. Such patients should be given N-acetylcysteine if the paracetamol dose exceeds 150 mg/kg body weight in any one 24-hour period or 75 mg/kg body weight in 'high-risk groups' (as shown in Fig. 3.3).

SALICYLATES (ASPIRIN)

Salicylate ingestion at doses greater than 150, 250 and 500 mg aspirin/kg body weight produces mild, moderate and severe poisoning respectively. Salicylate poisoning can also occur with ingestion of oil of wintergreen or when salicylic ointment (e.g. verruca remover) is applied extensively to skin. Aspirin overdose commonly produces nausea, vomiting, tinnitus and deafness. Direct stimulation of the respiratory centre produces hyperventilation. Peripheral vasodilatation with bounding pulses and profuse sweating occurs in moderately severe poisoning. Petechiae and subconjunctival haemorrhages can occur due to reduced platelet aggregation but are self-limiting. Signs of serious salicylate poisoning include metabolic acidosis, renal failure and central nervous system (CNS) effects such as agitation, confusion, coma and fits. Rarely, pulmonary and cerebral oedema occur. Death can occur as a consequence of CNS depression and cardiovascular collapse. The development of a metabolic acidosis is a bad prognostic sign, not least because acidosis results in increased salicylate transfer across the blood–brain barrier.

It is important to measure a plasma salicylate concentration in all but the most trivial overdose. This is best undertaken at 6 hours or later after ingestion because of continued absorption of the drug. The salicylate concentration needs to be interpreted in conjunction with the clinical features and acid–base status of the patient. Any significant metabolic acidosis should be treated with intravenous sodium bicarbonate (8.4%), and the volume given titrated to give an arterial pH of 7.4–7.5. Patients are often very dehydrated, and it is important to replace fluid loss from vomiting and sweating. However, injudicious use of intravenous fluids may precipitate pulmonary oedema. The use of multiple doses of activated charcoal (see p. 168) in salicylate poisoning is controversial, but this approach is currently recommended until the salicylate concentration has peaked. Urinary alkalinisation (see Fig. 3.2, p. 169) is indicated for adult patients with salicylate concentrations of 600–800 mg/l. Haemodialysis is very effective at removing salicylate and correcting acid–base and fluid balance abnormalities and should be considered when serum concentrations are above 800 mg/l in adult patients and above 700 mg/l in the elderly. Other indications for haemodialysis in acute salicylate overdose are metabolic acidosis resistant to correction, severe CNS effects such as coma or convulsions, pulmonary oedema and acute renal failure.

NON-STEROIDAL ANTI-INFLAMMATORY DRUGS (NSAIDs)

Overdose of most NSAIDs usually causes little more than minor gastrointestinal upset including mild abdominal pain, vomiting and diarrhoea. However, 10–20% of such patients have convulsions; these are usually self-limiting and seldom need treatment other than airway protection and oxygen. Serious features include coma, prolonged fits, apnoea and bradycardia but these are very rare. Deaths have been reported after massive overdose of ibuprofen, but not with mefenamic acid. Rarely, renal failure ensues. Features of toxicity tend to occur early and are unlikely to develop later than 6 hours after the overdose. Liver and renal function may be affected, and therefore electrolytes, liver function tests and a full blood count should be taken in all but the most trivial overdoses. The half-lives of most NSAIDs are less than 12 hours, so elimination methods are not needed. Activated charcoal should be given if more than 100 mg/kg body weight of ibuprofen or more than 10 tablets of another NSAID have been taken in the last hour. Non-self-limiting seizures are treated with intravenous diazepam, and gastro-intestinal irritation with oral H_2-blockers (e.g. ranitidine).

CARDIOTOXIC DRUGS

An individual's response to a cardiotoxic drug overdose is highly variable, and those with cardiac disease are more at risk of toxicity, particularly of complications such as pulmonary oedema. Care should be taken to identify whether or not the preparation is modified-release since in such cases toxicity can be delayed and prolonged. The cardiac features and principles of management of poisoning with cardiotoxic drugs are shown in Figure 3.4. In many countries, the more cardiotoxic tricyclic antidepressants are being replaced with the less cardiotoxic selective serotonin re-uptake inhibitors (SSRIs) for the treatment of depression. However, in large doses SSRIs can still cause hypotension and arrhythmias.

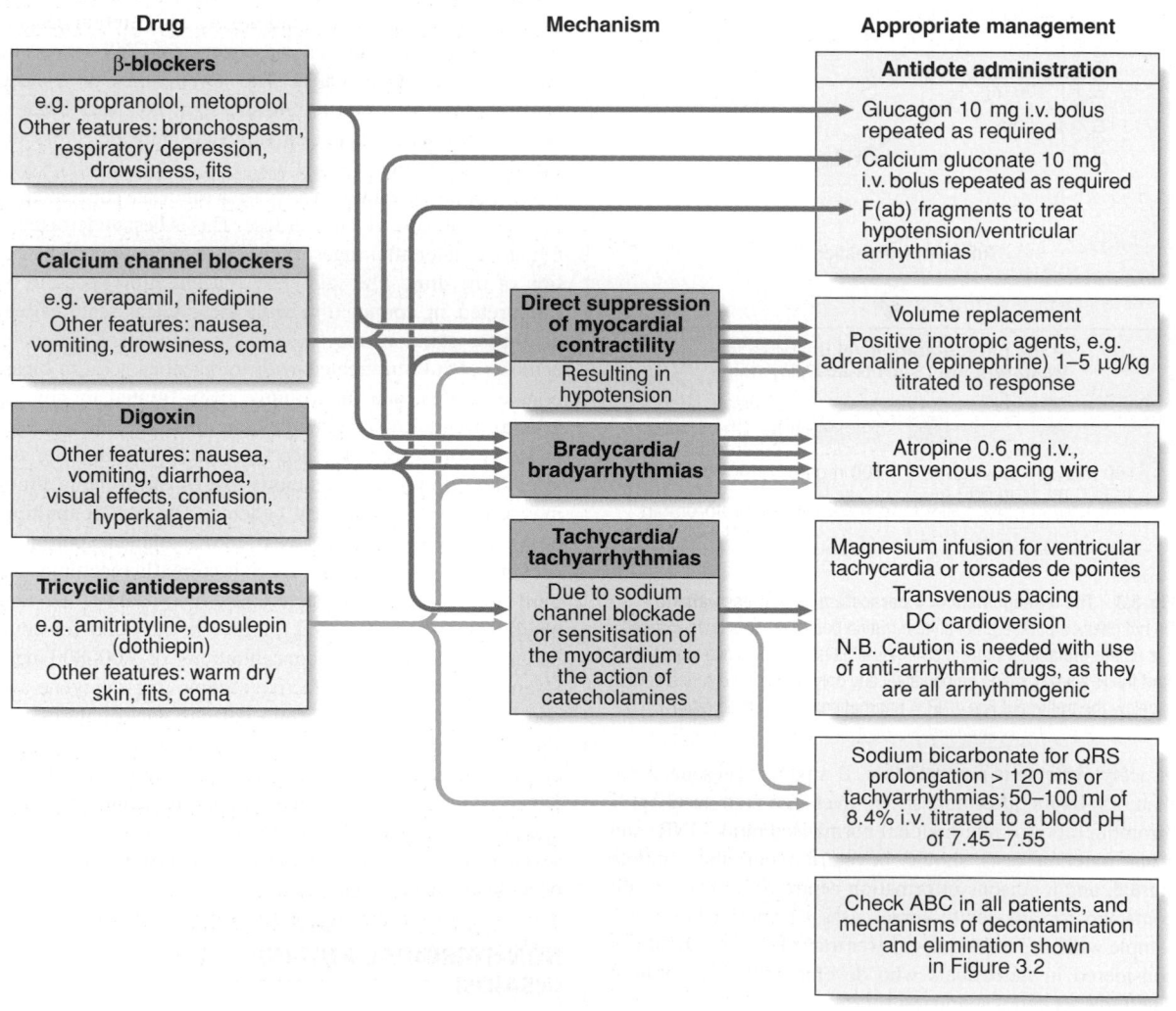

Fig. 3.4 Mechanisms and management of poisoning with cardiotoxic drugs.

ANTIMALARIALS

CHLOROQUINE

Symptoms and signs of chloroquine overdose usually start within 1 hour of ingestion and include nausea, vomiting, agitation, drowsiness, hypokalaemia, headaches and visual disturbances. After large ingestions coma, convulsions, hypotension (due to the negative inotropic effect) and arrhythmias (widened QRS and QT intervals, ventricular tachycardia—including torsade de pointes, and ventricular fibrillation) occur.

Activated charcoal should be given and gastric lavage considered in all patients who present within 1 hour of ingestion of more than 15 mg/kg chloroquine. Cardiovascular complications can be managed by the techniques shown in Figure 3.4. The plasma potassium should be monitored, although hypokalaemia may have a protective effect and should not be corrected in the early stages of poisoning. If hypokalaemia persists beyond 8 hours, potassium should be replaced with caution. High-dose diazepam (2 mg/kg body weight i.v. over 30 minutes) may have a protective effect in chloroquine poisoning, but respiratory support should be available before it is given.

QUININE

Quinine salts are widely used in the treatment of malaria and nocturnal cramps. The average fatal dose in an adult is 8 g, although deaths have been reported with as little as 1.5 g in an adult and 900 mg in a child. Quinine causes retinal vasoconstriction and also has a direct toxic effect on retinal photoreceptor cells. At 6–10 hours after ingestion, blurred vision and impaired colour perception start and can progress to constriction of the visual field, scotoma and complete blindness. The pupils become dilated and unresponsive to light, and fundoscopy shows retinal artery spasm progressing to disc pallor and retinal oedema. Visual loss can be permanent. Other features include nausea, vomiting, tinnitus, deafness, headache and tremor. In large overdoses ataxia, drowsiness, coma, respiratory depression, haemolysis and cardiac effects can occur. The latter include hypotension, ECG changes (prolongation of the QRS and corrected QT interval (QT_c), atrioventricular block) and arrhythmias (ventricular tachycardia—torsade de pointes and ventricular fibrillation).

Maintenance of the airway and ventilation is critical. Gastric lavage should be considered if a patient presents within 1 hour of ingestion of more than 15 mg/kg of quinine, and multiple-dose activated charcoal should be given to all patients who have ingested an amount of quinine above this threshold dose. All patients should have a 12-lead ECG, have blood taken for urea, electrolytes and glucose, and have cardiac monitoring. Visual effects of quinine are largely untreatable. In the past many measures were advocated, such as stellate ganglion block and retrobulbar or i.v. injections of vasodilators including nitrates; these measures are now obsolete. Cardiovascular complications can be managed by the techniques shown in Figure 3.4. Haemodialysis and haemoperfusion are ineffective in quinine poisoning.

ANTIDIABETIC AGENTS

These include the sulphonylureas (e.g. chlorpropamide, glibenclamide, gliclazide, glipizide, tolbutamide), biguanides (metformin) and insulin.

Antidiabetic agents can cause hypoglycaemia when taken in overdose, although insulin is non-toxic if ingested. The onset and duration of hypoglycaemia vary, but can last for several days with the longer-acting agents such as chlorpropamide and isophane and lente insulins. Hypoglycaemia may manifest as agitation, sweating, confusion, tachycardia, hypothermia, drowsiness, coma or convulsions (see p. 652). Permanent neurological damage can occur if the hypoglycaemia is prolonged. Metformin can cause a lactic acidosis in overdose, particularly when co-ingested with ethanol or in elderly patients and those with renal or hepatic impairment, and is associated with a high (> 50%) mortality. Other clinical effects observed after metformin overdose include nausea and vomiting, diarrhoea, abdominal pain, drowsiness, coma, hypotension and cardiovascular collapse.

Activated charcoal should be given (and gastric lavage considered) to all patients who present within 1 hour of ingestion of more than the normal therapeutic dose of an oral hypoglycaemic agent. Formal measurement of (venous) blood glucose (not just visually read strips or meter) and urea and electrolytes should be carried out and the tests repeated regularly. For medico-legal purposes, a blood sample may be required for subsequent measurement of insulin, pro-insulin and C-peptide levels. Hypoglycaemia should be corrected urgently with 50 ml 50% dextrose given i.v. if the patient is unconscious or with a sugary drink if the patient is conscious. This should be followed by an infusion of 10% or 20% dextrose titrated to the patient's blood glucose to prevent further hypoglycaemia. Patients may need dextrose infusions for several days, depending on the agent ingested/injected. Potassium replacement is necessary and should be guided by frequent measurement of urea and electrolytes. As a general rule, add 10–20 mmol potassium chloride to each litre of dextrose. Failure to regain consciousness within a few minutes of normalisation of the blood glucose can indicate that a CNS depressant has also been ingested, that the hypoglycaemia has been prolonged, that there is another cause for the coma (e.g. cerebral haemorrhage) or that the patient has cerebral oedema (see p. 846).

DRUGS LESS COMMONLY TAKEN IN OVERDOSE

Box 3.7 gives an overview of the clinical features and management of overdose of other drugs not discussed in detail above.

3.7 DRUGS TAKEN LESS COMMONLY IN OVERDOSE ⓘ

Drug	Features	Management
Anticonvulsants	Cerebellar signs Fits Coma Cardiovascular toxicity	Multiple-dose activated charcoal Cardiovascular support (as Fig. 3.4) I.v. diazepam for fits
Antihistamines	Drowsiness Cardiac arrhythmias	Activated charcoal within 1 hour Cardiovascular support (as Fig. 3.4)
Chlorpromazine/ haloperidol	Hypotension Drowsiness Fits	Single-dose activated charcoal Cardiovascular support (as Fig. 3.4) I.v. diazepam for fits
Iron tablets	Vomiting Haematemesis Abdominal pain Coma Convulsions Shock Metabolic acidosis Hepatic failure	Ingestion of < 30 mg elemental iron/kg body weight: no active treatment Ingestion of > 30 mg/kg: 　Check abdominal radiograph 　Perform gastric lavage/ whole bowel irrigation 　Check a serum iron concentration and above 90 μmol/l treat with i.v. desferrioxamine, especially if clinical features are present
Isoniazid	Peripheral neuropathy Fits	Activated charcoal I.v. pyridoxine I.v. diazepam for fits
Lithium	Nausea Vomiting Tremors Fits Confusion Coma	Does NOT bind to charcoal Whole bowel irrigation Increased hydration, avoid diuretics In severe cases: haemodialysis
Theophylline	Cardiac arrhythmias Fits Coma	Cardiovascular support (as Fig. 3.4) Multiple-dose activated charcoal I.v. diazepam for fits
Thyroxine	Tremor Tachycardia	Check thyroid function Treat symptomatically with propranolol p.o.
Zidovudine	Drowsiness Nausea Bone marrow suppression Fits	Activated charcoal Regular full blood count Diazepam for fits

---

ISSUES IN OLDER PEOPLE
POISONING BY SPECIFIC PHARMACEUTICAL AGENTS

- In salicylate poisoning in the elderly haemodialysis should be started at lower serum drug levels (see p. 171).
- Older people are more likely to develop lactic acidosis following metformin overdose.

DRUGS OF MISUSE

CANNABIS

The term 'cannabis' refers to all psychoactive substances derived from the dried leaves and flowers of the plant *Cannabis sativa*. Marijuana refers to any part of the plant used to induce effects, and hashish is the dried resin from the flower tops. Cannabis is usually dried and either smoked or eaten. Slang terms include grass, pot, ganja, spliff and reefer. When it is smoked, the onset of effect is 10–30 minutes; after ingestion the onset is 1–3 hours. The duration of effect is 4–8 hours. In low doses cannabis produces euphoria and perceptual alterations, followed by relaxation and drowsiness, hypertension, tachycardia, slurred speech and ataxia. High doses produce acute paranoid psychosis, anxiety, confusion, hallucinations and distortion of time and space. Intravenous misuse of the crude extract of cannabis may cause nausea and vomiting, diarrhoea, abdominal pain, fever, hypotension, pulmonary oedema, acute renal failure, disseminated intravascular coagulation and death.

Serious poisoning resulting from ingestion or smoking of cannabis is extremely rare. For patients with drug-induced psychosis reassurance is usually sufficient but i.v. diazepam may be used for sedation. Hypotension usually responds well to intravenous fluids. All patients who have injected cannabis should be admitted, and careful management of fluid and electrolyte balance is essential, owing to the risks of acute renal failure and pulmonary oedema.

BENZODIAZEPINES

In general, lone benzodiazepine overdoses are remarkably safe and near-full recovery takes place within 24 hours. Difficulties occur when other CNS depressants, such as tricyclic antidepressants, opioids or alcohol, are taken in addition or when an overdose occurs in susceptible groups such as the elderly or those with chronic obstructive pulmonary disease. Drowsiness and mid-position or dilated pupils are common and occur within 3 hours of ingestion. Ataxia, dysarthria, nystagmus and confusion are also observed. Coma may follow, but in lone benzodiazepine overdose a GCS grade below 10 (see p. 1143) is rare. Minor hypotension and respiratory depression may occur. Respiratory arrest is uncommon but can occur after shorter-acting agents such as midazolam.

Gastric lavage is not advised in pure benzodiazepine overdose. Activated charcoal, if required, can be given within 1 hour of the overdose, particularly in a mixed overdose. Impaired consciousness is treated conventionally, with particular attention to maintenance of the airway. Observation should be for at least 6 hours post-ingestion, or for 24 hours in more serious cases. Oxygen saturation monitoring using a pulse oximeter is useful for ascertaining the adequacy of ventilation if significant CNS depression is present. Flumazenil is a specific benzodiazepine antagonist but it is not used in the vast majority of cases of poisoning with benzodiazepines. Flumazenil must never be used in patients with a history of convulsions or toxin-induced cardiotoxicity, or in those who have co-ingested tricyclic antidepressants. In such circumstances, seizures and ventricular arrhythmias can be precipitated.

CRACK/COCAINE

Cocaine (hydrochloride) is usually purchased as a white crystalline powder or colourless crystals and may be sniffed into the nose (snorted) or injected intravenously. 'Crack' is cocaine that has been separated from the hydrochloride base (free-base), melted and smoked in a pipe or mixed with tobacco in a cigarette. Crack is usually sold in 'rocks' containing 150 mg of cocaine or as a 'line' of cocaine for snorting that contains 20–30 mg of the drug. While the toxic dose is very variable and depends on individual tolerance, the presence of other drugs and the route of administration, ingestion of any amount over 1 g is potentially fatal.

After intranasal use effects are experienced within minutes and tend to last 20–90 minutes. With intravenous use or oral intake the peak 'high' occurs within 10 and 45–90 minutes respectively. Smoking crack causes a peak 'high' within 10 minutes. In most cases the effects begin to resolve in about 20 minutes post-onset, except when taken intranasally. In fatal poisoning the onset and progression of symptoms are accelerated and death may occur in minutes. Survival beyond 3 hours indicates that the patient is unlikely to die.

Mild to moderate intoxication with cocaine causes euphoria, agitation, aggression, cerebellar signs (see p. 1135), dilated pupils, vomiting, pallor, headache, cold sweats, twitching, pyrexia, tachycardia, hallucinations and hypertension. Features of severe intoxication include convulsions, coma, muscular paralysis, severe hypertension and stroke. Coronary artery spasm may result in myocardial ischaemia or infarction, even in patients with normal coronary arteries, and this leads to hypotension, cyanosis and ventricular arrhythmias. Hyperthermia associated with rhabdomyolysis, acute renal failure and disseminated intravascular coagulation may also occur.

Activated charcoal should be given in any patient presenting within 1 hour of oral ingestion, irrespective of the amount taken. All patients should be observed with ECG monitoring for a minimum of 2 hours. Blood pressure, heart rate and body temperature should also be monitored and the patient observed carefully for the development of specific complications (see Box 3.8).

ECSTASY/AMPHETAMINES

MDMA (3,4-methylenedioxymethamphetamine, ecstasy) is a 'designer' amphetamine also known as E, Adam, white dove, white burger, or red and black. Amphetamines and the newer designer amphetamines are virtually indistinguishable in their clinical effects. Effects occur within 1 hour of ingestion and last 4–6 hours following doses of 75–150 mg but up to 48 hours after the ingestion of 100–300 mg. However, tolerance is common, and most regular users need to take considerably higher doses.

Supraventricular and ventricular arrhythmias are common and may cause death. Agitation or drowsiness is also common. Whilst the vast majority of patients who have taken ecstasy are profoundly dehydrated, a small proportion develop hyponatraemia, usually through drinking excessive amounts of water in the absence of sufficient exertion to sweat off the fluid. Antidiuretic hormone secretion may also contribute to the development of hyponatraemia. Other features of intoxication with amphetamines or ecstasy include nausea, hyper-reflexia, muscle pain, trismus (jaw-clenching), dilated pupils, blurred vision, sweating, dry mouth, agitation, visual hallucinations and anxiety. Severe intoxication is characterised by coma, convulsions, hypertension and cardiac arrhythmias. A hyperthermic (5-HT-like) syndrome may develop with rigidity, hyper-reflexia and hyperpyrexia (> 39°C) leading to hypotension, rhabdomyolysis, metabolic acidosis, acute renal failure, disseminated intravascular coagulation, hepatocellular necrosis, acute respiratory distress syndrome and cardiovascular collapse. In view of this it is important to measure urea and electrolytes, creatine kinase and blood glucose, carry out a full blood count and liver function tests, and observe all symptomatic cases with ECG, blood pressure and temperature monitoring for at least 6 hours post-exposure. A 12-lead ECG is required. The complications described above should be treated in the same way as for cocaine (see Box 3.8).

3.8 COMPLICATIONS AND MANAGEMENT OF ACUTE COCAINE INTOXICATION	
Complication	**Management**
Hypertension	Oral diazepam, nifedipine or doxazosin
Hypertension with encephalopathy, infarction, stroke or proteinuria	I.v. therapy: nitrates or sodium nitroprusside
Supraventricular tachycardia	I.v. verapamil; avoid β-blockers, which cause hypertension due to unopposed alpha stimulation
Cocaine-induced angina	I.v. or buccal nitrates are treatment of choice; avoid β-blockers
Cocaine-induced myocardial infarction	Use of thrombolytic agents usually not necessary because mechanism is spasm rather than thrombosis
Hyperthermia > 39°C	Cool i.v. fluids, dantrolene; paralyse and ventilate the patient if hyperthermia persists despite these measures
Agitation or psychosis	Oral diazepam; phenothiazines and haloperidol should be avoided as they lower the threshold for convulsions

Selective serotonergic antagonists (e.g. cyproheptadine/ketanserin) may become available for use in patients with a 5-HT-like syndrome to reduce temperature and rigidity by central mechanisms.

GAMMAHYDROXYBUTYRATE (GHB)

GHB is marketed illegally for body building and weight loss and as a replacement for L-tryptophan. Slang terms include liquid X, cherry meth, easy lay, scoop and GBH. It is commonly dissolved in water to produce a clear, colourless liquid that tastes of seaweed. Many misusers simply 'guzzle' it until they reach an adequate high, which is often achieved shortly before becoming unconscious. Owing to the drowsiness that may occur, it is sometimes mixed with amphetamines to prolong the 'high' for several hours. The severity and duration of effects seem to be dose-dependent. Doses of 10–30 mg/kg cause mild effects such as nausea, diarrhoea, confusion, vertigo, tremor, extrapyramidal signs, agitation and euphoria, whereas higher doses (30–50 mg/kg) cause drowsiness, coma, bradycardia, hypotension and respiratory depression. More than 50 mg/kg causes decreased cardiac output and increasingly severe respiratory depression, fits and coma. The effects are potentiated by other CNS depressants (e.g. alcohol, benzodiazepines, opioids and neuroleptic drugs). Bizarrely, patients often recover quickly (within 1–2 hours), with scenarios such as self-extubation and rapid reversal of coma seen. Coma usually resolves spontaneously within 2–4 hours, but may on occasion persist for as long as 96 hours.

Urea and electrolytes and glucose should be measured in all but the most trivial of cases. Activated charcoal treatment is recommended within 1 hour for ingestions of more than 20 mg/kg. All patients should be observed for a minimum of 2 hours, monitoring blood pressure, heart rate, respiratory rate and oxygenation. Patients who remain symptomatic after this time should be admitted and observed until symptoms resolve, but require supportive care only.

LSD

d-Lysergic acid diethylamide (LSD) is a synthetic hallucinogen. Common slang terms are acid, trips, dots, paper mushrooms or 'L'. LSD is usually ingested as small squares of impregnated absorbent paper, which are often printed with a distinctive design, or as 'microdots'. Patients presenting to hospital usually do so as a result of a 'bad trip', panic reaction, vivid visual hallucinations or aggression, or after a suicide attempt. The individual may be found wandering in a confused, agitated state. Dilated pupils are common. Peak effects are seen within 30–60 minutes of an oral dose. LSD itself is of low acute toxicity; fatalities are a result of behavioural changes induced by LSD, leading to accidents such as drowning. Flashbacks can occur within hours or months after acute or chronic misuse. These may be precipitated by physical or emotional stress.

Patients with psychotic reactions or CNS depression should be observed in hospital. The patient should be placed in a quiet, dimly lit room to minimise external stimulation. Where sedation is required, diazepam is the drug of choice; haloperidol is used as the second agent if diazepam is ineffective. The use of chlorpromazine has been associated with cardiovascular collapse in LSD intoxication.

OPIOIDS

These include heroin, morphine, methadone, codeine, pethidine, dihydrocodeine and dextropropoxyphene. The hallmarks of opioid analgesic poisoning are:

- depressed respiration
- pinpoint or small pupils
- depressed conscious level
- signs of intravenous drug misuse (e.g. needle track marks).

Severe poisoning is indicated by respiratory depression, hypotension, non-cardiogenic pulmonary oedema and hypothermia. Death occurs by respiratory arrest or from aspiration of gastric contents. Poisoning with dextropropoxyphene (the opioid moiety of co-proxamol) may also result in cardiac conduction effects, particularly QRS prolongation, ventricular arrhythmias and heart block. Unconscious patients should always have their paracetamol concentration checked because of the prevalence of combination opioid/paracetamol drugs. Symptoms of opioid poisoning can be prolonged for up to 48 hours, particularly after ingestion of methadone, which has a long half-life.

Steps should be taken to ensure a clear airway and, if necessary, provide respiratory support. Supplementary high-flow oxygen should be administered. The need for endotracheal intubation can often be avoided by prompt administration of adequate doses of the opioid antagonist naloxone (see below). Oxygen saturation monitoring and arterial blood gases demonstrate the adequacy of ventilation in those whose respiration has been compromised. The treatment of coma (see p. 1143), fits (see p. 1121) and hypotension (see Fig. 3.4, p. 172) is detailed elsewhere. Non-cardiogenic pulmonary oedema in severe cases does not usually respond to diuretic therapy, and CPAP and/or PEEP (see p. 204) may be required.

Naloxone is a specific opioid antagonist that reverses the above features of opioid toxicity. It should be used as a bolus dose (0.8–2 mg i.v.) in adults. This should be repeated every 2 minutes as necessary until the level of consciousness and respiratory rate increase and the pupils dilate. A total dose of as much as 10–20 mg may be required in some cases. Administration of too much naloxone should be avoided as it can precipitate a withdrawal reaction, characterised by gastrointestinal effects, sweating and fits. It is best to titrate repeat bolus doses, aiming for a GCS of 13–14 (not 15). After the initial i.v. bolus, an infusion of naloxone may be needed because the half-life of the antidote is much shorter than the half-lives of most opioids. As a guide, two-thirds of the bolus dose initially required to wake the patient should be infused each hour. Patients must be carefully observed for recurrence of coma and respiratory depression, usually for at least 18–24 hours. It is particularly important that patients are observed for recurrence of CNS depression for at least 4–6 hours after the last dose of naloxone is given. Naloxone has been reported to cause pulmonary oedema and ventricular arrhythmias, but such events are infrequent and not enough to outweigh its use.

MANAGEMENT OF BODYPACKERS

Bodypackers ingest drugs of misuse (particularly cocaine and heroin) wrapped in clingfilm or packed into condoms for the purpose of drug smuggling. It is important to ask the patient exactly what is in the packets and to obtain an abdominal radiograph to help establish where the packets are located and how many are present (see Fig. 3.5). If they are in the stomach, they can be removed endoscopically, taking extreme care not to rupture the packages. Alternatively, they can be allowed to pass through with the help of a laxative such as lactulose. Paraffin-based laxatives should not be used, as this may increase the risk of packet rupture. If packages are in the small or large bowel, either laxatives can be given, or whole bowel irrigation can be performed to aid their speedy recovery (see p. 170). Patients should be admitted and observed closely until all packets are recovered. Rupture of the packets can be fatal and rapid because of the large doses carried. Packets carried in the vagina or rectum should be removed manually.

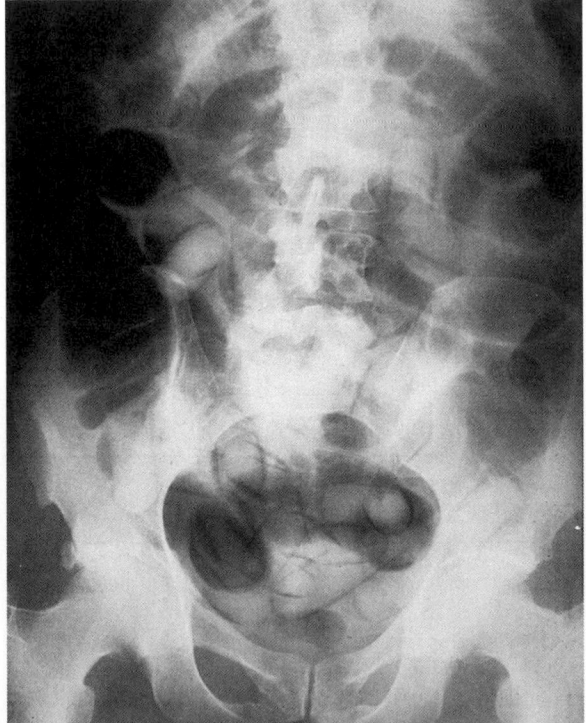

Fig. 3.5 Abdominal radiograph of a bodypacker showing multiple drug-filled condoms.

CHEMICALS AND PESTICIDES

Features of poisoning on clinical examination that point to the chemical, gas or pesticide responsible are shown in Figure 3.6.

CARBON MONOXIDE AND SMOKE

Carbon monoxide is a colourless, non-irritant, odourless gas; sources include smoke from fires, car exhausts and the incomplete burning of gas fires or cookers. The risk of carbon monoxide poisoning is greatest where ventilation is poor. As well as carbon monoxide, smoke produced in house fires contains a mixture of soot and organic particles, together with other gases such as hydrogen sulphide. Carbon monoxide is the major cause of death by poisoning in the United Kingdom and many other countries. It reduces the oxygen-carrying capacity of the blood by binding to haemoglobin to form carboxyhaemoglobin, and impairs the function of cytochrome oxidases. This impairs oxygen delivery from blood to tissues and its utilisation within tissues. Death may result from the acute cardiac and neurological sequelae, and there are also concerns over long-term effects from acute and chronic exposure.

The early clinical features of acute carbon monoxide poisoning are headache, nausea and vomiting, ataxia and nystagmus. Later features include drowsiness, hyperventilation, hyper-reflexia and shivering. Central and peripheral cyanosis occurs. Some patients are disinhibited, agitated or aggressive rather than drowsy. Convulsions, coma, hypotension, respiratory depression, ECG changes (ST segment depression, T-wave abnormalities, ventricular tachycardia or ventricular fibrillation) and cardiovascular collapse may occur in severe cases. Cerebral oedema is common and focal neurological signs can be present. Carbon monoxide-induced rhabdomyolysis leading to myoglobinuria and renal failure has been reported. Significant abnormalities on physical examination include impaired short-term memory and cerebellar signs (past-pointing and unsteadiness of gait, particularly heel-toe walking). Any one of these signs would classify the episode as severe. Rigidity, hyper-reflexia and extensor plantars may occur in mild, moderate or severe cases. Carbon monoxide poisoning in pregnancy is likely to cause miscarriage or premature labour due to fetal hypoxia. Patients recovering from carbon monoxide poisoning may suffer neurological sequelae including tremor, personality changes, memory impairment, visual loss, inability to concentrate and Parkinsonian features. Chronic carbon monoxide poisoning gives symptoms which are difficult to distinguish from influenza, i.e. nausea, vomiting, headache, lethargy, and aches and pains.

The carboxyhaemoglobin (COHb) concentration is of value in confirming the diagnosis of acute carbon monoxide poisoning, although it may not be elevated sufficiently to be diagnostic in chronic cases. However, the degree of COHb elevation does not correlate well with the severity

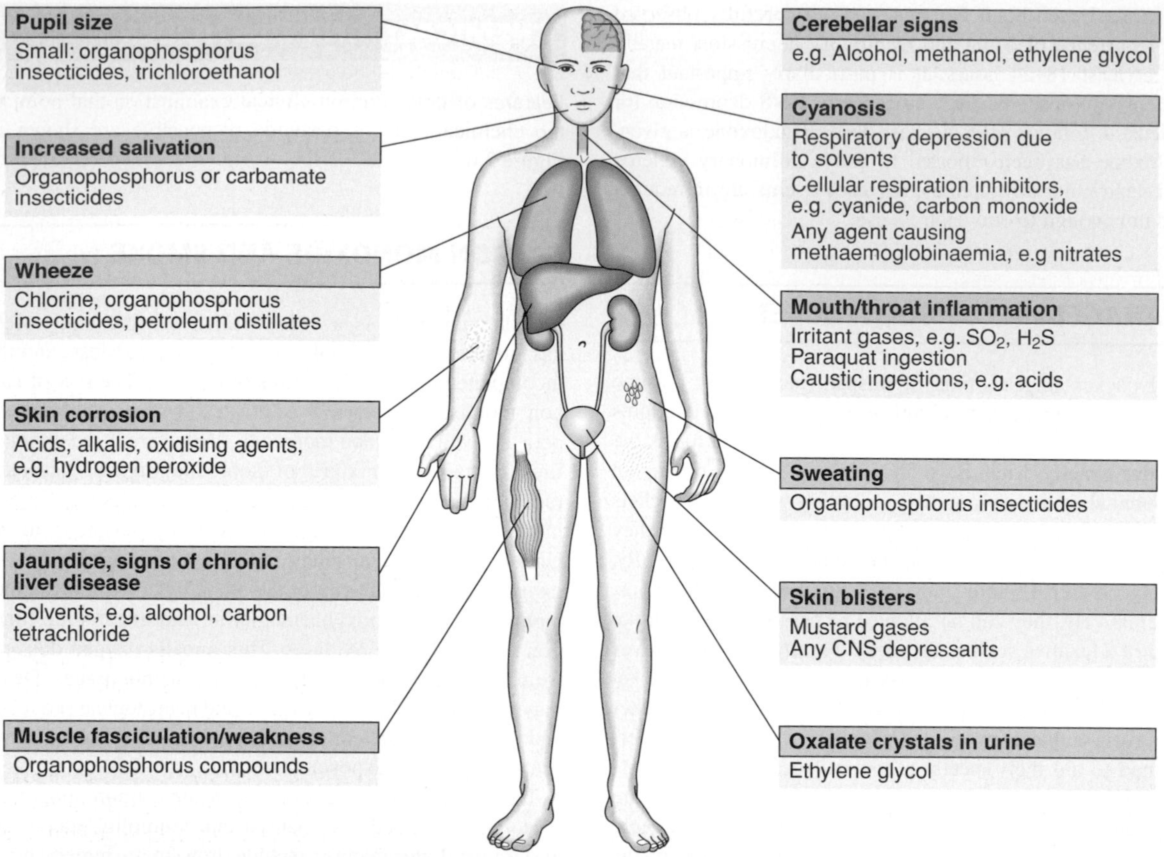

Pupil size
Small: organophosphorus insecticides, trichloroethanol

Increased salivation
Organophosphorus or carbamate insecticides

Wheeze
Chlorine, organophosphorus insecticides, petroleum distillates

Skin corrosion
Acids, alkalis, oxidising agents, e.g. hydrogen peroxide

Jaundice, signs of chronic liver disease
Solvents, e.g. alcohol, carbon tetrachloride

Muscle fasciculation/weakness
Organophosphorus compounds

Cerebellar signs
e.g. Alcohol, methanol, ethylene glycol

Cyanosis
Respiratory depression due to solvents
Cellular respiration inhibitors, e.g. cyanide, carbon monoxide
Any agent causing methaemoglobinaemia, e.g nitrates

Mouth/throat inflammation
Irritant gases, e.g. SO_2, H_2S
Paraquat ingestion
Caustic ingestions, e.g. acids

Sweating
Organophosphorus insecticides

Skin blisters
Mustard gases
Any CNS depressants

Oxalate crystals in urine
Ethylene glycol

Fig. 3.6   Clinical signs of poisoning by chemicals, pesticides or gases.

of poisoning, even acutely. Normal values are up to 3–5% and can be as high as 6–10% in smokers. An ECG should be performed in anyone with acute poisoning, especially in patients with pre-existing heart disease. Anyone with serious poisoning also requires arterial blood gas analysis. Oxygen saturation readings by pulse oximetry are misleading (see below).

The most important first step in treating carbon monoxide poisoning is to move the patient away from the source of exposure. It is vital to ensure that the airway, breathing and circulation are adequately maintained and give supplementary oxygen as soon as possible. Oxygen should be given in high flow, e.g. 12 litres per minute, ideally through a tightly fitting facemask such as a CPAP mask. It should be continued until the COHb is less than 5% and for at least 6 hours after exposure. Sometimes 12–20 hours are required for this to take place. Unfortunately, pulse oximeters measure both carboxyhaemoglobin and oxyhaemoglobin and so a normal saturation value does not give grounds for reassurance. The use of sodium bicarbonate intravenously should be avoided, as this will impair oxygen release to tissues. Care should be taken to avoid excessive intravenous fluid administration, particularly in the elderly, because of the risk of pulmonary oedema. Most deaths occur in those who have arrested at the scene or who are unconscious on arrival in hospital. Blood pressure should be monitored and convulsions controlled with

3.9 INDICATIONS FOR CONSIDERING HYPERBARIC OXYGEN THERAPY IN CARBON MONOXIDE POISONING

- Focal neurological signs, especially cerebellar ones
- COHb at any time > 40%
- Patient is pregnant
- Patient is unconscious at any time

diazepam. The use of hyperbaric oxygen is controversial; Box 3.9 lists the current indications for such therapy. The logistical difficulties of transporting sick patients to hyperbaric chambers should not be under-estimated.

ORGANOPHOSPHORUS INSECTICIDES/NERVE GASES

Organophosphorus compounds were initially developed as chemical warfare agents, e.g. sarin. Although they have numerous complex actions, their principal effect is inhibition of cholinesterase enzymes, particularly acetylcholinesterase (AChE) (see Fig. 3.7), which is very slow to 'age', yielding the active enzyme once again. This leads to accumulation of acetylcholine at muscarinic receptors (cholinergic effector cells), nicotinic receptors (skeletal neuromuscular junction and autonomic ganglia) and in the CNS. Organophosphorus compounds are well absorbed by ingestion and inhalation, and through the skin. The onset, severity and duration of poisoning depend on the route of exposure and the agent involved; onset can be as early as 5 minutes after exposure or be delayed for up to 12 hours.

Features of acute ingestion include muscarinic effects (vomiting, abdominal pain, diarrhoea, miosis, sweating, hypersalivation and dyspnoea due to bronchoconstriction and excessive bronchial secretions), nicotinic effects (muscle fasciculation, tremor and later weakness) and CNS effects (anxiety, headache, loss of memory, drowsiness and coma). Although bradycardia would be predicted from the mechanism of action, tachycardia occurs in about one-third of cases. Later, flaccid muscle paralysis with paralysis of limb muscles, respiratory muscles and sometimes extra-ocular muscles occurs. Respiratory muscle paralysis, bronchial constriction and the presence of copious respiratory secretions contribute to respiratory failure, but depression of respiratory drive is probably the single most important factor and respiratory complications are the major cause of death in severely poisoned patients. Coma is present in severely poisoned patients; rarely, hyperglycaemia, complete heart block and arrhythmias may occur.

A minority of patients develop the intermediate syndrome. This is characterised by cranial nerve and brain-stem lesions and a proximal neuropathy commencing 1–4 days after acute poisoning and lasting for approximately 3 weeks. Respiratory depression is a complication and ventilatory support is required as the intermediate syndrome is unresponsive to atropine and oximes.

Organophosphate-induced delayed neuropathy starts 2 weeks or more after exposure and is the result of degeneration of large myelinated motor and sensory fibres. Initial flaccidity and muscle weakness in the arms and legs give rise to a clumsy shuffling gait and are followed later by spasticity, hypertonicity, hyper-reflexia and clonus. In many

patients recovery is limited to the arms and hands, and damage to lower extremities, such as foot drop, is permanent. Not all organophosphorus compounds cause delayed neuropathy and those that do have been phased out in most developed countries.

If possible, the diagnosis should be confirmed by measuring AChE activity, preferably in both erythrocytes and plasma; the availability of this assay is limited and clinical features are more helpful than red cell cholinesterase measurements in determining the severity of intoxication. However, there is an approximate correlation between cholinesterase activity and clinical effects (~50% cholinesterase activity in subclinical poisoning, 20–50% activity in mild poisoning and less than 10% activity in severe poisoning). An ECG should be carried out in all patients, and urea, electrolytes and glucose monitored.

The management of acute organophosphorus poisoning includes clearing the airway, ensuring adequate ventilation and giving high-flow oxygen. For skin exposure, soiled clothing should be removed and placed in double-sealed bags, and the skin washed thoroughly with soap and water. If the compound has been ingested, gastric lavage may be undertaken within an hour of intake, followed by activated charcoal administered via nasogastric tube. Patients who are severely poisoned with organophosphorus compounds should be managed in an intensive care unit. Convulsions and twitching should be controlled with intravenous diazepam. Atropine (2 mg i.v. for an adult) reduces bronchorrhoea, bronchospasm, salivation and abdominal colic, and should be repeated every 10 minutes until secretions have dried up and bradycardia has been abolished. Atropine toxicity (flushed red skin, tachycardia, dilated pupils and dry mouth) should be avoided. Up to 30 mg of atropine, rarely more, may be required in the first 24 hours and the drug may have to be continued for a prolonged period.

Cholinesterase reactivators, such as the oximes pralidoxime (P2S) and obidoxime (toxogonin), are helpful if given before the organophosphorus-cholinesterase enzyme complex 'ages'. In the UK, pralidoxime is given in addition to atropine to every symptomatic patient at a dose of 30 mg/kg body weight by slow i.v. injection. Clinical improvement (cessation of convulsions and fasciculation, improved muscle power and recovery of consciousness) usually occurs within 30 minutes. The need for further therapy is guided by clinical improvement together with monitoring of cholinesterase activity. If necessary, further doses of pralidoxime can be given 4–6-hourly or by continuous infusion. Adverse effects are seen at high doses and include tachycardia, muscular rigidity, neuromuscular blockade, hypertension and laryngospasm. Haemoperfusion and haemodialysis are of no benefit.

CARBAMATE INSECTICIDES

Carbamate insecticides inhibit a number of tissue esterases, in particular cholinesterase enzymes and especially acetylcholinesterase (see Fig. 3.7). They have a very similar duration of action to organophosphorus compounds but it is

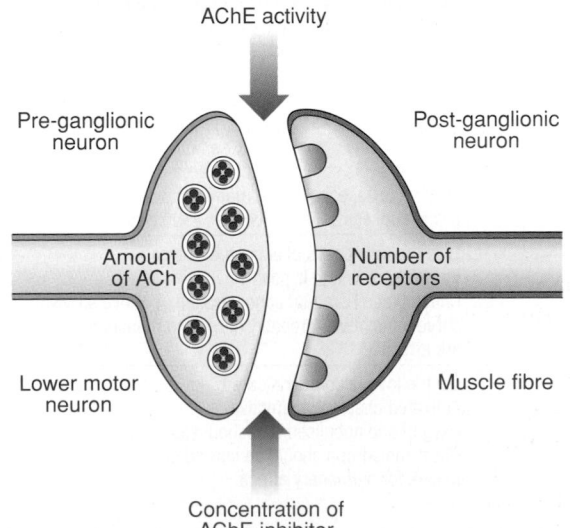

Fig. 3.7 Mechanism of action of acetylcholinesterase (AChE) and its inhibitors at the neuromuscular junction.

much shorter, as the carbamate/cholinesterase complex dissociates spontaneously with a half-life of 30–40 minutes. Since carbamate insecticides act in the same way as organophosphorus compounds, the features of poisoning are similar but not usually so severe. However, deaths have occurred. Delayed neurotoxicity has been reported following acute exposure to carbamate insecticide, particularly sensory loss and weakness in arms and legs, accompanied by peripheral axonal neuropathy.

The management of acute carbamate insecticide poisoning is identical to that for organophosphates, except that rapid recovery tends to occur with supportive therapy alone (including atropine), and the use of oximes is unnecessary and may be detrimental. In severe carbamate poisoning atropine may be given intravenously in frequent small doses (0.5–1.0 mg i.v. for an adult) until signs of atropinisation develop. Diazepam may be used to relieve anxiety.

3.10 CHEMICALS AND TOXINS TAKEN LESS COMMONLY IN OVERDOSE

Toxin	Features	Management
Acids and alkalis	Acid injures stomach but alkali injures oesophagus; aspiration causes pneumonitis Serious GI injury can result Later, strictures or malignant transformation can occur	Gastric lavage contraindicated Do not give neutralising chemicals Chest radiograph needed to exclude perforation Early endoscopy or Gastrografin studies advised to assess extent of damage and determine whether surgery is necessary
Button batteries containing lithium or mercury	Obstruction, corrosion of GI tract Heavy metal toxicity	Abdominal radiograph will locate position Remove endoscopically if obstruction/not passed from stomach within 24 hours
Bleach	Irritation around mouth Serious GI corrosion if an adult has deliberately ingested a large amount	Milk if small amounts have been ingested, e.g. accidental mouthful Endoscopy for adults as per acid (see above)
Essential oils, e.g. clove oil	Very toxic Fits and hepatotoxicity	Gastric lavage if even a few ml have been taken by a child
Ethanol, e.g. alcoholic drinks, mouthwashes, antiseptics, perfumes	Fatal dose of absolute ethanol is 6–10 ml/kg body weight in adults Blood alcohol concentrations of > 5 g/l associated with coma Convulsions, hypotension, and respiratory depression and/or circulatory failure may follow	Check blood alcohol concentration Protect airway to prevent aspiration; intubation and ventilation may be required Ensure patient is well hydrated; in a chronic alcoholic, give i.v. thiamine (Pabrinex) before dextrose Consider haemodialysis if blood ethanol concentration is > 5 g/l or arterial pH < 7
Methanol or ethylene glycol, e.g. antifreeze	Methanol metabolised to formate, causing profound metabolic acidosis and ocular toxicity Ethylene glycol metabolised to acids, causing metabolic acidosis; oxalate causes renal damage due to calcium oxalate crystals in urine	Ethylene glycol and methanol assays not widely available as an urgent assay Diagnosis usually made on presence of a high anion gap, osmolal gap (> 10 mOsm) and presence of oxalate crystals in urine (ethylene glycol in 50% of cases) Antidotal treatment inhibits alcohol dehydrogenase; includes oral ethanol, i.v. ethanol or i.v. 4-methylpyrazole (non-sedating) Haemodialysis should be considered in severe cases, especially if methanol or ethylene glycol concentration in blood is > 500 mg/l
Paraquat	Buccal ulceration Progressive respiratory fibrosis Respiratory failure Renal failure	Give multiple doses of activated charcoal if urine screen test is positive Check blood Paraquat concentration; if above survival curve, patient will probably die, as no measures are effective
Petroleum distillates, white spirit	Vomiting common Aspiration into lungs results in severe pulmonary complications: cough, choking, wheeze and dyspnoea, which peak in 24 hours and settle 3–4 days later In more severe cases chemical pneumonitis or lipoid pneumonia can develop; deaths have occurred	Gastric lavage contraindicated Activated charcoal ineffective Oxygen and nebulised bronchodilators Chest radiograph should be carried out to look for pulmonary effects

ALUMINIUM AND ZINC PHOSPHIDE

These are commonly used as rat poisons in South-east Asia. Aluminium phosphide has recently become the most common means of self-poisoning in Northern India, with a mortality rate of 60%.

When ingested, either compound reacts with water in the stomach to yield phosphine—a potent pulmonary toxicant. Hepatic toxicity and myocarditis have been reported after zinc phosphide ingestion. Many physicians will undertake gastric lavage in patients who have swallowed any amount of these tablets, as even a few can be fatal. Alternatively, lavage can be carried out with vegetable oil rather than water, in theory to reduce the generation of toxic phosphine. Sadly, most patients die, despite optimal supportive care.

CHEMICALS AND PESTICIDES LESS COMMONLY TAKEN IN OVERDOSE

Box 3.10 gives an overview of the clinical features and management for other chemicals not discussed above.

ENVENOMATION

SNAKE BITES

Snake bite is common in rural areas throughout the tropics; farmers, hunters and rice-pickers are at particular risk and prompt medical treatment is vital. Poisonous species of snake all fall into the following families (see Fig. 3.8):

- *Viperidae*—including true vipers such as Russell's viper, and the puff adder
- *Crotalidae*—often considered a subfamily of Viperidae; includes the pit vipers
- *Elapidae*—true elapids, including the cobras, kraits and coral snakes
- *Hydrophidae*—the sea snakes
- *Colubridae*—including the mangrove snake.

Pathogenesis

Snake venoms are complex mixtures of proteins and small polypeptides with enzymatic activity (e.g. the mitochondrial-damaging enzyme phospholipase A_2). Russell's viper venom

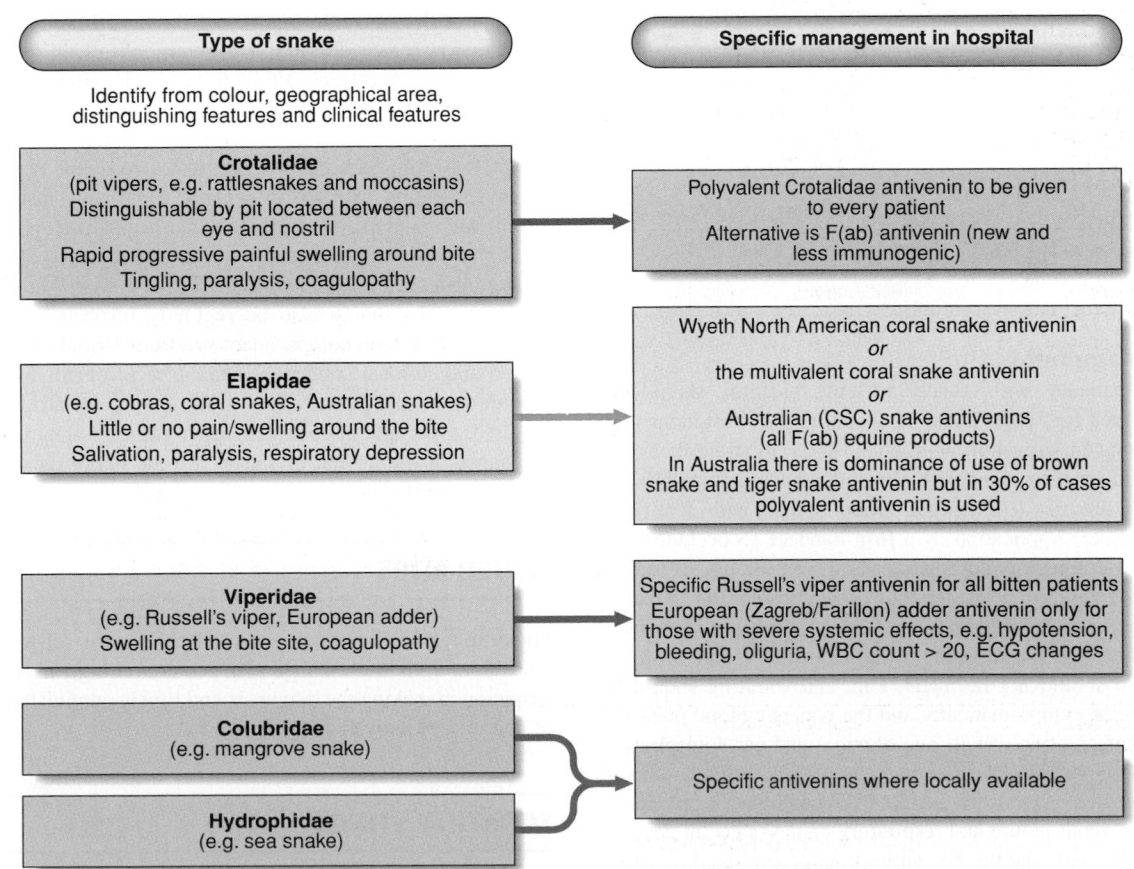

Fig. 3.8 The management of snake bites.

contains procoagulants; other venoms block transmission at the neuromuscular junction. The arbitrary grouping of snake venoms into neurotoxins, haemotoxins and cardiotoxins is toxicologically misleading and can result in serious management errors. This is because a so-called neurotoxin can produce marked cardiovascular or direct haematological effects.

Clinical features

Box 3.11 gives the geography of the common venomous snakes. Key questions to ask a victim are: Where were you bitten, how long ago and by what sort of snake? Friends and relatives will frequently bring the snake with the patients; the snake should be handled as little as possible since it may only be injured and not dead. The amount of venom injected via a bite is highly variable; it depends on the length of time since the snake last ate and on its aggression. Local swelling, ecchymosis and blistering occur at the site of the bite; vomiting, hypotension and shock then follow, particularly with viper bites. Neuromuscular weakness and respiratory muscle paralysis can occur. Bleeding and clotting disturbances are also a feature of viper and rattlesnake bites. Intravascular haemolysis is rare but may occur with bites from Russell's viper in India and Sri Lanka. Cobra bites may be followed by complement activation. Renal failure is rare; rhabdomyolysis is seen with tiger snakes, rattlesnakes, vipers and sea snakes.

3.11 VENOMOUS SNAKE DISTRIBUTION	
Area	Snake type
Africa	Vipers, adders, cobras, mambas
Middle East	Vipers, mambas
India/South-east Asia	Vipers, cobras, kraits
America	Rattlesnakes

Management

All patients with suspected envenomation should be observed for 12–24 hours, as the initial manifestations may be delayed, especially with elapid bites. First-aid measures should be directed at reassuring the patient, immobilising the bitten area to minimise venom spread, and identifying the snake. Application of a firm bandage to occlude lymphatic drainage is appropriate; however, the use of tourniquets is discouraged since they do not prevent the spread of venom and are frequently used inappropriately. Incisions at the bite site and attempts to suck out the venom with the mouth should not be made. Pain and vomiting should be managed symptomatically and the patient's blood pressure, and coagulation, renal, neurological and cardiorespiratory status monitored. A large-bore intravenous cannula should be inserted on an unaffected limb. Hypotension, anaphylactic shock, renal failure and respiratory distress may all develop rapidly and should be appropriately managed. Aspirin should not be used for analgesia since this may aggravate bleeding.

The most appropriate therapy for a snake bite is timely administration of the correct, species-appropriate antivenin (see Fig. 3.8); this should be given to patients with a severe or progressing local reaction, or clinical or laboratory features of systemic envenomation. Before starting antivenin therapy, enquiry must be made into any history of allergy and an intradermal sensitivity test performed by injecting 0.02 ml of saline-diluted antiserum at a site distant from the bite. The injection site is then observed for at least 10 minutes for the development of redness, hives, pruritus or other adverse effects. In general, the shorter the interval between injection and reaction, the greater the degree of sensitivity. A syringe containing 0.5 ml 1:1000 adrenaline (epinephrine) must be available whenever antivenin is administered. Unfortunately, a negative skin test does not always rule out a reaction following administration of the full antivenin dose. The rate of administration of antivenin should be based on the severity of the case and the patient's tolerance to the antivenin. The entire initial dose should be given as soon as possible and preferably within 4 hours of the bite. However, in severe envenomations, antivenin may be given up to 24 hours after the time of the bite and has been shown to reverse coagulation deficits even at 30 hours.

If an immediate hypersensitivity reaction to the venom occurs, administration of the antivenin should be immediately discontinued and the patient given an oral antihistamine or intramuscular adrenaline (epinephrine) as appropriate. If infusion of the antivenin is restarted, administration should be at a slower rate. Steroids are commonly given to treat serum sickness reactions, although their true value remains to be established. Bites by large snakes may need relatively high antivenin doses, particularly in children or small adults. If swelling continues to progress, if systemic features of envenomation increase in severity, or if new manifestations such as hypotension or reduced haematocrit appear, additional antivenin (e.g. the contents of 1–5 vials) should be administered.

Bitten limbs should also be regularly inspected; if the pulses are lost, then compartment syndrome should be suspected and surgical colleagues should be involved. Wound débridement and later skin grafting are occasionally required, especially in cobra and viper bites. Awareness and avoidance of the habitat of snakes are the major means of preventing snake bite.

SPIDER BITES

Spider bites are common, particularly in the USA and Australia. Optimum management requires a high index of suspicion in making the diagnosis and timely administration of appropriate antivenin (see Box 3.12).

SCORPION STINGS

The scorpion is characterised by its long segmented tail with a conspicuous stinger at the tip and can vary from 1.5 cm to

3.12 SPIDER BITES

Location/appearance of spider	Clinical response	Management
Black widow spider *(Lactrodectus mactans)* USA and Australia Jet-black body with red hourglass mark on underside of abdomen	Most bites painless; generalised pain in back or abdomen is most frequent presenting complaint Abdominal muscles become rigid, and severe cramps develop Nausea, vomiting, tremors, speech defects, sweating, periorbital oedema, skin rash, and rise in body temperature or blood pressure may be noted Severely poisoned patients may lapse into coma Respiratory muscle paralysis and cardiovascular collapse may also occur	Oxygen, i.v. access and cardiac monitoring indicated in symptomatic patients Oral diazepam may help with muscle cramps Black widow spider equine antivenin is given to those who have heart disease or respiratory distress, are pregnant, are < 16 or > 65 years of age, or show signs of envenomation or serious poisoning 1 vial of antivenin can be added to 15–100 ml of 0.9% (w/v) sodium chloride solution and then infused over 20–30 mins; normal dose is 1–2 vials Prompt resolution of features of poisoning characteristic within 1 hr
Funnel-web spider Australia	Venom is a neurotoxin causing widespread release of acetylcholine at motor end plates, and acetylcholine, adrenaline and noradrenaline (also calcium channel blockers in *Agelenopsis aperta*) through the autonomic nervous system Clinical features include neuromuscular paralysis and hypertension	Funnel-web spider antivenin covers the species *Atrax robustus*, *Hadronyche* and *Missulena*, and should be used for any patient developing more than a local bite reaction
Brown recluse spider *(Loxosceles reclusa)* USA Adults vary from yellow to dark brown; have dark, violin-shaped markings immediately behind eye	Venom induces injury to arteries and veins, which become occluded with thrombus and capillary stasis; tissue infarction ensues Clinical response varies from mild local stinging reaction to severe systemic involvement and death due to circulatory or renal failure Other features include urticaria, morbilliform rash, fever and haemolysis	Red blood cell transfusions, maintenance of good hydration and monitoring of renal function help ensure that haemoglobinuria does not cause renal failure A goat-derived specific antivenin to the brown recluse spider administered within 24 hrs of the bite prevents or markedly attenuates toxicity (*Titus phonentria*, *Loxosceles* spider antivenin)
Redback spider *(Latrodectus hasselti)* Often found in urban habitats in Australia	Bites can be painful and therefore bite and spider are recognised at the time of the bite	CSL redback spider antivenin is the most commonly used antivenin in Australia Reported as efficacious in 94% of cases 1 ampoule usually sufficient

20 cm in length. Movement and particularly situations in which the scorpion becomes trapped in clothing or shoes trigger the sting.

Two types of scorpion venom exist. The first, produced by species of the genera *Hadrurus*, *Vejovis* and *Uroctonus*, has local effects only. Such effects include sharp burning, swelling and discoloration at the skin site. Very rarely, anaphylaxis occurs. If local symptoms are present, such as swelling with or without discoloration, the sting is most likely from less lethal species. However, in *Leiurus* envenomation, which is common in the Middle East, localised reactions can occur in up to 90% of victims. Thus in countries where *Leiurus* species exist, more protracted surveillance is required, and if systemic manifestations develop, transfer to an area with better intensive care facilities should take place.

The second type of venom, produced by the genera of the poisonous varieties *Centruroides*, *Mesobuthus* and *Leiurus*, consists of protein and polypeptide neurotoxins. They block sodium channels, leading to spontaneous depolarisation of nerves of the parasympathetic and sympathetic systems, with resultant tachycardia, hypertension, pulmonary oedema (especially with *Mesobuthus* species) and seizures, as well as sweating, piloerection and hyperglycaemia. The sharp pain first produced by the sting is quickly followed by paraesthesiae and numbness in the sting area due to peripheral nerve effects, muscle fasciculations and finally drowsiness. With *Centruroides* and *Mesobuthus* species, there is no swelling at the sting site.

Local pain and paraesthesiae, both at the sting site and peripherally, are best treated with local compresses and oral analgesics. Patients with significant envenomation should be hospitalised for at least 12 hours and observed for cardiovascular and neurological sequelae of envenomation. More severe symptoms may require airway support, as well as 1–2 vials of intravenous antivenin. The use of antivenin is controversial because evidence of its effectiveness in the clinical setting is lacking, but its use is considered for the very young, the elderly or those individuals with severe hypertension. True anaphylaxis to the antivenin can occur but is rare.

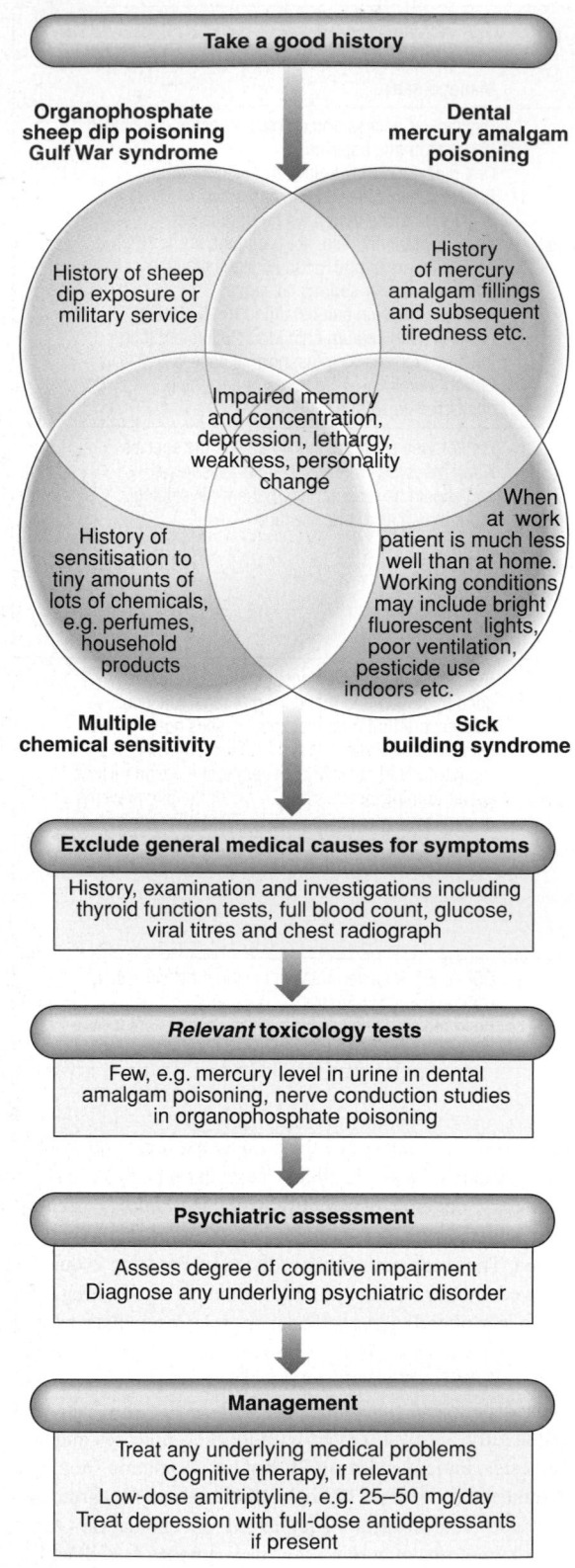

Fig. 3.9 **An approach to the management of environmental illness.**

Serum sickness is common after antivenin administration but is usually self-limited and easily controlled with steroids and histamines. Tachyarrhythmias can be treated with standard doses of intravenous metoprolol or esmolol, with the addition of α-adrenoceptor antagonists such as prazosin, if hypertension or pulmonary oedema develops. Other treatments, such as calcium or sympathomimetic drugs, have been shown to be of little value.

ENVIRONMENTAL POISONING AND ILLNESS

Various chronic illnesses can be categorised as being due to 'environmental stressors'. Such stressors involve having a combative role in the Gulf War, dental amalgam fillings etc. Figure 3.9 shows an overview of the assessment and management of such patients.

FURTHER INFORMATION

Jones AL, Dargan PI. Churchill's textbook of toxicology. Edinburgh: Churchill Livingstone; 2001.

www.aapcc.org *American Association of Poison Control Centers (AAPCC) home page.*
www.atsdr.cdc.gov *Agency for Toxic Substances and Disease Registry (ATSDR) home page: includes information on toxicological profiles, chemical-specific fact sheets, Hazdat (database of hazardous substance release and health effects) and ToxFaqS™, frequently asked questions about contaminants found at hazardous waste sites.*
www.spib.axl.co.uk *Toxbase, the clinical toxicology database of the UK National Poisons Information Service.*
www.toxnet.nlm.nih.gov *National Library of Medicine's Toxnet: a hazardous substances databank, including Toxline for references to literature on drugs and other chemicals.*

**POISONS CENTRE CONTACT NUMBERS
(dialling codes from the UK)**

• Australia (Sydney)	(61) 2 519 0466
• Canada (Vancouver)	(1) 604 682 2344
• China (Beijing)	(86) 1 771 9394
• Egypt (Cairo)	(20) 282 8212
• Eire (Dublin)	(353) 1 837 9964
• France (Paris)	(33) 1 40 37 04 04
• Germany (Munich)	(49) 89 19420
• India (New Delhi)	(91) 11 66 1123
• Malaysia (Penang)	(60) 4 877888
• Pakistan (Karachi)	(92) 21 529669
• South Africa (Johannesburg)	(27) 11 642 2417
• Spain (Madrid)	(34) 1 562 0420
• UK	0870 600 6266
• USA (Boston)	(1) 617 232 2120
• USA (San Francisco)	(1) 415 476 6600

Critical care

D.F. TREACHER • I.S. GRANT

Apart from elective surgical admissions, the majority of patients are admitted to general hospital wards via the accident and emergency department (A & E); they are initially managed by 'on-take' medical and surgical teams who mostly have specific 'organ-focused' expertise and have limited time to devote to each patient. This approach is not appropriate for the initial management of the critically ill patient who by definition is at risk of death; there is often no established diagnosis, history can be patchy or incomplete, and examination is frequently inconclusive. Moreover, the physical signs on which classical diagnosis depends tend to disappear as the patient approaches death.

The approach required and the priorities in managing the critically ill patient are:

- prompt resuscitation, adhering to advanced life support guidelines (see p. 404) and the principles of cardiorespiratory management that will be explained in this chapter
- urgent treatment of life-threatening emergencies such as hypotension, hypoxaemia, hyperkalaemia, hypoglycaemia and dysrhythmias
- analysis of the deranged physiology
- establishing the complete diagnosis in stages as further history and the results of investigations become available
- careful monitoring of the patient's condition and response to treatment.

Multiple expert opinions (surgeons, physicians, microbiologists etc.) are frequently appropriate but each will tend to adopt the 'parochial' perspective of 'their' specialty. The joy and challenge of critical care medicine are to synthesise these views and produce an integrated plan of management.

PROVISION OF CRITICAL CARE

ORGANISATION OF CRITICAL CARE

In countries where numbers of intensive care unit (ICU) beds are limited by resources there is a major gulf between the care available on the ICU and that possible on the general wards. The medical and nursing cover and expertise immediately available are frequently limited, particularly 'out of hours', and the patient's initial physical location is often determined by bed availability at the time of admission. The concept of progressive patient care addresses this problem by grouping patients together in units according to their severity of illness. Patients are transferred between these areas as their condition changes so that at all stages the provision of staff and technical support matches their specific needs as closely as possible. Four levels of care are described: intensive care, intermediate or high-dependency, general, and minimal or self-care. Critical care embraces the first two levels of care as practised within ICUs and

high-dependency units (HDUs). However, critically ill patients are also found in post-operative recovery areas, coronary care units (CCUs), the acute admission wards, and resuscitation areas within A & E departments where application of the principles of care described in this chapter is equally appropriate and, arguably, even better rewarded.

CRITICAL CARE 'OUTREACH'

The purpose of 'outreach' is to achieve earlier identification of critically ill patients on the wards so that assessment and, if appropriate, transfer to ICU/HDU is arranged before deterioration occurs to the point of imminent or actual cardiorespiratory arrest. Prompt identification and treatment may even avert the need for admission to ICU/HDU. Many hospitals are now setting up medical emergency teams or 'outreach'/'patient at risk' teams (PARTs). In some hospitals the medical emergency team may be the cardiac arrest team but with a wider remit, while in others this service is provided by the ICU or HDU team.

Criteria that identify deranged physiology (see Box 4.1) are used to alert the ward nursing and junior medical staff to impending problems so that they can summon the outreach team to assess the patient, institute initial resuscitation and supervise transfer to ICU or HDU as appropriate.

4.1 RECOGNISING THE CRITICALLY ILL PATIENT

Cardiovascular signs
- Cardiac arrest
- Pulse rate < 40 or > 140 bpm
- Systolic blood pressure (BP) < 100 mmHg
- Tissue hypoxia
    Poor peripheral perfusion
    Metabolic acidosis
    Hyperlactataemia
- Poor response to volume resuscitation
- Oliguria: < 0.5 ml/kg/hr (check urea, creatinine, K+)

Respiratory signs
- Threatened or obstructed airway
- Stridor, intercostal recession
- Respiratory arrest
- Respiratory rate < 8 or > 35/min
- Respiratory 'distress': use of accessory muscles; unable to speak in complete sentences
- SpO_2 < 90% on high-flow O_2
- Rising $PaCO_2$ > 8 kPa, or > 2 kPa above 'normal' with acidosis

Neurological signs
- Threatened or obstructed airway
- Absent gag or cough
- Failure to maintain normal PaO_2 and $PaCO_2$
- Failure to obey commands; Glasgow Coma Scale (GCS—see p. 1143) < 10
- Sudden fall in level of consciousness (GCS fall > 2 points)
- Repeated or prolonged seizures

ADMISSION GUIDELINES

Rigid rules to determine admission to ICU/HDU are destined to fail because every case must be evaluated on its own merits. Nevertheless, broad guidelines are required to avoid causing unnecessary suffering and the waste of valuable resources by admitting patients who have nothing to gain from intensive care because they are either too well or have no realistic prospect of recovery. The existence of an empty bed does not justify admission. The guiding principle when considering ICU/HDU admission should be the timely use of this resource in patients who have a realistic prospect of recovering to achieve a quality of life that they would value. Patients who do warrant admission should be identified early and admitted without delay since this improves survival and reduces the length of stay on the ICU. The wishes of the patient, if known, should be respected and whatever decision is made should be carefully explained to the patient's family.

If the appropriateness of admission remains uncertain, as may occur in the A & E department when little history is available, the patient should be given the benefit of the doubt and the indication for continued active treatment reviewed as further information becomes available (see Box 4.2).

There is now evidence that for patients undergoing high-risk elective or emergency surgery the mortality, morbidity and both ICU and hospital length of stay are reduced by pre-operative admission to ICU/HDU to improve their cardiorespiratory status ('pre-optimisation'). Such patients are often elderly with cardiorespiratory disease and poor physiological reserve, and benefit from a protocol of intensive perioperative care. At present many hospitals have major problems in implementing this strategy due to the current shortage of critical care beds.

Specific indications for admission to ICU and HDU are given in Box 4.3.

TRANSPORT OF THE CRITICALLY ILL PATIENT

Once identified, critically ill patients have to be transported to the most appropriate clinical area for their continuing care. Before intra- or interhospital transfer is undertaken, the patient's condition must be stabilised. Appropriate monitoring should be set up and if there is clinical evidence of progressive respiratory failure or inability to protect the airway, endotracheal intubation and ventilation are indicated. Intubation, while often essential, may be hazardous in the patient with cardiorespiratory failure, and full monitoring and resuscitation facilities must be available. Hypovolaemia and hypotension should be corrected and this will often require monitoring of the central venous pressure (CVP).

Transfer to another hospital may be necessary for further investigations (such as computed tomography—CT), for surgery or for specialist care—for example, on a liver failure, neurosurgical or cardiac surgical unit. The urgency of providing the specialist treatment has to be balanced against the stability of the patient's condition. It may be more appropriate to admit the patient to the local ICU for initial stabilisation before transfer to another hospital.

All critically ill patients should be accompanied during transfer by an appropriately trained medical escort.

4.2 FACTORS IN THE ASSESSMENT OF A POSSIBLE ICU ADMISSION

- Primary diagnosis and other active medical problems
- Prognosis of underlying condition
- Severity of physiological disturbance—is recovery still possible?
- Availability of the required treatment/technology
- Life expectancy and anticipated quality of life post-discharge
- Wishes of the patient and/or relatives

N.B. Age alone should not be a contraindication to admission.

4.3 ADMISSION CRITERIA FOR ICU AND HDU

Admission to ICU

- Patients requiring or likely to require endotracheal intubation and invasive mechanical ventilatory support
- Patients requiring support of two or more organ systems (e.g. inotropes and haemofiltration)
- Patients with chronic impairment of one or more organ systems (e.g. chronic obstructive pulmonary disease (COPD) *or* severe ischaemic heart disease (IHD)) who *also* require support for acute reversible failure of another organ system

Admission to HDU

- Patients who require far more detailed observation or monitoring than can be safely provided on a general ward
  Direct arterial BP monitoring
  Central venous pressure (CVP) monitoring
  Fluid balance
  Neurological observations, regular GCS recording
- Patients requiring support for a single failing organ system but excluding invasive ventilatory support
  Mask CPAP *or* non-invasive (mask) ventilation (NIPPV)—see Box 4.18, page 203
  Low- to medium-dose inotropic support
  Renal replacement therapy in an otherwise stable patient
- Patients no longer requiring intensive care but who cannot be safely managed in a general ward

MONITORING

GENERAL PRINCIPLES

On entering an ICU, relatives, students and even clinicians may be intimidated by the numerous tubes and cables attaching each patient to a battery of 'alarming' machines (see Fig. 4.1). Much of the bedside nurse's time is spent observing, recording and reacting to the information displayed by these monitors, particularly the electrocardiogram (ECG), CVP, arterial BP, temperature and ventilator data. The trends observed over time, interpreted in relation to changes in therapy, are an important guide to the patient's progress.

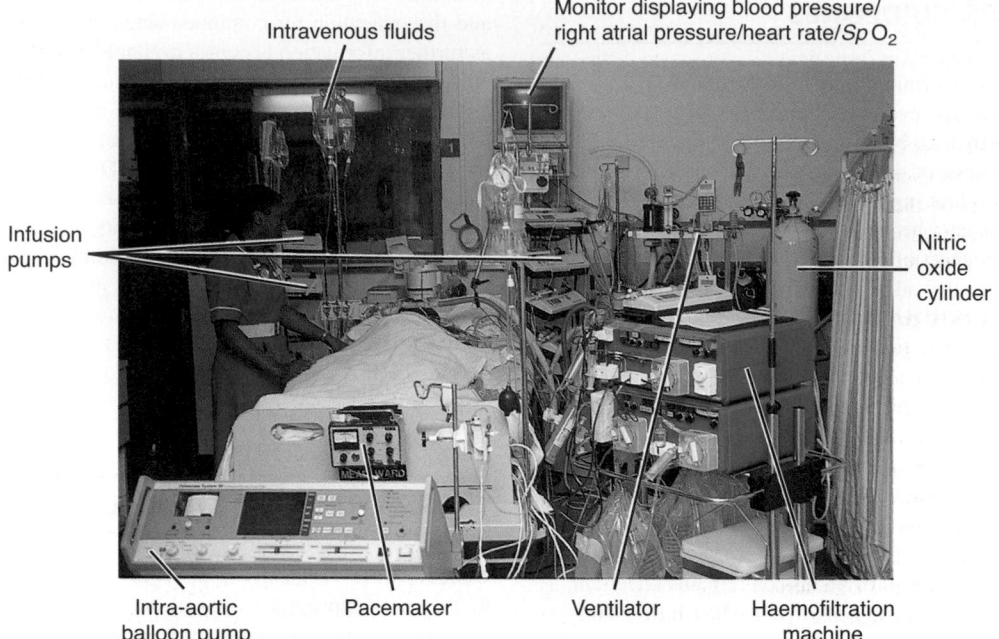

Intravenous fluids

Monitor displaying blood pressure/
right atrial pressure/heart rate/$Sp\,O_2$

Infusion
pumps

Nitric
oxide
cylinder

Intra-aortic
balloon pump

Pacemaker

Ventilator

Haemofiltration
machine

Fig. 4.1   A patient with multi-organ failure supported by haemodynamic monitoring, cardiac pacing, a counterpulsation aortic balloon pump, haemofiltration and nitric oxide therapy.

The critically ill patient should be monitored according to the following principles:

- Regular clinical examination should never be neglected.
- Simple physical signs such as respiratory rate, the appearance of the patient, restlessness, conscious level and indices of poor peripheral perfusion (pale, cold skin, delayed capillary refill in the nail bed) are just as important as a set of blood gases or numbers impressively displayed on expensive monitors.
- If there is conflict between clinical assessment and the information on a monitor, the monitor should be presumed to be wrong until all potential sources of error have been checked and eliminated. For example, CVP measurement may be erroneous because the line is blocked, the system has not been re-zeroed after a change in the patient's position, the tip of the cannula is lying in the right ventricle, or another infusion has been attached to the same central line.
- Changes and trends are more important than any single measurement.
- Many monitors have alarms which will activate if certain maximum and minimum values are breached. This is a crucial safety feature and may, for example, help to identify the fact that a patient has become disconnected from the ventilator. Despite the understandable desire to avoid extra noise, the alarm limits should always be set to define physiologically 'safe' limits for the variable being monitored.
- Sophisticated monitoring systems are often invasive and pose certain hazards, particularly infection (see Box 4.4). Always ask 'Is it necessary?', and cease monitoring as soon as possible.

4.4   COMPLICATIONS AND PITFALLS OF CENTRAL VENOUS AND PULMONARY ARTERY (PA) CANNULATION
At insertion
• Pneumothorax—more likely with subclavian than with internal jugular approach • Haematoma from accidental arterial puncture • Air embolism • Dysrhythmia • Damage to thoracic duct with left internal jugular or subclavian approach • Knotting of catheter* • Pulmonary artery rupture*
In situ
• Sepsis • Endocarditis • Thrombosis • Pulmonary infarct* • Pulmonary artery rupture* • Erroneous information • Inappropriate response to information
* Risk associated specifically with PA catheterisation.

MONITORING THE CIRCULATION

ECG

Standard monitors display a single-lead ECG, record heart rate and identify rhythm changes. More sophisticated machines can print out rhythm strips and monitor ST segment shift, which may be useful in patients with ischaemic heart disease.

Blood pressure

This may be measured intermittently using an automated sphygmomanometer but in critically ill patients continuous intra-arterial monitoring, using a line placed in the radial artery, is preferable. It is important to appreciate that when there is systemic vasoconstriction the mean arterial pressure may be normal or even high although the cardiac output is low. Conversely, if there is peripheral vasodilatation, as in sepsis, the mean arterial pressure may be low although the cardiac output is high.

Central venous pressure (CVP)

CVP or right atrial pressure (RAP) is monitored using a catheter inserted via either the internal jugular or the sub-clavian vein with the distal end sited in the upper right atrium. Although on general wards and some HDUs measurements may be made using a saline-filled manometer tube, in ICU the line is transduced as for arterial pressure measurement. The zero reference point used is normally the mid-axillary line (MAL), which approximates to the level of the tricuspid valve or mid-right atrium with the patient lying semi-supine. All intravascular pressures quoted in this chapter are referenced to that point. It is important to realise that classical bedside clinical examination uses the 'sternal angle' as the zero reference point and this lies approximately 6–8 cm (depending on the antero-posterior chest diameter) vertically above MAL. (Values of CVP measured from this reference point will therefore be 6–8 cm lower than values recorded from MAL.)

The CVP is a useful means of assessing the need for intravascular fluid replacement and the rate at which it should be given but, particularly when interpreting raised levels, it must be remembered that right heart function, intrathoracic pressure and venous 'tone' also influence CVP. The raised intrathoracic pressure associated with positive pressure ventilation may lead to marked swings in atrial pressures and blood pressure in time with respiration. Pressure measurements should be recorded at end-expiration or, if safe, off the ventilator because these values provide the most reliable measure of ventricular end-diastolic trans-mural pressure.

In severe hypovolaemia the RAP may be sustained by peripheral venoconstriction and transfusion may initially produce little or no change in the CVP (see Fig. 4.2).

Pulmonary artery 'wedge' pressure (PAWP) and PA catheterisation

In most situations the central venous pressure is an adequate guide to the filling pressures of both sides of the heart; however, certain conditions such as pulmonary hypertension or right ventricular dysfunction may lead to raised CVP levels even in the presence of hypovolaemia. If this is suspected, it may be appropriate to insert a pulmonary artery flotation catheter (see Fig. 4.3) so that pulmonary artery pressure and PAWP, which approximates to left atrial pressure, can be measured. The mean PAWP normally lies between 6 and 12 mmHg but in left heart failure it may be grossly elevated and exceed 30 mmHg. Provided the pulmonary capillary membranes are intact, the optimum

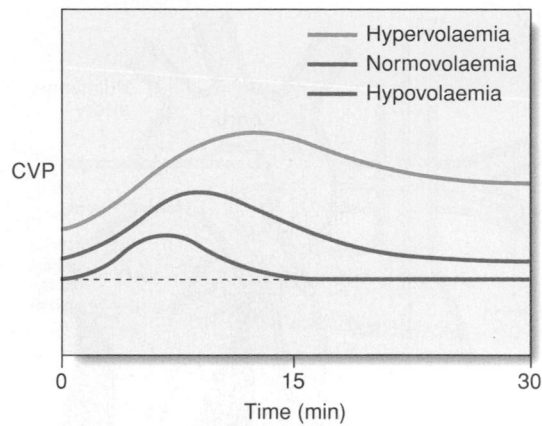

Fig. 4.2 The different responses observed in central venous pressure (CVP) after a fluid challenge of 250 ml, depending on the intravascular volume status of the patient.

PAWP in acute circulatory failure is generally 12–15 mmHg because this will ensure good left ventricular filling without risking hydrostatic pulmonary oedema.

These catheters may also be used to measure cardiac output, sample blood from the pulmonary artery ('mixed venous' samples) and, by oximetry, provide continuous monitoring of the mixed venous oxygen saturation (SvO_2). Measurement of SvO_2 gives an indication of the adequacy of cardiac output in relation to the body's metabolic requirements and is especially useful in low cardiac output states.

EBM

CRITICALLY ILL PATIENTS—role of pulmonary artery (PA) catheters

'The benefit of using PA catheters has been questioned by a controlled multicentre study that showed an increased mortality in critically ill patients managed with a PA catheter. With the demise of 'goal-directed' therapy (see EBM panel, p. 193) and the introduction of alternative non-invasive methods for assessing cardiac output and left ventricular filling, most units now use fewer PA catheters.'

- Connors AF, Speroff T, Dawson NV, et al. The effectiveness of right heart catheterisation in the initial care of critically ill patients. JAMA 1996; 276:889–897.
- Pulmonary Artery Catheter Consensus Conference. Consensus statement. Crit Care Med 1997; 25:910–925.
- Cooper AB, Doig DS, Sibbald WJ. Pulmonary artery catheters in the critically ill: an overview using the methodology of evidence-based medicine. Crit Care Clin 1996; 12:777–794.

Further information: 💻 www.biomednet.com/ccforum

Cardiac output

The most widely used method for cardiac output measurement is the thermodilution technique using a PA catheter. A bolus of cold 5% dextrose is rapidly injected into the right atrium via the CVP line and mixes with the total venous return in the right ventricle, producing a drop in the pulmonary artery temperature that is sensed by a thermistor at the tip of the PA catheter. The cardiac output is derived from the volume and temperature of the injectate and the resulting change in temperature measured in the pulmonary artery; it is inversely related to the area under the temperature–time curve. Although generally viewed as the 'gold standard' for

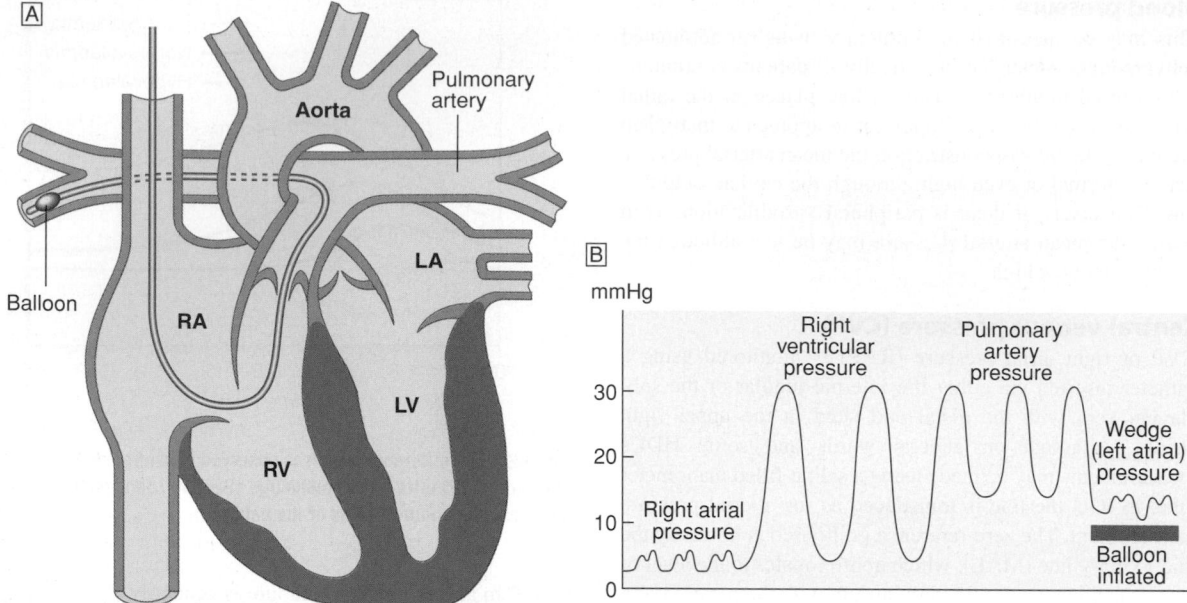

Fig. 4.3   A pulmonary artery catheter. [A] There is a small balloon at the tip of the catheter and pressure can be measured through the central lumen. The catheter is inserted via an internal jugular, subclavian or femoral vein and advanced through the right heart until its tip lies in the pulmonary artery. When the balloon is deflated the pulmonary artery pressure can be recorded. [B] Advancing the catheter while inflating the balloon will 'wedge' the catheter in the pulmonary artery. In this position blood cannot flow past the balloon so the tip of the catheter will now record the pressure transmitted from the pulmonary veins and left atrium. This is known as the pulmonary artery wedge pressure and provides an indirect measure of the left atrial pressure.

clinical measurement of cardiac output, the margin of error may be 10–15%.

Increasingly less invasive methods for monitoring cardiac output are being used. Oesophageal Doppler ultrasonography, lithium chloride dilution, analysis of the arterial pressure waveform and echocardiography can provide sufficiently accurate estimates of cardiac output and the adequacy of left ventricular filling to direct management and avoid the use of a PA catheter.

Urinary flow

This is a sensitive measure of renal perfusion, provided that the kidneys are not damaged (e.g. acute tubular necrosis) or affected by drugs (e.g. diuretics, dopamine), and can be monitored accurately if a urinary catheter is in place. It is normally measured hourly and the lower limit of normal is 0.5 ml/hour/kg body weight.

Fluid balance

Assessing fluid balance in critically ill patients is a difficult but important discipline. Weighing the patient daily can be helpful but is extremely difficult, and assessment is usually based on fluid balance charts which record:

- inputs: oral, nasogastric and intravenous, classified as crystalloid and colloid
- outputs: urine, nasogastric, fistulae, vomiting and diarrhoea.

The insensible loss from skin, respiration etc. is normally 500–1000 ml/day but can exceed 2 litres/day in a pyrexial patient with open wounds.

Peripheral/skin temperature

This is conventionally measured over the dorsum of the foot and reflects cutaneous blood flow and venous filling. The gradient between peripheral and central or 'core' temperature (from rectal, oesophageal or tympanic probes) may be used to assess peripheral perfusion; a difference of < 3°C suggests that both intravascular fluid replacement and tissue perfusion are adequate.

Blood lactate, hydrogen ion and base deficit

A metabolic acidosis with a base deficit > 5 mmol/l requires explanation. It often indicates increased lactic acid production in poorly perfused, hypoxic tissues and impaired lactate metabolism due to poor hepatic perfusion. Serial lactate measurements may therefore be helpful in monitoring tissue perfusion and the response to treatment. Other conditions such as acute renal failure, ketoacidosis and poisoning may be the cause of metabolic acidosis (see p. 289) in a critically ill patient.

MONITORING RESPIRATORY FUNCTION

Oxygen saturation (SpO_2)

This is measured by a probe that is usually attached to a finger or earlobe and uses spectrophotometric analysis to determine the relative proportions of saturated and desaturated haemoglobin. The technique is unreliable if peripheral perfusion is poor and may produce erroneous results in the presence of nail polish, excessive movement or high ambient light. In general, arterial oxygenation is satisfactory if SpO_2 is greater than 90%. In ICU sudden falls in SpO_2 may be caused by:

- pneumothorax
- displacement of the endotracheal tube
- disconnection from the ventilator
- lung collapse due to thick secretions blocking the proximal bronchial tree
- circulatory collapse causing a poor signal due to impaired peripheral perfusion
- error such as a detached probe.

Arterial blood gases

These are usually measured several times a day in a ventilated patient so that inspired oxygen (FIO_2) and minute volume can be adjusted to achieve the desired PaO_2 and $PaCO_2$ respectively. Analysis of arterial blood gas results is also a useful means of monitoring disturbances of acid–base balance (see Ch. 9).

Lung function

In ventilated patients lung function is monitored by:

- alveolar–arterial PO_2 gradient and hypoxaemia index (PaO_2/FIO_2), which are measures of gas exchange
- arterial and end-tidal CO_2, which are measures of alveolar ventilation
- tidal volume (V_T), respiratory rate (f), minute volume ($V_T \times f$), airway pressure and compliance, which reflect the adequacy of ventilation, 'stiffness' of the lungs and the required work of breathing.

Capnography

The CO_2 concentration in inspired gas is zero, but during expiration, after clearing the physiological dead space, it rises progressively to reach a plateau which represents the alveolar or end-tidal CO_2 concentration. This cyclical change in CO_2 concentration or capnogram is measured using an infrared sensor inserted between the ventilator tubing and the endotracheal tube. With normal lungs, the end-tidal CO_2 closely mirrors $PaCO_2$, and can be used to assess the adequacy of alveolar ventilation. However, with lung disease and impaired pulmonary perfusion (for example, due to hypovolaemia) there may be considerable discrepancies. Trends in end-tidal CO_2 are useful, especially for head injury management and during the transport of ventilated patients.

In combination with the gas flow and respiratory cycle data from the ventilator, CO_2 production and hence metabolic rate may be calculated.

PHYSIOLOGY OF THE CRITICALLY ILL PATIENT

OXYGEN TRANSPORT

The major function of the heart, lungs and circulation is the provision of oxygen and other nutrients to the various organs and tissues of the body. During this process carbon dioxide and the other waste products of metabolism are removed. The rate of supply and removal should match the specific metabolic requirements of the individual tissues. This requires adequate oxygen uptake in the lungs, global matching of delivery and consumption, and regional control of the circulation. Failure to supply sufficient oxygen to meet the metabolic requirements of the tissues is the cardinal feature of circulatory failure or 'shock'.

The transport of oxygen from the atmosphere to the mitochondria within individual cells is illustrated in Figure 4.4. The important points to note are that:

- The movement of oxygen from pulmonary capillary to systemic tissue capillary, referred to as the global oxygen delivery (DO_2), relies on convection or bulk flow and is the product of cardiac output and arterial oxygen content.
- The regional distribution of oxygen delivery is vital. If skin and muscle receive high blood flows but the splanchnic bed does not, the gut will become hypoxic even if overall oxygen delivery is high.
- The major determinants of the oxygen content of arterial blood are the arterial oxygen saturation of haemoglobin (SaO_2) and the haemoglobin concentration, since over 95% of oxygen carried in the blood is attached to haemoglobin (see Box 4.5).
- The movement of oxygen from tissue capillary to cell occurs by diffusion and depends on the gradient of oxygen partial pressures, diffusion distance and the ability of the cell to take up and use oxygen. Therefore microcirculatory, tissue diffusion and cellular factors, as well as DO_2, influence the oxygen status of the cell.

		PaO_2 (kPa)	SaO_2 (%)	Hb (g/l)	Dissolved O_2 (ml/l)	CaO_2 (ml/l)	CaO_2 (% change)
4.5 THE EFFECTS OF PROGRESSIVE INCREMENTS IN INSPIRED OXYGEN CONCENTRATION AND THEN TRANSFUSION ON THE OXYGEN CONTENT OF ARTERIAL BLOOD IN AN ANAEMIC, HYPOXAEMIC PATIENT							
	FIO_2						
Air	0.21	6	75	80	1.4	83	–
35% O_2	0.35	9.5	93	80	2.2	103	+24
60% O_2	0.60	16.5	98	80	3.8	110	+7
Transfusion	0.60	16.5	98	120	3.8	164	+48

(FIO_2 = inspired oxygen concentration; PaO_2 = arterial oxygen partial pressure; SaO_2 = arterial oxygen saturation; Hb = haemoglobin; CaO_2 = oxygen content of arterial blood)

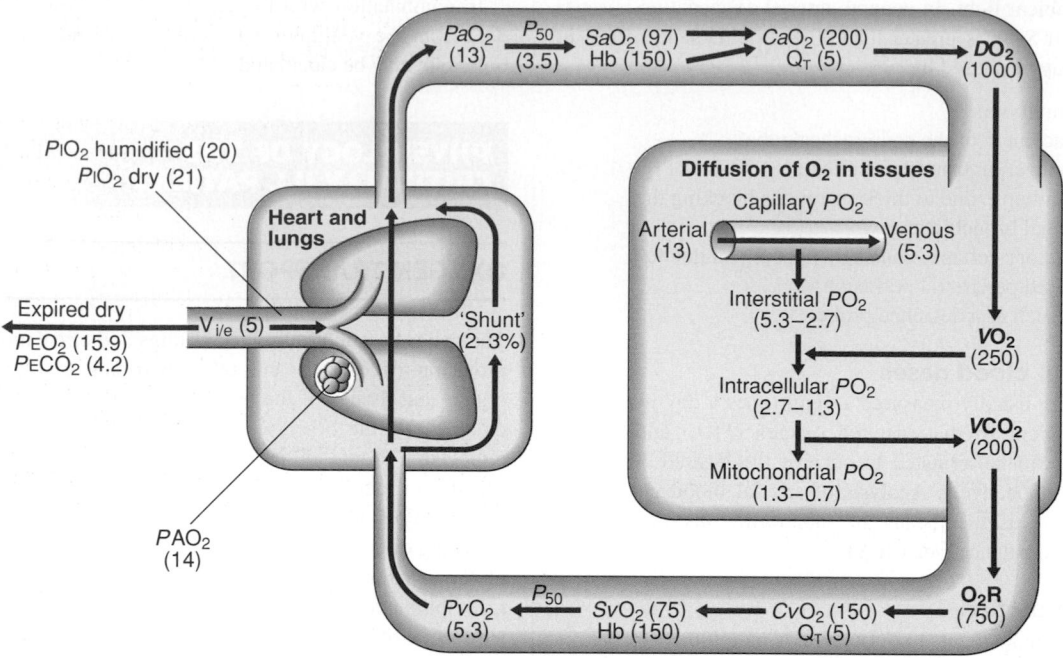

Calculations

$$CaO_2 = (Hb \times k \times SaO_2/100) + (PaO_2 \times 0.23) \qquad = 200\,ml\ O_2/l$$

$$k = \text{coefficient of haemoglobin oxygen-binding capacity} = 1.36\,ml\ O_2/gram\ of\ 100\%\ saturated\ Hb$$

$$PaO_2 \times 0.23 = \text{oxygen dissolved in plasma} \qquad = 3\,ml/l$$

$$DO_2 = Q_T \times CaO_2 \qquad = 1000\,ml/min$$

$$VO_2 = Q_T\,(CaO_2 - CvO_2) \qquad = 250\,ml/min$$

$$OER = VO_2/DO_2 \times 100 \qquad = 25\%$$

Fig. 4.4   Transport of oxygen from inspired gas to the cell, demonstrating the 'oxygen cascade', with equations for calculation of arterial oxygen content, global oxygen delivery, consumption and extraction. Values in parentheses for a normal 70 kg individual (body surface area: 1.67 m²) breathing air (FiO_2: 0.21) at standard atmospheric pressure (P_B: 101 kPa). Partial pressures of O_2, CO_2 in kPa; saturation in %; contents (CaO_2, CvO_2) in ml/litre; Hb in g/l; blood/gas flows (Q_T, $V_{i/e}$) in litre/min; oxygen transport (DO_2, O_2R), VO_2 and VCO_2 in ml/min.

CaO_2 = arterial O_2 content	O_2R = oxygen return	PiO_2 = inspired PO_2	SO_2 = oxygen saturation (%)
CvO_2 = mixed venous O_2 content	PaO_2 = arterial PO_2	PO_2 = oxygen partial pressure (kPa)	SvO_2 = mixed venous SO_2
DO_2 = oxygen delivery	PAO_2 = alveolar PO_2	PvO_2 = venous PO_2	VCO_2 = CO_2 production
Hb = haemoglobin	$PECO_2$ = mixed expired PCO_2	Q_T = cardiac output	$V_{i/e}$ = minute volume: inspired/expired
OER = oxygen extraction ratio	PEO_2 = mixed expired PO_2	SaO_2 = arterial SO_2	VO_2 = oxygen consumption

- Supranormal levels of oxygen delivery cannot compensate for diffusion problems between capillary and cell, nor for metabolic failure within the cell.

OXYHAEMOGLOBIN DISSOCIATION CURVE

The oxyhaemoglobin dissociation curve (see Fig. 4.5) describes the relationship between the saturation of haemoglobin (SO_2) and the partial pressure (PO_2) of oxygen in the blood. Due to the shape of the haemoglobin PaO_2–SaO_2 curve, a small drop in PaO_2 below 8 kPa will cause a marked fall in SaO_2. Its position and the effect of various physico-chemical factors are defined by the PO_2 at which 50% of the haemoglobin is saturated (P_{50}), which is normally 3.5 kPa.

A shift in this relationship will influence the uptake and release of oxygen by the Hb molecule; for example, if the curve moves to the right, the haemoglobin saturation will be lower for any given oxygen tension and therefore less oxygen will be taken up in the lungs but more will be released to the tissues. This increases unloading of oxygen in the tissues as capillary PCO_2 rises, a phenomenon known as the Bohr effect.

Traditionally, the optimum haemoglobin concentration for critically ill patients had been considered to be approximately 100 g/l, which represented a balance between maximising the oxygen content of the blood and avoiding regional microcirculatory problems due to increased viscosity. However, recent evidence suggests an improved outcome if the haemoglobin concentration is maintained between 70 and 90 g/l, with the exception of the elderly and patients with coronary artery disease, in whom a level of 100 g/l remains appropriate.

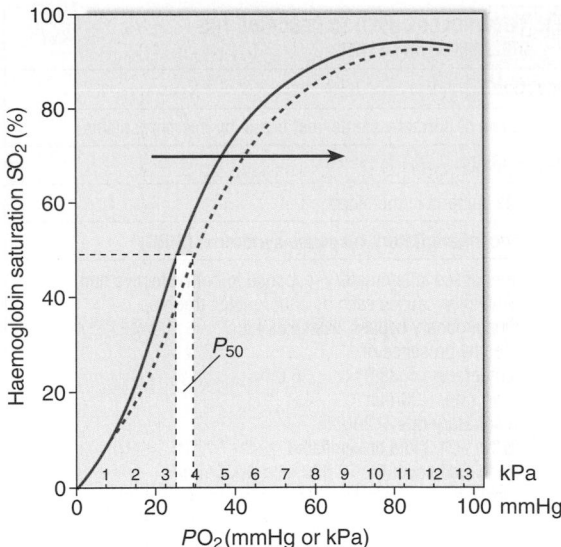

Fig. 4.5   The relationship between oxygen tension (PO_2) and percentage saturation of haemoglobin with oxygen (SO_2). The dotted line illustrates the rightward shift of the curve (i.e. P_{50} increases) caused by increases in temperature, $PaCO_2$, metabolic acidosis and 2,3,diphosphoglycerate (DPG).

OXYGEN CONSUMPTION

The sum of the oxygen consumed by the various organs represents the global oxygen consumption (VO_2) and is approximately 250 ml/min for an adult of 70 kg undertaking normal daily activities. VO_2 may be calculated from the product of cardiac output and the arterial mixed venous oxygen concentration difference, as shown in Figure 4.4, or from measurements of inspired and mixed-expired oxygen concentrations and expired minute volume.

The oxygen saturation in the pulmonary artery, otherwise known as the mixed venous oxygen saturation (SvO_2), represents a measure of the oxygen not consumed by the tissues (DO_2–VO_2). The saturation of venous blood from different organs varies considerably; for example, the hepatic venous saturation usually does not exceed 60% but the renal venous saturation may reach 90%, reflecting the great difference in both the metabolic requirements of these organs and the oxygen content of the blood delivered to them. The SvO_2 will be influenced by changes both in oxygen delivery (DO_2) and consumption (VO_2) and, provided the microcirculation and the mechanisms for cellular oxygen uptake are intact, can be used to monitor whether global oxygen delivery is adequate to meet overall demand.

The re-oxygenation of the blood that returns to the lungs and the resulting arterial saturation (SaO_2) will depend on how closely pulmonary ventilation and perfusion are matched. If part of the pulmonary blood flow perfuses non-ventilated parts of the lung, there will be 'shunting', and the blood entering the left atrium will be desaturated in proportion to the size of this shunt and the level of SvO_2.

RELATIONSHIP BETWEEN OXYGEN CONSUMPTION AND DELIVERY

The tissue oxygen extraction ratio (OER), which is 20–25% in a normal subject at rest, rises as consumption increases or supply diminishes (see Fig. 4.6). The maximum OER is approximately 60% for most tissues; at this point no further increase in extraction can occur and any further increase in oxygen consumption or decline in oxygen delivery will cause tissue hypoxia, anaerobic metabolism and increased lactic acid production.

In sepsis the slope of maximum OER decreases, reflecting the reduced ability of tissues to extract oxygen (DE cf. AB on Fig. 4.6), but the curve does not plateau and oxygen consumption continues to increase even at 'supranormal' levels of oxygen delivery. This concept encouraged some physicians to treat septic shock using vigorous intravenous

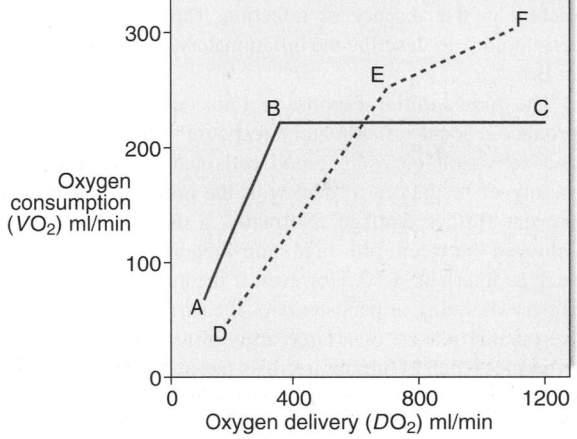

Fig. 4.6   The effects of changing oxygen delivery on consumption. The solid line (ABC) represents the normal relationship and the dotted line (DEF) the altered relationship believed to exist in sepsis.

EBM

OXYGEN DELIVERY IN CRITICALLY ILL PATIENTS

'Two RCTs have shown that for patients already on the ICU with established organ failure, treatment with aggressive volume-loading and inotropes in an attempt to achieve high levels of oxygen delivery ('goal-directed therapy') not only often fails to achieve these goals but also does not improve survival and may be harmful. However, a subsequent single-centre RCT applying goal-directed therapy *early* to patients with severe sepsis and septic shock in the A & E department before ICU admission and before they had developed established organ failure did reduce 28- and 60-day mortality.'

- Hayes MA, Yau EHS, Timmins AC, et al. Response of critically ill patients to treatment aimed at achieving supranormal oxygen delivery and consumption: relationship to outcome. Chest 1993;103:886–895.
- Gattinoni L, Brazzi L, Pelosi P, et al. A trial of goal orientated hemodynamic therapy in critically ill patients. N Engl J Med 1995; 333:1025–1032.
- Rivers E, Nguyen B, Havstad S, et al. Early goal-directed therapy in the treatment of severe sepsis and septic shock. N Engl J Med 2001; 345:1368–1377.

Further information: 🖥 www.nejm.org

fluid loading and inotropic support, usually with dobutamine, with the aim of achieving very high oxygen deliveries (> 600 ml/min/m²) in the belief that this strategy would increase oxygen consumption, relieve tissue hypoxia, prevent multiple organ failure and improve prognosis. However, several major studies have demonstrated no benefit from this approach in ICU patients with established organ failure and suggest that it may even be detrimental.

PATHOPHYSIOLOGY OF THE INFLAMMATORY RESPONSE

Fever, tachycardia and tachypnoea associated with a raised white cell count traditionally prompt a diagnosis of sepsis with the implication that the clinical picture is caused by invading microorganisms and their breakdown products. Although this may be correct, other conditions such as pancreatitis, trauma, tissue necrosis, aspiration, blood transfusion and drug reactions can all produce the same clinical picture in the absence of infection. The currently agreed terminology to describe the inflammatory response is shown in Box 4.6.

The body's initial response to a noxious local insult is to produce a local inflammatory response with sequestration and activation of white blood cells and the release of a variety of mediators to deal with the primary 'insult' and prevent further damage. Normally, a delicate balance is achieved between pro- and anti-inflammatory cytokines such as interleukin-10. However, if the inflammatory insult is overwhelming or persistent, local control is lost and there is systemic release of a large array of mediators including cytokines (such as tumour necrosis factor, interleukins 1 and 6, platelet activation factor), prostaglandins, leukotrienes, lysosomal enzymes and free oxygen radicals. These mediators trigger complex interactions between endothelial cells, platelets, coagulation pathways and white blood cells which become 'activated', express adhesion factors and adhere to and damage the vascular endothelium. Fluid and cells pass across the damaged endothelium into the interstitial spaces, causing oedema and further tissue inflammation. A vicious circle of endothelial injury, intravascular coagulation, microvascular occlusion, tissue damage and further release of inflammatory mediators ensues. All organs may become involved; in the lungs this manifests as the acute respiratory distress syndrome (ARDS), in the kidneys it manifests as acute tubular necrosis (ATN), and the widespread disruption of the coagulation system results in the clinical picture of disseminated intravascular coagulation (DIC—see p. 952). The endothelium itself produces a number of mediators that locally control blood vessel tone: endothelin 1, a potent vasoconstrictor, and prostacyclin and nitric oxide (NO) which are systemic vasodilators. Through its calcium-independent release triggered by inflammatory mediators, NO is implicated in myocardial depression, vasodilatation and the microcirculatory chaos that characterises septic

4.6 TERMINOLOGY USED TO DESCRIBE THE INFLAMMATORY STATE
Infection
• Invasion of normally sterile host tissue by microorganisms
Bacteraemia
• Viable bacteria in the blood
Systemic inflammatory response syndrome (SIRS)

• Encompasses inflammatory response to both infective and non-infective causes such as pancreatitis, trauma, cardiopulmonary bypass, vasculitis etc.
 • Defined by presence of
  Temperature > 38.0° or < 36.0°
  Heart rate > 90/min
  Respiratory rate > 20/min
  $PaCO_2$ < 4.3 kPa or ventilated
  White blood count > 12 000 or < 4000/mm²

Sepsis
• Systemic inflammatory response caused by documented infection
Severe sepsis/SIRS
• Sepsis/SIRS with evidence of early organ dysfunction *or* hypotension
Septic/SIRS shock
• Sepsis associated with organ failure *and* hypotension (systolic BP < 90 mmHg or > 40 mmHg fall from baseline) unresponsive to fluid resuscitation
Multiple organ dysfunction syndrome (MODS)
• Development of impaired organ function in critically ill patients with SIRS   • If prompt treatment of underlying cause and suitable organ support are not achieved, then multiple organ failure (MOF) will ensue

shock. A major component of the tissue damage in septic/SIRS shock is an inability to take up oxygen and use it at mitochondrial level irrespective of supranormal global oxygen delivery. This effective bypassing of the tissues is characterised by reduced arteriovenous oxygen difference, a low oxygen extraction ratio, a raised plasma lactate and a paradoxically high mixed venous oxygen saturation (SvO_2).

If both the precipitating cause and accompanying circulatory failure (hypotension and frequently severe hypovolaemia due to venodilatation and fluid loss through the leaky vascular endothelium) are promptly controlled before significant organ failure occurs ('early shock'), the prognosis should be good. However, if the global and peripheral circulatory failure are not corrected, and particularly if the underlying cause is not effectively treated, progressive deterioration in organ function occurs and multiple organ failure (MOF) will develop ('late shock'—see Fig. 4.7).

The mortality of MOF is high and increases with the number of organs that have failed, the duration of organ failure and the patient's age. Failure of four or more organs is associated with a mortality of up to 90%.

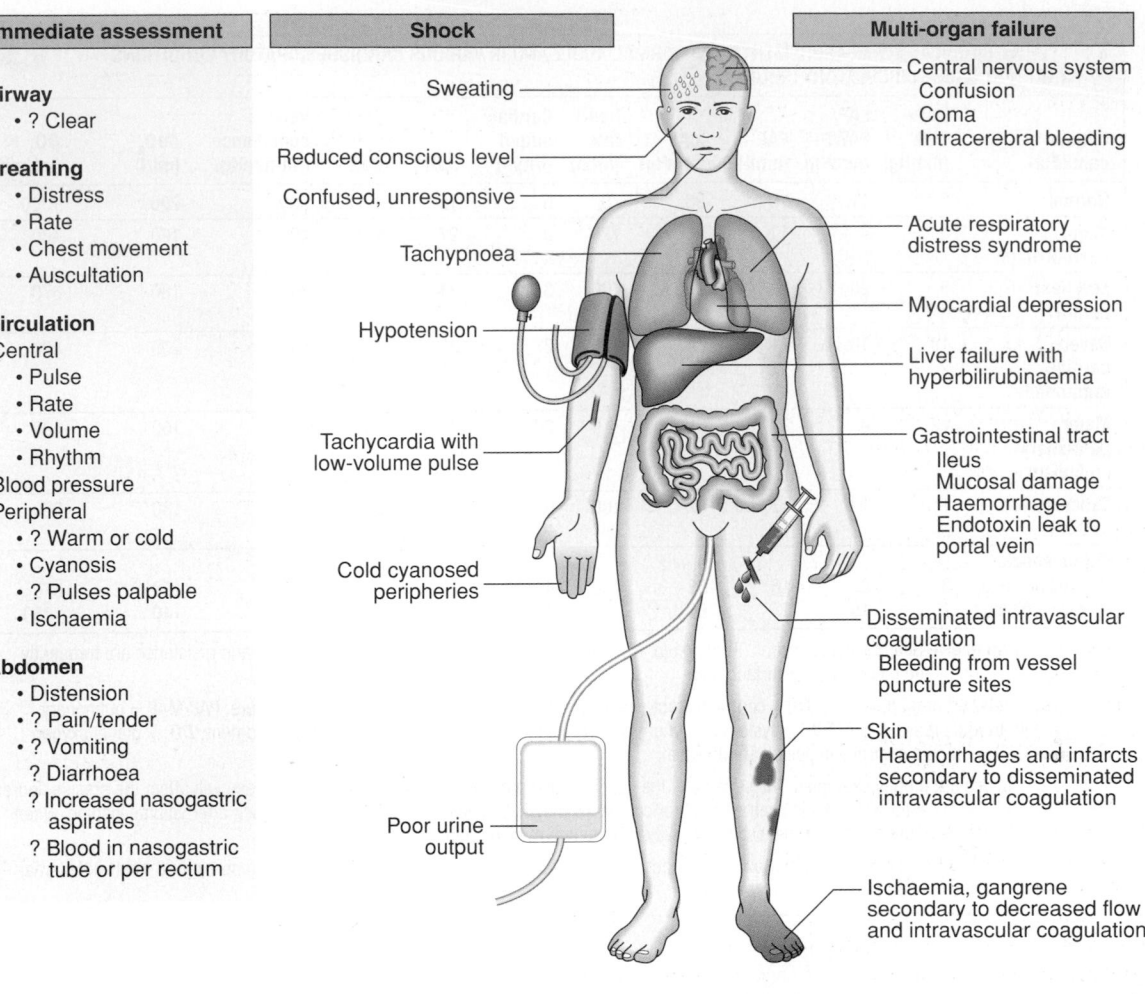

| Immediate assessment | Shock | Multi-organ failure |

Immediate assessment

Airway
- ? Clear

Breathing
- Distress
- Rate
- Chest movement
- Auscultation

Circulation
Central
- Pulse
- Rate
- Volume
- Rhythm
Blood pressure
Peripheral
- ? Warm or cold
- Cyanosis
- ? Pulses palpable
- Ischaemia

Abdomen
- Distension
- ? Pain/tender
- ? Vomiting
  ? Diarrhoea
  ? Increased nasogastric
   aspirates
  ? Blood in nasogastric
   tube or per rectum

Shock

Sweating

Reduced conscious level

Confused, unresponsive

Tachypnoea

Hypotension

Tachycardia with low-volume pulse

Cold cyanosed peripheries

Poor urine output

Multi-organ failure

Central nervous system
Confusion
Coma
Intracerebral bleeding

Acute respiratory distress syndrome

Myocardial depression

Liver failure with hyperbilirubinaemia

Gastrointestinal tract
Ileus
Mucosal damage
Haemorrhage
Endotoxin leak to portal vein

Disseminated intravascular coagulation
Bleeding from vessel puncture sites

Skin
Haemorrhages and infarcts secondary to disseminated intravascular coagulation

Ischaemia, gangrene secondary to decreased flow and intravascular coagulation

Fig. 4.7 Some features of shock. The early signs of shock are shown on the left and the organs affected in multi-organ failure are shown on the right.

MAJOR MANIFESTATIONS OF CRITICAL ILLNESS

CIRCULATORY FAILURE: 'SHOCK'

Circulatory failure or 'shock' exists when, despite a normal oxygen content of arterial blood, the oxygen delivery (DO_2) fails to meet the metabolic requirements of the tissues. In the context of critical illness, 'shock' is often considered to be synonymous with hypotension and to define the state of circulatory failure. While hypotension is a sinister development and requires urgent attention, it is most important to appreciate that hypotension is often a late manifestation of circulatory failure or shock and that the cardiac output and oxygen delivery may be critically low even though the blood pressure remains normal (see Box 4.7); the problem should be identified and treatment instituted before the blood pressure falls.

The many causes of circulatory failure or 'shock' may broadly be classified into:

- *hypovolaemic*—any condition provoking a major reduction in blood volume, e.g. internal or external haemorrhage, severe burns, dehydration (e.g. diabetic ketoacidosis)
- *cardiogenic*—any form of severe heart failure, e.g. myocardial infarction, acute mitral regurgitation, myocarditis
- *obstructive*—obstruction to blood flow around the circulation, e.g. major pulmonary embolism, cardiac tamponade, tension pneumothorax
- *neurogenic*—caused by major brain or spinal injury producing disruption of brain stem and neurogenic vasomotor control; may be associated with neurogenic pulmonary oedema

4.7 TYPICAL CIRCULATORY MEASUREMENTS IN A NORMAL ADULT AND IN VARIOUS CARDIORESPIRATORY CONDITIONS THAT MAY CAUSE CIRCULATORY 'SHOCK'

Clinical condition	RAP/ CVP (mmHg)	LAP/ PAWP (mmHg)	PAP (mmHg)	MAP (mmHg)	Heart rate (/min)	Cardiac output (l/min)	SVR*	PVR*	Venous compliance (ml/mmHg)	CaO_2 (ml/l)	DO_2 (ml/min)
Normal	6	11	16	96	70	5	18	1	300	200	1000
Major haemorrhage	0	4	11	81	120	3	27	2.3	40	160	480
Left heart failure	8	20	24	96	100	3.7	24	1	80	180	670
Severe cardiac tamponade	18	18	21	66	110	2	25	1.5	40	200	400
Major pulmonary embolism	12	6	36	81	110	2.5	28	12	40	160	400
Exacerbation of COPD	11	10	42	82	100	6	12	5	150	180	960
Septic shock Pre-volume load	3	8	16	55	130	4.5	12	1.3	340	150	675
Post-volume load	9	15	23	60	120	7.5	7	1.1	200	140	1050

* Multiply by 80 to give SI units: $dyn.sec.cm^{-5}$. To adjust for the size of the patient, the measurements of flow and resistance are frequently indexed by dividing by the patient's body surface area.

(RAP/LAP = right/left atrial pressure; CVP = central venous pressure; PAWP = pulmonary artery wedge pressure; PAP/MAP = pulmonary artery/mean arterial pressure; SVR/PVR = systemic/pulmonary vascular resistance; CaO_2 = arterial oxygen content; DO_2 = global oxygen delivery; COPD = chronic obstructive pulmonary disease)

Note These values are merely examples. The severity of the condition and pre-existing cardiorespiratory disease will affect the precise figures obtained in individual cases. Note that in contrast to other conditions the oxygen delivery is high in septic shock after volume loading. When the circulatory abnormalities have been defined in this way, appropriate management may be planned.

Pressures quoted referenced to zero at mid-axilla. Subtract vertical distance from mid-axilla to sternal angle (approx. 6–8 mmHg) if sternal angle used as reference point.

- *anaphylactic*—inappropriate vasodilatation triggered by an allergen (e.g. bee sting)
- *septic/SIRS*—infection or other causes of a systemic inflammatory response that produce widespread endothelial damage with vasodilatation, arteriovenous shunting, microvascular occlusion and tissue oedema, resulting in organ failure.

Clinical features and complications

Although dependent to some extent on the underlying cause, a range of clinical features are common to most cases (see Box 4.8 and Fig. 4.7).

Hypovolaemic, cardiogenic and obstructive types of the syndrome produce the 'popular' image of shock, with cold peripheries, weak central pulses and evidence of a low cardiac output. In contrast, neurogenic, anaphylactic and septic shock are usually associated with warm peripheries, bounding pulses and features of a high cardiac output. The central venous pressure (jugular venous pressure —JVP) is typically reduced in hypovolaemic and anaphylactic shock but elevated in cardiogenic and obstructive shock, and may be low, normal or high in neurogenic and

4.8 GENERAL FEATURES OF SHOCK

- Hypotension (systolic BP < 100 mmHg)
- Tachycardia (> 100/min)
- Cold, clammy skin
- Rapid, shallow respiration
- Drowsiness, confusion, irritability
- Oliguria (urine output < 30 ml/hr)
- Elevated or reduced central venous pressure (see text)
- Multi-organ failure (see Fig. 4.7)

septic shock. This is an important distinction and direct measurement of the central venous pressure or pulmonary artery wedge pressure (see Fig. 4.3, p. 190) may be very helpful if the physical signs are difficult to interpret. Figure 4.8 indicates how the likely diagnosis may be established by careful analysis of the CVP, peripheral perfusion, pulse volume and haematocrit. All forms of shock require early identification and treatment because, if inadequate regional tissue perfusion and cellular dysoxia persist, peripheral circulatory disruption will ensue and multiple organ failure will develop (see Fig. 4.7).

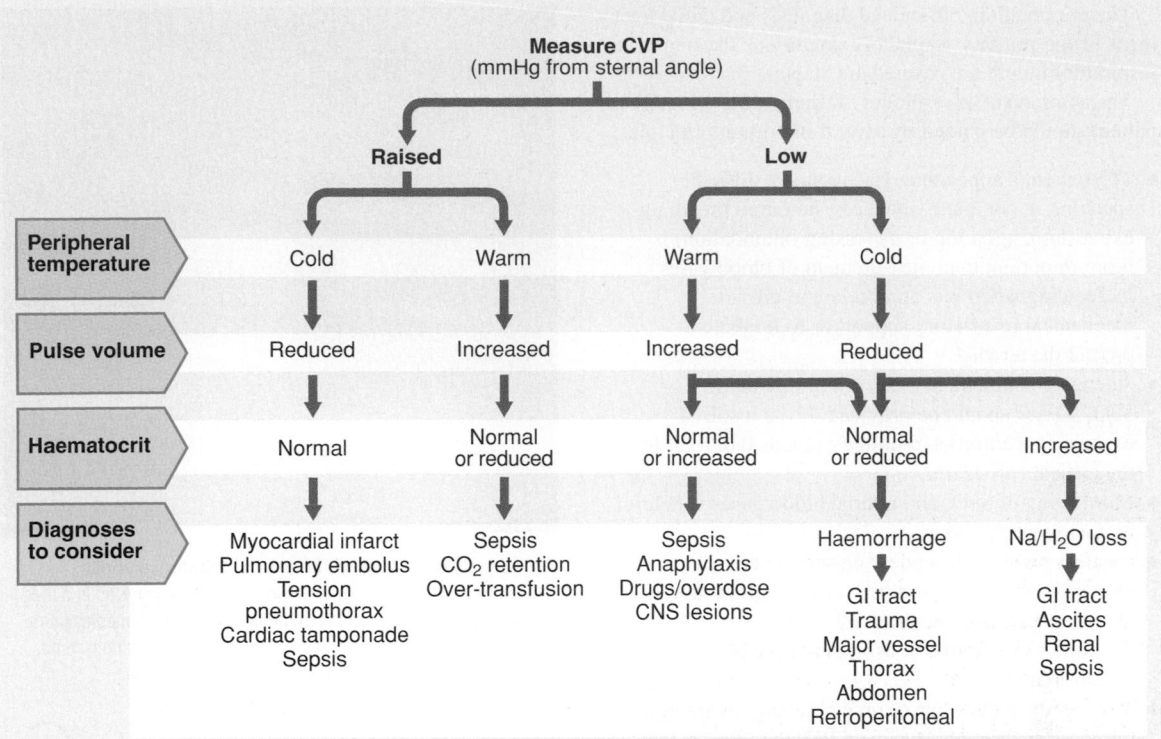

Fig. 4.8   A guide to the initial analysis and diagnosis of circulatory shock.

RESPIRATORY FAILURE

The majority of patients admitted to ICU/HDU will have respiratory problems either as the primary cause of their admission or secondary to pathology elsewhere. Respiratory failure is formally classified on the basis of blood gas analysis into:

- *type 1*—hypoxaemia (PaO_2 < 8 kPa when breathing air) without hypercapnia caused by a failure of gas exchange due to mismatching of pulmonary ventilation and perfusion
- *type 2*—hypoxaemia with hypercapnia ($PaCO_2$ > 6.5 kPa) due to alveolar hypoventilation which occurs when the respiratory muscles cannot perform sufficient effective work to clear the carbon dioxide produced by the body.

Although this distinction is conceptually useful, it cannot be applied too rigidly in critically ill patients since they may change from type 1 to 2 as their illness progresses. For example, hypercapnia may develop with progressive deterioration in pneumonia or pulmonary oedema as the patient tires and can no longer sustain the increased work of breathing.

Pulmonary problems in critically ill patients can also be divided according to the functional residual capacity (FRC, or the lung volume at the end of expiration). Examples of

low FRC include lung collapse, pneumonia and pulmonary oedema; examples of a high FRC (i.e. over-distended lungs) include asthma, COPD and bronchiolitis. This allows logical management directed at improving lung compliance and reducing the work of breathing.

The more common causes of acute respiratory failure presenting to ICU/HDU for respiratory support are shown in Box 4.9.

4.9 COMMON CAUSES OF RESPIRATORY FAILURE IN CRITICALLY ILL PATIENTS	
Type 1 respiratory failure	
• Pneumonia	• Lung collapse,* e.g. retained secretions
• Pulmonary oedema*	• Asthma
• Pulmonary embolism	• Pneumothorax
• Pulmonary fibrosis	• Pulmonary contusion (blunt chest trauma)
• ARDS*	
• Aspiration	
Type 2 respiratory failure	
• Reduced respiratory drive,* e.g. drug overdose, head injury	• COPD
• Peripheral neuromuscular disease, e.g. Guillain–Barré, myasthenia gravis	
• Upper airway obstruction (oedema, infection, foreign body)	• Flail chest injury
• Late severe acute asthma	• Exhaustion* (includes all type 1 causes)
Secondary complications of other diseases.	

The presentation, differential diagnosis and initial treatment of the primary respiratory conditions causing acute respiratory failure are covered in Chapter 13.

The assessment of respiratory failure in the critically ill patient should be guided by several important principles:

- The patient's appearance (tachypnoea, difficulty speaking in complete sentences, laboured breathing, exhaustion, agitation or increasing obtundation) is more important than measurement of blood gases in deciding when it is appropriate to provide mechanical respiratory support or to intubate to protect the airway.
- Adequate supplemental oxygen to maintain $SpO_2 > 94\%$ should be provided. If the inspired oxygen concentration required exceeds 0.6, refer to the critical care team.
- Monitoring of SpO_2 and arterial blood gases is helpful in documenting progress.
- Restless patients dependent on supplementary oxygen or with deteriorating conscious level are at risk. If they remove the mask or vomit, the resulting hypoxaemia or aspiration may be catastrophic.
- Try to reduce the work of breathing, e.g. by treating bronchoconstriction or using CPAP (see Box 4.18, p. 203).

ACUTE RESPIRATORY DISTRESS SYNDROME (ARDS)

This describes the acute, diffuse pulmonary inflammatory response to either direct (via airway or chest trauma) or indirect blood-borne insults that originate from extrapulmonary pathology. It is frequently associated with other organ dysfunction (kidney, heart, gut, liver, coagulation) as part of multiple organ failure. The term ARDS is often limited to patients requiring ventilatory support on the ICU, but less severe forms, conventionally referred to as acute lung injury (ALI) and with similar pathology, occur on acute medical and surgical wards. The clinical symptoms and signs are not specific, sharing many features with other pulmonary conditions. The criteria defining ARDS are:

- hypoxaemia, defined as PaO_2 (mmHg)/FiO_2 < 200 mmHg (26.7 kPa)
- chest radiograph showing diffuse bilateral infiltrates (see Fig. 4.9)
- absence of a raised left atrial pressure: PAWP < 15 mmHg
- impaired lung compliance.

The term ARDS has severe limitations as a diagnostic label since, like jaundice or a raised CVP, it represents a response to a variety of primary conditions (see Box 4.10).

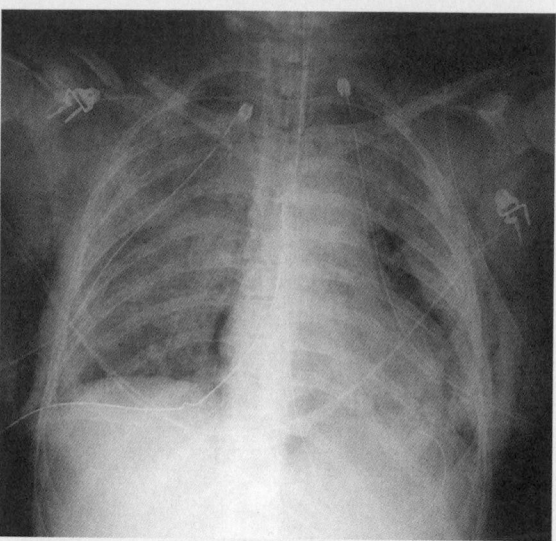

Fig. 4.9 Chest radiograph in acute respiratory distress syndrome (ARDS). This 22-year-old woman was involved in a road traffic accident. Note bilateral lung infiltrates, pneumomediastinum, pneumothoraces with bilateral chest drains, surgical emphysema, and fractures of the ribs, right clavicle and left scapula.

4.10 CONDITIONS PREDISPOSING TO ARDS	
Inhalation (direct)	
• Aspiration of gastric contents • Toxic gases/burn injury • Pneumonia	• Blunt chest trauma • Near-drowning
Blood-borne (indirect)	
• Sepsis • Necrotic tissue (particularly bowel) • Multiple trauma • Pancreatitis • Cardiopulmonary bypass • Severe burns • Drugs (heroin, barbiturates, thiazides)	• Major blood transfusion reaction • Anaphylaxis (wasp, bee, snake venom) • Fat embolism • Carcinomatosis • Obstetric crises (amniotic fluid embolus, eclampsia)

RENAL FAILURE

Oliguria is frequently an early sign of systemic problems in critical illness and successful resuscitation is associated with restoration of good urine output, an improving acid–base balance and correction of plasma potassium, urea and creatinine. Acute renal failure (see p. 594) developing in the context of critical illness usually results from pre-renal factors such as uncorrected hypovolaemia, hypotension or ischaemia causing acute tubular necrosis (ATN). Sepsis is frequently a compounding factor, causing both global hypotension and local ischaemia that is often associated with disseminated intravascular coagulation. In the presence of pre-existing chronic renal impairment or nephrotoxic drugs, acute renal failure may result from relatively minor ischaemic or hypotensive insults. While ATN is by far the most common cause of acute renal failure in the ICU, it is essential not to overlook other causes, such as renal tract obstruction (including a blocked urinary catheter), drug toxicity, acute glomerulonephritis and vasculitis associated with connective tissue diseases such as systemic lupus erythematosus. Appropriate investigations such as urinary microscopy, immunopathological tests and abdominal ultrasound to exclude renal tract obstruction need to be carried out at an early stage.

NEUROLOGICAL FAILURE (COMA)

Impaired consciousness or coma is often an early feature of severe systemic illness (see Box 4.11). Prompt assessment of conscious level and management of airway, breathing and circulation are essential to prevent further brain injury, to allow the diagnosis to be made and for definitive treatment to be instituted.

Impairment of conscious level is objectively graded according to the Glasgow Coma Scale (GCS—see p. 1143) and is used to monitor progress. Although necessarily limited, careful neurological examination is very important in the unconscious patient. Pupil size and reaction to light, presence or absence of neck stiffness, focal neurological signs and evidence of other organ impairment should be noted. After cardiorespiratory stability is achieved, the cause of the coma must be sought from history (family, witness, general practitioner), examination and investigation, particularly CT. The possibility of drug overdose should always be considered.

The direct neurological causes of coma are listed in Box 4.12 and further description of these conditions appears later in this chapter and in Chapter 22.

4.11 SYSTEMIC CAUSES OF COMA	
Cerebral hypoxia	
• Respiratory failure	
Cerebral ischaemia	
• Cardiac arrest	• Hypotension
Metabolic disturbance	
• Diabetes mellitus	• Uraemia
Hypoglycaemia	• Hepatic failure
Ketoacidosis	• Hypothermia
Hyperosmolar coma	• Drugs
• Hyponatraemia	• Sepsis

4.12 NEUROLOGICAL CAUSES OF COMA	
Trauma	
• Cerebral contusion	• Subdural haematoma
• Extradural haematoma	
Cerebrovascular disease	
• Subarachnoid/intracerebral haemorrhage	• Brain-stem stroke
	• Vasculitis
• Cerebral infarction	
Infection	
• Meningitis	• Abscess
• Encephalitis	
Others	
• Epilepsy	• Tumour

SEPSIS

The presentation may be dominated by any of the previously discussed major manifestations. Examination may reveal any or all of the features of SIRS (see Box 4.6, p. 194), together with an obvious focus of infection such as purulent sputum from the chest with shadowing on chest radiograph, erythema around an intravenous line, an acute abdomen or the characteristic rash of meningococcal sepsis (see Fig. 4.10). However, severe sepsis may present as unexplained hypotension (i.e. septic shock) and the speed of onset may simulate a major pulmonary embolus or myocardial infarction.

The appropriate terminology used to describe the critically ill patient with an inflammatory response is defined in Box 4.6, page 194; the term 'septicaemia' should now be abandoned.

The common sites of infection in critically ill patients and some of the appropriate investigations to consider are listed in Box 4.13.

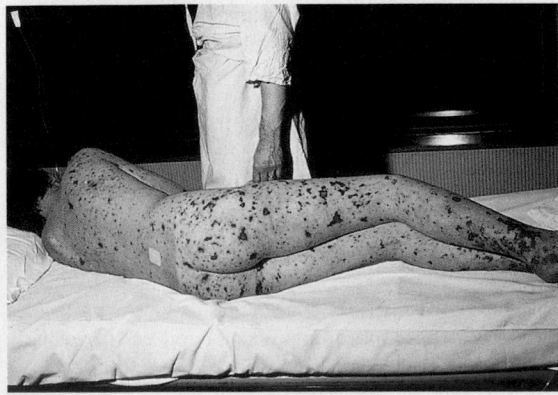

Fig. 4.10   The characteristic rash of meningococcal sepsis.

4.13 SITES OF INFECTION IN CRITICALLY ILL PATIENTS		
Sites of infection	**Investigations and comments**	
Major		
Intravenous lines (particularly central)	These should always be suspected; if the patient develops evidence of sepsis and the lines have not been changed for > 4 days, they must be replaced	
Lungs	The risk of nosocomial pneumonia is high in intubated patients. When the patient has been on the ICU for > 3–4 days, particularly if antibiotics have been administered, the nasopharynx becomes colonised with Gram-negative bacteria which migrate to the lower respiratory tract. Prophylaxis using a combination of parenteral and enteral antibiotics (selective decontamination of the digestive tract) has been shown to reduce incidence of nosocomial pneumonia	
Abdomen	Intra-abdominal abscesses or necrotic gut must be considered in patients who have had abdominal surgery. Pancreatitis or acute cholecystitis may develop as a complication of critical illness. Ultrasound, CT, aspiration of collections of fluid/pus and laparotomy are the relevant investigations	
Urinary tract	A catheter specimen of urine should always be taken in cases of unexplained sepsis but the lower urinary tract is a relatively unusual source of severe sepsis	
Other		
Heart valves	Transthoracic or transoesophageal echocardiogram	
Meninges	Lumbar puncture but check coagulation and platelet count first	
Joints and bones	Radiograph, gallium or technetium white cell scan	
Nasal sinuses, ears, retropharyngeal space	Clinical examination, plain radiograph, CT	
Genitourinary tract (particularly post-partum)	Per vaginam examination, ultrasound	
Gastrointestinal tract	Per rectum examination, stool culture, *Clostridium difficile* toxin, sigmoidoscopy	

The patient may be admitted with infection from home ('community-acquired') or may develop it after admission to the unit ('nosocomial'). The likely causative micro-organism and the antibiotic sensitivities will depend on this important distinction, which therefore directs the initial choice of antibiotics. Initial investigations should include:

● cultures of blood, sputum, intravascular lines, urine and any wound discharges
● coagulation profile, plasma lactate, arterial blood gases, urinalysis and chest radiograph.

As few as 10% of ICU patients with a clinical diagnosis of 'septic' shock will have positive blood cultures, due to the effects of prior antibiotic treatment and the fact that a patient with an inflammatory state is not necessarily infected.

Specific investigations will be driven by the history and examination. For example, erect/decubitus abdominal radiographs, ultrasound and CT might be considered in cases of suspected intra-abdominal sepsis (see Box 4.13).

The most important objective in management is to identify and treat the underlying cause. Nosocomial infections are an increasing problem on critical care units (see Box 4.14). Cross-infection is a major concern, particularly with regard to methicillin-resistant *Staphylococcus aureus* (MRSA) and multiresistant Gram-negative organisms, and if this is frequent it should prompt a review of the unit's infection control policies. The most important practice in

4.14 RISK FACTORS FOR NOSOCOMIAL INFECTION
● Mechanical ventilation ● Trauma ● Invasion with catheters—i.v., urinary, nasogastric tubes ● Stress ulcer prophylaxis with H_2-antagonists ● Prolonged length of stay

preventing cross-infection is thorough hand-washing after every patient contact.

DISSEMINATED INTRAVASCULAR COAGULATION

This is also known as consumptive coagulopathy and is one of the acquired disorders of haemostasis (see p. 952); it is common in critically ill patients and often heralds the onset of multi-organ failure. The condition is characterised by an increase in prothrombin time, partial thromboplastin time and fibrin degradation products, and a fall in platelets and fibrinogen. The clinically dominant feature may be either widespread bleeding from vascular access points, the gastrointestinal tract, bronchial tree and surgical wound sites, or widespread microvascular and even macrovascular thrombosis. Treatment is supportive with infusions of fresh frozen plasma and platelets.

GENERAL PRINCIPLES OF CRITICAL CARE MANAGEMENT

Critically ill patients should be assessed regularly and at least twice daily on morning and evening ward rounds. Initially, it seems daunting to perform such an assessment, particularly if there is multiple organ failure and no single unifying diagnosis. A systematic approach is required:

- Receive reports of progress from staff; review specialist opinions and medical/social history.
- Review charts.
- Examination: general (rashes, bleeding sites, line sites) and organ-specific.
- Assess information from monitors (check zeroing and calibration, determine whether they are still required).
- Fluid balance: note previous 24-hour balances, assess intra- and extravascular state of hydration and set targets for the bedside nurse for the next 24 hours, specifying crystalloid and colloid requirements, the route of administration (enteral or parenteral), and volume and filling pressure limits.
- Nutrition: review calorie intake, route of administration.
- Laboratory results: review haematology including coagulation, biochemistry and bacteriology.
- Review antibiotic therapy: note temperature, white count, line sites etc.
- Other drug therapy: review drug chart with ICU pharmacist to consider side-effects and interactions and to identify therapy that can be stopped.
- Review radiographs and other specialist investigations.
- Make an integrated management plan, specifying goals for each organ system.

MANAGEMENT OF MAJOR ORGAN FAILURE

CIRCULATORY SUPPORT

The key steps in the initial management of circulatory collapse or shock are listed in Box 4.15. In hypovolaemic shock the main priority is to resuscitate the patient by administering appropriate intravenous fluids at a rate dictated by the circulatory response to the infusion, while trying to identify and treat the source of fluid loss.

The management of tamponade is described on page 480 and the management of pulmonary embolism on page 565. Cardiac output (Q_T) is the product of stroke volume and heart rate ($Q_T = SV \times HR$) and therefore all measures to improve cardiac output are based on manipulation of rate and stroke volume. Three factors determine stroke volume: 'preload', 'afterload' and myocardial contractility.

PRELOAD

The atrial filling pressures (RAP or CVP, LAP or PAWP) or preload determine the end-diastolic ventricular volume

---

4.15 INITIAL MANAGEMENT OF SHOCK

- Measure blood gases
- Correct hypoxaemia
- Consider intubation if
  $PaCO_2 > 6.5$ kPa
  Respiratory rate > 25/min
  Impaired consciousness: GCS ≤ 7
- Correct acidaemia with i.v. bicarbonate if pH < 7.20 and $PaCO_2$ < 6 kPa (i.e. base excess > −10 mmol/l)
- Measure CVP (off ventilator)
  If CVP < +6 mmHg from mid-axillary line give volume challenge (250 ml normal saline or colloid)
  If CVP > +6 mmHg or poor ventricular function is suspected, use only 100 ml of fluid and consider insertion of PA catheter to direct further treatment with fluids and vasoactive agents

---

4.16 FACTORS INFLUENCING CENTRAL VENOUS PRESSURE

- Intravascular volume
- Venous tone
- Right heart function and 'afterload', i.e. PAP
- Intrathoracic pressure

---

which, according to Starling's Law and depending on the myocardial contractility, defines the force of the next cardiac contraction (see Fig. 12.23, p. 382). The predominant factor influencing preload is venous return, which is determined by the intravascular volume and the venous 'tone' (see Box 4.16).

When volume is lost (e.g. major haemorrhage), venous 'tone' increases and this helps to offset the consequent fall in atrial filling pressure and cardiac output. If the equivalent volume is returned slowly, over a few hours, the right atrial pressure will gradually return to normal as the intravascular volume is restored and the reflex increase in venous tone abates. However, if fluid is infused too rapidly there will be insufficient time for the venous and arteriolar tone to fall and pulmonary oedema may occur, even though the intravascular volume has only been restored to the pre-morbid level.

If the preload is low, volume loading (intravenous fluids) is the most appropriate means of improving cardiac output and oxygen delivery and should be the priority in circulatory resuscitation.

When the preload is high, due to excessive intravascular volume or impaired myocardial contractility, it is advisable to remove volume from the circulation (diuretics, venesection, haemofiltration) or increase the capacity of the vascular bed using venodilator therapy (glyceryl trinitrate, morphine).

AFTERLOAD

The tension in the ventricular myocardium during systole, or 'afterload', is determined by the resistance to ventricular outflow, which is a function of the peripheral arteriolar resistance. If the considerable assumption is made that flow in the circulation is linear and non-pulsatile, the resistance against which each ventricle works may be calculated as the pressure drop across the resistance bed divided by the flow:

Systemic vascular resistance (SVR) = (MAP – RAP)/Q_T
Pulmonary vascular resistance (PVR) = (PAP – LAP)/Q_T

If the pressures are measured in mmHg and flow in litres/min, these calculations give the resistances in simple or 'Wood' units; multiplication by 80 converts to SI units. For a normal 70 kg adult:

SVR = (90 – 0)/5 × 80 = 1440 dyn.sec.cm^{-5}
PVR = (10 – 5)/5 × 80 = 80 dyn.sec.cm^{-5}

Understanding the reciprocal relationship between pressure, flow and resistance is crucial for appropriate circulatory management. High resistances produce lower flows at higher pressures for a given amount of ventricular work. Therefore, a systemic vasodilator such as sodium nitroprusside will allow the same cardiac output to be maintained for less ventricular work but with a reduced arterial blood pressure. In hyperdynamic sepsis, the SVR and blood pressure are low but the cardiac output is high; therefore a vasoconstrictor (noradrenaline (norepinephrine), vasopressin) is appropriate to restore BP, albeit with some reduction in cardiac output.

MYOCARDIAL CONTRACTILITY

This determines the work that the ventricle performs under given loading conditions or, put another way, the stroke volume that the ventricle will generate against a given afterload for a particular level of preload.

The relationship between stroke work and filling pressure is shown in Figure 12.23, page 382. The ventricular stroke work is the external work performed by the ventricle with each beat and is calculated from the stroke volume (SV) and the pre- and afterload pressures:

Ventricular stroke work (VSW) = SV × (afterload – preload)
e.g. LVSW = SV × (MAP – LAP) ml.mmHg

Using the data for a normal adult shown in Box 4.7, page 196, and multiplying by 0.0136 to convert to SI units of gram.metres, LVSW and RVSW are 80 and 10 g.m respectively.

Consideration of ventricular work is important because it is desirable to maintain satisfactory perfusion and oxygen delivery to all organs at maximum cardiac efficiency and therefore minimise myocardial ischaemia. Myocardial contractility is frequently reduced in critically ill patients due to either pre-existing cardiac disease (usually ischaemic heart disease) or the disease process itself (particularly sepsis).

If the cardiac output is inadequate and myocardial contractility is poor, as defined by a flattened stroke work/filling pressure equation, the available treatment options are to:

- *Reduce afterload.* This can be achieved by using an arteriolar dilator (e.g. nitrates, ACE inhibitor) which may be limited by the consequent fall in systemic pressure. A counterpulsation balloon pump offers the ideal physiological treatment because it both reduces LV afterload and increases cardiac output, diastolic pressure and coronary perfusion; it is particularly valuable in treating myocardial ischaemia.
- *Increase preload.* However, if there is significant impairment of myocardial contractility, giving intravascular volume to increase filling pressures will only produce a small increase in stroke volume and cardiac output and risks precipitating pulmonary oedema.
- *Improve myocardial contractility.* Box 4.17 lists some of the characteristics of the commonly used inotropic agents.

4.17 CIRCULATORY EFFECTS OF COMMONLY USED VASOACTIVE DRUG INFUSIONS

Drug	Cardiac contractility	Heart rate	Blood pressure	Cardiac output	Splanchnic blood flow	SVR	PVR
Dopamine (< 5 mg/kg/min) (> 5 mg/kg/min)	↑ ↑↑	→/↑ ↑	→/↑ ↑	↑ ↑↑	→/↑ →	→/↑ ↑	→/↑ ↑
Adrenaline (epinephrine)	↑↑	↑	↑↑	↑↑↑	↓	↑	↑
Noradrenaline (norepinephrine)	→/↑	→/↓	↑↑	→/↓	→/↓	↑↑	↑↑
Isoprenaline	↑	↑↑	→/↓	↑	→/↑	→/↓	↓
Dobutamine	↑	↑	→/↓	↑↑	→	↓	↓
Dopexamine	↑	↑↑	→/↓	↑	↑	↓	↓
Glyceryl trinitrate	→	↑	↓	↑	↑	↓	↓
Nitroprusside	→	↑	↓	↑	↑	↓	↓
Epoprostenol (prostacyclin)	→	↑	↓	↑	↑	↓	↓
Milrinone	→/↑	↑	↓	↑↑	↑	↓	↓

Note These effects are guidelines only. The exact response will depend on the circulatory state of the patient and the dose of the drug.

- *Control heart rate and rhythm* (see pp. 405–419). The optimum heart rate is usually between 90 and 110 per minute. Correction of low serum potassium and magnesium concentrations should be the first stage in treating tachyarrhythmias in the critically ill.

RESPIRATORY SUPPORT

Respiratory support is indicated to maintain the patency of the airway, correct hypoxaemia and hypercapnia, and reduce the work of breathing. It ranges from oxygen therapy by facemask, through non-invasive techniques such as continuous positive airway pressure (CPAP—see Box 4.18) and non-invasive positive pressure ventilation (NIPPV), to full ventilation via an endotracheal tube or tracheostomy.

OXYGEN THERAPY

Oxygen is given to treat hypoxaemia and ensure adequate arterial oxygenation ($SpO_2 > 90\%$). It should initially be given by facemask or nasal cannulae and the inspired

4.18 MODES AND TERMS USED IN MECHANICAL VENTILATORY SUPPORT

Intermittent positive pressure ventilation (IPPV)

- Generic term for all types of ventilation using pressure above atmospheric pressure

Controlled mandatory ventilation (CMV)

• Most basic classic form of ventilation • Pre-set rate; pre-set ventilatory parameters; usually volume pre-set	• Does not allow spontaneous breaths • Appropriate for initial control of patients with little respiratory drive, severe lung injury or circulatory instability

Synchronised intermittent mandatory ventilation (SIMV)

• Pre-set rate of mandatory breaths with pre-set tidal volume • Allows spontaneous breaths between mandatory breaths	• Spontaneous breaths may be pressure-supported (PS) • Allows patient to settle on ventilator with less sedation

Pressure controlled ventilation (PCV)

• Pre-set rate; pre-set inspiratory pressure • Tidal volume depends on pre-set pressure, lung compliance and airways resistance	• Used in management of severe acute respiratory failure to avoid high airway pressure, often with prolonged inspiratory to expiratory ratio (pressure controlled inverse ratio ventilation—PCIRV)

Pressure support ventilation (PSV)

• Breaths are triggered by patient • Ventilator provides positive pressure to augment patient's breaths	• Useful for weaning • Usually combined with CPAP; may be combined with SIMV • Pressure support is titrated against tidal volume and respiratory rate

Positive end-expiratory pressure (PEEP)

• Positive airway pressure applied during expiratory phase in patients receiving mechanical ventilation	• Aids recruitment of atelectatic or oedematous lung; improves oxygenation • May impair venous return and reduce cardiac output

Continuous positive airways pressure (CPAP)

• Positive airway pressure applied throughout the respiratory cycle, via either an endotracheal tube or a tight-fitting facemask • Provided by a flow generator connected to a wall oxygen supply that entrains air to achieve the desired FiO_2 (between 30 and 100%)	• Aids recruitment of atelectatic or oedematous lung; improves oxygenation • Mask CPAP discourages coughing and clearance of lung secretions and may increase the risk of aspiration

Bi-level positive airway pressure (BiPAP/BIPAP)

• Describes situation of two levels of positive airway pressure (higher level in inspiration) • In fully ventilated patients, BIPAP is essentially the same as PCV with PEEP	• In partially ventilated patients, and especially if used non-invasively, BiPAP is essentially PSV with CPAP

Non-invasive intermittent positive pressure ventilation (NIPPV)

• Provides pressure support (typically 20–25 cm H_2O) at onset of inspiration, which ceases at onset of expiration • May be applied via a facemask or nasal mask • Benefits patients with an acute exacerbation of COPD or primary alveolar hypoventilation who are tiring and cannot generate sufficient work of breathing	• Oxygen can be added but it is difficult to achieve an $FiO_2 > 0.4$ • A lot of time has to be spent reassuring patients and matching the timing and trigger sensitivity to their respiratory pattern

Non-invasive intermittent negative pressure ventilation (NINPV)

• Operates by producing negative pressures within an external shell (cuirass), tank or iron lung that encases all or part of the thorax	• Developed following the polio epidemics of the 1950s and now largely superseded by NIPPV

oxygen concentration (FiO_2) can then be adjusted according to the results of pulse oximetry and arterial blood gas analysis. The risk of progressive hypercapnia in certain patients with COPD who are dependent on hypoxic drive has been overstated. If administration of oxygen to ensure $SpO_2 >$ 90% results in unacceptable hypercapnia, the patient almost certainly requires some form of mechanical respiratory support. The theoretical risks of oxygen toxicity are not relevant if the patient is acutely hypoxaemic. It is vital to maintain cerebral oxygenation even at the risk of pulmonary toxicity because hypoxic cerebral damage is irreversible. More detail on oxygen therapy is given on page 507.

NON-INVASIVE RESPIRATORY SUPPORT

If a patient remains hypoxaemic on high-flow oxygen, other measures are required to improve oxygenation and to reduce the work of breathing. If the patient has respiratory failure associated with lung collapse (low FRC), application of continuous positive airways pressure (CPAP—see Box 4.18) will both improve oxygenation by recruitment of underventilated alveoli, and reduce the work of breathing by improving lung compliance. CPAP is most successful in clinical situations where alveoli are readily recruited, such as in pulmonary oedema and post-operative collapse/ atelectasis. It is also helpful in treating pneumonia, especially in immunocompromised patients. The risk of nosocomial infection is reduced by avoiding endotracheal intubation. A CPAP mask often becomes uncomfortable and gastric distension may occur. Patients must therefore be cooperative, be able to protect their airway and have the strength to breathe spontaneously and cough effectively. NIPPV refers to ventilatory support by nasal or full facemask. It may avoid the need for endotracheal intubation in patients with type 2 respiratory failure, typically those with exacerbations of COPD, and it may be used during weaning from conventional ventilation. As with mask CPAP, NIPPV requires a patient who is conscious and cooperative.

ENDOTRACHEAL INTUBATION AND MECHANICAL VENTILATION

Over 60% of patients appropriately admitted to ICU require endotracheal intubation and mechanical ventilation, mostly for respiratory failure but also for other reasons (see Boxes 4.19 and 4.20).

The final decision to perform tracheal intubation and ventilate a patient should be taken on clinical grounds rather than as a response to the results of particular investigations. In the conscious patient intubation requires induction of anaesthesia and muscle relaxation, while in more obtunded patients sedation alone may be adequate. This can be hazardous in the critically ill patient with respiratory and often cardiovascular failure. Continuous monitoring, particularly of heart rate and BP (preferably invasively), is essential, and resuscitation drugs must be immediately available. Hypotension commonly follows sedation or anaesthesia because of direct cardiovascular effects of the drugs and loss of sympathetic drive, while positive pressure ventilation

---

4.19 CLINICAL CONDITIONS REQUIRING MECHANICAL VENTILATION

Post-operative

- e.g. After major abdominal or cardiac surgery

Respiratory failure

- ARDS
- Pneumonia
- COPD
- Acute severe asthma
- Aspiration
- Smoke inhalation, burns

Circulatory failure

- Following cardiac arrest
- Pulmonary oedema
- Low cardiac output—cardiogenic shock

Neurological disease

- Coma of any cause
- Status epilepticus
- Drug overdose
- Respiratory muscle failure (e.g. Guillain–Barré, poliomyelitis, myasthenia gravis)
- Head injury—to avoid hypoxaemia and hypercapnia, and to reduce intracranial pressure
- Bulbar abnormalities causing risk of aspiration (e.g. cerebrovascular accident, myasthenia gravis)

Multiple trauma—additional considerations

- Metabolic rate (ventilatory requirements rise as metabolic rate increases)
- Nutritional reserve (low potassium or phosphate reduces respiratory muscle power)
- Condition of the abdomen (distension due to surgery or tense ascites causes both discomfort and splinting of the diaphragm, compromising spontaneous respiratory effort and promoting bilateral basal lung collapse)

4.20 INDICATIONS FOR TRACHEAL INTUBATION AND MECHANICAL VENTILATION

- Protection of airway
- Removal of secretions
- Hypoxaemia ($PaO_2 < 8$ kPa; $SpO_2 < 90\%$) despite CPAP with $FiO_2 > 0.6$
- Hypercapnia if conscious level impaired or risk of raised intracranial pressure
- Vital capacity falling below 1.2 litres in patients with neuromuscular disease
- Removing the work of breathing in exhausted patients

---

compounds the problem by increasing intrathoracic pressure, thereby reducing venous return and hence cardiac output.

The different types of ventilatory support are illustrated in Figure 4.11. Modern ventilators allow considerable flexibility in the level of support from controlled mandatory ventilation to partial ventilatory support modes, and assisted spontaneous breathing which allows the ventilator to respond to patients' demands. Use of partial ventilatory support avoids the requirement for and hazards of paralysis and deep sedation, and allows the patient to be conscious and yet comfortable.

General considerations in the management of the ventilated/intubated patient

- Beware of the restless patient. Try to establish the cause of the problem before simply administering sedation. Possibilities include pneumothorax, hypoxaemia,

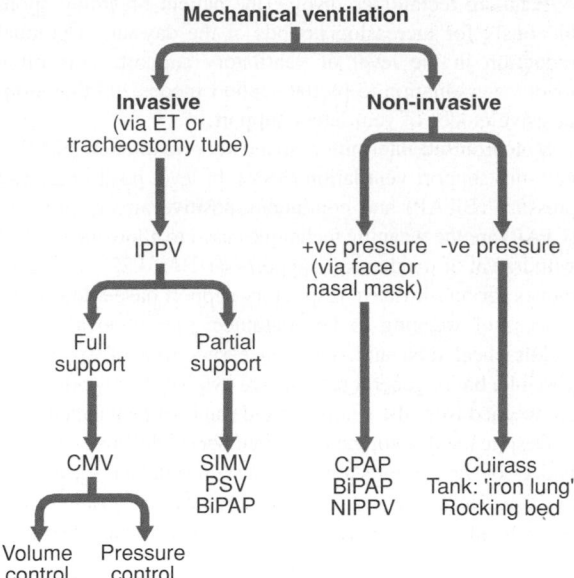

Mechanical ventilation

Invasive (via ET or tracheostomy tube)
- IPPV
  - Full support
    - CMV
      - Volume control
      - Pressure control
  - Partial support
    - SIMV
    - PSV
    - BiPAP

Non-invasive
- +ve pressure (via face or nasal mask)
  - CPAP
  - BiPAP
  - NIPPV
- -ve pressure
  - Cuirass
  - Tank: 'iron lung'
  - Rocking bed

Fig. 4.11 Different types of invasive and non-invasive ventilatory support. (See Box 4.18 for abbreviations; ET = endotracheal)

hypercapnia due to inadequate ventilation, pain, onset of sepsis, cardiac decompensation (pulmonary oedema, dysrhythmia, infarction) and proximal airway obstruction, e.g. secretions.

- Patients who are breathing spontaneously adjust their ventilation to compensate for metabolic derangements; this cannot occur in patients who are ventilated using mandatory modes so the clinician must either correct the underlying metabolic abnormality or make appropriate changes to the ventilator settings. For example, a patient with severe diabetic ketoacidosis will hyperventilate to compensate for the metabolic acidosis; if mechanical ventilation is instituted, there will be a potentially catastrophic fall in pH unless the acidosis is corrected by administering sodium bicarbonate or a high minute volume (artificial hyperventilation) is delivered.
- Ventilator alarms should be set to detect:
  —minimum acceptable minute volume to identify inadvertent disconnection
  —maximum acceptable airway pressure to prevent barotrauma.
- Humidify and warm inspired gas to prevent inspissation of secretions.
- Arrange regular positioning, physiotherapy and suctioning to clear secretions and prevent both proximal airway obstruction and distal alveolar collapse. The patient should generally be nursed in a 30° head-up position to avoid aspiration.
- Obtain a chest radiograph to check the position of the endotracheal tube following intubation (the appropriate position is 4 cm above the carina).
- Bronchoscopy should be readily available to:
  —investigate upper airways obstruction (plugging of the proximal bronchial tree by inspissated mucus is the most common cause)

—investigate lobar/segmental collapse, and aspirate mucus plug obstructing proximal bronchial tree
—assist in cases of difficult intubation or tracheostomy tube change
—obtain bronchoalveolar lavage specimens for microbiology
—identify the cause of haemoptysis (not always easy)
—exclude tracheobronchial disruption after thoracic trauma.

Ventilation strategy

The selection of ventilator mode and settings for tidal volume, respiratory rate, PEEP and inspiratory to expiratory ratio is dependent on the cause of the respiratory failure. The objectives should be to:

- improve gas exchange
- minimise damage to the lung by avoiding high lung volumes and F_IO_2
- avoid adverse circulatory effects
- make the patient comfortable without heavy sedation or muscle paralysis by reducing the work of breathing and ensuring harmonious interaction between the patient and the ventilator.

In asthma and conditions with increased lung volumes (high FRC) a prolonged expiratory phase is necessary to prevent progressive lung over-inflation; PEEP and large tidal volumes exacerbate over-distension, produce high alveolar pressures and increase the risk of pneumothorax. High intrathoracic pressures compromise circulatory function, particularly if there is intravascular volume depletion, so that oxygen delivery may actually fall in spite of improved arterial oxygenation.

In patients with alveolar collapse (low FRC), such as those with ARDS, it is appropriate to use a prolonged inspiratory to expiratory ratio and high levels of PEEP (+10 to +15 cm H_2O) to recruit alveoli and improve compliance and gas exchange (see Box 4.21). Recent studies have shown that in ARDS, damage to the lungs can be exacerbated by mechanical ventilation, possibly by over-distension of alveoli and repeated opening and closure of distal airways.

Other management strategies which may be of benefit in severe ARDS include prone ventilation, nitric oxide inhalation and corticosteroids.

EBM

ARDS—optimal ventilation strategy

'A large multicentre RCT has shown that in ARDS a 'lung-protective' ventilatory strategy using PEEP but limiting tidal volumes to 5–7 ml/kg and accepting higher $PaCO_2$ levels (permissive hypercapnia) improves outcome.'

- Acute Respiratory Distress Syndrome Network. Ventilation with lower tidal volumes as compared with traditional tidal volumes for acute lung injury and the acute respiratory distress syndrome. N Engl J Med 2000; 342:1301–1308.
- Amato MB, Barbas CS, Medeiros DM, et al. Effect of a protective ventilation strategy on mortality in the acute respiratory distress syndrome. N Engl J Med 1998; 338:347–354.

4.21 PRINCIPLES OF MECHANICAL VENTILATION IN ARDS

- Optimum ventilator settings are
  Pressure-controlled
  Long inspiratory to expiratory time
  Positive end-expiratory pressure (PEEP)
- Allow $Pa\text{CO}_2$ to rise (permissive hypercapnia) and tolerate lower oxygen saturations than normal (e.g. 88–90%)
- Avoid
  Large tidal volumes (ideally 6 ml/kg)
  Airway pressure of more than 35 cm H_2O
  $F\text{IO}_2$ of more than 0.8 if possible
- Remember that high intrathoracic pressures compromise circulatory function so oxygen delivery may actually fall in spite of improved oxygenation
- Management must be a balance between improving gas exchange, minimising the risk of subsequent pulmonary fibrosis due to lung injury, and avoiding adverse circulatory effects

Prone ventilation

Prone positioning improves oxygenation significantly in about two-thirds of patients with ARDS by matching ventilation to perfusion. However, the only multicentre trial performed to date has failed to demonstrate any beneficial effect on outcome.

Inhaled nitric oxide

Nitric oxide is a very short-acting pulmonary vasodilator. Delivered to the airway in concentrations of between 1 and 20 parts per million, it improves blood flow to ventilated alveoli, thus improving ventilation:perfusion matching. Oxygenation can be improved markedly in some patients but the evidence indicates that the benefit only lasts for 48 hours and outcome is not improved.

Pharmacological therapy

There is now considerable evidence that corticosteroids improve outcome if given in the fibroproliferative stage of ARDS. A trial of steroids is therefore indicated if a patient with ARDS has consistent gas exchange impairment and ventilator dependence at 7–10 days after diagnosis.

Weaning from respiratory support

This is the process of progressively reducing and eventually removing all external ventilatory support and associated apparatus. The majority of patients require mechanical ventilatory support for only a few days and do not need weaning. In these patients simple trials of breathing via the endotracheal tube will usually indicate whether the patient can be successfully extubated or not.

In contrast, patients who have required long-term ventilatory support for severe lung disease, e.g. ARDS, may initially be unable to sustain even a modest degree of respiratory work because of residual decreased lung compliance and hence increased work of breathing, compounded by respiratory muscle weakness. These patients therefore require weaning until respiratory muscle strength improves to the point that all support can be discontinued.

Weaning techniques involve the patient breathing spontaneously for increasing periods of the day and a gradual reduction in the level of ventilatory support. This often involves graduation to partial support modes and then non-invasive modes of ventilatory support.

Synchronised intermittent mandatory ventilation (SIMV), pressure support ventilation (PSV), bi-level positive airway pressure (BiPAP) and continuous positive airway pressure (CPAP) are the weaning techniques used to allow the gradual withdrawal of mechanical support (see Box 4.22). The techniques for non-invasive respiratory support have allowed the process of weaning to be continued after removal of the endotracheal tube and make an earlier trial of extubation possible, but in general patients are extubated only after they are weaned from the ventilator and can breathe unaided.

Despite the development of a number of objective tests and indices of the patient's ability to sustain spontaneous ventilation, the decision to extubate and the speed of weaning from mechanical ventilation still rely largely on clinical judgement.

4.22 FACTORS IN DECIDING WHETHER A VENTILATED PATIENT CAN BE WEANED AND SAFELY EXTUBATED

- Has the original indication for mechanical ventilation resolved?
- Is the respiratory pattern adequate with minimal pressure support (respiratory rate < 30/min; V_T > 5 ml/kg)?
- Is gas exchange satisfactory ($P\text{O}_2$ > 8 kPa on $F\text{IO}_2$ < 0.5; $P\text{CO}_2$ < 6 kPa)?
- Is the circulation stable, with a normal or reasonably low left atrial pressure?
- Is the patient conscious and able to cough and protect his/her airway?
- Is analgesia adequate?
- Are any metabolic problems well controlled?

Tracheostomy

Tracheostomy is usually performed electively when endotracheal intubation is likely to be prolonged (over 14 days). Tracheostomies have benefits in terms of patient comfort, aid weaning from ventilation (since sedation can be reduced or stopped), and allow access for tracheal toilet and intermittent respiratory support (see Box 4.23).

4.23 ADVANTAGES AND DISADVANTAGES OF TRACHEOSTOMY

Advantages

- Patient comfort
- Improved oral hygiene
- Reduced sedation requirement
- Enables speech with cuff deflated and a speaking valve attached
- Earlier weaning and ICU discharge
- Access for tracheal toilet
- Reduces vocal cord damage

Disadvantages

- Immediate complications: hypoxia, haemorrhage
- Tracheal damage; late stenosis
- Tracheostomy site infection

Tracheostomy is now usually carried out using a percutaneous technique in the ICU, which avoids the need for transfer to the operating theatre. This has led to earlier and more frequent use of tracheostomy.

Mini-tracheostomy

The passage of a smaller (4.5 mm internal diameter) tube through the cricothyroid membrane is a useful technique to clear airway secretions in spontaneously breathing patients with a poor cough effort. It can be particularly useful in the HDU and in post-operative patients.

RENAL SUPPORT

Oliguria (< 0.5 ml/kg/hr for 2–3 hours) requires explanation and early intervention to correct hypoxaemia, hypovolaemia, hypotension and renal hypoperfusion. There is little evidence that specific treatments aimed at inducing a diuresis, such as low-dose dopamine, furosemide (frusemide) or mannitol, have renoprotective action or additional beneficial value in restoring renal function beyond aggressive haemodynamic resuscitation to achieve normovolaemia, normotension and an appropriate cardiac output. Mannitol, an osmotic diuretic, is a physiological way of producing diuresis and is valuable in renal failure associated with intravenous contrast media and myoglobinuria due to rhabdomyolysis. Sepsis is frequently implicated in the development of acute renal failure and the focus must be promptly and adequately treated by surgical drainage and antibiotics if renal function is to be restored. Obstruction of the renal tract should always be excluded by abdominal ultrasound and, if present, should be relieved.

If renal function cannot be restored following resuscitation, renal replacement therapy (see p. 605) is indicated if there is:

- fluid overload and a risk of pulmonary oedema
- hyperkalaemia: potassium > 6 mmol/l despite treatment
- metabolic acidosis (pH < 7.25)
- uraemia: urea > 35–40 mmol/l.

The preferred renal replacement therapy in the ICU is pumped venovenous haemofiltration. This is associated with fewer osmotic fluid shifts and hence greater haemodynamic stability than haemodialysis. It is carried out using a double-lumen central venous catheter placed percutaneously. Haemofiltration should be continuous, preferably at a rate above 1.5 l/hour, because higher rates of filtration are associated with improved outcome. Intermittent treatment should only be used when the patient is recovering from the primary insult and awaiting the return of normal renal function. Provided the precipitating cause can be successfully treated, renal failure due to ATN usually recovers between 5 days and several weeks later.

Survival rates from multiple organ failure including acute renal failure have been around 50% for many years but recent evidence suggests that survival has improved as a result of modern haemofiltration techniques.

GASTROINTESTINAL AND HEPATIC SUPPORT

The gastrointestinal tract and liver play an important role in the evolution of multiple organ failure, even when the primary diagnosis is not related to the abdomen. Gastrointestinal symptoms such as nausea, vomiting and large nasogastric aspirates may be the earliest signs of regional circulatory failure and, when associated with a tender, distended, silent abdomen, indicate the probable site of the primary pathology. Ischaemic bowel is difficult to diagnose in the critically ill patient but, in the context of an otherwise unexplained lactic acidosis, hyperkalaemia and coagulopathy, urgent laparotomy must be considered. The gut has a very rapid cell turnover rate and fasting alone can produce marked changes in mucosal structure and function. In hypovolaemic and frank shock states, splanchnic vasoconstriction produces gut mucosal ischaemia, damaging the mucosal barrier and allowing toxins to enter the portal circulation and lymphatics. Although equipped to cope with moderate portal toxaemia, the liver may be overwhelmed and will then augment the inflammatory response itself by releasing cytokines into the systemic circulation. For this reason the gut has been described as the 'undrained abscess' or 'motor' of multiple organ failure.

Manifestations of MOF within the gastrointestinal tract include erosive gastritis, stress ulceration, bleeding and ischaemia, pancreatitis and acalculous cholecystitis. Adequacy of gastric mucosal perfusion can be assessed by gastric tonometry, a technique that uses a modified nasogastric tube with a balloon containing either saline or air to measure intramucosal pH (pHi) or PCO_2i. An increased difference between gastric PCO_2 and arterial PCO_2 or an intramucosal acidosis (pHi < 7.32) implies mucosal ischaemia.

Early institution of enteral nutrition is the most effective strategy for protecting the gut mucosa and providing nutritional support. There is evidence suggesting that nasogastric feeds supplemented with arginine, omega 3 fatty acids and nucleotides ('immunonutrition') may improve outcome in critical illness. Glutamine supplementation is logical, although not of proven benefit, since it is a 'conditionally essential' amino acid and the principal energy substrate used by the gut mucosa in critical illness. Total parenteral nutrition (TPN) should only be started if all attempts at implementing enteral feeding, including nasojejunal delivery, have failed; it should be necessary in fewer than 10% of general ICU patients.

Ranitidine and sucralfate are both used to reduce the risk of gastrointestinal haemorrhage, although ranitidine is the more effective. Both agents are associated with an increased incidence of nosocomial pneumonia. Treatment should be stopped when full enteral nutrition has been established and is probably only necessary in patients with a history of peptic ulcer and those who are ventilated or have a severe coagulopathy.

The hepatic circulation, 80% of which is derived from the portal venous system, is compromised by the same factors which lead to splanchnic vasoconstriction. Hepatic ischaemia leads to impaired filtering of endotoxin from the portal circulation and, as SIRS develops, inflammatory mediators (e.g. cytokines IL-1, IL-6 and TNF) are released from activated Kupffer cells (hepatic macrophages) into the systemic circulation, increasing the risk of acute renal failure and the other manifestations of MOF developing. Increased metabolic activity in the liver as a result of sepsis and the need for vasoconstricting agents to maintain blood pressure increase hepatic ischaemia. The synthetic inodilator dopexamine with dopaminergic 1 and 2 and beta-adrenergic effects may enhance splanchnic blood flow but has not yet been shown to improve outcome in patients with established or incipient MOF.

Two distinctive hepatic dysfunction syndromes occur in the critically ill:

- *Shock liver or ischaemic hepatitis* results from extreme hepatic tissue hypoxia and is characterised by centrilobular hepatocellular necrosis. Transaminase levels are often massively raised (> 1000–5000 IU/l) at an early stage, followed by moderate hyperbilirubinaemia (< 100 μmol/l). There is often associated hypoglycaemia, coagulopathy and lactic acidosis. Following successful resuscitation, hepatic function generally returns to normal.
- *Hyperbilirubinaemia ('ICU jaundice')* frequently develops following trauma or sepsis, particularly if there is inadequate control of the inflammatory process. There is a marked rise in bilirubin levels (predominantly conjugated) but only mild elevation of transaminase and alkaline phosphatase levels. It results from failure of bilirubin transport within the liver and has a histological appearance of intrahepatic cholestasis. Extrahepatic cholestasis must be excluded by abdominal ultrasound and potentially hepatotoxic drugs should be stopped. Treatment is non-specific and should include early institution of enteral feeding and avoiding therapy that compromises splanchnic blood flow, particularly high doses of vasoconstrictor agents.

NEUROLOGICAL SUPPORT

There is a diverse range of primary neurological and metabolic conditions that require management in the ICU (see Box 4.11, p. 199). Intensive care is required to:

- manage acute brain injury with control of raised intracranial pressure
- protect the airway, if necessary by endotracheal intubation
- provide respiratory support to correct hypoxaemia and hypercapnia
- treat circulatory problems, e.g. cardiac dysfunction, neurogenic pulmonary oedema in subarachnoid haemorrhage, autonomic disturbances in Guillain–Barré syndrome
- manage status epilepticus using anaesthetic agents such as thiopental or propofol, ensuring airway patency and preventing hypotension or hypoxaemia.

4.24 STRATEGIES TO CONTROL INTRACRANIAL PRESSURE
• Sedation, analgesia and occasionally paralysis to prevent coughing
• Nurse with 30° head-up tilt and avoid excessive flexion of the head or pressure around the neck that may impair cerebral venous drainage
• Control epileptiform activity with appropriate anticonvulsant therapy; an EEG may be necessary to ensure this is achieved
• Maintain strict glycaemic control with blood glucose between 4 and 8 mmol/l
• Aim for a core body temperature of between 36 and 37°C
• Maintain sodium > 140 mmol/l using i.v. normal saline
• Avoid dehydration or fluid overload
• Hyperventilation to reduce the PCO_2 to 4–4.5 kPa for the first 24 hours

The aim of management in acute brain injury is to optimise cerebral oxygen delivery by maintaining a normal arterial oxygen content and a cerebral perfusion pressure above 70 mmHg. Avoiding secondary insults to the brain such as hypoxaemia and hypotension improves outcome in head injury. Intracranial pressure (ICP) rises in acute brain injury as a result of haematoma, contusions or ischaemic swelling. Raised ICP is damaging both directly to the cerebral cortex and by producing downward pressure on the brain stem, and indirectly by reducing cerebral perfusion pressure, thereby threatening cerebral blood flow and oxygen delivery:

Cerebral perfusion pressure (CPP) = mean BP – ICP

ICP may be measured via pressure transducers inserted directly into the brain tissue or held in place on the dura. The normal upper limit for ICP is 15 mmHg and management should be directed at keeping ICP below 20 mmHg (see Box 4.24). Sustained pressures above 30 mmHg are associated with a poor prognosis.

Cerebral perfusion pressure should be maintained above 70 mmHg by ensuring adequate fluid replacement and if necessary by treating hypotension with a vasopressor such as noradrenaline (norepinephrine).

Complex neurological monitoring must be combined with frequent clinical assessment.

NEUROLOGICAL COMPLICATIONS IN INTENSIVE CARE

Neurological complications also occur as a result of systemic critical illness. Sepsis may be associated with an encephalopathy characterised by confusion/delirium and associated with cerebral oedema and loss of vasoregulation. Hypotension and coagulopathy may provoke cerebral infarction or haemorrhage. Neurological examination is very difficult if the patient is sedated or paralysed and it is important to stop sedation regularly to reassess the patient's underlying level of consciousness. The motor response to pain is a particularly important prognostic sign. No response or extension of the upper limbs is associated with severe injury, and unless there is improvement within a few days prognosis is very poor. A flexor response is encouraging and indicates that a good outcome is still possible. If there is evidence of a focal neurological deficit or a markedly declining level of consciousness, a CT of the brain should be performed.

Critical illness polyneuropathy is another potential complication in patients with sepsis and MOF. It results from peripheral nerve axonal loss rather than demyelination and can result in areflexia, gross muscle-wasting and failure to wean from the ventilator, thus prolonging the duration of intensive care.

MANAGEMENT OF SEPSIS

Prompt administration of appropriate antibiotics with a spectrum wide enough to cover probable causative organisms, based on an analysis of the likely site of infection, previous antibiotic therapy and the known resistance patterns on the unit, is essential. The haemodynamic changes in septic shock are very variable and are not specific for the Gram status of the infecting organism. The early stages of septic shock are often dominated by hypotension with relative volume depletion due to marked arteriolar and particularly venular dilatation. Sufficient intravenous fluid should be given to ensure that the intravascular volume is not the limiting factor in determining global oxygen delivery. The type of fluid that should be administered and what constitutes 'adequate' volume resuscitation remain controversial and it is inappropriate to use rigid protocols since the response to therapy is a crucial and frequently unpredictable factor. While the patient remains clinically volume-deplete, a continuous crystalloid infusion of at least 1–2 ml/kg/hr should be given, together with full enteral nutrition if tolerated to achieve the planned 24-hour crystalloid balance. Depending on haemoglobin concentration, blood or synthetic colloid should be given as 100–200 ml boluses to assess BP response to volume and to achieve CVP or PAWP targets. A recent meta-analysis has confirmed that albumin should not routinely be used in the resuscitation of critically ill patients (see p. 279).

The patient should be regularly reviewed and the nurses instructed to report any marked increase in inotropic support, volume administered or deterioration in gas exchange. It is now accepted that excessive fluid replacement in pursuit of 'supranormal' goals is not beneficial (see p. 193) and may be harmful, producing excessive tissue oedema.

Although ventricular function is frequently impaired, with a flat left ventricular stroke function curve (see Fig. 12.23, p. 382 and Fig. 12.26, p. 386), the characteristically low SVR ensures a high cardiac output (once adequately volume-resuscitated) albeit with low blood pressure.

The choice of the most appropriate vasoactive drug to use should be based on a full analysis of the circulation and knowledge of the different inotropic, dilating or constricting properties of these drugs (see Box 4.17, p. 202). In most cases a vasoconstrictor such as noradrenaline (norepi-

4.25 FACTORS THAT INFLUENCE METABOLIC RATE IN CRITICALLY ILL PATIENTS
• Fever (10–15% increase in VO_2 for every 1°C rise)
• Sepsis
• Trauma
• Burns
• Surgery
• Sympathetic activation (pain, agitation, shivering)
• Interventions (e.g. nursing procedures, physiotherapy, visitors)
• Drugs (e.g. β-adrenoceptor agonists, amphetamines, tricyclics)
N.B. Sedatives, analgesics and muscle relaxants will reduce metabolic rate.

nephrine) is necessary to increase SVR and blood pressure, while an inotrope may be necessary to maintain cardiac output and prevent regional ischaemia. In the later stages of severe sepsis the essential problem is at the level of the microcirculation. Oxygen uptake and utilisation are impaired due to failure of the regional distribution of flow and direct cellular toxicity despite adequate global oxygen delivery. Tissue oxygenation may be improved and aerobic metabolism sustained by reducing demand, i.e. metabolic rate (see Box 4.25).

SPECIFIC THERAPIES

Assessment of the pituitary–adrenal axis is difficult in the critically ill but up to 30% of patients in some series have evidence of adrenal insufficiency based on cortisol levels and the response to adrenocorticotrophic hormone (ACTH). Steroid replacement therapy is controversial and early studies showed no benefit. However, lower doses (hydrocortisone 100 mg 8-hourly) for longer periods (5 days) than previously used have now been shown to reduce vasoconstrictor requirements in hyperdynamic sepsis; despite encouraging trends, outcome benefit has yet to be demonstrated.

Until recently, numerous large multicentre trials using anticytokine and other novel drug therapies to interrupt the inflammatory cascade had all produced disappointing results. However, administration of activated protein C (levels of which frequently fall in critical illness) has recently been shown to produce a substantial reduction in mortality in patients with SIRS.

EBM
SEVERE SEPSIS—role of activated protein C
'A large multicentre RCT has shown a significant reduction in 28-day mortality (p < 0.005) in patients with severe sepsis who were treated with recombinant human activated protein C. The benefit was demonstrated even if multiple organ failure had already developed.'
• Bernard GR, Vincent JL, Laterre PF, et al. Efficacy and safety of recombinant human activated protein C for severe sepsis. N Engl J Med 2001; 344:699–709.
• Hartman DL, Bernard GR, Helterbrand JD, et al. Recombinant activated protein C (rhAPC) improves coagulation abnormalities associated with severe sepsis. Intensive Care Med 1998; 24:S77 (abstract).
• Taylor FB, Chang A, Esmon CT, et al. Protein C prevents the coagulopathic and lethal effects of Escherichia coli infusion in the baboon. J Clin Invest 1987; 79:918–925.

DISCHARGE FROM INTENSIVE CARE

Discharge is appropriate when the original indication for admission has resolved and the patient has sufficient physiological reserve to remain safe and continue his or her recovery without the facilities available in intensive care. For long-stay ICU patients who have been ventilator-dependent, 'step-down' to the HDU is appropriate. Due to the de-skilling of the general wards and frequent lack of suitable junior medical and nursing support out of hours and at weekends, discharges from ICU/HDU should preferably be within normal working hours.

The shortage of ICU and HDU beds in most hospitals in the UK creates pressure for early discharge but it has been shown that readmission rates and hospital mortality increase if discharge occurs prematurely or out of normal working hours.

The critical care team should give the receiving team a detailed handover, provide a written summary with relevant recent investigations, remain available for advice, and ideally should visit the patient on the ward within the 24 hours prior to discharge.

WITHDRAWAL OF CARE

Withdrawal of support is appropriate when it is clear that the patient has no realistic prospect of recovery or of surviving with a quality of life that the person would value. In these situations intensive care will only prolong the dying process and is therefore both futile and an inhumane waste of resources. Nevertheless, when active support is withdrawn, management should remain positive and be directed towards allowing the patient to die with dignity and as free from distress as possible. Patients' wishes in this regard are paramount but effective communication is rarely possible with a critically ill patient. However, increasing use is being made of advance directives or 'living wills'. Communication with the patient, if possible, with the family, with the referring clinicians and between members of the critical care team is crucial. Failure in this area damages working relations, causes stress and unrealistic expectations, and leads to subsequent unhappiness, anger and litigation.

BRAIN DEATH

The preconditions for considering brain-stem death and the criteria for establishing the diagnosis are listed on page 1144.

When formal brain-stem death criteria are met it is clearly futile to continue supporting life with mechanical ventilation and, at this stage, the possibility of organ donation should be considered. All intensive care clinicians have a responsibility to approach relatives to seek consent for organ donation, provided there is no contraindication to the use of the organs. This can be a very difficult task but it is easier if the patient carried an organ donor card. In the UK each region has a team of transplant coordinators who can help with the process and will provide information and advise about the necessary tests.

SCORING SYSTEMS IN CRITICAL CARE

Admission and discharge criteria vary between units so it is important to define the characteristics of the patients admitted (case mix) in order to assess the effects of the care provided on the outcome achieved (see Box 4.26).

4.26 USES OF CRITICAL CARE SCORING SYSTEMS

- Comparison of the performance of different units
- Assessment of new therapies
- Assessment of changes in unit policies and management guidelines
- Measurement of the cost-effectiveness of care

Two systems are widely used to measure severity of illness:

- 'APACHE' II—Acute Physiology Assessment and Chronic Health Evaluation
- 'SAPS' 2—Simplified Acute Physiology Score.

These scores include assessment of certain admission characteristics (e.g. age and pre-existing organ dysfunction) and a variety of routine physiological measurements (e.g. temperature, blood pressure, Glasgow Coma score) that reflect the response of the patient to his or her illness. Predicted mortality figures by diagnosis have been calculated from large databases generated from a range of ICUs. This allows a particular unit to evaluate its performance compared to the reference ICUs by calculating standardised mortality ratios (SMRs) for each diagnostic group:

SMR = observed mortality ÷ predicted mortality

A value of unity indicates the same performance as the reference ICUs while a value < 1 indicates a better than predicted outcome. A unit may have a high SMR in a certain diagnostic category and this would prompt investigation into how such patients were managed, with the intention of identifying aspects of care that could be improved.

When combined with the admission diagnosis, scoring systems have been shown to correlate well with the risk of hospital death. Such outcome predictions can never be 100% accurate and should be viewed as only one of many factors that the clinician considers when deciding whether or not further intervention is appropriate.

COSTS OF INTENSIVE CARE

Measuring the costs of intensive care is complex. The most widely used system is the Therapeutic Intervention Scoring System (TISS), which scores interventions and nursing activities for each day of admission and correlates reasonably well with detailed measurements of staff, equipment and drug costs incurred within the unit. Since it focuses on nurse-based interventions, TISS may also be used as an index of nurse dependency.

Current estimates of the daily cost of intensive care in the UK vary from £1000 to £2000, with high-dependency care approximately 50% and general ward care 20% of these costs. In the UK approximately 7% of gross domestic product (GDP) is spent on health care (7–10% in other Western European countries) but less than 2% of that total expenditure is spent on critical care.

OUTCOME FROM CRITICAL CARE

The most widely used measure to assess outcome from intensive care is mortality. This should be quoted at hospital discharge and at 28 days as mortality at the time of discharge from the unit will be influenced by the unit discharge policy. Mortality is also influenced by diagnostic case mix, length of stay and organisational aspects of the unit, as highlighted in a recent Audit Commission report.

The Kings Fund has emphasised the need to demonstrate long-term benefit to justify the increasing costs of critical care provision. Quality of life following discharge should be included in the evaluation of critical care but it is difficult to measure and interpret, not least because no objective pre-morbid assessment is possible with emergency admissions. However, several units in the UK now run follow-up clinics and have identified that there is a high incidence of physical and psychological problems affecting the patient and his or her family following ICU discharge.

ISSUES IN OLDER PEOPLE
THE CRITICALLY ILL OLDER PATIENT

- Increasing numbers of critically ill elderly patients are admitted to the ICU; over 50% of patients in many general ICUs are over 65 years old.
- Outcome is affected to some extent by age, as reflected in APACHE II, but age should not be used as the sole criterion for withholding or withdrawing ICU support.
- Age does affect outcome from cardiopulmonary resuscitation (CPR). Successful hospital discharge following in-hospital CPR is rare in patients over 70 years old in the presence of significant chronic disease.
- An ICU stay tends to be associated with loss of functional independence.
- Specific problems include:
  —Skin fragility and ulceration
  —Poor muscle strength: difficulty in weaning from ventilator, difficulty in mobilising
  —Confusion/delirium: compounded by sedatives and analgesics
  —High prevalence of underlying nutritional deficiency.

FURTHER INFORMATION

Bradley RD. Studies in acute heart failure. London: Edward Arnold; 1977.

Bradley RD, Treacher DF. Intensive care. In: Weatherall DJ, Ledingham JGG, Warrell DA, eds. Oxford textbook of medicine. 3rd edn. Oxford: Oxford University Press; 1996.

Hinds CJ, Watson D, eds. Intensive care: a concise textbook. 2nd edn. London: WB Saunders; 1996.

Oh TE. Intensive care manual. 4th edn. Oxford: Butterworth–Heinemann; 1997.

Shoemaker WC, Ayres SM, Grenvik A, Holbrook PR, eds. Textbook of critical care. 4th edn. London: WB Saunders; 1999.

Webb AR, Shapiro MJ, Singer M, Suter PM, eds. Oxford textbook of critical care. Oxford: Oxford University Press; 1999.

Oncology

D.A. CAMERON • J.F. SMYTH

Although other terms have been used, oncology, from the Greek words *onkos* (mass, tumour) and *logos* (study), best describes the study of malignant diseases. Amongst the available treatments for malignancy, surgery is the oldest, but more recently there has been an increasing role for physicians; this chapter will therefore look at non-surgical oncology, encompassing both radiotherapy (clinical oncology) and medical oncology.

Malignancy is surprisingly common, developing at some time in the life of more than one-third of the population, and it is the second most common cause of death in the Western world, after cardiovascular diseases. There is, however, significant variation with age, sex and geography in the incidence of the various types, as well as in the resources available for detection and treatment. Amongst the more common solid tumours, such as lung and breast cancer, the incidence is often higher in the developed world. For example, lung cancer is becoming increasingly common throughout the world, but at 14/100 000 in India the incidence is much lower than in the UK, where it is four times higher. Similarly, breast cancer, which accounts for around 20–25% of all female cancers in both India and the UK, has an incidence in the UK of 60/100 000 women, which is three times higher than in Mumbai. Yet the principles of management remain the same, and to illustrate many of the available treatments we have chosen breast cancer, since it poses a significant health care burden in every country of the world, and as a disease manifests most of the possible problems of patients with malignancy.

BIOLOGY

The key to understanding the clinical behaviour of cancers lies in their biology. Malignancies in general arise as a consequence of mutations in the DNA of at least one cell, which then no longer behaves like its normal neighbours. Most commonly, the mutations give malignant cells a growth advantage, so that mutated cells take up an increasing proportion of the tissue or organ of origin. Furthermore, most malignant cells acquire the ability to invade, causing both local spread beyond normal tissue boundaries and distant dissemination (or metastases). It is these properties of growth and invasion that give rise to the common presentations of cancers. However, almost all malignant cells retain some phenotypic properties of their original tissue, which is why lymphoma, sarcoma and breast cancer do not present or behave in the same manner.

Successful non-surgical treatment of malignancy also relies on tumour biology. Inherent to a cell's ability to reproduce is its ability to die, usually in a controlled or programmed manner known as apoptosis. Most of the current treatments for malignancy rely on this interplay between life and death and, by inducing DNA damage or interfering with growth factor pathways, trigger cell death. Mutations or altered expression of key proteins in this pathway, however, such as p53 and the bcl-2 family, may prevent cells from undergoing

apoptosis, and thus in part explain the limited sensitivity of cancer cells to DNA-damaging therapies. Normal human cells also possess this ability to die and therefore, particularly in tissues with a high cell turnover, many anticancer treatments cause some loss of normal cells which manifests as toxicity. This inherent non-specificity of cancer treatments often results in a narrow margin between efficacy and excessive toxicity, which is described as a 'narrow therapeutic index'. Indeed, the apparent inability of non-surgical treatments to cure some cancers is probably because of the dose-limiting effects of potential injury to healthy tissues. Much of the research during the latter part of the 20th century was therefore focused on methods of escalating treatment doses by preventing or reducing normal tissue damage. Autologous bone marrow support for such myelo-ablative chemotherapy has not, however, become an established treatment for solid tumours, although such approaches do find a role in haematological malignancies. There is now a shift in emphasis towards harnessing our increased understanding of the molecular biology of cancers to design targeted therapies, such as antibodies to proteins encoded for by key oncogenes like Her-2 *neu*, thereby avoiding toxicity.

DIAGNOSIS

The clinical picture (including history, examination and results of radiology and biochemistry) is always relevant to making a diagnosis of cancer, because it establishes the suspicion of malignancy and leads to the performance of appropriate further tests. However, a firm diagnosis of malignancy requires pathological examination of the abnormal tissue. The possibility of population screening for certain specific cancers now exists (see Box 5.1). Screening is a method of detecting cancer at a very early stage before it produces any signs or symptoms. The aim of screening is to reduce mortality. Mammography (see Fig. 5.1) is the most effective imaging presently available for breast cancer screening, which saves approximately 300 lives per year in the UK, set to rise to 1250 in 2010.

5.1 SCREENING		
Primary	**Technique**	**Standard?**
Breast	Mammography	Yes (women 50–65 years)
Cervix	Cervical smears	Yes
Gastric	Endoscopy	Only in Far East
Colon	Faecal occult blood Single flexible sigmoidoscopy	Not yet
Prostate	Serum prostate-specific antigen (PSA)	Not yet

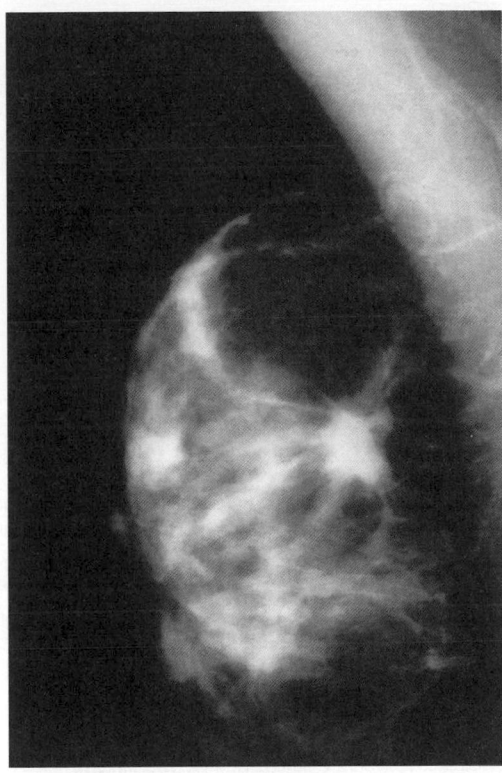

Fig. 5.1   Diagnostic mammogram showing a small breast cancer.

CLINICAL ASSESSMENT

In order to plan the management of a patient with malignancy, the doctor needs to know:

- the nature of the primary malignancy (site, type, pathology)
- the extent of the disease (stage)
- the patient's general condition and comorbid diseases
- the available treatment options (surgery, drugs, radiotherapy).

The presentation of a malignancy can involve both local and systemic features (see Boxes 5.2 and 5.3). The local signs or symptoms are usually due to mass effect or invasion of local tissues. In contrast, systemic features may be the result of metastases or the non-metastatic manifestations of disease.

In taking a history, details of the tumour-related problem should be established, along with potential risk factors. In breast cancer, family history, early menarche, late menopause and benign breast disease are associated with increased risk, while early full-term pregnancy reduces risk. An impression of the pace of the disease may help determine prognosis and treatment. Some indolent breast cancers can present as an inoperable lump without metastases simply because of years of neglect; the particularly aggressive inflammatory breast cancer presents with signs of inflammation but no lump, yet may have a worse outcome.

5.2 LOCAL FEATURES

Symptom	Site/tumour
Haemorrhage	Stomach, colon, bronchus, endometrium, bladder, kidney
Lump	Breast, lymph node (any site), testicle
Pain	Bone (primary sarcoma, secondary)
Skin abnormality	Melanoma, basal cell carcinoma (rodent ulcer)
Ulcer	Oesophagus, stomach, anus, skin
Obstruction Pain, cough, recurrent infection	Bronchus
Odynophagia, dysphagia, early satiety, vomiting	Gastro-oesophageal
Altered bowel habit, total obstruction (pain, distension)	Colon, rectum
Abdominal swelling (ascites)	Ovary, gastric cancer
Fracture	Metastatic cancer (breast, prostate, kidney)

5.3 NON-METASTATIC MANIFESTATIONS

Feature	Common associations
Weight loss and anorexia	Gastrointestinal tumours
Fatigue	Any
Hypercalcaemia	Myeloma, breast, renal
Prothrombotic tendency	Pancreas and other gastrointestinal tumours
Hormonal effects Syndrome of inappropriate antidiuretic hormone secretion (SIADH) Ectopic adrenocorticotrophic hormone (ACTH)	Small-cell lung cancer
Neuropathies and myopathies Eaton–Lambert Myasthenia-like syndrome Subacute cerebellar degeneration	Small-cell lung cancer
Skin abnormalities Acanthosis nigricans Dermatomyositis/polymyositis	Gastro-oesophageal Gastric, lung

A thorough clinical examination is essential to identify sites of metastases, and to identify any comorbid conditions that may have a bearing on the management plan.

The overall fitness of a patient can be evaluated using a variety of scales. One of the most common is the Eastern Cooperative Oncology Group (ECOG) performance scale (see Box 5.4). The outcome for patients with a performance status of 3 or 4 is worse in almost all malignancies than for patients with a good performance status of 1 or 2. Treatment decisions must take such assessments into account.

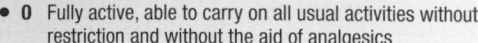

5.4 EASTERN COOPERATIVE ONCOLOGY GROUP (ECOG) PERFORMANCE STATUS SCALE

- **0** Fully active, able to carry on all usual activities without restriction and without the aid of analgesics
- **1** Restricted in strenuous activity but ambulatory and able to carry out light work or pursue a sedentary occupation. This group also contains patients who are fully active, as in grade 0, but only with the aid of analgesics
- **2** Ambulatory and capable of all self-care but unable to work. Up and about more than 50% of waking hours
- **3** Capable of only limited self-care, confined to bed or chair more than 50% of waking hours
- **4** Completely disabled, unable to carry out any self-care and confined totally to bed or chair

---

INVESTIGATIONS

Tumour imaging and sampling are required; for instance, a woman with a breast lump will almost always require mammography and biopsy. Sampling of other malignancies may be achieved under direct vision as at endoscopy, bronchoscopy or colonoscopy, or with ultrasound or computed tomography (CT) guidance. Superficial masses or lesions may be biopsied or fine-needle aspirates may be taken. In cases where treatment is initially or largely non-surgical, precise measurement of initial tumour size helps to assess subsequent response to therapy.

Special investigations such as serum tumour marker tests and a series of standard radiological tests to 'stage' the disease usually follow (see Boxes 5.6 and 5.7).

PATHOLOGY

The pathologist studying the tissue sample is seeking evidence of abnormality in the cells (reflecting mutations), such as:

- greater numbers than in normal tissue
- increased size
- a higher nuclear to cytoplasmic ratio
- a higher proliferation rate (evidenced by visible mitotic figures).

In addition, the cells may be in an abnormal location:

- cells which have penetrated (invaded) through the basement membrane
- cells which moved (metastasised) from their tissue of origin (e.g. to lymph nodes/liver).

There is, however, a continuum from benign to malignant (see Fig. 5.2).

IMMUNOHISTOCHEMISTRY

The pathologist may use antibodies (usually highly specific monoclonal antibodies) to various intracellular and cell-surface proteins to achieve a specific diagnosis (immuno-histochemistry—see Box 5.5). The uses of this technique include:

- determining the tissue of origin of a very undifferentiated tumour

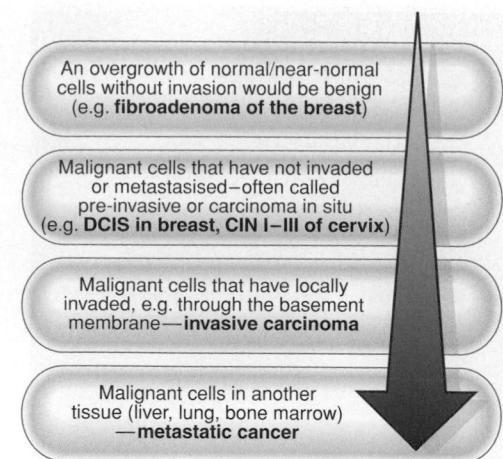

An overgrowth of normal/near-normal cells without invasion would be benign (e.g. **fibroadenoma of the breast**)

Malignant cells that have not invaded or metastasised–often called pre-invasive or carcinoma in situ (e.g. **DCIS in breast, CIN I–III of cervix**)

Malignant cells that have locally invaded, e.g. through the basement membrane—**invasive carcinoma**

Malignant cells in another tissue (liver, lung, bone marrow) —**metastatic cancer**

Fig. 5.2 Pathological progression from benign to malignant disease. (DCIS = ductal carcinoma in situ; CIN = cervical intraepithelial neoplasia)

5.5 IMMUNOHISTOCHEMISTRY MARKERS

Name	Oncogene?	Routine use?	Tumour type
S-100	No	Yes	Neural crest origin (e.g. melanoma)
Cam 5.2	No	Yes	Small-cell cancer (e.g. lung)
Carcinoembryonic antigen (CEA) (see p. 824)	No	Yes	Colon and other gastrointestinal tumours
CA-125	No	Yes	Ovary
Oestrogen receptor (ER)	No	Yes	Breast cancer (present in other tumours, e.g. ovary)
Her-2 neu	Yes	No	Breast cancer (present in other tumours, e.g. lung, ovary, gastric)

- identifying important subtypes of common cancers (small-cell, neuro-endocrine) which have different prognoses/therapies
- establishing the presence of oestrogen receptors in breast cancers (see Fig. 5.3—important in therapeutic decisions).

BIOCHEMISTRY AND TUMOUR MARKERS

In addition to classical pathological features, many tumours are associated with abnormalities in the clinical chemistry of peripheral blood. Often this is a result of the tumour secreting proteins into the circulation, which are detectable by routine tests (see Box 5.6). Many of these so-called tumour markers can be used in the diagnosis and in some types of cancer levels reflect the extent (stage) of the disease. Few are uniquely associated with the tumour, so that the currently available serum tumour markers are not as useful as one might wish. The main use of tumour markers is to assess a cancer's response to treatment and check for recurrence. Commonly, such markers are antigens that are usually only expressed in

5.6 TUMOUR MARKERS IN BLOOD

Name	Fetal antigen?	Normally detected?	Tumours
CEA	Yes	Yes	Gastrointestinal tract, lung, breast
CA-125	Yes	Yes	Ovary
Alphafetoprotein (αfp)	Yes	Yes (very low)	Hepatocellular carcinoma, germ cell tumours (teratoma, seminoma)
Lactate dehydrogenase (LDH)	No	Yes	Most, reflecting tumour burden or necrosis
PSA	No	Yes	Prostate, some breast cancers
Human chorionic gonadotrophin (HCG)	No	Only in pregnancy	Teratoma, choriocarcinoma, gastrointestinal tumours

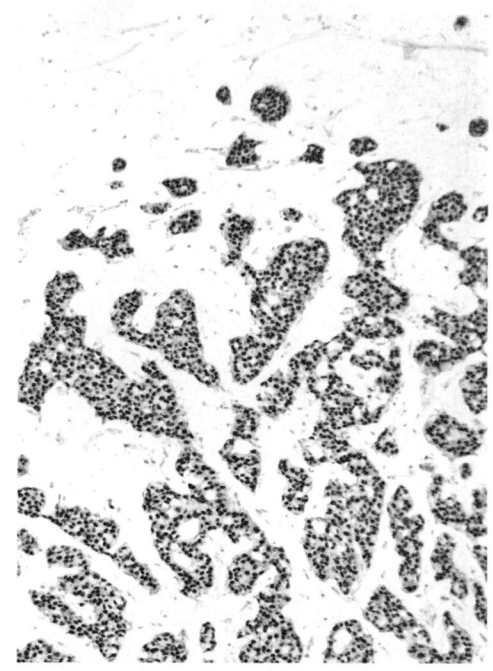

Fig. 5.3 Breast cancer specimen stained for the expression of oestrogen receptors using a monoclonal antibody. Note the heterogeneity of staining.

5.7 STAGING TESTS

Primary	Common	Less common/ geographical variation
Breast	Chest radiograph, bone scan	Bone marrow, CT of abdomen/thorax
Lymphoma	CT, bone marrow	Bone scan
Prostate	Bone scan, CT of pelvis	
Colon	Ultrasound, CT of liver	
Lung	Chest radiograph, CT	Bone marrow, bone scan

5.8 TNM CLASSIFICATION

T*	Extent of primary tumour
N*	Extent of regional lymph node involvement
M	Presence or absence of metastases

Extent of disease	
T0	Excised tumour
T1	
T2	Increases in primary tumour size
T3	

Increased involvement of nodes	
N1	
N2	Increases in involvement
N3	

Presence of metastases	
M0	Not present
M1	Present

* Exact criteria for size and region of nodal involvement have been defined for each anatomical site.

the fetus, but they can be produced by an adult tumour so that levels are much higher than normal. A notable exception to this is the production of hormones, both locally and systemically—for example, production of oestrogen by ovarian granulosa cell tumours, and human chorionic gonadotrophin (HCG) by choriocarcinomas and teratomas.

STAGING

This is the term applied to the determination of the extent of the malignancy. Staging entails clinical examination and investigations, usually radiological, which seek to establish possible sites or extent of disease involvement (see Fig. 5.4 and Box 5.7). The tests used depend on the likely patterns of spread. Once these tests have been performed, it is conventional to record the information using a standard staging system to enable comparisons to be made between different groups of patients. This allows therapeutic decisions and prognostic predictions to be made using the published evidence base for the disease. One of the most common of these systems is the T (tumour), N (regional lymph nodes) and M (metastatic sites) approach of the Union internationale contre le cancer (UICC) (see Box 5.8). For some tumours the most widely used system is not the UICC; colorectal cancer, for example, is often staged using the 'Dukes system' (see p. 825).

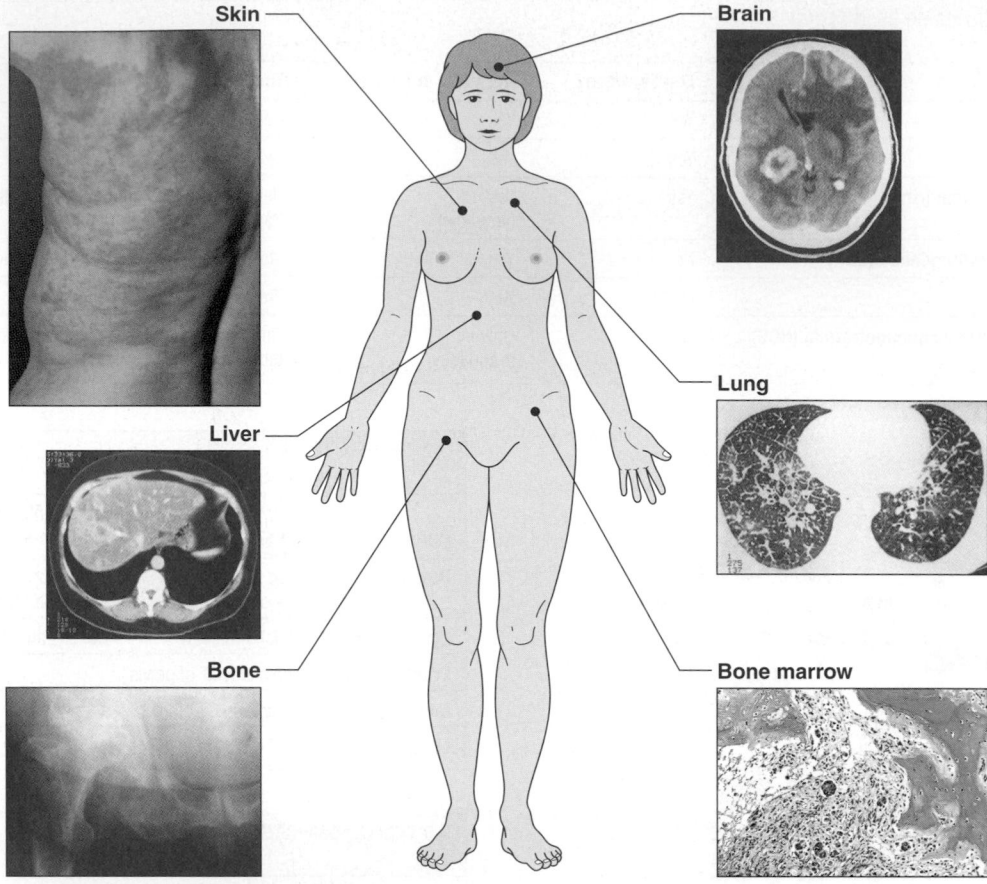

Fig. 5.4   Common sites of metastasis for breast and other cancers.

TREATMENT

In general, it is important for patients to be informed of their diagnosis and given some idea of stage and prognosis so that an informed discussion can follow about treatment options. It is not possible to foresee the future with certainty, and therefore all discussions with patients and relatives need to take account of the variabilities in outcome and response to treatment, but in a manner that does not undermine the patient's confidence. It is not helpful or indeed possible to give patients '6 months to live', or to describe a treatment as 'successful' when it is clear that residual disease may be present. It is better to have an initial consultation that is quiet, unhurried and empathetic, so that the patient's history, fears and concerns can be fully ascertained. By the same token, it is imperative that the doctor establishes a rapport with the patient so that good communication is established. In this way information and uncertainties to be transmitted to the patient will be better received. Patients' responses to the diagnosis of cancer and its implications vary from shock to denial, anxiety, depression or inappropriate fatalism. The challenge for oncologists is to remain sensitive to patients' needs and fears, yet still be able to discuss the appropriateness of starting and stopping treatment.

Integral to treatment planning for a patient with cancer is a decision about the aims of therapy (see Fig. 5.5 and Box 5.9). It should be clear to the doctor, and to patients and their relatives, whether treatment has the potential to be curative. Since most non-surgical treatments have a 'narrow therapeutic index' (see p. 148), it is not often worth risking serious and life-threatening toxicity unless cure or good

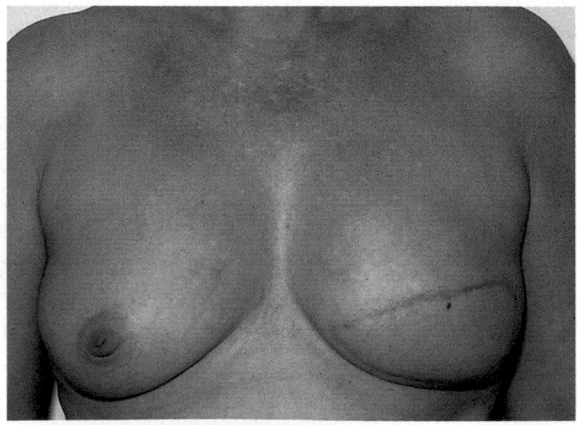

Fig. 5.5   Successful breast reconstruction after mastectomy for breast cancer.

5.9 TREATMENT GOALS

Curative	Radical, occasionally curative	Adjuvant	Palliative
Choriocarcinoma	Small-cell lung cancer	Breast cancer	Metastatic breast cancer
Teratoma	Stage III ovarian cancer	Stage I–II ovarian cancer	Stage IV ovarian cancer
Seminoma		Colorectal cancer	Advanced gastrointestinal cancers
High-grade lymphoma Cervical cancer Head and neck cancer		Osteogenic sarcoma	Metastatic sarcoma Metastatic prostate Advanced lung cancer

long-term control of the disease is possible. Furthermore, in most malignancies in which the primary treatment is surgical, patients remain at significant risk of relapse despite all evidence of macroscopic disease being removed. In some diseases, such as breast and colorectal cancer, additional subsequent treatment with drug therapy or radiotherapy reduces the risk of relapse and improves overall survival. Such treatment is termed adjuvant, and is presumed to work by killing microscopic foci of metastatic tumour.

If a cure is not realistic, the only alternative may be a palliative approach, which includes treatments targeted against the cancer and others to alleviate symptoms (see Ch. 6). There are several tumour types which therapy is unlikely to cure, but it may still significantly improve the outlook for patients and therefore justifies a radical approach. Sadly, there remain many situations where current treatments are not effective, and the emphasis of treatment must be on quality, rather than quantity, of life. Such therapy is termed palliative, but it should be remembered that the most effective way of reducing the symptoms caused by a cancer is usually to reduce the amount of cancer.

The non-surgical treatment of malignancy can be divided into three categories:

- treatment that kills cells via DNA-damaging techniques (often called cytotoxic treatments—including radiotherapy)
- hormonal approaches that manipulate the endocrine milieu which supports the growth/metastasis of cancer
- so-called biological therapies, including immunological approaches and drugs like bisphosphonates that target bony metastases.

Current drug development is focusing on further intracellular pathways that do not fall neatly into any of these groups. These will therefore be discussed separately.

CYTOTOXIC TREATMENTS

This approach relies on the propensity of cells to die when their DNA is damaged by therapeutic means. As a consequence of detecting extrinsically induced DNA damage, any cell, including a malignant one, will potentially induce its own death through apoptosis. Ionising radiation (from any source) and a number of chemicals can cause such DNA damage and hence be harnessed as a treatment for cancer.

RADIOTHERAPY

Conventional radiotherapy machines such as linear accelerators produce a targeted beam of high-energy photons, which penetrate the tissues and cause the release of electrons which travel with high energy and damage molecules within targeted tissues. The level of radiation doses used clinically causes most damage to DNA. Another method is to use a local source of radiation, such as compounds that emit γ rays. This technique is used in the treatment of cervical cancer, where radioactive sources are either directly placed in the tissue under anaesthetic (such as iridium implants), or remotely loaded via a catheter placed in the uterus/vagina. Irrespective of the source of the ionising radiation, the clinical effect relates to the ability of the electrons produced to damage cells, mostly as a consequence of DNA damage.

Practical aspects

As the ionising radiation is also damaging to normal tissues, radiotherapy is targeted to a specific area—normally the tumour and a surrounding margin to ensure optimal tumour control. The dose given is limited by the potential for 'bystander' injury to adjacent normal tissues, and the challenge for radiotherapists is to limit the normal tissue damage and yet achieve doses of radiation sufficient for curative therapy. This is usually done by 'fractionating' the radiotherapy over 4–6 weeks, either in small daily doses of around 2 gray (Gy), or by so-called 'hyperfractionation', when the radiotherapy is given two or three times daily. The side-effects experienced with radiotherapy depend on the area treated (see Fig. 5.6). With particularly radiosensitive malignancies, such as some of the haematological diseases, it is possible to irradiate the whole body (total body irradiation) and still achieve a significant antitumour effect, although bone marrow replacement will be necessary.

CHEMOTHERAPY

The potential for nitrogen mustard to destroy proliferating bone marrow and lymphoid cells was recognised in the 1940s, and rapidly led to the first use of alkylating cytotoxic agents. The second class of cytotoxics arose from research into the effects of altering folic acid metabolism in leukaemic cells, leading to the discovery of methotrexate, the first antimetabolite. In general, cytotoxic agents have a

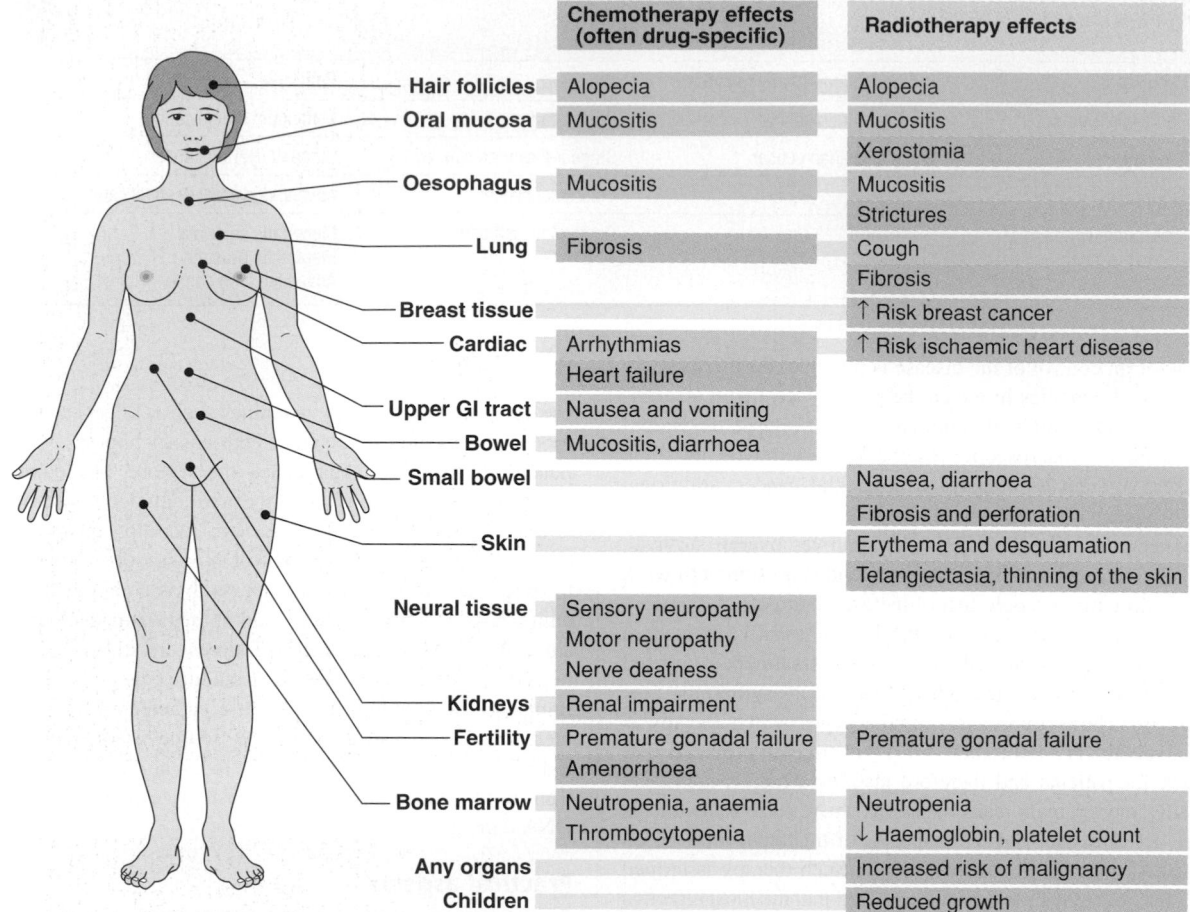

	Chemotherapy effects (often drug-specific)	Radiotherapy effects
Hair follicles	Alopecia	Alopecia
Oral mucosa	Mucositis	Mucositis
		Xerostomia
Oesophagus	Mucositis	Mucositis
		Strictures
Lung	Fibrosis	Cough
		Fibrosis
Breast tissue		↑ Risk breast cancer
Cardiac	Arrhythmias	↑ Risk ischaemic heart disease
	Heart failure	
Upper GI tract	Nausea and vomiting	
Bowel	Mucositis, diarrhoea	
Small bowel		Nausea, diarrhoea
		Fibrosis and perforation
Skin		Erythema and desquamation
		Telangiectasia, thinning of the skin
Neural tissue	Sensory neuropathy	
	Motor neuropathy	
	Nerve deafness	
Kidneys	Renal impairment	
Fertility	Premature gonadal failure	Premature gonadal failure
	Amenorrhoea	
Bone marrow	Neutropenia, anaemia	Neutropenia
	Thrombocytopenia	↓ Haemoglobin, platelet count
Any organs		Increased risk of malignancy
Children		Reduced growth

Fig. 5.6   Acute (in red) and late (in blue) effects of chemotherapy and radiotherapy.

broader range of intracellular effects than radiotherapy, although the biological aim is again to damage DNA. Chemotherapeutic drugs are classified by their mode of action. Box 5.10 lists some of the most commonly used. Most are effective only in actively proliferating tissues. They are not specifically designed to target malignant cells and therefore their common side-effects relate to these antiproliferative actions. Nausea and vomiting are common side-effects that used to be greatly feared. However, with modern antiemetics, usually the combination of dexamethasone and a highly selective 5-hydroxytryptamine (5-HT, serotonin) receptor antagonist, most patients now receive chemotherapy without any significant problems. However, other side-effects may be specific to a drug or to a class of drugs. Myelosuppression is common to almost all cytotoxics. This not only limits the dose of drug, but also can cause life-threatening complications.

Practical aspects

In order to overcome drug resistance and to limit the side-effects of different drugs, chemotherapy is most commonly given as a combination of agents. Combinations usually include drugs from different classes, each of which may be independently active and the combination of which

should not have additive deleterious effects. Drugs are conventionally given by intravenous injection every 3–4 weeks, thus allowing enough time for the patient to recover from short-term toxic effects (see Fig. 5.6) before the next dose. Patients are usually given between four and eight such cycles of treatment in total. More recently, a number of other strategies have been developed. For example, one of the oldest drugs still used, 5-fluorouracil (5-FU), which has a very short half-life, has recently been recognised as exerting increased efficacy when given by continuous intravenous infusion, using a semi-permanent in-dwelling intravenous catheter. The use of these catheters does, however, carry a number of risks, and further development is directed at the possible oral administration of 5-FU, or precursor molecules like capecitabine. Other oral chemotherapeutic agents have been developed over the past 30 years, although not many have replaced their intravenous counterparts. Schedules of administration at weekly or 2-weekly intervals have also found their place in the management of both solid and haematological malignancies.

Each tumour type has specific regimens that are used at various stages of the disease, and it is beyond the scope of this chapter to list the uses of each drug and combinations thereof.

5.10 COMMONLY USED CYTOTOXICS

Mode of action	Drug
Alkylating agents	Melphalan Cyclophosphamide Ifosfamide
Antimetabolites (target in parentheses)	Methotrexate (folic acid) 5-fluorouracil (uracIl) Cytarabine (cytidine) 6-mercaptopurine (hypoxanthine) 6-tioguanine (guanine)
Mitotic spindle poisons Vinca alkaloids	Vincristine Vindesine Vinorelbine
Taxanes	Docetaxel Paclitaxel
Topoisomerase antagonists Topo-I	Irinotecan
Topo-II	Doxorubicin (has other effects too) Epirubicin Daunorubicin Etoposide
Antibiotics	Bleomycin Mitomycin
Miscellaneous	Cisplatin Carboplatin Dacarbazine Procarbazine
Common combinations	Cyclophosphamide, methotrexate, 5-fluorouracil (CMF) Carboplatin and paclitaxel Cisplatin and 5-fluorouracil

EBM

ADVANCED COLORECTAL CANCER—role of chemotherapy

'Chemotherapy is effective in prolonging time to disease progression and survival in patients with advanced colorectal cancer. No age differences were found in the effectiveness of chemotherapy.'

• Cochrane Database of Systematic Reviews (2) CD001545, 2000.

Further information: 💻 www.cochrane.co.uk

HORMONAL TREATMENTS

In 1896 Beatson published the first example of women with breast cancer being treated with an artificially induced menopause. Since breast cancers arise from the epithelium of breast ducts, which are themselves sensitive to the female hormones oestrogen and progesterone, it is not surprising that breast cancers sometimes retain hormonal sensitivity. Dramatically reducing the circulating oestrogen can reduce the proliferation of cancer cells and increase their loss through apoptosis of breast cancer cells (see Fig. 5.7). Oestrogen synthesis can be inhibited by various means at different levels, including intratumoral production. The best predictor for the sensitivity of breast cancer to hormonal therapy is the presence of detectable levels of the intracellular

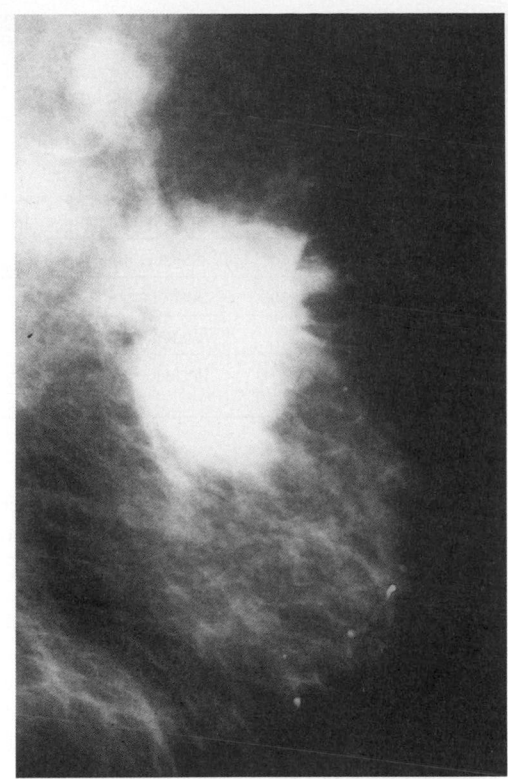

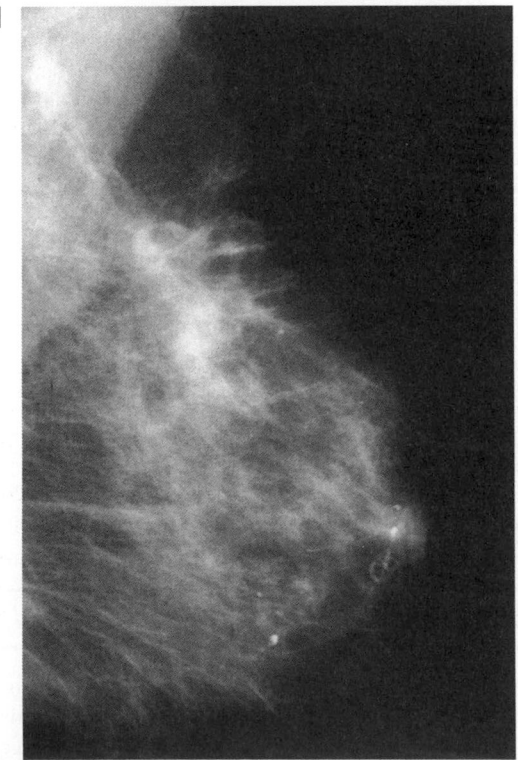

Fig. 5.7 Mammograms showing a breast cancer responding to hormone therapy. A Large tumour with involved axillary nodes before treatment. B After 3 months of hormone therapy alone, the tumour has shrunk significantly.

5.11 ENDOCRINOLOGICAL TREATMENTS

Drug/approach	Therapeutic target	Hormone	Disease
Luteinising hormone-releasing hormone (LHRH) agonists	Pituitary	LH, follicle-stimulating hormone (FSH) → secondary oestrogen secondary androgens	Breast cancer Prostate cancer
Ovarian ablation	Ovarian function	Oestrogen synthesis	Breast cancer
Testicular ablation	Testicular function	Androgen synthesis	Prostate cancer
Anti-oestrogens (e.g. tamoxifen)	Oestrogen receptor	Oestrogen function	Breast cancer
Aromatase inhibitors	Aromatase enzyme	Oestrogen synthesis	Breast cancer
Progestogens	Unclear	Oestrogen synthesis Direct on endometrium	Breast cancer Endometrial cancer

protein oestrogen receptor (ER-α), and assessment of serum levels of expression of this protein is now therefore a standard part of the pathological assessment of breast cancer.

The first ever randomised controlled trial of an anticancer therapy was conducted in the UK using an artificial menopause for women with breast cancer. Hormonal therapy of breast cancer is now well established and effective. In the correctly chosen patient (see EBM panel) adjuvant hormonal therapy reduces the risk of relapse and death at least as well as chemotherapy, and in advanced disease can induce stable disease behaviour and remissions that may last months to years, with acceptable toxicity. However, breast cancer is not the only disease for which hormonal manipulations may be effective (see Box 5.11). In prostate cancer, similar reductions in the level of the growth-promoting male hormones can provide good long-term control of advanced disease, but there is as yet no convincing evidence that it is an effective therapy following potentially curative surgery. Progestogens are active in the treatment of breast cancer and endometrial cancer.

EBM

EARLY BREAST CANCER—role of post-operative systemic therapy

'Post-operative systemic therapy reduces the risk of recurrence and death for women with early breast cancer. There is a clear benefit for the use of polychemotherapy, tamoxifen and, for women under the age of 50, ovarian ablation.'

- Early Breast Cancer Trialists' Collaborative Group (EBCTCG). Polychemotherapy for early breast cancer: an overview of the randomised trials. Lancet 1998; 352:930–942.
- EBCTCG. Tamoxifen for early breast cancer: an overview of the randomised trials. Lancet 1998; 351:1451–1467.
- EBCTCG. Ovarian ablation in early breast cancer: overview of the randomised trials. Lancet 1996; 348:1189–1196.

BIOLOGICAL TREATMENTS

Ever since Coley's observations of the beneficial effects of diphtheria toxin in the 19th century, it has been recognised that a profound stimulus to the patient's immune system can alter the natural history of a malignancy in some cases. Until the intricacies of the immune system were appreciated in the latter part of the 20th century, most such approaches were non-specific. For example, the use of the usually harmless bacille Calmette–Guérin (BCG) vaccine has been tried in many tumour types, with the best activity seen in superficial bladder cancers. More recently, the discovery and mass biosynthesis of interferons have stimulated much research. Although solid tumours show little benefit, interferons are clearly active in melanoma and lymphoma, and there is evidence that they are beneficial as adjuvants (after surgery and chemotherapy respectively) to delay recurrence. Whether interferon-induced stimulation of the immune system is capable of eradicating microscopic disease remains unproven. It is also clear that more powerful immune responses can be achieved with potent agents like interleukin-2 (IL-2), but the accompanying systemic toxicity is a problem at present.

The immune system is now being harnessed by the use of monoclonal antibodies directed against specific antigens carried by tumour cells. To date only two such antigens have been successfully targeted with antibodies that are licensed for clinical use: firstly, the common B-cell antigen CD-20 (its clinically used antibody is called Rhituximab). This agent provides effective palliation for B-cell lymphomas, and has recently been shown to enhance the benefit from first-line chemotherapy for non-Hodgkin's lymphoma. Secondly, the oncogene Her-2 *neu* is over-expressed in around one-third of breast cancers, as well as in a number of other solid tumours. The monoclonal antibody, herceptin, has been demonstrated to be an effective single-agent therapy, and also to improve survival in patients with advanced disease when it is given in conjunction with chemotherapy. Unfortunately, herceptin, by an as yet obscure biological mechanism, can induce cardiac failure, especially in combination with the potentially cardiotoxic cytotoxic drug doxorubicin.

Bisphosphonates (see p. 1033), which alter the normal behaviour of bone, have become routine for the treatment of bone metastases, commonly seen in advanced breast cancer and myeloma. Administration of bisphosphonates can inhibit osteoclast function, reducing bone turnover, bone pain and the risk of skeletal events, and there is some evidence to suggest that prophylactic use of these compounds may prevent skeletal complications in advanced (and potentially even early stage) breast cancer.

CASE STUDY

To illustrate the principles, a hypothetical case of breast cancer is outlined below.

A woman in her mid-50s, who is post-menopausal, presents with a lump in her right breast. She is quickly referred to a breast clinic, where she undergoes investigation:

- clinical examination—may help distinguish cyst from solid lump
- mammogram—may identify malignant calcification or other features of concern, or the presence of a cyst
- ultrasound—can complement mammography
- magnetic resonance imaging (MRI)—may help if other tests are equivocal
- pathological examination—cytology from fine-needle aspirate (FNA) and/or histopathology from a core biopsy.

An invasive cancer of no special type with its precursor lesion, non-invasive ductal carcinoma in situ (DCIS), is identified. Further staging tests are done, including a chest radiograph, bone scan, full clinical examination, routine haematology and biochemistry.

These are all normal, as is mammography of the opposite breast, so the surgeon offers the patient the option of surgery with breast conservation. The patient accepts and undergoes wide local excision and axillary node dissection (with or without sentinel node biopsy). The pathologist reports:

- an invasive cancer, grade 2, maximum dimension 21 mm
- surgical margins clear of both invasive and non-invasive disease
- strong staining for oestrogen receptors (ER +ve)
- 2 out of 16 lymph nodes containing metastatic cancer.

The patient is advised by an oncologist to have further adjuvant treatment, in the form of radiotherapy to the right breast, hormonal therapy (such as tamoxifen) and chemotherapy. Her chance of being cured of her breast cancer is estimated, with all these treatments, as being around 70%.

However, 7 years later she complains to her GP of pain in her back and legs. She is also rather breathless and tired. Investigation reveals that she has a palpable right supraclavicular lymph node, lung metastases, bone metastases and a high serum LDH and calcium. Biopsy of the supraclavicular lesion confirms recurrent breast cancer, similar in type to that she had 7 years previously.

What has gone wrong? The surgery was successful and, in conjunction with the accompanying radiotherapy, has probably completely removed all the cancer cells in her right breast. However, small numbers of breast cancer cells, already present in her axillary lymph nodes as detected by the pathologist, must have also been present in her supraclavicular fossa, lungs and bones, but in insufficient number to be detectable by clinical tests or examination. The chemotherapy will perhaps have killed some of these cells by inducing DNA damage but, either because the cells excreted the drugs before they could do enough damage, or because they had lost some of their ability to respond to the DNA damage by undergoing apoptosis, many cells survived the chemotherapy. The hormonal therapy similarly had insufficient impact to clear all the remaining micro-metastases, but the fact that it took 7 years before the cancer returned suggests that a significant proportion of the original tumour cells were sensitive to the therapy.

Now she is essentially incurable—but not necessarily terminal. Indeed, rehydration and bisphosphonates restore her calcium to normal, and the use of an aromatase inhibitor as second-line hormonal therapy keeps her disease under control for a further 3 years, during which time she leads a completely normal life. Subsequently, her breathlessness increases and she is found to have liver metastases. Further chemotherapy is given, and this keeps her disease stable for another 9–12 months. Gradually, over the following 2 years, her disease progresses and becomes less sensitive to conventional therapies, leading to increasing involvement of palliative care specialists and a terminal state.

ISSUES IN OLDER PEOPLE
ONCOLOGY

- Around 50% of cancers occur in 15% of the population: those aged over 65 years.
- Women aged over 65 in the UK are not invited to participate in breast cancer screening but may receive it on request. Uptake is low despite the increasing incidence with age.
- Presentation may be later for some cancers. Particularly when symptoms are non-specific, patients (and their doctors) may initially attribute them to age alone.
- The average life expectancy of an 80-year-old woman is 8 years, so cancer may still shorten life and an active approach therefore remains appropriate.
- Histology, stage at presentation and observation for even a brief period are better guides to prognosis than age alone.
- Some older patients experience a more indolent course of disease; this is not fully understood but may partly be due to a reduction in the effectiveness of angiogenesis with age, which may inhibit the development of metastases.
- Older people respond as well to treatment as younger people; this is well documented for a range of cancers and for the common modalities of treatment including surgery, radiotherapy, chemotherapy and hormonal therapy.
- Chronological age is of minor importance in selecting treatment compared to comorbid illness and patient choice.
- Although older patients can be treated effectively and safely, aggressive intervention with the goal of cure or long-term remission is not appropriate for all individuals. It may be decided that symptom control is all that is possible or desired by the patient.
- When discussing treatment options, it is important that the older patient understands that choosing a non-aggressive treatment option does not mean a grim, painful death. Reassurance that symptoms can be effectively controlled (see Ch. 6), whatever choice is made, is vital.

ONCOLOGICAL EMERGENCIES

The natural history of malignancy is progression resulting in increasing dysfunction of affected organs. Most of the treatments used above are given close to their tolerance, which may result in complications of disease and/or treatment that can be life-threatening and require urgent intervention and treatment. These problems can occur with rapid or insidious onset, and may present to a broad spectrum of clinical specialties. As they are described in detail in the specific system-based chapters indicated below, a brief outline only is given here.

HYPERCALCAEMIA

As a consequence of direct bone involvement with metastatic disease or ectopic tumour production of a hormone (almost always parathormone-related peptide, PTHrP), increased osteoclast activity produces a rise in serum calcium, which cannot be compensated for by the normal homeostatic mechanisms. The clinical manifestations are essentially the same as for any other cause of elevated serum calcium (see p. 715), except that the duration is usually shorter so that renal stone formation is rare. The basic physiological problem is dehydration, consequent upon the diuretic effect of the elevated urinary calcium, and the key to successful management is fluid replacement as well as prevention of further calcium release (see p. 716).

NEUTROPENIC SEPSIS/FEVER

Fever of 38°C for over 1 hour in a patient with a neutrophil count $< 1.0 \times 10^9$/l indicates possible septicaemia (see p. 905). This can be a complication of the disease but is most commonly a complication of chemotherapy, usually in leukaemias but very occasionally in metastatic solid tumours with extensive bone marrow replacement. Irrespective of the cause, the problem is life-threatening and requires urgent assessment and therapy. Presenting symptoms include obvious infection (fever, chills, influenza-like myalgia, headache), non-specific malaise and profound shock (see p. 195). Management should be by a specialist unit or an intensive care unit for a patient with shock and multi-organ failure, and should follow agreed protocols for the use of antibiotics that reflect local sensitivity patterns (see p. 200).

SPINAL CORD COMPRESSION

This is an oncological emergency that is difficult to treat effectively. The spinal cord resides within a confined bony framework, so that tumour tissue quickly causes a space-occupying lesion which damages nerve tissue directly by pressure or indirectly by interfering with blood supply. Pain and sensory symptoms vary according to the level of the cord compressed, and full details are given on page 1187.

Immediate diagnosis and therapy are essential. Plain radiographs may show bony destruction. MRI is the investigation of choice. Needle biopsy may be appropriate to establish the histological nature of the tumour. Treatment should be commenced with dexamethasone 4 mg 6-hourly. Urgent radiotherapy is the mainstay of therapy, but surgical decompression may be appropriate in some patients (see p. 1188). Useful function can be regained if treatment starts within 24 hours of the development of weakness or sphincter disturbance. However, despite treatment, many patients remain paraplegic with considerable morbidity. Tragically, warning signs of a band-like pain just below the lesion, or early evidence of neurological damage distal to the lesion, are often missed by patients and clinicians alike.

BRAIN METASTASES

Metastasis to the brain (see Fig. 5.8) may be the first presentation of some cancers. The prognosis in the majority of patients is poor. The clinical features of headache, local effects and seizures are described in detail on page 1204. The diagnosis should also be considered when a patient with cancer develops persistent nausea and vomiting. The diagnosis is made by CT or MRI. In those with a single lesion, surgical biopsy should be considered, as a tissue diagnosis may be important for management and prognosis.

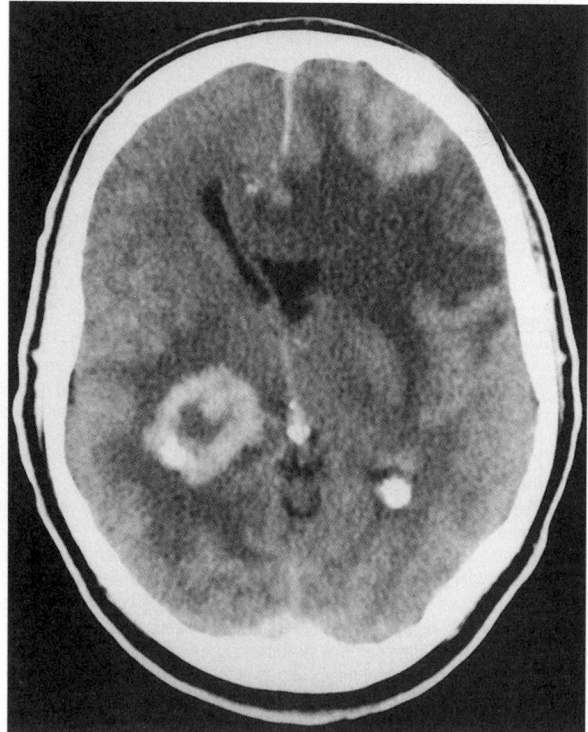

Fig. 5.8   CT showing multiple cerebral metastases.

The mainstay of treatment is dexamethasone to reduce the oedema and possibly to protect the brain during radiotherapy. Most patients are treated with palliative radiotherapy, although there is little definitive evidence for this approach (see p. 1205). For some patients with brain metastases, especially those with single lesions and/or low-volume or indolent extracranial metastases, a neurosurgical opinion should be sought as to whether surgical resection would be appropriate.

SUPERIOR VENA CAVAL OBSTRUCTION

Obstruction of the superior vena cava (SVCO) in the mediastinum reduces the filling of the right atrium and ventricle and causes venous engorgement and later oedema in the head, neck, arms and upper thorax. The symptoms are breathlessness (see p. 494), blackouts, and headaches which are worse on leaning forwards. Clinically, the venous engorgement is usually obvious, with fixed dilated external jugular veins.

The majority of cases (> 85% in the UK) are due to malignancy, but there are benign causes such as mediastinal fibrosis, so unless the patient is already known to have cancer a tissue diagnosis is necessary before treatment begins. The mainstay of treatment for SVCO due to malignant disease is radiotherapy, and two of the more common causes, small-cell lung cancer and lymphoma, are often exquisitely radiosensitive. In many patients secondary thrombosis within the superior vena cava occurs and therefore, particularly in recurrent SVCO, percutaneous insertion of a stent within the SVC may be necessary.

CARDIAC TAMPONADE

Occlusion of the pericardial space with fluid causes cardiac compression, which results in a dramatic reduction in cardiac output (see p. 379). Patients present with breathlessness, collapse, tachycardia and hypotension. Clinical signs are described in full on page 380. Plain chest radiograph may reveal an enlarged and globular heart, and echocardiogram confirms the presence of a significant pericardial effusion. Treatment involves aspiration of the pericardial fluid through a catheter placed under echocardiographic guidance, and a sample of fluid should be sent for cytological examination (see p. 480). Recurrent pericardial tamponade is fortunately uncommon but, if it occurs, surgical intervention with drainage into the left pleural cavity or peritoneal cavity may be necessary.

FURTHER INFORMATION

Franks LM, Teich NM. Introduction to the cellular and molecular biology of cancer. Oxford: Oxford University Press; 1997.

Kfir N, Slevin M. Challenging cancer: from chaos to control. London: Tavistock/Routledge; 1991.

Souhami R, Tobias J. Cancer and its management. 3rd edn. Oxford: Blackwell Science; 1998.

Tannock IF, Hill RP. The basic science of oncology. Oxford: Pergamon; 1987.

www.breastcancer.org *An American non-profit-making site for the public with data on adjuvant therapies etc.*

www.cancerworld.org/progetti/cancerworld/start/pagine/Homeframe.html *Website for protocols/evidence for the management of particular cancers, produced and maintained by the European School of Oncology.*

Palliative care and pain management

M. FALLON • I. POWER

This chapter discusses palliative care for patients with malignant disease, although clearly many of these principles are applicable to chronic non-malignant disease. In addition, cancer pain control and non-malignant pain control are described, showing similarities and differences in approaches between chronic malignant and non-malignant pain and acute pain.

PALLIATIVE CARE

Palliative care consists of:

- symptom control
- rehabilitation
- continuity of care
- terminal care.

The term palliative care used to be synonymous with terminal care and was considered when all other treatment approaches had failed. Now modern palliative care is focused on the patient rather than on the stage of disease. Symptom control, rehabilitation and continuity of care are integral parts of the care of all patients with cancer. While much of this care is given by oncologists and the primary health-care team, palliative care specialists can be called in at any point to help with difficult problems. Terminal care is now very active, rather than passive, in its approach. Through an interdisciplinary approach it seeks to achieve optimum symptom control and psychosocial care. Through all the stages of disease, palliative care requires a holistic assessment (see Fig. 6.1).

Palliative care can be provided at home, in hospital and in hospices. It should be available wherever patients are,

at any point in their illness. Clearly, each member of the interdisciplinary team will have a more prominent role at different times: for example, doctor and nurse specialist at times of difficult pain control, physiotherapist during periods of immobility, and a palliative care social worker whenever there are difficult social and communication problems.

GENERAL PRINCIPLES OF PAIN

The International Association for the Study of Pain (IASP) has defined pain as 'an unpleasant sensory and emotional experience associated with actual or potential tissue damage or described in terms of such damage'. It is clear from this definition that tissue damage and pain perception are not necessarily correlated, and the patient's account of pain should be accepted as his or her own perception of the problem. Moreover, pain perception is the sum of complex sensory, emotional and cognitive processes, represented by the biopsychosocial model of pain, which applies to both malignant and chronic non-malignant pain (see Fig. 6.2).

Effective pain treatment should be an integral part of medical practice, but good analgesia also facilitates recovery from injury or surgery, aids rapid recovery of function, and may minimise chronic pain and disability. Clearly, in cancer pain control we hope to ease some of the physical and psychological distress and contribute to improved quality of life. Unfortunately, there may be obstacles to the delivery of good pain relief, including poor assessment, attitudinal barriers and 'opioid phobias'.

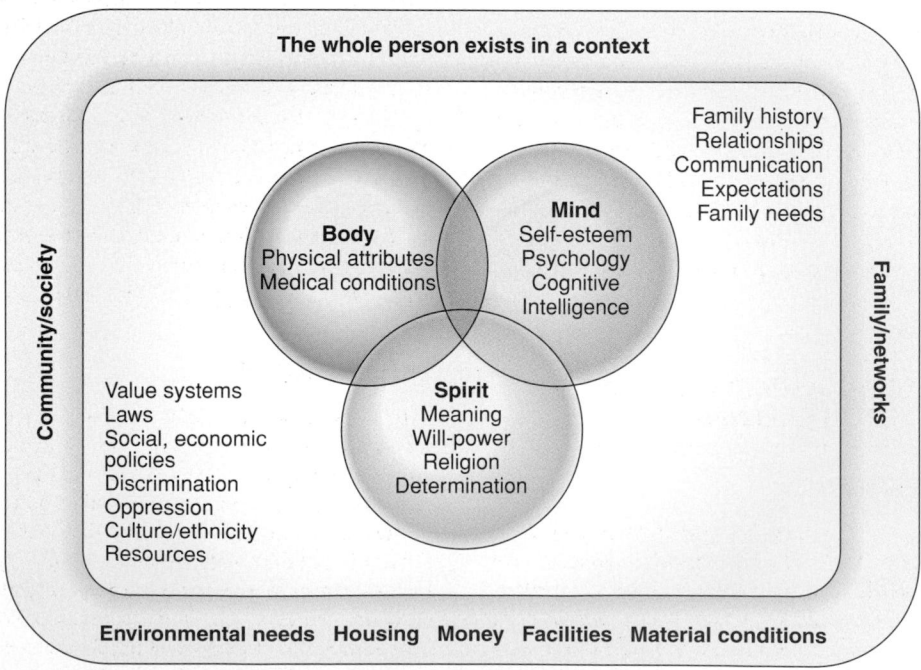

Fig. 6.1   A framework for holistic assessment.

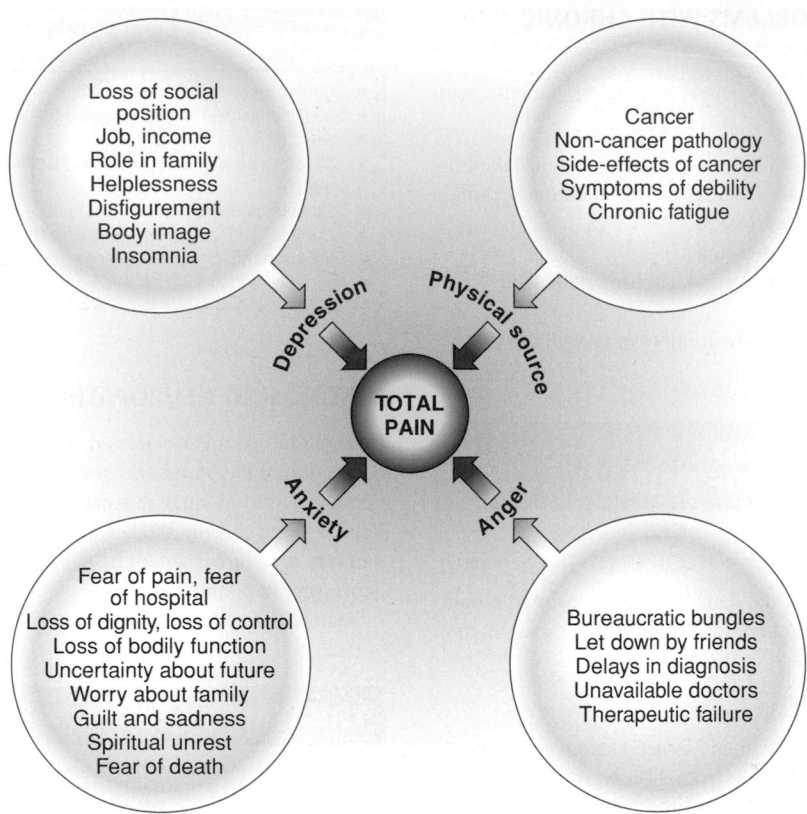

Fig. 6.2   Components of pain (WHO).

PAIN MECHANISMS

The 'pain pathway' was viewed in the past as a simple hard-wired circuit of nerves connecting tissue pain receptors to the brain. That theory is outdated and it is now accepted that there is considerable plasticity in all the peripheral and central components of the pain pathway, with several areas of modulation within the system (see p. 1142). In addition, it is also known that chronic pain can affect this neuroplasticity in a very detrimental way, making pain more difficult to control. Hence, early and appropriate treatment of pain is important.

PSYCHOLOGICAL ASPECTS OF CHRONIC PAIN AND CHRONIC ILLNESS

CHRONIC PAIN

Figures 6.1 and 6.2 show how the perception of pain can be influenced by factors other than the painful stimulus. (This model can be applied to any other chronic physical problem.) It is clear that previous models which regard pain as either physical or psychogenic in origin are less useful in clinical practice, as most patients with chronic pain will suffer emotional sequelae while, by the same token, emotional stress can exacerbate physical pain. The keystone to effective pain management is full clinical assessment, including signs and symptoms of anxiety and/or depression, which represent an integral part of the overall analysis (see Ch. 8).

Sometimes appropriate management of the pain alone will resolve anxiety and/or depression; however, in some cases concomitant management of depression/anxiety with a combination of drugs and psychotherapeutic approaches may be necessary. It is important not to assume that depression is 'understandable' because of a difficult physical symptom and therefore has no solution other than removing the symptom. Such anxiety/depression may still be amenable to therapy even if the underlying physical problem remains.

CHRONIC ILLNESS

Symptoms of anxiety and/or depression are common when a serious illness is diagnosed. This common psychological response to physical illness is known as an 'adjustment disorder' (see p. 255). Symptoms usually start within a month of diagnosis and tend to parallel the course of the illness. Clearly in patients with life-threatening progressive illness, such as cancer, depression or anxiety, psychological symptoms are unlikely to resolve spontaneously, and specific interventions with drugs and psychotherapeutic techniques are indicated. Between 20 and 40% of patients with cancer will suffer from depression at some point in their diagnosis.

ATTITUDINAL PROBLEMS WITH CHRONIC ILLNESS

Common pitfalls for physicians managing patients with chronic diseases are:

- a failure to recognise physical problems and mislabelling the patient as 'anxious', 'depressed' or 'attention-seeking'
- under-diagnosis of depression
- under-treatment of depression
- under-treatment of anxiety and labelling patients as 'anxious personalities'
- an assumption that drugs will improve everything.

ASSESSMENT AND MEASUREMENT OF PAIN

ASSESSMENT

Accurate assessment of the patient is the first step in providing good analgesia and should include history, examination and investigations.

History

An overall history of the patient's general health status should be taken along with a specific 'pain' history. A diagram of the body for the patient to mark the pain site can be helpful.

Examination

A full examination of the patient should include careful assessment of the painful area, seeking specific sensory signs, abnormal neurological conditions requiring urgent treatment such as spinal cord compression, or pain as a sign of a medical condition such as multiple sclerosis. In patients with cancer it is important not to assume that all pains are due to the cancer or its metastases.

Appropriate investigations

Investigations should be directed towards diagnosis of an underlying cause, remembering possible reversible causes, even in patients with terminal cancer. Radiological imaging may be indicated.

MEASUREMENT

Although pain measurement is subjective, it is an essential part of the overall assessment of the patient and the effect of treatment.

Verbal rating scale

Different verbal descriptions can be used to rate pain—'no pain', 'mild pain', 'moderate pain' and 'severe pain'.

Visual analogue scale (VAS)

A 10 cm line may be used which has 'no pain' on the left and 'worst possible pain' on the right. The patient makes a mark along the line. The 'VAS' score is the distance from 'no pain' to the patient's mark.

6.1 FEATURES OF NEUROPATHIC PAIN

- Burning, stabbing or pulsing pain
- Spontaneous pain, without ongoing tissue damage
- Pain in an area of sensory loss
- The presence of a major neurological deficit (e.g. spinal cord trauma)
- Pain in response to non-painful stimuli—'allodynia'
- Increased pain in response to painful stimuli—'hyperalgesia'
- Unpleasant abnormal sensations—'dysaesthesias'
- Poor relief with opioids alone

DIAGNOSING NEUROPATHIC PAIN

Neuropathic pain is associated with injury, disease or surgical section of the peripheral or central nervous system, and it is important to identify this early because it is very difficult to treat in the chronic state. Specific drug therapy is required with an anticonvulsant (e.g. gabapentin) or tricyclic antidepressant (e.g. amitriptyline).

Features of neuropathic pain are listed in Box 6.1.

TREATMENT OF PAIN

Treatment can be divided into pharmacological, non-pharmacological and alternative. It is essential to discuss treatment options with the patient at the earliest stage to ensure good compliance. It is also fundamental to cancer pain management that a patient's fears about opioids are explored. Patients should be reassured that when using opioids for cancer pain psychological dependence and tolerance are not a concern. Opioids can also be used safely in chronic non-malignant pain under appropriate supervision.

PHARMACOLOGICAL TREATMENTS

NON-OPIOIDS

Paracetamol

Paracetamol is effective when taken alone or in combination for mild to moderate pain. For severe pain it is inadequate alone, but remains a useful and well-tolerated adjunct.

Non-steroidal anti-inflammatory drugs (NSAIDs)

NSAIDs are effective in the treatment of mild to moderate pain, and are also useful adjuncts in the treatment of severe pain. Adverse effects (see p. 989) may be serious, especially in the elderly.

CANCER PAIN CONTROL, OPIOIDS AND THE 'WHO ANALGESIC LADDER'

Opioids, such as morphine, are the mainstay of management of severe pain. An outline of acute pain management is given in Figure 6.3.

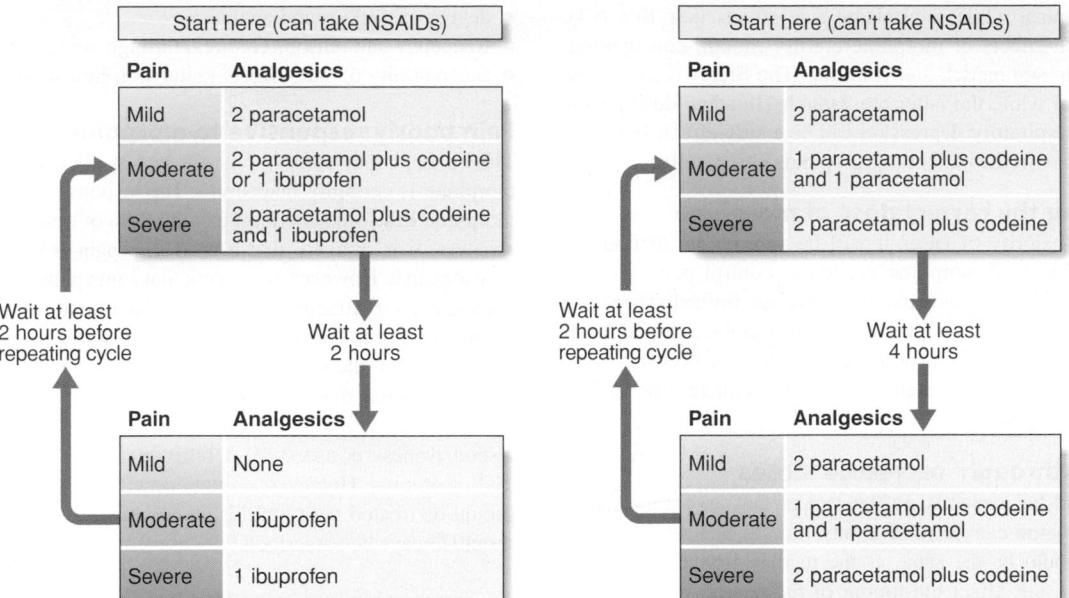

Fig. 6.3 Acute pain management. (Doses: 1 paracetamol tablet is paracetamol 500 mg; 1 codeine is codeine 30 mg; 1 ibuprofen is ibuprofen 400 mg; 1 paracetamol plus codeine is paracetamol 500 mg and codeine 30 mg. Parenteral opioids may be required for more severe pain)

CONTROL OF PAIN IN PATIENTS WITH CANCER	EBM

'Systematic reviews of single-dose studies show NSAIDs to be very potent analgesics and paracetamol/weak opioid compounds to be more potent than either paracetamol or a weak opioid alone.'

- Doyle D, Hanks GWC, MacDonald M. Oxford textbook of palliative medicine. Oxford: Oxford University Press; 1999.
- McQuay H, Moore A. An evidence-based resource for pain relief. Oxford: Oxford University Press; 1998.

The basic principle underlying the use of the World Health Organisation (WHO) analgesic ladder (see Fig. 6.4) is that the choice of drug therapy depends on the severity of pain. Generally, a patient with mild pain starts with a non-opioid analgesic drug, e.g. paracetamol 1 g 6-hourly. If the maximum recommended dose is not sufficient or the patient has moderate pain, a weak opioid, e.g. codeine 60 mg 6-hourly, is added. If adequate pain relief is still not achieved with the maximum recommended dosages or if the patient has severe pain, a strong opioid is substituted for the weak opioid. This is step three of the analgesic ladder. It is important not to move sideways on a particular step of the ladder in an attempt to control pain. Strong opioid analgesics should be prescribed when the severity of pain dictates. Morphine is by definition both an opiate and an opioid and is not only the archetypal compound, but is also the reference compound with which all other compounds with morphine-like activity are compared. The actions of morphine can be divided into three groups: namely, those with effects on the central nervous system, peripheral actions and other actions.

Morphine has a predictable onset of action, duration of action and side-effect profile (see Box 6.2). When this knowledge is shared with the patient the outcome can be rapid

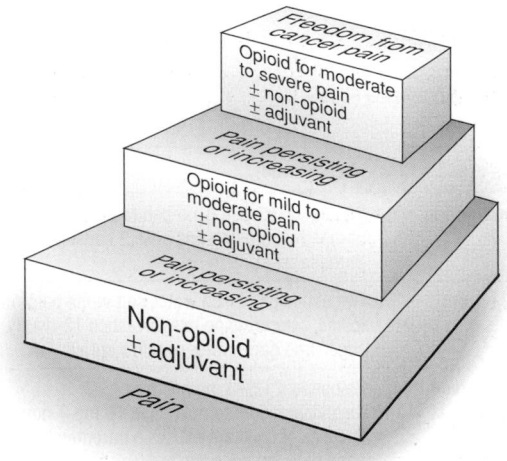

Fig. 6.4 The WHO analgesic ladder.

6.2 PHARMACODYNAMICS/EFFECTS OF MORPHINE

	Onset of action	Duration of action
Immediate-release (IR) morphine Morphine sulphate tablets Morphine elixir Morphine suppositories	20 mins	4 hrs
Controlled-release (CR) morphine Morphine sulphate tablets Morphine sulphate suspension	4 hrs	12 hrs
Parenteral morphine Subcutaneous diamorphine Intravenous diamorphine/morphine	5 mins	4 hrs

pain control while minimising side-effects (see Box 6.3). The side-effects of morphine are dry mouth, constipation, sedation, and nausea and vomiting. The first two are almost universal while the latter are variable. In acute dosing situations respiratory depression can be a side-effect; however, this is rare in the patient using opioids chronically.

Finding the correct dose of morphine
In the majority of cases it will be appropriate to find the correct dose of morphine needed to control pain, without unacceptable side-effects, by using an immediate-release (IR) oral morphine preparation in either tablet or liquid form. The advantages of this approach are increased sensitivity of analgesic dose, increased safety and a shorter time to find the dose required.

'Breakthrough' or 'rescue' doses
It should be explained to the patient that an extra dose of IR morphine can be used at any time to control pain. The dose should be the same as the regular 4-hourly dose and it should not affect the timing of the regular doses, which should remain fixed. The patient/carer should note the timing of any breakthrough doses and the reason they were needed (see Box 6.4). Every 24 hours this should be analysed and then the regular 4-hourly dose for the next 24 hours decided on the basis of:

- degree of background analgesia
- frequency and reasons for breakthrough analgesia
- acceptability of side-effects to the morphine dose.

Pain poorly responsive to morphine
The concept that some pains are not at all responsive to morphine is certainly inaccurate. The response of a pain to morphine lies somewhere on a continuum of opioid responsiveness; it is unlikely that a particular pain is completely unresponsive. However, we accept that some pains seem less amenable to treatment with opioids. Neuropathic pains are commonly put in this category; however, many neuropathic pains actually show a response to opioids. It should also be remembered that in cancer patients many pains are of a mixed aetiology. We advocate that the degree of opioid responsiveness is assessed in retrospect after an adequate trial of opioids. However, no patient with neuropathic pain should be treated with opioids alone; an adjuvant analgesic should always be prescribed.

NEUROPATHIC PAIN SYNDROMES—role of gabapentin EBM
'Evidence from two RCTs indicates that the anticonvulsant gabapentin is effective in the treatment of post-herpetic neuralgia and diabetic neuropathy. This evidence points to a potential role for this agent in the treatment of other neuropathic pain syndromes.'
• Doyle D, Hanks GWC, Macdonald M. Oxford textbook of palliative medicine. Oxford: Oxford University Press; 1999. • McQuay H, Moore A. An evidence-based resource for pain relief. Oxford: Oxford University Press; 1998.

Alternatives to morphine
Diamorphine, oxycodone, transdermal fentanyl, hydromorphone and occasionally methadone are alternatives to morphine in chronic pain management. Pethidine is used in acute pain management but should never be used to manage chronic pain.

Adjuvant analgesics
An adjuvant analgesic is a drug with a primary indication other than pain but which is analgesic in some painful conditions (see Box 6.5). At each step of the WHO analgesic ladder, an adjuvant analgesic should be considered, the choice depending on the type of pain.

NON-PHARMACOLOGICAL TREATMENTS

Surgery
It may be obvious at the time of initial assessment that surgery is required: for example, in a patient with known cancer who presents with a pathological fracture of the femur.

Physiotherapy
One of the key aims of pain management is to alleviate suffering and restore function. Thus physiotherapy and active mobilisation must be considered early in the assessment.

6.3 OPIOID SIDE-EFFECTS

Side-effect	Management
Constipation	Regular laxative, e.g. co-danthramer or co-danthrusate (starting dose 2 capsules o.d.; titrate laxative)
Dry mouth	Frequent sips of iced water, soft white paraffin to lips, chlorhexidine mouthwashes 12-hourly, sugar-free gum, water or saliva sprays
Nausea/vomiting	Haloperidol 1.5–3 mg nocte or metoclopramide/domperidone 10 mg 8-hourly. In cases of constant nausea a parenteral antiemetic is necessary to break the nausea cycle
Sedation	Explanation very important. Expect to settle in about 2–3 days. Avoid other sedating medication where possible. Ensure appropriate use of adjuvant analgesics which can have an opioid-sparing effect

6.4 CONVERSION TO CR MORPHINE FROM IR MORPHINE

- **Day 1** Morphine sulphate IR (tablets or liquids) 10 mg 4-hourly + breakthrough doses of 10 mg × 3
- **Day 2** Morphine sulphate IR 15 mg 4-hourly + breakthrough doses of 15 mg × 2
- **Day 3** Morphine sulphate IR 20 mg 4-hourly (no breakthrough dose required)
- **Day 4** Morphine sulphate CR 60 mg 12-hourly + breakthrough doses of morphine sulphate IR 20 mg p.r.n.

6.5 ADJUVANT ANALGESICS[1]

Drug	Dosage	Indications	Side-effects[2]
NSAIDs e.g. diclofenac	50 mg oral 8-hourly (SR 75 mg 12-hourly) 100 mg per rectum once a day	Bone metastases, soft tissue infiltration, liver pain, inflammatory pain	Gastric irritation and bleeding, fluid retention, headache; caution in renal impairment
Steroids e.g. dexamethasone	8–16 mg per day; use morning; titrate down to lowest dose which controls pain	Raised intracranial pressure, nerve compression, soft tissue infiltration, liver pain	Gastric irritation if used together with NSAID, fluid retention, confusion, Cushingoid appearance, candidiasis, hyperglycaemia
Gabapentin	100–300 mg nocte (starting dose) (titrate to 600 mg 8-hourly)	Nerve pain of any aetiology	Mild sedation, tremor, confusion
Amitriptyline (evidence for all tricyclics)	25 mg nocte (starting dose) 10 mg (elderly)	Nerve pain of any aetiology	Sedation, dizziness, confusion, dry mouth, constipation, urinary retention; avoid in cardiac disease
Carbamazepine (evidence for all anticonvulsants)	100–200 mg nocte (starting dose)	Nerve pain of any aetiology	Vertigo, sedation, constipation, rash

[1] Drugs with a primary indication other than pain, but analgesic when used as above.
[2] In the elderly all drugs can cause confusion.

Radiotherapy

Radiotherapy should be considered for all patients with painful bone metastases.

Other physical treatments

Pain may respond to spinal manipulation, massage, application of heat or cold, and exercise. For example, immediate cold application (e.g. through ice packs) reduces subsequent swelling and inflammation after sports injury.

ALTERNATIVE TREATMENTS

In some patients the use of non-pharmacological interventions may be helpful.

Psychological techniques

Psychological techniques such as cognitive behavioural therapies include simple relaxation, hypnosis and biofeedback. These methods focus on overt behaviour and underlying cognitions, and train the patient in coping strategies and behavioural techniques. This is clearly of more use in chronic non-malignant pain than in cancer pain.

Stimulation therapies

Acupuncture
Acupuncture has been used successfully in Eastern medicine for centuries. There does seem to be a scientific basis for acupuncture, with release of endogenous analgesics within the spinal cord.

Transcutaneous electrical nerve stimulation (TENS)
TENS may have a similar mechanism of action to acupuncture, and can be used in both acute and chronic pain.

Herbal medicine and homeopathy

These are widely used for pain, but often with little evidence for efficacy. Safety regulations for these treatments are limited compared with conventional drugs, and the doctor should be wary of unrecognised side-effects which may result.

CASE STUDY

A 45-year-old woman with metastatic breast carcinoma in bones and liver presents with the following symptoms:

- pain in the 7th–9th thoracic vertebrae
- right hip pain
- right upper quadrant pain
- pain in the lower abdomen
- constipation
- nausea
- poor mobility
- insomnia
- weight loss
- general weakness.

At presentation she has just completed palliative radiotherapy to painful bony metastasis in the right hip. Unfortunately, recent attempts at palliative chemotherapy have failed to control either disease or symptoms. She is married with three school-age children and is very anxious to return home to her family as soon as possible. She wishes to be less disabled by her symptoms so that she can retain her important role in family life for as long as is possible. On admission, co-codamol strong (codeine 60 mg/paracetamol 1 g) 6-hourly was stopped and morphine was commenced.

Current medication consists of:

- IR morphine 10 mg 4-hourly
- IR morphine 10 mg, as required (uses 3 times per 24 hours)
- co-danthrusate, 2 capsules 12-hourly
- diclofenac sustained-release (SR) 75 mg 12-hourly.

Approach

1. Analyse symptoms.
2. Reverse the reversible.
3. Palliate the irreversible with appropriate medication, depending on severity and type of pain, remembering non-pharmacological approaches, e.g. physiotherapy, occupational therapy, radiotherapy, TENS, anaesthetic techniques and relaxation techniques.
4. Anticipate and minimise drug side-effects.
5. Assess and reassess response to drugs.
6. Deal with non-physical problems.

Analysis of symptoms

Like most patients with cancer, this patient suffers from several sources of pain. She has local pain in her right hip and in her thoracic vertebrae which is constant but worse on movement. Both pains keep her awake at night; however, at rest they respond completely to IR morphine 10 mg within 30 minutes of administration, and this relief lasts for 2 hours. Pain on movement is only partially relieved by extra IR morphine 30 minutes before movement. Importantly, the vertebral pain is localised not radicular, and is not associated with any neurological symptoms or signs which might herald a spinal cord compression. Radiotherapy can take between 5 days and 5 weeks to have an analgesic effect; therefore her right hip pain may still respond.

The right upper quadrant pain is liver capsule pain, confirmed on clinical examination, and is responsive to morphine as assessed by IR morphine and showing improvement with the use of diclofenac SR 75 mg 12-hourly. Steroids are an alternative to NSAIDs for liver capsule pain.

The lower abdominal gaseous distension and palpable stool in the left iliac fossa are due to constipation and clearly should be reversible with increased oral laxative (using an increased dose of co-danthrusate, e.g. 3 capsules 12-hourly). If hard stool is blocking faecal flow (as established by per rectum or abdominal radiographic examination), then suppositories for rectal impaction or high enema for higher impaction should be used. Generally, once disimpacted of stool, patients can be successfully maintained on oral laxative.

Pain actions

The thoracic pain caused by vertebral metastases should be treated with radiotherapy. Meanwhile, the dose of morphine required to control the vertebral, hip and liver pain should be found by titration against the pain (see Fig. 6.4, p. 231).

The success of opioid titration lies in regular review of the balance between analgesia and any unwanted opioid effects.

Control of morphine side-effects

In control of acute pain respiratory depression is a risk but with chronic opioid use there are four common side-effects (see Box 6.3): sedation, constipation, dry mouth, and nausea and vomiting. These should always be anticipated.

Constipation and nausea

This patient has all the risk factors for constipation: immobility, opioid medication, nausea and poor oral intake. All patients with cancer and any of these risk factors should have a combination laxative (i.e. stimulant and softener), and the dose should be increased as necessary.

Nausea is a very distressing symptom and its control can be the keystone to the management of other symptoms. Nausea causes gastric stasis and impaired drug absorption even in the absence of vomiting. To break this cycle parenteral administration of an antiemetic is initially required. For this patient metoclopramide is the drug of choice. In addition to its action against opioid-induced emesis, it is a prokinetic, therefore useful in constipation.

Haloperidol is useful for its central action in opioid-induced nausea and vomiting; however, it has no prokinetic effect.

If this patient's nausea were secondary to raised intracranial pressure or secondary to a bowel aetiology (e.g. obstruction), then cyclizine would be the drug of choice. In patients unable to take analgesia by mouth, the subcutaneous route is preferred for diamorphine.

Insomnia

A careful history should establish the aetiology of insomnia. This patient presented with uncontrolled pain but other factors must be excluded. When asked why she could not sleep, she volunteered that she was worried about her family and needed help to speak with her children. The palliative care team helped the patient and her husband to understand how to approach the subject and with help they had a gentle but honest conversation with their children. Through dealing with a combination of physical symptoms and anxiety, insomnia is frequently helped. Sometimes an underlying depressive illness may coexist, requiring appropriate treatment with a combination of antidepressants and psychotherapeutic techniques.

Weight loss and general weakness

These symptoms require very careful analysis; some patients lose weight and develop weakness as a direct result of biomodulation of metabolism by the tumour, which is called cancer cachexia syndrome. In this syndrome calories cannot be utilised in the usual way. NSAIDs and megestrol acetate have some evidence for use in cancer cachexia. Recent studies suggest significant benefit to cancer cachexia patients from the combination of the fish oil extract eicosapentanoic acid (EPA) with high-protein supplements. In advanced cancer NSAIDs and megestrol acetate or EPA are unlikely to be effective but a short course of corticosteroids can temporarily boost appetite and general well-being. Steroids cause false weight gain by promoting fluid retention. While they can improve appetite and elevate mood, they need careful use. In addition to their physical side-effects, steroids can cause neuropsychiatric disturbances.

In summary, the patient we have described had lost 5 kg in 2 weeks because of constant nausea and vomiting. In addition her pain made her anorectic. She was generally weak because of weight loss and muscle disuse secondary to her pain. Clearly, control of pain, nausea and vomiting was a key element in optimising her disease management. Physiotherapy would now be crucial in the patient's rehabilitation following such a period of poor symptom control.

ISSUES IN OLDER PEOPLE
PRINCIPLES OF PAIN CONTROL

- Pain assessment in the cognitively impaired patient relies on good team-working and careful observation; grimacing, agitation, abnormal movements, and exacerbating and relieving factors should all be noted.
- Physical therapies such as TENS are important.
- Drugs should be used with caution; however, they will invariably be required, especially in cancer pain.
- NSAIDs should be used with care; when they are used, gastro-protection should also be prescribed.
- Opioids should be used at lower starting doses and, if renal impairment is present, at longer dosing intervals to prevent adverse reactions.
- Alternative opioids to morphine such as oxycodone or hydromorphone should be considered if cognitive impairment or hallucinations occur with morphine.
- Adjuvant analgesics should be considered as appropriate to the pain syndrome; however, the starting dose should be lower and rate of titration slower.

FURTHER INFORMATION

Doyle D, Hanks GWC, MacDonald M. Oxford textbook of palliative medicine. Oxford: Oxford University Press; 1999.
McQuay H, Moore A. An evidence-based resource for pain relief. Oxford: Oxford University Press; 1998.

Frail older people

N.R. COLLEDGE

Geriatric medicine takes much of the knowledge and clinical skills of the organ-based specialties and applies these to a particularly complex group: frail older people. This group is defined by the frequent presence of multiple pathology and the atypical way in which illness can present with confusion, falls, or loss of mobility and day-to-day functioning. Frail older people are also particularly prone to adverse drug reactions, partly because of polypharmacy and partly because of age-related changes in responses to drugs and their elimination (see p. 156).

The older population is extremely diverse. Many older people are not frail and enjoy a healthy active life into advanced old age. A substantial proportion of 90-year-olds live alone and manage with little support, while some 70-year-olds are severely disabled due to the ravages of disease or smoking. The terms 'chronological' and 'biological' ageing have been coined to try and define such differences, and increasingly 'biological' rather than 'chronological' age is used as a basis for decision-making in terms of investigation and intervention.

DEMOGRAPHY

There has been a striking change in the demography of developed countries over the past hundred years. In the UK population, the proportion of people aged over 65 years has risen from 5% to 16%, and is projected to increase steadily to 24% in 2061. In contrast, the proportion of those aged under 16 years in the UK is falling. By 2015 there will be approximately equal proportions of people aged under 16 and over 65 years of age, and thereafter people aged over 65 will outnumber those under 16.

Since the early 1980s there has been a particularly steep rise in the numbers of those aged 80 and over, and this trend is expected to continue (see Fig. 7.1). Life expectancy in the developed world is now significant (see Box 7.1). Women aged 80 years can expect to live for a further 9 years.

These changes are having a major impact on health and social services as there is an exponential increase in disability and mental and physical morbidity in people aged over 75 years. In the UK, the estimated prevalence of those with severe disability is less than 1% in those aged 50–59, but 13% in those aged over 80 years.

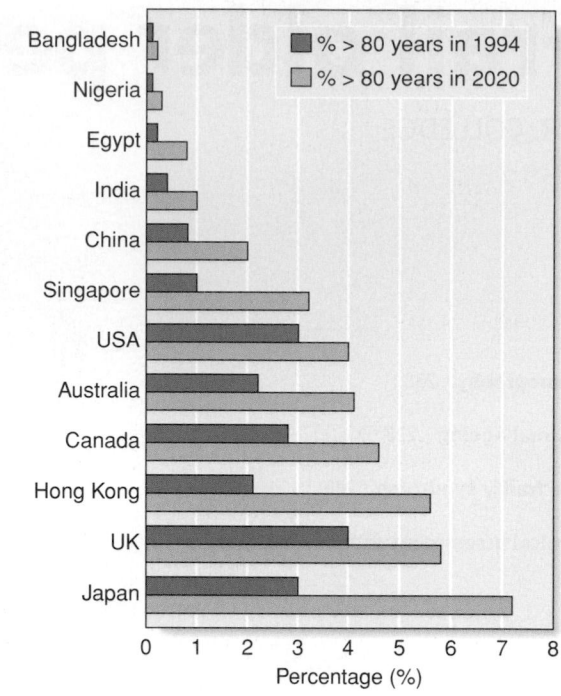

Fig. 7.1   Percentage of populations aged 80 and over, 1994 and 2020.

NORMAL AGEING

Knowledge of the features of normal ageing is needed in order to gauge the importance of symptoms and signs in elderly people. However, very few people reach old age completely free of disease. 'Normal' ageing is thus something of a misnomer, as its features have been established from a biologically elite population. There is a sharp increase in variation in function with ageing; an organ's function may appear to undergo a moderate decline with age on a population basis, but this may mask the fact that it remains unchanged in some older people while becoming so severely impaired in others that serious problems result. The effects of ageing are usually not enough to interfere with organ function under normal conditions, but reserve capacity is reduced.

Some features of ageing are age-determined; that is, they are inevitable. Others are age-related and result from an accumulation of factors such as lack of exercise or poor diet, or are accelerated by habits such as cigarette smoking, heavy alcohol consumption or over-exposure to sunlight. Age-related changes can therefore be slowed or prevented by a healthy lifestyle, and this remains worth encouraging even when old age has been reached.

Some of the changes of ageing are of no major clinical significance, such as depigmentation of the hair. Figure 7.2 shows the important changes and their clinical consequences.

7.1 LIFE EXPECTANCY IN THE DEVELOPED WORLD		
	Males	**Females**
At birth	75 years	80 years
At 60 years	20 years	23 years
At 70 years	13 years	15.5 years
At 80 years	7.5 years	9 years

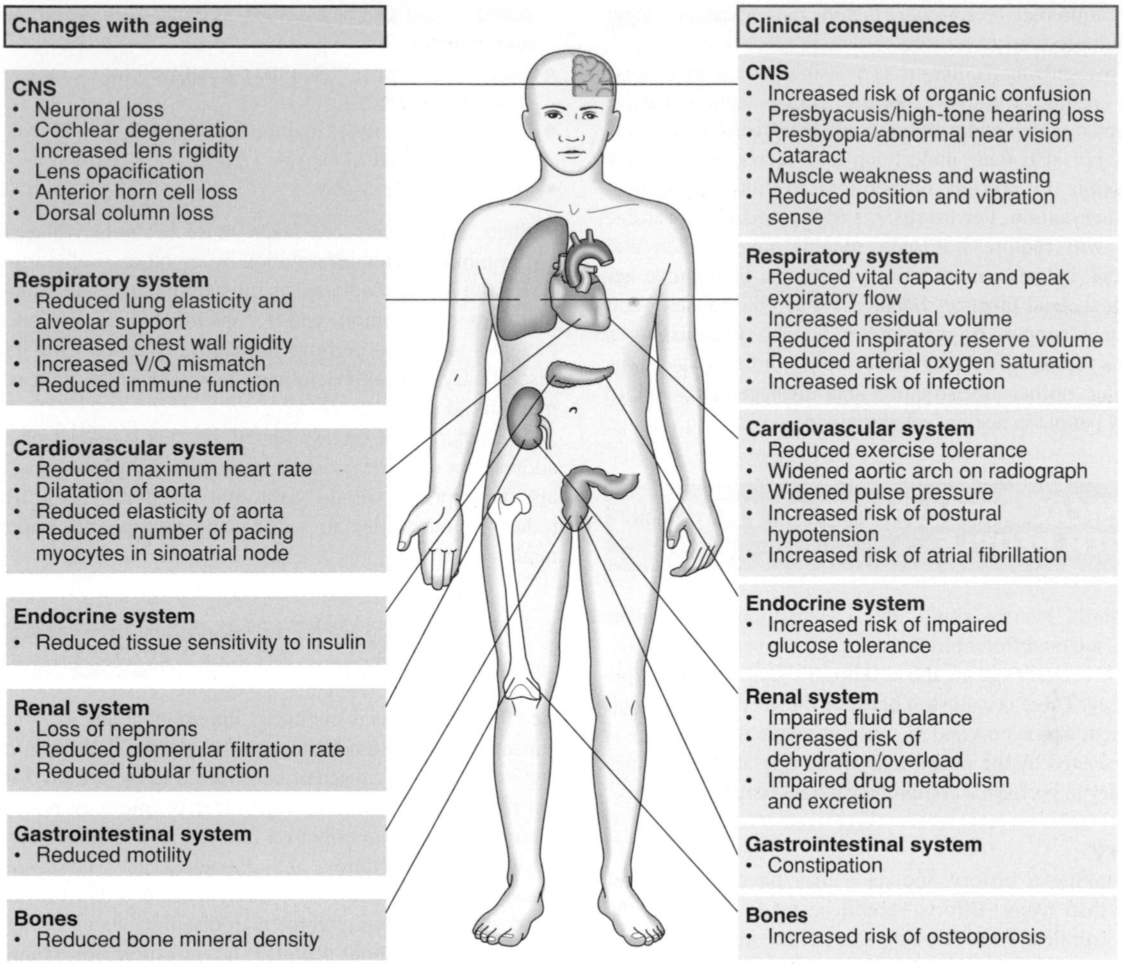

Changes with ageing		Clinical consequences

CNS
- Neuronal loss
- Cochlear degeneration
- Increased lens rigidity
- Lens opacification
- Anterior horn cell loss
- Dorsal column loss

Respiratory system
- Reduced lung elasticity and alveolar support
- Increased chest wall rigidity
- Increased V/Q mismatch
- Reduced immune function

Cardiovascular system
- Reduced maximum heart rate
- Dilatation of aorta
- Reduced elasticity of aorta
- Reduced number of pacing myocytes in sinoatrial node

Endocrine system
- Reduced tissue sensitivity to insulin

Renal system
- Loss of nephrons
- Reduced glomerular filtration rate
- Reduced tubular function

Gastrointestinal system
- Reduced motility

Bones
- Reduced bone mineral density

CNS
- Increased risk of organic confusion
- Presbyacusis/high-tone hearing loss
- Presbyopia/abnormal near vision
- Cataract
- Muscle weakness and wasting
- Reduced position and vibration sense

Respiratory system
- Reduced vital capacity and peak expiratory flow
- Increased residual volume
- Reduced inspiratory reserve volume
- Reduced arterial oxygen saturation
- Increased risk of infection

Cardiovascular system
- Reduced exercise tolerance
- Widened aortic arch on radiograph
- Widened pulse pressure
- Increased risk of postural hypotension
- Increased risk of atrial fibrillation

Endocrine system
- Increased risk of impaired glucose tolerance

Renal system
- Impaired fluid balance
- Increased risk of dehydration/overload
- Impaired drug metabolism and excretion

Gastrointestinal system
- Constipation

Bones
- Increased risk of osteoporosis

Fig. 7.2   Features and consequences of normal ageing.

THE FRAILTY SYNDROME

Frailty is defined as the loss of a person's ability to withstand minor environmental stresses because of reduced reserves in the physiological function of several organ systems. As a consequence frail people are at increased risk of death and disability from minor external stresses such as an infection or the addition of a new drug, because they do not have the reserves to respond and maintain adequate homeostasis. The same stresses would cause little disturbance in a fit person of the same age.

Unfortunately, the term 'frail' is often used rather vaguely, sometimes to justify a lack of adequate investigation and intervention in older people. Frailty is indicated by impairments in the function or status in several specific domains (see Box 7.2). These are all essential for an appropriate response to changes in the internal or external environment but are commonly reduced by disease, illness and indeed age. Their function can none the less be improved by specific intervention. In clinical practice, frailty per se is

rarely measured formally, but a comprehensive assessment would include an assessment of each domain.

It is important to understand the difference between disability and frailty as although they frequently coexist, they are separate entities. Disability indicates actual loss of function while frailty indicates increased vulnerability to loss of function. Disability may arise from a single pathological event such as a stroke in an otherwise healthy individual. After recovery minor fluctuations in function may occur, but overall it is stable and the patient may otherwise be in good health. When frailty and disability coexist, function fluctuates markedly in response to any minor illness, and the

7.2 DOMAINS IMPAIRED IN FRAILTY

- Musculoskeletal function
- Aerobic capacity, i.e. cardiorespiratory function
- Cognitive function
- Integrative neurological function (such as balance and gait)
- Nutritional status

deterioration may be so severe that the patient can no longer cope independently.

By recognising frailty, it is possible to identify those elderly people who will benefit from a comprehensive assessment which addresses not only the precipitating acute illness, but also their underlying loss of reserves. It may be possible to prevent further loss of function through early intervention. For instance, a frail woman with cardiac failure will require not only specific investigation and treatment, but also an exercise programme to improve her musculoskeletal function, balance and aerobic capacity, and nutritional support to restore lost weight. Establishing a patient's level of frailty also helps inform decisions regarding further investigation and management, and to identify people in need of rehabilitation.

CLINICAL ASSESSMENT OF FRAIL OLDER PEOPLE

As regards history-taking and examination, most older patients are no different from younger patients. They become more of a challenge in those who are frail with multiple pathology. There is a tension between the need to identify all the patient's problems and the need to ensure that he or she is not exhausted by the process. To avoid this, it is sometimes necessary to perform a comprehensive assessment in stages.

History
When taking a history, the pace may have to be rather slower than usual. Efforts should be made to ensure the patient can hear what is being said. There may not be one predominant symptom but rather a collection of vague complaints which seem unrelated at first, but frequently reflect the interaction of several comorbidities. The following information is particularly useful:

- the speed of onset of the illness
- a drug history, especially any recent prescriptions
- a full past medical history, even from many years previously
- patients' usual function
  —Can they walk normally?
  —Are they ever confused?
  —Can they perform all household tasks?
- their home circumstances and any help they have there.

It is helpful to confirm this information with a member of the patient's family or carer, and the general practitioner, particularly if the patient is confused or unable to communicate.

Examination
If all the relevant comorbidities are to be identified, the examination has to be thorough but also tailored to the patient's stamina and ability to cooperate. Over and above the usual examination, additional information required includes:

- *Mental state*. Cognitive function can be checked using the Mini-Mental State Examination (see p. 248);

mood should also be assessed, as depression is common and treatable.
- *Gait and balance*. Watch the patient walking (see pp. 960–961).
- *Nutrition*. Obesity or malnourishment may be obvious (see pp. 301 and 312).
- *Hearing and eyesight*.

Such assessments are made more accurate when they are combined with information from other professionals: for example, physiotherapists on stamina, gait and balance, dietitians on nutrition, and occupational therapists on the patient's ability to perform normal daily tasks. This interdisciplinary or multidisciplinary approach is key to assessment in old age.

The outcome of the assessment is a management plan to address not only the patient's acute presenting problems, but also to improve overall health and function. This aims to reduce vulnerability to subsequent illness and improve quality of life.

DECISIONS ABOUT INVESTIGATION

Accurate diagnosis is obviously important at any age, but is particularly so in frail older people because their problems are so commonly caused or contributed to by several different pathologies. However, frail older people may not have sufficient stamina or cognitive function to withstand lengthy or invasive procedures, and diagnoses may be revealed which cannot be treated for similar reasons. On the other hand, there is nothing worse than disability being accepted as due to age without adequate investigation; for example, the patient no longer able to climb stairs is supplied with a stair lift, when simple tests would have revealed osteoarthritis of a hip or vitamin D deficiency, and appropriate treatment might have restored sufficient function to allow the patient to climb stairs once more.

So how is it decided when and how far to investigate? For simple blood tests or plain radiographs, there is no issue in most cases. It becomes more difficult with complex or invasive investigations. The principal factors are as described below.

The patient's general health
Evidence of frailty will have been identified by a full clinical assessment. Do patients have the physical and mental capacity to tolerate the proposed investigation? Would they be able to manoeuvre on a radiograph table as required for a barium enema? Do they have the aerobic capacity to undergo bronchoscopy?

Whether the investigation will alter management
Would the patient be fit for or benefit from the treatment that would be indicated if investigation proved positive? This may be a particular issue if surgery is a possibility. If a patient with severe heart failure and a previous disabling stroke presents with a suspicious mass lesion on chest radiograph, detailed

investigation and staging are not appropriate if he or she is not fit for surgery, radical radiotherapy or chemotherapy. On the other hand, if the same patient presented with a pyrexia, detailed investigation for underlying infection would be important, as he or she would be able to tolerate the appropriate treatment.

The presence of comorbidity is more important than age itself in determining a patient's likely benefit from specific interventions. The more pathologies a patient has, the less likely he or she will be able to withstand an invasive or aggressive intervention.

The views of the patient and, where appropriate, the family

Older people often have strong views about their management, and these should be actively sought from the outset when assessing the risks and benefits of investigation and treatment. If the patient wishes, the views of relatives should also be taken into account. If the patient is not able to express a view, then relatives' input becomes particularly helpful. They should be asked what they think the patient would have wanted under the circumstances. Relatives should never be made to feel responsible for difficult decisions.

MAJOR MANIFESTATIONS OF DISEASE IN FRAIL OLDER PEOPLE

There are a number of special characteristics of disease in old age:

- the atypical way in which illness presents
- the late presentation of illness
- the presence of multiple pathologies and comorbidities.

The concept that illnesses as diverse as acute myocardial infarction, pneumonia, urinary tract infection and anaemia can all present with falls, confusion or incontinence rather than more specific signs and symptoms is fundamental to geriatric medicine. The reasons for these atypical presentations are not always easy to explain. Perception of pain is altered in old age (see p. 235), which may explain why myocardial infarction presents in other ways. The pyretic response is blunted in old age so that infection may not be obvious at first. Comorbidities may also alter more typical presentations.

Many people (of all ages) accept ill health as a consequence of ageing and thus may tolerate symptoms for lengthy periods before seeking medical advice. Comorbidities may be important; for example, in a patient whose mobility is limited by stroke disease, angina may take longer to present as the person cannot exercise sufficiently to cause symptoms in early disease.

Multiple pathology means that frequently a number of causes contribute to a single symptom. A patient may fall because of osteoarthritis of the knees, postural hypotension due to diuretic therapy for hypertension, and poor vision due to cataracts. All will have to be addressed in order to resolve the problem. A wide knowledge of adult medicine is required, as disease in any and often many of the organ systems has to be managed.

When assessing an elderly patient with non-specific problems such as falls or confusion, it is very difficult to know whether an acute illness has been the precipitant until it is established whether the patient's present state is a change from his or her usual level of function. It is unlikely that investigation for an acute illness will be fruitful in a patient whose mobility has been deteriorating over several months, whereas if it has suddenly become impaired such investigation would be appropriate.

The following section describes falls, one of the most common presentations in old age, as a specific example of a non-specific manifestation of disease. Patients often present with multiple problems, particularly confusion, incontinence and loss of mobility. Such manifestations often share underlying causes and may precipitate each other.

FALLS

Falls and unsteadiness are very common in older people. Around 30% of those aged 65 and over fall each year, rising to over 40% in those aged over 80 years. Although only 10–15% of falls result in serious injury, they are the principal cause of fractured neck of femur in this age group. Falls also lead to loss of confidence and fear, and are frequently the 'final straw' that makes an older person decide to move to institutional care.

The four main causes of falls are shown in Box 7.3. Those who have simply tripped may not require detailed assessment unless they have sustained an injury. It is important to establish whether the patient in fact lost consciousness, and, if so, perform appropriate investigations (see Figs 12.30, p. 398 and 22.10, p. 1121).

Acute illness

A proportion of older people who 'fall' have in fact collapsed as a result of an acute illness; falling is one of the classic atypical presentations of illness in the frail. This may be because of reduced reserves in older people's integrative neurological function and thus in their ability to maintain their balance when reserves are challenged by acute illness. Suspicion of this should be especially high in those in whom frequent falls have occurred suddenly over a period of a few days. Common underlying illnesses include infection, stroke disease, metabolic disturbance and heart failure. Thorough examination and investigation may be required to identify such problems and should include in the first instance:

- full blood count
- urea and electrolytes, liver function tests and glucose

7.3 CAUSES OF FALLS

Simple trip or accident

Blackout

Collapse due to acute illness

Multiple risk factors

Disease
- Cerebrovascular disease
- Alzheimer's disease
- Parkinson's disease
- Depression
- Arthropathy of weight-bearing joints
- Postural hypotension

Disabilities
- Poor balance
- Muscle weakness
- Gait abnormalities
- Visual impairment
- Cognitive impairment

Drugs
- Polypharmacy (four or more drugs)
- Drugs associated with sedation: benzodiazepines, phenothiazines, antidepressants
- Digoxin
- Diuretics
- Type I anti-arrhythmics

FALLS—interventions to prevent falls in older people

'Programmes that combine interventions, such as reduction in the number of drugs taken, balance and gait training, and attention to postural hypotension, reduce falls in those at risk.'

- Gillespie LD, Gillespie WJ, Cumming R, et al. Interventions for preventing falls in the elderly (Cochrane Review). Cochrane Library, issue 3, 2001. Oxford: Update Software.
- Tinetti ME, Baker DI, McAvay G, et al. A multifactorial intervention to reduce the risk of falling among elderly people living in the community. N Engl J Med 1994; 331:821–827.

Further information: 🖥 www.cochrane.co.uk

7.4 INTERVENTIONS TO PREVENT FALLS

- Identification and treatment of cause(s) of poor balance and gait disturbance
- Correction of postural hypotension
- Rationalisation of medication
- Correction of visual impairment
- Balance and strength training
- Environment safety check
- Safety education

- chest radiograph
- electrocardiogram (ECG)
- urinalysis for leucocytes or nitrites; if positive, urine culture.

It is also important to establish whether any drug has been started recently, which might have precipitated the deterioration. Once the underlying illness has been treated, falls may no longer be a problem.

Multiple risk factors

This leaves a large group in whom the immediate cause of falling may not be obvious. Such patients are often frail, with multiple medical problems and chronic disabilities. Their tendency to fall is caused by a number of risk factors, now well established from prospective studies (see Box 7.3). The risk of falling increases linearly with the number of risk factors present. Obviously such patients may present with a fall resulting from an acute illness or a syncope as above, but they will remain at risk of further falls even when the specific illness has resolved. It has been shown that the most effective way of preventing further falls in this group is multiple risk factor intervention (see EBM panel). A menu of these interventions is shown in Box 7.4 and these must be tailored to each individual's specific risk factors. Several interventions will be needed to reduce the risk of falling and a team of professionals is usually required to achieve this (see below).

When assessing a patient with recurrent falls, the cause of any disability such as loss of strength or gait disturbance has to be established, so that specific treatment can be given to improve it. For example, a patient's quadriceps muscles may be weak due to osteoarthritis of the hip, which will improve with adequate analgesia and physiotherapy. Gait disturbance due to Parkinson's disease will improve with appropriate drug treatment and physiotherapy. Rationalising medication may help to reduce postural hypotension or sedation. Other measures to reduce postural hypotension include correcting dehydration, tilting up the head of the bed and fitting support stockings, although elderly patients struggle to get these on. Non-steroidal anti-inflammatory drugs may be helpful; these cause salt and water retention, thus increasing the circulating volume. Fludrocortisone works by the same mechanism but is sometimes poorly tolerated as it may cause excessive fluid retention and thus provoke cardiac failure.

Simple interventions such as providing new glasses or chiropody can have a surprising impact on function. Although most falls are due to problems intrinsic to the patient, it is important to ensure the environment is safe, and this is best assessed by an occupational therapist visiting the patient's home. Personal alarms can be provided so that patients can summon help, should they fall again.

Bone protection

Osteoporosis prophylaxis should be considered in frail older patients who have recurrent falls, particularly if they have already sustained a fracture (see p. 1029). In this group, the most effective therapy is calcium and vitamin D_3. Devices known as hip protectors have been shown to reduce the risk of hip fracture by more than 50% in nursing home residents, although compliance tends to be poor. They consist of polypropylene pads fixed in special underwear to keep them positioned over the greater trochanters. Should patients fall on their hip, the pads disperse the force of the fall away from bone to soft tissues.

OTHER MANIFESTATIONS

It will be clear that there is a vast range of possible presentations in older people, and that they may present to any and every specialty. Relevant sections in other chapters are referenced in Box 7.5.

Within each chapter you will also find 'Issues in Older People' panels to highlight the areas in which presentation or management differs in this age group from younger or more robust individuals. An example for infection is shown below.

7.5 OTHER MAJOR MANIFESTATIONS IN FRAIL OLDER PEOPLE

• Infection	pp. 15 and 49
• Fluid balance problems	p. 283
• Poor nutrition	p. 325
• Hypothermia	p. 333
• Heart failure	p. 386
• Hypertension	p. 394
• Dizziness and blackouts	pp. 397 and 1121
• Atrial fibrillation	p. 402
• Urinary incontinence	pp. 594 and 1158
• Diabetes mellitus	p. 681
• Peptic ulceration	p. 788
• Anaemia	p. 914
• Painful joints	p. 974
• Bone disease and fracture	pp. 1025–1033
• Immobility	p. 1134
• Acute confusional states	p. 1144
• Stroke	p. 1168
• Dementia	p. 1177

ISSUES IN OLDER PEOPLE
INFECTION

- Humoral and cell-mediated immunity decline with advancing age, partly because of the associated burden of chronic disease.
- Infection is the most frequent reason for hospital admission in old age.
- Infection often presents with atypical or non-specific symptoms such as acute confusion or loss of mobility.
- There is an increase in the incidence of pneumonia, tuberculosis, urinary and soft tissue infection with age.
- Mortality and complications from infection rise with advancing age.
- Immunisation against influenza in those aged over 65 years has been shown to be highly cost-effective.

REHABILITATION

Rehabilitation aims to improve the ability of people with chronic disease to perform day-to-day activities. The prevalence of disability is strongly related to age. Acute illness in older people is often associated with loss of their usual ability to function, and common disabling conditions such as stroke, fractured neck of femur, arthritis and cardiorespiratory disease become increasingly prevalent with advancing age. The International Classification of Functioning and Disability provides a useful framework for rehabilitation (see Box 7.6). Doctors tend to be familiar with recognising pathology and impairments, but patients tend to be more concerned with their effects: disability and handicap.

Rehabilitation is a problem-solving process focused on a patient's function. This includes not only physical function, but psychological and social functioning too. The process includes:

- *Assessment.* The nature and extent of the patient's problems should be identified using the framework in Box 7.6.
- *Goal-setting.* Goals should be specific to the patient's problems, realistic and agreed by the patient with the rehabilitation team.
- *Intervention.* This includes active treatments to achieve the goals set but also support to maintain the patient's health and quality of life.
- *Reassessment.* There should be ongoing re-evaluation of the patient's function and progress toward the goals set, with modification of the interventions if necessary. This requires regular review with all members of the rehabilitation team, the patient and the carer.

7.6 INTERNATIONAL CLASSIFICATION OF FUNCTIONING AND DISABILITY

Pathology
- The underlying disease, e.g. stroke, osteoarthritis

Impairment
- The symptoms or signs of the pathology, e.g. hemiparesis, visual impairment

Disability (or activity limitation)
- The resultant loss of function, e.g. walking, dressing

Handicap (or participation restriction)
- The resultant loss of social function, e.g. going shopping, driving, sporting activities

The rehabilitation team includes several professional disciplines (see Box 7.7). Good communication and coordinated team-work are essential.

The interventions used in rehabilitation can be divided into 'hard', i.e. hands-on treatment by therapists using a functional, task-orientated approach to improve day-to-day activities, and 'soft' interventions, i.e. psychological support and education, often just as important to progress (see Fig. 7.3). The emphasis on the two types of intervention will be different depending on the patient's disabilities, psychological status and progress. The patient is a very active participant in the process, striving to overcome disability with the support of the rehabilitation team.

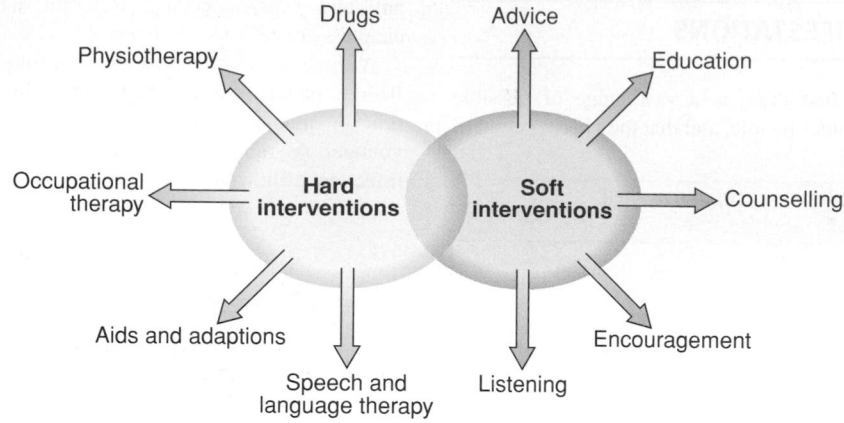

Fig. 7.3 'Hard' and 'soft' interventions in rehabilitation.

7.7 ROLES OF THE REHABILITATION TEAM	
Team member	**Role**
Physiotherapist	Promotion of balance, mobility and upper limb function
Occupational therapist	Promotion of activities of day-to-day living, e.g. dressing, cooking Assessment of home environment
Speech and language therapist	Management of speech and swallowing disorders
Dietitian	Management of nutrition
Social worker	Organisation of home support services or institutional care
Nurse	Reinforcement of rehabilitation programme Communication with relatives and other professionals
Doctor	Management of medical problems Coordinator of rehabilitation programme

STROKE—role of organised rehabilitation EBM

'Specialised stroke units reduce the risk of death, dependency and the need for long-term institutional care compared with care on a general medical ward, and benefits are not restricted to any particular subgroup of patients.'

- Stroke Unit Triallists' Collaboration. Collaborative systematic review of the randomized trial of organized inpatient (stroke unit) care after stroke. BMJ 1997; 314:1151–1159.
- Langhorne P, Williams BO, Gilchrist W, et al. Do stroke units save lives? Lancet 1993; 342:395–398.

Further information: 🖥 www.clinicalevidence.org

FURTHER INFORMATION

American Geriatrics Society, British Geriatrics Society and American Academy of Orthopedic Surgeons Panel on Falls Prevention. Guideline for the prevention of falls in older persons. J Am Geriatr Soc 2001; 49:664–672. *Can be downloaded from the BGS website.*
Campbell AJ, Buchner DM. Unstable disability and the fluctuations of frailty. Age Ageing 1997; 26:315–318.
Grimley Evans J, Williams FT, Beattie LB, et al., eds. Oxford textbook of geriatric medicine. 2nd edn. Oxford: Oxford University Press; 2000.

www.bgs.org.uk *British Geriatrics Society: useful publications, guidelines and links.*
www.nia.nih.gov *American National Institute on Ageing: a wealth of general information on illnesses in old age in the site index.*

Effective rehabilitation has a major impact on reducing disability in older patients, whether after acute illness or after emergency or elective surgery. There is also good evidence that rehabilitation improves functional outcome after stroke, in those with chronic obstructive pulmonary disease and following myocardial infarction. In addition, rehabilitation reduces mortality after stroke (see EBM panel).

Medical psychiatry

G.G. LLOYD • M.C. SHARPE

Psychiatric illnesses are fundamentally no different from medical illnesses. Historically, illnesses in which there was prominent disturbance of psychological function or behaviour and no obvious pathology came to be regarded as 'psychiatric'. However, we now know that there is demonstrably altered brain function in many psychiatric disorders. We also know that psychological disturbance is common in medical illness. Hence regarding psychiatric illness as 'mental' as opposed to 'physical' is incorrect. Psychiatric illness is no less real or less deserving of care than are medical conditions.

Diagnosis in psychiatry, as in much of medicine, is based mainly on identifying recognised patterns of subjective symptoms. These symptoms involve abnormalities of behaviour, mood, perception, thinking and intellectual function. When severe, these abnormalities may lead to patients being a danger to themselves or to other people. This is recognised in law, and in the United Kingdom the Mental Health Act gives doctors the authority to treat patients against their will in these cases (see p. 269). However, the great majority of 'psychiatric' patients are managed in general practitioners' surgeries, mental health centres or hospital outpatient clinics in much the same way as patients with any other medical condition. The prevalence of psychiatric illness in different UK populations is shown in Box 8.1. Figures are similar in most other countries.

The average general practitioner (GP) can expect to be consulted by 1 in 7 of his or her patients each year because of a psychiatric disorder. Physicians and GPs see a greater proportion of patients with neurotic illnesses and relatively few with psychotic illnesses; their patients are less severely ill than those attending a psychiatrist, and are more likely to present with somatic complaints.

This chapter does not aim at a comprehensive account of psychiatric disorders but concentrates on those areas of psychiatry which are most relevant to general physicians.

8.1 PREVALENCE OF PSYCHIATRIC ILLNESS IN DIFFERENT POPULATIONS IN THE UK

- Community — 15–20%
- General practice attenders — 30%
- General hospital outpatients — 20–30%
- General hospital inpatients — 25–40%

CLASSIFICATION OF PSYCHIATRIC DISORDERS

The two main classification systems currently in use are the American Psychiatric Association's Diagnostic and Statistical Manual (4th edition), usually abbreviated to DSM-IV, and the World Health Organisation's International Classification of Disease (10th edition), known as ICD-10. The two systems are very similar but ICD-10 is the more widely accepted outside the United States. The classification of clinical syndromes used in this chapter will be based on ICD-10, an outline of which is shown in Box 8.2.

8.2 CLASSIFICATION OF PSYCHIATRIC DISORDERS

Organic
- Acute, e.g. delirium
- Chronic, e.g. dementia

Substance misuse

Schizophrenia and delusional disorders

Affective (mood) disorders
- Depression
- Mania and bipolar disorder

Neurotic, stress-related and somatoform disorders

Reaction to severe stress
- Acute stress disorder
- Adjustment disorder
- Post-traumatic stress disorder

Anxiety disorders
- Generalised anxiety
- Phobic anxiety
- Panic disorder

Obsessive-compulsive disorder

(Medically unexplained somatic complaints)
- Somatoform disorders
- Neurasthenia
- Dissociative (conversion) disorder

Behavioural syndromes associated with physiological disturbance
- Eating disorders
- Sleep disorders
- Sexual dysfunction
- Puerperal mental disorders

Disorders of adult personality and behaviour
- Personality disorder
- Factitious disorder

AETIOLOGICAL FACTORS IN PSYCHIATRIC DISORDERS

As with most illnesses, psychiatric disorder commonly has multiple causes. Causal factors may be usefully categorised as predisposing, precipitating or perpetuating—'the three Ps' (see Box 8.3).

8.3 CLASSIFICATION OF AETIOLOGICAL FACTORS IN PSYCHIATRIC DISORDERS

Predisposing
- Increase susceptibility to psychiatric disorder
- Established in utero or in childhood
- Operate throughout patient's lifetime (e.g. genetic factors, congenital defects, chronic physical illness, disturbed family background)

Precipitating
- Trigger an episode of illness
- Determine its time of onset (e.g. stressful life events, acute physical illness)

Perpetuating
- Delay recovery from illness (e.g. lack of social support, chronic physical illness)

Genetic factors

These are important in several psychiatric disorders, including schizophrenia and affective illness, as evidenced by the following:

- a higher prevalence among first-degree relatives than in the general population
- a higher concordance rate in monozygotic than in dizygotic twins, even if the monozygotic twins have been reared apart
- a higher prevalence rate for children of mentally ill parents who are brought up by healthy adoptive parents.

Some disorders are due to single gene transmission, such as Huntington's chorea (autosomal dominant, see p. 346) and some uncommon causes of mental retardation (e.g. fragile X syndrome). However, for the majority of psychiatric disorders in which heredity plays a role, no single gene has been isolated and it is assumed that several genes have an influence on the development of the condition.

Family background

Many patients with psychiatric disorders report an unhappy childhood and it seems likely that a traumatic upbringing predisposes to future psychiatric illness. Important factors are loss of a parent in childhood, due to either death or separation, parental disharmony and physical, especially sexual, abuse.

Physical illness and chronic ill health

Both predispose to psychiatric disorder. There is an especially well-established link between brain injury and subsequent schizophrenic and depressive illness. Physical illness of acute onset can give rise to psychiatric disorder due either to its effect on cerebral anatomy and physiology or to its emotional significance and implications for the patient's future well-being.

Stressful life events

These can precipitate episodes of illness in vulnerable people. They usually involve a sense of loss or threat of loss, and include death of a close relative, marital breakdown, redundancy, retirement and major financial crisis.

Social isolation

Many psychiatrically ill patients are socially isolated and this often appears to be a contributory factor in their illness. Particularly important is the lack of a close, confiding relationship. Social deprivation is associated with various conditions, such as attempted suicide, alcoholism and drug dependence.

THE CLINICAL INTERVIEW AND MENTAL STATE EXAMINATION

The aims of the interview and topics covered are shown in Boxes 8.4 and 8.5. Whilst a psychiatrist may spend an hour on a full history and so-called 'mental state examination', an abbreviated psychiatric examination will be part of the assessment of all patients. A physical examination, paying particular attention to the neurological system, is also necessary. If possible, the doctor should also ask to see a reliable informant, who should be interviewed separately.

Several aspects of the patient's mental state will have become apparent while the history was being recorded. However, it is always necessary to ask specifically about current symptoms. Areas to be covered are listed in Box 8.6.

8.4 AIMS OF INTERVIEW

- Establish a positive relationship with the patient
- Elicit the symptoms and history and examine the mental state
- Provide information, reassurance and advice

8.5 TOPICS COVERED DURING INTERVIEW

Presenting problem

Reason for referral
- Why the patient has been referred and by whom

Presenting complaints
- The patient should be asked to describe the symptoms for which help is requested

History of present illness
- The patient should then be asked to describe the course of the illness from the time when symptoms were first noticed. The interviewer asks direct questions to determine the nature, duration and severity of symptoms and factors associated with them

Background

Family history
- Description of parents and siblings, and a record of mental illness in relatives

Personal history
- Birth history, major events in childhood, schooling, higher education, occupational history, relationships, marriage, children, current social circumstances and forensic problems

Previous medical and psychiatric history
- Previous health, accidents and operations; use of alcohol, tobacco and other drugs. Direct questions may be needed concerning previous psychiatric history since this may not be volunteered: 'Have you ever been treated for depression or nerves?' or 'Have you ever suffered a nervous breakdown?'

Previous personality
- The characteristic patterns of behaviour and thinking which determine a person's adjustment to the environment—including attitudes, moral values, interests, quality of relationships with other people and reactions to stress. The most useful information can be obtained from a description given by an informant who has known the patient well for many years

---

8.6 ASPECTS OF MENTAL STATE TO BE EXAMINED

- General appearance and behaviour
- Speech
- Mood
- Thought content
- Abnormal beliefs
- Abnormal perceptions
- Cognitive function
- Patient's own understanding of illness

GENERAL APPEARANCE AND BEHAVIOUR

Describe the patient's appearance, dress and general tidiness. Is there avoidance of eye contact or uncooperative behaviour with the examiner? Note any abnormalities of alertness and motor behaviour: for example, restlessness or retardation.

SPEECH

Speed and fluency of speech should be noted. Is there retardation of speech or difficulty finding words? Does the patient speak rapidly and is it difficult to interrupt the flow? Are there rapid changes in the topic of the conversation? Is it difficult to follow the patient's train of thought?

MOOD

Does the patient appear agitated, depressed or elated? This can be judged by facial expression, posture and other motor movements. The patient's subjective mood should be elicited. Some patients find it difficult to describe their mood in terms of anxiety or depression. Useful questions for depression are whether they have lost the ability to enjoy themselves (anhedonia) or whether they have lost interest in themselves and those around them. Other symptoms of depression include low self-esteem, guilt and worthlessness. It is also important to determine how they see their future. They should be asked about suicidal ideas: for example, 'Do you ever feel that life is not worth living?' Patients who reply positively need to be asked whether they have suicidal thoughts or plans for putting an end to their lives. Elated patients should be asked about feelings of grandiosity and self-importance.

THOUGHT CONTENT

Patients should be asked about their main preoccupations. This is best done by asking them to describe what is on their mind at present or what their main worries are. Is worry excessive? Is there evidence of phobic symptoms? A phobia is defined as an abnormal fear of an object or situation, the fear being sufficiently intense to lead to avoidance of the particular stimulus. Are there any obsessional symptoms? These are defined as thoughts, impulses or actions which enter the patient's mind repeatedly against his/her resistance but which nevertheless are recognised as his/her own thoughts. They are often associated with compulsive behaviours such as repeated hand-washing or checking.

ABNORMAL BELIEFS

Where there is reason to suspect the patient may have delusional beliefs, these should also be sought: for example, by asking whether he or she believes anything unusual is going on. Delusions are abnormal beliefs which are held with conviction and cannot be argued away, but which are out of keeping with the patient's social, cultural and educational background. They may be persecutory, grandiose or depressive in nature.

ABNORMAL PERCEPTIONS

Almost all medical patients will report bodily symptoms, and clear descriptions of these should be sought. Where suspected, abnormal perception should be directly asked about with questions such as 'Have you had any strange experiences recently?' or 'Do you ever hear people talking about you even though there is no one near you at the time?' Abnormalities of perception include depersonalisation, derealisation, illusions and hallucinations.

8.7 MINI-MENTAL STATE EXAMINATION (MMSE)

Patient name _____

Date of birth _____ Date of test _____

Max. points	Patient score	
		Orientation
5	( )	What is the (year) (season) (date) (day) (month)?
5	( )	Where are we (country) (county) (town/city) (building) (floor)?
		Registration
3	( )	Name three common objects (e.g. 'apple', 'table', 'penny'). Take 1 second to say each. Then ask the patient to repeat all three after you have said them. Give 1 point for each correct answer. Then repeat them until he/she learns all three. Count trials and record. Trials ( )
		Attention
5	( )	Spell 'world' backwards. The score is the number of letters in the correct order. (D_L_R_O_W_)
		Recall
3	( )	Ask for the three objects repeated above. Give 1 point for each correct answer. *(Note: recall cannot be tested if all three objects were not remembered during registration)*
		Language
2	( )	Name a 'pencil' and a 'watch'. *(2 points)*
1	( )	Repeat the following: 'No ifs, ands or buts.' *(I point)*
3	( )	Follow a three-stage command: 'Take a paper in your right hand, fold it in half, and put it on the floor.' *(3 points)*
1	( )	Read and obey the following: *(1 point)* CLOSE YOUR EYES
1	( )	Write a sentence. *(1 point)*
1	( )	Copy the following design. (Give 1 point if no construction problem)

30	( )	Total

Examiner _____ Notes

Depersonalisation refers to an unpleasant subjective feeling in which the patient's body is perceived as if it is changed, lifeless or unreal. It is often accompanied by derealisation, a sensation that the external world seems changed in that it appears grey, unreal or two-dimensional.

Illusions are abnormal perceptions of normal external stimuli. They occur most commonly in the auditory and visual modalities. Sounds appear distorted, muffled or louder than usual. Objects may be seen as larger (macropsia) or smaller (micropsia) than normal, distorted in shape or more vividly coloured.

Hallucinations are sensory perceptions which occur in the absence of external stimuli. They can also occur in any sensory modality. It is important to establish whether the patient perceives the sensation as emanating from within the mind or from the outside world. It is also important to establish the degree of insight into the experience. Hallucinations regarded as originating from within the patient's mind are known as 'pseudo-hallucinations'. Auditory hallucinations are characteristic of schizophrenia and affective psychoses. Visual, olfactory, gustatory and tactile hallucinations usually indicate organic mental disorder.

COGNITIVE FUNCTION

Intellectual abilities can be gauged from the history of the patient's educational background and attainments but can also be assessed during the interview from the patient's fluency, vocabulary and grasp of the interviewer's questions. The Mini-Mental State Examination (MMSE) is a useful screening questionnaire to detect cognitive impairment (see Box 8.7). A score of less than 24 out of a maximum of 30 is taken to indicate cognitive impairment.

The level of consciousness should be noted, especially in the assessment of possible delirium. Does the patient remain alert throughout the interview or is there a tendency to drift off and lose the ability to concentrate on what is being asked? Asking the patient to perform a simple repetitive task, such as subtracting 7 from 100 serially or repeating the months of the year backwards, can assess concentration more thoroughly.

Memory should be assessed under several headings. Recall of recent and distant events is determined by the patient's ability to describe details of personal history, dating back to childhood. It is also important to determine the ability to recall events occurring during the last few days and weeks. Registration is determined by presenting the patient with simple new information such as a name and address and then asking for this to be repeated immediately. The ability to consolidate and recall the information is checked by asking for the information to be repeated 5 minutes later, during which time the patient's attention should be diverted to other tasks.

Orientation is assessed by asking the patient about his or her exact location (orientation in place) and what day, date, month and year it is now (orientation in time). Orientation in person refers to the patient's ability to describe details of personal identity—that is, name, date of birth, marital status, address and other intimate details. It should be remembered that the degree of cognitive impairment in delirium typically fluctuates and may be missed by a single assessment.

PATIENT'S UNDERSTANDING OF ILLNESS

All patients should be asked what they think their symptoms are due to and what they fear might happen to them. Unjustified anxiety about disease may indicate hypochondriasis. It is also important to understand patients' views of the appropriateness of treatments (for example, referral to a psychologist or psychiatrist) before trying to implement these.

MAJOR MANIFESTATIONS OF PSYCHIATRIC ILLNESS

DISTURBED AND AGGRESSIVE BEHAVIOUR

Unfortunately, disturbed and aggressive behaviour is commonly encountered in hospitals. It is often alarming and sometimes dangerous.

Differential diagnosis
In many cases aggression may be a characteristic of the individual. In others it is associated with intoxication with drugs or alcohol or with delirium. In a small number of cases the person may be suffering from a functional psychosis such as schizophrenia.

Management
The first step is to ensure the safety of the patient and others (see Fig. 8.1). Dangerous behaviour must be controlled. This is best done by a calm approach but with enough staff available to provide 'overwhelming force' if necessary. If it is necessary to prevent harm to the patient or to others, forcible restraint may have to be used. Restraint may be applied in such circumstances under common law.

Rapid assessment is required. Two main decisions need to be taken. Firstly, is the behavioural disturbance due to psychiatric illness? If not, the patient may have to be dealt with by the police. The police should always be involved if the patient is armed or causing actual physical harm. If the patient is psychiatrically ill, the second decision is whether it is an organic or functional illness. A full history and mental state examination may be out of the question. As much information as possible should be obtained from informants, including details of recent mood change, paranoid ideas or other psychiatric symptoms. There may be a history of previous psychiatric illness, recent physical illness, head injury or drug abuse. When assessing the patient's mental state the key elements are

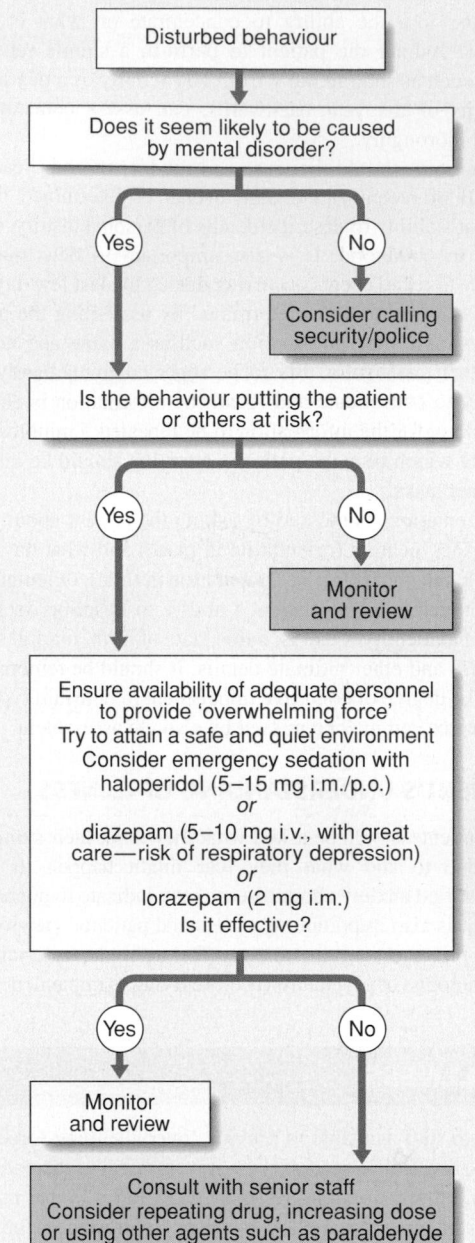

Fig. 8.1 Acute management of disturbed behaviour.

evidence of cognitive impairment, paranoid delusions, and aggressive or suicidal intent. It is also important to understand any triggering events which have precipitated the emergency.

Many aggressive and over-active patients are frightened because their behaviour is a response to paranoid experiences. They can be calmed by a confident, non-threatening approach. It is helpful if they feel the doctor understands what has brought on their distress.

Once restraints have been imposed it is likely that sedation will be required. Haloperidol is the drug of choice.

It can be given intramuscularly at an initial dose of 5–10 mg; this can be repeated if necessary until the patient is calmed. A decision can then be taken about the next stage in management, depending on the nature of any associated psychiatric disorder.

Priority must then be given to seeking the cause of the behaviour and in particular evidence of delirium or other psychiatric illness. If it is necessary either to stop patients leaving the ward or to transfer them to another ward against their will, they may need to be detained under mental health legislation (see p. 269).

DELUSIONS AND HALLUCINATIONS

Delusions and hallucinations (see p. 262) are diagnostic of psychosis.

Differential diagnosis
The main differential diagnosis of psychotic symptoms is:

- organic psychosis
  —delirium (including intoxication)
  —dementia and other chronic organic brain syndromes
- functional psychosis
  —severe depression
  —mania
  —schizophrenia.

Organic states are the most commonly encountered psychoses in medical patients. The elderly and medically ill are particularly at risk of delirium.

The key features of delirium are fluctuating impairment of consciousness and disorientation that is worse at night. Hallucinations are usually visual and transient in nature. Disturbed behaviour (for example, attempting to remove infusions or get into bed with other patients) is common, but the patient may also be quiet and withdrawn. It is always important to consider an organic explanation for psychosis, as urgent medical intervention may be required to correct the cause.

Drug and alcohol intoxication and withdrawal are important causes of delirium. Delirium associated with alcohol withdrawal is called delirium tremens ('DTs'). Chronic organic brain syndromes such as dementia may also present with hallucinations and delusions. The main way to differentiate an acute from a chronic organic brain syndrome is to obtain a history from the GP or other informant. However, remember that mild dementia is a risk factor for delirium and the patient may have both.

Functional psychosis may arise at any age. There will commonly be a history of previous episodes. Auditory hallucinations are most common, although visual, olfactory and tactile hallucinations may occur. The hallucinations are commonly accompanied by delusions. The type of delusion and hallucination and associated mood and behavioural disturbance offer important clues to the diagnosis. In severe depression the delusions and hallucinations tend to involve gloomy themes of guilt, wickedness, punishment and disease and there is usually a reduction in overall activity. In mania or pathologically elevated mood the delusions are typically grandiose with themes of self-importance or special powers. The manic person is usually over-active with rapid speech about changing and loosely linked topics. In schizophrenia the delusions and hallucinations may have a variety of themes but are not clearly associated with a persistent mood disturbance.

Certain types of delusion and hallucination are so characteristic as to be almost diagnostic of schizophrenia, such as the belief that one's thoughts are being interfered with or broadcast, and so-called third person auditory hallucinations (that is, hearing a voice or voices commenting on or talking about one).

Initial management

Aggressive behaviour may require management as outlined above. Patients are best managed in a side room. Those with delirium are generally better managed in a medical ward and require treatment of identifiable causes as well as sedation. Complicated alcohol withdrawal including Wernicke's encephalopathy requires specific treatment, as described on page 1173. For other psychoses appropriate nursing care and treatment with antipsychotics are appropriate, as outlined on page 257. The decision to transfer to a psychiatric ward should be based on the patient's needs, not the convenience of staff.

DEPRESSIVE SYMPTOMS

Depression is present in a quarter to a half of all medical patients. Symptoms of depression can be divided into psychological and somatic (see Box 8.8). It is important to note that the diagnosis of depression may be missed because it presents with somatic rather than psychological symptoms. The key psychological symptoms are depressed mood and loss of interest and/or pleasure.

8.8 SYMPTOMS OF DEPRESSIVE DISORDER	
Psychological	
• Depressed mood	• Loss of interest
• Reduced self-esteem	• Loss of enjoyment (anhedonia)
• Pessimism	• Suicidal thinking
• Guilt	
Somatic	
• Reduced appetite	• Loss of libido
• Weight change	• Bowel disturbance
• Disturbed sleep	• Retardation
• Fatigue	

Differential diagnosis

Depressed mood is usually a consequence of adverse circumstances in vulnerable persons. It is important to differentiate an adjustment disorder with depressed mood (see p. 263) from a depressive disorder. Adjustment disorders are transient reactions to adversity such as hospital admission and treatment-associated disability, disfigurement and loss. Depressive disorders (see p. 262) are characterised by more severe and persistent mood disturbance. In some people, depression may be a presenting symptom of a medical condition as a result of a direct effect on neurotransmitter function or interruption of anatomical pathways in the brain, or as a consequence of treatment with certain drugs. In such cases the depression may be referred to as an organic mood disorder (see Box 8.9).

8.9 ORGANIC AFFECTIVE DISORDERS: DISEASES THAT MAY CAUSE AFFECTIVE DISORDERS BY DIRECT ACTION ON THE BRAIN	
Neurological	
• Cerebrovascular disease	• Huntington's chorea
• Cerebral tumour	• Alzheimer's disease
• Multiple sclerosis	• Epilepsy
• Parkinson's disease	
Endocrine	
• Hypothyroidism	• Addison's disease
• Hyperthyroidism	• Hyperparathyroidism
• Cushing's syndrome	
Infections	
• Glandular fever	• Typhoid
• Herpes simplex	• Toxoplasmosis
• Brucellosis	
Connective tissue disease	
• Systemic lupus erythematosus	
Malignant disease	
Drugs	
• Reserpine, methyldopa	• Corticosteroids, oral
• Phenothiazines, phenylbutazone	contraceptives
	• Interferon

Initial management

Many cases of depression in medical settings are missed. It is therefore important to ask all patients about symptoms. Depression is the main risk factor for suicide and patients with depression should be asked about suicidal ideas and plans. The first step in managing depression is to find out the patient's concerns and provide an appropriate explanation and reassurance where possible. For example, it may emerge that he or she has an unjustifiably negative understanding of prognosis or treatment. If depression is persistent, specific treatment should be considered, as described on page 262.

ANXIETY SYMPTOMS

Anxiety is a common emotion and is typically a response to a perceived threat, such as an impending operation. It is a common emotion during the early stages of illness when a patient does not know what to expect and may fear the worst. Like depression, anxiety is common in medical patients and occurs in a similar proportion. It may be transient, persistent, episodic or limited to specific situations. Symptoms of anxiety can be divided into two groups: psychological and somatic (see Box 8.10).

8.10 SYMPTOMS OF ANXIETY DISORDER	
Psychological	
• Apprehension	• Irritability
• Fear of impending disaster	• Depersonalisation
Somatic	
• Tremor	• Dizziness
• Sweating	• Diarrhoea
• Palpitations	• Frequency of micturition
• Chest pain	• Initial insomnia
• Breathlessness	• Poor concentration
• Headache	

Differential diagnosis

Anxiety is usually transient as part of an adjustment disorder and subsides without treatment. Generalised anxiety (chronic anxiety associated with worry, see p. 262) and panic disorder (acute severe episodic anxiety, see p. 262) are important causes of medically unexplained somatic complaints. Phobic anxiety (see p. 262) is characterised by avoidance of the feared situation. Generalised avoidance or agoraphobia is a common association of panic disorder and causes profound disability. Anxiety may occasionally be a manifestation of a medical condition such as thyrotoxicosis (see Box 8.11).

8.11 MEDICAL CONDITIONS WHICH MAY MIMIC ANXIETY DISORDER	
• Hyperthyroidism	• Paroxysmal arrhythmias
• Phaeochromocytoma	• Alcohol withdrawal
• Hypoglycaemia	• Temporal lobe epilepsy

Initial management

The initial management of anxiety is to elicit the patient's concerns and worries, and provide appropriate reassurance. If anxiety is persistent or severe, drug treatment may be required; this is described on page 262. Specific psychological therapy is also effective. For patients who are phobic of medical procedures (such as being in a brain scanner) sedation with a benzodiazepine can be helpful. If the phobia concerns a procedure they will need to encounter many times (such as needles in a diabetic), cognitive behavioural therapy (CBT, see p. 256) that includes discussion, graded exposure and relaxation is preferable.

DELIBERATE SELF-HARM AND SUICIDAL IDEATION

Deliberate self-harm (DSH) is a very common reason for presentation to medical services. The term 'attempted suicide' is potentially misleading in that the majority of patients are not unequivocally trying to kill themselves. Most suicide attempts involve overdose, either of prescribed or non-prescribed drugs (see Ch. 3). Other less common methods include wrist-slashing, asphyxiation, drowning, hanging, jumping from a height or in front of a moving vehicle, and using firearms. Methods which carry a high chance of being fatal are more likely to be associated with serious psychiatric illness. There was a steady increase in hospital admissions for suicide attempts from the early 1960s so that by the end of the 1970s there were over 100 000 admissions annually in the UK. (The trend varies between countries.) Since then there has been a slight decrease but attempted suicide is still one of the most common reasons for acute medical admission.

Suicide attempts are more common in women than in men, and in young adults than in the elderly. In contrast, completed suicide is more common in men and in the elderly, although there has recently been an increased rate of suicide in young adults. There is a higher incidence of suicide attempts among the lower socio-economic groups, particularly those living in crowded, socially deprived urban areas. Patients often have a deprived family background due to early loss of a parent through death or separation. There are also links with alcohol misuse, child abuse, unemployment and recently broken relationships.

Differential diagnosis

The main differential diagnosis of DSH is from accidental poisoning. This may occur as a result of attempts to self-medicate in a person using analgesics or an accidental overdose in persons misusing drugs. DSH is not a diagnosis but a presentation. Any psychiatric diagnosis may be associated with DSH but the most common are adjustment disorders, substance and alcohol misuse, depressive disorders and personality disorders.

Initial management

A thorough psychiatric and social assessment must be carried out in all cases (see Fig. 8.2). In most hospitals this involves an interview with a psychiatrist. This need not always be the case because it is now recognised that junior physicians, nurses and social workers can assess these patients competently if properly trained and supervised. The assessment should be undertaken after emergency medical treatment has been completed. In

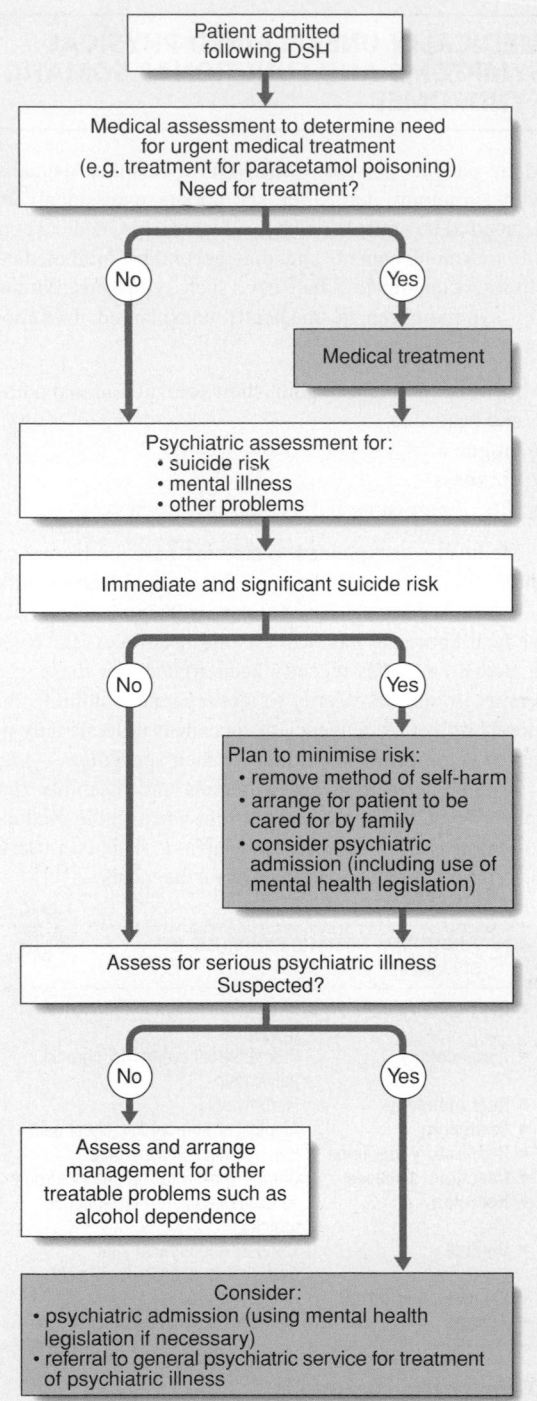

Fig. 8.2   Assessment of patients admitted following deliberate self-harm (DSH).

- limit damage from self-harm including poisoning
- establish the short-term risk of suicide
- identify modifiable factors such as psychiatric illness.

Topics to be covered when assessing a patient are listed in Box 8.12. The patient should be asked about events occurring immediately before the act and whether the attempt had been planned beforehand. In some cases there will be clear evidence that suicide was intended; the patient may have recently made a will, disposed of treasured possessions, gone to considerable effort to avoid discovery or left an explicit suicide note. The interviewer also needs to assess the severity of any current symptoms of psychiatric illness and to assess what personal and social supports would be available if the patient were to leave hospital. The majority of patients have depressive and anxiety symptoms, which are reactive to an acute life crisis superimposed on a background of chronic social and personal difficulties. Associated alcohol misuse is common. These patients do not require psychotropic medication or specialised psychiatric treatment. They do need emotional support and practical advice. A social worker or community psychiatric nurse may be the most appropriate person to provide this help. Admission to a psychiatric ward is necessary only for patients who have a major psychiatric illness, who remain intent on suicide or who require temporary respite from intolerable domestic circumstances. Admission should also be arranged when further information is needed to clarify the patient's mental state.

Approximately 20% make a repeat attempt during the following 12 months and 1% succeed in killing themselves. Factors that are known to be associated with an increased risk of suicide after DSH are listed in Box 8.13.

8.12 ASSESSMENT OF PATIENTS AFTER ATTEMPTED SUICIDE	

Current attempt

- How do they explain the attempt?
- What was the degree of suicide intent?
- Is there evidence of psychiatric illness?

Background

- Have they made previous suicide attempts?
- Family and personal history
- Social support available to patients
- Patients' usual ability to cope with stress

8.13 RISK FACTORS FOR SUICIDE AFTER DELIBERATE SELF-HARM	

- Psychiatric illness (depressive illness, schizophrenia)
- Age over 45
- Male sex
- Living alone
- Unemployed
- Recently bereaved, divorced or separated
- Chronic physical ill health
- Drug or alcohol misuse
- Violent method used (e.g. hanging, jumping)
- Suicide note written
- History of previous attempts

patients who have taken drug overdoses it is important that sufficient time has elapsed to allow the toxic effects of the drug to wear off.

When assessing a patient who has harmed himself or herself or has expressed ideas of doing so, a systematic approach is essential. The main tasks are to:

ALCOHOL MISUSE AND WITHDRAWAL

Alcohol misuse may present with intoxication, withdrawal or complications of excessive use. Intoxication will usually be obvious from behaviour and the smell of alcohol on the breath. It is important, however, not to assume that a person who is drunk does not also have a medical condition. Medical patients who have not presented as intoxicated may be reluctant to admit to excessive alcohol use. A history from the GP or other informant can therefore be helpful.

Alcohol withdrawal presents with tremor, sweating and feelings of tension. Less common but more serious withdrawal symptoms are seizures and delirium tremens. Delirium tremens is a potentially important medical condition that should be considered in the differential diagnosis of delirium developing soon after admission: for example, in fit young men admitted to orthopaedic wards after accidents.

Wernicke's encephalopathy should be suspected when the symptoms of delirium are associated with impaired ability to recall recent events and physical examination reveals a horizontal nystagmus, evidence of external ocular palsies, ataxia and peripheral neuropathy (see pp. 260 and 1173).

Benzodiazepines are commonly used to minimise withdrawal symptoms and the risk of fits (see p. 260). In suspected cases of Wernicke's encephalopathy immediate treatment with thiamin 50 mg i.v. is essential to minimise permanent damage. Further details on the management of alcohol misuse are given on page 260.

MISUSE OF DRUGS OTHER THAN ALCOHOL

The fact that patients are misusing drugs may be obvious; they may freely admit their habit or may reveal it by demanding drugs such as opiates. However, it may not be so obvious and they may present with symptoms of withdrawal, or with a complication of misuse such as hepatitis or HIV infection. There may be injection marks on examination.

Initial management

The first step is to discuss the problem with the patient and determine whether he or she wishes to stop using the drug. Some people do not, in which case advice about how to minimise the damage they do to themselves and others is appropriate. If they do want to stop, formal support will be required to help them withdraw from the drug (see p. 261). It should be noted that opiate-dependent individuals who have severe pain require higher doses of analgesic opiates to achieve analgesia.

MEDICALLY UNEXPLAINED PHYSICAL SYMPTOMS AND FUNCTIONAL SOMATIC SYNDROMES

Many patients present to their GP or hospital specialist with symptoms that, after appropriate assessment, are deemed to be unexplained by an identifiable medical condition. Among patients attending general hospital medical clinics, a quarter to a half have such symptoms. Almost any symptom can be medically unexplained. Common examples include:

- pain (including back pain, chest pain, abdominal pain and headache)
- fatigue
- dizziness
- 'fits', funny turns and feelings of weakness.

Medically unexplained symptoms have both medical and psychiatric classifications. The medical classification is in terms of system-based 'functional' syndromes. Each medical specialty has at least one; examples are listed in Box 8.14. It has recently been argued that these syndromes do not necessarily reflect separate conditions but merely reflect the tendency of specialists to focus only on those symptoms most pertinent to their specialty.

Another term used for symptoms and disability that appear to be disproportionate to the identifiable medical condition is abnormal illness behaviour. This is a useful description of behaviour but is not a diagnosis.

8.14 FUNCTIONAL SOMATIC SYNDROME BY SPECIALTY	
● **Gastroenterology**	Irritable bowel syndrome, non-ulcer dyspepsia
● **Gynaecology**	Premenstrual syndrome, chronic pelvic pain
● **Rheumatology**	Fibromyalgia
● **Cardiology**	Atypical or non-cardiac chest pain
● **Respiratory medicine**	Hyperventilation syndrome
● **Infectious diseases**	Chronic (post-viral) fatigue syndrome
● **Neurology**	Tension headache, non-epileptic attacks
● **Dentistry**	Temporo-mandibular joint dysfunction, atypical facial pain
● **Ear, nose and throat**	Globus syndrome
● **Allergy**	Multiple chemical sensitivity

Differential diagnosis

The main medical differential diagnosis is from symptoms due to organic disease. Difficulties are likely to involve unusual presentations of common diseases and rare diseases. Missing serious organic disease is always a concern. However, once a patient has been carefully assessed, the emergence of a 'missed' disease is the exception rather than the rule. The psychiatric classification is based on the number of somatic symptoms and associated psychological symptoms (see Box 8.15).

8.15 THE MAIN PSYCHIATRIC CATEGORIES OF MEDICALLY UNEXPLAINED SYMPTOMS

- Predominant worry about disease—hypochondriasis
- Predominant concern about symptoms—somatisation
  - Somatic presentation of depression and anxiety
  - Small number of symptoms—simple somatoform disorders
  - Chronic multiple symptoms—somatisation disorder (Briquet's syndrome)
- Loss of function—conversion disorder
- Dislike of body parts—body dysmorphic disorder

A full physical and psychiatric assessment should be completed to determine whether a medical or psychiatric diagnosis could be made (see Fig. 8.3). Physical examination and investigations should be arranged according to the pattern of symptoms. However, once the doctor is satisfied that relevant organic disease has been reasonably excluded, no further investigations should be undertaken. Further management is described on pages 265–267.

PSYCHIATRIC AND PSYCHOLOGICAL ASPECTS OF CHRONIC AND PROGRESSIVE DISEASE

Much of medical practice is concerned with managing chronic disease, such as arthritis and diabetes, or progressive diseases, such as cancer and multiple sclerosis. As well as ensuring appropriate medical diagnosis and medical treatment, the psychological care of such patients is important for quality of life, adherence to medical treatment and outcome. It is therefore essential that all such patients are regularly assessed for psychological and psychiatric problems as well as for the progress of biological aspects of their condition. Psychological problems are most likely to arise when there is deterioration in the patient's condition.

The most common psychiatric diagnoses are adjustment

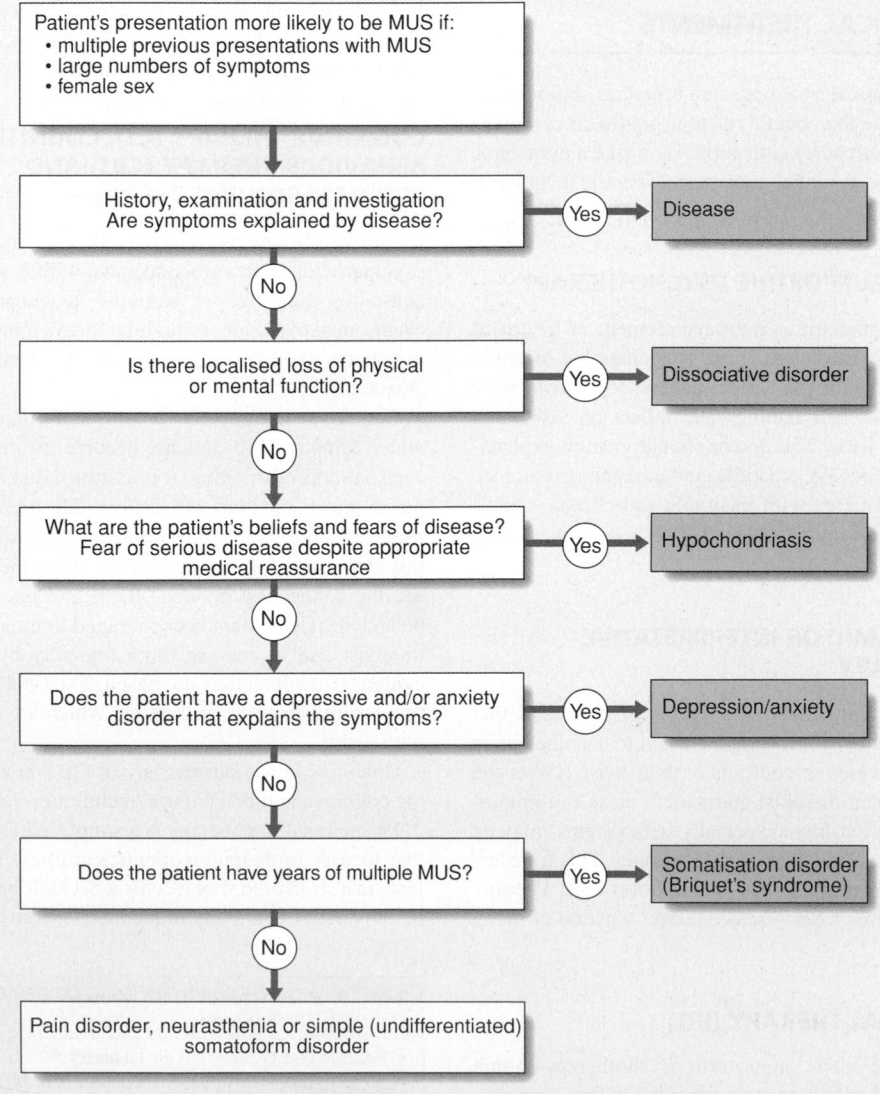

Fig. 8.3 Diagnosis of medically unexplained symptoms (MUS).

disorders and depressive disorders. These should not simply be regarded as 'understandable' but should be actively treated using psychological and pharmacological treatments, as described below.

Patients who develop adjustment disorders in response to demanding treatment such as chemotherapy or to the threat of imminent death can be greatly helped by an opportunity to discuss these matters either with their doctor or with a nurse. Those with more severe problems will benefit from appropriate psychological treatment.

Depressive disorders in patients with chronic illness are commonly missed, increased symptoms (such as increased pain) and disability being ascribed to deterioration in the medical condition rather than to depression. Conventional treatment for depression, as outlined on page 262, is effective. Care is required in prescribing to avoid exacerbating troublesome symptoms or producing interactions with other drugs.

TREATMENTS USED IN PSYCHIATRY

Some of the treatment approaches in psychiatry are unfamiliar in other branches of medicine so they will be summarised here.

PSYCHOLOGICAL TREATMENTS

Specific psychological treatments are based on communication, advice and the therapeutic relationship that is central to all good doctor–patient relationships. They take a number of forms based on the duration, contact and specific techniques used.

GENERAL OR SUPPORTIVE PSYCHOTHERAPY

Supportive psychotherapy is a crucial element in treatment throughout clinical medicine. It involves empathic listening during which the doctor encourages patients to describe their symptoms, express their feelings and reflect on associated problems in their lives. The doctor should give an explanation of symptoms, advice, practical guidance and reassurance as indicated. In patients with incurable and chronic conditions it forms a vital source of emotional support over many years.

PSYCHODYNAMIC OR INTERPRETATIVE PSYCHOTHERAPY

Interpretative psychotherapy is a specialist treatment that aims to help patients by encouraging them to become aware of traumatic memories or conflicts in their lives. It uses the relationship between therapist and patient as an example of how previous relationships (especially with parents) may be transferred inappropriately on to current ones. This transference may occur in all doctor–patient relationships. Therapy traditionally requires weekly sessions over a period of many months.

INTERPERSONAL THERAPY (IPT)

There is a trend to adapt longer-term psychotherapy so that it can be given in brief courses of 6 months or less. One specific form of such brief therapy that focuses on the patient's interpersonal relationships and problems is called interpersonal therapy (IPT). IPT is an effective treatment for mild and moderate depression.

BEHAVIOURAL THERAPIES

Behaviour therapy aims to help patients by showing them how to change their behaviour. If a person with a phobia (for example, of needles) is gradually exposed to the feared object, the associated anxiety initially increases and then subsides with resolution of the phobia.

COGNITIVE THERAPY (CT), COGNITIVE BEHAVIOUR THERAPY (CBT) AND PROBLEM-SOLVING THERAPY

Cognitive therapy is based on the assumption that some psychiatric disorders are associated with systematic errors in conscious thinking: for example, a tendency to interpret events negatively or as unduly threatening. In depression a negative triad of such thinking has been described (see Box 8.16).

Cognitive therapy is a problem-orientated approach which aims to help patients become aware of and modify such patterns of thinking; it is assumed that improvements in mood and behaviour will follow. The treatment has been used for depression, anxiety and eating disorders. The therapist has to identify the negative thoughts and help the patient see the connection between them and his or her mood or behaviour. The patient is encouraged to monitor the negative thoughts and to analyse them logically by examining the evidence on which they are based. The final step is to substitute positive patterns of thinking which are more in keeping with reality.

Cognitive behaviour therapy or CBT is a combination of the cognitive and behavioural techniques described above.

Problem-solving therapy is a simplified brief form of CBT that focuses on helping patients learn how to address problems in a structured way (see Box 8.17). It has been shown to be of benefit in mild and moderately severe depression.

8.16 THE NEGATIVE COGNITIVE TRIAD ASSOCIATED WITH DEPRESSION

- Negative view of self (e.g. 'I am no good')
- Negative view of current life experiences (e.g. 'My life is worthless')
- Negative view of the future (e.g. 'The future is hopeless')

8.17 STAGES OF PROBLEM-SOLVING THERAPY

- Define and list problems
- Choose one to work on
- List possible solutions
- Evaluate these and choose the best
- Try it out
- Evaluate the result

Repeat until problems are resolved

PHYSICAL TREATMENTS

DRUGS

Drugs used to treat psychiatric disorders are known collectively as psychotropic agents. They are classified according to their main mode of action (see Box 8.18). It should be noted, however, that drugs can have more than one application: for example, antidepressants are effective in anxiety and anticonvulsants are used as mood stabilisers. Drugs used in the management of Alzheimer-type dementia are described on page 1173.

8.18 CLASSIFICATION OF PSYCHOTROPIC DRUGS

Action	Main groups	Clinical use
Antipsychotic	Phenothiazines Butyrophenones Thioxanthenes Diphenylbutylpiperidines Substituted benzamides Dibenzodiazepine Benzisoxazole Thienobenzodiazepines	Schizophrenia Mania Acute confusion
Antidepressant	Tricyclics and related drugs	Depressive illness Obsessive-compulsive disorder
	Monoamine oxidase inhibitors	Depressive illness Phobic disorders
	Amine precursors	Depressive illness (in combination)
	Noradrenergic and 5-HT re-uptake inhibitors	Depressive illness
Mood-stabilising	Lithium	Prophylaxis of manic depression Acute mania
	Carbamazepine	Prophylaxis of manic depression
	Sodium valproate	Prophylaxis of manic depression
Anti-anxiety	Benzodiazepines	Anxiety disorders Insomnia Alcohol withdrawal
	β-adrenoceptor antagonists (β-blockers)	Anxiety (somatic symptoms)
	Azapirone	Anxiety disorders

Antipsychotic drugs

The essential mechanism of many of these drugs (see Box 8.19), which are also known as neuroleptics, is their ability to block central dopamine receptors. Antipsychotics are used to treat acute schizophrenia and mania, and to prevent relapse in chronic schizophrenia. They are also useful in the management of disturbed behaviour due to acute confusional states.

Side-effects of antipsychotics are shown in Box 8.20. Clozapine can produce agranulocytosis and its use is restricted to schizophrenic patients registered with a haematological monitoring service.

8.19 ANTIPSYCHOTIC DRUGS

Group	Drug	Usual dose
Phenothiazines	Chlorpromazine Trifluoperazine Fluphenazine	100–1500 mg daily 5–30 mg daily 20–100 mg fortnightly
Butyrophenones	Haloperidol	5–30 mg daily
Thioxanthenes	Flupentixol	40–200 mg fortnightly
Diphenylbutylpiperidines	Pimozide	4–30 mg daily
Substituted benzamides	Sulpiride	600–1800 mg daily
Dibenzodiazepine	Clozapine	25–900 mg daily
Benzisoxazole	Risperidone	2–16 mg daily
Thienobenzodiazepines	Olanzapine	5–20 mg daily

8.20 SIDE-EFFECTS OF ANTIPSYCHOTIC DRUGS

Weight gain due to increased appetite

Due to dopamine blockade*

- Parkinsonism
- Akathisia (motor restlessness)
- Acute dystonia
- Tardive dyskinesia
- Gynaecomastia
- Galactorrhoea

Due to cholinergic blockade

- Dry mouth
- Blurred vision
- Constipation
- Urinary retention
- Impotence

Hypersensitivity reactions

- Cholestatic jaundice
- Photosensitive dermatitis
- Blood dyscrasias (neutropenia with clozapine)

Ocular complications (long-term use)

- Corneal and lens opacities

* Less severe with clozapine, risperidone and olanzapine because of strong 5-HT-blocking effect and relatively weak dopamine blockade.

Antidepressant drugs

These are effective in moderately severe and severe depression, and can also be useful in anxiety disorders and unexplained symptoms such as pain (see Box 8.21).

8.21 ANTIDEPRESSANT DRUGS		
Group	**Drug**	**Usual dose**
Tricyclics	Amitriptyline	75–150 mg daily
	Imipramine	75–150 mg daily
	Dosulepin (dothiepin)	75–150 mg daily
	Clomipramine	75–150 mg daily
5-HT re-uptake inhibitors	Citalopram	20–60 mg daily
	Fluoxetine	20 mg daily
	Fluvoxamine	100–300 mg daily
	Sertraline	50–100 mg daily
	Paroxetine	20–50 mg daily
Monoamine oxidase inhibitors	Phenelzine	60–90 mg daily
	Tranylcypromine	20–40 mg daily
	Moclobemide	300–600 mg daily
Noradrenergic and 5-HT re-uptake inhibitors	Venlafaxine	75–375 mg daily
	Nefazodone	300–600 mg daily
Selective noradrenaline re-uptake inhibitor	Reboxetine	8–12 mg daily
Noradrenergic and specific serotonergic inhibitor	Mirtazapine	15–45 mg daily

Tricyclic antidepressants (TCAs). These have well-established efficacy, and are the most effective antidepressants for treating chronic pain. They inhibit the re-uptake of amines—noradrenaline and 5-hydroxytryptamine (5-HT, serotonin)—at synaptic clefts. There is a delay of 2–3 weeks between the start of treatment and the onset of therapeutic effect. Side-effects can be particularly troublesome during this period; they include anticholinergic effects, postural hypotension, lowering of the seizure threshold and cardio-toxicity.

Selective serotonin re-uptake inhibitors (SSRIs). Less cardiotoxic, less sedative and with fewer anticholinergic effects than tricyclics, these can still cause headache, nausea, anorexia and sexual dysfunction.

Monoamine oxidase inhibitors (MAOIs). These increase the availability of neurotransmitters at synaptic clefts by inhibiting metabolism of noradrenaline and 5-HT. MAOIs have important interactions with drugs such as amphetamines and opiates, and foods rich in tyramine such as cheese, pickled herrings, degraded protein and red wine. Amines accumulate in the systemic circulation causing a hypertensive crisis and rarely fatalities have occurred from cerebral haemorrhage. Patients taking MAOIs should be given a card listing all the substances to be avoided. Moclobemide is a reversible and selective inhibitor of monoamine oxidase subtype A, which causes minimal potentiation of the pressor response to dietary tyramine.

Newer antidepressants
A variety of newer antidepressant agents are available. They include venlafaxine, nefazodone, mirtazapine and reboxetine. They have different profiles of action and adverse effects but none has been shown to be more effective than the more established agents listed above.

Mood-stabilising drugs
These are used as prophylaxis against relapse in bipolar affective disorder.

Lithium carbonate. This is the main drug used in the prophylaxis of affective disorders. Lithium is also used for acute mania and in combination with a tricyclic as an adjuvant treatment for resistant depression. It has a narrow therapeutic range so regular blood monitoring is required to maintain a serum level of 0.5–1.0 mmol/l. This is usually achieved with a daily dose of 800–1200 mg.

Toxic effects include nausea, vomiting, tremor and convulsions. With long-term treatment, weight gain, hypothyroidism, nephrogenic diabetes insipidus and renal failure can occur. Thyroid and renal function should be checked before treatment is started and every 6 months thereafter. Lithium has a significant teratogenic effect and should never be prescribed during the first trimester of pregnancy. Take care if stopping lithium as it may result in relapse of affective disorder.

Carbamazepine and sodium valproate. These are established anticonvulsant drugs that have been used successfully as prophylaxis in manic depression. Common side-effects with carbamazepine are drowsiness, ataxia, headache, rashes and nausea; with valproate, common side-effects are nausea, ataxia and tremor.

Anti-anxiety drugs
Examples of commonly used anti-anxiety drugs are shown in Box 8.22. It should be noted that the so-called antidepressant drugs are also indicated for anxiety disorders.

Benzodiazepines. These have been used widely for the treatment of insomnia and anxiety-related disorders. They have the potential for dependence, and withdrawal symptoms may occur in some patients who have taken them for 6 weeks or more (see Box 8.23). These symptoms occur especially with short-acting benzodiazepines and if medication is stopped abruptly.

8.22 ANTI-ANXIETY DRUGS		
Group	**Drug**	**Usual dose**
Benzodiazepines	Diazepam	2–30 mg daily
	Chlordiazepoxide	5–30 mg daily
	Nitrazepam	5–10 mg daily
	Temazepam	10–20 mg at night
β-blockers	Propranolol	20–80 mg daily
Azapirone	Buspirone	10–45 mg daily

8.23 BENZODIAZEPINE WITHDRAWAL SYMPTOMS
• Anxiety • Heightened sensory perception • Hallucinations • Epileptic seizures • Ataxia • Paranoid delusions

Buspirone. Unrelated to any other psychotropic drug, buspirone is claimed not to have withdrawal effects; nor does it have sedative or muscle relaxant properties. Its mode of action is slow, over 3 or 4 weeks, and this is obviously a disadvantage when a quick response is required.

Beta-blockers. Beta-blockers such as propranolol have a limited role in the treatment of anxiety where somatic symptoms such as tremor and palpitations are prominent.

ELECTROCONVULSIVE THERAPY (ECT)

Electroconvulsive therapy involves the administration of high-voltage, brief direct current impulses to the head while the patient is anaesthetised and paralysed by muscle relaxants. It is effective for severe depressive illness. It is remarkably safe and has few side-effects. There may be amnesia for events occurring a few hours before ECT (retrograde) and after (anterograde). Permanent anterograde amnesia has been claimed to occur but is infrequent.

CLINICAL SYNDROMES

ORGANIC SYNDROMES

Organic disorders result from identifiable organic abnormalities within the brain or acting on the brain from a focus elsewhere in the body. The most common syndromes are delirium (see p. 250), dementia (see p. 250) and organic mood disorders (see p. 251).

SUBSTANCE MISUSE

ALCOHOL MISUSE

High levels of alcohol consumption are associated with social, psychological and physical problems. The criteria for 'alcohol dependence', a more restricted term, are shown in Box 8.24. Approximately one-quarter of male patients in general hospital medical wards in the UK have a current or previous alcohol problem.

Aetiology

Availability and social patterns of use appear to be the most important factors. Genetic factors may play some part in

---

8.24 CRITERIA OF ALCOHOL DEPENDENCE

- Narrowing of the drinking repertoire
- Priority of drinking over other activities
- Tolerance of effects of alcohol
- Repeated withdrawal symptoms
- Relief of withdrawal symptoms by further drinking
- Subjective compulsion to drink
- Reinstatement of drinking behaviour after abstinence

---

predisposition to dependence. The majority of alcoholics do not have an associated psychiatric illness, but a few drink heavily in an attempt to relieve anxiety or depression.

Problems caused by alcohol

Many patients' alcohol problems are not detected by their doctors. A high index of suspicion is important, particularly when there are repeated consultations for vague symptoms or minor accidents. The patient should be asked to describe a typical week's drinking quantified in terms of units of alcohol (one unit contains approximately 9 g of alcohol and is the equivalent of half a pint of beer, a single measure of spirits or a glass of table wine). Current opinion is that drinking becomes hazardous at levels above 21 units weekly for men and 14 units weekly for women. Conversely, there is some evidence that regular, modest consumption of alcohol may have a protective effect against the development of coronary artery disease. Laboratory tests can be useful in confirming alcohol misuse. Mean cell volume (MCV) or gamma-glutamyl transferase (γ-GT) is raised in approximately 50% of problem drinkers. Although the low sensitivity of these tests makes them unsuitable for population screening, they are useful for monitoring treatment response in individual cases where their values were elevated originally.

Social problems

These include absenteeism from work, unemployment, marital tensions, child abuse, financial difficulties and problems with the law, such as violence and traffic offences.

Psychological problems

Depression is common and is usually reactive to the numerous social problems which heavy drinking creates. Alcohol also has a direct depressant effect. Attempted suicide and completed suicide are often associated with alcohol misuse.

Anxiety is relieved by alcohol. People who are socially anxious may consequently use alcohol in this way and may develop dependence. Conversely, alcohol withdrawal increases anxiety.

Alcoholic hallucinosis is a rare condition in which alcoholic individuals experience auditory hallucination in clear consciousness.

Alcohol withdrawal is described on page 254. Symptoms usually become severe about 2 days after the last drink.

Delirium tremens is a form of delirium associated with alcohol withdrawal. Convulsions can occur with alcohol withdrawal.

Effects on the brain

These cause the familiar features of drunkenness. In very heavy drinkers there are periods of amnesia (alcoholic blackouts) for events which occurred during bouts of intoxication. When alcoholism has been established for several years, cortical atrophy can occur and the clinical picture of dementia develops. Indirect effects on behaviour can result from head injury, hypoglycaemia and portosystemic encephalopathy.

Wernicke–Korsakoff syndrome results from damage to the mamillary bodies, dorsomedial nuclei of the thalamus and adjacent areas of grey matter. It is caused by a deficiency of thiamin (vitamin B_1). In those who die in the acute stage, microscopic examination of the brain shows hyperaemia, petechial haemorrhages and astrocytic proliferation. For further details, including management, see page 1173.

Effects on other bodily organs

These are protean and can affect virtually any organ in the body; alcohol has replaced syphilis as the great mimic of disease. The effects are shown in Figure 8.4 and are discussed in detail in the relevant chapters.

Management

Straightforward advice about the harmful effects of alcohol and safe levels of consumption is often all that is needed. In more serious cases patients may have to be advised to alter leisure activities or change jobs if these are contributing to the problem. Supportive psychotherapy is often crucial in helping the patient effect the necessary changes in lifestyle. Psychological treatment is used for patients who have recurrent relapses. Treatment of this type is available at specialised centres and is also provided by voluntary organisations such as Alcoholics Anonymous (AA) in the UK.

Drug therapy also has a role in treatment. Benzodiazepines are the drugs of choice for withdrawal symptoms and can be given safely in large doses (e.g. diazepam 20 mg 6-hourly), tailed off over a period of 5–7 days as symptoms subside. It is usual to give high-dose vitamins during withdrawal treatment because of the possibility of thiamine deficiency. Disulfiram (200–400 mg daily) can be given as a deterrent to patients who have difficulty resisting sudden impulses to drink after becoming abstinent. The drug blocks the metabolism of alcohol, causing acetaldehyde to accumulate in the body. When alcohol is consumed, there follows an unpleasant reaction consisting of headache, flushing, nausea and laboured breathing. Knowledge that this reaction will occur can provide the patient with an insurance against drinking and even remove craving. Disulfiram is always an adjunct to other treatments, especially supportive psychotherapy. Acamprosate (666 mg 8-hourly) has recently been introduced to maintain abstinence by reducing craving for alcohol. Only rarely are antidepressants required; the depressive symptoms, if present, usually resolve with abstinence. Phenothiazines (e.g. chlorpromazine 100 mg 8-hourly) are required for alcoholic hallucinosis.

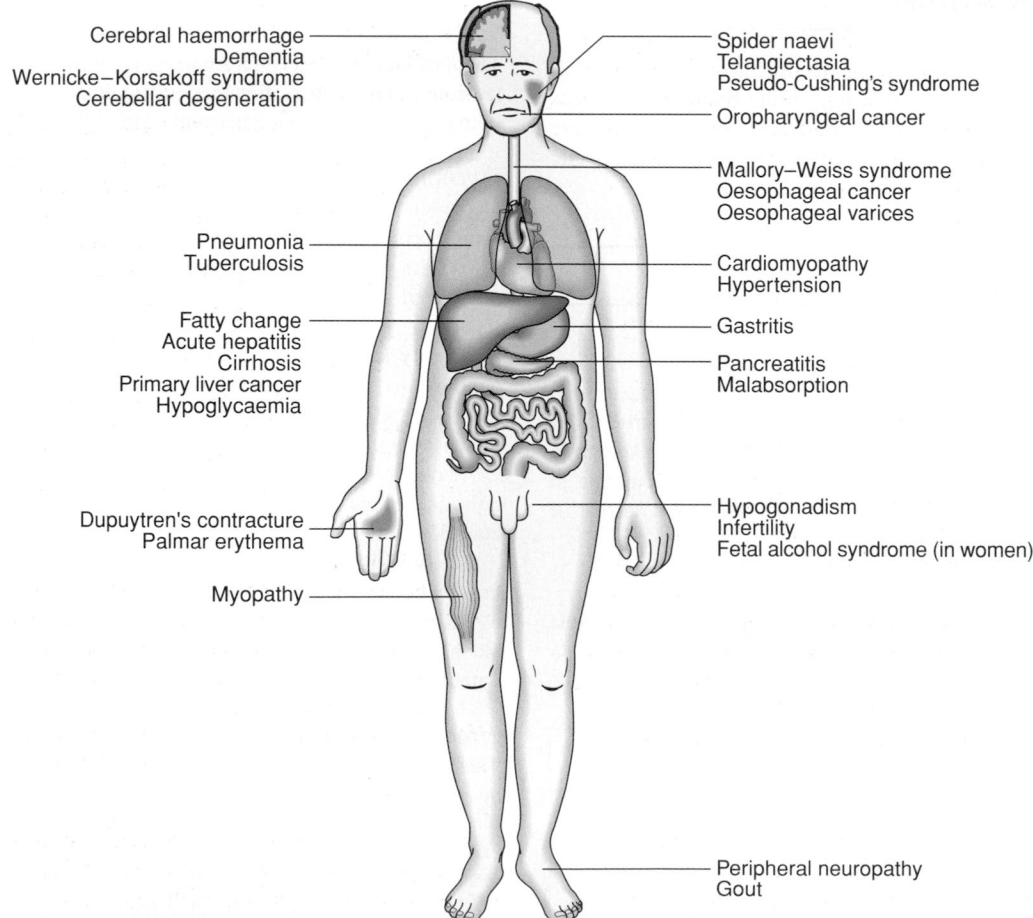

Cerebral haemorrhage
Dementia
Wernicke–Korsakoff syndrome
Cerebellar degeneration

Spider naevi
Telangiectasia
Pseudo-Cushing's syndrome

Oropharyngeal cancer

Mallory–Weiss syndrome
Oesophageal cancer
Oesophageal varices

Pneumonia
Tuberculosis

Cardiomyopathy
Hypertension

Fatty change
Acute hepatitis
Cirrhosis
Primary liver cancer
Hypoglycaemia

Gastritis

Pancreatitis
Malabsorption

Dupuytren's contracture
Palmar erythema

Hypogonadism
Infertility
Fetal alcohol syndrome (in women)

Myopathy

Peripheral neuropathy
Gout

Fig. 8.4   Physical effects of alcohol misuse.

DRUG MISUSE

Dependence on illegal and prescribed drugs is a major problem in Western countries. In the UK there are now 50 000–100 000 opiate addicts. Many of the aetiological factors which apply to alcohol misuse are also relevant to drug dependence. The main factors are cultural pressures, particularly within a peer group, and availability of a drug. In the case of some drugs, medical over-prescribing has increased availability, but there has also been a relative decline in price. Many drug users take a range of drugs—'polydrug' misuse.

Benzodiazepines

Dependence most commonly results from over-prescription. They are also misused by polydrug users.

Cannabis

Derived from the plant *Cannabis sativa*, cannabis is usually smoked mixed with tobacco. It quickly produces a sensation of relaxation and well-being; psychological dependence is common but tolerance and withdrawal symptoms are unusual. It is probably the most common illegal drug taken in the UK and is often the only drug with which young people experiment. The extent of its use cannot be estimated reliably. A toxic confusional state occurs after heavy consumption and acute psychotic episodes are well recognised.

Barbiturates

Now rarely prescribed, barbiturates have been replaced as hypnotics by the benzodiazepines. However, they are still taken by some people who manage to obtain them indirectly from doctors. They soon cause dependence, and sudden withdrawal is very likely to cause epileptic fits. Barbiturates are very dangerous in overdose because of their depressant effect on respiration.

Opiates

Morphine, heroin and codeine are the main drugs in this group; heroin has become especially prominent recently. Taken orally, intravenously or by inhalation, heroin gives a rapid, intensely pleasurable experience, often accompanied by heightened sexual arousal. Physical dependence occurs within a few weeks of regular high-dose injection; as a result, the dose is escalated and the addict's life becomes increasingly centred around obtaining and taking the drug. Intravenous users are prone to bacterial infections, hepatitis B and human immunodeficiency virus (HIV) infection through needle contamination. Accidental overdose is common. The withdrawal syndrome, which can start within 12 hours, can present with intense craving, rhinorrhoea, lacrimation, yawning, perspiration, shivering, piloerection, vomiting, diarrhoea and abdominal cramps. Examination shows a tachycardia, hypertension, mydriasis and facial flushing.

Amphetamines

These have a stimulating central effect and are taken to produce increased energy, elevated mood and greater capacity for concentration. There is also a suppression of appetite, an effect that accounts for their use in obesity. Amphetamines are taken orally or intravenously. Physical dependence is unusual but withdrawal of the drug results in rebound depression, anxiety and fatigue. Chronic ingestion can cause a syndrome identical to paranoid schizophrenia.

Ecstasy

Ecstasy, the popular name for a synthetic amphetamine analogue, has become fashionable among young people for recreational use at dance parties or 'raves'. It has both stimulant and hallucinogenic properties, thus producing feelings of euphoria and emotional intimacy together with distorted sensory perceptions. There is no evidence that it is addictive but there are several reports of physical complications. Fatalities have occurred from cardiac arrhythmias, hyperthermia, disseminated intravascular coagulation, acute renal failure and cerebral haemorrhage. Paranoid psychoses have also been reported.

Cocaine

Increasingly popular, cocaine is taken either intravenously or by sniffing or 'snorting' the powder into the nostrils through a tube. Absorption occurs through the nasal mucous membranes and gives a rapid stimulating effect similar to amphetamine. Cocaine hydrochloride may be converted by a simple chemical process into freebase or 'crack' cocaine, which can be smoked, giving a rapid onset of effect similar to intravenous use. A toxic psychosis occurs with high levels of consumption, and tactile hallucinations (formication) may be prominent. Chronic cocaine sniffing can cause ulceration of the nasal mucosa.

Hallucinogenic drugs

Lysergic acid diethylamide (LSD) and psilocybin (magic mushroom) are among the most commonly used hallucinogens. Perceptual changes occur within 40 minutes of oral ingestion. Vision is affected most often; the subject experiences heightened visual awareness of objects, especially colours. Images may be distorted in shape or size and true hallucinations occur. These may be pleasurable but also terrifying in nature, the experience then being referred to as a 'bad trip'. There may also be distorted perception of time, sounds and tactile sensations. Flashback experiences can occur several months after the last dose; during these the psychotic experiences of LSD are experienced again with their original intensity. A chronic psychotic illness has also been reported after regular LSD use.

Organic solvents

Solvent inhalation (glue sniffing) is popular in some adolescent groups. Solvents produce acute intoxication characterised by euphoria, excitement, dizziness and a floating sensation. Further inhalation leads to loss of consciousness; death can occur from the direct toxic effect of the solvent or from asphyxiation if the substance is inhaled from a plastic bag.

Management

For details on the features and management of overdose with drugs of misuse, see Chapter 3. The first step is to determine whether the patient wishes to stop using the drug. If not, patients need advice about 'harm minimisation': for example, advice to use clean needles for those who inject.

If they do want to stop, initial management is to help them withdraw from the drug. When there are signs of severe physical dependence, withdrawal is best undertaken in hospital, which also enables physical complications such as infections to be treated. Decreasing doses of the relevant drug are given over a period of 1–3 weeks, titrated against objective withdrawal symptoms. Oral methadone is used as a substitute for heroin in patients with opiate dependence. The withdrawal period may need to be extended to several months for some drugs, such as benzodiazepines.

In some cases complete opiate withdrawal is not successful and the patient functions better if maintained on regular doses of oral methadone as an outpatient. This decision should only be taken by a specialist, and long-term supervision requires the patient to attend a specialist drug treatment centre.

Long-term support is often necessary. Good results can be achieved if doctors strike up a rapport with the patient. Complicated or relapsing patients should be referred to specialist drug misuse services. Support can also be provided by self-help groups and voluntary bodies such as Narcotics Anonymous in the UK.

SCHIZOPHRENIA AND DELUSIONAL DISORDERS

Schizophrenia is a psychosis characterised by delusions and hallucinations occurring in clear consciousness. The delusions are various and may concern interference with and broadcasting of one's thoughts. The hallucinations are usually auditory and include voices talking about or commenting on the person's actions. Hallucinations may also occur in any modality. Mood disturbance can be present but is not predominant. The peak age of onset is young adulthood and the life risk of suffering it is 1%. Genetic factors account for 80% of the liability to schizophrenia but no major genes have yet been identified. There is also evidence of structural brain abnormalities. Episodes can be precipitated by stressful life events and by substance misuse. The differential diagnosis is considered on page 250.

Delusional disorders are characterised by delusions in the absence of both mood disturbance and other symptoms of schizophrenia. In such cases the delusion often concerns persecution or marital infidelity. The person may otherwise function normally.

Management
Acute symptoms generally respond well to antipsychotic drugs (see Box 8.19, p. 257). Adherence to drug therapy is often poor, however. Depot drug treatment and compulsory treatment may therefore be required.

CBT may also reduce symptoms. Both CBT and family therapy may improve patients' adherence to drug therapy. The relapse rate is high and many patients become chronically ill with poor social and occupational functioning, and require ongoing care. The lifetime risk of suicide is 10–15%.

The treatment of delusional disorders is as for schizophrenia.

AFFECTIVE (MOOD) DISORDERS

DEPRESSIVE DISORDERS

Depression is common and may be mild, moderate or severe. Clinically significant depression is often referred to as major depressive disorder (MDD). Depression is a major cause of disability and of suicide. It can be both a complication of a medical condition and a cause for medically unexplained symptoms (see below). The fact that it has somatic as well as psychological symptoms means that it may be difficult to distinguish from a medical condition. Hence there is a risk both of under-diagnosing it by erroneously attributing the symptoms to a medical condition, and of over-diagnosing by erroneously attributing the symptoms of a medical condition to depression. In cases of doubt it is helpful to seek the psychological symptoms of depression, particularly loss of interest and anhedonia. In practice depression is under-diagnosed.

Physical examination is essential in patients presenting with a new episode of psychiatric illness, and an associated medical condition should be considered, particularly in the circumstances listed in Box 8.25.

Medically unexplained symptoms that may result from depression include chronic fatigue, chronic widespread pain, weight loss and cognitive impairment (depressive pseudodementia).

Depression comorbid with a medical condition magnifies any associated disability, diminishes adherence to medical treatment and rehabilitation, and may even shorten life expectancy. Recent research suggests that patients who have a major depressive disorder soon after myocardial infarction or stroke die sooner than those who do not, even when disease severity is controlled.

8.25 POINTERS TO AN ORGANIC CAUSE FOR PSYCHIATRIC DISORDER

- Late age of onset of psychiatric illness
- No previous history of psychiatric illness
- No family history of psychiatric illness
- No apparent psychological precipitant

Management
The options should be discussed with the patient and include drug and psychological treatment. If a drug treatment is to be used, it should be chosen with care to avoid exacerbating the patient's illness and causing dangerous interactions with other treatments. Severe depression complicated by psychosis, risk of starvation or intractable suicide risk may require treatment with ECT.

Antidepressant drugs are effective in patients whose depression is a complication of disease as well as in those where it is the primary problem (see EBM panel). These agents are all effective in moderately severe and severe depression and also have application in anxiety. Commonly used antidepressants are shown in Box 8.21 (see p. 258). Tricyclic antidepressants are sometimes poorly tolerated by

**DEPRESSION IN THE MEDICALLY ILL
—do antidepressants work?**   EBM

'A systematic review found relatively few RCTs of antidepressant drugs in depressed patients who were also physically ill; the available trials do, however, support the effectiveness of antidepressant drugs in this group.'

- Gill D, Hatcher S. Antidepressants for depression in people with physical illness (Cochrane Review). Cochrane Library, issue 2, 2001. Oxford: Update Software.
- van Heeringen K, Zivkov M. Pharmacological treatment of depression in cancer patients: a placebo-controlled study of mianserin. Br J Psychiatry 1996; 169:440–443.

Further information: 🖳 www.cochrane.co.uk

people who have coexisting medical conditions. They may be contraindicated in the presence of heart disease, glaucoma and prostatism. Newer agents such as SSRIs are the drugs of choice in such cases. Close collaboration between physician and psychiatrist is essential for optimal management. Depending on the circumstances, the hospital doctor may either initiate treatment or inform the patient's GP.

Psychological treatment has also been shown to be effective in depression. Both CBT and interpersonal therapy are as effective as antidepressants for mild to moderately severe depression. Antidepressant drugs are, however, preferred for more severe depression. They can be used in combination with psychological treatment.

BIPOLAR DISORDER (MANIC DEPRESSION)

Bipolar disorder is a relapsing mood disturbance with periods of both elevated mood or mania and depressed mood or depression. Psychosis may occur in both depressive and manic phases, with delusions and hallucinations that are usually in keeping with the mood disturbance. In mania the patients may be irritable, disinhibited, over-active and grandiose. The depression is similar to unipolar depression as described above. The typical age of onset and lifetime risk are similar to those of schizophrenia. The aetiology is also largely genetic but as with schizophrenia no major genes have yet been identified. The relapse rate is very high, although patients may be perfectly well between episodes.

Management
Mania usually responds well to antipsychotic drugs (see Box 8.19, p. 257). Depression is treated as described above. Prophylaxis to prevent recurrent episodes is important. The main drugs used are lithium, carbamazepine and sodium valproate (see p. 258). Caution must be exercised when stopping these prophylactic drugs as a relapse may follow. There is a substantially increased risk of suicide.

NEUROTIC, STRESS-RELATED AND SOMATOFORM DISORDERS

REACTIONS TO STRESS, PHYSICAL ILLNESS AND ITS TREATMENT

Most medical patients experience psychological upset. Illness and its treatment may be alarming and may affect relationships, occupation and lifestyle. This disruption is usually temporary, but chronic illness may require long-term readjustment. In some cases the emotional impact of illness is sufficiently profound to precipitate psychiatric disorders requiring special attention from the physician or psychiatrist. Risk factors for depression are a previous history of depression, poor social support and a medical condition or treatment that is disfiguring, disabling or life-threatening.

Acute stress reaction
Following an exceptionally stressful event some people develop a characteristic pattern of symptoms, which include a sense of bewilderment, anxiety, anger, depression, over-activity and withdrawal. The symptoms are transient; they start to subside within a few hours and usually completely resolve within 3 days of their onset. Precipitating events include a traumatic diagnosis such as that of AIDS or cancer, death of a family member, a major accident, assault and rape.

Adjustment disorder
A more common psychological response to physical illness is a less severe but prolonged emotional reaction. The predominant symptom is depression or anxiety, or both, but this is not sufficiently intense to justify the diagnosis of an affective or anxiety disorder. The individual may also manifest anger and aggressive behaviour, and excessive alcohol use. These symptoms develop within a month of the onset of physical illness, and their duration and severity reflect the course of the underlying physical condition, resolution tending to occur with physical recovery.

Grief reactions are a particular type of adjustment disorder. The bereaved usually experiences a brief period of emotional numbing, followed by a period of distress lasting several weeks, during which sorrow, tearfulness, sleep disturbance, loss of interest and a sense of futility are common. Perceptual distortions may occur, including misinterpreting sounds as the dead person's voice or sensing the deceased's presence. The distinction between normal and abnormal grief is an arbitrary one. Considerable importance is given to the intensity and duration of symptoms and associated social dysfunction. Symptoms considered to indicate abnormal grief include persistent suicidal ideas, denial of the loss, guilt and the development of symptoms similar to those manifested by the deceased person.

Management of stress reactions
Ongoing contact with and support from a doctor or other who can listen, reassure, explain and advise are the main forms of management. Most patients do not require psychotropic medication, although benzodiazepines can help to reduce arousal in acute stress reaction and can aid sleep in adjustment disorders. Skilled psychotherapy is, however, required for some patients: for example, those with abnormal grief reactions.

Post-traumatic stress disorder (PTSD)
This is a delayed and protracted response to a stressful event of an exceptionally threatening or catastrophic nature, defined as being outside the range of everyday human experience and which would cause distress in almost everyone.

Such events include natural disasters, terrorist activity, serious accidents and witnessing violent deaths. It may also occur after distressing medical treatments. There is usually a delay ranging from a few days to several months between the traumatic event and the onset of symptoms. Typical symptoms are recurrent intrusive memories (flashbacks) of the traumatic event, as well as sleep disturbance, nightmares, autonomic arousal, emotional blunting and avoidance of any situation which evokes memories of the trauma. Anxiety and depression are associated features and excessive use of alcohol or drugs may complicate the clinical picture. The condition runs a fluctuating course. Most people recover within 2 years, although in a small proportion the symptoms become chronic.

Management

There has been a vogue for immediate counselling for those who have survived a major catastrophe, with the aim of preventing the development of PTSD. However, recent trials have suggested that this practice is potentially harmful for some people (see EBM panel). Such post-disaster counselling should therefore only be given to those who request it. The main aims are to provide support, direct advice and the opportunity for catharsis by reliving the trauma. In established PTSD structured psychological approaches (particularly cognitive therapy) and antidepressant medication are both effective.

EBM

POST-TRAUMATIC STRESS DISORDER (PTSD) —place of debriefing

'At present the routine use of individual debriefing in the aftermath of individual trauma cannot be recommended. The practice of compulsory debriefing should cease pending further evidence. Early counselling has been found to be unhelpful and possibly even harmful.'

- Rose S, Wessely S, Bisson J. Brief psychological interventions ('debriefing') for trauma-related symptoms and prevention of post-traumatic stress disorder (Cochrane Review). Cochrane Library, issue 2, 2001. Oxford: Update Software.

Further information: 💻 www.cochrane.co.uk

ANXIETY DISORDERS

Generalised anxiety disorder

Anxiety and worry are universal human experiences and only assume medical significance if they are disproportionate to stresses or persist after these have been resolved. Anxiety is common during the early stages of illness but usually subsides. Persistent anxiety is distressing, interferes with medical management and may require specific attention. Symptoms of anxiety can be divided into psychological and somatic (see Box 8.10, p. 252). These symptoms can complicate the presentation of underlying physical illness, and several physical conditions can initially manifest with anxiety before other symptoms and signs develop.

Phobic anxiety disorder

A phobia is an abnormal or excessive fear of a particular object or situation, which leads to avoidance of it. A more generalised phobia of going out alone or being in crowded places is called agoraphobia. Phobic responses can develop to medical interventions including venepuncture, hypodermic injections, and chemotherapy or radiotherapy. Phobic symptoms may be so severe that the patient abandons further treatment.

Panic disorder

The symptoms of panic disorder are due to episodic attacks of severe anxiety, which are not restricted to any particular situation or circumstances and are therefore unpredictable. Somatic symptoms of anxiety, such as chest pain, palpitations, breathlessness, dizziness and paraesthesiae, are prominent. The symptoms are in part due to involuntary over-breathing (hyperventilation). Patients often fear they are suffering from a serious acute illness such as a heart attack or stroke, and may therefore seek emergency medical care. Panic attacks are often associated with agoraphobia.

Management of the anxiety disorders

Explanation and reassurance are essential in the management of all forms of anxiety. The nature of the symptoms should be explained and the patient reassured that they form part of a recognised illness. Reassurance is also needed to allay fears of physical illness, if this can be given after appropriate assessment. Specific treatment for anxiety includes relaxation for those who do not respond to reassurance, graded exposure (desensitisation) to feared situations for phobic disorders, and cognitive therapy for panic.

Benzodiazepines are useful in treating anxiety when symptoms can be expected to last no more than a few weeks. A β-blocking drug such as propranolol can help when the peripheral somatic symptoms of anxiety are prominent. Antidepressant drugs are also effective for anxiety. Phobic disorders usually require exposure treatment as well as drug therapy.

OBSESSIVE-COMPULSIVE DISORDER

Obsessive-compulsive disorder (OCD) is characterised by obsessive thoughts which are recurrent, unwanted and usually anxiety-provoking, and by compulsions, repeated acts which relieve feelings of tension. An example is repeated hand-washing because of recurrent thoughts of contamination.

Management

OCD usually responds to antidepressant drugs and to CBT but relapses are common.

MEDICALLY UNEXPLAINED SOMATIC COMPLAINTS

Somatoform disorders

The essential feature of this group of disorders is medical consultation for physical symptoms which have no basis in disease, and which are not better diagnosed as part of a depressive or anxiety disorder. In many cases a psychiatric assessment will reveal that the physical symptoms have a relationship with stressful life events, although many patients may be reluctant to accept this. Several syndromes are described within somatoform disorders; there is considerable overlap between these, in both aetiology and clinical presentation.

The cause of many somatoform disorders is incompletely understood, but contributory factors can usually be identified. These factors include depression or anxiety, the erroneous interpretation of somatic symptoms as evidence of disease, and preoccupation with illness. A family history or previous history of a particular condition may have shaped concerns about illness. Patients may also selectively emphasise somatic symptoms to doctors because they do not want to see their problems as psychiatric. A doctor who either dismisses the complaints as non-existent or over-emphasises the possibility of disease may unwittingly reinforce the focus on somatic symptoms.

Somatisation disorder (Briquet's syndrome)

This syndrome runs a chronic and fluctuating course over many years. Symptoms start in early adult life, are more frequent in women and may be referred to any part of the body. Common complaints include pain, vomiting, nausea, headache, dizziness, menstrual irregularities and sexual dysfunction. By the time the patient is referred to a psychiatrist there is usually a multitude of negative investigations and unhelpful operations, particularly hysterectomy and cholecystectomy.

Hypochondriacal disorder

This is an anxious preoccupation with the possibility of having a serious physical illness. Patients have a persistent fear or belief that they have a serious, often fatal, disease that persists despite appropriate medical reassurance. They characteristically seek many medical opinions and investigations in a futile attempt to gain reassurance.

In a small proportion of cases conviction of disease reaches delusional intensity, the best-known example being the conviction of parasitic infestation ('delusional parasitosis'), which leads patients to consult dermatologists. Antipsychotic drugs have been claimed to be effective for this syndrome. A preoccupation with bodily disfigurement (body dysmorphic disorder) leads to inappropriate requests for cosmetic surgery.

Somatoform autonomic dysfunction

This includes symptoms that are referable to organs which are largely under autonomic control. The most common examples involve the cardiovascular system (cardiac neurosis), respiratory system (psychogenic hyperventilation) and gut (psychogenic vomiting and irritable bowel syndrome).

Somatoform pain disorder

This is used to describe severe, persistent pain which cannot be explained by pathology.

Neurasthenia

Also known as chronic fatigue syndrome (CFS), this is characterised by excessive fatigue after minimal physical or mental exertion, poor concentration, dizziness and muscular aches. There may also be various autonomic symptoms affecting the cardiovascular or gastrointestinal systems. The sleep pattern is frequently altered, with frequent waking or

hypersomnia. This pattern of symptoms may follow a viral infection such as infectious mononucleosis, influenza or hepatitis. However, in most cases there is no convincing evidence of viral infection, either from the history or from antibody titres. Symptoms overlap considerably with those of depression and anxiety. There is substantial evidence that many patients improve with CBT.

Dissociative (conversion) disorder

This has replaced the term 'hysteria' in the ICD-10 classification. It defines a syndrome characterised by a loss or distortion of neurological function not fully explained by organic disease. Although, by definition, the symptoms of hysteria are not themselves caused by organic disease, there is coexisting disease of the nervous system in a proportion of cases. The most common symptoms of dissociative disorder mimic lesions in the motor or sensory nervous system (see Box 8.26).

Dissociative disorder can also involve higher mental functions, especially memory and general intelligence.

The aetiology of dissociation is unknown. It has been considered to result from unconscious psychological processes. There is an association with adverse childhood experiences including physical and sexual abuse. Organic disease may facilitate dissociative mechanisms and provide a model for symptoms; thus, for example, pseudoseizures in patients with epilepsy. Recently, there has been renewed interest in the neurological mechanisms of conversion which is being pursued using modern functional imaging techniques.

8.26 COMMON PRESENTATIONS OF DISSOCIATIVE (CONVERSION) DISORDER	
• Gait disturbance	• Pseudoseizures
• Loss of function in limbs	• Sensory loss
• Aphonia	• Blindness

Management of medically unexplained complaints

The management of the various syndromes of medically unexplained complaints described above is based on general principles with specific measures for individual syndromes (see Box 8.27).

Reassurance

Giving appropriate reassurance is an important part of the medical consultation. It is most effective if based on

8.27 GENERAL MANAGEMENT PRINCIPLES FOR MEDICALLY UNEXPLAINED SYMPTOMS
• Take a full, sympathetic history
• Exclude disease but avoid unnecessary investigation or referral
• Seek specific treatable psychiatric syndromes
• Demonstrate to patients that you believe their complaints
• Establish a collaborative relationship
• Give the patient a positive explanation including but not over-emphasising psychological factors
• Encourage a return to normal functioning

patients' actual concerns so it is important to ask them what they are most worried about first. Many patients report a physical examination as particularly reassuring. A detailed explanation of what any laboratory tests do and do not show can also help. Clearly it may be unwise to state categorically that the patient has no disease but it can be emphasised as unambiguously as possible that the probability of having the feared disease is very low. If the patient repeatedly asks for reassurance about the same issue, he or she may have hypochondriasis. In this case, repeated reassurance can actually perpetuate the patient's illness concerns. Rather patients should be encouraged to focus on non-illness activities. If reassurance-seeking persists, CBT is effective.

Explanation

Patients need a positive explanation for their symptoms. It is nearly always unhelpful to explain to a patient that the symptoms are 'just psychological' or 'all in the mind'. Such statements are likely to reduce their confidence in the doctor and may paradoxically increase their concern about missed disease. On the other hand, it is potentially harmful to collude with the patient's idea that he or she has a disease when this is not true. This may lead to inappropriate coping behaviour, such as obtaining a wheelchair rather than seeking rehabilitation.

It is more useful to describe a plausible physiological mechanism for the symptom that emphasises the link with psychosocial factors and demonstrates that the symptoms are reversible. For example, it can be explained that in irritable bowel syndrome, psychological stress results in increased activation of the autonomic nervous system that leads to constriction of smooth muscle in the gut wall, which in turn causes pain. Therefore the symptoms may be perpetuated by a vicious circle in which pain leads to anxiety and anxiety leads to further pain, but this mechanism is reversible by targeting these perpetuating factors.

It is helpful to offer an optimistic prognosis. However, an unrealistically precise prediction ('you will be better next week') is unwise as it is likely to lead to loss of faith in the doctor if not fulfilled.

Advice

A plan of action that specifies both what the patient can change and what the doctor can do is helpful. An aim of improving functioning can be agreed. This is especially important in dissociative disorder. The patient is advised on how to overcome probable perpetuating factors—for example, by resolving stress-causing social problems or by practising relaxation. The doctor can offer to review progress, to prescribe (e.g. an 'antidepressant' drug) and, if appropriate, to refer (e.g. to physiotherapy or psychology). Action by the doctor gives the patient a sense of being taken seriously and not being dismissed, as may have been experienced before. Writing to the patient as well as to the GP to summarise the conclusions of the medical assessment and the proposed plan reinforces messages that may otherwise be forgotten. The attitudes of close relatives may need to be addressed if they have adopted an over-protective role, unwittingly reinforcing the patient's disability.

'Antidepressant' drugs

Antidepressant drugs are most useful when the patient is depressed (see EBM panel) but may also help when there is no overt mood disorder. An explanation of why they are being prescribed, which minimises blame and stigma, is needed if they are to be acceptable to the patient. There are two possible approaches. The first is to explain that the term 'antidepressant' is a misnomer, and that the drugs are broad-spectrum 'nervous tonics' of proven value for sleep and pain as well as for depression. The second is to be explicit that the drugs are being prescribed for depression, but to emphasise that this is understandable, given the somatic symptoms the patient is suffering.

> **EBM**
> **MEDICALLY UNEXPLAINED SOMATIC SYMPTOMS —role of antidepressant drugs**
>
> 'A systematic review of antidepressant drugs for medically unexplained symptoms found such therapy to be moderately effective overall; the odds ratio for improvement with antidepressant treatment compared with placebo was 3.4.'
>
> - O'Malley PG, Jackson JL, Santoro J, et al. Antidepressant therapy for unexplained symptoms and symptom syndromes. J Fam Pract 1999; 48:980–990.
> - van Heeringen K, Zivkov M. Pharmacological treatment of depression in cancer patients: a placebo-controlled study of mianserin. Br J Psychiatry 1996; 169:440–443.

Psychological therapies

Where explanation, reassurance and advice prove to be insufficient, they can be reinforced by formal psychological treatment. The most widely used is behavioural or cognitive behavioural treatment (see EBM panel and p. 256) although other psychological treatments may have a role.

> **EBM**
> **MEDICALLY UNEXPLAINED SOMATIC SYMPTOMS —role of cognitive behavioural therapy (CBT)**
>
> 'A systematic review of CBT for medically unexplained symptoms found that in 70% of trials such therapy was significantly superior to non-specific treatment.'
>
> - Kroenke K, Swindle R. Cognitive behavioral therapy for somatization and symptom syndromes: a critical review of controlled clinical trials. Psychother Psychosom 2000; 69:205–215.
> - Speckens AE, van Hemert AM, Spinhoven P, et al. Cognitive behavioural therapy for medically unexplained physical symptoms: a randomised controlled trial. BMJ 1995; 311:1328–1332.

The decision to refer will be based on the doctor's assessment of the patient and an appraisal of the available services. Reasons to refer include:

- very severe disability, e.g. dissociative disorder with paraparesis
- suspected somatisation disorder
- specific service available, e.g. for chronic pain or chronic fatigue syndrome
- patient remains distressed despite explanation and reassurance
- suicide risk.

When explaining the referral to the patient it is wise to:

- emphasise the reality of the patient's symptoms
- be positive about the service you are referring the patient to
- avoid implying that you think the origin of their complaint is imaginary.

A patient is more likely to attend for a referral if the doctor has given an appropriate reason.

Rehabilitation

Where there is chronic associated disability, conventional physical rehabilitation may be the best approach. This is especially the case where there is loss of motor function in dissociative disorder.

Shared care with the GP

For patients with chronic intractable symptoms, ongoing care is required as it is for any chronic illness. This will be the case for all patients with somatisation disorder. Scheduled appointments with the same specialist; interspersed with visits to the GP, are probably the best way to avoid unnecessary re-referral for investigation, to ensure that treatable aspects of the patient's problems such as depression are actively managed, and also to prevent the GP from becoming demoralised by feelings of helplessness. The specialist reviews the patient's condition and encourages him or her towards improved function.

BEHAVIOURAL SYNDROMES ASSOCIATED WITH PHYSIOLOGICAL DISTURBANCE

EATING DISORDERS

Anorexia nervosa

This is a condition in which there is marked weight loss as a result of self-starvation. It typically develops during adolescence and predominantly affects girls. Theories about aetiology are speculative. Current social pressures to maintain a slim figure are thought to have caused a recent increased incidence. Some girls have a history of obesity and embark on an extreme course of dieting after being teased about their fatness. The diagnostic criteria are listed in Box 8.28.

Emaciation may be disguised by wearing loosely fitting clothes and hiding heavy objects in the clothing when weight is checked on scales. Subjects are often physically over-active; they may use laxatives or induce vomiting secretly after meals. Other physical signs include a downy lanugo hair on the trunk and limbs, hypotension, bradycardia and peripheral cyanosis.

Management

The first objective is to restore normal body weight, which is most likely to be achieved if a trusting relationship can be established. Treatment can be conducted on an outpatient or

8.28 DIAGNOSTIC CRITERIA FOR ANOREXIA NERVOSA

- Weight loss of at least 25% of total body weight (or weight 25% below norm for age and height)
- Avoidance of high-calorie foods
- Distortion of body image so that patients regard themselves as fat even when grossly underweight
- Amenorrhoea for at least 3 months

day patient basis unless there is a risk of suicide or serious medical complications. A series of target weights should be set, with the final target within the normal range for the patient's age and height. Psychotherapy is an essential part of management.

The short-term prognosis is good if this programme is followed but the long-term outlook is less favourable. Approximately 20% make a full recovery, 20% remain chronically ill and 60% have recurring episodes of anorexia. Death occurs from suicide or physical complications in 5% of cases.

Bulimia nervosa

This is a condition in which there is alternating self-starving with self-induced vomiting, and eating large amounts of food. It is related to anorexia nervosa but weight is normal. It is almost exclusively confined to women and the age of onset is slightly older than for anorexia. Prevalence has been estimated at 1% of women in their early twenties. The clinical features are listed in Box 8.29.

Physical complications from vomiting and purgation include erosion of dental enamel, hypokalaemia and metabolic alkalosis. Electrolyte and fluid disturbances can cause cardiac arrhythmias or renal damage. A bilateral enlargement of the parotid glands is seen in some patients.

8.29 DIAGNOSTIC CRITERIA FOR BULIMIA NERVOSA

- Recurrent bouts of binge eating
- Lack of self-control over eating during binges
- Self-induced vomiting, purgation or dieting after binges
- Weight maintained within normal limits

Management

Cognitive behaviour therapy is the currently preferred approach, the central component being self-monitoring of eating behaviour. It can be undertaken on an outpatient basis and may need to be continued for several months. Short-term results are encouraging but the long-term prognosis of the condition is not known.

SLEEP DISORDERS

Sleep has a restorative function and is important for conservation of energy and growth (see p. 1133).

Insomnia

This is a condition of inadequate quantity or quality of sleep. It may be a symptom of a depressive illness, an anxiety disorder or some other psychiatric condition. More commonly it arises at a time of increased life stress; some people then become preoccupied with lack of sleep and fear trying to get to sleep. This establishes a vicious circle which perpetuates the problem.

Management

When insomnia results from a definite psychiatric illness treatment should be directed towards this. Sleep disturbance is a particularly distressing symptom of depressive illness; in this case an antidepressant drug with marked sedative properties (e.g. amitriptyline, trazodone or dosulepin (dothiepin)) taken at night may help. Hypnotic drugs, such as the benzodiazepine temazepam (10–20 mg), are useful for short-term treatment of insomnia. When insomnia is a chronic condition, drugs are less appropriate. Advice on 'sleep hygiene' should be given, with emphasis on avoiding meals, alcohol and caffeine during the evening, taking regular exercise, and avoiding sleep during the day.

PUERPERAL DISORDERS

There are three common psychiatric complications of childbirth.

Post-partum 'blues'

These are characterised by irritability, labile mood and tearfulness. Most women are affected to some degree. These symptoms begin soon after childbirth, peak on about the fourth day and then resolve. They may be related to hormonal or psychological changes associated with childbirth. No treatment is required other than reassurance.

Post-partum depression

This occurs in 10–15% of women. Women with a previous history of depression are at risk. Psychological and drug treatments for depression should be considered as well as practical help with childcare.

Puerperal psychosis

This is a psychotic state with onset usually in the first 2 weeks after childbirth. It affects about 1 in 500 women after childbirth and usually takes the form of a manic or depressive psychosis, although a schizophrenic psychosis also occurs. Delirium is rare with modern obstetrics but should still be considered. The management is as for the type of psychosis presented. In addition it is important to consider the baby and especially to establish whether the mother has ideas of harming it. Most women recover but are at increased risk of puerperal psychosis with subsequent pregnancies. Admission to a psychiatric mother and baby unit may be required.

DISORDERS OF ADULT PERSONALITY AND BEHAVIOUR

PERSONALITY DISORDER

Personality refers to ways of thinking and behaving that are long-term characteristics of the individual. Extreme behaviours that result in distress to the person (e.g. extreme obsessiveness) or to others (e.g. tendency to violent behaviour) are regarded as 'personality disorders'. Different types of personality disorder have been described. Personality disorder does not have a single cause and results from an interaction of genetics and upbringing, particularly early experience.

Management

Personality disorder cannot be easily modified and psychotherapy aimed at such modification is a long-term process. In the short term, treatment of psychiatric illnesses and substance misuse may be beneficial.

FACTITIOUS DISORDER

This term is used to describe patterns of behaviour in individuals who repeatedly and deliberately induce the signs or symptoms of disease. It is often difficult to understand the underlying motives other than as an attempt to gain access to the role of patient and to fool doctors. It is differentiated from malingering (see below), in which illness is feigned to obtain an identifiable practical benefit.

Factitious disorder is uncommon. Persons found to be fabricating illness are often young women working in nursing or a profession allied to medicine. These patients surreptitiously fabricate the signs of disease: for example, by regularly taking hormone preparations or by inducing anaemia by repeated bleeding. Other presentations include chronic ulcerating skin lesions (dermatitis artefacta), pyrexia of unknown origin and hypoglycaemia.

Münchausen's syndrome

This is a particularly severe but rare form of factitious disorder. Patients present with dramatic symptoms of a medical emergency such as myocardial infarction or intraabdominal catastrophe. The history may be convincing and persuade an unsuspecting doctor to undertake investigations or exploratory surgery. If suspicions are aroused it may be possible to trace the patient's history showing that he or she has presented similarly at several other hospitals, often changing name several times during the course of these travels. Some accident and emergency departments hold lists of such patients.

Management

Gentle but firm confrontation with clear evidence of the fabrication of illness, together with an offer of psychological support, is probably the best approach. Treatment is usually declined but it is important to recognise the syndrome to avoid causing further iatrogenic harm.

MALINGERING

This refers to the conscious simulation of signs of disease and disability. There is always a motive of which the patient is aware, often avoidance of a responsibility such as a court appearance, or financial gain such as compensation after an accident or the award of a pension for retirement on medical grounds. Malingering can be hard to detect at clinical assessment. Suggestive factors are evasion or inconsistency in the history. The only definitive way to identify malingering is if the person admits what he or she has been doing. Observation of behaviour that is inconsistent with the described disability is a strong indicator. If malingering is suspected, the best approach is a sympathetic but firm discussion of the observations suggesting this.

ISSUES IN OLDER PEOPLE
MEDICAL PSYCHIATRY

- Organic psychiatric disorders are especially common; cognitive function should always be assessed and an associated medical condition or adverse drug effect suspected.
- The most common cause of disturbed behaviour in the frail elderly is delirium.
- Depression is common in old age. Just because a person is old and frail does not mean that depression is 'to be expected' and that it should not be treated.
- Older people respond as well to antidepressant therapy as younger people, and the prognosis for depression is no different in old age.
- Deliberate self-harm is associated with an increased risk of completed suicide.
- Medically unexplained symptoms are common in old age and often associated with depressive disorder.
- Loneliness, poverty and lack of social support are issues to be considered in the management of older people.

LEGAL ASPECTS OF PSYCHIATRY

Psychiatric illness sometimes impairs judgement to the extent that patients are not considered fully responsible for their actions. This has implications for consent to treatment, for ability to manage personal and financial affairs, and for detention of patients against their will. In general, legislation should be used to aid rather than replace professional judgement. All countries have specific laws to deal with assessment of capacity to consent to or refuse treatment and the treatment of mental illness. The Mental Health Act 1983 governs the law in England and Wales but is currently under revision.

FURTHER INFORMATION

Bass C, Benjamin S. The management of chronic somatisation. Br J Psychiatry 1993; 162:472–480.

Hawton K, Arensman E, Townsend E, et al. Deliberate self harm: systematic review of efficacy of psychosocial and pharmacological treatments in preventing repetition. BMJ 1998; 317:441–447.

Johnstone EC, Freeman C, Zealley A, eds. Companion to psychiatric studies. 6th edn. Edinburgh: Churchill Livingstone; 1998.

Katon WJ. The impact of major depression on chronic medical illness. Gen Hosp Psychiatry 1996; 18:215–219.

cebmh.warne.ox.ac.uk/cebmh/ *Centre for evidence-based mental health.*
www.depressionalliance.org *Depression.*
www.mja.com.au/public/mentalhealth/articles/singh/singh.html#box5 *Somatisation.*
www.niaaa.nih.gov/ *Alcoholism.*
www.nimh.nih.gov/practitioners/ *General information on depression, anxiety etc.*
www.nimh.nih.gov/publicat/schizoph.htm *Schizophrenia.*
www.rcpsych.ac.uk/info/index.htm *Royal College of Psychiatrists: mental health information.*
www.who.int/mental_health/ *WHO mental health and brain disorders.*

Water, electrolyte and acid–base imbalance

A. CUMMING • W. PLANT

Disturbances of water, electrolyte and acid–base balance may present with a myriad of symptoms, often of a subtle nature. These disturbances may mimic other disease states, as illustrated by some examples in Box 9.1. Evaluation of fluid, electrolyte and acid–base balance should be central to the assessment of any unwell patient.

The kidneys play an important part in maintaining normal water, electrolyte and acid-base balance. The anatomy of the kidney and the physiology of glomerular function are described in Chapter 14.

9.1 WAYS IN WHICH WATER, ELECTROLYTE AND ACID–BASE DISTURBANCES MAY MIMIC OTHER CONDITIONS		
Disorder	**Manifestations**	**May mimic**
Hyponatraemia	Drowsiness Confusion Seizures	Hypoglycaemia Poisoning Intracerebral disease Psychiatric illness
Hypokalaemia	Tachyarrhythmia Muscle weakness	Cardiac disease Neurological disease
Acidosis	Tachypnoea Hypotension	Asthma Cardiac failure

PHYSIOLOGY OF WATER AND ELECTROLYTES

PRINCIPLES OF HOMEOSTASIS

In health, water, electrolyte and acid-base levels are maintained within a very narrow range. This is achieved by balanced variations in input and elimination, and also by differential movement of these substances within different body compartments. Disturbances of these mechanisms are common problems encountered in general medical and surgical practice. Some are trivial, but others are associated with a high mortality and require urgent assessment and treatment.

Recognition of three key principles is central to the successful management of these conditions:

- *Homeostasis.* Healthy, functioning internal organs best achieve homeostasis. Resuscitation of the unwell patient to re-establish normal cardiorenal function is often all that is required to correct even the most complex-seeming fluid and electrolyte problem.
- *Adaptation.* Disturbances in water and electrolyte balance are rapidly followed by adaptation. This may lead to the maintenance of a new steady state, which prevents further changes but does not restore the body to normal. Examples include the compensatory mechanisms occurring in response to acid–base disturbances, and the expanded extracellular fluid volume response to cardiac failure. Therapies must correct the deficit/excess before the steady state returns to a normal value.

- *Ageing.* It is a feature of the normal ageing process that homeostatic mechanisms react more slowly (and sometimes incompletely) to stresses disturbing water, electrolyte and acid–base balance. Unsuspected diminished renal function is present in up to two-thirds of patients aged 70 years or over (see 'Issues in Older People' panel, p. 283).

NORMAL DISTRIBUTION OF WATER AND ELECTROLYTES

Water

Total body water (TBW) is a function of gender, age and body habitus. Nearly 75% of the body weight of a neonate is water. This falls to 60% in healthy adult males; females have proportionately more body fat than males and TBW is about 55% of dry weight. As we age, muscle and bone mass decline whilst fat increases; thus TBW becomes an even smaller proportion of dry weight.

In health, about 70% of TBW is distributed to the intracellular fluid (ICF) compartment and 30% to the extracellular fluid (ECF) compartment. About 75% of ECF water is in the interstitial space, with 25% as intravascular water.

Water enters and leaves the body through the gastrointestinal tract, and is lost through the lungs, the skin and the kidneys. The distribution of water in a 'typical' adult male is illustrated in Figure 9.1.

Electrolytes

Electrolytes are dissolved in body water. However, concentrations differ between different body compartments, particularly between the ICF and the ECF (see Fig. 9.2). This difference is maintained by the permeability characteristics of the cell membrane, and by a wide range of active and passive transport mechanisms such as the ubiquitous Na^+/K^+ adenosine triphosphatase (ATPase). Many vital cellular processes, including cell depolarisation, depend upon this difference in concentration. The effective osmolality

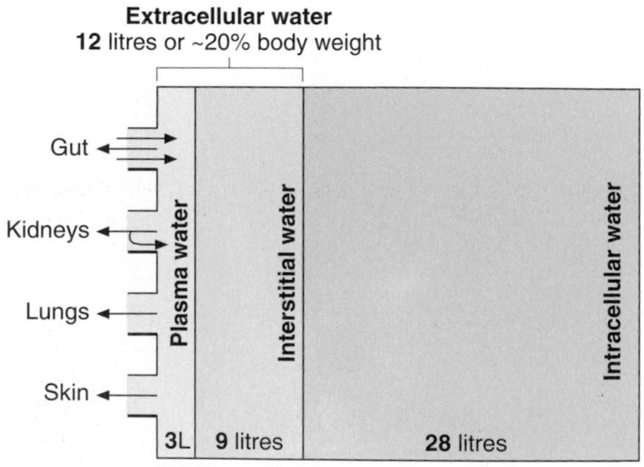

Fig. 9.1 Distribution of water in a 65 kg man. The vascular compartment is in contact with the environment at four portals. Net gain or loss of water and electrolytes occurs by these routes.

(tonicity) of plasma and interstitial fluid is determined by the concentrations of sodium (Na^+) and chloride (Cl^-), whilst that of the ICF is determined by the concentrations of potassium (K^+), magnesium (Mg^{++}), phosphate (PO_4^{-2}) and sulphate (SO_4^{-2}). The amount of hydrogen ion (H^+) in the ECF is tiny (40 nmol/l) and can be buffered by cationic proteins such as albumin and haemoglobin.

The concentration of electrolytes also varies between different body fluids, and this factor must be taken into account when replacing lost fluid. Some illustration of this is given in Box 9.2.

NEPHRON SEGMENTS AND FUNCTIONS

The kidneys play a central role in the maintenance of homeostasis, so it is important to appreciate the functional sequence of transport processes along the length of the nephron. Figure 9.3 gives an overview of the net fluxes at different sites. A schematic representation of each nephron segment will be presented below as we move through different disorders of homeostasis. It is important to recognise the key role of the glomerular filtration rate (GFR). This is the basic volume flow; the various constituents of the filtrate are then affected by the function of the tubules. Furthermore, 'downstream' segments of the nephron respond and react to events occurring 'upstream' (e.g. loop diuretic-induced losses of sodium from the thick ascending loop of Henle will lead to increased sodium reabsorption in the distal convoluted tubule and cortical collecting duct).

DISORDERS OF VOLUME STATUS

As the most abundant cation, total body sodium is the principal determinant of ECF volume. The interrelationship between ECF volume and mean arterial pressure (MAP) underlies the clinical manifestations of most disorders of sodium metabolism. These disorders therefore manifest predominantly as disorders of volume status. Evaluation is primarily dependent upon clinical examination. Disorders of sodium metabolism commonly coexist with disorders of water, potassium and acid–base homeostasis; laboratory tests are more helpful in the evaluation of these disorders.

EXTRACELLULAR FLUID VOLUME OVERLOAD

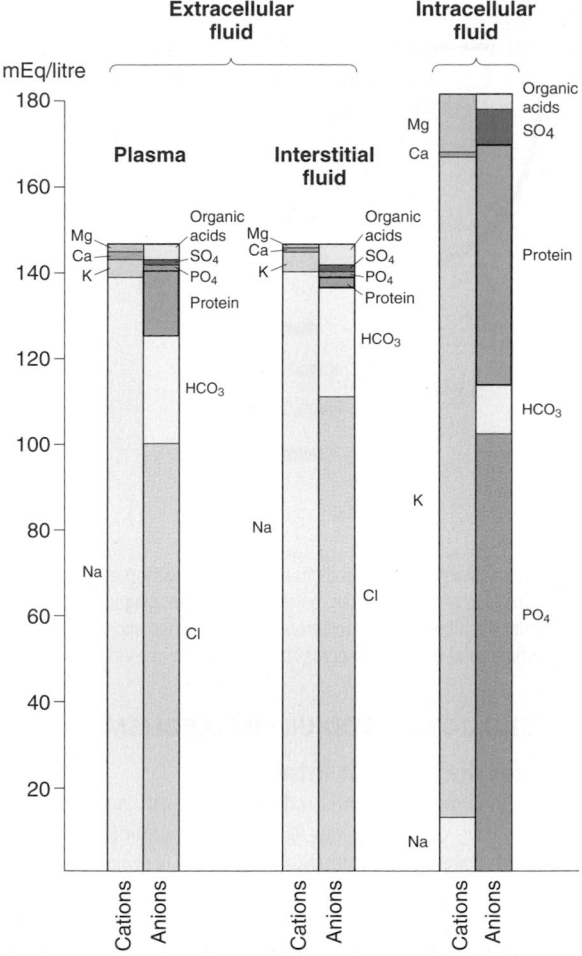

Fig. 9.2 Distribution of electrolytes in plasma, interstitial fluid and cell fluid. Note that values are given as milliequivalents not millimoles.

❓ Case example A

A 55-year-old man with a history of two myocardial infarctions presents with orthopnoea and dyspnoea. On examination he is found to have an extra heart sound, pulmonary crackles and peripheral oedema. Blood pressure is 90/65 mmHg. Plasma electrolytes are normal. Blood urea is 15 mmol/l and creatinine 180 µmol/l. Why has this patient developed signs of ECF volume overload?

9.2 TYPICAL ELECTROLYTE CONCENTRATIONS IN BODY FLUIDS					
	[Na^+] (mmol/l)	[K^+] (mmol/l)	[Cl^-] (mmol/l)	[HCO_3^-] (mmol/l)	[H^+] (nmol/l)
Gastric secretions	25–80	5–20	100–150	Nil	40–60
Biliary secretions	120–140	5–15	80–120	30–50	Nil
Small bowel secretions	120–140	5–15	90–130	20–40	Nil

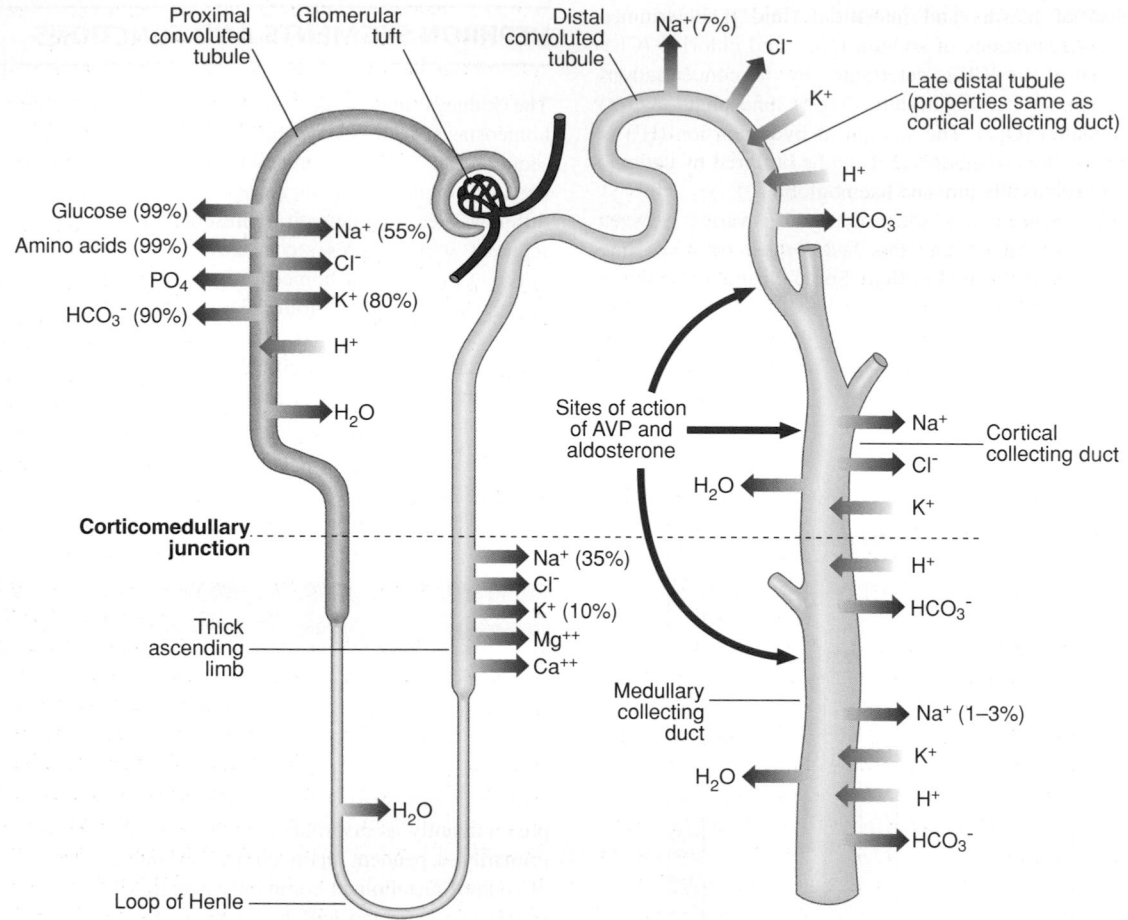

Fig. 9.3 Transport of water and electrolytes. In the proximal tubule approximately two-thirds of filtered sodium and water is reabsorbed, together with glucose, amino acids, phosphate and bicarbonate. In the thick ascending limb of the loop of Henle sodium, potassium, calcium, magnesium and chloride are reabsorbed, whilst in the cortical collecting duct sodium is reabsorbed under the influence of aldosterone with associated excretion of potassium and hydrogen ions. Water is reabsorbed from the distal nephron under the influence of arginine vasopressin (AVP) and the hypertonic medulla.

Additional signs of ECF volume overload are listed in Box 9.3. GFR is reduced, while total body salt and total body water are both increased. Oedema appears when the ECF volume has increased by about 15% and reflects:

- a change in the forces acting upon the microcirculation, which determine the distribution of water and electrolytes between intravascular and interstitial fluid
- renal retention of Na^+ and water, causing increased body Na^+ and expansion of the ECF.

There may or may not be an associated abnormality of sodium concentration. If there is, this usually represents a disorder of water metabolism.

Normal sodium homeostasis requires a balance between salt intake and salt excretion.

9.3 ADDITIONAL SIGNS OF ECF VOLUME OVERLOAD

- Hypertension
- Tachycardia
- Raised jugular venous pressure
- Displaced apex beat
- Pleural effusion
- Ascites

PHYSIOLOGY OF SODIUM METABOLISM

Normal dietary salt intake

In biological terms, healthy individuals require no more than 50 mmol/day of dietary salt to remain in balance. 'Healthy' diets in developed countries normally contain 80–100 mmol/day, but many individuals consume substantially more than this (200–300 mmol/day). Most dietary salt is added in food preservation or processing. An assessment of the patient's dietary salt intake is therefore important. If the patient described above were found to be taking approximately 180 mmol of sodium daily, an excretion of sodium substantially in excess of this would be required to restore normal homeostasis.

Normal sodium excretion

In the absence of unusual losses of sodium-containing fluids from the gastrointestinal tract, the kidney almost exclusively controls salt excretion. The final urinary sodium excretion (natriuresis) depends upon the GFR and the interrelated actions of specific segments of the nephron (see Fig. 9.3).

Relationship between mean arterial pressure and natriuresis

In health, a rise in mean arterial pressure (MAP) leads to increased (pressure) natriuresis; a drop in MAP leads to decreased natriuresis. This reciprocal relationship tends to return both ECF volume and MAP to baseline in the face of a primary disturbance in either parameter. In disease states such as cardiac failure, a reduction in cardiac output and hence MAP reduces sodium excretion by both physical and neuro-endocrine mechanisms (see below). This limits the fall in blood pressure but is often at the expense of ECF volume expansion. By contrast, in disease states such as primary renal failure there is initially sodium retention leading to an increased natriuresis which keeps the ECF volume stable, but at the price of an increased MAP.

Renal sodium handling

Sodium is freely filtered at the glomerulus. At a normal GFR of 150 ml/min and a normal plasma sodium concentration of 140 mmol/l, 21 mmol/min (30 240 mmol/day) of sodium enter the nephron. As a consequence of decreased cardiac output and renal blood flow, the patient described above has a GFR of approximately 50 ml/min. Therefore his filtered load of sodium is only 7 mmol/min (10 080 mmol/day). In normal circumstances, less than 1% of the filtered sodium load escapes reabsorption (the fractional sodium excretion). Figure 9.4 illustrates the relative contribution of different sites along the nephron to this process. The activity of the basolateral ATP-requiring 3 Na$^+$/2K$^+$ exchange pump (Na$^+$/K$^+$ ATPase) is the common driving force for sodium reabsorption. However, all segments of the nephron differ in the kinds of luminal transport mechanisms for sodium that operate there, in the regulatory factors which act upon them, and in their permeability to water.

A wide range of neuro-endocrine mechanisms have been shown to influence renal handling of sodium. Those that promote sodium retention include the renin-angiotensin-aldosterone system, the sympathetic nervous system and renal nerves, thromboxanes and endothelins; those that promote natriuresis include atrial natriuretic peptide, dopamine, the kallikrein-kinin system and prostaglandins. Interactions between these are complex and variable. This account illustrates how the renin-angiotensin-aldosterone system, the sympathetic nervous system, renal nerves and dopamine operate in particular segments of the nephron.

Proximal convoluted tubule

This segment, illustrated in Figure 9.5, has a high capacity for sodium reabsorption. The basolateral Na$^+$/K$^+$ ATPase provides the 'driving force'. Increased activity of the efferent renal sympathetic nerves, and angiotensin II (via the AT1 receptor) increase the activity of the basolateral Na$^+$/K$^+$ ATPase. Locally generated dopamine decreases this activity (via the DA1 receptor). As a result of his cardiac impairment, the patient described above is likely to be in a state of sympathetic hyperactivity and to have elevated circulating levels of angiotensin II.

Sodium crosses the proximal tubular wall by a number of mechanisms. Some sodium is reabsorbed by cotransport with reabsorption of filtered glucose, amino acids and phosphate. Most is reabsorbed in exchange for hydrogen ion (the sodium-hydrogen antiporter). Angiotensin II increases the expression of this antiporter. In order for this system to work, intracellular hydrogen ions must be generated. Carbonic acid is formed from carbon dioxide and water, both freely available in the tubular cell, under the influence of carbonic anhydrase. Being a relatively strong acid, carbonic acid naturally dissociates to generate hydrogen ions. In parallel, bicarbonate is generated and passes back into the body via the basolateral membrane. Drugs such as acetazolamide, which inhibit carbonic anhydrase, interfere with this mechanism and therefore inhibit proximal tubular sodium reabsorption.

Water is reabsorbed both transcellularly and paracellularly and follows solute reabsorption in a passive fashion. Transcellular water transport is via aquaporin-1 (AQP-1) water channels, which are constitutively expressed in this segment of the nephron.

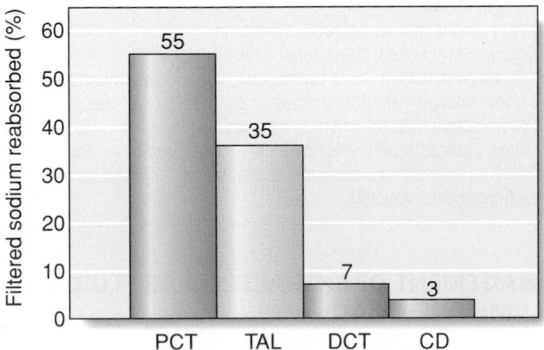

Fig. 9.4 Sites at which filtered Na$^+$ is reabsorbed along the nephron. Less than 1% is normally excreted. Important regulatory factors are the glomerular filtration rate; intratubular and peritubular hydraulic and oncotic pressures; flow rate of tubular fluid; and neuro-endocrine mechanisms as outlined above. (PCT = proximal convoluted tubule; TAL = thick ascending loop of Henle; DCT = distal convoluted tubule; CD = cortical collecting duct)

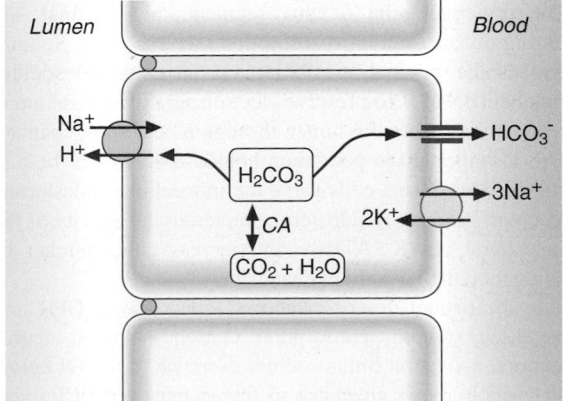

Fig. 9.5 Important factors in sodium reabsorption in the proximal convoluted tubule. Sodium cotransport with glucose, amino acids and phosphate is not represented. (CA = carbonic anhydrase)

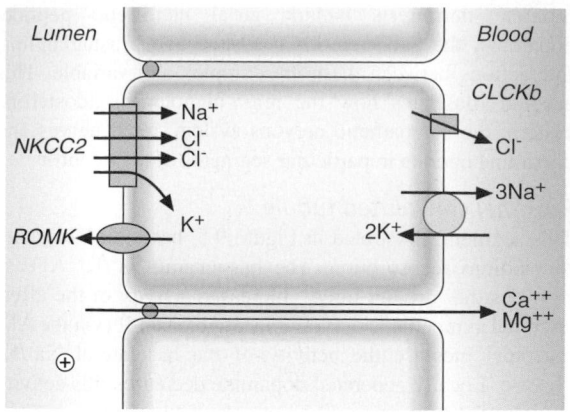

Fig. 9.6 **The thick ascending loop of Henle.** K^+ recycling renders the lumen electropositive relative to the blood. This drives the paracellular reabsorption of Ca^{++} and Mg^{++}. (NKCC2 = sodium-potassium-2-chloride transporter; ROMK = outward-rectifying potassium channel; CLCKb = kidney chloride channel b)

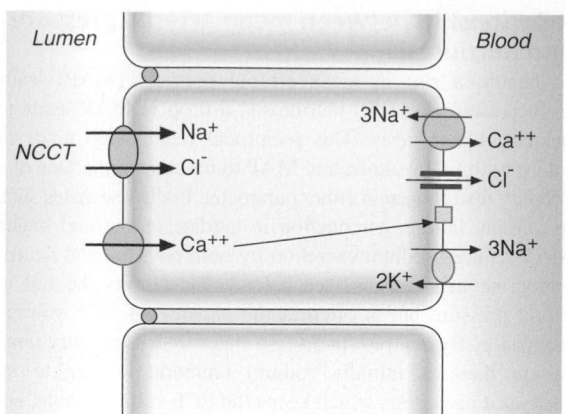

Fig. 9.7 **The distal convoluted tubule.** This segment has an important role in transcellular reabsorption of Ca^{++}. (NCCT = electroneutral sodium/chloride cotransporter)

Thick ascending limb of loop of Henle

This segment is illustrated in Figure 9.6. The drive for sodium reabsorption is again the basolateral Na^+/K^+ ATPase. Luminal reabsorption of sodium occurs via a sodium-potassium-2-chloride transporter (NKCC2). As the concentration of potassium in the tubular lumen is much lower than the sodium and chloride concentrations, there is a need for potassium to be recycled in this segment. This occurs through a potassium channel called ROMK. Aquaporin is not expressed in this segment, which is therefore impermeable to water.

Distal convoluted tubule/connecting segment

This segment (see Fig. 9.7) has a lower capacity for sodium reabsorption than the segments above it, but shows considerable capacity to adapt in the face of increased sodium delivery from the earlier parts of the nephron. The specific luminal sodium transporter at this site is the electroneutral sodium/chloride cotransporter (NCCT).

Cortical collecting duct

The principal cells of this segment are the final site for significant sodium reabsorption (see Fig. 9.8). Sodium crosses the luminal membrane via an epithelial sodium channel (ENaC). To preserve electroneutrality, potassium is secreted back into the lumen through a potassium channel. This is important in potassium homeostasis, as will be discussed later. These cells carry the intracellular aldosterone receptor. Binding of aldosterone increases the activity of the basolateral Na^+/K^+ ATPase and increases the number of luminal epithelial sodium channels.

In the patient described above, a decrease in GFR and increased sodium reabsorption consequent upon neuro-humoral activation limits sodium excretion to a level below that which allows clearance of the accumulated ECF overload, and may lead to progressive total body salt increase with a normal or increased dietary intake. In this case, cardiac failure with associated renal impairment is the underlying cause. A similar clinical pattern may be seen in the conditions in Box 9.4. Figure 9.9 provides a schematic overview.

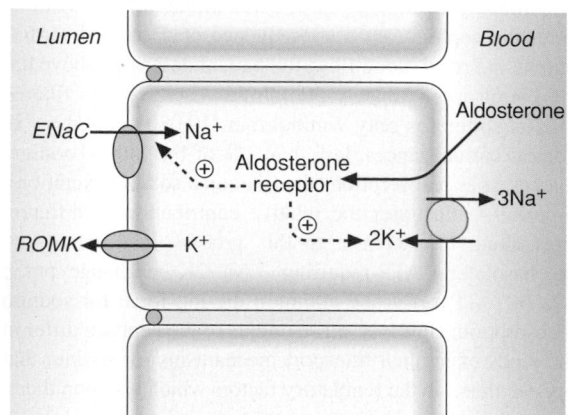

Fig. 9.8 **The principal cell of the cortical collecting duct.** (ENaC = epithelial sodium channel)

9.4 CONDITIONS ASSOCIATED WITH GENERALISED OEDEMA

- Cardiac failure
- Nephrotic syndrome; nephritic syndrome
- Chronic renal failure; acute renal failure
- Chronic liver failure; acute liver failure; hepatic vein thrombosis
- Protein-energy malnutrition; thiamin deficiency ('wet beri-beri')
- Premenstrual fluid retention; pregnancy
- Drugs: corticosteroids; non-steroidal anti-inflammatory drugs (NSAIDs); oestrogens; calcium channel blockers; vasodilators; carbenoxolone; liquorice

MANAGEMENT OF EXTRACELLULAR FLUID VOLUME OVERLOAD

Treatment of ECF volume overload involves:

- restriction of dietary sodium to 100 mmol/day ('no added salt') or 50 mmol/day in severe cases
- diuretics
- specific treatment directed at the cause, e.g. angiotensin-converting enzyme (ACE) inhibitor in heart failure, corticosteroids in minimal-change nephropathy.

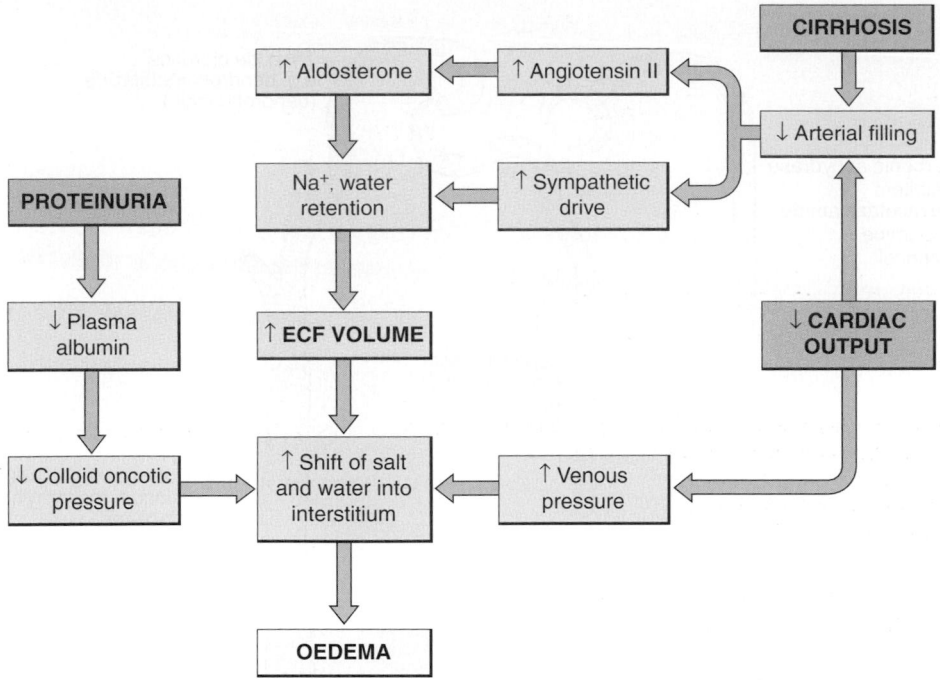

Fig. 9.9 The main forces acting to increase renal sodium and water reabsorption are shown for proteinuria, heart failure and cirrhosis.

Diuretics

General principles of diuretic therapy

Different diuretics inhibit sodium reabsorption at specific sites along the nephron (see Fig. 9.10). Their efficacy is influenced by:

- pharmacokinetic factors influencing rate of delivery to sites of action (diuretic resistance)
- pharmacodynamic factors at sites along the nephron (diuretic blunting).

Loop diuretics (furosemide (frusemide), bumetanide, torasemide). These are organic anions. Oral bioavailability varies from 40–60% (furosemide) to 90% (bumetanide). Oedema and heart failure are associated with reduced absorption of diuretics from the gut. In hypoalbuminaemia, the volume of distribution increases and the amount delivered to the kidneys is reduced; a higher dosage may therefore be necessary. Loop diuretics enter the tubular lumen by secretion in the proximal convoluted tubule. Secretion may be impaired in the presence of accumulated organic anions (as occurs in chronic renal failure and chronic liver failure). Cimetidine and trimethoprim also compete for this secretion pathway. Once in the tubular lumen, these agents bind to the chloride-binding sites of the NKCC2 transporter in the thick ascending loop of Henle (see Fig. 9.6), inhibiting its action. As this segment is responsible for a substantial proportion of sodium reabsorption in the nephron, these are relatively powerful diuretic agents.

Thiazides. Thiazide diuretics (bendroflumethiazide (bendrofluazide), hydrochlorothiazide) are also organic anions and are secreted in the proximal tubule. Their affinity is for the chloride-binding sites of the NCCT transporter of the distal convoluted tubule (see Fig. 9.7). Because of their site of action they are relatively weak agents. As these agents (and loop diuretics) increase sodium delivery to the distal nephron, they lead to increased sodium reabsorption in the cortical collecting duct, which indirectly raises potassium excretion.

Amiloride and triamterene. These are organic cations which are also secreted in the proximal tubule, and which block the epithelial sodium channel (ENaC) in the cortical collecting duct (see Fig. 9.8). As a consequence potassium excretion is diminished, so these are often described as potassium-sparing diuretics.

Spironolactone. This is the only diuretic which reaches its site of action from the basolateral side of the tubule, where it blocks the action of aldosterone on the intracellular aldosterone receptor in the cortical collecting duct. Because sodium is 'exchanged' for potassium at this site, spironolactone is a potassium-sparing diuretic (see Fig. 9.8).

Carbonic anhydrase inhibitors, dopamine and mannitol. All of these act to decrease sodium reabsorption in the proximal tubule (see Fig. 9.5). However, the downstream presence of the thick ascending loop of Henle segment, with its medium/high capacity for sodium reabsorption, limits their potency.

Diuretic resistance

Natriuresis is initiated when the delivery of diuretic to its site of action exceeds its therapeutic threshold. Oral bioavailability, hypoalbuminaemia, decreased renal blood

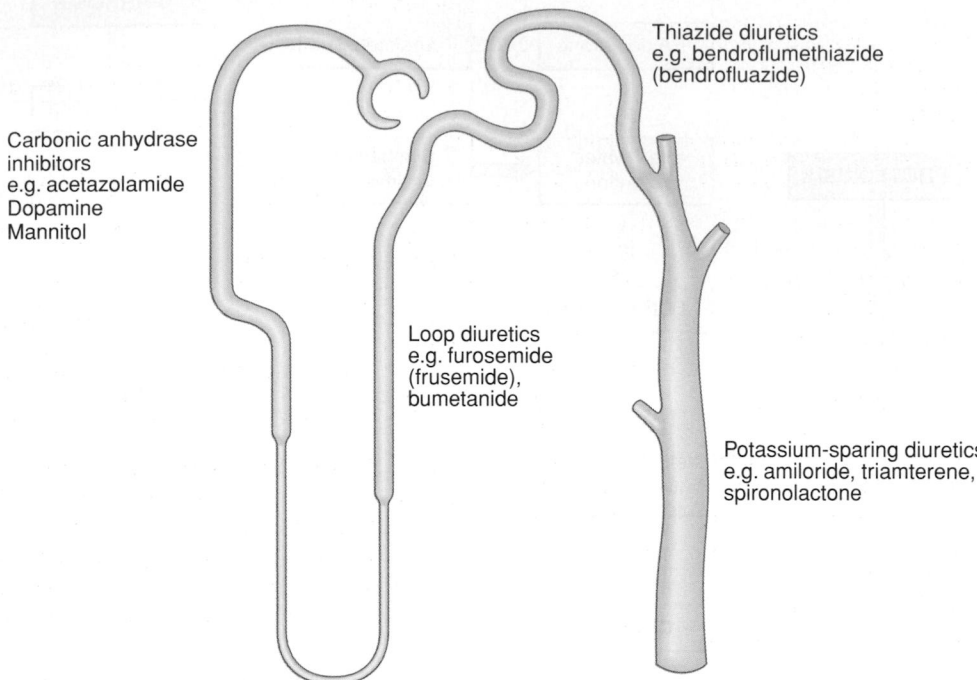

Fig. 9.10 Sites of action in the nephron of different types of diuretic.

flow and competition for secretion are all barriers requiring an increased initial dose or a change to the intravenous route.

Diuretic blunting

Within 3–5 days of the onset of diuretic-induced natriuresis, there is a compensatory increase in sodium reabsorption at the segments distal to the site of action of the diuretic. Studies indicate that the initial natriuretic response is preserved for longer and with greater total sodium loss when intravenous loop diuretic therapy is switched from an intermittent bolus regime to a continuous infusion. More significantly, the addition of agents acting more distally in the nephron decreases the blunting effect. Even in states of advanced cardiac or renal failure, the addition of thiazide and potassium-sparing diuretics to loop diuretics will therefore increase total natriuresis.

✔ Case example A: follow-up

The man described on page 273 has developed cardiac failure. The high venous pressure causes a shift of fluid to the interstitium. Blood pressure is low; this activates the renin-angiotensin-aldosterone and sympathetic nervous systems, leading to increased tubular reabsorption of sodium.

The patient responded well to dietary restriction of sodium (100 mmol/day), a loop diuretic (furosemide (frusemide) 80 mg daily) and an ACE inhibitor.

EXTRACELLULAR FLUID VOLUME DEPLETION

❓ Case example B

A 73-year-old woman living alone is brought to accident and emergency with a 5-day history of profuse watery diarrhoea. On examination she has a pulse rate of 120/min and blood pressures of 105/75 mmHg lying, 85/60 mmHg erect. There is reduced skin turgor and she is oliguric (20 ml/hr). Investigations show urea 25 mmol/l, creatinine 160 µmol/l, plasma sodium 138 mmol/l, potassium 4.8 mmol/l and bicarbonate 19 mmol/l. What has happened?

This patient exhibits the signs and symptoms of extracellular fluid volume depletion (see Box 9.5). She has lost isotonic bowel contents due to infective diarrhoea and this has exceeded her ability to ingest salt and water, leading to a reduction in blood volume. Compensatory mechanisms in the circulation limit the fall in blood pressure. The kidney responds appropriately by retaining sodium and water.

The low blood volume leads to reduced renal blood flow and GFR. The renin-angiotensin system is activated by the low blood pressure. Angiotensin II constricts the post-glomerular arteriole preferentially. This helps to maintain glomerular filtration by increasing the filtration fraction (GFR as a fraction of renal plasma flow). The increased

9.5 CONSEQUENCES OF ECF VOLUME DEPLETION

- Reduced blood volume and arterial pressure
- Renal renin release; increased sympathetic activity
- Systemic vasoconstriction
- Reduced renal blood flow
- Reduced GFR (ameliorated by angiotensin II-mediated efferent arteriolar vasoconstriction leading to increased filtration fraction)

filtration fraction leads to a greater plasma protein concentration in the peritubular capillaries, which provides an oncotic pressure gradient favouring sodium reabsorption. In the proximal convoluted tubule, increased renal nerve activation stimulates basolateral Na^+/K^+ ATPase and Na^+/H^+ antiporter activity (see Fig. 9.5, p. 275). Angiotensin II also enhances Na^+/H^+ antiporter activity. In the distal nephron (see Fig. 9.8, p. 276), aldosterone (synthesised by the adrenal cortex in response to increased angiotensin II) stimulates basolateral Na^+/K^+ ATPase activity and increases the number of epithelial sodium channels. The net result is a reduction in the percentage of filtered sodium which is excreted (fractional excretion of sodium).

Causes of sodium and water depletion are listed in Box 9.6. Clinical evaluation is outlined in Box 9.7.

Management

Homeostasis is best re-established by restoring perfusion of vital organs and replacing accumulated deficits of salt and water. This can be achieved by the administration of isotonic fluids. Crystalloids or colloids may be used, depending on

9.6 CAUSES OF SODIUM AND WATER DEPLETION

Loss from alimentary tract

External loss
- Vomiting
- Aspiration of GI contents
- Fistulae
- Diarrhoea
- Villous adenoma of large bowel

Sequestration of fluid in bowel
- Ileus
- Intestinal obstruction

Loss in urine

Extrarenal factors acting on kidney
- Osmotic diuresis
  - Diabetes mellitus
  - Mannitol
- Diuretics
- Metabolic acidosis
- Adrenocortical insufficiency

Renal disease
- Diuretic phase acute tubular necrosis
- Post-obstructive diuresis
- Chronic renal insufficiency
- Proximal renal tubular acidosis
- Medullary cystic disease
- Congenital polycystic disease
- Chronic interstitial nephritis

Loss in sweat
- Fever
- Hot environment

Loss in exudates and transudates, 'third' space losses

Loss from body surfaces
- Burns
- Extensive dermatitis

Loss into body cavities or soft tissues
- Ascites
- Peritonitis
- Acute pancreatitis
- Rhabdomyolysis
- Inferior vena cava thrombosis

9.7 CLINICAL EVALUATION OF SALT AND WATER DEPLETION

Mild (< 2 litres in adult)
- Thirst
- Concentrated urine

Moderate (2–3 litres in adult)

As above, plus:
- Dizziness, weakness
- Oliguria (< 400 ml/day)
- Postural hypotension > 20 mmHg systolic
- Low jugular venous pressure

Severe (> 3 litres in adult)

As above, plus:
- Confusion, stupor
- Systolic BP < 100 mmHg
- Tachycardia (not in elderly), low pulse volume
- Cold extremities, poor capillary return
- Reduced skin turgor ('doughy')

the clinical state of the patient and the type of fluid deficit (see EBM panel). Crystalloids include 0.9% NaCl solution, 1.26% sodium bicarbonate solution and 'normal-formula' products such as Hartmann's (compound sodium lactate solution). These differ in the concentration of electrolytes that they contain. Colloids include albumin (see EBM panel) and

EXTRACELLULAR FLUID VOLUME REPLACEMENT— crystalloids or colloids?

'Two meta-analyses of published studies have compared the use of crystalloid solutions (such as isotonic saline) with colloids (e.g. hetastarch, gelatin, dextrans) for ECF and plasma volume replacement.

One study found that, compared with crystalloids, use of colloids was associated with an increase in absolute risk of mortality of 4%. The other study found no apparent difference, with a trend in favour of crystalloids in trauma patients, but the power of the aggregated data was such that small but important effects could be missed.

Crystalloid solutions such as isotonic saline are safe and adequate in most situations. Where urgent restoration of plasma volume is necessary, synthetic colloid solutions have a more rapid effect and are retained in the circulation for longer.'

- Schierhout G, Roberts I. Fluid resuscitation with colloid or crystalloid solutions in critically ill patients: a systematic review of randomised trials. BMJ 1998; 316:961–964.
- Choi PT, Yip G, Quinonez LG, Cook DJ. Crystalloids vs. colloids in fluid resuscitation: a systematic review. Crit Care Med 1999; 27:200–210.
- Hankeln KB, Beez M. Haemodynamic and oxygen transport correlates of various volume substitutes in critically ill in-patients with various aetiologies of haemo-dynamic instability. Int J Intensive Care 1998; 5:8–14.

EXTRACELLULAR FLUID VOLUME REPLACEMENT— use of albumin solutions

'A meta-analysis of published studies found evidence of increased mortality in critically ill patients who had received infusions of human albumin to restore ECF volume and blood pressure. This meta-analysis has been extended recently and the findings have been confirmed. There is no evidence of a beneficial effect, even in patients with burns or hypoalbuminaemia from other causes, compared with the use of crystalloid solutions such as isotonic saline or synthetic colloid solutions.'

- Petros A, Schindler M, Pierce C, et al. Human albumin administration in critically ill patients. BMJ 1998; 317:882.
- Alderson P, Bunn F, Lefebvre C, et al. Human albumin solution for resuscitation and volume expansion in critically ill patients. Cochrane Library, issue 4, 2001. Oxford: Update Software.

Further information: 🖳 www.cochrane.org/cochrane/revabstr/ ab0001208.htm

plasma substitutes such as dextrans, gelatins and etherified starches—macromolecules that are slowly metabolised. Colloids restore the plasma volume rapidly but are not free of side-effects. Guidelines for the replacement of volume deficit are given in Box 9.8.

Depending on the stability of the patient, invasive monitoring using a central venous pressure line may be indicated. This will help to avoid over-transfusion and pulmonary oedema (see p. 381).

9.8 GUIDELINES FOR REPLACEMENT OF VOLUME DEFICIT
Mild
• 0.9% saline 1 litre i.v. 6–12-hourly
Moderate
• 0.9% saline 1 litre i.v. over 2–4 hours • 0.9% saline 1–2 litres i.v. 6–8-hourly
Severe
• Gelatin or starch solution 0.5–1 litre over 1 hour • 0.9% saline 2 litres i.v. over 4–6 hours • 0.9% saline 1 litre 6-hourly until replaced

N.B. Initial treatment must be reviewed frequently to ensure satisfactory improvement and to avoid precipitating cardiac failure. Central venous pressure monitoring is often indicated in patients with a history of heart disease or in the elderly. Maintenance treatment depends on the nature and amount of continuing losses which should be measured—potassium, calcium and magnesium may be needed.

✓ Case example B: follow-up

The patient described on page 278 has developed severe ECF volume depletion as a result of her diarrhoea. She is hypotensive with 'pre-renal' renal failure (see p. 594). A central venous pressure measurement was low at –5 cm water.

She was given 4 litres of normal saline over 24 hours, and a further 3 litres thereafter. Blood pressure, urine output and plasma biochemistry returned to normal.

DISORDERS OF WATER METABOLISM: DYSNATRAEMIAS

Total body water (TBW) is carefully regulated in health by maintaining a balance between variable intake (controlled by thirst) and variable excretion (regulated by renal control of urinary concentration and dilution). Water is also generated from metabolism (typically 350–500 ml/day) and excreted by non-renal means: skin, stool and lungs (typically 500 ml/day).

As we have seen, about 60% of the dry weight of an adult male is water (55% of an adult female), two-thirds of which is distributed to the intracellular space. This is proportionately greater in neonates and children, but falls with increasing age.

Disturbances of water metabolism are clinically manifest by disturbances in plasma sodium concentration (dysnatraemias). Sodium is the ion which has the greatest influence on plasma tonicity and usually plasma osmolality. The regulatory systems controlling water metabolism act to maintain plasma osmolality (Posm) at a level between 285 and 290 mOsm/kg. Dysnatraemias often coexist with disturbances of ECF volume.

The vast majority of filtered water is reabsorbed, two-thirds in the proximal tubule. This is driven by solute absorption and occurs paracellularly through the tight junctions and transcellularly via aquaporin-1 (AQP-1) channels constitutively expressed on the luminal surface of the tubular cells. The amount of water reabsorption in this segment is an important determinant of the ultimate concentrating/diluting capacity of the kidney. Conditions such as cardiac failure, ECF volume depletion and nephrotic syndrome lead to an increase in isotonic proximal tubular fluid reabsorption which limits the volume available for subsequent modification.

Solutes are reabsorbed independently of water in the thick ascending loop of Henle (see Fig. 9.6, p. 276) where no AQP-1 can be detected. A dilute luminal fluid is thus generated. Conditions such as tubulo-interstitial disease and drugs such as loop diuretics, which interfere with this function, can seriously compromise the ability to excrete dilute urine.

Finally, water can be reabsorbed through the collecting ducts, but only in the presence of antidiuretic hormone (ADH). The drive for water reabsorption comes from the concentrated medullary tonicity (itself generated by the cycling of urea through the tubules and ascending vasa rectae and by trapping of sodium chloride). ADH acts by binding to basolateral V2 receptors. This binding leads to the exocytic insertion of AQP-2 channels, normally stored in cytoplasmic vesicles, into the cell membrane, rendering the luminal surface permeable to water. Disorders in ADH release, damage to tubular segments or medullary blood vessels, and a number of drugs interfere with this process.

ADH is released from the posterior pituitary. Secretion is enhanced by an increase in plasma osmolality (the threshold for release is 280–290 mOsm/kg), by decreased ECF volume and by a number of other stimuli (nausea, pain and pregnancy). ADH has a half-life of 15–20 minutes before it is metabolised by the liver and kidney. Small changes in plasma osmolality are rapidly followed by changes in ADH secretion. ADH release is less sensitive to changes in ECF volume but much higher levels of ADH may be achieved in response to this stimulus.

Thirst is integral to the regulation of water intake. Small changes (2–3%) in osmolality lead to an immediate increase in the sensation of thirst (a phenomenon which blunts with increasing age). The threshold for increased thirst appears to be 290–295 mOsm/kg, slightly higher than that for ADH release. Equilibrium is usually achieved at a plasma osmolality midway between these values.

HYPONATRAEMIA

Abnormalities of plasma sodium concentration and hypo-natraemia are almost always due to disturbances in water metabolism. Because the sodium concentration is measured in whole serum, spuriously low values are seen if a high proportion of the serum volume is free of water, e.g. severe hyperlipidaemia or hyperproteinaemia. This is termed pseudo-hyponatraemia, and should be detected in the laboratory. Translocational hyponatraemia occurs when an increase in extracellular osmolality leads to a shift of water from cells to ECF. The most common cause is hyperglycaemia due to uncontrolled diabetes mellitus. Administration of low molecular weight solutes which do not readily permeate cells, such as mannitol, glycerol or methanol, has the same effect, particularly if they are not excreted as a result of kidney failure.

Hyponatraemia is commonly due to a decrease in the diluting capacity of the kidney. This is often multifactorial in origin. GFR declines with age, and is reduced in renal disease, cardiac and hepatic failure, nephrotic syndrome and ECF volume depletion. All lead to a decrease in the volume of filtrate delivered to the diluting segment (thick ascending loop of Henle; see Fig. 9.6, p. 276). Administration of loop diuretics and tubulo-interstitial disease may compromise this segment, and a variety of disturbances of ADH release/action may be encountered.

Clinical evaluation of the hyponatraemic patient should focus on four aspects:

- the ECF volume status of the patient
- the symptoms and signs present
- the rate at which hyponatraemia has developed
- the severity of the hyponatraemia.

Box 9.9 summarises the problems, causes and treatment of different patterns of hyponatraemia. Total body sodium status (TBNa) is assessed by clinical examination.

Symptoms and signs depend upon rate of change and severity. At plasma sodium above 120 mmol/l, neurological symptoms are uncommon compared with gastrointestinal symptoms (anorexia, nausea and vomiting) but increasing levels of neurological dysfunction, moving through apathy, lethargy and absent reflexes to seizures and coma, will occur if the onset has been rapid and plasma sodium level falls below 120 mmol/l. Children and young menstruant females who develop acute hyponatraemia due to injudicious post-operative hypotonic fluid management are at greatest risk of death or permanent neurological deficit. As well as the risks associated with hyponatraemia itself, there are hazards associated with treatment. Over-aggressive treatment has been associated with development of an acute demyelinating syndrome. This was termed 'central pontine myelinolysis', but is now known to affect extrapontine tissues as well. This leads to permanent neurological impairment and carries a high mortality; it is more common after correction of chronic hyponatraemia than acute. Older male patients, and particularly alcoholics, seem to be at particular risk. Current guidelines on treatment are shown in the EBM panel.

EBM

HYPONATRAEMIA—guidelines on correction

'As a rule, chronic hyponatraemia without symptoms can be corrected slowly over 2–3 days, often by water restriction alone, whereas severe hyponatraemia (generally < 120 mmol/l) of rapid onset with symptoms requires urgent correction. A target value of 130 mmol/l is appropriate. This should be done in a high-dependency setting with frequent careful monitoring. Hypertonic saline may be used with caution in severe acute cases.

The rate of rise in the plasma sodium should not exceed 0.5 mmol/l/hr (12 mmol/l/day) in order to minimise the risk of myelinolysis (see above).'

- Gross P, Reimann D, Henschkowski J, Damian M. Treatment of severe hyponatraemia: conventional and novel aspects. J Am Soc Nephrol 2001; 12:S10–S14.
- Kumar S, Berl T. Sodium. Lancet 1998; 352:220–228.
- Beck LH. Changes in renal function with aging. Clin Geriatr Med 1998; 14:199–209.

9.9 PATTERNS OF DISTURBANCE IN SODIUM AND WATER METABOLISM CAUSING HYPONATRAEMIA

Disturbance	Causes	Clinical features	Treatment
Body water ↓ Total body sodium ↓↓	Extra-renal losses—vomiting, diarrhoea, burns, pancreatitis Renal losses—diuretic excess, osmotic diuresis due to hyperglycaemia, tubulo-interstitial disease Cerebral salt wasting	Low jugular/central venous pressure, signs of ECF depletion (see Box 9.7)	Volume replacement with isotonic fluid—normal saline or, if severe, synthetic colloid initially (see Box 9.7) Avoid excess water intake
Body water ↑ Total body sodium normal	Psychogenic water drinking Iatrogenic water excess—i.v. dextrose solutions, absorption of hypotonic bladder irrigation fluid after prostatectomy Syndrome of inappropriate secretion of ADH (SIADH—see Boxes 9.10 and 9.11)	Normal jugular venous pressure (JVP), no signs of ECF depletion/excess	Water restriction (e.g. 500 ml/day) Severe cases may require hypertonic saline, with extreme care and specialist advice
Body water ↑↑ Total body sodium ↑	Cardiac failure Renal failure Liver failure Nephrotic syndrome	JVP ↑ in cardiac failure, renal failure; may be normal or low in liver failure and nephrotic syndrome because of underfilling of vascular compartment Tissue oedema common	Diuretic therapy Avoid excess water intake

SYNDROME OF INAPPROPRIATE ADH SECRETION

The syndrome of inappropriate ADH secretion (SIADH) is an important cause of hyponatraemia. It occurs when, in spite of water overload, hyponatraemia and a low plasma osmolality—which should suppress ADH secretion and produce a very dilute urine—there is either persistent secretion of ADH by the posterior pituitary, or ectopic production of ADH by a tumour. The presence of ADH leads to inappropriate concentration of the urine and retention of water. A urine osmolality above that of plasma is diagnostic (see Box 9.10). Serum urea concentration is often unusually low because of dilution by the extra water and an associated rise in GFR. Other serum chemistry is usually normal. The diagnosis requires that the patient is euvolaemic and does not have cardiac, hepatic, renal, thyroid or adrenal disease, all of which may cause impaired water excretion.

Causes of SIADH are listed in Box 9.11.

9.10 TYPICAL BIOCHEMICAL VALUES IN SIADH
• Plasma sodium 124 mmol/l (normal 135–145 mmol/l)
• Serum urea 2.3 mmol/l (normal 4–6 mmol/l)
• Plasma osmolality 260 mOsm/kg (normal ≈ 285 mOsm/kg)
• Urine osmolality 430 mOsm/kg (should be < 150 mOsm/kg in face of low plasma osmolality)

9.11 CONDITIONS ASSOCIATED WITH THE SYNDROME OF INAPPROPRIATE SECRETION OF ADH (SIADH)	
Neoplasm	
• Carcinoma of bronchus (small cell), pancreas, duodenum, ureter, bladder, prostate, lymphoma, thymoma, mesothelioma	
Disorders of CNS	
• Meningitis	• Cerebral vascular accident
• Encephalitis	• Hydrocephalus
• Brain abscess	• Cerebral or cerebellar atrophy
• Head injury	• Delirium tremens, psychosis
• Cerebral tumour	• Guillain–Barré syndrome
Non-malignant pulmonary lesions	
• Tuberculosis	• Pneumonia (bacterial, viral)
Drugs	
• Hypoglycaemic agents—chlorpropamide, tolbutamide	
• Antidepressants—amitriptyline, fluoxetine	
• Major tranquillisers—fluphenazine, haloperidol	
• Anti-epileptic drugs—carbamazepine	
• Chemotherapeutic drugs—cyclophosphamide*, vincristine, vinblastine	
• Thiazide diuretics and metolazone	
• Opiates—morphine	
• NSAIDs*	
Miscellaneous	
• Pain, post-operative period, nausea	
* Potentiate effect of ADH (vasopressin, AVP) on collecting duct.	

HYPERNATRAEMIA

Hypernatraemia occurs when a decreased water intake or increased water excretion or both leads to a decrease in TBW. Box 9.12 summarises the important causes. These are most commonly found in elderly patients with intercurrent illness. Because the fluid loss in these conditions is 'shared' between the ICF and ECF, signs of ECF volume depletion may be subtle and much less prominent than with equivalent losses

9.12 CAUSES OF PURE OR PREDOMINANT WATER DEPLETION	
Reduced intake	
• Water unavailable	• Coma
• Voluntary water intake reduced, e.g. in infants, the elderly, people who are depressed or apathetic	• Inability to swallow
	• Nausea
	• Primary hypodipsia
Increased loss from skin	
• Fever	• Hot environment
• Hyperthyroidism	
Increased loss from respiratory tract	
• Hyperventilation	• High altitudes
• Fever	
Increased loss in urine due to marked impairment of urinary concentrating mechanism	
Deficiency of vasopressin (ADH) (central diabetes insipidus)	
• Idiopathic	• CNS infection (encephalitis, meningitis)
• Brain-stem tumours (primary or secondary)	• Head injury
• Post-surgical (hypophysectomy, removal of craniopharyngioma or hypothalamic tumour)	• Brain-stem stroke
	• Cerebral aneurysm
Renal tubular unresponsiveness to AVP (nephrogenic diabetes insipidus)	
• Hypercalcaemia	• Medullary cystic disease
• K+ depletion	• Drugs, e.g. lithium
• Chronic interstitial nephritis	• Congenital
• Amyloidosis, obstructive uropathy	
Solute diuresis	
• Diabetes mellitus	
• Enteral or parenteral feeds with high solute concentration	

9.13 CLINICAL FEATURES OF PREDOMINANT WATER DEPLETION	
Mild (1–2 litres in adult)	
• Thirst	• Concentrated urine
Moderate (2–4 litres in adult)	
• Marked thirst, difficulty swallowing	• Oliguria, concentrated urine
• Dizziness, mild confusion/ aggression and weakness	• Rising plasma urea and Na+
Severe (4–10 litres in adult)	
• Severe thirst	• Tachycardia, low BP
• Confusion, coma, muscle weakness	• Oliguria, concentrated urine
• 'Doughy' skin and tissues	• Raised plasma urea, Na+ and haemoglobin

of isotonic fluid that predominantly affect the ECF (see Box 9.13). Treatment is with appropriate hypotonic fluid. The deficit may often be large (e.g. 5–10 litres in total).

POLYURIA

An inappropriately high urine volume may be solute-led—as in hyperglycaemia and natriuresis—or may represent a pure water diuresis. Free water clearance, i.e. water free of solute, may be calculated by measuring osmotic clearance:

Osmotic clearance = urine volume × Uosm/Posm

Free water clearance = urine volume – osmotic clearance

Polyuria with increased free water clearance in the absence of an excessive intake represents a deficit in urinary concentrating ability. This may be due to one of the forms of diabetes insipidus (DI). Central DI exists when a patient fails to concentrate the urine in conditions of water deprivation, but does so following administration of supraphysiological doses of the ADH analogue, 1-desamino-8-D-arginine vasopressin (dDAVP). Nephrogenic DI shows no urine concentration in response to water restriction and does not respond to dDAVP administration.

Approximately 50% of cases of central DI are idiopathic, with the bulk of the remainder due to CNS mass lesions, infections or trauma. Two inherited forms are recognised. The most common has an autosomal dominant pattern; there is also a very rare autosomal recessive condition known as DIDMOAD (diabetes insipidus, diabetes mellitus, optic atrophy and deafness). Most cases of nephrogenic diabetes insipidus are acquired, occurring in chronic renal failure, sickle-cell disease, drug therapy (lithium, amphotericin, foscarnet), hypokalaemia, hypercalcaemia or protein malnutrition. An X-linked form with abnormal V2 receptors is known, as is a very rare X-linked form with mutations in the gene encoding for AQP-2.

Hypernatraemia is an unusual feature of DI if patients have access to water. Problems may develop if they suffer from an intercurrent illness or become ECF volume-depleted.

DISORDERS OF POTASSIUM METABOLISM: DYSKALAEMIAS

Potassium is the major intracellular cation. Changes in the prevailing plasma potassium concentration have an important influence on neuromuscular transmission and membrane potentials, most significantly in the heart as a cause of cardiac arrest.

Potassium is pumped into cells in exchange for sodium by the ubiquitous Na^+/K^+ ATPase, in a ratio of 3 sodium to 2 potassium ions. This creates a negative intracellular voltage. The intracellular potassium concentration remains constant at around 150 mmol/l because of passive leakage from cells through ion-selective potassium channels. Na^+/K^+ ATPase is stimulated by insulin and β-adrenergic agonists—an effect which is exploited to treat hyperkalaemia. It is inhibited by acidosis, and hyperkalaemia is commonly associated with metabolic acidosis. Approximately 3500 mmol (50 mmol/kg) of potassium are intracellular, mostly in muscle, and 65 mmol are extracellular (see Fig. 9.11). The plasma potassium is therefore very sensitive to factors influencing the shift of potassium between extracellular and intracellular compartments.

Most of the dietary intake of potassium (approximately 100 mmol, 0.75–1.25 mmol/kg/day) is excreted in the urine, with small losses in the stool and sweat. In the kidney, about 90% of filtered potassium is reabsorbed actively in the proximal tubule and thick ascending limb. About 10% escapes reabsorption and, if the GFR is normal, this amount is adequate to maintain potassium balance. For this reason, hyperkalaemia is very uncommon in the presence of normal renal function. However, if the GFR is reduced, then active secretion of potassium by the distal nephron is necessary to avoid progressive accumulation of potassium and eventual hyperkalaemia. Although basal K^+ secretion occurs without aldosterone, this active secretion is mediated primarily by aldosterone, which stimulates the basolateral Na^+/K^+ ATPase and opens luminal sodium and potassium channels to facilitate sodium reabsorption and potassium secretion (see Fig. 9.8, p. 276 and Fig. 9.11). In health, the plasma aldosterone level rises as the plasma potassium increases. The other major stimulus to aldosterone synthesis is angiotensin II. Thus, any factors that inhibit the renin-angiotensin system will blunt the hormonal and renal response to rising plasma potassium. These include ACE inhibitors (by inhibiting

---

ISSUES IN OLDER PEOPLE
AGE-RELATED PHYSIOLOGICAL CHANGES IN SODIUM AND WATER METABOLISM

- Older people are at high risk of fluid and electrolyte disorders because of several physiological changes that occur with ageing.
- Older people have a greater proportion of fat to lean muscle mass than younger people; as there is less water in fat than in muscle, the older have a greater loss of water for any given reduction in body weight.
- There is an impaired thirst response to hypovolaemia and hyperosmolality, which means that thirst cannot be relied upon to compensate for water deficits in dehydrated older patients, and fluid may have to be prescribed.
- There is a reduction in glomerular filtration rate, which reduces ability to excrete an acute sodium load; this is compounded by the high prevalence of congestive cardiac failure in this age group.
- Renal concentrating ability is reduced due to a relative increase in medullary blood flow secondary to preferential loss of cortical glomeruli. This results in a 'washout' of medullary hypertonicity and reduced concentrating capacity.
- Renin and aldosterone levels are decreased, which leads to impaired sodium conservation.
- Reduced renal responsiveness to vasopressin may result in excessive water loss.

ISSUES IN OLDER PEOPLE
COMMON FLUID AND ELECTROLYTE DISTURBANCES IN OLDER PEOPLE

- Infections such as pneumonia and urinary tract infection account for a disproportionate amount of dehydration in this age group.
- People with dementia are especially prone to dehydration because of impaired thirst and inability to obtain or ask for water.
- Hyponatraemia is the most common electrolyte abnormality in old age and is associated with a high mortality.
- Older people are more likely to take medication (e.g. thiazide diuretics) which causes hyponatraemia or to have diseases associated with hyponatraemia.

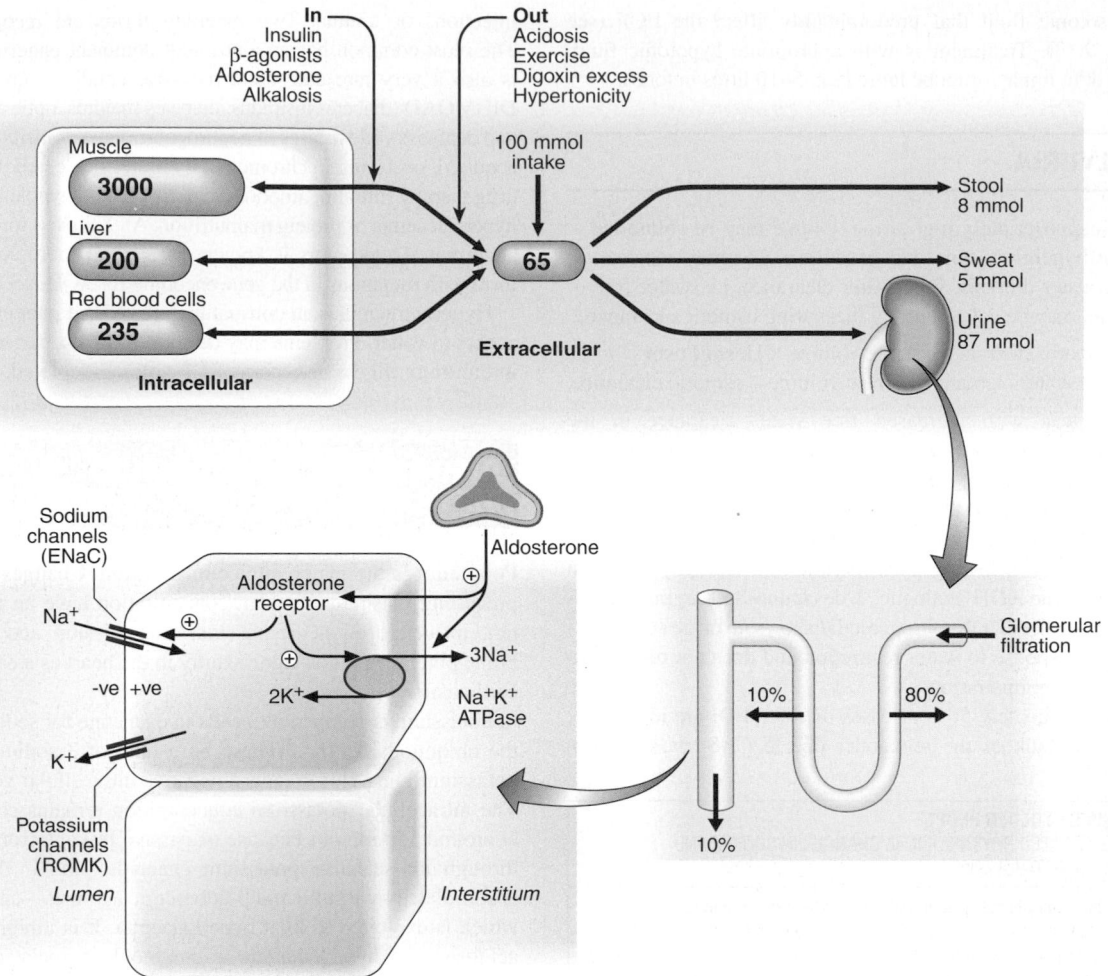

Fig. 9.11 **Total body potassium metabolism, renal potassium handling and distal tubular mechanisms for secretion of potassium.**
The tubular cell illustrated is the principal cell of the cortical collecting duct (see Fig. 9.8, p. 276).

conversion of angiotensin I to angiotensin II), non-steroidal anti-inflammatory drugs (NSAIDs; by blocking prostaglandin-mediated renin release) and β-adrenoceptor antagonists (β-blockers; by inhibiting renin release mediated by the renal nerves). Drugs which block the action of aldosterone (e.g. spironolactone, amiloride) also cause hyperkalaemia, particularly if the GFR is low.

HYPERKALAEMIA

❓ Case example C

A 75-year-old man is brought to accident and emergency, having collapsed at home. He lives alone and has not been seen by neighbours for 2 days. Clinical examination shows general muscle weakness, but with neurological signs of a right hemiplegia and facial weakness. Pulse is 42/min and irregular, and blood pressure 90/50 mmHg. An urgent serum analysis shows: urea 18.5 mmol/l, sodium 148 mmol/l, potassium 8.9 mmol/l, total CO_2 11 mmol/l. What has happened?

Hyperkalaemia can result from a shift of potassium out of cells or a reduction in renal excretion of potassium. In many cases these phenomena coexist. The normal plasma potassium concentration is in the range 3.7–5.2 mmol/l. Hyperkalaemia reduces the threshold for initiation of action potentials; cardiac complications of hyperkalaemia are likely at values over 7 mmol/l and, in general, values greater than 6 mmol/l should be acted upon. The principal factors contributing to the development of hyperkalaemia are given in Box 9.14.

In diabetic ketoacidosis, hyperkalaemia is relatively common because of metabolic acidosis (shift of potassium out of cells), hypoinsulinaemia and hypovolaemia (impaired K^+ excretion), despite an overall K^+ deficit accumulated during the preceding period of osmotic diuresis. During treatment with insulin, hyperkalaemia rapidly resolves and may be followed by significant hypokalaemia (see p. 666).

Spurious hyperkalaemia is caused by the release of K^+ in vitro from abnormal or damaged cells, such as the abnormal white blood cells in acute leukaemia. It is also common in poorly handled blood specimens that have been left for too long at room temperature before separation and analysis.

9.14 FACTORS CONTRIBUTING TO HYPERKALAEMIA

Increased intake of K⁺

- Intravenous therapy with K⁺
- High-potassium foods or drugs

Cell death with release of intracellular K⁺

- Bleeding into GI tract, soft tissues or body cavities—lysis of red blood cells
- Intravascular haemolysis
- Rhabdomyolysis
- Tissue necrosis due to ischaemia/hypoxia
- Catabolic states, e.g. fasting

Shift of K⁺ out of cells

- Acidosis
- Insulin deficiency (diabetic ketoacidosis)
- β-blockers
- Reduced plasma aldosterone concentration
- Hypertonicity of ECF (water depletion)
- Digoxin (in toxic doses)
- Strenuous exercise
- Tissue hypoxia
- Primary hyperkalaemic periodic paralysis

Impaired renal excretion of K⁺

Reduced GFR

- Acute renal failure
- Chronic renal failure (GFR < 15 ml/min)
- Urinary tract obstruction
- Reduced renal blood flow, e.g. hypovolaemia, circulatory failure

Impaired tubular secretion of K⁺

Reduced plasma aldosterone concentration

- Adrenal gland disorders
  Addison's disease
  Primary hypoaldosteronism
  Other adrenal enzyme deficiencies
- Reduced stimulus to aldosterone synthesis
  Hyporeninaemic hypoaldosteronism
  ACE inhibitors
  NSAIDs
  β-blockers
  Ciclosporin
  Heparin

Tubular resistance to action of aldosterone

- Drugs
  Spironolactone
  Amiloride
- Tubular disorders
- Systemic lupus erythematosus
- Transplanted kidneys
- Amyloidosis
- Sickle-cell disease

Spurious

- Tissue damage during venepuncture
- Incorrect blood sample handling
- Abnormally fragile red cells
- Marked erythrocytosis, thrombocytosis or leucocytosis

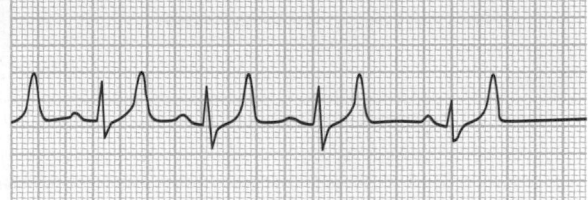

Fig. 9.12   Changes in the ECG associated with hyperkalaemia.
The T waves are tall, peaked and tent-like, and the PR interval and QRS complexes are lengthened. In severe cases, the P wave disappears and the QRS complex widens further, with loss of the T wave.

and ileus. However, they are more likely to present with collapse due to a dangerous cardiac arrhythmia, which may be the first and only sign of hyperkalaemia. An urgent electrocardiogram (ECG) should be performed. Typical ECG changes are shown in Figure 9.12.

The emergency management of acute hyperkalaemia is shown in Box 9.15. The necessity for such treatment can be avoided by appropriate preventative measures, based on an awareness of the contributing factors. These include dietary restriction of foods rich in K⁺ in patients with renal failure, aiming for a daily intake of around 70 mmol. Oral sodium bicarbonate can be used to control metabolic acidosis, and regular Calcium Resonium 15 g 2–3 times daily may be helpful in at-risk patients.

☑ Case example C: follow-up

The 75-year-old man discussed on page 284 has suffered a left-sided cerebral haemorrhage and has been lying incapacitated for up to 48 hours. With no access to fluids, he has developed significant, acute ECF volume depletion, causing a shift of K⁺ out of cells.

Because of the ECF depletion and consequent hypotension, there is renal vasoconstriction and a fall in GFR (reduced filtered load of potassium), causing the high urea and metabolic acidosis (shift of K⁺ out of cells).

History from the patient's daughter indicates that he was on an ACE inhibitor for hypertension prior to this event (reduced angiotensin II and aldosterone levels, reduced distal tubular potassium secretion).

An alert senior house officer notices a 'woody' feeling to the muscles in the patient's left calf and the very dark colour of the small amount of urine that is being passed. He suspects rhabdomyolysis, secondary to direct pressure on the muscle and ischaemia (massive release of potassium and hydrogen ions from dying muscle). Plasma analysis confirms a very high plasma concentration of creatine kinase (CK) at 25 000 units/ml.

Treatment consisted of emergency measures as in Box 9.15, including 500 ml 1.26% sodium bicarbonate over 3 hours; several litres of i.v. saline replacement; stopping the ACE inhibitor; and surgery to decompress the muscle compartments in the left calf.

Hyperkalaemia must be suspected in any of the circumstances outlined in Box 9.14, and confirmed by urgent analysis of plasma. Patients with acute or chronic renal failure are at particular risk, and may experience rapid increments in plasma potassium. Most patients with hyperkalaemia are asymptomatic. In severe cases (> 7 mmol/l) they may complain of tingling around the lips or in the fingers, or develop severe muscular weakness resulting in a flaccid paralysis, loss of tendon jerks, abdominal distension

9.15 MANAGEMENT OF ACUTE HYPERKALAEMIA

Action	Effect
Establish ECG monitoring and reliable i.v. access	
Inject 10 ml 10% calcium gluconate i.v. over 5 mins (reopens fast Na^+ channels which have closed in response to changes in resting membrane potential)	Onset in 5–10 mins Repeat if no change in ECG after 15 mins
Inject 50 ml 50% (25 g) dextrose with 5 units of soluble insulin i.v. over 10–15 mins; monitor plasma glucose—risk of hypoglycaemia, especially if ratio of insulin:dextrose exceeds 1 unit:5 g	Onset in 30–60 mins Peak effect at 90 mins Effect lasts for about 6 hrs Reduction of 0.7–1.2 mmol/l
Alternative or adjunctive: salbutamol 0.5 mg i.v. in 5% dextrose over 15 mins, or 5–10 mg by nebulised inhaler over 10 mins; risk of tachycardia	Onset in 60 mins Peak effect at 90 mins Effect lasts for about 6 hrs Reduction of 0.6–1.0 mmol/l Additive effect with insulin
Start infusion of 10 or 20% dextrose 500 ml 4–6-hourly (to minimise rebound ↑ K^+)—maintain until underlying problem corrected	Minimises further rise
Calcium Resonium (exchange resin, binds K^+ in exchange for Ca^{++}); 15–30 g orally; 30 g by rectal enema	Relatively ineffective in acute situation; better in chronic 1 g binds 1 mmol K^+
If metabolic acidosis present, infuse sodium bicarbonate 1.26% 500 ml 6–8-hourly i.v. until plasma HCO_3 in normal range **N.B.** Watch for circulatory overload	Onset in 30–60 mins Most effective in severe acidosis Reduction of 0.2–0.4 mmol/l
Identify and treat underlying cause (see Box 9.14). In particular, correct volume depletion, hypotension and acidosis if present. Aim to restore urine volume if patient oliguric	
Use haemodialysis, haemofiltration or peritoneal dialysis if the above fail, or if the underlying cause is not immediately correctable	Removes K^+ from plasma Specialist prescription

HYPOKALAEMIA

❓ Case example D

A 36-year-old woman with a long history of dyspepsia and proven gastric ulceration presents with severe muscle weakness, such that she cannot climb stairs at home. She gives a history of repeated vomiting for 3–4 weeks prior to presentation. Plasma analysis shows: urea 12.5 mmol/l, sodium 130 mmol/l, potassium 1.8 mmol/l, total CO_2 43 mmol/l. What has happened?

Hypokalaemia can be caused by a shift of potassium into cells (see Fig. 9.8, p. 276) or by potassium depletion. Both of these may be present.

When potassium intake is very low, reabsorption of potassium in the nephron is enhanced, and urinary excretion falls gradually to about 5 mmol/day, but this small continuing loss, together with the daily stool and sweat losses of 8–15 mmol, can result in K^+ depletion and eventual hypokalaemia. If potassium reabsorption is impaired, urinary losses will be greater.

Excretion of potassium in urine rises whenever there is increased delivery of sodium to the distal tubule. A proportion of the sodium is reabsorbed 'in exchange' for potassium, which is lost in the urine. This applies if there is a high urine flow rate (e.g. in uncontrolled diabetes) or if reabsorption of sodium in an earlier nephron segment is reduced (e.g. inhibited by a diuretic such as furosemide (frusemide)).

Excretion of potassium in urine is also increased whenever there are high concentrations of aldosterone, which promotes avid reabsorption of sodium in the distal tubule and hence loss of potassium. In patients with protracted, relatively mild ECF volume depletion, there are high plasma levels of renin, angiotensin I and II, and aldosterone. The GFR is maintained by angiotensin II-mediated efferent arteriolar constriction, so that distal sodium delivery is relatively preserved, but aldosterone drives the urinary losses of K^+. This is often termed 'contraction alkalosis'—increased sodium reabsorption in the proximal tubule leads to increased bicarbonate generation; it is usually associated with chloride depletion which interferes with sodium reabsorption in the loop of Henle and the distal convoluted tubule (see Figs 9.5–9.7, pp. 275–276). Consequently, distal sodium delivery remains high, with increased potassium loss. This is corrected by restoring the ECF volume and correcting the chloride deficit. Classically this afflicts patients with protracted vomiting (where the direct potassium losses in the vomitus make matters worse).

Any factor which moves potassium into cells (see Fig. 9.11) will cause the intracellular $[K^+]$, including that in the cells of the distal tubule, to rise; this enhances the secretion of potassium and hence urinary losses. This mechanism operates in alkalosis (from any cause); alkalosis and hypokalaemia are commonly associated.

9.16 FACTORS CONTRIBUTING TO POTASSIUM DEPLETION	
Reduced intake	
• Inadequate dietary intake	• Potassium-free intravenous fluids
Losses from the gastrointestinal tract	
External losses	
• Vomiting	• Diarrhoea
• Aspiration of upper GI contents	Acute
• Fistulae	Chronic, e.g. laxative
• Villous adenoma of colon	abuse, malabsorption
• Ureterosigmoid anastomosis	
Sequestration of fluid in bowel	
• Ileus	• Intestinal obstruction
Increased losses in urine	
Defective proximal reabsorption of potassium	
• Recovery phase of acute tubular necrosis	• Proximal renal tubular acidosis
• After relief of urinary tract obstruction	• Tubular damage by drugs, e.g. amphotericin
High urine flow rate and distal sodium delivery	
• Loop diuretics and thiazides	• Bartter's syndrome
• Uncontrolled diabetes	• Gitelman's syndrome
Mediated by mineralocorticoid receptor	
• Primary aldosteronism (Conn's syndrome)*	• Cushing's syndrome*
	• Steroid therapy*
• Secondary aldosteronism	• Carbenoxolone*, liquorice*
ECF depletion	
Renal artery stenosis*	
Accelerated hypertension*	
Cirrhosis	
Cardiac failure	
Nephrotic syndrome	
Shift of potassium into cells	
• Metabolic alkalosis	
• Liddle's syndrome (distal tubular dysfunction—mutated epithelial sodium channel causing increased sodium reabsorption)	
* Associated with hypertension.	

Clinical factors contributing to potassium depletion are given in Box 9.16.

Diagnosis

Hypokalaemia increases the threshold for initiation of action potentials. The diagnosis may be suggested by tiredness and muscular weakness. In extreme cases the patient may be unable to walk or climb stairs. Reduced intestinal motility or paralytic ileus may occur. Cardiac effects include ventricular arrhythmia or asystole, and potentiation of the adverse effects of digitalis. Typical ECG changes occur (see Fig. 9.13). Long-standing hypokalaemia damages renal tubular structures and results in a failure of the antidiuretic response to ADH (acquired nephrogenic diabetes insipidus). Patients with hypokalaemia may therefore present with nocturia or polyuria and polydipsia.

In most cases of K^+ depletion the plasma $[K^+]$ is low, but in some cases the factors that move K^+ out of cells (see Fig. 9.11, p. 284) may help to maintain a normal plasma $[K^+]$—for example, in untreated diabetic ketoacidosis. Conversely, patients with metabolic alkalosis, or who have been taking

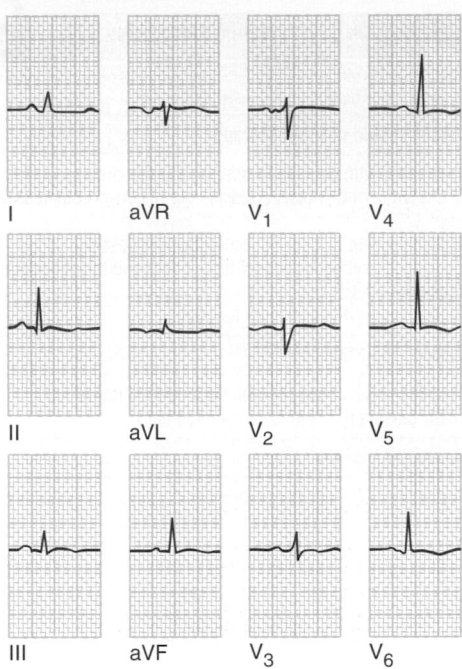

Fig. 9.13 Changes in the ECG associated with hypokalaemia. Sinus rhythm with normal QRS complexes. The T waves are flattened and U waves (a broad, low-amplitude deflection following the T wave) are present in most leads.

excessive insulin or β-adrenoceptor agonists, may have a low plasma $[K^+]$ despite a normal total body K^+ content, because of movement of K^+ into cells. In defining the cause of hypokalaemia, measurement of the urinary K^+ excretion may be helpful; a value of < 20 mmol/day makes abnormal renal K^+ loss unlikely, whilst a urinary K^+ excretion > 50 mmol/day in the presence of hypokalaemia suggests a renal cause.

Bartter's and Gitelman's syndromes are rare, familial and often asymptomatic renal potassium-losing conditions. Both have features of sodium-wasting, potassium-wasting and magnesium-wasting. Hypocalciuria occurs in Gitelman's syndrome, whereas hypercalciuria occurs in Bartter's syndrome. The clinical features mimic the effect of treatment with loop diuretics (Bartter's) or thiazide diuretics (Gitelman's). The genetic defects causing Bartter's syndrome affect those genes coding for the NKCC2 receptor, the ROMK potassium channel and basolateral chloride channel in the thick ascending loop of Henle cells (see Fig. 9.6, p. 276). The defect in many kindreds with Gitelman's syndrome affects the NCCT transporter in the distal convoluted tubule (see Fig. 9.7, p. 276). Blood pressure is normal, which helps to distinguish these conditions from primary aldosteronism. Most patients require life-long oral potassium supplements or potassium-sparing diuretics.

Management

Giving a K^+ salt orally or intravenously treats potassium depletion. The oral route is preferable because it is safer. Oral KCl (1 g = 13.4 mmol K^+) is satisfactory unless a metabolic acidosis is present, in which case potassium bicarbonate can be used. These preparations may cause gastrointestinal

9.17 PREVENTION OF POTASSIUM DEPLETION

Awareness of patients at risk (see Box 9.16)

Loop and thiazide diuretic therapy

- Combination with potassium-sparing diuretic may be useful
- ACE inhibitors and β-blockers also help to conserve potassium (see p. 277)
- Supplement with KCl 20–60 mmol/day if necessary
- Potassium excretion especially high if loop and thiazide diuretic combined
- Monitor plasma [K⁺] and renal function

Intravenous fluid therapy

- Most patients will need 60 mmol KCl over 24 hours
- Monitor plasma [K⁺] and renal function daily

Corticosteroid therapy

- Some patients on high doses need oral potassium supplements

irritation; oesophageal and small bowel erosions and strictures are rare complications. A diet rich in K⁺ is helpful; bananas, citrus fruits, milk and chocolate contain significant amounts.

In ill patients and those with marked clinical features, intravenous KCl is needed. Any associated salt and water deficiency should be treated, and intravenous administration of potassium avoided until urine output is established. Between 80 and 100 mmol K⁺/day is usually sufficient. No more than 20 mmol of K⁺ should be given in any 3-hour period.

If hypokalaemia is found to be difficult to correct in patients who have had diuretics, there may be an associated magnesium deficiency; correction of this may be necessary before the hypokalaemia returns to normal.

Strategies for the prevention of potassium depletion are shown in Box 9.17.

☑ Case example D: follow-up

The woman described on page 285 developed gastric outlet obstruction as a complication of peptic ulcer disease. This was confirmed by a gastrografin meal.

She has lost potassium in the gastric contents, leading to a potassium deficit. There is also a deficit of sodium, with ECF volume contraction, chloride depletion and alkalosis. Avid distal tubular sodium reabsorption, under the influence of aldosterone, causes an increased intracellular positive charge, which promotes loss of potassium and hydrogen ions into the urine. The alkalosis causes a shift of potassium into cells, including distal nephron cells, which also promotes distal tubular K⁺ secretion.

Treatment consisted of intravenous saline (4 litres over 24 hours); correction of the ECF volume contraction allowed the kidney to react appropriately by conserving potassium. The patient was given 60 mmol of KCl over the first 24 hours to correct the body deficit, following which further supplements were unnecessary. After correction of the electrolyte abnormalities, corrective gastric surgery was performed.

ACID–BASE DISORDERS

Acid–base disturbances occur when disease processes cause disruption of normal homeostatic mechanisms or when the acid or (more rarely) alkali burden presented exceeds the adaptive capacity of these mechanisms.

- Normal arterial pH ranges from 7.36 to 7.42; it is maintained by intracellular and extracellular buffers, and by renal and respiratory regulatory mechanisms.
- Intracellular pH ranges from 6.40 to 7.35.
- pH is $-\log_{10}$ of the hydrogen ion concentration, [H⁺].
- pH of 7.4 represents [H⁺] of 40 nmol/l.
- pH rising to 7.5 represents a drop in [H⁺] to 32 nmol/l.
- pH of 7.0 is equal to [H⁺] of 100 nmol/l.

Central to an understanding of acid–base disturbances is the carbonic acid-bicarbonate buffer pairing. This is expressed in the Henderson–Hasselbalch equation:

$$[H^+] = 181 \times PaCO_2/[HCO_3^-]$$

(181 is the dissociation coefficient of carbonic acid in the presence of carbonic anhydrase.)

The acidity of the blood is therefore directly related to the ratio between carbon dioxide tension and the plasma bicarbonate concentration. This buffer pairing is ubiquitous, is the dominant physiological buffer system in man and, most importantly, is in equilibrium with all other buffer systems in the body.

A condition in which hydrogen ion concentration rises, or would rise in the absence of compensatory mechanisms, is termed 'acidosis'. The converse is termed 'alkalosis'. When the primary disturbance is in the control of the carbon dioxide tension, it is termed 'respiratory', but when the primary disturbance is in control of the plasma bicarbonate concentration, it is termed 'metabolic'. The difference between the actual plasma bicarbonate and the normal value is termed the base deficit (in metabolic acidosis) or excess (in metabolic alkalosis)—see page 190. Mixed disturbances are common, and chronic acid–base disturbances usually lead to compensatory changes which modulate the shift in hydrogen ion concentration.

RENAL CONTROL OF ACID EXCRETION

When H⁺ is secreted into the proximal tubule, it binds with filtered HCO₃⁻. The resultant carbonic acid is dehydrated by carbonic anhydrase to H₂O and CO₂. H₂O is excreted and CO₂ diffuses back into the blood, to be excreted by the lungs. This sequence, intimately associated with proximal tubule sodium reabsorption, prevents bicarbonate loss but causes no net acid excretion.

The important distal nephron site of H⁺ secretion in the kidney is the α-intercalated cell of the collecting duct (see Fig. 9.14). H⁺ secreted into the tubular lumen also binds with non-bicarbonate buffers such as urate, creatinine and, most importantly, phosphate. The increased production of NaH₂PO₄ contributes to net urinary acid excretion and is quantified as the 'titratable acidity'. Ammonia is produced

9.18 CHARACTERISTIC CHANGES IN ARTERIAL [H⁺], PaCO₂ AND PLASMA BICARBONATE IN ACID–BASE DISTURBANCES*

Disorder	[H⁺]	nmol/l	PaCO₂	kPa	[HCO₃⁻]	mmol/l
Metabolic acidosis						
Acute	↑	60	→	5.3	↓↓	12
Compensated (by increased ventilation)	↗ or →	48	↓	4.0	↓↓	13
Metabolic alkalosis						
Acute	↓	28	→	5.4	↑	42
Compensated (by decreased ventilation)	↘ or →	35	↑	8.0	↑	40
Respiratory acidosis						
Acute	↑	65	↑↑	9.3	→	28
Compensated (by renal retention of bicarbonate)	↗ or →	44	↑↑	9.0	↑	39
Respiratory alkalosis						
Acute	↓	24	↓↓	2.7	→	22
Compensated (by renal excretion of bicarbonate)	↘ or →	36	↓	4.0	↓	14

* Normal [H⁺] = 36–44 nmol/l; normal $PaCO_2$ = 4.4–6.1 kPa; normal plasma [HCO₃⁻] = 21–28 mmol/l. Examples of typical values are shown in italics.

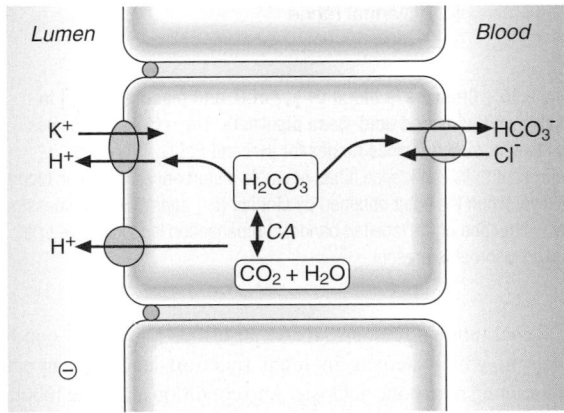

Fig. 9.14 Cortical collecting duct (α-intercalated cell). Some H⁺ secretion occurs in exchange for K⁺; there is an energy-requiring H⁺-ATPase which secretes against the concentration gradient.

in the tubular cells and diffuses into the lumen. Secreted H⁺ binds with ammonia to form the ammonium ion (NH₄⁺). Ammonium ions are trapped within the lumen and excreted.

Total acid excretion (TAE) by the kidney is the sum of titratable acidity and urinary ammonium excretion. Net acid excretion (NAE) is the sum of these, minus any excreted bicarbonate. NAE approximates to 1 mmol/kg/day. It is influenced by the pH, $PaCO_2$ and potassium concentration of body fluids, by the effective circulating volume, by the action of mineralocorticoids and by the level of renal function.

Characteristic changes in arterial blood [H⁺], $PaCO_2$ and plasma [HCO₃⁻] in acid–base disturbances are shown in Box 9.18.

CLINICAL ASSESSMENT OF ACID–BASE DISORDERS

Disturbances in acid–base balance may be accompanied by central nervous system dysfunction and abnormalities of respiration. The history, particularly of chronic diseases such as diabetes or obstructive airways disease, and of recent acute illness or drug ingestion, is important. Often the cause is obvious because acid–base disturbances accompany a variety of serious acute disorders. Assessment of volume status is also important in these patients, as it will help to guide therapy. Arterial blood gas analysis is essential for precise characterisation.

METABOLIC ACIDOSIS

❓ Case example E
A 32-year-old man is admitted in a very ill state. He had been drinking with friends, but had not been seen for some hours. On admission he is barely conscious and is breathing heavily. His arterial blood gases are [H⁺] 98 nmol/l, $PaCO_2$ 2.7 kPa, [HCO₃⁻] 6 mmol/l, PaO_2 13 kPa. What is the likely diagnosis, how should it be confirmed, and what treatment is required?

Metabolic acidosis is characterised by a reduction in plasma bicarbonate and a rise in [H⁺]. The $PaCO_2$ is reduced secondarily by hyperventilation, which mitigates the rise in [H⁺] (see Box 9.18).

The source of hydrogen ions may be volatile acids or fixed acids. Volatile acids such as lactate, acetoacetic acid, hydroxybutyric acid and free fatty acids are produced in variable amounts and normally have relatively little renal excretion. They are normally removed by cellular metabolism in the liver and kidney with regeneration of bicarbonate. Fixed acids including hydrochloric, sulphuric and phosphoric acids can only be eliminated by renal excretion.

Insight into the overall buffering capacity of the body may be gained by calculating the anion gap. This represents those negative ions not normally measured in clinical practice, including phosphate, sulphate, lactate, ketoacids and albumin. A convenient formula is:

Anion gap = plasma [Na⁺] – (plasma [Cl⁻] + plasma [HCO₃⁻])

Values for the anion gap in health range from 8 to 14 mmol/l. Where excessive acid is added to the plasma, either by disordered metabolism or by addition of exogenous acid, or there is failure of acid excretion, the anion gap is increased. A useful mnemonic for the causes of a raised anion gap recalls Kussmaul, who described the classic breathing pattern of metabolic acidosis:

- K—ketosis (diabetes, alcoholism, malnutrition)
- U—uraemia
- SS—salicylate poisoning
- M—methanol poisoning
- A—ethylene (formerly spelt æthylene) glycol poisoning
- U—uraemia
- L—lactic acidosis.

On the other hand, metabolic acidosis with a normal anion gap is usually due to loss of bicarbonate (e.g. in diarrhoea) or the group of conditions known as renal tubular acidosis. In these conditions, plasma chloride rises.

Aetiology

The physiological disturbances that give rise to metabolic acidosis are shown in Box 9.19, and conditions in which these develop are listed in Box 9.20. Changes in [H⁺] in different types of acid–base disturbance are represented in Figure 9.15. In most situations, metabolic acidosis is accompanied by sodium and water depletion.

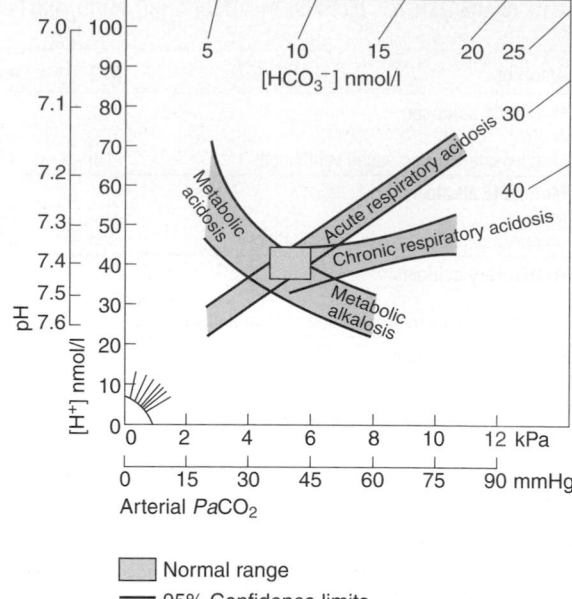

Fig. 9.15   **Changes in blood [H⁺], $PaCO_2$ and plasma [HCO₃⁻] in stable compensated acid–base disorders.** The rectangle indicates limits of normal reference ranges for [H⁺] and $PaCO_2$. The bands represent 95% confidence limits of single disturbances in human blood in vivo. When the point obtained by plotting [H⁺] against $PaCO_2$ does not fall within one of the labelled bands, compensation is incomplete or a mixed disorder is present.

9.19 DISTURBANCES WHICH GIVE RISE TO METABOLIC ACIDOSIS

- Over-production of acids other than H_2CO_3
- Ingestion of acids or potential acids
- Failure to excrete acids other than H_2CO_3 at a rate equal to their generation
- Loss of the base bicarbonate in urine or from the GI tract

Renal tubular acidosis (RTA) describes a group of conditions in which defects in renal function lead to a hyperchloraemic metabolic acidosis. Any condition affecting tubular function can lead to RTA. Three variants are described:

- proximal hypokalaemic RTA (formerly type II)—defective bicarbonate regeneration

---

9.20 METABOLIC ACIDOSIS

Mechanism	Clinical disorders	Accumulating acid	Anion gap
Addition of excessive acid to extracellular fluid			

Organic acidoses	Ketoacidosis
	  Diabetic
	  Alcoholism
	  Starvation
		Acetoacetic
		β-hydroxybutyric
			Increased

	Lactic acidosis	Lactic	Increased
Poisoning	Methanol poisoning	Formic	Increased
	Ethylene glycol poisoning	Glycolic and oxalic	Increased
	Salicylate poisoning	Salicylic and lactic	Increased
Failure to excrete acid at a normal rate			
Decreased GFR and inadequate renal ammonia production	Acute or chronic renal failure	Sulphuric, phosphoric, hydrochloric	Increased
Failure of the distal tubular H⁺ secretory system	Distal renal tubular acidosis	Hydrochloric	Normal
Loss of bicarbonate			
In urine	Proximal renal tubular acidosis	Hydrochloric	Normal
	Carbonic anhydrase inhibitors	Hydrochloric	Normal
From gastrointestinal tract	Diarrhoea, fistulae Ureterosigmoid anastomosis	Hydrochloric	Normal

9.21 CAUSES OF LACTIC ACIDOSIS

Group A—associated with tissue hypoxia	
• Shock from any cause (septic shock most common) • Respiratory failure	• Poisoning with cyanide or carbon monoxide • Severe anaemia

Group B—impaired mitochondrial function	
• Diabetes mellitus • Hepatic failure • Severe infection	• Drugs (biguanides such as metformin, salicylates, isoniazid, sorbitol) • Toxins (ethanol, methanol) • Congenital enzyme defects

• distal hypokalaemic RTA (formerly type I)—defective hydrogen ion secretion

• distal hyperkalaemic RTA (formerly type IV)—defective hydrogen ion secretion.

Systemic acidosis is most severe in distal hypokalaemic RTA, and is sometimes not present at all in distal hyperkalaemic RTA (which usually causes problems due to hyperkalaemia). Hypercalciuria, renal stones and nephrocalcinosis occur in up to 50% of those with distal hypokalaemic RTA. Fanconi's syndrome (see p. 623) often coexists with proximal hypokalaemic RTA. Patients with distal RTA are unable to lower urine pH below 5.3 in the face of systemic acidaemia.

One of the most common types of metabolic acidosis is lactic acidosis, which occurs when the rate of production of lactic acid from pyruvate in muscle, skin, brain and erythrocytes exceeds the rate of removal by liver and kidney. Causes of lactic acidosis are shown in Box 9.21. Group A causes are associated with hypotension and/or severe tissue hypoxia. Disorders of group B are not, but are associated instead with impaired mitochondrial respiration and increased lactate production. Diabetic ketoacidosis is discussed on page 651. In chronic renal failure, the most important factor limiting H^+ excretion is reduced production of NH_4^+ by the diminished mass of tubules (see p. 602).

Clinical features

Severe metabolic acidosis is clinically manifest as hyperventilation (Kussmaul's respiration), respiratory distress and fatigue, reduced cardiac output and arterial blood pressure, and cardiac dysrhythmias. Patients are frequently confused or drowsy. Insulin resistance, increased protein catabolism and hyperkalaemia frequently coexist. In many cases the clinical picture is dominated by the underlying disorder and the presence of sodium and water depletion.

Management

The cause of acidosis should be identified whenever possible. Organic acidoses such as ketoacidosis and lactic acidosis should be treated by:

• correction of the underlying abnormality (insulin deficiency, shock), which will diminish further production of organic acids (treatment of diabetic ketoacidosis and of lactic acidosis in diabetes is

described on pages 667–668; treatment of shock is described on page 195)

• resuscitation with appropriate colloids and/or crystalloids, which will allow cellular metabolism of the organic anions in the liver and kidney, with regeneration of water and bicarbonate.

Poisoning and metabolic acidosis due to fixed acid accumulation require treatment which increases their elimination, either by native kidney function or by extracorporeal therapies such as dialysis or haemofiltration (see p. 605).

Administration of extraneous buffer as sodium bicarbonate in the management of metabolic acidosis is controversial. Risks include hypervolaemia due to excessive sodium load, and overshoot alkalosis in the recovery period (particularly in organic acidoses). If it is used, blood $[H^+]$ and $[HCO_3^-]$ as well as the anion gap should be monitored closely.

In chronic renal failure, oral sodium bicarbonate supplements may be required on a long-term basis (see p. 604).

✓ Case example E: follow-up

The patient described on page 289 has severe acute metabolic acidosis, due to poisoning. His drink had probably been 'spiked' with methanol, which is metabolised to formic acid. Low $PaCO_2$ reflects partial respiratory compensation. Blood and urine should be sent to the laboratory for toxicology analysis—measurement of lactate, methanol and ethylene glycol.

The patient requires intravenous 1.26% sodium bicarbonate to restore safe $[H^+]$ ($\approx$ 70 nmol/l) over 12–24 hours. Intravenous fluids will establish a diuresis, and facilitate renal excretion of methanol and formic acid. If blood methanol level is high, oral ethanol is given to slow competitively the metabolism of methanol. Haemodialysis should be considered if there is any evidence of renal failure.

METABOLIC ALKALOSIS

❓ Case example F

A 44-year-old woman with a long history of indigestion begins to vomit at home. She becomes unwell after 4 days and is admitted to hospital because of marked muscle weakness. Her arterial blood gases are $[H^+]$ 28 nmol/l, $PaCO_2$ 6.5 kPa, $[HCO_3^-]$ 40 mmol/l, PaO_2 10.3 kPa, plasma potassium 2.1 mmol/l. What is the likely diagnosis and what treatment is required?

Metabolic alkalosis is less common than metabolic acidosis. It is characterised by an increase in plasma bicarbonate, a fall in blood $[H^+]$, and a small compensatory rise in $PaCO_2$ (see Fig. 9.15 and Box 9.18). In health, when plasma $[HCO_3^-]$ rises above normal, urinary excretion of HCO_3^- increases rapidly. It is therefore very unusual to observe metabolic alkalosis in the presence of normal renal function.

Aetiology

Commonly, several factors contribute to the development of metabolic alkalosis. It is convenient to consider an initiation phase, in which plasma $[HCO_3^-]$ increases, and a maintenance phase during which the raised plasma $[HCO_3^-]$ is sustained because of altered renal function (see Box 9.22).

There are important relationships between tubular handling of sodium, potassium and hydrogen ions. In particular, in the cortical collecting duct, where final adjustments of the urine composition are made, reabsorption of sodium via the ENaC channels generates an electrochemical gradient which effectively drives both potassium and hydrogen ions from the tubular cell into the lumen (see Fig. 9.8, p. 276). Thus, if the kidney is avidly retaining sodium, it cannot also retain potassium or hydrogen ions. If in addition the intracellular potassium concentration is low because of potassium depletion, the obligatory secretion of H^+ ions is even greater (and vice versa). When present in excess, aldosterone and other mineralocorticoids which drive tubular sodium reabsorption have a similar effect.

Chloride is also relevant because at various sites in the nephron, sodium can be reabsorbed along with either chloride or bicarbonate. If chloride is deficient, there is preferential reabsorption of bicarbonate, which will make an alkalosis worse and will prevent the additional excretion of bicarbonate by the distal tubule which is necessary to correct an established metabolic alkalosis.

The classic paradigm for metabolic alkalosis is sustained vomiting of gastric contents (e.g. pyloric stenosis). In health, when H^+ ions are secreted into the gastric lumen, bicarbonate from parietal cells is added to the blood; this is subsequently neutralised by reabsorption of the secreted H^+ in the small bowel. In sustained vomiting, the initial loss of H^+ ions from the body initiates the alkalosis. The kidney is unable to restore homeostasis by retaining H^+ ions because of the accumulating deficit of sodium and water, causing enhanced tubular sodium reabsorption. Because potassium is also lost in the vomit and there is an intracellular potassium deficit, the effect on tubular H^+ secretion is magnified and the alkalosis sustained. Chloride is also lost in the vomit, so there is enhanced bicarbonate reabsorption.

Use of diuretics, particularly if it is over-aggressive leading to ECF volume depletion, may have similar consequences. High renin, angiotensin and aldosterone levels drive distal sodium reabsorption, and because sodium reabsorption more proximally is inhibited by the drug, more sodium is delivered to the cortical collecting duct to undergo reabsorption 'in exchange' for H^+ and K^+.

The most common causes of metabolic alkalosis are shown in Box 9.23, and the pathogenesis is illustrated in Figure 9.16.

9.23 MOST COMMON CAUSES OF METABOLIC ALKALOSIS	
Loss of Na$^+$, Cl$^-$, H$^+$ and water (ECF depletion)	
• Vomiting or aspiration of gastric contents • Congenital chlorodiarrhoea[1]	• Administration of diuretics (thiazides, furosemide (frusemide), bumetanide)
Potassium depletion, excessive mineralocorticoid activity	
• See Box 9.16, page 287[2] • Primary aldosteronism • Cushing's syndrome • Bartter's syndrome	• Adrenal enzyme defects • Secondary aldosteronism • Administration of liquorice, carbenoxolone
Administration of exogenous alkali	
• Oral or i.v. HCO$_3^-$, citrate[3] • Administration of gluconate, acetate, lactate	

[1] A rare disorder associated with loss of H$^+$ and Cl$^-$ in diarrhoeal stools.
[2] Alkalosis is uncommon in K$^+$ depletion due to primary renal disease.
[3] Present in transfused blood.

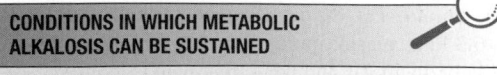

9.22 CONDITIONS IN WHICH METABOLIC ALKALOSIS CAN BE SUSTAINED

• Strong stimulus to reabsorb sodium (i.e. hypovolaemia), particularly in the presence of a low plasma chloride, and thus reduced filtered chloride*
• Increased secretion of H$^+$ by renal tubular cells:
    Increased delivery of sodium to the distal nephron (e.g. by loop diuretics)
    High PaCO$_2$ (e.g. chronic respiratory failure)
    Tubular cell K$^+$ depletion
    Increased mineralocorticoid activity

* Increased proportion of filtered sodium reabsorbed with bicarbonate.

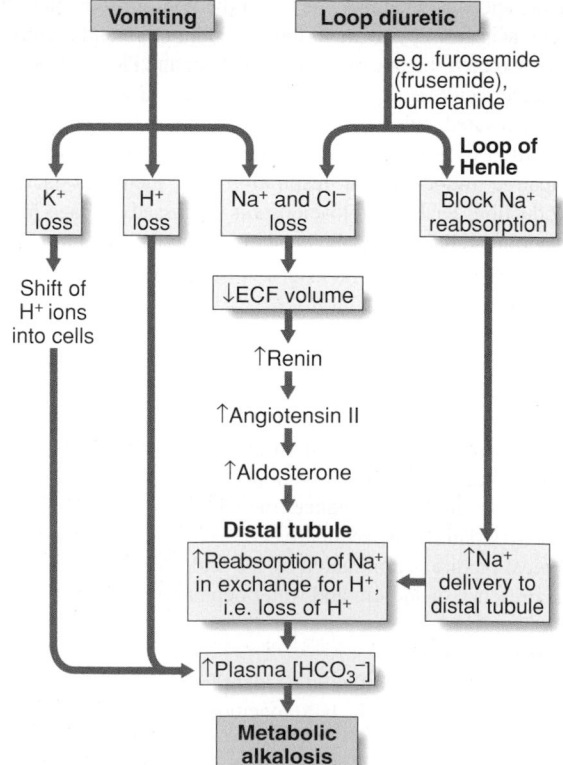

Fig. 9.16 Simplified scheme showing pathogenesis of metabolic alkalosis. Metabolic alkalosis can be due to loss of gastric contents or to use of loop diuretics.

Consequences of metabolic alkalosis

The alkalosis causes reduced ventilation and hence an increase in $PaCO_2$ which shifts [H^+] towards normal (respiratory compensation). CO_2 enters tubular cells freely and leads to enhanced H^+ secretion/bicarbonate reabsorption in the proximal tubule (see Fig. 9.5, p. 275). In some cases this means that the urine remains paradoxically acidic rather than alkaline.

Clinical features

Alkalosis rarely causes specific clinical symptoms. Acute alkalosis may cause tetany, either spontaneous or induced by Trousseau's manoeuvre (see p. 717) due to the acute fall in plasma ionised calcium. Apathy, confusion and drowsiness may occur in severe cases, although this is often multifactorial. Severe long-standing alkalosis may be associated with reduced renal function and uraemia.

Management

In patients without renal disease, restoration of the ECF volume and the plasma chloride and potassium concentrations will remove the stimulus to renal H^+ secretion and allow renal excretion of the excess bicarbonate. In patients who have lost gastric contents, e.g. in pyloric outlet obstruction, this should be done with isotonic (0.9%) sodium chloride solution (3–6 litres per 24 hours) and sufficient KCl to restore the K^+ deficit (40–60 mmol/day). Both strategies also serve to replace chloride losses. Patients who require continuous aspiration of gastric contents in preparation for surgery should have the volume of aspirate replaced by intravenous infusion of an equal amount of isotonic sodium chloride solution containing KCl (20 mmol/l).

Alkalosis associated with K^+ deficiency is corrected by sufficient KCl to restore body K^+ to normal. Diuretic-induced alkalosis can be difficult to correct. If possible, the diuretic should be stopped for a few days and the intake of sodium chloride increased. Any K^+ deficit must be corrected. When alkalosis is due to mineralocorticoid excess, the underlying disorder must be treated.

✔ Case example F: follow-up

The patient described on page 291 has a metabolic alkalosis, due to pyloric stenosis, caused in turn by a chronic duodenal ulcer. Vomiting has caused loss of potassium, H^+, sodium and chloride. There is a total body deficit of sodium, which stimulates tubular sodium reabsorption in the distal tubule (which can only be in exchange for either H^+ or K^+). The kidney therefore cannot conserve H^+ or K^+. Also, because of chloride deficit, more bicarbonate is reabsorbed than normal.

Isotonic (0.9%) sodium chloride solution, 3–6 litres per day, is required to correct the sodium chloride deficit. This removes the stimulus to sodium reabsorption and allows the kidney to conserve H^+ and K^+. Some intravenous K^+ will also be necessary (40–60 mmol/day). Surgery will be required to correct pyloric stenosis.

RESPIRATORY ACIDOSIS

❓ Case example G

A 56-year-old man, who has smoked heavily for many years, develops a worsening cough with purulent sputum, and is admitted to hospital because of difficulty in breathing. He is drowsy and cyanosed. His arterial blood gases are [H^+] 65 nmol/l, $PaCO_2$ 9.5 kPa, [HCO_3^-] 28 mmol/l, PaO_2 6.2 kPa. What is the likely diagnosis and what treatment is required?

Respiratory acidosis arises when the effective alveolar ventilation fails to keep pace with the rate of CO_2 production. As a result, $PaCO_2$, blood [HCO_3^-] and [H^+] all rise (see Fig. 9.15, p. 290).

The kidney responds by increased H^+ secretion, so that the urine becomes acid and bicarbonate is added to the blood. The distinction between respiratory acidosis and metabolic alkalosis can usually be made from knowledge of the cause of the disturbance, and the fact that, characteristically, [H^+] is raised in respiratory acidosis and reduced in metabolic alkalosis (see Box 9.18, p. 289).

Conditions acting to depress respiration are the most common causes of respiratory acidosis.

✔ Case example G: follow-up

The patient described above has acute respiratory acidosis, due to an infective exacerbation of obstructive pulmonary disease. If his respiratory failure became chronic, with a persistent rise in $PaCO_2$, the kidney would compensate by retaining bicarbonate, e.g. [H^+] 43 nmol/l, $PaCO_2$ 8.5 kPa, [HCO_3^-] 38 mmol/l, PaO_2 8.1 kPa.

The treatment aims to improve respiratory function —nebulised bronchodilators, physiotherapy, antibiotics, controlled low-flow oxygen (e.g. 28%).

RESPIRATORY ALKALOSIS

❓ Case example H

A 13-year-old schoolboy is brought to the casualty department, having become acutely unwell in the headmaster's office. He is alert and agitated, the respiratory rate is 35/min, and he complains of tingling in his hands. His arterial blood gases are [H^+] 29 nmol/l, $PaCO_2$ 2.8 kPa, [HCO_3^-] 22 mmol/l, PaO_2 16 kPa. What is the likely diagnosis and what treatment is required?

Respiratory alkalosis occurs when there is excessive loss of CO_2 due to over-ventilation of the lungs. $PaCO_2$ and H^+ fall. The low $PaCO_2$ results in reduced renal Na^+/H^+ exchange, loss of bicarbonate in the urine, and a fall in plasma bicarbonate which mitigates the fall in blood H+. Common causes include pregnancy, pulmonary embolus, hysterical over-breathing and excessive assisted ventilation.

☑ Case example H: follow-up

The patient described above has acute respiratory alkalosis, due to hyperventilation induced by anxiety. The tingling is due to a fall in plasma ionised calcium caused by the alkalosis.

He needs to be calmed down using reassurance and discussion, and by persuading him to breathe slowly.

MIXED ACID–BASE DISORDERS

Particularly in very ill patients, there may be both metabolic and respiratory factors contributing to an acid-base disturbance. The most common pattern is a mixed metabolic and respiratory acidosis. Management involves the treatments described above for each element of the disturbance.

DISORDERS OF DIVALENT ION METABOLISM

Calcium metabolism in health and disease is discussed on pages 714–715 and 1030.

PHOSPHATE

Phosphate is absorbed via a sodium-phosphate transporter in the jejunum and ileum. The proportion of dietary intake absorbed depends upon the amount of natural phosphate binders in the diet (phytates). Phosphate is freely filtered at the glomerulus, with 85% of this reabsorbed in the proximal tubule. Excess levels of parathyroid hormone decrease this reabsorption, leading to hypophosphataemia in primary hyperparathyroidism.

HYPOPHOSPHATAEMIA

Most body phosphate (80%) is in the bony skeleton; around 20% is in cells, predominantly muscle. Phosphate molecules are critical to many biochemical processes, including cell energetics (adenosine triphosphate, ATP), intracellular signalling (cyclic adenosine monophosphate, cAMP) and nucleic acid synthesis. A body deficit of phosphate therefore has widespread effects. In the presence of a plasma phosphate lower than 0.4 mmol/l (normal range 0.8–1.4 mmol/l), widespread cell dysfunction and death may occur. Rapid changes in plasma phosphate usually reflect redistribution from plasma to cells. In this respect, phosphate behaves similarly to potassium, and enters cells in association with insulin-stimulated carbohydrate metabolism. In clinical

9.24 CONSEQUENCES OF HYPOPHOSPHATAEMIA AND PHOSPHATE DEPLETION

- Muscle pain and weakness, increased plasma creatine kinase
- Respiratory muscle weakness
- Cardiac arrhythmias
- Neuroencephalopathy—confusion, convulsions, coma
- Haemolysis
- Hypercalciuria, hypermagnesuria

9.25 CAUSES OF REDUCED PLASMA PHOSPHATE CONCENTRATION*

Hyperparathyroidism (by increased urinary excretion)

- Primary
- Secondary
  e.g. Vitamin D deficiency/osteomalacia
  Malabsorption
  Familial hypophosphataemic rickets

Increased carbohydrate metabolism and insulin action (by shift into cells)

- Intravenous glucose infusions
- Insulin infusion
- Treatment of diabetic ketoacidosis
- Parenteral nutrition
- Nutritional recovery syndrome

Alkalosis (by shift into cells)

- Metabolic, e.g. bicarbonate infusion
- Respiratory, e.g. artificial hyperventilation

Reduced oral absorption of phosphate

- Oral phosphate-binding agents, e.g. aluminium hydroxide
- Starvation (only minor reduction because of ↓ carbohydrate metabolism)
- Chronic alcoholism, alcohol withdrawal

Phosphate removal

- Haemodialysis
- Peritoneal dialysis

Extracellular fluid volume expansion

* **N.B.** Hypophosphataemia is often multifactorial in origin.

situations where carbohydrate is administered acutely, with a background of impaired nutrition and a total body phosphate deficit, severe hypophosphataemia may ensue, with the consequences shown in Box 9.24. This is referred to as the nutritional recovery syndrome. Alkalosis also stimulates a shift into cells. Causes of hypophosphataemia are shown in Box 9.25.

Management

In many cases, and particularly if there is no prior body phosphate depletion, hypophosphataemia is transient and of no clinical significance. The duration and severity should be taken into account when deciding on treatment. Sustained values of < 0.4 mmol/l require therapy. Oral treatment is preferred. Milk is a good source (up to 2 litres/day) or oral supplements such as Phosphate-Sandoz (16 mmol phosphate, 20 mmol sodium, 3 mmol potassium per tablet), one 4–8-hourly. Intravenous therapy should be given with care, and in general should not exceed 18 mmol/24 hours of a mixed phosphate solution. Plasma concentrations of calcium, phosphate, potassium and magnesium must be closely monitored during treatment.

HYPERPHOSPHATAEMIA

This is most commonly seen in acute or chronic renal failure, or in states of massive cell necrosis (acute rhabdomyolysis, acute haemolysis or tumour lysis syndrome). Sustained hyperphosphataemia is associated with a risk of metastatic calcification, secondary stimulation of the parathyroid glands, and symptoms such as pruritus. Treatment with oral phosphate binders and/or dialysis may be required (see p. 605).

MAGNESIUM

Disorders of magnesium metabolism are almost unknown in isolation, and symptoms are usually attributable to accompanying changes in potassium, calcium or acid–base status.

Aetiology of magnesium depletion

The important causes of magnesium depletion are shown in Box 9.26.

Clinical features of magnesium depletion

These are predominantly neuromuscular, with tremor and choreiform movements. Depression, confusion, agitation, epileptic fits and hallucinations also occur. Cardiac arrhythmias, particularly torsades de pointes (see p. 411), may occur. The diagnosis can be confirmed by finding a plasma magnesium concentration of less than 0.7 mmol/l. Since most magnesium is intracellular, a body deficit can be present with a normal plasma concentration.

Up to 60% of patients with hypomagnesaemia will also be hypokalaemic, and up to 40% will be hypocalcaemic. The clinical manifestations of these disturbances may dominate.

Gitelman's syndrome is characterised by hypokalaemia and hypomagnesaemia and is caused by a mutation in the thiazide-sensitive NaCl cotransporter in the distal tubule (see Fig. 9.7, p. 276).

Management of magnesium depletion

Magnesium is very poorly absorbed orally and oral supplements are of little value. In the presence of significant symptoms the condition is best treated by giving magnesium

9.26 CAUSES OF MAGNESIUM DEPLETION

Reduced intake
- Protein-energy malnutrition (PEM)
- Prolonged administration of Mg++-free intravenous fluids

Loss from GI tract
- Vomiting
- Chronic diarrhoea (malabsorption, laxative abuse)
- Fistulae; aspiration of GI contents

Losses in urine

Extrarenal factors acting on the kidney
- Drugs, e.g. loop diuretics, gentamicin, cisplatin
- Ketoacidosis
- Chronic alcoholism
- Hyperparathyroidism
- Primary or secondary aldosteronism

Renal disease
- Gitelman's syndrome
- Post-obstructive diuresis
- Diuretic phase of acute tubular necrosis
- Renal tubular acidosis

Miscellaneous
- Acute pancreatitis
- Excessive lactation

chloride intravenously. Caution is necessary; rates exceeding 1 mmol/hr should only be given in closely supervised environments. When renal function is impaired the amount of magnesium should be reduced; this is almost the only situation in which hypermagnesaemia can occur, presenting with symptoms similar to hyperkalaemia. Treatment involves improving renal function.

FURTHER INFORMATION

Abraham WT, Schrier RW. Body fluid volume regulation and health in disease. Adv Intern Med 1994; 39:23–47.
Arieff AI. Management of hypernatraemia. BMJ 1993; 307:305–308.
Brater DC. Diuretic therapy. New Engl J Med 1998; 339:387–395.
Gennari FJ. Hypokalaemia. New Engl J Med 1998; 339:451–458.
He FJ, MacGregor GA. Beneficial effects of potassium. BMJ 2001; 323:497–501.
Latta K, Hisano S, Chan JC. Perturbations in potassium balance. Clin Lab Med 1993; 13:149–156.
Narins RG, ed. Clinical disorders of fluid and electrolyte metabolism. 5th edn. New York: McGraw-Hill; 1994.
Pearce SH. Straightening out the renal tubule: advances in the molecular basis of the inherited tubulopathies. QJM 1998; 91:5–12.
Preuss HG. Fundamentals of clinical acid–base evaluation. Clin Lab Med 1993; 13:103–116.

Nutritional, metabolic and environmental disease

C. SUMMERTON • P. SHETTY • L.N. SANDLE • S. WATT

There can be little doubt about the influence of nutritional factors on human health and disease. Obesity, with all its attendant consequences, is increasing both in the developed world and in urban centres in developing countries. In contrast, numerous adults and children die each year from the effects of famine and starvation. In developed countries, inappropriate dietary intakes have been linked with diseases such as coronary heart disease and cancer. In other parts of the world, deficiencies of simple vitamins lead to avoidable conditions such as blindness in children. The individual clinician may feel daunted by such global problems. However, a proper understanding of nutrition is essential in order to deal with the needs of individual patients and to inform the decisions of public policy-makers.

This chapter also covers two specific metabolic diseases—namely, porphyria and amyloidosis—and a range of common environmental disorders related to diving, altitude and exposure to high or low temperatures.

NUTRITIONAL ASSESSMENT AND NUTRITIONAL NEEDS

Nutrient goals have been devised by international committees, to assist governments in setting strategies to influence patterns of food consumption. Such goals have been based on systematic reviews and represent the appropriate average intake of individuals, to ensure the optimal health of a population (see Box 10.1). The upper and lower limits have been chosen to take account of the existing range seen in different healthy populations.

10.1 POPULATION NUTRIENT GOALS		
	Limits for population average intakes	
Nutrient	**Lower**	**Upper**
Total fat (% of total energy)	15	30
Saturated fatty acids (% total energy)	0	10
Polyunsaturated fatty acids (% total energy)	3	7
Dietary cholesterol (mg/day)	0	300
Total carbohydrate (% total energy)	55	75
Complex carbohydrate (% total energy)	50	70
Dietary fibre (g/day)		
As non-starch polysaccharides	16	24
As total dietary fibre	27	40
Free sugars (% total energy)	0	10
Protein (% total energy)	10	15
Salt (g/day)	ND	6
ND = not defined.		

NUTRITIONAL ASSESSMENT

A systematic investigation of an individual's nutritional health normally consists of four components: dietary history, clinical examination, anthropometry and laboratory investigations.

DIETARY HISTORY

In medical use this is usually qualitative: for example, has the patient been eating too little food, or omitting any major foods, or has an unusual diet been taken? Quantitative nutrient intake is best assessed by a dietitian, who is skilled in the area of dietary assessment. Estimates of intake can be made using a number of methods. These include taking a dietary history or asking the patient to recall food intake over a 24-hour period. Patients may also be instructed to keep a food diary or to complete a food frequency questionnaire. By using food tables, usually in computer form, the daily intake of the major nutrients can be obtained. This can then be compared with tables of recommended nutrient intake.

CLINICAL EXAMINATION

Thinness, oedema, pallor, weakness and other signs described in this chapter may be found in patients with nutritional deficiency but it is important not to wait for the classic features of a deficiency disease to develop before intervening with nutritional support. Coexisting illness may obscure or confuse signs of malnutrition.

Body mass index

Body mass index (BMI) is calculated by measuring a person's weight in kilograms and then dividing by that person's height in metres squared (kg/m^2). For example, an adult weighing 70 kg with a height of 1.75 metres has a BMI of $70/1.75^2 = 22.9$. The advantage of using this index, rather than weight alone, is that it is height-independent, such that tall and short people of similar proportions have a similar BMI. The internationally accepted range of BMIs in adults is shown in Box 10.2.

10.2 BODY MASS INDEX (WEIGHT/HEIGHT²)	
• Underweight	< 18.5
• Normal	18.5–24.9
• Overweight	25.0–29.9
• Obese	30.0–39.9
• Extremely obese	> 40

ANTHROPOMETRY

Changes of body weight reflect the water and/or energy (calorie) balance. If there is no unusual loss of water, each kilogram lost corresponds to 25–29.3 MJ (6000–7000 kcal) of energy (mostly adipose tissue). If there is increased protein catabolism, the energy value of the weight lost is less. Thus, regular weighing of patients is valuable in management. Wasting of both subcutaneous fat and muscle mass should also be monitored. If weighing is impractical, these observations are more critical. Clinical observation can be made more objective by measuring mid-arm circumference and triceps skinfold thickness. The relative contributions of fat and muscle can be calculated (mid-arm muscle circumference = arm circumference − triceps skinfold), but accurate measurement of skinfold thickness requires special callipers.

LABORATORY INVESTIGATIONS

Investigations can provide information about protein deficiency and can also indicate specific micronutrient deficiencies.

While the plasma albumin concentration can be used to assess visceral protein depletion, this value reflects synthetic rate, distribution in body pools and tissue catabolism or loss of protein from the body; hence it is important not to equate hypoproteinaemia with protein malnutrition. Injury, inflammation and the presence of liver disease all reduce the plasma albumin concentration. The ratio of C-reactive protein (see p. 970) to albumin therefore provides a better estimate of protein depletion. Plasma transferrin and pre-albumin are sometimes used as more sensitive indices of visceral protein status but both can be influenced by other conditions. Urinary nitrogen (or urea nitrogen) reveals the degree of protein catabolism.

Specific biochemical tests for micronutrient deficiencies are available in most hospital laboratories. These include the measurement of serum vitamin B_{12}, red cell folate levels and serum ferritin (see p. 1219).

NUTRIENT AND ENERGY REQUIREMENTS

All foods provide both nutrients and energy. If energy requirements are not being met, then it is highly unlikely that nutrient supply will be adequate, unless the diet has been carefully managed and computed, such as in a diet prescribed for weight loss. Hence meeting energy requirements is the fundamental goal of nutritional support.

NUTRIENT REQUIREMENTS

Various expert bodies have drawn up dietary reference values for the normal individual. These include the UK Department of Health, the European Union and the World Health Organisation. The recommendations apply to groups of healthy people and do not refer to situations where medical treatment of deficiency is required. The values suggested for different nutrients are found in the publications detailed on page 336.

ENERGY REQUIREMENTS

The largest component of energy expenditure is attributed to the lean body mass and is known as the basal metabolic rate (BMR). The lean body mass (related to weight and height) declines with age and is lower in women than in men. Extra energy is required for growth, for pregnancy and lactation, for muscular activity and during a febrile illness. There is some variation in energy expended between individuals of the same size, age, sex and activity. Adaptation occurs to an inadequate energy intake and, to a lesser degree, to excess energy intake. The largest variable in determining energy requirements is the energy attributed to exercise and movement. Approximate daily energy requirements are listed in Box 10.3.

10.3 DAILY ENERGY REQUIREMENTS

Circumstances	Requirements	
	Healthy adult females	Healthy adult males
At rest	6.7 MJ (1600 kcal)	8.4 MJ (2000 kcal)
Light work	8.4 MJ (2000 kcal)	11.3 MJ (2700 kcal)
Heavy work	9.4 MJ (2250 kcal)	14.6 MJ (3500 kcal)

ENERGY-YIELDING NUTRIENTS

Three nutrients can act as energy substrates: carbohydrates, fat and protein. Protein has a profoundly negative effect on appetite and its use as an energy substrate should not be contemplated for this and other biochemical reasons. Carbohydrates and fat are the most important energy substrates and have additional functional roles.

Carbohydrates

A classification of the different carbohydrates is shown in Box 10.4, based on the degree of polymerisation of monosaccharide units. The 'available' carbohydrates (starches and sugars) supply the major part of the energy in a normal diet. No individual carbohydrate is an essential nutrient as the body can make it for itself from protein. However, if the available carbohydrate intake is less than 100 g per day, ketosis is likely to occur. Sugars are found in fruits, milk (lactose) and some vegetables. Starches are mostly found in cereals, root vegetables and legumes.

Sugars

Sugars are classified as intrinsic (naturally incorporated in the cellular structure of fruits, milk etc.) or extrinsic (extracted, refined or concentrated, e.g. beet or cane sucrose). Intrinsic sugars and the foods that contain them are thought to be more acceptable nutritionally than extrinsic sugars because they are associated with other nutrients naturally present in the food.

Dietary goals. There is little doubt that the ingestion of free refined sugar is a major factor leading to dental caries. Excessive consumption of sugar also leads to hyperinsulinaemia. This has been associated with the development of hyperlipoproteinaemia, atherosclerosis and the formation

10.4 DIETARY CARBOHYDRATES

Class	Components	Examples
Free sugars	Monosaccharides Disaccharides	Glucose, fructose Sucrose, lactose, maltose
Short-chain carbohydrates	Oligosaccharides	Maltodextrins, fructo-oligosaccharides
Starch	Rapidly digestible starch Slowly digestible starch Resistant starch	
Non-starch polysaccharides	Plant cell wall NSP Other NSP	Cellulose Pectin

and increased growth of certain tumours (e.g. breast and colonic carcinomas). It is for these reasons that the recommended intake of refined sugar has been set at between 0% and 15% of total energy intake.

Starches

Starches are found in cereal foods (wheat, rice), root foods (potatoes, cassava) and legumes. They are the nutrients which provide the largest proportion of calories in most diets around the world. Although all starches are polymers of glucose, linked by the same 1–4 glycosidic linkages, they do not all behave in the same way when they are eaten.

Some starches are digested promptly by salivary and then pancreatic amylase and produce a steep rise in blood glucose. Other starches are more slowly digested because they are protected in the structure of the food, because of the crystal structure or because the molecule is unbranched (amylose). After ingestion, the blood glucose rise is flatter and lower. The glycaemic index (see Box 10.5) quantifies the effect of different carbohydrates on the blood glucose after a test meal. A small percentage of dietary starch may completely escape digestion in the small intestine and pass unchanged into the large intestine, where it is fermented by the resident bacteria. This resistant starch thus behaves in much the same way as dietary fibre and is thought to confer a beneficial effect on the intestinal mucosa.

Non-starch polysaccharides

Non-starch polysaccharides (NSP), also known as dietary fibre, constitute the natural packing of plant foods. They can be defined as those parts of food which are not digested by human enzymes. The principal classes of NSP are cellulose, hemicelluloses, lignins, pectins and gums. These are all polysaccharides except lignin, which occurs with cellulose in the structure of plants. Pectins and gums are viscous not fibrous.

Some types of NSP, notably the hemicellulose of wheat, increase the water-holding capacity of colonic contents and the bulk of faeces. They relieve simple constipation, appear to prevent diverticulosis and may reduce the risk of cancer of the colon. Other viscous, indigestible polysaccharides like pectin and guar gum have greater effect in the upper gastrointestinal tract. They tend to slow gastric emptying, contribute to satiety, and may flatten the glucose tolerance curve and reduce plasma cholesterol concentration.

NSP or dietary fibre (and resistant starch) is partly fermented in the large intestine by resident bacterial flora, yielding a small quantity of volatile fatty acids, which are absorbed through the colonic mucosa. Flatus formation is common.

Dietary goals. These have been calculated largely from studies of the effect of fibre on bowel action. On a worldwide basis, 16–24 g/day of NSP is the recommended intake.

Fats

With their high calorie value (38 KJ or 9 kcal/g), fats are useful to people with large energy requirements. However, their high energy density makes them an insidious cause of obesity for sedentary people. Fats are described as saturated if there are no double bonds between any of the carbon atoms. A monounsaturated fatty acid has one double bond and a polyunsaturated fatty acid has two or more (see Fig. 10.1 for nomenclature). Saturated fats, especially those containing myristic (14:0) and palmitic (16:0) acids, increase plasma low-density lipoproteins and total cholesterol. Polyunsaturated fatty acids can be divided into two main groups, depending on the distance of their first double bond (see Fig. 10.1) from the methyl ($-CH_3$, ω) end of the molecule. The $\omega6$ group of polyunsaturated fatty acids consists of linoleic acid (18:2 $\omega6$), the principal polyunsaturated fatty acid in plant seed oils, γ-linolenic acid (18:3 $\omega6$) and

---

10.5 GLYCAEMIC INDEX

- The glycaemic index is the incremental area under the 2-hour plasma glucose curve after eating the amount of a food containing 50 g carbohydrate
- The glycaemic index is high for bread, potatoes and glucose, and lower for pasta, legumes and wholegrain cereals. The index may be useful in constructing therapeutic diets for diabetes

---

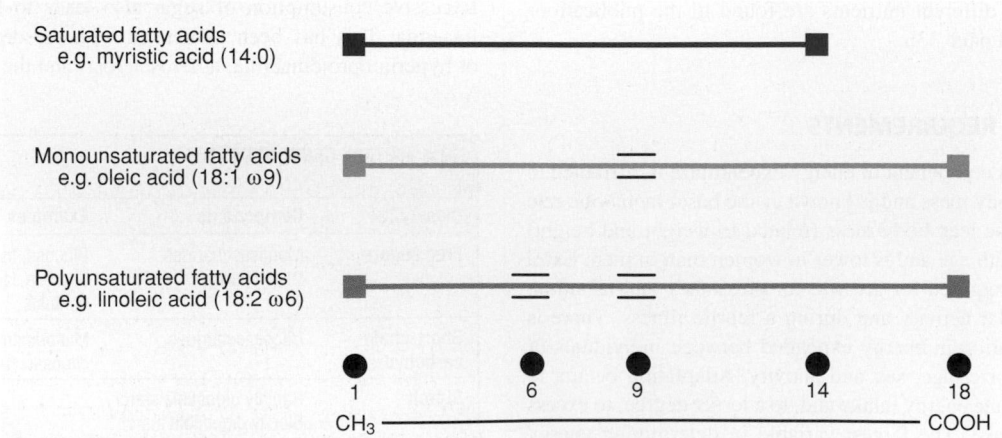

Fig. 10.1 Schematic representation of fatty acids. A standard nomenclature is used whereby the number of carbon atoms is specified and the number and position of the double bond relative to the methyl (-CH$_3$, ω) end of the molecule indicated after a colon.

arachidonic acid (20:4 ω6). The ω3 series of polyunsaturated fatty acids (e.g. docosahexanoic, 22:6 ω3) occur in fish oils and in the lipids of the human brain and retina. They are inhibitors of thrombosis and appear to act as competitive antagonists of thromboxane A_2 formation. Purified fish oils (e.g. ω3 marine triglycerides) may reduce the tendency to thrombosis in people with coronary heart disease. They also lower plasma triglyceride levels.

Linoleic acid (18:2 ω6) and α-linolenic acid (18:3 ω3) are termed essential fatty acids as they cannot be synthesised in the body and have to be obtained from the diet. Linoleic acid is a precursor of certain prostaglandins and leukotrienes.

Essential fatty acid deficiency is rare in humans but has been reported in patients fed solely by total parenteral nutrition (TPN) for long periods without fat emulsions. Free fatty acid mobilisation from adipose tissue is inhibited and tissues in the rest of the body become depleted. The main clinical manifestation is a scaly dermatitis.

Dietary goals. The dietary goals for fat consumption take account of the impact of fat intake on the development of coronary heart disease, the development of obesity and the increased risk of cancers. The figures for the recommended dietary intake are summarised in Box 10.1 (see p. 298).

Proteins

Proteins form the main structural component of body cells and an adequate intake is essential for health. Proteins are made up of some 20 different amino acids, of which nine are indispensable for normal synthesis of the different proteins in the body and for maintaining nitrogen balance in adults (also referred to as essential amino acids; see Box 10.6). These nine cannot be synthesised within the body and can only be obtained from dietary sources. Another group of amino acids are described as conditionally essential, which means that they can be synthesised from one or more of the essential amino acids, as long as there is an adequate dietary supply (see Box 10.7). The dispensable (or non-essential) amino acids can be synthesised in the body by transamination, provided there is a sufficient supply of amino groups.

The nutritional value of different proteins depends on the relative proportions of indispensable amino acids they contain (sometimes referred to as the biological value). Proteins of animal origin, particularly from eggs, milk and meat, are generally of higher biological value than the proteins of vegetable origin, which are low in one or more of the indispensable amino acids. However, when two different vegetable proteins are eaten together (e.g. a cereal and a legume), their amino acid patterns can complement one another and produce a mix of indispensable amino acids

10.6 INDISPENSABLE (OR ESSENTIAL) AMINO ACIDS* ℹ
• Tryptophan   • Valine
• Histidine   • Phenylalanine
• Methionine   • Lysine
• Threonine   • Leucine
• Isoleucine
* In approximate ascending order of dietary requirement.

10.7 PRECURSORS OF CONDITIONALLY ESSENTIAL AMINO ACIDS ℹ	
Amino acid	**Precursors**
Cysteine	Methionine, serine
Tyrosine	Phenylalanine
Arginine	Glutamine/glutamate, aspartate
Proline	Glutamate
Glycine	Serine, choline

with an adequate protein nutritive value. This is the principle of protein supply in a vegan or totally vegetarian diet.

Dietary goals. The usual recommendation for an adequate protein intake is 10% of the total calories, i.e. about 65 g per day for the average adult. The minimum requirement is around 40 g of protein with a high proportion of indispensable amino acids or a high biological value.

NUTRITIONAL AND METABOLIC DISORDERS

OBESITY

Obesity is an increasing problem in the developed world and has substantial health effects. In the United Kingdom, 50% of the adult population are overweight (BMI 25–29.9) and 20% are obese (BMI ≥ 30; see p. 298 for calculation of BMI). Fat deposition results from the discrepancy between energy consumption and expenditure. A small excess consumption of only 0.2–0.8 MJ (50–200 kcal) daily will lead to a weight gain of 2–20 kg over a period of 4–10 years. Excess weight gain usually starts when individuals are aged between 20 and 40, with maximum body weight being achieved in middle age. Weight tends to stabilise when the increased metabolic demands of the body balance the energy intake. Once weight has been gained, it is very unusual to lose it spontaneously before the age of 65. If there is significant unexpected weight loss, a careful search should be made for underlying illness (see p. 769).

Aetiology

In a few cases of obesity, specific causal factors can be identified and treated (see Box 10.8). However, for the most part, the aetiology of obesity arises from a complex interplay of behavioural and genetic factors.

Behavioural factors

There has been a substantial increase in the prevalence of obesity in developed countries over the past 20 years. However, studies of reported food intake in the UK show that individuals are consuming no more in the way of energy than they did 20 years ago. The major factor leading to obesity in the population therefore seems to be an overall decrease in activity levels. Thus, public health measures to reduce obesity in the population might be more appropriately targeted in this area, rather than simply on a reduction of

10.8 SPECIFIC CAUSES OF WEIGHT GAIN

Endocrine factors

- Hypothyroidism
- Cushing's syndrome
- Hypothalamic tumours or injury
- Insulinoma

Drug treatments

- Tricyclic antidepressants
- Sulphonylurea drugs
- Oral contraceptive pill (some agents)
- Corticosteroids
- Sodium valproate

Genetic

- Prader–Willi syndrome (childhood obesity with abnormal appearance and CNS function)

In the general population, there is confirmation from twin and adoption studies of a genetic influence on obesity. The pattern of inheritance suggests a polygenic disorder, with small contributions from a number of different genes. Overall estimates of the contribution of genetic factors to weight gain range from 25 to 70%. Genetic probes have been used to scan the human genome for loci associated with obesity. To date, there has been little success in describing any genetic predisposition to common obesity.

In obese individuals, two distinct phenotypes are apparent: generalised obesity and abdominal obesity (see Fig. 10.2). Abdominal obesity is recognised by measuring waist circumference or waist:hip ratio. These subgroups have different clinical problems and health risks. Abdominal obesity is a strong indicator for the development of coronary artery disease. This phenotype is also associated with insulin resistance and the development of type 2 diabetes mellitus.

food intake. A difference in physical activity accounts for the higher prevalence of obesity in lower social classes. The increase in weight with age is also a reflection of the reduction in activity levels.

Other important behavioural factors predisposing to obesity are:

- High-fat diets, since these do not switch off appetite as well as carbohydrates and protein. Also fat consumption induces very little energy expenditure as most is stored. Studies have shown that the prevalence of obesity is greatest in those eating proportionally more fats.
- Snacking and the loss of formalised meal patterns, which reduce the conscious recognition of foods eaten.
- Consumption of energy-dense foods (and drinks), often high in fat and sugar but low in bulk. This increases energy intake substantially.
- Alcohol consumption, which promotes weight gain by providing substantial energy. It can also stimulate appetite and loosen restraint.
- Giving up smoking, which induces a fall in energy expenditure and leads to an average weight gain of 2.8 kg in males and 3.8 kg in females. Nevertheless, the risk of smoking is so substantial that a rise in weight of 11 kg would be required to negate the benefit of giving up smoking 20 cigarettes per day.

Genetic factors

A few rare single gene disorders have been identified which lead to a symptom complex including obesity. These include mutations of the melanocortin-4 receptor (MC4R) that accounts for approximately 5% of severe early-onset obesity, the Prader–Willi syndrome (see p. 343) and mutations in the leptin gene. Leptin is an adipose-derived hormone, which acts on the hypothalamus and was originally thought to be a powerful homeostatic factor for maintaining body weight. Plasma leptin levels correlate with fat stores and respond to changes in energy balance. However, the initial view of leptin as a simple anti-obesity hormone has been superseded by an appreciation of its more complex effects in energy balance and a recognition of its involvement in the control of neuro-endocrine factors, immunity and development.

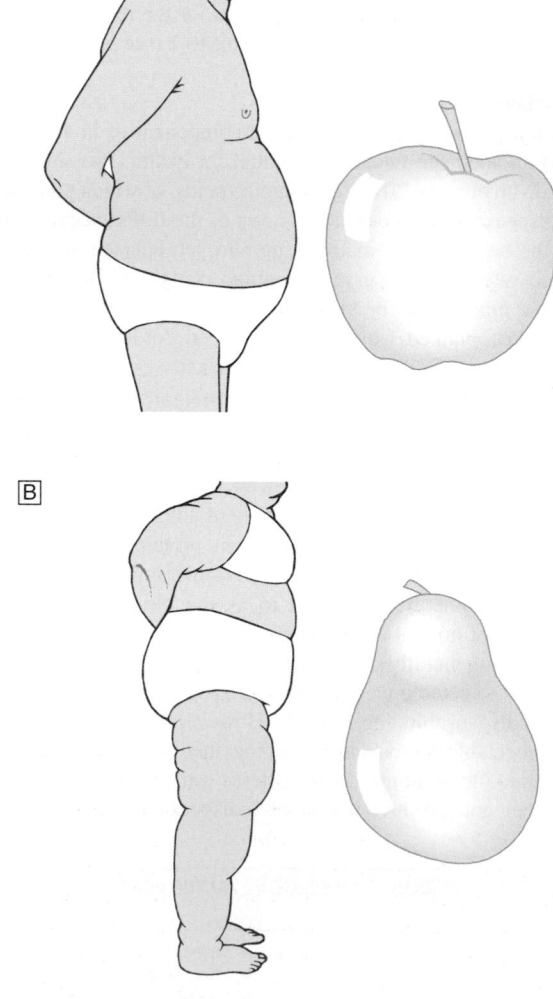

Fig. 10.2   Abdominal obesity and generalised obesity.
A Abdominal obesity (apple shape). B Generalised obesity where fat deposition is mainly on the hips and thighs (pear shape).

Complications of weight gain

Obesity has effects on both mortality and morbidity. Changes in mortality are difficult to analyse due to the compound effects of cigarette smoking. However, it is clear that the lowest mortality rates are seen in individuals with a BMI of 18.5–24. Data from population studies, such as that in Framingham, USA, show a clearly increased risk of death with increasing weight. For individuals aged between 30 and 42, the risk of death increases by 1% for each 0.5 kg weight rise. For individuals between the ages of 50 and 62, this figure becomes 2% for each 0.5 kg weight rise. Coronary heart disease is the major cause of death but cancer rates are also increased in the overweight, especially colorectal cancer in males and cancer of the gallbladder, biliary tract, breast, endometrium and cervix in females. Problems of morbidity increase steadily as the BMI increases above 25. Box 10.9 summarises the many medical complications of obesity. The only medical benefit of obesity is seen in osteoporosis, where bone density increases in response to excess weight (see p. 1026). Obesity may lead to profound psychological consequences for individuals. Society also suffers from the effects of obesity-related disability and early retirement.

Effects of weight reduction

In obese individuals, there is considerable health benefit from a moderate weight reduction (see Box 10.10). It is not necessary to return to an 'ideal weight' to achieve these benefits. Indeed, to have this as a therapeutic goal is generally unrealistic and will only lead to frustration and demoralisation for patient and health-care worker alike. There are some adverse consequences of losing weight. In one study women who lost 14 kg in weight had a 44% increased risk of clinically relevant gallstone disease. Bone density is typically reduced by weight loss, although there is no information regarding the consequences of this on overall fracture rate. Overall, the benefits of weight loss considerably outweigh these disadvantages.

Strategies for the management of obesity

Obesity cannot be treated in isolation and other risk factors must also be borne in mind: for example, smoking, the consumption of excess alcohol, and the presence of hyperlipidaemia or hypertension. Most overweight and obese patients will be encountered and managed in a primary health-care or community care setting.

Figure 10.3 outlines a suggested strategy for weight management in primary health care. Some patients will enter the programme through self-referral, while others might be identified by a practice audit of waist circumference and BMI or by opportunistic screening. Calculation of the BMI, together with an assessment of risk factors, will identify those patients who should be encouraged to enter a weight reduction programme. Smoking cessation (see p. 511) should be a priority goal for all patients. Unfortunately, stopping smoking increases appetite and decreases metabolic rate. Thus, to prevent such weight gain dietary advice on healthy eating should be given to all patients giving up smoking.

10.9 MEDICAL COMPLICATIONS OF WEIGHT GAIN

- Type 2 diabetes mellitus
- Hypertension
- Stroke
- Hyperlipidaemia
- Coronary heart disease
- Gallstones
- Increased risk of certain cancers
- Breathlessness and respiratory disease
- Menstrual abnormalities and hirsutism
- Pregnancy complications
- Weight-related musculoskeletal disorders and arthritis
- Stress incontinence
- Obstructive sleep apnoea

10.10 BENEFITS OF MODERATE WEIGHT LOSS

A 10 kg loss in weight will lead to the following health improvements:

Mortality

- > 20% fall in total mortality
- > 30% fall in diabetes-related deaths
- > 40% fall in obesity-related cancer deaths

Blood pressure

- Fall of 10 mmHg systolic blood pressure
- Fall of 20 mmHg diastolic blood pressure

Diabetes mellitus

- Fall of 50% in fasting glucose

Lipids

- Fall of 10% in total cholesterol
- Fall of 15% in low-density lipoprotein cholesterol
- Fall of 30% in triglycerides
- Increase of 8% in high-density lipoprotein cholesterol

A successful weight loss programme will have a number of components:

- Support from a trained health-care professional in a group setting since greater weight loss is achieved using groups than with individual consultations. This may reflect the interplay and mutual support of the individuals in the group.
- A diet consisting of a moderate reduction in energy intake of about 2.5 MJ (600 kcal) less than expenditure assessed on weight, sex and age. This actually produces a greater weight loss than stricter diets (e.g. 4.2 MJ/1000 kcal) due to improved compliance. Most diets aim to reduce fat intake. Starvation diets are potentially dangerous due to a risk of sudden death from heart disease exacerbated by profound loss in muscle mass and the development of arrhythmias secondary to elevated free fatty acids and deranged electrolytes. To be most effective, the dietary change should involve the patient's entire household.
- Behavioural modification therapy which is designed to support a process of change in the individual's attitude, perception and behaviour as regards food intake, lifestyle and physical activity.

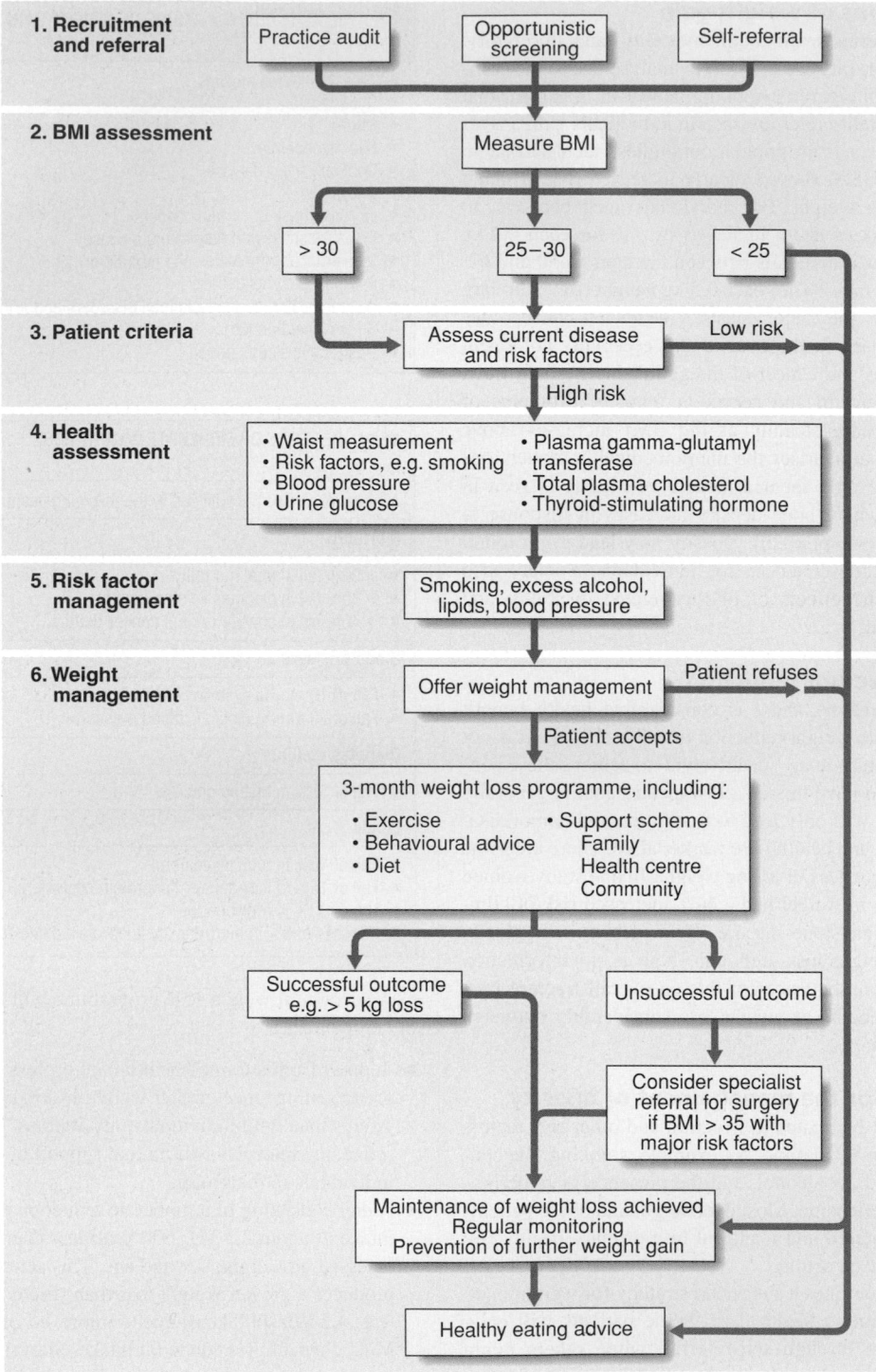

Fig. 10.3 Algorithm for weight management in primary or community care.

● Promotion of increased physical activity, which can be maintained in the long term. Such exercise need not be over-strenuous because health gain is achieved at modest levels of exercise, as long as these are maintained. Walking briskly for 30 minutes each day can result in an additional weight loss of 1 kg per month.

Specialist management of obesity

Individuals may require specialist management if their obesity is extreme or life-threatening. Other indications for referral of these individuals would include the presence of complications and risk factors or failure of community-based management.

Drug therapy

Historically, two groups of appetite suppressant drugs were available: namely, those affecting the hypothalamic catecholaminergic pathway (e.g. amphetamines, diethylpropion, phentermine and mazindol) and those affecting the hypothalamic serotinergic system (fenfluramine, dexfenfluramine). However, due to the cerebral stimulant properties of the first group and the high incidence of valvular heart disease and pulmonary hypertension seen in patients taking fenfluramine, dexfenfluramine and phentermine, these agents, even if available, are not recommended.

Two new drugs are now available. Orlistat (see EBM panel) inhibits pancreatic and gastric lipases and thereby decreases the hydrolysis of ingested triglycerides. This produces a 30% reduction in dietary fat absorption which can contribute to a caloric deficit of about 0.8 MJ (200 kcal) per 24 hours. The drug is not absorbed and adverse side-effects mainly relate to the effect of the resultant fat malabsorption on the gut, namely loose stools, oily spotting, faecal urgency, flatus and the potential for malabsorption of fat-soluble vitamins. The second drug is sibutramine, which reduces food intake through β_1-adrenoceptor and 5-HT$_{2A/2C}$ receptor agonist activity. Metabolic rate may also be enhanced via stimulation of peripheral β_3-adrenoceptors. Weight loss achieved with this agent is 3–5 kg better than placebo with 6 months' therapy and is associated with an improvement in lipid profile. Side-effects include dry mouth, constipation and insomnia; the noradrenergic effects of the drug can increase heart rate and blood pressure in some.

OBESITY—role of orlistat | EBM

'One SR and three subsequent RCTs have found that orlistat in combination with a low-calorie diet causes a modest increase in weight loss in obese adults compared with placebo plus diet.'

- Lindrade F. The effect of orlistat on body weight and coronary heart disease risk profile in obese patients: the Swedish Multi Morbidity Study. J Intern Med 2000; 248:245–254.
- Arterburn D, Hitchcock-Noël P. Obesity: extracts from clinical evidence. BMJ 2001; 322:1406–1409.

Further information: 🖥 www.nice.org.uk

A recent appraisal by the National Institute for Clinical Excellence in the UK recommends that orlistat be used in the following circumstances:

- Patients should have lost at least 2.5 kg in weight in the month before starting the drug.
- The drug should only be prescribed if the BMI is greater than 30 (or 28 if there are other risk factors).
- It should be used only in patients aged between 18 and 75.
- Other weight management steps should be used in conjunction with drug prescription.
- Treatment should be stopped after 3 months unless there is evidence of at least 5% weight loss.
- Treatment should be stopped after 6 months unless there is evidence of at least 10% weight loss.
- Treatment should never be continued beyond 24 months.

Treatment of depression in obese patients with tricyclic antidepressants often produces weight gain, resulting in drug non-compliance. The new class of antidepressants which inhibit serotonergic uptake (e.g. fluoxetine) also reduce weight. Weight is lost for about 6 months on this class of drug but then is regained for reasons unknown; these drugs are therefore not recommended for the treatment of obesity without depression. Bulk-forming drugs (e.g. methylcellulose) and diuretics should not be used to enhance weight loss. Thyroid replacement therapy should only be used in the obese person when there is definite biochemical evidence of hypothyroidism.

Very low calorie diets

In the UK very low calorie diets (VLCDs) are occasionally used in patients with a BMI > 30. Such diets produce weight losses of 1.5–2.5 kg/week compared to 0.5 kg on conventional regimes and hence require the supervision of an experienced physician and nutritionist. Unfortunately, most patients regain weight after stopping such a diet, so VLCDs are mainly used for short-term rapid weight loss. The composition of the diet should ensure a minimum of 50 g of protein each day for men and 40 g of protein for women to minimise muscle degradation. Energy content should be a minimum of 1.65 MJ (400 kcal) for women of height < 1.73 m and 2.1 MJ (500 kcal) for all men and for women taller than 1.73 m. Side-effects tend to be a problem in the early stages of the diet and include orthostatic hypotension, headache, diarrhoea and nausea.

Surgical management

Two procedures have traditionally dominated surgical practice: namely, vertical banded gastroplasty and gastric bypass. Vertical banded gastroplasty involves the construction of a small stomach pouch fashioned by vertical stapling to restrict both gastric outlet and size (see Fig. 10.4A). Gastric bypass (Roux-en-Y) involves fashioning a pouch of low

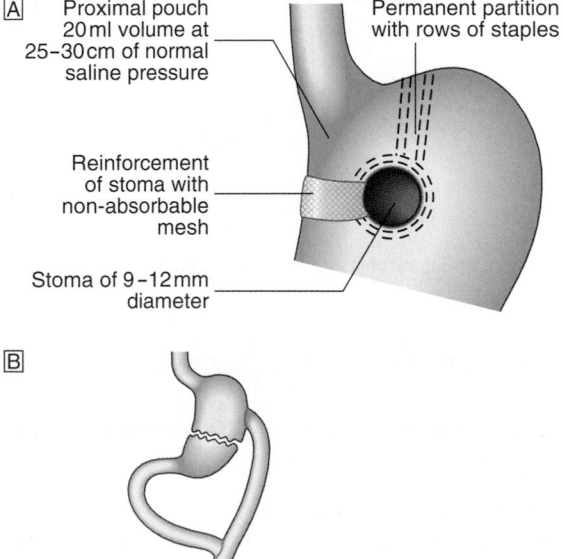

Fig. 10.4 **Bariatric surgical procedures.** Ⓐ Vertical banded gastroplasty. Ⓑ Roux-en-Y gastric bypass.

volume (less than 30 ml) by stapling across the stomach and then connecting a limb of small intestine as a conduit for food, hence bypassing the distal stomach, duodenum and upper jejunum (see Fig. 10.4B). The following recommendations apply:

- Most patients seeking such surgery should have a BMI > 40 but those with a BMI > 35 may be considered if there is a high-risk, life-threatening comorbid condition or severe physical incapacity.
- All patients should be given the opportunity to lose weight on a supervised, expert-run programme.
- Multidisciplinary team evaluation is essential and surgery should only be contemplated in well-informed and motivated patients.
- Surgery should be undertaken by an experienced surgeon in a setting which incorporates expert medical surveillance and access to intensive care facilities.
- Life-long medical surveillance after surgery is a necessity.

Mortality is low in experienced centres but post-operative respiratory problems, wound infection and dehiscence, staple leaks, stomal stenosis, marginal ulcers and venous thrombosis are common. Additional problems may arise at a later stage, such as pouch and distal oesophageal dilatation, persistent vomiting, dumping and micronutrient deficiencies, particularly of folate, vitamin B_{12} and iron which are of concern especially to women contemplating pregnancy. However, hypertension, hyperlipidaemia and diabetic glycaemic control are markedly improved.

Jaw wiring with the use of milk and other liquid diets can be most efficacious but rapid weight regain is usual once the jaws are unwired. This technique is therefore usually reserved for those needing to lose weight rapidly for some operation or life event. Apronectomy is usually advocated to remove an overhang of abdominal fat, especially if infected or ulcerated. This operation is of no value for long-term weight reduction if food intake remains unrestricted. Jejuno-ileal bypass has an unacceptable mortality and morbidity and is no longer recommended.

LIPOPROTEIN DISORDERS

Lipoprotein metabolism

Cholesterol and triglyceride are indispensable structural and metabolic components of all animal cells. Since they are hydrophobic they require to be transported through the aqueous environment of the plasma encapsulated (see Fig. 10.5) in a shell of phospholipid and special proteins (called apolipoproteins), forming a family of lipid-protein particles or lipoproteins (see Box 10.11). The apolipoproteins play an essential role not only in maintaining the structure of the particles but also in directing their metabolism by acting

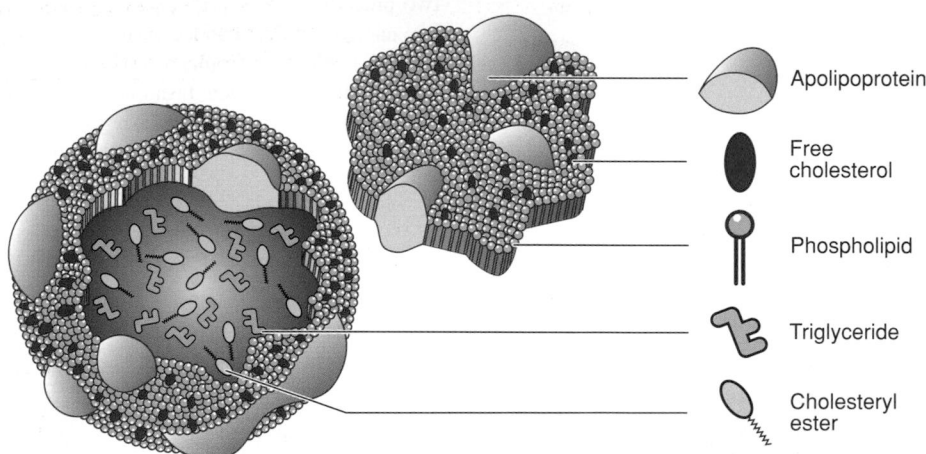

Apolipoprotein

Free cholesterol

Phospholipid

Triglyceride

Cholesteryl ester

Fig. 10.5 Structural characteristics of a typical lipoprotein.

10.11 STRUCTURE AND FUNCTIONS OF THE FOUR MAIN LIPOPROTEINS		
Lipoprotein	**Main apolipoproteins**	**Functions**
Chylomicron (CM)	B_{48}, AI, CII, E	Main transporter of dietary triglyceride, synthesised in the gut after a meal; not present in normal fasting plasma
Very low-density lipoprotein (VLDL)	B_{100}, CII, E	Main carrier of endogenous triglyceride synthesised in liver, precursor of LDL
Low-density lipoprotein (LDL)	B_{100}	Main cholesterol-carrier in blood, generated from VLDL in the blood stream
High-density lipoprotein (HDL)	AI, AII	Smallest but most abundant lipoprotein; transports cholesterol from peripheral tissues to liver for excretion; cardioprotective

as recognition proteins for a variety of plasma enzymes and cell membrane receptors (see Box 10.12).

Lipoprotein metabolism can be thought of in terms of three interconnected transport pathways focusing on the liver (see Fig. 10.6). One, the exogenous pathway, is responsible for the digestion, absorption and tissue dissemination of dietary fat. About 100 g of triglyceride and 0.5 g of cholesterol flow through it each day. Digestive enzymes in the intestinal lumen hydrolyse these fats to free cholesterol, fatty acids and mono- and diglycerides, which combine with bile salts to form the water-soluble micelles responsible for carrying the lipids to absorptive sites in the small intestine (see p. 751). Under normal circumstances triglyceride

absorption is virtually complete, while only about 50% of the cholesterol is taken up, the rest being lost in the faeces.

Following their absorption into the intestinal enterocytes, the component parts of the dietary fat are reconstituted to reform triglyceride and cholesteryl ester which are packaged in chylomicrons (CMs) and secreted into the intestinal lymphatics, through which they reach the blood stream via the thoracic duct. In the circulation triglyceride is gradually removed by the action of the enzyme lipoprotein lipase (LPL), located on the endothelial surface of capillary beds in adipose tissue and cardiac and skeletal muscle. This process eviscerates the chylomicron, causes some of its surface phospholipid and protein to be shed into the plasma as a precursor

10.12 PROPERTIES OF SOME HUMAN APOLIPOPROTEINS

Apolipoprotein	Molecular weight	Site of synthesis	Functions
AI	28 000	Liver, intestine	Main HDL protein Activates lecithin-cholesterol acyltransferase (LCAT)
B_{100}	549 000	Liver	Main structural protein of VLDL and LDL Involved in triglyceride and cholesterol transport Binds to LDL receptor
B_{48}	254 000	Intestine	N-terminal 50% of B_{100} Lacks LDL receptor binding site Main structural protein of chylomicrons
CII	8850	Liver	Activates lipoprotein lipase (LPL) Directs chylomicron and VLDL triglyceride hydrolysis
E	34 000	Liver, intestine, macrophages, glial cells	Binds to LDL receptor and probably also to another specific liver receptor Important in brain lipid transport

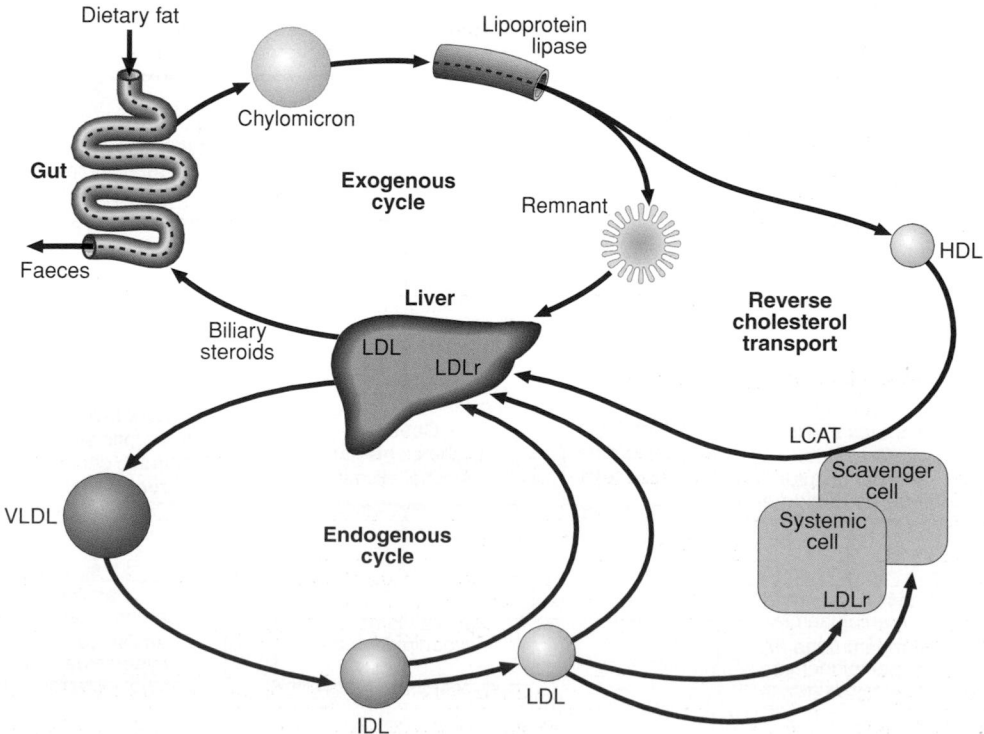

Fig. 10.6 Lipid transport through the plasma. (See text for abbreviations)

of high-density lipoprotein (HDL), and leaves a remnant which is taken up rapidly by the liver; in the process, dietary cholesterol is deposited in that organ. There the sterol may be incorporated into hepatocyte membranes, oxidised to bile acids or repackaged into the endogenous triglyceride-rich counterpart of the chylomicron, the very low-density lipoprotein (VLDL).

Among its many synthetic activities, the liver is responsible for the continuous production of VLDL, which, in the fasting state, represents the body's primary source of circulating triglyceride energy. This particle is subject to the same lipase-mediated digestion process as the chylomicron, except that in this case the resulting particle (intermediate-density lipoprotein—IDL) is not cleared rapidly by the liver. Instead, it undergoes additional remodelling to produce a cholesterol-enriched particle (low-density lipoprotein—LDL) which has a plasma half-life of about 3 days. LDL is ultimately removed from the circulation by the high-affinity LDL receptor pathway, or by other less well understood scavenger mechanisms thought to lead to the incorporation of LDL-cholesterol into atheromatous plaques. LDL particles contain most of the circulating cholesterol in humans. Raised levels of LDL-cholesterol predispose to coronary heart disease (CHD).

In contrast to LDL, cholesterol-rich HDL particles protect against CHD. They are synthesised in the liver and intestine and also generated in part by lipolysis of chylomicra and VLDL. Defective triglyceride lipolysis in the blood stream, which results in hypertriglyceridaemia, is also associated with low circulating HDL levels. One function of HDL is to remove cholesterol from peripheral tissues through the action of the plasma enzyme, lecithin-cholesterol acyltransferase (LCAT), and transport it centripetally for hepatic excretion ('reverse cholesterol transport'). This process is thought to be anti-atherogenic, consistent with the observation that raised levels of circulating HDL reduce the risk of CHD.

Disorders of lipoprotein metabolism

Lipoprotein disorders or dyslipidaemias are among the most common metabolic diseases seen in clinical practice. They are important because they may lead to a number of sequelae including CHD, dermatological manifestations (xanthelasmata and xanthomata), pancreatitis and (more rarely) neurological and ocular anomalies. Both hyper- and hypolipidaemias are recognised.

THE HYPERLIPIDAEMIAS

Hyperlipidaemia is common and either results from a primary abnormality in lipid metabolism or is a secondary manifestation of some other condition (see Fig. 10.7). In the latter case, the hyperlipidaemia usually disappears when the underlying condition is treated.

Classification

In the 1970s, Fredrickson and colleagues introduced a classification of the primary hyperlipidaemias, based on lipoprotein ultracentrifugation and electrophoresis (see Box 10.13). Although adopted by the World Health Organisation (WHO), these analytical techniques are beyond the capacity of most routine laboratories and patients with a particular genetic defect may fall into two or more of the five WHO

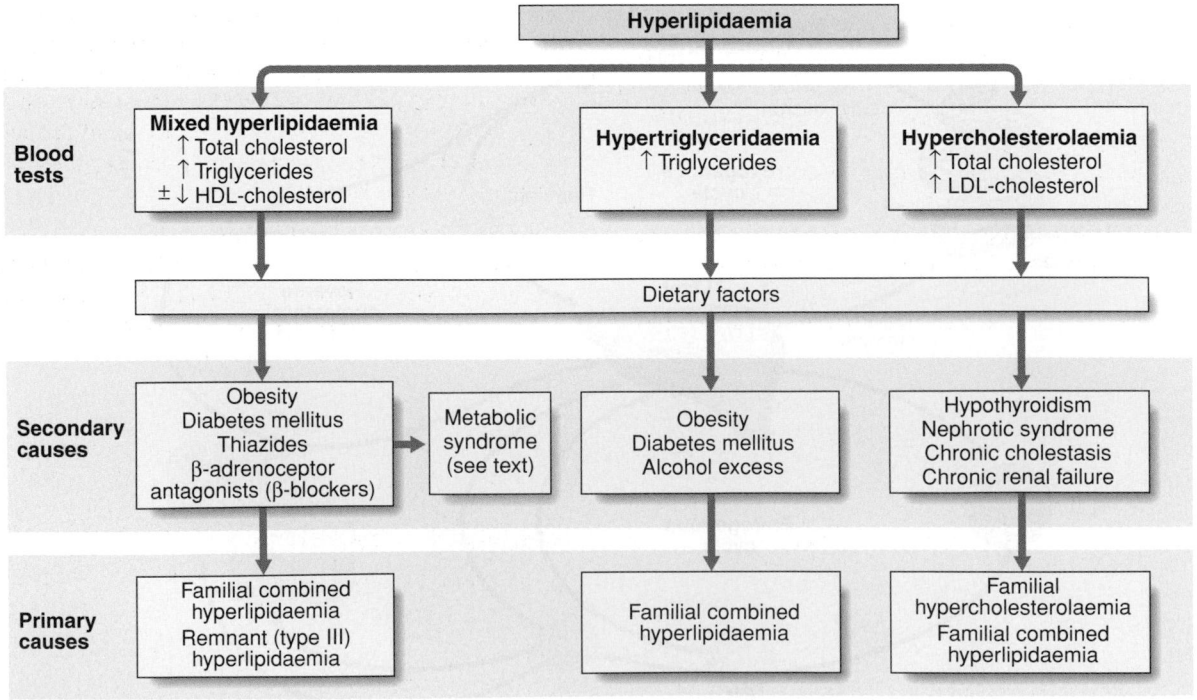

Fig. 10.7 **An approach to the classification of hyperlipidaemia into primary and secondary causes, using commonly available blood tests and clinical data.**

10.13 CLASSIFICATION OF THE HYPERLIPOPROTEINAEMIAS

Fredrickson type	Genetic classification	Defect	Clinical sequelae
I	Lipoprotein lipase deficiency Apo CII deficiency	Mutated or absent LPL Mutated LPL activator	Pancreatitis
II	Familial hypercholesterolaemia Apo B$_{3500}$ defect Familial combined hyperlipidaemia	Deficient LDL receptor binding Reduced LDL catabolism Over-production of B$_{100}$-containing particles	CHD
III	Apo E$_2$ homozygosity	Mutated apo E plus precipitating environmental factor	CHD and PVD
IV	Familial combined hyperlipidaemia	Over-production of B$_{100}$-containing particles	CHD
V	Familial hypertriglyceridaemia	Unknown	Pancreatitis

(CHD = coronary heart disease; PVD = peripheral vascular disease)

categories. Moreover, dietary manipulation, drug treatment or progression of the condition may cause a patient to move from one category to another. Hence from a practical viewpoint it is now more usual to divide the hyperlipidaemias according to the pattern of abnormality on blood testing: namely, hypercholesterolaemia, hypertriglyceridaemia or mixed hyperlipidaemia (see Fig. 10.7).

The principal primary hyperlipidaemias encountered in clinical practice are familial hypercholesterolaemia, familial combined hyperlipidaemia and remnant (Fredrickson type III) hyperlipidaemia. These are genetic in origin and with appropriate vigilance are easily recognisable clinical entities. Such vigilance includes a family history of hyperlipidaemia or early CHD which should be sought in individuals with a substantially raised plasma cholesterol or triglyceride.

Primary hyperlipidaemias

Familial hypercholesterolaemia
In familial hypercholesterolaemia functional LDL receptors are reduced or absent due to a defect in the LDL receptor gene (over 700 defects have been identified so far). A mutation in apo B$_{100}$ (called the B3500 defect since amino acid 3500 is mutated) produces a similar clinical picture since the mutant protein fails to bind to the LDL receptor.

Hypercholesterolaemia is seen at or soon after birth. Typical concentrations are around 10 mmol/l in heterozygotes (who number about 1 in 500 in Caucasian populations) and upwards of 20 mmol/l in the rare homozygote. Excessive tissue deposits may be seen around the eyes (xanthelasmata:

see Fig. 10.8) and in the cornea (corneal arcus: see Fig. 10.9). Those in the extensor tendons over pressure points (xanthomata: see Fig. 10.10) typically feel hard on palpation. Heterozygotes may present with the onset of CHD in the fourth or fifth decade. In homozygotes the above lesions and CHD both appear much earlier, with CHD, and often aortic stenosis, established in the teenage years.

Familial combined (mixed) hyperlipidaemia
In this condition LDL-cholesterol, triglyceride or both may be elevated (see Fig. 10.7). All three states may occur simultaneously in different family members, and the pattern of abnormality may change with time. It is not known whether this condition is monogenic or polygenic. The disorder, which occurs in approximately 1 in 250 people, results from over-production of the apo B$_{100}$-containing VLDL in the liver in combination with a partial defect in triglyceride lipolysis. Plasma HDL-cholesterol levels are usually low. Total cholesterol is elevated, though usually less markedly than in familial hypercholesterolaemia, and fasting triglyceride concentrations are usually only mildly increased. CHD is common, but there are no specific features to facilitate diagnosis in any given family. The occurrence of different types of lipid abnormality in one family and the absence of peripheral stigmata suggest the diagnosis.

Remnant (type III) hyperlipidaemia
This condition affects 1 in 1000 people and is the only WHO type identifiable as a distinct clinical and genotypic entity (see Box 10.13). It occurs in subjects who are homozygous

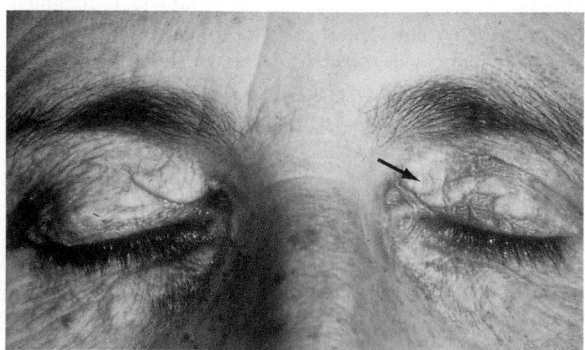

Fig. 10.8 Xanthelasma (arrow).

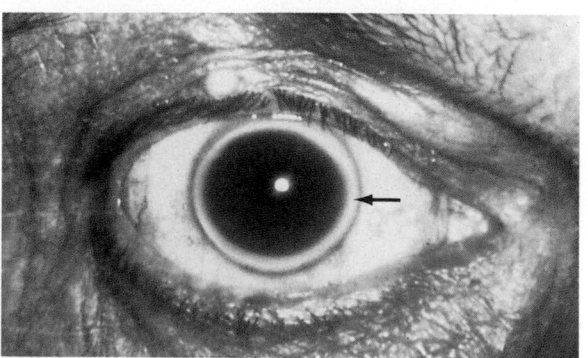

Fig. 10.9 Corneal arcus (arrow).

309

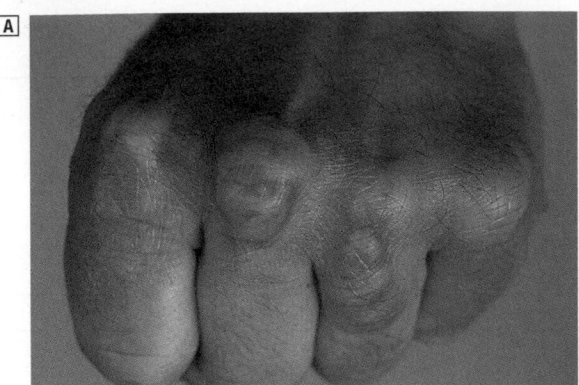 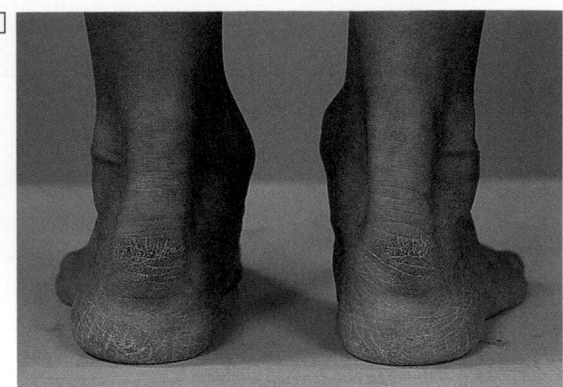

Fig. 10.10   Tendon xanthomata. A Xanthomata in the extensor tendons of the hand. B Achilles tendon xanthomata.

for the rare apo E_2 isoform, and in whom an additional risk factor (e.g. obesity, diabetes mellitus, hypothyroidism) causes decreased clearance, and hence accumulation, of CM and VLDL remnants. Plasma cholesterol and triglyceride levels are elevated, each often exceeding 20 mmol/l. The disorder is characterised by CHD and peripheral vascular disease, and the presence of tuberoeruptive and palmar xanthomata (see Fig. 10.11). In contrast to the xanthomata seen in familial hypercholesterolaemia these are soft and, being triglyceride-rich, irritant when deposited under the skin. The base of the lesions may be reddened due to inflammation and scratch marks may be seen.

The plurimetabolic syndrome (metabolic syndrome, syndrome X)

This is a cluster of variables, first suggested by Reaven in 1988, all of which place the individual at high risk from macrovascular disease. These include elevated VLDL, reduced HDL-cholesterol, a preponderance of small, dense LDL, insulin resistance and hyperinsulinism, glucose intolerance and hypertension. The one constant is that the variables are all related to insulin resistance. The syndrome reaches its full expression in patients with overt type 2 diabetes mellitus.

Hyperalphalipoproteinaemia

This term is applied to a group of disorders where HDL-cholesterol is above the 90th centile. Some families show an autosomal pattern of inheritance, whereas in others there are polygenic and environmental influences. This disorder underlines the need to perform a full lipid profile before initiating drug treatment, as this condition is associated with longevity and those affected need reassurance rather than medication.

Management of hyperlipidaemia

Hyperlipidaemia is one of a number of modifiable risk factors for CHD (see Appendix) and as such should be managed to reduce risk. Non-modifiable risk factors such as a strong family history may serve to justify more aggressive treatment. Recent guidelines from the UK, New Zealand and Europe use these risk factors to help define which patients should be treated and the targets for treatment. Most such guidelines use data from large epidemiological surveys such as the Framingham, MRFIT and PROCAM studies.

Dietary management

Most patients who present with hyperlipidaemia have a polygenic predisposition to raised blood lipids aggravated or unmasked by dietary or lifestyle indiscretion. Diets rich in cholesterol or saturated fat tend to raise blood (LDL) cholesterol, while high carbohydrate intake or excessive alcohol consumption may increase plasma (VLDL) triglyceride. Any treatment plan for hyperlipidaemia must exclude common causes of secondary hyperlipidaemia such as diabetes and (particularly in women) hypothyroidism. In hyperlipidaemia associated with diabetes it is the diabetes which needs to be controlled first. In hypothyroidism the hypercholesterolaemia should respond, albeit slowly, to treatment of the hypothyroidism.

All patients with hyperlipidaemia should be managed with a fat-modified diet, initially as the sole form of therapy for 3–6 months, before drug therapy is considered. It is the mainstay of long-term management of these patients, and in a minority may result in a dramatic improvement in lipid profiles, which may obviate the need for drug treatment. The principal dietary guidelines are shown in Box 10.14. In summary, dietary manipulation should aim to reduce intake of red meat, dairy produce and refined sugar whilst increasing the intake of vegetables, fruit and pulses. Other sources of protein such as fish should be encouraged, particularly oily fish such as mackerel, salmon or trout. These improve

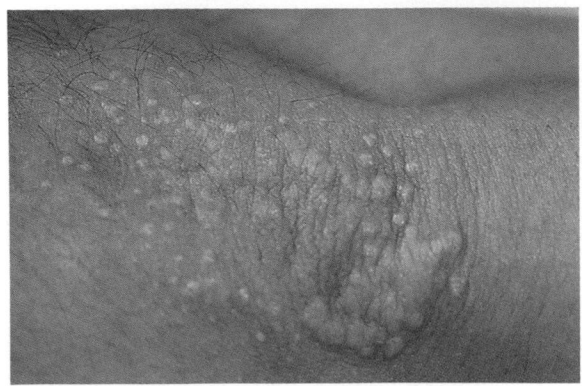

Fig. 10.11   Tuberoeruptive xanthomata.

the lipid profile due to the content of ω3 polyunsaturated fats (see p. 301). Increased physical activity should be encouraged as, together with reduction to ideal body weight, this will improve glucose, blood pressure and lipid profiles. Avoidance of cigarette smoking is essential in these patients.

Drug therapy

Drugs to lower blood lipid levels should be considered for all patients who remain hyperlipidaemic despite the above dietary measures and treatment of secondary causes of dyslipidaemia. There are several groups of lipid-lowering drugs with different actions (see Box 10.15). Generally, the first line of treatment is a statin if the LDL-cholesterol is elevated, and a fibrate if the HDL-cholesterol is low or if hypertriglyceridaemia is present (see Fig. 10.12). The bile acid sequestrants are less well tolerated and tend to be used only in pre-menopausal women (as both the statins and fibrates are contraindicated at the time of conception and throughout pregnancy) or as an adjunct to statin treatment. A number of clinical trials have now demonstrated the benefit of statins in patients with established vascular disease

10.15 DRUG THERAPY FOR HYPERLIPIDAEMIA

Drug group	Principal actions
HMG CoA reductase inhibitors (e.g. simvastatin, pravastatin, atorvastatin)	Inhibit cholesterol biosynthesis in the liver Activate hepatic LDL receptor Increase LDL catabolism Lower plasma and LDL-cholesterol
Bile acid sequestrant resins (e.g. colestyramine, colestipol)	Block intestinal reabsorption of bile acids Divert hepatic cholesterol into bile acid production Activate hepatic LDL receptors Lower plasma and LDL-cholesterol
Fibrates (e.g. bezafibrate, fenofibrate)	Activate LPL Increase VLDL lipolysis Lower plasma triglyceride and raise HDL; reduce plasma LDL
Nicotinic acid and its derivatives	Inhibit lipolysis within adipocytes Reduce plasma free fatty acid levels Lower hepatic VLDL synthesis and secretion Lower triglyceride and increase HDL

(secondary prevention; e.g. 4S, CARE and LIPID) or in patients at high risk of vascular disease (primary prevention; e.g. AFCAPS/TEXCAPS and WOSCOPS); similar data also exist for the fibrates (e.g. the Helsinki Heart and VA-HIT studies). Figure 10.12 shows a paradigm to help decide which patients should receive hypolipidaemic drugs. There are now a number of tables or computer programs available

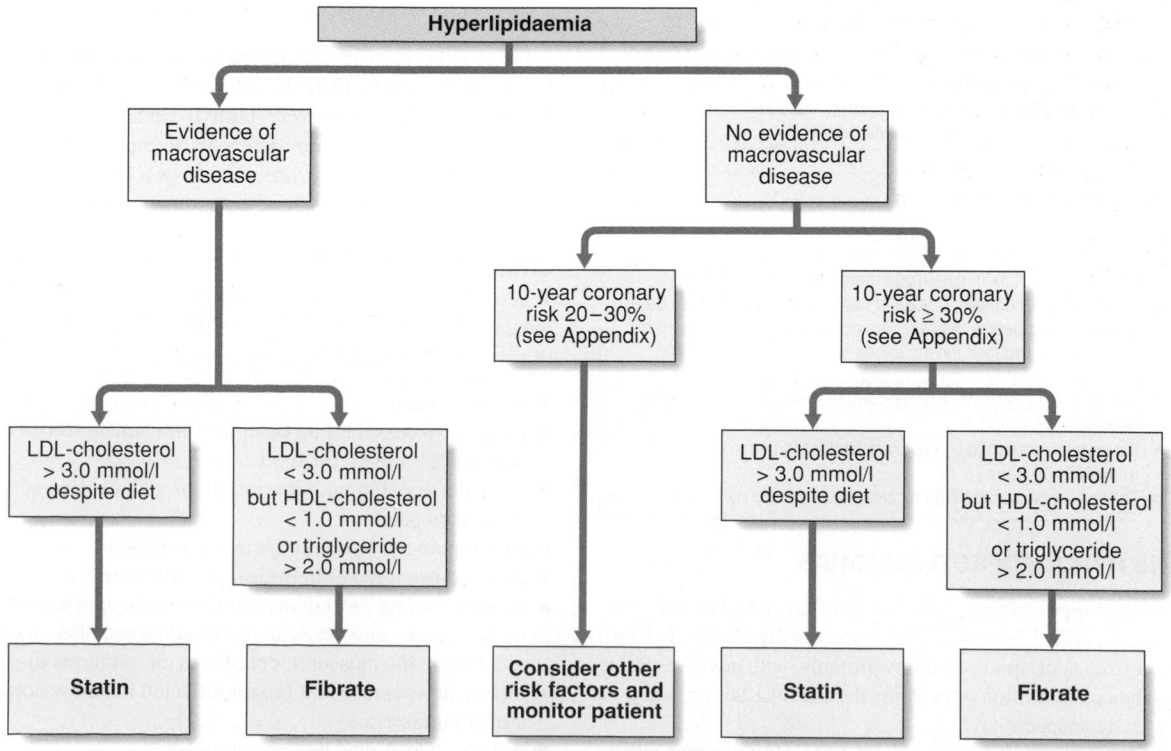

Fig. 10.12 An approach to the use of lipid-lowering drugs.

to help calculate vascular risk, based on lipid and other risk factors (see 'Further information' in EBM panel and the Appendix). Renal and liver function and creatine kinase should be measured prior to the start of drug therapy and then monitored thereafter; additionally, patients should be warned to seek medical advice if they develop muscle pains while taking hypolipidaemic drugs. The primary aim of therapy is to reduce the LDL-cholesterol to < 3.0 mmol/l; secondary aims are an HDL-cholesterol > 1.0 mmol/l, a total cholesterol of < 5.0 mmol/l and fasting triglycerides < 2.0 mmol/l. Referral to a lipid clinic should be considered if patients have a primary genetic hyperlipidaemia, especially if severe, if there is inadequate control with monotherapy or if there are troublesome side-effects.

Though the landmark clinical trials (see EBM panel) relate to individual drugs, treatment guidelines do not distinguish between different drugs in the same group, thus suggesting the interchangeability of drugs in the same group that is now reflected in routine clinical practice.

EBM

HYPERCHOLESTEROLAEMIA—use of statins

Primary prevention
'In men aged 45–64 with moderate hypercholesterolaemia (LDL-cholesterol of 4.0–6.0 mmol/l) but without a history of previous myocardial infarction (MI) pravastatin reduces the incidence of MI and death from cardiovascular causes.'

Secondary prevention
'In patients with a history of angina or previous MI and a serum cholesterol of 5.5–8.0 mmol/l and triglycerides > 2.5 mmol/l despite dietary treatment, long-term simvastatin is well tolerated and improves survival.'

- West of Scotland Coronary Prevention Study (WOSCOPS). Prevention of coronary heart disease with pravastatin in men with hypercholesterolaemia. N Engl J Med 1995; 333:1301–1307.
- 4S (Scandinavian Simvastatin Survival Study). Randomised trial of cholesterol lowering in 4444 patients with coronary heart disease. Lancet 1994; 344:1383–1389.

Further information: 🖥 www.bcs.com/publications/
pubbscsother.html

ISSUES IN OLDER PEOPLE
HYPERLIPIDAEMIA

- Absolute risk of atherosclerotic disease is greater in the elderly; thus risk reduction is potentially more beneficial.
- Few trials of treatment to prevent cardiovascular events (to date) have included people over the age of 65. However, treatment of hypertension reduces the incidence of cardiovascular events, and especially stroke, up to the age of 85 years.
- For secondary prevention, upper age limit for initiation of statin therapy is 75 years.
- For primary prevention, upper age limit for initiation of statin therapy is 69 years.
- There is no upper age limit for treatment already commenced.

THE HYPOLIPOPROTEINAEMIAS

The hypolipoproteinaemias are rare but present with spectacular clinical features. They can broadly be divided into deficiencies of apo B or apo A proteins, with adverse effects on the concentration of proteins the size of LDL or larger, or on HDL, respectively.

Abetalipoproteinaemia or hypobetalipoproteinaemia results from the defective synthesis of apo B_{100} in the liver or apo B_{48}

in intestinal cells. The principal clinical features are fat malabsorption, acanthocytosis of red blood cells, retinitis pigmentosa and ataxic neuropathy. The steatorrhoea responds to dietary fat restriction, and vitamin E supplementation (up to 10 000 mg/day) can prevent the onset of retinal or neurological disease. Supplementation of other fat-soluble vitamins (A and K) may also be helpful. Tangier disease is an autosomal recessive disorder of HDL particles. Reverse cholesterol transport is markedly reduced (see p. 308), and sterol esters accumulate in unusual peripheral sites within the reticulo-endothelial system and cornea. The characteristic features are orange tonsils, neuropathy, low cholesterol and abnormal or elevated triglyceride levels.

Low lipid levels also occur in end-stage parenchymal liver disease and severe malabsorption or malnutrition.

PROTEIN-ENERGY MALNUTRITION (PEM)

PEM IN ADULTS

The predominant form of PEM in adults is undernutrition, i.e. the result of a sustained negative energy (calorie) balance. This may be due to:

- insufficient food supply (e.g. in situations of famine)
- persistent regurgitation or vomiting
- anorexia
- malabsorption (e.g. small intestinal disease)
- increased energy requirements (e.g. thyrotoxicosis, trauma and febrile illnesses)
- increased energy losses (e.g. loss of calories in glycosuria secondary to diabetes mellitus).

Gross features of protein deficiency are rare in starvation, but are seen where there is excessive turnover or loss of body protein (e.g. in severe burns). Undernutrition often leads to associated vitamin deficiencies, especially thiamin, folate and vitamin C. Diarrhoea is also seen in cases of PEM, leading to depletion of sodium, potassium and magnesium.

Clinical features

When assessing the patient, consideration should be given to the causes and consequences of PEM. The clinical features of severe undernutrition in adults include:

- loss of weight
- thirst, weakness, feeling cold, nocturia, amenorrhoea and impotence, craving for food
- lax, pale, dry skin with loss of turgor and, occasionally, pigmented patches
- hair thinning or loss (except in adolescents)
- cold and cyanosed extremities, pressure sores
- muscle-wasting (best demonstrated by the appearance of the temporalis and periscapular muscles and also reflected in the measurement of arm circumference)
- loss of subcutaneous fat (again reflected in below normal arm circumference)
- oedema, which may be present without hypoalbuminaemia ('famine oedema')

10.16 INFECTIONS ASSOCIATED WITH PEM

Patients with starvation have increased susceptibility to:
- Gastroenteritis and Gram-negative septicaemia
- Respiratory infections, especially bronchopneumonia
- Certain viral diseases, especially measles and herpes simplex
- Tuberculosis
- Streptococcal and staphylococcal skin infections
- Helminthic infestations

- subnormal body temperature, slow pulse, low blood pressure and small heart
- distended abdomen, with diarrhoea
- diminished tendon jerks
- apathy, loss of initiative, depression, introversion, aggression if food is nearby
- susceptibility to infections (see Box 10.16).

The high mortality rate in famine situations is often due to infections, e.g. typhus or cholera epidemics. The usual signs of infection may not appear. In advanced starvation, patients become completely inactive and may assume a flexed, fetal position. In the last stage of starvation, death comes quietly and often quite suddenly. The very old are most vulnerable. All organs are atrophied at necropsy, except the brain, which tends to maintain its weight.

Investigations
In a famine it is usually only possible to measure the body weight, estimate the patient's height and grade the severity of undernutrition by calculating the BMI. Measurement of the arm circumference is also helpful for rapid diagnosis. Where other investigations are possible, plasma free fatty acids are found to be increased; there is ketosis and a mild metabolic acidosis. Plasma glucose is low but albumin concentration is often maintained because the liver still functions normally. Insulin secretion is diminished, glucagon and cortisol tend to increase and reverse T_3 replaces normal triiodothyronine. The resting metabolic rate falls, partly because of reduced lean body mass. The urine has a fixed specific gravity and creatinine excretion becomes low. There may be a mild anaemia, leucopenia and thrombocytopenia. The erythrocyte sedimentation rate is normal unless there is infection. Tests of delayed skin sensitivity, e.g. to tuberculin, can be falsely negative. The electrocardiogram (ECG) shows sinus brachycardia and low voltage.

Management
Whether in a famine or in wasting secondary to disease, individuals need to be graded according to BMI. People with mild starvation are in no danger; those with moderate starvation need extra feeding. People who are severely underweight need hospital-type care. Between 6.3 and 8.4 MJ/day (1500 and 2000 kcal/day) will prevent the downward progress of undernutrition.

In severe starvation there is atrophy of the intestinal epithelium and of the exocrine pancreas, and the bile is dilute. When food becomes available, it should therefore be given in small amounts at first. Food should be palatable and similar to the usual staple meal—for example, a cereal with some sugar, milk powder and oil. Salt should be restricted and a micronutrient supplement provided (e.g. potassium, magnesium, zinc and multivitamins). During refeeding, a weight gain of 5% body weight per month indicates satisfactory progress.

Circumstances and resources are different in every famine but many problems are non-medical and concern organisation, infrastructure, liaison, politics, procurement, security and ensuring that food is distributed on the basis of need. Lastly, plans must be made for prevention and/or earlier intervention should similar circumstances prevail in the future.

PEM IN YOUNG CHILDREN

Malnutrition in young children is endemic in many developing countries, where severe PEM affects around 2% and mild to moderate forms affect a much larger and variable proportion of children in the community. PEM is the result of inadequacy of food (both quantitative and qualitative), frequent infections, and neglect or lack of proper care.

Assessment of subclinical PEM in the community is based on indicators such as weight-for-age (underweight) and height-for-age (stunting). Inappropriately low weight-for-height, which is an indicator of 'wasting', signals severe PEM. The clinical presentation of severe PEM may be either as 'kwashiorkor' or as 'marasmus'. Some young children with severe PEM show clinical features of both types; in this situation it is referred to as 'marasmic kwashiorkor'. Box 10.17 outlines the Wellcome classification of severe PEM.

10.17 WELLCOME CLASSIFICATION OF SEVERE PEM IN CHILDREN

Weight-for-age*	Oedema Present	Oedema Absent
80–60% of standard	Kwashiorkor	Undernutrition
< 60% of standard	Marasmic kwashiorkor	Marasmus

* Expected weight-for-age of Harvard standards.

Kwashiorkor
Kwashiorkor describes childhood malnutrition manifesting with oedema. The term means 'the sickness of the older child when the next baby is born'. It occurs most often in the second year of life in a child weaned from the breast on to a starchy diet very low in protein. A typical diet would consist of cassava, yam, plantain, sweet potato or a cereal that has been refined and diluted. Such a child may appear in moderate health until its nutrient requirements are increased by an infection, e.g. gastroenteritis, measles or malaria.

The aetiopathogenesis of kwashiorkor is summarised in Figure 10.13. Kwashiorkor develops when the diet has a low protein to energy ratio, which may result in protein being a limiting factor for some children. Such a diet leads to high plasma insulin levels and low plasma cortisol levels. This in turn promotes the uptake of amino acids by muscle, diverting

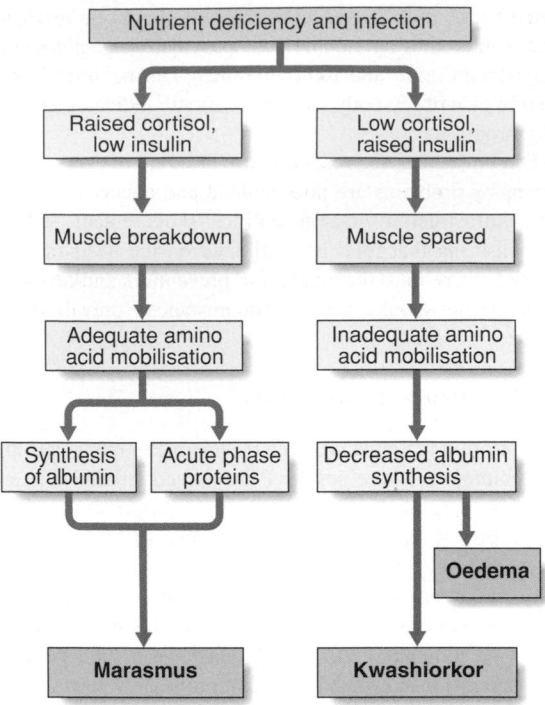

Fig. 10.13 Schematic outline of the aetiopathogenesis of severe PEM in children.

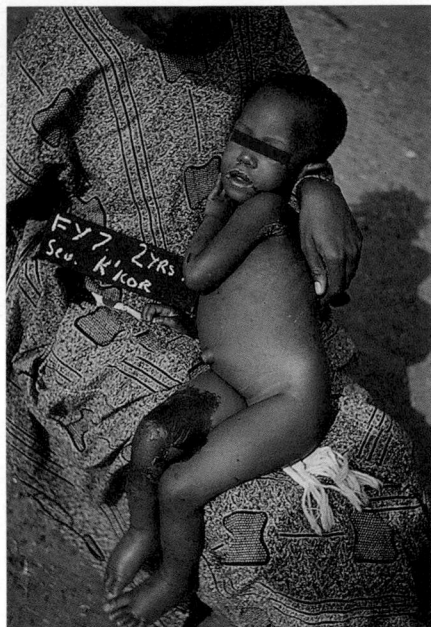

Fig. 10.14 Severe kwashiorkor. West African child with bilateral oedema, 'flaky-paint' dermatosis and upper body wasting typical of severe kwashiorkor.

these substrates away from the liver. As a consequence, there is a reduced synthesis of albumin (resulting in hypo-albuminaemia, which causes oedema). There is also a reduced synthesis of lipoproteins predisposing to a fatty liver. The presence of infections may divert amino acids into the synthesis of acute phase proteins and thus contribute further to reduced hepatic synthesis of albumin. Free radicals have also been implicated in the causation of kwashiorkor. It is thought that the imbalance between the production of these toxic radicals and their safe disposal results in the characteristic occurrence of oedema and skin lesions seen in children with kwashiorkor.

Clinically, the child presents with bilateral pitting oedema and is miserable, apathetic and often anorexic (see Fig. 10.14). There is some wasting, particularly in the shoulders and upper arms. The child may have a 'moon face' and even a 'pot belly', the latter due to weakness of the abdominal muscles. There are symmetrical skin changes in the buttocks, inner thighs and perineum. These areas are at first pigmented and thickened, then cracks appear and lead to denuded areas of shallow pigmentation. Confluent areas with this characteristic dermatosis have been termed 'flaky-paint' or 'crazy-paving' dermatosis. The hair alters colour from black to blond, reddish or grey, becomes thin, sparse and loose and can be easily plucked.

Marasmus

The term marasmus is derived from the Greek word *marasmos,* meaning 'dying away', and is applied to severe malnutrition in infants. The aetiology of marasmus seems to be different from that of kwashiorkor. When energy in the diet is limited due to inadequate food intake, a hormonal response opposite to that seen in kwashiorkor emerges. Low insulin and high plasma cortisol result in amino acids being released from muscle, leading to their availability for hepatic synthesis of protein and in particular albumin. This results in severe muscle-wasting, with normal albumin levels and hence no oedema. Absence of oedema in the presence of severe muscle-wasting is characteristic of marasmus. Thus 'the marasmic infant lives on his own meat'.

The child is very thin and wasted, with no subcutaneous fat and wasted muscles. The abdomen shows distension, and diarrhoea is usual. Body weight is severely reduced below 60% of the international (National Center for Health Statistics/World Health Organisation) standard. In contrast to kwashiorkor, there is no oedema, and skin and hair changes are mild or absent. The child is not usually anorexic (see Box 10.18).

Marasmic kwashiorkor

When a child presents with wasting of muscles and fat characteristic of marasmus along with oedema as in kwashiorkor, the child has a severe form of PEM called marasmic kwashiorkor.

10.18 CLINICAL FEATURES OF SEVERE PEM IN CHILDREN	
Kwashiorkor	**Marasmus**
• Oedema; bilateral and pitting	• No oedema
• Variable muscle-wasting	• Severe muscle-wasting
• Subcutaneous fat present	• Subcutaneous fat minimal
• Low serum albumin	• Serum albumin near normal
• 'Moon face'	• Severe wasting

Management of marasmus or kwashiorkor

The principles of management of severely malnourished children are given in Box 10.19. The management is in two phases (see Fig. 10.15). The first phase is stabilisation, which may last up to 7 days; phase two is rehabilitation. Hypoglycaemia, hypothermia, dehydration and electrolyte disturbances should be corrected during the stabilisation phase, together with the treatment of infection. Malnourished children are very susceptible to a number of infections and may not exhibit the usual responses of pyrexia and leucocytosis. Hence it is advisable to administer broad-spectrum antibiotics routinely.

Cautious feeding is commenced in the stabilisation phase and the amount and type of food are both important. Refeeding should consist of small, frequent feeds of milk-based starter

10.19 STEPS IN THE MANAGEMENT OF A SEVERELY MALNOURISHED CHILD DURING THE STABILISATION PHASE

1. Treat or prevent hypoglycaemia
- 10% glucose or sucrose or a feed, frequently every 2 hours, day and night

2. Treat or prevent hypothermia
- Keep child warm and feed frequently

3. Treat or prevent dehydration
- Do not use i.v. fluids or oral rehydration salts (ORS) solutions; use modified rehydration solutions with electrolyte and mineral solution

4. Correct electrolyte imbalance
- Use modified ORS with less sodium and with extra potassium and magnesium

5. Treat infections
- Administer broad-spectrum antibiotics as a routine

6. Correct micronutrient deficiencies
- Give multivitamin supplements, folic acid and zinc; avoid iron until child starts gaining weight

7. Start feeds cautiously: small, frequent, milk-based feeds
- 0.4 MJ/kg (100 kcal/kg) energy and 1–1.5 g protein/kg per day; encourage breastfeeding

formula, gradually increasing energy intake to 0.4 MJ/kg (100 kcal/kg) and protein to 1–1.5 g/kg per day. The feeds given are essentially the same for both types of severe PEM but in kwashiorkor the child's anorexia necessitates more intensive hand feeding. Feeds vary in different centres but are usually based on dried skimmed milk mixed with flour, sugar and oil and given 5–6 times (or more) during the day and also at night time. Potassium, magnesium, zinc and a multivitamin mixture are also administered. Associated conditions, including vitamin A deficiency, severe anaemia, dermatosis and diarrhoea, need appropriate medical attention.

Severe PEM is associated with a high mortality (20–50%) even in well-equipped hospitals. However, it has been shown that meticulous adherence to the above steps can reduce mortality dramatically (by 2–5%).

MALNUTRITION IN THE HOSPITAL POPULATION

In developed countries malnutrition is a common problem in the hospital setting. Studies have shown that approximately one-third of patients admitted are affected by moderate or severe malnutrition. Once in hospital, many patients lose weight due to factors such as poor appetite, concurrent illness, inadequate intake due to specific feeding difficulties, and even being kept 'nil by mouth' for investigations. However, this situation should not be accepted fatalistically. It has been shown that this deterioration can be prevented with proper monitoring and with the involvement of an appropriate multidisciplinary team. Malnutrition is still poorly recognised in hospital and has serious consequences, both for the individual patient and in the consumption of medical resources. Significant malnutrition leads to impaired immunity and muscle weakness, which in turn affect cardiac and respiratory function. The malnourished patient is often apathetic and withdrawn. This is often mistaken for a depressive illness and can affect cooperation with treatment. Poor nutrition leads to delayed wound healing after surgery and these patients are also more likely to develop post-operative infection. As a consequence of all

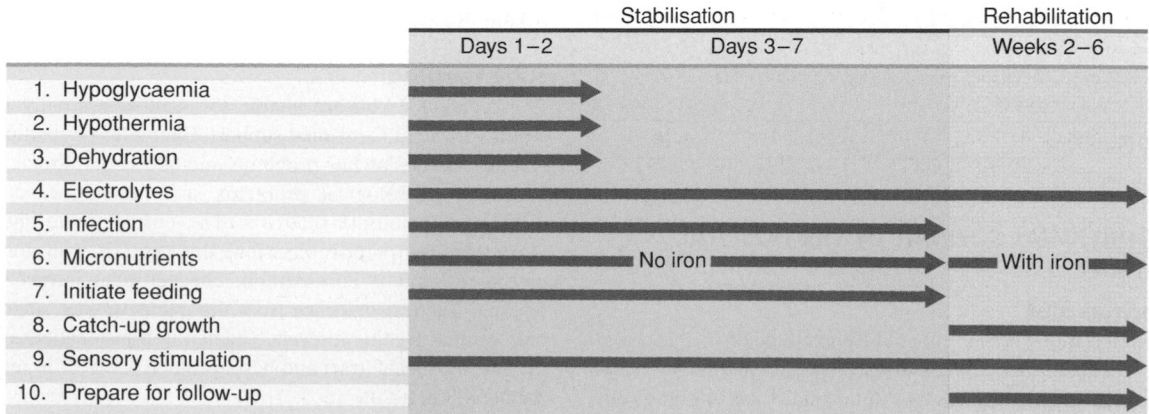

Fig. 10.15   Time frame for the management of a child with PEM.

these factors, malnutrition leads to increased morbidity, mortality and length of hospital stay. It has been estimated that the National Health Service in the UK could save £266 million per year by adopting appropriate nutritional management.

IDENTIFYING PATIENTS AT RISK

As a minimum standard, all patients should be weighed on admission to hospital. For patients undergoing a prolonged admission, weight should be rechecked on a weekly basis. A number of scoring systems have been developed to enable staff to identify malnourished patients. An example is given in Box 10.20. The interpretation of this score, together with recommended action, is detailed in Figure 10.16.

10.20 NUTRITION RISK SCORE

Criterion	Score
1. Weight loss in last 3 months (unintentional)	
No weight loss	0
0–3 kg weight loss	1
3–6 kg weight loss	2
> 6 kg weight loss	3
2. BMI (weight/height²)	
> 20	0
18–19	1
15–17	2
< 15	3
3. Appetite	
Good (manages most of three meals per day)	0
Poor (leaves more than half of meals provided)	2
Nil or virtually nil	3
4. Ability to eat and retain food	
No difficulties; no diarrhoea; no vomiting	0
Problems handling food; mild diarrhoea or vomiting	1
Difficulty with swallowing or chewing; moderate diarrhoea or vomiting	2
Unable to take food orally; severe diarrhoea or vomiting	3
5. Stress factor	
No stress factor	0
Mild (e.g. minor surgery or infection)	1
Moderate (e.g. chronic disease, major surgery, inflammatory bowel disease etc.)	2
Severe (multiple injuries; severe sepsis; malignant disease etc.)	3
TOTAL SCORE	**0–15**

NUTRITIONAL SUPPORT OF THE HOSPITAL PATIENT

Normal diet

As a first step, patients should be encouraged to eat a normal and adequate diet. This is often neglected and there is evidence of substantial wastage in hospital food. A significant proportion of patients are able to consume normal food but do not take adequate amounts. This situation must be moni-

Nutrition risk score (see Box 10.20)	Action required
0–3 Low risk	• No action necessary • Check weight weekly
4–5 Needs monitoring	• Check weight weekly • Encourage eating and drinking • Replace missed meals with supplements (check with dietitian if a special diet is needed) • Repeat score after 1 week and refer to dietitian if there is no improvement
6–15 High risk	• Refer to dietitian

Also refer to dietitian if:
• The patient needs a special diet not available on the normal menu or
• Advice is required about a special diet

Fig. 10.16 Analysis of nutrition risk score. Complete on admission and weekly if patient's condition has changed.

tored carefully on the ward. Inadequate intake may be due to the unpalatability of food, or to cultural and religious factors requiring patients to follow a specified diet. Patients who have been deemed to be at risk of malnutrition should be on a regular food chart, to record the quantities of food eaten. Hospital catering departments have an important role in providing acceptable and adequate meals.

Dietary supplements

If a patient is unable to achieve sufficient nutritional intake from normal diet alone, then dietary supplements should be used. These are drinks with a high energy and protein content. Supplements are available in cartons as manufactured, flavoured products but can also be made in the hospital kitchen from milk products and egg. To ensure that such supplements are taken on a regular basis, it is best if these are prescribed and administered by the nursing staff rather than simply being placed on the hospital bedside locker. Taking dietary supplements does not significantly affect the patient's consumption of normal food.

Tube feeding

Those patients who are unable to swallow normally may require artificial nutritional support. Examples of conditions leading to swallowing problems include acute stroke and long-term neurological problems such as motor neuron disease and multiple sclerosis. The enteral route should always be used if possible, since this accords with normal physiology and is considerably cheaper than intravenous feeding. There is evidence from the intensive care situation that enteral feeding prevents bacterial translocation from the gastrointestinal tract and has a protective effect in multiorgan failure.

If the need for artificial nutritional support is thought to be a short-term requirement, then feeding is instituted using a fine-bore nasogastric tube. Specially prepared liquid feeds are then administered either by continuous infusion or by using a bolus technique. If the patient fails to absorb the administered feed or vomits it up, this may indicate gastric outlet obstruction or gastric stasis. This problem can be overcome by placing a nasojejunal tube, using an endoscopic or radiological technique.

Where there is a need for long-term feeding, a percutaneous endoscopic gastrostomy (PEG) should be sited. The placement technique is summarised in Figure 10.17. A PEG tube is more comfortable for the patient, since there is no irritation to the nasal mucosa and the tube is less likely to become displaced or pulled out. Thus the feed can be given in a more consistent and reliable manner. However, inserting a gastrostomy is an invasive procedure and is associated with complications such as local infection and inadvertent puncture of other intra-abdominal viscus. It takes approximately 10 days for a fibrous tract to form around the PEG tube. If the PEG tube is displaced or removed during that time, there is a high risk of peritonitis. If a problem occurs with food absorption, a jejunal extension can be placed through the PEG tube and liquid feed administered directly into the small bowel.

Parenteral nutrition

In circumstances where the intestine cannot be used, nutrition is given via the intravenous route. In circumstances of active treatment, no patient should be allowed to starve for longer than 1 week.

Peripheral venous feeding

When there is a short-term need for artificial nutritional support, lipid-containing nutrient mixes can be infused via a peripheral vein. The main complication of this technique is peripheral vein thrombosis. This is minimised by using a small-gauge cannula sited in a large vein and by applying glyceryl trinitrate patches to the cannula site. Adding heparin and hydrocortisone to the infusion also delays the onset of thrombophlebitis.

Central venous feeding

This is the best option for long-term feeding needs. Typically, an 'all in one' mixture is infused through a central venous cannula. The main energy source in the feed is provided by carbohydrate, usually as glucose. The solution also contains amino acids, lipid emulsion, electrolytes, trace elements and vitamins. The most significant complication is line infection. Thus, the central line should be inserted under full aseptic conditions. In handling the line on the ward—for example, when infusion changes are made—strict aseptic precautions must also be observed. The nutrients to be infused are normally mixed as a large bag in a sterile environment within the pharmacy department. If the patient develops fever or other features of septicaemia, it should be assumed that there is a line infection. Blood cultures should be taken. The existing line should be removed and the tip sent for bacteriological analysis. A new line is normally inserted using a guidewire technique.

LEGAL AND ETHICAL ASPECTS OF ARTIFICIAL NUTRITIONAL SUPPORT

The ability to intervene with artificial nutritional support raises many legal and ethical dilemmas. Starvation will inevitably lead to death but the inability to eat may be part of the natural course of a disease process. Difficult decisions are raised by situations such as stroke, where swallowing ability is lost. The institution of feeding may speed recovery and lead to better functional outcome. On the other hand, in severe

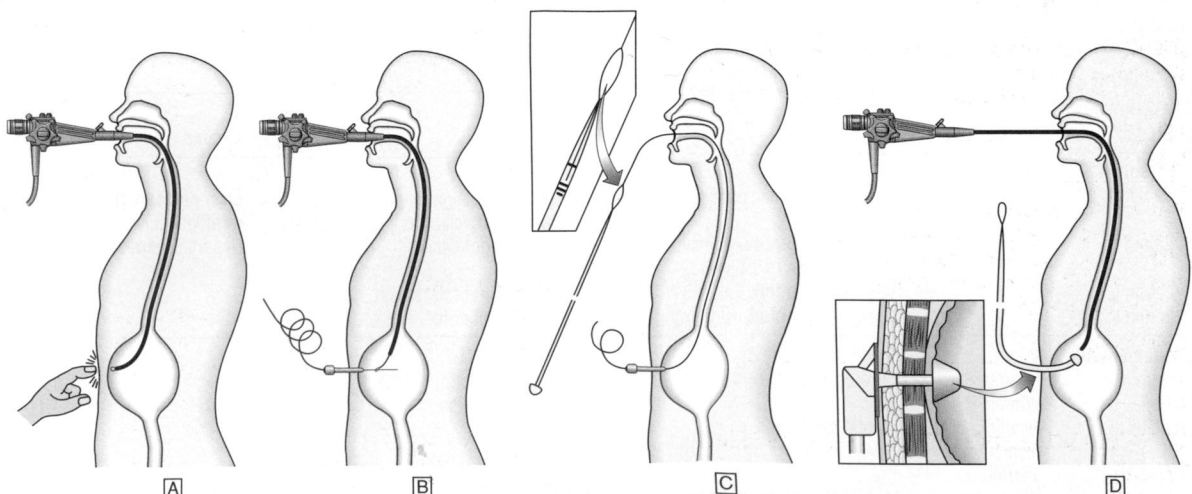

Fig. 10.17 Percutaneous endoscopic gastrostomy placement. A Finger pressure on anterior abdominal wall noted by endoscopist. B Following insertion of a cannula through the anterior abdominal wall into the stomach a guidewire is threaded through the cannula and grasped by the endoscopic forceps or snare. C The endoscope is withdrawn with the guidewire. The gastrostomy tube is then attached to the guidewire. D The guidewire and tube are pulled back through the mouth, oesophagus and stomach to exit on the anterior abdominal wall, and the endoscope is repassed to confirm the site of placement of the retention device. The latter closely abuts the gastric mucosa; its position is maintained by an external fixation device (see inset).

stroke feeding might prolong the process of dying. There will be different approaches to these decisions, depending on the local availability of resources as well as on cultural and religious influences. Some guidelines are given in Box 10.21.

10.21 ETHICAL AND LEGAL CONSIDERATIONS IN THE MANAGEMENT OF ARTIFICIAL NUTRITIONAL SUPPORT*

- Care of the sick involves the duty of providing adequate fluid and nutrients
- Food and fluid should not be withheld from a patient who expresses a desire to eat and drink, unless there is a medical contraindication (e.g. risk of aspiration)
- A treatment plan should include consideration of nutritional issues and should be agreed by all members of the health-care team
- In a situation of palliative care, tube feeding should only be instituted if it is needed to relieve symptoms
- Tube feeding is usually regarded in English law as a medical treatment. Like other treatments, the need for such support should be reviewed on a regular basis and changes made in the light of clinical circumstances
- A competent adult patient must give consent for any invasive procedures, including the passage of a nasogastric tube or the insertion of a central venous cannula
- If a patient is unable to give consent, the health-care team should act in that person's best interest, taking into account any previously expressed wishes of the patient and the views of family
- Under certain specified circumstances (e.g. anorexia nervosa), it will be appropriate to provide artificial nutritional support to the unwilling patient

* Based on British Association for Parenteral and Enteral Nutrition guidelines.

VITAMINS AND MINERALS

VITAMINS

Vitamins are organic substances in food, which are required in very small amounts but are not synthesised in the body. They occur naturally in food and are essential for health. Vitamins are broadly categorised into those that are fat-soluble (vitamins A, D, E and K) and those that are water-soluble (vitamins of the B complex group and vitamin C). This is an important clinical distinction, since deficiency of fat-soluble vitamins is seen in conditions of fat malabsorption (e.g. biliary obstruction). Twelve vitamins have been demonstrated to have clinical effects in humans (see Box 10.22).

Deficiencies of vitamins still occur in developed countries, e.g. of folate, thiamin and vitamins D and C. Some of these deficiencies are induced by diseases or drugs. In developing countries vitamin deficiency diseases are more prevalent; for example, vitamin A deficiency is a major cause of blindness in children. Thiamin deficiency and scurvy are seen in situations such as refugee camps. Some vitamins also have pharmacological actions well above the intake levels that normally prevent deficiency disease, e.g. the use of vitamin A (with precautions) for acne.

Taking vitamin tablets is fashionable in affluent countries and some individuals take very high doses of such supplements. Doctors therefore need to know the features of both deficiency and overdosage of the major vitamins. Side-effects or toxicity are most serious with high dosage of vitamins A, B_6 and D.

10.22 VITAMIN SUMMARY

Recommended name	Alternative name(s)	Sources	Deficiency	Excess
Fat-soluble				
Vitamin A		Liver, milk, butter, cheese, fish oils	Xerophthalmia, night blindness, keratomalacia, follicular hyperkeratosis	Liver damage, bone damage, teratogenesis
Vitamin D		Mainly manufactured in skin under the influence of sunlight	Rickets, osteomalacia	Hypercalcaemia
Vitamin E		Vegetables, seed oils	Haemolytic anaemia, ataxia	
Vitamin K		Green vegetables, dairy products	Coagulation disorder	
Water-soluble				
Thiamin	Vitamin B_1	Cereals, grains, beans, pork	Beri-beri, Wernicke–Korsakoff syndrome	
Riboflavin	Vitamin B_2	Milk	Glossitis, stomatitis	
Niacin	Nicotinic acid, nicotinamide, vitamin B_3	Plants, meat, fish	Pellagra	
Vitamin B_6	Pyridoxine	Meat, fish, potatoes, bananas	Polyneuropathy	Polyneuropathy
Biotin		Liver, egg yolk, cereals, yeast	Dermatitis, alopecia, paraesthesiae	
Folate		Liver	Anaemia	
Vitamin B_{12}	Cobalamin	Animal products	Anaemia, neurological degeneration	
Vitamin C	Ascorbic acid	Fresh fruit, fresh vegetables	Scurvy	

FAT-SOLUBLE VITAMINS

Vitamin A (retinol)

Retinol itself is found only in foods of animal origin; liver is the richest source. However, vitamin A is also produced in the intestine by the splitting of carotenes, which are present in green vegetables, carrots and some fruits. Two-thirds of vitamin A intake in the UK (and total intake in vegans) comes from carotenes (chiefly β-carotene). The functions of retinol include the following:

- In vision, 11-*cis* retinaldehyde is the initial part of the photoreceptor complex in rods of the retina.
- Another form of the vitamin, retinoic acid, induces differentiation of epithelial cells by binding to specific nuclear receptors, which turn on responsive genes. In vitamin A deficiency, mucus-secreting cells are replaced by keratin-producing cells.
- Vitamin A is necessary for normal growth, fetal development, fertility, haemopoiesis and immune function. Deficient children suffer more severe respiratory infections and gastroenteritis, and have increased morbidity and mortality rates.

Deficiency

On the world scale, the most important consequence of vitamin A deficiency is blindness. Each year, approximately 500 000 new cases of blindness occur in young children, mostly in Asia, and WHO is now giving high priority to the prevention of vitamin A deficiency. The ocular features of vitamin A deficiency pass through a number of stages.

Night blindness is the earliest sign of deficiency and results from an impairment of the dark adaptation process. The diagnosis is supported by a low plasma retinol concentration and is confirmed by marked improvement in dark adaptation following therapeutic doses of retinol. The next phase in the process involves the loss of the normal mucous cells from the cornea, which takes on a dull, hazy, lacklustre appearance due to keratinisation. This abnormality is described as xerophthalmia. Bitot's spots may also be seen. These are glistening white plaques of desquamated thickened conjunctival epithelium, usually triangular in shape and firmly adherent to the underlying conjunctiva (see Fig. 10.18A). The final consequence of deficiency is the development of keratomalacia (see Fig. 10.18B), leading to corneal ulceration, scarring and irreversible blindness.

Immediately following the diagnosis of vitamin A deficiency a single large dose of 60 mg retinol as palmitate or acetate (200 000 IU) should be given orally or, if there is vomiting or severe diarrhoea, by intramuscular injection. The oral dose should be repeated the next day and again prior to discharge or at a follow-up visit. Prevention is also important; in countries where vitamin A deficiency is endemic, pregnant women should be advised to eat dark-green leafy vegetables and yellow fruits to build up stores of retinol in the fetal liver. Babies should also be given such vegetables or locally available carotene-rich fruits. In communities where xerophthalmia is endemic, single prophylactic oral doses of 60 mg retinol (200 000 IU) as palmitate

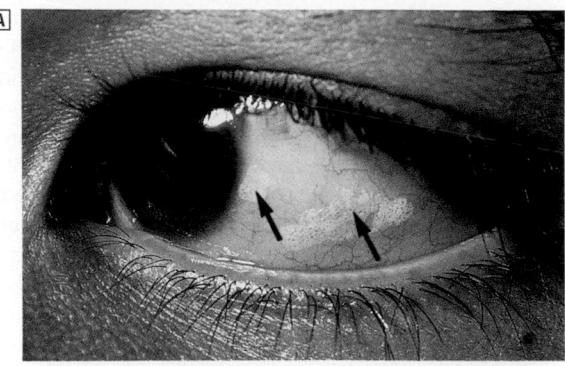
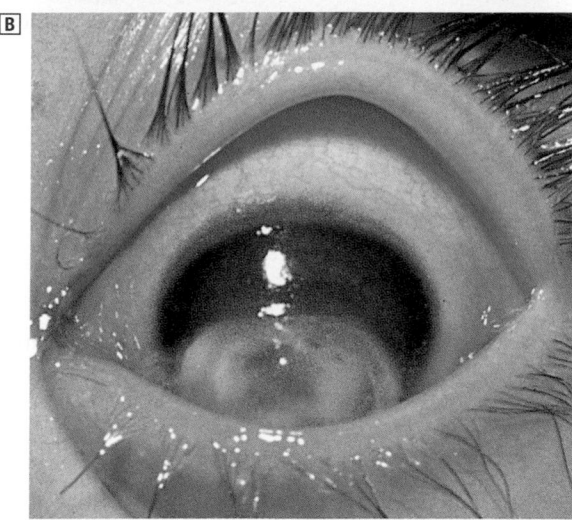

Fig. 10.18 Eye signs of vitamin A deficiency. A Bitot's spots showing the white triangular plaques (arrows). B Keratomalacia secondary to vitamin A deficiency in a 14-month-old child. There is liquefactive necrosis affecting the greater part of the cornea. The relative sparing of the superior aspect of the cornea is typical.

given to pre-school children significantly reduce mortality from gastroenteritis and respiratory infections; a similar large dose is indicated in any child with measles. Oral administration of periodic high doses of vitamin A (60 mg retinol or 200 000 IU) is now used to reduce vitamin A deficiency in developing countries. Dosing at 4–6-month intervals is sufficient to prevent serious consequences of vitamin A deficiency.

Toxicity

Single large doses in children, as described above, are well tolerated. The most serious side-effects of repeated moderate or high doses of retinol are liver damage, hyperostosis and teratogenicity. Women in developed countries who are pregnant are therefore advised not to take vitamin A supplements. Acute overdose leads to nausea and headache, increased intracranial pressure and skin desquamation. Excessive intake of carotene can cause a benign condition in which pigmentation of the skin occurs (hypercarotenosis); this gradually fades when the excessive intake is stopped.

Vitamin D

The natural form of vitamin D, cholecalciferol, is a modified steroid. It is formed in the skin by the action of ultraviolet (UV) light on 7-dehydrocholesterol, a minor companion of cholesterol (see Fig. 10.19). This is the major source of vitamin D. The natural dietary sources include egg yolk, oily fish, butter and milk, but these contribute very little to the body's requirements. The pharmaceutical form of pure vitamin D is (ergo)calciferol, made by the action of UV light on ergosterol (a sterol found in fungi). Ergocalciferol is added (in controlled amounts) to margarines and (in North America) to milk.

Cholecalciferol itself is not biologically active, and is converted in the liver to 25-hydroxycholecalciferol ($25(OH)D_3$) which is further hydroxylated in the kidneys mainly to 1,25-dihydroxycholecalciferol ($1,25(OH_2)D_3$). This second product is the active form of vitamin D (see Fig. 16.13, p. 715). Vitamin D has important effects upon the uptake of calcium from the gut and in bone formation. Deficiency leads to poor bone mineralisation, causing rickets in children and osteomalacia in adults (see p. 1030). This could occur in a number of circumstances. Older people and dark-skinned people make less vitamin D in their skin. In chronic intestinal diseases there can be malabsorption of vitamin D, and in chronic kidney disease production of the active form is impaired.

Vitamin D is toxic in large dosage, where it causes hypercalcaemia.

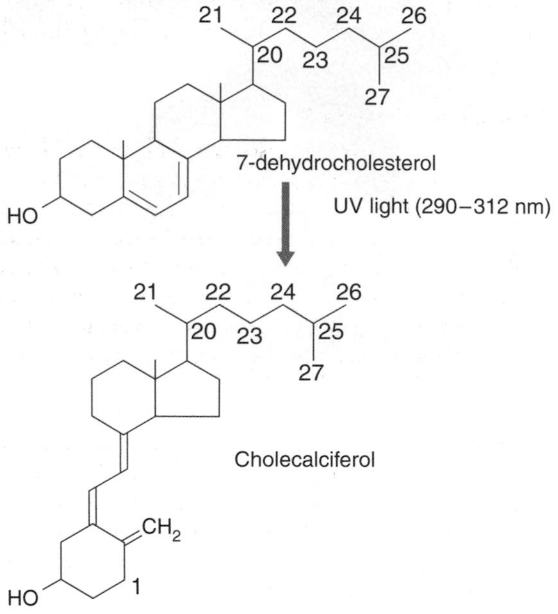

Vitamin E

There are actually eight related fat-soluble substances with vitamin E activity. The most important dietary form is alpha-tocopherol. Rich sources include vegetable oils, wholegrain cereals and nuts. Vitamin E is an important antioxidant, preventing oxidation of polyunsaturated fatty acids in cell membranes by free radicals. It has other roles, unrelated to antioxidant activity, including the maintenance of cell membrane structure and effects on DNA synthesis and cell signalling. It is also involved in the anti-inflammatory and immune systems.

In animal studies, vitamin E deficiency leads to myopathies, neuropathies and liver necrosis. This results from the effects of cell membrane damage with consequent cell leakage. Human deficiency states are rare and have only been described in premature infants and in malabsorption. The first feature of human deficiency is a mild haemolytic anaemia. In chronic fat malabsorption, ataxia and visual scotomas occur which respond to vitamin E.

As regards beneficial effects, vitamin E intake confers protection against coronary heart disease. A number of population studies have shown that the dietary intake of vitamin E is inversely related to the incidence of ischaemic heart disease (see Fig. 10.20). This effect is probably due to vitamin E protecting low-density lipoprotein from oxidation and hence reducing atherogenesis. It has not yet been established whether taking vitamin E supplements contributes towards primary or secondary prevention of ischaemic heart disease.

Fig. 10.19 Biochemical pathway of vitamin D synthesis.

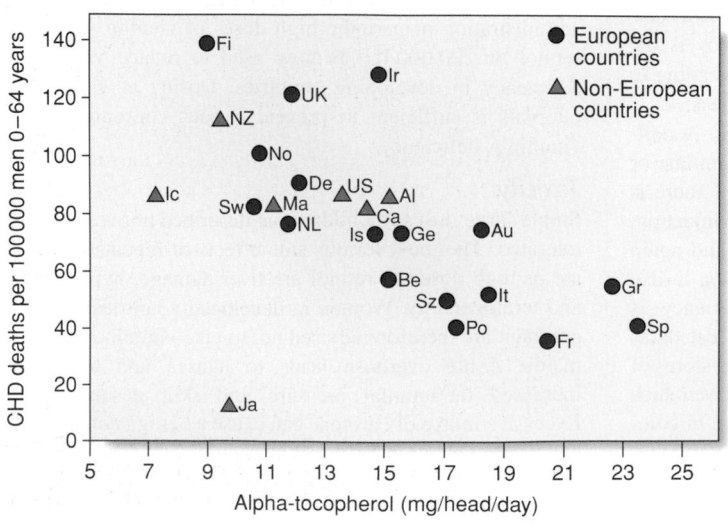

Fig. 10.20   The relation between vitamin E ingestion and the prevalence of coronary heart disease. (Al = Australia; Au = Austria; Be = Belgium; Ca = Canada; De = Denmark; Fr = France; Fi = Finland; Ge = Germany; Gr = Greece; Ic = Iceland; Ir = Ireland; Is = Israel; It = Italy; Ja = Japan; Ma = Malta; NL = Netherlands; No = Norway; NZ = New Zealand; Po = Portugal; Sp = Spain; Sw = Sweden; Sz = Switzerland; UK = United Kingdom; US = United States)

Vitamin K

Vitamin K is required for the synthesis of clotting factors and hence deficiency leads to prolonged coagulation and bleeding. Vitamin K is a cofactor in the production of an unusual amino acid, γ-carboxyglutamic acid (gla). Gla residues are part of the protein molecule of four of the coagulation factors, II, VII, IX and X. The gla residues confer on these proteins the capacity to bind to phospholipid surfaces in the presence of calcium.

Adequate amounts are normally supplied in the average diet (leafy vegetables and liver) or synthesised by bacteria in the colon. Vitamin K has important roles in three situations:

- In the newborn, primary deficiency can occur because placental transfer of vitamin K is inefficient, the neonatal bowel has not yet acquired bacteria and breast milk contains little of the vitamin. Vitamin K is given routinely to newborn babies to prevent haemorrhagic disease of the newborn. On a world-wide basis the latter remains a significant cause of infant mortality and morbidity.
- In obstructive jaundice, dietary vitamin K is not absorbed and it is very important to administer this vitamin in parenteral form before surgery.
- Warfarin and related anticoagulants (see p. 955) act by antagonising vitamin K.

WATER-SOLUBLE VITAMINS

Thiamin (vitamin B$_1$)

Thiamin pyrophosphate (TPP) is involved in carbohydrate metabolism. It is an essential coenzyme for the decarboxylation of pyruvate to acetylcoenzyme A. This is the bridge between anaerobic glycolysis and the tricarboxylic acid (Krebs) cycle. TPP is also the coenzyme for transketolase in the hexose monophosphate shunt pathway and for decarboxylation of α-ketoglutarate to succinate in the Krebs cycle. Consequently, when thiamin is deficient:

- Cells cannot metabolise glucose aerobically; this is likely to affect the nervous system first, since this organ depends largely on glucose for its energy requirements.
- There is accumulation of pyruvic and lactic acid, which produce vasodilatation and increased cardiac output.

Thiamin is widely distributed in foods of both vegetable and animal origin, although cereals are the main source. In the developed world, thiamin deficiency is mainly encountered in chronic alcoholics. Poor diet together with impaired absorption, storage and phosphorylation of thiamin in the liver and the increased requirements for thiamin due to the high energy in ethanol all contribute to the manifestation of deficiency. In the developing world, deficiency usually arises as a consequence of a diet consisting only of polished rice. The body has very limited stores of thiamin, so deficiency starts after about a month on a thiamin-free diet.

Thiamin deficiency leads to beri-beri, which may manifest in a number of clinical presentations:

- infantile beri-beri seen in exclusively breastfed infants of deficient mothers, a condition which is invariably fatal
- dry (or neurological) beri-beri which manifests in chronic peripheral neuropathy, with wrist and/or foot drop, and may manifest with Korsakoff's psychosis and Wernicke's encephalopathy (see p. 1173)
- wet (or cardiac) beri-beri with generalised oedema due to biventricular heart failure with pulmonary congestion.

Management of thiamin deficiency

In dry beri-beri the response to thiamin is not uniformly good. However, multivitamin therapy seems to produce some improvement, suggesting that other vitamin deficiencies may be involved. Wernicke's encephalopathy should be treated without delay with 50–100 mg thiamin hydrochloride by slow i.v. injection followed by 50–100 mg i.m. daily for a week. The response is both rapid (within 2–3 days) and dramatic and this confirms the diagnosis. The memory disorder (Korsakoff's psychosis) takes longer to improve and some degree of memory impairment often persists. Wet beri-beri is an acute medical emergency requiring treatment with i.v. thiamin.

Riboflavin (vitamin B$_2$)

Riboflavin is a flavoprotein and is part of the oxidation chain in the mitochondria, acting as a coenzyme in oxidation-reduction reactions. Riboflavin is widely distributed in animal and vegetable foods. The richest source of riboflavin is milk and its non-fat products. Levels of the vitamin are low in staple cereals but germination increases its content. It is a yellow-green fluorescent compound soluble in water. It is decomposed under alkaline conditions by heat and is also destroyed by exposure to UV light.

Clinical deficiency is rare in developed countries. Deficiency mainly affects the tongue and lips and manifests as glossitis, angular stomatitis and cheilosis. The genitals may be affected as well as the facial skin areas rich in sebaceous glands, where deficiency causes nasolabial or facial dyssebacea. Rapid recovery usually follows administration of riboflavin 10 mg daily by mouth.

Niacin (nicotinic acid and nicotinamide)

Nicotinic acid and nicotinamide have equal biological activity and are considered together in foods under the generic term 'niacin'. Both are water-soluble and resistant to heat. Nicotinamide is an essential part of the two important pyridine nucleotides, nicotinamide adenine dinucleotide (NAD) and nicotinamide adenine dinucleotide phosphate (NADP), which play a key role in intermediate metabolism. NAD is also the coenzyme for alcohol dehydrogenase. A special feature of this vitamin is that it is normally synthesised in the body in limited amounts from tryptophan. Eggs and cheese are examples of foods that contain little pre-formed niacin but provide niacin equivalents from tryptophan.

Pellagra

Pellagra is a nutritional disease resulting from deficiency of niacin and was formerly endemic among the poor whose diet subsisted chiefly of maize. The reason for this is that maize contains niacytin, a form of niacin that the body is unable to utilise. Pellagra can develop within 8 weeks in individuals eating diets that are deficient in niacin and tryptophan. It remains a problem in parts of Africa and is occasionally seen in developed countries in alcoholics and patients with chronic small intestinal disease. Pellagra can also occur in Hartnup's disease, a genetic disorder characterised by impaired absorption of several amino acids including tryptophan, and in carcinoid syndrome (see p. 801), where tryptophan is utilised for the production of 5-hydroxytryptamine (5-HT, serotonin), rather than being available for the synthesis of niacin.

Pellagra has been called 'the disease of the three Ds':

- *Dermatitis.* Characteristically, there is erythema resembling severe sunburn, appearing symmetrically over the parts of the body exposed to sunlight, particularly the limbs and especially on the neck but not the face (Casal's necklace; see Fig. 10.21). The skin lesions may progress to vesiculation, cracking, exudation and crusting with ulceration, and secondary infection may develop.
- *Diarrhoea.* This is often associated with anorexia, nausea, glossitis and dysphagia. It reflects the presence of a non-infective inflammation that extends throughout the gastrointestinal tract.
- *Dementia.* In severe deficiency, delirium occurs acutely, with dementia developing in chronic cases.

Treatment is with nicotinamide, given in a dose of 100 mg 8-hourly by mouth or by the parenteral route. The response is usually rapid; within 24 hours skin erythema diminishes, diarrhoea ceases and a striking improvement occurs in the patient's behaviour and mental attitude.

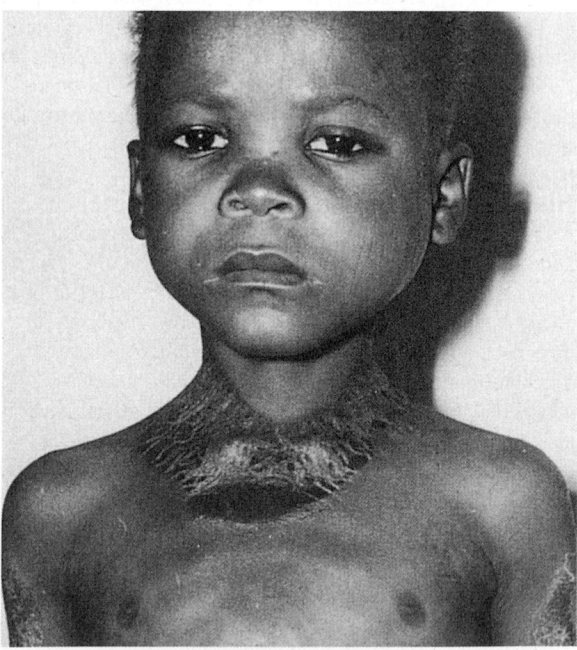

Fig. 10.21 Dermatitis due to pellagra (niacin deficiency).
The lesions appear in those parts of the body exposed to sunlight. The classic 'Casal's necklace' can be seen around the neck and upper chest. Note also the hyper-pigmentation in the arms and hands.

Vitamin B6 (pyridoxine)

Pyridoxine, pyridoxal and pyridoxamine are three closely related compounds with similar physiological actions. The active form of the vitamin in humans is pyridoxal 5-phosphate, the coenzyme for a large number of different enzyme systems involved in the metabolism of amino acids. Vitamin B6 is available in most foods, but rich sources include meat, fish, potatoes and bananas.

Dietary deficiency seems to be rare. However, certain drugs, such as isoniazid and penicillamine, act as chemical antagonists to pyridoxine and cause deficiency. Isoniazid causes peripheral neuropathy, which responds to B6 administration. Some cases of sideroblastic anaemia also respond to treatment with pyridoxine.

Large doses of vitamin B6 have an antiemetic effect in radiotherapy-induced nausea. It has also become popular for patients to take vitamin B6 supplements for the treatment of nausea in pregnancy, carpal tunnel syndrome and premenstrual syndrome; however, there is no convincing evidence of benefit. Megavitamin doses of vitamin B6 taken for several months can cause a sensory polyneuropathy.

Biotin

Biotin functions as a coenzyme in carbohydrate, fatty acid and amino acid metabolism. Biotin deficiency rarely occurs on a natural diet but is occasionally seen in patients consuming large quantities of raw eggs. Avidin in raw eggs binds to biotin in the intestine and inactivates it. The clinical features of deficiency include scaly dermatitis, alopecia and paraesthesia. A form of seborrhoeic dermatitis in infants responds to biotin.

Vitamin B12 and folate

These vitamins and the haematological disorders due to their deficiency are discussed on pages 918–920. Although the requirements for vitamin B12 are very small, it is only found in animal products and hence vegans are at particular risk of deficiency. The normal liver contains enough stores to cover requirements for several years. Infestation due to fish tapeworm *(Diphyllobothrium latum)* occurs in some communities that live around large lakes and may interfere with absorption of the vitamin.

Vitamin B12 and the nervous system

Severe prolonged vitamin B12 deficiency may cause megaloblastic anaemia and/or neurological degeneration. In some cases the neurological disease predominates; this may be because a good intake of folate maintains erythropoiesis. Vitamin B12, but not folate, is needed for the integrity of myelin. In severe deficiency there is insidious, diffuse and uneven demyelination. It may be clinically manifest as peripheral neuropathy or spinal cord degeneration affecting both posterior and lateral columns ('subacute combined degeneration of the spinal cord'), or there may be cerebral manifestations (resembling dementia) or optic atrophy. Treatment with hydroxocobalamin is usually beneficial but improvement may be slow.

Folic acid in the prevention of neural tube defects

Three major birth defects (spina bifida, anencephaly and encephalocele) result from imperfect closure of the neural tube, which takes place 3–4 weeks after conception. Folic acid has been shown to be of benefit in preventing neural tube defects (see EBM panel). Folate is involved directly in DNA and RNA synthesis and it seems that a higher than normal level is required during embryonic development. The UK Department of Health (1991) advises that women who have experienced a pregnancy affected by a neural tube defect should take 5 mg of folic acid daily from before conception and throughout the first trimester of pregnancy. In addition, all women planning a pregnancy are advised to include good sources of folate in their diet. Liver is the richest source of folate but an alternative source is advised in early pregnancy because of its high vitamin A content.

EBM

PREVENTING NEURAL TUBE DEFECTS—effect of periconceptional folate supplementation

'In a combined analysis of four RCTs, periconceptional folate supplementation at doses between 0.36 and 4 mg/day significantly reduced the incidence of neural tube defects (odds ratio 0.28, 95% confidence interval 0.15 to 0.53).'

- MRC Vitamin Study Research Group. Prevention of neural tube defects: results of the Medical Research Council Vitamin Study. Lancet 1991; 338:131–137.
- Lumley J, Watson L, Watson M, Bower C. Periconceptional supplementation with folate and/or multivitamins for preventing neural tube defects (Cochrane Review). Cochrane Library, issue 1, 2001. Oxford: Update Software.

Further information: 💻 www.cochrane.co.uk

Vitamin C (ascorbic acid)

Ascorbic acid is the most active reducing agent in the aqueous phase of living tissues. It is involved in intracellular electron transfer, since it is readily oxidised and reversibly reduced. Vitamin C is necessary for the formation of collagen and in connective tissue takes part in the hydroxylation of protocollagen proline and lysine to collagen hydroxyproline and hydroxylysine. While ascorbic acid is present in significant amounts in fresh fruit and vegetables, it is easily destroyed by heat, increased pH and light, and is very soluble in water. Hence many traditional cooking methods reduce or eliminate it.

It has been suggested that high-dose vitamin C improves immune function (including resistance to the common cold) and cholesterol turnover but such effects remain unproven in controlled trials. Daily intakes of more than 1 g have been reported to cause diarrhoea and increase the formation of renal oxalate stones.

Scurvy

Ascorbic acid deficiency results in defective formation of collagen and there is in consequence impaired healing of wounds, capillary haemorrhage and subnormal platelet adhesiveness (normal platelets are rich in ascorbate). Scurvy is the clinical manifestation of vitamin C deficiency. It is seen in people who have eaten no fruit or vegetables for 2–3 months. Infants fed on boiled milk are at risk of deficiency, as are adults with an inadequate diet. Trauma, surgery and burns, infections, smoking and certain drugs (e.g. adrenocortical steroids, aspirin, indometacin and tetracycline) all increase the requirement for vitamin C. Consequently, hospital patients often require more than the recommended intake.

The clinical features of scurvy are as follows:

- The pathognomonic clinical sign is swollen and spongy gums, which bleed easily.
- There may be perifollicular, petechial or spontaneous bruising.
- Haemorrhage may occur into a joint or into the gastrointestinal tract.
- The patient is usually anaemic.
- Fresh wounds fail to heal.

For treatment, a dose of 250 mg vitamin C 8-hourly by mouth should saturate the tissues quickly. The general deficiencies of the patient's former diet also need to be corrected. If the patient is anaemic, iron and sometimes folic acid are indicated.

INORGANIC NUTRIENTS

Sixteen or more inorganic elements are essential for humans (see Box 10.23). Deficiency disease is seen where there is inadequate dietary intake or excessive loss from the body. Toxic effects have also been observed from self-medication and disordered absorption or excretion. Clinical manifestations of toxicity are readily seen with excess of iron (haemochromatosis or haemosiderosis), fluoride (fluorosis, seen in India), copper (Wilson's disease) and selenium (selenosis, seen in parts of China).

Calcium

Calcium is the most abundant cation in the body and powerful homeostatic mechanisms exist for maintaining circulating ionised calcium levels (see pp. 714–715 and 1030). The main dietary sources are listed in Box 10.24. If calcium intake is truly inadequate, bone mineralisation may be impaired in

---

10.23 ESSENTIAL INORGANIC NUTRIENTS

- Sodium (see p. 274)
- Potassium (see p. 283)
- Chloride, magnesium (see p. 295)
- Calcium
- Phosphorus
- Iron
- Zinc
- Copper
- Chromium
- Selenium
- Manganese
- Molybdenum
- Iodine
- Fluoride
- Cobalt[1]
- Sulphur[2]

[1] Physiologically active in the form of vitamin B_{12}.
[2] Required in the form of the amino acids methionine and cysteine.

10.24 DIETARY SOURCES OF CALCIUM

- Milks, cheeses, yoghurt, eggs
- Fish eaten with bone, e.g. sardines, pilchards
- Some shellfish
- Some nuts, e.g. almonds, peanuts
- Some legumes, e.g. chick peas, beans
- Bread (if fortified)

children and bone loss accelerated in adults. Calcium absorption may be impaired in the following circumstances:

- vitamin D deficiency (see p. 320)
- malabsorption secondary to small intestinal disease
- where foods contain oxalate (e.g. spinach) or phytate (wholegrain cereals) that tends to form insoluble salts with calcium. In this way, the calcium is not available for absorption.

The potential benefits of a high calcium intake in osteoporosis are discussed on page 1026.

Phosphorus

Dietary deficiency of phosphorus is rare since it is present in nearly all foods and phosphates are added to a number of processed foods. Phosphate deficiency occurs:

- in premature infants fed on human milk
- in patients with renal tubular phosphate loss
- due to prolonged high dosage of aluminium hydroxide
- sometimes when alcoholic patients are fed with high-carbohydrate foods
- in patients on TPN if not enough phosphate is provided.

The features of deficiency are hypophosphataemia and muscle weakness secondary to adenosine triphosphate (ATP) deficiency.

Iron

Iron is needed by the body for the formation of haemoglobin. It is also involved in the transport of electrons within cells and in a number of enzyme reactions. The major consequence of iron deficiency is anaemia (see pp. 916–918). This is one of the most important nutritional causes of ill health world-wide, in both developed and developing countries.

There is no physiological mechanism for the excretion of iron, so homeostasis depends on the regulation of iron absorption. The normal daily loss of iron is 1 mg, arising from desquamated surface cells and intestinal losses. Since absorption is relatively inefficient, a daily intake of 8 mg is needed to match this amount. A regular loss of only 2 ml of blood per day doubles the iron requirement. On average 30 mg of iron is lost during menstruation and hence premenopausal women require about twice as much iron as men, i.e. 15 mg/day.

10.25 DIETARY SOURCES OF IRON
Haem iron
• Muscle meat (red more than white) • Organ meat (e.g. liver) • Fish and shellfish
Non-haem iron
• Oatmeal • Legumes (peas, beans), nuts, dried fruit • Wholemeal bread • Iron-fortified cereal foods • Red wine • Chocolate
N.B. Foods or meals rich in vitamin C enhance iron absorption.

Absorption of haem iron in foods of animal origin is usually high, whereas the non-haem iron in cereals and vegetables is poorly absorbed. The addition of a small quantity of meat to a large helping of cereal-based food results in much greater absorption of iron from the diet. Fruits and vegetables with a high vitamin C content will enhance iron absorption, while the tannins present in tea will reduce it. Foods rich in iron are listed in Box 10.25. The dietary requirement for iron is about 10 times the body's physiological requirements.

Dietary iron overload is occasionally observed and results in iron accumulation in the liver and, rarely, cirrhosis. Haemochromatosis results from an inherited increase in iron absorption and is described on page 870.

Iodine

Iodine is present in sea fish, seaweed and most plant foods grown near the sea. The amount of iodine in soil and water influences the iodine content of most foods. Iodine is, however, lacking in the high mountain areas of the world, e.g. the Alps and the Himalayas, and in the soil of flood plains (e.g. in Bangladesh). About a billion people in the world are estimated to have an inadequate iodine intake and hence are at risk of iodine deficiency disorder (IDD). Goitre is the most common form of IDD (see p. 702), affecting 200 million people world-wide, while 20 million have preventable brain damage due to iodine deficiency.

In those areas where most women have endemic goitre, 1% or more of the babies are born with congenital hypothyroidism (characterised by mental and physical retardation). There is a higher prevalence than usual of deafness, slowed reflexes and poor learning in the remaining population. The best way of preventing neonatal congenital hypothyroidism is by ensuring adequate levels of iodine during pregnancy. Intramuscular injections with 1–2 ml of iodised poppy seed oil (475–950 mg iodine) to women of childbearing age every 3–5 years may be one strategy. Administration of iodised oil orally at 6-monthly or yearly intervals may also be a useful approach for both adults and children. A more sustainable method to ensure adequate intakes of iodine and to reduce IDD is to make iodised salt widely available.

Zinc

Zinc is present in most foods of vegetable and animal origin. It is an essential component of many enzymes including carbonic anhydrase, alcohol dehydrogenase and alkaline phosphatase. Acute zinc deficiency has been reported in patients receiving prolonged zinc-free parenteral alimentation, and causes diarrhoea, mental apathy, a moist eczematoid dermatitis, especially round the mouth, and loss of hair. Zinc deficiency is responsible for the clinical features seen in the very rare congenital disorder known as acrodermatitis enteropathica (growth retardation, hair loss and chronic diarrhoea). In the Middle East chronic deficiency has been described in association with dwarfism and hypogonadism. Zinc deficiency has also been observed secondary to PEM, malabsorption syndromes, alcoholism and alcoholic liver disease. In PEM, associated zinc deficiency causes thymic atrophy, and zinc supplements may accelerate the healing of skin lesions, promote general well-being, improve appetite and reduce the morbidity associated with the malnourished state.

Selenium

Selenium is part of the enzyme glutathione peroxidase, which helps prevent free radical damage to cells. Some of the functions of selenium and vitamin E overlap. Selenium is also part of the enzyme responsible for the conversion of thyroxine to triiodothyronine in liver microsomes. This function is responsible for the infrequent occurrence of hypothyroidism seen in selenium-deficient areas. Selenium deficiency has been reported to cause cardiomyopathy in children and a more generalised myopathy in adults. A cardiomyopathy termed Keshan's disease is seen in some parts of China where soil selenium and the selenium content of food are depleted.

Other minerals

Copper metabolism is abnormal in Wilson's disease (see p. 871). Deficiency occasionally occurs in young children; the main features are a microcytic hypochromic anaemia, neutropenia, retarded growth, skeletal rarefaction and dermatosis.

Chromium facilitates the action of insulin. Deficiency presents as hyperglycaemia and has been reported in some children with PEM and as a rare complication of prolonged parenteral nutrition.

Fluoride

Fluoride has an important influence on the prevention of dental caries. If the water supply of a locality contains more than 1 part per million (ppm) of fluoride, the incidence of dental caries is low. Soft waters usually contain no fluoride, whilst very hard waters may contain over 10 ppm. The benefit of fluoride is greatest when it is taken before the permanent teeth erupt, while their enamel is being laid down; this increases the resistance of the enamel to acid attack. The deliberate addition of traces of fluoride (at 1 ppm) to public water supplies is now a standard public health practice in many countries.

Chronic fluoride poisoning is occasionally seen in localities where the water supply contains more than 10 ppm fluoride. It can also occur in workers handling cryocite (sodium ammonium fluoride), used in smelting aluminium. Excessive fluoride ingestion increases bone density and causes calcification of ligaments and the tendinous insertions of muscles. Excess fluoride can also affect the dental enamel and can cause mottling, pitting and pigmentation.

Sodium, potassium and magnesium

The roles of sodium, potassium and magnesium are discussed in Chapter 9.

OTHER METABOLIC DISORDERS

PORPHYRIAS

The porphyrins are chemical compounds, formed by the linkage of four pyrol rings. They include haem and its biosynthetic precursors. The metabolic pathway of haem synthesis involves a number of steps, each governed by a particular enzyme. Deficiencies of these enzymes give rise to an increased concentration of the precursor of that particular step. Increased levels of these chemicals cause the diseases known as the porphyrias. The pathway is summarised in Figure 10.22.

There are seven main types of porphyria classified according to the site of the enzyme defect (see Box 10.26 and Fig. 10.22). In hepatic porphyrias, the problem lies within the liver. In erythropoietic porphyrias, the problem is in the erythrocytes in the bone marrow. However, a more useful clinical classification specifies whether they cause acute symptoms, cutaneous features or a mixed picture (see Box 10.26).

ACUTE PORPHYRIAS

These conditions are characterised by intermittent attacks of abdominal pain. Neurological and psychiatric symptoms are also common, including proximal myopathy and motor and sensory neuropathies. Patients often experience constipation, nausea, vomiting and postural hypotension. Acute attacks may be precipitated by various triggers, including many prescribed medications (e.g. general anaesthetic agents, barbiturates, sulphonamides, griseofulvin, antidepressants and oral contraceptives).

The diagnosis is established by sending a urine sample to the laboratory at the time of an acute attack. The urine needs

---

ISSUES IN OLDER PEOPLE
NUTRITION

- Body composition changes with advancing age. There is a loss of muscle mass, and fat constitutes a greater percentage of total body weight than in youth.
- These changes affect nutritional needs. Energy requirements fall due to the decrease in energy expenditure that results from decreasing lean body mass.
- Calculation of BMI becomes difficult in old age as original height diminishes due to loss of vertebral bone, reduced disc spaces and increased laxity of the vertebral support ligaments. It is also difficult to measure height in those with postural abnormalities such as kyphosis. Alternatives include arm demispan and knee height, for which formulae exist to convert to actual height.
- Appetite declines with age and satiety occurs more rapidly, perhaps because of reduced rates of gastric emptying. Reduced smell and taste may also adversely affect appetite.
- Although energy requirements fall, the requirements for other nutrients remain unchanged, so with decreasing dietary intake micronutrient deficiencies become more likely and the diet of older people needs to be nutrient-rich to compensate for this.
- Reduced levels of vitamin D are found in frail older people, due to reduced dietary intake, decreased sun exposure and less efficient skin conversion. This can lead to bone loss and fractures. Supplements should be given to those at particular risk.
- There is a decline in immune function with advancing age. An adequate intake of antioxidant vitamins and minerals is important to preserve this function.
- Subclinical or overt vitamin deficiency may account for declining cognitive function in old age. Vitamin B_{12} is especially important for central nervous system function and should be replaced intramuscularly in all those with deficiency.

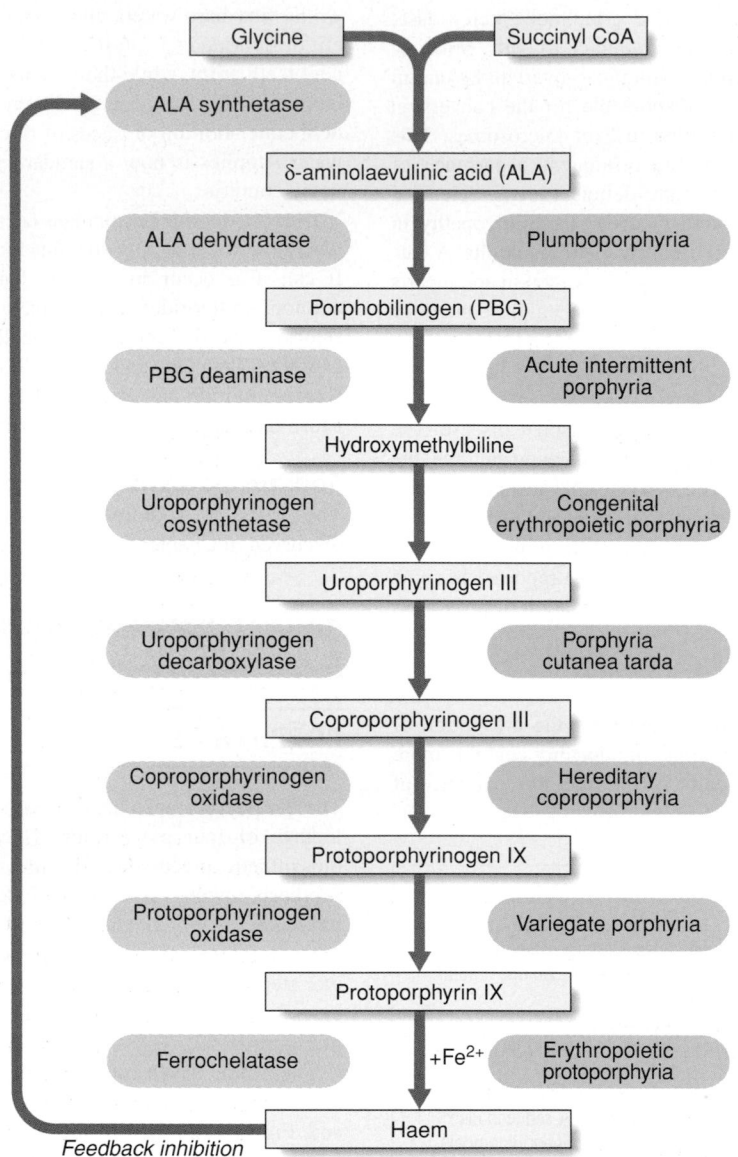

Fig. 10.22 Pathways of porphyrin synthesis. The enzyme responsible for each step is detailed on the left. The condition arising from the deficiency is shown on the right.

to be protected from light; the finding of a raised amino-laevulinic acid (ALA) and porphobilinogen (PBG) establishes the diagnosis. Between attacks, the concentration of these substances in the urine is usually normal.

Acute attacks are treated by the administration of glucose and haem arginate (3 mg/kg once daily for 4 days by i.v. infusion—maximal dose 250 mg/day). Together, these substances reduce the synthesis of aminolaevulinic acid, resulting in clinical improvement. If seizures occur in the context of an acute attack, these are notoriously difficult to control. Gabapentin and vigabatrin are appropriate treatments and do not predispose towards an acute attack of porphyria.

CUTANEOUS PORPHYRIAS

These conditions are characterised by the development of photosensitivity. In the majority of these conditions, patients develop subepidermal bullae and hypertrichosis. The skin is fragile and sustains damage on minor trauma. The lesions are slow to heal and often form extensive scarring. In erythropoietic protoporphyria, the situation is slightly different. Here, the affected individual develops a burning sensation affecting light-exposed parts of the skin.

In the diagnosis of cutaneous porphyria, porphyrins should be checked in both urine and faeces. The routes of

10.26 LABORATORY TESTS IN PORPHYRIA

	Urinary porphobilinogen (PBG) and aminolaevulinic acid (ALA)	Urinary porphyrins	Faecal porphyrins
Acute porphyrias			
Acute intermittent porphyria	PBG and ALA increased (very high during acute attack)	Mild increase (very high during acute attack)	Normal
Plumboporphyria	Raised ALA	Coproporphyrinogen III	Normal
Mixed porphyrias			
Hereditary coproporphyria	PBG and ALA raised during acute attack (normal in quiescent phase)	Coproporphyrinogen III	Coproporphyrinogen III
Variegate porphyria	PBG and ALA raised during acute attack (normal in quiescent phase)	Coproporphyrinogen III	Protoporphyrin IX > coproporphyrinogen III and porphyrin X
Cutaneous porphyrias			
Congenital erythropoietic porphyria	Normal	Uroporphyrinogen I > coproporphyrinogen I	Coproporphyrinogen I
Erythropoietic protoporphyria	Normal	Normal	Protoporphyrin increased or decreased
Porphyria cutanea tarda	Normal	Uroporphyrinogen > heptacarboxylate	Isocoproporphyrinogen, heptacarboxylate

excretion vary in different versions of cutaneous porphyria (see Box 10.26).

In all forms of cutaneous porphyria exposure to light should be avoided or effective blocking agents used. In porphyria cutanea tarda there is usually excessive iron accumulation within the body and regular venesection may be helpful.

AMYLOIDOSIS

Amyloidosis is a term applied to a number of conditions of varying aetiology characterised by the deposition of insoluble fibrillar proteins in organs and tissues. The protein deposition can affect many sites and give rise to a multisystem disorder. The diagnosis should be considered in all cases of unexplained nephrotic syndrome, cardiomyopathy and peripheral neuropathy.

Amyloidosis may be the consequence of an acquired or inherited condition. The classification of these disorders is based on the type of protein deposited. The more common varieties are summarised in Box 10.27. The aetiology, clinical features and treatment of the different forms of amyloidosis vary and will be described in turn.

AL amyloidosis
Typically, this is a rapidly progressive condition with amyloid deposition in numerous sites. The amyloid protein consists of fragments of immunoglobulin light chains, produced by a monoclonal population of plasma cells in the bone marrow. AL amyloidosis is more common in males and rarely presents before the age of 40. The most common initial feature is nephrotic syndrome, with urinary protein loss often > 20 g/day. Cardiac abnormalities are also common. The patient usually presents with symptoms of biventricular cardiac failure. Echocardiography reveals thickening of the walls of both ventricles, together with a small chamber size. Neurological features may also be found, including carpal tunnel syndrome resulting from median nerve compression due to amyloid deposits, peripheral neuropathy and autonomic neuropathy. This in turn can lead to manifestations such as diarrhoea, constipation and early satiety. Periorbital purpura due to capillary fragility is virtually pathognomonic of AL amyloidosis. However, it is only seen in 15% of patients. Another typical feature is macroglossia, although it is found in only 10% of patients.

Familial amyloidosis
These are inherited conditions, almost invariably arising from mutations in the transthyretin protein. Certain amino

10.27 AMYLOIDOSIS

Fibril-forming protein	Location of deposits	Clinical presentation
Immunoglobulin light chain (AL)	Kidney, heart, gut, nerves	AL amyloidosis
Transthyretin (ATTR)	Variable	Familial and senile amyloidosis
Amyloid A protein (AA)	Kidney, other	Secondary amyloidosis and familial Mediterranean fever
β2 microglobulin	Bones, joints, other	Dialysis-associated amyloid (carpal tunnel syndrome)
β-amyloid precursor	Brain	Alzheimer's disease

acid substitutions predispose the protein to form amyloid deposits. More than 60 substitutions have been described to date. All of these variants have a characteristic age of onset and clinical picture. However, the most common presentations are with peripheral and autonomic neuropathy. Cardiac problems can occur but renal involvement is rare. A positive family history would be a strong pointer towards the diagnosis.

Secondary amyloidosis

This form of amyloidosis arises as a consequence of chronic inflammatory conditions, most commonly tuberculosis, bronchiectasis and osteomyelitis. In such conditions, patients develop elevated levels of serum amyloid A (SAA) protein. This is an acute phase protein, which has a propensity for a fibrillar deposition. Secondary amyloidosis may also occur in familial Mediterranean fever.

Other forms of amyloidosis

There are other rarer forms of amyloidosis, including a condition seen in patients having chronic haemodialysis. In this situation, β2 microglobulin forms the precursor protein. Carpal tunnel syndrome is a common presentation. Amyloid protein (Aβ) is also found in the cerebral plaques of Alzheimer's disease.

Diagnosis of amyloidosis

Diagnosis is usually established by biopsy of an affected organ. Amyloidosis gives typical microscopic appearances. When viewed with haematoxylin and eosin staining, amyloid deposits appear pink in colour. With Congo red staining the deposits normally appear red but demonstrate an apple-green appearance upon the application of polarised light. Other methods of diagnosis include aspiration of subcutaneous fat, which reveals evidence of the condition in approximately 85% of cases. The presence of urinary Bence Jones protein (see p. 588) would suggest the diagnosis of AL amyloidosis. Quantitative scintigraphy can be performed with ^{123}I-labelled serum amyloid P component and

allows the progression and regression of AL, ATTR and AA amyloidosis to be monitored.

Management

Treatment strategies are summarised in Box 10.28. General measures are aimed at supporting the function of any affected organ. Specific treatments are designed to decrease the amount of precursor protein and to prevent further amyloid deposition.

ENVIRONMENTAL DISORDERS

DIVING ILLNESS

Recreational scuba diving is becoming increasingly popular in many parts of the world. Symptoms of decompression illness usually present during or soon after a dive but can also be provoked by flying; as a result, patients may present to medical services at sites far removed from the dive.

Ambient pressure underwater increases by 1 atmosphere (760 torr) for every 10 metres seawater (msw) depth. Under normal circumstances the diver breathes compressed air delivered via a demand valve at the diver's exact ambient pressure. 100% oxygen can only be used at very shallow depths (< 5 msw) due to the toxic effects to the lung and brain when the oxygen pressure exceeds 1.5 atmospheres. At depths over 50 msw mixtures of helium and oxygen (heliox) with less than 20% oxygen are used to avoid both oxygen toxicity and the narcotic effects of nitrogen.

The physiological impact of the gas laws (as demonstrated in Box 10.29) dictates that as divers descend they breathe air with increased partial pressures of nitrogen and oxygen and at increased density, which imposes a restriction on ventilation.

DECOMPRESSION ILLNESS AND PULMONARY BAROTRAUMA

Exposure of individuals to increased partial pressures of nitrogen results in additional nitrogen being dissolved in

10.28 TREATMENT OF AMYLOIDOSIS	
Condition	**Treatment**
General measures	
Congestive cardiac failure	Salt restriction, diuretics etc.
Heart block	Pacemaker
Nephrotic syndrome	Salt restriction, increased dietary protein
Renal failure	Dialysis
Postural hypotension	Increased salt intake, elastic stockings, fludrocortisone treatment
Gastric atony	Small frequent meals, metoclopramide treatment
Diarrhoea	Dietary changes, antidiarrhoeal medications
Specific treatments	
AL amyloidosis	Cyclical melphalan and prednisolone
AA amyloidosis	Treatment of underlying infection, surgical removal of source of infection if possible, colchicine for familial Mediterranean fever
ATTR amyloidosis	Orthotopic liver transplantation

10.29 PHYSICS OF BREATHING COMPRESSED AIR WHEN DIVING					
	Depth (m)				
	Surface	**10**	**20**	**30**	**50**
Pressure (ata)	1	2	3	4	6
Pressure (kPa)	100	200	300	400	600
Volume effect (ml)	1000	500	333	250	166
Partial pressure N₂ (kPa)	79	158	237	316	474
Partial pressure O₂ (kPa)	21	42	63	84	126
Gas density (g/l)	1.2	2.4	3.6	4.8	7.2

body tissues. On ascent, the tissues became supersaturated with nitrogen, and this places the diver at risk of producing a critical quantity of gas phase (bubbles) in tissues if the ascent is too fast. This is the cause of decompression illness. The gas so formed may cause symptoms locally, by distant embolic effects or by bubbles passing through the pulmonary vascular bed (see Box 10.30). Although there is often an obvious provoking dive-related factor, decompression illness may occur after apparently safe and well-conducted dives.

During the ascent phase of a dive, the gas in the diver's lungs expands due to the decreasing pressure. The diver must therefore ascend slowly and breathe regularly; if ascent is rapid or the diver holds his/her breath, the expanding gas may cause lung rupture (pulmonary barotrauma). This can result in pneumomediastinum, pneumothorax or arterial gas embolism due to gas passing through the pulmonary venous system. Symptoms of gas embolism present immediately or very soon after a dive and are cerebral in nature; in practice, however, these may be difficult to distinguish from bubble embolic disease related to dissolved gas.

Decompression illness varies in severity from a mild rash or musculoskeletal pain to life-threatening circulatory collapse. The majority of patients develop symptoms within 4 hours unless exposed to altitude during an aircraft flight or road travel, which may provoke symptoms up to 48 hours after diving. The clinical course tends to be unpredictable in the first 24 hours, with spontaneous remission, progression and relapse all common outcomes. As a result it is important that even minor symptoms are recognised and treated early.

10.30 SYMPTOMS OF DECOMPRESSION ILLNESS	
Symptom/sign	**Cause/comment**
Itch or urticaria	Gas diffusing through the skin
Oedema or other rash	Lymphatic or vascular obstruction by gas
Joint pain	Often large joints, especially wrist, elbow, shoulder
Malaise, fatigue, nausea	Non-specific constitutional symptoms
Paraesthesiae, low back pain	Spinal cord disease
Muscle weakness, incoordination, poor balance	Spinal cord or cerebral involvement
Loss of sphincter control	Often detected late because of dehydration
Vertigo	Inner ear involvement
Poor concentration, lightheadedness	Cerebral involvement
Haemoconcentration	Indicates significant intravascular bubble load
Breathlessness, cough, haemoptysis	Major embolisation of pulmonary capillary bed
Convulsion, hemiplegia, cortical blindness	Suggestive of cerebral arterial gas embolism
Hypotension	Circulatory collapse

Management

Treatment consists of:

- *Intravenous fluid replacement* (with 0.9% saline or Hartmann's solution) to correct the intravascular fluid loss from endothelial bubble injury and the dehydration associated with immersion. Maintenance of an adequate peripheral circulation is important for the excretion of excess dissolved gas.
- *High-flow oxygen*, given by a tight-fitting mask using a rebreathing bag. This assists in the washout of excess inert gas (nitrogen) and may reduce the extent of local tissue hypoxia resulting from focal embolic injury.
- *Recompression*, requiring transfer of the patient to a recompression chamber facility as soon as is appropriate to the patient's condition. Transfer may be by air or surface provided that the altitude remains low (< 2000 ft) and the patient continues to breathe 100% oxygen. Recompression reduces the volume of gas within tissues and puts nitrogen back into solution.

The prognosis with treatment is generally good, the majority of patients making a complete recovery. However, a small but significant number of patients with neurological disease are left with varying degrees of disability.

OTHER BAROTRAUMA

Barotrauma can affect the lung, middle ear and paranasal sinuses. The latter two cases are usually the result of blockage of the eustachian tube or sinus ostia, which prevents the equalisation of pressures in the middle ear and sinuses. Earache, facial pain or headache during the dive is the usual symptom; vertigo may occur during or after the dive and a blood-stained nasal discharge is common after sinus barotrauma. Rupture of the round or oval window causes perilymph leak into the middle ear and results in vertigo and deafness. This is a rare manifestation of barotrauma but is an ENT emergency.

NITROGEN NARCOSIS

When compressed air is breathed below 25 msw the increasing partial pressure of nitrogen results in narcosis. This causes impaired cerebral function with changes in mood and performance. Nitrogen narcosis is a common contributing factor to accidents underwater but is rapidly reversible on ascent.

Various other problems may occur underwater such as equipment failure, entrapment or vomiting, and these may lead to water inhalation and drowning, often the final events in many diving fatalities. Key messages for divers are listed in Box 10.31.

In the UK two organisations provide advice on the clinical management of diving illness and the availability of the nearest recompression facility: the Royal Navy (tel. 44-07831-151523) and Aberdeen Royal Infirmary (tel. 44-1224-681818; hyperbaric doctor on call).

10.31 DIVING: KEY MESSAGES

- Any symptom occurring within 24 hours of a dive may be due to decompression illness
- Decompression symptoms may be provoked by flying after a dive
- Even minor symptoms may progress to disabling neurological disease
- Decompression illness can occur even after well-conducted 'safe' dives
- Divers usually have a 'buddy' but decompression illness frequently only affects one diver
- If in any doubt seek advice from a recompression or hyperbaric medical facility

HYPERTHERMIA AND HEAT ILLNESS

Hyperthermia or the state of an elevated core body temperature above 37°C in a hot environment represents a failure of the body's normal thermoregulatory mechanisms. Heat production results from cellular metabolism and increases with the level of exertion. Heat loss occurs through the skin by vasodilatation and sweating, through expired air and in urine and faeces. The main mechanism for increasing heat loss is through sweating which occurs when the ambient temperature rises above 32.5°C or during exercise (see Box 10.32).

When heat gain exceeds the body's capacity for heat loss, core temperature rises. Heat illness occurs either when the environmental temperature is high, or when sweating is impaired or its efficacy as a heat loss mechanism is reduced by high ambient humidity. Three heat exposure syndromes are recognised.

HEAT CRAMPS

These painful muscle cramps occur most commonly in the legs of young people following vigorous exercise in hot weather. There is no elevation of core temperature. The mechanism is considered to be extracellular sodium depletion following electrolyte loss as a result of persistent sweating with replacement of water but not salt. The syndrome is also encountered in miners undertaking heavy physical work in hot conditions with very limited ventilation, which impairs the effect of evaporative heat loss from sweating. Symptoms usually respond rapidly to salt replacement.

HEAT EXHAUSTION

Heat exhaustion occurs when there is an elevation in core (rectal) temperature to between 37°C and 40°C and is usually seen when an individual is undertaking vigorous physical work in a hot environment. A high work rate, extreme ambient temperature or impairing evaporative heat loss due to high humidity or inappropriate clothing may all combine to overcome thermoregulatory control. The diagnosis is based on the finding of an elevated core temperature associated with hyperventilation and symptoms of tiredness or fatigue, muscular weakness, dizziness and collapse. Blood analyses may show evidence of dehydration with mild elevation of the blood urea, sodium concentration and haematocrit.

Treatment involves removal of the patient from the heat, active cooling using cool sponging, and fluid replacement. This may be achieved by using oral rehydration mixtures containing both salt and water or intravenous isotonic saline. Proprietary oral rehydration mixtures are effective if given in adequate volumes. Adult patients may require 5 litres or more positive fluid balance in the first 24 hours. Frequent monitoring of blood electrolytes is important, especially in those patients receiving intravenous fluid replacement.

HEAT STROKE

Heat stroke occurs when the core body temperature rises above 40°C and is a severe and life-threatening condition provoked by a failure of heat regulatory mechanisms. The symptoms of heat exhaustion (see above) progress to include headache, nausea and vomiting. Neurological manifestations include a coarse muscle tremor and confusion, which may progress to loss of consciousness. The patient's skin feels very hot, and sweating is often absent due to failure of thermoregulatory mechanisms. The condition may progress from heat exhaustion or present acutely in a patient who has become progressively dehydrated without symptoms. Coincidental illness, age and drug therapy, particularly phenothiazines, diuretics and alcohol, may be important contributory factors.

Complications include hypovolaemic shock, lactic acidosis, disseminated intravascular coagulation, rhabdomyolysis, hepatic and renal failure, and cerebral oedema.

10.32 THERMOREGULATION IN A HOT ENVIRONMENT		
Heat source/exchange	**Impact on core temperature**	**Factors altering effect**
Metabolic heat production	+	Basal metabolic rate Activity increases heat production
Radiant and conductive heat exchange	+ or −	Dependent on relative skin and ambient temperatures—cutaneous vasodilatation increases heat loss until ambient temperature exceeds core temperature
Convective heat exchange	+ or −	Dependent on relative skin and ambient temperatures and air movement
Evaporative heat exchange	−	Sweating is the main source of heat loss but its effectiveness reduces as ambient humidity increases

The patient should be managed in an intensive care unit with rapid cooling using ice packs, careful fluid replacement and appropriate intravascular monitoring. Investigations reflect the complications and include coagulation studies and muscle enzymes in addition to routine haematology and biochemistry.

ACCLIMATISATION

A considerable degree of acclimatisation occurs over a period of several weeks in individuals who move to a hot climate or who regularly work in a hot environment. Adaptive mechanisms include stimulation of the sweating mechanism with increased sweat volume and reduced sweat sodium content. The risk of heat-related illness falls as acclimatisation occurs.

Key messages on heat illness are listed in Box 10.33.

10.33 HEAT: KEY MESSAGES
• Dehydration can cause few symptoms at an early stage and its extent is often underestimated • The development of a heat syndrome in a previously fit individual indicates considerable negative fluid balance • Following initial recovery it may take several days for an individual to return to normal fluid balance; patients are therefore at considerably increased risk of recurrence if they return to the same environment or work conditions within a few days of recovery

HYPOTHERMIA

Hypothermia exists when the body's normal thermal regulatory mechanisms are unable to maintain sufficient heat production in a cold environment and core temperature falls below 35°C.

Protective mechanisms to avoid hypothermia include cutaneous vasoconstriction (which is effective in the limbs but less so over the trunk and scalp) and shivering (which generates additional heat through increased muscle activity). However, any muscle activity which involves movement may promote heat loss by increasing convective loss from the skin and increasing respiratory heat loss by stimulating ventilation (see Box 10.34).

Hypothermia occurs in a number of different clinical situations. The very young are susceptible because they have poor thermoregulation and a high body surface area to weight ratio. The elderly are also at risk because of often limited financial resources to maintain adequate ambient temperature and poor thermoregulatory mechanisms that may impair shivering in response to a fall in body temperature. Hypothyroidism is a common contributory factor in the elderly and needs active exclusion in all such patients presenting with hypothermia. Alcohol or other drugs may also impede the thermoregulatory response. In these circumstances core body temperature may fall slowly over many hours or days. More rarely, hypothermia is secondary to Addison's disease, myxoedema, stroke, hepatic failure, hypoglycaemia or in patients receiving phenothiazine drugs.

The alternative scenarios involve normal individuals whose thermoregulatory mechanisms are unable to cope with the intensity of the thermal stress. Typical situations include immersion in cold water, where core temperature may fall very rapidly, and exposure to extreme climates: for example, in Arctic and Antarctic travellers and climbers.

Clinical features

Diagnosis is dependent on the recognition of the environmental circumstances and a core (rectal) body temperature below 35°C. It is important that the true core temperature is recorded (using a low-reading thermometer) since

10.35 CLINICAL FEATURES OF HYPOTHERMIA	
Core temperature	**Clinical features**
36°C	Increased metabolic rate, vasoconstriction
35°C (hypothermia)	Shivering maximal, impaired judgement
34°C	Uncooperative, dehydrated
33°C	Depressed conscious level
28–32°C (severe hypothermia)	Progressive depression of conscious level, muscle stiffness Failure of vasoconstrictor response and shivering Bradycardia, hypotension, J waves present on ECG, risk of dysrhythmias
<28°C	Coma, patient may appear dead, absent pupillary and tendon reflexes Spontaneous ventricular fibrillation
20°C	Cardiac standstill

10.34 THERMOREGULATION IN A COLD ENVIRONMENT		
Heat source/exchange	**Impact on core temperature**	**Factors altering effect**
Metabolic heat production	+	Basal metabolic rate falls with core temperature Activity increases heat production Shivering increases heat production
Radiant and conductive heat exchange	–	Dependent on relative skin and ambient temperatures Vasoconstriction in peripheries reduces skin temperature and hence heat loss
Convective heat exchange	–	Dependent on relative skin and ambient temperatures and on air movement
Evaporative heat exchange	–	Evaporative loss associated with breathing increases as ambient temperature falls

measurement of tympanic membrane temperature is less accurate and cutaneous or oral temperatures are misleading. Clinical features depend on the degree of hypothermia (see Box 10.35).

Investigations

Haemoconcentration and metabolic acidosis are common. The ECG may show characteristic J waves which occur at the junction of the QRS complex and the ST segment (see Fig. 10.23). Abnormalities of cardiac rhythm occur, including ventricular fibrillation. Although the arterial oxygen tension may be normal when measured at room temperature, it should be remembered that the arterial PO_2 falls by 7% for each °C fall in core temperature. Serum aspartate aminotransferase and creatine kinase may be elevated secondary to muscle damage and the serum amylase is often high due to subclinical pancreatitis.

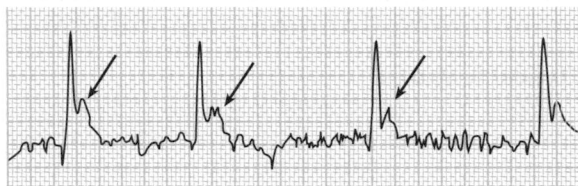

Fig. 10.23 Electrocardiogram showing J waves (arrows) in a hypothermic patient.

Management

The objectives of management are to rewarm the patient in a controlled manner, while treating the associated hypoxia, fluid and electrolyte disturbance, and cardiovascular abnormalities, particularly dysrhythmias. The most appropriate method depends partly on severity and partly on the circumstances leading to hypothermia. In situations where the core temperature is only modestly reduced (> 32°C) and the patient is conscious, passive rewarming is appropriate. Patients should be maintained in a warm room, with additional thermal insulation (blankets and/or space film blanket). They should be given warm fluids to drink and an adequate calorie intake. Core temperature will rise slowly over a few hours as a result of normal metabolic heat production. Associated conditions such as hypothyroidism should be treated promptly with tri-iodothyronine 10 µg i.v. 8-hourly (see p. 699).

Severe hypothermia (core temperature < 32°C) is associated with substantial metabolic disturbance, and dysrhythmias are a common complication. Immersion victims whose core temperature may have fallen rapidly can be rewarmed in a bath of warm water at 40°C. In patients whose temperature has fallen more gradually, rewarming should take place more slowly. The patient should be insulated as above and nursed in a warm room, preferably in an intensive care unit, with the aim of increasing core temperature by 1°C per hour. Rapid rewarming or any movement of the patient may provoke dysrhythmia. In addition to supplementary oxygen, warm intravenous fluids should be given. Monitoring of cardiac rhythm and arterial blood gases including pH is essential. Significant acidosis may require correction (see p. 289).

Very occasionally, more active rewarming measures are required. These include the administration of warm humidified oxygen, lavage of the stomach, peritoneal cavity or rectum with warm fluid, haemodialysis and cardiac bypass. The latter has the considerable advantage of allowing control of cardiac output despite rhythm disturbance and hence permits very rapid rewarming.

Severely hypothermic patients may appear to have no cardiac activity or output and hence be considered dead. Resuscitative measures should always continue until the core temperature is normal and only then should a diagnosis of brain death be considered (see p. 1143).

FROSTBITE

Frostbite represents the direct freezing of body tissues and usually affects the extremities, in particular the fingers, toes, ears and face. The tissues may become anaesthetised before freezing and as a result the injury is often not recognised until later, e.g. when boots are removed. Frostbitten tissue is initially pale and doughy to the touch and insensitive to pain. Once frozen, the tissue is hard.

Rewarming should not be attempted if there is any further risk of freezing as refreezing substantially increases the ultimate injury. Rewarming may be active using warm water and is associated with considerable pain. Thereafter management involves protection of the injured tissue and avoidance of infection. After initial blistering, recovery proceeds over weeks or months. Surgery to remove dead tissue may ultimately be necessary but should be delayed as surprisingly good recovery may occur over an extended period.

NON-FREEZING COLD INJURY (TRENCH FOOT OR IMMERSION FOOT)

This is a less severe form of cold injury resulting from prolonged exposure to cold and usually damp conditions. Initially the limb (usually foot) appears cold, ischaemic and numb but there is no freezing of the tissue. On rewarming the limb appears mottled and thereafter becomes hyperaemic, swollen and painful. Recovery may take many months, during which there may be chronic pain and sensitivity to cold. The pathology remains uncertain but probably involves endothelial injury. Gradual rewarming is associated with less pain than rapid rewarming. The pain and associated paraesthesia may be difficult to control with normal analgesics and if persistent may require the addition of amitriptyline.

Key messages on hypothermia are listed in Box 10.36.

10.36 HYPOTHERMIA: KEY MESSAGES

- The diagnosis of hypothermia requires a low-reading thermometer to record core (rectal or body cavity) temperature
- Severely hypothermic patients appear lifeless and resuscitation should be continued until core temperature is normal
- Movement and handling of hypothermic patients should be restricted because of the risk of provoking cardiac dysrhythmias

DROWNING/NEAR-DROWNING

Drowning refers to death due to asphyxiation following immersion in water. It remains a common cause of accidental death throughout the world and is particularly common in young children (see Box 10.37). In about 10% of cases no water enters the lungs and death follows intense laryngospasm ('dry' drowning). Following inhalation of water, there is a rapid onset of ventilation-perfusion imbalance with hypoxaemia, and the development of diffuse pulmonary oedema. Fresh water (hypotonic fluid), although rapidly absorbed, impairs surfactant function and leads to alveolar collapse and hence right-to-left shunt. Absorption of large amounts of hypotonic fluid can result in haemolysis. Salt water (hypertonic fluid) inhalation tends to provoke alveolar oedema but the overall clinical effect is virtually identical to that of fresh-water drowning. Infection may develop later, particularly after inhalation of contaminated water.

10.37 AETIOLOGY OF DROWNING BY AGE	
Infants/young children	
• Domestic baths	• Garden pools
Adolescents	
• Swimming pools	• Rivers, other bathing sites
Adults	
• Water sports, boating, fishing etc.	• Occupational
Older people	
• Domestic baths	

Clinical features

Those rescued alive (near-drowning) are often unconscious and not breathing. Hypoxaemia and a metabolic acidosis are inevitable features. Some recover spontaneous ventilation and consciousness rapidly. The acute lung injury (see Fig. 10.24) usually resolves rapidly over 48–72 hours unless infection occurs. Early complications include dehydration, hypotension, haemoptysis and cardiac dysrhythmias. A small number of patients, mainly the more severely ill, progress to develop the acute respiratory distress syndrome (see p. 198).

It is important to recognise that survival may be possible after immersion for periods of up to 30 minutes in very cold water without suffering brain damage. Overall there is a relationship between long-term outcome and the duration of immersion, delay in resuscitation, intensity of acidosis and the presence of cardiac arrest. Long-term outcome depends mainly on the severity of the cerebral hypoxic injury. However, outcomes are variable, and recovery with normal cerebral function is possible despite these poor prognostic indicators. The rapid development of hypothermia after immersion in very cold water may be protective and remarkable recoveries have been reported after prolonged immersion, particularly in children.

Management

Initial management requires standard cardiopulmonary resuscitation with administration of oxygen and maintenance of the circulation (see p. 404). It is important to clear the airway of foreign bodies. Attempts to drain the lungs physically are misdirected since there is unlikely to be any fluid remaining and such efforts simply delay resuscitation. Patients are inevitably hypoxaemic and require supplementary oxygen until blood gas analysis proves it is no longer required. Continuous positive airway pressure (CPAP, see p. 203) is particularly useful in maintaining arterial oxygenation for spontaneously breathing patients. Observation is

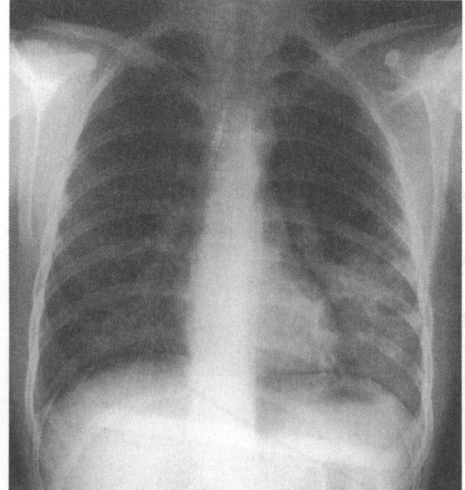

Fig. 10.24   Near-drowning. Chest radiograph of a 39-year-old farmer 2 weeks following immersion in a polluted fresh-water ditch for 5 minutes before rescue. The radiograph shows airspace consolidation and cavities in the left lower lobe reflecting secondary staphylococcal pneumonia and abscess formation.

required for a minimum of 24 hours after the event. Prophylactic antibiotic treatment is only required if exposure was to obviously contaminated water.

IMMERSION ACCIDENTS

Death after immersion may result from several mechanisms. A small proportion of people accidentally immersed in cold water die very rapidly despite a recognised ability to swim. This may be the result of an acute cardiac event or an inability to suppress breathing on immersion due to sudden cold exposure. At a later stage drowning may result from incapacitation (e.g. muscle stiffness) due to the cold and an inability to protect the airway. Later still, a fall in core temperature (hypothermia) may result in loss of consciousness and water inhalation. Immersion victims are dehydrated and hypotensive. Rescue from the water in the upright position may cause profound hypotension due to sudden removal of hydrostatic pressure and result in marked clinical deterioration. As a consequence, it is normal practice to remove immersion victims from the water in a horizontal position.

Key messages on drowning and near-drowning are listed in Box 10.38.

10.38 DROWNING AND NEAR-DROWNING: KEY MESSAGES

- Resuscitation of the drowned patient requires standard cardiopulmonary resuscitation and rapid administration of oxygen
- Victims of near-drowning are always hypoxaemic
- Acute respiratory distress syndrome may occur after near-drowning; hence patients require careful monitoring and observation

---

HIGH-ALTITUDE ILLNESS

The partial pressure of ambient air falls with increasing altitude due to the reduced mass of the atmospheric air above. The relationship between barometric pressure and altitude is not quite linear since air is compressible (see Fig. 10.25). Hence the partial pressure of ambient and alveolar oxygen

falls with altitude (see Fig. 10.26), with the partial pressure of oxygen being reduced by 50% at 5000 m. While most modern commercial aircraft fly at cruising altitudes of 10 000–13 000 m, the aircraft cabin is pressurised to a maximum cabin altitude of 2400 m. The reduced partial pressure of alveolar oxygen results in a fall in arterial oxygen saturation. The extent to which oxygen saturation falls is dictated by the sigmoid shape of the oxygen-haemoglobin dissociation curve and the extent of pre-existing hypoxaemia. The degree of arterial desaturation also depends upon the ventilatory response and degree of resultant respiratory alkalosis and these factors can vary considerably even in normal subjects. Approximate levels of oxygen saturation expected in fit adults at altitude are shown in Figure 10.27.

Below 2500 m the reduction in oxygen saturation is small and few symptoms occur other than some exertional breathlessness. Above 2500 m a number of altitude syndromes occur.

Sudden ascent to altitudes above 6000 m, as experienced by aviators, balloonists and astronauts, may result in decompression illness with the same clinical features as seen in divers (see p. 328). Rapid ascent to altitudes above 7000 m may result in loss of consciousness. Despite this, most altitude illness occurs in travellers or mountaineers.

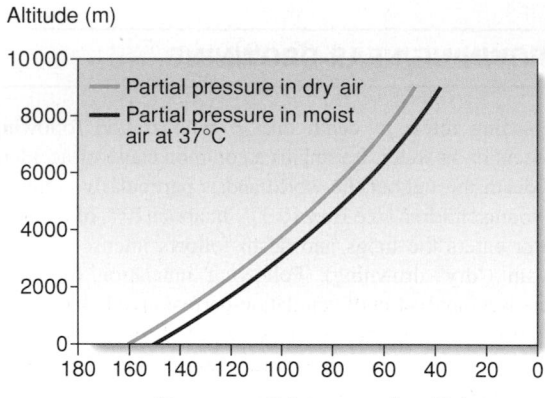

Fig. 10.26   Oxygen availability and altitude.

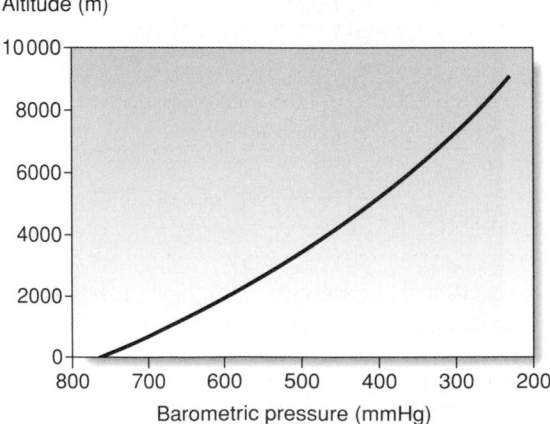

Fig. 10.25   Relationship between barometric pressure and altitude.

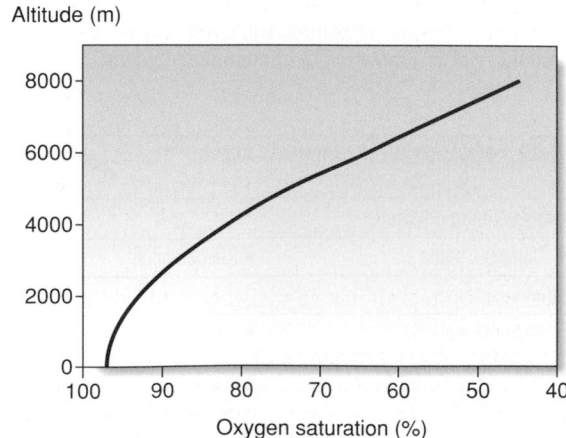

Fig. 10.27   Approximate changes in oxygen saturation in normal individuals at altitude.

ACUTE MOUNTAIN SICKNESS (AMS)

AMS is a syndrome comprising headache (the principal symptom) together with fatigue, anorexia, nausea and vomiting, difficulty sleeping and dizziness. Ataxia and peripheral oedema may be present. Symptoms occur within 6–24 hours of an ascent and vary in severity from trivial to completely incapacitating. The incidence in travellers to 3000 m may be 40–50%, depending on the rate of ascent.

Treatment consists of rest and simple analgesia; symptoms usually resolve after 12–48 hours at a stable altitude but may recur with further ascent. Persistent symptoms may respond to acetazolamide, a carbonic anhydrase inhibitor which induces a metabolic acidosis and stimulates ventilation. Steroids can also be effective but descent is the best option.

HIGH-ALTITUDE PULMONARY OEDEMA (HAPE)

HAPE is a serious and potentially fatal condition, which occurs rarely at altitude. Following a recent ascent, symptoms of dry cough, breathlessness and extreme fatigue develop. Later, the cough becomes productive of bloody sputum. It is associated with crepitations in both lung fields, profound hypoxaemia, pulmonary hypertension and radiological evidence of diffuse alveolar oedema. It is unknown whether the alveolar oedema is a result of mechanical stress on the pulmonary capillaries associated with the high pulmonary arterial pressure or an effect of hypoxia on capillary permeability. It appears to occur in susceptible subjects and such individuals are at particular risk of further episodes with future ascents. Other predisposing factors include youth, rapidity of ascent, the presence of mountain sickness and heavy exertion.

Treatment is directed at reversal of hypoxia with descent wherever possible and administration of oxygen. Reduction of pulmonary arterial pressure with nifedipine has also proved helpful and this agent has been used for prophylaxis in susceptible subjects.

HIGH-ALTITUDE CEREBRAL OEDEMA (HACE)

HACE is also a rare but serious and potentially fatal condition associated with recent ascent. It usually follows AMS and may represent a severe manifestation. It is most likely above altitudes of 3500 m. The presentation is with rapidly progressive cerebral symptoms, which may include hallucination or behavioural change, confusion, visual loss and ultimately loss of consciousness. Ataxia is usually present, papilloedema and retinal haemorrhages are common, and focal neurological signs may be found. The pathology is of diffuse cerebral oedema and the mechanism appears to be related to the rapid increase in cerebral blood flow and related increase in capillary permeability.

As with HAPE, treatment is directed at improving oxygenation. Descent is the single most important intervention. Administration of oxygen may help. High-dose steroids, diuretics and mannitol have all been used but efficacy is difficult to assess as these treatments are usually administered in field conditions.

MANAGEMENT

Descent is the most important treatment for all forms of mountain illness. Dramatic improvement may occur with relatively little descent; for example, while a 1000 m descent may have a small effect on alveolar oxygen partial pressure, it has a far greater impact on the disease than administration of oxygen without descent. Portable pressurised bags (Gamow bags) provide a means of temporarily increasing the patient's ambient pressure and are used to relieve symptoms where immediate descent is impossible.

Acclimatisation

Because of the difficulty in managing these disorders in the field, prevention is essential. Gradual ascent without excessive exertion allows the normal processes of acclimatisation to occur and reduces the risk of altitude illness. Acclimatisation results in an increase in ventilation over a few days, associated with a respiratory alkalosis and renal compensation, and a slower rise in haemoglobin. These changes promote the availability of oxygen to tissues. Above 3000 m, an ascent rate of no more than 300 m per day should permit acclimatisation. However, this ascent rate is too slow for many travellers' plans and impractical in some situations.

Prophylaxis for mountain illness

Acetazolamide taken in a dose of 250 mg 8-hourly commencing 24–48 hours before ascent reduces the incidence and severity of symptoms of acute mountain sickness at a cost of some minor side-effects of peripheral paraesthesiae. As a result of its effect on AMS, acetazolamide may also reduce the risk of HAPE and HACE but there is no evidence to support such an effect. There is evidence that nifedipine provides protection against HAPE in susceptible subjects, but it has no effect on AMS symptoms.

Key messages on altitude sickness are listed in Box 10.39.

10.39 ALTITUDE ILLNESS: KEY MESSAGES

- The best preventative measure is slow ascent to allow acclimatisation. No more than 300 m per day when above 3000 m is a sensible ascent rate
- Descent is the best treatment for any altitude illness
- Prophylactic treatment with acetazolamide is of value in reducing the symptoms of acute mountain sickness
- Susceptible subjects tend to have similar symptoms on subsequent ascents

RADIATION EXPOSURE

Radiation includes ionising and non-ionising radiations, i.e. UV, visible light, laser, infrared and microwave.

IONISING RADIATIONS

These either are high-energy electromagnetic radiations such as X-rays and gamma rays, or consist of subatomic particles such as alpha and beta particles and neutrons. They

10.40 PROPERTIES OF IONISING RADIATIONS

	Range in air	Range in tissue	Protection
Alpha particles	Few centimetres	No penetration	Paper
Beta particles	Few metres	Few millimetres	Aluminium sheet
X-rays/ gamma rays	Kilometres	Passes through	Lead
Neutrons	Kilometres	Passes through	Concrete or thick polythene

are characterised by their ability to interact in a physico-chemical manner on contact with matter or tissue. The clinical effects of different forms of radiation depend upon their range in air and tissue penetration (see Box 10.40).

Dosage

The dose of radiation is based upon the energy absorbed by a unit mass of tissue and is measured in grays (Gy), with 1 Gy representing 1 J/kg. This unit is useful in assessing high-dose exposures to specific organ systems. However, to take account of differences between the behaviour of different radiations and the differences in sensitivity of various tissues, weighting factors are used to produce a unit of effective dose measured in sieverts (Sv). This value therefore reflects the absorbed dose weighted for the damaging effects of the particular form of radiation. This unit is valuable in assessing chronic low-dose or whole-body exposures.

Natural background radiation

Radioactivity of naturally occurring substances on earth (e.g. radon gas) together with cosmic radiation (neutrons from outer space) produces an average individual dose of approximately 2.4 mSv per year.

Effects of radiation exposure

Effects may occur in both exposed individuals and their offspring through effects on the exposed individual's germ cells. Effects on the individual are classified as either deterministic or stochastic.

Deterministic effects show increasing severity of effect with dose and a threshold effect. Examples are the side-effects of radiotherapy, such as skin erythema or gastrointestinal effects, and the effects of accidental high-dose exposure.

Stochastic effects show increasing probability of occurring with dose but severity is independent of dose. Carcinogenesis represents a stochastic effect.

Deterministic effects

Tissues with actively dividing cells are particularly sensitive to ionising radiation. Hence the bone marrow and gastrointestinal mucosa are most sensitive. Lymphocyte depletion is the most sensitive marker of bone marrow injury and after exposure to a fatal dose marrow aplasia is a likely cause of death. However, gastrointestinal mucosal toxicity may cause earlier death due to profound diarrhoea, vomiting, dehydration and sepsis. The gonads are highly radiosensitive and radiation may result in temporary or permanent sterility. Eye

exposure can result in cataract. The lung and central nervous system are subject to acute inflammatory reactions, which may proceed to pulmonary fibrosis and permanent neurological deficit. The skin is subject to radiation burns. The thyroid is not inherently sensitive but accumulation of radioactive iodine isotopes may result in a high local dose.

Management

This is essentially supportive. Assessment of exposure dose from which the outcome can be predicted may be possible with the aid of changes in the peripheral lymphocyte count.

The principal problems after large-dose exposures are maintenance of adequate hydration, control of sepsis and the management of marrow aplasia which may require transplantation. Associated conventional injuries such as thermal burns or other trauma should be managed in the normal way. Exposure to radioisotopes that accumulate in the bone (e.g. ^{90}-strontium) should be treated with sodium calcium edetate or other equivalent chelating agents and high doses of oral calcium. Immediate administration of potassium iodide (133 mg/day) is an important intervention in patients with radio-iodine contamination as this substantially reduces the extent of radio-iodine uptake by the thyroid gland. The psychological impact of radiation exposure should not be forgotten.

Stochastic effects

Epidemiological studies of the appearance of malignancy after radiation exposure in various situations are used to calculate the predicted risk after exposure. With acute exposures leukaemia may arise after an interval of about 2 years and solid tumours after an interval of about 10 years. Thereafter the incidence rises with time. Hence an individual's risk depends on the dose received, the time to accumulate the total dose and the interval following exposure.

NON-IONISING RADIATIONS

Ultraviolet radiation may cause skin burn (sunburn) and corneal injury, as in 'arc eye' suffered by welders. Infrared radiation may cause thermal burns if intense, but lower levels of exposure can lead to cataract formation. Various forms of laser may cause thermal or retinal injury.

FURTHER INFORMATION

Department of Health. Report on health and social subjects 41. Dietary reference values for food energy and nutrients for the United Kingdom. Committee on Medical Aspects of Food Policy. London: HMSO; 1991.

EC Scientific Committee for Food. Nutrient and energy intakes for the European Community. Luxembourg: Directorate-General, Industry; 1993 (31st series).

Guidance on the use of sibutramine for the treatment of obesity in adults. Technology appraisal guidance no. 31. National Institute for Clinical Excellence; Oct 2001.

Hackett PH, Roach RC. High-altitude illness. N Engl J Med 2001; 245:107–114.

Johnson R. Clinical aviation medicine: safe travel by air. Clin Med 2001; 1:385–388.

Waterlow JC. Protein energy malnutrition. London: Edward Arnold; 1992.

World Health Organisation. Diet, nutrition and the prevention of chronic diseases. Technical report series 797. Geneva: WHO; 1990.

World Health Organisation. Management of the child with serious infection or severe malnutrition. Geneva: WHO; 2000.

Clinical genetics

R.N. SANDFORD

This chapter provides an overview of the types of disorder seen in the medical genetics clinic, the spectrum of genetic alterations that give rise to these diseases, and the role of genetic counselling in their management. The reader is directed to other texts for a fuller explanation of the molecular and cellular basis of these diseases and descriptions of the very varied nature of genetic disease (see 'Further information', p. 353).

Genetic disease is very common. Up to half of all major childhood disability and mortality has a genetic cause. Clinicians from all medical and surgical specialties will be involved in the management of genetic disease, and the role of genetic variation in common diseases such as hypertension, diabetes and cancer is certain to become much clearer in the near future. The Human Genome Project is having an enormous impact on our understanding of both normal physiology and the pathogenesis of a wide spectrum of disease. With advances in DNA and protein technology it is likely that the range of tests for genetic disease will increase considerably. Our experience with the use of currently available tests in the genetics clinic will be invaluable in ensuring that all these tests will be used appropriately in the future. They have the potential not only to provide individuals with a secure diagnosis and accurate information about the consequences of having or developing a disease but also to indicate the risks of transmitting it to offspring and the choices regarding screening, prevention and treatment.

THE ROLE OF THE CLINICAL GENETICIST

Medical genetics is concerned with the diagnosis and management of all types of developmental abnormality and diseases with a likely or proven genetic basis. It is therefore not restricted by organ system, disease process or age group. A medical geneticist will be involved in the management of an extremely diverse range of clinical problems, from antenatal diagnosis of a congenital defect through to late-onset familial neurodegenerative disorders. The role of the medical geneticist is also not simply concerned with the estimation of risk or the investigation, diagnosis and treatment of an individual but with the broader understanding of the role of genetics in disease. This is illustrated by the fact that medical genetics frequently deals with families and not just individuals.

An accurate diagnosis is required for providing information to a family about the risk of developing and transmitting disease and methods for screening, diagnosis and prevention; it also forms the basis for making the often very difficult decisions concerning major life events such as planning a family. This process is usually described as genetic counselling and forms the basis of the consultation in the medical genetics clinic. Medical genetics also employs its own set of investigative tools, cytogenetics and molecular genetics, alongside the more traditional ones of haematology, biochemistry, pathology and radiology. So whilst the majority of

patients will be managed in the long term by an appropriate specialist, genetic counselling is normally offered by the medical geneticist.

Clinical geneticists usually work within regional centres together with genetic counsellors and scientists to provide genetic services to a large population. The clinical responsibilities of a clinical geneticist are detailed in Box 11.1.

In addition to such responsibilities, the clinical geneticist has a major role in education, development of genetic services and genetic testing, maintenance of disease registers and research. Medical genetics is one of the few specialties where research may be rapidly translated into clinical practice. For example, the identification of a gene for a particular disorder and the development of a reliable method for mutation detection might permit molecular diagnosis, carrier detection, predictive testing and prenatal diagnosis where previously a diagnosis was made on clinical findings alone (see Box 11.2).

11.1 THE ROLE OF THE CLINICAL GENETICIST

- Diagnosis of all types of genetic disease, birth defects and developmental abnormalities
- Assessment of genetic risk
- Genetic counselling
- Predictive testing for genetic disease, especially late-onset disorders
- Follow-up and screening for certain genetic disorders
- Provision of genetic services to extended families

11.2 EXAMPLES OF GENETIC DISEASES FOR WHICH DIRECT GENE TESTING IS AVAILABLE

Disease	Gene/protein
Point mutations	
Haemochromatosis	HFE
Neurofibromatosis type 1 and 2	NF1 and NF2 (neurofibromin and merlin)
Tuberous sclerosis	TSC1 and TSC2 (hamartin and tuberin)
Von Hippel–Lindau syndrome	VHL
Achondroplasia	FGFR
Marfan's syndrome	FBN1 (fibrillin)
Familial breast cancer	BRCA1 and BRCA2
Deletions/point mutations	
Cystic fibrosis	CFTR
Incontinentia pigmenti	NEMO
Duchenne/Becker muscular dystrophy	DMD (dystrophin)
Gene duplication	
Hereditary motor and sensory neuropathy type 1	PMP22
Triplet repeat expansion	
Myotonic dystrophy	DMPK
Huntington's chorea	Huntingtin
Fragile X syndrome	FMR1
Friedreich's ataxia	FRDA1 (frataxin)
Ataxia-telangiectasia	ATM

THE ANATOMY OF THE HUMAN GENOME

Our understanding and investigation of genetic disease require knowledge of the most important 'unit' of genetics, the gene. The Human Genome Project has provided highly accurate sequence information on the 3×10^9 base pairs (3000 megabases) of deoxyribonucleic acid (DNA) present in the human genome. Within its sequence are all the genes and functional and structural elements that determine the development of a normal human being. Whilst a considerable amount of further work is required to identify and ascribe function to all these sequences, the estimated total number of genes—30 000–35 000—is far below some previous estimates of 100 000. If an average gene has a coding length of 1400 base pairs and spans 30 kilobases of genomic DNA, only 1.5% of the genome represents primary coding sequence with one-third transcribed in genes. While this number of genes is only about twice that found in the worm and fly, differential regulation of expression, the use of different exons within the same gene (alternative splicing) and other mechanisms dictate that these genes are likely to produce considerably more than 30 000 different proteins. These proteins in turn can be modified by a number of processes such as glycosylation (i.e. the addition of sugar side-chains to amino acid residues) such that the total number of different proteins may exceed hundreds of thousands. Work to define the human proteome has already started.

DNA, chromosomes and genes

Cellular DNA contains all of the genetic information required for the orchestrated development of cells into tissues, organs and a complete organism such as a human being. DNA forms a double-stranded helical structure through hydrogen bonding (see Fig. 11.1). Only two base pairings are possible: G–C and A–T. The double-stranded DNA unit of two nucleotides is referred to as a base pair (bp). The double-stranded DNA helix is coiled around chromosomal proteins called histones to form nucleosomes; these also adopt a coiled structure to form a chromatin fibre which on further coiling forms the chromosome.

Chromosomes

Virtually all human cells contain 46 chromosomes, 22 pairs of autosomes and the two sex chromosomes, X and Y (see Fig. 11.2). One of each pair is derived from each parent. These 46 chromosomes are the diploid number seen in somatic cells. Only germ cells (sperm and ova) have the haploid number of 23 chromosomes, 22 autosomes and either an X or a Y chromosome. The X and Y chromosomes are known as the sex chromosomes because they determine the sex of an individual: XY in the male and XX in the female, with the Y chromosome containing the testis-determining factor. One special property of the X chromosome in females is referred to as X inactivation (lyonisation). One of the two X chromosomes in a cell is inactive, so in a similar manner to males females only express one copy of genes on the X chromosome. The process of inactivation is random. This can have a bearing on the expression of diseases which are due to mutations in genes on the X chromosome, as either the normal or the mutant gene may be inactivated.

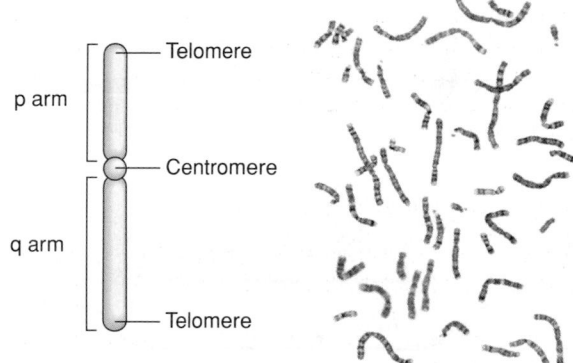

Fig. 11.2 A normal human male karyotype. Special stains enable each chromosome to be identified. A chromosome comprises a centromere and a long (q) and a short (p) arm. The end of each chromosome is called the telomere.

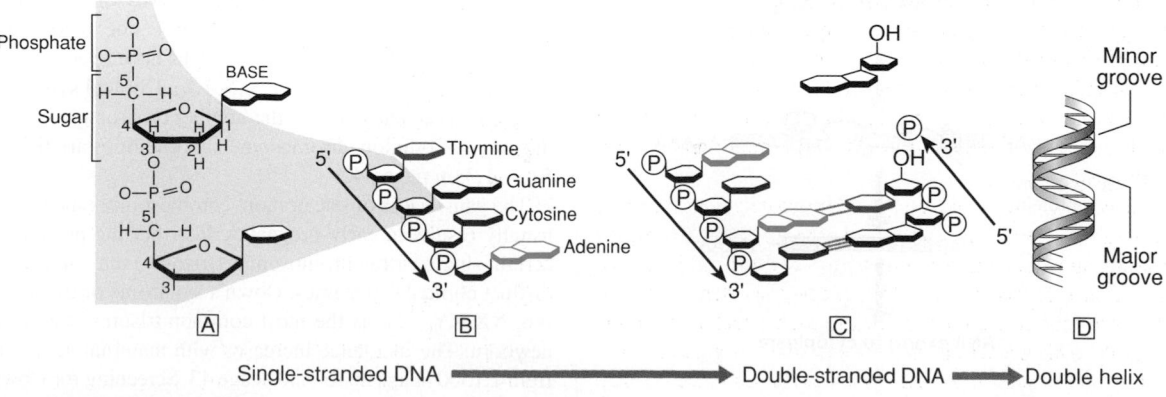

Fig. 11.1 DNA structure. A Biochemical structure of DNA indicating the relationship of base, sugar and phosphate in two adjacent nucleotide units. B Single-stranded DNA with bases colour-coded. Note the base ring structures. C The formation of double-stranded DNA. Base ring structures and hydrogen bonding generate strict pairings between T–A and C–G. D Spiralling of the double-stranded DNA molecule creates the double helix.

The genetic code, genes and loci

The genetic code by which DNA directs the synthesis of protein is a series of codons running 5′ to 3′ along the linear coding strand of DNA. Each codon is a three-nucleotide unit which specifies a particular amino acid to be incorporated into the mature protein, e.g. methionine: ATG. There are 4^3 (64) different triplets; 61 specify one of the 20 amino acids. Three—TAA, TAG and TGA—are 'nonsense' codons which do not specify an amino acid and instead terminate the growing polypeptide chain. Therefore some amino acids are specified by more than one codon.

As outlined above, only a very small fraction of the human genome codes for proteins; these protein coding regions are referred to as genes (see Fig. 11.3). A locus refers to any area of the genome. Not all of the DNA within a gene codes for the eventual protein; sequences within the gene include coding regions (exons), non-coding regions (introns) and regulatory sequences. DNA is not decoded directly into protein; during transcription, chromosomal DNA remains in the nucleus, whereas protein synthesis is associated with ribosomes in the cytoplasm. The conversion of DNA sequence to protein is mediated by ribonucleic acid (RNA).

Individuals inherit a unique pattern of DNA sequences. Despite the fact that the sequence of the genome is greater than 99.9% identical between individuals, this still enables many millions of different base-pair variations or polymorphisms to be present. Much of this natural variation in DNA occurs in non-coding regions and is of no direct relevance to development and function. Other variants may occur within genes leading to alterations in protein sequence and possibly function. If a particular variation results in sufficient impairment of protein function to bring about a deleterious effect, a genetic disease may result.

TYPES OF GENETIC DISEASE

We can only recognise diseases in which the genetic abnormality has been sufficiently 'mild' to permit early development; other genetic abnormalities may impair more vital processes whereby embryogenesis cannot proceed. The genotype of individuals refers to their genetic make-up, i.e. the sequence of their genes. The phenotype describes any aspect of structure, development or pathophysiology in an individual. Diseases may result from purely genetic or purely environmental factors, or, more frequently, a combination of the two (see Fig. 11.4). Common mechanisms of genetic disease are illustrated in Figure 11.5.

CHROMOSOMAL DISORDERS

Approximately 50% of spontaneous miscarriages are due to chromosome abnormalities and the majority of pregnancies with a chromosome abnormality will not reach term. Approximately 90 per 10 000 live births have a recognisable chromosome abnormality (i.e. 0.5–1%). Clinical syndromes arise due to an alteration in the number or structure of chromosomes. Common chromosome abnormalities are listed in Box 11.3 on page 342.

The gain or loss of one or more chromosomes (aneuploidy) usually results in early pregnancy loss, but the presence of certain single extra chromosomes (trisomy) may give rise to distinct clinical syndromes. Down's syndrome or trisomy 21 (46, XX/XY, +21) is the most common trisomy seen in the newborn. The incidence increases with maternal age, rising from 1:1500 at age 20 to 1:50 at age 43. Screening for Down's syndrome during pregnancy is now routinely offered in most developed countries using serum screening, fetal ultrasound and amniocentesis (see p. 352). An additional sex chromosome (X or Y) usually has less severe clinical effects.

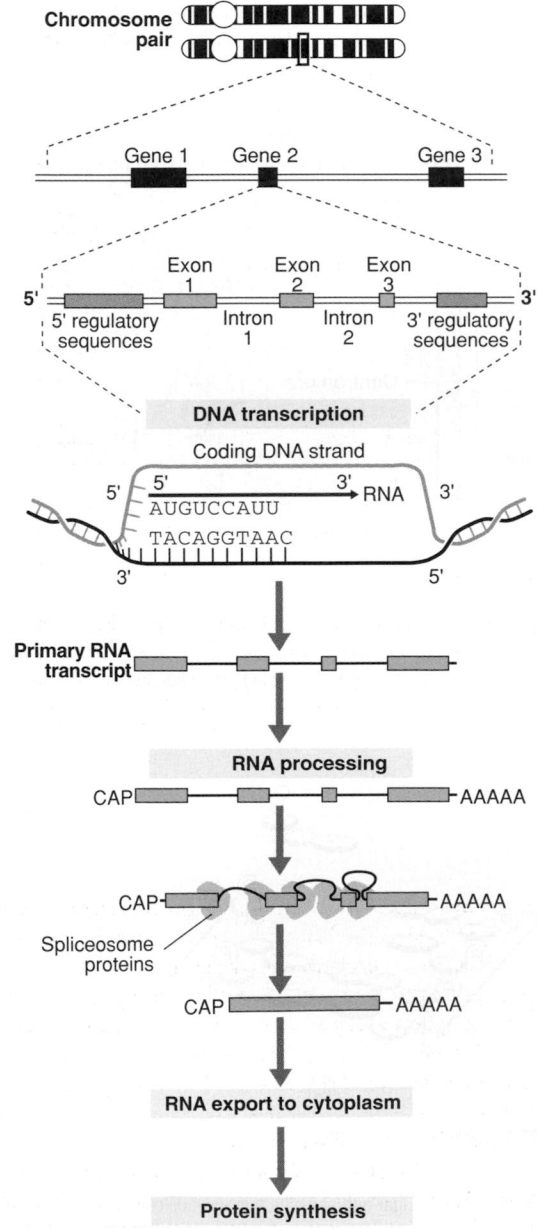

Fig. 11.3 **RNA synthesis and its translation into protein.**

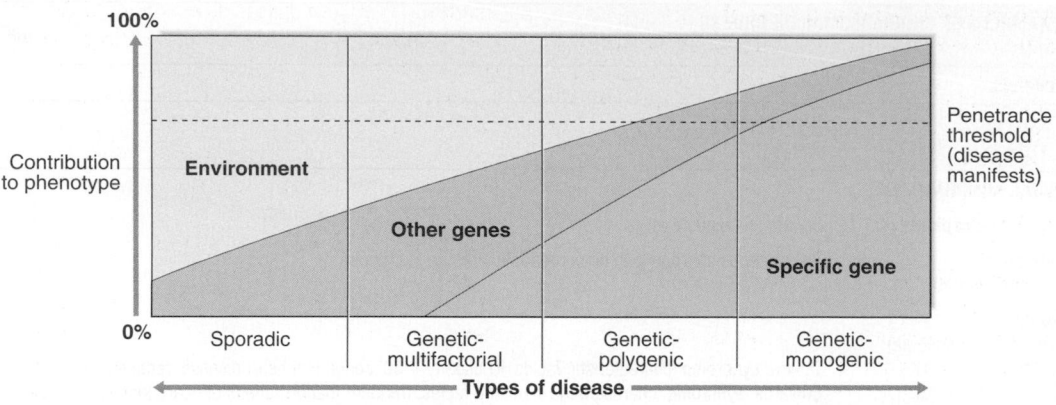

Fig. 11.4   The spectrum of genetic disease: how the genotype influences the phenotype. A particular characteristic or disease in an individual may be due to a specific genetic abnormality (monogenic disease), or may reflect several predisposing genes (polygenic disease). In each case, environmental factors may further influence the phenotype; in their absence, genetic factors alone may be insufficient to allow the disease to develop, resulting in non-penetrance (see p. 347).

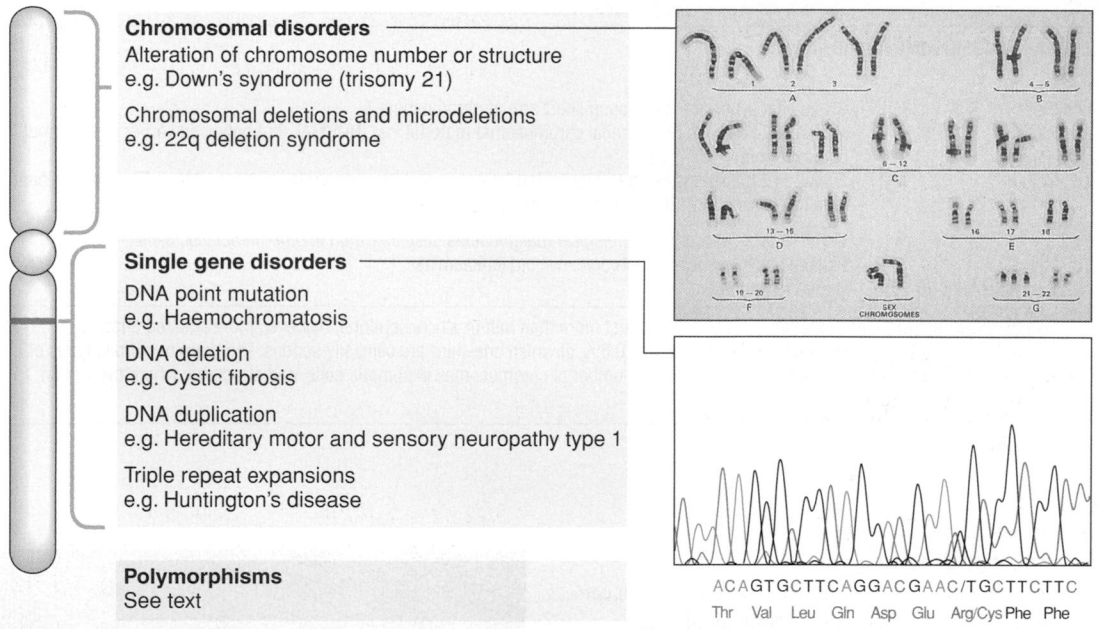

Fig. 11.5   Common mechanisms in genetic disease.

The loss of a chromosome (monosomy) is confined to the X or Y chromosome. 45, X produces a condition known as Turner's syndrome (see Box 11.3).

Abnormal chromosome structure may be due to translocations, deletions, duplications or inversions. Translocations are due to the exchange of genetic material between different chromosomes. The exchange of material between two different chromosomes is referred to as a reciprocal translocation and is balanced if there is no net loss. Such translocations are usually unique to an individual and can be inherited. They are relatively common, being found in about 1:500 individuals. Translocations may cause disease if the chromosome breakpoint disrupts a gene (e.g. the Philadelphia (Ph)

chromosome, see p. 935), or if loss of genetic material occurs during meiosis; in the latter case the translocation is said to be unbalanced. Unbalanced translocations frequently give rise to severe developmental defects or early pregnancy loss. A special type of translocation, the Robertsonian translocation, involves two of chromosomes 13, 14, 15, 21 or 22. The involvement of chromosome 21 in this type of translocation may result in a pregnancy with Down's syndrome and a relatively high risk of recurrence.

The loss of part of a chromosome or deletion may be 'microscopic' and visible using standard chromosome preparations, or 'submicroscopic' where special techniques are required for identification. The most useful investigation

11.3 EXAMPLES OF CHROMOOOMAL DISORDERS

Chromosomes	Result
2n (46, XX)	Normal female
2n (46, XY)	Normal male

NUMERICAL ABNORMALITIES

Triploidy (3n), **tetraploidy** (4n)	Spontaneous abortion
Parthenogenesis (2n from same parent)	Spontaneous abortion (can be compatible with life in chimera)
Aneuploidy (2n + specific chromosome)	
Trisomy 21 (47, XY, +21)	Down's syndrome (characteristic facies, IQ usually < 50, congenital heart disease, reduced life expectancy)
Trisomy 18 (47, XY, +18)	Edwards' syndrome (characteristic skull and facies, frequent malformations of heart, kidney and other organs)
Trisomy 13 (47, XY, +13)	Patau's syndrome (cleft lip and palate, polydactyly, small head, frequent congenital heart disease)
Sex chromosome aneuploidies	
Phenotypically male	
47, XXY	Klinefelter's syndrome (infertility, gynaecomastia, small testes)
47, XYY	XYY male (usually asymptomatic, often tall)
Phenotypically female	
47, XXX	Trisomy X (usually asymptomatic, 20% mentally handicapped)
45, XO	Turner's syndrome (short stature, webbed neck, primary amenorrhoea)

STRUCTURAL CHROMOSOME ABERRATIONS

Inherited	
46, XY,del(5p)	Cri du chat syndrome, deletion of short arm of chromosome 5
45, XY,t(14;21)	Fusion of 14 and 21, no essential chromosomal material lost (NORMAL, but balanced carrier of abnormal chromosome)
46, XY,t(14;21)	Fused 14;21 chromosome has segregated into gamete with normal chromosome 21, and fertilisation has generated trisomy 21 (Down's syndrome)
Acquired	*Occur in over 50% of haematological malignancies; also common in other neoplastic cells*
46, XY,t(9,22)	Philadelphia chromosome (chronic myeloid leukaemia)
46, XY,t(2,8) or t(8,14) or t(8,22)	Burkitt's lymphoma

Chromosomal disorders are extremely common and probably affect more than half of all conceptions. However, most affected offspring spontaneously miscarry, so that the live-born frequency is about 0.6%, of which one-third are clinically serious. There are two broad types of chromosome aberration: numerical, where there is an incorrect number of chromosomes in somatic cells; and structural, where there is an alteration in the structure of one or more chromosomes.

DiGeorge syndrome

- The most common microdeletion syndrome which can be transmitted as an autosomal dominant disorder. Most cases (90%) appear sporadic.
- Incidence 1:4000.
- Clinical features—neonatal hypocalcaemia arising from parathyroid hypoplasia, susceptibility to infection due to thymic hypoplasia, palatal dysfunction/clefting and cardiac outflow tract defects including tetralogy of Fallot, truncus arteriosus and interrupted aortic arch. Facial dysmorphism is usually seen. Other features reported include paranoid schizophrenia and major depressive illness. Clinical features seen more rarely include hypothyroidism, cleft lip and deafness. The syndrome may be very variable even within the same family.
- Diagnosis is made using routine molecular cytogenetic techniques. Screening for other family members can be offered (see Fig. 11.6).

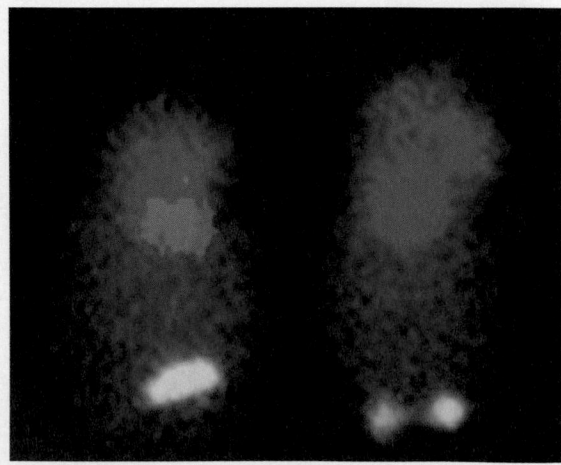

Fig. 11.6 Detection of a chromosome 22q11.2 microdeletion using fluorescent in situ hybridisation (FISH). A DNA probe labelled red identifies the missing region in one chromosome.

11.4 DISEASES DUE TO CHROMOSOMAL MICRODELETIONS

Disease	Chromosome	Clinical features
DiGeorge syndrome	22	Facial dysmorphism, congenital heart disease, absent parathyroids (also isolated congenital heart disease), palatal abnormalities
Williams' syndrome	7	Supravalvular aortic stenosis, facial dysmorphism, learning difficulties, hypercalcaemia
WAGR	11	Wilms' tumour, aniridia, genitourinary abnormalities, mental retardation
Angelman's/Prader–Willi syndrome	15	Abnormal movements, ataxia, mental retardation/hypotonia, marked obesity, mental retardation

is fluorescent in situ hybridisation (FISH—see Fig. 11.6 and DiGeorge syndrome—see panel). Many clinical syndromes due to microscopic and submicroscopic deletions have been identified and are usually the result of loss of one copy of several adjacent genes (see Box 11.4).

Many other types of structural chromosome abnormality have been described. The clinical and developmental consequences are dependent on the amount of genetic material lost or gained.

MUTATIONS

By convention, a mutation is recognised as a disease-causing DNA alteration, whereas sequence changes which do not result in a disease state are referred to as polymorphisms (see p. 347). A disease-causing mutation results in a variation in DNA sequence which alters the protein product in such a way as to contribute to, or cause, a disease process.

Point mutations, insertions, deletions and duplications occur in nuclear and mitochondrial DNA. They may be inherited if present in the germ line, although mitochondrial mutations can only be transmitted maternally.

Mutations may be divided into several broad categories.

Point mutations

Point mutations are single nucleotide changes. The change of one nucleotide for another, also called a substitution, is the most common type of mutation. It may alter a codon, resulting in an amino acid change in the protein (a mis-sense mutation) or introduce a premature stop codon truncating the protein (a nonsense mutation). The premature truncation of a protein is likely to result in loss of function, whereas the change of a single amino acid can have a variety of effects including loss of function or occasionally gain of a novel function. Examples of diseases commonly caused by point mutations are familial adenomatous polyposis coli and autosomal dominant polycystic kidney disease (see panels).

Familial adenomatous polyposis coli (FAP)
- A rare autosomal dominant colorectal cancer syndrome.
- Incidence 1:13 000.
- Clinical features—see page 821.
- The disease shows almost complete penetrance but striking variation in expression, with a very high rate of colorectal cancer by the age of 45. Annual screening

of the large bowel is therefore mandatory for all at-risk individuals from the age of 10–12 years.
- Mutations in the APC gene are found in FAP. Predictive testing for this condition may be offered to children and adults. A positive result confirms the need for screening but a negative result will spare a child years of invasive screening tests.
- See Box 11.5 for some other familial cancer syndromes.

11.5 OTHER FAMILIAL CANCER SYNDROMES

Disease	Inheritance*	Gene	Tumour(s)	Page reference
Retinoblastoma	AD	RB1	Retinoblastoma, osteosarcoma	–
Familial breast/ovarian cancer	AD	BRCA1 and BRCA2	Breast, ovary	Ch. 5
Hereditary non-polyposis colorectal cancer (HNPCC)	AD	hMSH2, hMLH1, hPMS1, hPMS2	Colorectal, endometrial, stomach, breast, urinary tract	822
Von Hippel–Lindau syndrome	AD	VHL	CNS haemangioblastoma, renal, phaeochromocytoma	1207
Peutz–Jeghers syndrome	AD	STK11	Gastrointestinal, endometrial, breast, ovary	822
Li–Fraumeni syndrome	AD	p53	Sarcoma, brain, breast, leukaemia, adrenal	–
* AD = autosomal dominant.				

Autosomal dominant polycystic kidney disease (ADPKD)

- A common autosomal dominant disorder.
- Incidence 1:1000.
- Clinical features—see page 622.
- Mutations in two genes, PKD1 (85% of cases) and PKD2 (15% of cases), cause the same clinical features. Disease due to mutations in PKD2 is milder, with a mean age of renal failure of 69 compared to 52 for PKD1-linked disease.
- Difficulties in the analysis of the PKD1 gene have prevented the widespread use of DNA testing for this condition. Careful renal ultrasound scanning after the age of 18 will detect > 95% of affected individuals and

is the best screening test. Linkage analysis may occasionally be used to exclude a diagnosis confidently in a young adult with a normal scan.

- The increased incidence of intracranial aneurysms (ICA) in ADPKD (10%) has also prompted the use of magnetic resonance angiography as a screening test. It is used only when a proven diagnosis of ICA has been made in a family member; in this case the risk of having an ICA rises from 10% to about 20%. Screening is only carried out after careful counselling and consultation with a neurosurgeon about possible therapeutic options.
- Hepatic cysts are a common feature of ADPKD. Rarely, massive polycystic liver disease may occur, most usually in multiparous females (see Figs 11.7 and 11.8). A separate disease of polycystic liver disease without polycystic kidneys has also been described.

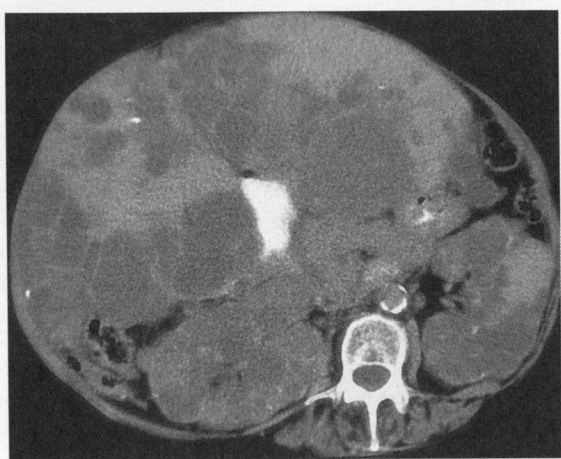

Fig. 11.7 CT scan of polycystic kidney disease with extensive hepatic cysts.

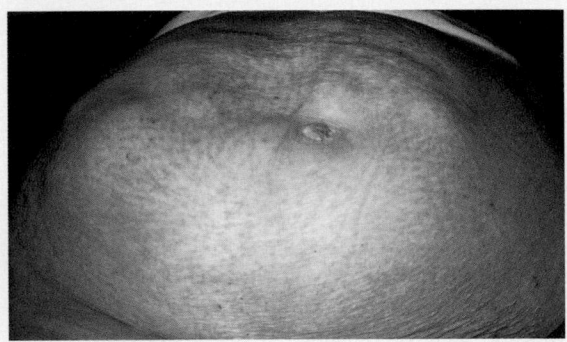

Fig. 11.8 Abdominal distension due to polycystic kidney and polycystic liver disease.

Insertions and deletions

One or more nucleotides may be inserted or deleted in a DNA strand. When this occurs in a gene it may result in abnormal splicing or alteration of the reading frame (frameshift mutation). The insertion or deletion of a single nucleotide will alter the following coding sequence. This will cause an abnormal protein to be synthesised and may also create a premature stop codon. Larger insertions or deletions also occur. Many examples of this type of mutation exist. Perhaps the most common is the ΔF508 mutation in the cystic fibrosis gene, CFTR (see panel).

Cystic fibrosis

- A common autosomal recessive disorder affecting children and young adults.
- Incidence 1:2500 in Western Europe.
- Clinical features—see page 523.
- Mutations found in the CFTR gene. A common three base-pair deletion at the 508th codon causes the loss of a phenylalanine (F) residue (ΔF508). ΔF508 accounts for about 70% of all CFTR mutations although wide geographic variation occurs. This mutation causes abnormal folding of the protein that prevents it reaching its normal cell surface location.

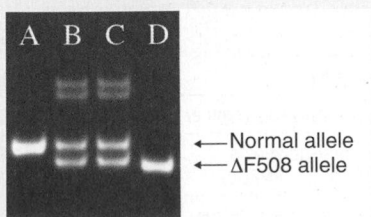

Fig. 11.9 Analysis of the cystic fibrosis gene using the polymerase chain reaction to demonstrate the common ΔF508 mutation. (A = normal individual; B and C = ΔF508 heterozygote; D = ΔF508 homozygote affected with cystic fibrosis)

Up to 90% of CFTR mutations can now be routinely detected. Approximately 1:22 of the population is a carrier of a CFTR mutation.

- Mutation detection is widely employed as a diagnostic test for cystic fibrosis, in prenatal diagnosis and for carrier detection. Carrier detection can be offered to relatives of an affected individual or carrier in a process known as cascade screening. Population screening can also be carried out—for example, in pregnant women and neonates (see Fig. 11.9).

Some deletions may be extremely large and completely remove one or more adjacent genes. At one extreme these may become visible by examination of the chromosomes either by microscopy or by FISH. The majority of deletions ranging from only a few base pairs to several megabases can be detected by direct analysis of a DNA sample (e.g. in Duchenne muscular dystrophy).

Duplications

A region of DNA may be duplicated. This may occur due to the presence of repeated DNA sequences resulting in misalignment during DNA replication. If an entire gene is duplicated, then the increased amount of gene product may have a deleterious effect. This is the mechanism involved in hereditary motor and sensory neuropathy (HMSN type 1) (see Box 11.6 and p. 1180).

Triplet repeat mutations

This recently discovered class of mutation has been identified in a variety of inherited diseases, and interestingly results mainly in neurological diseases; this provides an explanation for some of their clinical features (see Box 11.7).

11.6 DISEASE-CAUSING MUTATIONS

Disease	Inheritance*	Gene	Mutation	Carrier frequency	Effect on coding sequence
Point mutations					
Haemochromatosis	AR	HFE	G–A at position 845	10%	Cys to Tyr at position 282
α_1-antitrypsin deficiency	AR	PI	G–A at position 1197	3%	Glu-Lys at position 342
Familial adenomatous polyposis coli	AD	APC	Multiple, e.g. C–T at position 904	–	Arg-stop codon
Achondroplasia	AD	FGFR3	G–A at position 1138	–	Arg to Gly at position 380
Insertions/deletions					
Cystic fibrosis	AR	CFTR	Deletion of codon 508 (TTT)	23%	Deletion of Phe (ΔF508)
Duplications					
Hereditary motor and sensory neuropathy type 1	AD	PMP22	Duplication		

* AR = autosomal recessive; AD = autosomal dominant.

11.7 DISEASES ASSOCIATED WITH TRIPLET AND OTHER REPEAT SEQUENCES

Disease	Repeat	No. of repeats Normal	No. of repeats Mutant	Gene	Gene location	Inheritance
Coding repeat expansion						
Huntington's disease	[CAG]	6–34	> 35	Huntingtin	4p16	AD
Spinocerebellar ataxia (type 1)	[CAG]	6–39	> 40	Ataxin	6p22–23	AD
Spinocerebellar ataxia (types 2, 3, 6, 7)	[CAG]			Various	Various	AD
Dentatorubral-pallidoluysian atrophy	[CAG]	7–25	> 49	Atrophin	12p12–13	AD
Machado–Joseph disease	[CAG]	12–40	> 67	MJD	14q32	AD
Spinobulbar muscular atrophy	[CAG]	11–34	> 40	Androgen receptor	Xq11–12	XL recessive
Non-coding repeat expansion						
Myotonic dystrophy	[CTG]	5–37	> 50	DMPK-3′UTR	19q13	AD
Friedreich's ataxia	[GAA]	7–22	> 200	Frataxin-intronic	9q13	AD
Progressive myoclonic epilepsy	[---]$_{4-6}$	2–3	> 25	Cystatin B-5′UTR	21q	AR
Fragile X mental retardation	[CGG]	5–52	> 200	FMR1-5′UTR	Xq27	XL dominant
Fragile site mental retardation 2 (FRAXE)	[GCC]	6–35	> 200	FMR2	Xq28	XL, probably recessive

The triplet repeat diseases fall into two major groups: those with disease resulting from expansion of [CAG]n repeats in coding DNA, resulting in polyglutamine tracts, and those with non-coding repeats. The latter tend to be longer. Parents usually display 'pre-mutation' allele lengths that are just above the normal range, and may encroach on a stability threshold for trinucleotides of approximately 144–156 bp. (UTR = untranslated region; AD = autosomal dominant; AR = autosomal recessive; XL = X-linked)

Triplet repeat mutations are unstable mutations and consist of a variable number of triplet (three nucleotide) repeats. They represent expansions from a normal number of repeats. In normal DNA the triplets may encode amino acids in a gene, may be located in the 5′ or 3′ untranslated region of a gene, or may have a less understood association with a gene. Disease occurs when the number of triplet repeats expands beyond a certain limit (see Box 11.7). This increase occurs over several generations and is the genetic explanation for the phenomenon of anticipation. Anticipation is said to occur when the onset of disease occurs at a younger age or when the disease severity increases in subsequent generations. When triplet expansions exceed a certain size they often give rise to very early-onset disease (apparent in the neonatal period or in childhood) in a condition that is usually considered to be adult-onset. In some conditions the risk of an expansion increasing in size is influenced by whether it was inherited from the mother or father. In juvenile Huntington's disease (see panel) the expansion is usually inherited from the father, whilst in myotonic dystrophy the severe neonatal form usually occurs when the mutation is inherited from the mother (see p. 1186).

Huntington's disease

- A rare, mainly adult-onset autosomal dominant disorder.
- Incidence 1:15 000.
- Clinical features—see page 1177.
- Disease is caused by expansion of a CAG triplet repeat in the Huntingtin gene producing a polyglutamine tract. Expansion size is readily determined by molecular testing. Disease is caused by more than 35 repeats. Expansion is more likely to increase when inherited from the father. Large expansions may cause juvenile Huntington's disease.
- Predictive testing can be offered following strict guidelines, although the uptake is only about 20% of at-risk individuals (see Fig. 11.10).

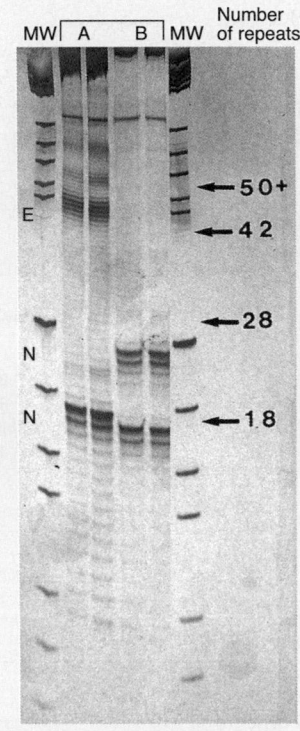

Fig. 11.10 Molecular analysis of the Huntington's disease gene. Lanes marked A represent duplicate samples from an affected patient showing both normal-sized (N) and expanded (E) alleles. The lanes marked B are from a normal individual and show two normal-sized alleles only. (MW = molecular weight markers)

Genomic imprinting

The term 'genomic imprinting' refers to where the effect of a gene depends on whether it is inherited from the mother or father, a parent of origin effect (see Box 11.8). If an imprinted gene carries a mutation, then the manifestation of any resultant disease will vary according to which parent transmitted the mutation. For example, a critical region on chromosome 15q contains several genes in which only the paternal or maternal allele is transcriptionally active. Deletion of these genes on the paternal chromosome causes Prader–Willi syndrome, whereas deletion of the maternal chromosome causes Angelman's syndrome (see Box 11.8).

THE EFFECTS OF MUTATIONS

Mutations may produce one of a number of effects (see Box 11.9).

Loss of function is caused by a change in protein sequence that results in reduced or absent functional activity. This is the effect of the majority of mutations in autosomal recessive disorders. The alteration of a key functional or structural residue in a protein produced from both alleles will result in the complete absence of normal protein. If the mutation is present on only one allele (in the heterozygous state), then both normal and mutant protein will be present. If the mutant protein interferes with the function of the normal protein it is said to have a dominant-negative effect. This is seen in proteins that form part of a complex or form multimers such as collagens. This is called haploinsufficiency if having only half the normal amount of protein causes disease. Gain-of-function mutations give a protein a novel function. This may be caused by an increase in activity due to increased expression or reduced degradation, or activation and resultant loss of regulation.

11.8 IMPRINTED GENES IMPLICATED IN HUMAN DISEASE

Chromosome	Gene(s)	Disease example
6q26	IGF2R	Tumour suppressor—inactivated by inappropriate imprinting
11p13	WT1	Wilms' tumour: WT1 gene mutated in 10–15% of cases
11p15	p57KIP2 HASH2, INS2 IGF2, H19	Beckwith–Wiederman syndrome: General 'over-growth', advanced ageing and increased childhood tumours. Probably due to mutations in p57KIP2
	WT2	Wilms' tumour
15q11–13	SNRPN Necdin and others	Prader–Willi syndrome: Obesity, hypogonadism and varying degrees of mental retardation. Lack of paternal contribution (due to deletion of paternal 15q11–q13, or inheritance of both chromosome 15q11–q13 regions from the mother). Currently thought to be a contiguous gene syndrome, due to loss of at least SNRPN and necdin
	Ubiquitin protein ligase E3A (UBE3A)	Angelman's syndrome (AS): Severe mental retardation, ataxia, epilepsy and inappropriate laughing bouts due to mutations in the UBE3A gene inherited from the patient's mother. The neurological phenotype results because most tissues express both maternal and paternal alleles of UBE3A, whereas the brain expresses predominantly the maternal allele
X chromosome		Duchenne muscular dystrophy: If, by chance, a sufficient number of the X chromosomes containing the normal gene are inactivated in muscle, even heterozygotes may have symptoms. Conversely, if a higher proportion of the disease gene-carrying chromosome is inactivated, a carrier female may test negative on biochemical screening for elevated creatine kinase levels

11.9 EFFECTS OF GENE MUTATIONS

- Loss of function
- Dominant-negative effect
- Haploinsufficiency
- Gain of function

POLYMORPHISMS

A genetic polymorphism represents a change in DNA sequence that does not result in an overt disease state. Small DNA sequence changes may be functionally silent if they:

- are located in non-coding DNA (which constitutes the majority of the genome)
- do not alter the amino acid inserted in a given protein (for example, there are six serine codons)
- result in a novel amino acid which is able to perform the same function as the original, even if the two are distinguishable (e.g. polymorphisms at the ABO blood group).

One of the major discoveries of the Human Genome Project has been the degree of genetic variation, or polymorphism, that exists between individuals. We all share genome sequences that are 99.9% identical. The remaining 0.1% is therefore responsible for all the genetic diversity between individuals. This is now readily determined by examining single nucleotide polymorphisms (SNPs). These single-base changes occur very frequently in the genome and hold great potential for locating genes involved in common diseases. The association of particular SNPs with disease in groups of affected individuals is being used to identify the causative genes which must lie close to the SNP marker.

GENETIC FACTORS IN COMMON DISEASES

Susceptibility to many common diseases is influenced by genetic factors. This is often recognised by an increased incidence of the disease in first-degree relatives of affected individuals but not in a pattern typical of classical single gene disorders. Asthma/atopy, hypertension, diabetes, ischaemic heart disease and many infectious diseases show this pattern. Genes that act together with environmental influences giving rise to this susceptibility are being studied intensively.

INHERITANCE PATTERNS

The common modes of inheritance are shown in Figure 11.11.

Penetrance and expression

Individuals who inherit a particular disease mutation rarely demonstrate an identical phenotype since they may not share the other genetic or environmental factors that predispose or unmask the full effect of the mutation in question. Penetrance is defined as the proportion of individuals who develop the disease phenotype. The mutation is said to be fully penetrant if all individuals who inherit it develop the associated disease phenotype. If additional environmental factors are needed, the gene may display late-onset penetrance, or even be non-penetrant if the individual is never exposed to sufficient additional factors (see Fig. 11.4, p. 341). Disease expression describes the degree to which the severity of the disease phenotype may vary.

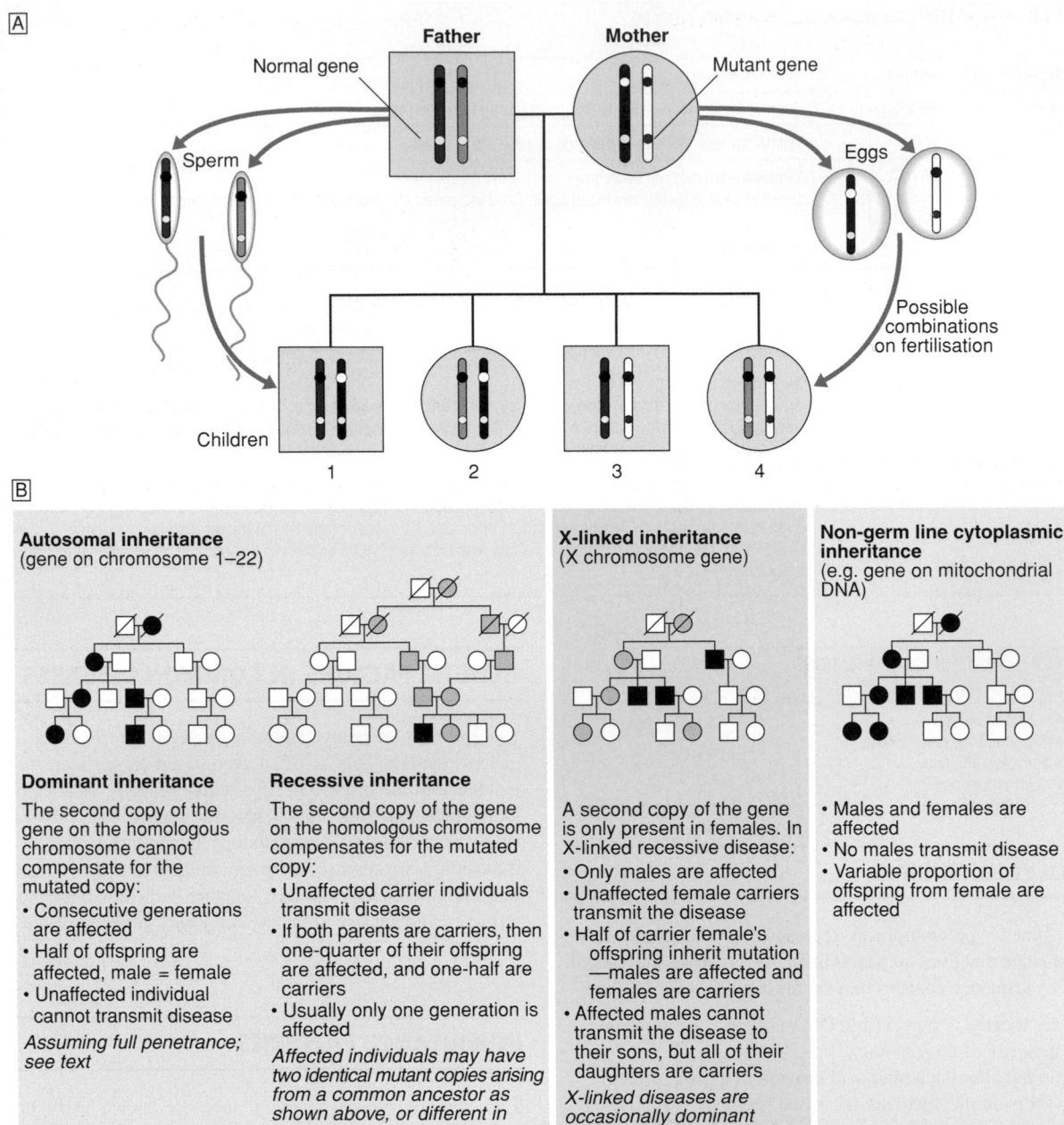

Fig. 11.11 Principles of inheritance. A Mendelian transmission of a single pair of autosomes, where the mother has a single mutant gene (red circle) on the chromosome shown in white. B Inheritance of a mutant gene using conventional symbol designation (male: square; female: circle; unaffected: white; affected: black; unaffected carrier: stippled; deceased: strike-through; see Fig. 11.12 for full explanation of symbols used in family pedigrees), with characteristic features of resulting genetic diseases.

COMMON PRESENTATIONS OF GENETIC DISEASE

Due to the very varied nature of genetic alterations that underlie clinical disease (see p. 343), genetic disease may present at any age from early development to old age and in any tissue or organ system (see Box 11.10). Frequently, several systems are involved either as a primary feature of the disease or due to secondary complications. Certain types of disease presentation are commonly seen in the genetics clinic and these are listed in Box 11.11.

11.10 COMMON MONOGENIC DISORDERS AFFECTING MAJOR ORGAN SYSTEMS

System	Disease	Inheritance
Multisystem	Neurofibromatosis	AD
	Tuberous sclerosis	AD
Respiratory	α_1-antitrypsin deficiency	AR
	Cystic fibrosis	AR
	Kartagener's syndrome	AR
Cardiovascular	Hypertrophic cardiomyopathy	AD
	Long QT syndromes	AD and AR
	22q deletion syndrome	AD
Renal	Polycystic kidney disease	AD
	Alport's syndrome	XL
	Finnish nephropathy	AR
	Renal tubular acidosis	AR
	Haemolytic-uraemic syndrome	AR
	Benign familial haematuria	AD
Gastrointestinal	Hereditary pancreatitis	AD
	Cystic fibrosis	AR
	Familial adenomatous polyposis coli	AD
Hepatic	Gilbert's disease	AD
	Haemochromatosis	AR
	Wilson's disease	AR
	α_1-antitrypsin deficiency	AR
	Polycystic liver disease	AD
Metabolic	Phenylketonuria	AR
	Familial hypercholesterolaemia	AD
	Acute intermittent porphyria	AD
	Galactosaemia	AR
	Glycogen storage diseases	AR
	Homocystinuria	AR
Endocrine	Congenital adrenal hyperplasia	AR
	Multiple endocrine neoplasia	AD
	Kallmann's syndrome	XL
Haematological	Sickle-cell disease	AR
	Alpha- and beta-thalassaemia	AR
	Haemophilia A and B	XL
	Glucose-6-phosphate dehydrogenase deficiency	AR
Neuromuscular	Duchenne muscular dystrophy	XL
	Myotonic dystrophy	AD
	Spinal muscular atrophy	AR
	Hereditary motor and sensory neuropathy type 1	AD
Central nervous system	Huntington's disease	AD
	Familial Alzheimer's disease	AD
	Friedreich's ataxia	AR
	Hereditary spastic paraplegia	Mainly AD
Connective tissue	Ehlers–Danlos syndrome	AD
	Marfan's syndrome	AD
	Osteogenesis imperfecta	Mostly AD
	Achondroplasia	AD
Skin	Albinism	AR
	Epidermolysis bullosa	AD
	Neurofibromatosis	AD
	Xeroderma pigmentosum	AR
Eye	Retinitis pigmentosa	AR, AD, XL
	Ocular albinism	XL
	Colour blindness	XL
	Leber's optic atrophy	Mitochondrial

11.11 COMMON PRESENTATIONS OF GENETIC DISEASE

- Healthy individuals with a known family history
- Organ-specific disease and recognised genetic diseases e.g. Cancers, dementia, polycystic kidney disease
- Abnormal antenatal scan/pregnancy screening result
- Pregnancy loss/neonatal death associated with severe malformations
- Congenital abnormalities (dysmorphology)
- Developmental delay
- Deafness/blindness

INVESTIGATION OF GENETIC DISEASE

The diagnosis and investigation of genetic disease are no different from those of any other disease in that they require an accurate history, thorough clinical examination and the appropriate use of diagnostic tests. These include haematology, biochemistry, radiology and histopathology as well as more specialised investigations depending on the disease: for example, electrophysiology in suspected neuropathies. In addition to these, the clinical geneticist uses chromosome and DNA analysis to confirm or exclude a diagnosis. Modern techniques of chromosome and DNA analysis have had a dramatic effect on the number of genetic diseases that can be tested for. For example, the polymerase chain reaction (PCR) can amplify virtually any gene sequence for analysis by gel electrophoresis or DNA sequencing (see Fig. 11.9, p. 344).

Despite the identification of the gene or genes responsible for a disorder, it may not be possible to search routinely for mutations in individuals or families due to technical problems. Whilst some diseases such as cystic fibrosis are mainly due to a single mutation in a large gene for which a test can be readily developed, other diseases are due to a wide variety of mutations (in either the same or a different gene), necessitating the screening of all exons and adjacent sequences. Whilst such screening can be undertaken in dedicated research laboratories this level of investigation is often impossible in hospital diagnostic laboratories that have to offer tests for a wide variety of common and rare disorders. Even with current developments in DNA technology (including high-throughput sequencing and DNA 'chips'), routine laboratory testing for many diseases is not currently available.

GENETIC COUNSELLING AND TESTING

Genetic counselling can be defined as the effective communication and provision of information to an individual or family concerning the diagnosis of, or risk of inheriting, a genetic disease (see Box 11.12). It should be considered to be an essential part of the management of individuals and families with genetic disease.

Collecting genetic information is the most fundamental part of genetic counselling. This is usually achieved by constructing a pedigree or family tree. All information is relevant as it provides a permanent record for that particular family and may be updated accordingly. Strict patient confidentiality should be observed at all times and information from medical records obtained only with prior consent. It is usually the responsibility of the individual (consultand) seeking genetic counselling to obtain further family details or the consent of relatives to provide such information, but help and support for this process is often provided within the framework of the genetics clinic.

CONSTRUCTING A PEDIGREE

Genetic information is usually documented in a family tree or pedigree. The basic symbols and nomenclature used in drawing a pedigree are given in Figure 11.12. The family history taken in a routine medical clerking should be presented in this manner. It will often reveal important genetic risks in a family that otherwise might not have been appreciated. This is especially true when taking a family history relating to cancer.

A pedigree must include details from both sides of the family, any history of pregnancy loss or infant death, consanguinity, and details of all medical conditions in family members. Other significant information includes dates of birth and age at death.

Most importantly, accurate genetic counselling can only be provided once a firm clinical diagnosis has been achieved. An accurate diagnosis may be available from patient records, from pathology reports or from a detailed clinical examination. A death certificate may be the only available record. It is also important to be aware that a diagnosis given by a family member or death certificate may be wrong. This is often true in cases of cancer where 'stomach' may mean any part of the bowel, and 'brain' may refer to secondary deposits or be used where the primary site has not been identified. Incomplete and inaccurate records concerning diagnosis may lead to incorrect reassurance or risk estimates being given, and/or inappropriate screening or invasive investigations being offered.

RISK CALCULATION

Not only can the calculation of risk in a genetic disease be complicated, but communicating this risk clearly and effectively to a patient may also be difficult. A 5% (or 1:20) risk

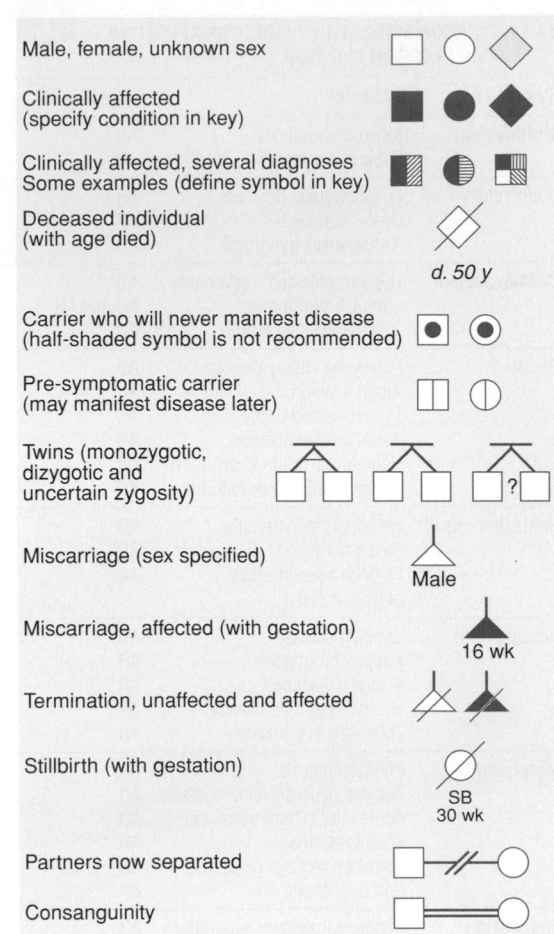

Fig. 11.12 **Common symbols used in constructing a pedigree.**

of a child being affected may be perceived by some individuals as low, but to a couple who already have a severely affected child this may be unacceptably high. Many factors determine how someone perceives risk. In a family with a highly penetrant autosomal dominant disorder in which there are many affected individuals, a 50% (1:2) risk may be readily accepted. In the case of a severely affected child born to a very mildly affected parent who was not aware of the diagnosis, a 50% risk for each subsequent child may be devastating. Therefore the concept of high or low risk supported with a precise risk figure will be interpreted very differently by different individuals and will be modified by the severity of the disease and their previous experience of it.

Risk can be calculated in many different ways and the details of such calculations are beyond the scope of this chapter. Several excellent books describing risk estimation are listed on page 353. It is also necessary to be aware that there are many pitfalls in providing accurate risks and any risk given by a non-specialist should be discussed at the earliest opportunity with a medical geneticist. One exception is when an empiric risk is given (see Box 11.13). An empiric risk is based on observational data obtained from a population comparable to the one the patient is from (e.g. the maternal age-related incidence of trisomy 21 in live-born

11.13 EMPIRIC SIBLING RECURRENCE RISKS FOR SOME COMMON CLINICAL DISORDERS*	
• Bilateral cleft lip and palate	5.7%
• Severe childhood deafness (unknown cause)	10%
• Neural tube defects	3%
• Congenital heart disease	2–3%
• Severe mental retardation (unknown cause)	3%
• Vesico-ureteric reflux	10%
• Epilepsy	5%
• Schizophrenia	9%
• Manic-depressive illness	13%
• Type II diabetes	10%
• Alzheimer's disease (< 65 years)	4–12%

*Parents normal.

INFORMATION AND SUPPORT

The genetic counselling clinic is an important opportunity to obtain information from, and provide information to, an individual or family. Patients may bring their own information obtained from a variety of sources, including the Internet. With such access it is quite usual for the patient to come to the clinic having already read a considerable amount about a particular condition. This may or may not be accurate or relevant and frequently concerns the more severe aspects of the disease. An important part of the counselling process is therefore effective communication of information. This must be provided in a non-directive and non-judgemental manner. The information may be distressing and several appointments may be necessary. For many people further support is necessary and this may be offered by telephone or in a home visit.

Many special problems may be encountered in genetic counselling, including adoption and the risk of a child having a genetic disorder, consanguinity and the increase in genetic risks, and non-paternity as an incidental finding. These and many other situations require a high degree of skill to manage effectively without causing distress to individuals, couples and families.

infants, see p. 340). Empiric risks have been derived for many conditions which have either multifactorial inheritance (e.g. neural tube defects) or an identical clinical phenotype without a specific diagnosis (e.g. profound childhood sensorineural hearing loss).

In the case of a fully penetrant Mendelian disorder it may also be possible to give accurate risks. For example, children of a healthy individual who has a sibling with an autosomal recessive disorder will be at negligible risk of being affected, although they will have a 25% (1:4) chance of being a carrier for the disorder. The pregnancy of a couple who have had a child previously affected with an autosomal recessive disorder will have a 25% (1:4) risk of being affected, and the child of an individual affected with an autosomal dominant disorder will be at 50% (1:2) risk.

However, even Mendelian risks can be modified. Thus an individual at 50% risk of inheriting an autosomal dominant disease may have a lower risk if he or she remains well beyond an age where the majority of affected individuals would be expected to be symptomatic (age-related penetrance). The 50% risk is the prior genetic risk and it has to be modified by conditional information to give a new modified risk. It is essential to consider such conditional information if it is available.

Bayes' theorem is commonly used to calculate such modified risks. This enables all information to be used in calculating a risk figure. A very simple Bayesian calculation is illustrated. Consider a woman who is at risk of being a carrier of an X-linked recessive disease. Her grandfather and brother are affected, which makes her mother an obligate gene carrier. Her risk of being a carrier is therefore 50%. However, she has two unaffected sons. This information can be used to modify her risk. The prior probability that she is a carrier is 1:2 and that she is not a carrier also 1:2. The conditional probability that she would have two normal sons if she were a carrier is $1/2 \times 1/2$ or 1/4. If she were not a carrier, the probability of having normal sons is 1. From this the joint probability for each outcome can be calculated (the prior risk × the conditional risk): $1/2 \times 1/4$ (1/8) for being a carrier and $1/2 \times 1$ (1/2) for not being a carrier. The final risk or relative probability for each outcome can then be obtained by dividing the joint probability for that outcome by the sum of the joint probabilities. The probability that she is a carrier is therefore $1/8/(1/8 + 1/2) = 1/5$ (20%).

THE MEDICAL GENETICS CLINIC

The key requirement of a genetic counselling clinic is the provision of adequate time in a quiet place free of disturbance. This may be hard to achieve in a busy medical outpatient clinic or hospital ward. A 1-hour initial consultation will usually allow most aspects of the counselling process to be carried out. Follow-up visits may be shorter. Genetic counselling is usually provided by a medical geneticist and a specialist nurse counsellor. It may also be provided by a clinician with particular skills in this area, such as an obstetrician or pediatrician. Contact outside the clinic is also important. This often takes the form of pre-clinic visits or telephone calls to explain the purpose of the appointment and to identify concerns and issues that may not be obvious in the referral letter, as well as follow-up after the clinic visit to obtain further information and samples and to give support. Great value is also placed on providing information in a written form. This may involve the use of information leaflets or more commonly a post-clinic letter summarising the important points discussed. This permanent record given to the patient will prevent important information from being forgotten and may also be used to inform other family members.

GENETIC TESTING

Genetic testing or the identification of individuals who have a child with a genetic disease, or who are at risk of developing or having one, uses several methods:

- The identification of markers of the disease. These may be clinical, biochemical, haematological or radiological. They may detect subclinical features of a disease in autosomal dominant disorders such as renal cysts in polycystic kidney disease, or identify a carrier in X-linked or autosomal recessive disorders (e.g. raised creatine kinase in muscular dystrophy).
- Karyotyping (e.g. trisomy 21 or Down's syndrome).
- Direct DNA testing (e.g. CAG expansion in Huntington's disease).

Tests may be used to screen for genetic disease; to detect carriers who themselves either do not manifest any signs of the disease or have only very mild features but who may have severely affected offspring; or to aid in diagnosis or prediction.

Genetic screening

This is usually carried out on populations or at-risk groups. Examples include screening for phenylketonuria and cystic fibrosis in the newborn, prenatal screening for neural tube defects (NTD) and Down's syndrome in pregnant women (see EBM panel), and screening for carriers of haemoglobinopathies and Tay–Sachs disease in at-risk populations.

DOWN'S SYNDROME—triple repeat testing `EBM`

'Antenatal maternal serum screening is an effective method for identifying pregnancies at risk of being affected by Down's syndrome other than on the basis of maternal age alone.'

- Wald NJ, Kennard A, Densem JW, et al. Antenatal maternal serum screening for Down's syndrome: results of a demonstration project. BMJ 1992; 305:391–394.

Further information: 🖥 www.omni.ac.uk

Maternal serum screening for NTD and Down's syndrome is now widely available. This test is offered at 15 weeks and involves measurement of α-fetoprotein for NTD and α-fetoprotein, unconjugated oestradiol and human chorionic gonadotrophin (the triple test) for Down's syndrome. It may be combined with other measurements such as nuchal translucency on ultrasound to provide an age-related risk. Direct testing with amniocentesis may then be offered. Genetic counselling must be offered and all issues surrounding possible termination of pregnancy discussed.

Prenatal testing

Direct invasive testing of a pregnancy for a specific condition, usually one severe enough to cause early infant death or severe disability, may be offered after careful explanation of the risks involved where a positive result will be used to decide about termination of pregnancy. Some indications for testing are listed in Box 11.14; methods used are summarised in Box 11.15.

Non-invasive ultrasound scanning is usually offered to all pregnant couples and is particularly important if there is a previous history of serious developmental abnormalities. As the range of tests for genetic diseases increases, demand for prenatal testing is likely to rise. A considerable ethical

11.14 SOME INDICATIONS FOR PRENATAL TESTING

- Advanced maternal age and a high-risk serum screening result
- A previous child with a detectable chromosome abnormality or a parent with a chromosome abnormality such as a balanced translocation
- A parent or child with a genetic disease for which testing is available

11.15 METHODS USED IN PRENATAL TESTING

Test	Gestation	Comments
Ultrasound	1st trimester onwards	Increased nuchal translucency (an oedematous flap of skin at the base of the neck) for trisomies and Turner's; all major abnormalities such as neural tube defects (NTDs), congenital heart disease
Chorionic villus biopsy	From 11 weeks	2% risk of miscarriage; used for early chromosomal, DNA and biochemical analysis; a specialised test
Amniocentesis	From 14 weeks	< 1% risk of miscarriage; used for chromosomal and some biochemical analysis, e.g. α-fetoprotein for NTD
Cordocentesis	From 19 weeks	2–3% risk of miscarriage; a highly specialised test; used for chromosomal and DNA analysis

debate is taking place about the types of disease for which prenatal testing is appropriate.

Diagnostic tests

In the presence of symptoms or signs of a particular disease a genetic test may be used to confirm the clinical diagnosis —a diagnostic test.

Predictive tests

In the absence of symptoms or signs of disease but in an individual usually at 50% risk of inheriting a genetic disease, a genetic test can be used to determine whether that individual carries the disease-causing mutation—a presymptomatic or predictive test. Predictive tests are usually carried out for adult-onset disorders such as familial cancer syndromes (see Box 11.5, p. 343) and neurodegenerative disorders such as Huntington's disease (see Box 11.16). However, many complicated ethical issues are raised and such tests should only be carried out by clinicians experienced in their use. Most experience with predictive testing has been gained with Huntington's disease; however, the guidelines can be applied for testing for other diseases. Exceptions include predictive testing in children for some diseases such as familial polyposis coli (see p. 343), which can be carried out where screening and therapeutic options will be changed depending on the result.

Whilst a negative predictive test is clearly viewed as a favourable outcome, a positive test may have significant consequences. These should have been explained in the counselling process and include difficulties in obtaining life and health insurance, employment discrimination and psychological effects. Evidence suggests that serious psychological sequelae are uncommon.

ETHICAL ISSUES IN GENETIC TESTING

Genetic tests have great value in the diagnosis of disease when clinical features are present. Their use in predictive testing when governed by carefully constructed protocols, e.g. in Huntington's disease, has also been widely accepted. Their wider use has caused considerable controversy, as illustrated by concerns about the use of results of genetic tests by the insurance industry. However, certain rules and ethical considerations cover the use of genetic tests and the disclosure of their results to anyone but the individual undergoing the test. These are widely employed and have prevented the inappropriate use of genetic tests, but as with any 'ethical' issue they may be open to different interpretations. Genetic testing should only be carried out by health professionals fully trained in their application and in the interpretation of results. These are usually clinical geneticists, genetic counsellors and specialists in obstetrics and fetal medicine.

Particular concerns have also been raised about the use of genetic tests in children. Testing is clearly appropriate if the condition is present or usually occurs in childhood or when proven treatments are available, e.g. testing a child for cystic fibrosis if he or she presents with symptoms or has an affected sibling. However, testing for late-onset disorders where the child is healthy and no benefit from early intervention exists is not normally carried out. In this situation families should be encouraged to discuss testing openly, with the help of genetic counselling, so that the child can make his or her own informed decision, taking into account medical, emotional, family and social consequences usually as a young adult (British Society of Human Genetics report into the genetic testing of children).

As genetic tests become available for a wide range of conditions their potential use for prenatal diagnosis and subsequent decisions regarding termination of pregnancy must also be considered. This raises many issues, including what abnormality should be considered severe enough to justify termination, parental rights, the rights of the unborn child and the acceptance of disability in society. As methods for screening for fetal abnormality improve, e.g. fetal ultrasound and serum screening, it is vital that appropriate counselling be provided and consent obtained before the test is performed.

FURTHER INFORMATION

Harper PS. Practical genetic counselling. 5th edn. Oxford: Butterworth Heinemann; 1998.

Lewin B. Genes VII. Oxford: Oxford University Press; 2000.

Young ID. Introduction to risk calculation in genetic counselling. 2nd edn. Oxford: Oxford University Press; 1999.

www.ncbi.nlm.nih.gov/Omim/ *Online Mendelian Inheritance in Man (OMIM).*

www.nhgri.nih.gov *Human Genome Project.*

Part 2
SYSTEM-BASED DISEASES

Cardiovascular disease

N.A. BOON • K.A.A. FOX • P. BLOOMFIELD • A. BRADBURY

CLINICAL EXAMINATION OF THE CARDIOVASCULAR SYSTEM

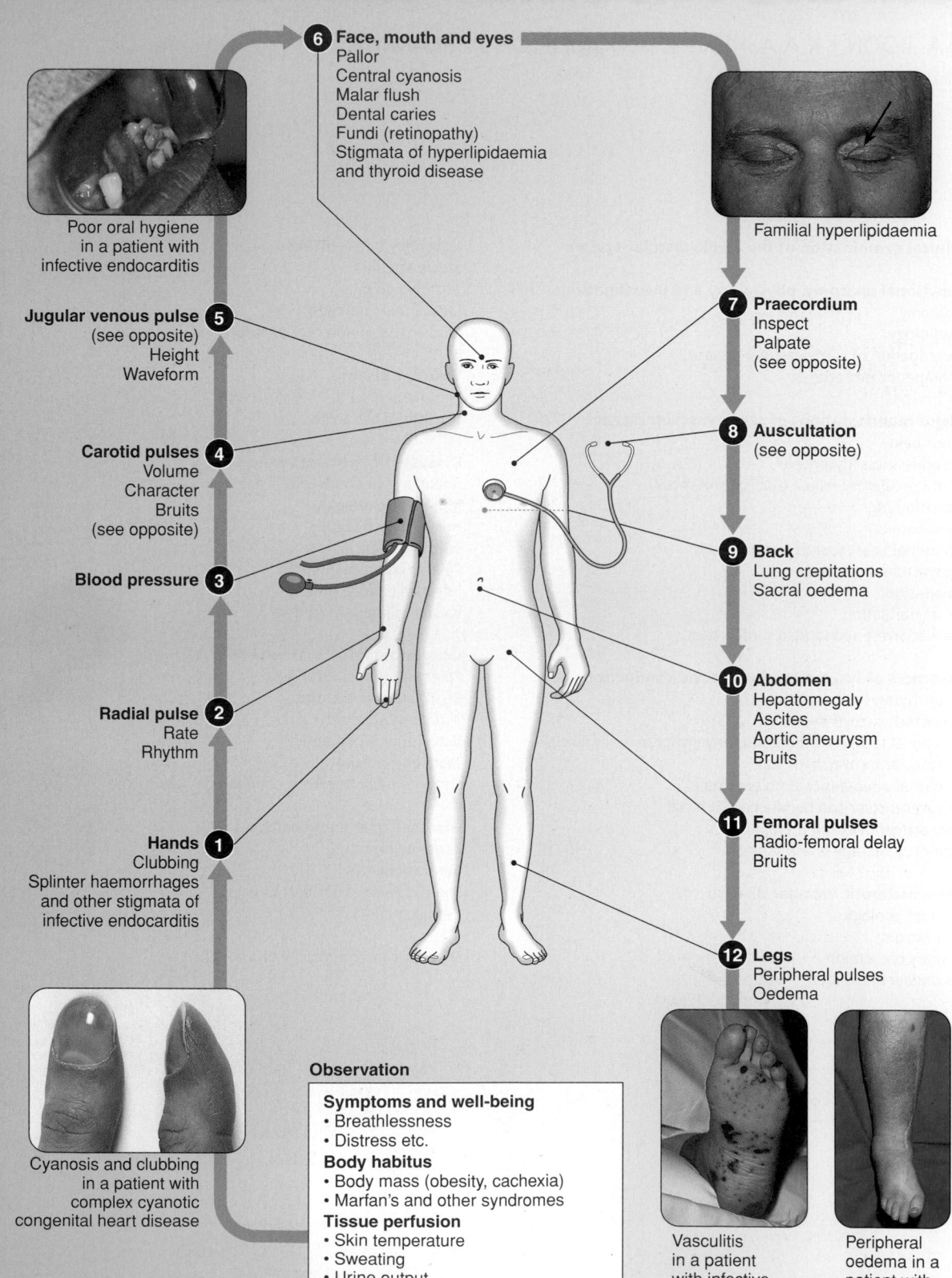

6 Face, mouth and eyes
Pallor
Central cyanosis
Malar flush
Dental caries
Fundi (retinopathy)
Stigmata of hyperlipidaemia
and thyroid disease

Poor oral hygiene
in a patient with
infective endocarditis

Familial hyperlipidaemia

Jugular venous pulse **5**
(see opposite)
Height
Waveform

7 Praecordium
Inspect
Palpate
(see opposite)

Carotid pulses **4**
Volume
Character
Bruits
(see opposite)

8 Auscultation
(see opposite)

Blood pressure **3**

9 Back
Lung crepitations
Sacral oedema

10 Abdomen
Hepatomegaly
Ascites
Aortic aneurysm
Bruits

Radial pulse **2**
Rate
Rhythm

11 Femoral pulses
Radio-femoral delay
Bruits

Hands **1**
Clubbing
Splinter haemorrhages
and other stigmata of
infective endocarditis

12 Legs
Peripheral pulses
Oedema

Cyanosis and clubbing
in a patient with
complex cyanotic
congenital heart disease

Observation

Symptoms and well-being
• Breathlessness
• Distress etc.
Body habitus
• Body mass (obesity, cachexia)
• Marfan's and other syndromes
Tissue perfusion
• Skin temperature
• Sweating
• Urine output

Vasculitis
in a patient
with infective
endocarditis

Peripheral
oedema in a
patient with
congestive
cardiac failure

SYMPTOMS

A close relationship between symptoms and exercise is the hallmark of heart disease. The New York Heart Association (NYHA) functional classification is often used to grade disability:

- Class I — No limitation during ordinary activity
- Class II — Slight limitation during ordinary activity
- Class III — Marked limitation of normal activities without symptoms at rest
- Class IV — Unable to undertake physical activity without symptoms; symptoms may be present at rest.

➍ EXAMINATION OF THE ARTERIAL PULSE

- The character of the pulse is determined by both stroke volume and arterial compliance and should be assessed by palpating the carotid arteries.
- Anaemia, aortic regurgitation and other causes of a large stroke volume typically produce a bounding pulse with a wide amplitude.
- Poor left ventricular function, mitral stenosis and other causes of a low stroke volume may produce a thin, thready, weak pulse.
- Aortic stenosis impedes ventricular emptying and may cause a slow rising, weak and delayed pulse.
- Arteries are elastic and so absorb or dampen the pulse wave; if they become non-compliant (stiff and rigid), due to the effects of ageing, hypertension or atherosclerosis, they may amplify the pulse wave. A prominent pulse can therefore be a feature of widespread arterial disease. Moreover, the relatively common combination of poor left ventricular function and widespread arterial disease can produce a seemingly normal pulse.

FEATURES THAT DISTINGUISH VENOUS FROM ARTERIAL PULSATION IN THE NECK

- Venous pulse has two peaks in each cardiac cycle (arterial has one).
- Venous pulse varies with respiration (falls on inspiration) and position.
- Abdominal compression causes the venous pulse to rise.
- Venous pulse is not palpable and can be occluded by light pressure.

➎ EXAMINATION OF THE JUGULAR VENOUS PULSE (JVP)

- The height of the JVP is determined by right atrial pressure and is therefore elevated in right heart failure and reduced in hypovolaemia.
- The *a* wave is caused by atrial systole and is absent in atrial fibrillation but exaggerated in tricuspid stenosis, all forms of right ventricular hypertrophy (e.g. pulmonary hypertension, pulmonary stenosis) and other conditions that cause a stiff, non-compliant right ventricle (e.g. right ventricular infarction).
- The relationship between atrial and ventricular systole is disturbed in a variety of arrhythmias. Giant cannon waves may be visible if the right atrium contracts when the tricuspid valve is closed or only partially open and can be intermittent (e.g. complete heart block) or regular (e.g. nodal rhythm).
- Tricuspid regurgitation produces giant *v* waves that coincide with ventricular systole.
- The JVP is grossly elevated and fixed in superior vena cava obstruction and may show a paradoxical rise during inspiration in tamponade or constrictive pericarditis.

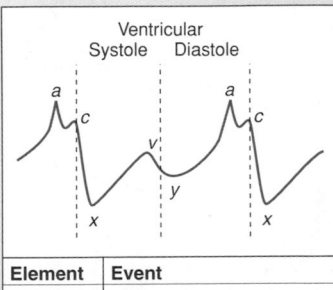

Element	Event
a wave	Right atrial contraction
c wave	Transmitted carotid impulse at onset of systole (not usually visible)
v wave	Passive atrial filling against closed tricuspid valve in systole
x descent	Right atrial relaxation and descent of tricuspid valve in systole
y descent	Passive filling of right ventricle at start of diastole
N.B. The two peaks of the *a* and *v* wave are the most easily seen.	

Waveform of the jugular venous pulse.

➐ PALPATION OF THE PRAECORDIUM

Technique

- Place heel of hand over left sternal edge and fingertips over apex, then feel the aortic and pulmonary areas by placing fingers in the rib spaces.

Common abnormalities of the apex beat

- Volume overload, e.g. mitral regurgitation: displaced, active, rocking
- Pressure overload, e.g. aortic stenosis: discrete, thrusting
- Dyskinetic, e.g. coronary disease/ aneurysm: displaced, incoordinate

Other abnormalities

- Palpable S1 (tapping apex beat— mitral stenosis)
- Palpable P2 (severe pulmonary hypertension)
- Right ventricular hypertrophy (right ventricular heave or lift) felt by heel of hand
- Aortic aneurysm

➑ AUSCULTATION OF THE HEART

- Optimise acoustics
  —Ensure the ear pieces of the stethoscope fit perfectly.
  —Experiment with different degrees of pressure on the head of the stethoscope.
- Time the sounds by feeling the carotid pulse.
- Use the bell to examine low-pitched noises
  —1st, 2nd, 3rd and 4th heart sounds, mid-diastolic murmurs.
- Use the diaphragm for high-pitched noises
  —Pansystolic murmurs, early diastolic murmurs.
- Listen to the noises like a piece of music
  —What tune or cadence can you hear?
  —Analyse each sound separately.

The haemodynamic effects of respiration are discussed on page 364.

See pages 395–397 for analysis and interpretation of heart sounds and murmurs.

Cardiovascular disease is the most frequent cause of adult death in the Western world; in the UK one-third of men and one-quarter of women will die as a result of ischaemic heart disease. In many Western countries the incidence of ischaemic heart disease has been falling for the last two or three decades, but it is rising in Eastern Europe and on the Indian subcontinent, and this has led to predictions that cardiovascular disease will soon become the leading cause of death on all continents. Strategies for the treatment and prevention of heart disease can be highly effective and have been subjected to rigorous evaluation in many randomised controlled trials. The evidence base for the treatment of cardiovascular disease is stronger than for almost any other disease group.

Valvular heart disease is common, but the aetiology varies in different parts of the world. On the Indian subcontinent it is predominantly due to rheumatic fever, whereas degenerative disease of the aortic valve is the most common problem in the West.

Prompt recognition of the development of heart disease is limited by two key factors. Firstly, it is very commonly latent. For example, disease of the coronary arteries can proceed to an advanced stage before the patient notices any symptoms. Secondly, the diversity of symptoms attributable to heart disease is limited and it is common for many different pathologies to present through a common symptomatic pathway.

FUNCTIONAL ANATOMY, PHYSIOLOGY AND INVESTIGATIONS

ANATOMY

The heart acts as two separate pumps operating in parallel; the right heart generates the circulation to the lungs and the left heart feeds the rest of the body. The right atrium drains deoxygenated blood from the superior and inferior venae cavae and discharges blood to the right ventricle, which in turn pumps it into the pulmonary artery. The left atrium drains oxygenated blood from the lungs through four pulmonary veins and discharges blood into the left ventricle, which in turn pumps it into the aorta (see Fig. 12.1). During ventricular contraction the two atrioventricular valves close (the tricuspid valve in the right heart and the mitral valve in the left heart), and the pulmonary and aortic valves open. In diastole the pulmonary and aortic valves close, and the two atrioventricular valves open.

The pressures in the left ventricle are normally at least four times greater than those in the right, and the wall of the left ventricle is usually at least 1 cm thick compared with 2–3 mm for the right. The atria lie within the mediastinum anterior to the oesophagus and the descending aorta. The ventricles lie anterior to the atria and taper towards the apex

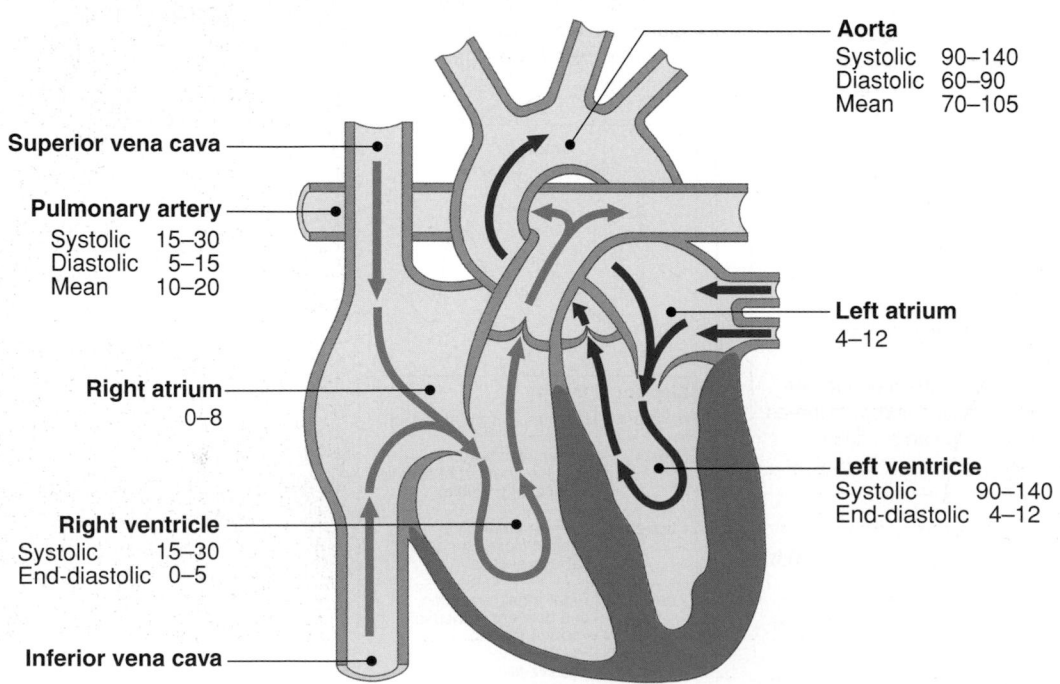

Fig. 12.1 Direction of blood flow through the heart. The blue arrows show unoxygenated blood moving through the right heart to the lungs. The red arrows show oxygenated blood moving from the lungs to the systemic circulation. The normal pressures are shown for each chamber in mmHg.

Aorta
Systolic   90–140
Diastolic   60–90
Mean   70–105

Superior vena cava

Pulmonary artery
Systolic   15–30
Diastolic   5–15
Mean   10–20

Left atrium
4–12

Right atrium
0–8

Left ventricle
Systolic   90–140
End-diastolic   4–12

Right ventricle
Systolic   15–30
End-diastolic   0–5

Inferior vena cava

of the heart, which lies to the left of the midline. The right ventricle lies immediately below the sternum and is not only to the right of, but also anterior to, the left ventricle.

The normal heart occupies less than 50% of the transthoracic diameter in the frontal plane, as seen on a chest radiograph. On the patient's left, the cardiac silhouette is formed by the aortic arch, the pulmonary trunk, the left atrial appendage and left ventricle (LV). On the right, the right atrium (RA) is joined by superior and inferior venae cavae, and the lower right border is made up by the right ventricle (RV; see Fig. 12.2A). In disease states or congenital cardiac abnormalities the silhouette may change as a result of hypertrophy or dilatation.

Echocardiography images the heart in two-dimensional slices so that individual chamber sizes and valve abnormalities can be seen (see Fig. 12.2C).

The coronary circulation

The left main and right coronary arteries arise from the left and right coronary sinuses, just distal to the aortic valve (see Fig. 12.3). Within 2.5 cm of its origin the left main coronary divides into the left anterior descending artery (LAD), which runs in the anterior interventricular groove, and the left circumflex artery (CX), which runs posteriorly in the atrioventricular groove. The LAD gives branches to supply the anterior part of the septum (septal perforators) and the anterior wall and apex of the left ventricle. The CX gives marginal branches that supply the lateral, posterior and inferior segments of the left ventricle. The right coronary artery (RCA) runs in the right atrioventricular groove, giving branches that supply the right atrium, right ventricle and infero-posterior aspects of the left ventricle. The posterior descending artery runs in the posterior interventricular groove and supplies the back of the heart. This vessel is a branch of the RCA in approximately 90% of people (dominant right system) and is supplied by the CX in the remainder (dominant left system). The exact coronary anatomy varies greatly from person to person and there are many 'normal variants'.

The right coronary artery supplies the sinoatrial (SA) node in about 60% of individuals, and the atrioventricular (AV) node in about 90%. Proximal occlusion of the RCA therefore often results in sinus bradycardia, and may also cause electrical conduction block of the AV node. Abrupt occlusions in the RCA, due to coronary thrombosis, result in infarction of the inferior part of the left ventricle and often the right ventricle. Abrupt occlusion of the LAD or CX causes infarction in the corresponding territory of the left ventricle, and occlusion of the left main coronary artery is usually fatal.

The venous system mainly follows the coronary arteries but drains to the coronary sinus in the inferior atrioventricular groove, and then to the right atrium. An extensive lymphatic system drains into vessels which travel with the coronary vessels and then into the thoracic duct.

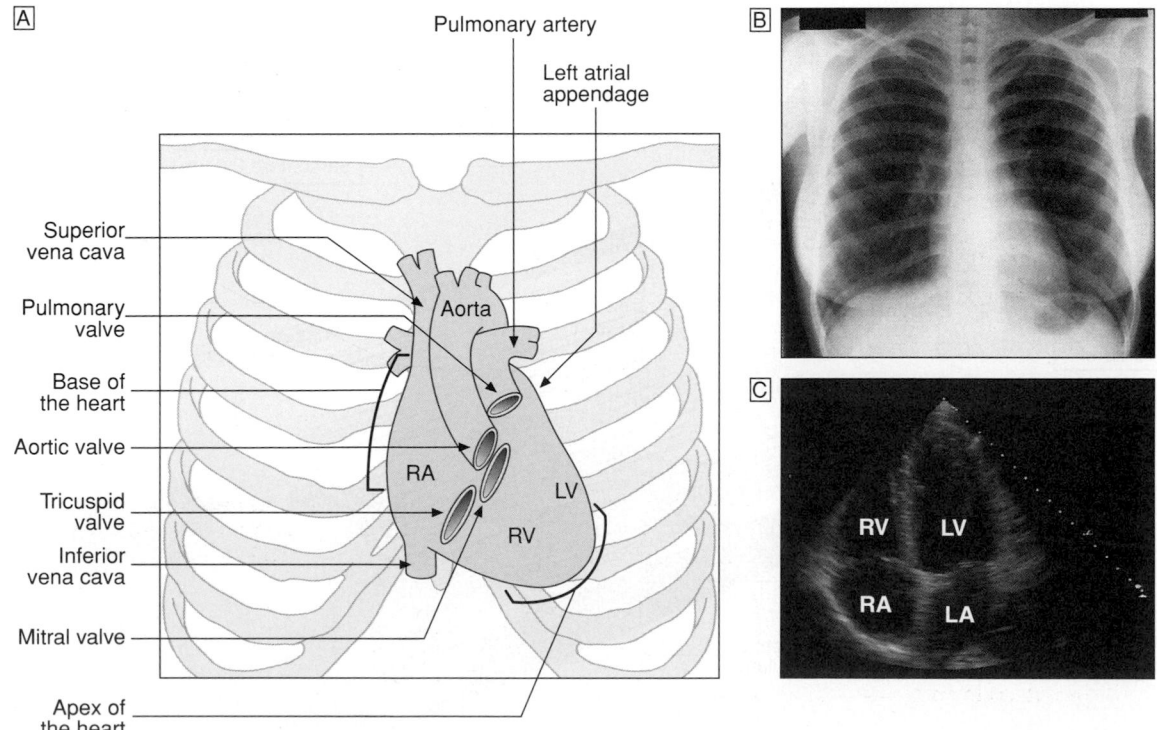

Fig. 12.2 Imaging of the heart. A Radiological outline of the heart. The positions of the major cardiac chambers and heart valves are shown. B Radiograph of the chest showing the silhouette of the heart. C Echocardiogram displaying the chambers of the heart in the four-chamber view, which does not correspond to the schematic.

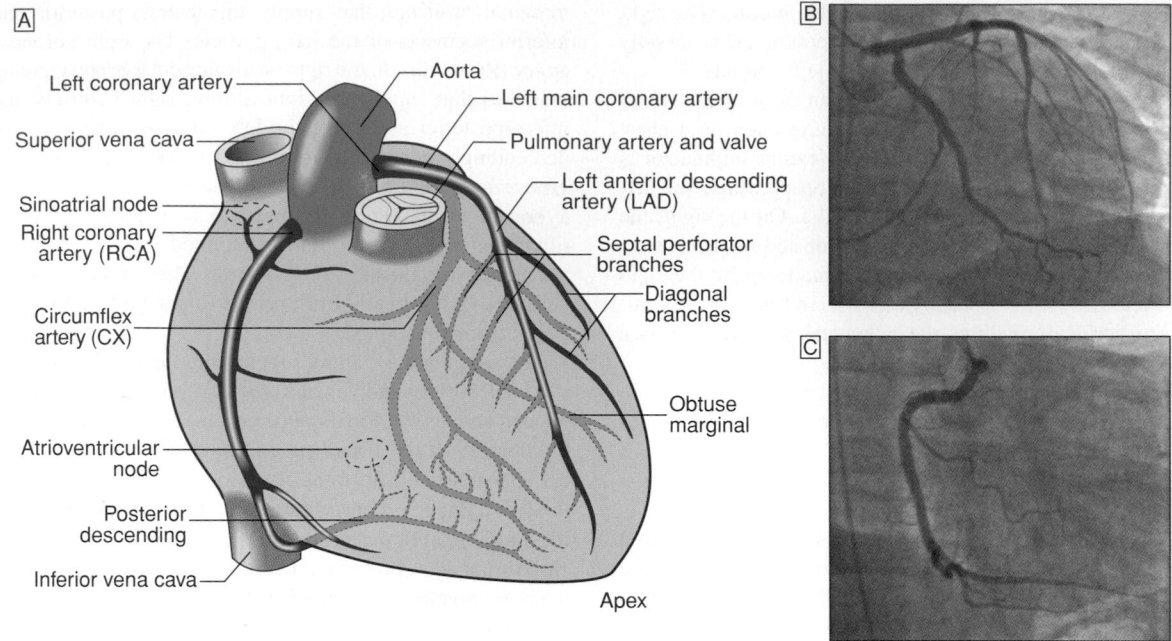

A
- Left coronary artery
- Superior vena cava
- Sinoatrial node
- Right coronary artery (RCA)
- Circumflex artery (CX)
- Atrioventricular node
- Posterior descending
- Inferior vena cava
- Aorta
- Left main coronary artery
- Pulmonary artery and valve
- Left anterior descending artery (LAD)
- Septal perforator branches
- Diagonal branches
- Obtuse marginal
- Apex

Fig. 12.3 The coronary arteries of the heart. [A] Diagram of the anterior view. [B] Corresponding coronary angiogram of the left coronary artery. [C] Right coronary artery.

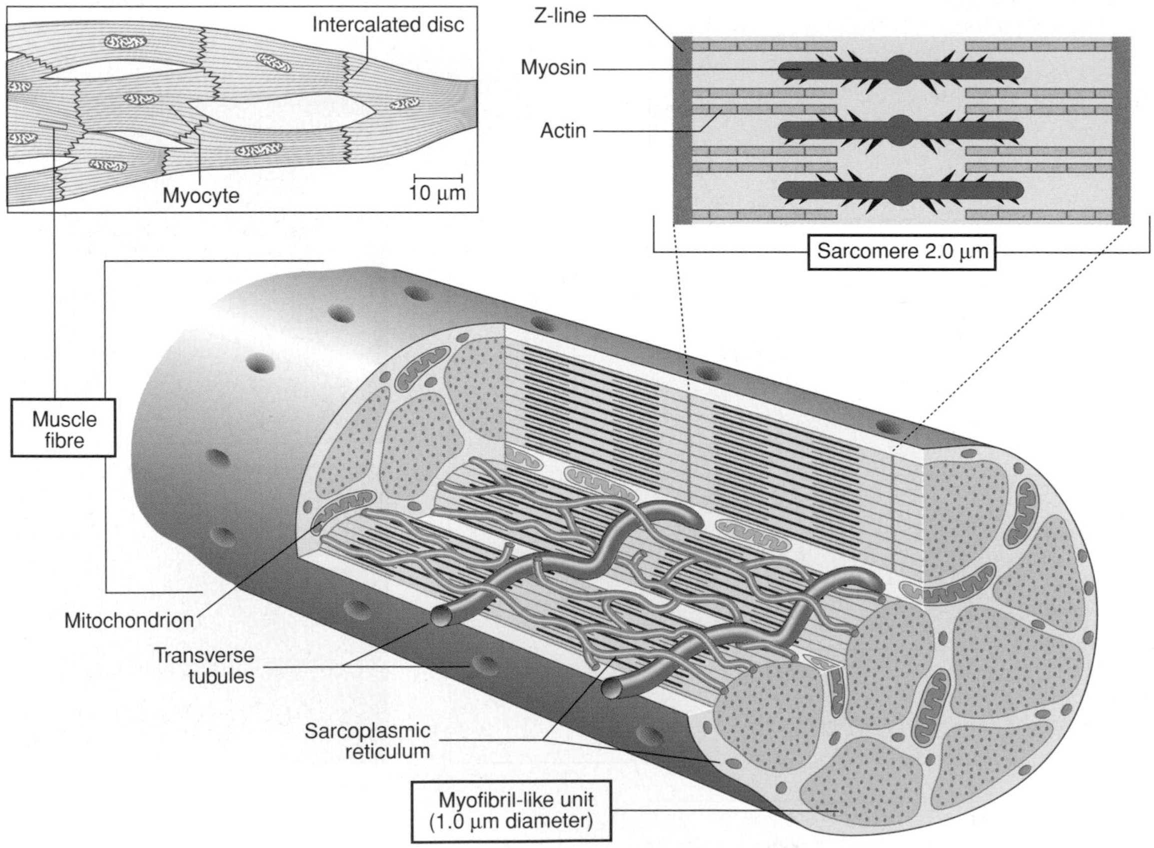

Intercalated disc
Myocyte
10 μm

Z-line
Myosin
Actin
Sarcomere 2.0 μm

Muscle fibre
Mitochondrion
Transverse tubules
Sarcoplasmic reticulum
Myofibril-like unit (1.0 μm diameter)

Fig. 12.4 Schematic of myocytes and a muscle fibre. The arrangement of myofibrils, and longitudinal and transverse tubules extending from the sarcoplasmic reticulum are shown. The expanded section shows a schematic of an individual sarcomere with thick filaments composed of myosin and thin filaments composed primarily of actin.

Nerve supply of the heart

The heart is innervated by both sympathetic and parasympathetic supply. Adrenergic nerves supply muscle fibres in the atria and ventricles and the electrical conducting system. Positive inotropic and chronotropic effects are mediated predominantly by β_1-adrenoceptors; β_2-adrenoceptors predominate in vascular smooth muscle and mediate vasodilatation. Parasympathetic pre-ganglionic fibres and sensory fibres reach the heart through the vagus nerve. Cholinergic nerves supply the AV and SA nodes via muscarinic (M2) receptors. Under resting conditions vagal inhibitory fibres predominate and the heart rate is slow. Adrenergic stimulation associated with exercise, emotional stress, fever and so on causes the heart rate to increase. In disease states the nerve supply to the heart may be affected. For example, in patients with heart failure the sympathetic system may be up-regulated, and in patients with diabetes the nerves themselves may be damaged so that there is little variation in heart rate.

The electrical conduction system is described in detail on page 365.

PHYSIOLOGY

Myocardial contraction

Myocardial cells (myocytes) are about 50–100 µm long; each cell branches and interdigitates with adjacent cells. An intercalated disc permits electrical conduction (via gap junctions) and mechanical conduction (via the fascia adherens) to adjacent cells. The basic unit of contraction is the sarcomere (2 µm in length), which is aligned to those of adjacent myofibrils, giving a striated appearance due to the Z-lines (see Fig. 12.4). Actin filaments (molecular weight 47 000) are attached at right angles to the Z-lines and interdigitate with thicker parallel myosin filaments (molecular weight 500 000). The cross-links between actin and myosin molecules contain myofibrillar ATPase, which breaks down adenosine triphosphate (ATP) to provide the energy for contraction. Two chains of actin molecules form a helical structure, with a second molecule, tropomyosin, in the grooves of the actin helix, and a further molecule, troponin, attached to every seventh actin molecule (see Fig. 12.5).

During contraction, shortening of the sarcomere results from the interdigitation of the actin and myosin molecules, without altering the length of either molecule. Contraction is initiated when calcium is made available during the plateau phase of the action potential by calcium ions entering the cell and being mobilised from the sarcoplasmic reticulum. As its concentration rises, calcium binds to troponin, precipitating contraction. The force of cardiac muscle contraction, or inotropic state, is regulated by the influx of calcium ions through 'slow calcium channels'. The extent to which the sarcomere can shorten determines stroke volume of the ventricle. It is maximally shortened in response to powerful inotropic drugs or severe exercise. However, the enlargement of the

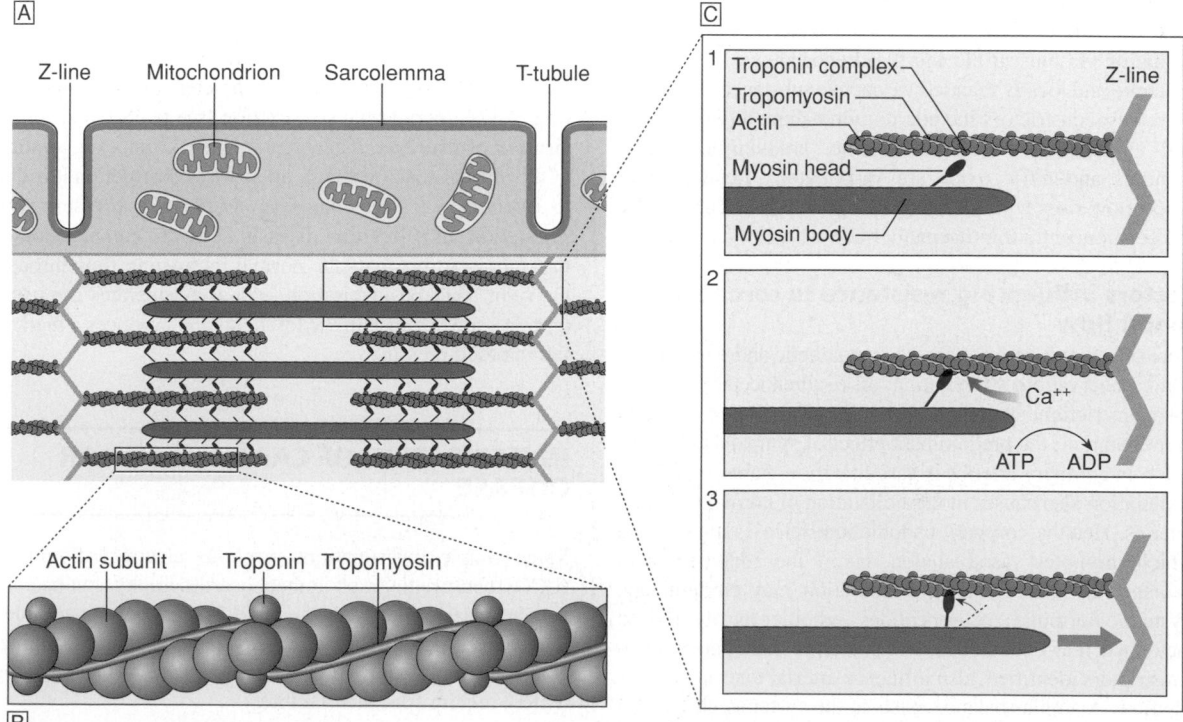

Fig. 12.5   Contraction process within the muscle fibre. [A] Schematic of a sarcomere showing the overlapping of actin and myosin filaments. [B] Enlarged diagram of the structure of an actin filament. [C] The three stages of contraction resulting in shortening of the sarcomere. 1. The actin binding site is blocked by tropomyosin. 2. ATP-dependent release of calcium ions which bind to troponin, displacing tropomyosin. The binding site is exposed. (ADP = adenosine diphosphate; ATP = adenosine triphosphate) 3. Tilting of the angle of attachment of the myosin head, resulting in fibre shortening.

heart seen in heart failure is due to slippage of the myofibrils and adjacent cells rather than lengthening of the sarcomere.

Factors influencing cardiac output

Cardiac output is determined by the product of stroke volume and heart rate. Stroke volume is dependent upon end-diastolic pressure (preload) and peripheral vascular resistance (afterload).

Stretch of cardiac muscle (arising from an increment in end-diastolic volume or preload) results in the increased force of contraction, producing an increase in stroke volume. This relationship is known as Starling's Law of the heart (see Fig. 12.23, p. 382).

Afterload falls as blood pressure is reduced and this allows greater shortening of the muscle fibres and hence increased stroke volume. The contractile state of the myocardium is controlled, in part, by the neuro-endocrine system; it is also influenced by various inotropic drugs and their antagonists. Determination of the response to a physio-logical change or to a drug can be predicted on the basis of its combined influence on preload, afterload and contrac-tility (see p. 201).

Factors influencing resistance to systemic blood flow

Systemic blood flow is critically dependent upon vascular resistance, which varies with the fourth power of the radius of the resistance vessel. Thus small changes in calibre have a marked influence on blood flow. Metabolic and mechanical factors control arteriolar tone. Neurogenic constriction oper-ates via α-adrenoceptors on vascular smooth muscle, and dilatation via muscarinic and β_2-adrenoceptors. In addition, systemic and locally released vasoactive substances influence tone; vasoconstrictors include noradrenaline, angiotensin II and endothelin, whereas adenosine, bradykinin, prosta-glandins and nitric oxide are vasodilators. Resistance to blood flow rises with viscosity, and is mainly influenced by red cell concentration (haematocrit).

Factors influencing resistance to coronary blood flow

Coronary blood vessels receive sympathetic and parasympa-thetic innervation. Stimulation of α-adrenoceptors causes vasoconstriction; stimulation of β_2-adrenoceptors causes vasodilatation; the predominant effect of sympathetic stimu-lation in coronary arteries is vasodilatation. Parasympathetic stimulation also causes modest dilatation of normal coronary arteries. Healthy coronary endothelium releases nitric oxide which promotes vasodilatation, but if the endothelium is damaged by atheroma, vasoconstriction may predominate. Systemic hormones, neuropeptides and other locally derived factors such as endothelins, which are the most potent vaso-constrictors identified, also influence arterial tone and coron-ary flow. A similar balance exists in the systemic circulation and influences peripheral vascular tone and blood pressure.

As a result of vascular regulation, an atheromatous narrowing (stenosis) in a coronary artery does not limit flow, even during exercise, until the cross-sectional area of the vessel is reduced by at least 70%.

12.1 HAEMODYNAMIC EFFECTS OF RESPIRATION

	Inspiration	Expiration
Jugular venous pressure	Falls	Rises
Blood pressure	Falls (up to 10 mmHg)	Rises
Heart rate	Accelerates	Slows
Second heart sound	Splits*	Fuses*

* Inspiration prolongs RV ejection, delaying P2, and shortens LV ejection, advancing A2; expiration produces the opposite effects.

The haemodynamic effects of respiration

There is a fall in intrathoracic pressure during inspiration which tends to suck blood into the chest, producing an increase in the flow of blood through the right heart. However, a substantial volume of blood is sequestered in the chest as the lungs expand; the increase in the capacitance of the pulmonary vascular bed usually exceeds any increase in the output of the right heart and there is therefore a reduction in the flow of blood into the left heart during inspiration. In contrast, expiration is accompanied by a fall in venous return to the right heart, a reduction in the output of the right heart, a rise in the venous return to the left heart (as blood is squeezed out of the lungs) and an increase in the output of the left heart.

The net effect of these changes in the normal heart is summarised in Box 12.1.

Pulsus paradoxus

This term is used to describe the dramatic fall in blood pres-sure during inspiration that is characteristic of tamponade (see p. 379), pericardial constriction (see p. 480) and severe airways obstruction. The phenomenon is an exaggeration of the normal state of affairs. In airways obstruction it is due to accentuation of the change in intrathoracic pressure with respiration. In pericardial disease, however, compression of the right heart prevents the normal increase in flow through the right heart on inspiration, which exaggerates the usual drop in venous return to the left heart and produces a marked fall in blood pressure.

INVESTIGATION OF CARDIOVASCULAR DISEASE

Some simple investigations, such as electrocardiography (ECG), chest radiograph and echocardiography, can be con-veniently performed at the bedside; however, more complex procedures, such as cardiac catheterisation, nuclear scanning, computed tomography (CT) and magnetic resonance imaging (MRI), require specialist facilities.

ELECTROCARDIOGRAPHY (ECG)

Electrocardiography is used to elucidate cardiac arrhythmias and conduction defects, and to diagnose and localise myocardial hypertrophy, ischaemia or infarction. It may also give information about electrolyte imbalance and the toxicity of certain drugs.

The fundamental basis for electrocardiography is that the electrical activation of a heart muscle cell causes a depolarisation of its membrane. The depolarisation is propagated along the length of the cell or fibre, and transmitted to adjoining cells. The result is a moving wave front of depolarisation, which passes through the heart and sets up electrical currents; these can be detected by surface electrodes, amplified and displayed as the electrocardiogram. From the electrical point of view the heart acts as if it has only two chambers because the two atria and then the two ventricles contract together. In the electrical conduction system the sinoatrial (sinus) node is situated at the junction of the superior vena cava and right atrium and is the origin of the impulses responsible for heart rhythm under normal conditions ('sinus rhythm'). Depolarisation of the sinoatrial node triggers a wave front of depolarisation which travels through the atria. Conduction directly to the ventricles is prevented by the annulus fibrosus, which insulates the atria from the ventricles. The AV node, which is normally the only route of conduction from the atria to the ventricles, is situated beneath the right atrial endocardium at the lower end of the interatrial septum; it conducts slowly and regulates the frequency of conduction to the ventricles. The bundle of His passes from the AV node through the annulus fibrosus and divides into right and left bundle branches, which pass down the respective sides of the ventricular septum (see Fig. 12.6A) and radiate out as the Purkinje network. The left bundle branch is subdivided into anterior and posterior fascicles. Injury to one of the main bundles may manifest on the electrocardiogram as right or left bundle branch block, whereas selective injury of one of the left fascicles (hemiblock—see p. 414) produces deviation of the electrical axis. Abnormalities of cardiac rhythm are discussed on pages 405–415.

The standard 12-lead ECG (see Box 12.2)

Normally, cardiac activation starts in the sinoatrial node, but this cannot be detected on the ECG. Depolarisation then spreads through the atria, creating the P wave and triggering atrial contraction. The PR interval represents the delay from the onset of atrial depolarisation to the onset of ventricular depolarisation (see Fig. 12.6). Electrical activity then spreads rapidly through the bundle of His and the bundle branches, triggering ventricular contraction and creating the QRS complex. The muscle mass of the ventricles is much larger than that of the atria, and the QRS complex is therefore correspondingly larger than the P wave. Repolarisation is a slower process that occurs in the opposite direction, from the epicardium to the endocardium, and produces the T wave. The QT interval (see Fig. 12.6) represents the total duration of depolarisation and repolarisation.

The 12-lead electrocardiogram is generated from chest and limb electrodes which view the heart from different directions. There are four limb electrodes: one on each wrist and one on each ankle, connected to a central terminal

---

12.2 ECG CONVENTIONS AND INTERVALS

- Depolarisation towards electrode: positive deflection
- Depolarisation away from electrode: negative deflection
- Sensitivity: 10 mm = 1 mV
- Paper speed: 25 mm per second
- Each large (5 mm) square = 0.2 s
- Each small (1 mm) square = 0.04 s
- Heart rate = 1500/R-R interval (mm)
  (i.e. 300 ÷ number of large squares between beats)

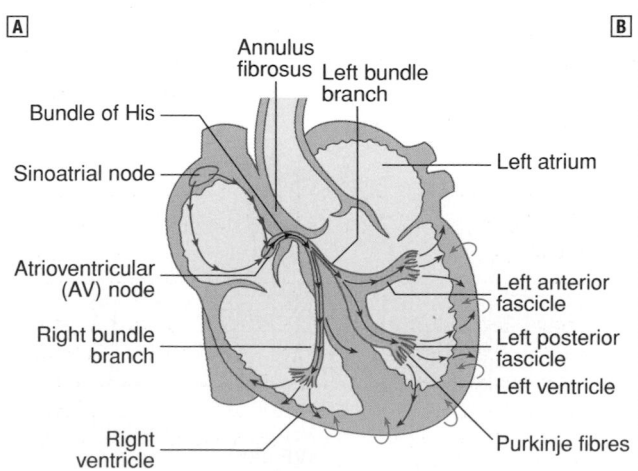

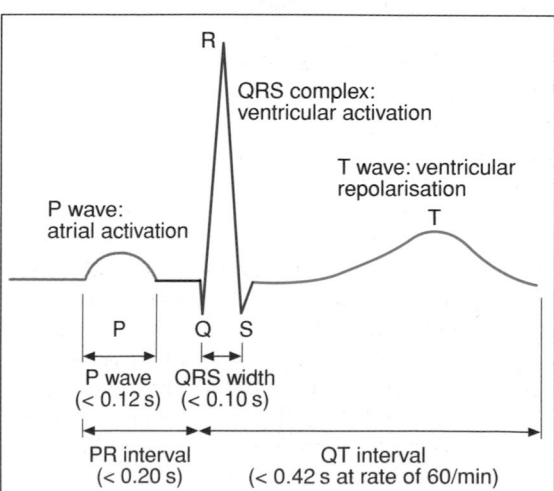

Fig. 12.6 The cardiac conduction system. **A** Depolarisation starts in the sinoatrial node and spreads through the atria and then through the AV node (black arrows). Depolarisation then reaches the ventricles via the bundle of His and the bundle branches (blue arrows). Repolarisation is in the opposite direction (green arrows). **B** The components of the ECG correspond to depolarisation and repolarisation as depicted in part A. The upper limit of the normal range for each interval is given in brackets.

which is electrically neutral. The signal recorded from the exploring electrode on the left wrist is augmented relative to the central terminal and is therefore designated lead aVL (see Fig. 12.7). Similarly augmented signals are obtained from the right arm (aVR) and left leg (aVF). These leads record the electrical activity of the heart within the frontal plane, with each lead 120° apart. Readings for leads I, II and III (the bipolar leads) are generated by subtraction of the signals from two adjacent leads. Lead I is the left arm minus the right arm, lead II is the left leg minus right arm, and lead III the left leg minus left arm. By convention lead I is designated as 0° within the frontal plane axis. The other leads are referenced from this point so that aVF becomes +90, aVL −30° etc.

When depolarisation spreads towards an electrode it produces a positive deflection in that lead; when it moves away a negative deflection is registered. The principal direction of depolarisation in the heart is known as the main vector or axis. When the vector is at right angles to a lead the depolarisation in that lead is equally negative and positive. In the example in Figure 12.7 the QRS complex is isoelectric in aVL, negative in aVR and most strongly positive in lead II; the main vector or axis of depolarisation is therefore 60°. The normal cardiac axis lies between −30° and +90°. Examples of left and right axis deviation are shown in Figure 12.8.

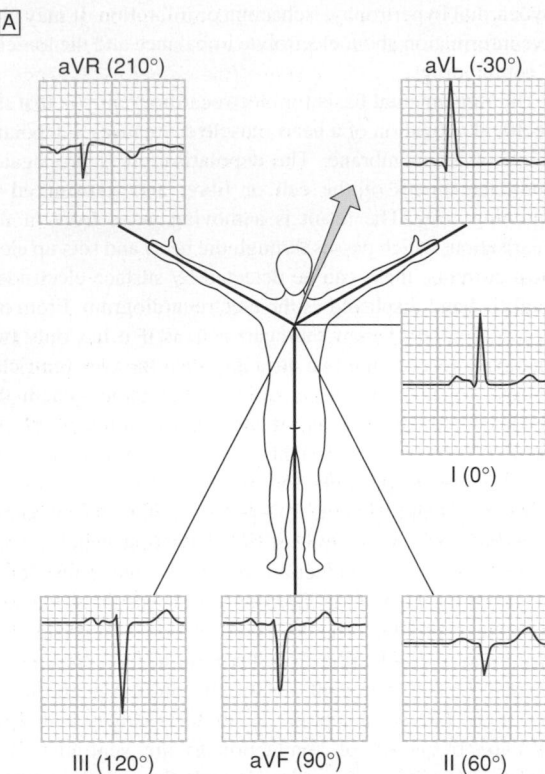

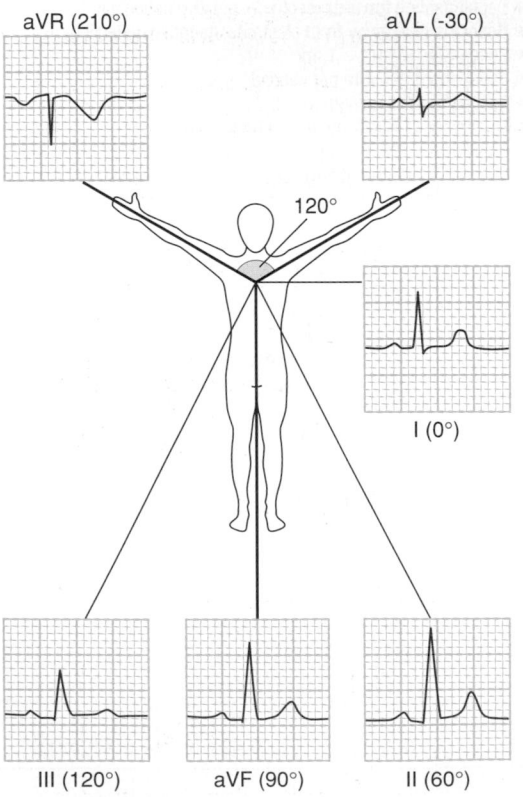

Fig. 12.7   The appearance of the ECG from various recording positions in the frontal plane.

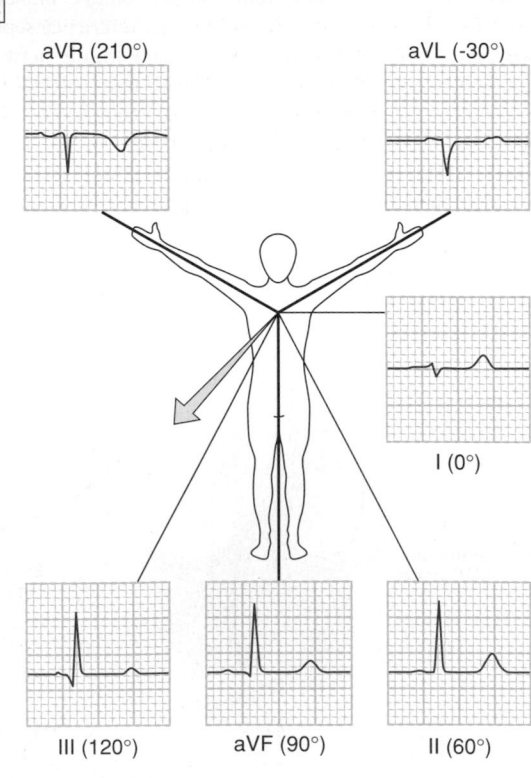

Fig. 12.8   The QRS axis. The large arrow indicates the main QRS axis. [A] Left axis deviation. [B] Right axis deviation.

There are six chest leads, V_1–V_6, from exploring electrodes placed on the anterior and lateral side of the chest over the heart. Leads V_1 and V_2 lie approximately over the right ventricle, leads V_3 and V_4 over the interventricular septum, and V_5 and V_6 over the left ventricle. The left ventricle has the greater muscle mass and contributes the major component of the QRS complex. Depolarisation of the interventricular septum occurs first and moves from left to right; this generates an initial negative deflection in V_6 (Q wave) and an initial positive deflection in V_2 (R wave). The second phase of depolarisation is activation of the body of the left ventricle, which creates a large positive deflection or R wave in V_6 (with reciprocal changes in V_2). The third and final phase of depolarisation involves the right ventricle and produces a small negative deflection or S wave in V_6 (see Fig. 12.9).

The ECG in infarction and ischaemia

When an area of the myocardium is ischaemic or undergoing infarction, repolarisation and depolarisation become abnormal relative to the surrounding myocardium. In transmural infarction there is initial ST segment elevation (the current of injury) in the leads facing or overlying the infarct; Q waves (negative deflections) will then appear as the entire thickness of the myocardial wall becomes electrically neutral relative to the adjacent myocardium. The changes occurring in infarction are described in more detail on page 435. Figures 12.73–12.76, pages 435–436 are examples of some common patterns of infarction. In myocardial ischaemia the ECG typically shows ST segment depression and/or T wave inversion; it is usually the subendocardium which most readily becomes ischaemic. Other conditions, such as left ventricular hypertrophy and electrolyte disturbances, can cause similar ST and T wave changes.

Exercise (stress) ECG

A 12-lead ECG is recorded during exercise on a treadmill or bicycle. The limb leads are placed on the shoulders and hips rather than the wrists and ankles. The Bruce Protocol has been well validated and is the most widely used test format for treadmill testing (see Box 12.3). Blood pressure is recorded and symptoms assessed regularly throughout the test. Common indications for exercise testing are shown in Box 12.4. A test is positive if anginal pain occurs and/or there

12.3 THE BRUCE PROTOCOL FOR EXERCISE TOLERANCE TESTING		
	Speed (mph)	Gradient (% incline)
Stage 1	1.7	10
Stage 2	2.5	12
Stage 3	3.4	14
Stage 4	4.2	16
Stage 5	5.0	18
Each stage lasts for 3 minutes.		

12.4 INDICATIONS FOR EXERCISE TESTING

- To confirm the diagnosis of angina
- To evaluate stable angina
- To assess prognosis following myocardial infarction
- To assess outcome after coronary revascularisation, e.g. coronary angioplasty
- To diagnose and evaluate the treatment of exercise-induced arrhythmias

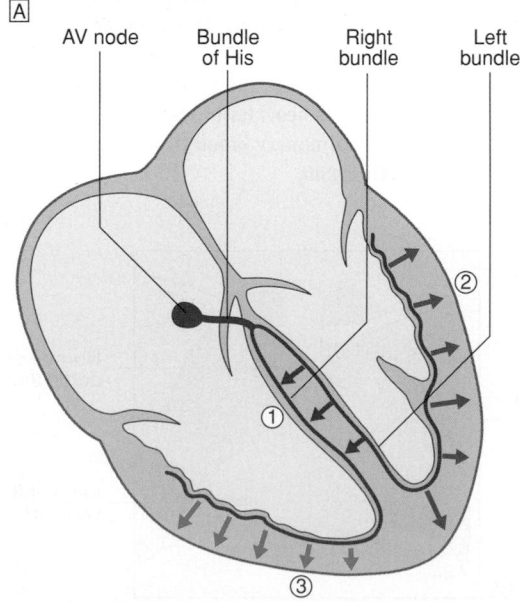

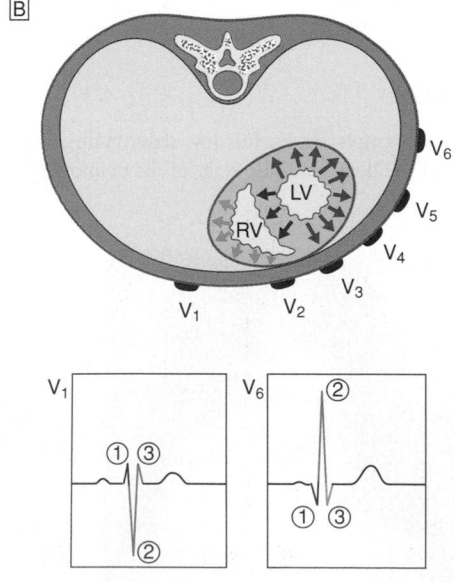

Fig. 12.9 The sequence of activation of the ventricles. A Activation of the septum occurs first (red arrows) followed by spreading of the impulse through the left ventricle (blue arrows) and then the right ventricle (green arrows). B Normal electrocardiographic complexes from leads V_1 and V_6.

12.5 EXERCISE TEST: HIGH-RISK FINDINGS

- Low threshold for ischaemia (i.e. within stage 1 or 2 of the Bruce Protocol)
- Fall in BP on exercise
- Widespread, marked or prolonged ischaemic ECG changes
- Exercise-induced arrhythmia

is ST segment depression of more than 1 mm (see Fig. 12.62, p. 426). The results of an exercise tolerance test (ETT) are not always conclusive. Some patients with a negative test will have underlying coronary disease (false negative) and, conversely, some with a positive test will not have coronary disease (false positive). Exercise testing is an unreliable screening tool because in a low-risk population (e.g. asymptomatic middle-aged women) an abnormal response is more likely to represent a false positive than a true positive test. Nevertheless, certain findings on exercise testing are predictive of severe underlying ischaemic heart disease (see Box 12.5).

Stress tests are contraindicated in the presence of unstable angina, decompensated heart failure, severe hypertension or severe LV outflow obstruction (e.g. aortic stenosis).

Ambulatory ECG (Holter monitoring)

Continuous recordings of one or more ECG leads may be obtained by attaching them to a small portable solid state or tape recorder. This technique is useful for detecting transient episodes of arrhythmia or ischaemia, which seldom occur fortuitously during the short time taken for routine 12-lead ECG recordings (see Fig. 12.50, p. 412). A variety of hand-held or implantable patient-activated devices can be used to record the ECG during symptomatic episodes and are particularly suitable for investigating patients with infrequent but potentially serious symptoms. Many of these devices have the facility to transmit ECG recordings to a cardiac centre through the telephone.

RADIOLOGY

A chest radiograph is useful for determining the size and shape of the heart, and the state of the pulmonary blood vessels and lung fields. Most information is given by a postero-anterior (PA) projection taken in full inspiration. Antero-posterior (AP) projections are convenient when the patient is confined to bed (e.g. in intensive care units) but result in magnification of the cardiac shadow because of the divergence of the radiograph beam.

An estimate of overall heart size can be made by comparing the maximum width of the cardiac outline with the maximum internal transverse diameter of the thoracic cavity. This 'cardiothoracic ratio' should be less than 0.5 and the transverse cardiac diameter should be less than 15.5 cm. Enlargement of the cardiac silhouette occurs in pericardial effusion. Apparent or artefactual cardiomegaly may be due to a mediastinal mass or pectus excavatum, and cannot be reliably assessed from an AP film.

Dilatation of individual cardiac chambers can be recognised by the characteristic alterations they cause to the cardiac silhouette (see Figs 12.10 and 12.11):

- Left atrial dilatation results in prominence of the left atrial appendage, creating the appearance of a straight left heart border, a double cardiac shadow to the right of the sternum, and widening of the angle of the carina (bifurcation of the trachea) as the left main bronchus is pushed upwards.
- Right atrial enlargement projects from the right heart border towards the right lower lung field.
- Left ventricular dilatation causes prominence of the left lower heart border and enlargement of the cardiac silhouette. LV hypertrophy produces rounding of the left heart border.
- Right ventricular dilatation increases heart size, displaces the apex upwards and straightens the left heart border.

Lateral or oblique projections may be useful in detecting aortic or mitral valve calcification, which may be obscured by the spine on the PA view. However, echocardiography is much more sensitive.

The lung fields on the chest radiograph may show congestion and oedema in heart failure (see Fig. 12.22, p. 380), and an increase in pulmonary blood flow ('pulmonary plethora') in left-to-right shunt.

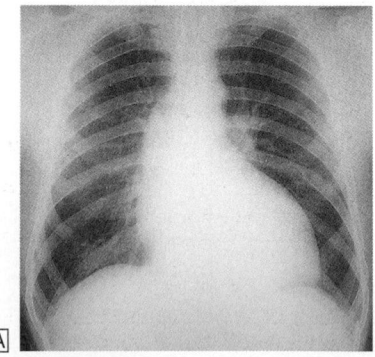
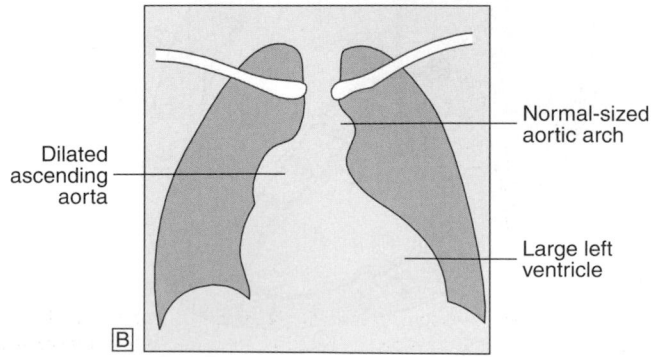

Dilated ascending aorta

Normal-sized aortic arch

Large left ventricle

Fig. 12.10 A patient with aortic regurgitation, left ventricular enlargement and dilatation of the ascending aorta. Ⓐ Chest radiograph. Ⓑ The position of major structures.

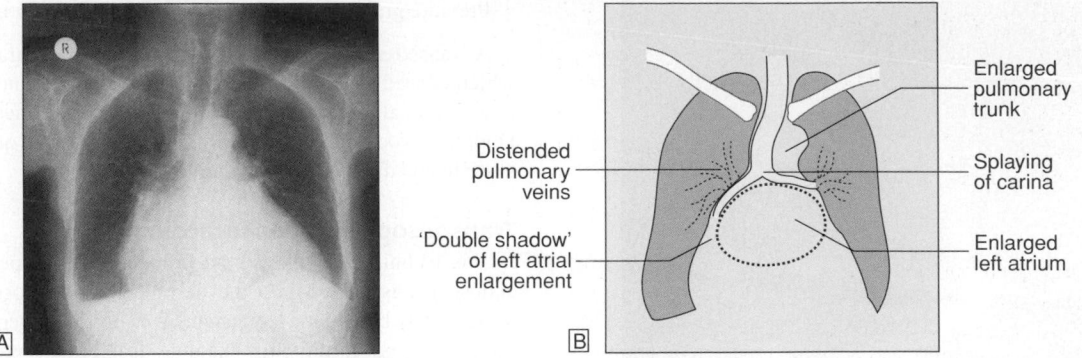

Fig. 12.11   A patient with mitral stenosis and regurgitation indicating enlargement of the left atrium and prominence of the pulmonary artery trunk. A Chest radiograph. B The major structures.

ECHOCARDIOGRAPHY (ECHO)

Two-dimensional echocardiography

Echocardiography is similar to other forms of ultrasound imaging and allows the structures of the heart to be visualised as a two-dimensional 'slice'. Images are obtained by placing the ultrasound transducer on the chest wall, so it is a non-invasive procedure. Contraction of the ventricles can easily be seen in 'real time' and this technique is the simplest available for assessing ventricular function (see Box 12.6). The valves are easily imaged, abnormalities of their structure and function can be demonstrated, and vegetations may be seen in endocarditis. The technique is also valuable for detecting intracardiac masses, such as thrombi or tumours, and can be used to define complex structural abnormalities in congenital heart disease.

Doppler echocardiography

This technique depends on the fundamental principle that sound waves reflected from moving objects, such as intracardiac red blood cells, undergo a frequency shift. The speed and direction of movement of the red cells, and thus of blood, can be detected in the heart chambers and great vessels. The greater the frequency shift, the faster the blood is moving. The derived information can be presented either as a plot of blood velocity against time for a particular point in the heart (see Fig. 12.12) or as a colour overlay on a two-dimensional real-time echo picture (colour flow Doppler; see Fig. 12.13). Doppler echocardiography is valuable in

12.6 COMMON INDICATIONS FOR ECHOCARDIOGRAPHY
• Assessment of left ventricular function
• Diagnosis and quantification of severity of valve disease
• Identification of vegetations in endocarditis
• Identification of structural heart disease in atrial fibrillation
• Detection of pericardial effusion
• Identification of structural heart disease in systemic embolism

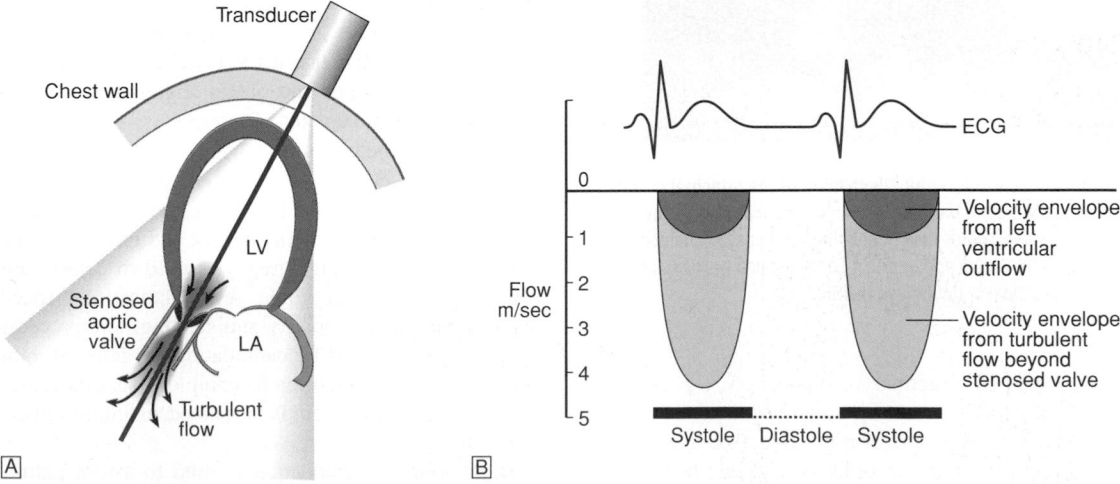

Fig. 12.12   Doppler echocardiography in aortic stenosis. A The aortic valve is imaged in a 'two-chamber' view and a Doppler beam passed directly through the left ventricular outflow tract and the aorta into the turbulent flow beyond the stenosed valve. B The velocity of the blood cells is recorded to determine the maximum velocity and hence the pressure gradient across the valve. The ratio of velocities from before the valve (left ventricular outflow) to beyond the valve (maximum velocity) indicates the degree of acceleration of blood and hence the severity of stenosis. A ratio of more than 4:1 indicates severe stenosis, as in this example.

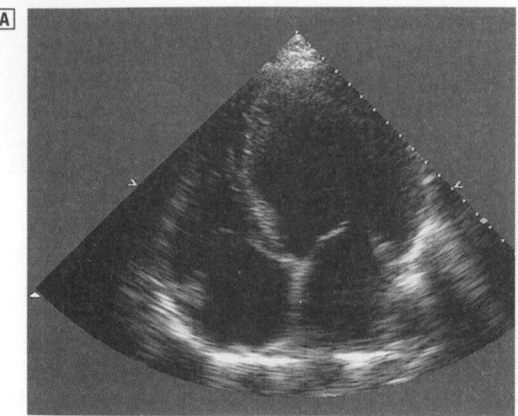

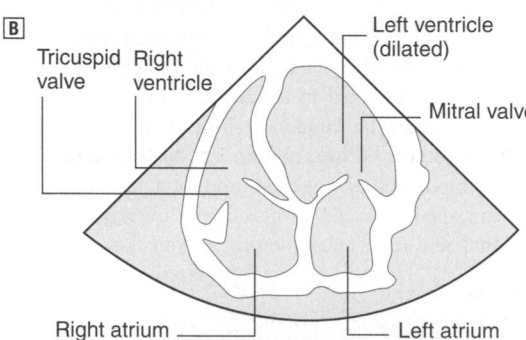

Tricuspid valve
Right ventricle
Left ventricle (dilated)
Mitral valve
Right atrium
Left atrium

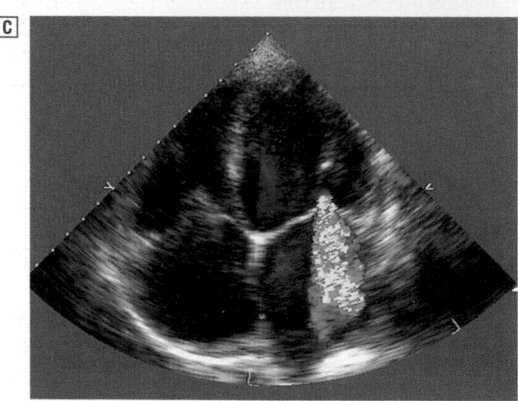

Fig. 12.13 Echocardiographic illustration of the principal cardiac structures in the 'four-chamber' view. [A] Late diastole. [B] The major features. [C] Systole: colour-flow Doppler has been used to demonstrate mitral regurgitation which appears as a flame-shaped (yellow/blue) turbulent jet into the left atrium (see p. 456).

detecting abnormal directions of blood flow, e.g. aortic or mitral reflux, and in estimating pressure gradients, e.g. the gradient across a stenosed aortic valve (see Fig. 12.12). Normal velocities are in the order of 1 m/sec; however, in the presence of a stenosis, flow velocity is increased. For example, in severe aortic stenosis the peak (maximum) aortic velocity may be increased to 5 m/sec. An estimate of the pressure gradient across a valve or lesion is given by the modified Bernoulli equation:

$$\text{Pressure gradient (mmHg)} = 4 \times (\text{peak velocity in m/sec})^2$$

Advanced echo techniques include intravascular ultrasound, which is used to define vessel wall abnormalities and guide interventional treatment of the coronary arteries, and Doppler myocardial imaging, which can be used to quantify systolic and diastolic myocardial function.

Transoesophageal echocardiography
In this technique an ultrasound probe, in the shape of an endoscope, is passed into the oesophagus and positioned immediately behind the left atrium. This produces very clear images; in endocarditis, for example, it is often possible to see vegetations that are too small to be detected by ordinary echocardiography. The high-quality images that can be obtained make the technique particularly valuable for investigating patients with prosthetic (especially mitral) valve dysfunction, patients with congenital abnormalities (e.g. atrial septal defect), and patients with systemic embolism in whom a cardiac defect is suspected but cannot be identified by transthoracic echocardiography.

Computed tomographic (CT) imaging
This is useful for imaging the chambers of the heart, the great vessels, the pericardium and surrounding structures. In practice it is most useful for imaging the aorta in suspected aortic dissection (see Fig. 12.84, p. 450).

Magnetic resonance imaging (MRI)
MRI requires no ionising radiation and can be used to generate multiple 'slices' of the chambers and great vessels of the heart. It has many growing applications and is particularly useful for imaging the aorta (see Fig. 12.83, p. 450).

CARDIAC CATHETERISATION

In this technique a specially designed catheter is inserted into a vein or artery and advanced into the heart under radiographic fluoroscopic guidance. This allows the operator to measure intracardiac pressures, take samples from individual cardiac chambers, and obtain angiograms by injecting contrast media into an area of interest.

Left heart catheterisation is mainly used to assess coronary artery disease but is also used to evaluate disease of the mitral valve, aortic valve and aorta. Left ventricular angiography is used to determine the size and function of the left ventricle; coronary angiography is used to detect stenoses (see Fig. 12.14) and guide revascularisation procedures such as balloon angioplasty and stenting. The procedure is usually accomplished by cannulating the femoral, brachial or radial artery. It can often be completed as a day case, and is safe, with serious complications occurring in fewer than 1 in 1000 cases.

Right heart catheterisation is used to assess pulmonary artery pressure and can also be used to detect intracardiac shunts by measuring oxygen saturation in different chambers. For example, a step up in oxygen saturation from 65% in the right atrium to 80% in the pulmonary artery is indicative of a large left-to-right shunt that might be due to a ventricular

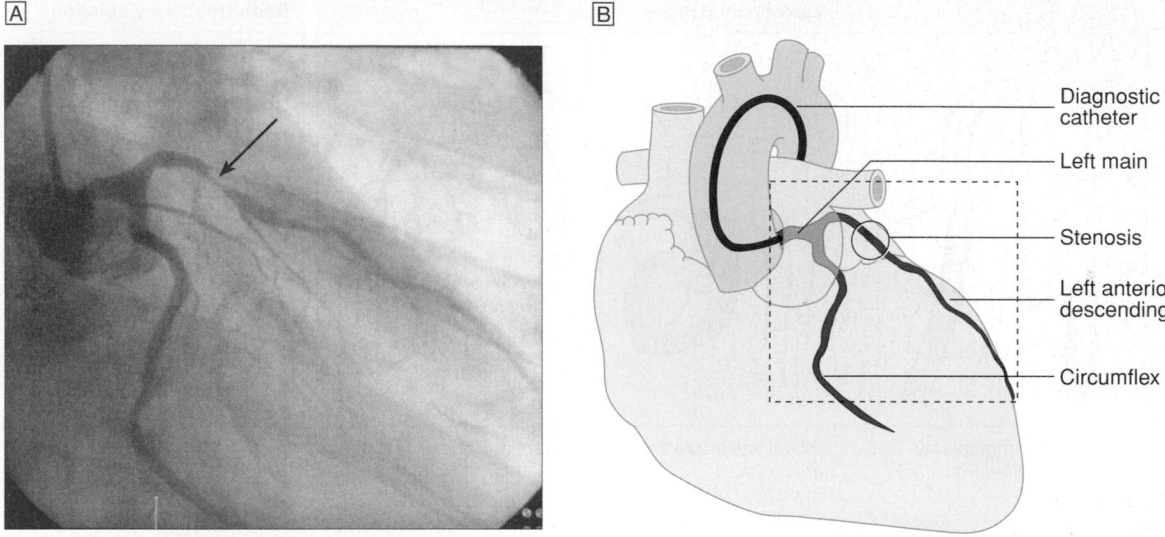

Fig. 12.14   The left anterior descending and circumflex coronary arteries with a stenosis in the left anterior descending vessel. [A] Coronary artery angiogram. [B] Schematic of the vessels and branches.

septal defect. Cardiac output can also be measured using dye dilution or thermodilution techniques. Left atrial pressure can be measured directly by puncturing the interatrial septum, from the right atrium, with a special catheter. However, for most purposes a satisfactory approximation to left atrial pressure can be obtained by 'wedging' an end-hole or balloon catheter in a branch of the pulmonary artery. Swan–Ganz balloon catheters are often used to monitor pulmonary 'wedge' pressure as a guide to left heart filling pressure in critically ill patients (see Fig. 4.3, p. 190).

RADIONUCLIDE IMAGING

The availability of gamma-emitting radionuclides with a short half-life has made it possible to use radionuclides for studying cardiac function non-invasively. The gamma rays are detected by means of a planar or tomographic camera and permit images of the heart to be reconstructed. Two techniques are available.

Blood pool imaging to assess ventricular function

The isotope is injected intravenously and mixes with the circulating blood. The gamma camera detects the amount of isotope-emitting blood in the heart at different phases of the cardiac cycle, and also the size and 'shape' of the cardiac chambers. By linking the gamma camera to the ECG it is possible to collect information over multiple cardiac cycles, allowing 'gating' of the systolic and diastolic phases of the cardiac cycle; the left (and right) ventricular ejection fraction (the proportion of blood ejected during each beat) can then be calculated. The normal value for left ventricular ejection fraction varies from centre to centre but is usually greater than 50–65%.

Myocardial perfusion imaging

This technique involves obtaining scintiscans of the myocardium at rest and during stress after the administration of an intravenous radioactive isotope such as ^{201}thallium or tetrafosmin (see Fig. 12.63, p. 427). More sophisticated quantitative information is available with positron emission tomography (PET), but this is only available in a few centres.

THERAPEUTIC PROCEDURES

See Figure 12.15.

Catheters can be passed under radiographic control from the femoral or brachial artery into the heart to permit balloon dilatation and/or stenting of diseased coronary arteries; stenosed valves (particularly the mitral valve) can sometimes be dilated in a similar way. Coarctation of the aorta (see p. 471) can also be treated by dilating the narrowing in the aorta with a large balloon.

Patients with congenital heart defects such as atrial septal defect and patent ductus arteriosus can have these closed by devices delivered to the heart via a catheter.

Pacemakers are implanted to correct bradycardias or heart block. Automatic implantable defibrillators have similar capabilities to pacemakers and, in addition, can deliver an internal shock to defibrillate the heart if a catastrophic rhythm like ventricular fibrillation occurs.

Recurrent arrhythmias can be treated by transcatheter radiofrequency ablation, in which a catheter placed adjacent to an area of abnormal electrical conduction can precisely deliver an impulse to ablate conduction through that area of the heart.

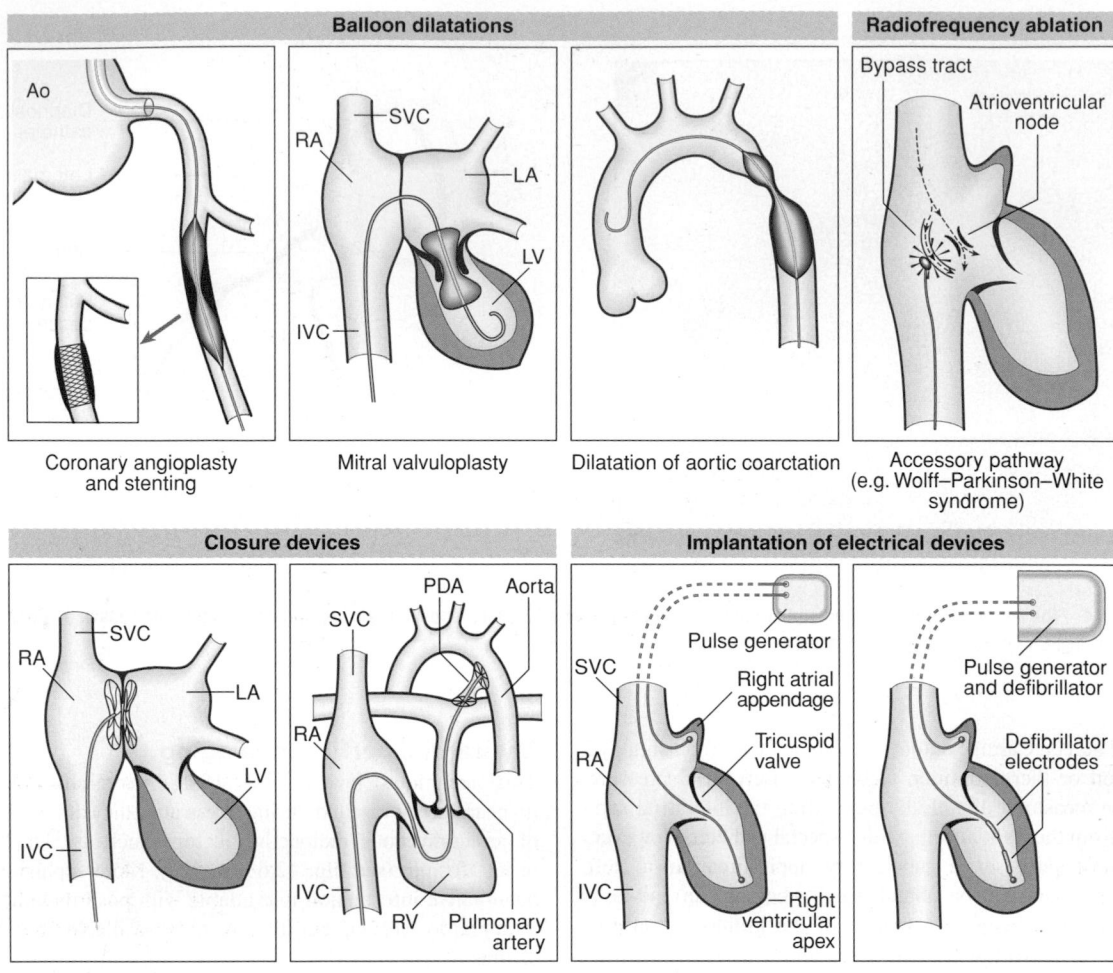

Fig. 12.15 Therapeutic procedures in cardiology. (Ao = aorta; RA = right atrium; LA = left atrium; SVC = superior vena cava; IVC = inferior vena cava; LV = left ventricle; RV = right ventricle; PDA = posterior descending artery)

MAJOR MANIFESTATIONS OF CARDIOVASCULAR DISEASE

Cardiovascular disease gives rise to a relatively limited range of symptoms. Differential diagnosis therefore often depends on careful analysis of the factors that provoke the symptoms, the subtle differences in how they are described by the patient, the clinical findings and appropriate investigations.

CHEST PAIN

Chest pain is a common presentation of cardiac disease, but can also be a manifestation of anxiety or of disease of the lungs, the musculoskeletal system or the gastrointestinal system (see Box 12.7, p. 375).

CHARACTERISTICS OF ISCHAEMIC CARDIAC PAIN

A number of key characteristics help to distinguish cardiac pain from that of other causes (see Fig. 12.16). Diagnosis may be difficult and it is often helpful to classify discomfort as possible, probable or definite ischaemic cardiac pain based on the balance of evidence (see Fig. 12.17).

Site of origin of pain
Cardiac pain is typically located in the centre of the chest because of the derivation of the nerve supply to the heart and mediastinum.

Radiation
Ischaemic cardiac pain, especially when severe, may radiate to the neck, jaw, and upper or even lower arms.

Fig. 12.16 Typical ischaemic cardiac pain. Characteristic hand gestures used to describe cardiac pain. Typical radiation of pain is shown in the schematic.

Occasionally, cardiac pain may be experienced only at the sites of radiation or in the back. Pain situated over the left anterior chest and radiating laterally may have many causes, including pleural or lung disorders, musculoskeletal problems and anxiety.

Character of the pain

Cardiac pain is typically dull, constricting, choking or 'heavy' and is usually described as squeezing, crushing, burning or aching but not sharp, stabbing, pricking or knife-like. The sensation can be described as breathlessness and the victim may complain of discomfort rather than pain. Patients typically use characteristic hand gestures (e.g. open hand or clenched fist) when describing ischaemic pain (see Fig. 12.16).

Provocation

Anginal pain occurs during (not after) exertion and is promptly relieved (in less than 5 minutes) by resting. The pain may also be brought on or exacerbated by emotion and tends to occur more readily during exertion after a large meal or in a cold wind. In crescendo or unstable angina similar pain may be precipitated by minimal exertion and may occur at rest. The increase in venous return or preload induced by lying down may also be sufficient to provoke pain in vulnerable patients (decubitus angina). The pain of myocardial infarction may be preceded by a period of stable or unstable angina but may occur de novo.

   In contrast, pleural or pericardial pain is usually described as a 'sharp' or 'catching' sensation that is exacerbated by breathing, coughing or movement. However, pain associated with a specific movement (bending, stretching, turning) is likely to be musculoskeletal in origin.

Pattern of onset

The pain of myocardial infarction typically takes several minutes or even longer to develop; similarly, angina builds up gradually in proportion to the intensity of exertion. Pain that occurs after rather than during exertion is usually musculoskeletal or psychological in origin. The pain of aortic dissection, massive pulmonary embolism or pneumothorax is usually very sudden or instantaneous in onset.

Associated features

The pain of myocardial infarction, massive pulmonary embolus or aortic dissection is often accompanied by autonomic disturbance including sweating, nausea and vomiting. Breathlessness, due to pulmonary congestion arising from transient ischaemic left ventricular dysfunction, is often a prominent, and occasionally the dominant, feature of myocardial infarction or angina. Breathlessness may also accompany any of the respiratory causes of chest pain and may be associated with cough, wheeze or other respiratory symptoms. Classical gastrointestinal symptoms (oesophageal reflux, oesophagitis, peptic ulceration or biliary disease) may provide the clue to the source of non-cardiac chest pain but effort-related 'indigestion' is usually due to heart disease.

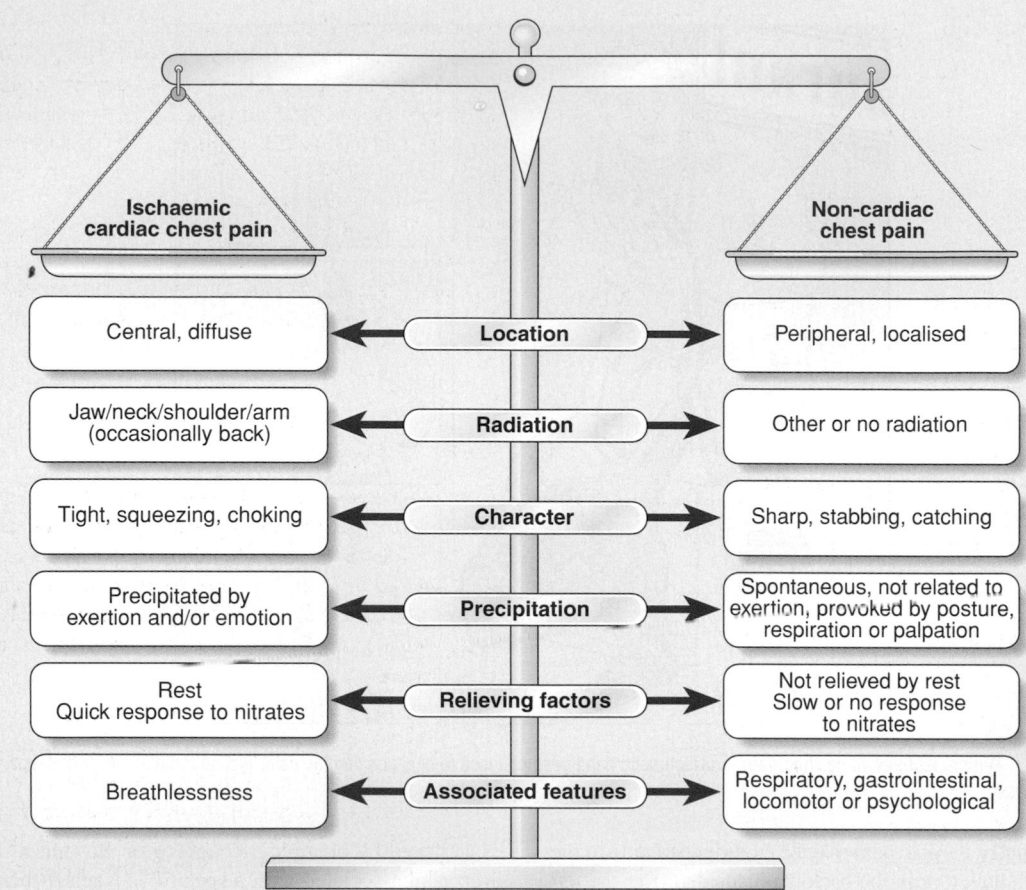

Fig. 12.17 Identifying ischaemic cardiac pain: the 'balance' of evidence.

THE DIFFERENTIAL DIAGNOSIS OF CARDIAC PAIN

The conditions labelled [1] in Box 12.7 are discussed here; the differential diagnosis of peripheral or pleural chest pain is discussed on page 499.

Psychological aspects of chest pain

Emotional distress is a very common cause of atypical chest pain (see p. 252). This diagnosis should be considered if there are features of anxiety or neurosis, and the pain lacks a predictable relationship with exercise. However, it is important to remember that the prospect of heart disease is a frightening experience, particularly when it has been responsible for the death of a close friend or relative; psychological and organic features therefore often coexist. Anxiety may amplify the effects of organic disease and this can create a very confusing picture. Patients who believe they are suffering from heart disease are sometimes afraid to take exercise and this may make it difficult to establish their true effort tolerance; assessment may also be complicated by the impact of physical deconditioning.

Myocarditis and pericarditis

These conditions may cause pain that is felt retrosternally, to the left of the sternum, or in the left or right shoulder, and characteristically varies in intensity with movement and the phase of respiration. The pain is usually described as 'sharp' and may 'catch' the patient during inspiration or coughing; there is occasionally a history of a prodromal viral illness.

Mitral valve prolapse

Sharp left-sided chest pains that are suggestive of a musculoskeletal problem may be a feature of mitral valve prolapse (see p. 456).

Aortic dissection

This pain is severe, sharp and tearing, often felt in or penetrating through to the back, and is typically very abrupt in onset (see p. 448).

Oesophageal pain

Oesophageal pain can mimic that of angina very closely, is sometimes precipitated by exercise and may be relieved by nitrates; however, it is usually possible to elicit a history relating chest pain to eating, drinking or oesophageal reflux.

12.7 SOME COMMON CAUSES OF CHEST PAIN

Central

Anxiety/emotion[1] (may also cause peripheral chest pain)

Cardiac
- Myocardial ischaemia (angina)[1]
- Myocardial infarction[1]
- Myocarditis[1]
- Pericarditis[1]
- Mitral valve prolapse syndrome[1]

Aortic
- Aortic dissection[1]
- Aortic aneurysm[1]

Oesophageal
- Oesophagitis
- Oesophageal spasm[1]
- Mallory–Weiss syndrome

Massive pulmonary embolus

Mediastinal
- Tracheitis
- Malignancy

Peripheral

Lungs/pleura
- Pulmonary infarct
- Pneumonia
- Pneumothorax
- Malignancy
- Tuberculosis
- Connective tissue disorders (rare)

Musculoskeletal[2]
- Osteoarthritis
- Rib fracture/injury
- Intercostal muscle injury
- Costochondritis (Tietze's syndrome)[1]
- Epidemic myalgia (Bornholm disease)[1]

Neurological[2]
- Prolapsed intervertebral disc
- Herpes zoster
- Thoracic outlet syndrome

[1] Discussed in the text.
[2] Can sometimes cause central chest pain.

Musculoskeletal chest pain

This is a common problem that is very variable in site and intensity but does not usually fall into any of the patterns described above. The pain may vary with posture or movement of the upper body and is sometimes accompanied by local tenderness over a rib or costal cartilage. There are numerous causes of chest wall pain, including arthritis, costochondritis, intercostal muscle injury and Coxsackie viral infection (epidemic myalgia or Bornholm disease). Many minor soft tissue injuries are related to everyday activities such as driving, manual work and sport.

INITIAL EVALUATION OF SUSPECTED CARDIAC PAIN

A careful history is crucial to the process of determining whether pain is cardiac or not. Although the physical findings and subsequent investigations may help to confirm the diagnosis, they are of more value in determining the nature and extent of any underlying heart disease, the risk of a serious adverse event and the best course of management.

Stable angina

Effort-related chest discomfort is the hallmark of stable angina (see Fig. 12.18). The reproducibility of the pain and its relationship to physical exertion (and occasionally emotion) are the most important features of the history. The duration of symptoms should be noted because patients with recent-onset angina are at greater risk than those with long-standing and unchanged symptoms.

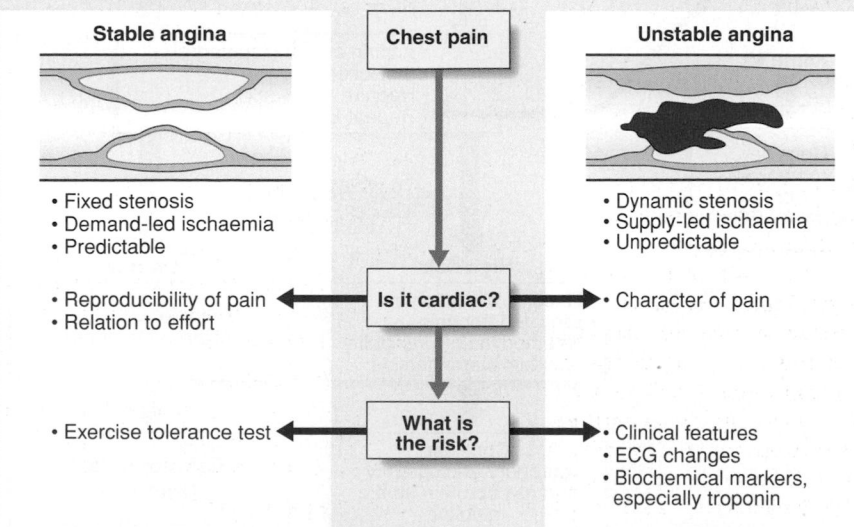

Fig. 12.18 Evaluation of suspected stable and unstable angina. The variables that help to identify cardiac pain and risk differ between the two conditions.

Physical examination is often normal but may reveal evidence of important risk factors (e.g. hyperlipidaemia, diabetes), left ventricular dysfunction (e.g. dyskinetic apex beat, gallop rhythm), other manifestations of arterial disease (e.g. bruits, signs of peripheral vascular disease) and unrelated conditions that may exacerbate angina (e.g. anaemia, thyroid disease). Stable angina is usually a symptom of coronary artery disease but may be a manifestation of other forms of heart disease, particularly aortic valve disease and hypertrophic cardiomyopathy. The discovery of a heart murmur, or other features of these conditions, may therefore merit echocardiography.

A full blood count, fasting blood glucose, lipids, thyroid function tests and a 12-lead ECG are the most important baseline investigations. Exercise testing may help to confirm the diagnosis and is also used to identify high-risk patients who require further investigation and treatment (see p. 425).

Acute coronary syndromes

Prolonged and severe cardiac chest pain may be due to unstable angina (which comprises recent-onset limiting angina, rapidly worsening or crescendo angina, and angina at rest) or acute myocardial infarction; these are known collectively as the acute coronary syndromes. Although there may be a history of antecedent chronic stable angina, an episode of chest pain at rest is often the first presentation of coronary disease. In this situation, the diagnosis depends heavily on an analysis of the character of the pain and its associated features. Physical examination may reveal signs of important comorbidity (e.g. peripheral and/or cerebrovascular disease), autonomic disturbance such as pallor or sweating, and complications such as arrhythmia or heart failure.

Patients presenting with symptoms that are consistent with an acute coronary syndrome require urgent evaluation because these conditions carry a high risk of potentially avoidable serious adverse events such as sudden death and myocardial infarction. Signs of haemodynamic compromise (hypotension, heart failure), ECG changes (ST elevation or depression), and biochemical markers of cardiac damage such as troponin I and T are the most powerful indicators of short-term risk. A 12-lead ECG is mandatory and is the most useful method of initial triage (see Fig. 12.19). The release of biochemical markers such as creatine kinase, troponin and myoglobin is relatively slow (see p. 436) and, although bedside analysis systems are available, these tests are seldom used to guide immediate treatment.

If the diagnosis is not clear, patients with a suspected acute coronary syndrome should be observed in hospital. Repeated ECG recordings are valuable, particularly if a

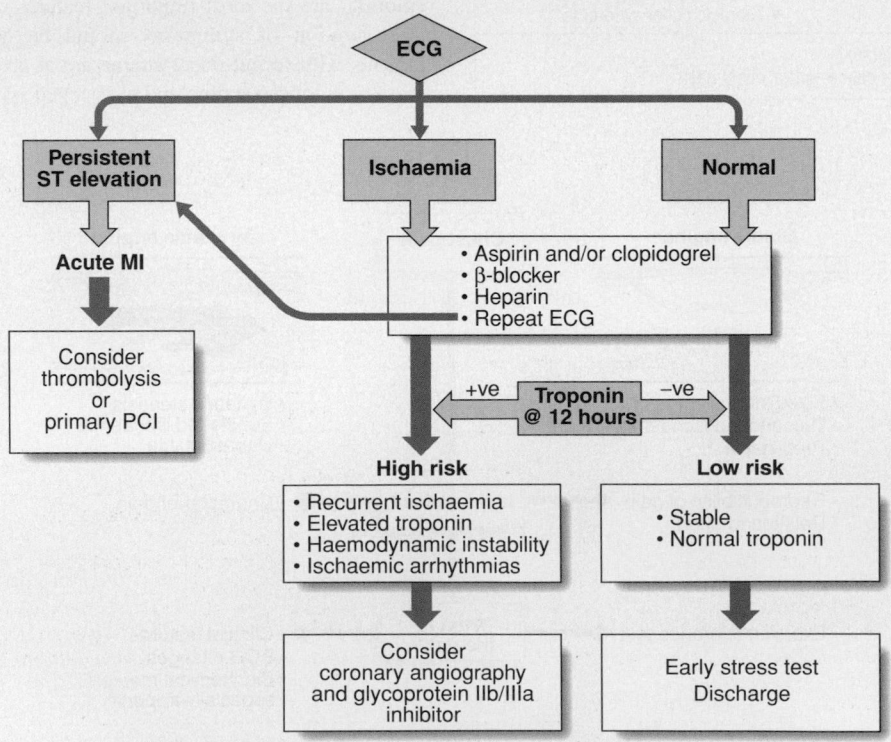

Fig. 12.19 The initial management of an acute coronary syndrome. The algorithm is based on the physical examination, ECG and blood test results.

trace can be obtained during an episode of pain. Plasma troponin should be measured and, if normal, the test should be repeated a minimum of 12 hours after the onset of symptoms. New ECG changes or the elevation of troponin confirm the diagnosis of an acute coronary syndrome. The subsequent management of myocardial infarction and unstable angina is described in detail on pages 433–443.

If the pain has not recurred 12 hours after the onset of symptoms, cardiac troponin tests are negative and there are no new ECG changes, the patient may be discharged from hospital. However, it may be advisable to arrange an exercise test in order to confirm or refute a diagnosis of underlying coronary disease at this stage.

BREATHLESSNESS (DYSPNOEA)

Dyspnoea of cardiac origin may vary in severity from an uncomfortable awareness of breathing to a frightening sensation of 'fighting for breath'. The sensation of dyspnoea originates in the cerebral cortex and, although the precise pathways that mediate it remain poorly defined, they include stimuli arising from receptors in the lungs, upper airways and respiratory muscles (see Box 12.8 and Ch. 13).

There are three forms of cardiac dyspnoea: acute pulmonary oedema, chronic heart failure and angina equivalent.

ACUTE PULMONARY OEDEMA

Acute left heart failure may be triggered by a major event such as myocardial infarction in a previously healthy heart, or a relatively minor event such as the onset of atrial fibrillation in a diseased heart. An increase in the left ventricular diastolic pressure causes the pressure in the left atrium, pulmonary veins and pulmonary capillaries to rise. When the hydrostatic pressure of the pulmonary capillaries exceeds the oncotic pressure of plasma (about 25–30 mmHg) fluid moves from the capillaries into alveoli. This stimulates respiration, through the vagus nerve and the Hering–Breuer reflex, producing rapid, shallow respiration. Congestion of the bronchial mucosa may cause wheeze (cardiac asthma).

Acute pulmonary oedema is a terrifying experience and patients will often describe the sensation of 'fighting for breath'. Sitting upright or standing may provide some relief by helping to reduce congestion at the apices of the lungs. The patient may be unable to speak and is typically distressed, agitated, cyanosed, sweaty and pale. Respiration is rapid with recruitment of accessory muscles, coughing and wheezing. Sputum may be profuse, frothy and blood-streaked or pink. Extensive crepitations and rhonchi are usually audible in the chest and there may also be signs of right heart failure.

CHRONIC HEART FAILURE

Chronic heart failure is the most common cardiac cause of chronic dyspnoea. Symptoms may first present on moderately severe exertion, such as walking up a steep hill, and may be described as a difficulty in 'catching my breath'. As heart failure progresses, the dyspnoea is provoked by lesser exertion and ultimately the patient may be breathless walking from room to room, washing, dressing or trying to hold a conversation.

Orthopnoea
Lying down increases the venous return to the heart and may provoke breathlessness (orthopnoea) in patients with heart failure.

12.8 SOME CAUSES OF DYSPNOEA		
System	**Acute dyspnoea at rest**	**Chronic exertional dyspnoea**
Cardiovascular system	*Acute pulmonary oedema	*Chronic congestive cardiac failure Myocardial ischaemia
Respiratory system	*Acute severe asthma *Acute exacerbation of chronic obstructive pulmonary disease *Pneumothorax *Pneumonia Pulmonary embolus Acute respiratory distress syndrome Inhaled foreign body (especially in the child) Lobar collapse Laryngeal oedema (e.g. anaphylaxis)	*Chronic obstructive pulmonary disease *Chronic asthma Chronic pulmonary thromboembolism Bronchial carcinoma Interstitial lung diseases: sarcoidosis, fibrosing alveolitis, extrinsic allergic alveolitis, pneumoconiosis Lymphatic carcinomatosis (may cause intolerable dyspnoea) Large pleural effusion(s)
Others	Metabolic acidosis (e.g. diabetic ketoacidosis, lactic acidosis, uraemia, overdose of salicylates, ethylene glycol poisoning) Hysterical hyperventilation	Severe anaemia Obesity
* Denotes a common cause.		

Paroxysmal nocturnal dyspnoea

In patients with severe heart failure, fluid shifts from the interstitial tissues in the peripheries to the circulation within 1–2 hours of lying down in bed. Pulmonary oedema (paroxysmal nocturnal dyspnoea) may supervene, causing the patient to wake and sit upright, 'fighting for breath'.

Cheyne–Stokes respiration

This cyclic pattern of respiration is due to reduced sensitivity of the respiratory centre to carbon dioxide and may occur in left ventricular failure. The pattern of slowly diminishing respiration, leading to apnoea, followed by progressively increasing respiration and hyperventilation, may be accompanied by a sensation of breathlessness and panic during the period of hyperventilation. The Cheyne–Stokes cycle length is a function of the circulation time. The condition can also occur in more diffuse cerebral atherosclerosis, stroke or head injury and may be exaggerated by sleep, barbiturates and narcotics.

ANGINA EQUIVALENT

The sensation of breathlessness is a common feature of angina. Patients will sometimes describe chest tightness as 'breathlessness'. However, myocardial ischaemia may also induce true breathlessness by provoking transient left ventricular dysfunction or heart failure. When breathlessness is the dominant or sole feature of myocardial ischaemia it is known as 'angina equivalent'. A history of chest tightness, the close correlation with exercise, and objective evidence of myocardial ischaemia from stress testing may all help to establish the diagnosis.

ACUTE CIRCULATORY FAILURE (CARDIOGENIC SHOCK)

Shock is a loosely defined term used to describe the clinical syndrome that develops when there is critical impairment of tissue perfusion due to some form of acute circulatory failure.

There are numerous causes of shock, and the condition is described in detail on page 195. However, the important features of acute heart failure or cardiogenic shock will be described here. Examples of some common causes are illustrated in Figure 12.20. Echocardiography is very helpful when the diagnosis is in doubt.

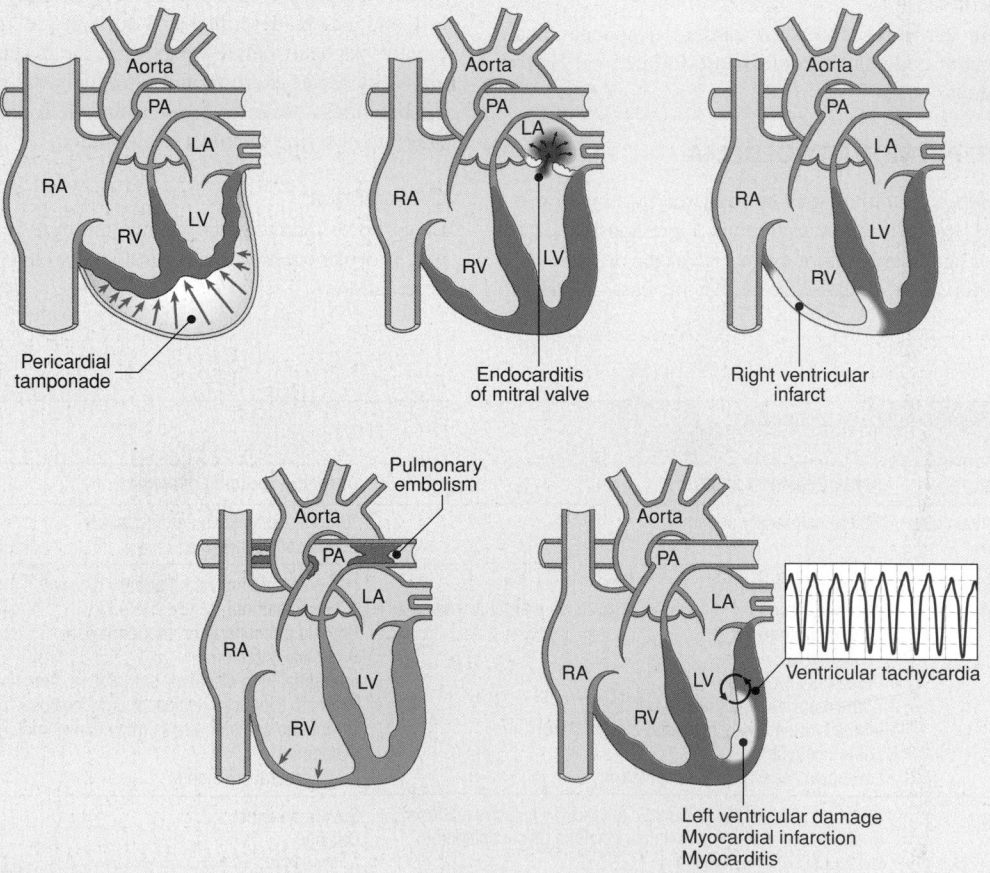

Fig. 12.20   Some examples of the common causes of acute circulatory failure (cardiogenic shock).

Myocardial infarction

Shock in acute myocardial infarction is usually (more than 70% of cases) due to left ventricular dysfunction. However, it may also be due to infarction of the right ventricle and a variety of mechanical complications, including tamponade (due to infarction and rupture of the free wall), an acquired ventricular septal defect (due to infarction and rupture of the septum) and acute mitral regurgitation (due to infarction or rupture of the papillary muscles).

Severe myocardial systolic dysfunction causes a fall in cardiac output, blood pressure and thereby coronary perfusion pressure. Diastolic dysfunction causes a rise in left ventricular end-diastolic pressure, pulmonary congestion and oedema, leading to hypoxia which further worsens myocardial ischaemia. These factors combine to create the 'downward spiral' of cardiogenic shock (see Fig. 12.21).

Hypotension, oliguria, confusion and cold, clammy peripheries are the manifestations of a low cardiac output, whereas breathlessness, hypoxia, cyanosis and inspiratory crackles at the lung bases are features of pulmonary oedema. A chest radiograph (see Fig. 12.22) may reveal signs of pulmonary congestion when clinical examination is normal. If necessary, a Swan–Ganz catheter can be used to measure the pulmonary artery wedge (PAW) pressure (see Fig. 4.3, p. 190).

These findings can be used to divide patients with acute myocardial infarction into four haemodynamic subsets (see Box 12.9).

The viable myocardium surrounding a fresh infarct may contract poorly for a few days and then recover. This phenomenon is known as myocardial stunning and means that, in this setting, it is often worth treating acute heart failure energetically in the hope and expectation that overall cardiac function will improve.

Acute massive pulmonary embolism

This may complicate leg or pelvic vein thrombosis and usually presents with sudden collapse. The clinical features are discussed on page 562.

Bedside echocardiography may be very helpful and usually demonstrates a small vigorous left ventricle with a dilated right ventricle; it is sometimes possible to see thrombus in the right ventricular outflow tract or main pulmonary artery. Spiral CT of the chest with contrast will usually provide a definitive diagnosis and is preferable to pulmonary angiography, which may be hazardous.

Treatment (see p. 565) is with high-flow oxygen and anticoagulation with heparin. Thrombolytic therapy is valuable in selected cases and surgical embolectomy may be needed on rare occasions.

Pericardial tamponade

This condition is due to a collection of fluid or blood in the pericardial sac compressing the heart; the effusion may be small and is sometimes less than 100 ml. Sudden deterioration is frequently due to bleeding into the pericardial space.

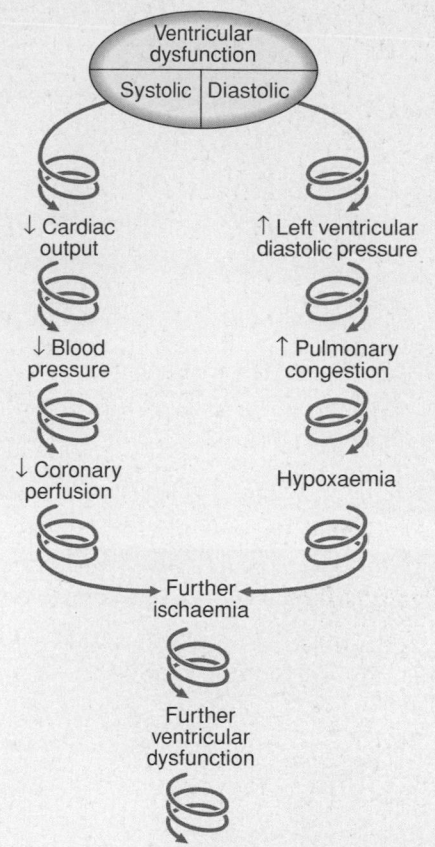

Fig. 12.21 The downward spiral of cardiogenic shock. Systolic dysfunction leads to falling cardiac output and coronary perfusion, and diastolic dysfunction to hypoxaemia. These combine to generate further ischaemia and worsening ventricular dysfunction.

12.9 ACUTE MYOCARDIAL INFARCTION: PATIENT SUBSETS
Normal cardiac output. No pulmonary oedema
• The normal state of affairs; carries a good outlook and requires no treatment for heart failure
Normal cardiac output. Pulmonary oedema
• Usually due to moderate left ventricular dysfunction; should be treated with diuretics and vasodilators
Low cardiac output. No pulmonary oedema
• Often caused by a combination of right ventricular infarction and hypovolaemia due to a reduced oral intake of fluids, vomiting and inappropriate diuretic therapy. Such patients are easier to manage if a Swan–Ganz catheter is inserted and i.v. fluids given to raise the PAW pressure to between 14 and 16 mmHg
Low cardiac output. Pulmonary oedema
• Usually due to extensive left ventricular damage and carries a very poor prognosis. The patient may benefit from treatment with diuretics, vasodilators and inotropes (see pp. 202 and 386)

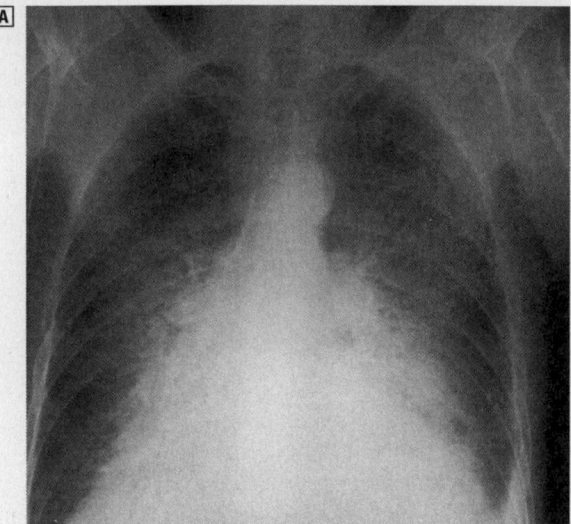

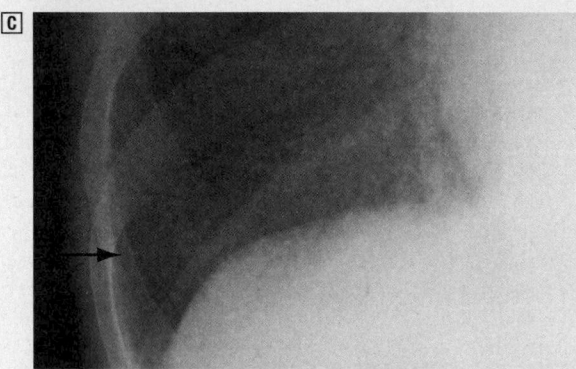

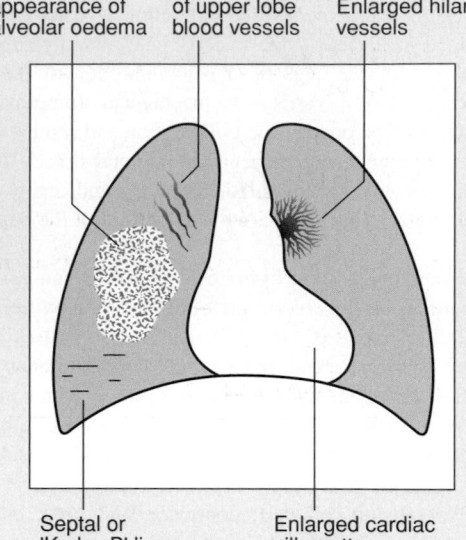

Fig. 12.22 Radiological features of heart failure.
A Chest radiograph of a patient with pulmonary oedema.
B Schematic highlighting the radiological features of
heart failure. C Enlargement of lung base showing septal
or 'Kerley B' lines (arrow).

Tamponade may complicate any form of pericarditis and is often due to malignant disease. Other causes include trauma and rupture of the free wall of the myocardium following myocardial infarction.

The important clinical features of the condition are listed in Box 12.10.

An ECG may show features of the underlying disease, e.g. pericarditis or acute myocardial infarction. When there is a large pericardial effusion, the ECG complexes are small and there may be electrical alternans (a changing axis with alternate beats caused by the heart moving in the bag of fluid). A chest radiograph may show an enlarged globular heart but can look normal. Echocardiography, which may be done at the bedside, is the best way of confirming the diagnosis, and helps to identify the optimum site for aspiration of the fluid.

Prompt recognition of tamponade is important because the patient usually responds dramatically to percutaneous pericardiocentesis (see p. 480) or surgical drainage.

Valvular heart disease

Acute left ventricular failure may be due to the sudden onset of aortic regurgitation, mitral regurgitation or prosthetic valve dysfunction. Some of the common causes of these problems are listed in Box 12.11.

The clinical diagnosis of acute valvular dysfunction is sometimes difficult. Murmurs are often unimpressive because there is usually a tachycardia with a low cardiac output. Transthoracic echocardiography will establish the diagnosis in most cases; however, transoesophageal echocardiography is sometimes required to identify prosthetic mitral valve regurgitation.

12.10 CLINICAL FEATURES OF PERICARDIAL TAMPONADE

- Dyspnoea
- Collapse
- Tachycardia
- Hypotension
- Gross elevation of the venous pressure
- Soft heart sounds with an early third heart sound
- Pulsus paradoxus (a large fall in blood pressure during inspiration when the pulse may be impalpable)
- Kussmaul's sign (a paradoxical rise in the jugular venous pressure during inspiration)

12.11 CAUSES OF ACUTE VALVE FAILURE

Aortic regurgitation

- Aortic dissection
- Infective endocarditis
- Ruptured sinus of Valsalva

Mitral regurgitation

- Papillary muscle rupture due to acute myocardial infarction
- Infective endocarditis
- Rupture of chordae due to myxomatous degeneration or blunt chest wall trauma

Prosthetic valve failure

- Mechanical valves: fracture, jamming, thrombosis, dehiscence
- Biological valves: degeneration with cusp tear

Patients with acute valve failure usually require cardiac surgery and should be referred for urgent assessment in a cardiac centre.

Aortic dissection may cause shock by causing aortic regurgitation, coronary dissection, tamponade or blood loss (see p. 448).

The chest radiograph in left heart failure

A rise in pulmonary venous pressure from left-sided cardiac failure first shows on the chest radiograph (see Fig. 12.22) as an abnormal distension of the upper lobe pulmonary veins (with the patient in the erect position). The vascularity of the lung fields becomes more prominent and the right and left pulmonary arteries dilate. Subsequently, interstitial oedema causes thickened interlobular septa and dilated lymphatics. These are evident as horizontal lines in the costophrenic angles (septal or 'Kerley B' lines). More advanced changes due to alveolar oedema cause a hazy opacification spreading from the hilar regions, and pleural effusions.

Management of acute pulmonary oedema

This is a feature of acute left heart failure and needs urgent treatment:

- Sit the patient up in order to reduce pulmonary congestion.
- Give oxygen (high flow, high concentration).
- Use morphine (10 mg intravenously, in 2 mg aliquots) to alleviate breathlessness and reverse reflex peripheral vasoconstriction.
- Administer one of the powerful diuretics such as furosemide (frusemide) 40–80 mg i.v.; these drugs provide rapid relief because they are also vasodilators.
- Administer nitrates, e.g. i.v. glyceryl trinitrate 10–200 μg/min titrated upwards every 10 minutes, until clinical improvement occurs or blood pressure falls to < 110 mmHg.

If these immediate measures prove inadequate, one may try to stimulate the heart using inotropic agents, or to reduce left ventricular load by using more powerful vasodilators.

Management of shock

The management of shock is discussed in detail in Chapter 4 (see p. 201).

HEART FAILURE

Heart failure is an imprecise term used to describe the state that develops when the heart cannot maintain an adequate cardiac output or can do so only at the expense of an elevated filling pressure. In the mildest forms of heart failure, cardiac output is adequate at rest and becomes inadequate only when the metabolic demand increases during exercise or some other form of stress.

In practice, heart failure may be diagnosed whenever a patient with significant heart disease develops the signs or symptoms of a low cardiac output, pulmonary congestion or systemic venous congestion.

Almost all forms of heart disease can lead to heart failure and it is important to appreciate that, like anaemia, the term refers to a clinical syndrome rather than a specific diagnosis. Good management depends on an accurate aetiological diagnosis, partly because in some situations a specific remedy may be available, but mainly because a clear understanding of the pathophysiology is essential to logical drug therapy. The possible mechanisms and some causes of heart failure are shown in Box 12.12.

Heart failure is frequently due to coronary artery disease, tends to affect elderly subjects and often leads to prolonged disability. The prevalence of heart failure rises from around 1% in the age group 50–59 years to between 5 and 10% of those aged 80–89 years. In the United Kingdom most patients admitted to hospital with heart failure are more than 65 years old and remain inpatients for a week or more.

Although the outlook depends to some extent on the underlying cause of the problem, heart failure carries a very poor prognosis; approximately 50% of patients with severe heart failure due to left ventricular dysfunction will die within 2 years. Many patients die suddenly from malignant ventricular arrhythmias or myocardial infarction.

Pathophysiology

The cardiac output is a function of the preload (the volume and pressure of blood in the ventricle at the end of diastole), the afterload (the arterial resistance) and myocardial contractility. The interaction of these variables is shown in Figure 12.23, which is based on Starling's Law of the heart.

In patients without valvular disease the primary abnormality in heart failure is impairment of ventricular function

12.12 MECHANISMS OF HEART FAILURE

Cause	Examples	Features
Reduced ventricular contractility	Myocarditis/cardiomyopathy (global dysfunction) Myocardial infarction (segmental dysfunction)	Progressive ventricular dilatation In coronary artery disease 'akinetic' or 'dyskinetic' segments contract poorly and may impede the function of the normal segments by distorting their contraction and relaxation patterns
Ventricular outflow obstruction (pressure overload)	Hypertension, aortic stenosis (left heart failure) Pulmonary hypertension, pulmonary valve stenosis (right heart failure)	Initially concentric ventricular hypertrophy allows the ventricle to maintain a normal output by generating a high systolic pressure. However, secondary changes in the myocardium and increasing obstruction eventually lead to failure with ventricular dilatation and rapid clinical deterioration
Ventricular inflow obstruction	Mitral stenosis, tricuspid stenosis Endomyocardial fibrosis and other disorders that cause a stiff myocardium, e.g. left ventricular hypertrophy Constrictive pericarditis	Small vigorous ventricle, dilated hypertrophied atrium. Atrial fibrillation is common and often causes marked deterioration because ventricular filling depends heavily on atrial contraction
Ventricular volume overload	LV volume overload (e.g. mitral or aortic regurgitation) RV volume overload (e.g. atrial septal defect) Ventricular septal defect Increased metabolic demand (high output)	Dilatation and hypertrophy allow the ventricle to generate a high stroke volume and help to maintain a normal cardiac output. However, secondary changes in the myocardium eventually lead to impaired contractility and worsening heart failure
Arrhythmia	Atrial fibrillation Tachycardia cardiomyopathy Complete heart block	Tachycardia does not allow for adequate filling of the heart, resulting in reduced cardiac output and back pressure Incessant tachycardia causes myocardial fatigue Bradycardia may limit cardiac output even if stroke volume is normal

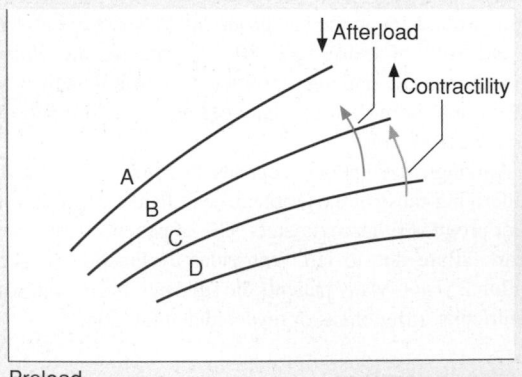

Cardiac output or ventricular performance

Fig. 12.23 Starling's Law. Normal (A), mild (B), moderate (C) and severe (D) heart failure. Ventricular performance is related to the degree of myocardial stretching. An increase in preload (end-diastolic volume, end-diastolic pressure, filling pressure or atrial pressure) will therefore enhance function; however, overstretching causes marked deterioration. In heart failure the curve moves to the right and becomes flatter. An increase in myocardial contractility or a reduction in afterload (arterial resistance/blood pressure) will shift the curve upwards and to the left.

leading to a fall in cardiac output. This activates counter-regulatory neurohormonal mechanisms which in normal physiological circumstances would support cardiac function, but in the setting of impaired ventricular function can lead to a deleterious increase in both afterload and preload (see Fig. 12.24). A vicious circle may be established because any additional fall in cardiac output will cause further neurohormonal activation and increasing peripheral vascular resistance.

Stimulation of the renin-angiotensin-aldosterone system leads to vasoconstriction, salt and water retention and sympathetic activation mediated by angiotensin II, which is a potent vasoconstrictor of efferent arterioles both in the kidney and systemic circulation (see Fig. 12.25). Activation of the sympathetic system may initially maintain cardiac output through an increase in myocardial contractility, heart rate and peripheral vasoconstriction. However, prolonged sympathetic stimulation leads to cardiac myocyte apoptosis (cell death), hypertrophy and focal myocardial necrosis. Salt and water retention is promoted by the release of aldosterone, endothelin (a potent vasoconstrictor peptide with marked effects on the renal vasculature) and, in severe heart failure, antidiuretic hormone (ADH). Natriuretic peptides are released from

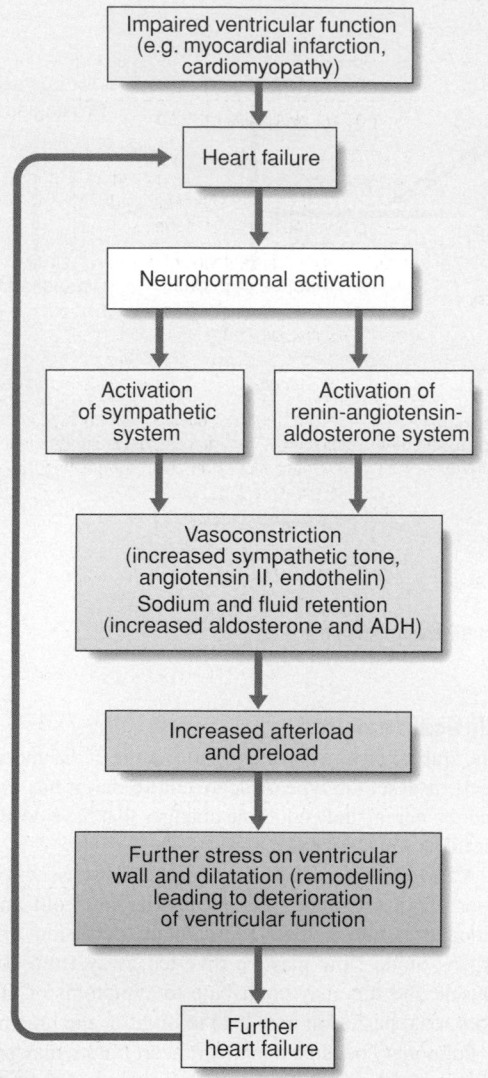

Fig. 12.24 Neurohormonal activation and compensatory mechanisms in heart failure. There is a vicious circle in progressive heart failure.

the atria, in response to atrial stretch, and act as physiological antagonists to the fluid-conserving effect of aldosterone; however, they have a short half-life in the circulation.

After myocardial infarction cardiac contractility is impaired and neurohormonal activation may lead to hypertrophy of non-infarcted segments with thinning, dilatation and expansion of the infarcted segment (remodelling, see Fig. 12.79, p. 441). This may lead to further deterioration in ventricular function and worsening heart failure.

The onset of pulmonary and/or peripheral oedema is due to high atrial pressures compounded by salt and water retention caused by impaired renal perfusion and secondary aldosteronism.

Types of heart failure

Heart failure can be described or classified in several ways.

Acute and chronic heart failure

Heart failure may develop suddenly, as in myocardial infarction, or gradually, as in progressive valvular heart disease. When there is gradual impairment of cardiac function, a variety of compensatory changes may take place.

The phrase 'compensated heart failure' is sometimes used to describe a patient with impaired cardiac function in whom adaptive changes have prevented the development of overt heart failure. A minor event, such as an intercurrent infection or development of atrial fibrillation, may precipitate overt or acute heart failure in this type of patient (see Box 12.13). Patients with chronic heart failure commonly experience a relapsing and remitting course, with periods of stability and episodes of decompensation leading to worsening symptoms which may necessitate hospitalisation.

> **12.13 FACTORS THAT MAY PRECIPITATE OR AGGRAVATE HEART FAILURE IN PATIENTS WITH PRE-EXISTING HEART DISEASE**
>
> - Myocardial ischaemia or infarction
> - Intercurrent illness (e.g. infection)
> - Arrhythmia (e.g. atrial fibrillation)
> - Inappropriate reduction of therapy
> - Administration of a drug with negative inotropic properties (e.g. β-blocker) or fluid-retaining properties (e.g. non-steroidal anti-inflammatory drugs, corticosteroids)
> - Pulmonary embolism
> - Conditions associated with increased metabolic demand (e.g. pregnancy, thyrotoxicosis, anaemia)
> - Intravenous fluid overload (e.g. post-operative i.v. infusion)

Left, right and biventricular heart failure

The left side of the heart is a term for the functional unit of the left atrium and left ventricle, together with the mitral and aortic valves; the right heart comprises the right atrium, right ventricle, tricuspid and pulmonary valves.

Left-sided heart failure. In this condition there is a reduction in the left ventricular output and/or an increase in the left atrial or pulmonary venous pressure. An acute increase in left atrial pressure may cause pulmonary congestion or pulmonary oedema; a more gradual increase in left atrial pressure, however, may lead to reflex pulmonary vasoconstriction, which protects the patient from pulmonary oedema at the cost of increasing pulmonary hypertension.

Right-sided heart failure. In this condition there is a reduction in right ventricular output for any given right atrial pressure. Causes of isolated right heart failure include chronic lung disease (cor pulmonale), multiple pulmonary emboli and pulmonary valvular stenosis.

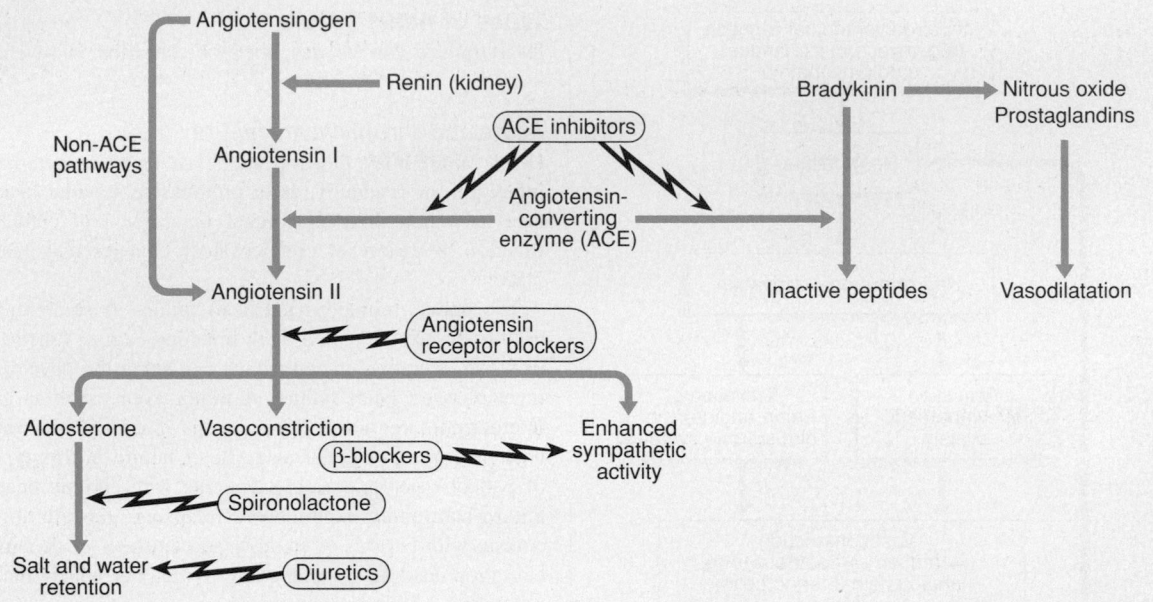

Fig. 12.25 Neurohormonal activation and sites of action of drugs used in the treatment of heart failure.

Biventricular heart failure. Failure of the left and right heart may develop because the disease process (e.g. dilated cardiomyopathy or ischaemic heart disease) affects both ventricles, or because disease of the left heart leads to chronic elevation of the left atrial pressure, pulmonary hypertension and subsequent right heart failure.

Forward and backward heart failure

In some patients with heart failure the predominant problem is an inadequate cardiac output (forward failure), whilst other patients may have a normal or near-normal cardiac output with marked salt and water retention causing pulmonary and systemic venous congestion (backward failure) (see Fig. 12.26).

Diastolic and systolic dysfunction

Heart failure may develop as a result of impaired myocardial contraction (systolic dysfunction) but can also be due to poor ventricular filling and high filling pressures caused by abnormal ventricular relaxation (diastolic dysfunction). The latter is commonly found in patients with left ventricular hypertrophy and occurs in many forms of heart disease, notably hypertension and ischaemic heart disease. Systolic and diastolic dysfunction often coexist, particularly in patients with coronary artery disease.

High-output failure

Conditions that are associated with a very high cardiac output (e.g. a large AV shunt, beri-beri, severe anaemia or thyrotoxicosis) can occasionally cause heart failure. In such cases additional causes of heart failure are often present.

Clinical features

The clinical picture depends on the nature of the underlying heart disease, the type of heart failure that it has evoked, and the neural and endocrine changes that have developed (see Box 12.12, p. 382).

A low cardiac output causes fatigue, listlessness and a poor effort tolerance; the peripheries are cold and the blood pressure is low. To maintain perfusion of vital organs blood flow may be diverted away from skeletal muscle and this may contribute to symptoms of fatigue. Poor renal perfusion may lead to oliguria and uraemia.

Pulmonary oedema due to left heart failure may present with breathlessness, orthopnoea, paroxysmal nocturnal dyspnoea and inspiratory crepitations over the lung bases. The chest radiograph shows characteristic abnormalities (see Fig. 12.22, p. 380) and is usually a more sensitive indicator of pulmonary venous congestion than the physical signs.

In contrast, right heart failure produces a high jugular venous pressure, with hepatic congestion and dependent peripheral oedema. In ambulant patients the oedema affects the ankles, whereas in bed-bound patients it collects around the thighs and sacrum. Massive accumulation of fluid may cause ascites or pleural effusion.

Heart failure is not the only cause of oedema (see Box 12.14).

Chronic heart failure is sometimes associated with marked weight loss (cardiac cachexia) caused by a combination of anorexia and impaired absorption due to gastrointestinal congestion; poor tissue perfusion due to a low cardiac output; and skeletal muscle atrophy due to immobility. Increased circulating levels of cytokine tumour necrosis factor have been found in patients with cardiac cachexia.

12.14 DIFFERENTIAL DIAGNOSIS OF PERIPHERAL OEDEMA

- **Cardiac failure** (right or combined left and right heart failure, pericardial constriction, cardiomyopathy)
- **Chronic venous insufficiency** (varicose veins)
- **Hypoalbuminaemia** (nephrotic syndrome, liver disease, protein-losing enteropathy)
  Often widespread, can affect arms and face
- **Drugs**
  Sodium retention (fludrocortisone, non-steroidal anti-inflammatory agents)
  Increasing capillary permeability (nifedipine, amlodipine)
- **Idiopathic** (women > men)
- **Chronic lymphatic obstruction**

Complications

In advanced heart failure a number of non-specific complications may occur.

Uraemia. This reflects poor renal perfusion due to the effects of diuretic therapy and a low cardiac output. Treatment with vasodilators or dopamine may improve renal perfusion.

Hypokalaemia (see p. 286). This may be the result of treatment with potassium-losing diuretics or hyperaldosteronism caused by activation of the renin-angiotensin system and impaired aldosterone metabolism due to hepatic congestion. Most of the body's potassium is intracellular, and there may be substantial depletion of potassium stores even when the plasma potassium concentration is in the normal range.

Hyperkalaemia (see p. 284). This may be due to the effects of drug treatment, particularly the combination of ACE inhibitors and spironolactone (which both promote potassium retention), and renal dysfunction.

Hyponatraemia (see p. 281). This is a feature of severe heart failure and may be caused by diuretic therapy, inappropriate water retention, or failure of the cell membrane ion pump.

Impaired liver function. Hepatic venous congestion and poor arterial perfusion frequently cause mild jaundice and abnormal liver function tests; reduced synthesis of clotting factors may make anticoagulant control difficult.

Thromboembolism. Deep vein thrombosis and pulmonary embolism may occur due to the effects of a low cardiac output and enforced immobility, whereas systemic emboli may be related to arrhythmias, particularly atrial fibrillation, or intracardiac thrombus complicating conditions such as mitral stenosis or LV aneurysm.

Arrhythmias. Atrial and ventricular arrhythmias are very common and may be related to electrolyte changes (e.g. hypokalaemia, hypomagnesaemia), the underlying structural heart disease, and the pro-arrhythmic effects of increased circulating catecholamines and some drugs (e.g. digoxin). Sudden death occurs in up to 50% of patients with heart failure and is often due to a ventricular arrhythmia. Frequent ventricular ectopic beats and runs of non-sustained ventricular tachycardia are common findings in patients with heart failure and are associated with an adverse prognosis.

Investigations

Simple tests (e.g. urea, electrolytes, haemoglobin, thyroid function, ECG, chest radiograph) may help to establish the nature and severity of the underlying heart disease and detect any complications.

Echocardiography is a very useful investigation and should be considered in all patients with significant heart failure in order to:

- confirm the diagnosis
- detect hitherto unsuspected valvular heart disease (e.g. occult mitral stenosis) and other conditions that may be amenable to specific remedies
- identify patients who will benefit from long-term therapy with an ACE inhibitor (see below).

Management of heart failure

General measures

Effective education of patients and their relatives about the causes and treatment of heart failure can help adherence to a management plan (see Box 12.15). Some patients may need to weigh themselves and adjust their diuretic therapy accordingly on a daily basis.

In patients with coronary heart disease secondary preventative measures such as low-dose aspirin and lipid-lowering therapy are appropriate (see p. 424).

Drug therapy

Cardiac function can be improved by increasing contractility, optimising preload or decreasing afterload. The

12.15 GENERAL MEASURES FOR THE MANAGEMENT OF HEART FAILURE
Education
- Explanation of nature of disease, treatment and self-help strategies
Diet
- Good general nutrition and weight reduction for the obese - Avoidance of high-salt foods and added salt, especially for patients with severe congestive heart failure
Alcohol
- Moderate alcohol consumption. Alcohol-induced cardiomyopathy requires abstinence
Smoking
- Giving up
Exercise
- Regular moderate exercise within limits of symptoms
Vaccination
- Influenza and pneumococcal vaccination should be considered

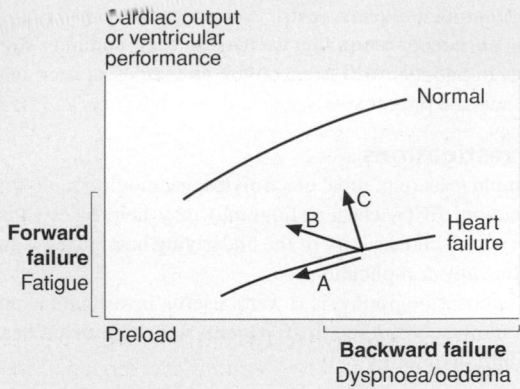

Fig. 12.26 The effect of treatment on ventricular performance curves in heart failure. Diuretics and venodilators (A), angiotensin-converting enzyme inhibitors and mixed vasodilators (B), and positive inotropic agents (C).

ISSUES IN OLDER PEOPLE
CONGESTIVE CARDIAC FAILURE

- The incidence of heart failure rises with age so that the condition affects 5–10% of people in their eighties.
- Heart failure in the elderly is most commonly caused by coronary artery disease, but hypertension and calcific degenerative valvular disease are also common causes.
- Diastolic dysfunction is often a prominent feature, particularly in those with a history of hypertension.
- ACE inhibitors improve symptoms and mortality but sometimes cause postural hypotension, because of pre-existing age-related reductions in plasma volume and baroreceptor responsiveness, incompetent venous valves and changes in the autoregulation of cerebral blood flow.
- Loop diuretics are usually required but may be poorly tolerated in patients with urinary incontinence and men with prostate enlargement.

---

effects of these measures are illustrated in Figure 12.26. Drugs that reduce preload are most appropriate in patients with high end-diastolic filling pressures and evidence of pulmonary or systemic venous congestion (backward failure); drugs that reduce afterload or increase myocardial contractility are particularly valuable in patients with signs and symptoms of a low cardiac output (forward failure).

Diuretics. These are usually the first line of treatment. The main types, mode of action and side-effects of these drugs are described on page 277. In heart failure, diuretics produce an increase in urinary sodium excretion, leading to a reduction in blood and plasma volume, and may also cause a small but significant degree of arterial and venous dilatation. Diuretic therapy will, therefore, reduce preload and improve pulmonary and systemic venous congestion; it may also cause a small reduction in afterload and ventricular volume leading to a fall in wall tension and increased cardiac efficiency.

Although a fall in preload (ventricular filling pressure) tends to reduce cardiac output, the 'Starling curve' in heart failure is flat so there may be a substantial and beneficial fall in filling pressure with little change in cardiac output (see Fig. 12.23, p. 382 and Fig. 12.26). Nevertheless, excessive diuretic therapy may cause an undesirable fall in cardiac output, with a rising blood urea, hypotension and increasing lethargy.

In some patients with severe chronic heart failure, particularly in the presence of chronic renal impairment, oedema may persist despite oral loop diuretics. In such patients an intravenous infusion of furosemide (frusemide), 10 mg per hour for example, can initiate a diuresis. Also combining a loop diuretic with a thiazide, e.g. bendroflumethiazide (bendrofluazide) 5 mg daily, or a thiazide-like diuretic, e.g. metolazone 5 mg daily, may prove effective; however, such combinations can produce an excessive diuresis. Spironolactone, a specific aldosterone antagonist, is of particular benefit in patients with heart failure but, as this drug causes potassium retention, care must be taken to avoid hyperkalaemia, particularly at doses above 50 mg per day.

Vasodilators. The use of vasodilators in acute circulatory failure is described on page 202. These drugs are also valuable in chronic heart failure; venodilators (e.g. organic nitrates) reduce preload, and arterial dilators (e.g. hydralazine) reduce afterload (see Fig. 12.26). However, their use is limited by pharmacological tolerance and hypotension.

Angiotensin-converting enzyme (ACE) inhibitors. The advent of these drugs has been a major advance in the treatment of heart failure. They interrupt the vicious circle of neurohormonal activation that is characteristic of moderate and severe heart failure by preventing the conversion of angiotensin I to angiotensin II, thereby counteracting salt and water retention, peripheral arterial and venous vasoconstriction, and activation of the sympathetic nervous system (see Fig. 12.25). They also prevent the undesirable activation of the renin-angiotensin system caused by diuretic therapy.

The major benefit of ACE inhibitor therapy in heart failure is a reduction in afterload; however, there may also be an advantageous reduction in preload and a modest increase in the plasma potassium concentration. Treating heart failure with a combination of a potassium-losing diuretic and an ACE inhibitor therefore has many potential advantages.

Clinical trials have shown that in moderate and severe heart failure ACE inhibitors can produce a substantial improvement in effort tolerance and in mortality. ACE inhibitors can also improve outcome and prevent the onset of overt heart failure in patients with poor residual left ventricular function following myocardial infarction (see EBM panels).

Unfortunately, these drugs can cause profound hypotension with postural symptoms and a deterioration in renal function (especially in patients with bilateral renal artery stenosis or pre-existing renal disease). Moreover, there may be a potentially catastrophic fall in blood pressure following the first dose of an ACE inhibitor, particularly if

EBM

CHRONIC HEART FAILURE—use of ACE inhibitors

'Meta-analysis of 32 RCTs examining the effects of ACE inhibitors in patients with chronic heart failure due to ventricular dysfunction has shown significantly reduced mortality and readmission rates with use of ACE inhibitor therapy. Average NNT for 1 year to prevent one death = 16. (Reduction in mortality was greatest in the RCTs that investigated the sickest patients.) Average NNT for the combined endpoint of death or readmission = 10.'

- Garg R, Yusuf S, for the Collaborative Group on ACE inhibitor trials. Overview of randomized trials of angiotensin converting enzyme inhibitors on mortality and morbidity in patients with heart failure. JAMA 1995; 273:1450–1456.
- Acute Infarction Ramipril Efficacy (AIRE) Study Investigators. Effect of ramipril on mortality and morbidity of survivors of acute myocardial infarction with clinical evidence of heart failure. Lancet 1993; 342:821–828.

Further information: www.sign.ac.uk

PREVENTION OF THE DEVELOPMENT OF HEART FAILURE—use of ACE inhibitors

'RCTs have found good evidence that ACE inhibitors can delay the development of symptomatic heart failure and reduce the frequency of cardiovascular events (death, myocardial infarction, hospitalisation) in patients with asymptomatic left ventricular systolic dysfunction, and in patients with other cardiovascular risk factors for heart failure. NNT for 2 years to prevent one death = 17.'

- SOLVD Investigators. Effect of enalapril on mortality and the development of heart failure in asymptomatic patients with reduced left ventricular ejection fractions. N Engl J Med 1992; 327:685–691.
- Flather M, Kober L, Pfeffer MA, et al. Meta-analysis of individual patient data from trials of long term ACE inhibitor treatment after acute myocardial infarction (SAVE, AIRE and TRACE studies). Circulation 1997; 96:1–706.

Further information: www.clinicalevidence.org

the drug is started in the presence of hypotension, hypovolaemia or hyponatraemia due to prior diuretic therapy. In stable patients without hypotension (systolic BP > 100 mmHg) ACE inhibitors can usually be started in the community without problems. However, in other patients it is usually advisable to withhold diuretics for 24 hours before starting treatment with a low dose, while the patient is supine and under observation. If hypotension occurs, this can be counteracted by elevating the foot of the bed and administering intravenous saline or, in extreme circumstances, intravenous angiotensin II. Renal function must be monitored and should be checked 1–2 weeks after starting therapy. Typical starting doses and target doses for commonly used ACE inhibitors are shown in Box 12.16.

12.16 ACE INHIBITOR DOSAGES IN HEART FAILURE

	Starting dose	Target dose
Captopril	12.5 mg 8-hourly	50 mg 8-hourly
Enalapril	2.5 mg 12-hourly	10 mg 12-hourly
Lisinopril	5 mg daily	20 mg daily
Ramipril	2.5 mg 12-hourly	5 mg 12-hourly

Angiotensin II receptor antagonists (e.g. losartan 50–100 mg once daily or valsartan 80–160 mg daily). These drugs act by blocking the action of angiotensin II on the heart, peripheral vasculature and kidney; in heart failure, they produce beneficial haemodynamic changes that are similar to the effects of ACE inhibitors (see Fig. 12.25, p. 384). They appear to have similar effects on mortality to ACE inhibitors but have not been as well tested in randomised trials. In contrast to ACE inhibitors, they have no effect on the breakdown of bradykinin within the lungs so do not cause cough, and are a useful alternative for patients who cannot tolerate ACE inhibitors. Unfortunately, they share all the more serious adverse effects of ACE inhibitors.

Beta-adrenoceptor antagonists (*'β-blockers'*). These drugs may help to counteract the deleterious effects of enhanced sympathetic stimulation and may prevent arrhythmias and sudden death. When initiated in standard doses they may precipitate acute on chronic heart failure, but when given in very small incremental doses (e.g. bisoprolol started at a dose of 1.25 mg daily and increased gradually over a 12-week period to a target maintenance dose of 10 mg daily) under carefully monitored conditions they can increase ejection fraction, improve symptoms, reduce the frequency of hospitalisation, and reduce mortality in patients with chronic heart failure (see EBM panel).

CHRONIC HEART FAILURE—use of β-blockers

'There is strong evidence from systematic reviews of RCTs that adding oral β-blockers gradually in small incremental doses to standard therapy including ACE inhibitors in people with heart failure reduces the rate of death or hospital admission. NNT for 1 year to prevent one death = 24.'

- Lechat P, Packer M, Chalon S, et al. Clinical effects of beta adrenergic blockade in chronic heart failure. A meta-analysis of double-blind, placebo-controlled, randomized trials. Circulation 1998; 98:1184–1191.
- McMurray JJV. Major β-blocker mortality trials in chronic heart failure: a critical review. Heart 1999; 82:14–22.

Further information: www.escardio.org

Digoxin. This should be used as first-line therapy in patients with heart failure and atrial fibrillation, when it will usually provide adequate control of the ventricular rate together with a small positive inotropic effect. The dosage and side-effects are discussed on page 418.

The role of digoxin in the treatment of patients with heart failure and sinus rhythm is less certain. In a recent large randomised controlled trial among this patient population, treatment with digoxin had no effect on overall survival but did reduce the need for hospitalisation.

Amiodarone (see p. 417). This is a potent anti-arrhythmic drug which has little negative inotropic effect and may be valuable in patients with poor left ventricular function. Clinical trials of amiodarone in heart failure, however, have produced conflicting results and the drug is usually used to treat patients with symptomatic arrhythmias.

Revascularisation

Coronary artery bypass surgery or percutaneous coronary intervention may improve function in areas of the myocardium that are 'hibernating' because of inadequate blood supply and can be used to treat very carefully selected patients with heart failure and coronary artery disease. If necessary, 'hibernating' myocardium can be identified by stress echocardiography and a variety of specialised nuclear techniques.

Heart transplantation

Cardiac transplantation is an established and very successful form of treatment for patients with intractable heart failure. Coronary artery disease and dilated cardiomyopathy are the most common reasons for transplantation. The introduction of ciclosporin for immunosuppression has improved survival, which now exceeds 90% at 1 year. The use of transplantation is limited by the availability of donor hearts so it is generally reserved for young patients with severe symptoms.

Conventional heart transplantation is contraindicated in patients with pulmonary vascular disease due to long-standing left heart failure, complex congenital heart disease (e.g. Eisenmenger's syndrome) or primary pulmonary hypertension, because the right ventricle of the donor heart may fail in the face of increased pulmonary vascular resistance. However, heart–lung transplantation is an option for such patients and has also been used in the treatment of terminal respiratory disease such as cystic fibrosis.

Although cardiac transplantation usually produces a dramatic improvement in the recipient's quality of life, serious complications may occur:

- *Rejection*. In spite of routine therapy with ciclosporin A, azathioprine and corticosteroids, episodes of rejection are common and may present with heart failure, arrhythmias or subtle ECG changes; cardiac biopsy is often used to confirm the diagnosis before starting treatment with high-dose steroids.
- *Accelerated atherosclerosis*. Recurrent heart failure is often due to progressive atherosclerosis in the coronary arteries of the donor heart. This is not confined to patients who were transplanted for coronary artery disease and is probably a manifestation of chronic rejection. Angina is rare because the heart has been denervated.
- *Infection*. Opportunistic infection with organisms such as cytomegalovirus or aspergillus remains a major cause of death in transplant recipients.

HYPERTENSION

Definition

High blood pressure is a trait as opposed to a specific disease and represents a quantitative rather than a qualitative deviation from the norm. Any definition of hypertension is therefore arbitrary.

Systemic blood pressure rises with age, and the incidence of cardiovascular disease (particularly stroke and coronary artery disease) is closely related to average blood pressure at all ages, even when blood pressure readings are within the so-called 'normal range'. Moreover, a series of randomised controlled trials have demonstrated that antihypertensive therapy can reduce the incidence of stroke and, to a lesser extent, coronary artery disease (see EBM panel, p. 393).

The cardiovascular risks associated with a given blood pressure are dependent upon the combination of risk factors in the specific individual. These include age, gender, weight, physical inactivity, smoking, family history, blood cholesterol, diabetes mellitus and pre-existing vascular disease. Effective management of hypertension therefore requires a holistic approach that is based on the identification of those at highest cardiovascular risk and the adoption of multifactorial interventions, targeting not only blood pressure but all modifiable cardiovascular risk factors.

In light of these observations a useful and practical definition of hypertension is 'the level of blood pressure at which the benefits of treatment outweigh the costs and hazards'.

Target organ damage

The adverse effects of hypertension principally involve the blood vessels, the central nervous system, the retina, the heart and the kidneys, and can often be detected by simple clinical means.

Blood vessels

In larger arteries (over 1 mm in diameter) the internal elastic lamina is thickened, smooth muscle is hypertrophied and fibrous tissue is deposited. The vessels dilate and become tortuous and their walls become less compliant. In smaller arteries (under 1 mm) hyaline arteriosclerosis occurs in the wall, the lumen narrows and aneurysms may develop. Widespread atheroma develops and may lead to coronary and/or cerebrovascular disease, particularly if other risk factors (e.g. smoking, hyperlipidaemia, diabetes) are present.

These structural changes in the vasculature often perpetuate and aggravate hypertension by increasing peripheral vascular resistance and reducing renal function.

Hypertension is also implicated in the pathogenesis of aortic aneurysm and aortic dissection (see pp. 447–450).

Central nervous system

Stroke is a common complication of hypertension and may be due to cerebral haemorrhage or cerebral infarction. Carotid atheroma and transient cerebral ischaemic attacks are more common in hypertensive patients. Subarachnoid haemorrhage is also associated with hypertension.

Hypertensive encephalopathy is a rare condition characterised by high blood pressure and neurological symptoms, including transient disturbances of speech or vision, paraesthesiae, disorientation, fits and loss of consciousness. Papilloedema is common. A CT scan of the brain often shows haemorrhage in and around the basal ganglia; however, the neurological deficit is usually reversible if the hypertension is properly controlled.

Retina
The optic fundi reveal a gradation of changes linked to the severity of hypertension; fundoscopy can, therefore, provide an indication of the arteriolar damage occurring elsewhere (see Box 12.17).

'Cotton wool' exudates are associated with retinal ischaemia or infarction, and fade in a few weeks (see Fig. 12.27A). 'Hard' exudates (small, white, dense deposits of lipid) and microaneurysms ('dot' haemorrhages) are more characteristic of diabetic retinopathy (see Fig. 15.17, p. 671).

Hypertension is also associated with central retinal vein thrombosis (see Fig. 12.27B).

12.17 HYPERTENSIVE RETINOPATHY

- **Grade 1** Arteriolar thickening, tortuosity and increased reflectiveness ('silver wiring')
- **Grade 2** Grade 1 plus constriction of veins at arterial crossings ('arteriovenous nipping')
- **Grade 3** Grade 2 plus evidence of retinal ischaemia (flame-shaped or blot haemorrhages and 'cotton wool' exudates)
- **Grade 4** Grade 3 plus papilloedema

Heart
The excess cardiac mortality and morbidity associated with hypertension is largely due to a higher incidence of coronary artery disease.

High blood pressure places a pressure load on the heart and may lead to left ventricular hypertrophy with a forceful apex beat and fourth heart sound. ECG or echocardiographic evidence of left ventricular hypertrophy is highly predictive of cardiovascular complications and these tests are therefore particularly useful in risk assessment.

Atrial fibrillation is common and may be due to diastolic dysfunction caused by left ventricular hypertrophy or the effects of coronary artery disease.

Severe hypertension can cause left ventricular failure in the absence of coronary artery disease, particularly when renal function, and therefore sodium excretion, is impaired.

Kidneys
Long-standing hypertension may cause proteinuria and progressive renal failure (see p. 609) by damaging the renal vasculature.

'Malignant' or 'accelerated' phase hypertension
This rare condition may complicate hypertension of any aetiology and is characterised by accelerated microvascular damage with necrosis in the walls of small arteries and arterioles ('fibrinoid necrosis') and intravascular thrombosis. The diagnosis is based on evidence of high blood pressure and rapidly progressive end organ damage such as retinopathy (grade 3 or 4), renal dysfunction (especially proteinuria) and/or hypertensive encephalopathy (see above). Left ventricular failure may occur and, if this is untreated, death occurs within months.

Aetiology
In more than 95% of cases a specific underlying cause of hypertension cannot be found. Such patients are said to have essential hypertension.

The pathogenesis of essential hypertension is not clearly understood. Different investigators have proposed the kidney, the peripheral resistance vessels and the sympathetic nervous system as the seat of the primary abnormality. In reality the problem is probably multifactorial. Hypertension is more common in some ethnic groups, particularly American Blacks and Japanese, and approximately 40–60% is explained by genetic factors. Important environmental factors include a high salt intake, heavy consumption of alcohol, obesity, lack of exercise and impaired intrauterine growth. There is very little evidence that 'stress' causes hypertension.

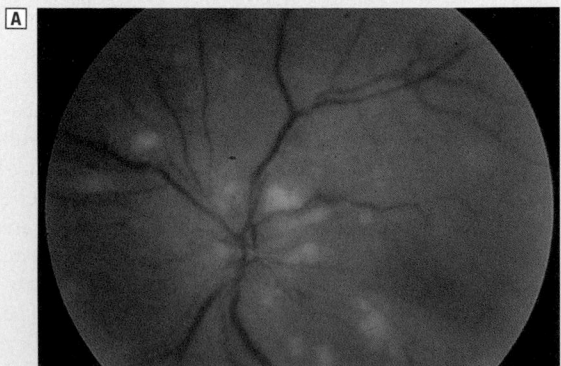 

Fig. 12.27 Retinal changes in hypertension. A Grade 4 hypertensive retinopathy showing swollen optic disc, retinal haemorrhages and multiple cotton wool spots (infarcts). B Central retinal vein thrombosis showing swollen optic disc and widespread fundal haemorrhage, commonly associated with systemic hypertension.

12.18 CAUSES OF SECONDARY HYPERTENSION
Alcohol
Pregnancy (pre-eclampsia)
Renal disease (see Ch. 14)
• Renal vascular disease • Parenchymal renal disease, particularly glomerulonephritis • Polycystic kidney disease
Endocrine disease (see Ch. 16)
• Phaeochromocytoma • Cushing's syndrome • Primary hyperaldosteronism (Conn's syndrome) • Hyperparathyroidism • Acromegaly • Primary hypothyroidism • Thyrotoxicosis • Congenital adrenal hyperplasia due to 11-β-hydroxylase or 17-hydroxylase deficiency • Liddle's syndrome • 11-β-hydroxysteroid dehydrogenase deficiency
Drugs
• e.g. Oral contraceptives containing oestrogens, anabolic steroids, corticosteroids, non-steroidal anti-inflammatory drugs, carbenoxolone, sympathomimetic agents
Coarctation of the aorta (see p. 471)

12.19 MEASUREMENT OF BLOOD PRESSURE
• Use a machine that has been validated, well maintained and properly calibrated • Measure sitting BP routinely, with additional standing BP in the elderly and diabetics • Remove tight clothing from the arm • Support arm at level of the heart • Use cuff of appropriate size (bladder must encompass > two-thirds of arm) • Lower mercury slowly (2 mm per second) • Read BP to the nearest 2 mmHg • Use phase V (disappearance of sounds) to measure diastolic BP • Take two measurements at each visit

In about 5% of unselected cases, hypertension can be shown to be a consequence of a specific disease or abnormality leading to sodium retention and/or peripheral vasoconstriction (secondary hypertension; see Box 12.18).

Approach to newly diagnosed hypertension

Hypertension occasionally causes headache but, provided there are no complications, most patients remain asymptomatic. Accordingly, the diagnosis is usually made at routine examination or when a complication arises. A blood pressure check is advisable every 5 years in adults.

The objectives of the initial evaluation of a patient with high blood pressure readings are:

• to obtain accurate and representative measurements of blood pressure
• to identify contributory factors and any underlying cause (secondary hypertension)
• to assess other risk factors and quantify cardiovascular risk
• to detect any complications (target organ damage) that are already present
• to identify comorbidity that may influence the choice of antihypertensive therapy.

These goals can usually be attained by a careful history, clinical examination and some simple investigations.

Measurement of blood pressure

A decision to embark upon antihypertensive therapy effectively commits the patient to life-long treatment, so it is vital that the blood pressure (BP) readings on which this decision is based are as accurate as possible.

Measurements should be made, to the nearest 2 mmHg, in the sitting position with the arm supported, and repeated after 5 minutes' rest if the first recording is high (see Box 12.19). In addition, the standing BP should be measured in elderly subjects, diabetics and those who may be suffering from postural hypotension. To avoid spuriously high recordings in obese subjects, the cuff should contain a bladder that encompasses at least two-thirds of the circumference of the arm. The diastolic pressure should be recorded at Korotkoff phase V (disappearance of sounds) and not phase IV (muffling of sounds).

Home and ambulatory blood pressure recordings

Exercise, anxiety, discomfort and unfamiliar surroundings can all lead to a transient rise in BP. Sphygmomanometry, particularly when performed by a doctor, can cause an unrepresentative surge in BP which has been termed 'white coat' hypertension, and as many as 20% of patients with apparent hypertension in the clinic may have a 'normal BP' when it is recorded by automated devices used in their own home. The risk of cardiovascular disease in these patients is less than that observed in patients with sustained hypertension but greater than that seen in normotensive subjects.

A series of automated ambulatory BP measurements, obtained over 24 hours or longer, provides a better profile than a limited number of clinic readings. Indeed, ambulatory BP measurements correlate more closely with evidence of target organ damage than casual BP measurements. However, treatment thresholds and targets must be adjusted downwards because ambulatory BP readings are systematically lower (approximately 12/7 mmHg) than clinic measurements (see Box 12.23); the average ambulatory day-time (not 24-hour or night-time) BP should be used to guide management decisions.

Patients can also measure their own BP at home using a range of variable-quality semi-automatic devices; the real value of such measurements is not well established but similar considerations apply.

Home or ambulatory BP measurements may be particularly helpful in patients with unusually labile blood pressure, those with refractory hypertension, those who may be experiencing symptomatic hypotension, and those in whom white coat hypertension is suspected.

Clinical assessment and investigations

History
Family history, lifestyle (exercise, diet, smoking habit) and other risk factors should be recorded. A careful history will also identify those patients with drug- or alcohol-induced hypertension and may elicit the symptoms of other causes of secondary hypertension such as phaeochromocytoma (paroxysmal headache, palpitation and sweating) or complications such as coronary artery disease (e.g. angina, breathlessness).

Examination
Radio-femoral delay (coarctation of the aorta), enlarged kidneys (polycystic kidney disease), abdominal bruits (renal artery stenosis) and the characteristic facies and habitus of Cushing's syndrome are all examples of physical signs that may help to identify one of the causes of secondary hypertension (see Box 12.18). Examination may also reveal features of important risk factors such as central obesity and hyperlipidaemia (tendon xanthomas etc.). Nevertheless, the majority of abnormal signs are due to the complications of hypertension.

Non-specific findings may include left ventricular hypertrophy (apical heave), accentuation of the aortic component of the second heart sound, and a fourth heart sound. The optic fundi are often abnormal (see Fig. 12.27) and there may be evidence of generalised atheroma or specific complications such as aortic aneurysm or peripheral vascular disease.

Investigations
All hypertensive patients should undergo a limited number of investigations. Additional investigations are appropriate in selected patients (see Boxes 12.20 and 12.21).

Management

Quantification of cardiovascular risk
The sole objective of antihypertensive therapy is to reduce the incidence of adverse cardiovascular events, particularly coronary heart disease, stroke and heart failure. The relative benefit of antihypertensive therapy (approximately 30% reduction in risk of stroke and 20% reduction in risk of coronary heart disease—see EBM panel, p. 393) is similar in all patient groups, so the absolute benefit (total number of events prevented) of treatment is greatest in those at highest risk. For example, extrapolating from the Medical Research Council (MRC) Mild Hypertension Trial (1985), one would have to treat 566 young patients with bendroflumethiazide (bendrofluazide) for 1 year to prevent 1 stroke (the equivalent figure for propranolol was 1423 patient years); in the MRC trial of antihypertensive treatment in the elderly (1992), 1 stroke was prevented for every 286 patients treated for 1 year.

A formal estimate of absolute cardiovascular risk may help to determine whether the likely benefits of therapy will outweigh its costs and hazards. This should take account of all the relevant risk factors and not just the blood pressure. A variety of computer programs and risk charts are available for this purpose (a chart issued by the Joint British Societies can be found in the Appendix of this book). Most of the excess morbidity and mortality associated with hypertension is attributable to coronary heart disease and many treatment guidelines are therefore based on estimates of the 10-year coronary heart disease risk. Total cardiovascular risk can be estimated by multiplying coronary heart disease (CHD) risk by 4/3 (i.e. if CHD risk is 30%, cardiovascular risk is 40%).

The value of this approach can be illustrated by comparing two hypothetical cases. A 65-year-old man with an average blood pressure of 150/90 mmHg, who smokes, has diabetes, a total:HDL cholesterol of 8, and ECG changes of left ventricular hypertrophy, will be found to have a 10-year CHD risk of 68% (Joint British Societies risk assessor). Antihypertensive therapy (assuming 20% relative risk reduction) would therefore be expected to prevent 14 coronary events for every 1000 patient years of treatment and would be advisable. In contrast a 55-year-old woman with exactly the same blood pressure, who does

---

12.20 HYPERTENSION: INVESTIGATION OF ALL PATIENTS

- Urinalysis for blood, protein and glucose
- Blood urea, electrolytes and creatinine
  N.B. Hypokalaemic alkalosis may indicate primary hyperaldosteronism but is usually due to diuretic therapy
- Blood glucose
- Serum total and high-density lipoprotein (HDL) cholesterol
- 12-lead ECG (left ventricular hypertrophy, coronary artery disease)

12.21 HYPERTENSION: INVESTIGATION OF SELECTED PATIENTS

- Chest radiograph: to detect cardiomegaly, heart failure, coarctation of the aorta
- Ambulatory BP recording: to assess borderline or 'white coat' hypertension
- Echocardiogram: to detect or quantify left ventricular hypertrophy
- Renal ultrasound: to detect possible renal disease
- Renal angiography: to detect or confirm presence of renal artery stenosis
- Urinary catecholamines: to detect possible phaeochromocytoma (see p. 730)
- Urinary cortisol and dexamethasone suppression test: to detect possible Cushing's syndrome (see pp. 724–725)
- Plasma renin activity and aldosterone: to detect possible primary aldosteronism (see p. 729)

12.22 MANAGEMENT OF HYPERTENSION: BRITISH HYPERTENSION SOCIETY GUIDELINES

Blood pressure (mmHg)	Major risk factor(s) present • Target organ damage • Diabetes • Cardiovascular disease • 10-year CHD risk ≥ 15%	Recommended action (advise all patients to institute non-pharmacological measures)
< 135/85	±	Reassess in 5 years
135–139/85–89	±	Reassess annually
140–159/90–99	−	Remeasure monthly Reassess CHD risk yearly Treat if 10-year CHD risk exceeds 15%
140–159/90–99	+	Confirm over 12 weeks and treat
160–199/100–109	−	Remeasure weekly for 4–12 weeks Treat if BP remains this high
160–199/100–109	+	Confirm over 3–4 weeks and treat
200–219/110–119	±	Confirm over 1–2 weeks and treat
> 220/120	±	Treat immediately

not smoke, is not diabetic, has a total:HDL cholesterol of 6 and a normal ECG, has a predicted 10-year CHD risk of less than 14%; treatment in this case might therefore prevent fewer than 3 events per 1000 patient years of treatment and would be questionable.

Threshold for intervention

Systolic blood pressure and diastolic blood pressure are both powerful predictors of cardiovascular risk. The British Hypertension Society management guidelines therefore utilise both readings, and treatment should be initiated if either systolic or diastolic pressure exceeds the given threshold (see Box 12.22).

Diabetics are at particularly high risk and the threshold for initiating antihypertensive therapy is therefore lower (≥ 140/90) in this patient group. Target blood pressures for diabetics are also lower (see below). The thresholds for treatment in the elderly are the same as for younger patients (see 'Issues in Older People' panel, p. 394).

Treatment targets

In the hypertension optimal treatment (HOT) trial the optimum blood pressure for reduction of major cardiovascular events was found to be 139/83 mmHg, and even lower in patients with diabetes; moreover, reducing blood pressure below this level caused no harm. Unfortunately, it seems clear that, despite best practice, the targets suggested by the British Hypertension Society (see Box 12.23) will not be achievable in many patients. In the UK the rule of halves has been observed: only half of all hypertensives are diagnosed, only half of these patients are on treatment, and blood pressure is well controlled in only half of those receiving therapy.

Patients taking antihypertensive therapy require follow-up, typically at 3-month intervals, to monitor blood pressure, minimise side-effects and reinforce lifestyle advice.

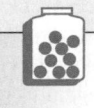

12.23 OPTIMAL TARGET BLOOD PRESSURES DURING ANTIHYPERTENSIVE TREATMENT: BRITISH HYPERTENSION SOCIETY GUIDELINES

	No diabetes	Diabetes
Clinic measurements	< 140/85	< 140/80
Mean day-time ambulatory or home measurement	< 130/80	< 130/75

N.B. Both systolic and diastolic values should be attained.

Non-drug therapy

Appropriate lifestyle measures may obviate the need for drug therapy in patients with borderline hypertension, reduce the dose and/or the number of drugs required in patients with established hypertension, and directly reduce cardiovascular risk.

Correcting obesity, reducing alcohol intake, restricting salt intake, taking regular physical exercise and increasing consumption of fruit and vegetables can all lower blood pressure. Moreover, quitting smoking, eating oily fish and adopting a diet that is low in saturated fat may produce further reductions in cardiovascular risk (see 'Primary prevention', p. 423).

Antihypertensive drugs

Thiazide and other diuretics (see p. 277). The mechanism of action of these drugs is incompletely understood, and it may take up to a month for the maximum effect to be observed. A daily dose of 2.5 mg bendroflumethiazide (bendrofluazide) or 0.5 mg cyclopenthiazide is appropriate. More potent loop diuretics, such as furosemide (frusemide) 40 mg daily or bumetanide 1 mg daily, have few advantages over thiazides in the treatment of hypertension unless there is substantial renal impairment or they are used in conjunction with an ACE inhibitor.

Beta-adrenoceptor antagonists (β-blockers). Metoprolol (100–200 mg daily), atenolol (50–100 mg daily) and bisoprolol (5–10 mg daily) are cardioselective and therefore preferentially block the cardiac β1-adrenoceptors, as opposed to the β2-adrenoceptors which mediate vasodilatation and bronchodilatation.

Labetalol. Labetalol (200 mg–2.4 g daily in divided doses) is a combined β- and α-adrenoceptor antagonist which is sometimes more effective than pure β-blockers and can be used as an infusion in malignant phase hypertension.

Angiotensin-converting enzyme (ACE) inhibitors. These drugs (e.g. captopril 25–75 mg twice daily, enalapril 20 mg daily, ramipril 5–10 mg daily or lisinopril 10–20 mg daily) inhibit the conversion of angiotensin I to angiotensin II and are usually well tolerated. They should be used with particular care in patients with impaired renal function or renal artery stenosis because they can reduce the filtration pressure in the glomeruli and precipitate renal failure. Side-effects include first-dose hypotension, cough, rash, hyperkalaemia, renal dysfunction and dysgeusia (an unpleasant metallic taste). Note that electrolytes and creatinine should be checked before and 1–2 weeks after commencing therapy.

Angiotensin II receptor antagonists. These drugs (e.g. losartan 50–100 mg daily, valsartan 40–160 mg daily) block the AT I angiotensin II receptor and have similar effects to ACE inhibitors; however, they do not influence bradykinin metabolism and do not therefore cause cough.

Calcium antagonists. The dihydropyridines (e.g. amlodipine 5–10 mg daily, nifedipine 30–90 mg daily) are effective and usually well-tolerated antihypertensive drugs that are particularly useful in the elderly. Side-effects include flushing, palpitations and fluid retention. The rate-limiting calcium antagonists (e.g. diltiazem 200–300 mg daily, verapamil 240 mg daily) can be useful when hypertension coexists with angina but they may cause bradycardia. The main side-effect of verapamil is constipation.

Other drugs. A variety of vasodilators are used to treat hypertension. These include the α1-adrenoceptor antagonists (α-blockers), such as prazosin (0.5–20 mg daily in divided doses), indoramin (25–100 mg twice daily) and doxazosin (1–4 mg daily), and drugs that act directly on vascular smooth muscle, such as hydralazine (25–100 mg 12-hourly) and minoxidil (10–50 mg daily). Side-effects include first-dose and postural hypotension, headache, tachycardia and fluid retention. Minoxidil also causes increased facial hair and is therefore unsuitable for female patients.

Centrally acting drugs, such as methyldopa (initial dose 250 mg 8-hourly) and clonidine (0.05–0.1 mg 8-hourly), are effective antihypertensive drugs but cause fatigue and are usually poorly tolerated.

Choice of antihypertensive drug

Trials that have compared the major classes of antihypertensive drug (thiazides, β-blockers, calcium antagonists, ACE inhibitors and α-blockers) have shown no consistent or important differences in outcome, efficacy, side-effects or quality of life. The choice of antihypertensive therapy is therefore usually dictated by cost, convenience, the response to treatment and freedom from side-effects. Nevertheless, comorbid conditions may have an important influence on initial drug selection (see Box 12.24); for example, a β-blocker might be the most appropriate treatment for a patient with angina unless there is also a history of asthma. Thiazide diuretics and dihydropyridine calcium antagonists are the most suitable drugs for the treatment of high blood pressure in elderly people.

Although some patients can be satisfactorily treated with a single antihypertensive drug, a combination of drugs is often required to achieve optimal blood pressure control. Combination therapy may be desirable for other reasons; for example, low-dose therapy with two or three drugs may produce fewer unwanted effects than treatment with the maximum dose of a single drug. Moreover, some drugs have complementary or synergistic actions (see Box 12.25); for example, thiazides increase renin production while β-blockers depress it.

The emergency treatment of accelerated phase or malignant hypertension

In accelerated phase hypertension it is unwise to lower blood pressure too quickly because this may compromise tissue perfusion (due to altered autoregulation) and can cause cerebral damage, including occipital blindness, and precipitate coronary or renal insufficiency. Even in the presence of cardiac failure or hypertensive encephalopathy a controlled reduction, to a level of about 150/90, over a period of 24–36 hours is ideal.

In most patients it is possible to avoid parenteral therapy and bring blood pressure under control with bed rest and oral drug therapy. Intravenous or intramuscular labetalol

12.24 THE INFLUENCE OF COMORBIDITY ON THE CHOICE OF ANTIHYPERTENSIVE DRUG THERAPY

Comorbid condition	Drug therapy	
	Favourable effects	Undesirable effects
Atrial fibrillation	β-blockers Rate-limiting calcium antagonists	
Bronchospasm		β-blockers
Coronary artery disease Angina Previous MI	β-blockers Calcium antagonists ACE inhibitors	
Depression		β-blockers
Diabetes	ACE inhibitors	
Erectile dysfunction		β-blockers Thiazides
Essential tremor	β-blockers	
Gout and hyperuricaemia		Diuretics
Heart block		β-blockers Rate-limiting calcium antagonists
Heart failure	ACE inhibitors Diuretics	Most calcium antagonists
Peripheral vascular disease		β-blockers
Prostatism	α-blockers	
Raynaud's phenomenon	Nifedipine	β-blockers
Renovascular disease		ACE inhibitors Angiotensin II receptor antagonists

12.25 LOGICAL ANTIHYPERTENSIVE DRUG COMBINATIONS

- Diuretic   plus   β-blocker
                                   ACE inhibitor
- β-blocker   plus   Diuretic
                                   Calcium antagonist
                                   α-blocker
- ACE inhibitor plus   Diuretic
                                   Calcium antagonist

(2 mg/min to a maximum of 200 mg), intravenous glyceryl trinitrate (0.6–1.2 mg/hour), intramuscular hydralazine (5 or 10 mg aliquots repeated at half-hourly intervals), and intravenous sodium nitroprusside (0.3–1.0 mg/kg body weight per minute) are all effective remedies but require careful supervision, preferably in an intensive care unit.

Refractory hypertension

The common causes of treatment failure in hypertension are non-compliance with drug therapy, inadequate therapy, and failure to recognise an underlying cause such as renal artery stenosis or phaeochromocytoma; of these, the first is by far the most prevalent. There is no easy solution to compliance problems, but simple treatment regimens, attempts to improve rapport with the patient and careful supervision may all help.

Adjuvant drug therapy

Aspirin. Antiplatelet therapy is a powerful means of reducing cardiovascular risk but may cause bleeding, particularly intracerebral haemorrhage, in a small number of patients. The benefits of aspirin therapy are thought to outweigh the risks in hypertensive patients aged 50 or over who have well-controlled blood pressure and either target organ damage, diabetes or a 10-year coronary heart disease risk of more than 15%.

Statins. Treating hyperlipidaemia can also produce a substantial reduction in cardiovascular risk. Cost is the main constraint on statin therapy in many health-care

ISSUES IN OLDER PEOPLE
TREATMENT OF HYPERTENSION

- More than half of all people over the age of 60 have hypertension (including isolated systolic hypertension).
- Hypertension is the most important risk factor for myocardial infarction, heart failure and stroke in older people.
- The absolute benefit of antihypertensive treatment is greatest in the elderly (at least up to 80 years).
- Target BP should be similar to that for younger patients.
- Older patients tolerate antihypertensive treatment as well as younger patients.
- Low-dose thiazides are the drug of choice, but in the presence of coexistent disease (e.g. angina, diabetes) other agents may be more appropriate.

systems. Nevertheless, these drugs are strongly indicated in patients who have a total serum cholesterol of > 5 mmol/l and established vascular disease, or hypertension with a high (> 30% in 10 years) risk of developing coronary heart disease (see pp. 422–424).

ABNORMAL HEART SOUNDS AND MURMURS

The first clinical manifestation of heart disease may be the discovery of an abnormal sound on auscultation (see Box 12.26). Such a finding may be incidental—for example, during a routine childhood examination—or may be prompted by symptoms of heart disease. Clinical evaluation is always helpful but an echocardiogram is often necessary to confirm the nature of an abnormal heart sound or murmur.

Is the sound cardiac?

Additional heart sounds and murmurs demonstrate a consistent relationship to a specific part of the cardiac cycle, but extracardiac sounds (e.g. pleural rub or venous hum) do not. Pericardial friction produces a characteristic scratching or crunching noise, which often has two components corresponding to atrial and ventricular systole and may vary with posture and respiration.

Is the sound pathological?

Pathological sounds and murmurs are the product of turbulent blood flow or rapid ventricular filling due to abnormal loading conditions.

Some added sounds are physiological but may also occur in pathological conditions; for example, a third sound is common in young people and in pregnancy but is also a feature of heart failure (see Box 12.26). Similarly, a systolic murmur due to turbulence across the right ventricular outflow tract may occur in hyperdynamic states (e.g. anaemia, pregnancy) but may also be due to pulmonary stenosis or an intracardiac shunt leading to volume overload of the right ventricle (e.g. atrial septal defect).

Benign (physiological) murmurs do not occur in diastole (see Box 12.27), and systolic murmurs that radiate or are associated with a thrill are almost always pathological.

12.26 NORMAL AND ABNORMAL HEART SOUNDS				
Sound	**Timing**	**Characteristics**	**Mechanisms**	**Variable features**

First heart sound (S1)	Onset of systole	Usually single or narrowly split	Closure of mitral and tricuspid valves	Loud
				  Hyperdynamic circulation (anaemia, pregnancy, thyrotoxicosis)
				  Mitral stenosis
				Soft
				  Heart failure
				  Mitral regurgitation

Second heart sound (S2)	End of systole	Split on inspiration Single on expiration (see p. 364)	Closure of aortic and pulmonary valve A_2 first P_2 second	Fixed wide splitting with atrial septal defect Wide but variable splitting with delayed right heart emptying (e.g. right bundle branch block) Reversed splitting due to delayed left heart emptying (e.g. left bundle branch block)

Third heart sound (S3)	Early in diastole, just after S2	Low pitch, often heard as 'gallop'	From ventricular wall due to abrupt cessation of rapid filling	Physiological
				  Young people
				  Pregnancy
				Pathological
				  Heart failure
				  Mitral regurgitation

Fourth heart sound (S4)	End of diastole, just before S1	Low pitch Always a pathological finding	Ventricular origin (stiff ventricle and augmented atrial contraction) related to atrial filling	Absent in atrial fibrillation A feature of severe left ventricular hypertrophy (e.g. hypertrophic cardiomyopathy)
Systolic clicks	Early or mid-systole	Brief, high-intensity sound	Valvular aortic stenosis Valvular pulmonary stenosis Floppy mitral valve Prosthetic heart sounds from opening and closing of normally functioning mechanical valves	Click may be lost when stenotic valve becomes thickened or calcified Prosthetic clicks lost when valve obstructed by thrombus or vegetations
Opening snap (OS)	Early in diastole	High pitch, brief duration	Opening of stenosed leaflets of mitral valve Prosthetic heart sounds	Moves closer to S2 as mitral stenosis becomes more severe. May be absent in calcific mitral stenosis

12.27 FEATURES OF A BENIGN OR INNOCENT HEART MURMUR

- Soft
- Mid-systolic
- Heard at left sternal edge
- No radiation
- No other cardiac abnormalities

Auscultatory evaluation of a heart murmur

Timing, intensity, location, radiation and quality are all useful clues to the origin and nature of a heart murmur (see Box 12.28). Radiation of a murmur is determined by the direction of turbulent blood flow and is only detectable when there is a high-velocity jet, e.g. in mitral regurgitation (radiation from apex to axilla) or aortic stenosis (radiation from base to neck). Similarly, the pitch and quality of the sound can help to distinguish the murmur, e.g. the 'blowing' murmur of mitral regurgitation or the 'rasping' murmur of aortic stenosis.

The position of a murmur in relation to the cardiac cycle should be assessed by timing it with the heart sounds, carotid pulse and apex beat; this is a very valuable discriminant (see Figs 12.28 and 12.29).

Systolic murmurs (see Box 12.29) associated with ventricular outflow tract obstruction occur in mid-systole and have a crescendo-decrescendo pattern reflecting the changing velocity of blood flow. Pansystolic murmurs maintain a constant intensity and extend from the first

12.28 AUSCULTATORY FEATURES OF HEART MURMURS

When does it occur?

- Time the murmur using heart sounds, carotid pulse and the apex beat. Is it systolic or diastolic?
- Does the murmur extend throughout systole or diastole or is it confined to a shorter part of the cardiac cycle?

How loud is it? (intensity)

- Grade 1   Very soft (only audible in ideal conditions)
- Grade 2   Soft
- Grade 3   Moderate
- Grade 4   Loud with associated thrill
- Grade 5   Very loud
- Grade 6   Heard without stethoscope

N.B. Diastolic murmurs are sometimes graded 1–4.

Where is it heard best? (location)

- Listen over the apex and base of the heart including the aortic and pulmonary areas

Where does it radiate?

- Evaluate radiation to the neck, axilla or back

What does it sound like? (pitch and quality)

- Pitch is determined by flow (high pitch indicates high-velocity flow)
- Is the intensity constant or variable?

heart sound throughout systole (up to and beyond the second heart sound). They occur when blood leaks from a ventricle into a low-pressure chamber at an even or constant velocity; mitral regurgitation, tricuspid regurgitation and ventricular septal defect are the only causes of a pansystolic murmur. Late systolic murmurs are unusual but may occur in mitral valve prolapse (if the mitral regurgitation is confined to late systole) and hypertrophic cardiomyopathy (if dynamic obstruction occurs late in systole).

Mid-diastolic murmurs are due to accelerated or turbulent flow across the mitral or tricuspid valves. They are low-pitched noises that are often difficult to hear and should be evaluated with the bell of the stethoscope. A mid-diastolic murmur may be due to mitral stenosis

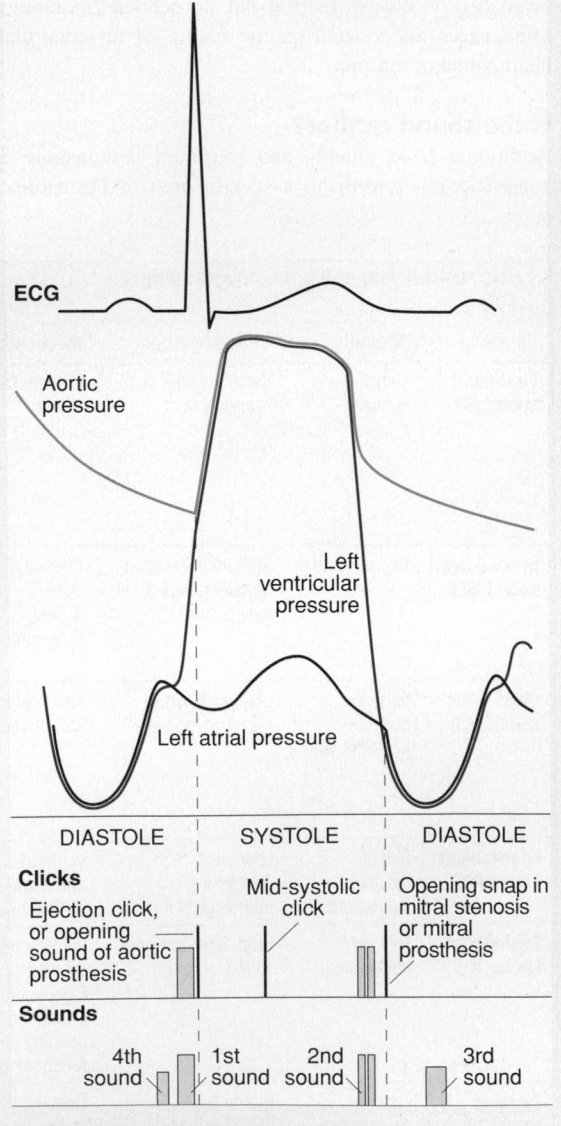

Fig. 12.28 The relationship of the cardiac cycle to the electrocardiogram, the left ventricular pressure wave and the position of heart sounds.

12.29 FEATURES OF SOME COMMON SYSTOLIC MURMURS

Condition	Timing and duration	Intensity and quality	Location and radiation	Associated features
Aortic stenosis	Mid-systolic	Loud rasping	Base and left sternal edge, radiating to suprasternal notch and carotids	Single second heart sound Ejection click (in young patients) Slow rising pulse Left ventricular hypertrophy (pressure overload)
Mitral regurgitation	Pansystolic	Loud blowing	Apex, radiating to axilla	Soft first heart sound Third heart sound Left ventricular hypertrophy (volume overload)
Ventricular septal defect (VSD)	Pansystolic	Harsh	Lower left sternal edge, radiating to whole praecordium	Thrill Biventricular hypertrophy
Benign	Mid-systolic	Soft	Left sternal edge, no radiation	No other signs of heart disease

(located at the apex and axilla), tricuspid stenosis (located at the left sternal edge), increased flow across the mitral valve (e.g. the to and fro murmur of severe mitral regurgitation) or increased flow across the tricuspid valve (e.g. left-to-right shunt through a large atrial septal defect). Early diastolic murmurs have a soft, blowing quality with a decrescendo pattern and should be evaluated with the diaphragm of the stethoscope; they are due to regurgitation across the aortic or pulmonary valves and are best heard at the left sternal edge with the patient sitting forward in held expiration.

Continuous murmurs result from a combination of systolic and diastolic flow (e.g. persistent ductus arteriosus) and must be distinguished from extracardiac noises such as bruits from arterial shunts, venous hums (high rates of venous flow in children) and pericardial friction rubs.

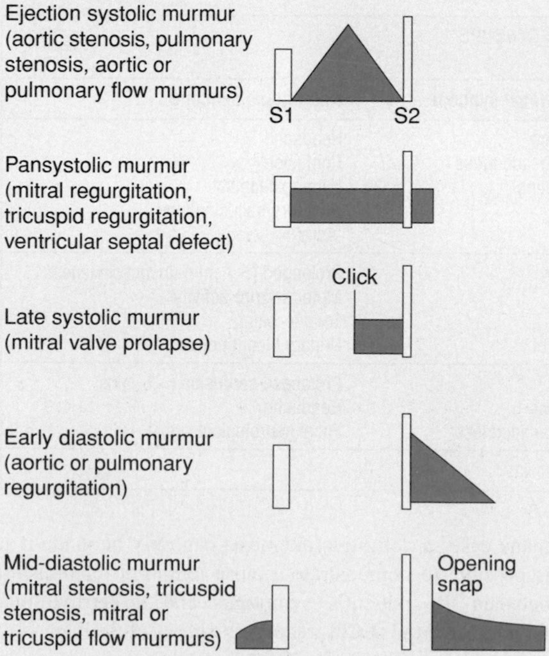

Ejection systolic murmur (aortic stenosis, pulmonary stenosis, aortic or pulmonary flow murmurs)

Pansystolic murmur (mitral regurgitation, tricuspid regurgitation, ventricular septal defect)

Late systolic murmur (mitral valve prolapse)

Early diastolic murmur (aortic or pulmonary regurgitation)

Mid-diastolic murmur (mitral stenosis, tricuspid stenosis, mitral or tricuspid flow murmurs)

Fig. 12.29 The timing and pattern of cardiac murmurs.

The characteristics of specific valve defects and congenital anomalies are described in the relevant sections later in the chapter.

PRESYNCOPE AND SYNCOPE

A wide variety of cardiovascular disorders can cause an abrupt fall in cerebral perfusion that may manifest as recurrent or isolated episodes of presyncope (lightheadedness) and syncope (sudden loss of consciousness).

Differential diagnosis

The common causes of blackouts and funny turns are listed in Figure 12.30. Diagnosis may be difficult but the probable mechanism of the patient's symptoms can usually be determined by careful analysis of the history. For example, a history of vertigo is suggestive of a labyrinthine or central vestibular disorder (see p. 1121).

Whenever possible, an accurate description of the attack should be obtained from the patient and a witness. Particular attention should be paid to possible precipitants or triggers such as medication, exercise and alcohol, the unconscious period and the recovery phase. In cardiac syncope (arrhythmia and structural heart disease), recovery is usually rapid; in contrast, patients with vasovagal syncope often feel nauseated and unwell for several minutes, and patients with neurogenic syncope usually take more than 5 minutes to recover. Some useful discriminants which can help to identify the likely mechanism of syncope are listed in Box 12.30.

A careful history, clinical examination and simple tests will often reveal the cause of recurrent syncope without recourse to complex and expensive investigations. In the remaining cases the pattern and description of the patient's symptoms should indicate the probable mechanism of syncope and will therefore determine subsequent investigations (see Fig. 12.31).

Arrhythmia

Lightheadedness may occur at the onset of a wide variety of arrhythmias but blackouts (Adams–Stokes attacks, see

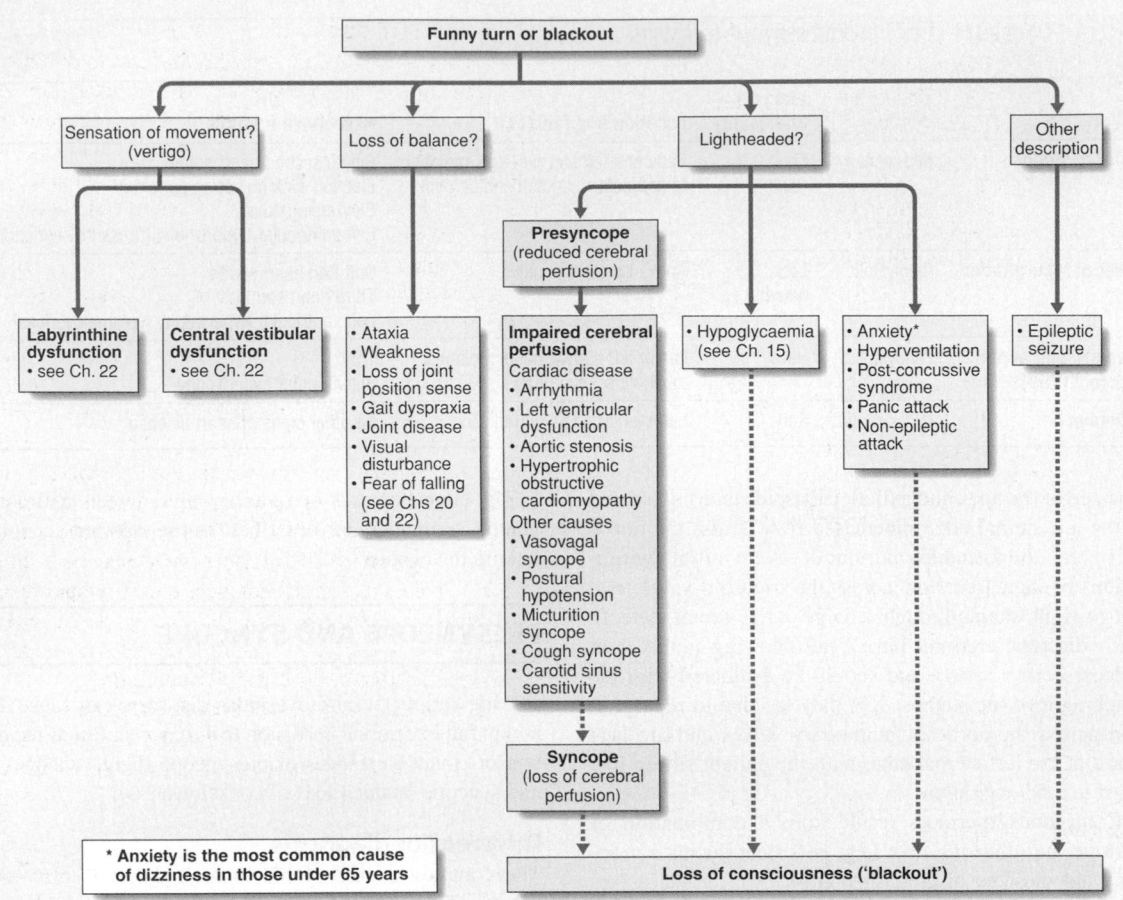

Fig. 12.30 The differential diagnosis of syncope and presyncope.

12.30 TYPICAL FEATURES OF CARDIAC, VASOVAGAL AND NEUROGENIC SYNCOPE			
	Cardiac syncope	**Vasovagal syncope**	**Neurogenic syncope**
Premonitory symptoms	Lightheadedness Palpitation Chest pain Breathlessness	Nausea Lightheadedness Sweating	Headache Confusion Hyperexcitability Olfactory hallucinations 'Aura'
Unconscious period	Extreme 'death-like' pallor	Pallor	Prolonged (> 1 min) unconsciousness Motor seizure activity* Tongue-biting Urinary incontinence
Recovery	Rapid recovery (< 1 min) Flushing	Slow Nausea Lightheadedness	Prolonged confusion (> 5 mins) Headache Focal neurological signs
*N.B. Cardiac syncope can also cause convulsions by inducing cerebral anoxia.			

p. 414) are usually due to profound bradycardia or malignant ventricular tachyarrhythmias. Prolonged ambulatory ECG recordings may help to establish the diagnosis but are of limited value unless the patient experiences typical symptoms while the recorder is in place. Minor rhythm disturbances are common in the healthy population and in many cases a definitive diagnosis can only be made if it is possible to demonstrate a close temporal relationship between the patient's symptoms and an arrhythmia. Patient-activated ECG recorders are useful diagnostic aids, and in particularly difficult cases tiny implantable ECG recorders may be used.

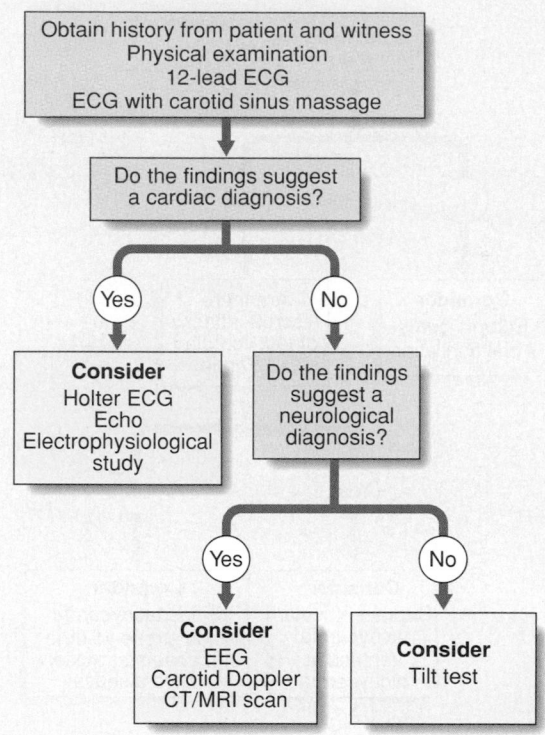

Fig. 12.31 A simple guide to the investigation and diagnosis of recurrent presyncope and syncope.

Structural heart disease

Severe aortic stenosis, hypertrophic obstructive cardiomyopathy and critical coronary artery disease can cause lightheadedness or syncope on exertion. This is usually mediated by profound hypotension due to the combination of a reduction in cardiac output and a drop in peripheral vascular resistance, but may also be the consequence of an arrhythmia.

Hypersensitive carotid sinus syndrome

Hypersensitivity of the carotid baroreceptors can cause recurrent episodes of altered consciousness by promoting inappropriate bradycardia and vasodilatation. The diagnosis can be established by monitoring the ECG and blood pressure during carotid sinus massage; however, this should not be attempted in patients with suspected or proven carotid vascular disease. A positive cardio-inhibitory response is defined as a sinus pause of 3 seconds or more; a positive vasodepressor response is defined as a fall in systolic blood pressure of more than 50 mmHg. Carotid sinus massage will produce positive findings in about 10% of elderly subjects but fewer than 25% of these individuals will report spontaneous syncope. Symptoms should not therefore be attributed to the hypersensitive carotid sinus syndrome unless they are reproduced by carotid sinus massage. Dual-chamber pacing may relieve symptoms that are due to bradycardia.

Vasovagal syncope

This is mediated by the Bezold–Jarisch reflex and is usually triggered by a reduction in venous return due to prolonged standing, excessive heat or a large meal. Concomitant sympathetic activation then leads to vigorous contraction of the relatively underfilled ventricles and engages the reflex by stimulating ventricular mechanoreceptors. This produces parasympathetic (vagal) activation and sympathetic withdrawal causing bradycardia, vasodilatation or both. Head-up tilt testing, which involves asking the patient to lie on a table that is then tilted to an angle of 70° for up to 45 minutes while the ECG and blood pressure are monitored, can be used to confirm the diagnosis. A positive test is characterised by profound bradycardia (cardio-inhibitory response) and/or hypotension (vasodepressor response) that is associated with typical symptoms. Treatment is often unnecessary but in severe cases β-blockers (which inhibit the initial sympathetic activation) or disopyramide (a vagolytic agent) may be helpful. A dual-chamber pacemaker can be useful if symptoms are predominantly due to bradycardia. Finally, the subgroup of patients with a urinary sodium excretion of less than 170 mmol/24 hours may respond to salt loading.

Some variants of vasovagal syncope occur in the presence of identifiable triggers (e.g. cough syncope, micturition syncope) and are known collectively as situational syncope.

Postural hypotension

Symptomatic postural hypotension is caused by a failure of the normal compensatory mechanisms. Relative hypovolaemia (often due to excessive diuretic therapy), sympathetic degeneration (diabetes, Parkinson's disease, ageing) and drug therapy (vasodilators, antidepressants) can all cause or aggravate the problem. Treatment is often ineffective; however, withdrawing unnecessary medication while advising the patient to wear graduated elastic stockings and get up slowly may be helpful. Treatment with non-steroidal anti-inflammatory drugs and fludrocortisone may also be of value.

PALPITATION

Palpitation is a very common and sometimes frightening symptom. Patients may use the term to describe a wide variety of sensations including an unusually erratic, fast, slow or forceful heart beat and even chest pain or breathlessness. Initial evaluation should concentrate on determining the likely mechanism of the symptom and whether or not there is significant underlying heart disease.

A detailed description of the sensation is essential and it is often helpful to ask patients to illustrate their experience by tapping out the heart beat on their chest or a table top. A provisional diagnosis can usually be made on the basis of a careful and thorough history (see Box 12.31 and Fig. 12.32) and investigations are often unnecessary;

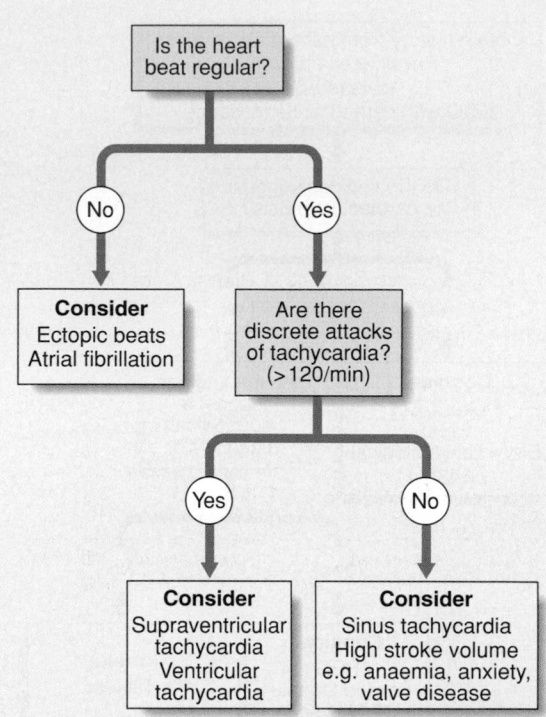

Fig. 12.32 A simple approach to the diagnosis of palpitation.

however, it may be necessary to obtain an ECG recording during an attack of typical palpitation to make a definitive diagnosis.

Recurrent but short-lived bouts of an irregular heart beat are usually due to atrial or ventricular extrasystoles (ectopic beats). Some patients will describe the experience as a 'flip' or a 'jolt' in the chest, while others report dropped or missed beats. Extrasystoles are often more frequent during periods of stress or debility; they may also be triggered by alcohol and some foodstuffs such as strong cheese or chocolate.

Poorly defined attacks of a pounding, forceful and relatively fast (90–120/min) heart beat are a common manifestation of anxiety. This sort of symptom complex may also be a manifestation of other forms of a hyperdynamic circulation such as anaemia, pregnancy and thyrotoxicosis, and can occur in some forms of valve disease (e.g. aortic regurgitation).

Discrete bouts of a very rapid (> 120/min) heart beat are more likely to be due to a paroxysmal arrhythmia. Atrial, junctional and ventricular tachycardias may all present in this way. In contrast, episodes of atrial fibrillation typically present with a characteristically irregular and chaotic tachycardia.

Palpitation is usually benign and, even if the patient's symptoms are due to an arrhythmia, the outlook is good if there is no underlying structural heart disease. Most cases are due to an awareness of the normal heart beat, a sinus tachycardia or benign extrasystoles that have been triggered by stress, an intercurrent illness, or the effects of caffeine, alcohol and nicotine. Nevertheless, the experience is often unpleasant and frightening. In these situations a careful explanation and reassurance may be all that is required. However, if the patient continues to experience distressing symptoms a spell of treatment with a low dose of a β-blocker may be helpful.

The diagnosis and management of individual arrhythmias are considered in detail on pages 405–420.

ATRIAL FIBRILLATION

Atrial fibrillation (AF) is the most common sustained cardiac arrhythmia, with an overall prevalence of 0.5% in the adult population of the UK. It can be classified as paroxysmal (discrete self-terminating episodes), persistent (prolonged episodes that can be terminated by electrical or chemical cardioversion) or permanent. However, it may be difficult to identify which form of the arrhythmia is present in patients with asymptomatic or recent-onset AF. Moreover, more than one form may occur in the same patient at different times; for example, permanent AF is often preceded by bouts of paroxysmal AF and one or more episodes of persistent AF.

During episodes of AF, the atria beat rapidly, chaotically and ineffectively while the ventricles respond at irregular intervals, producing the characteristic 'irregularly irregular' pulse. The ECG (see Fig. 12.33) shows normal but irregular QRS complexes; there are no P waves but the baseline may show irregular fibrillation waves.

AF may be the first manifestation of many forms of heart disease (see Box 12.32), particularly those that are associated with enlargement or dilatation of the atria. Alcohol, hyperthyroidism and chest disease are also common causes of AF. Multiple aetiological factors often coexist (e.g. alcohol, hypertension and coronary disease); nevertheless, 50% of all patients with paroxysmal AF and 20% of patients with persistent or permanent AF have

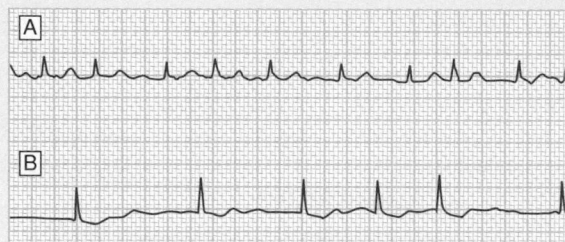

Fig. 12.33 Two examples of atrial fibrillation. The QRS complexes are irregular and there are no P waves. **A** There is usually a fast ventricular rate, often between 120 and 160/min, at the onset of atrial fibrillation. **B** However, in chronic atrial fibrillation the ventricular rate may be much slower due to the effects of medication and AV nodal fatigue.

12.32 COMMON CAUSES OF ATRIAL FIBRILLATION

- Coronary artery disease (including acute myocardial infarction)
- Valvular heart disease, especially rheumatic mitral valve disease
- Hypertension
- Sinoatrial disease (see p. 412)
- Hyperthyroidism
- Alcohol
- Cardiomyopathy
- Congenital heart disease
- Chest infection
- Pulmonary embolism
- Pericardial disease
- Idiopathic (lone AF)

---

otherwise normal hearts (an entity sometimes known as 'lone atrial fibrillation').

The onset of AF can cause palpitation, and may precipitate or aggravate cardiac failure in patients with an abnormal heart, especially those with mitral stenosis or poor left ventricular function. A fall in blood pressure may cause lightheadedness, and chest pain may occur in patients with underlying coronary disease. Symptoms tend to be most troublesome at the outset and may improve if the arrhythmia persists. AF is often completely asymptomatic, in which case it is usually discovered as the result of a routine examination or ECG.

AF is associated with a twofold increase in mortality and significant morbidity which are largely attributable to the effects of the underlying heart disease and the risk of cerebral embolism. Careful assessment, risk stratification and therapy can improve the outlook considerably.

Management
The optimal assessment of newly diagnosed AF includes a full history, clinical examination, 12-lead ECG, echocardiogram and thyroid function tests. Additional investigations such as exercise testing may be required to determine the nature and extent of any underlying heart disease. Biochemical evidence of hyperthyroidism will be found in approximately 10% of patients with otherwise unexplained AF.

When AF complicates an acute illness (e.g. chest infection, pulmonary embolism) effective treatment of the primary disorder will usually restore sinus rhythm. In other situations the main objectives of treatment are to restore sinus rhythm as soon as possible, prevent recurrent episodes of AF, optimise the heart rate during periods of AF, minimise the risk of thromboembolism and treat any underlying disease.

Paroxysmal atrial fibrillation
Occasional attacks that are well tolerated do not necessarily require treatment, but β-blockers and class 1c drugs such as flecainide and propafenone (see p. 417) are the drugs of first choice if symptoms are troublesome. Beta-blockers may have particular advantages in patients with underlying structural heart disease or hypertension and in those who are prone to develop AF during exertion or at times of stress. Digoxin is not effective but amiodarone is a useful second-line drug. Permanent atrial pacing may help to maintain sinus rhythm in patients with bradycardia-related AF, which is often a manifestation of sinoatrial disease (see p. 412). Some forms of paroxysmal AF can be treated by radiofrequency ablation (see p. 419).

Persistent atrial fibrillation
Rate control and cardioversion are both acceptable treatment options. An attempt to restore sinus rhythm is particularly appropriate if the arrhythmia has precipitated troublesome symptoms and there is a modifiable or treatable underlying cause. Electrical cardioversion (see p. 418) is initially successful in three-quarters of patients but relapse is frequent (25–50% at 1 month and 70–90% at 1 year). Attempts to restore and maintain sinus rhythm are most successful if AF has been present for less than 3 months, the patient is young, and there is no important structural heart disease.

Immediate DC cardioversion, after the administration of intravenous heparin, is appropriate if AF has been present for less than 48 hours. An attempt to restore sinus rhythm by infusing intravenous flecainide is a safe and attractive alternative to electrical cardioversion if there is no underlying heart disease. In other situations DC cardioversion should be deferred until the patient has been established on warfarin, with an international normalised ratio (INR) of between 2 and 3:1, for a minimum of 3 weeks, and any underlying problems, such as hyperthyroidism, have been dealt with. Anticoagulation should be maintained for at least 1 month and ideally for 6 months following successful cardioversion; if relapse occurs, a second (or third) cardioversion may be appropriate. Concomitant anti-arrhythmic therapy with drugs such as amiodarone or β-blockers may reduce the risk of recurrence.

Permanent atrial fibrillation
If sinus rhythm cannot be restored, treatment should be directed towards maintaining an appropriate heart rate. Digoxin, β-blockers or rate-limiting calcium antagonists such as verapamil or diltiazem (see pp. 415–418) will reduce the ventricular rate by increasing the degree of AV

block. This alone may produce a striking improvement in overall cardiac function, particularly in patients with mitral stenosis. Beta-blockers and rate-limiting calcium antagonists are often more effective than digoxin at controlling the heart rate during exercise and may have additional benefits in patients with hypertension and/or structural heart disease. Combination therapy (e.g. digoxin + atenolol) is often advisable.

In exceptional cases, poorly controlled and symptomatic AF can be treated by deliberately inducing complete heart block with transvenous catheter radiofrequency ablation; a permanent pacemaker must be implanted at the same time.

Prevention of thromboembolism

Ineffective atrial contraction and left atrial dilatation predispose to stasis and may lead to thrombosis and systemic embolism, particularly stroke. The annual risk of stroke or systemic embolism in all forms of AF is approximately 5% but this is influenced by many factors (see Box 12.33) and may range from 0 to 15% (see Box 12.34).

Several large randomised trials have shown that treatment with adjusted-dose warfarin (target INR 2–3:1) reduces the risk of stroke by about two-thirds, at the cost of an annual risk of bleeding of approximately 1–1.5%,

whereas treatment with aspirin reduces the risk of stroke by only one-fifth (see EBM panel). Nevertheless, the patients in these trials were often highly selected and may not be representative of patients encountered in routine clinical practice where also the risks of anticoagulant treatment may be higher than experienced in the setting of a tightly controlled clinical trial.

ATRIAL FIBRILLATION—use of warfarin to reduce ischaemic stroke EBM

'Systematic reviews have found that anticoagulation with warfarin reduces the risk of ischaemic stroke in non-rheumatic atrial fibrillation by about 62% (absolute risk reduction 2.7% for primary prevention and 8.4% for secondary prevention), while aspirin reduces the risk by only 22% (absolute risk reduction 1.5% for primary prevention and 2.5% for secondary prevention). NNT for 1 year (warfarin vs placebo) = 18.'

- Hart RG, Benavente O, McBride R, Pearce LA. Antithrombotic therapy to prevent stroke in patients with atrial fibrillation: a meta-analysis. Ann Intern Med 1999; 131:492–501.
- Benavente O, Hart R, Koudstaal P, et al. Oral anticoagulants for preventing stroke in patients with non-valvular atrial fibrillation and no previous history of stroke or transient ischaemic attacks (Cochrane Review). Cochrane Library, issue 4, 2000. Oxford: Update Software.

Further information: 💻 www.sign.ac.uk

A careful assessment of the risk of embolism will help to define the possible benefits of antithrombotic therapy (see Box 12.34), which must be balanced against the potential hazards of treatment. Echocardiography is a valuable aid in risk stratification. Warfarin is indicated in patients at high or very high risk of stroke, unless anticoagulation poses unacceptable risks. Comorbid conditions that may be complicated by bleeding, such as peptic ulcer, uncontrolled hypertension, poor drug compliance and potential drug interactions, are all relative contraindications to warfarin. Patients at moderate risk of stroke may be treated with warfarin or aspirin after discussing the balance of risk and benefit with the individual. Young patients (under 65 years) with no evidence of structural heart disease have a very low risk of stroke; they do not require warfarin but may benefit from aspirin treatment.

12.33 RISK FACTORS FOR THROMBOEMBOLISM IN ATRIAL FIBRILLATION

- Previous ischaemic stroke or transient ischaemic attack
- Mitral valve disease
- Age over 65
- Hypertension
- Diabetes mellitus
- Heart failure
- Echocardiographic features of:
  - Left ventricular dysfunction
  - Mitral annular calcification

12.34 EFFECT OF RISK STATUS AND TREATMENT ON THE ANNUAL RISK OF STROKE IN NON-RHEUMATIC ATRIAL FIBRILLATION

Risk group	Untreated	Aspirin	Warfarin
Very high Previous stroke or transient ischaemic attack	12%	10%	5%
High Age > 65 and one other risk factor (see Box 12.33)	6.5%	5%	2.5%
Moderate Age > 65, no other risk factors Age < 65, other risk factors	4%	3%	1.5%
Low Age < 65 and no other risk factors	1.2%	1%	0.5%

N.B. In most studies the annual risk of significant bleeding during warfarin therapy is between 1.0 and 1.5%.

ISSUES IN OLDER PEOPLE
ATRIAL FIBRILLATION

- The prevalence of AF rises with age, reaching more than 10% in those over 75 years of age.
- Although sometimes asymptomatic, it is often accompanied by diastolic heart failure.
- AF may be the dominant feature of otherwise silent or occult hyperthyroidism.
- Cardioversion is followed by high rates (~70% at 1 year) of recurrent AF.
- AF is an important preventable cause of stroke (cerebral embolism). It is found in 15% of all stroke patients and 2–8% of patients with transient ischaemic attacks.
- Although the risk of thromboembolism rises with age, the hazards of anticoagulation also rise because of increased comorbidity, particularly falls and cognitive impairment.
- If anticoagulation is recommended, a target INR of 1.6–2.5 may represent the best balance of benefit and risk in those over the age of 75.

CARDIAC ARREST AND SUDDEN CARDIAC DEATH

Cardiac arrest describes the sudden and complete loss of cardiac function. There is no pulse, the patient loses consciousness and respiration ceases almost immediately; death is virtually inevitable unless effective treatment is given promptly.

Sudden and unexpected cardiac death is usually due to the development of a catastrophic arrhythmia and accounts for 25–30% of the people who die from cardiovascular disease, claiming an estimated 70 000 to 90 000 lives each year in the UK. Arrhythmias may complicate many types of heart disease and may sometimes occur in the absence of recognisable structural abnormalities (see Box 12.35). Sudden death is also occasionally due to an acute mechanical catastrophe such as cardiac rupture or aortic dissection (see p. 448).

Coronary artery disease is the most common cause of arrhythmic sudden death. One-third of all people developing myocardial infarction die before reaching hospital, many within an hour of the onset of acute symptoms, and the cardiac rhythm in the majority of these cases is ventricular fibrillation or pulseless ventricular tachycardia. Defibrillation is the only effective treatment for both of these arrhythmias, but the chances of a successful outcome fall by about 7–10% with each minute's delay. When cardiac arrest occurs outside hospital death is inevitable unless a defibrillator can be brought promptly to the patient.

The aim of basic life support is to maintain the circulation until more definitive treatment with advanced life support can be administered (see below). This has led to the concept of a 'chain of survival' which, like all chains, is only as strong as its weakest link (see Fig. 12.34). A victim of cardiac arrest is most likely to survive if all links in the chain are strong, i.e. if the arrest is witnessed, help is called immediately, basic life support is administered by a trained individual, the emergency medical services respond promptly, and defibrillation is achieved within a few minutes. Good training in both basic and advanced life support is essential to the practice of medicine and should be maintained by attending regular refresher courses.

12.35 COMMON CAUSES OF SUDDEN ARRHYTHMIC CARDIAC DEATH
Coronary artery disease (85%)
• Myocardial ischaemia
• Myocardial infarction
• Prior MI with myocardial scarring
Structural heart disease (10%)
• Aortic stenosis (see p. 458)
• Hypertrophic cardiomyopathy (see p. 476)
• Dilated cardiomyopathy (see p. 475)
• Arrhythmogenic right ventricular dysplasia (see p. 477)
• Congenital heart disease (see p. 467)
No structural heart disease (5%)
• Long QT syndrome (see p. 411)
• Brugada syndrome (see p. 412)
• Wolff–Parkinson–White syndrome (see p. 409)
• Adverse drug reactions (torsades de pointes—see p. 411)
• Severe electrolyte abnormalities

Aetiology of cardiac arrest

Cardiac arrest may be due to ventricular fibrillation, pulseless ventricular tachycardia, asystole or electromechanical dissociation.

Ventricular fibrillation and pulseless ventricular tachycardia

This is the most common and most easily treatable cause of sudden death. Ventricular fibrillation produces rapid, ineffective, uncoordinated movement of the ventricles, which therefore produce no pulse. The ECG (see Fig. 12.35) shows chaotic, bizarre, irregular complexes. Ventricular tachycardia (see p. 410) may also cause loss

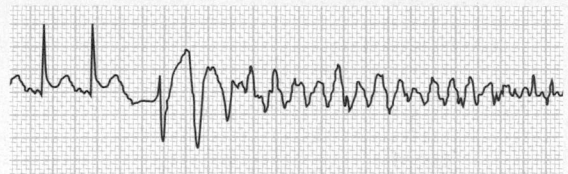

Fig. 12.35 Ventricular fibrillation. A bizarre chaotic rhythm initiated in this case by two ectopic beats in rapid succession.

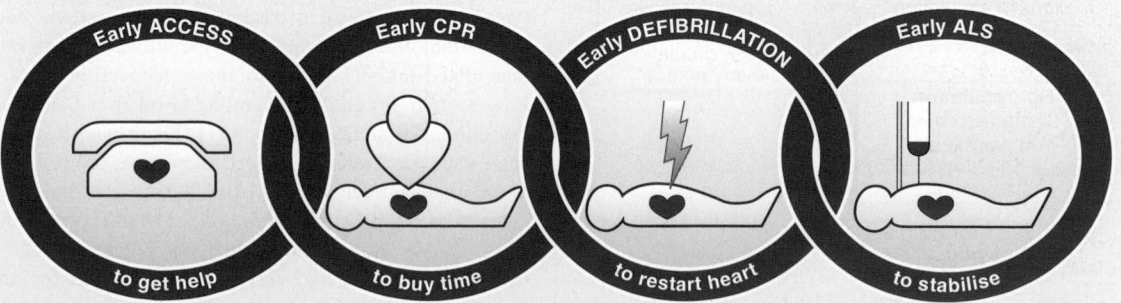

Fig. 12.34 The chain of survival in cardiac arrest. (CPR = cardiopulmonary resuscitation; ALS = advanced life support)

of cardiac output (pulseless ventricular tachycardia) and cardiac arrest, and may degenerate into ventricular fibrillation.

Ventricular asystole

This occurs when there is no electrical activity of the ventricles and is usually due to failure of the conducting tissue or massive ventricular damage complicating myocardial infarction. Cardiac massage or a blow to the chest can sometimes restore cardiac activity, although an artificial pacemaker may be needed to prevent further attacks.

Electromechanical dissociation

This occurs when there is no effective cardiac output despite the presence of normal or near-normal electrical activity. It may be caused by treatable conditions such as hypovolaemia or tension pneumothorax (see below) but is often due to cardiac rupture or massive pulmonary embolism and therefore carries a poor prognosis.

Management of cardiac arrest

Basic life support (BLS)

The management of the collapsed patient requires prompt assessment and restoration of the airway, breathing and circulation (ABC) using basic life support (see Fig. 12.36), with the aim of maintaining the circulation until more

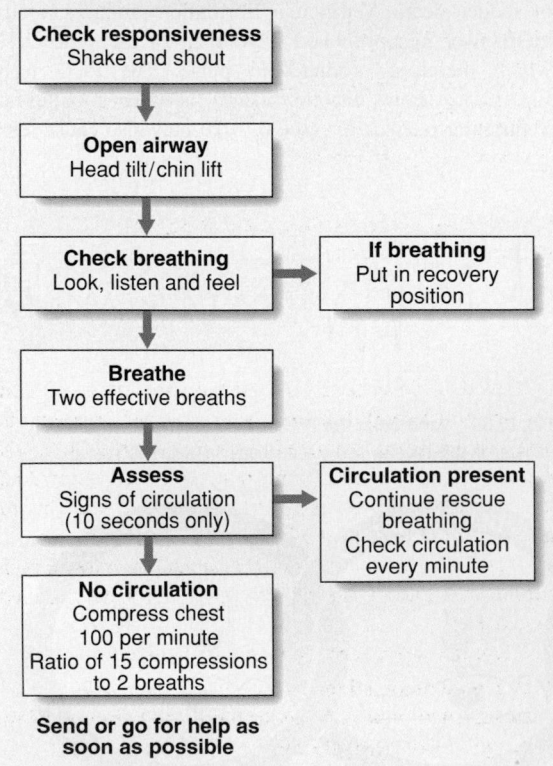

Send or go for help as soon as possible

Fig. 12.36 Algorithm for adult basic life support. For further information see www.resus.org.uk.

definitive treatment with advanced life support can be administered.

Advanced life support (ALS)

Advanced life support (see Fig. 12.37) aims to restore normal cardiac rhythm by defibrillation when the cause of cardiac arrest is due to a tachyarrhythmia, and/or to restore cardiac output by correcting other reversible causes of cardiac arrest. ALS provides support to the circulation additional to BLS by administering intravenous drugs, and by passing an endotracheal tube to administer positive pressure ventilation.

If cardiac arrest is witnessed, a praecordial thump may sometimes convert ventricular fibrillation or tachycardia to normal rhythm, but this is futile if cardiac arrest has lasted longer than a few seconds.

The priority in ALS is to assess the patient's cardiac rhythm by attaching a defibrillator/monitor. The most common arrhythmias causing cardiac arrest in adults are ventricular fibrillation (VF) or pulseless ventricular tachycardia (VT), and with prompt defibrillation these can usually be successfully treated. Defibrillation is firstly with 200 joules; if normal rhythm is not restored, a further shock of 200 joules is given; if unsuccessful, this is followed by a third shock of 360 joules. If these three shocks are unsuccessful, 1 mg of adrenaline (epinephrine) intravenously and a further 1 minute of cardiopulmonary resuscitation should be given before trying a further sequence of up to three shocks each at 360 joules.

Cardiac arrest may be due to asystole which can occasionally be mimicked by ventricular fibrillation of low amplitude, or 'fine VF'. If asystole cannot be confidently diagnosed, the patient should be regarded as having 'fine VF', and should be defibrillated. If an electrical rhythm is present which would be expected to produce a cardiac output, 'electromechanical dissociation' is present. There are several potentially reversible causes which can be easily remembered as a list of four Hs and four Ts (see green box, Fig. 12.37). In practical terms, electromechanical dissociation or definite asystole is treated without defibrillation by maintaining cardiopulmonary resuscitation (CPR) whilst seeking potentially reversible causes, i.e. following the 'non-VF/VT' limb of the ALS algorithm.

Survivors of cardiac arrest

Patients who survive a cardiac arrest caused by acute myocardial infarction need no specific treatment other than that routinely given to those recovering from an infarct; their prognosis is similar to other patients with myocardial infarction (see p. 437). Those with reversible causes such as exercise-induced ischaemia (see p. 425) or aortic stenosis (see p. 458) should have the underlying cause treated if possible. Survivors for whom no reversible cause can be found and treated are potentially at risk of another episode and should be considered for anti-arrhythmic therapy or implantation of an implantable cardioverter-defibrillator (see p. 419).

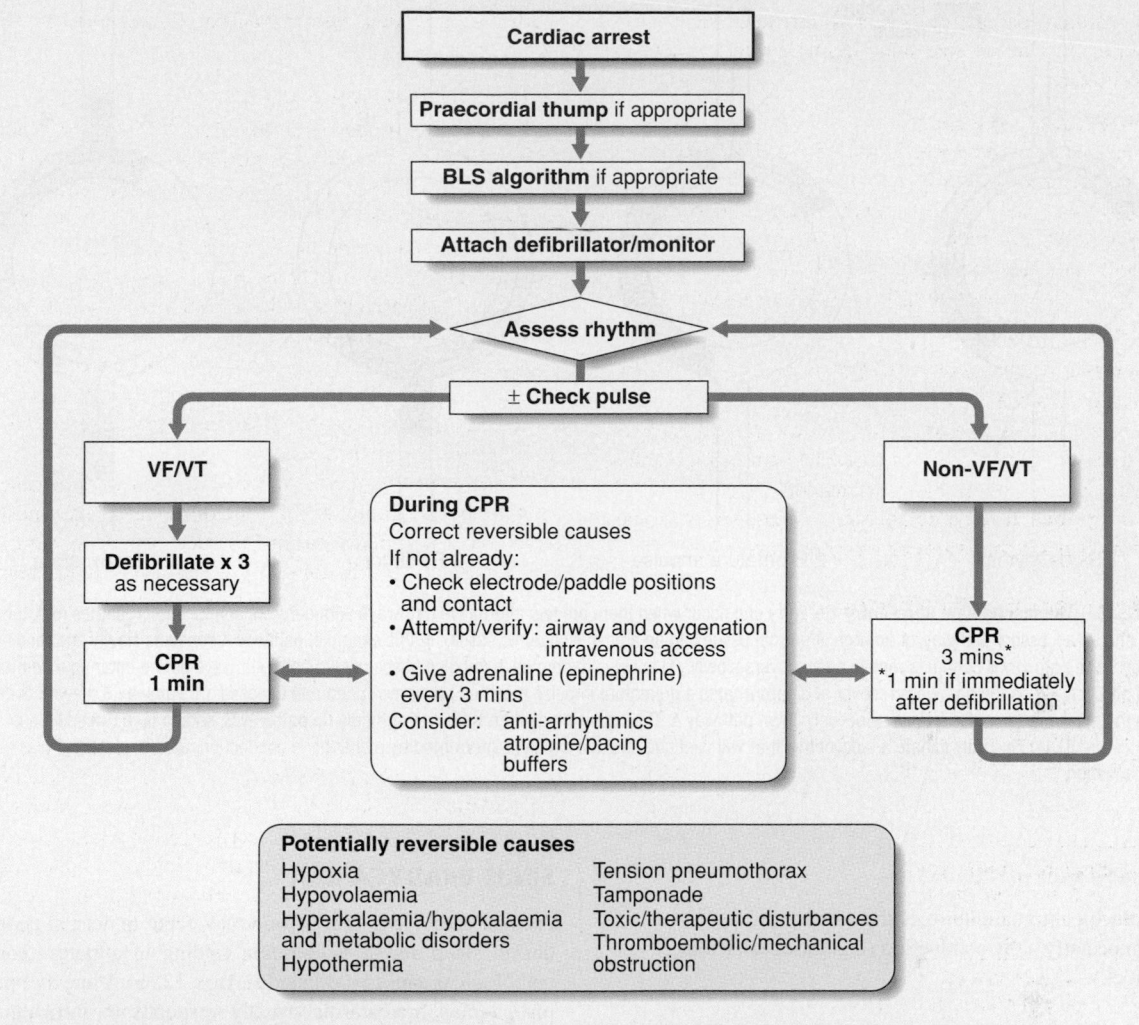

Fig. 12.37 Algorithm for adult advanced life support. For further information see www.resus.org.uk. (BLS = basic life support; VF = ventricular fibrillation; VT = pulseless ventricular tachycardia; CPR = cardiopulmonary resuscitation)

DISORDERS OF HEART RATE, RHYTHM AND CONDUCTION

The heart beat is normally initiated by an electrical discharge from the sinoatrial (sinus) node. The atria and ventricles then depolarise sequentially as electricity passes through the specialised conducting tissue (see Fig. 12.6, p. 365). The sinus node acts as a pacemaker and has its own intrinsic rate that is regulated by the autonomic nervous system; vagal activity slows the heart rate, and sympathetic activity accelerates it.

If the sinus rate becomes unduly slow, a lower centre may assume the role of pacemaker. This is known as an escape rhythm and may arise in the AV node (nodal rhythm) or the ventricles (idioventricular rhythm).

A cardiac arrhythmia is a disturbance in the electrical rhythm of the heart; this may be paroxysmal or continuous, and may cause sudden death, syncope, heart failure, light-headedness, palpitations or no symptoms at all. Arrhythmias are often a manifestation of structural heart disease but may also occur in the context of an otherwise normal heart.

A heart rate of more than 100/minute is called a tachycardia and a heart rate of less than 60/minute is called a bradycardia.

There are two mechanisms of tachycardia:

- increased automaticity—when the tachycardia is sustained by repeated spontaneous depolarisation of an ectopic focus or single cell
- re-entry—when the tachycardia is initiated by an ectopic beat but sustained by a closed loop or re-entry circuit (see Fig. 12.38). Most tachyarrhythmias are due to re-entry.

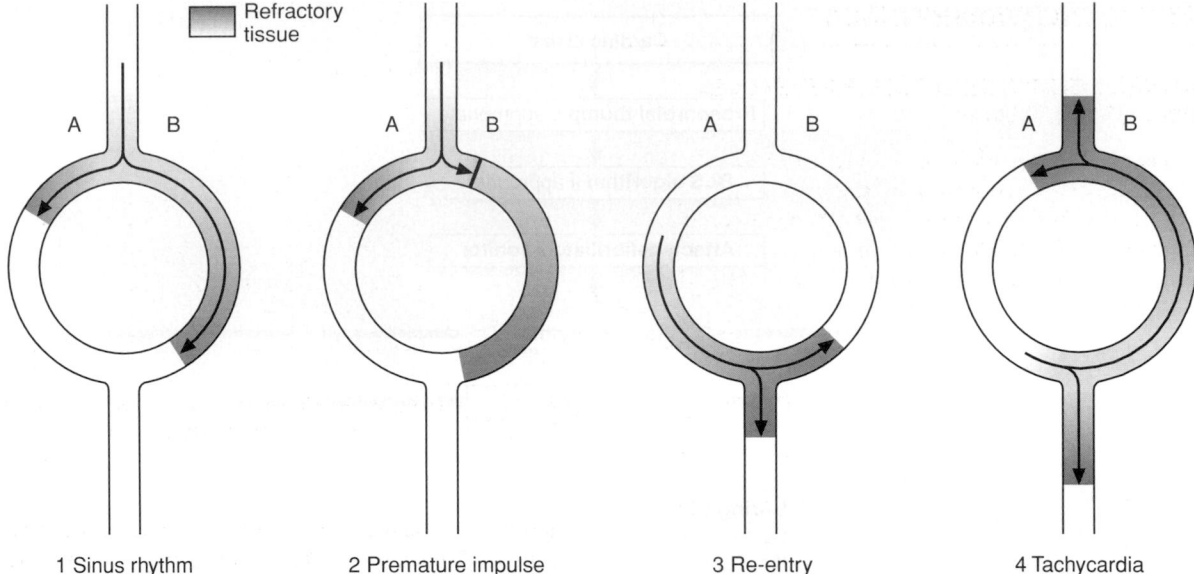

1 Sinus rhythm   2 Premature impulse   3 Re-entry   4 Tachycardia

Fig. 12.38 The mechanism of re-entry. Re-entry can occur when there are two alternative pathways with different conducting properties (e.g. the AV node and an accessory pathway, or an area of normal tissue and an area of ischaemic tissue). In this example, pathway A conducts slowly and recovers quickly while pathway B conducts rapidly and recovers slowly. (1) In sinus rhythm each impulse passes down both pathways before entering a common distal pathway. (2) As the pathways recover at different rates a premature impulse may find pathway A open and B closed. (3) Pathway B may recover while the premature impulse travels selectively down pathway A. The impulse may then travel retrogradely up pathway B, setting up a closed loop or re-entry circuit. (4) This may initiate a tachycardia that will continue until the circuit is interrupted by a change in conduction rates or electrical depolarisation.

Bradycardia may be due to:

• reduced automaticity (e.g. sinus bradycardia)
• abnormally slow conduction (e.g. atrioventricular block).

An arrhythmia may be supraventricular (sinus, atrial or junctional) or ventricular. Supraventricular rhythms usually produce narrow QRS complexes because the ventricles are depolarised normally through the AV node and bundle of His. In contrast, ventricular rhythms produce broad bizarre QRS complexes because the ventricles are activated through an abnormal pathway. However, occasionally a supraventricular rhythm can produce broad or wide QRS complexes due to coexisting bundle branch block or the presence of accessory conducting tissue (see below).

SINUS RHYTHMS

SINUS ARRHYTHMIA

Phasic alteration of the heart rate during respiration (the sinus rate increases during inspiration and slows during expiration) is a manifestation of normal autonomic nervous activity and is often particularly pronounced in children. A complete absence of this normal variation in heart rate with breathing or with changes in posture may be a feature of autonomic neuropathy.

SINUS BRADYCARDIA

A sinus rate of less than 60/min may occur in normal people during sleep and is a common finding in athletes. Some pathological causes are listed in Box 12.36. Acute symptomatic sinus bradycardia usually responds to intravenous atropine 0.6 mg.

SINUS TACHYCARDIA

This is defined as a sinus rate of more than 100/min, and is usually due to an increase in sympathetic activity associated with exercise, emotion or pathology (see Box 12.36). The rate seldom exceeds 160/min, except in infants.

12.36 SOME PATHOLOGICAL CAUSES OF SINUS BRADYCARDIA AND TACHYCARDIA 	
Sinus bradycardia	

• Myocardial infarction
• Sinus node disease
  (sick sinus syndrome)
• Hypothermia
• Hypothyroidism
	• Cholestatic jaundice
	• Raised intracranial pressure
	• Drugs, e.g. β-blocker, digoxin,
	  verapamil

Sinus tachycardia	
• Anxiety • Fever • Pregnancy • Anaemia • Heart failure	• Thyrotoxicosis • Phaeochromocytoma • Drugs, e.g. β-adrenoceptor agonists (bronchodilators)

ATRIAL TACHYARRHYTHMIAS

ATRIAL ECTOPIC BEATS (EXTRASYSTOLES, PREMATURE BEATS)

These usually cause no symptoms but can give the sensation of a missed beat or an abnormally strong beat. The ECG (see Fig. 12.39) shows a premature but otherwise normal QRS complex; if visible, the preceding P wave has a different configuration because the impulse starts at an abnormal site. Beyond reassurance no treatment is necessary.

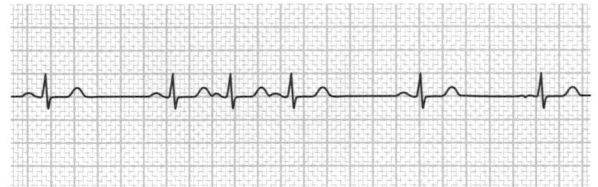

Fig. 12.39   Atrial ectopic beats. The first, second and fifth complexes are normal sinus beats. The third, fourth and sixth complexes are atrial ectopic beats with identical QRS complexes and abnormal (sometimes barely visible) P waves.

ATRIAL TACHYCARDIA

An ectopic atrial tachycardia due to increased automaticity is rare but is sometimes a manifestation of digitalis toxicity. The ECG shows an atrial rate of 140–220/min with abnormal P waves often accompanied by atrioventricular block (e.g. 2:1, 3:1 or variable). Management is similar to that for atrial flutter (see below).

ATRIAL FLUTTER

In this arrhythmia the atrial rate is approximately 300/min. It is usually associated with 2:1, 3:1, 4:1 atrioventricular block (with corresponding heart rates of 150, 100, 75); however, the degree of AV block often varies and occasionally every beat is conducted, producing a heart rate of 300/min. The ECG shows characteristic saw-toothed flutter waves (see Fig. 12.40). When there is regular 2:1 AV block it may be difficult to distinguish atrial flutter from supraventricular or

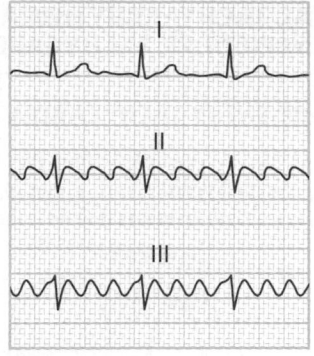

Fig. 12.40   Atrial flutter. Simultaneous recording showing atrial flutter with 3:1 block; flutter waves are only visible in leads II and III.

sinus tachycardia because alternate flutter waves are buried in the QRS complexes. This should always be suspected when there is a narrow complex tachycardia of 150/min. Carotid sinus massage or intravenous adenosine may help to establish the diagnosis by temporarily increasing the degree of AV block and revealing the flutter waves (see Fig. 12.41).

Management

Digoxin, β-blockers or verapamil can be used to control the ventricular rate (see pp. 417–418). However, in many cases it may be preferable to try and restore sinus rhythm by atrial overdrive pacing, direct current (DC) cardioversion or drug therapy. Amiodarone, propafenone or flecainide may be effective and can also be used to prevent recurrent episodes of atrial flutter (see p. 417). Radiofrequency catheter ablation (see p. 419) offers a high chance of complete cure and has become the treatment of choice for patients with persistent and troublesome symptoms.

ATRIAL FIBRILLATION

In this rhythm disorder there is rapid activation of the atria by multiple meandering wavelets, there is no coordinated contraction and only a proportion of impulses are conducted to the ventricles. The arrhythmia is extremely common and is discussed in detail on pages 400–402.

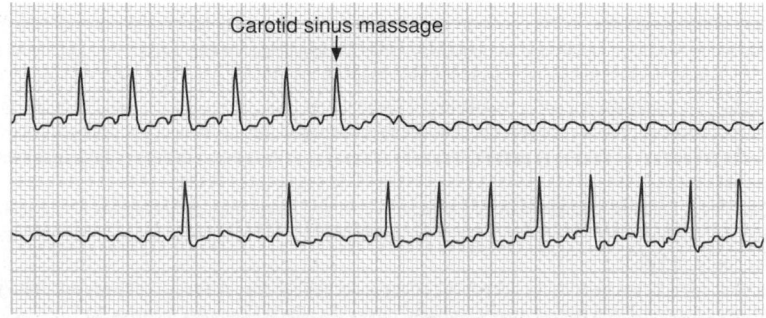

Carotid sinus massage

Fig. 12.41   Carotid sinus massage in atrial flutter: continuous trace. In this example, the diagnosis of atrial flutter with 2:1 block was established when carotid sinus massage produced temporary AV block revealing the flutter waves.

JUNCTIONAL TACHYARRHYTHMIAS (SUPRAVENTRICULAR TACHYCARDIA)

AV NODAL RE-ENTRY TACHYCARDIA

This rhythm is due to re-entry within the AV node and produces a regular tachycardia with a rate of between 140 and 220; it tends to occur in hearts that are otherwise normal

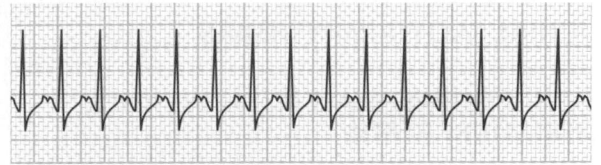

Fig. 12.42 Supraventricular tachycardia. The rate is 180/min and the QRS complexes are normal.

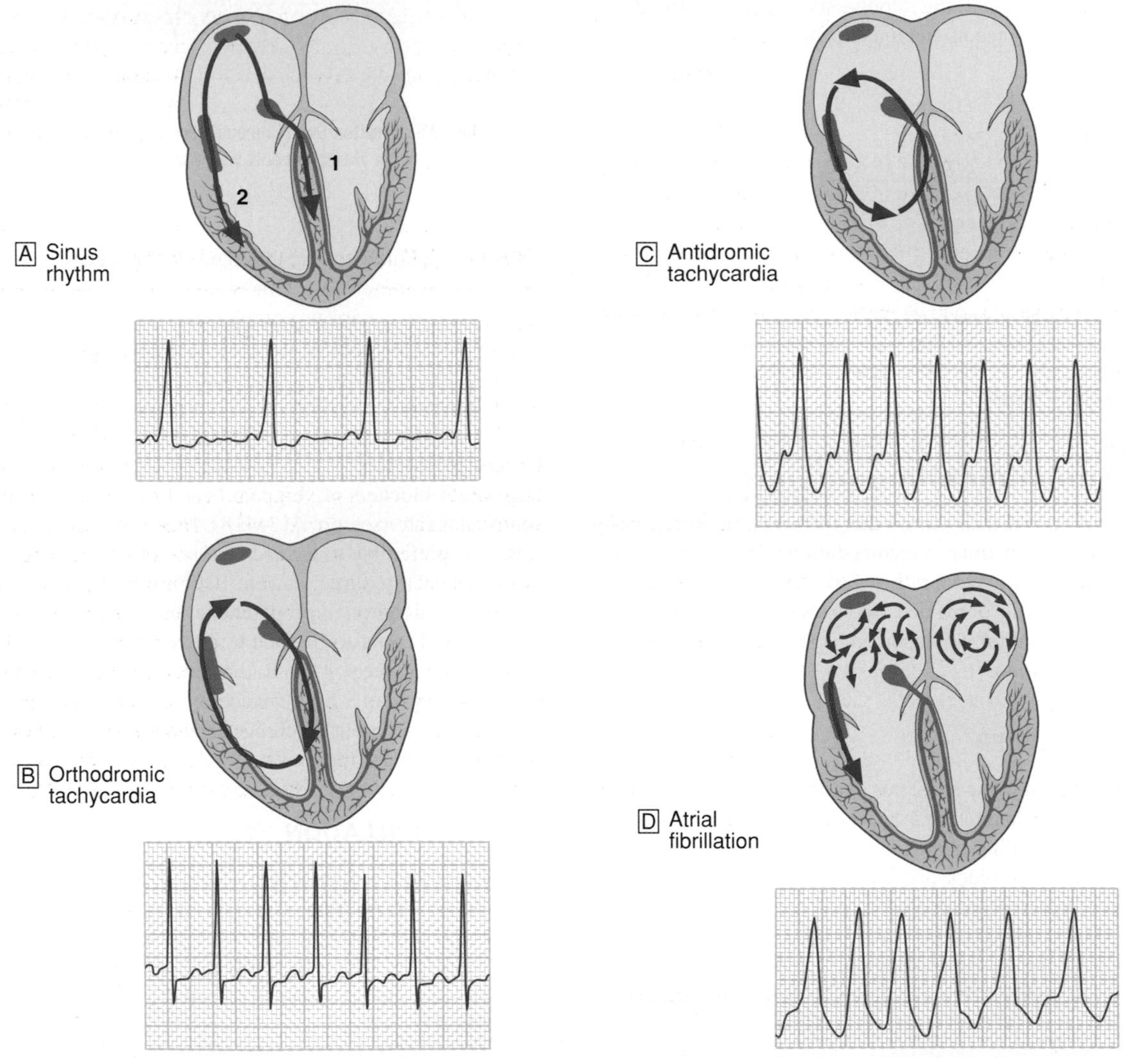

A Sinus rhythm

C Antidromic tachycardia

B Orthodromic tachycardia

D Atrial fibrillation

Fig. 12.43 Wolff–Parkinson–White syndrome. In this condition there is a strip of accessory conducting tissue that allows electricity to bypass the AV node and spread from the atria to the ventricles rapidly and without delay. When the ventricles are depolarised through the AV node (1) the ECG is normal but when the ventricles are depolarised through the accessory conducting tissue (2) the ECG shows a very short PR interval and a broad QRS complex.

A **Sinus rhythm.** In sinus rhythm the ventricles are partly depolarised through the AV node, and partly through the accessory pathway, producing an ECG with a short PR interval and broadened QRS complexes; the characteristic slurring of the upstroke of the QRS complex is known as a delta wave. The degree of pre-excitation (the proportion of electricity passing down the accessory pathway) and therefore the ECG appearances may vary a lot, and at times the ECG can look normal.

B **Orthodromic tachycardia.** This is the most common form of tachycardia in WPW. The re-entry circuit passes antegradely through the AV node and retrogradely through the accessory pathway. The ventricles are therefore depolarised in the normal way, producing a narrow-complex tachycardia that is indistinguishable from other forms of SVT.

C **Antidromic tachycardia.** Occasionally the re-entry circuit passes antegradely through the accessory pathway and retrogradely through the AV node. The ventricles are then depolarised through the accessory pathway, producing a broad-complex tachycardia.

D **Atrial fibrillation.** In this rhythm the ventricles are largely depolarised through the accessory pathway, producing an irregular broad-complex tachycardia which is often more rapid than the example shown.

and may last from a few seconds to many hours. The patient is usually aware of a fast heart beat and may feel faint or breathless. Polyuria, due to the release of atrial natriuretic peptide, is sometimes a feature, and cardiac pain or heart failure may occur if there is coexisting structural heart disease. The ECG (see Fig. 12.42) usually shows a tachycardia with normal QRS complexes but occasionally there may be rate-dependent bundle branch block.

Management

Treatment is not always necessary. However, an attack may be terminated by carotid sinus massage or other measures that increase vagal tone (e.g. Valsalva manoeuvre). Intravenous adenosine or verapamil will restore sinus rhythm in most cases. Suitable alternative drugs include β-blockers, disopyramide and digoxin. In an emergency (severe haemodynamic compromise) the tachycardia should be terminated by DC cardioversion (see p. 418).

If attacks are frequent or otherwise disabling, prophylactic oral therapy with a β-blocker, verapamil, disopyramide or digoxin may be indicated. However, radiofrequency ablation (see p. 419) offers the prospect of a complete cure and is usually preferable to long-term drug treatment.

WOLFF–PARKINSON–WHITE (WPW) SYNDROME

In this condition there is an abnormal band of atrial tissue which connects the atria and ventricles and can electrically bypass the AV node. In normal sinus rhythm conduction takes place partly through the AV node and partly through the more rapidly conducting bypass tract. The ECG shows shortening of the PR interval and a 'slurring' of the QRS complex called a delta wave (see Fig. 12.43A). As the AV node and bypass tract have different conduction speeds and refractory periods, a re-entry circuit (see Fig. 12.38, p. 406) can develop, causing paroxysms of tachycardia (see Figs 12.43B and 12.43C). Carotid sinus massage or intravenous adenosine will often terminate an episode of this form of

tachycardia. The onset of atrial fibrillation may produce very rapid ventricular rates because the bypass pathway lacks the rate-limiting properties of the normal AV node (see Fig. 12.43D). Atrial fibrillation is potentially a very dangerous arrhythmia in these patients and may cause collapse, syncope and even death; it should therefore be treated as a medical emergency, usually with DC cardioversion.

Prophylactic anti-arrhythmic drug therapy is only indicated in symptomatic patients and is aimed at slowing the conduction rate and prolonging the refractory period of the bypass tract, using agents such as flecainide, disopyramide or amiodarone (see pp. 417–418); digoxin and verapamil increase conduction in the bypass tract and should be avoided. Transvenous radiofrequency catheter ablation (see p. 419) of the bypass tract offers the prospect of a lifetime cure and is the treatment of choice for most patients.

VENTRICULAR TACHYARRHYTHMIAS

VENTRICULAR ECTOPIC BEATS (EXTRASYSTOLES, PREMATURE BEATS)

The ECG shows premature broad, bizarre QRS complexes which may be unifocal (identical beats arising from a single ectopic focus) or multifocal (varying morphology with multiple foci—see Fig. 12.44). 'Couplet' and 'triplet' are terms used to describe two or three successive ectopic beats, whereas a run of alternate sinus and ectopic beats is known as 'bigeminy'. Ectopic beats produce a low stroke volume because left ventricular contraction is premature and ineffective. The pulse is therefore irregular, with weak or missed beats (see Fig. 12.44). Patients are often asymptomatic but may complain of an irregular heart beat, missed beats or abnormally strong beats (due to the increased output of the post-ectopic sinus beat). The significance of ventricular ectopic beats (VEBs) depends on the nature of any underlying heart disease.

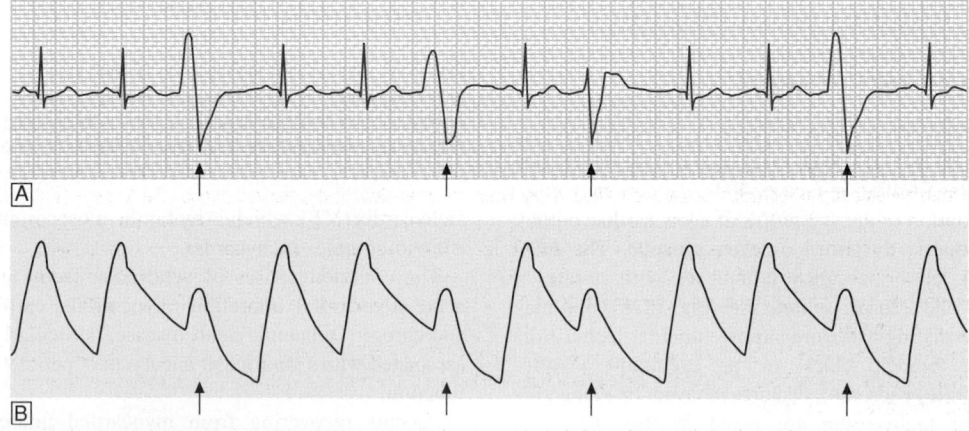

Fig. 12.44 Ventricular ectopic beats. A There are broad bizarre QRS complexes with no preceding P wave (arrows) in between normal sinus beats. Their configuration varies, so these are multifocal ectopics. B A simultaneous arterial pressure trace is shown. The ectopic beats result in a weaker pulse (arrows), which may be perceived as a 'dropped beat'.

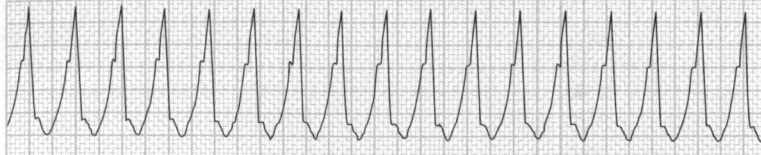

Fig. 12.45   Ventricular tachycardia: rhythm strip. Typical broad bizarre QRS complexes with a rate of 160/min.

Ventricular ectopic beats in otherwise healthy subjects

VEBs are frequently found in normal people, and their prevalence increases with age. Ectopic beats in patients with otherwise normal hearts are often more prominent at rest, and tend to disappear with exercise. The outlook is excellent and treatment is unnecessary, although low-dose β-blocker treatment is sometimes used to suppress anxiety and palpitation.

VEBs are sometimes a manifestation of otherwise subclinical heart disease, particularly coronary artery disease. There is no evidence that anti-arrhythmic therapy is merited in such patients but the discovery of frequent VEBs might reasonably prompt some general cardiac investigations.

Ventricular ectopic beats associated with heart disease

Frequent VEBs are often observed during acute myocardial infarction but are of no prognostic significance and require no treatment. However, persistent frequent (> 10/hour) ventricular ectopic beats in patients who have survived the acute phase of myocardial infarction are indicative of a poor long-term outcome. Unfortunately, anti-arrhythmic therapy does not improve, and may even worsen, the prognosis in these patients.

VEBs are common in patients with heart failure, when they are associated with an adverse prognosis, but again the outlook is no better if they are suppressed with anti-arrhythmic drugs. Effective treatment of the heart failure may suppress the ectopic beats.

VEBs are also a feature of digoxin toxicity, are sometimes found in mitral valve prolapse, and may occur as 'escape beats' in the presence of an underlying bradycardia. Treatment should always be directed at the underlying condition.

VENTRICULAR TACHYCARDIA

This is a grave arrhythmia because it is nearly always associated with serious heart disease and may degenerate into ventricular fibrillation (see p. 403). Patients may complain of palpitation or the symptoms of a low cardiac output, such as dizziness, dyspnoea or even syncope. The ECG shows broad, abnormal QRS complexes with a rate of between 140 and 220 per minute (see Fig. 12.45) and may be difficult to distinguish from supraventricular tachycardia with bundle branch block or pre-excitation (Wolff–Parkinson–White syndrome). Features in favour of a diagnosis of ventricular tachycardia are listed in Box 12.37. A 12-lead (see Fig. 12.46), intracardiac (see Fig. 12.47) or oesophageal ECG may help to establish the diagnosis. When there is doubt it is safer to manage the problem as ventricular

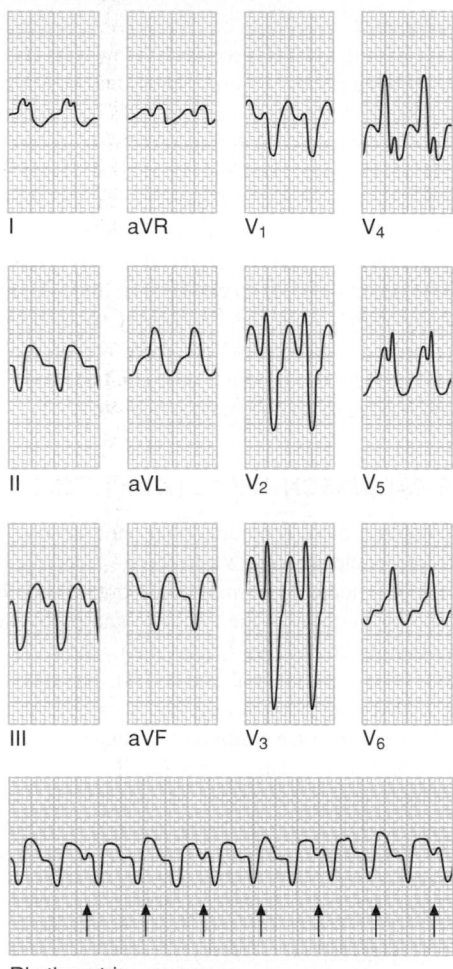

I   aVR   V₁   V₄

II   aVL   V₂   V₅

III   aVF   V₃   V₆

Rhythm strip

Fig. 12.46   Ventricular tachycardia: 12-lead ECG. The morphology of this tachycardia is typical of VT, with very broad QRS complexes and marked left axis deviation. In addition, there is AV dissociation; some P waves are visible and others are buried in the QRS complexes (arrows).

tachycardia (VT), which is by far the most common cause of a broad-complex tachycardia.

The common causes of ventricular tachycardia include acute myocardial infarction, myocarditis, cardiomyopathy and chronic ischaemic heart disease, particularly when it is associated with a ventricular aneurysm or poor left ventricular function.

Patients recovering from myocardial infarction sometimes have periods of idioventricular rhythm ('slow' ventricular tachycardia) at a rate only slightly above the preceding sinus rate. These episodes are usually self-limiting and

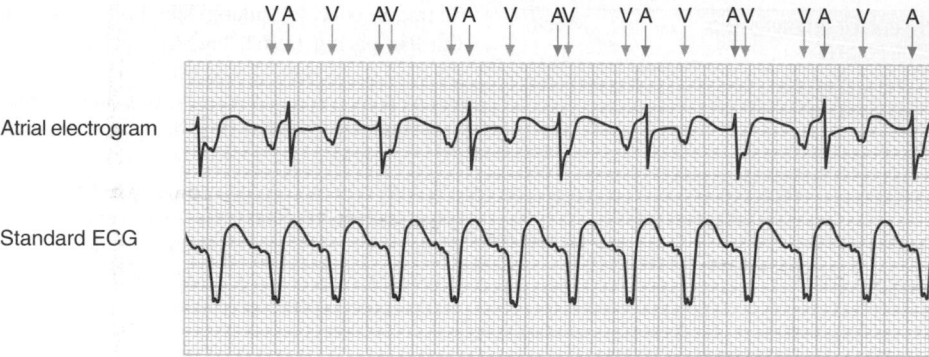

Fig. 12.47 Ventricular tachycardia: intracardiac ECG. A simultaneous recording of an atrial electrogram, obtained by placing a pacing lead in the right atrium, and an ordinary rhythm strip illustrating ventricular tachycardia with AV dissociation. Although the standard ECG shows a broad-complex tachycardia with no visible P waves, dissociated atrial activity is clearly visible in the atrial electrogram. (A = atrial depolarisation; V = ventricular depolarisation)

> **12.37 FEATURES IN FAVOUR OF VENTRICULAR TACHYCARDIA IN THE DIFFERENTIAL DIAGNOSIS OF BROAD-COMPLEX TACHYCARDIA**
>
> - A history of myocardial infarction
> - AV dissociation (pathognomonic)
> - Capture/fusion beats (pathognomonic—see Fig. 12.48)
> - Extreme left axis deviation
> - Very broad QRS complexes (> 140 ms)
> - No response to carotid sinus massage or i.v. adenosine

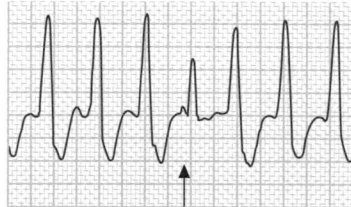

Fig. 12.48 Ventricular tachycardia: fusion beat (arrow). In ventricular tachycardia there is independent atrial and ventricular activity. Occasionally a P wave is conducted to the ventricles through the AV node. This may produce a normal sinus beat in the middle of the tachycardia (a capture beat); however, more commonly the conducted impulse fuses with an impulse from the tachycardia (a fusion beat). This phenomenon can only occur when there is AV dissociation and is therefore diagnostic of ventricular tachycardia.

asymptomatic, and do not require treatment. Other forms of ventricular tachycardia, if they last for more than a few beats, will require treatment, often as an emergency.

Management

Prompt action to restore sinus rhythm is required and in most cases should be followed by prophylactic therapy. DC cardioversion is often the initial treatment of choice but if this is not available or if the arrhythmia is well tolerated, intravenous lidocaine (lignocaine) may be given as a bolus followed by an intravenous infusion (see p. 417). Mexiletine, flecainide, disopyramide and amiodarone are suitable alternatives (see p. 417). Hypokalaemia, hypomagnesaemia and acidosis must be corrected.

Oral prophylactic therapy with either mexiletine, disopyramide, propafenone or amiodarone (see p. 417) is often necessary. The efficacy of such drug therapy should always be assessed by ambulatory ECG monitoring, exercise testing or invasive electrophysiological studies. If drug therapy fails, alternative treatments include the use of an automatic implantable cardioverter-defibrillator (see p. 419), or surgery to identify and resect the area of diseased myocardium which is responsible for the arrhythmia.

TORSADES DE POINTES (TWISTING POINTS)

This form of polymorphic ventricular tachycardia is a complication of prolonged ventricular repolarisation (prolonged QT interval). The ECG shows rapid irregular complexes that oscillate from an upright to an inverted position and seem to twist around the baseline as the mean QRS axis changes (see Fig. 12.49). The arrhythmia is usually non-sustained and repetitive but may degenerate into ventricular fibrillation. During periods of sinus rhythm the ECG will usually show a prolonged QT interval.

Some of the common causes are listed in Box 12.38. The arrhythmia is more common in women and is often triggered by a combination of aetiological factors (e.g. multiple medications and hypokalaemia). The congenital long QT syndromes are a family of genetic disorders that are

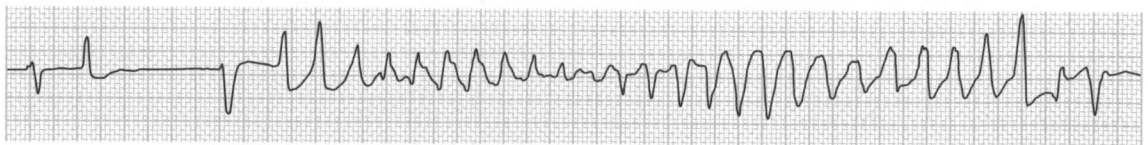

Fig. 12.49 Torsades de pointes. A bradycardia with a long QT interval is followed by polymorphic ventricular tachycardia that is triggered by an R on T ectopic.

12.38 CAUSES OF LONG QT INTERVAL AND TORSADES DE POINTES
Bradycardia
• Sinus node disease • Complete heart block
Electrolyte disturbance
• Hypokalaemia • Hypomagnesaemia • Hypocalcaemia
Drugs
• Disopyramide (and other class Ia anti-arrhythmic drugs—   see p. 417) • Sotalol, amiodarone (and other class III anti-arrhythmic drugs) • Amitriptyline (and other tricyclic antidepressants) • Chlorpromazine (and other phenothiazines) • Erythromycin (and other macrolides) … plus many more
Congenital syndromes
• Romano–Ward syndrome (autosomal dominant) • Jervell and Lange-Nielson's syndrome (autosomal recessive,   associated with congenital deafness)

characterised by specific functional abnormalities of the sodium channel. The Brugada syndrome is a related genetic disorder that may present with polymorphic ventricular tachycardia or sudden death; it is characterised by a defect in sodium channel function, and an abnormal ECG (right bundle branch block and ST elevation in V_1 and V_2, but not usually prolongation of the QT interval).

Treatment should be directed at the underlying cause. Intravenous magnesium (8 mmol over 15 minutes, then 72 mmol over 24 hours) should be given in all cases. Cardiac pacing (atrial, but ventricular or dual-chamber in the case of AV block) will usually suppress the arrhythmia. Intravenous isoprenaline is a reasonable alternative to pacing but should be avoided in patients with the congenital long QT syndrome.

Long-term therapy may not be necessary if the underlying cause can be removed. Beta-blockers or left stellate ganglion block may be of value in patients with one of the congenital long QT syndromes. An implantable cardioverter-defibrillator is often advisable.

SINOATRIAL DISEASE (SICK SINUS SYNDROME)

Sinoatrial disease can occur at any age, but is most common in the elderly. The underlying pathology is not understood but may involve fibrosis, degenerative changes and/or ischaemia of the sinoatrial (sinus) node. The condition is characterised by a variety of arrhythmias (see Box 12.39) and may present with palpitation, dizzy spells or syncope, due to intermittent tachycardia, bradycardia, or pauses (sinoatrial block or sinus arrest) with no atrial or ventricular activity (see Fig. 12.50).

12.39 COMMON FEATURES OF SINOATRIAL DISEASE
• Sinus bradycardia • Sinoatrial block (sinus arrest) • Paroxysmal supraventricular tachycardia • Paroxysmal atrial fibrillation • Atrioventricular block

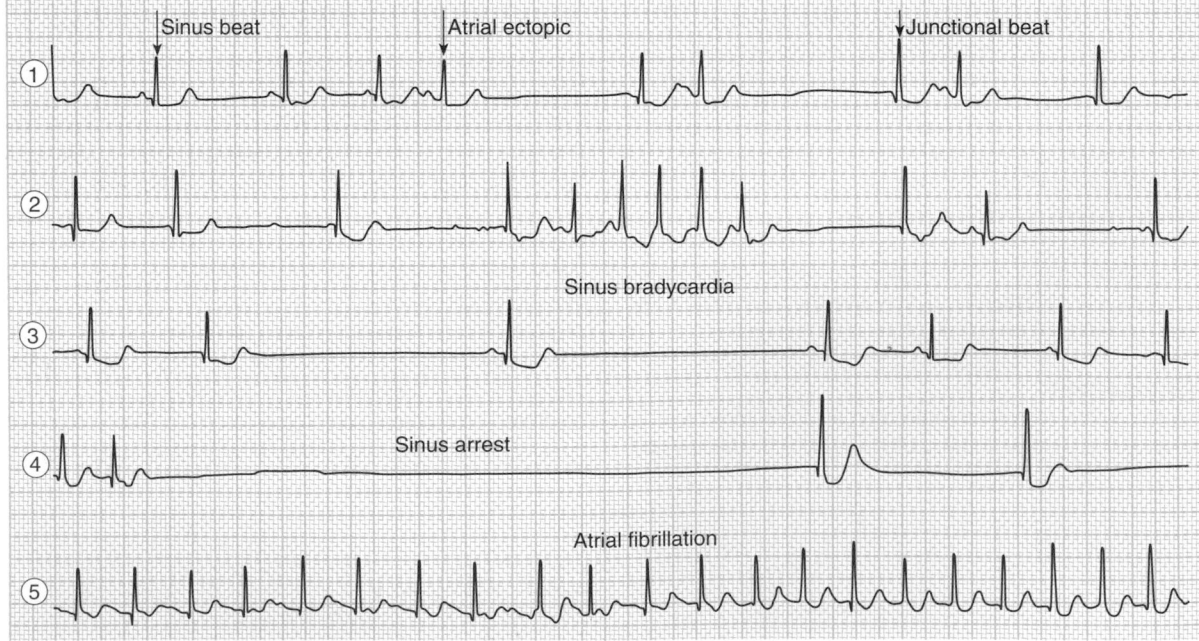

Fig. 12.50 Sinoatrial disease (sick sinus syndrome). A continuous rhythm strip from a 24-hour ECG tape recording illustrating periods of sinus rhythm, atrial ectopics, junctional beats, sinus bradycardia, sinus arrest and paroxysmal atrial fibrillation.

A permanent pacemaker may benefit patients with troublesome symptoms due to spontaneous bradycardias, or those with symptomatic bradycardias induced by drugs required to prevent tachyarrhythmias. Pacing the atrium may help to prevent episodes of atrial fibrillation; however, permanent pacing does not improve prognosis and is not indicated in patients who are asymptomatic.

ATRIOVENTRICULAR AND BUNDLE BRANCH BLOCK

ATRIOVENTRICULAR (AV) BLOCK

Atrioventricular conduction is influenced by autonomic activity. AV block can therefore be intermittent and may only be evident when the conducting tissue is stressed by a rapid atrial rate. Accordingly, atrial tachyarrhythmias are often associated with AV block (see Fig. 12.40, p. 407).

First-degree AV block
In this condition AV conduction is delayed so the PR interval is prolonged beyond the upper limit of normal (0.20

seconds). There are no symptoms and the diagnosis can only be made from the ECG (see Fig. 12.51).

Second-degree AV block
In this condition dropped beats occur because some impulses from the atria fail to get through to the ventricles.

In Mobitz type I second-degree AV block (see Fig. 12.52) there is progressive lengthening of successive PR intervals culminating in a dropped beat. The cycle then repeats itself. This is known as Wenckebach's phenomenon and is usually due to impaired conduction proximal to the bundle of His. The phenomenon may be physiological and is sometimes observed at rest or during sleep in athletic young adults with high vagal tone.

In Mobitz type II second-degree AV block (see Fig. 12.53) the PR interval of the conducted impulses remains constant but some P waves are not conducted. This is usually caused by disease below the bundle of His and is more serious than Mobitz type I.

In 2:1 AV block (see Fig. 12.54) alternate P waves are conducted so it is impossible to distinguish between Mobitz type I and type II block.

Third-degree (complete) AV block
When AV conduction fails completely, the atria and ventricles beat independently (AV dissociation—see Fig. 12.55). Ventricular activity is maintained by an escape rhythm arising in the bundle of His (narrow QRS complexes) or the distal conducting tissues (broad QRS complexes). Distal escape rhythms tend to be slower and less reliable.

The aetiology is shown in Box 12.40.

Complete heart block produces a slow (25–50/min), regular pulse that, except in the case of congenital complete heart

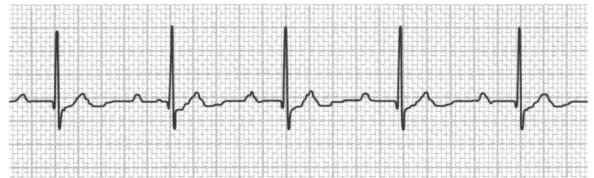

Fig. 12.51 First-degree heart block. The PR interval is prolonged and measures 0.26 seconds.

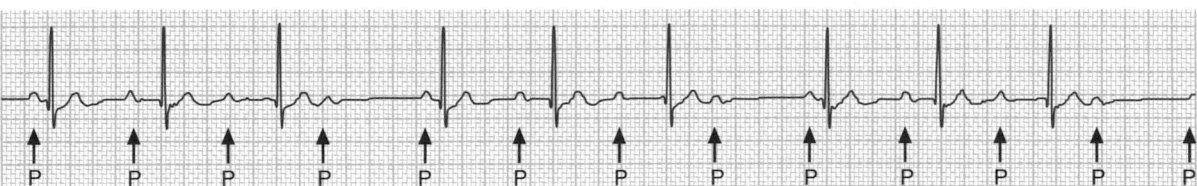

Fig. 12.52 Second-degree heart block (Mobitz type I—Wenckebach's phenomenon). The PR interval progressively increases until a P wave is not conducted. The cycle then repeats itself. In this example conduction is at a ratio of 4:3, leading to groupings of three ventricular complexes in a row.

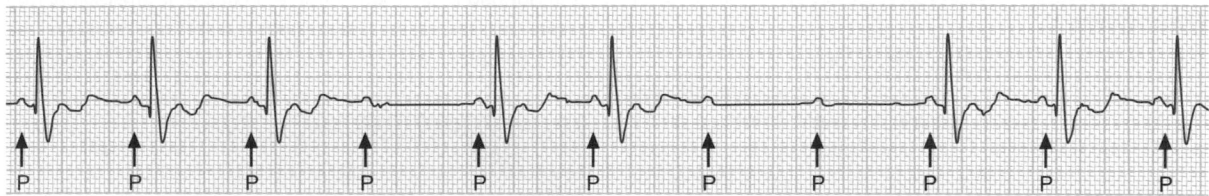

Fig. 12.53 Second-degree heart block (Mobitz type II). The PR interval of conducted beats is normal but some P waves are not conducted. The constant PR interval distinguishes this from Wenckebach's phenomenon.

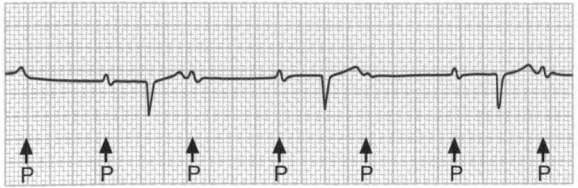

Fig. 12.54 Second-degree heart block with fixed 2:1 block. Alternate P waves are not conducted. This may be due to Mobitz type I or II block.

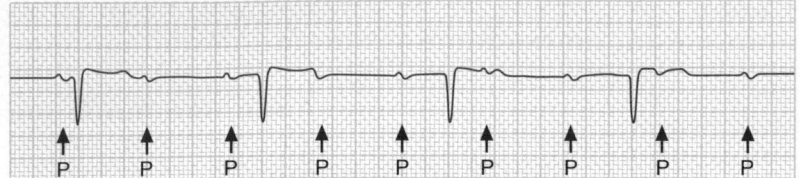

Fig. 12.55 Complete (third-degree) AV block. There is complete dissociation of atrial and ventricular complexes. The atrial rate is 80/min and the ventricular rate is 38/min.

12.40 AETIOLOGY OF COMPLETE HEART BLOCK
Congenital
Acquired

• Idiopathic fibrosis
• Myocardial infarction/ischaemia
• Inflammation
  Acute (e.g. aortic root abscess in infective endocarditis)
  Chronic (e.g. sarcoidosis—see p. 552, Chagas disease—
  see p. 60)
• Trauma (e.g. cardiac surgery)
• Drugs (e.g. digoxin, β-blocker)

block, does not vary with exercise. There is usually a compensatory increase in stroke volume with a large-volume pulse and systolic flow murmurs. Cannon waves may be visible in the neck and the intensity of the first heart sound varies due to the loss of AV synchrony.

Adams–Stokes attacks

Episodes of ventricular asystole may complicate complete heart block or Mobitz type II second-degree AV block, and can also occur in patients with sinoatrial disease (see Fig. 12.50). This may cause recurrent syncope or 'Adams–Stokes' attacks.

A typical episode is characterised by a sudden loss of consciousness, which frequently occurs without warning and may result in a fall. Convulsions (due to cerebral ischaemia) can occur if there is prolonged asystole. There is pallor and a death-like appearance during the attack, but when the heart starts beating again there is a characteristic flush. In contrast to epilepsy, recovery is rapid.

The hypersensitive carotid sinus syndrome and the vasovagal syndrome (see pp. 397–399) may cause similar symptoms.

Management

AV block complicating acute myocardial infarction

Acute inferior myocardial infarction is often complicated by transient AV block because the right coronary artery supplies the junctional tissues and bundle of His. However, there is usually a reliable escape rhythm and if the patient remains well no treatment is required. Clinical deterioration due to second-degree or complete heart block may respond to atropine (0.6 mg intravenously, repeated as necessary) or, if this fails, a temporary pacemaker. In the vast majority of cases the AV block will resolve within 7–10 days.

Second-degree or complete heart block complicating acute anterior myocardial infarction is usually a sign of extensive myocardial damage and therefore carries a poor prognosis. Asystole may ensue and a temporary pacemaker should be inserted as soon as possible. If the patient presents

with asystole, atropine (0.6 mg intravenously, repeated if necessary) and isoprenaline (1–5 mg in 500 ml 5% dextrose, infused intravenously at the minimum rate needed to produce a satisfactory heart rhythm) may help to maintain the circulation until a temporary pacing electrode can be inserted.

Chronic AV block

Patients with symptomatic bradyarrhythmias associated with AV block should receive a permanent pacemaker (see below).

Asymptomatic first-degree or Mobitz type I second-degree AV block (Wenckebach's phenomenon) does not require treatment but may be an indication of serious underlying heart disease.

A permanent pacemaker is usually indicated in patients with asymptomatic Mobitz type II second-degree or complete heart block because there is evidence that pacing can improve their prognosis. An exception may be made in young asymptomatic patients with congenital complete heart block who have a mean day-time heart rate of more than 50 per minute.

BUNDLE BRANCH BLOCK AND HEMIBLOCK

Interruption of the right or left branch of the bundle of His delays activation of the appropriate ventricle, broadens the QRS complex (0.12 seconds or more) and produces the characteristic alterations in QRS morphology shown in Figures 12.56 and 12.57.

Right bundle branch block (RBBB) is a common normal variant but left bundle branch block (LBBB) usually signifies important underlying heart disease. Both forms of bundle branch block may be due to conducting tissue disease but are also features of other types of heart disease (see Box 12.41).

The left branch of the bundle of His divides into an anterior and a posterior fascicle. Damage to the conducting tissue at this point (hemiblock) does not broaden the QRS complex, but alters the mean direction of ventricular

12.41 COMMON CAUSES OF BUNDLE BRANCH BLOCK
RBBB
• Normal variant • Right ventricular hypertrophy or strain, e.g. pulmonary embolism • Congenital heart disease, e.g. atrial septal defect • Coronary artery disease
LBBB
• Coronary artery disease • Hypertension • Aortic valve disease • Cardiomyopathy

depolarisation (mean QRS axis), causing left axis deviation in left anterior hemiblock and right axis deviation in left posterior hemiblock (see Fig. 12.8, p. 366). The combination of right bundle branch and left anterior or posterior hemiblock is known as bifascicular block.

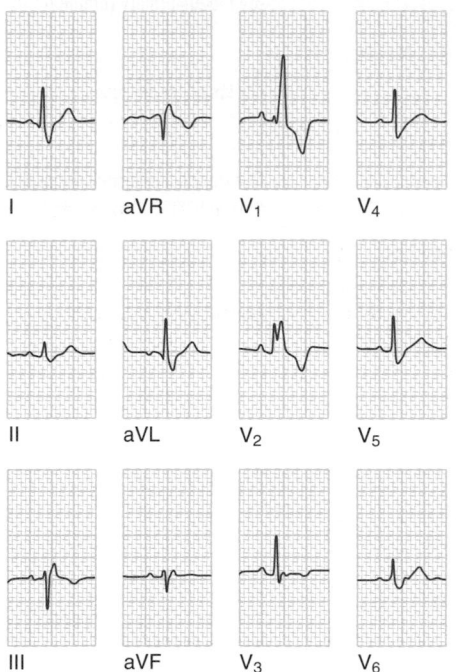

Fig. 12.56 Right bundle branch block. Note the wide QRS complexes with 'M'-shaped configuration in leads V₁ and V₂ and a wide S wave in lead I.

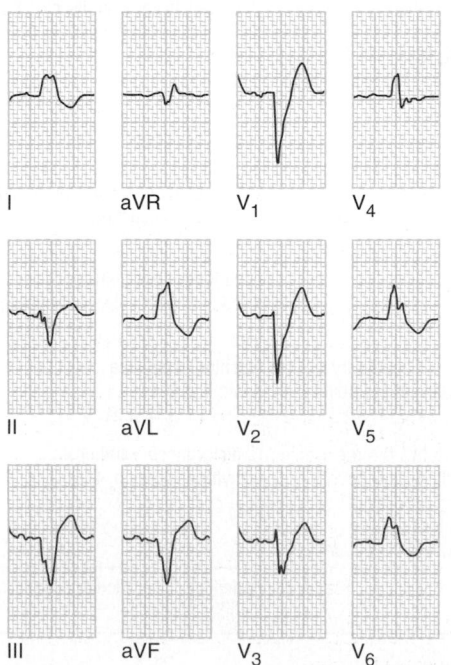

Fig. 12.57 Left bundle branch block. Note the wide QRS complexes with the loss of the Q wave or septal vector in lead I and 'M'-shaped QRS complexes in V₅ and V₆.

ANTI-ARRHYTHMIC DRUG THERAPY

THE CLASSIFICATION OF ANTI-ARRHYTHMIC DRUGS

Some of the drugs used to treat individual arrhythmias have already been mentioned. These agents may be classified according to their mode of action or their main site of action (see Box 12.42 and Fig. 12.58). The main uses, dosages and side-effects of the most widely used drugs are summarised in Box 12.43, and principles of use are outlined in Box 12.44.

12.42 CLASSIFICATION OF ANTI-ARRHYTHMIC DRUGS ACCORDING TO THEIR EFFECT ON THE INTRACELLULAR ACTION POTENTIAL
Class I—membrane-stabilising agents (fast sodium channel blockers)
(a) Block Na⁺ channel and prolong action potential   • Quinidine, disopyramide   (b) Block Na⁺ channel and shorten action potential   • Lidocaine (lignocaine), mexiletine   (c) Block Na⁺ channel with no effect on action potential   • Flecainide, propafenone
Class II—β-adrenoceptor antagonists (β-blockers)
• Atenolol, bisoprolol, metoprolol, l-sotalol
Class III—drugs whose main effect is to prolong the action potential
• Amiodarone, d-sotalol
Class IV—slow calcium channel blockers
• Verapamil, diltiazem
N.B. Some drugs (e.g. digoxin and adenosine) have no place in this classification, while others have properties in more than one class (e.g. amiodarone, which has actions in all four classes).

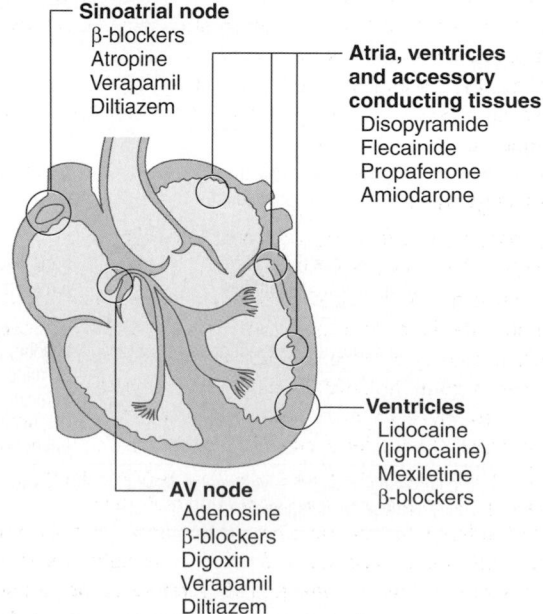

Fig. 12.58 Classification of anti-arrhythmic drugs by site of action.

12.43 THE MAIN USES, DOSAGES AND SIDE-EFFECTS OF THE MOST WIDELY USED ANTI-ARRHYTHMIC DRUGS

Drug	Main uses	Route	Dose (adult)	Important side-effects
CLASS I **Disopyramide**	Prevention and treatment of all tachyarrhythmias	I.v. Oral	2 mg/kg at 30 mg/min then 0.4 mg/kg/hr (max 800 mg/day) 300–800 mg daily in divided dosage	Myocardial depression, hypotension, dry mouth, urinary retention
Lidocaine **(lignocaine)**	Treatment and short-term prevention of VT and VF	I.v.	Bolus 50–100 mg 4 mg/min for 30 mins, then 2 mg/min for 2 hrs, then 1 mg/min for 24 hrs	Confusion, convulsions
Mexiletine	Prevention and treatment of ventricular tachyarrhythmias	I.v. Oral	Loading dose: 100–250 mg at 25 mg/min then 250 mg in 1 hr then 250 mg in 2 hrs Maintenance therapy: 0.5 mg/min 200–250 mg 8-hourly	GI irritation, confusion, dizziness, tremor, nystagmus, ataxia
Flecainide	Prevention and treatment of all tachyarrhythmias	I.v. Oral	2 mg/kg over 10 mins then 1.5 mg/kg/hr for 1 hr then 0.1 mg/kg/hr 50–100 mg 12-hourly	Myocardial depression, dizziness
Propafenone	Prevention and treatment of all tachyarrhythmias	Oral	150 mg 8-hourly for 1 week then 300 mg 12-hourly	Myocardial depression, dizziness
CLASS II **Atenolol**	Treatment and prevention of SVT and AF Prevention of VEs and exercise-induced VT	I.v. Oral	2.5 mg at 1 mg/min repeated at 5 min intervals (max 10 mg) 50–100 mg daily	Myocardial depression, bradycardia, bronchospasm, fatigue, depression, nightmares, cold peripheries
Bisoprolol		Oral	5–10 mg daily	
Metoprolol		I.v. Oral	5 mg over 2 mins to a maximum of 15 mg 50–100 mg 8- or 12-hourly	
Sotalol		I.v. Oral	10–20 mg slowly 40–160 mg 12-hourly	Sotalol can cause torsades de pointes (see p. 411)
CLASS III **Amiodarone**	Serious atrial and ventricular tachyarrhythmias	I.v. Oral	5 mg/kg over 20–120 mins then up to 15 mg/kg/24 hrs Initially 600–1200 mg/day then 100–200 mg daily	Photosensitivity, skin discoloration, corneal deposits, thyroid dysfunction, alveolitis, nausea and vomiting, hepatotoxicity, peripheral neuropathy, torsades de pointes (see p. 411); potentiates digoxin and warfarin
CLASS IV **Verapamil**	Treatment of SVT, control of AF	I.v. Oral	5–10 mg over 30 secs 40–120 mg 8-hourly or 240 mg SR daily	Myocardial depression, hypotension, bradycardia, constipation
OTHER **Atropine**	Treatment of bradycardia and/or hypotension due to vagal overactivity	I.v.	0.6–3 mg	Dry mouth, thirst, blurred vision, atrial and ventricular extrasystoles
Adenosine	Treatment of SVT, aid to diagnosis in unidentified tachycardia	I.v.	3 mg over 2 secs, followed if necessary by 6 mg then 12 mg at intervals of 1–2 mins	Flushing, dyspnoea, chest pain Avoid in asthma
Digoxin	Treatment and prevention of SVT, control of AF	I.v. Oral	Loading dose: 0.5–1 mg (total), 0.5 mg over 30 mins then 0.25–0.5 mg 4- to 8-hourly to maximum total of 1 mg, assessing response before each additional dose 0.5 mg 6-hourly then 0.125–0.25 mg daily	GI disturbance, xanthopsia, arrhythmias (see p. 418)

(VT = ventricular tachycardia; VF = ventricular fibrillation; SVT = supraventricular tachycardia; AF = atrial fibrillation; VE = ventricular ectopic; SR = sustained-release formulation)

Class I drugs

Class I drugs act principally by suppressing excitability and slowing conduction in atrial or ventricular muscle.

Quinidine

Quinidine can cause torsades de pointes, hypersensitivity and unpleasant gastrointestinal side-effects; it has been shown to increase mortality in patients with paroxysmal atrial fibrillation and should be avoided.

Disopyramide

Disopyramide has weak atropine-like effects and may cause urinary retention or precipitate glaucoma. It has a depressant effect on ventricular function and should be avoided in cardiac failure. If it is used in patients with atrial flutter and AV block, there is a risk of a paradoxical increase in heart rate as the atria slow and 2:1 block changes to 1:1 conduction; this can be prevented by pre-treatment with digoxin.

Lidocaine (lignocaine)

Lidocaine must be given parenterally and has a very short plasma half-life, so plasma concentration will depend on the rate of infusion. It is mainly used for the urgent treatment or prophylaxis of ventricular tachycardia or fibrillation.

Mexiletine

Mexiletine can be given intravenously or orally and is used for the treatment or prophylaxis of ventricular arrhythmias. Side-effects include nausea, vomiting, confusion, dizziness, tremor, nystagmus and ataxia. Metabolism is mainly hepatic and the drug may accumulate in liver disease.

Flecainide

Flecainide can be given intravenously or orally for the treatment or prophylaxis of supraventricular or ventricular arrhythmias and may be useful in the management of Wolff–Parkinson–White syndrome. Unfortunately, it is a potent myocardial depressant and cannot, therefore, be used safely in patients with poor left ventricular function. Like all anti-arrhythmic drugs it can in some circumstances be proarrhythmic and has been found to be hazardous in patients with a history of myocardial infarction.

Propafenone

Propafenone is indicated for the treatment or prophylaxis of all tachyarrhythmias and is particularly useful in paroxysmal atrial fibrillation, ventricular tachycardia and the Wolff–Parkinson–White syndrome. Propafenone is a class Ic drug but also has some β-blocker (class II) properties and may precipitate heart failure or heart block in susceptible patients. Important interactions with digoxin, warfarin and cimetidine have been described.

Class II drugs

This group comprises the β-adrenoceptor antagonists (β-blockers). The agents used most commonly are as follows.

Atenolol, bisoprolol and metoprolol

These are cardioselective β-blockers that are usually well tolerated.

Sotalol

This is a racemic mixture of two isomers with non-selective β-blocker (mainly l-sotalol) and class III (mainly d-sotalol) activity. It has a long half-life and may cause torsades de pointes.

Propranolol

This is not cardioselective and is subject to extensive first-pass metabolism in the liver. The effective oral dose is therefore unpredictable and must be titrated after treatment is started with a small dose.

Class III drugs

Class III drugs act by prolonging the plateau phase of the action potential, thus lengthening the refractory period.

Amiodarone

Amiodarone is the principal drug in this class although both disopyramide and sotalol have class III activity. Amiodarone has unusual pharmacokinetics and is effective against a wide variety of atrial and ventricular arrhythmias. It is probably the most effective drug currently available for controlling paroxysmal atrial fibrillation and the arrhythmias associated with the Wolff–Parkinson–White syndrome. Furthermore, it is very useful in preventing episodes of recurrent ventricular tachycardia, particularly in patients with poor left ventricular function. Amiodarone has an extraordinarily long tissue half-life (25–110 days). This means that the onset of action after oral and intravenous therapy is delayed; indeed, it may take several months to reach steady state. For the same reason the drug's effects may last for weeks or months after treatment has been stopped. Side-effects are frequent (up to one-third of patients), numerous and potentially serious; they include photosensitisation, corneal deposits, gastrointestinal problems, thyroid dysfunction (see p. 689), liver disease, pulmonary fibrosis and torsades de pointes. Drug interactions are also common; for example, the effects of digoxin and warfarin are potentiated by amiodarone.

Class IV drugs

These block the 'slow calcium channel' which is particularly important for impulse generation and conduction in atrial and nodal tissue, although it is also present in ventricular muscle.

Verapamil

This is the most widely used anti-arrhythmic drug in this class; however, diltiazem has similar properties. Intravenous verapamil may cause profound bradycardia and/or hypotension and should not be used in conjunction with oral or intravenous β-blockers.

Other anti-arrhythmic drugs

Atropine sulphate

Atropine sulphate (0.6 mg i.v., repeated if necessary to a maximum of 3 mg) increases the sinus rate and sinoatrial and AV conduction, and is the treatment of choice for severe bradycardia and/or hypotension due to vagal overactivity (vasovagal syndrome—see p. 399). It may also be of value in the initial management of symptomatic bradyarrhythmias complicating the early stages of inferior myocardial infarction and cardiac arrest due to asystole. Repeat dosing may be necessary because the drug disappears rapidly from the circulation after parenteral administration. Side-effects include dry mouth, thirst, blurred vision and both atrial and ventricular extrasystoles.

Adenosine

Adenosine must be given intravenously; like carotid sinus massage, it produces transient AV block lasting a few seconds. Accordingly, it may be used to terminate junctional tachycardias when the AV node is part of the re-entry circuit or to help establish the diagnosis in difficult arrhythmias such as atrial flutter with 2:1 AV block (see Fig. 12.41, p. 407) or broad-complex tachycardia (see Boxes 12.43 and 12.45).

Adenosine is given as an intravenous bolus according to an ascending dosage schedule. The initial dose is 3 mg given over 2 seconds. If there is no response after 1–2 minutes, 6 mg should be given and if necessary the physician should wait another 1–2 minutes before administering the maximum dose of 12 mg. Patients should be warned that they may experience short-lived and sometimes distressing side-effects of flushing, breathlessness and chest pain. Adenosine can cause bronchospasm and should be avoided in asthmatics; its effects are greatly potentiated by dipyridamole and inhibited by theophylline and other xanthines.

12.45 RESPONSE TO INTRAVENOUS ADENOSINE

Arrhythmia	Response
Supraventricular junctional tachycardia	Termination
Atrial fibrillation, atrial flutter	Transient AV block
Ventricular tachycardia	No effect

12.46 DIGOXIN TOXICITY

Extracardiac manifestations

- Anorexia, nausea, vomiting
- Diarrhoea
- Altered colour vision (xanthopsia)

Cardiac manifestations

- Bradycardia
- Multiple ventricular ectopics
- Ventricular bigeminy (alternate ventricular ectopics)
- Atrial tachycardia (with variable block)
- Ventricular tachycardia
- Ventricular fibrillation

Digoxin

Digoxin is a purified glycoside from the European foxglove, *Digitalis lanata*, which slows conduction and prolongs the refractory period in the AV node. This effect helps to control the ventricular rate in atrial fibrillation and will often interrupt re-entry tachycardias involving the AV node. On the other hand, digoxin tends to shorten refractory periods and enhance excitability and conduction in other parts of the heart (including accessory conduction pathways); it may therefore increase atrial and ventricular ectopic activity and can lead to more complex atrial and ventricular tachyarrhythmias.

Digoxin is largely excreted by the kidneys, and the maintenance dose (see Box 12.43) should be reduced in children, the elderly and those with renal impairment. It is widely distributed and has a long tissue half-life so that effects may persist 24–36 hours after the last dose. Measurements of plasma digoxin concentration are useful in demonstrating that the dose is inadequate and in confirming a clinical impression of toxicity (see Box 12.46).

NON-DRUG THERAPY OF ARRHYTHMIAS

EXTERNAL DEFIBRILLATION AND CARDIOVERSION

The heart can be completely depolarised by passing a sufficiently large electrical current through it from an external source. This will interrupt any arrhythmia and produce a brief period of asystole which is usually followed by the resumption of normal sinus rhythm. Defibrillators deliver a direct current (DC), high-energy, short-duration shock via two metal paddles coated with conducting jelly or a gel pad, positioned over the upper right sternal edge and the apex.

Energy applied during a critical period around the peak of the T wave may provoke ventricular fibrillation, so when this technique is used to treat organised rhythms such as atrial fibrillation or ventricular tachycardia the shock should be synchronised with the ECG, and is normally given 0.02 seconds after the peak of the R wave. The precise timing of the discharge is not important in ventricular fibrillation.

In ventricular fibrillation and other emergencies the energy of the first shock should be 200 joules; there is no need for an anaesthetic if the patient is unconscious.

Elective cardioversion requires a general anaesthetic. High-energy shocks may cause myocardial damage, so if there is no urgency it is appropriate to begin with a low-amplitude shock (e.g. 50–100 joules), going on to larger shocks if necessary.

Digoxin toxicity increases the risk of untoward arrhythmias after cardioversion so it is conventional practice to withhold the drug for 24 hours before elective cardioversion. Patients with long-standing atrial arrhythmias are at risk of systemic embolism before and after cardioversion, so it is wise to ensure that the patient is adequately anticoagulated for at least 4 weeks either side of the procedure.

IMPLANTABLE CARDIOVERTER-DEFIBRILLATORS (ICDs)

These sophisticated and expensive devices can automatically sense and terminate life-threatening ventricular arrhythmias using tiered sequences of treatments, including competitive pacing, synchronised cardioversion with a low-energy shock, and defibrillation with a higher-energy shock (which can be painful if the patient is still conscious); they can also pace the ventricles in the event of bradycardia (see Fig. 12.15, p. 372). ICDs are implanted transvenously like a permanent pacemaker and are subject to similar complications (e.g. infection, erosion—see below). Clinical trials among high-risk patients have shown that the devices are more effective than anti-arrhythmic drugs in preventing sudden death (see EBM panel). An ICD may be used to treat patients who, in the absence of acute myocardial infarction or any other

---

EBM

VENTRICULAR ARRHYTHMIAS—use of implantable cardioverter-defibrillators (ICDs)

'A meta-analysis has found that ICD therapy is superior to anti-arrhythmic drug therapy (typically amiodarone) for the prevention of death among the survivors of ventricular fibrillation or sustained ventricular tachycardia. NNT for 3 years = 10.'

- Connolly SJ, Hallstrom AP, Cappato R, et al. Meta-analysis of the implantable cardioverter defibrillator secondary prevention trials. Eur Heart J 2000; 21:2071–2078.
- Anti-arrhythmic Versus Implantable Defibrillators (AVID) Investigators. A comparison of anti-arrhythmic drug therapy with implantable defibrillators in patients resuscitated from near-fatal ventricular arrhythmia. N Engl J Med 1997; 337:1576–1583.

Further information: 🖥 www.nice.org.uk

---

treatable cause, present with a cardiac arrest due to VT or VF, sustained VT causing syncope or severe haemodynamic compromise, or sustained VT associated with poor left ventricular function (LV ejection fraction < 35%). The devices may also be used prophylactically in selected patients who are thought to be at high risk of sudden cardiac death (e.g. long QT syndrome, hypertrophic cardiomyopathy, arrhythmogenic right ventricular dysplasia—see pp. 475–477).

RADIOFREQUENCY CATHETER ABLATION

The aim of this technique is to interrupt a re-entry circuit by selectively damaging endocardial tissue with radiofrequency energy delivered through a steerable catheter that is passed into the heart from a peripheral artery or vein (see Fig. 12.15,

p. 372). The procedure does not require an anaesthetic but is often time-consuming and the patient may experience some discomfort during the ablation itself. Serious complications are rare (< 1%) and include inadvertent complete heart block and cardiac rupture. Nevertheless, radiofrequency ablation is a very attractive form of treatment because it offers the prospect of a lifetime cure, thereby eliminating the need for long-term drug therapy.

The technique has revolutionised the management of many arrhythmias and is now the treatment of choice for ectopic atrial tachycardias, AV nodal re-entry tachycardia and the Wolff–Parkinson–White syndrome. Atrial flutter can also be eliminated by radiofrequency ablation, although some patients continue to experience attacks of atrial fibrillation. The applications of the technique are expanding and it has been used to treat some forms of ventricular tachycardia. Focal atrial fibrillation (a rare form of AF that originates from a focus close to the pulmonary veins) can also be treated by radiofrequency ablation.

Exceptionally troublesome AF and other refractory atrial tachyarrhythmias can be treated by using radiofrequency ablation to induce complete heart block deliberately; a permanent pacemaker must be implanted as well.

ARTIFICIAL CARDIAC PACEMAKERS

Temporary pacemakers

Transcutaneous pacing is administered by delivering an electrical stimulus that is sufficient to induce cardiac contraction through two large adhesive gel pad electrodes placed over the apex and upper right sternal edge, or over the praecordium and back. It has the advantage of being easy and quick to set up but may cause discomfort and skeletal muscle contraction. Some sophisticated ECG monitor/defibrillator machines incorporate a transcutaneous pacing system which can be used as a temporary measure until transvenous pacing is established.

Transvenous pacing is administered by inserting a bipolar pacing electrode via an antecubital, subclavian or femoral vein and positioning it under fluoroscopic control in the apex of the right ventricle. The electrode is then connected to an external pulse generator which can be adjusted to alter the energy output or pacing rate. The threshold is the lowest output that will reliably pace the heart and should be less than 1 volt at implantation. The generator should be set to deliver an output that is at least twice this figure, and may require daily adjustment because the threshold tends to rise, due to inflammation and oedema around the tip of the electrode.

Temporary pacing may be indicated in the management of transient heart block and other arrhythmias complicating acute myocardial infarction, as a safety measure in patients with heart block or sinoatrial disease (that does not require permanent pacing) who are undergoing a general anaesthetic, or as a prelude to permanent pacing. Complications include pneumothorax and other forms of trauma related to the insertion of the wire, local infection or septicaemia (usually *Staphylococcus aureus*), and pericarditis. Failure of the system may be due to lead displacement or a progressive

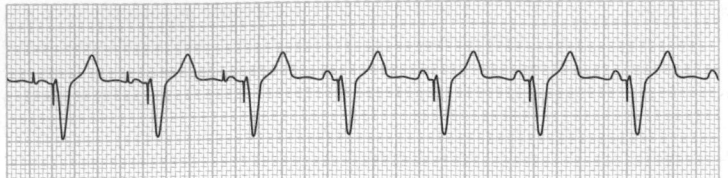

Fig. 12.59 Dual-chamber pacing. The first three beats show atrial and ventricular pacing with narrow pacing spikes in front of each P wave and QRS complex. The last four beats show spontaneous P waves with a different morphology and no pacing spike; the pacemaker senses or tracks these P waves and maintains AV synchrony by pacing the ventricle after an appropriate interval.

increase in the threshold (exit block). The complication and failure rates increase with time and it is seldom wise to use a temporary pacing system for more than 7–10 days.

The ECG of a patient whose rhythm is controlled by an artificial ventricular pacemaker placed in the right ventricle shows regular broad QRS complexes with a left bundle branch block pattern. Each complex is immediately preceded by a 'pacing spike' (see Fig. 12.59). Nearly all pulse generators are used in the 'demand' mode so that a spontaneously generated QRS complex will inhibit the pacemaker.

Permanent pacemakers

Permanent artificial pacemakers utilise the same principles, but the pulse generator is implanted under the skin. Electrodes can be placed in the apex of the right ventricle, the right atrial appendage or both (see Fig. 12.15, p. 372).

Most permanent pacemakers are programmable so the rate, output, mode etc. can be altered by an external programmer using radiofrequency or magnetic signals. This facility allows the cardiologist to prolong the life of the pacemaker by choosing optimum settings and may provide the means to overcome a wide range of pacing problems. For example, programming can be used to increase output in the face of an unexpected increase in threshold, or to alter sensitivity if the pacemaker is inappropriately inhibited by electrical potentials generated in the pectoral muscles (myopotential inhibition).

Atrial pacing may be appropriate for patients with sinoatrial disease without AV block, and ventricular pacing is the only suitable mode for patients with continuous atrial fibrillation. In dual-chamber (atrial and ventricular) pacing the atrial electrode can be used to detect spontaneous atrial activity and trigger ventricular pacing (see Fig. 12.59), thereby preserving atrioventricular synchrony and allowing the ventricular rate to increase together with the atrial rate during exercise and other forms of stress. Dual-chamber pacing is more expensive but has many advantages when compared to simple ventricular pacing; these include superior haemodynamics leading to a better effort tolerance, a lower prevalence of atrial arrhythmias in patients with sinoatrial disease, and the ability to prevent or cure the 'pacemaker syndrome' (a fall in blood pressure and dizziness precipitated by the start of ventricular pacing).

A three-letter code is used to signify the pacing mode (see Box 12.47). For example, a system that paces the atrium, senses the atrium, and is inhibited if it senses spontaneous activity is designated AAI. A system that both paces and senses the ventricle, both paces and senses the atrium, is inhibited if it senses activity in the ventricle and can trigger

12.47 INTERNATIONAL GENERIC PACEMAKER CODE

Chamber paced	Chamber sensed	Response to sensing
O = none	O = none	O = none
A = atrium	A = atrium	T = triggered
V = ventricle	V = ventricle	I = inhibited
D = both	D = both	D = both

an impulse (in the ventricle) if it senses activity in the atrium is designated DDD.

There are also 'rate-responsive' pacemakers which react (by changing the pacing rate) to parameters such as respiration or physical movement. This type of pacemaker helps to maintain an optimum heart rate and can be used in patients who are not suitable for atrial triggered pacing, e.g. those with atrial fibrillation.

The immediate complications of permanent pacing include pneumothorax, trauma, infection and lead displacement; long-term problems include infection (which can usually only be treated satisfactorily by explanting the pacing system), erosion of the generator or lead, and occasionally electromagnetic interference.

ATHEROSCLEROTIC VASCULAR DISEASE

Atherosclerotic vascular disease may manifest as coronary heart disease (e.g. angina, myocardial infarction, sudden death), cerebrovascular disease (e.g. stroke and transient ischaemic attack) or peripheral vascular disease (e.g. claudication and critical limb ischaemia). These entities often coexist and the pathogenesis of the disease is similar in all affected vessels. Occult coronary artery disease is common in those who present with other forms of atherosclerotic vascular disease (e.g. intermittent claudication or erectile dysfunction of vascular origin) and is an important cause of subsequent morbidity and mortality in such patients.

PATHOPHYSIOLOGY

Atherosclerosis is a progressive inflammatory disorder of the arterial wall that is characterised by focal lipid-rich deposits of atheroma that remain clinically silent until they become large enough to impair arterial perfusion or until ulceration or disruption of the lesion results in thrombotic occlusion or embolisation of the affected vessel. These mechanisms are common to the entire vascular tree and the clinical manifestations of atherosclerosis depend upon the site of the lesion and the vulnerability of the organ supplied.

Atherosclerosis is a disorder that begins early in life; abnormalities of arterial endothelial function have been detected among high-risk children and adolescents (e.g. cigarette smokers and those with familial hyperlipidaemia or hypertension), and fatty streaks (early atherosclerotic lesions) have been found in the arteries of victims of accidental death in the second and third decades of life. Nevertheless, clinical manifestations often do not appear until the sixth, seventh or eighth decade.

Early atherosclerosis

Fatty streaks tend to occur at sites of altered arterial shear stress such as bifurcations and are associated with abnormal endothelial function. They develop when inflammatory cells, predominantly monocytes, bind to receptors expressed by endothelial cells, migrate into the intima, take up oxidised low-density lipoprotein (LDL) from the plasma and become lipid-laden foam cells or macrophages. Extracellular lipid pools appear in the intimal space when these foam cells die and release their contents (see Fig. 12.60). Smooth muscle cells then migrate from the media of the arterial wall into the intima, in response to cytokines and

growth factors produced by the activated macrophages, and change from a contractile to a repair phenotype in an attempt to stabilise the atherosclerotic lesion. If they are successful, the lipid core will be covered by smooth muscle cells and matrix, producing a stable atherosclerotic plaque that will remain asymptomatic until it becomes large enough to obstruct arterial flow.

Advanced atherosclerosis

In an established atherosclerotic plaque macrophages mediate inflammation and smooth muscle cells promote repair; if inflammation predominates, the plaque becomes active or unstable and may be complicated by ulceration and super-added thrombosis. Cytokines such as interleukin-1, tumour necrosis factor-α, interferon gamma, platelet-derived growth factors, and matrix metalloproteinases are released by activated macrophages and may cause the intimal smooth muscle cells overlying the plaque to become senescent, resulting in thinning of the protective fibrous cap; they may also digest collagen cross-struts within the plaque. These changes make the lesion vulnerable to the effects of mechanical stress and may lead to erosion, fissuring or rupture of the plaque surface (see Fig. 12.60). Any breach in the integrity of the plaque will expose its contents to circulating blood and may trigger platelet aggregation and

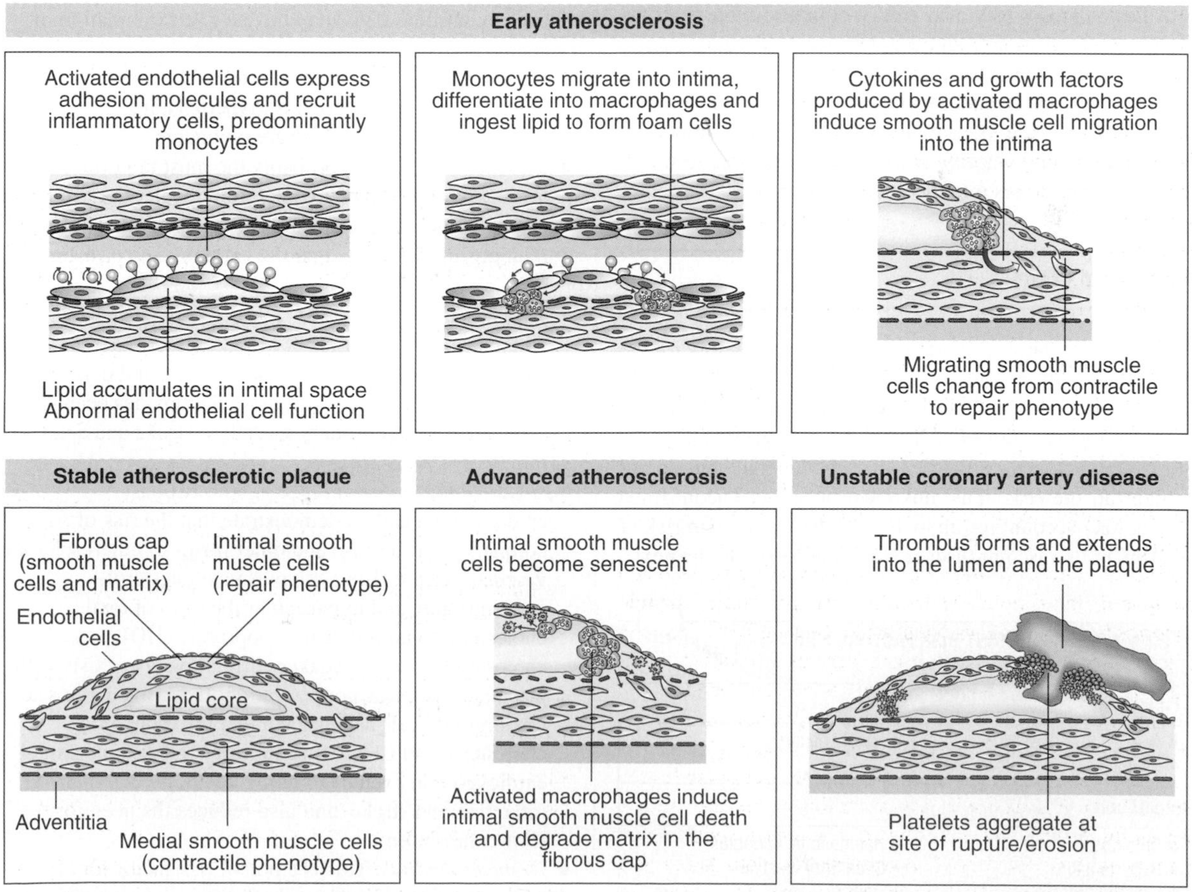

Fig. 12.60 The pathogenesis of atherosclerosis.

thrombosis that extends into the atheromatous plaque and the arterial lumen. This type of plaque event may cause partial or complete obstruction at the site of the lesion and/or distal embolisation resulting in infarction or ischaemia of the affected organ. It is the common mechanism that underlies many of the acute manifestations of atherosclerotic vascular disease (e.g. acute lower limb ischaemia, myocardial infarction and stroke).

The number and complexity of arterial plaques increase with age and with systemic risk factors (see below) but the rate of progression of individual plaques is variable. There is a complex and dynamic interaction between mechanical wall stress and atherosclerotic lesions. 'Vulnerable plaques' are characterised by a lipid-rich core, a thin fibrocellular cap, an increase in inflammatory cells, and the release of specific cytokines that degrade matrix proteins. In contrast, safe or stable plaques are typified by a small lipid pool, a thick fibrous cap and plentiful collagen cross-struts. Lipid-lowering therapy may help to stabilise vulnerable plaques. Fissuring or rupture tends to occur at sites of maximal mechanical stress, particularly the margins of an eccentric plaque, and may be triggered by a surge in blood pressure (e.g. during exercise or emotional upset). Surprisingly, plaque events are often subclinical and may heal spontaneously; however, this may allow thrombus to be incorporated into the lesion, producing plaque growth and further obstruction to flow in the arterial lumen.

Atherosclerosis may also induce complex changes in the media that lead to arterial remodelling; thus, some arterial segments may slowly constrict (negative remodelling) whilst others may gradually enlarge (positive remodelling). These changes are poorly understood but are important because they may amplify or minimise the degree to which atheroma encroaches into the arterial lumen.

RISK FACTORS

The role and relative importance of many risk factors for the development of coronary, peripheral and cerebrovascular disease have been defined in experimental animal studies, epidemiological studies and clinical interventional trials. Some key factors (see Box 12.48) have emerged but do not explain all the risk; thus, unknown or as yet unconfirmed factors may account for up to 40% of the variation in risk of atheromatous vascular disease from one person to the next.

12.48 SOME IMPORTANT RISK FACTORS FOR ATHEROSCLEROSIS	
Fixed	
• Age	• Family history
• Male sex	
Modifiable	
• Smoking	• Haemostatic variables
• Hypertension	• Sedentary lifestyle
• Lipid disorders	• Obesity
• Diabetes mellitus	• Diet

The impact of genetic risk is illustrated by twin studies; for example, a monozygotic twin of an affected individual has an eightfold increased risk, and a dizygotic twin a fourfold increased risk (compared to the general population) of dying from coronary heart disease.

The effect of risk factors is multiplicative rather than additive. People with a combination of risk factors (e.g. smoking, hypertension and diabetes) are at greatest risk and assessment should therefore be based on a holistic approach that takes account of all identifiable risk factors. It is also important to distinguish between relative risk (the proportional increase in risk) and absolute risk (the actual chance of an event). Thus, a man of 35 with a plasma cholesterol of 7 mmol/l who smokes 40 cigarettes a day is relatively much more likely to die from coronary disease within the next decade than a non-smoking woman of the same age with a normal cholesterol, but the absolute likelihood of his dying during this time is still small (high relative risk, low absolute risk).

- *Age and gender.* Age is the most powerful independent risk factor for atherosclerosis. Pre-menopausal women have much lower rates of disease than age- and risk-matched males; however, the gender difference disappears rapidly after the menopause. Randomised trials of hormone replacement therapy have not, so far, produced convincing evidence of benefit.
- *Family history.* Atherosclerotic vascular disease often runs in families. This may be due to a combination of shared genetic, environmental and lifestyle (e.g. smoking, exercise and diet) factors. The most common inherited risk characteristics (hypertension, hyperlipidaemia, diabetes) are polygenic.
- *Smoking.* Smoking is probably the most important avoidable cause of atherosclerotic vascular disease; for example, there is a strong, consistent and dose-linked relationship between cigarette smoking and ischaemic heart disease.
- *Hypertension* (see pp. 388–394). The incidence of atherosclerosis increases as blood pressure rises and the excess risk is related to both systolic and diastolic blood pressure. Antihypertensive therapy has been shown to reduce coronary mortality, stroke and heart failure.
- *Hypercholesterolaemia* (see p. 309). Robust epidemiological data demonstrate that the risk of coronary heart disease and other forms of atherosclerotic vascular disease rises with plasma cholesterol concentration, and in particular the ratio of total cholesterol to high-density lipoprotein (HDL) cholesterol. A much weaker correlation also exists with plasma triglyceride concentration. Extensive large-scale randomised trials have shown that lowering total cholesterol and LDL concentrations reduces the risk of cardiovascular events including death, myocardial infarction and stroke, and also reduces the need for revascularisation.
- *Diabetes mellitus.* This is a potent risk factor for all forms of atherosclerotic vascular disease and is often associated with diffuse disease that is difficult to treat.

Insulin resistance (normal glucose homeostasis with high levels of insulin) is associated with obesity and physical inactivity, and is also a potent risk factor for coronary heart disease. Glucose intolerance accounts for a major part of the high incidence of ischaemic heart disease in certain ethnic groups (e.g. South Asians).

- *Haemostatic factors*. Platelet activation and high levels of fibrinogen and factor VII are associated with an increased risk of myocardial infarction (coronary thrombosis). Other coagulation disorders (deficiencies of protein C, protein S, factor V Leiden) are associated with an increased risk of venous and arterial thrombosis.
- *Physical activity*. Physical inactivity roughly doubles the risk of coronary heart disease and is a major risk factor for stroke. Regular exercise (brisk walking, cycling or swimming for 20 minutes two or three times a week) appears to have a protective effect which may be related to increased HDL cholesterol, lower blood pressure, reduced blood clotting, and collateral vessel development.
- *Obesity* (see p. 301). Obesity, particularly if central or truncal, is an independent risk factor, although it is often associated with other adverse factors such as hypertension, diabetes and physical inactivity.
- *Alcohol*. A moderate intake of alcohol (2–4 units a day) appears to offer some protection from coronary disease; however, heavy drinking is associated with hypertension and excess cardiac events.
- *Other dietary factors*. Diets deficient in fresh fruit, vegetables and polyunsaturated fatty acids are associated with an increased risk of vascular disease. Low levels of vitamin C, vitamin E and other antioxidants may enhance the production of oxidised LDL. Hyperhomocysteinaemia is associated with accelerated atherosclerosis including stroke and peripheral vascular disease. Low dietary folate, vitamin B_{12} and vitamin B_6 can elevate homocysteine concentrations.
- *Mental stress and personality*. Certain personality traits are associated with an increased risk of coronary disease. Nevertheless, there is little or no evidence to support the popular belief that stress is a major cause of coronary artery disease.

PRIMARY PREVENTION

Two complementary strategies can be used to prevent atherosclerosis in apparently healthy but at-risk individuals.

The population strategy aims to modify the risk factors of the whole population through diet and lifestyle advice on the basis that even a small reduction in smoking or average cholesterol, or modification of exercise and diet will produce worthwhile benefits (see Box 12.49). Some risk factors for atheroma, such as obesity and smoking, are also associated with a high risk of other diseases and should be actively discouraged through public health measures.

In contrast, the targeted strategy aims to identify and treat high-risk individuals, who usually have a combination of

---

12.49 POPULATION ADVICE TO PREVENT CORONARY DISEASE

- Do not smoke
- Take regular exercise (minimum of 20 mins, three times a week)
- Maintain 'ideal' body weight
- Eat a mixed diet rich in fresh fruit and vegetables
- Aim to get no more than 30% of energy intake from saturated fat

---

EBM

PRIMARY PREVENTION OF ATHEROSCLEROTIC VASCULAR DISEASE—physical activity and smoking

'There is strong observational evidence that moderate to high levels of physical activity reduce the risk of coronary heart disease and stroke (relative risk reduction 30–50%). Observational studies have found that the risk of death and cardiovascular events falls when people stop smoking.'

- Doll R, Peto R, Wheatley K, et al. Mortality in relation to smoking: 40 years' observations on male British doctors. BMJ 1994; 309:901–911.
- Wannamethee G, Shaper AG. Physical activity and stroke in British middle-aged men. BMJ 1992; 304:597–601.

Further information: 🖥 www.clinicalevidence.org.uk

EBM

PREVENTION OF ATHEROSCLEROTIC DISEASE— lowering cholesterol

Primary prevention
'A systematic review of two large primary prevention trials in patients *without evidence of coronary disease* but with high cholesterol levels showed that cholesterol-lowering with statins did not significantly lower mortality but did significantly lower coronary events (angina and myocardial infarction).'

Secondary prevention
'A systematic review of three large secondary prevention trials in patients *with established coronary disease* (MI or angina) showed that cholesterol-lowering with statins substantially reduced morbidity and mortality. Benefit depended on initial risk in the population studied. NNTs for 5 years to prevent one death, in individual trials, = 31, 63 and 90.'

- LaRosa JC, He J, Vupputuri S. Effect of statins on risk of coronary disease: a meta-analysis of randomised controlled trials. JAMA 1999; 282:2340–2346.
- Scandinavian Simvastatin Survival Study Group. Randomised trial of cholesterol-lowering in 4444 patients with coronary heart disease: Scandinavian Simvastatin Survival Study (4S). Lancet 1994; 344:1383–1389.

Further information: 🖥 www.sign.ac.uk

---

risk factors and can be identified by using composite scoring systems (see p. 391 and Appendix). It is important to consider the absolute risk of atheromatous cardiovascular disease that any one individual is facing before contemplating specific antihypertensive or lipid-lowering therapy because this will help to determine whether the possible benefits of intervention are likely to outweigh the expense, inconvenience and possible side-effects of treatment. Using the same example shown on page 391 under the treatment of hypertension, a 65-year-old man with an average blood pressure of 150/90 mmHg, who smokes and has diabetes, a total:HDL cholesterol of 8 and left ventricular hypertrophy on ECG, will have a 10-year risk of CHD of 68% and a 10-year risk of any cardiovascular event of 90%. Lowering his cholesterol will reduce these risks by 30% and lowering his blood pressure will produce a further 20% reduction; both treatments would obviously be worth while. Conversely, the 55-year-old woman who has an identical blood pressure, is a non-smoker, is not diabetic and has a normal ECG and a total:HDL cholesterol of 6 has a much better outlook, with a predicted CHD risk of 14% and cardiovascular risk of 19% over the next 10 years. Although lowering her cholesterol and blood pressure would also reduce risk by 30% and 20% respectively, the value of both forms of treatment would clearly be questionable.

SECONDARY PREVENTION

Patients who already have evidence of atheromatous vascular disease (e.g. peripheral vascular disease or myocardial infarction) are at high risk of another vascular event and can be offered a variety of treatments and measures that have been shown to improve their outlook (secondary prevention). The energetic correction of risk factors, particularly smoking, hypertension and hypercholesterolaemia, is particularly important in this patient group because the absolute risk of further vascular events is very high. There has been considerable debate over what level of cholesterol should be treated, as there is some evidence of benefit at all levels; nevertheless, most physicians now aim to reduce total cholesterol concentrations to less than 5.0 mmol/l. Blood pressure should be treated to a target of 140/80, or 130/80 in those with diabetes (see p. 392). Aspirin is of benefit to all patients with evidence of vascular disease. Beta-blockers

---

SECONDARY PREVENTION IN PATIENTS WITH ATHEROSCLEROTIC VASCULAR DISEASE—use of aspirin **EBM**

'A collaborative review has shown that in patients with established ischaemic heart disease, peripheral vascular disease or thrombotic stroke, aspirin is effective in reducing morbidity and mortality (non-fatal myocardial infarction, stroke and cardiovascular death). Overall relative risk reduction = 27%.'

- Antiplatelet Trialists' Collaboration. Collaborative overview of randomised trials of antiplatelet therapy I: prevention of death, myocardial infarction, and stroke by prolonged antiplatelet therapy in various categories of people. BMJ 1994; 308:81–106.
- Hennekens C, Buring JE, Sandercock P, et al. Aspirin and other anti-platelet agents in the secondary and primary prevention of cardiovascular disease. Circulation 1989; 80:749–756.

Further information: 🖥 www.clinicalevidence.org

---

and ACE inhibitors will benefit patients with a history of myocardial infarction (see p. 442). Long-term therapy with ACE inhibitors may also reduce the risk of vascular events and death among unselected patients with vascular disease and diabetics.

Many clinical events offer an unrivalled opportunity to introduce effective secondary preventive measures. For example, patients who have just survived a myocardial infarction or undergone bypass surgery are usually keen to help themselves and may be particularly receptive to appropriate lifestyle advice, such as weight reduction, stopping smoking etc.

ISSUES IN OLDER PEOPLE
ATHEROSCLEROTIC VASCULAR DISEASE

- Atherosclerosis is not considered part of the normal ageing process, but in developed countries its prevalence is related almost exponentially to age.
- The evidence suggests that hypertension, smoking and raised cholesterol remain risk factors for adverse cardiovascular outcomes in old age and that treating these lowers risk.
- Frail older people frequently present with advanced multisystem arterial disease, along with a host of other comorbidities.
- In the very frail with extensive disease and limited life expectancy, the risks of surgical intervention may outweigh the benefits, and symptomatic care is all that should be offered.

CORONARY HEART DISEASE

Coronary heart disease (CHD) is the most common form of heart disease and the single most important cause of premature death in Europe, the Baltic states, Russia, North and South America, Australia and New Zealand. By 2020 it is estimated that it will become the major cause of death in all regions of the world.

In the UK (population 54 million) 1 in 3 men and 1 in 4 women die from CHD, an estimated 330 000 people have a myocardial infarct each year and approximately 1.3 million people have angina. The death rates from CHD in the UK are amongst the highest in Western Europe (more than 140 000 people in 1997) but are falling, particularly in younger age groups; in the last 10 years CHD mortality has fallen by 42% among UK men and women aged 16–64.

Disease of the coronary arteries is almost always due to atheroma and its complications, particularly thrombosis; the common clinical manifestations and pathological correlates of CHD are shown in Box 12.50. Occasionally, the coronary arteries are involved in other disorders such as aortitis, polyarteritis and other connective tissue disorders.

12.50 CORONARY HEART DISEASE: CLINICAL MANIFESTATIONS AND PATHOLOGY

Clinical problem	Pathology
Stable angina	Ischaemia due to fixed atheromatous stenosis of one or more coronary arteries
Unstable angina	Ischaemia caused by dynamic obstruction of a coronary artery due to plaque rupture with superimposed thrombosis and spasm
Myocardial infarction	Myocardial necrosis caused by acute occlusion of a coronary artery due to plaque rupture and thrombosis
Heart failure	Myocardial dysfunction due to infarction or ischaemia
Arrhythmia	Altered conduction due to ischaemia or infarction
Sudden death	Ventricular arrhythmia, asystole or massive myocardial infarction

STABLE ANGINA

Angina pectoris is the symptom complex caused by transient myocardial ischaemia and constitutes a clinical syndrome rather than a disease; it may occur whenever there is an imbalance between myocardial oxygen supply and demand (see Box 12.51). Coronary atheroma is by far the most common cause of angina; however, the symptom may also be a manifestation of other forms of heart disease, particularly aortic valve disease and hypertrophic cardiomyopathy.

This section describes the features of 'stable' angina pectoris which occurs when coronary perfusion is impaired by fixed or stable atheroma of the coronary arteries.

Clinical features

The history is by far the most important factor in making the diagnosis; the features of cardiac pain and the differential diagnosis of chest pain are discussed on pages 372–377.

Stable angina is characterised by central chest pain, discomfort or breathlessness that is precipitated by exertion or other forms of stress (see Box 12.52), and is promptly relieved by rest (see Figs 12.16 and 12.17, pp. 373–374). Some patients find that the pain comes when they start walking and that later it does not return despite greater effort ('start-up angina').

Physical examination is frequently negative, but should include a careful search for evidence of valve disease (particularly of the aortic valve), important risk factors (e.g. hypertension, diabetes), left ventricular dysfunction (e.g.

cardiomegaly, gallop rhythm), other manifestations of arterial disease (e.g. carotid bruits, peripheral vascular disease) and unrelated conditions that may exacerbate angina (e.g. anaemia, thyrotoxicosis).

Investigations

Resting ECG

The ECG may show evidence of previous myocardial infarction but is often normal even in patients with left main or severe three-vessel coronary artery disease. Occasionally, there is T-wave flattening or inversion in some leads, providing non-specific evidence of myocardial ischaemia or damage.

The most convincing ECG evidence of myocardial ischaemia is obtained by demonstrating reversible ST segment depression or elevation, with or without T-wave inversion, at the time the patient is experiencing symptoms (whether spontaneous or induced by exercise testing).

Exercise ECG

A formal exercise tolerance test (ETT) is usually performed using a standard treadmill or bicycle ergometer protocol (see p. 367) while monitoring the patient's ECG, blood pressure and general condition. Planar or down-sloping ST segment depression of 1 mm or more is indicative of ischaemia (see Fig. 12.61); up-sloping ST depression is less specific and often occurs in normal individuals.

Exercise testing can be used to confirm or refute a diagnosis of angina and is also a useful means of assessing the severity of coronary disease and identifying high-risk individuals (see Box 12.53). For example, the amount of exercise which can be tolerated and the extent and degree

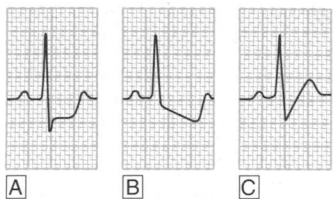

Fig. 12.61 Forms of exercise-induced ST depression. [A] Planar ST depression is usually indicative of myocardial ischaemia. [B] Down-sloping depression also usually indicates myocardial ischaemia. [C] Up-sloping depression, however, may be a normal finding.

12.51 FACTORS INFLUENCING MYOCARDIAL OXYGEN SUPPLY AND DEMAND

Oxygen demand

Cardiac work
- Heart rate
- Blood pressure
- Myocardial contractility
- Left ventricular hypertrophy

Oxygen supply

Coronary blood flow
- Duration of diastole
- Coronary perfusion pressure (aortic diastolic minus coronary sinus or right atrial diastolic pressure)
- Coronary vasomotor tone
- Oxygenation
   Haemoglobin
   Oxygen saturation

N.B. Coronary blood flow occurs mainly in diastole.

12.52 ACTIVITIES PRECIPITATING ANGINA

Common
- Physical exertion
- Cold exposure
- Heavy meals
- Intense emotion

Rare
- Lying flat (decubitus angina)
- Vivid dreams (nocturnal angina)

12.53 A GUIDE TO RISK STRATIFICATION IN STABLE ANGINA

High risk	Low risk
Post-infarct angina	Predictable exertional angina
Poor effort tolerance	Good effort tolerance
Ischaemia at low workload	Ischaemia only at high workload
Left main or three-vessel disease	Single-vessel or minor two-vessel disease
Poor LV function	Good LV function

N.B. Patients may fall between these categories.

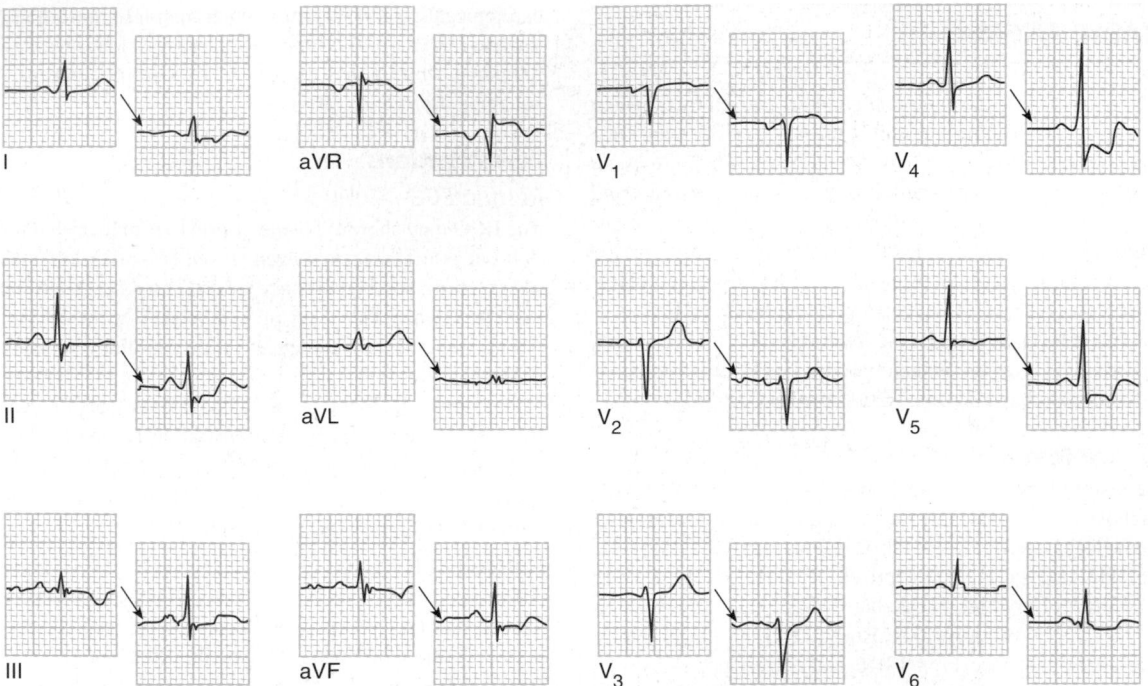

Fig. 12.62   A positive exercise test. The resting 12-lead ECG shows some minor T wave changes in the inferolateral leads but is otherwise normal. After 3 minutes' exercise on a treadmill there is marked planar ST depression in leads II, V$_4$ and V$_5$ (right offset). Subsequent coronary angiography revealed critical three-vessel coronary artery disease.

of any ST segment change (see Fig. 12.62) provide a useful guide to the likely extent of coronary disease.

Exercise testing is not infallible and may produce false positive results in the presence of digoxin therapy, left ventricular hypertrophy, left bundle branch block or Wolff–Parkinson–White syndrome. The predictive accuracy of exercise testing is lower in women than men. The test should be classed as non-contributory (and not negative) if the patient cannot achieve an adequate level of exercise because of locomotor or other non-cardiac problems.

Other forms of stress testing

Myocardial perfusion scanning. This may be helpful in the evaluation of patients with an equivocal or uninterpretable exercise test and those who are unable to exercise; its predictive accuracy is higher than that of the exercise ECG. The technique involves obtaining scintiscans of the myocardium at rest and during stress after the administration of an intravenous radioactive isotope such as [201]thallium ([201]T1) or tetrafosmin. It may be used in conjunction with conventional exercise testing or some form of pharmacological stress such as a controlled infusion of dobutamine. Thallium and tetrafosmin are taken up by viable perfused myocardium. A perfusion defect present during stress but not rest provides evidence of reversible myocardial ischaemia (see Fig. 12.63), whereas a persistent perfusion defect seen during both phases of the study is usually indicative of previous myocardial infarction.

Stress echocardiography. This is an alternative to myocardial perfusion scanning and with an experienced operator can achieve similar predictive accuracy (superior to exercise ECG). The technique uses transthoracic echocardiography to identify ischaemic segments of myocardium and areas of infarction. The former characteristically exhibit reversible defects in contractility during pharmacological stress (for example, with dobutamine infusion); the latter typically do not contract at rest or during stress.

Coronary arteriography

This provides detailed information about the extent and nature of coronary artery disease (see Fig. 12.64), and is usually performed with a view to coronary bypass grafting or percutaneous coronary intervention (PCI—see p. 429). In some patients, diagnostic coronary angiography may be indicated when non-invasive tests have failed to elucidate the cause of atypical chest pain. The procedure is performed under local anaesthesia and requires specialised radiological equipment, cardiac monitoring and an experienced operating team.

Management

The management of angina pectoris involves:

● a careful assessment of the likely extent and severity of arterial disease
● the identification and control of significant risk factors (e.g. smoking, hypertension, hyperlipidaemia)
● the use of measures to control symptoms
● the identification of high-risk patients and application of treatment to improve life expectancy.

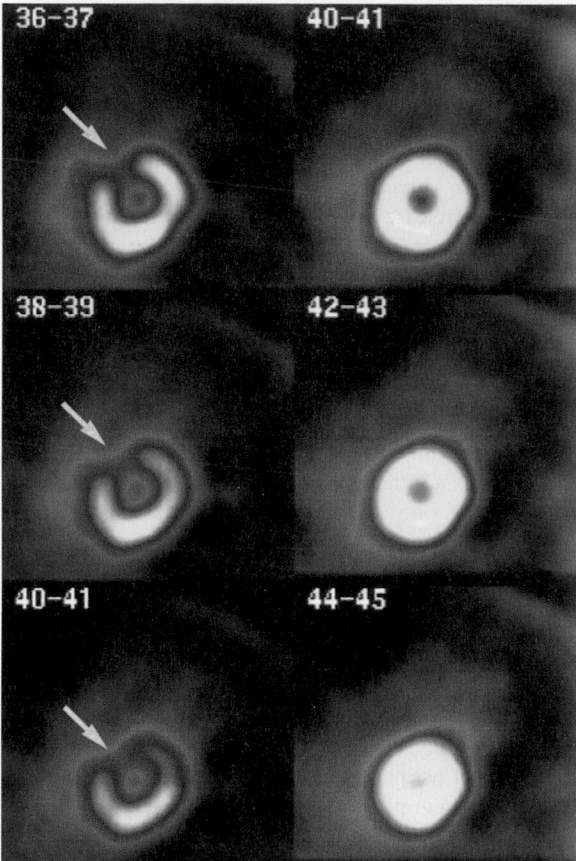

Fig. 12.63 A thallium scan showing reversible anterior myocardial ischaemia. The images are cross-sectional tomograms of the left ventricle. The resting scans (right) show even uptake of thallium and look like doughnuts; during stress (in this case a dobutamine infusion) there is reduced uptake of thallium, particularly along the anterior wall (arrows), and the scans look like crescents (left).

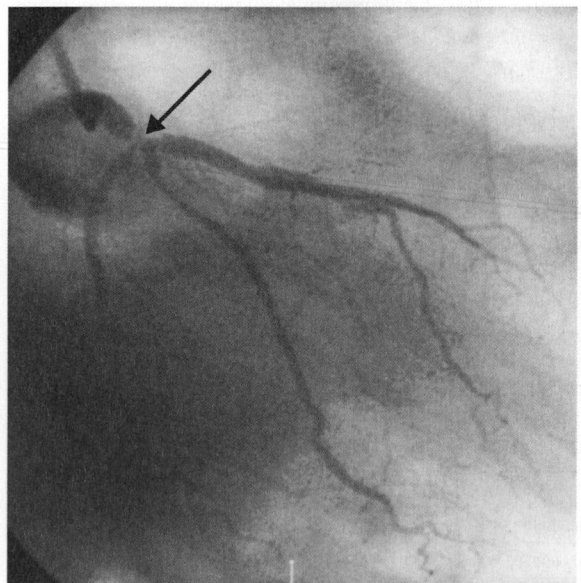

Fig. 12.64 Coronary angiogram from a patient with stable angina. There is severe stenosis of the left main stem (arrow).

Symptoms alone are a poor guide to the extent of coronary artery disease; exercise or pharmacological stress testing is therefore advisable in all patients who are potential candidates for revascularisation. An algorithm for the investigation and treatment of patients with stable angina is shown in Figure 12.65.

Treatment should start with a careful explanation of the problem and a discussion of the potential lifestyle and medical interventions that may relieve symptoms and improve prognosis (see Box 12.54). Anxiety and misconceptions often contribute to disability; for example, some patients avoid all forms of exertion because they believe that each attack of

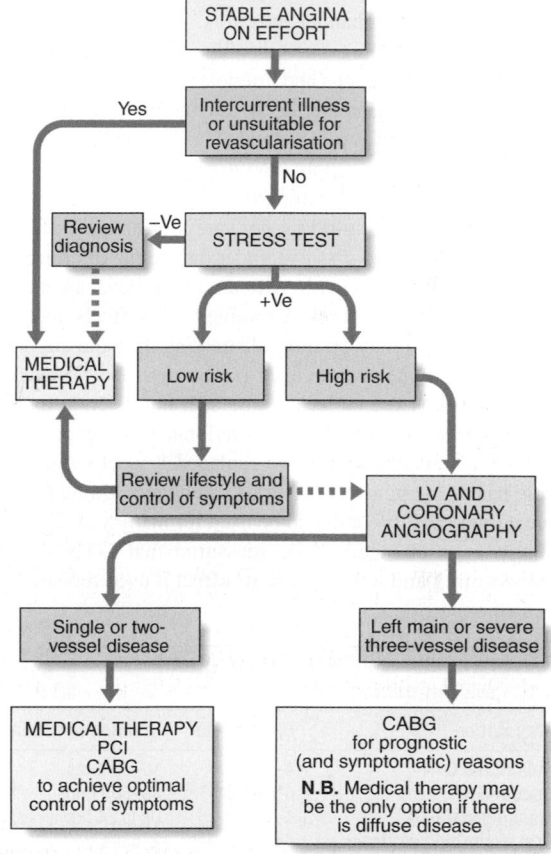

Fig. 12.65 A schema for the investigation and treatment of stable angina on effort. (PCI = percutaneous coronary intervention; CABG = coronary artery bypass grafting)

12.54 ADVICE TO PATIENTS WITH STABLE ANGINA

- Do not smoke
- Aim at ideal body weight
- Take regular exercise (exercise up to, but not beyond, the point of chest pain is beneficial and may promote collateral vessels)
- Avoid severe unaccustomed exertion, and vigorous exercise after a heavy meal or in very cold weather
- Take sublingual nitrate before undertaking exertion that may induce angina

angina is a 'mini heart attack' that results in permanent damage. Effective management of these psychological factors can make a huge difference to the patient's quality of life.

Antiplatelet therapy

Low-dose (75–150 mg) aspirin reduces the risk of adverse events such as myocardial infarction and should be prescribed for all patients with coronary artery disease indefinitely (see EBM panel, p. 424). Clopidogrel (75 mg daily) is an equally effective but more expensive antiplatelet agent that can be prescribed if aspirin causes troublesome dyspepsia or other side-effects.

Anti-anginal drug treatment

Four groups of drugs are used to help relieve or prevent the symptoms of angina: nitrates, β-blockers, calcium antagonists and potassium channel activators.

Nitrates. These drugs act directly on vascular smooth muscle to produce venous and arteriolar dilatation; their beneficial effects in angina are due to a reduction in myocardial oxygen demand (lower preload and afterload) and an increase in myocardial oxygen supply (coronary vasodilatation).

Sublingual glyceryl trinitrate (GTN) administered from a metered-dose aerosol (400 µg per spray) or as a tablet (300 or 500 µg) allowed to dissolve under the tongue or crunched and retained in the mouth will usually relieve an attack of angina in 2–3 minutes. Unwanted side-effects include headache (which may be more distressing than the angina), symptomatic hypotension and, rarely, syncope. To avoid these symptoms the tablet may be spat out as soon as the angina is relieved. GTN tablets deteriorate when exposed to the atmosphere and should be replaced 8 weeks after the bottle has been opened; in contrast, sublingual nitrate sprays have a long shelf life and can be used for many years.

Patients often need to be reassured that GTN is not habit-forming and will not lose its effect if used repeatedly.

They should also be encouraged to use the drug prophylactically before engaging in exercise that is liable to provoke symptoms.

Sublingual GTN has a short duration of action (see Box 12.55); however, a variety of alternative nitrate preparations can provide a more prolonged therapeutic effect. GTN can be given percutaneously as a patch (5–10 mg daily), or as a slow-release buccal tablet (1–5 mg 6-hourly). GTN is subject to extensive first-pass metabolism in the liver and is therefore virtually ineffective when swallowed; however, other nitrates such as isosorbide dinitrate (10–20 mg 8-hourly) and isosorbide mononitrate (20–60 mg once or twice a day) can be given by mouth. Headache is common but tends to diminish if the patient perseveres with the treatment. Continuous nitrate therapy causes pharmacological tolerance and this should be avoided by using a regimen that includes a nitrate-free period of 6–8 hours every day. A variety of once-daily proprietary preparations with a built-in nitrate-free period are available. It is usually advisable to schedule the medication so that drug levels are low during the night when the patient is inactive; however, if nocturnal angina is a prominent symptom, long-acting nitrates can be given at the end of the day instead.

Beta-blockers. These drugs lower myocardial oxygen demand by reducing heart rate, blood pressure and myocardial contractility. Unfortunately, they can exacerbate the symptoms of peripheral vascular disease and may provoke bronchospasm in patients with obstructive airways disease. The properties and side-effects of β-blockers are discussed on pages 416–417.

In theory, non-selective β-blockers may aggravate coronary vasospasm by blocking the coronary artery β_2-adrenoceptors and it is usually advisable to use a once-daily cardioselective preparation (e.g. atenolol 50–100 mg daily, slow-release metoprolol 200 mg daily, bisoprolol 5–10 mg daily).

A β-blocking drug should not be withdrawn abruptly because this may precipitate dangerous arrhythmias, worsening angina or myocardial infarction (the β-blocker withdrawal syndrome).

Calcium antagonists. These drugs inhibit the slow inward current caused by the entry of extracellular calcium through the cell membrane of excitable cells, particularly cardiac and arteriolar smooth muscle, and lower myocardial oxygen demand by reducing blood pressure and myocardial contractility.

12.55 DURATION OF ACTION OF SOME NITRATE PREPARATIONS

Preparation	Peak action	Duration of action
Sublingual GTN	4–8 mins	10–30 mins
Buccal GTN	4–10 mins	30–300 mins
Transdermal GTN	1–3 hrs	Up to 24 hrs
Oral isosorbide dinitrate	45–120 mins	2–6 hrs
Oral isosorbide mononitrate	45–120 mins	6–10 hrs

12.56 CALCIUM ANTAGONISTS USED FOR THE TREATMENT OF ANGINA

Drug	Dose	Feature
Nifedipine	5–20 mg 8-hourly*	May cause marked tachycardia
Nicardipine	20–40 mg 8-hourly	May cause less myocardial depression than the other drugs in this group
Amlodipine	2.5–10 mg daily	Ultralong-acting
Verapamil	40–80 mg 8-hourly*	Commonly causes constipation; useful anti-arrhythmic properties (see p. 418)
Diltiazem	60–120 mg 8-hourly*	Similar anti-arrhythmic properties to verapamil
*Once- or twice-daily slow-release preparations are available.		

Nifedipine, nicardipine and amlodipine often cause a reflex tachycardia; this may be counterproductive and it is often best to use these drugs in combination with a β-blocker. In contrast, verapamil and diltiazem are particularly suitable for patients who are not receiving a β-blocker because they inhibit conduction through the AV node and tend to cause a bradycardia. The calcium antagonists may reduce myocardial contractility and can aggravate or precipitate heart failure. Other unwanted effects include oedema, flushing, headache and dizziness.

The dosage and some of the distinguishing features of these drugs are listed in Box 12.56.

Potassium channel activators. These drugs (e.g. nicorandil 10–30 mg 12-hourly orally) have arterial and venous dilating properties but do not exhibit the tolerance seen with nitrates.

Although each of these groups of drug has been shown to be superior to placebo in relieving the symptoms of angina, there is little convincing evidence that one group is more effective than another. Moreover, many commonly used combinations of anti-anginal drugs have not been evaluated in well-controlled clinical trials. Nevertheless, it is conventional to start therapy with low-dose aspirin, sublingual

GTN and a β-blocker, and then add a calcium channel antagonist or a long-acting nitrate later, if necessary. The goal is the control of angina with minimum side-effects and the simplest possible drug regimen. There is little or no evidence that prescribing multiple anti-anginal drugs is of benefit, and revascularisation should be considered if an appropriate combination of two drugs produces an unsatisfactory symptomatic response.

Invasive treatment

The most widely used invasive options for the treatment of ischaemic heart disease include percutaneous coronary intervention (PCI), also known as percutaneous transluminal coronary angioplasty (PTCA), reversed saphenous vein bypass grafting and internal mammary artery grafting (coronary artery bypass grafting, or CABG).

Percutaneous coronary intervention (PCI)

This is performed by passing a fine guidewire across a coronary stenosis under radiographic control and using it to position a balloon which is then inflated to dilate the stenosis (see Fig. 12.15, p. 372 and Fig. 12.66). A coronary stent is a piece of coated metallic 'scaffolding' that can be deployed

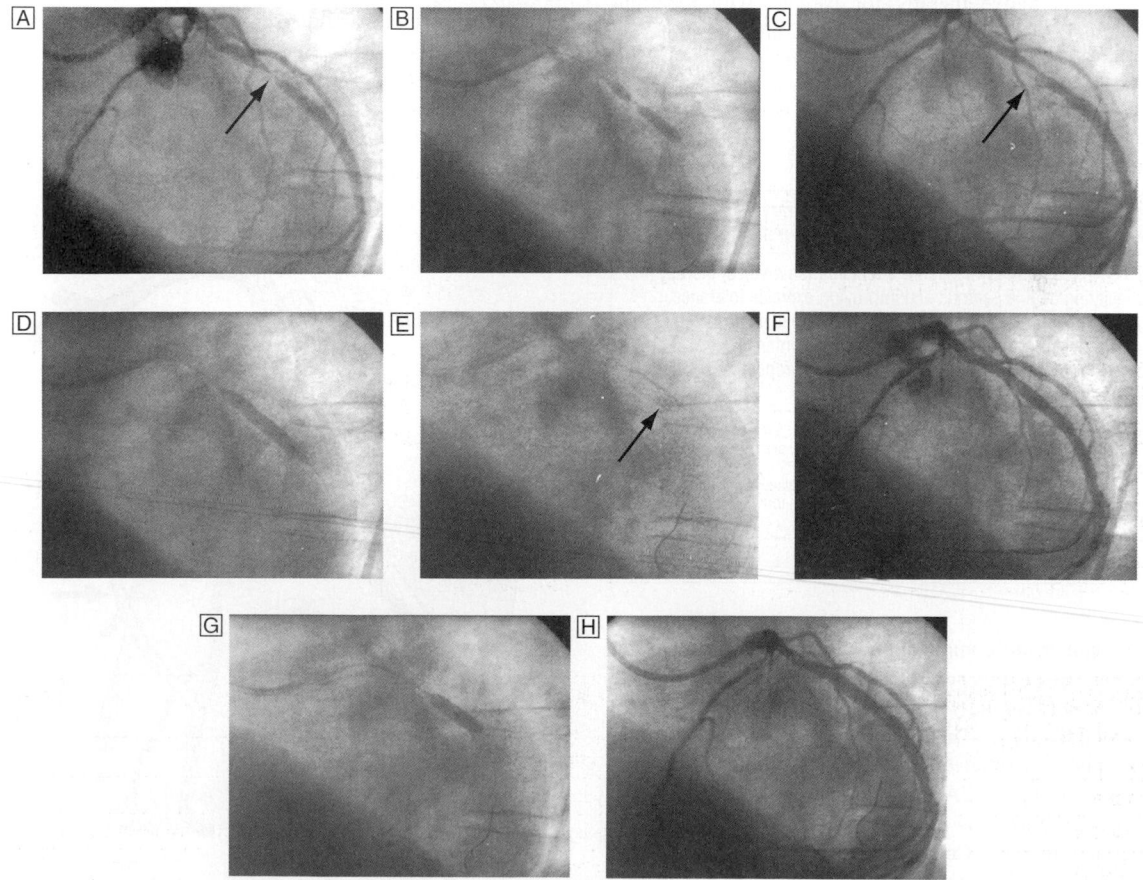

Fig. 12.66 Percutaneous coronary intervention. A sequence of images from a 58-year-old woman with stable angina. A Severe stenosis of the circumflex artery (arrow). B A balloon has been advanced into the stenosis, over a guidewire, and has been inflated. (Note the waisting caused by the lesion.) C Residual stenosis and dissection (tramline shadow—arrow) after balloon dilatation. D A stent is deployed on a balloon. E The stent is visible on plain fluoroscopy (arrow). F Angiogram after stenting. G A short balloon is used to dilate the stent at high pressure. H Final result.

on a balloon and used to maximise and maintain dilatation of a stenosed vessel. The routine use of stents, in appropriate vessels, reduces both acute complications and the incidence of clinically important restenosis.

PCI provides an effective symptomatic treatment for chronic stable angina but there is no evidence that it improves survival. PCI is mainly used in single or two-vessel disease; stenoses in bypass grafts can be dilated as well as those in the native coronary arteries, and the technique is often used to provide palliative therapy for patients with recurrent angina after CABG. Coronary surgery is usually the preferred option in patients with three-vessel or left main disease, but recent trials have demonstrated that PCI is also feasible in such patients.

The main acute complications of PCI are occlusion of the target vessel or a side branch by thrombus or a loose flap of intima (coronary artery dissection), and consequent myocardial damage. This occurs in about 2–5% of procedures and can often be corrected by deploying a stent; however, emergency CABG is sometimes required. Minor myocardial damage, as indicated by elevation of sensitive intracellular markers (troponins), occurs in up to 10% of cases. The main long-term complication of PCI is restenosis, which occurs in up to one-third of cases; this is due to a combination of elastic recoil and smooth muscle proliferation and tends to occur within 3 months. Stenting substantially reduces the risk of restenosis, probably because it

allows the operator to achieve more complete dilatation in the first place. Recurrent angina (approximately 15–20% in stented patients at 6 months) may require further PCI or bypass grafting.

The risk of complications and the likely success of the procedure are closely related to the morphology of the stenoses, the experience of the operator and the presence of important comorbidity (e.g. diabetes, peripheral arterial disease). A good outcome is less likely if the target lesion is complex, long, eccentric or calcified, lies on a bend or within a tortuous vessel, involves a branch or contains acute thrombus.

Adjunctive therapy with potent platelet inhibitors (clopidogrel and glycoprotein IIb/IIIa inhibitors) in addition to aspirin and heparin has been shown to improve the outcome of PCI, with lower short- and long-term rates of death and myocardial infarction.

Coronary artery bypass grafting (CABG)

The internal mammary arteries or reversed segments of the patient's own saphenous vein can be used to bypass coronary artery stenoses (see Fig. 12.67). This usually involves major surgery under cardiopulmonary bypass but in some cases grafts can be applied to the beating heart. The operative mortality is approximately 1.5%, but risks are higher in elderly patients and those with poor left ventricular function.

Approximately 90% of patients are free of angina a year after surgery but fewer than 60% of patients are asymptomatic 5 or more years after CABG. Early post-operative angina is

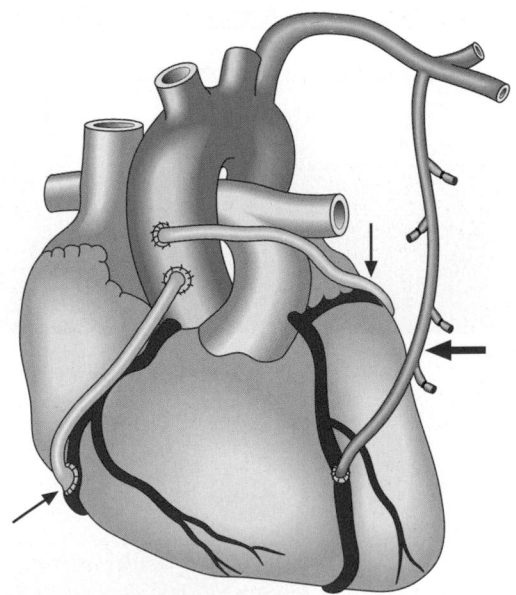

Fig. 12.67   A triple coronary artery bypass graft operation.
Reversed saphenous vein grafts have been placed on the circumflex and right coronary arteries (small arrows) and the left internal mammary artery has been used to graft the left anterior descending coronary artery (large arrow).

usually due to graft failure arising from technical problems during the operation or poor 'run off' due to disease in the distal native coronary vessels. Late recurrence of angina may be due to progressive disease in the native coronary arteries or graft degeneration. Less than 50% of vein grafts are patent 10 years after surgery, although internal mammary artery grafts last much longer.

Aspirin (75–150 mg daily) and clopidogrel (75 mg daily) have both been shown to improve graft patency and should be prescribed indefinitely if well tolerated. Aggressive lipid-lowering therapy has also been shown to slow the progression of disease in the native coronary arteries and bypass grafts and to reduce clinical cardiovascular events; total blood cholesterol should therefore be reduced to at least 5.0 mmol/l (see EBM panel, p. 423). There is substantial excess cardiovascular morbidity and mortality in patients who continue to smoke after bypass grafting. Persistent smokers are twice as likely to die in the 10 years following surgery compared with those who give up at surgery.

CABG has been shown to improve survival in patients with left main coronary stenosis, and symptomatic patients with three-vessel coronary disease (i.e. involving left anterior descending, circumflex and right coronary arteries) or two-vessel disease involving the proximal left anterior descending coronary artery. Improvement in survival is most marked in those who have undergone left internal mammary artery grafting and those with impaired left ventricular function prior to surgery.

Neurological complications are common, with a 1–5% risk of perioperative stroke. Between 30 and 80% of patients develop short-term cognitive impairment that is often mild and typically resolves within 6 months. There are also reports of long-term cognitive decline which may be evident in more than 30% of patients at 5 years.

Coronary angioplasty and CABG are compared in Box 12.57 and the EBM panel.

12.57	COMPARISON OF PERCUTANEOUS CORONARY INTERVENTION (PCI) AND CORONARY ARTERY BYPASS GRAFTING (CABG)	

	PCI	CABG
Death	0.5%	1.5%
Myocardial infarction*	2%	10%
Hospital stay	12–36 hrs	5–8 days
Return to work	2–5 days	6–12 weeks
Recurrent angina	30% at 6 months	10% at 1 year
Repeat revascularisation	20% at 2 years	2% at 2 years
Neurological complications	Rare	Common (see text)
Other complications	Emergency CABG Vascular damage related to access site	Diffuse myocardial damage Infection (chest, wound) Wound pain

* Defined as CK-MB > 2 x normal—see page 437.

STABLE ANGINA—use of coronary artery bypass grafting (CABG) EBM

'A systematic review of RCTs has shown benefit of CABG compared with medical treatment at 5, 7 and 10 years after surgery. Greatest benefit occurred in those with a significant stenosis in the left main coronary artery or those with three-vessel disease and impaired ventricular function. These RCTs were carried out up to the mid-1980s and may not be relevant to current practice as both medical and surgical treatment have improved. A recent RCT showed clear benefit of revascularisation (CABG or angioplasty) compared with optimal medical therapy.'

- Yusuf S, Zucker D, Pedozzi P, et al. Effect of coronary bypass graft surgery on survival: overview of 10 year results from randomised trials by the coronary artery bypass graft surgery trialists collaboration. Lancet 1994; 344:563–570.
- Davies RF, Goldberg AD, Forman S, et al. Asymptomatic cardiac ischaemia pilot (ACIP) study two-year follow up; outcomes of patients randomised to initial strategies of medical therapy versus revascularisation. Circulation 1997; 95:2037–2043.

Further information: www.sign.ac.uk

STABLE ANGINA—comparison of percutaneous coronary intervention (PCI) and coronary artery bypass grafting (CABG) EBM

'In low- to medium-risk patients a systematic review has found no difference in death, myocardial infarction and quality of life. However, PCI was associated with a greater need for repeat procedures. The trials reported pre-dated the routine use of intracoronary stents (which improve long-term results) and so may not be of relevance to current practice. One large trial found that at 5 years mortality in patients with diabetes was lower with CABG than PCI (19.4% vs 34.5%, p = 0.003).'

- Pocock SJ, Henderson RA, Rickards AF, et al. Meta-analysis of randomised trials comparing coronary angioplasty with bypass surgery. Lancet 1995; 346:1184–1189.
- Bypass Angioplasty Revascularisation Investigation (BARI) Investigators. Comparison of coronary bypass surgery with angioplasty in multivessel disease. N Engl J Med 1996; 335:217–225.

Further information: www.sign.ac.uk

Prognosis

Symptoms are a poor guide to prognosis; nevertheless the 5-year mortality of patients with severe angina (NYHA class III or IV—see p. 359) is nearly double that of patients with mild symptoms. Exercise testing and other forms of stress testing are much more powerful predictors of mortality; for example, in one study the 4-year mortality of patients with stable angina and a negative exercise test was 1%, compared to more than 20% in those with a strongly positive test.

In general the prognosis of coronary artery disease is related to the number of diseased vessels (one-, two- or three-vessel coronary artery disease) and the degree of left ventricular dysfunction. A patient with single-vessel disease and good LV function has an excellent outlook (5-year survival > 90%), whereas a patient with severe LV dysfunction and extensive three-vessel disease has a poor prognosis (5-year survival < 30%) without revascularisation.

Spontaneous symptomatic improvement due to the development of collateral vessels is common.

ANGINA WITH NORMAL CORONARY ARTERIES

Approximately 10% of patients who report stable angina on effort will be found to have angiographically normal coronary arteries. Many of these patients are women and the mechanism of their symptoms is often difficult to establish.

Coronary artery spasm

Vasospasm in coronary arteries may coexist with atheroma, especially in unstable angina (see below); however, occasionally (< 1% of all cases of angina) vasospasm may occur without angiographically detectable atheroma. This form of angina is sometimes known as variant angina and may be accompanied by spontaneous and transient ST elevation on the ECG (Prinzmetal's angina). Calcium antagonists, nitrates and other coronary vasodilators (e.g. nicorandil) are the most useful therapeutic agents.

Syndrome X

The constellation of typical angina on effort, objective evidence of myocardial ischaemia on stress testing, and angiographically normal coronary arteries is sometimes known as syndrome X. This disorder is poorly understood but carries a good prognosis and may respond to treatment with calcium antagonists.

UNSTABLE ANGINA

Unstable angina is a clinical syndrome that is characterised by rapidly worsening angina (crescendo angina), angina on minimal exertion or angina at rest. The condition shares common pathophysiological mechanisms with acute myocardial infarction (see Fig. 12.60, p. 421) and the term 'acute coronary syndrome' is used to describe both disorders. These entities comprise a spectrum of disease that encompasses ischaemia with no myocardial damage, ischaemia with minimal myocardial damage, partial thickness (non-Q wave) myocardial infarction, and full thickness (Q wave) myocardial infarction (see Fig. 12.68).

An acute coronary syndrome may present as a new phenomenon or against a background of chronic stable angina. The culprit lesion is usually a complex ulcerated or fissured atheromatous plaque with adherent platelet-rich thrombus and local coronary artery spasm (see Fig. 12.60, p. 421 and Fig. 12.69). In contrast to stable angina (which is related to a fixed obstruction), episodes of myocardial ischaemia are due to an abrupt reduction in coronary blood flow caused by thrombosis or spasm (supply-led ischaemia). It is important to appreciate that this is a dynamic process whereby the degree of obstruction may either increase by accretion and changes in plaque morphology, sometimes leading to complete occlusion of the vessel, or regress, sometimes only temporarily, due to the effects of platelet disaggregation and endogenous thrombolysis.

Diagnosis and risk stratification

The assessment of acute chest pain is described in detail on pages 374–377 and depends heavily on an analysis of the character of the pain and its associated features, evaluation of the ECG, and serial measurements of biochemical markers of cardiac damage, such as troponin I and T. A 12-lead ECG is mandatory and is the most useful method of initial triage (see Fig. 12.19, p. 376). Evolving transmural infarction is characterised by persistent ST elevation, new Q waves or new left bundle branch block, and is discussed in

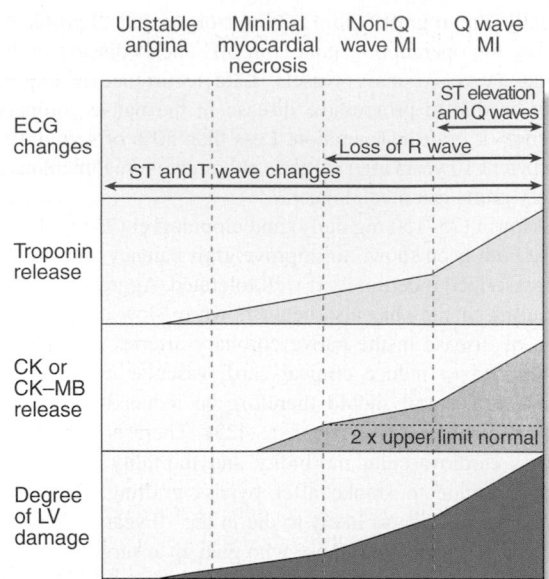

Fig. 12.68   The spectrum of acute coronary syndromes. The relation between ECG changes, biochemical markers of damage and the extent of myocardial necrosis. (CK = creatine kinase)

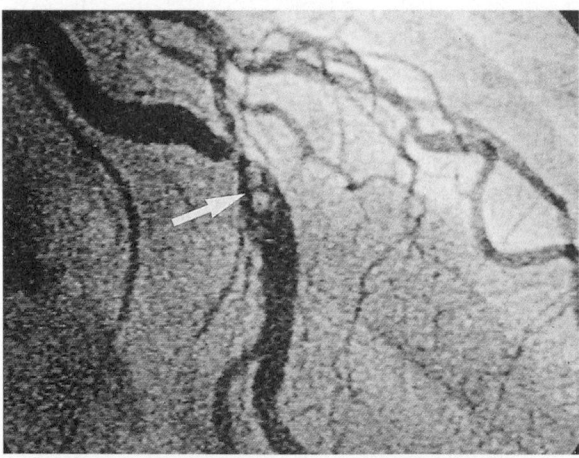

Fig. 12.69   Coronary angiogram from a patient with unstable angina. The angiogram demonstrates a complex stenosis of the circumflex coronary artery with a filling defect due to adherent thrombus (arrow).

the next section. In patients with unstable angina or partial thickness (non-Q wave or non-ST elevation) myocardial infarction, the ECG may show ST/T wave changes including ST depression, transient ST elevation and T wave inversion; the T wave changes are sometimes prolonged.

Approximately 12% of patients with well-characterised unstable angina or non-ST segment elevation myocardial infarction progress to acute infarction or death, and almost a third will suffer a recurrence of severe ischaemic pain, within 6 months of the index event. The risk markers that are indicative of an adverse prognosis include recurrent ischaemia, extensive ECG changes at rest or during pain, the release of biochemical markers (creatine kinase or troponin—see p. 436), arrhythmias and haemodynamic complications (e.g. hypotension, mitral regurgitation) during episodes of

12.58 UNSTABLE ANGINA: RISK STRATIFICATION

	High risk	Low risk
Clinical	Post-infarct angina Recurrent pain at rest Heart failure	No history of MI Rapid resolution of symptoms
ECG	Arrhythmia ST depression Transient ST elevation Persistent deep T wave inversion	Minor or no ECG changes
Biochemistry	Troponin T > 0.1 µg/l	Troponin T < 0.1 µg/l

N.B. There is a 5- to 10-fold difference in risk between the lowest and highest risk groups.

ischaemia; those who experience unstable angina following acute myocardial infarction are also at increased risk. Risk stratification is important because it guides the use of more complex pharmacological and interventional treatment (see Box 12.58 and Fig. 12.19, p. 376).

Management

Patients should be admitted urgently to hospital because there is a significant risk of death or acute myocardial infarction during the unstable phase and appropriate medical therapy can reduce the incidence of adverse events by at least 50%.

The initial treatment should include bed rest, antiplatelet therapy (aspirin 75–325 mg daily and/or clopidogrel 75 mg daily—see first EBM panel) and a β-blocker (e.g. atenolol 50–100 mg daily or metoprolol 50–100 mg 12-hourly). A dihydropyridine calcium antagonist (e.g. nifedipine or

amlodipine) can be added to the β-blocker, but may cause an unwanted tachycardia if used alone; verapamil or diltiazem is therefore the calcium antagonist of choice if a β-blocker is contraindicated. An intravenous infusion of unfractionated heparin, with dose adjusted according to the thrombin time, or subcutaneous low molecular weight heparin—for example, enoxaparin 1 mg/kg 12-hourly—should be given. If pain persists or recurs, infusions of intravenous nitrates (e.g. GTN 0.6–1.2 mg/hr or isosorbide dinitrate 1–2 mg/hr) or buccal nitrates may help, but such patients should also be considered for revascularisation.

Most low-risk patients stabilise with aspirin, heparin and anti-anginal therapy, and can be gradually mobilised. If there are no contraindications, exercise testing should be performed prior to or shortly following discharge. Coronary arteriography with a view to revascularisation should be considered in patients at high risk, including those who fail to settle on medical therapy, those with extensive ECG changes, those with an elevated plasma troponin and those with severe pre-existing stable angina. This often reveals disease that is amenable to PCI (see Fig. 12.70); however, if the lesions are not suitable for PCI the patient should be considered for urgent CABG. High-risk patients, particularly those who undergo PCI, should also be considered for treatment with an intravenous glycoprotein IIb/IIIa inhibitor such as abciximab, tirofiban or eptifibatide.

UNSTABLE ANGINA—use of oral antiplatelet agents **EBM**

'A systematic review has found that aspirin alone (75–325 mg/day) reduces the risk of death and myocardial infarction in patients with unstable angina. NNT = 20. A large RCT has shown that the combination of clopidogrel (75 mg daily) and aspirin is superior to aspirin alone. NNT for death, MI and stroke = 45.'

- Antiplatelet Trialists Collaboration. Collaborative overview of randomised trials of antiplatelet therapy I: prevention of death, myocardial infarction, and stroke by prolonged antiplatelet therapy in various categories of patients. BMJ 1994; 308:81–106.
- The Clopidogrel in Unstable Angina to prevent Recurrent Events (CURE) trial investigators. Effects of clopidogrel in addition to aspirin in preventing major vascular events in patients with acute coronary syndromes. N Engl J Med 2001; 345:494–502.

Further information: ⌨ www.acc.org

UNSTABLE ANGINA—use of low molecular weight heparin **EBM**

'RCTs have found that treating patients with unstable angina with aspirin plus low molecular weight heparin is more effective than aspirin alone (reduction in combined endpoint of death, myocardial infarction, refractory angina and urgent need for revascularisation).'

- Antman EM, Cohen M, Radley D, et al. for the TIMI IIB (Thrombolysis in Myocardial Infarction) and ESSENCE (Efficacy and Safety of Subcutaneous Enoxaparin in Non-Q-wave Coronary Events) Investigators. Assessment of the treatment effect of enoxaparin for unstable angina/non-Q-wave myocardial infarction. TIMI IIB-ESSENCE meta-analysis. Circulation 1999; 100:1602–1608.
- Eikelboom JW, Anand SS, Malmberg K, et al. Unfractionated heparin and low-molecular weight heparin in acute coronary syndrome without ST elevation: a meta-analysis. Lancet 2000; 355:1936–1942.

Further information: ⌨ www.acc.org

ACUTE CORONARY SYNDROMES—use of intravenous glycoprotein IIb/IIIa inhibitors **EBM**

'A meta-analysis of randomised trials involving 32 135 patients with acute coronary syndromes showed that antiplatelet treatment with i.v. glycoprotein IIb/IIIa inhibitors was associated with a reduction in the combined endpoint of death or myocardial infarction (predominantly MI). Most benefit was seen in the context of percutaneous coronary intervention and there was no convincing evidence of benefit in patients who were treated without revascularisation. NNT (death or MI) = 50; NNT (death, MI or revascularisation) = 33.'

- Kong DF, Califf RM, Miller DP, et al. Clinical outcomes of therapeutic agents that block the platelet glycoprotein IIb/IIIa integrin in ischemic heart disease. Circulation 1998; 2829–2835.
- Bertrand ME, Simoons ML, Fox KAA, et al. Management of acute coronary syndromes: acute coronary syndromes without persistent ST segment elevation. Recommendations of the Task Force of the European Society of Cardiology. Eur Heart J 2000; 21:1406–1432.

Further information: ⌨ www.nice.org.uk

ISSUES IN OLDER PEOPLE
ANGINA

- The prevalence of coronary artery disease increases with age and among the elderly affects women almost as often as men.
- Comorbid conditions such as anaemia and thyroid disease are common and may worsen angina.
- Calcific aortic stenosis is common and should be sought in all old people with angina.
- When myocardial ischaemia occurs, age-related changes in autonomic function, myocardial compliance and diastolic relaxation can cause the presentation to be with symptoms of heart failure such as breathlessness, rather than with chest pain.
- Angioplasty and coronary artery bypass surgery can provide symptomatic relief, although with increased procedure-related morbidity and mortality. Outcome is determined by the number of diseased vessels, severity of myocardial dysfunction and the number of concomitant diseases as much as by age itself.

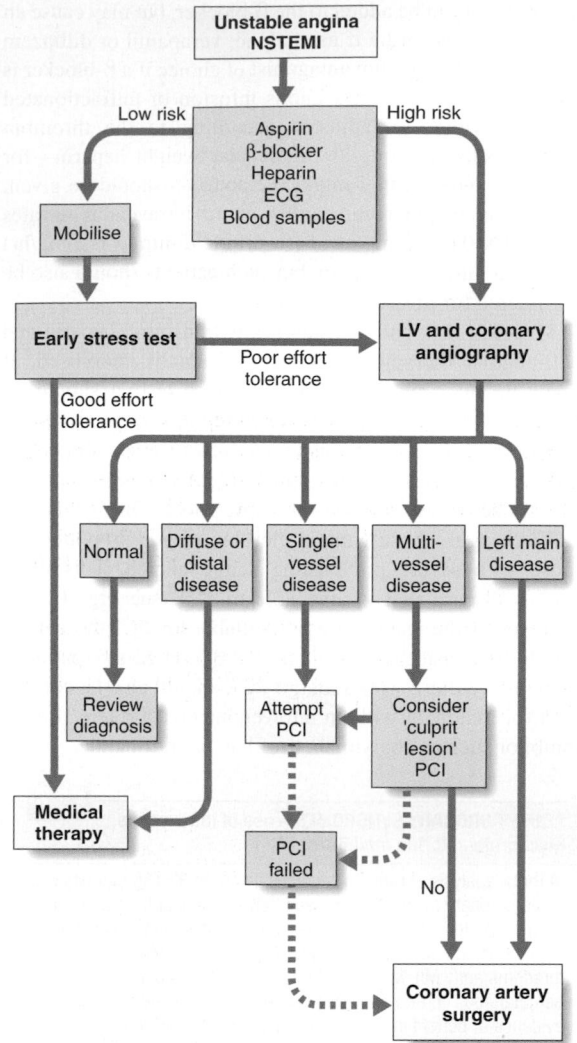

Unstable angina
NSTEMI

Fig. 12.70   A guide to the investigation and treatment of unstable angina and non-ST segment elevation myocardial infarction (NSTEMI). See Figure 12.19 on page 376, Box 12.58 and text for identification of high- and low-risk patients.

MYOCARDIAL INFARCTION

Myocardial infarction (MI) is almost always due to the formation of occlusive thrombus at the site of rupture or erosion of an atheromatous plaque in a coronary artery (see Fig. 12.60, p. 421). The thrombus often undergoes spontaneous lysis over the course of the next few days, although by this time irreversible myocardial damage has occurred. Without treatment the infarct-related artery remains permanently occluded in 30% of patients. The process of infarction progresses over several hours and therefore most patients present when it is still possible to salvage myocardium and improve outcome (see Fig. 12.71).

Clinical features

Pain is the cardinal symptom of MI, but breathlessness, vomiting, and collapse or syncope are common features (see Box 12.59). The pain occurs in the same sites as angina but is usually more severe and lasts longer; it is often described as a tightness, heaviness or constriction in the chest. At its worst the pain is one of the most severe which can be experienced and the patient's expression and pallor may vividly convey the seriousness of the situation.

Most patients are breathless and in some this is the only symptom. Indeed, some myocardial infarcts pass unrecognised. Painless or 'silent' myocardial infarcts are particularly common in elderly and diabetic patients. If syncope occurs, it is usually due to an arrhythmia or profound hypotension. Vomiting and sinus bradycardia are often due to vagal stimulation and are particularly common in patients with inferior MI. Nausea and vomiting may also be caused or aggravated by opiates given for pain relief. Sometimes infarction occurs in the absence of physical signs.

Sudden death, from ventricular fibrillation or asystole, may occur immediately, and many deaths occur within the first hour. If the patient survives this most critical stage, the liability to dangerous arrhythmias remains, but diminishes as each hour goes by. The development of cardiac failure reflects the extent of myocardial damage and is the major cause of death in those who survive the first few hours of infarction.

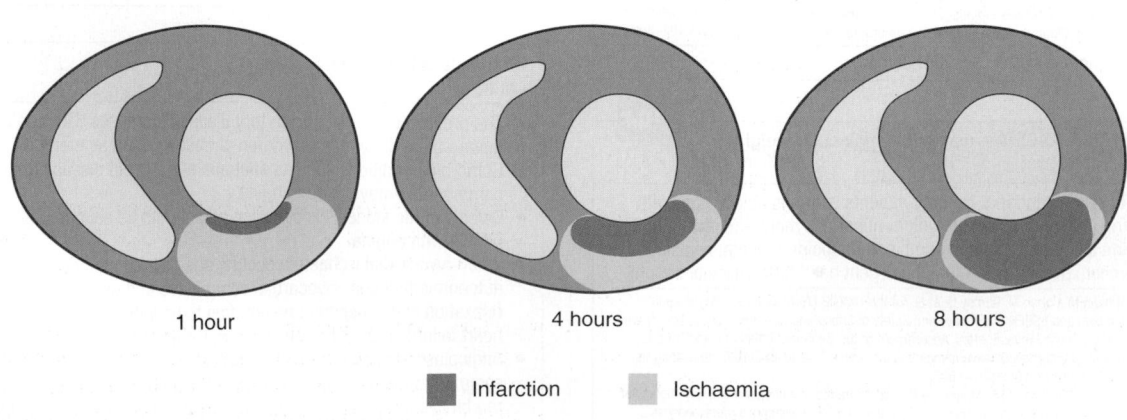

1 hour   4 hours   8 hours

■ Infarction   ■ Ischaemia

Fig. 12.71   The time course of myocardial infarction. The relative proportion of ischaemic, infarcting and infarcted tissue slowly changes over a period of 12 hours. In the early stages of myocardial infarction a significant proportion of the myocardium in jeopardy is potentially salvageable.

12.59 CLINICAL FEATURES OF MYOCARDIAL INFARCTION

Symptoms

- Prolonged cardiac pain
    Chest, throat, arms, epigastrium or back
- Anxiety
    Fear of impending death
- Nausea and vomiting
- Breathlessness
- Collapse/syncope

Physical signs

- Signs of sympathetic activation
    Pallor, sweating, tachycardia
- Signs of vagal activation
    Vomiting, bradycardia
- Signs of impaired myocardial function
    Hypotension, oliguria, cold peripheries
    Narrow pulse pressure
    Raised jugular venous pressure
    Third heart sound
    Quiet first heart sound
    Diffuse apical impulse
    Lung crepitations
- Signs of tissue damage
    Fever
- Signs of complications
    e.g. Mitral regurgitation, pericarditis (see below)

Differential diagnosis

The differential diagnosis is wide and includes most causes of central chest pain or collapse (see p. 374).

Investigations

Electrocardiography

The ECG is usually a sensitive and specific way of confirming the diagnosis; however, it may be difficult to interpret if there is bundle branch block or evidence of previous MI. Only rarely is the initial ECG entirely normal, but in up to one-third of cases the initial ECG changes may not be diagnostic.

The earliest ECG change is usually ST elevation; later on there is diminution in the size of the R wave, and in transmural (full thickness) infarction a Q wave begins to develop. One explanation for the Q wave is that the myocardial infarct acts as an 'electrical window', transmitting the changes of potential from within the ventricular cavity and allowing the ECG to 'see' the reciprocal R wave from the other walls of the ventricle. Subsequently, the T wave becomes inverted because of a change in ventricular repolarisation; this change persists after the ST segment has returned to normal. These features are shown diagrammatically in Figure 12.72 and their sequence is sufficiently reliable for the approximate age of the infarct to be deduced.

In contrast to transmural lesions, partial thickness or subendocardial infarction causes ST/T wave changes (see Fig. 12.73) without Q waves or prominent ST elevation; this is often accompanied by some loss of the R waves in the leads facing the infarct and is also known as non-Q wave or non-ST elevation myocardial infarction (see above).

The ECG changes are best seen in the leads which 'face' the infarcted area. When there has been anteroseptal

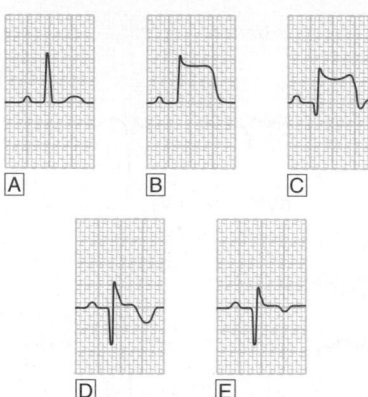

Fig. 12.72   The serial evolution of ECG changes in full thickness myocardial infarction. [A] Normal ECG complex. [B] Acute ST elevation ('the current of injury'). [C] Progressive loss of the R wave, developing Q wave, resolution of the ST elevation and terminal T wave inversion. [D] Deep Q wave and T wave inversion. [E] Old or established infarct pattern—the Q wave tends to persist but the T wave changes become less marked.

The rate of evolution is very variable but, in general, stage B appears within minutes, stage C within hours, stage D within days and stage E after several weeks or months. This diagrammatic representation should be compared with the actual ECGs in Figures 12.74, 12.75 and 12.76.

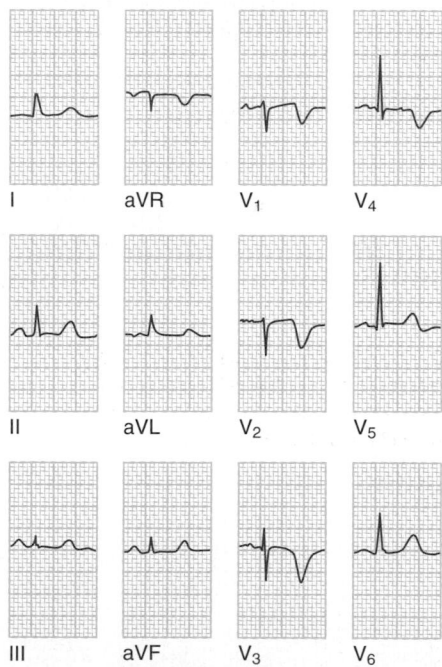

Fig. 12.73   Recent anterior subendocardial (partial thickness) infarction. There is deep symmetrical T wave inversion together with a reduction in the height of the R wave in leads V_1, V_2, V_3 and V_4.

infarction, abnormalities are found in one or more leads from V_1 to V_4, while anterolateral infarction produces changes from V_4 to V_6, in aVL and in lead I. Inferior infarction is best shown in leads II, III and aVF, while at the same time leads I, aVL and the anterior chest leads may show 'reciprocal' changes of ST depression (see Figs 12.74, 12.75 and 12.76).

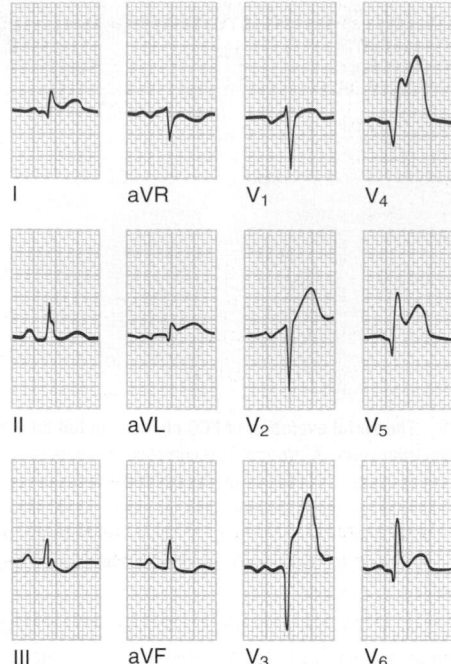

Fig. 12.74   Acute full thickness anterior myocardial infarction. This ECG was recorded from a 48-year-old man who had developed severe chest pain 6 hours earlier. There is ST elevation in leads I, aVL, V_2, V_3, V_4, V_5 and V_6, and there are Q waves in leads V_3, V_4 and V_5. Anterior infarcts with prominent changes in leads V_2, V_3 and V_4 are sometimes called 'anteroseptal' infarcts, as opposed to 'anterolateral' infarcts where the ECG changes are predominantly found in V_4, V_5 and V_6.

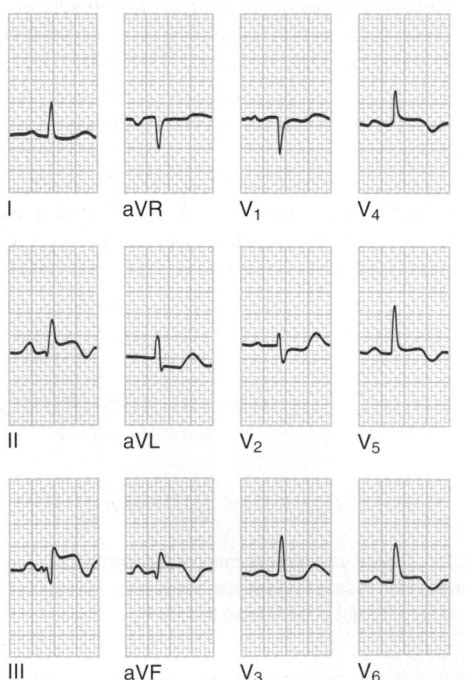

Fig. 12.75   Acute full thickness inferolateral myocardial infarction. This ECG was recorded from a 55-year-old woman who had developed severe chest pain 4 hours earlier. There is ST elevation in the inferior leads II, III and aVF and the lateral leads V_4, V_5 and V_6. There is also 'reciprocal' ST depression in leads aVL and V_2.

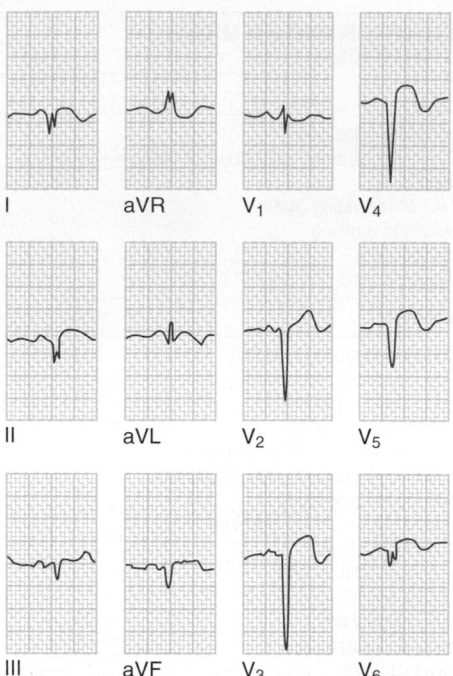

Fig. 12.76   Established anterior and inferior full thickness infarction. This ECG was recorded from a 70-year-old man who had presented with an acute anterior infarct 2 days earlier and had been treated for an inferior myocardial infarct 11 months before then. There are Q waves in the inferior leads (II, III and aVF) and Q waves with some residual ST elevation in the anterior leads (I and V_2–V_6).

Infarction of the posterior wall of the left ventricle does not cause ST elevation or Q waves in the standard leads, but can be diagnosed by the presence of reciprocal changes (ST depression and a tall R wave in leads V_1–V_4). Some infarctions (especially inferior) also involve the right ventricle; this may be identified by recording from additional leads placed over the right praecordium.

Plasma biochemical markers

MI causes a detectable rise in the plasma concentration of enzymes and proteins that are normally concentrated within cardiac cells. The biochemical markers that are most widely used in the detection of MI are creatine kinase (CK), a more sensitive and cardiospecific isoform of this enzyme—CK-MB, and the cardiospecific proteins troponins T and I. The troponins are also released, to a minor degree, in unstable angina with minimal myocardial damage (see Fig. 12.68, p. 432). Serial (usually daily) estimations are particularly helpful because it is the change in plasma concentrations of these markers that is of diagnostic value (see Fig. 12.77).

CK starts to rise at 4–6 hours, peaks at about 12 hours and falls to normal within 48–72 hours. CK is also present in skeletal muscle, and a modest rise in CK (but not CK-MB) may sometimes be due to an intramuscular injection, vigorous physical exercise or, in old people particularly, a fall. Defibrillation causes significant release of CK but not CK-MB or troponins. The most sensitive markers of myocardial cell damage are the cardiac troponins T and I, which are released within 4–6 hours and remain elevated for up to 2 weeks.

CORONARY HEART DISEASE **12**

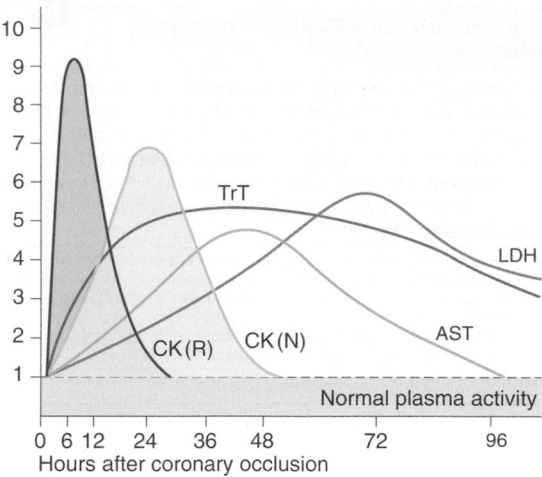

Fig. 12.77 Changes in plasma enzyme concentrations after myocardial infarction. Creatine kinase (CK) and troponin T (TrT) are the first to rise, followed by aspartate aminotransferase (AST) and then lactate (hydroxybutyrate) dehydrogenase (LDH). In patients treated with a thrombolytic agent reperfusion is usually accompanied by a rapid rise in plasma creatine kinase (curve CK (R)) due to a washout effect; if there is no reperfusion, the rise is less rapid but the area under the curve is often greater (curve CK (N)).

The American College of Cardiology and the European Society of Cardiology have redefined MI as 'a typical rise in cardiac troponin T or I, or CK-MB, above the 99th centile for normal, with at least one of the following: ischaemic symptoms, development of pathological Q waves on the ECG, ischaemic ECG changes (ST depression or elevation) or coronary artery intervention (e.g. PCI)'. This definition therefore includes non-ST segment elevation MIs as well as those that evolve through ST segment elevation and Q wave development.

Other blood tests

A leucocytosis is usual, reaching a peak on the first day. The erythrocyte sedimentation rate becomes raised and may remain so for several days. C-reactive protein (CRP) is also elevated in acute MI.

Chest radiography

This may demonstrate pulmonary oedema which is not evident on clinical examination (see Fig. 12.22, p. 380). The heart size is often normal but there may be cardiomegaly due to pre-existing myocardial damage.

Cardiac ultrasound

Echocardiography can be performed at the bedside and is a very useful technique for assessing left and right ventricular function and for detecting important complications such as cardiac rupture, ventricular septal defect, mitral regurgitation and pericardial effusion.

EARLY MANAGEMENT

Patients with suspected acute MI require immediate access to medical/paramedical care and defibrillation facilities. In the UK ambulances are equipped with semi-automatic advisory defibrillators. A patient with severe chest pain also

12.60 EARLY MANAGEMENT OF ACUTE MYOCARDIAL INFARCTION
Provide facilities for defibrillation
Immediate measures
● High-flow oxygen ● I.v. access ● ECG monitoring ● 12-lead ECG ● I.v. analgesia (opiates) and antiemetic
Reperfusion
● Aspirin plus thrombolytic or primary PCI
Detect and manage acute complications
● Arrhythmias ● Ischaemia ● Heart failure

requires urgent medical assessment and analgesia, so it is often appropriate to summon an ambulance and a general practitioner at the same time.

The essentials of the immediate management of acute MI are listed in Box 12.60.

Patients are usually managed in a dedicated cardiac unit because this offers a convenient way of concentrating the necessary expertise, monitoring and resuscitation facilities. If there are no complications, the patient can be mobilised from the second day and discharged from hospital on the fifth or sixth day.

Analgesia

Adequate analgesia is essential not only to relieve severe distress, but also to lower adrenergic drive and thereby reduce pulmonary and systemic vascular resistance and susceptibility to ventricular arrhythmias. Intravenous opiates (initially morphine sulphate 10 mg or diamorphine 5 mg) and antiemetics (initially cyclizine 50 mg or prochlorperazine 12.5 mg) should be administered through an intravenous cannula and titrated against the response by giving repeated small aliquots until the patient is comfortable. Intramuscular injections should be avoided because the clinical effect may be delayed by poor skeletal muscle perfusion and a painful haematoma may form following thrombolytic therapy.

Aspirin

Oral administration of 75–300 mg aspirin daily improves survival (30% reduction in mortality) on its own, and

EBM
ACUTE MYOCARDIAL INFARCTION—use of aspirin
'A systematic review of RCTs has found that, in people with acute myocardial infarction, aspirin reduces mortality (NNT = 40), reinfarction (NNT = 100) and stroke (NNT = 300). The optimal dose of aspirin is 160–325 mg acutely, followed by a maintenance dose of 75 mg daily.'
● Second International Study of Infarct Survival (ISIS 2) Collaborative Group. Randomized trial of intravenous streptokinase, oral aspirin, both or neither among 17,187 cases of suspected acute myocardial infarction. Lancet 1988; ii:349–360. ● Antiplatelet Trialists' Collaboration. Collaborative overview of randomised trials of antiplatelet therapy I: prevention of death, myocardial infarction, and stroke by prolonged antiplatelet therapy in various categories of people. BMJ 1994; 308:81–106.
Further information: 💻 www.escardio.org

437

enhances the effect of thrombolytic therapy. The first tablet (300 mg) should be given in a soluble or chewable form and the therapy should be continued indefinitely if there are no unwanted effects.

Acute reperfusion: thrombolysis and primary percutaneous coronary intervention

Thrombolysis. Coronary thrombolysis helps restore coronary patency (see Fig. 12.78), preserves left ventricular function and improves survival. Successful thrombolysis leads to reperfusion with relief of pain, resolution of acute ST elevation and sometimes transient arrhythmias (e.g. idioventricular rhythm). The sooner the patient is treated, the better the results will be; any delay will only increase the extent of myocardial damage—'minutes mean muscle'.

Clinical trials have shown that the appropriate use of these drugs can reduce the hospital mortality of myocardial infarction by between 25% and 50% (see EBM panel) and follow-up studies have demonstrated that this survival advantage is maintained for at least 10 years. The benefit is greatest in those patients who receive treatment within the first few hours, and choice of agent is less important than speed of treatment. Pre-hospital thrombolysis may be appropriate if transfer times are prolonged (> 30 mins) and the necessary expertise and ECG facilities are available.

Streptokinase, 1.5 million units in 100 ml of saline given as an intravenous infusion over 1 hour, is a widely used regimen. Streptokinase is relatively cheap (approximately £60 per dose in the UK) but is antigenic and occasionally causes serious allergic manifestations. The drug may also cause hypotension, which can often be managed by stopping the infusion and restarting at a slower rate. Circulating neutralising antibodies are formed following treatment with streptokinase and may persist for 5 years or more. These antibodies can render subsequent infusions of streptokinase ineffective so it is advisable to use another non-antigenic agent if the patient requires further thrombolysis in the future.

EBM

ACUTE MYOCARDIAL INFARCTION—thrombolytic treatment

'A systematic review of RCTs has found that prompt thrombolytic treatment (within 12 hours, and particularly within 6 hours, of the onset of symptoms) reduces mortality in patients with acute myocardial infarction and ECG changes of ST elevation or new bundle branch block (NNT = 56). Intracranial haemorrhage was more common in people given thrombolysis with one additional stroke for every 250 people treated.'

- Fibrinolytic Therapy Trialists' (FTT) Collaborative Group. Indications for fibrinolytic therapy in suspected acute myocardial infarction: collaborative overview of early mortality and major morbidity results from all randomised trials of more than 1000 patients. Lancet 1994; 343:311–322.
- Collins R, Peto R, Baigent BM, Sleight P. Aspirin, heparin and fibrinolytic therapy in suspected acute myocardial infarction. N Engl J Med 1997; 336:847–860.

Further information: 💻 www.escardio.org

Alteplase (human tissue plasminogen activator or tPA) is a genetically engineered drug and is approximately 7–10 times more expensive than streptokinase; it is not antigenic and seldom causes hypotension. The standard regimen is given over 90 minutes (bolus dose of 15 mg, followed by 0.75 mg/kg body weight, but not exceeding 50 mg, over 30 minutes and then 0.5 mg/kg body weight, but not exceeding 35 mg, over 60 minutes). Many units only use tPA if streptokinase is contraindicated by virtue of allergy, previous exposure or profound hypotension. However, there is evidence that the drug may produce better survival rates than streptokinase, particularly among high-risk patients (e.g. large anterior infarct), but with a slightly higher risk of intracerebral bleeding (10 per 1000 increased survival, but 1 per 1000 more non-fatal stroke).

Large-scale trial data have demonstrated that bolus administration of tenecteplase (TNK) is as effective as alteplase in relation to the risk of major cardiac events including death and MI. Intracerebral bleeding risks are similar. However, other major bleeding and transfusion risks are lower and the practical advantages of bolus administration

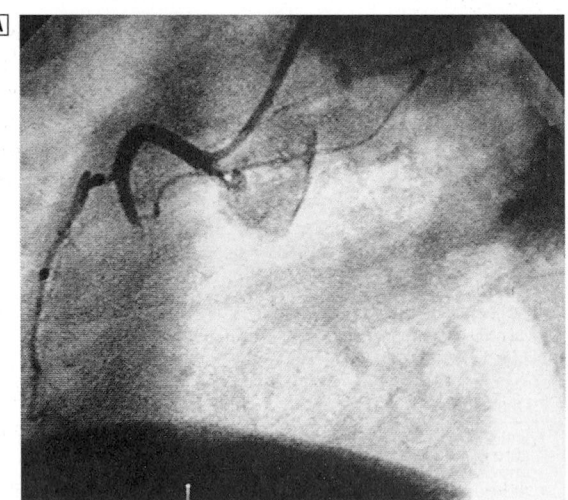 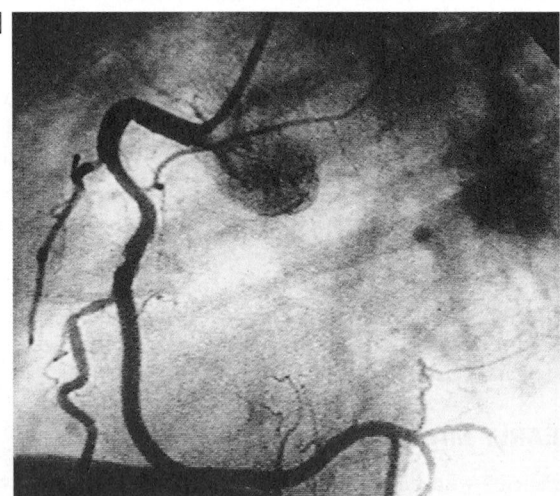

Fig. 12.78 Coronary angiograms from a patient with acute inferior myocardial infarction. [A] Complete occlusion of the proximal right coronary artery. [B] Appearance of the right coronary artery following successful thrombolytic therapy.

may provide opportunities for prompt treatment in the emergency department or in the pre-hospital setting.

Reteplase (rPA) is administered as a double bolus and trial data indicate a similar outcome to that achieved with alteplase, although some of the bleeding risks appear slightly higher. The double bolus administration may provide practical advantages over the infusion of alteplase.

An overview of all the large randomised trials confirms that thrombolytic therapy significantly reduces short-term mortality in patients with suspected MI if it is given within 12 hours of the onset of symptoms and the ECG shows bundle branch block or characteristic ST segment elevation of greater than 1 mm in the limb leads or 2 mm in the chest leads. Thrombolysis appears to be of little net benefit in other patient groups, specifically those who present more than 12 hours after the onset of symptoms and those with a normal ECG or ST depression. In patients with ST elevation or bundle branch block the absolute benefit of thrombolysis plus aspirin is approximately 50 lives saved per 1000 patients treated within 6 hours and 40 lives saved per 1000 patients treated between 7 and 12 hours after the onset of symptoms.

The major hazard of thrombolytic therapy is bleeding. Cerebral haemorrhage causes 4 extra strokes per 1000 patients treated and the incidence of other major bleeds is between 0.5% and 1%. Accordingly, it may be wise to withhold the treatment if there is a significant risk of serious bleeding. Some potential contraindications to thrombolytic therapy are outlined in Box 12.61.

12.61 RELATIVE CONTRAINDICATIONS TO THROMBOLYTIC THERAPY (POTENTIAL CANDIDATES FOR PRIMARY ANGIOPLASTY)

- Active internal bleeding
- Previous subarachnoid or intracerebral haemorrhage
- Uncontrolled hypertension
- Recent surgery (within 1 month)
- Recent trauma (including traumatic resuscitation)
- High probability of active peptic ulcer
- Pregnancy

The potential benefits and risks of thrombolytic therapy must be assessed in every case. For example, it would be reasonable to give thrombolytic therapy to a patient who presents early with evidence of extensive anterior infarction despite a history of active peptic ulceration. On the other hand, the risks of thrombolysis would probably exceed the benefits in a patient with a similar history of peptic ulceration who presents late with evidence of limited inferior myocardial infarction.

Primary percutaneous coronary intervention (PCI). Immediate or primary angioplasty (without thrombolysis) of the infarct-related coronary artery is a safe and effective alternative to thrombolytic therapy (when performed promptly, in experienced high-volume centres). This form of treatment is particularly suitable for patients in whom the hazards of thrombolysis are high, but it is not widely available.

Although rescue angioplasty is sometimes undertaken in patients who do not respond to thrombolytic therapy, the benefits of this form of treatment have not yet been established in randomised trials.

Anticoagulants

Subcutaneous heparin (12 500 units twice daily), given in addition to oral aspirin, may prevent reinfarction after successful thrombolysis and reduce the risk of thromboembolic complications. Clinical trials have shown that this form of therapy, when given for 7 days or until discharge from hospital, produces a small reduction in short-term mortality (approximately 5 lives saved per 1000 patients treated) but also increases the risk of cerebral haemorrhage (0.56% versus 0.4%) and of other bleeding complications (1% versus 0.8%). Intravenous heparin should be given for 48–72 hours following thrombolysis with alteplase, TNK or reteplase. Recent trial data suggest that low molecular weight heparin can be used in place of unfractionated heparin and with similar safety.

A period of treatment with warfarin should be considered if there is persistent atrial fibrillation or evidence of extensive anterior infarction, or if echocardiography shows mobile mural thrombus, because these patients are at increased risk of systemic thromboembolism.

Beta-blockers

Intravenous β-blockers (e.g. atenolol 5–10 mg given over 5 minutes or metoprolol 5–15 mg given over 5 minutes) relieve pain, reduce arrhythmias and improve short-term mortality in patients who present within 12 hours of the onset of symptoms, but should be avoided if there is heart failure, heart block or severe bradycardia. Chronic oral β-blocker therapy improves long-term survival and should be given to all patients who can tolerate it (see p. 417).

Nitrates and other agents

Sublingual glyceryl trinitrate (300–500 µg) is a valuable first-aid measure in threatened infarction, and intravenous nitrates (nitroglycerin 0.6–1.2 mg/hour or isosorbide dinitrate 1–2 mg/hour) are useful for the treatment of left ventricular failure and the relief of recurrent or persistent ischaemic pain.

Large-scale trials have shown that there is no evidence of a survival advantage from the routine use of oral nitrate therapy, oral calcium antagonists or intravenous magnesium in patients with acute MI.

Complications of infarction

Arrhythmias

Nearly all patients with acute MI have some form of arrhythmia; in many cases this is transient and of no haemodynamic or prognostic significance. Various degrees of heart block (see pp. 413–415) are also common. Some common arrhythmias are listed in Box 12.62; diagnosis and management are discussed in detail on pages 405–418.

Pain relief, rest, reassurance and the correction of hypokalaemia can all play a major role in the prevention of arrhythmias.

Ventricular fibrillation. This occurs in about 5–10% of patients who reach hospital, and is thought to be the major cause of death in those who die before receiving medical attention. Prompt defibrillation will usually restore sinus rhythm. Moreover, the prognosis of patients who are successfully resuscitated in this way is identical to the prognosis of patients with acute MI that is not complicated by ventricular fibrillation. The need to recognise and treat ventricular fibrillation quickly is one of the main foundations on which the policy of acute coronary care is built. Prompt pre-hospital resuscitation and defibrillation have the potential to save many more lives than thrombolysis.

Atrial fibrillation. This is common, frequently transient, and may not require treatment. However, if the arrhythmia causes a rapid ventricular rate with severe hypotension or circulatory collapse, cardioversion by means of an immediate synchronised DC shock should be considered. In other situations digoxin (see p. 418) is usually the treatment of choice. Atrial fibrillation (due to acute atrial stretch) is often a feature of impending or overt left ventricular failure, and therapy may be ineffective if heart failure is not recognised and treated appropriately. Anticoagulation may be required.

Sinus bradycardia. This does not usually require treatment, but if there is hypotension or haemodynamic deterioration atropine (0.6 mg i.v.) may be given.

Heart block (see section on AV block complicating acute MI, p. 414). Heart block complicating inferior infarction is usually temporary and often resolves following thrombolytic therapy; it may also respond to atropine (0.6 mg i.v. repeated as necessary). However, if there is clinical deterioration due to second-degree or complete heart block, a temporary pacemaker should be considered. Heart block complicating anterior infarction is more serious because asystole may suddenly supervene; it constitutes an indication for the insertion of a prophylactic temporary pacemaker (see p. 419).

Ischaemia

Post-infarct angina occurs in up to 50% of patients. Most patients have a residual stenosis in the infarct-related vessel despite successful thrombolysis, and this may cause angina if there is still viable myocardium downstream; nevertheless, there is no evidence that routine angioplasty improves outcome after thrombolysis. In some patients occlusion of a vessel may precipitate angina by disturbing a system of collateral flow that was compensating for disease in another vessel.

Patients who develop angina at rest or on minimal exertion following MI should be managed in the same way as patients with unstable angina who are thought to be at high risk (see pp. 432–434). Intravenous nitrates (e.g. nitroglycerin 0.6–1.2 mg/hour or isosorbide dinitrate 1–2 mg/hour) and either intravenous heparin (1000 units/hour, adjusted according to the thrombin time) or low molecular weight heparin may be helpful, and early coronary angiography with a view to angioplasty of the 'culprit' lesion should be considered. Glycoprotein IIb/IIIa inhibitors are of benefit in selected patients, particularly those undergoing PCI.

Acute circulatory failure

Acute circulatory failure usually reflects extensive myocardial damage and indicates a bad prognosis. All the other complications of MI are more likely to occur when acute heart failure is present.

The assessment and management of heart failure complicating acute MI are discussed in detail on pages 378–379.

Pericarditis

This may occur at any stage of the illness but is particularly common on the second and third days. The patient may recognise that a different pain has developed, even though it is at the same site, and often finds that the pain is positional and tends to be worse, or sometimes only appears, on inspiration. A pericardial rub may be audible.

The post-myocardial infarction syndrome (Dressler's syndrome) is characterised by persistent fever, pericarditis and pleurisy and is probably due to autoimmunity. The symptoms tend to occur a few weeks or even months after the infarct and often subside after a few days; prolonged or severe symptoms may require treatment with high-dose aspirin, an NSAID or even corticosteroids.

Mechanical complications

Part of the necrotic muscle in a fresh infarct may tear or rupture, with devastating consequences:

- Papillary muscle damage may cause acute pulmonary oedema and shock due to the sudden onset of severe mitral regurgitation with a loud pansystolic murmur and third heart sound. The diagnosis can be confirmed by Doppler echocardiography, and emergency mitral valve replacement may be necessary. Lesser degrees of mitral regurgitation are common and may be transient.
- Rupture of the interventricular septum may cause left-to-right shunting through a ventricular septal defect. This usually presents with sudden haemodynamic deterioration accompanied by a new loud pansystolic murmur, and may be difficult to distinguish from acute mitral regurgitation. However, patients with an acquired

ventricular septal defect tend to develop right heart failure rather than pulmonary oedema. Doppler echocardiography and right heart catheterisation will confirm the diagnosis. Without prompt surgery the condition is usually fatal.

- Rupture of the ventricle may lead to cardiac tamponade and is usually fatal (see p. 479), although it may be possible to support a patient with an incomplete rupture until emergency surgery is performed.

Embolism

Thrombus often forms on the endocardial surface of freshly infarcted myocardium; this may lead to systemic embolism and occasionally causes a stroke or ischaemic limb.

Venous thrombosis and pulmonary embolism may occur but have become less common due to the use of prophylactic anticoagulants and early mobilisation.

Impaired ventricular function, remodelling and ventricular aneurysm

Acute full thickness MI is often followed by thinning and stretching of the infarcted segment (infarct expansion); this leads to an increase in wall stress with progressive dilatation and hypertrophy of the remaining ventricle (ventricular remodelling—see Fig. 12.79). As the ventricle dilates, it becomes less efficient and heart failure may supervene. Infarct expansion occurs over a few days and weeks but ventricular remodelling may take years; heart failure may therefore develop many years after acute MI. ACE inhibitor therapy reduces late ventricular remodelling and can prevent the onset of heart failure (see EBM panel, p. 387).

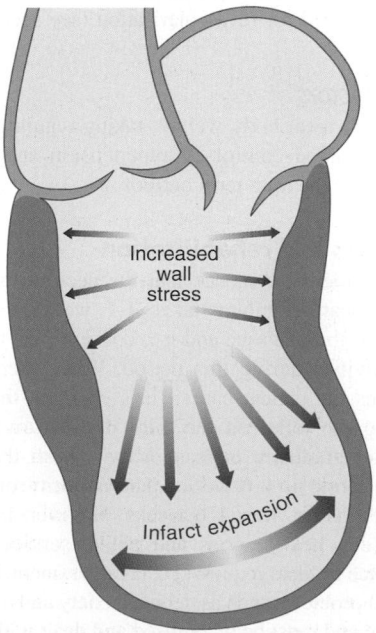

Fig. 12.79 Infarct expansion and ventricular remodelling. Full thickness myocardial infarction causes thinning and stretching of the infarcted segment (infarct expansion), which leads to increased wall stress with progressive dilatation and hypertrophy of the remaining ventricle (ventricular remodelling).

A left ventricular aneurysm develops in approximately 10% of patients and is particularly common when there is persistent occlusion of the infarct-related vessel. Heart failure, ventricular arrhythmias, mural thrombus and systemic embolism are all recognised complications of aneurysm formation. Other clinical features include a paradoxical impulse on the chest wall, persistent ST elevation on the ECG, and sometimes an unusual bulge from the cardiac silhouette on the chest radiograph. Echocardiography is usually diagnostic. Surgical removal of a left ventricular aneurysm carries a high morbidity and mortality but is sometimes necessary.

LATE MANAGEMENT

Patients who have survived an MI are at risk of further ischaemic events; any management strategy should therefore aim to identify those patients at high risk and introduce effective secondary prevention measures (see Box 12.63).

Risk stratification and further investigation

The prognosis of patients who have survived an acute MI is related to the degree of myocardial damage, the extent of any residual myocardial ischaemia and the presence of significant ventricular arrhythmias.

Left ventricular function

The degree of left ventricular dysfunction can be crudely assessed from the physical findings (tachycardia, third heart sound, crackles at the lung bases, elevated venous pressure etc.), the ECG changes and the size of the heart on chest radiograph. However, formal measurements using echocardiography or radionuclide imaging are often valuable.

Ischaemia

Patients with early post-MI ischaemia should be managed in the same way as patients with high-risk unstable angina (see pp. 432–434). Patients without spontaneous ischaemia who are suitable candidates for revascularisation should undergo an exercise tolerance test approximately 4 weeks after the infarct; this will help to identify those individuals with significant residual myocardial ischaemia who require further investigation, and may help to boost the confidence of the remainder.

12.63 LATE MANAGEMENT OF MYOCARDIAL INFARCTION

Risk stratification and further investigation (see text)

Lifestyle modification
- Stop smoking
- Regular exercise
- Diet (weight control, lipid-lowering)

Secondary prevention drug therapy
- Antiplatelet therapy (aspirin or clopidogrel)
- β-blocker
- ACE inhibitor
- Statin
- Additional therapy for control of diabetes and hypertension

Rehabilitation

If the exercise test is negative and the patient has a good effort tolerance, the outlook is good, with a 1–4% chance of an adverse event in the next 12 months. In contrast, patients with residual ischaemia in the form of chest pain or ECG changes at low exercise levels are at high risk, with a 15–25% chance of suffering a further ischaemic event in the next 12 months.

Coronary arteriography, with a view to angioplasty or bypass grafting, should therefore be considered in any patient with spontaneous ischaemia, significant angina on effort, or a strongly positive exercise tolerance test.

Arrhythmias

The presence of ventricular arrhythmias during the convalescent phase of MI may be a marker of poor ventricular function and may herald sudden death. Although empirical anti-arrhythmic treatment appears to be of no value and may even be hazardous, selected patients may benefit from sophisticated electrophysiological testing and specific anti-arrhythmic therapy (including the implantation of a cardioverter-defibrillator (ICD)—see p. 419).

Recurrent ventricular arrhythmias are sometimes manifestations of myocardial ischaemia or impaired LV function and may respond to appropriate treatment directed at the underlying problem.

Secondary prevention

Aspirin

Low-dose aspirin therapy reduces the risk of further infarction and other vascular events by approximately 25% and should be continued indefinitely if there are no unwanted effects. Clopidogrel is a suitable alternative.

Beta-blockers

Continuous treatment with an oral β-blocker has been shown to reduce long-term mortality by approximately 25% among the survivors of acute MI (see EBM panel). Unfortunately, a significant minority of patients do not tolerate β-blockers because of bradycardia, heart block, hypotension, overt cardiac failure, asthma, chronic obstructive airways disease or peripheral vascular disease.

EBM

SECONDARY PREVENTION AFTER MYOCARDIAL INFARCTION—use of β-blockers

'Systematic reviews of RCTs (usual follow-up 1 year) have found that β-blockers reduce the risk of all causes of mortality (NNT = 48), sudden death (NNT = 63) and non-fatal reinfarction (NNT = 56) in patients after myocardial infarction. The greatest benefit was seen in those at highest risk and about a quarter of patients suffered adverse events.'

- Yusuf S, Peto R, Lewis J, et al. Beta blockade during and after myocardial infarction: an overview of the randomised trials. Prog Cardiovasc Dis 1985; 27:335–371.
- Beta-blocking pooling project research group. The beta blocker pooling project (BBPP): subgroup findings from randomised trials in post infarction patients. Eur Heart J 1988; 9:8–16.

Further information: 🖥 www.sign.ac.uk

ACE inhibitors

Several clinical trials have shown that long-term treatment with an ACE inhibitor (e.g. captopril 50 mg 8-hourly, enalapril 10 mg 12-hourly or ramipril 2.5–5 mg 12-hourly)

can counteract ventricular remodelling, prevent the onset of heart failure, improve survival and reduce hospitalisation. The benefit of treatment is greatest in those with overt heart failure (clinical or radiological) but extends to patients with asymptomatic LV dysfunction. This form of therapy should therefore be considered in any patient who has sustained a myocardial infarct complicated by transient heart failure or poor residual left ventricular function (e.g. LV ejection fraction < 40%). Caution must be exercised in hypovolaemic or hypotensive patients because the introduction of an ACE inhibitor may exacerbate hypotension and impair coronary perfusion.

Smoking

The 5-year mortality of patients who continue to smoke cigarettes is double that of those who quit smoking at the time of their infarct. Giving up smoking is the single most effective contribution a patient can make to his or her own future.

Hyperlipidaemia

Convincing evidence from large-scale randomised clinical trials has demonstrated the importance of lowering plasma cholesterol following MI. The aim is to reduce total cholesterol to less than 5.0 mmol/l and/or low-density lipoprotein (LDL) cholesterol to less than 3.0 mmol/l. Lipids should be measured within 24 hours of presentation because there is often a transient and unrepresentative fall in blood cholesterol in the 3 months following infarction. Dietary advice should be given but is often ineffective. HMG CoA reductase enzyme inhibitors ('statins') can produce marked reductions in total (and LDL) cholesterol and have been shown to reduce the subsequent risk of death, reinfarction, stroke and the need for revascularisation (see second EBM panel, p. 423).

Other risk factors

Maintaining an ideal body weight, taking regular exercise, and achieving good control of hypertension and diabetes may all improve the long-term outlook.

Mobilisation and rehabilitation

There is histological evidence that the necrotic muscle of an acute myocardial infarct takes 4–6 weeks to become replaced with fibrous tissue and it is conventional to restrict physical activities during this period. When there are no complications the patient can sit in a chair on the second day, walk to the toilet on the third day, return home in 5–7 days and gradually increase activity with the aim of returning to work in 4–6 weeks. The majority of patients may resume driving after 4–6 weeks; however, in the UK vocational (e.g. heavy goods and public service vehicle) driving licence holders require special assessment.

Emotional problems such as denial, anxiety and depression are common, and must be recognised and dealt with accordingly. Many patients are severely and even permanently incapacitated as a result of the psychological rather than the physical effects of MI, and all benefit from thoughtful explanation, counselling and reassurance at every stage of the illness. Many patients mistakenly believe that 'stress' was the cause of their heart attack and may restrict their activity inappropriately. The patient's spouse or partner will also require emotional support, information and counselling.

Formal rehabilitation programmes based on graded exercise protocols with individual and group counselling are often very successful, and in some cases have been shown to improve the long-term outcome.

Prognosis

In almost a quarter of all cases of MI death occurs within a few minutes without medical care. Half the deaths from MI occur within 24 hours of the onset of symptoms and about 40% of all affected patients die within the first month. The prognosis of those who survive to reach hospital is much better, with a 28-day survival of more than 80%.

Early death is usually due to an arrhythmia but later on the outcome is determined by the extent of myocardial damage. Unfavourable features include poor left ventricular function, heart block and persistent ventricular arrhythmias. The prognosis is worse for anterior than for inferior infarcts. Bundle branch block and high enzyme levels both indicate extensive myocardial damage. Old age, depression and social isolation are also associated with a higher mortality. In the absence of unfavourable features, the outlook is as good for those who survive ventricular fibrillation as for the others.

Of those who survive an acute attack, more than 80% live for a further year, about 75% for 5 years, 50% for 10 years and 25% for 20 years.

ISSUES IN OLDER PEOPLE
MYOCARDIAL INFARCTION

- Presentation is often atypical, and the dominant symptom may be dyspnoea, fatigue or weakness rather than chest pain.
- The case fatality of MI rises steeply with age. Hospital mortality exceeds 25% in those who are over 75 years old (five times greater than that seen in patients less than 55 years old).
- The relative survival benefit of most evidence-based treatments is not influenced by age; the absolute benefit of these treatments may therefore be greatest in the elderly.
- The hazards of most evidence-based treatments (e.g. the risk of intracerebral bleeding after thrombolysis) rise with age due partly to increased comorbidity.
- Elderly patients, particularly those with significant comorbidity, were under-represented in many of the RCTs that have helped to establish the treatment of MI. The balance of risk and benefit for many treatments (e.g. thrombolysis, primary PCI) in older people is therefore uncertain.

CARDIAC RISK OF NON-CARDIAC SURGERY

Non-cardiac surgery, particularly major vascular, abdominal or thoracic surgery, can precipitate serious perioperative cardiac complications, such as MI and death, in patients with coronary artery and other forms of heart disease. Careful preoperative cardiac assessment may help to determine the balance of benefit versus risk, on an individual patient basis, and identify measures that can be used to minimise the operative risk (see Box 12.64).

12.64 MAJOR RISK FACTORS FOR CARDIAC COMPLICATIONS OF NON-CARDIAC SURGERY

- Recent (< 6 months) MI or unstable angina
- Severe stable angina on effort
- Poorly controlled heart failure
- Severe valvular heart disease (especially aortic stenosis)

A hypercoagulable state is part of the normal physiological response to surgery and may promote coronary thrombosis leading to an acute coronary syndrome (unstable angina or MI) in the early post-operative period. Patients with a history of recent unstable angina or MI are at greatest risk and, whenever possible, elective non-cardiac surgery should be avoided for 3, and preferably 6, months after such an event. Beta-blockers reduce the risk of perioperative MI in patients with coronary artery disease and should be prescribed throughout the perioperative period.

Careful attention to fluid balance during and after surgery is particularly important in patients with impaired left ventricular function and valvular heart disease because antidiuretic hormone is released as part of the normal physiological response to surgery, and in these circumstances the over-zealous administration of intravenous fluids can easily precipitate heart failure. Patients with severe valvular heart disease, particularly aortic stenosis and mitral stenosis, are also at increased risk because they may not be able to increase their cardiac output in response to the stress of surgery.

Atrial fibrillation may be triggered by hypoxia, myocardial ischaemia or heart failure (atrial stretch) and is a common post-operative complication in patients with pre-existing heart disease. The arrhythmia usually terminates spontaneously when the precipitating factors have been eliminated but it may be advisable to prescribe digoxin or β-blockers to slow the heart rate.

VASCULAR DISEASE

PERIPHERAL ARTERIAL DISEASE

In developed countries, almost all peripheral arterial disease (PAD) is due to atherosclerosis, which is discussed on pages 420–424. The pathology of PAD is similar to coronary artery disease and the most important risk factors are smoking, diabetes, hyperlipidaemia and hypertension. Plaque rupture is responsible for the most serious manifestations of the disease, and often occurs in a plaque that hitherto has been asymptomatic.

Approximately 20% of middle-aged (55–75 years) people in the UK have PAD but only a quarter of such individuals will have symptoms. The clinical manifestations depend upon the anatomical site, the presence or absence of a collateral supply, the speed of onset and the mechanism of injury (see Box 12.65).

12.65 FACTORS INFLUENCING THE CLINICAL MANIFESTATIONS OF PERIPHERAL ARTERIAL DISEASE

Anatomical site

Cerebral circulation
- Transient ischaemic attack (TIA), amaurosis fugax, vertebro-basilar insufficiency

Renal arteries
- Hypertension and renal failure

Mesenteric arteries
- Mesenteric angina, acute intestinal ischaemia

Limbs (legs >> arms)
- Intermittent claudication, critical limb ischaemia, acute limb ischaemia

Collateral supply

- In a patient with a complete circle of Willis, occlusion of one carotid artery may be asymptomatic
- In a patient without cross-circulation, stroke is likely

Speed of onset

- Where PAD develops slowly a collateral supply will develop
- By contrast, sudden occlusion of a previously normal artery is likely to cause severe distal ischaemia

Mechanism of injury

Haemodynamic
- Plaque must reduce arterial diameter by 70% ('critical stenosis') to reduce flow and pressure at rest. On exertion—for example, walking—a much lesser stenosis may become 'critical'. This type of mechanism tends to have a relatively benign course due to collateralisation

Thrombotic
- Occlusion of a long-standing critical stenosis may be asymptomatic due to collateralisation. However, acute rupture and thrombosis of a non-haemodynamically significant plaque usually has severe consequences

Atheroembolic
- Symptoms depend upon embolic load and size
- Carotid (TIA, amaurosis fugax or stroke) and peripheral arterial (blue toe/finger syndrome) plaque are common examples

Thromboembolic
- Usually secondary to atrial fibrillation
- The clinical consequences are usually dramatic as the thrombus load is often large and tends to occlude a major, previously healthy, non-collateralised artery suddenly and completely

CHRONIC LOWER LIMB ARTERIAL DISEASE

PAD affects the leg eight times more often than the arm. The lower limb arterial tree comprises the aorto-iliac ('inflow'), femoropopliteal and infra-popliteal ('outflow') segments. One or more segments may be affected in a variable and asymmetric manner. Lower limb ischaemia presents as two distinct clinical entities: namely, intermittent claudication and critical limb ischaemia. The presence and severity of ischaemia can be determined by clinical examination (see Box 12.66) and measurement of the ankle:brachial pressure index (ABPI), the ratio between the (highest systolic) ankle and brachial blood pressures. In health the ABPI is > 1.0, in intermittent claudication typically 0.5–0.9, and in critical limb ischaemia usually < 0.5.

12.66 FEATURES OF CHRONIC LOWER LIMB ISCHAEMIA

- Pulses—diminished or absent
- Bruits—denote turbulent flow but bear no relationship to the severity of the underlying disease
- Reduced skin temperature
- Pallor on elevation and rubor on dependency (Buerger's sign)
- Superficial veins that fill sluggishly and empty ('gutter') upon minimal elevation
- Muscle-wasting
- Skin and nails—dry, thin and brittle
- Loss of hair

Intermittent claudication

Ischaemic pain of the leg muscles precipitated by walking and relieved by rest is known as intermittent claudication (IC). The pain is usually felt in the calf muscles because the disease tends to affect the superficial femoral artery. However, the pain may be felt in the thigh or buttock if the iliac arteries are involved. Typically, the pain comes on after a reasonably constant 'claudication distance', and rapidly and completely subsides on cessation of walking. Resumption of walking leads to a return of the pain. Most patients describe a cyclical pattern of exacerbation and resolution due to the progression of disease and the subsequent development of collaterals.

Approximately 5% of middle-aged men report IC. Provided patients comply with 'best medical therapy' (see Box 12.67), only 1–2% per year will deteriorate to a point where amputation and/or revascularisation are required. However, the annual mortality rate exceeds 5%, which is 2–3 times higher than an age- and sex-matched non-claudicant population. This excess mortality is due to the fact that IC is nearly always found in association with widespread atherosclerosis. Indeed, most claudicants succumb to myocardial infarction or stroke. General measures to reduce cardiovascular mortality, many of which may also improve the functional status of the limb, are central to patient management. Intervention (angioplasty, stenting, endarterectomy or bypass) is usually only considered once best medical therapy has been instituted and given at least 6 months to effect symptomatic improvement, and then only in those patients who are severely disabled or whose livelihood is threatened by their disability.

12.67 BEST MEDICAL THERAPY FOR PERIPHERAL ARTERIAL DISEASE

- Cessation of smoking
- Regular exercise (in a typical claudicant this would entail 30 minutes of walking three times per week)
- Antiplatelet agent (aspirin 75 mg daily or clopidogrel 75 mg daily)
- Reduction of total cholesterol to less than 5.0 mmol/l (diet ± statin therapy)
- Diagnosis and treatment of diabetes mellitus (every patient should undergo measurement of fasting glucose)
- Diagnosis and treatment of frequently associated conditions (e.g. hypertension, anaemia, heart failure)

All patients with any manifestation of peripheral arterial disease should be considered candidates for best medical therapy.

Critical limb ischaemia

Critical limb ischaemia (CLI) is defined as rest (night) pain, requiring opiate analgesia, and/or tissue loss (ulceration or gangrene), present for more than 2 weeks, in the presence of an ankle blood pressure of less than 50 mmHg (see Fig. 12.80). Rest pain and no tissue loss with ankle pressures above 50 mmHg is sometimes known as subcritical limb ischaemia (SCLI). The term severe limb ischaemia (SLI) is often used to describe both entities. Whereas IC is usually due to single-segment plaque, CLI is always due to multilevel disease.

Intra-arterial digital subtraction angiography (IA-DSA) remains the investigation of choice, although in a minority of centres patients are imaged by means of duplex ultrasonography. Many patients with CLI have not previously sought medical advice for IC, principally because they often have other comorbidity that prevents them from walking to a point where claudication pain might develop. In contrast to IC, patients with CLI are at risk of losing their limb, sometimes their life, in a matter of weeks or months without surgical bypass or endovascular revascularisation. However, treatment is difficult because such patients represent end-stage disease, have severe multilevel disease, are usually elderly and nearly always have significant multisystem comorbidity.

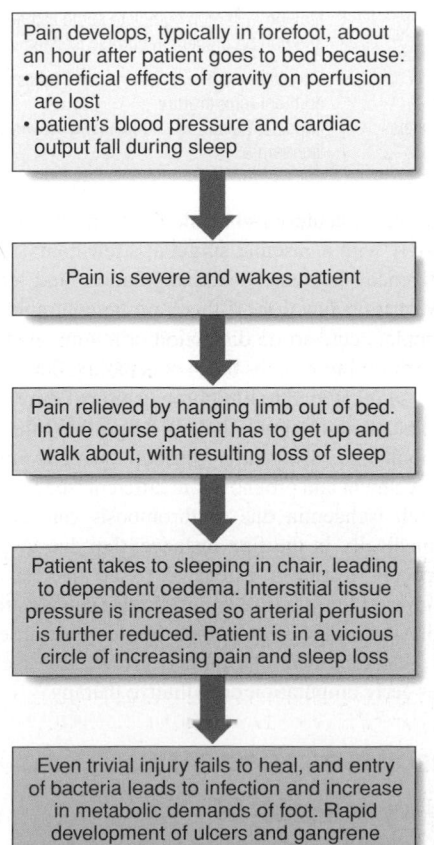

Fig. 12.80 Progressive night pain and the development of tissue loss.

12.68 DIABETIC VASCULAR DISEASE: THE 'DIABETIC FOOT'	
Feature	**Difficulty**
Arterial calcification	Spuriously high ABPI due to incompressible ankle vessels Inability to clamp arteries for the purposes of bypass surgery Resistant to angioplasty
Immunocompromise	Prone to rapidly spreading cellulitis, gangrene and osteomyelitis
Multisystem arterial disease	Coronary and cerebral arterial disease increases the risks of intervention
Distal disease	Diabetic vascular disease has a predilection for the crural vessels. Although vessels in the foot are often spared, the technical challenge of performing a satisfactory bypass or angioplasty to these small vessels is considerable
Sensory neuropathy	Even severe ischaemia and/or tissue loss that would lead a sensate patient to seek urgent medical advice may be completely painless. Diabetic patients often present late with extensive destruction of the foot. Loss of proprioception leads to abnormal pressure loads and exacerbates joint destruction (Charcot's joints)
Motor neuropathy	Weakness of the long and short flexors and extensors leads to abnormal foot architecture, abnormal pressure loads, callus formation and ulceration
Autonomic neuropathy	This leads to a dry foot deficient in sweat that normally lubricates the skin and contains antibacterial substances. Scaling and fissuring create a portal of entry for bacteria. Abnormal blood flow in the bones of the ankle and foot may also contribute to osteopenia and bony collapse

Diabetic vascular disease

Approximately 5–10% of patients with PAD have diabetes but this proportion increases to 30–40% in those with CLI. Although critical limb ischaemia was thought to be caused by an obstructive microangiopathy at the capillary level, this is now known to be incorrect, and diabetes is not a contraindication per se to lower limb revascularisation. Nevertheless, the 'diabetic foot' does pose a number of particular problems (see Box 12.68 and Ch. 15). If the blood supply is adequate, then dead tissue can be excised in the expectation that healing will occur, provided infection is controlled and the foot is protected from pressure. However, if ischaemia is also present the priority is to revascularise the foot, if possible. Sadly, many diabetic patients present late with extensive tissue loss, which accounts for the high amputation rate.

Buerger's disease (thromboangiitis obliterans)

This is an inflammatory obliterative arterial disease that is distinct from atherosclerosis. It is rare in the UK but more common in people from the Mediterranean and North

Africa. It is likely that there is a strong genetic element. Buerger's disease usually presents in young (20–30 years) male smokers and characteristically affects the peripheral arteries, giving rise to claudication in the feet or rest pain in the fingers or toes. The condition also affects the veins, and superficial thrombophlebitis is common. Wrist and ankle pulses are usually absent, but brachial and popliteal pulses are characteristically palpable. Arteriography shows narrowing or occlusion of arteries below the knee but relatively healthy vessels above that level.

The condition often remits if the patient stops smoking; sympathectomy and prostaglandin infusions may be helpful. If amputation is required it can often be limited to the digits at first. However, bilateral below-knee amputation is the most frequent outcome if patients continue to smoke.

CHRONIC UPPER LIMB ARTERIAL DISEASE

The subclavian artery is the most common site of disease, which may manifest as:

● *Arm claudication* (rare).
● *Atheroembolism* (blue finger syndrome). Small emboli lodge in digital arteries and may be confused with Raynaud's phenomenon (see below), except that in this case the symptoms are unilateral. Failure to make the diagnosis may eventually lead to amputation.
● *Subclavian steal.* When the arm is used, blood is 'stolen' from the brain via the vertebral artery. This leads to vertebro-basilar ischaemia, which is characterised by dizziness, cortical blindness and/or collapse (see p. 1164).

Most subclavian artery disease should be treated by means of angioplasty with or without stenting, as the results are good and surgery (carotid-subclavian bypass) is difficult.

RAYNAUD'S PHENOMENON AND RAYNAUD'S DISEASE

Raynaud's phenomenon
Cold and sometimes emotional stimuli may trigger vasospasm in the peripheral arteries. Raynaud's phenomenon describes the characteristic sequence of digital pallor due to vasospasm, followed by cyanosis due to the presence of deoxygenated blood, and then rubor due to reactive hyperaemia.

Primary Raynaud's phenomenon
This is also called Raynaud's disease and affects 5–10% of young women in temperate climates. The condition is often familial and usually appears between the ages of 15 and 30 years. It does not progress to ulceration or infarction and significant pain is unusual. No investigation is necessary and the patient should be reassured and advised to avoid exposure to cold, in the first instance. Treatment with a long-acting preparation of nifedipine may also be helpful. The underlying cause is unclear. Sympathectomy is not indicated.

Secondary Raynaud's phenomenon
This is also known as Raynaud's syndrome and tends to occur in older people in association with connective tissue disease (most commonly systemic sclerosis or the CREST

syndrome—see p. 1036), vibration-induced injury (from the use of power tools) and thoracic outlet obstruction (e.g. cervical rib). In contrast to primary disease the condition is associated with fixed obstruction of the digital arteries; fingertip ulceration and necrosis are often present and pain is usual. The fingers must be protected from cold and trauma, infection requires treatment with antibiotics, and surgery should be avoided if possible. Vasoactive drugs have no clear benefit. Sympathectomy helps for a year or two. Prostacyclin infusions are sometimes beneficial.

ACUTE LIMB ISCHAEMIA

Acute limb ischaemia is most frequently caused by acute thrombotic occlusion of a pre-existing stenotic arterial segment, thromboembolism and trauma, which may be iatrogenic. Apart from paralysis (inability to wiggle toes/fingers) and paraesthesia (loss of light touch over the dorsum of the foot/hand), the so-called 'Ps of acute ischaemia' (see Box 12.69) are non-specific for ischaemia and/or inconsistently related to its severity. Pain on squeezing the calf indicates muscle infarction and impending irreversible ischaemia.

12.69 SYMPTOMS AND SIGNS OF ACUTE LIMB ISCHAEMIA	
Symptoms/signs	**Comment**
Pain Pallor Pulselessness	May be absent in complete acute ischaemia, and can be present in chronic ischaemia
Perishing cold	Unreliable, as the ischaemic limb takes on the ambient temperature
Paraesthesia Paralysis	Important features of impending irreversible ischaemia

All suspected acutely ischaemic limbs must be discussed immediately with a vascular surgeon; a few hours can make the difference between death/amputation and complete recovery of limb function. If there are no contraindications (for example, acute aortic dissection or trauma, particularly head injury), an intravenous bolus of heparin (3000–5000 IU) should be administered to limit propagation of thrombus and protect the collateral circulation. Distinguishing thrombosis from embolism is frequently difficult but it is important because treatment and prognosis are different (see Box 12.70). Acute limb ischaemia due to thrombosis can usually be treated medically in the first instance; that due to embolus will normally result in extensive tissue necrosis within 6 hours unless the limb is revascularised. The indications for thrombolysis remain controversial but, in general, enthusiasm for this treatment is waning. Irreversible ischaemia mandates early amputation or palliative therapy.

CEREBROVASCULAR DISEASE

This is discussed on pages 1159–1168.

RENOVASCULAR DISEASE

This is discussed on pages 609–611.

12.70	ACUTE LIMB ISCHAEMIA: DISTINGUISHING FEATURES OF EMBOLISM AND THROMBOSIS IN SITU	
Clinical features	**Embolism**	**Thrombosis in situ**
Severity	Complete (no collaterals)	Incomplete (collaterals)
Onset	Seconds or minutes	Hours or days
Limb	Leg 3:1 arm	Leg 10:1 arm
Multiple sites	Up to 15%	Rare
Embolic source	Present (usually AF)	Absent
Previous claudication	Absent	Present
Palpation of artery	Soft, tender	Hard, calcified
Bruits	Absent	Present
Contralateral leg pulses	Present	Absent
Diagnosis	Clinical	Angiography
Treatment	Embolectomy, warfarin	Medical, bypass, thrombolysis
Prognosis	Loss of life > loss of limb	Loss of limb > loss of life

ISCHAEMIC GUT INJURY

This is discussed on pages 819–820.

DISEASES OF THE AORTA

Three types of condition may affect the aorta: aneurysm, dissection and aortitis (see Fig. 12.81).

AORTIC ANEURYSM

An aortic aneurysm is an abnormal dilatation of the aortic wall. Aortic dissection has a different pathology and is considered separately.

Aetiology and types of aneurysm

Non-specific aneurysms

Although there are important clinical and pathological differences between occlusive atheromatous and aneurysmal arterial disease, these conditions share similar risk factors (e.g. smoking and hypertension) and often coexist. Why some patients develop occlusive and others aneurysmal disease remains unclear; however, unlike occlusive disease, what is now termed 'non-specific' aneurysmal disease tends to 'run in families', and genetic factors are undoubtedly important. The most common site for 'non-specific' aneurysm formation is the infrarenal abdominal aorta. The suprarenal abdominal aorta and a variable length of the descending thoracic aorta may be affected in 10–20% of patients but the ascending aorta is usually spared.

Marfan's syndrome

This connective tissue disorder is inherited as an autosomal dominant trait and is caused by mutations in the fibrillin

gene on chromosome 15. There is considerable phenotypic variation but the major features involve the skeleton (arachnodactyly, joint hypermobility, scoliosis, chest deformity and high arched palate), the eyes (dislocation of the lens) and the cardiovascular system (aortic disease and mitral regurgitation). Weakening of the aortic media leads to progressive dilatation of the ascending aorta that may be complicated by aortic regurgitation and aortic dissection (see below). Pregnancy is particularly hazardous. Chest radiography, echocardiography, MRI or CT may detect aortic dilatation at an early stage and can be used to monitor the disease.

Treatment with β-blockers reduces the rate of aortic dilatation and the risk of rupture. Elective replacement of the ascending aorta may be considered in patients with evidence of progressive aortic dilatation but carries a mortality of 5–10%.

Aortitis

Syphilis is a rare cause of aortitis that characteristically produces saccular aneurysms of the ascending aorta containing calcification. Other conditions that can cause aortitis and aneurysm formation include Takayasu's disease, Reiter's syndrome, giant cell arteritis and ankylosing spondylitis (see pp. 1008–1010 and 1041–1042).

Thoracic aneurysms

Thoracic aortic aneurysms may produce chest pain similar to cardiac pain, associated with expansion of the aneurysm. If they extend proximally they may cause aortic valve regurgitation. They can also cause symptoms by compressing the trachea, main bronchus or superior vena cava. Occasionally, they may erode into the adjacent structures, causing haemorrhage, tamponade and death.

Abdominal aortic aneurysm (AAA)

AAAs are present in 5% of men aged over 60 years and 80% are confined to the infrarenal segment. Men are affected three times more commonly than women. AAA can present in a number of ways (see Box 12.71). The median age at presentation is 65 years for elective and 75 years for emergency cases. About two-thirds of AAAs are sufficiently calcified to show up on a plain abdominal radiograph. Ultrasound is the best way of establishing the diagnosis; an approximate size may be obtained, and the technique can be used to follow up patients with asymptomatic aneurysms that are not yet large enough to warrant surgical repair. CT will provide much more accurate information about the size and extent of the aneurysm, the surrounding structures and whether there is any other intra-abdominal pathology, and is the standard pre-operative investigation; however, it is not suitable for surveillance. Arteriography is usually only indicated if there are concerns about associated lower limb, renal and/or visceral occlusive disease.

Management

Until an asymptomatic AAA has reached a maximum of 5.5 cm in diameter, the risks of surgery generally outweigh the risks of rupture. All symptomatic AAAs should be considered for repair, not only to rid the patient of symptoms but also because pain often predates rupture. Distal embolisation is a strong indication for repair, regardless of size,

12.71 ABDOMINAL AORTIC ANEURYSM: COMMON PRESENTATIONS

Incidental

- Most AAAs are detected incidentally on physical examination, plain radiograph or, most commonly, abdominal ultrasound
- Even large ones can be difficult to feel, which explains why so many remain undetected until they rupture
- Studies are currently under way to determine whether screening will reduce the number of deaths from rupture

Pain

- AAAs may cause pain in the central abdomen, back, loin, iliac fossa or groin

Thromboembolic complications

- Thrombus within the aneurysm sac may be a source of emboli to the lower limbs
- Less commonly, the aorta may undergo thrombotic occlusion

Compression

- AAAs may also compress surrounding structures such as the duodenum (obstruction and vomiting) and the inferior vena cava (oedema and deep vein thrombosis)

Rupture

- AAAs may rupture into the retroperitoneum, the peritoneal cavity or surrounding structures (most commonly the inferior vena cava, leading to an aortocaval fistula)

12.72 FACTORS THAT MAY PREDISPOSE TO AORTIC DISSECTION

- Hypertension (80% of cases)
- Aortic atherosclerosis
- Non-specific aortic aneurysm
- Aortic coarctation
- Collagen disorders (e.g. Marfan's syndrome, Ehlers–Danlos syndrome)
- Fibromuscular dysplasia
- Previous aortic surgery (e.g. CABG, aortic valve replacement)
- Pregnancy (usually third trimester)
- Trauma
- Iatrogenic (e.g. cardiac catheterisation, intra-aortic balloon pumping)

because otherwise limb loss is common. Most patients with a ruptured AAA do not survive to reach hospital, but if they do, and surgery is thought to be appropriate, there must be no delay in getting them to the operating theatre to clamp the aorta.

Open AAA repair is the established treatment of choice in both the elective and the emergency setting and entails replacing the aneurysmal segment with a prosthetic (usually Dacron) graft. The 30-day mortality for this procedure is approximately 5–8% for elective asymptomatic AAA, 10–20% for emergency symptomatic AAA, and 50% for ruptured AAA. However, patients who survive operation to leave hospital have a long-term survival which approaches that of the normal population. Some AAAs may be treated with a covered stent placed via a femoral arteriotomy under radiological guidance.

AORTIC DISSECTION

In this dramatic condition a breach in the integrity of the aortic wall allows arterial blood to burst into the media of the aorta which is then split into two layers, creating a 'false lumen' alongside the existing or 'true lumen' (see Fig. 12.81). The aortic valve may be damaged and the branches of the aorta may be compromised. Typically the false lumen eventually re-enters the true lumen creating a double-barrelled or biluminal aorta, but it may also rupture into the left pleural space or pericardium with fatal consequences.

The primary event is often a spontaneous or iatrogenic tear in the intima of the aorta; multiple tears or entry points are common. On the other hand, many dissections appear to be triggered by a haemorrhage in the media of the aorta

which then ruptures, through the intima, into the true lumen. This form of spontaneous bleeding from the vasa vasorum is sometimes confined to the aortic wall, when it may present as a painful intramural haematoma.

Disease of the aorta and hypertension are the most important aetiological factors but a variety of other conditions may be implicated (see Box 12.72). Chronic dissections may lead to aneurysmal dilatation of the aorta, and thoracic aneurysms may be complicated by dissection; it is therefore sometimes difficult to determine which was the primary pathology.

The peak incidence is in the sixth and seventh decades of life but dissection can occur in younger patients, most commonly in association with Marfan's syndrome, pregnancy or trauma; men are twice as frequently affected as women.

Aortic dissection is classified anatomically and for management purposes into type A, which involves the ascending aorta, and type B, which involves only the descending aorta distal to the left subclavian artery (see Fig. 12.81). Type A dissections account for two-thirds of cases and frequently extend into the descending aorta.

Clinical features

The patient usually presents with severe 'tearing' chest pain that frequently radiates to the back between the shoulder blades. The onset of pain is typically very abrupt and collapse is common. Unless there is frank rupture, the patient is invariably hypertensive. There may be asymmetry of the brachial, carotid or femoral pulses, and the signs of aortic reflux may be present in type A dissections. Occlusion of aortic branches may cause a variety of complications including myocardial infarction (coronary), paraplegia (spinal), mesenteric infarction with an acute abdomen (coeliac and superior mesenteric), renal failure (renal) and acute limb (usually leg) ischaemia.

Investigations

The chest radiograph characteristically shows broadening of the upper mediastinum and distortion of the aortic 'knuckle', but these findings are variable and are absent in 40% of cases. A left-sided pleural effusion is common. The ECG may show left ventricular hypertrophy in patients with hypertension, or changes of acute myocardial infarction (usually inferior). Doppler echocardiography may show aortic regurgitation, a dilated aortic root and, occasionally, the flap of the dissection (see Fig. 12.82). Transoesophageal

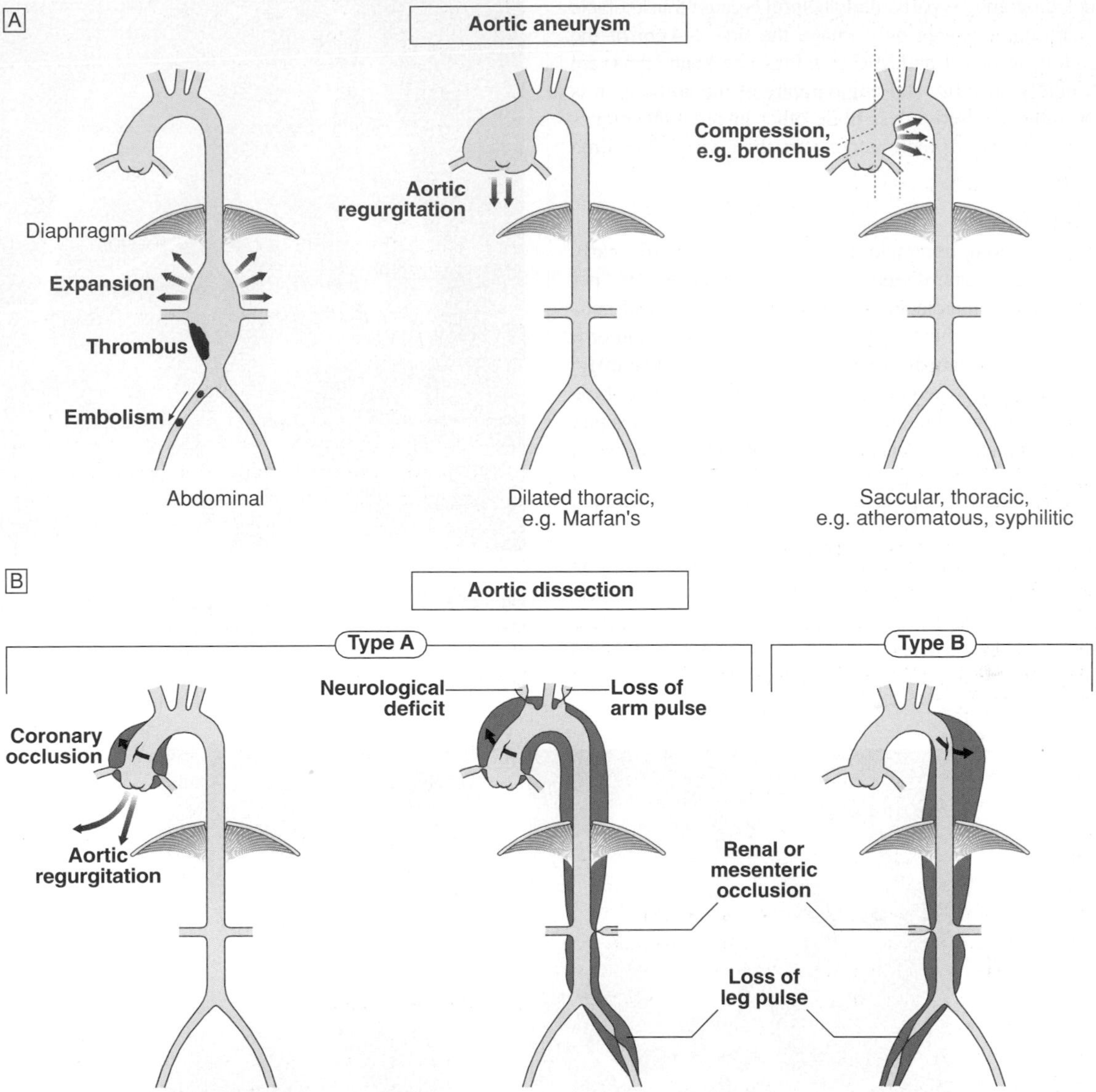

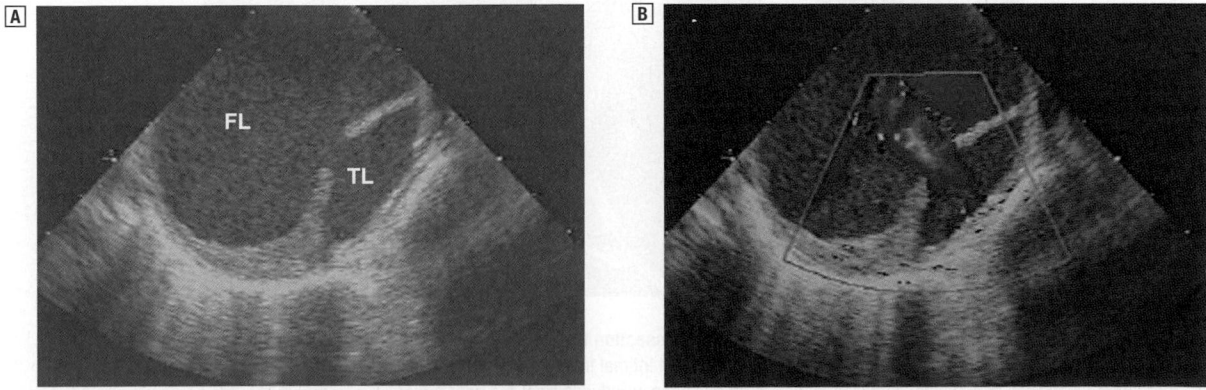

A Aortic aneurysm

Diaphragm
Expansion
Thrombus
Embolism

Abdominal

Aortic regurgitation

Dilated thoracic, e.g. Marfan's

Compression, e.g. bronchus

Saccular, thoracic, e.g. atheromatous, syphilitic

B Aortic dissection

Type A

Coronary occlusion
Aortic regurgitation

Neurological deficit
Loss of arm pulse
Renal or mesenteric occlusion
Loss of leg pulse

Type B

Fig. 12.81   Types of aortic disease and their complications. A Types of aortic aneurysm. B Types of aortic dissection.

A
FL
TL

B

Fig. 12.82   Echocardiograms from a patient with a chronic aortic dissection demonstrating the communication between the two lumens.
The false lumen (FL) is typically larger than the true lumen (TL) in chronic disease. A Transoesophageal echocardiogram. B Colour-flow Doppler study.

echocardiography is particularly helpful because transthoracic echocardiography can only image the first 3–4 cm of the ascending aorta. CT and MRI (see Figs 12.83 and 12.84) are both highly specific, and angiography of the aortic arch is not usually required unless these other imaging techniques are not available or there is concern about visceral or limb perfusion.

Management

Assessment and treatment are urgent because the early mortality of acute dissection is approximately 1% per hour. Initial management comprises pain control and anti-hypertensive treatment with sodium nitroprusside and/or a β-blocker to maintain the systolic pressure below 100 mmHg. Type A dissections require emergency surgical repair. Type B aneurysms can be treated medically unless there is actual or impending external rupture, or vital organs (gut, kidneys) or limbs are ischaemic. Surgery involves replacing the affected part with a Dacron graft; aortic valve replacement is sometimes necessary.

Percutaneous or minimal access endoluminal repair is possible in some cases and involves either 'fenestrating' (per-forating) the intimal flap so that blood can return from the false to the true lumen (so decompressing the former), or implanting a stent graft placed from the femoral artery (see Fig. 12.84).

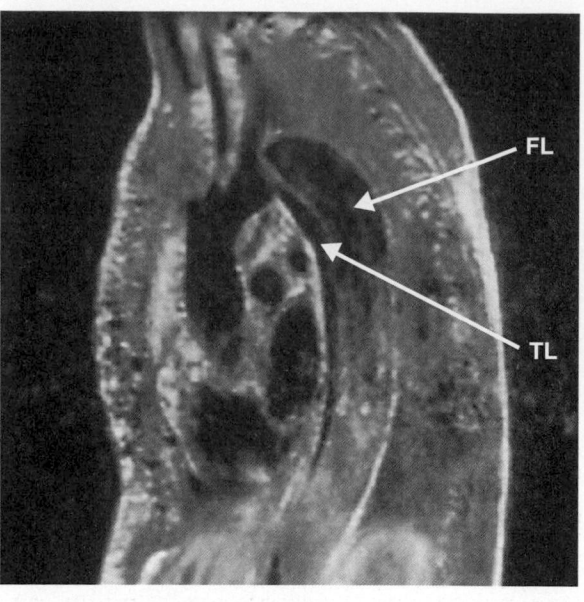

Fig. 12.83 Sagittal view of an MRI scan from a patient with long-standing aortic dissection illustrating a biluminal aorta. There is sluggish flow in the false lumen (FL) which accounts for its grey appearance. (TL = true lumen)

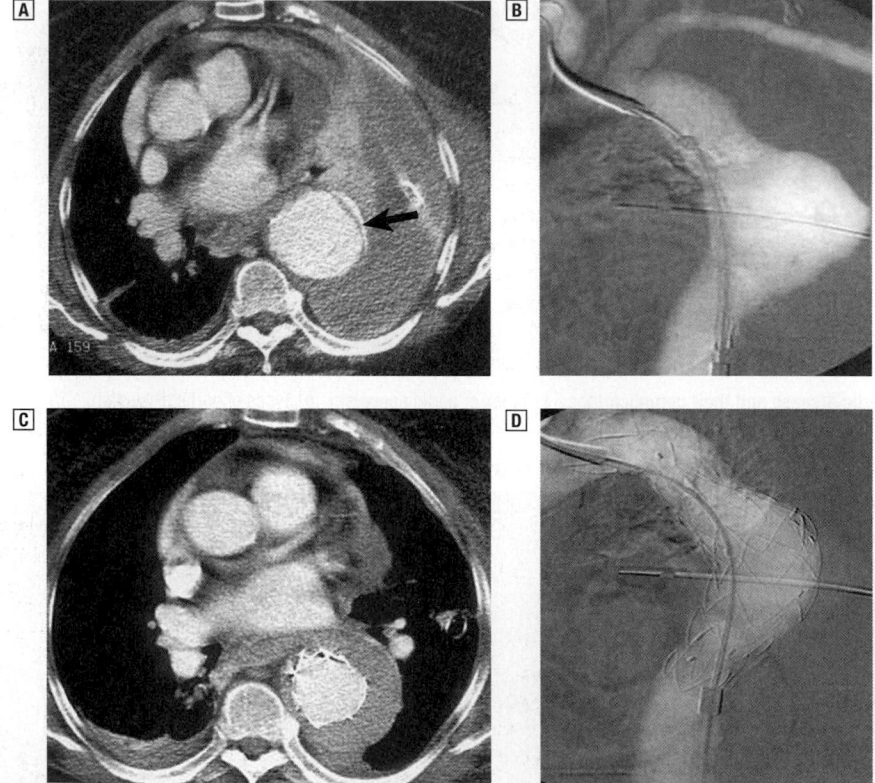

Fig. 12.84   Images from a patient with an acute type B aortic dissection that had ruptured into the left pleural space and was repaired by deploying an endoluminal stent graft. [A] CT scan illustrating an intimal flap (arrow) in the descending aorta and a large pleural effusion. [B] Aortogram illustrating aneurysmal dilatation; a stent graft has been introduced from the right femoral artery and is about to be deployed. [C] CT scan after endoluminal repair. The pleural effusion has been drained but there is a haematoma around the descending aorta. [D] Aortogram illustrating the stent graft.

DISEASES OF THE HEART VALVES

A diseased valve may be narrowed (stenosed) or it may fail to close adequately, and thus permit regurgitation of blood. The term 'incompetence' may be used synonymously with regurgitation or reflux, but the latter descriptions are preferable. The principal causes of valve disease are summarised in Box 12.73.

12.73 PRINCIPAL CAUSES OF VALVE DISEASE	
Valve regurgitation	
• Congenital	• Traumatic valve rupture
• Acute rheumatic carditis	• Senile degeneration
• Chronic rheumatic carditis	• Damage to chordae and
• Infective endocarditis	papillary muscles (e.g. MI)
• Syphilitic aortitis	
• Valve ring dilatation	
(e.g. dilated cardiomyopathy)	
Valve stenosis	
• Congenital	• Senile degeneration
• Rheumatic carditis	

Doppler echocardiography is the most useful technique for assessing patients with valvular heart disease (see p. 369), but it should be appreciated that this is a very sensitive technique that often detects minor, unimportant and even 'physiological' abnormalities, such as trivial regurgitation of the mitral valve. Disease of the heart valves may progress with time and selected patients require regular review, usually every 1 or 2 years, to ensure that deterioration is detected before complications such as heart failure ensue. Patients with valvular heart disease are susceptible to bacterial endocarditis which can be prevented by attention to good dental hygiene and the use of antibiotic prophylaxis at times of bacteraemia such as dental extraction (see p. 466).

The aetiology of individual valve lesions is considered separately below.

RHEUMATIC HEART DISEASE

ACUTE RHEUMATIC FEVER

Incidence and pathogenesis

Acute rheumatic fever usually affects children (being most common between 5 and 15 years) or young adults, and has become very rare in Western Europe and North America. Nevertheless, it remains endemic in parts of Asia, Africa and South America, with an annual incidence in some countries of more than 100 per 100 000; it is still the most common cause of acquired heart disease in childhood and adolescence.

The condition is triggered by an abnormal response to infection with specific strains of group A streptococci that possess antigens which may cross-react with cardiac myosin and sarcolemmal membrane protein. Antibodies produced against the streptococcal antigens mediate inflammation in the endocardium, myocardium and pericardium as well as the joints and skin. Histologically, fibrinoid degeneration can be seen in the collagen of connective tissues of these organs. The Aschoff nodule, which occurs only in the heart, is pathognomonic and is composed of multinucleated giant cells surrounded by macrophages and T lymphocytes.

Clinical features

Rheumatic fever is a multisystem disorder that typically follows an episode of streptococcal pharyngitis and usually presents with fever, anorexia, lethargy and joint pains. Symptoms characteristically occur 2–3 weeks after the initial attack of pharyngitis but the patient may give no history of sore throat. Arthritis occurs in approximately 75% of patients; other features include skin rashes, carditis and neurological changes (see Fig. 12.85). The diagnosis according to the revised Jones criteria is based upon two or more major manifestations, or one major and two or more minor manifestations; evidence of preceding streptococcal infection is also required (see Box 12.74). Only about 25% of patients will have a positive culture for group A streptococcus at the time of diagnosis because there is a latent period between infection and presentation; serological evidence of recent streptococcal infection such as a raised antistreptolysin O (ASO) antibody titre may therefore be helpful.

Carditis

This is a 'pancarditis' that involves the endocardium, myocardium and pericardium to varying degrees; its incidence declines with increasing age, ranging from 90% at 3 years to around 30% in adolescence. Carditis may manifest as breathlessness (due to heart failure or pericardial effusion), palpitations or chest pain (usually due to pericarditis or pancarditis). Other features include tachycardia, cardiac enlargement and new or changed cardiac murmurs. A soft systolic murmur due to mitral regurgitation is very common. A soft mid-diastolic murmur (the Carey Coombs murmur)

12.74 JONES CRITERIA FOR THE DIAGNOSIS OF RHEUMATIC FEVER	
Major manifestations	
• Carditis	• Erythema marginatum
• Polyarthritis	• Subcutaneous nodules
• Chorea	
Minor manifestations	
• Fever	• Leucocytosis
• Arthralgia	• First-degree or second-degree
• Previous rheumatic fever	AV block
• Raised ESR or C-reactive	
protein	
PLUS	
• Supporting evidence of preceding streptococcal infection: recent scarlet fever, raised antistreptolysin O or other streptococcal antibody titre, positive throat culture	
N.B. Evidence of recent streptococcal infection is particularly important if there is only one major manifestation.	

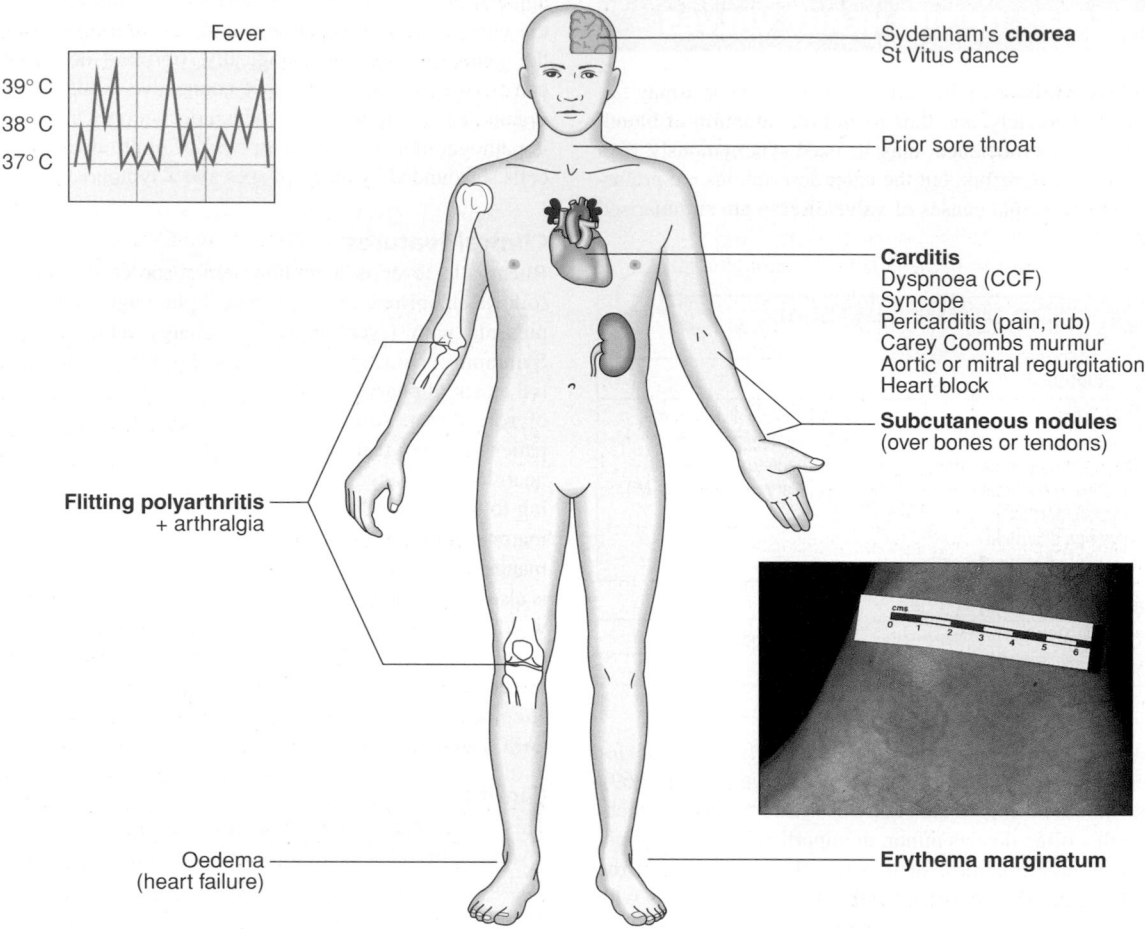

Fever

39° C
38° C
37° C

Sydenham's **chorea**
St Vitus dance

Prior sore throat

Carditis
Dyspnoea (CCF)
Syncope
Pericarditis (pain, rub)
Carey Coombs murmur
Aortic or mitral regurgitation
Heart block

Subcutaneous nodules
(over bones or tendons)

Flitting polyarthritis
+ arthralgia

Oedema
(heart failure)

Erythema marginatum

Fig. 12.85   Clinical features of rheumatic fever. Bold labels indicate Jones major criteria. (CCF = congestive cardiac failure)

is typically due to valvulitis, with nodules forming on the mitral valve leaflets. Aortic regurgitation occurs in about 50% of cases but the tricuspid and pulmonary valves are rarely involved in the acute process. Pericarditis may cause chest pain, a pericardial friction rub and praecordial tenderness. Cardiac failure may be due to myocardial dysfunction and/or mitral or aortic regurgitation. Electro-cardiographic changes are common and include ST and T wave changes; conduction defects sometimes occur and may cause syncope.

Sydenham's chorea (St Vitus dance)

This is a late neurological manifestation that typically appears at least 3 months after the episode of acute rheumatic fever when all the other signs may have disappeared. It occurs in up to one-third of cases and is more common in females. Emotional lability may be the first feature and is typically followed by characteristic purposeless involuntary choreiform movements of the hands, feet or face. Speech may be explosive and halting. Spontaneous recovery usually occurs within a few months. Approximately one-quarter of patients with Sydenham's chorea will go on to develop chronic rheumatic valve disease.

Arthritis

This is usually an early feature of the illness that tends to occur when streptococcal antibody titres are high. It is characterised by acute, painful, asymmetric and migratory inflammation of the large joints (typically the knees, ankles, elbows and wrists). The joints are involved in quick succession and are usually red, swollen and tender for between a day and a week. The pain characteristically responds to aspirin; if it does not, the diagnosis is in doubt.

Skin lesions

Erythema marginatum occurs in less than 10% of patients. The lesions start as red macules (blotches) which fade in the centre but remain red at the edges and occur mainly on the trunk and proximal extremities but not on the face. The resulting red rings or 'margins' may coalesce or overlap (see Fig. 12.85).

Subcutaneous nodules occur in 10–15% of patients. They are small (0.5–2.0 cm), firm and painless, and are best felt over bone or tendons. Nodules typically appear more than 3 weeks after the onset of other manifestations and are therefore a feature that helps to confirm rather than make the diagnosis.

Other systemic manifestations are rare, but include pleurisy, pleural effusion and pneumonia.

Investigations

These are listed in Box 12.75. The ESR and CRP are non-specific markers of systemic inflammation, and are useful for monitoring progress of the disease. ASO titres are normal in about one-fifth of adult cases of rheumatic fever and most cases of chorea. Echocardiography typically shows mitral regurgitation with dilatation of the mitral annulus and prolapse of the anterior mitral leaflet; other common findings are aortic regurgitation and pericardial effusion.

12.75 INVESTIGATIONS IN ACUTE RHEUMATIC FEVER

Evidence of a systemic illness (non-specific)

- Leucocytosis, raised ESR, raised CRP

Evidence of preceding streptococcal infection (specific)

- Throat swab culture: group A β-haemolytic streptococci (also from family members and contacts)
- Antistreptolysin O antibodies (ASO titres): rising titres, or levels of > 200 units (adults) or > 300 units (children)

Evidence of carditis

- Chest radiograph: cardiomegaly; pulmonary congestion
- ECG: first- and second-degree heart block; features of pericarditis; T wave inversion; reduction in QRS voltages
- Echocardiography: cardiac dilatation and valve abnormalities

Treatment of the acute attack

Benzathine penicillin 1.2 million units i.m. or oral phenoxy-methylpenicillin 250 mg 6-hourly for 10 days should be given on diagnosis in order to eliminate any residual streptococcal infection. Treatment of acute rheumatic fever is then directed towards limiting cardiac damage and relieving symptoms.

Bed rest and supportive therapy

Bed rest is important as it lessens joint pain and reduces cardiac workload in patients with carditis. The duration of bed rest should be guided by symptoms and markers of inflammation (e.g. temperature, leucocyte count and ESR) and should be continued until these indices of disease activity have settled. In patients who have had carditis, it is conventional to recommend bed rest for 2–6 weeks after the ESR and temperature have returned to normal. Prolonged bed rest, particularly in children or adolescents, produces problems of boredom and depression that need to be anticipated and managed.

Cardiac failure should be treated as necessary (see pp. 381–388). Some patients, particularly those in early adolescence, develop a fulminant form of the disease with severe mitral regurgitation and sometimes concomitant aortic regurgitation. If heart failure does not respond to medical treatment in these cases valve replacement may be necessary and is often associated with a dramatic decline in rheumatic activity. Heart block is seldom progressive, and pacemaker therapy is rarely needed.

Aspirin

Aspirin will usually relieve the symptoms of arthritis rapidly and a prompt response (within 24 hours) helps to confirm the diagnosis. A reasonable starting dose is 60 mg/kg body weight per day, divided into six doses. In adults, 120 mg/kg per day may be needed up to the limits of tolerance or a maximum of 8 g per day. Mild toxic effects include nausea, tinnitus and deafness; more serious ones are vomiting, tachypnoea and acidosis. Aspirin should be continued until the ESR has fallen, and then gradually tailed off.

Corticosteroids

These produce more rapid symptomatic relief than aspirin, and are indicated in cases with carditis or severe arthritis. There is no evidence that long-term steroids are beneficial. Prednisolone 1.0–2.0 mg/kg per day in divided doses should be continued until the ESR is normal, then gradually tailed off.

Secondary prevention

Patients are susceptible to additional attacks of rheumatic fever if further streptococcal infection occurs, and long-term prophylaxis with penicillin should be given as benzathine penicillin 1.2 million units i.m. monthly (if compliance is in doubt) or oral phenoxymethylpenicillin 250 mg 12-hourly. Erythromycin may be used if the patient is allergic to penicillin. Further attacks of rheumatic fever are unusual after the age of 21, at which age treatment may be stopped. However, treatment should be extended if an attack has occurred in the last 5 years, or the patient lives in an area of high prevalence, or has an occupation (e.g. teaching) with high exposure to streptococcal infection. It is important to appreciate that long-term antibiotic prophylaxis is intended to prevent another attack of acute rheumatic fever and does not protect against infective endocarditis.

CHRONIC RHEUMATIC HEART DISEASE

Chronic valvular heart disease develops in at least half of those affected by rheumatic fever with carditis. Two-thirds of cases occur in women. Some episodes of rheumatic fever may pass unrecognised and it is only possible to elicit a history of rheumatic fever or chorea in about half of all patients with chronic rheumatic heart disease.

The mitral valve is affected in more than 90% of cases; the aortic valve is the next most frequently affected valve, followed by the tricuspid and then the pulmonary valve. Isolated mitral stenosis accounts for about 25% of all cases of rheumatic heart disease and an additional 40% have mixed mitral stenosis and regurgitation.

Valve disease may be symptomatic during fulminant forms of acute rheumatic fever, but may remain asymptomatic for many years.

Pathology

In contrast to the destructive lytic process of acute rheumatic fever, the main pathological process in chronic rheumatic heart disease is progressive fibrosis. The heart valves are predominantly affected but involvement of the pericardium and myocardium may contribute to heart failure and conduction disorders. Fusion of the mitral valve commissures and short-ening of the chordae tendineae may lead to mitral stenosis with or without regurgitation. Similar changes in the aortic and tricuspid valves produce distortion and rigidity of the cusps, leading to stenosis and/or regurgitation. Once a valve has been damaged, the altered haemodynamic stresses perpetuate and extend the damage, even in the absence of a continuing rheumatic process.

MITRAL VALVE DISEASE

MITRAL STENOSIS

Aetiology and pathophysiology

Mitral stenosis is almost always rheumatic in origin. In the elderly, however, heavy calcification of the mitral valve apparatus can produce a form of mitral stenosis. There is also a rare form of congenital mitral stenosis.

In rheumatic mitral stenosis the mitral valve orifice is slowly diminished by progressive fibrosis, calcification of the valve leaflets, and fusion of the cusps and subvalvular apparatus. The flow of blood from left atrium to left ventricle is therefore restricted and left atrial pressure rises, leading to pulmonary venous congestion and breathlessness. There is dilatation and hypertrophy of the left atrium, and left ventricular filling becomes more dependent on left atrial contraction.

Any increase in heart rate shortens diastole (the time the mitral valve is open) and produces a further rise in left atrial pressure; situations that demand an increase in cardiac output will also increase left atrial pressure. Exercise and pregnancy are therefore poorly tolerated.

The mitral valve orifice is normally about 5 cm² in diastole and may be reduced to 1 cm² or less in severe mitral stenosis. Patients usually remain asymptomatic until the stenosis is at least moderately severe (approximately 2 cm² or less). At first, symptoms occur only on exercise; however, in severe stenosis left atrial pressure is permanently elevated and symptoms may occur at rest. Reduced lung compliance, due to chronic pulmonary venous congestion, contributes to breathlessness, and a low cardiac output may cause fatigue.

Atrial fibrillation due to progressive dilatation of the left atrium is very common. The onset of atrial fibrillation often precipitates pulmonary oedema because the accompanying tachycardia and loss of atrial contraction frequently lead to marked haemodynamic deterioration with a rapid rise in left atrial pressure. In contrast, a more gradual rise in left atrial pressure tends to cause an increase in pulmonary vascular resistance, which leads to pulmonary artery hypertension that may protect the patient from pulmonary oedema.

A minority of patients (less than 20%) remain in sinus rhythm; many of these individuals have a small fibrotic left atrium and severe pulmonary hypertension.

All patients with mitral stenosis, and particularly those with atrial fibrillation, are at risk from left atrial thrombosis and systemic thromboembolism. Prior to the advent of anticoagulant therapy, emboli caused a quarter of all deaths in this condition.

Clinical features

The main features of mitral stenosis are shown in Boxes 12.76 and 12.77.

Symptoms

Effort-related dyspnoea is usually the dominant symptom. Exercise tolerance typically diminishes very slowly over many years and patients often do not appreciate the extent of their disability. Eventually symptoms occur at rest. Acute pulmonary oedema or pulmonary hypertension can lead to haemoptysis. Systemic embolism is sometimes a presenting feature.

Signs

The forces that open and close the mitral valve increase as left atrial pressure rises. The first heart sound (S1) is therefore often unusually loud and may even be palpable (tapping apex beat). An opening snap may be audible and moves closer to the second sound (S2) as the stenosis becomes more severe and left atrial pressure rises. However, the first heart sound and opening snap may be inaudible if the valve is heavily calcified.

Turbulent flow produces the characteristic low-pitched mid-diastolic murmur and sometimes a thrill (see Fig. 12.86). The murmur is accentuated by exercise and during atrial systole (pre-systolic accentuation). Early in the disease a pre-systolic murmur may be the only auscultatory abnormality but in patients with symptoms the murmur usually extends from the opening snap to the first heart sound. Coexisting mitral regurgitation causes a pansystolic murmur which radiates towards the axilla.

If pulmonary hypertension supervenes there may be a right ventricular heave at the left sternal edge (due to right ventricular hypertrophy) and accentuation of the pulmonary component of the second heart sound. Tricuspid regurgitation secondary to right ventricular dilatation causes a systolic murmur and systolic waves in the venous pulse.

12.76 SYMPTOMS OF MITRAL STENOSIS

- Breathlessness (pulmonary congestion)
- Fatigue (low cardiac output)
- Oedema, ascites (right heart failure)
- Palpitation (atrial fibrillation)
- Haemoptysis (pulmonary congestion, pulmonary embolism)
- Cough (pulmonary congestion)
- Chest pain (pulmonary hypertension)
- Symptoms of thromboembolic complications (e.g. stroke, ischaemic limb)

12.77 SIGNS OF MITRAL STENOSIS

- Atrial fibrillation
- Mitral facies
- Auscultation
  Loud first heart sound, opening snap
  Mid-diastolic murmur
- Signs of raised pulmonary capillary pressure
  Crepitations, pulmonary oedema, effusions
- Signs of pulmonary hypertension
  RV heave, loud P_2

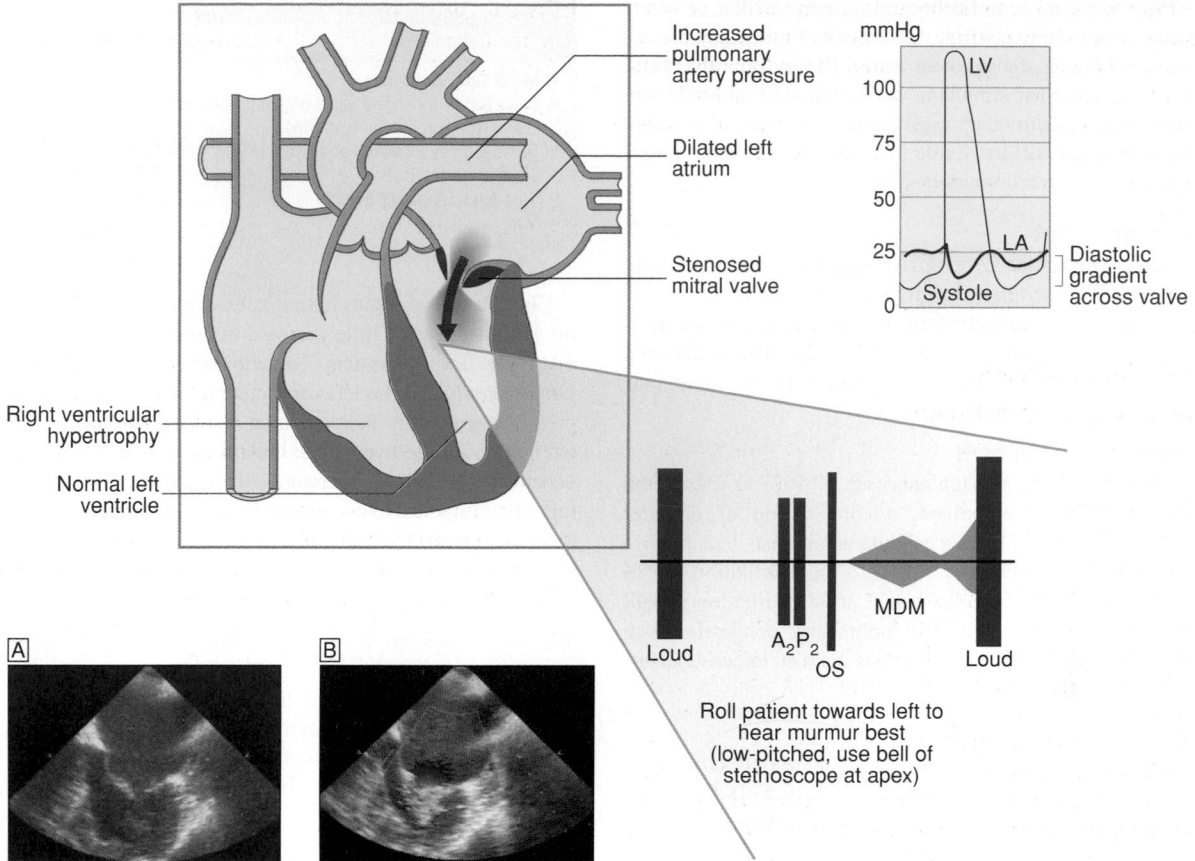

Fig. 12.86   Mitral stenosis: murmur and illustration of the diastolic pressure gradient between left atrium and left ventricle. (Mean gradient is reflected by the area between LA and LV in diastole.) The first heart sound is loud, there is an opening snap (OS) and mid-diastolic murmur (MDM) with pre-systolic accentuation. A Echocardiogram showing reduced opening of the mitral valve in diastole. B Colour Doppler showing turbulent flow.

The physical signs of mitral stenosis are often found before symptoms develop, and their recognition is of particular importance in pregnancy.

Investigations

The ECG (see Box 12.78) may show either the bifid P waves (P mitrale) associated with left atrial hypertrophy, or atrial fibrillation. There may also be evidence of right ventricular hypertrophy (pulmonary hypertension). The chest radiograph (see Fig. 12.11, p. 369) may show enlargement of the left atrium and its appendage, enlargement of the main pulmonary artery, and features of pulmonary venous congestion (enlargement of the upper pulmonary veins and horizontal linear shadows in the costophrenic angles).

Doppler echocardiography can provide the definitive evaluation of mitral stenosis; apart from confirming the diagnosis, it allows an assessment of its severity and also provides information on the rigidity and degree of calcification of the valve cusps, the size of the left atrium, pulmonary artery pressure and the state of left ventricular function (see Fig. 12.86).

12.78 INVESTIGATIONS IN MITRAL STENOSIS
ECG
• Left atrial hypertrophy (if not in AF)   • Right ventricular hypertrophy
Chest radiograph
• Enlarged left atrium   • Signs of pulmonary venous congestion
Echo
• Thickened immobile cusps   • Reduced valve area   • Reduced rate of diastolic filling of LV
Doppler
• Pressure gradient across mitral valve   • Pulmonary artery pressure
Cardiac catheterisation
• Pressure gradient between LA (or pulmonary wedge) and LV

Prior to the advent of echocardiography, cardiac catheterisation was used to confirm the severity of mitral stenosis by measurement of the gradient across the mitral valve from pressures recorded simultaneously in the left ventricle and left atrium (or pulmonary capillary wedge position). Cardiac catheterisation still has a role in assessing coexisting mitral regurgitation and coronary disease.

Management

Patients with minor symptoms should be treated medically, but the definitive treatment of mitral stenosis is by balloon valvuloplasty, mitral valvotomy or mitral valve replacement. Intervention should be considered if the patient remains symptomatic despite medical treatment or if severe pulmonary hypertension develops.

Medical management

This consists of anticoagulants (see p. 402) to reduce the risk of systemic embolism, a combination of digoxin, β-blockers or rate-limiting calcium antagonists (see p. 401) to control the ventricular rate in atrial fibrillation (or to prevent a rapid ventricular rate if atrial fibrillation should develop), diuretics to control pulmonary congestion (see p. 386), and antibiotic prophylaxis against infective endocarditis (see Box 12.95, p. 467).

Mitral balloon valvuloplasty

This is the treatment of choice if the appropriate criteria are fulfilled (see Box 12.79 and Fig. 12.15, p. 372). Closed or open mitral valvotomy may be used if the facilities or expertise for valvuloplasty are not available. Patients who have undergone mitral valvuloplasty or valvotomy should practise antibiotic prophylaxis against infective endocarditis and should be followed up at 1–2-yearly intervals because restenosis may occur. Clinical symptoms and signs are a guide to the severity of mitral restenosis, but Doppler echocardiography provides a more accurate assessment.

12.79 CRITERIA FOR MITRAL VALVULOPLASTY

- Significant symptoms
- Isolated mitral stenosis
- No (or trivial) mitral regurgitation
- Mobile, non-calcified valve/subvalve apparatus on echo
- Left atrium free of thrombus

For further information see www.acc.org, which has comprehensive guidelines on valvular heart disease.

Mitral valve replacement

Valve replacement is indicated if there is substantial mitral reflux, or if the valve is rigid and calcified (see p. 467).

MITRAL REGURGITATION

Aetiology and pathophysiology

Rheumatic disease is the principal cause of mitral regurgitation in countries where rheumatic fever is common, but elsewhere, including in the UK, other causes are more important (see Box 12.80). Mitral regurgitation may also follow successful relief of mitral stenosis by valvotomy or valvuloplasty.

12.80 CAUSES OF MITRAL REGURGITATION

- Mitral valve prolapse
- Dilatation of the mitral valve ring (e.g. rheumatic fever, coronary artery disease, cardiomyopathy)
- Damage to valve cusps and chordae (e.g. rheumatic heart disease, endocarditis)
- Damage to papillary muscle
- Myocardial infarction

Chronic mitral regurgitation causes gradual dilatation of the left atrium with little increase in pressure and therefore relatively few symptoms. Nevertheless, the left ventricle dilates slowly and the left ventricular diastolic and left atrial pressures gradually increase as a result of chronic volume overload of the left ventricle; breathlessness and pulmonary oedema eventually supervene. In contrast, acute mitral regurgitation tends to cause a rapid rise in left atrial pressure (because left atrial compliance is normal) and marked symptomatic deterioration.

Mitral valve prolapse

This is also known as 'floppy' mitral valve and is one of the more common causes of mild mitral regurgitation. It is caused by congenital anomalies or degenerative myxomatous changes and is sometimes a feature of connective tissue disorders such as Marfan's syndrome.

In the mildest forms of mitral prolapse the valve remains competent but bulges back into the atrium during systole, causing a mid-systolic click but no murmur. Occasionally, multiple clicks are audible. In the presence of a regurgitant valve the click is followed by a late systolic murmur which lengthens as the regurgitation becomes more severe. A click is not always audible and the physical signs may vary with both posture and respiration.

Progressive elongation of the chordae tendineae may lead to increasing mitral regurgitation, and if chordal rupture occurs regurgitation may suddenly become severe. These complications are rare before the fifth or sixth decade of life.

Haemodynamically significant mitral valve prolapse can predispose to infective endocarditis, and requires antibiotic prophylaxis. Mitral valve prolapse is also associated with a variety of typically benign arrhythmias, atypical chest pain and a very small risk of embolic stroke or transient ischaemic attack. Nevertheless, the overall long-term prognosis is good. An echocardiogram of mitral valve prolapse is shown in Figure 12.87.

Other causes of mitral regurgitation

The mitral valve depends for its proper function on the chordae tendineae and their papillary muscles; dilatation of the left ventricle distorts the geometry of these supporting structures and may cause mitral regurgitation. Dilated cardiomyopathy and the impaired ventricular function that results from coronary artery disease are common causes of so-called 'functional' mitral regurgitation. Ischaemia or infarction of the papillary muscles may also cause mitral regurgitation. Endocarditis may lead to distortion or perforation of the valve leaflets and is an important cause of acute mitral regurgitation.

Clinical features

These are summarised in Box 12.81.

The symptoms depend on how suddenly the regurgitation develops. Chronic mitral regurgitation produces a symptom complex that is similar to that of mitral stenosis, but sudden-onset mitral regurgitation usually presents with acute pulmonary oedema.

The regurgitant jet causes an apical systolic murmur (see Fig. 12.87) which often radiates into the axilla, and may be accompanied by a thrill. The first heart sound is quiet because valve closure is abnormal. Increased forward flow through the mitral valve may give rise to a loud third heart sound and even a short mid-diastolic murmur. The apex beat feels active and rocking (left ventricular volume overload) and is usually displaced to the left as a result of dilatation of the left ventricle.

12.81 CLINICAL FEATURES OF MITRAL REGURGITATION
Symptoms
• Dyspnoea (pulmonary venous congestion)
• Fatigue (low cardiac output)
• Palpitation (AF, increased stroke volume)
• Oedema, ascites (right heart failure)
Signs
• Atrial fibrillation/flutter
• Cardiomegaly—displaced hyperdynamic apex beat
• Apical pansystolic murmur ± thrill
• Soft S1, apical S3
• Signs of pulmonary venous congestion (crepitations, pulmonary oedema, effusions)
• Signs of pulmonary hypertension and right heart failure

Investigations

The radiograph and ECG may show features of left atrial and/or left ventricular hypertrophy (see Box 12.82). Atrial fibrillation is common, as a consequence of atrial dilatation. Echocardiography provides information about the state of the mitral valve, left ventricular function and left atrial size but Doppler echocardiography is required to estimate the extent of regurgitation. At cardiac catheterisation the severity of mitral regurgitation may be indicated by the size of the v (systolic) waves in the left atrial or PAW pressure trace, or

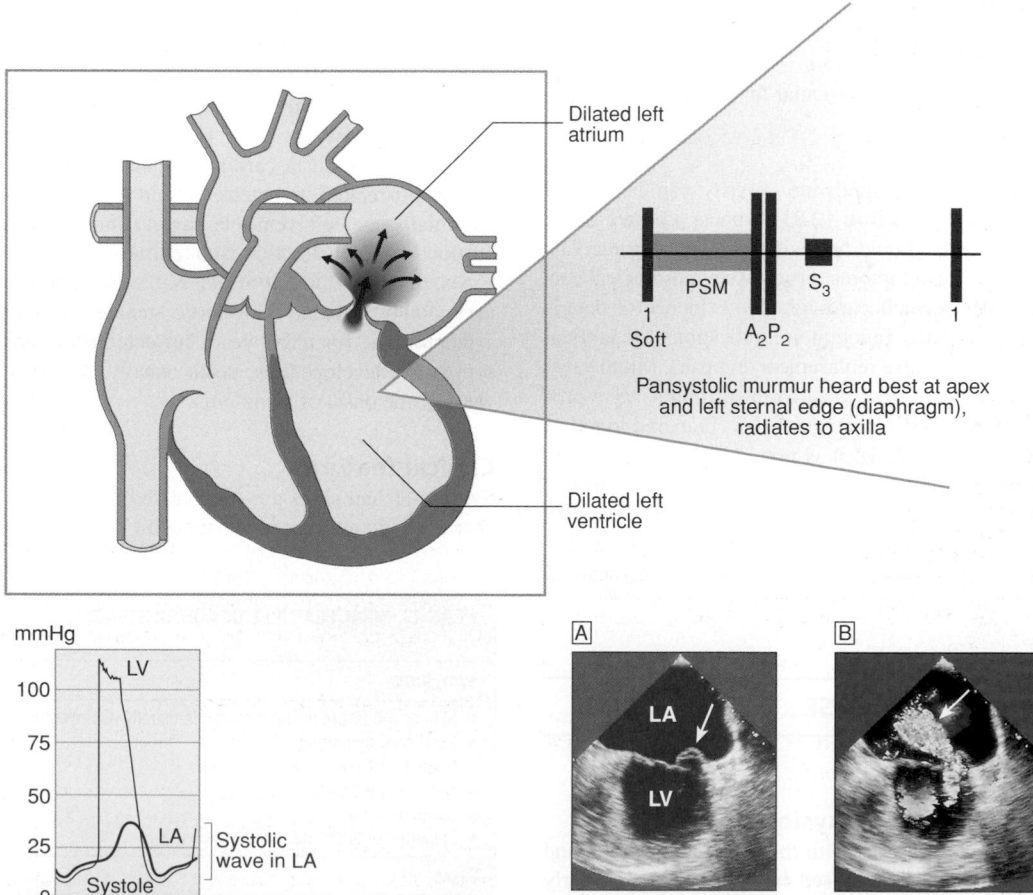

Fig. 12.87 Mitral regurgitation: radiation of the murmur to the axilla and illustration of systolic wave in left atrial pressure. The first sound is normal or soft and merges with a pansystolic murmur (PSM) extending to the second heart sound. A third heart sound occurs with severe regurgitation. The left atrium and ventricle become dilated. **A** A transoesophageal echocardiogram shows an example of mitral valve prolapse, with one leaflet bulging towards the left atrium (LA; arrow). **B** This results in a jet of mitral regurgitation on colour Doppler (arrow).

12.82 INVESTIGATIONS IN MITRAL REGURGITATION
ECG
• Left atrial hypertrophy (if not in AF) • Left ventricular hypertrophy
Chest radiograph
• Enlarged left atrium   • Pulmonary venous congestion • Enlarged left ventricle   • Pulmonary oedema (if acute)
Echo
• Dilated LA, LV • Dynamic LV (unless myocardial dysfunction predominates) • Structural abnormalities of mitral valve (e.g. prolapse)
Doppler
• Detects and quantifies regurgitation
Cardiac catheterisation
• Dilated LA, dilated LV, mitral regurgitation • Pulmonary hypertension • Coexisting coronary artery disease

12.83 MEDICAL MANAGEMENT OF MITRAL REGURGITATION
• Diuretics • Vasodilators, e.g. ACE inhibitors (see p. 386) • Digoxin if atrial fibrillation is present • Anticoagulants if atrial fibrillation is present • Antibiotic prophylaxis against infective endocarditis

12.84 CAUSES OF AORTIC STENOSIS
Infants, children, adolescents
• Congenital aortic stenosis • Congenital subvalvular aortic stenosis • Congenital supravalvular aortic stenosis
Young adults to middle-aged
• Calcification and fibrosis of congenitally bicuspid aortic valve • Rheumatic aortic stenosis
Middle-aged to elderly
• Senile degenerative aortic stenosis • Calcification of bicuspid valve • Rheumatic aortic stenosis

by left ventricular angiography; however, this is not always reliable, as left atrial compliance may vary. In practice, a common and difficult problem lies in deciding on the extent to which cardiac failure is due to mitral regurgitation as opposed to impaired left ventricular function.

Management

Mitral regurgitation of moderate severity can be treated medically, as shown in Box 12.83. Patients who are being managed medically should be reviewed at regular intervals because worsening symptoms, progressive radiological cardiac enlargement or echocardiographic evidence of deteriorating left ventricular function are indications for surgical intervention (mitral valve replacement or repair). Mitral valve repair can be used to treat most forms of mitral valve prolapse and offers many advantages when compared to mitral valve replacement. Indeed, it is now advocated for severe regurgitation even in asymptomatic patients because results are excellent and early repair has been shown to prevent irreversible left ventricular damage. When mitral regurgitation is due to left ventricular dilatation caused by myocardial disease, treatment should be directed to the latter.

AORTIC VALVE DISEASE

AORTIC STENOSIS

Aetiology and pathophysiology

The likely aetiology varies with the age of the patient, and possible causes are summarised in Box 12.84. In elderly patients aortic stenosis and coronary atheroma frequently coexist.

Aortic stenosis develops slowly, except in the congenital forms, and cardiac output is initially maintained at the cost of a steadily increasing pressure gradient across the aortic valve. The left ventricle becomes increasingly hypertrophied and coronary blood flow may then be inadequate; patients may therefore develop angina, even in the absence of concomitant coronary disease. The fixed outflow obstruction limits the increase in cardiac output required on exercise, and effort-related hypotension and syncope may occur. Eventually the left ventricle can no longer overcome the outflow tract obstruction and pulmonary oedema supervenes. In contrast to mitral stenosis, which tends to progress very slowly, patients with aortic stenosis typically remain asymptomatic for many years but deteriorate rapidly when symptoms develop; thus, death usually ensues within 3–5 years of the onset of symptoms.

Clinical features

Symptoms and signs are summarised in Box 12.85 and the characteristic murmur is illustrated in Figure 12.88.

12.85 CLINICAL FEATURES OF AORTIC STENOSIS
Symptoms
• Mild or moderate aortic stenosis is usually asymptomatic • Exertional dyspnoea • Angina • Exertional syncope • Sudden death • Episodes of acute pulmonary oedema
Signs
• Ejection systolic murmur • Slow-rising carotid pulse • Narrow pulse pressure • Thrusting apex beat (LV pressure overload) • Signs of pulmonary venous congestion (e.g. crepitations)

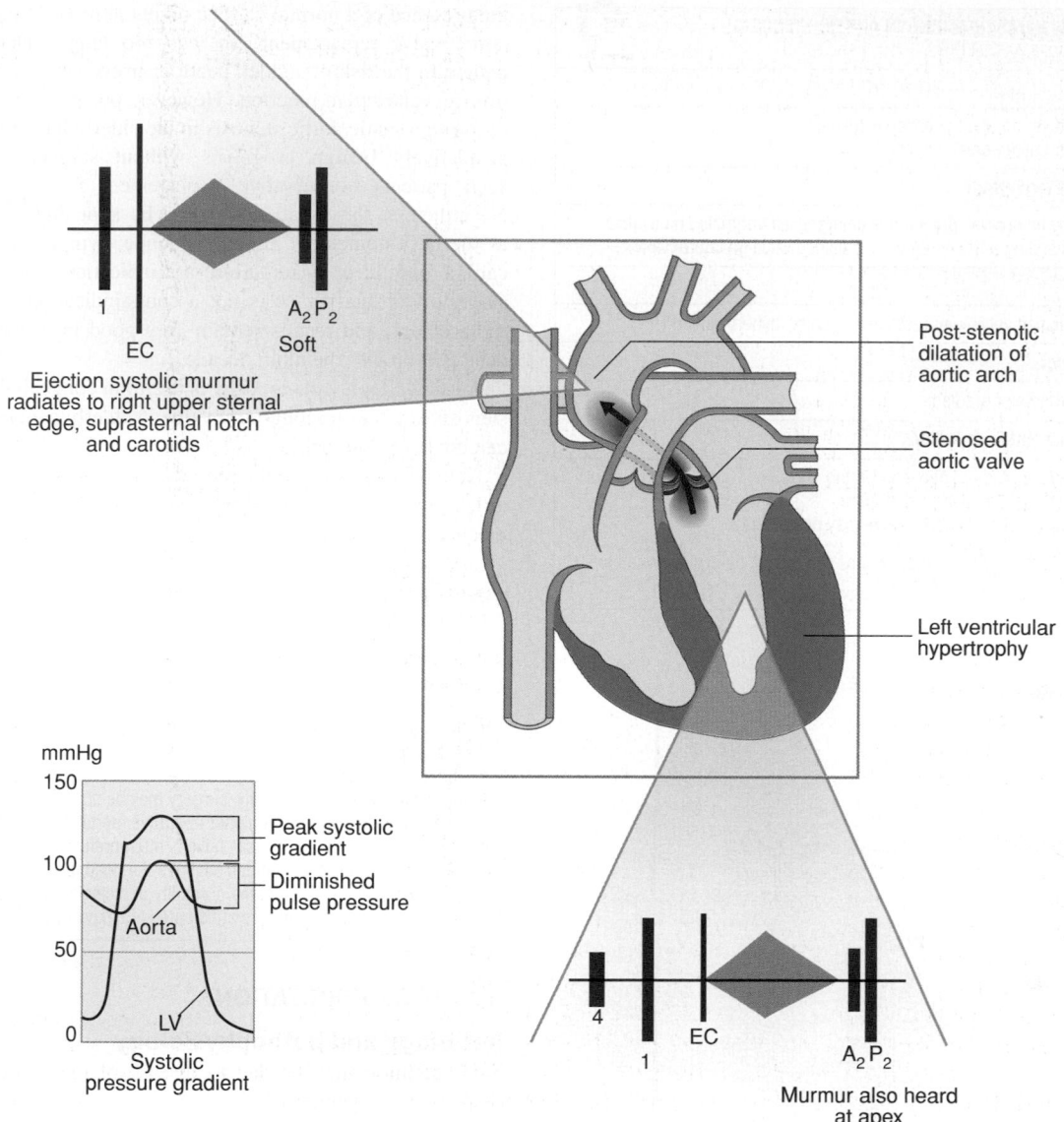

Fig. 12.88 Aortic stenosis. Pressure traces show the systolic gradient between left ventricle and aorta. The carotid pulse is low-volume and slow-rising. The 'diamond shape' murmur may be heard best with the diaphragm in the aortic outflow and also at the apex. The aortic component of the second heart sound (A₂) is quiet or inaudible. An ejection click (EC) may be present in young patients with bicuspid aortic valve but not in older patients with calcified valves. Aortic stenosis may lead to left ventricular hypertrophy with a fourth sound at the apex and post-stenotic dilatation of the aortic arch. The typical Doppler signal with aortic stenosis is illustrated in Figure 12.12, page 369.

Investigations

The ECG may show left ventricular hypertrophy and ST changes; left bundle branch block is also common (see Box 12.86). In advanced cases features of hypertrophy are often gross (see Fig. 12.89), and down-sloping ST segments and T inversion ('strain pattern') may be seen in leads reflecting the left ventricle. Nevertheless, especially in the elderly, the ECG can be normal despite severe stenosis. The postero-anterior chest radiograph is frequently normal, but may show left ventricular enlargement and post-stenotic dilatation of the ascending aorta. A lateral radiograph or magnetic resonance image may show valve calcification, but the diagnosis is more readily made on echocardiography.

Echocardiography will show an abnormal aortic valve, which may be heavily calcified and disorganised, and a hypertrophied left ventricle. Doppler echocardiography permits calculation of the systolic gradient across the aortic valve from the velocity of the ejected jet of blood, and detects the presence or absence of aortic regurgitation (see Fig. 12.12, p. 369). Cardiac catheterisation is indicated if the ultrasound studies are unsatisfactory or if it is necessary to assess the state of the coronary arteries.

Management

Patients with symptomatic aortic stenosis and a valve gradient indicative of moderate or severe stenosis (i.e. > 50 mmHg in

.459

12.86 INVESTIGATIONS IN AORTIC STENOSIS

ECG

- Left ventricular hypertrophy (usually)
- Left bundle branch block

Chest radiograph

- May be normal. Sometimes enlarged left ventricle and dilated ascending aorta on PA view, calcified valve on lateral view

Echo

- Calcified valve with restricted opening, hypertrophied LV

Doppler

- Estimate of gradient

Cardiac catheterisation

- Systolic gradient between LV and aorta
- Post-stenotic dilatation of aorta
- Regurgitation of aortic valve may be present

N.B. Cardiac catheter may only be required to determine whether coronary disease is present.

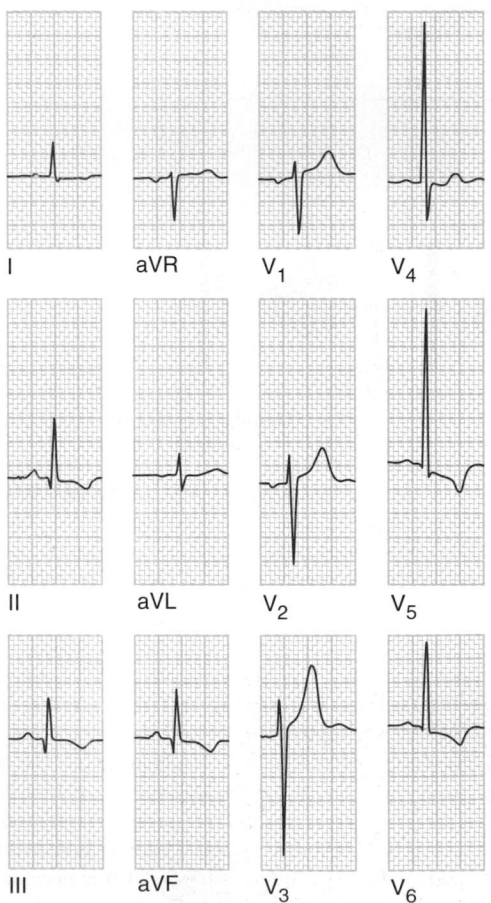

Fig. 12.89 Left ventricular hypertrophy: QRS complexes in limb leads have increased amplitude with a very large R wave in V$_5$ and S wave in V$_2$. There is ST depression and T wave inversion in leads II, III, aVF, V$_5$ and V$_6$: a 'left ventricular strain' pattern.

the presence of a normal cardiac output at rest) should have aortic valve replacement. To wait too long exposes the patient to the risk of sudden death or irreversible deterioration in ventricular function. However, prospective studies of asymptomatic aortic stenosis in the elderly have revealed a relatively benign prognosis without surgery, and in such patients conservative management is appropriate. Nevertheless, these patients should be kept under review, as the development of angina, syncope, symptoms of low cardiac output, or heart failure are indications for prompt surgery. Old age per se is not a contraindication to valve replacement, and results remain very good in experienced centres even into the ninth decade.

Aortic balloon valvuloplasty is useful in congenital aortic stenosis but is of no long-term value in elderly patients with calcific aortic stenosis.

Anticoagulants are only required in patients who have atrial fibrillation or have had a valve replacement with a mechanical prosthesis.

ISSUES IN OLDER PEOPLE
AORTIC STENOSIS

- Aortic stenosis is a common cause of syncope, angina and heart failure, and is the most common form of valve disease in the very old.
- Because of increased arterial stiffness, a low pulse pressure and a slow rising pulse may not be present.
- The prognosis without surgery after the onset of symptoms is poor.
- In the absence of comorbidity, surgery may be advisable in those aged 80 or over, but has a higher operative mortality.
- Replacement with a biological valve is often preferable to a mechanical valve because this obviates the need for anticoagulation; moreover, the durability of biological valves usually exceeds the patient's anticipated life expectancy.

AORTIC REGURGITATION

Aetiology and pathophysiology

This condition may be due to disease of the aortic valve cusps (e.g. congenital bicuspid valve, rheumatic heart disease, infective endocarditis) or dilatation of the aortic root (see Box 12.87).

The left ventricle dilates and hypertrophies to compensate for the regurgitation; the stroke output of the left ventricle may eventually be doubled or trebled and the major arteries are then conspicuously pulsatile. As the disease progresses left ventricular diastolic pressure rises, at first only with exercise, and breathlessness develops.

12.87 CAUSES OF AORTIC REGURGITATION

Congenital

- Bicuspid valve or disproportionate cusps

Acquired

- Rheumatic disease
- Infective endocarditis
- Trauma
- Aortic dilatation (Marfan's syndrome, aneurysm, dissection, syphilis, ankylosing spondylitis)

Clinical features

Until the onset of breathlessness, the only symptom may be an awareness of the heart beat, particularly when lying on the left side; this results from the increased stroke volume (see Box 12.88). Paroxysmal nocturnal dyspnoea is sometimes the first symptom and peripheral oedema, or angina, may occur. The characteristic murmur is illustrated in Figure 12.90. Although it is usually best heard to the left of the sternum, it is sometimes louder to the right; a thrill is rare. A systolic murmur due to the increased stroke volume is common and does not necessarily indicate stenosis. When the leak is small the murmur will be heard only if the steps shown in Figure 12.90 are followed; this is of crucial importance in the early detection of infective endocarditis affecting the aortic valve. However, when the leak is large the diagnosis is usually easy, with gross pulsation in the large arteries, a collapsing pulse, a low diastolic and an increased pulse pressure, a heaving apical impulse (volume overload), a pre-systolic impulse and a fourth heart sound. The regurgitant jet causes fluttering and, if severe, partial closure of the anterior mitral leaflet; this may render the mitral valve functionally stenotic leading to a soft mid-diastolic (Austin Flint) murmur.

12.88 CLINICAL FEATURES OF AORTIC REGURGITATION (AR)
Symptoms
Mild to moderate AR   • Often asymptomatic   • Awareness of heart beat, 'palpitations'
Severe AR   • Breathlessness   • Angina
Signs
Pulses   • Large-volume or 'collapsing' pulse   • Bounding peripheral pulses   • Capillary pulsation in nail beds—Quincke's sign   • Femoral bruit ('pistol shot')—Duroziez's sign   • Head nodding with pulse—de Musset's sign
Murmurs   • Early diastolic murmur   • Systolic murmur (increased stroke volume)   • Austin Flint murmur (soft mid-diastolic)
Other signs   • Displaced, rocking apex beat (volume overload)   • Fourth heart sound   • Pulmonary venous congestion (crepitations)

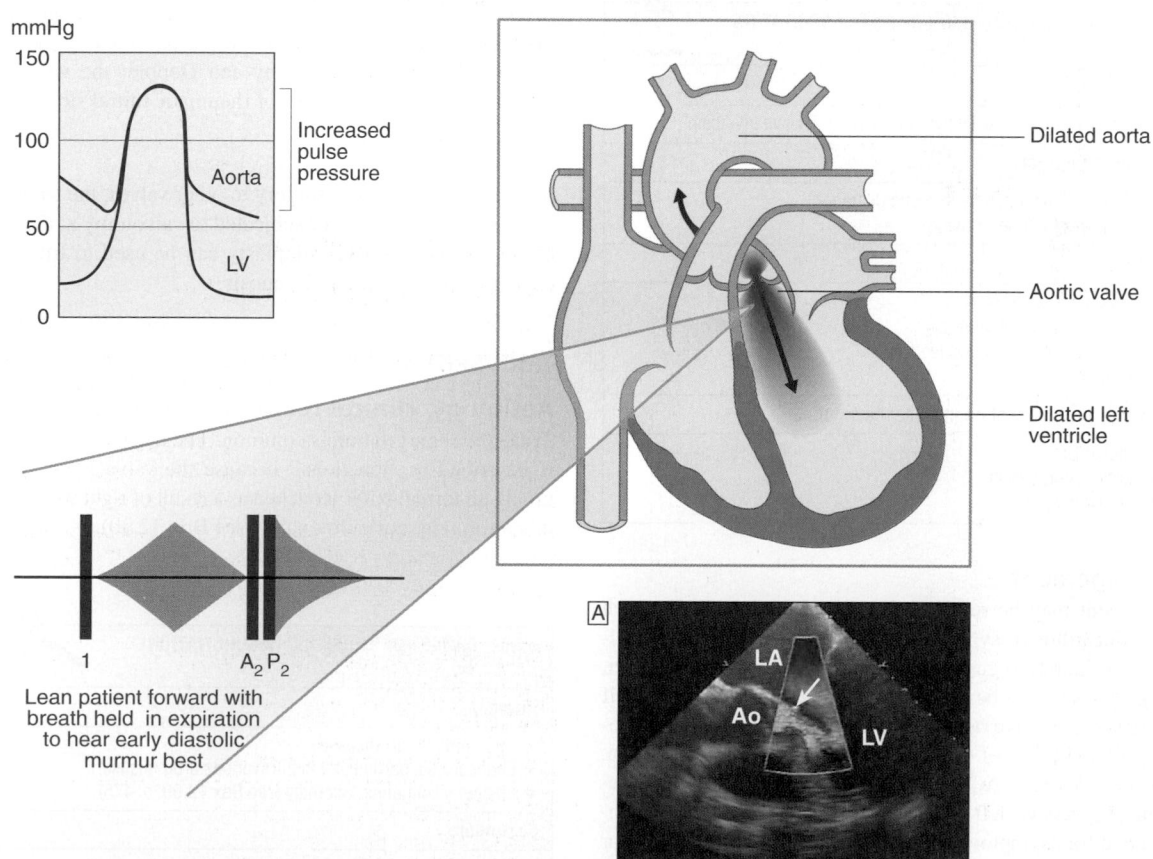

Fig. 12.90   Aortic regurgitation. The early diastolic murmur is best heard at the left sternal edge and may be accompanied by an ejection systolic murmur due to the enlarged stroke volume ('to and fro' murmur). Aortic regurgitation may lead to dilatation of the aortic arch and left ventricle.
A An echocardiogram with the regurgitant jet on colour Doppler (arrow). (LV = left ventricle; LA = left atrium; Ao = aorta)

In acute severe regurgitation (e.g. perforation of aortic cusp in endocarditis) there may be no time for compensatory left ventricular hypertrophy and dilatation to develop and the features of heart failure may predominate. Moreover, in this situation the classical signs of aortic regurgitation may be masked by tachycardia and an abrupt rise in LV end-diastolic pressure; thus, the pulse pressure is often narrow and the diastolic murmur may be short or even absent.

Investigations

The chest radiograph characteristically shows cardiac and aortic dilatation, together with signs of left heart failure (see Box 12.89). When regurgitation is marked, the ECG may show left ventricular hypertrophy and ST changes. Echocardiography in aortic regurgitation typically shows a dilated left ventricle with vigorous contraction (until heart failure ensues). There may be fluttering of the anterior mitral leaflet in the regurgitant jet and vegetations may be visible in infective endocarditis. Regurgitation is readily detected by Doppler echocardiography. In severe acute aortic regurgitation the rapid rise in LV diastolic pressure may cause premature mitral valve closure. Cardiac catheterisation and aortography can be helpful in assessing the severity of regurgitation, and dilatation of the aorta.

12.89 INVESTIGATIONS IN AORTIC REGURGITATION
ECG
• Initially normal, later LV hypertrophy and T wave inversion
Chest radiograph
• Cardiac dilatation, maybe aortic dilatation • Features of left heart failure
Echo
• Dilated left ventricle • Hyperdynamic left ventricle • Fluttering anterior mitral leaflet • Doppler detects reflux
Cardiac catheterisation (may not be required)
• Dilated LV • Aortic regurgitation • Dilated aortic root

Management

Treatment may be required for underlying conditions such as endocarditis or syphilis. Aortic valve replacement is indicated if aortic regurgitation causes symptoms. However, surgery may also be advisable in asymptomatic patients if there is progressive radiological cardiomegaly or echocardiographic evidence of deteriorating left ventricular function. Vasodilators (e.g. ACE inhibitors) have been shown to prevent progressive left ventricular dilatation and are recommended for asymptomatic patients. The latter require regular echocardiographic assessment, usually on an annual basis, to detect early signs of ventricular dilatation. When aortic root dilatation is the cause of aortic regurgitation (e.g. Marfan's syndrome) aortic root replacement may be necessary.

TRICUSPID VALVE DISEASE

TRICUSPID STENOSIS

Aetiology

Tricuspid stenosis is usually rheumatic in origin, and is therefore seldom seen in Western countries. Clinically evident tricuspid disease occurs in fewer than 5% of patients with rheumatic heart disease and nearly always occurs in association with mitral and aortic valve disease. Isolated rheumatic tricuspid stenosis is very rare. Tricuspid stenosis and regurgitation are also features of the carcinoid syndrome (see p. 801).

Clinical features and investigations

Usually the symptoms of the associated mitral and aortic valve disease predominate; however, tricuspid stenosis may cause symptoms of right heart failure including hepatic discomfort and peripheral oedema.

The main clinical feature is a raised jugular venous pressure with a prominent *a* wave, and a slow *y* descent due to the loss of normal rapid RV filling (see p. 359). There is also a mid-diastolic murmur usually best heard at the lower left or right sternal edge; this is usually higher-pitched than the murmur of mitral stenosis and is increased by inspiration. Right heart failure may give rise to hepatomegaly with pre-systolic pulsation (large *a* wave), ascites and peripheral oedema. On echocardiography and Doppler the valve has similar appearances to those of rheumatic mitral stenosis.

Management

In patients who require surgery to other valves, the tricuspid valve is either replaced or subjected to valvotomy at the time of surgery. Balloon valvuloplasty can be used to treat rare cases of isolated tricuspid stenosis.

TRICUSPID REGURGITATION

Aetiology, clinical features and investigations

Tricuspid regurgitation is common. The most frequent cause is described as 'functional' because the valve is not structurally abnormal but is stretched as a result of right ventricular dilatation (e.g. cor pulmonale—see Box 12.90).

12.90 CAUSES OF TRICUSPID REGURGITATION
Primary
• Rheumatic heart disease • Endocarditis, particularly in intravenous drug misusers • Ebstein's congenital anomaly (see Box 12.99, p. 475)
Secondary
• Right ventricular dilatation due to chronic left heart failure ('functional tricuspid regurgitation') • Right ventricular infarction • Pulmonary hypertension (e.g. cor pulmonale)

Symptoms are usually non-specific, and relate to reduced forward flow (tiredness) and venous congestion (oedema, hepatic enlargement). The most prominent clinical feature is a large systolic wave in the jugular venous pulse (a *cv* wave replaces the normal *x* descent). Other features include a pansystolic murmur at the left sternal edge and systolic pulsation of the liver. Echocardiography may reveal dilatation of the right ventricle; if the valve has been affected by rheumatic disease the leaflets will appear thickened, and in endocarditis vegetations may be seen. Ebstein's anomaly (see Box 12.99, p. 475) is a congenital abnormality of the tricuspid valve in which the valve is displaced towards the right ventricular apex, with consequent enlargement of the right atrium; it is commonly associated with tricuspid regurgitation.

Management

Tricuspid regurgitation that is due to right ventricular dilatation gets better when the cause of right ventricular overload is corrected (e.g. by mitral valve replacement or by diuretic and vasodilator treatment of congestive cardiac failure).

Patients with a normal pulmonary artery pressure tolerate isolated tricuspid reflux well, and valves damaged by endocarditis do not always need to be replaced. However, a few patients with organic tricuspid valve damage and elevated pulmonary artery pressure require tricuspid valve repair (annuloplasty) or replacement.

PULMONARY VALVE DISEASE

PULMONARY STENOSIS

Aetiology

The condition can occur in the carcinoid syndrome but is usually congenital, when it may be isolated or associated with other abnormalities such as Fallot's tetralogy (see p. 474).

Clinical features, investigations and management

The principal finding on examination is an ejection systolic murmur, loudest to the left of the upper sternum and radiating towards the left shoulder. There may be a thrill, best felt when the patient leans forward and breathes out. The murmur is often preceded by an ejection sound (click). Delay in right ventricular ejection may cause wide splitting of the second heart sound. Severe pulmonary stenosis is characterised clinically by a loud harsh murmur, an inaudible pulmonary closure sound (P_2), an increased right ventricular heave, prominent *a* waves in the jugular pulse, ECG evidence of right ventricular hypertrophy, and post-stenotic dilatation in the pulmonary artery on the chest radiograph. Doppler echocardiography is the investigation of choice.

Mild to moderate isolated pulmonary stenosis is relatively common, does not usually progress, and does not require treatment; it is a low-risk lesion for infective endocarditis.

Severe pulmonary stenosis (resting gradient > 50 mmHg with a normal cardiac output) is treated by percutaneous pulmonary balloon valvuloplasty or, if unavailable, by surgical valvotomy. Long-term results are very good. Post-operative pulmonary regurgitation is common but benign.

PULMONARY REGURGITATION

Pulmonary regurgitation is rarely an isolated phenomenon and is usually associated with pulmonary artery dilatation due to pulmonary hypertension. It may, for example, complicate mitral stenosis, producing an early diastolic decrescendo murmur at the left sternal edge that is difficult to distinguish from aortic regurgitation (Graham Steell murmur). The pulmonary hypertension may also be secondary to other disease of the left side of the heart, to primary pulmonary vascular disease or to Eisenmenger's syndrome (see p. 470). Trivial pulmonary regurgitation is a frequent Doppler finding in normal individuals that is of no clinical significance.

INFECTIVE ENDOCARDITIS

Infective endocarditis is due to microbial infection of a heart valve (native or prosthetic), the lining of a cardiac chamber or blood vessel, or a congenital anomaly (e.g. septal defect). The causative organism is usually a bacterium, but may be a rickettsia (*Coxiella burnetii*—Q fever endocarditis), chlamydia or fungus.

Pathophysiology

Infective endocarditis typically occurs at sites of pre-existing endocardial damage. However, infection with particularly virulent or aggressive organisms (e.g. *Staphylococcus aureus*) can cause endocarditis in a previously normal heart; for example, staphylococcal endocarditis of the tricuspid valve is a common complication of intravenous drug misuse. A wide variety of acquired and congenital cardiac lesions are vulnerable to endocarditis. Defects associated with jet lesions (areas of endocardial damage caused by a high-pressure jet of blood) such as ventricular septal defect, mitral regurgitation and aortic regurgitation, many of which are haemodynamically insignificant, are particularly susceptible. In contrast the risk of endocarditis at the site of many haemodynamically important low-pressure lesions (e.g. a large atrial septal defect) is negligible.

Infection tends to occur at sites of endothelial damage because these areas attract deposits of platelets and fibrin, which are vulnerable to colonisation by blood-borne organisms. The avascular valve tissue and presence of fibrin aggregates help to protect proliferating organisms from host defence mechanisms. When the infection is established vegetations, composed of organisms, fibrin and platelets, grow and may become large enough to cause obstruction; they may also break away as emboli. Adjacent tissues are destroyed and abscesses may form; valve regurgitation may develop or increase if the affected valve is damaged by tissue distortion, cusp perforation or disruption of chordae. Extracardiac manifestations such as vasculitis and skin lesions are due to emboli or immune complex deposition. Mycotic aneurysms may develop in arteries at the site of infected emboli. At postmortem it is common to find infarction of the spleen and kidneys, and sometimes an immune glomerulonephritis.

Microbiology

The viridans group of streptococci (*Strep. mitis*, *Strep. sanguis*, α-haemolytic streptococci) are commensals in the upper respiratory tract that may enter the blood stream on chewing, teeth-brushing or at the time of dental treatment, and are common causes of subacute endocarditis (see Box 12.91). Other organisms, including *Enterococcus faecalis*, *E. faecium*, *Strep. milleri* and *Strep. bovis*, may enter the blood from the bowel or urinary tract. *Strep. milleri* and *Strep. bovis* endocarditis is sometimes associated with large-bowel neoplasms.

Staph. aureus is a common cause of acute endocarditis, originating from skin infections, abscesses or vascular access sites (e.g. intravenous and central lines), or from intravenous drug misuse. It is a highly virulent and invasive organism, usually producing florid vegetations, rapid valve destruction and abscess formation. Other causes of acute endocarditis include *Strep. pneumoniae* and *Neisseria gonorrhoeae*.

Post-operative endocarditis follows cardiac surgery and may affect native or prosthetic heart valves or other prosthetic materials. The most common organism is a coagulase-negative staphylococcus (*Staph. epidermidis*), which is a normal skin contaminant. There is frequently a history of post-operative wound infection with the same organism. *Staph. epidermidis* occasionally causes endocarditis in patients who have not had cardiac surgery and its presence in blood cultures may be erroneously dismissed as contamination. Another coagulase-negative staphylococcus, *Staph. lugdenensis*, has recently been recognised as a cause of rapidly destructive acute endocarditis that is frequently associated with multiple emboli and often affects previously normal valves. Unless accurately identified and speciated, it may also be overlooked as a contaminant.

In Q fever endocarditis the patient often has a history of contact with farm animals. The aortic valve is usually affected and there may be hepatic complications and purpura. Prolonged (life-long) antibiotic therapy may be required.

Gram-negative bacteria of the so-called HACEK group are slow-growing fastidious organisms that may only be revealed after prolonged culture and may be resistant to penicillin.

Brucella is associated with a history of contact with goats or cattle and often affects the aortic valve.

Yeasts and fungi (*Candida*, *Aspergillus*) may attack previously normal or prosthetic valves. Abscesses and emboli are common, therapy is difficult (surgery is often required) and the mortality is high. Concomitant bacterial infection may be present.

Incidence

The incidence of infective endocarditis in community-based studies ranges from 2 to 5 cases per 100 000 per annum. In a large British study, the underlying heart disease was rheumatic heart disease in 24% of patients, congenital heart disease in 19%, and some other cardiac abnormality (e.g. calcified AV, floppy MV) in 25%. The remainder (32%) were not thought to have a pre-existing cardiac abnormality. More than 50% of patients with infective endocarditis are more than 60 years of age.

Clinical features

Possible clinical features in endocarditis, and their frequency, are shown in Figure 12.91.

The clinical course of endocarditis

Endocarditis can be divided into an acute and a more insidious 'subacute' form. However, there is considerable overlap because the clinical pattern is influenced not only by the organism, but also by the site of infection, prior antibiotic therapy and the presence of a valve or shunt prosthesis. Furthermore, the subacute form may abruptly develop acute life-threatening complications such as valve disruption or emboli.

Subacute endocarditis. This should be suspected when a patient known to have congenital or valvular heart disease develops a persistent fever, complains of unusual tiredness, night sweats or weight loss, or develops new signs of valve dysfunction or heart failure. Less often, it presents as an embolic stroke or peripheral arterial embolism. Other features include purpura and petechial haemorrhages in the skin and mucous membranes, and splinter haemorrhages under the finger or toe nails. Osler's nodes are painful tender swellings at the fingertips that are probably the product of vasculitis; they are rare. Digital clubbing is a late sign. The spleen is frequently palpable; in *Coxiella* infections the spleen and the liver may be considerably enlarged. Microscopic haematuria is common. The finding of any of these features in a patient with persistent fever or malaise is an indication for re-examination to detect hitherto unrecognised heart disease.

Acute endocarditis. This usually presents as a severe febrile illness with prominent and changing heart murmurs and petechiae. Clinical stigmata of chronic endocarditis are usually absent. Embolic events are common, and cardiac or renal failure may develop rapidly. Abscesses may be detected on echocardiography. Partially treated acute endocarditis behaves like subacute endocarditis.

Post-operative endocarditis. Any unexplained fever in a patient who has had heart valve surgery should be investigated for possible endocarditis. The infection usually

12.91 INFECTIVE ENDOCARDITIS ON NATIVE VALVES: PREVALENCE OF ORGANISMS IN EUROPE AND NORTH AMERICA (% OF CASES)	
Bacteria	
• Streptococci	
Viridans group	30–40%
Enterococci	10–15%
Other streptococci	20–25%
• Staphylococci	
Staph. aureus	9–27%
Coagulase-negative	1–3%
• Gram-negative bacilli	
• Haemophilus	Total 3–8%
• Anaerobes	
Other organisms	
• Rickettsiae, fungi	Less than 2%

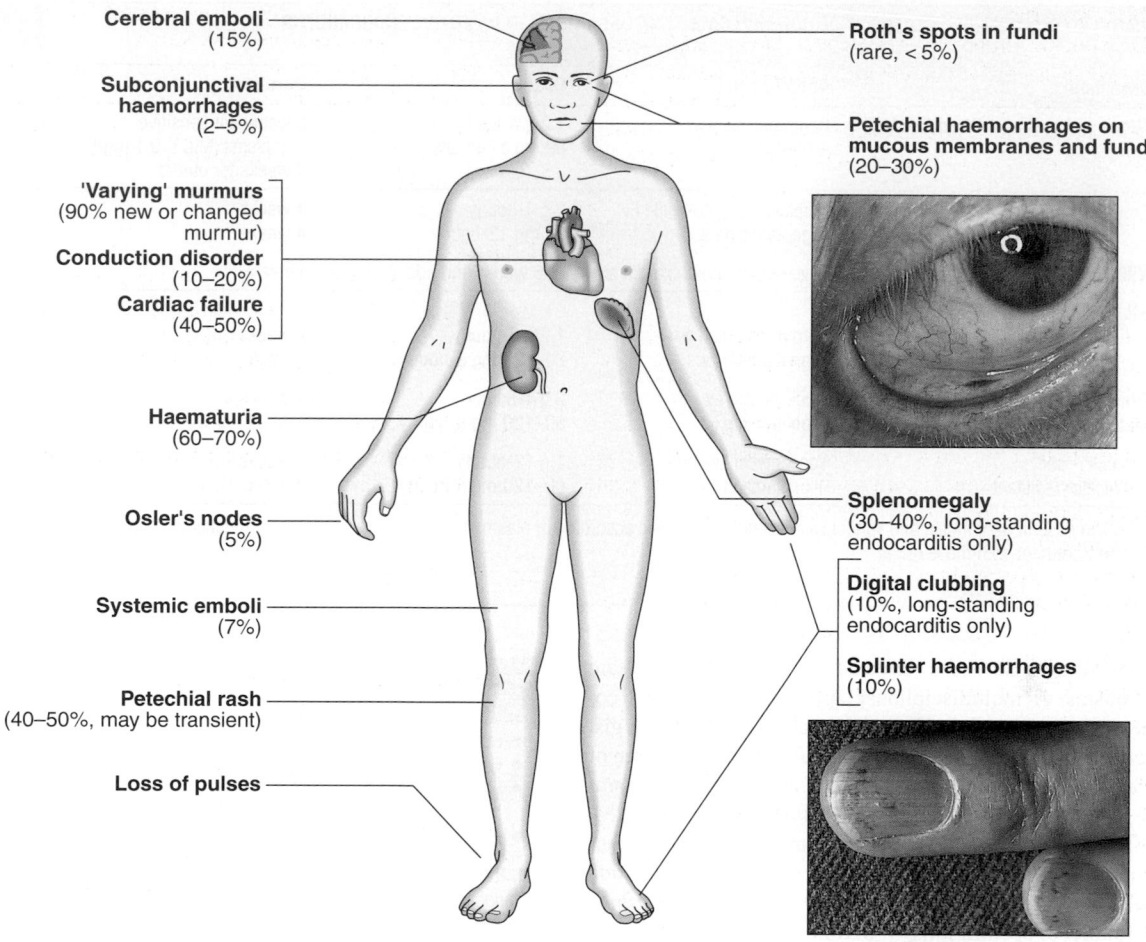

Cerebral emboli (15%)

Subconjunctival haemorrhages (2–5%)

'Varying' murmurs (90% new or changed murmur)

Conduction disorder (10–20%)

Cardiac failure (40–50%)

Haematuria (60–70%)

Osler's nodes (5%)

Systemic emboli (7%)

Petechial rash (40–50%, may be transient)

Loss of pulses

Roth's spots in fundi (rare, < 5%)

Petechial haemorrhages on mucous membranes and fundi (20–30%)

Splenomegaly (30–40%, long-standing endocarditis only)

Digital clubbing (10%, long-standing endocarditis only)

Splinter haemorrhages (10%)

Fig. 12.91   Clinical features which may be present in endocarditis.

affects the valve ring and may resemble subacute or acute endocarditis, depending on the virulence of the organism. Morbidity and mortality are high and redo surgery is often required. The range of organisms is similar to that seen in native valve disease but when endocarditis occurs during the first few weeks after surgery it is usually due to infection with a coagulase-negative staphylococcus that was introduced during the perioperative period.

Investigations

Blood culture is the crucial investigation because it may identify the infection and guide antibiotic therapy. Three specimens should be taken prior to commencing therapy, and these need not wait for episodes of pyrexia. The first two specimens will detect bacteraemia in 90% of culture-positive cases. Aseptic technique is essential and the risk of contaminants should be minimised by sampling from different venepuncture sites. An in-dwelling line should not be used for cultures. Aerobic and anaerobic cultures are required. A knowledge of prior antibiotic treatment may allow an inactivating enzyme to be added to the culture in order to facilitate growth.

Echocardiography is the key investigation for detecting and following the progress of vegetations, for assessing valve damage and for detecting abscess formation. Vegetations as

small as 3–5 mm can be detected by transthoracic echo, and even smaller ones (1–1.5 mm) can be visualised by transoesophageal echo, which is particularly valuable for identifying abscess formation and investigating patients with prosthetic heart valves. Vegetations may be difficult to distinguish in the presence of an abnormal valve; the sensitivity of transthoracic echo is approximately 65% but that of transoesophageal echo is more than 90%. Failure to detect vegetations does not exclude the diagnosis and should not delay treatment.

Elevation of the ESR, a normocytic, normochromic anaemia and leucocytosis are common but not invariable, and thrombocytopenia may be present. Measurement of plasma CRP is more reliable than the ESR in monitoring progress. Proteinuria may occur and microscopic haematuria is usually present.

The ECG may show the development of conduction defects (due to abscess formation) and occasionally infarction due to emboli. The chest radiograph may show evidence of cardiac failure and cardiomegaly.

Management

The case fatality of bacterial endocarditis is approximately 20% and even higher in those with prosthetic valve

12.92 ANTIMICROBIAL TREATMENT OF COMMON CAUSATIVE ORGANISMS IN INFECTIVE ENDOCARDITIS

Organism	Antimicrobial	Dose	Duration
Strep. viridans and *Strep. bovis*	Benzylpenicillin i.v. + gentamicin i.v.	1.2 g 4-hourly 80 mg 12-hourly	2 weeks for sensitive organisms (MIC ≤ 0.1 mg/l)* 4 weeks for others
Enterococci	Ampicillin or amoxicillin i.v. + gentamicin i.v.	2 g 4-hourly 80 mg 12-hourly	4 weeks 4 weeks

N.B. For gentamicin-resistant organisms give ampicillin/amoxicillin alone for 6 weeks and add streptomycin if sensitive.

Staphylococci Penicillin-sensitive	Benzylpenicillin i.v. + gentamicin i.v.	1.2 g 4-hourly 80–120 mg 8-hourly	4 weeks 1 week
Penicillin-resistant Methicillin-sensitive	Flucloxacillin i.v. + gentamicin i.v.	2 g 4-hourly 80–120 mg 8-hourly	4 weeks 1 week
Penicillin- and methicillin-resistant	Vancomycin i.v. + gentamicin i.v.	1 g 12-hourly 80–120 mg 8-hourly	4 weeks 1 week

N.B. The dose of gentamicin and vancomycin should be adjusted according to plasma drug concentrations. Renal function should be monitored during treatment with these drugs.

* See Box 12.93.

endocarditis and those infected with antibiotic-resistant organisms. A multidisciplinary approach with careful co-operation between the physician, surgeon and bacteriologist increases the chance of a successful outcome. Any source of infection should be removed as soon as possible; for example, a tooth with an apical abscess should be extracted. Isolation of the organism allows minimum inhibitory concentration (MIC) and minimum bactericidal concentration (MBC) of the antimicrobial drug to be measured. Plasma antibiotic concentrations 4–8 times the MIC/MBC will usually eradicate the infection.

Some common antimicrobial treatment regimens for common causative organisms are shown in Box 12.92. For patients allergic to penicillins a glycopeptide (e.g. vancomycin) may be substituted. Vancomycin plus gentamicin is recommended for staphylococcal endocarditis.

A 2-week treatment regimen may be sufficient for fully sensitive strains of *Strep. viridans* and *Strep. bovis*, provided certain conditions are met (see Box 12.93). For the empirical treatment of bacterial endocarditis, penicillin plus gentamicin is the regimen of choice for most patients; however, when staphylococcal infection is suspected vancomycin plus gentamicin is recommended.

Cardiac surgery (débridement of infected material and valve replacement) is advisable in a substantial proportion

12.94 INDICATIONS FOR CARDIAC SURGERY IN INFECTIVE ENDOCARDITIS

- Heart failure due to valve damage
- Failure of antibiotic therapy (persistent or uncontrolled infection)
- Large vegetations on left-sided heart valves with evidence or 'high risk' of systemic emboli
- Abscess formation

N.B. Patients with prosthetic valve endocarditis or fungal endocarditis often require cardiac surgery.

of patients, particularly those with *Staph. aureus* and fungal infections (see Box 12.94); antimicrobial therapy must be started before surgery.

Prevention

Patients with valvular or congenital heart disease may be susceptible to infective endocarditis. These individuals should be made aware of the risk of endocarditis, the need to avoid bacteraemia and the importance of maintaining good dental health. Any potential source of infection in susceptible individuals should be treated promptly and invasive procedures that may cause transient bacteraemia should be accompanied by appropriate antibiotic prophylaxis. The chosen drug regimen should be sufficient to kill the likely organism, and should only be given shortly before the anticipated bacteraemia in order to reduce the risk of resistance (see Box 12.95).

12.93 CONDITIONS TO BE MET FOR THE SHORT-COURSE TREATMENT OF *STREP. VIRIDANS* AND *STREP. BOVIS* ENDOCARDITIS

- Native valve infection
- MIC < 0.1 mg/l
- No adverse prognostic factors (e.g. heart failure, aortic regurgitation, conduction defect)
- No evidence of thromboembolic disease
- No vegetations > 5 mm diameter
- Clinical response within 7 days

ISSUES IN OLDER PEOPLE
ENDOCARDITIS

- The diagnosis may not be suspected because symptoms and signs (confusion, weight loss, malaise and weakness) are non-specific.
- Enterococci (often from the urinary tract) and *Strep. bovis* (from a colonic source) are more common causative organisms than in younger people.
- Morbidity and mortality are much higher in older patients.

12.95 ANTIBIOTIC PROPHYLAXIS AGAINST ENDOCARDITIS

Procedure	Antibiotic regimen
Dental or upper respiratory tract procedures under local anaesthetic	Amoxicillin 3 g orally 1 hr before
If allergic to or received penicillin in last month	Clindamycin 600 mg orally 1 hr before
N.B. Previous endocarditis: treat as special-risk (see below).	
Dental or upper respiratory tract procedures under general anaesthetic	Amoxicillin 1 g i.v. at induction *plus* amoxicillin 0.5 g orally 6 hrs later
If allergic to or received penicillin in last month	Vancomycin 1 g i.v. infusion over at least 100 mins *plus* gentamicin 120 mg i.v. at induction
Special-risk patients, i.e. prosthetic valve or previous endocarditis Genitourinary procedures	Amoxicillin 1 g i.v. *plus* gentamicin 120 mg i.v. at induction *plus* amoxicillin 0.5 g orally 6 hrs later
If allergic to or received penicillin in last month	Vancomycin 1 g i.v. infusion over at least 100 mins *plus* gentamicin 120 mg i.v. at induction
N.B. Obstetric and gynaecological procedures or gastrointestinal surgery/instrumentation—treat only prosthetic valve patients (as for special-risk patients above).	

VALVE REPLACEMENT SURGERY

Diseased heart valves can be replaced with mechanical or biological prostheses. The three most commonly used types of mechanical prosthesis are the ball and cage, tilting single disc and tilting bileaflet valves. All generate prosthetic sounds or clicks on auscultation. Pig valves mounted on a supporting stent are the most commonly used biological valves. They generate normal heart sounds. All prosthetic valves used in the aortic position produce a systolic flow murmur.

All mechanical valves require long-term anticoagulation because they may develop thrombus around the valve, causing obstruction to flow and/or embolism (see Box 12.96); the prosthetic clicks may become inaudible if the valve malfunctions. Biological valves have the advantage of not requiring anticoagulants to maintain proper function; however, many patients undergoing valve replacement surgery, especially mitral valve replacement, will have atrial fibrillation that requires anticoagulation anyway. Biological valves are less durable than mechanical valves and may degenerate

12.96 PROSTHETIC HEART VALVES: OPTIMAL ANTICOAGULANT CONTROL

Mechanical valves	Target INR
Ball and cage (e.g. Starr–Edwards) Tilting disc (e.g. Bjork–Shiley)	3.5
Bileaflet (e.g. St Jude)	3.0
Biological valves with atrial fibrillation	2.5

7 or more years after implantation, particularly when used in the mitral position.

Symptoms or signs of unexplained heart failure in a patient with a prosthetic heart valve may be due to valve dysfunction and require urgent cardiological assessment.

CONGENITAL HEART DISEASE

Congenital heart disease usually manifests in childhood but may pass unrecognised and not present until adult life. Defects which are well tolerated, e.g. atrial septal defect, may cause no symptoms until adult life or may first be detected incidentally on routine examination or chest radiograph. Congenital defects that previously may have been fatal in childhood can now be corrected, or at least partially corrected, so that survival to adult life is now the norm. Such patients may remain well for many years and subsequently re-present in later life with related problems such as arrhythmia or ventricular dysfunction (see Box 12.97).

The fetal circulation

Understanding the fetal circulation helps to understand how some forms of congenital heart disease occur. The fetus has only a small flow of blood through the lungs, as it obviously cannot breathe in the uterus. The fetal circulation therefore allows oxygenated blood from the placenta to pass directly to the left side of the heart through the foramen ovale without having to flow through the lungs (see Fig. 12.92).

Congenital defects may arise if the changes from fetal circulation to the extrauterine circulation are not properly completed. Atrial septal defects occur at the site of the foramen ovale. A patent ductus arteriosus may remain if it fails to close after birth. Failure of the aorta to develop at the point of the aortic isthmus can lead to narrowing or coarctation of the aorta.

In fetal development, the heart develops as a single tube which folds back on itself and then divides into two separate circulations. Failure of separation can lead to some forms of atrial and ventricular septal defects. Failure of alignment of the great vessels with the ventricles contributes to transposition of the great arteries, tetralogy of Fallot and truncus arteriosus.

12.97 PRESENTATION OF CONGENITAL HEART DISEASE THROUGHOUT LIFE

Birth and neonatal period

- Cyanosis
- Heart failure

Infancy and childhood

- Cyanosis
- Heart failure
- Arrhythmia
- Murmur
- Failure to thrive

Adolescence and adulthood

- Heart failure
- Murmur
- Arrhythmia
- Cyanosis due to shunt reversal (Eisenmenger's syndrome)
- Hypertension (coarctation)
- Late consequences of previous cardiac surgery, e.g. arrhythmia, heart failure

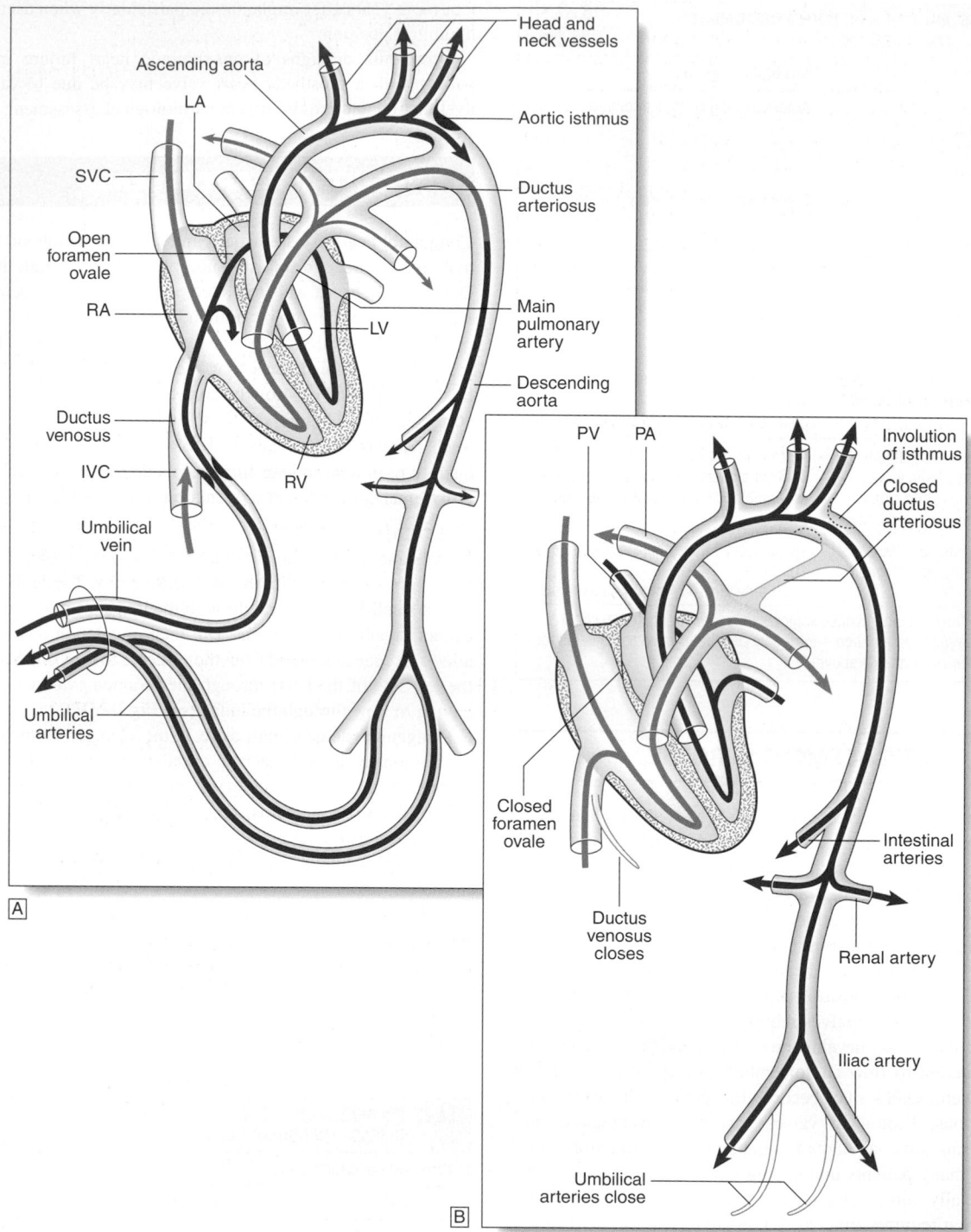

Fig. 12.92 Changes in the circulation at birth. A In the fetus oxygenated blood comes through the umbilical vein where it enters the inferior vena cava via the ductus venosus (red). The oxygenated blood streams from the right atrium through the open foramen ovale to the left atrium and via the left ventricle into the aorta. Venous blood from the superior vena cava (blue) crosses under the main blood stream into the right atrium and then, partly mixed with oxygenated blood (purple), into the right ventricle and pulmonary artery. The pulmonary vasculature has a high resistance and so little blood passes to the lungs; most blood passes through the ductus arteriosus to the descending aorta. The aortic isthmus is a constriction in the aorta that lies in the aortic arch before the junction with the ductus arteriosus and limits the flow of oxygen-rich blood to the descending aorta. This configuration means that less oxygen-rich blood is supplied to organ systems that take up their function mainly after birth, e.g. the kidneys and intestinal tract.
B At birth, the lungs expand with air and pulmonary vascular resistance falls so that blood now flows to the lungs and back to the left atrium. The left atrial pressure rises above right atrial pressure and the flap valve of the foramen ovale closes. The umbilical arteries and the ductus venosus close.
In the next few days the ductus arteriosus closes under the influence of hormonal changes (particularly prostaglandins) and the aortic isthmus expands.

Aetiology and incidence

The incidence of haemodynamically significant congenital cardiac abnormalities is about 0.8% of live births (see Box 12.98). Maternal infection or exposure to drugs or toxins may cause congenital heart disease. Maternal rubella infection is associated with persistent ductus arteriosus, pulmonary valvular and/or artery stenosis, and atrial septal defect. Maternal alcohol misuse is associated with septal defects, and maternal lupus erythematosus is associated with congenital complete heart block. Genetic or chromosomal abnormalities such as Down's syndrome may cause septal defects, and gene defects have also been identified as causing specific abnormalities, e.g. Marfan's and DiGeorge's syndromes.

Clinical features

Symptoms may be absent, or the child may be breathless or fail to attain normal growth and development. All degrees of severity occur. Some defects are not compatible with extrauterine life, or only for a short time. Clinical signs vary with the anatomical lesion. Cerebrovascular accidents and cerebral abscesses are complications of severe cyanotic congenital disease.

12.98 INCIDENCE AND RELATIVE FREQUENCY OF CONGENITAL CARDIAC MALFORMATIONS	
Lesion	% of all CHD defects
Ventricular septal defect	30
Atrial septal defect	10
Patent ductus arteriosus	10
Pulmonary stenosis	7
Coarctation of aorta	7
Aortic stenosis	6
Tetralogy of Fallot	6
Complete transposition of great arteries	4
Others	20

Early diagnosis is important because many types of congenital heart disease are amenable to surgical treatment, but this opportunity may be lost if secondary changes—for example, pulmonary vascular damage—occur.

Principal features are illustrated in Figure 12.93.

Central cyanosis and digital clubbing

Central cyanosis of cardiac origin occurs when desaturated blood enters the systemic circulation without passing through the lungs (i.e. there is a right-to-left shunt). In the neonate, the most common cause is transposition of the

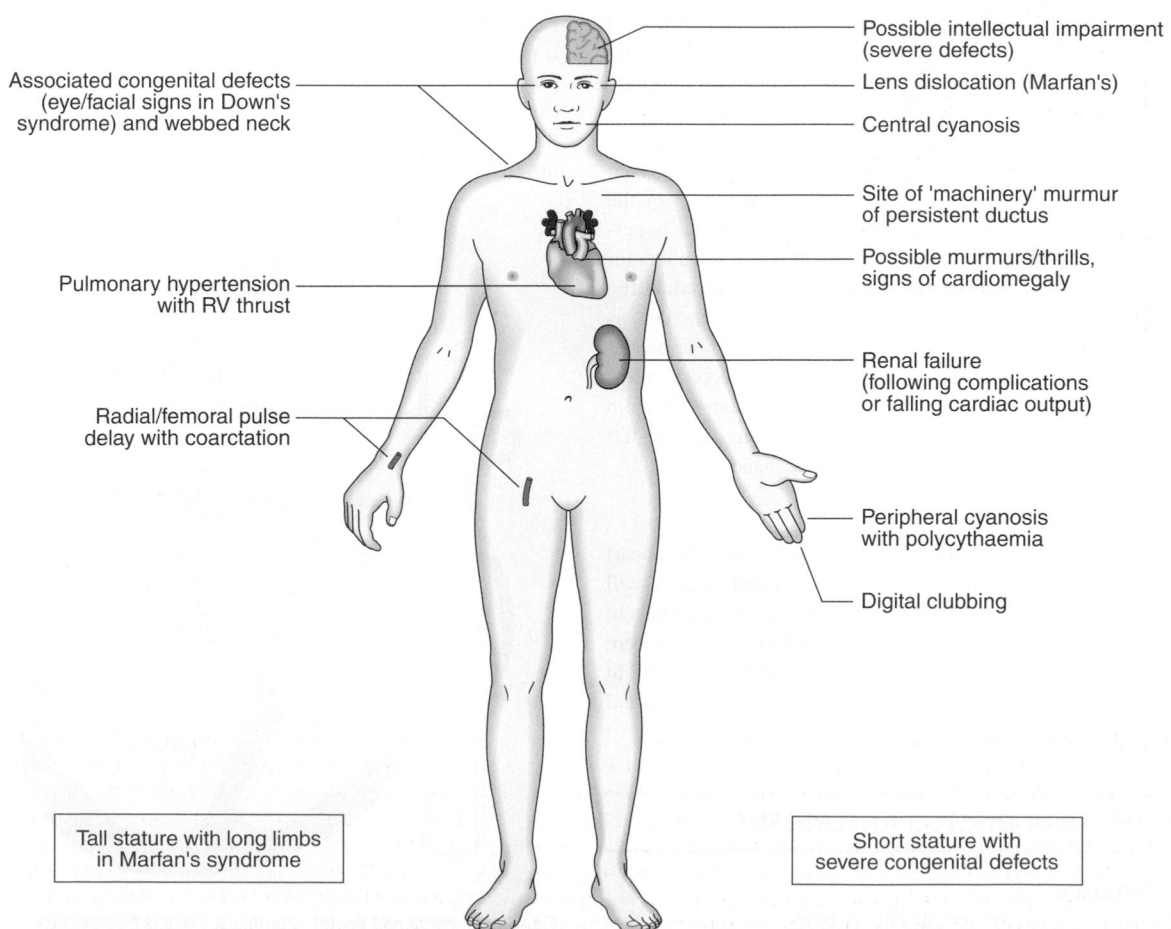

Fig. 12.93 Clinical features which may be present in various forms of congenital heart disease.

great arteries, in which the aorta arises from the right ventricle and the pulmonary artery from the left. In older children, cyanosis is usually the consequence of a ventricular septal defect combined with severe pulmonary stenosis (tetralogy of Fallot) or with pulmonary vascular disease (Eisenmenger's syndrome). Prolonged cyanosis is associated with finger and toe clubbing (see p. 358).

Growth retardation and learning difficulties

These may be a feature with large left-to-right shunts at ventricular or great arterial level but can also occur with other defects, especially if they form part of a genetic syndrome. Major intellectual impairment is uncommon in children with isolated congenital heart disease; however, minor learning difficulties can occur and may also be the consequence of cardiac surgery.

Syncope

In the presence of increased pulmonary vascular resistance or severe left or right ventricular outflow obstruction, exercise may provoke syncope. (Systemic vascular resistance falls on exercise but pulmonary vascular resistance may rise, worsening right-to-left shunting and cerebral oxygenation.)

Pulmonary hypertension and Eisenmenger's syndrome

Persistently raised pulmonary flow (e.g. with left-to-right shunt) leads to increased pulmonary resistance followed by pulmonary hypertension. Progressive changes (including obliteration of distal vessels) take place in the pulmonary vasculature and, once established, the increased pulmonary resistance is irreversible. Central cyanosis appears and digital clubbing develops. The chest radiograph shows enlarged central pulmonary arteries and peripheral 'pruning' of the pulmonary vessels. The ECG shows right ventricular hypertrophy. If severe pulmonary hypertension develops, a left-to-right shunt may reverse, resulting in right-to-left shunting and marked cyanosis (Eisenmenger's syndrome). This is more common with large ventricular septal defects or persistent ductus arteriosus than with atrial septal defects. Patients with Eisenmenger's syndrome are at particular risk from abrupt changes in afterload that exacerbate right-to-left shunting (vasodilatation, anaesthesia, pregnancy).

Pregnancy

Most patients with surgically corrected congenital heart disease and many with palliated or untreated disease will tolerate pregnancy well. However, pregnancy is hazardous in the presence of conditions associated with cyanosis or severe pulmonary hypertension. For example, maternal mortality in patients with Eisenmenger's syndrome is more than 50% and sterilisation is usually recommended in such patients.

PERSISTENT DUCTUS ARTERIOSUS

Aetiology

During fetal life, before the lungs begin to function, most of the blood from the pulmonary artery passes through the ductus arteriosus into the aorta (see Fig. 12.92). Normally

the ductus closes soon after birth but sometimes it fails to do so. Persistence of the ductus may be associated with other abnormalities and is much more common in females.

Since the pressure in the aorta is higher than that in the pulmonary artery (PA), there will be a continuous arteriovenous shunt, the volume of which depends on the size of the ductus. As much as 50% of the left ventricular output may be recirculated through the lungs, with a consequent increase in the work of the heart.

Clinical features

With small shunts there may be no symptoms for years, but when the ductus is large, growth and development may be retarded. Usually there is no disability in infancy but cardiac failure may eventually ensue, dyspnoea being the first symptom. A continuous 'machinery' murmur is heard with late systolic accentuation, maximal in the second left intercostal space below the clavicle (see Fig. 12.94). It is frequently accompanied by a thrill. Enlargement of the pulmonary artery may be detected radiologically. The ECG is usually normal.

A large left-to-right shunt in infancy may cause a considerable rise in pulmonary artery pressure, and sometimes this leads to progressive pulmonary vascular damage. Pulses are increased in volume.

Persistent ductus with reversed shunting

If pulmonary vascular resistance increases, pulmonary artery pressure rises and may continue to do so until it equals or exceeds aortic pressure. The shunt through the defect may then reverse, causing central cyanosis (Eisenmenger's syndrome), which may be more apparent in the feet and toes

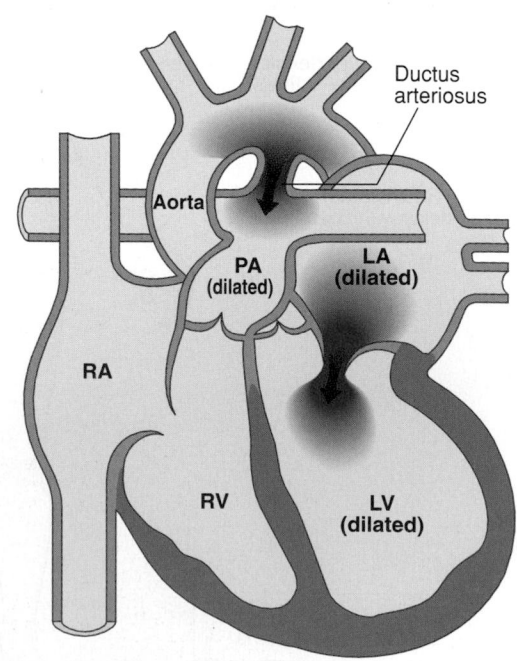

Fig. 12.94 Persistent ductus arteriosus. There is a connection between the aorta and the pulmonary artery with left-to-right shunting and dilatation of the pulmonary artery, left atrium and left ventricle.

than in the upper part of the body. The murmur becomes quieter, may be confined to systole or may disappear. The ECG shows evidence of right ventricular hypertrophy.

Management

It is now usual practice to close a patent ductus at cardiac catheterisation with an implantable occlusive device (see Fig. 12.15, p. 372). Closure should be undertaken in infancy if the shunt is significant and pulmonary resistance not elevated, but this may be delayed until later childhood in those with smaller shunts for whom closure remains advisable to reduce the risk of endocarditis.

Pharmacological treatment in the neonatal period

When the ductus is structurally intact, a prostaglandin synthetase inhibitor (indometacin (indomethacin) or ibuprofen) may be used in the first week of life to induce closure. However, in the presence of a congenital defect with impaired lung perfusion (e.g. severe pulmonary stenosis and left-to-right shunt through the ductus), it may be advisable to improve oxygenation by keeping the ductus open with prostaglandin treatment. Unfortunately, these treatments do not work if the ductus is intrinsically abnormal.

COARCTATION OF THE AORTA

Aetiology

Narrowing of the aorta most commonly occurs in the region where the ductus arteriosus joins the aorta, i.e. at the isthmus just below the origin of the left subclavian artery (see Fig. 12.92, p. 468 and Fig. 12.95). The condition is twice as common in males as in females and occurs in 1 in 4000 children. It is associated with other abnormalities, of which the most frequent are bicuspid aortic valve and 'berry' aneurysms of the cerebral circulation. Acquired coarctation of the aorta is rare but may follow trauma or occur as a complication of a progressive arteritis (Takayasu's disease, see p. 1042).

Clinical features

Aortic coarctation is an important cause of cardiac failure in the newborn, but symptoms are often absent when it is detected in older children or adults. Headaches may occur from hypertension proximal to the coarctation, and occasionally weakness or cramps in the legs may result from decreased circulation in the lower part of the body. The blood pressure is raised in the upper body but normal or low in the legs. The femoral pulses are weak, and delayed in comparison with the radial pulse. A systolic murmur is usually heard posteriorly, over the coarctation. There may also be an ejection click and systolic murmur in the aortic area due to a bicuspid aortic valve. As a result of the aortic narrowing, collaterals form, mainly involving the periscapular, internal mammary and intercostal arteries. These may result in localised bruits.

Radiological examination in early childhood is often normal but at a later age may show changes in the contour of the aorta (indentation of the descending aorta, '3 sign') and notching of the under-surfaces of the ribs from collaterals. MRI is ideal for demonstrating the lesion (see Fig. 12.96). The ECG may show left ventricular hypertrophy.

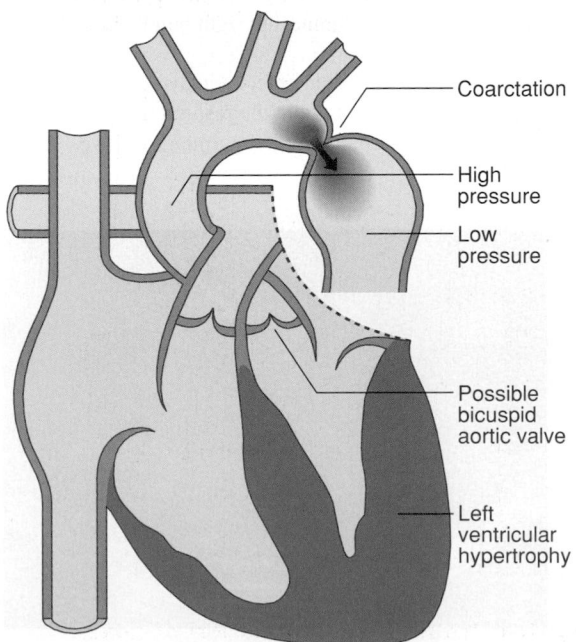

Fig. 12.95 Coarctation of the aorta.

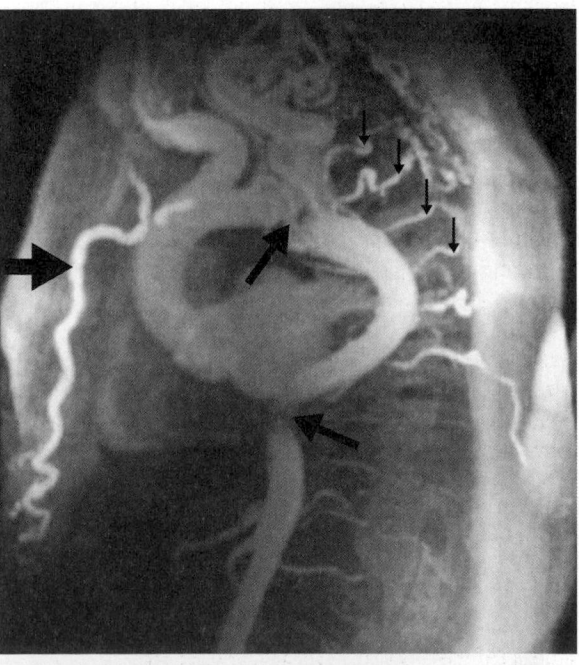

Fig. 12.96 MRI scan of coarctation of the aorta. The aorta is severely narrowed just beyond the arch at the start of the descending aorta (upper medium arrow). Extensive collaterals have developed with a large internal mammary artery shown (large arrow), and several intercostal arteries (small arrows). Unusually, in this case there is also a coarctation of the abdominal aorta (lower medium arrow).

Management

In untreated cases, death may occur from left ventricular failure, dissection of the aorta or cerebral haemorrhage. Surgical correction is advisable in all but the mildest cases. If this is done sufficiently early in childhood persistent hypertension can be avoided. Patients repaired in late childhood or adult life often remain hypertensive or develop recurrent hypertension later in life. Recurrence of stenosis may occur as the child grows, and this may be managed by balloon dilatation, which can also be used as the primary treatment in some cases (see Fig. 12.15, p. 372). Coexistent bicuspid aortic valve, which occurs in over 50% of cases, may lead to progressive aortic stenosis or regurgitation and also requires long-term follow-up.

ATRIAL SEPTAL DEFECT

Aetiology

Atrial septal defect is one of the most common congenital heart defects, and occurs twice as frequently in females. Most are 'ostium secundum' defects, involving the fossa ovalis which in uterine life was the foramen ovale (see Fig. 12.92, p. 468). 'Ostium primum' defects result from a defect in the atrioventricular septum and are associated with a 'cleft mitral valve' (split anterior leaflet).

Since the normal right ventricle is much more compliant than the left, a large volume of blood shunts through the defect from the left to the right atrium and then to the right ventricle and pulmonary arteries (see Fig. 12.97). As a result there is gradual enlargement of the right side of the heart and of the pulmonary arteries. Pulmonary hypertension and shunt reversal sometimes complicate atrial septal defect, but are less common and tend to occur later in life than with other types of left-to-right shunt.

Clinical features

Most children are free of symptoms for many years and the condition is often detected at routine clinical examination or following a chest radiograph. Dyspnoea, chest infections,

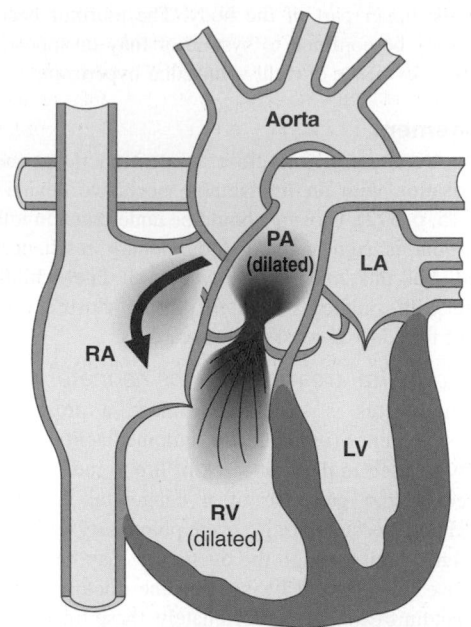

Fig. 12.97   Atrial septal defect. Blood flows across the atrial septum (arrow) from left to right. The murmur is produced by increased flow velocity across the pulmonary valve, as a result of left-to-right shunting and a large stroke volume. The density of shading is proportional to velocity of blood flow.

cardiac failure and arrhythmias, especially atrial fibrillation, are other possible modes of presentation. The characteristic physical signs are the result of the volume overload of the right ventricle:

- wide fixed splitting of the second heart sound
  —wide because of delay in right ventricular ejection (increased stroke volume and right bundle branch block)
  —fixed because the septal defect equalises left and right atrial pressures throughout the respiratory cycle
- a systolic flow murmur over the pulmonary valve.

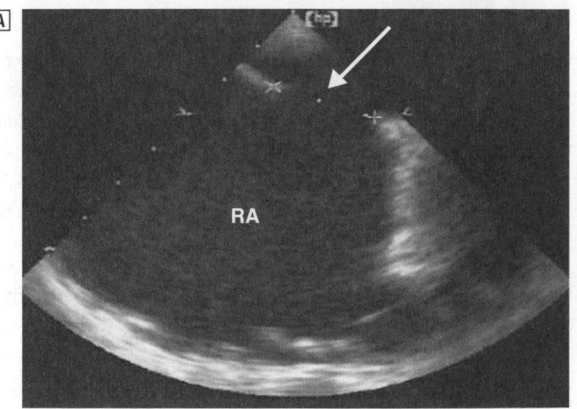
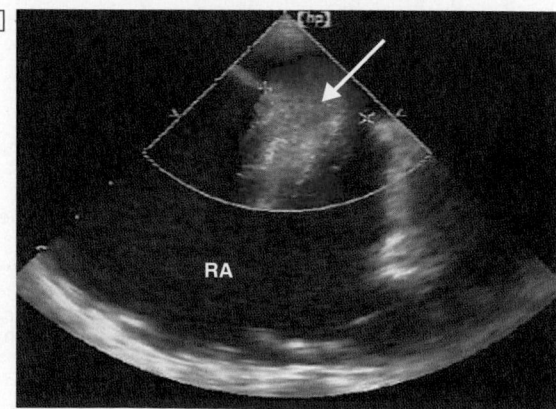

Fig. 12.98   Transoesophageal echocardiograph of an atrial septal defect (ASD). [A] The defect is clearly seen between the left atrium and the right atrium (RA). [B] Doppler colour-flow imaging shows flow across the defect.

In children with a large shunt there may be a diastolic flow murmur over the tricuspid valve. Unlike a mitral flow murmur, this diastolic murmur is usually high-pitched.

The chest radiograph typically shows enlargement of the heart and the pulmonary artery as well as pulmonary plethora. The ECG usually shows incomplete right bundle branch block because right ventricular depolarisation is delayed as a result of ventricular dilatation (with a 'primum' defect there is also left axis deviation). Echocardiography can directly demonstrate the defect and typically shows RV dilatation, RV hypertrophy and pulmonary artery dilatation. The precise size and location of the defect can be shown by transoesophageal echocardiography (see Fig. 12.98).

Management

Atrial septal defects in which pulmonary flow is increased 50% above systemic flow (i.e. flow ratio of 1.5:1) are often large enough to be clinically recognisable and should be closed surgically. Closure can also be accomplished at cardiac catheterisation using implantable closure devices (see Fig. 12.15, p. 372). The long-term prognosis thereafter is excellent unless pulmonary hypertension has developed. Severe pulmonary hypertension and shunt reversal are both contraindications to surgery.

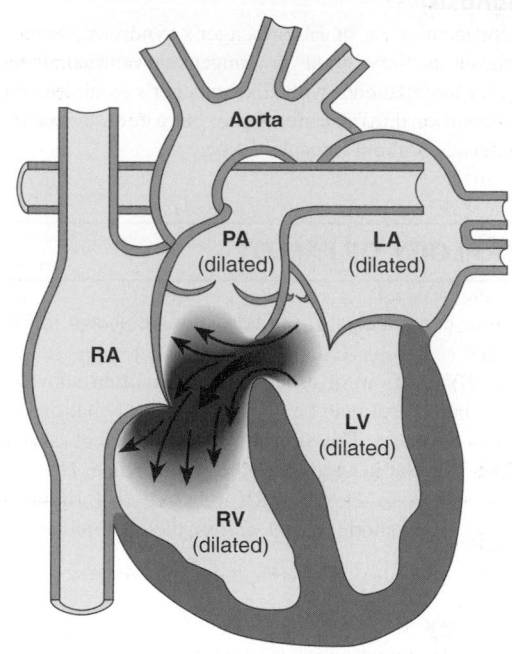

Fig. 12.99 Ventricular septal defect. In this example a large left-to-right shunt (arrows) has resulted in chamber enlargement.

VENTRICULAR SEPTAL DEFECT

Aetiology

Congenital ventricular septal defect occurs as a result of incomplete septation of the ventricles. Embryologically, the interventricular septum has a membranous and a muscular portion, and the latter is further divided into inflow, trabecular and outflow portions. Most congenital defects are 'perimembranous', i.e. at the junction of the membranous and muscular portions.

Ventricular septal defects are the most common congenital cardiac defect, occurring once in 500 live births. The defect may be isolated or part of complex congenital heart disease. Acquired ventricular septal defect may result from rupture as a complication of acute myocardial infarction (see p. 440), or rarely from trauma.

Clinical features

Flow from the high-pressure left ventricle to the low-pressure right ventricle during systole produces a pansystolic murmur usually heard best at the left sternal edge but radiating all over the praecordium (see Fig. 12.99). A small defect often produces a loud murmur (maladie de Roger) in the absence of other haemodynamic disturbance. Conversely, a large defect may produce a softer murmur, particularly if pressure in the right ventricle is elevated. This may be found to be the case immediately after birth, while pulmonary vascular resistance remains high, or when the shunt is reversed—Eisenmenger's syndrome (described above).

Congenital ventricular septal defect may present as cardiac failure in infants, as a murmur with only minor haemodynamic disturbance in older children or adults, or rarely as Eisenmenger's syndrome. In a proportion of infants, the murmur gets quieter or disappears due to spontaneous closure of the defect.

If cardiac failure complicates a large defect it is usually absent in the immediate postnatal period and becomes apparent in the first 4–6 weeks of life. In addition to the murmur, there is prominent parasternal pulsation, tachypnoea and indrawing of the lower ribs on inspiration. The chest radiograph shows pulmonary plethora and the ECG shows right and left ventricular hypertrophy.

Management

Small ventricular septal defects require no specific treatment apart from endocarditis prophylaxis. Cardiac failure caused by a ventricular septal defect in infancy is initially treated medically with digoxin and diuretics. Persisting failure is an indication for surgical repair of the defect. Closure devices to be delivered at cardiac catheterisation are being developed.

Doppler echocardiography helps to predict the small septal defects that are likely to close spontaneously. Eisenmenger's syndrome is avoided by monitoring (serial ECG and echocardiography) for signs of rising pulmonary resistance and carrying out surgical repair when appropriate. Surgical closure is contraindicated in fully developed Eisenmenger's syndrome when heart-lung transplantation may be the only effective method of treatment.

Prognosis

Except in the case of Eisenmenger's syndrome, long-term prognosis is very good in congenital ventricular septal defect. Many patients with Eisenmenger's syndrome die in the second or third decade of life, but a few survive to the fifth decade without transplantation.

TETRALOGY OF FALLOT

The four components of the tetralogy are shown in Figure 12.100.

The RV outflow obstruction is most often subvalvular (infundibular), but may be valvular, supravalvular or a combination of these. The ventricular septal defect is usually large and similar in aperture to the aortic orifice. The combination results in elevated RV pressure and right-to-left shunting of cyanotic blood across the ventricular septal defect.

Aetiology

The embryological cause is abnormal development of the bulbar septum which separates the ascending aorta from the pulmonary artery, and which normally aligns and fuses with the outflow part of the interventricular septum. The defect occurs in about 1 in 2000 births and is the most common cause of cyanosis in infancy after the first year of life.

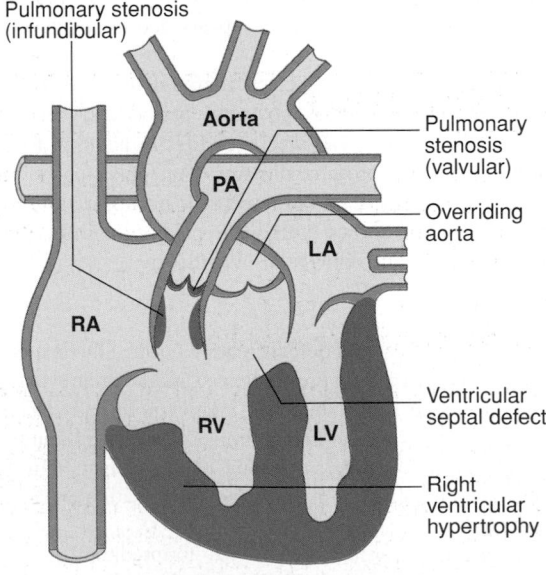

Fig. 12.100   Tetralogy of Fallot. The tetralogy comprises (1) pulmonary stenosis, (2) overriding of the ventricular septal defect by the aorta, (3) a ventricular septal defect and (4) right ventricular hypertrophy.

Clinical features

Children are usually cyanosed but cyanosis may not be present in the neonate because it is only when right ventricular pressure rises to equal or exceed left ventricular pressure that a large right-to-left shunt develops. The subvalvular component of the RV outflow obstruction is dynamic, and may increase suddenly under adrenergic stimulation. The affected child suddenly becomes increasingly cyanosed, often after feeding or a crying attack, and may become apnoeic and unconscious. These attacks are called 'Fallot's spells'. In older children Fallot's spells are uncommon, but cyanosis becomes increasingly apparent, with stunting of growth, digital clubbing and polycythaemia. Some children characteristically obtain relief by squatting after exertion (this increases the afterload of the left heart and reduces the right-to-left shunting). The natural history before the development of surgical correction was variable, but most patients died in infancy or childhood.

On examination the most characteristic feature is the combination of cyanosis with a loud ejection systolic murmur in the pulmonary area (as for pulmonary stenosis). However, cyanosis may be absent in the newborn, or in patients with only mild right ventricular outflow obstruction ('acyanotic tetralogy of Fallot').

Investigations

ECG shows right ventricular hypertrophy, and the chest radiograph shows an abnormally small pulmonary artery and a 'boot-shaped' heart. Echocardiography is diagnostic and demonstrates that the aorta is not continuous with the anterior ventricular septum.

Management

The definitive management is total correction of the defect by surgical relief of the pulmonary stenosis and closure of the ventricular septal defect. Primary surgical correction may be undertaken prior to age 5, unless the pulmonary arteries are too hypoplastic, when a palliative shunt may be performed (for example, an anastomosis between the pulmonary artery and subclavian artery). The shunt improves pulmonary blood flow and pulmonary artery development and may facilitate definitive correction at a later stage.

The prognosis after total correction is good, especially if the operation is performed in childhood. Follow-up is needed to identify residual shunting, recurrent pulmonary stenosis and rhythm disorders.

OTHER CAUSES OF CYANOTIC CONGENITAL HEART DISEASE

Other causes of cyanotic congenital heart disease are summarised in Box 12.99. Echocardiography is usually the definitive diagnostic procedure, supplemented if necessary by cardiac catheterisation.

12.99 OTHER CAUSES OF CYANOTIC CONGENITAL HEART DISEASE	
Defect	**Features**
Tricuspid atresia	Absent tricuspid orifice, hypoplastic RV RA to LA shunt, VSD shunt, other anomalies Surgical correction *may* be possible
Transposition of the great vessels	Aorta arises from the morphological RV, pulmonary artery from LV Shunt via atria, ductus and possibly VSD Palliation by balloon atrial septostomy/enlargement Surgical correction possible
Pulmonary atresia	Pulmonary valve atretic and pulmonary artery hypoplastic RA to LA shunt, pulmonary flow via ductus Palliation by balloon atrial septostomy Surgical correction may be possible
Ebstein's anomaly	Tricuspid valve is dysplastic and displaced into RV, right ventricle 'atrialised' Tricuspid regurgitation and RA to LA shunt Wide spectrum of severity Arrhythmias Surgical repair possible, but significant risks

DISEASES OF THE MYOCARDIUM

Although the myocardium is involved in most types of heart disease, the terms 'myocarditis' and 'cardiomyopathy' are usually reserved for conditions that primarily affect the heart muscle.

ACUTE MYOCARDITIS

This is an acute inflammatory and potentially reversible condition that may complicate a wide variety of infections; inflammation may be due to infection of the myocardium or the effects of circulating toxins. Viral infection is the most common cause and the main culprits are the Coxsackie viruses (35 cases per 1000 infections) and influenza viruses A and B (25 cases per 1000 infections). Myocarditis may occur several weeks after the initial viral infection and susceptibility is increased by corticosteroid treatment, immunosuppression, radiation, previous myocardial damage and exercise. Some bacterial and protozoal infections may be complicated by myocarditis; for example, approximately 5% of patients with Lyme disease (*Borrelia burgdorferi*; see p. 21) develop myopericarditis, which is often associated with variable degrees of atrioventricular block.

The clinical picture ranges from a symptomless disorder, sometimes recognised by the presence of an inappropriate tachycardia or abnormal ECG, to fulminant heart failure. ECG changes are common but non-specific. Plasma troponin and cardiac enzyme concentrations are elevated in proportion to the extent of damage. Echocardiography may reveal left ventricular dysfunction which is sometimes regional and, if necessary, the diagnosis can be confirmed by endomyocardial biopsy.

In most patients the disease is self-limiting and the immediate prognosis is excellent. However, death may occur, due to a ventricular arrhythmia or rapidly progressive heart failure. Myocarditis has been reported as a cause of sudden and unexpected death in young athletes. There is strong evidence that some forms of myocarditis may lead to chronic low-grade myocarditis or dilated cardiomyopathy (see below); for example, in Chagas disease (see p. 60) the patient frequently recovers from the acute infection but goes on to develop a chronic dilated cardiomyopathy 10 or 20 years later.

Specific antimicrobial therapy may be used if a causative organism has been identified; however, this is rare and in most cases only supportive therapy is available. Treatment for cardiac failure or arrhythmias may be required and patients should be advised to avoid intense physical exertion because there is some evidence that this can induce potentially fatal ventricular arrhythmias. Clinical trials have failed to demonstrate any benefit from treatment with corticosteroids and immunosuppressive agents.

Giant cell myocarditis is a rare disease that is characterised by the presence of multinucleated giant cells in the myocardium and may resemble viral myocarditis. The aetiology is not known but the condition is associated with certain systemic diseases (e.g. sarcoidosis, systemic lupus erythematosus and thymomas) and may represent an autoimmune reaction. Most cases are rapidly fatal and early transplantation may be indicated. Unfortunately, the disease may recur in the donor heart.

CARDIOMYOPATHY

The aetiology of most intrinsic disorders of the myocardium has not been elucidated and a functional classification is therefore the most appropriate means of describing these diseases (see Fig. 12.101).

DILATED CARDIOMYOPATHY

This condition is characterised by dilatation and impaired contraction of the left (and sometimes the right) ventricle; left ventricular mass is increased but wall thickness is normal or reduced (see Fig. 12.101). The histological changes are variable but include myofibrillary loss, interstitial fibrosis and T-cell infiltrates. The differential diagnosis includes coronary artery disease and many specific disorders of heart muscle (see below), and a diagnosis of dilated cardiomyopathy should only be offered when these conditions have been excluded.

The pathogenesis is not clear but dilated cardiomyopathy probably encompasses a heterogenous group of conditions.

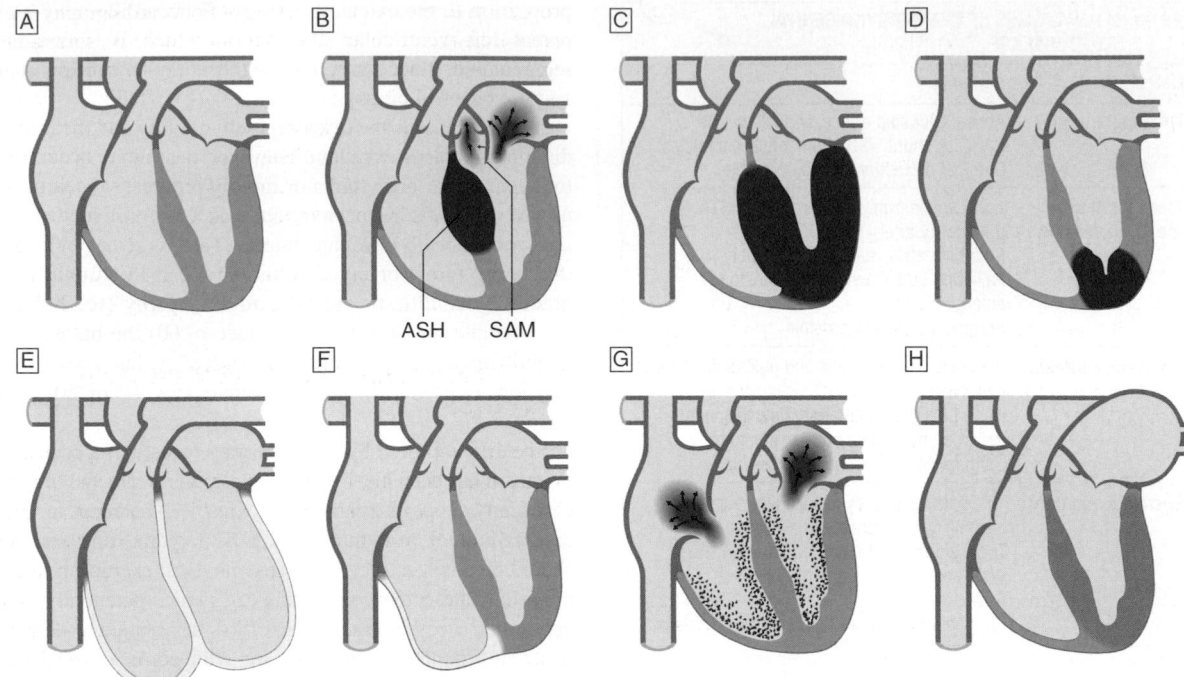

Fig. 12.101 Types of cardiomyopathy. A Normal. B Hypertrophic cardiomyopathy: asymmetric septal hypertrophy (ASH) with systolic anterior motion of the mitral valve (SAM), causing mitral reflux and dynamic LV outflow tract obstruction. C Hypertrophic cardiomyopathy: concentric hypertrophy. D Hypertrophic cardiomyopathy: apical hypertrophy. E Dilated cardiomyopathy. F Arrhythmogenic right ventricular dysplasia. G Obliterative cardiomyopathy. H Restrictive cardiomyopathy.

Alcohol appears to be an important aetiological factor in a significant proportion of patients. At least 25% of cases are inherited as an autosomal dominant trait and a variety of single gene mutations have been identified. Most of these mutations affect proteins in the cytoskeleton of the myocyte (e.g. dystrophin, lamin A and C, emerin and metavinculin) and many are associated with minor skeletal muscle abnormalities. Moreover, the majority of the X-linked inherited skeletal muscular dystrophies (e.g. Becker and Duchenne—see p. 1186) are associated with heart disease. Finally, a late autoimmune reaction to viral myocarditis is thought to be the main aetiological factor in a substantial subgroup of patients with dilated cardiomyopathy; a similar mechanism is thought to be responsible for the heart muscle disease that occurs in up to 10% of patients with advanced HIV infection.

In North America and Europe symptomatic dilated cardiomyopathy has an incidence of 20 per 100 000 and a prevalence of 38 per 100 000. Men are affected more than twice as often as women. Most patients present with heart failure or are found to have the condition as a result of a routine test. Arrhythmia, thromboembolism and sudden death are common and may occur at any stage; sporadic chest pain is a surprisingly frequent symptom. The ECG usually shows non-specific changes but echocardiography is useful in establishing the diagnosis. Treatment is aimed at controlling the resulting heart failure. Although some patients remain well for many years, the prognosis is variable and cardiac transplantation may be indicated.

HYPERTROPHIC CARDIOMYOPATHY

This is the most common form of cardiomyopathy, with a prevalence of approximately 100 per 100 000, and is characterised by inappropriate and elaborate left ventricular hypertrophy with malalignment of the myocardial fibres. The hypertrophy may be generalised or confined largely to the interventricular septum (asymmetric septal hypertrophy—see Fig. 12.101) or other regions (e.g. apical hypertrophic cardiomyopathy, a variant which is common in the Far East).

Heart failure may develop because the stiff non-compliant ventricles impede diastolic filling. Hypertrophy of the septum may also cause dynamic left ventricular outflow tract obstruction (HOCM—hypertrophic obstructive cardiomyopathy) and mitral regurgitation due to abnormal systolic anterior motion of the anterior mitral valve leaflet. Effort-related symptoms (angina and breathlessness), arrhythmia and sudden death are the dominant clinical problems.

The condition is a genetic disorder with autosomal dominant transmission, a high degree of penetrance and variable expression. In most patients the disease appears to be due to a single point mutation in one of the genes that encode sarcomeric contractile proteins. There are three common groups of mutation with different phenotypes. Beta-myosin heavy chain mutations are associated with elaborate ventricular hypertrophy. Troponin mutations are associated with little, and sometimes even no, hypertrophy but marked myocardial fibre disarray, an abnormal vascular response (e.g. exercise-induced hypotension) and a high risk of sudden death. Myosin-binding protein C mutations tend to present late in life and are often associated with hypertension and arrhythmia.

Symptoms and signs are similar to those of aortic stenosis, except that in hypertrophic cardiomyopathy the character of the arterial pulse is jerky (see Box 12.100).

The ECG is usually abnormal and may show the features of left ventricular hypertrophy with a wide variety of often bizarre abnormalities (e.g. pseudo-infarct pattern, deep T-wave inversion). Echocardiography is usually diagnostic; however, diagnosis may be difficult when another cause of left ventricular hypertrophy is present (e.g. physical training—athletes' heart, hypertension) but the degree of hypertrophy is greater than expected. Genetic testing may facilitate diagnosis in the future.

The natural history is variable but clinical deterioration is often slow. The annual mortality from sudden death is 2–3% among adults and 4–6% in children and adolescents (see Box 12.101). Sudden death typically occurs during or just after vigorous physical activity; indeed, hypertrophic cardiomyopathy is the most common cause of sudden death in young athletes. Ventricular arrhythmias are thought to be responsible for many of these deaths.

Beta-blockers and the rate-limiting calcium antagonists (e.g. verapamil) can help to relieve angina and sometimes prevent syncopal attacks; however, there is no pharmacological treatment that is definitely known to improve prognosis. Arrhythmias are common and often respond to treatment with amiodarone. Dual-chamber pacing and surgery (partial resection of the septum or mitral valve replacement) are useful in selected patients, particularly those with outflow tract obstruction. Digoxin and vasodilators may increase outflow tract obstruction and should be avoided.

Patients thought to be at high risk of sudden death (e.g. those with three or more risk factors—see Box 12.101) may be offered an implantable cardioverter-defibrillator (ICD).

ARRHYTHMOGENIC RIGHT VENTRICULAR DYSPLASIA

In this condition patches of the right ventricular myocardium are replaced with fibrous and fatty tissue (see Fig. 12.101). The disease is inherited as an autosomal dominant trait and is particularly common in some parts of Italy. The prevalence in the UK is thought to be approximately 10 per 100 000. The dominant clinical problems are ventricular arrhythmias and sudden death. The ECG typically shows inverted T waves in the right praecordial leads. MRI is a useful diagnostic tool and is often used to screen the first-degree relatives of affected individuals. Patients at high risk of sudden death can be offered an ICD.

OBLITERATIVE CARDIOMYOPATHY

This disease involves the endocardium of one or both ventricles. The pathogenesis is not clear but some form of endocardial damage appears to trigger thrombosis and elaborate fibrosis which gradually obliterates the ventricular cavities (see Fig. 12.101). The mitral and tricuspid valves are often involved and may become regurgitant. Heart failure and pulmonary and systemic embolism are prominent features. In temperate climates the endocardial damage is usually attributable to some form of eosinophilia (e.g. eosinophilic leukaemia, Churg–Strauss syndrome—see p. 1043) but this does not seem to be the case in tropical countries, where the disease can be responsible for up to 10% of cardiac deaths. Treatment is unsatisfactory and mortality is high (50% at 2 years). Anticoagulation and antiplatelet therapy are usually advisable and diuretics may help to treat the symptoms of heart failure. Surgery (tricuspid and/or mitral valve replacement with decortication of the endocardium) may be helpful in selected cases.

RESTRICTIVE CARDIOMYOPATHY

In this rare condition ventricular filling is impaired because the ventricles are 'stiff' (see Fig. 12.101). This leads to high atrial pressures with atrial hypertrophy, dilatation and later atrial fibrillation. Amyloidosis is the most common cause of restrictive physiology in the UK. However, other forms of infiltration (e.g. glycogen storage diseases), idiopathic perimyocyte fibrosis and a familial form of restrictive cardiomyopathy can present with this form of heart disease.

12.100 CLINICAL FEATURES OF HYPERTROPHIC CARDIOMYOPATHY
Symptoms
• Angina on effort
• Dyspnoea on effort
• Syncope on effort
• Sudden death
Signs
• Jerky pulse*
• Palpable left ventricular hypertrophy
• Double impulse at the apex (palpable fourth heart sound due to left atrial hypertrophy)
• Mid-systolic murmur at the base*
• Pansystolic murmur (due to mitral regurgitation) at the apex
* Signs of left ventricular outflow tract obstruction which may be augmented by standing up (reduced venous return), inotropes and vasodilators (e.g. sublingual nitrate).

12.101 RISK FACTORS FOR SUDDEN DEATH IN HYPERTROPHIC CARDIOMYOPATHY
• A history of previous cardiac arrest or sustained ventricular tachycardia
• Recurrent syncope
• An adverse genotype and/or family history
• Exercise-induced hypotension
• Multiple episodes of non-sustained ventricular tachycardia on ambulatory ECG monitoring
• Marked increase in left ventricular wall thickness

Diagnosis can be very difficult and may require complex Doppler echocardiography, CT or MRI, and endomyocardial biopsy. Treatment is symptomatic but the prognosis is usually poor and transplantation may be indicated.

SPECIFIC DISEASES OF HEART MUSCLE

Many forms of specific heart muscle disease produce a clinical picture that is indistinguishable from dilated cardiomyopathy (e.g. connective tissue disorders, sarcoidosis, haemochromatosis, alcoholic heart muscle disease—see Box 12.102). In contrast, amyloidosis and eosinophilic heart disease produce symptoms and signs similar to those found in restrictive or obliterative cardiomyopathy, whereas the heart disease associated with Friedreich's ataxia (see p. 1178) can mimic hypertrophic cardiomyopathy.

Treatment and prognosis are determined by the underlying disorder. Abstention from alcohol may lead to a dramatic improvement in patients with alcoholic heart muscle disease.

12.102 SPECIFIC DISEASES OF HEART MUSCLE
Infections
• Viral, e.g. Coxsackie A and B, influenza, HIV • Bacterial, e.g. diphtheria, *Borrelia burgdorferi* • Protozoal, e.g. trypanosomiasis
Endocrine and metabolic disorders
• e.g. Diabetes, hypo- and hyperthyroidism, acromegaly, carcinoid syndrome, phaeochromocytoma, inherited storage diseases
Connective tissue diseases
• e.g. Systemic sclerosis, systemic lupus erythematosus, polyarteritis nodosa
Infiltrative disorders
• e.g. Haemochromatosis, haemosiderosis, sarcoidosis, amyloidosis
Toxins
• e.g. Doxorubicin, alcohol, cocaine, irradiation
Neuromuscular disorders
• e.g. Dystrophia myotonica, Friedreich's ataxia

CARDIAC TUMOURS

Primary cardiac tumours are rare (< 0.2% of autopsies), but the heart and mediastinum may be the site of metastases.

Most primary tumours are benign (75%), and of these the majority are myxomas. The remainder are fibromas, lipomas, fibroelastomas and haemangiomas.

ATRIAL MYXOMA

Myxomas most commonly arise in the left atrium, as single or multiple polypoid tumours, attached by a pedicle to the interatrial septum. They are usually gelatinous but may be solid and even calcified, with superimposed thrombus.

The tumour may be detected incidentally (on echocardiography), or following investigation of pyrexia, syncope, arrhythmias or emboli. Occasionally the condition presents with malaise and features suggestive of a connective tissue disorder, including a raised ESR.

On examination the first heart sound is usually loud, and there may be a murmur of mitral regurgitation with a variable diastolic sound (tumour 'plop') due to prolapse of the mass through the mitral valve.

The diagnosis is made on echocardiography and treatment is by surgical excision. If the pedicle is removed, fewer than 5% of tumours recur.

DISEASES OF THE PERICARDIUM

The normal pericardial sac contains about 50 ml of fluid, similar to lymph, which lubricates the surface of the heart. The pericardium limits distension of the heart, contributes to the haemodynamic interdependence of the ventricles, and acts as a barrier to infection. Nevertheless, congenital absence of the pericardium does not appear to result in significant clinical or functional limitations.

ACUTE PERICARDITIS

Aetiology
Pericardial inflammation may be due to infection, immunological reaction, trauma or neoplasm (see Box 12.103) and sometimes remains unexplained. Pericarditis and myocarditis often coexist, and all forms of pericarditis may produce a pericardial effusion (see below) which, depending on the aetiology, may be fibrinous, serous, haemorrhagic or purulent.

A fibrinous exudate may eventually lead to varying degrees of adhesion formation, whereas serous pericarditis often produces a large effusion of turbid, straw-coloured fluid with a high protein content.

A haemorrhagic effusion is often due to malignant disease, particularly carcinoma of the breast, carcinoma of the bronchus and lymphoma.

Purulent pericarditis is rare and may occur as a complication of septicaemia, by direct spread from an intrathoracic infection, or from a penetrating injury.

12.103 AETIOLOGY OF ACUTE PERICARDITIS	
Common	
• Acute myocardial infarction	• Viral (e.g. Coxsackie B, but often not identified)
Less common	
• Uraemia • Malignant disease	• Trauma (e.g. blunt chest injury) • Connective tissue disease (e.g. SLE)
Rare (in UK)	
• Bacterial infection • Rheumatic fever	• Tuberculosis

Clinical features

The characteristic pain of pericarditis is retrosternal, radiates to the shoulders and neck and is typically aggravated by deep breathing, movement, a change of position, exercise and swallowing. A low-grade fever is common.

A pericardial friction rub is a high-pitched superficial scratching or crunching noise produced by movement of the inflamed pericardium, and is diagnostic of pericarditis; it is usually heard in systole but may also be audible in diastole and frequently has a 'to-and-fro' quality.

Investigations

The ECG shows ST elevation with upward concavity (see Fig. 12.102) over the affected area, which may be widespread. Later, there may be T-wave inversion, particularly if there is a degree of myocarditis.

Management

The pain can usually be relieved by aspirin (600 mg 4-hourly), but a more potent anti-inflammatory agent such as indometacin (25 mg 8-hourly) may be required. Corticosteroids may suppress symptoms but there is no evidence that they accelerate cure.

In viral pericarditis recovery usually occurs within a few days or weeks, but there may be recurrences (chronic relapsing pericarditis). Purulent pericarditis requires treatment with antimicrobial therapy, paracentesis and, if necessary, surgical drainage.

PERICARDIAL EFFUSION

If a pericardial effusion develops there is sometimes a sensation of retrosternal oppression. An effusion is difficult to detect clinically; although the heart sounds may become quieter, pericardial friction is not always abolished.

The QRS voltages on the ECG are often reduced in the presence of a large effusion. Serial chest radiographs may show a rapid increase in the size of the cardiac shadow over days or even hours, and when there is a large effusion the heart often has a globular or pear-shaped appearance. Echocardiography is the definitive investigation for pericardial effusion (see Fig. 12.103).

Cardiac tamponade

This term is used to describe acute heart failure due to compression of the heart by a large or rapidly developing effusion. Atypical presentations may occur when the effusion is loculated as a result of previous pericarditis or cardiac surgery. See also page 379.

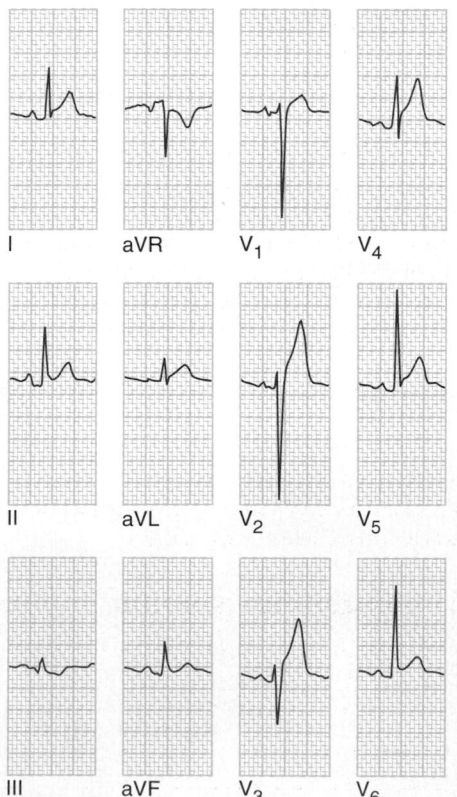

Fig. 12.102 ECG from a young man with viral pericarditis.
Widespread ST elevation (leads I, II, aVL and V_1–V_6) is shown. The upward concave shape of the ST segments (see leads II and V_6) and the unusual distribution of changes (involving anterior and inferior leads) may help to distinguish pericarditis from acute myocardial infarction.

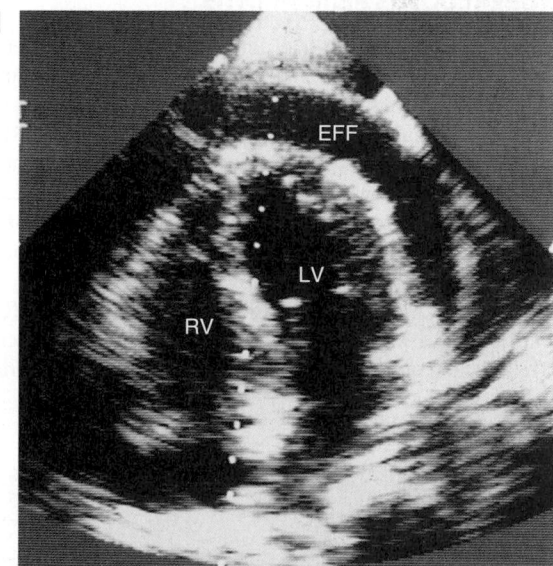

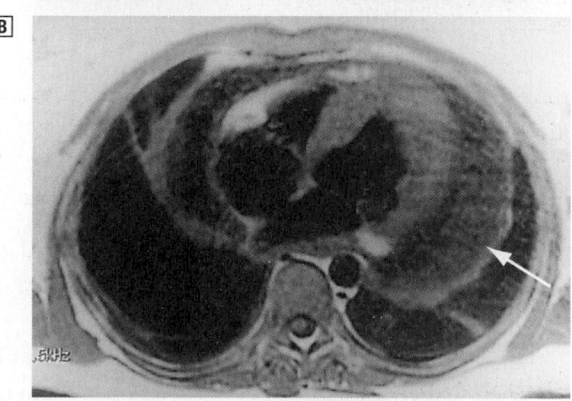

Fig. 12.103 Pericardial effusion. A Echocardiogram (apical view) (effusion is marked EFF). B MRI scan (effusion is marked with an arrow).

Pericardial aspiration

Aspiration of a pericardial effusion may be indicated for diagnostic purposes or for the treatment of cardiac tamponade. It may be accomplished by introducing a needle just medial to the cardiac apex or by inserting a needle below the xiphoid process and directing it towards the left shoulder; the procedure should be guided by simultaneous echocardiography. The route of choice will depend on the experience of the operator, the shape of the patient and the position of the effusion. A few millilitres of fluid aspirated through the needle may be sufficient for diagnostic purposes; however, if therapeutic drainage is required, it may be safer to use a plastic cannula inserted over a needle or guidewire.

Complications of pericardiocentesis include arrhythmias, damage to a coronary artery, and bleeding with exacerbation of tamponade as a result of injury to the right ventricle. When tamponade is due to cardiac rupture or aortic dissection pericardial aspiration may precipitate further, potentially fatal bleeding and in these situations emergency surgery is usually the treatment of choice. A viscous, loculated or recurrent effusion may also require formal surgical drainage.

TUBERCULOUS PERICARDITIS

Tuberculous pericarditis may complicate pulmonary tuberculosis but may also be the first manifestation of the infection. In Africa a tuberculous pericardial effusion is a common feature of the acquired immunodeficiency syndrome (AIDS).

The condition typically presents with chronic malaise, weight loss and a low-grade fever. An effusion usually develops and the pericardium may become thick and unyielding, leading to pericardial constriction or tamponade. An associated pleural effusion is often present.

The diagnosis may be confirmed by aspiration of the fluid and direct examination or culture for tubercle bacilli. Treatment requires specific antituberculous chemotherapy

(see p. 538); in addition, a 3-month course of prednisolone (initial dose 60 mg a day, tapering down rapidly) has been shown to improve outcome.

CHRONIC CONSTRICTIVE PERICARDITIS

Constrictive pericarditis is due to progressive thickening, fibrosis and calcification of the pericardium. In effect, the heart is encased in a solid shell and cannot fill properly; the calcification may extend into the myocardium, so there may also be impaired myocardial contraction.

The condition often follows an attack of tuberculous pericarditis but can also complicate haemopericardium, viral pericarditis, rheumatoid arthritis and purulent pericarditis. It is often impossible to identify the original insult.

Clinical features

The symptoms and signs of systemic venous congestion are the hallmarks of constrictive pericarditis; atrial fibrillation is common and there is often dramatic ascites and hepatomegaly (see Box 12.104). Breathlessness is not a prominent symptom because the lungs are seldom congested.

12.104 CLINICAL FEATURES OF CONSTRICTIVE PERICARDITIS
• Fatigue
• Rapid, low-volume pulse
• Pulsus paradoxus (an excessive fall in blood pressure during inspiration)
• Elevated jugular venous pulse (JVP) with a rapid *y* descent
• Kussmaul's sign (a paradoxical rise in the JVP during inspiration)
• Loud early third heart sound or 'pericardial knock'
• Hepatomegaly
• Ascites
• Peripheral oedema

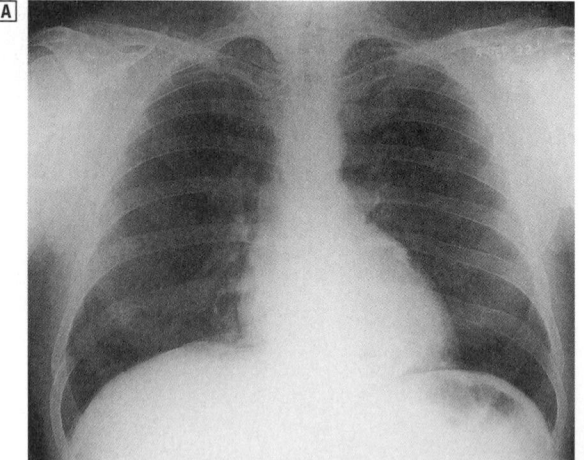
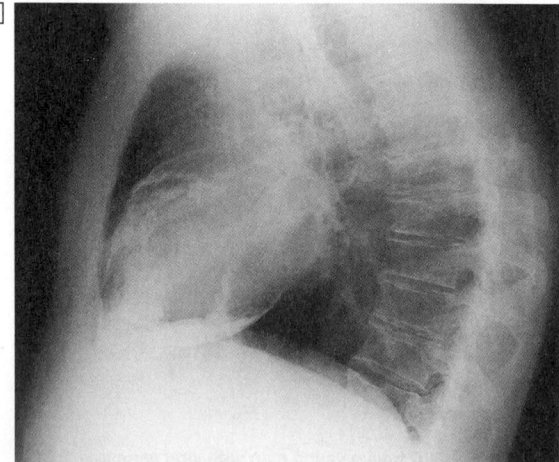

Fig. 12.104 Chest radiographs from a patient with severe heart failure due to chronic constrictive pericarditis. The heart is not enlarged and there is heavy calcification of the pericardium that is most visible on the lateral film. A PA radiograph. B Lateral radiograph.

The condition is sometimes overlooked and should be suspected in any patient with unexplained right heart failure and a small heart. A chest radiograph, which may show pericardial calcification (see Fig. 12.104), and echocardiography often help to establish the diagnosis. CT and MRI are also useful techniques for imaging the pericardium.

Constrictive pericarditis is often difficult to distinguish from restrictive cardiomyopathy and the final diagnosis may depend on complex echo-Doppler studies and cardiac catheterisation.

Management

Surgical resection of the diseased pericardium can lead to a dramatic improvement but carries a high morbidity and produces disappointing results in up to 50% of patients.

FURTHER INFORMATION

Bayer AS, Bolger AF, Taubert KA, et al. Diagnosis and management of infective endocarditis and its complications. Circulation 1998; 98:2938–2948.

Bennett DH. Cardiac arrhythmias. 5th edn. Oxford: Butterworth–Heinemann; 1997.

Brickner ME, Hillis LD, Lange RA. Congenital heart disease in adults. N Engl J Med 2000; 342:256–263, 334–342.

Carabello BA, Crawford FA. Valvular heart disease. N Engl J Med 1997; 337:32–41.

Cleland JG. Heart failure. Lancet 1998; 352(suppl 1):1–41. *A collection of up-to-date reviews dealing with all aspects of heart failure.*

Davies MJ. The cardiomyopathies: an overview. Heart 2000; 83:469–474.

Hampton JR. The ECG in practice. 3rd edn. Edinburgh: Churchill Livingstone; 1997.

Hampton JR. The ECG made easy. 5th edn. Edinburgh: Churchill Livingstone; 1997.

Hart RG, Benavente O, McBride R, Pearce LA. Antithrombotic therapy to prevent stroke in patients with atrial fibrillation: a meta-analysis. Ann Intern Med 1999; 131:492–501.

Mills P. Education in *Heart*, vol. 1. London: BMJ Books; 2001. *A collection of excellent review articles from the journal Heart. These articles were written for specialists in training, and cover all aspects of heart disease. They are strongly recommended and can also be accessed through the journal itself.*

Munro JF, Campbell IW. Macleod's clinical examination. 10th edn. Edinburgh: Churchill Livingstone; 2000.

Yeghiazarians Y, Braunstein JB, Askari A, Stone PH. Unstable angina pectoris. N Engl J Med 2000; 342:101–114.

www.acc.org *This and the following websites provide access to useful national and international guidelines.*
www.bcs.org
www.bhf.org
www.escardio.org
www.sign.ac.uk

Respiratory disease

C. HASLETT • E.R. CHILVERS • P.A. CORRIS

CLINICAL EXAMINATION OF THE RESPIRATORY SYSTEM

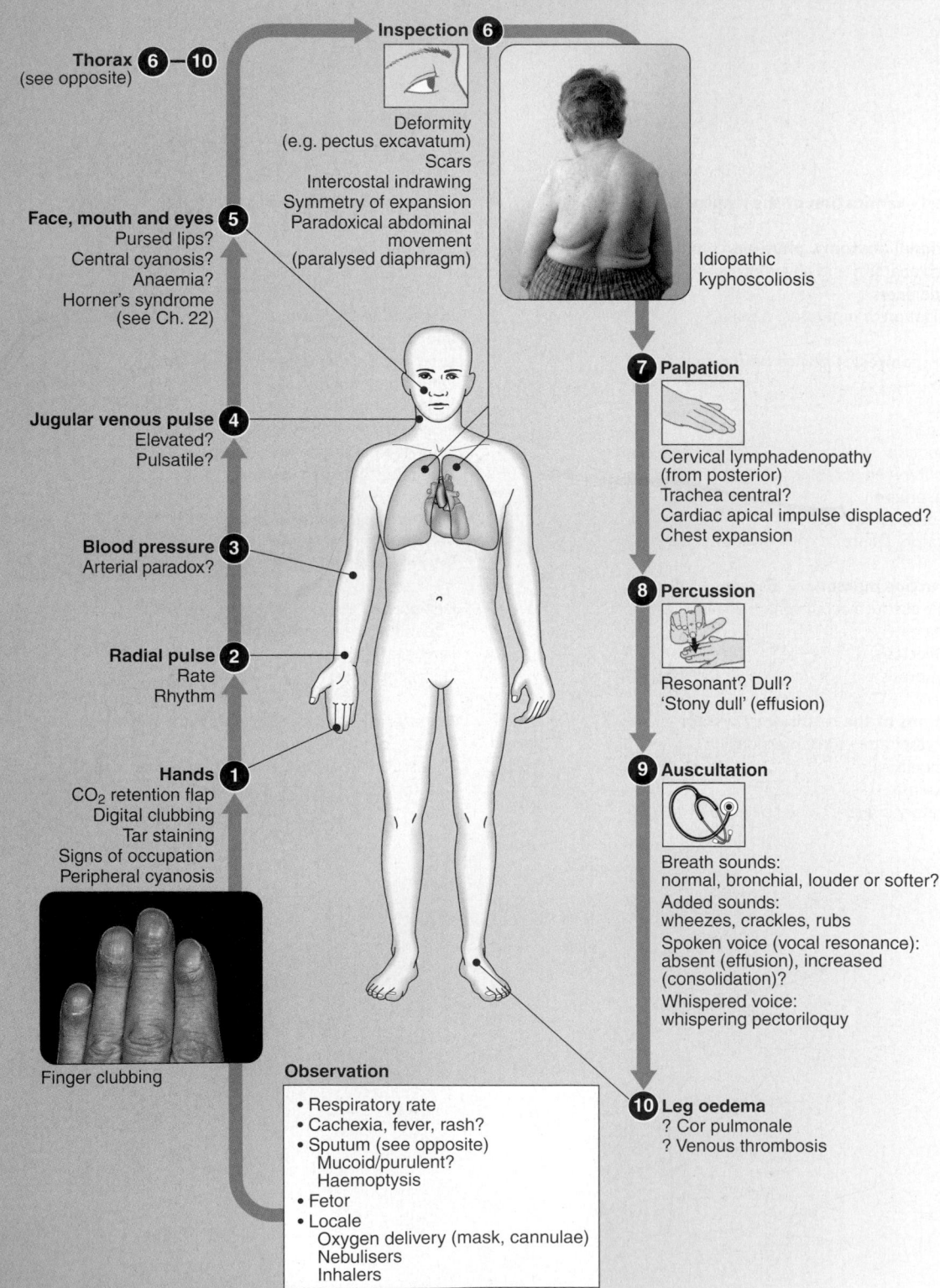

Thorax 6 — 10
(see opposite)

Inspection 6

Deformity
(e.g. pectus excavatum)
Scars
Intercostal indrawing
Symmetry of expansion
Paradoxical abdominal
movement
(paralysed diaphragm)

Idiopathic
kyphoscoliosis

Face, mouth and eyes 5
Pursed lips?
Central cyanosis?
Anaemia?
Horner's syndrome
(see Ch. 22)

Jugular venous pulse 4
Elevated?
Pulsatile?

7 Palpation

Cervical lymphadenopathy
(from posterior)
Trachea central?
Cardiac apical impulse displaced?
Chest expansion

Blood pressure 3
Arterial paradox?

8 Percussion

Resonant? Dull?
'Stony dull' (effusion)

Radial pulse 2
Rate
Rhythm

9 Auscultation

Breath sounds:
normal, bronchial, louder or softer?
Added sounds:
wheezes, crackles, rubs
Spoken voice (vocal resonance):
absent (effusion), increased
(consolidation)?
Whispered voice:
whispering pectoriloquy

Hands 1
CO_2 retention flap
Digital clubbing
Tar staining
Signs of occupation
Peripheral cyanosis

Finger clubbing

Observation

- Respiratory rate
- Cachexia, fever, rash?
- Sputum (see opposite)
  Mucoid/purulent?
  Haemoptysis
- Fetor
- Locale
  Oxygen delivery (mask, cannulae)
  Nebulisers
  Inhalers

10 Leg oedema
? Cor pulmonale
? Venous thrombosis

PHYSICAL FINDINGS IN COMMON RESPIRATORY CONDITIONS

Sputum

SPUTUM	
Appearance	**Cause**
Serous Clear, watery, frothy, may be pink	Acute pulmonary oedema Bronchoalveolar cell carcinoma (rare)
Mucoid Clear, grey, white, may be frothy or black (soot)	Chronic bronchitis, COPD, asthma
Mucopurulent or purulent Yellow, green, brown	All types of bronchopulmonary infection
Rusty Rusty, golden-yellow	Pneumococcal pneumonia

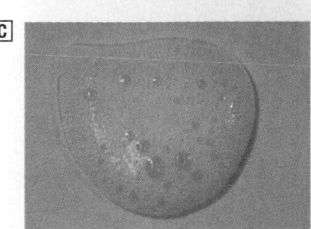

Appearances of sputum in respiratory disease. A Mucopurulent sputum. B Purulent sputum. C Sample from patient with fulminant pulmonary oedema.

❻–❿ Key features on examination of common respiratory conditions

Chronic obstructive pulmonary disease

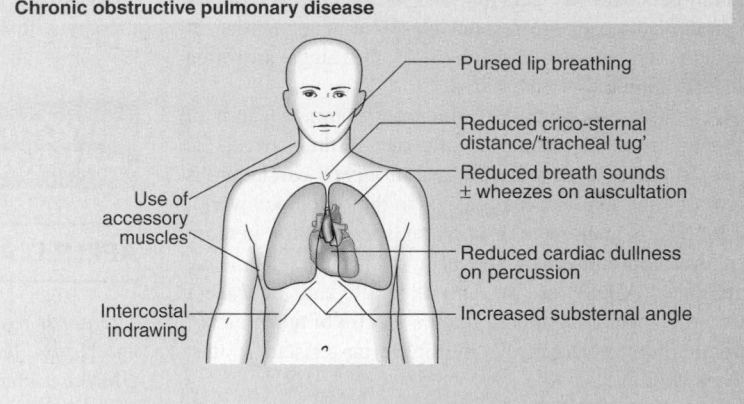

- Pursed lip breathing
- Reduced crico-sternal distance/'tracheal tug'
- Reduced breath sounds ± wheezes on auscultation
- Reduced cardiac dullness on percussion
- Increased substernal angle
- Use of accessory muscles
- Intercostal indrawing

Fibrosing alveolitis

Hands
  Finger clubbing (common in cryptogenic fibrosing alveolitis and asbestosis)
  Signs of occupation
  Central cyanosis (if severe)
  JVP↑ + ankle oedema (if severe)

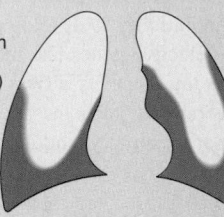

Inspection
  ↑ Respiratory rate (on mild exertion)
  ↓ Chest expansion
Palpation
  ↓ Expansion at lung bases
Percussion
  Dull at lung bases
Auscultation
  Bilateral crepitations

Right middle lobe pneumonia

Febrile ± rigors
In pain (if pleurisy)
Central cyanosis (if severe)
Tachycardia
Blood-stained sputum

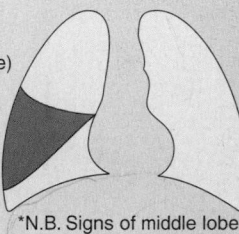

*N.B. Signs of middle lobe pneumonia are most apparent in the right axilla

Inspection
  ↑ Respiratory rate
  ↓ Chest expansion due to pain
Palpation
  ↓ Chest expansion on right
***Percussion**
  Dull right mid-zone
***Auscultation**
  Bronchial breath sounds
  Pleural rub
  ↑ Vocal resonance
  Whispering pectoriloquy

Right-sided pleural effusion

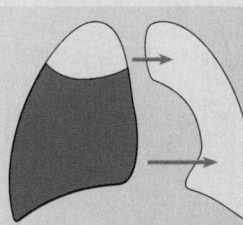

Inspection
  ↑ Respiratory rate
  ↓ Chest expansion on right
Palpation
  Mediastinal shift to left (trachea and apex beat)
Percussion
  'Stony' dull in right mid- and lower zone
Auscultation
  Reduced/absent breath sounds
  ↓ Vocal resonance

The lungs, with their combined surface area of greater than 500 m², are directly open to the external environment. Thus structural, functional or microbiological changes within the lungs can be closely related to epidemiological, environmental, occupational, personal and social factors. Primary respiratory diseases are responsible for a major burden of morbidity and untimely deaths, and the lungs are often affected in multisystem diseases.

Respiratory symptoms are the most common cause of presentation to the family practitioner. Asthma occurs in more than 10% of British children; bronchial carcinoma is the most common fatal malignancy in the developed world; the lung is the major site of opportunistic infection in those immunocompromised by the acquired immunodeficiency syndrome (AIDS) or by anti-allograft and anticancer chemotherapeutic regimens; and the spectre of tuberculosis, particularly the emergence of multiple drug-resistant strains, is back with us.

A number of important research advances have occurred in recent years. The discovery of the genetic mechanism of cystic fibrosis provides a novel opportunity to develop gene therapy strategies to replace the defective gene. The lung is especially favoured for gene therapy since its airway epithelial cells are accessible to nebulised particles and the extensive microvascular pulmonary capillary endothelium is available to intravenously delivered agents. Finally, recent advances in our understanding of the cellular and molecular mechanisms underlying diseases such as asthma and the acute (formerly adult) respiratory distress syndrome (ARDS) are likely to lead to rational, mechanism-based therapy within the foreseeable future.

FUNCTIONAL ANATOMY, PHYSIOLOGY AND INVESTIGATIONS

APPLIED ANATOMY AND PHYSIOLOGY

The upper respiratory tract includes the nose, nasopharynx and larynx. It is lined by vascular mucous membranes with ciliated epithelium on their surfaces. The lower respiratory tract includes the trachea and bronchi. These form an interconnecting tree of conducting airways eventually joining, via around 64 000 terminal bronchioles, with the alveoli to form the acini. The lower respiratory tract is lined with ciliated epithelium as far as the terminal bronchioles. The larynx and large bronchi are supplied with sensory nerve receptors involved in the cough reflex.

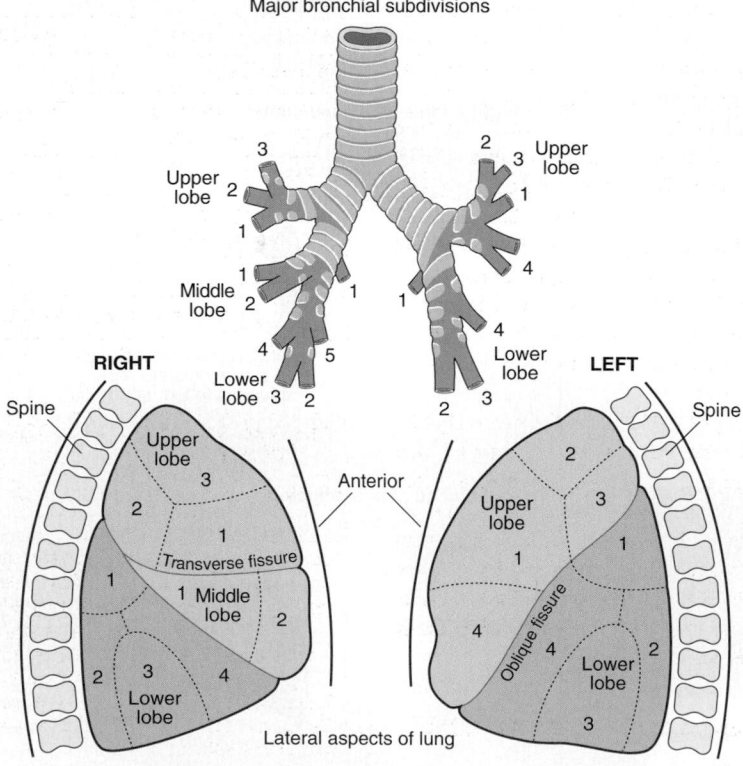

Fig. 13.1 The major bronchial divisions and the fissures, lobes and segments of the lungs. The position of the oblique fissure is such that the left upper lobe is largely anterior to the lower lobe. On the right side the transverse fissure separates the upper from the anteriorly placed middle lobe which is matched by the lingular segment on the left side. The site of the lobe determines whether physical signs are mainly anterior or posterior. Each lobe is composed of two or more bronchopulmonary segments, i.e. the lung tissue supplied by the main branches of each lobar bronchus. BRONCHOPULMONARY SEGMENTS: **Right**—*Upper lobe* (1) Anterior (2) Posterior (3) Apical. *Middle lobe* (1) Lateral (2) Medial. *Lower lobe* (1) Apical (2) Posterior basal (3) Lateral basal (4) Anterior basal (5) Medial basal. **Left**—*Upper lobe* (1) Anterior (2) Apical (3) Posterior (4) Lingular. *Lower lobe* (1) Apical (2) Posterior basal (3) Lateral basal (4) Anterior basal.

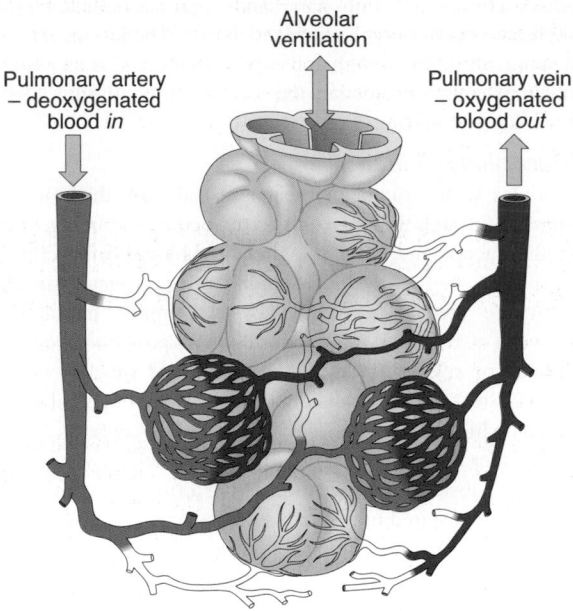

Fig. 13.2   The acinus—the basic gas exchange unit of the lung.

Some knowledge of the patterns of branching of the lobar and segmental bronchi is necessary for interpreting investigations, including chest radiographs and CT scans. Major bronchial and pulmonary divisions are shown in Figure 13.1. (See also bronchoscopic appearances in Fig. 13.8, p. 492.)

The acinus is the gas exchange unit of the lung (see Fig. 13.2) and comprises branching respiratory bronchioles leading to clusters of alveoli. The alveoli are lined mostly with flattened epithelial cells (type I pneumocytes), but there are some, more cuboidal, type II pneumocytes. The latter produce surfactant, a mixture of phospholipids, which acts to reduce surface tension and counteract the tendency of alveoli to collapse. Type II pneumocytes also display a remarkable capacity to divide and reconstitute the type I pneumocytes after lung injury.

The right ventricle pumps blood against the relatively low pulmonary vascular resistance. Blood flows through a rich capillary network, intimately adjacent to alveoli (see Fig. 13.2), facilitating gas exchange. Increased pulmonary vascular resistance—due, for example, to thromboembolism (see p. 562) or to destructive changes caused by chronic obstructive pulmonary disease (COPD, see p. 508)—results in right ventricular hypertrophy, and eventually right heart failure (cor pulmonale) ensues.

GAS EXCHANGE, VENTILATION, BLOOD FLOW AND DIFFUSION

Gas exchange in the lungs is suboptimal unless there is sufficient ventilation, distributed uniformly to different parts of the lungs and matched by uniform distribution of blood flow. Furthermore, abnormal diffusion of oxygen or carbon dioxide across the alveolar-capillary membrane impairs gas exchange.

In clinical practice the important consequences of impaired gas exchange are hypoxaemia and hypercapnia.

Hypercapnia ($PaCO_2 > 6$ kPa) is generally caused by conditions resulting in alveolar hypoventilation or ventilation-perfusion mismatch (see Box 13.1). Hypoventilation may be caused by depression of the respiratory centre in the medulla; in contrast, stimulation of the respiratory centre causes hypocapnia and respiratory alkalosis (see Box 13.2). Ventilation-perfusion mismatch is thought to be largely responsible for the hypercapnia of COPD and severe asthma.

Causes of hypoxaemia are shown in Box 13.3. Blood flow wasted on perfusing poorly ventilated lung is probably the most important of these and contributes to the hypoxaemia found, for example, in bronchial obstruction (due to secretions, mucosal oedema, bronchoconstriction or tumours), destruction of elastic tissue (e.g. emphysema), pulmonary collapse, consolidation, fibrosis or oedema, and chest wall deformities. In conditions where the area of alveolar-capillary interface available for gas exchange is reduced (e.g. emphysema), impaired diffusion may contribute to

13.1 COMMON CAUSES OF HYPERCAPNIA (RAISED $PaCO_2$)	
Central	
• Brain-stem lesion	• Central sleep apnoea
Neuromuscular	
• Peripheral neuropathy • Myasthenia gravis	• Myopathy
Chest wall	
• Kyphoscoliosis • Ankylosing spondylitis	• Trauma
Pulmonary	
• Chronic obstructive airways disease (COPD)	

13.2 SOME INFLUENCES ON THE RESPIRATORY CENTRE	
Mechanism	**Example**
Stimulant	
Voluntary	Over-breathing
Upper brain-stem lesions	Central neurogenic hyperventilation
Input from receptors	Pain; muscles and joints; pulmonary afferents
Increased $PaCO_2$	Via central and peripheral chemoreceptors
Increased arterial [H$^+$]	Via peripheral chemoreceptors
Decreased PaO_2 (< 8 kPa at rest)	Via peripheral chemoreceptors
Pyrexia	
Depressant	
Voluntary	Breath-holding
Brain-stem lesions	
Sedative drugs	Opiates, benzodiazepines
Hypothermia	
Hypothyroidism	

hypoxaemia. This effect may not be significant at rest, but may limit the amount of oxygen which can be taken up during exercise.

Hypoxaemia due to ventilation-perfusion mismatch, hypoventilation or diffusion impairment is reversed by giving oxygen. In right-to-left shunts—as, for example, in congenital heart diseases and pulmonary vascular anomalies—blood does not pass through alveolar capillaries and therefore oxygen does not fully correct the hypoxaemia. Hypoxaemia also occurs if the oxygen-carrying capacity of the blood is reduced—as, for example, in anaemia or carbon monoxide poisoning.

The normal arterial PaO_2 is over 12 kPa at the age of 20 and falls to around 11 kPa at 60. Above this age a further fall in PaO_2 of up to 1.3 kPa may occur on lying down because of closure of small airways in the dependent regions of the lungs.

Under physiological conditions hypoxaemia and hypercapnia both stimulate ventilation. In some patients with COPD, tolerance to chronic hypercapnia ensues, and in such patients administration of high concentrations of oxygen removes the remaining hypoxaemic stimulus for ventilation, resulting in worsening hypercapnia. Patients with COPD who have chronic hypercapnia should therefore receive, if required, low concentrations of oxygen (e.g. 24–28%), adjusted according to arterial blood gas analysis (see p. 512). Patients with pure asthma do not have chronic hypercapnia and it is therefore safe, and indeed important, to give high concentrations of oxygen during exacerbations of asthma (see p. 520).

LUNG DEFENCES

Each day our lungs are directly exposed to more than 7000 litres of air which contain varying amounts of inorganic and organic particles as well as potentially lethal bacteria and viruses. In general terms, physical mechanisms including cough are particularly important in defence of the upper airways, whereas the lower airways are protected by complex mucociliary mechanisms, by the antimicrobial properties of surfactant and the lung-lining fluids, and by resident alveolar macrophages.

Physical defences

Most large particles are removed from inspired air by the nose, which is composed of a 'stack' of fine aerodynamic filters comprising fine hairs and columnar ciliated epithelium which cover the turbinate bones. The larynx acts as a sphincter during cough and expectoration and is an essential mechanism protecting the lower airways during swallowing and vomiting.

Mucociliary clearance

Particles with a diameter greater than 0.5 μm that survive passage through the nose will be trapped by the lining fluid of the trachea and bronchi and cleared by the 'mucociliary escalator' (see Fig. 13.3). This highly effective small particle clearance mechanism works by a complex interaction between cilia, which are a series of small projections on the surface of respiratory epithelial cells, and mucus, which forms a 'raft' on top of the cilia. Particles are trapped by the mucus which is then swept by the cilia in a cephalic direction. Other important functions of mucus include dilution of noxious substances, lubrication of the airways, and humidification of inspired air. Mucus is mostly secreted by goblet cells within the respiratory epithelium and is composed of the mucus glycoproteins and a variety of other proteins (see Box 13.4) which, although present in low concentrations, play an important role in the defence of the bronchial tree. A number of factors reduce mucociliary clearance by interfering with ciliary function or by causing actual ciliary damage. These include pollutants, cigarette smoke, local and general anaesthetic agents, bacterial products and viral

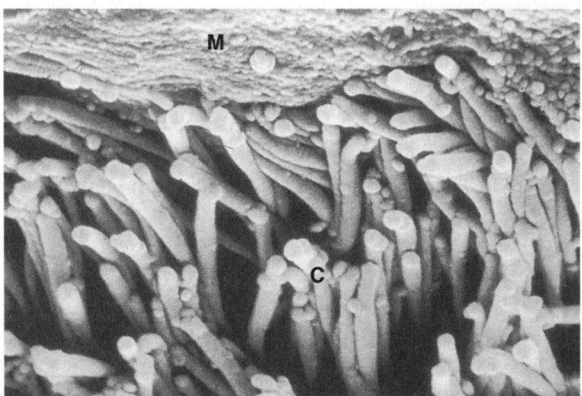

Fig. 13.3 The mucociliary escalator. Scanning electron micrograph of the respiratory epithelium showing large numbers of cilia (C) overlaid by the mucus 'raft' (M).

13.4 PROTECTIVE AGENTS IN THE LUNG-LINING FLUID

- Surfactant proteins—bacterial opsonisation
- Immunoglobulins (IgA, IgG, IgM)—bacterial opsonisation, generation of the immune response
- Complement—bacterial opsonisation, generation of the inflammatory response
- Bactericidal proteins—bacterial killing
- Proteinase inhibitors—protection of host tissues during the inflammatory response

infection. There is also a rare autosomal recessive condition (1 in 30 000 live births) called primary ciliary dyskinesia, which is characterised by repeated sinusitis and respiratory tract infections which progress to persistent lung suppuration and bronchiectasis, thus reinforcing the importance of ciliary clearance in antibacterial lung defences.

Surfactant and other defensive proteins

In addition to its surface active properties which are so important in lung mechanics, surfactant contains a number of proteins, including surfactant protein A, which can opsonise bacteria and other particles, rendering them susceptible to phagocytosis by macrophages. Lung-lining fluids also contain other defensive proteins (see Box 13.4) including immunoglobulins, complement, defensins (powerful antibacterial peptides) and a variety of antiproteinases (including α_1-antitrypsin) which play an important role in protecting healthy tissues from damage which would be incurred by the release of proteinases from inflammatory cells during the inflammatory response.

Alveolar macrophages

These multipotent cells normally patrol the interior of the alveoli (see Fig. 13.4), where they display a formidable array of mechanisms by which they recognise and destroy bacteria and other foreign particles. The remarkably versatile resident macrophage can also 'call in reinforcements' by generating mediators which cause an inflammatory response and attract granulocytes and monocytes. It may also generate an immune response by presenting antigens and by releasing specific lymphokines. Finally, the alveolar macrophage exerts important scavenging functions in the clearance of dead bacteria and other cells during the aftermath of infection and inflammation. Nevertheless, it is important to appreciate that the excessive or uncontrolled release of some of these powerful macrophage products may cause disordered inflammation or scarring responses which are likely to be important in the pathogenesis of a variety of inflammatory diseases including asthma, COPD and other inflammatory/scarring conditions of the lung, e.g. fibrosing alveolitis.

Fig. 13.4   Alveolar macrophages. Scanning electron micrograph showing alveolar macrophages (arrow) patrolling the alveolar spaces of the lung.

> **ISSUES IN OLDER PEOPLE**
> RESPIRATORY FUNCTION
>
> - The vast reserve capacity of the respiratory system means a significant reduction in function can occur with ageing with only minimal effect on normal breathing, but the ability to combat acute respiratory disease is reduced.
> - Lung volumes fall gradually with age; the FEV_1/VC ratio falls by around 0.2% per year from 70% at the age of 40–45 years. The decline is less rapid in men.
> - There are reduced ventilatory responses to hypoxia and hypercapnia in old age, so older people may be less tachypnoeic for any given fall in PaO_2 or rise in $PaCO_2$.
> - Reduced numbers of glandular epithelial cells lead to a reduction in protective mucus and thus impaired defences against infection.
> - Maximum oxygen uptake declines with age due to a combination of changes in the respiratory and cardiovascular systems. This leads to a reduction in cardiorespiratory reserve and exercise capacity.
> - The chest wall becomes less mobile due to reduced intervertebral disc spaces and ossification of the costal cartilages; respiratory muscle strength and endurance also decline. These changes only become important in the presence of other respiratory disease.
> - Ageing leads to reduced elastic recoil in the small airways, which causes a tendency for these to collapse during expiration, particularly in dependent areas of the lungs, thus reducing ventilation and increasing ventilation-perfusion mismatch.

INVESTIGATION OF RESPIRATORY DISEASE

It is essential to take a detailed history from the patient, and much can be learned from a careful physical examination (see Box 13.5). Routine haematological and biochemical investigations can provide indices of infection, immunosuppression and evidence of metastasis of lung tumours, but a number of special investigations are often required in the diagnosis and monitoring of lung disease.

IMAGING

The 'plain' chest radiograph

Many diseases, including bronchial carcinoma and pulmonary tuberculosis, cannot be detected at an early stage without a radiograph of the chest. A lateral film provides additional information about the likely nature and situation of a pulmonary, pleural or mediastinal abnormality. Comparison with previous radiographs may help to distinguish between a 'new' or progressive change which is thus potentially serious, and 'old' or static abnormalities which may be of no importance. In some diseases, such as COPD and asthma, there is often no radiographic abnormality. In these diseases functional assessment (see p. 493) is of much more value in detecting abnormality.

Computed tomography (CT)

This has virtually taken over from conventional tomography in centres where it is available. Conventional tomography was valuable in determining the position and size of a pulmonary nodule or mass and whether calcification or cavitation was present. It was also useful in localising lesions for percutaneous needle biopsy and in assessing the mediastinum and thoracic cage. In all of these examples, however, computed tomography is more sensitive and accurate.

13.5 SUMMARY OF TYPICAL PHYSICAL SIGNS IN THE MORE COMMON RESPIRATORY DISEASES

Pathological process	Movement of chest wall	Mediastinal displacement	Percussion note	Breath sounds	Vocal resonance	Added sounds
Consolidation (as in lobar pneumonia)	Reduced on side affected	None	Dull	High-pitched bronchial	Increased; whispering pectoriloquy	Fine crepitations[1] early; coarse crepitations later
Collapse due to obstruction of a major bronchus	Reduced on side affected	Towards lesion	Dull	Diminished or absent	Reduced or absent	None
Collapse due to peripheral bronchial obstruction	Reduced on side affected	Towards lesion	Dull	High-pitched bronchial	Increased; whispering pectoriloquy	None early; coarse crepitations later
Localised fibrosis and/or bronchiectasis	Slightly reduced on side affected	Towards lesion	Impaired	Low-pitched bronchial	Increased	Coarse crepitations
Cavitation (usually associated with consolidation or fibrosis)	Slightly reduced on side affected	None, or towards lesion	Impaired	Bronchial	Increased; whispering pectoriloquy	Coarse crepitations
Pleural effusion Empyema	Reduced or absent (depending on size) on side affected	Towards opposite side	Stony dull	Diminished or absent (occasionally bronchial)	Reduced or absent (occasionally increased)	Pleural rub in some cases (above effusion)
Pneumothorax	Reduced or absent (depending on size) on side affected	Towards opposite side	Normal or hyper-resonant	Diminished or absent (occasionally faint bronchial)	Reduced or absent	Tinkling crepitations when fluid present
Bronchitis (acute or chronic)	Normal or symmetrically diminished	None	Normal	Vesicular with prolonged expiration	Normal	Rhonchi,[2] usually with some coarse crepitations
Bronchial asthma	Symmetrically diminished	None	Normal	Vesicular with prolonged expiration	Normal or reduced	Rhonchi, mainly expiratory and high-pitched
Bronchopneumonia	Symmetrically diminished	None	May be impaired	Usually harsh vesicular with prolonged expiration	Normal	Rhonchi and coarse crepitations
Diffuse pulmonary emphysema	Symmetrically diminished	None	Normal or hyper-resonant	Diminished vesicular with prolonged expiration	Normal or reduced	Expiratory rhonchi
Interstitial lung disease	Symmetrically diminished	None	Normal	Harsh vesicular with prolonged expiration	Usually increased	End-inspiratory crepitations not influenced by coughing

[1] Crepitations = crackles.
[2] Rhonchi = wheeze.

CT is now routinely used in the pre-operative assessment of patients with lung cancer, particularly for assessing mediastinal spread, and the presence of metastases in the liver or adrenals. Its value in imaging the mediastinum can be greatly enhanced by using an intravenous contrast which outlines the mediastinal vessels. High-resolution CT is particularly useful in diagnosing interstitial fibrosis, and in identifying bronchiectasis (see Fig. 13.5).

Ventilation-perfusion imaging
The main value of this technique is in the detection of pulmonary thromboemboli. ^{133}Xe gas is inhaled (the ventilation scan) and ^{99m}Tc-labelled macroaggregates of albumin, or albumin microspheres, are injected intravenously, the particles becoming transiently trapped in pulmonary micro-vessels and providing the 'perfusion' scan. Pulmonary emboli can be detected as a 'filling defect' in the perfusion scan (see Fig. 13.6), but patients with asthma, COPD or other forms of obstructive airways disease may also have disordered pulmonary vascular distribution. However, in these patients the ventilation scan shows defects which match the areas of reduced perfusion on the perfusion scan, whereas the perfusion defects in pulmonary embolism are not matched to defects on the ventilation scan. Ventilation-perfusion scanning is also useful in pre-operative assessment of the functional effects of lung cancer and bullae.

Positron emission tomography (PET)

Whole-body PET with [18]-fluorodeoxyglucose (FDG) is showing considerable utility in the investigation of pulmonary nodules and in staging mediastinal lymph node involvement and distal metastatic disease in patients with lung cancer. Recent studies have shown that FDG-PET can prevent unnecessary surgery in 20% of patients with non-small-cell lung cancer.

Pulmonary angiography

This is the definitive method of diagnosing pulmonary emboli, particularly in the acutely ill and shocked patient or when ventilation-perfusion scans are equivocal. Conventional pulmonary angiography is performed by passing contrast medium down a catheter inserted via the femoral vein into the main pulmonary artery. This catheter can also be used to measure pulmonary artery pressure and instil thrombolytic agents such as streptokinase. Digital subtraction angiography (DSA) is a technique whereby images obtained before contrast injection are digitised and subtracted from post-contrast images, thus removing bones and other background structures from the final digital images. This technique is more sensitive and requires much less contrast to obtain high-quality images (see Fig. 13.7). Other techniques for imaging the pulmonary arteries include the use of contrast-enhanced spiral CT—'CT pulmonary angiography'—which is increasingly used in the diagnosis of pulmonary thrombo-embolism (see p. 562).

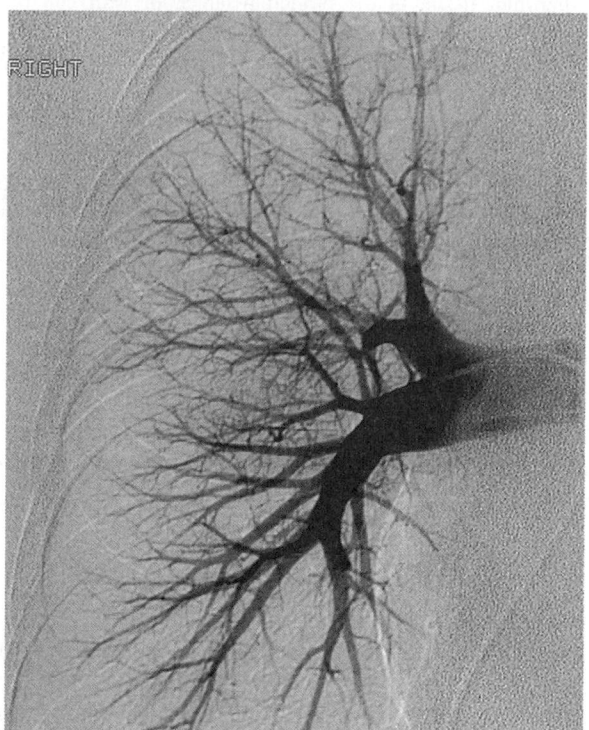

Fig. 13.7   Normal digital subtraction pulmonary angiogram of the right lung.

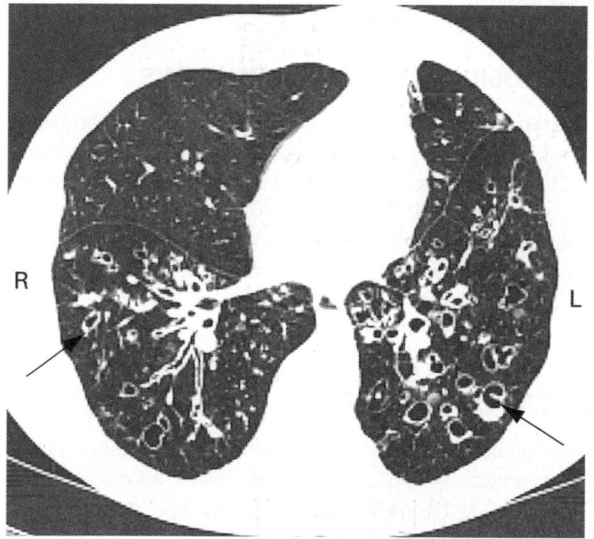

Fig. 13.5   Computed tomography of the thorax. This scan shows extensive dilatation of the bronchi (bronchiectasis) with thickened walls (arrows) in both lower lobes.

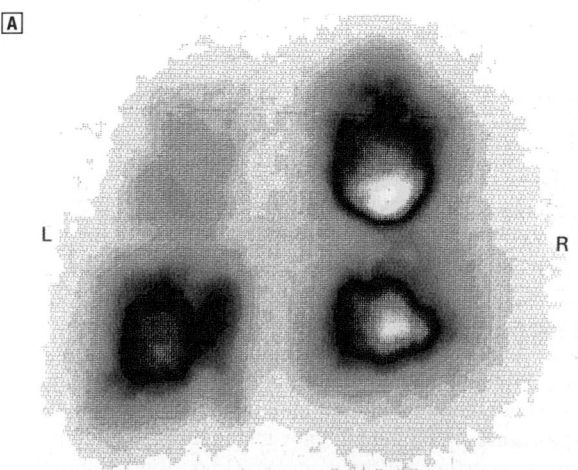

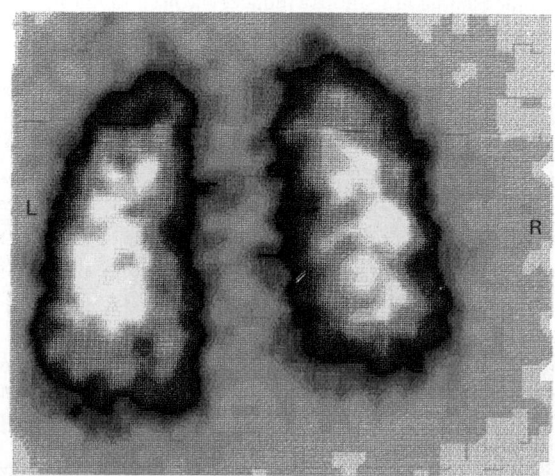

Fig. 13.6   Lung ventilation and perfusion scintigraphy. [A] Multiple perfusion defects present in left upper zone and right mid-zone of perfusion scan. [B] Normal ventilation scan. The appearances in [A] indicate a high probability of recent pulmonary embolism.

ENDOSCOPIC EXAMINATION

Laryngoscopy

The larynx may be inspected indirectly with a mirror or directly with a laryngoscope. Fibreoptic instruments allow a magnified view to be obtained.

Bronchoscopy

The trachea (see Fig. 13.8) and larger bronchi are inspected by a bronchoscope of flexible fibreoptic or rigid type. Rigid bronchoscopy usually requires general anaesthesia. Structural changes, such as distortion or obstruction, can be seen. Abnormal tissue in the bronchial lumen or wall can be biopsied, and bronchial brushings, washings or aspirates can be taken for cytological or bacteriological examination. The range of vision is limited by the calibre of the subsegmental bronchi, but peripheral lesions can sometimes be reached by flexible biopsy forceps directed under fluoroscopic control. Small biopsy specimens of lung tissue taken by forceps passed through the bronchial wall (transbronchial biopsies) may reveal sarcoid granulomata or malignant diseases and may be helpful in diagnosing certain bronchocentric disorders (e.g. extrinsic allergic alveolitis, cryptogenic organising pneumonia), but are generally too small to be of diagnostic value in diffuse interstitial lung disease (see p. 552).

Mediastinoscopy

The mediastinoscope is introduced through a small incision at the suprasternal notch to give a view of the upper mediastinum. Biopsy of some mediastinal nodes is possible, which may be of value in obtaining a diagnosis and in determining whether a bronchial carcinoma has spread to the mediastinum and is, therefore, inoperable.

Pleural aspiration and biopsy

Pleural aspiration and biopsy using an Abram's needle is a 'blind' procedure but often provides histological evidence of the cause of a pleural effusion. Transthoracic needle biopsy (with radiological guidance) may be useful in obtaining a cytological diagnosis from a peripheral lung lesion. In difficult cases, thoracoscopy may be necessary to obtain diseased tissue; the recent introduction of video-assisted thoracoscopic lung biopsy reduces the need for thoracotomy in cases of interstitial lung disease when lung biopsy is required (see p. 552).

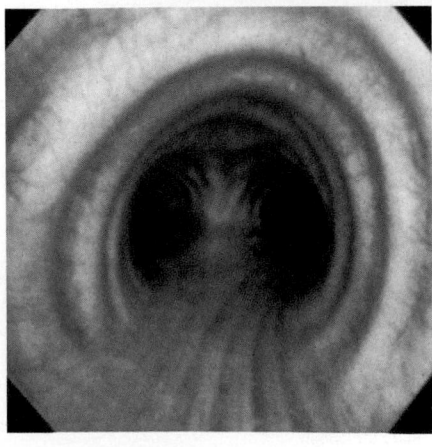

Fig. 13.8 Bronchoscopic appearances of the lower trachea, carina and the right and left main bronchi.

SKIN TESTS

The tuberculin test (see p. 537) may be of value in the diagnosis of tuberculosis. Skin hypersensitivity tests are useful in the investigation of allergic diseases.

IMMUNOLOGICAL AND SEROLOGICAL TESTS

The presence of pneumococcal antigen (revealed by counter-immunoelectrophoresis) in sputum, blood or urine may be of diagnostic importance. Exfoliated cells colonised by influenza A virus (see p. 525) can be detected by fluorescent antibody techniques. In blood, high or rising antibody titres to specific organisms (such as *Legionella*, *Mycoplasma*, *Chlamydia* or viruses) may eventually clinch a diagnosis suspected on clinical grounds. Precipitating antibodies may be found as a reaction to fungi such as *Aspergillus* (see p. 540) or to antigens involved in allergic alveolitis (see p. 556).

MICROBIOLOGICAL INVESTIGATIONS

Sputum, pleural fluid, throat swabs, blood and bronchial washings and aspirates can be examined for bacteria, fungi and viruses. In some cases, as when *Mycobacterium tuberculosis* is isolated, the information is diagnostically conclusive but in other circumstances the findings must be interpreted in conjunction with the results of clinical and radiological examination.

HISTOPATHOLOGICAL AND CYTOLOGICAL EXAMINATION

Histopathological examination of biopsy material (obtained from pleura, lymph node or lung) often allows a 'tissue diagnosis' to be made. This is of particular importance in suspected malignancy or in elucidating the pathological changes in interstitial lung disease (see p. 550). Important causative organisms, such as *M. tuberculosis*, *Pneumocystis carinii* or fungi, may be identified in bronchial washings, brushings or transbronchial biopsies.

Cytological examination of exfoliated cells in sputum, pleural fluid or bronchial brushings and washings or of fine-needle aspirates from lymph nodes or pulmonary lesions can support a diagnosis of malignancy but a tissue biopsy is necessary in most cases to confirm the diagnosis. Cellular patterns in bronchial lavage fluid may help to distinguish pulmonary changes due to sarcoidosis (see p. 552) from those caused by fibrosing alveolitis (see p. 555) or allergic alveolitis (see p. 556).

LUNG FUNCTION TESTING

Pulmonary function tests are used to aid diagnosis, assess functional impairment and monitor treatment or progression of disease. Common abbreviations used in pulmonary function testing are shown in Box 13.6. Simple spirometry should be a routine procedure carried out by all doctors when assessing a patient who is breathless.

13.6 ABBREVIATIONS USED IN PULMONARY FUNCTION TESTING	
Abbreviation	**Stands for**
FEV$_1$	Forced expiratory volume in 1 second
FVC	Forced vital capacity
VC	Vital capacity (relaxed)
PEF	Peak (maximum) expiratory flow
TLC	Total lung capacity
FRC	Functional residual capacity
RV	Residual volume
TLCO	Gas transfer factor for carbon monoxide
KCO	Transfer coefficient for carbon monoxide

13.7 PATTERNS OF ABNORMAL VENTILATORY CAPACITY			
	Asthma	**Emphysema**	**Lung fibrosis**
FEV$_1$	Low	Low	Low
VC	Low	Low	Low
FEV$_1$/VC	Low	Low	Normal
DLCO	Normal	Low	Low
KCO	Normal	Low	Low
TLC	High	High	Low
RV	High	High	Low

Spirometry and peak flow

The forced expiratory volume in 1 second (FEV$_1$) and vital capacity (VC) are obtained from maximal forced and relaxed expirations into a spirometer. The results are compared with predicted values based on age, sex, height and ethnic group. The FEV$_1$/VC ratio is also a useful diagnostic aid, with values of less than 70% defining airflow obstruction (see Box 13.7). Acute reversibility testing using inhaled short-acting β$_2$-adrenoceptor agonists (e.g. salbutamol or terbutaline) should be carried out when airflow obstruction is seen; full reversibility is diagnostic of asthma (see p. 513). Peak expiratory flow (PEF) monitored via a small portable meter can be usefully recorded by patients at home or at work in order to assess asthma control on an objective basis. Peak flow monitoring can be used by patients as a basis for self-management plans. Serial measures show any circadian changes, and responses to occupational exposure or therapy are of value in both the diagnosis and the management of asthma.

Flow–volume curves

The plotting of flow versus volume during both maximal expiratory and inspiratory manoeuvres is of major help in differentiating central airflow obstruction (leading to stridor) from diffuse airflow obstruction as seen in COPD and asthma.

Lung volumes

Measurement of total lung capacity and residual volume is best performed using a whole body plethysmograph, but can be measured by a helium dilution method. In general, restrictive defects lead to reduced values, and obstructive defects to increased values (see Box 13.7 and Fig. 13.9).

Measurement of diffusing capacity

The diffusing capacity (DLCO) is a measure of the lung's ability to transfer gas from alveoli to blood. The test utilises uptake of carbon monoxide from a single breath of 0.3% mixture in air; this gas is chosen because it combines rapidly with haemoglobin and provides a true estimate of diffusion across the alveolar capillary membrane. The diffusing capacity is reduced in patients with disease principally affecting alveoli such as fibrosing alveolitis or emphysema. The transfer coefficient (KCO) is a measure of diffusing capacity expressed per volume of ventilated lung during the single breath test and is useful to confirm that a low DLCO is due to alveolar disease rather than maldistribution of ventilation. High values of DLCO may be seen in alveolar haemorrhage.

Arterial blood gases and oximetry

The measurement of hydrogen ion concentration, PaO_2 and $PaCO_2$, and derived bicarbonate concentration of arterial blood is essential in assessing the degree and type of respiratory failure and for measuring overall acid–base status. Use of

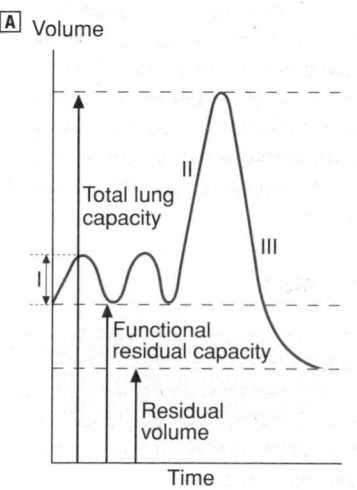

A Volume

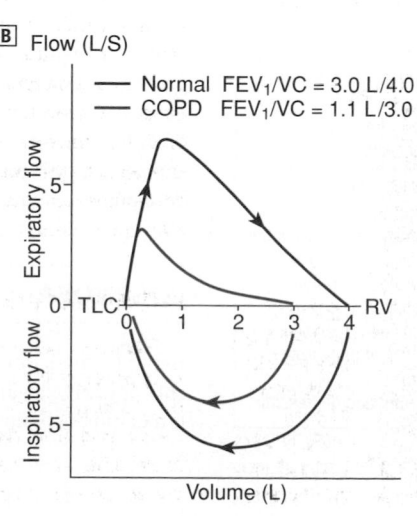

B Flow (L/S)

— Normal FEV$_1$/VC = 3.0 L/4.0 L
— COPD   FEV$_1$/VC = 1.1 L/3.0 L

Fig. 13.9 Normal lung volumes and schematic tidal flow-volume curves.
A Volume-time plot during tidal breathing (I), forced inspiration (II) and forced expiration (III). B Schematic tidal flow-volume curve in a normal subject and in a patient with COPD and moderate airflow obstruction.

a pulse oximeter allows a non-invasive continuous method of assessing oxygen saturation in patients who require continuous monitoring in order to assess hypoxaemia and its response to therapy, including supplemental oxygen.

Exercise tests

Formal exercise testing with measurement of metabolic gas exchange and respiratory and cardiac responses using cycle ergometry or treadmill exercise is useful in providing a detailed analysis of both pulmonary and cardiac function in the breathless patient. Exercise challenge with measurement of spirometry before and after can also be helpful in demonstrating exercise-induced asthma. Finally, the 6-minute walk test or 'shuttle' test can provide a simple but objective assessment of disability and response to treatment.

MAJOR MANIFESTATIONS OF LUNG DISEASE

COUGH

Cough is the most frequent symptom of respiratory disease. It is caused by stimulation of sensory nerves in the mucosa of the pharynx, larynx, trachea and bronchi. Sensitisation of the normal cough reflex is also observed following viral infections, oesophageal reflux, post-nasal drip, 'cough variant' asthma and in 10–15% of patients (particularly women) taking angiotensin-converting enzyme (ACE) inhibitors. Rarely, cough may also arise following stimulation of the parietal pleura: for example, during the aspiration of a pleural effusion. The nature and characteristics of cough originating at various levels of the respiratory tract are given in Box 13.8.

The explosive quality of a normal cough is lost in patients with severe airflow obstruction, respiratory muscle paralysis or vocal cord palsy. Paralysis of a single vocal cord gives rise to a prolonged, low-pitched, inefficient 'bovine' cough accompanied by hoarseness. Patients with sensitisation of the cough reflex typically have symptoms induced by changes in air temperature or exposure to cigarette smoke or perfumes. Coexistence of stridor indicates partial obstruction of a major airway (e.g. laryngeal oedema, tumour or an inhaled foreign body) and requires urgent investigation and treatment. Sputum production is common in patients with acute or chronic cough and its nature and appearance can provide valuable clues as to the aetiology (see p. 485).

Acute or transient cough most commonly relates to viral-induced lower respiratory tract infection, post-nasal drip resulting from rhinitis or sinusitis, or throat-clearing secondary to laryngitis or pharyngitis. Acute cough occurring in the context of more serious diseases such as pneumonia, aspiration, congestive heart failure or pulmonary embolism is usually easy to diagnose due to the presence of other clinical features.

Patients with chronic cough often represent more of a diagnostic challenge, especially those individuals with a normal examination, chest radiograph and lung function studies. In this context, most cough can be explained by post-nasal drip secondary to nasal or sinus disease; asthma, where cough may be the principal or exclusive clinical manifestation; or gastro-oesophageal reflux. The latter cause may require ambulatory pH monitoring or a prolonged trial of anti-reflux therapy (see p. 775) to diagnose. *Bordetella pertussis* infection in adults can also result in protracted cough and should always be suspected in those in close contact with children. While less than 1% of patients with a bronchogenic carcinoma have a normal chest radiograph on presentation, fibreoptic bronchoscopy or spiral CT of the airways is advisable in most adults with otherwise unexplained cough of recent onset (especially in smokers) as this may reveal a small intrabronchial tumour or unexpected foreign body (see Fig. 13.10).

DYSPNOEA

Breathlessness or dyspnoea can be defined as an unpleasant subjective awareness of the sensation of breathing. It is a common symptom of cardiac and respiratory disease,

13.8 COUGH		
Origin	**Common causes**	**Nature/characteristics**
Pharynx	Post-nasal drip	Usually persistent
Larynx	Laryngitis, tumour, whooping cough, croup	Harsh, barking, painful, persistent, often associated with stridor
Trachea	Tracheitis	Painful
Bronchi	Bronchitis (acute) and COPD	Dry or productive, worse in mornings
	Asthma	Dry or productive, worse at night
	Bronchial carcinoma	Persistent (often with haemoptysis)
Lung parenchyma	Tuberculosis	Productive, often with haemoptysis
	Pneumonia	Dry initially, productive later
	Bronchiectasis	Productive, changes in posture induce sputum production
	Pulmonary oedema	Often at night (may be productive of pink, frothy sputum)
	Interstitial fibrosis	Dry, irritant and distressing

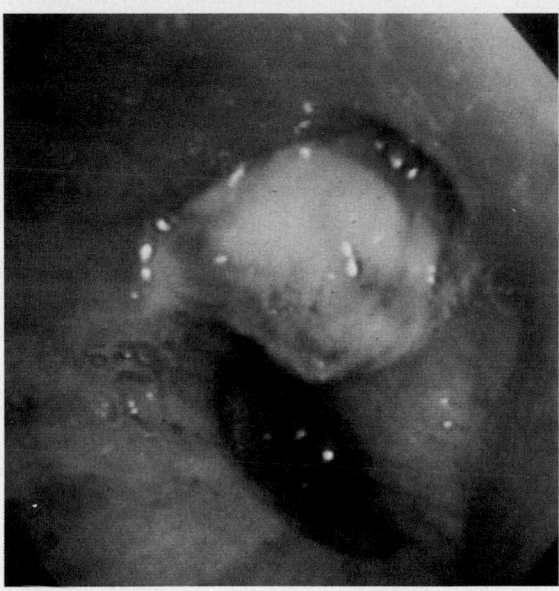

Fig. 13.10 Bronchoscopic appearances of inhaled foreign body (tooth) with a covering mucous film.

but it may occur as a result of disorders of other systems, e.g. diabetic ketoacidosis or severe anaemia.

Breathless patients with asthma or COPD often also describe a 'tight chest'. Pleural pain (see p. 499) of any cause is associated with limitation of breathing.

In broad physiological terms, patients usually perceive discomfort either from an increased ventilatory rate or drive, which can be provoked by a variety of factors, or from any disease which causes sufficient reduction of

---

13.9 PHYSIOLOGICAL BASIS OF DYSPNOEA

Increased ventilatory drive

- ↑ $Pa\mathrm{CO_2}$—e.g. COPD
- ↓ $Pa\mathrm{O_2}$—e.g. cyanotic congenital heart disease, asthma, COPD
- Acidaemia—e.g. diabetic ketoacidosis, lactic acidosis
- Exercise
- Fever

Reduced ventilatory capacity

- ↓ Lung volume, e.g. restrictive lung diseases—pneumonia, pulmonary oedema, interstitial lung diseases
- Pleural pain
- ↑ Resistance to airflow, e.g. asthma, COPD, upper airway or laryngeal obstruction

---

ventilatory capacity (see Box 13.9). Other factors, however, including the stimulation of intrapulmonary receptors (e.g. J receptors), augment the ventilatory response in many bronchopulmonary disorders.

It follows that dyspnoea often has a multifactorial aetiology, e.g. acute respiratory infections may stimulate the respiratory rate as a consequence of fever, hypoxaemia and, in severe cases, by acidaemia or hypercapnia. They may also reduce ventilatory capacity by increasing bronchial resistance and by restricting ventilation because of pleural pain.

While it is useful to understand the physiological basis of dyspnoea, patients often present either as an emergency with acute breathlessness (with prominent symptoms even at rest) or with chronic dyspnoea on exertion, and it is useful therefore to describe the causes of dyspnoea in this fashion (see Box 13.10).

13.10 SOME CAUSES OF DYSPNOEA

System	Acute dyspnoea at rest	Chronic exertional dyspnoea
Cardiovascular	*Acute pulmonary oedema (see p. 377) Myocardial ischaemia (angina equivalent) (see p. 378)	Chronic heart failure (see p. 377) Myocardial ischaemia (angina equivalent) (see p. 378)
Respiratory	*Acute severe asthma *Acute exacerbation of COPD *Pneumothorax *Pneumonia *Pulmonary embolus Acute respiratory distress syndrome Inhaled foreign body (especially in the child) Lobar collapse Laryngeal oedema (e.g. anaphylaxis)	*COPD *Chronic asthma Bronchial carcinoma Interstitial lung disease (sarcoidosis, fibrosing alveolitis, extrinsic allergic alveolitis, pneumoconiosis) Chronic pulmonary thromboembolism Lymphatic carcinomatosis (may cause intolerable dyspnoea) Large pleural effusion(s)
Others	Metabolic acidosis (e.g. diabetic ketoacidosis, lactic acidosis, uraemia, overdose of salicylates, ethylene glycol poisoning) Psychogenic hyperventilation (anxiety or panic-related)	Severe anaemia Obesity
* Denotes a common cause.		

AN APPROACH TO THE DIFFERENTIAL DIAGNOSIS IN THE PATIENT WITH CHRONIC EXERTIONAL DYSPNOEA

Chronic obstructive pulmonary disease (COPD)

There is usually a history of exertional dyspnoea, often associated with wheeze, over many months or years, with a steady decline in exercise capacity (e.g. initially breathlessness on hills and stairs, but eventually after walking a few paces on the flat). Chronic cough productive of sputum, usually most troublesome in the mornings, is the rule and there is often a history of recurrent acute exacerbations, usually in the winter months. In late disease orthopnoea, nocturnal breathlessness and ankle swelling may supervene as a result of the development of cor pulmonale.

Central cyanosis at rest or after minimal exertion, wheeze and pursing of the lips during expiration, and intercostal indrawing during inspiration are common examination findings. The antero-posterior diameter of the chest may be increased (barrel chest) and there may be a reduced crico-sternal distance with a 'tracheal tug' on inspiration.

The chest radiograph may show signs of hyperinflation and/or bullae; arterial blood gases may reveal hypoxaemia, hypercapnia and a raised plasma bicarbonate, indicating compensated type II respiratory failure. It is important to note that patients presenting with type II respiratory failure (see p. 506) may not be distressed by breathlessness. There will often be a severe obstructive defect on spirometry, with a low FEV_1 and little, if any, improvement after bronchodilator therapy.

Heart disease

It is often difficult to differentiate breathlessness due to heart disease from that caused by lung disease. A history of cough, wheezing and nocturnal breathlessness may occur in cardiac failure as well as in patients with lung disease. A history of angina or hypertension may be useful in implicating a cardiac cause (see Fig. 13.11).

On examination, an increase in heart size as judged by a displaced apex beat, a raised jugular venous pressure (JVP) and cardiac murmurs may implicate cardiac disease (although these signs can occur in severe cor pulmonale). The chest radiograph may show cardiomegaly and an ECG may provide evidence of left ventricular disease. Arterial blood gases may be of value, since in the absence of an intracardiac shunt or obvious pulmonary oedema the PaO_2 in cardiac disease is not usually reduced significantly and the $PaCO_2$ is low or normal.

Interstitial or alveolar disease of the lung

A large number of conditions can cause interstitial lung disease (see p. 550), which may be difficult to distinguish from other conditions including infiltrating malignancy and certain opportunistic lung infections (see Box 13.74, p. 551). It is imperative to elicit a detailed history, including lifetime occupation and exposure to birds and other sources of organic agents which may provoke lung disease.

The chest radiograph is nearly always abnormal, but early changes may be very subtle. Pulmonary function tests usually show a restrictive defect (reduced vital capacity) and reduced gas transfer. Arterial blood gases may show hypoxaemia, or haemoglobin desaturation may be detected by oximetry, particularly during formal exercise testing, which may be valuable in early disease; the $PaCO_2$ is seldom elevated, even in advanced disease.

Diseases of the chest wall or respiratory muscles

These are usually obvious on history, examination and chest radiography. Other rarer causes of alveolar hypoventilation, e.g. brain-stem defects, primary alveolar hypoventilation and alveolar hypoventilation in gross obesity, may cause disordered breathing and cyanosis, but these conditions are not usually associated with breathlessness. Bilateral diaphragmatic weakness or palsy results in breathlessness that is characteristically worse on lying; this is associated with a drop in the vital capacity. Patients with major chest wall abnormalities, or problems with ventilatory drive or muscle strength tend to develop problems initially during sleep, with nocturnal hypoxaemia and hypercapnia which resolve during the day.

Pulmonary thromboembolism

As will be considered below, pulmonary thromboembolism often presents with acute breathlessness with or without chest pain. However, chronic pulmonary thromboembolic disease (see p. 562) should be suspected in patients who present with more gradual onset of breathlessness, in particular those with a previous history of thromboembolic events or those with marked exertional breathlessness but a relatively normal chest radiograph. Leg swelling and an elevated JVP may arouse suspicion but clearly can also occur in cardiac failure.

Psychogenic breathlessness

Breathlessness which is not caused by organic disease of the heart or lungs is also relatively common. It creates a particularly difficult clinical problem when it occurs in patients with pre-existing disease, such as asthma or heart disease. It is possible in most patients to ascertain by careful questioning whether the sensation of breathlessness is different from that caused by exertion in the past, or dyspnoea associated with any pre-existing lung or heart disease.

Psychogenic breathlessness is usually described as an 'inability to get enough air into the lung' and this leads to extra deep breaths having to be taken. This form of breathlessness rarely disturbs sleep, but may be present after waking for another reason. Symptoms occur predominantly at rest and may even be relieved by exercise. Specialist centres use a number of features to develop a 'points' score in the assessment of this problem, often called anxiety-related hyperventilation—see Box 13.11. Occasionally, formal exercise testing may be required to be confident that patients have breathlessness which does not have an organic cause.

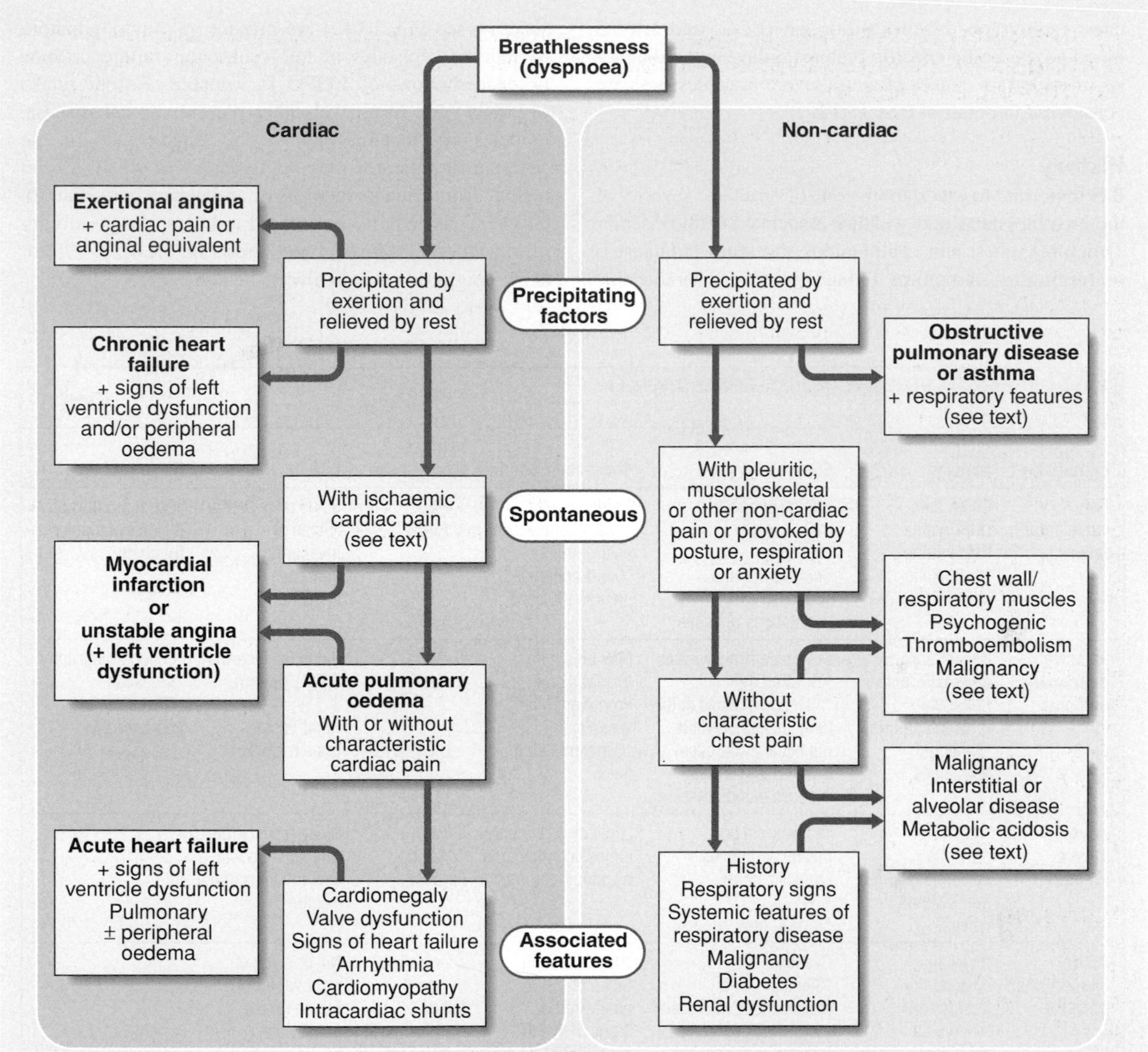

Breathlessness
(dyspnoea)

Cardiac | **Non-cardiac**

Precipitating factors

Precipitated by exertion and relieved by rest → **Exertional angina** + cardiac pain or anginal equivalent

Precipitated by exertion and relieved by rest → **Obstructive pulmonary disease or asthma** + respiratory features (see text)

Chronic heart failure + signs of left ventricle dysfunction and/or peripheral oedema

Spontaneous

With ischaemic cardiac pain (see text)

With pleuritic, musculoskeletal or other non-cardiac pain or provoked by posture, respiration or anxiety

Myocardial infarction or unstable angina (+ left ventricle dysfunction)

Chest wall/ respiratory muscles Psychogenic Thromboembolism Malignancy (see text)

Acute pulmonary oedema With or without characteristic cardiac pain

Without characteristic chest pain

Malignancy Interstitial or alveolar disease Metabolic acidosis (see text)

Acute heart failure + signs of left ventricle dysfunction Pulmonary ± peripheral oedema

Cardiomegaly Valve dysfunction Signs of heart failure Arrhythmia Cardiomyopathy Intracardiac shunts

Associated features

History Respiratory signs Systemic features of respiratory disease Malignancy Diabetes Renal dysfunction

Fig. 13.11   Features that can distinguish cardiac from non-cardiac dyspnoea. N.B. Non-cardiac dyspnoea may coexist with occult or symptomatic heart disease. Psychological factors may amplify cardiac or non-cardiac symptoms or occur in isolation.

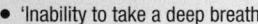

13.11 SOME FACTORS POINTING TO PSYCHOGENIC HYPERVENTILATION

- 'Inability to take a deep breath'
- Frequent sighing/erratic ventilation at rest
- Short breath-holding time in the absence of severe respiratory disease
- Difficulty in performing/inconsistent spirometry manoeuvres
- High score on Nijmegen anxiety questionnaire
- Induction of symptoms during submaximal hyperventilation
- Resting end-tidal $CO_2 < 4.5\%$

Overt 'hysterical' or panic-related hyperventilation is associated with paraesthesia in the hands and feet, cramps and carpopedal spasm due to acute respiratory alkalosis; it can present as a respiratory emergency but rarely creates a diagnostic problem. It must always,

however, be included in the differential diagnosis of acute-onset breathlessness (see Box 13.10). It is best treated with oxygen and reassurance delivered in a quiet environment rather than by rebreathing into a bag as formerly suggested.

AN APPROACH TO THE PATIENT WITH ACUTE SEVERE DYSPNOEA

Acute severe breathlessness is one of the most common medical emergencies. The presentation is often dramatic and it is easy for the inexperienced clinician to be disconcerted. Although there are usually a number of possible causes, attention to the history and a rapid but careful examination will usually suggest a diagnosis which can often be confirmed by routine investigations, including chest radiograph, electrocardiogram (ECG) and arterial blood gases. Some specific features aiding in the diagnosis of important causes of acute severe breathlessness are considered in detail in Box 13.12.

History

It is important to ascertain the rate of onset and severity of the breathlessness and whether associated cardiovascular symptoms (chest pain, palpitations, sweating and nausea) or respiratory symptoms (cough, wheeze, haemoptysis, stridor—see Fig. 13.12) are present. A previous history of repeated episodes of left ventricular failure, asthma or exacerbations of COPD is valuable. Recent intake of drugs or a history of other diseases (renal disease, diabetes or anaemia) should be established. In the severely ill patient it may be necessary to obtain a brief history from friends, relatives or ambulance personnel. In children, particularly pre-school toddlers, the possibility of inhalation of a foreign body (see Fig. 13.10, p. 495) or acute epiglottitis should always be considered.

13.12 DIFFERENTIAL DIAGNOSIS OF ACUTE SEVERE DYSPNOEA

Condition	History	Signs	Chest radiography	Arterial blood gases	ECG	Other tests
Left ventricular failure	Chest pain Orthopnoea Palpitations *A previous cardiac history	Central cyanosis JVP ($\rightarrow$ or $\uparrow$) *Sweating Cool extremities *Dullness and crepitations at bases	Cardiomegaly *Upper zone vessel enlargement *Overt oedema/ pleural effusions	$\downarrow PaO_2$ $\downarrow PaCO_2$	Sinus tachycardia *Signs of myocardial infarction Arrhythmia	*Echocardiography ($\downarrow$ left ventricular function)
Massive pulmonary embolus	Recent surgery or other risk factors Chest pain Previous pleurisy *Syncope *Dizziness	Severe central cyanosis *Elevated JVP *Absence of signs in the lung (unless previous pulmonary infarction) Shock (tachycardia, reduced blood pressure)	May be subtle changes only Prominent hilar vessels *Oligaemic lung fields	$\Downarrow PaO_2$ $\Downarrow PaCO_2$	Sinus tachycardia $S_1Q_3T_3$ pattern $\downarrow T (V_1–V_4)$ Right bundle-branch block	*Echocardiography *V̇/Q̇ scan *CT pulmonary angiography
Acute severe asthma	*History of previous episodes, asthma medications, wheeze	Tachycardia and pulsus paradoxus Cyanosis (late) *JVP $\rightarrow$ *$\Downarrow$ peak flow, rhonchi	*Hyperinflation only (unless complicated by pneumothorax)	$\downarrow PaO_2$ $\downarrow PaCO_2$ (until late)	Sinus tachycardia (bradycardia with severe hypoxaemia —late)	
Acute exacerbation of COPD	*Previous episodes (admissions) If in type II respiratory failure, may not be distressed	Cyanosis *Signs of COPD (barrel chest, intercostal indrawing, pursed lips, tracheal tug) *Signs of CO_2 retention (warm periphery, flapping tremor, bounding pulses)	*Hyperinflation Signs of emphysema Signs of events precipitating exacerbation	$\downarrow$ or $\Downarrow PaO_2$ In type II failure $PaCO_2 \uparrow$, with $\uparrow [H^+]$ and $\uparrow$ bicarbonate	Nil, or signs of right ventricular failure (in cor pulmonale)	
Pneumonia	*Prodromal illness *Fever *Rigors *Pleurisy	Fever, confusion *Pleural rub *Consolidation Cyanosis (only if severe)	*Pneumonic consolidation	$\downarrow PaCO_2$ $\downarrow PaO_2$	Tachycardia	$\uparrow$ CRP $\uparrow$ White cell count Sputum and blood culture
Metabolic acidosis	*Evidence of diabetes/renal disease *Overdose of aspirin or ethylene glycol	Fetor (ketones) *Hyperventilation without physical signs in heart or lungs *Dehydration Air hunger (Kussmaul's respiration)	Normal	*PaO_2 normal $\Downarrow PaCO_2$ $\Downarrow$ pH ($\uparrow H^+$)		
Psychogenic (a diagnosis of *exclusion*)	Previous episodes	*_Not_ cyanosed *_No_ heart signs *_No_ lung signs Carpopedal spasm	Normal	*PaO_2 normal $\Downarrow PaCO_2$ *pH normal or $\uparrow$ ($H^+ \downarrow$)		End-tidal $PaCO_2$ *Low exercise tolerance test

* Denotes a valuable discriminatory feature.

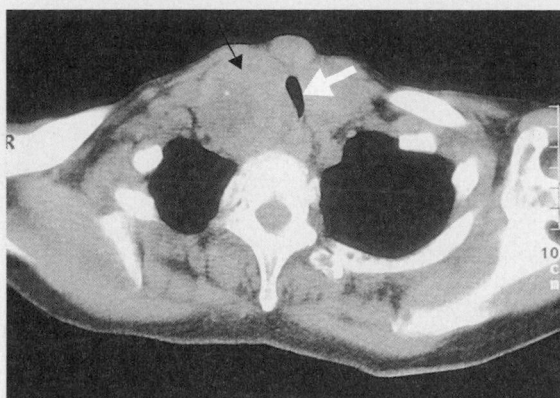

Fig. 13.12 CT showing retrosternal multinodular goitre (small arrow) causing acute severe breathlessness and stridor due to tracheal compression (large arrow).

13.13 DIFFERENTIAL DIAGNOSIS OF CHEST PAIN	
Central	
Cardiac	
• Myocardial ischaemia (angina)	• Myocarditis
• Myocardial infarction	• Pericarditis
	• Mitral valve prolapse syndrome
Aortic	
• Aortic dissection	• Aortic aneurysm
Oesophageal	
• Oesophagitis	• Mallory–Weiss syndrome
• Oesophageal spasm	
Massive pulmonary embolus	
Mediastinal	
• Tracheitis	• Malignancy
Anxiety/emotion[1]	
Peripheral	
Lungs/pleura	
• Pulmonary infarct	• Malignancy
• Pneumonia	• Tuberculosis
• Pneumothorax	• Connective tissue disorders
Musculoskeletal[2]	
• Osteoarthritis	• Costochondritis (Tietze's syndrome)
• Rib fracture/injury	
• Intercostal muscle injury	• Epidemic myalgia (Bornholm disease)
Neurological[2]	
• Prolapsed intervertebral disc	• Herpes zoster
	• Thoracic outlet syndrome

[1] May also cause peripheral chest pain.
[2] Can sometimes cause central chest pain.

Examination

The severity of the condition should be assessed immediately by the level of consciousness, degree of central cyanosis, evidence of anaphylaxis (urticaria or angio-oedema), patency of the upper airway, ability to speak (in single words or sentences), and the cardiovascular status assessed by heart rate and rhythm, blood pressure and degree of peripheral perfusion. Examination should then be targeted on digital clubbing, clinical evidence of anaemia or polycythaemia, and any clinical features of diabetes, renal failure or any other chronic disease. A detailed examination of the respiratory system should include the respiratory rate, clinical evidence of CO_2 retention, pattern of breathing, position of the trachea, degree and symmetry of chest expansion, and whether there are areas of hyper-resonance or dullness on percussion. Breath sounds should be compared on each side of the chest and at the bases, and the presence of abnormal sounds noted. The peak expiratory flow should be measured whenever possible. Leg swelling may suggest cardiac failure or venous thrombosis.

CHEST PAIN

Chest pain is a major and frequent manifestation of both cardiac and respiratory disease and is considered in detail on page 372. In general, however, lung disease only gives rise to chest pain when there is pleural or chest wall involvement and hence tends to be predominantly peripheral (see Box 13.13). Central chest pain or tightness is a feature of acute airways obstruction in asthma and COPD or may reflect disorders of the oesophagus (see p. 775) or thoracic aorta (see p. 448). Tracheitis produces severe upper chest pain worse on coughing. Persistent dull central chest pain is also a feature of malignant disease affecting the mediastinum.

HAEMOPTYSIS

Coughing up blood, irrespective of the amount, is an alarming symptom and nearly always brings the patient to the doctor. A clear history should be taken to establish that it is true haemoptysis and not haematemesis or epistaxis (nosebleed). Haemoptysis must always be assumed to have a serious cause until appropriate investigations have excluded bronchial carcinoma, thrombo-embolic disease, tuberculosis etc. (see Box 13.14).

Many episodes of haemoptysis are unexplained, even after full investigation, and are likely to be caused by simple bronchial infection. A history of repeated small haemoptyses, or blood-streaking of sputum, is highly suggestive of bronchial carcinoma. Chronic fever and weight loss may suggest tuberculosis. Pneumococcal pneumonia is often the cause of 'rusty'-coloured sputum but can cause frank haemoptysis, as can all the pneumonic infections which lead to suppuration or abscess formation (see p. 530). Bronchiectasis and intracavitary aspergilloma (see p. 541) can cause catastrophic bronchial haemorrhage and

13.14 CAUSES OF HAEMOPTYSIS

Bronchial disease

- Carcinoma*
- Bronchiectasis*
- Acute bronchitis*
- Bronchial adenoma
- Foreign body

Parenchymal disease

- Tuberculosis*
- Suppurative pneumonia
- Lung abscess
- Parasites (e.g. hydatid disease, flukes)
- Trauma
- Actinomycosis
- Aspergilloma

Lung vascular disease

- Pulmonary infarction*
- Polyarteritis nodosa
- Goodpasture's syndrome (see p. 614)
- Idiopathic pulmonary haemosiderosis

Cardiovascular disease

- Acute left ventricular failure*
- Mitral stenosis
- Aortic aneurysm

Blood disorders

- Leukaemia
- Haemophilia
- Anticoagulants

* More common causes.

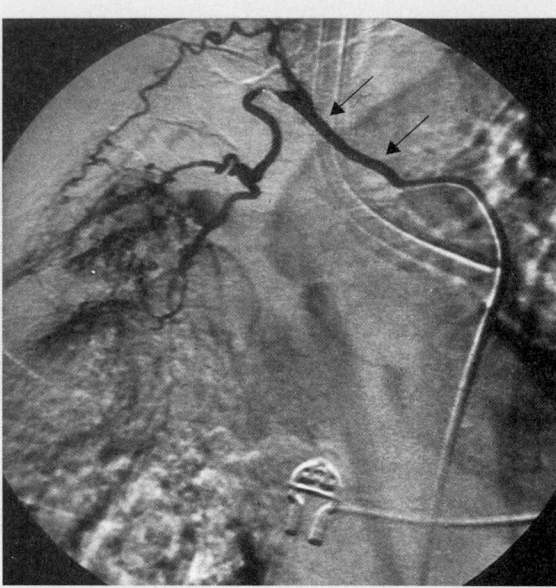

Fig. 13.13 Bronchial artery angiography. An angiography catheter has been passed via the femoral artery and aorta into an abnormally dilated right bronchial artery (arrows). Contrast is seen flowing into the lung. This patient had post-tuberculous bronchiectasis affecting the right upper lobe and presented with massive haemoptysis. Bronchial artery embolisation was successfully carried out.

in these patients there may be a history of previous tuberculosis or pneumonia in early life. Pulmonary thromboembolism is a common cause of haemoptysis and should always be considered. Major risk factors include immobilisation, malignant disease of any organ, cardiac failure and pregnancy.

Physical examination may reveal clues as to the underlying diagnosis, e.g. finger clubbing in bronchial carcinoma or bronchiectasis; other signs of malignancy such as cachexia, hepatomegaly, lymphadenopathy etc.; fever or signs of consolidation and pleurisy in pneumonia or pulmonary infarction; leg signs of deep venous thrombosis in a minority of patients with pulmonary infarction; and signs of systemic diseases including rash, purpura, haematuria, splinter haemorrhages, lymphadenopathy or splenomegaly in the uncommon systemic diseases which may be associated with haemoptysis.

Management

In catastrophic acute haemoptysis, the patient should be nursed on the side of the suspected source of bleeding, haemodynamically resuscitated and then bronchoscoped. Ideally this is performed under general anaesthesia using a rigid bronchoscope which allows optimal bronchial suction and can be used to maintain adequate ventilation during anaesthesia. Angiography and bronchial arterial embolisation (see Fig. 13.13), or even emergency pulmonary surgery, can be life-saving in the acute situation.

In the vast majority of cases, however, the haemoptysis itself is not life-threatening and it is possible to follow a logical sequence of investigations which include:

- Chest radiograph, which may give clear evidence of a localised lesion including pulmonary infarction, a tumour (malignant or benign), pneumonia or tuberculosis.
- Full blood count and other haematological tests including clotting screen.
- Bronchoscopy, which will often be necessary to exclude a central bronchial carcinoma (not visible on the chest radiograph) and to provide a tissue diagnosis in other cases of suspected bronchial neoplasia.
- Ventilation-perfusion ($\dot{V}/\dot{Q}$) lung scan, which is helpful in establishing a diagnosis of suspected pulmonary thromboembolic disease. CT pulmonary angiography may be necessary in patients with pre-existing lung disease where interpretation of the $\dot{V}/\dot{Q}$ scan can be difficult.
- CT, which is particularly useful in investigating peripheral lesions seen on the chest radiograph which may not be accessible to bronchoscopy and facilitates accurate percutaneous needle biopsy where indicated.

THE SOLITARY RADIOGRAPHIC PULMONARY LESION

Patients frequently present because they have been found to have an abnormal chest radiograph. A common clinical problem is created by the adult with few or no symptoms, who has been found to have a single peripheral lesion (nodule) detected by chest radiography. There are many causes of the 'peripheral radiograph shadow', some of which are shown in Box 13.15. Primary bronchial carcinoma is the most likely cause in a middle-aged or elderly adult, particularly if a smoker.

13.15 THE SOLITARY PULMONARY NODULE	
Common causes	
• Bronchial carcinoma • Single metastasis • Localised pneumonia	• Lung abscess • Tuberculoma • Pulmonary infarct
Uncommon causes	

• Benign tumours
• Lymphoma
• Arteriovenous malformation
• Hydatid cyst
• Bronchogenic cyst
• Rheumatoid nodule
• Pulmonary sequestration
	• Pulmonary haematoma
	• Wegener's granuloma
	• 'Pseudotumour'—fluid
	  collection in a fissure
	• Aspergilloma (usually
	  surrounded by air 'halo')

Investigations

Radiography

The single most important investigation is examination of previous radiographs, if they exist, since if a lesion has been present for more than 2 years and has not changed, it can be assumed to be non-malignant. If there are no previous radiographs or if previous films are normal, CT can be of great value in defining the lesion more precisely, demonstrating the presence of calcification and cavitation within it, and identifying whether other smaller lesions exist in other areas of the lung which may not be apparent on the conventional radiograph. The injection of intravenous contrast medium at the time of the CT provides information regarding the vascularity of the lesion, with malignant tumours tending to show greatest contrast enhancement. CT will also show hilar and mediastinal lymphadenopathy, which is important in the staging of a primary bronchial carcinoma. A positive [18]FDG-PET scan (see p. 491) is also suggestive of a malignant lesion.

Invasive procedures

Bronchoscopy is unlikely to allow direct inspection of a peripheral lesion, but a diagnosis of malignant disease or infection can be achieved by examination of bronchial washings and brushings obtained from the segment of lung in which the lesion is seen on the chest radiograph or CT. Biopsy of the lesion via the bronchoscope may be possible with the aid of radiographic screening. Percutaneous needle biopsy under CT guidance has proved to be the most effective procedure for the diagnosis of solitary pulmonary nodules with few complications (pneumothorax and haemorrhage). On occasion, a definitive diagnosis can only be made by surgical resection.

Whenever bacterial infection is included in the clinical differential diagnosis, an antibiotic should be given during the period in which the investigations are being performed; the patient should then undergo a repeat radiograph to see whether there has been a reduction in size of the opacity. In elderly patients in whom a primary malignant lesion is suspected, but who are considered unfit for any form of curative treatment, observation by repeat radiograph at intervals of a few weeks may be the most appropriate management decision.

PLEURAL EFFUSION

This term is used when serous fluid accumulates in the pleural space. The presence of frank pus (empyema) or blood (haemothorax) in the pleural space represents separate conditions; empyema is considered elsewhere (see p. 569). In general, pleural fluid accumulates as a result of either increased hydrostatic pressure or decreased osmotic pressure ('transudative effusion', as seen in cardiac, liver and renal failure), or from increased microvascular permeability due to disease of the pleural surface itself or injury in the adjacent lung ('exudative effusion'). Some causes of pleural effusion are shown in Boxes 13.16 and 13.17.

Pleural effusion may be unilateral or bilateral. Bilateral effusions often occur in cardiac failure, but are also seen in patients with connective tissue diseases and hypoproteinaemia. The likely cause of the majority of pleural effusions can usually be identified if a careful history is taken and a comprehensive clinical examination performed.

Particular attention should be paid to recent history of respiratory infection, the presence of heart, liver or renal disease, smoking history, occupation—for example, exposure to asbestos, contact with tuberculosis, and risk factors for thromboembolism such as recent immobilisation or operation.

13.16 CAUSES OF PLEURAL EFFUSION	
Common	

• Pneumonia ('para-pneumonic
  effusion')
• Tuberculosis
• Pulmonary infarction
• Malignant disease
	• Cardiac failure
	• Subdiaphragmatic disorders
	  (subphrenic abscess,
	  pancreatitis etc.)

Uncommon	

• Hypoproteinaemia (nephrotic
  syndrome, liver failure,
  malnutrition)
• Connective tissue diseases
  (particularly systemic lupus
  erythematosus and
  rheumatoid arthritis)
• Acute rheumatic fever
• Post-myocardial infarction
  syndrome
	• Meigs' syndrome (ovarian
	  tumour plus pleural
	  effusion)
	• Myxoedema
	• Uraemia
	• Asbestos-related benign
	  pleural effusion

13.17 PLEURAL EFFUSION: MAIN CAUSES AND FEATURES

Cause	Appearance of fluid	Type of fluid	Predominant cells in fluid	Other diagnostic features
Tuberculosis	Serous, usually amber-coloured	Exudate	Lymphocytes (occasionally polymorphs)	Positive tuberculin test Isolation of *M. tuberculosis* from pleural fluid (20%) Positive pleural biopsy (80%)
Malignant disease	Serous, often blood-stained	Exudate	Serosal cells and lymphocytes Often clumps of malignant cells	Positive pleural biopsy (40%) Evidence of malignant disease elsewhere
Cardiac failure*	Serous, straw-coloured	Transudate	Few serosal cells	Other evidence of left ventricular failure Response to diuretics
Pulmonary infarction*	Serous or blood-stained	Exudate (rarely transudate)	Red blood cells Eosinophils	Evidence of pulmonary infarction Source of embolism Factors predisposing to venous thrombosis
Rheumatoid disease*	Serous Turbid if chronic	Exudate	Lymphocytes (occasionally polymorphs)	Rheumatoid arthritis; rheumatoid factor in serum Cholesterol in chronic effusion; very low glucose in pleural fluid
Systemic lupus erythematosus (SLE)*	Serous	Exudate	Lymphocytes and serosal cells	Other manifestations of SLE Antinuclear factor or anti-DNA in serum
Acute pancreatitis	Serous or blood-stained	Exudate	No cells predominate	High amylase in pleural fluid (greater than in serum)
Obstruction of thoracic duct	Milky	Chyle	None	Chylomicrons

* Effusion often bilateral.

Clinical features

Symptoms and signs of pleurisy often precede the development of an effusion, especially in patients with underlying pneumonia, pulmonary infarction or connective tissue disease. Frequently, however, the onset is insidious. Breathlessness is the only symptom related to the effusion and the severity depends on the size and rate of accumulation of the fluid. The physical signs in the chest are those of fluid in the pleural space—namely, reduced chest wall movement on the affected side, stony dullness on percussion, and reduced or absent breath sounds and vocal resonance. Large effusions cause displacement of the trachea and mediastinum to the opposite side.

Investigations

Radiological examination

The chest radiograph shows a dense uniform opacity in the lower and lateral parts of the hemithorax, shading off above and medially into translucent lung (see Fig. 13.14). Occasionally, the fluid is localised below the lower lobe ('subpulmonary effusion'), the appearances simulating an elevated hemidiaphragm. A localised opacity may be seen when the effusion is loculated—for example, in an interlobar fissure.

Ultrasonography

This investigation is invaluable in differentiating between a loculated pleural effusion and pleural tumour and allows examination of the diaphragm and subdiaphragmatic space. It also helps to localise an effusion prior to aspiration and pleural biopsy.

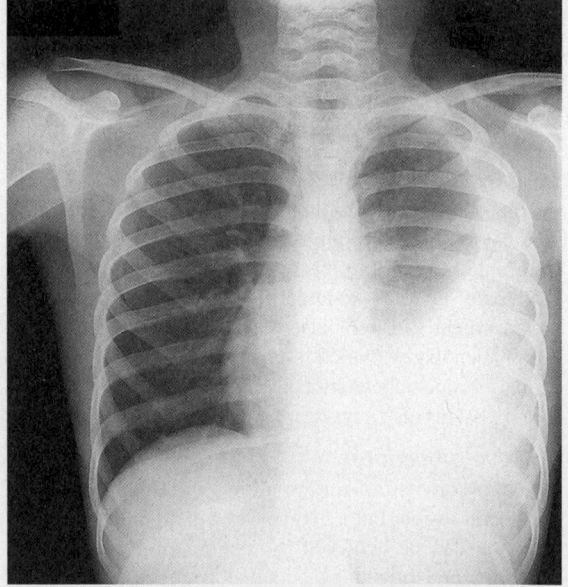

Fig. 13.14 Pleural effusion. Chest radiograph showing the characteristic opacification of a large left-sided effusion.

Pleural aspiration and pleural biopsy

Absolute proof that an effusion is present can be obtained only by the aspiration of fluid. Since the chances of obtaining a diagnosis from pleural biopsy material are much greater than by examination of the pleural liquid alone, pleural biopsy is always indicated whenever a diagnostic aspiration of pleural fluid is performed. Ideally, ultrasound or CT should be used to indicate the most appropriate site for pleural aspiration and biopsy. If these are not readily available, the pleural biopsy needle should be inserted through an intercostal space at the area of maximum dullness on percussion and at the site of maximum radiological opacity as shown by postero-anterior and lateral films. At least 50 ml of fluid should be withdrawn initially, aliquots being placed in separate containers for microbiological examination (including culture for tuberculosis), cytology and biochemical examination. Whenever there is a strong suspicion of tuberculosis, a large volume of pleural liquid should be submitted to the laboratory. Pleural biopsies should be taken after the initial pleural fluid sample has been aspirated for diagnostic purposes and before further drainage is undertaken.

The appearance of the fluid can be straw-coloured, blood-stained, purulent or chylous. Knowledge of the biochemical characteristics of pleural fluid can be very valuable in determining the aetiology of a pleural effusion. The most useful indices to measure are protein, lactate dehydrogenase, glucose and pH (see Fig. 13.15). The predominant cell type (neutrophil, eosinophil, lymphocyte, red blood cell) provides useful information, and fluid should always be examined for malignant cells.

Other investigations

Estimation of the total and differential peripheral blood leucocyte count, a tuberculin test and examination of the sputum for tubercle bacilli should be routine in most situations. A chest radiograph may disclose an underlying pulmonary lesion and indicate its nature. If the lung is obscured by a massive effusion, the radiograph should be repeated after the fluid has been aspirated. Other investigations which may be of help include bronchoscopy, biopsy or aspiration of enlarged regional lymph nodes, thoracoscopy and serological tests for antinuclear and rheumatoid factors.

The main diagnostic features and more important causes of pleural effusion are shown in Box 13.17.

Management

Aspiration of pleural fluid may be necessary to relieve breathlessness. It is inadvisable to remove more than 1 litre on the first occasion because 're-expansion' pulmonary oedema occasionally follows the aspiration of larger amounts. A pneumothorax may be produced even by a careful operator, and a chest radiograph must always be taken after the procedure.

Treatment of the underlying cause—for example, heart failure, pneumonia, pulmonary embolism or subphrenic abscess—will often be followed by resolution of the effusion. However, certain conditions require special measures as detailed below.

Para-pneumonic pleural effusion

Pleural effusions complicating pneumonia require complete and often repeated aspiration to ensure that an empyema

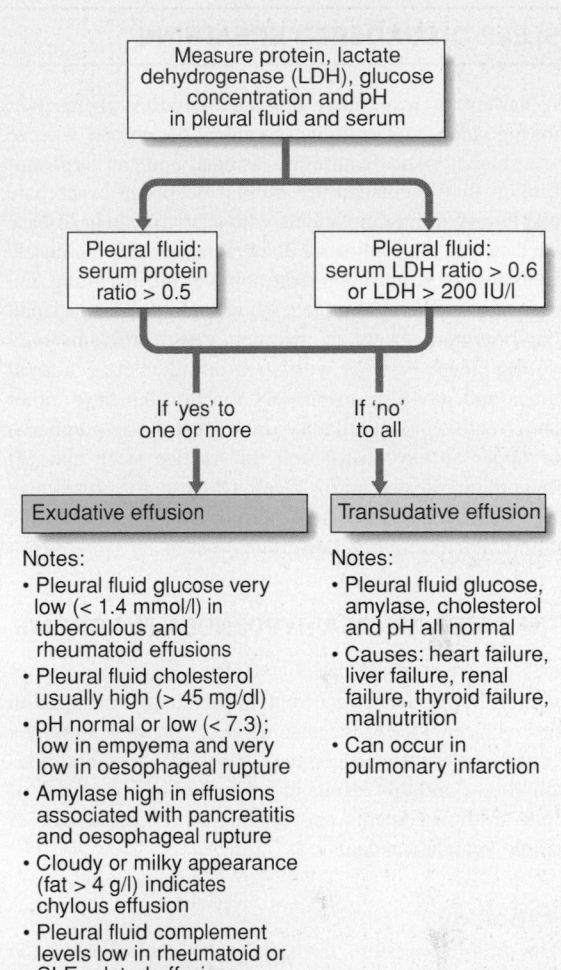

Fig. 13.15   Pleural effusion. Biochemical characteristics.

has not developed and that one does not develop, and to reduce the extent of pleural thickening.

Tuberculous pleural effusion

Patients with tuberculous effusions should always receive antituberculosis chemotherapy (see p. 538). Aspiration is required initially if the effusion is large and causing breathlessness. The addition of prednisolone 20 mg daily by mouth for 4–6 weeks in patients with large effusions will promote rapid absorption of the fluid, obviate the need for further aspiration and may prevent fibrosis.

Malignant effusions

Effusions caused by malignant infiltration of the pleural surfaces usually reaccumulate rapidly. To avoid the distress of repeated aspirations, an attempt should be made to drain all fluid via an intercostal tube and then obliterate the pleural space (pleurodesis) by the injection of substances which produce an inflammatory reaction and extensive pleural adhesions. The agents most frequently used are talc and tetracycline.

SLEEP-DISORDERED BREATHING

A variety of respiratory disorders manifest themselves during sleep. For example, nocturnal cough and wheeze are characteristic features of asthma, and the hypoventilation that occurs during normal sleep can exacerbate respiratory failure in patients with restrictive lung disease such as kyphoscoliosis, diaphragmatic palsy, muscle weakness (e.g. muscular dystrophy) or intrinsic lung disease (e.g. COPD, pulmonary fibrosis). In contrast, a small but important group of disorders cause problems only during sleep. Patients with such disorders have normal lungs and day-time respiratory function but have either abnormalities of ventilatory drive (central sleep apnoea) or upper airway obstruction (obstructive sleep apnoea) that are manifested during sleep. Of these, the obstructive sleep apnoea/hypopnoea syndrome is by far the most common and important disorder.

THE SLEEP APNOEA/HYPOPNOEA SYNDROME

It is now recognised that 2–4% of the middle-aged population suffer from recurrent upper airway obstruction during sleep. Due to the ensuing sleep fragmentation they experience day-time sleepiness, especially in monotonous situations, and this results in a threefold increased risk of road traffic accidents and a ninefold increased risk of single-vehicle accidents.

Aetiology

The problem results from recurrent occlusion of the pharynx during sleep, most often starting at the level of the soft palate. On inspiration the pressure in the throat is subatmospheric. During wakefulness upper airway dilating muscles—including the palatoglossus and genioglossus—actively contract during each inspiration to preserve airway patency. During sleep, muscle tone declines and the ability of the upper airway dilating muscles to maintain pharyngeal patency falls. In most people sufficient tone persists to result in uncompromised breathing during sleep. However, in those who for some reason have a narrow throat when awake, upper airway muscle tone is more important and when it falls during sleep the airway narrows. If the narrowing is slight, turbulent flow and vibration occur, resulting in snoring; around 40% of middle-aged men and 20% of middle-aged women snore. If the upper airway narrowing progresses to the point of occlusion or near-occlusion, sleeping subjects increase respiratory effort to try to breathe until the increased effort transiently awakens them, so briefly that they have no recollection, but long enough for the upper airway dilating muscles to open the airway again. Then a series of deep breaths are taken before the subject rapidly returns to sleep, snores and becomes apnoeic once more. This recurrent cycle of apnoea, awakening, apnoea, awakening etc. may repeat itself many hundreds of times per night and result in severe sleep fragmentation. The awakenings are associated with surges in blood pressure which may lead to an increased frequency of hypertension, ischaemic heart disease and stroke.

Predisposing factors to the sleep apnoea/hypopnoea syndrome include being male, which doubles the risk, probably due to a testosterone effect on the upper airway, and obesity, found in about half the patients and having the effect of narrowing the throat by parapharyngeal fat deposits. Nasal obstruction or anomalies of the upper airway can further exacerbate the problem. Acromegaly and hypothyroidism also predispose individuals to this condition by causing submucosal infiltration and narrowing of the upper airway. The condition is often familial, and in these families the maxilla and mandible are back-set, thus narrowing the upper airway. Alcohol and sedatives predispose to snoring and apnoeas by relaxing the upper airway dilating muscles.

Clinical features

Excessive day-time sleepiness is the principal symptom and snoring is virtually universal. The patient usually feels that he or she has been asleep all night but wakes unrefreshed. Bed partners report loud snoring in all body positions and will often have noticed multiple breathing pauses (apnoeas). Difficulty with concentration, impaired cognitive function and work performance, depression, irritability and nocturia are other features.

Investigations

Provided that the sleepiness does not result from inadequate time in bed or from shift work etc., any person who falls asleep during the day when not in bed, who complains that his or her work is impaired by sleepiness, or who is a habitual snorer with multiple witnessed apnoeas should be referred to a sleep or respiratory specialist. A more quantitative assessment of day-time sleepiness can be obtained by questionnaire (see Box 13.18).

Overnight studies of breathing, oxygenation and sleep quality are diagnostic (see Fig. 13.16) but the level of

---

13.18 EPWORTH SLEEPINESS SCALE

How likely are you to doze off or fall asleep in the situations described below? Use the following scale to choose the most appropriate number for each situation:

0 = would never doze
1 = slight chance of dozing
2 = moderate chance of dozing
3 = high chance of dozing

- Sitting and reading
- Watching TV
- Sitting, inactive in a public place (e.g. a theatre or a meeting)
- As a passenger in a car for an hour without a break
- Lying down to rest in the afternoon when circumstances permit
- Sitting and talking to someone
- Sitting quietly after a lunch without alcohol
- In a car, while stopped for a few minutes in the traffic

Normal subjects average 5.9 (S.D. 2.2) and patients with severe obstructive sleep apnoea average 16.0 (S.D. 4.4)

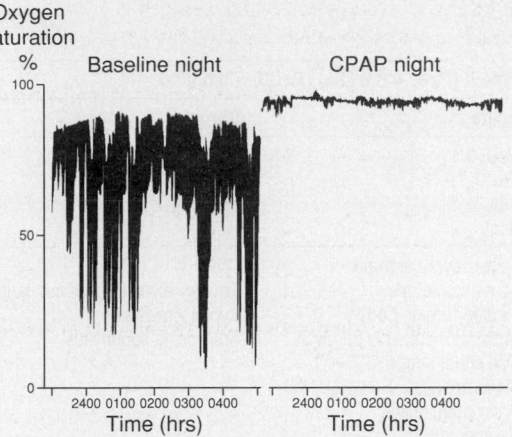

Fig. 13.16 **Sleep apnoea/hypopnoea syndrome: overnight oxygen saturation trace.** The left panel shows the trace of a 46-year-old patient during a night when he slept without continuous positive airway pressure (CPAP) and had 53 apnoeas plus hypopnoeas/hour, 55 brief awakenings/hour and marked oxygen desaturation. The right panel shows the next night when he slept with a CPAP of 10 cm H_2O delivered through a tight-fitting nasal mask which abolished his breathing irregularity and awakenings and improved his oxygenation.

complexity of investigations will vary depending on the probability of diagnosis, differential diagnosis and resources. The current threshold for diagnosing the sleep apnoea/hypopnoea syndrome is 15 apnoeas/hypopnoeas per hour of sleep, where an apnoea is a 10-second or longer breathing pause and a hypopnoea a 10-second or longer 50% reduction in breathing.

Differential diagnosis
A number of other conditions can cause day-time sleepiness but these can usually be excluded by a careful history (see Box 13.19). Narcolepsy is a rare cause of sleepiness,

13.19 DIFFERENTIAL DIAGNOSIS OF PERSISTENT SLEEPINESS
Lack of sleep
• Inadequate time in bed • Extraneous sleep disruption (e.g. babies/children) • Shift work • Excessive caffeine intake • Physical illness (e.g. pain)
Sleep disruption
• Sleep apnoea/hypopnoea syndrome • Periodic limb movement disorder (recurrent limb movements during non-REM sleep, frequent nocturnal awakenings)
Sleepiness with relatively normal sleep
• Narcolepsy • Idiopathic hypersomnolence (rare) • Neurological lesions (e.g. hypothalamic or upper brain-stem infarcts or tumours) • Drugs
Psychological/psychiatric
• Depression

occurring in 0.05% of the population (see p. 1133), and is associated with cataplexy (when muscle tone is lost in fully conscious people in response to emotional triggers and they may flop over—see p. 1133), hypnagogic hallucinations (hallucinations at sleep onset) and sleep paralysis. Idiopathic hypersomnolence occurs in younger individuals and is characterised by long nocturnal sleeps.

Management
In a few patients advice to avoid evening alcohol and lose weight suffices, but most need to use continuous positive airway pressure (CPAP) delivered by a nasal mask every night at home. CPAP keeps the throat open by making the upper airway pressure above atmospheric. The pressure for CPAP is set in the laboratory to the lowest that will prevent apnoeas, hypopnoeas and awakenings. The effect is often dramatic (see Fig. 13.16) and CPAP results in improvements in symptoms, day-time performance, quality of life and survival. Unfortunately, 30–50% of patients are poorly compliant or do not tolerate such therapy. There is no evidence that upper airway surgery has any role in the management of this condition but mandibular advancement devices may be effective in some patients.

RESPIRATORY FAILURE

Respiratory failure results from a disorder in which lung function is inadequate for the metabolic requirements of the individual. Its classification into type I and type II relates to the absence or presence of hypercapnia (raised $PaCO_2$). A summary of respiratory failure and its characteristic blood gas abnormalities is shown in Box 13.20.

Management of acute type I respiratory failure
The most common causes of acute type I respiratory failure ($PaO_2 < 8.0$ kPa) are listed in Box 13.21.

All patients should be treated with a high-concentration ($\geq 35\%$) of oxygen delivered by an oronasal mask. Young children may need to be treated in oxygen tents, since few of them tolerate masks. Very ill patients may require immediate ventilatory support, often involving tracheal intubation and mechanical ventilation (see p. 204). Effective management requires prompt diagnosis and treatment of the underlying disorder. Close monitoring is essential and arterial blood gases taken on presentation should be repeated within 20 minutes to establish that treatment has achieved acceptable PaO_2 levels. If there is no improvement despite treating the underlying condition, an early decision about mechanical ventilation is necessary. In acute left ventricular failure, in massive pulmonary embolism and when pulmonary infarction or pneumonia is the cause of pleural pain, treatment with opiates is entirely appropriate, but these drugs should never be used in asthma or COPD, except immediately prior to and during assisted mechanical ventilation.

13.20 RESPIRATORY FAILURE

	Type I (PaO_2 < 8.0 kPa) ($PaCO_2$ < 6.6 kPa)		Type II (PaO_2 < 8.0 kPa) ($PaCO_2$ > 6.6 kPa)	
	Acute	**Chronic**	**Acute**	**Chronic**
Typical blood gases	$PaO_2\downarrow\downarrow$ $PaCO_2\leftrightarrow$ or $\downarrow$ pH $\leftrightarrow$ or $\downarrow\downarrow$ $HCO_3\leftrightarrow$	$PaO_2\downarrow$ $PaCO_2\leftrightarrow$ pH $\leftrightarrow$ $HCO_3\leftrightarrow$	$PaO_2\downarrow$ $PaCO_2\uparrow$ pH$\downarrow$ $HCO_3\leftrightarrow$	$PaO_2\downarrow$ $PaCO_2\uparrow$ pH$\downarrow$ or $\leftrightarrow$ $HCO_3\uparrow$
Causes	Acute asthma Pulmonary embolus Pulmonary oedema ARDS Pneumothorax Pneumonia	Emphysema Lung fibrosis Lymphangitis carcinomatosa Right-to-left shunts Anaemia	Acute severe asthma Acute epiglottitis Inhaled foreign body Respiratory muscle paralysis Flail chest injury Sleep apnoea Brain-stem lesion Narcotic drugs	COPD Primary alveolar hypoventilation Kyphoscoliosis Ankylosing spondylitis
Therapy	Treat underlying disorder High-concentration O_2 Mechanical ventilation if necessary	Treat underlying disorder Controlled long-term O_2	Treat underlying disorder Controlled low-concentration O_2 Mechanical ventilation (or tracheostomy) if necessary	Treat underlying disorder Controlled long-term O_2 Mechanical ventilatory support if necessary

13.21 COMMON CAUSES OF ACUTE TYPE I RESPIRATORY FAILURE

- Acute severe asthma (causes type II failure when life-threatening)—see page 519
- Acute exacerbation of COPD (also causes type II failure)—see page 512
- Left ventricular failure and other causes of pulmonary oedema—see page 377
- Pulmonary embolism—see page 562
- Pneumonia—see page 526
- Pneumothorax—see page 570
- ARDS—see page 198

13.22 SOME CAUSES OF 'ACUTE ON CHRONIC' TYPE II RESPIRATORY FAILURE

- Retention of secretions
- Infection
- Bronchospasm
- Pulmonary embolus
- Cardiac failure
- Rib fractures/intercostal muscle tears
- Pneumothorax
- Central nervous system depression (narcotic drugs)

Management of type II respiratory failure

Acute

In acute type II respiratory failure, also known as asphyxia, CO_2 retention occurs ($PaCO_2$ > 6.6 kPa) and causes severe acute respiratory acidosis (see Box 13.20). Treatment is aimed at immediate or very rapid reversal of the precipitating event—e.g. dislodgement of a laryngeal foreign body or tracheostomy, fixation of ribs in a flail chest injury, reversal of narcotic poisons, treatment of acute severe asthma etc. In some cases it will be necessary to support ventilation temporarily by means of non-invasive ventilation (see p. 204) or intubation and mechanical ventilation if the condition causing respiratory failure cannot immediately be reversed.

Chronic

The most common cause of chronic type II respiratory failure is COPD. Here CO_2 retention may occur on a chronic basis, the potential for acidaemia being corrected by renal conservation of bicarbonate, which results in the plasma pH remaining within the normal range. The status quo is often maintained until there is a further pulmonary insult (see Box 13.22), such as an exacerbation of COPD which precipitates an episode of 'acute on chronic' respiratory failure.

The further acute increase in $PaCO_2$ results in acidaemia and worsening hypercapnia, and may lead to drowsiness and eventually coma. The principal aim of treatment in type II respiratory failure is to achieve a safe PaO_2 (PaO_2 > 7.0 kPa) without inducing extremes of $PaCO_2$ or pH while identifying and treating the precipitating condition (see Box 13.22). It is important to note that in the patient who already has severe lung disease, only a small insult may be required to tip the balance towards catastrophic respiratory failure. Moreover, in contrast to acute severe asthma, a patient with type II respiratory failure due to COPD may not be overtly distressed despite being critically ill with severe hypoxaemia, hypercapnia and acidaemia.

In the initial assessment it is important to evaluate the patient's conscious level and his or her ability to respond to commands, particularly the ability to cough effectively. This may give a preliminary indication of whether intubation and tracheal suction may be necessary to clear secretions or whether physiotherapy will be helpful. The decision regarding mechanical ventilation can be complex and difficult. Ideally, an early decision should be made, based mainly on whether there is a potentially remediable precipitating condition (see Box 13.22) and whether the patient is likely to regain an acceptable quality of life. It is important to remember that while physical signs of CO_2 retention (confusion, flapping tremor, bounding pulses etc.) can be helpful if present, they are often unreliable; there is no substitute for arterial blood gases in the assessment of initial severity and response to treatment.

Prompt intervention may occasionally be necessary for some precipitating conditions, e.g. intercostal tube drainage of pneumothoraces or injection with local anaesthetic for fractured ribs and torn muscles; such interventions can result in a dramatic improvement of respiratory function (see Box 13.23). Generally, however, treatment is empirical and includes low-concentration controlled oxygen therapy (24–28% oxygen), physiotherapy, bronchodilators, broad-spectrum antibiotics and diuretics (see p. 512). While the dangers of hypercapnia should not be under-estimated, it is important to recognise that severe hypoxaemia must be reversed if the patient is not to suffer potentially fatal arrhythmias or severe cerebral complications. The aim of oxygen therapy is not necessarily to achieve a normal PaO_2; even a small increment of increase in the PaO_2 will often have a greatly beneficial

effect on oxygen delivery to tissues since the arterial values of these patients are often on the very steep part of the oxygen saturation curve. If controlled oxygen treatment causes an increase in the $PaCO_2$ associated with a reduction in pH, invasive or non-invasive ventilatory support (see p. 203) may be required. Doxapram (1.5–4 mg min^{-1}) by slow intravenous infusion should only be used as a respiratory stimulant where non-invasive ventilation is not available or is poorly tolerated, or in those with reduced respiratory drive due to sedatives or anaesthetic agents. Even in these circumstances this agent provides only minor and transient improvements in arterial blood gas parameters.

OXYGEN THERAPY

The delivery of oxygen to tissue mitochondria is controlled by factors exerting influences at various levels, including: inspired oxygen concentration (FiO_2); alveolar ventilation; ventilation-perfusion distribution within the lung; haemoglobin and concentrations of agents such as carbon monoxide which may bind to haemoglobin; influences on the oxygen-haemoglobin dissociation curve (see p. 192); cardiac output; and distribution of capillary blood flow within the tissues.

Many of the causes of hypoxaemia (see Box 13.21) are corrected by increasing the FiO_2, but right-to-left shunting, either through circulatory channels bypassing the lung or through parts of the lung in which the alveoli are inaccessible to inspired oxygen, is less susceptible to such therapeutic approaches. The increased amount of dissolved oxygen carried by the blood which has perfused alveoli with a high PaO_2 can saturate the haemoglobin in small quantities of shunted blood, but persistence of cyanosis when 100% oxygen is breathed indicates that the shunt is larger than 20% of the cardiac output.

The consequences of severe hypoxaemia include: systemic hypotension, pulmonary hypertension, polycythaemia, tachycardia, and undesirable cerebral consequences ranging from confusion to coma.

The objectives of oxygen therapy are:

- to overcome the reduced partial pressure and quantity of oxygen in the blood
- to increase the quantity of oxygen carried in solution in the plasma, even when the haemoglobin is fully saturated.

Adverse effects

100% oxygen is both irritant and toxic if inhaled for more than a few hours. Premature infants develop retrolental fibroplasia and blindness if exposed to excessive concentrations. In adults, pulmonary oxygen toxicity (as manifested by pulmonary oedema) would not be expected to occur unless the patient had been treated with inappropriately high concentrations of oxygen for more than 24 hours.

13.23 ASSESSMENT AND MANAGEMENT OF 'ACUTE ON CHRONIC' TYPE II RESPIRATORY FAILURE

Initial assessment

N.B. Patient may not appear distressed despite being critically ill.

- Conscious level (response to commands, ability to cough)
- CO_2 retention (warm periphery, bounding pulses, flapping tremor)
- Airways obstruction (wheeze, intercostal indrawing, pursed lips, tracheal 'tug')
- Right heart failure (peripheral oedema, raised JVP, hepatomegaly, ascites)
- Background functional status and quality of life
- Signs of precipitating event (see Box 13.22)

Investigations

- Arterial blood gases (severity of hypoxaemia, hypercapnia and acidaemia)
- Chest radiograph

Management

- Maintenance of airway
- Treatment of specific precipitating event (see Box 13.22)
- Frequent physiotherapy ± pharyngeal suction
- Nebulised bronchodilators
- Controlled oxygen therapy
  Start with 24% controlled-flow mask
  Aim for a $PaO_2 \geq 7$ kPa (a $PaO_2 < 5$ is very dangerous)
- Antibiotics
- Diuretics

Progress

- If $PaCO_2$ continues to rise or patient cannot achieve a safe PaO_2 without severe hypercapnia and acidaemia, respiratory stimulants (e.g. doxapram) or mechanical ventilatory support may be required

Administration

Oxygen should always be prescribed in writing with clearly specified flow rates or concentrations.

- *High concentrations for short periods*, such as 60% oxygen via a high-flow mask, are particularly useful in acute type I respiratory failure such as commonly occurs in pneumonia or asthma.
- *Low concentrations*, via a 24% or 28% controlled-flow mask, are the most accurate method of delivering controlled oxygen therapy, particularly in type II respiratory failure. However, when a low concentration of oxygen is required continuously for more than a few hours, 1–2 litres per minute delivered via nasal double cannulae allows patients to eat and to undergo physiotherapy etc. while continuing to receive oxygen. When high-flow masks are used, the oxygen should be humidified by passing it over warm water. This is not necessary with low-flow masks or nasal cannulae, as a high proportion of atmospheric air is mixed with oxygen.
- *Chronic oxygen delivery* from cylinders delivered to the home, or more conveniently from an oxygen concentrator, is often given via a low-concentration mask or nasal cannulae. Assessment for long-term oxygen therapy requires that patients should have a PaO_2 of less than 7.3 kPa breathing air and an FEV_1 of less than 1.5 litres in the steady state (i.e. at least 1 month since the previous exacerbation) (see p. 512). Long-term oxygen delivery has also been achieved by transtracheal microcatheters which have proved to be both oxygen-saving and of cosmetic benefit.

MECHANICAL VENTILATION

Patients with initially severe respiratory failure (type I or type II) or those who fail to improve despite optimal medical therapy may require mechanical ventilation. The various types of invasive (via an endotracheal tube) or non-invasive (via a face or nasal mask) ventilation are detailed on page 204. In many patients with respiratory failure, intermittent positive pressure ventilation (IPPV) with full sedation is indicated but nasal positive pressure ventilation (NPPV), delivered by a nasal mask, has proved to be of great value in the treatment of acute on chronic and chronic respiratory failure. Patients who benefit most from long-term (usually nocturnal) NPPV are those with skeletal deformity, especially kyphoscoliosis, and neuromuscular disease. However, NPPV can also be of value in some patients with central alveolar hypoventilation. It is now in widespread use in the acute situation in patients with COPD and type II respiratory failure, usually to try to avoid tracheal intubation and IPPV, but also in weaning such patients from mechanical ventilation.

LUNG TRANSPLANTATION

Lung transplantation is now an established treatment for carefully selected patients with advanced cardiopulmonary disease unresponsive to medical treatment. Transplantation of both heart and lungs was the first successful approach for many disorders (see Box 13.24). However, improved surgical techniques and the shortage of donor organs have led to the development of isolated lung transplantation using double or single lungs. More recently, living lobar transplantation has been introduced. Single-lung transplantation is best applied for older patients with emphysema and patients with intrapulmonary restrictive disorders such as lung fibrosis. It is contraindicated in patients with chronic bilateral pulmonary infection, such as cystic fibrosis and bronchiectasis, where bilateral lung transplantation is the favoured option. Combined transplantation of the heart and lungs remains necessary for the treatment of patients with advanced congenital heart disease such as Eisenmenger's syndrome and is preferred by some surgeons for the treatment of primary pulmonary hypertension unresponsive to prostenoid therapy.

13.24 SOME INDICATIONS FOR HEART-LUNG TRANSPLANTATION	
Parenchymatous lung disease	
• Cystic fibrosis	• Langerhans cell histiocytosis
• Emphysema	• Lymphangioleiomyomatosis
• Pulmonary fibrosis	• Obliterative bronchiolitis
Pulmonary vascular disease	
• Primary pulmonary hypertension	• Veno-occlusive disease
• Thromboembolic pulmonary hypertension	• Eisenmenger's syndrome (see p. 470)

OBSTRUCTIVE PULMONARY DISEASES

CHRONIC OBSTRUCTIVE PULMONARY DISEASE (COPD)

Chronic obstructive pulmonary disease is the internationally preferred term encompassing chronic bronchitis and emphysema. By definition COPD is a chronic, slowly progressive disorder characterised by airflow obstruction ($FEV_1 < 80\%$ predicted and FEV_1/VC ratio $< 70\%$) which does not change markedly over several months. The impairment of lung function is largely fixed but may be partially reversible by bronchodilator therapy. Historically, the term 'chronic bronchitis' was used to define any patient who coughed up sputum on most days of at least 3 consecutive months for more than 2 successive years (provided other causes of cough had been excluded) and 'emphysema' referred to the pathological process of a permanent destructive enlargement of the airspaces distal to the terminal bronchioles. Although 'pure' forms of these two conditions do exist, there is considerable overlap in the vast majority of patients.

The death rate from COPD currently exceeds 25 000/year (> 20-fold higher than asthma) in England and Wales and this condition accounts for over 10% of all hospital medical admissions in the United Kingdom.

Aetiology and natural history

The single most important cause of COPD is cigarette smoking although in developing countries exposure to smoke from biomass and solid fuel fires is also important. Smoking is thought to have its effect by inducing persistent airway inflammation and causing a direct imbalance in oxidant/antioxidant capacity and proteinase/antiproteinase load in the lungs. Individual susceptibility to smoking is, however, very wide, with only 15% of smokers likely to develop clinically significant COPD. Recent studies have also emphasised the strong familial risks associated with the development of COPD, with the incidence of disease in an individual who smokes and has an affected sibling being 4.7 times that of matched controls. A small additional contribution to the severity of COPD has been reported in patients exposed to dusty or polluted air. An association also exists between low birth weight, bronchial hyper-responsiveness and the development of COPD. Alpha$_1$-antitrypsin deficiency can cause emphysema in non-smokers but this risk is increased dramatically in enzyme-deficient patients who smoke. Stopping smoking slows the average rate of the decline in FEV$_1$ from 50–70 ml/year to 30 ml/year (i.e. equal to non-smokers) (see Fig. 13.17). Interestingly, there is no evidence that acute exacerbations or drug therapy affect the rate of decline of the FEV$_1$.

Pathology

Most patients develop airway wall inflammation, hypertrophy of the mucus-secreting glands and an increase in the number of goblet cells in the bronchi and bronchioles with a consequent decrease in ciliated cells. There is, therefore,

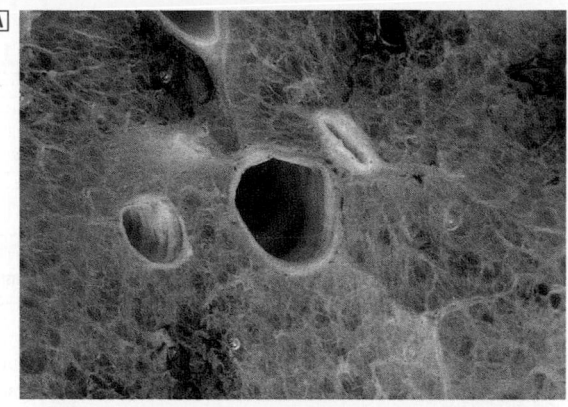

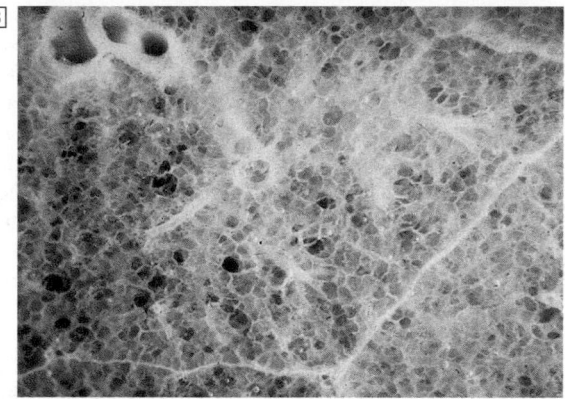

Fig. 13.18   The pathology of emphysema. A Normal lung. B Emphysematous lung showing gross loss of the normal surface area available for gas exchange.

less efficient transport of the increased mucus in the airways. Airflow limitation reflects both mechanical obstruction in the small airways and loss of pulmonary elastic recoil. Loss of alveolar attachments around such airways makes them more liable to collapse during expiration.

Emphysema is usually centriacinar, involving respiratory bronchioles, alveolar ducts and centrally located alveoli. More rarely, panacinar emphysema (see Fig. 13.18) or paraseptal emphysema develops, with the latter responsible for blebs on the lung surface and/or giant bullae. Pulmonary vascular remodelling caused by persistent hypoxaemia results in pulmonary hypertension and right ventricular hypertrophy and dilatation.

Clinical features

The clinical state is dictated largely by the severity of disease (see Box 13.25). The initial symptoms are usually repeated attacks of productive cough, usually after colds during the winter months, which show a steady increase in severity and duration with successive years until cough is present all the year round. Thereafter, patients suffer recurrent respiratory infections, exertional breathlessness, regular morning cough, wheeze and occasionally chest tightness. Sputum may be scanty, mucoid, tenacious and occasionally streaked with blood during infective exacerbations. Frankly

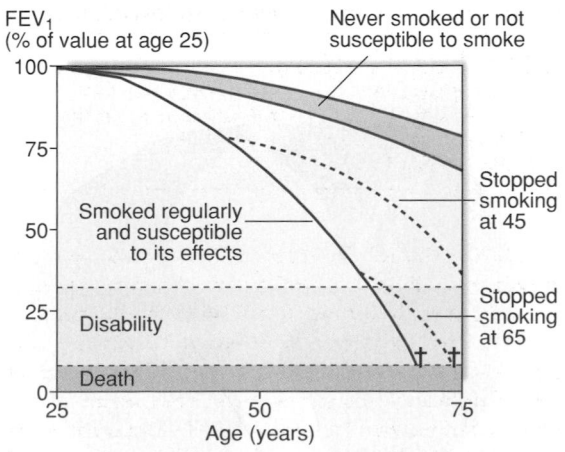

Fig. 13.17   Model of annual decline in FEV$_1$ with accelerated decline in susceptible smokers. When smoking is stopped, subsequent loss is similar to that in healthy non-smokers.

13.25 CLASSIFICATION AND DIAGNOSIS OF COPD		
Severity	**Spirometry**	**Symptoms**
Mild	FEV$_1$ 60–79% predicted	Smoker's cough ± exertional breathlessness
Moderate	FEV$_1$ 40–59% predicted	Exertional breathlessness ± wheeze, cough ± sputum
Severe	FEV$_1$ < 40% predicted	Breathlessness, wheeze and cough prominent, swollen legs

purulent sputum is indicative of bacterial infection, which often occurs in these patients. Breathlessness is aggravated by infection, excessive cigarette smoking and adverse atmospheric conditions.

In patients with mild to moderate disease the respiratory examination may be normal. However, variable numbers of inspiratory and expiratory rhonchi, mainly low- and medium-pitched, are audible in most patients. Crepitations (crackles) which usually, but not always, disappear after coughing may be audible over the lower zones.

Physical signs associated with severe disease are outlined in Box 13.26. These reflect pulmonary hyperinflation, hypoxaemia, the development of cor pulmonale (pulmonary hypertension and right heart failure) and polycythaemia.

Complications

Pulmonary bullae are thin-walled airspaces created by rupture of alveolar walls. They may be single or multiple, large or small, and tend to be situated subpleurally. Rupture of subpleural bullae may cause pneumothorax (see p. 570), and occasionally bullae increase in size, compress functioning lung tissue and further embarrass pulmonary ventilation. Respiratory failure and cor pulmonale are generally late complications in COPD patients.

Investigations

Pulmonary function tests

The diagnosis and classification of COPD rest on objective demonstration of airways obstruction by spirometric testing (see Box 13.25). An abnormal FEV$_1$ (< 80% predicted), with an FEV$_1$/VC ratio of < 70% and little variation in serial PEF, strongly suggests COPD. A normal FEV$_1$ excludes the diagnosis. The relationship between FEV$_1$ and PEF is poor in COPD, and PEF in particular may under-estimate the degree of airflow obstruction in these patients.

Reversibility testing to salbutamol and ipratropium bromide is necessary to detect patients with substantial increases in FEV$_1$ who really have asthma, and to establish the post-bronchodilator FEV$_1$ which is the best predictor of long-term prognosis. Significant reversibility is defined as a 15% and at least 200 ml increase in FEV$_1$. Evidence of a similar objective response to a course of oral prednisolone (30 mg daily for 2 weeks) should also be performed in all patients with COPD.

Lung volumes show an increase in total lung capacity (TLC) and residual volume (RV) due to gas trapping; the carbon monoxide transfer factor and coefficient are markedly

13.26 CLINICAL ABNORMALITIES IN PATIENTS WITH ADVANCED AIRFLOW OBSTRUCTION
• Rhonchi, especially on forced expiration • A reduction in the length of the trachea palpable above the sternal notch • Tracheal descent during inspiration (tracheal 'tug') • Contraction of the sternomastoid and scalene muscles on inspiration • Excavation of the suprasternal and supraclavicular fossae during inspiration, together with indrawing of the costal margins and intercostal spaces • Increased antero-posterior diameter of the chest relative to the lateral diameter; loss of cardiac dullness • Loss of weight common (often stimulates unnecessary investigation) • Pursed lip breathing—physiological response to decrease air trapping • Central cyanosis • Flapping tremor and bounding pulse (due to hypercapnia) • Peripheral oedema which may indicate cor pulmonale • Raised JVP, right ventricular heave, loud pulmonary second sound, tricuspid regurgitation

reduced in patients with a severe emphysema component. Alveolar underventilation causes a fall in PaO_2 and often a permanent increase in $PaCO_2$, especially in severe cases. Measurement of arterial blood gases should be performed in all patients with severe COPD (FEV$_1$ < 40% predicted).

Exercise tests are of little diagnostic value but can provide an objective assessment of exertional dyspnoea.

Imaging

COPD cannot be diagnosed on a chest radiograph but this investigation is useful in excluding other pathology. In moderate and severe COPD the chest radiograph typically shows hypertranslucent lung fields with disorganisation of the vasculature, low flat diaphragms or 'terracing' of the hemidiaphragms and prominent pulmonary artery shadows at both hila. Bullae may also be observed. CT can be used to quantify the extent and distribution of emphysema (see Fig. 13.19) but its clinical value is currently restricted to the assessment of bullous emphysema and the potential for lung volume reduction surgery or lung transplantation (see p. 508). Patients with α_1-antitrypsin deficiency typically display basal

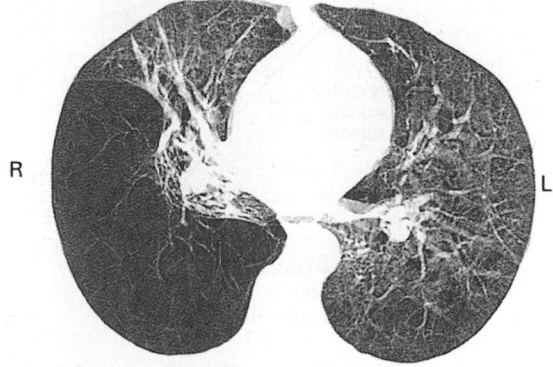

Fig. 13.19 Gross emphysema. High-resolution CT showing emphysema most evident in the right lower lobe.

disease, compared with the predominantly apical disease seen in smokers with normal α_1-antitrypsin levels.

Haematology

Polycythaemia (see p. 904) may develop but should not be assumed to be secondary without measurement of PaO_2. Venesection may be considered if the haematocrit is above 0.55.

Management

The treatment of patients with stable COPD is outlined in Figure 13.20.

Reduction of bronchial irritation

It is of extreme importance that the patient who smokes should stop completely and permanently. Participation in an active smoking cessation programme, together with the use of nicotine replacement therapy, leads to a higher quit rate. In well-motivated patients bupropion (150 mg once daily increasing to 150 mg 12-hourly on day 7) commenced 1–2 weeks prior to stopping smoking is also a valuable adjunct to smoking cessation. Bupropion is contraindicated in those patients with a history of epilepsy or known CNS tumour and should only be used for 7–9 weeks (see Box 13.27).

Telephone advice for patients wanting to stop smoking is available in the UK on:

- NHS Smoking Helpline: 0800 1690169
- QUIT: 0800 002200.

13.27 RECOMMENDATIONS FOR USING ANTI-SMOKING INTERVENTIONS*
Smokers who are not motivated to try to stop smoking
• Record smoking status at regular intervals • Anti-smoking advice • Encourage change in attitude regarding smoking to improve motivation
Motivated light smokers (< 10/day)
• Anti-smoking advice • Involve in anti-smoking support programme
Motivated heavy smokers (10–15/day)
• As above plus nicotine replacement therapy (NRT) (minimum 8 weeks)
Motivated heavy smokers (> 15/day)
• As above plus bupropion if NRT and behavioural support unsuccessful and patient remains motivated

Dusty and smoke-laden atmospheres should be avoided; this may involve a change of occupation.

Treatment of respiratory infection

Respiratory infection should be treated promptly because it aggravates breathlessness and may precipitate type II respiratory failure in patients with severe airflow obstruction. Purulent sputum is treated with amoxicillin 250 mg 8-hourly (clarithromycin 250–500 mg 12-hourly if

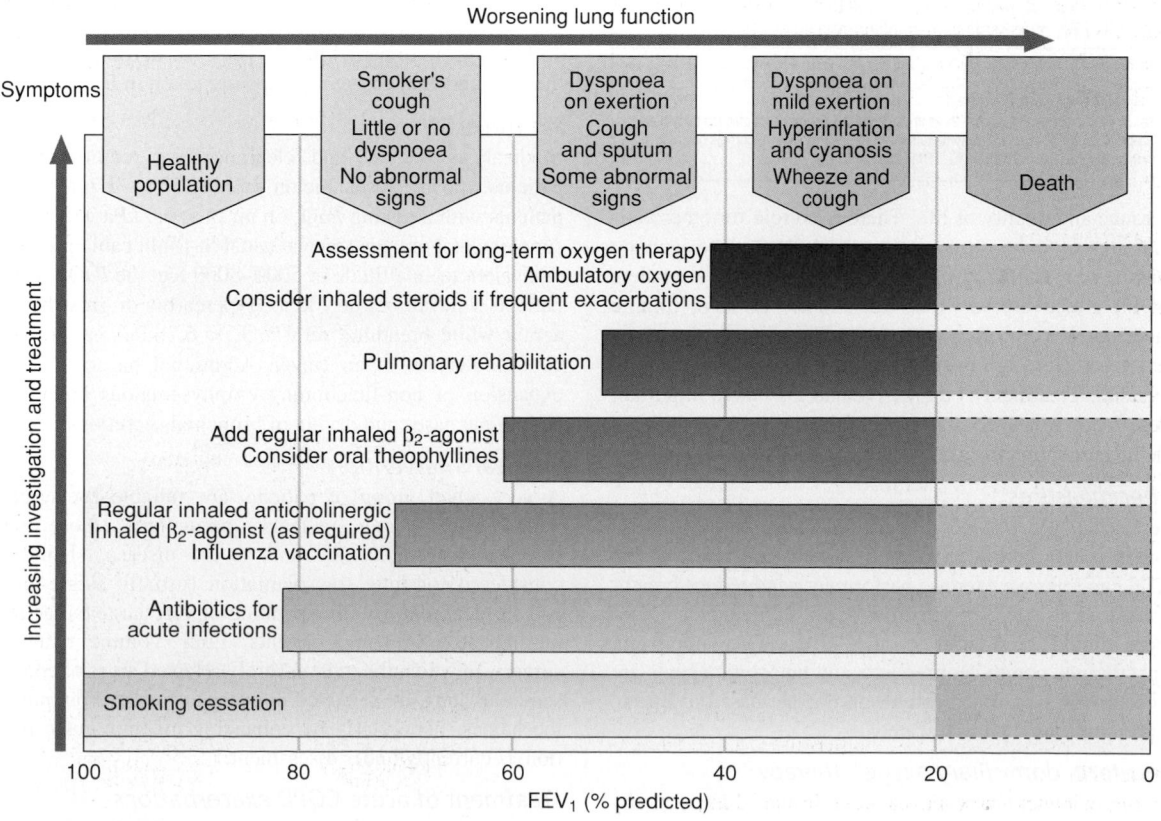

Fig. 13.20 Summary of management of COPD.

penicillin-sensitive) pending sputum culture results. Co-amoxiclav 375 mg 8-hourly should be used if there is no response or if a β-lactamase-producing organism is cultured. The usual causative organisms are *Streptococcus pneumoniae* or *Haemophilus influenzae*. A 5–10-day course of treatment is usually effective. Well-informed, reliable patients can be given a supply of one of these drugs and start a course of treatment on their own initiative when the need arises.

Continuous suppressive antibiotic treatment is not advised as it is apt to promote the emergence of drug-resistant organisms within the respiratory tract. Influenza immunisation should be offered to all patients each year.

Bronchodilator and anti-inflammatory therapy

Bronchodilator therapy with regular inhaled anticholinergic agents and short-acting β$_2$-agonists taken as required provides useful symptomatic relief in the majority of patients. In moderate and severe COPD these agents should be used regularly and in combination, and low-dose inhaled steroids considered in patients with severe COPD and frequent exacerbations requiring hospital admission. These latter agents should not be used routinely (see EBM panel). Theophyllines and long-acting β$_2$-adrenoceptor agonists are of limited value in COPD but may produce small increases in exercise

---

COPD—role of regular inhaled corticosteroids **EBM**

'Several large RCTs have found no evidence for a long-term beneficial effect of inhaled corticosteroid therapy on the annual decline in FEV$_1$ in patients with smoking-related COPD.'

- Pauwels RA, Lofdahl CG, Laitinen LA, et al. Long-term treatment with inhaled budesonide in persons with mild chronic obstructive pulmonary disease who continue to smoke. N Engl J Med 1999; 340:1948–1953.
- Burge PS, Calvertey PM, Jones PW, et al. Randomised, double blind, placebo controlled study of fluticasone propionate in patients with moderate to severe chronic obstructive pulmonary disease: the ISOLDE trial. BMJ 2000; 320:1297–1303.

---

tolerance and quality of life. There is no role for other anti-inflammatory drugs. It is vital to check inhaler use as many patients with COPD struggle to use metered-dose inhalers (MDIs) effectively; dry powder inhalers or large-volume spacer devices are often preferable. The use of home nebulisers to deliver high doses of bronchodilator drugs is controversial. Treatment is expensive and may have important side-effects; however, a few patients may show significant objective or subjective improvements with such treatment.

Other measures

Exercise should be encouraged and outpatient-based pulmonary rehabilitation programmes, while not affecting the FEV$_1$, can improve exercise performance and reduce breathlessness. Obesity, poor nutrition, depression and social isolation should be identified and, if possible, improved. Expectorants, cough suppressants and mucolytic agents are of no proven benefit. Sedatives and opiate-based analgesic preparations are contraindicated.

Long-term domiciliary oxygen therapy

Long-term low-concentration oxygen therapy (2 litres/min by nasal cannulae) decreases pulmonary hypertension, reduces secondary polycythaemia, improves neuropsychological

---

13.28 PRESCRIPTION OF LONG-TERM OXYGEN THERAPY (LTOT) IN COPD

- Arterial blood gases measured in clinically stable patient on optimal medical therapy on at least two occasions 3 weeks apart
- PaO$_2$ < 7.3 kPa irrespective of PaCO$_2$ and FEV$_1$ < 1.5 litres
- PaO$_2$ 7.3–8 kPa plus pulmonary hypertension, peripheral oedema or nocturnal hypoxaemia
- Patient stopped smoking

  Use at least 15 hours/day at 2–4 litres/min to achieve PaO$_2$ > 8 kPa without an unacceptable rise in PaCO$_2$

COPD—role of long-term domiciliary oxygen therapy (LTOT) **EBM**

'Two RCTs have demonstrated that long-term oxygen therapy (used for ≥ 15 hours/day) in patients with COPD and chronic and severe hypoxaemia improves survival, reduces secondary polycythaemia and prevents the progression of pulmonary hypertension. LTOT did not improve survival in patients with moderate hypoxaemia or in those with arterial desaturation occurring only at night.'

- Nocturnal Oxygen Therapy Trial Group. Continuous or nocturnal oxygen therapy in hypoxaemic chronic obstructive lung disease. A clinical trial. Ann Intern Med 1980; 93:391–398.
- MRC Working Group. Long term domiciliary oxygen therapy in chronic hypoxic cor pulmonale complicating chronic bronchitis and emphysema. Lancet 1981; 1:681–686.
- Crockett AJ, Cranston JM, Moss JR, Alpers JH. Domiciliary oxygen for COPD (Cochrane Review). Cochrane Library, issue 4, 2000. Oxford: Update Software.

Further information: www.brit-thoracic.org.uk

---

health and, most importantly, prolongs life in hypoxaemic COPD patients. The most efficient method of providing oxygen in this way is by an oxygen concentrator. Low-concentration oxygen should be administered for 15 hours or more per 24 hours. The criteria for the prescription of long-term oxygen therapy are given in Box 13.28.

Air travel

Medical assessment and clearance are required in all patients who are dyspnoeic on walking 50 m. In practice, all patients with a resting PaO$_2$ on air of < 9.0 kPa will require supplemental oxygen since at usual in-flight cabin pressures equivalent to an altitude of 5000–8000 feet the PaO$_2$ of such patients will fall below 7 kPa. Hypercarbia or gross hypoxaemia while breathing air (PaO$_2$ < 6.7 kPa) is a relative contraindication to air travel. Additional hazards include expansion of non-functioning emphysematous bullae and abdominal gases and drying of bronchial secretions.

Surgical intervention

A very small group of patients are suitable for surgical intervention. Young patients, particularly those with α$_1$-antitrypsin deficiency and severe disease, should be considered for lung transplantation (usually single-lung), and surgical removal of expanding or very large bullae may be indicated in some patients. Lung volume reduction surgery, in which the most severely affected areas of emphysematous lung are removed in order to improve pulmonary mechanics, particularly by enhancing diaphragmatic function, is currently under assessment.

Treatment of acute COPD exacerbations

The assessment and management of type I and type II respiratory failure are detailed on page 505. Acute exacerbations

13.29 MANAGEMENT OF ACUTE COPD EXACERBATIONS

In the community

- Add or increase bronchodilator therapy
- Antibiotics (see p. 511)
- Oral corticosteroids *if* patient already on oral corticosteroids, *if* previous response to such treatment, *if* airflow obstruction fails to respond to bronchodilator therapy or *if* first presentation of disease (prednisolone 30 mg daily for 1 week)

In hospital

- Check arterial blood gases (ABGs), chest radiograph, ECG, full blood count, urea and electrolytes; measure FEV_1 + peak flow; send sputum for culture
- Oxygen: 24–28% via mask, 2 litres/min by nasal prongs; check ABGs within 60 mins and adjust according to PaO_2 (try to keep ≥ 7.5 kPa) and $PaCO_2$/pH
- Bronchodilators: nebulised β_2-adrenoceptor agonist (+ ipratropium bromide if severe) 4–6-hourly. If no response consider i.v. aminophylline infusion
- Oral corticosteroids: indicated as above
- Diuretics: indicated if JVP elevated and oedema present
- If pH < 7.35 and $PaCO_2$ > 6, consider ventilatory support (invasive or non-invasive IPPV, see p. 508). If patient continuing to deteriorate despite non-invasive ventilation support, and endotracheal intubation not indicated (e.g. previous poor quality of life, significant comorbidity), doxapram can be considered
- Prophylactic subcutaneous low molecular weight heparin

N.B. All patients should be reviewed 4–6 weeks after hospital discharge to assess ability to cope at home, FEV_1, inhaler technique and understanding of treatment, and the potential need for LTOT or a home nebuliser.

of COPD can present as increased sputum volume and purulence, increased breathlessness and wheeze, chest tightness and sometimes fluid retention. The differential diagnosis includes pneumonia, pneumothorax, left ventricular failure, pulmonary embolism, lung cancer and upper airway obstruction. The management of an acute COPD exacerbation is outlined in Box 13.29. Any patient with severe breathlessness, cyanosis, worsening oedema, impaired conscious level or poor social circumstances should be referred for hospital admission.

COPD EXACERBATIONS—role of non-invasive ventilation EBM

'RCTs have demonstrated that the early use of non-invasive ventilation of patients with an acute exacerbation of COPD associated with mild to moderate respiratory acidosis (arterial pH 7.25–7.35, $PaCO_2$ > 6 kPa) reduces the need for endotracheal intubation, the length of hospital stay and the in-hospital mortality.'

- Brochard L, Mancebo J, Wysocki M, et al. Non-invasive ventilation for acute exacerbations of chronic obstructive pulmonary disease. N Engl J Med 1995; 333:817–822.
- Plant PK, Owen JL, Elliott MW. Early use of non-invasive ventilation for acute exacerbations of chronic obstructive pulmonary disease on general respiratory wards: a multicentre randomised controlled trial. Lancet 2000; 355:1931–1935.

Prognosis

The best guide to the progression of COPD is the decline in FEV_1 over time (normally 30 ml/year). The prognosis is inversely related to age and directly related to the post-bronchodilator FEV_1. Patients with atopy have a significantly better survival but to date no drug treatment (aside from long-term oxygen therapy) has been shown to affect

disease outcome. Pulmonary hypertension in COPD implies a poor prognosis. The mean survival of patients admitted with an acute exacerbation of COPD associated with an elevated $PaCO_2$ that reverts to normal on recovery is 3 years.

ASTHMA

Asthma is defined as a disorder characterised by chronic airway inflammation and increased airway responsiveness resulting in symptoms of wheeze, cough, chest tightness and dyspnoea. It is characterised functionally by the presence of airflow obstruction which is variable over short periods of time or is reversible with treatment. It is not a uniform disease but rather a dynamic clinical syndrome which has a number of clinical patterns. Many patients with well-controlled asthma are asymptomatic with normal lung function between exacerbations, although even these patients have evidence of chronic airway inflammation and hyper-responsiveness. By contrast, in some patients with chronic asthma the asthma progresses, leading to irreversible obstruction of the airways (see Box 13.30).

13.30 CARDINAL PATHOPHYSIOLOGICAL FEATURES OF ASTHMA

Airflow limitation

- Usually reverses spontaneously or with treatment

Airway hyper-responsiveness

- Exaggerated bronchoconstriction to a wide range of non-specific stimuli, e.g. exercise, cold air

Airway inflammation

- Eosinophils, lymphocytes, mast cells, neutrophils; associated oedema, smooth muscle hypertrophy and hyperplasia, thickening of basement membrane, mucous plugging and epithelial damage (see Fig. 13.22, p. 515)

Prevalence

Asthma is common and its prevalence is increasing. Studies using objective measurements of lung function, airway responsiveness and symptoms suggest that about 7% of adults and up to 15% of children in the UK have asthma. There is considerable interest in the reasons for the increase in the prevalence of asthma, most probably relating to changes in the indoor environment including early exposure to air allergens and cigarette smoke, fewer childhood infections and changes in diet. There is a wide variability in the geographical prevalence of asthma, with the highest rates observed in New Zealand, Australia and the UK, and the lowest in countries such as China and Malaysia.

Pathophysiology

Asthma is multifactorial in origin, arising from the interaction of both genetic and environmental factors. Airway inflammation characterising asthma occurs when genetically susceptible individuals are exposed to environmental factors, but the exact processes may vary from patient to patient. The timing, intensity and mode of exposure to aero-allergens are important environmental factors which stimulate the production of IgE.

Genetic susceptibility

It has long been known that asthma and atopy run in families. Asthma which begins in childhood generally occurs in atopic individuals who produce significant amounts of IgE on exposure to small amounts of common antigens. This contrasts with those patients who develop asthma in adult life and who are non-atopic, so-called 'intrinsic' or late-onset asthma. First-degree relatives of asthmatic patients have a higher prevalence of asthma when compared to relatives of non-asthmatic patients. Atopic individuals demonstrate positive reactions to antigens delivered in skin prick tests and have a high prevalence of asthma, allergic rhinitis, urticaria and eczema. Several potential gene linkages (e.g. chromosome 11q13) to asthma and atopy have been suggested; however, the genetic contribution to asthma remains poorly defined. It possibly involves polygenic inheritance with several genes contributing to the asthmatic tendency in any one individual, and genetic heterogeneity where different combinations of genes lead to asthma in different individuals.

Environmental factors

The importance of environmental factors in the aetiology of asthma has been particularly evident in studies of populations who have migrated from one country to another. The change to a modern, urban, economically developed society seems to be particularly associated with the development of asthma.

Indoor. The indoor environment is a particularly important cause of asthma in children since allergen exposure early in life appears to be important in determining sensitisation. House dust mites abound in carpets, soft furnishings and bedding, and pet-derived allergens are widespread in houses where dogs or cats are kept. Other allergens of relevance are fungal spores and cockroach antigens. Pollutants such as nitrogen dioxide are found in higher concentrations indoors than outside as a result of gas cookers. Sulphur dioxide and particulate pollutants are released from open fires. Passive exposure to cigarette smoke immediately following birth increases the risk of developing asthma.

Outdoor. Experimental and population studies have shown that nitrogen dioxide, ozone, sulphur dioxide and airborne particulates exacerbate asthma symptoms. The predominant source of nitrogen dioxide comprises motor vehicle emissions and fuel-burning industries. Nitrogen dioxide reacts with sunlight and oxygen in a photochemical reaction to produce ozone. Sulphur dioxide is created by the burning of fossil fuels and emissions from diesel-powered vehicles. Such vehicles also contribute to the development of air-borne particulates. Finally, levels of grass and flower pollens vary considerably according to the atmospheric conditions, as do allergens from rapeseed, soya bean and other crops. Interactions between atmospheric pollutants, aero-allergens and climate will have important effects on asthma, with some studies showing exposure to air pollution increasing airway responsiveness to allergens. Several epidemics of acute asthma have been associated with thunderstorms in patients sensitised to both pollen and fungal antigens.

Work. Many agents encountered in the workplace may induce occupational asthma, e.g. isocyanates, epoxy resins and wood dust.

Drugs

Beta$_2$-adrenoceptor antagonists (β-blockers) can induce bronchoconstriction even when administered in the form of eye drops. Hence β-blockers should be avoided in patients with asthma or COPD. Approximately 10% of asthmatic patients develop bronchoconstriction when given salicylates (e.g. aspirin) or non-steroidal anti-inflammatory agents.

Infections

Many viral and bacterial infections of the respiratory system produce a transient increase in airway responsiveness in asthmatic patients. Viruses in particular are an important cause of asthma exacerbations.

Smoking

Smoking during pregnancy is thought to increase the risk of developing atopic disease in infancy, and passive exposure to smoking has an adverse effect on asthma and other respiratory diseases.

Anxiety and psychosocial factors

Any cause of severe anxiety or stress (see p. 252) can exacerbate asthma, and acute emotion may provoke an acute attack, but there is no evidence that asthmatics are primarily psychologically disturbed.

Pathology

The inhalation of an allergen in a sensitised atopic asthmatic patient results in a two-phase bronchoconstrictor response (see Fig. 13.21). The inhaled allergen rapidly interacts with mucosal mast cells via an IgE-dependent mechanism, resulting in the release of mediators such as histamine and the cysteinyl leukotrienes which lead to bronchoconstriction. A full spectrum of inflammatory cells, however, are involved in the perpetuation of the chronic inflammatory reaction in

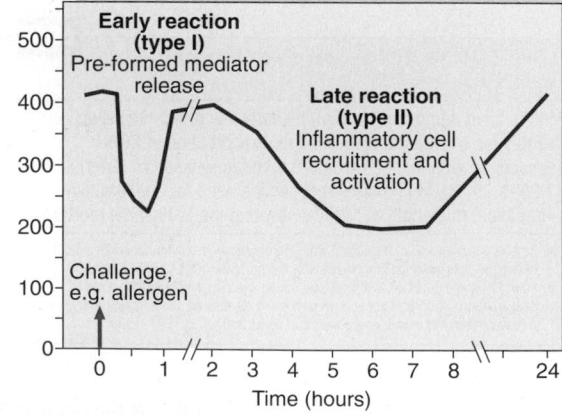

Fig. 13.21 Changes in peak flow following allergen challenge. A similar biphasic response is observed following a variety of different challenges. Occasionally an individual will develop an isolated late response with no early reaction.

the bronchial wall which characterises asthma. It is now known that epithelial and smooth muscle cells are also capable of releasing inflammatory mediators rather than acting solely as passive targets. All of these cells are also involved in the initiation of asthma in non-atopic patients. T lymphocytes are present in increased numbers in asthmatic airways and have an important role in the regulation of the inflammatory response. They are programmed to release inflammatory cytokines amongst which IL-4 and IL-5 are of importance since they both recruit eosinophils to the airway and delay apoptosis of these cells. This pattern of cytokine release, which also includes IL-15, GM-CSF and IL-10, identifies the T cells as being of TH2 subtype. Eosinophils are characteristically present in increased numbers in the airway. These cells release bioactive lipid mediators and oxygen radicals; their granules also contain toxic basic proteins including major basic protein, eosinophil cationic protein, eosinophil-derived neurotoxin and eosinophil peroxidase. The number of airway macrophages is also increased in asthma and these cells may be activated by a number of mechanisms including a low affinity IgE receptor. Epithelial shedding (see Fig. 13.22) is commonly

observed in airway biopsies from asthmatic patients. This has long been recognised as a feature of fatal asthma. Microvascular leakage is also a feature and may be triggered by many inflammatory mediators. This results in plasma exudation into the lumen of the airways, contributing to mucous plugging, decreased mucociliary clearance, release of kinins and complement fragments and oedema of the airway wall which facilitates epithelial stripping. The increase in airway smooth muscle bulk around the airways appears to be a particularly important contributory factor in airflow obstruction. Likewise, airway inflammation induces an imbalance between cholinergic and peptidergic neuronal control, causing exaggerated bronchoconstrictor responses. As a result of the ongoing airway inflammation, therefore, the asthmatic airway wall is thickened by oedema, cellular infiltration, increased smooth muscle mass and hypertrophy of mucus-secreting glands. With increasing severity and chronicity of the disease, remodelling of the airway occurs, leading to fibrosis of the airway wall, fixed narrowing of the airway and a reduced response to bronchodilator medication. Although in clinical practice patients with asthma are sometimes classified as having 'extrinsic' asthma (occurring

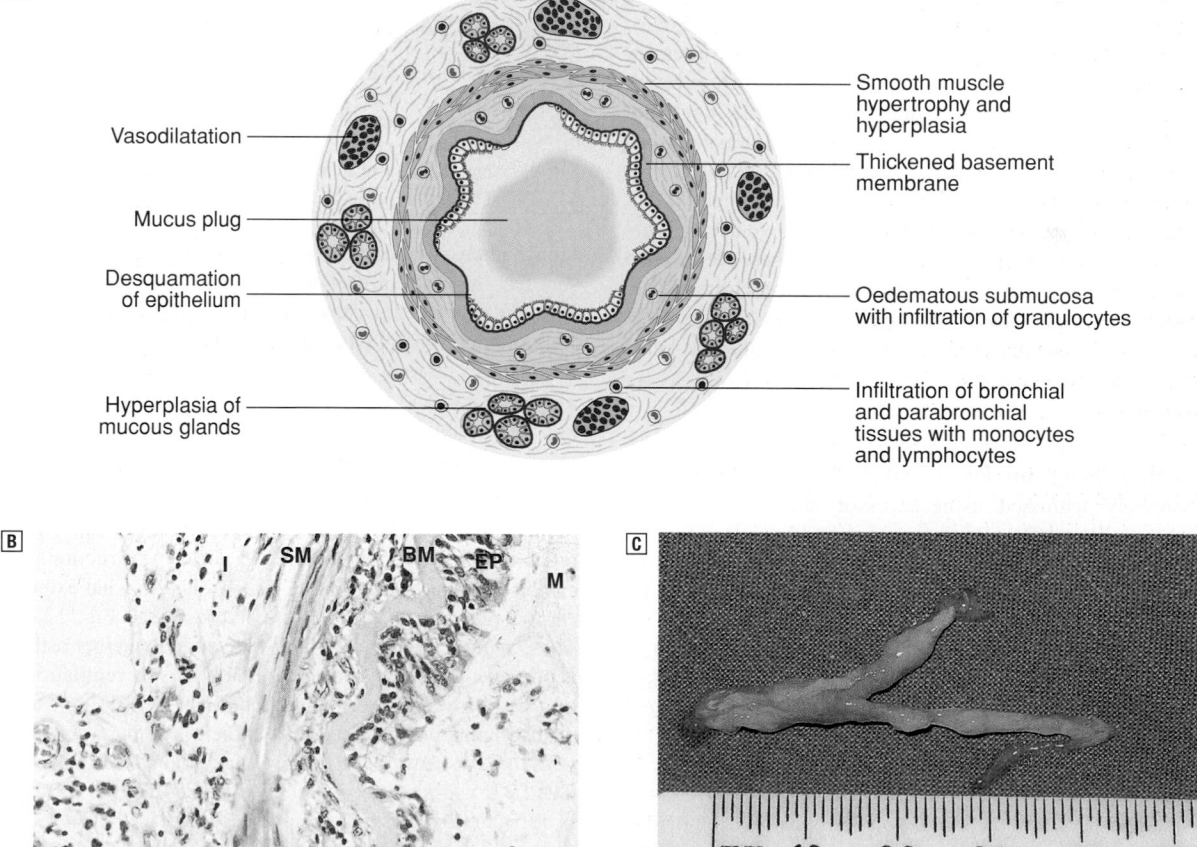

Fig. 13.22 Pathological changes in asthma. Ⓐ Pathological changes seen in the bronchus of an asthmatic. Ⓑ Histological section of bronchus in a patient with asthma, demonstrating pathological changes as illustrated in A. (I = inflammatory cells in bronchial tissues; SM = smooth muscle; BM = basement membrane; EP = epithelium; M = mucus in airway lumen) Ⓒ Mucus plug expectorated by patient with acute severe asthma.

in relation to inhalation of environmental antigens) or 'intrinsic' asthma (occurring without any definable relationship to an environmental antigen), the pathological features of the airway inflammation are identical. It is likely that the inflammatory cascade of asthma can be initiated by a variety of different factors in different patients.

Clinical features

Typical symptoms of asthma comprise wheeze, breathlessness, cough and a sensation of chest tightness. These symptoms may occur for the first time at any age, and may be episodic or persistent. Patients with episodic asthma are usually asymptomatic between exacerbations, which occur during viral respiratory tract infections or after exposure to allergens. This pattern of asthma is commonly seen in children or young adults who are atopic. In other patients the clinical pattern is of persistent asthma with chronic wheeze and breathlessness. This may sometimes make it difficult to distinguish from wheeze due to COPD or more unusual causes, e.g. cardiac failure. (Note that acute pulmonary oedema or an inhaled foreign body in a child can cause acute wheeze which can mimic acute severe asthma—see below.) This pattern is more common in older patients with adult-onset asthma who are non-atopic and typifies intrinsic asthma. The variable nature of symptoms is a characteristic feature. Typically, there is a diurnal pattern (see Fig. 13.23), with symptoms and peak expiratory flow measurement being worse in the early morning. Symptoms such as cough and wheeze often disturb sleep and the term 'nocturnal asthma' emphasises this. Cough may be the dominant symptom and the lack of wheeze or breathlessness may lead to a delay in making the diagnosis of so-called 'cough variant asthma'. Symptoms may be specifically provoked by exercise ('exercise-induced asthma'). All of these descriptive clinical terms are useful in emphasising the characteristic features of asthma particular to each patient and highlight the fact that asthma is not a uniform static disease but a broad dynamic syndrome.

Acute severe asthma

This term has replaced status asthmaticus as a description of life-threatening attacks of asthma. Patients are usually extremely distressed, using accessory muscles of respiration, are hyperinflated and tachypnoeic. Respiratory symptoms are accompanied by tachycardia, pulsus paradoxus (loss of pulse pressure on inspiration due to reduced cardiac return as a consequence of severe hyperinflation) and sweating. In very severe asthma central cyanosis occurs and airflow may have become so restrictive that rhonchi are no longer produced. The presence of a silent chest and bradycardia in such patients is an ominous sign.

Investigations

A diagnosis of asthma is made on the basis of a compatible clinical history plus a demonstration of variable airflow obstruction (see Box 13.31) which may classically be seen as 'morning dipping' of the peak expiratory flow (see Fig. 13.23).

In more difficult situations where the above tests are negative, an exercise test, a histamine or methacholine

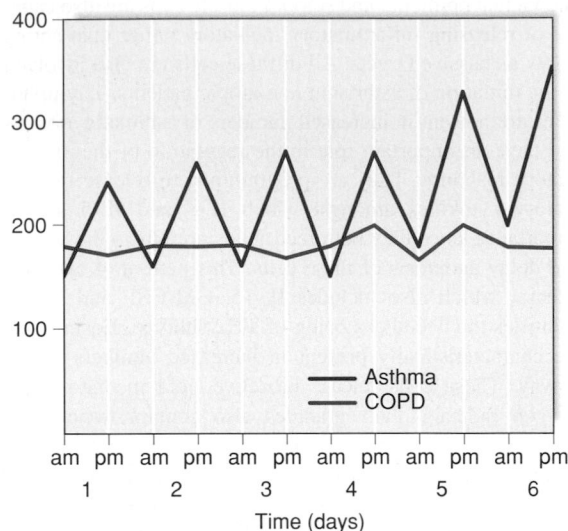

Fig. 13.23 **'Morning dipping'.** Serial recordings of peak expiratory flow (PEF) in patients with COPD and asthma. Note sharp overnight fall (morning dip) and subsequent rise during the day in patients with asthma, which does not occur in patients with COPD.

13.31 MAKING A DIAGNOSIS OF ASTHMA

Compatible clinical history *plus either/or*:
- ≥ 15% improvement in FEV$_1$ or PEF following administration of a bronchodilator (see Fig. 13.24) *or*
- ≥ 15% spontaneous change in PEF during 1 week of home monitoring (see Fig. 13.23)

bronchial provocation test (see p. 517), an occupational exposure test or a trial of oral corticosteroids (e.g. prednisolone 30 mg daily for 2 weeks) may be required. An elevated sputum or peripheral blood eosinophil count, or an increased serum level of total or allergen-specific IgE (radioallergosorbent test—RAST) may also be helpful. It is particularly important, however, to be aware that wheeze is audible in many conditions other than asthma.

Pulmonary function tests

Measurement of the FEV$_1$/VC ratio or PEF provides a fairly reliable indication of the degree of airflow obstruction, and can also be used to determine whether and to what extent it can be relieved by bronchodilator drugs (see Fig. 13.24). These parameters are also used to examine whether asthma is provoked by exercise (see Fig. 13.25), hyperventilation or occupational exposure. Serial recordings of PEF are useful in distinguishing patients with chronic asthma from those with fixed or irreversible airflow obstruction associated with COPD. In asthma there is usually a marked diurnal variation in PEF, the lowest values being recorded in the mornings ('morning dipping') (see Fig. 13.23). Serial PEF recordings are also invaluable in the assessment of a patient's response to corticosteroid therapy and in the long-term monitoring of patients with poorly controlled disease. They are also essential in monitoring response to treatment in acute severe asthma.

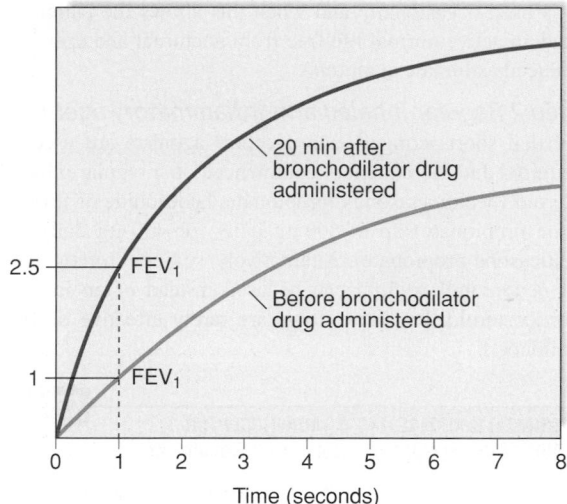

Volume expired (litres)

Fig. 13.24   Reversibility test. Forced expiratory manoeuvres before and 20 minutes after inhalation of a β_2-adrenoceptor agonist. Note the increase in FEV_1 from 1.0 to 2.5 litres.

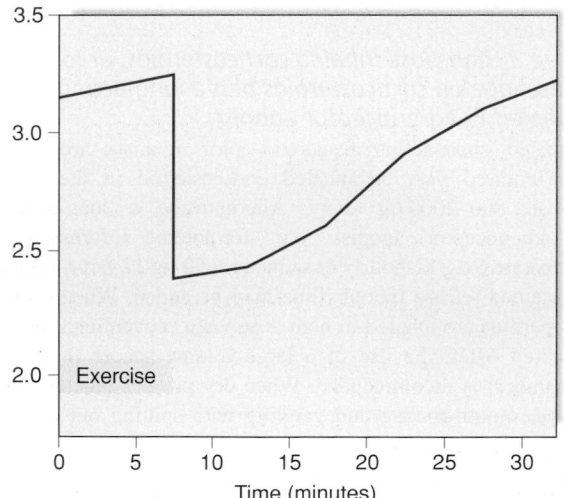

FEV_1 (litres)

Fig. 13.25   Exercise-induced asthma. Serial recordings of forced expiratory volume in 1 second (FEV_1) in a patient with bronchial asthma before and after 6 minutes of strenuous exercise. Note initial slight rise on completion of exercise, followed by sudden fall and gradual recovery. Adequate warm-up exercise or pre-treatment with a β_2-adrenoceptor agonist, nedocromil sodium or a leukotriene antagonist (e.g. montelukast sodium) often protects against exercise-induced symptoms.

Measurement of bronchial reactivity can be of value in diagnosing asthma and in assessing the effects of treatment. This can be achieved by administering increasing concentrations of substances such as histamine and methacholine by inhalation until there is a 20% fall in FEV_1 or PEF. This concentration is called the PC_{20}. Patients with asthma show evidence of bronchoconstriction at much lower concentrations than normal subjects.

Radiological examination

In an acute attack of asthma the lungs appear hyperinflated. Between episodes the chest radiograph is usually normal. In long-standing chronic cases the appearances may be indistinguishable from hyperinflation caused by emphysema and a lateral view may demonstrate a 'pigeon chest' deformity. Occasionally, when a large bronchus is obstructed by tenacious mucus, there is an opacity caused by lobar or segmental collapse.

A chest radiograph should be performed in all patients with acute severe asthma. This is especially important if there is poor response to treatment and assisted ventilation is being contemplated, since pneumothorax is a rare but potentially fatal complication. The chest radiograph may rarely show mediastinal, pericardial or subcutaneous emphysema in patients with acute severe asthma.

Allergic bronchopulmonary aspergillosis may complicate chronic persisting asthma (see p. 540) and produce areas of segmental/subsegmental collapse and proximal bronchiectasis.

Arterial blood gas analysis

Measurements of arterial blood gas pressures (PaO_2 and $PaCO_2$) are indispensable in the management of patients with acute severe asthma.

Management

Patient education

Successful management of asthma mandates that the patient or parents of a child with asthma understand the nature of the condition and its treatment. Patient education should begin at the time of diagnosis and be revisited in every subsequent consultation between patient, doctor or nurse. Education involves the patient understanding the nature of asthma, the practical skills necessary to manage asthma successfully and the adoption of appropriate actions in response to deteriorating asthma. It is important for patients to appreciate differences between reliever (bronchodilator) and preventer (anti-inflammatory) medications and patients should be fully capable of using their inhaler devices. Use of a peak flow meter provides patients with an objective measure of airway obstruction and allows them to monitor the effect of treatment and the severity of exacerbations. There is clear evidence that the development of a personalised asthma action plan for patients improves outcome and this should be discussed individually with patients.

 EBM

ASTHMA—role of self-management plans

'Self-management plans advising asthmatic patients how to respond to worsening symptoms or PEF lead to less need for emergency medical care, less time off work and a better quality of life.'

- Lahdensno A, Halahtela T, Herals J, et al. Randomised comparison of guided self-management and traditional treatment of asthma over one year. BMJ 1996; 312:748–752.
- Ignacio-Garcia J, Gonzalez-Santos P. Asthma self-management education program by home monitoring of peak expiratory flow. Am J Respir Crit Care Med 1995; 151:353–359.

Avoidance of precipitating factors

There are few instances in which a single agent can be identified as a cause of an asthma exacerbation; however, where possible, measures can be taken to prevent or reduce allergen exposure, such as avoiding contact with household pets.

Desensitisation is a highly specialised technique in which repeated injections of an allergen are given in an attempt to produce blocking antibody of IgG type which can prevent the allergen from binding to specific IgE on mast cells. It is most commonly used in well-documented life-threatening anaphylactic reactions to insect stings; there is little evidence of its benefit in asthma and this form of therapy has largely been abandoned in the UK because of the attendant risks.

Management of chronic persistent asthma

Treatment should be stepped up or down as required, with PEF monitoring being key to such decisions. The patient should be allowed to select the best inhaler device for himself or herself, and compliance and inhaler technique must be checked at every opportunity. All metered dose inhalers (MDIs) which remain the most cost-effective inhaler devices will be reformulated over the next few years to replace conventional chlorofluorocarbon (CFC) propellants with hydrofluoroalkanes (HFAs). While these products are equally effective and as safe as current CFC-containing MDIs, the aerosol characteristics are different and this may be noticed by patients. In patients with mild to moderate asthma (on step 1–3 medication—see below and Fig. 13.26) the aim of treatment should be to abolish or minimise all symptoms, permit unrestricted exercise and prevent exacerbations. In patients with more severe disease (on step 4–5 medication) the aim should be to achieve the best possible and most stable PEF, to improve symptoms and exercise capacity, and to reduce the need for bronchodilator drug use as far as possible with the least adverse effects from the drugs used.

Step 1 Occasional use of inhaled short-acting β_2-adrenoceptor agonist bronchodilators

Short-acting bronchodilators, such as salbutamol or terbutaline, are used by inhalation as required for the relief of occasional minor symptoms. If the patient is using β_2-adrenoceptor agonists more than once daily, move to step 2. Beta$_2$-adrenoceptor agonist therapy alone is only recommended if it is used occasionally and when this allows the patient to lead an active normal life free from nocturnal and exercise-induced asthmatic symptoms.

Step 2 Regular inhaled anti-inflammatory agents

Inhaled short-acting β_2-adrenoceptor agonists are used as required and the patient is commenced on a regular inhaled steroid (beclometasone dipropionate, budesonide or fluticasone propionate) up to 800 μg daily (or 400 μg daily for fluticasone propionate). Alternatively, sodium cromoglicate or nedocromil sodium can be used instead of an inhaled corticosteroid, but these drugs are rarely effective outside childhood.

EBM

INHALED SHORT-ACTING β_2-ADRENOCEPTOR AGONISTS—regular versus as-needed treatment

'Systematic review of 24 RCTs found that regularly scheduled as opposed to as-needed use of short-acting inhaled β_2-adrenoceptor agonists in people with mild intermittent asthma provides no additional clinical benefit.'

- Drazen JM, Israel E, Boushey HA, et al. Comparison of regularly scheduled with as-needed use of albuterol [salbutamol] in mild asthma. Asthma Clinical Network. N Engl J Med 1996; 335:841–847.
- Walters EH, Walters J. Inhaled short-acting beta2-agonist use in asthma: regular vs as needed treatment (Cochrane Review). Cochrane Library, issue 4, 2000. Oxford: Update Software.

Step 3 High-dose inhaled corticosteroids, or low-dose inhaled corticosteroids plus a long-acting inhaled β_2-adrenoceptor agonist

Inhaled short-acting β_2-adrenoceptor agonists are used as required *plus* an inhaled corticosteroid in the dose range 800–2000 μg daily. Alternatively, a long-acting β_2-adrenoceptor agonist (e.g. formoterol (eformoterol) fumarate 6 μg 12-hourly or salmeterol 50 μg 12-hourly) or a sustained-release theophylline may be added. When corticosteroids are inhaled in high dose via a conventional pressurised MDI, the use of a large-volume spacer (holding chamber) is recommended. When dry powder inhalers are used, mouth-rinsing and gargling with spitting out of the

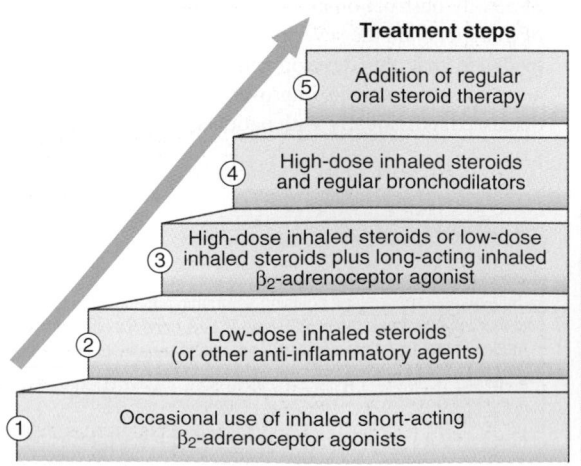

Treatment steps

⑤ Addition of regular oral steroid therapy

④ High-dose inhaled steroids and regular bronchodilators

③ High-dose inhaled steroids or low-dose inhaled steroids plus long-acting inhaled β_2-adrenoceptor agonist

② Low-dose inhaled steroids (or other anti-inflammatory agents)

① Occasional use of inhaled short-acting β_2-adrenoceptor agonists

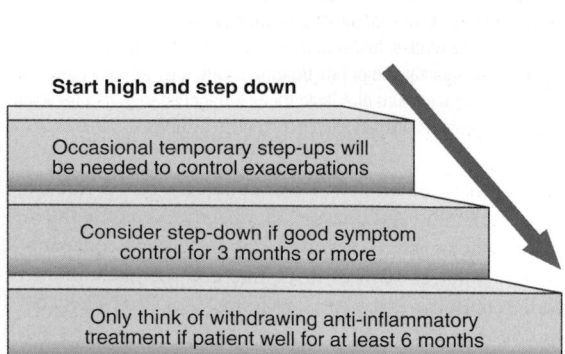

Start high and step down

Occasional temporary step-ups will be needed to control exacerbations

Consider step-down if good symptom control for 3 months or more

Only think of withdrawing anti-inflammatory treatment if patient well for at least 6 months

Fig. 13.26   Concept of step-up and step-down drug treatment in asthma.

rinsing liquid after each treatment should be encouraged. Spacers and mouth-rinsing are recommended to decrease gastrointestinal absorption of swallowed drug, and to lower the risk of developing the local side-effect of oropharyngeal candidiasis. Recent studies have suggested that the addition of a long-acting β_2-adrenoceptor agonist is more effective in improving symptoms, improving lung function and reducing exacerbations than increasing the dose of inhaled corticosteroids.

EBM

CHRONIC ASTHMA—role of long-acting β_2-adrenoceptor agonists

'RCTs have found that in patients whose asthma is poorly controlled by inhaled corticosteroids, the addition of a long-acting β_2-adrenoceptor agonist improves symptoms and lung function and reduces exacerbations.'

- Greening AP, Ind PW, Northfield M, Shaw G. Added salmeterol versus higher-dose corticosteroid in asthma patients with symptoms on existing inhaled corticosteroid. Lancet 1994; 344:219–224.
- Pauwels RA, Lofdahl C-G, Postma DS, et al. Effect of inhaled formoterol and budesonide on exacerbations of asthma. N Engl J Med 1997; 387:1405–1411.

Further information: 🖥 www.brit-thoracic.org.uk

Step 4 High-dose inhaled corticosteroids and regular bronchodilators

Inhaled short-acting β_2-adrenoceptor agonists are used as required with an inhaled corticosteroid (800–2000 µg daily) *plus* a sequential therapeutic trial of one or more of:

- inhaled long-acting β_2-adrenoceptor agonist (e.g. salmeterol 50 µg 12-hourly or formoterol fumarate (eformoterol fumarate) 12 µg 12-hourly)
- leukotriene receptor antagonist (e.g. montelukast sodium)
- inhaled ipratropium bromide or oxitropium bromide
- long-acting oral β_2-adrenoceptor agonist (sustained-release salbutamol or terbutaline preparations)
- high-dose inhaled β_2-adrenoceptor agonists
- sodium cromoglicate or nedocromil sodium.

The role of anti-IgE antibody therapy in patients with severe atopic asthma is under evaluation.

Step 5 Addition of regular oral corticosteroid therapy

Step 4 treatment is given *plus* regular prednisolone tablets prescribed in the lowest amount necessary to control symptoms as a single daily dose in the mornings.

Using this 'stepwise' approach to asthma management (see Fig. 13.26), the initial treatment for each patient should be chosen individually depending upon severity of disease. In general, it is better to start with a treatment regimen which is likely to achieve disease control rapidly and then 'step down' rather than to start with inadequate treatment and then have to 'step up'. Patient compliance is also likely to be better when symptom control is achieved rapidly. Regular review is important and if there has been good symptomatic control for 3–6 months a step down should be made. This is of particular importance in those taking oral and high-dose inhaled corticosteroids (steps 3–5).

Short-course oral corticosteroid treatments

Short courses of 'rescue' oral corticosteroids are often required to regain control of symptoms. For adults, 30–60 mg of prednisolone can be given initially and the same dose continued in a single daily dose each morning until 2 days after control is re-established. In children, a dose of 1–2 mg/kg body weight can be used. Tapering of the dose to withdraw treatment is not necessary unless given for more than 3 weeks. Indications for 'rescue' courses include:

- symptoms and PEF progressively worsening day by day
- fall of PEF below 60% of the patient's personal best recording
- onset or worsening of sleep disturbance by asthma
- persistence of morning symptoms until midday
- progressively diminishing response to an inhaled bronchodilator
- symptoms severe enough to require treatment with nebulised or injected bronchodilators.

Increase in dose of inhaled corticosteroid

Doubling the dose of inhaled corticosteroids is often advised to control minor exacerbations of asthma not severe enough to warrant treatment with oral prednisolone. This appears to be effective in many cases.

Management of acute severe asthma

The aims of management are to prevent death, to restore pulmonary function to the patient's best as quickly as possible, to maintain optimal pulmonary function and to prevent early relapse. The features of acute severe asthma are shown in Box 13.32.

PEF should be recorded immediately in all patients unless they are too ill to cooperate. PEF measurements are most easily interpreted when expressed as a percentage of the predicted normal value or of the previous best value obtained on optimal treatment. When neither of these is known, decisions have to be made on the absolute value recorded,

13.32 IMMEDIATE ASSESSMENT OF ACUTE SEVERE ASTHMA
Features of severity
<ul><li>Pulse rate > 110 per min</li><li>Pulsus paradoxus</li><li>Unable to speak in sentences</li><li>PEF < 50% of expected</li></ul>
N.B. *Apparent* distress and respiratory rate may be misleading.
Life-threatening features
<ul><li>Cannot speak</li><li>Central cyanosis</li><li>Exhaustion, confusion, reduced conscious level</li><li>Bradycardia</li><li>'Silent chest'</li><li>Unrecordable PEF</li></ul>
Arterial blood gases in life-threatening asthma
<ul><li>A normal (5–6 kPa) or high CO_2 tension</li><li>Severe hypoxaemia (< 8 kPa), especially if being treated with oxygen</li><li>A low pH or high [H+]</li></ul>

remembering that normal values vary with age, sex and height. In a previously fit asthmatic patient, recordings of < 200 l/min are indicative of severe disease, and values of < 100 l/min must be taken as evidence of life-threatening asthma.

Immediate treatment (see Fig. 13.27)

Oxygen. Oxygen should be given at the highest concentration available (usually 60%). High-concentration oxygen therapy does not cause or aggravate carbon dioxide retention in asthma, and the presence of carbon dioxide retention must not be interpreted as a contraindication for the use of high-concentration oxygen treatment. Thereafter, the concentration of oxygen used can be adjusted according to the arterial blood gas measurements. A PaO_2 of > 8.5–9 kPa should be maintained if possible.

High doses of inhaled β_2-adrenoceptor agonists. When possible, β_2-adrenoceptor agonists should be nebulised using oxygen. Salbutamol 2.5–5 mg or terbutaline 5–10 mg should be given initially and repeated within 30 minutes if necessary. When treatment is given outside hospital and oxygen is not available, an air compressor can be used to drive the nebuliser. An alternative method of giving high doses of β_2-adrenoceptor agonists in general practice is multiple actuations of an MDI into a large-volume spacer device.

Systemic corticosteroids. Systemic corticosteroids are necessary for the treatment of all cases of acute severe asthma. Oral prednisolone 30–60 mg (or intravenous hydrocortisone 200 mg if the patient is unable to swallow or vomiting) should be given initially.

ACUTE ASTHMA—use of intravenous aminophylline

'Two SRs of RCTs examining the effect of adding intravenous aminophylline to initial standard therapy with nebulised β_2-adrenoceptor agonists and systemic corticosteroids in acute asthma failed to demonstrate any beneficial effect of aminophylline. The frequency of adverse effects was also higher with aminophylline.'

- Parameswaran K, Beida J, Rowe BH. Addition of intravenous aminophylline to beta2-agonists in adults with acute asthma (Cochrane Review). Cochrane Library, issue 4, 2000. Oxford: Update Software.
- Hart SP. Should aminophylline be abandoned in the treatment of acute asthma in adults? QJM 2000; 93:761–765.

Use of intravenous aminophylline is not recommended (see EBM panel).

Subsequent management

All patients must be closely supervised and oxygen therapy continued. If features of severity persist, additional measures may be required (see Box 13.33). Systemic corticosteroid

---

13.33 CONTINUED MANAGEMENT OF ACUTE SEVERE ASTHMA

If features of severity persist:

- Ipratropium bromide 0.5 mg should be added to the nebulised β_2-adrenoceptor agonist
- Continue nebulised β_2-adrenoceptor agonist treatment every 15–30 minutes as necessary. Reduce to 4-hourly once clear clinical response
- Magnesium sulphate (25 mg/kg i.v., maximum 2 g)
- Mechanical ventilation

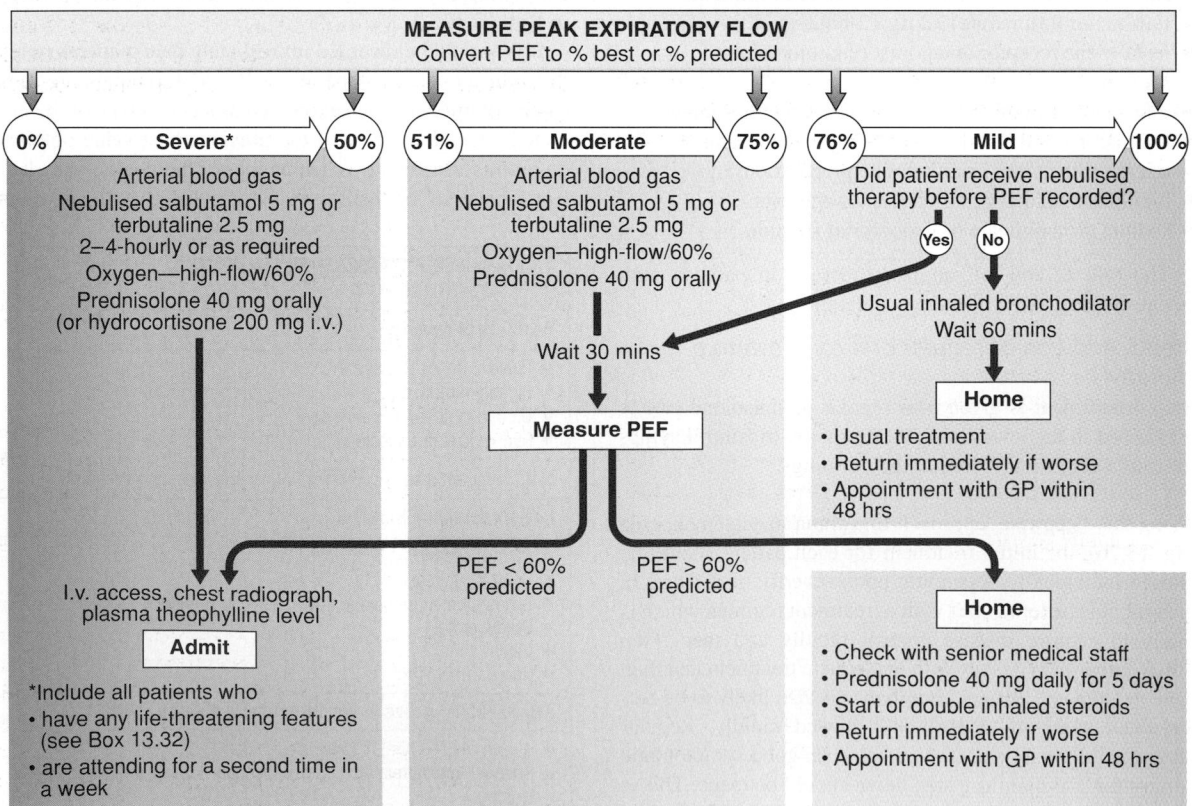

Fig. 13.27   Immediate treatment of patients with acute severe asthma.

13.34 INDICATIONS FOR ASSISTED VENTILATION IN ACUTE SEVERE ASTHMA
• Coma
• Respiratory arrest

• Deterioration of arterial blood gas tensions despite optimal therapy
   $PaO_2 < 8$ kPa and falling
   $PaCO_2 > 6$ kPa and rising
   pH low and falling (H^+ high and rising)

• Exhaustion, confusion, drowsiness

treatment with oral prednisolone 30–60 mg daily is recommended for patients responding to treatment, but intravenous hydrocortisone 200 mg 6-hourly should be continued in the seriously ill. Mechanical ventilation is necessary as a life-saving procedure in a few patients. Indications for endotracheal intubation and intermittent positive pressure ventilation are shown in Box 13.34.

Monitoring of treatment

PEF recordings should be made every 15–30 minutes to assess early response and as necessary thereafter. In hospital PEF values should be charted 4–6-hourly before and after inhaled bronchodilator treatments throughout the period of hospital stay.

Repeat measurement of arterial blood gas tensions and pH or H^+ within 1–2 hours is necessary in all patients if the first arterial sample showed features of life-threatening disease (see Box 13.33). Continuous monitoring of oxygen saturation by pulse oximetry is valuable in all patients to help assess response. Oximetry may also prevent the need to repeat an arterial puncture in some patients.

Prognosis

The prognosis of individual asthma attacks is generally good. There is occasionally a fatal outcome, especially if treatment is inadequate or delayed. Spontaneous remission is fairly common in episodic asthma, particularly in children, but rare in chronic asthma. Seasonal fluctuations can occur in both types of asthma. Atopic subjects with episodic asthma are usually worse in the summer when they are more heavily exposed to antigens, while chronic asthmatic patients are usually worse in winter months because of the increased frequency of viral infections.

Prior to discharge from hospital, patients should have been taking discharge medication (i.e. changed from nebulised drugs) for 24 hours and have a PEF of 75% predicted or personal best over that period. They should also have their own PEF meter, a written self-management plan, an adequate supply of medication and an appointment to be reviewed by their GP within 7 days.

BRONCHIECTASIS

Aetiology and pathogenesis

Bronchiectasis is the term used to describe abnormal dilatation of the bronchi. It is usually acquired (see Box 13.35) but may result from an underlying congenital defect of immune or ciliary function.

In the UK the symptoms of bronchiectasis can often be tracked back to a severe bacterial infection in childhood

13.35 CAUSES OF BRONCHIECTASIS
Congenital

• Ciliary dysfunction syndromes
   Primary ciliary dyskinesia (immotile cilia syndrome)
   Kartagener's syndrome
   Young's syndrome

• Cystic fibrosis
• Primary hypogammaglobulinaemia (see p. 795)
Acquired—children
• Pneumonia (complicating whooping cough or measles)
• Primary tuberculosis
• Foreign body
Acquired—adults
• Suppurative pneumonia
• Pulmonary tuberculosis
• Allergic bronchopulmonary aspergillosis (see p. 540)
• Bronchial tumours

consequent upon whooping cough or measles. World-wide, pulmonary tuberculosis remains the most common cause of bronchiectasis.

Bronchiectasis may be due to bronchial distension resulting from the accumulation of pus beyond a lesion obstructing a major bronchus, such as compression by tuberculous hilar lymph nodes, an inhaled foreign body or a bronchial tumour. Recurrent infection and chronic obstruction by viscid mucus are both factors in causing bronchiectasis in cystic fibrosis (see p. 522). Rarely, it may be the result of congenital dysfunction of the cilia, which is a feature of, for example, Kartagener's syndrome (bronchiectasis, sinusitis and transposition of the viscera), or immunoglobulin deficiency.

Pathology

The bronchiectatic cavities may be lined by granulation tissue, squamous epithelium or normal ciliated epithelium. There may also be inflammatory changes in the deeper layers of the bronchial wall and hypertrophy of the bronchial arteries. Chronic inflammatory and fibrotic changes are usually found in the surrounding lung tissue.

Clinical features

Bronchiectasis may involve any part of the lungs but the more efficient drainage by gravity of the upper lobes usually produces less serious symptoms and complications than when bronchiectasis involves the lower lobes.

The groups of clinical features that occur in more severe cases are shown in Box 13.36.

Physical signs in the chest may be unilateral or bilateral. If the bronchiectatic airways do not contain secretions and there is no associated lobar collapse, there are no abnormal physical signs. When there are large amounts of sputum in the bronchiectatic spaces numerous coarse crepitations can be heard over the affected areas. When collapse is present the character of the physical signs depends on whether or not the proximal bronchus supplying the collapsed lobe is patent (see Box 13.5, p. 490).

13.36 SYMPTOMS OF BRONCHIECTASIS

Due to accumulation of pus in dilated bronchi

- Chronic productive cough usually worse in mornings and often brought on by changes of posture. Sputum often copious and persistently purulent in advanced disease

Due to inflammatory changes in lung and pleura surrounding dilated bronchi

- Fever, malaise and increased cough and sputum volume when spread of infection causes pneumonia, which is frequently associated with pleurisy. Recurrent pleurisy in the same site often occurs in bronchiectasis

Haemoptysis

- Can be slight or massive and is often recurrent. Usually associated with purulent sputum or an increase in sputum purulence. Can, however, be the only symptom in so-called 'dry bronchiectasis'

General health

- When disease is extensive and sputum persistently purulent a decline in general health occurs with weight loss, anorexia, lassitude, low-grade fever, and failure to thrive in children. In these patients digital clubbing is common

Investigations

Bacteriological and mycological examination of sputum

This is necessary in all patients but is especially important in bronchiectasis associated with cystic fibrosis and in any patient who has had numerous courses of antibiotics.

Radiological examination

Bronchiectasis, unless very gross, is not usually apparent on a chest radiograph. In advanced disease the cystic bronchiectatic spaces may be visible. Abnormalities produced by associated pulmonary infection and/or collapse are evident. A diagnosis of bronchiectasis can only be made with certainty by CT (see Fig. 13.5, p. 491).

Assessment of ciliary function

A screening test can be performed in patients suspected of having a ciliary dysfunction syndrome by assessing the time taken for a small pellet of saccharin placed in the anterior chamber of the nose to reach the pharynx, when the patient can taste it. This time should not exceed 20 minutes and is greatly prolonged in patients with ciliary dysfunction. It is also possible to assess ciliary function by measuring ciliary beat frequency using biopsies taken from the nose. If ciliary function is thought to be impaired, the ciliary ultrastructure should also be determined by electron microscopy.

Management

Postural drainage

In addition to optimising treatment with inhaled bronchodilators and corticosteroids to enhance airway patency, the aim of this measure is to keep the dilated bronchi empty of secretions. Efficiently performed, it is of great value both in reducing the amount of cough and sputum and in preventing recurrent episodes of bronchopulmonary infection. In its simplest form, postural drainage consists of adopting a position in which the lobe to be drained is uppermost, thereby allowing secretions in the dilated bronchi to gravitate towards the trachea, from which they can readily be cleared by vigorous coughing. 'Percussion' of the chest wall with cupped hands aids dislodgement of sputum, and a number of mechanical devices are available which cause the chest wall to oscillate, thus achieving the same effect as postural percussion and chest wall compression. The optimum duration and frequency of postural drainage depend on the amount of sputum but 5–10 minutes once or twice daily is a minimum for most patients. Forced expiratory manoeuvres ('huffing and puffing') are of help in augmenting the expectoration of sputum.

Antibiotic therapy

The policy governing the use of antibiotics in most patients with bronchiectasis is the same as that in COPD (see p. 511). Some, especially those with cystic fibrosis, present difficult therapeutic problems because of secondary infection with bacteria such as staphylococci and Gram-negative bacilli, in particular *Pseudomonas* species. In these circumstances antibiotic therapy should be guided by the microbiological results but frequently requires the use of oral ciprofloxacin (250–750 mg twice daily) or ceftazidime by intravenous injection or infusion (100–150 mg/kg daily in three divided doses). The bronchi of some patients with cystic fibrosis also become colonised by *Aspergillus fumigatus*.

Surgical treatment

Surgery is only indicated in a small minority of individuals. These are usually young patients in whom the bronchiectasis is unilateral and confined to a single lobe or segment as demonstrated by CT. Unfortunately, many of the patients in whom medical treatment proves unsuccessful are also unsuitable for pulmonary resection because of either extensive bronchiectasis or coexisting chronic lung disease. Resection of areas of bronchiectatic lung has no role in the management of the progressive forms of bronchiectasis—for example, those associated with ciliary dysfunction and cystic fibrosis.

Prognosis

The disease is progressive when associated with ciliary dysfunction and cystic fibrosis, and inevitably causes respiratory failure and right ventricular failure. In other patients the prognosis can be relatively good if postural drainage is performed regularly and antibiotics are used judiciously.

Prevention

As bronchiectasis commonly starts in childhood following measles, whooping cough or a primary tuberculous infection, it is essential that these conditions receive adequate prophylaxis and treatment. The early recognition and treatment of bronchial obstruction are also particularly important.

CYSTIC FIBROSIS

Epidemiology and pathogenesis

Cystic fibrosis (CF) is the most common severe autosomal recessive disease in Caucasians, occurring with a carrier rate

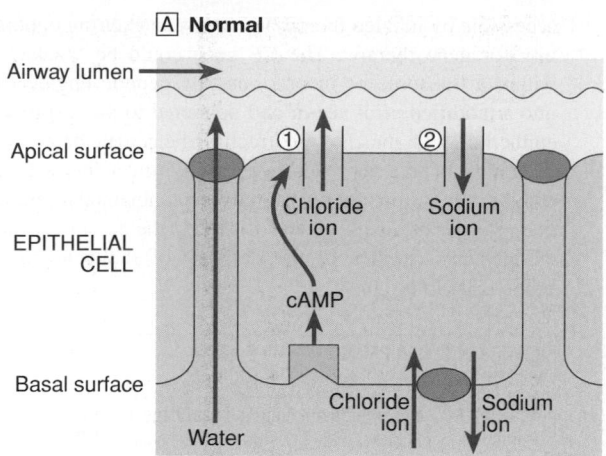
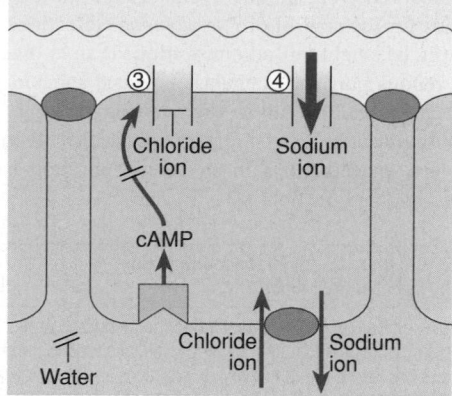

β₂-adrenoceptor

Fig. 13.28 Cystic fibrosis: basic defect in the pulmonary epithelium. $\boxed{A}$ The CF gene codes for a chloride channel (1) in the apical (luminal) membrane of epithelial cells in the conducting airways. This channel is normally controlled by cyclic adenosine monophosphate (cAMP) and indirectly by β-adrenoceptor stimulation. It is one of several apical ion channels which together control the quantity and solute content of airway-lining fluid. Normal channels appear to inhibit the adjacent epithelial sodium channels (2). $\boxed{B}$ In CF, one of many CF gene defects causes absence or defective function of this chloride channel (3). This leads to reduced chloride secretion and loss of inhibition of sodium channels with excessive sodium resorption (4) and dehydration of the airway lining. The resulting abnormal airway-lining fluid is believed to predispose to infection by mechanisms which are not fully understood.

of 1 in 25 and an incidence of about 1 in 2500 live births (see p. 344). CF is the result of mutations affecting a gene (located on the long arm of chromosome 7) which encodes for a chloride channel known as cystic fibrosis transmembrane conductance regulator (CFTR), which is essential for the regulation of salt and water movement across cell membranes. The most common CFTR mutation in northern European and American populations is Δ508, but numerous mutations have now been identified in this region. The genetic defect causes an increased sodium chloride content in sweat and increased electrical potential difference across the respiratory epithelium which can be detected in the nose (see Fig. 13.28). This results in much increased viscosity of secretions in the lung and other organs, which causes ciliary dysfunction and chronic bronchial infection. Recurrent exacerbations of bronchial infection predispose to bronchial wall damage, eventually causing bronchiectasis, often predominantly in the upper lobes initially but subsequently in all areas of both lungs, with the end result of death from respiratory failure. There are also disorders in the gut epithelium, and in the pancreas and liver (causing intestinal malabsorption, diabetes and hepatic cirrhosis). Most men with CF are infertile due to failure of development of the vas deferens. Population carrier screening is feasible but unlikely to affect overall patient numbers significantly. However, early diagnosis can be achieved by neonatal screening, and in some cases by amniocentesis.

Clinical features

Lung function is normal at birth, which leads to the hope that if the basic defect can be corrected by gene therapy many of the sequelae (see Box 13.37) might be avoided. Bronchiectasis, however, usually develops at a young age. Initially, the bacteria associated with CF are those expected

13.37 COMPLICATIONS OF CYSTIC FIBROSIS	
Respiratory	
• Spontaneous pneumothorax	• Respiratory failure
• Haemoptysis	• Cor pulmonale
• Nasal polyps	
Gastrointestinal	
• Malabsorption	• Biliary cirrhosis
• Distal intestinal obstruction syndrome	• Increased frequency of gallstones
Others	
• Diabetes (11% of adults)	• Psychosocial problems
• Delayed puberty	• Amyloidosis
• Male infertility	• Arthropathy

in bronchiectasis of other causes (see p. 521), but infection with *Staphylococcus aureus* tends to be early in CF and the majority have *Pseudomonas* infection at an early age. Repeated lung infections, inflammation and scarring almost inevitably lead to respiratory failure and death.

Management

The management of established cystic fibrosis is that of severe bronchiectasis (see opposite). All patients with cystic fibrosis who produce sputum should have regular chest physiotherapy, which should be performed more frequently during exacerbations. Lung infections are usually predominantly caused by *Pseudomonas* species and *Staph. aureus*. Unfortunately, the bronchi of many CF patients eventually become colonised with pathogens which are resistant to most antibiotics; *Pseudomonas aeruginosa* and *Burkholderia cepacia* (previously known as *Pseudomonas cepacia*) are the main culprits. Infections with *Haemophilus influenzae* can be treated with a number of antibiotics and *Staph. aureus* should be treated with flucloxacillin or erythromycin. Patients requiring frequent courses of intravenous antibiotics for the control of *Pseudomonas* infections can, with benefit, be taught self-administration via an in-dwelling central venous port and cannula, implanted subcutaneously in the chest wall to allow intravenous therapy at home. Nebulised antibiotic therapy, mainly with colistin, is used between exacerbations in an attempt to suppress chronic pseudomonal infection.

EBM

CYSTIC FIBROSIS—role of nebulised anti-pseudomonal antibiotics

'Meta-analysis of RCTs demonstrates that nebulised anti-pseudomonal antibiotic therapy improves lung function and decreases the risk of infective exacerbations and hospitalisation in patients with cystic fibrosis and *Pseudomonas aeruginosa* infection. The long-term benefit and impact of such treatment on quality of life and survival remain to be determined.'

- Ramsey BW, Pepe MS, Quan JM, et al. Intermittent administration of inhaled tobramycin in patients with cystic fibrosis. N Engl J Med 1999; 340:23–30.
- Ryan G, Mukhopadhyay S, Singh M. Nebulised anti-pseudomonal antibiotics for cystic fibrosis (Cochrane Review). Cochrane Library, issue 4, 2000. Oxford: Update Software.

Further information: 💻 www.update-software.com/ccweb/cochrane/revabstr/ab001021.htm

---

Treatment with nebulised recombinant human DNAase (rhDNAase) has been available since 1994. The aim of this therapy is to solubilise DNA derived from disintegrated inflammatory cells, which is a major contributor to the viscosity of bronchial secretions in CF, in which it is present in abundance. This therapy has been shown to improve pulmonary function and increase well-being in a subgroup of patients, and perhaps also to reduce the number of infective exacerbations. There is also some evidence that it can reduce the neutrophil elastase load and, therefore, decelerate bronchial wall tissue damage. It has to be emphasised that this treatment is very expensive and is not of benefit to all patients, which makes clinical selection of patients for such treatment difficult. Aerosol α_1-antitrypsin treatment has been used to reduce the neutrophil elastase load, but this form of therapy is even less established than rhDNAase.

A number of patients with cystic fibrosis develop symptoms of bronchospasm, which can be treated effectively with bronchodilators following appropriate reversibility tests. Allergic bronchopulmonary aspergillosis (see p. 540) is also a well-recognised complication of CF. It is also common for 'atypical mycobacteria' to be cultured from the sputum of CF patients, but it is frequently difficult to determine whether these organisms are causing disease, or are benign 'colonisers' of the bronchiectatic airways which do not require specific therapy.

The prognosis of CF has greatly improved in the last decade, mainly because of better control of bronchial sepsis and maintenance of nutrition. The median survival of patients with CF is now predicted to be at least 40 years for children born in the 1990s. Organ transplantation remains last-resort therapy for patients with end-stage disease.

The potential for somatic gene therapy

The discovery of the CF gene and the fact that the lung defect is located in the respiratory epithelium (which is accessible by inhaled therapy) presents an exciting opportunity for gene therapy. The CF gene could be 'packaged' within a liposome or incorporated by genetic engineering into a modified viral vector and delivered to the respiratory epithelium with the aim of correcting the genetic defect. The feasibility of this approach is currently under investigation and initially promising results have been obtained in preliminary studies of the CF gene delivered to the nasal mucosa of CF patients. Studies of the delivery of the gene to the bronchi are in progress.

ISSUES IN OLDER PEOPLE
OBSTRUCTIVE PULMONARY DISEASE

- Both COPD and asthma are common in old age and are not mutually exclusive. A bias towards misdiagnosis of COPD rather than asthma is well recognised in elderly men and those of lower socio-economic class.
- Older people with poor vision have difficulty reading PEF meters.
- Older people perceive acute bronchoconstriction less well than younger patients, so their description of symptoms is not a reliable indicator of severity, and 'on demand' bronchodilators may not be appropriate as a first step in treatment.
- The beneficial effects of stopping smoking on the rate of loss of lung function decline with age but remain valuable up to the age of 80.
- Most older people cannot use metered dose inhalers because of difficulty coordinating and triggering the device. Even mild cognitive impairment virtually precludes their use. Spacer devices are much preferred by patients. Frequent demonstration and reinstruction in the use of all devices are required.
- Mortality rates for acute asthma are higher in old age, partly because patients under-estimate the severity of bronchoconstriction and develop less tachycardia and pulsus paradoxus for the same degree of bronchoconstriction.
- Advanced age in itself is not a barrier to intensive care or mechanical ventilation in an acute episode of asthma or COPD, but a decision about this can be difficult and should be shared with the patient (if possible), relatives and general practitioner.

INFECTIONS OF THE RESPIRATORY SYSTEM

Infections of the upper and lower respiratory tract continue to be a major cause of morbidity and mortality throughout the world, with patients at the extremes of age or with pre-existing lung disease or immune suppression being at particular risk. Viruses are the most frequent cause of upper respiratory illnesses, with bacteria being responsible for the majority of community- and hospital-acquired pneumonia in adults. Organisms such as *Mycoplasma*, *Coxiella* and *Chlamydia* are less common causes of severe pneumonia. Pulmonary infection by *Mycobacterium tuberculosis*, atypical mycobacteria and fungi results in diseases of a more chronic type. These are described separately.

UPPER RESPIRATORY TRACT INFECTIONS

The clinical features, complications and management of the common and most important upper respiratory tract infections are summarised in Box 13.38. The vast majority of

13.38 THE COMMON AND MOST IMPORTANT UPPER RESPIRATORY TRACT INFECTIONS: CLINICAL FEATURES, COMPLICATIONS AND MANAGEMENT

Infection	Clinical features	Complications	Management
Acute coryza (common cold)	Rapid onset. Burning and tickling sensation in nose. Sneezing. Sore throat. Blocked nose with watery discharge. Discharge usually green/yellow after 24–48 hrs. Nasal allergy can give rise to similar clinical features	Sinusitis. Lower respiratory tract infection (bronchitis/pneumonia). Hearing impairment, otitis media (due to blockage of eustachian tubes)	Most do not require treatment. Paracetamol 0.5–1 g 4–6-hourly for relief of systemic symptoms. Nasal decongestant in some cases. Antibiotics not necessary in uncomplicated coryza
Acute laryngitis	Often a complication of acute coryza. Dry sore throat. Hoarse voice or loss of voice. Attempts to speak cause pain. Initially, painful and unproductive cough. Stridor in children (croup) because of inflammatory oedema leading to partial obstruction of a small larynx	Complications rare. Chronic laryngitis. Downward spread of infection may cause tracheitis, bronchitis or pneumonia	Rest voice. Paracetamol 0.5–1 g 4–6-hourly for relief of discomfort and pyrexia. Steam inhalations may be of value. Antibiotics not necessary in simple acute laryngitis
Acute laryngo-tracheobronchitis (croup)*	Initial symptoms like common cold. Sudden paroxysms of cough accompanied by stridor and breathlessness. Contraction of accessory muscles and indrawing of intercostal spaces. Cyanosis and asphyxia in small children, if appropriate treatment not given	Asphyxia. Death. Superinfection with bacteria, especially *Strep. pneumoniae* and *Staph. aureus*. Viscid secretions may occlude bronchi	Inhalations of steam and humidified air/high concentrations of oxygen. Endotracheal intubation or tracheostomy to relieve laryngeal obstruction and allow clearing of bronchial secretions. Intravenous antibiotic therapy for seriously ill (co-amoxiclav or erythromycin). Maintain adequate hydration
Acute epiglottitis	Fever and sore throat, rapidly leading to stridor because of swelling of epiglottis and surrounding structures (infection with *H. influenzae*). Stridor and cough in absence of much hoarseness may distinguish acute epiglottitis from other causes of stridor	Death from asphyxia which may be precipitated by attempts to examine the throat—*avoid using a tongue depressor or any instrument* unless facilities for endotracheal intubation or tracheostomy are immediately available	Intravenous antibiotic therapy essential. Co-amoxiclav or chloramphenicol. Other measures as for acute laryngotracheobronchitis
Acute bronchitis and tracheitis	Often follows acute coryza. Initially irritating unproductive cough accompanied by retrosternal discomfort of tracheitis. Chest tightness, wheeze and breathlessness when bronchi become involved. Tracheitis causes pain on coughing. Sputum is initially scanty or mucoid. After a day or so sputum becomes mucopurulent, more copious and, in tracheitis, often blood-stained. Acute bronchial infection may be associated with a pyrexia of 38–39°C and a neutrophil leucocytosis. Spontaneous recovery occurs over a few days	Bronchopneumonia. Exacerbation of chronic bronchitis which often results in type II respiratory failure in patients with severe COPD. Acute exacerbation of bronchial asthma	Specific treatment rarely necessary in previously healthy individuals. Cough may be eased by pholcodine 5–10 mg 6–8-hourly. In patients with COPD (see p. 508) and asthma (see p. 513) aggressive treatment of exacerbations may be required. Amoxicillin 250 mg 8-hourly should be given to previously healthy patients who are thought to be developing bronchopneumonia (see also p. 526)
Influenza (a specific acute illness caused by a group of myxoviruses—two common types, A and B)	Sudden onset of pyrexia associated with generalised aches and pains, anorexia, nausea and vomiting. Degree of ill health ranges from mild to rapidly fatal. Usually harsh unproductive cough. Most patients do not develop complications and acute symptoms subside within 3–5 days, but may be followed by 'post-influenzal asthenia' which can persist for several weeks. During epidemics the diagnosis is usually easy. Sporadic cases may have to be diagnosed by virus isolation, fluorescent antibody techniques or serological tests for specific antibodies	Tracheitis, bronchitis, bronchiolitis and bronchopneumonia. Secondary bacterial invasion by *Strep. pneumoniae, H. influenzae* and *Staph. aureus* may occur. Toxic cardiomyopathy may cause sudden death (rare). Encephalitis, demyelinating encephalopathy and peripheral neuropathy are also rare complications	Bed rest is advisable until fever has subsided. Paracetamol 0.5–1 g 4–6-hourly can be used to relieve headache and generalised pains. Pholcodine 5–10 mg 6–8-hourly may be given to suppress cough. Specific treatment for pneumonia (see p. 528) may be necessary

* Whooping cough (caused by *Bordetella pertussis*) is often considered a disease of non-immunised children but it also occurs in sporadic 'epidemics' in middle life when immunisation effectiveness has waned. After a short, febrile tracheobronchitis (which itself is responsive to antibiotics), severe episodic paroxysmal coughing bouts, associated with laryngospasm and often leading to intercostal muscle tears or fractured ribs, may persist for many weeks.

13.39 RESPIRATORY INFECTIONS CAUSED BY VIRUSES	
Clinical syndrome	**Usual cause (other causes in parentheses)**
Epidemic influenza	Influenza A and B
'Influenza-like' illness	Adenoviruses, rhinoviruses (enteroviruses)
Sore throat	Adenoviruses (enteroviruses, parainfluenza viruses, influenza A and B in partially immune)
Common cold (coryza)	Rhinoviruses (coronaviruses, enteroviruses, adenoviruses, respiratory syncytial virus)
'Feverish' cold	Rhinoviruses, enteroviruses (influenza A and B, parainfluenza viruses, respiratory syncytial virus)
Croup	Parainfluenza 1, 2, 3 (rhinoviruses, enteroviruses)
Bronchitis	Rhinoviruses, adenoviruses (influenza A and B)
Bronchiolitis	Respiratory syncytial virus (parainfluenza 3)
Pneumonia	Influenza A and B, chickenpox (respiratory syncytial virus, parainfluenza, measles and adenoviruses in children and elderly)

these illnesses, of which acute coryza (common cold) is by far the most common, are caused by viruses (see Box 13.39). Immunity is short-lived and virus-specific. Other viral infections include acute laryngitis and acute laryngotracheobronchitis. Bacterial infection is the usual cause of acute tonsillitis, otitis media and epiglottitis.

Most patients with upper respiratory tract infections recover rapidly and specific investigation is indicated only in more severe illness. The possibility of acute epiglottitis, which represents a medical emergency, must be considered at all times (see Box 13.38). Viruses can be isolated from exfoliated cells collected on throat swabs, and may be identified retrospectively by serological tests. Certain viruses can be identified in exfoliated cells by the fluorescent antibody technique, allowing the pathogen to be identified more rapidly. Throat swabs may also be helpful if streptococcal pharyngitis is suspected, and examination of the blood will

---

EBM

ACUTE UNCOMPLICATED UPPER RESPIRATORY TRACT INFECTIONS—role of antibiotics

'Two SRs of RCTs have found no evidence that antibiotics have a clinically important effect in patients with acute undifferentiated upper respiratory tract infections. Antibiotics can prevent the non-suppurative complications of β-haemolytic streptococcal pharyngitis.'

- Arrol B, Kenealy T. The use of antibiotics versus placebo in the common cold (Cochrane Review). Cochrane Library, issue 3, 1999. Oxford: Update Software.
- Fahey T, Stocks N, Thomas T. Systematic review of the treatment of upper respiratory tract infection. Arch Dis Child 1998; 79:225–230.

EBM

INFLUENZA VACCINE—use in elderly people

'One SR of cohort studies and several recent RCTs have found that influenza vaccination reduces the risk of influenza and death in elderly people.'

- Gross PA, Hermogenes AW, Sacks HS, et al. The efficacy of influenza vaccine in elderly persons: a meta-analysis and review of the literature. Ann Intern Med 1995; 123:518–527.
- Nichol KL, Margolis KL, Wuorenma J, Von Sternberg T. The efficacy of influenza vaccination in elderly persons living in the community. N Engl J Med 1994; 31:778–784.

Further information: 💻 www.clinicalevidence.org

---

identify infectious mononucleosis (see p. 16). Radiographic examination may be required if an underlying chronic infection involving the sinuses is suspected.

PNEUMONIA

Pneumonia is defined as an acute respiratory illness associated with recently developed radiological pulmonary shadowing which either is segmental or affects more than one lobe. As the setting in which a pneumonia develops has such major implications for the likely organisms involved and hence dictates the immediate choice of antibiotics, pneumonias are now classified as community-acquired, hospital-acquired, or those occurring in the immunocompromised host or damaged lung (including suppurative and aspirational pneumonia).

COMMUNITY-ACQUIRED PNEUMONIA

This form of pneumonia is responsible for over 1 000 000 admissions per year in the UK. Infection is usually spread by droplet inhalation and, while most patients affected are previously well, cigarette smoke, alcohol and corticosteroid therapy all impair ciliary and immune function. Other risk factors include old age, recent influenza infection, pre-existing lung disease and, for certain forms of pneumonia, contact with sick birds (*Chlamydia psittaci*) or farm environments (*Coxiella burnetii*). Knowledge of the patient's recent travel history and local epidemics is also valuable. Appropriate investigation allows a microbiological diagnosis to be made in approximately 60% of patients with pneumonia. 'Lobar pneumonia' is a radiological and pathological term referring to homogeneous consolidation (red hepatisation) of one or more lung lobes, often with associated pleural inflammation; bronchopneumonia refers to more patchy alveolar consolidation associated with bronchial and bronchiolar inflammation often affecting both lower lobes.

Clinical features

Patients present with a short illness of cough, fever and malaise, often associated with pleuritic chest pain which is occasionally referred to the shoulder or anterior abdominal wall. The cough is characteristically short, painful and at first dry, but later becomes productive and may become rust-coloured or even frankly blood-stained. The sudden onset of a high fever can result in rigors or, in children, vomiting or a febrile convulsion. Appetite is usually lost and headache is a frequent accompanying symptom. In patients with severe pneumonia confusion can be an early and dominant problem. Certain features may suggest a particular microbiological diagnosis (see Box 13.40).

Physical signs include a significant pyrexia, tachycardia, tachypnoea, evidence of hypoxaemia and, not infrequently, hypotension and confusion. Pleurisy often results in diminution of respiratory movement and a pleural rub on the affected side. At a variable time after onset, generally within 2 days, signs of consolidation appear, with impairment of

13.40 CLINICAL AND RADIOLOGICAL CHARACTERISTICS OF COMMUNITY-ACQUIRED PNEUMONIAS CAUSED BY SPECIFIC ORGANISMS

Organism	Frequency*	Clinical features	Radiological features
Common organisms			
Streptococcus pneumoniae	30%(+)	Young to middle-aged, rapid onset, high fever, rigors, pleuritic chest pain, herpes simplex labialis, 'rusty' sputum	Lobar consolidation, one or more lobes
Chlamydia pneumoniae	10%	Young to middle-aged, large-scale epidemics or sporadic, often mild, self-limiting disease. Associated sinusitis, pharyngitis, laryngitis. White cell count often normal, liver transaminases elevated. Usually diagnosed on serology	Small segmental infiltrates
Mycoplasma pneumoniae	9%	Children and young adults, autumn and 3–4-yearly cycles. Insidious onset, headaches, systemic features, often few signs in chest. Erythema nodosum, myocarditis, pericarditis, meningoencephalitis, rash, haemolytic anaemia	Patchy or lobar consolidation, hilar lymphadenopathy may be seen
Legionella pneumoniae	5%	Middle to old age, recent travel, local epidemics around point source, e.g. cooling tower. Headache, malaise, myalgia, high fever, dry cough, gastrointestinal symptoms. Confusion, hepatitis, hyponatraemia, hypoalbuminaemia	Shadowing may spread despite antibiotics and often slow to resolve
Uncommon organisms			
Haemophilus influenzae	3%	Often underlying lung disease, purulent sputum	Bronchopneumonia
Staphylococcus aureus	< 1%	Coexistent debilitating illness. Often complicates viral pneumonia. Can arise from, or cause, abscesses in other organs, e.g. osteomyelitis	Lobar or segmental. Abscess formation, residual cysts
Chlamydia psittaci	< 1%	Contact with sick birds. Malaise, low-grade fever, protracted illness. Hepatosplenomegaly	Patchy lower lobe consolidation
Coxiella burnetii		Farm or abattoir contact. Chronic course, influenza-like illness, dry cough, conjunctivitis, hepatomegaly, endocarditis	Multiple segmental opacities
Klebsiella pneumoniae	< 1%	Systemic disturbance marked, widespread consolidation, often in upper lobes, purulent dark sputum, high mortality	Expansion of affected lobes
Actinomyces israelii	< 1%	Mouth commensal. Cervicofacial, abdominal or pulmonary infection, empyema, chest wall sinuses, pus with 'sulphur grains'	Abscesses, pleural effusions and bone involvement
Primary viral pneumonias		Influenza, parainfluenza and measles can cause pneumonia commonly complicated by bacterial infection. Respiratory syncytial virus seen mainly in infancy. Varicella (chickenpox) can cause severe pneumonia	Chickenpox produces multiple miliary nodular shadows which may calcify

* No microbiological diagnosis established in approximately 40% of patients with community-acquired pneumonia admitted to hospital.

the percussion note and high-pitched bronchial breath sounds. When resolution begins, numerous coarse crepitations are heard, indicating liquefaction of the alveolar exudate. If a para-pneumonic pleural effusion develops, physical signs of fluid in the pleural space are usually found, but bronchial breath sounds can persist and the presence of an empyema (see p. 569) may be suspected only from the recurrence or persistence of pyrexia. Upper abdominal tenderness is sometimes apparent in patients with lower lobe pneumonia or if there is associated hepatitis.

Investigations

The main objectives of investigating patients with a clinically based diagnosis of pneumonia are:

- to obtain a radiological confirmation of the diagnosis
- to exclude other conditions that may mimic pneumonia (see Box 13.41)
- to obtain a microbiological diagnosis
- to assess the severity of the pneumonia
- to identify the development of complications.

Radiological examination

In lobar pneumonia, the chest radiograph shows a homogeneous opacity localised to the affected lobe or segment; this usually appears within 12–18 hours of the onset of the illness (see Fig. 13.29). Radiological examination is also particularly helpful if a complication such as pleural effusion, intrapulmonary abscess formation or empyema is suspected. Hilar lymphadenopathy is occasionally seen in mycoplasma pneumonia, and lung cavities are more frequently observed in patients with staphylococcal or pneumococcal serotype 3 pneumonia. Follow-up radiological examination is essential as failure of a pneumonia to resolve may indicate underlying bronchial obstruction (e.g. a foreign body or carcinoma).

13.41 DIFFERENTIAL DIAGNOSIS OF PNEUMONIA

Pulmonary infarction

- Often presents like bacterial pneumonia, but pyrexia usually less, cough not as troublesome, haemoptysis much more common and the source of embolism may be apparent

Pulmonary/pleural tuberculosis

- Acute pulmonary tuberculosis can simulate pneumonia, but patients seldom as acutely ill. Tuberculous pleurisy may also present like a bacterial pleural infection

Pulmonary oedema

- Pulmonary oedema, especially if unilateral and localised, may be difficult to distinguish from pneumonia on the chest radiograph. Absence of fever and presence of heart disease favour a diagnosis of oedema

Inflammatory conditions below the diaphragm

- Conditions such as cholecystitis, perforated peptic ulcer, subphrenic abscess, acute pancreatitis and hepatic amoebiasis may be mistaken for lower lobe pneumonia associated with diaphragmatic pleurisy

Rare disorders

- Pulmonary eosinophilia, intrathoracic manifestations of connective tissue disorders, acute allergic alveolitis, Wegener's granulomatosis

Microbiological investigations

Every effort should be made to establish a microbiological diagnosis, as such information is invaluable in tailoring antibiotic therapy and in managing any complications. The identification of organisms such as *Legionella pneumophila* also has important public health implications. Rapid results can sometimes be obtained with 'bedside' complement fixation tests for antigen levels (for example, of *H. influenzae* and *Pneumocystis carinii*) in urine and other body fluids. In patients who are severely ill a microbiological diagnosis becomes essential and, if sputum cannot be obtained, an attempt should be made to aspirate secretions or washings from the trachea or lower respiratory tract either by bronchoscopy or by inserting a needle through the cricothyroid membrane. Some patients can be induced to produce sputum by the administration of nebulised hypertonic saline. A summary of the microbiological investigations required in patients with community-acquired pneumonia is provided in Box 13.42; see also Figure 13.30.

Arterial blood gas measurements

These should be measured in all patients admitted to hospital with a diagnosis of pneumonia.

General blood tests

A high neutrophil leucocytosis favours a diagnosis of bacterial (particularly pneumococcal) pneumonia; patients with pneumonia caused by atypical agents tend to have a marginally raised or normal white cell count. A marked leucopenia indicates either a viral aetiology or an overwhelming bacterial infection.

Assessment of disease severity

It is essential that in every patient with a clinical diagnosis of pneumonia an assessment is made to determine the severity

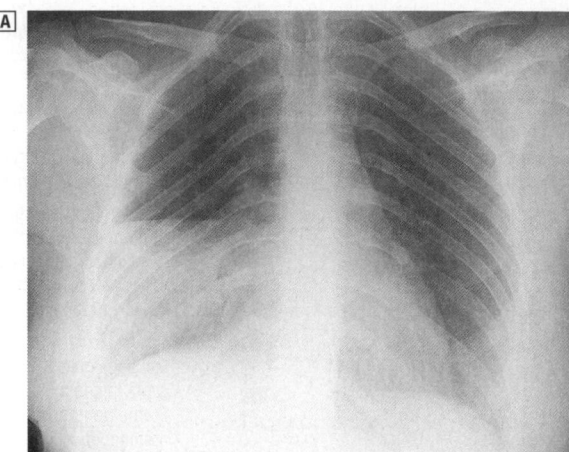

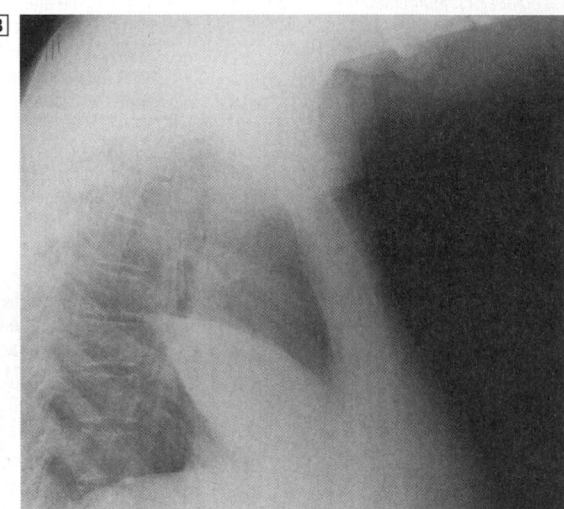

Fig. 13.29 Pneumonia of the right middle lobe. A Postero-anterior (PA) view: consolidation in right middle lobe with characteristic opacification beneath the horizontal fissure and loss of normal contrast between the right heart border and lung. B Lateral view: consolidation confined to the anteriorly situated middle lobe.

of the disease. The use of simple clinical and laboratory parameters can determine very accurately those at high risk of death (see Box 13.43) and forms an important guide to the level of patient monitoring required. This assessment also has an important bearing on antibiotic choice. As a simple guide, patients with two or more of the four cardinal markers of severity, namely a respiratory rate ≥ 30, a diastolic blood pressure ≤ 60 mmHg, a serum urea ≥ 7 mmol/l or the presence of confusion, have a 36-fold higher risk of dying compared with those patients without such features. Likewise, it is important to appreciate that a higher proportion of patients with mycoplasma pneumonia die compared to those with pneumococcal pneumonia and that in the latter condition coexistent septicaemia increases the mortality rate significantly.

Management

With appropriate intervention most patients respond promptly to antibiotic treatment. Delayed recovery suggests either that some complication such as empyema has developed or that

13.42 MICROBIOLOGICAL INVESTIGATIONS IN PATIENTS WITH COMMUNITY-ACQUIRED PNEUMONIA

All patients

- Sputum—direct smear by Gram (see Fig. 13.30) and Ziehl–Neelsen stains. Culture and antimicrobial sensitivity testing
- Blood culture—frequently positive in pneumococcal pneumonia
- Serology—acute and convalescent titres to diagnose *Mycoplasma*, *Chlamydia*, *Legionella* and viral infections. Pneumococcal antigen detection in serum

Severe community-acquired pneumonia

The above tests *plus* consider:
- Tracheal aspirate, induced sputum, bronchoalveolar lavage, protected brush specimen or percutaneous needle aspiration. Direct fluorescent antibody stain for *Legionella* and viruses
- Serology—*Legionella* antigen in urine. Pneumococcal antigen in sputum and blood. Immediate IgM for *Mycoplasma*
- Cold agglutinins—positive in 50% of patients with *Mycoplasma*

Selected patients

- Throat/nasopharyngeal swabs—helpful in children or during influenza epidemic
- Pleural fluid—should always be sampled when present in more than trivial amounts, preferably with ultrasound guidance

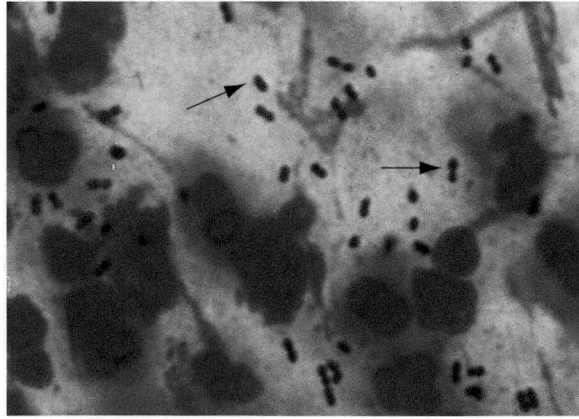

Fig. 13.30   Gram stain of sputum showing Gram-positive diplococci characteristic of *Strep. pneumoniae* (arrows).

the diagnosis is incorrect. Alternatively, the pneumonia may be secondary to a proximal bronchial obstruction or recurrent aspiration which delays recovery.

Oxygen

Oxygen should be administered to all hypoxaemic patients, and high concentrations ($\geq 35\%$) should be used in all patients who do not have hypercapnia associated with advanced COPD. Assisted ventilation should be considered at an early stage in all patients who remain significantly hypoxaemic despite adequate oxygen therapy. Most patients with moderate to severe pneumonia also require intravenous fluids and occasionally inotrope support (see p. 203).

Antibiotic treatment

Antibiotics should be given as soon as a clinical diagnosis of pneumonia is made. If possible, culture specimens should be sent prior to starting antibiotics but such treatment should

13.43 FEATURES ASSOCIATED WITH A HIGH MORTALITY IN PNEUMONIA

Clinical

- Age 60 years or older
- Respiratory rate > 30/min
- Diastolic blood pressure 60 mmHg or less
- Confusion
- More than one lobe involved on chest radiograph
- Presence of underlying disease

Laboratory

- Hypoxaemia ($PaO_2 < 8$ kPa)
- Leucopenia (white blood cells $< 4000 \times 10^9$/litre)
- Leucocytosis (white blood cells $> 20\,000 \times 10^9$/litre)
- Raised serum urea (> 7 mmol/l)
- Positive blood culture
- Hypoalbuminaemia

not be delayed if, for example, a sputum sample is not readily available. The antibiotic regimens currently recommended in uncomplicated and severe community-acquired pneumonia are detailed in Box 13.44. If *Strep. pneumoniae* is identified as the causative organism, benzylpenicillin 1–2 g 6-hourly (i.v.) can be used in place of amoxicillin. Oral cephalosporins should not be used in the management of community-acquired pneumonia as they do not penetrate well into sputum or bronchial fluids and do not cover likely organisms. Patients with proven *Klebsiella* pneumonia should be treated with gentamicin (dose according to patient age, weight, creatinine clearance and intended frequency of use) plus either ceftazidime 1 g 8-hourly (i.v.) or ciprofloxacin 200 mg 12-hourly (i.v. infusion). *Chlamydia pneumoniae* is a somewhat difficult organism to culture and hence most cases are diagnosed late or retrospectively on serological grounds. In proven or suspected (epidemic) cases, erythromycin or tetracycline is recommended. Psittacosis is treated with tetracycline 500 mg 6-hourly orally or 500 mg 12-hourly i.v., or erythromycin at an equivalent dose. Actinomycosis, which is now regarded as

13.44 ANTIBIOTIC TREATMENT FOR COMMUNITY-ACQUIRED PNEUMONIA (CAP)

Uncomplicated CAP

- Amoxicillin 500 mg 8-hourly orally
- *If patient allergic to penicillin*
  Clarithromycin 500 mg 12-hourly orally *or*
  Erythromycin 500 mg 6-hourly orally
- *If Staphylococcus is cultured or suspected*
  Flucloxacillin 1–2 g 6-hourly i.v. *plus*
  Clarithromycin 500 mg 12-hourly i.v.
- *If Mycoplasma or Legionella is suspected*
  Clarithromycin 500 mg 12-hourly orally or i.v. *or*
  Erythromycin 500 mg 6-hourly orally or i.v. *plus*
  Rifampicin 600 mg 12-hourly i.v. in severe cases

Severe CAP

- Clarithromycin 500 mg 12-hourly i.v. *or*
  Erythromycin 500 mg 6-hourly i.v. *plus*
- Co-amoxiclav 1.2 g 8-hourly i.v. *or*
  Ceftriaxone 1–2 g daily i.v. *or*
  Cefuroxime 1.5 g 8-hourly i.v. *or*
  Amoxicillin 1 g 6-hourly i.v. *plus* flucloxacillin 2 g 6-hourly i.v.

an anaerobic bacterial infection, responds best to benzyl-penicillin 2–4 g 6-hourly (i.v.). Chickenpox pneumonia is usually treated with oral aciclovir 200 mg five times daily for 5 days.

In most cases of uncomplicated pneumococcal pneumonia a 7–10-day course of treatment is usually adequate, although treatment is usually required for 14 days or longer in patients with *Legionella*, staphylococcal or *Klebsiella* pneumonia.

Treatment of pleural pain

It is important to relieve pleural pain in order to allow the patient to breathe normally and cough efficiently. Mild analgesics such as paracetamol are rarely adequate and most patients require pethidine 50–100 mg or morphine 10–15 mg by intramuscular or intravenous injection. Opiates, however, must be used with extreme caution in patients with poor respiratory function.

Physiotherapy

Formal physiotherapy is not indicated in patients with community-acquired pneumonia; however, assisted coughing is important in patients who suppress cough because of pleural pain. The administration of analgesic drugs should be coordinated with this form of physiotherapy to optimise patient cooperation.

Complications

Assessing progress can be difficult in patients with pneumonia. Although the response to antibiotics may be rapid and dramatic, fever may persist for several days and the chest radiograph often takes several weeks or even months to resolve, especially in the elderly. Failure to respond to therapy may indicate use of the wrong antibiotic, mixed infection, bronchial obstruction, the wrong diagnosis (e.g. pulmonary thromboembolism) or the development of a complication (see Box 13.45).

13.45 COMPLICATIONS OF PNEUMONIA

- Para-pneumonic effusion—common
- Empyema—see page 569
- Retention of sputum causing lobar collapse
- Development of thromboembolic disease
- Pneumothorax—particularly with *Staph. aureus*
- Suppurative pneumonia/lung abscess—see below
- ARDS, renal failure, multi-organ failure
- Ectopic abscess formation (*Staph. aureus*)
- Hepatitis, pericarditis, myocarditis, meningoencephalitis
- Pyrexia due to drug hypersensitivity

SUPPURATIVE AND ASPIRATIONAL PNEUMONIA (INCLUDING PULMONARY ABSCESS)

Suppurative pneumonia is the term used to describe a form of pneumonic consolidation in which there is destruction of the lung parenchyma by the inflammatory process. Although microabscess formation is a characteristic histological feature of suppurative pneumonia, it is usual to restrict the term 'pulmonary abscess' to lesions in which

there is a fairly large localised collection of pus, or a cavity lined by chronic inflammatory tissue, from which pus has escaped by rupture into a bronchus.

Suppurative pneumonia and pulmonary abscess may be produced by infection of previously healthy lung tissue with *Staph. aureus* or *Klebsiella pneumoniae*. These are, in effect, primary bacterial pneumonias associated with pulmonary suppuration. More frequently, suppurative pneumonia and pulmonary abscess develop after the inhalation of septic material during operations on the nose, mouth or throat under general anaesthesia, or of vomitus during anaesthesia or coma. In such circumstances gross oral sepsis may be a predisposing factor. Additional risk factors for aspiration pneumonia include bulbar or vocal cord palsy, achalasia or oesophageal reflux and alcoholism. Intravenous drug users are at particular risk of developing lung abscess, often in association with endocarditis affecting the pulmonary and tricuspid valves. Aspiration into the lungs of acid gastric contents can give rise to a severe haemorrhagic pneumonia often complicated by the acute respiratory distress syndrome (ARDS, see p. 198). The clinical features of a suppurative pneumonia are summarised in Box 13.46.

Bacterial infection of a pulmonary infarct or of a collapsed lobe may also produce a suppurative pneumonia or a lung abscess. The organism(s) isolated from the sputum include *Strep. pneumoniae*, *Staph. aureus*, *Strep. pyogenes*, *H. influenzae* and, in some cases, anaerobic bacteria. In many cases, however, no pathogens can be isolated, particularly when antibiotics have been given.

13.46 CLINICAL FEATURES OF SUPPURATIVE PNEUMONIA

Onset
- Acute or insidious

Symptoms
- Cough productive of large amounts of sputum which is sometimes fetid and blood-stained
- Pleural pain common
- Sudden expectoration of copious amounts of foul sputum occurs if abscess ruptures into a bronchus

Clinical signs
- High remittent pyrexia
- Profound systemic upset
- Digital clubbing may develop quickly (10–14 days)
- Chest examination usually reveals signs of consolidation; signs of cavitation rarely found
- Pleural rub common
- Rapid deterioration in general health with marked weight loss can occur if disease not adequately treated

Chest radiograph features

There is a homogeneous lobar or segmental opacity consistent with consolidation or collapse. A large, dense opacity, which may later cavitate and show a fluid level, is the characteristic finding when a frank lung abscess is present. Occasionally, a pre-existing emphysematous bulla becomes infected and appears as a cavity containing an air-fluid level.

Management

In many patients oral treatment with amoxicillin 500 mg 6-hourly is effective. If an anaerobic bacterial infection is suspected (e.g. from fetor of the sputum), oral metronidazole 400 mg 8-hourly should be added. Antibacterial therapy should be modified according to the results of microbiological examination of the sputum. Prolonged treatment for 4–6 weeks may be required in some patients with lung abscess. Removal or treatment of any obstructing endobronchial lesion is essential.

In contrast to uncomplicated community-acquired pneumonia, physiotherapy is of great value, especially when large abscess cavities have formed. It may not be possible to drain lower lobe cavities without postural coughing.

In most patients there is a good response to treatment and although residual fibrosis and bronchiectasis are common sequelae, these seldom give rise to serious morbidity. Abscesses that fail to resolve despite optimal medical therapy require surgical intervention.

HOSPITAL-ACQUIRED PNEUMONIA

Hospital-acquired or nosocomial pneumonia refers to a new episode of pneumonia occurring at least 2 days after admission to hospital. The term includes post-operative and certain forms of aspiration pneumonia, and pneumonia or bronchopneumonia developing in patients with chronic lung disease, general debility or those receiving assisted ventilation.

Aetiology

The factors predisposing to the development of pneumonia in a hospitalised patient are listed in Box 13.47. The elderly are particularly at risk and this condition now occurs in 2–5% of all hospital admissions.

13.47 FACTORS PREDISPOSING TO NOSOCOMIAL PNEUMONIA
Reduced host defences against bacteria
• Reduced immune defences (e.g. corticosteroid treatment, diabetes, malignancy) • Reduced cough reflex (e.g. post-operative) • Disordered mucociliary clearance (e.g. anaesthetic agents) • Bulbar or vocal cord palsy
Aspiration of nasopharyngeal or gastric secretions
• Immobility or reduced conscious level • Vomiting, dysphagia, achalasia or severe reflux • Nasogastric intubation
Bacteria introduced into lower respiratory tract
• Endotracheal intubation/tracheostomy • Infected ventilators/nebulisers/bronchoscopes • Dental or sinus infection
Bacteraemia
• Abdominal sepsis • Intravenous cannula infection • Infected emboli

The most important distinction between hospital- and community-acquired pneumonia is the difference in the spectrum of pathogenic organisms, with the majority of hospital-acquired infections caused by Gram-negative bacteria. These include *Escherichia*, *Pseudomonas* and *Klebsiella* species. Infections caused by *Staph. aureus* (including multidrug-resistant—MRSA—forms) are also common in hospital, and anaerobic organisms are much more likely than in pneumonia acquired in the community. This profile of organisms in part reflects the high rate of colonisation of the nasopharynx of hospital patients with Gram-negative bacteria, together with the poor host defences and general inability of the severely ill or semiconscious patient to clear upper airway and respiratory tract secretions.

Clinical features

The clinical features and investigation of patients with hospital-acquired pneumonia are very similar to community-acquired pneumonia (see pp. 526–528). In the elderly or debilitated patient who develops acute bronchopneumonia (or 'hypostatic pneumonia') symptoms of acute bronchitis are followed after 2 or 3 days by increased cough and sputum purulence associated with a rise in temperature. Breathlessness and central cyanosis may then appear, but pleural pain is uncommon. In the early stages the physical signs are those of acute bronchitis followed by the development of crepitations. There is a neutrophil leucocytosis and the chest radiograph shows mottled opacities in both lung fields, chiefly in the lower zones.

Management

Adequate Gram-negative coverage is usually obtained with:

- a third-generation cephalosporin (e.g. cefotaxime) *plus* an aminoglycoside (e.g. gentamicin)
- imipenem *or*
- a monocyclic β-lactam (e.g. aztreonam) *plus* flucloxacillin.

Aspiration pneumonia can be treated with co-amoxiclav 1.2 g 8-hourly plus metronidazole 500 mg 8-hourly. The nature and severity of most hospital-acquired pneumonias dictate that these antibiotics are all given intravenously, at least initially.

Physiotherapy is of particular importance in the immobile and elderly, and adequate oxygen therapy, fluid support and monitoring are essential. The mortality from hospital-acquired pneumonia is high (approximately 30%).

PNEUMONIA IN THE IMMUNOCOMPROMISED PATIENT

Pulmonary infection is common in patients receiving immunosuppressive drugs and in those with diseases causing defects of cellular or humoral immune mechanisms. For example, patients with AIDS are susceptible to many types of pneumonia, in particular *Pneumocystis carinii* (see p. 120). It is important to recognise, however, that the common pathogenic bacteria are responsible for the majority of lung infections in immunocompromised patients (see Box 13.48). Despite this, the Gram-negative bacteria, especially

13.48 **COMMON CAUSES OF IMMUNE SUPPRESSION: ASSOCIATED LUNG INFECTION**

	Cause	Lung infection
Neutropenia	Cytotoxic drugs Agranulocytosis Acute leukaemia	*Staph. aureus* Gram-negative bacteria *Candida albicans* *Aspergillus fumigatus*
T cell defect (± B cell defect)	Lymphoma Chronic lymphocytic leukaemia (CLL) Immunosuppressive drugs Bone marrow transplants Splenectomy	*C. albicans* *Mycobacterium tuberculosis* *Pneumocystis carinii* Cytomegalovirus Gram-negative bacteria *Staph. aureus* *Strep. pneumoniae* *H. influenzae*
Antibody production	CLL Myeloma	*Strep. pneumoniae* *H. influenzae*

Pseudomonas aeruginosa, are more of a problem than Gram-positive organisms, and unusual organisms or those normally considered to be of low virulence or non-pathogenic may become 'opportunistic' pathogens. Likewise, infection is often due to more than one organism. *Pneumocystis carinii* and other fungi such as *Aspergillus fumigatus* (see pp. 540–542), viral infections, cytomegalovirus (see p. 30), herpesviruses, and infections with *M. tuberculosis* and other types of mycobacteria (see opposite) are all common causes of infection in patients who are immunocompromised.

Clinical features

The patient usually presents with fever, cough, breathlessness and infiltrates on the chest radiograph. Patients may develop non-specific symptoms, and a high index of suspicion is required to determine the site and nature of the infection. In general, the onset of symptoms tends to be less rapid in patients with opportunistic organisms such as *Pneumocystis carinii* and mycobacterial infections. In *Pneumocystis carinii* pneumonia symptoms of cough and breathlessness can be present several days or weeks before the onset of systemic symptoms or even a chest radiograph abnormality.

Diagnosis

Lung biopsy offers the greatest chance of establishing a diagnosis if examination of sputum or bronchoalveolar lavage fluid has not revealed a pathogen. This, however, is a relatively high-risk and invasive procedure and should be reserved for patients in whom less invasive procedures fail to establish a diagnosis and in whom there has been no response to broad-spectrum antibiotic treatment. Some patients who cannot produce sputum can be induced to do so by the inhalation of nebulised hypertonic saline. Fibreoptic bronchoscopy should be performed early since a diagnosis can often be established by examination of lavage fluid, bronchial brushings or transbronchial biopsies.

Management

Whenever possible, treatment should be based on an established aetiological diagnosis. In practice, however, the cause of the pneumonia is frequently not known when treatment has to be started. Hence, broad-spectrum antibiotic therapy is required (e.g. a third-generation cephalosporin, or a quinolone, plus an antistaphylococcal antibiotic, or an antipseudomonal penicillin plus an aminoglycoside) and this treatment is thereafter tailored according to the results of investigations and the clinical response. The management of *P. carinii* infection is detailed on page 121.

TUBERCULOSIS

Epidemiology

Tuberculosis (TB) remains the most common infectious disease in the world, with an estimated one-third of the population infected and 2.5 million deaths annually. In the mid-1980s, the falling global incidence reversed in both developed and developing nations (see Box 13.49). In 1999 there were an estimated 8.4 million new cases of tuberculosis world-wide (up 5% from 1997), with 3 million occurring in South-east Asia and 2 million in Africa (where two-thirds are HIV-infected). By 2005, WHO predicts there will be 10.2 million new cases and Africa will have more cases than any other region (up 10% annually). In England and Wales there has been a 21% increase in notifications since 1987. Annual rates of tuberculosis are highest amongst non-white ethnic groups (Indian subcontinent, black African and Chinese) and in urban areas. In 1998, over half of all notified patients were born outside the UK, one-third of cases occurred in young adults and an estimated 3.3% were HIV-coinfected. Apart from HIV, several other factors are recognised to increase the risk of individuals developing tuberculosis (see Box 13.50).

Mycobacterium tuberculosis belongs to a complex of organisms with *M. bovis* (reservoir cattle) and African and Asian variants (reservoir humans); all cause clinical tuberculosis. In addition, other species of environmental mycobacteria (often termed 'atypical') may cause human

13.49 REASONS FOR THE INCREASING INCIDENCE OF PULMONARY TUBERCULOSIS

Developed countries

- HIV (mainly urban)
- Immigration from high prevalence areas
- Increasing life expectancy of the elderly
- Social deprivation (injection drug use, homelessness, poverty)
- Drug resistance (MDRTB)*
- Reduced priority for TB control

Developing countries

- HIV (mainly urban)
- Population increase (75% predicted increase in India over 30 years)
- Lack of access to health care
- Poverty, civil unrest
- Ineffective control programmes
- Drug resistance (MDRTB)*

* MDRTB = multiple drug-resistant tuberculosis (rifampicin/isoniazid resistance with/without additional drug).

13.50 FACTORS INCREASING THE RISK OF TUBERCULOSIS

Patient-related

- Age (children > young adults)
- First-generation immigrants from high prevalence countries
- Close contacts of patients with smear-positive pulmonary tuberculosis
- Chest radiograph evidence of self-healed tuberculosis
- Primary infection < 1 year previously

Associated diseases

- HIV
- Silicosis
- Immunocompromise
- Malignancy (especially lymphoma, leukaemia)
- Type 1 diabetes mellitus
- Chronic renal failure
- Gastrointestinal disease associated with malnutrition (gastrectomy, jejuno-ileal bypass, cancer of the pancreas, malabsorption)

13.51 SITE-SPECIFIC MYCOBACTERIAL DISEASE

	Major	Less common
Pulmonary	M. tuberculosis	M. bovis M. xenopi M. kansasii M. malmoense MAC
Lymph node	M. tuberculosis MAC	M. malmoense M. fortuitum M. bovis M. chelonei
Soft tissue/skin	M. leprae M. ulcerans (prevalent in Africa, northern Australia and South-east Asia)	M. tuberculosis M. marinum M. fortuitum M. chelonei
Disseminated (seen in immunodeficiency states)	MAC (HIV-associated)	M. haemophilum M. genavense M. fortuitum M. chelonei BCG

(MAC = Mycobacterium avium complex—M. scrofulaceum, M. intracellulare and M. avium)

disease (see Box 13.51). The sites commonly involved are the lungs, lymph nodes, skin and soft tissues. With the advent of HIV, disseminated infection with *Mycobacterium avium complex* (MAC) has become common when severe immunodeficiency exists (CD4 count < 50 cells/ml—see p. 121). Environmental mycobacteria are low-grade pathogens (with the exception of *M. malmoense* and *M. ulcerans*), tending to cause disease in the setting of immunocompromise or scarred lungs. The significance of an isolate depends on the species, site of isolation, number of isolates and whether or not there is a recognised association with the clinical presentation. Where the isolate is from a non-sterile site, multiple positive cultures are usually required to confirm infection.

Pathology and pathogenesis

Infection with *M. tuberculosis* occurs most frequently through inhalation of infected droplets, with the primary infection occurring in the lung (see Fig. 13.31). Occasionally, the tonsil, intestine or skin may be the site of primary disease. Following inhalation of *M. tuberculosis*, a small subpleural lesion (the Ghon focus) develops with rapid transport of bacilli to the regional (hilar) lymph nodes and the development of the primary complex. Non-specifically activated macrophages that have ingested the bacilli then aggregate and the lesions enlarge. At 2–4 weeks, two distinct T cell-mediated immune responses start. A delayed-type hypersensitivity reaction destroys non-activated macrophages containing bacilli but also results in tissue necrosis and caseation. Cell-mediated immunity results in macrophages being activated into epithelioid cells with the formation of granulomas seen at the periphery of the caseation. The virulence factors of *M. tuberculosis* have not been fully elucidated. The organism is versatile, with the ability to multiply rapidly outside cells within cavities, survive inside macrophages preventing fusion between the lysosome and phagosome, and survive in a relatively inactive state with only infrequent bursts of division.

In 85–90% of cases the primary complex heals spontaneously in 1–2 months and the tuberculin skin test becomes positive. In 10–15%, multiplication of *M. tuberculosis* is not contained and lymph node enlargement results in either local pressure effects, lymphatic spread to the pleura or pericardium, or rupture into an adjacent bronchus or pulmonary blood vessel. Where dissemination has occurred, disease may progress rapidly to the development of miliary and meningeal tuberculosis. Also, foci of infection may be set up in bone, the lung, the genitourinary and gastrointestinal tracts, or lymph nodes, which may progress to clinical disease (see Box 13.52). However, 85–90% of patients develop

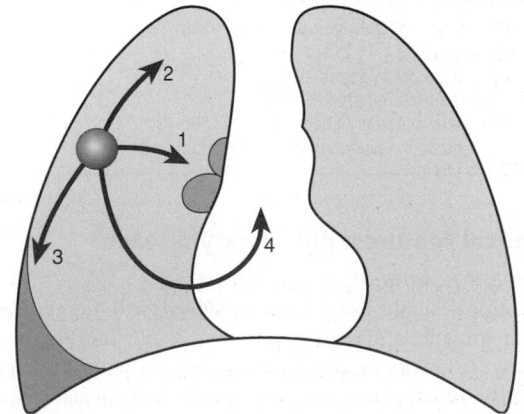

Fig. 13.31 Primary pulmonary tuberculosis. (1) Spread from the primary focus to hilar and mediastinal lymph glands to form the 'primary complex', which in most cases heals spontaneously. (2) Direct extension of the primary focus—'progressive pulmonary tuberculosis'. (3) Spread to the pleura—tuberculous pleurisy and pleural effusion. (4) Blood-borne spread: *few bacilli*—pulmonary, skeletal, renal, genitourinary infection often months or years later; *massive spread*—miliary tuberculosis and meningitis.

13.52 TIMETABLE OF TUBERCULOSIS

Time from infection	Manifestations
3–8 weeks	Primary complex, positive tuberculin skin test
3–6 months	Meningeal, miliary and pleural disease
Up to 3 years	Gastrointestinal, bone and joint, and lymph node disease
Around 8 years	Renal tract disease
From 3 years onwards	Post-primary disease due to reactivation or reinfection

latent infection (positive tuberculin test or radiographic evidence of self-healed tuberculosis). Within this group 5–10% reactivate during their life-time, resulting in post-primary disease. This is predominantly pulmonary (75%) and infectious (50% smear-positive). Re-exposure to smear-positive pulmonary tuberculosis may result in post-primary disease and accounts for up to one-third of all cases. The likelihood of infection after exposure (30%), development of progressive primary disease (30%) and reinfection from other infectious cases (50%) are all increased in HIV-infected individuals. Where good immune function is retained in HIV, clinical disease resembles classical post-primary tuberculosis. However, where significant immunodeficiency has occurred, the presentation is more likely to be disseminated or extrapulmonary (see Box 13.53 and opposite).

13.53 TUBERCULOSIS IN HIV

- More likely:
  Infection after exposure
  Progressive primary disease after infection
  Reactivation of latent infection
  Reinfection with new strain
- Reduced smear-positive rates in pulmonary TB
- Less cavitation
- Atypical chest radiograph appearance
- Increased disseminated disease
- More extrapulmonary infection
- Greater risk of adverse drug reactions

Clinical features: pulmonary disease

Primary pulmonary tuberculosis

Infection usually occurs in childhood and is generally asymptomatic; a few patients develop a self-limiting febrile illness. A history of contact with a person with active pulmonary tuberculosis is often obtained. Clinical disease results either from the development of a hypersensitivity reaction or from the infection pursuing a progressive course (see Box 13.54). Erythema nodosum may be the presenting feature of primary tuberculosis and is associated with a strongly positive tuberculin skin test. Progressive primary disease may appear during the course of the initial illness or after a latent interval of weeks or months. The features depend on the site affected (see below).

13.54 FEATURES OF PRIMARY TUBERCULOSIS

Infection (4–8 weeks)

- Influenza-like illness
- Skin test conversion
- Primary complex

Disease

- Lymphadenopathy (hilar (often unilateral), paratracheal or mediastinal)
  Collapse (especially right middle lobe)
  Consolidation (especially right middle lobe)
  Obstructive emphysema
  Cavitation (rare)
- Pleural effusion
- Endobronchial
- Miliary
- Meningitis
- Pericarditis

Hypersensitivity

- Erythema nodosum
- Phlyctenular conjunctivitis
- Dactylitis

Miliary tuberculosis

This is a severe infection often diagnosed late. The disease may start suddenly but more frequently there is a period of 2–3 weeks when fever, night sweats, anorexia, weight loss and a dry cough are present. Hepatosplenomegaly may be present (25%) and the presence of headache may indicate coexistent tuberculous meningitis. Auscultation of the chest is frequently normal, although with more advanced disease widespread crackles are evident. Choroidal tubercles occur in 5–10%. The chest radiograph reveals fine 1–2 mm lesions (millet seeds) throughout the lungs, although occasionally the appearances are coarser. Anaemia and leucopenia may be present. An unusual presentation seen usually in the elderly is 'cryptic' miliary tuberculosis (see Box 13.55).

13.55 PRESENTATION OF CRYPTIC TUBERCULOSIS

- Age over 60 years
- Intermittent low-grade pyrexia of unknown origin
- Unexplained weight loss, general debility (hepatosplenomegaly in 25–50%)
- Normal chest radiograph
- Blood dyscrasias; leukaemoid reaction, pancytopenia
- Negative tuberculin skin test
- Confirmation by biopsy (granulomata and/or acid-fast bacilli demonstrated) of liver or bone marrow

Post-primary pulmonary tuberculosis

Disease in adults is usually a result of post-primary disease. A subacute illness characterised by cough, haemoptysis, dyspnoea, anorexia and weight loss associated with fevers and night sweats is typical. Other clinical presentations are listed in Box 13.56. Auscultation of the chest frequently reveals localising signs but may be normal. The earliest radiological change is typically an ill-defined opacity situated in one of the upper lobes. Disease often involves two or more areas of lung and may be bilateral; as disease progresses,

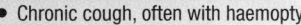

13.56 CLINICAL PRESENTATION OF PULMONARY TUBERCULOSIS

- Chronic cough, often with haemoptysis
- Pyrexia of unknown origin
- Unresolved pneumonia
- Exudative pleural effusion
- Asymptomatic (diagnosis on chest radiograph)
- Weight loss, general debility
- Spontaneous pneumothorax

13.57 CHRONIC COMPLICATIONS OF PULMONARY TUBERCULOSIS

Pulmonary

- Massive haemoptysis
- Cor pulmonale
- Fibrosis/emphysema
- Atypical mycobacterial infection
- Aspergilloma
- Lung/pleural calcification
- Obstructive airways disease
- Bronchiectasis
- Bronchopleural fistula

Non-pulmonary

- Empyema necessitans
- Laryngitis
- Enteritis*
- Anorectal disease*
- Amyloidosis
- Poncet's polyarthritis

*From swallowed sputum.

consolidation, collapse and cavitation develop to varying degrees (see Fig. 13.32). The presence of a miliary pattern or cavitation indicates active disease although there is a wide differential. In extensive disease, collapse may be marked

and result in significant displacement of the trachea and mediastinum. Occasionally, a caseous lymph node may drain into an adjoining bronchus, resulting in tuberculous pneumonia. The complications of pulmonary tuberculosis are shown in Box 13.57.

Clinical features: extrapulmonary disease

Lymphadenitis

The most common extrapulmonary site of disease is the lymph nodes. Cervical and mediastinal glands are affected most frequently, followed by axillary and inguinal; in 5% of patients, more than one region is involved. Disease may represent primary infection, spread from contiguous sites or reactivation of infection. Supraclavicular lymphadenopathy is usually a result of spread from mediastinal disease. The nodes are usually painless and initially mobile but become matted together with time. When caseation and liquefaction occur, the swelling becomes fluctuant and may discharge through the skin with the formation of a 'collar-stud' abscess and sinus formation. Approximately half of patients fail to show any constitutional features such as fevers and night sweats. The tuberculin skin test is usually strongly positive. During or after treatment, paradoxical enlargement, development of new nodes and suppuration may all occur but without evidence of continued infection; rarely, surgical excision is necessary. In non-immigrant children in the UK, most mycobacterial lymphadenitis is caused by environmental (atypical) mycobacteria, especially of the *M. avium complex* (see Box 13.51).

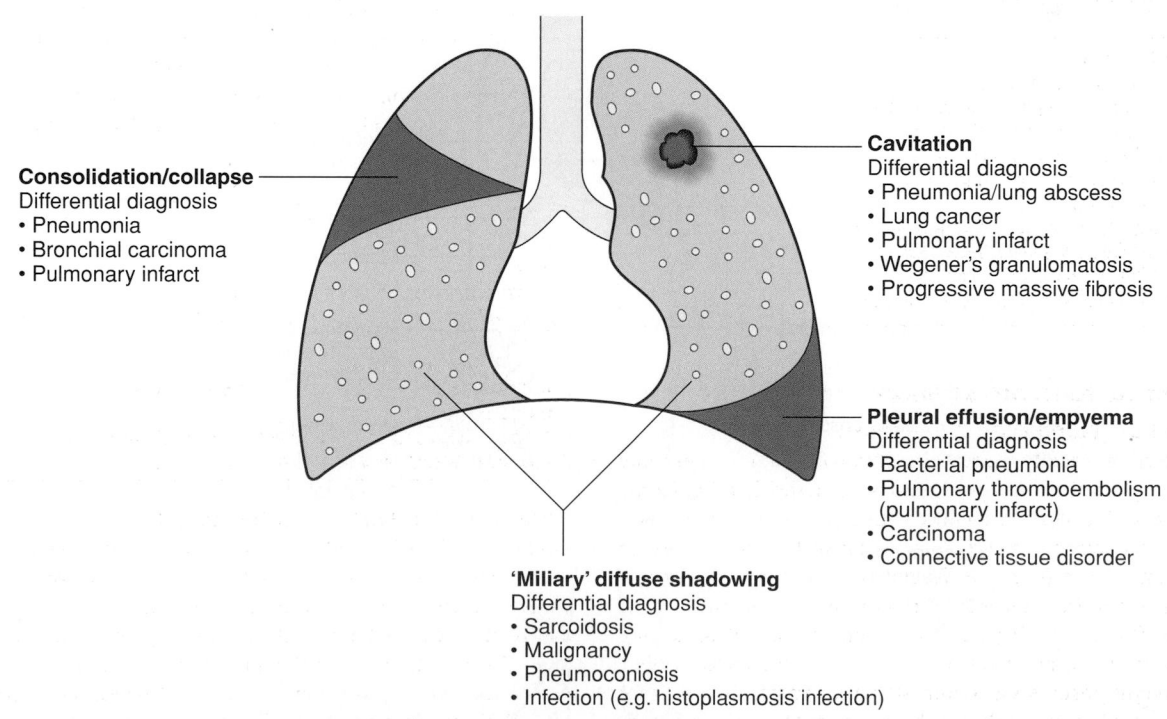

Consolidation/collapse
Differential diagnosis
- Pneumonia
- Bronchial carcinoma
- Pulmonary infarct

Cavitation
Differential diagnosis
- Pneumonia/lung abscess
- Lung cancer
- Pulmonary infarct
- Wegener's granulomatosis
- Progressive massive fibrosis

Pleural effusion/empyema
Differential diagnosis
- Bacterial pneumonia
- Pulmonary thromboembolism (pulmonary infarct)
- Carcinoma
- Connective tissue disorder

'Miliary' diffuse shadowing
Differential diagnosis
- Sarcoidosis
- Malignancy
- Pneumoconiosis
- Infection (e.g. histoplasmosis infection)

Fig. 13.32   Chest radiograph: major manifestations and differential diagnosis of pulmonary tuberculosis. Less common manifestations include pneumothorax, ARDS (see p. 198), cor pulmonale and localised emphysema.

Gastrointestinal tuberculosis

Tuberculosis can affect any part of the bowel and patients may present with a wide range of symptoms and signs (see Fig. 13.33). Upper gastrointestinal tract involvement is rare and is usually an unexpected histological finding in an endoscopic or laparotomy specimen. Ileocaecal disease accounts for approximately half of abdominal tuberculosis cases. Fever, night sweats, anorexia and weight loss are usually prominent and a right iliac fossa mass may be palpable. Up to 30% of cases present with an acute abdomen. Ultrasound or CT may reveal thickened bowel wall, abdominal lymphadenopathy, mesenteric thickening or ascites. Barium enema and small bowel enema reveal narrowing, shortening and distortion of the bowel with caecal involvement predominating. Diagnosis rests on obtaining histology by either colonoscopy or mini-laparotomy. The main differential diagnosis is Crohn's disease (see p. 808). Tuberculous peritonitis is characterised by abdominal distension, pain and constitutional symptoms. The ascitic fluid is exudative and cellular with a predominance of lymphocytes. Laparoscopy reveals multiple white 'tubercles' over the peritoneal and omental surfaces. Low-grade hepatic dysfunction is common in miliary disease when biopsy reveals granulomata. Occasionally, patients may be frankly icteric with a mixed hepatic/cholestatic picture.

Pericardial disease

Disease occurs in two main forms (see Fig. 13.33 and p. 478): pericardial effusion and constrictive pericarditis. Fever and night sweats are rarely prominent and the presentation is usually insidious with breathlessness and abdominal swelling. Pulsus paradoxus, a very raised JVP, hepatosplenomegaly, prominent ascites and the absence of peripheral oedema are common to both types of disease. Pericardial effusion is associated with increased pericardial dullness and a globular enlarged heart on chest radiograph. Constriction is associated with atrial fibrillation (< 20%), an early third heart sound and pericardial calcification in 25%. Diagnosis is on clinical, radiological and echocardiographic grounds. The pericardial effusion is blood-stained in 85% of cases. Coexistent pulmonary disease is very rare, with the exception of pleural effusion. Open pericardial biopsy can be performed in patients with effusion where there is doubt about the diagnosis. The addition of corticosteroids has been shown to be beneficial when added to antituberculosis treatment (see below) for both.

Central nervous system disease

By far the most important form of central nervous system tuberculosis is meningeal disease. This is life-threatening and may be rapidly fatal if not diagnosed early. Clinical features, investigations and management are dealt with on page 1192.

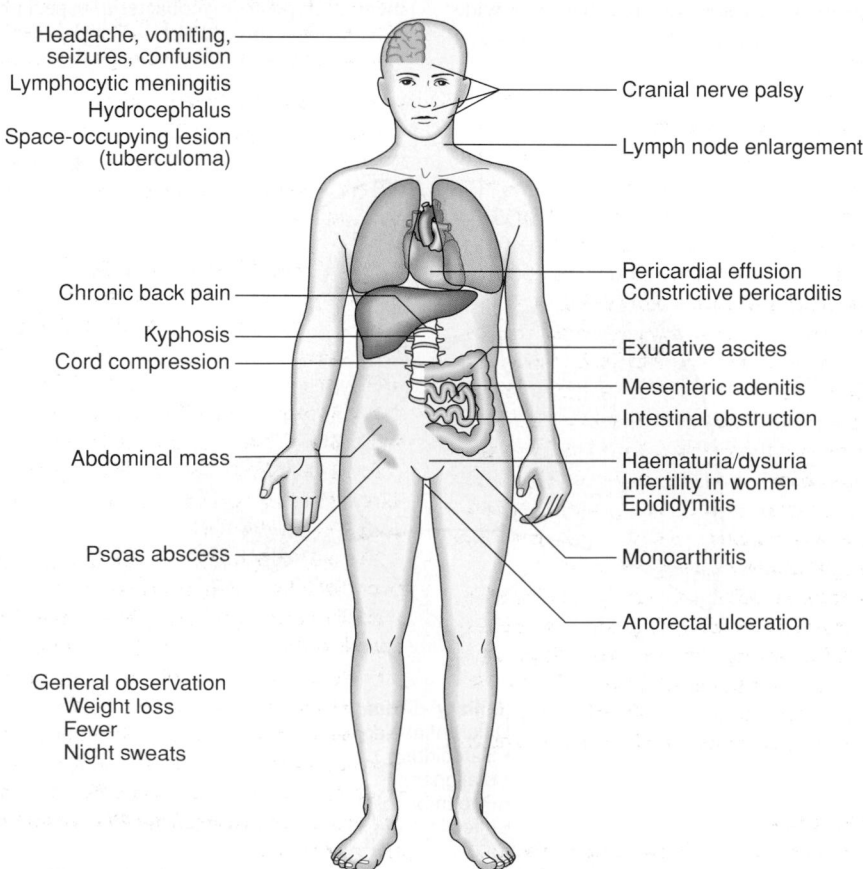

Headache, vomiting, seizures, confusion
Lymphocytic meningitis
Hydrocephalus
Space-occupying lesion (tuberculoma)

Cranial nerve palsy

Lymph node enlargement

Chronic back pain

Kyphosis
Cord compression

Pericardial effusion
Constrictive pericarditis

Exudative ascites

Mesenteric adenitis
Intestinal obstruction

Abdominal mass

Haematuria/dysuria
Infertility in women
Epididymitis

Psoas abscess

Monoarthritis

Anorectal ulceration

General observation
Weight loss
Fever
Night sweats

Fig. 13.33 Systemic presentations of extrapulmonary tuberculosis.

Bone and joint disease

Tuberculosis of the spine usually presents with chronic back pain and typically involves the lower thoracic and lumbar spine (see Fig. 13.33). The infection starts as a discitis and then spreads along the spinal ligaments to involve the adjacent anterior vertebral bodies, causing angulation of the vertebrae with subsequent kyphosis. Paravertebral and psoas abscess formation is common. CT is valuable in gauging the extent of disease, the amount of cord compression, and the site for needle biopsy or open exploration if required. The major differential diagnosis is malignancy, which tends to affect the vertebral body and leave the disc intact. In the absence of spinal instability or cord compression, patients can be treated as outpatients. Tuberculosis can affect any joint, but most frequently involves the hip or knee. Presentation is usually insidious with pain and swelling; fever and night sweats are uncommon. Radiological changes are often non-specific but, as disease progresses, reduction in joint space and erosions appear.

Genitourinary disease

Fever and night sweats are rare with renal tract tuberculosis and patients are often only mildly symptomatic for many years. Haematuria, frequency and dysuria are often present, with sterile pyuria found on urine microscopy and culture. In women, infertility from endometritis, or pelvic pain and swelling from salpingitis or a tubo-ovarian abscess may occur infrequently. In men, genitourinary tuberculosis may present as epididymitis or prostatitis.

Diagnosis (see Box 13.58)

Mycobacterial infection can be confirmed by direct microscopy of samples (Ziehl–Neelsen or auramine staining) and culture. Confirmation of the isolate as *M. tuberculosis* is obtained through standard culture methods (growth characteristics, pigment production and biochemical tests) or molecular DNA technology (hybridisation probes, polymerase chain reaction amplification). After decontamination, samples should be cultured on solid medium as well as into liquid medium, which provides more rapid growth. Drug susceptibility profiles can be obtained within 1–2 weeks of growth using the BACTEC system. Where MDRTB is suspected, molecular methods allow the detection of rifampicin resistance (a marker for multidrug resistance) in primary specimens as well as cultures. If a cluster of cases suggests a common source, fingerprinting of isolates with restriction-fragment length polymorphism (RFLP) or DNA amplification can help confirm this.

Primary tuberculosis in children is rarely confirmed by culture. In adults, direct microscopy is positive in 60% of pulmonary and 5–25% of extrapulmonary cases (highest for lymph node and lowest for meningeal disease). In 10–20% of patients with pulmonary disease and 40–50% of patients with extrapulmonary disease, culture is also negative and the diagnosis is clinical.

Control and prevention

BCG (the Calmette–Guérin bacillus) is an attenuated vaccine derived from *M. bovis*, which was developed in 1921 (see pp. 1213–1214). Its protective efficacy is up to 80% for

---

13.58 DIAGNOSIS OF TUBERCULOSIS

Specimen

Respiratory
- Sputum* (induced with nebulised hypertonic saline if not expectorating)
- Gastric washing* (mainly used for children)
- Bronchoalveolar lavage
- Transbronchial biopsy

Non-respiratory
- Fluid examination (cerebrospinal, ascitic, pleural, pericardial, joint)
- Tissue biopsy (from affected site; also bone marrow/liver may be diagnostic in patients with disseminated disease)

Diagnostic test
- Circumstantial (ESR, C-reactive protein, anaemia etc.)
- Tuberculin skin test (low sensitivity/specificity; useful only in primary or deep-seated infection)
- Stain
  Ziehl–Neelsen
  Auramine fluorescence
- Nucleic acid amplification
- Culture
  Solid (Löwenstein–Jensen, Middlebrook)
  Liquid (e.g. BACTEC)
- Response to empirical antituberculous drugs (usually seen after 5–10 days)

* 3 × early morning samples.

10–15 years and is greatest for preventing disseminated disease in children. In the UK it is recommended for the following tuberculin skin test-negative groups:

- all children 10–14 years of age
- contacts < 2 years old
- immigrants from countries where tuberculosis is endemic
- infants in high prevalence ethnic groups
- health-care workers at risk.

Only those who do not respond to tuberculin are vaccinated. Grade 3–4 tuberculin skin test responders should be referred for clinical and radiological examination. Tuberculin skin testing is usually performed using the Heaf or Mantoux technique (see Box 13.59 and Fig. 13.34). Some countries do not use BCG because they value the diagnostic sensitivity of the tuberculin skin test as a measure of recent primary infection. Occasional complications include a local BCG abscess and disseminated infection in immunocompromised persons.

Chemoprophylaxis is given to prevent infection progressing to clinical disease. It is recommended for children aged less than 16 years with strongly positive Heaf tests, children aged less than 2 years in close contact with smear-positive pulmonary disease, those in whom recent tuberculin conversion has been confirmed, and babies of mothers with pulmonary tuberculosis. It should be considered for HIV-infected close contacts of a patient with smear-positive disease. Rifampicin and isoniazid for 3 months, rifampicin and pyrazinamide for 2 months, or isoniazid for 6 months are all effective.

In the UK an active contact-screening programme operates, beginning with compulsory notification of all tuberculosis

13.59 SKIN TESTING IN TUBERCULOSIS	

Tests using purified protein derivative (PPD)	False negatives
Heaf (read at 3–7 days) Multipuncture method Grade 1: 4–6 papules Grade 2: Confluent papules forming ring Grade 3: Central induration Grade 4: > 10 mm induration **Mantoux** (read at 2–4 days) Using 10 tuberculin units: positive when induration 5–14 mm (equivalent to Heaf grade 2) and > 15 mm (Heaf grade 3–4)	Severe TB (25% of cases negative) Newborn and elderly HIV (if CD4 count < 200 cells/ml) Recent infection (e.g. measles) or immunisation Malnutrition Immunosuppressive drugs Malignancy Sarcoidosis

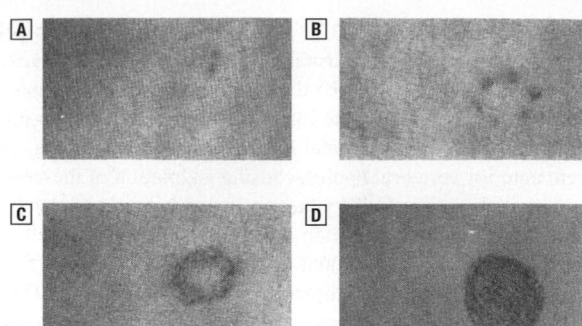

Fig. 13.34 Gradings of the Heaf test response.
A Negative. B Grade 1.
C Grade 2. D Grade 3.
E Grade 4.

cases. The aim of contact tracing is to identify a possible index case with clinical disease, other cases infected by the same index patient (with or without evidence of disease), and close contacts who should receive BCG vaccination. Approximately 10–20% of close contacts of patients with smear-positive pulmonary tuberculosis and 2–5% of those with smear-negative, culture-positive disease have evidence of tuberculosis infection. Close contacts of patients with pulmonary disease are seen in dedicated clinics where their BCG and clinical status is reviewed, Heaf tests are performed (except in those below 16 years of age), and the need for radiography is assessed. Outcomes include chemotherapy (for active disease), chemoprophylaxis (to prevent infection progressing to active disease), BCG immunisation or discharge.

Chemotherapy

Short-course therapy with 2 months of four drugs (rifampicin, isoniazid, pyrazinamide, and either ethambutol or streptomycin) followed by 4 months of rifampicin and isoniazid is now recommended for all patients with new-onset, uncomplicated pulmonary or extrapulmonary tuberculosis (see Box 13.60). The fourth drug (ethambutol or streptomycin) can be omitted in patients in whom isoniazid resistance is unlikely (previously untreated white patients, presumed HIV-negative individuals and those having no contact with a possible patient with drug-resistant disease). Streptomycin is now rarely used in the UK but it is an important component of short-course treatment regimens in developing nations. Drugs should be given as a single daily dose before breakfast. Patients should be considered for longer treatment (9–12 months) where meningeal disease is present, there is HIV coinfection, or drug intolerance occurs and a second-line agent is substituted. Relapse is rare when the strain is fully sensitive (< 2%) and adherence to drug therapy is complete. In patients with a history of past treatment, four drugs must be used until the sensitivity results are obtained. In the UK drug resistance in newly diagnosed patients is uncommon (overall < 5%) and is more frequently

13.60 TREATMENT OF TUBERCULOSIS AND DISSEMINATED MAC				
	Initial	Months	Continuation	Months
New cases	HRZE	2	HR	4
New cases: resource-poor settings	HRZS or HRZE	2	HT[1] or HE	6
Relapses and treatment failures	HRZE[2]	2+	≥ 2 drugs[3]	6–10
MDRTB	≥ 5 drugs[4]	24		
Disseminated MAC	≥ 4 drugs[5]	2–6	2 drugs[6]	12+

First-line drugs[7]: Ethambutol (E), isoniazid (H), rifampicin (R), pyrazinamide (Z), streptomycin (S), rifabutin, thiacetazone (T)[1]

Second-line drugs: Clarithromycin (or azithromycin), ofloxacin (or ciprofloxacin), protionamide (or ethionamide), cycloserine, capreomycin, para-aminosalicylic acid (PAS)

[1] Thiacetazone is bacteriostatic and contraindicated in HIV.
[2] Additional second-line agents may be indicated until sensitivities are known.
[3] Guided by sensitivity results.
[4] Dependent on sensitivities.
[5] Ciprofloxacin, ethambutol, azithromycin, rifabutin is a recommended regimen.
[6] When CD4 count > 100 cells/ml reduction to azithromycin and one other drug is safe.
[7] HRZE and S can all be given by intermittent dosing (directly observed therapy).

observed in isolates from ethnic minority patients. The treatment of MDRTB is complex and depends on the sensitivity of the isolate. Five or more drugs are used and the patient must be admitted to a negative-pressure isolation room for treatment until deemed non-infectious.

Most patients can be treated at home, although where there is uncertainty about the diagnosis, intolerance of medication, questionable compliance, a background of adverse social conditions or a significant risk of MDRTB (culture positive after 2 months on treatment, contact with known MDRTB), patients should be admitted. Where drug resistance is not expected, patients can be assumed to be non-infectious after 2 weeks of quadruple therapy including rifampicin and isoniazid. Combined drug preparations (including rifampicin and isoniazid with or without pyrazinamide) reduce tablet load and allow relatively simple screening for compliance as the urine can be assessed visually for an orange-red colour. Directly observed therapy (DOT) is recommended where patients are unlikely to comply (alcoholics, injection drug users, the mentally ill and patients failing previous therapy), where there is multidrug resistance (as part of the continuation phase) and where there are language difficulties. In developing nations, DOT dispenses with the need for initial hospitalisation to receive streptomycin, is cost-effective and is less disruptive to patients' lives. Most importantly, it improves adherence. All the first-line agents can be given thrice weekly. Currently, WHO recommends DOT therapy for all patients with tuberculosis at a global level.

In choosing a suitable drug regimen, it is important to bear in mind underlying comorbidity (renal and hepatic dysfunction, eye disease, peripheral neuropathy and HIV as well as the potential for drug interactions (rifampicin is a potent cytochrome inducer). Baseline liver function and subsequent regular monitoring are important for patients with underlying liver disease treated with standard therapy including rifampicin, isoniazid and pyrazinamide, all of which are potentially hepatotoxic. Patients treated with the first-line drug rifampicin should always be warned that their urine, tears and other secretions will develop a bright orange/red coloration. Ethambutol should be used with caution in patients with renal failure, with appropriate dose reduction and monitoring of drug levels.

Corticosteroids are recommended in tuberculous pericarditis as they reduce the need for pericardiectomy in constrictive pericarditis and repeat aspiration or open surgical drainage in pericardial effusion. They are also advised for moderate to severe tuberculous meningitis. In patients with ureteric disease, pleural effusion, primary endobronchial disease or severe disseminated disease, corticosteroids should be considered, although the evidence is less certain. Surgery is still occasionally required (e.g. for massive haemoptysis, loculated empyema, constrictive pericarditis, lymph node suppuration, spinal disease with cord compression), but usually only after a full course of antituberculosis treatment.

PULMONARY TUBERCULOSIS—optimal choice of antituberculous drugs

'Two large RCTs have shown that 6 months of treatment are as effective as longer courses if a four-drug combination (isoniazid, rifampicin, pyrazinamide and ethambutol, or isoniazid, rifampicin, pyrazinamide and streptomycin) is used for 2 months followed by isoniazid and rifampicin for 4 months. One RCT has shown no difference between streptomycin and ethambutol as the fourth drug. One SR shows no difference between daily and thrice-weekly short course regimens.'

- Global Tuberculosis Programme. Treatment of tuberculosis. Geneva: World Health Organisation; 1997 (WHO/TB/97.220).
- British Thoracic Society. A controlled trial of 6 months' chemotherapy in pulmonary tuberculosis: results during the 36 months after the end of chemotherapy and beyond. Br J Dis Chest 1984; 78:330–336.
- Mwandumba HC, Squire SB. Fully intermittent dosing with drugs for tuberculosis (Cochrane Review). Cochrane Library, issue 1, 2001. Oxford: Update Software.

Further information: www.clinicalevidence.org www.cochrane.co.uk

CHEMOTHERAPY FOR TUBERCULOSIS—optimal duration of therapy

'RCTs have found no evidence of a difference in relapse rates between 6 and 9 months' chemotherapy in people with pulmonary tuberculosis. In contrast, SR of 9 trials comparing 6 months of treatment with shorter-duration regimens demonstrates consistently higher relapse rates (range 1–8%) in the shorter treatment arms. On the basis of such data, WHO recommends 6 months of treatment in all patients with active pulmonary tuberculosis infection.'

- Gelband H. Regimens of less than six months for treating tuberculosis (Cochrane Review). Cochrane Library, issue 4, 2000. Oxford: Update Software.
- Joint Tuberculosis Committee of the British Thoracic Society. Chemotherapy and management of tuberculosis in the United Kingdom: recommendations 1998. Thorax 1998; 53:536–548.

Further information: www.cochrane.co.uk

13.61 MAIN ADVERSE REACTIONS OF FIRST-LINE ANTITUBERCULOUS DRUGS

	Isoniazid	Rifampicin	Pyrazinamide	Streptomycin	Ethambutol
Mode of action	Cell wall synthesis	DNA transcription	Unknown	Protein synthesis	Cell wall synthesis
Major adverse reactions	Peripheral neuropathy[1] Hepatitis[2] Rash	Febrile reactions Hepatitis Rash Gastrointestinal disturbance	Hepatitis Gastrointestinal disturbance Hyperuricaemia	8th nerve damage Rash	Retrobulbar neuritis[3] Arthralgia
Less common adverse reactions	Lupoid reactions Seizures Psychoses	Interstitial nephritis Thrombocytopenia Haemolytic anaemia	Rash Photosensitisation Gout	Nephrotoxicity Agranulocytosis	Peripheral neuropathy Rash

[1] 2–5%; reduced to 0.2% with supplementary pyridoxine.
[2] 1.5%; increased with age, slow acetylator status, rifampicin use and alcohol.
[3] Reduced visual acuity and colour vision with higher doses; usually reversible.

Adverse drug reactions occur in 10% of patients but are significantly more common where there is HIV coinfection (see Box 13.61).

Prognosis

In the absence of major complications, short-course therapy using four drugs initially is curative. Occasionally, patients die of overwhelming infection (usually miliary disease or bronchopneumonia) and some patients succumb to the later complications of tuberculosis (e.g. cor pulmonale). A few patients die unexpectedly soon after commencing therapy and it is possible that some of these individuals have sub-clinical hypoadrenalism that is unmasked by a rifampicin-induced increase in steroid metabolism. In HIV-associated tuberculosis, mortality is increased but mainly as a result of superimposed bacterial infection.

RESPIRATORY DISEASES CAUSED BY FUNGI

Most fungi encountered by humans are harmless sapro-phytes but some species may, in certain circumstances, infect human tissue or promote damaging allergic reactions.

The term 'mycosis' is applied to disease caused by fungal infection. Predisposing factors include metabolic disorders such as diabetes mellitus, toxic states (for example, chronic alcoholism), diseases in which immunological responses are disturbed such as AIDS, treatment with corticosteroids and immunosuppressive drugs, and radiotherapy. Local factors such as tissue damage by suppuration or necrosis and the elimination of the competitive influence of a normal bacterial flora by antibiotics may also facilitate fungal infection.

Diagnosis

The diagnosis of fungal disease of the respiratory system is usually made by mycological examination of sputum—microscopic examination of stained films for fungal hyphae being extremely important—supported by serological tests and in some cases by skin sensitivity tests.

ASPERGILLOSIS

Most cases of bronchopulmonary aspergillosis are caused by *Aspergillus fumigatus*, but other members of the genus (*A. clavatus*, *A. flavus*, *A. niger* and *A. terreus*) occasionally cause disease. The conditions associated with *Aspergillus* species are listed in Box 13.62.

13.62 CLASSIFICATION OF BRONCHOPULMONARY ASPERGILLOSIS

- Atopic (allergic) asthma (see p. 514)
- Allergic bronchopulmonary aspergillosis (asthmatic pulmonary eosinophilia)
- Extrinsic allergic alveolitis (*Aspergillus clavatus*)
- Intracavitary aspergilloma
- Invasive pulmonary aspergillosis

ALLERGIC BRONCHOPULMONARY ASPERGILLOSIS (ABPA)

This is caused by hypersensitivity reactions to *A. fumigatus* involving the bronchial wall and peripheral parts of the lung. In the vast majority of patients it is associated with bronchial asthma, but it can occur in non-asthmatic patients and is a recognised complication of cystic fibrosis. It is one of the causes of pulmonary eosinophilia (see p. 560), since it is characterised by fleeting radiographic abnormalities associated with peripheral blood eosinophilia.

Clinical features

Fever, breathlessness, cough productive of bronchial casts and worsening of asthmatic symptoms can all be manifestations of ABPA, but frequently the diagnosis is suggested by abnormalities on routine chest radiographs of patients whose asthmatic symptoms are no worse than usual. When repeated episodes of ABPA have caused bronchiectasis, the symptoms and complications of that disease often overshadow those of asthma.

Investigations

The disease is characterised by recurrent transient radiograph abnormalities of two main types: diffuse pulmonary infiltrates and lobar or segmental pulmonary collapse. Permanent radiographic changes of bronchiectasis ('tram-line', ring and 'gloved-finger' shadows) are seen predominantly in the upper lobes in patients with advanced disease.

The diagnostic features are shown in Box 13.63. Not all are required to make a confident diagnosis.

13.63 DIAGNOSTIC FEATURES OF ALLERGIC BRONCHOPULMONARY ASPERGILLOSIS

- Asthma (in the majority of cases)
- Peripheral blood eosinophilia > 0.5 × 10⁹/litre
- Presence or history of chest radiograph abnormalities
- Positive skin test to an extract of *A. fumigatus*
- Serum precipitating antibodies to *A. fumigatus*
- Elevated total serum IgE
- Fungal hyphae of *A. fumigatus* on microscopic examination of sputum

Management

In the absence of safe and effective antifungal agents which can be given long-term, the main aims of therapy are:

- suppression of the immunopathological responses to *A. fumigatus* with low-dose oral corticosteroid therapy (prednisolone 7.5–10 mg daily)
- optimal control of associated asthma
- prompt, effective management of exacerbations associated with new chest radiograph changes—prednisolone 40–60 mg daily and physiotherapy. If lobar collapse persists for more than 7–10 days, bronchoscopy to remove impacted mucus should be performed to prevent the development of bronchiectasis.

INTRACAVITARY ASPERGILLOMA

Inhaled air-borne spores of *A. fumigatus* may lodge and germinate in damaged pulmonary tissue, and an 'aspergilloma' (a ball of *Aspergillus* fungus) can form in any area of damaged lung in which there is a persistent abnormal space. The most common cause of such pulmonary damage is tuberculosis (see Fig. 13.35), but an aspergilloma can develop in an abscess cavity, a bronchiectatic space or even a cavitated tumour. Most, but not all, are caused by *A. fumigatus*.

Clinical features

An aspergilloma often produces no specific symptoms but may be responsible for recurrent haemoptysis, which is often severe. The presence of a fungus ball in the lung can also give rise to non-specific systemic features such as lethargy and weight loss.

Investigations

The development of a fungal ball within a cavity produces a tumour-like opacity on radiograph. An aspergilloma can usually be distinguished from a peripheral bronchial carcinoma by the presence of a crescent of air between the fungal ball and the upper wall of the cavity. Aspergillomata may be multiple.

Diagnosis

The diagnosis is usually suspected because of the chest radiograph findings. Serum precipitins to *A. fumigatus* can be demonstrated in virtually all patients. Sputum contains hyphal fragments on microscopy which are often only scanty, and is usually positive on culture. Less than 50% of patients exhibit skin hypersensitivity to extracts of *A. fumigatus*.

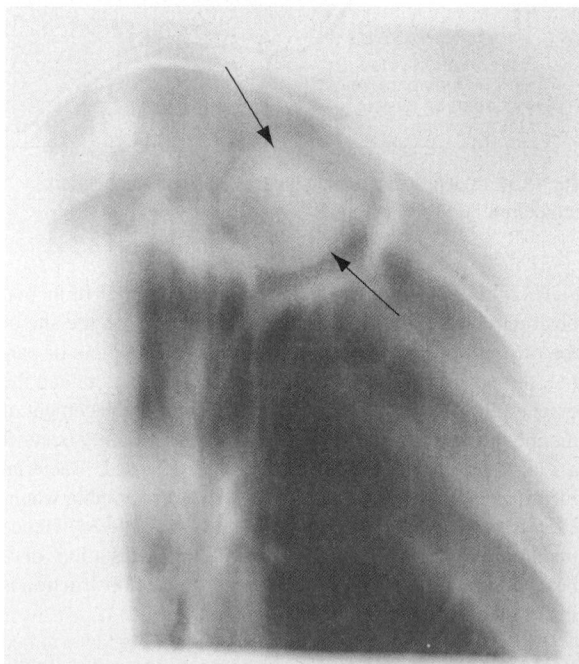

Fig. 13.35   Aspergilloma in left upper lobe cavity. Aspergilloma demonstrated using conventional tomography. Rounded fungal ball (arrows) separated from the wall of the cavity by a 'halo' of air.

Management

Specific antifungal therapy is of no value. Surgical removal of the aspergilloma is indicated in patients who have massive haemoptysis and in whom thoracotomy is not contraindicated because of poor respiratory reserve. Bronchial artery embolisation is an alternative approach to the management of recurrent haemoptysis.

INVASIVE PULMONARY ASPERGILLOSIS

Invasion of previously healthy lung tissue by *A. fumigatus* is uncommon but can produce a serious and often fatal condition which usually occurs in patients who are immunocompromised by either drugs or disease. The source of the infection can be an aspergilloma but this is by no means always so.

Clinical features

Spread of the disease to the lungs is usually rapid, with the production of consolidation, necrosis and cavitation. There is grave systemic disturbance. The formation of multiple abscesses is associated with the production of copious amounts of purulent sputum which is often blood-stained.

A much more indolent form of invasive pulmonary aspergillosis is now recognised.

Diagnosis

Invasive pulmonary aspergillosis should be suspected in any patient thought to have severe suppurative pneumonia (see p. 530) which has not responded to antibiotic therapy. The diagnosis can be established by the demonstration of abundant fungal elements in stained smears of sputum. Serum precipitins can be demonstrated in some, but not all, patients.

Management

If the diagnosis is established at an early stage, antifungal therapy can be successful. Amphotericin 0.25–1 mg/kg

---

ISSUES IN OLDER PEOPLE
RESPIRATORY INFECTION

- In the developed world the vast majority of deaths from pneumonia occur in the elderly.
- Older people are at increased risk of and from respiratory infection because of reduced immune responses, reduced respiratory muscle strength and endurance, altered mucus layer, poor nutritional status and the increased prevalence of chronic lung disease.
- Influenza has a much higher complication rate, morbidity and mortality in old age. Vaccination significantly reduces morbidity and mortality in old age but uptake is poor.
- Other medical conditions may also predispose to infection; for example, swallowing difficulties due to stroke increase the risk of aspiration pneumonia.
- Elderly patients are more likely to present with atypical symptoms, especially confusion.
- Most cases of tuberculosis in old age represent reactivation of previous, often unrecognised disease and may be precipitated by steroid therapy, diabetes mellitus and the factors above. Cryptic miliary tuberculosis is an occasional alternative presentation. Older people more commonly suffer adverse effects from antituberculous chemotherapy and require close monitoring.

daily by slow intravenous infusion over 6 hours should be given in combination with flucytosine 150–200 mg/kg daily by mouth or by intravenous infusion, in four divided doses. The combination of flucytosine and amphotericin prevents resistance to flucytosine developing and allows a smaller daily dose of amphotericin to be used than would be possible if this drug was used on its own. Liposomal amphotericin is recommended when toxicity precludes the use of conventional amphotericin. Itraconazole has been used successfully in the treatment of invasive aspergillosis.

Histoplasmosis, coccidioidomycosis, blastomycosis and cryptococcosis
See pages 93–95.

TUMOURS OF THE BRONCHUS AND LUNG

Between 1995 and 1996 there were more than 36 000 lung cancer deaths in the UK (see Box 13.64). Bronchial carcinoma is by far the most common (> 90%) lung tumour; by comparison, benign tumours of the lung are rare. Primary carcinomas of other organs, in particular the breast, kidney, uterus, ovary, testes and thyroid, may give rise to metastatic pulmonary deposits, as may an osteogenic or other sarcoma. Bronchial tumours also represent the most common cause of obstruction to a major bronchus (see Box 13.65).

13.64 THE BURDEN OF LUNG CANCER
• 36 000 deaths/year in the UK • 25% of all cancer deaths • 8% of all male deaths and 4% of all female deaths • More than threefold increase in deaths since 1950 • Most rapidly increasing cause of cancer death in women • Most common cause of cancer death in men • After breast cancer, the second most common cause of cancer death in women in England and Wales

13.65 CAUSES OF LARGE BRONCHUS OBSTRUCTION
Common
• Bronchial carcinoma or adenoma (see Box 13.70) • Enlarged tracheobronchial lymph nodes (malignant or tuberculous) • Inhaled foreign bodies (especially right lung and in children) • Bronchial casts or plugs consisting of inspissated mucus or blood clot (especially asthma, haemoptysis, debility) • Collections of mucus or mucopus retained in the bronchi as a result of ineffective expectoration (especially post-operative following abdominal surgery)
Rare
• Aortic aneurysm • Giant left atrium • Pericardial effusion • Congenital bronchial atresia • Fibrous bronchial stricture (e.g. following tuberculosis)

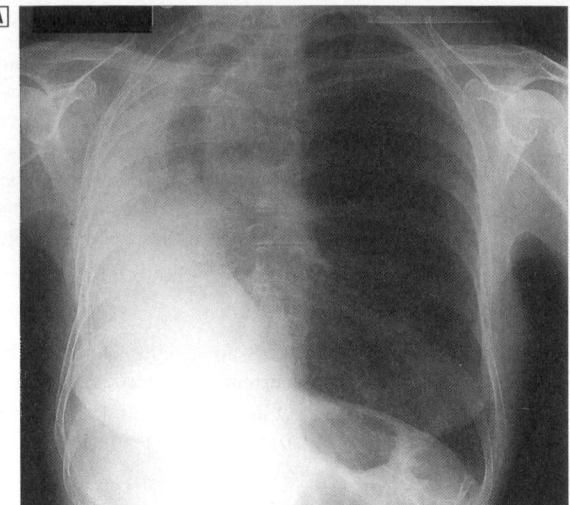

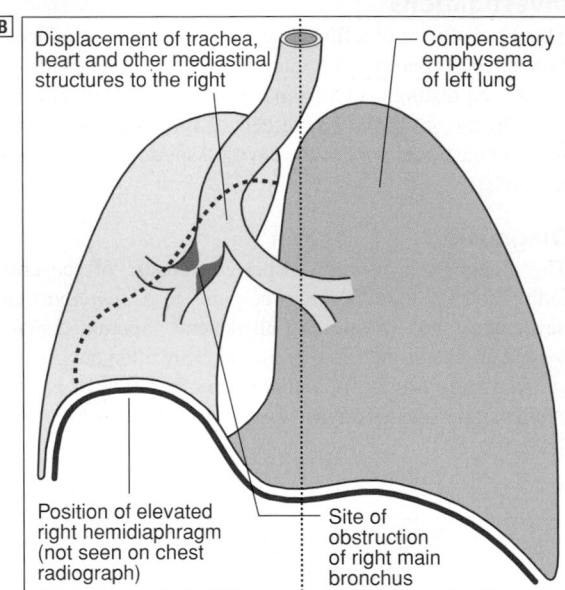

Fig. 13.36   Collapse of the right lung: effects on neighbouring structures. A Chest radiograph. B Artist's impression.

The clinical and radiological manifestations of bronchial obstruction (see Figs 13.36 and 13.37) depend on the site of the obstruction, whether the obstruction is complete or partial, the presence or absence of secondary infection, and the extent of pre-existing lung disease. Signs of displacement of the mediastinum or elevation of the diaphragm only occur if a major portion of the lung becomes collapsed. Bacterial infection affecting the distal lung is almost inevitable whenever a major bronchus is significantly obstructed. Hence pneumonia is often the first clinical manifestation of a bronchial carcinoma, even when the degree of obstruction is insufficient to cause collapse.

The cause of bronchial obstruction should be determined at bronchoscopy; this procedure also enables biopsy of abnormal tissue and the removal of foreign bodies, mucus plugs or tenacious secretions.

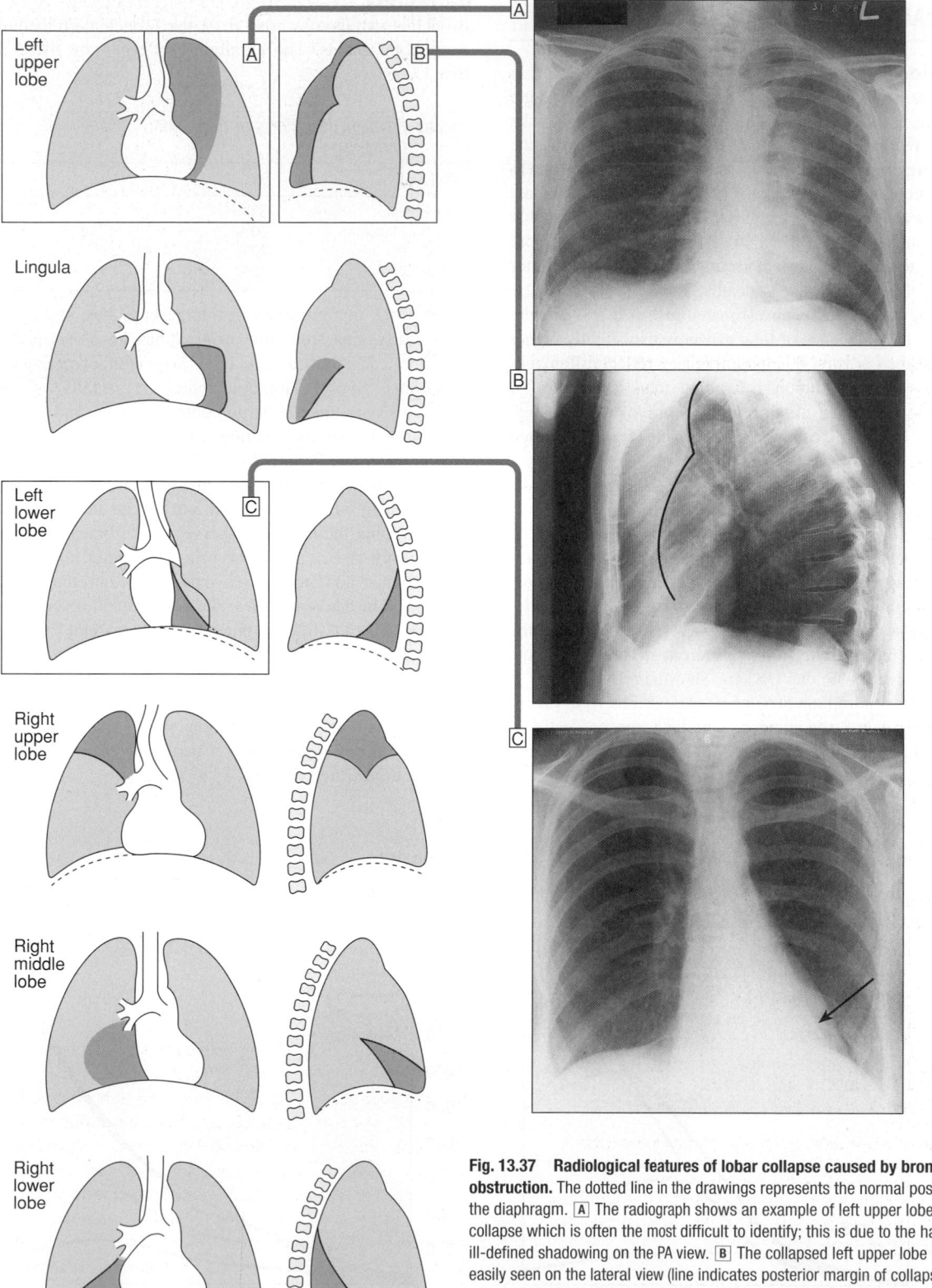

Left upper lobe

Lingula

Left lower lobe

Right upper lobe

Right middle lobe

Right lower lobe

Fig. 13.37 Radiological features of lobar collapse caused by bronchial obstruction. The dotted line in the drawings represents the normal position of the diaphragm. **A** The radiograph shows an example of left upper lobe collapse which is often the most difficult to identify; this is due to the hazy, ill-defined shadowing on the PA view. **B** The collapsed left upper lobe is more easily seen on the lateral view (line indicates posterior margin of collapsed left upper lobe). **C** Radiograph of collapsed left lower lobe (arrow) causing increased density behind heart and loss of normal clarity between lung and both the left hemidiaphragm and descending thoracic aorta.

PRIMARY TUMOURS OF THE LUNG

Aetiology

Cigarette smoking is by far the most important single factor in the causation of lung cancer. It is thought to be directly responsible for at least 90% of lung carcinomas, the risk being directly proportional to the amount smoked and to the tar content of cigarettes. For example, the death rate from the disease in heavy cigarette smokers is 40 times that in non-smokers. The effect of 'passive' smoking is more difficult to quantify but is currently believed to be a factor in 5% of all lung cancer deaths. Exposure to naturally occurring radon has been estimated to cause 5% of lung cancers. The incidence of lung cancer is also slightly higher in urban than in rural dwellers; this may reflect differences in atmospheric pollution (including tobacco smoke) or occupation since a number of industrial products (e.g. asbestos, beryllium, cadmium and chromium) are associated with lung cancer.

BRONCHIAL CARCINOMA

The incidence of bronchial carcinoma increased dramatically during the 20th century (see Fig.13.38) and it is now the most common fatal malignancy in the developed world, with escalating incidences in the less developed world as the prevalence of cigarette smoking increases. The current data for lung cancer in the UK are shown in Box 13.64. It accounts for more than 50% of all male deaths from malignant disease and the incidence of lung cancer deaths is expected to climb over the next 10 years, with an increasing number unrelated to smoking.

Pathology

Bronchial carcinomas arise from the bronchial epithelium or mucous glands. The common cell types are listed in Box 13.66.

13.66 COMMON CELL TYPES OF BRONCHIAL CARCINOMA	
Cell type	**%**
Squamous	35%
Adenocarcinoma	30%
Small-cell	20%
Large-cell	15%

When the tumour arises in a large bronchus, symptoms arise early, but tumours originating in a peripheral bronchus can attain a very large size without producing symptoms. Such a tumour, which is usually of the squamous type, may undergo central necrosis and cavitation, when it may have similar radiographic features to a lung abscess (see Fig. 13.39).

Bronchial carcinoma may involve the pleura either directly or by lymphatic spread and extend into the chest wall, invading the intercostal nerves or the brachial plexus and causing severe pain. The primary tumour, or tumour within lymph node metastases, may spread into the mediastinum and invade or compress the pericardium, oesophagus, superior vena cava, trachea, phrenic or left recurrent laryngeal nerves. Lymphatic spread to supraclavicular and mediastinal lymph nodes is also frequently observed. Blood-borne metastases occur most commonly in liver, bone, brain, adrenals and skin. Even a small primary tumour may cause widespread metastatic deposits and this is a particular characteristic of small-cell-type lung cancers.

A Males

Deaths per million/year

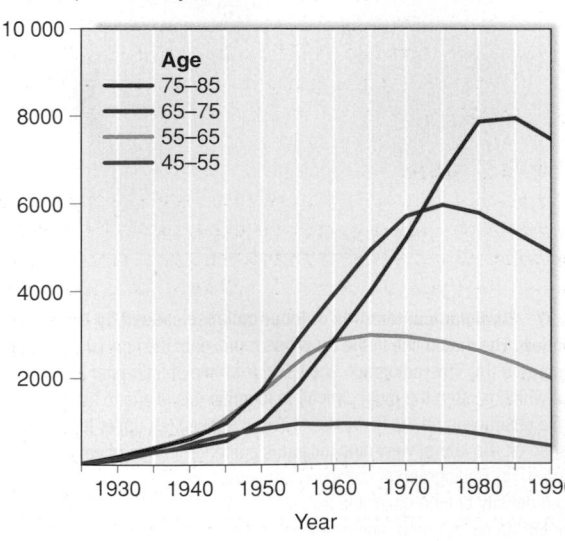

B Females

Deaths per million/year

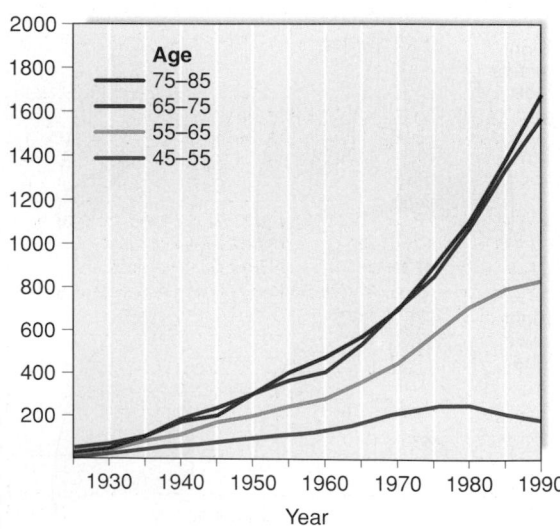

Fig. 13.38   Mortality trends from lung cancer in England and Wales, 1921–90 by age and year of death. **A** Males. **B** Females. Note the decline in mortality from lung cancer in men towards the end of this period, reflecting a change in smoking habit.

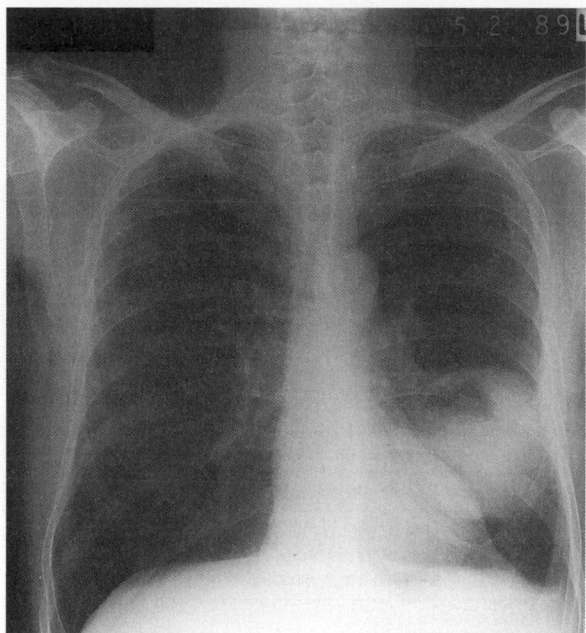

Fig. 13.39 Large cavitated bronchial carcinoma in left lower lobe.

Clinical features

Lung cancer may present in a number of different ways. Most commonly, symptoms reflect local involvement of the bronchus, but may also arise from spread to the chest wall or mediastinum, from distant blood-borne spread or, less commonly, as a result of a variety of non-metastatic paraneoplastic syndromes (see Box 13.67).

Cough is the most common early symptom; sputum is purulent if there is secondary infection. Bronchial obstruction may lead to pneumonia, and a recurrent pneumonia at the same site or one which is slow to respond to treatment, particularly in a cigarette smoker, should immediately suggest the possibility of bronchial carcinoma. A lung abscess may sometimes develop, leading to cough productive of large volumes of purulent sputum. A change in the character of the 'regular' cough of a smoker, particularly if it is associated with other new respiratory symptoms, should always alert the clinician to the possibility of bronchial carcinoma.

Haemoptysis is a common symptom, especially in tumours arising in large bronchi. Occasionally, central tumours invade large vessels, causing massive haemoptysis which may be fatal. Repeated episodes of scanty haemoptysis or blood-streaking of sputum in a smoker are highly suggestive of bronchial carcinoma and should always be investigated.

Breathlessness may reflect occlusion of a large bronchus, resulting in collapse of a lobe or lung or the development of a large pleural effusion. Stridor may occur where spread of the tumour to the subcarinal and paratracheal glands causes compression of the main bronchi or lower end of the trachea or, rarely, where the trachea is the site of the primary tumour.

Pleural pain usually reflects malignant invasion of the pleura, although it can reflect distal infection. Involvement of the intercostal nerves or brachial plexus may cause pain in the chest or upper limb along the appropriate nerve root distribution. Bronchial carcinoma in the apex of the lung ('superior sulcus tumour') may cause Horner's syndrome (ipsilateral partial ptosis, enophthalmos, a small pupil and hypohidrosis of the face) due to involvement of the sympathetic chain at or above the stellate ganglion, and/or Pancoast's syndrome (pain in the shoulder and inner aspect of the arm) caused by involvement of the lower part of the brachial plexus. Mediastinal spread may result in dysphagia.

The patient may also present with symptoms due to blood-borne metastases, such as focal neurological defects, epileptic seizures, personality change, jaundice, bone pain or skin nodules. Lassitude, anorexia and weight loss usually indicate the presence of metastatic spread. Finally, the patient may present with symptoms referable to the presence of a number of non-metastatic extrapulmonary manifestations (see Box 13.67). Hypercalcaemia is usually caused by squamous carcinoma and causes polyuria, nocturia, fatigue, constipation, confusion and occasionally coma. The most frequently encountered endocrine syndromes (inappropriate antidiuretic hormone (ADH) secretion and ectopic adrenocorticotrophic hormone (ACTH) secretion) are usually associated with small-cell lung cancer. Associated neurological syndromes may occur with any type of bronchial carcinoma.

Physical signs

Examination is usually normal unless there is significant bronchial obstruction, or the tumour has spread to the pleura or mediastinum. A tumour obstructing a large bronchus produces the physical signs of collapse (or occasionally obstructive emphysema) and may give rise to pneumonia that is characterised by a relative absence of physical signs and a slow response to treatment. A monophonic or unilateral rhonchus (wheeze) suggests the presence of a fixed bronchial obstruction, and the presence of stridor indicates obstruction at or above the level of the main carina. A hoarse voice associated with an ineffectual or 'bovine' cough usually indicates left recurrent laryngeal nerve palsy. Phrenic nerve paralysis causes unilateral diaphragmatic palsy and hence dullness to percussion and absent breath sounds at a lung base. Involvement of the pleura produces the physical

13.67 NON-METASTATIC EXTRAPULMONARY MANIFESTATIONS OF BRONCHIAL CARCINOMA	
Endocrine	
• Inappropriate antidiuretic hormone (ADH) secretion causing hyponatraemia • Ectopic adrenocorticotrophic hormone (ACTH) secretion	• Hypercalcaemia due to secretion of parathyroid hormone (PTH)-related peptides • Carcinoid syndrome (see p. 801) • Gynaecomastia
Neurological	
• Polyneuropathy • Myelopathy • Cerebellar degeneration	• Myasthenia (Eaton–Lambert syndrome, see p. 1185)
Other	
• Digital clubbing • Hypertrophic pulmonary osteoarthropathy • Nephrotic syndrome	• Polymyositis and dermatomyositis • Eosinophilia

signs of pleurisy or of pleural effusion (see p. 501). Bronchial carcinoma is also the most common cause of the superior vena cava syndrome, which presents initially as bilateral engorgement of the jugular veins and later as oedema affecting the face, neck and arms. Digital clubbing is often seen and may be a component part of a syndrome called hypertrophic pulmonary osteoarthropathy (HPOA), which is characterised by periostitis of the long bones, most commonly the distal tibia, fibula, radius and ulna. This gives rise to pain and tenderness in the affected joints and often pitting oedema over the anterior aspect of the shin. Radiographs of the painful bone show subperiosteal new bone formation. HPOA, while most frequently associated with bronchial carcinoma, can occur with other tumours and has been described in association with cystic fibrosis.

Investigations

The main aims of investigation are to confirm the diagnosis, establish the histological cell type and define the extent of the disease.

The common radiological features of bronchial carcinoma are illustrated in Figure 13.40. Further investigation to obtain a histological diagnosis and determine operability is nearly always indicated.

Bronchoscopy is usually the most useful investigation as it can provide tissue (biopsies and bronchial brush samples) for pathological examination and allow direct assessment of the proximity of central tumours to the main carina (see Fig. 13.41). If abnormal tissue is not visible at bronchoscopy, bronchial washings and directed biopsies can be taken from the lung segment in which the tumour is shown to be located on radiological examination. In patients who are not fit enough for a bronchoscopy, examination of sputum cytology can be a valuable diagnostic aid (see Fig. 13.42). Pleural biopsy is indicated in all patients with pleural effusions. If bronchoscopy fails to obtain a cytological diagnosis, percutaneous needle biopsy under CT guidance is appropriate for peripheral tumours or mediastinoscopy for patients with suspected mediastinal involvement. Not infrequently, thoracoscopy or thoracotomy is required to obtain a definitive histological diagnosis. In patients with metastatic disease the diagnosis can often be confirmed by needle aspiration or biopsy of enlarged lymph nodes, skin lesions, where indicated, liver or bone marrow.

13.68 COMMON RADIOLOGICAL PRESENTATIONS OF BRONCHIAL CARCINOMA
1 Unilateral hilar enlargement
• Central tumour. Hilar glandular involvement. Beware—peripheral tumour in apical segment of a lower lobe can look like an enlarged hilar shadow on the PA radiograph
2 Peripheral pulmonary opacity (see p. 500)
• Usually irregular but well circumscribed. May have irregular cavitation within it. Can be very large
3 Lung, lobe or segmental collapse
• Usually caused by tumour within the bronchus causing occlusion. Lung collapse can be produced by compression of the main bronchus by enlarged lymph glands
4 Pleural effusion
• Usually indicates tumour invasion of pleural space; very rarely a manifestation of infection in collapsed lung tissue distal to a bronchial carcinoma
5–7 Broadening of mediastinum, enlarged cardiac shadow, elevation of a hemidiaphragm
• Paratracheal lymphadenopathy may cause widening of the upper mediastinum. A malignant pericardial effusion will cause enlargement of the cardiac shadow. If a raised hemidiaphragm is caused by phrenic nerve palsy, screening will show it to move paradoxically upwards when patient sniffs
8 Rib destruction
• Direct invasion of the chest wall or blood-borne metastatic spread can cause osteolytic lesions of the ribs

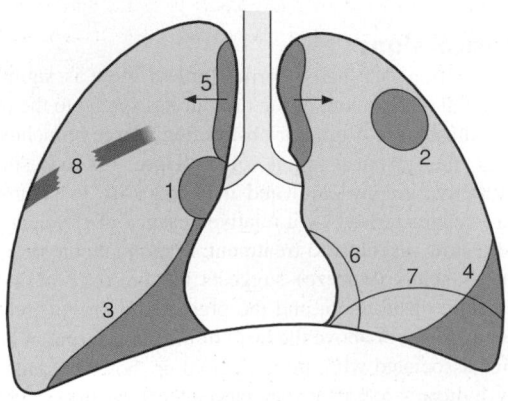

Fig. 13.40   Common radiological presentations of bronchial carcinoma. (See Box 13.68 for details.)

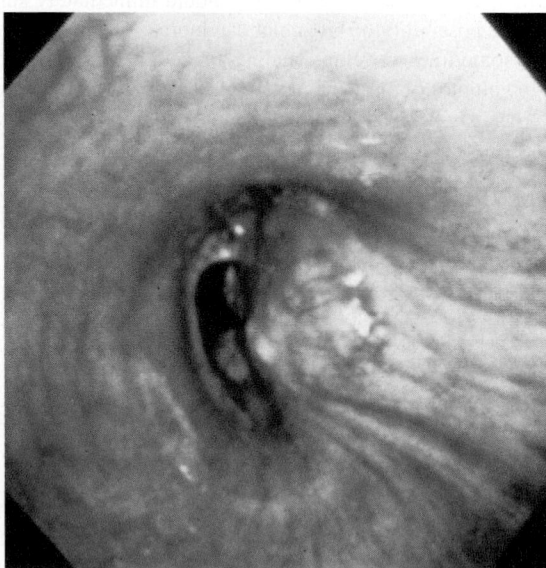

Fig. 13.41   Bronchoscopic view of a bronchogenic carcinoma.
There is distortion of mucosal folds, partial occlusion of the airway lumen and abnormal tumour tissue.

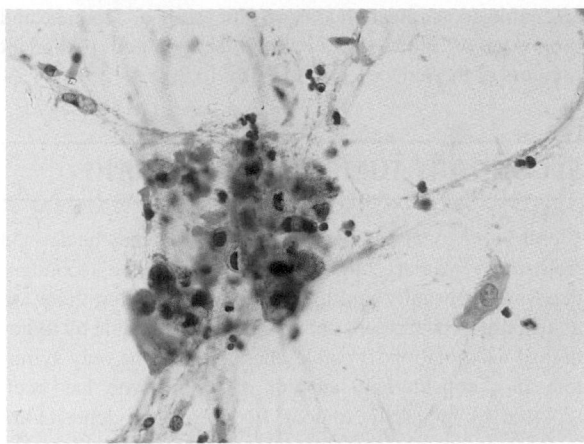

Fig. 13.42 Sputum sample showing a cluster of carcinoma cells.
There is keratinisation, showing orangeophilia of the cytoplasm, and
non-keratinised forms are also seen. The nuclei are large and 'coal-
black' in density. These are the features of squamous cell bronchogenic
carcinoma.

After establishing a histological diagnosis, investigations
should focus on determining whether the tumour is opera-
ble. This requires excluding involvement of central mediastinal structures or spread of tumour to distant sites and
ensuring that the patient's respiratory and cardiac function is
sufficient to allow surgical treatment (see Box 13.69). The
propensity of small-cell lung cancer to metastasise early dictates that very few patients with this tumour type are suitable
for surgical intervention and that more detailed pre-
operative staging is advisable before resection is contemplated. Head CT, radionuclide bone scanning, liver ultrasound and bone marrow biopsy can be reserved for patients
with clinical, haematological or biochemical evidence of
tumour spread to such sites.

Management
Cure can only be achieved by surgical resection.
Unfortunately, in the majority of cases (approximately 85%)
surgery is not possible or appropriate, and such patients can
only be offered palliative therapy. Radiotherapy, and in some
cases chemotherapy, can relieve distressing symptoms.

Surgical treatment
As discussed, careful staging is essential prior to surgical
resection and equal attention must be given to the patient's
respiratory reserve and cardiac status. This, coupled with
improvements in surgical and post-operative care, now
offers 5-year survival rates of > 75% in stage I disease (N0,
tumour confined within visceral pleura) and 55% in stage II
disease, which includes resection in patients with ipsilateral
peribronchial or hilar node involvement.

Radiotherapy
While much less effective than surgery, radical radiotherapy
can offer long-term survival in certain patients with
bronchial carcinoma. It is of greatest value, however, in the
palliation of distressing complications such as superior vena
caval obstruction, recurrent haemoptysis, and pain caused
by chest wall invasion or by skeletal metastatic deposits.

**13.69 CONTRAINDICATIONS TO SURGICAL
RESECTION IN BRONCHIAL CARCINOMA**

- Distant metastasis (M1)
- Invasion of central mediastinal structures including heart, great
  vessels, trachea and oesophagus (T4)
- Malignant pleural effusion (T4)
- Contralateral mediastinal nodes (N3)
- $FEV_1 < 0.8$ litres
- Severe or unstable cardiac or other medical condition

N.B. In otherwise fit individuals, direct extension of tumour into the
chest wall, diaphragm, mediastinal pleura or pericardium or to within
2 cm of the main carina does not exclude surgery. Though surgically
resectable, patients with N2 (ipsilateral mediastinal) nodes may
require neoadjuvant or adjuvant therapy.

Obstruction of the trachea and main bronchi can also be
relieved temporarily by radiotherapy. Radiotherapy can be
used in conjunction with chemotherapy in the treatment of
small-cell carcinoma and is particularly efficient at preventing
the development of brain metastasis in patients who have had
a complete response to chemotherapy. Continuous hyperfrac-
tionated accelerated radiotherapy (CHART), in which a similar total dose is given in smaller but more frequent fractions,
offers better survival prospects than conventional schedules.

Chemotherapy
The treatment of small-cell carcinoma with combinations of
cytotoxic drugs, sometimes in combination with radiotherapy,
can increase the median survival of patients with this highly
malignant type of bronchial carcinoma from 3 months to
well over a year. Combination chemotherapy leads to better
outcomes than single-agent treatment. In particular, oral
etoposide leads to more toxicity and worse survival than
standard combination chemotherapy. Current recommendations include i.v. cyclophosphamide, doxorubicin and vincristine or i.v. cisplatin and etoposide. The above regimens
are given every 3 weeks for 3–6 cycles. Nausea and vomiting peak for 3 days after each cycle of chemotherapy and are
best treated with 5-HT$_3$ receptor antagonists (see p. 220).

The use of combinations of chemotherapeutic drugs
requires considerable medical skill and expertise and it is
recommended that such treatment should only be given
under the supervision of clinicians experienced in such
treatment. In general, chemotherapy is far less effective in
non-small-cell bronchial cancers. However, recent studies in
such patients using platinum-based chemotherapy regimens
have shown a 30% response rate associated with a small
increase in survival.

EBM

**SMALL-CELL LUNG CANCER—role of prophylactic
cranial irradiation**

'Meta-analysis of seven RCTs has found that prophylactic cranial
irradiation reduces the risk of developing brain metastases and
improves survival in patients with small-cell lung cancer in complete
remission.'

- Auperin A, Arriagada R, Pignon J-P, et al. Prophylactic cranial irradiation for people with
  small-cell lung cancer in complete remission. N Engl J Med 1999; 341:476–484.
- Cranial irradiation for preventing brain metastases of small cell lung cancer in patients in
  complete remission (Cochrane Review). Cochrane Library, issue 4, 2000. Oxford: Update
  Software.

Further information: 🖥 www.cochrane.co.uk

Laser therapy

Laser treatment via a fibreoptic bronchoscope is essentially palliative, the aim being to destroy tumour tissue occluding major airways to allow re-aeration of collapsed lung. The best results are achieved in tumours of the main bronchi.

General aspects of management

As in other forms of carcinoma, effective communication, pain relief and attention to diet are important (see Ch. 5). Lung tumours can cause clinically significant depression and anxiety, and these may need specific therapy. Hypercalcaemia (see p. 715) is an uncommon but important complication of lung cancer, particularly squamous cell carcinoma. Treatment in the acute situation involves intravenous rehydration, maintenance of a good urine output and administration of bisphosphonates. Thereafter, steroids may be effective and mithramycin may be necessary to maintain a normal blood calcium. Demeclocycline can be useful for controlling inappropriate ADH secretion in patients with small-cell lung cancer. The management of malignant pleural effusions is outlined on page 503.

<table>
<tr><td>STAGE IV NON-SMALL-CELL LUNG CANCER—role of palliative chemotherapy</td><td>EBM</td></tr>
</table>

'Four SRs of RCTs have found that chemotherapy significantly prolongs 1-year survival in patients with stage IV non-small-cell lung cancer. The survival benefit is greatest with regimens containing cisplatin. Quality of life issues remain undefined.'

- Non-Small Cell Lung Cancer Collaborative Group. Chemotherapy in non-small cell lung cancer: a meta-analysis using updated individual patient data from 52 randomised clinical trials. BMJ 1995; 311:899–909.
- Marino P, Pampallona S, Preatoni A, et al. Chemotherapy versus supportive care in advanced non-small cell lung cancer: results of a meta-analysis of the literature. Chest 1994; 106:861–865.

Further information: 🖥 www.meds.com/pdq/nonsmallcell_pro.html

Prognosis

The overall prognosis in bronchial carcinoma is very poor, with around 80% of patients dying within a year of diagnosis and less than 6% of patients surviving 5 years after diagnosis. The best prognosis is with well-differentiated squamous cell tumours which have not metastasised and are amenable to surgical treatment. The clinical features and prognosis of other less common benign and malignant tumours of the lung are given in Box 13.70.

SECONDARY TUMOURS OF THE LUNG

Blood-borne metastatic deposits in the lungs may be derived from many primary tumours (see p. 542). The secondary deposits are usually multiple and bilateral. Often there are no respiratory symptoms and the diagnosis is made by radiological examination. Breathlessness may be the only symptom if a considerable amount of lung tissue has been replaced by metastatic tumour. Endobronchial deposits are uncommon but can cause haemoptysis and lobar collapse.

PULMONARY LYMPHATIC CARCINOMATOSIS

Lymphatic infiltration may develop in patients with carcinoma of the breast, stomach, bowel, pancreas or bronchus. This grave condition causes severe and rapidly progressive breathlessness associated with marked hypoxaemia. The diagnosis is often suggested by the chest radiograph, which shows diffuse pulmonary shadowing radiating from the hilar regions, often associated with septal lines.

TUMOURS OF THE MEDIASTINUM

The mediastinum can be divided into four major compartments with reference to the lateral chest radiograph (see Fig. 13.43):

- superior mediastinum—above a line drawn between the lower border of the 4th thoracic vertebra and the upper end of the body of the sternum
- anterior mediastinum—in front of the heart
- middle mediastinum—between the anterior and posterior compartments
- posterior mediastinum—behind the heart.

13.70 RARER TYPES OF LUNG TUMOUR

Tumour	Status	Histology	Typical presentation	Prognosis
Adenosquamous carcinoma	Malignant	Tumours with areas of unequivocal squamous and adeno-differentiation	Peripheral or central lung mass	Stage-dependent
Carcinoid tumour (see p. 801)	Low-grade malignant	Neuro-endocrine differentiation	Bronchial obstruction, cough	95% 5-year survival with resection
Bronchial gland adenoma	Benign	Salivary gland differentiation	Tracheobronchial irritation/obstruction	Local resection curative
Bronchial gland carcinoma	Low-grade malignant	Salivary gland differentiation	Tracheobronchial irritation/obstruction	Local recurrence occurs
Hamartoma	Benign	Mesenchymal cells, cartilage	Peripheral lung nodule	Local resection curative
Bronchoalveolar carcinoma	Malignant	Tumour cells line alveolar spaces	Alveolar shadowing, productive cough	Variable, worse if multifocal

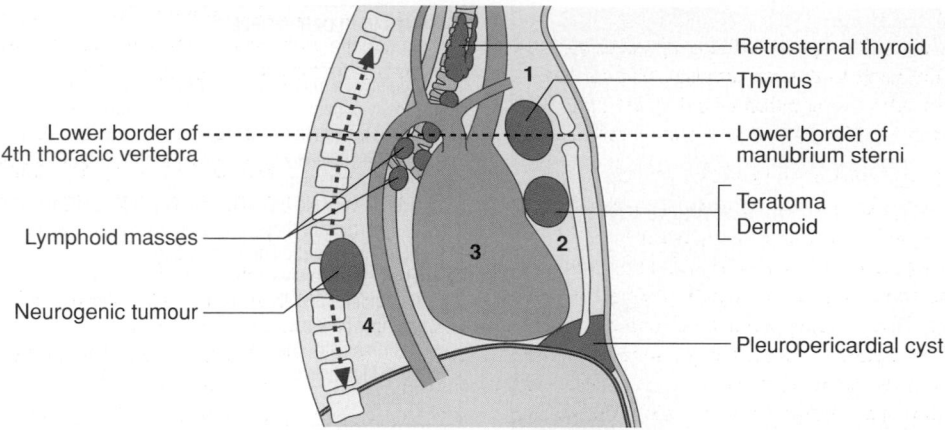

Fig. 13.43   The divisions of the mediastinum described in the diagnosis of mediastinal masses. (1) Superior mediastinum. (2) Anterior mediastinum. (3) Middle mediastinum. (4) Posterior mediastinum. Sites of the more common mediastinal tumours are also illustrated.

13.71 SOME CAUSES OF A MEDIASTINAL MASS	
Superior mediastinum	

• Retrosternal goitre
• Vascular lesion
  Persistent left superior
  vena cava
  Prominent left
  subclavian artery
	• Thymic tumour
	• Dermoid cyst
	• Lymphoma
	• Aortic aneurysm

Anterior mediastinum	

• Retrosternal goitre
• Dermoid cyst
• Thymic tumour
• Lymphoma
• Aortic aneurysm
	• Germ cell tumour
	• Pericardial cyst
	• Hernia through the
	  diaphragmatic foramen
	  of Morgagni

Posterior mediastinum	
• Neurogenic tumour • Paravertebral abscess • Oesophageal lesion	• Aortic aneurysm • Foregut duplication
Middle mediastinum	
• Bronchial carcinoma • Lymphoma • Sarcoidosis	• Bronchogenic cyst • Hiatus hernia

13.72 SYMPTOMS AND SIGNS PRODUCED BY MALIGNANT INVASION OF THE STRUCTURES OF THE MEDIASTINUM
Trachea and main bronchi
• Stridor, breathlessness, cough, pulmonary collapse
Oesophagus
• Dysphagia, oesophageal displacement or obstruction on barium swallow examination
Phrenic nerve
• Diaphragmatic paralysis
Left recurrent laryngeal nerve
• Paralysis of left vocal cord giving rise to hoarseness and 'bovine' cough
Sympathetic trunk
• Horner's syndrome
Superior vena cava
• SVC obstruction results in non-pulsatile distension of neck veins, oedema and cyanosis of head, neck, hands and arms. Dilated anastomotic veins on chest wall
Pericardium
• Pericarditis and/or pericardial effusion

A variety of conditions can present radiologically as a mediastinal mass (see Box 13.71).

Benign tumours and cysts arising within the mediastinum are frequently diagnosed when radiological examination of the chest is undertaken for some other reason. In general, they do not invade vital structures but may cause symptoms by compressing the trachea or occasionally the superior vena cava. A dermoid cyst may very occasionally rupture into a bronchus.

Malignant mediastinal tumours are distinguished by their power to invade as well as compress structures such as bronchi and lungs (see Box 13.72). As a result, even a small malignant tumour can produce symptoms, although as a rule the tumour has attained a considerable size before this happens. Included in this category are mediastinal lymph node metastases, lymphomas, leukaemia, malignant thymic tumours and germ-cell tumours. Aortic and innominate aneurysms have destructive features resembling those of malignant mediastinal tumours.

Investigations

Radiological examination

A benign mediastinal tumour generally appears as a sharply circumscribed opacity situated mainly in the mediastinum but often encroaching on one or both lung fields (see Fig. 13.44). A malignant mediastinal tumour seldom has a clearly defined margin and often presents as a general broadening of the mediastinal shadow. CT together with MRI are the investigations of choice for mediastinal tumours.

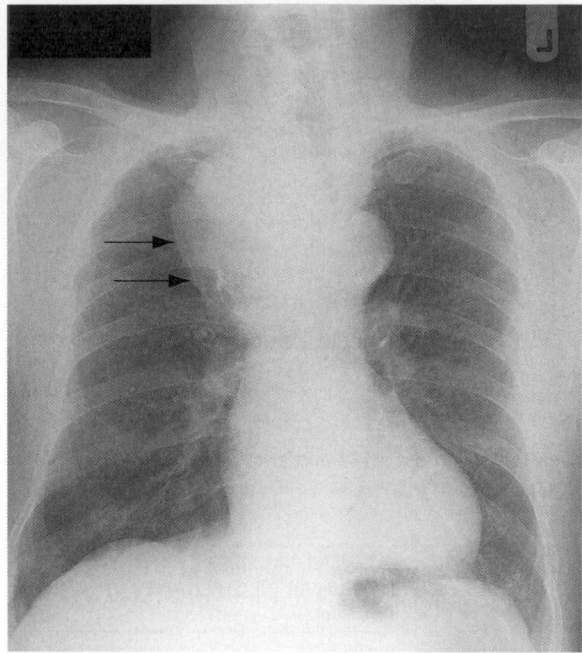

Fig. 13.44 Large mass (intrathoracic goitre—arrows) extending from right upper mediastinum.

Bronchoscopy

Bronchoscopy should be carried out in most patients because bronchial carcinoma is a common cause of mediastinal tumour by secondary lymphatic spread.

Surgical exploration

If enlarged lymph nodes are suspected in the anterior mediastinum, tissue from these nodes can be removed for histological examination by mediastinoscopy. However, surgical exploration of the chest with removal of part or all of the tumour is often required to obtain a histological diagnosis.

Management

Benign mediastinal tumours should be removed surgically because most produce symptoms sooner or later. Some of them, particularly cysts, may become infected, while others, especially neural tumours, have the potential to undergo malignant transformation. The operative mortality is low provided there is not a relative contraindication to surgical treatment, such as coexisting cardiovascular disease, COPD or extreme age.

The treatment of lymphoma and leukaemia is described on pages 931 and 939 respectively. The management of malignant thymomas is surgical. Lymph node metastases from bronchial carcinoma often respond well, though temporarily, to radiotherapy or, in the case of small-cell carcinoma, to chemotherapy. Complications such as superior vena caval and tracheal obstruction can also be treated with radiotherapy or a combination of radiotherapy and chemotherapy, and the placement of internal stents is now possible for localised obstruction of both these structures.

INTERSTITIAL AND INFILTRATIVE PULMONARY DISEASES

INTERSTITIAL PULMONARY DISEASES

Interstitial lung diseases are a heterogeneous group of conditions caused by diffuse thickening of the alveolar walls with inflammatory cells and exudate (e.g. the acute respiratory distress syndrome—ARDS), granulomas (e.g. sarcoidosis), alveolar haemorrhage (e.g. Goodpasture's syndrome, see p. 614) and/or fibrosis (e.g. fibrosing alveolitis). Some are the result of exposure to known agents (e.g. asbestos), whereas in others, such as sarcoidosis, the cause is unknown. Lung disease may occur in isolation, or as part of a systemic connective tissue disorder—for example, in rheumatoid arthritis and systemic lupus erythematosus. Interstitial lung diseases may present acutely, as in acute drug reactions and ARDS, but more often the natural history is one of slowly progressive loss of alveolar-capillary gas exchange units over months or even years. This relentless progression of increased lung stiffness, disordered matching of ventilation and perfusion, and defects in gas transfer results in worsening exertional dyspnoea which, in many cases, eventually progresses to respiratory failure, pulmonary hypertension and death.

Aetiology

There is a very wide range of causes of interstitial lung disease (see Box 13.73). Some, like sarcoidosis, are quite common whereas others are rare. Despite the different causes and pathological processes involved, many interstitial lung diseases give rise to similar symptoms, physical signs, radiological changes and disturbances of pulmonary function and are therefore worthy of collective consideration. Nevertheless, the various underlying aetiologies present very different implications for prognosis and therapy. Moreover, interstitial lung diseases may be confused with other conditions with similar clinical and radiological features (see Box 13.74). Therefore a general approach to interstitial lung disease will be considered before a more detailed description of some specific disorders.

13.73 SOME CAUSES OF INTERSTITIAL LUNG DISEASE

- Sarcoidosis
- Cryptogenic fibrosing alveolitis
- Exposure to organic dusts, e.g. farmer's lung, bird fancier's lung
- Exposure to inorganic dusts, e.g. asbestosis, silicosis
- As part of systemic inflammatory disease, e.g. ARDS, fibrosing alveolitis in connective tissue disorders
- Some forms of pulmonary eosinophilia
- Exposure to irradiation and drugs
- Rare disorders, e.g. alveolar proteinosis, Langerhans cell histiocytosis

13.74 CONDITIONS WHICH MIMIC INTERSTITIAL LUNG DISEASES

Infection
- Viral pneumonia
- *Pneumocystis carinii*
- *Mycoplasma pneumoniae*
- Tuberculosis
- Parasites, e.g. filariasis
- Fungal infection

Malignancy
- Leukaemia and lymphoma
- Lymphatic carcinomatosis
- Multiple metastases
- Bronchoalveolar carcinoma

Pulmonary oedema

Aspiration pneumonitis

Diagnosis of interstitial lung disease: a general approach

The first task is to differentiate the disorder from other conditions which can mimic interstitial lung diseases (ILDs) (see Box 13.74), and then to determine which of the many causes of ILD is implicated. Establishing a diagnosis is important for a number of reasons. Firstly, there are prognostic implications; for example, sarcoidosis is frequently self-limiting (see p. 552), whereas cryptogenic fibrosing alveolitis (CFA, see p. 555) is most often fatal. Secondly, establishing a specific diagnosis will avoid inappropriate treatment; for example, the powerful immunosuppressive regimens used for some cases of cryptogenic fibrosing alveolitis would be undesirable if the underlying condition was asbestosis or extrinsic allergic alveolitis (see p. 556). Thirdly, some ILDs can be expected to respond better than others to treatment, e.g. a good symptomatic response to corticosteroids could be predicted in sarcoidosis, whereas the prognosis would need to be much more guarded in cryptogenic fibrosing alveolitis. Finally, a lung biopsy taken when the patient is already established on empirical immunosuppressive therapy is not only associated with a higher morbidity and mortality, but the tissue obtained is more difficult to interpret histologically; it is desirable, therefore, to be confident about the diagnosis before starting any therapy.

Establishing a diagnosis often presents a considerable clinical challenge, necessitating meticulous attention to the history and physical signs together with the judicious and selective use of investigations (see Fig. 13.45).

History

The duration of disease may sometimes be difficult to ascertain. In the early stages particularly, gradually progressive shortness of breath on exertion may be the only symptom, and hence the patient may not present clinically until there is quite extensive lung pathology. It is clearly important to elicit a detailed history of exposure to organic dusts, inorganic dusts and drugs, including the degree and duration of such exposure. A 'lifetime' occupational history is essential for this purpose. Contact with birds at home or in the working environment is the cause of the most common form of

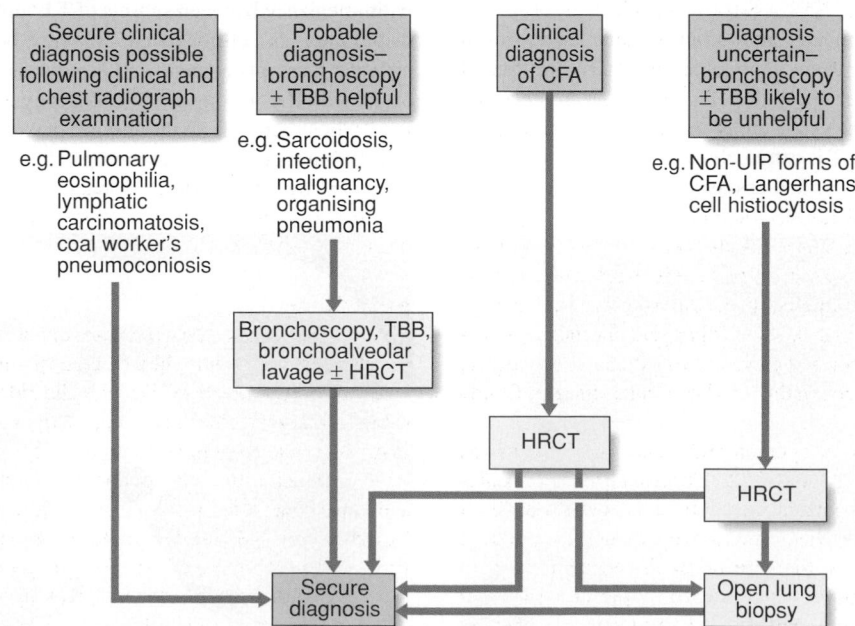

Fig. 13.45 **Algorithm for the investigation of patients with interstitial lung disease following initial clinical and chest radiograph examination.** (CFA = cryptogenic fibrosing alveolitis; UIP = usual interstitial pneumonia; TBB = transbronchial biopsy; HRCT = high-resolution CT)

extrinsic allergic alveolitis, but such enquiry is easily over-looked. A history of rashes, joint pains or renal disease may suggest an underlying connective tissue disorder or vasculitis (see Ch. 20).

Physical signs

In many cases, especially in early disease, there may be few, if any, physical signs. In advanced disease tachypnoea and cyanosis may be obvious at rest, and there may be signs of pulmonary hypertension and right heart failure. Digital clubbing may be prominent, particularly in cryptogenic fibrosing alveolitis or asbestosis. There may be restriction of lung expansion and showers of end-inspiratory crepitations on auscultation over the lower zones posteriorly and later-ally. Extrapulmonary signs, including lymphadenopathy or uveitis, may be present in sarcoidosis (see Box 13.75) and arthropathies or rashes may suggest an ILD occurring as a manifestation of a connective tissue disorder (see p. 559).

Investigations

Laboratory investigations

No single blood test is diagnostic for a particular interstitial lung disease. Some laboratory tests may be useful in indicat-ing systemic disease or providing crude indices of disease activity. The ESR and C-reactive protein may be non-specifically elevated. Serological tests may be of value: anti-nuclear antibodies, rheumatoid factor etc. in connective tissue diseases, and antiglomerular basement membrane antibodies in Goodpasture's syndrome (see p. 614). Serum levels of angiotensin-converting enzyme (ACE) may be elevated in sarcoidosis, but the test is not specific for this condition.

Radiology

The chest radiograph may show a fine reticular shadowing, a reticulonodular or even a nodular pattern of infiltration at the bases and periphery (see Fig. 13.46A). In advanced disease there may be cystic areas and honeycombing.

High-resolution CT is extremely valuable in detecting early interstitial lung disease and assessing the extent and type of involvement (see Fig. 13.46B), and is also helpful in identify-ing hilar and paratracheal lymphadenopathy, particularly in sarcoidosis.

Bronchoalveolar lavage

Bronchoalveolar lavage is not often of diagnostic value, but there are some important exceptions (see Fig. 13.45). Increased numbers of lymphocytes in bronchoalveolar lavage fluid occur in sarcoidosis and extrinsic allergic alveo-litis, whereas a neutrophilia is suggestive of cryptogenic fibrosing alveolitis or pneumoconiosis. In the rare disease, alveolar proteinosis (see p. 562), copious lipoproteinaceous material is recovered in the lavage fluid and large numbers of iron-laden macrophages are seen in pulmonary haemosiderosis (see Box 13.84, p. 562).

Lung biopsy

Examination of biopsy material is an important diagnostic procedure in most cases. Bronchial and transbronchial biop-sies obtained via the fibreoptic bronchoscope will usually establish the diagnosis in sarcoidosis and in some conditions which mimic ILDs, such as lymphatic carcinomatosis and certain infections. However, this approach provides only a small sample of tissue, and in less specific disorders such as cryptogenic fibrosing alveolitis a larger surgical biopsy sam-ple is often necessary to yield a confident diagnosis. This can be obtained by limited thoracotomy or video-assisted thoracoscopy (VATS).

SARCOIDOSIS

Sarcoidosis is a multisystem granulomatous disease. It is most common in colder climates (e.g. Scandinavian coun-tries). The lung is affected in over 90% of cases. While the aetiology of sarcoidosis remains uncertain, it is associated with imbalance between subsets of T lymphocytes and other disturbances of cell-mediated immunity, but the relationship between these phenomena and sarcoidosis has not yet been explained. The lesions are histologically similar to tubercu-lous follicles, apart from the absence of caseation and tubercle bacilli, but there is no convincing evidence that the disease is caused by any of the mycobacteria. Chronic beryllium

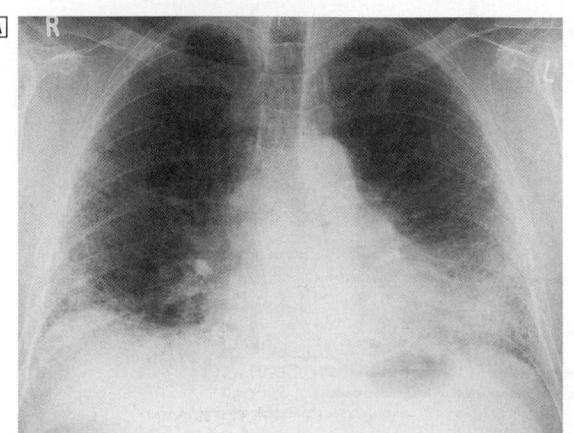
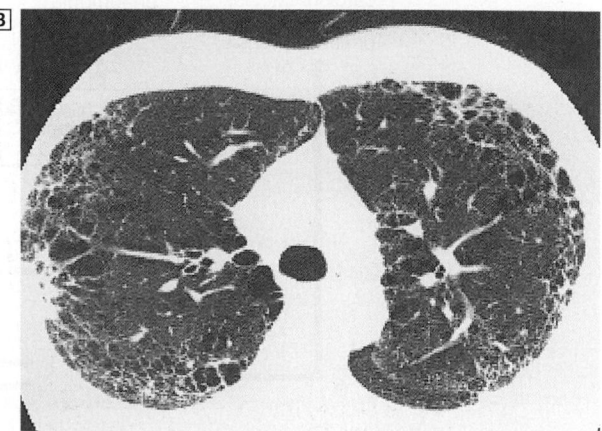

Fig. 13.46 Cryptogenic fibrosing alveolitis. Ⓐ Chest radiograph showing bilateral, predominantly lower zone and peripheral coarse reticulonodular shadowing and small lungs. Ⓑ The CT shows honeycombing and scarring which is most marked peripherally.

poisoning produces a disease which mimics sarcoidosis both pathologically and clinically but exposure to beryllium is now extremely uncommon. Histological changes resembling those of sarcoidosis are occasionally seen in individual organs, such as lymph nodes, in conditions such as carcinoma and fungal infections, but these localised 'sarcoid reactions' are not associated with systemic sarcoidosis.

Pathology

The mediastinal and superficial lymph nodes, lungs, liver, spleen, skin, eyes, parotid glands and phalangeal bones are most frequently affected, but all tissues may be involved (see Figs 13.47 and 13.48). The characteristic histological feature consists of non-caseating epithelioid granulomas which usually resolve spontaneously; fibrosis occurs in up to 20% of cases of pulmonary sarcoidosis and it is impossible at present to identify this group of patients prospectively. The overall mortality rate of sarcoidosis is low (1–5%) and usually relates to the involvement of vital organs, particularly the heart. Calcium metabolism may be disturbed, causing hypercalciuria, hypercalcaemia and, rarely, nephrocalcinosis.

Clinical features

Since sarcoid lesions can develop in almost any tissue, the mode of presentation can be quite variable (see Box 13.75). Patients can present with an 'acute' form of sarcoidosis with erythema nodosum, peripheral arthropathy, uveitis, bilateral hilar lymphadenopathy, lethargy and occasionally fever. Alternatively, the disease has a more insidious onset and presents with cough, exertional breathlessness or one of the protean extrapulmonary manifestations. Clubbing and

13.75 PRESENTATION OF SARCOIDOSIS

- Asymptomatic—abnormal routine chest radiograph (c. 30%) or abnormal liver function tests
- Respiratory and constitutional symptoms (20–30%)
- Erythema nodosum and arthralgia (20–30%)
- Ocular symptoms (5–10%)
- Skin sarcoid (including lupus pernio) (5%)
- Superficial lymphadenopathy (5%)
- Other (1%), e.g. hypercalcaemia, diabetes insipidus, cranial nerve palsies, cardiac arrhythmias, nephrocalcinosis

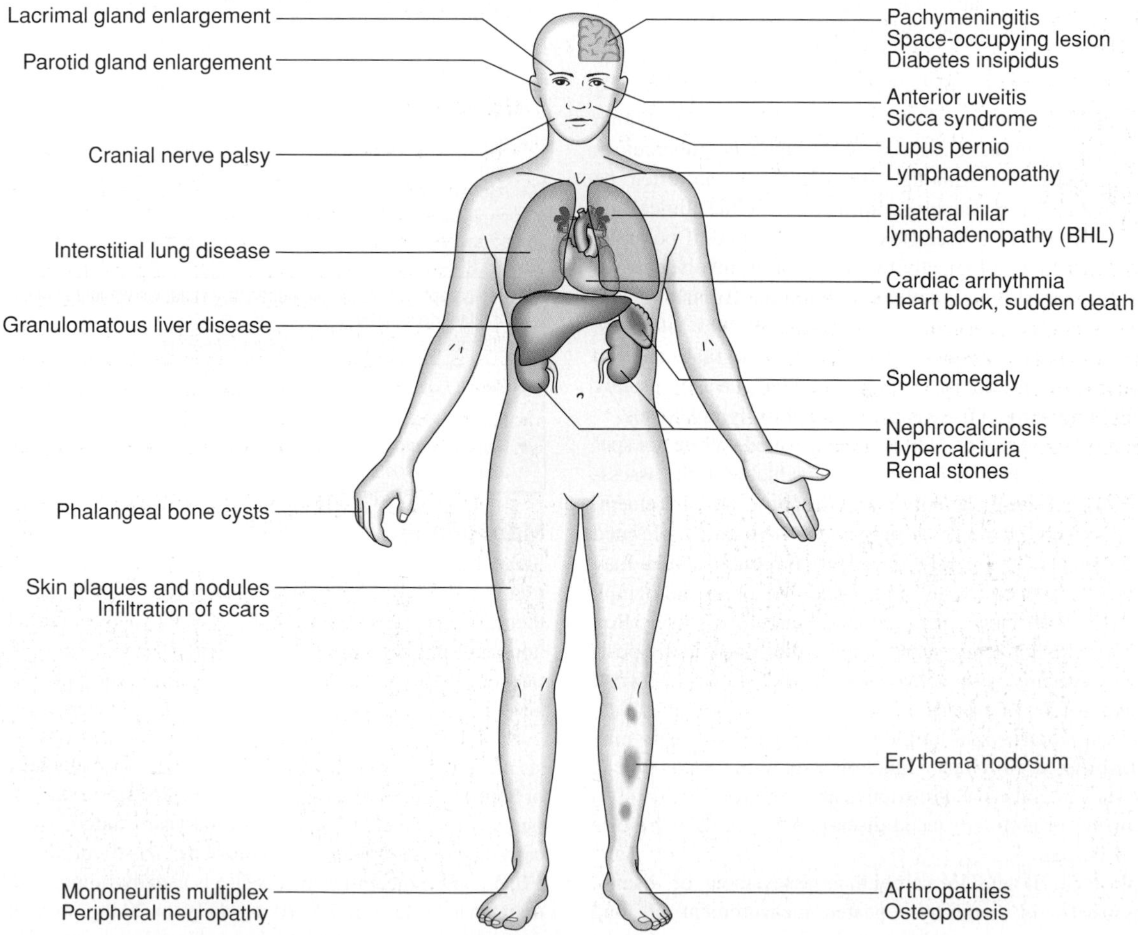

Lacrimal gland enlargement

Parotid gland enlargement

Cranial nerve palsy

Interstitial lung disease

Granulomatous liver disease

Phalangeal bone cysts

Skin plaques and nodules
Infiltration of scars

Mononeuritis multiplex
Peripheral neuropathy

Pachymeningitis
Space-occupying lesion
Diabetes insipidus

Anterior uveitis
Sicca syndrome

Lupus pernio
Lymphadenopathy

Bilateral hilar
lymphadenopathy (BHL)

Cardiac arrhythmia
Heart block, sudden death

Splenomegaly

Nephrocalcinosis
Hypercalciuria
Renal stones

Erythema nodosum

Arthropathies
Osteoporosis

Fig. 13.47 **The range of possible systemic involvement in sarcoidosis.**

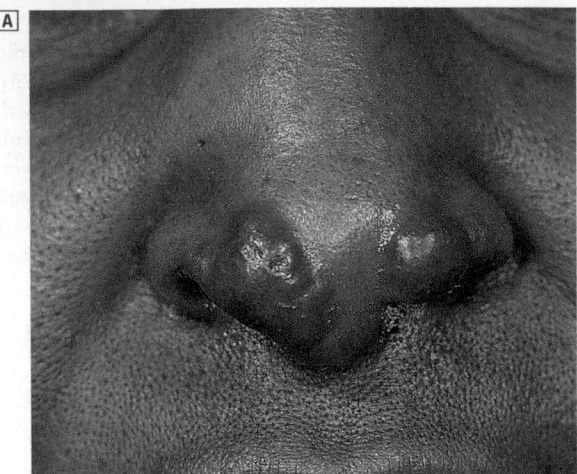

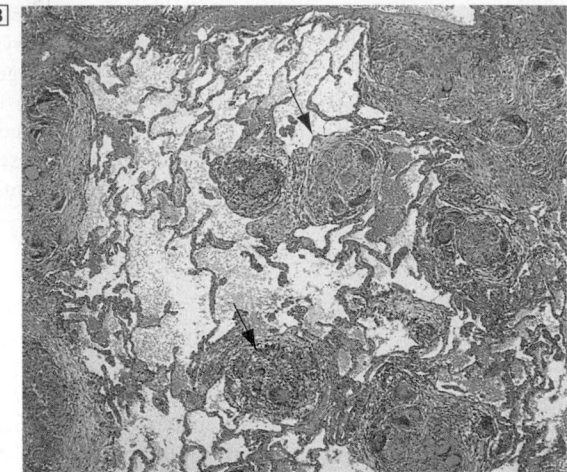

Fig. 13.48 Pathological lesions in sarcoidosis. A Nasal cutaneous sarcoid lesions. B Histology of sarcoidosis in the lung, showing non-caseating granulomas (arrows).

cyanosis are unusual even in advanced pulmonary disease and, in contrast to cryptogenic fibrosing alveolitis, inspiratory crepitations are not a prominent feature.

Investigations

Skin sensitivity to tuberculin is depressed or absent in most (but not all) patients, and the Mantoux reaction is, therefore, a useful 'screening' test; a strongly positive reaction to one tuberculin unit virtually excludes sarcoidosis. The presence of 'rim enhancement' with central necrosis in the lymph nodes on contrast-enhanced CT suggests tuberculous lymphadenopathy. Although the diagnosis can often be made with a fair measure of confidence from the clinical and radiological features (see Box 13.75), it should, if possible, be confirmed histologically by biopsy of an involved organ (e.g. superficial lymph node or skin lesion). Transbronchial lung biopsy confirms the diagnosis in 80–90% of cases, even in those with a normal chest radiograph and no pulmonary symptoms. Bronchoalveolar lavage usually yields fluid with an increased proportion of lymphocytes.

The plasma level of ACE is often elevated. While not specific for sarcoidosis, this test may be valuable in the assessment of disease activity and response to treatment. Lymphopenia, hypercalciuria and a moderately elevated ESR are also frequently observed. Hypercalcaemia may occur but seldom causes symptoms. The chest radiograph features have been used to stage sarcoidosis (see Box 13.76). A radionuclide scan using [67]gallium is usually positive in patients with active disease and shows abnormal uptake in affected organs.

When parenchymal lung disease is significant there may be disordered pulmonary function tests with a reduction in gas transfer and typical restrictive abnormalities (see p. 493) occurring in more advanced disease, particularly if fibrosis has occurred.

In stage III and IV sarcoidosis assessment of disease progression is made by repeated measurement of lung volumes, carbon monoxide transfer factor and serial chest radiographs.

13.76 CHEST RADIOGRAPH CHANGES IN SARCOIDOSIS

Stage I

- Radiograph shows bilateral hilar enlargement, usually symmetrical; paratracheal nodes often enlarged
- Spontaneous resolution within 1 year in the majority of cases. Often asymptomatic, but may be associated with erythema nodosum and arthralgia

Stage II

- Radiograph shows a combination of hilar glandular enlargement and pulmonary opacities which are often diffuse
- Patients are breathless or have a cough. Spontaneous improvement occurs in the majority

Stage III

- Radiograph shows diffuse pulmonary shadows without evidence of hilar adenopathy
- Disease less likely to resolve spontaneously

Stage IV

- Pulmonary fibrosis
- Can cause progressive ventilatory failure, pulmonary hypertension and cor pulmonale

Management

Stage I and II disease usually resolves spontaneously and treatment is seldom required. Patients with persistent erythema nodosum, pyrexia and arthralgia may benefit from non-steroidal anti-inflammatory drugs. Short-term oral corticosteroid therapy is occasionally required for patients with severe systemic features, anterior uveitis or hypercalcaemia.

Symptomatic stage III pulmonary sarcoidosis and sarcoidosis involving the eyes or other vital organs (especially the heart or brain) usually need to be treated with corticosteroids, which may have to be continued for several years. Sarcoidosis typically responds rapidly to prednisolone 20–40 mg daily (see EBM panel); thereafter the disease is usually suppressed by a maintenance dose of 7.5–10 mg daily, or 20 mg on alternate days. Methotrexate and hydroxychloroquine are effective second-line or steroid-sparing agents.

PULMONARY SARCOIDOSIS—role of systemic steroids

'RCTs indicate that oral steroids improve symptoms, respiratory function and radiographic appearance in patients with stage II and III pulmonary sarcoidosis. However, these effects are small and there are no data beyond 2 years to indicate whether such therapy influences long-term disease progression.'

- Gibson GJ, Prescott RJ, Muers MF, et al. The British Thoracic Society Sarcoidosis Study: effects of long term corticosteroid treatment. Thorax 1996; 51:238–247.
- Paramothayan NS, Jones PW. Corticosteroids for pulmonary sarcoidosis (Cochrane Review). Cochrane Library, issue 4, 2000. Oxford: Update Software.

CRYPTOGENIC FIBROSING ALVEOLITIS

Cryptogenic fibrosing alveolitis (CFA; also referred to as idiopathic pulmonary fibrosis in North America) exemplifies many of the typical features of interstitial lung disease. By definition this form of fibrosing alveolitis is not associated with an overt systemic or connective tissue disorder. The Epstein–Barr virus and exposure to metal and wood dusts have been reported to be associated with the disease. CFA has an incidence of 6–10 per 100 000 per year and is about twice as common among cigarette smokers as in non-smokers. Men are also more commonly affected than women.

CFA is probably not a single disease entity and other forms of idiopathic interstitial lung disease are now recognised both clinically and pathologically (see Box 13.77). Such differentiation is important as many of these conditions have a much better response to corticosteroid therapy and a better prognosis.

Macroscopically, the lungs show subpleural fibrosis and a honeycomb appearance, predominantly in the lower lobes and basolateral pleural regions. Microscopically, there is architectural disruption with temporal heterogeneity and characteristic fibroproliferative lesions representing the site of healing alveolar injury. There is variable mononuclear cell infiltration of the alveolar walls, fibrosis and smooth muscle proliferation.

Clinical features

CFA is predominantly a disease of the elderly, with a mean age at presentation of 69 years. Progressive exertional breathlessness is usually the presenting symptom, often accompanied by persistent dry cough. In 60% of patients digital clubbing is observed. Chest expansion may be poor and numerous bilateral end-inspiratory crepitations are audible on auscultation, particularly over the lower zones posteriorly.

Investigations

Blood tests are of no value in confirming a diagnosis of CFA. However, rheumatoid factor and antinuclear factor can be detected in 30–50% of patients. The ESR and lactate dehydrogenase are elevated in most cases.

The chest radiograph shows diffuse pulmonary opacities which are usually most obvious in the lower zones and peripherally (see Fig. 13.46A, p. 552). The hemidiaphragms are high and the lungs appear small. In advanced disease the chest radiographs may show a 'honeycomb' appearance, in which diffuse pulmonary shadowing is interspersed with small cystic translucencies. 'Honeycomb lung' is also a characteristic feature of rare diseases such as Langerhans cell histiocytosis and tuberous sclerosis (see Box 13.84, p. 562). High-resolution CT can reveal a characteristic

13.77 HISTOLOGICAL SUBCLASSIFICATION OF IDIOPATHIC FORMS OF INTERSTITIAL LUNG DISEASE

Histological diagnosis	Clinical diagnosis	Notes
Usual interstitial pneumonia (UIP)	Cryptogenic fibrosing alveolitis (CFA)	See text Poor response to corticosteroids Poor prognosis
Non-specific interstitial pneumonia (NSIP)	NSIP	Uniform fibrosis and thickening of alveolar walls Associated with underlying connective tissue disease and HIV infection Good response to corticosteroids Better prognosis than CFA
Respiratory bronchiolitis	Respiratory bronchiolitis (interstitial lung disease)	Invariable association with cigarette smoking Accumulation of pigment-laden macrophages in respiratory bronchioles and adjacent alveoli Good prognosis on stopping smoking
Diffuse alveolar damage (DAD)	Acute interstitial pneumonia (AIP)	Proteinaceous alveolar exudate, interstitial oedema and fibrosis, hyaline membranes Poor prognosis
Desquamative interstitial pneumonia (DIP)	DIP	Alveolar wall thickening and mononuclear cell infiltration; alveoli filled with alveolar macrophages Good initial response to corticosteroid therapy
Organising pneumonia	Cryptogenic organising pneumonia (COP)	Intraluminal organising fibrosis of distal airspaces, patchy distribution, preservation of lung architecture Good response to corticosteroids Good prognosis

picture (see p. 552) and is particularly useful in early disease when chest radiograph changes may be slight or absent.

Pulmonary function tests show a restrictive ventilatory defect with proportionate reduction in VC and FEV_1. The carbon monoxide transfer factor is low and there is an overall reduction in lung volume. In early disease there is arterial hypoxaemia on exercise; later, arterial hypoxaemia and hypocapnia are present at rest.

A firm diagnosis of CFA can usually be achieved on the basis of the history, clinical findings and characteristic high-resolution CT appearance (see Fig. 13.46B, p. 552). If doubt exists, an open lung biopsy is indicated. Bronchoalveolar lavage and transbronchial biopsy are generally unhelpful and do not allow the pathologist to differentiate between CFA and other forms of pulmonary fibrosis.

Management

CFA has a high mortality rate, with survival beyond 5 years unusual; there are no RCTs of corticosteroids (or alternative immunosuppressive agents) in CFA but a proportion of patients do respond in terms of symptoms (50%) and lung function (25%) (see Box 13.77 for further details). Currently, such therapy is recommended in patients who are highly symptomatic or have rapidly progressive disease, have a predominantly 'ground-glass' appearance on CT or have a sustained fall of > 15% in their FVC or gas transfer over a 3–6-month period. The recommended initial treatment is combined therapy with prednisolone (0.5 mg/kg) and azathioprine (2–3 mg/kg).

Assessment of response to this treatment is by repeat measurement of lung volumes, transfer factor and chest radiograph. Immunosuppressive therapy should be withdrawn over a few weeks if there is no response. Should objective evidence of improvement be demonstrated the prednisolone dose can be reduced gradually to a maintenance dose of 10–12.5 mg daily.

Prognosis

The median survival time of patients with CFA is about 3.5 years. Most deaths occur in patients over the age of 55, with males predominating. The rate of disease progression varies considerably from death within a few months to survival with minimal symptoms for many years. Occasionally, the disease process may 'burn out', but in the majority of patients the disease is progressive, even in those who have responded to treatment. Lung transplantation (see p. 508) should be considered in young patients with advanced disease.

LUNG DISEASES DUE TO ORGANIC DUSTS

A wide range of organic agents may cause respiratory disorders (see Box 13.78). Disease results from a local immune response to animal proteins (e.g. bird fancier's lung) or fungal antigens in mouldy vegetable matter. The most common presentation has been termed extrinsic allergic alveolitis.

13.78 SOME EXAMPLES OF LUNG DISEASES CAUSED BY ORGANIC DUSTS		
Disorder	Source	Antigen/agent
Farmer's lung*	Mouldy hay, straw, grain	*Micropolyspora faenae* *Aspergillus fumigatus*
Bird fancier's lung*	Avian excreta, proteins and feathers	Avian serum proteins
Malt worker's lung*	Mouldy maltings	*Aspergillus clavatus*
Byssinosis	Textile industries	Cotton, flax, hemp dust
Inhalation ('humidifier') fever	Contamination of air conditioning	Thermophilic actinomycetes
Cheese worker's lung*	Mouldy cheese	*Aspergillus clavatus* *Penicillium casei*
Maple bark stripper's lung*	Bark from stored maple	*Cryptostroma corticale*

* Denotes lung disease presenting as extrinsic allergic alveolitis.

EXTRINSIC ALLERGIC ALVEOLITIS

In this condition the inhalation of certain types of organic dust produces a diffuse immune complex reaction in the walls of the alveoli and bronchioles.

The pathogenic mechanisms concerned in the production of extrinsic allergic alveolitis (EAA) are not fully understood. It is thought that the disease develops in sensitised individuals mainly through a type III Arthus reaction, although type IV mechanisms are probably also important. When the antigen is inhaled, the immune complexes formed in antibody excess are precipitated very rapidly. Deposition of these immune complexes results in complement activation, causing a localised inflammatory reaction in the alveolar walls. Immunofluorescence has shown IgG, IgA and complement to be fixed in the pulmonary tissues when biopsy specimens are examined in the acute stages. The presence of granulomata in the alveolar walls provides some evidence for a type IV response also being involved. Bronchoalveolar lavage fluid from patients with extrinsic allergic alveolitis usually shows an increase in the number of lymphocytes.

Some of the agents which produce EAA, their source, and the names given to the resulting disease are shown in Box 13.78. In the UK, 50% of reported cases of EAA occur in farm workers. If patients with this disorder continue to be exposed to the relevant antigen, they develop progressive lung fibrosis, leading to severe respiratory disability, pulmonary hypertension and cor pulmonale.

Clinical features

EAA should be suspected when anyone who is regularly or intermittently exposed to organic dust complains, within a few hours of re-exposure to the same dust, of influenza-like symptoms. These include headache, muscle pains, malaise, pyrexia, dry cough and breathlessness without wheeze. When exposure is continuous, as is the case with an indoor pet bird at home, the presentation can be with breathlessness without systemic symptoms, and if the cause is not recognised this may result in the formation of irreversible pulmonary fibrosis. For reasons that remain uncertain, there is a lower incidence of EAA in smokers compared to non-smokers.

Investigations

In the acute stage of the disease widespread end-inspiratory crepitations are the rule and the chest radiograph shows diffuse micronodular shadowing, often more pronounced in the upper zones. High-resolution CT in patients with acute EAA shows bilateral areas of consolidation superimposed on small centrilobar nodular opacities and air-trapping on expiration. In more chronic disease, features of fibrosis with linear opacities and architectural distortion predominate. Pulmonary function studies reveal a restrictive ventilatory defect with preservation of (or an increase in) the FEV_1/FVC ratio. The PaO_2 is reduced and the $PaCO_2$ is often below normal because of over-ventilation. Diffusion capacity is impaired.

The diagnosis of EAA is usually based on the characteristic clinical and radiological features, together with the identification of a potential source of antigen at the patient's home or place of work. Reduction in the carbon monoxide transfer factor is the most sensitive functional abnormality. The diagnosis may be supported by a positive precipitin test or by more sensitive serological tests based on the enzyme-linked immunosorbent assay (ELISA) technique. However, it is also important to recognise that the great majority of farmers with positive precipitins do not have farmer's lung, and up to 15% of pigeon breeders may have positive serum precipitins and yet remain healthy. Where the diagnosis is suspected but the cause is not readily apparent, it may be helpful to visit the patient's home or workplace. Occasionally, such as when a new agent is suspected, it may be necessary to prove the diagnosis by a provocation test; if positive, the inhalation of the relevant antigen is followed after 3–6 hours by pyrexia and a reduction in VC and gas transfer factor. Open lung biopsy may be necessary to establish a diagnosis.

Management

Mild forms of extrinsic allergic alveolitis rapidly subside when exposure to the antigen ceases. In acute cases prednisolone should be given for 3–4 weeks, starting with an oral dose of 40 mg per day. Severely hypoxaemic patients may require high-concentration oxygen therapy initially. Most patients recover completely, but the development of interstitial fibrosis causes permanent disability when there has been prolonged exposure to antigen.

BYSSINOSIS

Not all inhaled organic dusts cause interstitial infiltration. In byssinosis the initial lesion caused by cotton dust inhalation is acute bronchiolitis associated with symptoms and signs of generalised airflow obstruction, more in keeping with asthma. Initially, symptoms tend to recur after the weekend break ('Monday fever') but eventually become continuous. There is usually no radiological abnormality. Recovery usually follows removal from the dust hazard. Smokers have a greater incidence of byssinosis than non-smokers.

INHALATION ('HUMIDIFIER') FEVER

Inhalation fever is characterised by self-limiting fever and breathlessness following exposure to organism-contaminated water from humidifiers or air-conditioning systems. An identical syndrome can also develop after disturbing an accumulation of mouldy hay, compost or mulch.

LUNG DISEASES DUE TO INORGANIC DUSTS

In certain occupations, the inhalation of inorganic dusts, fumes or other noxious substances may give rise to specific pathological changes in the lungs. The risk of these forms of occupational lung disease is highest in spray painters, shipyard and dock workers, miners and quarrymen, welders, electronic assembly workers and those that work in the construction industry or in chemical processing. Generally, prolonged exposure to inorganic dusts (see Box 13.79) leads to diffuse pulmonary fibrosis (the pneumoconioses), although

13.79 SOME LUNG DISEASES CAUSED BY EXPOSURE TO INORGANIC DUSTS			
Cause	**Occupation**	**Description**	**Characteristic pathological features**
Coal dust Silica	Coal mining Mining, quarrying, stone dressing, metal grinding, pottery, boiler scaling	Coal worker's pneumoconiosis Silicosis	Focal and interstitial fibrosis, centrilobular emphysema, progressive massive fibrosis
Asbestos	Demolition, ship breaking, manufacture of fireproof insulating materials and brake-pads, pipe and boiler lagging	Asbestos-related disease	Interstitial fibrosis, pleural disease, carcinoma of larynx and bronchus
Iron oxide	Arc welding	Siderosis	Mineral deposition only
Tin oxide	Tin mining	Stannosis	
Beryllium	Aircraft, atomic energy and electronics industries	Berylliosis	Granulomata, interstitial fibrosis

13.80 SOME LUNG DISEASES CAUSED BY INORGANIC GASES AND FUMES		
Cause	Occupation	Disease
Irritant gases (chlorine, ammonia, phosgene, nitrogen dioxide)	Various (industrial accidents)	Acute lung injury ARDS
Cadmium	Welding and electroplating	COPD
Isocyanates (e.g. epoxy resins, paints)	Plastic, paints; manufacture of epoxy resins and adhesives	Bronchial asthma Eosinophilic pneumonia

berylliosis causes an interstitial granulomatous disease similar to sarcoidosis. The dusts themselves cause little direct damage to the lung parenchyma and the pathological result depends largely on the inflammatory and fibrotic responses to the particular dust. The fibrogenic properties of mineral dusts vary, silica being markedly fibrogenic whereas iron and tin are almost inert. The most important types of pneumoconiosis are coal worker's pneumoconiosis, silicosis and asbestosis.

Industrial inorganic gases and fumes can cause other, often more acute, respiratory diseases including pulmonary oedema and asthma (see Box 13.80).

Clearly, it is essential to elicit a detailed occupational history, both present and past, since a diagnosis of occupational lung disease can easily be overlooked and the patient may be eligible for compensation. It must also be emphasised that in many types of pneumoconiosis a long period of dust exposure is required before radiological changes appear, and these may precede clinical symptoms.

Notes on diagnosis and claims for benefits in pneumoconiosis, occupational asthma and other related occupational disease in Britain are contained in government pamphlets. New industrial processes are constantly being introduced and it is necessary to remain alert to the possibility that they may be associated with occupational lung disease.

COAL WORKER'S PNEUMOCONIOSIS

This disease follows prolonged inhalation of coal dust. The condition is subdivided into simple pneumoconiosis and progressive massive fibrosis for both clinical purposes and certification. It must be emphasised that for certification purposes in Britain the diagnosis rests at present on radiological and not clinical features.

Simple coal worker's pneumoconiosis

This is categorised radiologically into three grades, depending on the size and extent of the nodulation present. It does not progress if the miner leaves the industry.

Progressive massive fibrosis

In this form of the disease, large dense masses, single or multiple, occur mainly in the upper lobes. These may be irregular in shape and may cavitate. Tuberculosis may be a complication. The disease can be disabling, may shorten life expectancy and may progress even after the miner leaves the industry.

Cough and sputum from associated chronic bronchitis are frequently present. The sputum may be black (melanoptysis). Progressive breathlessness on exertion occurs in the later stages, and respiratory and right ventricular failure supervene as terminal events. There may be no abnormal physical signs in the chest but when present they are those of chronic obstructive airways disease.

Antinuclear factor is present in the serum of about 15% of patients with coal worker's pneumoconiosis. Rheumatoid factor is present in some patients in whom rheumatoid arthritis coexists, with rounded fibrotic nodules 0.5–5 cm in diameter. These are mainly in the periphery of the lung fields and the association is known as Caplan's syndrome. This syndrome may also occur in other types of pneumoconiosis.

SILICOSIS

This disease is becoming rare as the standards of industrial hygiene improve. It is caused by the inhalation of fine free crystalline silicon dioxide (silica) dust or quartz particles.

Silica is a most fibrogenic dust and causes the development of hard nodules which coalesce as the disease progresses. Tuberculosis may modify the silicotic process with ensuing caseation and calcification. The radiological features are similar to those seen in coal worker's pneumoconiosis, though the changes tend to be more marked in the upper zones. The hilar shadows may be enlarged; 'egg-shell' calcification in the hilar lymph nodes is a distinctive feature but does not occur in all patients. The disease progresses even when exposure to dust ceases. The patient should, therefore, be removed from the offending environment as soon as possible. Clinical features are also similar to those of coal worker's pneumoconiosis.

Intense exposure to very fine crystalline silica dust can cause a more acute disease similar to alveolar proteinosis (see p. 562) with over-production of surfactant by type II alveolar pneumocytes.

ASBESTOSIS

The main types of the fibrous mineral, asbestos, are chrysotile (white asbestos), which accounts for 90% of the world's production, crocidolite (blue asbestos) and amosite (brown asbestos). Exposure occurs in the mining and milling of the mineral and in a variety of occupations (see Box 13.79).

Asbestos exposure is a recognised risk factor for the development of a number of respiratory diseases (see Fig. 13.49), including carcinoma of the lung and larynx. Asbestos-related pleural disease is covered on page 572. Asbestosis itself is defined as diffuse fibrosis of the lungs caused by inhalation of asbestos particles. This condition may or may not be associated with fibrosis of the parietal or visceral layer of the pleura. Together with asbestos-related diffuse pleural fibrosis and mesothelioma, it qualifies an individual in the UK for industrial injury benefit. In contrast to the other forms of asbestos-related respiratory disease, asbestosis tends to develop in individuals exposed to significant levels of asbestos dust over a number of years.

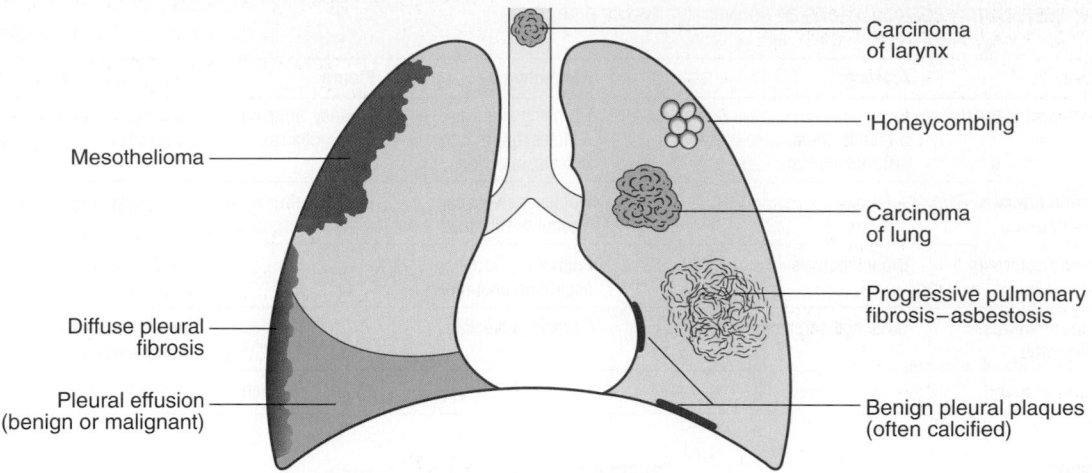

Fig. 13.49   Asbestos: the range of possible effects on the respiratory tract.

Asbestosis usually has an indolent course and may be present subclinically for many years before becoming symptomatic in late middle age with dyspnoea, digital clubbing and inspiratory crepitations audible over the lower zones of both lungs. The chest radiograph shows bi-basal reticular nodular shadowing and occasionally 'honeycombing'. Other features of asbestos exposure may also be present (e.g. pleural plaques). Pulmonary function abnormalities are a restrictive defect with decreased lung volumes and reduced gas transfer factor. The risk of bronchial carcinoma is extremely high, especially in patients who also smoke.

The diagnosis is usually easy to establish from the history of exposure to asbestos and the above clinical, radiological and pulmonary function abnormalities. Lung biopsy may be required to confirm the diagnosis (and exclude other treatable causes of interstitial lung disease) but should not be undertaken solely for the purpose of allowing patients to claim benefit.

Management

No specific treatment is available. Corticosteroids are of no value in the management of asbestosis. Respiratory failure and cor pulmonale should be treated appropriately.

Prevention

Improvements in standards of industrial hygiene are now enforced by law in many countries; such measures as wearing respirators, damping dust and efficient ventilation systems are already proving effective in a number of industries.

LUNG DISEASES DUE TO SYSTEMIC INFLAMMATORY DISEASE

THE ACUTE RESPIRATORY DISTRESS SYNDROME

See page 198.

RESPIRATORY INVOLVEMENT IN CONNECTIVE TISSUE DISORDERS

Fibrosing alveolitis is a recognised complication of most connective tissue diseases. The clinical features are usually indistinguishable from cryptogenic fibrosing alveolitis (see p. 555) and the response to immunosuppressive drugs is similarly unpredictable. Connective tissue disorders may also cause disease of the pleura, diaphragm and chest wall muscles (see Box 13.81 and Ch. 20). Pulmonary hypertension and cor pulmonale may result from advanced fibrosing alveolitis associated with connective tissue disorders and is particularly common in patients with systemic sclerosis.

Indirect associations between connective tissue disorders and respiratory complications include those due to disease in other organs, e.g. thrombocytopenia causing haemoptysis; pulmonary toxic effects of drugs used to treat the connective tissue disorder (e.g. gold and methotrexate); and secondary infection due to the disease itself, neutropenia or immunosuppressive drug regimens.

Rheumatoid disease

Fibrosing alveolitis is the most common pulmonary manifestation (rheumatoid lung). The clinical features, investigations, treatment and prognosis are similar to those of cryptogenic fibrosing alveolitis, although a rare variant of localised upper lobe fibrosis and cavitation has been described.

Pleural effusion is common, especially in men with seropositive disease. Effusions are usually small and unilateral but can be large and bilateral. Most resolve spontaneously. Biochemical testing shows an exudative effusion (see p. 501) with markedly reduced glucose levels and raised protein lactate dehydrogenase (LDH). Effusions that fail to resolve spontaneously may respond to a short course of oral prednisolone (30–40 mg daily) but some become chronic.

Rheumatoid pulmonary nodules do not usually cause symptoms and are detected on chest radiographs performed for other reasons. They are usually multiple and subpleural

13.81 RESPIRATORY COMPLICATIONS OF CONNECTIVE TISSUE DISORDERS

Disorder	Airways	Parenchyma	Pleura	Diaphragm and chest wall
Rheumatoid arthritis	Bronchitis, obliterative bronchiolitis, bronchiectasis, crico-arytenoid arthritis, stridor	Fibrosing alveolitis, nodules, upper lobe fibrosis, infections	Pleurisy, effusion, pneumothorax	Poor healing of intercostal drain sites
Systemic lupus erythematosus	–	Fibrosing alveolitis, 'vasculitic' infarcts	Pleurisy, effusion	'Shrinking lungs'
Systemic sclerosis	Bronchiectasis	Pulmonary fibrosis, aspiration pneumonia	–	'Hidebound chest'
Dermatomyositis/ polymyositis	Bronchial carcinoma	Fibrosing alveolitis	–	Intercostal and diaphragmatic myopathy
Rheumatic fever	–	Pneumonia	Pleurisy, effusion	–

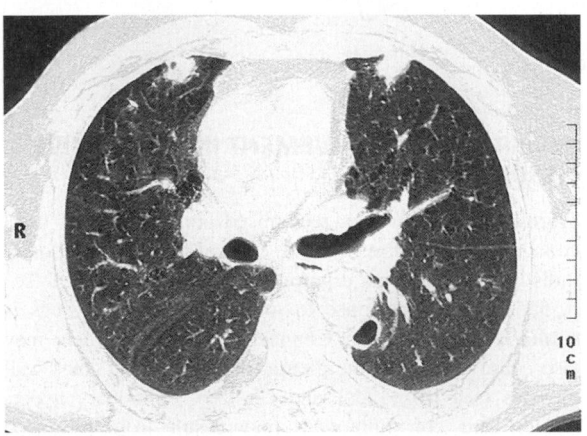

Fig. 13.50 Rheumatoid (necrobiotic) nodules. Thoracic CT just below the level of the main carina showing the typical appearance of peripheral, pleural-based nodules. The nodule in the left lower lobe shows characteristic cavitation.

in site (see Fig. 13.50). Solitary nodules can mimic primary bronchial carcinoma and when multiple the differential diagnosis includes pulmonary metastatic disease. Cavitation of nodules can raise the possibility of tuberculosis and cause pneumothorax. The combination of rheumatoid nodules and pneumoconiosis is known as Caplan's syndrome (see p. 558).

Bronchitis and bronchiectasis are both more common in rheumatoid patients. Rarely, the potentially fatal condition, obliterative bronchiolitis, may develop.

Systemic lupus erythematosus

Fibrosing alveolitis is a relatively uncommon manifestation of systemic lupus erythematosus (SLE). Pleuropulmonary involvement is more common in lupus than in any other connective tissue disorder. Up to two-thirds of patients have repeated episodes of pleurisy, with or without effusions. Effusions may be bilateral and involve the pericardium.

Some patients with SLE present with exertional dyspnoea and orthopnoea but without overt signs of fibrosing alveolitis. The chest radiograph reveals elevated diaphragms, and pulmonary function testing shows reduced lung volumes. This condition has been described as 'shrinking lungs' and is thought to be caused by diaphragmatic myopathy.

Systemic sclerosis

Most patients with systemic sclerosis eventually develop diffuse pulmonary fibrosis; at necropsy more than 90% have evidence of lung fibrosis. In some patients it is indolent, but when progressive, like cryptogenic fibrosing alveolitis, the median survival time is around 4 years. Pulmonary fibrosis is rare in the CREST variant of progressive systemic sclerosis but isolated pulmonary hypertension may develop.

Other pulmonary complications include recurrent aspiration pneumonias secondary to oesophageal disease. Rarely, sclerosis of the skin of the chest wall may be so extensive and cicatrising as to restrict chest wall movement seriously—the so-called 'hidebound chest'.

PULMONARY EOSINOPHILIA AND VASCULITIDES

This term is applied to a group of disorders of different aetiology in which lesions in the lungs produce a chest radiograph abnormality associated with an increase in the number of the eosinophil leucocytes in the peripheral blood. There is no satisfactory classification of this disparate group of disorders, but they can be divided into two main categories (see Box 13.82).

Some causes of extrinsic pulmonary eosinophilia are also given in the box. The most common disorder of this type in developed countries is allergic bronchopulmonary aspergillosis (see p. 540); in tropical countries the presence of microfilariae in the pulmonary capillaries (see p. 73) has to be considered.

CRYPTOGENIC EOSINOPHILIC PNEUMONIA

Cryptogenic eosinophilic pneumonia is more common in middle-aged females, and usually presents with malaise, fever, breathlessness and unproductive cough. The chest radiograph can show abnormal parenchymal shadowing which tends to be bilateral, peripheral and upper lobe in distribution. Unless corticosteroids have been given, the peripheral blood eosinophil count is almost always very high, and the ESR and total serum IgE are elevated. Bronchoalveolar lavage reveals a high proportion of

13.82 PULMONARY EOSINOPHILIA

Extrinsic (cause known)

- Helminths
  e.g. *Ascaris*, *Toxocara*, *Filaria*
- Drugs
  Nitrofurantoin, para-aminosalicylic acid (PAS), sulfasalazine, imipramine, chlorpropamide, phenylbutazone
- Fungi
  e.g. *Aspergillus fumigatus* causing allergic bronchopulmonary aspergillosis (see p. 540)

Intrinsic (cause unknown)

- Cryptogenic eosinophilic pneumonia
- Churg–Strauss syndrome (diagnosed on the basis of four or more of the following features: asthma, peripheral blood eosinophilia of > 10%, mononeuropathy or polyneuropathy, pulmonary infiltrates, paranasal sinus disease or eosinophilic vasculitis on biopsy of an affected site)
- Hypereosinophilic syndrome
- Polyarteritis nodosa (see p. 1042; rare)

13.83 DRUG-INDUCED RESPIRATORY DISEASE

Non-cardiogenic pulmonary oedema (ARDS)

- Hydrochlorothiazide
- Thrombolytics (streptokinase)
- I.v. β-adrenoceptor agonists (e.g. treatment of premature labour)
- Aspirin and opiates (in overdose)

Non-eosinophilic alveolitis

- Amiodarone, flecainide, gold, nitrofurantoin, cytotoxic agents— especially bleomycin, busulfan, mitomycin C, methotrexate

Pulmonary eosinophilia

- Antimicrobials (nitrofurantoin, penicillin, tetracyclines, sulphonamides, nalidixic acid)
- Antirheumatic agents (gold, aspirin, penicillamine, naproxen)
- Cytotoxic drugs (bleomycin, methotrexate, procarbazine)
- Psychiatric drugs (chlorpromazine, dosulepin (dothiepin), imipramine)
- Anticonvulsants (carbamazepine, phenytoin)
- Others (sulfasalazine, nadolol)

Pleural disease

- Bromocriptine, amiodarone, methotrexate, methysergide
- Via induction of SLE—phenytoin, hydralazine, isoniazid

Asthma

- Via pharmacological mechanism (β-blockers, cholinergic agonists, aspirin and NSAIDs)
- Idiosyncratic reaction (tamoxifen, dipyridamole)

eosinophils in the lavage fluid. Response to prednisolone (20–40 mg daily) is usually dramatic. Prednisolone treatment can usually be withdrawn after a few weeks without relapse, but long-term low-dose therapy is occasionally necessary to control the disease.

LUNG DISEASES DUE TO IRRADIATION AND DRUGS

RADIOTHERAPY

The lungs are exposed during radiotherapy treatment of lung tumours and also tumours of the breast, spine and oesophagus. The pulmonary effects of radiation (see p. 219) are exacerbated by treatment with cytotoxic drugs, oxygen delivery and previous radiotherapy. Radiotherapy may cause acute damage to the lung, and also a chronic insidious scarring disease.

After pulmonary irradiation, acute radiation pneumonitis may present with cough and dyspnoea within 6–12 weeks. This acute form of lung damage may resolve spontaneously or respond to corticosteroid treatment. Chronic interstitial fibrosis presents later, usually with symptoms of exertional dyspnoea and cough. Established post-irradiation fibrosis does not usually respond to corticosteroid treatment.

DRUGS

Drugs may cause a number of parenchymal reactions, including ARDS (see Box 13.83), eosinophilic reactions and diffuse interstitial inflammation/scarring. Drugs can also cause other lung disorders including asthma (see p. 514), haemorrhage (e.g. anticoagulants, penicillamine) and occasionally pleural effusions and pleural thickening (e.g. hydralazine, isoniazid, methysergide). An ARDS-like syndrome of acute non-cardiogenic pulmonary oedema may present with dramatic onset of breathlessness, severe hypoxaemia and signs of alveolar oedema on the chest radiograph. This syndrome has been reported most frequently in cases of

opiate overdose in drug addicts (see p. 176) but also after salicylate overdose, and there are occasional reports of its occurrence after therapeutic doses of drugs including hydrochlorothiazides and some cytotoxic drugs.

Pulmonary fibrosis may occur in response to a variety of drugs, but is seen most frequently with bleomycin, methotrexate, amiodarone and nitrofurantoin. Eosinophilic pulmonary reactions can also be caused by drugs. The pathogenesis may

ISSUES IN OLDER PEOPLE
INTERSTITIAL LUNG DISEASE

- Cryptogenic fibrosing alveolitis is the most common interstitial lung disease in old people and has a worse prognosis.
- Chronic aspiration pneumonitis must always be considered in elderly patients presenting with bilateral basal shadowing on a chest radiograph.
- Wegener's granulomatosis is a rare condition but is more common in old age. Renal involvement is more common at presentation and upper respiratory problems are fewer in older people.
- The symptoms of asbestosis may appear for the first time in old age because of the prolonged latent period between exposure and the development of disease.
- Drug-induced interstitial lung disease is more common in old age, presumably because of the increased chance of exposure to multiple drugs.
- Sarcoidosis, idiopathic pulmonary haemosiderosis, alveolar proteinosis and eosinophilic pneumonia rarely present in old age.
- Coexistent muscle weakness, chest wall deformity (e.g. thoracic kyphosis) and deconditioning may all exacerbate the extent of dyspnoea associated with interstitial lung disease.
- Open lung biopsy is often inappropriate in the very frail and a diagnosis therefore frequently depends on clinical and high-resolution CT findings alone.

13.84 RARE INTERSTITIAL LUNG DISEASES

Disease	Presentation	Chest radiograph	Course
Idiopathic pulmonary haemosiderosis	Haemoptysis, breathlessness, anaemia	Bilateral infiltrates often perihilar Diffuse pulmonary fibrosis	Rapidly progressive in children Slow progression or remission in adults Death from massive pulmonary haemorrhage or cor pulmonale and respiratory failure
Alveolar proteinosis	Breathlessness and cough Occasionally fever, chest pain and haemoptysis	Diffuse bilateral shadowing, often more pronounced in the hilar regions Air bronchogram	Spontaneous remission in one-third Whole lung lavage or granulocyte macrophage-colony stimulating factor (GM-CSF) therapy may be effective
Langerhans cell histiocytosis (histiocytosis X)	Breathlessness, cough, pneumothorax	Diffuse interstitial shadowing progressing to honeycombing	Progressive leading to respiratory failure Poor response to immunosuppressive therapy Smoking cessation is important and may result in significant improvement
Neurofibromatosis	Breathlessness and cough in a patient with multiple organ involvement with neurofibromas including skin	Bilateral reticular nodular shadowing of diffuse interstitial fibrosis	Slow progression to death from respiratory failure Poor response to corticosteroid therapy
Alveolar microlithiasis	No symptoms Breathlessness and cough	Diffuse calcified micronodular shadowing more pronounced in the lower zones	Slowly progressive to cor pulmonale and respiratory failure May stabilise in some Disodium etidronate may be effective
Lymphangioleiomyomatosis	Haemoptysis, breathlessness, pneumothorax and chylous effusion in females	Diffuse bilateral shadowing CT shows characteristic thin-walled cysts with well-defined walls throughout both lungs	Progressive to death within 10 years Oestrogen ablation and progesterone therapy of doubtful value Lung transplantation
Pulmonary tuberous sclerosis	Very similar to lymphangioleiomyomatosis except occasionally occurs in men		

be an immune reaction similar to that in extrinsic allergic alveolitis, which specifically attracts large numbers of eosinophils into the lungs. This type of reaction is well described as a rare reaction to a variety of antineoplastic agents (e.g. bleomycin), antibiotics (e.g. sulphonamides), sulfasalazine and the anticonvulsants phenytoin and carbamazepine. Patients usually present with breathlessness, cough and fever. The chest radiograph characteristically shows patchy shadowing. Most cases resolve completely on withdrawal of the drug, but if the reaction is severe, rapid resolution can be obtained with corticosteroids.

RARE INTERSTITIAL LUNG DISEASES

See Box 13.84.

PULMONARY VASCULAR DISEASE

VENOUS THROMBOEMBOLISM

Deep venous thrombosis (DVT, see pp. 953–956) and pulmonary embolism (PE) can be usefully considered under the heading venous thromboembolism (VTE); 75% of pulmonary emboli derive from DVT in the lower limb and

60% of patients with DVT will have evidence of PE on scanning even in the absence of symptoms. Rarely, PE may occur due to amniotic fluid, placenta, air, fat, tumour (especially choriocarcinoma) and septic emboli from endocarditis affecting tricuspid or pulmonary valves. Pulmonary emboli occur in 1% of patients admitted to hospital and are responsible for about 5% of all hospital deaths. The prophylaxis of VTE is the same as DVT (see p. 956). Clinical presentation, physical signs and treatment of PE are best understood when classified on the basis of size, site and speed of onset (see Box 13.85).

Clinical features

Acute massive pulmonary embolism
The clinical features are of acute haemodynamic collapse with central chest pain, apprehension, a low cardiac output and syncope. The pathophysiology is due to acute obstruction of more than 50% of either the main or the proximal pulmonary artery, leading to an acute reduction of cardiac output and right ventricular dilatation. On examination there is a sinus tachycardia, hypotension and peripheral vasoconstriction. Tachypnoea is typically present with cyanosis and an elevated JVP. A right ventricular gallop may be heard with wide-splitting of the second heart sound. Other signs of pulmonary hypertension are not expected in acute massive pulmonary embolism.

13.85 CATEGORISATION OF PULMONARY THROMBOEMBOLI

	Acute massive PE	Acute small/medium PE	Chronic PE
Pathophysiology	Major haemodynamic effects: ↓ cardiac output; acute right heart failure; disordered ventilation-perfusion ratio	Occlusion of segmental pulmonary artery → infarction ± effusion	Chronic occlusion of pulmonary microvasculature; pulmonary hypertension, right heart failure
Symptoms	Sudden syncope, faintness, central chest pain, apprehension, severe dyspnoea	Pleurisy, restricted breathing, haemoptysis	Exertional dyspnoea Late—exertional syncope, symptoms of right ventricular (RV) failure
Signs Cardiovascular	Major circulatory collapse; tachycardia; hypotension; ↑ jugular venous pressure; gallop rhythm; P_2 widely split (late)	Tachycardia	May be minimal early in disease Late—RV heave, loud, split P_2 Terminal—signs of RV failure
Respiratory	Severe cyanosis, otherwise no local signs	Pleural rub, raised hemidiaphragm, crepitations, effusion (usually blood-stained)	
Other	↓ Urine output	Low-grade fever	
Investigations Chest radiograph	Often subtle; oligaemic lung fields, slight ↑ hilar shadows	Pleuropulmonary opacities; pleural effusion; linear shadows; raised hemidiaphragm	Enlarged pulmonary artery trunk; enlarged heart, prominent RV
ECG	$S_1Q_3T_3$ (see Fig. 13.52) T wave ↓ V_1–V_4 Right bundle-branch block	Sinus tachycardia	Signs of RV hypertrophy and 'strain'
Blood gases	↓ PaO_2; ↓ $PaCO_2$	(↓ $PaCO_2$)	Exertional ↓ PaO_2 or desaturation (on formal exercise testing)
V̇/Q̇ scan	Major areas of ↓ perfusion	Perfusion defect(s) not matched on the ventilation scan	May be no abnormality
Pulmonary angiography	Definitive diagnosis	Definitive diagnosis	Usually diagnostic; may need lung biopsy to confirm diagnosis

Acute minor pulmonary embolism

The majority of patients will present with so-called 'pulmonary infarction syndrome' with pleurisy, shortness of breath and haemoptysis. Clinically, there may be a pleural rub and signs of a pleural effusion. The chest radiograph (see Fig. 13.51) may show wedge-shaped opacity due to haemorrhage, pleural effusion or an elevated diaphragm. Some cases present with isolated breathlessness and these patients tend to have more extensive central thrombus if pulmonary angiography is performed.

Acute embolism in patients with chronic cardiopulmonary disease

Patients with a small degree of cardiopulmonary reserve may demonstrate a major and sudden deterioration in their clinical state even with small pulmonary emboli. The clinical

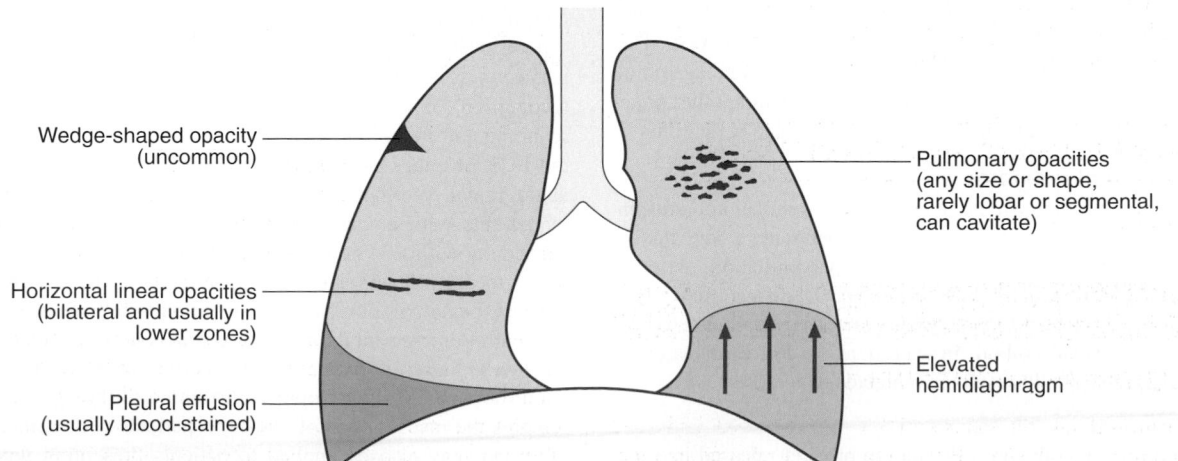

Wedge-shaped opacity (uncommon)

Horizontal linear opacities (bilateral and usually in lower zones)

Pleural effusion (usually blood-stained)

Pulmonary opacities (any size or shape, rarely lobar or segmental, can cavitate)

Elevated hemidiaphragm

Fig. 13.51 Features of pulmonary thromboembolism/infarction on chest radiograph.

features of PE may be obscured by the clinical features of the underlying disease and diagnosis can be difficult in this important situation. A high index of suspicion is required if successful investigation and management in this group of patients are to be achieved.

Chronic venous thromboembolism leading to thromboembolic pulmonary hypertension

This is a relatively rare but important condition which arises without a history of previous acute PE in over 50% of cases. Patients typically present with a history of exertional breathlessness, syncope and chest pain developing over months or years. On examination there are signs of pulmonary hypertension with a loud pulmonary component to the second heart sound and a right ventricular heave. The JVP is raised and there may be *v* waves indicating tricuspid regurgitation (see p. 462). Patients with severe pulmonary hypertension secondary to chronic pulmonary emboli should be considered for thromboendarterectomy, an operation that involves removal of the organised obstructing thrombus via an endarterectomy. The operation should be carried out in specialist centres; despite a significant operative mortality (10–20%), it has a high degree of success.

Investigations

All patients presenting with suspected pulmonary embolism should undergo basic investigations including chest radiography, electrocardiography and arterial blood gases.

Chest radiography

Although the chest radiograph may be normal or show non-specific changes, it is extremely valuable in excluding other diagnoses such as heart failure, pneumonia, pneumothorax or tumour. The common findings in PE include focal infiltrates, segmental collapse, raised hemidiaphragm and pleural effusion (see Fig. 13.51). A wedge-shaped pleural-based opacity, though well described, is rare. Hypovascularity as described in a large embolism is often difficult to detect. A normal chest radiograph in an acutely breathless and hypoxaemic patient increases the likelihood of PE.

Electrocardiography

ECG abnormalities in PE are common but usually comprise non-specific changes in the ST segment and/or T wave. The classic $S_1Q_3T_3$ pattern (see Fig. 13.52) is rare and again not specific for PE. ECG is also useful in excluding other diagnoses such as acute myocardial infarction and pericarditis.

Arterial blood gases

Pulmonary embolism is characterised by ventilation-perfusion mismatch and reduced cardiac output with a low mixed venous oxygen saturation and hyperventilation. Arterial blood gases typically show reduced PaO_2 and a normal or low $PaCO_2$. Normal PaO_2 and $PaCO_2$ values may be found, particularly in small emboli. In acute massive PE, cardiovascular collapse typically results in a metabolic acidosis.

D-dimers

D-dimer is a specific degradation product released into the circulation when cross-linked fibrin undergoes endogenous fibrinolysis (see p. 900). In patients with suspected PE a

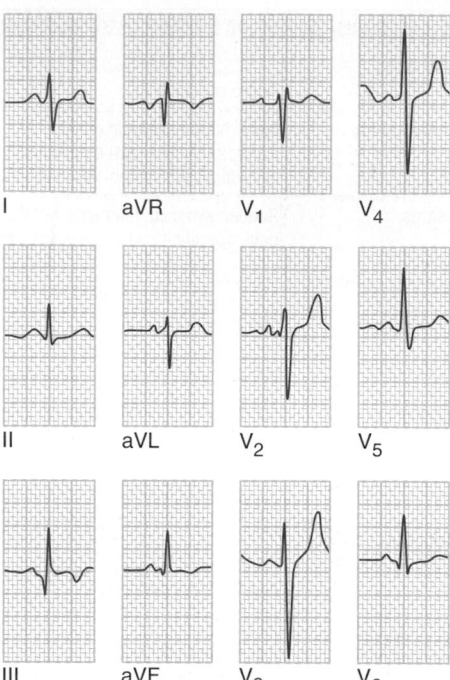

Fig. 13.52   ECG from a patient with pulmonary embolism showing '$S_1Q_3T_3$' pattern. S wave in lead I, Q wave and inverted T wave in lead III.

low plasma D-dimer (< 500 mg/ml measured by ELISA) has a 95% predictive power for excluding PE and hence the D-dimer can be used as an initial screening investigation (see Fig. 13.53). A positive D-dimer, however, does not positively diagnose PE since raised levels may be seen in a whole range of inflammatory conditions including pneumonia.

Imaging

Ventilation-perfusion ($\dot{V}/\dot{Q}$) lung scanning (see p. 490) has been the most popular method of attempting to confirm the presence of PE by demonstrating the presence of 'non-matched' defects of perfusion. In practice, however, many patients presenting with a suspected PE have pre-existing chronic cardiopulmonary disease (such as COPD) which can seriously impair the diagnostic efficacy of ventilation-perfusion scanning and lead to indeterminate reports. The recognition of an over-reliance on ventilation-perfusion scanning and the recent acquisition of spiral CT imaging in most UK hospitals has led to increased use of CT pulmonary angiography. Ventilation-perfusion scanning remains useful in patients with no previous lung disease and should be carried out within 24 hours of presentation since some scans revert to normal very quickly and 50% do so by 1 week. Spiral CT angiography has good sensitivity and specificity for central or segmental thrombi and this is now considered the investigation of choice in patients presenting with isolated dyspnoea. Colour Doppler ultrasound of the leg veins remains the investigation of choice in patients with clinical DVT but may also be applied to patients presenting with features of PE alone since many will have identifiable proximal thrombus in the lower limbs. It is important to note

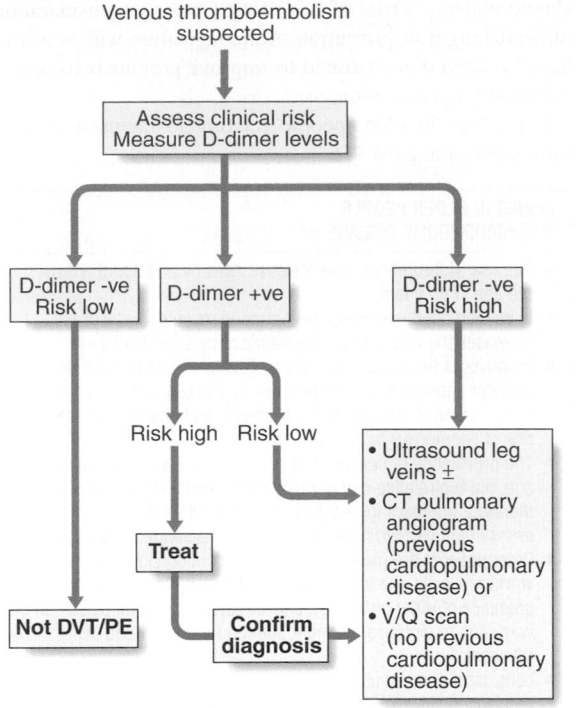

Venous thromboembolism suspected

↓

Assess clinical risk
Measure D-dimer levels

D-dimer -ve
Risk low

D-dimer +ve

D-dimer -ve
Risk high

Risk high   Risk low

Treat

Not DVT/PE

Confirm
diagnosis

- Ultrasound leg
  veins ±
- CT pulmonary
  angiogram
  (previous
  cardiopulmonary
  disease) or
- V̇/Q̇ scan
  (no previous
  cardiopulmonary
  disease)

Fig. 13.53 **Algorithm for the investigation of patients with suspected pulmonary thromboembolism.** Clinical risk is based on the presence of risk factors for VTE and the probability of another diagnosis.

that the sensitivity and specificity of ventilation-perfusion scanning in ruling pulmonary embolism in or out can be increased by the use of a simple clinical probability score indicating high or low clinical risk.

Echocardiography

Echocardiography can be used to diagnose a major central PE and is valuable for excluding other conditions such as myocardial infarction, aortic dissection and pericardial tamponade. Changes only occur when there has been significant obstruction to the pulmonary circulation and this investigation should therefore be carried out only in patients with systemic hypotension. Accuracy can be increased by using the transoesophageal route, which is much more likely to show clot in either the right heart or the main pulmonary arteries.

Pulmonary angiography

Although conventional pulmonary angiography is said to be the 'gold standard' for the diagnosis of PE, there may be difficulties in interpretation, even with an experienced radiologist. While there are no absolute contraindications, particular care should be exercised in patients with known sensitivity to contrast media.

Management
General measures

Opiates may be necessary to relieve pain and distress but should be used with great caution in the hypotensive patient. Resuscitation by external cardiac massage may be successful in the moribund patient by dislodging and breaking up a large central embolus. Oxygen should be given to all hypoxaemic patients in a concentration necessary to restore arterial oxygen saturation to over 90%. Diuretics and vasodilators should be avoided in the acute setting. Likewise, in the shocked patient inotropic agents are of limited value since in massive PE the hypoxic dilated right ventricle is near maximally stimulated by endogenous catecholamines.

Anticoagulation

Heparin should be given to all patients with a high clinical suspicion of PE whilst confirmatory test results are awaited. Low molecular weight heparin given subcutaneously has been demonstrated to be as effective as intravenous unfractionated heparin and it is much easier to administer (see p. 955). The dose is standardised for the weight of the patient and does not require monitoring by tests of coagulation. Heparin is effective in reducing mortality in PE by reducing the potential of further emboli. It should be administered for at least 5 days and anticoagulation continued using oral warfarin. Heparin should not be discontinued until the INR is over 2. The duration of warfarin therapy is under considerable discussion but should be continued for a minimum of 6 weeks for patients who have an identifiable and reversible cause for their DVT such as hip surgery, and for 3 months in patients with no identified cause. Patients with an underlying prothrombotic risk or a history of previous emboli should be anticoagulated for life. (For all anticoagulation control, see p. 955.)

EBM

ACUTE VENOUS THROMBOEMBOLISM (VTE)—use of subcutaneous low molecular weight heparins

'Low molecular weight heparins given subcutaneously in a weight-adjusted dosage are the treatment of choice for acute VTE.'

- Columbus Investigations. Low molecular weight heparin in the treatment of patients with venous thromboembolism. N Engl J Med 1997; 337:657–662.
- Simonneau G, Sors H, Charbonnier B, et al. A comparison of low molecular weight heparin with unfractionated heparin for acute pulmonary embolism. N Engl J Med 1997; 337:663–669.

Further information: 🖥 www.acponline.org/journals/annals/15jun98/lmwhepar.htm
🖥 http://dacc.bsd.uchicago.edu/drug/Bulletins/No399.html

Thrombolytic therapy

Patients with an acute massive PE and evidence of right ventricular dysfunction on echocardiography or of hypotension should be considered for urgent thrombolytic therapy when the diagnosis is confirmed. Streptokinase or alteplase (human tissue plasminogen activator or tPA) can be used. The latter is more expensive but less likely to lead to systemic side-effects and hypotension. A dose of 60 mg i.v. administered over 15 minutes is sufficient. Heparin should be given subsequently.

Caval filters

Patients with recurrent PE despite adequate anticoagulation control benefit from the insertion of a filter placed in the inferior vena cava below the origin of the renal vessels. Such filters may also be placed in patients with PE in whom anticoagulation is contraindicated (e.g. immediately following neurosurgery).

SEVERE PULMONARY HYPERTENSION

Although respiratory failure due to intrinsic pulmonary disease is the most common cause of pulmonary hypertension (see p. 505), severe pulmonary hypertension may occur as a primary disorder or as a result of chronic repeated thromboembolic events. The primary disorder may be familial, sporadic or associated with an underlying cause such as previous ingestion of appetite suppressant drugs, HIV infection or underlying connective tissue disease, particularly limited cutaneous systemic sclerosis (see p. 1036).

The pathological features include hypertrophy of both the media and intima of the vessel wall, and the so-called plexiform lesion which represents a clonal expansion of endothelial cells. There is marked narrowing of the vessel lumen and this, together with the frequently observed in situ thrombosis, leads to an increase in pulmonary vascular resistance and pulmonary hypertension. The gene responsible for familial pulmonary hypertension has recently been identified as a member of the TGF-β superfamily, BMPR2. Up to 30% of patients with sporadic pulmonary hypertension have also been found to have mutations in this gene.

Patients usually present with an insidious history of breathlessness on exertion and commonly the diagnosis is delayed for up to 2 years until the presence of severe pulmonary hypertension and right heart failure is evident. The prognosis of primary pulmonary hypertension was, until recently, very poor, with the majority of patients dying within 3 years of diagnosis unless they underwent heart-lung transplantation. The introduction of epoprostenol (prostacyclin) or iloprost therapy, given either as a continuous intravenous infusion through a central venous catheter or via the nebulised route, has dramatically improved exercise performance, symptoms and prognosis. All patients should undergo a trial of this therapy prior to consideration of heart-lung transplantation. Anticoagulation with warfarin has also been demonstrated to improve prognosis in severe pulmonary hypertension.

For issues in older people relating to haemostasis and thrombosis, see page 956.

DISEASES OF THE NASOPHARYNX, LARYNX AND TRACHEA

DISEASES OF THE NASOPHARYNX

ALLERGIC RHINITIS

This is a disorder in which there are episodes of nasal congestion, watery nasal discharge and sneezing. It may be seasonal or perennial.

Aetiology

Allergic rhinitis is due to an immediate hypersensitivity reaction in the nasal mucosa. The antigens concerned in the seasonal form of the disorder are pollens from grasses, flowers, weeds or trees. Grass pollen is responsible for hay fever (pollenosis), the most common type of seasonal allergic rhinitis in northern Europe; in the UK this disorder is at its peak between May and July.

Perennial allergic rhinitis may be a specific reaction to antigens derived from house dust, fungal spores or animal dander but similar symptoms can be caused by physical or chemical irritants—for example, pungent odours or fumes, including strong perfumes, cold air and dry atmospheres. The term 'vasomotor rhinitis' is often used for this type of nasal problem because in this context the term 'allergic' is a misnomer.

Clinical features

In the seasonal type there are frequent sudden attacks of sneezing, with profuse watery nasal discharge and nasal obstruction. These attacks last for a few hours and are often accompanied by smarting and watering of the eyes and conjunctival infection. In the perennial variety the symptoms are similar but more continuous and generally less severe. Skin hypersensitivity tests with the relevant antigen are usually positive in seasonal allergic rhinitis and are thus of diagnostic value, but these tests are less useful in perennial rhinitis.

Management
The following symptomatic measures, singly or in combination, are usually effective in both seasonal and perennial allergic rhinitis:

- an antihistamine drug such as loratadine 10 mg daily by mouth
- sodium cromoglicate nasal spray, one metered dose of a 2% solution into each nostril 4–6-hourly
- beclometasone dipropionate or budesonide aqueous nasal spray, one or two doses of 50 μg into each nostril 12-hourly.

Patients failing to respond to these measures may obtain symptomatic relief from intramuscular injection of a long-acting corticosteroid preparation; this form of treatment should be reserved for occasional use in patients whose symptoms are very severe and seriously interfere with school, business or social activities. Vasomotor rhinitis is often difficult to treat, but may respond to ipratropium bromide, administered into each nostril 6–8-hourly.

Prevention
In the seasonal type an attempt should be made to reduce exposure to pollen—for example, by avoiding country districts and keeping indoors as much as possible with windows closed during the pollen season, especially when pollen counts are reported to be high. The prevention of perennial rhinitis consists of avoiding, as far as possible, exposure to any identifiable aetiological factors but this is often difficult or impossible.

LARYNGEAL DISORDERS

Acute infections have already been described (see Box 13.38, p. 525). Other disorders of the larynx include chronic laryngitis, laryngeal tuberculosis, laryngeal paralysis and laryngeal obstruction. Tumours of the larynx are relatively common. For detailed information on these conditions, the reader should refer to a textbook of diseases of the ear, nose and throat.

CHRONIC LARYNGITIS

The common causes of this condition are listed in Box 13.86.

Clinical features
The chief symptom is hoarseness and the voice may be lost completely (aphonia). There is irritation of the throat and a

---

13.86 SOME CAUSES OF CHRONIC LARYNGITIS

- Repeated attacks of acute laryngitis
- Excessive use of the voice, especially in dusty atmospheres
- Heavy tobacco smoking
- Mouth-breathing from nasal obstruction
- Chronic infection of nasal sinuses

spasmodic cough. The disease pursues a chronic course frequently uninfluenced by treatment, and in long-standing cases the voice is often permanently impaired.

Differential diagnosis
The causes of chronic hoarseness are listed in Box 13.87.

These conditions must be considered in the differential diagnosis if hoarseness does not improve within a few weeks. In some patients a chest radiograph may bring to light an unsuspected bronchial carcinoma or pulmonary tuberculosis. If no such abnormality is found, laryngoscopy should be performed, usually by a specialist in otolaryngology.

13.87 CAUSES OF CHRONIC HOARSENESS

If hoarseness persists for more than a few days, consider:
- Tumour of the larynx
- Tuberculosis
- Laryngeal paralysis
- Inhaled corticosteroid treatment

Management
The voice must be rested completely. This is particularly important in public speakers. Smoking should be prohibited. Some benefit may be obtained from frequent inhalations of medicated steam.

LARYNGEAL PARALYSIS
Aetiology
Paralysis is due to interference with the motor nerve supply of the larynx. It is nearly always unilateral and, by reason of the intrathoracic course of the left recurrent laryngeal nerve, usually left-sided. One or both recurrent laryngeal nerves may be damaged at thyroidectomy or by carcinoma of the thyroid. Rarely, the vagal trunk itself is involved by tumour, aneurysm or trauma.

Clinical features
Hoarseness
This always accompanies laryngeal paralysis, whatever its cause. Paralysis of organic origin is seldom reversible but when only one vocal cord is affected hoarseness may improve or even disappear after a few weeks, following a compensatory adjustment whereby the unparalysed cord crosses the midline and approximates with the paralysed cord on phonation.

'Bovine cough'
A characteristic feature of organic laryngeal paralysis is a cow-like cough which results from the loss of the explosive

phase of normal coughing consequent upon the failure of the cords to close the glottis. Difficulty in bringing up sputum, which some patients experience, is also explained on the same basis. A normal cough in patients with partial loss of voice or aphonia virtually excludes laryngeal paralysis.

Stridor

Stridor is occasionally present but is seldom severe, except when laryngeal paralysis is bilateral.

Diagnosis

Laryngoscopy is necessary to establish the diagnosis of laryngeal paralysis with certainty. The paralysed cord lies in the so-called 'cadaveric' position, midway between abduction and adduction.

Management

The cause of laryngeal paralysis should be treated if that is possible. In unilateral paralysis the voice may be improved by the injection of Teflon into the affected vocal cord. In bilateral organic paralysis, tracheal intubation, tracheostomy or a plastic operation on the larynx may be necessary.

PSYCHOGENIC HOARSENESS AND APHONIA

Psychogenic causes of hoarseness or complete loss of voice may be suggested by associated symptoms in the history (see p. 254). However, laryngoscopy may be necessary to exclude a physical cause of the voice abnormality. In psychogenic aphonia only the voluntary movement of adduction of the vocal cords is seen to be impaired.

LARYNGEAL OBSTRUCTION

Laryngeal obstruction is more liable to occur in children than in adults because of the smaller size of the glottis. Some important causes are given in Box 13.88.

13.88 CAUSES OF LARYNGEAL OBSTRUCTION

- Inflammatory or allergic oedema, or exudate
- Spasm of laryngeal muscles
- Inhaled foreign body
- Inhaled blood clot or vomitus in an unconscious patient
- Tumours of the larynx
- Bilateral vocal cord paralysis
- Fixation of both cords in rheumatoid disease

Clinical features

Sudden complete laryngeal obstruction by a foreign body produces the clinical picture of acute asphyxia—violent but ineffective inspiratory efforts with indrawing of the intercostal spaces and the unsupported lower ribs, accompanied by cyanosis. Unrelieved, the condition progresses rapidly to coma and death within a few minutes. When, as in most cases, the obstruction is incomplete at first, the main clinical features are progressive breathlessness accompanied by stridor and cyanosis. There is indrawing of the intercostal spaces and lower ribs on both sides with each inspiratory effort. In

such cases the great danger is that complete laryngeal obstruction may occur at any time and result in sudden death.

Management

Transient attacks of laryngeal obstruction due to exudate and spasm, which may occur with acute laryngitis in children (see p. 525) and with whooping cough, are potentially dangerous but can usually be relieved by the inhalation of steam.

Laryngeal obstruction from all other causes carries a high mortality and demands prompt treatment. The following measures may have to be employed.

Relief of obstruction by mechanical measures

When a foreign body is known to be the cause of the obstruction in children it can often be dislodged by turning the patient head downwards and squeezing the chest vigorously. In adults this is often impossible, but a sudden forceful compression of the upper abdomen (Heimlich manoeuvre) may be effective. In other circumstances the cause of the obstruction should be investigated by direct laryngoscopy which may also permit the removal of an unsuspected foreign body, or the insertion of a tube past the obstruction into the trachea. Tracheostomy must be performed without delay if these procedures fail to relieve laryngeal obstruction, but except in dire emergencies this operation should be performed in an operating theatre by a surgeon.

Treatment of the cause

In cases of diphtheria, antitoxin should be administered, and for other infections the appropriate antibiotic should be given. In angio-oedema complete laryngeal occlusion can usually be prevented by treatment with adrenaline (epinephrine) 0.5–1 mg (0.5–1 ml of 1:1000) intramuscularly, chlorphenamine maleate 10–20 mg by slow intravenous injection and intravenous hydrocortisone sodium succinate 200 mg.

TRACHEAL DISORDERS

ACUTE TRACHEITIS

See Box 13.38, page 525.

TRACHEAL OBSTRUCTION

External compression by enlarged mediastinal lymph nodes containing metastatic deposits, usually from a bronchial carcinoma, is a more frequent cause of tracheal obstruction than the uncommon primary benign or malignant tumours. Rarely, the trachea may be compressed by an aneurysm of the aortic arch, or in children by tuberculous mediastinal lymph nodes. Tracheal stenosis is an occasional complication of tracheostomy, prolonged intubation, Wegener's granulomatosis or trauma.

Clinical features

Stridor can be detected in every patient with severe tracheal narrowing. Endoscopic examination of the trachea should be undertaken without delay to determine the site, degree and nature of the obstruction.

Management

Localised tumours of the trachea can be resected, but reconstruction after resection may present complex technical problems. Endobronchial laser therapy, tracheal stents and radiotherapy are alternatives to surgery. The choice of treatment depends upon the nature of the tumour and the general health of the patient. Radiotherapy or chemotherapy may temporarily relieve compression by malignant lymph nodes, and tracheal stents introduced bronchoscopically may be of temporary value. Benign tracheal strictures can sometimes be dilated but may have to be resected.

TRACHEO-OESOPHAGEAL FISTULA

This may be present in newborn infants as a congenital abnormality. In adults it is usually due to malignant lesions in the mediastinum, such as carcinoma or lymphoma, eroding both the trachea and oesophagus to produce a communication between them. Swallowed liquids enter the trachea and bronchi through the fistula and provoke coughing.

Management

Surgical closure of a congenital fistula, if undertaken promptly, is usually successful. There is usually no curative treatment for malignant fistulae and death from overwhelming pulmonary infection rapidly supervenes.

DISEASES OF THE PLEURA, DIAPHRAGM AND CHEST WALL

DISEASES OF THE PLEURA

PLEURISY

Pleurisy is not a diagnosis but simply a term used to describe the result of any disease process involving the pleura and giving rise to pleuritic pain or evidence of pleural friction. Pleurisy is a common feature of pulmonary infarction and may be an early manifestation of pleural invasion by pulmonary tuberculosis or a bronchogenic carcinoma.

Clinical features

Pleural pain is the characteristic symptom. On examination rib movement is restricted and a pleural rub is present. This may only be heard in deep inspiration or near the pericardium, where a so-called pleuro-pericardial rub may be present. The other clinical features depend upon the nature of the disease causing the pleurisy. Loss of the pleural rub and diminution in the chest pain may indicate recovery or herald the development of a pleural effusion.

Every patient must have a chest radiograph but a normal radiograph does not exclude a pulmonary cause for the pleurisy. A preceding history of cough, purulent sputum and pyrexia is presumptive evidence of a pulmonary infection which may not have been severe enough to produce a radiographic abnormality or which may have resolved before the chest radiograph was taken.

Management

The primary cause of pleurisy must be treated. The symptomatic treatment of pleural pain is described on page 530.

PLEURAL EFFUSION

See page 501.

EMPYEMA

This term describes the presence of pus in the pleural space. The pus may be as thin as serous fluid or so thick that it is impossible to aspirate even through a wide-bore needle. Microscopically, neutrophil leucocytes are present in large numbers. The causative organism may or may not be isolated from the pus. An empyema may involve the whole pleural space or only part of it ('loculated' or 'encysted' empyema) and is almost invariably unilateral.

Aetiology

Empyema is always secondary to infection in a neighbouring structure, usually the lung. The principal infections liable to produce empyema are the bacterial pneumonias and tuberculosis. Over 40% of patients with community-acquired pneumonia develop an associated pleural effusion ('parapneumonic' effusion) and about 15% of these become secondarily infected. Other causes are infection of a haemothorax and rupture of a subphrenic abscess through the diaphragm. Despite the widespread availability of effective antibacterial therapy for patients with pneumonia, empyema continues to be a significant cause of morbidity and mortality even in developed countries. All too often, this reflects a delay in the diagnosis or instigation of appropriate therapy.

Pathology

Both layers of pleura are covered with a thick, shaggy inflammatory exudate. The pus in the pleural space is often under considerable pressure and if the condition is not adequately treated pus may rupture into a bronchus causing a bronchopleural fistula and pyopneumothorax, or track through the chest wall with the formation of a subcutaneous abscess or sinus.

The only way in which an empyema can heal is by eradication of the infection, obliteration of the empyema space and apposition of the visceral and parietal pleural layers. This cannot occur unless re-expansion of the compressed lung is secured at an early stage by removal of all the pus from the pleural space. This cannot take place if:

- the visceral pleura becomes grossly thickened and rigid due to delayed treatment or inadequate drainage of the infected pleural fluid
- the pleural layers are kept apart by air entering the pleura through a bronchopleural fistula
- there is underlying disease in the lung, such as bronchiectasis, bronchial carcinoma or pulmonary tuberculosis preventing re-expansion.

In all these circumstances an empyema tends to become chronic, and healing may not take place without surgical intervention.

Clinical features

An empyema should be suspected in patients with pulmonary infection if there is persistence or recurrence of pyrexia despite the administration of a suitable antibiotic. In other cases the illness produced by the primary infective lesion may be so slight that it passes unrecognised and the first definite clinical features are due to the empyema itself.

Once an empyema has developed, two separate groups of clinical features are found. These are shown in Box 13.89.

13.89 CLINICAL FEATURES OF EMPYEMA
Systemic features
• Pyrexia, usually high and remittent • Rigors, sweating, malaise and weight loss • Polymorphonuclear leucocytosis, high CRP
Local features
• Pleural pain; breathlessness; cough and sputum usually because of underlying lung disease; copious purulent sputum if empyema ruptures into a bronchus (bronchopleural fistula) • Clinical signs of fluid in the pleural space

Investigations

Radiological examination

The appearances are often indistinguishable from those of pleural effusion. When air is present in addition to pus (pyo-pneumothorax), a horizontal 'fluid level' marks the interface between the liquid and air. Ultrasound and CT are extremely valuable in defining the extent of pleural thickening and location of the fluid, and in the case of CT assessing the underlying lung parenchyma and patency of the major bronchi.

Aspiration of pus

This confirms the presence of an empyema. Ultrasound or CT is recommended to identify the optimal place to undertake pleuracentesis, which is best performed using a wide-bore needle. The pus is frequently sterile when antibiotics have already been given; the distinction between tuberculous and non-tuberculous disease can be difficult and often requires pleural histology and culture.

Management

Treatment of non-tuberculous empyema

When the patient is acutely ill and the pus is thin an intercostal tube should be inserted under ultrasound CT guidance into the most dependent part of the empyema space and connected to a water-seal drain system. If the initial aspirate reveals turbid fluid or frank pus, or if loculations are seen on ultrasound, the tube should be put on suction (5–10 cm water) and flushed regularly with 20 ml normal saline. Although intrapleural fibrinolytic therapy is widely used in such situations there is currently insufficient evidence to support its routine use (see EBM panel). Finally, an antibiotic directed against the organism causing the empyema should be given for 2–4 weeks.

An empyema can often be aborted if these measures are started early. If, however, the intercostal tube is not providing adequate drainage, which can happen when the pus is

thick or loculated, surgical intervention is required. The empyema cavity is cleared of pus and adhesions, and a wide-bore tube inserted to allow optimal drainage. Surgical 'decortication' of the lung may also be required if gross thickening of the visceral pleura has developed and is preventing re-expansion of the lung.

Treatment of tuberculous empyema

Antituberculosis chemotherapy must be started immediately (see p. 538) and the pus in the pleural space aspirated through a wide-bore needle until it ceases to reaccumulate. Intercostal tube drainage is often required. In many patients no other treatment is necessary but surgery is occasionally required to ablate a residual empyema space.

SPONTANEOUS PNEUMOTHORAX

Pneumothorax is the presence of air in the pleural space; it can either occur spontaneously, or result from iatrogenic injury or trauma to the lung or chest wall (see Box 13.90). The incidence of pneumothorax is highest in males aged 15–30 (see Fig. 13.54) where smoking, height and the presence of apical subpleural blebs appear to be the most important aetiological factors. Secondary pneumothorax is most common in older patients and those living in urban areas, and is associated with the highest mortality rates.

13.90 CLASSIFICATION OF PNEUMOTHORAX
Spontaneous
Primary • Without evidence of overt lung disease. Air is usually introduced into the pleural space through rupture of a small subpleural emphysematous bulla or pleural bleb, or the pulmonary end of a pleural adhesion
Secondary • Underlying lung disease, most commonly COPD and tuberculosis; also seen in asthma, lung abscess, pulmonary infarcts, bronchogenic carcinoma, all forms of fibrotic and cystic lung disease
Traumatic
• Iatrogenic (e.g. following thoracic surgery or biopsy) or non-iatrogenic

Clinical features

Most episodes of primary spontaneous pneumothorax occur while the individual is at rest. Virtually all patients experience sudden-onset unilateral chest pain or breathlessness. In those with underlying chest disease, breathlessness can be severe and does not resolve spontaneously. In patients with

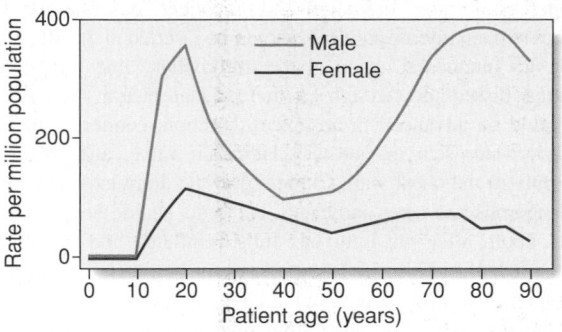

Fig. 13.54 Bimodal age distribution for hospital admissions for pneumothorax in England. The incidence of primary spontaneous pneumothorax peaks in males aged 15–30. Secondary spontaneous pneumothorax occurs mainly in males > 55 years.

a small pneumothorax the physical examination may be normal except for a tachycardia. A larger pneumothorax (> 15% of the hemithorax) results in decreased movement of the chest wall, a hyper-resonant percussion note and decreased or absent breath sounds.

A tension pneumothorax may develop if the communication between the pleura and lung persists but is small, and if it acts as a one-way valve which allows air to enter the pleural space during inspiration and coughing but prevents it from escaping. Very large amounts of air may be trapped in the pleural space and the intrapleural pressure may rise to well above atmospheric levels. This causes not only compression of the underlying deflated lung but also mediastinal displacement towards the opposite side, with consequent compression of the opposite lung and cardiovascular compromise (see Fig. 13.55C). Clinically, this results in rapidly progressive breathlessness associated with a marked tachycardia, hypotension and cyanosis.

Where the communication between the lung and pleural space seals off as the lung deflates and does not reopen, the pneumothorax is referred to as 'closed' (see Fig. 13.55A). In such circumstances the mean pleural pressure remains negative, spontaneous reabsorption of air and re-expansion of the lung occur over a few days or weeks, and infection is uncommon. This contrasts with an 'open' pneumothorax, where the communication fails to seal and air continues to transfer freely between the lung and pleural space (see Fig. 13.55B). An example of the latter is a bronchopleural fistula which, if large, can also facilitate the transmission of infection from the air passages into the pleural space, and empyema is a common complication. An open pneumothorax is most commonly seen following rupture of an emphysematous bulla, tuberculous cavity or lung abscess into the pleural space.

Investigations

The chest radiograph usually shows the sharply defined edge of the deflated lung with complete translucency between this and the chest wall and no lung markings (see Fig. 13.56). The practice of obtaining films in both inspiration and expiration

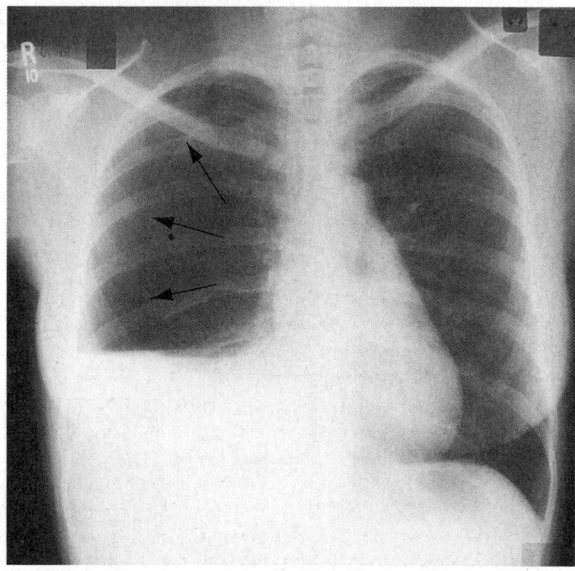

Fig. 13.56 Haemopneumothorax. Chest radiograph of a patient with a right traumatic haemopneumothorax showing the characteristic visceral pleural line displaced from the chest wall (arrows), together with free fluid within the pleural cavity (not seen in patients with uncomplicated spontaneous pneumothorax).

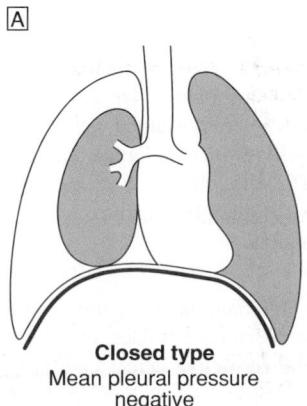

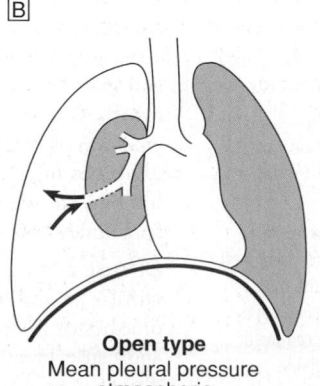

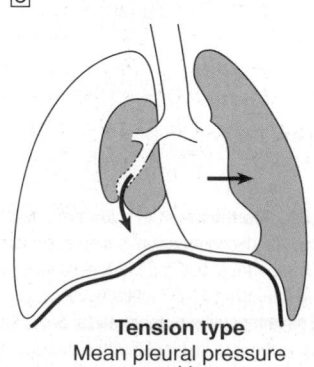

Closed type	**Open type**	**Tension type**
Mean pleural pressure negative	Mean pleural pressure atmospheric	Mean pleural pressure positive

Fig. 13.55 Types of spontaneous pneumothorax. A Closed type. B Open type. C Tension (valvular) type.

has been abandoned as the latter do not improve the diagnostic yield. Care must be taken to differentiate between a large pre-existing emphysematous bulla and a pneumothorax; where any doubt exists, an emergency thoracic CT is indicated. Radiographs also show the extent of any mediastinal displacement and give information regarding the presence or absence of pleural fluid and underlying pulmonary disease. It is important to note that the absence of mediastinal shift on a chest radiograph does not exclude the presence of a tension pneumothorax, the diagnosis of which is largely clinical.

Management

It is now recognised that percutaneous needle aspiration of air is a simple, effective and well-tolerated alternative to intercostal tube drainage in young patients presenting with a moderate or large spontaneous pneumothorax (see Fig. 13.57). However, even a small pneumothorax may cause severe respiratory failure in patients with underlying chronic lung disease, and hence all such patients require

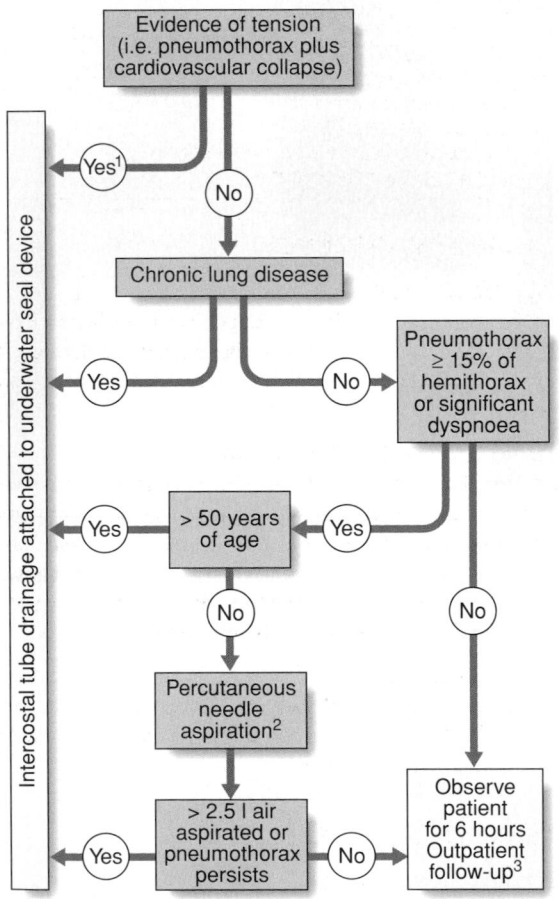

Fig. 13.57 Management of spontaneous pneumothorax.
(1) Immediate decompression is required prior to insertion of intercostal drain. (2) Aspirate in the 2nd intercostal space anteriorly in the mid-clavicular line using a 16 F cannula; discontinue if either resistance is felt, the patient coughs excessively, or > 2.5 litres of air are removed.
(3) Beware: the post-aspiration chest radiograph is not a reliable indicator of whether a pleural leak remains and hence all patients should be told to attend again immediately in the event of noticeable deterioration.

intercostal tube drainage and inpatient observation. If required, an intercostal drain should be inserted in the 4th, 5th or 6th intercostal space in the mid-axillary line following blunt dissection through to the parietal pleura. The tube should be advanced in an apical direction, connected to an underwater seal or one-way Heimlich valve, and secured firmly to the chest wall. Clamping of the drain is potentially dangerous and never indicated. The drain should be removed 24 hours after the lung has fully reinflated and bubbling stopped. If bubbling in the underwater bottle stops prior to full reinflation, the tube is either blocked, kinked or displaced. All patients should receive supplemental oxygen as this accelerates the rate at which air is reabsorbed by the pleura.

Patients presenting with a spontaneous pneumothorax should not fly or dive for 3 months following full reinflation of the lung. They should also be advised to stop smoking and be informed about the risks of a further attack.

Recurrent spontaneous pneumothorax

Due to the seriousness of this condition surgical pleurodesis is recommended in all presenting with a secondary pneumothorax. This can be achieved by pleural abrasion or parietal pleurectomy at thoracotomy or thoracoscopy. In patients with their first primary spontaneous pneumothorax the risk of recurrence is high (approximately 30–50%), particularly in women and those who continue to smoke. Currently, chemical or surgical pleurodesis is recommended in all such patients following a second pneumothorax (even if ipsilateral) or in patients following their first pneumothorax where there is a persistent air leak (> 7 days). Patients who plan to continue activities that increase the risk of complications developing following a pneumothorax (e.g. flying or diving) should also undergo preventative treatment after the first episode of a primary spontaneous pneumothorax.

ASBESTOS-RELATED PLEURAL DISEASE

Benign pleural plaques

These areas of pleural thickening do not produce clinical symptoms and are usually identified on routine chest radiograph. They are often calcified and in the early stage are best seen on oblique films. They are most commonly observed on the diaphragm and anterolateral pleural surfaces (see Fig. 13.58).

Benign pleural effusion

This is considered to be a specific asbestos-related entity and may be associated with pleural pain, fever and leucocytosis. The pleural liquid may be blood-stained, and differentiation of this benign condition from a malignant effusion caused by mesothelioma can be difficult. The disease is self-limiting but may cause considerable pleural fibrosis which sometimes leads to breathlessness.

Diffuse pleural fibrosis

Diffuse pleural fibrosis is an important pleural manifestation of asbestos fibre inhalation and can restrict chest expansion and cause breathlessness. The restrictive defect caused by diffuse pleural fibrosis tends to progress and, like asbestosis and mesothelioma, qualifies a patient for industrial injury benefit in the UK.

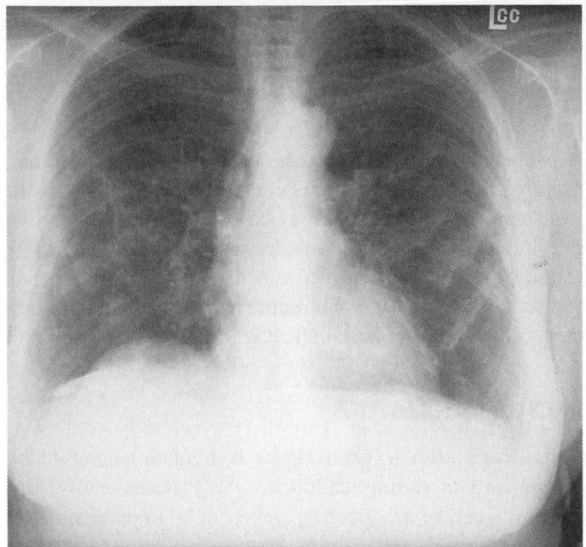

Fig. 13.58 Asbestos-related benign pleural plaques. Chest radiograph showing extensive calcified pleural plaques ('candle wax' appearance), particularly marked on the diaphragm and lateral pleural surfaces.

Mesothelioma of the pleura

Mesothelioma is a malignant tumour affecting the pleura (pleural mesothelioma) or, less commonly, the peritoneum (peritoneal mesothelioma). Blue asbestos (crocidolite) is thought to be the most potent cause of mesothelioma. A time lag of 20 years or more between asbestos exposure and the development of mesothelioma is typical. The incidence of this tumour has increased markedly over the past 20 years and this trend is predicted to continue until 2010. Asbestos exposure is also a recognised risk factor for the development of bronchogenic carcinoma.

Clinical presentation is frequently with chest pain. A pleural effusion, often blood-stained, may develop and cause breathlessness. Diagnosis rests on percutaneous or surgical biopsy of the pleura. Surgical resection is rarely indicated and most tumours are resistant to chemotherapy. Radiotherapy is, however, effective in preventing tumour growth through previous chest drain or biopsy sites. There is no curative treatment and chest wall pain is often difficult to control.

ISSUES IN OLDER PEOPLE
PLEURAL DISEASE

- Spontaneous pneumothorax in the elderly is invariably associated with underlying lung disease and has a significant mortality. Surgical or chemical pleurodesis is advised in all such patients.
- Rib fracture is a common cause of pleural-type pain in the elderly and underlying osteomalacia may contribute to poor healing, especially in the housebound with no exposure to sunlight.
- Tuberculosis should always be considered and actively excluded in any elderly patient presenting with a unilateral pleural effusion.
- Mesothelioma is more common in older than younger people due to a long latency between asbestos exposure (often > 40 years) and the development of disease.
- Frail older people are particularly sensitive to the respiratory depressant effects of opiate-based analgesia and careful monitoring is required when using these agents for pleural pain.

DISEASES OF THE DIAPHRAGM

Abnormalities of the diaphragm are common and may be congenital or acquired. Both hemidiaphragms are displaced downwards and functionally impaired by diseases which cause pulmonary hyperinflation, notably emphysema. Diaphragmatic function can also be impaired in a variety of neuromuscular and connective tissue diseases (e.g. Guillain–Barré syndrome and polymyositis—see pp. 1180 and 1038) and with skeletal deformities such as thoracic scoliosis (see Box 13.91). Unilateral diaphragmatic palsy results from injury or damage to the phrenic nerve and should always alert the clinician to the possibility of intrathoracic malignancy (see below).

13.91 CAUSES OF ELEVATION OF A HEMIDIAPHRAGM

- Phrenic nerve paralysis
- Eventration of the diaphragm
- Decrease in volume of one lung (e.g. lobectomy, unilateral pulmonary fibrosis)
- Severe pleuritic pain
- Pulmonary infarction
- Subphrenic abscess
- Large volume of gas in the stomach or colon
- Large tumours or cysts of the liver

CONGENITAL DISORDERS

Diaphragmatic hernias

Congenital defects of the diaphragm can allow herniation of abdominal viscera. Posteriorly situated hernias through the foramen of Bochdalek are more common than anterior hernias through the foramen of Morgagni.

Eventration of the diaphragm

Abnormal elevation or bulging of one hemidiaphragm, more often the left, results from total or partial absence of muscular development of the septum transversum. Most eventrations are asymptomatic and are detected by chance on radiograph in adult life, but severe respiratory distress can be caused in infancy if the diaphragmatic muscular defect is extensive.

Other diaphragmatic abnormalities

These include defects of the oesophageal hiatus, congenital absence and duplication. The diaphragm may be involved in most primary muscle disorders.

ACQUIRED DISORDERS

Diaphragmatic paralysis

Phrenic nerve damage leading to paralysis of a hemidiaphragm is most often produced by bronchial carcinoma but can also be idiopathic or the result of a number of neurological disorders, injury or disease of cervical vertebrae and tumours of the cervical cord. Trauma to the chest and neck, including road traffic and birth injuries, surgery and stretching of the phrenic nerve by mediastinal masses and aortic aneurysms may also lead to diaphragmatic paralysis.

Paralysis of one hemidiaphragm results in loss of approximately 20% of ventilatory capacity, but this is not usually noticed by otherwise healthy individuals.

Diagnosis is suggested by elevation of the hemidiaphragm on chest radiograph and is confirmed by screening or ultrasound examination, which show paradoxical movement of the paralysed hemidiaphragm on sniffing.

Other acquired diaphragmatic disorders

Hiatus hernia is common (see p. 775). Diaphragmatic rupture is usually caused by a crush injury and may not be detected until years later. Peripheral neuropathies of any type can involve the diaphragm, as can disorders affecting the anterior horn cells, e.g. poliomyelitis (see p. 1198). Connective tissue disorders such as systemic lupus erythematosus, and hypothyroidism and hyperthyroidism, may cause diaphragmatic weakness. Respiratory disorders which cause pulmonary hyperinflation, e.g. emphysema, and those which result in small stiff lungs, e.g. diffuse pulmonary fibrosis, decrease diaphragmatic efficiency and predispose to fatigue. Severe skeletal deformity, such as kyphosis, causes gross distortion of diaphragmatic muscle configuration and gross mechanical disadvantage.

DEFORMITIES OF THE CHEST WALL

THORACIC KYPHOSCOLIOSIS

Abnormalities of alignment of the dorsal spine and their consequent effects on thoracic shape may be caused by:

- congenital abnormality
- vertebral disease, including tuberculosis, osteoporosis and ankylosing spondylitis
- trauma
- neuromuscular disease such as poliomyelitis.

Simple kyphosis causes less pulmonary embarrassment than kyphoscoliosis.

Kyphoscoliosis, if severe, restricts and distorts expansion of the chest wall, causing maldistribution of the ventilation and blood flow in the lungs and impaired diaphragmatic function. Patients with severe deformity may develop type II respiratory failure (initially manifest during sleep), pulmonary hypertension and right ventricular failure; such patients can often be successfully treated with nocturnal and, if necessary, day-time, non-invasive ventilatory support (see p. 508).

PECTUS EXCAVATUM

In pectus excavatum (funnel chest) the body of the sternum, usually only the lower end, is curved backwards. The heart is displaced to the left and may be compressed between the sternum and the vertebral column; only rarely is there associated disturbance of cardiac function. The deformity may restrict chest expansion and reduce vital capacity. Operative correction is usually only indicated for cosmetic reasons.

PECTUS CARINATUM

Pectus carinatum (pigeon chest) is frequently caused by severe asthma during childhood. Very occasionally, this deformity can be produced by rickets or be idiopathic.

FURTHER INFORMATION

Beckett WS. Occupational respiratory diseases. N Engl J Med 2000; 342:406–413.

Fedullo PF, Auger WR, Kerr KM, Rubin LJ. Chronic thromboembolic pulmonary hypertension. N Engl J Med 2001; 345:1465–1472.

Global Initiative for Chronic Obstructive Lung Disease (GOLD guidelines). National Institutes of Health, April 2001.

Lim WS, Macfarlane JT. Hospital-acquired pneumonia. Clin Med 2001; 1:180–184.

Peppard PE, Young PT, Palta M, Skatrud J. Prospective study of the association between sleep-disordered breathing and hypertension. N Engl J Med 2000; 342:1378–1384.

Smoking cessation guidelines and their cost-effectiveness. Thorax 1998; 53(suppl).

Tattersfield AE, Harrison TW. Inhaled steroids for COPD? Thorax 2001; 56(suppl 11):ii2–6.

www.brit-thoracic.org.uk *British Thoracic Society website; has access to guidelines from recent years including community-acquired pneumonia, COPD, asthma, selection of patients with cancer for operation, pulmonary embolism etc.*

www.cancerlinks.usa.com/lung.htm *An American site which provides a good synopsis of thoracic oncology.*

www.cancernews.com/lung/htm *An American site which provides very good links to other relevant sites and is constantly updated.*

www.lunguk.org *British Lung Foundation site.*

www.sign.ac.uk/guidelines/published/index.htm/#cancer *Royal College site outlining the guidelines for the management of lung cancer, asthma, sleep etc.*

www.thoracic.org *Contains useful information and guidelines for management.*

www.thoraxjnl.com *Journal of the British Thoracic Society on-line*

Kidney and genitourinary disease

A.N. TURNER • J. SAVILL • L.H. STEWART • A. CUMMING

CLINICAL EXAMINATION OF THE KIDNEY AND GENITOURINARY SYSTEM

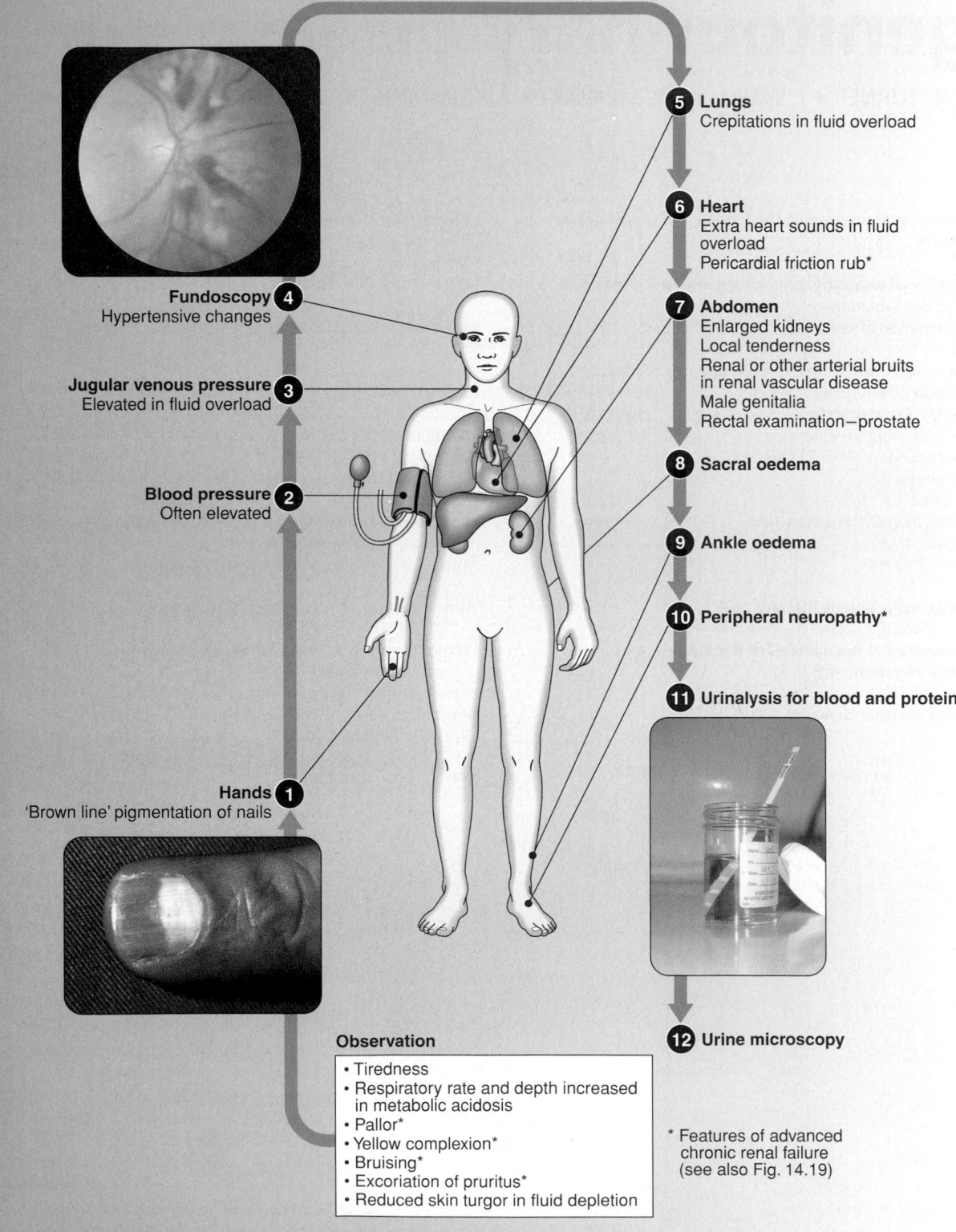

5 Lungs
Crepitations in fluid overload

6 Heart
Extra heart sounds in fluid overload
Pericardial friction rub*

7 Abdomen
Enlarged kidneys
Local tenderness
Renal or other arterial bruits in renal vascular disease
Male genitalia
Rectal examination—prostate

8 Sacral oedema

9 Ankle oedema

10 Peripheral neuropathy*

11 Urinalysis for blood and protein

12 Urine microscopy

Fundoscopy 4
Hypertensive changes

Jugular venous pressure 3
Elevated in fluid overload

Blood pressure 2
Often elevated

Hands 1
'Brown line' pigmentation of nails

Observation

- Tiredness
- Respiratory rate and depth increased in metabolic acidosis
- Pallor*
- Yellow complexion*
- Bruising*
- Excoriation of pruritus*
- Reduced skin turgor in fluid depletion

* Features of advanced chronic renal failure (see also Fig. 14.19)

Diseases of the kidneys and urinary tract are often clinically 'silent'. Detection then depends on biochemical testing—measurement of plasma creatinine or testing of urine for abnormal constituents. Severe renal disease may present with non-specific symptoms—tiredness or breathlessness due to renal failure and associated anaemia, or oedema due to fluid retention. In end-stage renal failure, a wide range of physical signs may be present, including some iatrogenic features, as seen opposite. In less severe disease, physical findings may be few.

CARDINAL SYMPTOMS OF DISEASE OF THE KIDNEYS AND URINARY TRACT

Symptoms referrable to the lower urinary tract

- Dysuria, frequency, urgency—dominant symptoms of lower urinary tract infection
- Impaired urinary flow, hesitancy, dribbling of urine, incomplete emptying of bladder—dominant symptoms of bladder outflow obstruction
- Urinary retention, incontinence/enuresis—dominant symptoms of sphincter or bladder wall dysfunction

Symptoms referrable to the upper urinary tract

- Loin pain/tenderness—seen with renal infection, glomerulonephritis, renal infarction or rarely obstruction
- Renal or ureteric colic—severe loin pain due to acute obstruction of the renal pelvis and ureter by calculus or blood clot; may radiate to the iliac fossa, groin and genitalia

Abnormal urine volume

- Anuria or oliguria—due to acute renal failure or obstruction to the flow of urine
- Polyuria or nocturia—due to failure of the kidneys to concentrate the urine (e.g. diabetes insipidus, chronic renal failure)

Abnormal urinary constituents

- Proteinuria—suggests disease affecting the glomeruli; oedema may be the consequence of massive proteinuria
- Haematuria—may indicate disease anywhere in the urinary tract

Hypertension

- May indicate acute or chronic parenchymal disease or renovascular disease

Uraemia

- A group of symptoms consequent upon advanced renal failure

Diseases of the testes and epididymis

- Local swelling, pain and tenderness; pain may be felt in the abdomen; inflammation and torsion are causes

❼ ABDOMEN

Technique for palpating the kidneys

- Lie the patient flat with the abdominal muscles relaxed.
- Use both hands—place one hand posteriorly just below the lower ribs and the other anteriorly over the upper quadrant.
- Push the two hands towards each other firmly but gently as the patient breathes out.
- Then feel for the lower pole of the kidney moving down between the hands as the patient breathes in.
- If palpable, push the kidney back and forwards between the two hands ('ballotting'). This helps to confirm that it is the kidney.
- Assess the size, surface and consistency of a palpable kidney; e.g. polycystic kidneys are often massively enlarged with an irregular, nodular surface and a firm consistency.

Local tenderness may reflect infection or inflammation.

The lower pole of a normal right kidney can often be palpated, especially in thin subjects.

Possible findings

- Transplanted kidney—palpable in the iliac fossa, with an overlying scar.
- Distension of the bladder—smooth midline mass arising from the pelvis, dull to percussion.
- Arterial bruits—heard on either side of the epigastrium; may arise from renal artery stenosis; there is usually also evidence of vascular disease elsewhere.
- Inspection of the male genitalia—looking particularly for testicular masses.
- Rectal examination—assesses extent and nature of prostatic enlargement. Benign enlargement is characteristically smooth and regular; an enlarged, hard, irregular prostate suggests prostatic cancer.

⓬ URINE MICROSCOPY

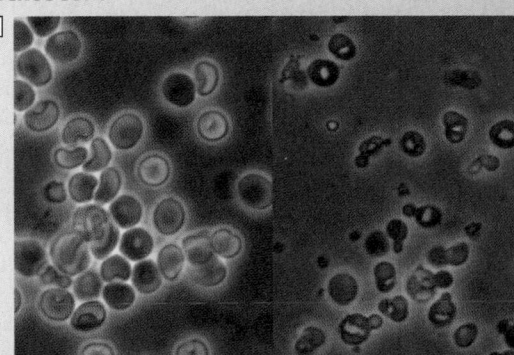

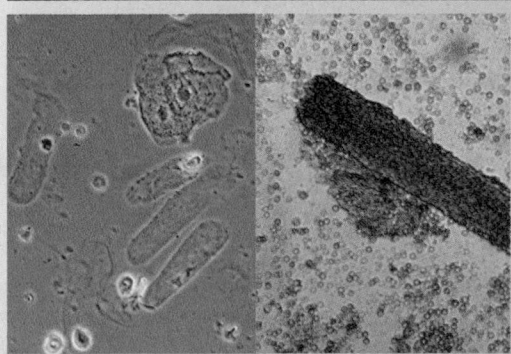

Urine microscopy. Ⓐ Phase contrast images of red blood cells (× 400) showing on the right glomerular bleeding with many dysmorphic forms including acanthocytes (teardrop forms), and on the left bleeding from lower in the urinary tract. Ⓑ On the left, phase contrast images show hyaline casts, a normal feature of urine (× 160). On the right, numerous red cells and a large red cell cast in acute glomerular inflammation (× 100, not phase contrast).

FUNCTIONAL ANATOMY, PHYSIOLOGY AND INVESTIGATIONS

Renal medicine ranges from the management of common conditions (e.g. urinary tract infection) to the use of complex technology to replace renal function. Since it has been possible to do this, the practice of nephrology has extended to involve the management of multisystem diseases where renal function is threatened or lost, and to transplantation, by which loss of renal function is most effectively replaced.

In health, the volume and composition of body fluids are tightly regulated and the kidneys are largely responsible for maintaining this state. This is achieved by making large volumes of an ultrafiltrate of plasma (120 ml/min, 170 l/day) at the glomerulus, and selectively reabsorbing components of the ultrafiltrate at points along the nephron. Most of these processes are tightly controlled and many represent the targets of drug action.

In addition, the kidney has a number of hormonal functions. Three of these are particularly important:

- The kidney is the main source of erythropoietin, which is produced by interstitial peritubular cells in response to hypoxia. Replacement of erythropoietin reverses the anaemia of chronic renal failure.
- The kidney is essential for vitamin D metabolism; it hydroxylates 25-hydroxycholecalciferol to the active form, 1,25-dihydroxycholecalciferol. Failure of this process contributes to the hypocalcaemia and bone disease of chronic renal failure (see p. 601).
- Renin is secreted from the juxtaglomerular apparatus in response to reduced afferent arteriolar pressure, stimulation of sympathetic nerves, and changes in the composition of fluid in the distal convoluted tubule at the macula densa. Renin generates angiotensin II. As well as causing constriction of the efferent arteriole of the glomerulus and, thereby increasing glomerular filtration pressure (see Fig. 14.1), this produces systemic vasoconstriction and hypertension. Thus renal ischaemia leads to systemic hypertension.

FUNCTIONAL ANATOMY

KIDNEYS

Adult kidneys are 11–14 cm (three lumbar vertebral bodies) in length, and are located retroperitoneally on either side of the aorta and inferior vena cava. The right kidney is usually a few centimetres lower because the liver lies above it. Both kidneys rise and descend several centimetres with respiration.

Each kidney contains approximately 1 million nephrons. There is a rich blood supply (20–25% of cardiac output)

although there is considerable physiological variation in this. Intralobular branches of the renal artery give rise to the glomerular afferent arterioles. Variations in the calibre of the afferent and efferent arterioles control the filtration pressure at the glomerular basement membrane (GBM). This is normally tightly regulated in order to maintain a constant glomerular filtration rate (GFR) despite varying systemic blood pressure and renal perfusion pressure. In response to a reduction in perfusion pressure, constriction of the efferent arteriole restores filtration pressure. The efferent arteriole's response is dependent on angiotensin II production. The efferent arteriole goes on to supply the distal nephron and medulla.

The glomerulus contains three main cell types (see Fig. 14.1D). The GBM is produced by fusion of the basement membranes of epithelial and endothelial cells. Both of these cells are specialised in structure and function. The glomerular capillary endothelial cells contain pores (fenestrae) which allow access of circulating molecules to the underlying GBM. On the outer side of the GBM, glomerular epithelial cells (podocytes) put out multiple long foot processes which interdigitate with those of adjacent epithelial cells. These are non-dividing cells whose integrity is critical to the structure and function of the glomerulus. The death of a podocyte may lead to adhesion of the underlying GBM to Bowman's capsule, followed by the formation of a focal glomerular scar. The normal filtration barrier (see Fig. 14.1E) requires integrity of the junctions between the epithelial cells, the epithelial slit diaphragm apparatus, as well as the GBM itself, and these structures are responsible for the size limit to glomerular filtration. The filtration barrier at the glomerulus is normally almost absolute to proteins the size of albumin (67 kDa) or larger, with those of 20 kDa or smaller able to filter freely. Between these sizes there is a gradient of clearance, the behaviour of individual molecules being influenced by their shape and charge. Anionic (negatively charged) proteins are relatively less freely filtered than cationic proteins. Little lipid is filtered.

Mesangial cells lie in the central region of the glomerulus. They have similarities to vascular smooth muscle cells (e.g. contractility), but also some macrophage-like properties. In health, bone marrow-derived macrophages are occasionally found in glomeruli and in the interstitium.

Tubular cells are polarised, with a brush border (proximal tubular cells) and specialised functions at both their basal and their apical surfaces. Regionally, in the proximal convoluted tubule (PCT), thick ascending limb of the loop of Henle (TAL), distal convoluted tubule (DCT) and collecting duct (CD) they serve distinct functions, and carry a specific complement of transporter, channel and receptor molecules (see Fig. 9.3, p. 274). Interstitial cells between tubules are less well understood. Fibroblast-like cells in the cortex are capable of producing erythropoietin in response to hypoxia. In the medulla, lipid-laden interstitial cells are believed to be important in prostaglandin production.

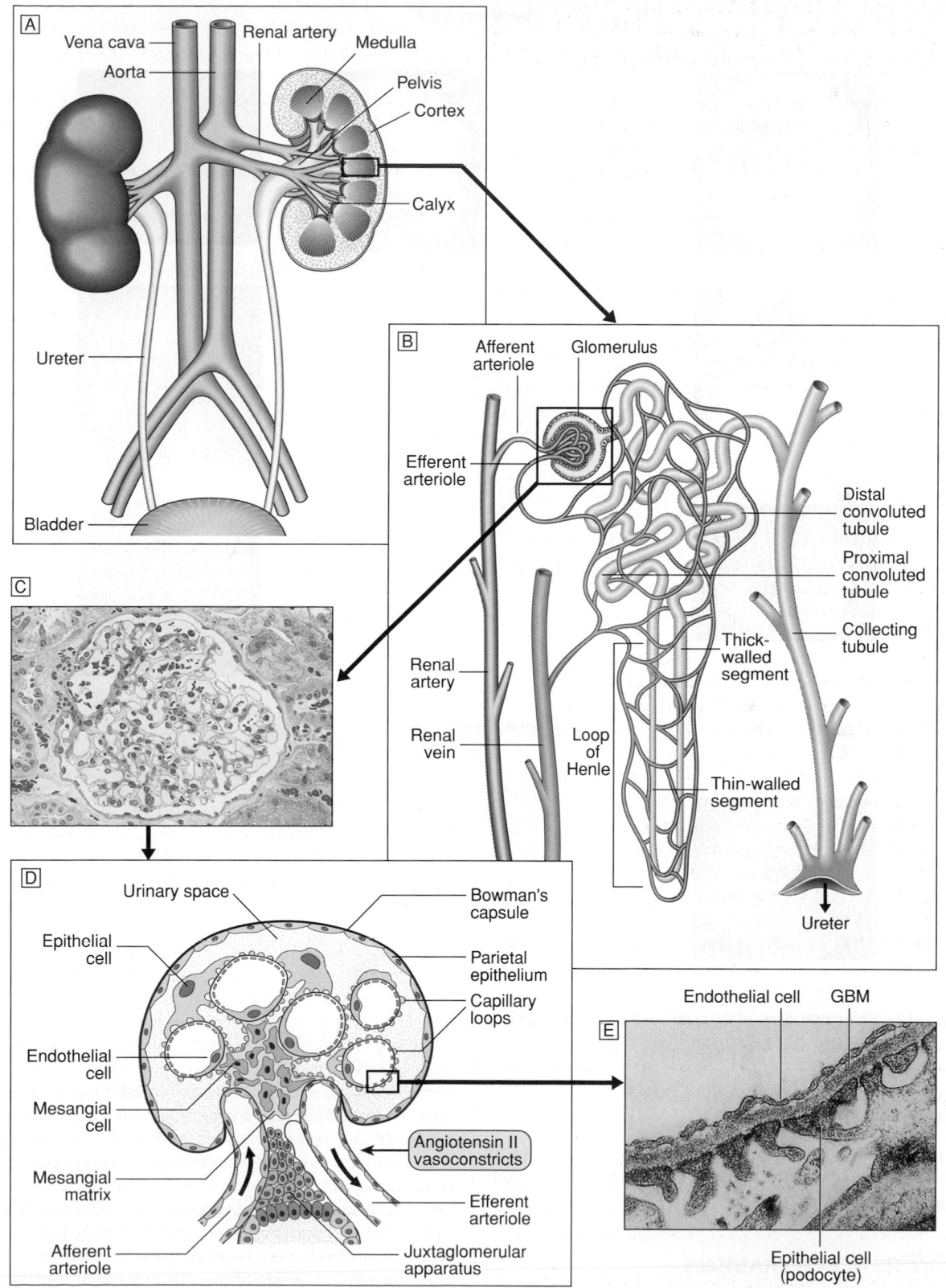

Fig. 14.1   Functional anatomy of the kidney. [A] Anatomical relationships of the kidney. [B] A single nephron. For the functions of different segments, see Figure 9.3, page 274. [C] Histology of a normal glomerulus. [D] Schematic cross-section of a glomerulus showing five capillary loops, to illustrate structure and show cell types. [E] Electron micrograph of the filtration barrier. (GBM = glomerular basement membrane)

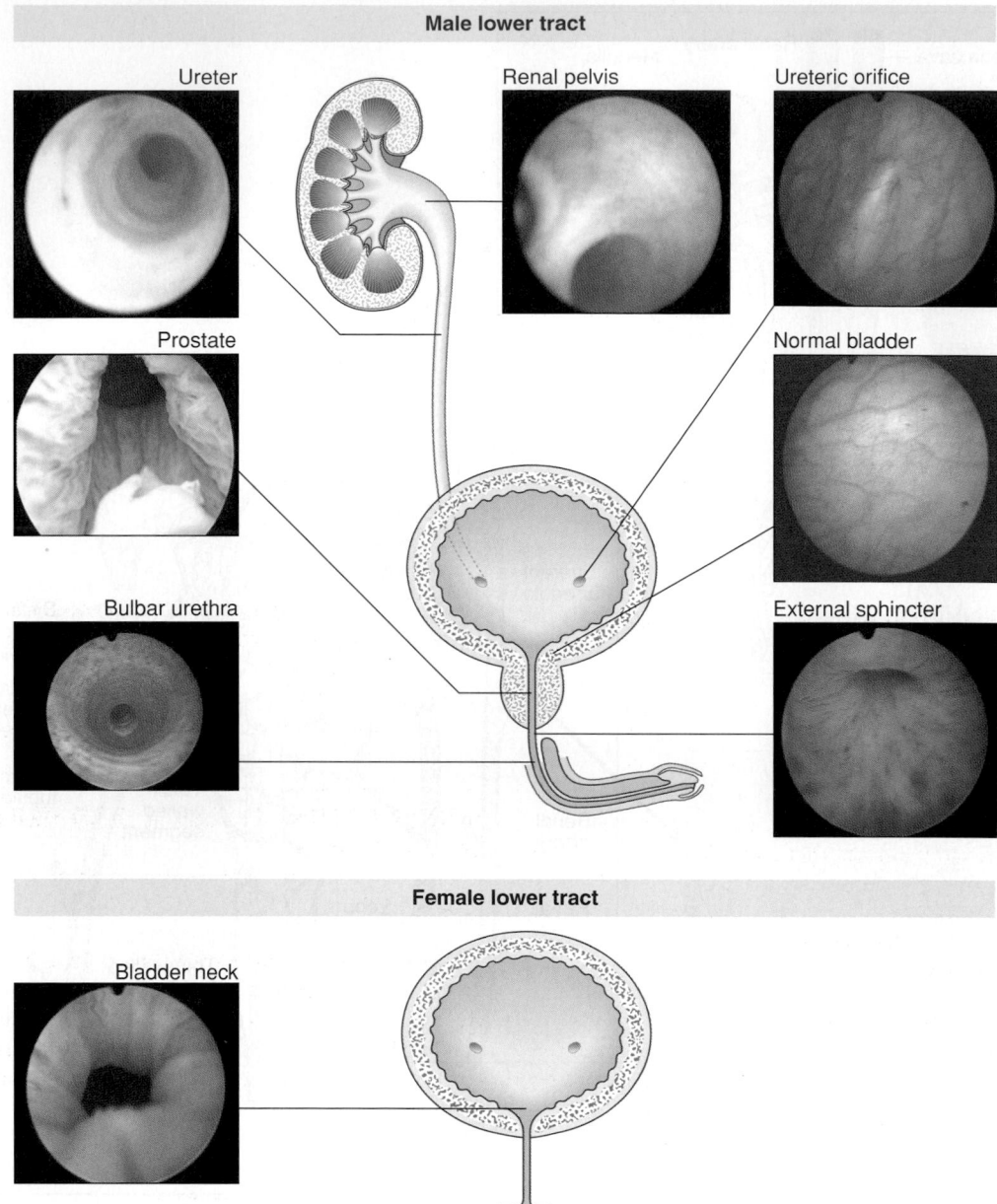

Fig. 14.2 Endoscopic views of the upper and lower urinary tract.

COLLECTING SYSTEM AND LOWER URINARY TRACT

This part of the urinary system is illustrated in Figure 14.2. It is subject to a variety of congenital anomalies, as outlined on page 608.

CONTINENCE MECHANISMS

Continence is dependent on the anatomical structures shown in Figure 14.2 and also on neurological and muscle (sphincter and detrusor) function. Parasympathetic nerves arising from S2–4 supply the detrusor muscle. These cholinergic nerves stimulate detrusor contraction, resulting in micturition. Sympathetic nerves arising from T10–L2 relay in the pelvic ganglia before reaching the detrusor and bladder neck. Stimulation of these noradrenergic nerves produces detrusor relaxation (via β-adrenoceptors) and contraction of the bladder neck (via α-adrenoceptors). This assists urine storage and continence during bladder filling. The distal sphincter mechanism is innervated from the sacral segments S2–4 by somatic motor fibres which reach the sphincter either by the pelvic plexus or via the pudendal nerves.

Afferent sensory impulses pass to the cerebral cortex which suppresses detrusor contractions. Their main function is to inhibit micturition until it is appropriate.

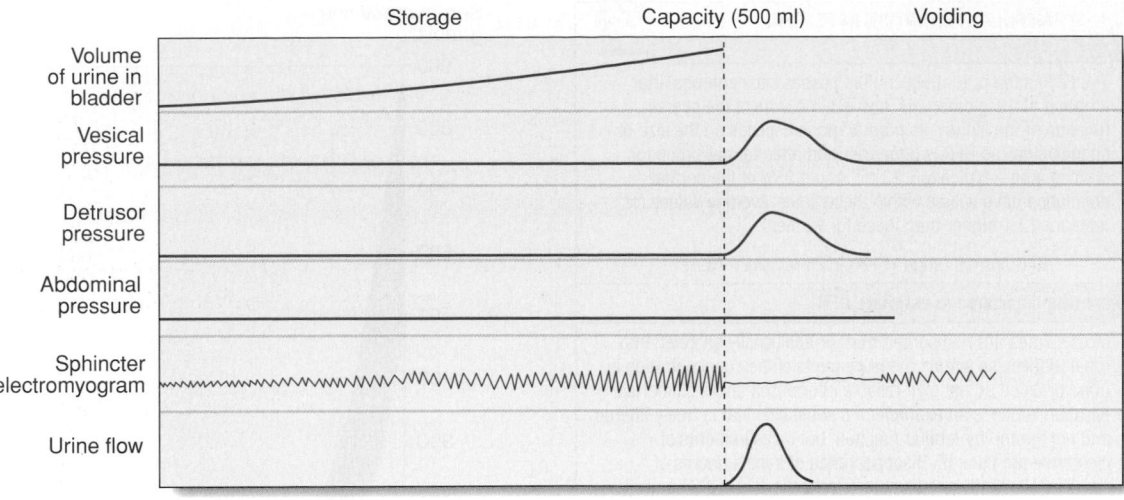

Fig. 14.3   Normal micturition cycle.

The micturition cycle

Storage (filling) phase

Due to the high compliance of the detrusor muscle the bladder fills steadily without a rise in intravesical pressure. As bladder volume increases, stretch receptors in its wall cause reflex bladder relaxation and increased sphincter tone. At approximately 75% bladder capacity there is a desire to void. Voluntary control is now exerted over the desire to void, which disappears temporarily. Compliance of the detrusor allows further increase in capacity until the next desire to void. Just how often this desire needs to be inhibited depends on many factors, not the least of which is finding a suitable place in which to void.

Voiding (micturition) phase

The act of micturition is initiated first by voluntary and then by reflex relaxation of the pelvic floor and distal sphincter mechanism, followed by reflex detrusor contraction. These actions are coordinated by the pontine micturition centre. Intravesical pressure remains greater than urethral pressure until the bladder is empty. Disorders of micturition may therefore be structural or neurogenic.

The normal micturition cycle is illustrated in Figure 14.3.

INVESTIGATION OF RENAL AND URINARY TRACT DISEASE

TESTS OF FUNCTION

Blood urea is a poor guide to renal function as it varies with protein intake, liver metabolic capacity and renal perfusion (see Fig. 14.4). Serum creatinine is a more reliable guide as it is produced from muscle at a constant rate and almost completely filtered at the glomerulus. As very little creatinine is secreted by tubular cells, the creatinine clearance

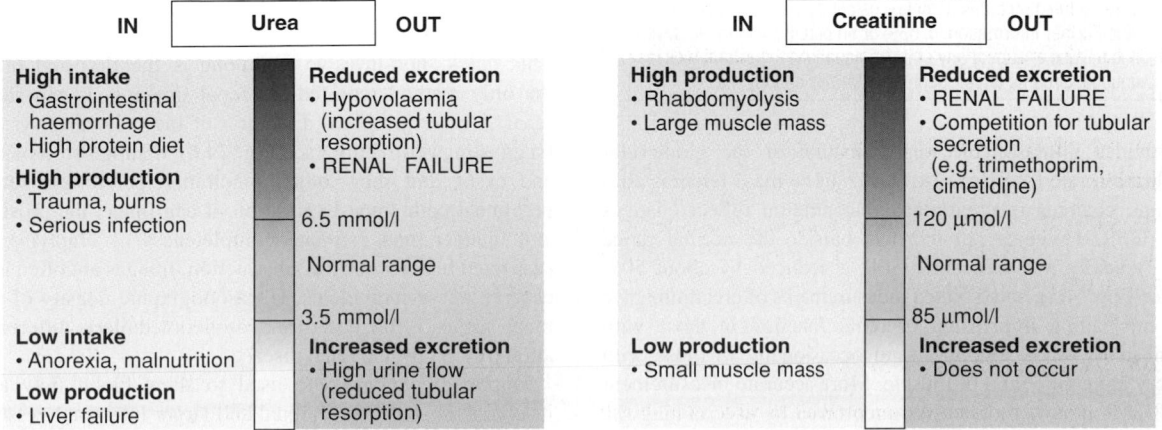

Fig. 14.4   Factors affecting blood levels of urea and creatinine. Factors affecting intake and production are shown to the left ('in'); those affecting excretion are shown to the right ('out'). Creatinine intake is omitted here as dietary creatinine (from meat) only rarely influences blood levels.

14.1 GLOMERULAR FILTRATION RATE (GFR)

- The GFR is the rate at which fluid passes into nephrons after filtration at the glomerulus, and is a measure of the overall function of the kidney. Its normal range depends on the size of an individual, so GFR is often reported after normalisation for surface area—typically 1.73 m^2. About 95% of the normal population have values within these limits. Average values for men are 12% higher than those for women:

    GFR normal range = 120 ± 25 ml/min/1.73 m^2

Measuring clearance to estimate GFR

- Most solutes are reabsorbed from or additionally secreted into renal tubules, so simple measurements of their concentration in urine or blood do not give reliable information about glomerular filtration. Inulin is an example of a substance that is freely filtered and not altered by tubular function, but measurements of clearance are difficult. Disappearance of trace amounts of radio-labelled ethylenediamine-tetraacetic acid (EDTA) from the blood can be measured more simply
- Creatinine clearance (CrCl) is relatively simple to measure, as no injections are required; measurements of serum concentration and the amount of creatinine in a 24-hour urine collection are needed. It is calculated as follows (care with units is required:

$$CrCl \text{ [mls/min]} = \frac{\text{amount of creatinine in urine [µmols]}}{\text{concentration in plasma [µmols/l]}} \times \frac{1000}{1440}$$

[1000 converts litres to mls; 1440 converts 24 hours to minutes]

However, CrCl exaggerates GFR when renal function is poor and may be affected by drugs that alter tubular creatinine secretion (e.g. trimethoprim, cimetidine). Its reliability also depends on accurate urine collection

Equations

- Equations have been shown to be a reliable and consistent way of assessing GFR from serum creatinine alone. The Cockcroft and Gault equation is widely used, and is reasonably accurate at normal to moderate renal function. However, it was designed to estimate CrCl, not GFR. Better equations have been developed for poorer levels of function (e.g. creatinine > 180 µmol/l):

    CrCl (Cockcroft and Gault) =

$$\frac{(140 - \text{age}) \times \text{lean body weight (kg)} \times (1.22 \text{ males } or \text{ } 1.04 \text{ females})}{\text{serum creatinine (µmol/l)}}$$

The Modification of Diet in Renal Disease (MDRD) study equation is particularly well proven in 'standard' patients at varying levels of renal function but is complex; calculators are available on-line (see Further information, p. 639) or on portable electronic devices. It is unwise to expect any of these equations to perform well in unusual circumstances, such as extremes of body mass

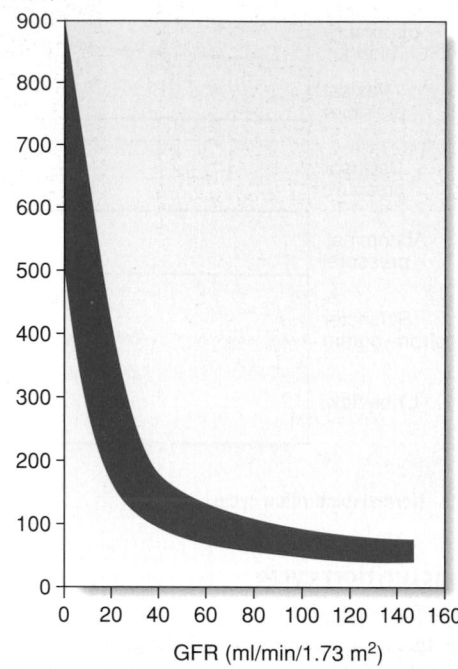

Fig. 14.5 Serum creatinine and the glomerular filtration rate (GFR). The inverse reciprocal relationship between GFR and serum creatinine is shown for a group of patients with renal disease. The red band indicates the range of values obtained. Note that some individuals have a GFR as low as 30–40 ml/min without serum creatinine rising out of the normal range.

Tests of tubular function, including concentrating ability, ability to excrete a water load and ability to excrete acid, are valuable in some circumstances.

IMAGING TECHNIQUES

Plain radiographs may show the renal outlines if perinephric fat and bowel gas shadows permit. Opaque calculi and calcification within the renal tract may also be shown.

Ultrasound

This quick, non-invasive technique is the first and often the only method required for renal imaging. It can show renal size and position, dilatation of the collecting system (suggesting obstruction, see Fig. 14.6), distinguish tumours and cysts, and show other abdominal, pelvic and retroperitoneal pathology. In addition, it can image the prostate and bladder, and estimate completeness of emptying in suspected bladder outflow obstruction. Images are often less clear in obese individuals. Ultrasonographic density of the renal cortex is increased and corticomedullary differentiation lost in chronic renal disease.

Doppler techniques are used to show blood flow and its characteristics in extrarenal and larger intrarenal vessels. The resistivity index is the ratio of peak systolic and diastolic velocities, and is influenced by the resistance to flow through small intrarenal arteries. It may be elevated in

provides a reasonable approximation of the glomerular filtration rate (see Box. 14.1). If muscle mass remains constant, changes in creatinine concentration reflect changes in GFR. However, an increase outside the normal range is typically not seen until GFR is reduced by about 50% (see Fig. 14.5), and isolated measurements of creatinine give a misleading impression of renal function in those with unusually small amounts (and occasionally in those with very large amounts) of muscle. More accurate measurement of GFR is now most easily undertaken by ascertaining the clearance of ^{51}Cr-labelled ethylenediamine-tetraacetic acid (EDTA). This has largely replaced estimation of inulin clearance in clinical practice.

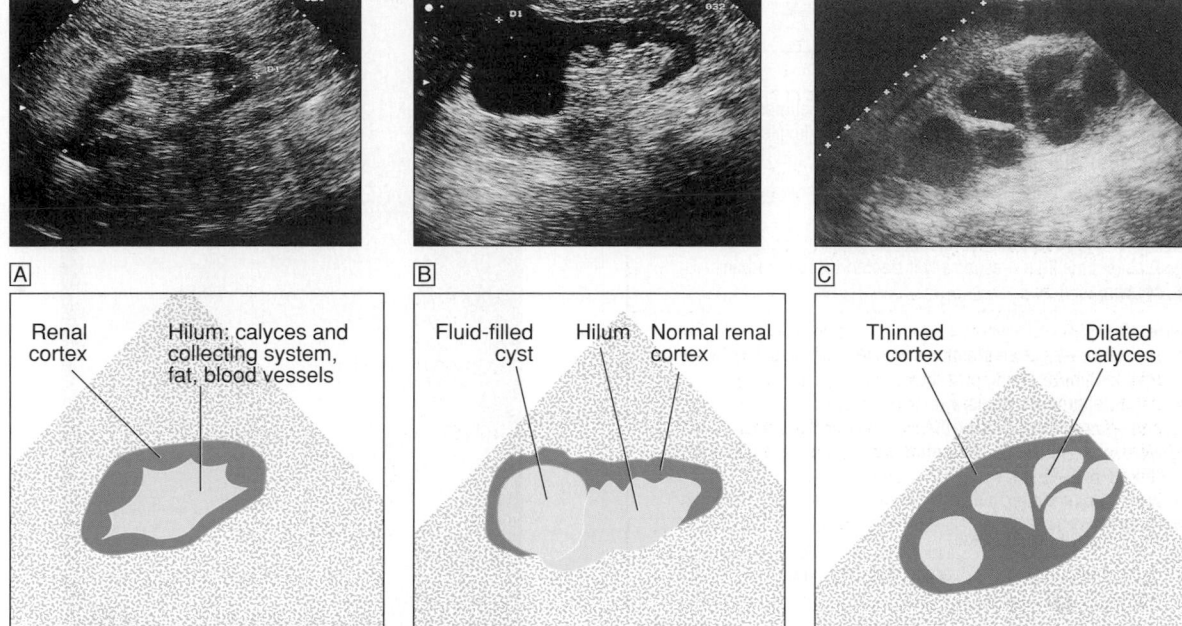

Fig. 14.6   Renal ultrasound. [A] Normal kidney. The normal cortex is less echo-dense (blacker) than the adjacent liver. [B] A simple cyst occupies the upper pole of an otherwise normal kidney. [C] The renal pelvis and calyces are dilated by a chronic obstruction to urinary outflow. The thinness and increased density of the remaining renal cortex indicate chronicity.

various diseases, including acute glomerulonephritis and rejection of a renal transplant. While severe renal artery stenosis causes damping of flow in intrarenal vessels, with high peak velocities, to date ultrasound has not proved to be a reliable technique for detecting renal artery stenosis.

The disadvantages of renal ultrasound are that it is operator-dependent and that the printed images convey only a fraction of the information gained by performing the investigation in real time.

Intravenous urography (IVU)

While intravenous urography has been largely replaced by ultrasound for routine renal imaging, this technique provides excellent definition of the collecting system and ureters, and remains superior to ultrasound for examining renal papillae, stones and urothelial malignancy (see Fig. 14.7). Radiographs are taken at intervals following administration of an intravenous bolus of an iodine-containing compound that is excreted by the kidney. An early image (1 minute

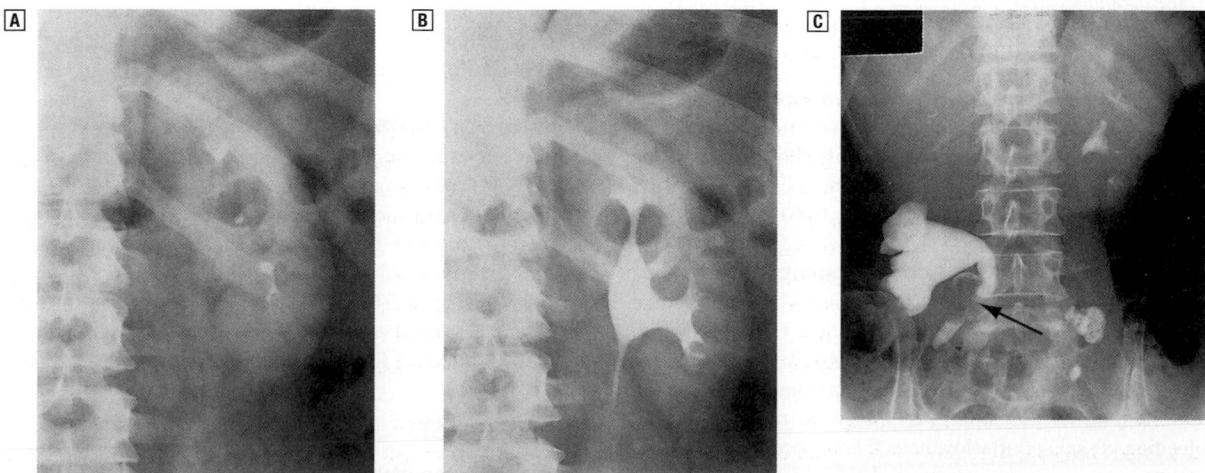

Fig. 14.7   Intravenous urograms. [A] Nephrogram phase at 1 minute. [B] Collecting system at 5 minutes. [C] Intravenous urogram showing a later view of a normal collecting system on the patient's left, with obstruction of the right system by a transitional cell carcinoma of the upper ureter, shown as a filling defect (arrow).

14.2 RENAL COMPLICATIONS OF RADIOLOGICAL INVESTIGATIONS

Contrast nephrotoxicity

- An acute deterioration in renal function, sometimes life-threatening, commencing within 24 hrs of administration of i.v. radiographic contrast media

Risk factors
- Pre-existing renal impairment
- Use of high-osmolality contrast media
- Diabetes mellitus—especially if treated with metformin
- Myeloma

Prevention
- Hydration—e.g. free oral fluids plus i.v. isotonic saline 500 ml then 250 ml/hr during procedure
- Avoid nephrotoxic drugs; withhold non-steroidal anti-inflammatory drugs (NSAIDs); omit metformin for 48 hrs
- Most other measures are ineffective or increase (e.g. diuretics) the risk
- If the risks are high, consider alternative methods of imaging

Cholesterol atheroembolism

- Typically follows days to weeks after intra-arterial investigations—see page 611

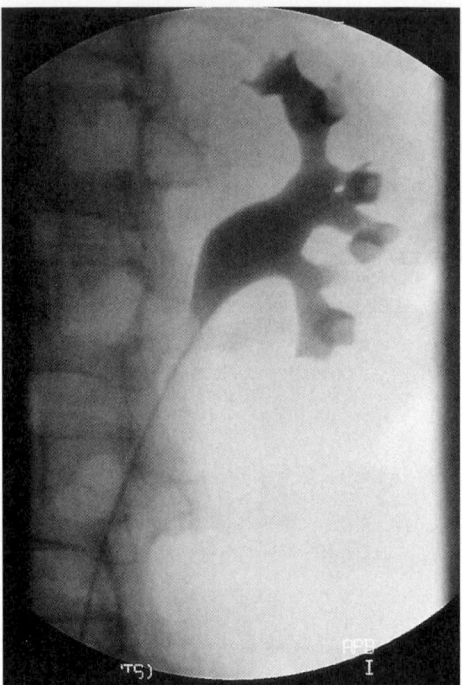

Fig. 14.8 Retrograde pyelography. The best views of the normal collecting system are shown by pyelography. A catheter has been passed into the left renal pelvis at cystoscopy. The anemone-like calyces are sharp-edged and normal. (Compare with the obstructed system shown in Figure 14.7C.)

after injection) will demonstrate the nephrogram phase of renal perfusion in patients with an adequate renal arterial supply. This is followed by contrast filling the collecting system, ureters and bladder. The disadvantages of this technique are the need for an injection, time requirement, dependence on adequate renal function for good images, and risk of exposure to contrast medium (see Box 14.2).

Pyelography

Pyelography (direct injection of contrast medium into the collecting system from above or below) offers the best views of the collecting system and upper tract, and is commonly used to identify the cause of urinary tract obstruction (see p. 590). Antegrade pyelography requires the insertion of a fine needle into the pelvicalyceal system under ultrasound or radiographic control. Contrast is injected to outline the collecting system, and particularly to localise the site of obstruction. This approach is much more difficult and hazardous in a non-obstructed kidney. In the presence of obstruction, percutaneous nephrostomy drainage can be established, and often stents can be passed through any obstruction. Retrograde pyelography can be performed by inserting catheters into the ureteric orifices at cystoscopy (see Fig. 14.8).

Renal arteriography and venography

The main indication for renal arteriography is to investigate suspected renal artery stenosis (see p. 609) or haemorrhage. In the absence of computed tomography it is also valuable for defining renal tumours. Therapeutic balloon dilatation and stenting of the renal artery may be undertaken, and bleeding vessels or arteriovenous fistulae occluded.

Computed tomography (CT)

While not routinely of greater value than ultrasound, CT is particularly useful for characterising mass lesions within the

kidney (see Fig. 14.40, p. 635), or combinations of cysts with masses. It gives clearer definition of the retroperitoneal anatomy and, unlike ultrasound, is aided by increased amounts of fat.

Spiral CT is a rapid-sequence technique, with images obtained immediately following a large bolus injection of intravenous contrast media to outline vascular structures. It produces high-quality images of the main renal vessels and, when used to screen for possible renal artery stenosis in secondary hypertension, has the advantage of providing renal and adrenal images at the same time. It is also a very useful technique for demonstrating renal stones.

Magnetic resonance imaging (MRI)

MRI offers excellent resolution and distinction between different tissues. Magnetic resonance angiography (MRA) uses gadolinium-based contrast media which are non-nephrotoxic, and avoids the risk of atheroemboli. It can produce good images of main renal vessels. These techniques are likely to develop further and find an important role in non-invasive screening for renal artery stenosis. The relative places of spiral CT and MRA for this condition have yet to be defined.

SPECIAL TESTS

Radionuclide studies

These studies require the injection of gamma ray-emitting radiopharmaceuticals which are taken up and excreted by the kidney, a process which can be monitored by an external

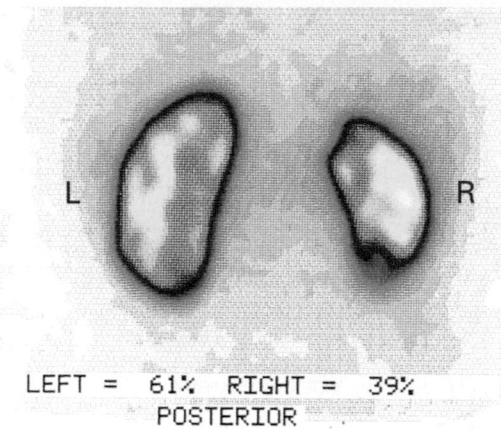

Fig. 14.9 DMSA isotope renogram. A posterior view is shown of a normal left kidney and a small right kidney (with evidence of cortical scarring at upper and lower poles) which contributes only 39% of total renal function.

gamma camera. In this way, the function of individual kidneys can be assessed.

Diethylenetriamine-pentaacetic acid labelled with technetium (^{99m}Tc-DTPA) is excreted by glomerular filtration. Following injection of DTPA, computer analysis of uptake and excretion can be used to provide information regarding the arterial perfusion of each kidney. In renal artery stenosis, transit time is prolonged, peak activity delayed and excretion reduced. In less severe but still significant stenosis, a single dose of an angiotensin-converting enzyme (ACE) inhibitor ('captopril renography') can, by inhibiting the compensatory efferent glomerular arteriolar constriction induced by angiotensin II, induce these changes in a kidney that previously perfused normally, although this is not a reliable enough technique for screening. In patients with significant obstruction of the outflow tract, persistence of the nuclide in the renal pelvis is seen (see Fig. 14.12, p. 591), and a loop diuretic fails to accelerate its disappearance.

Dimercaptosuccinic acid labelled with technetium (^{99m}Tc-DMSA) is filtered by glomeruli and partially bound to proximal tubular cells. Following intravenous injection, images of the renal cortex show the shape, size and function of each kidney (see Fig. 14.9). This is a sensitive method of demonstrating early cortical scarring that is of particular value in children with vesico-ureteric reflux and pyelonephritis. It is also possible to assess the relative contribution of each kidney to total function.

Renal biopsy

Renal biopsy is used to establish the nature and extent of renal disease in order to judge the prognosis and need for treatment. The indications, contraindications and complications are given in Box 14.3. The procedure is performed with ultrasound guidance to ensure accurate needle placement into a renal pole. Radiographic screening after contrast administration or other methods may also be used. Light microscopy, electron microscopy and immunohistological assessment of the specimen may all be required.

14.3 RENAL BIOPSY
Indications
• Acute renal failure that is not adequately explained • Chronic renal failure with normal-sized kidneys • Nephrotic syndrome or glomerular proteinuria in adults • Nephrotic syndrome in children that has atypical features or is not responding to treatment • Isolated haematuria with renal characteristics or associated abnormalities
Contraindications
• Disordered coagulation or thrombocytopenia • Uncontrolled hypertension • Kidneys < 60% predicted size • Solitary kidney (except transplants) (relative contraindication)
Complications
• Pain, usually mild • Bleeding into urine, usually minor but may produce clot colic and obstruction • Bleeding around the kidney, occasionally massive and requiring angiography with intervention, or surgery • Arteriovenous fistula, rarely clinically significant

MAJOR MANIFESTATIONS OF RENAL AND URINARY TRACT DISEASE

GENERAL MANIFESTATIONS OF RENAL DISEASE

The broad categories of renal and urinary tract disease, and the typical manifestations that they may cause, are indicated in Figure 14.10. Symptoms related directly to the kidneys are uncommon in intrinsic or pre-renal disorders, and identification of such diseases is further complicated by the fact that loss of renal function is, with some exceptions, only recognised clinically at a late stage. Exceptions include the polyuria or sodium-wasting of some tubular disorders. More commonly, sodium retention and fluid imbalance lead to hypertension and oedema.

While non-inflammatory and subacute inflammatory/proliferative glomerular disorders may present with substantial proteinuria resulting in nephrotic syndrome (see p. 589), inflammatory glomerular disorders more typically cause haematuria in association with early signs of disturbed renal function, such as hypertension.

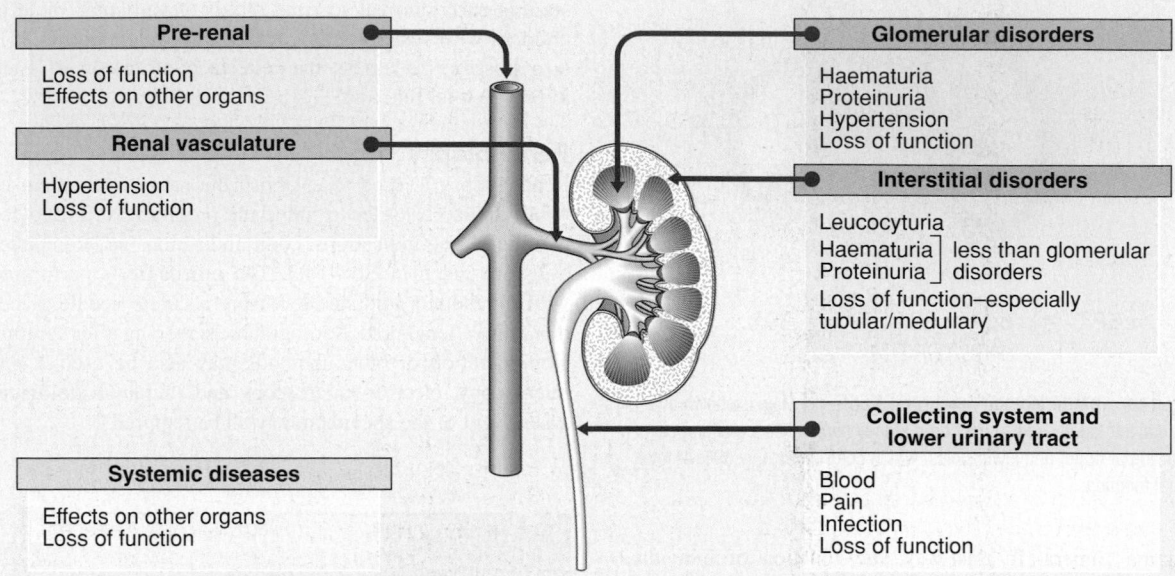

Fig. 14.10 Manifestations of renal and urinary tract disease.

If progressive, obvious signs of impaired excretion of water and solutes develop. The onset of these features in close succession has been described as the nephritic syndrome (see Box 14.6), but in pure form this condition is seen rarely, except in countries where post-infectious glomerulonephritis is common. Mixed inflammatory and nephrotic features are more common. It is important to recognise such disease, especially if renal impairment is progressing, as the inflammatory group includes some of the most treatable renal disorders.

Hypertension is a very common feature of renal parenchymal and vascular disease. Renal mechanisms are also likely to be important in essential hypertension. Most inherited causes of disordered blood pressure have been attributed to altered salt and water handling by the kidney. Hypertension is an early feature of glomerular disorders. In interstitial disorders, sodium loss (through reduced reabsorption from glomerular filtrate) may lead to hypotension. However, as GFR declines, hypertension becomes an increasingly common feature, regardless of the aetiology of the renal disease. When renal function is replaced by dialysis, control of hypertension often becomes easier as salt and volume balance are controlled. Obsessional attention to fluid balance in haemodialysis patients may reduce or remove the need for hypotensive drugs. Control of hypertension is very important in those with renal impairment because of its close relationship with further decline of renal function (see p. 391).

URINARY ABNORMALITIES

DISORDERS OF URINE VOLUME

Urine volume gives a poor guide to renal function unless it is inappropriate to the circumstances. On a normal diet, between 300 and 500 ml/day are needed to excrete solutes at maximum concentration. Complete anuria suggests either an acute vascular event or total urinary obstruction; even in the most severe intrinsic renal disorders some urine is usually still produced. Polyuria, which refers to the production of an excess volume of urine (> 3 l/day), may have a number of causes (see Box 14.4). Oliguria is discussed on pages 594–595.

14.4 CAUSES OF POLYURIA

- Excess fluid intake
- Osmotic, e.g. hyperglycaemia
- Cranial diabetes insipidus (loss of antidiuretic hormone—ADH) —see page 744
- Nephrogenic diabetes insipidus (tubular dysfunction)
  Genetic tubular cell defects: ADH receptor, aquaporin mutations
  Drugs/toxins: lithium, diuretics, hypercalcaemia
  Interstitial renal disease (see p. 618)

HAEMATURIA

Haematuria may indicate bleeding from anywhere in the renal tract (see Fig. 14.11). Dipstick tests are very sensitive and can identify all significant bleeding. Microscopy shows that normal individuals have occasional red cells in the urine, and positive tests may occur during menstruation, but persistent haematuria requires explanation, particularly in older age groups or others at risk of carcinoma of the bladder or other malignancy (see EBM panel). Macroscopic (visible) haematuria is particularly likely to be caused by tumours (see pp. 634–636). Urine microscopy (see p. 577) can be valuable in establishing the cause of bleeding. The presence of white blood cells and organisms may suggest infection; the presence of red cell casts indicates glomerular bleeding; a high proportion of dysmorphic erythrocytes (best seen by phase-contrast microscopy) likewise supports glomerular bleeding. In the absence of evidence of intrinsic renal disease, however, urological tract investigations should come first, at least in patients over 35 years of age.

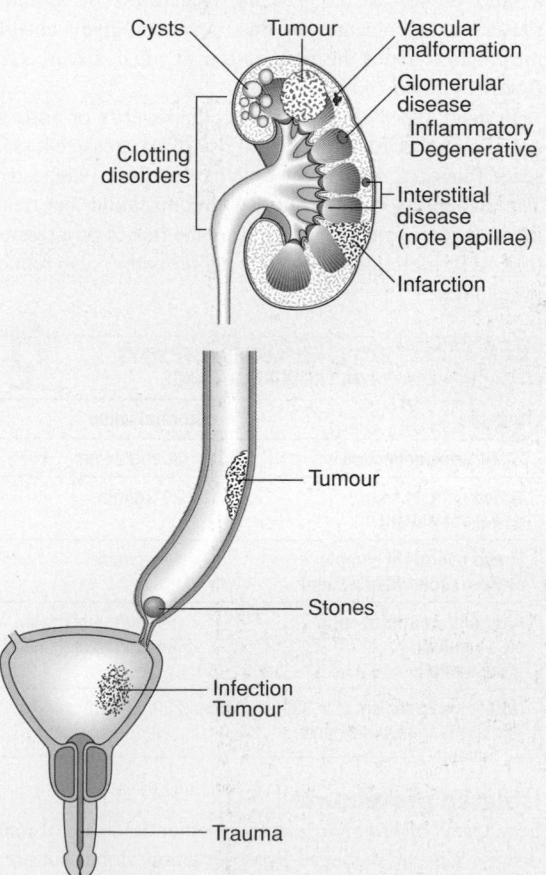

Fig. 14.11 Causes of haematuria. See Box 14.5 for other causes of red or dark urine.

ISOLATED HAEMATURIA—malignancy as an important cause

'In a large series of patients investigated for haematuria, 13% had urinary tract infections, 12% had bladder cancer and 2% had unsuspected renal stones. No basis for it was found in 61%. The likelihood of renal disease is low unless there are associated features, notably proteinuria, raised serum creatinine or hypertension.'

- Khadra MH, Pickard RS, Charlton M, et al. A prospective analysis of 1930 patients with hematuria to evaluate current diagnostic practice. J Urology 2000; 163:524–527.

Further information: 🖥 www.sign.ac.uk
🖥 www.edren.org

Glomerular bleeding implies that the GBM is fractured. It may be seen physiologically following very strenuous exertion. Other causes of red or dark urine may sometimes be confused with haematuria (see Box 14.5). If haematuria occurs with pointers to renal disease, further investigations should be directed towards looking for inflammatory renal disease, usually including renal biopsy. As noted, haematuria is an important feature of patients with the nephritic syndrome (see Box 14.6).

Isolated microscopic haematuria

Where there are no features of significant renal disease (no hypertension, normal renal function, insignificant amounts of protein in the urine) and malignancy has been excluded, patients with isolated microscopic haematuria may be managed by observation alone. Although this scenario occasionally gives warning of significant renal disease (e.g. Alport's syndrome, IgA nephropathy), it is commonly caused by the usually benign condition of thin GBM disease (see p. 612), insignificant vascular

14.5 CAUSES OF RED OR DARK URINE

- Haematuria
- Haemoglobinuria: red urine, stick test for blood positive, but no red cells on microscopy
- Myoglobinuria: in rhabdomyolysis. Very dark or black urine. Stick test for blood positive, but no red cells on microscopy
- Food dyes: beetroot (anthocyanins)
- Drugs: phenolphthalein (pink when alkaline), senna and other anthraquinones (orange), rifampicin (orange), levodopa (darkens on standing)
- Porphyria (urine turns dark on standing; see p. 325)
- Alkaptonuria

14.6 NEPHRITIC SYNDROME *

- Haematuria (brown urine)
- Oedema and generalised fluid retention
- Hypertension
- Oliguria

* Classically seen in post-infectious glomerulonephritis. In its complete form it may also be seen in acute IgA nephropathy and occasionally in other types of glomerulonephritis, although some features of it are common to many types.

malformations, renal cysts or renal stones. In 'loin pain-haematuria' syndrome, benign glomerular bleeding is associated with loin pain. Recurrent episodes of gross haematuria in association with respiratory infections are characteristic of IgA nephropathy (see p. 616).

PROTEINURIA

Patients are usually unaware of proteinuria, although it may make urine froth easily. Moderate amounts of low molecular weight protein are normally filtered at the glomerulus. These proteins are normally reabsorbed by tubular cells so that less than 150 mg/day should appear in the urine. Low molecular weight proteins appearing in the urine in larger quantities than this point to failure of reabsorption by damaged tubular cells, i.e. tubular proteinuria. This can be demonstrated by analysis of the size of excreted proteins or by specific assays for such proteins (e.g. β_2-microglobulin, molecular weight 12 kDa). The amounts of such protein rarely exceed 1.5–2 g/24 hrs, and proteinuria greater than this almost always indicates significant glomerular disease.

Glomerular lesions allow filtration of larger serum proteins. The presence of albumin in the urine is a sure sign of glomerular abnormality. Albumin is the dominant serum protein, with a molecular weight of 67 kDa. Assays for this protein can identify the very early stages of glomerular disease in disorders with a predictably progressive course, such as diabetic nephropathy.

Persistent microalbuminuria (below amounts detectable by dipstick testing) has also been associated with an increased risk of atherosclerosis and other diseases; neither the mechanism of proteinuria nor an explanation of these associations has yet been found.

Relatively minor leakage of albumin into the urine may also occur transiently after vigorous exercise, during fever, in heart failure, and in some other disease states, accounting for some positive stick tests in these circumstances. Such proteinuria should not reach nephrotic levels (see Box 14.7), and tests should be repeated once the stimulus is no longer present. Occasionally, proteinuria occurs only during the day, and the first morning sample

is negative. In the absence of other signs of renal disease, such 'orthostatic proteinuria' is usually regarded as benign.

Patients with a clone of B lymphocytes secreting free immunoglobulin light chains (molecular weight 25 kDa) filter these freely into the urine, and Bence Jones protein can then be identified in fresh urine samples. This may occur in amyloidosis (see p. 328) and other plasma cell dyscrasias, but is particularly important as a marker for myeloma (see p. 943). Some light chains are toxic to tubular cells and contribute to the damage seen in myeloma. Bence Jones protein is poorly identified by stick tests for urinary protein; specific tests (e.g. immunoelectrophoresis) must be performed. The sulphosalicylic acid precipitation test is positive in Bence Jones proteinuria but is less sensitive.

Twenty-four-hour collections of urine are arduous and often inaccurate. Use of the protein/creatinine ratio in single samples makes allowance for the variable degree of urinary dilution. For an individual with an average muscle mass and normal rate of creatinine generation, a ratio of 120 (derived from [urine protein] in mg/1 divided by the [urine creatinine] in mmol/1) corresponds to a protein excretion rate of approximately 1 g/24 hrs, and a ratio of 400 to 3.5 g/24 hrs. Regardless of absolute muscle mass, changes in this ratio can give valuable information about the progression of renal disease (see Boxes 14.7 and 14.8).

In many types of renal disease, the severity of proteinuria is a marker for an increased risk of progressive loss of renal function, and direct toxicity has been suggested. The evidence for this is mostly circumstantial, but treatments that are effective at lowering the risk of progression (e.g. ACE inhibitors in diabetic nephropathy) also reduce proteinuria.

14.8 ALBUMIN EXCRETION: ALTERNATIVE WAYS OF EXPRESSING THE NORMAL RANGE

Sample	Normal value
24-hr urine collection	< 30 mg/24 hrs
Timed sample from ambulant patient	< 20 µg/min
Timed overnight sample or from recumbent patient	< 10 µg/min
Albumin/creatinine ratio on a random urine sample	< 2.5 mg/mmol (male) < 3.5 mg/mmol (female)

Note A measurement of > 300 mg/24 hrs (200 µg/min) represents frank proteinuria.

Isolated proteinuria

Low levels of proteinuria without other evidence of renal disease may be managed by observation alone, but are a marker for later development of hypertension and overt renal disease. Nephrotic levels of proteinuria, or lesser levels in the presence of haematuria, hypertension or renal impairment, are usually an indication for renal biopsy.

14.7 PROTEINURIA

Excretion rate	Protein/creatinine (mg/mmol)*	Significance
< 0.15 g/24 hrs	< 15	Normal
0.3–0.5 g/24 hrs	15–50	Stick tests positive
0.5–2 g/24 hrs	50–200	Source equivocal
> 2.5 g/24 hrs	> 300	Glomerular disease likely
> 3.5 g/24 hrs	> 400	Nephrotic range: always glomerular

* [Urine protein] (mg/l)/[urine creatinine] (mmol/l).

Nephrotic syndrome

When substantial amounts of protein are lost in the urine, a series of secondary phenomena occur. It is these that constitute the nephrotic syndrome, although they begin to occur at levels of proteinuria lower than 'nephrotic range' (3.5 g/24 hrs). One formal definition of the nephrotic syndrome requires a serum albumin < 30 g/l, evidence of fluid retention or oedema, and more than 3.5 g of proteinuria/day. The diseases that cause nephrotic syndrome always affect the glomerulus (see Box 14.9) and tend to be non-inflammatory, or subacute examples of inflammatory glomerulonephritis.

There are important age-related differences in the incidence of different causes. In neonates congenital aetiologies are most common. Minimal change nephropathy is the dominant diagnosis in older children in Caucasian races; focal and segmental glomerulosclerosis (FSGS) is common in black races. In later life there is a progressive increase in the incidence of membranous nephropathy and FSGS. Diabetes mellitus and amyloidosis rarely cause nephrotic syndrome in childhood.

The consequences and complications of the nephrotic syndrome are listed in Box 14.10. Oedema accumulates predominantly in the lower limbs in adults, extending to the genitalia and lower abdomen as it becomes more severe. In the morning, the upper limbs and face may be more affected. In children, ascites occurs early and oedema is often seen only in the face. Blood volume may be normal, reduced or increased. Avid renal sodium retention is an early and universal feature.

Management of nephrotic syndrome has four elements:

- Establish the cause.
- Treat the cause if possible.
- Treat the symptoms.
- Prevent complications.

In children with nephrotic syndrome, initial management includes administration of high-dose corticosteroids. In older patients, and in children where this therapy is unsuccessful, a renal biopsy is essential unless there is strong evidence for a specific aetiology (e.g. a long history of diabetes, with other microvascular complications and a demonstrated progression from microalbuminuria, and with hypertension but no haematuria).

Symptomatic oedema is controlled by diuretics and a low-sodium diet (no added salt). In severe nephrotic syndrome very large doses of combinations of diuretic acting on different parts of the nephron (e.g. loop diuretic plus thiazide plus amiloride) may be required. In occasional patients with evidence of hypovolaemia, intravenous salt-poor albumin infusions may help to establish a diuresis. Over-diuresis risks secondary impairment of renal function through hypovolaemia. Venous thromboembolism is guarded against by anticoagulation and there is a case for routine anticoagulation in all patients with chronic or severe nephrotic syndrome. Hypercholesterolaemia is common and treated with lipid-lowering drugs (e.g. HMG CoA reductase inhibitors, see p. 311). However, controlled trials have not been reported for this patient group. The risk of infection with pneumococci is especially high in children, who should be offered immunisation.

14.9 COMMON CAUSES OF NEPHROTIC SYNDROME

Non-inflammatory glomerulonephritis

- Minimal change nephropathy
- Focal and segmental glomerulosclerosis (FSGS)
- Membranous nephropathy

Proliferative/inflammatory glomerulonephritis

- Mesangiocapillary glomerulonephritis (MCGN)
- Systemic lupus erythematosus (SLE) (with a variety of histopathological types)
- Other 'subacute' proliferative nephritis

Systemic diseases

- Diabetic nephropathy
- Amyloidosis

14.10 CONSEQUENCES AND COMPLICATIONS OF NEPHROTIC SYNDROME

Oedema

- Caused by avid sodium retention and hypoalbuminaemia

Hypercoagulability

- Presumed relative loss of inhibitors of coagulation and excessive production of coagulation factors
- Venous thromboembolism is common and sometimes fatal

Hypercholesterolaemia

- High rate of arterial occlusions and disease

Infection

- Especially by pneumococci
- Associated with hypogammaglobulinaemia

OEDEMA

APPROACH TO THE PATIENT WITH OEDEMA

Oedema may form locally or generally. There are three mechanisms, each of which acts on the 'Starling forces' that maintain tissue fluid volumes. Box 14.11 lists these mechanisms and gives major examples of each. In developed countries the most common causes are local venous problems and heart failure, but it is important to differentiate the others.

It is easy to mistake the first signs of generalised oedema for a local problem. Firstly, substantial volumes (litres) of extracellular fluid (ECF) may accumulate without any clinical signs. In adults dependent regions or immobile limbs are usually the first site of oedema formation. Ankle-swelling is characteristic, but oedema

14.11 OEDEMA

Lowered oncotic pressure of blood

Characterised by low serum albumin (a representative of total serum proteins and the major serum protein) because of reduced synthesis or increased loss. Many of these conditions are also associated with avid sodium retention by the kidney. All cause generalised oedema that is worse in dependent regions:

- Liver failure—particular tendency to form ascites
- Nephrotic syndrome—urine testing will be strongly positive for protein
- Malnutrition or malabsorption

Increased capillary permeability

Leakage of proteins into the interstitium reduces the osmotic pressure gradient that draws fluid back into the lymphatics and blood:

- Locally with infection or inflammation
- Systemically in severe sepsis—probably related to circulating cytokines
- Drug-related—e.g. calcium channel blockers

Increased hydrostatic pressure

Increased hydrostatic pressure in veins or lymphatics reduces fluid return to the circulation. Venous pressure is generally high in heart failure or with volume (or sodium) overload:

Venous—high venous pressure or obstruction
- Deep venous thrombosis or venous insufficiency—causes local oedema
- Other local causes of obstruction—pregnancy, tumour
- Heart failure—common cause of generalised oedema
- Renal failure with intravascular volume expansion

Lymphatic—lymphatic obstruction
Termed lymphoedema when chronic. Characteristically non-pitting; always localised:

- Infection—filariasis, lymphogranuloma venereum (see pp. 73 and 104)
- Malignancy
- Radiation injury
- Congenital abnormality

develops over the sacrum in bed-bound patients. It rises higher up the lower limbs with increasing severity, to affect the genitalia and abdomen. Ascites is common and often an earlier feature in children or young adults, and in liver disease. Pleural effusions are common and can be a feature of any cause of generalised oedema. Facial oedema on waking is common in adults with low oncotic pressure oedema. Like ascites, it is a more common feature of oedema in young patients.

Lower limb oedema is common in morbid obesity. Although venous obstruction may often be a problem, it may also be multifactorial—for example, right heart failure caused by sleep apnoea.

Diagnosis

The cause of oedema is usually apparent quite quickly from the history and from examination of the cardiovascular and gastrointestinal systems, followed by testing the urine for protein. A serum albumin level is also relevant. Where ascites or pleural effusions in isolation are causing diagnostic difficulty, aspiration of fluid with measurement of protein and glucose, and microscopy for cells, will usually give the answer (see pleural effusion, p. 501).

Management

Where a specific cause is apparent (e.g. venous thrombosis) this should be treated. Diuretics are commonly used, but also commonly abused, for oedema. Where there is sodium retention and generalised oedema, restriction of sodium (and sometimes fluid) intake is rational, along with diuretic treatment. However, in oedema caused by venous or lymphatic obstruction or by inflammation, diuretics are likely to be hazardous, as they will cause hypovolaemia. Local treatments, such as the use of compression either continuously (e.g. compression stockings) or intermittently (with a mechanical device), can be useful in these circumstances.

Mild fluid retention will respond to a thiazide or to a low dose of a loop diuretic such as furosemide (frusemide) or bumetanide. Withdrawing therapy when the cause has resolved can lead to transient 'rebound' oedema. In nephrotic syndrome, renal failure and severe cardiac failure, very large doses of diuretics, sometimes in combination, may be required to achieve a negative sodium and fluid balance.

OBSTRUCTION OF THE URINARY TRACT

UPPER TRACT OBSTRUCTION

Obstruction to the upper renal tract may be due to extrinsic, intrinsic or intraluminal pathology in the renal pelvis or ureter. Stones within the renal pelvis (see p. 632) and congenital abnormality of the pelvi-ureteric junction (PUJ) are the main causes of obstruction. More rarely, a sloughed renal papilla, blood clot, tumour (see pp. 635–636, and Fig. 14.7, p. 583), retroperitoneal fibrosis or chronic infection may obstruct either kidney or ureter (see Fig. 14.12).

Renal stones
Renal stones are described on page 632.

Pelvi-ureteric junction obstruction (idiopathic hydronephrosis)
This results from a functional obstruction at the junction of the ureter and renal pelvis despite normal muscle cells on electron microscopy. The aetiology is obscure. The abnormality is likely to be congenital and is often bilateral. It can be seen in very young children, but gross hydronephrosis may present at any age.

The common presentation is ill-defined renal pain or ache exacerbated by drinking large volumes of liquid.

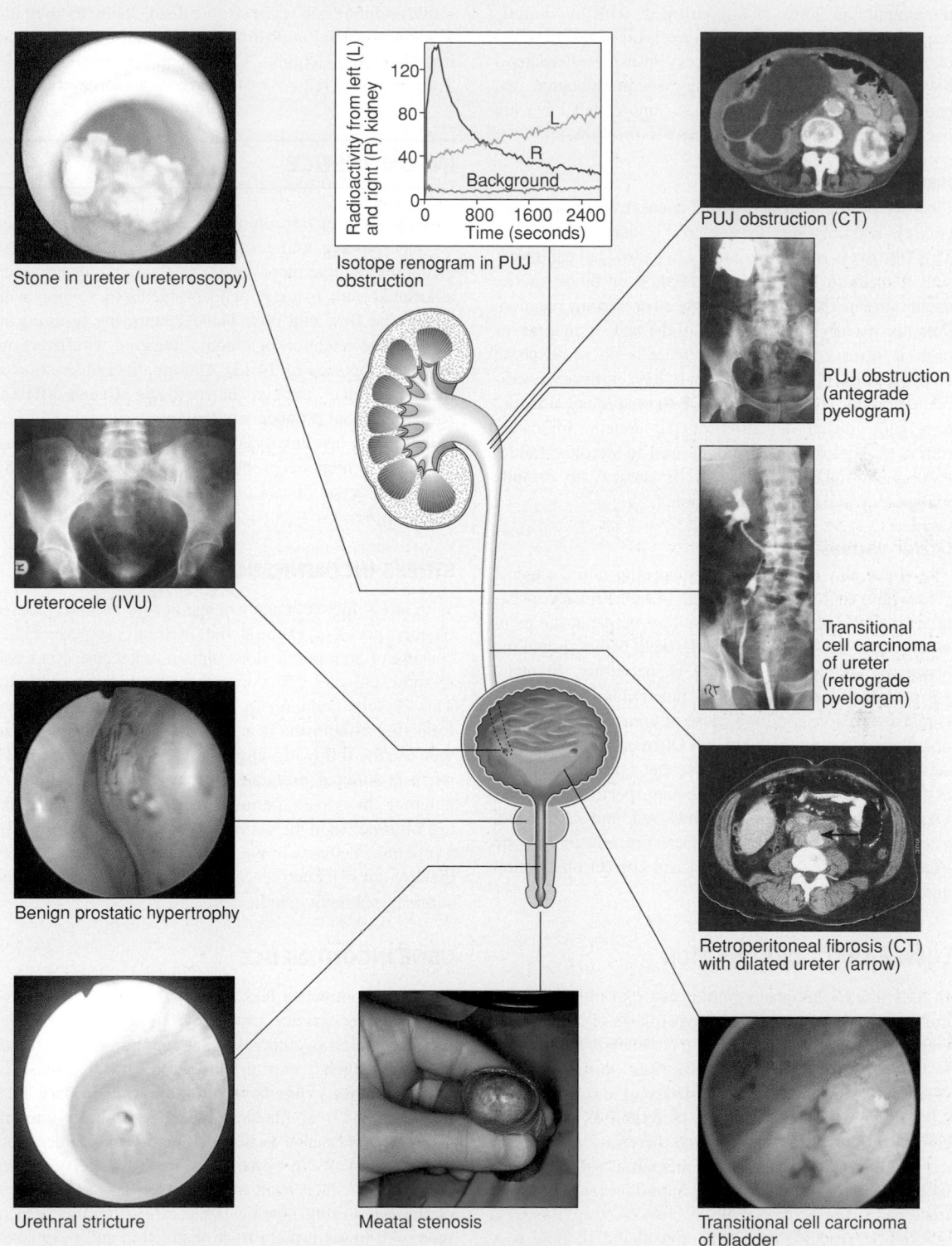

Stone in ureter (ureteroscopy)

Isotope renogram in PUJ obstruction

PUJ obstruction (CT)

PUJ obstruction (antegrade pyelogram)

Ureterocele (IVU)

Transitional cell carcinoma of ureter (retrograde pyelogram)

Benign prostatic hypertrophy

Retroperitoneal fibrosis (CT) with dilated ureter (arrow)

Urethral stricture

Meatal stenosis

Transitional cell carcinoma of bladder

Fig. 14.12　Urinary tract obstruction. Some common causes and their locations. Compare with images in Figure 14.2.

Rarely, it is asymptomatic. Diagnosis is suspected after ultrasound or IVU and confirmed with a diuretic renogram. Treatment is surgical excision of the PUJ and reanastomosis (pyeloplasty). Less invasive alternatives have been developed, including balloon dilatation and endoscopic pyelotomy. These are simpler but have not been evaluated over very long periods of follow-up.

Retroperitoneal fibrosis

Fibrosis of the retroperitoneal connective tissues may encircle and compress the ureter(s), causing obstruction. This fibrosis is most commonly idiopathic, but can represent a reaction to infection, radiation or blood (aortic aneurysm), or be caused by cancer or a drug reaction. Patients usually present with ill-defined symptoms of ureteric obstruction. Typically, there is an acute phase response (high C-reactive protein (CRP), erythrocyte sedimentation rate (ESR)). IVU or CT shows ureteric obstruction with medial deviation of the ureters. Idiopathic retroperitoneal fibrosis responds well to steroids; failure to respond indicates the need for surgery to exclude malignancy and relieve obstruction.

Other causes

The ureter may be obstructed by opening into a ureterocele within the bladder (see Fig. 14.12). Primary megaureter may be obstructive or non-obstructive at the point where the ureter enters the bladder wall. Narrowing of the ureter and reimplantation may be necessary. In many parts of the developing world tuberculosis or schistosomiasis is also a common cause of ureteric stricture and obstruction (see pp. 532 and 76). Often patients present in such an advanced state of disease that surgical treatment is not feasible. Both infections require specific drug treatment. When the ureters are involved and obstructed, a variety of reconstructive surgical procedures may be used to conserve renal function and correct obstruction and/or reflux.

LOWER TRACT OBSTRUCTION

In older males the most common cause of obstruction of the lower renal tract is benign hyperplasia of the prostate (see p. 636); in younger males the obstruction may be due to bladder neck dyssynergia. This can be managed by α-adrenoceptor antagonists but endoscopic surgical division of the bladder neck may be preferable as long as the risk of retrograde ejaculation and therefore infertility is not of concern to the patient. Carcinoma of the prostate (see p. 638) is a less frequent but important cause of lower tract obstruction.

Urethral stricture should be considered if there is a history of urethral infection, instrumentation (including catheterisation) or trauma. The flow pattern is distinctive (see Fig. 14.13). Treatment is by stretching, cutting or urethroplasty. Obstruction may also be the result of a tight phimosis, meatal stricture or of tight urethral valves.

In neurological disorders such as spinal injury, spina bifida and multiple sclerosis, the distal sphincter may fail to relax, resulting in obstruction. Specialised urodynamic investigation is required to make an accurate diagnosis. Treatment may require endoscopic sphincterotomy.

INCONTINENCE

Disorders of micturition may relate either to problems in urine storage that result in incontinence (e.g. stress incontinence, urge incontinence or continual incontinence associated with fistulae) or to problems in voiding with poor urine flow and poor bladder emptying resulting in either acute retention or chronic retention with overflow incontinence (see Fig. 14.13). Abnormalities of function of the lower urinary tract can be confusing because different pathologies can produce similar symptoms. Incontinence is defined as involuntary loss of urine sufficient to cause a social or hygiene problem. It may occur transiently during an acute illness or hospitalisation, especially in older people.

STRESS INCONTINENCE

With stress incontinence leakage occurs because passive bladder pressure exceeds the urethral pressure, either because of poor pelvic floor support or because of a weak urethral sphincter. Most often there is an element of both. This is very common in women and most often seen following childbirth. It is only rarely seen in men and then usually following surgery to the prostate. Urine leaks when abdominal pressure rises, e.g. when coughing or laughing. In women, perineal inspection may reveal leakage of urine when the patient coughs, and sometimes also a prolapse. Females in particular respond well to physiotherapy but if incontinence is persistent and troublesome surgical treatment is indicated.

URGE INCONTINENCE

In urge incontinence leakage usually occurs because of detrusor over-activity producing an increased bladder pressure which overcomes the urethral sphincter (motor urgency). Urgency may also be driven by a hypersensitive bladder (sensory urgency) resulting from urinary tract infection (UTI) or bladder stone. In the latter circumstances incontinence is less common. The incidence of urge incontinence in women increases with age, occurring in 15% of women aged over 65 years and around 50% of those requiring nursing home care. It is also seen in men with lower urinary tract obstruction and most often remits after the obstruction is relieved (see p. 637). In such patients the diagnosis is often made on the basis of symptoms and the exclusion of urinary retention by bladder ultrasound; confirmation requires urodynamic testing (see Fig. 14.13). The mainstay of treatment is bladder retraining

Abnormal micturition pattern

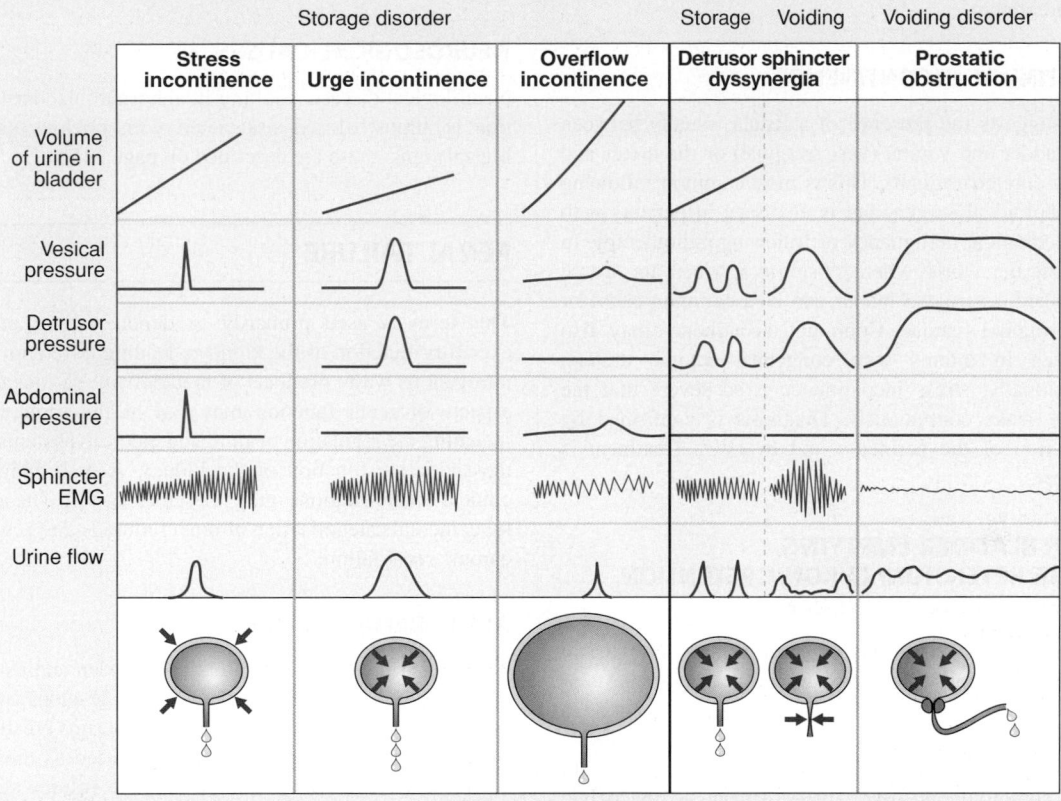

| | Storage disorder | | | Storage | Voiding | Voiding disorder |
| | Stress incontinence | Urge incontinence | Overflow incontinence | Detrusor sphincter dyssynergia | | Prostatic obstruction |

Rows (left labels): Volume of urine in bladder; Vesical pressure; Detrusor pressure; Abdominal pressure; Sphincter EMG; Urine flow

Flow rates and patterns

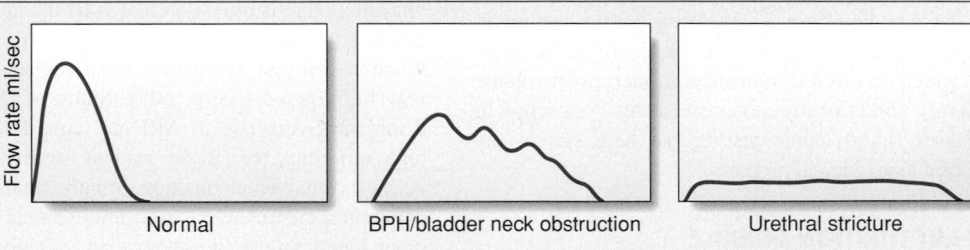

Normal   BPH/bladder neck obstruction   Urethral stricture

(Flow rate ml/sec)

Voiding diary

Normal pattern			Unstable bladder and urge incontinence		
	Time	Volume (ml)		Time	Volume (ml)
	0700	300		0700	150
	1200	400		0800	75
	1700	500		0915	25
	2300	300		1030	50
				1200	70
				1300	100
				1330	75
				1415 etc.	125 etc.
Total	**4 times**	**1.5 litres**	**Total**	**16 times**	**1.5 litres**

Fig. 14.13 **Urodynamic abnormalities in patients with urinary incontinence.** See Figure 14.3, page 581 for normal micturition cycle. (BPH = benign prostatic hyperplasia)

and anticholinergic medication. Surgery is restricted to patients who have severe day-time incontinence despite such treatment.

CONTINUAL INCONTINENCE

This suggests the presence of a fistula, usually between the bladder and vagina (vesicovaginal) or the ureter and vagina (ureterovaginal). This is most common following gynaecological surgery but is also seen in patients with gynaecological malignancy or following radiotherapy. In parts of the world where obstetric services are scarce prolonged obstructed labour can be a common cause of vesicovaginal fistulae. Continual incontinence may also be seen in infants with congenital ectopic ureters. Occasionally, stress incontinence is so severe that the patient leaks continuously. Diagnosis is confirmed by inspection of the perineum and by IVU. Treatment is surgical.

POOR BLADDER EMPTYING, ACUTE RETENTION, CHRONIC RETENTION, OVERFLOW INCONTINENCE

This group of conditions is most commonly seen in males and associated with benign prostatic hyperplasia or bladder neck obstruction (see p. 636), but may occur in either sex as a result of a failure of the detrusor muscle (atonic bladder). The latter state may be idiopathic but more commonly is the result of damage to the pelvic nerves either from surgery (commonly hysterectomy or rectal excision), trauma or infection or from compression of the cauda equina from disc prolapse, trauma or tumour. Incomplete bladder emptying can be identified by ultrasound, which reveals a significant post-micturition volume (> 100 ml). Outlet obstruction necessitates cystoscopy in most cases. Urodynamic testing can help clarify the nature of a neurological problem.

POST-MICTURITION DRIBBLE

This is very common in men, even in the relatively young. It is due to a small amount of urine becoming trapped in the U-bend of the bulbar urethra, which leaks out when

the patient moves. It is more pronounced if associated with a urethral diverticulum or urethral stricture.

NEUROLOGICAL CAUSES

Neurological disease resulting in abnormal bladder function is almost always associated with obvious neurological signs; these are described on page 1158.

RENAL FAILURE

This term is used primarily to denote failure of the excretory function of the kidneys, leading to retention of nitrogenous waste products of metabolism. Various other aspects of renal function may fail at the same time, including the regulation of fluid and electrolyte status and the endocrine function of the kidney. A wide range of clinical manifestations may therefore occur. The most fundamental categorisation of renal failure is into acute or chronic renal failure.

ACUTE RENAL FAILURE

Acute renal failure (ARF) refers to a sudden and usually reversible loss of renal function, which develops over a period of days or weeks. An increase in plasma creatinine concentration to > 200 μmol/l is often used as the biochemical definition. A reduction in urine volume occurs usually, but not always. There are many possible causes (see Fig. 14.14), and it is frequently multifactorial. The clinical picture is often dominated by the underlying condition. If the cause cannot be rapidly corrected and renal function restored, temporary renal replacement therapy may be required (see p. 605). Many of the underlying disorders giving rise to ARF are complex and carry a high mortality but, if the patient survives, normal or nearly normal renal function usually returns. The most common scenarios relate to haemodynamic disturbances, often interacting with exposure to infection and toxins, particularly drugs. When this is not immediately likely, it is important to remember other important disorders that may lead to rapid loss of renal function (see Box 14.12).

A typical biochemistry profile in a patient with ARF is shown in Figure 14.15.

REVERSIBLE PRE-RENAL ACUTE RENAL FAILURE

Pathogenesis
The kidney can regulate its own blood flow and GFR over a wide range of perfusion pressures. When the perfusion pressure falls, as in hypovolaemia, shock, heart failure or narrowing of the renal arteries, the resistance vessels in the kidney dilate to facilitate flow. This is partly mechanical, due to decreased stretch of the vessel walls, and partly neurohumoral. Vasodilator prostaglandins are important,

---

ISSUES IN OLDER PEOPLE
INCONTINENCE

- Urinary incontinence affects 15% of women and 10% of men aged over 65 years.
- It may be transient due to an acute confusional state, urinary infection, medication (such as diuretics), faecal impaction or restricted mobility, and these should be treated before embarking on further specific investigation.
- Established incontinence in old age is most commonly due to detrusor over-activity which may be caused by damage to central inhibitory centres or local detrusor muscle abnormalities.
- Poor manual dexterity or cognitive impairment may necessitate the help of a carer to assist with intermittent catheterisation.

and this mechanism is markedly impaired by NSAIDs (see p. 627). If autoregulation of blood flow fails, the GFR can still be maintained by means of selective constriction of the post-glomerular (efferent) arteriole. This is mediated through the release of renin and generation of angiotensin II, which preferentially constricts this vessel. ACE inhibitors interfere with this response.

More severe or prolonged under-perfusion of the kidney may lead to failure of these compensatory mechanisms. Blood flow and GFR decline. The renal tubules are intact, and become hyperfunctional—i.e. tubular reabsorption of sodium and water is increased, partly

through physical factors and partly through the influence of angiotensins, aldosterone and vasopressin. This leads to the formation of a low volume of urine which is concentrated (high osmolality) but low in sodium (see Box 14.13).

Clinical features

There may be a marked reduction of blood pressure and signs of poor peripheral perfusion, such as delayed capillary return. However, pre-renal ARF may occur without systemic hypotension. Postural hypotension (a fall in

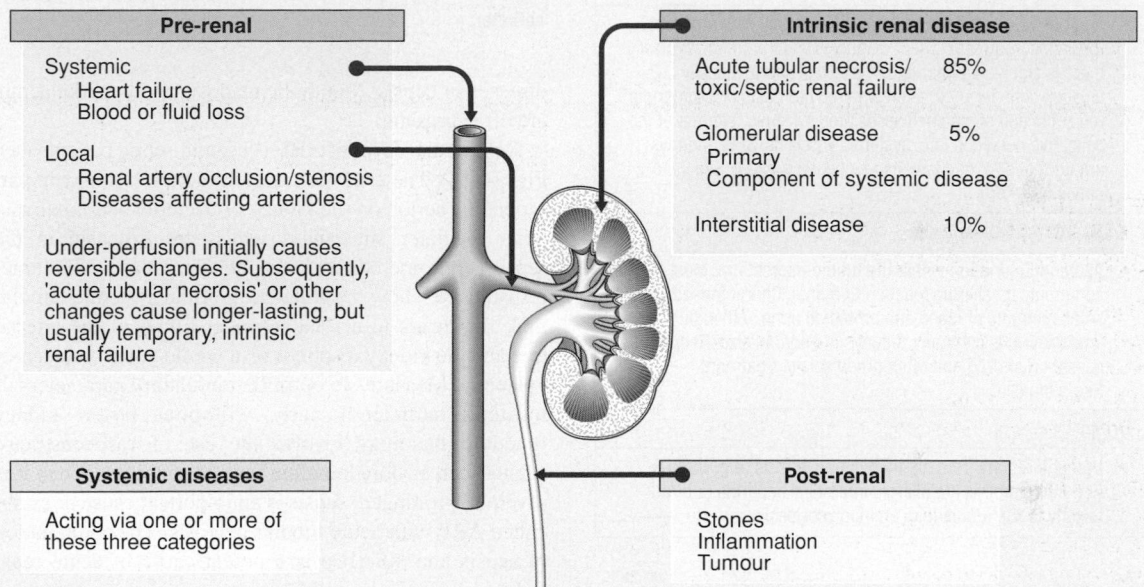

Fig. 14.14 Causes of acute renal failure.

Patient: Mr J.D.	D.O.B: 14.03.25	Drugs: Ibuprofen, enalapril
Date	11.08.2001	15.09.2001
Clinical information	Pre-operative assessment, hip replacement	Post-op—reduced urine output
Urea (mmol/l)	5.7	24
Sodium (mmol/l)	135	127
Potassium (mmol/l)	4.6	6.3
Total CO_2 (mmol/l)	29	17
Creatinine (μmol/l)	98	249
Calcium (mmol/l)	2.42	2.05
Phosphate (mmol/l)	1.14	1.86

Fig. 14.15 Typical biochemistry profile in a patient with acute renal failure.

blood pressure of ≥ 20/10 mmHg from lying to standing) is a valuable sign of hypovolaemia. The cause of the reduced renal perfusion may be obvious, but concealed blood loss can occur into the gastrointestinal tract, following trauma (particularly where there are fractures of the pelvis or femur) and into the pregnant uterus. Large volumes of intravascular fluid are lost into tissues after crush injuries or burns, or in severe inflammatory skin

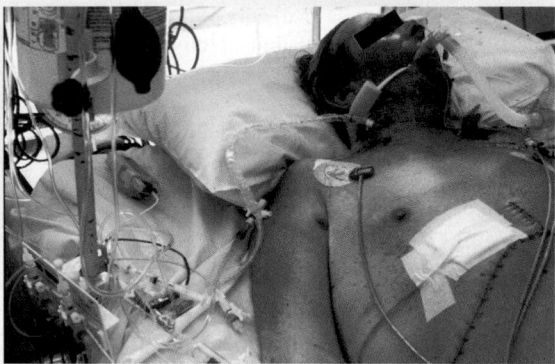

Fig. 14.16 Septic post-operative patient with pulmonary artery catheter.

diseases or sepsis. Metabolic acidosis and hyperkalaemia are often present.

A particular form of ARF is seen in septic patients (see Fig. 14.16). The causation is multifactorial. It may in part reflect the action on the kidney of bacterial endotoxin and other mediator substances which are activated in the sepsis syndrome. Most septic patients, if they are volume-resuscitated, show vasodilatation of the systemic circulation; this leads to a relative under-filling of the arterial tree and the kidney responds as it would to absolute hypovolaemia. Measures to optimise circulatory parameters, if instituted sufficiently early, will often restore kidney function; this may involve the use of vasoconstrictor agents such as noradrenaline (norepinephrine). When it is severe or prolonged, sepsis is an important cause of established ARF with acute tubular necrosis. The combination of sepsis and NSAIDs is a potent cause of acute renal failure.

Management

The underlying cause of the ARF must be established and corrected. When hypovolaemia is present, the blood volume must be restored as rapidly as possible, by replacement with blood, plasma or isotonic saline (0.9%), depending on what has been lost. If metabolic acidosis is severe, isotonic sodium bicarbonate (e.g. 500 ml of 1.26%) may be included as part of the replacement fluid. In most cases, however, restoration of blood volume will restore kidney function and allow correction of acidosis. It is often helpful to monitor the central venous pressure or pulmonary wedge pressure as an adjunct to clinical examination in determining the rate of administration of fluid. Recent trials do not support the use of low-dose dopamine in severely ill patients at risk of ARF (see EBM panel).

As well as optimisation of volume status, patients with cardiogenic or septic shock (see p. 195) may require invasive haemodynamic monitoring to assess cardiac output and systemic vascular resistance, and the use of inotropic drugs to restore an effective blood pressure.

ACUTE RENAL FAILURE—role of low-dose dopamine

'Dopamine at low, 'renal' doses has been used for many years in the belief that it may increase renal blood flow in critically ill patients (as it does in normal individuals) and prevent acute renal failure. There is minimal evidence for benefits from clinical trials, and suggestions that it may do harm. In an RCT including 328 patients in 23 intensive care units in Australia, dopamine 2 μg/kg/min was no different from placebo, doing neither harm nor good. There is no evidence to support the use of low-dose dopamine for prevention or modification of acute renal failure.'

- ANZICS Clinical Trials Group. Low-dose dopamine in patients with early renal dysfunction: a placebo-controlled randomised trial. Lancet 2000; 356:2139–2143.
- O'Leary MJ, Bihari DJ. Preventing renal failure in the critically ill. BMJ 2001; 322:1437–1438.

Prognosis

If treatment is given sufficiently early, renal function will usually return rapidly; in such circumstances residual renal impairment is unlikely. In some cases, however, treatment is ineffective and renal failure becomes established.

ESTABLISHED ACUTE RENAL FAILURE

Established ARF may develop following severe or prolonged under-perfusion of the kidney (pre-renal ARF). In such cases, the histological pattern of acute tubular necrosis is usually seen. Alternatively, patients may present de novo with established ARF, due to intrinsic disease of the kidney, rapidly progressive glomerulonephritis, or to obstruction of the urinary tract (see Fig. 14.14).

Acute tubular necrosis (ATN)

Acute necrosis of renal tubular cells (see Fig. 14.32, p. 618) may result from ischaemia or nephrotoxicity, caused by chemical or bacterial toxins. In practice, multiple factors are common.

Pathogenesis of acute tubular necrosis

Ischaemic tubular necrosis usually follows a period of shock, during which renal blood flow is greatly reduced. Measurements during the oliguric phase of ATN indicate that, even when the systemic circulation has been restored, renal blood flow remains at about 20% of normal. This is due to swelling of the endothelial cells of the glomeruli and peritubular capillaries, and oedema of the interstitium. Blood flow is further reduced by vasoconstrictors such as thromboxane, vasopressin, noradrenaline (norepinephrine) and angiotensin II, partly counterbalanced by the release of intrarenal vasodilator prostaglandins. Thus, in ischaemic ATN there is reduced oxygen delivery to the tubular cells, which are very active metabolically, particularly in the thick ascending limb of the loop of Henle. Their high oxygen requirement is largely driven by the active reabsorption of sodium, and even in health the renal medulla is critically balanced in terms of oxygen delivery and consumption.

The ischaemic insult causes peroxidation of cell membrane lipids, influx of calcium and cell swelling. Mitochondrial function is impaired, leading to anaerobic glycolysis and intracellular acidosis, and ultimately to lysosomal disruption, denaturation of proteins and DNA, and death of tubular cells (see Fig. 14.32, p. 618). There is loss of adhesion between tubular cells and the basement membrane, leading to shedding of cells into the tubular lumen, where they may contribute to tubular obstruction. Focal breaks in the tubular basement membrane develop; these allow tubular contents to leak into the interstitial tissue and cause interstitial oedema.

In nephrotoxic ATN a similar sequence occurs, but it is initiated by direct toxicity of the causative agent to tubular cells. Mechanisms of cell damage include the production of reactive oxygen species and peroxidation of membrane lipids, binding of toxins or drugs to target intracellular proteins to interfere with cellular respiration, and inhibition of cell protein synthesis. Examples include the aminoglycoside antibiotics, such as gentamicin, the cytotoxic agent cisplatin, and the antifungal drug amphotericin B.

Fortunately, tubular cells can regenerate and re-form the basement membrane. If the patient is supported during the regeneration phase, kidney function returns. There is often a diuretic phase where urine output increases rapidly and remains excessive for several days before returning to normal. This is due in part to loss of the medullary concentration gradient, which normally allows concentration of the urine in the collecting duct, and which depends on continued delivery of filtrate to the ascending limb of the loop of Henle and active tubular transport. Both factors are disturbed during ATN. The medullary concentration gradient is gradually 'washed out', and is not re-established until glomerular filtration and tubular function are restored. Not all patients have a diuretic phase, depending on the severity of the renal damage and the rate of recovery.

Rapidly progressive glomerulonephritis

Rapidly progressive glomerulonephritis (RPGN) is an extreme inflammatory nephritis which causes rapid loss of renal function over days to weeks. Renal biopsy shows crescent formation (see Fig. 14.30E, p. 615); indeed, 'crescentic nephritis' is another term for RPGN. It can occur in a number of diseases (see Box 14.14), some of which (e.g. vasculitis, SLE) may cause symptoms and signs in other systems, while others (e.g. anti-GBM disease) do not. Where there are other symptoms, differentiating these diseases from subacute infection (e.g. endocarditis) is very important.

Early recognition can salvage kidney function and prevent other serious consequences of underlying disease (see Box 14.14). Sometimes treatment can be commenced before the diagnosis is certain, if confirmatory tests will follow shortly.

14.14 RAPIDLY PROGRESSIVE GLOMERULONEPHRITIS (CRESCENTIC NEPHRITIS)

Recognition

- Rapid loss of renal function over days to weeks
- Urine contains blood and protein
- Normal or large unobstructed kidneys on ultrasound
- Possible evidence of systemic illness or of disease affecting other organs (but not always)

Defining the cause

- Blood tests: antineutrophil cytoplasmic antibodies (ANCA), antinuclear antibodies (ANA), anti-GBM antibodies, complement immunoglobulins
- Renal biopsy

Common causes

- Systemic vasculitis (focal necrotising glomerulonephritis)
- SLE
- Goodpasture's (anti-GBM) disease
- Aggressive phase of other inflammatory nephritis (e.g. IgA nephropathy, post-infectious (post-streptococcal) glomerulonephritis)

Management

- Immunosuppressive treatment, e.g. cyclophosphamide and prednisolone for most causes
- Supportive treatment, e.g. dialysis when indicated

Other causes of established ARF

Established ARF may also develop in conditions affecting the intrarenal arteries and arterioles, such as vasculitis, accelerated hypertension and disseminated intravascular coagulation. Acute allergic interstitial nephritis (see p. 617), which is often due to drugs, may cause ARF.

ARF can result from obstruction at any point in the urinary tract (see Fig. 14.12, p. 591). If there are two functioning kidneys, ureteric obstruction only causes uraemia if it is bilateral. A history of loin pain, haematuria, renal colic or difficulty in micturition suggests the diagnosis. Often the onset is clinically silent, and the obstruction is only discovered on investigation. An ultrasound examination of the kidneys and ureters should, therefore, be carried out in any patient with unexplained renal failure.

Clinical features

These reflect the causal condition, such as trauma, septicaemia or systemic disease, together with features associated with renal failure. Patients are usually oliguric (urine volume < 500 ml daily). Anuria (complete absence of urine) is rare and usually indicates acute urinary tract obstruction or vascular occlusion. In about 20% of cases, the urine volume is normal or increased, but with a low GFR and a reduction of tubular reabsorption (non-oliguric ARF). Excretion is inadequate despite good urine output, and the plasma urea and creatinine increase. In ARF, the rate of rise in plasma urea and creatinine is determined by the rate of catabolism (tissue breakdown). In ARF associated with severe infections, major

surgery or trauma, the daily rise in plasma urea often exceeds 5 mmol/l.

Disturbances of water, electrolyte and acid–base balance arise. Hyperkalaemia is common, particularly with massive tissue breakdown, haemolysis or metabolic acidosis (see p. 289). Patients may have dilutional hyponatraemia if they have received inappropriate amounts of intravenous dextrose or have continued to drink freely despite oliguria. Metabolic acidosis develops unless prevented by loss of hydrogen ions through vomiting or aspiration of gastric contents. Hypocalcaemia, due to reduced renal production of 1,25-dihydroxycholecalciferol, is common.

At first the patient may feel well but, unless dialysis is instituted, clinical features linked to the retention of metabolic waste products eventually appear. Initially, these are anorexia, nausea and vomiting. Later, drowsiness, apathy and confusion, muscle-twitching, hiccoughs, fits and coma occur. The respiratory rate is increased due to acidosis, pulmonary oedema or respiratory infection. Pulmonary oedema (see Fig. 14.17) may result from the administration of excessive amounts of fluids and because of increased pulmonary capillary permeability. Anaemia is common and due to excessive blood loss, haemolysis or decreased erythropoiesis. There is a bleeding tendency due to disordered platelet function and disturbances of the coagulation cascade. Gastrointestinal haemorrhage may occur, often late in the illness, although this is less common with effective dialysis and the use of agents that reduce gastric acid production. Severe infections may complicate ARF because humoral and cellular immune mechanisms are depressed.

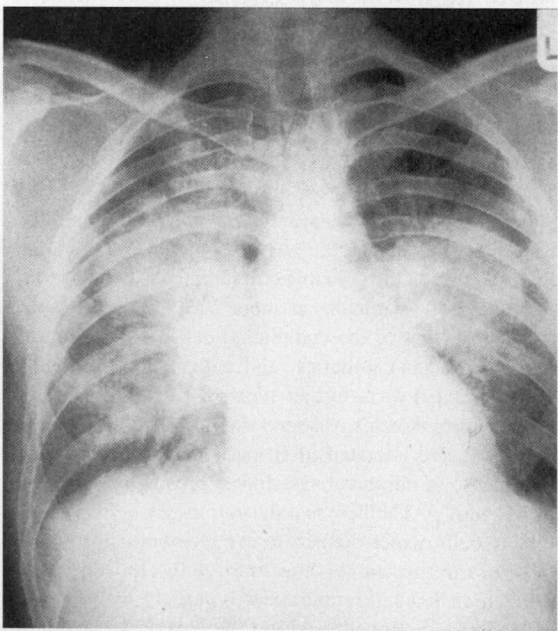

Fig. 14.17 Pulmonary oedema in acute renal failure. The appearances are indistinguishable from left ventricular failure but the heart size is usually normal. Blood pressure is often high.

Management

Emergency resuscitation

Hyperkalaemia (a plasma K^+ concentration > 6 mmol/l) must be treated to prevent the development of life-threatening cardiac arrhythmias. This is detailed on pages 284–286.

The circulating blood volume, if low, must be corrected by transfusion with appropriate fluids. This may require monitoring of central venous or pulmonary wedge pressure. Patients with pulmonary oedema usually require dialysis to remove sodium and water.

Determination of the cause of ARF and specific treatment of the underlying cause

The cause may be obvious or revealed by simple initial investigations (e.g. ultrasound showing obstruction). If not, a range of investigations, including renal biopsy, may be necessary. In many cases, more than one factor contributes to the renal dysfunction.

There is no specific treatment for acute tubular necrosis. Some other causes of ARF may require specific therapy. Obstruction should be relieved urgently. Corticosteroids and immunosuppressive drugs are of value in ARF due to systemic vasculitis and some other causes of RPGN (see Box 14.14). Corticosteroids may also be indicated in acute tubulo-interstitial nephritis (see p. 617). Control of blood pressure is critical in ARF due to accelerated hypertension (see p. 611). Plasma infusion and plasma exchange may be indicated in microangiopathic diseases (see p. 610).

If pelvic or ureteric dilatation is found, percutaneous nephrostomy is undertaken to decompress the urinary system (see p. 584). Dialysis can usually be avoided. Injection of dye through the nephrostomy tube (antegrade pyelography) reveals the site of the obstruction.

Once obstruction has been relieved and blood chemistry has returned towards normal, the underlying cause is identified and treated wherever possible (see p. 590). Sometimes obstruction is caused by pelvic malignancies, such as carcinoma of the cervix, uterus or colon, which are so advanced that intervention is inadvisable.

General management of established ARF

In established ARF the aims are to control fluid and electrolyte balance, maintain nutrition, control the biochemical abnormalities and protect the patient from infection. Drugs must be used with particular care. Renal replacement therapy may be required (see p. 605).

Fluid and electrolyte balance. After initial resuscitation, daily fluid intake should equal urine output, plus an additional 500 ml to cover insensible losses; such losses are higher in febrile patients and in tropical climates. Since sodium and potassium are retained, intake of these substances should be restricted. If abnormal losses occur, as in diarrhoea, additional fluid and electrolytes are required. The patient should be weighed daily. Large changes in body weight, or the development of oedema or signs of fluid depletion indicate that fluid intake should be reassessed.

Protein and energy intake. In patients where dialysis is likely to be avoided, dietary protein is restricted to about 40 g/day. Attempts are made to suppress endogenous protein catabolism by giving as much energy as possible in the form of fat and carbohydrate. Patients treated by dialysis may have more protein (70 g protein daily, 10–12 g nitrogen). In some patients, feeding via a nasogastric tube may be helpful. Parenteral nutrition (see p. 317) may be required because of vomiting or diarrhoea, or if the bowel is not intact, or to give adequate energy and nitrogen to hypercatabolic patients.

Recovery from acute renal failure

This is usually indicated by a gradual return of urine output, and subsequently a steady improvement in plasma biochemistry towards normal. Some patients, primarily those with acute tubular necrosis or after relief of chronic urinary obstruction, develop a 'diuretic phase'. Fluid should be given to replace the urine output as appropriate. Supplements of sodium chloride, sodium bicarbonate and potassium chloride, and sometimes calcium, phosphate and magnesium, may be needed to compensate for increased urinary losses. After a few days urine volume falls to normal as the concentrating mechanism and tubular reabsorption are restored.

Prognosis

In uncomplicated ARF, such as that due to simple haemorrhage or drugs, mortality is low even when renal replacement therapy is required. In ARF associated with serious infection and multiple organ failure, mortality is 50–70%. Outcome is usually determined by the severity of the underlying disorder and other complications, rather than by renal failure itself. Issues relating to ARF in older people are outlined below.

ISSUES IN OLDER PEOPLE
ACUTE RENAL FAILURE

- Nephrons decline in number from the age of 30; creatinine clearance declines at a rate of about 10 ml/min per decade after the age of 50 years.
- As muscle mass also falls with age, less creatinine is produced each day. Serum creatinine can thus be a misleading guide to renal function in poorly nourished older people with low muscle mass.
- The renal tubules also undergo age-related changes, leading to loss of urinary concentration, acidification and toxin secretion.
- Older people are more likely to take drugs which may contribute to loss of renal function, such as diuretics, ACE inhibitors and NSAIDs.
- Due to this reduction in function, older people are more prone to acute renal failure; infection, renal vascular disease, prostatic obstruction, hypovolaemia and severe cardiac dysfunction are common contributory causes.
- The most important cause of renal disease in older people is vascular, and the kidneys are thus highly susceptible to any hypotensive episode.
- The mortality from acute renal failure rises with age, primarily because of comorbid conditions.

CHRONIC RENAL FAILURE

Chronic renal failure (CRF) refers to an irreversible deterioration in renal function which classically develops over a period of years. Initially, it is manifest only as a biochemical abnormality. Eventually, loss of the excretory, metabolic and endocrine functions of the kidney leads to the development of the clinical symptoms and signs of renal failure, which are referred to as uraemia. When death is likely without renal replacement therapy it is called end-stage renal failure (ESRF).

The social and economic consequences of CRF are considerable. In the UK 85–95 new patients per million of the adult population are accepted for long-term dialysis treatment each year (see Fig. 14.18); the availability of dialysis and transplantation has transformed the outlook for such patients. The incidence of CRF is much higher in some other countries due to differences in regional and racial incidences of disease as well as because of differences in medical practice.

Aetiology

CRF may be caused by any condition which destroys the normal structure and function of the kidney. Important

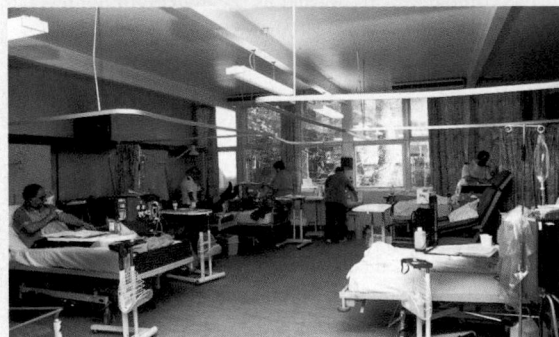

Fig. 14.18 Haemodialysis unit. Six of 19 stations, a mixture of beds and chairs, in an outpatient haemodialysis unit. Each station treats three patients daily and therefore six patients in total (each attending three times weekly).

causes are shown in Box 14.15. A presumptive diagnosis of a chronic form of glomerulonephritis may be made if there is proteinuria, haematuria and hypertension in the absence of any other cause of renal failure, but a precise diagnosis is not always established. Patients often have bilateral small kidneys, and in such a situation renal biopsy is usually inadvisable because of the difficulty in making a histological diagnosis in severely damaged kidneys and the fact that treatment is unlikely to improve renal function significantly.

Pathogenesis

Disturbances in water, electrolyte and acid–base balance contribute to the clinical picture in patients with chronic renal failure, but the exact pathogenesis of the clinical syndrome of uraemia is unknown. Many substances present in abnormal concentration in the plasma have been suspected as being 'uraemic toxins', and uraemia is probably caused by the accumulation of various intermediary products of metabolism.

Clinical features

Renal failure may present as a raised blood urea and creatinine found during routine examination, often accompanied by hypertension, proteinuria or anaemia. When renal function deteriorates slowly patients may remain asymptomatic until the GFR is 20 ml/min or less (normal range 80–120 ml/min; see Fig. 14.5, p. 582). Nocturia, due to the loss of concentrating ability and increased osmotic load per nephron, is often an early symptom. Thereafter, due to the widespread effects of renal failure, symptoms and signs may develop related to almost every body system (see Fig. 14.19). Patients may present with complaints which are not obviously renal in origin, such as tiredness or breathlessness.

In end-stage renal failure (creatinine clearance < 5 ml/min) patients appear ill and anaemic. They do not necessarily retain fluid, and may show signs of sodium and water depletion. There may be unusually deep respiration

14.15 IMPORTANT CAUSES OF CHRONIC RENAL FAILURE

Disease	Proportion of end-stage renal failure	Comments
Congenital and inherited	5%	e.g. Polycystic kidney disease, Alport's syndrome
Renal artery stenosis	5%	
Hypertension	5–25%	It is uncertain whether such variation is due to true racial differences or to differences in diagnostic labelling
Glomerular diseases	10–20%	IgA nephropathy is most common
Interstitial diseases	5–15%	
Systemic inflammatory diseases	5%	e.g. SLE, vasculitis
Diabetes mellitus	20–40%	Large racial and national differences exist—the higher rate is from the USA
Unknown	5–20%	

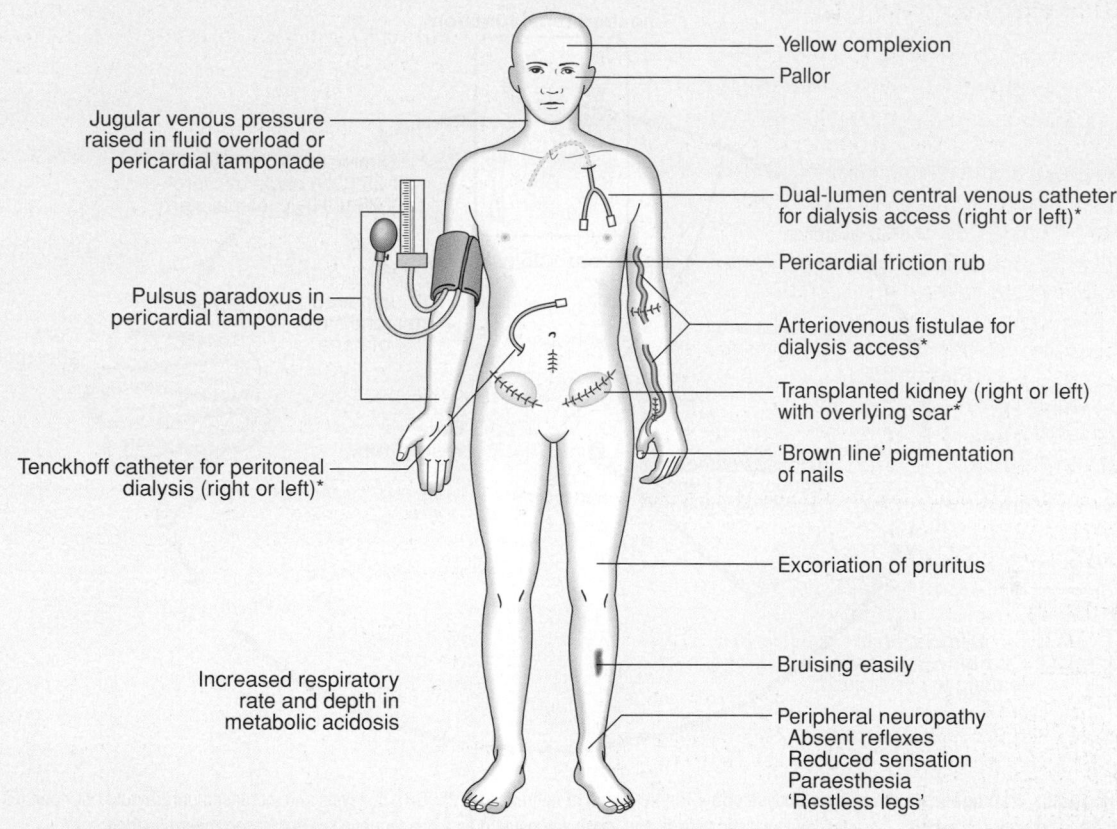

Yellow complexion
Pallor

Jugular venous pressure
raised in fluid overload or
pericardial tamponade

Dual-lumen central venous catheter
for dialysis access (right or left)*

Pericardial friction rub

Pulsus paradoxus in
pericardial tamponade

Arteriovenous fistulae for
dialysis access*

Transplanted kidney (right or left)
with overlying scar*

'Brown line' pigmentation
of nails

Tenckhoff catheter for peritoneal
dialysis (right or left)*

Excoriation of pruritus

Bruising easily

Increased respiratory
rate and depth in
metabolic acidosis

Peripheral neuropathy
Absent reflexes
Reduced sensation
Paraesthesia
'Restless legs'

Fig. 14.19   Physical signs in chronic renal failure. (* Features of renal replacement therapy)

related to metabolic acidosis (Kussmaul's respiration), anorexia and nausea. Later, hiccoughs, pruritus, vomiting, muscular twitching, fits, drowsiness and coma ensue.

Anaemia

Anaemia is common; it usually correlates to the severity of renal failure and contributes to many of the non-specific symptoms of CRF. Several mechanisms are implicated, including:

- relative deficiency of erythropoietin
- diminished erythropoiesis due to the toxic effects of uraemia on marrow precursor cells
- reduced red cell survival
- increased blood loss due to capillary fragility and poor platelet function
- reduced dietary intake and absorption of iron and other haematinics.

Plasma erythropoietin is usually within the normal range and thus inappropriately low for the degree of anaemia. In patients with polycystic kidneys, anaemia is often less severe or absent, and in some interstitial disorders it appears disproportionately severe for the degree of renal failure. This is probably because of the effects of these disorders on the interstitial fibroblasts that secrete erythropoietin.

Renal osteodystrophy

This metabolic bone disease which accompanies CRF consists of a mixture of osteomalacia, hyperparathyroid bone disease (osteitis fibrosa), osteoporosis and osteosclerosis (see Fig. 14.20). Osteomalacia (see p. 1029) results from diminished activity of the renal 1-α-hydroxylase enzyme, with failure to convert cholecalciferol to its active metabolite 1,25-dihydroxycholecalciferol. A deficiency of the latter leads to diminished intestinal absorption of calcium, hypocalcaemia and reduction in the calcification of osteoid. Osteitis fibrosa results from secondary hyperparathyroidism. The parathyroid glands are stimulated by the low plasma calcium, and also by hyperphosphataemia. In some patients tertiary or autonomous hyperparathyroidism with hypercalcaemia develops. Osteoporosis occurs in many patients, possibly related to malnutrition. Osteosclerosis is seen mainly in the sacral area, at the base of the skull and in the vertebrae; the cause of this unusual reaction is not known.

Myopathy

Generalised myopathy is due to a combination of poor nutrition, hyperparathyroidism, vitamin D deficiency and disorders of electrolyte metabolism. Muscle cramps are common, and quinine sulphate may be helpful. The 'restless leg syndrome', where the patient's legs are jumpy

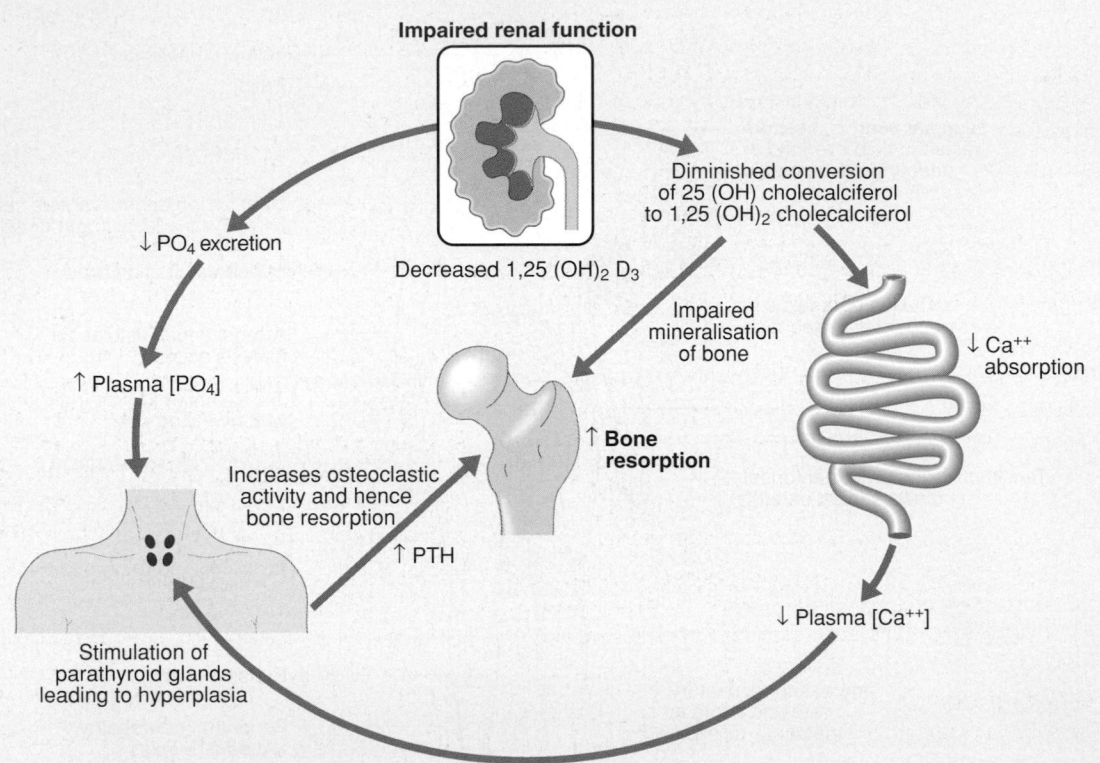

Fig. 14.20   Pathogenesis of renal osteodystrophy. The net result of decreased 1,25 $(OH)_2$ D_3 levels and increased parathyroid hormone (PTH) levels is bone which exhibits increased osteoclastic activity and increased osteoid as a consequence of decreased mineralisation.

during the night, may be troublesome and is often improved by clonazepam.

Neuropathy
This results from demyelination of medullated fibres with the longer fibres being involved at an earlier stage. Sensory neuropathy may cause paraesthesiae. Motor neuropathy may present as foot drop. Uraemic autonomic neuropathy may cause delayed gastric emptying, diarrhoea and postural hypotension. Clinical manifestations of neuropathy appear late in the course of chronic renal failure but may improve or even resolve once dialysis is established.

Endocrine function
A number of hormonal abnormalities may be present, of which the most important are hyperprolactinaemia and hyperparathyroidism. In women, amenorrhoea is common. In both sexes there is loss of libido and sexual function, at least in part related to hyperprolactinaemia and galactorrhoea (see p. 739). Treatment with bromocriptine is sometimes useful.

The half-life of insulin is prolonged in CRF due to reduced tubular metabolism of insulin; insulin requirements may therefore decline in diabetic patients in end-stage CRF. However, there is also a post-receptor defect in insulin action, leading to relative insulin resistance. This latter abnormality is improved by dialysis treatment.

Changes in carbohydrate metabolism depend on which factors predominate.

Cardiovascular disorders
Hypertension develops in approximately 80% of patients with CRF. In part, this is caused by sodium retention. Chronically diseased kidneys also tend to hypersecrete renin, leading to high circulating concentrations of renin, angiotensin II and aldosterone. This is exaggerated if there is renal under-perfusion related to renal vascular disease. Hypertension must be controlled, as it causes further vascular and glomerular damage and worsening of renal failure. Atherosclerosis is common and may be accelerated by hypertension. Vascular calcification may develop and be sufficiently severe to cause limb ischaemia. Pericarditis is common in untreated or inadequately treated end-stage renal failure. It may lead to pericardial tamponade and, later, constrictive pericarditis.

Acidosis
Declining renal function is associated with metabolic acidosis (see p. 289), which is often asymptomatic. Sustained acidosis results in protons being buffered in bone in place of calcium, thus aggravating metabolic bone disease. Acidosis may also contribute to reduced renal function and increased tissue catabolism. The plasma bicarbonate should be maintained above 18 mmol/l by giving sodium bicarbonate supplements. The dose is determined by

clinical trial, commencing with 1 g 8-hourly and increasing as required. The increased sodium intake may induce hypertension or oedema; calcium carbonate (up to 3 g daily) is an alternative agent that is also used to bind dietary phosphate.

Infection
Cellular and humoral immunity are impaired, with increased susceptibility to infection. Infections are the second most common cause of death in dialysis patients, after cardiovascular disease.

Bleeding
There is an increased bleeding tendency in renal failure which manifests in patients with advanced disease as cutaneous ecchymoses and mucosal bleeds. Platelet function is impaired and bleeding time prolonged. Adequate dialysis treatment partially corrects the bleeding tendency.

Gastrointestinal disorders
Anorexia followed by nausea and vomiting (especially in the morning) is commonly seen. There is a higher incidence of peptic ulcer disease in uraemic patients.

Management
There are several aspects to the management of CRF:

- Identify the underlying renal disease.
- Attempt to prevent further renal damage.
- Look for reversible factors which are making renal function worse (see Box 14.16).
- Attempt to limit the adverse effects of the loss of renal function.
- Institute renal replacement therapy (dialysis, transplantation) when appropriate.

At presentation the nature of the underlying disease should be determined, if possible, by history, examination, testing of biochemistry, immunology, radiology and biopsy. The degree of renal failure is assessed and complications are documented. In some cases the cause may be amenable to specific therapy, e.g. immunosuppression in some types of glomerulonephritis. A search is made for reversible factors, correction of which results in improved renal function (see Box 14.16).

14.16 REVERSIBLE FACTORS IN CHRONIC RENAL FAILURE
- Hypertension
- Reduced renal perfusion
  Renal artery stenosis
  Hypotension due to drug treatment
  Sodium and water depletion
  Poor cardiac function
- Urinary tract obstruction
- Urinary tract infection
- Other infections: increased catabolism and urea production
- Nephrotoxic medications

In patients with irreversible renal failure, various measures can reduce symptoms and may slow progression to end-stage renal failure.

Retarding the progression of CRF
Unless dialysis or transplantation is provided, CRF is eventually fatal. Once the plasma creatinine exceeds about 300 µmol/l, there is usually progressive deterioration in renal function, irrespective of aetiology. The rate of deterioration is very variable between patients but is relatively constant for an individual patient. A plot of the reciprocal of the plasma creatinine concentration against time allows the physician to predict when dialysis will be required and to detect any unexpected worsening of renal failure (see Fig. 14.21). Changes in the slope may reflect changes in treatment—for instance, blood pressure control or other interventions.

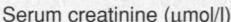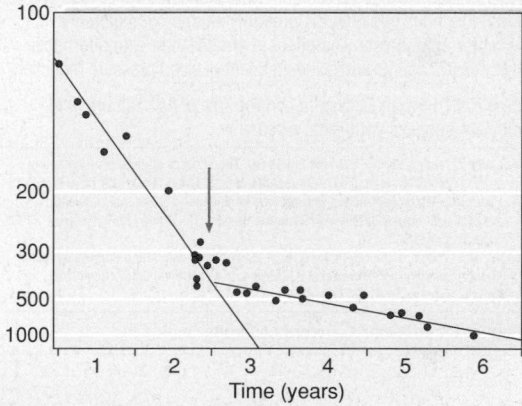

Fig. 14.21 Plot of the reciprocal of serum creatinine concentration against time over a 6-year period in a patient with progressive renal failure caused by membranous nephropathy. Serial plasma creatinine estimations permit prediction of the time to end-stage renal disease. The 'break point' (arrow) at which the gradient of the line is dramatically reduced was associated with a 6-month course of treatment with chlorambucil and prednisolone.

Control of blood pressure
In many types of renal disease, but particularly in diseases affecting glomeruli, control of blood pressure may retard the rate of deterioration of GFR. This has been proven for diabetic nephropathy, but is probably true for other diseases as well, particularly those associated with heavy proteinuria. No threshold for this effect has been found; reduction of any level of blood pressure is beneficial. Various target blood pressures have been suggested—for example, 130/85 mmHg for CRF alone, lowered to 125/75 mmHg for those with proteinuria greater than 1 g/day. Achieving these targets often requires multiple drugs and may be limited by toxicity or non-compliance. The very high incidence of left ventricular hypertrophy, heart failure and occlusive vascular disease in patients with long-standing renal disease also justifies vigorous efforts to control blood pressure.

ACE inhibitors have been shown to be more effective at retarding the progression of renal failure than other therapies giving an equal lowering of systemic blood pressure (see EBM panel). This may be because they reduce glomerular perfusion pressure by dilating the efferent arteriole, an effect which causes an immediate reduction in GFR when therapy is initiated. Reduction in proteinuria is a good prognostic sign, but it is not clear if this is causally related to prognosis. Apart from ACE inhibitors, angiotensin II receptor antagonists also reduce glomerular perfusion pressure, and the same effect may be achieved by certain non-dihydropyridine calcium antagonists.

EBM

CHRONIC RENAL FAILURE (CRF)—role of angiotensin-converting enzyme (ACE) inhibitors in non-diabetic patients

'In non-diabetic patients with hypertension, CRF and proteinuria, ACE inhibitors reduce proteinuria and slow the rate of loss of renal function. This effect is probably shared by angiotensin receptor antagonists. The effect is greater than with alternative hypotensive agents and is independent of blood pressure reduction.'

(See p. 674 for an EBM panel on the role of ACE inhibitors in diabetic subjects with renal disease.)

- Lewis EJ, Hunsicker LG, Bain RP, Rohde RD. The effect of angiotensin-converting enzyme inhibition on diabetic nephropathy. N Engl J Med 1993; 329:1456–1462.
- Lovell HG. Angiotensin-converting enzyme inhibitors in normotensive diabetic patients with microalbuminuria (Cochrane Review). Cochrane Library, issue 4, 2000. Oxford: Update Software.
- Ihle BU, Whitworth JA, Shahinfar S, et al. Angiotensin-converting enzyme inhibition in non-diabetic progressive renal insufficiency: a controlled double-blind trial. Am J Kidney Dis 1996; 27:489–495.

Further information: 💻 www.cochrane.co.uk

Diet

In experimental studies, progressive renal disease can be retarded by various manipulations of diet, most notably by restriction of dietary protein. In human studies results have been less clear-cut (see EBM panel); low-protein diets are difficult to adhere to and carry a risk of inducing

---

EBM

CHRONIC RENAL FAILURE—role of dietary protein restriction

'Although the single largest controlled trial did not demonstrate a significant overall effect, subsequent subgroup analysis and two meta-analyses of published RCTs suggest that restriction of dietary protein intake delays the progression of chronic renal failure in non-diabetic subjects and in insulin-dependent diabetes mellitus. In non-diabetic subjects the occurrence of end-stage renal failure is reduced by about 40% compared with unrestricted protein intake. Trials have used between 0.3 and 0.8 g/kg, and do not allow definition of the optimum intake.'

- Klahr S, Levey AS, Beck GJ, et al. The effects of dietary protein restriction and blood-pressure control on the progression of chronic renal disease. Modification of Diet in Renal Disease Study Group. N Engl J Med 1994; 330:877–884.
- Fouque D, Wang P, Laville M, Boissel JP. Low protein diets for chronic renal failure in non diabetic adults (Cochrane Review). Cochrane Library, issue 4, 2000. Oxford: Update Software.
- Waugh NR, Robertson AM. Protein restriction for diabetic renal disease (Cochrane Review). Cochrane Library, issue 4, 2000. Oxford: Update Software.

Further information: 💻 www.cochrane.co.uk

---

malnutrition. This remains a controversial area but, for most patients living in areas where renal replacement therapy is available, severe protein restriction is not generally recommended. Moderate restriction (to 60 g protein per day) should be accompanied by an adequate intake of calories to prevent malnutrition. Anorexia and muscle loss may indicate a need to commence dialysis treatment.

Lipids

Hypercholesterolaemia is almost universal in patients with significant proteinuria, and increased triglyceride levels are also common in patients with CRF. As well as influencing the development of vascular disease, it has been suggested that this may accelerate the progression of chronic renal disease. The introduction of HMG CoA reductase inhibitors (see p. 311) has made it possible to achieve substantial reductions in lipids in chronic renal disease, but there have been no long-term studies in this group of patients. However, many believe that the high incidence of vascular disease in CRF justifies the treatment of these abnormalities in advance of proof from controlled trials.

Electrolytes and fluid

Due to the reduced ability of the failing kidney to concentrate the urine, a relatively high urine volume is needed to excrete products of metabolism and a fluid intake of around 3 l/day is desirable. Some patients with so-called 'salt-wasting' disease may require a high sodium and water intake, including supplements of sodium chloride and sodium bicarbonate, to prevent fluid depletion and worsening of renal function. This is most often seen in patients with renal cystic disease, obstructive uropathy, reflux nephropathy or other tubulo-interstitial diseases and is not seen in patients with glomerular disease. These patients benefit from taking 5–10 g/day (85–170 mmol/day) of sodium chloride by mouth. It is usual to start with 2–3 g/day and increase the dose as required. The limit for additional salt is set by the development of peripheral or pulmonary oedema, or aggravation of hypertension. Sodium bicarbonate may be substituted in part for sodium chloride when acidosis requires correction.

Limitation of potassium intake (e.g. 70 mmol/day) and sodium intake (e.g. 100 mmol/day) may be required in late CRF if there is evidence of accumulation. Disproportionate fluid retention in milder renal failure, sometimes leading to episodic pulmonary oedema, is particularly associated with renal artery stenosis.

Anaemia

Recombinant human erythropoietin is effective in correcting the anaemia of CRF. Therapy is usually directed towards achieving a target haemoglobin of between 10 and 12 g/l. It must be injected, and subcutaneous administration is most effective. Complications of treatment include increased blood pressure, and adjustment of antihypertensive medication is often necessary. There is also an increase in blood coagulability and an increased incidence of thrombosis of the arteriovenous fistulae used for haemodialysis. If anaemia is corrected slowly, these effects are less common. Erythropoietin is less effective in the presence of iron deficiency, active inflammation or malignancy, or in patients with aluminium overload which may occur in dialysis. These factors should be sought and, if possible, corrected before treatment.

Osteodystrophy

Plasma calcium and phosphate should be kept as near to normal as possible. Hypocalcaemia is corrected by giving 1-α-hydroxylated synthetic analogues of vitamin D. The dose is adjusted to avoid hypercalcaemia. This will usually prevent or control osteomalacia, although it is sometimes resistant, presumably because of other factors inhibiting bone mineralisation. Hyperphosphataemia is controlled by dietary restriction of foods with high phosphate content (milk, cheese, eggs) and the use of phosphate-binding drugs. These agents form insoluble complexes with dietary phosphate and prevent its absorption (e.g. calcium carbonate 500 mg with each meal). Aluminium hydroxide also has a phosphate-binding effect (aluminium hydroxide capsules 300–600 mg before each meal). To prevent aluminium toxicity, the dose of aluminium hydroxide should be kept to a minimum and administered immediately before meals. Secondary hyperparathyroidism is usually prevented or controlled by these measures but, in severe bone disease with autonomous parathyroid function, parathyroidectomy may become necessary.

Prognosis

The tendency of renal impairment to progress was described above (see Fig. 14.21), along with ways of influencing that progression.

Information about the long-term prognosis for patients on dialysis or following transplantation is limited because these techniques have been available only for the past 30 years and technology is changing rapidly. Nevertheless, dialysis and transplantation can be considered as highly effective forms of treatment, with a 5-year survival of approximately 80% for home haemodialysis, 80% following renal transplantation, 60% for hospital haemodialysis and 50% for continuous ambulatory peritoneal dialysis (CAPD). These figures are not directly comparable because of patient selection—many older patients and those with systemic diseases such as diabetes mellitus are treated by CAPD. They also conceal a very large increase in death rates from certain causes, but particularly vascular disease, in comparison with an age-matched population. However, they indicate how the prognosis of end-stage renal disease is now much better than that of many other potentially fatal diseases.

RENAL REPLACEMENT THERAPY

Since the 1960s the facility to replace certain functions of the kidney by artificial means has been available to physicians. Initially, this was applied primarily in ARF, but it has now become routine in patients with end-stage renal failure, who account for the vast majority of treatments. These treatments do not replace the endocrine and metabolic functions of the kidney. They do, however, achieve control of plasma biochemistry and the facility to remove fluid from the circulation (ultrafiltration). The prototype renal replacement therapy was haemodialysis, which is still the most common modality, but a variety of other strategies have evolved, particularly for treating unstable patients with ARF (see Box 14.17).

RENAL REPLACEMENT IN ACUTE RENAL FAILURE

The indications for renal replacement therapy in ARF are as follows:

- *Increased plasma urea:* in general, a plasma urea greater than 30 mmol/l and creatinine greater than 600 μmol/l are undesirable, but much depends on factors such as the rate of biochemical deterioration and the risks of dialysis for the patient involved.
- *Hyperkalaemia:* while this can usually be controlled by medical measures in the short term (see pp. 285–286), dialysis is often required for definitive control.
- *Fluid overload:* if not controlled by fluid restriction and diuretics.
- *Uraemic pericarditis* (uncommon in ARF).

The principal options for renal replacement in ARF are haemodialysis, high-volume haemofiltration, continuous arteriovenous or venovenous haemofiltration, and peritoneal dialysis.

Haemodialysis

Although continuous techniques are being used increasingly in the management of ARF, intermittent haemodialysis is still an important treatment modality in most renal units. In ARF most patients can be treated by 3–4 hours of haemodialysis, either daily in catabolic patients or on alternate days. Dialysis regimens are adjusted to maintain a pre-dialysis urea concentration less than 30 mmol/l, adequate control of potassium and phosphate, and normal ECF volume status.

Vascular access is most often obtained by means of a double-lumen catheter placed in a major vein, commonly the internal jugular, subclavian or femoral. The lifespan of these catheters is often limited due to thrombosis or infection. The Scribner shunt is now rarely used. This consisted of Teflon tips and siliconised rubber tubing placed to connect an artery

14.17 TYPES OF ARTIFICIAL RENAL REPLACEMENT THERAPY

	Application	Typical duration	Typical frequency	Dialysis membrane	Access device
Treatments involving circulation of blood outside the body, regulated by machine					
Haemodialysis	ARF	3–5 hrs	Often daily, sometimes alternate days	Synthetic polymer	Dual-lumen central vein catheter
	CRF	3–5 hrs	3 times per week	Synthetic polymer	Dual-lumen central vein catheter or peripheral arteriovenous fistula
High-volume haemofiltration	ARF	4–6 hrs (15–30 l of filtrate replaced)	Often daily, sometimes alternate days	High-flux synthetic polymer	Dual-lumen central vein catheter
Continuous venovenous haemofiltration (CVVH)	ARF (unstable patients, e.g. in intensive care unit)	Continuous for as long as necessary	1–2 l of filtrate replaced per hour	High-flux synthetic polymer	Dual-lumen central vein catheter
Continuous arteriovenous haemofiltration (CAVH)	ARF (unstable patients, e.g. in intensive care unit)	Continuous for as long as necessary	Continuous— 1–2 l of filtrate replaced per hour	High-flux synthetic polymer	Peripheral arterial and venous cannulae
Treatments involving instillation of fluid into the peritoneal cavity					
Continuous ambulatory peritoneal dialysis (CAPD)	CRF	Continuous	4–5 × 2 l fluid exchanges daily	Peritoneal membrane	Soft intraperitoneal catheter ('Tenckhoff' catheter)
Automated peritoneal dialysis	CRF	Overnight (often with single day-time exchange too)	4–5 fluid exchanges by machine	Peritoneal membrane	'Tenckhoff' catheter
Acute peritoneal dialysis	ARF	Continuous	Hourly fluid exchanges manually or by machine	Peritoneal membrane	Rigid peritoneal catheter

and a vein at the ankle or wrist. The tubing was then separated for connection to the dialyser.

Anticoagulation is required to prevent clotting of the extracorporeal circuit. Haemodialysis machines are equipped to infuse heparin; the efficiency of anticoagulation is monitored by the activated clotting time (ACT). Recent studies have suggested that the use of epoprostenol (prostacyclin) for anticoagulation is associated with a lower risk of bleeding on dialysis, and many units use this in selected patients.

High-volume haemofiltration

This technique involves the rapid removal and replacement of 15–30 l of plasma ultrafiltrate over 3–5 hours, using an artificial membrane with a very high ultrafiltration capacity, on a daily or alternate-day basis. The fluid removed is replaced by haemofiltration fluid. It is claimed that this technique induces less circulatory instability than haemodialysis.

Continuous techniques

These include continuous arteriovenous haemofiltration (CAVH) and continuous venovenous haemofiltration (CVVH —see Fig. 14.22). These systems cause less haemodynamic disturbance than conventional haemodialysis, and are widely used in patients with ARF who are unstable and require intensive care (see Fig. 14.16, p. 596). In CAVH the extracorporeal blood circuit is driven by the arteriovenous pressure difference. Poor filtration rates and clotting of the filter

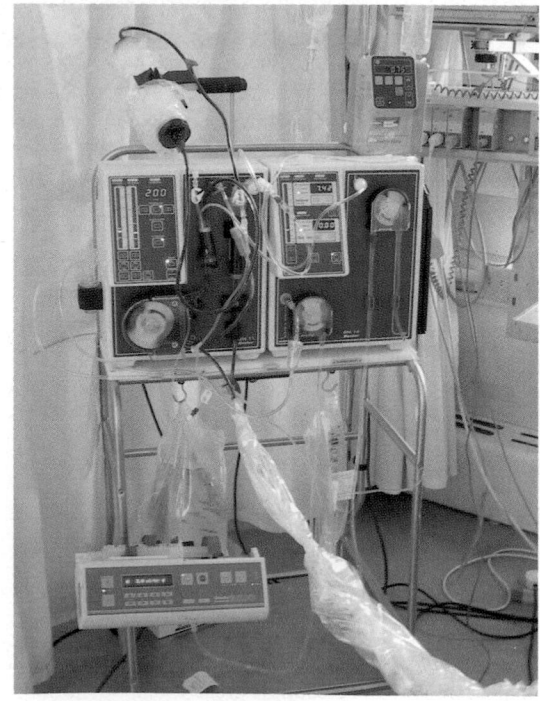

Fig. 14.22 Continuous venovenous haemofiltration (CVVH) on an intensive care unit. In this hypothermic patient the haemofilter and blood lines have been wrapped to reduce heat loss.

may result from low arterial pressure and/or elevated central venous pressure. CVVH is pump-driven, allowing a reliable extracorporeal circulation. Most patients are managed by removal and replacement of 1–2 l of filtrate per hour (equivalent to a GFR of 15–30 ml/min).

Peritoneal dialysis

In ARF, this technique has been supplanted in most centres by those outlined above. It is less efficient than haemodialysis, and seldom achieves good biochemical control, especially in catabolic patients. It is not feasible after recent abdominal surgery, but can be useful in patients with cardiovascular instability (e.g. after cardiac surgery). A trocar and cannula system is used for acute peritoneal access, and 0.5–2 l volumes of peritoneal dialysis fluid are infused and drained cyclically. Flow can be regulated manually or by an automatic cycler. Cloudy effluent indicates the development of peritonitis, in which case the catheter should be removed immediately and appropriate antibiotics given (e.g. vancomycin or gentamicin).

RENAL REPLACEMENT IN CHRONIC RENAL FAILURE

Haemodialysis

Intermittent haemodialysis is the standard blood purification therapy in end-stage renal failure (ESRF—see Fig. 14.23). Haemodialysis should be started when, despite adequate medical treatment, the patient has advanced renal failure, and before he or she develops serious complications. This often occurs with a plasma creatinine of 600–800 µmol/l. Vascular access is required; an arteriovenous fistula should be formed, usually in the forearm, when the serum creatinine is around 400 µmol/l, so that it has time to become established. After 4–6 weeks, increased pressure in the veins leading from the fistula will have caused distension and thickening of the vessel wall (arterialisation). Large-bore

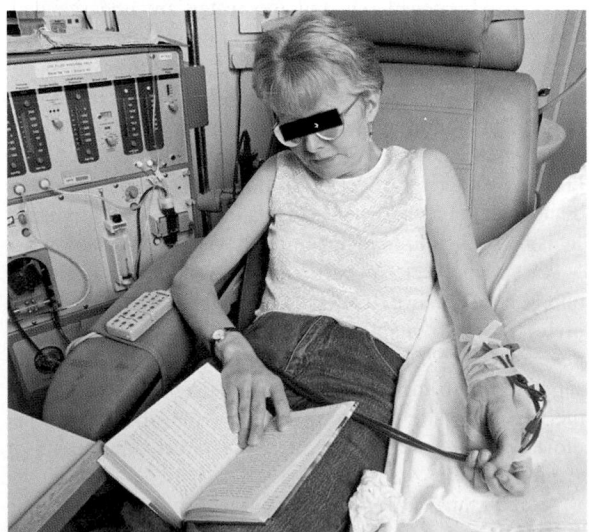

Fig. 14.23 Haemodialysis. A patient receiving haemodialysis through a forearm subcutaneous fistula (a Brescia–Cimino fistula). She subsequently received a live related transplant.

needles can then be inserted into the vein to provide access for each haemodialysis treatment (see Fig. 14.23). If this is not possible, plastic cannulae in central veins can be used for short-term access. Haemodialysis is usually carried out for 3–5 hours three times weekly. Most patients notice a gradual improvement in symptoms during the first 6 weeks of treatment. Plasma urea and creatinine are lowered by each treatment but do not return to normal. Accepted standards of dialysis adequacy, which relate the clearance of urea to total body water, are adhered to in most units. Some patients are able to carry out their treatment at home. Many patients lead normal and active lives, and patient survival for more than 20 years is commonplace.

Continuous ambulatory peritoneal dialysis (CAPD)

CAPD is a form of long-term dialysis involving insertion of a permanent Silastic catheter into the peritoneal cavity. Two litres of sterile, isotonic dialysis fluid are introduced and left in place for a period of approximately 6 hours. During this time, metabolic waste products diffuse from peritoneal capillaries into the dialysis fluid down a concentration gradient. The fluid is then drained and fresh dialysis fluid introduced. This cycle is repeated four times daily, during which time the patient is mobile and able to undertake normal daily activities. It is particularly useful in young children, in elderly patients with cardiovascular instability and in patients with diabetes mellitus. Its long-term use may be limited by episodes of bacterial peritonitis, but some patients have been treated successfully for more than 10 years.

The use of automated peritoneal dialysis (APD) is now widespread. This system is similar to CAPD but uses a mechanical device to perform the fluid exchanges during the night, leaving the patient free or with only a single exchange to perform during the day.

Renal transplantation

This offers the possibility of restoring normal kidney function and correcting all the metabolic abnormalities of CRF. The kidney graft is taken from a cadaver donor or from a relative. ABO (blood group) compatibility between donor and recipient is essential, and it is usual to select donor kidneys on the basis of human leucocyte antigen (HLA) matching as this improves graft survival. Immune-mediated graft rejection is the major cause of failure. Results of kidney transplantation have improved significantly in recent years. Three-year graft survival is in the region of 80%, while 3-year patient survival is approximately 90%.

Long-term immunosuppressive therapy is required following renal transplantation. Many therapeutic regimens have been used, but the most common involves a combination of prednisolone, ciclosporin A and azathioprine. There is concern about the long-term nephrotoxicity of ciclosporin. The role of newer immunosuppressive agents such as tacrolimus (FK506), mycophenolate mofetil and rapamycin is currently being established by clinical trials.

Immunosuppression is associated with an increased incidence of infection, particularly opportunistic, and an increased risk of malignant neoplasms, especially of the skin. Approximately 50% of white patients will have developed skin malignancy by 15 years post-transplant. Lymphomas are rare but occur early and are often related to infection with herpes virus, especially Epstein–Barr virus (see p. 16). Despite these drawbacks, transplantation offers the best hope of complete rehabilitation and is the most cost-effective of the treatment options for chronic renal failure.

ISSUES IN OLDER PEOPLE
RENAL REPLACEMENT THERAPY

- Age itself is not a barrier to good quality of life on renal replacement therapy.
- The high prevalence of coexisting cardiovascular disease in old age can make dialysis difficult; the elderly are more sensitive to fluid balance changes, predisposing to hypotension during dialysis with rebound hypertension between dialyses. In addition the ischaemic heart cannot cope with fluid overload and pulmonary oedema easily develops.
- This means that only hospital-provided haemodialysis is suitable and older patients require more medical and nursing time.
- Survival on dialysis is difficult to predict for an individual patient, but is independently correlated with age, functional ability (e.g. Barthel or Karnofsky score) and comorbid disease.
- Withdrawal from dialysis is a common cause of death in older patients with comorbid disease.
- Relative risks of surgery and immunosuppression, and limited organ availability exclude most older people from transplantation.
- Conservative therapy, i.e. without dialysis but with adequate support, may be a popular option for patients at high risk of complications from dialysis, who have a limited prognosis and little hope of functional recovery.

CONGENITAL ABNORMALITIES OF THE KIDNEYS AND URINARY SYSTEM

Congenital anomalies of the urinary tract (see Fig. 14.24) affect more than 10% of infants and, if not immediately lethal, may lead to complications in later life. About 1 in 500 infants are born with only one kidney. Although usually compatible with normal life, this is often associated with other abnormalities. Polycystic kidney disease (see p. 621) is the most common inherited cause of severe renal disease. The next most common, Alport's syndrome, is considered on page 611 and other cystic diseases on page 622. Other inherited disorders affecting the kidney include tumour syndromes (see p. 635) and conditions caused by mutations in transporter or exchanger molecules (see p. 623).

Hypospadias is caused by a failure of fusion of embryonic folds and results in abnormal placing of the external urinary meatus on the ventral surface of the penis. The opening may be coronal, penile, scrotal or even perineal. With opening in these latter sites, the corpus spongiosum is scarred and fibrosed, leading to a ventral curvature or chordee of the penis. The aim of treatment is to correct the chordee by excising the fibrosis and then to perform a plastic surgical operation to make a new urethral opening in the normal position on the glans. This procedure should be completed before the boy reaches school age.

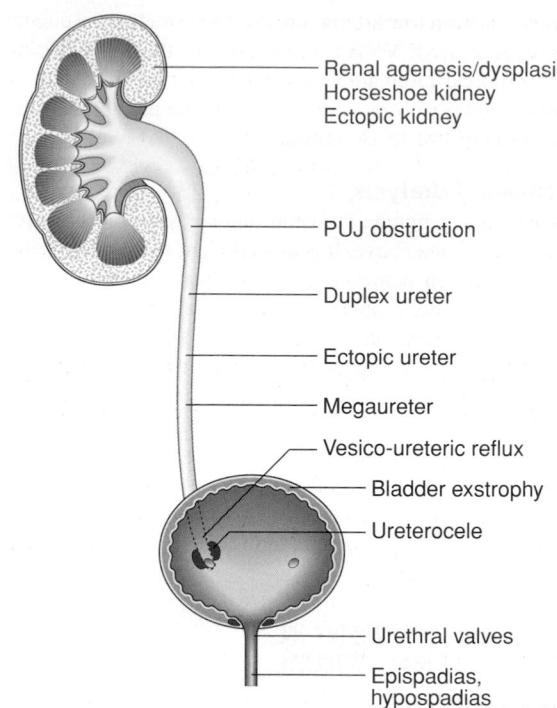

Fig. 14.24   **Congenital abnormalities of the urinary tract.**

- Renal agenesis/dysplasia
  Horseshoe kidney
  Ectopic kidney
- PUJ obstruction
- Duplex ureter
- Ectopic ureter
- Megaureter
- Vesico-ureteric reflux
- Bladder exstrophy
- Ureterocele
- Urethral valves
- Epispadias, hypospadias

Epispadias refers to a condition where the external urinary meatus opens on the dorsal surface of the penis. The extent of the malformation varies from an isolated penile abnormality to a gross failure in the development of the bladder and urethra. Severe deformity results from extension of the cloacal membrane on to the lower abdominal wall, preventing the two halves of the wall from closing over the developing bladder. As a result, the mucosa of the bladder and the ureteric orifices are exposed and form the infra-umbilical part of the abdominal wall (exstrophy). The urethra lies opened out and the testes are undescended; additional abnormalities include separation of the symphysis pubis and rectal prolapse. Reconstruction of these deformities is not always successful and urinary incontinence may remain a major problem and require urinary diversion.

A ureterocele (see Fig. 14.12, p. 591) develops behind a pin-hole ureteric orifice; the intramural part of the ureter dilates and bulges into the bladder, and can become very large. Incision of the pin-hole opening relieves the obstruction.

An ectopic ureter occurs with congenital duplication of one or both kidneys (duplex kidneys). Developmentally, the ureter has two main branches and, if this arrangement persists, the two ureters of the duplex kidneys may drain separately into the bladder. One ureter enters normally on the trigone, while the ectopic ureter (from the upper renal moiety) enters the bladder or, more rarely, the vagina or seminal vesicle.

A ureter that is ectopic and drains into the bladder is liable to have an ineffective valve mechanism so that urine passes up the ureter on voiding (vesico-ureteric reflux, see p. 620). Reflux can occur in normally sited ureters if the intramural ureter fails to act as a valve. The pressure of refluxing urine behaves as an intermittent obstruction which in children may lead to serious renal damage. The management of vesico-ureteric reflux and associated reflux nephropathy is outlined on page 621.

In primary obstructive megaureter there is dilatation of the ureter in all but its terminal segment without obvious cause and without vesico-ureteric reflux. Radiographic and pressure/flow studies may be needed to determine whether there is obstruction to urine flow. Narrowing of the ureter and reimplantation may be necessary.

RENAL VASCULAR DISEASES

Adequate blood supply is critical for all aspects of renal function. Hence, diseases which affect the renal blood vessels can cause any and all of the clinical manifestations of renal disease. They are particularly likely to cause acute or chronic renal failure and secondary hypertension.

RENAL ARTERY STENOSIS

While disease of the renal arteries is a well-known cause of secondary hypertension, it is also an increasingly recognised cause of renal failure, particularly in the elderly—a condition known as ischaemic nephropathy.

Pathology

The most common cause is atherosclerosis, especially in older patients; it is usually associated with clinically significant atherosclerosis elsewhere, and is particularly likely if there are symptoms or signs of disease affecting the lower limbs. In younger patients (< 50 years), fibromuscular dysplasia is a more likely cause. This is a congenital band of fibrous tissue around the artery, which, as the patient grows, causes progressive narrowing of the vessel. It most commonly presents with hypertension in patients aged 15–30 years. In both types, if the stenosis is haemodynamically significant, an area of post-stenotic dilatation develops distal to the narrowed area. Stenosis is classed as ostial, proximal or distal according to the part of the vessel affected, and is quantified in terms of the degree of narrowing. Stenosis of less than 50% is not usually considered to be haemodynamically significant. In simple, unilateral disease the unaffected kidney will show changes of hypertensive nephrosclerosis; the renal parenchyma on the stenosed side may be relatively protected from the effects of hypertension, but will have a reduced GFR due to under-perfusion. In atherosclerosis the picture is often complicated by small-vessel disease in the kidneys that may be related to subclinical atheroemboli, hypertension or other disease.

Investigations

If the stenosis is long-standing, a reduction in kidney size occurs which can be detected by ultrasound. Since renal artery stenosis is often asymmetrical or unilateral, a discrepancy in size between the two kidneys on ultrasound is a useful (but insensitive and late) pointer to the diagnosis, along with hypertension, renal impairment or vascular disease elsewhere (see Box 14.18). Renal isotope scanning may

---

14.18 RENAL ARTERY STENOSIS

Renal artery stenosis is more likely if:

- Hypertension is severe, *or* of recent onset, *or* difficult to control
- Kidneys are asymmetrical in size
- There is evidence of vascular disease elsewhere (especially in lower limbs)

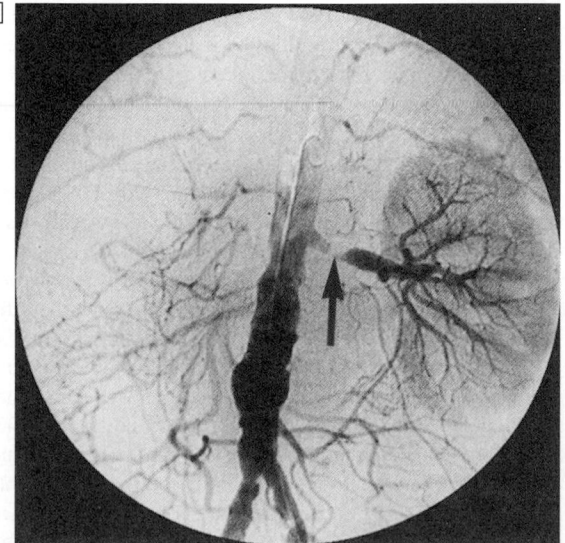

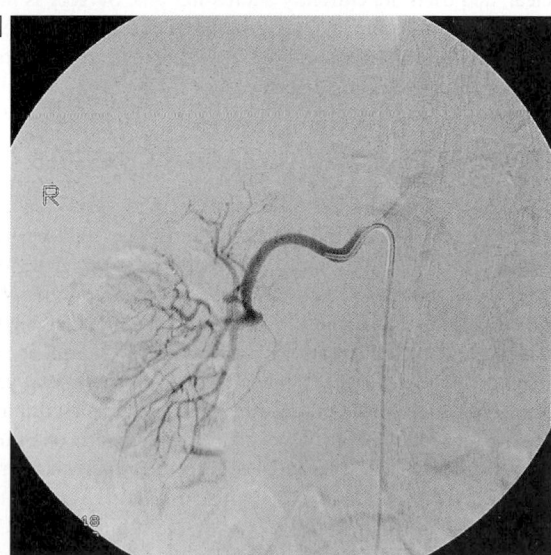

Fig. 14.25   Renal artery stenosis. **A** Digital subtraction arteriogram following injection of contrast material into the aorta showing renal artery stenosis. The abdominal aorta is severely irregular and atheromatous. The right renal artery is absent. The left renal artery is stenosed (arrow), but contrast medium has passed the stenosis and the developing nephrogram can be seen. **B** In another patient, a catheter has been passed beyond a stenosis at the ostium of the right renal artery in preparation for balloon dilatation/stenting.

show delayed uptake of isotope and reduced excretion by an affected kidney. The definitive investigation is renal arteriography (see Fig. 14.25) and this is required before treatment is undertaken.

Management and prognosis

Untreated, atheromatous renal artery stenosis will progress to complete arterial occlusion and loss of kidney function in about 15% of cases; this figure is increased with more severe degrees of stenosis. If the progression is gradual, collateral vessels may develop and some function may be preserved. Even if the main arterial supply is lost, the kidney receives some blood supply from capsular blood vessels. These will not support kidney function, but may be sufficient to prevent infarction and loss of kidney structure. Fibromuscular dysplasia does not usually cause complete occlusion of the renal artery, and will usually stabilise once the patient stops growing.

Treatment options are as follows:

- medical treatment (antihypertensive therapy, low-dose aspirin and lipid-lowering drugs if appropriate)
- angioplasty, with or without mechanical stenting after balloon dilatation
- surgical resection of the stenosed segment and reanastomosis.

At present there are no conclusive data to indicate the overall superiority of one approach over another. Angioplasty is widely used, usually with stenting to improve the patency rate. However, there may be substantial risks to these procedures in patients with atherosclerosis—of contrast nephropathy (see Box 14.2, p. 584), of renal artery occlusion and renal infarction, and of atheroemboli (see p. 611) from manipulations in a severely diseased aorta. The overall effect on renal function and on patient survival is far from clear, and trials are currently addressing this. Surgery is now much less commonly undertaken. Conservative medical treatment may be appropriate if there is widespread atheromatous disease of the aorta and elsewhere.

DISEASES OF SMALL INTRARENAL VESSELS

A number of conditions are associated with acute damage and occlusion of small blood vessels (arterioles and capillaries) in the kidney. They are associated to varying degrees with similar changes elsewhere in the body. A common feature of these syndromes is microangiopathic haemolytic anaemia, in which haemolysis occurs as a consequence of damage incurred during passage through the abnormal vessels. Fragmented red cells can be seen on a blood film and are a hallmark of small-vessel disease. The main conditions associated with damage and occlusion of small intrarenal vessels are given in Box 14.19.

Thrombotic microangiopathy

Haemolytic uraemic syndrome (HUS) and thrombotic thrombocytopenic purpura (TTP) are types of thrombotic microangiopathy. A common feature of both disorders is

14.19 MICROVASCULAR DISORDERS ASSOCIATED WITH ACUTE RENAL DAMAGE

- Thrombotic microangiopathy (haemolytic uraemic syndrome and thrombotic thrombocytopenic purpura)
    Associated with verotoxin-producing *Escherichia coli*
    Other (familial, drugs, cancer etc.)
- Disseminated intravascular coagulation (see p. 611)
- Malignant hypertension
- Small-vessel vasculitis (see p. 624)
- Systemic sclerosis (scleroderma; see p. 611)
- Atheroemboli ('cholesterol' emboli)

damage to endothelial cells of the microcirculation, which is followed by cell swelling, platelet adherence and thrombosis. The aetiology of the syndromes may be rather different, as are the manifestations, although there is substantial overlap. The kidney microcirculation tends to be most affected in HUS, with involvement of other organs (including the brain) in more severe cases. In TTP the brain is commonly affected and involvement of the kidney may be less. Both disorders are characterised by a severe microangiopathy causing a marked reduction in the platelet count and haemoglobin concentration. Other features of intravascular haemolysis—raised bilirubin and lactate dehydrogenase (LDH), decreased haptoglobins—are also present. A reticulocytosis is often seen.

Thrombotic microangiopathy associated with *E. coli* infection (especially O157 serotypes) is a relatively new condition associated with verotoxin-producing organisms (see p. 42). Although the bacteria live as commensals in the gut of cattle and other domestic livestock, they can cause haemorrhagic diarrhoea in humans when the infection is contracted from contaminated food products, water or other infected individuals. In a proportion of cases, verotoxin produced by the organisms enters the circulation and binds to specific glycolipid receptors that are expressed particularly on the surface of microvascular endothelial cells. In children, this causes diarrhoea-associated (D+)HUS, although in more severe cases the brain and other organs are also affected. D+HUS is now the most common cause of acute renal failure in children in developed countries. In adults, the disease may more closely resemble TTP; both adults and children usually recover, often after 5–15 days of dialysis. No specific treatments have been shown to help.

Other causes of thrombotic microangiopathy have a less certain outlook and are more likely to recur (sometimes after renal transplantation). Familial examples may reflect an abnormality of endothelial cell defence against damage or thrombosis, including complement factor H deficiency, and deficiency of von Willebrand protease (see p. 952). The disease may occur post-partum, in response to certain drugs (especially chemotherapy), after bone marrow transplantation, in malignancy and apparently spontaneously. Plasma exchange using fresh frozen plasma is effective at controlling the disease in many of these examples. There is evidence that it can in some circumstances replace a deficient substance (probably the von Willebrand protease).

Disseminated intravascular coagulation

In this condition, the most prominent abnormality is consumption of clotting factors due to uncontrolled thrombosis in the microvasculature, leading to severe deficiency of these proteins in the plasma and a tendency to haemorrhage from larger vessels (see p. 952). There may also be thrombocytopenia. Precipitating conditions include septic shock, in which bacterial endotoxin directly activates the coagulation cascade; obstetric complications; disseminated cancer; and other causes of massive internal bleeding or coagulation activation or depletion. Treatment consists of maintaining haemostasis with replacement of clotting factors as required and correcting the underlying condition.

Malignant hypertension

Malignant or accelerated hypertension (see p. 389) is of such severity as to cause acute damage to renal arterioles. It is often symptomatic, with headache, impaired vision and, finally, manifestations of renal failure (see Fig. 14.26). It is usually associated with the features of microangiopathy described above. In the absence of a previous history, it may be difficult to distinguish these patients from those with HUS and marked hypertension. Patients usually respond to effective control of blood pressure, although renal function is permanently lost in 20% of cases.

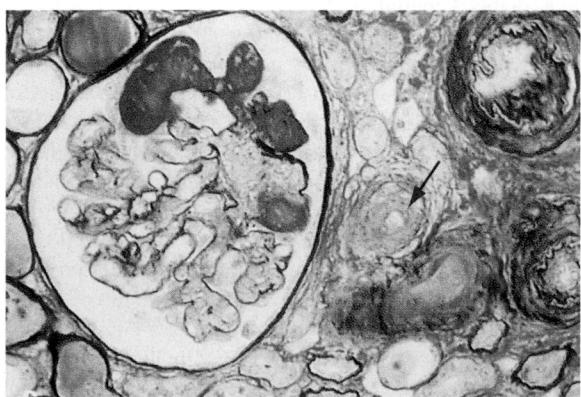

Fig. 14.26 **Glomerular capillary thrombosis in malignant hypertension.** Similar changes occur in thrombotic microangiopathy. The adjacent arteriole (arrow) shows gross intimal thickening.

Small-vessel vasculitis

Renal disease caused by small-vessel vasculitis is covered on page 624.

Systemic sclerosis (scleroderma)

This connective tissue disease is described on page 1036. Renal involvement is a serious feature, and is characterised by intimal cell proliferation and luminal narrowing of intrarenal arteries and arterioles. Clinically, it usually presents as 'scleroderma renal crisis', with severe hypertension, microangiopathic features and progressive oliguric renal failure. There is intense intrarenal vasospasm, and plasma renin activity is markedly elevated. Use of ACE inhibitors to control the hypertension has improved the 1-year survival from 20%

to 75%; however, about 50% of patients continue to require renal replacement therapy.

Atheroembolic renal disease ('cholesterol' emboli)

This is caused by showers of cholesterol-containing microemboli, arising in atheromatous plaques in major arteries. It occurs in patients with widespread atheromatous disease, usually after interventions such as surgery or arteriography. Clinical features are loss of renal function, haematuria and proteinuria, and sometimes eosinophilia and inflammatory features which may mimic a small-vessel vasculitis. Accompanying signs of microvascular occlusion in the lower limbs (e.g. ischaemic toes, livedo reticularis) are common but not invariable (see Fig. 14.27). There is no specific treatment.

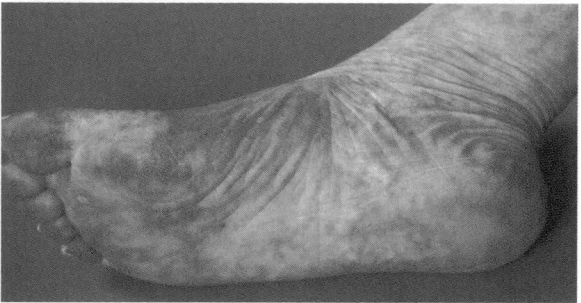

Fig. 14.27 **The foot of a patient who suffered extensive atheroembolism following coronary artery stenting.**

GLOMERULAR DISEASES

Glomerular diseases may cause any of a characteristic range of abnormalities including haematuria, proteinuria, loss of renal function and hypertension; they continue to be a major source of CRF in developed as well as developing countries (see Fig. 14.10, p. 586). While a few glomerular diseases are inherited, most are acquired. The acquired disorders can be divided into inflammatory/proliferative and non-inflammatory or non-immune types.

INHERITED GLOMERULAR DISEASES

ALPORT'S SYNDROME

A number of uncommon diseases may affect the glomerulus in childhood, but the most important disease affecting adults is Alport's syndrome (see Box 14.20). Most cases arise from a mutation or deletion of the COL4A5 gene on the X chromosome that results in a progressive degeneration of the GBM (see Fig. 14.28). Some other basement membranes containing the same collagen isoforms are similarly affected, notably in the cochlea.

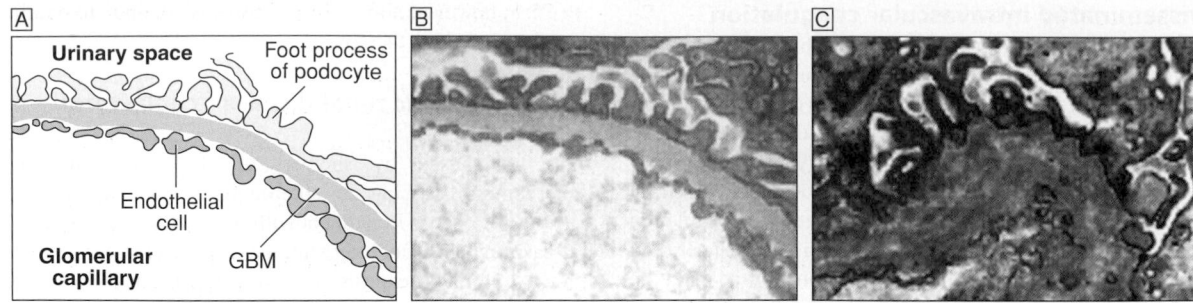

Fig. 14.28 Alport's syndrome. [A] Diagrammatic structure of the normal GBM. [B] The normal GBM (electron micrograph) contains mostly the tissue-specific α3, α4 and α5 chains of type IV collagen. [C] In Alport's syndrome this network is disrupted and replaced by α1 and α2 chains. Although the GBM appears structurally normal in early life, in time thinning appears, progressing to thickening, splitting and degeneration.

14.20 ALPORT'S SYNDROME

- The second most common inherited cause of renal failure (polycystic kidney disease being the most common)
- Hallmark is progressive degeneration of GBM (see Fig. 14.28)
- Caused by abnormalities of tissue-specific isoforms of type IV (basement membrane) collagen
- Associated with sensorineural deafness (to high tones first) and ocular abnormalities
- Most cases associated with mutations of COL4A5, encoding α5 (IV) collagen, located at Xq22

X-linked disease (COL4A5)

- Affected males progress from haematuria to end-stage renal failure in late teens or twenties
- Female carriers usually have haematuria but rarely develop significant renal disease

Autosomal recessive disease (COL4A3, COL4A4)

- Females and males equally affected
- Carriers may have microscopic haematuria and thin GBM disease

No treatment has been devised to slow the progress of this condition, but patients with Alport's syndrome are good candidates for renal replacement therapy as they are young and usually otherwise healthy. Some of these patients develop an immune response to the normal collagen antigens present in the GBM of a transplanted kidney, and in a small minority anti-GBM disease develops and destroys the allograft.

THIN GBM DISEASE

In 'thin GBM' disease there is glomerular bleeding, usually only at the microscopic or stick-test level, without associated hypertension, proteinuria or reduction of GFR. The glomeruli appear normal by light microscopy, but on electron microscopy the GBM is abnormally thin. The prognosis is good. This autosomal dominant condition accounts for a large proportion of 'benign familial haematuria', and has an excellent prognosis. Some families may be carriers of autosomal recessive Alport's syndrome, but this does not account for all cases.

GLOMERULONEPHRITIS

Although glomerulonephritis literally means 'inflammation of glomeruli', the term is used to include other types of glomerular disease (glomerulopathies) even though there is no histological evidence of inflammation. Glomerular damage may follow a number of insults: immunological injury, inherited error (e.g. Alport's syndrome), metabolic stress (e.g. diabetes mellitus), deposition of extraneous materials (e.g. amyloid), or other direct injury to glomerular cells.

Most glomerulonephritis is presumed to be immunologically mediated. For some diseases there is direct evidence of this—e.g. the anti-GBM antibodies seen in Goodpasture's disease. Deposition of antibody is seen in many types of glomerulonephritis (see Box 14.21). In many, the presumed mechanisms involve cellular immunity, which is more difficult to investigate and prove. The response of several types of glomerulonephritis to immunosuppressive drugs provides further indirect evidence. In most cases the targets of immunity are likely to be glomerular antigens (see Fig. 14.29).

Although deposition of circulating immune complexes was previously thought to be a common mechanism of glomerulonephritis, it now seems likely that most granular deposits of immunoglobulin within glomeruli are caused by 'in situ' formation of immune complexes about glomerular antigens, or about other antigens ('planted' antigens, e.g. viral or bacterial ones) that have localised in glomeruli.

Classifications of glomerulonephritis are largely histopathological and may appear daunting. How these pathological appearances arise is the subject of the next section. The major histopathological types are shown in Box 14.21 and Fig. 14.30, and clinically important examples are described in the text.

Responses to glomerular injury

Glomerular changes that occur following initiation of injury are limited to a small repertoire, and can be simplified to six processes.

Leucocyte infiltration

Generation of chemoattractants and other mediators following injury by immunological or other processes causes

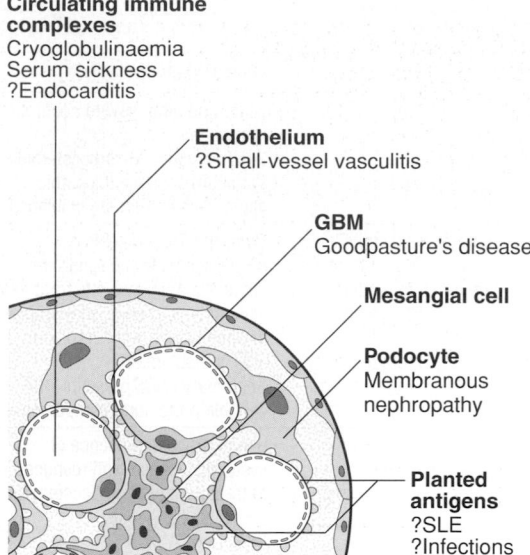

Circulating immune complexes
Cryoglobulinaemia
Serum sickness
?Endocarditis

Endothelium
?Small-vessel vasculitis

GBM
Goodpasture's disease

Mesangial cell

Podocyte
Membranous
nephropathy

Planted antigens
?SLE
?Infections

Fig. 14.29　Cells of the glomerulus and targets of immunity and autoimmunity. The diagram also shows where antibodies and antigen-antibody (immune) complexes may be seen: subepithelial, between podocyte and GBM; intramembranous, within the GBM; subendothelial, between endothelial cell and GBM; and mesangial, within the mesangial matrix (compare with Fig. 14.30).

endothelial cells to express adhesion molecules to which leucocytes bind. Leucocytes may also migrate towards high concentrations of chemoattractants (chemotaxis), crossing basement membranes by diapedesis. Monocytes can mature into secretory macrophages, which may exacerbate injury; however, monocytes may also play a major role in the resolution of inflammation by phagocytic clearance of apoptotic leucocytes. Current corticosteroid and cytotoxic therapies influence these processes.

Resident cell changes

Hydraulic stress upon mesangial cells, secretory macrophages and recruited platelets may all release mitogens such as platelet-derived growth factor (PDGF) or basic fibroblast growth factor (bFGF). These trigger proliferation of mesangial and endothelial cells and phenotypic change in these and in epithelial cells (podocytes). Such changes lead to alterations in matrix (see below). Resolution involves deletion of excess resident cells by apoptosis and restoration of the resident cell phenotype. Currently available therapies are not known to influence these processes directly, but PDGF and other mediators are potential targets.

Extracellular matrix changes

Secretory macrophages or mesangial cells stressed by (for example) hydraulic stimuli may release transforming growth factor-β_1 (TGF-β_1) that is locally activated. In turn, this fibrogenic cytokine causes mesangial cells to adopt a myofibroblastic phenotype, secreting both matrix components and inhibitors of metalloproteinases (TIMPs), leading to net accumulation of matrix. Similar mechanisms acting on podocytes or endothelial cells may lead to thickening

of GBM. Blockade of TGF-β function is being studied in human disease.

Crescent formation

Severe glomerular capillary injury, most likely mediated by leucocyte-derived reactive oxygen species and injurious proteins, causes breaches in capillary walls. Bleeding into Bowman's space and formation of fibrin clots stimulate the proliferation of parietal epithelial cells of Bowman's capsule. Infiltrating monocytes may join the crescent cells. The resultant crescent may compress capillaries (see Fig. 14.30). Glomerular loss is the rule but resolution may occur in some circumstances (e.g. post-streptococcal nephritis), particularly if Bowman's capsule is not breached. Modification of inflammation using cytotoxic agents and corticosteroids can rescue glomeruli affected by crescents in some other diseases, e.g. systemic vasculitis.

Glomerular capillary thrombosis

Platelet adherence to the glomerular capillary wall may reflect mediator generation within the glomerulus or from the blood, causing endothelial cell activation with adhesion molecule expression, or endothelial cell retraction leading to GBM exposure. Tufts in which glomerular capillaries are occluded usually die by ischaemic necrosis, but resolution is possible, as fibrinolysis can result in recanalisation of capillaries, which can be repaired by angiogenesis. Previous attempts to prevent thrombosis by using anticoagulants in human disease have not proven effective, but angiogenesis could potentially be promoted by therapy.

Glomerulosclerosis

Leucocyte accumulation, resident cell and matrix changes, and recruitment of extraglomerular fibroblasts set up a situation in which progressive and unscheduled apoptosis of resident cells leads to a featureless glomerular scar. This lesion can also arise because of podocyte injury and retraction; naked GBM then adheres to Bowman's capsule, this adhesion enlarges and glomerular filtration occurs directly into the paraglomerular space, causing periglomerular fibrosis, ultimately progressing to a functionless scar.

CRESCENTIC NEPHRITIS (RPGN)

Crescentic nephritis is described on pages 597–598.

MINIMAL CHANGE NEPHROPATHY AND PRIMARY FOCAL SEGMENTAL GLOMERULOSCLEROSIS (FSGS)

Patients with minimal change nephropathy and a subgroup of patients with FSGS can be seen as opposite ends of a spectrum of conditions causing the idiopathic nephrotic syndrome (see p. 589). Minimal change disease occurs at all ages but accounts for most cases of nephrotic syndrome in childhood and is the underlying diagnosis in about one-quarter of adult patients with nephrotic syndrome. Proteinuria usually remits on high-dose corticosteroid therapy (1 mg/kg prednisolone for 6 weeks), although some patients who respond incompletely or relapse frequently need maintenance corticosteroids, cytotoxic therapy or other

14.21 GLOMERULONEPHRITIS: TYPES, ASSOCIATIONS AND CAUSES

	Histology	Immune deposits	Pathogenesis	Association	Clinical features
Minimal change	Normal, except on electron microscopy, where fusion of podocyte foot processes is seen (occurs in many types of proteinuria)	None	Unknown	Atopy, HLA-DR7 Drugs	Acute and often severe nephrotic syndrome Good response to corticosteroids Dominant cause of idiopathic nephrotic syndrome in childhood
Focal segmental glomerulosclerosis (FSGS)	Segmental scars in some glomeruli No acute inflammation Podocyte foot process fusion seen in primary FSGS with nephrotic syndrome	Non-specific trapping in focal scars	Unknown; in some, circulating factors increase glomerular permeability Injury to podocytes may be a common feature	Healing of previous local glomerular injury HIV infection, heroin misuse, morbid obesity	*Primary FSGS* presents as idiopathic nephrotic syndrome but is less responsive to treatment than minimal change; may progress to renal impairment, can recur after transplantation *Secondary FSGS* presents with variable proteinuria and outcome
Focal segmental (necrotising) glomerulonephritis	Segmental inflammation and/or necrosis in some glomeruli May be crescent formation	Variable according to cause, but typically negative (or 'pauci-immune')	Small-vessel vasculitis	Primary or secondary small-vessel vasculitis	Usually implies presence of systemic disease, and responds to treatment with corticosteroids and cytotoxic agents Check ANCA, ANA
Membranous nephropathy	Thickening of GBM Progressing to increased matrix deposition and glomerulosclerosis	Granular subepithelial IgG	Antibodies to a podocyte surface antigen, with complement-dependent podocyte injury (presumed from animal model)	HLA-DR3 (for idiopathic) Drugs Heavy metals Hepatitis B virus Malignancy	Usually idiopathic; common cause of adult idiopathic nephrotic syndrome One-third progress; may respond to chlorambucil/prednisolone Associated HLA class II allele varies in different populations
IgA nephropathy	Increased mesangial matrix and cells Focal segmental nephritis in acute disease	Mesangial IgA	Unknown	Usually idiopathic Liver disease	Very common disease with range of presentations, but usually including haematuria and hypertension (see text)
Mesangiocapillary glomerulonephritis (MCGN) (= membranoproliferative glomerulonephritis, MPGN)					
Type I	Mesangial cells interpose between endothelium and GBM	Subendothelial	Deposition of circulating immune complexes or 'planted' antigens	Bacterial infection Hepatitis B virus Cryoglobulinaemia (± hepatitis C virus infection)	Usually proteinuria, may be haematuria Most common pattern found in association with subacute bacterial infection No proven treatments except where cause can be treated
Type II	Mesangial cells interpose between endothelium and GBM	Intramembranous dense deposits	Associated with complement consumption caused by autoantibodies	C3 nephritic factor and partial lipodystrophy	Also known as dense deposit disease
Post-infection	Diffuse (uniformly in all glomeruli) proliferation of endothelial and mesangial cells Infiltration by neutrophils and macrophages May be crescent formation	Subendothelial	Immune response to streptococcal infection Cross-reactive epitopes or other explanation	Streptococcal and other infections	Now rare in developed countries Presents with severe sodium and fluid retention, hypertension, haematuria, oliguria Usually resolves spontaneously
Goodpasture's disease (anti-GBM disease)	Usually crescentic nephritis	Linear IgG along GBM	Autoimmunity to α3 chain of type IV collagen	HLA-DR15 (previously known as DR2)	Associated with lung haemorrhage, but either may occur alone Treat with corticosteroids, cyclophosphamide and plasma exchange to remove circulating autoantibodies
Lupus nephritis	Almost any histological type	Always positive and often profuse Pattern varies according to type	Some anti-DNA antibodies also bind to glomerular targets	Complement deficiencies Complement consumption	Very variable presentation; sometimes as renal disease alone without systemic features Responds to cytotoxic therapy in addition to prednisolone

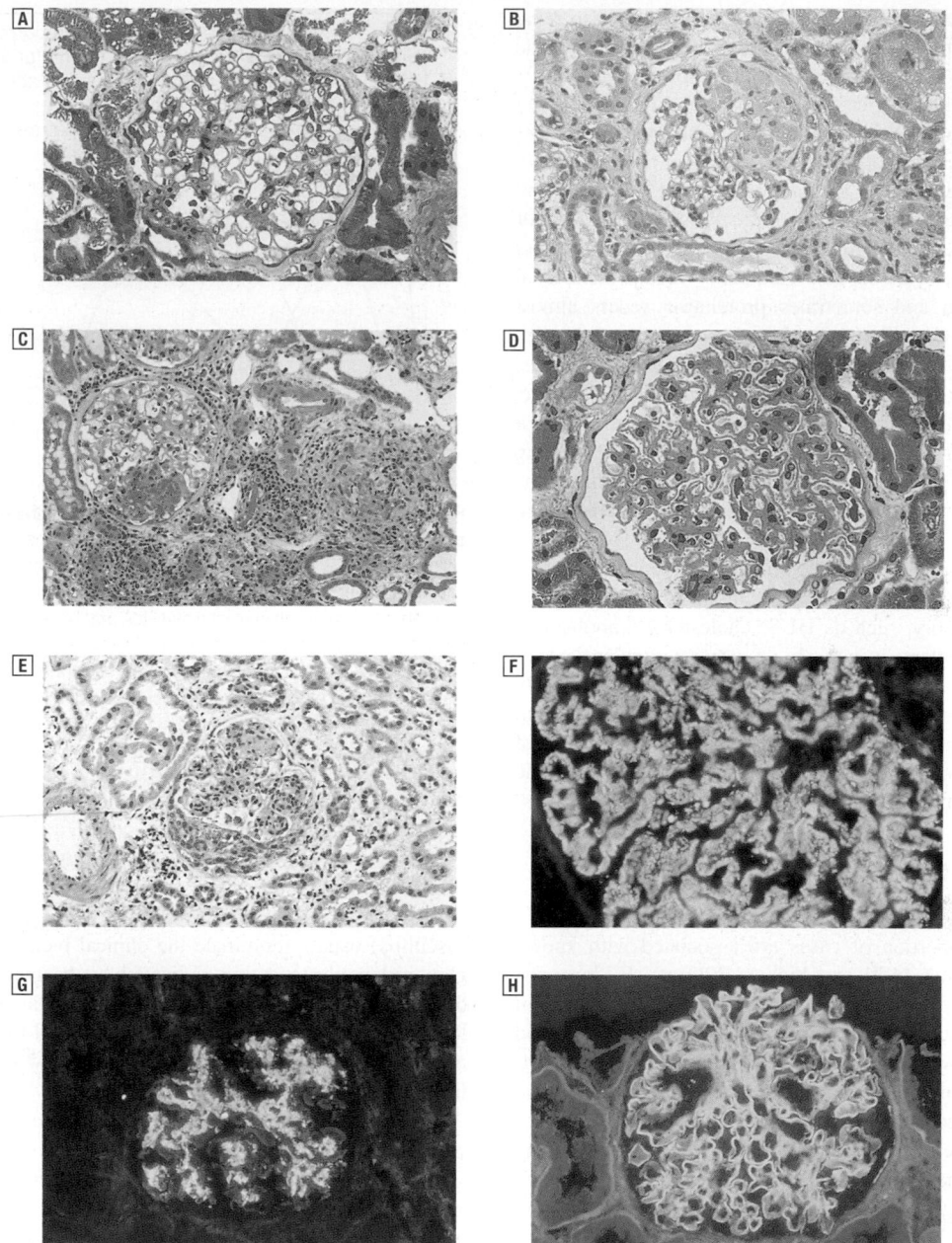

Fig. 14.30 Histopathology of glomerular disease. (A – E light microscopy)

A A normal glomerulus. Note the open capillary loops and thinness of their walls—'should look as if you could cut yourself on them'.

B Focal segmental glomerulosclerosis. The portion of the glomerulus at 2 o'clock shows loss of capillary loops and cells, which are replaced by matrix.

C Focal necrotising glomerulonephritis. The portion of the glomerulus at 6 o'clock is replaced by bright pink material with some 'nuclear dust'. Neutrophils may be seen elsewhere in the glomerulus. There is surrounding interstitial inflammation. Disease of this type is most commonly associated with small-vessel vasculitis (see text) and may progress to crescentic nephritis (see E). D Membranous nephropathy. The capillary loops are thickened (compare with the normal glomerulus) and there is expansion of the mesangial regions by matrix deposition. However, there is no gross cellular proliferation or excess of inflammatory cells. E Crescentic glomerulonephritis. The lower part of Bowman's space is occupied by a semicircular formation ('crescent') of large pale cells, compressing the glomerular tuft. This is usually seen in aggressive inflammatory types of glomerulonephritis.

Antibody deposition in the glomerulus. (F – H direct immunofluorescence)

F Granular deposits of IgG along the basement membrane in a subepithelial pattern, typical of membranous nephropathy. G IgA deposits in the mesangium, as seen in IgA nephropathy. H Ribbon-like linear deposits of anti-GBM antibodies along the GBM in Goodpasture's disease. Glomerular structure is well preserved in all of these examples.

agents. Minimal change disease does not progress to renal impairment; the main problems are those of the nephrotic syndrome (see p. 589) and complications of treatment.

FSGS is a histological description (see Fig. 14.30), and similar appearances are found in patients with a number of different causes of renal disease. The primary FSGS group that present with idiopathic nephrotic syndrome and no other cause of renal disease typically show no or a poor response to corticosteroid treatment and often progress to renal failure; the disease frequently recurs after renal transplantation and sometimes proteinuria recurs almost immediately. Cases between these extremes are common. A proportion of patients do show a response to steroids, and other treatments are used as for minimal change disease. As FSGS is a focal process, abnormal glomeruli may not be seen on renal biopsy if only a few are sampled, leading to an initial diagnosis of minimal change nephropathy. Juxtamedullary glomeruli are more likely to be affected in early disease.

In other patients with the histological appearances of FSGS, focal scarring reflects healing of previous focal glomerular injury, such as HUS, cholesterol embolism or vasculitis. In others, it seems to represent particular types of nephropathy—for instance, those associated with heroin misuse, human immunodeficiency virus (HIV) infection and massive obesity. Associations with numerous other forms of injury and renal disorders are reported. There is no specific treatment for most of these.

MEMBRANOUS NEPHROPATHY

This is the most common cause of nephrotic syndrome in adults. A proportion of cases are associated with known causes (see Box 14.21 and Figs 14.30D and F), but most are idiopathic. Of this group, approximately one-third remit spontaneously, one-third remain in a nephrotic state, and one-third show progressive loss of renal function. Short-term treatment with high doses of corticosteroids and alkylating agents may improve both the nephrotic syndrome and the long-term prognosis. However, because of the toxicity of these regimens, most nephrologists reserve such treatment for those with severe nephrotic syndrome or deteriorating renal function.

IgA NEPHROPATHY AND HENOCH–SCHÖNLEIN PURPURA

IgA nephropathy is the most commonly recognised type of glomerulonephritis and can present in many ways (see Fig. 14.31). Haematuria is almost universal, proteinuria usual, and hypertension very common. There may be severe proteinuria and nephrotic syndrome, or in some cases progressive loss of renal function. The disease is a common cause of end-stage renal failure. A particular hallmark of the disease in some individuals is acute exacerbations, often with gross haematuria, in association with minor respiratory infections. This may be so acute as to resemble acute post-infectious glomerulonephritis, with fluid retention, hypertension and oliguria with dark or red urine. Characteristically,

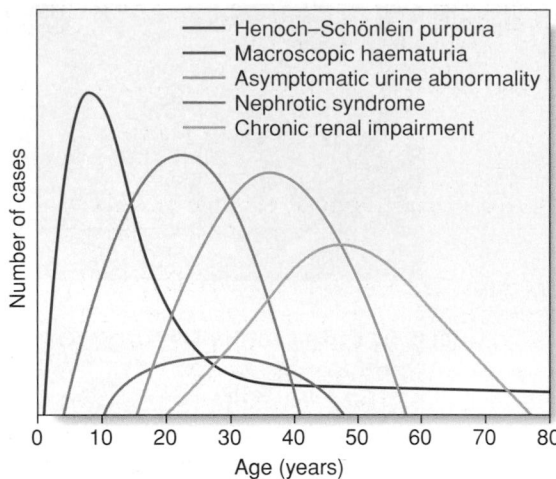

Fig. 14.31 Clinical presentations of IgA nephropathy in relation to age at diagnosis. Henoch–Schönlein purpura is most common in childhood but may occur at any age. Macroscopic haematuria is very uncommon over the age of 40 years. The importance of asymptomatic urine abnormality as the presentation of IgA nephropathy will depend on attitudes to routine urine testing and renal biopsy. It is uncertain whether those presenting with chronic renal impairment have a disease distinct from that of those presenting younger with macroscopic haematuria.

the latency from clinical infection to nephritis is short—a few days or less. These episodes usually subside spontaneously.

In children, and occasionally in adults, a systemic vasculitis occurring in response to similar infections is called Henoch–Schönlein purpura. A characteristic petechial rash (cutaneous vasculitis) and abdominal pain (gastrointestinal vasculitis) usually dominate the clinical picture, with mild glomerulonephritis being indicated by haematuria. When the disease occurs in older children or adults the glomerulonephritis is usually more prominent. Renal biopsy shows mesangial IgA deposition and appearances indistinguishable from acute IgA nephropathy.

Occasionally, IgA nephropathy progresses rapidly and crescent formation may be seen. The response to immunosuppressive therapy is usually poor. The management of less acute disease is largely directed towards the control of blood pressure in an attempt to prevent or retard progressive renal disease.

ACUTE POST-INFECTIOUS GLOMERULONEPHRITIS

This is most commonly seen following streptococcal infections, but can occur in response to other types. It is much more common in children than adults and is now rarely seen in the developed world. The latency is usually about 10 days after a throat infection, suggesting an immune mechanism rather than direct infection. The latency after skin infection is longer. As for rheumatic fever, only certain streptococcal strains are associated with this complication.

An acute nephritis of varying severity occurs with avid sodium retention and oedema, hypertension, reduction of GFR, proteinuria, haematuria and reduced urine volumes. Characteristically, this gives the urine a red or smoky

14.22 CAUSES OF GLOMERULONEPHRITIS ASSOCIATED WITH LOW SERUM COMPLEMENT

- Post-infection glomerulonephritis
- Subacute bacterial infection—especially endocarditis
- SLE
- Cryoglobulinaemia
- Mesangiocapillary glomerulonephritis—usually type II

appearance. There are low serum concentrations of C3 and C4 (see Box 14.22) and evidence of streptococcal infection (antistreptolysin O (ASO) titre, culture of throat swab, and other tests if skin infection is suspected).

Renal function begins to improve spontaneously within 10–14 days, and management by fluid and sodium restriction and use of diuretic and hypotensive agents is usually adequate. The renal lesion in almost all children and most adults seems to resolve completely despite the apparent severity of the glomerular inflammation and proliferation seen histologically.

GLOMERULONEPHRITIS ASSOCIATED WITH INFECTION

Bacterial infections, usually subacute (typically subacute bacterial endocarditis), may cause a variety of histological patterns of glomerulonephritis, but usually with plentiful immunoglobulin deposition, and often with evidence of complement consumption (low serum C3; see Box 14.21). In the developed world, hospital-acquired infections are now a common cause of these syndromes. World-wide, glomerulonephritis associated with malaria, hepatitis B, hepatitis C, schistosomiasis, leishmaniasis and other chronic infections is very common. The usual histological patterns are membranous and mesangiocapillary lesions, although many other types may be seen; FSGS associated with HIV infection is increasingly prevalent. Proving a causative relationship between renal disease and infection in individual cases is extremely difficult. Acute and chronic infections may also cause interstitial renal disease (see below).

OTHER GLOMERULAR DISEASES

Some diseases distort glomerular architecture and function by altering the structure or production of normal glomerular components, or by deposition of extraneous materials, without provoking inflammation. Some types of primary glomerulonephritis that do this (minimal change nephropathy, membranous nephropathy) have been discussed above. Almost all the other diseases in which this occurs are haematological or systemic disorders, in which the glomerulus is only one of the structures involved. In the nephropathy of diabetes mellitus (see p. 673) the GBM is thickened and the mesangial matrix expanded, often in a nodular pattern. In amyloidosis (see p. 327) fibrils are deposited in glomeruli and elsewhere. Both amyloidosis and diabetic nephropathy commonly present as nephrotic syndrome.

TUBULO-INTERSTITIAL DISEASES

Tubulo-interstitial disease refers to a heterogeneous group of conditions characterised by structural change and dysfunction of renal tubular structures and the surrounding interstitium. The clinical presentation is often renal failure, either acute and reversible, or chronic; electrolyte abnormalities are commonly observed, especially hyperkalaemia and acidosis. Proteinuria (and albuminuria) is rarely > 1 g/24 hrs but low molecular weight proteinuria is common (e.g. retinol-binding protein, β_2-microglobulin, lysozyme). Haematuria and pyuria are frequent in acute and chronic disease.

Acute tubular necrosis, the most common cause of the clinical syndrome of ARF, is described on page 597. Illustrations of tubulo-interstitial pathology are shown in Figure 14.32.

INTERSTITIAL NEPHRITIS

ACUTE INTERSTITIAL NEPHRITIS

Acute interstitial nephritis (AIN) refers to acute inflammation within the tubulo-interstitium. Precipitating causes include drugs and toxins, and a variety of systemic diseases and infections (see Box 14.23).

Renal biopsies (see Fig. 14.32) show intense inflammation, with polymorphonuclear leucocytes and lymphocytes surrounding tubules and blood vessels, and invading tubules (tubulitis) and occasional eosinophils (especially in drug-induced disease).

14.23 CAUSES OF ACUTE INTERSTITIAL NEPHRITIS

Allergic	
- Penicillins	- Allopurinol
- NSAIDs	- Many other drugs

Immune
- Autoimmune with uveitis or isolated

Infections	
- Acute bacterial pyelonephritis	- Tuberculosis
- Leptospirosis	- Hantavirus, cytomegalovirus

Toxic	
- Myeloma light chains	- Mushrooms (*Cortinarius*)

Diagnosis

Less than 30% of patients with drug-induced AIN have a generalised drug hypersensitivity reaction (e.g. fever, rash, eosinophilia), and dipstick testing of the urine is usually unimpressive. However, leucocyturia is common, and eosinophils are to be found in the urine in up to 70% of

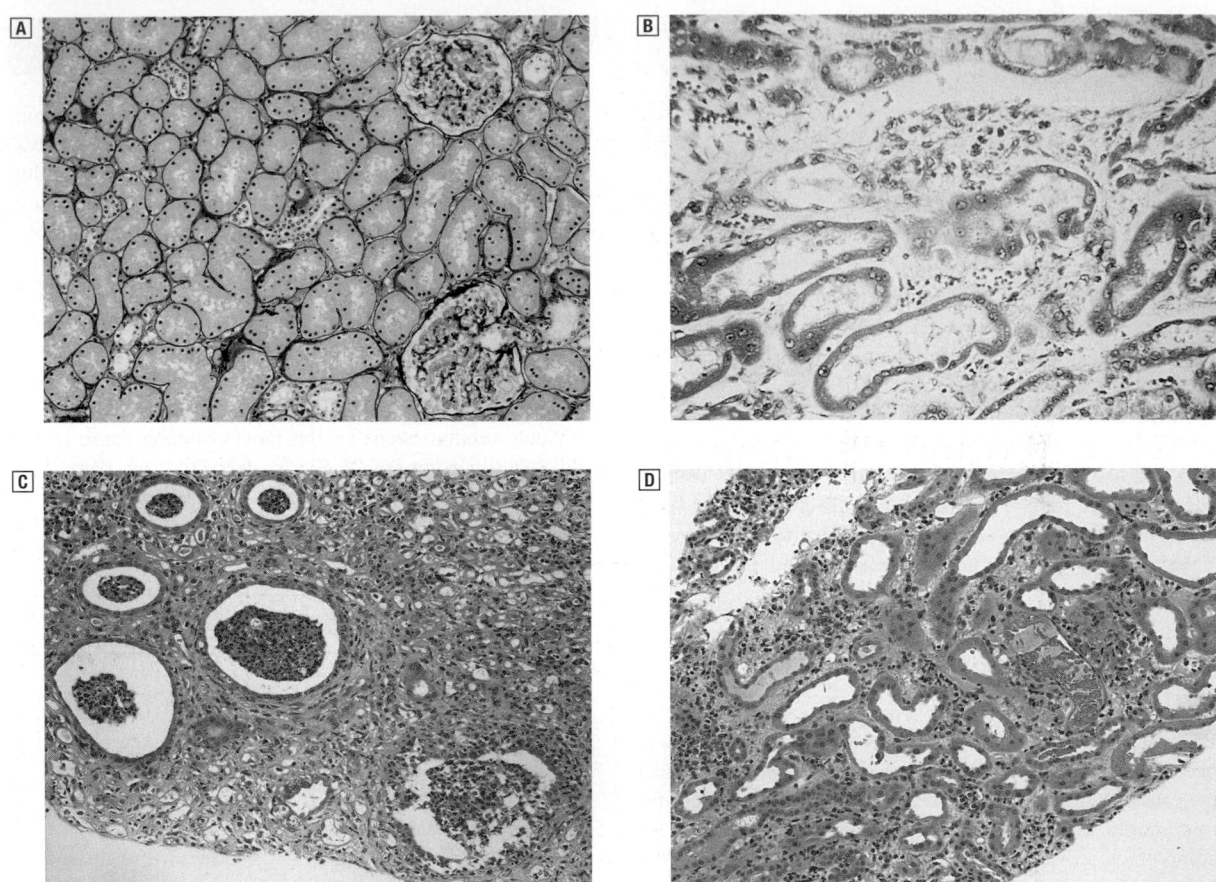

Fig. 14.32 Tubular histopathology. [A] Normal tubular histology. The tubules are back-to-back. Brush borders can be seen on the luminal borders of cells in the proximal tubule. [B] Acute tubular necrosis. There are scattered breaks in tubular basement membranes, swelling and vacuolation of tubular cells, and in places apoptosis and necrosis of tubular cells with shedding of cells into the lumen. During the regenerative phase there is increased tubular mitotic activity. The interstitium is oedematous and infiltrated by inflammatory cells. The glomeruli (not shown) are relatively normal, although there may be endothelial cell swelling and fibrin deposition. [C] Acute bacterial pyelonephritis. A widespread inflammatory infiltrate that includes many neutrophils is seen. Granulocyte casts are forming within some dilated tubules. Other tubules are scarcely visible because of the extent of the inflammation and damage. [D] Acute (allergic) interstitial nephritis. In this patient who received an NSAID, an extensive mononuclear cell infiltrate (no neutrophils) involving tubules is seen. This inflammation does not involve the glomeruli (not shown). Sometimes eosinophils are prominent. Transplant rejection looks similar to this.

patients. Deterioration of renal function in drug-induced AIN may be dramatic and resemble RPGN. Careful history, examination and specific tests may point to the diagnosis but renal biopsy is usually required. The degree of chronic inflammation in a biopsy is also a useful predictor of the eventual outcome for renal function. Many patients are not oliguric despite moderately severe ARF, and AIN should always be considered in patients with non-oliguric ARF.

Management

ARF can be managed conservatively (see p. 599); dialysis is only required for symptomatic or ill patients with a blood urea > 30 mmol/l. Many patients with drug-induced AIN recover following withdrawal of the drug alone, but cortico-steroids (1 mg/kg/day) accelerate recovery and may prevent long-term scarring. Other specific causes (see Box 14.23) should be treated where possible.

CHRONIC INTERSTITIAL NEPHRITIS

Aetiology

Chronic interstitial nephritis (CIN) is caused by a hetero-geneous group of diseases, summarised in Box 14.24. However, it is quite common for the condition to be diag-nosed late and for no aetiology to be apparent.

Clinical features

Most patients present in adult life with CRF, hypertension and small kidneys. CRF is often moderate (urea < 25 mmol/l) but, because of tubular dysfunction, electrolyte abnormali-ties are typically more severe (e.g. hyperkalaemia, acidosis). Urinalysis is non-specific. A minority of patients present with hypotension, polyuria and features of sodium and water depletion (e.g. low blood pressure and jugular venous pres-sure) suggesting severe damage to collecting ducts ('salt-losing nephropathy'). Impairment of urine-concentrating

14.24 CAUSES OF CHRONIC INTERSTITIAL NEPHRITIS

Acute interstitial nephritis

• Any of the causes of AIN if persistent

Glomerulonephritis

• Varying degrees of interstitial inflammation occur in association with most types of inflammatory glomerulonephritis

Immune/inflammatory

• Sarcoidosis
• Sjögren's syndrome
• SLE, primary autoimmune
• Chronic transplant rejection

Toxic

• Mushrooms
• Lead
• Chinese herbs
• Balkan nephropathy (see text)

Drugs

• All drugs causing AIN
• Lithium toxicity
• Analgesic nephropathy
• Ciclosporin, tacrolimus

Infection

• Consequence of severe pyelonephritis

Congenital/developmental

• Vesico-ureteric reflux— is associated; causation not clear
• Renal dysplasias—often associated with reflux
• Inherited—now well recognised but mechanisms unclear
• Other—Wilson's disease, medullary sponge kidney, sickle-cell nephropathy

Metabolic and systemic diseases

• Hypokalaemia, hyper-calciuria, hyperoxaluria
• Amyloidosis

ability and sodium conservation places patients with CIN at risk of superimposed ARF with even moderate salt and water depletion during an acute illness.

The combination of interstitial nephritis and tumours of the collecting system is seen in Balkan nephropathy, so called because of where cases are found, and has been attributed to ingestion of fungal toxins, particularly ochratoxin A, present in food made from stored grain. A plant toxin, aristolochic acid, has been blamed for a rapidly progressive syndrome caused by Chinese herbs. Hyperkalaemia may be disproportionate in CIN or in diabetic nephropathy because of hyporeninaemic hypoaldosteronism (see p. 624). Renal tubular acidosis is seen most often in myeloma, sarcoidosis and amyloidosis.

Management

CRF will require conservative management (see p. 603). A full diagnostic workup for the conditions in Box 14.24 may help to identify a specific drug or toxin which can be withdrawn or suggest a specific diagnosis for treatment. Acidosis can be corrected with oral sodium bicarbonate. Hyperkalaemia will require further measures (see p. 284).

ANALGESIC NEPHROPATHY

Long-term ingestion of analgesic drugs can cause renal papillary necrosis and CIN. In animals, lesions can be induced with almost any NSAID. In humans, mixtures containing aspirin and phenacetin were historically important, and recent surveys show a fall in the incidence of this condition following withdrawal of phenacetin. Dehydration, which reduces medullary blood flow and results in concentration of the drugs in the renal medulla, is probably an important contributory factor.

Clinical features

Patients have usually taken prescribed or over-the-counter analgesic preparations for many years for headaches, backache, rheumatoid arthritis or osteoarthrosis. Asymptomatic disease may be disclosed when abnormalities of blood or urine are found during medical examination. Patients with moderate renal impairment present with malaise, thirst and polyuria due to impaired urinary concentration. Recurrent urinary infection is common. Approximately 60% of patients are hypertensive but 10% may be 'salt-losing'. Renal damage is predominantly tubular; failure to conserve sodium and renal tubular acidosis are common. Acute papillary necrosis is common, and is probably the initial lesion in most cases. Renal colic, ureteric obstruction and acute renal failure may be caused by the passage of fragments of necrotic papillae, which can be recognised by microscopic examination of the urine. ARF may also follow urinary infection or a sudden increase in the intake of analgesics. However, many cases present with established CRF. A recognised complication is the development of carcinoma of the uroepithelium (renal pelvis, ureter or bladder).

Investigations

Apart from the history of drug ingestion, the diagnosis can sometimes be made on the basis of radiological findings and biochemical evidence of tubular dysfunction. The appearance of the papillae on IVU or retrograde pyelography is often diagnostic. The contrast medium appears as a small tract within the papillary substance; later, the papillae may separate, giving rise to a ring shadow. The urine usually contains red cells, and sterile pyuria is common. Proteinuria rarely exceeds 1 g/24 hrs at presentation, but tends to increase as renal failure develops. Renal biopsy shows diffuse interstitial fibrosis and tubular atrophy.

Management

Analgesic preparations must be discontinued; otherwise irreversible renal failure develops. This results in recovery of function in approximately 25% of patients. Treatment also consists of maintaining a fluid intake of 2–3 l/day, treating hypertension and infections, and providing supplements of sodium chloride and sodium bicarbonate to restore ECF volume and correct metabolic acidosis where necessary. Regular follow-up is essential. When renal function is severely impaired, the regimen for management of CRF should be instituted (see p. 603).

SICKLE-CELL NEPHROPATHY

The longer survival of patients with sickle-cell disease (see p. 926) means that a larger proportion live to develop chronic complications of microvascular occlusion. In the kidney these changes are most pronounced in the medulla, where the vasa recta are the site of sickling because of hypoxia and hypertonicity. Loss of urinary concentrating ability and polyuria are the earliest changes; distal renal tubular acidosis and impaired potassium excretion are typical. Papillary necrosis (as seen in analgesic nephropathy) is very common. A minority of patients develop end-stage renal failure. This is managed according to the usual principles, but response to recombinant erythropoietin is understandably poor. Patients with sickle trait have an increased incidence of unexplained microscopic haematuria, and occasionally overt papillary necrosis.

REFLUX NEPHROPATHY (CHRONIC PYELONEPHRITIS)

This is a chronic interstitial nephritis associated with vesico-ureteric reflux (VUR) in early life, and with the appearance of 'scars' in the kidney, as demonstrated by various imaging techniques. The incidence of reflux nephropathy is not known. About 12% of patients in Europe requiring treatment for end-stage renal disease are said to have renal scarring, but the precise diagnostic criteria are variable.

Pathogenesis

VUR is closely associated with recurrent urinary tract infection (UTI) in childhood, and until recently it was widely assumed that this relationship was critical to the association of VUR with progressive renal damage. However, modern imaging techniques have shown that renal scars can be first seen in utero, in the absence of infection. Furthermore, epidemiological surveys and controlled trials have found that efforts to reduce progression to ESRF by surgical or other means have not been effective.

It is now clear that susceptibility to VUR has a large genetic component, and that it may be associated with renal dysplasia and other abnormalities of the urinary tract. It usually occurs from an apparently normal bladder but it may be associated with outflow obstruction, usually caused by urethral valves. Regardless of other lesions, it is associated with a susceptibility to UTI.

It is clearly true that episodes of severe pyelonephritis may occasionally cause permanent renal damage in adults and children. However, in the absence of other urinary tract abnormalities, acute pyelonephritis in patients over the age of 5 years rarely leads to detectable new scars or renal impairment. Permanent renal damage may occur in association with urinary tract obstruction or other abnormal anatomy (e.g. after renal transplantation). It is not clear that lesser degrees of urine infection are associated with progressive renal damage, though this has not as yet been rigorously disproved.

Reflux diminishes as the child grows, and usually disappears. It is often not demonstrable in an adult with a scarred kidney.

Pathology

The changes, which are not diagnostic, may be unilateral or bilateral and of any grade of severity. Gross scarring of the kidneys, commonly at the poles, is seen with reduced size and narrowing of the cortex and medulla. Renal scars are juxtaposed to dilated calyces. Histologically, there is patchy fibrosis with chronic inflammatory cell infiltration, tubular atrophy, periglomerular fibrosis and eventual disappearance of nephrons. The arteries and arterioles may show sclerosis and narrowing. In patients who develop heavy proteinuria and hypertension, renal biopsies show glomerulomegaly and focal glomerulosclerosis (see p. 616), probably as a secondary change.

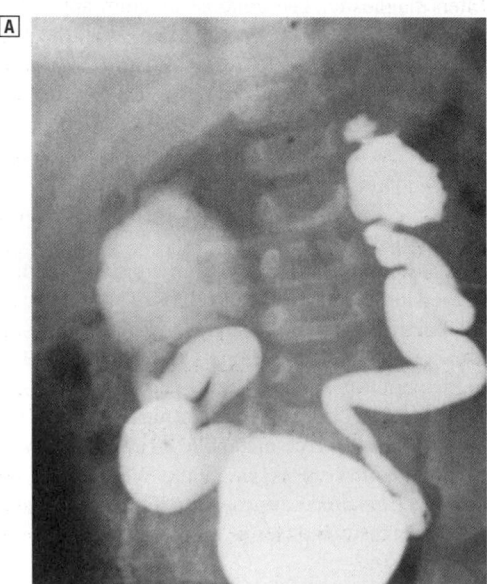 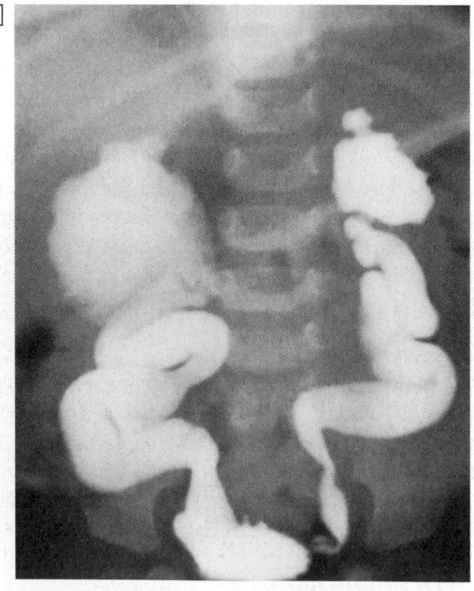

Fig. 14.33 Vesico-ureteric reflux (grade IV) shown by micturating cystogram. [A] The bladder has been filled by contrast medium through a urinary catheter. Even before micturition there was gross vesico-ureteric reflux into widely distended ureters and pelvicalyceal systems. [B] The bladder is now empty except for a small residual pool, but contrast medium is retained in both collecting systems.

Clinical features

In many cases no symptoms arise directly from the renal lesions, and the patient presents very late with only vague symptoms of renal failure. Discovery of hypertension or proteinuria on routine examination may be the first indication of the disease in individuals with no history of overt UTI. A small proportion of patients with severely scarred kidneys will develop hypertension (sometimes severe) and CRF as teenagers. Symptoms arising from the urinary tract may also be present and include frequency of micturition, dysuria and aching lumbar pain. Occasionally, weakness and fainting result from salt loss in the urine. Pyuria and proteinuria < 1 g/24 hrs are common but not invariable. Renal calculi are more common.

A number of women present with hypertension and/or proteinuria in pregnancy. In some patients a positive family history is obtained with an autosomal dominant pattern of inheritance.

Investigations

In mild cases (grades I, II) small amounts of urine pass a short distance up the ureter during voiding, returning to the bladder after cessation of micturition to form residual urine. In severe cases (grades III, IV) reflux occurs up the entire length of the ureter (see Fig. 14.33) and presumably into the renal parenchyma. The IVU shows the diagnostic features. The kidneys are reduced in size and there is localised contraction of the renal substance associated with clubbing of the adjacent calyces (see Fig. 14.34). Culture of the urine is mandatory. Investigations, notably renal ultrasound and radionuclide scanning, are performed to identify any abnormality causing obstruction to the flow of urine. DMSA scans are especially useful to demonstrate scarring (see Fig. 14.9, p. 585). A radionuclide renogram with post-micturition scanning or a micturating cysto-urethrogram will demonstrate VUR. Renal function should be assessed by estimation of the blood urea and creatinine, plasma electrolytes and creatinine clearance.

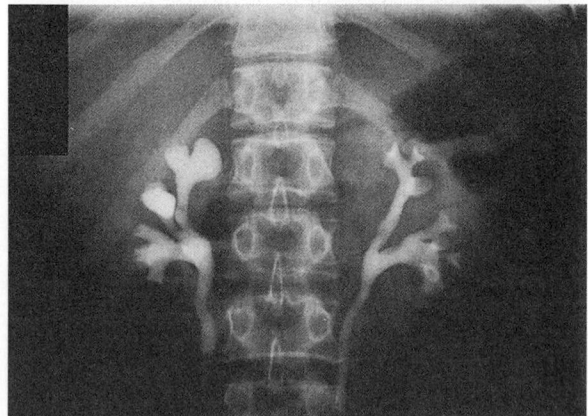

Fig. 14.34   Reflux nephropathy (chronic pyelonephritis).
Intravenous urogram revealing clubbing of the calyces which is particularly marked in the upper right pole. The appearances on the left are virtually normal.

Management

If infection is present, it should be treated (see EBM panel) and, if recurrent, preventative measures and prophylactic therapy may be given as described for UTI (see p. 629). If pyonephrosis develops or unilateral renal infection or pain persists, nephrectomy or other measures may be indicated.

The usual principles regarding the management of CRF apply (see p. 603). A salt-losing state may develop in reflux nephropathy and other tubulo-interstitial disorders, and these features should be managed as described on page 604. However, hypertension is common. Rarely, hypertension is cured by the removal of a diseased kidney.

As most childhood reflux tends to disappear spontaneously, and trials have shown small or no benefits from anti-reflux surgery, such intervention is uncommon although it may be considered if there is recurrent pyelonephritis. Local treatments (e.g. the subureteric injection of biocompatible material) are under investigation.

UTI AND URETERIC REFLUX—medical and surgical management

'Recurrent UTIs are associated with vesico-ureteric reflux and renal scarring or dysplasia. Prophylactic antibiotics reduce recurrences of UTI but there is no evidence for or against their ability to protect against further renal scarring or impairment. There is no evidence that surgery to correct vesico-ureteric reflux reduces UTI or renal scarring, despite their close association.'

- Smellie JM, Barrat TM, Gordon I, et al. Medical versus surgical treatment in children with severe bilateral vesicoureteric reflux and bilateral nephropathy: a randomised trial. Lancet 2001; 357:1329–1333.

Further information: 🖥 www.clinicalevidence.org

Prognosis

Children and adults with small or unilateral scars have a good prognosis, provided renal growth is normal. With significant unilateral scars there is usually compensatory hypertrophy of the contralateral kidney.

In patients with more severe bilateral disease prognosis correlates with measures of renal function, and with hypertension and proteinuria. If the serum creatinine is normal and hypertension and proteinuria are absent, then the long-term prognosis is usually good.

CYSTIC KIDNEY DISEASES

POLYCYSTIC KIDNEY DISEASE

Infantile polycystic kidney disease is rare; inherited as an autosomal recessive trait, it is associated with hepatic fibrosis and is often fatal in the first year of life due to renal or hepatic failure.

Adult polycystic kidney disease (APKD) is a more common condition and inherited as an autosomal dominant trait. The genetic basis and molecular pathogenesis of this disorder are detailed on page 344.

Pathology

Small cysts lined by proximal tubular epithelium are present in infancy and enlarge at a variable rate. In fully developed APKD the kidneys are asymmetrically enlarged and contain numerous cysts. These differ in size and are surrounded by a variable amount of parenchyma which often shows extensive fibrosis and arteriolosclerosis.

Clinical features

Affected subjects are usually asymptomatic until later life. After the age of 20 there is often insidious onset of hypertension, which may or may not be associated with deterioration of renal function. Common clinical features are shown in Box 14.25.

Often one or both kidneys can be palpated and the surface may be nodular. Other diseases in which the kidneys may be palpably enlarged are hydronephrosis/pyonephrosis, solitary cyst, compensatory hypertrophy in a single kidney, renal tumours and renal amyloid. The right kidney, and occasionally the lower pole of the left kidney, may be felt on clinical examination in normal slim adults.

About 30% of patients with APKD have hepatic cysts (see Fig. 11.7, p. 344), but disturbance of liver function is rare. Berry aneurysms of cerebral vessels are an associated feature, especially in patients with a family history of this condition, and about 10% of patients have a subarachnoid haemorrhage. Mitral and aortic regurgitation are frequent but rarely severe, and colonic diverticula and abdominal wall hernias are recognised associations. There is a gradual reduction in renal function. However, the mean age of starting dialysis treatment in patients heterozygous for the PKD1 mutation is 52 years; 50% of patients never require dialysis.

14.25 ADULT POLYCYSTIC KIDNEY DISEASE: COMMON CLINICAL FEATURES
• Vague discomfort in loin or abdomen due to increasing mass of renal tissue • Acute loin pain or renal colic due to haemorrhage into a cyst • Hypertension • Haematuria (with little or no proteinuria) • Urinary tract infection • Renal failure

Investigations

The diagnosis is made on the basis of clinical findings, family history and ultrasound, which is a sensitive method for demonstrating cysts. Now that the gene defects responsible for APKD have been identified, it is sometimes possible to make a specific genetic diagnosis (see p. 344).

Management

Good control of blood pressure is important, since uncontrolled hypertension accelerates the development of renal failure. Urinary infections must be treated promptly. Patients with impaired ability to conserve sodium ('salt-losing') require supplements of sodium chloride and sodium bicarbonate. The regimen for management of CRF will be needed as renal function deteriorates (see p. 603).

Screening and counselling

See page 351.

CYSTIC DISEASES OF THE RENAL MEDULLA

Cysts predominantly in the renal medulla are found in two different conditions. In medullary sponge kidney (see Fig. 14.35) the cysts are confined to the papillary collecting ducts. The condition is not usually genetic and its aetiology is unknown. Affected patients, usually adults, present with pain, haematuria, stone formation or urinary infection. The diagnosis is made by ultrasound or IVU. Contrast medium is seen to fill dilated or cystic tubules, which are sometimes calcified. The prognosis is generally good.

In medullary cystic diseases (sometimes referred to as nephronophthisis in children) small cortical cysts are also present, and these lead to progressive destruction of the nephron. These conditions, characterised by thirst and polyuria (due to nephrogenic diabetes insipidus), are usually diagnosed in younger patients, and there is often a family history. Sometimes affected patients are 'salt-losing', which aggravates the degree of renal failure. Even when treated appropriately, serious renal failure is usual. The genetic basis of these disorders is complex but gradually becoming clearer.

Patients with a very long history of renal impairment (usually on long-term dialysis) often develop multiple renal

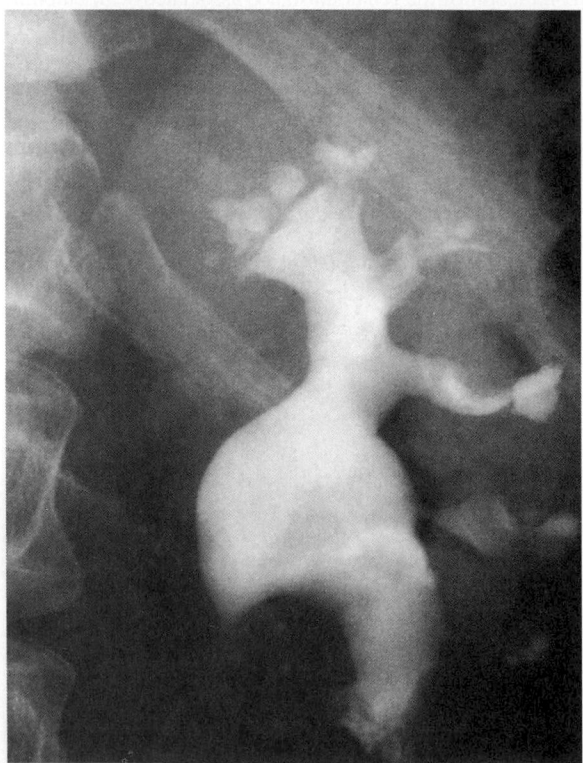

Fig. 14.35 Medullary sponge kidney. Intravenous pyelogram showing contrast medium filling both the collecting system and cavities arising from collecting ducts, especially within papillae of the upper pole. The cavities have been likened to bunches of grapes. A plain abdominal radiograph may show calcification in the same regions.

cysts—acquired cystic kidney disease. These are associated with increased erythropoietin production, and sometimes with the development of renal cell carcinoma.

ISOLATED DEFECTS OF TUBULAR FUNCTION

An increasing number of disorders are now known to be due to specific defects of transporter molecules or other functions in renal tubular cells. More emerge regularly, and only a significant few are mentioned here.

Renal glycosuria is a benign defect of tubular reabsorption of glucose and is usually inherited as an autosomal recessive trait. Glucose appears in the urine in the presence of a normal blood glucose concentration.

Cystinuria is a rare condition in which reabsorption of filtered cystine, ornithine, arginine and lysine is defective. The high concentration of cystine in urine leads to cystine stone formation (see p. 632). Other uncommon tubular disorders include vitamin D-resistant rickets, in which reabsorption of filtered phosphate is reduced; nephrogenic diabetes insipidus (see p. 744), in which the tubules are resistant to the effects of vasopressin; and Bartter's and Gitelman's syndromes, in which there is sodium-wasting and hypokalaemia (see p. 287).

The term 'Fanconi's syndrome' is used to describe generalised proximal tubular dysfunction. Notable abnormalities include low blood phosphate and uric acid, the finding of glucose and amino acids in urine, and proximal renal tubular acidosis (see below). In addition to the causes of interstitial nephritis described above, some congenital metabolic disorders are associated with Fanconi's syndrome, notably Wilson's disease, cystinosis and hereditary fructose intolerance.

RENAL TUBULAR ACIDOSIS (RTA)

RTA results from either a defect in reabsorption of bicarbonate in the proximal tubule or a failure of acidification of the urine in the distal tubule. There may be little or no overall reduction in renal function. In both types, gene defects are described; otherwise the causes are diseases affecting the renal interstitium (see Box 14.24, p. 619), or the specific effects of toxins or drugs. Some disorders and toxins predominantly affect the distal tubule and are associated with distal RTA. These include hypercalciuria (see below), hyperoxaluria, amphotericin, solvents, medullary sponge kidney, sickle-cell disease and chronic urinary obstruction.

Distal renal tubular acidosis (classical or type 1)
In this condition the ability to form a very acid urine is lost, and the urine pH cannot be reduced to less than 5.3 even in the presence of severe systemic acidosis. This defect is due to failure of the collecting ducts to secrete hydrogen ions or to sustain the gradient for hydrogen ions between the luminal fluid and the tubular cell. Two types have been described. In complete distal RTA there is persistent hyperchloraemic acidosis. In the incomplete form, the plasma bicarbonate is normal, but the urine pH does not fall to less

than 5.3 after ammonium chloride administration. Anorexia and fatigue are common, and there is hypercalciuria, hyperphosphaturia, and consequent stone formation and nephrocalcinosis. Loss of Na^+/H^+ exchange in collecting ducts leads to loss of sodium in urine and fluid depletion. Osteomalacia develops in part through increased calcium loss. Children present with failure to thrive, polyuria and thirst.

Management consists of determining and dealing with the underlying cause where possible. Bicarbonate supplements should be given in a dose sufficient to keep the plasma bicarbonate in excess of 18 mmol/l. Large doses may be required, starting with a dose of 1 g of sodium bicarbonate 8-hourly and increasing the dose until the desired plasma bicarbonate is achieved and there are no signs of sodium depletion. When hypokalaemia is present, a mixture of sodium and potassium bicarbonate should be given. Initially, about half of the total bicarbonate supplement is given as the potassium salt. The proportion of potassium bicarbonate is determined by regular monitoring of plasma potassium. Patients with osteomalacia may require 1α-hydroxycholecalciferol (alfacalcidol) or calcitriol.

Proximal renal tubular acidosis (type 2)
This may occur as an isolated defect (primary proximal RTA). More commonly, it occurs as part of Fanconi's syndrome (see above). Proximal tubular Na^+/H^+ exchange is impaired, resulting in decreased bicarbonate reabsorption, large losses of bicarbonate in the urine and a marked reduction in plasma bicarbonate. Once the plasma bicarbonate has fallen to about 12 mmol/l, the reduced filtered load can be reabsorbed by the proximal tubular cells, and the amount of bicarbonate reaching the distal tubule is negligible. In these circumstances, it is possible to show that the collecting duct cells can secrete hydrogen ions against a gradient, so that the urine pH falls to less than 5.3. There is frequently associated hyperchloraemia, potassium depletion and hypocalcaemia. Distinction of proximal and distal RTA requires special tests not considered here.

Any underlying cause should be treated if possible. The plasma bicarbonate should be maintained at a level greater than 18 mmol/l with oral sodium bicarbonate. Very large amounts of bicarbonate are needed, and it is recommended that the starting dose should be 1 mmol/kg daily. A 500 mg sodium bicarbonate capsule provides 6 mmol of bicarbonate. In those patients with hypokalaemia, a proportion of the dose, determined by monitoring plasma potassium, is given as potassium bicarbonate. Where necessary, calcium supplements and 1α-hydroxycholecalciferol are given.

RENAL INVOLVEMENT IN SYSTEMIC DISORDERS

The kidneys may be directly involved in a number of multisystem diseases or secondarily affected by diseases of other organs. Involvement may be at a pre-renal, glomerular, interstitial or post-renal level. Many of the diseases are described in other sections of this chapter or in other chapters of the book. Diabetes mellitus, systemic vasculitis, SLE, cancer and pregnancy are considered in further detail here.

DIABETES MELLITUS

In patients with diabetes, the steady advance from micro-albuminuria to dipstick-positive proteinuria, the development of hypertension and the progression to frank nephrotic syndrome are described on pages 673–674. Not all patients require renal biopsy to establish the diagnosis, but non-diabetic renal disease causes proteinuria in up to 8% of diabetic patients and hence other treatable causes of renal disease should be considered.

Once overt diabetic nephropathy has developed, hypo-tensive agents reduce the rate of loss of renal function. ACE inhibitors have an effect over and above that caused by reduction of blood pressure, by reducing intraglomerular pressure (see EBM panel, p. 674). Some non-dihydropyridine calcium antagonists have similar effects on proteinuria, and may therefore be useful if ACE inhibitors or angiotensin receptor antagonists cannot be used. Blood pressure-lowering should be aggressive. Beneficial effects have been shown at all levels of blood pressure and multiple agents may be required.

Management of nephrotic syndrome is according to the usual principles (see p. 589). However, the presence of other diabetic complications often makes the management of nephrotic syndrome and renal impairment more difficult, and fluid retention is often particularly severe. Associated cardiac and peripheral vascular disease and autonomic neuropathy make changes in fluid balance associated with hypoproteinaemia, oedema and renal impairment more difficult to tolerate, and drug side-effects often compound this. Hyperkalaemia may be a prominent feature because of hyporeninaemic hypoaldosteronism, in which reduced renin production from pro-renin and reduced release of aldosterone occur. Volume expansion and atrial natriuretic peptide may contribute to this. Gastroparesis and disordered bowel motility are frequently exacerbated, and irregular intake and absorption of food, plus alterations in the bio-availability of insulin due to a reduction in its elimination

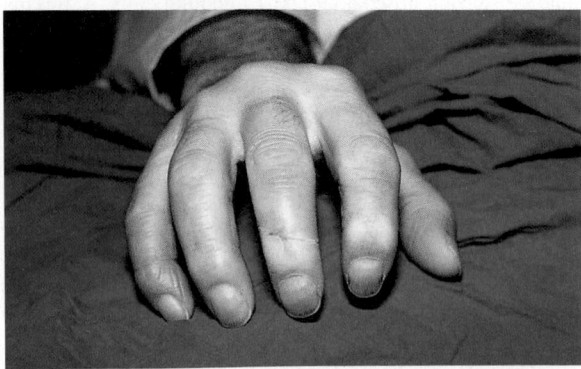

Fig. 14.36 The ischaemic hand of a diabetic patient with end-stage renal disease (ESRD). Symptoms and signs were precipitated by formation of an arteriovenous fistula for haemodialysis. The photograph illustrates the difficulties of managing ESRD in diabetic patients.

and other changes in metabolism that occur as renal function declines, usually lead to a deterioration of blood glucose control. Hypoglycaemic episodes are common in diabetic patients with renal failure. For these reasons, patients with diabetes commonly benefit from commencing renal replacement therapy at an earlier stage than other patients with ESRF, as this permits control of fluid balance and blood pressure with fewer drugs and enables some stabilisation to be achieved. Although the mortality of diabetic patients on dialysis and with renal transplants remains higher than that of other patients and management is often more difficult (see Fig. 14.36), survival rates are improving and their quality of life, especially following renal transplantation, can be good.

SYSTEMIC VASCULITIS

The varieties and classification of systemic vasculitis are considered on page 1040. Renal involvement is most commonly associated with small-vessel vasculitis (SVV), in which capillaritis may profoundly affect glomerular function. This causes an inflammatory glomerulonephritis that is focal in nature; focal necrosis is characteristic (see Box 14.21, p. 614 and Fig. 14.30, p. 615), and often occurs with crescentic changes in the glomeruli. The most important causes of this syndrome, microscopic polyangiitis and Wegener's granulomatosis, are usually associated with antibodies to neutrophil granule enzymes (ANCA, see p. 1043). Vasculitis in other organs may give clues to the underlying systemic disorder and its subtype—e.g. ear, nose and throat involvement and lung disease in Wegener's granulomatosis. The similarity of alveolar and glomerular capillaries means that pulmonary haemorrhage, the consequence of capillaritis affecting alveoli, frequently occurs, together with rapidly progressive glomerulonephritis (see p. 597). In some patients a focal glomerulonephritis with or without crescent formation may occur alone, with ANCA, as a kidney-limited form of systemic vasculitis. Importantly, ANCA have been described in a number of chronic infections associated with renal disease, including endocarditis, HIV and tuberculosis, and hence ANCA alone are not diagnostic of SVV. Inappropriate immunosuppression in these circumstances may be disastrous.

Treatment of the primary types of SVV with cyclophosphamide and corticosteroids is life-saving (see p. 1043). Death from extrarenal manifestations of the disease is prevented, and renal function can be salvaged in acute disease, even if the glomerulonephritis is so severe as to cause oliguria.

Henoch–Schönlein purpura (HSP) and IgA nephropathy are discussed on page 616. HSP is another form of SVV, in which similar focal nephritis is seen by light microscopy. However, instead of being pauci-immune (minimal or no immunoglobulin deposition in the glomeruli), mesangial deposits of IgA are seen, as in IgA nephropathy. ANCA are not usually detected. The disease is usually episodic and self-limiting, but severe progressive renal (or other) disease sometimes justifies the use of immunosuppressive treatment.

In addition to these common disorders, SVV sometimes occurs in the setting of other systemic inflammatory disorders, and the kidneys may be affected in these. SLE and rheumatoid arthritis are the most common examples of this, although SLE usually involves the kidney in different ways (see below).

Medium- to large-vessel vasculitis (e.g. classical polyarteritis nodosa, p. 1042), in the absence of involvement of small vessels, only causes renal disease when arterial involvement leads to hypertension or renal infarction.

Systemic lupus erythematosus (SLE)

Renal involvement in SLE occurs in approximately 30% of patients within 1 year of diagnosis and a further 20% of patients by 5 years. Although it is clinically silent in many, it usually manifests as glomerulonephritis; serologically, and sometimes clinically, overlapping syndromes (e.g. mixed connective tissue disorder, Sjögren's syndrome) may be associated with interstitial nephritis. As indicated in Box 14.21 (see p. 614), SLE can produce almost any histological pattern of glomerular disease and an accordingly wide range of clinical features ranging from florid RPGN (see p. 597) to chronic nephrotic syndrome.

Most typically, patients present with subacute disease, with inflammatory features (haematuria, hypertension, variable renal impairment) accompanied by heavy proteinuria that often reaches nephrotic levels. In severely affected patients the most common histological pattern is an inflammatory, diffusely proliferative glomerulonephritis with distinct features to suggest lupus. Controlled trials have shown that the risk of ESRF in this type of disease is significantly reduced by cyclophosphamide treatment, often given as regular intravenous pulses (see EBM panel, p. 1036).

Significant renal involvement has traditionally been described as a poor prognostic factor in SLE. It usually signifies a need for more powerful (and therefore more hazardous) immunosuppressive therapy but, in most, renal failure can be prevented. Drug side-effects are important; over-reliance on high doses of corticosteroids to control disease leads to substantial toxicity over many years. Cytotoxic agents carry the predictable risks of bone marrow suppression, infection, infertility and secondary malignancy. The risks of teratogenic effects and loss of fertility are particularly important, as many patients are young women.

Many patients go into relative remission from SLE once ESRF has developed. This may be because ESRF itself is an immunosuppressed state, as indicated by the higher incidence of bacterial infections in ESRF from all causes. Patients with ESRF caused by SLE are usually good candidates for dialysis and transplantation. Although it is one of the diseases that may recur in renal allografts, the immunosuppression required to prevent allograft rejection usually keeps SLE suppressed at the same time.

MALIGNANT DISEASES

Cancer may affect the kidney in many ways (see Box 14.26).

PREGNANCY

Pregnancy has important physiological effects on the renal system and is associated with a number of distinct disorders.

14.26 RENAL EFFECTS OF MALIGNANCIES
Direct involvement
• Kidney: hypernephroma, lymphoma • Urinary tract: e.g. urothelial tumours, cervical carcinoma
Immune reaction
• Glomerulonephritis: especially membranous nephropathy • Systemic vasculitis (rarely): usually ANCA-negative
Metabolic consequences
• Hypercalcaemia • Uric acid crystal formation in tubules: usually in tumour lysis syndromes
Remote effects of tumour products
• Light chains in myeloma, amyloidosis • Antibodies in cryoglobulinaemia

Physiological adaptations begin in the first few weeks. Peripheral vascular resistance declines, blood volume, cardiac output and GFR increase, and there is usually a reduction in blood pressure and plasma creatinine and urea values in the first trimester. Recordings of blood pressure and urine testing from the first clinic visit are valuable if problems arise later.

Some conditions are more common in pregnancy, the manifestations of others are modified by the physiological changes of pregnancy, and a few diseases are unique to pregnancy (see Box 14.27). Pyelonephritis is more common, perhaps because of dilatation of the urinary collecting system and ureters. Asymptomatic bacteriuria should be treated in pregnancy (see EBM panel). Proteinuria caused by glomerular disease is always exacerbated, and nephrotic

14.27 FEATURES AND COMPLICATIONS OF PRE-ECLAMPSIA AND RELATED DISEASES
Clinical syndromes
• Eclampsia: severe hypertension, encephalopathy and fits • Disseminated intravascular coagulation • Thrombotic microangiopathy: may also occur post-partum (post-partum HUS) • Acute fatty liver of pregnancy • 'HELLP' syndrome: haemolysis, elevated liver enzymes, low platelets (thrombotic microangiopathy with abnormal liver function)
Clinical signs
• Hypertension • Proteinuria • Oedema • Other evidence of the clinical syndromes listed above
Investigations
• Uric acid levels increased (before renal impairment apparent) • Platelets decreased • Reduced GFR (late) • Fetus small for dates and growing slowly • Fetal distress (late)

syndrome may develop without any alteration in the underlying disease in individuals who had only slight proteinuria before pregnancy. This gives a particular risk of venous thromboembolism, which is now the leading cause of maternal deaths in developed countries.

Systemic autoimmune diseases are typically relatively quiescent during pregnancy, but tend to relapse in the first few weeks and months following delivery. Patients with such diseases who may become pregnant should be aware of the extra associated risks. Drugs used should be safe in pregnancy wherever possible. During pregnancy, therapy should not usually be stopped, but blood pressure targets may be modified (after discussion with the patient) and agents altered to those of proven safety.

Pre-existing renal disease increases the fetal and maternal risk involved in pregnancy, to a degree dependent on the level of renal function, proteinuria and hypertension. Similar consideration should be given to counselling and therapy.

Pre-eclampsia and related disorders

Pre-eclampsia is a systemic disorder that occurs in or near the third trimester of pregnancy. Its aetiology is unknown, although a number of risk factors are described (see Box 14.28).

Pre-eclampsia is traditionally defined by the triad of oedema, proteinuria and hypertension. However, oedema is common in late pregnancy, proteinuria is a late sign and, while hypertension is usually present, it may be relative, mild, or even absent in certain variants of pre-eclampsia. Furthermore, all these features occur in renal disease that may be exacerbated by pregnancy. Differentiating the two may be important, as pre-eclampsia is a progressive disease presenting increasing risk to the fetus and the mother, whereas in renal disease continuing the pregnancy may permit delivery of a healthier, more mature baby. Proteinuria

14.28 RISK FACTORS FOR PRE-ECLAMPSIA

• First pregnancy
• First pregnancy with a new partner
• Pre-eclampsia in previous pregnancies
• Age < 20 years or > 35 years
• Multiple pregnancy (singleton < twin < triplets etc.)
• Pre-existing hypertension
• Pre-existing renal disease

and hypertension in the early part of pregnancy suggest pre-existing renal disease.

The only effective management for pre-eclampsia is delivery. The role of antiplatelet therapy remains controversial (see first EBM panel). Hypertension is a consequence not the cause of the disorder, and treatment is only justified to lower it from severe and immediately dangerous levels (e.g. higher than 180/110). Treating lower levels has been shown to confer no benefit, and exposes the fetus to additional drugs. If life-threatening complications are not present and the baby is immature, corticosteroids may be given to induce maturation of fetal lungs, and delivery postponed while mother and baby are closely observed. Magnesium sulphate has been shown to reduce the incidence of eclamptic convulsions (see second EBM panel).

Acute renal failure may occur in the setting of most of these syndromes. Cortical necrosis (irreversible infarction of the renal cortex) is more likely to occur in pregnancy as a complication of some of these disorders.

DRUGS AND THE KIDNEY

PRESCRIBING IN RENAL DISEASE

Many drugs and drug metabolites are excreted by the kidney. The presence of renal impairment alters the required dose and frequency of those which are affected. This is discussed on page 154.

DRUG-INDUCED RENAL DISEASE

The susceptibility of the kidney to damage by drugs stems from the fact that it is the route of excretion of many water-soluble compounds, including drugs and their metabolites. Some may reach high concentrations in the renal cortex as a result of proximal tubular transport mechanisms. Others are concentrated in the medulla by the operation of the counter-current system. The same applies to certain toxins.

Toxic renal damage may occur by a variety of mechanisms (see Box 14.29). Very commonly, drugs contribute as one of multiple insults to the development of acute tubular necrosis. Haemodynamic renal impairment, acute tubular necrosis, and allergic reactions if recognised early enough are usually reversible. However, other types, especially those associated with extensive fibrosis, are less likely to be reversible. Numerically, reactions to NSAIDs and ACE inhibitors are the most important.

Non-steroidal anti-inflammatory drugs (NSAIDs)

NSAIDs have the predictable effect of impairing renal function in individuals where compensatory mechanisms are maintaining renal function (e.g. heart failure, cirrhosis, sepsis and renal impairment of almost any type), and may precipitate acute tubular necrosis in susceptible patients. This is a class effect that is related to alteration of essential prostaglandin-mediated vasodilatation. In addition, idiosyncratic immune reactions may occur: minimal change nephrotic syndrome and acute interstitial nephritis (see p. 617)—and these may occur together. Analgesic nephropathy (see p. 619) is an occasional complication of long-term use.

Angiotensin-converting enzyme (ACE) inhibitors

ACE inhibitors abolish the compensatory angiotensin II-mediated vasoconstriction of the glomerular efferent arteriole

14.29 MECHANISMS AND EXAMPLES OF DRUG- AND TOXIN-INDUCED RENAL DISEASE/DYSFUNCTION

Mechanism	Drug or toxin	Comments
Haemodynamic	NSAIDs	Especially as a cofactor. Via inhibition of prostaglandin synthesis
	ACE inhibitors	Reduce efferent glomerular arteriolar tone. Toxic in the presence of renal artery stenosis and other conditions of renal hypoperfusion
	Radiographic contrast media	Effect mediated via intense vasoconstriction, but this may not be the primary effect of these drugs
Acute tubular necrosis	Aminoglycosides, amphotericin	In most examples there is evidence of direct tubular toxicity, but haemodynamic and other factors probably contribute
	Paracetamol	May occur with or without serious hepatotoxicity
	Others	Drugs often act as one of several cofactors
	Radiographic contrast media	May be secondary to precipitation in tubules. Furosemide (frusemide) is a cofactor
Loss of tubular/collecting duct function	Lithium	Dose-related, partially reversible loss of concentrating ability
	Cisplatin	
	Aminoglycosides, amphotericin	At lower exposures than cause ATN
Immune (glomerular)	Penicillamine, gold	Membranous nephropathy
	Mercury and heavy metals	Membranous nephropathy
	Penicillamine	Crescentic or focal necrotising glomerulonephritis in association with ANCA and systemic small-vessel vasculitis
	NSAIDs	Minimal change nephropathy
Immune (interstitial)	NSAIDs, penicillins, many others	Acute interstitial nephritis
Chronic interstitial nephritis (alone)	Lithium	As a consequence of acute toxicity. Otherwise controversial
	Ciclosporin, tacrolimus	The major problem with these drugs
	Lead, cadmium	Consequence of chronic toxicity
	Bence Jones protein	Only some light chains are nephrotoxic
	Ochratoxin and other fungal toxins	Produced by *Aspergillus* species. Putative cause of Balkan nephropathy (see p. 619)
	Aristolochic acid and other plant toxins	Found in *Aristolochia* clematis. Putative cause of 'Chinese herb' nephropathy
Chronic interstitial nephritis (with papillary necrosis)	Various analgesics	(See p. 618)
Obstruction (crystal formation)	Aciclovir	Crystals of the drug form in tubules. Aciclovir is now more common than the original example of sulphonamides
	Chemotherapy	Uric acid crystals forming as a consequence of tumour lysis (typically a first-dose effect in haematological malignancy)
Retroperitoneal fibrosis	Methysergide*, practolol*	Idiopathic is more common (see p. 592)

* These drugs are no longer in use in the UK.

that occurs to maintain glomerular perfusion pressure distal to a renal artery stenosis (see Fig. 14.1, p. 579). If the stenosis is bilateral, or occurs in a single functioning kidney, an acute deterioration in renal function occurs. These drugs are increasingly used in patient groups at high risk of atherosclerotic renal artery stenosis, so the reaction is common, and monitoring of renal function before and after initiation of therapy is essential.

INFECTIONS OF THE KIDNEY AND URINARY TRACT

INFECTIONS OF THE LOWER URINARY TRACT

When the urinary tract is anatomically and physiologically normal, and local and systemic defence mechanisms are intact, bacteria are confined to the lower end of the urethra. Urinary tract infection (UTI) implies multiplication of organisms in the urinary tract.

It is usually associated with the presence of more than 100 000 organisms/ml in a midstream sample of urine (MSU). However, contamination can also lead to high bacterial counts, which should therefore be interpreted with caution in the absence of pyuria. Such infections are much more common in women, about one-third of whom have a UTI at some time. The prevalence of UTI in women is about 3% at the age of 20, increasing by about 1% in each subsequent decade. In males UTI is uncommon except in the first year of life and in men over 60, in whom a degree of urinary tract obstruction due to prostatic hypertrophy is common. UTI causes considerable morbidity and, in a small minority of cases, renal damage and chronic renal failure.

Pathogenesis

UTI may be uncomplicated or complicated (see Box 14.30). Complicated infections may result in permanent renal damage, whereas uncomplicated infections rarely (if ever) do so. Uncomplicated infections are almost invariably due to a single strain of organism.

Outside hospitals, E. coli derived from the faecal reservoir accounts for about 75% of infections, the remainder being

14.30 PATHOGENESIS OF URINARY TRACT INFECTION

Uncomplicated

- Anatomically and physiologically normal urinary tract
- Normal renal function
- No associated disorder which impairs defence mechanisms

Complicated

- Abnormal urinary tract, e.g. obstruction, calculi, vesico-ureteric reflux, neurological abnormality, in-dwelling catheter, chronic prostatitis, cystic kidney, analgesic nephropathy, renal scarring
- Associated disorder or treatment that predisposes to UTI (e.g. diabetes mellitus)

due to *Proteus*, *Pseudomonas* species, streptococci or *Staphylococcus epidermidis*. In hospital a greater proportion of infections are due to organisms such as *Klebsiella* or streptococci, but faecal *E. coli* still predominates. Certain strains of *E. coli* have a particular propensity to invade the urinary tract.

The first stage in the development of UTI is colonisation of the periurethral zone with pathogenic, usually faecal, organisms. The urothelium of susceptible persons may have more receptors to which virulent strains of *E. coli* become adherent. In women, the ascent of organisms into the bladder is facilitated by the short urethra and absence of bactericidal prostatic secretions. Sexual intercourse causes minor urethral trauma and may transfer bacteria from the perineum into the bladder. Instrumentation of the bladder may also introduce organisms. Multiplication of organisms then depends on a number of factors, including the size of the inoculum and virulence of the bacteria.

Residual urine left after voiding increases the potential for bacterial multiplication; thus, patients with bladder outflow obstruction, gynaecological abnormalities, pelvic floor weakness or neurological problems are susceptible to infection. In those with vesico-ureteric reflux (see p. 620) urine expelled into the ureters during voiding returns to the bladder when it relaxes, again leading to incomplete voiding. Injury to the mucosa and the presence of a foreign body in the bladder also increase the risk of infection.

Clinical features

The varying clinical presentation of UTI is outlined in Box 14.31. There is often an abrupt onset of frequency of micturition and dysuria. Scalding pain is felt in the urethra during micturition. Cystitis may give rise to suprapubic pain during and after voiding. After the bladder has been emptied, there may be an intense desire to pass more urine due to spasm of the inflamed bladder wall. Systemic symptoms are usually slight or absent. Suprapubic tenderness is often present. The urine may have an unpleasant odour and appear cloudy. Gross haematuria may occur. The diagnosis depends on:

- the characteristic clinical features
- demonstration of a significant growth of organisms in an MSU (see Box 14.34)
- the presence of neutrophils in the urine (pyuria).

The presence of neutrophils is almost invariable in symptomatic infections, but is not universal. The number of organisms amounting to a 'significant' culture is based on probabilities. Urine taken by a sterile technique from a ureter or by suprapubic aspiration should be sterile, so the presence

14.31 CLINICAL PRESENTATION OF URINARY TRACT INFECTION

- Asymptomatic bacteriuria
- Symptomatic acute urethritis and cystitis
- Acute prostatitis
- Acute pyelonephritis
- Septicaemia (usually Gram-negative bacteria)

14.32 ANTIBIOTIC REGIMENS FOR TREATMENT OF URINARY TRACT INFECTIONS IN ADULTS

Drug	Treatment of presumed urinary tract infection		Treatment of presumed pyelonephritis		Treatment of acute prostatitis		Prophylactic or suppressive therapy
	Dose	Duration of course	Dose	Duration of course	Dose	Duration of course	Dose
Trimethoprim	300 mg daily	3 days	300 mg daily	7–14 days	200 mg 12-hourly	4–6 weeks	100 mg/night
Co-amoxiclav	250 mg 8-hourly	3 days	250–500 mg 8-hourly	7–14 days			250 mg/night
Gentamicin[1]			3–5 mg/kg i.v. daily[1]	7–14 days			
Cefuroxime[2]			250 mg 12-hourly oral *or* 750 mg 6–8-hourly i.v.	7–14 days Start treatment i.v. in seriously ill patient			
Ciprofloxacin[2]	250–500 mg 12-hourly	3 days	250–500 mg 12-hourly oral *or* 100 mg 12-hourly i.v.	7–14 days	250 mg 12-hourly	4–6 weeks	
Cefalexin							250 mg/night
Erythromycin					250 mg 6-hourly	4–6 weeks	

[1] Dose determined by plasma [creatinine] and [gentamicin].
[2] Modification of dosage is necessary when renal function is severely impaired.

of any organisms is significant. In the presence of symptoms and pyuria, a small number of organisms is significant. In asymptomatic patients, more than 10^5/ml organisms is usually taken as significant (covert bacteriuria, see below).

Management

A fluid intake of at least 2 l/day is helpful. Box 14.32 shows recommended antibiotic regimens for the treatment of UTI in adults. Ideally, results of urine culture and sensitivities should be available before treatment, but if the patient is in discomfort treatment may be started while awaiting the result. Ampicillin and amoxicillin are no longer the drugs of choice for empirical treatment because of the widespread emergence of resistance among *E. coli*. Trimethoprim is still useful in domiciliary practice although resistant organisms are being encountered with increasing frequency. Nitrofurantoin or co-amoxiclav remain effective in terms of bacterial sensitivity, but nitrofurantoin should not be used for pyelonephritis because of its poor serum and tissue levels. Penicillins and cephalosporins are safe to use in pregnancy but trimethoprim, sulphonamides, quinolones and tetracyclines should be avoided.

Failure to eradicate an organism suggests that one of the complicating factors listed above is present. Investigations should be performed to diagnose the underlying problem, which should be treated appropriately. Failing this, after a further course of antibiotics, suppressive antibiotic therapy can be used to prevent recurrent symptoms, septicaemia and renal damage as outlined in Box 14.32. Urine is cultured regularly and the antibiotic changed as required.

Reinfection with another organism, or with the same organism after an interval, is not uncommon, particularly in sexually active women. Simple measures may prevent recurrence (see Box 14.33). If these fail, freedom from attacks

14.33 PROPHYLACTIC MEASURES TO BE ADOPTED BY WOMEN WITH RECURRENT URINARY INFECTIONS

- Fluid intake of at least 2 l/day
- Regular emptying of bladder (3-hour intervals by day and before sleep)
- Complete emptying of bladder
- Double micturition if reflux present (The patient should be advised, particularly before retiring for the night, to empty the bladder and then attempt to empty the bladder a second time approximately 10–15 minutes later)
- Emptying bladder before and after intercourse

The above regimen is started after completion of a curative course of treatment and continued for several months.

may be achieved by taking a single nightly dose of a suitable antibiotic after voiding and before going to bed, as above.

All individuals with signs of pyelonephritis or systemic infection must be more fully investigated, as shown in Box 14.34. Men and children with recurrent simple infections should also be investigated. In women, recurrent infections are so common that this is only justified if infections are frequent or severe.

COVERT OR ASYMPTOMATIC BACTERIURIA

This is defined as more than 10^5/ml organisms in the MSU of apparently healthy asymptomatic patients. Approximately 1% of children under the age of 1, 1% of schoolgirls, 0.03% of schoolboys and men, 3% of non-pregnant adult women and 5% of pregnant women have covert bacteriuria. There is no evidence that this condition causes chronic renal scarring in non-pregnant adults with normal urinary tracts. When it occurs in infants or in pregnant women, treatment is

14.34 INVESTIGATION OF PATIENTS WITH ACUTE URINARY TRACT INFECTION	
Investigation	**Indications**
Culture of MSU or urine obtained by suprapubic aspiration	All patients
Microscopic examination of urine for white cells, red cells and casts	All patients
Dipstick examination of urine for blood, protein and glucose	All patients
Full blood count	Infants; children; adults with acute pyelonephritis or prostatitis
Plasma urea, electrolytes, creatinine	Infants; children; acute pyelonephritis; recurrent UTI
Blood culture	Fever, rigors or evidence of septic shock
Pelvic examination	Women with recurrent UTI
Rectal examination	Men (to examine prostate)
Renal ultrasonography	To identify obstruction, cysts, calculi Infants, children, men after single UTI, and women who have (1) acute pyelonephritis; (2) recurrent UTI after urinary tract treatment; (3) had UTI or covert bacteriuria in pregnancy (IVU 6 weeks after delivery)
Intravenous urography (IVU) including film of bladder after voiding, to identify physiological and anatomical abnormalities	Alternative to ultrasound, particularly to image collecting system and ureter
Micturating cysto-urethrography (MCU) to identify and quantitate vesico-ureteric reflux and disturbed bladder emptying	Infants; children with abnormal IVU; any patient thought to have a disturbance of bladder emptying
Cystoscopy	Patients with chronic haematuria; patients with a suspected bladder lesion

required, and subsequent investigation may be indicated. In the presence of urinary tract abnormalities, covert bacteriuria may again be more significant and require intervention.

URETHRAL SYNDROME

Some patients, usually female, have symptoms suggestive of urethritis and cystitis but no bacteria are cultured from the urine. Possible explanations include infection with organisms not readily cultured by ordinary methods (e.g. *Chlamydia*, certain anaerobes), irritation by or allergy to toilet preparations or disinfectants, symptoms related to sexual intercourse, or post-menopausal atrophic vaginitis. Antibiotics are not indicated.

CATHETER-RELATED BACTERIURIA

In hospital patients catheter-related bacteriuria increases the risk of Gram-negative bacteraemia by a factor of five. However, bacteriuria becomes almost universal after 30 days of catheterisation, and should not be treated in asymptomatic patients as it promotes the emergence of antibiotic resistance. Prevention is all-important and depends on sterile insertion, closed drainage systems and prompt catheter removal when not required.

ACUTE PROSTATITIS

This is often accompanied by perineal pain and considerable systemic disturbance. The prostate is usually very tender.

The diagnosis is confirmed by a positive culture from urine or from urethral discharge obtained after prostatic massage. The treatment of choice is trimethoprim or erythromycin, which penetrates prostatic secretions. A 4–6-week course is required (see Box 14.32).

INFECTIONS OF THE UPPER URINARY TRACT AND KIDNEY

The proportion of patients with cystitis or bacteriuria in whom the kidney is involved is unknown, but a figure of 50% has been suggested. Clinically, it is often impossible to know if renal infection is present.

Pathogenesis

Bacterial infection of the renal parenchyma is usually due to ascent of organisms via the ureter, although it can be blood-borne. About 75% of infections are due to *E. coli*, the remainder to *Proteus* species, *Klebsiella*, staphylococci or streptococci. One or more complicating factors are commonly present (see Box 14.30) but in infants and women infection can occur in the absence of such factors. Stasis within the urinary tract compromises its defences. Renal cysts or scars facilitate infection. The renal medulla may be particularly susceptible to infection because the low oxygen tension, high osmolality and high concentrations of H^+ and ammonia interfere with the function of leucocytes. The high osmolality probably favours conversion of bacteria to antibiotic-resistant L-forms.

ACUTE PYELONEPHRITIS

Pathology

The renal pelvis is inflamed and small abscesses are often evident in the renal parenchyma. Histological examination shows focal infiltration by neutrophils, which can often be seen within the tubules. These cells are uncommon in other pathological conditions.

Clinical features

There is sudden onset of pain in one or both loins, radiating to the iliac fossae and suprapubic area. About 30% of patients have dysuria due to associated cystitis. Features suggesting renal infection may be absent, particularly in the elderly. Fever is usually present, and rigors and vomiting may occur. Septicaemia with hypotension may supervene. Tenderness and guarding are usually present in the lumbar region. There is a leucocytosis. Examination of urine reveals pyuria, organisms, red cells and tubular epithelial cells.

Acute pyelonephritis in infants and children may present as fever without localising symptoms. The initial feature may be a convulsion; apathy, abdominal distension and diarrhoea may occur. In a febrile child, the urine should always be examined for pus cells and organisms.

Rarely, acute papillary necrosis follows an attack of acute pyelonephritis. Fragments of renal papillae are excreted in the urine and can be identified histologically. This complication, which may lead to acute renal failure, is particularly liable to occur in patients with diabetes mellitus or chronic urinary obstruction. It is also seen (in the absence of infection) in analgesic nephropathy and sickle-cell disease.

Differential diagnosis

Acute pyelonephritis should be distinguished from acute appendicitis, diverticulitis, cholecystitis and salpingitis, and also from perinephric abscess. In this condition there is marked pain and tenderness in the renal region, and often bulging of the loin on the affected side. Patients are extremely ill, with fever, leucocytosis and positive blood cultures. Urinary symptoms are absent, and the urine contains neither pus cells nor organisms.

EBM

PYELONEPHRITIS IN NON-PREGNANT WOMEN— optimum antibiotic regimens

'RCTs have consistently found that oral antibiotic treatment with trimethoprim–sulfamethoxazole, amoxicillin–clavulanic acid or a fluoroquinolone is effective in female outpatients with uncomplicated infection.'

'There is limited evidence that intravenous antibiotics are effective in women admitted to hospital with uncomplicated infection, and that ampicillin should not be used alone to treat infection with *E. coli* because of antimicrobial resistance.'

'Two RCTs of oral versus intravenous antibiotics found no significant difference in effectiveness.'

- Cooper B, Chew L, Fihn S. Pyelonephritis in non-pregnant women. Clinical Evidence 2000; 3:955–960.
- Pinson AG, Philbrick JT, Lindbeck GH, Schorling JB. Oral antibiotic therapy for acute pyelonephritis: a methodologic review of the literature. J Gen Intern Med 1992; 7:544–553.

Further information: www.clinicalevidence.org

Management

Box 14.34 outlines the necessary investigations. Diagnosis depends on the clinical features and results of urine culture. Renal tract ultrasound should be performed without delay. Severe cases require intravenous antibiotic therapy (e.g. with a cephalosporin or gentamicin; see Box 14.32 and EBM panel), later switching to an appropriate oral agent. In less severe cases oral antibiotics can be used throughout. Penicillins and cephalosporins are safe in pregnancy; other antibiotics should usually be avoided. Treatment should be given for 7–14 days. Urine culture should be repeated during the course of antibiotics, and 7 and 21 days after treatment.

RENAL TUBERCULOSIS

Tuberculosis of the kidney is invariably secondary to tuberculosis elsewhere (see p. 532) and occurs as a result of blood-borne infection. The initial lesion develops in the renal cortex and, if untreated, may ulcerate into the pelvis, with consequent involvement of the bladder, epididymis, seminal vesicles and prostate. The disease tends to occur in young people, and may present with recurrent haematuria and dysuria due to secondary involvement of the bladder. In addition, the general features of tuberculosis, i.e. malaise, fever, lassitude and weight loss, may be present. Chronic renal failure may result from destruction of kidney tissue, or be due to obstruction of the urinary tract when lesions heal by fibrosis. Culture of the urine by ordinary methods may be sterile in spite of pyuria, and indeed sterile pyuria is an indication to perform special cultures for tubercle bacilli. The extent of the infection with regard to the lower urinary tract should be ascertained by cystoscopic examination.

ISSUES IN OLDER PEOPLE
URINARY INFECTION

- The prevalence of asymptomatic bacteriuria rises with age; amongst the frailest in institutional care it rises to approximately 40% in women and 30% in men.
- Factors contributing to this may include an increased prevalence of underlying structural abnormalities, post-menopausal oestrogen deficiency and increased residual urine (in women), and prostatic hypertrophy with reduced bactericidal activity of prostatic secretions (in men).
- The urinary tract is the most frequent source of bacteraemia in older patients admitted to hospital.
- New or increased incontinence is a common presentation of urinary tract infection in older women.
- There is no evidence that urinary infection in old age presents with subtle changes in mental state or function, without clinical findings localised to the urinary tract.
- Post-menopausal women with acute lower urinary tract symptoms have a relatively poorer response to short courses of antibiotics, and may require longer than 3 days' therapy.
- There is little evidence for the benefit of treating asymptomatic bacteriuria in old age; it does not improve symptoms of chronic incontinence, nor does it decrease episodes of morbidity from symptomatic urinary infection or mortality.
- Treatment of asymptomatic bacteriuria may simply lead to adverse effects from the antibiotic and promote the emergence of resistant organisms.

URINARY TRACT CALCULI AND NEPHROCALCINOSIS

Aetiology

Urinary calculi consist of aggregates of crystals containing small amounts of proteins and glycoprotein. Different types occur with different frequencies in different parts of the world, probably as a consequence of dietary and environmental factors, but genetic factors may also make a significant contribution. In Europe, renal stones in which the crystalline component consists of calcium oxalate are the most common, and stones containing calcium as oxalate, phosphate or both comprise about 80% of the total. About 15% contain magnesium ammonium phosphate (struvite; these are often associated with infection), and small numbers of pure cystine or uric acid stones are found. Rarely, drugs may form stones (e.g. indinavir, ephedrine).

In developing countries, bladder stones are common, particularly in children. In developed countries the incidence of childhood bladder stones is low, and renal stones in adults are more common. In a North American survey, 12% of men and 5% of women had experienced a renal stone by the age of 70 years. It is surprising that stones and nephrocalcinosis are not more common, since some of the constituents are present in urine in concentrations which exceed their maximum solubility in water. However, urine contains proteins, glycosaminoglycans, pyrophosphate and citrate which may help to keep otherwise insoluble salts in solution.

A number of risk factors and predisposing conditions are known for renal stone formation (see Box 14.35). However, in developed countries most calculi occur in healthy young men in whom investigations reveal no clear single predisposing cause.

14.35 KIDNEY STONES: PREDISPOSING FACTORS AND CONDITIONS

Environmental and dietary

- Low urine volumes: high ambient temperatures, low fluid intake
- Diet: high protein intake, high sodium, low calcium
- High sodium excretion
- High oxalate excretion
- High urate excretion
- Low citrate excretion

Other medical conditions

- Hypercalcaemia of any cause (see p. 715)
- Ileal disease or resection (leads to increased oxalate absorption and urinary excretion)
- Renal tubular acidosis type I (distal) (e.g. in Sjögren's syndrome)

Congenital and inherited conditions

- Familial hypercalciuria
- Medullary sponge kidney
- Cystinuria
- Renal tubular acidosis type I (distal)
- Primary hyperoxaluria

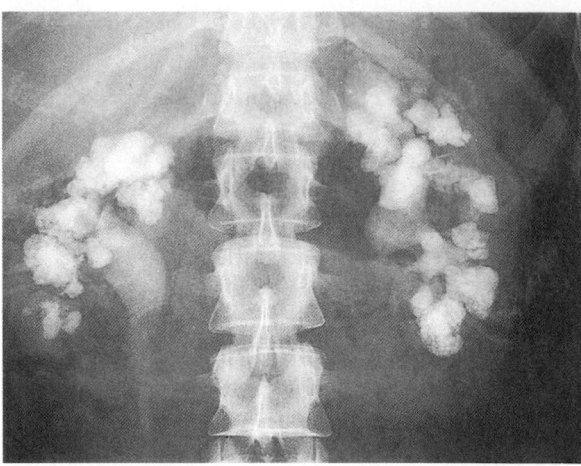

Fig. 14.37 Bilateral staghorn calculi. The intravenous pyelogram demonstrates that, while some dye is being excreted by the right kidney, there is little function on the left.

Pathology

Urinary concretions vary greatly in size. There may be particles like sand anywhere in the urinary tract, or large round stones in the bladder. Staghorn calculi fill the whole renal pelvis and branch into the calyces (see Fig. 14.37); they are usually associated with infection and composed largely of struvite. Deposits of calcium may be present throughout the renal parenchyma, giving rise to nephrocalcinosis. This is especially liable to occur in patients with renal tubular acidosis, hyperparathyroidism, vitamin D intoxication and healed renal tuberculosis.

Clinical features

These vary according to the size, shape and position of the stone, and the nature of any underlying condition. Renal calculi or nephrocalcinosis may be present for years without giving rise to symptoms, and may be discovered during radiological examination for another disorder. More commonly, patients present with pain, recurrent urinary infection or clinical features of urinary tract obstruction. Protein, red cells or leucocytes may appear in the urine.

When a stone becomes impacted in the ureter, an attack of renal colic develops. The patient is suddenly aware of pain in the loin, which radiates round the flank to the groin and often into the testis or labium, in the sensory distribution of the first lumbar nerve. The pain steadily increases in intensity to reach a maximum in a few minutes. The patient is restless, and generally tries unsuccessfully to obtain relief by changing position or pacing the room. There is pallor, sweating and often vomiting, and the patient may groan in agony. Frequency, dysuria and haematuria may occur. The intense pain usually subsides within 2 hours, but may continue unabated for hours or days. The pain is usually constant during attacks, though slight fluctuations in severity may occur. Contrary to general belief, attacks rarely consist of intermittent severe pains coming and going every few minutes.

Subsequent to an attack of renal colic there may be intermittent dull pain in the loin or back. It is therefore often suspected that such pains in patients who have not had renal colic may be related to renal stones. Unfortunately, this is frequently not the case, and it is presumed that in most cases this discomfort is musculoskeletal in origin.

Investigations

The diagnosis of renal colic is usually made easily from the history and by finding red cells in the urine. Any patient suspected of having stones should have investigations to identify the site of the stone and degree of obstruction. About 90% of stones are seen on a plain abdominal radiograph. When the stone is in the ureter an IVU shows delayed excretion of contrast from the kidney and a dilated ureter down to the stone (see Fig. 14.38). IVU is very accurate and remains the most commonly used investigation world-wide, but spiral CT gives the most accurate assessment and will identify non-opaque stones (e.g. uric acid).

Patients with a first renal stone should have a minimum set of investigations; the yield of more detailed investigation is low, and hence usually reserved for those with recurrent or multiple stones, or those with complicated or unexpected presentations (e.g. in the very young; see Box 14.36).

14.36 INVESTIGATIONS FOR RENAL STONES		First stone	Recurrent stones
Sample	**Test**		
Stone	Chemical composition—most valuable when possible	✓	✓
Blood	Calcium	✓	✓
	Phosphate	✓	✓
	Uric acid	✓	✓
	Urea and electrolytes	✓	✓
	Parathyroid hormone—only if calcium or calcium excretion high		(✓)
Urine	Dipstick test for protein, blood, glucose	✓	✓
	Amino acids		✓
24-hr urine	Urea		✓
	Creatinine clearance		✓
	Sodium		✓
	Calcium		✓
	Oxalate		✓
	Uric acid		✓

Management

The immediate treatment of renal pain or renal colic is bed rest, and application of warmth to the site of pain. Renal colic is often unbearably painful and demands powerful analgesia, e.g. morphine (10–20 mg), pethidine (100 mg) intramuscularly or diclofenac as a suppository (100 mg). Patients are advised to drink 2 litres per day. Around 90% of stones less than 4 mm in diameter will pass spontaneously but only 10% of stones of more than 6 mm will pass and may require active intervention. Immediate action is required if anuria or severe infection occurs in the stagnant urine proximal to the stone (pyonephrosis).

While attempts to dissolve stones have failed, most can now be fragmented by extracorporeal shock wave lithotripsy (ESWL; see Fig. 14.39). Using this apparatus shock waves generated outside the patient's body are focused on to the stone, breaking it into small pieces which can pass easily down the ureter. The technique requires free drainage of the distal urinary tract.

Endoscopic surgery is still often required for stones but open surgery is now almost never needed except for large bladder stones (see Box 14.37). All stones are potentially infected and surgery should be covered with appropriate antibiotics.

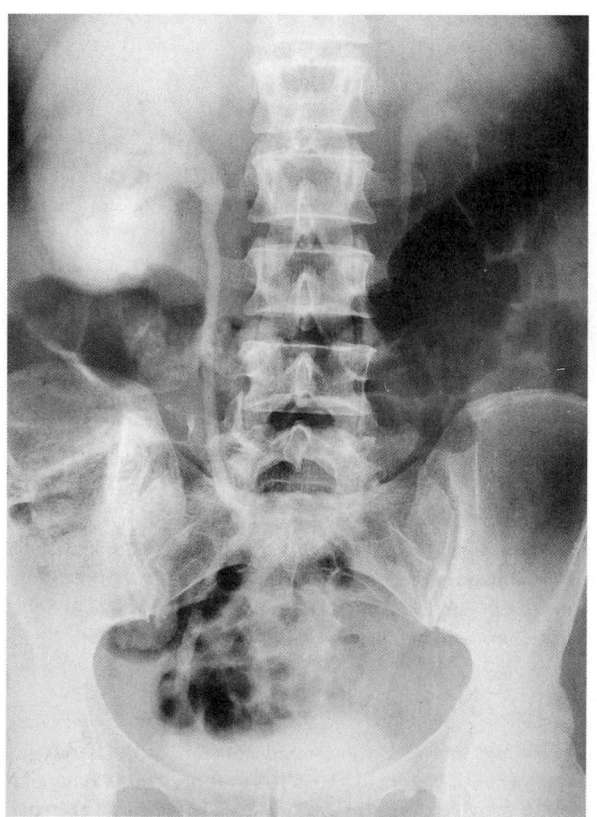

Fig. 14.38 Unilateral obstruction. Intravenous urogram of a patient with a stone (not visible) at the lower end of the right ureter. This film, taken 2 hours post-contrast injection, demonstrates persistence of contrast medium in the right kidney, pelvicalyceal system and ureter, whereas only a small amount remains visible in the normal left pelvicalyceal system.

14.37 OPERATIVE INTERVENTION IN STONE DISEASE	
• Obstructive anuria or severe infection (pyonephrosis)	→ Emergency percutaneous nephrostomy only
• Severe pain or solitary kidney	→ Urgent ESWL or surgery
• Pain and failure of the stone to move	→ Elective ESWL or surgery

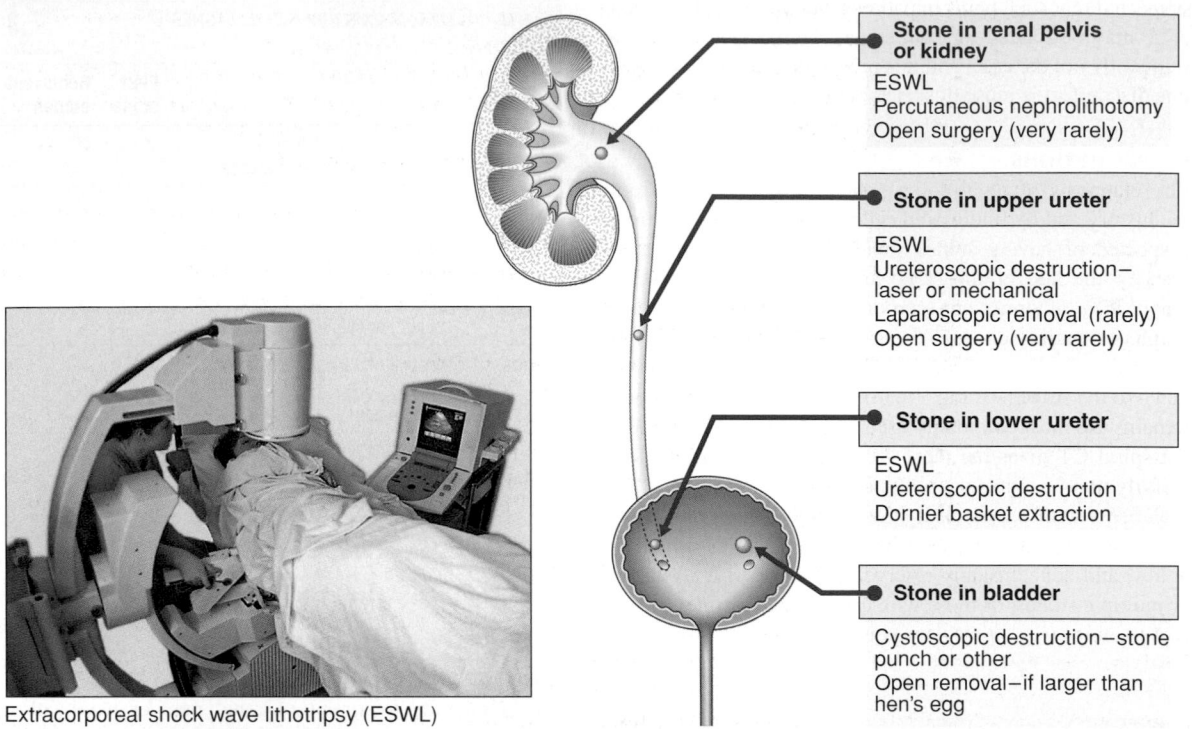

Stone in renal pelvis or kidney
ESWL
Percutaneous nephrolithotomy
Open surgery (very rarely)

Stone in upper ureter
ESWL
Ureteroscopic destruction—laser or mechanical
Laparoscopic removal (rarely)
Open surgery (very rarely)

Stone in lower ureter
ESWL
Ureteroscopic destruction
Dornier basket extraction

Stone in bladder
Cystoscopic destruction—stone punch or other
Open removal—if larger than hen's egg

Extracorporeal shock wave lithotripsy (ESWL)

Fig. 14.39 Surgical options for urinary stones.

Management to prevent further stone formation should be guided by the results of the investigations in Box 14.36, but some general principles apply to almost every patient with calcium-containing stones (see Box 14.38). More specific measures apply to some stone types. Urate stones can be prevented by allopurinol, and indeed this may also reduce calcium stone formation in patients with a high urate excretion. Stones formed in cystinuria can be reduced by penicillamine therapy. Attempts to alter urine pH with ammonium chloride (low pH discourages phosphate stone formation) or sodium bicarbonate (high pH discourages urate and cystine stone formation) may be made in the face of particular problems.

14.38 GENERAL MEASURES TO PREVENT CALCIUM STONE FORMATION
Diet
• Fluid—at least 2 l output per day (intake 3–4 l)—check with 24-hr urine collections—with intake distributed throughout the day (especially before bed)
• Sodium—restrict intake
• Protein—moderate; not high
• Calcium—plenty in diet (because calcium forms an insoluble salt with dietary oxalate, lowering oxalate excretion) but avoid supplements away from meals (increase calcium excretion without reducing oxalate excretion)
• Oxalate—avoid foods that are very rich in oxalate (e.g. rhubarb)
N.B. Citrate supplementation of unproven value.
Drugs
• Thiazide diuretics—reduce calcium excretion; valuable in recurrent stone formers and patients with hypercalciuria
• Allopurinol—if urate excretion high
• Avoid (or carefully monitor) vitamin D supplements as they increase calcium absorption and excretion

TUMOURS OF THE KIDNEY AND GENITOURINARY TRACT

TUMOURS OF THE KIDNEY

Tumours of the kidney account for 3% of all malignancies, and a variety of benign, malignant and secondary tumours can occur. Renal adenocarcinoma is by far the most common adult tumour, and nephroblastoma (Wilms' tumour) most common in children.

RENAL ADENOCARCINOMA

This is the most common malignant tumour of the kidney in adults with an incidence of 16 cases per 100 000 population. It is twice as common in males as in females. The peak incidence is between 65 and 75 years of age and it is uncommon before 40. The tumour arises from renal tubules. Haemorrhage and necrosis give a characteristic mixed golden-yellow and red appearance to the cut surface. Microscopically, there are clear and granular cell types; the former are more common. There is early spread of the tumour into the renal pelvis, causing haematuria. Invasion of the renal vein, often extending into the inferior vena cava, also occurs early. Direct spread into perinephric tissues is common. Lymphatic spread occurs to para-aortic nodes, while blood-borne metastases (which may be solitary) may develop almost anywhere in the body.

Clinical features

About 60% of cases present with haematuria, 40% with loin pain and only 25% with a mass. The triad of pain, haematuria and a mass is an important but late feature occurring in only 15% of cases. A remarkable range of systemic effects may occur, including fever, raised ESR, polycythaemia, disorders of coagulation, and abnormalities of plasma proteins and liver function tests. The patient may present with pyrexia of unknown origin or, rarely, with neuropathy. Systemic effects may be due to tumour secretion of products such as renin, erythropoietin, parathormone and gonadotrophins. The effects disappear when the tumour is removed but may reappear when metastases develop, and so can be used as markers of tumour activity.

Investigations

The initial investigation is ultrasound, which allows differentiation between solid tumour and simple renal cysts. Thereafter, a contrast-enhanced CT of the abdomen and chest should be performed for staging (see Fig. 14.40).

Management and prognosis

Radical nephrectomy that includes the perirenal fascial envelope and ipsilateral para-aortic lymph nodes is performed whenever possible. Renal adenocarcinoma is resistant to radiotherapy and chemotherapy but some benefit has been seen with immunotherapy using interferon and interleukin-2. Even when metastases are present, nephrectomy should always be considered. Not only may systemic effects disappear, but there may even be regression of any metastases.

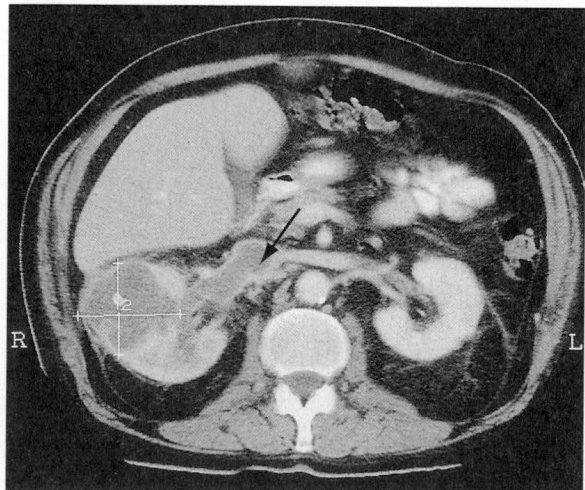

Fig. 14.40 Renal adenocarcinoma. In this CT, the right kidney is expanded by a low-density tumour which fails to take up contrast material. Tumour is shown extending into the renal vein and inferior vena cava (arrow).

Solitary metastases tend to remain single for long periods and excision is often worth while.

If the tumour is confined to the kidney, the 5-year survival is 75%. This falls to only 5% when there are distant metastases.

NEPHROBLASTOMA

Nephroblastoma is the most common childhood urological malignancy with an incidence of 7 per million children per year. It usually occurs in children under 4 years of age. The tumour is probably derived from embryonic mesodermal tissue and microscopically has a mixed appearance of spindle cells, epithelial cells and muscle fibres. Growth is rapid and there is early local spread, including invasion of the renal vein. Invasion of the renal pelvis occurs late, so haematuria is seen in only 15% of cases. Distant metastases most commonly appear in the lungs, liver and bones. Tumours presenting in the first year of life have a better prognosis.

Clinical features

The cardinal sign is a large abdominal mass. Some of the unusual clinical features associated with a renal carcinoma in adults, such as fever or hypertension, may be present.

Investigations

A CT of the abdomen and chest is essential for diagnosis and staging. The main differential diagnosis is from a neuroblastoma affecting the adrenal, but other causes of a large kidney, such as hydronephrosis and cystic disease, must be considered. The tumour is bilateral in 5–10% of cases.

Management

Transabdominal nephrectomy with wide excision of the mass is carried out after preliminary ligation of the renal pedicle. This is followed by chemotherapy using dactinomycin and vincristine. Radiotherapy is reserved for residual disease. As a result of this treatment, the 5-year survival rate has improved from 10% to 80%.

TUMOUR SYNDROMES

Two uncommon autosomal dominant inherited conditions are associated with the formation of multiple renal tumours in adult life. In tuberous sclerosis (see p. 1097) replacement of renal tissue by multiple angiomyolipomas (tubers) may occasionally cause renal failure in adult life. Other organs affected include the skin (adenoma sebaceum on the face) and brain (causing seizures and mental retardation). The von Hippel–Lindau syndrome (see p. 1207) is associated with the formation of multiple renal cysts, renal adenomas and renal adenocarcinoma. Other organs affected include the CNS (haemangioblastomas) and the adrenals (phaeochromocytoma).

TUMOURS OF THE RENAL PELVIS, URETERS AND BLADDER

The vast majority of these tumours arise from the urothelium or transitional cell lining. The urothelium is exposed to chemical carcinogens excreted in the urine such as naphthylamines and benzidine which were extensively used in the chemical and dye industries until their carcinogenic properties were recognised. The bladder is more susceptible to urinary carcinogens as urine is stored in the bladder for relatively long periods of time. Almost all tumours are transitional cell carcinomas. Squamous carcinoma may occur in urothelium that has undergone metaplasia, usually due to chronic inflammation or irritation due to a stone or schistosomiasis.

The incidence of transitional cell carcinoma in the bladder in the UK is 45 cases per 100 000 population, and is three times more common in men than women. The appearance of a transitional cell tumour ranges from a delicate papillary structure to a solid ulcerating mass (see Fig. 14.41). The appearance correlates well with subsequent behaviour, in that papillary tumours are relatively benign cancers while those which ulcerate are much more aggressive.

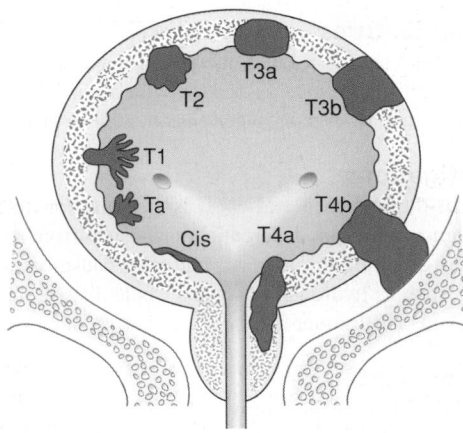

Fig. 14.41 Transitional cell carcinoma of the bladder. Stages are shown from carcinoma in situ (Cis) to invasive tumour progressing beyond the bladder and prostate (T4b).

Clinical features

More than 80% of patients have haematuria, which is usually visible and painless. It should be assumed that such bleeding is from a tumour until proved otherwise. A tumour at the lower end of a ureter or a bladder tumour involving the ureteric orifice may cause obstructive symptoms. Examination is usually unhelpful. Rectal examination detects only very advanced tumours.

Investigations

Imaging of the whole of the urinary tract is essential; when the bleeding is macroscopic this is best performed by IVU. If there is any suspicious defect in the ureter or renal pelvis, a retrograde ureteropyelogram is required. Cystoscopy is mandatory as small bladder tumours are easily missed on IVU. Solid invasive tumours need to be staged by CT of the abdomen, pelvis and chest. Microscopic haematuria carries a lower risk of malignancy, and a common strategy is to undertake flexible cystoscopy, ultrasound examination (rather than IVU) and urine cytology, and perform a plain radiograph of the kidneys, ureters and bladder.

Management

Small, large and even multiple superficial bladder tumours can be treated endoscopically by transurethral resection of the tumour(s) (TURT). Intravesical chemotherapy (e.g. epirubicin, mitomycin C) is useful to treat multiple low-grade bladder tumours and to reduce their recurrence rate. Regular 'check' cystoscopies are required and recurrences can usually be controlled by diathermy; only rarely will cystectomy be required for superficial disease.

Carcinoma in situ (Cis) may occur in association with a proliferative tumour (often in an apparently normal mucosa), or as a separate entity, when there may be only a generalised redness (malignant cystitis). Untreated patients with Cis have a high risk of progression to invasive cancer. The tumour responds well to intravesical bacille Calmette–Guérin (BCG) treatment but if there is any doubt about the response, and especially if there is any pathological evidence of progression, more aggressive treatment is needed (see below).

The management of invasive bladder tumours is debated. Radical cystectomy is recommended for patients under 70 years of age. The morbidity and mortality associated with such a radical procedure increase with age and radical radiotherapy may be a better option in older patients. Unfortunately, this may not always cure the tumour and 'salvage' cystectomy may be needed for recurrence or for symptoms such as intractable bleeding.

Cystectomy necessitates urinary diversion. In favourable cases, however, where the urethra can be retained, it may be possible to construct a new bladder from colon or small bowel (orthotopic bladder replacement). In such cases the patient may retain normal continence. Alternatively, a continent urinary diversion can be constructed. In less favourable circumstances an ileal conduit should be performed. In some countries where a stoma is not acceptable, the ureters can be implanted into the sigmoid colon (ureterosigmoidostomy), but renal infection and metabolic disturbances can be serious complications.

Transitional cell carcinoma of the renal pelvis and ureter is usually treated by nephroureterectomy and regular surveillance of the bladder, but if the tumour is solitary and low-grade it may be treated endoscopically; surveillance remains problematic.

Prognosis

The prognosis of bladder tumours depends on tumour stage and grade. The 5-year survival rate varies from 50–60% in those with superficial tumours to 20–30% for those with deep muscle invasion. Overall, about one-third of patients survive for 5 years.

PROSTATIC DISEASE

BENIGN PROSTATIC HYPERPLASIA

From 40 years of age the prostate increases in volume by 2.4 cm^3 per year on average. The process begins in the periurethral (central) zone of the prostate and involves both glandular and stromal tissue to a variable degree. Associated symptoms are common from 60 years, and some 50% of men over 80 years of age will have lower urinary tract symptoms associated with benign prostatic hyperplasia (BPH).

Clinical features

The primary symptoms of BPH are due to the prostate obstructing the urethra and consist of hesitancy, poor prolonged flow and a sensation of incomplete emptying. Secondary (irritative) symptoms comprising urinary frequency, urgency of micturition and urge incontinence are not specific to BPH.

Patients may present more dramatically with acute urinary retention where they are suddenly unable to micturate and develop a painful distended bladder. This is often precipitated by excessive alcohol intake, constipation or prostatic infection. This is an emergency and requires the bladder to be drained by a catheter to relieve the retention. In chronic retention the bladder slowly distends due to inadequate emptying over a long period of time. This condition is characterised by pain-free bladder distension; this may cause back pressure on the kidneys over a prolonged time and result in hydroureter, hydronephrosis and renal failure. Patients with chronic retention can also develop acute retention: so-called acute on chronic retention. They require careful management because of their renal failure.

Investigations

Symptoms are scored on the international prostate symptom score (IPSS, see Box 14.39) which serves as a valuable starting point for the assessment of urinary problems. Once a baseline value is established any improvement/deterioration may be assessed on subsequent visits. Flow rates are accurately measured with a flow meter and prostate volume can be estimated by rectal examination or more accurately by transrectal ultrasound scan (TRUS). Assessment of obstruction is only possible by urodynamics (see Fig. 14.13, p. 593).

Management

Mild to moderate symptoms can be treated by medication (see EBM panel and Box 14.40). Alpha-adrenoceptor

---

BENIGN PROSTATIC HYPERPLASIA—role of medical management **EBM**

'Oral α-adrenoceptor blocker therapy causes prostatic relaxation and rapid improvement in urinary flow in 60–70% of patients. The 5α-reductase inhibitor finasteride causes slow shrinkage of large prostate glands with improvement in symptoms.'

- Caine M, Perlberg S, Meretyk S. A placebo-controlled double-blind study of the effect of phenoxybenzamine in benign prostatic obstruction. Brit J Urol 1978; 50:551–554.
- Clifford GM, Farmer RD. Medical therapy for benign prostatic hyperplasia: a review of the literature. Eur Urol 2000; 38:2–19.
- Boyle P, Gould AL, Roehrborn CG. Prostate volume predicts outcome of treatment of benign prostate hyperplasia with finasteride: meta-analysis of randomised clinical trials. Urology 1996; 48:398–405.

Further information: 🖥 www.cochrane.co.uk

14.40 TREATMENT FOR BENIGN PROSTATIC HYPERTROPHY

Medical

- Prostate < 40 cm³ α-adrenoceptor blockers
- Prostate > 40 cm³ finasteride (5α-reductase inhibitor)

Non-surgical intervention

- Thermotherapy

Surgical

- TURP
- Holmium laser enucleation
- Open prostatectomy

---

blockers (e.g. alfuzosin, tamsulosin) reduce the tone in the prostate, thereby reducing the obstruction. Finasteride (a 5α-reductase inhibitor) stops the conversion of testosterone to dihydrotestosterone in the prostate and so causes the prostate to shrink. Severe symptoms require surgical removal of some of the obstructing prostate tissue. Transurethral resection of the prostate (TURP) still remains the gold standard treatment but enucleation of the prostate by holmium laser appears as effective with potentially fewer complications. Open surgery is rarely required except in very large glands (> 100 cm³). Thermotherapy, where the

---

14.39 DETERMINING THE INTERNATIONAL PROSTATE SYMPTOM SCORE (IPSS): A WORKING EXAMPLE FOR A PATIENT WITH MODERATE SYMPTOMS

IPSS	Not at all	Less than 1 time in 5	Less than half the time	About half the time	More than half the time	Almost always	Your score
1. Straining	0	1	②	3	4	5	
2. Weak stream	0	1	②	3	4	5	
3. Intermittency	0	1	②	3	4	5	
4. Incomplete emptying	0	1	②	3	4	5	
5. Frequency	0	1	②	3	4	5	
6. Urgency	0	1	②	3	4	5	
7. Nocturia (times per night)	0	①	2	3	4	5	
Total IPSS score							**13**

	Delighted	Pleased	Satisfied	Mixed	Dissatisfied	Unhappy	Terrible
Quality of life	0	1	2	③	4	5	6

Key Scores: 0–7 = mild symptoms; 8–19 = moderate symptoms; 20–35 = severe symptoms.

prostate is heated by microwaves of radio frequency through a urethral catheter, is little better than medication but may have a place in the patient unfit for surgery.

PROSTATE TUMOURS

Prostatic cancer is common in northern Europe and the US (particularly in the black population) but rare in China and Japan. In the UK it is the third most common malignancy in males, with an incidence of 50 cases per 100 000 population and increasing in frequency. It is the second most common cause of cancer death in men in the UK. It rarely occurs before the age of 50 and is uncommon before the age of 60. The mean age at presentation is 70 years. The aetiology is unknown.

Prostate cancers arise within the peripheral zone of the prostate and almost all are carcinomas. Metastatic spread to pelvic lymph nodes occurs early and metastases to bone, mainly the lumbar spine and pelvis, are common. Prostatic specific antigen (PSA) is a good tumour marker for this malignancy and 40% of patients with a serum PSA > 4.0 ng/ml will have prostate cancer on biopsy. This has led to the introduction of screening programmes, principally in the USA, despite a lack of consensus about their utility.

Clinical features

Most patients present with lower urinary tract symptoms indistinguishable from BPH. Symptoms and signs due to metastases are much less common and include back pain, weight loss, anaemia and obstruction of the ureters. On rectal examination the prostate feels nodular and stony hard, and the median sulcus may be lost. However, 10–15% of tumours are not palpable.

Investigations

Since most patients present with outflow tract obstruction, an ultrasound scan and serum creatinine determination are used to assess the urinary tract. A plain radiograph of the pelvis and lumbar spine (to investigate backache) may show osteosclerotic metastases as the first evidence of prostatic malignancy.

Whenever possible, the diagnosis is confirmed by needle biopsy, usually aided by transrectal ultrasound scan (see Fig. 14.42), or by histological examination of tissue removed by endoscopic resection if this is needed to relieve outflow obstruction.

The patient is assessed for distant metastases by a radio-isotope bone scan but high levels of serum PSA (> 100 ng/ml) almost always indicate distant bone metastases. PSA is also useful for monitoring response to treatment and disease progression.

Management

Tumour confined to the prostate is potentially curable by either radical prostatectomy or radical radiotherapy, and these options should be considered in all patients with more than 10 years' life expectancy. A small focus of tumour found incidentally at TURP does not significantly alter life expectancy and only requires follow-up.

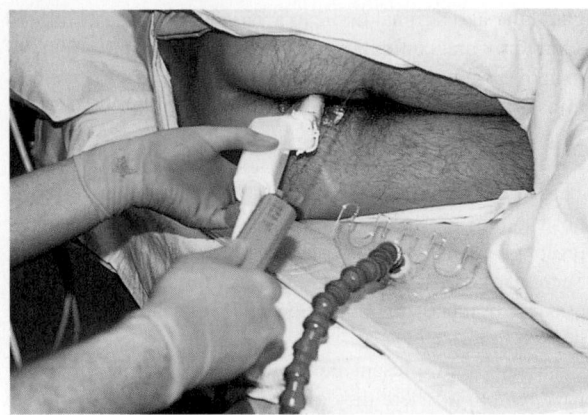

Fig. 14.42 Transrectal ultrasound of the prostate (TRUS) and needle biopsy. Scanning alone will miss 40% of cancers and biopsy is mandatory.

Approximately half of the men with prostate cancer will have metastatic disease at the time of diagnosis. Prostatic cancer, like breast cancer, is sensitive to hormonal influences; locally advanced or metastatic prostate cancer is treated by androgen depletion either by surgery (orchidectomy) or more commonly now by androgen-suppressing drugs (see EBM panel). Anti-androgen drugs such as cyproterone acetate act by preventing dihydrotestosterone binding to the tumour cells, so preventing cell growth. Luteinising hormone-releasing hormone analogues such as goserelin act by binding irreversibly to pituitary receptors. This initially causes an increase in testosterone before producing a prolonged reduction, and for this reason the initial dose must be covered with an anti-androgen to prevent a tumour flare.

EBM

PROSTATE CANCER—role of hormone manipulation in treatment

'Prostate cancer is hormone-sensitive, and reducing circulating testosterone levels to castrate levels (either by castration or by medication) results in a 70% initial response rate. Further reduction by blocking adrenal testosterone (maximal androgen blockade) produces a small but significant increase in survival but with poorer quality of life.'

- Huggins C, Hodges CV. Studies on prostate cancer: the effect of castration, of estrogen and of androgen injection on serum phosphatases in metastatic carcinoma of the prostate. Cancer Res 1941; 1:293–297.
- Schmitt B, Bennett C, Seidenfeld J, et al. Maximal androgen blockade for advanced prostate cancer (Cochrane Review). Cochrane Library, issue 4, 2000. Oxford: Update Software.

Further information: 💻 www.cochrane.co.uk

A small proportion of patients fail to respond to endocrine treatment. A larger number respond for a year or two, but then the disease progresses. Other oestrogens or progesterones are of limited value but chemotherapy with 5-fluorouracil, cyclophosphamide or nitrogen mustard can be effective. Radiotherapy is useful treatment for localised bone pain. For severe generalised bone pain, hemi-body radiotherapy, or [89]strontium may give effective palliation but the basis of treatment remains pain control by analgesia (see p. 228).

Prognosis

The life expectancy of a patient with an incidental finding of focal carcinoma of the prostate is that of the normal population. With tumours localised to the prostate, a 10-year survival rate of 50% can be expected, but if metastases are present this falls to 10%.

TESTICULAR TUMOURS

Tumours of the testes are uncommon, with an incidence of 5 cases per 100 000 population, but they occur in men between the age of 20 and 40 years. These tumours secrete tumour markers which provide good indices for both diagnosis and prognosis. Seminoma and teratoma account for 85% of all tumours of the testis.

Seminomas arise from seminiferous tubules and represent a relatively low-grade malignancy. Metastases occur mainly via the lymphatics and may involve the lungs. Teratomas arise from primitive germinal cells. They may contain cartilage, bone, muscle, fat and a variety of other tissues, and are classified according to the degree of differentiation. Well-differentiated tumours are the least aggressive; at the other extreme, trophoblastic teratoma is highly malignant. Occasionally, teratoma and seminoma occur together.

Clinical features

The common presentation is incidental discovery of a painless testicular lump although some patients complain of a testicular ache. The peak age for a teratoma is 20–30 years and for a seminoma 30–40 years, but either may occur at any age.

Investigations

All suspicious scrotal lumps should be imaged by ultrasound which provides a high degree of accuracy. As soon as a tumour is suspected, and before orchidectomy, serum levels of alphafetoprotein (AFP) and β-human chorionic gonadotrophin (β-HCG) should be determined. The levels of these 'tumour markers' are increased in extensive disease. Accurate staging is based on CT of the lungs, liver and retroperitoneal area, and renal and pulmonary function should be assessed.

Management

Through an inguinal incision the cord is ligated and divided at the internal ring, and the testis is removed. Subsequent treatment depends on the histological type and stage. Radiotherapy is the treatment of choice for early stage seminoma since this tumour is very radiosensitive. The management of a teratoma depends on the stage of the disease. Early disease confined to the testes may be managed without further treatment provided that there is close surveillance for at least 2 years; tumour progression is treated by chemotherapy. More advanced cancers are managed initially by chemotherapy, usually the combination of bleomycin, etoposide and cisplatin. Follow-up is by CT and assessment of AFP and β-HCG. Retroperitoneal lymph node dissection is now only performed for residual or recurrent nodal masses.

Prognosis

The 5-year survival rate for patients with seminoma is 90–95%. The more variable prognosis of teratomas depends on tumour type, stage and volume. With more favourable tumours the 5-year survival rate may be as high as 95%, but in more advanced cases 60–70% is more usual.

FURTHER INFORMATION

Bihl G, Meyers A. Recurrent renal stone disease—advances in pathogenesis and clinical management. Lancet 2001; 358:651–656.

Brater DC. Drug therapy: diuretic therapy. N Engl J Med 1998; 339:387–395. *Review articles.*

Bushinsky DA. Nephrolithiasis. Am J Kidney Dis 1998; 9:917–924.

Davison JM. Management of pre-existing disorders in pregnancy: renal disease. Prescribers' Journal 1997; 37:46–53.

Johnson RJ, Feehally JF, eds. Comprehensive clinical nephrology. London: Harcourt Brace; 1999.

Short A, Cumming AD. ABC of intensive care: renal support. BMJ 1999: 319:41–44.

Walker R. General management of end-stage renal disease. BMJ 1997; 315:1429–1432.

www.edren.org *Website of the Renal Unit, Royal Infirmary of Edinburgh; information about individual diseases, protocols for immediate in-hospital management and a list of educational resources, including key cases; extensive links to other resources.*

www.nephron.com *The links under 'professional resources' are particularly good and include useful urology links; includes an MDRD calculator for estimating GFR from serum creatinine; extensive links to other resources.*

www.sign.ac.uk *Scottish Intercollegiate Guidelines Network; management of haematuria, proteinuria, diabetic renal disease.*

www.sin-italia.org/imago/sediment/sed-htm *Italian Society of Nephrology website; analysis of urinary sediment.*

Diabetes mellitus

B.M. FRIER • B.M. FISHER

CLINICAL EXAMINATION OF THE PATIENT WITH DIABETES

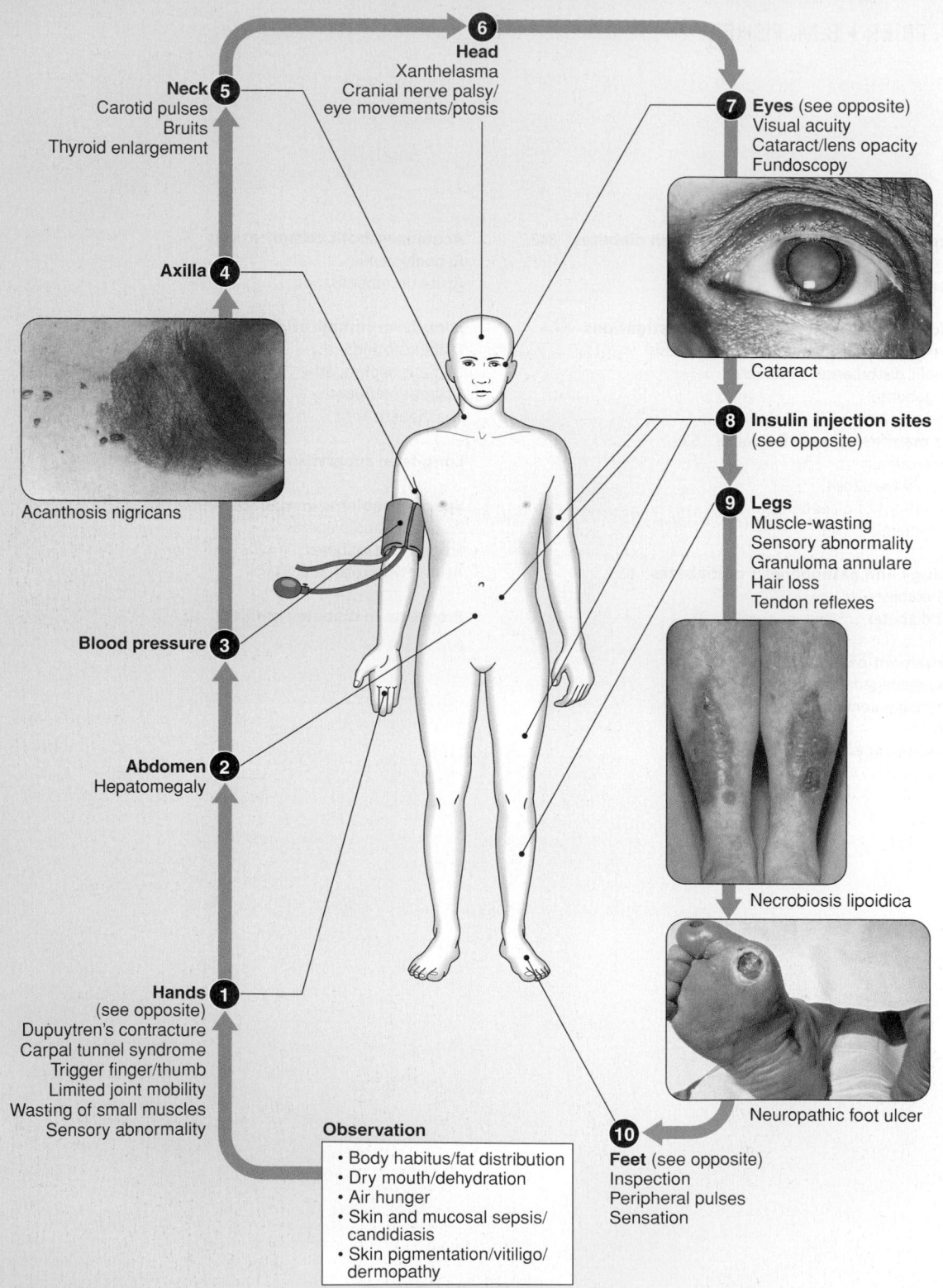

6 Head
Xanthelasma
Cranial nerve palsy/
eye movements/ptosis

5 Neck
Carotid pulses
Bruits
Thyroid enlargement

4 Axilla

Acanthosis nigricans

7 Eyes (see opposite)
Visual acuity
Cataract/lens opacity
Fundoscopy

Cataract

8 Insulin injection sites
(see opposite)

9 Legs
Muscle-wasting
Sensory abnormality
Granuloma annulare
Hair loss
Tendon reflexes

Necrobiosis lipoidica

3 Blood pressure

2 Abdomen
Hepatomegaly

Neuropathic foot ulcer

1 Hands
(see opposite)
Dupuytren's contracture
Carpal tunnel syndrome
Trigger finger/thumb
Limited joint mobility
Wasting of small muscles
Sensory abnormality

Observation
• Body habitus/fat distribution
• Dry mouth/dehydration
• Air hunger
• Skin and mucosal sepsis/
  candidiasis
• Skin pigmentation/vitiligo/
  dermopathy

10 Feet (see opposite)
Inspection
Peripheral pulses
Sensation

SIGNS ASSOCIATED WITH DIABETES

- Weight loss (insulin deficiency)
- Obesity—may be abdominal (insulin resistance)
- White spots on shoes (glycosuria)
- Dry mouth and tongue
- Deep sighing respiration (Kussmaul breathing)
- Skin infections—boils, candidiasis

❶ EXAMINATION OF THE HANDS

- Limited joint mobility (sometimes called 'cheiroarthropathy') may be present; this is the inability to extend (to 180°) the metacarpophalangeal or interphalangeal joints of at least one finger bilaterally. The effect can be demonstrated in the 'prayer sign'. It causes painless stiffness in the hands, and occasionally affects the wrists and shoulders.
- Dupuytren's contracture (see p. 978) is common in diabetes and may include nodules or thickening of the skin and knuckle pads.
- Carpal tunnel syndrome (see p. 1182) is common in diabetes and presents with wrist pain radiating into the hand.
- Trigger finger (flexor tenosynovitis) may be present in people with diabetes.
- Muscle-wasting/sensory changes may be present as features of a peripheral sensorimotor neuropathy, although this is more common in the lower limbs.

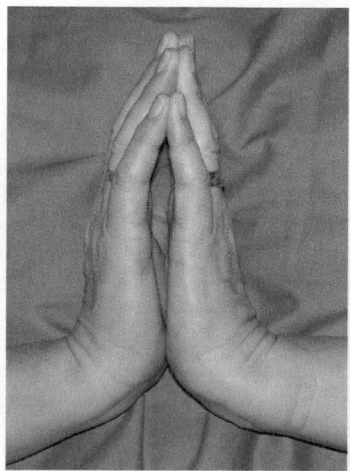

'Prayer sign'.

❼ EXAMINATION OF THE EYES

Visual acuity
- Distance vision using Snellen chart at 6 metres.
- Near vision using standard reading chart.
- Impaired visual acuity may indicate the presence of diabetic eye disease, and serial decline may suggest development or progression in severity.

Lens opacification
- Look for the red reflex using the ophthalmoscope held 30 cm from the eye.
- The presence of lens opacities or cataract should be noted.

Fundal examination
- The pupils must be dilated with a mydriatic (e.g. tropicamide) and examined in a darkened room.
- Features of diabetic retinopathy (see p. 670) should be noted, including evidence of previous laser treatment which leaves photocoagulation scars.

❽ INSULIN INJECTION SITES

Main areas used
- Anterior abdominal wall
- Upper thighs/buttocks
- Upper outer arms

Inspection
- Bruising
- Lumps (lipodystrophy)
- Subcutaneous fat deposition (lipohypertrophy)
- Subcutaneous fat loss (lipoatrophy; associated with injection of unpurified animal insulins—now rare)
- Erythema, infection (rare)

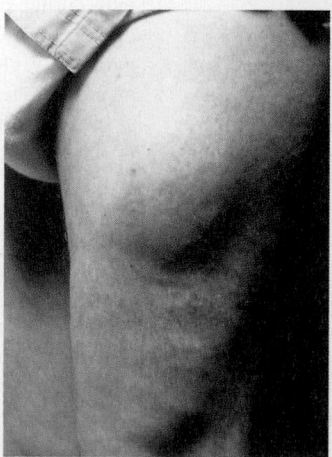

Lipohypertrophy.

❿ EXAMINATION OF THE FEET

Inspection
- Look for evidence of callus formation on weight-bearing areas, clawing of the toes (a feature of neuropathy), loss of the plantar arch, discoloration of the skin (ischaemia), localised infection and the presence of ulcers.
- Deformity of the feet may be present, especially in Charcot neuroarthropathy.
- Fungal infection may affect skin between toes, and nails.

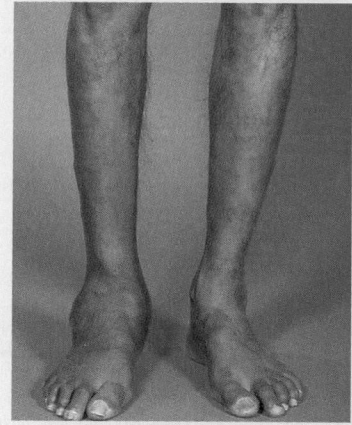

Charcot neuroarthropathy.

Circulation
- Peripheral pulses, skin temperature and capillary refill should be tested.

Sensation
- Light touch: use monofilaments.
- Vibration sense: use 128 Hz tuning fork over big toe/malleoli.
- Pin-prick: use pin.
- Pain: pressure over Achilles tendon.
- Proprioception: test position of big toe.
- Test for distal anaesthesia/hyperaesthesia in stocking distribution.

Reflexes
- Test plantar and ankle reflexes.

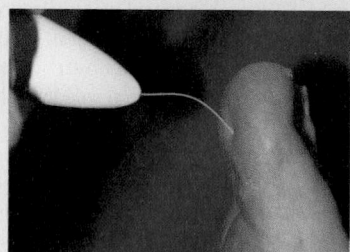

Monofilaments.

Diabetes mellitus is a clinical syndrome characterised by hyperglycaemia due to absolute or relative deficiency of insulin. This can arise in many different ways (see Box 15.1). Lack of insulin affects the metabolism of carbohydrate, protein and fat, and causes a significant disturbance of water and electrolyte homeostasis. Death may result from acute metabolic decompensation, while long-standing metabolic derangement is frequently associated with permanent and irreversible functional and structural changes in the cells of the body, with those of the vascular system being particularly susceptible. These changes lead to the development of well-defined clinical entities, the so-called 'complications of diabetes' which characteristically affect the eye, the kidney and the nervous system.

15.1 AETIOLOGICAL CLASSIFICATION OF DIABETES MELLITUS

Type 1 diabetes
- Immune-mediated
- Idiopathic

Type 2 diabetes

Other specific types
- Genetic defects of β-cell function (see Box 15.13, p. 654)
- Genetic defects of insulin action
- Pancreatic disease (e.g. pancreatitis, pancreatectomy, neoplastic disease, cystic fibrosis, haemochromatosis, fibrocalculous pancreatopathy)
- Excess endogenous production of hormonal antagonists to insulin (e.g. growth hormone—acromegaly; glucocorticoids—Cushing's syndrome; glucagon—glucagonoma; catecholamines—phaeochromocytoma; thyroid hormones—hyperthyroidism)
- Drug-induced (e.g. corticosteroids, thiazide diuretics, phenytoin)
- Viral infections (e.g. congenital rubella, mumps, Coxsackie virus B)
- Uncommon forms of immune-mediated diabetes
- Associated with genetic syndromes (e.g. Down's syndrome; Klinefelter's syndrome; Turner's syndrome; DIDMOAD (Wolfram's syndrome)—diabetes insipidus, diabetes mellitus, optic atrophy, nerve deafness; Friedreich's ataxia; myotonic dystrophy)

Gestational diabetes

EPIDEMIOLOGY

Epidemiological studies of whole populations have shown that the distribution of blood glucose concentration is unimodal, with no clear division between normal and abnormal values. However, hyperglycaemia represents an independent risk factor for the development of disease of both small and large blood vessels. Diagnostic criteria for diabetes (see p. 649) have therefore been selected on the basis of identifying those who have a degree of hyperglycaemia which, if untreated, is associated with a significantly increased risk of developing vascular disease. The implication of these criteria is that there is no such thing as 'mild' diabetes not requiring effective treatment.

Diabetes is world-wide in distribution and the incidence of both type 1 and type 2 diabetes is rising. It is estimated that, in the year 2000, 150 million people world-wide had diabetes, and this is expected to double by 2010. This global pandemic principally involves type 2 diabetes, and is associated with several contributory factors including increased longevity, obesity, unsatisfactory diet, sedentary lifestyle and increasing urbanisation. However, the prevalence of both types of diabetes varies considerably around the world, and is related to differences in genetic and environmental factors. A pronounced rise in prevalence occurs in migrant populations to industrialised countries, e.g. Asian and Afro-Caribbean immigrants to the United Kingdom. The prevalence of known diabetes in Britain is around 2–3%. Many more cases of type 2 diabetes remain undetected. In Europe and North America the ratio of type 2:type 1 is approximately 7:3. In northern Europe the prevalence of type 1 diabetes in children has doubled in the last 20 years, with a particular increase in children under 5 years of age. Type 2 diabetes is also commencing at an earlier age in many populations, and in some ethnic groups, such as Hispanic and Afro-Americans, is now being observed in children and adolescents.

PHYSIOLOGY, PATHOPHYSIOLOGY AND INVESTIGATIONS

NORMAL GLUCOSE METABOLISM AND HOMEOSTASIS

In humans, blood glucose is tightly regulated by homeostatic mechanisms and maintained within a narrow range of 3.5–6.5 mmol/l. A balance is preserved between the entry of glucose into the circulation from the liver, supplemented by intestinal absorption after meals, and glucose uptake by peripheral tissues, particularly skeletal muscle. A continuous supply of glucose is essential for the brain, which uses glucose as its principal metabolic fuel.

When intestinal glucose absorption declines between meals, hepatic glucose output is increased in response to the counter-regulatory hormones glucagon and adrenaline, and it falls during prolonged starvation as other metabolic fuels derived from fat become more important. The liver produces glucose by gluconeogenesis and glycogen breakdown. The main substrates for gluconeogenesis are shown in Figure 15.1.

Insulin is the only anabolic hormone and it has profound effects on the metabolism of carbohydrate, fat and protein (see Box 15.2). Insulin is secreted from pancreatic beta cells (see Fig. 15.2) into the portal circulation, with a brisk increase in response to a rise in blood glucose (e.g. after meals). A glucose sensor has been identified in the portal vein which modulates insulin secretion via neural mechanisms. Some characteristics of normal insulin secretion are shown in Figure 15.3. Insulin lowers blood glucose by suppressing hepatic glucose production and stimulating peripheral glucose uptake in skeletal muscle and fat, mediated by the glucose transporter, GLUT 4.

Adipocytes (and the liver) synthesise triglyceride from non-esterified fatty acids (NEFAs) and glycerol. Insulin

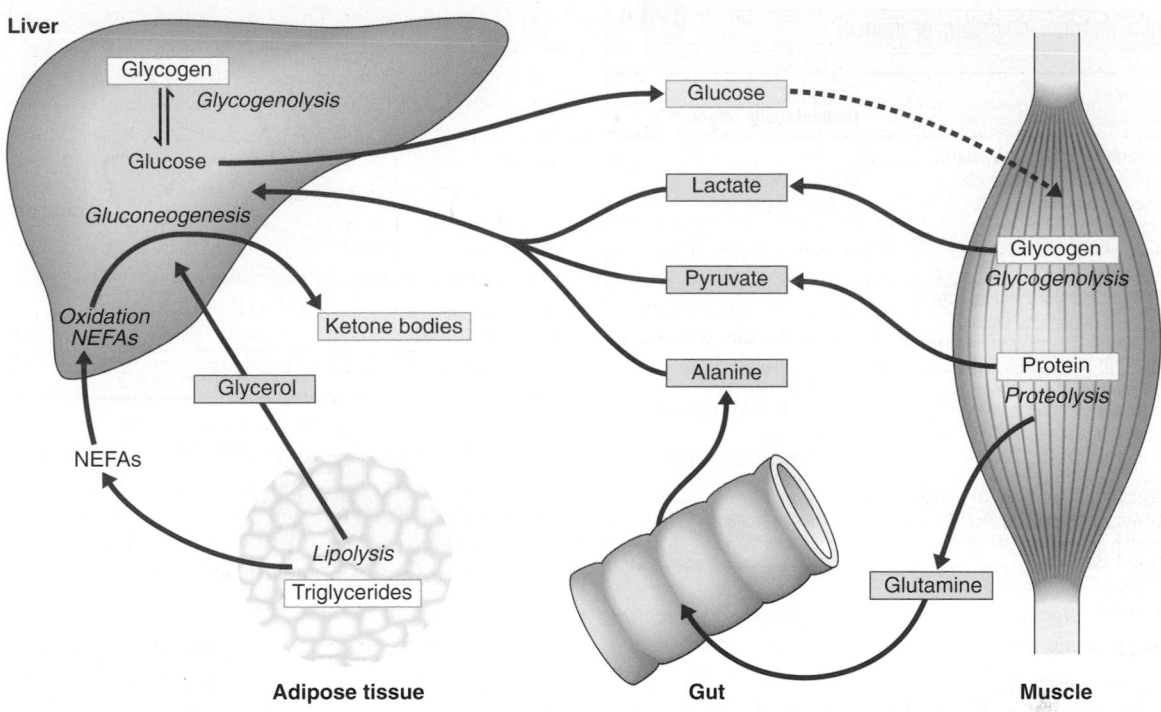

Fig. 15.1 Major gluconeogenic substrates and their tissues of origin. Insulin suppresses gluconeogenesis and promotes glycogen synthesis and storage. It promotes the peripheral uptake of glucose, particularly in skeletal muscle, and encourages storage (as muscle glycogen) and protein synthesis. It also promotes lipogenesis and suppresses lipolysis. These processes are reversed in the absence of insulin. (NEFAs = non-esterified fatty acids)

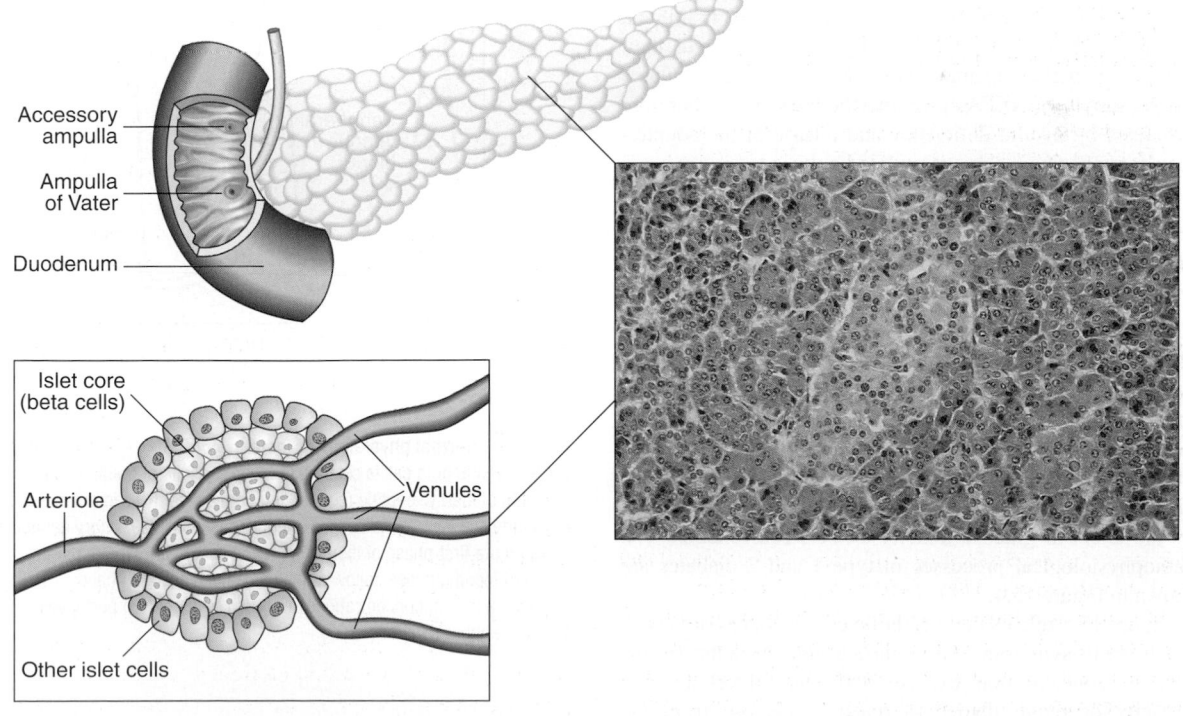

Fig. 15.2 Pancreatic structure and endocrine function. The normal adult pancreas contains about 1 million islets which are scattered throughout the exocrine parenchyma. On staining with haematoxylin and eosin the islet in the centre is identified by its distinct morphology and lighter staining than the surrounding exocrine tissue. The core of each islet consists of beta cells that produce insulin, and is surrounded by a cortex of endocrine cells that produce other hormones including glucagon (alpha cells), somatostatin (delta cells) and pancreatic polypeptide (PP cells).

15.2 METABOLIC ACTIONS OF INSULIN	
Increase **(anabolic effects)**	**Decrease** **(anticatabolic effects)**
Carbohydrate metabolism Glucose transport (muscle, adipose tissue) Glucose phosphorylation Glycogenesis Glycolysis Pyruvate dehydrogenase activity Pentose phosphate shunt	Gluconeogenesis Glycogenolysis
Lipid metabolism Triglyceride synthesis Fatty acid synthesis (liver) Lipoprotein lipase activity (adipose tissue)	Lipolysis Lipoprotein lipase (muscle) Ketogenesis Fatty acid oxidation (liver)
Protein metabolism Amino acid transport Protein synthesis	Protein degradation

stimulates lipogenesis and inhibits lipolysis, so preventing fat catabolism. Lipolysis, mediated by triglyceride lipase, is stimulated by catecholamines and liberates NEFAs which can be oxidised by many tissues. Their partial oxidation in the liver provides energy to drive gluconeogenesis and also produces ketone bodies (acetoacetate, which can be reduced to 3-hydroxybutyrate or decarboxylated to acetone) which are generated in hepatocyte mitochondria. Ketone bodies are organic acids which, when formed in small amounts, are oxidised and utilised as metabolic fuel. However, the rate of utilisation of ketone bodies by peripheral tissues is limited, and when the rate of production by the liver exceeds their removal, hyperketonaemia results. Ketogenesis is regulated by the supply of NEFAs reaching the liver and is therefore enhanced by insulin deficiency and release of the counter-regulatory hormones that stimulate lipolysis.

METABOLIC DISTURBANCES IN DIABETES

The hyperglycaemia of diabetes develops because of an absolute (type 1 diabetes) or a relative (type 2 diabetes) deficiency of insulin, resulting in decreased anabolic and increased catabolic effects. In both type 1 and type 2 diabetes, the actions of insulin are also impaired by insensitivity of target tissues. While this is a fundamental defect in type 2 diabetes, hyperglycaemia can also reduce insulin secretion by the effect of glucose toxicity on beta cell function. The pathophysiological processes in type 1 and 2 diabetes are shown in Figure 15.4.

Figure 15.5 relates the metabolic consequences of lack of insulin to its symptoms. Glycosuria occurs when the plasma glucose concentration exceeds the renal threshold (the capacity of renal tubules to reabsorb glucose from the glomerular filtrate) at approximately 10 mmol/l. The severity of the classical osmotic symptoms of polyuria and polydipsia is related to the degree of glycosuria. If hyperglycaemia develops slowly over months or years, as in type

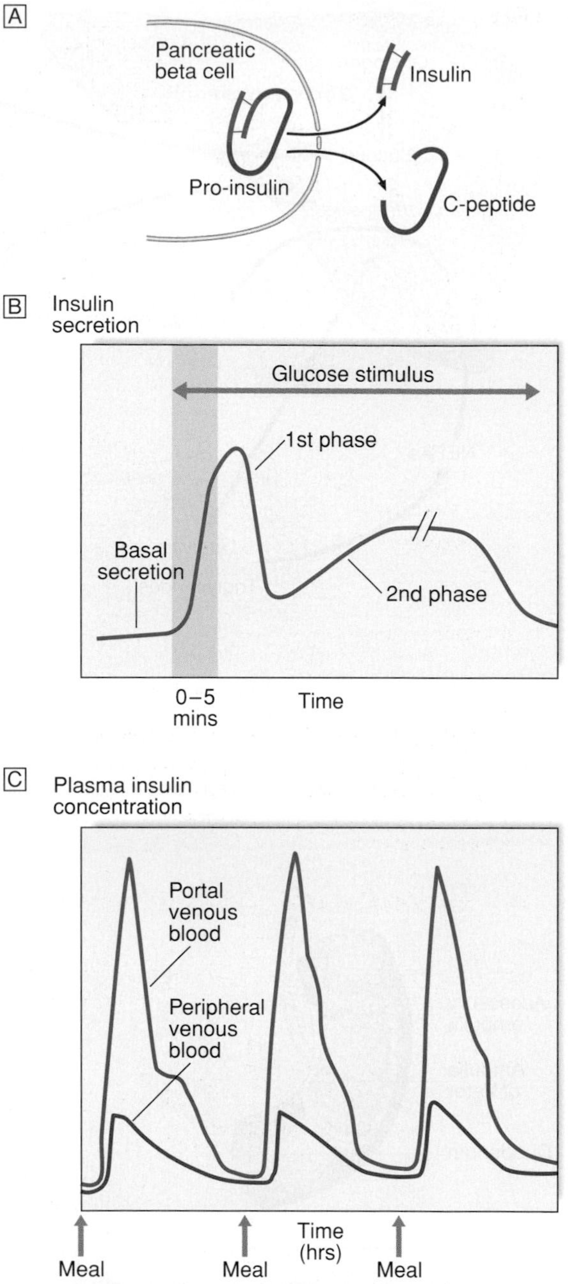

Fig. 15.3 Normal physiology of insulin secretion. [A] Pro-insulin in the pancreatic beta cell is cleaved to release insulin and equimolar amounts of inert C-peptide (connecting peptide). Measurement of C-peptide can be used to assess endogenous insulin secretory capacity. [B] An acute first phase of insulin secretion occurs in response to an elevated blood glucose, followed by a sustained second phase. [C] Plasma insulin concentrations are much higher in the portal vein than in peripheral venous blood.

2 diabetes, the renal threshold for glucose rises, and the symptoms of diabetes are mild. This is one reason for the large number of undetected cases of type 2 diabetes, many of which are discovered coincidentally.

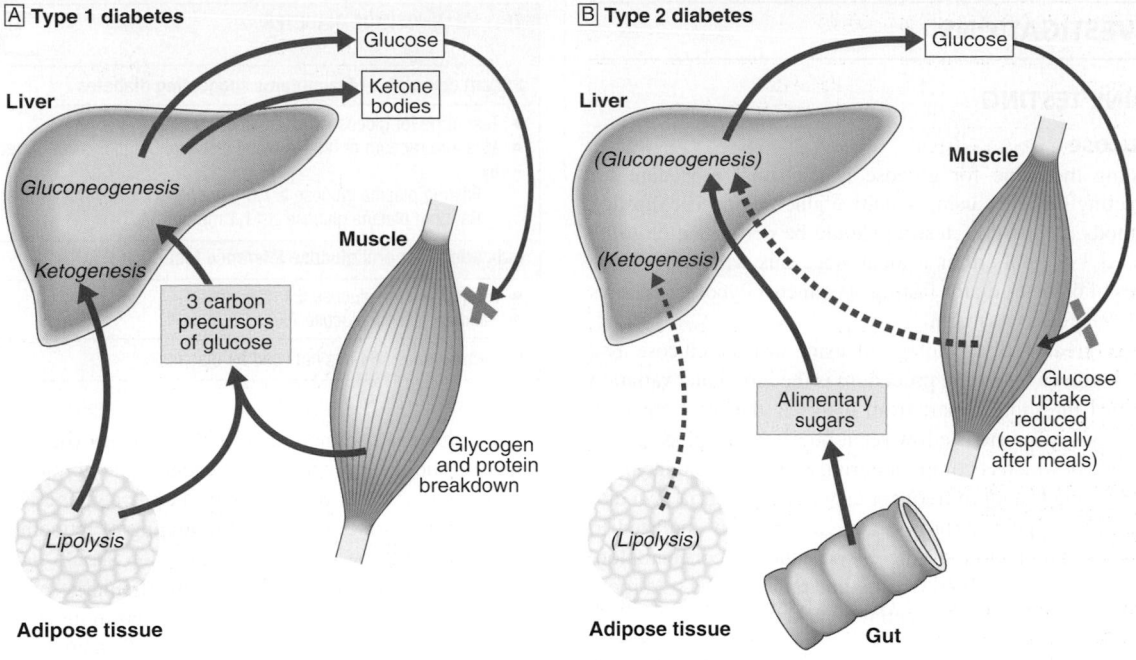

A Type 1 diabetes

• No insulin (severe deficiency)
• Increased counter-regulatory hormones
  —Unrestrained gluconeogenesis, lipolysis and ketogenesis
  —Peripheral glucose utilisation blocked
• Leads to ketoacidosis
• Protein catabolism with muscle-wasting and negative nitrogen balance

B Type 2 diabetes

• Insulin resistance
  —Hepatic and peripheral
  —Insulin-stimulated (post-prandial) glucose uptake impaired, especially in skeletal muscle
• Increased glucagon
  —Enhanced hepatic glucose output, impaired peripheral utilisation
• Ketoacidosis rarely develops

Fig. 15.4   Pathophysiological processes in diabetes mellitus. A Type 1 diabetes. B Type 2 diabetes.

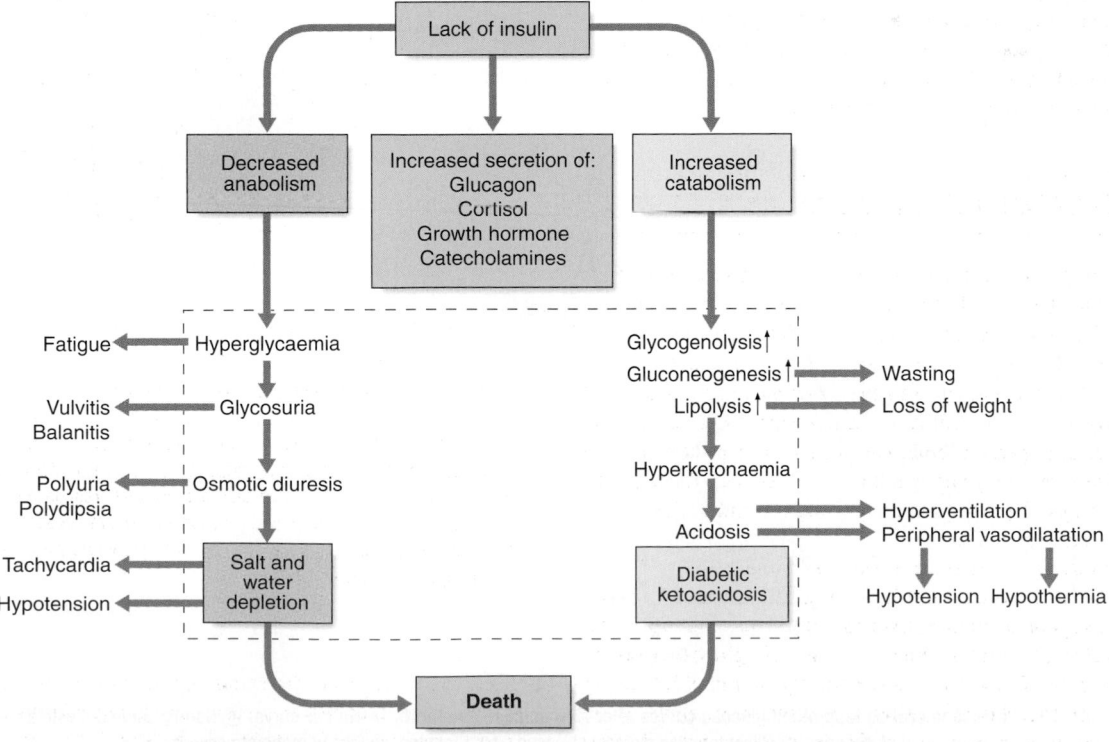

Fig. 15.5   Pathophysiological basis of the symptoms and signs of untreated or uncontrolled diabetes mellitus.

INVESTIGATIONS

URINE TESTING

Glucose

Testing the urine for glucose is the usual procedure for detecting diabetes, using sensitive glucose-specific dipstick methods. If possible, testing should be performed on urine passed 1–2 hours after a meal since this will detect more cases of diabetes than a fasting specimen. Glycosuria always warrants full assessment.

The greatest disadvantage of using urinary glucose as a diagnostic or screening procedure is the individual variation in renal threshold. Apart from diabetes, the most common cause of glycosuria is a low renal threshold for glucose (see Fig. 15.6), which is common during pregnancy and in young people, and is a more frequent cause of glycosuria than diabetes. Renal glycosuria is a benign condition unrelated to diabetes. Estimation of the blood glucose concentration, using an accurate laboratory method rather than a side-room technique, is therefore essential in making the diagnosis (see Box 15.3).

In some individuals a rapid but transitory rise of blood glucose follows a meal and the concentration exceeds the normal renal threshold; during this time glucose will be present in the urine. This response to an oral glucose load is benign and is described as a 'lag storage' blood glucose curve, although alimentary glycosuria is a better term (see Fig. 15.6C). It may occur in normal people or after gastric surgery, when it is caused by rapid gastric emptying and more rapid absorption of glucose into the circulation, and is sometimes observed in patients with hyperthyroidism, peptic ulceration or hepatic disease.

15.3 DIAGNOSIS OF DIABETES	

Patient complains of symptoms suggesting diabetes

- Test urine for glucose and ketones
- Measure random or fasting blood glucose. Diagnosis confirmed by:
  Fasting plasma glucose ≥ 7.0 mmol/l
  Random plasma glucose ≥ 11.1 mmol/l

Indications for oral glucose tolerance test

- Fasting plasma glucose 6.1–6.9 mmol/l
- Random plasma glucose 7.0–11.0 mmol/l

N.B. HbA_{1c} (see p. 649) is not used for diagnosis.

Glycosuria is common in normal pregnancy (because the renal threshold for glucose falls secondary to an increase in the glomerular filtration rate), and in late pregnancy lactose appears in the urine. However, the finding of reducing substances in the urine of a pregnant woman should never be ignored and in all cases blood glucose should be measured to identify gestational diabetes. Since even minimal hyperglycaemia in pregnancy is associated with increased perinatal mortality and morbidity, it is important to detect and treat these cases effectively.

Ketones

Ketone bodies can be identified by the nitroprusside reaction, which is primarily specific for acetoacetate. The test is conveniently carried out using tablets or dipsticks for ketones. Ketonuria may be found in normal people who have been fasting or exercising strenuously for long periods, who have been vomiting repeatedly, or who have been eating a diet high in fat and low in carbohydrate. Ketonuria is

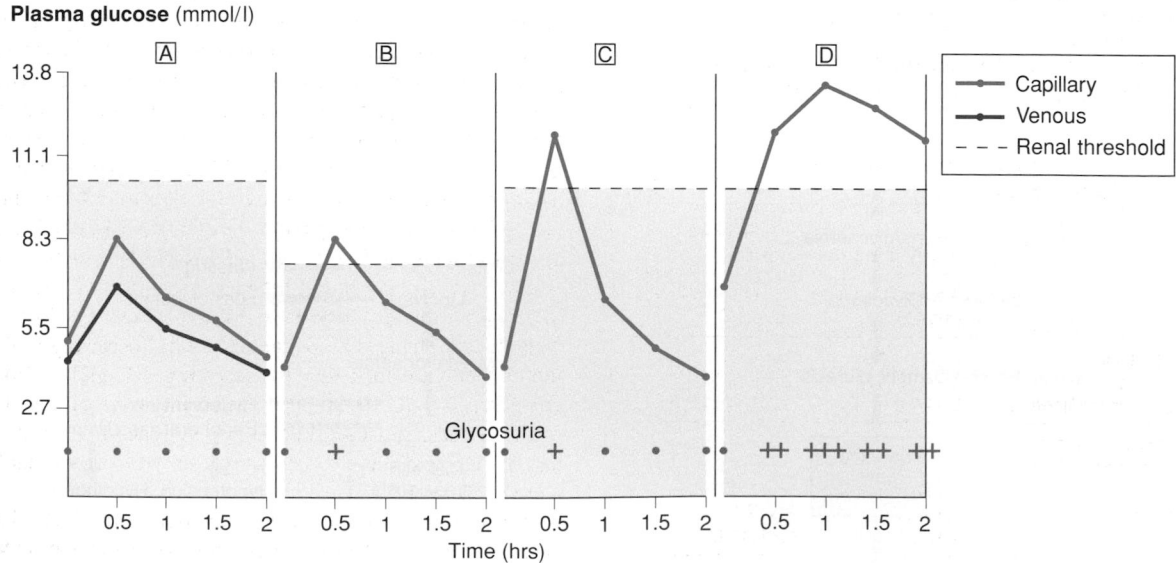

Fig. 15.6   The glucose tolerance test: blood glucose curves after 75 g glucose by mouth. Ⓐ Normal curve. Ⓑ Normal curve but with a low renal threshold leading to renal glycosuria. Ⓒ Alimentary (lag storage) glycosuria. Ⓓ Diabetes mellitus of moderate severity.

therefore not pathognomonic of diabetes but, if associated with glycosuria, the diagnosis of diabetes is highly likely. In diabetic ketoacidosis (see p. 651), ketones can be detected in plasma using dipsticks.

Protein

Dipstick testing for albumin is a standard procedure to identify the presence of renal disease (or urinary infection) in people with diabetes. This will detect urinary albumin greater than 300 mg/l. Smaller amounts of urinary albumin (microalbuminuria) can be measured and these provide indicators of risk of developing diabetic nephropathy and/or macrovascular disease (see Box 15.36, p. 674).

BLOOD TESTING

Glucose

When symptoms suggest diabetes, the diagnosis may be confirmed by a random blood glucose concentration greater than 11 mmol/l. When random blood glucose values are elevated but are not diagnostic of diabetes, glucose tolerance is usually assessed either by a fasting blood glucose estimation or by the oral glucose tolerance test (see Box 15.4).

The diagnostic criteria for diabetes mellitus (and normality) recommended by the World Health Organisation (WHO) in 2000 are shown in Boxes 15.3 and 15.5. The values are based on the threshold for risk of developing vascular disease. Diabetes is defined by a fasting plasma glucose of 7.0 mmol/l or above, or a random plasma glucose of 11.1 mmol/l or above, or an abnormal oral glucose tolerance test. Intermediate readings on the glucose tolerance test are

classified as 'impaired glucose tolerance' (IGT) and indicate the need for further evaluation. Many patients with IGT progress to frank diabetes with time, and it may therefore be necessary to keep such patients under review and to repeat the OGTT at a later date.

Another abnormal finding is 'fasting hyperglycaemia' or 'impaired fasting glucose', when the fasting plasma glucose is between 6.1 and 6.9 mmol/l. Patients with impaired fasting glucose have an increased risk of developing vascular disease. Reliance on fasting blood glucose values alone, as advocated by the American Diabetes Association, will miss some cases of type 2 diabetes which are revealed by the OGTT.

In some people, in whom an OGTT is usually normal, an abnormal result is observed under conditions which impose a burden on the pancreatic beta cells, e.g. during pregnancy, infection, myocardial infarction or other severe stress, or during treatment with diabetogenic drugs such as corticosteroids. This 'stress hyperglycaemia' usually disappears after the acute illness has resolved, but blood glucose should be remeasured.

The diagnostic criteria for diabetes in pregnancy are more stringent than those recommended for non-pregnant subjects. Pregnant women with abnormal glucose tolerance should be referred urgently to a specialist unit for full evaluation.

Glycated haemoglobin

Glycated haemoglobin provides an accurate and objective measure of glycaemic control over a period of weeks to months. This can be utilised as an assessment of glycaemic control in a patient with known diabetes, but is not sufficiently sensitive to make a diagnosis of diabetes and is usually normal in patients with impaired glucose tolerance. Several minor components of adult haemoglobin (HbA_1) can be separated from unmodified haemoglobin (HbA_0) by ion-exchange chromatography, and these haemoglobin moieties are increased in diabetes by the slow non-enzymatic covalent attachment of glucose and other sugars (glycation). Currently, laboratories report glycated haemoglobin as total glycated haemoglobin (GHb), HbA_{1c} or HbA_1. In the UK, HbA_{1c} is now the preferred measurement. The rate of formation of HbA_{1c} is directly proportional to the ambient blood glucose concentration; a rise of 1% in HbA_{1c} corresponds to an approximate average increase of 2 mmol/l in blood glucose. The close relationship between HbA_{1c} and mean blood glucose is shown in Figure 15.7. Although HbA_{1c} concentration reflects the integrated blood glucose control over the lifespan of the erythrocyte (120 days), the estimate is weighted by changes in glycaemic control occurring in the month before measurement (representing 50% of the HbA_{1c} concentration). As HbA_{1c} is affected more by recent than by earlier events, a large shift in blood glucose control is rapidly accompanied by a change in HbA_{1c}, detectable within 2–3 weeks.

Various assay methods can be used to measure HbA_{1c}, but because of a current lack of consensus on a suitable reference method and the non-standardisation of methodology, a local non-diabetic reference range must be ascertained, and this precludes direct comparison of HbA_{1c} values between

---

15.4 ORAL GLUCOSE TOLERANCE TEST (OGTT)

- Unrestricted carbohydrate diet for 3 days before test
- Fasted overnight
- Rest before test (30 mins); no smoking; seated for duration of test
- Plasma glucose measured before 75 g glucose load and at 2 hrs

---

15.5 ORAL GLUCOSE TOLERANCE TEST: WHO DIAGNOSTIC CRITERIA

	Plasma glucose	Whole blood glucose
	Venous (capillary) (mmol/l)	Venous (capillary) (mmol/l)
Diabetes		
Fasting	≥ 7.0 (≥ 7.0)	≥ 6.1 (6.1)
2 hrs after glucose load	≥ 11.1 (≥ 12.2)	≥ 10.0 (≥ 11.1)
Impaired glucose tolerance		
Fasting	< 7.0 (< 7.0)	< 6.1 (6.1)
2 hrs after glucose load	7.8–11.0 (8.9–12.1)	6.7–9.9 (7.8–11.0)

N.B. Venous blood glucose concentration is lower than capillary blood. Whole blood glucose is lower than plasma because red blood cells contain relatively little glucose.

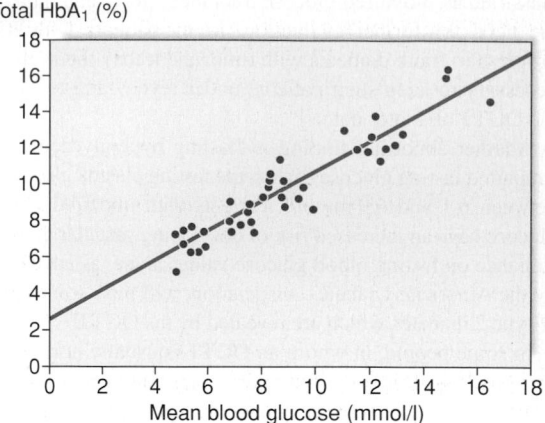

Total HbA₁ (%)

Fig. 15.7 The relationship between glycated haemoglobin (shown as HbA₁) and mean blood glucose levels in the previous 3 months. Each dot represents the mean blood glucose concentration for a single patient. Each patient collected capillary blood samples before and 2 hours after each main meal for 24 hours every 2 weeks for 3 months. Glycated haemoglobin is expressed here as total HbA₁, but HbA₁c is often reported alone and has a non-diabetic range that is lower than total HbA₁.

laboratories. HbA₁c estimates may be erroneously diminished in people with anaemia or during pregnancy, and with some assay methods may be difficult to interpret in patients who have uraemia or a haemoglobinopathy. In clinical practice, HbA₁c is usually measured once or twice yearly to assess glycaemic control, permitting appropriate changes in treatment and identifying inconsistency with the patient's record of home blood glucose monitoring. HbA₁c also provides an index of risk for developing diabetic complications.

Glycated serum proteins ('fructosamine') can be measured and, because of their shorter half-life, give an indication of glycaemic control over the preceding 2 weeks. Other than diabetic pregnancy, this is generally too short a period to make clinical decisions on therapeutic management.

Blood lipids

The concentration of serum lipids—total cholesterol, low-density and high-density lipoprotein (LDL and HDL) cholesterol and triglyceride—is another important index of overall metabolic control in diabetic patients and should be measured at diagnosis and regularly thereafter. Ideally, the triglyceride concentration should be measured in the fasting state.

MAJOR MANIFESTATIONS OF DISEASE

HYPERGLYCAEMIA

Hyperglycaemia is a very common biochemical abnormality. It is frequently detected on routine biochemical analysis of asymptomatic patients, and is found during conditions which impose a burden on pancreatic beta cells, such as pregnancy, severe illness or treatment with drugs such as corticosteroids ('stress hyperglycaemia').

Hyperglycaemia can present with the chronic symptoms described in Box 15.6. Occasionally, patients present as an acute emergency with metabolic decompensation due to ketoacidosis (see below).

Clinical features

The clinical features of the two main types of diabetes are compared in Box 15.7. While the distinction between type 1

and type 2 diabetes is broadly true in relation to the features listed, overlap occurs particularly in age at onset, duration of symptoms and family history. A few young people have a form of diabetes designated 'maturity onset diabetes of the young' (MODY; see Box 15.13, p. 654), while some middle-aged and elderly people present with typical autoimmune type 1 diabetes. Some people with apparent type 2 diabetes have evidence of autoimmune activity against pancreatic beta cells, and may have a

15.6 SYMPTOMS OF HYPERGLYCAEMIA ASSOCIATED WITH DIABETES

- Thirst, dry mouth
- Polyuria
- Nocturia
- Tiredness, fatigue, irritability, apathy
- Recent change in weight
- Blurring of vision
- Pruritus vulvae, balanitis (genital candidiasis)
- Nausea; headache
- Hyperphagia; predilection for sweet foods

15.7 COMPARATIVE CLINICAL FEATURES OF TYPE 1 AND TYPE 2 DIABETES

	Type 1	Type 2
Age at onset	< 40 years	> 50 years
Duration of symptoms	Weeks	Months to years
Body weight	Normal or low	Obese
Ketonuria	Yes	No
Rapid death without treatment with insulin	Yes	No
Autoantibodies	Yes	No
Diabetic complications at diagnosis	No	25%
Family history of diabetes	Uncommon	Yes
Other autoimmune disease	Yes	Uncommon

slowly evolving variant of type 1 diabetes (latent auto-immune diabetes in adults—LADA). Insulin-deficient forms of type 2 diabetes in middle-aged patients may be difficult to identify at diagnosis, and classification of the type of diabetes can be difficult.

The classical symptoms of thirst, polyuria, nocturia and rapid weight loss are prominent in type 1 diabetes, but are often absent in patients with type 2 diabetes, many of whom are asymptomatic or have non-specific complaints such as chronic fatigue and malaise. Uncontrolled diabetes is associated with an increased susceptibility to infection and patients may present with skin sepsis (boils) and genital candidiasis, and complain of pruritus vulvae or balanitis.

Patients with type 1 diabetes often have no physical signs attributable to diabetes, but weight loss is common.

The physical signs in patients with type 2 diabetes at diagnosis depend on the mode of presentation. More than 70% are overweight, and obesity may be central (truncal or abdominal). Obesity is less common in developing countries. Hypertension is present in 50% of patients with type 2 diabetes. Although hyperlipidaemia is also common, skin lesions such as xanthelasma and eruptive xanthomata are relatively rare.

Investigations

When symptoms suggest diabetes, the diagnosis may be confirmed by a random blood glucose concentration greater than 11 mmol/l (see Box 15.3). When random blood glucose values are elevated but not diagnostic of diabetes, glucose tolerance is usually assessed either by a fasting blood glucose estimation, or by the glycaemic response to oral ingestion of a glucose load (see Boxes 15.4 and 15.5). Hyperglycaemia during pregnancy is abnormal and requires careful assessment (see p. 678).

In those with stress hyperglycaemia the blood glucose should be remeasured on recovery from the acute illness, when it should have returned to normal.

When a diagnosis of diabetes is confirmed, other investigations should include urea, creatinine, electrolytes, liver function tests, cholesterol and triglycerides, and urine testing for protein or microalbuminuria.

Management

Three methods of treatment are available for the management of diabetes: diet alone, oral hypoglycaemic agents and insulin. Full details are given on pages 656–663.

DIABETIC KETOACIDOSIS

The biochemistry and pathophysiology of this are described in detail on page 666. Marked hyperglycaemia causes a profound osmotic diuresis leading to dehydration and electrolyte loss, particularly of sodium and potassium. A significant number of new patients still present in diabetic ketoacidosis. In established diabetes a common course of events is that patients develop an intercurrent infection, lose their appetite, and either stop or drastically reduce their dose of insulin in the mistaken belief that under these circumstances less insulin is required. Any form of stress, particularly that produced by infection, may precipitate severe ketoacidosis, even in patients with type 2 diabetes. Although some deaths from ketoacidosis are associated with severe medical conditions such as acute myocardial infarction or septicaemia, others are the consequence of delays in diagnosis and management errors. No obvious precipitating cause can be found in many cases.

Clinical features

The clinical features of ketoacidosis are listed in Box 15.8. In the fulminating case the striking features are those of salt and water depletion, with loss of skin turgor, furred tongue and cracked lips, tachycardia, hypotension and reduced intra-ocular pressure. Breathing may be deep and sighing, the breath is usually fetid, and the sickly-sweet smell of acetone may be apparent. Mental apathy, confusion or a reduced conscious level may be present. The state of consciousness is very variable in patients with diabetic ketoacidosis; coma is uncommon. A patient with dangerous ketoacidosis requiring urgent treatment may walk into the consulting room. For this reason the term 'diabetic ketoacidosis' is to be preferred to 'diabetic coma', which implies that there is no urgency until unconsciousness supervenes. In fact, it is imperative that energetic treatment is started at the earliest possible stage.

Abdominal pain is sometimes a feature of diabetic ketoacidosis, particularly in children. Serum amylase may be elevated but rarely indicates coexisting pancreatitis. Although leucocytosis invariably occurs, this represents a stress response and does not necessarily indicate infection; pyrexia may not be present initially because of vasodilatation secondary to acidosis.

15.8 CLINICAL FEATURES OF DIABETIC KETOACIDOSIS	
Symptoms	
• Polyuria, thirst	• Leg cramps
• Weight loss	• Blurred vision
• Weakness	• Abdominal pain
• Nausea, vomiting	
Signs	
• Dehydration	• Smell of acetone
• Hypotension	• Hypothermia
• Tachycardia	• Confusion, drowsiness,
• Air hunger (Kussmaul breathing)	coma (10%)

Investigations

The following are important but should not delay the institution of intravenous fluid and insulin replacement:

- urea and electrolytes, blood glucose
- arterial blood gases to assess the severity of acidosis
- urinalysis for ketones
- full blood count
- infection screen: blood and urine culture, chest radiograph.

Management

Diabetic ketoacidosis is a medical emergency which should be treated in hospital, preferably in a high-dependency area. Full details of management are given on page 666.

The principal components of treatment are:

- the administration of short-acting (soluble) insulin
- fluid replacement
- potassium replacement
- the administration of antibiotics if infection is present.

Details of other causes of acute decompensation, such as non-ketotic hyperosmolar coma and lactic acidosis, are given on page 668.

COMPLICATIONS OF DIABETES

In the context of a patient with long-standing type 1 diabetes, there will be little doubt as to the cause of the development of a foot ulcer, renal impairment, sensory loss or retinopathy, but occasionally one of these may be the presenting finding in a new case of diabetes. In

15.9 COMPLICATIONS OF DIABETES
Microvascular/neuropathic
Retinopathy, cataract • Impaired vision
Nephropathy • Renal failure
Peripheral neuropathy • Sensory loss • Motor weakness
Autonomic neuropathy • Postural hypotension • GI problems
Foot disease • Ulceration • Arthropathy
Macrovascular
Coronary circulation • Myocardial ischaemia/infarction
Cerebral circulation • Transient ischaemic attack • Stroke
Peripheral circulation • Claudication • Ischaemia

addition, diabetes may be detected for the first time when a patient presents with hypertension or vascular disease such as an acute myocardial infarction or stroke. Blood glucose should thus be checked in all patients presenting with such pathology (see Box 15.9).

Further details of the investigation and management of these problems are given on page 668.

HYPOGLYCAEMIA

This is described in detail on page 663. Hypoglycaemia (i.e. a blood glucose < 3.5 mmol/l) is a result of the treatment of diabetes rather than a manifestation of the disease itself. It occurs often in those treated with insulin but relatively infrequently in those taking a sulphonylurea drug. Most patients recognise the symptoms of hypoglycaemia and can take appropriate remedial action; others are less aware of these and, if action is not taken, neuroglycopenia and reduced consciousness ensue. Full details of awareness of symptoms are given on page 664.

Hypoglycaemia can occur in people without diabetes, when it is known as spontaneous hypoglycaemia. The causes and investigation of this are described on page 732.

Clinical features

Common symptoms of hypoglycaemia are listed in Box 15.10. They comprise two main groups: those related to acute activation of the autonomic nervous system and those secondary to glucose deprivation of the brain (neuroglycopenia). Symptoms of hypoglycaemia are idiosyncratic and differ with age. The ability to recognise their onset is an important aspect of the initial education of diabetic patients treated with insulin. Mood changes such as tense-tiredness, irritability and anger also occur, and behavioural change is common in children. Management is with oral carbohydrate or intravenous glucose, depending on the patient's conscious level and ability to swallow (see p. 665).

15.10 COMMON SYMPTOMS OF HYPOGLYCAEMIA	
Autonomic	
• Sweating • Trembling • Pounding heart	• Hunger • Anxiety
Neuroglycopenic	
• Confusion • Drowsiness • Speech difficulty	• Inability to concentrate • Incoordination
Non-specific	
• Nausea • Tiredness	• Headache
N.B. Age-specific differences in symptoms occur. Children have behavioural changes and elderly people have more prominent neurological features.	

AETIOLOGY AND PATHOGENESIS OF DIABETES

Although the precise aetiology of both main types of diabetes is uncertain, environmental factors interact with a genetic susceptibility to determine which of those people with the genetic predisposition develop the clinical syndrome, and the timing of its onset. However, both the pattern of inheritance and the environmental factors differ between type 1 and type 2 diabetes.

TYPE 1 DIABETES

Genetics

Genetic factors account for about one-third of the susceptibility to type 1 diabetes, the inheritance of which is polygenic. Over 20 different regions of the human genome show some linkage with type 1 diabetes but most interest has focused on the human leucocyte antigen (HLA) region within the major histocompatibility complex on the short arm of chromosome 6; this locus is designated IDDM 1. The HLA haplotypes DR3 and/or DR4 are associated with increased susceptibility to type 1 diabetes in Caucasians. These DR3 and DR4 alleles are in 'linkage disequilibrium', i.e. they tend to be transmitted together with the neighbouring alleles of the HLA-DQA1 and DQB1 genes, and the latter may be the main determinants of the genetic susceptibility.

HLA class II antigens (which are coded by the HLA class II genes) on the surface of cells present foreign and self-antigens to T lymphocytes and play a key role in initiating the autoimmune response. Some polymorphisms of the HLA-DQB1 gene that result in specific amino acid substitutions in the β chains of class II antigens may affect the ability of the class II molecule to accept and present autoantigens derived from pancreatic islet beta cells, and will so determine whether or not autoimmune damage will take place. Variants of the DQ β chain which carry an uncharged amino acid residue (e.g. alanine, serine or valine) at position 57 appear to be diabetogenic, whereas the presence of aspartate is protective against type 1 diabetes, at least in Caucasian populations.

The region of the insulin gene on chromosome 11p (designated IDDM 2) is also linked with type 1 diabetes. Insulin or its precursors may act as a beta cell autoantigen; alternatively, the level of insulin production could determine the activity of the beta cell and its expression of other autoantigens. Other weaker diabetes susceptibility loci include IDDM 3, IDDM 4 and IDDM 5, which lie on chromosomes 15q, 11q and 6q respectively, but their gene products and modes of action are unknown.

Environmental factors

Although genetic susceptibility appears to be a prerequisite for the development of type 1 diabetes, the concordance rate between monozygotic twins is less than 40% (see Box 15.11), and environmental factors have an important role in promoting clinical expression of the disease. It has been

15.11 RISK OF DEVELOPING TYPE 1 DIABETES IN AN INDIVIDUAL WHO HAS A FIRST-DEGREE RELATIVE WITH TYPE 1 DIABETES

Relative with type 1 diabetes	% overall risk
Identical twin	35
Non-identical twin	20
HLA-identical sibling	16
Non-HLA-identical sibling	3
Father	9
Mother	3
Both parents	Up to 30

proposed that lack of exposure to pathogenic organisms in early childhood limits maturation of the immune system and increases susceptibility to autoimmune disease ('the hygiene hypothesis').

Viruses

The evidence that viral infection might cause some forms of type 1 diabetes is derived from studies where virus particles known to cause cytopathic or autoimmune damage to beta cells have been isolated from the pancreas. Several viruses have been implicated, including mumps, Coxsackie B4, retroviruses, rubella (in utero), cytomegalovirus and Epstein–Barr virus, although the putative mechanisms by which they may induce type 1 diabetes differ.

Diet

Circumstantial evidence supports the proposition that dietary factors may, at least in certain circumstances, influence the development of type 1 diabetes. Bovine serum albumin (BSA), a major constituent of cow's milk, has been implicated in triggering type 1 diabetes. It has been shown that children who are given cow's milk early in infancy are more likely to develop type 1 diabetes than those who are breastfed. BSA may cross the neonatal gut and raise antibodies which, because of the close homology between BSA, the β chain of HLA class II antigens and a heat-shock protein expressed by beta cells, could cross-react with and cause damage to beta cell components.

Various nitrosamines (found in smoked and cured meats) and coffee have been proposed as potentially diabetogenic factors. In susceptible animals such as the diabetes-prone BB rat, various dietary proteins (e.g. gluten) may be essential for the expression of clinical type 1 diabetes.

Stress

Stress may progress the development of type 1 diabetes by stimulating the secretion of counter-regulatory hormones and possibly by modulating immune activity.

Immunological factors

Type 1 diabetes is a slow T cell-mediated autoimmune disease. Family studies have produced evidence that destruction of the insulin-secreting cells in the pancreatic islets takes place over many years. Hyperglycaemia accompanied by the classical symptoms of diabetes occurs only when 70–90% of beta cells have been destroyed. In humans and animals with spontaneous type 1 diabetes the immune system retains the capacity to recognise and destroy transplanted pancreatic beta cells indefinitely.

Pancreatic pathology

The pathological picture in the pre-diabetic pancreas in type 1 diabetes is characterised by:

- 'insulitis' (see Fig. 15.8)—that is, infiltration of the islets with mononuclear cells containing activated macrophages, helper cytotoxic and suppressor T lymphocytes, natural killer cells and B lymphocytes
- the initial patchiness of this lesion with, until a very late stage, lobules containing heavily infiltrated islets seen adjacent to unaffected lobules
- the striking beta cell specificity of the destructive process, with the glucagon and other hormone-secreting cells in the islet invariably remaining intact.

Islet cell antibodies can be detected before the clinical development of type 1 diabetes, have a variable predictive value as a marker of disease, and disappear with increasing

duration of diabetes. At present these antibodies are not suitable for screening or diagnostic purposes, but glutamate decarboxylase (GAD) antibodies may have a role in identifying late-onset type 1 diabetes in middle-aged people.

Type 1 diabetes is associated with other autoimmune disorders, including thyroid disease, coeliac disease, Addison's disease, pernicious anaemia and vitiligo.

TYPE 2 DIABETES

Type 2 diabetes commonly occurs in subjects who are obese and insulin-resistant, but these two factors alone are insufficient to cause diabetes unless accompanied by impaired beta cell function.

Genetics

Genetic factors are more important in the aetiology of type 2 than type 1 diabetes, as shown by studies in monozygotic twins where concordance rates for type 2 diabetes approach 100%.

The majority of cases of type 2 diabetes are multifactorial in nature, with interaction of environmental and genetic factors (see Box 15.12). The nature of the genetic contribution is largely unknown, but it is evident that several genes are involved. In this polygenic model, inheritance of variation in individual genes would not be sufficient to cause type 2

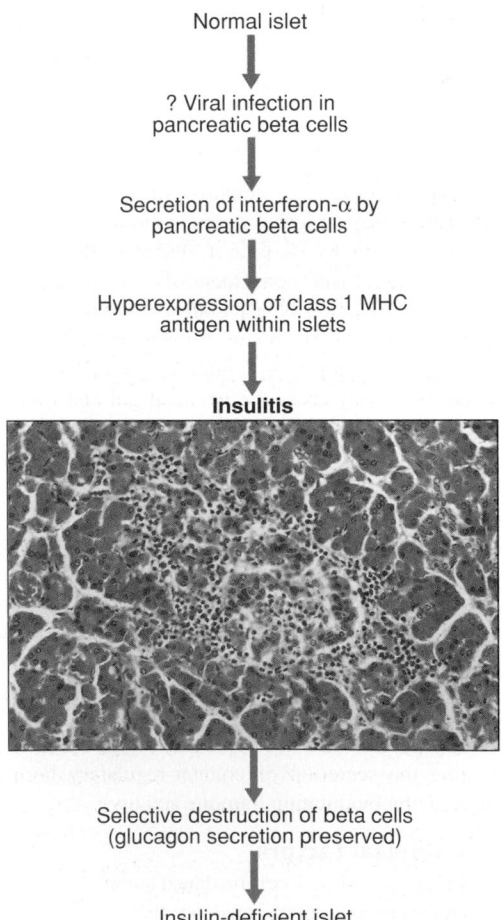

Insulitis

Normal islet

↓

? Viral infection in pancreatic beta cells

↓

Secretion of interferon-α by pancreatic beta cells

↓

Hyperexpression of class 1 MHC antigen within islets

↓

Insulitis

↓

Selective destruction of beta cells (glucagon secretion preserved)

↓

Insulin-deficient islet

Fig. 15.8 Proposed pathogenesis of type 1 diabetes. Proposed sequence of events in the development of type 1 diabetes. In insulitis, a chronic inflammatory cell infiltrate is seen in a pancreatic islet. (MHC = major histocompatibility complex)

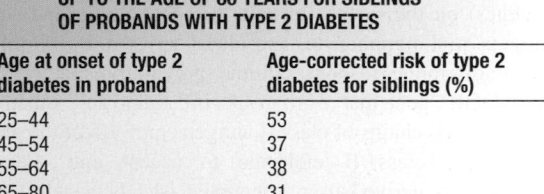

15.12	RISK OF DEVELOPING TYPE 2 DIABETES UP TO THE AGE OF 80 YEARS FOR SIBLINGS OF PROBANDS WITH TYPE 2 DIABETES	
Age at onset of type 2 diabetes in proband	**Age-corrected risk of type 2 diabetes for siblings (%)**
25–44	53
45–54	37
55–64	38
65–80	31

15.13	SINGLE GENE DEFECTS OF PANCREATIC BETA CELL FUNCTION CAUSING MATURITY ONSET DIABETES OF THE YOUNG (MODY)		
Gene	**Inheritance**	**Clinical features**
Glucokinase (GCK)	Autosomal dominant	10% of MODY in UK. Mild hyperglycaemia from birth, stable and managed by diet alone
Hepatic nuclear factor 1α (HNF1α)	Autosomal dominant	65% of MODY in UK. Diabetes presents during adolescence, progressive with requirement for oral agents or insulin
Hepatic nuclear factor 4α (HNF4α)	Autosomal dominant	5% of MODY in UK. Similar to HNF1α but age at diagnosis may be later
Insulin promoter factor 1 (IPF1)	Autosomal dominant	Rare, presentation before 25 years is unusual
Hepatic nuclear factor 1β (HNF1β)	Autosomal dominant	Rare, early-onset diabetes, renal cysts, proteinuria, renal failure

diabetes directly, but would confer an increased (or decreased) susceptibility. Over 200 candidate susceptibility genes have been investigated, such as insulin, the insulin receptor, glucose transporters and glycogen synthase, but there has not been consistent association of variants in candidate genes with type 2 diabetes. Genome-wide searches have identified susceptibility genes on chromosome 1q, 12q and 20q, but the underlying genes have not been identified.

Molecular genetics has allowed the identification of certain specific and clinically identifiable forms of diabetes, which are caused by single gene defects (see Box 15.1, p. 644 and Box 15.13). However, these subtypes, such as maturity onset diabetes of the young (MODY), are uncommon and constitute less than 5% of all cases of diabetes. Determining the molecular genetic aetiology can help to define the prognosis, optimum treatment, and risk of diabetes in relatives.

Environmental factors

Lifestyle
Epidemiological studies of type 2 diabetes provide evidence that overeating, especially when combined with obesity and underactivity, is associated with the development of this type of diabetes. Other more direct studies have shown that middle-aged people with diabetes eat significantly more and are fatter and less active than their non-diabetic siblings. Although the majority of middle-aged diabetic people are obese, only a few obese people develop diabetes. Obesity probably acts as a diabetogenic factor (through increasing resistance to the action of insulin) in those genetically predisposed to develop type 2 diabetes.

Malnutrition in utero
Retrospective analysis of the birth weight of males born in England in the 1930s has demonstrated an inverse relationship between weight at birth and at 1 year, and the development of type 2 diabetes in late adulthood. It is proposed (but not yet proven) that malnutrition in utero may programme beta cell development and metabolic functions at a critical period, so predisposing to type 2 diabetes later in life. Smoking during pregnancy has also been implicated.

Age
Age is an important risk factor for type 2 diabetes. In Britain over 70% of all cases of diabetes occur after the age of 50 years. Type 2 diabetes is principally a disease of the middle-aged and elderly, affecting 10% of the population over the age of 65.

Pregnancy
During normal pregnancy, insulin sensitivity is reduced through the action of placental hormones and this affects glucose tolerance. The insulin-secreting cells of the pancreatic islets may be unable to meet this increased demand in women genetically predisposed to develop diabetes. The term 'gestational diabetes' refers to hyperglycaemia occurring for the first time during pregnancy (see p. 679). Repeated pregnancy may increase the likelihood of developing irreversible diabetes, particularly in obese women; 80% of women with gestational diabetes ultimately develop permanent clinical diabetes requiring treatment.

Pathogenesis of type 2 diabetes

Insulin resistance
Increased hepatic production of glucose and resistance to the action of insulin in muscle are invariable in both obese and non-obese patients with type 2 diabetes. Insulin resistance may be due to any one of three general causes: an abnormal insulin molecule, an excessive amount of circulating antagonists, or target tissue defects. The last is the most common cause of insulin resistance in type 2 diabetes and seems to be the predominant abnormality in those with more severe hyperglycaemia.

A characteristic feature of type 2 diabetes is that it is often associated with other medical disorders including obesity, hypertension and hyperlipidaemia. It has been suggested that this cluster of conditions, all of which predispose to cardiovascular disease, is a specific entity (the 'insulin resistance syndrome' or 'metabolic syndrome'), with insulin resistance being the primary defect (see Box 15.14).

> **15.14 SOME FEATURES OF INSULIN RESISTANCE (METABOLIC) SYNDROME**
>
> - Hyperinsulinaemia
> - Type 2 diabetes or impaired glucose tolerance
> - Hypertension
> - Low HDL cholesterol; elevated triglycerides
> - Central (visceral) obesity
> - Microalbuminuria
> - Increased fibrinogen
> - Increased plasminogen activator inhibitor-1
> - Elevated plasma uric acid
>
> **Note** This constellation of features is also known as Reaven's syndrome and syndrome X, and is strongly associated with atherosclerosis. This is manifested by macrovascular disease (coronary, cerebral, peripheral) and an excess mortality.

Pancreatic beta cell failure
In type 2 diabetes there is only moderate reduction in the total mass of pancreatic islet tissue which is consistent with a measurable fall in plasma insulin concentration when related to the blood glucose level. However, some pathological changes are typical of type 2 diabetes, the most consistent of which is deposition of amyloid. This is accompanied by atrophy of the normal tissue, particularly islet epithelial cells. Islet amyloid is composed of insoluble fibrils formed from islet amyloid polypeptide (also known as amylin). Small quantities of islet amyloid are very common in elderly non-diabetic patients, and the role of islet amyloid in the pathogenesis of type 2 diabetes is uncertain. Deposition of amyloid is probably not a cause of diabetes but rather reflects a pathological process which is increased in type 2 diabetes. More extensive amyloidosis is, however, found in patients who have progressed to insulin replacement therapy, suggesting that islet function may become compromised by amyloid deposition.

While beta cell numbers are reduced by 20–30% in type 2 diabetes, alpha cell mass is unchanged and glucagon secretion is increased, which may contribute to the hyperglycaemia. Insulin resistance tends to raise blood glucose and this stimulates insulin secretion to prevent hypergly-caemia (see Fig. 15.9). When the maximal insulin secretory capacity has been exceeded, any further increase in fasting blood glucose levels causes a decline in insulin generation (see Fig. 15.10). Possible mechanisms for beta cell decompensation include glucotoxicity, an intrinsic failure of insulin production, a switch to abnormal processing pathways producing biologically inactive products and chronic degranulation of the beta cell.

Some people with type 2 diabetes, most of whom are not overweight, have advanced pancreatic beta cell failure at the time of presentation and require early treatment with insulin.

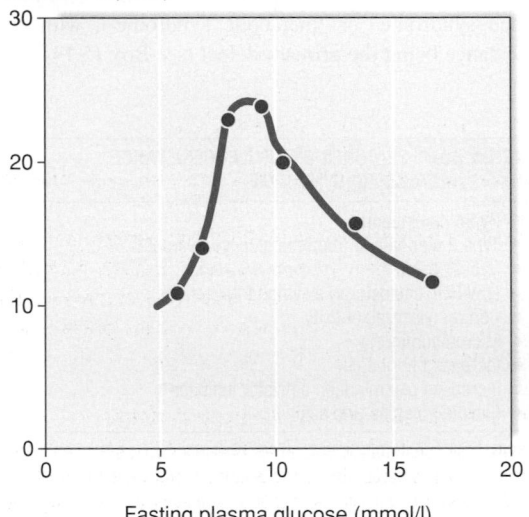

Fasting plasma insulin concentration (mU/l)

Fasting plasma glucose (mmol/l)

Fig. 15.9 **Insulin secretory capacity in type 2 diabetes.** In the natural history of pancreatic beta cell function in type 2 diabetes, insulin secretion initially increases to compensate for insulin resistance, but eventually fails, leading to type 2 diabetes. The fasting plasma insulin concentrations associated with the fasting plasma glucose are shown. This profile has been termed the 'Starling curve of the pancreas'.

MANAGEMENT OF DIABETES

Three methods of treatment are available for diabetic patients: diet alone, oral hypoglycaemic drugs, and insulin. Approximately 50% of new cases of diabetes can be controlled adequately by diet alone, 20–30% will need an oral hypoglycaemic drug, and 20–30% will require insulin. Regardless of aetiology, the type of treatment required is determined by the circulating plasma insulin concentration. In clinical practice the age and weight of the patient at diagnosis are closely related to the plasma insulin and usually indicate the type of treatment required (see Fig. 15.11). However, in each individual case the regimen adopted is effectively chosen by therapeutic trial.

The importance of lifestyle changes such as taking regular exercise, observing a healthy diet and reducing alcohol consumption should not be under-estimated in improving glycaemic control, but many people, particularly the middle-aged and elderly, find them difficult to sustain. Patients should also be encouraged to stop smoking.

THERAPEUTIC GOALS

The aim of treatment is to achieve as near normal metabolism as is practicable. The nearer the body weight approaches the ideal level and the closer the blood glucose concentration is kept to normal, the more the total metabolic profile is improved and the lower the incidence of vascular disease and specific diabetic complications (see p. 669).

The ideal management for diabetes would allow the patient to lead a completely normal life, to remain not only symptom-free but in good health, to achieve a normal metabolic state and to escape the long-term complications of diabetes. Although a few diabetic patients die from acute metabolic complications (ketoacidosis and hypoglycaemia), the major problem is the excess mortality and serious morbidity suffered as a result of the long-term complications of diabetes; the factors associated with these are listed in Box 15.15. As indicated in Box 15.16, the cost to the community and to the individual patient is enormous.

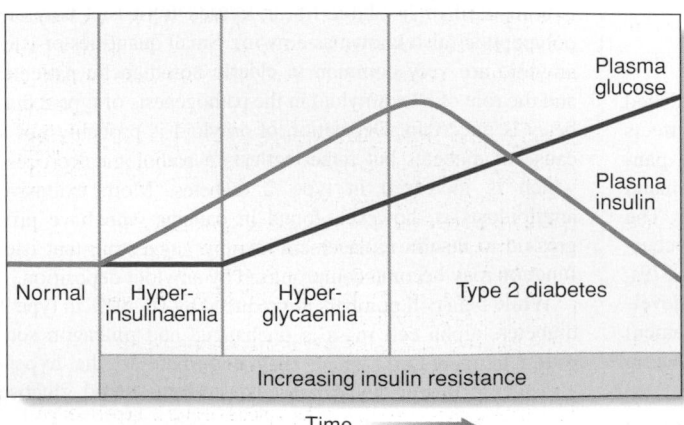

Normal | Hyper-insulinaemia | Hyper-glycaemia | Type 2 diabetes

Plasma glucose

Plasma insulin

Increasing insulin resistance

Time

Fig. 15.10 **Natural history of type 2 diabetes.** In the early stage of the disorder the response to progressive insulin resistance is an increase in insulin secretion by the pancreatic cells, causing hyperinsulinaemia. Eventually the beta cells are unable to compensate adequately and blood glucose rises, producing hyperglycaemia. With further beta cell failure (type 2 diabetes) glycaemic control deteriorates and treatment requirements escalate.

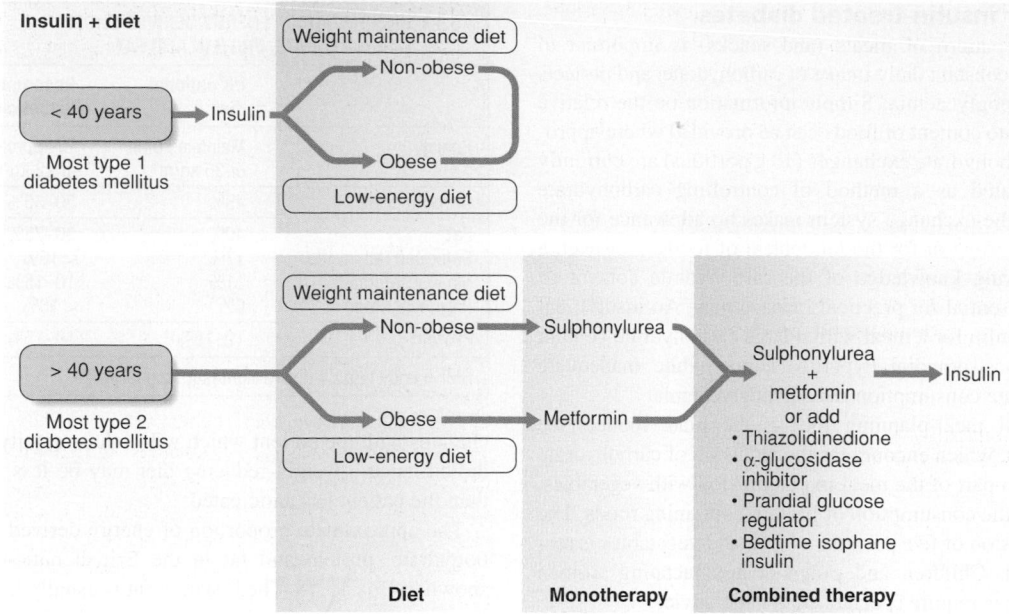

Fig. 15.11 Long-term treatment of diabetes. The treatment required by any individual can be determined by considering age and weight at diagnosis.

15.15 FACTORS ASSOCIATED WITH INCREASED MORTALITY AND MORBIDITY IN DIABETIC PATIENTS

- Duration of diabetes
- Early age at onset of disease
- High glycated Hb (HbA$_{1c}$)
- Raised blood pressure
- Proteinuria; microalbuminuria
- Obesity
- Hyperlipidaemia

15.16 THE CURRENT COST OF DIABETES IN THE UK

- 30% reduction in life expectancy
- Most common cause of blindness in age group 20–65 years
- 600 patients per annum reach end stage renal failure in UK
- Lower limb amputation rate increased 25-fold
- Use of hospital beds increased sixfold
- 4–5% of total National Health Service budget

DIETARY MANAGEMENT

Dietary measures are required in the treatment of all diabetic patients to achieve the overall therapeutic goal: normal metabolism. The aims of dietary treatment are set out in Box 15.17.

TYPES OF DIABETIC DIET

Two basic types of diet are used in the treatment of diabetes: low-energy, weight-reducing diets and weight maintenance diets. The beneficial effect of weight reduction on the mortality rate of obese non-diabetic people is well known and applies even more strikingly to the obese diabetic patient. Management of obese people (both diabetic and non-diabetic) with a diet low in refined carbohydrate and high in unrefined carbohydrate, and restricted in total energy content results in increased insulin sensitivity. This promotes a

decline in blood glucose in the obese diabetic patient. The precise mechanism of this effect is uncertain. Reduction in body weight increases this effect, encouraging a rise in the plasma insulin concentration in many patients so that additional therapy can often be avoided.

Low-energy, weight-reducing diets

Dietary prescriptions which cause a daily deficit of 500 kcal provide a realistic diet and induce a weekly weight loss of around 0.5 kg. Rapid weight reduction may provoke loss of lean body tissue, and care must be taken in the elderly to avoid the omission of essential nutrients, vitamins and minerals. Caloric restriction is essential for the obese diabetic patient treated with insulin and most oral agents, to try to minimise the weight gain which these can promote. In such individuals, the omission of snacks between meals is often necessary.

Weight maintenance diets

These are necessary for individuals with a normal body mass index (BMI, see Box 15.18, p. 658) and ideally should be high in carbohydrate and low in fat, with particular attention being paid to the type of fat ingested. While total energy intake remains constant, the percentage of energy from macronutrients should be altered as described in Box 15.18.

15.17 AIMS OF DIETARY MANAGEMENT

- Abolish symptoms of hyperglycaemia
- Reduce overall blood glucose and minimise fluctuations
- Achieve weight reduction in obese patients to reduce insulin resistance, hyperglycaemia and dyslipidaemia
- Avoid hypoglycaemia associated with therapeutic agents (insulin, sulphonylureas)
- Avoid weight gain associated with therapeutic agents (insulin, sulphonylureas, thiazolidinediones)
- Avoid 'atherogenic' diets or those which may aggravate diabetic complications (e.g. high protein intake in nephropathy)

Diets for insulin-treated diabetes

A regular pattern of meals (and snacks) is important to maintain a constant daily intake of carbohydrate, and protects against hypoglycaemia. Simple information on the relative carbohydrate content of foods can be provided where appropriate. Carbohydrate exchanges (10 g portions) are currently not advocated as a method of controlling carbohydrate intake, as the exchange system makes no allowance for the glycaemic effect or for the fat content of foods. However, a good working knowledge of the carbohydrate content of foods is essential for practical management. An insufficient dose of insulin for a meal with a large carbohydrate content leads to post-prandial hyperglycaemia, while inadequate carbohydrate consumption risks hypoglycaemia.

A useful meal-planning tool is the plate model (see Fig. 15.12), which encourages the inclusion of carbohydrate as the main part of the meal in conjunction with vegetables, and limits the consumption of protein-containing foods. The daily inclusion of five portions of fruit and vegetables is recommended. Children and pregnant and lactating women with diabetes require specialised dietetic advice.

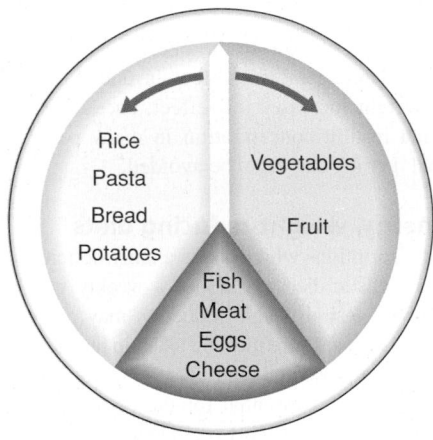

Fig. 15.12 A 'plate model' for meal planning. The plate is divided into three sections. The smallest section (one-fifth of total area) is for the meat, fish, eggs or cheese, and the remainder divided in roughly equal proportions between the staple food (rice, pasta, potatoes, bread etc.) and vegetables or fruit.

DAILY ENERGY INTAKE

It is important that all diabetic patients consume a diet containing an appropriate energy content as this greatly influences glycaemic control. An individual patient's daily energy requirement involves consideration of factors such as age, sex, actual weight in relation to desirable weight, activity and occupation. However, although a dietary history is useful to establish an individual's habitual eating pattern and to assess what types of food are consumed regularly, it is not essential that all patients have their dietary energy content quantified formally. Formulae are available for estimating total energy expenditure and this information may be of value when prescribing a realistic diet for the obese patient. One successful approach is to agree appropriate dietary

15.18 PROPORTION OF ENERGY DERIVED FROM CARBOHYDRATE, PROTEIN AND FAT		
	UK national diet	Recommended diabetic diet
Energy	Maintains BMI of 25 kg/m²	To approach BMI of 22 kg/m²
Carbohydrate	45%	50–55%
Fat	40%	30–35%
Saturated fatty acids	17%	<10%
Monounsaturated	11%	10–15%
Polyunsaturated	6%	<10%
Protein	12–15%	10–15%
BMI = body mass index (weight [kg]/height² [m²])		

changes with the patient which will induce a daily 500 kcal deficit; such a weight-reducing diet may be less restrictive than the patient has anticipated.

The approximate proportion of energy derived from carbohydrate, protein and fat in the British national diet is shown in Box 15.18. The intake of fat is usually high, with a large proportion consisting of saturated fat, and is considered to be atherogenic; in the diabetic patient it is recommended that the percentage of calories derived from carbohydrate should be increased and that from fat reduced. It is important to explain to the individual patient that the 'diabetic diet' is principally a 'healthy diet' that is recommended for the population in general (see p. 299).

CARBOHYDRATE AND NON-STARCH POLYSACCHARIDE (DIETARY FIBRE)

A suitable diet for diabetic people should have 50% of the daily caloric intake derived from carbohydrate, of which significant amounts should be in the form of non-starch polysaccharide (NSP), as dietary fibre. This can be subdivided into soluble and insoluble types. The consumption of 15 g soluble fibre (present in beans, peas, pulses, oats, fruit and vegetables) can produce a 10% reduction in fasting blood glucose, glycated haemoglobin and LDL cholesterol. However, sustaining this indefinitely requires a high level of motivation, and is difficult to achieve if the daily intake is less than 1500 kcal. The inclusion of insoluble NSP (in wholemeal bread and breakfast cereals) aids satiety and may benefit weight control but the effect on lowering blood glucose is minimal. The most useful effect of a high-carbohydrate diet is to facilitate the maintenance of a much less atherogenic low-fat diet.

Restricted consumption of mono- and disaccharides (fructose, sucrose and glucose) is advised as part of healthy eating guidelines. Foods which contain a lot of sucrose are often high in fat and their intake should be limited. Sugar-free drinks should be used and unsweetened fruit juices avoided. Confectionery, puddings, biscuits and cakes should be restricted, as should quenching thirst with milk when appetite is normal.

Classification of foods according to their acute effect on the blood glucose concentration ('glycaemic index'—see p. 300) has been suggested as a means of determining the optimal carbohydrate foods for diabetic patients, but this system is not widely used.

FAT

As diabetes is a risk factor for macrovascular disease, the intake of fat should be restricted to 30–35% of energy with less than 10% as saturated fat, less than 10% as polyunsaturated fat, and 10–15% as monounsaturated fat. The latter is associated with an improved plasma lipid profile (reduction in total and LDL cholesterol without lowering HDL cholesterol) in type 2 diabetes. The use of monounsaturated oils (e.g. olive oil) in the diet is also beneficial. Weight loss in obese patients with type 2 diabetes greatly assists in lowering plasma lipids, but many patients find the reduction of dietary fat intake very difficult to achieve.

ALCOHOL

In general, diabetic individuals should take the same precautions regarding alcohol intake as the general population. However, account must be taken of:

- the energy and carbohydrate content of alcoholic drinks
- the inhibition of gluconeogenesis by alcohol, which may potentiate the hypoglycaemic action of sulphonylureas and insulin
- the similarity of the features of inebriation and hypoglycaemia which may be confused by observers
- the tendency of alcohol to predispose towards the development of lactic acidosis in patients taking metformin
- the fact that alcohol can induce a 'disulfiram type' of reaction in some patients taking chlorpropamide.

Abstinence should be encouraged if obesity, hypertension or hypertriglyceridaemia is present.

SALT

Diabetic patients should follow the advice given to the general population: namely, to reduce sodium intake to no more than 6 g daily. Further restriction of sodium intake (to less than 3 g daily) is important in the management of hypertensive diabetic patients.

DIABETIC FOODS AND SWEETENERS

Low-calorie and sugar-free drinks are useful for patients with diabetes. These drinks usually contain non-nutritive sweeteners. Many 'diabetic foods' contain sorbitol or fructose which are relatively high in energy, may be expensive and may have gastrointestinal side-effects. They are not recommended as part of the diabetic diet.

The non-nutritive sweeteners saccharin, aspartame, sucramate and acesulphame K are the most widely used and provide means for reducing energy intake without loss of palatability.

ORAL HYPOGLYCAEMIC DRUGS

Various drugs are effective in reducing hyperglycaemia in patients with type 2 diabetes (see Fig. 15.13). Although their mechanisms of action are different, most depend upon a supply of endogenous insulin and they therefore have no hypoglycaemic effect in patients with type 1 diabetes. The sulphonylureas and the biguanides have been the mainstay of treatment for many years but novel agents are now available, such as the insulin-enhancing agents, the thiazolidinediones, the α-glucosidase inhibitors, which delay carbohydrate digestion and absorption of glucose, and the prandial glucose regulators which stimulate endogenous insulin secretion. Adherence to prescribed medication is best when few drugs are used, preferably with once-daily administration. The effects of these drugs are compared in Box 15.19.

SULPHONYLUREAS

Mechanism of action

The principal effect of sulphonylureas is mediated through stimulation of the release of insulin from the pancreatic beta cell (insulin secretagogues), but they also exert extrapancreatic effects, particularly in reducing the hepatic release of glucose.

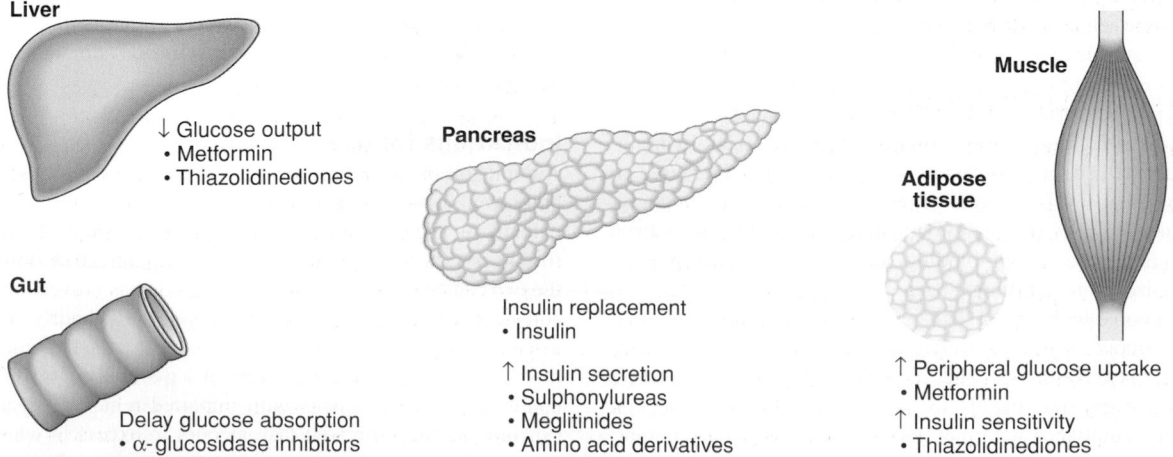

Fig. 15.13 Principal modes and sites of action of pharmacological treatments for type 2 diabetes.

15.19 EFFECTS OF HYPOGLYCAEMIC DRUGS USED IN THE TREATMENT OF TYPE 2 DIABETES

	Insulin	Sulphonyl-ureas	Metformin	Acarbose	Thiazoli-dinediones	Meglitinides and amino acid derivatives
Reduce basal glycaemia	Yes	Yes	Yes	Slight	Yes	?
Reduce post-prandial glycaemia	Yes	Yes	Yes	Yes	Yes	Yes
Raise plasma insulin	Yes	Yes	No	No	No	Yes
Increase body weight	Yes	Yes	No	No	Yes	Yes
Improve lipid profile	Yes	No	Slight	Slight	Variable	?
Risk of hypoglycaemia	Yes	Yes	No	No	No	Yes
Tolerability	Good	Good	Moderate	Moderate	Good	Good

Indications for use

Sulphonylureas are valuable in the treatment of non-obese patients with type 2 diabetes who fail to respond to dietary measures alone. Although sulphonylureas will lower the blood glucose concentration of obese patients with type 2 diabetes, such patients should be treated energetically in the first instance by dietary measures alone since treatment with sulphonylureas is often associated with an increase in weight, which will increase insulin resistance and eventually aggravate the total disability. This leads to secondary failure to respond to the drugs, and progression to treatment with insulin. The main differences between the individual compounds lie in their potency, duration of action and cost.

Tolbutamide, the mildest of the first-generation sulphonyl-ureas, is very well tolerated and rarely causes toxic reactions. Its duration of action is relatively short, it is usually administered 8- or 12-hourly, and is a useful drug in the elderly in whom the risk and the consequences of inducing hypo-glycaemia are greater. Chlorpropamide has a biological half-life of about 36 hours and is taken once daily, but may cause severe and prolonged hypoglycaemia. It is now rarely used.

Of the second-generation sulphonylureas, gliclazide and glipizide cause few side-effects, but glibenclamide is prone to induce severe hypoglycaemia and should be avoided in the elderly. Newer long-acting preparations such as glimepiride and a modified-release form of gliclazide can be administered once daily with no apparent increased risk of hypoglycaemia. The dose-response of all sulphonylureas is most effective at low dosage; little additional hypogly-caemic benefit is obtained when the dose is increased to maximal levels. Several drugs can potentiate the hypogly-caemic effect of sulphonylureas by displacing them from their plasma protein-binding sites, e.g. salicylates, phenyl-butazone and antifungal agents.

People with type 2 diabetes who fail to respond to initial treatment with sulphonylureas are considered 'primary treatment failures'. The incidence of primary treatment failure depends mainly on the criteria for initial selection and compliance with diet. Patients with 'secondary failure' (i.e. after a period of satisfactory glycaemic control) are not a homogeneous group; they include some with late-onset type 1 diabetes who develop an absolute deficiency of insulin, some with insulin-deficient diabetes who present as type 2 diabetes, and others with significant circulating plasma insulin levels who are usually obese and have failed to lose weight while supposedly taking a low-energy diet. Failure to adhere to the recommended diet is the most common precipitant of secondary treatment failure. With continuing follow-up, 'secondary failure' affects 3–10% of patients each year.

BIGUANIDES

Metformin is the only biguanide available. The long-term benefit of metformin was shown in the United Kingdom Prospective Diabetes Study (UKPDS; see p. 669), but it is less widely used than the sulphonylureas because of a higher incidence of side-effects, particularly gastrointestinal symptoms.

Mechanism of action

The mechanism of action of metformin has not been precisely defined. It has no hypoglycaemic effect in non-diabetic individuals, but in diabetes, insulin sensitivity and periph-eral glucose uptake are increased. There is some evidence that it also impairs glucose absorption by the gut and inhibits hepatic gluconeogenesis. Although secretion of some endogenous insulin is mandatory for its hypogly-caemic action, it does not increase insulin secretion or cause hypoglycaemia.

Indications for use

Administration of metformin is not associated with a rise in body weight and it is therefore preferred for the obese patient. In addition, as the hypoglycaemic effect of met-formin is synergistic with that of the sulphonylurea drugs, the two can be combined when either alone has proved inad-equate. Metformin is given with food 8- or 12-hourly. The usual starting dose is 500 mg 12-hourly, with a gradual increase as required to a maximum of 1 g 8-hourly. Its use is contraindicated in patients with impaired renal or hepatic function and in those who take alcohol in excess in whom the risk of lactic acidosis is significantly increased. It should be discontinued, at least temporarily, if any other serious medical condition develops, especially one causing severe shock or hypoxaemia. In such circumstances, treatment with insulin should be substituted.

ALPHA-GLUCOSIDASE INHIBITORS

The alpha-glucosidase inhibitors delay carbohydrate absorption in the gut by selectively inhibiting disaccharidases. Acarbose or miglitol is available and is taken with each meal. Both lower post-prandial blood glucose and modestly improve overall glycaemic control. They can be combined with a sulphonylurea. The main side-effects are flatulence, abdominal bloating and diarrhoea.

THIAZOLIDINEDIONES

These novel drugs (also called TZD drugs, 'glitazones' or PPARγ agonists) bind and activate peroxisome proliferator-activated receptor γ, a nuclear receptor that regulates the expression of several genes involved in metabolism, and work by enhancing the actions of endogenous insulin. Insulin sensitivity (mainly in adipose tissue) is improved only in patients with insulin resistance; plasma insulin concentrations are not increased and hypoglycaemia is not a problem. Rosiglitazone or pioglitazone should be prescribed with either a sulphonylurea or metformin; they have few side-effects, although they promote weight gain and fluid retention and are contraindicated in people who have cardiac failure.

MEGLITINIDES AND AMINO ACID DERIVATIVES

These drugs are oral prandial glucose regulators. Repaglinide directly stimulates endogenous insulin secretion and is taken immediately before food. It is less likely to cause hypoglycaemia than sulphonylureas. Nateglinide has a similar mode of action, restores first-phase insulin secretion, and is prescribed with metformin.

COMBINED ORAL HYPOGLYCAEMIC THERAPY AND INSULIN

In diabetic patients who are requiring increasing doses of a sulphonylurea or biguanide, either alone or in combination with each other or with a thiazolidinedione, the introduction of a single dose of an intermediate-acting insulin (usually isophane), administered at bedtime, may improve glycaemic control and delay the development of overt pancreatic beta cell failure. The exogenous insulin suppresses hepatic glucose output during the night and lowers fasting blood glucose. This treatment is ineffective in diabetic patients who have no residual endogenous insulin secretion, i.e. those who are C-peptide-negative. The combination of bedtime isophane insulin with metformin has been shown to be the regimen least likely to promote weight gain. For patients who are approaching secondary failure to oral medication, this provides a simple and effective introduction to self-treatment with insulin with little risk of hypoglycaemia.

INSULIN

MANUFACTURE AND FORMULATION

Insulin was discovered in 1921 and transformed the management of type 1 diabetes, until then a fatal disorder. Until the 1980s insulin was obtained by extraction and purification from pancreata of cows and pigs (bovine and porcine insulins) and some people continue to use animal insulins. The use of recombinant DNA technology has enabled large-scale production of human insulin. Recently, rDNA and protein engineering techniques that alter the amino acid sequence of insulin have been used to produce 'monomeric' analogues of insulin, which are more rapidly absorbed from the site of injection (e.g. insulin lispro or aspart).

The duration of action of short-acting, unmodified insulin ('soluble' or 'regular' insulin), which is a clear solution, can be extended by the addition of protamine and zinc at neutral pH (isophane or NPH insulin) or excess zinc ions (lente insulins). These modified 'depot' insulins are cloudy preparations. Pre-mixed formulations containing short-acting and isophane insulins in various proportions are available. The time characteristics of insulins are shown in Box 15.20.

In many countries, the insulin concentrations in available formulations have been standardised at 100 units/ml.

15.20 DURATION OF ACTION (IN HOURS) OF INSULIN PREPARATIONS			
Insulin	**Onset**	**Peak**	**Duration**
Fast-acting (insulin analogue)	< 0.5	0.5–2.5	3–4.5
Short-acting (soluble, regular)	0.5–1	1–4	4–8
Intermediate-acting (isophane, lente)	1–3	3–8	7–14
Long-acting (bovine ultralente)	2–4	6–12	12–30
Long-acting (insulin analogue-glargine)	1–2	None	24

INSULIN DELIVERY

Insulin is injected subcutaneously into the anterior abdominal wall, upper arms, outer thighs and buttocks (see Box 15.21). Accidental intramuscular injection often occurs in children and thin adults. The rate of absorption of insulin may be influenced by many factors other than the insulin formulation, including the site, depth and volume of injection, skin temperature (warming), local massage and exercise.

15.21 TECHNIQUE OF INSULIN INJECTION

- Needle sited at right angle to the skin
- Subcutaneous (not intramuscular) injection (depth of injection, needle size)
- Delivery devices—glass syringe (requires resterilisation), plastic syringe (disposable), pen device, infusion pump

Absorption is delayed from areas of lipohypertrophy at injection sites (see p. 643), which results from the local trophic action of insulin, so repeated injection at the same site should be avoided. Other routes of administration (intravenous and intraperitoneal) are reserved for specific circumstances.

Insulin is administered using a disposable plastic syringe with a fine needle (which can be reused several times) in preference to the traditional glass syringe and metal needle which require repeated sterilisation. Pen injectors with insulin in cartridge form are popular and convenient and are also available as pre-loaded disposable pens. They do not necessarily improve glycaemic control but may increase compliance.

'Open-loop' systems are battery-powered portable pumps providing continuous subcutaneous or intravenous infusion of insulin, delivered at variable rates without reference to the blood glucose concentration. In practice, the 'loop' is closed by the patient performing blood glucose estimations, and the use of these devices requires a high degree of patient motivation; they are prone to pump failure and patients may experience rapid onset of ketoacidosis. These increasingly sophisticated systems can achieve excellent glycaemic control but will not be adopted for widespread therapeutic use until they are less expensive and incorporate a miniaturised glucose sensor.

Short-acting insulin has to be injected at least 30 minutes before a meal to allow adequate time for absorption. Many patients find this inconvenient and ignore this requirement. However, the rapidly absorbed fast-acting insulin analogues can be administered immediately before food, or even after meals, and their peak action coincides more closely with the post-prandial rise in blood glucose (see Box 15.20).

Once absorbed into the blood stream, insulin has a half-life of a few minutes. It is cleared mainly by the liver and also the kidneys; plasma insulin concentrations are elevated in patients with liver disease or renal failure. The rate of clearance is also affected by binding to insulin antibodies (associated with the use of animal insulins).

INSULIN REGIMENS

Various insulin regimens are used in the treatment of diabetes. The choice of regimen depends on the desired degree of glycaemic control, the patient's lifestyle and his or her ability to adjust the insulin dose. Most people require two or more injections of insulin daily. Once-daily injections rarely achieve satisfactory glycaemic control and are reserved either for some elderly patients or for those who retain significant endogenous insulin secretion and have a low insulin requirement.

Twice-daily administration of a short-acting and intermediate-acting insulin (usually soluble and isophane insulins), given in combination before breakfast and the evening meal, is the simplest and most commonly used regimen. Individual requirements vary considerably but usually two-thirds of the total daily requirement of insulin is given in the morning in a ratio of 1:2, short:intermediate-acting insulins. The remaining third is given in the evening, and doses are adjusted according to blood glucose monitoring.

Several pre-mixed formulations are available containing different proportions of soluble and isophane insulins (e.g. 30:70 and 50:50). These are of value in patients who have difficulty mixing insulins, but are inflexible as the individual components cannot be adjusted independently.

Multiple injection regimens are popular, with short-acting insulin being taken before each meal, and intermediate-acting insulin being injected at bedtime (basal-bolus regimen). This type of regimen allows greater freedom of timing of meals and is of value to individuals with variable day-to-day activities, but snacks may have to be taken between meals to prevent hypoglycaemia. The use of pen injectors has improved the acceptability of multiple injection regimens. The time-action profile of different insulin regimens, compared to the secretory pattern of insulin in the non-diabetic state, is shown in Figure 15.14. Fast-acting insulin analogues may be used before meals, and are particularly useful if the evening meal is late, as they do not induce nocturnal hyperinsulinaemia. However, a long interval between meals allows the blood glucose to rise, and may require injection of additional isophane insulin before breakfast.

The management of children and teenagers presents particular problems which should be addressed in specialised clinics.

The complications of insulin therapy are listed in Box 15.22; the most important of these is hypoglycaemia.

15.22 SIDE-EFFECTS OF INSULIN THERAPY
• Hypoglycaemia
• Weight gain
• Peripheral oedema (insulin treatment causes salt and water retention in the short term)
• Insulin antibodies (animal insulins)
• Local allergy (rare)
• Lipodystrophy at injection sites

EDUCATING PATIENTS ABOUT INSULIN

It is essential that people with diabetes learn to handle all aspects of their management as quickly as possible, and this can be done on an outpatient basis. However, patients requiring insulin have to be seen daily at first and, if this is not practicable, admission to hospital may be necessary.

Everybody with type 1 diabetes who is capable of learning must be taught how to perform capillary blood glucose estimations and test for urinary ketones, to keep a record of the results and to understand their significance.

Those requiring insulin need to learn how to measure their dose of insulin accurately with an insulin syringe or pen device, to give their own injections and to adjust the dose themselves on the basis of blood glucose values and other factors such as illness, exercise and hypoglycaemic episodes. They must be familiar with the symptoms associated with hypoglycaemia (see Box 15.10, p. 652). They must therefore have a working knowledge of diabetes and also ready access to medical advice when the need arises.

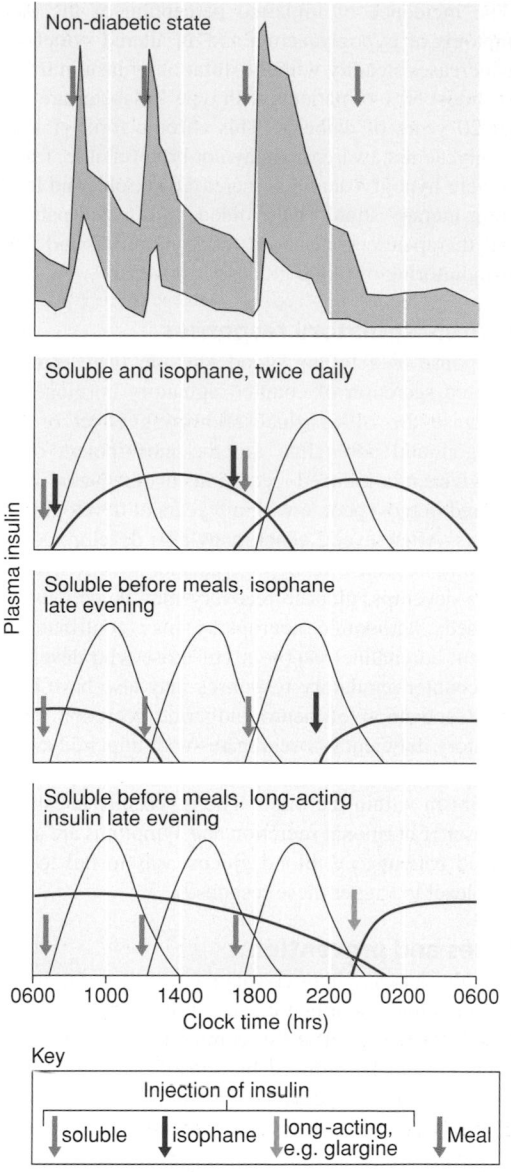

Key

Injection of insulin			
↓ soluble	↓ isophane	↓ long-acting, e.g. glargine	↓ Meal

Fig. 15.14 Profiles of plasma insulin associated with different insulin regimens. The profiles are compared to the normal secretory pattern in a non-diabetic person (top panel). These are theoretical patterns of plasma insulin and may differ considerably in magnitude and duration of action amongst individuals.

Information should be provided about driving (statutory regulations and practical advice; see Box 15.23). Provision of such education is time-consuming but only in this way can patients safely undertake normal activities while maintaining good control.

It is a wise precaution for diabetic patients who are taking insulin or an oral hypoglycaemic drug to carry a card stating their name and address, the fact that they have diabetes, the nature and dose of any insulin or other drugs they may be taking, and the name, address and telephone number of their family doctor and any specialist diabetes clinic they attend.

SELF-ASSESSMENT OF GLYCAEMIC CONTROL

Urine testing

Semi-quantitative pre-prandial urine testing to assess blood glucose control has major limitations, particularly in people with type 1 diabetes, but also in those with type 2 diabetes where a raised renal threshold for glucose may mask persistent hyperglycaemia. Negative urine tests fail to distinguish between normal and low blood glucose levels, which is a particular disadvantage since the aim of treatment is a normal blood glucose level while avoiding hypoglycaemia. However, urine glucose testing with visually read strips is still used by many people with type 2 diabetes and is satisfactory in those treated with diet alone or in those taking oral therapy who have stable glycaemic control.

Blood testing

Wherever possible, patients (particularly those treated with insulin) should be taught to perform capillary blood glucose measurements at home, using blood glucose test strips read either visually or with a glucose meter. The great advantage of self-monitoring of capillary blood glucose concentration is that information is available immediately and permits the well-informed and motivated patient to make appropriate adjustments in treatment (particularly in insulin dose) on a day-to-day basis. Thus ketoacidosis can be avoided, compliance with dietary measures encouraged and a normal or near-normal metabolism achieved while avoiding frequent and disabling hypoglycaemia. Single random blood glucose estimations obtained at routine clinic visits are of limited value and the main disadvantage of profiles measured in hospital is that they are obtained in a highly artificial situation.

ACUTE METABOLIC COMPLICATIONS

HYPOGLYCAEMIA

Hypoglycaemia (blood glucose < 3.5 mmol/l) occurs often in diabetic patients treated with insulin but relatively infrequently in those taking a sulphonylurea drug. The risk of hypoglycaemia is the most important single factor limiting the attainment of the therapeutic goal, namely near-normal glycaemia.

Severe hypoglycaemia, defined as 'hypoglycaemia requiring the assistance of another person for recovery', can result in serious morbidity (see Box 15.24) and has a recognised mortality of 2–4% in insulin-treated patients. The unrecognised mortality may be higher. Occasionally, sudden death occurs during sleep in otherwise healthy young patients with type 1 diabetes ('dead-in-bed syndrome'); hypoglycaemia-induced cardiac arrhythmia or acute respiratory arrest with impaired baroreflex sensitivity has been implicated.

In most instances the patient has no difficulty in recognising the symptoms of hypoglycaemia and can take appropriate remedial action. Clinical features are described on page 652. However, in certain circumstances (e.g. during sleep or during periods of strict glycaemic control) and in certain types of patient (e.g. patients with long duration of type 1 diabetes), warning symptoms are not always perceived by the patient even when awake, so that appropriate action is not taken and neuroglycopenia with reduced consciousness ensues.

Awareness of symptoms

Severe hypoglycaemia is very disruptive and impinges on many aspects of the patient's life, including employment, driving and sport.

If short-acting (soluble) insulin is administered to a normal person, symptoms of hypoglycaemia are usually experienced when the venous or capillary blood glucose is around 2.5–3.0 mmol/l. In diabetic patients who are chronically hyperglycaemic the same symptoms may develop at a higher blood glucose level; conversely, patients who have strict glycaemic control (HbA$_{1c}$ within the non-diabetic range) or who experience frequent hypoglycaemia may not experience any symptoms even when the blood glucose is well below 2.5 mmol/l. This is a manifestation of cerebral adaptation to blood glucose concentrations. Therapy-induced impaired awareness of hypoglycaemia is usually reversible if glycaemic control is relaxed and hypoglycaemia avoided.

The incidence of impaired perception of the onset of symptoms of hypoglycaemia and an altered symptom profile increases steadily with the duration of insulin treatment, and almost 50% of patients with type 1 diabetes are affected after 20 years of diabetes. This chronic form of impaired hypoglycaemia awareness may not be reversible; frequency of severe hypoglycaemia is increased sixfold, and intensive insulin therapy should be avoided. In affected patients the usual therapeutic goals need to be modified and frequent self-monitoring of blood glucose is mandatory.

Counter-regulatory responses

In response to a falling blood glucose, there is normally increased secretion of counter-regulatory hormones which antagonise the blood glucose-lowering effect of insulin. Glucagon and adrenaline are the most potent of these. Hypoglycaemia-induced secretion of glucagon becomes impaired in most people within 5 years of developing type 1 diabetes. After several years many also develop a defective adrenaline response to hypoglycaemia so that if hypoglycaemia develops, glucose recovery may be seriously compromised. Autonomic neuropathy may contribute to the deficient adrenaline response, but those who develop deficient counter-regulatory responses may also have impaired central activation of neuro-endocrine secretion. Counter-regulatory deficiency cosegregates with impaired awareness of hypoglycaemia, suggesting a common pathogenetic mechanism within the brain. The glycaemic thresholds for the onset of hormonal secretion and symptoms are altered in affected patients, i.e. blood glucose has to fall to a much lower level to trigger these responses.

Causes and prevention

The main causes of hypoglycaemia in patients taking insulin or a sulphonylurea drug are listed in Box 15.25.

The incidences of most common causes of hypoglycaemia can all be reduced by adequate patient education. Exercise-induced hypoglycaemia (see Fig. 15.15) occurs in well-controlled, insulin-treated diabetic patients because a key factor in the normal adaptation to exercise, namely decreased secretion of endogenous insulin, does not occur. Patients should be taught that, if strenuous or protracted exercise is anticipated, the preceding dose of insulin should

15.25 CAUSES OF HYPOGLYCAEMIA

- Missed, delayed or inadequate meal
- Unexpected or unusual exercise
- Alcohol
- Errors in oral hypoglycaemic agent or insulin dose/schedule/ administration
- Poorly designed insulin regimen, particularly if predisposing to nocturnal hyperinsulinaemia
- Lipohypertrophy
- Gastroparesis due to autonomic neuropathy
- Malabsorption, e.g. coeliac disease
- Dumping
- Unrecognised other endocrine disorder, e.g. Addison's disease
- Factitious (deliberately induced)

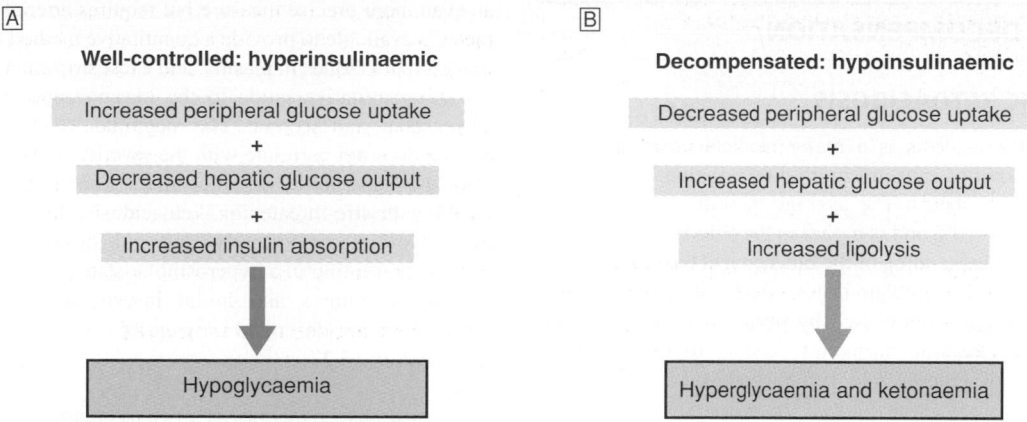

Fig. 15.15   The effect of exercise in diabetic patients being treated with insulin. A Well-controlled hyperinsulinaemic patients. B Decompensated hypoinsulinaemic patients.

be reduced (the degree of reduction varying widely in individual patients but often being substantial) and extra carbohydrate ingested. All patients taking insulin should carry glucose tablets at all times.

The incidence of nocturnal hypoglycaemia in patients with type 1 diabetes treated conventionally with a twice-daily injection regimen is difficult to establish but is certainly high. As nocturnal hypoglycaemia does not usually waken the sleeping patient, and the usual warning symptoms are not perceived, it is often undetected. However, on direct questioning, patients may admit to poor quality of sleep, morning headaches, 'hangover', chronic fatigue and vivid dreams or nightmares. Sometimes a relative may observe sweating (which may be profuse), restlessness, twitching or even convulsions. The only reliable way to make the diagnosis is to measure the blood glucose during the night. The common problem is that many insulin regimens in current use produce inappropriate nocturnal hyperinsulinaemia. When an intermediate-acting depot insulin such as isophane is taken before the main evening meal at 1700–1900 hrs, its peak action will coincide with the period of maximum sensitivity to insulin, namely 2300–0200 hrs. Short-acting insulin administered before a late evening meal also causes early nocturnal hypoglycaemia. With a basal-bolus regimen the times of maximum risk of biochemical hypoglycaemia are between 2300 and 0200 hrs and between 0500 and 0700 hrs. To reduce the risk of nocturnal hypoglycaemia, administration of the evening dose of depot intermediate-acting insulin should be deferred until bedtime (after 2300 hrs) or a fast-acting insulin analogue used before the evening meal. It is a sensible precaution for patients to measure the blood glucose before they go to bed and to take additional carbohydrate if the reading is less than 6.0 mmol/l.

Management

Treatment of acute hypoglycaemia depends on the severity of the hypoglycaemia and whether the patient is conscious and able to swallow. Treatment may simply require oral carbohydrate if hypoglycaemia is recognised early. If the adult patient is unable to swallow, intravenous glucose (30–50 ml of 50% dextrose) or glucagon (1 mg by intramuscular injection) should be administered. The recommended dose of intravenous dextrose in children is 0.2 g/kg. A commercial viscous gel solution can be applied into the buccal cavity in children, although jam or honey may be just as effective, but should not be used if the patient is unconscious.

As soon as the patient is able to swallow, glucose should be given orally. Full recovery may not occur immediately and reversal of cognitive impairment is not complete until 60–90 minutes after normoglycaemia is restored. Further, when hypoglycaemia has occurred in a patient using a long- or intermediate-acting insulin or a long-acting sulphonylurea, such as glibenclamide, the possibility of recurrence should be anticipated and to prevent this a 10% dextrose infusion, titrated to the patient's glucose, may be necessary.

The development of cerebral oedema should be considered in patients who fail to regain consciousness after blood glucose is restored to normal. Other causes of impaired consciousness, such as alcoholic intoxication, a post-ictal state or cerebral haemorrhage, should be excluded. Cerebral oedema has a high mortality and morbidity, and requires urgent treatment with mannitol and high-dose oxygen.

Following recovery it is important to try to identify a cause and make appropriate adjustments to the patient's therapy. Unless the reason for a hypoglycaemic episode is clear, the patient should reduce the next dose of insulin by 20% and seek medical advice about further adjustments in dose. Patient education on the potential risks of inducing hypoglycaemia and on its treatment, including the need to have an accessible supply of glucose (and glucagon) and regular blood glucose monitoring, are fundamental to the prevention of this potentially dangerous side-effect of treatment. Relatives and friends also need to be familiar with the symptoms and signs of hypoglycaemia and should be instructed as to how this should be managed (including how to give an intramuscular injection of glucagon).

The management of self-poisoning with oral hypoglycaemic agents is given on page 173.

ACUTE DECOMPENSATION

DIABETIC KETOACIDOSIS

Diabetic ketoacidosis is a major medical emergency and remains a serious cause of morbidity, principally in people with type 1 diabetes. The average mortality in developed countries is 5–10% and is higher in the elderly.

A clear understanding of the biochemical basis and pathophysiology of this problem is essential for its efficient treatment. Ketoacidosis is caused by insulin deficiency and an increase in catabolic hormones, leading to hepatic overproduction of glucose and ketone bodies (see Fig. 15.5, p. 647).

The cardinal biochemical features of diabetic ketoacidosis are:

- hyperglycaemia
- hyperketonaemia
- metabolic acidosis.

The hyperglycaemia causes a profound osmotic diuresis leading to dehydration and electrolyte loss, particularly of sodium and potassium. The metabolic acidosis forces hydrogen ions into cells, displacing potassium ions, which may be lost in urine or through vomiting.

The average loss of fluid and electrolytes in moderately severe diabetic ketoacidosis in an adult is shown in Box 15.26. About half the deficit of total body water is derived from the intracellular compartment and occurs comparatively early in the development of acidosis with relatively few clinical features; the remainder represents loss of extracellular fluid sustained largely in the later stages. It is at this time that marked contraction of the size of the extracellular space occurs, with haemoconcentration, a decreased blood volume, and finally a fall in blood pressure with associated renal ischaemia and oliguria.

Every patient in diabetic ketoacidosis is potassium-depleted, but the plasma concentration of potassium gives very little indication of the total body deficit. Plasma potassium may even be raised initially due to disproportionate loss of water and catabolism of protein and glycogen. However, soon after insulin treatment is started there is likely to be a precipitous fall in the plasma potassium due to dilution of extracellular potassium by administration of intravenous fluids, the movement of potassium into cells as a result of treatment with insulin, and the continuing renal loss of potassium.

The severity of ketoacidosis can be assessed rapidly by measuring the plasma bicarbonate; less than 12 mmol/l indicates severe acidosis. The hydrogen ion concentration gives

an even more precise measure but requires arterial blood. A meter is available to provide a quantitative method for determination of ketones in plasma, and a test strip can be used as a semi-quantitative guide to the plasma concentration of acetoacetate and acetone. The magnitude of the hyperglycaemia does not correlate with the severity of the metabolic acidosis; moderate elevation of blood glucose may be associated with life-threatening ketoacidosis. In some cases, hyperglycaemia predominates and acidosis is minimal, with patients presenting in a hyperosmolar state.

Clinical features and initial investigation of diabetic ketoacidosis are described on page 651. Complications are listed in Box 15.27.

15.27 COMPLICATIONS OF DIABETIC KETOACIDOSIS

- Cerebral oedema
  May be caused by rapid reduction of blood glucose, use of hypotonic fluids and/or bicarbonate
  High mortality
  Treat with mannitol, oxygen
- Acute respiratory distress syndrome (see p. 198)
- Thromboembolism
- Disseminated intravascular coagulation (rare)
- Acute circulatory failure

Management

Guidelines for the management of ketoacidosis are shown in Boxes 15.28 and 15.29. Treatment must be monitored by laboratory measurement of plasma glucose, urea and electrolytes, and arterial pH (H^+ concentration) and bicarbonate, estimated initially at intervals of 1–2 hours.

The principal components of treatment are:

- the administration of short-acting (soluble) insulin
- fluid replacement
- potassium replacement
- the administration of antibiotics if infection is present.

Insulin

If an intravenous infusion of insulin (see Box 15.28) is not possible, a loading dose of 10–20 units of soluble insulin can be given by intramuscular injection, immediately followed by 5 units hourly thereafter. The blood glucose concentration should fall by 3–6 mmol/l per hour. A more rapid fall in blood glucose should be avoided, as hypoglycaemia can be precipitated and the serious complication of cerebral oedema may develop. If blood glucose does not fall within 2 hours of commencing treatment, the dose of insulin should be doubled until a satisfactory response is obtained. Ketosis, dehydration, acidaemia, infection and stress combine to produce severe insulin resistance in some cases but most will respond to a low-dose insulin regimen. When the blood glucose concentration has fallen to 10–15 mmol/l the dose of insulin should be reduced to 1–4 units hourly. Restoration of insulin by subcutaneous injection should not be instituted until the patient is able to eat and drink normally. Sliding scales of insulin administration should not be used.

15.26 AVERAGE LOSS OF FLUID AND ELECTROLYTES IN ADULT DIABETIC KETOACIDOSIS OF MODERATE SEVERITY

- Water: 6 litres
- Sodium: 500 mmol
- Chloride: 400 mmol
- Potassium: 350 mmol

15.28 PROTOCOL FOR THE MANAGEMENT OF DIABETIC KETOACIDOSIS

Time (hrs)	Insulin (use only short-acting (soluble) insulin)	Fluid (i.v.)	Potassium (i.v.)	Other
0	Start i.v. insulin infusion 5 U/hr (Alternatively, 10–20 U i.m. followed by 5 U/hr i.m. thereafter)	Start i.v. 0.9% saline infusion, 1 litre in 30 mins		Check capillary blood glucose. If ≥ 17 mmol/l, obtain venous blood for urgent laboratory measurement of glucose, Na, K, Cl, CO_2, urea and pH or [H^+]. Test urine for ketones
0.5	Continue insulin 5 U/hr i.v.	0.5 litre of 0.9% saline in 30 mins	If plasma K^+ > 5.5 mmol/l, give no KCl; 3.5–5.5 mmol/l, give 20 mmol KCl/l of infused fluid; < 3.5 mmol/l, give 40 mmol KCl/l of infused fluid	If plasma Na^+ > 155 mmol/l, give 0.45% rather than 0.9% saline until Na^+ falls to 140 mmol/l. If pH < 7.0 ([H^+] > 100 nmol/l), give 300 ml 1.26% sodium bicarbonate over 30 mins into large vein
1	Continue insulin 5 U/hr i.v.	0.5 litre of 0.9% saline in 1 hr	As above	Recheck biochemistry
2	Continue insulin 5 U/hr i.v. (higher rate if fall in blood glucose < 3 mmol/hr)	0.5 litre of 0.9% saline in 2 hrs	As above	Recheck biochemistry
	When blood glucose < 15 mmol/l Reduce rate of insulin infusion to 1–4 U/hr	Change to 5% glucose infusion 0.5 litre/2 hrs	Continue i.v. K^+ supplements	Continue to check biochemistry every 2–4 hrs

Continue with regimen until fluid deficit replaced, ketonuria abolished and adequate oral intake of carbohydrate feasible.

N.B. These guidelines for a typical 'average' case should be modified appropriately in the individual patient after considering the blood biochemistry and clinical features, e.g. see page 668 for information on treatment of non-ketotic hyperosmolar diabetic coma.

15.29 OTHER ISSUES IN THE MANAGEMENT OF DIABETIC KETOACIDOSIS

Fluid replacement

- 6 litres deficit
  3 litres from extracellular compartment: replaced by saline
  3 litres from intracellular compartment: replaced by dextrose

Capillary blood glucose measurement

- An accurate laboratory measurement of blood glucose should be taken at an early stage
- A capillary blood glucose measurement of ≥ 17 mmol/l using visually read glucose strips can be very misleading since the actual blood glucose concentration is often considerably higher when measured accurately in the laboratory; therefore an accurate measurement should be taken at an early stage

Additional procedures

- Catheterisation if no urine passed after 3 hrs
- Nasogastric tube to keep stomach empty in unconscious or semiconscious patients
- Central venous line if cardiovascular system compromised so that fluid replacement can be adjusted accurately
- Plasma expander if BP does not rise with i.v. saline
- Antibiotic if infection demonstrated or suspected

Monitoring

- Blood glucose and electrolytes hourly for 3 hrs and every 2–4 hrs thereafter
- Temperature, pulse, respiration, BP hourly
- Urinary output and ketones
- ECG, plasma osmolality, arterial pH in some cases

Fluid replacement

Intravenous fluid replacement is required since, even when the patient is able to swallow, fluids given by mouth may be poorly absorbed. The extracellular fluid deficit should be replenished by infusing isotonic saline (0.9% NaCl). Early and rapid rehydration is essential, otherwise the administered insulin will not reach the poorly perfused tissues. If the plasma sodium is greater than 155 mmol/l, 0.45% saline may be given initially instead of 0.9%.

The intracellular water deficit must be replaced by using 5% or 10% dextrose and not by more saline. It is best given when the blood glucose concentration approaches normal. An accurate record of fluid balance must be maintained.

Potassium

As the plasma potassium is often high at presentation, treatment with intravenous potassium chloride should be started cautiously (see Box 15.28) and carefully monitored. Sufficient should be given to maintain a normal plasma concentration and large amounts may be required (100–300 mmol in the first 24 hours). Cardiac rhythm should be monitored in severe cases because of the risk of electrolyte-induced cardiac arrhythmia.

Bicarbonate

In patients who are severely acidotic (pH < 7.0, [H^+] > 100 nmol/l) the infusion of sodium bicarbonate (300 ml 1.26%

over 30 minutes into a large vein) should be considered, with the simultaneous administration of potassium. Its use is controversial, however, and should only be considered in exceptional circumstances. Complete correction of the acidosis should not be attempted.

Antibiotics

Infections must be carefully sought and vigorously treated since it may not be possible to abolish ketosis until they are controlled.

NON-KETOTIC HYPEROSMOLAR DIABETIC COMA

This condition is characterised by severe hyperglycaemia (> 50 mmol/l) without significant hyperketonaemia or acidosis. Severe dehydration and pre-renal uraemia are common. This condition usually affects elderly patients, many with previously undiagnosed diabetes. Mortality is over 40%. Its treatment differs from that of ketoacidosis in two main respects. Firstly, these patients are usually relatively sensitive to insulin and approximately half the dose of insulin recommended for the treatment of ketoacidosis should usually be employed. Secondly, the plasma osmolality should be measured or, less accurately, calculated using the following formula based on plasma values in mmol/l:

Plasma osmolality = $2[Na^+] + 2([K^+] + [glucose] + [urea])$

The normal value is 280–300 mmol/kg and the conscious level is depressed when it is high (> 340 mmol/kg). The patient should be given 0.45% saline until the osmolality approaches normal, when 0.9% should be substituted. The rate of fluid replacement should be regulated on the basis of the central venous pressure, and plasma sodium concentration checked frequently. Thromboembolic complications are common, and prophylactic subcutaneous heparin is recommended.

LACTIC ACIDOSIS

In coma due to lactic acidosis the patient is likely to be taking metformin for type 2 diabetes and is very ill and overbreathing but not so profoundly dehydrated as is usual in coma due to ketoacidosis. The patient's breath does not smell of acetone, and ketonuria is mild or even absent, yet the plasma bicarbonate and pH are markedly reduced (pH < 7.2). The diagnosis is confirmed by a high (usually > 5.0 mmol/l) concentration of lactic acid in the blood. Treatment is with intravenous sodium bicarbonate sufficient to raise the plasma pH to above 7.2, along with insulin and glucose. Despite energetic treatment, the mortality in this condition is > 50%. Sodium dichloroacetate may be given to lower blood lactate.

ACUTE CIRCULATORY FAILURE

Acute circulatory failure occurring in any of these types of acute metabolic decompensation should be treated as described on page 201.

LONG-TERM COMPLICATIONS OF DIABETES

The long-term results of treatment of diabetes are disappointing in many patients. As shown in Boxes 15.30 and 15.31, the excess mortality incurred by diabetic patients is mainly caused by large blood vessel disease, which accounts for about 70% of all deaths, mostly from myocardial infarction and stroke. The pathological changes associated with atherosclerosis in diabetic patients are similar to those seen in the non-diabetic population but they occur earlier in life and are more extensive and severe. Diabetes enhances the effects of the other major cardiovascular risk factors: smoking, hypertension and hyperlipidaemia (see Fig. 15.16). Hyperinsulinaemia may promote atherogenic changes in blood lipids and blood coagulability and raise arterial blood pressure. A metabolic (insulin resistance) syndrome has been described in which the cosegregation of various conditions is associated with premature and severe macrovascular disease (see Box 15.14, p. 655). However, randomised controlled trials have shown that aggressive management of diabetic patients with cardiovascular disease can improve outcome (see EBM panels).

Disease of small blood vessels is a specific complication of diabetes and is termed diabetic microangiopathy. It contributes to mortality by causing renal failure due to diabetic nephropathy.

Both types of vascular disease also cause substantial morbidity and disability: for example, blindness due to diabetic retinopathy; difficulty in walking, chronic ulceration of the feet, bowel and bladder dysfunction due to autonomic neuropathy; and angina, cardiac failure, intermittent claudication and gangrene due to atherosclerosis.

15.30 MORTALITY IN DIABETES	
	Mortality ratio (diabetics vs matched controls)
Overall	2.6 (p < 0.001)
Coronary heart disease **Cerebrovascular disease** **Peripheral vascular disease**	2.8 (p < 0.001)
All other causes, including renal failure	2.7 (p < 0.05)

15.31 CAUSES OF DEATH IN TREATED DIABETIC PATIENTS*	
• Cardiovascular disease	70%
• Renal failure	10%
• Cancer	10%
• Infections	6%
• Diabetic ketoacidosis	1%
• Other	3%
* These figures are approximate.	

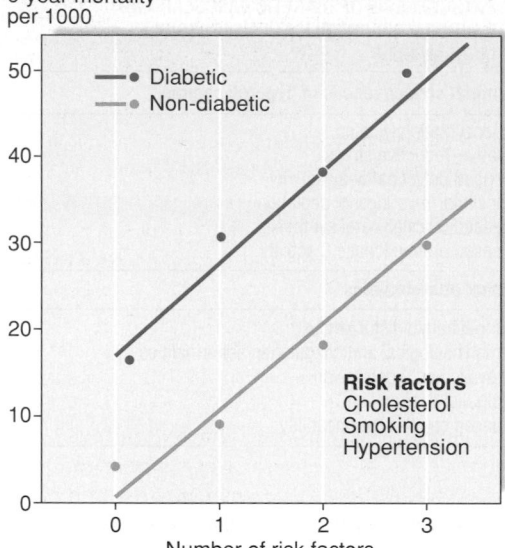

6-year mortality
per 1000

Fig. 15.16 Diabetes mellitus as a risk factor for coronary heart disease (CHD). Three major factors—smoking, hypertension and raised cholesterol—are associated with risk of CHD in the general population. The presence of diabetes mellitus produces an increment in risk in addition to these conventional factors.

METABOLIC CONTROL AND DEVELOPMENT OF LONG-TERM COMPLICATIONS

A graded relationship has been demonstrated between the duration and degree of sustained hyperglycaemia, however caused and at whatever age it develops, and the risk of vascular disease.

The possibility of reversing early vascular disease by improving metabolic control has been examined in several prospective randomised controlled clinical trials involving patients with early background retinopathy and minimal proteinuria. None of these studies produced any evidence of reversal of either retinopathy or nephropathy, and in some cases retinopathy worsened abruptly soon after control was improved. Despite this, in the long term the rate of progression of both retinopathy and nephropathy was reduced by continuing better control. These studies stimulated a search for markers of early reversible retinal, renal and neural dysfunction, and shifted the emphasis in the management of diabetes to primary prevention of complications.

The Diabetes Control and Complications Trial (DCCT) was a large study that lasted 9 years in type 1 diabetic patients to answer the question: are diabetic complications preventable? The trial demonstrated a 60% overall reduction in the risk of developing diabetic complications in those on intensive therapy with strict glycaemic control (mean HbA$_{1c}$ around 7%), compared with those on conventional therapy (mean HbA$_{1c}$ around 9%–see EBM panel). No single factor other than glycaemic control had a significant effect on outcome.

The conclusions which can be drawn are:

- Diabetic complications are preventable.
- The aim of treatment should be 'near-normal' glycaemia, while at the same time avoiding severe hypoglycaemia in insulin-treated patients.

In the patients with strict glycaemic control in the DCCT, weight gain was common and severe hypoglycaemic episodes occurred three times more often. Although there was no associated increase in deaths, major macrovascular events or neurological/cognitive defects, this increased risk of hypoglycaemia may alter the risk:benefit ratio of good control in certain patients. Thus less intensive treatment may be indicated in:

- those with impaired awareness of hypoglycaemia
- those with severe macrovascular disease (particularly if they have a past history of myocardial infarction or cerebrovascular accident)
- those who are very old and frail
- very young (pre-school) children.

A large study of patients with type 2 diabetes, UKPDS, has shown that the frequency of diabetic complications is lower and progression slower with good glycaemic control and effective treatment of hypertension, irrespective of the type of therapy used (see EBM panels). This study has indicated that the target HbA_{lc} should be 7% or less and blood pressure less than 140/80. This often requires the use of multiple medications, with the potential problem of patient adherence to therapy.

TYPE 2 DIABETES—role of control of blood pressure EBM

'The micro- and macrovascular complications of type 2 diabetes can be minimised by strict control of blood pressure, with a target of less than 140/80 mmHg. Several hypotensive agents may be required in combination to achieve target levels.'

- UK Prospective Diabetes Study (UKPDS) Group. Tight blood pressure control and risk of macrovascular and microvascular complications in type 2 diabetes (UKPDS 38). BMJ 1998; 317:703–713.
- Hanson L, Zanchetti A, Carruthers SG, et al. (HOT Study Group). Effects of intensive blood-pressure lowering and low-dose aspirin in patients with hypertension: principal results of Hypertension Optimal Treatment (HOT) randomised trial. Lancet 1998; 351:1755–1762.

Further information: 🖥 www.dtu.ox.ac.uk/ukpds/

TYPE 2 DIABETES—role of glycaemic control EBM

'The microvascular complications of type 2 diabetes can be minimised by strict glycaemic control (mean HbA_{lc} around 7%) using either oral hypoglycaemic agents or insulin.'

- UK Prospective Diabetes Study (UKPDS) Group. Intensive blood-glucose control with sulphonylureas or insulin compared with conventional treatment and risk of complications in patients with type 2 diabetes (UKPDS 33). Lancet 1998; 352:837–853.
- UK Prospective Diabetes Study (UKPDS) Group. Effect of intensive blood-glucose control with metformin on complications in overweight patients with type 2 diabetes (UKPDS 34). Lancet 1998; 352:854–865.

Further information: 🖥 www.dtu.ox.ac.uk/ukpds/

Pathophysiology

Some of the numerous biochemical and functional abnormalities found in long-standing, poorly controlled diabetes are listed in Box 15.32.

The histopathological hallmark of diabetic microangiopathy is thickening of the capillary basement membrane, with associated increased vascular permeability throughout the body. The development of the characteristic clinical syndromes of diabetic retinopathy, nephropathy, neuropathy and atherosclerosis is thought to result from additional anatomical, haemodynamic and metabolic organ- and tissue-specific factors on the generalised vascular injury. For example, in the wall of large vessels, increased permeability of arterial endothelium, particularly when combined with hyperinsulinaemia and hypertension, will increase the deposition of atherogenic lipoproteins.

The precise mechanisms linking hyperglycaemia to the pathological changes underlying the clinical syndromes are not yet fully defined. However, it is thought that increased metabolism of glucose to sorbitol via the polyol pathway is of central importance in pathogenesis, since haemodynamic, vascular permeability and structural changes in capillaries are prevented in diabetic animals by treatment with a variety of structurally different aldose-reductase inhibitors which inhibit this process. Glycation of structural proteins and the production and deposition of advanced glycation end-products in various tissues, along with possible free radical-mediated damage, may underlie some of the structural and functional abnormalities of diabetic complications.

15.32 PATHOGENESIS OF DIABETIC VASCULAR AND NEUROPATHIC COMPLICATIONS: POSSIBLE MECHANISMS ℹ

Biochemical consequences of hyperglycaemia

- Non-enzymatic glycation
- Oxidative-reductive stress
- Increased polyol pathway activity
- Intracellular *myo*-inositol depletion
- Increased diacylglycerol synthesis
- Increased protein kinase C activity

Functional abnormalities

- Haemodynamic disturbances
- Haemorrheological and coagulation abnormalities
- Microvascular hypertension
- Endothelial dysfunction
- Increased capillary permeability

Likewise, an increase in glycolytic metabolites within the cell contributes to enhanced synthesis of diacylglycerol which has been linked via the activation of protein kinase C to the various functional abnormalities listed in Box 15.32.

Whatever the mechanism of the noxious effect of long-standing hyperglycaemia, it has been shown that the nearer the overall blood glucose concentration is to normal, the fewer and less severe are the abnormalities listed in Box 15.32, and the lower the incidence of the clinical syndromes arising from micro- and macroangiopathy.

DIABETIC RETINOPATHY

Diabetic retinopathy is the most common cause of blindness in adults between 30 and 65 years of age in developed countries. Retinal photocoagulation is an effective treatment, provided it is given at a relatively early stage when the patient is usually symptomless. This means that regular examination of the fundi, with the pupils fully dilated, is mandatory in all diabetic patients.

Pathogenesis

Hyperglycaemia increases retinal blood flow and metabolism and has direct effects on retinal endothelial cells and pericytes, loss of which impairs vascular autoregulation. The resulting uncontrolled blood flow increases production of vasoactive substances and endothelial cell proliferation, resulting in capillary closure. This causes chronic retinal hypoxia and stimulates production of growth factors, including vascular endothelial growth factor (VEGF). VEGF acts via protein kinase C to stimulate endothelial cell growth (causing new vessel formation) and increased vascular permeability (causing exudative damage).

Clinical features

The clinical features characteristic of diabetic retinopathy are listed in Box 15.33. These occur in varying combinations in different patients. Abnormalities of the capillary bed, which are not visible clinically, are the earliest lesions. They include capillary dilatation and closure.

15.33 CLINICAL FEATURES OF DIABETIC RETINOPATHY	
• Microaneurysms	• Neovascularisation
• Retinal haemorrhages	• Pre-retinal haemorrhage
• Exudates	• Vitreous haemorrhage
• Cotton wool spots	• Fibrosis
• Venous changes	

Microaneurysms

In most cases these are the earliest clinical abnormality detected. They appear as tiny, discrete, circular, dark red spots near to, but apparently separate from, the retinal vessels (see Fig. 15.17A). They look like tiny haemorrhages but photographs of injected preparations of retina show that they are in fact minute aneurysms arising mainly from the venous end of capillaries near areas of capillary closure.

Haemorrhages

These most characteristically occur in the deeper layers of the retina and hence are round and regular in shape and described as 'blot' haemorrhages (see Fig. 15.17A). The smaller ones may be difficult to differentiate from microaneurysms and the two are often grouped together as 'dots and blots'. Superficial flame-shaped haemorrhages may also occur, particularly if the patient is hypertensive.

Exudates

These are characteristic of diabetic retinopathy. They vary in size from tiny specks to large confluent patches and tend to occur particularly in the perimacular area (see Fig. 15.17B). They result from leakage of plasma from abnormal retinal capillaries and overlie areas of neuronal degeneration.

Cotton wool spots

These are similar to those seen in hypertension, and also occur particularly within five disc diameters of the optic disc. They represent arteriolar occlusions causing retinal ischaemia and hence are a feature of pre-proliferative diabetic retinopathy; they are most often seen in rapidly advancing retinopathy or in association with uncontrolled hypertension.

Intraretinal microvascular abnormalities

Intraretinal microvascular abnormalities (IRMA) are dilated, tortuous capillaries which represent the remaining patent capillaries in an area where most have been occluded.

Neovascularisation

This may arise from the venous circulation on the optic disc or the retina in response to areas of ischaemic retina. The earliest appearance is that of fine tufts of delicate vessels forming arcades on the surface of the retina (see Fig. 15.17C). As they grow, they may extend forwards towards the vitreous.

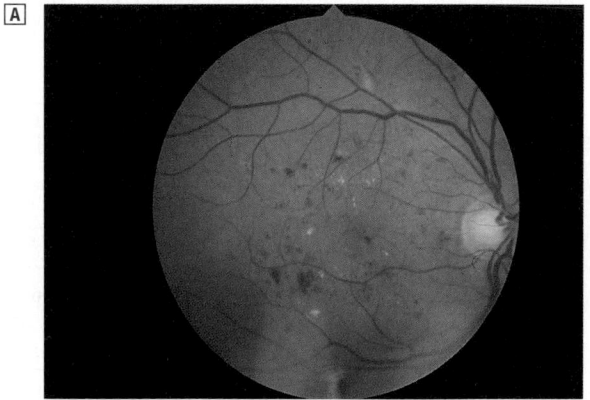
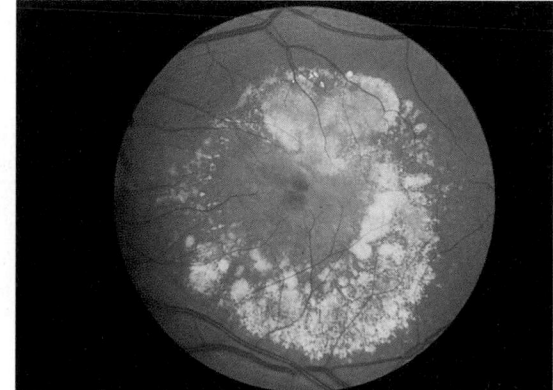
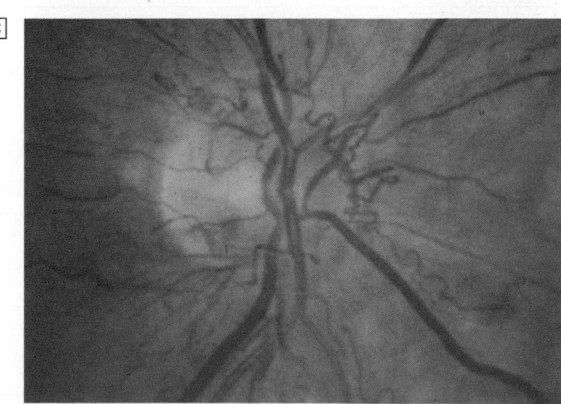
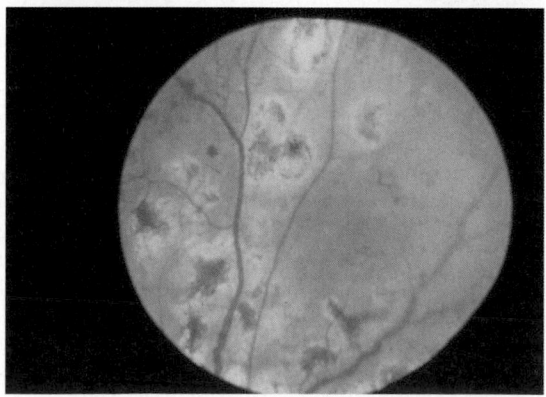

Fig. 15.17 Examples of diabetic eye disease. [A] Background diabetic retinopathy showing dot and blot haemorrhages and a few hard exudates. [B] Diabetic maculopathy with ring of exudates surrounding macula. [C] Proliferative diabetic retinopathy showing new vessels at upper and lower edges of optic discs. [D] Photocoagulation scars in retina treated with laser therapy.

They are fragile and leaky and are liable to rupture, causing haemorrhage which may be intraretinal, pre-retinal ('sub-hyaloid') or into the vitreous. Serous products leaking from these new vessel systems stimulate a connective tissue reaction, retinitis proliferans. This first appears as a white, cloudy haze among the network of new vessels. As it extends, the new vessels may be obliterated and the surrounding retina covered by a dense white sheet. At this stage, bleeding is less common but retinal detachment can occur due to contraction of adhesions between the vitreous and the retina.

Venous changes

These include venous dilatation (an early feature probably representing increased blood flow), 'beading' (sausage-like changes in calibre) and increased tortuosity including 'oxbow lakes' or loops. These latter changes indicate widespread capillary non-perfusion and are a feature of advanced pre-proliferative retinopathy.

Classification

A classification of diabetic retinopathy, based on prognosis for vision and indications for specialist referral, is shown in Box 15.34.

Microaneurysms, abnormalities of the veins, and small blot haemorrhages and exudates situated in the periphery will not interfere with vision unless they are associated with macular oedema in the perimacular or macular area. This is not easy to detect by ophthalmoscopy but should be suspected, particularly if there is impairment of visual acuity in association with mild peripheral non-proliferative retinopathy and no other obvious pathology.

New vessels may be symptomless until visual symptoms occur with floaters or sudden visual loss occurs from a pre-retinal or vitreous haemorrhage. Although these frequently resolve, the risk of recurrence is high, and the more frequent the haemorrhage, the slower and less complete the recovery. Fibrous tissue may seriously interfere with vision by obscuring the retina and/or causing further retinal haemorrhage or detachment.

Prevention

Glycaemic control

Good glycaemic control, particularly in the early years following the development of diabetes, reduces the risk of developing retinopathy. Early diagnosis followed by effective treatment is particularly important for those with type 2 diabetes, 30% of whom present with established retinopathy. In others, retinopathy is diagnosed only when the patient is referred for a specialist opinion after years of ineffective treatment of type 2 diabetes. Hyperglycaemia promotes retinal hyperperfusion, so a rapid reduction in blood glucose may cause an initial deterioration of retinopathy by causing relative ischaemia. Improvement in glycaemic control should therefore be effected gradually. The rate of progression of

15.34 CLASSIFICATION OF DIABETIC RETINOPATHY BASED ON PROGNOSIS FOR VISION		
Type of retinopathy	**Prognosis**	**Action required**

Non-proliferative 'background' retinopathy without maculopathy
Venous dilatation
Peripheral
  Microaneurysms
  Blot haemorrhages
  Exudates
	No immediate threat to vision	Maximise control of blood glucose, lipids and blood pressure
		Give advice to stop smoking and reduce intake of alcohol
		Observe carefully, i.e. fundoscopy with dilated pupils every 6–12 months
		Refer for specialist opinion if rate of progression increases significantly

Maculopathy Exudation Haemorrhage Ischaemia Macular oedema	Sight-threatening	Refer for specialist opinion Medical review of risk factors, glycaemic control, blood pressure and lipid levels
Pre-proliferative retinopathy Venous loops and beading Clusters/sheets of microaneurysms and small blot haemorrhages and/or large retinal haemorrhages Intraretinal microvascular abnormalities Multiple cotton wool spots Macular oedema with reduced visual acuity Perimacular exudates ± retinal haemorrhages of any size	Sight-threatening	Refer for specialist opinion At this stage rapid lowering of the blood glucose may result in abrupt worsening of retinopathy with the appearance of cotton wool spots and an increased number of haemorrhages; it may be safer to lower the blood glucose gradually over a period of months
Proliferative retinopathy Pre-retinal haemorrhage Neovascularisation Fibrosis Exudative maculopathy	Sight-threatening	Urgent review and treatment by specialist mandatory

retinopathy is still significantly slower in intensively treated patients than in matched control subjects, and blood pressure lowering is of proven benefit in hypertensive patients.

Screening

Regular screening for retinopathy is essential in all diabetic patients but is particularly important in those with risk factors. These include early onset, long duration of diabetes, hypertension, poor glycaemic control, pregnancy, use of the oral contraceptive pill, smoking, excessive alcohol consumption, and evidence of microangiopathy elsewhere, particularly in patients with neuropathy and proteinuria. Screening should be undertaken by trained personnel in an organised and audited programme, by the patient's GP if sufficiently experienced, or by trained optometrists. The preferred options are digital imaging photographic systems or ophthalmoscopy by stereo biomicroscopy. The problem remains that many people with diabetes do not attend for screening and receive no regular supervision.

Management

Severe non-proliferative and proliferative retinopathy can be treated with retinal photocoagulation and has been shown to reduce severe visual loss by 85% and maculopathy by 50%. Photocoagulation is used:

- to destroy areas of retinal ischaemia (since it is thought that this plays a major role in the development of neovascularisation) and reduce growth factor production (e.g. VEGF)
- to seal leaking microaneurysms and reduce macular oedema
- to obliterate new vessels directly on the retinal surface (but not on the optic disc).

Laser photocoagulation is usually of argon green for pan-retinal photocoagulation but the diode laser is also used for treatment of macular oedema. This simple procedure can be carried out under local anaesthesia, and in skilled hands carries little risk and can be very effective. Pan-retinal photocoagulation results in new vessel elimination, with vision being maintained in up to 90% of patients who have new vessels on the retina and/or disc; macular oedema is also successfully treated in many patients with focal laser therapy. Patients must be reviewed regularly to check for further development of new vessels and/or maculopathy. Extensive photocoagulation scarring can cause significant visual field loss, which may interfere with driving ability and reduce night vision.

Vitrectomy may be used in selected cases with advanced diabetic eye disease where visual loss is due to recurrent vitreous haemorrhage which has failed to clear, or retinal detachment resulting from retinitis proliferans.

The more severe types of retinopathy may be accompanied by the development of new vessels on the anterior surface of the iris: 'rubeosis iridis'. These vessels may obstruct the drainage angle of the eye and the outflow of aqueous fluid, causing secondary glaucoma. The main method of management is the prevention of extension of the rubeosis by early pan-retinal photocoagulation.

OTHER CAUSES OF VISUAL LOSS IN PEOPLE WITH DIABETES

Around 50% of visual loss in people with type 2 diabetes is due to causes other than diabetic retinopathy. These include age-related macular degeneration, retinal vein occlusion, retinal arterial occlusion, non-arteritic ischaemic optic neuropathy and glaucoma. These conditions are to be expected in this group as they relate to cardiovascular risk factors (e.g. hypertension, hyperlipidaemia, smoking) which are prevalent in people with type 2 diabetes.

Cataract

Cataract is a permanent lens opacity and is the most common cause of visual deterioration in the elderly population. The lens thickens and opacifies with age, and the increased metabolic insult to the lens in people with diabetes causes these changes to accelerate and occur prematurely. Very rarely, a type of cataract specific to diabetes occurs in young patients with poorly controlled diabetes, called a 'snowflake' cataract. This does not usually affect vision but tends to make fundal examination difficult.

The indications for cataract extraction are similar to those for the non-diabetic population and depend on the degree of visual impairment caused by the cataract. An additional indication in diabetes is when adequate assessment of the fundus, or laser treatment to the retina, is prevented. The extracapsular method of extraction is preferable in diabetes, with implantation of an intra-ocular lens.

DIABETIC NEPHROPATHY

Diabetic nephropathy is an important cause of morbidity and mortality, and is now among the most common causes of end-stage renal failure (ESRF) in developed countries. As it occurs with other microvascular and macrovascular complications, management is frequently difficult and the benefits of prevention are very great.

About 30% of patients with type 1 diabetes have developed diabetic nephropathy after 20 years, but the risk after this time falls to less than 1% per year, and from the outset the risk is not equal in all patients (see Box 15.35). Epidemiological data have suggested that the overall incidence is declining as standards of control have improved.

The pattern of progression of renal abnormalities in diabetes is shown schematically in Figure 15.18. Pathologically, the first changes (seen at the time of microalbuminuria) are thickening of the glomerular basement membrane

15.35 RISK FACTORS FOR DEVELOPING DIABETIC NEPHROPATHY

- Poor control of blood glucose
- Long duration of diabetes
- Presence of other microvascular complications
- Ethnicity (e.g. Asian races, Pima Indians)
- Pre-existing hypertension
- Family history of diabetic nephropathy
- Family history of hypertension

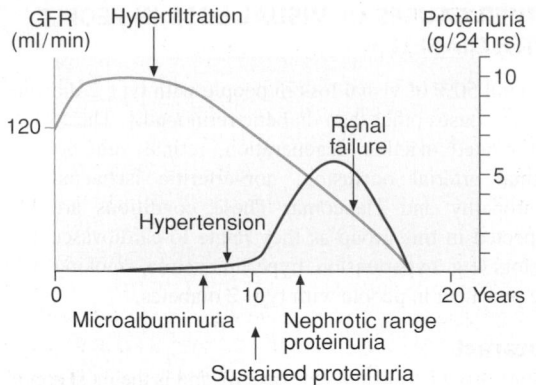

Fig. 15.18 Natural history of diabetic nephropathy. In the first few years of type 1 diabetes mellitus there is hyperfiltration which declines fairly steadily to return to a normal value at approximately 10 years (blue line). After about 10 years there is sustained proteinuria and by approximately 14 years it has reached the nephrotic range (red line). Renal function continues to decline, with the end stage being reached at approximately 16 years.

and accumulation of matrix material in the mesangium. Subsequently, nodular deposits (see Fig. 15.19) are characteristic, and glomerulosclerosis worsens (heavy proteinuria develops) until glomeruli are progressively lost and renal function deteriorates.

Microalbuminuria (see Box 15.36) is an important indicator of risk of developing overt diabetic nephropathy, although it is also found in other conditions. It is therefore most reliable as an indicator of diabetic nephropathy within the first 10 years of type 1 diabetes (the majority will progress to overt nephropathy within a further 10 years), and less reliable in older patients with type 2 diabetes, in whom it may be accounted for by other diseases. Progressively increasing albuminuria, or albuminuria accompanied by hypertension, is much more likely to be due to early diabetic nephropathy.

If there is evidence of incipient nephropathy, vigorous efforts should be made to reduce the risk of progression by:

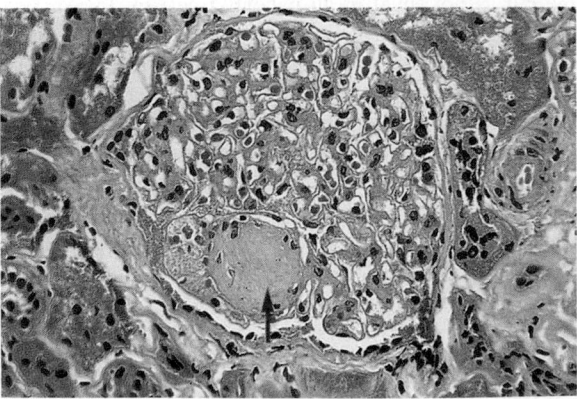

Fig. 15.19 Nodular diabetic glomerulosclerosis. There is thickening of basement membranes and mesangial expansion, and a Kimmelstiel–Wilson nodule (arrow).

15.36 SCREENING FOR MICROALBUMINURIA

- Identifies nephropathy in type 1 diabetes; independent predictor of macrovascular disease in type 2 diabetes
- Risk factors include increased blood pressure, poor glycaemic control, smoking
- Measured as albumin excretion rate (AER) of 20–200 µg/min (30–300 mg/24 hrs); requires timed collection of urine (overnight or 24 hrs)
- Random urine sample can estimate urinary albumin:creatinine ratio (3–30 mg/mmol) (abnormal values: male >2.5, female > 3.5)

Who to screen

- Type 1 diabetes annually from 5 years after diagnosis
- Type 2 diabetes annually from time of diagnosis

Abnormal tests

- Exclude recent (24 hrs) vigorous exercise, fever, heart failure, urine infection, prostatitis, menstruation
- Confirm observation twice within 3–6 months
- Look for hypertension (or increased blood pressure within the normal range)

EBM

MICROALBUMINURIA—role of angiotensin-converting enzyme inhibitors

'Microalbuminuria in type 1 diabetes indicates the presence of diabetic nephropathy and should be treated with ACE inhibitors regardless of whether blood pressure is elevated or not.'

- Lewis EJ, Hunsickler LG, Bain RP, Rohde RD (Collaborative Study Group). The effect of angiotensin-converting enzyme inhibition on diabetic nephropathy. N Engl J Med 1993; 329:1450–1462.
- Microalbuminuria Captopril Study Group. Captopril reduces the risk of nephropathy in IDDM patients with microalbuminuria. Diabetologia 1996; 39:587–593.

- improved control of blood glucose
- aggressive reduction of blood pressure
- institution of angiotensin-converting enzyme inhibitor (ACE-I) therapy (see EBM panel).

ACE inhibitors have been shown to provide greater benefit than equal blood pressure reduction achieved with other drugs (see p. 393). Recent studies have shown similar benefits from angiotensin II receptor antagonists. There may be particular problems with the use of either in diabetic nephropathy because of hyperkalaemia (see p. 284) and renal artery stenosis. Non-dihydropyridine calcium antagonists (diltiazem, verapamil) may be suitable alternatives in these circumstances.

Diabetic control becomes difficult as renal impairment progresses. Treatment with metformin should be abandoned when creatinine is higher than 150 µmol/l as the risk of lactic acidosis is increased. Long-acting sulphonylureas should be replaced by short-acting agents that are metabolised rather than excreted.

Renal replacement therapy (see p. 605) may benefit diabetic patients at an earlier stage than other patients with ESRF, although it may carry additional difficulties. Renal transplantation can dramatically improve the life of many, although large blood vessel disease causing cardiac failure and peripheral vascular disease, and microvascular disease causing neuropathy and retinopathy show continued progression. The progression of recurrent diabetic nephropathy in the allograft is usually too slow to be a serious problem. Coronary heart disease is the major cause of death. Pancreatic transplantation (generally carried out at the same time as renal transplantation) can produce insulin independence and can slow or reverse microvascular disease, but the supply of organs is very limited and this is available to few. For further information on management, see Chapter 14.

DIABETIC NEUROPATHY

This is a relatively early and common complication affecting approximately 30% of diabetic patients. Although in a few patients it can cause severe disability, it is symptomless in the majority. Like retinopathy, it occurs secondary to metabolic disturbance, and prevalence is related to the duration of diabetes and the degree of metabolic control. Although there is evidence that the central nervous system is affected in long-term diabetes, the clinical impact of diabetes is mainly manifest on the peripheral nervous system.

Pathology
The main pathological features are listed in Box 15.37. They can occur in motor, sensory and autonomic nerves.

Classification
Various classifications of diabetic neuropathy have been proposed. One is shown in Box 15.38. None of the proposed classifications is entirely satisfactory since motor, sensory and autonomic nerves may be involved in varying combinations so that clinically mixed syndromes usually occur.

15.37 DIABETIC NEUROPATHY: HISTOPATHOLOGY

- Axonal degeneration of both myelinated and unmyelinated fibres
  Early: axon shrinkage
  Later: axonal fragmentation; regeneration
- Thickening of Schwann cell basal lamina
- Patchy, segmental demyelination
- Thickening of basement membrane and microthrombi in intraneural capillaries

15.38 CLASSIFICATION OF DIABETIC NEUROPATHY

Somatic
- Polyneuropathy
  Symmetrical, mainly sensory and distal
  Asymmetrical, mainly motor and proximal (including amyotrophy)
- Mononeuropathy (including mononeuritis multiplex)

Visceral (autonomic)
- Cardiovascular
- Gastrointestinal
- Genitourinary
- Sudomotor
- Vasomotor
- Pupillary

Clinical features
Symmetrical sensory polyneuropathy
This is frequently asymptomatic. The most common signs found on physical examination are diminished perception of vibration sensation distally, 'glove-and-stocking' impairment of all other modalities of sensation, and loss of tendon reflexes in the lower limbs. Sensory abnormalities dominate the clinical presentation. Symptoms include paraesthesiae in the feet and, rarely, in the hands, pain in the lower limbs (dull, aching and/or lancinating, worse at night, and mainly felt on the anterior aspect of the legs), burning sensations in the soles of the feet, cutaneous hyperaesthesia and an abnormal gait (commonly wide-based), often associated with a sense of numbness in the feet. Muscle weakness and wasting develop only in advanced cases, but subclinical motor nerve dysfunction is common. The toes may be clawed with wasting of the interosseous muscles, which results in increased pressure on the plantar aspects of the metatarsal heads with the development of callus skin at these and other pressure points. Electrophysiological tests (see p. 1109) demonstrate slowing of both motor and sensory conduction, and tests of vibration sensitivity and thermal thresholds are abnormal. A diffuse small-fibre neuropathy causes altered perception of pain and temperature and is associated with symptomatic autonomic neuropathy; characteristic features include foot ulcers and Charcot neuroarthropathy.

Asymmetrical motor diabetic neuropathy
Sometimes called diabetic amyotrophy, this presents as severe and progressive weakness and wasting of the proximal muscles of the lower (and occasionally the upper) limbs. It is commonly accompanied by severe pain, mainly felt on the anterior aspect of the leg, and hyperaesthesia and paraesthesiae are common. Sometimes there may also be marked loss of weight ('neuropathic cachexia'). The patient may look extremely ill and may be unable to get out of bed. Tendon reflexes may be absent on the affected side(s). Sometimes there are extensor plantar responses and the cerebrospinal fluid protein is often raised. This condition is thought to involve acute infarction of the lower motor neurons of the lumbosacral plexus. Other lesions involving this plexus, such as neoplasms and lumbar disc disease, must be excluded. Although recovery usually occurs within 12 months, some deficits become permanent. Management is mainly supportive.

Mononeuropathy
Either motor or sensory function can be affected within a single peripheral or cranial nerve. Unlike the gradual progression of distal symmetrical and autonomic neuropathies, mononeuropathies are severe and of rapid onset; they eventually recover. The nerves most commonly affected are the 3rd and 6th cranial nerves, resulting in diplopia, and the femoral and sciatic nerves. Rarely, involvement of other single nerves results in paresis and paraesthesiae in the thorax and trunk (truncal radiculopathies). Nerve compression palsies commonly affect the median nerve, giving the clinical picture of carpal tunnel compression syndrome, and less commonly the ulnar nerve. Lateral popliteal nerve compression occasionally causes foot drop.

Autonomic neuropathy

This is not necessarily associated with peripheral somatic neuropathy. Either parasympathetic or sympathetic nerves may be predominantly affected in any one system or more. Although autonomic neuropathy can affect virtually all bodily systems in any one patient, involvement tends to be patchy. The symptoms and signs arising from autonomic neuropathy affecting the various systems are listed in Box 15.39. Tests of autonomic function are listed in Box 15.40. The development of autonomic neuropathy is less clearly related to poor metabolic control than somatic neuropathy, and improved control rarely results in amelioration of symptoms. Within 10 years of developing overt symptoms of autonomic neuropathy, 30–50% of patients are dead—many from sudden cardiorespiratory arrest, the cause of which is unknown. Patients with postural hypotension (a drop in systolic pressure of ≥ 20 mmHg on standing from the supine position) have the highest subsequent mortality.

Erectile dysfunction

Erectile failure (impotence) affects 30% of diabetic males and is often multifactorial. Although neuropathy and vascular causes are common, psychological factors, including depression, anxiety and reduced libido, may be partly responsible. Alcohol and antihypertensive drugs such as thiazide diuretics and β-adrenoceptor antagonists (β-blockers) may cause sexual dysfunction and, rarely, patients may have an endocrine cause such as testosterone deficiency or hyperprolactinaemia. For further information, see page 707.

Management

Management of peripheral sensorimotor and autonomic neuropathies is outlined in Box 15.41.

15.39 CLINICAL FEATURES OF AUTONOMIC NEUROPATHY

Cardiovascular

- Postural hypotension
- Resting tachycardia
- Fixed heart rate

Gastrointestinal

- Dysphagia, due to oesophageal atony
- Abdominal fullness, nausea and vomiting, unstable diabetes, due to delayed gastric emptying ('gastroparesis')
- Nocturnal diarrhoea ± faecal incontinence (see p. 829)
- Constipation, due to colonic atony

Genitourinary

- Difficulty in micturition, urinary incontinence, recurrent infection, due to atonic bladder
- Impotence and retrograde ejaculation

Sudomotor

- Gustatory sweating
- Nocturnal sweats without hypoglycaemia
- Anhidrosis; fissures in the feet

Vasomotor

- Feet feel cold, due to loss of skin vasomotor responses
- Dependent oedema, due to loss of vasomotor tone and increased vascular permeability
- Bullous formation

Pupillary

- Decreased pupil size
- Resistance to mydriatics
- Delayed or absent reflexes to light

15.40 TESTS OF CARDIOVASCULAR AUTONOMIC FUNCTION

Simple cardiovascular reflex tests

- Heart rate variation during deep breathing
- Heart rate response to standing
- Heart rate changes during the Valsalva manoeuvre
- Blood pressure response to standing
- Blood pressure response to sustained hand grip

Other tests

- Baroreflex sensitivity using power spectral analysis of heart rate
- Time-domain analysis of heart rate and blood pressure variations
- MIBG (meta-iodobenzylguanidine) scan of the heart

15.41 MANAGEMENT OF PERIPHERAL SENSORIMOTOR AND AUTONOMIC NEUROPATHIES

Condition	Management
Pain and paraesthesiae from peripheral somatic neuropathies	Intensive insulin therapy (strict glycaemic control) Tricyclic antidepressants (amitriptyline, imipramine) Anticonvulsants (carbamazepine, phenytoin, gabapentin) Capsaicin (topical)
Postural hypotension	Support stockings Fludrocortisone α-adrenoceptor agonist (midodrine*) Non-steroidal anti-inflammatory drugs (NSAIDs)
Gastroparesis	Dopamine agonists (metoclopramide, domperidone) Erythromycin
Diarrhoea (see p. 767)	Loperamide Broad-spectrum antibiotics Clonidine Octreotide
Constipation	Stimulant laxatives (senna)
Atonic bladder	Intermittent self-catheterisation (see p. 1159)
Excessive sweating	Anticholinergic drugs (propantheline, poldine*) Clonidine Topical antimuscarinic agent (glycopyrrolate*)
Erectile dysfunction (impotence)	Phosphodiesterase inhibitor (sildenafil) Papaverine or prostaglandin E1 (alprostadil) injected into corpus cavernosum Vacuum tumescence devices Implanted penile prosthesis Psychological counselling

*Named patients only.

THE DIABETIC FOOT

The foot is a frequent site for complications in patients with diabetes and for this reason foot care is particularly important. The clinical features are listed in Box 15.42.

Tissue necrosis in the feet is a common reason for hospital admission in diabetic patients. Such admissions tend to be prolonged and often end with amputation.

Aetiology

Foot ulceration occurs as a result of trauma (often trivial) in the presence of neuropathy and/or peripheral vascular disease (see p. 443), with infection occurring as a secondary phenomenon following ulceration of the protective epidermis. In most cases all three components are involved but sometimes neuropathy or ischaemia may predominate. The clinical features of these two types of foot are compared in Box 15.42. Pure ischaemia accounts for a minority of foot ulcers in diabetic patients, with most being either neuropathic or neuro-ischaemic in type.

The main factors involved in the development of foot ulceration are shown in Figure 15.20. The most common cause of ulceration is a plaque of callus skin beneath which tissue necrosis occurs. This eventually breaks through to the surface.

Management

The main components of medical management are listed in Box 15.43. Removal of callus skin with a scalpel is usually best done by a chiropodist (podiatrist) who has specialist training and experience in diabetic foot problems. Effective treatment of local infection with appropriate antibiotics is essential, and may have to be continued for protracted periods; osteomyelitis may be extremely difficult to eradicate.

15.42 CLINICAL FEATURES OF THE DIABETIC FOOT

Neuropathy	Ischaemia
Symptoms	
None	None
Paraesthesiae	Claudication
Pain	Rest pain
Numbness	
Structural damage	
Ulcer	Ulcer
Sepsis	Sepsis
Abscess	Gangrene
Osteomyelitis	
Digital gangrene	
Charcot joint	

15.43 MANAGEMENT OF DIABETIC FOOT ULCERS

- Remove callus skin
- Treat infection
- Avoid weight-bearing
- Ensure good diabetic control
- Control oedema
- Undertake angiogram to assess feasibility of vascular reconstruction where indicated

Charcot neuroarthropathy with disorganisation of joints may cause serious deformity. Angiography may be necessary if the foot is ischaemic or ulcers are very slow to heal. Measures to improve glycaemic control may be necessary to promote healing. Amputation may be unavoidable if there is extensive tissue and/or bony destruction or intractable ischaemic pain at rest in a limb in which vascular reconstruction has failed or is impossible due to extensive large

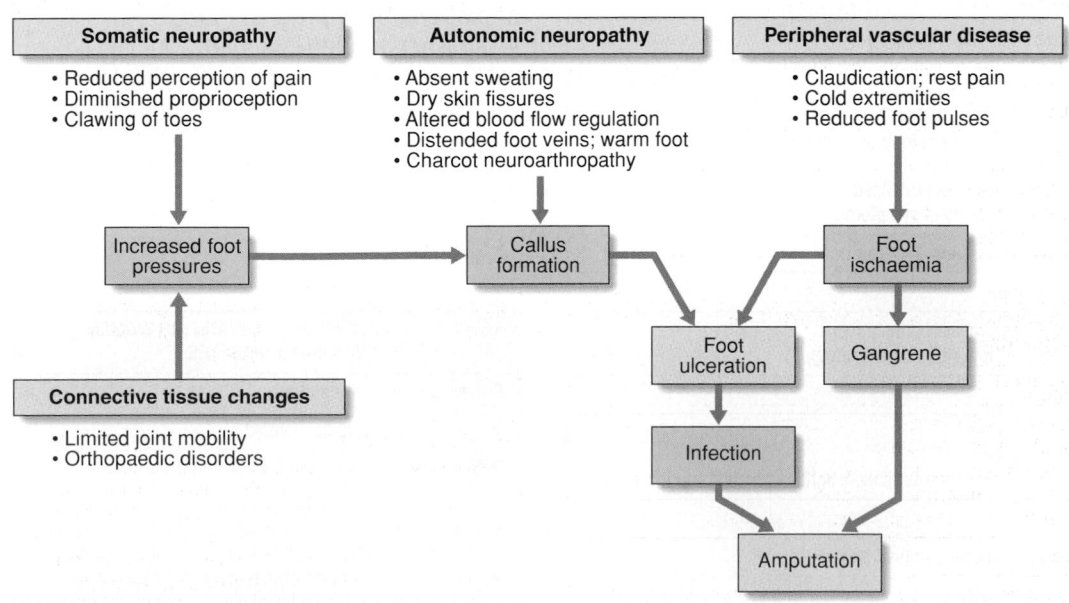

Fig. 15.20 Pathways leading to foot ulceration and amputation in diabetic foot disease. Interrelationships of aetiological factors and principal clinical features are shown.

blood vessel disease. Further information is given on the management of peripheral arterial disease on page 445. Preventative measures are shown in Box 15.44.

15.44 DIABETIC FOOT: PRACTICE POINTS

- Prevention is the most effective way of dealing with the problem of tissue necrosis in the diabetic foot
- A specialist chiropodist (podiatrist) is an integral part of the diabetes team to ensure regular and effective chiropody and to educate patients in care of the feet
- Specially manufactured and fitted orthotic footware is required to prevent recurrence of ulceration and protect feet of patients with Charcot neuroarthropathy

---

LONG-TERM SUPERVISION

Diabetes is a complex disorder which progresses in severity with time, so people with diabetes should be seen at regular intervals for the remainder of their lives, either at a specialist diabetic clinic or by their GP, provided he or she has a particular interest and training in diabetes. A checklist for follow-up visits is given in Box 15.45. The frequency of visits is very variable, ranging from weekly during pregnancy

---

15.45 CHECKLIST FOR FOLLOW-UP OF PATIENTS WITH DIABETES MELLITUS

Body weight (body mass index)

Urinalysis

- Analyse fasting specimen for glucose, ketones, albumin (both macro- and microalbuminuria)

Glycaemic control

- Glycated haemoglobin (HbA_{1c})
- Inspection of home blood glucose monitoring record

Hypoglycaemic episodes

- Number of severe (requiring assistance for treatment) and mild (self-treated) episodes
- Time when 'hypos' experienced
- Nature and intensity of symptoms

Blood pressure (supine and erect)

Eye examination

- Visual acuities (near and distance)
- Ophthalmoscopy (with pupils dilated)

Lower limbs

- Peripheral pulses
- Tendon reflexes
- Perception of vibration sensation, light touch and proprioception

Feet

- Callus skin indicating pressure areas
- Nails
- Need for chiropody
- Ulceration
- Deformity

---

to annually in the case of patients with well-controlled type 2 diabetes.

'Brittle diabetes' is generally considered not to exist, and use of this term should be discouraged. Most studies have shown that this problem (mostly affecting young women) is not a pathological process, but is associated with persistent manipulation of therapy (stopping insulin or taking excessive doses) to induce recurrent diabetic ketoacidosis or severe hypoglycaemia requiring hospital admission. This attention-seeking behaviour may be a manifestation of psychological disturbance, is factitious, and is not a specific phenomenon peculiar to some aspect of diabetes or its management in susceptible individuals (see p. 268 for management of factitious disorders).

SPECIAL PROBLEMS IN MANAGEMENT

PREGNANCY AND DIABETES

Problems in diabetic pregnancy

Hyperglycaemia in early pregnancy can cause fetal malformations, and will promote increased somatic growth later in gestation. Pregnancy in diabetic women is associated with an increased perinatal mortality rate (that is, stillbirths and neonatal deaths within the first week of life). The main causes are intrauterine death in the third trimester of pregnancy, prematurity (due to a high incidence of spontaneous premature labour and of elective premature delivery in an attempt to avoid late intrauterine death), low birth weight and congenital malformation. Birth trauma is also more common due to a high incidence of excessively large, macrosomic babies.

Management of pregnancy in established diabetic women

All the above problems are directly related to poor metabolic control and largely disappear if near-normoglycaemia is maintained before and at conception and during pregnancy and delivery. The therapeutic goals and the components of a successful diabetic pregnancy are listed in Box 15.46.

15.46 MANAGEMENT OF PREGNANCY IN WOMEN WITH ESTABLISHED DIABETES

Pre-pregnancy counselling

- Pregnancy should be planned

Before and at conception and during pregnancy

- Folic acid supplementation
- Maintain strict glycaemic control, i.e. HbA_{1c} close to the non-diabetic range by use of 3–4 injections of insulin daily
- Do not strive for normoglycaemia at the expense of hypoglycaemia. Check blood glucose during the night periodically
- Check overnight sample of urine for ketones regularly; increase intake of carbohydrate and dose of insulin to abolish ketonuria

---

Gestational diabetes

Gestational diabetes, defined as hyperglycaemia diagnosed for the first time in pregnancy, is a common problem. It occurs in individuals who have an inherited predisposition to develop diabetes and may take the form of either type 1 or type 2 diabetes. The hyperglycaemia may not disappear after delivery. It is associated not only with increased rates of perinatal mortality and neonatal morbidity but also with a high incidence (possibly as great as 80% at 25 years postpartum) of subsequent clinical diabetes (both type 1 and type 2) in the mother. Normalisation of metabolism, whether by treatment with dietary measures alone or, more commonly, with additional treatment in the form of insulin, undoubtedly reduces the fetal risk; its effect on diminishing the maternal risk of subsequent diabetes is less certain.

Screening for gestational diabetes by the measurement of true venous plasma glucose concentration 1 hour after a 50 g oral glucose load, followed by a formal 3-hour 100 g oral glucose tolerance test in suspicious cases, has been validated but is complicated. An accurate laboratory measurement of the basal (i.e. fasting or more than 3 hours after a meal) prevailing venous plasma glucose concentration can be recommended for the following reasons:

- It is a simple test which avoids the need for special preparation and can be incorporated readily as part of routine antenatal care, thus encouraging assessment two or three times during pregnancy in all pregnant women.
- It is more physiological and relevant to the clinical problem, since the prevailing maternal blood glucose concentration is the important measurement as far as the fetus is concerned.

This measurement selects those in need of treatment. The basal plasma glucose concentrations which indicate the need to consider treatment are shown in Box 15.47.

Glycated haemoglobin is unreliable as a screening test for gestational diabetes and for assessing glycaemic control during pregnancy because:

- It is too insensitive.
- It changes too slowly.
- It is affected by things other than changes in the blood glucose concentration, such as the influx of new red cells into the circulation.
- It reflects the overall integrated mean blood glucose concentration; it gives no information about fluctuations in the blood glucose level and may therefore be misleading.

Although measurements of glycated serum proteins ('fructosamine') may be more useful than glycated haemoglobin in pregnancy (since its rate of turnover is of the order of 2–4 weeks), it complements rather than substitutes for measurement of the blood glucose concentration.

Management of diabetes at delivery

Due to the risk of sudden intrauterine death in the third trimester, diabetic women traditionally were delivered at 36–38 weeks' gestation. Today, improved metabolic control

15.47 SCREENING FOR GESTATIONAL DIABETES	
Gestation	Basal (fasting) venous plasma glucose concentration
Up to 20 weeks	> 5.5 mmol/l
20–40 weeks	> 6.5 mmol/l

makes later delivery possible and most are now delivered between 38 and 39 weeks' gestation after induction of labour, or if necessary by caesarean section; an increasing number also proceed to spontaneous vaginal delivery at term.

On the morning of delivery the usual breakfast and insulin should be replaced by an intravenous infusion of 10% dextrose with 10 units of short-acting (soluble) insulin added to each 500 ml, given at a rate of 100 ml hourly. The blood glucose concentration should be monitored at intervals of 1–2 hours and the concentration of insulin adjusted to keep the blood glucose concentration within the range of 5–6 mmol/l. An alternative, easier and better method is to give the insulin separately from the glucose infusion by means of a constant rate infusion pump at a rate of 1–2 units hourly. Whichever method is used, administration of insulin should be stopped immediately on delivery and subcutaneous insulin resumed according to need, as determined by capillary blood glucose estimations. Little or no insulin may be required for 12 hours after delivery. Thereafter, the pre-pregnancy dose of subcutaneously administered insulin can be gradually resumed. Lactating diabetic mothers require additional dietary carbohydrate to avoid hypoglycaemia.

SURGERY AND DIABETES

Surgery, whether performed electively or in an emergency, causes catabolic stress and secretion of cortisol, catecholamines, glucagon and growth hormone both in normal and in diabetic subjects. This results in increased glycogenolysis, gluconeogenesis, lipolysis, proteolysis and insulin resistance, while the release of endogenous insulin is suppressed. In the non-diabetic person these metabolic effects lead to a secondary increase in the secretion of insulin, which exerts a restraining and controlling influence. In diabetic patients there is either absolute deficiency of insulin (type 1 diabetes) or insulin secretion is delayed and impaired (type 2 diabetes), so that in untreated or poorly controlled diabetes the uptake of metabolic substrate is significantly reduced, catabolism is increased and ultimately metabolic decompensation in the form of diabetic ketoacidosis may develop in both types of diabetes. Starvation will exacerbate this process. In addition, hyperglycaemia impairs phagocytic function (leading to reduced resistance to infection) and wound healing. Thus surgery must be carefully planned and managed in the diabetic patient, with particular emphasis on good metabolic control and avoidance of hypoglycaemia, particularly dangerous in the unconscious or semiconscious patient.

Pre-operative assessment

Careful pre-operative assessment is mandatory and is summarised in Box 15.48. Much of this can be done on an outpatient basis but, if cardiovascular or renal function is impaired, there are signs of neuropathy (particularly autonomic), diabetic control is poor or alterations need to be made to the patient's usual treatment, then admission to hospital some days before operation will be required.

15.48 PRE-OPERATIVE ASSESSMENT IN DIABETIC PATIENTS
• Assess cardiovascular and renal function
• Check for features of neuropathy, particularly autonomic
• Assess glycaemic control
Measure HbA$_{1c}$
Monitor pre-prandial and bedtime blood glucose
• Review treatment of diabetes
Replace long-acting with intermediate and short-acting insulins
Stop metformin and long-acting sulphonylureas; replace with insulin if necessary

Perioperative management

The management of diabetic patients undergoing surgery requiring general anaesthesia is summarised in Figure 15.21. Post-operatively, the glucose/insulin/potassium infusion should be continued until the patient's intake of food is adequate, when the normal insulin or tablet regimen can be resumed. If the intravenous infusion has to be continued for more than 24 hours, plasma electrolytes and urea should be measured and urinary ketones checked daily. If the infusion is prolonged, the concentration of potassium may require adjustment, and if dilutional hyponatraemia occurs, a parallel saline infusion may be necessary. If fluids need to be restricted, e.g. in patients with cardiovascular or renal disease, the rate of infusion can be halved by using a 20% dextrose solution and doubling the concentration of insulin and potassium. The insulin requirement is likely to be higher than that indicated in Figure 15.21 in patients with hepatic disease, obesity or sepsis and in those being treated with corticosteroids or undergoing cardiopulmonary bypass surgery.

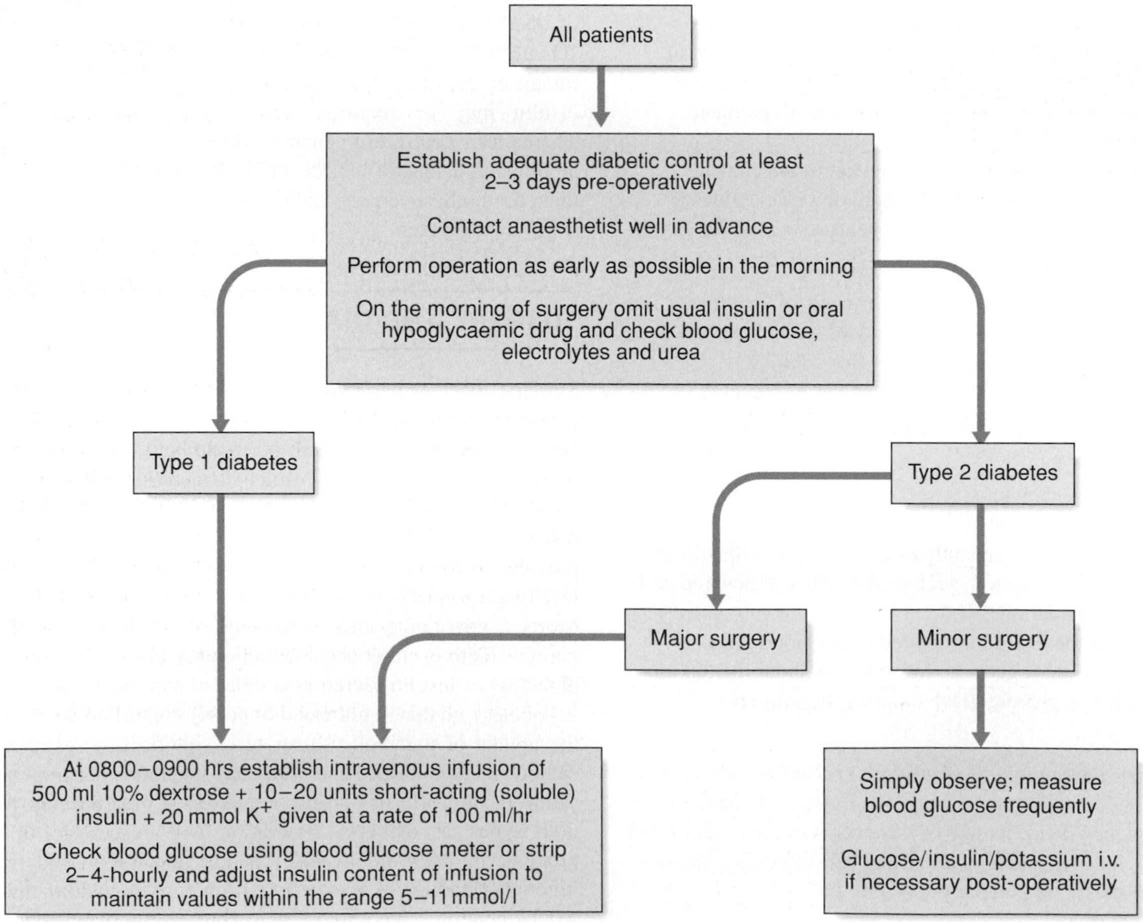

All patients

↓

Establish adequate diabetic control at least 2–3 days pre-operatively

Contact anaesthetist well in advance

Perform operation as early as possible in the morning

On the morning of surgery omit usual insulin or oral hypoglycaemic drug and check blood glucose, electrolytes and urea

Type 1 diabetes   Type 2 diabetes

Major surgery   Minor surgery

Type 1 / Major surgery:
At 0800–0900 hrs establish intravenous infusion of 500 ml 10% dextrose + 10–20 units short-acting (soluble) insulin + 20 mmol K^{+} given at a rate of 100 ml/hr

Check blood glucose using blood glucose meter or strip 2–4-hourly and adjust insulin content of infusion to maintain values within the range 5–11 mmol/l

Minor surgery:
Simply observe; measure blood glucose frequently

Glucose/insulin/potassium i.v. if necessary post-operatively

Fig. 15.21 **Management of diabetic patients undergoing surgery and general anaesthesia.**

Surgical emergencies

If the patient is significantly hyperglycaemic and/or keto-acidotic, this should be corrected first with an intravenous infusion of saline and/or glucose plus insulin, 6 units per hour, and potassium as required. Subsequently, treatment is as described in Figure 15.21.

Emergency surgery in a patient with well-controlled insulin-treated diabetes depends on when the last subcutaneous injection of insulin was given. If this was recent, an infusion of glucose alone may be sufficient, but frequent monitoring is essential.

ACUTE MYOCARDIAL INFARCTION

There is much that can be done to reduce mortality from myocardial infarction in those with diabetes (see Box 15.49). Hyperglycaemia is often found in patients who have sustained an acute myocardial infarction. In some, this represents stress hyperglycaemia, some have previously undiagnosed diabetes, and many have established diabetes. Hyperglycaemia should be treated with insulin and, in patients with type 2 diabetes, oral hypoglycaemic agents should be stopped in the peri-infarct period. Recent studies have suggested that conversion to insulin therapy in type 2 patients with acute myocardial infarction may reduce their long-term mortality from coronary heart disease (see EBM panel).

15.49 POSSIBLE TREATMENTS TO REDUCE MORTALITY FROM MYOCARDIAL INFARCTION IN PEOPLE WITH DIABETES

Primary prevention of myocardial infarction

- Strict glycaemic control
- Aggressive control of hypertension
- ? Cholesterol reduction with statins

Immediate measures in acute myocardial infarction

- Thrombolysis/fibrinolysis
- Aspirin
- Intravenous insulin
- β-blockers
- ACE inhibitors

Secondary prevention of myocardial infarction

- Aspirin
- β-blockers
- ACE inhibitors
- Subcutaneous insulin
- Cholesterol reduction with statins

ISSUES IN OLDER PEOPLE
DIABETES

- The prevalence of diabetes increases with age, affecting approximately 10% of people over 65 years. Half of these people will be unaware that they have the disorder.
- Impaired glucose-induced insulin release and resistance to insulin-mediated glucose disposal contribute to this high prevalence.
- The mortality rate of older people with diabetes is more than double that of age-matched non-diabetic people, largely because of increased deaths from cardiovascular disease.
- The renal threshold for glucose rises with age, so glycosuria may not develop until the blood glucose concentration is markedly raised.
- Older people have reduced symptomatic awareness of hypoglycaemia and limited knowledge of symptoms, and are at greater risk of and from hypoglycaemia.
- The optimal degree of glycaemic control in older people has yet to be determined. Improving glycaemic control can benefit cognitive and affective function in older people.
- A team approach can improve glycaemic control, adherence to therapy and quality of life.

PROSPECTS IN DIABETES MELLITUS

MANAGEMENT

There are exciting developments in the search for better methods of treating diabetes. Whole pancreas transplantation presents particular problems relating to the exocrine pancreatic secretions, and long-term immunosuppression is necessary. While results are steadily improving, they remain less favourable than for renal transplantation. Xenotransplantation with a porcine pancreas may be an alternative approach. However, it is questionable whether it will ever be considered justifiable to transplant young diabetic patients before vascular disease is clinically apparent.

Transplantation of isolated pancreatic islets (usually into the liver via the portal vein) has now been achieved in a small number of humans; it is safe and the problem of the exocrine secretions is avoided. Progress is being made towards meeting the needs of supply, purification and storage of islets but the problems of bioincompatibility, rejection and autoimmune destruction remain. Nevertheless, the development of methods of inducing tolerance to transplanted islets and the use of stem cells or transformation of hepatocytes to make insulin by genetic engineering means that this may still prove the most promising approach in the long term.

MYOCARDIAL INFARCTION—role of glycaemic control `EBM`

'Diabetic patients who sustain a myocardial infarction should be considered for immediate treatment with intravenous insulin, and post-infarct, with subcutaneous insulin for at least 3 months.'

- Malmberg K, Ryden L, Efendic S, et al. on behalf of the DIGAMI (Diabetes Mellitus, Insulin Glucose Infusion in Acute Myocardial Infarction) Study Group. Randomized trial of insulin-glucose infusion followed by subcutaneous insulin treatment in diabetic patients with acute myocardial infarction (DIGAMI Study): effects on mortality at 1 year. J Am Coll Cardiol 1995; 26:57–65.
- Malmberg K for the DIGAMI Study Group. Prospective randomised study of intensive insulin treatment on long-term survival after acute myocardial infarction in patients with diabetes mellitus. BMJ 1997; 314:1512–1515.

Further information: 💻 www.diabetes-mellitus.org

Alternative methods and routes of insulin delivery are being sought other than subcutaneous injection which has the disadvantage of delivering insulin into the systemic and not the portal circulation. A wider range of insulin analogues, including long-acting preparations, is being developed, inhaled insulin is under trial and other routes of delivery including oral and transcutaneous (utilising patch technology) are being explored. Other therapeutic agents such as glucagon-like peptide (GLP-1) are promising, and several novel oral drugs are being evaluated.

PRIMARY PREVENTION OF DIABETES

From a public health standpoint the only cost-effective way of dealing with diabetes is to prevent it.

Type 2 diabetes is associated with an affluent lifestyle that is likely to arise in genetically predisposed individuals who eat too much and exercise too little. Effective health education has shown promising results in the primary prevention of type 2 diabetes, while screening for diabetes (particularly in high-risk groups such as the first-degree relatives of known cases) and more vigorous and early treatment of impaired glucose tolerance could reduce the incidence of serious vascular disease in these patients.

In type 1 diabetes, the fact that the islet insulin-secreting cells are destroyed slowly over several years before clinical presentation offers the hope that, in the future, it may be possible to prevent type 1 diabetes. This depends on:

- the availability of accurate, predictive markers for the development of clinical diabetes in genetically predisposed individual subjects
- an understanding of the precise sequence of events leading to pancreatic beta cell destruction
- the development of methods of intervention based

on specifically targeted immunomodulation which could be applied early in the pre-diabetic period before most of the insulin-secreting cells have been destroyed. One such drug which halts the autoimmune destruction of pancreatic beta cells (DiaPep 277) is undergoing clinical trials.

TREATMENT OF DIABETIC COMPLICATIONS

Treatment with aminoguanidine, an inhibitor of the formation of advanced glycation end-products, has been shown to prevent damage to the retina, kidney, nerve and artery in diabetic animals. It has low toxicity and is undergoing preliminary trials in humans with chronic diabetic complications. Protein kinase C inhibitors have been shown to limit diabetic retinopathy in humans and will soon be available for clinical use.

FURTHER INFORMATION

Atkinson MA, Eisenbarth GS. Type 1 diabetes: new perspectives on disease pathogenesis and treatment. Lancet 2001; 358:221–229.

Frier BM, Fisher BM, eds. Hypoglycaemia in clinical diabetes. Chichester: John Wiley; 1999.

Herlitz J, Malmberg K. How to improve the cardiac prognosis for diabetes. Diabetes Care 1999; 22:B89–96.

Pickup J, Williams G, eds. Textbook of diabetes. 2nd edn. Oxford: Blackwell Scientific; 1997.

www.cdc.gov/diabetes *Diabetes Public Health Resource*
www.diabetes.org/ *American Diabetes Association*
www.diabetes.org.uk *Diabetes UK*
www.diabetologists-abcd.org.uk/ *Association of British Clinical Diabetologists*
www.idf.org *International Diabetes Federation*
www.jdrf.org *Juvenile Diabetes Research Foundation*
www.joslin.org *Joslin Diabetes Center*
www.mendosa.com/faq.htm *Online Diabetes Resources*
www.sign.ac.uk *Scottish Intercollegiate Guidelines Network*

Endocrine disease

B.R. WALKER • A.D. TOFT

CLINICAL EXAMINATION OF ENDOCRINE DISEASE

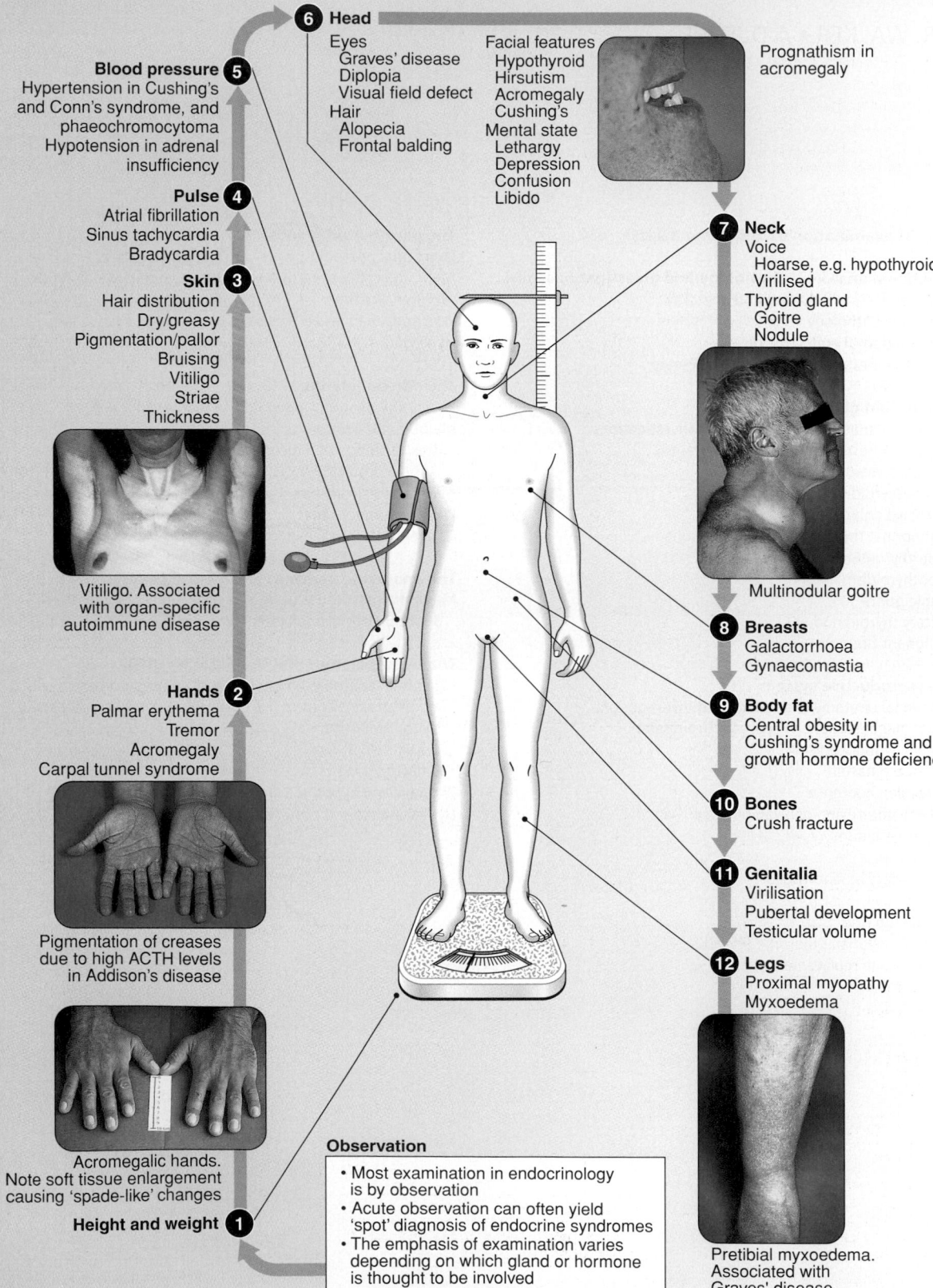

6 Head

Eyes
  Graves' disease
  Diplopia
  Visual field defect
Hair
  Alopecia
  Frontal balding

Facial features
  Hypothyroid
  Hirsutism
  Acromegaly
  Cushing's
Mental state
  Lethargy
  Depression
  Confusion
  Libido

Prognathism in acromegaly

5 Blood pressure
Hypertension in Cushing's and Conn's syndrome, and phaeochromocytoma
Hypotension in adrenal insufficiency

4 Pulse
Atrial fibrillation
Sinus tachycardia
Bradycardia

3 Skin
Hair distribution
Dry/greasy
Pigmentation/pallor
Bruising
Vitiligo
Striae
Thickness

Vitiligo. Associated with organ-specific autoimmune disease

2 Hands
Palmar erythema
Tremor
Acromegaly
Carpal tunnel syndrome

Pigmentation of creases due to high ACTH levels in Addison's disease

Acromegalic hands. Note soft tissue enlargement causing 'spade-like' changes

1 Height and weight

7 Neck
Voice
  Hoarse, e.g. hypothyroid
  Virilised
Thyroid gland
  Goitre
  Nodule

Multinodular goitre

8 Breasts
Galactorrhoea
Gynaecomastia

9 Body fat
Central obesity in Cushing's syndrome and growth hormone deficiency

10 Bones
Crush fracture

11 Genitalia
Virilisation
Pubertal development
Testicular volume

12 Legs
Proximal myopathy
Myxoedema

Pretibial myxoedema. Associated with Graves' disease

Observation
- Most examination in endocrinology is by observation
- Acute observation can often yield 'spot' diagnosis of endocrine syndromes
- The emphasis of examination varies depending on which gland or hormone is thought to be involved

CLINICAL PRESENTATION

- The manner in which patients with endocrine disease present is extremely varied, reflecting the protean effects of hormone excess or deficiency.
- Most patients with endocrine disease present with non-specific symptoms. Often patients are first referred to other specialist clinics—for example, dermatology (pruritus of hyperthyroidism), cardiology (dysrhythmia of hyperthyroidism or phaeochromocytoma), diabetes (glycosuria of Cushing's syndrome or acromegaly) or psychiatry (depression of Cushing's syndrome).
- Duration of symptoms before diagnosis is also variable. The average duration of symptoms before consultation in Graves' thyrotoxicosis is ~6 months; young patients often present more acutely. Most endocrine syndromes are insidious in onset, and are often diagnosed by chance (e.g. routine blood tests may detect hypercalcaemia or hypothyroidism), when a change in appearance is noted by a friend or relative who has not seen the patient for some time (e.g. in acromegaly or

Cushing's syndrome), or when an acute complication arises (e.g. a hypoadrenal 'crisis' in Addison's disease or hypopituitarism, or pain following bleeding into a nodule in multinodular goitre).

- Apart from thyroid disease and diabetes mellitus, endocrine disease is relatively rare. So, although headache may be a presenting complaint in patients with pituitary tumours, not every patient with headache is harbouring a macroadenoma stretching the diaphragma sellae. Similarly, obesity is much more likely to be idiopathic than to be caused by hypothyroidism or Cushing's syndrome.

ASYMPTOMATIC ENDOCRINE DISEASE

This may be detected as a result of screening or indiscriminate biochemical testing, the most common being:

- subclinical hypothyroidism (raised serum TSH, normal T_4)
- hyperglycaemia (see Ch. 15)
- mild primary hyperparathyroidism with serum calcium concentrations between 2.70 and 2.90 mmol/l.

INFLUENCE OF GENDER

- Endocrine disease is more common, and often more obvious, in women. Hyperprolactinaemia causes galactorrhoea, amenorrhoea/oligo-menorrhoea and infertility in the female and, as these symptoms usually prompt an early visit to the general practitioner, any underlying pituitary tumour (prolactinoma) is likely to be small.
- In the male the only symptom of hyperprolactinaemia may be impotence and, because of embarrassment or an acceptance that the problem may be age-related, any pituitary tumour is usually large at the time of presentation with headache, features of hypopituitarism or compression of surrounding structures, such as the optic chiasm.

INVESTIGATIONS

Most diagnoses in endocrinology are based on results of biochemical investi-gations. A clear understanding of these tests is crucial, guided by the principles outlined in the box.

COMMON PRESENTING SYMPTOMS OF ENDOCRINE DISEASE	
Symptom	**Most likely endocrine disorder(s)**
Lethargy and depression	Hypothyroidism, diabetes mellitus, hyperparathyroidism, hypogonadism, adrenal insufficiency, Cushing's syndrome
Weight gain	Hypothyroidism, Cushing's syndrome
Weight loss	Hyperthyroidism, adrenal insufficiency, diabetes mellitus
Amenorrhoea/ oligomenorrhoea	Menopause, polycystic ovarian syndrome, hyperprolactinaemia, hyperthyroidism, premature ovarian failure, Cushing's syndrome
Polyuria and polydipsia	Diabetes mellitus, diabetes insipidus, hyperparathyroidism, Conn's syndrome
Heat intolerance	Hyperthyroidism, menopause
Palpitations	Hyperthyroidism, phaeochromocytoma
Thyroid nodule	Solitary thyroid nodule, dominant nodule in multinodular goitre
Generalised thyroid enlargement	Simple goitre (nodular or diffuse), Graves' disease, Hashimoto's thyroiditis
Pain over thyroid	Haemorrhage into nodule, de Quervain's thyroiditis, rarely Hashimoto's thyroiditis
Prominence of eyes	Graves' disease
Hirsutism	Idiopathic, polycystic ovarian syndrome, congenital adrenal hyperplasia, Cushing's syndrome
Galactorrhoea	Hyperprolactinaemia
Impotence	Hyperprolactinaemia, hypogonadism, diabetes mellitus
Visual dysfunction	Pituitary tumour
Headache	Acromegaly, pituitary tumour, phaeochromocytoma
Muscle weakness (usually proximal)	Hyperthyroidism, Cushing's syndrome, hypokalaemia (e.g. Conn's syndrome), hyperparathyroidism, hypogonadism
Paraesthesiae and tetany	Hypoparathyroidism
Recurrent ureteric colic	Hyperparathyroidism
Coarsening of features	Acromegaly, hypothyroidism

PRINCIPLES OF ENDOCRINE INVESTIGATION

Timing of measurement

- Release of many hormones is rhythmical (e.g. pulsatile, circadian or monthly), so random measurement may be invalid and sequential or dynamic tests may be required

Choice of dynamic biochemical tests

- Abnormalities are often characterised by loss of normal regulation of hormone secretion
- If hormone deficiency is suspected, choose a stimulation test
- If hormone excess is suspected, choose a suppression test
- The more tests there are to choose from, the less likely it is that any single test is infallible, so do not interpret one result in isolation

Imaging

- Secretory cells also take up substrates, which can be labelled
- Most endocrine glands have a high prevalence of 'incidentalomas', so do not scan unless the biochemistry confirms endocrine dysfunction or the primary problem is a tumour

Biopsy

- Many endocrine tumours are difficult to classify histologically (e.g. adrenal carcinoma and adenoma)

Endocrinology concerns the synthesis, secretion and action of hormones. These are chemical messengers which have diverse molecular structures, are released from endocrine glands and coordinate the activities of many different cells. Endocrine disease therefore has a wide range of manifestations affecting many other major organs. This chapter describes the principles of endocrinology before dealing with diseases of each gland in turn.

Some endocrine diseases are common, particularly those of the thyroid gland, reproductive system and β cells of the pancreas (see Ch. 15). For example, thyroid dysfunction occurs in more than 10% of the population in areas with iodine deficiency, e.g. the Himalayas, and 4% of women aged 20–50 years in the UK. Many rare endocrine syndromes present a particular diagnostic challenge to primary care clinicians who may see very few such patients during their working lives. These are described later in the chapter.

Endocrinology is mostly practised in outpatient clinics rather than in hospital wards. This is another reason why many endocrine syndromes are unfamiliar to general physicians. Students are advised to attend a specialist endocrinology clinic to gain an appreciation of common endocrine problems.

Few endocrine therapies have been evaluated by randomised controlled trials, in part because hormone replacement therapy (e.g. with thyroxine) has obvious clinical benefits and placebo-controlled trials would be unethical, and in part because many endocrine syndromes are rare. Recommendations for 'evidence-based medicine' are, therefore, relatively scarce. They relate mainly to use of therapy which is 'optional' and/or recently available, e.g. oestrogen replacement in post-menopausal women, adrenal androgen and growth hormone replacement.

FUNCTIONAL ANATOMY, PHYSIOLOGY AND INVESTIGATIONS

MAJOR ENDOCRINE FUNCTIONS AND ANATOMY

Although some endocrine glands (e.g. parathyroid glands and pancreas) respond directly to metabolic signals, most are controlled by hormones released from the pituitary gland. Anterior pituitary hormone secretion is controlled in turn by substances produced in the hypothalamus and released into portal blood which drains directly down the pituitary stalk (see Fig. 16.1). Posterior pituitary hormones are synthesised in the hypothalamus and transported down nerve axons to be released from the posterior pituitary. Hormone release in the hypothalamus and pituitary is regulated by numerous stimuli of nervous, metabolic, physical or hormonal origin, in particular feedback control by hormones produced by the target glands (thyroid, adrenal cortex and gonads). These integrated endocrine systems are called 'axes', and are listed in Figure 16.2. The characteristics of each axis are described in relation to individual glands later in this chapter.

A wide variety of molecules act as hormones. Peptides (e.g. insulin), glycoproteins (e.g. thyroid-stimulating hormone,

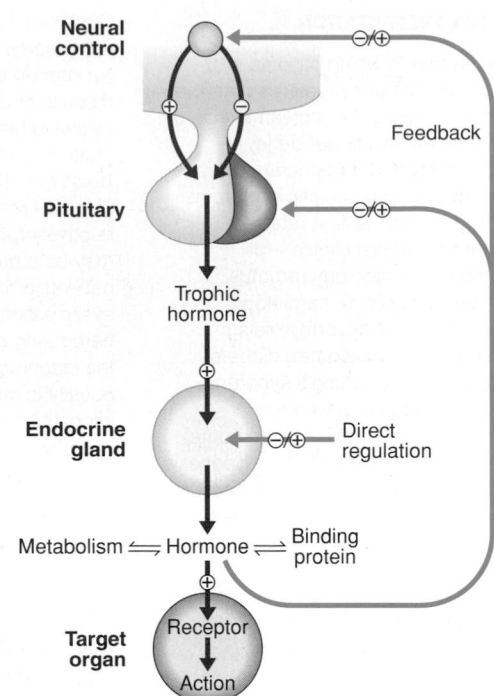

Fig. 16.1 An archetypal endocrine axis. Regulation by negative feedback and direct control is shown along with the equilibrium between active circulating free hormone and bound or metabolised hormone.

TSH) and amines (e.g. noradrenaline) act on specific cell surface receptors which signal through G-proteins and/or enzymes on the cytosolic side of the plasma membrane. Other hormones (e.g. steroids, thyroid hormones and vitamin D) bind to specific intracellular receptors which in turn bind to response elements on DNA to regulate gene transcription.

The classical model of endocrine function involves hormones which are synthesised in endocrine glands, released into the circulation, and act at sites distant from those of secretion (as in Fig. 16.1). However, additional levels of complex regulation have now been recognised. Thus, most major organs also secrete hormones or contribute to the peripheral metabolism and activation of prohormones; many hormones act on adjacent cells (paracrine system, e.g. neurotransmitters), or even back on the cell of origin (autocrine system); and the sensitivity of target tissues is regulated in a tissue-specific fashion. The clinical implications of this complexity of hormone action are only now being appreciated.

ENDOCRINE PATHOLOGY

For each endocrine axis or major gland in this chapter, diseases can be classified as shown in Box 16.1. Note that pathology arising within the gland is often called 'primary' disease (e.g. primary hypothyroidism in Hashimoto's thyroiditis) while abnormal stimulation of the gland is often called 'secondary' disease (e.g. secondary hypothyroidism in patients with pituitary tumour and TSH deficiency). In

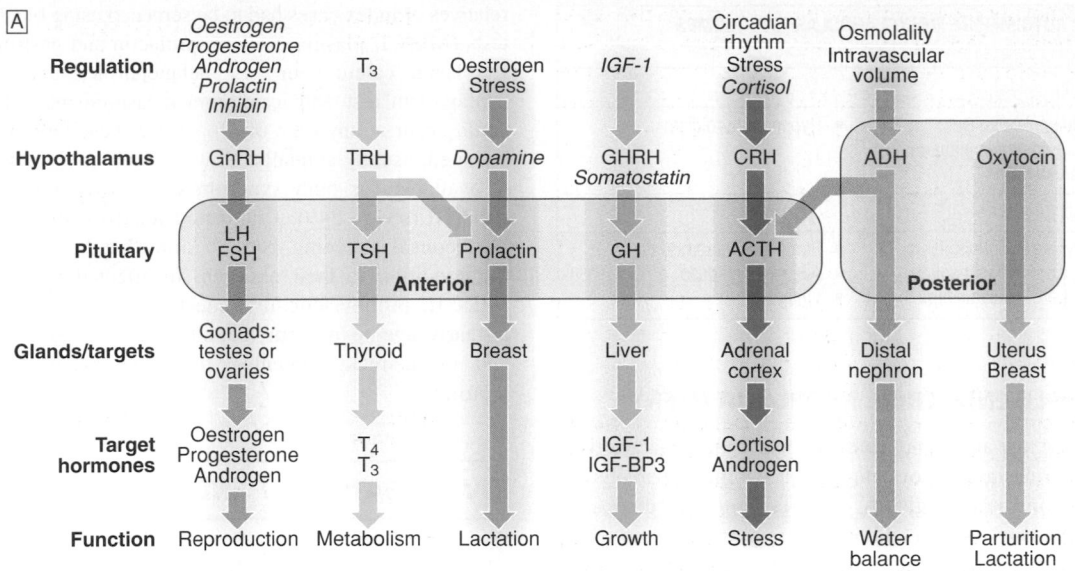

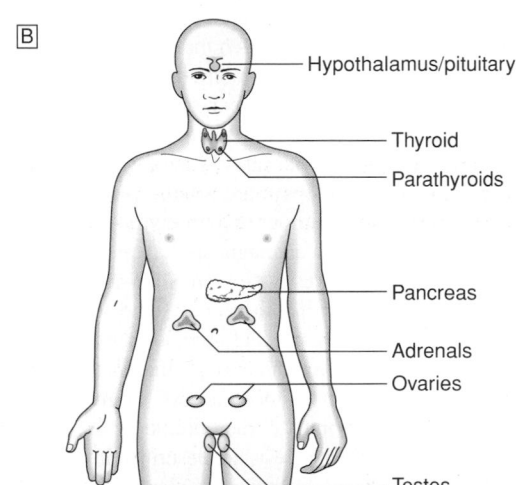

Fig. 16.2   The principal endocrine 'axes' and glands. A Endocrine axes. Some major endocrine glands are not controlled by the pituitary. These include the parathyroid glands (regulated by calcium concentrations—see p. 714), the adrenal zona glomerulosa (regulated by the renin-angiotensin system—see p. 720) and the endocrine pancreas (see Ch. 15 and p. 732). Italics show negative regulation. (ACTH = adrenocorticotrophic hormone; ADH = antidiuretic hormone, arginine vasopressin; CRH = corticotrophin-releasing hormone; FSH = follicle-stimulating hormone; GH = growth hormone; GHRH = growth hormone-releasing hormone; GnRH = gonadotrophin-releasing hormone; IGF-1 = insulin-like growth factor-1; IGF-BP3 = IGF-binding protein-3; LH = luteinising hormone; T_3 = triiodothyronine; T_4 = thyroxine; TRH = thyrotrophin-releasing hormone; TSH = thyroid-stimulating hormone) B Endocrine glands.

16.1 CLASSIFICATION OF ENDOCRINE DISEASE
Hormone excess
• Primary gland over-production • Secondary to excess trophic substance
Hormone deficiency
• Primary gland failure • Secondary to deficient trophic hormone
Hormone hypersensitivity
• Failure of inactivation of hormone • Target organ over-activity/hypersensitivity
Hormone resistance
• Failure of activation of hormone • Target organ resistance
Non-functioning tumours

addition to these gland-specific disorders, there are two pathologies which affect multiple glands: organ-specific autoimmune diseases (which are common) and multiple endocrine neoplasia (which is rare).

AUTOIMMUNE DISEASE

From an endocrinology perspective, autoimmune disorders cluster into two syndromes, as shown in Box 16.2. In patients who present with one gland affected, the likelihood of developing further endocrine deficiency is variable, and can be predicted only in part by the detection of circulating antibodies against antigens in other glands. Primary hypothyroidism (see p. 691) is the only autoimmune endocrine disorder which is sufficiently prevalent to justify routine screening when antibodies are detected in the absence of any other affected gland. The annual incidence of hypothyroidism in patients with circulating antimicrosomal and antithyroglobulin antibodies is ~2%.

16.2 AUTOIMMUNE 'POLYGLANDULAR' SYNDROMES	
Type 1	
• Addison's disease • Chronic mucocutaneous candidiasis	• Hypoparathyroidism
Type 2	
• Primary hypothyroidism • Primary hypogonadism • Diabetes mellitus type 1	• Pernicious anaemia • Addison's disease • Vitiligo

MULTIPLE ENDOCRINE NEOPLASIA (MEN)

These are rare autosomal dominant syndromes characterised by hyperplasia and formation of adenomas or malignant tumours in multiple glands. They fall into two groups, as shown in Box 16.3. In addition, there are families in which single tumours are more prevalent, e.g with acromegaly or phaeochromocytoma. Also, other genetic diseases affecting tumour suppressor genes may be manifest as endocrine tumours (e.g. phaeochromocytoma in von Hippel–Lindau syndrome, see p. 1207).

MEN syndromes should be considered in all patients with two or more of the relevant disorders (e.g. hypercalcaemia and pituitary tumour) and in patients with solitary tumours who report other endocrine tumours in their family.

Important advances have been made in recent years to establish the genetic causes of these syndromes. MEN I results from inactivating mutations in 'menin', a tumour suppressor gene. In MEN II, mutations in the RET proto-oncogene cause constitutive activation of a membrane-associated tyrosine kinase. RET controls the development of cells which migrate from the neural crest, and different mutations causing loss of function of the RET kinase are associated with Hirschsprung's disease. Somatic mutations of these genes have been described in sporadic tumours, e.g. menin mutations in parathyroid adenomas and RET mutations in papillary thyroid carcinomas.

As these are autosomal dominant disorders with full penetrance, there is a 50% chance that first-degree relatives of patients with MEN will carry the affected gene. Previously,

16.3 MULTIPLE ENDOCRINE NEOPLASIA (MEN) SYNDROMES
MEN I (Werner's syndrome)
• Primary hyperparathyroidism • Pituitary tumours • Pancreatic tumours (e.g. insulinoma, gastrinoma)
MEN II (Sipple's syndrome)
• Primary hyperparathyroidism • Medullary carcinoma of thyroid • Phaeochromocytoma
In addition, in MEN IIb syndrome there are phenotypic changes (including marfanoid habitus, skeletal abnormalities, abnormal dental enamel, multiple mucosal neuromata)

relatives of index cases had to be screened using biochemical tests (MEN I: plasma calcium, prolactin and gastrin; MEN II: plasma calcium, urinary metanephrines, and calcium-pentagastrin test with calcitonin measurements). Tumours could occur at any time of life so that these tests had to be repeated, usually annually. Now, accurate genetic diagnosis is available for both syndromes. Genetic counselling is required (see p. 349). Unaffected relatives not only avoid biochemical screening, but also know that they will not pass the condition to their children. In affected relatives with MEN II, prophylactic thyroidectomy is recommended at an early age to prevent medullary carcinoma of thyroid, and biochemical screening for other manifestations is performed.

INVESTIGATION OF ENDOCRINE DISEASE

An understanding of biochemical investigations is important in endocrinology. Most hormones can be measured in blood, but the circumstances in which the sample is taken are often crucial, especially for hormones with pulsatile secretion (e.g. growth hormone) or marked physiological variation (e.g. diurnal variation of cortisol, or monthly variation of sex steroids in pre-menopausal women). Other investigations (e.g. imaging and biopsy) are usually reserved for patients who present with a tumour (e.g. in thyroid or pituitary) or in whom the biochemical diagnosis has already been made. The principles of investigation are shown on page 685. The choice of test is often pragmatic; some tests are intellectually attractive, but clinical studies have shown them to have poor predictive value (e.g. the metyrapone test in Cushing's syndrome); local access to reliable sampling facilities and laboratory measurements is an important consideration. Specific tests are described in relation to individual glands in the following sections. Approximate adult reference values for hormone concentrations in plasma are given in the Appendix.

MAJOR MANIFESTATIONS OF ENDOCRINE DISEASE

As described above (see p. 685), endocrine diseases present in many different ways. Classical syndromes are described in relation to individual glands in the following sections. The most common classical presentations are of thyroid disease, reproductive disorders and hypercalcaemia. In addition, endocrine diseases are often part of the differential diagnosis of common complaints discussed in other chapters of this book, including electrolyte abnormalities (see Ch. 9), hypertension (see Ch. 12), obesity (see Ch. 10) and osteoporosis (see Ch. 20). Although diseases of the adrenal glands, hypothalamus and pituitary are relatively rare, their diagnosis often relies on astute clinical observation in a patient with non-specific complaints so that it is important that clinicians are familiar with their key features.

THE THYROID GLAND

The thyroid axis is involved in the regulation of metabolism. Thyroid disease in its various forms is common, affecting some 5% of the population, predominantly females.

FUNCTIONAL ANATOMY, PHYSIOLOGY AND INVESTIGATIONS

Thyroid physiology is illustrated in Figure 16.3 and diseases are classified in Box 16.4. The thyroid secretes predominantly thyroxine (T_4), and only a small amount of tri-iodothyronine (T_3); approximately 85% of T_3 is produced by monodeiodination of T_4 in other tissues such as liver, muscle and kidney. T_4 is probably not metabolically active until converted to T_3, and may be regarded as a prohormone. T_3 and T_4 circulate in plasma almost entirely (> 99.9%) bound to transport proteins, mainly thyroxine-binding globulin (TBG). It is the minute fraction of unbound or free hormone

16.4 CLASSIFICATION OF THYROID DISEASE		
	Primary	**Secondary**
Hormone excess	Graves' disease Multinodular goitre Adenoma Subacute thyroiditis	Pituitary TSHoma
Hormone deficiency	Hashimoto's thyroiditis Atrophic hypothyroidism	Hypopituitarism
Hormone hypersensitivity	–	
Hormone resistance	Thyroid hormone resistance syndrome 5'-monodeiodinase deficiency	
Non-functioning tumours	Differentiated carcinoma Medullary carcinoma Lymphoma	

which diffuses into tissues and exerts its metabolic action. While it is possible to measure the concentration of total or

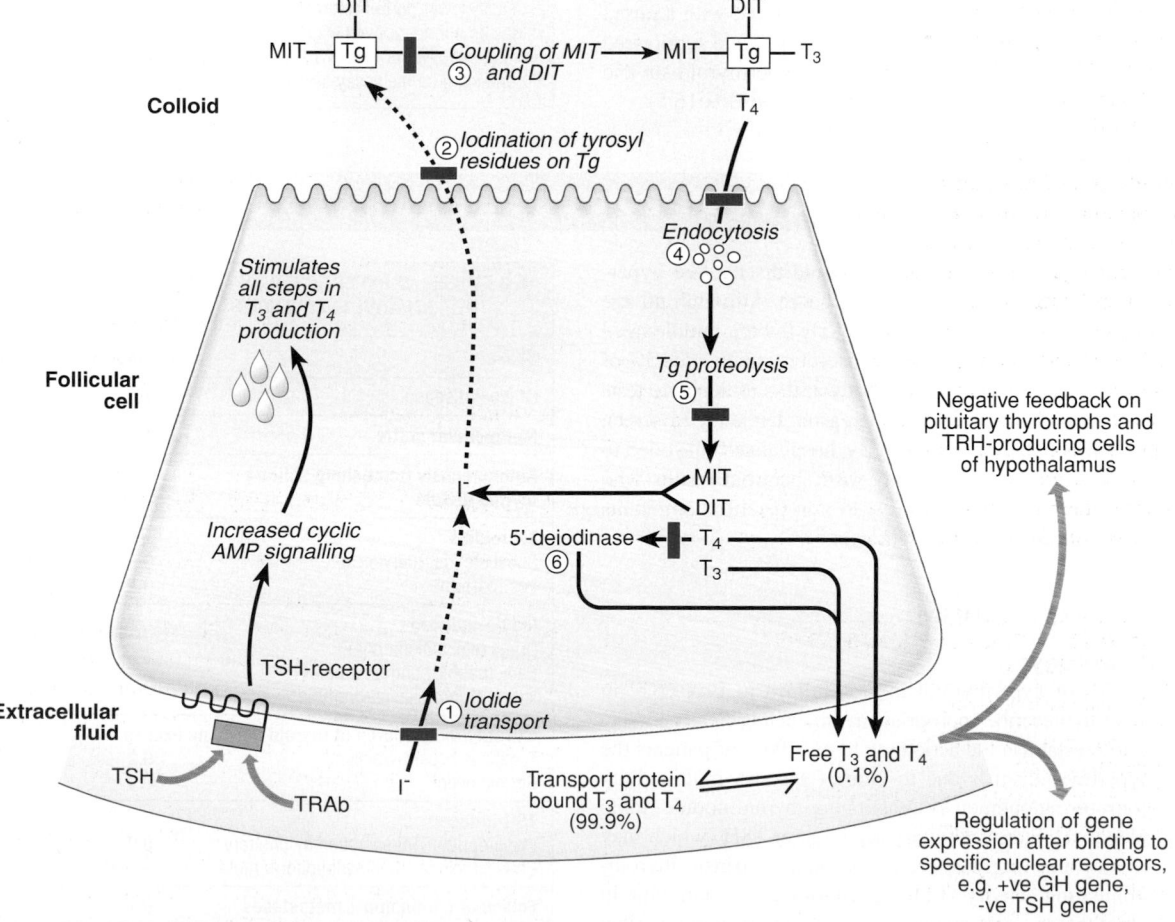

Fig. 16.3 Thyroid hormone synthesis and secretion, and sites of inhibition by antithyroid drugs. Sites of action of antithyroid drugs are as follows: 1. Potassium perchlorate; 2. and 3. Carbimazole, propylthiouracil; 4. Lithium, iodide; 5. Iodide; 6. Propylthiouracil. (Tg = thyroglobulin; MIT = monoiodotyrosine; DIT = diiodotyrosine; TRH = thyrotrophin-releasing hormone; TRAb = TSH-receptor antibody present in patients with Graves' disease)

free T_3 and T_4 in plasma, the advantage of the free hormone measurements is that they are not influenced by changes in the concentration of binding proteins; in pregnancy, for example, TBG levels are increased and total T_3 and T_4 may be raised, but free thyroid hormone levels are normal.

Production of T_3 and T_4 in the thyroid is stimulated by thyrotrophin (thyroid-stimulating hormone, TSH), a glycoprotein released from the thyrotroph cells of the anterior pituitary in response to the hypothalamic tripeptide, thyrotrophin-releasing hormone (TRH; see p. 687). A circadian rhythm of TSH secretion can be demonstrated with a peak at 0100 hrs and trough at 1100 hrs, but the variation is small and does not influence the timing of blood sampling when assessing thyroid function.

There is a negative feedback of thyroid hormones on the thyrotrophs such that in hyperthyroidism, when plasma concentrations of T_3 and T_4 are raised, TSH secretion is suppressed, and in hypothyroidism due to disease of the thyroid gland low T_3 and T_4 are associated with high circulating TSH levels. The anterior pituitary is very sensitive to minor changes in thyroid hormone levels within the normal range. Although the reference range for total T_4 is 60–150 nmol/l, a rise or fall of 20 nmol/l in an individual in whom the level is usually 100 nmol/l would be associated on the one hand with undetectable TSH, and on the other hand with a raised TSH. The combination of 'normal' T_3 and T_4 and suppressed or raised TSH is known as subclinical hyperthyroidism and subclinical hypothyroidism respectively (see Box 16.5).

16.5 PATTERNS OF THYROID FUNCTION TEST RESULTS IN PATIENTS WITH THYROID DISEASE

Type of disease	T_4	T_3	TSH
Conventional hyperthyroidism (95% of cases)	Raised	Raised	Undetectable
T_3-hyperthyroidism (5% of cases)	Normal[1]	Raised	Undetectable
Subclinical hyperthyroidism	Normal[1]	Normal[1]	Undetectable
Primary hypothyroidism	Low	Not indicated[2]	Raised (usually > 20 mU/l)
Subclinical hypothyroidism	Normal[3]	Not indicated[2]	Raised
Secondary hypothyroidism i.e. pituitary or hypothalamic disease	Low	Not indicated[2]	Usually undetectable[4]
Non-thyroidal illness	Raised	Low, normal or raised[5]	Usually undetectable

[1] Usually upper part of reference range.
[2] Measurement of T_3 is not a sensitive indicator of hypothyroidism and should not be requested.
[3] Usually lower part of reference range.
[4] May be normal or even slightly raised due to the production of immunoreactive forms of TSH which have no biological activity.
[5] Depending on the assay system.

MAJOR MANIFESTATIONS OF THYROID DISEASE

The major manifestations of thyroid disease are hyperthyroidism, hypothyroidism and goitre. Although no age group is exempt, the patient is likely to be a middle-aged female, and collectively these disorders affect some 5% of the population. In addition, ready access to accurate tests of thyroid function and an increasing tendency to screen certain populations (e.g. elderly, hospitalised) have led to the identification of patients with abnormal results who are either asymptomatic or with non-specific complaints such as tiredness and weight gain.

HYPERTHYROIDISM

Aetiology

Causes of hyperthyroidism are outlined in Box 16.6; in order to prescribe appropriate treatment it is clearly important to establish the aetiology. In over 90% of patients the hyperthyroidism is due to Graves' disease, multinodular goitre or autonomously functioning thyroid nodule (toxic adenoma). Excess pituitary secretion of TSH (which may or may not originate from a tumour), intrinsic thyroid-stimulating activity of human chorionic gonadotrophin in hydatidiform mole and choriocarcinoma, ovarian teratoma containing thyroid tissue (struma ovarii), and metastatic differentiated carcinoma of the thyroid are so rare that they are unlikely to be met outside specialist practice.

16.6 CAUSES OF HYPERTHYROIDISM AND THEIR RELATIVE FREQUENCIES

Cause	Frequency[1] (%)
Graves' disease	76
Multinodular goitre	14
Autonomously functioning solitary thyroid nodule	5
Thyroiditis Subacute (de Quervain's)[2] Post-partum[2]	3 0.5
Iodide-induced Drugs (e.g. amiodarone)[2] Radiographic contrast media[2] Iodine prophylaxis programme[2]	1 – –
Extrathyroidal source of thyroid hormone excess Factitious hyperthyroidism[2] Struma ovarii[2]	0.2 –
TSH-induced Inappropriate TSH secretion by pituitary Choriocarcinoma and hydatidiform mole	0.2 –
Follicular carcinoma ± metastases	0.1

[1] In a series of 2087 patients presenting to the Royal Infirmary, Edinburgh, over a 10-year period.
[2] Characterised by a negligible radio-iodine uptake test result.

16.7 CLINICAL FEATURES OF HYPERTHYROIDISM

Goitre

- Diffuse ± bruit[1]
- Nodular (see p. 684)

Gastrointestinal

- Weight loss despite normal or increased appetite[2]
- Hyperdefaecation[2]
- Diarrhoea and steatorrhoea
- Anorexia[3]
- Vomiting

Cardiorespiratory

- Palpitations[2], sinus tachycardia, atrial fibrillation[3]
- Increased pulse pressure
- Ankle oedema in absence of cardiac failure
- Angina, cardiomyopathy and cardiac failure[3]
- Dyspnoea on exertion[2]
- Exacerbation of asthma

Neuromuscular

- Nervousness, irritability, emotional lability[2], psychosis
- Tremor
- Hyper-reflexia, ill-sustained clonus
- Muscle weakness, proximal myopathy, bulbar myopathy[3]
- Periodic paralysis (predominantly Chinese)

Dermatological

- Increased sweating[2], pruritus
- Palmar erythema, spider naevi
- Onycholysis
- Alopecia
- Pigmentation, vitiligo[1]
- Digital clubbing[1]
- Pretibial myxoedema[1] (see p. 684)

Reproductive

- Amenorrhoea/oligomenorrhoea
- Infertility, spontaneous abortion
- Loss of libido, impotence

Ocular

- Lid retraction, lid lag[1] (see p. 694)
- Grittiness[1], excessive lacrimation[2]
- Chemosis[1]
- Exophthalmos[1], corneal ulceration[1]
- Ophthalmoplegia[1], diplopia[1]
- Papilloedema[1], loss of visual acuity[1]

Other

- Heat intolerance[2]
- Fatigue[2], apathy[3]
- Gynaecomastia
- Lymphadenopathy[1]
- Thirst
- Osteoporosis[3]

[1] Features of Graves' disease only.
[2] The most common symptoms of hyperthyroidism, irrespective of its cause.
[3] Features found particularly in elderly patients.

Clinical features

These are shown in Box 16.7. The most common symptoms are weight loss with a normal or increased appetite, heat intolerance, palpitations, tremor and irritability. Although a clinical diagnosis can usually be made, it is important to confirm the impression biochemically by more than one test of thyroid function in view of the likely need for prolonged medical treatment or destructive therapy.

Investigations

Serum T_3 and T_4 are elevated in the majority, but T_4 is in the upper part of the normal range and T_3 raised (T_3-thyrotoxicosis) in 5% of patients, particularly those with recurrent hyperthyroidism, following surgery or a course of antithyroid drugs. In primary hyperthyroidism serum TSH is undetectable at less than 0.1 mU/l (see Box 16.5). Other non-specific abnormalities are listed in Box 16.8. Further tests which may be required to establish the aetiology of hyperthyroidism include measurement of TSH-receptor antibodies (TRAb, elevated in Graves' disease), isotope scanning and uptake tests (see Box 16.6 and Fig. 16.6, p. 697).

16.8 NON-SPECIFIC BIOCHEMICAL ABNORMALITIES IN HYPERTHYROIDISM

Hepatic dysfunction
- Slightly raised concentrations of bilirubin, alanine aminotransferase and gamma-glutamyl transferase; elevated alkaline phosphatase derived from bone and liver

Mild hypercalcaemia (5%)

Glycosuria
- Associated diabetes mellitus
- 'Lag storage' (see p. 648)

HYPOTHYROIDISM

Aetiology

The prevalence of primary hypothyroidism is 1:100 but increases to 5:100 if patients with subclinical hypothyroidism (normal T_4, raised TSH) are included. The female:male ratio is approximately 6:1. There are various causes of primary hypothyroidism (see Box 16.9), but spontaneous atrophic hypothyroidism, thyroid failure following ^{131}I or surgical treatment of hyperthyroidism, and the hypothyroidism of Hashimoto's thyroiditis account for over 90% of cases in those parts of the world which are not significantly iodine-deficient.

16.9 CLASSIFICATION OF PRIMARY HYPOTHYROIDISM

- Spontaneous atrophic
- Post-ablative (post-^{131}I)
- Subclinical
- Transient
- Congenital
- Goitrous
  - Hashimoto's thyroiditis
  - Drug-induced
  - Iodine deficiency
  - Dyshormonogenesis

Clinical features

These depend on the duration and severity of the hypothyroidism. In the patient in whom complete thyroid failure has developed insidiously over months or even years many of the clinical features listed in Box 16.10 are likely to be present. A consequence of prolonged hypothyroidism is the infiltration of many body tissues by the mucopolysaccharides, hyaluronic acid and chondroitin sulphate, resulting in a low-pitched voice, poor hearing, slurred speech due to a large tongue, and compression of the median nerve at the wrist. Infiltration of the dermis gives rise to non-pitting oedema or myxoedema which is most marked in the skin of the hands, feet and eyelids. The resultant periorbital puffiness is often striking and, when combined with facial pallor due to vasoconstriction and anaemia, or a lemon-yellow tint to the skin due to carotenaemia, purplish lips and malar flush, the clinical diagnosis is simple. Most cases of hypothyroidism are not so obvious, however, and unless the diagnosis is positively entertained in the middle-aged woman complaining of tiredness, weight gain or depression, or with carpal tunnel syndrome an opportunity for early treatment will be missed.

Investigations

In the most common form of hypothyroidism, namely primary hypothyroidism resulting from an intrinsic disorder of the thyroid gland, serum T_4 is low and TSH elevated, usually in excess of 20 mU/l. Serum T_3 concentrations do not discriminate reliably between euthyroid and hypothyroid patients and should not be measured. Other non-specific abnormalities include elevation of the enzymes lactate dehydrogenase (LDH) and creatine kinase, raised cholesterol and triglyceride concentrations, and low serum sodium. In severe prolonged hypothyroidism the electrocardiogram classically demonstrates sinus bradycardia with low voltage complexes and ST segment and T wave abnormalities. In the rare secondary hypothyroidism there is atrophy of an inherently normal thyroid gland caused by failure of TSH secretion in a patient with hypothalamic or anterior pituitary disease, e.g. pituitary macroadenoma. Serum T_4 is low but TSH may be low, normal or even slightly elevated. It follows therefore that screening for thyroid disease by measurement of TSH alone, an increasingly common laboratory policy, will result in missing cases of secondary hypothyroidism with potentially serious consequences. Antibodies against thyroid peroxidase suggest spontaneous atrophic hypothyroidism or, in the presence of goitre, Hashimoto's thyroiditis (see pp. 699–701). Further investigations are rarely required, provided there is no suspicion of transient hypothyroidism (see pp. 699 and 701).

THYROID ENLARGEMENT

Palpable thyroid enlargement is common, affecting about 5% of the population, although it is the minority who seek medical attention, often because a friend or relative has noticed a lump in the neck. There are several causes, ranging from the soft diffuse goitre of puberty and youth to the multinodular goitre of middle age and beyond (see p. 702) which may progress to hyperthyroidism, and the solitary nodule which can present at any age. Whereas diffuse and multinodular goitre are almost invariably benign, there is a 1:20 chance of malignancy in the truly solitary lesion (see p. 702).

16.10 CLINICAL FEATURES OF HYPOTHYROIDISM

General

- Tiredness, somnolence
- Weight gain
- Cold intolerance
- Hoarseness
- Goitre

Cardiorespiratory

- Bradycardia, hypertension, angina, cardiac failure*
- Xanthelasma
- Pericardial and pleural effusion*

Neuromuscular

- Aches and pains, muscle stiffness
- Delayed relaxation of tendon reflexes
- Carpal tunnel syndrome, deafness
- Depression, psychosis*
- Cerebellar ataxia*
- Myotonia*

Haematological

- Macrocytosis
- Anaemia
  Iron deficiency (pre-menopausal women)
  Normochromic
  Pernicious

Dermatological

- Dry, flaky skin and hair, alopecia
- Purplish lips and malar flush, carotenaemia
- Vitiligo
- Erythema ab igne (Granny's tartan)
- Myxoedema

Reproductive

- Menorrhagia
- Infertility
- Galactorrhoea*
- Impotence*

Gastrointestinal

- Constipation
- Ileus*
- Ascites*

* Rare but well-recognised features.

ABNORMAL THYROID FUNCTION TEST RESULTS

One of the most common problems in medical practice is how to manage patients with abnormal thyroid function tests who have no obvious signs or symptoms of thyroid disease. For practical purposes these can be divided into three categories.

Subclinical hyperthyroidism

Here the serum TSH is undetectable and the serum T_3 and T_4 lie in the upper parts of their respective reference ranges. This combination is most often found in patients with nodular goitre. These patients are at increased risk of atrial fibrillation and osteoporosis and hence the consensus view is that such patients have mild hyperthyroidism and require therapy, usually with ^{131}I. Otherwise annual review is essential as the conversion rate to overt hyperthyroidism with elevated T_4 and/or T_3 concentrations is 5% each year.

Subclinical hypothyroidism

The serum TSH is raised and the serum T_3 and T_4 concentrations are usually in the lower part of their respective reference ranges. It is most often encountered after ^{131}I or surgical treatment of hyperthyroidism and may persist for many years, although there is an inexorable progression to overt thyroid failure, particularly if antibodies are present in the serum directed against thyroid peroxidase. The view is that these patients are mildly hypothyroid, however asymptomatic, and it is better to treat the thyroid failure early rather than risk loss to follow-up and subsequent

presentation with profound hypothyroidism. Thyroxine should be given in a dose of 50–150 µg daily, sufficient to restore the serum TSH concentration to normal.

Non-thyroidal illness

In ill patients (e.g. myocardial infarction, pneumonia) not only is there a decreased peripheral conversion of T_4 to T_3, but also alterations of binding proteins and their affinity for thyroid hormones. In addition, serum TSH concentrations may be subnormal as a result of the illness itself or the use of drugs such as dopamine or corticosteroids. The most common combination is a low serum TSH, raised T_4 and normal or low T_3, but many patterns of thyroid function tests can be seen, dependent upon the type of assay used. During convalescence serum TSH concentrations may increase to levels found in primary hypothyroidism. It follows that biochemical assessment of thyroid function should not be undertaken in patients with non-thyroidal illness, unless there is good evidence of concomitant thyroid disease, e.g. goitre, exophthalmos. If an abnormal result is found, no treatment should be given and the tests repeated after recovery.

HYPERTHYROIDISM

GRAVES' DISEASE

Graves' disease is distinguished clinically from other forms of hyperthyroidism by the presence of diffuse thyroid enlargement, ophthalmopathy and rarely pretibial myxoedema (see p. 684). It can occur at any age but is unusual before puberty and most commonly affects the 30–50-year-old age group.

Pathogenesis

Graves' disease is the major immunologically mediated form of hyperthyroidism, the other being post-partum thyroiditis (see p. 697). The hyperthyroidism results from the production of IgG antibodies directed against the TSH-receptor on the thyroid follicular cell which stimulates thyroid hormone production and, in the majority, goitre formation. These antibodies are termed thyroid-stimulating immunoglobulins or TSH-receptor antibodies (TRAb) and can be detected in the serum of most patients with Graves' disease.

In Caucasians there is an association of Graves' disease with HLA-B8, DR3 and DR2, and with inability to secrete

the water-soluble glycoprotein form of the ABO blood group antigens coded for on chromosomes 6 and 19 respectively. Family studies show that 50% of monozygotic twins are concordant for hyperthyroidism as opposed to 5% of dizygotic twins.

The trigger for the development of hyperthyroidism in genetically susceptible individuals may be infection with viruses or bacteria, although there is no proof. However, certain strains of the gut organisms *Escherichia coli* and *Yersinia enterocolitica* possess cell membrane TSH-receptors. The production of antibodies to these microbial antigens which might cross-react with the TSH-receptor on the host thyroid follicular cell could result in the development of hyperthyroidism. Stress is usually dismissed as aetiologically unimportant but many experienced endocrinologists are impressed from time to time by the temporal relationship between the onset of hyperthyroidism and a major life event such as the death of a close relative. In regions of iodine deficiency, iodine supplementation may result in the development of hyperthyroidism, but only in those with pre-existing subclinical Graves' disease. Smoking is weakly associated with Graves' hyperthyroidism but strongly linked with the development of ophthalmopathy.

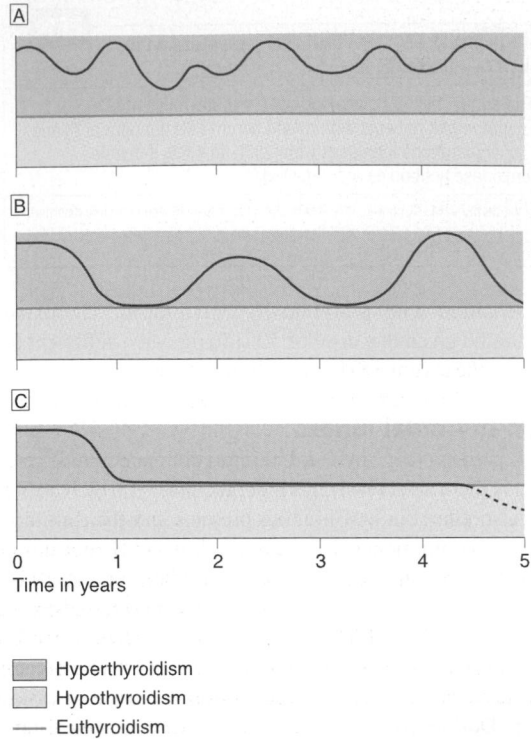

Time in years

■ Hyperthyroidism
□ Hypothyroidism
— Euthyroidism

Fig. 16.4 Natural history of the hyperthyroidism of Graves' disease.
A and B The majority (60%) of patients have either prolonged periods of hyperthyroidism of fluctuating severity, or periods of alternating relapse and remission. C It is the minority who experience a single short-lived episode followed by prolonged remission and, in some cases, by the eventual onset of hypothyroidism.

The concentration of TRAb in the serum is presumed to fluctuate because of the natural history of Graves' disease (see Fig. 16.4). The ultimate thyroid failure seen in some patients is thought to result from the presence of yet another immunoglobulin, a blocking antibody against the TSH-receptor, and from tissue destruction by cytotoxic antibodies and cell-mediated immunity.

The pathogenesis of the ophthalmopathy and dermopathy is less well understood. Both are immunologically mediated but the autoantigen(s) which causes the local accumulation of lymphocytes has not been identified. Within the orbit (and the dermis) there is cytokine-mediated proliferation of fibroblasts which secrete hydrophilic glycosaminoglycans. The resulting increased interstitial fluid content, combined with a chronic inflammatory cell infiltrate, causes marked swelling of the extraocular muscles (see Fig. 16.5) and a rise in retrobulbar pressure. The eye is displaced forwards (proptosis, exophthalmos) and in more severe cases there is optic nerve compression. Ultimately, there is fibrosis of the extraocular muscles.

Clinical features

Goitre
The diffusely enlarged gland is usually 2–3 times the normal volume, and increased blood flow may be manifest by a

thrill or bruit. In some patients, particularly the elderly, no thyroid enlargement is palpable or the gland may be nodular. The largest goitres tend to occur in young men.

Ophthalmopathy
This is only present in 50% of patients when first seen but may develop after successful treatment of the hyperthyroidism of Graves' disease, or precede its development by many years (exophthalmic Graves' disease). As noted, it is more common in cigarette smokers. The most frequent presenting symptoms are related to increased exposure of the cornea, resulting from proptosis and lid retraction. There may be excessive lacrimation made worse by wind and bright light, and pain due to conjunctivitis or corneal ulceration. In addition, there may be loss of visual acuity and/or visual field resulting from corneal oedema or optic nerve compression. If the extraocular muscles are involved and do not act in concert, diplopia will result.

Pretibial myxoedema
This infiltrative dermopathy takes the form of raised pink-coloured or purplish plaques on the anterior aspect of the

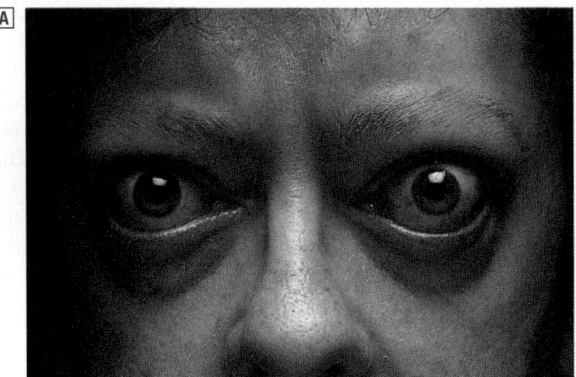

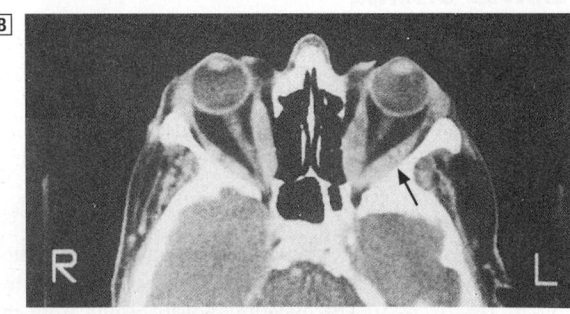

Fig. 16.5 Graves' disease. A Bilateral ophthalmopathy in a 42-year-old man, developing 2 years after successful treatment of hyperthyroidism with [131]I. The main symptoms were those of diplopia in all directions of gaze and reduced visual acuity in the left eye. The periorbital swelling is due to retrobulbar fat prolapsing into the eyelids, and increased interstitial fluid as a result of raised intraorbital pressure. B Transverse CT of the orbits of the same patient, showing the extraocular muscles enlarged to three times their normal bulk. This is most obvious at the apex of the left orbit (arrow), causing compression of the optic nerve and reduced visual acuity.

leg, extending on to the dorsum of the foot (see p. 684). The lesions may be itchy and the skin may have a 'peau d'orange' appearance with growth of coarse hair; less commonly, the face and arms may be affected.

Management of hyperthyroidism of Graves' disease

The different treatment options are compared in Box 16.11. If it were possible to predict with confidence the natural history of the hyperthyroidism in an individual patient at presentation, it would be appropriate to give an antithyroid drug for 12–18 months to those in whom a single episode was anticipated, and to advise destructive therapy with ^{131}I or surgery for those likely to experience recurrent disease. With the exception of young men with large goitres and those with severe hyperthyroidism, such a prediction is not possible. For patients under 40 years of age many centres adopt the empirical approach of prescribing a course of carbimazole and recommending surgery if relapse occurs. Although there is no evidence that thyroid carcinoma or leukaemia is induced by therapeutic ^{131}I, or that its use results in an increased frequency of congenital malformation among subsequent offspring, radioactive iodine treatment is usually reserved in the UK for patients over the age of 40. In many countries, however, ^{131}I is used more extensively.

Antithyroid drugs

The most commonly used are carbimazole (see Box 16.12) and its active metabolite, methimazole (not available in the UK). Propylthiouracil is equally effective. These drugs reduce the synthesis of new thyroid hormones by inhibiting the iodination of tyrosine (see Fig. 16.3, p. 689). Carbimazole also has an immunosuppressive action, leading to a reduction in serum TRAb concentrations, but this is not enough to influence the natural history of the hyperthyroidism significantly.

There is subjective improvement within 10–14 days of starting carbimazole and the patient is usually clinically and biochemically euthyroid at 3–4 weeks. The maintenance dose is determined by measurement of T_4 and TSH, attempting to keep both hormones within their respective reference ranges. In most patients it can be taken as a single daily dose and is continued for 18–24 months in the hope that during this period permanent remission will occur. Unfortunately, hyperthyroidism recurs in at least 50%, usually within 2 years of stopping treatment. Rarely, despite good drug compliance, T_4 and TSH levels fluctuate between those of hyperthyroidism and hypothyroidism at successive review appointments, presumably due to rapidly changing concentrations of TRAb. In such patients satisfactory control can be achieved by blocking thyroid hormone synthesis with carbimazole 30 mg daily and adding T_4 150 µg daily as replacement therapy when the patient is euthyroid.

The adverse effects of the antithyroid drugs develop within 7–28 days of starting treatment. Agranulocytosis cannot be predicted by routine measurement of white blood cell count, and is fortunately reversible. Patients should be warned to stop the drug and contact their medical attendant immediately should a severe sore throat or fever develop. Cross-sensitivity between the antithyroid drugs is relatively unusual and another member of the group can be substituted with good effect.

16.12 CARBIMAZOLE

Dosage

- 0–3 weeks: 40–60 mg daily
- 4–8 weeks: 20–40 mg daily
- Maintenance: 5–20 mg daily for 18–24 months

Adverse effects

- Rash (2%)
- Agranulocytosis (0.2%)
- Jaundice (extremely rare)

16.11 COMPARISON OF THE DIFFERENT TREATMENTS FOR THE HYPERTHYROIDISM OF GRAVES' DISEASE

Management	Indications	Contraindications	Disadvantages/complications
Antithyroid drugs e.g. carbimazole	First episode in patients < 40 yrs	Hypersensitivity Breastfeeding (propylthiouracil suitable)	> 50% relapse rate usually within 2 years of stopping drug
Subtotal thyroidectomy	1. Recurrent hyperthyroidism after course of antithyroid drugs in patients < 40 yrs 2. Initial treatment in males with large goitres and in those with severe hyperthyroidism, i.e. total T_3 > 9.0 nmol/l 3. Poor drug compliance	Previous thyroid surgery Dependence upon voice, e.g. opera singer, lecturer[1]	Transient hypocalcaemia (10%) Hypoparathyroidism (1%) Recurrent laryngeal nerve palsy[1] (1%)
Radio-iodine	1. Patients > 40 yrs[2] 2. Recurrence following surgery irrespective of age 3. Other serious comorbidity	Pregnancy or planned pregnancy within 6 months of treatment	Hypothyroidism, approx. 40% in first year, 80% after 15 years Most likely treatment to result in exacerbation of exophthalmos

[1] It is not only vocal cord palsy due to recurrent laryngeal nerve damage which alters the voice following thyroid surgery; the superior laryngeal nerves are frequently transected and result in minor changes in voice quality.
[2] In certain parts of the world, ^{131}I is used more liberally and prescribed for young women in the 20–40 age group.

GRAVES' DISEASE—antithyroid drug therapy **EBM**

'Remission rates in patients with Graves' disease are not improved by combining thyroxine with antithyroid drugs (block and replace therapy).'

- McIver B, Rae P, Beckett GJ, et al. Lack of effect of thyroxine in patients with Graves' hyperthyroidism who are treated with an antithyroid drug. N Engl J Med 1996; 334:220–224.

Further information: 🖥 www.endocrinology.org

Subtotal thyroidectomy

Patients must be rendered euthyroid before operation. The antithyroid drug is stopped 2 weeks before surgery and replaced by potassium iodide (Lugol's solution) 60 mg 8-hourly orally. This maintains euthyroidism in the short term by inhibiting thyroid hormone release and reduces the size and vascularity of the gland, making surgery technically easier. Complications of surgery are rare (see Box 16.11). One year after surgery 80% of patients are euthyroid, 15% are permanently hypothyroid and 5% remain thyrotoxic. Thyroid failure within 6 months of operation may be temporary. Long-term follow-up of patients treated surgically is necessary, as the late development of hypothyroidism and recurrence of thyrotoxicosis are well recognised.

Radioactive iodine

^{131}I acts either by destroying functioning thyroid cells or by inhibiting their ability to replicate. The variable radiosensitivity of the gland means that the choice of dose is empirical. In most centres 185–370 MBq (5–10 mCi) is given orally, the dose depending upon clinical assessment of goitre size. This regimen is effective in 75% of patients within 4–12 weeks. During the lag period symptoms can be controlled by a β-adrenoceptor antagonist (β-blocker) or, in more severe cases, by carbimazole starting 48 hours after radio-iodine administration. If hyperthyroidism persists after 12–24 weeks, a further dose of ^{131}I should be employed. The disadvantage of ^{131}I treatment is that the majority of patients eventually develop hypothyroidism and long-term follow-up is therefore necessary.

Beta-blockers

A non-selective β-blocker, such as propranolol (160 mg daily) or nadolol (40–80 mg daily), will alleviate but not abolish symptoms of hyperthyroidism within 24–48 hours. Beta-blockers cannot be recommended for long-term treatment, but they are extremely useful in the short term, e.g. for patients awaiting hospital consultation or following ^{131}I therapy. Propranolol alone or in combination with iodine has been used in the preparation of patients for subtotal thyroidectomy, but this treatment cannot be recommended as standard practice.

Management of ophthalmopathy

The majority of patients require no treatment other than reassurance. Lid retraction will usually resolve when the patient becomes euthyroid, and exophthalmos usually lessens gradually over a period of 2–3 years. For those with symptomatic ophthalmopathy, methylcellulose eye drops will counter the gritty discomfort of dry eyes, and tinted glasses or side shields attached to spectacle frames will reduce the excessive lacrimation triggered by sun or wind. Corneal ulceration is an indication for a lid-lengthening procedure. Persistent diplopia can be corrected by extraocular muscle surgery but this should be delayed until the degree of diplopia is stable.

Papilloedema, loss of visual acuity or visual field defect requires urgent treatment with prednisolone 60 mg daily if blindness is to be prevented. Close cooperation between the endocrinologist and ophthalmologist is necessary and, if significant improvement is not evident within 7–10 days, orbital decompression is indicated. Radiotherapy to the orbits in association with prednisolone may be effective in some patients.

GRAVES' OPHTHALMOPATHY—effect of antithyroid therapy **EBM**

'Development or worsening of mild ophthalmopathy in patients with Graves' disease is more common following ^{131}I administration than with surgery or antithyroid drugs.'

- Tallstedt L, Lundell G, Torring O, et al. Occurrence of ophthalmopathy after treatment for Graves' hyperthyroidism. N Engl J Med 1992; 326:1733–1738.
- Bartelena L, Marcocci C, Bogazzi F, et al. Relation between therapy for hyperthyroidism and the course of Graves' ophthalmopathy. N Engl J Med 1998; 338:73–78.

Further information: 🖥 www.endocrinology.org

Management of dermopathy

The pretibial myxoedema of Graves' disease rarely requires to be treated. Local injections of triamcinolone or the application of betamethasone ointment under occlusive dressings may be effective.

TOXIC MULTINODULAR GOITRE

Like Graves' disease, this form of hyperthyroidism is more common in women. The mean age of presentation is 60 years. Thyroid hormone levels are usually only slightly elevated but, as an older age group is affected, cardiovascular features such as atrial fibrillation or cardiac failure tend to predominate. Treatment is usually with a large dose of ^{131}I (555–1850 MBq, 15–50 mCi), as the gland is relatively resistant to radiation. Hypothyroidism is less common than after treatment of Graves' disease. If there is tracheal compression or retrosternal extension of the goitre, partial thyroidectomy is indicated. Long-term treatment with antithyroid drugs is not appropriate as relapse is invariable after drug withdrawal.

TOXIC ADENOMA

The presence of a toxic solitary nodule is the cause of less than 5% of all cases of hyperthyroidism. The nodule is a follicular adenoma which autonomously secretes excess thyroid hormones and inhibits endogenous TSH secretion with subsequent atrophy of the rest of the thyroid gland. The adenoma is usually greater than 3 cm in diameter. In some cases spontaneous resolution of hyperthyroidism has occurred as a result of infarction of the adenoma.

Most patients are female and over 40 years of age. Although most nodules are palpable, the diagnosis can be made with certainty only by isotope scanning (see Fig. 16.6C). The hyperthyroidism is usually mild and in almost 50% of patients the plasma T_3 alone is elevated (T_3-thyrotoxicosis). Treatment is by hemithyroidectomy or

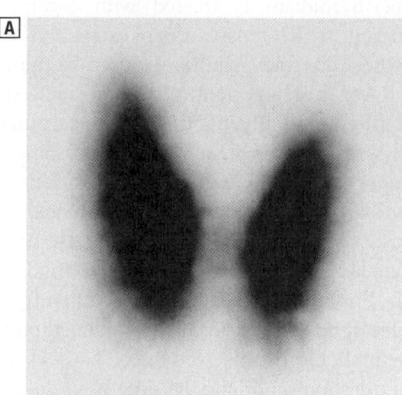

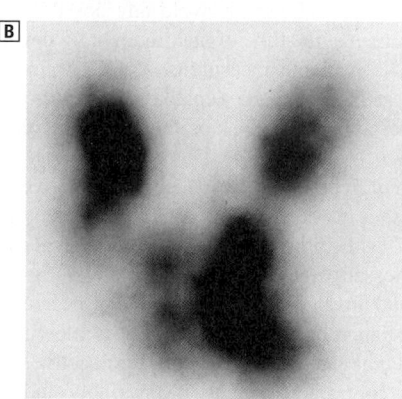

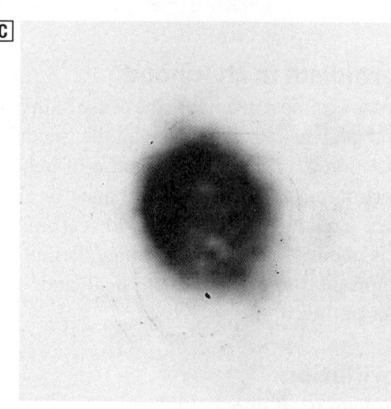

Fig. 16.6 ^{99m}Technetium scans of patients with hyperthyroidism. A Graves' disease, showing diffuse uptake of isotope. B Multinodular goitre with maximum activity confined to individual nodules; such an appearance is not always associated with a palpable thyroid. C Right-sided toxic adenoma with lack of uptake of isotope by normal dormant gland due to suppression of serum TSH. Isotope thyroid scanning is of value in determining the cause of hyperthyroidism in patients with no palpable goitre or other indicators such as exophthalmos or pretibial myxoedema.

by ^{131}I (555–1110 MBq, 15–30 mCi). Permanent hypothyroidism does not occur following surgery and is unusual after treatment with ^{131}I, since the atrophic cells surrounding the nodule will have received little or no irradiation.

HYPERTHYROIDISM ASSOCIATED WITH A LOW IODINE UPTAKE

In patients with hyperthyroidism the thyroid uptake of ^{131}I is usually high but a low or negligible uptake of iodine occurs in some rarer causes (see Box 16.6, p. 690). If a radioactive iodine uptake test is not routinely performed in patients with thyrotoxicosis who do not have obvious Graves' disease or nodular goitre, the correct diagnosis may not be made and inappropriate treatment may be given.

Subacute (de Quervain's) thyroiditis

Subacute thyroiditis is a virus-induced (Coxsackie, mumps or adenovirus) inflammation of the thyroid gland which results in release of colloid and its constituents into the circulation.

This form of hyperthyroidism is characterised by pain in the region of the thyroid gland which may radiate to the angle of the jaw and the ears and is made worse by swallowing, coughing and movement of the neck. The thyroid is usually palpably enlarged and tender. Systemic upset is common. Affected patients are usually females aged 20–40 years.

Thyroid hormone levels are raised for 4–6 weeks until the pre-formed colloid is depleted. The iodine uptake is low because the damaged follicular cells are unable to trap iodine and because endogenous TSH secretion is suppressed. Low-titre thyroid autoantibodies appear transiently in the serum, and the erythrocyte sedimentation rate (ESR) is usually raised. The hyperthyroidism is followed by a period of hypothyroidism which is usually asymptomatic, and finally by full recovery of thyroid function within 4–6 months. The pain and systemic upset usually respond to simple measures such as aspirin or other non-steroidal anti-inflammatory drugs. Occasionally, however, it may be necessary to prescribe prednisolone 40 mg daily for 3–4 weeks. The hyperthyroidism is mild and treatment with propranolol 160 mg daily is usually adequate. Antithyroid drugs are of no benefit.

Post-partum thyroiditis

The maternal immune response which is modified during pregnancy to allow survival of the fetal homograft is enhanced after delivery and may unmask previously unrecognised subclinical autoimmune thyroid disease. Surveys have shown that transient biochemical disturbances of thyroid function, i.e. hyperthyroidism, hypothyroidism, and hyperthyroidism followed by hypothyroidism, lasting a few weeks occur in 5–10% of women within 6 months of delivery. Those affected are likely to possess antithyroid peroxidase (microsomal) antibodies in the serum in early pregnancy. Thyroid biopsy shows a lymphocytic thyroiditis. Symptoms of thyroid dysfunction are rare and there is no association between postnatal depression and abnormal thyroid function tests. However, symptomatic hyperthyroidism presenting for the first time within 6 months of childbirth is unlikely to be due to Graves' disease, and the diagnosis of post-partum thyroiditis can be confirmed by a negligible radio-iodine uptake.

If treatment of the hyperthyroid phase is necessary, a β-blocker should be prescribed and not an antithyroid drug. Post-partum thyroiditis tends to recur after subsequent pregnancies and eventually patients progress over a period of years to permanent hypothyroidism.

A similar painless form of thyroiditis, unrelated to pregnancy, has been increasingly recognised in North America and Japan, and accounts in these countries for up to 20% of all cases of hyperthyroidism.

Iodine-induced hyperthyroidism

The administration of iodine, either in prophylactic iodinisation programmes in iodine-deficient parts of the world or as a radiographic contrast medium, may result in the development of hyperthyroidism which is usually mild and self-limiting. Affected individuals are thought to have underlying thyroid autonomy, such as nodular goitre or Graves' disease in remission. This form of hyperthyroidism is now most often seen as a result of treatment with the anti-arrhythmic agent, amiodarone, which contains significant amounts of iodine. In some patients amiodarone causes a thyroiditis-like picture and mild transient hyperthyroidism which may require treatment with β-blockers. Most patients have underlying thyroid autonomy where severe thyrotoxicosis may be precipitated. Such patients may even present for the first time up to 6 months after the drug has been stopped, due to its slow release from adipose tissue. Treatment of thyroid autonomy is with an antithyroid drug for as long as amiodarone is prescribed.

Assessment of thyroid function may be difficult in patients taking amiodarone, as the drug inhibits the peripheral conversion of T_4 to T_3. As a result, in euthyroid individuals it is not uncommon to record markedly elevated serum T_4 concentrations and even suppressed serum TSH, but serum T_3 is usually in the lower part of the normal range. In those developing hyperthyroidism, serum T_3 is clearly elevated but, if the value is equivocal, the decision to treat will depend upon the presence of other features of thyroid disease, such as goitre and ophthalmopathy.

Factitious hyperthyroidism

This uncommon condition occurs when someone takes excessive amounts of a thyroid hormone preparation, most often thyroxine. The exogenous T_4 suppresses pituitary TSH secretion and hence iodine uptake, serum thyroglobulin and release of endogenous thyroid hormones. As a result the T_4:T_3 ratio (approximately 30:1 in conventional hyperthyroidism) is increased to approximately 70:1 because circulating T_3 in factitious thyrotoxicosis is derived exclusively from the peripheral monodeiodination of T_4. The combination of negligible iodine uptake, high T_4:T_3 ratio and a low or undetectable thyroglobulin is diagnostic and has made what was often a difficult diagnosis much simpler. The condition often reflects underlying psychological or psychiatric illness that may require specialist help (see p. 268).

SPECIAL PROBLEMS OF HYPERTHYROIDISM

Hyperthyroidism in pregnancy

The coexistence of pregnancy and hyperthyroidism is unusual as anovulatory cycles are common in thyrotoxic patients and autoimmune disease tends to remit during pregnancy. The hyperthyroidism is almost always caused by Graves' disease.

The hyperthyroidism is treated with carbimazole or propylthiouracil, which crosses the placenta and also treats the fetus, whose thyroid gland is exposed to the action of maternal TRAb. It is important to use the smallest dose of antithyroid drug (optimally less than 15 mg carbimazole per day) which will maintain maternal (and presumably fetal) free hormones and TSH within their respective normal ranges in order to avoid fetal hypothyroidism and goitre. An association has been claimed between the use of carbimazole in pregnancy and a skin defect in the child known as aplasia cutis. For this reason some physicians prefer to advise propylthiouracil before and during any planned pregnancy.

The patient should be reviewed every 4 weeks and it is a wise precaution to discontinue the drug 4 weeks before the expected date of delivery to avoid any possibility of fetal hypothyroidism at the time of maximum brain development. If the assay is available, measurement of TRAb in the maternal serum at this stage is valuable; a high titre identifies those fetuses at particular risk of developing neonatal hyperthyroidism.

If maternal hyperthyroidism occurs after delivery and the patient wishes to continue breastfeeding, propylthiouracil (see p. 695) is the drug of choice as it is excreted in the milk to a much lesser extent than carbimazole.

If subtotal thyroidectomy is necessary because of poor drug compliance or hypersensitivity, it is most safely performed in the middle trimester. Radioactive iodine is absolutely contraindicated as it invariably induces fetal hypothyroidism.

Hyperthyroidism in childhood

Graves' disease is almost invariably the cause of thyrotoxicosis in childhood and usually presents in the second decade. Medical attention may be sought because of behaviour disorders, deteriorating academic performance or a premature growth spurt. Treatment should be with carbimazole until the patient is about 18 years of age in an attempt to guarantee the important stages in the physical and educational development of the child.

Atrial fibrillation

Hyperthyroidism is an important cause of atrial fibrillation. Characteristically, the ventricular rate is little influenced by digoxin but responds to the addition of a β-blocker. The dysrhythmia is present in about 10% of all patients with thyrotoxicosis but the incidence increases with age so that almost half of all males over the age of 60 are affected (see Fig. 16.7). It is increasingly recognised that subclinical hyperthyroidism may be a risk factor for atrial fibrillation. Cardioversion will establish stable sinus rhythm in up to 50% of patients but should not be contemplated until serum

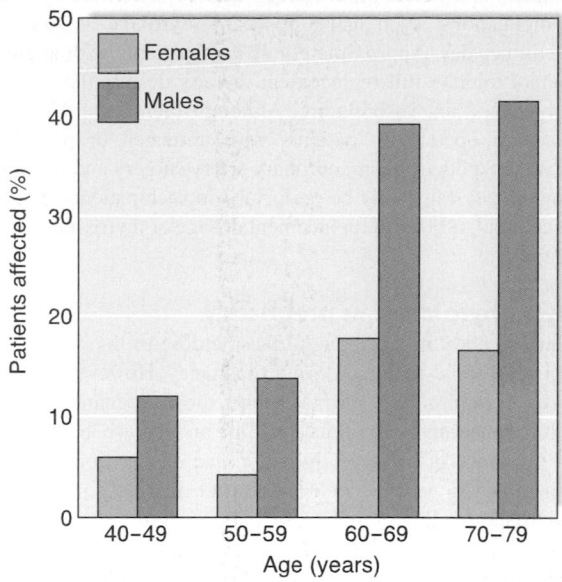

Fig. 16.7 Age-related incidence of atrial fibrillation in patients with hyperthyroidism.

thyroid hormone and TSH concentrations have been restored to normal. Anticoagulation is required with warfarin unless contraindicated, in which case aspirin should be used (see p. 402).

Hyperthyroid crisis

This is a rare and life-threatening increase in the severity of the clinical features of hyperthyroidism. The most prominent signs are fever, agitation, confusion, tachycardia or atrial fibrillation and, in the older patient, cardiac failure. It is a medical emergency and, despite early recognition and treatment, the mortality rate is 10%. Thyrotoxic crisis is most commonly precipitated by infection in a patient with previously unrecognised or inadequately treated hyperthyroidism. It may also develop shortly after subtotal thyroidectomy in an ill-prepared patient or within a few days of ^{131}I therapy when acute irradiation damage may lead to a transient rise in serum thyroid hormone levels.

Patients should be rehydrated and given a broad-spectrum antibiotic. Propranolol is rapidly effective orally (80 mg 6-hourly) or intravenously (1–5 mg 6-hourly). Sodium iopodate 500 mg per day orally will restore serum T_3 levels to normal in 48–72 hours. This is a radiographic contrast medium which not only inhibits the release of thyroid hormones, but also reduces the conversion of T_4 to T_3 and is therefore more effective than potassium iodide or Lugol's solution. Oral carbimazole 40–60 mg daily inhibits the synthesis of new thyroid hormone. If the patient is unconscious or uncooperative, carbimazole can be administered rectally with good effect, but no preparation is available for parenteral use. Sodium iopodate and propranolol can be withdrawn after 10–14 days and the patient maintained on carbimazole.

Subclinical hyperthyroidism
See page 693.

HYPOTHYROIDISM

SPONTANEOUS ATROPHIC HYPOTHYROIDISM

This form of primary hypothyroidism increases in incidence with age and, like Graves' disease and Hashimoto's thyroiditis, is an organ-specific autoimmune disorder. There is destructive lymphoid infiltration of the thyroid, ultimately leading to fibrosis and atrophy. There is also evidence for the presence of TSH-receptor antibodies which block the effects of endogenous TSH. In some patients there is a history of Graves' disease treated with antithyroid drugs 10–20 years earlier and, very occasionally, patients with this form of hypothyroidism develop Graves' disease. As with any of the immunologically mediated thyroid disorders, patients are at risk of developing other organ-specific autoimmune conditions such as type 1 diabetes mellitus, pernicious anaemia and Addison's disease, and autoimmune disease is not uncommon in first- and second-degree relatives (see p. 687).

Investigations

Serum T_4 is low and TSH raised (see pp. 691–692). Antibodies against thyroid peroxidase may be detected. In symptomatic patients no further investigation is necessary. If the clinical features suggest a transient cause of hypothyroidism (such as non-thyroidal illness, neck pain suggesting subacute thyroiditis or recent pregnancy), repeat measurements after a few weeks may be required before embarking on long-term thyroxine therapy.

Management

Hypothyroidism should be treated with thyroxine; it is customary to start slowly and a dose of 50 μg per day should be given for 3 weeks, increasing thereafter to 100 μg per day for a further 3 weeks and finally to 150 μg per day. Thyroxine should always be taken as a single daily dose as it has a plasma half-life of approximately 7 days.

Patients feel better within 2–3 weeks. Reduction in weight and periorbital puffiness occurs quickly, but the restoration of skin and hair texture and resolution of any effusions may take 3–6 months.

EBM

HYPOTHYROIDISM—thyroid hormone therapy

'Neuropsychological testing has shown that some patients with primary hypothyroidism benefit from treatment with a combination of T_4 and T_3 when compared to T_4 alone. However, no satisfactory synthetic combination preparation currently exists and animal thyroid extract has too variable a potency to be recommended.'

- Bunevicius R, Kazanavicius G, Zalinkevicius R, Prange AJ. Comparative effects of thyroxine versus thyroxine plus triiodothyronine in patients with hypothyroidism. N Engl J Med 1999; 340:424–429.
- Toft AD. Thyroid hormone replacement—one hormone or two? N Engl J Med 1999; 340:469–470.

Further information: 🖥 www.endocrinology.org

Monitoring therapy

The correct dose of thyroxine in most patients is that which restores serum TSH to the lower part of the reference range when serum T_4 will be normal or even slightly raised. In some patients a sense of well-being is only achieved by taking an extra 25–50 μg of thyroxine, resulting in a suppressed serum TSH concentration. This is acceptable only if serum T_3 is unequivocally normal.

Patients often fail to take long-term medication in the recommended dose and thyroxine is no exception. It is, therefore, important to measure thyroid function every 1–2 years once the dose of thyroxine is stabilised and at each visit to reinforce the need for regular medication. In some poorly compliant patients thyroxine is taken diligently or even in excess for a few days prior to a clinic visit, resulting in the seemingly anomalous combination of a high serum T_4 and high TSH.

Occasionally, patients who have been taking the same dose of thyroxine for some time show biochemical evidence of over-treatment or under-treatment. The various causes of a change in requirements are shown in Box 16.13.

16.13 SITUATIONS IN WHICH AN ADJUSTMENT OF THE DOSE OF THYROXINE MAY BE NECESSARY	
Increased dose required	
Use of other medication Phenobarbital Phenytoin Carbamazepine Rifampicin Sertraline* Chloroquine*	Increase thyroxine clearance
Colestyramine Sucralfate Aluminium hydroxide Ferrous sulphate Dietary fibre supplements Calcium carbonate	Interfere with intestinal absorption
Pregnancy or oestrogen therapy	Increases concentration of serum thyroxine-binding globulin
After surgical or ^{131}**I ablation of Graves' disease**	Reduces thyroidal secretion with time
Malabsorption, e.g. coeliac disease	
Decreased dose required	
Ageing	Decreases thyroxine clearance
Graves' disease developing in patient with long-standing primary hypothyroidism	Switch from production of blocking to stimulating TSH-receptor antibodies
* Mechanism not fully established.	

SPECIAL PROBLEMS OF HYPOTHYROIDISM

Ischaemic heart disease

Around 5% of patients with long-standing hypothyroidism complain of angina at presentation or develop it during treatment with thyroxine. Although angina may remain unchanged in severity or paradoxically disappear with restoration of metabolic rate, exacerbation of myocardial ischaemia, infarction and sudden death are well-recognised complications, even using doses of thyroxine as low as 25 μg per day. Approximately 40% of patients with angina cannot tolerate full replacement therapy despite the use of β-blockers and vasodilators. Although there is still reluctance to operate on patients with untreated or partially treated hypothyroidism, coronary artery surgery and balloon angioplasty can safely be performed in such patients and, if successful, allow full replacement dosage of thyroxine in the majority.

Hypothyroidism in pregnancy

Until recently it was thought that the dose of thyroxine did not need to be changed during pregnancy. However, on the basis of serum TSH measurements most pregnant women with primary hypothyroidism require an increase in the dose of thyroxine of some 50 μg daily. One explanation for this phenomenon is the well-recognised increase in serum thyroxine-binding globulin concentration during pregnancy, resulting in a decrease in serum free thyroid hormone concentrations which cannot be compensated for by thyroidal secretion. Serum TSH and free T_4 should be measured during each trimester and the dose of thyroxine adjusted to maintain a normal TSH.

Myxoedema coma

This is a rare presentation of hypothyroidism in which there is a depressed level of consciousness, usually in an elderly patient who appears myxoedematous. Body temperature may be as low as 25°C, convulsions are not uncommon and cerebrospinal fluid (CSF) pressure and protein content are raised. The mortality rate is 50% and survival depends upon early recognition and treatment of hypothyroidism and other factors contributing to the altered consciousness level, e.g. drugs such as phenothiazines, cardiac failure, pneumonia, dilutional hyponatraemia, hypoxaemia and hypercapnia due to hypoventilation.

Myxoedema coma is a medical emergency and treatment must begin before biochemical confirmation of the diagnosis. Thyroxine is not usually available for parenteral use and triiodothyronine is given as an intravenous bolus of 20 μg followed by 20 μg 8-hourly until there is sustained clinical improvement. In survivors there is a rise in body temperature within 24 hours and, after 48–72 hours, it is usually possible to substitute oral thyroxine in a dose of 50 μg per day. Unless it is apparent that the patient has primary hypothyroidism, e.g. thyroidectomy scar or goitre, the thyroid failure should be assumed to be secondary to hypothalamic or pituitary disease and treatment given with hydrocortisone sodium succinate 100 mg i.m. 8-hourly, pending the results of T_4, TSH and cortisol concentrations (see p. 727). Other measures include slow rewarming (see p. 332), cautious use of intravenous fluids, broad-spectrum antibiotics and high-flow oxygen. Occasionally, assisted ventilation may be necessary.

Inappropriate thyroxine therapy

In some patients treatment with thyroxine may have been started in the past, without biochemical confirmation of the diagnosis, for a variety of complaints such as obesity, tiredness or alopecia, or may have been given for many years to patients in whom thyroid failure could have been short-lived, e.g. post-partum thyroiditis. Thyroxine should be stopped and serum T_4 and TSH concentrations measured 4–6 weeks later. This period allows for any thyroxine-induced suppression of pituitary thyrotrophs to recover and a biochemical distinction to be made between primary and secondary hypothyroidism.

GOITROUS HYPOTHYROIDISM

The following conditions are not always associated with hypothyroidism and should therefore be included in the differential diagnosis of a euthyroid patient with goitre.

Hashimoto's thyroiditis

This is the most common cause of goitrous hypothyroidism. It typically affects 20–60-year-old women who present with a small or moderately sized diffuse goitre which is characteristically firm or rubbery in consistency. The goitre may be soft, however, and impossible to differentiate from simple goitre by palpation alone. Thyroid status depends upon the relative degrees of lymphocytic infiltration, fibrosis and follicular cell hyperplasia within the gland but 25% of patients are hypothyroid at presentation. In the remainder, serum T_4 is normal and TSH normal or raised but these patients are at risk of developing overt hypothyroidism in future years. In 90% of patients with Hashimoto's thyroiditis thyroid peroxidase antibodies are present in the serum. In those under the age of 20 years the antinuclear factor (ANF) may also be positive.

Thyroxine therapy is indicated not only for hypothyroidism but also for goitre shrinkage. In this context the dose of thyroxine should be sufficient to suppress serum TSH to undetectable levels without inducing hyperthyroidism (usually 150–200 μg daily).

Drug-induced hypothyroidism

Lithium carbonate

This is widely used for the treatment of bipolar affective disorder (see p. 263). Like iodide, lithium inhibits the release of thyroid hormones (see Fig. 16.3, p. 689). Although the most common evidence of thyroid dysfunction is a raised serum TSH, some (usually those with underlying auto-immune thyroiditis) develop goitre and hypothyroidism.

Iodine

When taken for prolonged periods iodine may cause goitrous hypothyroidism in patients with underlying auto-immune thyroiditis. This is usually seen in patients with chronic respiratory diseases given expectorants containing potassium iodide, or in those receiving amiodarone, which contains a significant amount of iodine.

Iodine deficiency

In certain parts of the world, such as the Andes, the Himalayas and central Africa, where there is dietary iodine deficiency, thyroid enlargement is common (more than 10%

of the population) and is known as endemic goitre. Most patients are euthyroid and have normal or raised TSH levels. In general the more severe the iodine deficiency, the greater the incidence of hypothyroidism.

Dyshormonogenesis

Dyshormonogenesis is an unusual genetically determined defect in thyroid hormone synthesis. The mode of inheritance is autosomal recessive. Although several forms have been described, the most common results from deficiency of the intrathyroidal peroxidase enzyme. Homozygous individuals present with congenital hypothyroidism; heterozygotes present in the first two decades of life with goitre, normal thyroid hormone levels and a raised TSH. The combination of dyshormonogenetic goitre and nerve deafness is known as Pendred's syndrome.

TRANSIENT HYPOTHYROIDISM

This is often observed during the first 6 months after subtotal thyroidectomy or ^{131}I treatment of Graves' disease, in the post-thyrotoxic phase of subacute thyroiditis and in post-partum thyroiditis (see Fig. 16.8). In these conditions thyroxine treatment should not be necessary as the patient is usually asymptomatic during the short period of thyroid failure. In some neonates transplacental passage of TSH-receptor-blocking antibodies from a mother with auto-immune thyroid disease is a cause of hypothyroidism which, like neonatal thyrotoxicosis, is temporary.

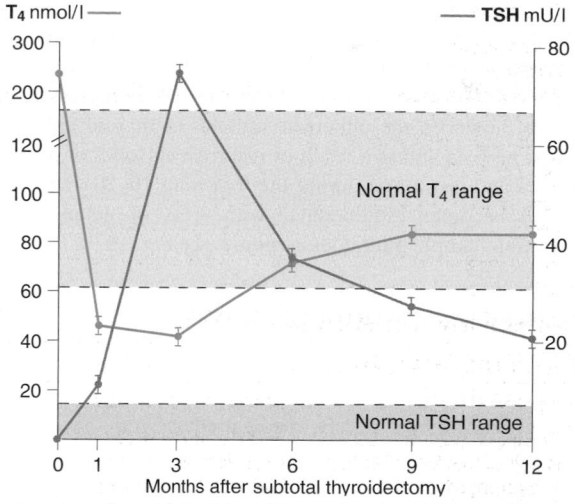

Fig. 16.8 Total T_4 and TSH levels before and after subtotal thyroidectomy in a series of patients with temporary hypothyroidism.

CONGENITAL HYPOTHYROIDISM

It has long been recognised that early treatment with thyroxine is essential to prevent irreversible brain damage in children with congenital hypothyroidism. Thyroid failure, however, is difficult to diagnose clinically in the first few weeks of life. Routine screening of TSH levels in blood spot samples obtained 5–7 days after birth has revealed an incidence of approximately 1 in 3000, resulting either from thyroid agenesis, ectopic or hypoplastic glands, or from dyshormonogenesis. Congenital hypothyroidism is thus six times more common than phenylketonuria. It is now possible to start thyroid replacement therapy within 2 weeks of birth. Developmental assessment of infants treated at this early stage has revealed no differences between cases and controls in most children.

SIMPLE GOITRE

This is the term used to describe diffuse or multinodular enlargement of the thyroid which occurs sporadically and is of unknown aetiology. It is likely, however, that suboptimal dietary iodine intake, minor degrees of dyshormonogenesis and stimuli such as epidermal growth factor and growth-stimulating immunoglobulins are important in the development of simple goitre. Affected patients are euthyroid, are usually female and often have a family history of goitre.

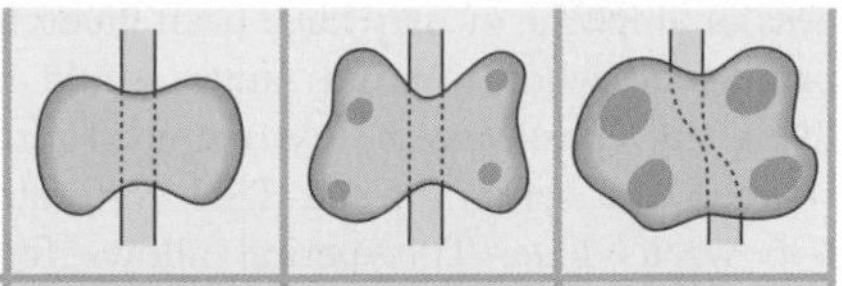

SIMPLE DIFFUSE GOITRE

This form of goitre usually presents between the ages of 15 and 25 years, often during pregnancy, and tends to be noticed not by the patient but by friends and relatives. Occasionally, there is a tight sensation in the neck, particularly when swallowing. The goitre is soft and symmetrical and the thyroid is enlarged to two or three times its normal size. There is no tenderness, lymphadenopathy or overlying bruit. Concentrations of T_3, T_4 and TSH are normal and no thyroid autoantibodies are detected in the serum. No treatment is necessary and in most cases the goitre regresses. In some, however, the unknown stimulus to thyroid enlargement persists and as a result of recurrent episodes of hyperplasia and involution during the following 10–20 years the gland becomes multinodular with areas of autonomous function (simple multinodular goitre; see Fig. 16.9).

SIMPLE MULTINODULAR GOITRE

Presentation is rare before middle age. The patient may have been aware of a goitre for many years, perhaps slowly increasing in size. Rarely, medical advice may have been sought because of painful swelling lasting a few days caused by haemorrhage into a nodule or cyst. The goitre is nodular or lobulated on palpation and may extend retrosternally. Very large goitres may cause mediastinal compression with stridor, dysphagia and obstruction of the superior vena cava. Hoarseness due to recurrent laryngeal nerve palsy can occur but is far more suggestive of thyroid carcinoma. Serum T_3 and T_4 are normal and in the majority are associated with normal TSH. In approximately 25%, thyroid hormone levels are in the upper part of their respective normal ranges and TSH is undetectable (subclinical hyperthyroidism, see

Age (in years)	15–25	35–55	> 55
Goitre	Diffuse	Nodular	Nodular
Tracheal compression/ deviation	No	Minimal	Yes
T_3, T_4	Normal	Normal	Raised
TSH	Normal	Normal or undetectable	Undetectable

Fig. 16.9 Natural history of simple goitre.

p. 693). CT of the thoracic inlet will show tracheal displacement or compression, intrathyroidal calcification and the extent of retrosternal extension. A flow-volume loop (see p. 493) will detect cases with significant tracheal compression.

If the goitre is small, no treatment is necessary other than annual review, as the natural history is progression to a toxic multinodular goitre. Partial thyroidectomy is indicated for large goitres which cause mediastinal compression or which are cosmetically unattractive. [131]I can result in a significant reduction in thyroid size after 1–2 years and may be of value in elderly patients. Unfortunately, recurrence 10–20 years later is not uncommon and is not prevented by thyroxine, which may serve only to aggravate any associated hyperthyroidism.

SOLITARY THYROID NODULE

In those who seek medical attention it is important to determine whether the nodule is benign, e.g. cyst or colloid nodule, or malignant. With the exception of haemorrhage into a cyst when thyroid enlargement is of rapid onset and painful, or the presence of cervical lymphadenopathy which is highly suggestive of carcinoma, it is rarely possible to make this distinction on clinical grounds alone. However, a solitary nodule presenting in childhood or adolescence, particularly if there is a past history of head and neck irradiation, or presenting in the elderly should raise the suspicion of malignancy. Very occasionally, a secondary deposit from a renal, breast or lung carcinoma presents as a painful, rapidly growing solitary thyroid nodule.

Investigations

The most useful is fine-needle aspiration of the nodule. This is performed in the outpatient clinic using a standard 21-gauge venepuncture needle and a 20 ml syringe. Aspiration may be therapeutic in the small proportion of patients in whom the swelling is a pure cyst, although recurrence on more than one occasion is an indication for surgery. Usually, two to three aspirates are taken from the nodule. Cytological examination will differentiate benign (80%) from suspicious or definitely malignant nodules (20%), of which half are confirmed as cancer at surgery. The advantage of fine-needle aspiration over long-established tests such as isotope and ultrasound scanning is that a much higher proportion of patients avoid surgery. The limitation of the method is that it cannot differentiate between follicular adenoma and carcinoma.

It is important to measure serum T_3, T_4 and TSH in all patients with a solitary thyroid nodule. The finding of undetectable TSH is very suggestive of an autonomously functioning thyroid adenoma which can only be confirmed by thyroid isotope scanning (see Fig. 16.6, p. 697), and is for practical purposes always benign.

MALIGNANT TUMOURS

Primary thyroid malignancy is rare, accounting for less than 1% of all carcinomas, and has a prevalence of 25 per million. As shown in Box 16.14, it can be classified according to the cell type of origin. With the exception of medullary carcinoma, thyroid cancer is always more common in females.

DIFFERENTIATED CARCINOMA

In most patients, presentation is with a palpable solitary nodule.

Papillary carcinoma

This is the most common of the malignant thyroid tumours and accounts for 90% of irradiation-induced thyroid cancer. It may be multifocal, and spread is to regional lymph nodes.

Some patients present with cervical lymphadenopathy and no apparent thyroid enlargement, and the primary lesion may be less than 10 mm in diameter.

Follicular carcinoma

This is always a single encapsulated lesion. Spread to cervical lymph nodes is rare. Metastases are blood-borne and are most often found in bone, lungs and brain.

Management

This is usually by total thyroidectomy followed by a large dose of ^{131}I (3000 MBq, ~80 mCi) in order to ablate any remaining thyroid tissue, normal or malignant. Thereafter, long-term treatment with thyroxine in a dose sufficient to suppress TSH (usually 150–200 µg daily) is important, as there is some evidence that differentiated thyroid carcinomas may be TSH-dependent. Follow-up is by measurement of serum thyroglobulin which should be low or undetectable in patients taking a suppressive dose of thyroxine. A level in

---

DIFFERENTIATED THYROID CANCER—identifying recurrent or metastatic disease `EBM`

'Recombinant human TSH administration is a safe and effective means of stimulating radio-iodine uptake in patients undergoing evaluation for thyroid cancer persistence and recurrence, and compares favourably with thyroid hormone withdrawal.'

- Haugen BK, Pacini F, Reiners C, et al. A comparison of recombinant human thyrotropin and thyroid hormone withdrawal for the detection of thyroid remnant or cancer. J Clin Endocrinol Metab 1999; 84:3877–3885.

Further information: www.endocrinology.org

---

excess of 15 µg/l is strongly suggestive of tumour recurrence or metastases which may be detected by whole-body scanning with ^{131}I and may respond to further radio-iodine therapy. For meaningful results, isotope scanning requires serum TSH concentrations to be elevated (> 20 mU/l). In the past this has been achieved by stopping thyroxine for 4–6 weeks. By using recombinant human TSH to stimulate radio-iodine

---

16.14 MALIGNANT THYROID TUMOURS

Origin of tumour	Type of tumour	Frequency (%)	Usual age of presentation (years)	Approximate 20-year survival (%)
Follicular cells	Differentiated carcinoma			
	Papillary	70	20–40	95
	Follicular	10	40–60	60
	Undifferentiated carcinoma			
	Anaplastic	5	> 60	< 1
Parafollicular C cells	Medullary carcinoma	5–10	> 40*	50
Lymphocytes	Lymphoma	5–10	> 60	10

* Patients with medullary carcinoma as part of multiple endocrine neoplasia type II (see p. 688) may present in childhood.

uptake, thyroxine does not need to be discontinued and therefore symptomatic hypothyroidism is avoided.

Prognosis

Most patients have an excellent prognosis when treated appropriately. Those under 50 years of age with papillary carcinoma can anticipate a near-normal life expectancy if the tumour is less than 2 cm in diameter, confined to the thyroid and cervical nodes, and of low-grade malignancy histologically. Even for patients with distant metastases at presentation, the 10-year survival is approximately 40%.

ANAPLASTIC CARCINOMA AND LYMPHOMA

These two conditions are difficult to distinguish clinically but this is made easier with cytological examination or cutting needle biopsy. Patients are usually elderly women in whom there is rapid thyroid enlargement over 2–3 months. The goitre is hard and symmetrical. There is usually stridor due to tracheal compression and hoarseness due to recurrent laryngeal nerve palsy. There is no effective treatment of anaplastic carcinoma although radiotherapy may afford temporary relief of mediastinal compression. The prognosis for lymphoma, which may arise from pre-existing Hashimoto's thyroiditis, is better. External irradiation often produces dramatic goitre shrinkage and, when combined with chemotherapy, may result in survival for 5 years or more.

MEDULLARY CARCINOMA

This tumour arises from the parafollicular C cells of the thyroid. In addition to calcitonin, the tumour may secrete 5-hydroxytryptamine (5-HT, serotonin), various peptides of the tachykinin family, ACTH and prostaglandins. As a consequence carcinoid syndrome (see p. 801) and Cushing's syndrome (see p. 722) have been described in association with medullary carcinoma.

Patients usually present in middle age with a firm thyroid mass. Cervical lymphadenopathy is common, but distant metastases are rare initially. Serum calcitonin levels are raised and are useful in monitoring response to treatment. Despite the very high levels of calcitonin found in some patients, hypocalcaemia is extremely rare.

Treatment is by total thyroidectomy with removal of affected cervical nodes. Since the C cells do not concentrate iodine there is no role for ^{131}I therapy. Prognosis is very variable, some patients surviving 20 years or more and others less than 1 year.

Medullary carcinoma of the thyroid may be part of the multiple endocrine neoplasia type II syndrome (see p. 688).

RIEDEL'S THYROIDITIS

This is not a form of thyroid cancer but the presentation is similar and the differentiation can usually only be made by thyroid biopsy. It is an exceptionally rare condition of unknown aetiology in which there is extensive infiltration of the thyroid and surrounding structures with fibrous tissue. There may be associated mediastinal and retroperitoneal fibrosis. Presentation is with a slow-growing goitre which is irregular and stony-hard. There is usually tracheal and oesophageal compression necessitating partial thyroidectomy. Other recognised complications include recurrent laryngeal nerve palsy, hypoparathyroidism and eventually hypothyroidism.

ISSUES IN OLDER PEOPLE
THE THYROID GLAND

Hyperthyroidism
- Hyperthyroidism is commonly due to nodular goitre and those with Graves' disease often have no thyroid enlargement.
- Symptoms may be significantly different from those in younger patients, with apathy, anorexia, proximal myopathy, atrial fibrillation and cardiac failure predominating.
- Presentation may be late as patients equate weight loss with malignant disease and, not wishing their worst fears to be confirmed, avoid seeking medical attention.
- Interpretation of thyroid function tests may be difficult due to the effects of other non-thyroidal illnesses.

Hypothyroidism
- Some of the clinical features such as constipation, dry skin and slowing down both mentally and physically are often attributed to increasing age and the diagnosis is delayed for months or even years.
- Because of the possibility of exacerbating latent or established heart disease, the starting dose of thyroxine should be 25 μg daily.
- Thyroxine requirements fall with increasing age and few patients will need more than 100 μg daily.
- Other medication (see Box 16.13, p. 700) may interfere with absorption or metabolism of thyroxine, necessitating an increase in dose.

THE REPRODUCTIVE SYSTEM

Clinical practice in reproductive medicine is shared between several specialties, including gynaecology, urology, psychiatry and endocrinology. The following section focuses on aspects that are commonly managed by endocrinologists.

FUNCTIONAL ANATOMY, PHYSIOLOGY AND INVESTIGATIONS

The physiology of male and female reproductive function is illustrated in Figures 16.10 and 16.11. Pathways of synthesis of sex steroids are shown in Figure 16.16 on page 721. In the male, the testis subserves two principal functions: synthesis of testosterone by the interstitial Leydig cells under the control of luteinising hormone (LH), and spermatogenesis

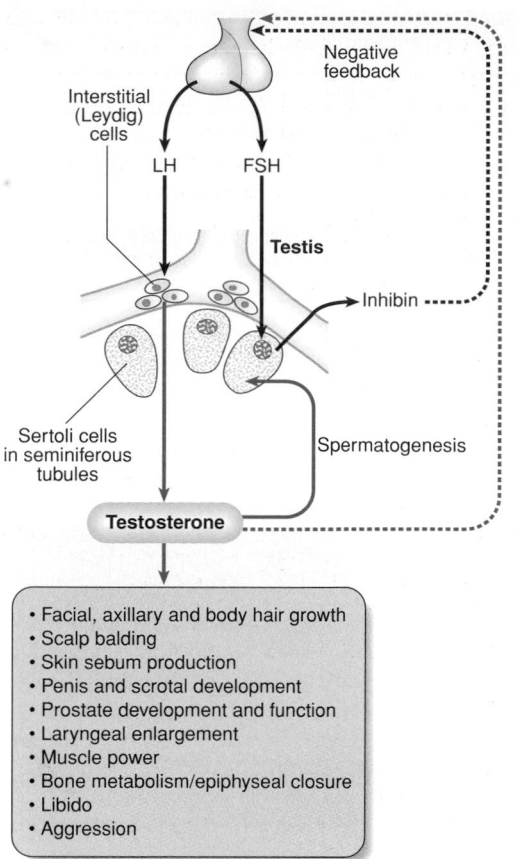

• Facial, axillary and body hair growth
• Scalp balding
• Skin sebum production
• Penis and scrotal development
• Prostate development and function
• Laryngeal enlargement
• Muscle power
• Bone metabolism/epiphyseal closure
• Libido
• Aggression

Fig. 16.10   Male reproductive physiology.

by Sertoli cells under the control of follicle-stimulating hormone (FSH) (but also requiring adequate testosterone). Negative feedback suppression of LH and FSH secretion is mediated principally by testosterone and another hormone from the testis, inhibin, respectively. The axis can be assessed easily by a random blood sample for testosterone, LH and FSH. Testosterone is largely bound in plasma to sex hormone-binding globulin, and this can also be measured to calculate the 'free androgen index'. Testicular function can also be tested by semen analysis.

In the female, physiology is complicated by variations in function during the normal menstrual cycle. FSH produces growth and development of ovarian follicles during the first 14 days after the menses. This leads to a gradual increase in oestradiol production from granulosa cells, which initially suppresses FSH secretion (negative feedback) but then, above a certain level, stimulates an increase in both the frequency and amplitude of gonadotrophin-releasing hormone (GnRH) pulses, resulting in a marked increase in LH secretion (positive feedback). The mid-cycle 'surge' of LH induces ovulation. After release of the ovum the follicle differentiates into a corpus luteum which secretes progesterone. Withdrawal of progesterone results in menstrual bleeding. Circulating levels of oestrogen and progesterone in pre-menopausal women are, therefore, critically dependent on the time of the cycle. The most useful 'test' of ovarian function is a careful menstrual history. In addition, ovulation can be confirmed by measuring progesterone levels during the luteal phase.

The pathophysiology of male and female reproductive function is summarised in Box 16.15.

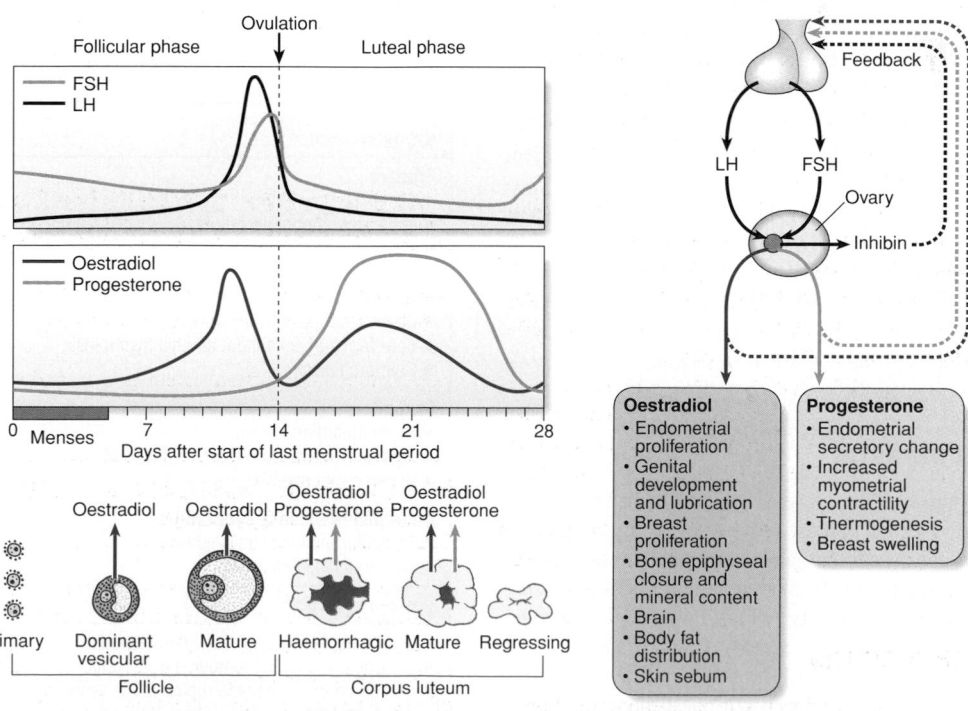

Fig. 16.11   Female reproductive physiology and the normal menstrual cycle.

16.15 CLASSIFICATION OF DISEASES OF THE REPRODUCTIVE SYSTEM

	Primary	Secondary
Hormone excess	Polycystic ovarian syndrome Granulosa cell tumour Leydig cell tumour	Pituitary gonadotrophinoma
Hormone deficiency	Menopause Hypogonadism (see Box 16.16) Turner's syndrome (45, XO female) Klinefelter's syndrome (47, XXY male)	Hypopituitarism Kallmann's syndrome (isolated GnRH deficiency) Severe systemic illness, including anorexia nervosa
Hormone hypersensitivity	–	
Hormone resistance	Androgen resistance syndrome ('testicular feminisation' or Reifenstein's syndrome) 5α-reductase deficiency	
Non-functioning tumours	Ovarian cysts Carcinoma	

MAJOR MANIFESTATIONS OF REPRODUCTIVE DISEASE

MALE HYPOGONADISM

Causes of hypogonadism are listed in Box 16.16. The clinical features of primary (failure of the testis) and secondary (failure of the hypothalamus or anterior pituitary) hypogonadism are identical. These include loss of libido, lethargy with muscle weakness, and decreased frequency of shaving. Patients commonly present with gynaecomastia, erectile impotence, infertility or delayed puberty. Clinical assessment of each of these presentations is detailed below.

Male hypogonadism is confirmed by demonstrating a low serum testosterone level. The distinction between primary and secondary hypogonadism is made by measurement of random LH and FSH. Patients with hypogonadotrophic hypogonadism (i.e. secondary hypogonadism) should be investigated as described for pituitary disease on pages 735–736. Patients with hypergonadotrophic hypogonadism (i.e. primary hypogonadism) should have the testes examined for cryptorchidism (see p. 709) or tumours, measurement of serum ferritin (to exclude haemochromatosis) and a karyotype (to identify Klinefelter's syndrome, i.e. 47, XXY). If there is no obvious cause, then no further investigations are necessary.

Treatment of men with testosterone deficiency is described on page 713.

GYNAECOMASTIA

Gynaecomastia is the presence of glandular breast tissue in males. Normal breast development in women is oestrogen-dependent but androgens oppose this effect. Gynaecomastia results from an imbalance between androgen and oestrogen activity, which may reflect androgen deficiency or oestrogen excess. Causes are listed in Box 16.16. Prolactin stimulates milk production in breast tissue which has been primed with oestrogen, but hyperprolactinaemia is rarely associated with gynaecomastia

and galactorrhoea in men; if present, it is explained by the androgen deficiency which results from suppression of LH and FSH by prolactin, and not by the prolactin excess itself.

16.16 CAUSES OF GYNAECOMASTIA

Idiopathic

Physiological/peripubertal

Drug-induced
- Cimetidine
- Digoxin
- Spironolactone
- Anti-androgen therapies for prostatic carcinoma
- Some exogenous anabolic steroids, e.g. diethylstilbestrol

Hypogonadism

Primary
- Klinefelter's syndrome
- Autoimmune gonadal failure
- Mumps orchitis
- Haemochromatosis
- Tuberculosis
- Chemotherapy or irradiation
- Rare forms of congenital adrenal hyperplasia
- Cryptorchidism

Secondary
- Hypopituitarism
- Kallmann's syndrome (GnRH deficiency)
- Hyperprolactinaemia

Androgen resistance syndromes
- Testicular feminisation syndrome
- 5α-reductase deficiency

Oestrogen excess
- Liver failure (impaired steroid metabolism)
- Oestrogen-secreting tumour, e.g. of testis
- Human chorionic gonadotrophin (hCG)-secreting tumour, e.g. of testis

Clinical assessment

A drug history is important. Palpation allows gynaecomastia to be distinguished from the prominent adipose tissue around the nipple often seen in obesity. Unilateral gynaecomastia should be considered to be breast carcinoma unless proved otherwise. Features of hypogonadism should be sought (see above).

Investigations and management

A random blood sample should be taken for testosterone, LH, FSH, oestradiol, prolactin and human chorionic gonadotrophin. If these tests are normal, and no drug is responsible, then there is no useful endocrine therapy. Surgical excision may be justified for cosmetic reasons, except in young boys with a short history in whom gynaecomastia may resolve. The surgical approach should be through a small incision around the nipple, and is best performed by a specialist in plastic surgery.

ERECTILE IMPOTENCE

Causes of erectile failure are shown in Box 16.17. With the exception of diabetes mellitus, endocrine causes are relatively uncommon, vascular, neuropathic and psychological causes being most common. From experience gained in diabetes clinics, impotence is a markedly underdiagnosed problem. It is important to be able to discuss issues frankly with the patient, and to establish whether there are associated features of hypogonadism (see above), and whether erections occur at any other time (i.e. whether the patient ever has an erection on wakening in the morning, a feature that makes vascular and neuropathic causes much less likely).

are sufficient to allow erections to occur during sleep; intracavernosal injection of papaverine or prostaglandin E_1 to test the adequacy of blood supply; internal pudendal artery angiography; and tests of autonomic and peripheral sensory nerve conduction.

Management

Hypogonadism should be treated as described on page 713. Psychotherapy which includes the sexual partner is most useful for psychological problems. Neuropathy and vascular disease are unlikely to improve, but several treatments are available. First-line therapy is usually with oral sildenafil, a phosphodiesterase inhibitor which potentiates the vasodilator action of nitric oxide on cyclic guanosine monophosphate (cGMP). Coadministration of sildenafil with nitric oxide donors ('nitrate' drugs) is contraindicated because of the risk of severe hypotension. Caution should also be exercised in patients with chronic disease including ischaemic heart disease, principally because the unaccustomed stress of sexual activity may precipitate cardiac ischaemia or dysrhythmia. Other treatments for impotence include self-administered intracavernosal injection or urethral gel administration of prostaglandin E_1; vacuum devices which achieve an erection which is maintained by a tourniquet around the base of the penis; and prosthetic implants, either of a fixed rod or of an inflatable reservoir. Many patients elect not to use these methods, but unfortunately even more are unaware of their availability.

SHORT STATURE AND DELAYED PUBERTY

Patients with short stature usually present during their teenage years. In most, failure to grow is associated with

16.17 CAUSES OF IMPOTENCE
With reduced libido
• Hypogonadism (see Box 16.16) • Depression
With intact libido
• Psychological problems, including anxiety • Vascular insufficiency (atheroma) • Neuropathic (e.g. diabetes mellitus, alcohol excess, multiple sclerosis) • Drugs (e.g. β-blockers, thiazide diuretics)

Investigations

Blood should be taken for glucose, glycated haemoglobin, prolactin, testosterone, LH and FSH. A number of further tests are available but are rarely employed because they do not usually influence management. These tests include nocturnal tumescence monitoring (using a plethysmograph placed around the shaft of the penis overnight) to establish whether blood supply and nerve function

16.18 CAUSES OF SHORT STATURE
With delayed puberty
• Constitutional/familial • Systemic illness (e.g. asthma, malabsorption, coeliac disease, cystic fibrosis, renal failure) • Psychological stress • Anorexia nervosa • Excessive physical exercise • Hypogonadism (see Box 16.16; also Turner's syndrome in girls) • Other endocrine disease (e.g. Cushing's syndrome, primary hypothyroidism, pseudohypoparathyroidism)
Without delayed puberty
• Isolated growth hormone deficiency • Previous precocious puberty with closure of epiphyses (e.g. congenital adrenal hyperplasia, Langerhans cell histiocytosis, McCune–Albright syndrome) • Prior problem restricting growth now resolved (e.g. intrauterine growth restriction, congenital heart disease) • Skeletal abnormality (e.g. achondroplasia, mucopolysaccharidoses)

delayed puberty, although there are exceptions (see Box 16.18). Although the mechanisms which initiate puberty are not fully understood and are in part genetic, there is probably a threshold of body weight which acts as a trigger for normal puberty in boys (mean ± 2 SD for stage 1 is 12 ± 2.5 years) and girls (stage 1 at 11.2 ± 2 years; menarche at 13 ± 1.9 years). Youngsters with delayed puberty are often underweight at presentation and have been small as children. Rarely, patients present later in life in whom failure to progress into puberty was not investigated. In this situation, the long bone epiphyses are not closed by sex steroids. These individuals have characteristic 'eunuchoid proportions', i.e. they are tall rather than short and have long arms and legs relative to trunk height.

Clinical assessment

Patients with short stature and delayed puberty require a general history and examination. Current weight and height and assessment of pubertal development should be charted against centiles for normals (see Fig. 16.12). The heights of the parents and older siblings and the age of their pubertal development may support a diagnosis of constitutional pubertal delay. In 95% of normal children final height is within 8.5 cm of the mean parental height. Previous growth measurements in childhood, which can usually be obtained from the school health records, are useful since growth hormone-deficient children usually have always been small, whereas a change in growth velocity resulting in 'crossing the centiles' is more likely to reflect recent pathology. Patients with growth hormone

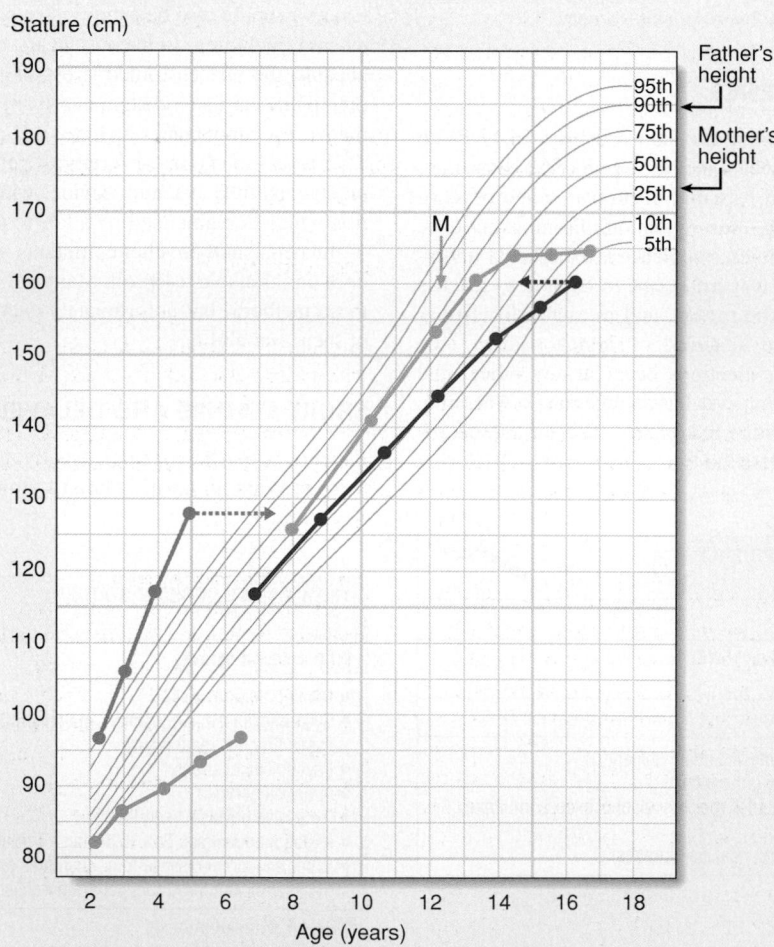

Fig. 16.12 **Differential diagnosis of short stature from growth charts.** The dots mark height measured at the chronological age shown. The mother's and father's heights are shown. Corresponding bone ages from wrist radiographs are plotted as arrowheads. Typical patterns are shown for childhood short stature (in green; due to congenital growth hormone deficiency); early accelerated growth with premature fusion of the epiphyses (in blue; due to precocious puberty, e.g. in congenital adrenal hyperplasia); late short stature with delayed puberty (in red; due to constitutional pubertal delay, but also consistent with hypogonadism or other causes shown in Box 16.18); and interrupted puberty (in light brown, where M marks the onset of periods at menarche, e.g. due to acquired hypopituitarism in craniopharyngioma, but also consistent with another severe systemic illness, e.g. anorexia nervosa).

deficiency are characteristically 'chubby', with increased subcutaneous fat, and so are short but not underweight. The presence of anosmia suggests possible Kallmann's syndrome due to isolated GnRH deficiency. Some light axillary and pubic hair may develop because of adrenal androgen production, even though the patient is hypogonadal.

The psychological impact of short stature and sexual immaturity on the young patient needs careful consideration since this is the principal determinant of whether specific treatment is appropriate.

Investigations

Before blood sampling, ask the patient to exercise (e.g. by running up and down the stairs or round the car park until breathless) to stimulate growth hormone secretion (normal > 15 mU/l). Measure growth hormone, testosterone (in boys), oestradiol (in girls), LH and FSH, and perform screening tests for systemic illness, including haematology, renal function, liver function and thyroid function. Antigliadin and antimyosin antibodies are a useful screen for coeliac disease. A plain radiograph of the wrist should be compared with a set of standard films to obtain a bone age. Bone age is delayed in pubertal delay and hypogonadism and is advanced in other conditions, e.g. following precocious puberty.

Further tests if growth hormone deficiency or hypogonadotrophic hypogonadism is suspected are described on pages 735–736. Note that normal growth hormone responses to stimulation in peripubertal children require priming of the pituitary with sex steroids for a few days beforehand, and that growth hormone secretion is impaired by any other systemic illness. The demonstration of hypergonadotrophic hypogonadism should be followed by chromosomal analysis to establish Turner's (45, XO with female phenotype) or Klinefelter's (47, XXY with male phenotype) syndrome.

Management

Treatments of specific endocrine abnormalities are discussed elsewhere. In patients with constitutional delay, puberty can be induced using low doses of oral oestrogen in girls (e.g. ethinylestradiol 2 μg daily) or testosterone in boys (e.g. depot testosterone ester injections 50 mg i.m. each month). Higher doses carry a risk of early fusion of epiphyses. This therapy should be given in a specialist clinic and progress monitored until endogenous puberty is established and priming therapy can be discontinued, usually in less than a year.

Isolated growth hormone deficiency is treated by daily subcutaneous injection of growth hormone. Growth hormone also has an established role in Turner's syndrome and in chronic renal failure. Its use in short children without a demonstrable endocrine abnormality is controversial; although it accelerates current growth, it does not result in an increase in final height.

Patients who have already gone through puberty and whose epiphyses have fused cannot be induced to grow further.

CRYPTORCHIDISM

Cryptorchidism (undescended testis) usually occurs in otherwise normal boys but may be the presenting feature of hypogonadotrophic hypogonadism. Highly retractile testes, particularly in an obese boy, may be mistaken for cryptorchidism. If the testes remain in the inguinal canal, they are more liable to trauma than if situated in the scrotum. The seminiferous tubules will fail to develop in an undescended gland and, if the condition is bilateral, sterility will follow. However, even in testes which remain undescended into adult life, the interstitial cells can function normally, so that secondary sex characteristics may develop in the usual way. In a minority of patients with cryptorchidism, the testis has taken an abnormal route of descent during development and lies ectopically either retroperitoneally or within the pelvis. This is called 'maldescent' and carries a significant risk of testicular malignancy, so maldescended testes need to be located by cross-sectional imaging or ultrasound, and excised.

Human chorionic gonadotrophin or intranasal GnRH can induce descent in about 40% of children but, if this fails or the condition is discovered in adulthood, then the testis or testes should be either removed or placed in the scrotum surgically.

HIRSUTISM

Hirsutism refers to the excessive growth of thick terminal hair in an androgen-dependent distribution in women (upper lip, chin, chest, back, lower abdomen, thigh, forearm) and is one of the most common presentations of endocrine disease. It should be distinguished from hypertrichosis, which is generalised excessive growth of vellus hair. The aetiology of androgen excess is shown in Box 16.19.

Clinical assessment

The severity of hirsutism is subjective. Some women suffer profound embarrassment from a degree of hair growth which others would not consider remarkable. Other important observations are a drug and menstrual history, calculation of body mass index, measurement of blood pressure, examination for virilisation (clitoromegaly, deep voice, balding, breast atrophy), and associated features including acne vulgaris or Cushing's syndrome (see p. 723). Hirsutism of recent onset associated with virilisation is suggestive of an androgen-secreting tumour, but these are rare.

Investigations

A random blood sample should be taken for testosterone, prolactin, LH and FSH. If there are clinical features of Cushing's syndrome, an overnight 1 mg dexamethasone suppression test should be performed (see p. 724).

If testosterone levels are elevated above twice the upper limit of the normal female range, especially if this is associated with low LH and FSH, then causes other than

16.19 CAUSES OF HIRSUTISM

Cause	Clinical features	Investigation findings	Treatment
Idiopathic	Often familial Mediterranean or Asian background	Normal	Cosmetic measures Anti-androgens
Polycystic ovarian syndrome (see Box 16.22)	Obesity Oligomenorrhoea or secondary amenorrhoea Infertility	LH:FSH ratio > 2.5:1 Minor elevation of androgens* Mild hyperprolactinaemia	Weight loss Cosmetic measures Anti-androgens (Insulin sensitising drugs may be useful)
Congenital adrenal hyperplasia (95% 21-hydroxylase deficiency)	Pigmented History of salt-wasting in childhood, ambiguous genitalia, or adrenal crisis when stressed Jewish background	Elevated androgens* which suppress with dexamethasone Abnormal rise in 17OH-progesterone with ACTH	Glucocorticoid replacement administered in reverse rhythm to suppress early morning ACTH
Exogenous androgen administration	Athletes Virilised	Low LH and FSH Androgens depend on which steroid is being taken	Stop steroid misuse
Androgen-secreting tumour of ovary or adrenal cortex	Rapid onset Virilisation: clitoromegaly, deep voice, balding, breast atrophy	High androgens* which do not suppress with dexamethasone or oestrogen Low LH and FSH CT demonstrates a tumour	Surgical excision
Cushing's syndrome	Clinical features of Cushing's syndrome (see p. 723)	Normal or mild elevation of adrenal androgens* See investigations, page 724	Treat the cause (see p. 725)

* E.g. serum testosterone levels in women: < 2 nM is normal; 2–5 nM is mild elevation; > 5 nM is high and requires further investigation.

idiopathic hirsutism and polycystic ovarian syndrome are more likely, and the source of the androgen excess should be established. Congenital adrenal hyperplasia due to 21-hydroxylase deficiency is diagnosed by a short ACTH stimulation test with measurement of 17OH-progesterone (see p. 731). In patients with androgen-secreting tumours, serum testosterone does not suppress following dexamethasone (either as an overnight or a 48-hour low-dose suppression test) or oestrogen (30 μg daily for 7 days). The tumour should then be sought by CT or MRI of the adrenals and ovaries.

Management

This depends on the cause (see Box 16.19). Similar options are available for the treatment of polycystic ovary syndrome and idiopathic hirsutism. These are described on page 712.

SECONDARY AMENORRHOEA

Primary amenorrhoea describes a patient who has never menstruated, i.e. who has not had a menarche. Secondary amenorrhoea describes the cessation of menstruation. The causes of this common problem are shown in Box 16.20.

Clinical assessment

Associated clinical features depend on the age of the patient and the underlying cause. Women of menopausal age (see p. 711) are unlikely to present unless they are considering hormone replacement therapy or are troubled by 'menopausal' symptoms such as flushing (see Box 16.21). Note, however, that these symptoms may occur in patients of any age with oestrogen deficiency of any cause. A premature menopause is defined, arbitrarily, as occurring before 40 years of age. If there is weight loss, then this may be primary as in anorexia nervosa (see p. 267), or secondary to an underlying disease such as tuberculosis, malignancy or hyperthyroidism. Weight gain may suggest hypothyroidism, Cushing's syndrome or, very rarely, a hypothalamic lesion. Hirsutism, obesity and long-standing irregular periods suggest the polycystic ovarian syndrome. The breasts should be examined for galactorrhoea. The presence of other autoimmune disease raises the possibility of autoimmune premature ovarian failure.

Investigations

Blood should be taken for LH, FSH, oestradiol, prolactin and TSH. In the absence of a menstrual cycle these can be taken at any time. High levels of LH and FSH with low or low to normal oestradiol suggest primary ovarian failure, including the menopause. Elevated LH with normal oestradiol is common in the polycystic ovarian syndrome. Investigation of hyperprolactinaemia is described on page 740. Low levels of LH, FSH and oestradiol suggest hypothalamic or pituitary disease. Assessment of bone mineral density, e.g. by DXA scan (see p. 972), is appropriate in patients with low androgen and oestrogen levels.

16.20 CAUSES OF SECONDARY AMENORRHOEA

Hypothalamic dysfunction
- See page 737; also anorexia nervosa, excessive exercise, psychogenic

Pituitary disease
- See page 737; especially hyperprolactinaemia

Ovarian dysfunction
- Polycystic ovarian syndrome
- Androgen-secreting tumours
- Autoimmune (premature menopause)
- Turner mosaic
- Menopause (see below)

Adrenal disease
- Cushing's syndrome, congenital adrenal hyperplasia, androgen-secreting tumours

Thyroid disease
- Hypo- and hyperthyroidism

Other conditions
- Severe systemic disease, e.g. renal failure, endometrial tuberculosis

16.21 MENOPAUSAL SYMPTOMS

Vasomotor effects
- Hot flushes
- Sweating

Psychological
- Anxiety
- Irritability
- Emotional lability

Genitourinary
- Dyspareunia ('senile vaginitis')
- Urgency of micturition
- Vaginal infections ↑

Management

This depends on the cause. In oestrogen-deficient patients it is usually appropriate to offer hormone replacement therapy for symptomatic improvement and/or to prevent osteoporosis (see p. 713).

INFERTILITY

Around 10% of couples have difficulty in conceiving children. This is attributable in roughly equal thirds to infertility in the female, infertility in the male, and idiopathic cases. So, although it is common for women to present with this problem, early assessment of both partners is essential to avoid unnecessary investigations and delay. This should include establishing that the couple are having intercourse when the woman is likely to be fertile.

Further assessment of women includes a menstrual history. Oligomenorrhoea suggests that the cycles are anovulatory. This can be confirmed by measurement of serum progesterone 21 days after the start of the last menstrual period (ovulation indicated by level > 15 nmol/l). Subsequent tests are similar to those for secondary amenorrhoea above. If the woman has regular menses, and no abnormality is found in the man, then further gynaecological investigation may be required.

The male should be examined for a varicocele or other testicular abnormality. A semen analysis should be performed. If he has oligospermia, then blood should be taken for prolactin, testosterone, FSH and LH and these interpreted as described for male hypogonadism above. If the only biochemical abnormality is a high FSH, then an irreversible failure of spermatogenesis is likely (the FSH rises because of lack of β-inhibin). Testicular biopsy is rarely indicated.

In patients with gonadotrophin deficiency, fertility can be induced over several months, as described on page 714. This is usually performed once, and sperm stored for subsequent artificial insemination.

THE MENOPAUSE

The cessation of menstruation in women in most developed countries occurs at a median age of 50.8 years. In the 5 years before there is a gradual increase in the number of anovulatory cycles. This period is referred to as the climacteric. Oestrogen and inhibin secretion falls and negative feedback results in increased pituitary secretion of LH and FSH. Levels of serum LH and FSH > 30 U/l in the presence of low oestradiol confirm the diagnosis.

Clinical features

Clinical features are listed in Box 16.21. Irregular periods commonly precede the menopause and hence its exact timing can only be recognised in retrospect (e.g. 6 months after the last period). Menopausal symptoms relate to oestrogen

deficiency. In some patients they are relatively minor but in others they are a major problem. The flushes may start when the patient still has regular periods and in about 25% of women they go on for more than 5 years. Their precise cause remains unknown but they are associated with an LH pulse. In the longer term, the fall in oestrogen secretion is associated with increased bone resorption and a risk of osteoporosis (see p. 1025). Before the menopause, women have lower rates of cardiovascular disease than men, but this advantage is substantially reduced after the menopause.

Management

Many women seek explanation and reassurance rather than treatment.

Oestrogen replacement therapy (usually called HRT) is discussed on page 713. In patients who decide against such therapy (e.g. strong family history of breast cancer) vasomotor symptoms may respond to clonidine. Vaginal and urinary symptoms may be helped by topical oestrogen cream. If anxiety or emotional problems associated with the menopause do not respond to HRT, they may need treatment in their own right.

POLYCYSTIC OVARIAN SYNDROME (PCOS)

Clinical features

PCOS describes a constellation of clinical and biochemical features, for which the aetiology remains poorly understood. It is probably the common endpoint of a heterogeneous group of pathologies, characterised by loss of coordinate control of the menstrual cycle. PCOS often affects several family members and is aggravated by obesity. Clinical and biochemical features are shown in Box 16.22, though patients vary in the severity of each feature. Some definitions of PCOS require the demonstration of multiple cysts in the ovaries, which are most readily detected by transvaginal ultrasound. However, the presence of ovarian cysts does not usually alter management, and does not always predict other features of PCOS, so ultrasound examination is arguably not a cost-effective test in this setting.

Management

This depends on the clinical problem. Infertility may be treated under specialist supervision with clomifene or exogenous gonadotrophins. Although patients with PCOS may have amenorrhoea, hormone replacement therapy is not required to prevent osteoporosis since they have elevated, rather than low, circulating levels of oestrogens and androgens.

For hirsutism, most patients will have used cosmetic measures such as bleaching and waxing before consulting a doctor. Electrolysis is effective for small areas, e.g. upper lip and chest hair, but is expensive. The pathophysiology of the common causes of hirsutism is poorly understood, but insulin resistance may be an important factor in PCOS. Weight loss is a vital step to enhance insulin sensitivity and reduce the peripheral conversion of androgens to oestrogens by the aromatase enzyme in adipose tissue. If these conservative measures have been tried and have failed, then anti-androgen therapy may be employed, as shown in Box 16.23. The life cycle of each hair follicle is at least 3 months so that no improvement is likely to be noticed before this time, when previous follicles have all shed their hair and replacement hair growth has been suppressed. In addition, insulin-sensitising drugs such as the thiazolidinediones and

16.22 FEATURES OF POLYCYSTIC OVARIAN SYNDROME	
Mechanisms*	**Manifestations**
Pituitary dysfunction	High serum LH High serum prolactin
Anovulatory menstrual cycles	Oligomenorrhoea Secondary amenorrhoea Cystic ovaries Infertility
Androgen excess	Hirsutism Acne
Obesity	Hyperglycaemia
Insulin resistance	Dyslipidaemia Hypertension

* These mechanisms are interrelated—it is not known which, if any, is primary. PCOS probably represents the common endpoint of several different pathologies.

16.23 ANTI-ANDROGEN THERAPY			
Mechanism of action	**Drug**	**Dose**	**Hazards**
Androgen receptor antagonists	Cyproterone acetate	2, 50 or 100 mg on days 1–11 of 28-day cycle with ethinylestradiol 30 µg on days 1–21	Hepatic dysfunction Feminisation of male fetus Progesterone receptor agonist Dysfunctional uterine bleeding
	Spironolactone	100–200 mg daily	Electrolyte disturbance Carcinogenic in rats
	Flutamide	Not recommended	Hepatic dysfunction
5α-reductase inhibitors (prevent conversion of testosterone to active dihydrotestosterone)	Finasteride	Not recommended	Unproven efficacy
Suppression of ovarian steroid production	Oestrogen	See combination with cyproterone acetate above or Conventional oestrogen-containing contraceptive	Venous thromboembolism Hypertension Weight gain Dyslipidaemia Increased breast and endometrial carcinoma
Suppression of adrenal androgen production	Exogenous glucocorticoid to suppress ACTH	e.g. Hydrocortisone 5 mg at 0900 hrs and dexamethasone 0.5 mg at 2200 hrs	Cushing's syndrome

biguanides (see Ch. 15) may have a role but require specialist supervision. Unless the patient has lost weight, the hirsutism will return if therapy is discontinued. The patient should be aware that prolonged exposure to some of these agents may not be desirable, that they should be discontinued in advance of pregnancy, and that the prescription should be reviewed at least every 6 months.

SEX HORMONE REPLACEMENT THERAPY

In males

Testosterone replacement is indicated in hypogonadal adults to prevent osteoporosis, and restore muscle power and libido. It is also sometimes used in adolescents with pubertal delay (see p. 709). Routes of testosterone administration are shown in Box 16.24. First-pass hepatic metabolism of testosterone is highly efficient, so bioavailability of oral preparations is poor. Doses of systemic testosterone can be titrated against symptoms; circulating testosterone levels provide only a rough guide to dosage because they are highly variable. It is prudent to avoid testosterone administration in men with androgen-dependent prostatic carcinoma; prostate-specific antigen (PSA) should be measured before and a few weeks after commencing testosterone therapy in men older than 50 years.

In females

Oestrogen replacement is indicated in women with pituitary disease or premature ovarian failure to prevent osteoporosis (see EBM panel). In pre-menopausal females the treatment is cyclical oestrogen therapy on days 1–21 and progestogen on days 14–21. This is administered most conveniently as an oral contraceptive pill. If oestrogenic side-effects (fluid retention, weight gain, hypertension, thrombosis and family history of breast cancer) are a concern, then a lower-dose oral or transdermal cyclical HRT is appropriate.

In post-menopausal females HRT is effective for menopausal symptoms and prevents osteoporotic fractures (see EBM panel). Initial observations suggested that HRT prevents cardiovascular disease, but randomised controlled trials show that combined HRT increases the risk of coronary events and stroke. HRT also increases the risk of breast and endometrial cancer and of venous thromboembolism. Unlike the higher doses of oestrogen used for contraception, HRT probably has no adverse effect on blood pressure.

MENAPAUSE—use of hormone replacement therapy (HRT) EBM

'RCTs show that conventional oestrogen therapy (combined with progestogen in women with an intact uterus) is effective in preventing loss of bone mineral density and osteoporotic fractures. HRT also reduces menopausal symptoms. However, RCTs also show that combined HRT also increases the risk of breast cancer, endometrial cancer, coronary heart disease, stroke and venous thromboembolism. The risks are small; the Women's Health Initiative study predicts that 5 years of continuous combined HRT to 10 000 unselected women aged 50–79 years results in 8 extra cases of breast cancer, 8 extra cases of pulmonary embolus, 7 extra episodes of coronary heart disease and 8 extra strokes while preventing 5 hip fractures and 6 cases of colorectal cancer.'

- Turgerson DJ, Bell–Syer SE. Hormone replacement therapy and prevention of nonvertebral fractures: a meta-analysis of randomized trials. JAMA 2001; 285:2891–2897.
- Hulley SB, Grady D, Bush T, et al. Randomized trial of estrogen plus progestin for secondary prevention of coronary heart disease in postmenopausal women. JAMA 1998; 280:605–613.
- Writing Group for the Women's Health Initiative Investigators. Risks and benefits of estrogen plus progestin in healthy postmenopausal women. JAMA 2002; 288:321–333.

Further information: www.cochrane.co.uk

The decision on whether to use HRT must be made on an individual basis, weighing up risk factors for these various benefits and complications, especially family history. Patients with a menopause before the age of 45 years should be encouraged to take HRT.

Oestrogen should not be given 'unopposed' (i.e. without progesterone) in women who have not had a hysterectomy as there is then a high risk of endometrial cancer. However, although theoretically better, it is no longer considered essential to induce withdrawal bleeds, and combined oestrogen and progesterone can be given continuously. Both oestrogen and progesterone can be given either orally or as dermal patches.

In addition to conventional oestrogen/progestogen combinations, selective oestrogen receptor modulators (SERMs) are available. These drugs interact with sites on the oestrogen receptor which are involved in interactions with tissue-specific transcription factors. As a result, they are oestrogen agonists in some sites and antagonists in others. Examples include tamoxifen (antagonist in breast, partial agonist in bone) and raloxifene (antagonist in breast and uterus, full agonist in bone). Unlike conventional HRT, these agents reduce rather than enhance the risk of breast cancer. Raloxifene is likely to be used increasingly in the prevention and treatment of osteoporosis. However, it does not relieve menopausal symptoms.

16.24 OPTIONS FOR ANDROGEN REPLACEMENT THERAPY

Preparation	Dose	Route of administration	Frequency	Comment
Depot testosterone esters	250–500 mg	I.m. injection	Every 2–4 weeks	Tends to wear off before next dose is due
Transdermal patches	5–10 mg	To skin	Daily	Consistent circulating testosterone levels but 10% incidence of skin hypersensitivity
Testosterone undecanoate	40–120 mg	Oral	12-hourly	Variable blood levels and risk of liver dysfunction
Testosterone implant	600–800 mg	Subcutaneous	Every 3–6 months	Effective but causes scarring at site of implantation

It is often difficult to say how long to continue HRT, since the benefits regress after discontinuing therapy, but the risks are proportional to the duration of therapy. As a rough guide, patients presenting with oestrogen deficiency before the age of 45 years should be encouraged to take HRT until at least the age of 50 years, and may continue if they wish until the age of 60 years. Patients with a normal menopause may be offered treatment for 10 years or until the age of 60 years, whichever comes sooner.

MENOPAUSE—role of raloxifene `EBM`

'RCTs show that raloxifene, a selective oestrogen receptor modulator, prevents loss of bone mass, prevents osteoporotic fracture, and reduces the risk of oestrogen receptor-positive breast cancer. Raloxifene does not affect the risk of developing endometrial cancer. However, it is ineffective for menopausal symptoms, and— like combined HRT—does increase the risk of thromboembolic disease.'

- Ettinger B, Black D, Mitlak BH, et al. Reduction of vertebral fracture risk in postmenopausal women with osteoporosis treated with raloxifene. JAMA 1999; 282:637–645.
- Cummings SR, Eckert S, Krueger KA, et al. The effect of raloxifene on risk of breast cancer in postmenopausal women. JAMA 1999; 281:2189–2197.

Further information: 💻 www.endocrinology.org

In patients desiring fertility

Sex steroid replacement does not stimulate ovulation or spermatogenesis. Patients wishing fertility are usually given injections of gonadotrophins several times a week (hCG for LH action and human or equine extracted FSH). If there is a hypothalamic cause for the hypopituitarism, then pulsatile GnRH therapy with a portable infusion pump is an alternative. Note that the pituitary GnRH receptors respond to pulsatile stimulation; continuous administration of GnRH or its analogues will suppress rather than stimulate LH/FSH secretion. The duration of gonadotrophin therapy depends on the duration and cause of hypogonadism. In both sexes the treatment requires specialist supervision, especially in females in whom there is a risk of multiple ovulation and the hyperstimulation syndrome, characterised by capillary leak with circulatory shock, pleural effusions and ascites.

THE PARATHYROID GLANDS

Parathyroid hormone (PTH) is a key controller of calcium metabolism which interacts with vitamin D in kidney and bone. Consequences of altered vitamin D in gut and renal disease are discussed in Chapters 17 and 14, respectively. Other metabolic bone disease is discussed in Chapter 20. Here, we address primary disorders of the parathyroid glands. The most common is hyperparathyroidism resulting in hypercalcaemia, which can be mimicked by release of PTH-like peptides, e.g. in malignancies.

FUNCTIONAL ANATOMY, PHYSIOLOGY AND INVESTIGATIONS

The four parathyroid glands lie behind the lobes of the thyroid. The parathyroid glands are not regulated by the pituitary gland, but respond directly to changes in ionised calcium concentrations. PTH is a single-chain polypeptide of 84 amino acids which is synthesised by the chief cells and released in response to a fall in serum ionised calcium concentration. This hormone interacts with vitamin D and its metabolites in regulating calcium absorption and excretion. Its actions are shown in Figure 16.13.

In summary, PTH has direct effects which promote reabsorption of calcium from renal tubules and bone. PTH also has indirect effects, mediated by increasing conversion of 25-hydroxycholecalciferol (i.e. 25-hydroxy-vitamin D) to the more potent hormone 1,25-dihydroxycholecalciferol, which results in increased calcium absorption from food and enhanced mobilisation of calcium from bone. PTH plays a central role in regulating calcium homeostasis because vitamin D and dietary calcium are rarely deficient. Moreover, 99% of total body calcium is in bone, but this pool is in dynamic equilibrium with the extracellular fluid by processes of bone resorption and deposition. The initial effect of PTH on bone is to stimulate osteolysis, returning calcium from bone to the extracellular fluid. Prolonged exposure of bone to PTH is associated with increased osteoclastic activity, extensive bone remodelling and osteoblastic repair.

Investigation of calcium metabolism is usually straightforward. Most laboratories measure total calcium in serum. About 50% of circulating calcium is bound to organic ions

---

ISSUES IN OLDER PEOPLE
REPRODUCTIVE MEDICINE

- The major physiological change with ageing is the menopause in women. Although testosterone levels do fall with age, no qualitative 'male menopause' exists.
- Many older people remain sexually active, so problems such as dyspareunia (due to post-menopausal vaginal dryness) or erectile dysfunction should receive careful attention.
- Post-menopausal osteoporosis is a major public health problem in old age. Appropriate use of HRT after the menopause is an important preventative measure.
- Preliminary evidence suggests that oestrogen therapy prevents cognitive dysfunction in elderly women. Further trials may establish the value of HRT in preventing dementia.
- The risks of oestrogen therapy are increased by prolonged use and increasing age. Hence HRT should not usually be prescribed beyond the age of 60 years.
- There is no evidence that replacement of testosterone in mildly hypogonadal elderly men is of benefit, and it may induce prostatic hyperplasia and cancer.
- Some common disorders of reproductive function become less troublesome after the menopause, including hirsutism in polycystic ovarian syndrome. However, very old women may suffer idiopathic hirsutism and balding which, if very severe or rapidly progressive, may represent significant pathological androgen excess, e.g. from an ovarian tumour.

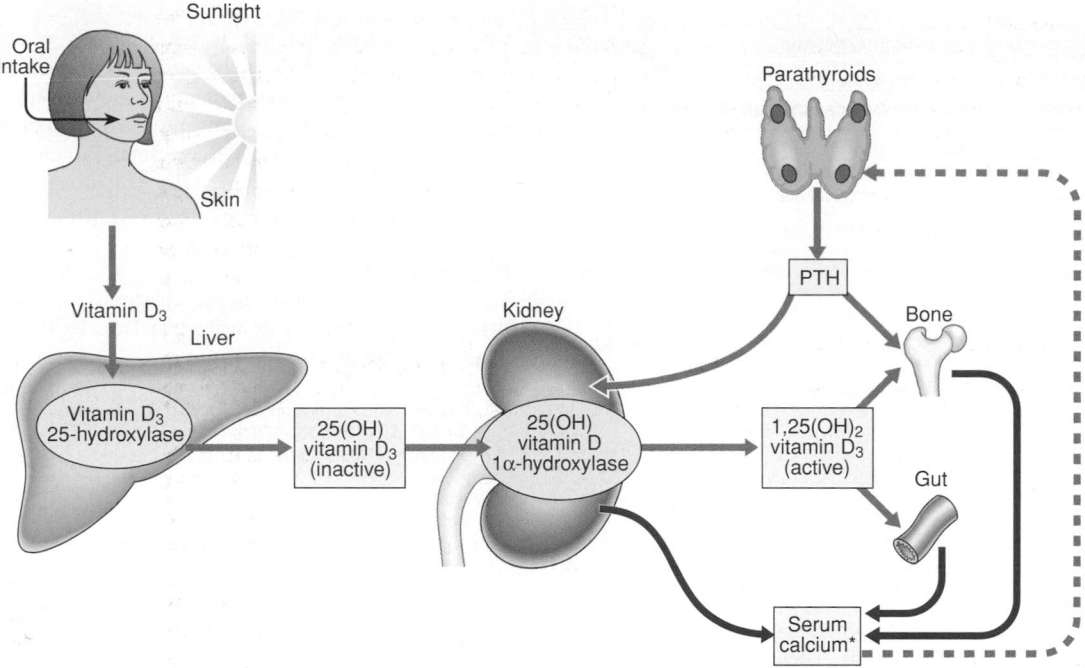

Fig. 16.13 Outline of calcium homeostasis showing interactions between parathyroid hormone (PTH) and vitamin D. * Calcium in serum exists as 50% ionised (Ca++), 10% non-ionised or complexed with organic ions such as citrate and phosphate, and 40% protein-bound, mainly to albumin. It is the ionised calcium concentration which regulates PTH production.

such as citrate or phosphate and to proteins. Total calcium measurements need to be corrected if the serum albumin is low, by adjusting the value for calcium upwards by 0.1 mmol/l for each 6 g/l reduction in albumin. Differential diagnosis of disorders of calcium metabolism requires measurement of phosphate, alkaline phosphatase and sometimes PTH (for which the blood sample has to be taken to the laboratory 'on ice' and centrifuged rapidly).

In some species calcitonin, a hormone secreted from the parafollicular C cells of the thyroid gland, also regulates calcium metabolism. However, although calcitonin is a useful tumour marker in medullary carcinoma of thyroid (see p. 704) and can be administered therapeutically in Paget's disease of bone (see p. 1031), its release from the thyroid is of no clinical relevance to calcium homeostasis in humans.

Disorders of the parathyroid glands are summarised in Box 16.25.

16.25 CLASSIFICATION OF DISEASES OF THE PARATHYROID GLANDS

	Primary	Secondary
Hormone excess	Primary hyper-parathyroidism (adenoma, hyperplasia, occasionally carcinoma) Tertiary hyperparathyroidism	Secondary hyper-parathyroidism
Hormone deficiency	Post-surgical Autoimmune	
Hormone hypersensitivity	–	
Hormone resistance	Pseudohypoparathyroidism	
Non-functioning tumours	Parathyroid carcinoma	

MAJOR MANIFESTATIONS OF DISEASES OF THE PARATHYROID GLANDS

HYPERCALCAEMIA

Hypercalcaemia is one of the most common biochemical abnormalities. (For other electrolyte disturbances, see Ch. 9.) It is detected most frequently during routine biochemical analysis in asymptomatic patients. However, it can present with chronic symptoms as described below, and occasionally patients present as acute emergencies with severe hypercalcaemia and dehydration.

Causes of hypercalcaemia are listed in Box 16.26. Of these, primary hyperparathyroidism and malignant hypercalcaemia are by far the most common.

Clinical assessment

Symptoms and signs of hypercalcaemia include polyuria and polydipsia, renal colic, lethargy, anorexia, nausea, dyspepsia and peptic ulceration, constipation, depression, drowsiness and impaired cognition. Patients with malignant

16.26 CAUSES OF HYPERCALCAEMIA
With normal or elevated (i.e. inappropriate) PTH levels
• Primary or tertiary hyperparathyroidism • Lithium-induced hyperparathyroidism • Familial hypocalciuric hypercalcaemia
With low (i.e. suppressed) PTH levels
• Malignancy (e.g. lung, breast, renal, ovarian, colonic and thyroid carcinoma) • Multiple myeloma • Elevated 1,25(OH)$_2$ vitamin D$_3$ (e.g. intoxication or sarcoidosis) • Thyrotoxicosis • Paget's disease with immobilisation • Milk-alkali syndrome • Thiazide diuretics • Addison's disease

hypercalcaemia can have a rapid onset of symptoms and may have clinical features which help to localise their tumour.

Patients with primary hyperparathyroidism may have a chronic, non-specific history. Their symptoms are brought to mind by the adage 'bones, stones and abdominal groans'. However, about 50% of patients with primary hyperparathyroidism are asymptomatic. In others, symptoms may go unrecognised until patients present with renal calculi (5% of first stone formers and 15% of recurrent stone formers have primary hyperparathyroidism), with or without impaired renal function, or acute dehydration and profound hypercalcaemia. Hypertension is common in hyperparathyroidism. Parathyroid tumours are almost never palpable.

A family history of renal tract stones and/or neck surgery raises the possibility of multiple endocrine neoplasia (see p. 688). Familial hypocalciuric hypercalcaemia is a rare but important catch for the unwary. This autosomal dominant disorder is associated with a defective calcium receptor in the parathyroid gland, but is almost always asymptomatic and uncomplicated. Occasionally, these patients have had their parathyroid glands removed unnecessarily.

Investigations

Low plasma phosphate and elevated alkaline phosphatase support a diagnosis of primary hyperparathyroidism or malignancy. High plasma phosphate and alkaline phosphatase accompanied by renal impairment suggest tertiary hyperparathyroidism (see p. 601). Hypercalcaemia may cause nephrocalcinosis and renal tubular impairment resulting in hyperuricaemia and hyperchloraemia.

The most discriminant investigation is the measurement of PTH using a specific immunoradiometric assay. Older assays were not able to distinguish PTH from PTH-related peptide. If PTH is normal or elevated and urinary calcium is elevated, then hyperparathyroidism is confirmed. If PTH is low and no other cause is apparent, then malignancy with or without bony metastases is likely. PTH-related peptide

can be measured, but this is not generally necessary. Unless the source is obvious, the patient should be screened for malignancy with a chest radiograph, isotope bone scan, myeloma screen (ESR, serum protein electrophoresis, immunoglobulins and urinary Bence Jones protein), serum angiotensin-converting enzyme (elevated in sarcoidosis), and further imaging as appropriate.

Management

Treatment of malignant hypercalcaemia and primary hyperparathyroidism is described in Box 16.27 and on page 718, respectively.

16.27 TREATMENT OF MALIGNANT HYPERCALCAEMIA
Rehydration with normal saline To replace as much as a 4–6 l deficit May need monitoring with central venous pressure in old age or renal impairment
Bisphosphonates, e.g. pamidronate 90 mg i.v. over 4 hours Causes a fall in calcium which is maximal at 2–3 days and lasts a few weeks Unless the cause is removed, follow up with an oral bisphosphonate
Additional rapid therapy may be required in very ill patients Forced diuresis with saline and furosemide (frusemide) Glucocorticoids, e.g. prednisolone 40 mg daily Calcitonin Haemodialysis
Treat the cause

HYPOCALCAEMIA

Aetiology

Hypocalcaemia is much less common than hypercalcaemia. Its differential diagnosis is shown in Box 16.28. Although almost all laboratories routinely report total serum calcium concentrations, it is the ionised concentration which is biologically important. The most common cause of hypocalcaemia is a low serum albumin with normal ionised calcium concentration. Correction of total serum calcium concentration for serum albumin is described on page 715. Conversely, ionised calcium may be low in the face of normal total serum calcium if the serum is alkalotic—for example, as a result of hyperventilation (see Ch. 9).

The most common cause of hypoparathyroidism is damage to the parathyroid glands (or their blood supply) during thyroid surgery, although this complication is only permanent in 1% of thyroidectomies. Transient hypocalcaemia develops in 10% of patients 12–36 hours following subtotal thyroidectomy for Graves' disease.

Idiopathic hypoparathyroidism may develop at any age, and is sometimes associated with autoimmune disease of the adrenal, thyroid or ovary, especially in young people (see Box 16.2).

Pseudohypoparathyroidism is usually an autosomal dominant syndrome in which there is tissue resistance to

16.28 DIFFERENTIAL DIAGNOSIS OF HYPOCALCAEMIA

	Total serum calcium concentration	Ionised serum calcium concentration	Serum phosphate concentration	Serum PTH concentration	Comments
Hypoalbuminaemia	↓	→	→	→	Adjust calcium upwards by 0.1 mmol/l for each 6 g/l reduction in albumin
Alkalosis Respiratory, e.g. hyperventilation Metabolic, e.g. Conn's syndrome	→	↓	→	→ or ↑	See Chapter 9
Vitamin D deficiency	↓	↓	↓	↑	See Chapter 20
Chronic renal failure	↓	↓	↑	↑	Due to impaired vitamin D hydroxylation Serum creatinine ↑
Hypoparathyroidism Post-surgical Idiopathic Infantile	↓	↓	↑	↓	See text
Pseudohypoparathyroidism	↓	↓	↑	↑	Characteristic phenotype
Acute pancreatitis	↓	↓	→ or ↓	↑	Usually clinically obvious Serum amylase ↑

the effects of PTH. The PTH-receptor is normal but there is a defective post-receptor mechanism.

Clinical features

Tetany occurs in all syndromes in which ionised calcium concentrations are low. Additional features are specific to different aetiologies.

Tetany

Low ionised calcium concentrations cause increased excitability of peripheral nerves. In the absence of alkalosis, tetany usually occurs in adults only if total serum calcium is < 2.0 mmol/l. Children are more sensitive than adults. Magnesium depletion should also be considered as a possible contributing factor, particularly in malabsorption, diuretic therapy or alcohol excess.

In children a characteristic triad of carpopedal spasm, stridor and convulsions occurs, though one or more of these may be found independently of the others. The hands in carpal spasm adopt a characteristic position. The metacarpophalangeal joints are flexed, the interphalangeal joints of the fingers and thumb are extended, and there is opposition of the thumb ('main d'accoucheur'). Pedal spasm is much less frequent. Stridor is caused by spasm of the glottis. Adults complain of tingling in the hands and feet and around the mouth. Less often there is painful carpopedal spasm, while stridor and fits are rare.

Latent tetany may be present when signs of overt tetany are lacking. It is best recognised by eliciting Trousseau's sign. Inflation of a sphygmomanometer cuff on the upper arm to more than the systolic blood pressure is followed by carpal spasm within 3 minutes. A less specific sign of hypocalcaemia is that described by Chvostek, in which tapping over the branches of the facial nerve as they emerge from the parotid gland produces twitching of the facial muscles.

Other features

Prolonged hypocalcaemia in hypoparathyroidism may cause grand mal epilepsy, psychosis, cataracts, calcification of basal ganglia and papilloedema. In addition, there is an association with mucocutaneous candidiasis. In pseudohypoparathyroidism there is no associated mucocutaneous candidiasis, but patients may have mental retardation and characteristically there are skeletal abnormalities such as short stature and short 4th and 5th metacarpals and metatarsals. The term 'pseudo-pseudohypoparathyroidism' is used in connection with patients exhibiting the above skeletal abnormalities but in whom serum calcium concentration and other biochemistry are normal.

Management

To control tetany, alkalosis can be reversed acutely if arterial PCO_2 is increased by rebreathing expired air in a paper bag or administering 5% CO_2 in oxygen. Injection of 20 ml of a 10% solution of calcium gluconate slowly into a vein will raise the serum calcium concentration immediately. An intramuscular injection of 10 ml may also be given to obtain a more prolonged effect. In severe cases of alkalotic tetany, intravenous calcium gluconate often relieves the spasm, while specific treatment of the alkalosis, which will vary with the cause, is being applied (see Ch. 9). If tetany is not relieved by giving calcium, the administration of magnesium may be required.

For chronic control of hypocalcaemia, commercial preparations of PTH are unsatisfactory because they have to be given by frequent injections, and soon become ineffective due to antibody formation. Substitution therapy for persistent hypoparathyroidism and for pseudohypoparathyroidism is provided by 1α-hydroxycholecalciferol (alfacalcidol) which is hydroxylated in the liver to 1,25-dihydroxycholecalciferol (calcitriol).

HYPERPARATHYROIDISM

It is customary to distinguish three categories of hyper-parathyroidism, as shown in Box 16.29. In primary hyper-parathyroidism there is autonomous secretion of PTH, usually by a single parathyroid adenoma varying in size from a few millimetres to several centimetres in diameter. Secondary hyperparathyroidism is present when there is increased PTH secretion to compensate for prolonged hypocalcaemia and is associated with hyperplasia of all parathyroid tissue. Its effect is to restore serum calcium levels at the expense of the stores of calcium in bone. In a very small proportion of cases of secondary hyperparathyroidism continuous stimulation of the parathyroids may result in adenoma formation and autonomous PTH secretion. This is known as tertiary hyperparathyroidism.

Primary hyperparathyroidism is the most common of the parathyroid disorders with a prevalence of about 1 in 800. It is two to three times more common in women than men and 90% of patients are over 50 years of age. It also occurs in all of the familial multiple endocrine neoplasia syndromes, as described on page 688, when hyperplasia rather than adenoma is more likely. Its clinical presentation is described under hypercalcaemia on page 715.

Skeletal and radiological changes in primary hyperparathyroidism

These features are rarer with earlier use of surgical para-thyroidectomy (see below). Osteitis fibrosa results from increased bone resorption by osteoclasts with fibrous replacement in the lacunae. This may present as bone pain and tenderness, fracture and deformity. Chondrocalcinosis is due to deposition of calcium pyrophosphate crystals within articular cartilage. This typically affects the menisci at the knees and can result in secondary degenerative arthritis or predispose to attacks of acute pseudogout.

There are characteristic changes on plain radiographs. In the early stages there may be demineralisation, with sub-periosteal erosions and terminal resorption in the phalanges (see Fig. 16.14). A 'pepper-pot' appearance may be seen on lateral radiographs of the skull. In nephrocalcinosis, scattered opacities may be visible within the renal outline. There may be soft tissue calcification in arterial walls, in soft tissues of the hands, and in the cornea. However, changes on plain radiographs are features of long-standing hyperpara-thyroidism, and these investigations are not required either to confirm the diagnosis or as a criterion for surgery.

Localisation of parathyroid tumours

If primary hyperparathyroidism is confirmed biochemically, imaging to locate the adenoma or differentiate adenomas from hyperplasia is not necessary. In over 90% of patients an experienced surgeon will locate the adenoma without difficulty. If surgical exploration has been unsuccessful, however, ultrasonography, selective neck vein catheterisation with PTH measurements, CT and subtraction imaging may prove useful. In this last technique the neck is imaged during the successive injections of two short-lived isotopes: [201]thallium (taken up by

16.29 HYPERPARATHYROIDISM		
Type	Serum calcium	PTH
Primary Single adenoma (90%) Multiple adenomata (4%) Nodular hyperplasia (5%) Carcinoma (1%)	Raised	Not suppressed
Secondary Chronic renal failure Malabsorption Osteomalacia and rickets	Low	Raised
Tertiary	Raised	Not suppressed

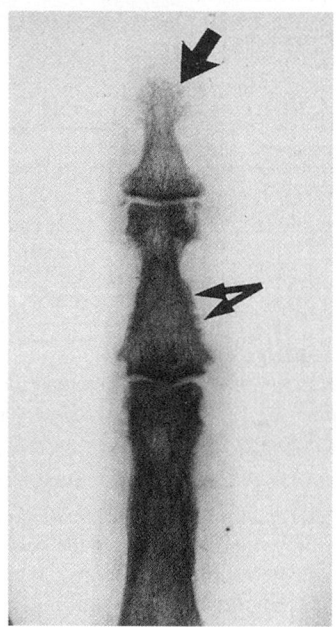

Fig. 16.14 Radiograph of subperiosteal erosions (lower arrows) in a phalanx with terminal resorption (top arrow) in a patient with primary hyperparathyroidism.

thyroid and parathyroid), followed by [99m]technetium (taken up by thyroid only). Computer subtraction of the two images leaves a solitary parathyroid image if an adenoma is present.

Treatment of primary hyperparathyroidism

Treatment of severe hypercalcaemia in hyperparathyroidism is as for malignant hypercalcaemia (see Box 16.27). Note that hypercalcaemia in patients with primary hyperparathy-roidism responds less well to glucocorticoids and bisphos-phonates than in malignancy. Urgent neck surgery is occasionally required, but strenuous attempts should be made to replace fluid deficits and lower the serum calcium concentration before administering an anaesthetic.

Most patients do not require urgent treatment. The only long-term therapy is surgery, with excision of a solitary parathyroid adenoma or debulking of hyperplastic glands. In hyperplasia, all four glands may be removed and some of the excised tissue transplanted to the forearm. If hypercalcaemia returns, part of the transplant can be removed under local anaesthetic. Post-operative hypocalcaemia is not uncommon during the first 2 weeks while residual suppressed parathyroid tissue recovers.

As detailed in the EBM panel, the selection of patients with primary hyperparathyroidism that require surgery is not always straightforward. Surgery is indicated for those with clear-cut symptoms or documented complications such as peptic ulceration, renal stones, renal impairment or osteopenia. However, a large number of patients have only vague symptoms or are asymptomatic. Younger patients are being operated on more frequently, but older patients with contra-indications to surgery can be reviewed every 6–12 months, with assessment of symptoms, renal function, serum calcium and bone mineral density. They should be encouraged to maintain a high oral fluid intake to avoid renal stones.

EBM

PRIMARY HYPERPARATHYROIDISM—role of parathyroidectomy in asymptomatic patients

'In asymptomatic patients, primary hyperparathyroidism is progressive in fewer than 25% of cases over a 10-year period. Parathyroid surgery is therefore reserved for patients who either are symptomatic; are younger than 50 years; have a serum calcium > 0.4 mM above the normal range; have a creatinine clearance < 70% of predicted; or have a bone mineral density < 2 SD below the age-adjusted mean.'

- Silverberg SJ, Shane E, Jacobs TP, et al. A 10-year prospective study of primary hyperparathyroidism with or without parathyroid surgery. N Engl J Med 1999; 341:1249–1255.
- NIH conference: diagnosis and management of asymptomatic primary hyperparathyroidism; consensus development conference statement. Ann Intern Med 1991; 114:593–597.

Further information: 🖥 www.endocrinology.org

ISSUES IN OLDER PEOPLE
THE PARATHYROID GLANDS

- Primary hyperparathyroidism becomes more common with increasing age. Most elderly patients can be observed and surgical intervention avoided.
- However, hypercalcaemia causes confusion in older people. In a patient with otherwise asymptomatic primary hyperparathyroidism, confusional states may improve following parathyroidectomy.
- Vitamin D deficiency is a common cause of hypocalcaemia in older patients, because of poor diet and limited exposure to the sun.
- In patients with osteoporotic fractures, metabolic bone disease including osteomalacia and hyperparathyroidism should be excluded by biochemical screening.

THE ADRENAL GLANDS

The adrenals function as several separate endocrine glands within one anatomical structure. The adrenal medulla is an extension of the sympathetic nervous system which secretes catecholamines. Most of the adrenal cortex is made up of cells which secrete cortisol and adrenal androgens, and form part of the hypothalamic-pituitary-adrenal axis. The small outer glomerulosa of the cortex secretes aldosterone under the control of the renin-angiotensin system. These functions are important in the integrated control of cardiovascular, metabolic and immune responses to stress.

Subtle alterations in adrenal function may be important in common diseases, including hypertension, obesity and type 2 diabetes mellitus. However, classical syndromes of adrenal hormone deficiency and excess are relatively rare.

FUNCTIONAL ANATOMY, PHYSIOLOGY AND INVESTIGATIONS

Adrenal anatomy and function are shown in Figure 16.15. Histologically, the cortex is divided into three zones, but these function as two units (zona glomerulosa and zonae fasciculata/reticularis) which produce corticosteroids in response to humoral stimuli. Pathways for the biosynthesis of corticosteroids are shown in Figure 16.16. Investigation of adrenal function is described under specific diseases below. Pathologies are classified in Box 16.30.

Glucocorticoids

Cortisol is the major glucocorticoid in humans. Levels are highest in the morning on waking and lowest in the middle of the night. Cortisol rises dramatically during stress, including any illness. This elevation protects key metabolic functions at the expense of others (e.g. maintaining cerebral glucose supply during starvation) and puts an important 'brake' on potentially damaging inflammatory responses to infection and injury. The clinical importance of cortisol deficiency is therefore most obvious at times of stress.

16.30 CLASSIFICATION OF DISEASES OF THE ADRENAL GLANDS

	Primary	Secondary
Hormone excess	Non-ACTH-dependent Cushing's syndrome (see Box 16.33, p. 723) Primary hyperaldosteronism (see Box 16.38, p. 728) Phaeochromocytoma	ACTH-dependent Cushing's syndrome Secondary hyperaldosteronism
Hormone deficiency	Addison's disease (see Box 16.35, p. 726) Congenital adrenal hyperplasia	Hypopituitarism
Hormone hypersensitivity	11β-hydroxysteroid dehydrogenase deficiency Liddle's syndrome	
Hormone resistance	Pseudohypoaldosteronism Glucocorticoid resistance syndrome	
Non-functioning tumours	Carcinoma (usually functioning) Metastatic tumours	

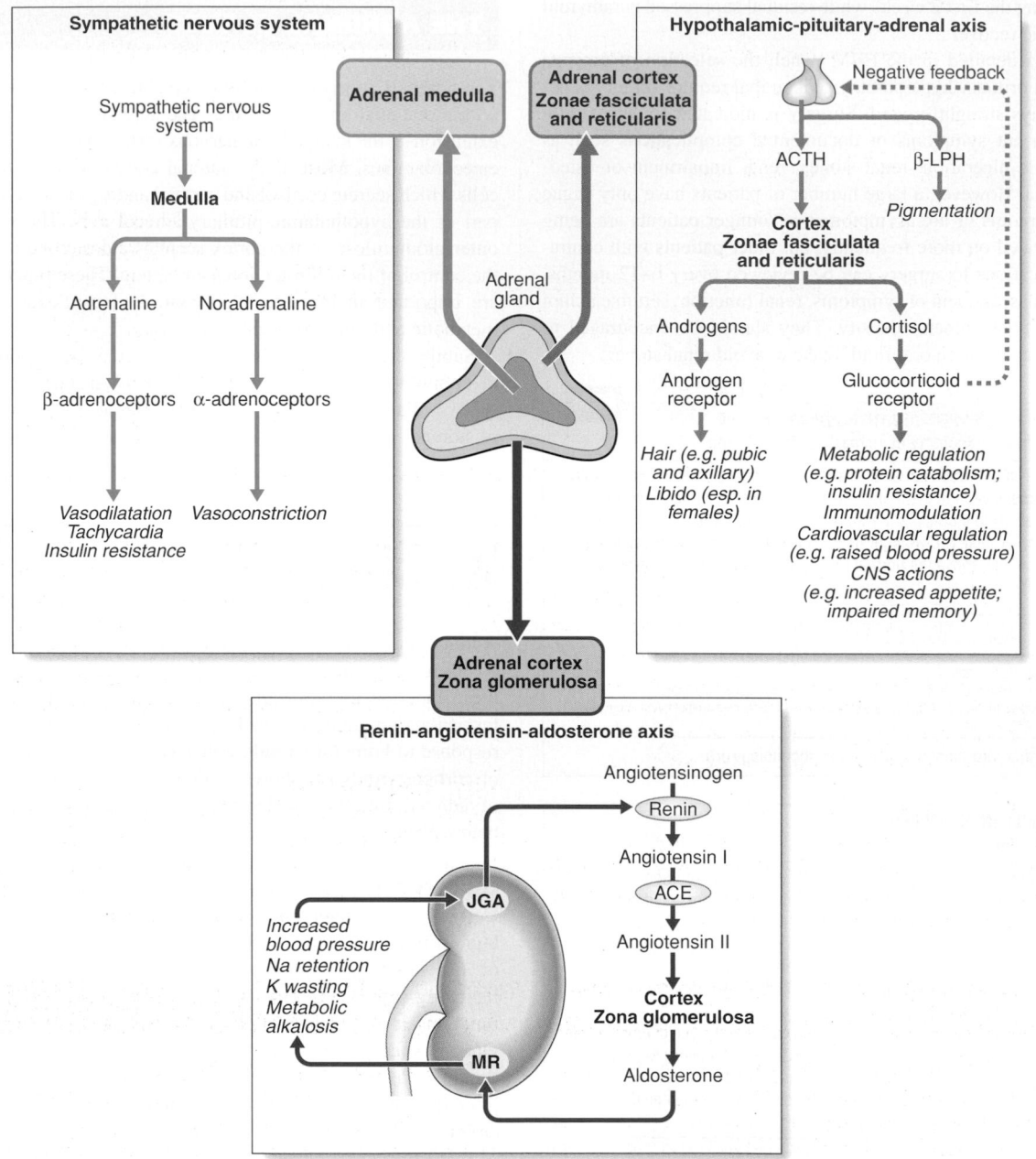

Fig. 16.15 Structure and function of the adrenal glands. (ACE = angiotensin-converting enzyme; JGA = juxtaglomerular apparatus; MR = mineralocorticoid receptor; β-LPH = β-lipotrophic hormone, a fragment of the ACTH precursor peptide pro-opiomelanocortin which contains melanocyte-stimulating hormone activity)

In the circulation more than 95% of cortisol is bound to protein, principally cortisol-binding globulin. It is the free fraction which is biologically active via glucocorticoid receptors which regulate the transcription of many genes in many cells. Cortisol can also activate mineralocorticoid receptors, but it does not normally do so because most cells containing mineralocorticoid receptors also express an enzyme, 11β-hydroxysteroid dehydrogenase type 2 (11β-HSD), which converts cortisol to its inactive metabolite, cortisone. Loss of this protection of mineralocorticoid receptors by

inhibition of 11β-HSD (e.g. by liquorice) results in cortisol acting like aldosterone as a potent sodium-retaining steroid.

Mineralocorticoids

Aldosterone is the body's most important sodium-retaining hormone, which acts via mineralocorticoid receptors. Sodium is retained at the expense of increased excretion of potassium. Increased potassium in the lumen of the distal nephron also results in increased exchange with protons and metabolic alkalosis. The principal stimulus to aldosterone

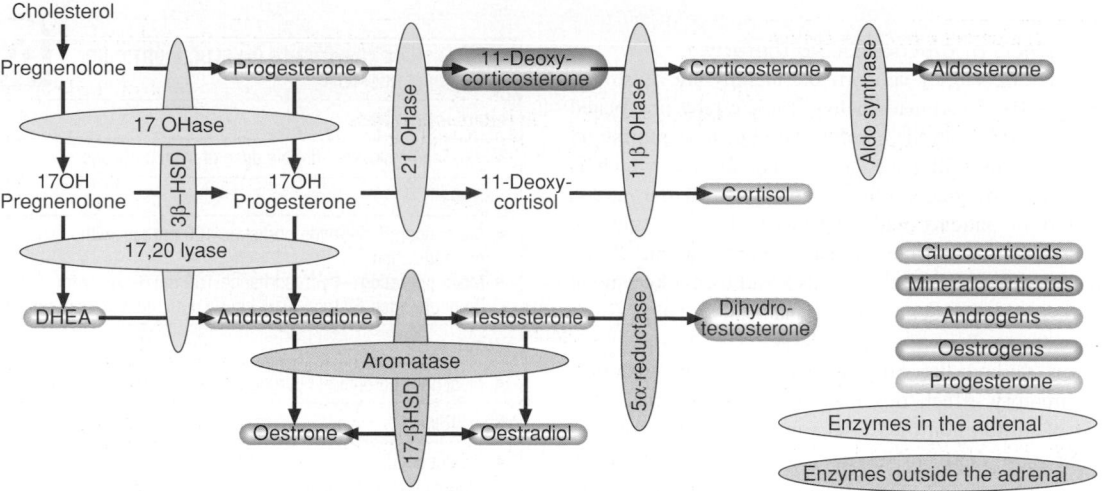

Fig. 16.16 The major pathways of synthesis of steroid hormones. (DHEA = dehydroepiandrosterone; OHase = hydroxylase; HSD = hydroxysteroid dehydrogenase)

secretion is angiotensin II, a peptide produced by activation of the renin-angiotensin system (see Fig. 16.15). Renin secretion from the juxtaglomerular apparatus in the kidney is stimulated by low perfusion pressure in the afferent arteriole, low sodium filtration leading to low sodium concentrations at the macula densa, or increased sympathetic nerve activity. As a result, renin is increased in hypovolaemia and renal artery stenosis, and standing levels of renin are about double those when lying down.

Catecholamines

In humans, only a small proportion of circulating noradrenaline is derived from the adrenal medulla; much more is released from other nerve endings. However, the methyltransferase enzyme responsible for the conversion of noradrenaline to adrenaline is induced by glucocorticoids. Blood flow in the adrenal is centripetal so that the medulla is bathed in high concentrations of cortisol and is the major source of circulating adrenaline. However, in the absence of functioning adrenal medullae, e.g. after bilateral adrenalectomy, there appear to be no clinical consequences attributable to deficiency of circulating catecholamines.

Adrenal androgens

Adrenal androgens are secreted in response to ACTH and are the most abundant steroids in the blood stream. They are probably important in the initiation of puberty (the adrenarche). The adrenals are also the major source of androgens in adult females, and may be important in female libido.

MAJOR MANIFESTATIONS OF ADRENAL DISEASE

Adrenal diseases are rare but they often need to be considered because they are encountered in the context of common complaints (see p. 685). Classical syndromes of adrenal disease are described below. Disorders of the adrenal glands are also diagnosed in childhood (congenital adrenal hyperplasias), in patients presenting with hypertension (see Ch. 12; primary hyperaldosteronism, phaeochromocytoma), or in women with hirsutism (see p. 709; late-onset congenital adrenal hyperplasia).

THE 'CUSHINGOID' PATIENT

Cushing's syndrome is caused by excessive activation of glucocorticoid receptors. By far the most common cause is iatrogenic, due to prolonged administration of synthetic glucocorticoids such as prednisolone. Non-iatrogenic Cushing's syndrome is rare, although it presents by many diverse routes and is often a 'spot diagnosis' made by an astute clinician.

Iatrogenic Cushing's syndrome

The remarkable anti-inflammatory properties of glucocorticoids have led to their use in a wide variety of clinical conditions, but the hazards are significant. Equivalent doses of commonly used glucocorticoids are listed in Box 16.31. Topical preparations (dermal, rectal and inhaled) can also be absorbed into the systemic circulation. Although this rarely occurs to a sufficient degree to produce clinical features of Cushing's syndrome, it can result in significant suppression of endogenous ACTH and cortisol secretion (see below).

16.31 EQUIVALENT DOSES OF GLUCOCORTICOIDS: ANTI-INFLAMMATORY POTENCY

- Hydrocortisone: 20 mg
- Cortisone acetate: 25 mg
- Prednisolone: 5 mg
- Dexamethasone: 0.75 mg

Side-effects of glucocorticoid therapy

The side-effects of glucocorticoid therapy are illustrated in Figure 16.17 and listed below. These effects are related to dose which should therefore be kept to a minimum. Some patients will have pre-existing disease which is exacerbated by glucocorticoid therapy; particular care is required in patients with diabetes mellitus or glucose intolerance, to avoid symptomatic hyperglycaemia. Rapid changes in cortisol levels can also lead to marked mood disturbance, either depression or mania (see pp. 262–263), and insomnia.

Even though the drug is being used for its anti-inflammatory effect, this may produce problems. Thus signs of perforation of a viscus may be masked and the patient may show no febrile response to an infection. Gastric erosions are more common, probably because of impaired prostaglandin synthesis. Hence the combination of corticosteroid with analgesic drugs such as aspirin may lead to haemorrhage from the stomach or duodenum. Latent tuberculosis may be reactivated and patients on corticosteroids should be advised to avoid contact with varicella zoster if they are not immune.

Osteoporosis is a particularly difficult problem in post-menopausal women who require long-term corticosteroids. There is evidence that both sex hormone replacement therapy and bisphosphonates protect the bones in this setting (see p. 1028).

PROLONGED GLUCOCORTICOID THERAPY— prevention of osteoporosis [EBM]

'Patients receiving prolonged courses of immunosuppressive glucocorticoid therapy (i.e. > 6 months) should be considered for primary prevention of osteoporotic fractures with either calcium and vitamin D or bisphosphonate drugs. This is especially important in post-menopausal women and in patients with pre-existing osteopenia. Calcitonin is an effective but less practical alternative therapy.'

- Homik J, Cranney A, Shea B, et al. Bisphosphonates for steroid-induced osteoporosis (Cochrane Review). Cochrane Library, issue 1, 2001. Oxford: Update Software.
- Homik J, Suarez-Almazor ME, Shea B, et al. Calcium and vitamin D for corticosteroid-induced osteoporosis (Cochrane Review). Cochrane Library, issue 1, 2001. Oxford: Update Software.

Further information: 💻 www.cochrane.co.uk

Withdrawal of glucocorticoid therapy

All glucocorticoid therapy, even if inhaled or applied topically, can suppress the hypothalamic-pituitary-adrenal axis (HPA). In practice, this is only likely to result in a crisis due to adrenal insufficiency if glucocorticoids have been administered orally or systemically for longer than 3 weeks, if repeated courses have been prescribed within the previous year, or if the dose is higher than the equivalent of 40 mg prednisolone per day. In these circumstances, the drug, when it is no longer required for the underlying condition, must be withdrawn slowly with the rate dictated by the duration of treatment. If glucocorticoid therapy has been prolonged, then it may take many months for the HPA to recover. All patients must be advised to avoid sudden drug withdrawal. They should be

16.32 ADVICE TO PATIENTS ON GLUCOCORTICOID REPLACEMENT

Intercurrent stress
- e.g. Febrile illness—double dose of hydrocortisone

Surgery
- Minor operation—hydrocortisone 100 mg i.m. with premedication
- Major operation—hydrocortisone 100 mg 6-hourly for 24 hours, then 50 mg i.m. 6-hourly until ready to take tablets

Vomiting
- Must have parenteral hydrocortisone if unable to take by mouth

Steroid card
- Patient should carry this at all times. Should give information regarding diagnosis, steroid, dose and doctor

Bracelet
- Patients should be encouraged to buy one of these and have it engraved with the diagnosis and a reference and phone number for a centrally held database

---

issued with a steroid card and/or wear an engraved bracelet (see Box 16.32).

It should help the axis to recover if there is no exogenous glucocorticoid present during the nocturnal surge in ACTH secretion, i.e. if the glucocorticoid is given in the morning or even on alternate days. Giving ACTH to stimulate adrenal recovery is of no value as the pituitary remains suppressed.

In patients who have received glucocorticoids for longer than a few weeks, it is often valuable to confirm that the HPA is recovering during glucocorticoid withdrawal. Once the dose of glucocorticoid is reduced to a minimum (e.g. 4 mg prednisolone or 0.5 mg dexamethasone per day), then measure plasma cortisol at 0900 hrs before the next dose. If this is detectable, then perform an ACTH stimulation test (see p. 727) to confirm that glucocorticoids can be withdrawn completely.

Spontaneous, non-iatrogenic Cushing's syndrome

Aetiology

Causes are shown in Box 16.33. Amongst endogenous causes, pituitary-dependent cortisol excess (by convention, called Cushing's disease) accounts for ~80% of cases. Both Cushing's disease and adrenal tumour are four times more common in women than men. In contrast, ectopic ACTH syndrome (often due to a small-cell carcinoma of the bronchus) is more common in men.

Clinical features

The diverse manifestations of glucocorticoid excess are indicated in Figure 16.17. Many of these are not specific to Cushing's syndrome and, because spontaneous Cushing's syndrome is rare, the positive predictive value of any one feature alone is low. Moreover, some common disorders can be confused with Cushing's syndrome because they are associated with alterations in cortisol secretion: for example, obesity and depression (see Box 16.33). Features which have the best predictive value

(see Box 16.33)

16.33 CLASSIFICATION OF CUSHING'S SYNDROME
ACTH-dependent
• Pituitary-dependent bilateral adrenal hyperplasia (i.e. Cushing's disease)   • Ectopic ACTH syndrome (e.g. bronchial carcinoid, small-cell lung carcinoma, pancreatic carcinoma)   • Iatrogenic (ACTH therapy)
Non-ACTH-dependent
• Iatrogenic (chronic glucocorticoid therapy, e.g. for asthma)   • Adrenal adenoma   • Adrenal carcinoma
Pseudo-Cushing's syndrome, i.e. cortisol excess as part of another illness
• Alcohol excess (biochemical and clinical features)   • Major depressive illness (biochemical features only, some clinical overlap—see p. 262)   • Primary obesity (mild biochemical features, some clinical overlap)

in favour of Cushing's syndrome in an obese patient are bruising, myopathy and hypertension. Any clinical suspicion of cortisol excess is best resolved by further investigation.

Some clinical features are more common in ectopic ACTH syndrome. Unlike pituitary tumours secreting ACTH, ectopic tumours have no residual negative feedback sensitivity to cortisol, and both ACTH and cortisol levels are usually higher than with other causes. Very high ACTH levels are associated with marked pigmentation. Very high cortisol levels overcome the barrier of 11β-HSD in the kidney (see p. 720) and cause hypokalaemic alkalosis. Hypokalaemia aggravates both myopathy and hyperglycaemia (by inhibiting insulin secretion). When the tumour secreting ACTH is malignant (e.g. pancreatic or small-cell lung carcinomas), then the onset is usually rapid and may be associated with cachexia. For these reasons, the classical features of Cushing's syndrome are less common in ectopic ACTH syndrome, and if present suggest that a benign tumour (e.g. bronchial carcinoid) is responsible.

In Cushing's disease the pituitary tumour is almost always a microadenoma (< 10 mm in diameter); hence other features of a pituitary macroadenoma (hypopituitarism, visual failure or disconnection hyperprolactinaemia, see p. 737) are rare.

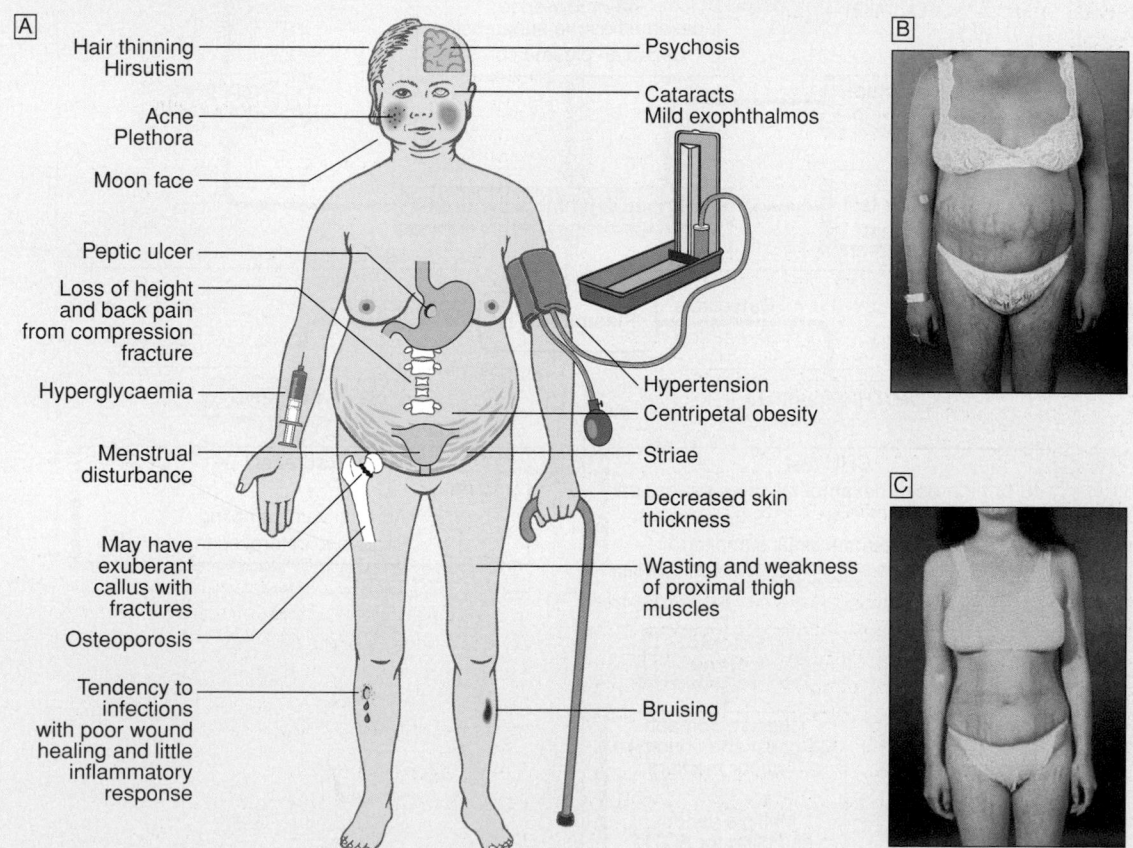

Fig. 16.17 **Cushing's syndrome.** A Clinical features common to all causes. B A patient with Cushing's disease before treatment. C The same patient 1 year after the successful removal of an ACTH-secreting pituitary microadenoma by trans-sphenoidal surgery.

Investigations

The large number of tests available for Cushing's syndrome reflects the fact that no single test is infallible and several are needed to establish the diagnosis. It is useful to divide investigations into those which establish whether the patient has Cushing's syndrome, and those which are used subsequently to elucidate the aetiology.

A recommended sequence of investigations is shown in Figure 16.18 and the interpretation of these tests is shown in Box 16.34. Some additional tests are useful in all cases of Cushing's syndrome, including plasma electrolytes, glucose, glycosylated haemoglobin and bone mineral density measurement.

Does the patient have Cushing's syndrome?

Plasma cortisol levels are highly variable in healthy subjects so that patients with Cushing's syndrome often have day-time values within the normal range. For this reason, there is no place for a random measurement of daytime plasma cortisol in the clinic in either supporting or refuting a diagnosis of Cushing's syndrome. Cushing's syndrome is confirmed by the demonstration of increased secretion of cortisol (measured in urine) which fails to suppress with relatively low doses of dexamethasone (measured in plasma or urine) (see Box 16.34). Loss of diurnal variation, with elevated evening plasma cortisol, is also characteristic of Cushing's syndrome, but samples are awkward to obtain.

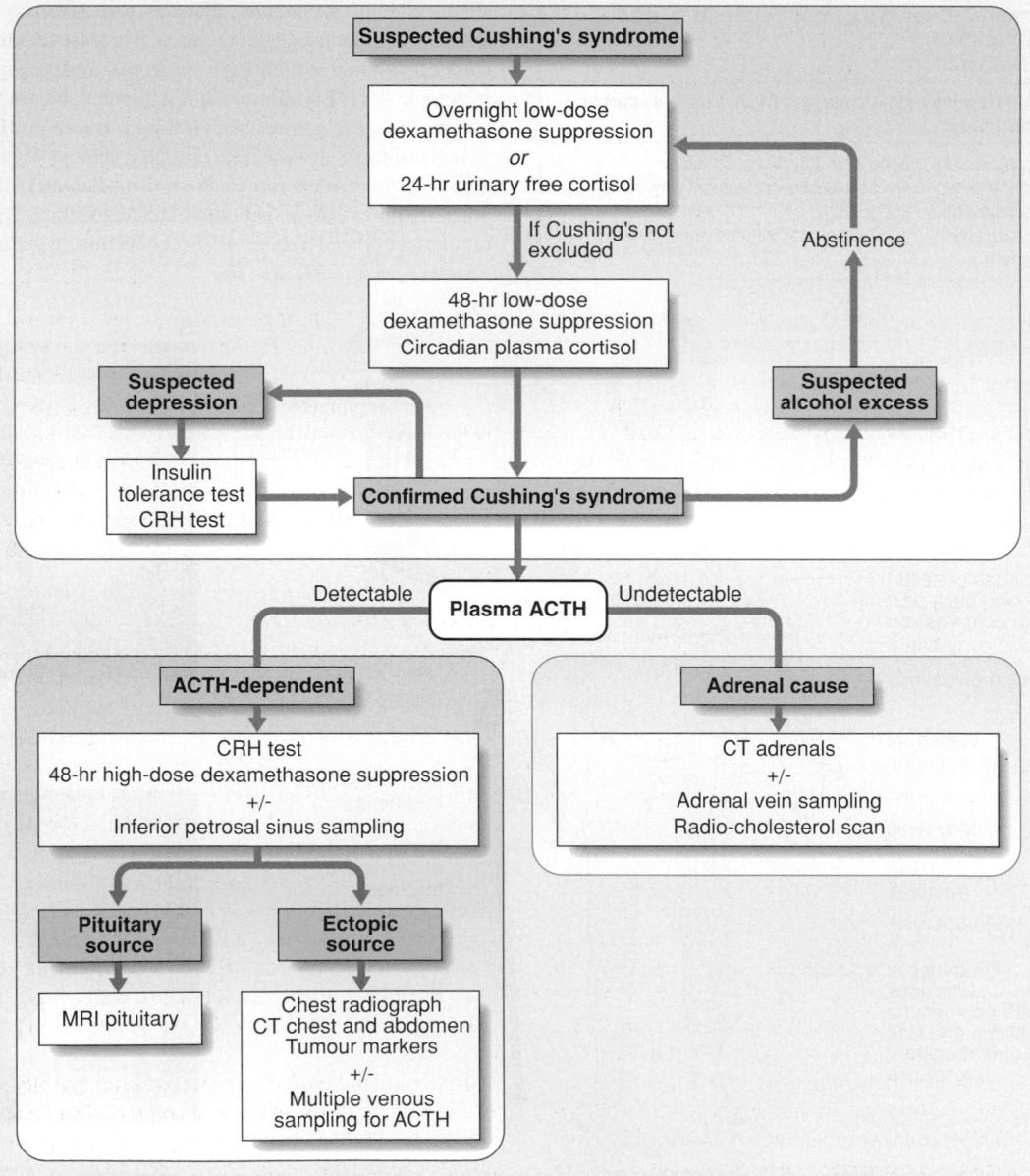

Fig. 16.18   Sequence of investigations in suspected spontaneous Cushing's syndrome. (CRH = corticotrophin-releasing hormone)

16.34 TESTS FOR CUSHING'S SYNDROME

Test	Protocol	Interpretation
Urine free cortisol	24-hr timed collection (some centres use overnight collections corrected for creatinine)	Normal range depends on assay
Overnight dexamethasone suppression test	1 mg orally at midnight; measure plasma cortisol at 0800–0900 hrs	Plasma cortisol < 60 nmol/l excludes Cushing's
Diurnal rhythm of plasma cortisol	Sample for cortisol at 0900 hrs and at 2300 hrs (requires acclimatisation to ward for at least 48 hrs)	Evening level > 75% of morning level in Cushing's
Low-dose dexamethasone suppression test	0.5 mg 6-hourly for 48 hrs; sample 24-hr urine cortisol during second day and 0900-hr plasma cortisol after 48 hrs	Urine cortisol < 100 nmol/day or plasma cortisol < 60 nmol/l excludes Cushing's
Insulin tolerance test	See Box 16.47, page 738	Peak plasma cortisol > 120% of baseline excludes Cushing's
High-dose dexamethasone suppression test	2 mg 6-hourly for 48 hrs; sample 24-hr urine cortisol at baseline and during second day	Urine cortisol < 50% of basal suggests pituitary-dependent disease; > 50% basal suggests ectopic ACTH syndrome
Corticotrophin-releasing hormone test	100 μg ovine CRH i.v. and monitor plasma ACTH and cortisol for 2 hrs	Peak plasma cortisol > 120% and/or ACTH > 150% of basal values suggests pituitary-dependent disease; lesser responses suggest ectopic ACTH syndrome
Inferior petrosal sinus sampling	Catheters placed in both inferior petrosal sinuses and simultaneous sampling from these and peripheral blood for ACTH; may be repeated 10 minutes after peripheral CRH injection	ACTH in either petrosal sinus > 200% peripheral ACTH suggests pituitary-dependent disease; < 150% suggests ectopic ACTH syndrome

Dexamethasone is used for suppression testing because, unlike prednisolone, it does not cross-react in radio-immunoassays for cortisol. However, metabolism of dexamethasone may be altered by drugs, e.g. enzyme-inducers such as oestrogen or phenytoin. Also, the hypothalamic-pituitary-adrenal axis may 'escape' from suppression by dexamethasone if a more potent influence such as psychological stress supervenes.

There is a rare syndrome of cyclical Cushing's syndrome in which the excessive secretion of cortisol is episodic. If there is a strong clinical suspicion of Cushing's syndrome but initial screening tests are normal, then weekly 24-hour urine cortisol measurements for up to 3 months are sometimes justified.

What is the cause of the Cushing's syndrome?

Once the presence of Cushing's syndrome is established, measurement of plasma ACTH is key in establishing the differential diagnosis. In the presence of excess cortisol secretion, an undetectable ACTH indicates an adrenal tumour while any detectable ACTH is pathological. Tests to discriminate pituitary from ectopic sources of ACTH rely on the fact that pituitary tumours, but not ectopic tumours, retain some features of normal regulation of ACTH secretion. Thus, in Cushing's disease ACTH secretion is suppressed by dexamethasone, albeit at a higher dose than in health, and ACTH is stimulated by corticotrophin-releasing hormone (CRH).

Techniques for localisation of tumours secreting ACTH or cortisol are listed in Figure 16.18. MRI with gadolinium contrast enhancement detects around 70% of pituitary microadenomas secreting ACTH. Venous catheterisation with measurement of inferior petrosal sinus ACTH (i.e. draining directly from the pituitary) may be helpful in confirming Cushing's disease if the MRI does not show a microadenoma. CT or MRI detects most adrenal adenomas. Adrenal carcinomas are usually large (> 5 cm). If CT does not demonstrate a unilateral tumour, then lateralisation may be possible either with selective adrenal vein catheterisation and sampling for cortisol, or by functional adrenal scanning using [75]selenium-labelled cholesterol.

Management

This is essential, as untreated Cushing's syndrome has a 50% 5-year mortality. Most patients are treated surgically with medical therapy given for a few weeks prior to operation. The type of surgery depends on the cause.

Medical therapy. A number of drugs are used to inhibit corticosteroid biosynthesis, including metyrapone, aminoglutethimide and ketoconazole. The dose of these agents is best titrated against 24-hour urine free cortisol.

Cushing's disease. Trans-sphenoidal surgery with selective removal of the adenoma is the treatment of choice. Experienced surgeons can identify microadenomas which were not detected by MRI and cure about 80% of patients. If the operation is unsuccessful or the diagnosis is not certain, then bilateral adrenalectomy is an alternative.

If bilateral adrenalectomy is used in patients with pituitary-dependent Cushing's syndrome, then there is a risk that the pituitary tumour will grow in the absence of the negative feedback suppression previously provided by the elevated cortisol levels. This can result in Nelson's syndrome, with an aggressive pituitary macroadenoma and very high ACTH levels causing pigmentation. Nelson's syndrome can be prevented by pituitary irradiation.

External pituitary irradiation alone is of little value in adults but is surprisingly effective in children with Cushing's disease.

Adrenal tumours. Adrenal adenomas are removed via laparoscopy or a loin incision. Adrenal carcinomas are resected if possible, the tumour bed irradiated and the patient given the adrenolytic drug o',p'-DDD (mitotane).

Ectopic ACTH syndrome. Benign tumours causing this syndrome (e.g. bronchial carcinoid) should be removed. During treatment or palliation of other malignancies, it is important to reduce the severity of the Cushing's syndrome using medical therapy (see above).

ADRENAL INSUFFICIENCY

Adrenal insufficiency results from inadequate secretion of cortisol and/or aldosterone. It is potentially fatal and notoriously variable in its presentation. A high index of suspicion is therefore required in patients with unexplained fatigue, hyponatraemia or hypotension.

Aetiology

Causes are shown in Box 16.35. The most common is ACTH deficiency (i.e. secondary adrenocortical failure), usually because of inappropriate withdrawal of chronic glucocorticoid therapy or a pituitary tumour. Congenital adrenal hyperplasias and Addison's disease (i.e. primary adrenocortical failure) are rare, although in areas where AIDS and tuberculosis are common associated Addison's disease is increasing in prevalence.

16.35 CAUSES OF ADRENOCORTICAL INSUFFICIENCY
Secondary (↓ACTH)
• Withdrawal of suppressive glucocorticoid therapy • Hypothalamic or pituitary disease
Primary (↑ACTH)

Addison's disease
Common causes
• Autoimmune
    Sporadic
    Polyglandular syndromes (see p. 687)
• Tuberculosis
• HIV/AIDS
• Metastatic carcinomas
• Bilateral adrenalectomy
 	
Rare causes
• Lymphoma
• Intra-adrenal haemorrhage (Waterhouse–Friedrichsen syndrome following meningococcal septicaemia)
• Amyloidosis
• Haemochromatosis
 	
Corticosteroid biosynthetic enzyme defects
• Congenital adrenal hyperplasias
• Drugs
    Aminoglutethimide, metyrapone, ketoconazole, etomidate etc.

Clinical features

Features of adrenal insufficiency are shown in Box 16.36. In Addison's disease, either glucocorticoid or mineralocorticoid deficiency may come first, but eventually all patients fail to secrete both classes of corticosteroid. Similar features occur in different combinations with other causes of adrenocortical insufficiency.

16.36 CLINICAL AND BIOCHEMICAL FEATURES OF ADRENAL INSUFFICIENCY				
	Glucocorticoid insufficiency	**Mineralocorticoid insufficiency**	**ACTH excess**	**Adrenal androgen insufficiency**
Withdrawal of exogenous glucocorticoid	✓	X	X	✓
Hypopituitarism	✓	X	X	✓
Addison's disease	✓	✓	✓	✓
Congenital adrenal hyperplasia (21-OHase deficiency)	✓	✓	✓	X
Clinical features	Weight loss Malaise Weakness Anorexia Nausea Vomiting Gastrointestinal—diarrhoea or constipation Postural hypotension Shock Hypoglycaemia Hyponatraemia Hypercalcaemia	Hypotension Shock Hyponatraemia Hyperkalaemia	Pigmentation Sun-exposed areas Pressure areas, e.g. elbows, knees Palmar creases, knuckles Mucous membranes Conjunctivae Recent scars	Decreased body hair and loss of libido, especially in female

Patients may present with chronic features and/or in acute circulatory shock. With a chronic presentation, initial symptoms are often misdiagnosed (e.g. as chronic fatigue syndrome or depression). Adrenocortical insufficiency should also be considered in patients with hyponatraemia, even in the absence of symptoms (see Ch. 9). Vitiligo occurs in 10–20% of patients with autoimmune Addison's disease (see p. 684).

Features of an acute adrenal crisis include circulatory shock with severe hypotension, hyponatraemia, hyperkalaemia and, in some instances, hypoglycaemia and hypercalcaemia. Muscle cramps, nausea, vomiting, diarrhoea and unexplained fever may be present. The crisis is often precipitated by intercurrent disease, surgery or infection.

Investigations

In patients presenting with chronic illness the investigations below should be performed before any treatment. In patients with suspected acute adrenal crisis treatment should not be delayed pending results. A random blood sample should be stored for measurement of cortisol, and it may be appropriate to spend 30 minutes performing a short ACTH stimulation test (see Box 16.37), but investigations may need to be performed after recovery.

Assessment of glucocorticoids

Random plasma cortisol is usually low in patients with adrenal insufficiency, but it may be within the normal reference range yet inappropriately low for a seriously ill patient. Random measurement of plasma cortisol cannot therefore be used to confirm or refute the diagnosis unless the value is high, i.e. > 550 nmol/l.

More useful is the short ACTH stimulation test (also called the tetracosactide or short Synacthen test) described in Box 16.37. Cortisol levels fail to increase in response to exogenous ACTH in patients with primary or secondary adrenal insufficiency. These can be distinguished by measurement of ACTH (which is low in ACTH deficiency and high in Addison's disease). If an ACTH assay is unavailable, then a long ACTH stimulation test can be used (1 mg depot ACTH i.m. daily for 3 days). In secondary adrenal insufficiency there is a progressive increase in plasma cortisol with repeated ACTH administration, whereas in Addison's disease cortisol remains less than 700 nmol/l at 8 hours after the last injection.

In a patient who is already receiving glucocorticoids, the short ACTH stimulation test can be performed first thing in the morning > 12 hours after the last dose of glucocorticoid, or the treatment can be changed to a synthetic steroid such as dexamethasone (0.75 mg daily), which does not cross-react in the plasma cortisol radioimmunoassay.

Assessment of mineralocorticoids

Plasma electrolyte measurements are insufficient to assess mineralocorticoid secretion in patients with suspected Addison's disease. Hyponatraemia occurs in both aldosterone and cortisol deficiency (see Box 16.36 and p. 737). Hyperkalaemia is common, but not universal, in aldosterone deficiency. Plasma renin activity and aldosterone should be measured in the supine position. In mineralocorticoid deficiency, plasma renin activity is high, with plasma aldosterone being either low or normal.

Other tests to establish the cause

Patients with unexplained secondary adrenocortical insufficiency should be investigated as described in the section on pituitary disease on page 736. In patients with elevated ACTH, further tests are required to establish the cause of Addison's disease. In those who have autoimmune adrenal failure, antibodies can often be measured against steroid-secreting cells (adrenal and gonad), thyroid antigens, pancreatic β cells and parietal cells. Thyroid function tests, full blood count (to screen for pernicious anaemia), plasma glucose, and tests of gonadal function (see p. 705) and serum calcium should be performed. Other causes of adrenocortical disease are usually obviously clinically, particularly if health is not fully restored by corticosteroid replacement therapy. Tuberculosis causes adrenal calcification, visible on plain radiograph or ultrasound scan. A chest radiograph and early morning urine for culture should also be taken. An HIV test may be appropriate if risk factors for infection are present. Imaging of the adrenals by CT or MRI to identify metastatic malignancy may also be appropriate.

Management

Patients with adrenocortical insufficiency always need glucocorticoid replacement therapy and usually, but not

---

16.37 ACTH STIMULATION TEST
Use
• Diagnosis of primary or secondary adrenal insufficiency
• Assessment of hypothalamic-pituitary-adrenal axis in patients taking suppressive glucocorticoid therapy
• Relies on ACTH-dependent adrenal atrophy in secondary adrenal insufficiency, so may not detect acute ACTH deficiency (e.g. in pituitary apoplexy, see p. 736)
Dose
• 250 μg ACTH$_{1-24}$ (Synacthen) by i.m. injection at any time of day
Blood samples
• 0 and 30 minutes for plasma cortisol
• 0 minutes also for ACTH (on ice) if Addison's disease is being considered (i.e. patient not known to have pituitary disease or to be taking exogenous glucocorticoids)
Results
• Normal subjects plasma cortisol > 550 nmol/l either at baseline or at 30 minutes
• Incremental change in cortisol is not a criterion

always, mineralocorticoid. Other treatments depend on the underlying cause.

Glucocorticoid replacement

Cortisol (hydrocortisone) is the drug of choice. In the past, cortisone acetate was given but this has to be converted to cortisol in the liver and in some patients this process may be impaired. In someone who is not critically ill cortisol should be given by mouth, 15 mg on waking and 5 mg at ~1800 hrs. The precise dose may need to be adjusted for the individual patient, but this is subjective. Excess weight gain usually indicates over-replacement, whilst persistent lethargy may be due to an inadequate dose. Measurement of plasma cortisol levels is unhelpful, because the dynamic interaction between cortisol and glucocorticoid receptors is not predicted by measurements such as the maximum or minimum plasma cortisol level after each dose. Advice to patients dependent on glucocorticoid replacement is given in Box 16.32, page 722. These are physiological replacement doses which should not cause Cushingoid side-effects.

An adrenal crisis is a medical emergency and requires intravenous hydrocortisone succinate 100 mg and intravenous fluid (normal saline and 10% dextrose for hypoglycaemia). Parenteral hydrocortisone should be continued (100 mg i.m. 6-hourly) until gastrointestinal symptoms abate before starting oral therapy. The precipitating cause should be sought and, if possible, treated.

Mineralocorticoid replacement

Aldosterone is not readily available and fludrocortisone (i.e. 9α-fluoro-hydrocortisone) is the mineralocorticoid used. The halogen group prevents fludrocortisone from being metabolised by 11β-HSD and thereby confers a longer half-life and access to mineralocorticoid receptors. The usual dose is 0.05–0.1 mg daily. Adequacy of replacement can be assessed objectively by measurement of blood pressure, plasma electrolytes and plasma renin activity.

In adrenal crisis, however, rapid replacement of sodium deficiency is more important than administration of fludrocortisone. Intravenous saline should be infused as required to normalise haemodynamic indices. In severe hyponatraemia (< 125 mmol/l) caution should be exercised to avoid too rapid normalisation, which risks pontine demyelination.

EBM

HRT IN ADRENOCORTICAL INSUFFICIENCY—use of adrenal androgens

'Glucocorticoid and mineralocorticoid replacement therapy have not been studied in RCTs. One RCT in 39 patients shows that replacement therapy with the adrenal androgen dehydroepiandrosterone (DHEA) improves mood and fatigue in patients with Addison's disease.'

● Hunt PJ, Gurnell EM, Huppert FA, et al. Improvement in mood and fatigue after dehydroepiandrosterone replacement in Addison's disease in a randomized, double blind trial. J Clin Endocrinol Metab 2000; 85:4650–4656.

MINERALOCORTICOID EXCESS AND PRIMARY HYPERALDOSTERONISM

Aetiology

Causes of excessive activation of mineralocorticoid receptors are shown in Box 16.38. Most often, this results from enhanced secretion of renin (secondary hyperaldosteronism) in response to inadequate renal perfusion (e.g. in heart failure, hypoalbuminaemia or renal artery stenosis). Secondary hyperaldosteronism is described on page 855 and is not dealt with here. Less commonly, mineralocorticoid excess occurs in the face of suppressed renin secretion (primary hyperaldosteronism and rare disorders of mineralocorticoid action). These disorders are usually diagnosed in patients presenting with hypertension. Indications to test for primary hyperaldosteronism in hypertensive patients include hypokalaemia (including hypokalaemia induced by thiazide diuretics), poor control of blood pressure with conventional therapy, or presentation at a young age.

The prevalence of primary hyperaldosteronism is controversial. If only hypertensive patients with hypokalaemia are investigated, then fewer than 1% of patients with hypertension will be found to have primary hyperaldosteronism. Around half of these have an adrenal adenoma secreting aldosterone (Conn's syndrome). However, recent studies in which hypertensive patients have been screened using aldosterone/renin ratios (see below) suggest that the prevalence may be as high as 5%. Most of these 'extra' patients have bilateral adrenal hyperplasia rather than Conn's syndrome, and many have normal plasma potassium. Although spironolactone would be the antihypertensive agent of choice in such patients, it remains to be determined whether investigation of all hypertensive patients for bilateral adrenal hyperplasia is worth while.

Glucocorticoid suppressible hyperaldosteronism is a rare autosomal dominant disorder caused by translocation of two homologous genes, such that the ACTH-regulated

---

16.38 CAUSES OF MINERALOCORTICOID EXCESS

With renin high and aldosterone high (secondary hyperaldosteronism)

● E.g. diuretic therapy, cardiac failure, liver failure, nephrotic syndrome, renal artery stenosis

With renin low and aldosterone high (primary hyperaldosteronism)

● Adrenal adenoma secreting aldosterone (Conn's syndrome)
● Idiopathic bilateral adrenal hyperplasia
● Glucocorticoid suppressible hyperaldosteronism (rare)

With renin low and aldosterone low (rare)

● Ectopic ACTH syndrome
● Liquorice misuse (inhibition of 11β-HSD)
● Liddle's syndrome
● 11-deoxycorticosterone-secreting adrenal tumour
● Rare forms of congenital adrenal hyperplasia and 11β-HSD deficiency

promoter of one gene (11β-hydroxylase) is linked with the coding exons of another (aldosterone synthase—see Fig. 16.16, p. 721). The result is inappropriate secretion of aldosterone from the adrenal in response to normal levels of ACTH, despite suppression of renin and angiotensin II levels. Treatment is by suppression of ACTH, e.g. with dexamethasone.

In a few conditions, the mineralocorticoid receptor pathway in the distal nephron is activated even though aldosterone levels are low. Either the receptors are activated by cortisol (ectopic ACTH syndrome or 11β-HSD deficiency) or 11-deoxycorticosterone (rare congenital adrenal hyperplasias or tumours), or post-receptor mechanisms are inappropriately activated (e.g. the epithelial sodium channel in Liddle's syndrome).

Clinical features

Many patients are asymptomatic, but they may have features of sodium retention or potassium loss. Sodium retention causes oedema, while hypokalaemia causes muscle weakness (or even paralysis, especially in Chinese), polyuria (secondary to renal tubular damage which produces nephrogenic diabetes insipidus), and occasionally tetany (because of associated metabolic alkalosis and low ionised calcium). Hypertension is almost invariable in primary hyperaldosteronism.

Investigations

Biochemical

Plasma electrolytes may show hypokalaemia and elevated bicarbonate. Plasma sodium is usually towards the upper end of the normal range in primary hyperaldosteronism but is characteristically low in secondary hyperaldosteronism (because low plasma volume stimulates ADH release and high angiotensin II levels stimulate thirst).

The key measurements are plasma renin activity and aldosterone (see Box 16.38). Almost all antihypertensive drugs interfere with these hormones (e.g. β-blockers inhibit whilst thiazide diuretics stimulate renin secretion), so these should be stopped for at least 6 weeks beforehand. If this is not possible, then antihypertensives which have minimal effects on the renin-angiotensin system, such as bethanidine or debrisoquine, should be employed.

If renin is low and aldosterone levels are high, then Conn's adenoma can be differentiated from bilateral adrenal hyperplasia by tests of aldosterone response to angiotensin II. (In Conn's adenoma aldosterone does not rise on standing or with furosemide (frusemide) administration.) In the rare circumstance when renin and aldosterone are both low, further tests include measurement of urinary cortisol and its metabolites, and 11-deoxycorticosterone.

Localisation

The only cause of primary hyperaldosteronism which is usually treated by surgery is Conn's adenoma. Abdominal CT is often the only test required to localise the tumour (see Fig. 16.19), but it is important to recognise that non-functioning adrenal adenomata are present in about 20% of patients with essential hypertension, and adrenal CT should only be performed when the biochemistry supports the diagnosis of adrenal tumour. If the scan is inconclusive, then adrenal vein catheterisation with measurement of aldosterone (and cortisol to confirm positioning of the catheters) or selenocholesterol scanning may be helpful.

Ⓐ **35-year-old male**

- Mild polyuria
- Blood pressure 188/104 mmHg

Plasma biochemistry

- Na 144 mmol/l (132–144)
- K 3.1 mmol/l (3.3–4.7)
- HCO₃⁻ 29 mmol/l (21–27)

Lying at 0900 hrs
- Renin activity < 0.5 (0.4–1.5*)
- Aldosterone 850 pmol/l (30–440*)

Standing at 1200 hrs
- Renin activity < 0.5 (1.0–2.5*)
- Aldosterone 750 pmol/l (110–860*)

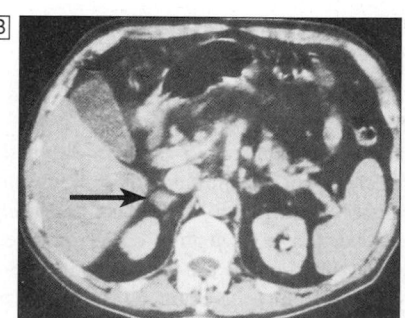

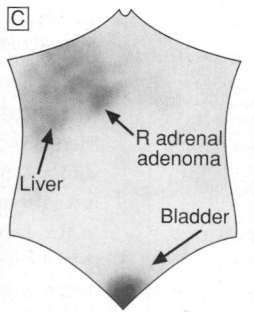

Ⓒ
Liver
R adrenal adenoma
Bladder

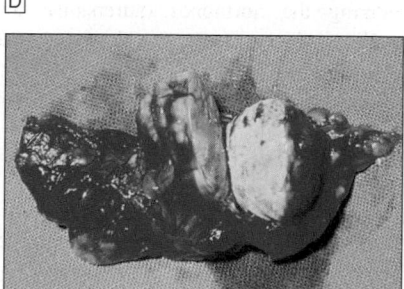

Fig. 16.19 Conn's adenoma causing primary hyperaldosteronism. Ⓐ Characteristic biochemical results: hypernatraemia, hypokalaemic metabolic alkalosis, suppressed plasma renin activity, and high supine aldosterone which is not under angiotensin II control and so does not rise on standing. Normal ranges for biochemical results are shown in brackets. * Normal ranges for renin activity (in μg angiotensin I generated/ml/hr) and aldosterone vary widely according to the assay used. Ⓑ CT appearance showing adenoma in right adrenal (arrow). Ⓒ Unilateral uptake of radio-labelled cholesterol in right adrenal. Ⓓ Lipid-laden macroscopic appearance after adenomectomy.

Management

The mineralocorticoid receptor antagonist spironolactone is valuable in treating both hypokalaemia and hypertension in all forms of mineralocorticoid excess. High doses (up to 400 mg/day) may be required. Up to 20% of males develop gynaecomastia on spironolactone. Amiloride (10–40 mg/day), which blocks the epithelial sodium channel regulated by aldosterone, can be used when such problems arise.

In patients with Conn's adenoma, spironolactone is usually given for a few weeks to normalise whole-body electrolyte balance before unilateral adrenalectomy. Laparoscopic surgery cures the biochemical abnormality but hypertension remains in as many as 70% of cases, probably because of irreversible damage to the systemic microcirculation.

PHAEOCHROMOCYTOMA

This is a rare tumour of chromaffin tissue which secretes catecholamines and is responsible for less than 0.1% of cases of hypertension. There is a useful 'rule of tens' in this condition: ~10% are malignant; ~10% are extra-adrenal (i.e. elsewhere in the sympathetic chain); and ~10% are familial.

Clinical features

These depend on the pattern of catecholamine secretion and are listed in Box 16.39.

Some patients may present with a complication of the hypertension, e.g. accelerated phase hypertension, stroke, myocardial infarction, left ventricular failure or hypertensive retinopathy. Occasionally, patients are hypotensive (especially those with dopamine-secreting tumours). There may be features of the familial syndromes associated with phaeochromocytoma including neurofibromatosis, von Hippel–Lindau syndrome and multiple endocrine neoplasia type II (see p. 688).

Investigations

Biochemical

Excessive secretion of catecholamines can be confirmed by measuring the hormones (adrenaline, noradrenaline

---

and dopamine) in plasma or their metabolites (e.g. vallinyl-mandelic acid, VMA; conjugated metanephrine and nor-metanephrine) in urine. However, catecholamine secretion is usually paroxysmal and sometimes the paroxysms are infrequent; in a patient with classical symptoms, phaeochromocytoma can only be excluded if the 24-hour urinary catecholamine excretion is normal on a day on which symptoms have occurred.

Increased urinary catecholamine excretion occurs in stressed patients (e.g. after myocardial infarction or major surgery) and is induced by some drugs (notably β-blockers and antidepressants). For this reason, a suppression test may be valuable. Normal adrenomedullary secretion is suppressed by administration of drugs which interfere with sympathetic outflow, such as clonidine or pentolinium. In phaeochromocytoma these drugs do not suppress plasma catecholamines. Provocative tests of catecholamine release should not be used.

Localisation

Phaeochromocytomas are usually identified by abdominal CT (see Fig. 16.20). Difficulty can arise with the localisation of extra-adrenal tumours. Scintigraphy using meta-iodobenzyl guanidine (MIBG) can be useful; MIBG labelled with radioactive iodine is taken up by both benign and malignant phaeochromocytomas. If the tumour cannot be localised, then selective venous sampling with measurement of plasma noradrenaline may be required.

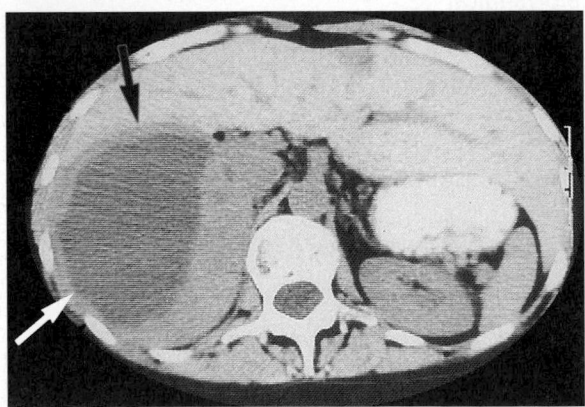

Fig. 16.20   CT of abdomen showing large right phaeochromocytoma (arrows).

Management

Medical therapy is required to prepare the patient for surgery, preferably for a minimum of 6 weeks to allow restoration of normal plasma volume. The most useful drug in the face of very high circulating catecholamines is the α-blocker phenoxybenzamine (10–20 mg orally 6–8-hourly) because it is a non-competitive antagonist, unlike prazosin or doxazosin. If α-blockade produces a marked tachycardia, then a β-blocker (e.g. propranolol) or combined α- and β-antagonist (e.g. labetalol) can be added. On no account should the β-antagonist be given before the α-antagonist, as vasoconstriction due to unopposed α-adrenoceptor activity may occur with a further increase in blood pressure.

16.39 CLINICAL FEATURES OF PHAEOCHROMOCYTOMA	

- Hypertension (usually paroxysmal; often postural drop of blood pressure)
- Attacks with
  - Pallor (occasionally flushing)
  - Palpitations
  - Sweating
  - Headache
  - Anxiety (fear of death—angor animi)
- Abdominal pain, vomiting
- Constipation
- Weight loss
- Glucose intolerance

During surgery sodium nitroprusside and the short-acting α-antagonist phentolamine are useful in controlling hypertensive episodes which may result from anaesthetic induction or tumour mobilisation. Post-operative hypotension may occur and require volume expansion and, very occasionally, noradrenaline infusion. This is uncommon if the patient has been prepared with phenoxybenzamine for at least 6 weeks.

CONGENITAL ADRENAL HYPERPLASIA

Aetiology and clinical features

Defects in the cortisol biosynthetic pathway result in impaired negative feedback and increased ACTH secretion. ACTH then stimulates the production of steroids up to the enzyme block. This produces adrenal hyperplasia and a combination of clinical features which depend on the severity and site of the defect in biosynthesis. All of these enzyme abnormalities are inherited as autosomal recessive traits. There is therefore a 1:4 chance that the sibling of an affected child will also have the disease, but a low risk of passing the disease to the next generation.

The most common enzyme defect is 21-hydroxylase deficiency. In about one-third of cases this defect is severe, producing all of the features outlined in Figure 16.21. In the other two-thirds, mineralocorticoid secretion is not affected but there may be features of cortisol insufficiency and/or androgen excess. Sometimes the mildest enzyme defects are not apparent until adult life, when females may present with amenorrhoea and/or hirsutism (see p. 709). This is called 'non-classical' or 'late-onset' congenital adrenal hyperplasia.

Defects of all the other enzymes have been described but are much rarer. Both 17-hydroxylase and 11β-hydroxylase deficiency may produce hypertension due to excess production of 11-deoxycorticosterone, a mineralocorticoid.

Investigations

High levels of plasma 17OH-progesterone are found in 21-hydroxylase deficiency. In late-onset cases this may only be demonstrated after ACTH administration. To avoid salt-wasting crises in infancy, 17OH-progesterone is routinely measured in heel prick blood spot samples taken from all infants in the first week of life. Assessment is otherwise as described for adrenal insufficiency on page 726.

In siblings of affected children, antenatal genetic diagnosis can be made by amniocentesis or chorionic villous sampling. This allows prevention of virilisation of affected female fetuses by administration of dexamethasone to the mother.

Management

The aim is to replace deficient corticosteroids, and also suppress ACTH and hence adrenal androgen production. In contrast with glucocorticoid replacement therapy in other forms of cortisol deficiency (see p. 728), it is usual to give

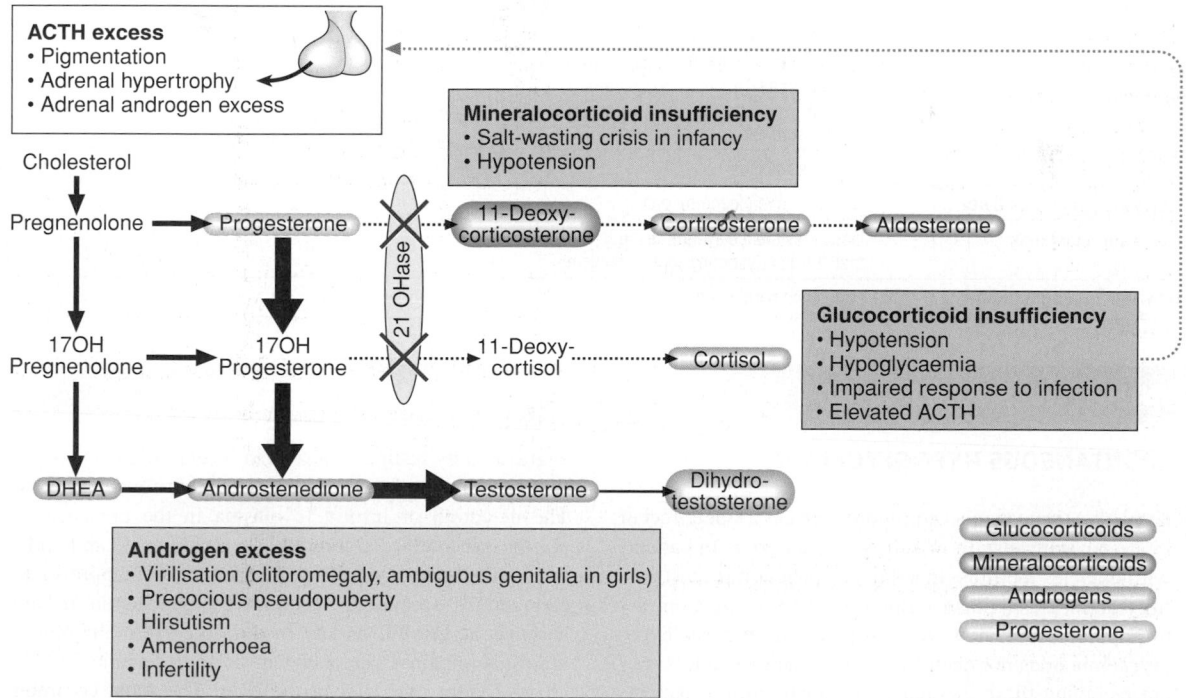

Fig. 16.21   Manifestations of congenital adrenal hyperplasia due to 21-hydroxylase deficiency. The enzyme block leads to insufficiency of hormones 'distal' to the block (glucocorticoids and mineralocorticoids; see Box 16.36, p. 726), and impaired negative feedback suppression of ACTH leading to accumulation of precursor hormones 'proximal' to the block which 'spill over' into the adrenal androgen biosynthetic pathway. The severity of the mutation in the 21-hydroxylase (21 OHase) gene determines which features are present. The most severely affected 'classical' patients present in infancy (salt-wasting in boys; ambiguous genitalia in girls). The least severely affected 'late-onset' patients present as adults (hirsutism in women). (DHEA = dehydroepiandrosterone)

'reverse' treatment, i.e. a larger dose of a long-acting synthetic glucocorticoid just before going to bed to suppress the early morning ACTH peak, and a smaller dose in the morning. A careful balance is required between adequate suppression of adrenal androgen excess and excessive glucocorticoid replacement resulting in features of Cushing's syndrome. In children, growth velocity is the most useful measurement since either under- or over-replacement with glucocorticoids suppresses growth. In adults, clinical features (menstrual cycle, hirsutism, weight gain, blood pressure) and biochemical profiles (plasma renin activity and 17OH-progesterone levels) provide a guide.

Patients with late-onset 21-hydroxylase deficiency may not require corticosteroid replacement. If hirsutism is the main problem, anti-androgen therapy may be just as effective (see p. 712).

THE ENDOCRINE PANCREAS AND GASTROINTESTINAL TRACT

A series of hormones are secreted from cells distributed throughout the gastrointestinal tract and pancreas. Functional anatomy is described in Chapters 15 and 17. Pathology of these hormones is listed in Box 16.40. They account for one extremely common condition, diabetes mellitus, and a handful of rare conditions. Diabetes mellitus is discussed in detail in Chapter 15. Other pancreatic tumours, including gastrinoma (causing Zollinger–Ellison syndrome) and neuro-endocrine tumours causing diarrhoea (e.g. VIPoma), are discussed in Chapter 17. Outside the pancreas, the most common secretory tumour of the gastrointestinal tract causes carcinoid syndrome, which is also discussed in Chapter 17.

ISSUES IN OLDER PEOPLE
THE ADRENAL GLANDS

- Presentation of adrenal disease is often insidious, and may be especially difficult to spot in elderly patients with multiple pathology.
- Anti-inflammatory glucocorticoid therapy is especially hazardous in older patients, who are relatively immunocompromised and susceptible to osteoporosis, hyperglycaemia etc.
- Poor compliance with glucocorticoid therapy, combined with increased prevalence of 'stressful' illness in the elderly, increases the risk of adrenal crisis. Careful explanation of the treatment, and provision of a steroid card and/or 'medicalert' bracelet are important.

16.40 CLASSIFICATION OF ENDOCRINE DISEASES OF THE PANCREAS AND GASTROINTESTINAL TRACT

	Primary	Secondary
Hormone excess	Insulinoma Gastrinoma (Zollinger–Ellison syndrome) Carcinoid syndrome (secretion of 5-hydroxytryptamine (5-HT, serotonin) etc.) Glucagonoma VIPoma Somatostatinoma	Hypergastrinaemia of achlorhydria
Hormone deficiency	Diabetes mellitus	
Hormone hypersensitivity	Rare, e.g. pseudoacromegaly	
Hormone resistance	Insulin resistance syndromes (e.g. type 2 diabetes mellitus, lipodystrophy, leprechaunism)	
Non-functioning tumours	Pancreatic carcinoma	

MAJOR MANIFESTATIONS OF DISEASE OF THE ENDOCRINE PANCREAS

SPONTANEOUS HYPOGLYCAEMIA

Hypoglycaemia is most commonly seen as a side-effect of treatment with insulin or sulphonylurea drugs in patients with diabetes mellitus. In a diabetic patient it is most usefully defined as a plasma glucose < 3.5 mmol/l. Contrary to popular belief, however, for practical purposes hypoglycaemia does not occur in diabetic patients unless they are receiving these therapies and, apart from in patients with alcohol intoxication, is rare in non-diabetic patients. In non-diabetic patients it is defined as a plasma glucose < 2.2 mmol/l, although plasma glucose < 2.5 mmol/l may be pathological in some circumstances.

Causes of spontaneous hypoglycaemia are shown in Figure 16.22. In all these conditions, hypoglycaemia is aggravated by fasting. Causes can be classified according to the circulating insulin and/or C-peptide concentrations. The detection of insulin in plasma in the presence of plasma glucose < 2.5 mmol/l is pathological, and indicates either exogenous administration or an inappropriate endogenous source of insulin. Hypoglycaemia in the absence of insulin, or any insulin-like factor in blood, indicates impaired gluconeogenesis and/or availability of glucose from glycogen in the liver. The most common cause is inhibition of gluconeogenic enzymes by alcohol.

Hypoglycaemia may also occur without fasting as part of a dumping syndrome in patients with previous gastric surgery, in whom rapid small bowel absorption of oral carbohydrate is thought to induce an inappropriately brisk secretion of insulin. However, it is now thought that a

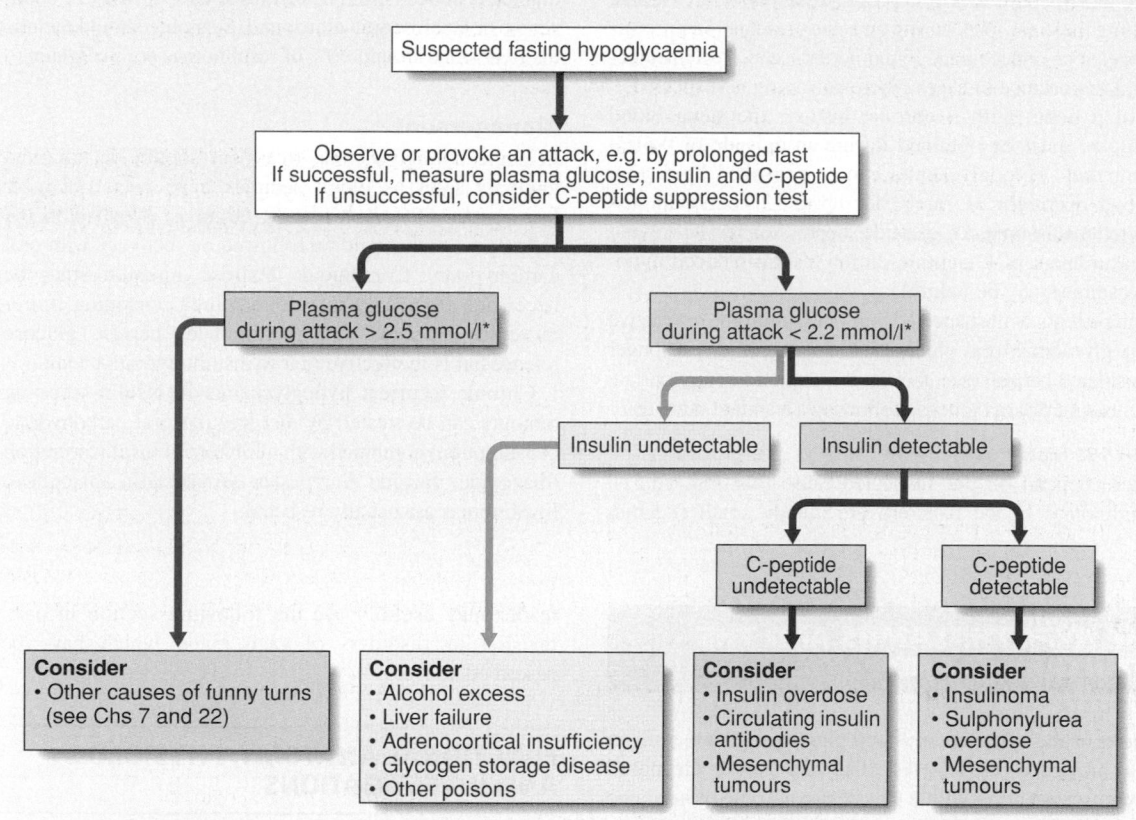

Fig. 16.22   Differential diagnosis of spontaneous hypoglycaemia. * Plasma glucose 2.2–2.5 mmol/l with undetectable insulin and no symptoms is likely to be normal, but with detectable insulin and/or symptoms is likely to be pathological as for plasma glucose < 2.2 mmol/l.

more important mechanism for symptoms of dumping is the osmotic effect of rapid delivery of oral carbohydrate to the small bowel (see p. 786). Indeed, whether hypoglycaemia occurs at all in the dumping syndrome has been questioned. Similarly, at one time, 'reactive' hypoglycaemia was commonly diagnosed in patients reporting post-prandial symptoms including sweating, lightheadedness and lethargy. In some of these patients, plasma glucose falls below 3.0 mmol/l during a glucose tolerance test. However, this is also an occasional finding in healthy subjects undergoing glucose tolerance tests and is poorly predictive of symptoms.

Clinical features

Patients usually present either in the outpatient clinic with a history of unexplained 'attacks' or as an acute emergency with convulsions, collapse or confusion.

Clinical features are described in the section on insulin-induced hypoglycaemia on page 652. Like insulin-treated diabetic patients with recurrent hypoglycaemia, patients with chronic spontaneous hypoglycaemia often have attenuated autonomic responses, and may present with a wide variety of features of neuroglycopenia, including odd behaviour and convulsions. Symptoms are almost always episodic, and key questions include whether they are more frequent on fasting or exercise, and whether they are relieved by consumption of refined carbohydrate.

Investigations

Establishing the diagnosis

Hypoglycaemia is confirmed by a venous plasma glucose concentration < 2.2 mmol/l. Values of 2.2–2.5 mmol/l in the presence of symptoms may also be pathological.

In an acute presentation, suspected hypoglycaemia is usually tested first of all with capillary blood glucose strips and automated meters, used for monitoring glycaemic control in diabetic patients. However, while these tests are sufficient to exclude hypoglycaemia in the presence of symptoms, they do not confirm it as they are not sufficiently accurate in the hypoglycaemic range. Also, whole capillary blood glucose concentrations are 15% lower than plasma glucose concentrations. In patients not known to be receiving insulin or sulphonylurea therapy, hypoglycaemia must always be confirmed before treatment is administered by formal laboratory glucose measurement in a venous or capillary sample. At the same time, a blood sample should be immediately chilled on ice and centrifuged promptly for later measurement of insulin, C-peptide and, if appropriate, sulphonylurea levels. Taking these samples during an acute presentation prevents subsequent unnecessary dynamic tests and is of medico-legal importance in cases where poisoning is suspected.

In patients with a chronic history, the same blood samples must be obtained during an episode of typical symptoms. Hypoglycaemia can be provoked by fasting (either overnight or, rarely, for up to 72 hours). In suspected insulinoma, a C-peptide suppression test (involving measurement of C-peptide during insulin-induced hypoglycaemia) may be helpful.

In patients with suspected dumping syndrome or reactive hypoglycaemia, oral glucose tolerance tests are no longer considered helpful (see above). It is sometimes appropriate to measure plasma glucose following a standard meal test.

Further tests

These depend on the suspected cause (see Fig. 16.22). Insulinomas in the pancreas are usually small (< 5 mm

diameter) but can often be identified by CT, MRI, or endoscopic or laparoscopic ultrasound. Scanning should include the liver since around 10% of insulinomas are malignant.

Management

In acute hypoglycaemia, treatment should be administered as soon as blood samples have been obtained. Intravenous 50% dextrose 30–50 ml is effective in the short term, and should be followed on recovery with oral carbohydrate. Continuous dextrose infusion may be necessary, especially in sulphonylurea poisoning. Intramuscular glucagon (1 mg) stimulates hepatic glucose release but is ineffective in low-insulin hypoglycaemia.

Chronic recurrent hypoglycaemia in insulin-secreting tumours can be treated by diet (regular oral carbohydrate consumption) combined with inhibitors of insulin secretion (diazoxide, thiazide diuretics or somatostatin analogues). Insulinomas are usually resected.

THE HYPOTHALAMUS AND THE PITUITARY GLAND

Diseases of the hypothalamus and pituitary are rare, with an annual incidence of ~1:50 000. They are usually diagnosed in patients presenting with a classical syndrome of hormone excess (e.g. acromegaly or prolactinoma), hormone deficiency (e.g. hypopituitarism, isolated secondary hypogonadism or adrenal insufficiency) or a space-occupying lesion (headache and/or visual disturbance). The pituitary plays a central role in several major endocrine axes, so that investigation and treatment involve several other glands. The

reader may usefully use the following section in part as revision of disorders of each gland which have been described above.

FUNCTIONAL ANATOMY, PHYSIOLOGY AND INVESTIGATIONS

The anatomy of the pituitary is shown in Figure 16.23 and its numerous functions are shown in Figure 16.2 on page 687. The pituitary gland is enclosed in the sella turcica and bridged over by a fold of dura mater called the diaphragma sellae, with the sphenoidal air sinuses below and the optic

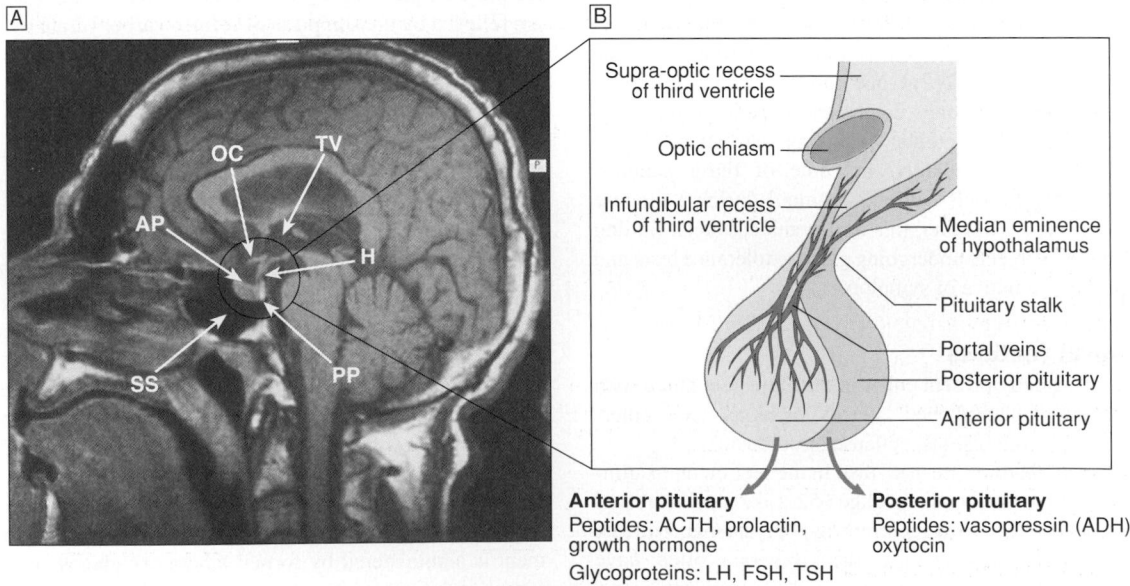

Fig. 16.23 Anatomical relationships and function of the pituitary and hypothalamus. See also Figure 16.2, page 687. A MRI. (SS = sphenoid sinus; AP = anterior pituitary; OC = optic chiasm; TV = third ventricle; H = hypothalamus; PP = posterior pituitary) B Close-up of the central area of the MRI.

chiasm above. The cavernous sinuses are lateral to the pituitary fossa and contain the 3rd, 4th and 6th cranial nerves and the internal carotid arteries. The gland is composed of two lobes, anterior and posterior, and is connected to the hypothalamus by the infundibular stalk, which has portal vessels carrying blood from the median eminence of the hypothalamus to the anterior lobe and nerve fibres to the posterior lobe.

Diseases of the hypothalamus and pituitary are classified in Box 16.41. By far the most common disorder is a benign adenoma of the anterior pituitary gland. Pituitary tumours of any size may be associated with hypersecretion (most commonly of prolactin or growth hormone). Larger tumours are associated with local mechanical complications and/or hyposecretion (of any anterior pituitary hormone).

16.41 CLASSIFICATION OF DISEASES OF THE PITUITARY AND HYPOTHALAMUS

	Primary	Secondary
Hormone excess		
Anterior pituitary	Prolactinoma Acromegaly Cushing's syndrome Rare TSH-, LH- and FSHomas	Disconnection hyperprolactinaemia
Hypothalamus and posterior pituitary	Syndrome of inappropriate antidiuretic hormone (SIADH; see Ch. 9)	
Hormone deficiency		
Anterior pituitary	Hypopituitarism	e.g. GnRH deficiency (Kallmann's syndrome)
Hypothalamus and posterior pituitary	Cranial diabetes insipidus	
Hormone hypersensitivity	–	–
Hormone resistance	Growth hormone resistance (Laron dwarfism) Nephrogenic diabetes insipidus	
Non-functioning tumours	Pituitary adenoma Craniopharyngioma Metastatic tumours	

16.42 INVESTIGATION OF PATIENTS WITH PITUITARY AND HYPOTHALAMIC DISEASE

Identify hypopituitarism

ACTH deficiency
- Short ACTH stimulation test (see Box 16.37, p. 727)
- Only if uncertainty in interpretation of short ACTH stimulation test (e.g. acute presentation) then insulin tolerance test (see Box 16.47, p. 738)

LH/FSH deficiency
- In the male, measure random serum testosterone, LH and FSH
- In the pre-menopausal female, ask if she has regular menses
- In the post-menopausal female, measure random serum LH and FSH (which would normally be > 30 mU/l)

TSH deficiency
- Measure random serum thyroxine
- Note that TSH is often detectable in pituitary disease, due to inactive isoforms in the blood

Growth hormone deficiency
(Only investigate if growth hormone replacement therapy is being contemplated; see p. 738)
- Measure immediately after exercise
- Consider other stimulatory tests (see Box 16.46, p. 738)

Cranial diabetes insipidus
(Only investigate if patient complains of polyuria/polydipsia, which may be masked by ACTH or TSH deficiency)
- Exclude other causes with blood glucose, potassium and calcium measurements
- Water deprivation test (see Box 16.53, p. 745) or 5% saline infusion test

Identify hormone excess

- Measure random serum prolactin
- Investigate for acromegaly (glucose tolerance test) or Cushing's syndrome (see p. 724) if there are clinical features

Establish the anatomy and diagnosis

- Consider visual field testing
- Image the pituitary and hypothalamus by MRI or CT

Investigations

Although pituitary disease presents with diverse manifestations (see below), the approach to the patient is similar in all cases. Clinical assessment is described below. Investigations follow the outline in Box 16.42.

Anterior pituitary gland

Tests for hormone excess vary according to the hormone in question. For example, prolactin is not secreted in pulsatile fashion, although it rises with significant mental stress. Assuming that the patient was not distressed by venepuncture, a random measurement of serum prolactin is sufficient to diagnose hyperprolactinaemia. In contrast, growth hormone is secreted in a pulsatile fashion. A high random level does not confirm acromegaly; the diagnosis is only confirmed by failure of growth hormone to be suppressed (by the insulin-induced rise in insulin-like growth factor-1) during an oral glucose tolerance test. Similarly, in suspected ACTH-dependent Cushing's disease (see p. 724), random measurement of plasma cortisol is unreliable and the diagnosis is usually made by a dexamethasone suppression test.

The means of testing for hypopituitarism also differs between hormones. A common test, which is still employed in some centres, involves the simultaneous administration of thyrotrophin-releasing hormone (TRH), gonadotrophin-releasing hormone (GnRH) and insulin (to induce hypoglycaemic stress and stimulate ACTH and growth hormone). However, this is a potentially hazardous procedure and there is evidence that assessment of the target glands for most of these hormones provides equally reliable results. Details of each test are given in the sections on individual glands above and in Box 16.42.

Local compression by a large pituitary tumour most commonly results in compression of the optic pathway. The resulting visual field defect can be documented by formal charting (e.g. a Goldman's perimetry chart). Viewing the pituitary gland by MRI reveals 'abnormalities' of the pituitary fossa in as many as 10% of middle-aged patients. It should therefore be performed only if there is a clear biochemical abnormality or in a patient who presents with clinical features of pituitary tumour (see below). Functional imaging (e.g. with radio-labelled octreotide, a somatostatin analogue) is rarely used.

Surgical biopsy is usually only performed as part of a therapeutic operation. Conventional staining identifies pituitary tumours as either chromophobe, acidophil or basophil. Classically, acidophil tumours are associated with growth hormone or prolactin excess, basophil tumours are associated with ACTH hypersecretion, and chromophobe tumours are non-functioning. However, many chromophobe tumours are associated with hormonal excess. Immunohistochemistry using specific antisera against the pituitary hormones is more valuable in identifying the hormone(s) secreted by specific pituitary cells. It is not possible for histology to identify the rare pituitary tumours which regrow rapidly and invade local structures.

Posterior pituitary and hypothalamus

Patients with hypothalamic disease are at risk of anterior pituitary dysfunction and require assessment as above. In addition, these patients may have posterior pituitary dysfunction. Note that the posterior pituitary is rarely affected by pituitary tumours, and dysfunction most commonly occurs following pituitary surgery. In practice, the only posterior pituitary function requiring investigation is deficiency of vasopressin resulting in diabetes insipidus (see p. 744).

MAJOR MANIFESTATIONS OF HYPOTHALAMIC AND PITUITARY DISEASE

Routes of presentation of pituitary and hypothalamic disease are shown in Box 16.43. All patients should be assessed clinically as in Figure 16.24, and biochemically as in Box 16.42. Younger women with pituitary disease commonly present with secondary amenorrhoea (see p. 710) or galactorrhoea (in hyperprolactinaemia). Postmenopausal women and men of any age are less likely to report symptoms of hypogonadism (see p. 706) and so commonly present late with larger tumours causing visual field defects.

HYPOPITUITARISM

Hypopituitarism describes combined deficiency of any of the anterior pituitary hormones. Causes include any pathology of the hypothalamus and pituitary gland, as shown in Box 16.44.

Clinical features

The presentation is highly variable and depends on the underlying lesion. Congenital defects of the hypothalamus

usually present with short stature (see p. 707). With progressive lesions of the pituitary there is a characteristic sequence of loss of pituitary hormone secretion. Growth

16.43 COMMON PRESENTING COMPLAINTS IN HYPOTHALAMIC/PITUITARY DISEASE
(See Fig. 16.24)
Chronic presentations
• Secondary amenorrhoea
• Galactorrhoea
• Visual field defect
• Incidental finding on skull radiograph or CT performed for another reason
• 'Spot' diagnosis of acromegaly or Cushing's syndrome
• Short stature
• Sexual dysfunction/infertility
• Unexplained fatigue (hypopituitarism)
Acute presentations
• Pituitary apoplexy (headache, cavernous sinus involvement with diplopia, visual dysfunction, hypopituitarism)
• Adrenal insufficiency (shock precipitated by intercurrent illness)

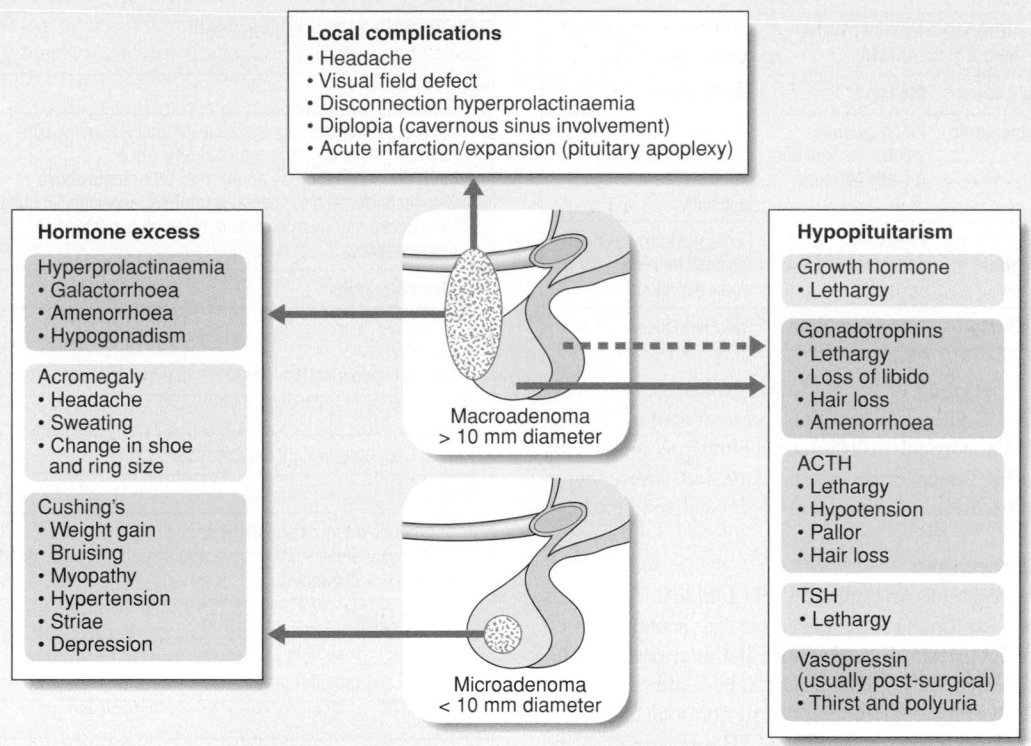

Local complications
• Headache
• Visual field defect
• Disconnection hyperprolactinaemia
• Diplopia (cavernous sinus involvement)
• Acute infarction/expansion (pituitary apoplexy)

Hormone excess

Hyperprolactinaemia
• Galactorrhoea
• Amenorrhoea
• Hypogonadism

Acromegaly
• Headache
• Sweating
• Change in shoe and ring size

Cushing's
• Weight gain
• Bruising
• Myopathy
• Hypertension
• Striae
• Depression

Macroadenoma
> 10 mm diameter

Microadenoma
< 10 mm diameter

Hypopituitarism

Growth hormone
• Lethargy

Gonadotrophins
• Lethargy
• Loss of libido
• Hair loss
• Amenorrhoea

ACTH
• Lethargy
• Hypotension
• Pallor
• Hair loss

TSH
• Lethargy

Vasopressin
(usually post-surgical)
• Thirst and polyuria

Fig. 16.24   Common symptoms and signs to consider in a patient with suspected pituitary disease.

16.44 CAUSES OF HYPOPITUITARISM

Site of lesion	Common deficiencies/causes	Rare deficiencies/causes
Hypothalamus		
Acquired	Craniopharyngioma	Sarcoidosis
	Head injury	Tuberculosis
	Surgery	Langerhans cell
	Radiotherapy	histiocytosis
		Primary or secondary
		tumour
		Syphilis
		Encephalitis
Congenital	GnRH (Kallmann's	TRH
	syndrome)	CRH
	GHRH	
Pituitary		
Structural	Pituitary tumour	Secondary tumour
	Surgery	Post-partum necrosis
	Radiotherapy	(Sheehan's syndrome)
	Head injury	Autoimmune
	Local meningioma	Haemorrhage (apoplexy)
		Haemochromatosis
Functional	Anorexia nervosa	
	Malnutrition	

hormone secretion is often the earliest to be lost. In adults, this produces lethargy, muscle weakness and increased fat mass but these features are not obvious in isolation. Next, gonadotrophin (LH and FSH) secretion becomes impaired

with, in the male, loss of libido and impotence and, in the female, oligomenorrhoea or amenorrhoea. Later, in the male there may be gynaecomastia and decreased frequency of shaving. In both sexes axillary and pubic hair eventually become sparse or even absent. The skin becomes characteristically finer and wrinkled.

The next hormone to be lost is usually ACTH, resulting in symptoms of cortisol insufficiency. In contrast to primary adrenal insufficiency (see p. 726), angiotensin II-dependent zona glomerulosa function is not lost and hence aldosterone secretion maintains normal plasma potassium. However, there may be postural hypotension and a dilutional hyponatraemia for three reasons:

● Failure of vasoconstriction in the absence of cortisol results in pooling of blood in the legs on standing.
● Antidiuretic hormone (ADH) release is enhanced by hypotension and cortisol deficiency.
● Cortisol is required for normal water excretion by the kidney.

In contrast to the pigmentation of Addison's disease a striking degree of pallor is usually present, principally because of lack of stimulation of melanocytes by β-lipotrophic hormone (β-LPH, a fragment of the ACTH precursor peptide) in the skin.

Finally, TSH secretion is lost with consequent secondary hypothyroidism. This contributes further to apathy and cold intolerance. In contrast to primary hypothyroidism frank myxoedema is not seen.

16.45 COMA IN A PATIENT WITH HYPOPITUITARISM

Possible cause	Measure	Mechanism
Hypoglycaemia	Blood glucose, insulin, cortisol and growth hormone	Lack of growth hormone and cortisol causing increased sensitivity to insulin
Water intoxication	Plasma Na^+, K^+ and urea—all low	Cortisol and thyroxine required for renal water excretion
Hypothermia	Rectal temperature	Hypothyroidism

The onset of all of the above symptoms is notoriously insidious. Sometimes, patients present acutely unwell with adrenocortical insufficiency, often precipitated by some mild infection or injury. Untreated severe hypopituitarism eventually results in coma (see Box 16.45).

Investigations

The strategy of investigation of pituitary disease is described in Box 16.42, page 735. In acutely unwell patients the priority is to diagnose and treat cortisol deficiency (see p. 726). Other tests can be undertaken later. Specific dynamic tests for diagnosing hormone deficiency are described in Boxes 16.37 (ACTH—see p. 727) and 16.46 (growth hormone). More specialised biochemical tests, such as insulin tolerance tests (see Box 16.47), GnRH and TRH tests, are rarely required. All patients with biochemical evidence of pituitary hormone deficiency should have an MRI or a CT to identify pituitary or hypothalamic tumours.

Management

Treatment of acutely ill patients is similar to that described for adrenocortical insufficiency on page 728, except that sodium depletion is not an important component to correct. Chronic hormone replacement therapies are described below. Once the cause of hypopituitarism is established, specific treatment—of a pituitary macroadenoma, for example—may be required.

Cortisol replacement

Hydrocortisone (another name for cortisol) should be given if there is ACTH deficiency. Suitable doses are

16.46 TESTS OF GROWTH HORMONE SECRETION

GH levels are commonly undetectable, so a choice from the range of stimulation tests is required:

- 1 hour after going to sleep
- Frequent sampling during sleep
- Post-exercise
- Insulin-induced hypoglycaemia
- Arginine

Note that in pre-pubertal patients, priming with sex steroid is required before stimulation tests are performed.

16.47 INSULIN TOLERANCE TEST

Use

- Assessment of the hypothalamic-pituitary-adrenal axis
- Assessment of growth hormone deficiency
- Indicated when there is doubt from other tests above
- Usually performed in specialist centres, especially in children
- I.v. glucose and hydrocortisone must be available for resuscitation

Contraindications

- Ischaemic heart disease
- Epilepsy
- Severe hypopituitarism (0800 hrs plasma cortisol < 180 nmol/l)

Dose

- 0.15 U/kg body weight soluble insulin i.v.

Aim

- To produce adequate hypoglycaemia (signs of neuroglycopenia—tachycardia and sweating—with blood glucose < 2.2 mmol/l)

Blood samples

- 0, 30, 45, 60, 90, 120 minutes for blood glucose, plasma cortisol and growth hormone

Results

- Normal subjects GH > 20 mU/l
- Normal subjects cortisol > 550 nmol/l

described in the section on adrenal disease (see p. 727). Mineralocorticoid replacement is not required.

Thyroid hormone replacement

Thyroxine 0.1–0.15 mg once daily should be given. Unlike in primary hypothyroidism, measuring TSH is not helpful in adjusting the replacement dose, because patients with hypopituitarism often secrete glycoproteins which are measured in the TSH assays but are not bioactive. The aim is to maintain serum T_4 in the upper part of the reference range. This is required to ensure adequate levels of triiodothyronine (T_3), the active hormone, in target tissues, since all T_3 in these patients is derived from circulating T_4 and not secreted by the thyroid gland. It is dangerous to give thyroid replacement to patients with adrenal insufficiency without first giving glucocorticoid therapy, since this may precipitate adrenal crisis.

Sex hormone replacement

This is indicated if there is gonadotrophin deficiency in men of any age and in pre-menopausal women to restore normal sexual function and to prevent osteoporosis. See page 713.

Growth hormone replacement

Growth hormone (GH) is administered, by daily subcutaneous self-injection, to young patients with GH deficiency, renal failure or Turner's syndrome to assist them in attaining their growth potential. Until recently, GH was discontinued once the epiphyses had fused, and was not given to adults. However, although hypopituitary adults receiving 'full' replacement with hydrocortisone, thyroxine and sex steroids are usually much improved by these therapies, they often remain lethargic and unwell compared with a healthy population. Recent studies suggest that some of these patients feel better, and have objective improvements in their fat/muscle mass ratios and other metabolic parameters, if they are also given GH replacement. The principal side-effect is sodium retention, manifest as peripheral oedema or carpal tunnel syndrome. For this reason, GH replacement is started at a low dose, with monitoring of the response by measurement of serum insulin-like growth factor-1 (IGF-1) levels.

ADULT HYPOPITUITARISM—use of growth hormone (GH) replacement therapy `EBM`

'Short-term (6–12-month) RCTs show that GH improves quality of life and exercise capacity, and reduces central obesity and low-density lipoprotein-cholesterol levels. Beneficial effects on bone mineral density may occur after prolonged therapy but these results could be confounded by "selection bias". Longer-term studies are required to establish effects of GH therapy on cardiovascular disease, fracture, pituitary tumour recurrence and other malignancies. GH therapy is appropriate in patients who are incapacitated by lethargy and whose quality of life improves substantially with such treatment.'

- Carroll PV, Christ ER and the members of the Growth Hormone Research Society Scientific Committee. Growth hormone deficiency in adulthood and the effects of growth hormone replacement: a review. J Clin Endocrinol Metab 1998; 83:382–395.

Further information: www.endocrinology.org

VISUAL FIELD DEFECT

Compression of the neural connections between the retina and occipital cortex by a pituitary tumour leads to impaired visual fields. Although the classical visual field abnormalities associated with compression of the optic chiasm are bitemporal hemianopia or upper quadrantanopia, any type of visual field defect can result from suprasellar extension of a pituitary tumour because it may compress the optic nerve (unilateral loss of acuity or scotoma), the optic chiasm or the optic tract (homonymous hemianopia). Optic atrophy may be apparent on ophthalmoscopy. Diplopia and strabismus may follow pressure on the 3rd, 4th or 6th cranial nerves.

The differential diagnosis of visual field defects is wide, and includes neurological (see p. 1152) and orbital (e.g. glaucoma) disease. In the absence of any other clear explanation for a field defect, however, MRI or CT of the pituitary fossa should be performed to identify a pituitary tumour (see Fig. 16.25).

In patients with radiological evidence of a pituitary tumour, further clinical assessment and investigation should be performed as in Box 16.42 on page 735 and Figure 16.24.

Tumours causing visual field defects require urgent treatment, as described on page 741.

GALACTORRHOEA

Galactorrhoea describes lactation without breastfeeding. Some women exhibit physiological galactorrhoea, e.g. failing to stop lactation after ceasing breastfeeding or in

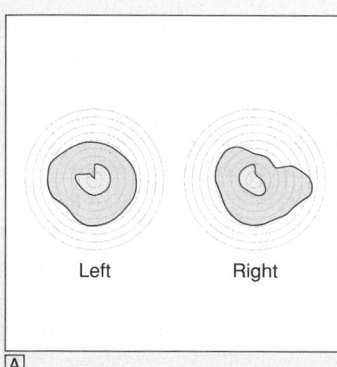
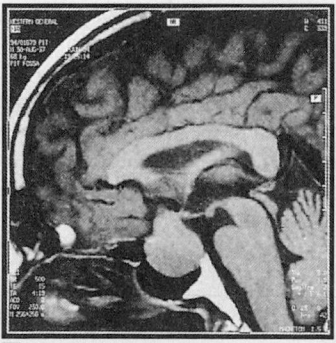
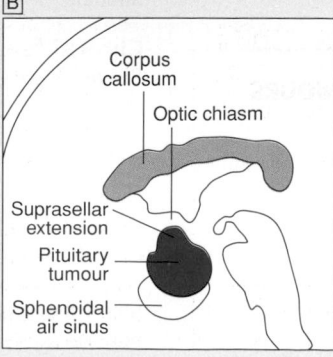
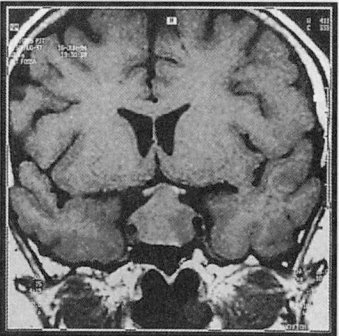
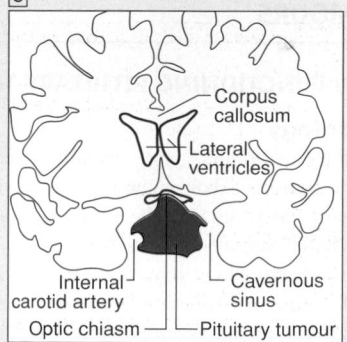

Left   Right

Fig. 16.25 Pituitary macroadenoma in a patient presenting with a visual field defect. A Bitemporal hemianopia visual field defect to red (red line) and white (black line) light. B Suprasellar extension of large pituitary tumour (sagittal view). C Coronal view of pituitary tumour showing compression of the optic chiasm.

Corpus callosum — Optic chiasm — Suprasellar extension — Pituitary tumour — Sphenoidal air sinus

Corpus callosum — Lateral ventricles — Internal carotid artery — Cavernous sinus — Optic chiasm — Pituitary tumour

response to a new baby in the house. The quantity of milk produced is variable, and it may be observed only by manual expression or in certain circumstances (e.g. in the heat or with nipple stimulation). Pathological galactorrhoea is caused by hyperprolactinaemia. The differential diagnosis is shown in Box 16.48.

Clinical assessment

Important points in the history include drug use, recent pregnancy and menstrual history. Significant hyperprolactinaemia usually results in amenorrhoea or irregular menses. Unilateral galactorrhoea may be confused with nipple discharge, and careful breast examination to exclude a malignancy is important. Further assessment follows the principles in Figure 16.24, page 737. Most prolactinomas are, however, microadenomas so that hypopituitarism is relatively uncommon.

Investigations

The upper limit of normal for many assays of serum prolactin is ~500 mU/l. During pregnancy and lactation physiological levels may reach 20 000 mU/l. In non-pregnant and non-lactating patients, levels of 500–1000 mU/l are likely to be induced by stress or drugs, and a repeat measurement is indicated. Levels between 1000 and 5000 mU/l are likely to be due to drugs, a microprolactinoma or disconnection hyperprolactinaemia (due to pressure on the infundibular stalk and loss of dopamine inhibition of prolactin secretion). Levels above 5000 mU/l are highly suggestive of a prolactinoma, and the higher the level, the bigger the tumour. Some macroprolactinomas cause levels as high as 100 000 mU/l.

Patients with prolactin excess should have tests of gonadal function (see p. 705), and T_4 and TSH measured to exclude primary hypothyroidism causing TRH-induced prolactin excess. Unless the prolactin falls after withdrawal of relevant drug therapy, a serum prolactin of > 1000 mU/l is an indication for an MRI or a CT of the hypothalamus and pituitary. Patients with macroadenomas also need tests for hypopituitarism (see Box 16.42, p. 735).

MRI will detect all macroadenomas and around 70% of microadenomas. In patients with a normal scan and no

16.48 CAUSES OF ELEVATED PLASMA PROLACTIN

Physiological

- Stress
- Pregnancy
- Lactation
- Chest wall reflex (e.g. nipple stimulation)
- Wet nursing reflex (e.g. baby crying)

Drugs

Dopamine antagonists
- Antipsychotics (phenothiazines and butyrophenones)
- Antidepressants
- Antiemetics (e.g. metoclopramide, domperidone)

Dopamine-depleting drugs
- Reserpine
- Methyldopa

Oestrogens
- Oral contraceptive pill

Pathological

Common
- Disconnection hyperprolactinaemia (e.g. non-functioning pituitary macroadenoma)
- Prolactinoma (usually microadenoma)
- Primary hypothyroidism
- Polycystic ovarian syndrome

Uncommon
- Hypothalamic disease
- Pituitary tumour secreting prolactin and growth hormone
- Renal failure

Rare
- Post-herpes zoster
- Ectopic source

other cause of prolactin excess, the presumptive diagnosis is a small microadenoma.

Management

Treatment of prolactinomas is described on page 742. Galactorrhoea will resolve on specific treatment of other causes of prolactin excess or withdrawal of the offending drug. Troublesome physiological galactorrhoea can be treated with dopamine agonists (see Box 16.50, p. 742).

PITUITARY AND HYPOTHALAMIC TUMOURS

NON-FUNCTIONING PITUITARY TUMOURS

Aetiology

Pituitary tumours are usually benign adenomas. Interpretation of their pathology is described on page 736. Primary carcinoma of the pituitary gland is rare, but a metastatic tumour from a primary in the breast, lung, kidney or elsewhere may occur in the hypothalamus and reduce pituitary function. Other tumours—for example, pinealoma, ependymoma or meningioma—may be associated with damage to the pituitary or hypothalamus.

Conditions such as sarcoidosis or syphilis may mimic pituitary tumours.

Clinical features

See the approach in Figure 16.24, page 737. Clinical features vary, depending on the type of lesion in the pituitary gland and the effect of that lesion on surrounding structures. Tumours which do not secrete excess hormones—non-functioning adenomas—present with hypopituitarism or features resulting from local expansion of the tumour. Headache is the most common but least specific symptom. Pituitary tumours only cause features of hypothalamic or posterior pituitary dysfunction if they expand sufficiently to impinge on the hypothalamus, since pressure on the posterior pituitary does not interfere with its function. Visual field defects are common (see p. 739).

Although hydrocephalus is described with pituitary tumours, it is important to recognise that these do not behave like 'brain tumours', in that they are usually slowly progressive, and exceedingly rarely cause neurological impairment or raised intracranial pressure. This is an important concept to get across to patients at an early stage.

Investigations
All patients with pituitary tumours should have the tests described in Box 16.42, page 735. If the clinical features suggest hormonal hypersecretion, then this must also be assessed. The imaging technique with the highest resolution is MRI (see Fig. 16.25, p. 739), which will establish whether the tumour is a macroadenoma (> 10 mm diameter) or a microadenoma (< 10 mm diameter). If this is not available, CT is reliable for identifying macroadenomas. The distinction of size of tumour is important mainly because microadenomas are not associated with hypopituitarism or compression of local structures and are only treated if they are secreting excess hormones.

Management
Modalities of treatment for pituitary tumours are shown in Box 16.49.

If there is evidence of pressure on visual pathways, then urgent treatment is required. The chances of recovery of a visual field defect are proportional to the duration of symptoms; full recovery is unlikely if the defect has been present for longer than 4 months. The only medical therapy which reliably shrinks macroadenomas is dopamine agonists for macroprolactinomas (see below). It is crucial that serum prolactin is measured before emergency surgery is performed. If the prolactin is > 4000 mU/l, then a therapeutic trial of a dopamine agonist for just a few days may successfully shrink the tumour and make surgery unnecessary.

Most operations on the pituitary are performed by the trans-sphenoidal approach. The pituitary fossa is approached via the sphenoid sinus from an incision under the upper lip or through the nose. Transfrontal surgery via a craniotomy is reserved for very large tumours and craniopharyngiomas. It is uncommon to be able to resect a macroadenoma completely.

Following decompression, imaging is repeated after a few months and, if there is any residual tumour, external radiotherapy is given to reduce the risk of recurrence. Radiation therapy is not useful in patients requiring urgent therapy because it takes many months or years to be effective and there is a risk of acute swelling of the tumour.

All operations on the pituitary carry a risk of damaging normal endocrine function; this risk increases with the size of the primary tumour. Radiation therapy carries a life-long risk of hypopituitarism (50–70% in the first 10 years) and annual pituitary function tests are required. There is also concern that radiotherapy, which is delivered through the temporal lobes, might impair cognitive function and even induce primary brain tumours, but these side-effects have not been quantified and are likely to be rare.

Non-functioning tumours are followed up by repeated imaging at intervals which depend on the size of the tumour and on whether or not radiotherapy has been administered.

PROLACTINOMA
Aetiology
Elevation of plasma prolactin levels is a common finding and may arise from a variety of causes, as listed in Box 16.48. Even though the list is long, it is usually possible to reach a presumptive diagnosis by taking a careful history, especially with regard to drug therapy.

Clinical features
Hippocrates was one of the first to observe that milk secretion was associated with decreased gonadal function. The cardinal features of hyperprolactinaemia are galactorrhoea (see p. 739) and hypogonadism. In women hypogonadism causes secondary amenorrhoea, oligomenorrhoea or menorrhagia, and anovulation with infertility. In men there is decreased libido, erectile impotence, reduced shaving frequency and lethargy. Men usually present with symptoms at a later stage than women and are more likely to have a macroadenoma.

Patients with macroadenomas may also have any of the clinical features of non-functioning pituitary tumours (see Fig. 16.24, p. 737).

16.49 THERAPEUTIC MODALITIES FOR HYPOTHALAMIC AND PITUITARY TUMOURS

	Surgery	Radiotherapy	Medical	Comment
Non-functioning pituitary macroadenoma	1st line	2nd line	–	
Prolactinoma	2nd line	2nd line	1st line: Dopamine agonists	Dopamine agonists usually cause macroadenomas to shrink
Acromegaly	1st line	2nd line	2nd line: Somatostatin analogues Dopamine agonists GH receptor antagonists	Medical therapy does not reliably cause macroadenomas to shrink
Cushing's disease	1st line	2nd line	–	Radiotherapy is used in children and to prevent Nelson's syndrome
Craniopharyngioma	1st line	2nd line	–	

Investigations
These are described under galactorrhoea on page 740 and the principles are outlined in Box 16.42, page 735.

Management
Medical
In almost all cases of hyperprolactinaemia dopamine agonist therapy will normalise prolactin levels with return of gonadal function. If gonadal function does not return despite effective lowering of prolactin, then there may be associated gonadotrophin deficiency or, in the female, the onset of the menopause. Several dopamine agonists are now available, as shown in Box 16.50.

Dopamine agonist therapy is likely to be long-term in the majority of patients. However, it has been possible to withdraw bromocriptine without recurrence of hyperprolactinaemia after 10 years' treatment in some patients with microadenoma. Also, after the menopause suppression of prolactin is only required in microadenomas if galactorrhoea is troublesome, since hypogonadism is then physiological and tumour growth highly unlikely. In patients with macroadenomas drugs can only be withdrawn after curative surgery or radiotherapy and under close supervision.

In general, patients with prolactin excess should avoid drugs which stimulate prolactin, including oestrogens.

Surgical
Dopamine agonists not only lower prolactin levels but shrink the majority of prolactin-secreting macroadenomas. Thus, surgical decompression is not usually necessary unless the macroadenoma is cystic. However, in patients who are intolerant of dopamine agonists, microadenomas can be removed selectively by trans-sphenoidal surgery with a cure rate of about 80%. The cure rate for surgery in macroadenomas is substantially lower.

Radiotherapy
External irradiation may be required for some macroadenomas to prevent regrowth if dopamine agonists are stopped.

Pregnancy
Hyperprolactinaemia often presents with infertility so dopamine agonist therapy is often followed by pregnancy.

Patients with microadenomas are advised to withdraw bromocriptine as soon as pregnancy is confirmed (e.g. by urinary human chorionic gonadotrophin (hCG) test on the third day after a missed period). In contrast, macroprolactinomas may enlarge rapidly under oestrogen stimulation and these patients continue dopamine agonist therapy and need measurement of prolactin levels and visual fields during pregnancy. All patients are advised to report headache or visual disturbance promptly.

ACROMEGALY
Acromegaly is caused by growth hormone (GH) secretion from a pituitary tumour, usually a macroadenoma.

Clinical features
If GH hypersecretion occurs before epiphyses have fused, then gigantism will result. More commonly, GH excess occurs in adult life, after epiphyseal closure, and acromegaly ensues. If hypersecretion starts in adolescence and persists into adult life, then the two conditions may be combined. The clinical features are listed in Box 16.51. The most common complaints are headache and sweating.

Further assessment follows the strategy in Figure 16.24. Macroadenomas may be associated with local complications of tumour expansion and with hypopituitarism.

Investigations
The clinical diagnosis must be confirmed by measuring GH levels during an oral glucose tolerance test (see Fig. 16.26). In normal subjects plasma GH suppresses to below 2 mU/l. In acromegaly it does not suppress and in about 50% of patients there is a paradoxical rise. The rest of pituitary function should be investigated as described in Box 16.42, page 735. In about 30% of patients prolactin levels are elevated.

The diagnosis of acromegaly is more difficult in patients with insulin deficiency, either type 1 or long-standing type 2 diabetes mellitus. GH may fail to suppress following a glucose load in these patients because inadequate insulin secretion results in failure of glucose to stimulate IGF-1 from the liver. It is IGF-1 which in turn suppresses GH secretion. This is important because acromegaly can cause diabetes

16.50 DOPAMINE AGONIST THERAPY: DRUGS USED TO TREAT PROLACTINOMAS

	Oral dose*	Advantages	Disadvantages
Bromocriptine	2.5–15 mg/day 8–12-hourly	Available for parenteral use Short half-life; useful in treating infertility Proven long-term efficacy	Ergotamine-like side-effects (nausea, headache, postural hypotension, constipation) Frequent dosing so poor compliance
Cabergoline	250–1000 µg/week 2 doses/week	Long-acting, so missed doses less important Reported to have fewer ergotamine-like side-effects	Unsuitable for treating infertility
Quinagolide	50–150 µg/day Once daily	A non-ergot with few side-effects in patients intolerant of the above	Untested in pregnancy
Pergolide			An older drug with bromocriptine-like side-effects; no longer used

* Tolerance develops for the side-effects. All of these agents, especially bromocriptine, must be introduced at low dose and increased slowly. If several doses of bromocriptine are missed, the process must start again.

16.51 CLINICAL FEATURES OF ACROMEGALY

Soft tissue changes

- Skin thickening
- Increased sweating
- Headache
- Increased sebum production
- Enlargement of lips, nose and tongue
- Increased heel pad thickness
- 'Acromegalic arthropathy'
- Myopathy
- Carpal tunnel syndrome
- Late-onset Raynaud's phenomenon
- Visceromegaly (e.g. thyroid, heart, liver)

Acral enlargement

- Large hands (difficult to remove rings—see p. 684)
- Large feet (increasing shoe size)

Other bone changes

- Growth of lower jaw—prognathism
- Skull growth—prominent supraorbital ridges with large frontal sinuses
- Kyphosis
- Osteoarthritis

Metabolic effects

- Glucose intolerance (25%)
- Diabetes mellitus (10%)
- Hypertension (25% associated with increased body sodium)

Long-term complications

- Atheromatous disease (two- to threefold relative risk)
- Colonic cancer (two- to threefold relative risk)

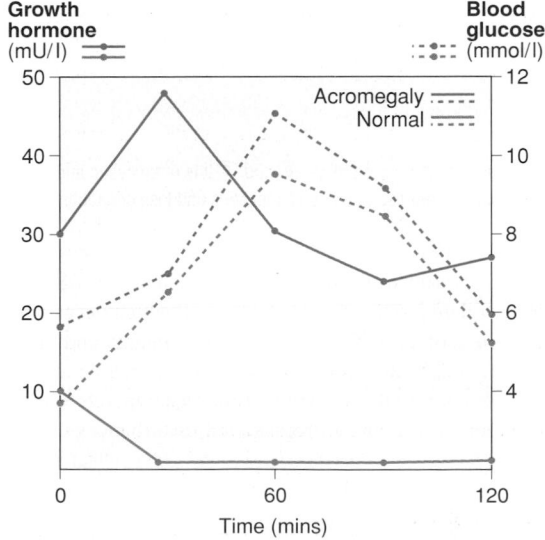

Fig. 16.26 Oral glucose tolerance tests in a normal subject and a patient with acromegaly with measurement of blood glucose and plasma growth hormone. Note the suppression of growth hormone secretion of < 2 mU/l in the normal subject, and failure to suppress (sometimes accompanied by paradoxical elevation) in acromegaly. Glucose tolerance may also be impaired in acromegaly.

mellitus by exacerbating insulin resistance. However, in diabetic patients without acromegaly, IGF-1 levels are low, while in acromegalic patients they are high.

Additional tests in acromegaly may include screening for colonic neoplasms with colonoscopy.

Management

Therapeutic modalities are described in Box 16.49.

Surgical

Trans-sphenoidal surgery is usually the first line of treatment and may result in cure of GH excess, especially in patients with microadenomas. More often, surgery serves to debulk the tumour and further second-line therapy is required, according to post-operative imaging and glucose tolerance test results.

Radiotherapy

External radiotherapy is usually employed as second-line treatment if acromegaly persists after surgery to stop tumour growth and lower GH levels. However, GH levels fall slowly (over many years) and there is a risk of hypopituitarism.

Medical

In patients with persisting acromegaly after surgery, most centres employ medical therapy to lower GH levels to < 5 mU/l (see EBM panel). Medical therapy may be discontinued after several years in patients who have received radiotherapy, since GH secretion continues to fall for many years after pituitary irradiation. Somatostatin analogues (e.g. octreotide or lanreotide) can be administered as intramuscular slow-release injections every few weeks. Importantly, octreotide does not reliably shrink GH-secreting tumours. Dopamine agonists are less potent in lowering GH but may be helpful, especially in patients with associated prolactin excess. Encouraging trials have also been performed with GH receptor antagonists (e.g. pegvisomant).

EBM

ACROMEGALY—therapeutic targets

'Observational data in 1362 acromegalic patients show a linear relationship between mean growth hormone (GH) levels during follow-up after surgery and radiotherapy, and mortality from colon cancer and cardiovascular disease. Attainment of GH < 5 mU/l was associated with normal survival. Therefore, in most patients, medical therapy, where required, is used to lower GH to < 5 mU/l.'

- Orme SM, McNally RJQ, Cartwright RA, Belchetz PE for the United Kingdom Acromegaly Study Group. Mortality and cancer incidence in acromegaly: a retrospective cohort study. J Clin Endocrinol Metab 1998; 83:2730–2734.

Further information: 💻 www.endocrinology.org

CRANIOPHARYNGIOMA

Craniopharyngiomas are benign tumours which develop in cell rests of Rathke's pouch, and may be located within the sella turcica, or commonly in the suprasellar space. They are often cystic and/or calcified (see Fig. 16.27). They occur more commonly in young people than do pituitary adenomas. They may present with pressure effects on adjacent structures, hypopituitarism or a hypothalamic syndrome, as described below. Craniopharyngiomas can rarely

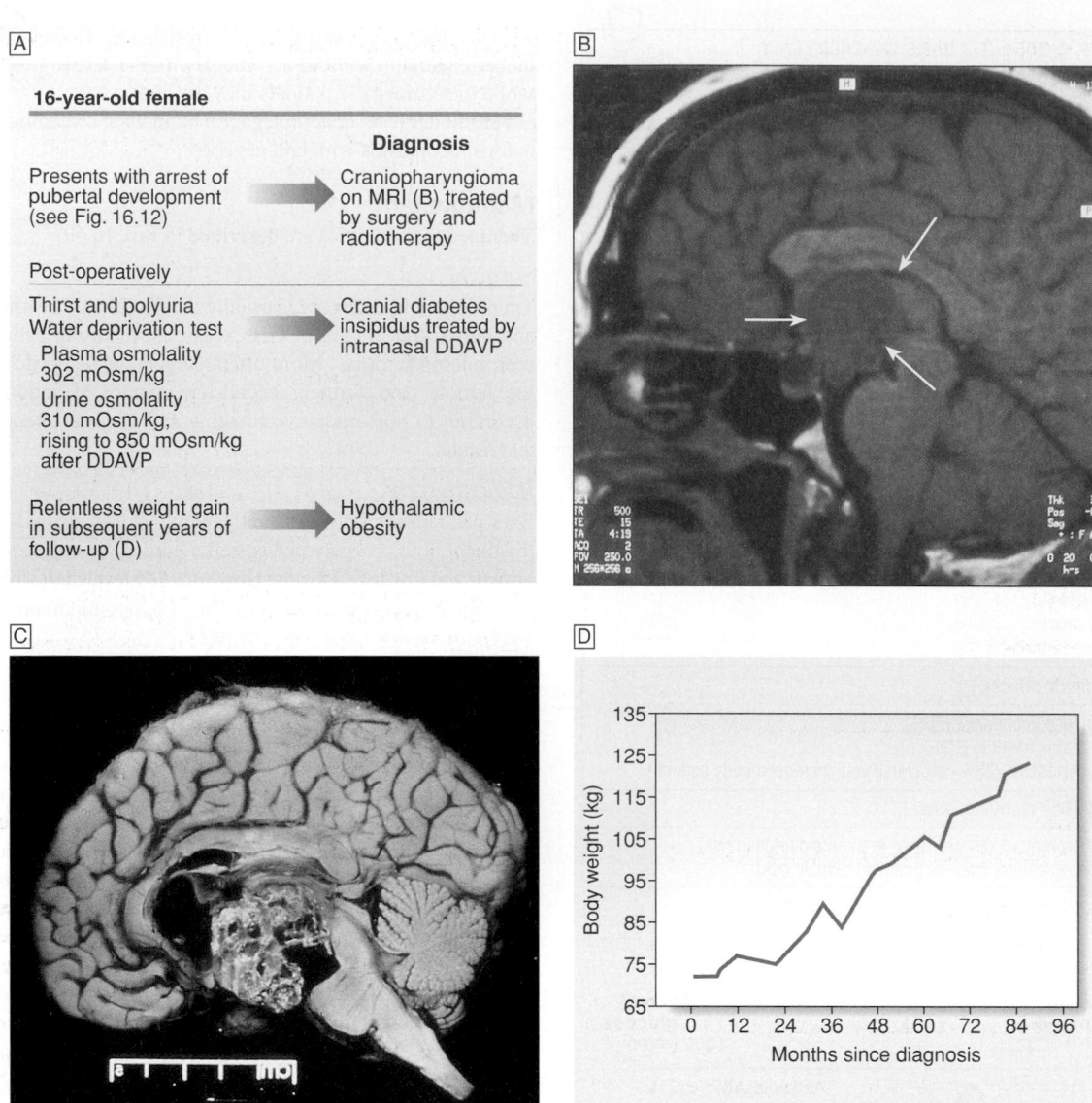

Fig. 16.27 Craniopharyngioma. [A] This hypothalamic tumour characteristically presents in younger patients. [B] and [C] It is often cystic and calcified, as shown in the MRI (arrows) and pathology specimen. [D] Hypothalamic damage is manifest as diabetes insipidus and loss of satiety leading to relentless weight gain. (For DDAVP, see text)

be reached by the trans-sphenoidal route, and surgery involves a craniotomy, with a relatively high risk of hypothalamic damage and other complications. Surgery is unlikely to be curative, and radiotherapy is usually given, although there is uncertainty about its efficacy. Unfortunately, craniopharyngiomas often recur, requiring repeated surgery and inevitably causing considerable morbidity, usually from hypothalamic obesity and/or visual failure.

HYPOTHALAMIC AND POSTERIOR PITUITARY DISEASE

Causes of hypothalamic disease are shown in Box 16.44 (see p. 737). Although commonly associated with anterior

pituitary dysfunction, there are clinical features which are directly related to the hypothalamus and which occasionally present in isolation. These include hyperphagia and obesity (see Fig. 16.27), disturbance of temperature regulation leading most commonly to hypothermia in temperate climates and hyperthermia in the tropics, and disturbances of water balance.

DIABETES INSIPIDUS

This uncommon disease is characterised by the persistent excretion of excessive quantities of dilute urine, and by thirst. Diabetes insipidus can be divided into cranial diabetes insipidus, in which there is deficient production of ADH, and nephrogenic diabetes insipidus, in which the renal tubules are unresponsive to ADH.

16.52 CAUSES OF DIABETES INSIPIDUS

Cranial

Hypothalamic or high stalk lesion
- E.g. craniopharyngioma, head injury, surgery, Langerhans cell histiocytosis, sarcoidosis, pituitary tumour with suprasellar extension, basal meningitis, encephalitis

Idiopathic

Genetic defect
- Dominant
- Recessive (DIDMOAD syndrome—association of diabetes insipidus with diabetes mellitus, optic atrophy, deafness)

Nephrogenic

Genetic defect
- Sex-linked recessive
- Cystinosis

Metabolic abnormality
- Hypokalaemia
- Hypercalcaemia

Drug therapy
- Lithium
- Demeclocycline

Poisoning
- Heavy metals

16.53 WATER DEPRIVATION TEST

Use

To establish a diagnosis of diabetes insipidus, and differentiate cranial from nephrogenic causes

Protocol

- No coffee, tea or smoking on the test day
- Free fluids until 0730 hrs on the morning of the test, but discourage patients from 'stocking up' with extra fluid in anticipation of fluid deprivation
- No fluids from 0730 hrs
- Attend at 0830 hrs for body weight, plasma and urine osmolality
- Record body weight, urine volume, urine and plasma osmolality and thirst score on a visual analogue scale every 2 hours for up to 8 hours
- Stop the test if the patient loses 3% of body weight
- If plasma osmolality reaches > 300 mOsm/kg and urine osmolality < 660 mOsm/kg, then administer DDAVP (see text) 2 µg i.m.

Interpretation

- Diabetes insipidus is confirmed by a plasma osmolality > 300 mOsm/kg with a urine osmolality < 660 mOsm/kg
- Cranial diabetes insipidus is confirmed if urine osmolality rises to > 660 mOsm/kg after DDAVP
- Nephrogenic diabetes insipidus is confirmed if DDAVP does not concentrate the urine

Aetiology

Causes of diabetes insipidus are listed in Box 16.52.

Clinical features

The most marked symptoms are polyuria and polydipsia. The patient may pass 5–20 litres or more of urine in 24 hours. This is of low specific gravity and osmolality. If the patient has an intact thirst mechanism, is conscious and has access to oral fluids, then he or she can maintain adequate fluid intake. However, in the unconscious patient or one with damage to the hypothalamic thirst centre, diabetes insipidus is potentially lethal. If there is associated cortisol deficiency, then diabetes insipidus may not be manifest until glucocorticoid replacement therapy is given. The differential diagnosis includes diabetes mellitus and primary polydipsia, a condition which is seen most often in patients with established psychiatric disease.

Investigations

Diabetes insipidus is confirmed if, in the face of elevated plasma osmolality (i.e. > 300 mOsm/kg), either ADH is not measurable in serum or the urine is not maximally concentrated (i.e. is < 660 mOsm/kg). Sometimes, random simultaneous samples of blood and urine will confirm the diagnosis, or refute the diagnosis by demonstrating a urine osmolality > 660 mOsm/kg. More often, a dynamic test is required. Most centres use a water deprivation test, described in Box 16.53. An alternative is to infuse hypertonic saline (5% saline) and measure ADH secretion in response to increasing plasma osmolality. Thirst can also be assessed during these tests on a visual analogue scale.

Anterior pituitary function and suprasellar anatomy should be assessed in patients with cranial diabetes insipidus as indicated in Box 16.42, page 735.

In primary polydipsia the urine may be excessively dilute because of chronic diuresis which 'washes out' the solute gradient across the loop of Henle, but plasma osmolality is low rather than high. DDAVP (see below) should not be administered to patients with primary polydipsia, since it will prevent excretion of water and risks severe water intoxication if the patient continues to drink fluid to excess.

In nephrogenic diabetes insipidus appropriate further tests include plasma electrolytes, calcium and investigation of the renal tract (see Chs 9 and 14).

Management

Treatment of cranial diabetes insipidus is with des-amino-des-aspartate-arginine vasopressin (desmopressin, DDAVP), an analogue of ADH with a longer half-life. Polyuria in nephrogenic diabetes insipidus is improved by thiazide diuretics (e.g. bendroflumethiazide (bendrofluazide) 2.5–5 mg/day), amiloride (5–10 mg/day) and non-steroidal anti-inflammatory drugs (e.g. indometacin 15 mg 8-hourly), although the last of these carries a risk of reducing glomerular filtration rate.

DDAVP

DDAVP is usually administered via the mucous membrane of the nose, either as a metered dose spray or using a manual aerosol device. It is also available as tablets, although bioavailability of peptides after oral administration is very low and rather unpredictable. In sick patients, DDAVP is given by intramuscular injection. The dose of DDAVP required to keep the patient in water balance must be determined by measuring plasma sodium concentrations and/or osmolality. The principal hazard is excessive treatment resulting in water intoxication and hyponatraemia.

ISSUES IN OLDER PEOPLE
THE PITUITARY AND HYPOTHALAMUS

- Pituitary tumours are slow-growing. In patients without visual dysfunction, treatment may not be necessary.
- Older patients may not recognise the usual early features of pituitary disease (e.g. amenorrhoea, galactorrhoea, sexual dysfunction) and are likely to present late with large pituitary tumours and visual dysfunction.
- Hyperprolactinaemia due to microadenoma is less hazardous after the menopause, when 'physiological hypogonadism' occurs anyway. However, macroadenomas should be actively treated at all ages.
- Growth hormone secretion falls with age, sometimes resulting in apparent biochemical GH deficiency. This should only be tested when clinically indicated (see Box 16.42, p. 735).

Inadequate treatment results in thirst and a compensatory increase in fluid intake in the conscious patient. The ideal dose prevents nocturia but allows a degree of polyuria from time to time before the next dose (e.g. DDAVP nasal dose 5 µg in the morning and 10 µg at night).

FURTHER INFORMATION

deGroot L, Jameson JL. Endocrinology. 4th edn. London: WB Saunders; 2000.

Trainer PJ, Besser GM. The Bart's endocrine protocols. Edinburgh: Churchill Livingstone; 1995. *Detailed protocols for dynamic endocrine tests.*

Wilson JD, Foster DW, Kronenberg HM, Larson PR. Williams textbook of endocrinology. 9th edn. London: WB Saunders; 1998.

www.endocrinology.org *Website of the British Society for Endocrinology; useful links to other resources.*

www.endo-society.org *Website of the American Endocrine Society; useful links to other resources.*

Alimentary tract and pancreatic disease

K.R. PALMER • I.D. PENMAN • S. PATERSON-BROWN

CLINICAL EXAMINATION OF THE GASTROINTESTINAL TRACT

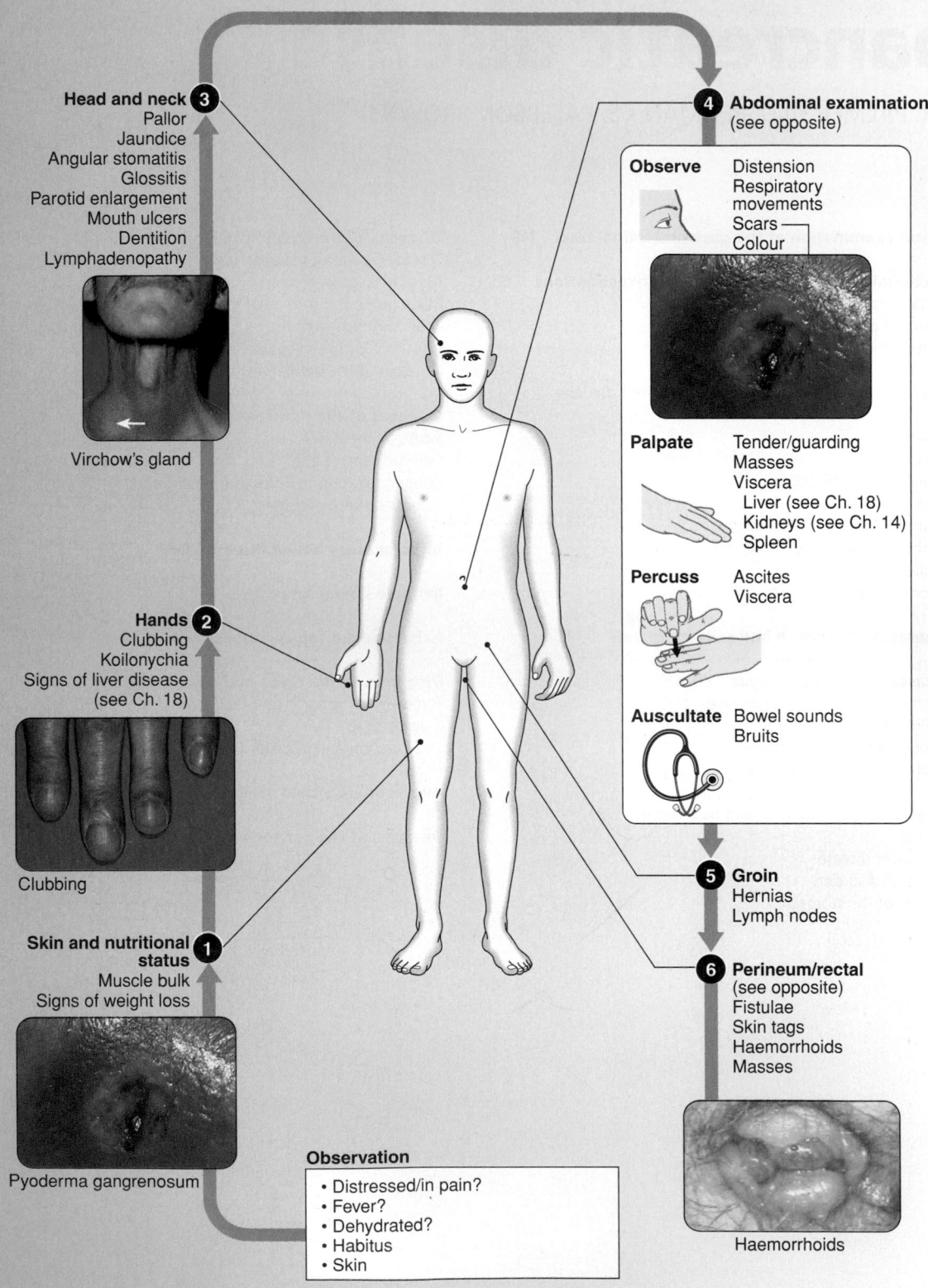

Head and neck **3**
Pallor
Jaundice
Angular stomatitis
Glossitis
Parotid enlargement
Mouth ulcers
Dentition
Lymphadenopathy

Virchow's gland

Hands **2**
Clubbing
Koilonychia
Signs of liver disease
(see Ch. 18)

Clubbing

Skin and nutritional status **1**
Muscle bulk
Signs of weight loss

Pyoderma gangrenosum

Observation
• Distressed/in pain?
• Fever?
• Dehydrated?
• Habitus
• Skin

4 **Abdominal examination**
(see opposite)

Observe
Distension
Respiratory movements
Scars
Colour

Palpate
Tender/guarding
Masses
Viscera
Liver (see Ch. 18)
Kidneys (see Ch. 14)
Spleen

Percuss
Ascites
Viscera

Auscultate
Bowel sounds
Bruits

5 **Groin**
Hernias
Lymph nodes

6 **Perineum/rectal**
(see opposite)
Fistulae
Skin tags
Haemorrhoids
Masses

Haemorrhoids

4 ABDOMINAL EXAMINATION: POSSIBLE FINDINGS

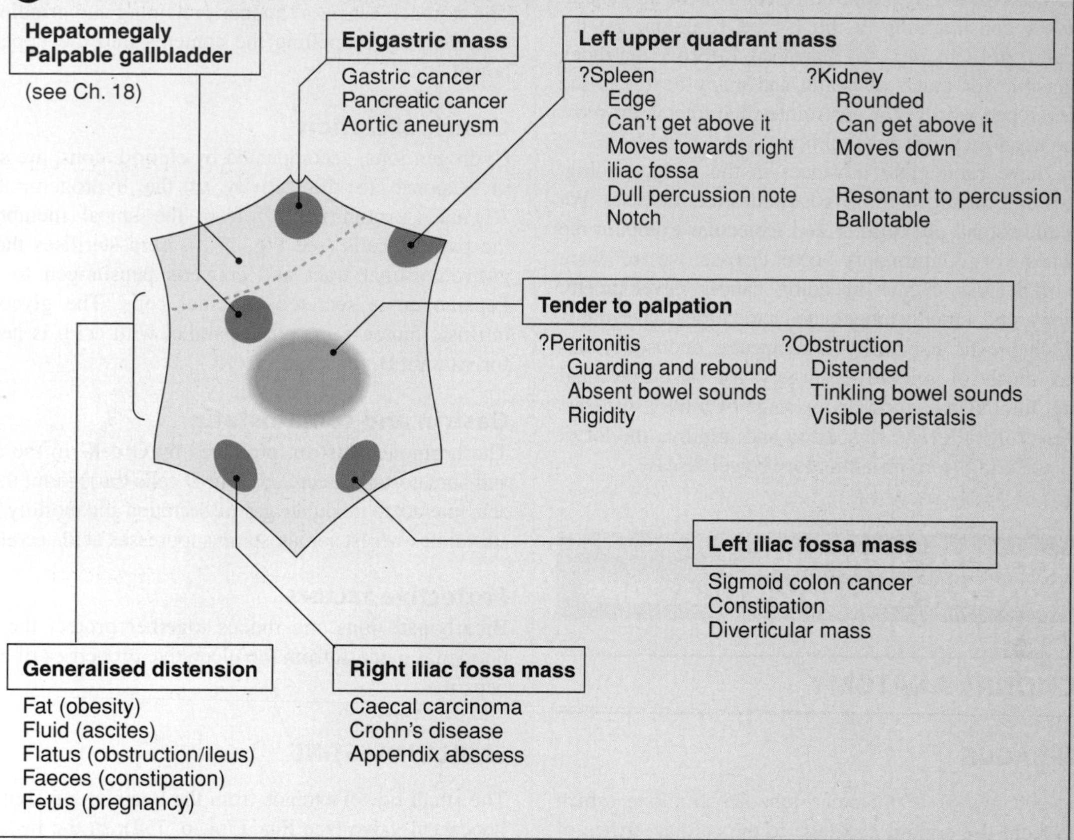

Hepatomegaly
Palpable gallbladder

(see Ch. 18)

Epigastric mass

Gastric cancer
Pancreatic cancer
Aortic aneurysm

Left upper quadrant mass

?Spleen	?Kidney
Edge	Rounded
Can't get above it	Can get above it
Moves towards right iliac fossa	Moves down
Dull percussion note	Resonant to percussion
Notch	Ballotable

Tender to palpation

?Peritonitis	?Obstruction
Guarding and rebound	Distended
Absent bowel sounds	Tinkling bowel sounds
Rigidity	Visible peristalsis

Left iliac fossa mass

Sigmoid colon cancer
Constipation
Diverticular mass

Generalised distension

Fat (obesity)
Fluid (ascites)
Flatus (obstruction/ileus)
Faeces (constipation)
Fetus (pregnancy)

Right iliac fossa mass

Caecal carcinoma
Crohn's disease
Appendix abscess

6 RECTAL EXAMINATION: COMMON FINDINGS

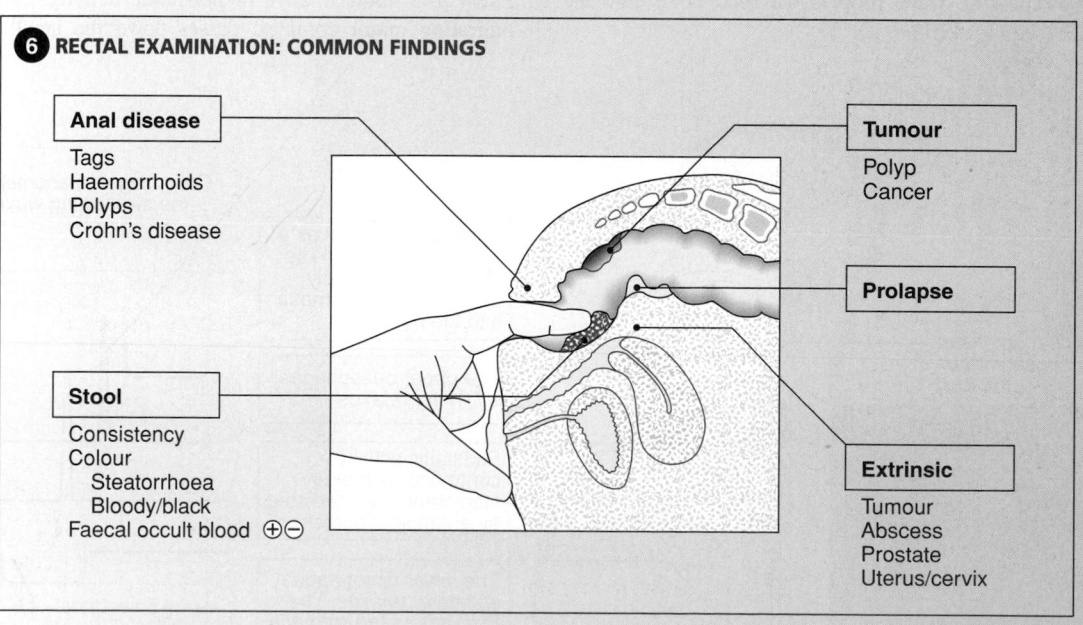

Anal disease

Tags
Haemorrhoids
Polyps
Crohn's disease

Tumour

Polyp
Cancer

Prolapse

Stool

Consistency
Colour
  Steatorrhoea
  Bloody/black
Faecal occult blood ⊕⊖

Extrinsic

Tumour
Abscess
Prostate
Uterus/cervix

Diseases of the gastrointestinal tract are a major cause of morbidity and mortality. Approximately 10% of all general practitioner consultations in the United Kingdom are for indigestion, and 1 in 14 is for diarrhoea. Infective diarrhoea is responsible for much ill health and many deaths in the underdeveloped world. The gastrointestinal tract is the most common site for cancer development.

There have been great advances in the understanding, diagnosis and management of gastrointestinal diseases. We largely understand the cellular and molecular events in the pathogenesis of inflammatory bowel disease; we are aware of the molecular events in colon cancer development. Endoscopy and other sophisticated modalities have transformed diagnostic capability. Therapeutic endoscopy has replaced much of operative surgery for gastrointestinal bleeding, tumour palliation and a range of biliary diseases. Powerful drugs alleviate dyspepsia and improve the lot of patients suffering from inflammatory bowel disease.

FUNCTIONAL ANATOMY, PHYSIOLOGY AND INVESTIGATIONS

FUNCTIONAL ANATOMY

OESOPHAGUS

The oesophagus is a muscular tube 25 cm long which extends from the cricoid cartilage to the cardiac orifice of the stomach. It has an upper and a lower sphincter. A peristaltic swallowing wave propels the food bolus into the stomach (see Fig. 17.1).

STOMACH AND DUODENUM (see Fig. 17.2)

The stomach acts as a 'hopper', retaining and grinding food, then actively propelling the contents into the upper small bowel.

Gastric secretion

Hydrogen ions, accompanied by chloride ions, are secreted in response to the activity of the hydrogen-potassium ATPase ('proton pump') from the apical membrane of the parietal cells (see Fig. 17.3). Acid sterilises the upper gastrointestinal tract and converts pepsinogen to pepsin. Pepsinogen is secreted by chief cells. The glycoprotein intrinsic factor, secreted in parallel with acid, is necessary for vitamin B_{12} absorption.

Gastrin and somatostatin

The hormones gastrin, produced by G cells in the antrum, and somatostatin, secreted from D cells throughout the stomach, interact to modulate gastric secretion and motility. Gastrin stimulates whilst somatostatin suppresses acid secretion.

Protective factors

Bicarbonate ions and mucus together protect the gastroduodenal mucosa from the ulcerative properties of acid and pepsin.

SMALL INTESTINE

The small bowel extends from the ligament of Treitz to the ileocaecal valve (see Fig. 17.4, p. 752). In the fasted state, muscular activity is absent for at least 80% of the time. Every 1–2 hours a wave of peristaltic activity, called the migrating motor complex, passes down the small bowel.

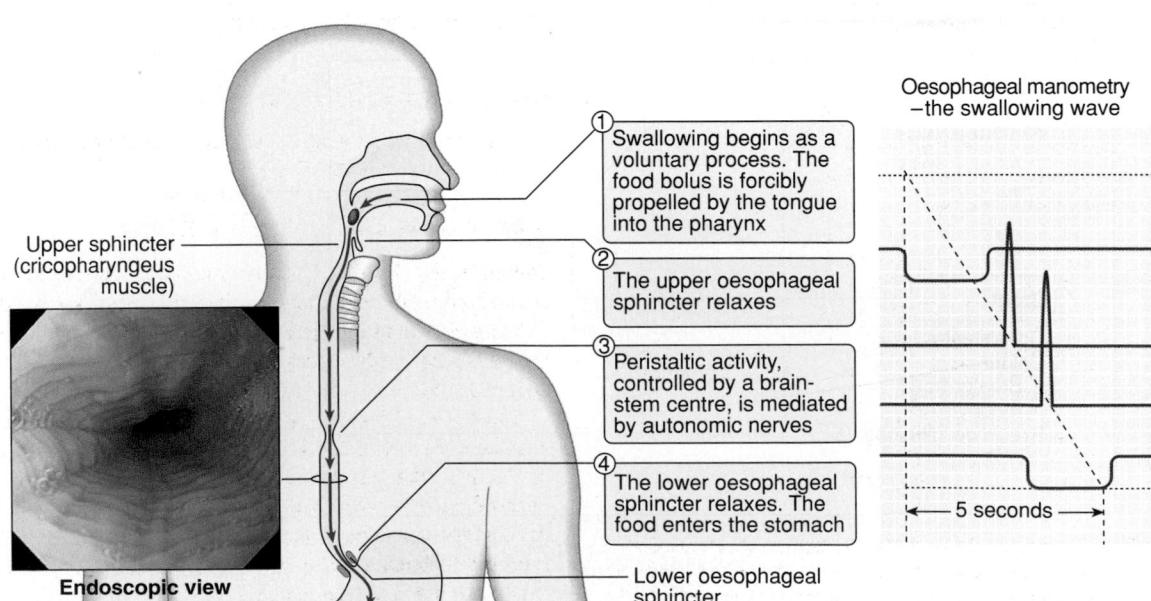

Upper sphincter (cricopharyngeus muscle)

Endoscopic view

① Swallowing begins as a voluntary process. The food bolus is forcibly propelled by the tongue into the pharynx

② The upper oesophageal sphincter relaxes

③ Peristaltic activity, controlled by a brain-stem centre, is mediated by autonomic nerves

④ The lower oesophageal sphincter relaxes. The food enters the stomach

Lower oesophageal sphincter

Oesophageal manometry –the swallowing wave

←— 5 seconds —→

Fig. 17.1 **The oesophagus: anatomy and function.** The swallowing wave.

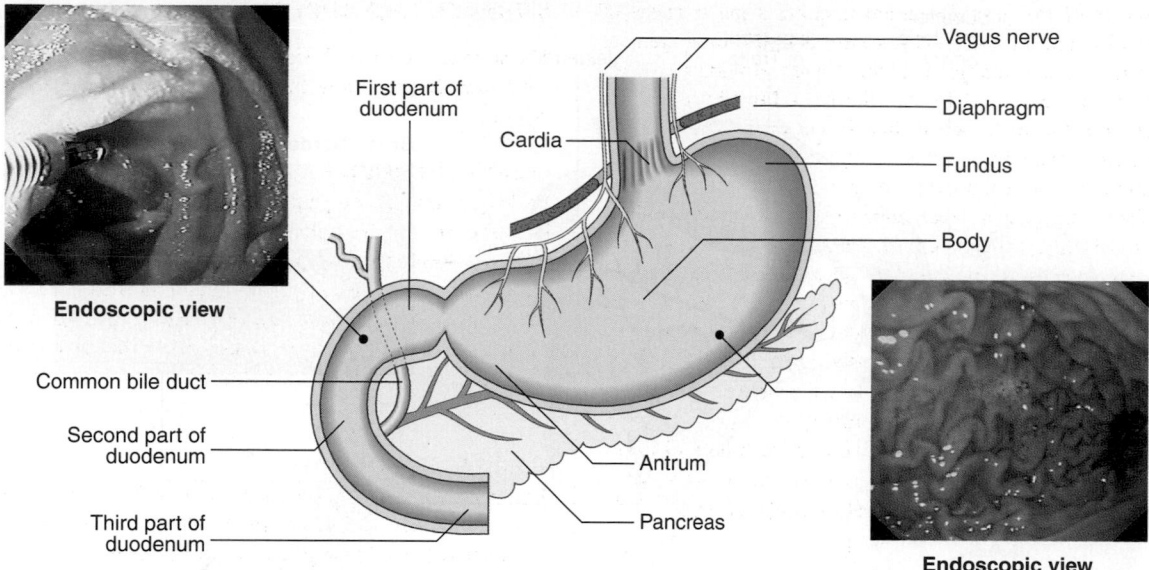

First part of duodenum

Cardia

Vagus nerve

Diaphragm

Fundus

Body

Endoscopic view

Common bile duct

Second part of duodenum

Third part of duodenum

Antrum

Pancreas

Endoscopic view

Fig. 17.2 Normal gastric and duodenal anatomy.

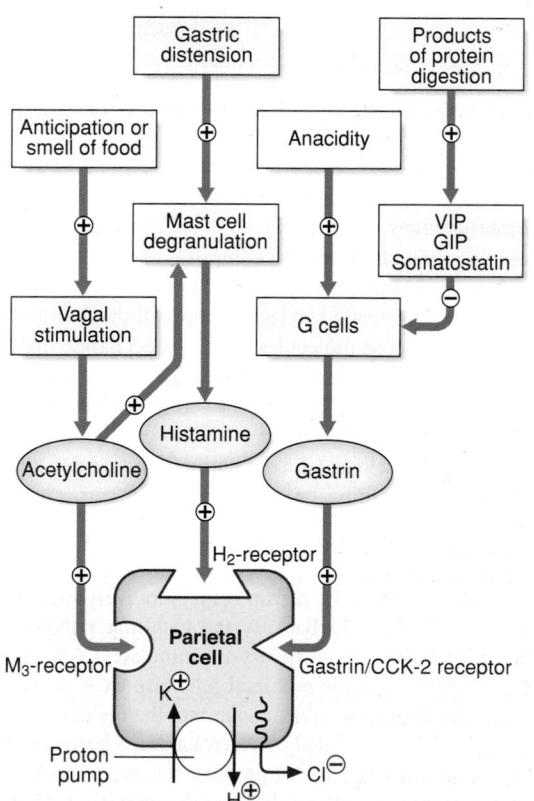

Fig. 17.3 Control of acid secretion. The parietal cell secretes acid in response to cholinergic activity, histamine and gastrin. Hydrogen ions are secreted in exchange for potassium ions from the apical membrane of the cell and chloride ions passively diffuse to maintain electroneutrality. (VIP = vasoactive intestinal polypeptide; GIP = gastric inhibitory polypeptide)

Entry of food into the gastrointestinal tract stimulates small bowel peristaltic activity.

Functions of the small intestine are:

- digestion
- absorption—the products of digestion, water, electrolytes and vitamins
- protection against ingested toxins—immunological, mechanical, enzymatic and peristaltic.

Digestion and absorption

Fat

Dietary fat comprises:

- long-chain triglycerides (a glycerol 'backbone' bound to three fatty acid molecules)
- cholesterol esters
- fat-soluble vitamins (A, D, K and E).

Digestion and absorption involve multiple, interrelated steps as food passes through the gastrointestinal tract (see p. 306).

Stomach. Churning activity emulsifies the fat. Limited hydrolysis of triglycerides to diglycerides and fatty acid occurs due to the activity of swallowed, lingual lipase.

Duodenum. Secretin is released in response to acid exposure. This stimulates pancreatic bicarbonate secretion, producing alkaline duodenal contents. Intraluminal fat releases cholecystokinin (CCK). This hormone stimulates gallbladder contraction and relaxes the sphincter of Oddi, resulting in entry of bile into the duodenum. Bile further emulsifies lipids to form chyme.

Upper jejunum. Pancreatic lipase and colipase hydrolyse triglycerides to monoglycerides and free fatty acids (see

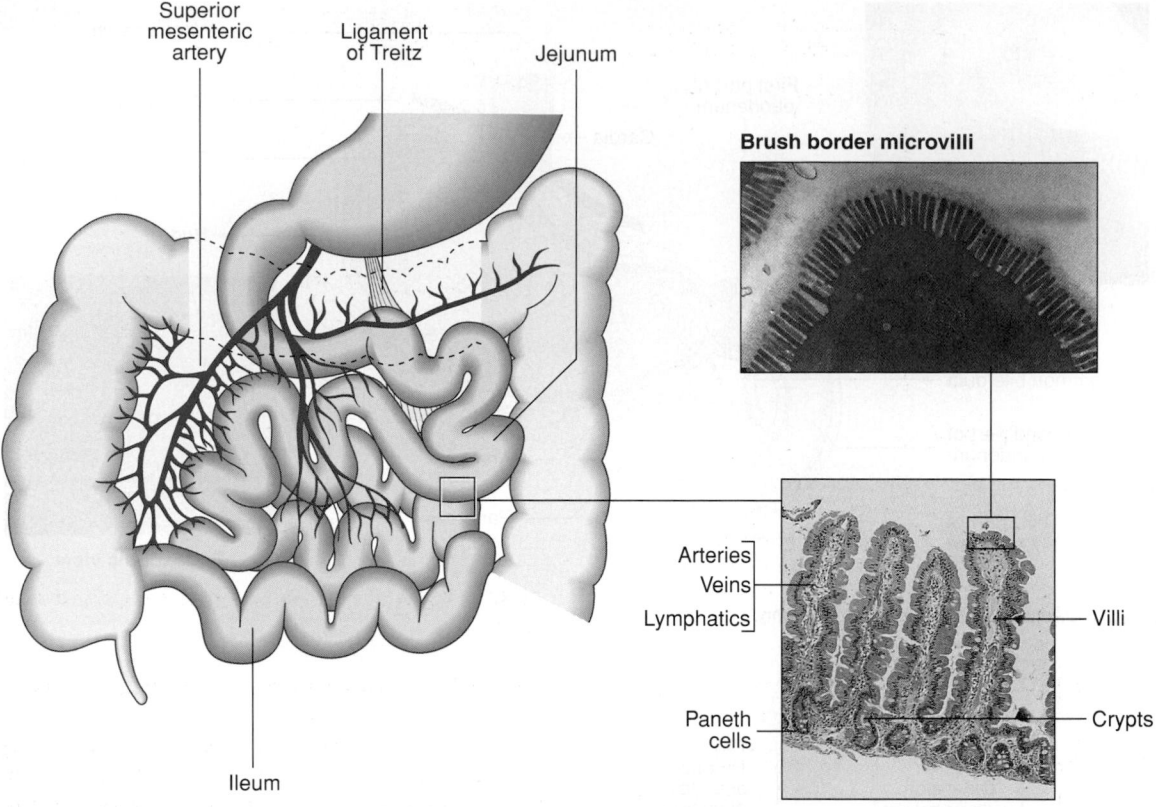

Fig. 17.4   Small intestine: anatomy. Epithelial cells are formed in crypts and differentiate as they migrate to the tip of the villi to form enterocytes (absorptive cells) and goblet cells.

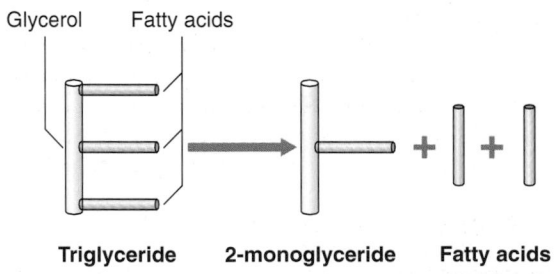

Fig. 17.5   Hydrolysis of triglycerides to monoglycerides and free fatty acids—the jejunal phase of fat digestion.

Fig. 17.5). Phospholipids and cholesterol esters are hydro- lysed by other pancreatic enzymes. The lipid mixture is now emulsified by the bile acids as 'mixed micelles'.

Distal small intestine. The lipid contents of the mixed micelles pass across cell membranes into enterocytes. Bile salts remain in the lumen and are absorbed in the terminal ileum, pass via the portal vein back to the liver and are then recycled (the enterohepatic circulation). Within enterocytes, fatty acids, monoglycerides and diglycerides are re-esterified to form triglycerides. These are coated with apoproteins, phospholipids and cholesterol in the endoplasmic reticulum to form chylomicrons which leave the cells by exocytosis and eventually enter the portal circulation via lymphatics.

Carbohydrates

Dietary carbohydrate largely comprises the polysaccharide starch, some sucrose and lactose. Starch is hydrolysed by salivary and pancreatic amylases to alpha-limit dextrins con- taining 4–8 glucose molecules; to the disaccharide maltose; and to the trisaccharide maltotriose.

Disaccharides are digested by enzymes fixed to the microvillous membrane to form the monosaccharides glucose, galactose and fructose. Glucose and galactose enter the cell by an energy-requiring process involving a carrier protein. Fructose enters by simple diffusion.

Protein

Intragastric digestion by pepsin is quantitatively modest but nevertheless important because the resulting polypeptides and amino acids are sufficient to stimulate CCK release from the mucosa of the proximal jejunum. CCK stimulates secretion of pancreatic trypsinogen into the duodenum.

Trypsinogen is activated by enterokinase, a hormone fixed to the duodenal mucosa, to produce the active proteolytic enzyme, trypsin. Trypsin subsequently activates a range of other pancreatic proenzymes and these digest proteins to form small polypeptides and amino acids. The enzymes com- prise the endopeptidases trypsin, chymotrypsin and elastase, which hydrolyse bonds within proteins, and exopeptidases, which hydrolyse the carboxyl terminus. Peptidases on the microvilli then digest polypeptides to form dipeptides and amino acids, which are absorbed by sodium-dependent

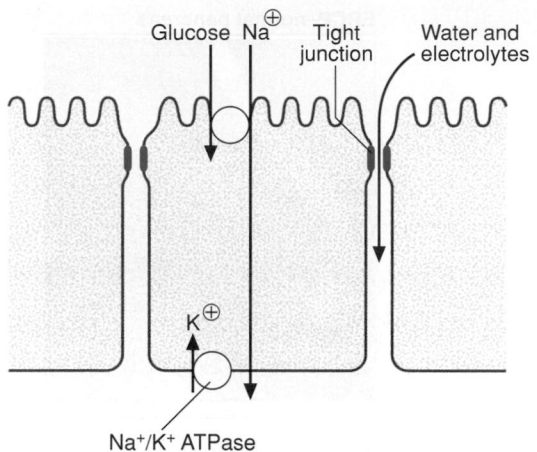

Fig. 17.6 Glucose/sodium cotransport. Glucose/sodium cotransport across the apical membrane of the enterocyte involving an energy-dependent pump on the basolateral membrane and a carrier for glucose and sodium on the apical membrane. Passive movement of water and electrolytes through tight junctions occurs as a consequence of electrochemical gradients.

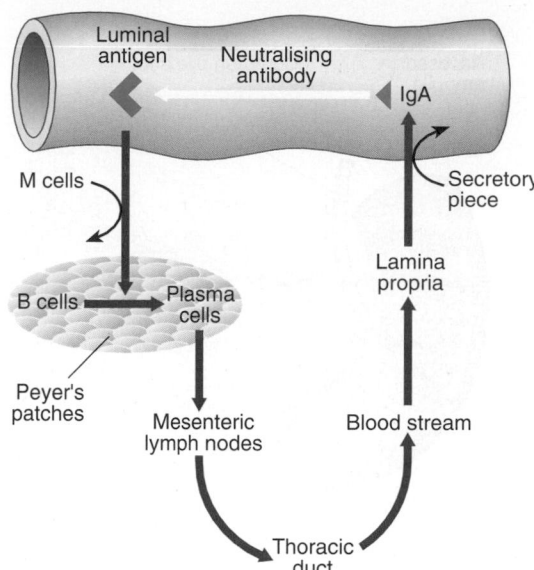

Fig. 17.7 Migration of gut lymphoid tissue in response to antigen exposure.

active transport systems. Within the enterocytes, cytosolic peptidases further digest dipeptides to amino acids.

Water and electrolytes

Both absorption and secretion of electrolytes and water occur throughout the intestine. Net transport is the difference between absorption and secretion; in health, absorption predominates. Electrolytes and water are transported by two pathways (see Fig. 17.6):

- the paracellular route, in which flow through tight junctions between cells is a consequence of osmotic, electrical or hydrostatic gradients
- the transcellular route across apical and basolateral membranes by energy-requiring specific active transport carriers (pumps).

Vitamins and trace elements

Water-soluble vitamins are absorbed throughout the intestine. The absorption of folic acid, vitamin B_{12}, calcium and iron is described on pages 322–324.

Protective function of the small intestine

Immunology

B and T lymphocytes, macrophages and mast cells are found throughout the gastrointestinal mucosa. Mucosa-associated lymphoid tissue (MALT) constitutes 25% of the total lymphatic tissue of the body.

Luminal macromolecules and viral particles are transported by specialised (M) cells to Peyer's patches (see Fig. 17.7). These comprise lymphoid follicles with a well-defined structure. B lymphocytes within Peyer's patches differentiate to plasma cells following exposure to the antigens, and these cells migrate to mesenteric lymph nodes, thence to the blood stream via the thoracic duct and then return to the lamina propria of the gut, bronchial tree and other lymph nodes. They subsequently release IgA, which is transported

into the lumen of the intestine after linkage to secretory piece. This neutralises the antigen.

The role of T lymphocytes is less clear, but these cells probably help localise the plasma cells to the site of antigen exposure as well as producing inflammatory mediators. Macrophages phagocytose foreign materials and secrete a range of cytokines which mediate inflammation. Activation of mast cell surface IgE receptors leads to degranulation and release of other molecules involved in inflammation.

Mucosal barrier

The epithelium of the gastrointestinal tract constitutes a barrier to luminal contents. This barrier comprises mucus, secreted by goblet cells, the membranes of the enterocytes and the tight junctions between them. These cells are constantly renewed, those of the small intestine every 48 hours.

PANCREAS (see Box 17.1)

The exocrine pancreas is necessary for the digestion of fat, protein and carbohydrate. Inactive proenzymes are secreted from acinar cells in response to circulating gastrointestinal hormones (see Fig. 17.8) and are then activated by trypsin.

17.1 PANCREATIC ENZYMES		
Enzyme	**Substrate**	**Product**
Amylase	Starch and glycogen	Limit dextrans Maltose Maltriose
Lipase **Colipase**	Triglycerides	Monoglycerides and free fatty acids
Proteolytic enzymes Trypsinogen Chymotrypsinogen Proelastase Procarboxypeptidases	Proteins and polypeptides	Short polypeptides

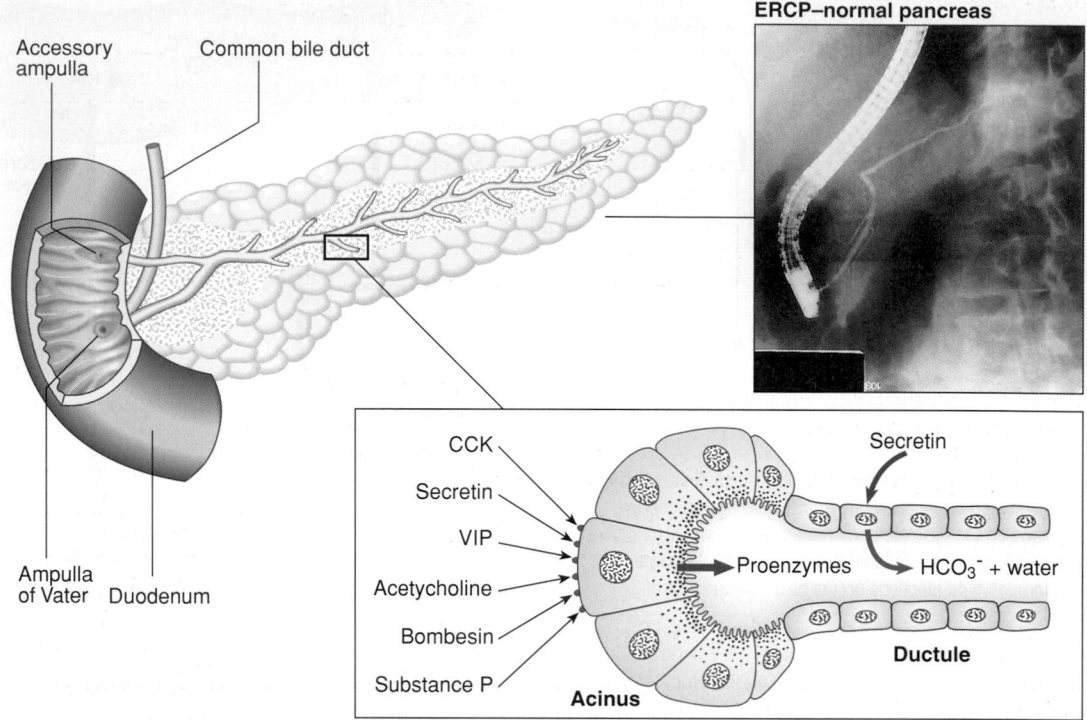

Fig. 17.8 **Pancreatic structure and function.** Ductular cells secrete alkaline fluid in response to secretin. Acinar cells secrete digestive enzymes from zymogen granules in response to a range of secretagogues. The photograph shows a normal pancreatic duct and side branches as defined at ERCP.

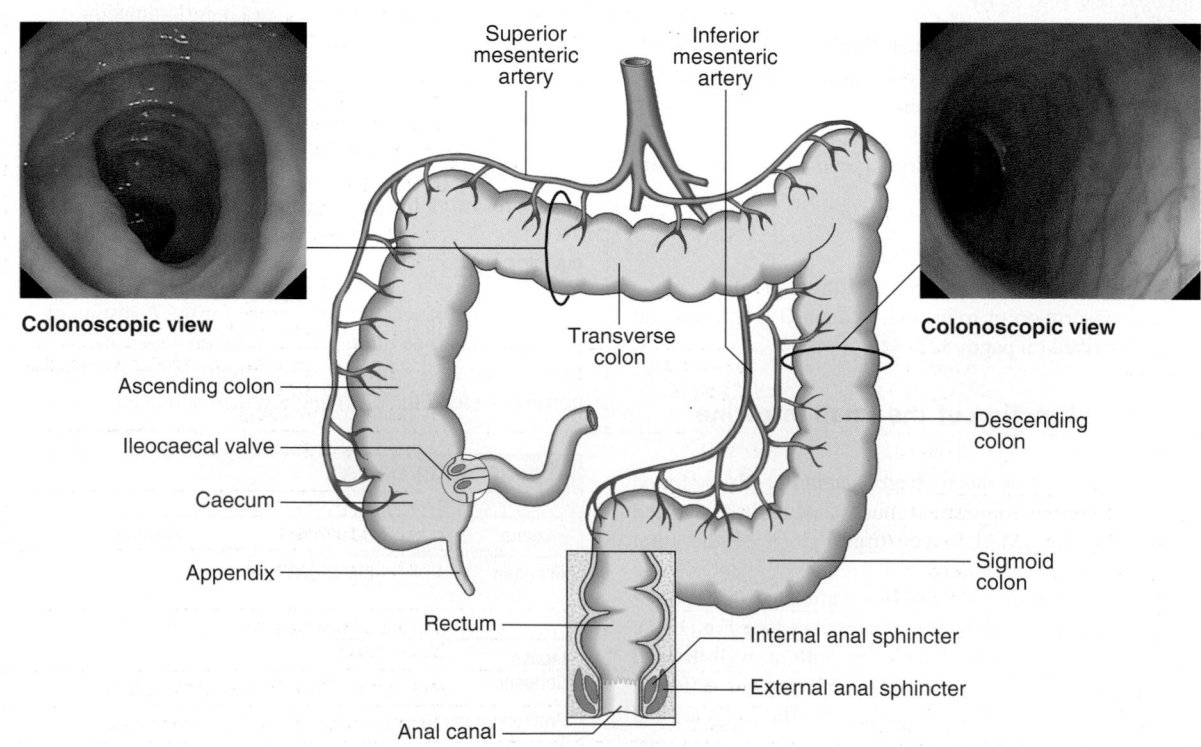

Fig. 17.9 **The normal colon, rectum and anal canal.**

Bicarbonate-rich fluid is secreted from ductular cells to produce an optimum, alkaline pH for enzyme activity.

COLON

The colon (see Fig. 17.9) absorbs water and electrolytes. It also acts as a storage organ and has contractile activity. Two types of contraction occur. The first of these is segmentation (ring contraction), which leads to mixing but not propulsion; this facilitates absorption of water and electrolytes. Propulsive (peristaltic contraction) waves cause mass movement several times a day and propel the faecal bolus to the rectum. All activity is stimulated after meals, probably in response to release of motilin and CCK.

Faecal continence depends upon maintenance of the anorectal angle and tonic contraction of the external anal sphincters. Relaxation of these muscles, increased intra-abdominal pressure from a Valsalva manoeuvre and contraction of abdominal muscles, with relaxation of the anal sphincters, result in defaecation.

CONTROL OF GASTROINTESTINAL FUNCTION

Secretion, absorption, motor activity, growth and differentiation are modulated by nervous and hormonal factors.

17.2 GUT NEUROPEPTIDES

Neuropeptide	Action
Opioids	Pain perception Decrease motility, regulate sphincter activity Increase acid secretion Modulate electrolyte and water absorption
Substance P	Propagates peristaltic activity Stimulates lower oesophageal sphincter Pain modulation
Vasoactive intestinal polypeptide (VIP)	Smooth muscle relaxation Vasodilatation
Gastrin-releasing polypeptide Bombesin	Mediate gastrin release
Cholecystokinin (CCK)	Controls satiety Release of acetylcholine and γ-aminobutyric acid (GABA) from myenteric plexus
Neuropeptide Y	Vasocontraction of splanchnic circulation Reduces small bowel secretions

17.3 GUT HORMONES

Hormone	Origin	Stimulus	Action
Gastrin	Stomach (G cell)	Products of protein digestion Suppressed by acid and somatostatin	Stimulates gastric acid secretion Stimulates growth of gastrointestinal mucosa
Somatostatin	Throughout GI tract (D cell)	Fat ingestion	Inhibits gastrin and insulin secretion Decreased acid secretion Decreased absorption
Cholecystokinin	Duodenum and jejunum	Products of protein digestion Fat and fatty acids Suppressed by trypsin	Stimulates pancreatic enzyme secretion Gallbladder contraction Sphincter of Oddi relaxation Satiety Decreased gastric acid secretion Reduced gastric emptying Regulates pancreatic growth
Secretin	Duodenum and jejunum	Duodenal acid Fatty acids	Stimulates pancreatic fluid and bicarbonate secretion Decreased acid secretion Reduced gastric emptying
Motilin	Duodenum and jejunum	Fasting Dietary fat	Regulates peristaltic activity
Gastric inhibitory polypeptide (GIP)	Duodenum and jejunum	Nutrients	Stimulates insulin release Inhibits acid secretion
Pancreatic polypeptide	Duodenum and jejunum	Protein digestive products Gastric distension	Inhibits pancreatic secretions
Enteroglucagon	Ileum and colon	Unknown	Modulates insulin release Trophic effect
Neurotensin	Ileum and colon	Unknown	May regulate ileal motility in response to fat
Peptide Y	Ileum and colon	Intestinal fat	Decreases pancreatic and gastric secretion
Vasoactive intestinal polypeptide (VIP)	Nerve fibres throughout GI tract	Unknown	Regulates blood flow

17.4 CONTRAST RADIOLOGY IN THE INVESTIGATION OF GASTROINTESTINAL DISEASE

	Barium swallow	Barium meal	Barium follow-through	Barium enema
Indications	Dysphagia Heartburn Chest pain Possible motility disorder	Dyspepsia Epigastric pain Anaemia Vomiting Possible perforation (non-ionic contrast)	Diarrhoea and abdominal pain of small bowel origin Possible obstruction by strictures etc.	Altered bowel habit Rectal bleeding Anaemia
Major uses	Strictures Hiatus hernia Gastro-oesophageal reflux and motility disorders, e.g. achalasia	Gastric, duodenal ulcers Gastric cancer Outlet obstruction Gastric emptying disorders	Malabsorption Crohn's disease	Neoplasia Diverticulosis Strictures, e.g. ischaemic Megacolon
Limitations	Risk of aspiration Poor mucosal detail Unable to biopsy	Low sensitivity for early cancer Unable to biopsy or assess *Helicobacter pylori*	Time-consuming Radiation exposure	Difficult in frail elderly or incontinent patients Uncomfortable Sigmoidoscopy also necessary to evaluate rectum Possibly misses polyps < 1 cm Less useful in inflammatory bowel disease

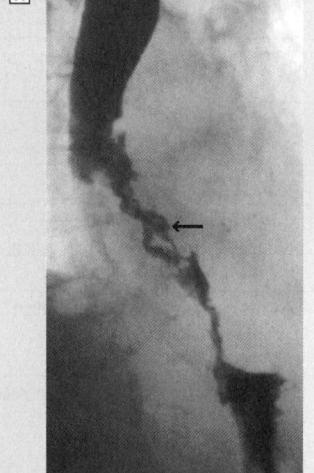
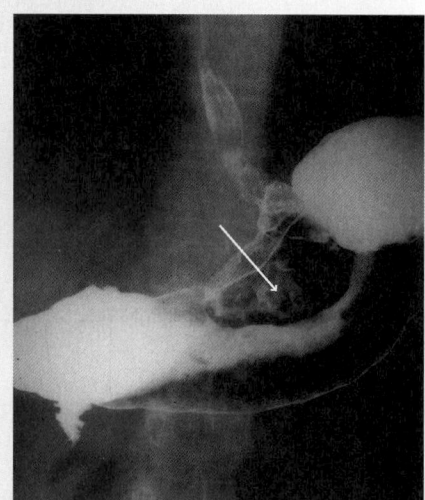
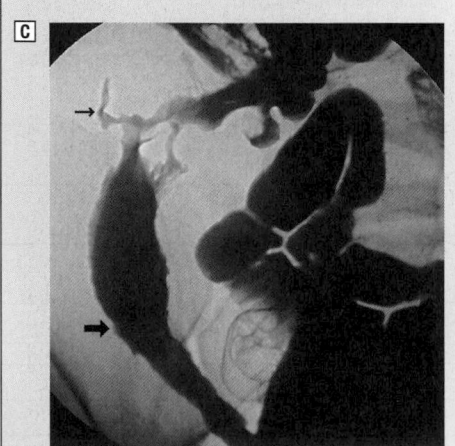
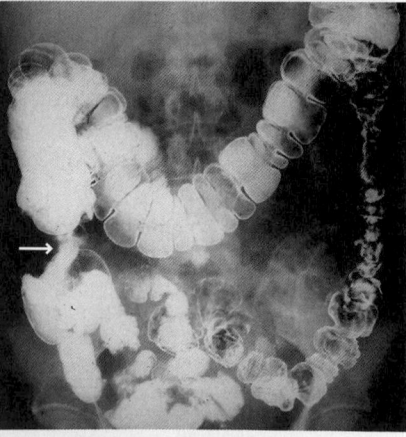

Fig. 17.10. Examples of contrast radiology. A A long irregular stricture (arrow) caused by oesophageal cancer. B A polypoid carcinoma demonstrated as a filling defect arising from the gastric body (arrow). C A long Crohn's stricture in the terminal ileum (large arrow) and also an adjacent fistulous tract (small arrow). D Colon cancer demonstrated as an 'apple core' stricture in the caecum (arrow).

THE ENTERIC NERVOUS SYSTEM

Extrinsic innervation is provided by sympathetic nerves which release noradrenaline, and by parasympathetic, vagal nerves which release acetylcholine. In general, sympathetic pathways stimulate contraction and secretion, whilst parasympathetic pathways are inhibitory.

Extrinsic nerves interact with the intrinsic plexuses of the gastrointestinal tract (Auerbach's and Meissner's plexuses). Neuropeptides produced by these nerves exert a wide range of activities (see Box 17.2) through neurocrine, paracrine and autocrine mechanisms; some (e.g. VIP, CCK) also have endocrine actions.

GUT HORMONES

The origin, action and control of the major gut hormones are summarised in Box 17.3.

INVESTIGATION OF GASTROINTESTINAL DISEASE

A wide range of tests are available for the investigation of patients with gastrointestinal symptoms. These can be classified broadly into tests of structure, tests of infection and tests of function.

TESTS OF STRUCTURE: IMAGING

Plain radiographs

Plain radiographs of the abdomen show the distribution of gas within the small and large intestines and are useful in the diagnosis of intestinal obstruction or paralytic ileus where dilated loops of bowel and (in the erect position) fluid levels

17.5 ULTRASOUND SCANNING, CT AND MRI IN GASTROENTEROLOGY

Investigation	Ultrasound	CT	MRI
Major uses	Abdominal masses, e.g. cysts, tumours, abscesses Organomegaly Ascites Biliary tract dilatation Gallstones Guided needle aspiration and biopsy of lesions	Assessment of pancreatic disease Hepatic tumour deposits Tumour staging Assessment of vascularity of lesions	Hepatic tumour staging Magnetic resonance cholangiopancreatography (MRCP) Pelvic/perianal Crohn's fistulae
Limitations	Low sensitivity for small lesions Little functional information Operator-dependent Gas and obesity may obscure view	Expensive High radiation dose May understage some tumours, e.g. oesophago-gastric	Role in gastrointestinal disease not fully established Limited availability Time-consuming 'Claustrophobic' for some Contraindicated in presence of metallic prosthesis, cardiac pacemaker

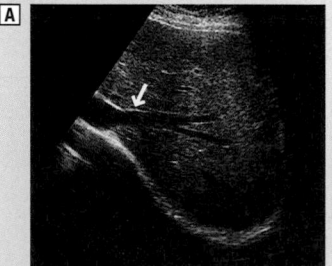 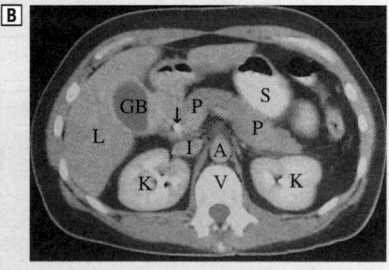 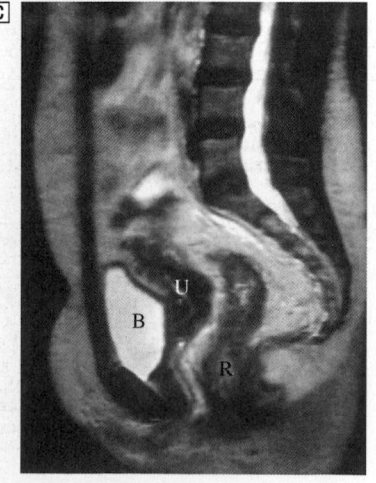

Fig. 17.11 Examples of ultrasound, CT and MRI. A Ultrasound of normal liver with hepatic veins entering the inferior vena cava (arrow). B CT showing a stent in the common bile duct (arrow). (L = liver; GB = gallbladder; K = kidneys; S = stomach; P = pancreas; V = vertebra; A = aorta; I = inferior vena cava) C Normal pelvic MRI (sagittal image). (B = bladder; R = rectum; U = uterus)

are seen. The outlines of soft tissues such as liver, spleen and kidneys may be visible, and calcification of these organs as well as pancreas, blood vessels, lymph nodes and calculi may be detected. Abdominal radiographs do not help in cases of gastrointestinal bleeding. A chest radiograph shows the diaphragm, and erect films may detect subdiaphragmatic free air in cases of perforation. Unexpected pulmonary problems such as pleural effusions will also be revealed.

Contrast studies

Barium sulphate is inert and provides good mucosal coating and excellent opacification. It can, however, solidify and impact proximal to an obstructive lesion. Water-soluble contrast is used to opacify bowel prior to abdominal computed tomography and in cases of suspected perforation but is less radio-opaque and is also irritant if aspirated into the lungs. Contrast studies are carried out under fluoroscopic control, which allows assessment of motility and correct patient positioning. The double contrast technique improves mucosal visualisation by using gas to distend the barium-coated intestinal surface.

Barium studies are useful for detecting filling defects, which may be intraluminal (e.g. food or faeces), intramural (e.g. carcinoma) or extramural (e.g. lymph nodes). Strictures, erosions, ulcers and motility disorders can all be detected.

The major uses and limitations of various contrast studies are shown in Box 17.4 and Fig. 17.10.

Ultrasound, computed tomography (CT) and magnetic resonance imaging (MRI)

These are increasingly used in the evaluation of intra-abdominal disease. They are non-invasive and offer detailed images of the abdominal contents. Their main applications are summarised in Box 17.5 and Fig. 17.11.

Endoscopy

In recent years video endoscopy has replaced fibreoptic endoscopes. Images are displayed on a colour monitor. Endoscopes have controls to allow steering of the tip and also possess channels for suction and insufflation of air and water. An increasing array of instruments can be passed down the endoscope to allow both diagnostic and therapeutic procedures, some of which are illustrated in Figure 17.12.

Upper gastrointestinal endoscopy

After the patient has fasted for at least 4 hours, this is performed under light intravenous benzodiazepine sedation, or using only local anaesthetic throat spray. With the patient in the left lateral position the entire oesophagus (excluding pharynx), stomach and first two parts of duodenum can be seen. Indications, contraindications and complications are given in Box 17.6.

Enteroscopy

Using a longer endoscope (enteroscope) it is possible to visualise a large portion of the small intestine. Enteroscopy

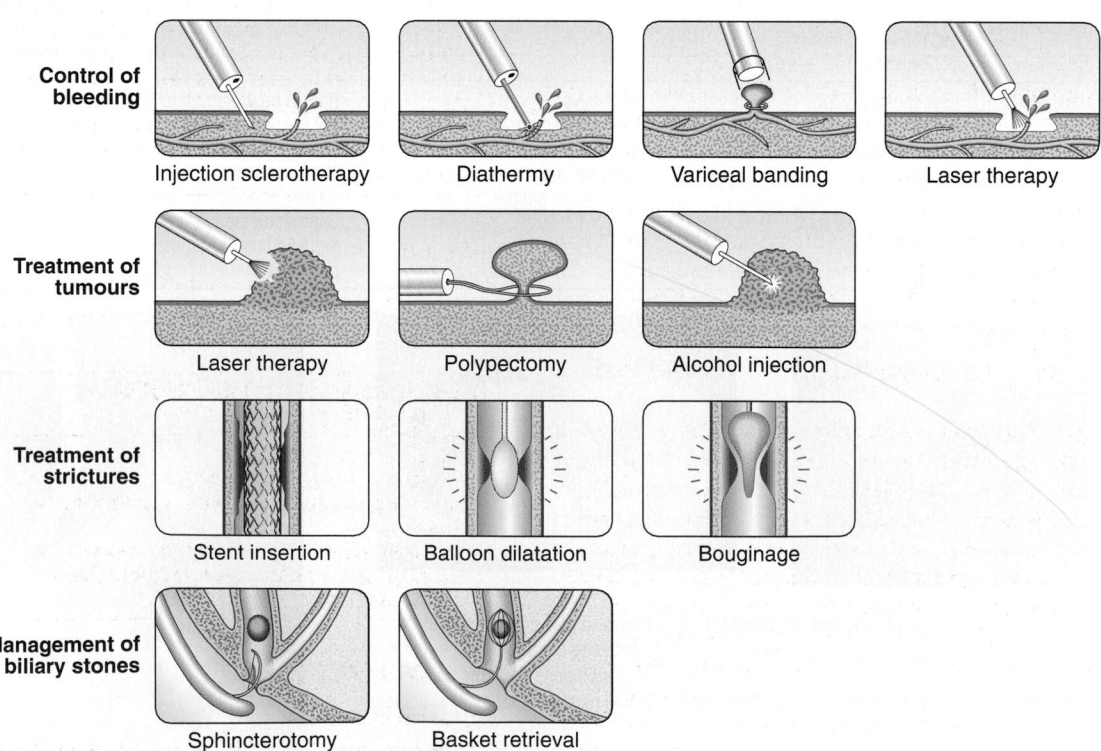

Control of bleeding	Injection sclerotherapy	Diathermy	Variceal banding	Laser therapy
Treatment of tumours	Laser therapy	Polypectomy	Alcohol injection	
Treatment of strictures	Stent insertion	Balloon dilatation	Bouginage	
Management of biliary stones	Sphincterotomy	Basket retrieval		

Fig. 17.12 **Examples of therapeutic techniques in endoscopy.**

17.6 UPPER GASTROINTESTINAL ENDOSCOPY

Indications

- Dyspepsia (especially aged over 55 years)
- Upper abdominal pain
- Atypical chest pain
- Dysphagia
- Vomiting
- Weight loss
- Acute or chronic gastrointestinal bleeding
- Suspicious barium meal
- Duodenal biopsies in the investigation of malabsorption

Contraindications

- Severe shock
- Recent myocardial infarction, unstable angina, cardiac arrhythmia*
- Severe respiratory disease*
- Atlantoaxial subluxation*
- Possible visceral perforation

* These are 'relative' contraindications; in experienced hands, endoscopy can be safely performed.

Complications

- Cardiorespiratory depression due to sedation
- Aspiration pneumonia
- Perforation
- Bleeding
- Infective endocarditis (use antibiotic prophylaxis in those with previous endocarditis or a prosthetic heart valve)

17.7 COLONOSCOPY

Indications

- Suspected inflammatory bowel disease
- Altered bowel habit
- Rectal bleeding or anaemia
- Assessment of abnormal barium enema
- Colorectal cancer surveillance
- Therapeutic procedures

Contraindications

- Severe shock
- Recent myocardial infarction, unstable angina, cardiac arrhythmia*
- Severe respiratory disease
- Possible visceral perforation
- Severe, active ulcerative colitis

* These are 'relative' contraindications; in experienced hands, colonoscopy can be safely performed.

Complications

- Cardiorespiratory depression due to sedation
- Perforation
- Bleeding
- Infective endocarditis (use antibiotic prophylaxis in those with previous endocarditis or a prosthetic heart valve)

ISSUES IN OLDER PEOPLE
ENDOSCOPY

- Endoscopic procedures are generally well tolerated even in very old people.
- Older people are more sensitive to side-effects from sedation with pethidine and/or midazolam; respiratory depression, hypotension and prolonged recovery times are more common.
- Bowel preparation for colonoscopy can be difficult in frail, immobile people. Sodium phosphate-based preparations can cause dehydration or hypotension and should be avoided in those with underlying cardiac or renal failure.
- Hyoscine should be avoided in those with glaucoma and can also cause tachyarrhythmias. Glucagon is preferred if an antiperistaltic agent is needed.

---

is of special value in the assessment of obscure, recurrent gastrointestinal bleeding.

Sigmoidoscopy and colonoscopy

Sigmoidoscopy can be carried out either in the outpatient clinic using a 20 cm rigid plastic sigmoidoscope or in the endoscopy suite using a 60 cm flexible instrument following a disposable enema for bowel preparation. When sigmoidoscopy is combined with proctoscopy, accurate detection of haemorrhoids, ulcerative colitis and distal colorectal neoplasia is possible. After full bowel cleansing it is possible to examine the entire colon and often the terminal ileum using a longer colonoscope. Indications, contraindications and complications of colonoscopy are listed in Box 17.7.

Endoscopic retrograde cholangiopancreatography (ERCP)

Using a side-viewing duodenoscope, it is possible to cannulate the main pancreatic duct and common bile duct. The procedure is valuable in defining the ampulla of Vater, biliary tree and pancreas. Its main uses include investigation of obstructive jaundice, biliary pain and suspected pancreatic disease, such as chronic pancreatitis and pancreatic cancer. Obstruction of the common bile duct by stones can be treated by stone extraction after sphincterotomy, and strictures may be stented. The procedure is technically demanding and carries a significant risk of pancreatitis (3–5%), haemorrhage (4% after sphincterotomy) and perforation (1%). Diagnostic ERCP is being replaced by magnetic resonance cholangiopancreatography (MRCP), which provides comparable images of the biliary tree and pancreas.

Histology

Biopsy material obtained during endoscopy or percutaneously can provide useful information (see Box 17.8).

17.8 REASONS FOR BIOPSY OR CYTOLOGICAL EXAMINATION

- Suspected malignant lesions
- Assessment of mucosal abnormalities
- Diagnosis of infection (e.g. *Candida*, *Helicobacter pylori*, *Giardia lamblia*)
- Measurement of enzyme contents (e.g. disaccharidases)
- Analysis of genetic mutations (e.g. oncogenes, tumour suppressor genes)

TESTS OF INFECTION

Bacterial cultures

Stool cultures are essential in the investigation of diarrhoea, especially when it is acute or bloody, to identify pathogenic organisms (see Ch. 1).

Serology

Detection of antibodies plays a limited role in the diagnosis of gastrointestinal infection caused by organisms such as *Helicobacter pylori*, *Salmonella* species and *Entamoeba histolytica*.

Breath tests

Non-invasive breath tests for *H. pylori* infection are discussed on page 761. Breath tests for suspected small intestinal bacterial overgrowth are discussed on page 795.

TESTS OF FUNCTION

A number of dynamic tests can be used to investigate aspects of gut function, including digestion, absorption, inflammation and epithelial permeability. Some of those more commonly used are listed in Box 17.9. In the assessment of suspected malabsorption, blood tests (full blood count, erythrocyte sedimentation rate (ESR), folate, B_{12}, iron status, albumin, calcium and phosphate) are essential. Endoscopy with distal duodenal biopsy is also indicated in most cases.

Gastrointestinal motility

A range of diverse radiological, manometric and radioisotopic tests exist for investigation of gut motility but many are research tests of limited value in daily clinical practice.

Oesophageal motility

A careful barium swallow can give useful information about oesophageal motility. Videofluoroscopy, with joint assessment by a speech and language therapist and a radiologist, may be necessary in difficult cases. Oesophageal manometry (see Fig. 17.1, p. 750), often in conjunction with 24-hour pH measurements, is of value in diagnosing cases of refractory gastro-oesophageal reflux, achalasia and non-cardiac chest pain.

Gastric emptying

Delayed gastric emptying (gastroparesis) may be responsible for some cases of persistent nausea, vomiting, bloating or early satiety. Endoscopy and barium studies are often normal. Calculating the amount of radioisotope retained in the stomach after a test meal containing solids and liquids labelled with different isotopes (see Fig. 17.13) is often useful.

17.9 DYNAMIC TESTS OF GASTROINTESTINAL FUNCTION

Process	Test	Principle	Comments
Absorption Fat	^{14}C-triolein breath test	Measurement of $^{14}CO_2$ in breath after oral ingestion of radio-labelled fat	Fast and non-invasive but not quantitative
	3-day faecal fat	Quantification of stool fat while patient ingests 100 g/day fat. Normally < 20 mmol/day	Non-invasive but slow and unpleasant for all
Lactose	Lactose H_2 breath test	Measurement of breath H_2 content after 50 g oral lactose. Undigested sugar is metabolised by colonic bacteria in hypolactasia, and expired hydrogen is measured	Non-invasive and accurate; may provoke pain and diarrhoea in sufferers
Bile acids	^{75}SeHCAT test	Isotopic quantification of 7-day whole-body retention of oral dose ^{75}Se-labelled homocholyltaurine (> 15% = normal, < 5% = abnormal)	Accurate and specific but requires two visits and involves radiation. Can be equivocal. Serum cholestenone is as sensitive and specific
Pancreatic exocrine function	Pancreolauryl test	Pancreatic esterases cleave fluoroscein dilaurate after oral ingestion. Fluoroscein is absorbed and quantified in urine	Accurate and avoids duodenal intubation. Takes 2 days. Accurate urine collection essential
	Faecal chymotrypsin or elastase	Immunoassay of pancreatic enzymes on stool sample	Simple, quick and avoids urine collection. Does not detect mild disease
Mucosal inflammation/ permeability	^{51}Cr-EDTA	Urinary quantification of label after oral dose. More is absorbed through 'leaky' mucosa	Relatively non-invasive and accurate but involves radioactivity; limited availability
	Sugar tests (lactulose: rhamnose)	Small intestine absorbs mono- but not disaccharides unless inflamed. Urinary excretion of oral dose of two sugars expressed as ratio (normal < 0.04)	Non-invasive test of small bowel mucosal integrity (e.g. coeliac, Crohn's). Accurate urine collection essential
	Calprotectin	A protein secreted non-specifically by neutrophils into the colon in response to inflammation or neoplasia	Useful screening test for colonic disease

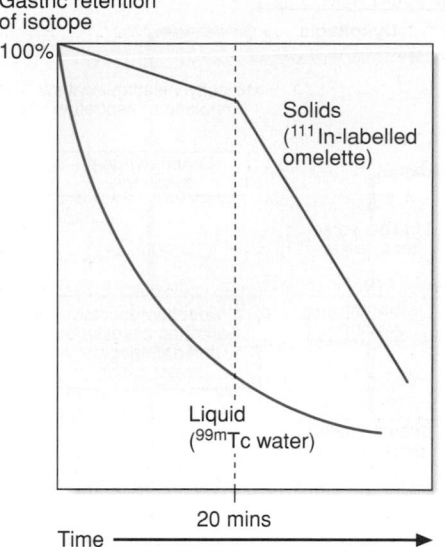

Fig. 17.13 Gastric emptying study. The body of the stomach churns solids into small particles which are then actively expelled by antral peristaltic activity. Gastric emptying is decreased by (a) fats, (b) high osmolality and (c) acid.

Small intestinal transit

This is much more difficult to quantify and is seldom necessary in clinical practice. Barium follow-through examination can give a rough estimate by noting the time taken for

contrast to reach the terminal ileum (normally 90 minutes or less). Orocaecal transit can be assessed by the lactulose-hydrogen breath test. Lactulose is a disaccharide which normally reaches the colon intact; here, breakdown by colonic bacteria results in hydrogen production. The time at which this occurs, as measured in expired air, is a measure of orocaecal transit.

Colonic and anorectal motility

A plain abdominal radiograph taken on day 5 after ingestion of different-shaped inert plastic pellets on days 1–3 gives an estimate of whole gut transit time. The test is useful in the evaluation of chronic constipation when the position of any retained pellets can be observed, and helps to differentiate cases of slow transit from those due to obstructed defaecation. The mechanism of defaecation and anorectal function can be assessed by anorectal manometry, electrophysiological tests and defaecating proctography.

RADIOISOTOPE TESTS

Many different radioisotope tests are used (see Box 17.10). In some, structural information is obtained, e.g. localisation of a Meckel's diverticulum or distribution of activity in inflammatory bowel disease. Others use radioisotopes for functional information, e.g. rates of gastric emptying or ability to reabsorb bile acids. Yet others are tests of infection and rely on the presence of bacteria to hydrolyse a radio-labelled test substance followed by detection of the radioisotope in expired air (e.g. urea breath test for *H. pylori*).

17.10 COMMONLY USED RADIOISOTOPE TESTS IN GASTROENTEROLOGY		
Test	**Isotope**	**Major uses and principle of test**
Gastric emptying study	^{99m}Tc-sulphur ^{111}In-DTPA	Used in assessment of gastric emptying, particularly for possible gastroparesis
Urea breath test	^{14}C- or ^{13}C-urea	Used in non-invasive diagnosis of *Helicobacter pylori*. Bacterial urease enzyme splits urea to ammonia and CO_2 which is detected in expired air
Meckel's scan	^{99m}Tc-pertechnate	Diagnosis of Meckel's diverticulum in cases of obscure GI bleeding. Isotope is injected i.v. and localises in ectopic parietal mucosa within diverticulum
Labelled red cell scan	^{51}Cr-labelled erythrocytes	Diagnosis of obscure and recurrent GI bleeding. Labelled erythrocytes seen extravasating into intestine from bleeding vessel
Labelled leucocyte scan	^{111}In- or ^{99m}Tc-HMPAO-labelled leucocytes	Localisation of abscess collections and distribution of activity in inflammatory bowel disease. Patient's white cells are labelled in vitro, are reinfused and migrate to site of inflammation or infection

MAJOR MANIFESTATIONS OF GASTROINTESTINAL DISEASE

DYSPHAGIA

Dysphagia is defined as difficulty in swallowing. It may coexist with heartburn or vomiting but should be distinguished from both globus sensation (in which anxious people feel a lump in the throat without organic cause)

and odynophagia (which refers to pain with swallowing, usually resulting from oesophagitis due to gastro-oesophageal reflux or candidiasis).

Dysphagia can be classified into oropharyngeal and oesophageal causes (see Fig. 17.14). Oropharyngeal disorders result from neuromuscular dysfunction affecting the initiation of swallowing by the pharynx and upper

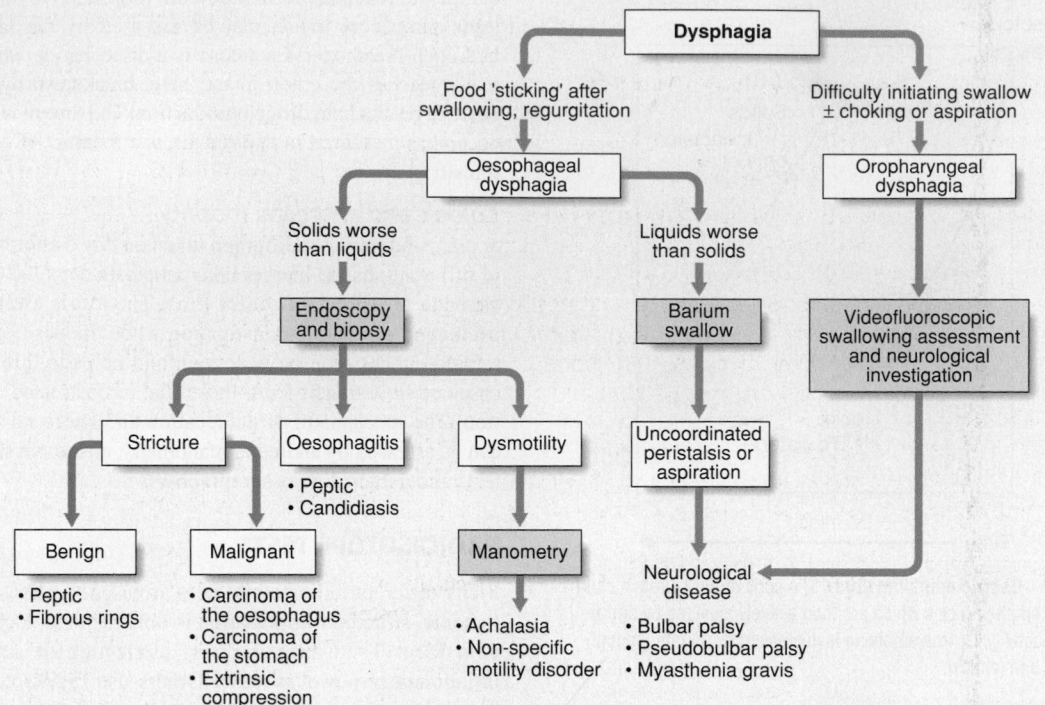

Fig. 17.14 Investigation of dysphagia.

oesophageal sphincter (e.g. bulbar or pseudobulbar palsy and myasthenia gravis). Patients with oropharyngeal dysphagia have difficulty initiating swallowing and develop choking, nasal regurgitation or tracheal aspiration. On examination, drooling, dysarthria, hoarseness and cranial nerve or other neurological signs may be present. Oesophageal causes include structural disease (benign or malignant strictures) and dysmotility of the oesophagus. Patients with oesophageal disease complain of food 'sticking' after swallowing, although the level at which this is felt correlates poorly with the true site of obstruction. Swallowing of liquids is normal until strictures become extreme.

Investigations

Dysphagia usually implies significant disease and should always be promptly investigated. Endoscopy is the investigation of choice because it facilitates detection, biopsy and dilatation of suspicious strictures. If no abnormality is found, then barium swallow, possibly with videofluoroscopic swallowing assessment, will detect most motility disorders. In a few cases oesophageal manometry is required. The algorithm (see Fig. 17.14) summarises an approach to patients with dysphagia and lists the major causes.

DYSPEPSIA

Dyspepsia ('indigestion') is a collective term for any symptoms thought to originate from the upper gastrointestinal tract. It encompasses many different symptoms and

17.11 CAUSES OF DYSPEPSIA
Upper gastrointestinal disorders
• Peptic ulcer disease
• Acute gastritis
• Gallstones
• Motility disorders, e.g. oesophageal spasm
• 'Functional' (non-ulcer dyspepsia and irritable bowel syndrome)
Other gastrointestinal disorders
• Pancreatic disease (cancer, chronic pancreatitis)
• Hepatic disease (hepatitis, metastases)
• Colonic carcinoma
Systemic disease
• Renal failure
• Hypercalcaemia
Drugs
• Non-steroidal anti-inflammatory drugs (NSAIDs)
• Iron and potassium supplements
• Corticosteroids
• Digoxin
Others
• Alcohol
• Psychological, e.g. anxiety, depression

disorders (see Box 17.11), including some arising outside the digestive system. Heartburn and other 'reflux' symptoms are separate entities and are considered elsewhere.

Although symptoms often correlate poorly with the underlying diagnosis, a careful history is important to:

- elicit symptoms classical of specific disorders, e.g. peptic ulcer
- detect 'alarm' features requiring urgent investigation (see Box 17.12)
- detect atypical symptoms more suggestive of other disorders, e.g. myocardial ischaemia.

Dyspepsia is extremely prevalent, affecting up to 80% of the population at some time, and very often no abnormality is discovered during investigation, especially in younger patients. Patients with 'alarm' symptoms, those over 55 years old with new dyspepsia and younger patients unresponsive to empirical treatment require prompt investigation to exclude serious gastrointestinal disease.

Examination may reveal important findings such as evidence of anaemia, weight loss, lymphadenopathy, abdominal masses or signs of liver disease. An algorithm for the investigation of dyspepsia is outlined in Figure 17.15.

17.12 'ALARM' FEATURES IN DYSPEPSIA
• Weight loss
• Anaemia
• Vomiting
• Haematemesis and/or melaena
• Dysphagia
• Palpable abdominal mass

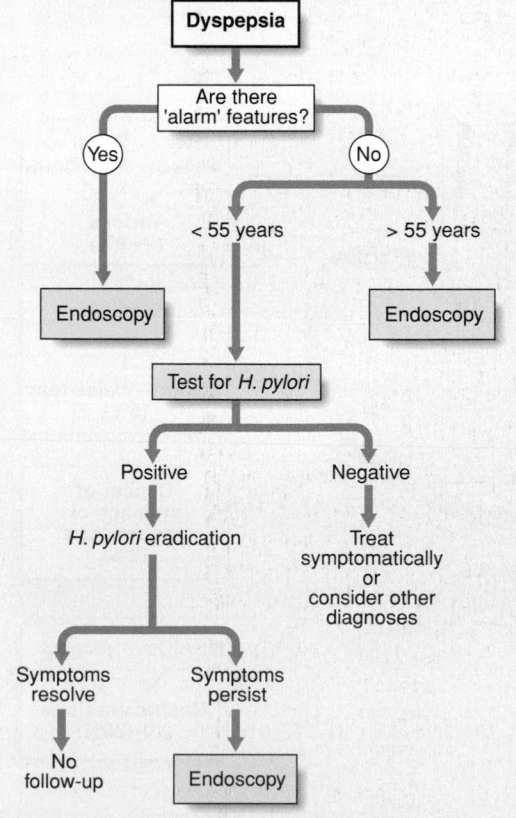

Fig. 17.15   Investigation of dyspepsia.

VOMITING

Vomiting is a highly integrated and complex reflex involving both autonomic and somatic neural pathways. Synchronous contraction of the diaphragm, intercostal muscles and abdominal muscles raises intra-abdominal pressure and, combined with relaxation of the lower oesophageal sphincter, results in forcible ejection of gastric contents.

Vomiting is usually associated with nausea, retching, salivation, anorexia or dyspepsia. It is important to distinguish true vomiting from regurgitation and to elicit whether the vomiting is acute or chronic (recurrent), as the underlying causes may differ. Associated symptoms of abdominal pain, fever, diarrhoea, relationship to food, drug ingestion, headache, vertigo and weight loss should be sought.

Examination may reveal signs of dehydration, fever and infection. Evidence of abdominal masses, peritonitis or intestinal obstruction must be sought, as should neurological signs including papilloedema, nystagmus, photophobia and neck stiffness. Other findings may suggest alcoholism, pregnancy or bulimia as the underlying diagnosis. The diagnostic approach will be dictated by the history and examination. The major causes of vomiting are listed in Box 17.13.

17.13 CAUSES OF VOMITING	
Infections	
• Gastroenteritis	• Urinary tract infection
• Hepatitis	
Drugs	
• NSAIDs	• Digoxin
• Antibiotics	• Cytotoxic drugs
• Opiates	
Gastroduodenal disease	
• Chronic peptic ulcer disease (± gastric outlet obstruction)	• Gastroparesis, e.g. diabetes, scleroderma, drugs
• Gastric cancer	
Acute abdominal disorders	
• Appendicitis	• Pancreatitis
• Cholecystitis	• Intestinal obstruction
CNS disorders	
• Vestibular neuronitis	• Raised intracranial pressure
• Migraine	
• Meningitis	
Metabolic	
• Diabetic ketoacidosis	• Addison's disease
• Uraemia	
Others	
• Any severe pain, e.g. myocardial infarction	• Alcoholism (see p. 259)
• Psychogenic (see p. 789)	

GASTROINTESTINAL BLEEDING

ACUTE UPPER GASTROINTESTINAL HAEMORRHAGE

This is the most common gastrointestinal emergency, accounting for 50–120 admissions to hospital per 100 000 of the population each year in the United Kingdom. Common causes are shown in Figure 17.16.

Clinical features

Haematemesis may be red with clots when bleeding is profuse, or black ('coffee grounds') when less severe. Syncope may occur and is due to hypotension from intravascular volume depletion. Symptoms of anaemia suggest chronic bleeding.

Melaena is the term used to describe the passage of black, tarry stools containing altered blood; this is usually due to bleeding from the upper gastrointestinal tract, although haemorrhage from the right side of the colon is occasionally responsible. The characteristic appearance is the result of the action of digestive enzymes and of bacteria upon haemoglobin. Severe acute upper gastrointestinal bleeding can sometimes cause maroon or bright red stool.

Management

1. *Intravenous access.* The first step is to gain intravenous access using at least one large-bore cannula.

2. *Initial clinical assessment.*
- Define circulatory status. Severe bleeding causes tachycardia with hypotension and oliguria. The patient is cold, sweating and may be agitated.
- Seek evidence of liver disease. Jaundice, cutaneous stigmata, hepatosplenomegaly and ascites may be present in decompensated cirrhosis.
- Define comorbidity. The presence of cardiorespiratory, cerebrovascular or renal disease is important, both because these may be worsened by acute bleeding and because these diseases increase the hazards of endoscopy and surgical operations.

3. *Blood tests.* These include:
- A full blood count. Chronic or subacute bleeding leads to anaemia, but the haemoglobin concentration may be normal after sudden, major bleeding until haemodilution occurs.
- Urea and electrolytes. This may show evidence of renal failure. The blood urea rises as the absorbed products of luminal blood are metabolised by the liver.
- Liver function tests.
- Prothrombin time, if there is clinical suggestion of liver disease or in anticoagulated patients.
- Cross-matching of at least 2 units of blood.

4. *Resuscitation* (see p. 201). Intravenous crystalloid fluids or colloid are given to restore the blood pressure. Blood is transfused when the patient is shocked or when the haemoglobin concentration is less than 100 g per litre.

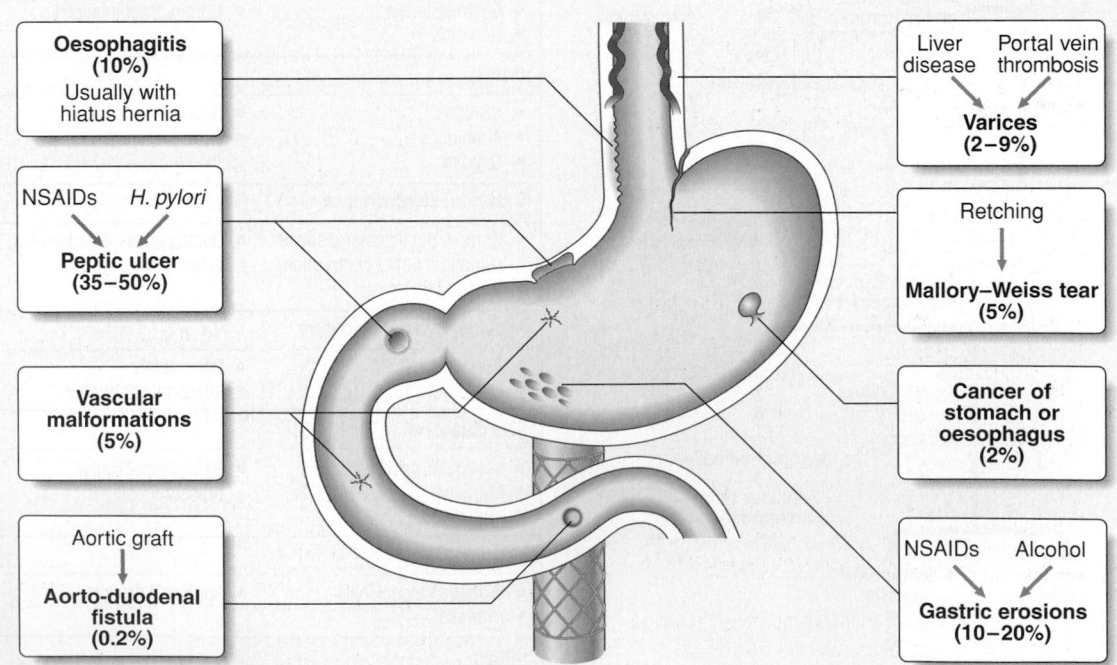

Fig. 17.16   **Causes of acute upper gastrointestinal haemorrhage.** (Frequency in parentheses.)

Normal saline should be avoided in patients with liver disease because it can cause ascites.

Central venous pressure (CVP) monitoring is used in severe bleeding, particularly in patients who have cardiac disease, to assist in defining the volume of fluid replacement and in identification of rebleeding.

5. *Oxygen*. This should be given by facemask to all patients in shock.

6. *Endoscopy*. This should be carried out after adequate resuscitation. A diagnosis will be achieved in 80% of cases. Patients who are found to have major endoscopic stigmata of recent haemorrhage (see Fig. 17.17) are treated endoscopically using a thermal modality such as a 'heater probe', by injection of dilute adrenaline (epinephrine) into the bleeding point, or by application of metallic clips. Endoscopic therapy may stop active bleeding and prevent rebleeding, avoiding the need for surgery in these patients. Endoscopic therapy is also used for varices (see p. 852), vascular malformations and occasionally for Mallory–Weiss tears.

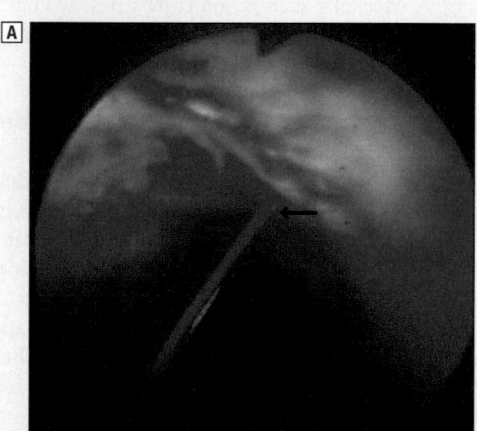

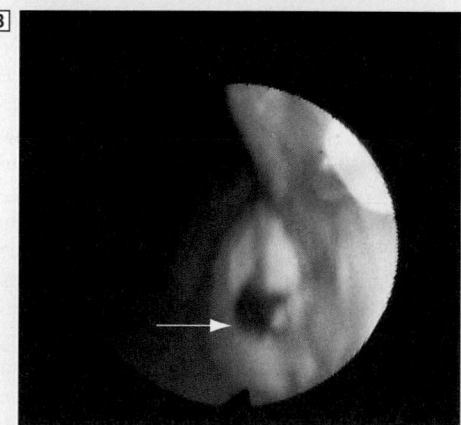

Fig. 17.17   Major stigmata of recent haemorrhage. [A] Active spurting haemorrhage (arrow) from a duodenal ulcer. When associated with shock, 80% of cases will continue to bleed or rebleed. [B] 'Visible vessel' (arrow). In reality, this is a pseudoaneurysm of the feeding artery seen here in a pre-pyloric peptic ulcer. It carries a 50% chance of rebleeding.

Radio-labelled red cell scanning or visceral angiography is done when endoscopy is normal and the patient is actively bleeding by at least 1 ml per minute. For bleeding of lesser severity, colonoscopy is the best option; vascular malformations are the most common cause. In young patients, a ^{99}Tc-pertechnate scan may show bleeding from a Meckel's diverticulum.

7. *Monitoring*. Patients are closely observed with hourly pulse, blood pressure and urine output measurements.

8. *Surgical operation*. An urgent surgical operation is undertaken when:

- endoscopic haemostasis fails to stop active bleeding
- rebleeding occurs on one occasion in an elderly or frail patient, or twice in younger, fitter patients.

The choice of operation depends on the site and diagnosis of the bleeding lesion. Duodenal ulcers are treated by under-running with or without pyloroplasty. Although under-running can also be carried out for gastric ulcers, excision, if possible, is more appropriate. Biopsies should always be taken to exclude carcinoma and, if there is any doubt or if simple excision is not possible, partial gastrectomy is indicated. Following successful surgery for ulcer bleeding, all patients should be treated with *H. pylori* eradication therapy if positive and should avoid non-steroidal anti-inflammatory drugs (NSAIDs) in the future. Duodenal ulcer patients need confirmation of successful eradication by urea breath testing.

Prognosis

The mortality of patients admitted to hospital following a diagnosis of acute upper gastrointestinal bleeding is

17.14 RISK FACTORS FOR DEATH IN PATIENTS WHO PRESENT WITH ACUTE UPPER GASTROINTESTINAL HAEMORRHAGE	
Factor	**Comments**
Increasing age	Risk increases over age 60 and especially in very elderly
Comorbidity	Advanced malignancy; renal and hepatic failure are associated with particularly high mortality
Shock	Defined as pulse > 100/min, BP < 100 mmHg
Diagnosis	Varices and cancer have the worst prognosis
Endoscopic findings	Active bleeding and a non-bleeding visible vessel at endoscopy are associated with a high risk of continuing bleeding
Rebleeding*	Associated with 10-fold rise in mortality

* Defined as fresh haematemesis or melaena associated with shock or a fall of Hb > 20 g/l over 24 hours.

approximately 10%. Risk factors for death are shown in Box 17.14. Improved mortality can be achieved by specialised units in which joint management by physicians and surgeons and adherence to agreed protocols for transfusion and surgery are applied.

LOWER GASTROINTESTINAL BLEEDING

This may be due to haemorrhage from the small bowel, colon or anal canal. It is useful to distinguish those patients who present with profuse, acute bleeding from those who present with chronic or subacute bleeding of lesser severity (see Box 17.15).

Severe acute lower gastrointestinal bleeding

This is an unusual medical emergency. Patients present with profuse red or maroon diarrhoea and with shock.

Diverticular disease is the most common cause. Acute bleeding is due to erosion of an artery within the mouth of a diverticulum and bleeding almost always stops spontaneously.

Angiodysplasia is a disease of the elderly in which vascular malformations develop in the proximal colon. It is most commonly seen in patients receiving anticoagulants following aortic valve replacement. Bleeding can be acute and profuse; it usually stops spontaneously but commonly recurs. Diagnosis is often difficult. Colonoscopy reveals characteristic vascular spots which are reminiscent of spider naevi. In acute bleeding, visceral angiography shows bleeding into the intestinal lumen and an abnormal large, draining vein. In some patients diagnosis is only achieved by laparotomy with on-table colonoscopy. The treatment of choice is endoscopic thermal ablation but right hemicolectomy is sometimes necessary in severe cases.

17.15 CAUSES OF LOWER GASTROINTESTINAL BLEEDING	
Severe acute	
• Diverticular disease	• Ischaemia
• Angiodysplasia	• Meckel's diverticulum
Moderate, chronic/subacute	
• Anal disease, e.g. fissure, haemorrhoids	• Large polyps
	• Angiodysplasia
• Inflammatory bowel disease	• Radiation enteritis
• Carcinoma	• Solitary rectal ulcer

Ischaemia is due to occlusion of the inferior mesenteric artery and presents with abdominal colic and rectal bleeding. It should be considered in patients (particularly the elderly) who have evidence of generalised atherosclerosis.

Meckel's diverticulum with ectopic gastric epithelium may ulcerate and erode into a major artery. The diagnosis should be considered in children or adolescents who present with profuse or recurrent lower gastrointestinal bleeding. A Meckel's scan is sometimes positive but the diagnosis is commonly made only by laparotomy, at which time the diverticulum is excised.

Subacute or chronic lower gastrointestinal bleeding

This is extremely common at all ages and is usually due to haemorrhoids or anal fissure. Haemorrhoidal bleeding is bright red and occurs during or after defaecation. Proctoscopy is used to make the diagnosis but in subjects who also have altered bowel habit and in all patients presenting over 40 years of age, colonoscopy or barium enema is necessary to exclude coexisting colorectal cancer. Anal fissure should be suspected when fresh rectal bleeding and anal pain occur during defaecation.

OCCULT GASTROINTESTINAL BLEEDING

'Occult' means that blood or its breakdown products are present in the stool but cannot be seen. Occult bleeding may reach 200 ml per day, cause iron deficiency anaemia and signify serious gastrointestinal disease. Any cause of gastrointestinal bleeding may be responsible but the most important is colorectal cancer, particularly carcinoma of the caecum which may have no gastrointestinal symptoms.

In clinical practice, investigation of the gastrointestinal tract should be considered whenever a patient presents with unexplained iron deficiency anaemia. Testing the stool for the presence of blood is unnecessary and should not influence whether or not the gastrointestinal tract is imaged because bleeding from tumours is often intermittent and a negative faecal occult blood (FOB) test does not exclude important gastrointestinal disease. Many colorectal cancer patients are FOB-negative at presentation, and the only value of FOB-testing relates to screening for colonic disease in asymptomatic populations (see p. 825).

DIARRHOEA

The bowel frequency of the normal population ranges from three bowel movements per day to one bowel action every third day, and a normal stool consistency ranges from porridge-like to hard and pellety. The term 'diarrhoea' means different things to different people. Many patients and doctors think of diarrhoea in terms of increased stool frequency, and loose or watery stools. Gastroenterologists define diarrhoea as the passage of more than 200 g of stool daily, and the measurement of stool volume is sometimes helpful in patient evaluation. The most severe symptom in many patients is urgency of defaecation, and faecal incontinence is a common event in acute and chronic diarrhoeal illnesses.

ACUTE DIARRHOEA

This is extremely common and usually due to faecal-oral transmission of bacterial toxins, viruses, bacteria or protozoan organisms (see Ch. 1). Infective diarrhoea is usually short-lived and patients who present with a history of diarrhoea lasting more than 10 days rarely have an infective cause. A variety of drugs, including antibiotics, cytotoxic drugs, proton pump inhibitors and NSAIDs, may be responsible for acute diarrhoea.

CHRONIC OR RELAPSING DIARRHOEA

The most common cause is irritable bowel syndrome (see p. 817), which can present with increased frequency of defaecation and loose, watery or pellety stools. Diarrhoea rarely occurs at night and is most severe before and after breakfast. At other times the patient is constipated and there are other characteristic symptoms of irritable bowel syndrome. The stool often contains mucus but never blood, and 24-hour stool volume is less than 200 g.

Chronic diarrhoea can be categorised as disease of the colon or small bowel, or malabsorption (see Box 17.16). Clinical presentation, examination of the stool, routine blood tests and imaging reveal a diagnosis in many cases. A series of negative investigations usually implies irritable bowel syndrome but some patients clearly have organic disease and need more extensive investigations.

MALABSORPTION

Digestion and absorption of nutrients is a complex, highly coordinated and extremely efficient process; normally, less than 5% of ingested carbohydrate, fat and protein is excreted in the faeces. Diarrhoea and weight loss in patients with a normal diet should always lead to the suspicion of malabsorption.

The symptoms of malabsorption are diverse in nature and variable in severity. A few patients have apparently normal bowel habit but diarrhoea is usual and may be watery and voluminous. Bulky, pale and offensive stools which float in the toilet (steatorrhoea) signify fat malabsorption. Abdominal distension, borborygmi, cramps, weight loss and undigested food in the stool may be present. Some patients complain only of malaise and lethargy. In others, symptoms related to deficiencies of specific vitamins, trace elements and minerals (e.g. calcium, iron, folic acid) may occur (see Fig. 17.18).

Aetiology and pathogenesis

Malabsorption results from abnormalities of the three processes which are essential to normal digestion:

1. *Intraluminal maldigestion* occurs when deficiency of bile or pancreatic enzymes results in inadequate solubil-

17.16 CHRONIC OR RELAPSING DIARRHOEA			
	Colonic	**Malabsorption**	**Small bowel**
Clinical features	Blood and mucus in stool Cramping lower abdominal pain	Steatorrhoea Undigested food in the stool Weight loss and nutritional disturbances	Large-volume, watery stool Abdominal bloating Cramping mid-abdominal pain

Some causes	Inflammatory bowel disease
	Neoplasia
		Pancreatic
		  Chronic pancreatitis
		  Cancer of pancreas
		  Cystic fibrosis
		Enteropathy
		  Coeliac disease
		  Tropical sprue
		  Lymphoma
		  Lymphangiectasia
			VIPoma
			Drug-induced
			  NSAIDs
			  Aminosalicylates
			  Selective serotonin re-uptake
			  inhibitors (SSRIs)

Investigations	Flexible sigmoidoscopy with biopsies and barium enema, or colonoscopy with biopsies	Ultrasound, CT and ERCP Small bowel biopsy Barium follow-through	Stool volume Gut hormone profile Barium follow-through

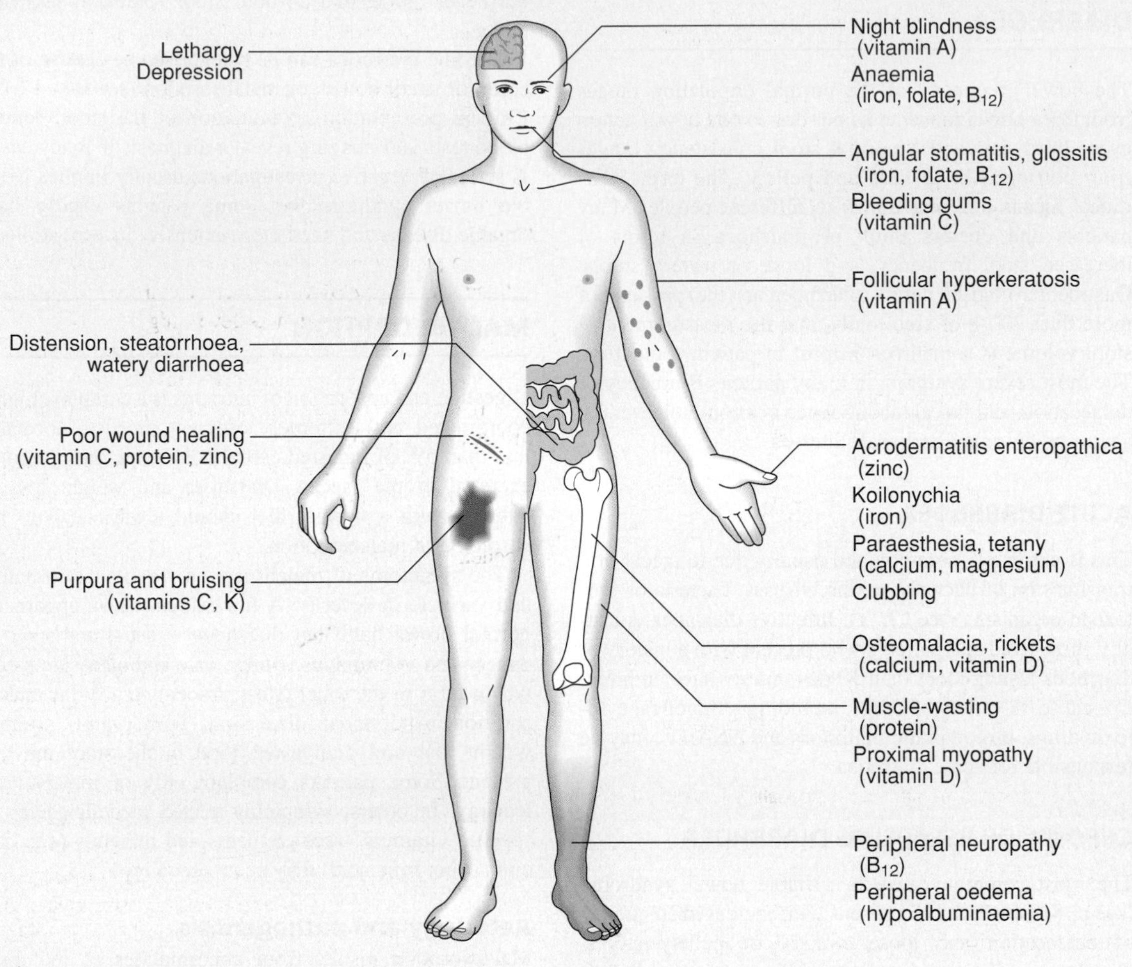

Lethargy
Depression

Night blindness
(vitamin A)
Anaemia
(iron, folate, B_{12})

Angular stomatitis, glossitis
(iron, folate, B_{12})
Bleeding gums
(vitamin C)

Follicular hyperkeratosis
(vitamin A)

Distension, steatorrhoea,
watery diarrhoea

Poor wound healing
(vitamin C, protein, zinc)

Acrodermatitis enteropathica
(zinc)
Koilonychia
(iron)
Paraesthesia, tetany
(calcium, magnesium)
Clubbing

Purpura and bruising
(vitamins C, K)

Osteomalacia, rickets
(calcium, vitamin D)

Muscle-wasting
(protein)
Proximal myopathy
(vitamin D)

Peripheral neuropathy
(B_{12})
Peripheral oedema
(hypoalbuminaemia)

Fig. 17.18 Possible physical consequences of malabsorption.

isation and hydrolysis of nutrients. Fat and protein malabsorption results. This may also occur in the presence of small bowel bacterial overgrowth.

2. *Mucosal malabsorption* results from small bowel resection or conditions which damage the small intestinal epithelium, thereby diminishing the surface area for absorption and depleting brush border enzyme activity.

3. *'Postmucosal' lymphatic obstruction* prevents the uptake and transport of absorbed lipids into lymphatic vessels. Increased pressure in these vessels results in leakage into the intestinal lumen, leading to protein-losing enteropathy.

Diagnosis and investigations

Investigations are performed to confirm that malabsorption is present and then to determine the cause. Routine blood tests may show one or more of the abnormalities listed in

17.17 ROUTINE BLOOD TESTS IN MALABSORPTION
Haematology
• Microcytic anaemia (iron deficiency)
• Macrocytic anaemia (folate or B_{12} deficiency)
• Increased prothrombin time (vitamin K deficiency)
Biochemistry
• Hypoalbuminaemia
• Hypocalcaemia and vitamin D deficiency
• Hypomagnesaemia
• Deficiencies of phosphate, zinc

Box 17.17. Tests to confirm fat and protein malabsorption are performed as described on page 760.

An approach to the investigation of malabsorption is shown in Figure 17.19.

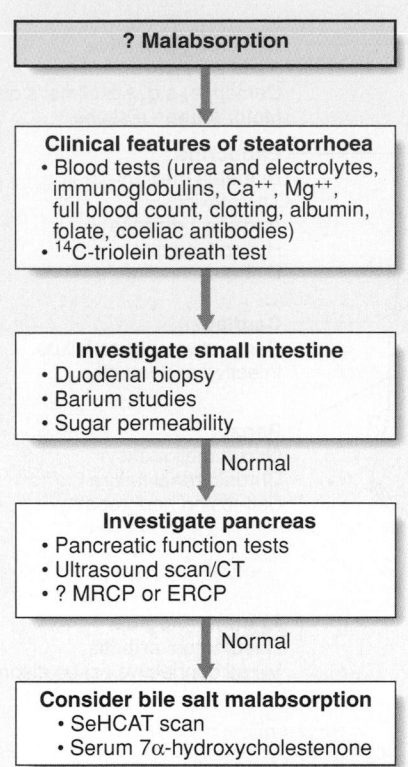

Fig. 17.19   Investigation for suspected malabsorption.

WEIGHT LOSS

Weight loss may be 'physiological' due to dieting, exercise, starvation, or the decreased nutritional intake which accompanies old age. Alternatively, weight loss may signify disease; that greater than 3 kg over 6 months is significant. Hospital and general practice weight records may be valuable, as may reweighing patients at intervals, as sometimes weight is regained or stabilises in those with no obvious cause.

In general pathological weight loss is due to psychiatric illness, systemic disease, gastrointestinal causes or advanced disease of any specific organ system (see Fig. 17.20).

History and examination

Weight loss occurring as an isolated symptom is seldom associated with serious organic disease; almost always a careful history, physical examination and simple laboratory tests will define other features which lead to a specific diagnosis.

'Physiological' weight loss

This may be obvious in cases of young individuals who describe changes in physical activity or social circumstances. It may be more difficult to be sure of this in older patients when a history of nutritional intake may be unreliable; professional help from a dietitian is often valuable.

Psychiatric illness

Features of anorexia nervosa, bulimia (see p. 267) and affective disorders (see p. 262) may only be apparent with formal psychiatric input. Alcoholic patients lose weight as a consequence of self-neglect and poor dietary intake.

Systemic diseases

Chronic infections including tuberculosis (see p. 532), recurrent urinary or chest infections, and a range of parasitic and protozoan infections (see Ch. 1) should be considered. A history of foreign travel, high-risk activities and specific features such as fever, night sweats, rigors, productive cough and dysuria is essential. Sensitive, appropriate questions regarding lifestyle (promiscuous sexual activity and drug misuse) may suggest HIV-related illness (see p. 108).

Weight loss is a late feature of disseminated malignancy (carcinoma, lymphoma or other haematological disorders). Specific symptoms, physical signs, relevant imaging, or biochemical or haematological abnormalities are almost invariable.

Gastrointestinal disease

Almost any disease of the gastrointestinal tract can cause weight loss. Dysphagia and gastric outflow obstruction (see p. 787) cause defective dietary intake. Malignancy at any site may cause weight loss by mechanical obstruction, anorexia or cytokine-mediated systemic effects. Malabsorption from pancreatic diseases (see p. 802) or small bowel causes may lead to profound weight loss with specific nutritional deficiencies (see Ch. 1). Inflammatory diseases such as Crohn's disease or ulcerative colitis (see p. 808) cause anorexia, fear of eating and loss of protein, blood and nutrients from the gut.

Specific diseases of any major organ system

These may be difficult to diagnose without a high index of suspicion. They may cause weight loss by a range of mechanisms, including altered metabolism in diabetes mellitus, Addison's disease and thyrotoxicosis (see Chs 10 and 15).

Weight loss occurs as a consequence of increased metabolic demands in patients with end-stage respiratory and cardiac diseases. Multiple mechanisms are responsible in many cases: for example, poor dietary intake, increased metabolic demands in Parkinson's disease (see p. 1174) and other neurodegenerative disorders. Patients with active or advanced rheumatological and collagen-vascular disorders (see p. 1005) lose weight from a combination of anorexia, physical disability, altered metabolic demands and the systemic effects of their conditions.

In many diseases anorexia and weight loss may be compounded by the effects of drug therapies (e.g. digoxin) which may cause nausea, dyspepsia, constipation or depression.

Some easily overlooked causes of weight loss are listed in Box 17.18.

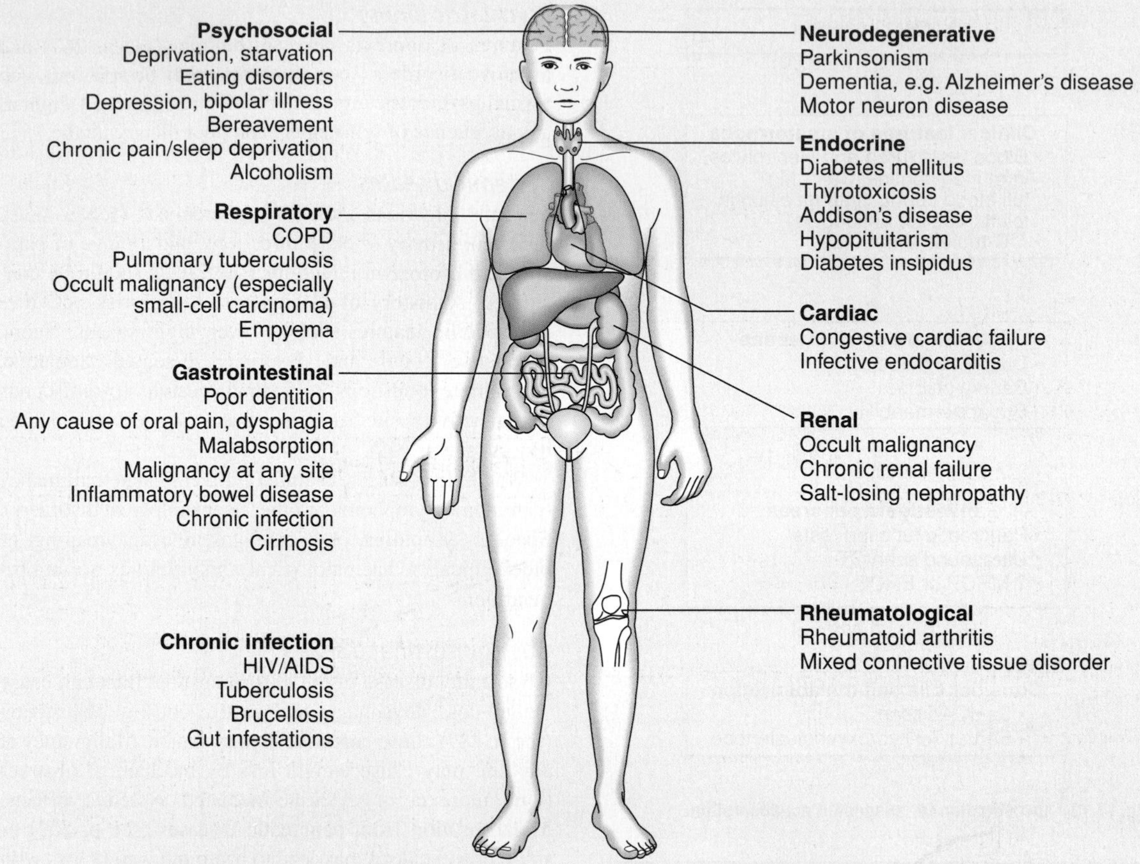

Psychosocial
Deprivation, starvation
Eating disorders
Depression, bipolar illness
Bereavement
Chronic pain/sleep deprivation
Alcoholism

Respiratory
COPD
Pulmonary tuberculosis
Occult malignancy (especially
small-cell carcinoma)
Empyema

Gastrointestinal
Poor dentition
Any cause of oral pain, dysphagia
Malabsorption
Malignancy at any site
Inflammatory bowel disease
Chronic infection
Cirrhosis

Chronic infection
HIV/AIDS
Tuberculosis
Brucellosis
Gut infestations

Neurodegenerative
Parkinsonism
Dementia, e.g. Alzheimer's disease
Motor neuron disease

Endocrine
Diabetes mellitus
Thyrotoxicosis
Addison's disease
Hypopituitarism
Diabetes insipidus

Cardiac
Congestive cardiac failure
Infective endocarditis

Renal
Occult malignancy
Chronic renal failure
Salt-losing nephropathy

Rheumatological
Rheumatoid arthritis
Mixed connective tissue disorder

Fig. 17.20   Some important causes of weight loss.

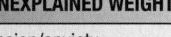

17.18 SOME EASILY OVERLOOKED CAUSES OF UNEXPLAINED WEIGHT LOSS
• Depression/anxiety • Chronic pain or sleep deprivation • Psychosocial deprivation/malnutrition in the elderly • Existing conditions, e.g. severe chronic obstructive pulmonary disease (COPD), cardiac failure • Diabetes mellitus/hyperthyroidism • Occult malignancy (e.g. proximal colon, renal, lymphoma) • Anorexia nervosa in atypical groups, e.g. young men • Rare endocrine disorders, e.g. Addison's disease, panhypopituitarism

Investigations

In cases where the cause of weight loss is not obvious after thorough history-taking and physical examination, or where it is considered that an existing condition is unlikely, the following investigations are indicated: urinalysis for sugar, protein and blood; blood tests including liver function tests, random blood glucose, and thyroid function tests; ESR (may be raised in unsuspected infections (e.g. tuberculosis), connective tissue disorders and malignancy). Sometimes invasive tests such as bone marrow aspiration or liver biopsy may be necessary to identify conditions like cryptic miliary tuberculosis (see p. 534).

Rarely, abdominal and pelvic imaging by CT may be necessary, but before embarking on invasive or very costly investigations it is always worth revisiting the patient's history and reweighing patients at intervals.

CONSTIPATION

Constipation is defined as infrequent passage of hard stools. Patients may also complain of straining, a sensation of incomplete evacuation and either perianal or abdominal discomfort. Constipation may be the end result of many gastrointestinal and other medical disorders (see Box 17.19).

The onset, duration and characteristics are important, e.g. a neonatal onset suggests Hirschsprung's disease, while a recent change in bowel activity in middle age should raise the suspicion of organic disorders such as colonic carcinoma. The presence of symptoms such as rectal bleeding, pain and weight loss is important, as are excessive straining, symptoms suggestive of irritable bowel syndrome, a history of childhood constipation and emotional distress.

Careful examination contributes more to the diagnosis than extensive investigation. A search should be made for

17.19 CAUSES OF CONSTIPATION	
Gastrointestinal disorders	
Dietary	
• Lack of fibre and/or fluid intake	
Motility	
• Slow-transit constipation (see p. 826)	• Drugs (see below)
• Irritable bowel syndrome	• Chronic intestinal pseudo-obstruction
Structural	
• Colonic carcinoma	• Hirschsprung's disease
• Diverticular disease	
Defaecation	
• Obstructed defaecation (see p. 826)	• Anorectal disease (Crohn's, fissures, haemorrhoids)
Non-gastrointestinal disorders	
Drugs	
• Opiates	• Iron supplements
• Anticholinergics	• Aluminium-containing antacids
• Calcium antagonists	
Neurological	
• Multiple sclerosis	• Cerebrovascular accidents
• Spinal cord lesions	• Parkinsonism
Metabolic/endocrine	
• Diabetes mellitus	• Hypothyroidism
• Hypercalcaemia	• Pregnancy
Others	
• Any serious illness with immobility, especially in the elderly	• Depression

general medical disorders as well as signs of intestinal obstruction. Neurological disorders, especially spinal cord lesions, should be sought. Perineal inspection and rectal examination are essential and may reveal abnormalities of the pelvic floor (e.g. abnormal descent, impaired sensation), anal canal or rectum (masses, faecal impaction, prolapse).

It is neither possible nor appropriate to investigate every person with this very common complaint. Most will respond to dietary fibre supplementation and the judicious use of laxatives. Middle-aged or elderly patients with a short history or worrying symptoms (rectal bleeding, pain or weight loss) must be investigated promptly, by either barium enema or colonoscopy. For those with simple constipation, investigation will usually proceed along the following lines.

Initial visit

Digital rectal examination, proctoscopy and sigmoidoscopy (to detect anorectal disease), routine biochemistry, including serum calcium and thyroid function tests, and a full blood count should be carried out. If these are normal, a 1-month trial of dietary fibre and/or laxatives is justified.

Next visit

If symptoms persist, then examination of the colon by barium enema or colonoscopy is indicated to look for structural disease.

Further investigation

If no cause is found and disabling symptoms are present, then specialist referral for investigation of possible dysmotility may be necessary. The problem may be one of infrequent desire to defaecate ('slow transit') or else may result from excessive straining ('obstructed defaecation', see p. 826). Intestinal marker studies, anorectal manometry, electrophysiological studies and defaecating proctography can all be used to define the problem.

ABDOMINAL PAIN

There are several types of abdominal pain:

- *Visceral*. Gut organs are insensitive to stimuli such as burning and cutting but are sensitive to distension, contraction, torsion and stretching. Pain from unpaired structures is usually but not always felt in the midline.
- *Parietal*. Parietal peritoneum is innervated by somatic nerves, and its involvement by disease processes, e.g. inflammation, infection or neoplasia, tends to produce sharp, well-localised and lateralised pain.
- *Referred pain*. (For example, gallbladder pain is referred to the back or shoulder tip.)
- *Psychogenic*. Cultural, emotional and psychosocial factors influence everyone's experience of pain. In some patients, no organic cause can be found despite investigation, and psychogenic causes may be responsible, e.g. depression or somatisation disorder (see pp. 262 and 265).

THE ACUTE ABDOMEN

This accounts for approximately 50% of all urgent admissions to general surgical units. The acute abdomen is a consequence of one or more pathological processes (see Box 17.20):

- *Inflammation*. Pain develops gradually, usually over several hours. It is initially rather diffuse until the parietal peritoneum is involved, when it becomes localised. Movement exacerbates the pain, and abdominal rigidity and guarding occur.
- *Perforation*. When a viscus perforates, pain starts abruptly; it is severe and leads to generalised peritonitis.
- *Obstruction*. Pain is colicky, with spasms which cause the patient to writhe around and double up. Colicky pain which does not disappear between spasms suggests complicating inflammation.

17.20 CAUSES OF ACUTE ABDOMINAL PAIN ('SURGICAL')

Inflammation

- Appendicitis
- Diverticulitis
- Cholecystitis
- Pelvic inflammatory disease
- Pancreatitis
- Pyelonephritis
- Intra-abdominal abscess

Perforation/rupture

- Peptic ulcer
- Diverticular disease
- Ovarian cyst
- Aortic aneurysm

Obstruction

- Intestinal obstruction
- Biliary colic
- Ureteric colic

Other (rare)

- See 'extraintestinal' causes (Box 17.21)

Management

Initial assessment

Following initial assessment, which must include a detailed history and examination, a differential diagnosis is reached. This should broadly follow the question: 'Are there signs of peritonitis?' If the answer is 'yes' (i.e. guarding and rebound tenderness with rigidity), minimal further investigations are required and, following adequate resuscitation, operation is arranged. If the answer is 'no', further investigations are organised in order to reach a diagnosis.

Investigations

In the majority of patients with acute abdominal pain full blood count (leucocytosis?), urea and electrolytes (dehydration?) and a serum amylase level (acute pancreatitis?) are measured. Further information can be obtained from an erect chest radiograph (air under the diaphragm?) and abdominal radiograph (obstruction?). Additional help can be provided by an abdominal ultrasound if acute gallstone disease (cholecystitis or cholangitis), ureteric colic or a soft tissue mass is suspected. Ultrasonography is also useful in the detection of free fluid and any possible intra-abdominal abscess. Contrast studies, by either mouth or anus, are useful in the further evaluation of intestinal obstruction, and essential in the differentiation of pseudo-obstruction from mechanical large bowel obstruction. Other investigations commonly used include CT (pancreatitis, retroperitoneal collections or masses, including an aortic aneurysm) and angiography (mesenteric ischaemia).

In those patients in whom the decision to operate remains in doubt and in whom the diagnosis has not been revealed by the appropriate investigations, diagnostic laparoscopy is advised. However, all patients must be carefully and regularly reassessed (every 2–4 hours) so that any change in condition which might alter both the suspected diagnosis and clinical decision can be observed and acted upon early.

Treatment

In general, and depending on the organ affected, perforations are closed, inflammatory conditions are treated with antibiotics or resection, and obstructions are relieved. The speed of intervention and the necessity for surgery depend on a number of factors, of which the presence or absence of peritonitis is the most important. A treatment summary of some of the more common surgical conditions follows.

Acute appendicitis

Although non-operative treatment can be successful in some patients, the risk of perforation and subsequent recurrent attacks means that surgery is carried out early.

Acute cholecystitis

The condition can be successfully treated non-operatively but the high risk of recurrent attacks and the low morbidity of surgery have resulted in early laparoscopic cholecystectomy becoming the recommended treatment of choice.

Acute diverticulitis

Non-operative treatment for uncomplicated cases is the usual course, but if perforation with abscess or peritonitis has occurred resection will be required. Depending on peritoneal contamination and the state of the patient, primary anastomosis is preferred to a Hartmann's procedure (oversew of rectal stump and end colostomy which are reversed at a later date).

Small bowel obstruction

If the cause is obvious and surgery inevitable (e.g. for an external hernia) early operation is arranged. If the suspected cause is adhesions from previous surgery non-operative treatment is attempted, reserving surgical intervention for those patients who do not resolve within the first 48 hours or who develop signs of strangulation (colicky pain becomes constant, peritonitis, tachycardia, fever, leucocytosis).

Large bowel obstruction

Pseudo-obstruction is treated non-operatively, with colonoscopic decompression in some patients, and mechanical obstruction managed by surgical resection, usually with primary anastomosis. The differentiation between the two is made by a water-soluble contrast enema which is a mandatory investigation in all patients with large bowel obstruction.

Perforated peptic ulcer

Although surgical closure of the perforation is standard practice, some patients without generalised peritonitis in whom a water-soluble contrast meal has confirmed spontaneous sealing of the perforation can be treated non-operatively. The most important consideration in patients with a suspected perforated peptic ulcer is adequate and aggressive resuscitation. Rushing elderly, shocked and under-resuscitated patients to theatre in the middle of the night is to be condemned. These patients, who usually have significant comorbidity, require careful preoperative assessment and optimal resuscitation before surgery.

For a more detailed discussion of acute abdominal pain the reader is referred to the sister volume of this text, *Principles and Practice of Surgery*.

ISSUES IN OLDER PEOPLE
ACUTE ABDOMINAL PAIN

- The severity and localisation of acute abdominal pain may blunt with age. Presentation may be atypical, even with perforation of a viscus.
- Cancer is a more common cause of acute pain in those over 70 years than in those under 50 years. Older people with vague abdominal symptoms should therefore be carefully assessed and serious pathology excluded.
- Intra-abdominal inflammatory conditions such as diverticulitis may present with non-specific symptoms such as acute confusion or anorexia and relatively little abdominal tenderness. The reasons for this are not clear but it may result from altered sensory perception.
- The outcome of abdominal surgery is determined by the degree of comorbid disease and whether surgery is elective or emergency, rather than by chronological age.

CHRONIC OR RECURRENT ABDOMINAL PAIN

A careful and detailed history is essential, with particular attention to the features of the pain and any associated symptoms (see Boxes 17.21 and 17.22).

Note should be made of the patient's general demeanour, mood and emotional state, signs of weight loss, fever, jaundice or anaemia. If thorough abdominal and rectal examination are normal, a careful search should be made for evidence of disease affecting other structures, particularly the vertebral column, spinal cord, lungs and cardiovascular system.

The initial choice of investigations will obviously depend on the clinical features elicited during the history and examination:

- Epigastric pain, dyspepsia and relationship to food suggest gastroduodenal or biliary disease. Endoscopy and ultrasound are indicated.
- Altered bowel habit, rectal bleeding or features of obstruction suggest colonic disease. Barium enema and sigmoidoscopy, or colonoscopy is indicated.
- Pain provoked by food in a patient with widespread atherosclerosis may indicate mesenteric ischaemia. Mesenteric angiography may be necessary.
- Young patients with a long history of pain relieved by defaecation, bloating and alternating bowel habit are likely to have irritable bowel syndrome (see p. 817). Simple investigations (blood tests and sigmoidoscopy) may be sufficient, but persistent symptoms require exclusion of colonic or small bowel disease by radiology or endoscopy.
- Upper abdominal pain radiating to the back, a history of alcohol misuse, weight loss and diarrhoea suggest

---

17.21 'EXTRAINTESTINAL' CAUSES OF CHRONIC OR RECURRENT ABDOMINAL PAIN

Retroperitoneal
- Aortic aneurysm
- Malignancy
- Lymphadenopathy
- Abscess

Psychogenic
- Depression
- Anxiety
- Hypochondriasis
- Somatisation

Locomotor
- Vertebral compression
- Abdominal muscle strain

Metabolic/endocrine
- Diabetes mellitus
- Addison's disease
- Acute intermittent porphyria
- Hypercalcaemia

Drugs/toxins
- Corticosteroids
- Azathioprine
- Lead
- Alcohol

Haematological
- Sickle-cell disease
- Haemolytic disorders

Neurological
- Spinal cord lesions
- Tabes dorsalis
- Radiculopathy

17.22 IMPORTANT FACTORS IN THE ASSESSMENT OF ABDOMINAL PAIN

- Duration
- Site and radiation
- Severity
- Precipitating and relieving factors (food, drugs, alcohol, posture, movement, defaecation)
- Nature (colicky, constant, sharp or dull, wakes patient at night)
- Pattern (intermittent or continuous)
- Associated features (vomiting, dyspepsia, altered bowel habit)

---

chronic pancreatitis or pancreatic cancer. Ultrasound, CT and pancreatic function tests are required.
- Recurrent attacks of pain in the loins or radiating to the flanks with urinary symptoms should prompt investigation for renal or ureteric stones by ultrasound and intravenous urography.
- A past history of psychiatric disturbance, repeated negative investigations or vague symptoms which do not fit any particular disease or organ pattern may point to a psychological origin for the patient's pain (see p. 254). Careful review of case notes and previous investigations, along with open and honest discussion with the patient, may reduce the need for further cycles of unnecessary and invasive tests. Care must always be taken, however, not to miss rare causes or atypical presentations of common diseases.

CONSTANT PAIN

Patients with chronic pain which is constant or nearly always present will usually have features to suggest the underlying diagnosis, e.g. malignancy (gastric, pancreatic, colonic), hepatic metastases, chronic pancreatitis or intra-abdominal abscess. In other patients the diagnosis is not initially obvious but will become so after appropriate investigation. In a minority no cause will be found despite thorough investigation. Once unusual or rare conditions and atypical presentations of common diseases have been ruled out, the diagnosis of 'chronic functional abdominal pain' is made. In these patients a psychological cause is highly likely (see p. 254) and the most important tasks are to provide symptom control, if not relief, and to minimise the effects of the pain on social, personal and occupational life. Patients are best managed in specialised pain clinics where, in addition to psychological support, appropriate use of drugs including amitriptyline, gabapentin, ketamine and opioids may be necessary.

DISEASES OF THE MOUTH AND SALIVARY GLANDS

APHTHOUS ULCERATION

Aphthous ulcers are superficial and painful; they occur in any part of the mouth. Recurrent ones afflict up to 30% of the population and are particularly common in women prior to menstruation. The aetiology is unknown, but in severe cases other causes of oral ulceration must be considered (see Box 17.23). Occasionally, biopsy is necessary for diagnosis.

17.23 CAUSES OF ORAL ULCERATION	
Aphthous	
• Idiopathic	• Premenstrual
Infection	
• Fungal, e.g. candidiasis • Viral, e.g. herpes simplex	• Bacterial, e.g. Vincent's angina, syphilis
Gastrointestinal diseases	
• Crohn's disease	• Coeliac disease
Dermatological conditions	
• Lichen planus • Pemphigoid	• Pemphigus
Drugs	
• Hypersensitivity, e.g. Stevens–Johnson syndrome (see p. 33)	• Cytotoxics
Systemic diseases	
• Systemic lupus erythematosus (see p. 1034)	• Behçet's syndrome (see p. 1044)
Neoplasia	
• Carcinoma • Leukaemia	• Kaposi's sarcoma

Topical corticosteroids (such as 0.1% triamcinolone in Orabase) or choline salicylate (8.7%) gel can effect healing. Symptomatic relief is achieved using local anaesthetic mouthwashes. A few patients have very severe, recurrent aphthous ulcers and need oral steroids.

VINCENT'S ANGINA

This is characterised by painful, deep, sloughing ulcers which principally affect the gums. It is due to invasion of the mucous membranes by organisms such as *Borrelia vincenti* and other commensals. Invasion occurs when host resistance is low and oral hygiene is poor. Malnutrition, general debility and the acquired immunodeficiency syndrome (AIDS) predispose. The illness is associated with halitosis, and many patients are feverish and systemically unwell. Local treatment with hydrogen peroxide mouthwashes and broad-spectrum antibiotics are required.

CANDIDIASIS

The yeast *Candida albicans* is a normal mouth commensal but it may proliferate to cause thrush. This occurs in babies, debilitated patients, patients receiving corticosteroid or antibiotic therapy, diabetics and immunosuppressed patients, especially those receiving cytotoxic therapy and patients with AIDS. White patches are seen on the tongue and buccal mucosa. Painful swallowing (odynophagia) or dysphagia suggests pharyngeal and oesophageal candidiasis. A clinical diagnosis is sufficient to instigate therapy, although brushings or biopsies can be obtained for mycological examination.

Oral thrush is treated using nystatin or amphotericin suspensions or lozenges. Resistant cases or immunosuppressed patients may require oral fluconazole.

PAROTITIS

Parotitis is due to viral or bacterial infection. Mumps causes a self-limiting acute parotitis (see p. 36). Bacterial parotitis usually occurs as a complication of major surgery. It is a consequence of dehydration and poor oral hygiene and can be avoided by good post-operative care. Patients present with painful parotid swelling and this can be complicated by abscess formation. Broad-spectrum antibiotics are required, whilst surgical drainage is necessary for abscesses. Other causes of salivary gland enlargement are listed in Box 17.24.

17.24 CAUSES OF SALIVARY GLAND SWELLING

• Infection
   Mumps
   Bacterial (post-operative)
• Calculi
• Tumours
   Benign: pleomorphic adenoma (95% of cases)
   Intermediate: mucoepidermoid tumour
   Malignant: carcinoma
• Sjögren's syndrome (see p. 1038)
• Sarcoidosis

- Around 40% of healthy older people complain of dry mouth.
- Gustatory and olfactory sensation declines with age and chewing power is diminished.
- Baseline salivary flow falls with age but stimulated salivation is unchanged.
- Root caries and periodontal disease are common in old age, partly because oral hygiene deteriorates with increasing frailty.
- In the very frail, Gram-negative anaerobic infection in the periodontal pockets can lead to bacteraemia and septicaemia.

DISEASES OF THE OESOPHAGUS

GASTRO-OESOPHAGEAL REFLUX DISEASE

Gastro-oesophageal reflux resulting in heartburn affects approximately 30% of the general population.

Pathophysiology

Occasional episodes of gastro-oesophageal reflux are common in health. Reflux is followed by oesophageal peristaltic waves which efficiently clear the gullet, alkaline saliva neutralises residual acid, and symptoms do not occur. Gastro-oesophageal reflux disease develops when the oesophageal mucosa is exposed to gastric contents for prolonged periods of time, resulting in symptoms and, in a proportion of cases, oesophagitis. Several factors are known to be involved (see Fig. 17.21).

Abnormalities of the lower oesophageal sphincter

In health, the lower oesophageal sphincter is tonically contracted, relaxing only during swallowing (see p. 750).

Some patients with gastro-oesophageal reflux disease have reduced lower oesophageal sphincter tone, permitting reflux when intra-abdominal pressure rises. In others, basal sphincter tone is normal but reflux occurs in response to frequent episodes of inappropriate sphincter relaxation.

Hiatus hernia

Hiatus hernia (see Box 17.25 and Fig. 17.22) causes reflux because the pressure gradient between the abdominal and

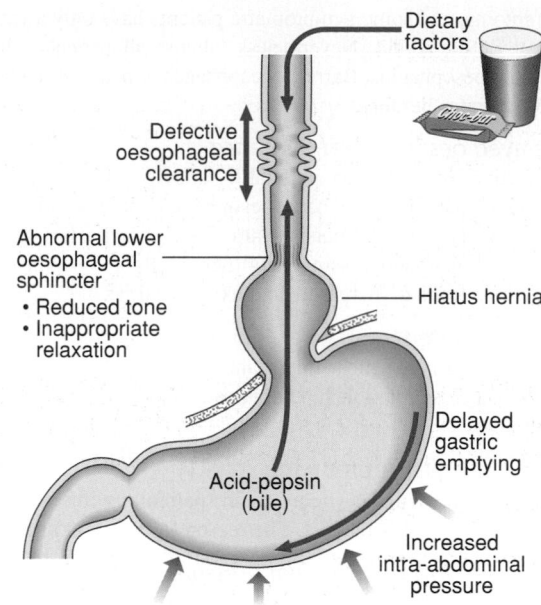

Fig. 17.21   Factors associated with the development of gastro-oesophageal reflux disease.

17.25 IMPORTANT FEATURES OF HIATUS HERNIA

- Occurs in 30% of the population over the age of 50 years
- Often asymptomatic
- Heartburn and regurgitation can occur
- Gastric volvulus may complicate large para-oesophageal hernias

thoracic cavities, which normally pinches the hiatus, is lost. In addition, the oblique angle between the cardia and oesophagus disappears. Many patients who have large hiatus hernias develop reflux symptoms, but the relationship between the presence of a hernia and symptoms is poor. Hiatus hernia is very common in individuals who have no

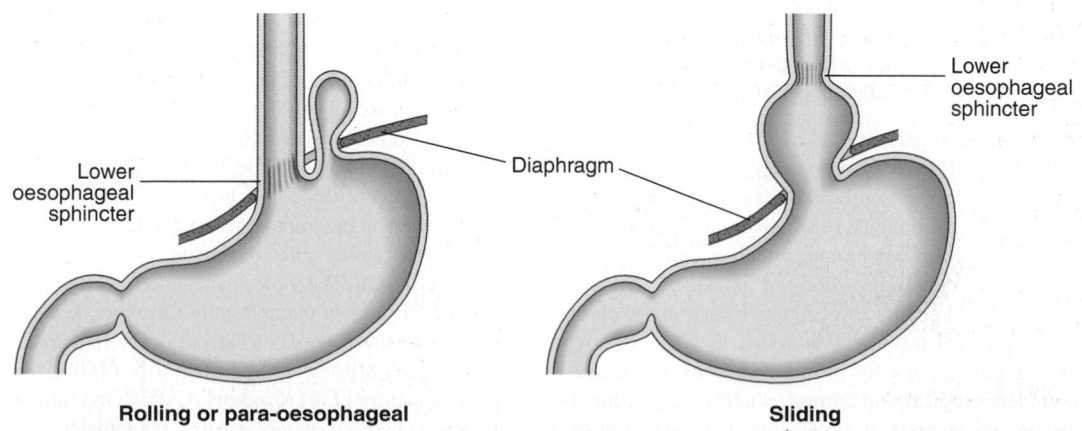

Rolling or para-oesophageal   Sliding

Fig. 17.22   Types of hiatus hernia.

symptoms, and some symptomatic patients have only a very small or no hernia. Nevertheless, almost all patients who develop oesophagitis, Barrett's oesophagus or peptic strictures have a hiatus hernia.

Delayed oesophageal clearance

Defective oesophageal peristaltic activity is commonly found in patients who have oesophagitis. It is a primary abnormality, since it persists after oesophagitis has been healed by acid-suppressing drug therapy. Poor oesophageal clearance leads to increased acid exposure time.

Gastric contents

Gastric acid is the most important oesophageal irritant and there is a close relationship between acid exposure time and symptoms.

Defective gastric emptying

Gastric emptying is delayed in patients with gastro-oesophageal reflux disease. The reason for this is unknown.

Increased intra-abdominal pressure

Pregnancy and obesity are established predisposing causes. Weight loss may improve symptoms.

Dietary and environmental factors

Dietary fat, chocolate, alcohol and coffee relax the lower oesophageal sphincter and may provoke symptoms. There is little evidence to incriminate smoking or NSAIDs as causes of gastro-oesophageal reflux disease.

Clinical features

The major symptoms are heartburn and regurgitation, often provoked by bending, straining or lying down. 'Waterbrash', which is salivation due to reflex salivary gland stimulation as acid enters the gullet, is often present. A history of weight gain is common. Some patients are woken at night by choking as refluxed fluid irritates the larynx. Others develop odynophagia or dysphagia. A few present with atypical chest pain which may be severe, can mimic angina and is probably due to reflux-induced oesophageal spasm.

Complications

Oesophagitis

A range of endoscopic findings, from mild redness to severe, bleeding ulceration with stricture formation, is recognised (see Fig. 17.23). There is a poor correlation between symptoms and histological and endoscopic findings. A normal endoscopy and normal oesophageal histology are perfectly compatible with significant gastro-oesophageal reflux disease.

Barrett's oesophagus

Background. Barrett's oesophagus ('columnar lined oesophagus'—CLO) is a pre-malignant glandular metaplasia of the lower oesophagus, in which the normal squamous lining is replaced by columnar mucosa composed of a cellular mosaic containing areas of intestinal metaplasia (see Fig. 17.24). It occurs as an adaptive response to chronic gastro-oesophageal reflux and is found in 10% of patients undergoing gastroscopy for reflux symptoms. Community-based epidemiological and autopsy studies suggest the true prevalence may be up to 20 times greater as the condition is

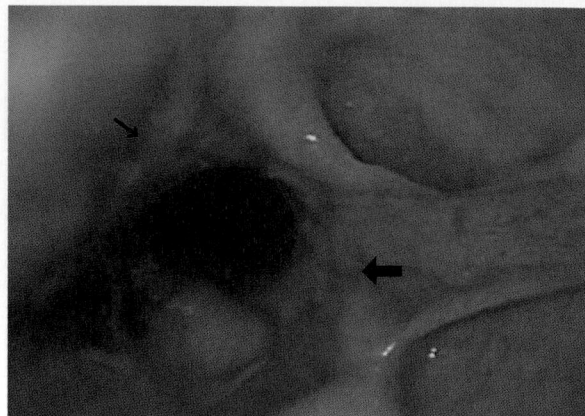

Fig. 17.23   Reflux oesophagitis. The gullet is inflamed and ulcerated (small arrows) and there is early stricturing (large arrow).

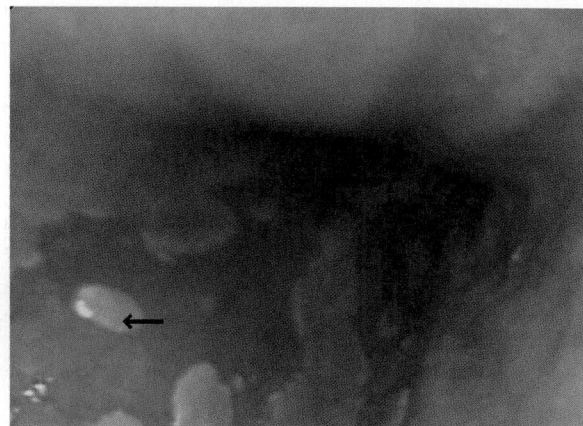

Fig. 17.24   Barrett's oesophagus. Pink columnar mucosa extends up the gullet. Small islands of squamous mucosa remain (arrow).

often asymptomatic until first discovered when the patient presents with oesophageal cancer. CLO principally occurs in Western Caucasian males and is rare in other racial groups. It is the major risk factor for oesophageal adenocarcinoma, with a lifetime cancer risk of around 10%. The cancer incidence is estimated at 1 in 200 patient years (0.5% per year). The absolute risk is low, however, and more than 95% of patients with CLO die of causes other than oesophageal cancer. The epidemiology and aetiology of CLO are poorly understood. The prevalence is increasing, and it is more common in men (especially white) and those over 50 years of age. It is weakly associated with smoking but not alcohol. Recent studies suggest that cancer risk is related to the severity and duration of reflux rather than the presence of CLO per se but this remains to be proven. Recent attention has focused on the importance of duodenogastro-oesophageal reflux, containing bile, pancreatic enzymes and pepsin in addition to acid. The molecular events underlying the progression of CLO from metaplasia to dysplasia to cancer are not well understood but E-cadherin polymorphisms, p53 mutations, transforming growth factor-β (TGF-β), epidermal growth factor (EGF) receptors, COX-2 and tumour necrosis factor-α (TNF-α) may play roles in neoplastic progression.

Diagnosis requires multiple systematic biopsies to maximise the chance of detecting intestinal metaplasia and/or dysplasia.

Management. Neither potent acid suppression nor anti-reflux surgery will stop progression or induce regression of CLO, and treatment is only indicated for symptoms of reflux or complications such as stricture. Endoscopic ablation therapy or photodynamic therapy can induce regression but 'buried islands' of glandular mucosa may persist underneath the squamous epithelium and cancer risk is not eliminated. At present these therapies remain experimental but show promise; they are used in patients with high-grade dysplasia (HGD) or early malignancy that is not suitable for surgery.

Regular endoscopic surveillance is often performed to detect dysplasia and prevent malignancy or diagnose it at a curable stage. Surveillance can detect tumours at earlier stages and improve 2-year survival but, because most CLO is undetected until cancer develops, surveillance strategies are unlikely to influence the overall mortality rate of oesophageal cancer. Surveillance is expensive and cost-effectiveness studies have been conflicting. Surveillance is currently recommended every 1–2 years for those without dysplasia and 6–12-monthly for those with low-grade dysplasia. Oesophagectomy is widely recommended for those with HGD as the resected specimen harbours cancer in up to 40%. This may be an over-estimate and recent data suggest that HGD often remains stable and may not progress to cancer, at least in the medium term. Close follow-up with biopsies every 3 months is an alternative strategy for those with HGD. Further studies are required to confirm recent evidence suggesting that more selective surveillance at longer intervals may be safe and more cost-effective.

Anaemia

Iron deficiency anaemia occurs as a consequence of chronic, insidious blood loss from long-standing oesophagitis. Almost all such patients have a large hiatus hernia. Nevertheless, hiatus hernia is very common and other causes of blood loss, particularly colorectal cancer, must be considered in anaemic patients, even when endoscopy reveals oesophagitis and a hiatus hernia.

Benign oesophageal stricture

Fibrous strictures develop as a consequence of long-standing oesophagitis. Most patients are elderly and have poor oesophageal peristaltic activity. They present with dysphagia which is worse for solids than for liquids. Bolus obstruction following ingestion of meat can lead to absolute dysphagia. A history of heartburn is common but not invariable; many elderly patients presenting with strictures have no preceding heartburn.

Diagnosis is made by endoscopy, and biopsies of the stricture are taken to exclude malignancy. Endoscopic balloon dilatation or bouginage is undertaken. Subsequently, long-term therapy with a proton pump inhibitor drug at full dose should be started to reduce the risk of recurrent oesophagitis and stricture formation. The patient should be advised to chew food thoroughly, and it is important to ensure adequate dentition.

Investigations

Young patients who present with typical symptoms of gastro-oesophageal reflux, without worrying features such as dysphagia, weight loss or anaemia, can be treated empirically.

Investigation is advisable if patients present in middle or late age, if symptoms are atypical or if a complication is suspected. Endoscopy is the investigation of choice. This is performed to exclude other upper gastrointestinal diseases which can mimic gastro-oesophageal reflux, and to identify complications. A normal endoscopy in a patient with compatible symptoms should not preclude treatment for gastro-oesophageal reflux disease.

When, despite endoscopy, the diagnosis is unclear or if surgical intervention is under consideration, 24-hour pH monitoring is indicated. This involves tethering a slim catheter with a terminal radiotelemetry pH-sensitive probe above the gastro-oesophageal junction. The intraluminal pH is recorded whilst the patient undergoes normal activities, and episodes of pain are noted and related to pH. A pH of less than 4 for more than 6–7% of the study time is diagnostic of reflux disease.

Management

Lifestyle advice, including weight loss, avoidance of dietary items which the patient finds worsen symptoms, elevation of the bed head in those who experience nocturnal symptoms, avoidance of late meals and giving up smoking are recommended but rarely needed.

Proprietary antacids and alginates, which are said to produce a protective mucosal 'raft' over the oesophageal mucosa, are taken with considerable symptomatic benefit by most patients. H_2-receptor antagonist drugs (see p. 786) help symptoms without healing oesophagitis. They are well tolerated, and the timing of medication and dosage should be tailored to individual need.

Proton pump inhibitors (see p. 786) are the treatment of choice for severe symptoms and for complicated reflux disease. Symptoms almost invariably resolve and oesophagitis heals in the majority of patients. Recurrence of symptoms is common when therapy is stopped and some patients require life-long treatment at the lowest acceptable dose.

Patients who fail to respond to medical therapy, those who are unwilling to take long-term proton pump inhibitors and those whose major symptom is severe regurgitation

---

EBM

GASTRO-OESOPHAGEAL REFLUX DISEASE—role of pharmacological intervention

'A meta-analysis of available RCT data indicates that proton pump inhibitors are significantly better than H_2-receptor antagonists in both healing oesophagitis and relieving symptoms. Proton pump inhibitors heal oesophagitis resistant to long-term therapy with H_2-receptor antagonists.'

- Chiba N, de Gara CJ, Wilkinson JM, et al. Speed of healing and symptom relief in grade II to IV gastroesophageal reflux disease: a meta-analysis. Gastroenterol 1997; 112:1798–1810.
- Bate CM, Green JR, Axon AT, et al. Omeprazole is more effective than cimetidine in the prevention of recurrence of GERD-associated heartburn and the occurrence of underlying oesophagitis. Aliment Pharmacol Ther 1998; 12:41–47.

Further information: www.bsg.org.uk
www.evidbasedgastro.com

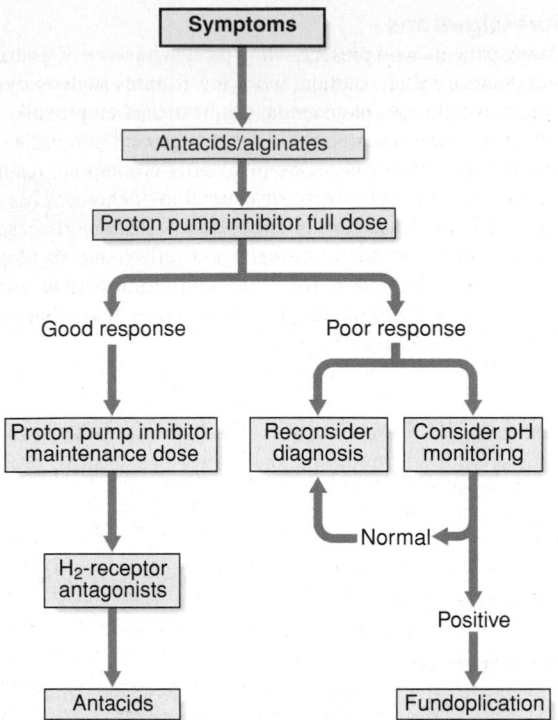

Fig. 17.25   Treatment of gastro-oesophageal reflux disease: a 'step-down' approach.

should be considered for anti-reflux surgery. This can be undertaken by an open operation but is increasingly being carried out laparoscopically. Although heartburn and regurgitation are alleviated in most patients, a proportion develop complications such as inability to vomit and abdominal bloating ('gas-bloat syndrome'). A treatment algorithm is outlined in Figure 17.25.

ISSUES IN OLDER PEOPLE
GASTRO-OESOPHAGEAL REFLUX DISEASE

- The prevalence of gastro-oesophageal reflux disease is higher in older people and complications are more common.
- The severity of symptoms does not correlate with the degree of mucosal inflammation in old age.
- Late complications such as peptic strictures or bleeding from oesophagitis are more common in older people.
- Aspiration from occult gastro-oesophageal reflux disease should be considered in older patients with recurrent pneumonia.

OTHER CAUSES OF OESOPHAGITIS

Infection

Oesophageal candidiasis occurs in debilitated patients and those taking broad-spectrum antibiotics or cytotoxic drugs. It is a particular problem in AIDS patients, who are also susceptible to a spectrum of oesophageal infections (see p. 116).

Corrosives

Suicide attempt by strong household bleach or battery acid is followed by painful burns of the mouth and pharynx and by extensive erosive oesophagitis. This is complicated by oesophageal perforation leading to mediastinitis and by stricture formation. At the time of presentation treatment is conservative, based upon analgesia and nutritional support. Vomiting should be avoided and endoscopy should not be carried out at this stage because of the high risk of oesophageal perforation. Following the acute phase, a barium swallow is performed to demonstrate the extent of stricture formation. Endoscopic dilatation is usually necessary, although it is difficult and hazardous because strictures are often long, tortuous and easily perforated.

Drugs

Potassium supplements and NSAIDs may cause oesophageal ulcers when the tablets are trapped above an oesophageal stricture. Liquid preparations of these drugs should be used in such patients. Bisphosphonates, especially alendronate, cause oesophageal ulceration and should be used with caution in patients with known oesophageal disorders.

MOTILITY DISORDERS

PHARYNGEAL POUCH

Incoordination of swallowing within the pharynx leads to herniation through the cricopharyngeus muscle and formation of a pouch. Most patients are elderly and have no symptoms, although regurgitation, halitosis and dysphagia can occur. Some notice gurgling in the throat after swallowing. A barium swallow demonstrates the pouch and reveals incoordination of swallowing, often with pulmonary aspiration. Endoscopy may be hazardous since the instrument may enter and perforate the pouch. Surgical myotomy and resection of the pouch are indicated in symptomatic patients.

ACHALASIA OF THE OESOPHAGUS

Pathophysiology

Achalasia is characterised by:

- a hypertonic lower oesophageal sphincter which fails to relax in response to the swallowing wave
- failure of propagated oesophageal contraction, leading to progressive dilatation of the gullet.

The cause is unknown, although failure of non-adrenergic, non-cholinergic (NANC) innervation related to abnormal nitric oxide synthesis within the lower oesophageal sphincter has been found. Degeneration of ganglion cells within the sphincter and the body of the oesophagus occurs. Loss of the dorsal vagal nuclei within the brain stem can be demonstrated in later stages.

Chagas disease (see p. 60) is endemic in South America; infestation with the protozoan organism *Trypanosoma cruzi* leads to myocarditis and a range of motility disorders of the gastrointestinal tract. Destruction of the myenteric plexus causes a syndrome which is clinically indistinguishable from achalasia.

Clinical features

Achalasia is an unusual disease affecting 1:100 000 people in Western populations. It usually develops in middle life but can occur at any age. Dysphagia develops slowly, and is initially intermittent. It is worse for solids and is eased by drinking liquids, standing and moving around after eating. Heartburn does not occur, since the closed oesophageal sphincter prevents gastro-oesophageal reflux. Some patients experience episodes of severe chest pain due to oesophageal spasm ('vigorous achalasia'). As the disease progresses dysphagia worsens, the oesophagus empties poorly and nocturnal pulmonary aspiration develops. Achalasia predisposes to squamous carcinoma of the oesophagus.

Investigations

A chest radiograph may be abnormal in late disease, with widening of the mediastinum from gross oesophageal dilatation and features of aspiration pneumonia. A barium swallow shows tapered narrowing of the lower oesophagus. In late disease the oesophageal body is dilated, aperistaltic and food-filled (see Fig. 17.26A). Endoscopy must always be carried out to distinguish these radiological appearances from carcinoma. A strategically placed carcinoma of the cardia can mimic the presentation and radiological and manometric features of achalasia ('pseudo-achalasia'). Manometry in achalasia confirms the high-pressure, non-relaxing lower oesophageal sphincter with poor contractility of the oesophageal body (see Fig. 17.26B).

Management

Endoscopic

Forceful pneumatic dilatation using a 30–35 mm diameter fluoroscopically positioned balloon disrupts the oesophageal sphincter and improves symptoms in 80% of patients. Some patients require more than one dilatation but those requiring frequent dilatation are best treated surgically. Endoscopically directed injection of botulinum toxin into the lower oesophageal sphincter induces clinical remission, but late relapse is common.

Surgical

Surgical myotomy ('Heller's operation') is done by open operation or by a laparoscopic approach and is an extremely effective although more invasive option. Both pneumatic dilatation and myotomy may be complicated by gastro-oesophageal reflux, and this can lead to severe oesophagitis because oesophageal clearance is so poor in these patients. For this reason Heller's myotomy is accompanied by a partial fundoplication anti-reflux operation. Acid-suppressing drug therapy, using a proton pump inhibitor, is often necessary following surgical or endoscopic intervention for achalasia to prevent oesophagitis.

OTHER OESOPHAGEAL MOTILITY DISORDERS

Diffuse oesophageal spasm presents in late middle age with episodic chest pain which may mimic angina, but is sometimes accompanied by transient dysphagia. Some cases occur in response to gastro-oesophageal reflux. Treatment is based upon the use of proton pump inhibitor drugs when gastro-oesophageal reflux is present. Oral or sublingual nitrates or nifedipine may relieve attacks of pain. Results of therapy are often disappointing and the alternatives of pneumatic dilatation and surgical myotomy are also poor.

'Nutcracker' oesophagus is a condition in which extremely forceful peristaltic activity leads to episodic chest pain and dysphagia. Treatment is based upon the use of nitrates or nifedipine.

Non-specific motility disorders represent a collection of oesophageal motility disorders which do not fall into a specific disease entity. Patients are usually elderly and present with dysphagia and chest pain. A range of manometric abnormalities from poor peristalsis to spasm occur.

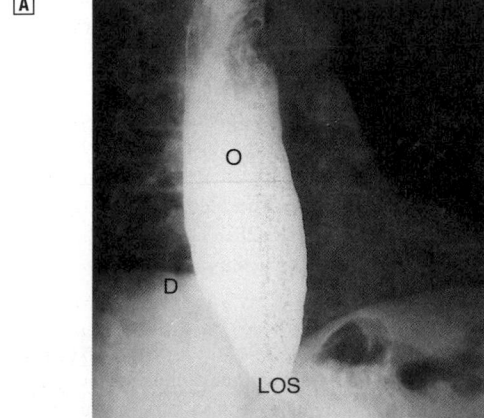

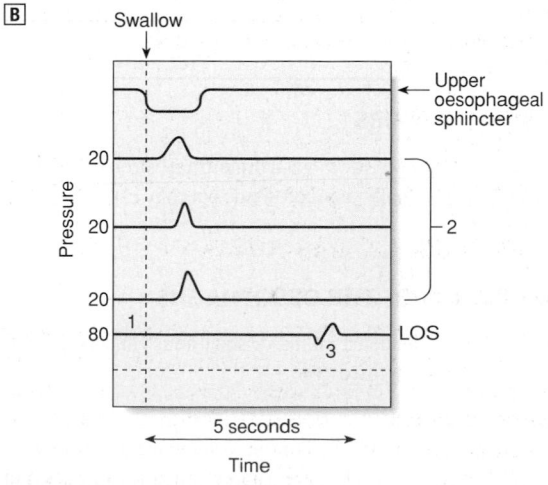

Fig. 17.26 Achalasia. Ⓐ Radiograph showing a dilated, barium-filled oesophagus (O) with tapering, and a closed lower oesophageal sphincter (LOS). (D = diaphragm) Ⓑ Oesophageal manometry demonstrates an elevated resting LOS pressure (1), low-amplitude, non-propagated contractions in the oesophageal body (2), and failure of the LOS to relax on swallowing (3). Compare with Figure 17.1, page 750.

SECONDARY CAUSES OF OESOPHAGEAL DYSMOTILITY

In systemic sclerosis the muscle of the oesophagus is replaced by fibrous tissue. Consequently, oesophageal peristalsis fails and this leads to heartburn and dysphagia. Oesophagitis is often severe, and benign fibrous strictures occur. Such patients require long-term therapy with proton pump inhibitor drugs. Dermatomyositis, rheumatoid arthritis and myasthenia gravis are other causes of dysphagia.

BENIGN OESOPHAGEAL STRICTURE

Benign oesophageal stricture is usually a consequence of gastro-oesophageal reflux disease (see Box 17.26) and occurs most often in elderly patients who have poor oesophageal clearance. Rings, due to submucosal fibrosis, occur at the oesophago-gastric junction ('Schatzki ring') and cause intermittent dysphagia, often starting in middle age. A post-cricoid web is a rare complication of iron deficiency anaemia (Paterson–Kelly or Plummer–Vinson syndrome), and may be complicated by development of squamous carcinoma.

Benign strictures are treated by endoscopic dilatation, in which wire-guided bougies or balloons are used to disrupt the fibrous tissue of the stricture.

17.26 CAUSES OF OESOPHAGEAL STRICTURE

- Gastro-oesophageal reflux disease
- Webs and rings
- Carcinoma of the oesophagus or cardia
- Extrinsic compression from bronchial carcinoma
- Corrosive ingestion
- Post-operative scarring following oesophageal resection
- Post-radiotherapy
- Following long-term nasogastric intubation

TUMOURS OF THE OESOPHAGUS

BENIGN TUMOURS

The most common is a gastrointestinal stromal tumour (GIST). This is usually asymptomatic but may cause bleeding or dysphagia.

CARCINOMA OF THE OESOPHAGUS

Almost all are adenocarcinoma or squamous cancers. Small-cell cancer is a rare third type.

Squamous cancer

In Western populations squamous oesophageal cancer (see Box 17.27) is relatively rare (approximately 4 cases per 100 000), whilst in Iran, South Africa and China it is common (200 per 100 000). Squamous cancer can arise in any part of the oesophagus from the post-cricoid region to the

---

17.27 SQUAMOUS CARCINOMA: AETIOLOGICAL FACTORS

- Smoking
- Alcohol excess
- Chewing betel nuts or tobacco
- Coeliac disease
- Achalasia of the oesophagus
- Post-cricoid web
- Post-caustic stricture
- Tylosis (familial hyperkeratosis of palms and soles)

---

cardia. Almost all tumours above the lower third of the oesophagus are squamous cancers.

Adenocarcinoma

This arises in the lower third of the oesophagus from Barrett's oesophagus or from the cardia of the stomach. The incidence of this tumour is increasing and is now approximately 5:100 000 in the UK; this is possibly because of the high prevalence of gastro-oesophageal reflux and Barrett's oesophagus in Western populations.

Clinical features

Most patients have a history of progressive, painless dysphagia for solid foods. Others present acutely because of food bolus obstruction. In late stages weight loss is often extreme; chest pain or hoarseness suggests mediastinal invasion. Fistulation between the oesophagus and the trachea or bronchial tree leads to coughing after swallowing, pneumonia and pleural effusion. Physical signs may be absent but even at initial presentation cachexia, cervical lymphadenopathy or other evidence of metastatic spread is common.

Investigations

The investigation of choice is upper gastrointestinal endoscopy (see Fig. 17.27) with cytology and biopsy. A barium swallow demonstrates the site and length of the stricture but adds little useful information.

Once a diagnosis has been achieved, investigations are performed to stage the tumour and define operability. Thoracic and abdominal CT are carried out to identify metastatic spread and local invasion. Invasion of the aorta and other local structures may preclude surgery. Unfortunately, CT tends to understage tumours and the most sensitive modality is endoscopic ultrasound (EUS), in which an ultrasound transducer is incorporated into the tip of a modified endoscope (see Fig. 17.28). These investigations will define the TNM stage of the disease (see Ch. 5).

Management

Despite modern treatment, the overall 5-year survival of patients presenting with oesophageal cancer is 6–9%. Survival following oesophageal resection depends on stage. Tumours which have extended beyond the wall of the oesophagus and have lymph node involvement (T3, N1) are associated with a 5-year survival of around 10% after surgery. However, this figure improves significantly if the tumour is confined to the oesophageal wall and there is

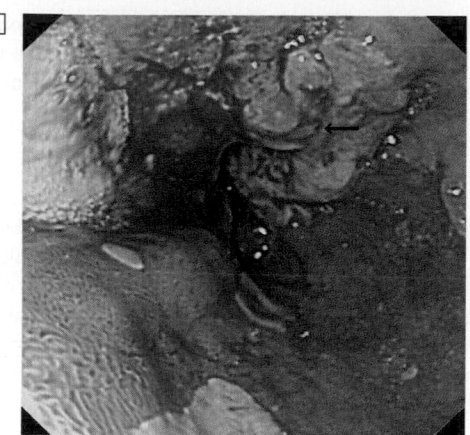

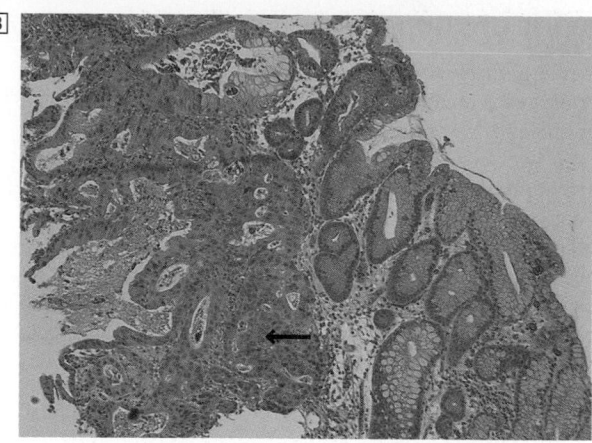

Fig. 17.27 Adenocarcinoma of the lower oesophagus. [A] Adenocarcinoma in association with Barrett's oesophagus (arrow). [B] Histology: clumps of invasive malignant cells are seen below areas of intestinal metaplasia (arrow).

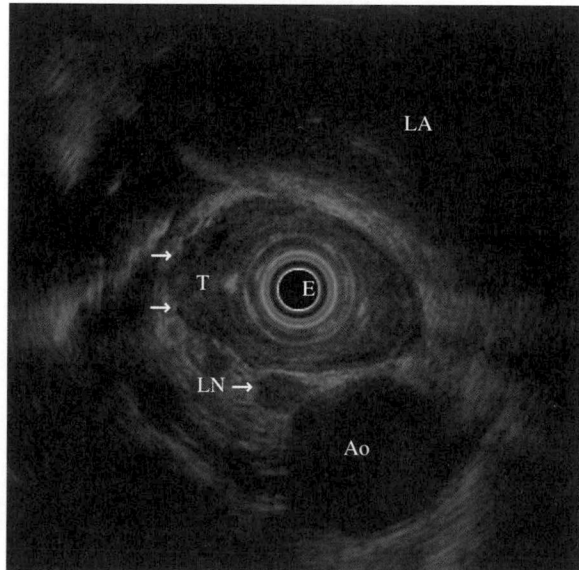

Fig. 17.28 Endoscopic ultrasound staging of oesophageal carcinoma. The tumour (T) has extended through the oesophageal wall (T3, arrows). A small peri-tumoral lymph node (LN) is also seen (arrow). (Ao = aorta; LA = left atrium; E = echoendoscope)

no spread to lymph nodes. Overall survival following 'potentially curative' surgery (all macroscopic tumour removed) is about 30% at 5 years, but recent studies have suggested that this can be improved by neoadjuvant (pre-operative) chemotherapy, including agents such as cisplatin and 5-fluorouracil. Although squamous carcinomas are radiosensitive, radiotherapy alone is associated with a 5-year survival of only 5%.

Approximately 70% of patients have extensive disease at presentation; in these, treatment is palliative and based upon relief of dysphagia and pain. Endoscopically directed tumour ablation using laser therapy or insertion of stents is the major method of improving swallowing. Palliative radiotherapy may induce shrinkage of both squamous cancers and adenocarcinomas but symptomatic response may be slow. Quality of life can be improved by nutritional support and appropriate analgesia.

PERFORATION OF THE OESOPHAGUS

The most common cause is iatrogenic perforation complicating dilatation or intubation. Malignant, corrosive or post-radiotherapy strictures are more likely to be perforated than peptic strictures. A perforated peptic stricture is usually managed conservatively using broad-spectrum antibiotics and parenteral nutrition; most heal within days. Malignant, caustic and radiotherapy stricture perforations require surgical resection or intubation.

Spontaneous oesophageal perforation ('Boerhaave's syndrome') results from forceful vomiting and retching. Severe chest pain and shock occur as oesophago-gastric contents enter the mediastinum and thoracic cavity. Subcutaneous emphysema, pleural effusions and pneumothorax develop. The diagnosis is made using a water-soluble contrast swallow and treatment is surgical. Delay in diagnosis is a key factor in the high mortality associated with this condition.

DISEASES OF THE STOMACH AND DUODENUM

GASTRITIS

Gastritis is a histological diagnosis, although it can sometimes be recognised at endoscopy.

ACUTE GASTRITIS

Acute gastritis is often erosive and haemorrhagic. Neutrophils are the predominant inflammatory cell in the superficial epithelium. Many cases result from aspirin or NSAID ingestion (see Box 17.28). Acute gastritis often produces no symptoms but may cause dyspepsia, anorexia, nausea or vomiting, haematemesis or melaena. Many cases resolve quickly and do not merit investigation; in others, endoscopy and biopsy may be necessary to exclude peptic ulcer or cancer. Treatment should be directed to the underlying cause. Short-term symptomatic therapy with antacids, acid suppression (e.g. H_2-receptor antagonists) or antiemetics (e.g. metoclopramide) may be necessary.

CHRONIC GASTRITIS DUE TO *HELICOBACTER PYLORI* INFECTION

The most common cause of chronic gastritis is *H. pylori* (see Box 17.28). The predominant inflammatory cells are lymphocytes and plasma cells. Correlation between symptoms and endoscopic or pathological findings is poor. Most patients are asymptomatic and do not require any treatment. Patients with dyspepsia and *H. pylori*-associated gastritis may benefit from *H. pylori* eradication.

AUTOIMMUNE CHRONIC GASTRITIS

This involves the body of the stomach, spares the antrum and results from autoimmune activity against parietal cells. The histological features are diffuse chronic inflammation, atrophy and loss of fundic glands, intestinal metaplasia and sometimes hyperplasia of enterochromaffin-like (ECL) cells. Circulating antibodies to parietal cell and intrinsic factor may be present. In some patients the degree of gastric atrophy is severe, and loss of intrinsic factor secretion leads to pernicious anaemia. The gastritis itself is usually asymptomatic but some patients have evidence of other organ-specific autoimmunity, particularly thyroid disease. There is a four-fold increase in the risk of gastric cancer development (see also p. 789).

MÉNÉTRIER'S DISEASE

In this rare condition the gastric pits are elongated and tortuous, with replacement of the parietal and chief cells by mucus-secreting cells. As a result, the mucosal folds of the body and fundus are greatly enlarged. Most patients are hypochlorhydric. Whilst some patients have upper gastrointestinal symptoms, the majority present in middle or old age with protein-losing enteropathy (see p. 798) due to exudation from the gastric mucosa. Barium meal shows enlarged, nodular and coarse folds which are also seen at endoscopy, although biopsies may not be deep enough to show all the histological features. Treatment with antisecretory drugs may reduce protein loss but unresponsive patients require partial gastrectomy.

PEPTIC ULCER DISEASE

The term 'peptic ulcer' refers to an ulcer in the lower oesophagus, stomach or duodenum, in the jejunum after surgical anastomosis to the stomach, or, rarely, in the ileum adjacent to a Meckel's diverticulum. Ulcers in the stomach or duodenum may be acute or chronic; both penetrate the muscularis mucosae but the acute ulcer shows no evidence of fibrosis. Erosions do not penetrate the muscularis mucosae.

GASTRIC AND DUODENAL ULCER

Although the prevalence of peptic ulcer is decreasing in many Western communities, it still affects approximately 10% of all adults at some time in their lives. The male to female ratio for duodenal ulcer varies from 5:1 to 2:1, whilst that for gastric ulcer is 2:1 or less.

Aetiology

Helicobacter pylori

In the industrialised world the prevalence of *H. pylori* infection in the general population rises steadily with age, and in the UK approximately 50% of those over the age of 50 years are infected. In many parts of the underdeveloped world infection is much more common and is often acquired in childhood. Up to 90% of the population are infected by adult life in some countries. The vast majority of colonised people remain healthy and asymptomatic and only a minority develop clinical disease. Around 90% of duodenal ulcer patients and 70% of gastric ulcer patients are infected with *H. pylori*; the remaining 30% of gastric ulcers are due to NSAIDs.

Pathogenesis and pathophysiology of infection. The organism's motility allows it to localise and live deep beneath the mucus layer closely adherent to the epithelial surface.

17.28 COMMON CAUSES OF GASTRITIS

Acute gastritis (often erosive and haemorrhagic)

- Aspirin, NSAIDs
- *H. pylori* (initial infection)
- Alcohol
- Other drugs, e.g. iron preparations
- Severe physiological stress, e.g. burns, multi-organ failure, CNS trauma
- Bile reflux, e.g. following gastric surgery
- Viral infections, e.g. cytomegalovirus (CMV), herpes simplex virus in AIDS (see pp. 115–117)

Chronic non-specific gastritis

- *H. pylori* infection
- Autoimmune (pernicious anaemia)
- Post-gastrectomy

Chronic 'specific' forms (rare)

- Infections, e.g. CMV, tuberculosis
- Gastrointestinal diseases, e.g. Crohn's disease
- Systemic diseases, e.g. sarcoidosis, graft-versus-host disease
- Idiopathic, e.g. granulomatous gastritis

Here the surface pH is close to neutral and any acidity is buffered by the organism's production of the enzyme urease. This produces ammonia from urea and raises the pH around the bacterium. Although it is non-invasive, the bacterium stimulates chronic gastritis by provoking a local inflammatory response in the underlying epithelium due to release of a range of cytotoxins (see Fig. 17.29). *H. pylori* exclusively colonises gastric-type epithelium and is only found in the duodenum in association with patches of gastric metaplasia.

In most people *H. pylori* causes antral gastritis associated with depletion of somatostatin (from D cells) and gastrin release from G cells. The subsequent hypergastrinaemia stimulates acid production by parietal cells, but in the majority of cases this has no clinical consequences. In a minority of patients (perhaps those who inherit a large parietal cell mass) this effect is exaggerated, leading to duodenal ulceration

(see Fig. 17.30). The role of *H. pylori* in the pathogenesis of gastric ulcer is less clear but *H. pylori* probably acts by reducing gastric mucosal resistance to attack from acid and pepsin. In approximately 1% of infected people, *H. pylori* causes a pangastritis leading to gastric atrophy and hypochlorhydria. This allows bacteria to proliferate within the stomach; these may produce mutagenic nitrites from dietary nitrates, predisposing to the development of gastric cancer (see Fig. 17.31). The reasons for different outcomes are unclear but bacterial strain differences and host genetic factors are both likely.

Diagnosis. Many different diagnostic tests for *H. pylori* infection are available (see Box 17.29). Some are invasive and require endoscopy; others are non-invasive. They vary in sensitivity and specificity. Overall, breath tests are best because of their accuracy, simplicity and non-invasiveness.

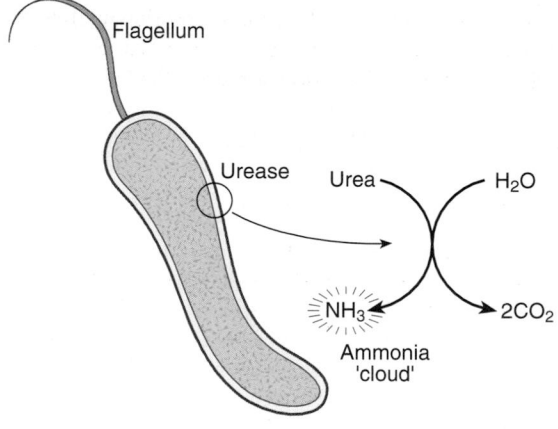

Other factors
- Vacuolating cytotoxin (vacA)
- Cytotoxin-associated gene (cagA)
- Adhesins
- Phospholipases, porins

Fig. 17.29   Some factors which may influence the virulence of *Helicobacter pylori*.

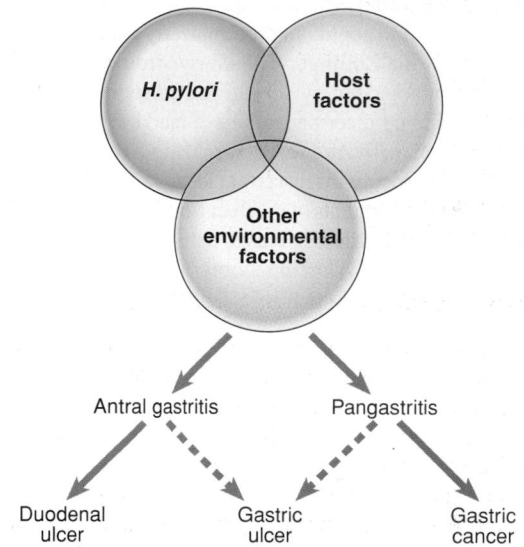

Fig. 17.31   Consequences of *H. pylori* infection.

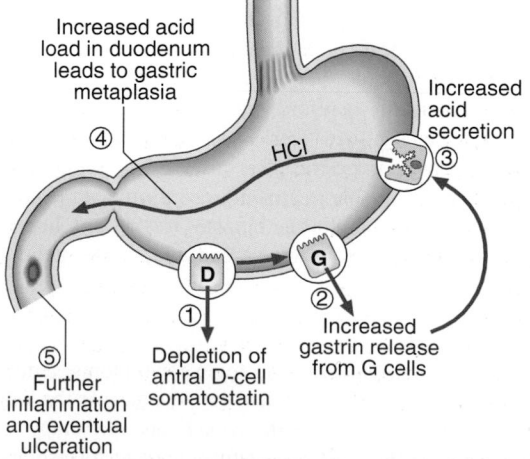

Fig. 17.30   Sequence of events in the pathophysiology of duodenal ulceration.

17.29 METHODS FOR THE DIAGNOSIS OF *HELICOBACTER PYLORI* INFECTION		
Test	**Advantages**	**Disadvantages**
Non-invasive		
Serology	Rapid office kits available Good for population studies	Lacks sensitivity and specificity Cannot differentiate current from past infection
Urea breath tests	High sensitivity and specificity	^{14}C uses radioactivity ^{13}C requires expensive mass spectrometer
Invasive (antral biopsy)		
Histology	Sensitivity and specificity	False negatives occur Takes several days to process
Rapid urease tests, e.g. CLO, Pyloritek	Cheap, quick Specificity	Lack sensitivity
Microbiological culture	'Gold standard' Defines antibiotic sensitivity	Slow and laborious culture Lacks sensitivity

Non-steroidal anti-inflammatory drugs (NSAIDs)
See page 989.

Smoking
Smoking confers an increased risk of gastric ulcer and, to a lesser extent, duodenal ulcer. Once the ulcer has formed, it is more likely to cause complications and less likely to heal on standard treatment regimens if the patient continues to smoke.

Acid-pepsin versus mucosal resistance
An ulcer forms when there is an imbalance between aggressive factors, i.e. the digestive power of acid and pepsin, and defensive factors, i.e. the ability of the gastric and duodenal mucosa to resist this digestive power (see Fig. 17.32). This mucosal resistance constitutes the gastric mucosal barrier. Ulcers occur only in the presence of acid and pepsin; they are never found in achlorhydric patients such as those with pernicious anaemia. On the other hand, severe intractable peptic ulceration nearly always occurs in patients with the Zollinger–Ellison syndrome (see p. 788), which is characterised by very high acid secretion.

Most duodenal ulcer patients have markedly exaggerated acid secretion in response to stimulation by gastrin, and *H. pylori* (as already discussed) leads to hypergastrinaemia. In gastric ulcer patients the effects of *H. pylori* are more complex, and impaired mucosal defence resulting from a combination of *H. pylori* infection, NSAIDs and smoking may have a more important role.

Pathology
Chronic gastric ulcer is usually single; 90% are situated on the lesser curve within the antrum or at the junction between body and antral mucosa. Chronic duodenal ulcer usually occurs in the first part of the duodenum just distal to the junction of pyloric and duodenal mucosa; 50% are on the anterior wall. Gastric and duodenal ulcers coexist in 10% of patients and more than one peptic ulcer is found in 10–15% of patients. A chronic ulcer extends to below the muscularis mucosa and the histology shows four layers: surface debris, an infiltrate of neutrophils, granulation tissue and collagen.

Clinical features
Peptic ulcer disease is a chronic condition with a natural history of spontaneous relapse and remission lasting for decades, if not for life. Although they are different diseases, duodenal and gastric ulcers share common symptoms which will be considered together.

The most common presentation is that of recurrent abdominal pain which has three notable characteristics: localisation to the epigastrium, relationship to food and episodic occurrence.

Occasional vomiting occurs in about 40% of ulcer subjects; persistent vomiting occurring daily suggests gastric outlet obstruction. In one-third of patients the history is less characteristic. This is especially true in elderly subjects under treatment with NSAIDs. In these patients pain may be absent or so slight that it is experienced only as a vague sense of epigastric unease. Occasionally, the only symptoms are anorexia and nausea, or a sense of undue repletion after meals. In some patients the ulcer is completely 'silent', presenting for the first time with anaemia from chronic undetected blood loss, as an abrupt haematemesis or as acute perforation; in others there is recurrent acute bleeding without ulcer pain between the attacks.

It should be noted that the diagnostic value of individual symptoms for peptic ulcer disease is poor, and the history is often a poor predictor of the presence of an ulcer.

Investigations
The diagnosis can be made by double-contrast barium meal examination or by endoscopy. Endoscopy is the preferred investigation because it is more accurate and has the enormous advantage that suspicious lesions and *H. pylori* status can be evaluated by biopsy. For those with a duodenal ulcer seen at barium meal, urea breath testing will accurately define *H. pylori* status. Very occasionally, a gastric ulcer may be malignant; therefore endoscopy and biopsy are mandatory when a gastric ulcer is detected on barium examination. Moreover, in gastric ulcer disease endoscopy must be repeated after suitable treatment to confirm that the ulcer has healed and to obtain further biopsies if it has not. In contrast, it is not necessary to repeat endoscopy after treating duodenal ulcers.

Management
The aims of management are to relieve symptoms, induce ulcer healing in the short term, and cure the ulcer in the long term. *H. pylori* eradication is the cornerstone of therapy for peptic ulcers, as this will successfully prevent relapse and eliminate the need for long-term therapy in the majority of patients.

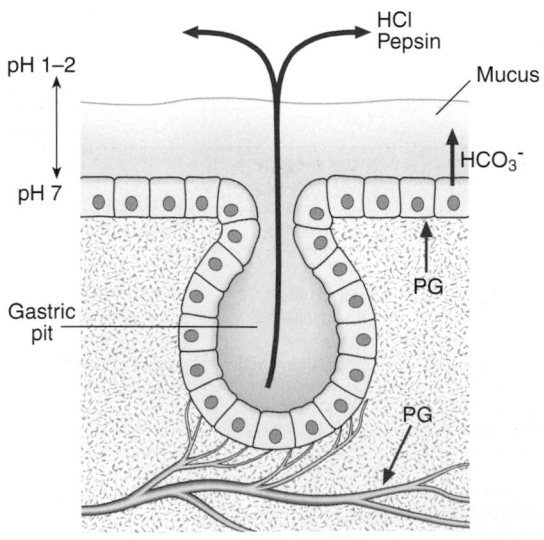

Fig. 17.32 Gastroduodenal mucosal protection. Prostaglandins (PG) stimulate bicarbonate and mucus secretion and increase mucosal blood flow. Bicarbonate ions are secreted into the unstirred mucus layer, neutralising hydrogen ions as they back-diffuse towards the epithelium. Rapid cell turnover and a rich mucosal blood supply are important protective elements.

H. pylori eradication

All patients with proven acute or chronic duodenal ulcer disease and those with gastric ulcers who are *H. pylori*-positive should be offered eradication therapy as primary therapy. Treatment is based upon a proton pump inhibitor taken simultaneously with two antibiotics (from amoxicillin, clarithromycin and metronidazole) for 7 days. Compliance, side-effects and metronidazole resistance influence the success of therapy (see Box 17.30).

Second-line therapy should be offered to those patients who remain infected after initial therapy once the reasons for failure of first-line therapy (e.g. compliance) have been established. For those who are still colonised after two treatments, the choice lies between a third attempt with quadruple therapy (bismuth, proton pump inhibitor and two antibiotics) or long-term maintenance therapy with acid suppression.

Other indications for *H. pylori* eradication are shown in Box 17.31.

17.30 COMMON SIDE-EFFECTS OF *H. PYLORI* ERADICATION THERAPY

- Diarrhoea
  30–50% of patients; usually mild but *Clostridium difficile*-associated colitis can occur
- Metronidazole
  Metallic taste (common), peripheral neuropathy (rare)
  Flushing and vomiting when taken with alcohol
- Nausea, vomiting
- Abdominal cramp
- Headache
- Rash

17.31 INDICATIONS FOR *H. PYLORI* ERADICATION

Definite

- Peptic ulcer
- MALToma

Not indicated

- Asymptomatic
- Gastro-oesophageal reflux disease

Uncertain

- Family history of gastric cancer
- Non-ulcer dyspepsia
- Long-term NSAID users

EBM

H. PYLORI ERADICATION—antibiotic regimens

'RCTs show that first-line therapy should include a proton pump inhibitor at standard dose (12-hourly), clarithromycin 500 mg 12-hourly, and amoxicillin 1 g 12-hourly or metronidazole 400 mg 12-hourly, for 7 days. In case of failure recommended second-line therapy is a proton pump inhibitor at standard dose (12-hourly), bismuth 120 mg 6-hourly, metronidazole 400 mg 12-hourly, and tetracycline 500 mg 6-hourly, for 7 days.'

- Lind T, Veldhuyzen van Zanten SJO, Unge P, et al. Eradication of *Helicobacter pylori* using one week triple therapies combining omeprazole with two antimicrobials—the MACH 1 study. Helicobacter 1996; 1:138–140.
- Megrand F, Lehn N, Lind T, et al. The MACH 2 study. *Helicobacter pylori* resistance to antimicrobial agents and its influence on clinical outcome. Gastroenterology 1997; 112:A216 (abstract).

Further information: 🖳 www.bsg.org.uk
🖳 www.evidbasedgastro.com

General measures

Cigarette smoking, aspirin and NSAIDs should be avoided. Alcohol in moderation is not harmful and no special dietary advice is required.

Short-term management

Many different drugs are available for the short-term management of acid peptic symptoms (see Box 17.32).

17.32 DRUGS COMMONLY USED IN PEPTIC ULCERS AND OTHER ACID DYSPEPTIC DISORDERS

Drugs	Short term	Maintenance	Side-effects
Drugs which inhibit acid secretion			
H₂-antagonists			
Cimetidine	400 mg 12-hourly or 800 mg at night	400 mg at night	Confusion, diarrhoea, interaction with warfarin, phenytoin, theophylline
Ranitidine	150 mg 12-hourly or 300 mg at night	150 mg at night	Confusion
H⁺/K⁺ ATPase inhibitors (proton pump inhibitors)			
Omeprazole	20–40 mg once daily	20 mg at night ⎱	Hypergastrinaemia, diarrhoea, interactions
Lansoprazole	30 mg once daily	15 mg at night ⎰	with warfarin, phenytoin
Pantoprazole	40 mg once daily	Not recommended ⎱	Hypergastrinaemia; fewer drug interactions,
Rabeprazole	20 mg once daily	Not recommended ⎰	headache, diarrhoea, rashes
Drugs which enhance mucosal defence and prokinetic agents			
Colloidal bismuth	125 mg 6-hourly	Not recommended	Blackens tongue, teeth and faeces; rarely, bismuth toxicity with prolonged use
Misoprostol	200 μg 6-hourly	200 μg 6-hourly	Abortifacient, contraindicated in women of childbearing age; diarrhoea in up to 20%
Sucralfate	2 g 12-hourly	Not recommended	May bind and reduce absorption of digoxin, warfarin, tetracycline, phenytoin; cramps, diarrhoea, extrapyramidal effects
Domperidone	10–20 mg 8-hourly	Not recommended	Hyperprolactinaemia and acute dystonia

Antacids. These are widely available for self-medication and are used for relief of minor dyspeptic symptoms. The majority are based on combinations of calcium, aluminium and magnesium salts, all of which have individual side-effects. Calcium compounds cause constipation, while magnesium-containing agents cause diarrhoea. Aluminium compounds block absorption of digoxin, tetracycline and dietary phosphates. Most have a high sodium content and can exacerbate congestive heart failure.

Histamine H_2-receptor antagonist drugs. These are competitive inhibitors of histamine at the H_2-receptor on the parietal cell. Dyspeptic symptoms remit promptly, usually within days of starting treatment, and 80% of duodenal ulcers will heal after 4 weeks. These drugs do not inhibit acid secretion to the same degree as the proton pump inhibitors but are useful for the short-term management of acid dyspeptic symptoms prior to investigation. They are moderately effective for the management of reflux disease. They have a proven safety record and several can now be purchased in the UK without prescription.

H^+/K^+ ATPase ('proton pump') inhibitors. These are substituted benzimidazole compounds that specifically and irreversibly inhibit the proton pump hydrogen/potassium ATPase in the parietal cell membrane. They are the most powerful inhibitors of gastric secretion yet discovered, with maximal inhibition occurring 3–6 hours after an oral dose. They have an excellent safety profile. After a few days of treatment virtual achlorhydria is achieved and rapid healing of both gastric and duodenal ulcers follows. Omeprazole and lansoprazole are important components of *H. pylori* eradication regimens. Proton pump inhibitors are also much more effective than H_2-antagonists for healing and maintenance of reflux oesophagitis.

Colloidal bismuth compounds. Colloidal bismuth sub-citrate (CBS) is an ammoniacal suspension of a complex colloidal bismuth salt. It has little, if any, effect on gastric acid secretion and its ulcer-healing effect is probably due to a combination of activity against *H. pylori* and enhancement of mucosal defence mechanisms.

Sucralfate. This is a basic aluminium salt of sucrose octasulphate. It has little effect on acid secretion but probably acts to protect the ulcer base from peptic activity in a number of ways. It binds to fibroblast growth factor and to the ulcer base, reducing the access of pepsin and acid. It may also enhance epithelial cell turnover. It should be taken 30–60 minutes before meals.

Synthetic prostaglandin analogues (misoprostol). Prostaglandins exert complex effects on the gastroduodenal mucosa. In low doses they protect against injury induced by aspirin and NSAIDs by enhancing mucosal blood flow, and by stimulating mucus and bicarbonate secretion and epithelial cell proliferation. At high doses acid secretion is inhibited. Misoprostol is effective for the prevention and treatment of NSAID-induced ulcers, but in clinical practice proton pump inhibitors are preferred, since they are at least as effective and have fewer side-effects.

Maintenance treatment

Continuous maintenance treatment should not be necessary after successful *H. pylori* eradication. For the minority who require maintenance treatment the lowest effective dose should be used.

Surgical treatment

The cure of most peptic ulcers by *H. pylori* eradication therapy and the availability of safe, potent acid-suppressing drugs have made elective surgery for peptic ulcer disease a rare event. The indications are listed in Box 17.33.

The operation of choice for a chronic non-healing gastric ulcer is partial gastrectomy, preferably with a Billroth I anastomosis, in which the ulcer itself and the ulcer-bearing area of the stomach are resected. The reason for this is to exclude an underlying cancer. Definitive anti-acid surgery in the form of vagotomy and drainage (pyloroplasty or gastroenterostomy) or highly selective vagotomy is no longer indicated for duodenal ulcer disease. In the emergency situation 'under-running' the ulcer for bleeding or 'oversewing' (patch repair) for perforation is all that is required. In the presence of giant duodenal ulcers partial gastrectomy using a 'Polya' or Billroth II reconstruction may be required.

17.33 INDICATIONS FOR SURGERY IN PEPTIC ULCER
Emergency
• Perforation • Haemorrhage
Elective
• Complications, e.g. gastric outflow obstruction • Recurrent ulcer following gastric surgery

Complications of gastric resection or vagotomy

Some degree of disability is seen in up to 50% of patients following peptic ulcer surgery. In most, the effects are minor but in 10% of cases they significantly impair quality of life.

Early satiety and vomiting. Rapid gastric emptying leads to distension of the proximal small intestine as the hypertonic contents draw fluid into the lumen. This leads to abdominal discomfort and diarrhoea after eating. Autonomic reflexes release a range of gastrointestinal hormones which lead to vasomotor features such as flushing, palpitations, sweating, tachycardia and hypotension ('early dumping'). Patients should therefore avoid large meals with high carbohydrate content.

Bile reflux gastritis. Duodenogastric bile reflux leads to chronic gastritis. This is usually asymptomatic but dyspepsia can occur. Symptomatic treatment with aluminium-containing antacids or sucralfate may be effective. A few patients require revisional surgery with creation of a Roux-en-Y loop to prevent bile reflux into the stomach.

Late dumping syndrome. Symptoms of dumping occur 90–180 minutes after eating. The pathogenesis is broadly similar to early dumping, but in addition reactive hypoglycaemia occurs and may cause mental confusion. Rapid emptying of carbohydrates into the proximal small intestine results in an exaggerated release of insulin with subsequent reactive hypoglycaemia. Other gut hormones and enteric peptides may also be involved. Treatment is similar to that of early dumping syndrome.

Diarrhoea and maldigestion. Diarrhoea may develop after any peptic ulcer operation and usually occurs 1–2 hours after eating. Poor mixing of food in the stomach, with rapid emptying, inadequate mixing with pancreatic biliary secretions, reduced small intestinal transit times and bacterial overgrowth, may lead to malabsorption.

Diarrhoea often responds to dietary advice to eat small, dry meals with a reduced intake of refined carbohydrates. Antidiarrhoeal drugs such as codeine phosphate (15–30 mg 4–6 times a day) or loperamide (2 mg after each loose stool) are often helpful.

Weight loss. Most patients lose weight shortly after surgery and 30–40% are unable to regain all the weight which is lost. The usual cause is reduced intake because of a small gastric remnant, but diarrhoea and mild steatorrhoea also contribute.

Anaemia. Anaemia is common many years after subtotal gastrectomy. Although iron deficiency is the most common cause, folic acid and B_{12} deficiency are also seen. Inadequate dietary intake of iron and folate, lack of acid and intrinsic factor secretion, mild chronic low-grade blood loss from the gastric remnant and recurrent ulceration are responsible.

Metabolic bone disease. Both osteoporosis and osteomalacia occur as a consequence of calcium and vitamin D malabsorption.

Gastric cancer. An increased risk of gastric cancer has been reported from several epidemiological studies. The risk is highest in those with hypochlorhydria, duodenogastric reflux of bile, smoking and *H. pylori* infection. Although the relative risk is increased, the absolute risk of cancer remains low and endoscopic surveillance is not indicated following gastric surgery.

Complications of peptic ulcer disease

These are perforation, gastric outlet obstruction and bleeding.

Perforation

When free perforation occurs, the contents of the stomach escape into the peritoneal cavity, leading to peritonitis. Perforation occurs more commonly in duodenal than in gastric ulcers, and usually in ulcers on the anterior wall. About one-quarter of all perforations occur in acute ulcers and NSAIDs are often incriminated.

Clinical features. Perforation is often the first sign of ulcer, and a history of recurrent epigastric pain is uncommon. The most striking symptom is sudden, severe pain; its distribution follows the spread of the gastric contents over the peritoneum. Pain initially develops in the upper abdomen and rapidly becomes generalised; shoulder tip pain is due to irritation of the diaphragm. The pain is accompanied by shallow respiration due to limitation of diaphragmatic movements, and by shock. The abdomen is held immobile and there is generalised 'board-like' rigidity. Intestinal sounds are absent and liver dullness to percussion decreases due to the presence of gas under the diaphragm. After some hours symptoms may improve, although abdominal rigidity remains. Later the patient's condition deteriorates as general peritonitis develops.

In at least 50% of cases an erect chest radiograph shows free air beneath the diaphragm. If not, a water-soluble contrast swallow will confirm leakage of gastroduodenal contents.

Management and prognosis. After resuscitation, the acute perforation is treated surgically, either by simple closure, or by converting the perforation into a pyloroplasty if it is large. On rare occasions a 'Polya' partial gastrectomy is required. Following surgery *H. pylori* is treated (if present) and NSAIDs are avoided.

Perforation carries a mortality of 25%. This high figure reflects the high age and comorbidity of this population.

Gastric outlet obstruction

The causes are shown in Box 17.34. The most common is an ulcer in the region of the pylorus.

Clinical features. Nausea, vomiting and abdominal distension are the cardinal features of gastric outlet obstruction. Large quantities of gastric content are often vomited, and food eaten 24 hours or more previously may be recognised.

Physical examination frequently shows evidence of wasting and dehydration. A succussion splash may be elicited 4 hours or more after the last meal or drink. Visible gastric peristalsis is diagnostic of gastric outlet obstruction.

Investigations. Loss of gastric contents leads to dehydration with low serum chloride and potassium, and raised serum bicarbonate and urea concentrations. This results in enhanced renal absorption of Na^+ in exchange for H^+ and paradoxical aciduria. Nasogastric aspiration of at least 200 ml of fluid from the stomach after an overnight fast suggests the diagnosis.

Endoscopy should be performed after the stomach has been emptied by a wide-bore nasogastric tube. Endoscopic balloon dilatation of benign stenoses may be possible in some patients. In gastroparesis the pylorus is normal and the endoscope can be passed easily into the duodenum.

Barium studies are rarely advisable because they cannot usually distinguish between peptic ulcer and cancer. Moreover, barium remains in the stomach and is difficult to remove.

Management. Nasogastric suction and intravenous correction of dehydration are undertaken. In severe cases at least 4 litres of isotonic saline and 80 mmol of potassium may

17.34 DIFFERENTIAL DIAGNOSIS AND MANAGEMENT OF GASTRIC OUTLET OBSTRUCTION	
Cause	**Management**
Fibrotic stricture from duodenal ulcer, i.e. 'pyloric stenosis'	Balloon dilatation or surgery
Oedema from pyloric channel or duodenal ulcer	Medical therapy
Carcinoma of antrum	Surgery
Adult hypertrophic pyloric stenosis	Surgery
Gastroparesis	Investigate cause, prokinetic drugs

be necessary during the first 24 hours. Correction of metabolic alkalosis is not required. In some patients proton pump inhibitor drugs heal ulcers, relieve pyloric oedema and overcome the need for surgery. In others partial gastrectomy is necessary although this is best done after a 7-day period of nasogastric aspiration which enables the stomach to return to normal size. A gastroenterostomy is an alternative operation but patients will then require long-term proton pump inhibitor therapy to prevent stomal ulceration unless a vagotomy is also carried out.

Bleeding
See pages 764–766.

ISSUES IN OLDER PEOPLE
PEPTIC ULCER DISEASE

- Gastroduodenal ulcers have a manyfold greater incidence, admission rate and mortality in older people.
- This results from the high prevalence of *H. pylori* and NSAID use, and impaired defence mechanisms.
- Pain and dyspepsia are frequently absent or atypical so older people develop complications such as bleeding or perforation more frequently.
- When bleeding does occur, older patients require more intensive management (including central venous pressure measurement) than younger patients because they tolerate hypovolaemic shock poorly.

ZOLLINGER—ELLISON SYNDROME

This is a rare disorder characterised by the triad of severe peptic ulceration, gastric acid hypersecretion and a non-beta cell islet tumour of the pancreas ('gastrinoma'). It probably accounts for about 0.1% of all cases of duodenal ulceration. The syndrome occurs in either sex at any age, although it is most common between 30 and 50 years of age.

Pathophysiology
The gastrinoma secretes large amounts of gastrin, which stimulates the parietal cells of the stomach to secrete acid to their maximal capacity and increases the parietal cell mass three- to sixfold. Pentagastrin does not increase the secretory rate much above basal values because the stomach is maximally secreting. The acid output may be so great that it reaches the upper small intestine, reducing the luminal pH to 2 or less. Pancreatic lipase is inactivated and bile acids are precipitated. Diarrhoea and steatorrhoea result.

Pathology
Around 90% of tumours occur in the pancreatic head or proximal duodenal wall, the latter site being more common. At least half are multiple, and tumour size can vary from 1 mm to 20 cm. Approximately one-half to two-thirds are malignant but are often slow-growing. Of these patients, 20–60% also have adenomas of the parathyroid and pituitary glands (multiple endocrine neoplasia, MEN type I; see p. 688).

Clinical features
Peptic ulcers are multiple, severe and may occur in unusual sites such as the post-bulbar duodenum, jejunum or oesophagus. There is a poor response to standard ulcer therapy. The

history is usually short; bleeding and perforations are common. The syndrome may present as severe recurrent ulceration following a standard operation for peptic ulcer. Diarrhoea is seen in one-third or more of patients and can be the presenting feature. The diagnosis should be suspected in all patients with unusual or severe peptic ulceration, especially if a barium meal shows abnormally coarse gastric mucosal folds.

Investigations
Hypersecretion of acid under basal conditions with little increase following pentagastrin may be confirmed by gastric aspiration. Serum gastrin levels are grossly elevated (10- to 1000-fold). Injection of the hormone secretin normally causes no change or a slight decrease in circulating gastrin concentrations, but in Zollinger–Ellison syndrome there is a paradoxical dramatic increase in gastrin. Tumour localisation is best achieved by endoscopic ultrasound and use of radio-labelled somatostatin receptor scintigraphy.

Management
Approximately 30% of small and single tumours can be localised and resected but many tumours are multifocal. Some patients present with metastatic disease and surgery is inappropriate. Proton pump inhibitors have made total gastrectomy unnecessary and in the majority of patients continuous therapy with omeprazole heals ulcers and alleviates diarrhoea. Larger doses (60–80 mg daily) than those used to treat duodenal ulcer are required. The synthetic somatostatin analogue, octreotide, given by subcutaneous injection, reduces gastrin secretion and is sometimes of value. Overall 5-year survival is 60–75% and all patients should be monitored for the later development of other manifestations of MEN I.

FUNCTIONAL DISORDERS

NON-ULCER DYSPEPSIA

This is defined as chronic dyspepsia (pain or upper abdominal discomfort) with no evidence of organic disease on investigation (which must include endoscopy). Other commonly reported symptoms include early satiety, fullness, bloating and nausea. 'Ulcer-like' and 'dysmotility-type' subgroups are reported, but there is great overlap between these and also with irritable bowel syndrome, which often coexists.

Aetiology
The condition of non-ulcer dyspepsia probably covers a spectrum of mucosal, motility and psychiatric disorders.

Clinical features
Patients are usually young (< 40 years) and women are affected twice as commonly as men. Abdominal pain is associated with a variable combination of other 'dyspeptic' symptoms, the most common being nausea and bloating after meals. Morning symptoms are characteristic and pain or nausea may occur on waking. Direct enquiry may elicit symptoms suggestive of irritable bowel syndrome. Peptic

ulcer disease must be considered, whilst in older subjects intra-abdominal malignancy is a prime concern.

There are no diagnostic signs, apart perhaps from inappropriate tenderness on abdominal palpation. Symptoms may appear disproportionate to clinical well-being and there is no weight loss. Patients often appear anxious and usually distraught, and it is sometimes possible to detect psychological symptoms.

A drug history should be taken and the possibility of a depressive illness should be considered. Pregnancy should be ruled out in young women before radiological studies are undertaken. Alcohol misuse should be suspected when early morning nausea and retching are prominent.

Investigations

The history will often suggest the diagnosis but in older subjects an endoscopy is necessary to exclude mucosal disease. While an ultrasound scan may detect gallstones, these are rarely responsible for dyspeptic symptoms.

Management

The most important elements are explanation and reassurance. Possible psychological factors should be explored and the concept of psychological influences on gut function should be explained. Idiosyncratic and restrictive diets are of little benefit, but fat restriction may help.

Drug treatment is not especially successful but merits trial. Antacids are sometimes helpful. Prokinetic drugs such as metoclopramide (10 mg 8-hourly) or domperidone (10–20 mg 8-hourly) may be given before meals if nausea, vomiting or bloating is prominent. Metoclopramide may induce extrapyramidal side-effects, including tardive dyskinesia in young subjects. H_2-receptor antagonist drugs may be tried if night pain or heartburn is troublesome. Low-dose amitriptyline is sometimes of value. The role of *H. pylori* eradication remains controversial, although a minority (up to 20%) may benefit.

Symptoms which can be associated with an identifiable cause of stress (impending marriage or divorce, or financial or employment difficulties, for example) resolve with appropriate counselling. Some patients have major chronic psychological disorders resulting in persistent or recurrent symptoms and need behavioural or other formal psychotherapy (see p. 256).

FUNCTIONAL CAUSES OF VOMITING

Psychogenic vomiting may occur in anxiety neurosis. It starts usually on wakening or immediately after breakfast; only rarely does it occur later in the day. The disorder is probably a reaction to facing up to the worries of everyday life; in the young it can be due to school phobia. There may be retching alone or the vomiting of gastric secretions or food. Although functional vomiting may occur regularly over long periods, there is little or no weight loss. Early morning vomiting also occurs in pregnancy, alcohol misuse and depression.

In all patients it is essential to exclude other common causes (see p. 763). Tranquillisers and antiemetic drugs (e.g.

metoclopramide 10 mg 8-hourly, domperidone 10 mg 8-hourly, prochlorperazine 5–10 mg 8-hourly) have only a secondary place in management. Antidepressants in full dose may be effective (see p. 257).

TUMOURS OF THE STOMACH

GASTRIC CARCINOMA

Although the incidence of gastric cancer in the UK has fallen markedly in recent years, it remains the leading cause of cancer death world-wide. There is marked geographical variation in incidence. It is extremely common in China, Japan and parts of South America (mortality rate 30–40 per 100 000), less common in the UK (12–13 deaths per 100 000) and uncommon in the USA. Studies of Japanese migrants to the USA have revealed a much lower incidence in second-generation migrants, confirming the importance of environmental factors. Gastric cancer is more common in men and the incidence rises sharply after 50 years of age.

Aetiology

H. pylori is associated with chronic atrophic gastritis and gastric cancer (see Fig. 17.33). *H. pylori* infection may be responsible for 60–70% of cases and acquisition of infection at an early age may be important. Although the majority of *H. pylori*-infected individuals have normal or increased acid secretion, a few become hypo- or achlorhydric and these people are thought to be at greatest risk. Chronic inflammation with generation of reactive oxygen species and depletion of the normally abundant antioxidant ascorbic acid are also important.

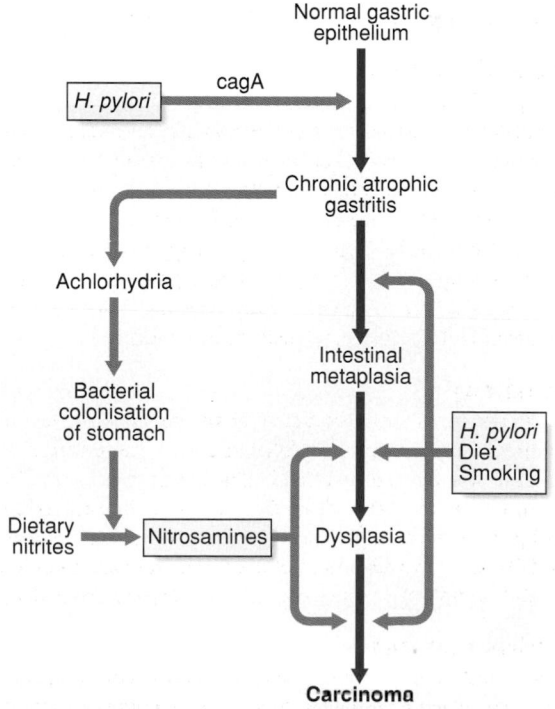

Fig. 17.33   Gastric carcinogenesis: a possible mechanism.

Diets rich in salted, smoked or pickled foods and the consumption of nitrites and nitrates are associated with cancer risk. Carcinogenic N-nitroso-compounds are formed from nitrates by the action of nitrite-reducing bacteria which colonise the achlorhydric stomach. Diets lacking fresh fruit and vegetables as well as vitamins C and A may also contribute.

Other recognised risk factors include smoking, heavy alcohol intake and a number of less common factors (see Box 17.35).

No predominant genetic abnormality has been identified, although cancer risk is increased two- to threefold in first-degree relatives of patients, and links with blood group A have been reported. Rare 'gastric cancer families' have also been described, in which diffuse gastric cancers occur in association with mutations of the E-cadherin gene. This is inherited as an autosomal dominant trait.

Pathology

Virtually all tumours are adenocarcinomas arising from mucus-secreting cells in the base of the gastric crypts. Most develop upon a background of chronic atrophic gastritis with intestinal metaplasia and dysplasia. Cancers are either 'intestinal', arising from areas of intestinal metaplasia with histological features reminiscent of intestinal epithelium, or 'diffuse', arising from normal gastric mucosa. Intestinal carcinomas are more common, and arise against a background of chronic mucosal injury. Diffuse cancers tend to be poorly differentiated and occur in younger patients.

Of gastric cancers, 50% occur in the antrum and 20–30% are situated in the gastric body, often on the greater curve. About 20% occur in the cardia and this type of tumour is becoming more common. Diffuse submucosal infiltration by a scirrhous cancer (linitis plastica) is uncommon. Macroscopically, tumours may be classified as polypoid, ulcerating, fungating or diffuse.

Early gastric cancer is defined as cancer confined to the mucosa or submucosa, regardless of lymph node involvement (see Fig. 17.34). It is often recognised in Japan, where widespread screening is practised. Over 80% of patients in the West present with advanced gastric cancer.

Clinical features

Early gastric cancer is usually asymptomatic but may occasionally be discovered during endoscopy for investigation of dyspepsia. Two-thirds of patients with advanced cancers have weight loss and 50% have ulcer-like pain. Anorexia and nausea occur in one-third, while early satiety, haematemesis, melaena and dyspepsia alone are less common features. Dysphagia occurs in tumours of the gastric cardia which obstruct the gastro-oesophageal junction. Anaemia from occult bleeding is also common.

Examination may reveal no abnormalities, but signs of weight loss, anaemia or a palpable epigastric mass are not infrequent. Jaundice or ascites may signify metastatic spread. Occasionally, tumour spread occurs to the supraclavicular lymph nodes (Troisier's sign), umbilicus ('Sister Joseph's

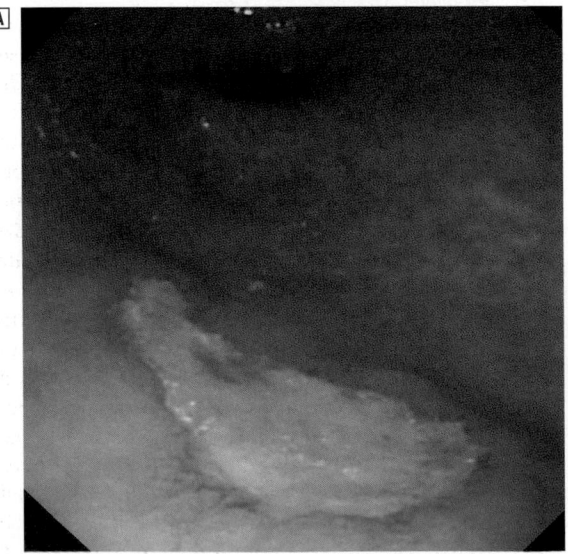

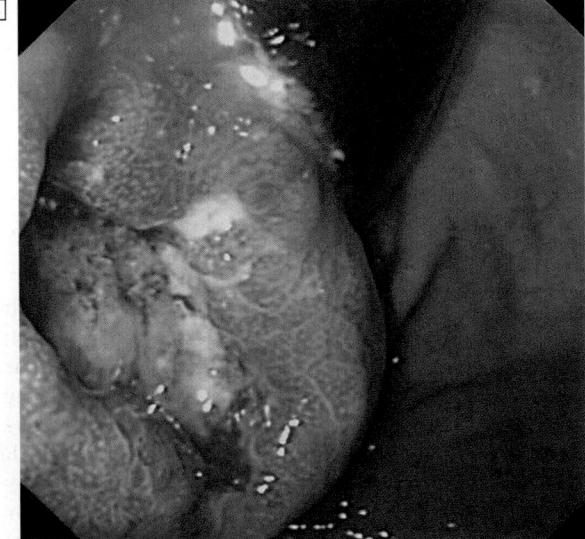

Fig. 17.34   Gastric carcinoma. A Endoscopic view of early cancer showing a shallow, depressed ulcer. B Advanced cancer seen as a large deep ulcer with rolled edges in the cardia.

nodule') or ovaries (Krukenberg tumour). Paraneoplastic phenomena, such as acanthosis nigricans, thrombophlebitis (Trousseau's sign) and dermatomyositis, occur rarely. Metastases occur most commonly in the liver, lungs, peritoneum and bone marrow.

Diagnosis and staging

There are no laboratory markers of sufficient accuracy for the diagnosis of gastric cancer. Upper gastrointestinal endoscopy is the investigation of choice and should be performed promptly in any dyspeptic patient with 'alarm features' (see p. 763). Multiple biopsies from the edge and base of a gastric ulcer are required and exfoliative brush cytology also improves the diagnostic yield. Barium meal is a poor alternative approach but any abnormalities must be followed by endoscopy to obtain biopsy. Once the diagnosis is made, further imaging is necessary for accurate staging and assessment of resectability. CT may not demonstrate small involved lymph nodes, but will show evidence of intra-abdominal spread or liver metastases. Even with these techniques, laparoscopy is required to determine whether the tumour is resectable as it is the only modality that will detect peritoneal spread.

Management

Surgery

Resection offers the only hope of cure, which can be achieved in 90% of patients with early gastric cancer. For the majority who have locally advanced disease radical and total gastrectomy with lymphadenectomy is the operation of choice, preserving the spleen if possible. Proximal tumours involving the oesophago-gastric junction require an associated distal oesophagectomy. Small distally sited tumours can be managed by a partial gastrectomy with lymphadenectomy and either a Billroth I or Roux-en-Y reconstruction. More extensive lymph node resection may increase survival rates but carries greater morbidity. Even for those who cannot be cured, palliative resection may be safely performed with low morbidity and may be necessary when patients present with bleeding or gastric outflow obstruction. Between 80 and 85% of tumours recur, particularly if serosal penetration has occurred, although complete removal of all macroscopic tumours combined with lymphadenectomy will achieve a 50–60% 5-year survival. Neoadjuvant chemotherapy (based on 5-fluorouracil) may improve survival rates, although post-operative radiotherapy has no value.

Unresectable tumours

The management of inoperable, locally advanced cancer is unsatisfactory. Modest palliation of symptoms can be achieved in some patients with chemotherapy using FAM (5-fluorouracil, doxorubicin and mitomycin C) or ECF (epirubicin, cisplatin and 5-fluorouracil). Endoscopic laser ablation of tumour tissue for control of dysphagia or recurrent bleeding benefits some patients. Carcinomas at the cardia may require endoscopic dilatation, laser therapy or insertion of expandable metallic stents to allow adequate swallowing.

Prognosis

Apart from patients with early gastric cancer overall prognosis remains very poor due to advanced stage at presentation, with less than 30% surviving 5 years. Thus the best hope for improved survival lies in greater detection of tumours at an earlier stage. The low incidence of gastric carcinoma in many Western countries makes widespread endoscopic screening impractical but urgent referral and investigation of patients with new-onset dyspepsia over the age of 55, or those with 'alarm' features, are essential. If the important association with *H. pylori* proves to be causal, this offers the possibility of gastric cancer prevention by widespread eradication of the infection.

GASTRIC LYMPHOMA

Primary gastric lymphoma accounts for less than 5% of all gastric malignancies. The stomach is, however, the most common site for extranodal non-Hodgkin's lymphoma and 60% of all primary gastrointestinal lymphomas occur at this site. Lymphoid tissue is not found in the normal stomach but lymphoid aggregates develop in the presence of *H. pylori* infection. Indeed, *H. pylori* infection is closely associated with the development of a low-grade lymphoma ('MALToma'). Superficial MALTomas may be cured by *H. pylori* eradication.

The clinical presentation is similar to that of gastric cancer and endoscopically the tumour appears as a polypoid or ulcerating mass. While initial treatment of low-grade MALTomas consists of *H. pylori* eradication and close observation, high-grade lymphomas are treated by combination chemotherapy, surgery and/or radiotherapy. The prognosis depends on the stage at diagnosis. Features predicting a favourable prognosis are stage I or II disease, small resectable tumours, those with low-grade histology, and age below 60 years.

OTHER TUMOURS OF THE STOMACH

Gastrointestinal stromal cell tumours (GIST) are occasionally found at upper gastrointestinal endoscopy. They are benign and usually asymptomatic but may occasionally be responsible for dyspepsia; they can also ulcerate and cause gastrointestinal bleeding. A variety of polyps occur. Hyperplastic polyps and fundic cystic gland polyps are common and of no consequence. Adenomatous polyps are rare; they may be pre-malignant and should be removed endoscopically.

Occasionally, gastric carcinoid tumours (see p. 801) are seen in the fundus and body in patients with long-standing pernicious anaemia. These benign tumours arise from enterochromaffin-like (ECL) or other endocrine cells, and are often multiple but rarely invasive. Unlike carcinoid tumours arising elsewhere in the gastrointestinal tract, they usually run a benign and favourable course. However, large (> 2 cm) carcinoids may metastasise and should be removed. Rarely, small nodules of ectopic pancreatic exocrine tissue are found. These 'pancreatic rests' may be mistaken for gastric neoplasms and usually cause no symptoms. Endoscopic ultrasound is the most useful investigation.

DISEASES OF THE SMALL INTESTINE

DISORDERS CAUSING MALABSORPTION

COELIAC DISEASE

Coeliac disease is an immunologically mediated inflammatory disorder of the small bowel occurring in genetically susceptible individuals. It can result in malabsorption and responds to a gluten-free diet. The condition occurs world-wide but is more common in northern Europe. The prevalence in the UK is between 1:1000 and 1:1500. Improved awareness of non-classical presentations and better serological tests for diagnosis, however, suggest that the true prevalence may be nearer 1:300 in northern Europe. Some of these are undiagnosed 'silent' cases and there are probably also many cases of 'latent' coeliac disease. These are asymptomatic, genetically susceptible people who may later develop clinical coeliac disease.

Pathogenesis

The precise mechanism of damage causing coeliac disease is unclear but immunological responses to gluten play a key role (see Fig. 17.35). As yet unidentified environmental agents probably trigger small bowel inflammation, allowing gluten peptides (gliadin) access to the enzyme tissue transglutaminase (TTG) in the lamina propria. TTG modifies gluten and this allows it to bind to the antigen-binding groove of major histocompatibility complex (MHC) class II molecules on the surface of antigen presenting cells (APC). In turn the modified gluten peptide is now recognised as antigenic by CD4+ T cells. A TH1 response ensues with release of pro-inflammatory cytokines (e.g. interleukin-1, TNF-α and interferon-γ). TTG is now recognised as the autoantigen for anti-endomysial antibodies.

Clinical features and associations

Coeliac disease presents at any age. In infancy it occurs after weaning on to cereals and often presents with classic features of diarrhoea, malabsorption and failure to thrive. It may be seen in older children with non-specific features such as delayed growth. Features of malnutrition are often found on examination and mild abdominal distension may be present. Affected children fail to thrive and have both growth and pubertal delay, leading to short stature in adulthood.

In adults peak onset is in the fifth decade and females are affected slightly more than males. The presentation is highly variable, depending on the severity and extent of small bowel involvement. Some patients have florid malabsorption while others develop non-specific symptoms such as tiredness, weight loss, folate deficiency or iron deficiency anaemia. Other recognised presentations include oral ulceration, dyspepsia and bloating.

Coeliac disease is associated with other human leucocyte antigen (HLA)-linked autoimmune disorders and with certain other diseases (see Box 17.36).

17.36 DISEASE ASSOCIATIONS OF COELIAC DISEASE

- Insulin-dependent diabetes mellitus (2–8%)
- Thyroid disease (5%)
- Primary biliary cirrhosis (3%)
- Sjögren's syndrome (3%)
- IgA deficiency (2%)
- Pernicious anaemia
- Inflammatory bowel disease
- Sarcoidosis
- Myasthenia gravis
- Neurological complications—encephalopathy, cerebellar atrophy, peripheral neuropathy, epilepsy

- Dermatitis herpetiformis
- Down's syndrome
- Enteropathy-associated T-cell lymphoma
- Small bowel carcinoma
- Squamous carcinoma of oesophagus
- Ulcerative jejunitis
- Pancreatic insufficiency
- Microscopic colitis
- Splenic atrophy

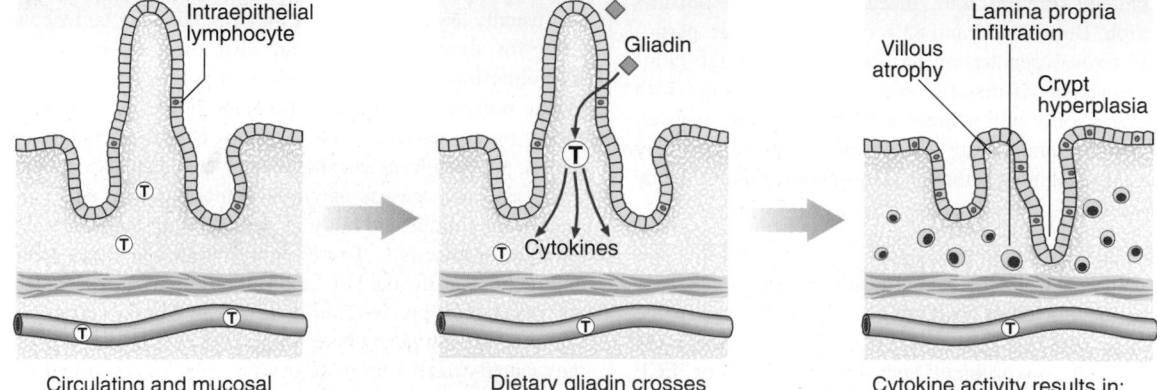

Circulating and mucosal T lymphocytes sensitised to gluten

Dietary gliadin crosses epithelium and interacts with T cells which release cytokines

Cytokine activity results in:
- Villous atrophy
- Crypt hyperplasia
- Increased intraepithelial lymphocytes
- Lamina propria infiltration

Fig. 17.35 Pathophysiology of coeliac disease.

Investigations

These are performed to confirm the diagnosis and to look for consequences of malabsorption.

Duodenal or jejunal biopsy

Endoscopic small bowel biopsy is the gold standard. The histological features are usually characteristic but other causes of villous atrophy should also be considered (see Box 17.37 and Fig. 17.36).

Antibodies

Serum antigliadin (especially IgA) and anti-endomysial antibodies are detectable in most untreated cases. IgA anti-endomysial antibodies are detected by immunofluorescence. They are not quantitative, but are more sensitive (85–95%) and specific (approximately 99%) for the diagnosis, except in very young infants. IgG antibodies, however, must be analysed in patients with coexisting IgA deficiency. TTG assays may replace other blood tests in the future as they are easier to perform, semi-quantitative and more accurate in patients with IgA deficiency. These antibody tests constitute valuable screening in patients with diarrhoea but are not a substitute for small bowel biopsy; they usually become negative with successful treatment.

Haematology and biochemistry

A full blood count may show microcytic or macrocytic anaemia from iron or folate deficiency and features of hyposplenism (target cells, spherocytes and Howell–Jolly

bodies). Biochemical tests may reveal reduced concentrations of calcium, magnesium, total protein, albumin or vitamin D.

Other investigations

These are usually unnecessary. Barium follow-through radiographs may show dilated loops of bowel, coarse or diminished folds and sometimes flocculation of contrast. Sugar tests of intestinal permeability are abnormal and a modest degree of fat malabsorption is usual. Newly diagnosed patients should undergo baseline measurement of bone density by dual energy X-ray absorptiometry (DEXA scan) to look for evidence of metabolic bone disease.

Management

The aims are to correct existing deficiencies of iron, folate, calcium and/or vitamin D, and to commence a life-long gluten-free diet. This requires the exclusion of wheat, rye, barley and initially oats although oats may be reintroduced safely in most patients. Rice, maize and potatoes are satisfactory sources of complex carbohydrates. Initially, frequent dietary counselling is required to make sure the diet is being observed, as the most common reason for failure to improve with dietary treatment is accidental or unrecognised gluten ingestion. Mineral and vitamin supplements are also given when indicated but are seldom necessary when a strict gluten-free diet is adhered to. Booklets produced by coeliac societies in many countries, containing diet sheets and recipes for the use of gluten-free flour, are of great value. Regular monitoring of symptoms, weight and nutrition is essential. Patients who have an excellent clinical response with disappearance of circulating anti-endomysial antibodies probably do not need to undergo repeat jejunal biopsies. These should be reserved for patients who do not symptomatically improve or whose antibodies remain persistently positive.

Rarely, patients are 'refractory' and require treatment with corticosteroids or immunosuppressive drugs to induce remission. Dietary compliance should be carefully assessed in patients who fail to respond but if their diet is satisfactory, other conditions such as pancreatic insufficiency or microscopic colitis should be sought, as should

17.37 IMPORTANT CAUSES OF SUBTOTAL VILLOUS ATROPHY 
• Coeliac disease
• Tropical sprue
• Dermatitis herpetiformis
• Lymphoma
• AIDS enteropathy
• Giardiasis
• Hypogammaglobulinaemia
• Radiation
• Whipple's disease
• Zollinger–Ellison syndrome

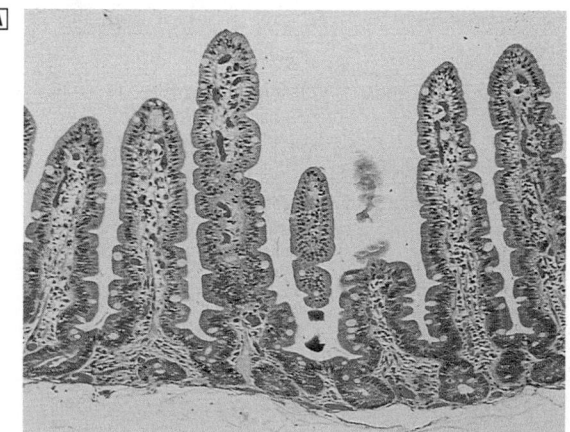

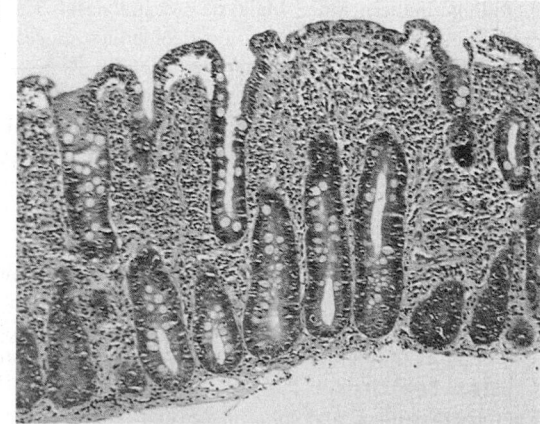

Fig. 17.36 Jejunal mucosa. [A] Normal. [B] Jejunum in coeliac disease showing subtotal villous atrophy and marked inflammatory infiltrate.

complications of coeliac disease such as ulcerative jejunitis or enteropathy-associated T-cell lymphoma.

Prognosis and complications

There is an increased risk of malignancy, particularly of enteropathy-associated T-cell lymphoma, small bowel carcinoma and squamous carcinoma of the oesophagus. A few patients develop ulcerative jejunoileitis characterised by deep ulcers in the jejunum with malabsorption. Fever, pain, obstruction or perforation may supervene. The diagnosis is rarely made by barium studies or enteroscopy, and laparotomy and full-thickness biopsy are necessary.

Treatment is difficult. Steroids are used with mixed success and some patients require surgical resection and parenteral nutrition. The course is often progressive and relentless.

Metabolic bone disease is common in patients with long-standing, poorly controlled coeliac disease and is a source of considerable morbidity. This complication is less common in patients who adhere strictly to a gluten-free diet.

DERMATITIS HERPETIFORMIS

This is characterised by crops of intensely itchy blisters over extensor surfaces of the limbs and back. Immunofluorescence shows granular or linear IgA deposition at the dermo-epidermal junction. Almost all patients have partial villous atrophy on jejunal biopsy, even though they usually have no gastrointestinal symptoms. In contrast, fewer than 10% of coeliac patients have evidence of dermatitis herpetiformis although both disorders are associated with the same histocompatibility antigen groups. The rash usually responds to a gluten-free diet but some patients require additional treatment with dapsone (100–150 mg daily).

TROPICAL SPRUE

Tropical sprue is defined as chronic, progressive malabsorption in a patient in or from the tropics, associated with abnormalities of small intestinal structure and function.

Aetiology

The disease occurs mainly in the West Indies and in Asia, including southern India, Malaysia and Indonesia. The epidemiological pattern and occasional epidemics suggest that an infective agent or agents may be involved. Although no single bacterium has been isolated, the condition often begins after an acute diarrhoeal illness. Small bowel bacterial overgrowth with *Escherichia coli*, *Enterobacter* and *Klebsiella* is frequently seen.

Pathology

The changes closely resemble those of coeliac disease. Partial villous atrophy is more common than subtotal villous atrophy.

Clinical features

There is diarrhoea, abdominal distension, anorexia, fatigue and weight loss. In visitors to the tropics the onset of severe diarrhoea may be sudden and accompanied by fever. When the disorder becomes chronic, the features of megaloblastic anaemia from folic acid malabsorption and other deficiencies are common. Remissions and relapses may occur. There may be oedema, glossitis and stomatitis.

The differential diagnosis in the indigenous tropical population is an infective cause of diarrhoea. The important differential diagnosis in visitors to the tropics is giardiasis (see p. 46).

Management

Tetracycline 250 mg 6-hourly for 28 days is the treatment of choice and brings about long-term remission or cure. In most patients pharmacological doses of folic acid (5 mg daily) improve symptoms and jejunal morphology. In some cases treatment must be prolonged before improvement occurs, and occasionally patients must leave the tropics.

SMALL BOWEL BACTERIAL OVERGROWTH ('BLIND LOOP SYNDROME')

The normal duodenum and jejunum contain less than 10^4/ml organisms which are usually derived from saliva. The count of coliform organisms never exceeds 10^3/ml. In bacterial overgrowth there may be 10^8–10^{10}/ml organisms, and these are bacteria which are normally found only in the colon. Disorders which impair the normal physiological mechanisms controlling bacterial proliferation in the intestine predispose to bacterial overgrowth (see Box 17.38). The most important are loss of gastric acidity, impaired intestinal motility and structural abnormalities which allow colonic bacteria to gain access to the small intestine or provide a secluded haven from the peristaltic stream.

Clinical features

The patient presents with watery diarrhoea and/or steatorrhoea with anaemia due to B_{12} deficiency. These arise because of deconjugation of bile acids, which impairs micelle formation, and because of bacterial utilisation of vitamin B_{12}. There may also be symptoms from the underlying intestinal cause.

17.38 CAUSES OF SMALL BOWEL BACTERIAL OVERGROWTH	
Mechanism	**Examples**
Hypo- or achlorhydria	Pernicious anaemia Partial gastrectomy Long-term proton pump inhibitor therapy
Impaired intestinal motility	Scleroderma Diabetic autonomic neuropathy Chronic intestinal pseudo-obstruction
Structural abnormalities	Gastric surgery (blind loop after Billroth II operation) Jejunal diverticulosis Enterocolic fistulae (e.g. Crohn's disease) Extensive small bowel resection Strictures (e.g. Crohn's disease)
Impaired immune function	Hypogammaglobulinaemia

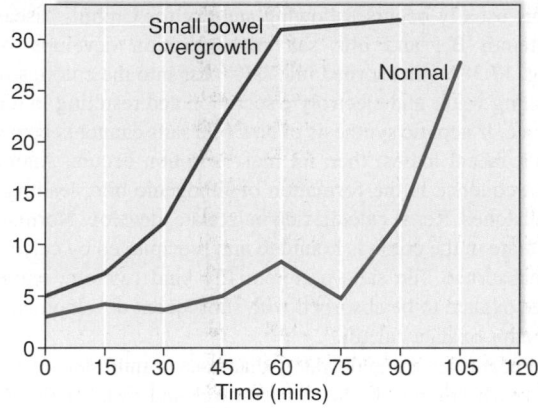

Breath H$_2$ (PPM)

Fig. 17.37 Early rise in breath hydrogen in small bowel bacterial overgrowth. Breath samples are analysed after ingestion of glucose. Bacteria within the small bowel release hydrogen as the glucose is digested.

Investigations

Serum vitamin B$_{12}$ concentration is low, whilst folate levels are normal or elevated because the bacteria produce folic acid. Barium follow-through or small bowel enema may reveal blind loops or fistulae. Endoscopic duodenal biopsies exclude mucosal disease such as coeliac disease. During endoscopy, aspiration of jejunal contents for bacteriological examination is carried out; the laboratory analysis requires anaerobic and aerobic culture techniques. The diagnosis can often be made non-invasively using the glucose hydrogen or ^{14}C-glycocholic acid breath tests. In these tests breath samples are serially measured after oral ingestion of the test material. Bacteria within the small bowel cause an early rise in breath hydrogen from glucose (see Fig. 17.37) or ^{14}C from ^{14}C-glycocholate.

Management

The underlying cause of small bowel bacterial overgrowth should be addressed. Tetracycline 250 mg 6-hourly for 7 days is the treatment of choice, although up to 50% of patients do not respond adequately. Metronidazole 400 mg 8-hourly or ciprofloxacin 250 mg 12-hourly are alternatives. Some patients require up to 4 weeks of treatment and, in a few, continuous rotating courses of antibiotics are necessary. Intramuscular vitamin B$_{12}$ supplementation is needed in chronic cases.

Some specific causes of bacterial overgrowth
(see Box 17.38)

Jejunal diverticulosis

This is sometimes seen on barium follow-through examinations in patients over the age of 50 years. The diverticula are usually asymptomatic but predispose to bacterial overgrowth and subsequent malabsorption. Rarely, they may cause acute or chronic gastrointestinal bleeding, obstruction or perforation.

Diabetic diarrhoea

This results from diabetic autonomic neuropathy (see p. 676), which reduces small bowel motility and affects enterocyte secretion. In some diabetic patients coexisting pancreatic insufficiency or coeliac disease may be responsible. The diarrhoea is watery. It may be continuous or interrupted by bouts of constipation. It is often worse at night, frequently associated with faecal incontinence and may be refractory to antidiarrhoeal drugs. Treatment with antibiotics may be helpful but antidiarrhoeal drugs (diphenoxylate 5 mg 8-hourly orally or loperamide 2 mg 4–6-hourly orally) or opiates are usually needed. The α$_2$-adrenergic agonist clonidine (50–100 μg 8-hourly) or the somatostatin analogue octreotide may benefit some patients.

Progressive systemic sclerosis (scleroderma)

The circular and longitudinal layers of the intestinal muscle are fibrosed, motility is abnormal and malabsorption due to bacterial overgrowth is common. The patient may also have features of chronic intestinal pseudo-obstruction (see p. 1037).

Hypogammaglobulinaemia

This rare disorder is characterised by a markedly reduced or absent IgA and IgM content in the serum and jejunal secretions. Chronic diarrhoea, malabsorption and respiratory infections are common. Diarrhoea is due to bacterial overgrowth and recurrent gastrointestinal infections (particularly giardiasis).

The diagnosis is made by measurement of serum immunoglobulins and by intestinal biopsy which shows reduced or absent plasma cells and nodules of lymphoid tissue (nodular lymphoid hyperplasia). Some patients have the histological features of coeliac disease. Treatment involves control of giardiasis (see p. 46) and, if necessary, regular parenteral replacement of immunoglobulins.

WHIPPLE'S DISEASE

This rare condition is characterised by infiltration of small intestinal mucosa by 'foamy' macrophages which stain positive with periodic acid-Schiff (PAS) reagent. The disease is a multisystem one and almost any organ can be affected, sometimes long before gastrointestinal involvement becomes apparent (see Box 17.39).

Electron microscopy reveals small Gram-positive bacilli (*Tropheryma whippelli*) within the macrophages. Villi are widened and flattened; densely packed macrophages occur in the lamina propria. These may obstruct lymphatic drainage, causing fat malabsorption.

Clinical features

Middle-aged men are most commonly affected and the presentation depends on the pattern of organ involvement. Low-grade fever is common and most patients have joint symptoms to some degree. Occasionally, neurological manifestations may predominate.

Management

Whipple's disease is often fatal if untreated but responds well, at least initially, to penicillin, tetracycline or sulphonamides.

17.39 CLINICAL FEATURES OF WHIPPLE'S DISEASE	
Gastrointestinal	
• Diarrhoea, steatorrhoea, weight loss, bloating, protein-losing enteropathy, ascites, hepatosplenomegaly (< 5%)	
Musculoskeletal	
• Seronegative large joint arthropathy, sacroiliitis	
Cardiac	
• Pericarditis (10%), myocarditis, endocarditis, coronary arteritis	
Neurological	
• Apathy, fits, dementia, myoclonus, meningitis, cranial nerve lesions	
Pulmonary	
• Chronic cough, pleurisy, pulmonary infiltrates	
Haematological	
• Anaemia, lymphadenopathy	
Other	
• Fever, pigmentation	

Symptoms resolve within a week and biopsy changes revert to normal in a few weeks. Long-term follow-up is essential, as relapse occurs in up to one-third of patients. This often occurs within the central nervous system, in which case 2 weeks of parenteral penicillin and co-trimoxazole, followed by 6–12 months of oral co-trimoxazole, are necessary.

INTESTINAL RESECTION

The long-term effects of small bowel resection depend on the site and the amount of intestine resected, and vary from trivial to life-threatening.

Ileal resection

This usually occurs following surgery for Crohn's disease. Vitamin B_{12} and bile salt malabsorption develops (see Fig. 17.38). Unabsorbed bile salts pass into the colon, stimulating water and electrolyte secretion and resulting in diarrhoea. If hepatic synthesis of new bile salts cannot keep pace with faecal losses, then fat malabsorption occurs. Another consequence is the formation of lithogenic bile, leading to gallstones. Renal calculi, rich in oxalate, develop. Normally, oxalate in the colon is bound to and precipitated by calcium. Unabsorbed bile salts preferentially bind calcium, leaving free oxalate to be absorbed with subsequent development of urinary oxalate calculi.

Patients have urgent watery diarrhoea or mild steatorrhoea. Contrast studies of the small bowel and tests of B_{12} and bile acid absorption (see pp. 760–761) are useful investigations. Parenteral vitamin B_{12} supplementation is necessary. Diarrhoea usually responds well to colestyramine, a resin which binds bile salts in the intestinal lumen. Aluminium hydroxide may also do this in those unable to tolerate colestyramine.

Massive resection (short bowel syndrome)

Short bowel syndrome is defined as malabsorption resulting from extensive small intestinal resection. Many factors determine the severity, including the extent and site of resection, the presence of underlying disease in the remaining intestine, the presence of the ileocaecal valve and the ability of the remaining small intestine to undergo 'adaptation'.

Aetiology and pathogenesis

The syndrome has many causes (see Box 17.40) but in adults it usually results from extensive surgery undertaken for Crohn's disease or mesenteric infarction.

Loss of surface area for digestion and absorption is the key problem. These processes are normally completed within the first 100 cm of jejunum, and enteral feeding is

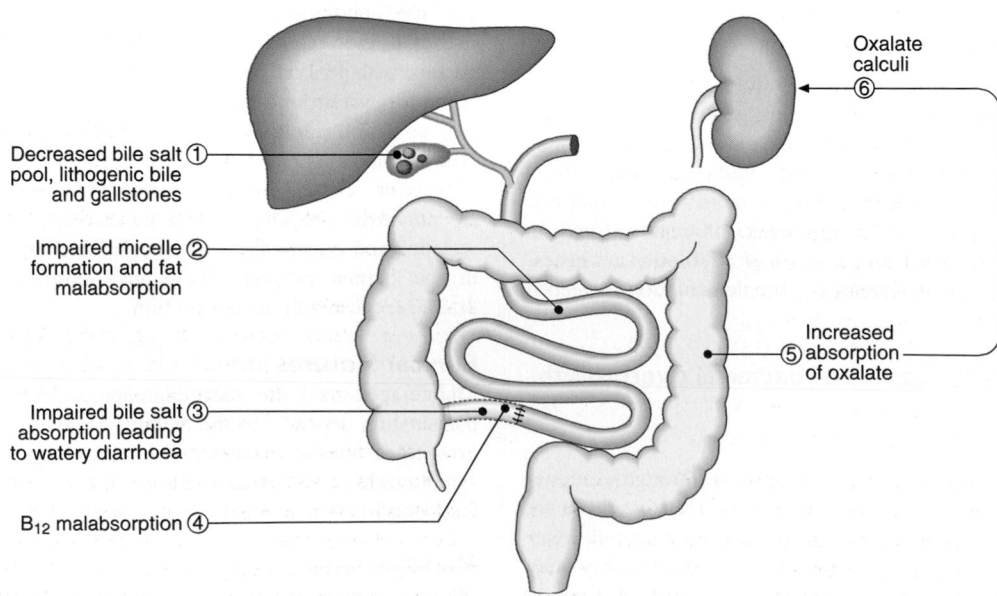

Fig. 17.38 Consequences of ileal resection.

option in some patients but rejection and 'graft-versus-host' disease (see p. 934) remain significant hurdles to be overcome.

17.40 AETIOLOGY OF SHORT BOWEL SYNDROME
Children

• Congenital anomalies (e.g. mid-gut volvulus, atresia)	• Necrotising enterocolitis

Adults	
• Crohn's disease	• Radiation enteritis
• Mesenteric infarction	• Volvulus

usually possible if this amount of small intestine remains. The proximal small bowel normally reabsorbs around 8 of the 9 litres of fluid it receives daily, and patients with a high jejunostomy are at great risk of hypovolaemia, dehydration and electrolyte losses. The presence of some or all of the colon may markedly improve these losses by increased water reabsorption. The presence of an intact ileocaecal valve ameliorates the clinical picture by slowing small intestinal transit and reducing bacterial overgrowth. The remaining small bowel mucosa undergoes 'adaptation', whereby mucosal hyperplasia over months or years increases the effective surface area for absorption.

Clinical features

Severely affected patients have large volumes of jejunostomy fluid losses or, if the colon is preserved, diarrhoea and steatorrhoea. Dehydration and signs of hypovolaemia are common, as are weight loss, loss of muscle bulk and malnutrition. Some patients remain in satisfactory but precarious fluid balance until a minor intercurrent illness or intestinal upset occurs, when they can rapidly become dehydrated.

Management

In the immediate post-operative period, total parenteral nutrition (TPN) is started. Proton pump inhibitor therapy is given to reduce gastric secretions. Enteral feeding is cautiously introduced after 1–2 weeks under careful supervision and is slowly increased as tolerated.

The principles of long-term management are:

- Detailed nutritional assessments at regular intervals.
- Monitoring of fluid and electrolyte balance. Patients can usually be taught how to do this for themselves. A readily available supply of oral rehydration solution is useful for intercurrent illness.
- Adequate calorie and protein intake. Fats are a good energy source and should be taken as tolerated. Medium-chain triglyceride supplements are often given first because they are more easily absorbed.
- Replacement of B_{12}, calcium, vitamin D, magnesium, zinc and folic acid.
- Antidiarrhoeal agents, e.g. loperamide (2–4 mg 6-hourly) or codeine phosphate (30 mg 4–6-hourly).

Some patients are unable to maintain positive fluid balance. Octreotide (50–200 μg 8–12-hourly by subcutaneous injection) reduces gastrointestinal secretions and is useful in such individuals. Despite these measures, some patients require long-term home TPN for survival and this is best managed in specialist centres. Small bowel transplantation is an

RADIATION ENTERITIS AND PROCTOCOLITIS

Intestinal damage occurs in 10–15% of patients undergoing radiotherapy for abdominal or pelvic malignancy. The risk varies with total dose, dosing schedule and the use of concomitant chemotherapy.

Pathology

The rectum, sigmoid colon and terminal ileum are most frequently involved. Radiation causes acute inflammation, shortening of villi, oedema and crypt abscess formation. These usually resolve completely but in some patients an obliterative endarteritis affecting the endothelium of submucosal arterioles develops over 2–12 months. Fibroblastic proliferation produces progressive ischaemic fibrosis over years and may lead to adhesions, ulceration, strictures, obstruction or fistula to adjacent organs.

Clinical features

In the acute phase there is nausea, vomiting, cramping abdominal pain and diarrhoea. When the rectum and colon are involved, rectal mucus, bleeding and tenesmus occur. The chronic phase develops after 5–10 years in some patients and produces one or more of the problems listed in Box 17.41.

17.41 CHRONIC COMPLICATIONS OF INTESTINAL IRRADIATION
• Proctocolitis
• Bleeding from telangiectasia
• Small bowel strictures
• Fistulae—rectovaginal, colovesical, enterocolic
• Adhesions
• Malabsorption—bacterial overgrowth, bile salt malabsorption (ileal damage)

Investigations

In the acute phase the rectal changes at sigmoidoscopy resemble those of ulcerative proctitis (see Fig. 17.50, p. 813). The extent of the lesion is determined by colonoscopy. Barium follow-through examination shows small bowel strictures, ulcers and fistulae.

Management

Diarrhoea in the acute phase is treated with codeine phosphate, diphenoxylate or loperamide in standard dosage. Local steroid enemas help proctitis, and antibiotics may be required for bacterial overgrowth. Nutritional supplements are necessary when malabsorption is present. Colestyramine (4 g as a single sachet) is useful for bile salt malabsorption. Endoscopic laser or argon plasma coagulation therapy may reduce bleeding from proctitis. Surgery should be avoided, if possible, because the injured intestine is difficult to resect and anastomose, but it may be necessary for obstruction, perforation or fistula.

ABETALIPOPROTEINAEMIA

This rare autosomal recessive disorder results from deficiency of apolipoprotein B and subsequent failure of chylomicron formation. It leads to fat malabsorption and deficiency of fat-soluble vitamins. Jejunal biopsy reveals enterocytes distended with resynthesised triglyceride and normal villous morphology. Serum cholesterol and triglyceride levels are low. A number of other abnormalities occur in this syndrome, including acanthocytosis, retinitis pigmentosa and a progressive neurological disorder with cerebellar and dorsal column signs. Symptoms may be improved by a low-fat diet supplemented with medium-chain triglycerides and vitamins A, D, E and K.

ISSUES IN OLDER PEOPLE
MALABSORPTION

- The following apply to coeliac disease in old age:
  — It tends to present with vague symptoms such as dyspepsia or isolated folate or iron deficiency; only 25% present classically with diarrhoea and weight loss.
  — Severe osteopenia and osteomalacia, or bleeding due to hypothrombinaemia are more common than in the young.
  — Small bowel lymphoma is more common when coeliac disease develops in the elderly.
- Small bowel bacterial overgrowth is more prevalent in older than younger people because:
  — atrophic gastritis resulting in hypo- or achlorhydria becomes more prevalent with age
  — jejunal diverticulosis is prevalent in old age
  — the long-term effects of gastric surgery for ulcer disease are now being seen in older people.

MOTILITY DISORDERS

CHRONIC INTESTINAL PSEUDO-OBSTRUCTION

Small intestinal motility is disordered in conditions which affect the smooth muscle or nerves of the intestine. Many cases are 'primary' (idiopathic), while others are 'secondary' to a variety of disorders or drugs (see Box 17.42).

Clinical features

There are recurrent episodes of nausea, vomiting, abdominal discomfort and distension, often worse after food.

17.42 CAUSES OF CHRONIC INTESTINAL PSEUDO-OBSTRUCTION
Primary or idiopathic
• Rare familial visceral myopathies or neuropathies
• Congenital aganglionosis
Secondary
• Drugs, e.g. opiates, tricyclic antidepressants, phenothiazines
• Smooth muscle disorders, e.g. scleroderma, amyloidosis, mitochondrial myopathies
• Myenteric plexus disorders, e.g. paraneoplastic syndrome in small-cell lung cancer
• CNS disorders, e.g. Parkinsonism, autonomic neuropathy
• Endocrine and metabolic disorders, e.g. hypothyroidism, phaeochromocytoma, acute intermittent porphyria

Alternating constipation and diarrhoea occur and weight loss results from malabsorption (due to bacterial overgrowth) and fear of eating. There may also be symptoms of dysmotility affecting other parts of the gastrointestinal tract, e.g. dysphagia, and, in primary cases, features of bladder dysfunction. Some patients have obscure but severe abdominal pain which is extremely difficult to manage.

Investigations

The diagnosis is often delayed and a high index of suspicion is needed. Plain radiographs show distended loops of bowel and air-fluid levels but barium studies demonstrate no mechanical obstruction. Laparotomy is sometimes performed to exclude obstruction and to obtain full-thickness biopsies of the intestine. Electron microscopy, histochemistry and special stains define rare, specific syndromes.

Management

This is often difficult. Underlying causes should be addressed and further surgery avoided if at all possible. Metoclopramide or domperidone may enhance motility, and antibiotics are given for bacterial overgrowth. Nutritional and psychological support are also necessary.

MISCELLANEOUS DISORDERS OF THE SMALL INTESTINE

PROTEIN-LOSING ENTEROPATHY

This term is used when there is excessive loss of protein into the gut lumen, sufficient to cause hypoproteinaemia. Less than 10% of plasma protein is normally lost from the gastrointestinal tract. Protein-losing enteropathy occurs in many gut disorders but is most common in those where ulceration occurs (see Box 17.43). In other disorders protein loss results from increased mucosal permeability or obstruction of intestinal lymphatic vessels.

Patients present with peripheral oedema and hypoproteinaemia in the presence of normal liver function and without proteinuria. There may also be features of the underlying cause.

17.43 CAUSES OF PROTEIN-LOSING ENTEROPATHY	
With mucosal erosions or ulceration	
• Crohn's disease	• Oesophageal, gastric or colonic cancer
• Ulcerative colitis	• Lymphoma
• Radiation damage	
Without mucosal erosions or ulceration	
• Ménétrier's disease	• Tropical sprue
• Bacterial overgrowth	• Eosinophilic gastroenteritis
• Coeliac disease	• Systemic lupus erythematosus
With lymphatic obstruction	
• Intestinal lymphangiectasia	• Lymphoma
• Constrictive pericarditis	• Whipple's disease

The diagnosis is confirmed by measurement of faecal clearance of α_1-antitrypsin or ^{51}Cr-labelled albumin after intravenous injection. Other investigations are performed to determine the underlying cause. Treatment is that of the underlying disorder, nutritional support and measures to control peripheral oedema.

INTESTINAL LYMPHANGIECTASIA

This may be primary, resulting from congenital malunion of lymphatics, or secondary to lymphatic obstruction due to lymphoma, filariasis or constrictive pericarditis. Impaired drainage of intestinal lymphatic vessels leads to discharge of protein and fat-rich lymph into the gastrointestinal lumen. The condition presents with peripheral lymphoedema, pleural effusions or chylous ascites, and steatorrhoea. Investigations reveal hypoalbuminaemia, lymphocytopenia and reduced serum immunoglobulin concentrations. Jejunal biopsies show greatly dilated lacteals, and lymphangiography shows lymphatic obstruction. Treatment consists of a low-fat diet with medium-chain triglyceride supplements.

ULCERATION OF THE SMALL INTESTINE

Small bowel ulcers are uncommon and are either idiopathic or secondary to underlying intestinal disorders (see Box 17.44).

Ulcers are more common in the ileum, and cause bleeding, perforation, stricture formation or obstruction. Barium studies and enteroscopy confirm the diagnosis.

17.44 CAUSES OF SMALL INTESTINAL ULCERS
• Idiopathic
• Inflammatory bowel disease, e.g. Crohn's
• Drugs, e.g. NSAIDs, enteric-coated potassium tablets
• Ulcerative jejunoileitis
• Lymphoma and carcinoma
• Infections, e.g. tuberculosis, typhoid, *Yersinia*
• Others, e.g. radiation, vasculitis

EOSINOPHILIC GASTROENTERITIS

This disorder of unknown aetiology can affect any part of the gastrointestinal tract; it is characterised by eosinophil infiltration affecting the gut wall in the absence of parasitic infection or eosinophilia of other tissues. Peripheral blood eosinophilia is present in 80% of cases.

Inflammation and destruction affect mucosal, muscular and/or serosal layers.

Clinical features

There are features of obstruction and inflammation, such as colicky pain, nausea and vomiting, diarrhoea and weight loss. Protein-losing enteropathy occurs and up to 50% of patients have a history of other allergic disorders. Serosal involvement may produce eosinophilic ascites.

Diagnosis and management

The diagnosis is made by histological assessment of multiple endoscopic biopsies, although full-thickness biopsies are occasionally required. Other investigations are performed to exclude parasitic infection and other causes of eosinophilia. A raised serum IgE concentration is often seen.

Dietary manipulations are rarely effective although elimination diets, especially of milk, may benefit a few patients. Severe symptoms are treated with prednisolone 20–40 mg daily and/or sodium cromoglicate, which stabilises mast cell membranes. The prognosis is good in the majority of patients.

MECKEL'S DIVERTICULUM

This is the most common congenital anomaly of the gastrointestinal tract and occurs in 0.3–3% of people. Most patients are asymptomatic. The diverticulum results from failure of closure of the vitelline duct, with persistence of a blind-ending sac arising from the antimesenteric border of the ileum; it usually occurs within 100 cm of the ileocaecal valve, and is up to 5 cm long. Approximately 50% contain ectopic gastric mucosa; rarely, colonic, pancreatic or endometrial tissue is present.

Complications most commonly occur in the first 2 years of life but are occasionally seen in young adults. Bleeding results from ulceration of ileal mucosa adjacent to the ectopic parietal cells and presents as recurrent melaena or altered blood per rectum. Diagnosis can be made by scanning the abdomen using a gamma counter following an intravenous injection of ^{99m}-technetium pertechnate, which is concentrated by ectopic parietal cells. Other complications include intestinal obstruction, diverticulitis, intussusception and perforation. Intervention is unnecessary unless complications occur. The vast majority of patients remain asymptomatic throughout life.

ADVERSE FOOD REACTIONS

Adverse food reactions are common and are subdivided into food intolerance and food allergy, the former being much more common.

FOOD INTOLERANCE

This involves adverse reactions to food which are not immune-mediated and result from a wide range of mechanisms. Contaminants in food, preservatives and lactase deficiency may all be involved.

LACTOSE INTOLERANCE

Human milk contains around 200 mmol/l of lactose which is normally digested to glucose and galactose by the brush border enzyme lactase prior to absorption. In most populations enterocyte lactase activity declines throughout childhood. The enzyme is deficient in up to 90% of adult Africans, Asians and South Americans, but only 5% of northern Europeans.

In cases of racially determined (primary) lactase deficiency, jejunal morphology is normal. 'Secondary' lactase deficiency occurs as a consequence of disorders which damage the jejunal mucosa, e.g. coeliac disease and viral gastroenteritis. Unhydrolysed lactose enters the colon, where bacterial fermentation produces volatile short-chain fatty acids, hydrogen and carbon dioxide.

Clinical features
In most people lactase deficiency is completely asymptomatic. However, some complain of colicky pain, abdominal distension, increased flatus, borborygmi and diarrhoea after ingesting milk or milk products. Irritable bowel syndrome is often suspected but the diagnosis is suggested by clinical improvement on lactose withdrawal. The lactose hydrogen breath test is a useful non-invasive confirmatory investigation.

Dietary exclusion of lactose is recommended, although most sufferers are able to tolerate small amounts of milk without symptoms. Addition of commercial lactase preparations to milk has been effective in some studies but is costly.

DIARRHOEA DUE TO OTHER SUGARS

'Osmotic' diarrhoea can be caused by sorbitol, an unabsorbable carbohydrate which is used as an artificial sweetener. Fructose may also cause diarrhoea if consumed in greater quantities (e.g. in fruit juices) than can be absorbed.

FOOD ALLERGY

Food allergies are immune-mediated disorders due to IgE antibodies and type 1 hypersensitivity reactions. Up to 20% of the population perceive themselves as suffering from food allergy but only 1–2% of adults have genuine food allergies. The most common culprits are peanuts, milk, eggs, soya and shellfish.

Clinical manifestations occur immediately on exposure and range from trivial to life-threatening or even fatal anaphylaxis. In the 'oral allergy syndrome' contact with certain fresh fruit juices results in urticaria and angio-oedema of the lips and oropharynx. 'Allergic gastroenteropathy' has features similar to eosinophilic gastroenteritis, while 'gastrointestinal anaphylaxis' consists of nausea, vomiting, diarrhoea and sometimes cardiovascular and respiratory collapse. Fatal reactions to trace amounts of peanuts are well documented.

The diagnosis of food allergy is difficult to prove or refute. Skin prick tests and measurements of antigen-specific IgE antibodies in serum have limited predictive value. Double-blind placebo-controlled food challenges are the gold standard, but are laborious and are not readily available. In many cases clinical suspicion and trials of elimination diets are used.

Treatment of proven food allergy consists of detailed patient education and awareness, strict elimination of the offending antigen and in some cases antihistamines or sodium cromoglicate. Anaphylaxis should be treated as a medical emergency with resuscitation, airway support and intravenous adrenaline (epinephrine). Teachers and other carers of affected children should be trained in this. Patients should wear an information bracelet and be taught to carry and use a preloaded adrenaline (epinephrine) syringe.

INFECTIONS OF THE SMALL INTESTINE

TRAVELLERS' DIARRHOEA
See page 47.

GIARDIASIS
See page 46.

AMOEBIASIS
See page 45.

ABDOMINAL TUBERCULOSIS

Mycobacterium tuberculosis is a rare cause of abdominal disease in Caucasians but must be considered in immigrants from the underdeveloped world and in AIDS patients. Gut infection usually results from human *M. tuberculosis* which is swallowed after coughing. Many patients have no pulmonary symptoms and a normal chest radiograph.

The area most commonly affected is the ileocaecal region; presentation and radiological findings may be very similar to those of Crohn's disease. Abdominal pain can be acute or of several months' duration, but diarrhoea is less common in tuberculosis (TB) than in Crohn's disease. Low-grade fever is common but not invariable. Like Crohn's disease, TB can affect any part of the gastrointestinal tract, and perianal disease with fistula is recognised. Peritoneal TB may result in peritonitis with exudative ascites, associated with abdominal pain and fever. Granulomatous hepatitis occurs.

Diagnosis
Abdominal TB causes an elevated erythrocyte sedimentation rate (ESR); a raised serum alkaline phosphatase concentration suggests hepatic involvement. Histological confirmation is sought by endoscopy, laparoscopy or liver biopsy. Caseation of granulomata is not always seen and acid- and alcohol-fast bacteria are often scanty. Culture may be helpful but identification of the organism may take 6 weeks.

Management
When the presentation is very suggestive of abdominal TB, chemotherapy with four drugs, isoniazid, rifampicin, pyrazinamide and ethambutol (see p. 538), should be commenced even if bacteriological or histological proof is lacking.

CRYPTOSPORIDIOSIS

Cryptosporidiosis and other protozoal infections, including isosporiasis (*Isospora belli*) and microsporidiosis, are dealt with on pages 47 and 118–119.

TUMOURS OF THE SMALL INTESTINE

The small intestine is rarely affected by neoplasia, and fewer than 5% of all gastrointestinal tumours occur here.

Benign tumours

The most common are adenomas, GIST, lipomas and hamartomas. Adenomas are most often found in the peri-ampullary region and are usually asymptomatic, although occult bleeding or obstruction due to intussusception may occur. Transformation to adenocarcinoma is rare. Multiple adenomas are common in the duodenum of patients with familial adenomatous polyposis (FAP), who merit regular endoscopic surveillance. Hamartomatous polyps with almost no malignant potential occur in Peutz–Jeghers syndrome (see p. 822).

Malignant tumours

These are rare and include, in decreasing order of frequency, adenocarcinoma, carcinoid tumour, malignant GIST and lymphoma. The majority occur in middle age or later. Kaposi's sarcoma is seen in patients with AIDS.

Adenocarcinomas occur with increased frequency in patients with FAP, coeliac disease and Peutz–Jeghers syndrome. The non-specific presentation and rarity of these lesions often lead to delay in diagnosis. Barium follow-through examination or small bowel enema studies will demonstrate most lesions of this type. Enteroscopy, mesenteric angiography and CT also play a role in investigation.

CARCINOID TUMOURS

These are derived from enterochromaffin cells and are most common in the ileum. Localised spread and the potential for metastasis to the liver increase with primary lesions over 2 cm in diameter. Carcinoid tumours also occur in the rectum and in the appendix; those in the latter are usually benign. Overall, these tumours are less aggressive than carcinomas and their growth is usually slow.

The term 'carcinoid syndrome' refers to the systemic symptoms produced when secretory products of the neoplastic enterochromaffin cells reach the systemic circulation (see Box 17.45). When produced by the primary tumour they are usually metabolised in the liver and do not reach the systemic circulation. The syndrome is therefore only seen when 5-hydroxytryptamine (5-HT, serotonin), bradykinin and other peptide hormones are released by hepatic metastases.

Management

The treatment of a carcinoid tumour is surgical resection. The treatment of carcinoid syndrome is palliative because hepatic metastases have occurred, although prolonged survival is common. Surgical removal of the primary tumour is usually attempted and the hepatic metastases can be excised as reduction of tumour mass improves symptoms. Hepatic artery embolisation retards growth of hepatic deposits. Octreotide 200 µg 8-hourly by subcutaneous injection is

---

17.45 CLINICAL FEATURES OF THE CARCINOID SYNDROME
• Small-bowel obstruction due to the tumour mass • Intestinal ischaemia (due to mesenteric infiltration or vasospasm) • Hepatic metastases causing pain, hepatomegaly and jaundice • Flushing and wheezing • Diarrhoea • Cardiac involvement (tricuspid regurgitation, pulmonary stenosis, right ventricular endocardial plaques) leading to heart failure • Facial telangiectasia
The diagnosis is made by detecting excess levels of the 5-HT metabolite, 5-HIAA, in a 24-hour urine collection.

used to reduce tumour release of secretagogues. Cytotoxic chemotherapy has only a minor role.

LYMPHOMA

Non-Hodgkin's lymphoma (see p. 940) may involve the gastrointestinal tract as part of more generalised disease or may rarely arise in the gut, with the small intestine being most commonly affected. Lymphomas occur with increased frequency in patients with coeliac disease, AIDS and other immunodeficiency states. Most are of B-cell origin, although lymphoma associated with coeliac disease is derived from T cells (enteropathy-associated T-cell lymphoma).

Colicky abdominal pain, obstruction and weight loss are the usual presenting features and perforation is also occasionally seen. Malabsorption is only a feature of diffuse bowel involvement and hepatosplenomegaly is rare.

The diagnosis is made by small bowel biopsy, radiological contrast studies and CT. Staging investigations are performed. Surgical resection where possible is the treatment of choice, with radiotherapy and combination chemotherapy reserved for those with advanced disease. The prognosis depends largely on the stage at diagnosis, cell type, patient age and the presence of 'B' symptoms.

IMMUNOPROLIFERATIVE SMALL INTESTINAL DISEASE (IPSID)

Also known as 'alpha heavy chain disease', this rare condition occurs mainly in the Mediterranean, Middle East, India and Pakistan, and North America. The aetiology is unknown but it may be a response to chronic stimulation by bacterial antigens. The condition varies in severity from relatively benign to frankly malignant.

The small intestinal mucosa is diffusely affected, especially proximally, by a dense lymphoplasmacytic infiltrate. Enlarged mesenteric lymph nodes are also common. Most patients are young adults who present with malabsorption, anorexia and fever. Serum electrophoresis confirms the presence of alpha heavy chains (from the Fc portion of IgA). Prolonged remissions can be obtained with long-term antibiotic therapy but chemotherapy is required for those who fail to respond or who have aggressive disease.

DISEASES OF THE PANCREAS

ACUTE PANCREATITIS

Acute pancreatitis accounts for 3% of all cases of abdominal pain admitted to hospital. It affects 2–28 per 100 000 of the population and may be increasing in incidence.

Pathophysiology

Acute pancreatitis is an acute inflammatory process of the pancreas with variable involvement of regional tissues and remote organ systems. It occurs as a consequence of premature activation of zymogen granules, releasing proteases which digest the pancreas and surrounding tissue (see Fig. 17.39). The normal pancreas has only a poorly developed capsule, and adjacent structures, including the common bile duct, duodenum, splenic vein and transverse colon, are commonly involved in the inflammatory process. The severity of acute pancreatitis is dependent upon the balance between activity of released proteolytic enzymes and antiproteolytic factors. The latter comprise an intracellular pancreatic trypsin inhibitor protein and circulating β_2-macroglobulin, α_1-antitrypsin and Cl-esterase inhibitors. Causes of acute pancreatitis are given in Box 17.46.

Acute pancreatitis may be mild, with minimal organ dysfunction and uneventful recovery. Alternatively, it may be severe and associated with local complications such as necrosis (often with infection), pseudocyst or abscess, and systemic complications leading to multi-organ failure.

17.46 CAUSES OF ACUTE PANCREATITIS	
Common (90% of cases)	
• Gallstones	• Idiopathic
• Alcohol	• Post-ERCP
Rare	
• Post-surgical (abdominal, cardiopulmonary bypass)	
• Trauma	
• Drugs (azathioprine, thiazide diuretics, sodium valproate)	
• Metabolic (hypercalcaemia, hypertriglyceridaemia)	
• Pancreas divisum (see p. 806)	
• Infection (mumps, Coxsackie virus)	
• Hereditary	
• Renal failure	
• Organ transplantation (kidney, liver)	
• Severe hypothermia	

Clinical features

Severe, constant upper abdominal pain which radiates to the back in 65% of cases builds up over 15–60 minutes. Nausea and vomiting are common. There is marked epigastric tenderness but in the early stages (and in contrast to a perforated peptic ulcer), guarding and rebound tenderness are absent because the inflammation is principally retroperitoneal. Bowel sounds become quiet or absent as paralytic ileus develops.

In severe cases the patient becomes hypoxic and develops hypovolaemic shock with oliguria. Discoloration of the flanks (Grey Turner's sign) or the periumbilical region (Cullen's sign) are features of severe pancreatitis with haemorrhage. The differential diagnosis includes a perforated viscus, acute cholecystitis and myocardial infarction.

Complications

These are listed in Box 17.47. An acute pancreatic pseudocyst is a localised extrapancreatic collection of pancreatic juice and debris which usually develops in the lesser sac following inflammatory rupture of the pancreatic duct. The pseudocyst is initially contained within a poorly defined, fragile wall of granulation tissue which matures over a 6-week period to form a fibrous capsule (see Fig. 17.40).

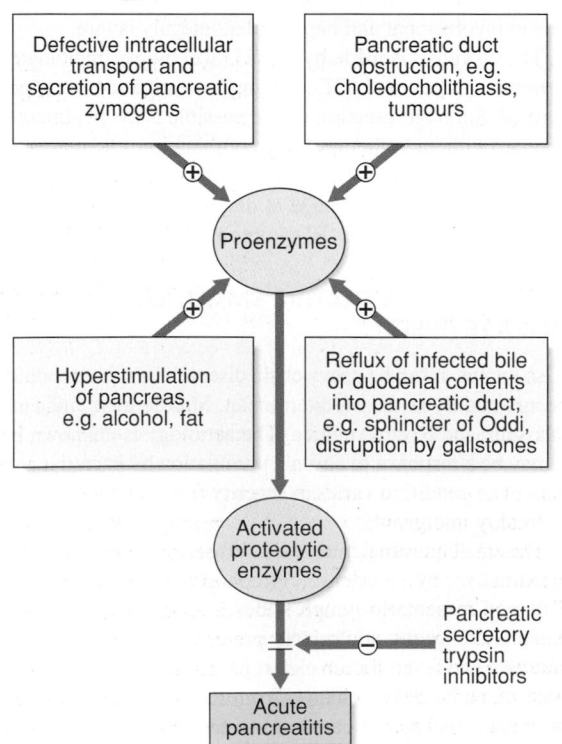

Fig. 17.39 Pathophysiology of acute pancreatitis.

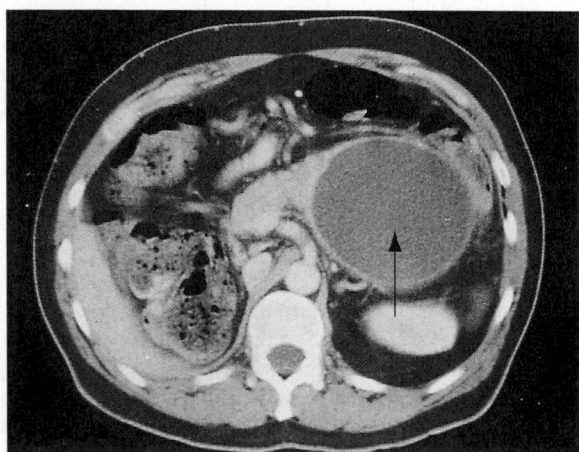

Fig. 17.40 CT showing large pancreatic pseudocyst (arrow) developing from the body of the pancreas.

17.47 COMPLICATIONS OF ACUTE PANCREATITIS

Complication	Cause
Systemic	
Systemic inflammatory response syndrome (SIRS): renal failure	Increased vascular permeability from cytokine, platelet aggregating factor and kinin release, paralytic ileus, vomiting
Hypoxia	Acute respiratory distress syndrome (ARDS) due to microthrombi in pulmonary vessels
Hyperglycaemia	Disruption of islets of Langerhans with altered insulin/glucagon axis
Hypocalcaemia	Sequestration of calcium in fat necrosis, fall in ionised calcium (? cause)
Reduced serum albumin concentration	Increased capillary permeability
Pancreatic	
Necrosis	Non-viable pancreatic tissue and peripancreatic tissue death; frequently infected
Abscess	Circumscribed collection of pus close to the pancreas and containing little or no pancreatic necrotic tissue
Pseudocyst	Disruption of pancreatic ducts
Pancreatic ascites or pleural effusion	Disruption of pancreatic ducts
Gastrointestinal	
Upper gastrointestinal bleeding	Gastric or duodenal erosions
Variceal haemorrhage Erosion into colon	Splenic or portal vein thrombosis
Duodenal obstruction	Compression by pancreatic mass
Obstructive jaundice	Compression of common bile duct

Small intrapancreatic cysts and pseudocysts are common features of both acute and chronic pancreatitis; they are usually asymptomatic and resolve as the pancreatitis recovers. Pseudocysts greater than 6 cm in diameter seldom disappear spontaneously. Large pseudocysts cause constant abdominal pain, can produce a palpable abdominal mass and may compress or erode surrounding structures including blood vessels to form pseudoaneurysms.

Pancreatic ascites occurs when fluid leaks from a disrupted pancreatic duct into the peritoneal cavity. Leakage into the thoracic cavity can result in a pleural effusion or a broncho-pancreatic fistula.

Diagnosis

The diagnosis of acute pancreatitis is based upon elevation of serum amylase or lipase concentrations and ultrasound or CT evidence of pancreatic swelling. Plain radiographs are taken to exclude other diagnoses such as perforation or obstruction and to identify pulmonary complications.

Amylase is efficiently excreted by the kidneys, and concentrations may have returned to normal if measured 24–48 hours after the onset of pancreatitis. In this situation the diagnosis can be made by demonstrating an elevated urinary amylase:creatinine ratio. A persistently elevated serum amylase concentration suggests pseudocyst formation. Peritoneal amylase concentrations are massively elevated in pancreatic ascites. Serum amylase concentrations are also elevated (but to a lesser extent) in intestinal ischaemia, perforated peptic ulcer and ruptured ovarian cyst, and the salivary isoenzyme of amylase is elevated in parotitis.

Ultrasound scanning confirms the diagnosis, although in the earlier stages the gland may not be grossly swollen. The ultrasound scan is also useful because it may show gallstones, biliary obstruction or pseudocyst formation.

CT between 3 and 10 days after admission is used to define the viability of the pancreas. Necrotising pancreatitis is associated with decreased pancreatic enhancement following intravenous injection of contrast material. The presence of gas within necrotic material suggests infection and impending abscess formation, in which case percutaneous aspiration of material for bacterial culture should be carried out. Involvement of the colon, blood vessels and other adjacent structures by the inflammatory process is best seen by CT.

Certain investigations stratify the severity of acute pancreatitis and have important prognostic value at the time of presentation (see Box 17.48). In addition, serial assessment of C-reactive protein (CRP) is a useful indicator of progress. A peak CRP > 210 mg/l in the first 4 days predicts severe acute pancreatitis with 80% accuracy. It is worth noting that the serum amylase concentration has no prognostic value.

Management

Management comprises several related steps:

- establishing the diagnosis and stratifying disease severity
- early treatment according to whether the disease is mild or severe
- detection and treatment of complications
- treating the underlying cause—specifically gallstones.

The initial management is based upon analgesia using pethidine and correction of hypovolaemia using normal saline and/or colloids. All severe cases should be managed in a high-dependency or intensive care unit. A central venous line or Swan–Ganz catheter and urinary catheter are used to monitor patients with shock. Hypoxic patients need oxygen and patients who develop ARDS may require ventilatory support. Hyperglycaemia is corrected using insulin, but it is not necessary to correct hypocalcaemia by intravenous calcium injection unless tetany occurs.

Nasogastric aspiration is only necessary if paralytic ileus is present. Enteral feeding via a nasoenteral tube should be started at an early stage in patients with severe pancreatitis. These patients are in a severely catabolic state and need nutritional support. In addition enteral feeding decreases endotoxaemia and thereby may reduce systemic complications. Prophylaxis of thromboembolism with low-dose subcutaneous heparin is also advisable. Prophylactic, broad-spectrum intravenous antibiotics such as imipenem or cefuroxime may improve outcome in severe cases.

Patients who present with cholangitis or jaundice in association with severe acute pancreatitis should undergo urgent ERCP to diagnose and treat choledocholithiasis. In less severe cases of gallstone pancreatitis ERCP may be carried out after the acute phase has resolved.

ACUTE PANCREATITIS—role of nutritional support **EBM**

'Clinical improvement in patients with acute pancreatitis is greater in those receiving nasojejunal tube feeding rather than total parenteral nutrition.'

- Windsor AC, Kanwar S, Li AG, et al. Compared with parenteral nutrition, enteral feeding attenuates the acute phase response and improves disease severity in acute pancreatitis. Gut 1998; 42:431–435.

Further information: 🖥 www.bsg.org.uk
🖥 www.evidbasedgastro.com

ACUTE PANCREATITIS—role of ERCP **EBM**

'Emergency ERCP with biliary sphincterotomy and stone extraction when stones are identified in the common bile duct improves outcome in severe acute pancreatitis. Greatest benefit occurs in those patients who have ascending cholangitis.'

- Neoptolemos JP, London NJ, James D, et al. Controlled trial of urgent endoscopic retrograde cholangiopancreatography and endoscopic sphincterotomy versus conservative treatment for acute pancreatitis due to gallstones. Lancet 1988; ii:979–983.
- Fan ST, Lai ECS, Mok FPT, et al. Early treatment of acute biliary pancreatitis by endoscopic papillotomy. N Engl J Med 1993; 328:278–282.
- Folsch UR, Nitsche R, Ludtke R, et al. Early ERCP and papillotomy compared with conservative treatment for acute biliary pancreatitis. N Engl J Med 1997; 336:237–242.

Further information: 🖥 www.bsg.org.uk
🖥 www.evidbasedgastro.com

Management of complications

Patients who have developed necrotising pancreatitis or pancreatic abscess require urgent surgical débridement of the pancreas, followed by drainage of the pancreatic bed. Pancreatic pseudocysts are treated by drainage into the stomach or duodenum. This is usually done after at least 6 weeks, once a pseudocapsule has matured, using open surgery or endoscopic methods.

Prognosis (see Box 17.48)

Despite recent advances in management, the mortality has remained unchanged at 10–15%. About 80% of all cases are mild with a mortality less than 5%; 98% of deaths occur in the 20% of severe cases. One-third occur within the first

17.48 ADVERSE PROGNOSTIC FACTORS IN ACUTE PANCREATITIS (GLASGOW CRITERIA)*

- Age > 55 years
- PO_2 < 8 kPa
- White blood cell count (WBC) > 15 × 10⁹/litre
- Albumin < 32 g/l
- Serum calcium < 2 mmol/l (corrected)
- Glucose > 10 mmol/l
- Urea > 16 mmol/l (after rehydration)
- Alanine aminotransferase (ALT) > 200 U/l
- Lactate dehydrogenase (LDH) > 600 U/l

* Severity and prognosis worsen as the number of these factors increases. More than three implies severe disease.

week, usually from multi-organ failure. After this time the majority of deaths result from sepsis, especially that complicating infected necrosis.

CHRONIC PANCREATITIS

Chronic pancreatitis is a chronic inflammatory disease characterised by fibrosis and destruction of exocrine pancreatic tissue. Diabetes mellitus occurs in advanced cases because the islets of Langerhans are involved.

Pathophysiology

Around 80% of cases in Western countries result from alcohol misuse (see Fig. 17.41). In southern India severe chronic calcific pancreatitis occurs in non-alcoholics, possibly as a result of malnutrition and dietary cassava consumption. Other causes are listed in Box 17.49.

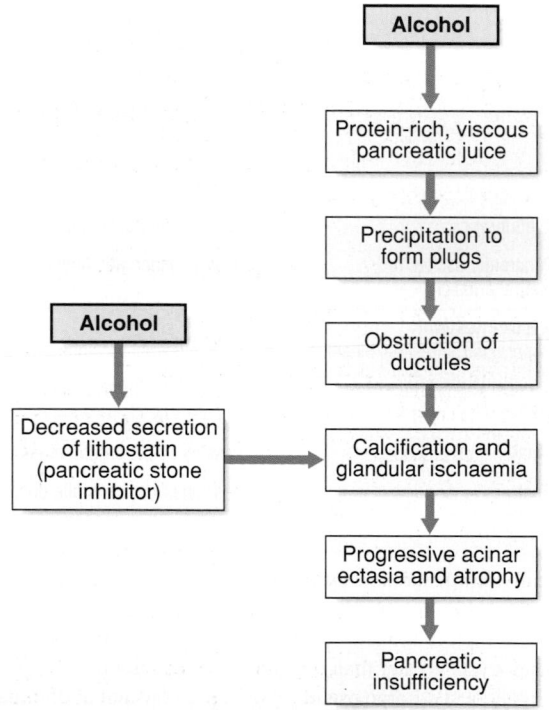

Fig. 17.41 Pathophysiology of chronic pancreatitis.

17.49 CAUSES OF CHRONIC PANCREATITIS

- Calcific
  Alcoholism
  Tropical
- Obstructive
  Stenosis of the ampulla of Vater
- Pancreas divisum (see p. 806)
- Cystic fibrosis
- Hereditary
- Idiopathic

N.B. Many patients have gallstones but these do not cause chronic pancreatitis.

Clinical features

Chronic pancreatitis predominantly affects middle-aged alcoholic men. Almost all present with abdominal pain. In 50% this occurs as episodes of 'acute pancreatitis', although each attack results in a degree of permanent pancreatic damage. Relentless, slowly progressive chronic pain without acute exacerbations affects 35% of patients, whilst the remainder have no pain but present with diarrhoea. Pain is due to a combination of increased pressure within the pancreatic ducts and direct involvement of pancreatic and peripancreatic nerves by the inflammatory process. Pain may be relieved by leaning forwards or by drinking alcohol. Approximately one-fifth of patients chronically consume opiate analgesics.

Weight loss is common and results from a combination of anorexia, avoidance of food because of post-prandial pain, malabsorption and/or diabetes. Steatorrhoea occurs when more than 90% of the exocrine tissue has been destroyed; protein malabsorption only develops in the most advanced cases. Overall, 30% of patients are diabetic, but this figure rises to 70% in those with chronic calcific pancreatitis.

Physical examination reveals a thin, malnourished patient with epigastric tenderness. Skin pigmentation over the abdomen and back is common and results from chronic use of a hot water bottle (erythema ab igne). Many patients have features of other alcohol- and smoking-related diseases.

Complications are listed in Box 17.50.

Investigations

Investigations (see Box 17.51) are carried out to:

- make a diagnosis of chronic pancreatitis

17.50 COMPLICATIONS OF CHRONIC PANCREATITIS

- Pseudocysts and pancreatic ascites, which occur in both acute and chronic pancreatitis
- Extrahepatic obstructive jaundice due to a benign stricture of the common bile duct as it passes through the diseased pancreas
- Duodenal stenosis
- Portal or splenic vein thrombosis leading to segmental portal hypertension and gastric varices
- Peptic ulcer

17.51 INVESTIGATIONS IN CHRONIC PANCREATITIS

Tests to establish the diagnosis

- Ultrasound
- CT (may show atrophy, calcification or ductal dilatation)
- Abdominal radiograph (may show calcification)
- ERCP only if non-invasive tests are negative or equivocal (see Fig. 17.42)
- Endoscopic ultrasound

Tests of pancreatic function

- Collection of pure pancreatic juice after secretin injection (gold standard but invasive and seldom used)
- Pancreolauryl or PABA test (see p. 760)
- Faecal pancreatic chymotrypsin or elastase
- Oral glucose tolerance test

Tests of anatomy prior to surgery

- ERCP (see Fig. 17.42)

- define pancreatic function
- demonstrate anatomical abnormalities prior to surgical intervention.

Management

Alcohol misuse

Alcohol avoidance is crucial in halting the progression of the disease and reducing pain. Unfortunately, counselling and psychiatric intervention are rarely successful and the majority of patients continue to drink alcohol.

Pain relief

A range of analgesic drugs, particularly NSAIDs, are valuable, but the severe and unremitting nature of the pain often leads to opiate use with the risk of addiction. Oral pancreatic enzyme supplements suppress pancreatic secretion and their regular use reduces analgesic consumption in some patients.

Patients who are abstinent from alcohol and who have severe chronic pain which is resistant to conservative measures are considered for surgical or endoscopic pancreatic therapy (see Box 17.52). Coeliac plexus neurolysis or

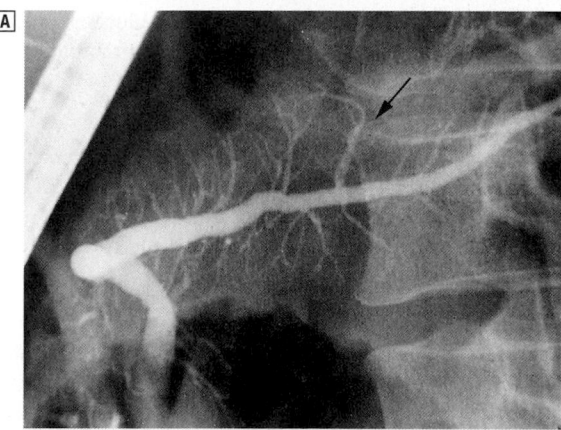

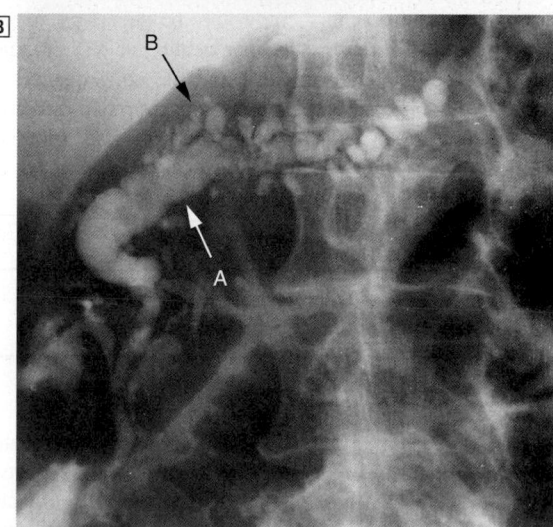

Fig. 17.42 ERCP in chronic pancreatitis. A Early pancreatitis with irregular dilated side branches (arrow). B Advanced disease. Dilated, irregular main duct (arrow A), with obstructed abnormal side branches (arrow B).

17.52 INTERVENTION IN CHRONIC PANCREATITIS
Endoscopic therapy
• Dilatation or stenting of main pancreatic duct • Removal of calculi (mechanical or shock-wave lithotripsy)
Surgical methods
• Partial pancreatic resection, preserving the duodenum • Pancreatico-jejunostomy

minimally invasive thoracoscopic splanchnicectomy sometimes produces long-lasting pain relief although relapse eventually occurs in the majority of cases.

In some patients ERCP does not show a surgically or endoscopically correctable abnormality and in these patients the only surgical approach is total pancreatectomy. Unfortunately, even after this operation, some patients will continue to experience pain. Moreover, the procedure causes diabetes which may be difficult to control, with a high risk of hypoglycaemia (since both insulin and glucagon release are absent), and this is a cause of significant morbidity and mortality.

Steatorrhoea

This is treated by dietary fat restriction (with supplementary medium-chain triglyceride therapy in malnourished patients) and oral pancreatic enzyme supplements. A proton pump inhibitor is added to optimise duodenal pH for pancreatic enzyme activity.

Diabetes

Diabetes requires carbohydrate restriction and insulin therapy.

Management of complications

Surgical or endoscopic therapy may be necessary for the management of pseudocysts, pancreatic ascites, common bile duct or duodenal stricture and the consequences of portal hypertension. Many patients with chronic pancreatitis also require treatment for other alcohol- and smoking-related diseases and for the consequences of self-neglect and malnutrition.

CONGENITAL ABNORMALITIES OF THE PANCREAS

PANCREAS DIVISUM

This is due to failure of the primitive dorsal and ventral ducts to fuse during embryonic development of the pancreas. As a consequence, most of the pancreatic drainage occurs through the smaller accessory ampulla rather than through the major ampulla.

Pancreas divisum occurs in 7–10% of the normal population and is usually asymptomatic. Some patients develop acute pancreatitis, chronic pancreatitis or atypical abdominal pain, possibly because drainage through the accessory papilla is restricted.

ANNULAR PANCREAS

In this congenital anomaly, the pancreas encircles the second/third part of the duodenum, leading to gastric outlet obstruction. Annular pancreas is associated with malrotation of the intestine, atresias and cardiac anomalies.

CYSTIC FIBROSIS

This disease is considered in detail on page 522. The gastrointestinal manifestations of cystic fibrosis are pancreatic insufficiency and meconium ileus. Peptic ulcer, and hepatic and biliary disease also occur.

In cystic fibrosis pancreatic secretions are protein- and mucus-rich. The resultant viscous juice forms plugs which obstruct the pancreatic ductules, leading to progressive destruction of acinar cells. Steatorrhoea is universal and the large-volume bulky stools predispose to rectal prolapse. Malnutrition is compounded by the metabolic demands of respiratory failure and by diabetes which develops in 40% of patients by adolescence.

The majority of patients now survive well into adulthood and heart/lung transplantation can further prolong life. Optimal treatment of the cystic fibrosis patient depends upon an assiduous team approach to respiratory, nutritional and hepatobiliary complications. Nutritional counselling and supervision are important to ensure intake of high-energy foods, providing 120–150% of the recommended intake for normal subjects. Fats are an important calorie source and, despite the presence of steatorrhoea, fat intake should not be restricted. Supplementary fat-soluble vitamins are also necessary.

High-dose oral pancreatic enzymes are necessary, in doses sufficient to control steatorrhoea and stool frequency. A proton pump inhibitor aids fat digestion by producing an optimal duodenal pH. Diabetic patients usually require insulin injections rather than oral hypoglycaemic agents.

Meconium ileus

Mucus-rich plugs within intestinal contents can obstruct the small or large intestine. Meconium ileus is treated by the mucolytic agent N-acetylcysteine given orally, by gastrografin enema or by gut lavage using polyethylene glycol. In resistant cases of meconium ileus surgical resection may be necessary.

TUMOURS OF THE PANCREAS

Pancreatic carcinoma affects 10–15 per 100 000 in Western populations, rising to 100 per 100 000 in those over the age of 70. Men are affected twice as often as women. The disease is associated with smoking and chronic pancreatitis. Between 5 and 10% of patients have a genetic predisposition (hereditary pancreatitis, MEN, hereditary non-polyposis colon cancer—HNPCC).

Pathology

Approximately 90% of pancreatic neoplasms are adenocarcinomas which arise from the pancreatic ducts. These tumours involve local structures and metastasise to regional lymph nodes at an early stage. The majority of patients have advanced disease at the time of presentation.

Ampullary or periampullary adenocarcinomas are rare neoplasms which arise from the ampulla of Vater or adjacent duodenum. These tumours are often polypoid and ulcerated. They infiltrate the duodenum but behave less aggressively than pancreatic adenocarcinoma.

Cystadenocarcinoma is a very rare, slowly growing tumour, usually arising from the head of the pancreas and characterised by mucinous cyst formation. It occurs most often in middle-aged women.

Clinical features

The clinical features of pancreatic cancer are pain, weight loss and obstructive jaundice (see Fig. 17.43). The pain results from invasion of the coeliac plexus and is characteristically incessant and boring. It often radiates from the upper abdomen through to the back and may be eased a little by bending forwards. Almost all patients lose weight and many are cachectic. Weight loss is the consequence of anorexia, steatorrhoea and metabolic effects of the tumour. Around 60% of tumours arise from the head of the pancreas, and involvement of the common bile duct results in the development of obstructive jaundice, often with severe pruritus.

A few patients present with diarrhoea, vomiting from duodenal obstruction, diabetes mellitus, recurrent venous thrombosis, acute pancreatitis or depression.

Physical examination reveals clear evidence of weight loss. An abdominal mass due to the tumour itself, a palpable gallbladder or hepatic metastasis is commonly found. A palpable gallbladder in a jaundiced patient is usually the consequence of distal biliary obstruction by a pancreatic cancer (Courvoisier's sign).

Investigations

When a patient presents with biochemically confirmed cholestatic jaundice the diagnosis is usually made by ultrasound and CT (see Fig. 17.44). Diagnosis in non-jaundiced patients is often delayed because presenting symptoms are relatively non-specific.

Fit patients with small localised tumours should undergo staging to define operability. Laparoscopy with laparoscopic ultrasound will define tumour size, involvement of blood vessels and metastatic spread. In patients unsuitable for

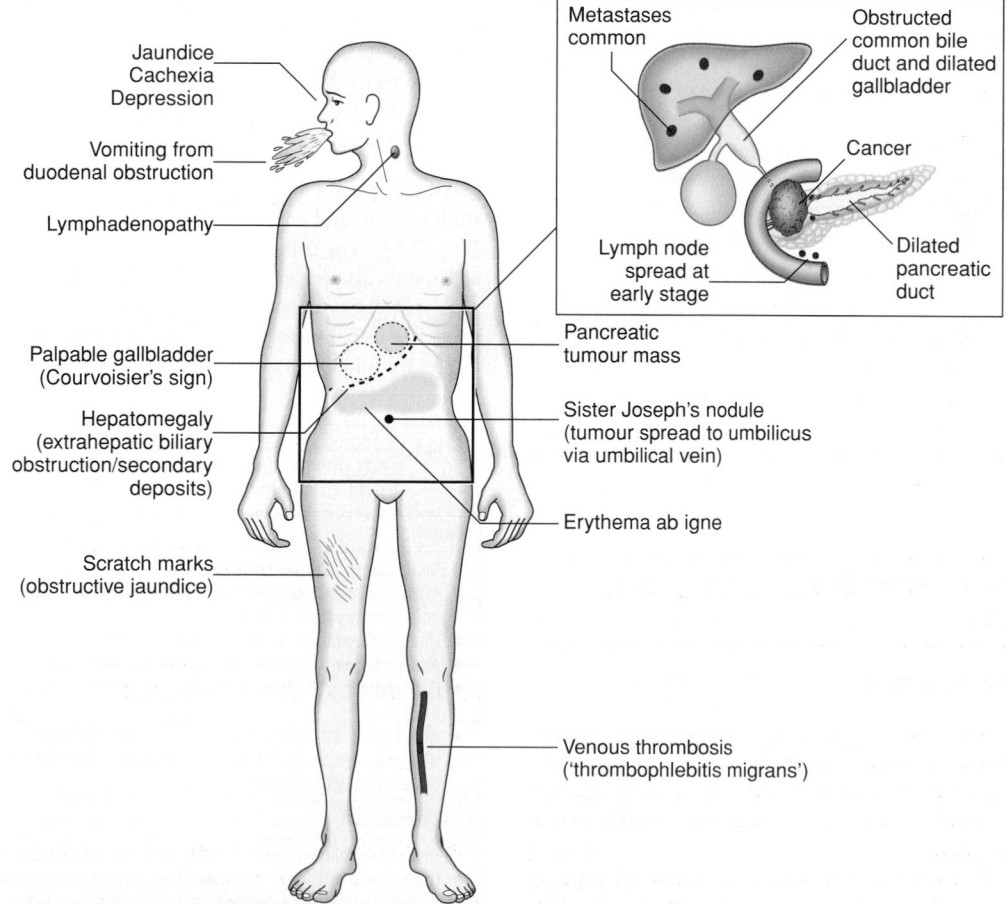

Fig. 17.43   Features of pancreatic cancer.

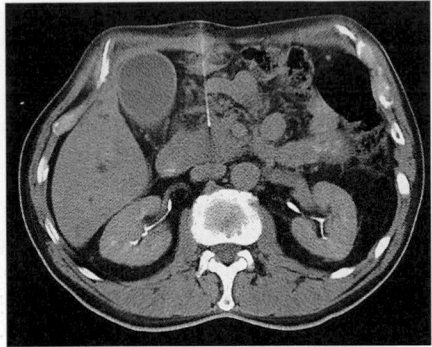

Fig. 17.44 Carcinoma of the pancreatic head. CT obtained during biopsy of mass in pancreatic head.

surgery because of advanced disease, frailty or comorbid disease, ultrasound or CT-guided cytology or biopsy may be used to confirm the diagnosis. Endoscopic ultrasound with fine-needle aspiration is used to define vascular invasion and obtain cytological proof of diagnosis.

ERCP is a sensitive method of diagnosing pancreatic cancer and is valuable when the diagnosis is in doubt, although differentiation between cancer and localised chronic pancreatitis can be difficult. The main role of ERCP is to insert a stent into the common bile duct to relieve obstructive jaundice.

Management

Surgical resection is the only method of effecting cure; adjuvant chemotherapy or radiotherapy confers no clear additional benefits. Unfortunately, a mere 15% of tumours are amenable to curative resection since most neoplasms are locally advanced at the time of diagnosis.

For the vast majority of patients therapy is based on palliation of pain and obstructive jaundice. Pain relief is achieved using analgesic drugs and, in some patients, coeliac plexus neurolysis by a percutaneous or endoscopic ultrasound-guided phenol injection. Jaundice is relieved by choledochojejunostomy in fit patients; percutaneous or endoscopic stenting is used in the elderly or in patients who have very advanced disease.

Around 25% of patients undergoing resection of ampullary or periampullary tumours survive for 5 years and this contrasts with 3–5% survival in patients who present with pancreatic ductal cancer.

ENDOCRINE TUMOURS

These arise from neuro-endocrine tissue within the pancreas. They may occur in association with parathyroid and pituitary adenomas (MEN I, see p. 688). The majority of endocrine tumours are non-secretory and, although malignant, grow slowly and metastasise late. Other tumours secrete hormones and present because of their endocrine effects (see Box 17.53). Neuro-endocrine pancreatic tumours may be single, but are frequently multifocal and arise from other clusters of neuro-endocrine cells derived from neural crest tissues. They are localised by CT and endoscopic ultrasound. ^{111}In-labelled DTPA is very sensitive in the diagnosis of glucagonoma.

17.53 ENDOCRINE PANCREATIC TUMOURS		
Tumour	**Hormone**	**Effects**
Gastrinoma	Gastrin	Peptic ulcer and steatorrhoea
Insulinoma	Insulin	Recurrent hypoglycaemia (see p. 732)
VIPoma	VIP	Watery diarrhoea and hypokalaemia
Glucagonoma	Glucagon	Diabetes mellitus, necrolytic migratory erythema
Somatostatinoma	Somatostatin	Diabetes mellitus and steatorrhoea

INFLAMMATORY BOWEL DISEASE

Ulcerative colitis and Crohn's disease are chronic inflammatory bowel diseases which pursue a protracted relapsing and remitting course, usually extending over years. The diseases have many similarities and it is sometimes impossible to differentiate between them. A crucial distinction is that ulcerative colitis only involves the colon, while Crohn's disease can involve any part of the gastrointestinal tract from mouth to anus.

The incidence of inflammatory bowel disease (IBD) varies widely between populations; Crohn's disease appears to be very rare in the underdeveloped world yet ulcerative colitis, although still unusual, is becoming more common. In the West, the incidence of ulcerative colitis is stable at 10 per 100 000 while that of Crohn's disease is increasing and is now 5–7 per 100 000. Both diseases most commonly start in young adults, with a second incidence peak in the seventh decade.

Pathogenesis

Both genetic and environmental factors are implicated (see Box 17.54). The cellular events involved in the pathogenesis of Crohn's disease and ulcerative colitis involve activation of macrophages, lymphocytes and polymorphonuclear cells with release of inflammatory mediators, and these events represent targets for future therapeutic intervention (see Fig. 17.45).

17.54 FACTORS ASSOCIATED WITH THE DEVELOPMENT OF INFLAMMATORY BOWEL DISEASE
Genetic
• More common in Ashkenazi Jews • 10% have a first-degree relative or at least one close relative with inflammatory bowel disease • High concordance between identical twins • Associated with autoimmune thyroiditis and SLE • Four regions of linkage on chromosomes 16, 12, 6 and 14 ('IBD 1–4') • HLA-DR103 associated with severe ulcerative colitis • Ulcerative colitis and Crohn's patients with HLA-B27 commonly develop ankylosing spondylitis
Environmental
• Ulcerative colitis—more common in non-smokers and ex-smokers • Crohn's—most patients are smokers (relative risk = 3) • Associated with low-residue, high refined sugar diet • Appendicectomy protects against ulcerative colitis

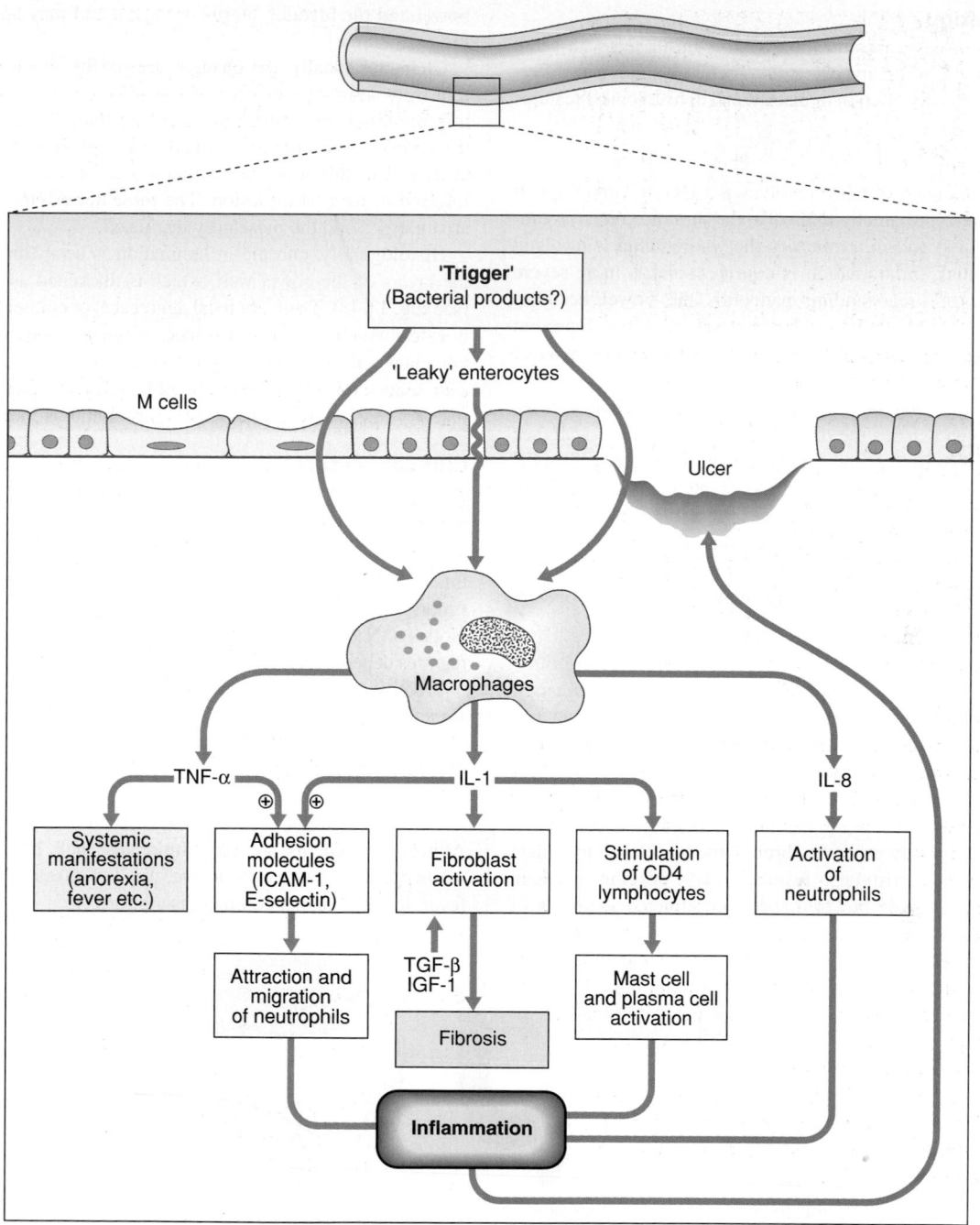

Fig. 17.45 Probable pathogenesis of inflammatory bowel disease. Dietary or bacterial antigens either are taken up by specialised *M cells*, pass between leaky epithelial cells or enter the lamina propria through ulcerated mucosa. Macrophages within Peyer's patches process the antigen and then secrete a series of cytokines. *Tumour necrosis factor-alpha (TNF-α)* up-regulates adhesion molecules (E-selectin and ICAM-1). These are localised on the vascular endothelium and cause circulating neutrophils to adhere to the endothelium and then pass through into the bowel wall. TNF-α is also largely responsible for the anorexia, malaise, fever and metabolic bone disease which characterise inflammatory bowel disease. *Interleukin-1 (IL-1)* also up-regulates adhesion molecules, thereby aiding neutrophil recruitment. In addition, IL-1 activates CD4 lymphocytes. These in turn secrete interleukins 3 and 4, which activate mast cells and plasma cells. Mast cells secrete molecules (platelet activating factor and leukotrienes), which are necessary for inflammation; plasma cells secrete IgG and IgE. IL-1 stimulates other CD4 cells to secrete gamma interferon (IFN-γ) and this results in expression of HLA-DR antigens on the intestinal mucosa. Lastly, in Crohn's disease but not ulcerative colitis, IL-1, TGF-β and IGF-1 (secreted from various sources) activate fibroblasts, thereby stimulating collagen metabolism, fibrosis and stricture formation. *Interleukin-8 (IL-8)* attracts, activates and degranulates neutrophils. Toxic proteases and reactive oxygen species are released; these are cytotoxic and cause ulceration. The regulatory cytokines IL-10 and transforming growth factor-β (TGF-β), produced by macrophages and mature T lymphocytes, down-regulate these inflammatory processes. These pathways occur in all normal individuals exposed to an inflammatory insult and this is self-limiting in healthy subjects. In genetically predisposed persons, dysregulation of these steps leads to chronic inflammatory bowel disease.

Pathology

In both diseases the intestinal wall is infiltrated with acute and chronic inflammatory cells. There are important differences in the distribution of disease and in histological features (see Fig. 17.46).

Ulcerative colitis

Inflammation invariably involves the rectum (proctitis). It may spread proximally to involve the sigmoid colon (proctosigmoiditis) and in a minority the whole colon is involved (pancolitis). Inflammation is confluent and is more severe distally. In long-standing pancolitis the bowel becomes shortened and 'pseudopolyps' develop; these represent normal or hypertrophied residual mucosa within areas of atrophy.

Histologically, the inflammatory process is limited to the mucosa and spares the deeper layers of the bowel wall (see Fig. 17.47). Both acute and chronic inflammatory cells infiltrate the lamina propria and the crypts ('cryptitis'). Crypt abscesses are typical. Goblet cells lose their mucus and in long-standing cases glands become distorted. Dysplasia, characterised by heaping of cells within the crypts, nuclear atypia and increased mitotic rate, may herald the development of colon cancer.

Crohn's disease

The sites most commonly involved, in order of frequency, are terminal ileum and right side of colon, colon alone, terminal ileum alone, ileum and jejunum. Characteristically, the entire wall of the bowel is oedematous and thickened. There are deep ulcers which often appear as linear fissures; thus the mucosa between them is described as 'cobblestone'. Deep ulcers may penetrate through the bowel wall to initiate abscesses or fistulae. Fistulae may develop between adjacent loops of bowel or between affected segments of bowel and the bladder, uterus or vagina and may appear in the perineum.

Characteristically, the changes are patchy. Even when a relatively short segment of bowel is affected, the inflammatory process is interrupted by islands of normal mucosa and the change from the affected part is abrupt. A small lesion separated in this way from a major area of involvement is referred to as a 'skip' lesion. The mesenteric lymph nodes are enlarged and the mesentery thickened.

Histologically, chronic inflammation is seen through all the layers of the bowel wall, which is thickened as a result (see Fig. 17.48). There are focal aggregates of epithelioid histiocytes, which may be surrounded by lymphocytes and contain giant cells. Lymphoid aggregates or microgranulomas are also seen, and when these are near to the surface of the mucosa they often ulcerate to form tiny aphthous-like ulcers.

Clinical features

Ulcerative colitis

The first attack is usually the most severe and thereafter the disease is followed by relapses and remissions. Only a minority of patients have chronic, unremitting symptoms. Emotional stress, intercurrent infection, gastroenteritis, antibiotics or NSAID therapy may provoke a relapse. The clinical features depend upon the site and activity of the disease.

Proctitis causes rectal bleeding and mucus discharge, sometimes accompanied by tenesmus. Some patients pass frequent, small-volume fluid stools, while others are constipated and pass pellety stools. Constitutional symptoms do not occur.

Proctosigmoiditis causes bloody diarrhoea with mucus. Almost all patients are constitutionally well but a small minority who have very active, limited disease develop fever, lethargy and abdominal discomfort.

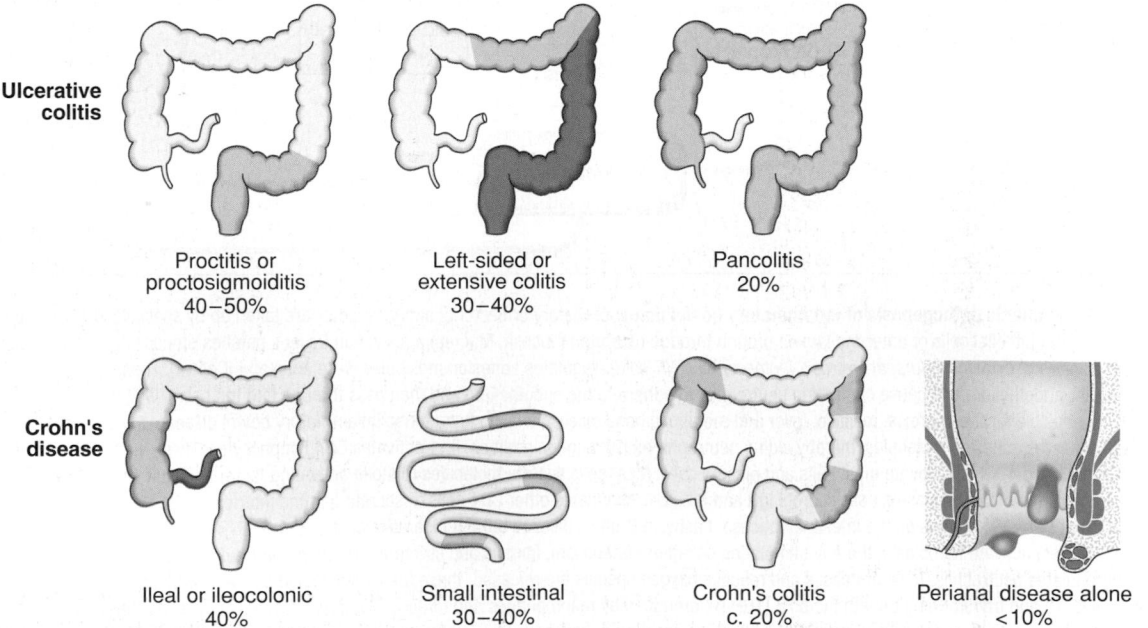

Ulcerative colitis

Proctitis or proctosigmoiditis 40–50%

Left-sided or extensive colitis 30–40%

Pancolitis 20%

Crohn's disease

Ileal or ileocolonic 40%

Small intestinal 30–40%

Crohn's colitis c. 20%

Perianal disease alone <10%

Fig. 17.46   Common patterns of disease distribution in inflammatory bowel disease. Overlap of distribution is common in Crohn's disease.

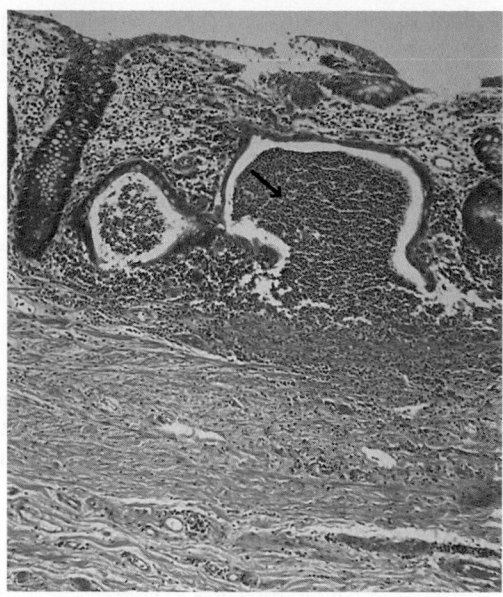

Fig. 17.47 Histology of ulcerative colitis. Inflammation is confined to the mucosa with excess inflammatory cells in the lamina propria, loss of goblet cells, and crypt abscesses (arrow).

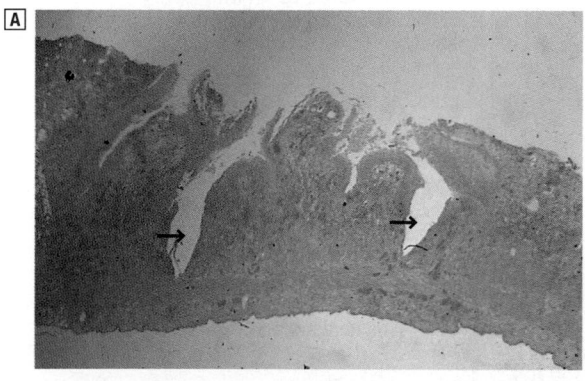

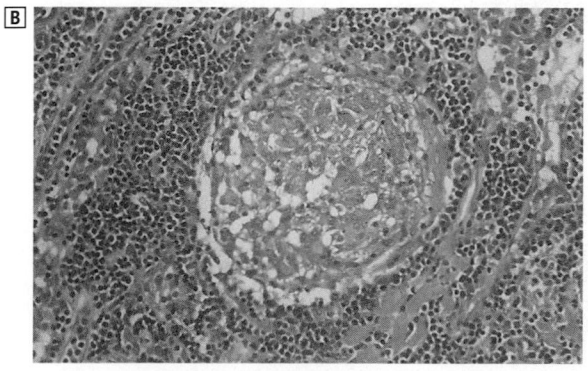

Fig. 17.48 Histology of Crohn's disease. A Inflammation is 'transmural'; there is ulceration with loss of surface epithelium and deep fissuring ulcers extending into the submucosa (arrows). B At higher power a characteristic non-caseating granuloma is seen.

17.55 DISEASE SEVERITY ASSESSMENT IN ULCERATIVE COLITIS		
	Mild	Severe
Daily bowel frequency	< 4	> 6
Blood in stools	+/–	+++
Stool volume (g/24 hrs)	< 200	> 400
Pulse (bpm)	< 90	> 90
Temperature (°C)	Normal	> 37.8, 2 days out of 4
Sigmoidoscopy	Normal or granular mucosa	Blood in lumen
Abdominal radiograph	Normal	Dilated bowel and/or mucosal islands
Haemoglobin (g/l)	Normal	< 100
ESR (mm/hr)	Normal	> 30
Serum albumin (g/l)	> 35	< 30

Extensive colitis causes bloody diarrhoea with passage of mucus. In severe cases anorexia, malaise, weight loss and abdominal pain occur, and the patient is toxic with fever, tachycardia and signs of peritoneal inflammation (see Box 17.55).

Crohn's disease
Presentation depends on the major site of disease involvement.

Ileal disease causes abdominal pain, principally because of subacute intestinal obstruction, although an inflammatory mass, intra-abdominal abscess or acute obstruction may be responsible. Pain is often associated with diarrhoea which is watery and does not contain blood or mucus. Almost all patients lose weight. This is usually because they avoid food since eating provokes pain. Weight loss may also be due to malabsorption, and some patients present with features of fat, protein or vitamin deficiencies.

Crohn's colitis presents in an identical manner to ulcerative colitis, with bloody diarrhoea, passage of mucus and constitutional symptoms including lethargy, malaise, anorexia and weight loss. Rectal sparing and the presence of perianal disease are features which favour a diagnosis of Crohn's disease rather than ulcerative colitis.

Many patients present with symptoms of both small bowel and colonic disease. A few have isolated perianal disease, vomiting from jejunal strictures or severe oral ulceration.

Physical examination often reveals evidence of weight loss, anaemia with glossitis and angular stomatitis. There is abdominal tenderness, most marked over the inflamed area. An abdominal mass due to matted loops of thickened bowel or an intra-abdominal abscess may occur. Perianal skin tags, fissures or fistulae are found in at least 50% of patients.

Complications
Intestinal
- *Severe, life-threatening inflammation of the colon.* This occurs in both ulcerative colitis and Crohn's disease. In the most extreme cases the colon dilates (toxic megacolon)

and bacterial toxins pass freely across the diseased mucosa into the portal then systemic circulation. This complication occurs most commonly during the first attack of colitis and is recognised by the features described in Box 17.55. An abdominal radiograph should be taken daily because when the transverse colon is dilated to more than 6 cm (see Fig. 17.54, p. 815) there is a high risk of colonic perforation and subsequent generalised peritonitis and death.

- *Perforation of the small intestine or colon*. This can occur without the development of toxic megacolon.
- *Life-threatening acute haemorrhage*. Haemorrhage due to erosion of a major artery is a rare complication of both conditions.
- *Fistula and perianal disease*. Fistulous connections between loops of affected bowel, or between bowel and bladder or vagina are specific complications of Crohn's disease and do not occur in ulcerative colitis. Enteroenteric fistulae cause diarrhoea and malabsorption due to blind loop syndrome. Enterovesical fistulation causes recurrent urinary infections and pneumaturia. An enterovaginal fistula causes a feculent vaginal discharge. Fistulation from the bowel may also cause perianal or ischiorectal

abscesses, fissures and fistulae. These may sometimes be extremely severe and can be the source of great morbidity.

- *Cancer*. Patients with extensive active colitis of more than 8 years' duration are at increased risk of colon cancer. The cumulative risk for ulcerative colitis may be as high as 20% after 30 years but is probably less for Crohn's colitis. Tumours develop in areas of dysplasia and may be multiple. Small bowel adenocarcinoma is a rare complication of long-standing small bowel Crohn's disease. Patients with long-standing, extensive colitis are therefore entered into surveillance colonoscopy programmes beginning 8–10 years after diagnosis. Multiple random biopsies are taken every 10 cm throughout the colon and additional biopsies are taken from raised or ulcerated areas. Dysplastic changes are graded by histopathologists as low-grade or high-grade. Assessment of biopsies is subjective and the presence of active inflammation makes analysis of dysplasia very difficult. Patients who have no evidence of dysplasia or only low-grade dysplasia are screened every year to every 2 years, while those with high-grade dysplasia should be considered for panproctocolectomy because of the high risk of colon cancer development.

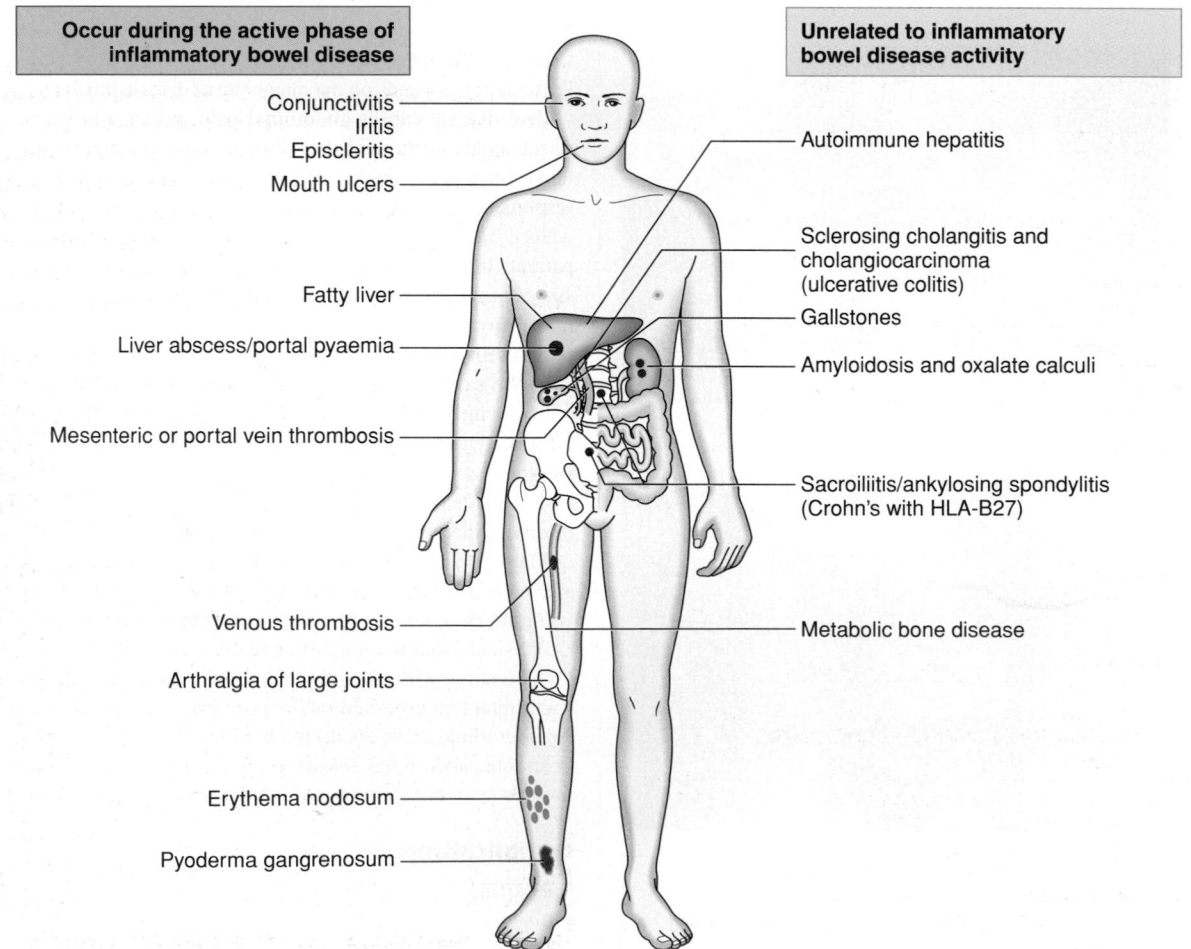

Occur during the active phase of inflammatory bowel disease

- Conjunctivitis
- Iritis
- Episcleritis
- Mouth ulcers
- Fatty liver
- Liver abscess/portal pyaemia
- Mesenteric or portal vein thrombosis
- Venous thrombosis
- Arthralgia of large joints
- Erythema nodosum
- Pyoderma gangrenosum

Unrelated to inflammatory bowel disease activity

- Autoimmune hepatitis
- Sclerosing cholangitis and cholangiocarcinoma (ulcerative colitis)
- Gallstones
- Amyloidosis and oxalate calculi
- Sacroiliitis/ankylosing spondylitis (Crohn's with HLA-B27)
- Metabolic bone disease

Fig. 17.49 Systemic complications of inflammatory bowel disease.

Extraintestinal

Inflammatory bowel disease can be considered as a systemic illness and in some patients extraintestinal complications dominate the clinical picture. Some of these occur during relapse of intestinal disease; others appear unrelated to intestinal disease activity (see Fig. 17.49).

Differential diagnosis (see Boxes 17.56 and 17.57)

Ulcerative colitis

The major diagnostic difficulty is to distinguish the first attack of acute colitis from infection. In general, diarrhoea lasting longer than 10 days in Western countries is unlikely to be the result of infection. A history of foreign travel, antibiotic exposure (pseudomembranous colitis) or homosexual contact suggests infection. Stool microscopy, culture and examination for *Clostridium difficile* toxin or for ova and cysts, sigmoidoscopy and rectal biopsy, blood cultures and serological tests for infection are useful.

Small bowel Crohn's disease

Crohn's disease can usually be diagnosed with confidence without histological confirmation in the appropriate clinical setting. Indium- or technetium-labelled white cell scanning may help identify inflamed intestinal segments. In atypical cases biopsy or surgical resection is necessary to exclude other diseases (see Box 17.57). This can often be done endoscopically by ileal intubation at colonoscopy, but sometimes laparotomy or laparoscopy with resection or full-thickness biopsy is necessary.

Investigations

These confirm the diagnosis, define disease distribution and activity, and identify specific complications.

Blood tests

Anaemia results from bleeding or malabsorption of iron, folic acid or vitamin B_{12}. Serum albumin concentration falls as a consequence of protein-losing enteropathy, reflecting active and extensive disease, or because of poor nutrition. The ESR is raised in exacerbations or because of abscess. Elevation of CRP concentration is helpful in monitoring Crohn's disease activity.

Bacteriology

Stool cultures are performed to exclude superimposed enteric infection in patients who present with exacerbations of inflammatory bowel disease. Blood cultures are also advisable in patients with known colitis or Crohn's disease who develop fever.

Endoscopy

Sigmoidoscopy with biopsies is a simple and essential investigation in all patients who present with diarrhoea (see Fig. 17.50). Rectal sparing, perianal disease and discrete ulcers suggest Crohn's disease rather than ulcerative colitis.

Colonoscopy may show active inflammation with pseudopolyps or a complicating carcinoma. Biopsies are taken to define disease extent, as this is underestimated by endoscopic appearances alone, and to seek dysplasia in patients with long-standing colitis. In ulcerative colitis the

17.56 CONDITIONS WHICH CAN MIMIC ULCERATIVE OR CROHN'S COLITIS	
Infective	
Bacterial	
• *Salmonella*	• *E. coli* 0:157
• *Shigella*	• Gonococcal proctitis
• *Campylobacter jejuni*	• Pseudomembranous colitis
Viral	
• Herpes simplex proctitis	• Cytomegalovirus
• *Chlamydia* proctitis	
Protozoal	
• Amoebiasis	
Non-infective	
Vascular	
• Ischaemic colitis	• Radiation proctitis
Idiopathic	
• Collagenous colitis	• Behçet's disease
Drugs	
• NSAIDs	
Neoplastic	
• Colonic carcinoma	
Other	
• Diverticulitis	

17.57 DIFFERENTIAL DIAGNOSIS OF SMALL BOWEL CROHN'S DISEASE

• Other causes of right iliac fossa mass
  Caecal carcinoma*
  Appendix abscess*
  Infection (tuberculosis, *Yersinia*, actinomycosis)

• Mesenteric adenitis
• Pelvic inflammatory disease
• Lymphoma
* Common; other causes are rare.

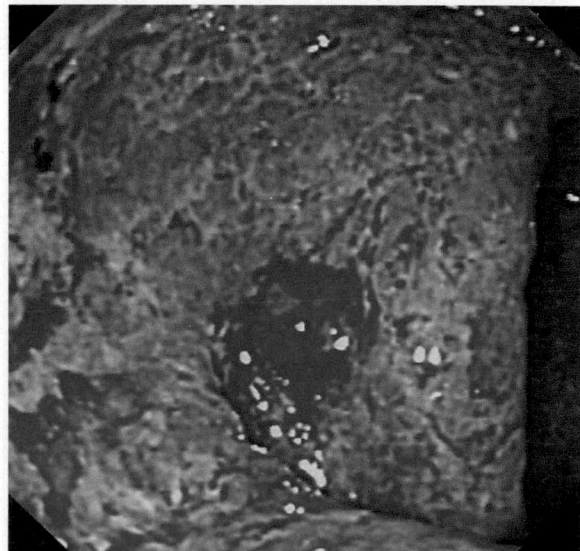

Fig. 17.50 Sigmoidoscopic view of moderately active ulcerative colitis. Mucosa is erythematous and friable with contact bleeding. Submucosal blood vessels are no longer visible.

macroscopic and histological abnormalities are confluent and most severe in the distal colon and rectum. Stricture formation does not occur in the absence of a carcinoma. In Crohn's colitis the endoscopic abnormalities are patchy, with normal mucosa between the areas of abnormality. Aphthoid or deeper ulcers and strictures are common.

Barium studies

Barium enema is a less sensitive investigation than colonoscopy for the investigation of colitis. In long-standing ulcerative colitis the colon is shortened and loses haustra to become tubular, and pseudopolyps are seen (see Fig. 17.51). In Crohn's colitis a range of abnormalities occur. The appearances may be identical to those of ulcerative colitis but skip lesions, strictures and deeper ulcers are characteristic (see Fig. 17.52). Reflux into the terminal ileum may show stricture and ulcers.

Contrast studies of the small bowel are normal in ulcerative colitis, but in Crohn's disease affected areas are narrowed and ulcerated; multiple strictures are common (see Fig. 17.53).

Plain radiographs

A straight abdominal radiograph is essential in the management of patients who present with severe active disease. In colitis dilatation of the colon (see Fig. 17.54), mucosal oedema ('thumb-printing') or evidence of perforation may be found. In small bowel Crohn's disease there may be evidence of intestinal obstruction or displacement of bowel loops by a mass.

Radionuclide scans

Radio-labelled white cell scans show areas of active inflammation. They are less accurate than other imaging modalities with poor specificity but may be useful in severely ill patients in whom invasive tests are best avoided.

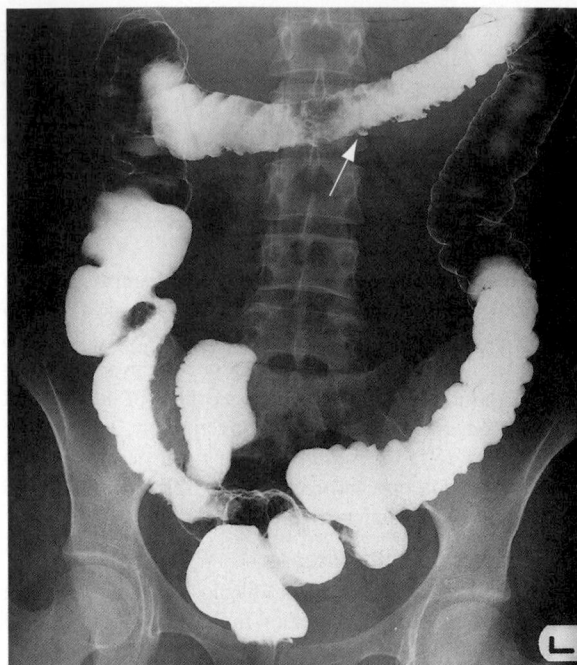

Fig. 17.52 Ileocolonic Crohn's disease. Barium enema showing normal rectum and sigmoid colon, typical aphthous ulceration in the descending colon, ulceration (arrow) and lack of haustra in the transverse colon. The ascending colon and caecum are normal and there is typical Crohn's disease affecting the terminal ileum, with coarse ulceration, rigidity and lack of mucosal folds.

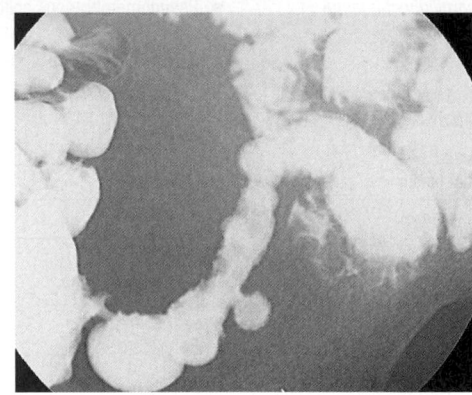

Fig. 17.53 Barium follow-through showing terminal ileal Crohn's disease.

MRI

MRI scans are very accurate in delineating pelvic or perineal involvement by Crohn's disease.

Management

Best treatment depends upon a team approach involving physicians, surgeons, radiologists and dietitians. Both ulcerative colitis and Crohn's disease are life-long conditions and have psychosocial implications; counsellors and patient support groups have important roles in education, reassurance and coping. The key aims are to:

- treat acute attacks
- prevent relapses

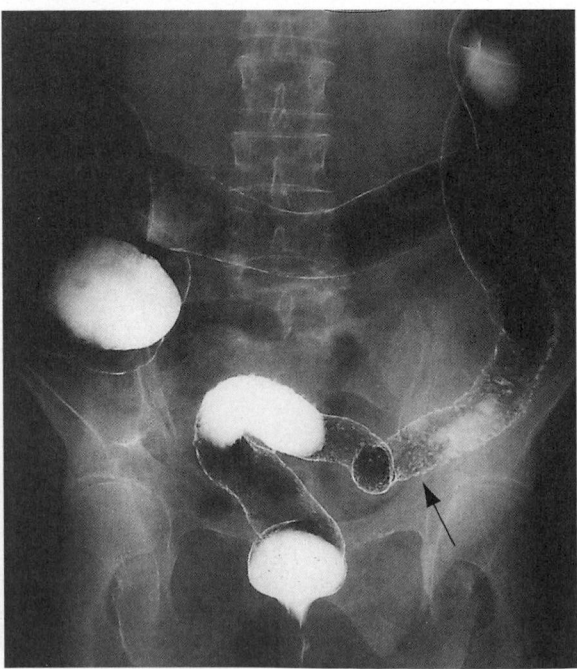

Fig. 17.51 Barium enema showing shortened colon, loss of haustra, pseudopolyps and fine ulceration (arrow).

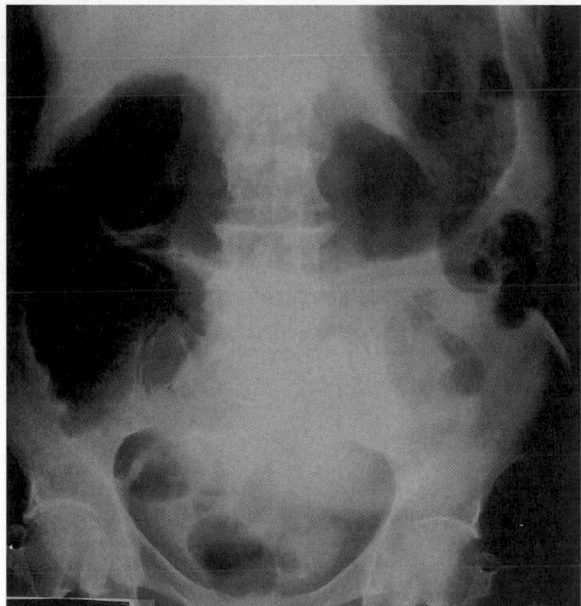

Fig. 17.54 **Plain abdominal radiograph showing a grossly dilated colon due to severe ulcerative colitis.**

- detect carcinoma at an early stage
- select patients for surgery.

Drug treatment of colitis

The principles of drug treatment are similar for ulcerative colitis and Crohn's colitis. They are based upon the treatment of active disease and prevention of relapse.

Active colitis. Corticosteroids are the first-line treatment. Active proctosigmoiditis should be managed by steroid foam or liquid retention enemas, from which systemic corticosteroid absorption is clinically insignificant. Patients with very active proctosigmoiditis, those who are unable to retain enemas and those who have active, extensive colitis need oral corticosteroids. Prednisolone (30–40 mg/day orally) is given for 2 weeks and then reduced slowly over 8 weeks. Severe active colitis can be treated with intravenous methylprednisolone (60 mg daily by infusion). Once improvement occurs, the patient is converted to a reducing regimen of oral prednisolone.

Systemic steroid complications, such as mood changes, acne, weight gain and dyspepsia, are common but these resolve as the dose is reduced. Long-term, high-dose therapy must be avoided because of risks of the more severe steroid complications such as metabolic bone disease and infection.

Patients who relapse frequently after courses of steroids or who require maintenance steroid therapy may be considered for azathioprine treatment (1.5–2 mg/kg body weight daily). This immunosuppressant drug exerts its maximal effect only after 6–12 weeks, and corticosteroid therapy may have to be continued until this time. Treatment is sometimes complicated by bone marrow suppression, nausea, vomiting, myalgia or acute pancreatitis.

Antidiarrhoeal agents (codeine phosphate, loperamide or diphenoxylate) are sometimes useful but should be avoided in severe active disease.

Maintenance of remission. This is based upon the use of 5-aminosalicylic acid (5-ASA) which acts by modulating intestinal inflammatory activity. High concentrations of 5-ASA are delivered to the colon using the preparations mesalazine or olsalazine and these have replaced sulfasalazine which has a worse side-effect profile. Mesalazine is an enteric-coated form in which 5-ASA is slowly released from a cellulose-based or pH-dependent coating. Olsalazine comprises two molecules of 5-ASA bound by an azo bond to optimise delivery to the colon. 5-ASA liquid or foam retention enemas are also available and are as effective as steroid enemas for treating active proctitis.

EBM

ULCERATIVE COLITIS—role of 5-aminosalicylic acid (5-ASA)

'Six RCTs including a total of 485 5-ASA-treated patients and 401 placebo-treated patients indicate that active therapy is better than placebo (Chi Square 2.39).'

- Jewell DP, Sutherland LR. Ulcerative colitis: diagnosis, prognosis and treatment. In: McDonald J, Burroughs A, Feagan B, eds. Evidence-based gastroenterology and hepatology. London: BMJ Books; 1999.

Further information: 💻 www.evidbasedgastro.org

Drug treatment of small bowel Crohn's disease

Drug treatment for active disease is based upon the use of oral corticosteroids (prednisolone 30–40 mg daily), reducing over 6–8 weeks. Patients who respond yet frequently relapse after stopping steroids, or who are steroid-dependent, are usually treated with azathioprine (1.5–2 mg/kg body weight daily). Steroid side-effects can be overcome by using budesonide; this is a potent synthetic corticosteroid which reduces mucosal inflammation. (9 mg is equivalent to 30 mg of prednisolone.) Following absorption, the drug undergoes extensive first-pass metabolism in the liver; adrenocortical suppression is minimised and steroid side-effects are reduced.

Some patients respond inadequately to steroids and azathioprine. In these, other immunosuppressive drugs such as methotrexate or immunomodulatory agents have a role. Antibodies to TNF-α ('infliximab') induce remission in 70–80% of patients whose disease is refractory to corticosteroids; this drug is particularly useful in healing fistulae associated with Crohn's disease. Unfortunately, most patients relapse after approximately 12 weeks and further infliximab infusions given at this time may cause anaphylactic reactions. Other genetically engineered immunomodulatory drugs, directed against other steps in the inflammatory cascade (see Fig. 17.45, p. 809), will inevitably be developed.

EBM

CROHN'S DISEASE—role of azathioprine

'Six RCTs examining the role of azathioprine in the maintenance of Crohn's disease (136 patients azathioprine, 183 patients placebo) have shown that active therapy is better than placebo (Chi Square 7.37).'

- Feagan BG, McDonald JWD. Crohn's disease: treatment. In: McDonald J, Burroughs A, Feagan B, eds. Evidence-based gastroenterology and hepatology. London: BMJ Books; 1999.

Further information: 💻 www.evidbasedgastro.org

17.58 INDICATIONS FOR SURGERY IN ULCERATIVE COLITIS

Impaired quality of life
- Loss of occupation or education
- Disruption of family life

Failure of medical therapy
- Dependence upon oral corticosteroids
- Complications of drug therapy

Fulminant colitis

Disease complications, unresponsive to medical therapy
- Arthritis
- Pyoderma gangrenosum

Colon cancer or severe dysplasia

Metabolic bone disease

Inflammatory bowel disease patients, particularly those needing frequent courses of steroids and those who are malnourished, have a significant risk of bone demineralisation leading to osteopenia and osteoporosis, and a high risk of fracture. Details of management are given on page 1027.

Nutritional therapy

Many patients embark upon 'elimination diets' in which specific foods are avoided. Although some colitic patients do improve on a milk-free diet and a few others respond to avoidance of wheat, the best advice for the majority of patients is to eat a well-balanced, healthy diet and to avoid only those foods which, by experience, are poorly tolerated. Exceptions include patients with small bowel strictures, who should avoid nuts, pulses, raw fruit and vegetables which may precipitate intestinal obstruction, and patients with a combination of proctitis and constipation who benefit from increased dietary fibre.

Many patients who have severe chronic inflammatory bowel disease are undernourished. They require dietary assessment and appropriate calorie, protein, vitamin and mineral supplements. This is particularly important in children.

Specific nutritional therapy can induce remission in active Crohn's disease but not in ulcerative colitis. Elemental diets which contain simple sugars, triglycerides, amino acids, vitamins and trace elements, and polymeric diets which contain oligopeptides rather than amino acids, are both effective. Normal food is avoided for the 2–4 weeks of treatment. Possible modes of action include improved nutrition, exclusion of dietary antigens and avoidance of dietary fibre. Unfortunately, nutritional therapy is expensive, is often poorly tolerated and is usually followed by disease relapse on return to a normal diet.

Surgical treatment

Ulcerative colitis. Up to 60% of patients with extensive ulcerative colitis eventually require surgery. The indications are listed in Box 17.58. Impaired quality of life, with impact upon occupation and on social and family life, is the most important of these.

Surgery involves removal of the entire colon and rectum and cures the patient. Before surgery, patients must be counselled by doctors, stoma nurses and patients who have undergone similar surgery. The choice of procedure is either panproctocolectomy with ileostomy or proctocolectomy with ileal-anal pouch anastomosis. Surgical textbooks should be consulted for further details.

Crohn's disease. The indications for surgery are similar to those for ulcerative colitis. Operations are often necessary to deal with fistulae, abscesses and perianal disease, and may also be required to relieve small or large bowel obstruction.

Up to 80% of patients eventually need some form of surgical intervention but, unlike ulcerative colitis, surgery does not cure the patients and disease recurrence is the rule. Surgical intervention should therefore be as conservative as possible in order to minimise loss of viable intestine and to avoid creation of a short bowel syndrome.

Patients who have localised segments of Crohn's colitis may be managed by segmental resection. Others who have extensive colitis require total colectomy but ileal-anal pouch formation should be avoided because of the high risk of disease recurrence within the pouch and subsequent fistula, abscess formation and pouch failure.

Patients who have perianal Crohn's disease are managed as conservatively as possible by drainage of abscess and avoidance of resection or reconstructive procedures. Obstructing or fistulating small bowel disease may require resection of affected tissue. Patients who have multiple or recurrent strictures are considered for strictureplasty in which the stricture is not resected but instead incised in its longitudinal axis and sutured transversely.

Management of complications

Fulminant colitis. This is a life-threatening complication which demands intensive medical and surgical management. Patients should be monitored frequently for clinical signs of peritonitis, fever and tachycardia. Stool frequency and volumes are documented and abdominal radiographs are taken daily to seek evidence of toxic dilatation or perforation. The patient must also be counselled about the possibility of surgery.

If improvement has not occurred within 5–7 days, or if the patient deteriorates, urgent colectomy should be undertaken. The lower rectum can be left in situ for subsequent ileo-anal pouch reconstruction. Key steps in the management of fulminant ulcerative colitis are listed in Box 17.59.

17.59 MANAGEMENT OF FULMINANT ULCERATIVE COLITIS
• Intravenous fluids • Transfusion if Hb < 100 g/l • I.v. methylprednisolone (60 mg daily) or hydrocortisone • Antibiotics for proven infection • Nutritional support • Subcutaneous heparin for prophylaxis of venous thromboembolism • Avoidance of opiates and antidiarrhoeal agents

Perianal disease. The treatment of perianal disease, including fissure, fistula and abscess formation, is based upon a conservative approach. For many patients symptoms are few, even when the visible disease is apparently severe. In these the benefits of medical or surgical intervention are few and the relative risks of complications are high. Patients who have painful or discharging perineal disease are managed jointly by surgeons and physicians. Metronidazole or ciprofloxacin therapy may relieve pain and eliminate sepsis. Abscesses require drainage but radical procedures risk damage to the anal sphincters and faecal incontinence. Infliximab may induce remission in resistant cases.

Inflammatory bowel disease in special circumstances

Childhood
Ulcerative colitis and Crohn's disease can develop before adolescence. Chronic ill health results in growth failure, metabolic bone disease and delayed puberty. Loss of schooling and social contact, as well as frequent hospitalisation, can have important psychosocial consequences. Treatment is similar to that described for adults and may require use of corticosteroids, immunosuppressive drugs and surgery. Monitoring of height, weight and sexual development is important.

Pregnancy
The activity of inflammatory bowel disease is not usually affected by pregnancy although relapse may be more common after parturition. Drug therapy including aminosalicylates, corticosteroids and azathioprine can be safely continued throughout the pregnancy.

Prognosis
Life expectancy in patients with inflammatory bowel disease is now similar to that of the general population. Although many patients require surgery and admission to hospital for other reasons, the majority have an excellent work record and pursue a normal life. Around 90% of ulcerative colitis patients have intermittent disease activity, whilst 10% have continuous symptoms. One-third of those with pancolitis undergo colectomy within 5 years of diagnosis. Around 80% of Crohn's patients undergo surgery at some stage, and 70% of these require more than one operation during their lifetime. Clinical recurrence following resectional surgery is present in 50% of all cases at 10 years.

MICROSCOPIC COLITIS
Some patients experience watery diarrhoea as a consequence of microscopic ('lymphocytic') colitis. The colonoscopic appearances are normal but histological examination of biopsies shows a range of abnormalities.

Collagenous colitis is characterised by the presence of a thick submucosal band of collagen; a chronic inflammatory infiltrate is usually seen. The disease is more common in women and is associated with rheumatoid arthritis, diabetes and coeliac disease. Patients have a history of intermittent watery diarrhoea and treatment is based upon the use of antidiarrhoeal drugs, bismuth, aminosalicylates and topical steroid enemas.

IRRITABLE BOWEL SYNDROME

Functional gastrointestinal disorders are extremely common. They are defined as disorders of gut function in the absence of structural pathology. Irritable bowel syndrome (IBS) is a functional bowel disorder in which abdominal pain is associated with defaecation or a change in bowel habit with features of disordered defaecation and distension.

Epidemiology
Approximately 20% of the general population fulfil diagnostic criteria for IBS but only 10% of these consult their doctors because of gastrointestinal symptoms. Nevertheless, IBS is the most common cause of gastrointestinal referral and accounts for frequent absenteeism from work and impaired quality of life. Young women are most often affected. There is wide overlap with non-ulcer dyspepsia, chronic fatigue syndrome, dysmenorrhoea and urinary frequency. A significant proportion of these patients have a history of physical or sexual abuse.

Aetiology
Irritable bowel syndrome encompasses a wide range of symptoms and a single cause is unlikely. It is generally believed that most patients develop symptoms in response to psychosocial factors, altered gastrointestinal motility, altered visceral sensation or luminal factors.

Psychosocial factors
Most patients seen in general practice do not have psychological problems but about 50% of patients referred to hospital meet criteria for a psychiatric diagnosis. A range of disturbances are identified, including anxiety, depression, somatisation and neurosis. Panic attacks are also common. Acute psychological stress and overt psychiatric disease are known to alter gastrointestinal motility in both irritable bowel patients and healthy people. There is an increased prevalence of abnormal illness behaviour with frequent consultations for minor symptoms (see p. 254).

Altered gastrointestinal motility
A range of motility disorders are found but none is diagnostic. Patients with diarrhoea as a predominant symptom exhibit clusters of rapid jejunal contraction waves, rapid intestinal

transit and an increased number of fast and propagated colonic contractions. Those who are predominantly constipated have decreased orocaecal transit and a reduced number of high-amplitude, propagated colonic contraction waves but there is no consistent evidence of abnormal motility.

Abnormal visceral perception

Irritable bowel syndrome is associated with increased sensitivity to intestinal distension induced by inflation of balloons in the ileum, colon and rectum, a consequence of altered CNS processing of visceral sensation.

Luminal factors

Between 10 and 20% of patients develop irritable bowel syndrome following an episode of gastroenteritis, while others may be intolerant of specific dietary components, particularly lactose and wheat.

Clinical features

The most common presentation is that of recurrent abdominal pain (see Box 17.60). This is usually colicky or 'cramping', is felt in the lower abdomen and is relieved by defaecation. Abdominal bloating worsens throughout the day; the cause is unknown but it is not due to excessive intestinal gas. The

bowel habit is variable. Most patients alternate between episodes of diarrhoea and constipation but it is useful to classify patients as having predominantly constipation or predominantly diarrhoea. The constipated type tend to pass infrequent pellety stools, usually in association with abdominal pain or proctalgia. Those with diarrhoea have frequent defaecation but produce low-volume stools and rarely have nocturnal symptoms. Passage of mucus is common but rectal bleeding does not occur.

Despite apparently severe symptoms, patients do not lose weight and are constitutionally well. Many have other 'functional' symptoms including dyspepsia, urinary frequency, headaches, backache, dyspareunia, poor sleep and chronic fatigue syndrome. Physical examination does not reveal any abnormalities, although abdominal bloating and variable tenderness to palpation are common.

Diagnosis

Investigations are normal. A positive diagnosis can confidently be made in patients under the age of 40 years without resort to complicated tests. Full blood count, ESR and sigmoidoscopy are usually done routinely, but barium enema or colonoscopy should only be undertaken in older patients to exclude colorectal cancer. Those who present atypically require investigations to exclude organic gastrointestinal disease. Diarrhoea-predominant patients justify investigations to exclude microscopic colitis (see p. 817), lactose intolerance (see p. 799), bile acid malabsorption (see p. 760), coeliac disease (see p. 792) and thyrotoxicosis. All patients who give a history of rectal bleeding should undergo colonoscopy or barium enema to exclude colonic cancer or inflammatory bowel disease.

17.60 FEATURES OF IRRITABLE BOWEL SYNDROME	

- Altered bowel habit
- Colicky abdominal pain
- Abdominal distension
- Rectal mucus
- Feeling of incomplete defaecation

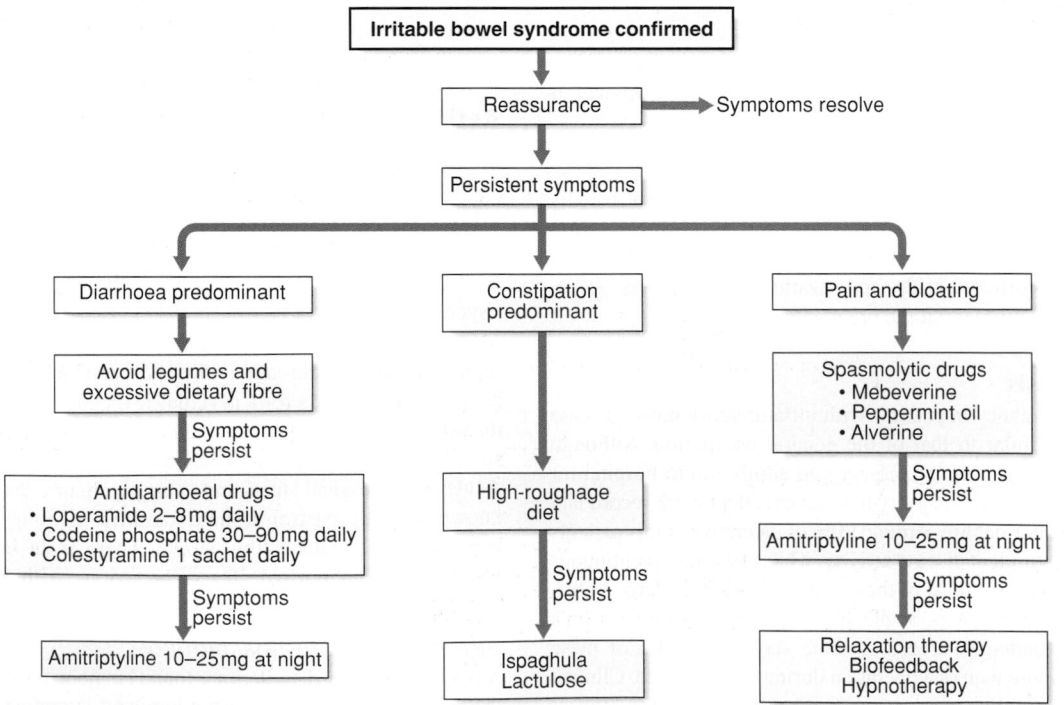

Fig. 17.55 **Management of irritable bowel syndrome.**

Management

The most important steps are to make a positive diagnosis and reassure the patient. Many patients are concerned that they have developed cancer, and a cycle of anxiety leading to colonic symptoms, which further heighten anxiety, can be broken by explanation that symptoms are not due to organic disease but are the result of altered bowel motility and sensation. In patients who fail to respond to reassurance, treatment is tailored to the predominant symptoms (see Fig. 17.55).

Patients with intractable symptoms sometimes benefit from several months of therapy with amitriptyline. This is given in doses (10–25 mg at night) which are much lower than those used to treat depression. Side-effects include dry mouth and drowsiness but these are usually mild and the drug is well tolerated. It may act by reducing visceral sensation and by altering gastrointestinal motility. Other drugs may overcome abnormalities of 5-HT signalling which have been identified in some IBS patients. These include 5-HT4 agonists. Hypnotherapy is reserved for the most difficult cases.

Most patients have a relapsing and remitting course. Exacerbations often follow stressful life events, occupational dissatisfaction and difficulties with interpersonal relationships.

IRRITABLE BOWEL SYNDROME—role of antidepressants **EBM**

'Six placebo-controlled RCTs have shown benefit for tricyclic antidepressant therapy in irritable bowel patients. Patients whose major symptoms are pain and diarrhoea benefit most; those with constipation as a predominant symptom benefit least.'

- Greenbaum DS, Magle JE, Vanegeren LE, et al. The effects of despiramine on IBS compared with atropine and placebo. Dig Dis Sci 1987; 32:257–266.
- Myren J, Lovland B, Larssen SE. A double blind study of the effect of trimipramine in patients with the irritable bowel syndrome. Scand J Gastroenterol 1984; 19:835–843.
- Ritchie JA, Tinelore SC. Comparisons of various treatments for irritable bowel syndrome. BMJ 1980; 281:257–266.
- Tripathi BM, Misra NP, Gupta AK. Evaluation of tricyclic compound (trimipramine) vis-à-vis placebo in irritable bowel syndrome. J Assoc Physicians India 1989; 31:201–203.

Further information: 💻 www.bsg.org.uk
💻 www.evidbasedgastro.com

AIDS AND THE GASTROINTESTINAL TRACT

See page 117.

ISCHAEMIC GUT INJURY

Ischaemic gut injury (see Fig. 17.56) is usually the result of arterial occlusion. Severe hypotension and venous insufficiency are less frequent causes (see p. 207).

ACUTE SMALL BOWEL ISCHAEMIA

An embolus from the heart to the superior mesenteric artery is responsible for 40–50% of cases. Non-occlusive ischaemia following hypotension results from myocardial infarction, heart failure, arrhythmias or sudden blood loss. The pathological spectrum ranges from a transient alteration of bowel function to transmural haemorrhagic necrosis and gangrene.

Patients usually have evidence of cardiac disease and arrhythmia. Almost all develop abdominal pain and this is characteristically more impressive than the physical findings. In the early stages the only physical sign is abdominal distension, and signs of peritonitis develop at a late stage as a consequence of necrotic intestine.

Leucocytosis, metabolic acidosis, hyperphosphataemia and hyperamylasaemia are typical. Plain abdominal radiographs show 'thumb-printing' due to mucosal oedema. Mesenteric angiography reveals an occluded or narrowed major artery with spasm of arterial arcades, although most patients undergo laparotomy on the basis of a clinical diagnosis without undergoing angiography.

The key steps in treatment are resuscitation, correction of cardiac disease and intravenous antibiotic therapy, followed

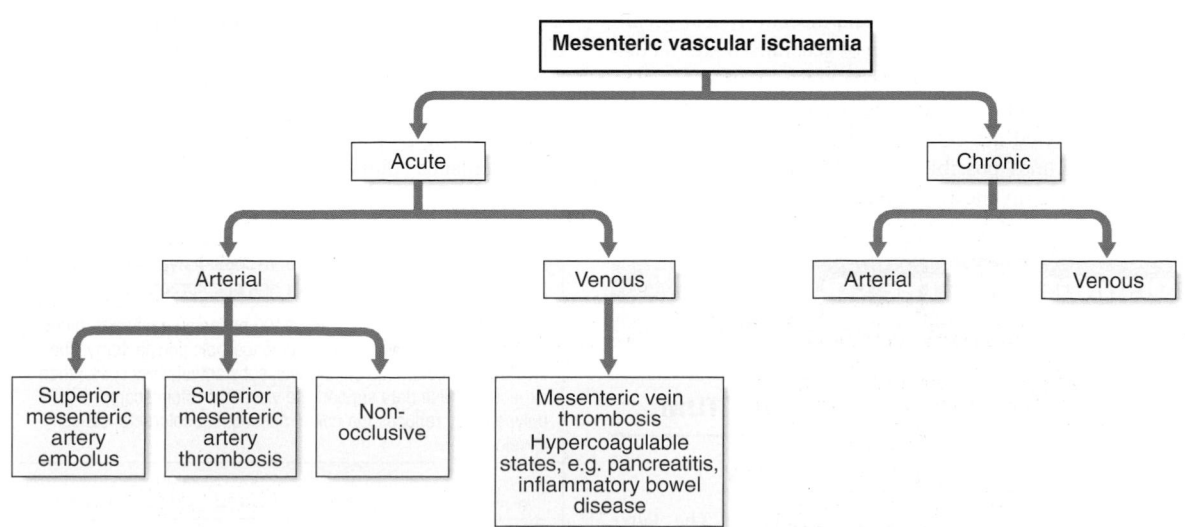

Fig. 17.56   Types of mesenteric vascular ischaemia.

by laparotomy. If this is done early enough, embolectomy and vascular reconstruction may salvage some small bowel. In these rare cases a 'second look' laparotomy is undertaken 24 hours later and further necrotic bowel resected. The results of therapy are dependent upon early intervention; patients treated at a late stage have a 75% mortality rate. Survivors often have nutritional failure from short bowel syndrome (see p. 796) and require intensive nutritional support, sometimes including home parenteral nutrition. Small bowel transplantation is a promising therapy in selected patients.

ACUTE COLONIC ISCHAEMIA

The splenic flexure and descending colon have little collateral circulation and lie in 'watershed' areas of arterial supply. A spectrum of injury ranging from reversible colopathy to transient colitis, colonic stricture, gangrene and fulminant pancolitis can occur. Arterial thromboembolism is usually responsible but colonic ischaemia can also occur following severe hypotension, colonic volvulus, strangulated hernia, systemic vasculitis or hypercoagulable states.

The patient is usually elderly and presents with sudden onset of cramping left-sided lower abdominal pain and rectal bleeding. In the majority of cases symptoms resolve spontaneously over 24–48 hours and healing occurs within 2 weeks. Some are left with a residual fibrous stricture or a segment of colitis. A minority develop gangrene and peritonitis. The diagnosis is established by colonoscopy or barium enema which should be performed within 48 hours of presentation because mucosal ulceration and oedema may have otherwise resolved.

CHRONIC MESENTERIC ISCHAEMIA

This results from atherosclerotic stenosis affecting at least two of the coeliac axis, superior mesenteric and inferior mesenteric arteries. The patient develops dull but severe mid- or upper abdominal pain approximately 30 minutes after eating. Patients lose weight because of reluctance to eat, and a proportion experience diarrhoea. Physical examination invariably shows evidence of generalised arterial disease. An abdominal bruit is sometimes audible but is a non-specific finding. Mesenteric angiography confirms at least two affected mesenteric arteries. Vascular reconstruction is sometimes possible. Left untreated, many patients eventually develop intestinal infarction.

DISORDERS OF THE COLON AND RECTUM

TUMOURS OF THE COLON AND RECTUM

POLYPS AND POLYPOSIS SYNDROMES

Polyps may be neoplastic or non-neoplastic. The latter include hamartomas, metaplastic ('hyperplastic') polyps and inflammatory polyps. These have no malignant potential.

Polyps may be single or multiple and vary from a few millimetres to several centimetres in size.

Colorectal adenomas are extremely common in the Western world and the prevalence rises with age; 50% of people over 60 years of age have adenomas, and in half of these the polyps are multiple. They are more common in the rectum and distal colon and are either pedunculated or sessile. Histologically, they are classified as either tubular, villous or tubulovillous, according to the glandular architecture.

Adenomas are usually asymptomatic and discovered incidentally. Occasionally, they cause bleeding and anaemia. Villous adenomas sometimes secrete large amounts of mucus, causing diarrhoea and hypokalaemia. The majority of cancers arise from adenomas ('adenoma-carcinoma sequence') over 5–10 years, although not all polyps carry the same degree of risk. Features associated with a higher risk of subsequent malignancy in colonic polyps are listed in Box 17.61.

17.61 RISK FACTORS FOR MALIGNANT CHANGE IN COLONIC POLYPS
• Large size (> 2 cm) • Multiple polyps • Villous architecture • Dysplasia

Discovery of a polyp at sigmoidoscopy is an indication for colonoscopy because proximal polyps are present in 40–50% of such patients. Colonoscopic polypectomy should be carried out wherever possible, as this considerably reduces subsequent colorectal cancer risk (see Fig. 17.57). Very large or sessile polyps which cannot be removed endoscopically require surgery. Once all polyps have been removed, patients should undergo surveillance colonoscopy at 3–5-year intervals, as new polyps develop in 50% of patients. Patients over 75 years of age do not require repeated colonoscopies, as their lifetime cancer risk is low.

Between 10 and 20% of polyps show histological evidence of malignancy. When cancer cells are found within 2 mm of the resection margin of the polyp, when the polyp cancer is poorly differentiated or when lymphatic invasion is present, segmental colonic resection is recommended because residual tumour or lymphatic spread may be present. Malignant polyps without these features can be followed up by surveillance colonoscopy.

EBM

COLONIC POLYPS—role of colonoscopic polypectomy in the reduction of subsequent risk of colorectal cancer

'In the US National Polyp Study, 1400 patients underwent follow-up for a mean of 5 years following colonoscopic polypectomy. The incidence of colorectal cancer was substantially less (75%) than expected; these data support the view that colonoscopic polypectomy reduces the risk of subsequent colorectal cancer development.'

• Winawer SJ, Zauber AG, Ho MN, et al. Prevention of colorectal cancer by colonoscopic polypectomy. National Polyp Study Workgroup. N Engl J Med 1993; 329:1977–1981.

Further information: 💻 www.bsg.org.uk
💻 www.evidbasedgastro.com

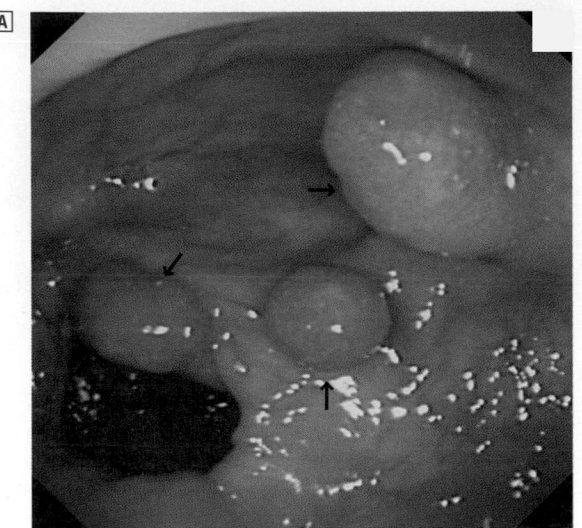 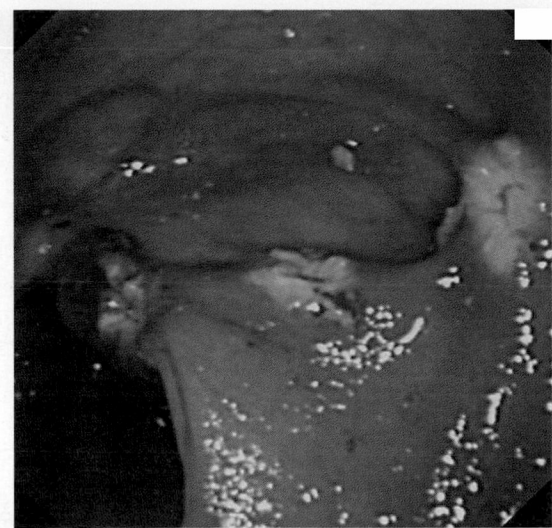

Fig. 17.57 Adenomatous colonic polyps. [A] Before colonoscopic polypectomy (arrows show polyps). [B] After polypectomy.

Polyposis syndromes are classified by histopathology (see Box 17.62). It should be noted that, while the hamartomatous polyps in Peutz–Jeghers syndrome and juvenile polyposis are not themselves neoplastic, these disorders are associated with an increased risk of certain malignancies, e.g. breast, colon, ovary and thyroid.

Familial adenomatous polyposis (FAP)

This uncommon (1 in 8000–14 000) autosomal dominant disorder results from germ-line mutation of the APC gene on the long arm of chromosome 5. One-third of cases arise as new mutations and have no family history. Hundreds to thousands of adenomatous colonic polyps will develop in 50% of patients by age 16 (see Fig. 17.58). Of those affected, 90% will develop colorectal cancer by the age of 45 years.

Adenomatous polyps are also frequently found in the stomach (50%) and duodenum (over 90%). The latter are most common around the ampulla of Vater and may undergo malignant transformation to adenocarcinoma. Many extraintestinal features are also seen in FAP and these are summarised in Box 17.63.

17.63 EXTRAINTESTINAL FEATURES OF FAMILIAL ADENOMATOUS POLYPOSIS

- Subcutaneous epidermoid cysts (extremities, face, scalp)
- Lipomas
- Benign osteomas, especially skull and angle of mandible
- Desmoid tumours
- Dental abnormalities (15–20%)
- Congenital hypertrophy of the retinal pigment epithelium (CHRPE)

17.62 GASTROINTESTINAL POLYPOSIS SYNDROMES					
	Neoplastic	**Non-neoplastic**			
	Familial adenomatous polyposis	Peutz–Jeghers syndrome	Juvenile polyposis	Cronkhite–Canada syndrome	Cowden's disease
Inheritance	Autosomal dominant	Autosomal dominant	Autosomal dominant in 1/3	None	Autosomal dominant
Oesophageal polyps	–	–	–	+	+
Gastric polyps	+	++	+	+++	+++
Small bowel polyps	++	+++	++	++	++
Colonic polyps	+++	++	++	+++	+
Other features	See text	See text	See text	Hair loss, pigmentation, nail dystrophy, malabsorption	Many congenital anomalies, oral and cutaneous hamartomas, thyroid and breast tumours

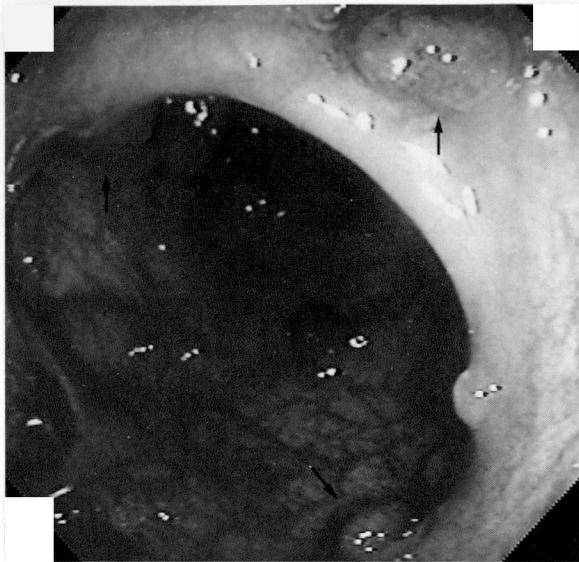

Fig. 17.58 Colonoscopic view in familial adenomatous polyposis. There are multiple small polyps throughout (arrows).

Desmoid tumours occur in 10% of patients and usually arise in the mesentery or abdominal wall. Although benign, they may become very large, may cause compression of adjacent organs and are difficult to remove. Congenital hypertrophy of the retinal pigment epithelium can be seen as dark, round, pigmented retinal lesions. When present in an at-risk individual, they are 100% predictive of the presence of FAP.

Clinically, several variants of FAP exist, including Gardner's syndrome, Turcot's syndrome and 'attenuated FAP', in which far fewer polyps are found and cancer development is delayed. In Gardner's syndrome, benign extra-intestinal features are prominent, notably epidermoid cysts and osteomas. Turcot's syndrome was formerly thought to be a distinct genetic entity but the majority of patients also have APC mutations. The syndrome is characterised by FAP with brain tumours (astrocytoma or medulloblastoma).

Diagnosis and management

In newly diagnosed cases with new mutations, genetic testing by DNA linkage analysis confirms the diagnosis, and all first-degree relatives should also undergo testing (see p. 343). In families with known FAP, at-risk family members undergo direct mutation testing at 13–14 years of age. This is less invasive than regular sigmoidoscopy which is reserved for those known to have the mutation. Affected individuals should undergo colectomy after school or college education has been completed. The operation of choice is ileal pouch-anal anastomosis. Periodic upper gastro-intestinal endoscopy is recommended to detect duodenal adenomas. Duodenal carcinoma is the most common cause of death in FAP patients who have undergone colectomy.

Peutz–Jeghers syndrome

This is characterised by multiple hamartomatous polyps in the small intestine and colon, as well as melanin pigmentation of the lips, mouth and digits (see Fig. 17.59). Most

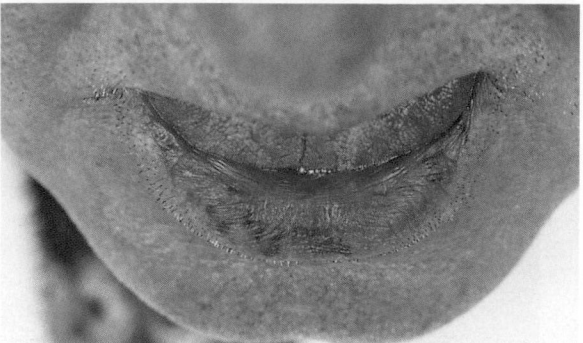

Fig. 17.59 Peutz–Jeghers syndrome. Typical lip pigmentation.

cases are asymptomatic, although chronic bleeding, anaemia or intussusception is seen. There is a small but significant risk of small bowel adenocarcinoma, and of cancer of the pancreas, ovary, breast and endometrium.

Juvenile polyposis

Tens to hundreds of mucus-filled hamartomatous polyps are found in the colon and rectum. One-third of cases are inherited in an autosomal dominant manner and up to 20% of patients develop colorectal cancer before the age of 40. Colonoscopy with biopsies should be performed every 1–3 years.

COLORECTAL CANCER

Although relatively rare in the underdeveloped world, colorectal cancer is the second most common internal malignancy and the second leading cause of cancer deaths in Western countries. In the UK the incidence is 50–60 per 100 000, equating to 30 000 cases per year. The condition becomes increasingly common over the age of 50.

Aetiology

Both environmental and genetic factors are important in colorectal carcinogenesis (see Fig. 17.60).

Environmental factors

Environmental factors probably account for 80% of all 'sporadic' colorectal cancers. This figure is based on the wide geographic variation in incidence and the decrease in risk seen in migrants who move from high- to low-risk countries. Dietary factors are believed to be most important and these are summarised in Box 17.64; other recognised risk factors are listed in Box 17.65.

Genetic factors

Colorectal cancer development results from the accumulation of multiple genetic mutations (see Fig. 17.61). Several important hereditary forms of colon cancer are recognised. Familial adenomatous polyposis (FAP) accounts for only 1% of cases of colonic cancer. In a further 10% there is a strong family history of colorectal cancer at an early age. Pedigrees of these families with 'hereditary non-polyposis colon cancer' (HNPCC, also known as Lynch's syndrome) indicate an autosomal dominant pattern of inheritance.

These patients have germ-line mutations in one or more genes (designated hMSH2, hMLH1, hPMS1 and hPMS2) involved in the repair of errors which normally occur during DNA replication. Failure of this DNA 'mismatch repair' system results in a genetically unstable phenotype and accumulation of multiple somatic mutations throughout the genome.

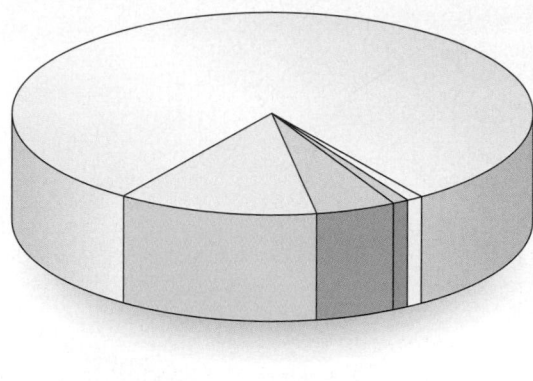

- ☐ 'Sporadic' (average risk) 75–80%
- ☐ Other family history 10–15%
- ☐ Hereditary non-polyposis colon cancer 5%
- ☐ Familial adenomatous polyposis 1%
- ☐ Inflammatory bowel disease 1%

Fig. 17.60   Risk factors in colon cancer development.

17.64 DIETARY RISK FACTORS FOR COLORECTAL CANCER DEVELOPMENT

Risk factor	Comments
Increased risk	
Red meat	High saturated fat and protein content Carcinogenic amines formed during cooking
Saturated animal fat	High faecal bile acid and fatty acid levels May affect colonic prostaglandin turnover
Decreased risk	
Dietary fibre	Effects vary with fibre type; shortened transit time, binding of bile acids and effects on bacterial flora proposed
Fruit and vegetables	Green vegetables contain anticarcinogens, e.g. glucosinolates and flavonoids. Little evidence for protection from vitamins A, C, E
Calcium	Binds and precipitates faecal bile acids
Folic acid	Reverses DNA hypomethylation

17.65 NON-DIETARY RISK FACTORS IN COLORECTAL CANCER

Medical conditions

- Colorectal adenomas (see p. 820)
- Long-standing extensive ulcerative colitis (see p. 808)
- Acromegaly
- Pelvic radiotherapy

Others

- Obesity and sedentary lifestyle—may be related to dietary factors
- Alcohol and tobacco (weak association)

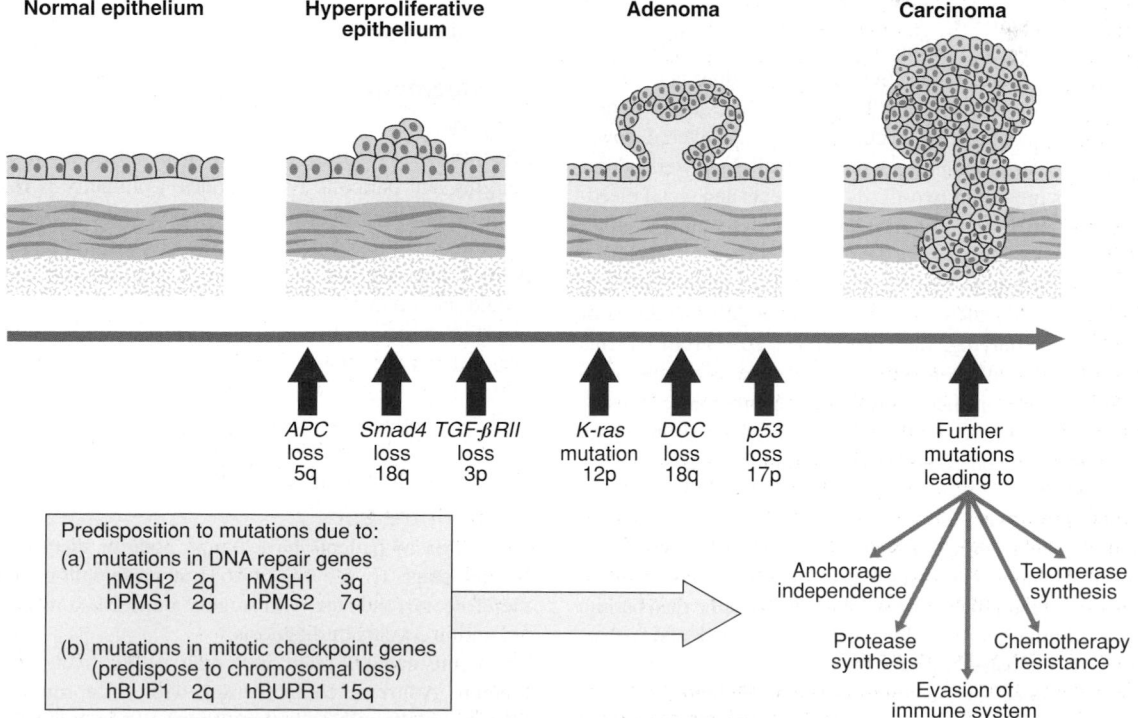

Fig. 17.61   The multistep origin of cancer: molecular events implicated in colorectal carcinogenesis.

The criteria necessary for diagnosing this condition are given in Box 17.66. The lifetime risk of colorectal cancer in affected individuals is 80%. The mean age of cancer development is 45 years, and two-thirds of tumours occur proximally, in contrast to sporadic colon cancer. In a subset of patients, there is also an increased incidence of cancers of the endometrium, urinary tract, stomach and pancreas.

Those who fulfil the criteria for diagnosis should be referred for pedigree assessment, genetic testing and colonoscopy. These should begin around 25 years of age or 5–10 years earlier than the youngest case of cancer in the family. Colonoscopy needs to be repeated every 1–2 years.

A further 10% of patients who do not have HNPCC still have a family history of colorectal cancer. The relative risks of cancer with one and two affected first-degree relatives are 1 in 12 and 1 in 6, respectively. The risk is even higher if relatives were affected at an early age. The genes mediating this increased risk are unknown.

Pathology

Most tumours arise from malignant transformation of a benign adenomatous polyp. Over 65% occur in the rectosigmoid and a further 15% recur in the caecum or ascending colon. Synchronous tumours are present in 2–5% of patients. Macroscopically, the majority of cancers are either polypoid and 'fungating', or annular and constricting. Spread occurs through the bowel wall. Rectal cancers may invade the pelvic viscera and side walls. Lymphatic invasion is common at presentation, as is spread through both portal and systemic circulations to reach the liver and, less commonly, the lungs. Tumour stage at diagnosis is the most important determinant of prognosis (see p. 217).

Clinical features

Symptoms vary depending on the site of the carcinoma. In tumours of the left colon, fresh rectal bleeding is common and obstruction occurs early. Tumours of the right colon present with anaemia from occult bleeding, or altered bowel habit, but obstruction is a late feature. Colicky lower abdominal pain is present in two-thirds of patients and rectal bleeding occurs in 50%. A minority present with features of either obstruction or perforation, leading to peritonitis, localised abscess or fistula formation. Carcinoma of the rectum usually causes early bleeding, mucus discharge or a feeling of incomplete emptying. Between 10 and 20% of all patients present solely with iron deficiency anaemia or weight loss.

On examination there may be a palpable mass, signs of anaemia or hepatomegaly from metastases. Low rectal tumours may be palpable on digital examination.

Investigations

Rigid sigmoidoscopy will detect approximately one-third of tumours. Colonoscopy (see Fig. 17.62) is the investigation of choice because it is more sensitive and specific than barium enema. Furthermore, lesions can be biopsied and polyps removed. Endoanal ultrasound or pelvic MRI stages rectal cancers accurately. CT colography ('virtual colonoscopy') is a promising non-invasive technique for diagnosing tumours and large polyps. CT is valuable for detecting hepatic metastases,

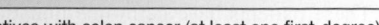

> **17.66 CRITERIA FOR THE DIAGNOSIS OF HEREDITARY NON-POLYPOSIS COLON CANCER**
>
> - Three or more relatives with colon cancer (at least one first-degree)
> - Colorectal cancer in two or more generations
> - At least one member affected under 50 years of age
> - Familial adenomatous polyposis (FAP) excluded

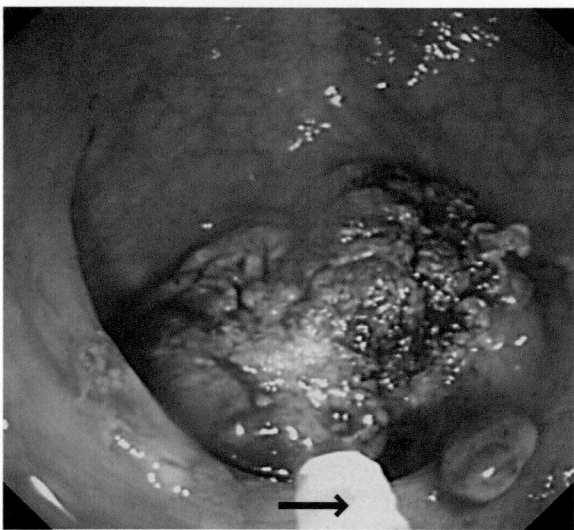

Fig. 17.62 Colonoscopic view of a polypoid rectal carcinoma undergoing laser therapy (arrow) in a patient unfit for surgery.

although intraoperative ultrasound is being used increasingly for this purpose. A proportion of patients have raised serum carcinoembryonic antigen (CEA) concentrations but this is variable and so of little use in diagnosis. Measurements of CEA are valuable, however, during follow-up and can help to detect early recurrence.

Management

Surgery

The tumour is removed, along with adequate resection margins and pericolic lymph nodes. Continuity is restored by direct anastomosis wherever possible. Carcinomas within a few centimetres of the anal verge may require abdominoperineal resection and formation of a colostomy. All patients should be counselled pre-operatively about the possible need for a stoma. Solitary hepatic metastases are sometimes resected at a later stage.

Post-operatively, patients should undergo colonoscopy after 6–12 months and periodically thereafter to search for local recurrence or development of new 'metachronous' lesions, which occur in 6% of cases.

Adjuvant therapy

Two-thirds of patients have lymph node or distant spread (Dukes stage C, see Fig. 17.63) at presentation and are, therefore, beyond cure with surgery alone. Most recurrences are within 3 years of diagnosis.

Colonic cancers recur in lymph nodes, liver and peritoneum. Adjuvant chemotherapy with 5-fluorouracil and folinic acid (to reduce toxicity) improves both disease-free and overall survival in patients with Dukes C colon cancer.

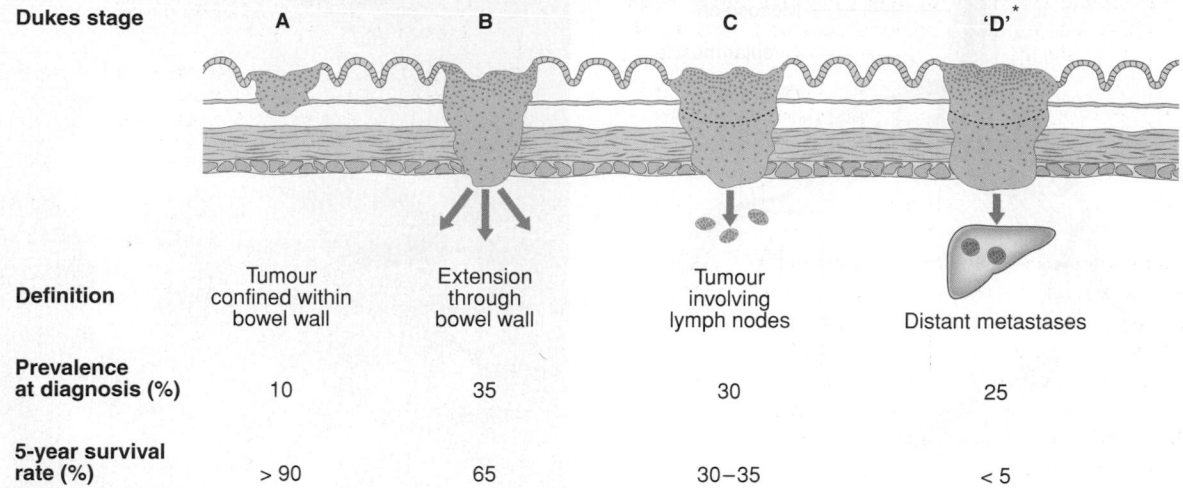

Dukes stage	A	B	C	'D'*
Definition	Tumour confined within bowel wall	Extension through bowel wall	Tumour involving lymph nodes	Distant metastases
Prevalence at diagnosis (%)	10	35	30	25
5-year survival rate (%)	> 90	65	30–35	< 5

Fig. 17.63 Staging and survival in colorectal cancer. (Modified Dukes classification.* Dukes' original staging only had stages A–C.)

This combination also provides useful palliation for patients with metastatic disease and is usually well tolerated. A short pre-operative course of radiotherapy is given to patients with large, fixed rectal cancers to 'down-stage' the tumour. Dukes C and some Dukes B rectal cancers are given post-operative radiotherapy to reduce the risk of recurrence.

Prevention and screening

Evidence suggests that colorectal cancer is preventable. At present there are no guidelines in the UK for primary prevention by dietary or lifestyle changes.

Chemoprevention

No effective, safe, long-term agent yet exists. The most promising agents at present are aspirin, calcium and folic acid. COX-2 is over-expressed in many polyps and most colorectal cancers where it has anti-apoptotic actions. Selective COX-2 inhibitors may be useful chemopreventive drugs with a superior safety profile to standard NSAIDs.

Secondary prevention

Secondary prevention aims to detect and remove lesions at an early or pre-malignant stage. Several potential methods exist:

- Widespread screening by regular *faecal occult blood (FOB) testing* reduces colorectal cancer mortality by 15–20% and increases the proportion of early cancers detected. These tests currently lack sensitivity and specificity and need to be improved. In the USA, annual FOB screening is recommended after the age of 50 years.
- *Colonoscopy* remains the gold standard but requires expertise, is expensive and carries risks; many countries lack the resources to offer this form of screening.
- *Flexible sigmoidoscopy* is an alternative option and has been shown to reduce overall colorectal cancer mortality by approximately 35% (70% for cases arising in the rectosigmoid). It is recommended in the USA every 5 years in all persons over the age of 50.
- Screening by *molecular genetic analysis* is an exciting prospect but is not yet available.

DIVERTICULOSIS

Diverticula are acquired and are most common in the sigmoid and descending colon of middle-aged people. Diverticulosis is present in over 50% of people above the age of 70 and is usually asymptomatic. Symptomatic or complicated diverticulosis ('diverticulitis') is much less common.

Aetiology

A life-long refined diet with a relative deficiency of fibre is widely thought to be responsible and the condition is rare in populations with a high dietary fibre intake, particularly in Africa and parts of Asia. It is postulated that small-volume stools require high intracolonic pressures for propulsion and this leads to herniation of mucosa between the taeniae coli (see Fig. 17.64).

Pathology

Diverticula consist of protrusions of mucosa covered by peritoneum. There is commonly hypertrophy of the circular muscle coat. Inflammation is thought to result from impaction of diverticula with faecoliths. This may resolve spontaneously or progress to cause perforation, local abscess formation,

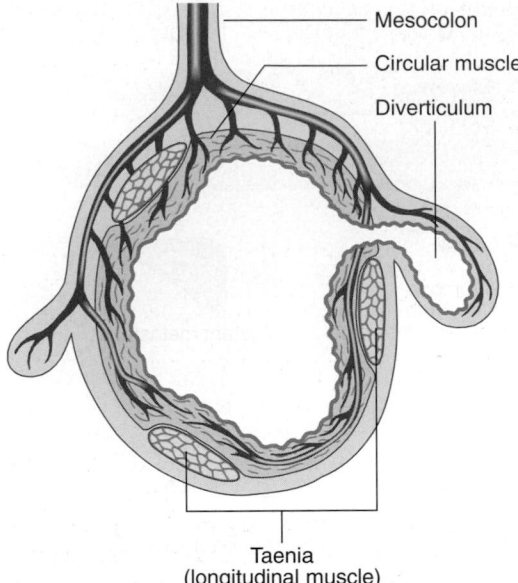

Fig. 17.64   The human colon in diverticulosis. The colonic wall is weak between the taeniae. The blood vessels that supply the colon pierce the circular muscle and weaken it further by forming tunnels. Diverticula usually emerge through these points of least resistance.

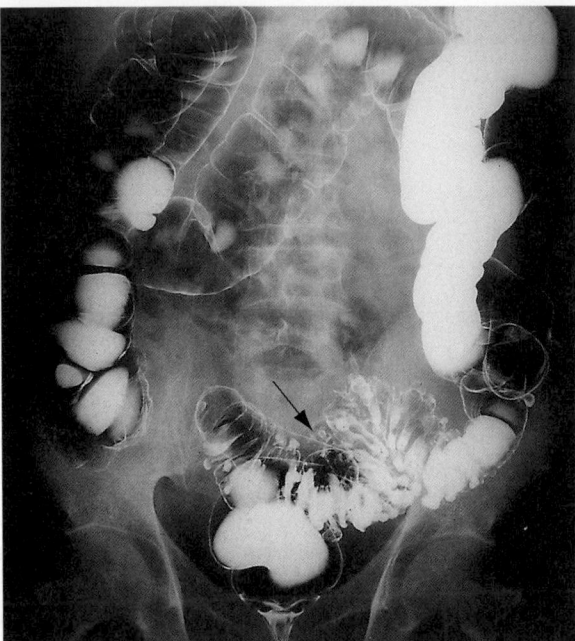

Fig. 17.65   Barium enema showing severe diverticular disease. There is tortuosity and narrowing of the sigmoid colon with multiple diverticula (arrow).

fistula and peritonitis. Repeated attacks of inflammation lead to thickening of the bowel wall, narrowing of the lumen and eventual obstruction.

Clinical features

Symptoms are usually the result of associated constipation or spasm. Colicky pain is usually suprapubic or felt in the left iliac fossa. The descending colon may be palpable and, in attacks of diverticulitis, there is local tenderness, guarding, rigidity and a palpable mass. During these episodes there may also be diarrhoea, rectal bleeding or fever. The differential diagnosis includes colorectal cancer, ischaemic colitis, inflammatory bowel disease and infection. Diverticular disease is complicated by perforation, pericolic abscess and acute rectal bleeding. These complications are more common in patients who take NSAIDs or aspirin.

Investigations

These are usually performed to exclude colorectal neoplasia. Barium enema confirms the presence of diverticula (see Fig. 17.65). Strictures and fistulae may also be seen. Flexible sigmoidoscopy is performed to exclude a coexisting neoplasm which is easily missed radiologically. Colonoscopy requires expertise and carries a risk of perforation. CT is used to assess complications.

Management

Diverticulosis which is asymptomatic and discovered co-incidentally requires no treatment. Constipation can be relieved by a high-fibre diet with or without a bulking laxative (ispaghula husk, 1–2 sachets daily) taken with plenty of fluids. Stimulants should be avoided.

An acute attack of diverticulitis requires 7 days of metronidazole (400 mg 8-hourly orally), along with either a cephalosporin or ampicillin (500 mg 6-hourly orally). Severe cases require intravenous fluids, analgesia and nasogastric suction. Emergency surgery is reserved for severe haemorrhage or perforation. Elective surgery is performed in patients after recovery from repeated acute attacks of obstruction, and resection of the affected segment with primary anastomosis is the procedure of choice.

CONSTIPATION AND DISORDERS OF DEFAECATION

The clinical approach to patients with constipation and its aetiology have been described on pages 770–771.

SIMPLE CONSTIPATION

This is extremely common and does not imply underlying organic disease. It usually responds to increased dietary fibre or the use of bulking agents; an adequate fluid intake is also essential. Many types of laxative are available, and these are listed in Box 17.67.

SEVERE IDIOPATHIC CONSTIPATION

This occurs almost exclusively in young women and often begins in childhood or adolescence. The cause is unknown but some have 'slow transit' with reduced motor activity in the colon. Others have 'obstructed defaecation' resulting

17.67 LAXATIVES	
Class	**Examples**
Bulk-forming	Ispaghula husk Methylcellulose
Stimulants	Bisacodyl Dantron (only for terminally ill patients) Docusate Senna
Faecal softeners	Docusate Arachis oil enema
Osmotic laxatives	Lactulose Lactitol Magnesium salts
Others	Polyethylene glycol (PEG)* Phosphate enema*
* Used mainly for bowel preparation prior to investigation or surgery.	

from inappropriate contraction of the external anal sphincter and puborectalis muscle (anismus).

The condition is often resistant to treatment. Bulking agents may exacerbate symptoms but prokinetic agents or balanced solutions of polyethylene glycol '3350' benefit some patients with slow transit. Glycerol suppositories and biofeedback techniques are used for those with obstructed defaecation. Rarely, subtotal colectomy is necessary as a last resort.

FAECAL IMPACTION

In faecal impaction a large, hard mass of stool fills the rectum. This tends to occur in disabled, immobile or institutionalised patients, especially the frail elderly or those with dementia. Constipating drugs, autonomic neuropathy and painful anal conditions also contribute. Megacolon, intestinal obstruction and urinary tract infections may supervene. Perforation and bleeding from pressure-induced ulceration are occasionally seen. Treatment involves adequate hydration and careful digital disimpaction after softening the impacted stool with arachis oil enemas. Stimulants should be avoided.

MELANOSIS COLI AND LAXATIVE MISUSE SYNDROMES

Long-term consumption of stimulant laxatives leads to accumulation of lipofuscin pigment in macrophages in the lamina propria. This imparts a brown discoloration to the colonic mucosa, often described as resembling 'tiger skin'. The condition is benign and resolves when the laxatives are stopped.

Prolonged laxative use may rarely result in megacolon or 'cathartic colon', in which barium enema demonstrates a featureless mucosa, loss of haustra and shortening of the bowel.

Surreptitious laxative misuse is a psychiatric condition seen in young women, some of whom have a history of bulimia or anorexia nervosa (see p. 267). They complain of refractory watery diarrhoea. Laxative use is usually denied and may continue even when patients are undergoing investigation. Screening of urine for laxatives may reveal the diagnosis.

MEGACOLON

Megacolon is characterised by dilatation of the colon and refractory constipation. It may be congenital (Hirschsprung's disease) or develop in later life (acquired megacolon).

Hirschsprung's disease
This is congenital aganglionosis of the large intestine, with an incidence of 1:5000. It may be local or diffuse and a family history is present in one-third of all cases. The condition results from failure of migration of neuroblasts into the gut wall during embryogenesis. Ganglion cells are absent from nerve plexuses, most commonly in a short segment of the rectum and/or sigmoid colon. As a result, the internal anal sphincter fails to relax. Constipation, abdominal distension and vomiting usually develop immediately after birth but a few cases do not present until childhood or adolescence. The rectum is empty on digital examination.

Barium enema shows a small rectum and colonic dilatation above the narrowed segment. Full-thickness biopsies are required to demonstrate nerve plexuses and confirm the absence of ganglion cells. Histochemical stains for acetylcholinesterase are also used. Anorectal manometry demonstrates failure of the rectum to relax with balloon distension. Treatment involves resection of the affected segment.

Acquired megacolon
This may develop in childhood as a result of voluntary withholding of stool during toilet training. In such cases it presents after the first year of life and is distinguished from Hirschsprung's disease by the urge to defaecate and the presence of stool in the rectum. It usually responds to osmotic laxatives.

In adults, acquired megacolon has several causes. It is seen in depressed or demented patients, either as part of the condition or as a side-effect of antidepressant drugs. Prolonged misuse of stimulant laxatives may cause degeneration of the myenteric plexus, while interruption of sensory or motor innervation may be responsible in a number of neurological disorders. Scleroderma and hypothyroidism are other recognised causes.

Most patients can be managed conservatively by treatment of the underlying cause, high-residue diets, laxatives and the judicious use of enemas. Prokinetics are helpful in a minority of patients. Subtotal colectomy is a last resort for the most severely affected patients.

ACUTE COLONIC PSEUDO-OBSTRUCTION (OGILVIE'S SYNDROME)

This condition has many causes (see Box 17.68) and is characterised by relatively sudden onset of painless, massive

17.68 CAUSES OF ACUTE COLONIC PSEUDO-OBSTRUCTION
• Trauma, burns
• Recent surgery
• Drugs, e.g. opiates, phenothiazines
• Respiratory failure
• Electrolyte and acid–base disorders
• Diabetes mellitus
• Uraemia

enlargement of the proximal colon accompanied by distension; there are no features of mechanical obstruction. Bowel sounds are normal or high-pitched rather than absent. Left untreated, it may progress to perforation, peritonitis and death.

Plain abdominal radiographs show colonic dilatation with air extending to the rectum. A caecal diameter greater than 10–12 cm is associated with a high risk of perforation. Single-contrast or water-soluble barium enemas demonstrate the absence of mechanical obstruction.

Management consists of treating the underlying disorder and correcting any biochemical abnormalities. The anticholinesterase, neostigmine, is often effective by enhancing parasympathetic activity and gut motility. Decompression either with a rectal tube or by careful colonoscopy may be effective but needs to be repeated until the condition resolves. In severe cases, surgical or fluoroscopic defunctioning caecostomy is necessary.

CLOSTRIDIUM DIFFICILE INFECTION

Antibiotic-associated diarrhoea, antibiotic-associated colitis and pseudomembranous colitis are part of the same disease spectrum which results from disturbance of the normal intestinal flora. *Cl. difficile* can be isolated from a variable proportion of patients and is thought to be the cause in most cases. The organism is a Gram-positive, anaerobic, spore-forming bacterium. It is commonly found in hospital wards.

Pathogenesis

Around 5% of healthy adults and up to 20% of elderly patients in long-term care carry *Cl. difficile*. Infection is usually hospital-acquired and becomes established when the normal colonic bacterial flora is disrupted by antibiotic treatment. It can also occur, however, in debilitated patients who have not been exposed to antibiotics. Although almost any antibiotic may be responsible, the most commonly implicated are cephalosporins, ampicillin, amoxicillin and clindamycin.

The organism produces two cytotoxic and inflammatory exotoxins (A and B), both of which contribute to virulence. It is not known why some people are asymptomatic carriers whilst others develop fulminant colitis. Host antibody responses to *Cl. difficile* toxin A may play a role in determining the clinical response to infection.

Pathology

Initially the mucosa shows focal areas of inflammation and ulceration. In severe cases the ulcers become covered by a creamy-white adherent 'pseudomembrane' composed of fibrin, debris and polymorphs.

Clinical features

Around 80% of cases occur in people over 65 years of age, many of whom are frail with comorbid diseases. Symptoms usually begin in the first week of antibiotic therapy but can occur at any time up to 6 weeks after treatment has finished. The onset is often insidious, with lower abdominal pain and diarrhoea which may become profuse and watery. The presentation may resemble acute ulcerative colitis with bloody diarrhoea, fever and even toxic dilatation and perforation. Ileus is also seen in pseudomembranous colitis.

Diagnosis

The diagnosis should be suspected in any patient who is currently taking or has recently taken antibiotics. The rectal appearances at sigmoidoscopy may be characteristic, with erythema, white plaques or an adherent pseudomembrane. At other times the appearances resemble those of ulcerative colitis. In some cases the rectum is spared and the changes predominantly affect the proximal colon. Biopsies are carried out routinely.

Stool cultures isolate *Cl. difficile* in 30% of patients with antibiotic-associated diarrhoea and over 90% of those with pseudomembranous colitis. As some healthy people may harbour *Cl. difficile*, isolation of toxins A and B by cell cytotoxicity assays is required to prove the diagnosis. Culture and toxin isolation can be difficult and may take up to 72 hours.

Management

The offending antibiotic should be stopped and the patient should be isolated. Supportive therapy with intravenous fluids and bowel rest is often needed. Ill patients and those with evidence of ileus, dilatation or pseudomembranous colitis should be treated with antibiotics. These are most effective when given orally and there is little to choose between metronidazole 400 mg 8-hourly and vancomycin 125 mg 6-hourly. Seven to ten days of therapy are usually effective, although relapses occur in 5–20% and require repeated treatment. Intravenous immunoglobulin is sometimes given in the most severe cases. Preventative measures include the responsible use of antibiotics and improved ward hygiene, hand-washing and disinfection policies.

ENDOMETRIOSIS

Ectopic endometrial tissue can become embedded on the serosal aspect of the intestine, most frequently in the sigmoid and rectum. The overlying mucosa is usually intact. Cyclical engorgement and inflammation result in pain, bleeding, diarrhoea, constipation and adhesions or obstruction.

Low backache is frequent. The onset is usually between 20 and 45 years and is more common in nulliparous women. Bimanual examination may reveal tender nodules in the pouch of Douglas. Endoscopic studies only reveal the diagnosis if carried out during menstruation, when a bluish mass with intact overlying mucosa is apparent. In some patients laparoscopy is required. Treatment options include laparoscopic diathermy and hormonal therapy with progestogens (e.g. norethisterone), gonadotrophin-releasing hormone analogues or danazol.

PNEUMATOSIS CYSTOIDES INTESTINALIS

In this rare condition multiple gas-filled submucosal cysts line the colonic and small bowel walls. The cause is unknown but the condition may be seen in patients with chronic cardiac or pulmonary disease, pyloric obstruction, scleroderma or dermatomyositis. Most patients are asymptomatic, although there may be abdominal cramp, diarrhoea, tenesmus, rectal bleeding and mucus discharge. The cysts are recognised on sigmoidoscopy, plain abdominal radiographs or barium enema. Fasting breath hydrogen levels are elevated and fall with treatment. Therapies reported to be effective include prolonged high-flow oxygen, elemental diets and antibiotics.

ISSUES IN OLDER PEOPLE
CONSTIPATION

- Particular attention should be paid to immobility, dietary fluid and fibre intake, drugs and depression in the evaluation of older people with constipation.
- Immobility predisposes to constipation by increasing the colonic transit time; the longer this is, the greater the fluid absorption and the harder the stool.
- In those with slow transit times, bulking agents can make matters worse and should be avoided.
- If faecal impaction develops, paradoxical overflow diarrhoea may occur. If antidiarrhoeal agents are given, the underlying impaction may worsen and result in serious complications such as stercoral ulceration and bleeding.

ANORECTAL DISORDERS

FAECAL INCONTINENCE

The normal control of anal continence is described on page 755. Common causes of incontinence are listed in Box 17.69.

Patients are often embarrassed to admit incontinence and may complain only of 'diarrhoea'. A careful history and examination, especially of the anorectum and perineum, may help to establish the underlying cause. Endoanal ultrasound is valuable for defining the integrity of the anal sphincters, while anorectal manometry and electrophysiology are also useful investigations if available.

17.69 CAUSES OF FAECAL INCONTINENCE

- Obstetric trauma—childbirth, hysterectomy
- Severe diarrhoea, faecal impaction
- Congenital anorectal anomalies
- Anorectal disease—haemorrhoids, rectal prolapse, Crohn's disease
- Neurological disorders—spinal cord or cauda equina lesions, dementia

---

Management

This is often very difficult. Underlying disorders should be treated and diarrhoea managed with loperamide, diphenoxylate or codeine phosphate. Pelvic floor exercises and biofeedback techniques help some patients, and those with confirmed anal sphincter defects may benefit from sphincter repair operations.

HAEMORRHOIDS ('PILES')

Haemorrhoids arise from congestion of the internal and/or external venous plexuses around the anal canal. They are extremely common in adults. The aetiology is unknown, although they are associated with constipation and straining and may develop for the first time during pregnancy. First-degree piles bleed, while second-degree piles prolapse but retract spontaneously. Third-degree piles are those which require manual replacement after prolapsing. Bright red rectal bleeding occurs after defaecation. Other symptoms include pain, pruritus ani and mucus discharge. Treatment involves measures to prevent constipation and straining. Injection sclerotherapy or band ligation is effective for most, but a minority of patients require haemorrhoidectomy, which is usually curative.

PRURITUS ANI

This is common and can result from many causes (see Box 17.70), most of which result in contamination of the perianal skin with faecal contents.

17.70 CAUSES OF PRURITUS ANI

Local anorectal conditions	
- Haemorrhoids - Fistula, fissures	- Poor hygiene
Infections	
- Threadworms	- Candidiasis
Skin disorders	
- Contact dermatitis - Psoriasis	- Lichen planus
Other	
- Diarrhoea or incontinence of any cause	- Irritable bowel syndrome - Anxiety

---

Itching may be trivial or severe and results in an itch-scratch-itch cycle which exacerbates the problem. When no underlying cause is found, all local barrier ointments and creams must be stopped. Good personal hygiene is essential, with careful washing after defaecation. The perineal area must be kept dry and clean. Bulk-forming laxatives may reduce faecal soiling.

SOLITARY RECTAL ULCER SYNDROME

This is most common in young adults and occurs on the anterior rectal wall. It is thought to result from localised chronic trauma and/or ischaemia associated with disordered puborectalis function and mucosal prolapse. The ulcer is seen at sigmoidoscopy and biopsies show a characteristic accumulation of collagen.

Symptoms include minor bleeding and mucus per rectum, tenesmus and perineal pain. Treatment is often difficult but avoidance of straining at defaecation is important and treatment of constipation may help. Marked mucosal prolapse is treated surgically.

ANAL FISSURE

In this common problem traumatic or ischaemic damage to the anal mucosa results in a superficial mucosal tear, most commonly in the midline posteriorly. Spasm of the internal anal sphincter exacerbates the condition. Severe pain occurs on defaecation and there may be minor bleeding, mucus discharge and pruritus. The skin may be indurated and an oedematous skin tag, or 'sentinel pile', adjacent to the fissure is common.

Avoidance of constipation with bulk-forming laxatives is important. Relaxation of the internal sphincter is normally mediated by nitric oxide, and 0.2% glyceryl trinitrate ointment, which donates nitric oxide, is effective in a proportion of patients. Manual dilatation under anaesthesia leads to long-term incontinence and has been superseded by lateral anal sphincterotomy for those requiring surgery.

ANORECTAL ABSCESSES AND FISTULAE

Perianal abscesses develop between the internal and external anal sphincters and may point at the perianal skin. Ischiorectal abscesses occur lateral to the sphincters in the ischiorectal fossa. They usually result from infection of anal glands by normal intestinal bacteria. Crohn's disease (see p. 808) is sometimes responsible.

Patients complain of extreme perianal pain, fever and/or discharge of pus. Spontaneous rupture may also lead to the development of fistulae. These may be superficial or may track through the anal sphincters to reach the rectum. Abscesses are drained surgically and fistulae are laid open with care to avoid sphincter damage.

DISEASES OF THE PERITONEAL CAVITY

PERITONITIS

Surgical peritonitis occurs as the result of a ruptured viscus (see surgical textbooks). Peritonitis may also complicate ascites (spontaneous bacterial peritonitis) or may occur in children in the absence of ascites, due to infection with pneumococci or β-haemolytic streptococci.

Chlamydial peritonitis is a complication of pelvic inflammatory disease. The affected woman presents with right upper quadrant abdominal pain, pyrexia and a hepatic rub (the Fitz-Hugh–Curtis syndrome).

TB may cause peritonitis and ascites.

TUMOURS

The most common is secondary adenocarcinoma from the ovary or gastrointestinal tract.

Mesothelioma is a rare tumour complicating asbestos exposure. It presents as a diffuse abdominal mass, due to omental infiltration, and with ascites. The prognosis is extremely poor.

FURTHER INFORMATION

Cotton PB, Williams CB. Gastrointestinal endoscopy: a practical approach. 4th edn. Oxford: Blackwell Science; 1996.

Feldman M, Scharschmidt BF, Sleisenger M. Sleisenger and Fordtran's gastrointestinal and liver disease. 6th edn. Philadelphia: WB Saunders; 1998.

McDonald J, Burroughs A, Feagan B. Evidence-based gastroenterology and hepatology. London: BMJ Books; 1999.

Shearman DJC, Finlayson NDC, Camilleri M, et al. Diseases of the gastrointestinal tract and liver. 3rd edn. Edinburgh: Churchill Livingstone; 1997.

www.bsg.org.uk *British Society of Gastroenterology website. Contains Society guidelines for many gastrointestinal disorders and their management (downloadable via Adobe Acrobat).*

www.coeliac.co.uk *Website of the UK Coeliac Society with links to other websites of the Association of European Coeliac Societies.*

www.evidbasedgastro.com *Website of the textbook (above).*

www.gastrohep.com *Comprehensive resource with access and links to many textbooks, journals and relevant websites. Other features include abstracts of recent major journal articles, libraries of endoscopic images and case studies.*

www.gastro.org *Website of the American Gastroenterological Association and the American Digestive Health Foundation. Useful site for information about many GI disorders and sections for patient information and advice.*

www.homepages.uel.ac.uk/C.P.Dancey/ibs.html *A site run by and for IBS sufferers, with input from leading medical experts.*

www.nacc.org.uk *The National Association for Colitis and Crohn's disease (NACC) is the UK's support, information and research-funding charity for people with Crohn's disease and colitis and their families.*

www.uegf.org *Home of the United European Gastroenterology Federation.*

Liver and biliary tract disease

P.C. HAYES • K.J. SIMPSON • O.J. GARDEN

CLINICAL EXAMINATION OF THE ABDOMEN FOR LIVER AND BILIARY DISEASE

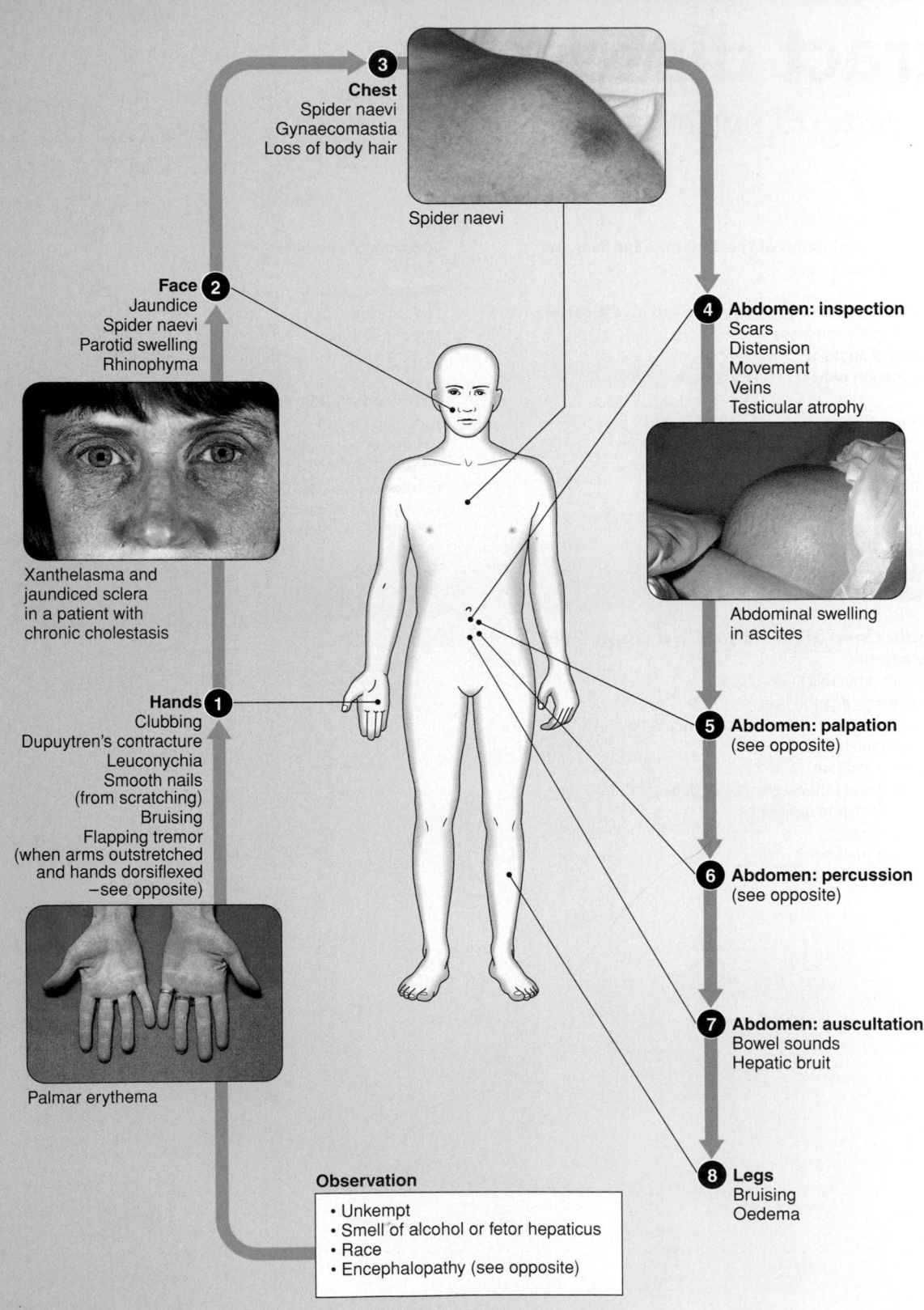

3 Chest
Spider naevi
Gynaecomastia
Loss of body hair

Spider naevi

Face 2
Jaundice
Spider naevi
Parotid swelling
Rhinophyma

Xanthelasma and
jaundiced sclera
in a patient with
chronic cholestasis

4 Abdomen: inspection
Scars
Distension
Movement
Veins
Testicular atrophy

Abdominal swelling
in ascites

Hands 1
Clubbing
Dupuytren's contracture
Leuconychia
Smooth nails
(from scratching)
Bruising
Flapping tremor
(when arms outstretched
and hands dorsiflexed
– see opposite)

Palmar erythema

5 Abdomen: palpation
(see opposite)

6 Abdomen: percussion
(see opposite)

7 Abdomen: auscultation
Bowel sounds
Hepatic bruit

8 Legs
Bruising
Oedema

Observation
- Unkempt
- Smell of alcohol or fetor hepaticus
- Race
- Encephalopathy (see opposite)

ENCEPHALOPATHY

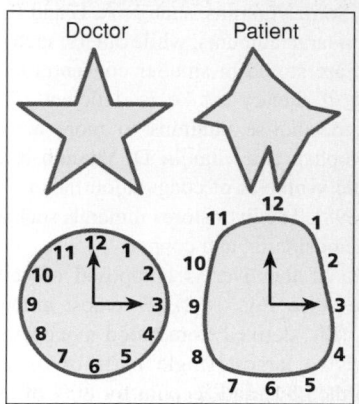

Doctor   Patient

Drawing stars and clocks may reveal marked abnormality.

❶ FLAPPING TREMOR

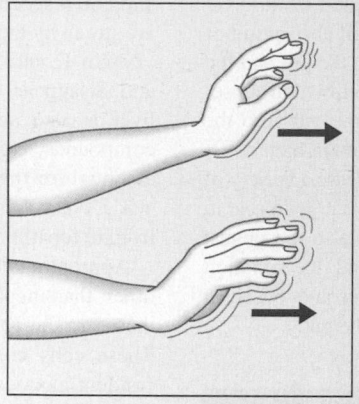

Jerky forward movements every 2–3 seconds.

❻ PERCUSSION OF THE ABDOMEN

Liver
- Always start percussion from resonant to dull; i.e. percuss lower border from beneath and upper border from above.
- Percuss the abdomen gently, the chest more firmly.
- Once the upper border of the liver is identified, confirm its position by counting down the ribs from the sternal angle (second intercostal space).

Shifting dullness
- Start around the umbilicus (resonant).
- Percuss at 1 cm intervals around to the left flank.

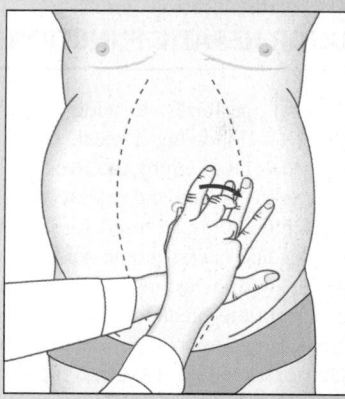

- Identify where dullness occurs.
- Roll the patient on to the left-hand side and note if the level of dullness moves towards the umbilicus.

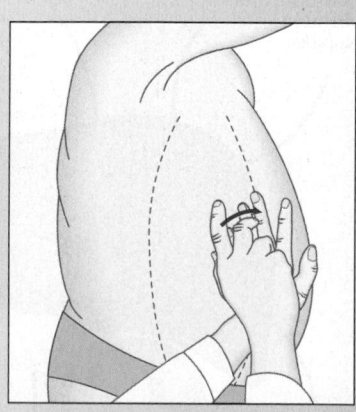

❺ PALPATION OF THE ABDOMEN

Liver
- Start in the right iliac fossa.
- Progress up the abdomen 2 cm with each breath (through open mouth).
- Confirm the lower border of the liver by percussion (see 6).

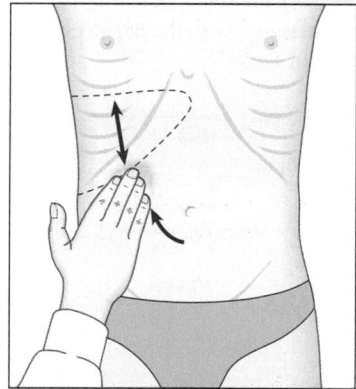

- Detect if smooth or irregular, tender or non-tender; ascertain shape.
- Identify the upper border by percussion (see 6).

Spleen
- Start again in the right iliac fossa.
- Progress towards the left upper quadrant at 2 cm intervals.
- Place the left hand around the lower lateral ribs as the costal margin is approached.

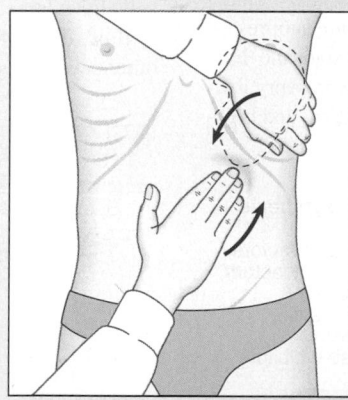

- Note the characteristics of the spleen
  —Notch
  —Superficial
  —Dull to percussion
  —Cannot get between ribs and spleen
  —Moves well with respiration.

The liver is one of the heaviest organs in the body (1.2–1.5 kg) and serves the principal function of maintaining the body's internal milieu. The anatomical position of the liver is key to fulfilling this function, as almost all absorption of foreign material into the body takes place in the gut and the portal blood draining the gut flows to the liver, which subsequently controls the release of absorbed nutrients into the systemic circulation. In addition to its function in metabolising nutrients, the liver is able to store and release a variety of substrates, vitamins and minerals, and plays a crucial role in drug and bilirubin metabolism. The liver is also the largest reticulo-endothelial organ in the body and its situation is important in removing infecting bacteria and bacterial products, which often enter the body from the gut.

FUNCTIONAL ANATOMY, PHYSIOLOGY AND INVESTIGATIONS

MAJOR HEPATIC FUNCTIONS

The liver performs a wide variety of functions (see Fig. 18.1). Following a meal, more than half the glucose absorbed is taken up by the liver and stored as glycogen or converted to lactate and released into the systemic circulation. Amino acids are used for hepatic and plasma protein synthesis and excess amino acids are catabolised to urea. In contrast, during fasting the liver releases glucose, derived either from the breakdown of glycogen or from gluconeogenesis using amino acids released from extrahepatic tissues such as muscle (see p. 644). Synthesis of urea, and endogenous protein and hepatic amino acid release are suppressed during fasting. In both the fed and fasting state the liver plays a central role in lipid metabolism, producing very low-density lipoproteins and further metabolising low- and high-density lipoproteins (see p. 306).

The liver plays a central role in the metabolism of bilirubin and bile salts, drugs and alcohol (see pp. 843 and 881, 868 and 866 respectively). Some vitamins, such as A, D and B_{12}, are stored by the liver in large amounts, while others, such as vitamin K and folate, are stored in smaller concentrations and disappear rapidly if dietary intake is deficient. The liver is also able to metabolise vitamins to more active compounds, e.g. tryptophan and vitamin D. Vitamin K is essential for the hepatic synthesis of coagulation factors II, VII, IX and X (see p. 898). The liver stores minerals such as iron, in ferritin and haemosiderin, and copper.

Approximately 15% of the liver is composed of cells other than hepatocytes (see Fig. 18.2). Foremost among these are the Kupffer cells, derived from blood monocytes. These cells constitute the largest single mass of tissue-resident monocytes in the body and account for 80% of the phagocytic capacity of this system. Kupffer cells remove aged and damaged red blood cells, bacteria, viruses, antigen-antibody complexes and endotoxin. In addition, these cells are able to produce a wide variety of inflammatory mediators that may act locally or may be released into the systemic circulation. Stellate cells are found in the space of Disse and play an important role in regulating blood flow through the liver. Following liver injury cytokines produced by Kupffer cells and hepatocytes activate the stellate cells. Activated stellate cells become transformed into a myofibroblast phenotype and are an important source of extracellular matrix components such as collagen during the genesis of cirrhosis. Endothelial cells line the hepatic sinusoids. These capillary vessels of the liver differ from other capillary beds in the body. There is no basement membrane visible by electron microscopy and the endothelial cells have large fenestrae (0.1 microns), allowing free flow of fluid and particulate matter across to the hepatocytes and other cells lining the space of Disse.

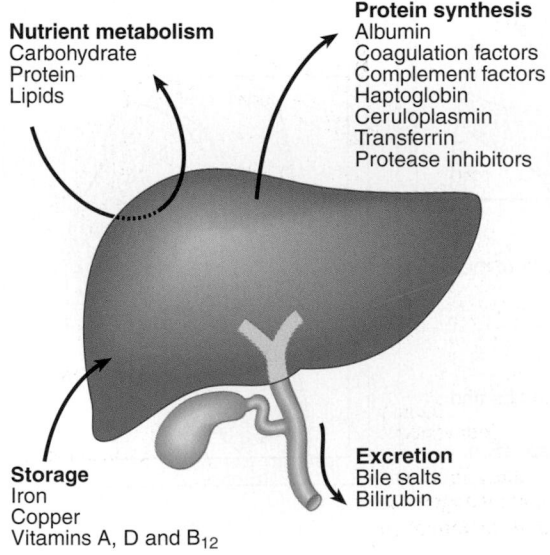

Fig. 18.1   Important liver functions.

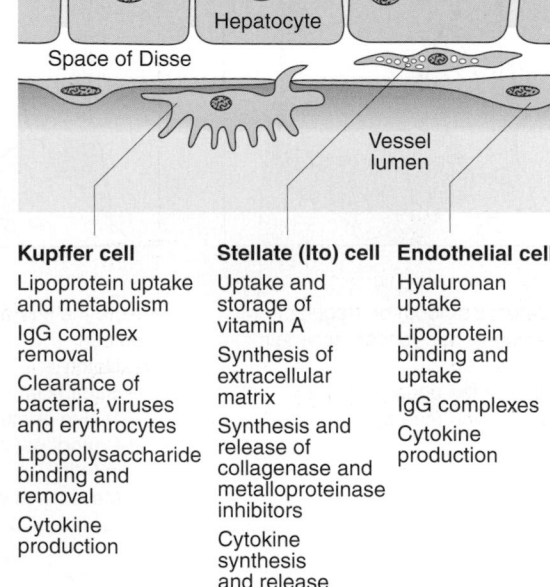

Fig. 18.2   Function of non-parenchymal liver cells.

FUNCTIONAL ANATOMY

The liver has traditionally been divided into the left and right lobes, by the falciform ligament, fissure of the ligamentum teres and fissure of the ligamentum venosum. Advances in hepatic surgery, however, have indicated a more useful division into right and left hemilivers based on the hepatic blood supply (see Fig. 18.3). The right and left hemilivers are further divided into a total of eight segments in accordance with subdivisions of the hepatic and portal veins. Each segment is made up of multiple smaller units known as lobules, comprised of a central vein, radiating sinusoids separated from each other by single liver cell (hepatocyte) plates and

peripheral portal tracts. However, the hepatic lobule has no functional significance. The functional unit of the liver is the hepatic acinus (see Fig. 18.4), which is anatomically almost the reverse of the hepatic lobule. Blood flows into the hepatic acinus via the single terminal branches of the portal vein and hepatic artery located in the portal tracts, and along the hepatic sinusoids; it then drains into several hepatic venous tributaries at the periphery of the acinus. In contrast, the flow of bile is in the opposite direction along the biliary canaliculi into terminal bile ductules (cholangioles) and subsequently into the interlobular bile ducts located in the portal tracts. The hepatocytes in each acinus can be divided functionally into three different zones, in accordance with their position relative to the terminal portal tract. The hepatocytes in zone 1 are closest to the terminal branches of the portal vein and hepatic artery and therefore are supplied firstly with oxygenated blood, and secondly with blood containing the highest concentration of nutrients and toxins. The hepatocytes in zone 3 are furthest from the portal tracts andclosest to the hepatic veins and are therefore relatively hypoxic compared with the hepatocytes in zone 1.

INVESTIGATION OF HEPATOBILIARY DISEASE

The aims of investigation in patients with suspected liver disease are shown in Box 18.1. When investigating patients with suspected liver disease various testing modalities are integrated along the pathways presented in the algorithm (see Fig. 18.5).

DETECTION OF HEPATIC ABNORMALITY

The clinical suspicion of liver disease usually leads to the measurement of the liver function tests or 'LFTs' (see Box 18.2). The LFTs are not truly function tests, provide

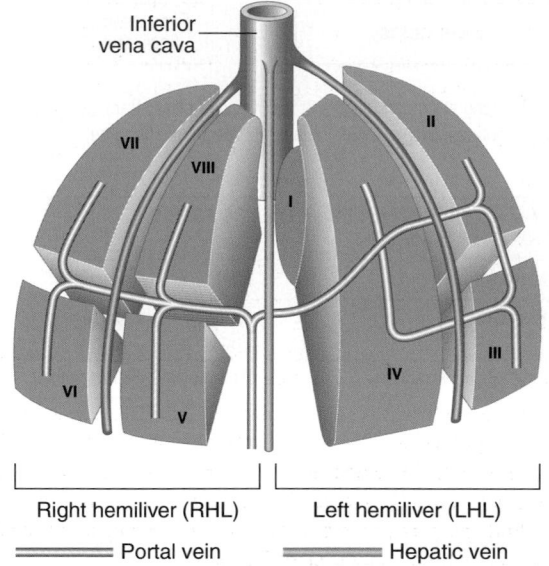

Fig. 18.3 **Schematic representation of the liver.**

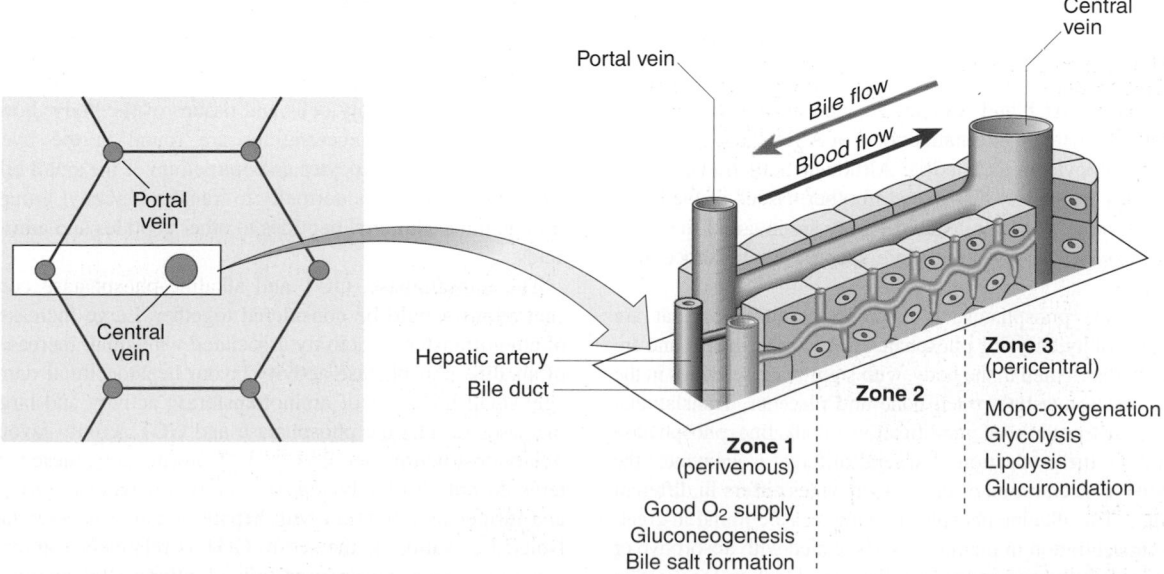

Fig. 18.4 **Hepatic acinus.** Functional unit of the liver.

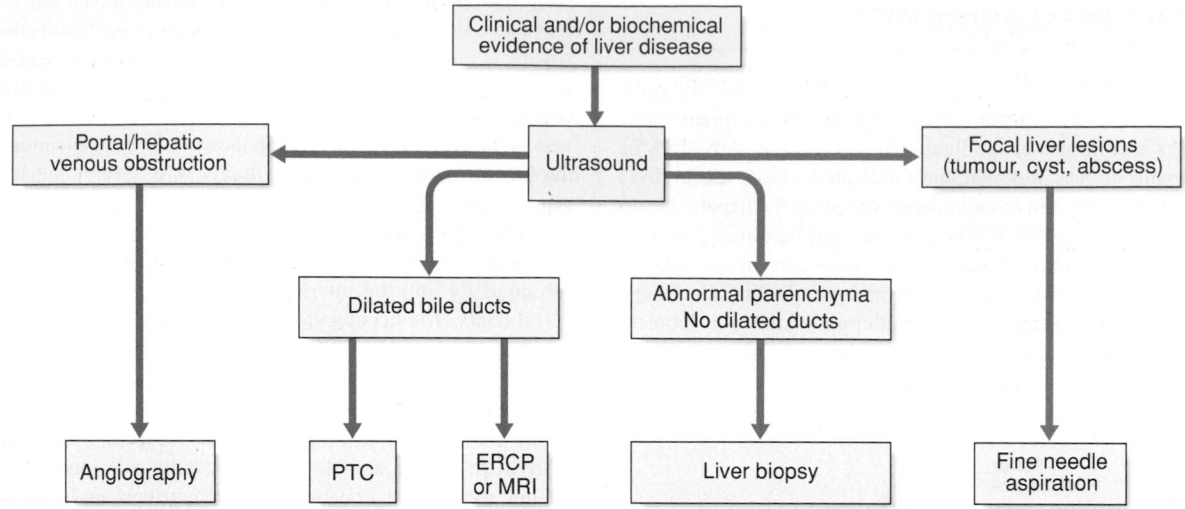

Fig. 18.5   Investigative procedures in liver disease. Suggested sequence for identifying structural lesions in the liver and biliary tract. (ERCP = endoscopic retrograde cholangiopancreatography; PTC = percutaneous transhepatic cholangiography; MRI = magnetic resonance imaging)

18.1 AIMS OF INVESTIGATIONS IN PATIENTS WITH SUSPECTED LIVER DISEASE
• Detect hepatic abnormality
• Measure the severity of liver damage
• Define the structural effects on the liver
• Identify the specific cause
• Investigate possible complications

18.2 LIVER FUNCTION TESTS USED TO ASSESS LIVER DISEASE		
Measurement	**Fluid**	**Assessment**
Bilirubin[1]	Plasma Urine	Transport
Aminotransferases[2]	Plasma	Hepatocellular damage
Alkaline phosphatase	Plasma	Biliary obstruction
Gamma-glutamyl transferase	Plasma	Enzyme induction
Proteins (total and albumin)	Plasma	Synthesis
Coagulation tests	Plasma	Synthesis

[1] Bilirubin detected in the urine identifies conjugated hyperbilirubinaemia and indicates hepatobiliary disease.
[2] Alanine aminotransferase is more specific for liver damage than aspartate aminotransferase.

little prognostic information and do not indicate a specific diagnosis, although they may point to an underlying pathological process and direct further investigation. Several serum enzymes are measured in these widely available biochemical tests.

The activities of one or two transaminase enzymes, alanine aminotransferase (ALT) and aspartate aminotransferase (AST), are often measured. These enzymes function normally to transfer the amino group from an amino acid, alanine in the case of ALT and aspartate in the case of AST, to a ketoacid, producing pyruvate and oxaloacetate respectively. Both ALT and AST are located in the cytoplasm of the hepatocyte; an alternative form of AST is also located in the hepatocyte mitochondria. Although both transaminase enzymes are widely distributed in other tissues of the body, the activities of ALT outside the liver are low and therefore this enzyme is considered more specific for hepatocellular damage.

Alkaline phosphatase is a group of enzymes that are capable of hydrolysing phosphate esters at alkaline pH and are widely distributed in the body, with significant activities in the liver, gastrointestinal tract, bone and placenta. Translational and post-translational modification of alkaline phosphatase results in the production of several different isoenzymes; the relative concentration of these isoenzymes differs in different tissues. The alkaline phosphatase enzymes are found in greatest concentration in membranes associated with absorptive or secretory functions; in the liver they are therefore localised in the sinusoidal and biliary canalicular membrane.

Gamma-glutamyl transferase (GGT) is a microsomal enzyme found in many cells and tissues of the body; however, the largest concentrations are found in the liver, localised in the hepatocytes and epithelium of the small bile ducts. GGT functions normally to transfer glutamyl groups from gamma-glutamyl peptides to other peptides and amino acids.

The transaminase, GGT and alkaline phosphatase concentrations should be considered together. Large increases of aminotransferase activity associated with small increases of alkaline phosphatase activity favour hepatocellular damage; small increases of aminotransferase activity and large increases of alkaline phosphatase and GGT activity favour biliary obstruction (see Box 18.3). Unfortunately, these patterns do not absolutely separate the two diagnostic groups and further investigation with hepatic imaging is essential. Isolated elevation of the serum GGT is relatively common and may occur during ingestion of microsomal enzyme-inducing drugs (see Box 18.4).

18.3 BIOCHEMICAL TESTS IN DIFFERENT CAUSES OF JAUNDICE			
Enzyme combination		Diagnostic likelihood	
Aminotransferase	Alkaline phosphatase	Hepatocellular jaundice	Biliary obstruction
> × 6	< × 2.5	90%	10%
< × 6	> × 2.5	10%	80%
Other combinations		No clear separation	

18.4 DRUGS INCREASING PLASMA GAMMA-GLUTAMYL TRANSFERASE	
• Barbiturates	• Isoniazid
• Carbamazepine	• Meprobamate
• Ethanol	• Phenytoin
• Glucocorticoids	• Primidone
• Griseofulvin	• Rifampicin

Other widely available biochemical tests may become altered in patients with liver disease. Hyponatraemia occurs in severe liver disease and is multifactorial in aetiology. Serum urea may be reduced due to impaired hepatic synthesis. Increased urea may occur following gastrointestinal haemorrhage, but when associated with a high serum creatinine and low urinary sodium excretion is indicative of hepatorenal failure, which carries a grave prognosis.

Haematological investigations are also commonly abnormal in patients with liver disease and may suggest the underlying diagnosis. The haemoglobin concentration, and white cell and platelet count may be normal. A normochromic normocytic anaemia can reflect acute upper gastrointestinal haemorrhage from oesophago-gastric varices or peptic ulcer disease, the latter being more common in liver disease than among the general population. Chronic blood loss from peptic ulcers or portal hypertensive gastropathy may produce a chronic hypochromic microcytic anaemia secondary to iron deficiency. A high erythrocyte mean cell volume (macrocytosis) is associated with alcohol misuse, but target cells in any jaundiced patient also result in a macrocytosis. Rarely, an erythrocytosis occurs in hepatocellular carcinoma due to ectopic secretion of erythropoietin. Leucopenia and thrombocytopenia may complicate portal hypertension and hypersplenism. In contrast, leucocytosis may occur with cholangitis, alcoholic hepatitis and hepatic abscesses. Atypical lymphocytes are seen in infectious mononucleosis, which may be complicated by an acute hepatitis. Thrombocytosis may occur in those with active gastrointestinal haemorrhage and, rarely, in association with hepatocellular carcinoma.

TESTS TO DETERMINE THE SEVERITY AND ACTIVITY OF LIVER DISEASE

Simple and widely available biochemical and haematological investigations can give important information on the severity of both acute and chronic liver failure and provide prognostic information in these clinical situations.

Biochemical tests

Requesting the liver function tests also routinely involves measurement of the serum bilirubin and albumin concentrations. These measurements are truly tests of liver function. Bilirubin metabolism is discussed on page 843. Albumin is one of the most important proteins involved in maintaining the normal colloidal oncotic pressure of the blood and is a major carrier of low molecular weight substances such as bilirubin, hormones and drugs. The liver produces 8–14 g of albumin per day, but the reduction in serum albumin observed with liver diseases involves changes in the volume of distribution of albumin, inaddition to reduction in synthesis.

Coagulation tests

The liver synthesises most coagulation factors, and requires vitamin K to activate factors II, VII, IX and X. Severe liver damage and prolonged biliary obstruction, the latter reducing vitamin K absorption, are associated with a reduced plasma fibrinogen concentration and prolongation of the prothrombin time. The prothrombin time depends on factors I, II, V, VII and X, and is prolonged when the plasma concentration of any of these factors falls below 30% of normal. The normal half-lives of the vitamin K-dependent coagulation factors in the blood are short (5–72 hours). Therefore changes in the prothrombin time occur relatively quickly following liver damage, and provide valuable prognostic information in patients with both acute and chronic liver failure. An increased prothrombin time is evidence of severe liver damage in chronic liver disease, provided that vitamin K (10 mg by slow i.v. injection) is given to exclude deficiency. Hypercoagulation can cause hepatic venous thrombosis and the Budd–Chiari syndrome (see p. 875).

Specific aetiological investigations

A variety of blood tests are available to determine the aetiology of hepatic disease (see Box 18.5), and are discussed under specific diseases. In certain clinical situations these blood tests may require further assessment by performing a liver biopsy.

LIVER BIOPSY

A liver biopsy can confirm the severity of liver damage and provide aetiological information; it is performed with a Trucut or Menghini needle, usually through an intercostal space, using local analgesia. Liver biopsy is a relatively safe procedure if the conditions detailed in Box 18.6 are met, but should never be undertaken lightly as the mortality rate is about 0.05%. The main complications are abdominal and/or shoulder pain, bleeding and, rarely, biliary peritonitis which usually occurs when a biopsy is performed in a patient with obstruction of a large bile duct. Liver biopsies can be carried out in patients with defective haemostasis if the defect is corrected with fresh frozen plasma and platelet transfusion, if the biopsy is obtained by the transjugular route, or if the procedure is conducted percutaneously under ultrasound control and the needle track is then plugged with procoagulant material. In patients with potentially resectable malignancy,

18.5 SPECIFIC AETIOLOGICAL INVESTIGATIONS

Disease	Test
Haemochromatosis	Serum ferritin Serum iron, iron-binding capacity, saturation Polymerase chain reaction (PCR) for genetic abnormality
Wilson's disease	Serum ceruloplasmin Serum, urine, liver copper estimations
Hepatitis A infections	IgM anti-hepatitis A virus
Hepatitis B infections	Hepatitis B surface antigen (HBsAg) Hepatitis Be antigen (HBeAg) Hepatitis B viral DNA (HBV-DNA) Anti-hepatitis B core (anti-HBc) Anti-hepatitis B surface (anti-HBs) Anti-hepatitis Be (anti-HBe)
Hepatitis C	Anti-hepatitis C virus antibodies (various) PCR for hepatitis C viral RNA
Hepatitis D	Anti-hepatitis D (IgM and IgG)
Hepatitis E	Anti-hepatitis E (anti-HEV)
Autoimmune chronic active hepatitis	Serum immunoglobulins Serum antinuclear factor, anti-smooth muscle and liver, kidney, microsomal (LKM) antibodies
Primary biliary cirrhosis	Serum immunoglobulins Serum antimitochondrial antibodies

18.6 CONDITIONS REQUIRED FOR SAFE LIVER BIOPSY

- Cooperative patient
- Prothrombin time < 4 seconds prolonged
- Platelet count > 100×10^9/l
- Exclusion of bile duct obstruction, localised skin infection, advanced chronic obstructive pulmonary disease, marked ascites and severe anaemia

biopsy should be avoided due to the potential risk of bleeding and tumour dissemination. Operative or laparoscopic liver biopsy may sometimes be valuable, as in the staging of lymphoma.

Histological assessment of hepatic biopsies

Histological assessment of liver biopsy tissue is enhanced by discussion between clinicians and pathologists. Although the pathological features of liver disease can be diverse and variable, with several features occurring together, liver disorders can be broadly classified histologically into fatty liver (steatosis), hepatitis and cirrhosis. The use of special histological stains can sometimes help in determining the aetiology of liver disorders. The clinical features and prognosis of these changes are dependent on the underlying aetiology, and are discussed in the relevant sections.

Steatosis

Hepatic steatosis results from accumulation of fat within hepatocytes. The accumulating lipid depends on the aetiology; for example, alcoholic steatosis is associated with increased cellular triacylglycerol. Mild steatosis involving less than

10% of hepatocytes is normal; more severe steatosis is seen in a number of disorders. Steatosis may be macrovesicular where a single fat globule fills the liver cell and pushes the nucleus to the periphery, or microvesicular where small fat vacuoles give the liver cell a foamy appearance and the nucleus remains central (see Fig. 18.6). In some patients macrovesicular steatosis occurs with associated neutrophilic infiltrate, liver cell death and, rarely, Mallory's hyaline. This histological change has been termed steatohepatitis.

Hepatitis

In this disorder there is inflammation of the liver which results in damage to hepatocytes, with subsequent cell death. Acute injury is generally followed by complete recovery. Prolonged inflammation may be accompanied by fibrosis and progression to cirrhosis. The most common causes of hepatitis are listed in Box 18.7. The histological appearances in hepatitis are generally classified as acute or chronic but they are not always readily separable and areas of overlap occur.

Acute hepatitis. The pathology of acute hepatitis depends on the cause of the damage. Lesions in acute viral hepatitis and most instances of acute damage due to drugs are similar. Cell damage occurs throughout the liver, particularly in centrilobular areas, though individual lobules are variably affected. Damaged hepatocytes are swollen and granular, while dead ones become shrunken and deeply stained acidophilic bodies. These changes, originally described in yellow fever (Councilman bodies), are strong indicators of acute hepatitis. The lobules may be infiltrated with mononuclear cells (lobulitis). Polymorphonuclear leucocytes and fatty change are features of alcoholic hepatitis or amiodarone hepatotoxicity. The portal tracts are enlarged and contain a predominantly mononuclear cell infiltrate (triaditis). More severe damage is accompanied by collapse of the reticulin framework, particularly between the central veins and portal tracts, which become linked to one another; this is known as bridging or subacute hepatic necrosis. Very severe damage destroys whole lobules (massive necrosis) and is the lesion underlying most instances of acute hepatic failure. Cholestasis is occasionally prominent.

18.7 CAUSES OF HEPATITIS

Viral infections

- Hepatitis A virus
- Hepatitis B virus
- Hepatitis C virus
- Hepatitis D virus

- Hepatitis E
- Epstein–Barr virus (EBV)
- Cytomegalovirus (CMV)
- Herpes simplex

Toxins

- Alcohol

- Drugs, e.g. methyldopa, isoniazid, halothane, amiodarone, herbal drugs

Miscellaneous

- Autoimmune hepatitis
- Wilson's disease

- α_1-antitrypsin deficiency
- Haemochromatosis

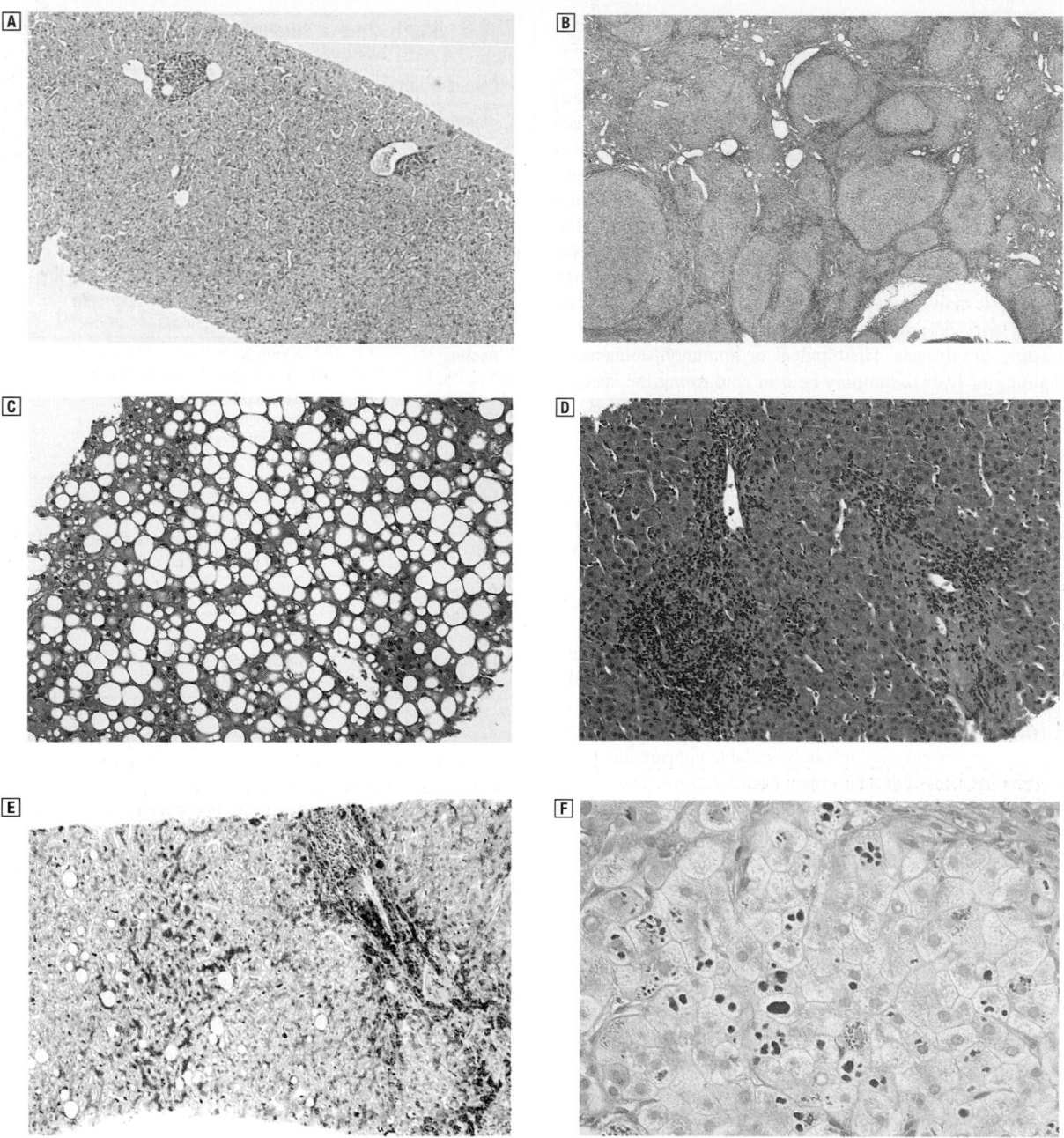

Fig. 18.6 Liver histology. **A** Normal liver. This van Gieson stain shows normal liver appearances. Columns of hepatocytes 1–2 cells thick radiate from the portal tracts to the central veins. The portal tract contains a normal intralobular bile duct branch of the hepatic artery and portal venous radical. There is little fibrous tissue which stains pink with this particular stain. **B** A cirrhotic liver. This van Gieson stain shows disruption of the liver architecture. The normal arrangement of portal tracts and hepatic veins is lost and nodules of proliferating hepatocytes are broken up by strands of pink-staining fibrous tissue. **C** Hepatitic steatosis. Haematoxylin and eosin-stained liver section shows expansion of hepatocytes with clear globules of fat. These globules are large enough to distort the hepatocytes, a change which is termed macrovesicular steatosis. **D** Hepatitis. This haematoxylin and eosin-stained section shows expansion of a normal portal tract with inflammatory cells. The majority are lymphocytes which are spilling over from the portal tract into the hepatic lobules surrounding single liver cells and destroying them by apoptosis. This change is known as interface hepatitis. There are also foci of inflammatory cells surrounding individual hepatocytes within the lobules (lobulitis). **E** Haemochromatosis. This Perls stain shows accumulating iron within hepatocytes which is stained blue. There is also accumulation of large fat globules in some hepatocytes (macrovesicular steatosis). As well as accumulating in hepatocytes, the iron is also found in Kupffer cells and biliary epithelial cells. **F** α_1-antitrypsin deficiency. Accumulation of periodic acid-Schiff-positive granules within individual hepatocytes is shown in this section from a patient with α_1-antitrypsin deficiency.

Chronic hepatitis. Chronic hepatitis is characterised by a mononuclear inflammatory cell infiltrate of the portal tracts (see Fig. 18.6). When this infiltrate is confined to the portal tract (a condition previously known as chronic persistent hepatitis) and is associated with a normal lobular architecture, the condition is regarded as mild, and progression to cirrhosis is uncommon. Invasion of inflammatory cells into the periportal parenchyma with loss of definition of the portal-periportal interface (limiting plate), damage to the periportal hepatocytes and formation of hepatocyte 'rosettes' is termed interface hepatitis (previously described as chronic active hepatitis). Interface hepatitis is often associated with progressive parenchymal damage and fibrosis leading to cirrhosis. Histological or immunohistochemical staining of liver tissue may help in confirming the specific aetiology of a chronic hepatitis, such as with hepatitis B.

Cirrhosis

Common causes of cirrhosis are listed in Box 18.8. The changes in cirrhosis affect the whole liver but not necessarily every lobule (see Fig. 18.6). They include progressive and widespread death of liver cells associated with inflammation and fibrosis, leading to loss of the normal lobular liver architecture. Destruction of the liver architecture causes distortion and loss of the normal hepatic vasculature with the development of portal-systemic vascular shunts, and the formation of nodules rather than lobules due to the proliferation of surviving hepatocytes. The evolution of cirrhosis is gradual and progressive, and consequently cirrhotic livers have an infinitely variable appearance, limiting the usefulness of anatomical classifications. The current classification includes micronodular cirrhosis, characterised by regular connective tissue septa, regenerative nodules approximating in size to the original lobules (1 mm in diameter), and involvement of every lobule; and macronodular cirrhosis, in which the connective tissue septa vary in thickness and the nodules show marked differences in size, with large ones containing histologically normal lobules. Micronodular cirrhosis tends to evolve gradually into macronodular cirrhosis, and intermediate mixed forms are seen. Hepatic cirrhosis contrasts histologically with congenital hepatic fibrosis and partial nodular transformation. In the former condition extensive fibrosis occurs in the absence of hepatocyte injury and nodular regeneration; in the latter nodular regeneration occurs without hepatic fibrosis.

18.8 CAUSES OF CIRRHOSIS	

- Any cause of chronic hepatitis
- Alcohol
- Primary biliary cirrhosis
- Primary sclerosing cholangitis
- Secondary biliary cirrhosis (stones, strictures)
- Haemochromatosis
- Wilson's disease
- α_1-antitrypsin deficiency
- Cystic fibrosis

18.9 INVESTIGATION OF COMPLICATIONS OF HEPATIC CIRRHOSIS	
Complication	**Investigations**
Hepatic encephalopathy	Investigation for any precipitating cause Psychometric tests Electroencephalogram (EEG) Sensory evoked potentials
Portal hypertension	Upper gastrointestinal endoscopy Barium swallow and meal Liver ultrasound Abdominal computed tomography (CT) Wedged hepatic venous pressure Venography of hepatic veins
Ascites	Ascitic fluid sampling (for protein concentration, white blood cell count, bacterial culture, cytological examination) Liver ultrasound Laparoscopy
Renal failure	Urine analysis Renal ultrasound Central venous pressure recording Renal biopsy
Hepatocellular carcinoma	α-fetoprotein Liver ultrasound Abdominal CT Hepatic angiogram Laparoscopy

INVESTIGATION OF THE POTENTIAL COMPLICATIONS OF LIVER DISEASE

Investigation of patients for specific complications is especially important in those who have cirrhosis of the liver. The investigations employed are summarised in Box 18.9 and are discussed in more detail in the relevant sections.

IDENTIFICATION OF STRUCTURAL LESIONS WITHIN THE LIVER (IMAGING TECHNIQUES)

Several complementary imaging techniques can be used to determine the site and general nature of structural lesions in the liver and biliary tree. Ultrasound requires a skilled operator but is safe and comfortable for the patient. Its most frequent use is the identification of gallstones (see Fig. 18.7) and biliary obstruction. Ultrasound is often used in the initial assessment of patients with liver disease to determine further investigation. However, it is often difficult to identify diffuse parenchymal diseases; moreover, focal lesions, such as tumours or metastatic disease, may not be resolved unless they are more than about 2 cm in diameter and have echogenic characteristics sufficiently different from normal liver tissue. The advent of colour Doppler ultrasound has allowed blood flow in the hepatic artery, portal vein and hepatic veins to be investigated. Endoscopic and laparoscopic ultrasound provides high-resolution images of the

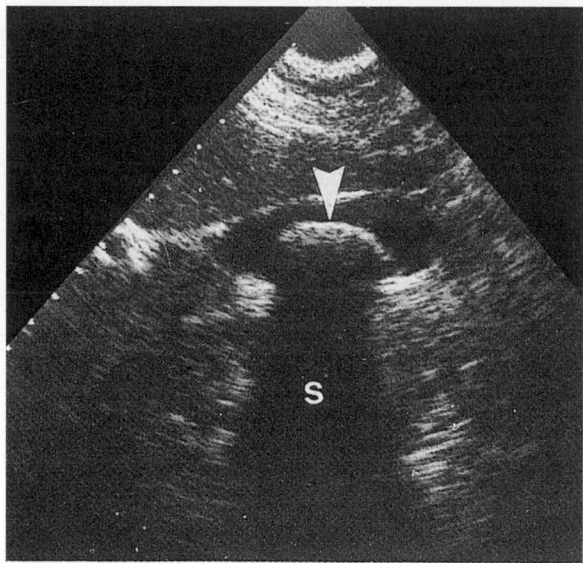

Fig. 18.7   Ultrasound showing stone in the gallbladder. Stone (arrow) with acoustic shadow (S).

pancreas, biliary tree and liver. Computed tomography (CT) can be used for the same purposes as ultrasound, but detects smaller focal lesions in the liver, especially when combined with contrast injection.

Cholangiography can also be undertaken via an endoscopic (endoscopic retrograde cholangiopancreatography, ERCP) or percutaneous (percutaneous transhepatic cholangiography, PTC) approach (see Fig. 18.8). The latter does

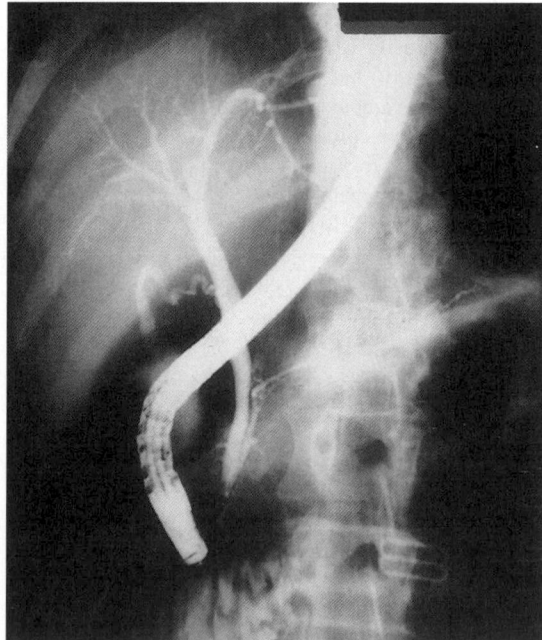

Fig. 18.8   ERCP showing normal biliary and pancreatic duct system.

not allow the ampulla of Vater or pancreatic duct to be imaged. Both endoscopic and percutaneous approaches allow therapeutic interventions such as the insertion of biliary stents across malignant bile duct strictures.

Magnetic resonance imaging (MRI) is increasingly used for the investigation of the liver and biliary tree. Magnetic resonance cholangiopancreatography (MRCP) is as good as ERCP at imaging the biliary tree and is less invasive, but does not allow therapeutic intervention (see Fig. 18.9).

Hepatic arteriography is most useful for localising focal liver lesions, particularly primary and secondary tumours, and is necessary in planning hepatic surgery. Hepatic portal venography is rarely performed, but imaging of the hepatic veins is necessary in patients with suspected Budd–Chiari syndrome (see Fig. 18.27, p. 876).

Plain abdominal radiographs, oral cholecystography and radionucleotide liver scanning are now rarely employed to investigate liver diseases.

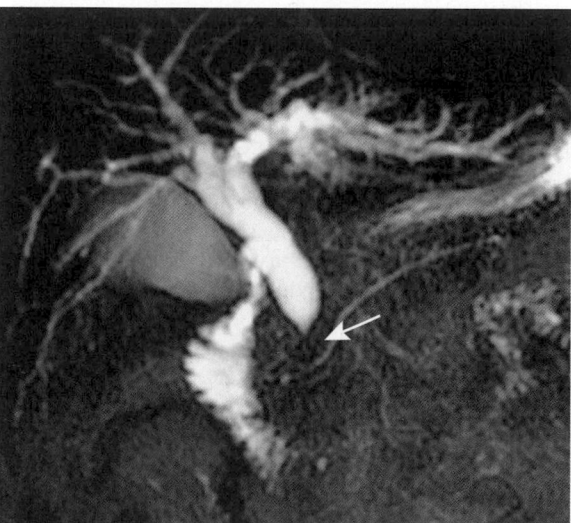

Fig. 18.9   A magnetic resonance cholangiopancreatogram (MRCP) showing a cholangiocarcinoma in the distal common bile duct (arrow). The proximal common bile duct is dilated but the pancreatic duct is normal.

ISSUES IN OLDER PEOPLE
INTERPRETATION OF LIVER FUNCTION TESTS

- There is a reduction in liver size and a decline in liver blood flow with age.
- Older people are more prone to drug hepatotoxicity, partly because of increased exposure to drugs. Up to a third of acute hepatitis in old age is drug-induced.
- There are no clinically relevant changes in liver function tests in older adults.
- Minor transient changes in liver function tests are not uncommon during acute infective illnesses or heart failure in old age.
- Persistent abnormalities of liver function in older patients are therefore a sign of possible liver disease.

MAJOR MANIFESTATIONS OF LIVER DISEASE

Liver disease produces a wide range of clinical manifestations. Jaundice is the main manifestation of acute liver disease, usually in association with systemic features of an acute illness. Severe acute liver disease can give rise to neuropsychiatric symptoms (encephalopathy) which characterise the rare syndrome of fulminant or acute hepatic failure. Chronic liver disease causes manifestations resulting from damage to the liver itself and from portal hypertension. Fluid retention (ascites and oedema) and hepatic encephalopathy are due mainly to a combination of these two processes and are features of chronic liver failure (or hepatic decompensation). The main manifestation of portal hypertension is bleeding from varices or gastropathy. In most countries the dominant cause of portal hypertension is hepatic cirrhosis and, although the underlying liver disease is always advanced, liver failure may or may not be present.

'ASYMPTOMATIC' ABNORMAL LIVER FUNCTION TESTS

The almost universal availability of automated biochemical analysis and the frequency of insurance, employment and health screening examinations have led increasingly to the identification of abnormal biochemical liver tests in asymptomatic people. Whilst the finding of abnormal biochemical liver tests may be indicative of a severe underlying liver disease, it is important to note that chronic liver disease may be associated with normal liver function tests; hence approximately 10% of patients with cirrhosis are identified unexpectedly at laparotomy or autopsy.

Investigation of patients with abnormal liver function tests starts with a clinical history and physical examination. Non-specific symptoms such as fatigue and weakness are common in patients with chronic liver disease. Clinical features of jaundice, pruritus, ascites, gastrointestinal bleeding and hepatic encephalopathy should be sought. The patient should be questioned regarding alcohol intake and previous drug exposure, including 'over the counter' or illegal drugs and herbal medicines. The physical examination specifically addresses whether or not there are cutaneous manifestations of chronic liver disease such as palmar erythema, spider telangiectasia and other skin changes. Abdominal examination may reveal hepatosplenomegaly and ascites. Features of hepatic encephalopathy, such as flapping tremor (asterixis) and constructional apraxia, should be sought. Measurement of height and weight allows calculation of the body mass index (BMI, see p. 298).

Often patients are truly asymptomatic or at most suffer from the non-specific symptoms described above. This situation is becoming more frequent in clinical practice

and fatty liver related to obesity is one of the most common causes. The pattern of abnormality of the liver function tests may suggest a specific disorder (see p. 837). Isolated elevation of the bilirubin is seen in Gilbert's disease (see p. 844). Significant elevation of the alkaline phosphatase and GGT occurs in cholestatic disorders such as primary biliary cirrhosis and primary sclerosing cholangitis (see p. 874) or gallstones (see p. 882). Isolated elevation of the GGT occurs in alcohol misuse and with some forms of drug therapy (see Box 18.4, p. 837). Predominant increases in the serum transaminases are suggestive of hepatitis which has many causes (see Box 18.3, p. 837 and Box 18.7, p. 838).

Raised transaminases have been reported in 2.4–8.8% of healthy blood donors and 0.5% of US military recruits. In approximately 33% of cases the elevated transaminases will resolve spontaneously, 33% resolve but subsequently recur, and 33% remain elevated. In the latter two groups a careful alcohol history, calculation of the BMI and specific aetiological blood tests as discussed above will usually identify the cause without recourse to liver biopsy, which is rarely necessary or helpful in investigating such patients.

JAUNDICE

Jaundice refers to the yellow appearance of the skin, sclerae and mucous membranes resulting from an increased bilirubin concentration in the body fluids. It is usually detectable clinically when the plasma bilirubin exceeds 50 µmol/l (3 mg/dl) but recognition of jaundice is often dependent on the ambient light available. Internal tissues and body fluids are coloured yellow but not the brain, as bilirubin does not cross the blood–brain barrier other than in the immediate neonatal period. Mechanisms leading to jaundice are shown in Box 18.10.

18.10 MECHANISMS PRODUCING JAUNDICE
Increased production of bilirubin
• Haemolysis
Impaired excretion of bilirubin
Congenital non-haemolytic hyperbilirubinaemia
• Gilbert's syndrome
• Crigler–Najjar type I and type II
• Dubin–Johnson syndrome
• Rotor's syndrome
Hepatocellular jaundice
• Acute parenchymal liver disease
• Chronic parenchymal liver disease
Cholestasis

- Haemoglobin breakdown
- Catabolism of other haem-containing proteins, e.g. myoglobin and cytochrome enzymes
- Ineffective erythropoiesis

Bilirubin metabolism

Unconjugated bilirubin is produced (425–510 mmol, 250–300 mg daily) from the catabolism of haem after removal of its iron component. The sources of unconjugated bilirubin are detailed in Box 18.11. Bilirubin in the blood is normally almost all unconjugated and, as it is not water-soluble, it is bound to albumin and does not pass into the urine. Further metabolism of bilirubin is shown in Figure 18.10. Unconjugated bilirubin is conjugated by the endoplasmic reticulum enzyme, glucuronyl transferase, into bilirubin mono- and diglucuronide. These bilirubin conjugates are water-soluble and exported into the bile via specific carriers on the hepatocyte membrane. Conjugated bilirubin is metabolised by colonic bacteria to form stercobilinogen, which may be further oxidised to stercobilin. Both stercobilinogen and stercobilin are then excreted in the stool. A small amount of stercobilinogen (4 mg/day) is absorbed from the bowel, passes through the liver and is excreted in the urine, where it is known as urobilinogen or, following further oxidisation, urobilin.

HAEMOLYTIC JAUNDICE

This results from increased destruction of red blood cells, or their precursors in the marrow, causing increased bilirubin production. Jaundice due to haemolysis is usually mild because a healthy liver can excrete a bilirubin load six times greater than normal before unconjugated bilirubin accumulates in the plasma. However, this does not apply to the newborn, in whom the hepatic bilirubin transport mechanism is immature, or to patients with liver disease.

Clinical features

There are often no stigmata of chronic liver disease other than jaundice. Increased excretion of bilirubin and hence stercobilinogen leads to normal-coloured or dark stools, and increased urobilinogen excretion causes the urine to turn dark on standing as urobilin is formed. Pallor due to anaemia and splenomegaly due to excessive reticulo-endothelial activity are usually present.

Investigations

The plasma bilirubin is usually less than 100 μmol/l (6 mg/dl) and the liver function tests are otherwise normal. There is no bilirubinuria because the hyperbilirubinaemia is predominantly unconjugated. The blood

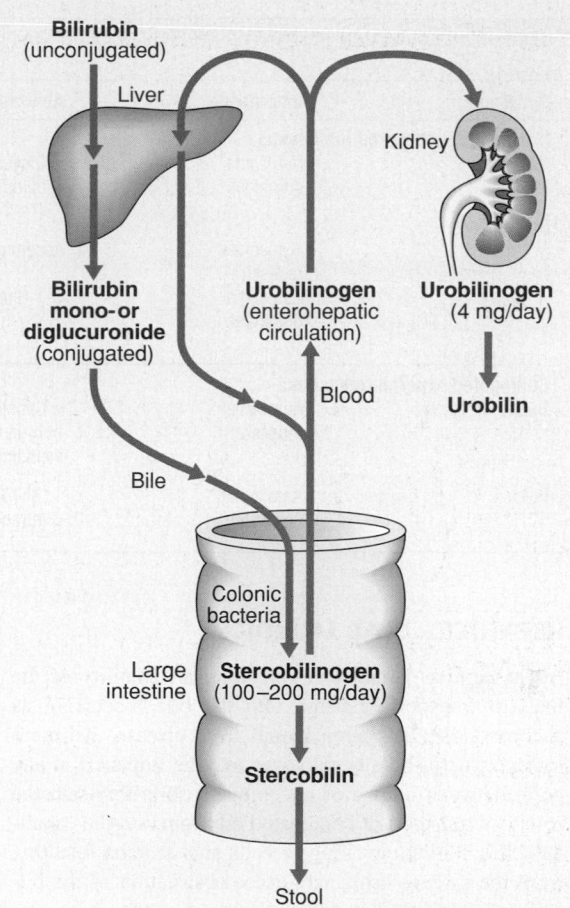

Fig. 18.10 **Pathway of bilirubin excretion.**

count and film may show evidence of haemolytic anaemia (see p. 921).

CONGENITAL NON-HAEMOLYTIC HYPERBILIRUBINAEMIA

Gilbert's syndrome is the only common form of congenital non-haemolytic hyperbilirubinaemia. All other forms are very rare (see Box 18.12). Familial cases of Gilbert's syndrome have been linked to a mutation in the promoter region of the UDP-glucuronyl transferase enzyme leading to reduced enzyme expression. This results in decreased conjugation of bilirubin, which accumulates as unconjugated bilirubin in the blood. The levels of unconjugated bilirubin increase during fasting and fall during treatment with phenobarbital (and can be used as confirmatory tests in difficult cases). The hyperbilirubinaemia is mild (< 100 μmol/l), and other liver function tests and hepatic histology are normal. The condition has an excellent prognosis, needs no treatment, and is clinically important only because it may be mistaken for more serious liver disease.

18.12 CONGENITAL NON-HAEMOLYTIC HYPERBILIRUBINAEMIA

Syndrome	Inheritance	Abnormality	Clinical features/treatment
Unconjugated hyperbilirubinaemia			
Gilbert's	Autosomal dominant	↓ Glucuronyl transferase ↓ Bilirubin uptake	Mild jaundice, especially with fasting No treatment necessary
Crigler–Najjar			
Type I	Autosomal recessive	Absent glucuronyl transferase	Rapid death in neonate (kernicterus)
Type II	Autosomal dominant	↓ ↓ Glucuronyl transferase	Presents in neonate Phenobarbital, ultraviolet light or liver transplant as treatment
Conjugated hyperbilirubinaemia			
Dubin–Johnson	Autosomal recessive	↓ Canalicular excretion of organic anions including bilirubin	Mild No treatment necessary
Rotor's	Autosomal dominant	↓ Bilirubin uptake ↓ Intrahepatic binding	Mild No treatment necessary

HEPATOCELLULAR JAUNDICE

Hepatocellular jaundice results from an inability of the liver to transport bilirubin into the bile, occurring as a consequence of parenchymal liver disease. Bilirubin transport across the hepatocytes may be impaired at any point between uptake of unconjugated bilirubin into the cells and transport of conjugated bilirubin into the canaliculi. In addition, swelling of cells and oedema resulting from the disease itself may cause obstruction of the biliary canaliculi. In hepatocellular jaundice the concentrations in the blood of both unconjugated and conjugated bilirubin increase, perhaps because of the variable way in which bilirubin transport is disturbed. The severity of jaundice, the other clinical features, and the investigation and treatment vary with the underlying disease and are considered later in this chapter.

CHOLESTATIC JAUNDICE

In unrelieved cholestasis jaundice tends to become progressively more and more severe because conjugated bilirubin is unable to enter the bile canaliculi and passes back into the blood, and also because there is a failure of clearance of unconjugated bilirubin arriving at the liver cells.

Aetiology

The causes of cholestatic jaundice are listed in Box 18.13. Cholestasis may be due to failure of the hepatocytes to generate bile flow, to obstruction of bile flow in the bile ducts in the portal tracts, or to obstruction of bile flow in the extrahepatic bile ducts between the porta hepatis and the papilla of Vater. Causes of cholestasis can operate at more than one of these levels. Those confined to the extrahepatic bile ducts may be amenable to surgical correction.

18.13 CAUSES OF CHOLESTATIC JAUNDICE

Intrahepatic

- Primary biliary cirrhosis
- Primary sclerosing cholangitis
- Alcohol
- Drugs
- Viral hepatitis
- Autoimmune hepatitis
- Severe bacterial infections
- Post-operative
- Hodgkin's lymphoma
- Pregnancy
- Idiopathic recurrent cholestasis

Extrahepatic

- Choledocholithiasis
- Carcinoma
  Ampullary
  Pancreatic
  Bile duct
  (cholangiocarcinoma)
  Secondary
- Cystic fibrosis
- Parasitic infection
- Traumatic biliary strictures

Clinical features

Clinical features in cholestatic jaundice include those due to cholestasis itself and those due to the development of infection (cholangitis) consequent to biliary obstruction (see Box 18.14). Other clinical features may point to a likely cause for the condition (see Box 18.15) and are discussed in greater detail in the relevant sections; none of these is pathognomonic of a particular cause, but each is more likely in some diseases than in others.

Investigations

The history and clinical findings determine investigations in individual patients. Usually, biochemical tests show greater elevation of the alkaline phosphatase and GGT compared with the aminotransferases, and an ultrasound is performed to identify any biliary dilatation. Subsequent investigation is shown in Figure 18.5, page 836.

18.14 CLINICAL FEATURES IN CHOLESTATIC JAUNDICE

Cholestasis

Early features
- Jaundice
- Dark urine
- Pale stools
- Pruritus

Late features
- Xanthelasma and xanthomata
- Malabsorption
  Weight loss
  Steatorrhoea
  Osteomalacia
  Bleeding tendency

Cholangitis
- Fever
- Rigors
- Pain
- Hepatic abscess

18.15 CLINICAL FEATURES SUGGESTING AN UNDERLYING CAUSE OF CHOLESTATIC JAUNDICE*

Clinical feature	Causes
Jaundice Static or increasing Fluctuating	Carcinoma Stone Stricture Pancreatitis Choledochal cyst
Abdominal pain	Stone Pancreatitis Choledochal cyst
Cholangitis	Stone Stricture Choledochal cyst
Abdominal scar	Stone Stricture
Irregular hepatomegaly	Hepatic carcinoma
Palpable gallbladder	Carcinoma below cystic duct (usually pancreas)
Abdominal mass	Carcinoma Pancreatitis (cyst) Choledochal cyst
Occult blood in stools	Papillary tumour

* Each of the diseases listed here can give rise to almost any of the clinical features shown. The more likely causes of each clinical feature are given.

Management

This depends on the underlying cause of the cholestasis and is discussed in detail in the relevant sections.

UNUSUAL FORMS OF CHOLESTASIS

Cholestasis of pregnancy

This is probably caused by an inherited susceptibility of the patient's liver cells to oestrogens; the condition may also be precipitated by oral contraceptives. Pruritus is the dominant symptom and jaundice occurs in about half of the patients. Itching almost always starts in the third trimester of pregnancy and remits within about 2 weeks of delivery. Some patients experience steatorrhoea. Pruritus can be relieved with colestyramine (see p. 874). There is an increased risk of premature delivery, fetal distress during delivery and stillbirth. Careful obstetric surveillance during the third trimester is essential and treatment with ursodeoxycholic acid may reduce the incidence of fetal complications.

Benign recurrent intrahepatic cholestasis

This is a rare condition in which episodes of cholestasis lasting from 1–6 months occur, starting in adolescence or early adult life. Genetic factors are probably important, as more than one family member may be affected. Episodes start with pruritus, and painless jaundice develops later. Liver function tests show the pattern of cholestasis; liver biopsy shows cholestasis during an episode but is normal between episodes. Treatment is required to relieve pruritus and the long-term prognosis is good.

ACUTE (FULMINANT) HEPATIC FAILURE

Acute or fulminant hepatic failure is a rare syndrome in which hepatic encephalopathy, characterised by mental changes progressing from confusion to stupor and coma, results from a sudden severe impairment of hepatic function. The syndrome is defined further as occurring within 8 weeks of onset of the precipitating illness, in the absence of evidence of pre-existing liver disease, to distinguish it from those instances in which hepatic encephalopathy represents a deterioration in chronic liver disease.

Aetiology

Any cause of liver damage can produce acute hepatic failure, provided it is sufficiently severe (see Fig. 18.11). Acute viral hepatitis is the most common cause worldwide; paracetamol toxicity (see p. 170) is the most frequent cause in the UK. Otherwise acute liver failure occurs occasionally with other drugs, or from *Amanita phalloides* (mushroom) poisoning, in pregnancy, in Wilson's disease, following shock (see p. 195) and, rarely, in extensive malignant disease of the liver.

Pathogenesis

Traditionally, cell death (including that of hepatocytes) has been described, mainly on morphological appearances, as occurring by apoptosis or necrosis. Apoptosis results in cell shrinkage, nuclear and cytoplasmic condensation, and cellular fragmentation into apoptotic bodies, which are phagocytosed by the surrounding immune and parenchymal cells. Cell membrane integrity is maintained during apoptosis and therefore inflammation is minimal.

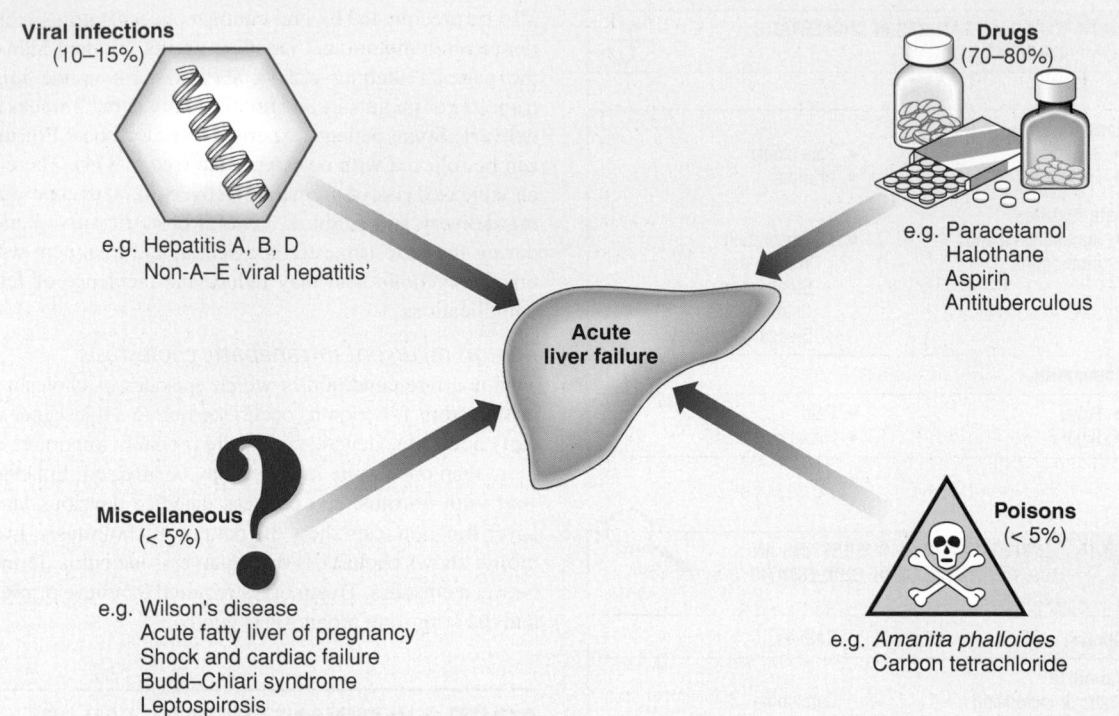

Fig. 18.11 Causes of acute liver failure in the UK. The relative frequency of different causes of liver failure varies according to geographical area.

In contrast, necrosis of cells leads to cellular swelling and rupture of the plasma membrane. The consequent release of cytoplasmic contents provokes an inflammatory response in the surrounding cells. Hepatocyte apoptosis can be induced by receptor-mediated (e.g. tumour necrosis factor, Fas, TRAIL) or mitochondrial (e.g. cellular stress and reactive oxygen intermediates) pathways which result in the activation of cytoplasmic caspase enzymes. These proteolytic enzymes exist as inactive zymogens but become activated during apoptosis and induce cellular destruction and the histological features of apoptosis. In contrast, necrotic stimuli lead to extensive mitochondrial damage and reduction in cellular adenosine triphosphate (ATP) levels. (ATP is required for the apoptotic process.)

However, this strict division of the types of cell death into either necrotic or apoptotic is now no longer appropriate; many types of injurious stimuli can lead to both forms of cell death. Although liver biopsy is often contraindicated by the severe coagulopathy, liver transplantation has allowed examination of liver tissue from patients with acute hepatic failure. These studies have shown that the histological and electron microscopic features of both hepatocyte apoptosis and necrosis occur in patients with acute hepatic failure. Activation of both receptor and mitochondrial apoptotic pathways has been implicated in the pathogenesis of acute hepatic failure induced by paracetamol overdose, viral hepatitis, Wilson's disease and other causes.

Clinical features

Cerebral disturbance (hepatic encephalopathy) is the cardinal manifestation of acute hepatic failure, but in the early stages this can be mild and episodic. The initial clinical features are often subtle and include reduced alertness and poor concentration, progressing through behavioural abnormalities such as restlessness, aggressive outbursts and mania, to drowsiness and coma (see Box 18.16). Confusion, disorientation, inversion of sleep rhythm, slurred speech, yawning, hiccup and convulsions may also occur. A flapping 'hepatic' tremor (asterixis) of the extended hands is characteristic but may be absent. Cerebral oedema can produce increased intracranial pressure causing unequal or abnormally reacting pupils,

18.16	CLINICAL GRADING OF HEPATIC ENCEPHALOPATHY
Clinical grade	**Clinical signs**
Grade 1	Poor concentration, slurred speech, slow mentation, disordered sleep rhythm
Grade 2	Drowsy but easily rousable, occasional aggressive behaviour, lethargic
Grade 3	Marked confusion, drowsy, sleepy but responds to pain and voice, gross disorientation
Grade 4	Unresponsive to voice, may or may not respond to painful stimuli, unconscious

fixed pupils, hypertensive episodes and bradycardia, hyperventilation, profuse sweating, local or general myoclonus, focal fits or decerebrate posturing. Papilloedema occurs rarely and is a late sign. More general symptoms include weakness, nausea and vomiting. Right hypochondrial pain is only an occasional feature.

Examination shows jaundice, which develops rapidly and is usually deep in subsequently fatal cases. Jaundice is not seen in Reye's syndrome, and death in other causes of acute hepatic failure occasionally occurs before jaundice develops. Fetor hepaticus can be present. The liver may be enlarged initially but later becomes impalpable. Splenomegaly is uncommon and never prominent. Ascites and oedema are late developments and may be a consequence of fluid therapy. Other features are related to the development of complications, which are considered below in the management of the condition.

Investigations

Investigations are used to determine the cause of the liver failure and the prognosis (see Boxes 18.17 and 18.18). The prothrombin time rapidly becomes prolonged as coagulation factor synthesis fails; this is the laboratory test of greatest prognostic value and it should be carried out at least twice daily. The plasma bilirubin reflects the degree of jaundice. Plasma aminotransferase activity is particularly high after paracetamol overdose, reaching 100 to 500 times the normal activity, but falls as liver damage progresses and is not helpful in determining prognosis. Plasma albumin concentration remains normal unless the course is prolonged. Percutaneous liver biopsy is contraindicated because of the severe coagulopathy, but biopsy can be undertaken by the transjugular route. Liver biopsy is particularly helpful in patients with suspected malignancy.

Management

A patient with acute hepatic damage should be observed in a high-dependency or intensive care unit as soon as a progressively prolonging prothrombin time or hepatic encephalopathy is identified (see Box 18.19) so that prompt treatment of complications can be initiated (see Box 18.20). Conservative treatment aims to maintain life in the hope that hepatic regeneration will occur, but early

---

18.17 INVESTIGATIONS TO DETERMINE THE CAUSE OF ACUTE HEPATIC FAILURE

- Toxicology screen of blood and urine
- IgM anti-HBc
- IgM anti-HAV
- Anti-HEV, HCV, CMV, herpes simplex, EBV
- Ceruloplasmin, serum copper, urinary copper
- Autoantibodies: ANF, AMA, ASMA, LKM
- Ultrasound of liver and Doppler of hepatic veins

See 'Investigation of hepatobiliary disease' (pp. 835–841) for abbreviations.

18.18 ADVERSE PROGNOSTIC CRITERIA IN ACUTE HEPATIC FAILURE*

Paracetamol overdose

- pH < 7.3 at or beyond 24 hours following the overdose
or
- Serum creatinine > 300 µmol/l, prothrombin time > 100 seconds and encephalopathy grade 3 or 4

Non-paracetamol cases

- Prothrombin time > 100 seconds
or
- Any three of the following:
  Jaundice to encephalopathy time > 7 days
  Age < 10 or > 40 years
  Indeterminate or drug-induced causes
  Bilirubin > 300 µmol/l
  Prothrombin time > 50 seconds

* Predict a mortality rate of ≥ 90%.

18.19 OBSERVATIONS IN FULMINANT HEPATIC FAILURE

Neurological

- Conscious level
- Pupils—size, equality, reactivity
- Fundi—papilloedema
- Plantar responses

Cardiorespiratory

- Pulse
- Blood pressure
- Central venous pressure
- Respiratory rate

Fluid balance

- Input—oral, intravenous
- Output
  Hourly urine output, 24-hour sodium output
  Vomiting, diarrhoea

Blood analyses

- Arterial blood gases
- Peripheral blood count (including platelets)
- Creatinine, urea
- Sodium, potassium, HCO_3^-, calcium, magnesium
- Glucose (2-hourly in acute phase)
- Prothrombin time

Infection surveillance

- Cultures—blood, urine, throat, sputum, cannula sites
- Chest radiograph
- Temperature

18.20 COMPLICATIONS OF ACUTE HEPATIC FAILURE

- Encephalopathy
- Cerebral oedema
- Respiratory failure
- Hypotension
- Hypothermia
- Infection
- Bleeding
- Pancreatitis
- Renal failure
- Metabolic
  Hypoglycaemia
  Hypokalaemia
  Hypocalcaemia
  Hypomagnesaemia
  Acid–base disturbance

transfer to a specialised transplant unit should always be considered. N-acetylcysteine therapy may improve outcome, particularly in patients with acute liver failure due to paracetamol poisoning (see EBM panel). Liver transplantation is an increasingly important treatment for acute hepatic failure, and criteria have been developed to identify patients unlikely to survive without a transplant. Patients should, wherever possible, be transferred to a transplant centre before these criteria are met to allow time for assessment of the patient and to maximise the time for a donor liver to become available. Survival following liver transplantation for acute liver failure is improving with increasing experience and 1-year survival rates of about 60% can be expected. Survival without transplantation is under 10%.

PARACETAMOL-INDUCED ACUTE LIVER FAILURE— role of N-acetylcysteine therapy

'In an RCT N-acetylcysteine (NAC) treatment in patients with paracetamol-induced acute liver failure was associated with a significant improvement in survival, less cerebral oedema and fewer episodes of hypotension requiring inotropic support.'

- Keays R, Harrison PM, Wendon JA, et al. Intravenous acetylcysteine in paracetamol-induced fulminant hepatic failure: a prospective controlled trial. BMJ 1991; 303:1026–1029.

CIRRHOSIS AND CHRONIC LIVER FAILURE

Cirrhosis and chronic liver failure are not synonymous terms, although the former can eventually lead to the latter. Chronic liver failure develops when the functional capacity of the liver can no longer maintain normal physiological conditions. The term 'hepatic decompensation' or 'decompensated liver disease' is often used when chronic liver failure occurs. Chronic liver failure is a syndrome complex that can occur as a consequence of insidious destruction of hepatocytes, but is more commonly precipitated by a number of events such as variceal haemorrhage or infection. It is characterised by a variety of clinical and laboratory features which may occur alone or more commonly in combination (see Box 18.21) and include hepatic encephalopathy, ascites and peripheral oedema, renal failure, jaundice, and hypoalbuminaemia and coagulation abnormalities due to defective protein synthesis.

Aetiology and pathogenesis

Hepatic cirrhosis can occur at any age and often causes prolonged morbidity. It frequently manifests itself in younger adults and is an important cause of premature death. Causes are listed in Box 18.8 on page 840. Any condition leading to persistent or recurrent hepatocyte death may lead to hepatic cirrhosis, e.g. viral hepatitis and alcohol. Prolonged biliary damage or obstruction, as can occur in primary biliary cirrhosis, sclerosing cholangitis and post-surgical biliary strictures, will also result in cirrhosis. Persistent blockage of the venous return from the liver, e.g. veno-occlusive disease and Budd–Chiari syndrome, will eventually result in

---

18.21 CLINICAL FEATURES OF HEPATIC CIRRHOSIS

Hepatomegaly (although liver may also be small)

Jaundice

Ascites

Circulatory changes
- Spider telangiectasia, palmar erythema, cyanosis

Endocrine changes
- Loss of libido, hair loss
- Men: gynaecomastia, testicular atrophy, impotence
- Women: breast atrophy, irregular menses, amenorrhoea

Haemorrhagic tendency
- Bruises, purpura, epistaxis, menorrhagia

Portal hypertension
- Splenomegaly, collateral vessels, variceal bleeding, fetor hepaticus

Hepatic (portosystemic) encephalopathy

Other features
- Pigmentation, digital clubbing, low-grade fever

---

liver cirrhosis. World-wide, the most common causes of cirrhosis are viral hepatitis and prolonged excessive alcohol consumption.

Common to all causes of liver cirrhosis is an activation of the hepatic stellate cells. These cells are widely distributed throughout the liver in the space of Disse. Following activation the quiescent fat-storing stellate cells become transformed into multifunctional cells, capable of collagen production, contraction and cytokine synthesis. This process is dependent on interaction with other cells in the liver, such as hepatocytes and Kupffer cells, and both paracrine and autocrine cytokine stimulation (see Fig. 18.12).

Chronic liver failure occurs when the functional capacity of the liver is exceeded. This situation may result following an increase in liver injury such as may occur in viral hepatitis or following an alcoholic binge. Alternatively, it may occur when certain clinical situations lead to increased metabolic demands on the liver, e.g. infection or gastrointestinal haemorrhage. Factors leading to the development of the clinical features of chronic liver failure, ascites, hepatic encephalopathy and jaundice are discussed under the appropriate sections.

Clinical features

These vary greatly and include any combination of the manifestations described below. Autopsy series have highlighted the fact that cirrhosis may be entirely asymptomatic, and in life may be found incidentally at surgery or may be associated with minimal features such as isolated hepatomegaly. Frequent complaints include weakness, fatigue, muscle cramps, weight loss and non-specific digestive symptoms such as anorexia, nausea, vomiting, upper abdominal discomfort and gaseous abdominal distension. Otherwise, clinical features are due mainly to hepatic insufficiency and portal hypertension.

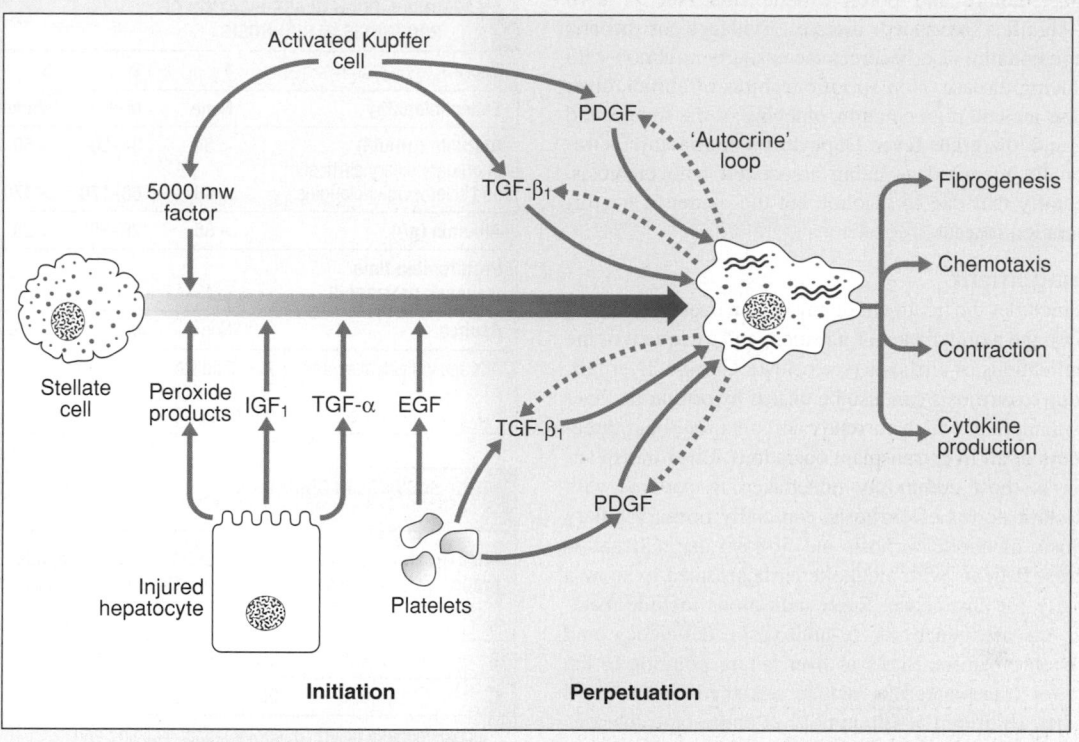

Fig. 18.12 Pathogenic mechanisms in hepatic fibrosis. The activation of hepatic stellate cells from a quiescent fat-storing cell into an activated myofibroblast-like cell occurs during the pathogenesis of hepatic fibrosis. Stellate cell activation occurs under the influence of cellular factors (cytokines) released from several different cell types within the liver. Injured hepatocytes release lipid peroxide products, insulin-like growth factor (IGF) and transforming growth factor-α (TGF-α); activated platelets release platelet-derived growth factor (PDGF), transforming growth factor-β₁ (TGF-β₁) and epidermal growth factor (EGF). Activated Kupffer cells also release PDGF and TGF-β₁, as well as an as yet uncharacterised 5000 mw factor which activates stellate cells. Once stellate cells become myofibroblast-like they can perpetuate their own activation by the synthesis of PDGF and TGF-β₁ in a series of autocrine activation loops. Activated stellate cells lose their fat-storing vesicles and become able to synthesise collagen matrix and inhibitors of collagen breakdown. They can migrate towards appropriate stimuli (chemotaxis) and contract under appropriate stimuli, as well as being able to synthesise cytokines.

Hepatomegaly is common, but progressive hepatocyte destruction and fibrosis gradually reduce liver size as the disease progresses. A reduction in liver size is especially common if the cause of cirrhosis is viral hepatitis. The liver is often hard, irregular and painless. Jaundice is usually mild when it first appears and is due primarily to a failure to excrete bilirubin. Mild haemolysis occurs in cirrhosis but is not important in the development of jaundice. Palmar erythema (see p. 832) can be seen early in the disease, but it is of limited diagnostic value as it occurs in many other conditions associated with a hyperdynamic circulation as well as in some normal people. Spider telangiectasia (see p. 832) are due to associated arteriolar changes and comprise a central arteriole (which occasionally raises the skin surface) from which small vessels radiate. They vary in size from 1–2 mm to 1–2 cm in diameter, are usually found only above the nipples, and can occur early in the disease. One or two small spider telangiectasia are found in about 2% of healthy people and they can occur transiently in greater numbers in the

third trimester of pregnancy, but otherwise they are a strong indicator of liver disease. Florid spider telangiectasia, gynaecomastia and parotid enlargement are most common in alcoholic cirrhosis. Pigmentation is most striking in haemochromatosis and in any cirrhosis associated with prolonged cholestasis. Pulmonary arteriovenous shunts also develop, leading to hypoxaemia and eventually to central cyanosis, but this is a late feature.

Endocrine changes are noticed more readily in men, who show loss of male hair distribution and testicular atrophy. Gynaecomastia is infrequent and can be due to drugs such as spironolactone. Easy bruising becomes more frequent as cirrhosis advances, and epistaxis is common and sometimes severe; it can mimic upper gastrointestinal bleeding if the blood is swallowed. Splenomegaly, collateral vessel formation and fetor hepaticus are features of portal hypertension, which occurs in more advanced disease (see p. 850). Haemorrhoids are often said to be more common in patients with portal hypertension but there is no evidence for this. Ascites is due to a combination of liver failure and portal hypertension (see p. 856) and signifies advanced disease. Evidence of hepatic encephalopathy also becomes increasingly common with advancing disease. Non-specific features of chronic liver disease include pigmentation, clubbing of the fingers and toes, and low-grade fever. Dupuytren's contracture is traditionally regarded as being associated with cirrhosis, especially that due to alcohol, but the evidence for this association is weak.

Management

This includes the treatment of any known cause (discussed below), the maintenance of nutrition, and treatment of the complications of cirrhosis (see below). Chronic liver failure due to cirrhosis can also be treated by orthotopic liver transplantation, which currently accounts for about three-quarters of all liver transplant operations. Liver transplantation is most commonly undertaken in patients with cholestatic forms of cirrhosis, especially primary biliary cirrhosis, alcoholic cirrhosis and cirrhosis due to hepatitis C virus. Patients with alcoholic cirrhosis need to show a capacity for abstinence. Rarer indications include metabolic diseases such as α_1-antitrypsin deficiency and haemochromatosis. Signs of liver failure pointing to the need for transplantation include sustained or increased jaundice (bilirubin > 100 mmol/l in cholestatic diseases such as primary biliary cirrhosis), ascites or hepatic encephalopathy not responding readily to medical therapy, and hypoalbuminaemia (< 30 g/l). Fatigue and lethargy affecting the quality of life, intractable itching in cholestatic disease, and recurrent variceal bleeding are additional indications. The main contraindications to transplantation are sepsis, the acquired immunodeficiency syndrome (AIDS), extrahepatic malignancy, active alcohol or other substance misuse, and marked cardiorespiratory dysfunction. Survival at 1 year after transplantation is about 80%, and the prognosis thereafter is good.

LIVER TRANSPLANTATION FOR CHRONIC LIVER FAILURE **EBM**

'RCTs of liver transplantation for chronic liver failure have not been reported. However, a survival benefit of transplantation has been shown in patients with liver failure secondary to primary biliary cirrhosis or alcoholic cirrhosis when compared with a simulated control population.'

- Markus BH, Dickson ER, Grambsch PM, et al. Efficacy of liver transplantation in patients with primary biliary cirrhosis. N Engl J Med 1989; 320:1709–1713.
- Poynard T, Naveau S, Doffoel M, et al. Evaluation of efficacy of liver transplantation in alcoholic cirrhosis using matched and simulated controls: 5-year survival. Multicentre group. J Hepatol 1999; 30:1130–1137.

Further information: 🖥 www.bsg.org.uk

Prognosis

The overall prognosis in cirrhosis is poor. Many patients present with advanced disease and/or serious complications that carry a high mortality. Overall, only 25% of patients survive 5 years from diagnosis but, where liver function is good, 50% survive for 5 years and 25% for up

18.22 CHILD–PUGH CLASSIFICATION OF PROGNOSIS IN CIRRHOSIS

Score	1	2	3
Encephalopathy	None	Mild	Marked
Bilirubin (μmol/l)	< 34	34–50	> 50
In primary biliary cirrhosis and sclerosing cholangitis	< 68	68–170	> 170
Albumin (g/l)	> 35	28–35	< 28
Prothrombin time (seconds prolonged)	< 4	4–6	> 6
Ascites	None	Mild	Marked

Add the individual scores: < 7 = Child's A
7–9 = Child's B
> 9 = Child's C

18.23 SURVIVAL IN CIRRHOSIS

Child–Pugh grade	Survival (%)			Hepatic deaths* (%)
	1 year	5 years	10 years	
A	82	45	25	43
B	62	20	7	72
C	42	20	0	85

* Include hepatic failure, gastrointestinal bleeding and hepatocellular carcinoma.

to 10 years. The prognosis is more favourable where the underlying cause of the cirrhosis can be corrected, as in alcohol misuse, haemochromatosis and Wilson's disease.

Laboratory tests give only a rough guide to prognosis in individual patients. Deteriorating liver function, as evidenced by jaundice, ascites or encephalopathy, indicates a poor prognosis unless a treatable cause such as infection is found. Increasing plasma bilirubin, falling plasma albumin or an albumin concentration < 30 g/l, marked hyponatraemia (< 120 mmol/l not due to diuretic therapy) and a prolonged prothrombin time are all bad prognostic signs (see Boxes 18.22 and 18.23). The course of cirrhosis is uncertain, as unforeseen complications such as variceal bleeding may lead to death unexpectedly.

PORTAL HYPERTENSION

Portal hypertension is characterised by prolonged elevation of the portal venous pressure (normally 2–5 mmHg). Patients developing clinical features or complications of portal hypertension usually have portal venous pressures above 12 mmHg.

Aetiology and pathogenesis

Portal venous pressure is determined by the portal blood flow and by the portal vascular resistance. Increased vascular resistance is usually the main factor producing portal hypertension, irrespective of its cause, and consequently the causes of portal hypertension are classified in accordance with the main sites of obstruction to blood flow in the portal venous system (see Fig. 18.13 and Box 18.24).

Extrahepatic portal vein obstruction is frequently the cause of portal hypertension in childhood and adolescence, while cirrhosis causes 90% or more of portal hypertension in adults in Western countries. Schistosomiasis is the most common cause of portal hypertension world-wide but it is infrequent outside endemic areas. Increased portal vascular resistance leads to a gradual reduction in the flow of portal blood to the liver and simultaneously to the development of collateral vessels, allowing portal blood to bypass the liver and enter the

systemic circulation directly. Increased portal blood flow may contribute to portal hypertension but is not the dominant factor. Collateral vessel formation is widespread but occurs particularly in the gastrointestinal tract, especially the oesophagus, stomach and rectum, in the anterior abdominal wall, and in the renal, lumbar, ovarian and testicular vasculature. Normally, virtually all the portal blood flows through the liver but, as collateral vessel formation progresses, half or more (and occasionally almost all) of the portal blood flow can be shunted directly to the systemic circulation.

Clinical features

The clinical features of portal hypertension result principally from portal venous congestion and from collateral vessel formation. Splenomegaly is a cardinal finding, and a diagnosis of portal hypertension is unlikely when splenomegaly cannot be detected clinically or by ultrasonography. The spleen is rarely enlarged more than 5 cm below the left costal margin in adults, but more marked splenomegaly can occur in childhood and adolescence. Hypersplenism is common and frequently results in thrombocytopenia. Platelet counts are usually around $100 \times 10^9/l$; values below $50 \times 10^9/l$ are rare. Leucopenia occurs occasionally, but anaemia can hardly ever be attributed to hypersplenism. Collateral vessels may be visible on the anterior abdominal wall and occasionally

Heart

Blood flow

Inferior vena cava

① Hepatic vein

Liver

②

③

④ ⑤ Portal vein

Blood flow

① Extrahepatic post-sinusoidal, e.g. Budd–Chiari syndrome

② Intrahepatic post-sinusoidal, e.g. veno-occlusive disease

③ Sinusoidal, e.g. cirrhosis

④ Intrahepatic pre-sinusoidal, e.g. sarcoidosis, schistosomiasis

⑤ Extrahepatic pre-sinusoidal, e.g. portal vein thrombosis

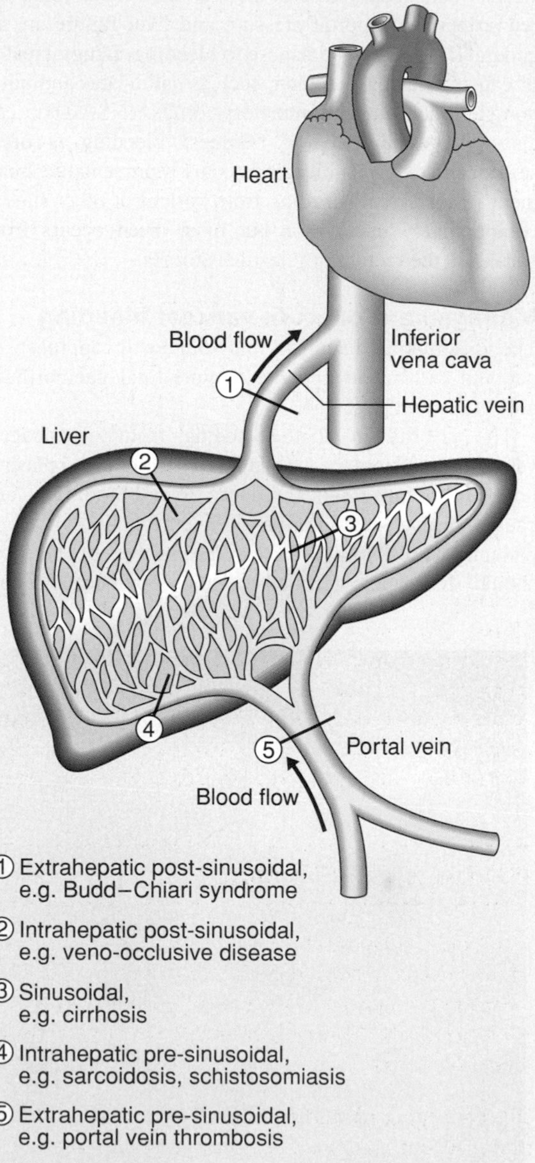

Fig. 18.13 Classification of portal hypertension according to site of vascular obstruction.

18.24 CAUSES OF PORTAL HYPERTENSION ACCORDING TO SITE OF ABNORMALITY
Extrahepatic post-sinusoidal
• Budd–Chiari syndrome
Intrahepatic post-sinusoidal
• Veno-occlusive disease
Sinusoidal
• Cirrhosis*
• Cystic liver disease
• Partial nodular transformation of the liver
• Metastatic malignant disease
Intrahepatic pre-sinusoidal
• Schistosomiasis*
• Sarcoidosis
• Congenital hepatic fibrosis
• Vinyl chloride
• Drugs
Extrahepatic pre-sinusoidal
• Portal vein thrombosis due to sepsis (umbilical, portal pyaemia)* or procoagulopathy (thrombotic diseases, oral contraceptives, pregnancy, secondary—cirrhosis)
• Abdominal trauma, including surgery
• Malignant disease of pancreas or liver
• Pancreatitis
• Congenital
* These are the most common causes (cirrhosis accounts for about 90% of portal hypertension).

several radiate from the umbilicus to form a caput medusae. Rarely, a large umbilical collateral vessel has a blood flow sufficient to give a venous hum on auscultation (Cruveilhier–Baumgarten syndrome). The most important collateral vessels occur in the oesophagus and stomach, where they can cause severe bleeding. Rectal varices also cause bleeding and are often mistaken for haemorrhoids, which are no more common in portal hypertension than in the general population. Fetor hepaticus results from portosystemic shunting of blood, which allows mercaptans to pass directly to the lungs.

Investigations

Radiological and endoscopic examination of the upper gastrointestinal tract can show varices. This establishes the presence of portal hypertension but not its cause (see Fig. 18.14). Imaging, particularly ultrasonography, can show features of portal hypertension, such as splenomegaly and collateral vessels, and can sometimes indicate the cause, such as liver disease or portal vein thrombosis. Portal venography demonstrates the site and often the cause of portal venous obstruction and is performed prior to surgical intervention. Portal venous pressure measurements are rarely needed but can be used to confirm portal hypertension and to differentiate sinusoidal and pre-sinusoidal forms.

Complications

Gastrointestinal bleeding from varices or from congestive gastropathy is the main complication (see Box 18.25). Hypersplenism is rarely severe enough to be clinically significant and portal hypertension is only one factor contributing to the development of ascites (see p. 855), renal failure (see p. 847) and hepatic encephalopathy (see p. 858).

18.25 COMPLICATIONS OF PORTAL HYPERTENSION
• Variceal bleeding   Oesophageal, gastric, other (rare) • Congestive gastropathy • Hypersplenism • Ascites • Renal failure • Hepatic encephalopathy

VARICEAL BLEEDING

Variceal bleeding occurs from oesophageal varices that are usually located within 3–5 cm of the oesophagogastric junction or from gastric varices. The size of the varices, endoscopic variceal features such as red spots and red stripes, high portal pressure and liver failure are all general factors that predispose to bleeding. Drugs capable of causing mucosal erosion, such as salicylates and other non-steroidal anti-inflammatory drugs (NSAIDs), can also precipitate bleeding. Variceal bleeding is often severe, and recurrent bleeding occurs if preventative treatment is not given. Bleeding from varices at other sites is comparatively uncommon but most often occurs from varices in the rectum or intestinal stomas.

Management of acute variceal bleeding

The differential diagnosis and diagnostic approach in patients with acute upper gastrointestinal haemorrhage are detailed on page 764.

The priority in acute bleeding from oesophageal varices is to restore the circulation with blood and plasma, not least because shock reduces liver blood flow and causes further deterioration of liver function. Even in patients with known varices, the source of bleeding should always be confirmed by endoscopy because about

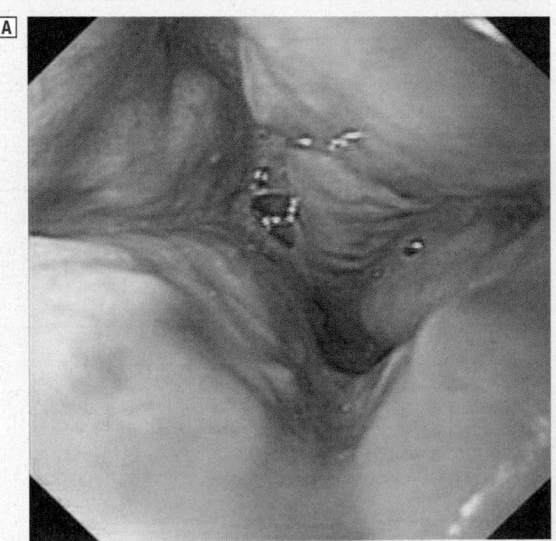

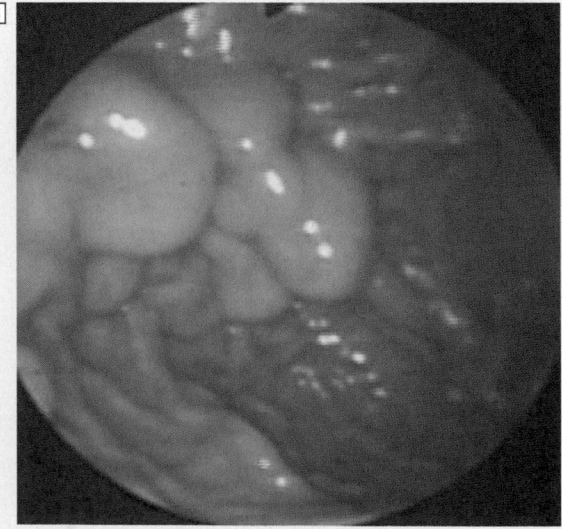

Fig. 18.14 Varices: endoscopic views. A Oesophageal varices at the lower end of the oesophagus. B Gastric varices.

20% of such patients are found to be bleeding from some other lesion, especially acute gastric erosions. Several treatments are available to stop acute variceal bleeding and to prevent its recurrence (see Box 18.26). Sclerotherapy and banding are the preferred initial means for treating variceal bleeding.

Reduction of portal venous pressure

Pharmacological reduction of portal pressure is less important than sclerotherapy or banding, is expensive and is not always used. Transjugular intrahepatic porto-systemic stent shunts (TIPSS) are increasingly being used for reducing portal pressure (see below).

Pharmacological treatment. Vasopressin constricts the splanchnic arterioles and reduces portal blood flow and hence portal pressure. It is best given by intravenous infusion 0.4 U/min until bleeding stops or for 24 hours, and then 0.2 U/min for a further 24 hours. Vasoconstriction also occurs in other vascular beds and can cause angina, arrhythmia and even myocardial infarction. Glyceryl trinitrate should be given transdermally or intravenously to combat these side-effects. Vasopressin should not be used in patients with ischaemic heart disease. Terlipressin is the current drug of choice because vasopressin is released from it over several hours in amounts sufficient to reduce the portal pressure without producing systemic effects. It is given in a dose of 2 mg i.v. 6-hourly until bleeding stops and then 1 mg 6-hourly for a further 24 hours.

Octreotide, the synthetic form of somatostatin, reduces the portal pressure and can stop variceal bleeding. It has few side-effects and is given in a dose of 50 μg intravenously, followed by an infusion of 50 μg hourly.

TIPSS and shunt surgery. TIPSS, described below, can be used for acute bleeding not responding to sclerotherapy or banding. Emergency portosystemic shunt surgery has a mortality of 50% or more and is now virtually never used for treating active variceal bleeding.

Local measures

The measures used to control acute variceal bleeding include sclerotherapy, banding, balloon tamponade and oesophageal transection.

Sclerotherapy or banding. This is the most widely used initial treatment and is undertaken if possible at the time of diagnostic endoscopy. It stops variceal bleeding in 80% of patients and can be repeated if bleeding recurs. Active bleeding at endoscopy may make sclerotherapy difficult; in such cases bleeding should be controlled by balloon tamponade prior to sclerotherapy. Banding can be used to stop acute variceal bleeding but it is less easy to apply than sclerotherapy in this situation (see Fig. 18.15).

Balloon tamponade. This technique employs a Sengstaken–Blakemore tube possessing two balloons which exert pressure in the fundus of the stomach and in the lower oesophagus respectively. Current modifications, such as the Minnesota tube, incorporate sufficient lumens to allow material to be aspirated from the stomach and from the oesophagus above the oesophageal balloon. The tube should be passed through the mouth and its presence in the stomach should be checked by auscultating the upper abdomen while injecting air into the stomach and by radiology. Gentle traction is used to maintain pressure on the varices. Initially, only the gastric balloon should be inflated as this will usually control bleeding. Inflation of the gastric balloon must be stopped if the patient experiences pain because inadvertent inflation in the oesophagus can cause oesophageal rupture. If the oesophageal balloon needs to be used because of continued bleeding, it should be deflated for about 10 minutes every 3 hours to avoid oesophageal mucosal damage. Balloon tamponade will almost always stop oesophageal and gastric fundal variceal bleeding, but only creates time for the use of more definitive therapy.

18.26 TREATMENTS TO STOP OESOPHAGEAL VARICEAL BLEEDING AND TO PREVENT RECURRENT BLEEDING
Local measures
• Sclerotherapy • Banding • Balloon tamponade • Oesophageal transection
Reduction of portal venous pressure
• Somatostatin (octreotide) • Vasopressin • Terlipressin
Prevention of recurrent bleeding
• Sclerotherapy/banding • Transjugular intrahepatic portosystemic stent shunt (TIPSS) • Portosystemic shunt surgery (unselective or selective) • Propranolol

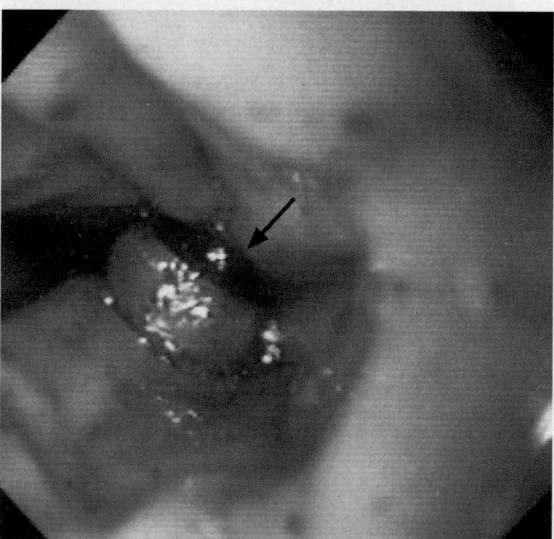

Fig. 18.15 Appearances of oesophageal varices following application of strangulating bands (band ligation, arrow).

Oesophageal transection. Transection of the varices can be performed with a stapling gun, although it carries some risk of subsequent oesophageal stenosis, and is normally combined with splenectomy. The operation is used when TIPSS is not available and when bleeding cannot be controlled by the other therapies described. The operative morbidity and mortality are considerable as hepatic failure is normally well established when other interventions have failed to control haemorrhage.

Prevention of recurrent bleeding

Recurrent bleeding is the rule rather than the exception in patients who have previously bled from oesophageal varices, and treatment to prevent this is needed.

EBM

VARICEAL BLEEDING IN PATIENTS WITH CIRRHOSIS—role of secondary prophylaxis

'Following control of active variceal bleeding, varices should be eradicated using endoscopic methods, with band ligation the current method of choice. While TIPSS is more effective than endoscopic treatment in reducing variceal rebleeding, it does not improve survival and is associated with more encephalopathy.'

- Jalan R, Hayes PC. UK guidelines on management of variceal haemorrhage in cirrhotic patients. Gut 2000; 6:1–15.
- Laine L. Ligation: endoscopic treatment of choice for patients with bleeding esophageal varices? Hepatology 1995; 22:663–665.

Further information: 🖳 www.bsg.org.uk/guidelines.html

Sclerotherapy

This is the most widely used method for preventing recurrent oesophageal variceal bleeding. Varices are injected with a sclerosing agent as soon as practicable after bleeding, and injections are repeated every 1–2 weeks thereafter until the varices are obliterated. Regular follow-up endoscopy is necessary to allow treatment of any recurrence of varices. The treatment is not free of risk as injections can cause transient chest or abdominal pain, fever, transient dysphagia and occasionally oesophageal perforation. Oesophageal strictures may develop. However, mortality is low even in those with poor liver function, and recurrent bleeding is largely prevented. Prolongation of life has been claimed but this remains to be proven.

Banding

This is a technique in which varices are sucked into an endoscope accessory, allowing them to be occluded with a tight rubber band. The occluded varix subsequently sloughs with variceal obliteration. The technique is applied in the same way as sclerotherapy, is generally more effective, has fewer side-effects and is becoming the treatment of choice.

TIPSS

This is a technique in which a stent is placed between the portal vein and the hepatic vein in the liver to provide a portosystemic shunt to reduce portal pressure (see Fig. 18.16). The procedure is carried out under radiological control via the internal jugular vein; prior patency of the portal vein must be determined angiographically, coagulation deficiencies may require correction with fresh frozen plasma, and antibiotic cover is provided. Successful shunt placement stops and prevents variceal bleeding. Further bleeding necessitates investigation and treatment (e.g. angioplasty) because it is usually associated with shunt narrowing or occlusion. Hepatic encephalopathy may occur following TIPSS and requires that the shunt diameter be reduced. The long-term value of the technique remains to be assessed.

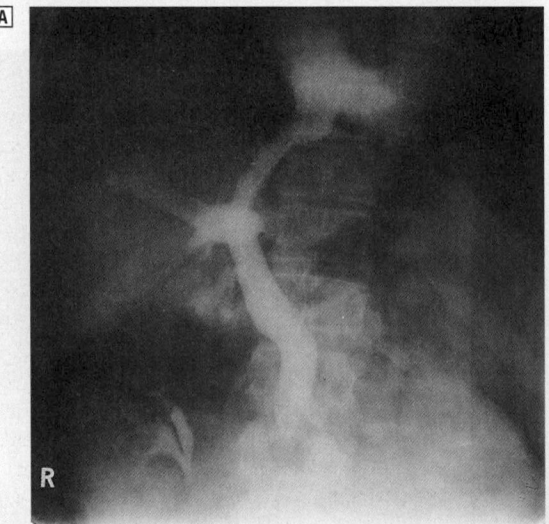
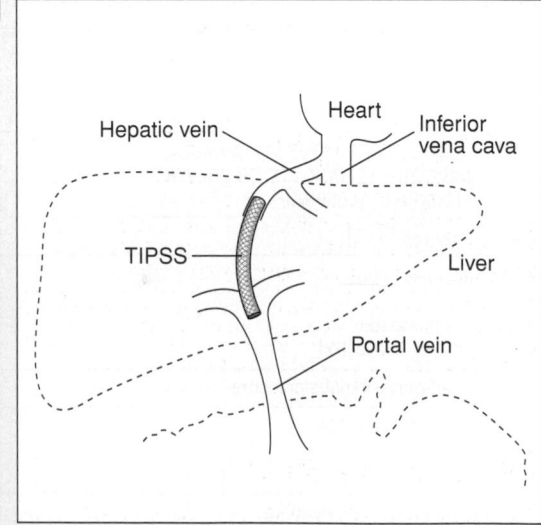

Fig. 18.16 Transjugular intrahepatic portosystemic stent shunt (TIPSS). Ⓐ Radiograph showing placement of TIPSS within the portal vein, allowing blood to flow from the right hepatic vein into the inferior vena cava. Note contrast within the superior mesenteric vein but not the splenic vein, which has collapsed with the reduction in portal pressure. Ⓑ Explanatory diagram.

Portosystemic shunt surgery

This used to be the treatment of choice because it effectively prevented bleeding, provided the shunt remained patent. However, the mortality associated with the procedure was high, especially in patients with poor liver function, and follow-up of patients showed that troublesome hepatic encephalopathy often supervened. Non-selective porta-caval shunts can divert the majority of the portal blood away from the liver. This diversion of blood renders patients liable to post-operative liver failure and hepatic encephalopathy. This led to the development of more selective shunts (such as the distal splenorenal (Warren) shunt) to decompress the oesophageal varices and preserve portal blood flow to the liver. Such shunts are associated with less post-operative encephalopathy, but with the passage of time liver portal blood flow falls and later encephalopathy may occur. Furthermore, survival is not prolonged, as death from liver failure occurs. In practice, portosystemic shunts are now reserved for patients in whom other treatments have not been successful and are offered only to those with good liver function.

Propranolol

Propranolol (80–160 mg/day) reduces the portal venous pressure in portal hypertension and has been used to prevent recurrent variceal bleeding; however, it is not widely used in secondary prevention and compliance may be poor.

Primary prophylaxis of initial variceal bleeding

In view of the mortality and morbidity associated with variceal haemorrhage, portosystemic shunts, sclerotherapy and propranolol have all been used to try to prevent initial bleeding from varices. Propranolol in a dose of 80–160 mg daily has given beneficial results and can be used for primary prevention (see EBM panel).

PRIMARY PREVENTION OF VARICEAL BLEEDING **EBM**

'Meta-analysis of RCTs of propranolol versus no therapy has demonstrated a 47% reduction in variceal bleeding (p = 0.0001), a reduction of 45% in deaths from bleeding (p = 0.017) and a 22% overall reduction in mortality (p = 0.052).'

• Hayes PC, Davies JM, Lewis JA, Bouchier IA. Meta-analysis of value of propranolol in prevention of variceal haemorrhage. Lancet 1990; 336:153–156.

Further information: 🖥 www.bsg.org.uk/guidelines.html

CONGESTIVE GASTROPATHY

Long-standing portal hypertension causes chronic gastric congestion recognisable at endoscopy as multiple areas of punctate erythema. Similar lesions occur rarely more distally in the gastrointestinal tract. These areas may become eroded, causing bleeding from multiple sites. Acute bleeding can occur, but repeated minor bleeding causing iron-deficiency anaemia is more common. Anaemia may be prevented by oral iron supplements but repeated blood transfusions can become necessary. Reduction of the portal pressure using propranolol 80–160 mg/day is the best initial treatment; if this is ineffective, a TIPSS procedure can be undertaken.

ASCITES

Ascites refers to the accumulation of free fluid in the peritoneal cavity. While cirrhosis is a common cause of ascites, there are many other causes, and these need to be considered even in a patient with chronic liver disease (see Box 18.27).

18.27 CAUSES OF ASCITES	
Common causes	

• Malignant disease
   Hepatic
   Peritoneal
	• Cardiac failure
	• Hepatic cirrhosis

Other causes	

• Hypoproteinaemia
   Nephrotic syndrome
   Protein-losing
   enteropathy
   Malnutrition
• Hepatic venous occlusion
   Budd–Chiari syndrome
   Veno-occlusive disease
• Pancreatitis
• Lymphatic obstruction
	• Infection
	   Tuberculosis
	   Spontaneous bacterial
	   peritonitis
	• Rare
	   Meigs' syndrome
	   Vasculitis
	   Hypothyroidism
	   Renal dialysis

Pathogenesis

Liver failure and portal hypertension in cirrhosis cause general sodium and water retention in the body, and localisation of fluid in the peritoneum due to the high venous pressure in the mesenteric circulation. The mechanism of sodium and water retention is unknown, but two general theories have been put forward. One explanation postulates that following the loss of fluid into the peritoneum there is compensatory renal retention of sodium and water ('underfilling theory'), while the other postulates a primary renal retention of sodium and water with eventual overspill of fluid into the peritoneum ('overflow' theory'). The most important pathogenic factor is probably splanchnic vasodilatation causing a reduction in effective circulating volume ('vasodilator theory'). This leads to activation of the renin-angiotensin system with secondary aldosteronism, increased sympathetic nervous activity, alteration of atrial natriuretic hormone secretion and altered activity of the kallikrein-kinin system (see Fig. 18.17).

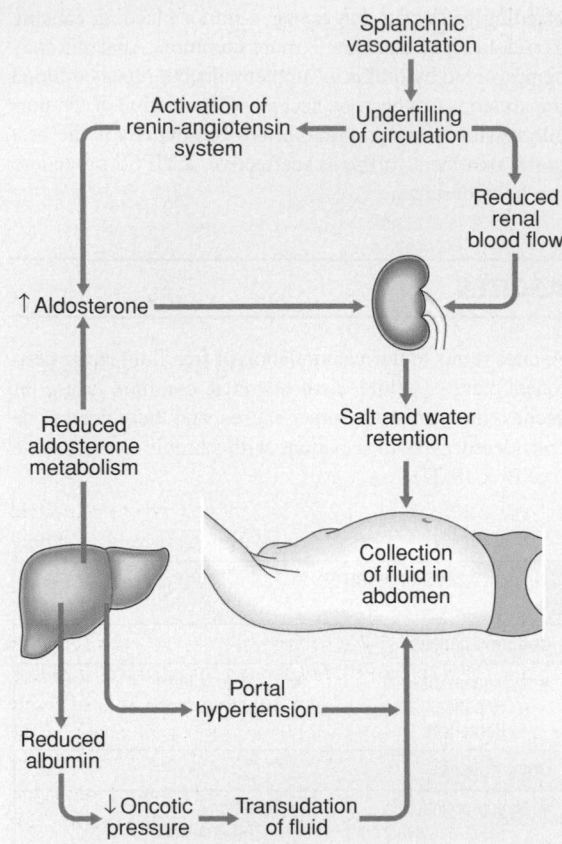

Fig. 18.17 Pathogenesis of ascites.

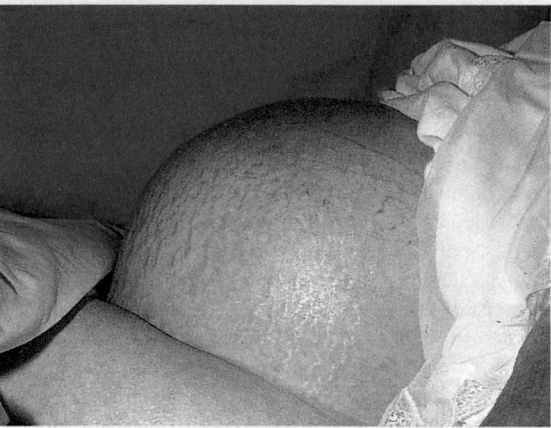

Fig. 18.18 Abdominal swelling in ascites.

18.28	APPEARANCES AND CAUSES OF ASCITES	
Cause		**Appearance**
Cirrhosis		Clear, straw-coloured or light green
Malignant disease		Bloody
Infection		Cloudy
Biliary communication		Heavy bile staining
Lymphatic obstruction		Milky-white (chylous)*
* Milky-white chylomicrons pass into supernatant on centrifugation.		

Clinical features

Ascites causes abdominal distension with fullness in the flanks, shifting dullness on percussion, and a fluid thrill when the ascites is marked (see Fig. 18.18). These signs do not appear until the ascites volume exceeds a litre even in thin patients, and much larger volumes can be hard to detect in the obese. Associated features of ascites include distortion or eversion of the umbilicus, herniae, abdominal striae, divarication of the recti and, occasionally, meralgia paraesthetica (see p. 1182) and scrotal oedema. Pleural effusions can be found in about 10% of patients, usually on the right side. Most are small and only identified on chest radiographs, but occasionally a massive hydrothorax occurs. Pleural effusions, particularly those on the left side, should not be assumed to be due to the ascites.

Investigations

Ultrasonography is the best means of confirming ascites, particularly in the obese and those with small volumes of fluid. Abdominal radiographs can show ascites, but they are insensitive and non-specific. Paracentesis can also be used to confirm the presence of ascites, but is most useful in obtaining ascitic fluid for analysis, if necessary under ultrasonic guidance. The appearance of the ascites may point to the underlying cause (see Box 18.28). The ascites protein concentration and the serum-ascites albumin gradient are used to separate ascites due to transudation from ascites due to exudation. Ascites with protein concentrations below 25 g/l or serum-ascites albumin gradients above 1.5 (transudates) are usually due to cirrhosis. Exudative ascites (ascites protein concentration above 25 g/l or serum-ascites albumin ratio below 1.5) raises the possibility of infection (especially tuberculosis), malignancy, hepatic venous obstruction, pancreatic ascites or, rarely, hypothyroidism. Ascites amylase activity above 1000 U/l identifies pancreatic ascites, and low ascites glucose concentrations suggest malignant disease or tuberculosis. Cytological examination can reveal malignant cells, and polymorphonuclear leucocyte counts above 250/mm³ strongly suggest infection (spontaneous bacterial peritonitis). Laparoscopy can be valuable in detecting peritoneal disease.

Diagnosis

In the great majority of patients ascites is caused by malignant disease, cirrhosis or cardiac failure; however, the presence of cirrhosis does not necessarily mean that this is the cause of the ascites. This is particularly so when liver function is good or when there is no evidence of portal hypertension, and in such patients a complication of cirrhosis, such as hepatocellular carcinoma or portal vein thrombosis, should be sought or an independent cause of ascites considered.

Management

Successful treatment of ascites relieves discomfort but does not prolong life, and if over-vigorous can produce serious disorders of fluid and electrolyte balance and precipitate hepatic encephalopathy (see p. 858). Conventional treatment aims to reduce body sodium and water by restricting intake, promoting urine output and, if necessary, removing ascites directly. The rate of loss of sodium and water is most easily measured by regular weighing. No more than 900 ml can be mobilised from the peritoneum daily so the body weight should not fall by more than 1 kg daily if fluid depletion in the rest of the body is to be avoided.

Sodium and water restriction

Restriction of dietary sodium intake is essential to achieving negative sodium balance in patients with ascites. Restriction to 80 mmol/day ('no added salt diet') may be adequate, but restriction to 40 mmol/day is necessary in more severe ascites and this requires close dietetic supervision. Drugs containing relatively large amounts of sodium and those promoting sodium retention such as non-steroidal analgesic agents must be avoided (see Boxes 18.29 and 18.30). Restriction of water intake to 0.5–1.0 litre/day is necessary only if the plasma sodium falls below 125 mmol/l. A few patients can be managed satisfactorily on this treatment alone.

Diuretic drugs

Most patients require diuretic drugs in addition to sodium restriction. Spironolactone (100–400 mg/day) is the drug of choice for long-term therapy because it is a powerful aldosterone antagonist, but it can cause painful gynaecomastia and hyperkalaemia. Some patients will also require powerful loop diuretics (e.g. furosemide (frusemide)), though these can cause fluid, electrolyte and renal function

18.29 SOME DRUGS CONTAINING RELATIVELY LARGE AMOUNTS OF SODIUM OR CAUSING SODIUM RETENTION
High sodium content

• Antacids	• Effervescent
• Alginates	preparations
• Antibiotics (see Box 18.30)	e.g. Aspirin
• Aspirin	Calcium
• Phenytoin	Paracetamol
• Sodium valproate	

Sodium retention	
• Carbenoxolone	• Metoclopramide
• Corticosteroids	• NSAIDs
• Diazoxide	• Oestrogens

18.30 SOME ANTIBIOTICS WITH A HIGH SODIUM CONTENT

• Amoxicillin	• Ceftazidime
• Ampicillin	• Cefuroxime
• Benzylpenicillin	• Chloramphenicol
• Cefotaxime	• Flucloxacillin
• Cefoxitin	• Piperacillin
• Cefradine	• Ticarcillin

Note Significant increases of sodium intake due to antibacterial therapy usually occur only during parenteral therapy when large (gram) amounts of drug are used. Maximum parenteral doses of the above drugs increase daily sodium intake by about 20–50 mmol. Drugs that do not themselves contain sodium increase sodium intake if they are infused in sodium-containing fluids. Oral antibacterial therapy rarely increases sodium intake but can occur with fucidin and para-aminosalicylate.

disorders. Diuresis is improved if patients are rested in bed while the diuretics are acting, perhaps because renal blood flow increases in the horizontal position.

Paracentesis

Paracentesis of 3–5 litres over 1–2 hours has always been used for immediate relief of cardiorespiratory distress due to gross ascites. Large-volume paracentesis alone has been regarded as a hazardous treatment; however, paracentesis to dryness or the removal of 3–5 litres daily is safe, provided the circulation is supported by giving a colloid such as human albumin solutions (6–8 g per litre of ascites removed) or another plasma expander. Total paracentesis can therefore be used as an initial therapy or when other treatments fail.

LeVeen shunt

The LeVeen shunt is a long tube with a non-return valve running subcutaneously from the peritoneum to the internal jugular vein in the neck, which allows ascitic fluid to pass directly into the systemic circulation. It is effective in ascites resistant to conventional treatment, but complications including infection, superior vena caval thrombosis, pulmonary oedema, bleeding from oesophageal varices and disseminated intravascular coagulopathy limit its use.

TIPSS

TIPSS (see p. 854) can relieve resistant ascites but does not prolong life. It can be used where liver function is reasonable or in patients awaiting liver transplantation. It should not be used in the terminally ill.

Prognosis

Ascites is a serious development in cirrhosis as only 10–20% of patients survive 5 years from its appearance. The outlook is not universally poor, however, and is best in those with well-maintained liver function and where the response to therapy is good. The prognosis is also better where a treatable cause for the underlying cirrhosis is present (see p. 850) or where a precipitating cause for ascites, such as excess salt intake, is found.

Complications

Ascites may be complicated by infections which are spontaneous (see below) or, more commonly, precipitated by invasive investigations or treatment, such as upper gastrointestinal endoscopy and injection sclerotherapy. Ascites can also be complicated by renal failure. Both of these complications have adverse prognostic significance and may prompt referral for transplantation.

SPONTANEOUS BACTERIAL PERITONITIS (SBP)

Patients with cirrhosis are very susceptible to infection of ascitic fluid as part of their general susceptibility to infection. SBP usually presents suddenly with abdominal pain, rebound tenderness, absent bowel sounds and fever in a patient with obvious features of cirrhosis and ascites. Abdominal signs are mild or absent in about one-third of patients, and in these patients hepatic encephalopathy and fever are the main features. Diagnostic paracentesis may show cloudy fluid, and an ascites neutrophil count above $250/mm^3$ almost invariably indicates infection. The source of infection cannot usually be determined, but most organisms isolated from ascitic fluid or blood cultures are of enteric origin and *Escherichia coli* is the organism most frequently isolated. Ascites culture in blood culture bottles gives the highest yield of organisms. SBP needs to be differentiated from other intra-abdominal emergencies, and the finding of multiple organisms on culture should arouse suspicion of a perforated viscus.

Treatment is started immediately with broad-spectrum antibiotics such as cefotaxime. Recurrence of SBP is common and may be reduced by norfloxacin (400 mg daily). Infections of other fluid collections that may occur in patients with cirrhosis, such as pleural and pericardial effusions, have been reported.

SPONTANEOUS BACTERIAL PERITONITIS (SBP)— treatment and prophylaxis	**EBM**

'Empirical antibiotic therapy improves outcome in patients with an ascitic fluid neutrophil count of greater than $250/mm^3$. Cefotaxime (> 2 g/12 hrs, 5 days' minimum duration), other cephalosporins or amoxicillin-clavulanic acid at standard doses are the recommended antibiotics. In patients with a previous episode of SBP norfloxacin 400 mg/day can prevent recurrence in patients with continued ascites.'

- Rimola A, Garcia-Tsao G, Navasa M, et al. Diagnosis, treatment and prophylaxis of spontaneous bacterial peritonitis: a consensus document. International Ascites Club. J Hepatol 2000; 32:142–153.
- Bernard B, Grange JD, Khac EN, et al. Antibiotic prophylaxis for the prevention of bacterial infections in cirrhotic patients with gastrointestinal bleeding: a meta-analysis. Hepatology 1999; 29:1655–1661.

HEPATIC (PORTOSYSTEMIC) ENCEPHALOPATHY

Hepatic encephalopathy is a neuropsychiatric syndrome caused by liver disease. It occurs most often in patients with cirrhosis but also occurs in acute hepatic failure.

Aetiology

Hepatic encephalopathy is thought to be due to a biochemical disturbance of brain function because it is reversible and does not cause marked pathological changes in the brain. Liver failure and portosystemic shunting of blood are two important factors underlying hepatic encephalopathy and the balance between these varies in different patients. Some degree of liver failure is a constant factor as portosystemic shunting of blood hardly ever causes encephalopathy if liver function is normal. Little is known of the biochemical 'neurotoxins' causing the encephalopathy, but they are thought to be mainly nitrogenous substances produced in the gut, at least in part by bacterial action, which are normally metabolised by the healthy liver so that they do not enter the systemic circulation. Ammonia has long been considered an important factor but much interest has centred recently on gamma-aminobutyric acid. Additional putative culprit substances include other false neurotransmitters such as octopamine, amino acids, mercaptans and fatty acids. Some factors appear to precipitate hepatic encephalopathy by increasing the availability of these substances; in addition, the brain in cirrhosis may be sensitised to other factors such as drugs that are able to precipitate hepatic encephalopathy (see Box 18.31). Disruption of the function of the blood–brain barrier is a feature of acute hepatic failure and may lead to cerebral oedema.

18.31 FACTORS PRECIPITATING HEPATIC ENCEPHALOPATHY

- Uraemia
  - Spontaneous, diuretic-induced
- Drugs
  - Sedatives, antidepressants, hypnotics
- Gastrointestinal bleeding
- Excess dietary protein
- Constipation
- Paracentesis (volumes > 3–5 litres)
- Hypokalaemia
- Infection
- Trauma (including surgery)
- Portosystemic shunts
  - Surgical, spontaneous (large)

Clinical features

These include changes of intellect, personality, emotions and consciousness, with or without neurological signs. When an episode develops acutely a precipitating factor may be found (see Box 18.31). The earliest features are very mild but, as the condition becomes more severe, apathy, inability to concentrate, confusion, disorientation, drowsiness, slurring of speech and eventually coma develop. Convulsions sometimes occur. Examination usually shows a flapping tremor (asterixis, see p. 833), inability to perform simple mental arithmetic tasks (see Fig. 18.19) or draw objects such as a star (constructional apraxia, see p. 833), and, as the condition progresses, hyper-reflexia and bilateral extensor plantar responses.

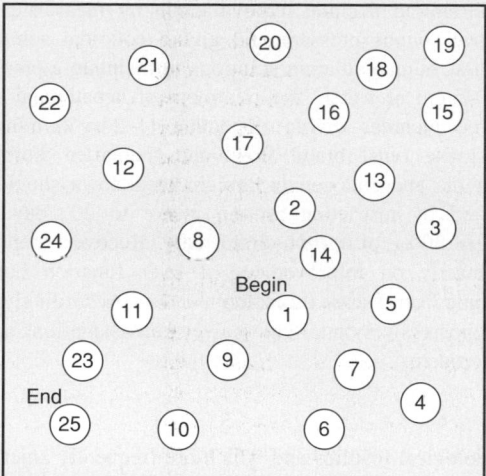

Fig. 18.19   Number connection test used in assessing encephalopathy. These 25 numbered circles can normally be joined together within 30 seconds. Serial observations may provide useful information as long as the position of the numbers is varied to avoid the patient learning their pattern.

Hepatic encephalopathy rarely causes focal neurological signs, and if these are present, other causes must be sought. Fetor hepaticus, a sweet musty odour to the breath, is usually present but is more a sign of liver failure and porto-systemic shunting than of hepatic encephalopathy. Rarely, chronic hepatic encephalopathy (hepatocerebral degeneration) gives rise to variable combinations of cerebellar dysfunction, Parkinsonian syndromes, spastic paraplegia and dementia.

Investigations

The diagnosis can usually be made clinically, but when doubt exists an electroencephalogram (EEG) shows diffuse slowing of the normal alpha waves with eventual development of delta waves. The arterial ammonia is usually increased in patients with hepatic encephalopathy. However, increased concentrations can occur in the absence of clinical encephalopathy so this investigation is of little or no diagnostic value. Other clinical conditions that may be confused with hepatic encephalopathy are listed in Box 18.32.

18.32 DIFFERENTIAL DIAGNOSIS OF HEPATIC ENCEPHALOPATHY
• Subdural haematoma
• Drug or alcohol intoxication
• Delirium tremens
• Wernicke's encephalopathy
• Primary psychiatric disorders
• Hypoglycaemia
• Neurological Wilson's disease

Management

Episodes of encephalopathy are common in cirrhosis and are usually readily reversible until the terminal stages occur. The principles of management are to treat or remove precipitating causes (see Box 18.31), to reduce protein intake, and to suppress production of neurotoxins by bacteria in the bowel. Dietary protein is reduced to less than 20 g/day, and glucose (300 g/day) is given orally or parenterally in severe cases. As encephalopathy improves, dietary protein is increased by 10–20 g/day every 48 hours to an intake of 40–60 g/day, which is usually the limit in cirrhotic patients. Lactulose (15–30 ml 8-hourly) is a disaccharide which is taken orally and reaches the colon intact to be metabolised by colonic bacteria. The dose is increased gradually until the bowels are moving twice daily. It produces an osmotic laxative effect, reduces the pH of the colonic content, thereby limiting colonic ammonia absorption, and promotes the incorporation of nitrogen into bacteria (see EBM panel). Lactitol is a rather more palatable alternative to lactulose, with a less explosive action on bowel function. Neomycin (1–4 g 4–6-hourly) is an antibiotic which acts by reducing the

TREATMENT OF HEPATIC ENCEPHALOPATHY   **EBM**
'Studies in small numbers of patients have shown lactulose to be of benefit in both acute and chronic hepatic encephalopathy but large RCTs are lacking.'
'Neomycin treatment is not significantly better than placebo in treating acute hepatic encephalopathy.'
'Current evidence does not support the use of branched-chain amino acid solutions in either acute or chronic hepatic encephalopathy.'
• Simmons F, Goldstein H, Boyle JD. A controlled clinical trial of lactulose in hepatic encephalopathy. Gastroenterology 1970; 59:827–832.   • Elkington SG, Floch MH, Conn HO. Lactulose in the treatment of chronic portal-systemic encephalopathy. A double-blind clinical trial. N Engl J Med 1969; 281:408–412.   • Strauss E, Tramote R, Silva EP, et al. Double-blind randomized clinical trial comparing neomycin and placebo in the treatment of exogenous hepatic encephalopathy. Hepatogastroenterology 1992; 39:542–545.   • Morgan MY. Branched chain amino acids in the management of chronic liver disease. Facts and fantasies. J Hepatol 1990; 11:133–141.

bacterial content of the bowel. It can be used in addition or as an alternative to lactulose if diarrhoea becomes troublesome. Neomycin is poorly absorbed from the bowel but sufficient gains access to the body to contraindicate its use when uraemia is present. It is less desirable than lactulose for long-term use; ototoxicity is the main deleterious effect. Chronic or refractory hepatic encephalopathy is one of the main indications for liver transplantation.

HEPATOPULMONARY SYNDROME

Many patients with cirrhosis are hypoxaemic due to a variety of factors including pulmonary hypertension, pleural effusions and the hepatopulmonary syndrome. The latter is characterised by resistant hypoxaemia and intrapulmonary vascular dilatation. Clinical features include digital clubbing, cyanosis, spider naevi, and a characteristic reduction in arterial oxygen saturation on standing. The hepatopulmonary syndrome is now considered an indication for liver transplantation.

HEPATORENAL FAILURE

Renal failure consequent on liver failure can occur in cirrhosis. The kidneys themselves are intrinsically normal and renal failure is thought to result from altered systemic blood flow including diminished renal blood flow. The condition is called 'functional renal failure of cirrhosis' or the 'hepatorenal syndrome'. It occurs in advanced cirrhosis, almost always with ascites, and is characterised by the absence of proteinuria or abnormal urinary sediment, a urine sodium excretion below 10 mmol/day and a urine/plasma osmolality ratio greater than 1.5. It is important to exclude hypovolaemia by measuring the central venous pressure and giving colloidal solutions such as human albumin solutions to maintain a pressure of 0–5 cm of water. The treatment of hepatorenal syndrome includes giving dopamine (1–2 µg/kg/min) to maximise renal blood flow, and thereafter diuretics. Uraemia and endogenous protein breakdown should be limited by restricting protein intake to 20 g/day and giving 300 g of carbohydrate daily. Recovery depends ultimately on improvement of liver function but in chronic liver disease this seldom occurs. Accordingly, the prognosis is very poor unless liver transplantation can be undertaken.

SPECIFIC CAUSES OF PARENCHYMAL LIVER DISEASE

VIRAL HEPATITIS

Viral hepatitis is almost always caused by one of the specific hepatitis viruses; hepatitis due to other viruses accounts for only about 1–2% of cases (see Box 18.33). All these viruses give rise to illnesses which are similar in their clinical and pathological features and which are frequently anicteric or asymptomatic. The features of the major hepatitis viruses are summarised in Box 18.34.

Clinical features

Prodromal symptoms usually precede the development of jaundice by a few days to 2 weeks. They are the common manifestations of an acute infectious disease and include chills, headache and malaise. Gastrointestinal symptoms may be prominent; anorexia and distaste for cigarettes are frequent, and nausea, vomiting and diarrhoea may follow. A steady upper abdominal pain, occasionally severe, occurs as a result of stretching of the peritoneum over the enlarged liver. Initially, physical signs are scanty; the liver is usually tender though not readily palpable, enlarged cervical lymph nodes may be found, and splenomegaly may occur, particularly in children. Patients with HBV infection often have arthralgia during the prodrome, and occasionally a 'serum sickness syndrome' with skin rashes (including urticaria) and polyarthritis occurs.

18.33 CAUSES OF VIRAL HEPATITIS	

- Hepatitis A virus (HAV)
- Hepatitis B virus (HBV)
- Hepatitis C virus (HCV)
- Hepatitis D virus (HDV)
- Hepatitis E virus (HEV)
- Non-A–E viral hepatitis
- Cytomegalovirus
- Epstein–Barr virus
- Herpes simplex virus
- Yellow fever virus

18.34 FEATURES OF THE MAIN HEPATITIS VIRUSES

	Hepatitis A	Hepatitis B	Hepatitis C	Hepatitis D	Hepatitis E
Virus					
Group	Enterovirus	Hepadna	Flavivirus	Incomplete virus	Calicivirus
Nucleic acid	RNA	DNA	RNA	RNA	RNA
Size (diameter)	27 nm	42 nm	30–38 nm	35 nm	27 nm
Incubation (weeks)	2–4	4–20	2–26	6–9	3–8
Spread					
Faeces	Yes	No	No	No	Yes
Blood	Uncommon	Yes	Yes	Yes	No
Saliva	Yes	Yes	Yes	?	?
Sexual	Uncommon	Yes	Uncommon	Yes	?
Vertical	No	Yes	Uncommon	Yes	No
Chronic infection	No	Yes	Yes	Yes	No
Prevention					
Active	Vaccine	Vaccine	No	Prevented by	No
Passive	Immune serum globulin	Hyperimmune serum globulin	No	hepatitis B vaccination	No

Note All body fluids are potentially infectious, though some (e.g. urine) are less infectious.

Dark urine and a yellow tint to the sclerae herald the onset of jaundice. As obstruction to the biliary canaliculi develops, the jaundice deepens, the stools become paler, the urine darker and the liver more easily palpable. At this time the appetite often improves and gastrointestinal symptoms diminish in intensity. Thereafter the jaundice recedes, the stools and urine regain their normal colour, the liver enlargement regresses, and in the course of 3–6 weeks the majority of patients recover. Mild illnesses may run an anicteric course recognised only because of known contact with a definite case or by the association of vague gastrointestinal complaints or malaise with bilirubinuria and biochemical evidence of hepatic dysfunction.

Investigations

A plasma aminotransferase activity exceeding 400 U/l, even before jaundice develops, is the most striking abnormality. The plasma bilirubin reflects the severity of the jaundice. The alkaline phosphatase activity rarely exceeds 250 U/l unless marked cholestasis develops, and the albumin concentration is normal. Prolongation of the prothrombin time is a reliable indication of severe liver damage. Bilirubinuria is an early finding, occurring in the prodromal phase and usually continuing into the convalescent period. Mild proteinuria may be present. The white cell count is normal or low in uncomplicated cases, sometimes with a relative lymphocytosis; this is of some value in differentiation from Weil's disease (see p. 20). Serological tests can identify HAV, HBV, HEV, cytomegalovirus and Epstein–Barr infection but are unreliable in acute HCV infection. Differential diagnosis is discussed on page 838.

Complications

While many complications of acute viral hepatitis are recognised (see Box 18.35), in practice serious complications are uncommon. Fatalities are rare and are usually attributable to acute hepatic failure (see p. 845). The return of symptoms and signs of acute hepatitis during recovery is characteristic of relapsing hepatitis and occurs in 5–15% of patients. Asymptomatic 'biochemical' relapses with increases of plasma aminotransferase activity are even more common. Relapsing hepatitis resolves spontaneously and does not imply a worse prognosis. Cholestasis can develop at any stage during the course of the illness, causing more severe

jaundice of a clinically and biochemically obstructive type. Liver biopsy shows the features of hepatitis with prominent cholestasis and no evidence of chronic liver damage. This cholestatic illness may continue for many months; however, the prognosis is good.

Debility for 2–3 months is common following clinical and biochemical recovery. Sometimes, particularly in anxious patients, there may be prolonged malaise, anorexia, nausea and right hypochondrial discomfort without clinical or biochemical evidence of liver disease. This phenomenon is known as the post-hepatitis syndrome.

Chronic HBV infection, with or without HDV superinfection, can cause chronic hepatitis and cirrhosis. Chronic HCV infection can also cause chronic hepatitis and cirrhosis. These chronic viral infections also predispose to hepatocellular carcinoma. Unconjugated hyperbilirubinaemia is sometimes found after acute viral hepatitis. Most instances are probably due to pre-existing Gilbert's syndrome.

Systemic complications are rare but include aplastic anaemia. This seems most common after non-A–E infection and may not become apparent for up to a year after the hepatic illness. Other complications are mostly related to HBV and HCV infection and include connective tissue disease, particularly polyarteritis nodosa (see p. 1042), and renal damage such as glomerulonephritis (see p. 612). Henoch–Schönlein purpura and papular acrodermatitis have been reported in children.

General management

Only the more severely affected patients require care in hospital, principally to allow early detection of developing acute hepatic failure. The post-hepatitis syndrome is treated by reassurance. Specific treatments are discussed below for the different viruses.

Diet

A nutritious diet containing 2000–3000 kcal daily is given. This is often not tolerated initially owing to anorexia and nausea, in which case a light diet supplemented by fruit drinks and glucose is usually acceptable. The content of the diet is dictated largely by the patient's wishes; however, a good protein intake should be encouraged. If vomiting is severe, intravenous fluid and glucose may be required.

Drugs

Drugs should be avoided if possible, especially in severe hepatitis, because many are metabolised in the liver. This applies especially to sedative and hypnotic agents. Alcohol must be avoided during the illness but can be taken once clinical and biochemical recovery have occurred. Oral contraceptives may be resumed after clinical and biochemical recovery.

Surgery

Surgery during acute viral hepatitis carries a significant risk of post-operative liver failure. Only life-saving operations should be carried out.

Liver transplantation

Liver transplantation may be required for acute or chronic liver failure due to hepatitis viruses.

18.35 COMPLICATIONS OF ACUTE VIRAL HEPATITIS	
• Acute hepatic failure	• Connective tissue disease
• Relapsing hepatitis	• Renal failure
Biochemical	• Henoch–Schönlein
Clinical	purpura
• Cholestatic hepatitis	• Papular acrodermatitis
• Post-hepatitis syndrome	• Chronic hepatitis
• Hyperbilirubinaemia	• Cirrhosis (hepatitis B, C)
(Gilbert's syndrome)*	• Hepatocellular carcinoma
• Aplastic anaemia	

* Gilbert's syndrome may be brought to light by follow-up of viral hepatitis.

Prognosis

This varies depending on the cause of the hepatitis (see below). The overall mortality of acute viral hepatitis is about 0.5% in otherwise well patients under 40 years of age, but mortality reaches about 3% in patients over 60 years and may be much higher in patients with other serious diseases, such as chronic liver disease, carcinoma or lymphoma.

VIROLOGY

The hepatitis viruses (A–E) all cause primarily hepatic illness in humans but otherwise are quite distinct and belong to separate virus groups.

Hepatitis A

The hepatitis A virus (HAV) belongs to the picornavirus group of enteroviruses and, although it can be cultured, this is only done for research purposes. HAV is highly infectious and is spread by the faecal-oral route by persons incubating or suffering from the disease. Infected persons excrete viruses in the faeces for about 2–3 weeks before the onset of the illness and for up to 2 weeks thereafter. Children are most commonly affected and conditions of overcrowding and poor sanitation facilitate spread. In occasional outbreaks water, milk and shellfish have been the vehicles of transmission. Though faeces are the usual source, a transient viraemia in the incubation period occasionally allows infection to be spread by blood and by homosexual activity, especially in men. A chronic carrier state, analogous to that for hepatitis B virus, does not occur.

Investigations

Only one HAV antigen has been found; individuals infected with HAV make an antibody to this antigen (anti-HAV). Anti-HAV is important in diagnosis as HAV is only present in the blood transiently during the incubation period. Excretion in the stools occurs for only 7–14 days after the onset of the clinical illness and the virus cannot be grown readily. Anti-HAV of IgM type, indicating a primary immune response, is already present in the blood at the onset of the clinical illness and is diagnostic of an acute HAV infection. Titres of this antibody fall to low levels within about 3 months of recovery. Anti-HAV of IgG type is of no diagnostic value as HAV infection is common and this antibody persists for years after infection, but it can be used to measure the prevalence of HAV infection. Its presence indicates immunity to HAV.

Prevention

Infection in the community is best prevented by improving social conditions, especially overcrowding and poor sanitation. Individuals can be given substantial protection from infection by active immunisation with an inactivated virus vaccine (Havrix). Immunisation should be considered for individuals with chronic hepatitis B or C infections. Immediate protection can be provided by immune serum globulin if this is given soon after exposure to the virus. This can be considered for those at particular risk such as close contacts, the elderly, those with other major disease and perhaps pregnant women. Immune serum globulin can be effective in an outbreak of hepatitis, in a school or nursery, as injection of those at risk prevents secondary spread to families. Persons travelling to endemic areas are best protected by vaccination, but where time is limited vaccine and immune serum globulin can be injected in separate sites to provide immediate and longer-term protection. The protective effect of immune serum globulin is attributed to its anti-HAV content; those with anti-HAV in the blood are protected naturally.

Prognosis

Acute hepatic failure is rare in HAV infection and chronic infection does not occur. However, HAV infection in patients with chronic hepatitis B or C may cause serious or life-threatening disease.

Hepatitis B

The hepatitis B virus (HBV) is the only hepadna virus causing infection in humans. It cannot yet be grown but can be transmitted to certain primates, such as the chimpanzee, in which it replicates. It comprises a capsule and a core containing DNA and a DNA polymerase enzyme (see Fig. 18.20). The virus, known as Dane particles, and an excess of its capsular material, hepatitis B surface antigen (HBsAg), circulate in the blood. Humans are the only source of infection. Individuals incubating or suffering from acute hepatitis are highly infectious for at least as long as the HBsAg is in the blood. Patients with chronic infections may be asymptomatic or have chronic liver failure. These individuals are most infectious when markers of continuing viral replication such as HBeAg, HBV-DNA or DNA polymerase are present in the blood, and are least infectious when these are absent

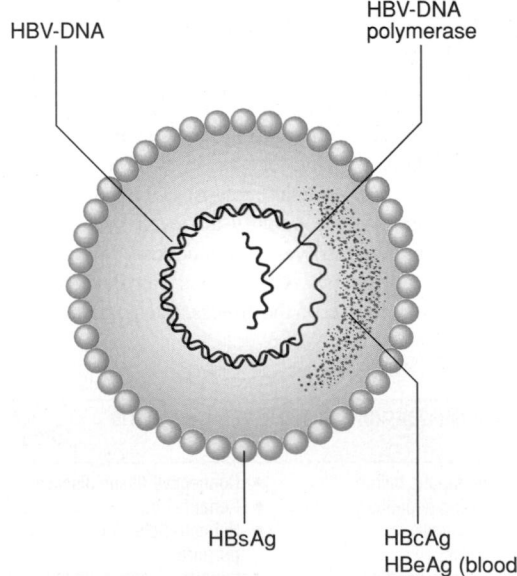

Fig. 18.20 Schematic diagram of hepatitis B virus. Hepatitis B surface antigen (HBsAg) is a protein which makes up part of the viral envelope; hepatitis B core antigen (HBcAg) is a protein which makes up the capsid or core part of the virus (found in the liver but not in blood); hepatitis B e antigen (HBeAg) is part of the HBcAg which can be found in the blood and indicates infectivity.

and only anti-HBe is present. Chronic hepatitis B affects about 300 million people around the world; infection is associated with cirrhosis and primary hepatocellular carcinoma. Chronic carrier rates of the virus following infection vary from 10–20% in Asia, Africa, the Middle East and the Pacific Islands, where most infections are acquired in infancy, to 2% in Europe and North America.

Blood is the main source of infection; spread may follow transfusion of infected blood or blood products, or result from injections with contaminated needles, a mode of spread most common among parenteral drug misusers who share needles or other injecting paraphernalia. Blood and blood products used for transfusion are no longer a major source of infection, provided that donor blood is tested for the virus, and less than 10% of all post-transfusion hepatitis is now attributable to HBV. However, only products such as albumin solutions and gamma-globulin which are pasteurised are wholly free of risk. Tattooing or acupuncture can also spread this disease if inadequately sterilised needles are used.

HBV can also cause sporadic infections which cannot be attributed to parenteral modes of spread. The means of non-parenteral transmission are uncertain, but the discovery of HBsAg or HBV-DNA in body fluids such as saliva, urine, semen and vaginal secretions suggests many mechanisms. Close personal contact seems necessary for transmission, and sexual intercourse, especially in male homosexuals, is an important route of infection. The virus may also be spread vertically from mother to child in the immediate perinatal period; this represents the chief source of infection globally.

Investigations

HBV contains several antigens to which infected persons can make immune responses (see Fig. 18.21); these antigens and their antibodies are important in identifying HBV infection (see Box 18.36).

In acute infection the hepatitis B surface antigen (HBsAg) is a reliable marker of HBV infection, and a negative test for HBsAg makes HBV infection very unlikely but not impossible (see Fig. 18.21). HBsAg appears in the blood late in the incubation period and before the prodromal phase of acute type B hepatitis; it may be present for only a few days, disappearing even before jaundice has developed, but usually lasts for 3–4 weeks and can persist for up to 5 months. Antibody to HBsAg (anti-HBs) usually appears after about 3–6 months and persists for many years or perhaps permanently. Anti-HBs implies either a previous infection, in which case anti-HBc (see below) is usually also present, or previous vaccination if anti-HBc is not present. The hepatitis B core antigen (HBcAg) is not found in the blood, but antibody to it (anti-HBc) appears early in the illness and rapidly reaches a high titre which then subsides gradually and persists. Anti-HBc is initially of IgM type with IgG antibody appearing later. Anti-HBc (IgM) can sometimes reveal an acute HBV infection when the HBsAg has disappeared and before anti-HBs has developed (see Fig. 18.21 and Box 18.36). The hepatitis Be antigen (HBeAg) appears only transiently at the outset of the illness and is followed by the production of antibody (anti-HBe). The HBeAg reflects active replication of the virus in the liver.

Chronic HBV infection (see p. 864) is marked by the presence of HBsAg and anti-HBc (IgG) in the blood. Rarely, anti-HBc (IgG) alone is the sole evidence of chronic infection. Usually, HBeAg or anti-HBe is also present; HBeAg indicates continued active replication of the virus in the liver while anti-HBe implies that replication is occurring at a much lower level or that HBV-DNA has become integrated into host hepatocyte DNA. Polymerase chain reactions (PCR) can show HBV-DNA in the blood, implying that viral replication is occurring. This is rarely needed for diagnosis but can be useful in selecting for, and measuring response to, therapy. Some rare mutant forms of the virus cannot synthesise the 'e' antigen and HBV-DNA is necessary for their detection.

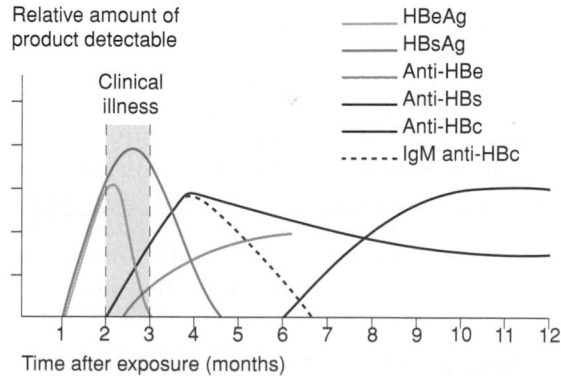

Fig. 18.21 Serological responses to hepatitis B virus infection. (HBsAg = hepatitis B surface antigen; anti-HBs = antibody to HBsAg; HBeAg = hepatitis B e antigen; anti-HBe = antibody to HBeAg; anti-HBc = antibody to hepatitis B core antigen)

18.36 INTERPRETATION OF MAIN INVESTIGATIONS USED IN THE SEROLOGICAL DIAGNOSIS OF HEPATITIS B VIRUS INFECTION				
		Anti-HBc		
Interpretation	HBsAg	IgM	IgG	Anti-HBs
Incubation period	+	+	–	–
Acute hepatitis				
Early	+	+	–	–
Established	+	+	+	–
Established (occasional)	–	+	+	–
Convalescence				
(3–6 months)	–	±	+	±
(6–9 months)	–	–	+	+
Post-infection				
> 1 year	–	–	+	+
Uncertain	–	–	+	–
Chronic infection				
Usual	+	–	+	–
Occasional	–	–	+	–
Immunisation without infection	–	–	–	+
+ = positive; – = negative; ± = present at low titre or absent.				

Management

Treatment of acute hepatitis B is supportive with close monitoring for acute liver failure. The role of lamivudine is currently unclear. Treatment of chronic hepatitis B is limited, with interferon and lamivudine being licensed drugs. Interferon is most effective in patients with high serum transaminase concentrations and active hepatitis on biopsy, who have not acquired infection at birth, and in those who are HIV-negative. Treatment consists of 5 MU daily or 10 MU three times per week for 16 weeks. Side-effects include influenza-like symptoms (fever and myalgia), depression, neutropenia, thrombocytopenia and thyroid abnormalities. Sustained loss of markers of viral replication (HBeAg and HBV-DNA) leads to biochemical, clinical and histological remission. A response to interferon is characterised by an increase in serum aminotransferases after 6–8 weeks of therapy. Great care is necessary, therefore, in treating patients with cirrhosis as liver failure may be induced. Long-term follow-up studies are scanty but indicate a significant improvement in survival among responders. Individuals with pre-core mutant virus, who lack HBeAg, respond poorly. Other unfavourable prognostic markers include high pre-treatment levels of HBV-DNA, male gender, cirrhosis on liver histology and origin in the Far East.

A number of anti-HBV nucleoside drugs are currently under evaluation; all these agents are inhibitors of HBV-DNA polymerase. The most promising at present is lamivudine which is now licensed and is used in a daily dose of 100 mg for 1 year. It has a low incidence of side-effects and causes complete suppression of serum HBV-DNA in 93–100% of patients, with significant improvements in liver histology. Seroconversion from HBeAg to anti-HBeAg is approximately 17% compared with 8% in controls, and this figure rises if therapy is prolonged. However, HBV replication recurs in many patients when treatment is stopped. Prolonged use leads to the emergence of a lamivudine-resistant strain of virus which is rapidly replaced by wild-type when treatment is withdrawn. There is evidence that lamivudine therapy may reduce or even reverse fibrosis.

CHRONIC HEPATITIS B INFECTION—role of antiviral therapy   **EBM**

'A meta-analysis of over 15 RCTs of interferon-alpha treatment of patients with chronic hepatitis B infection showed a significant response in the treated patients: HBeAg loss among 33% of those treated, compared with 12% of controls; HBV-DNA loss among 37% of those treated compared with 17% of controls. Randomised trials of lamivudine (100 mg/day for 52 weeks) showed significant response rates in both American and Chinese patients. An RCT of interferon and lamivudine therapy showed no additional benefit over interferon therapy alone.'

- Wong DK, Cheung AM, O'Rourke K, et al. Effect of alpha-interferon treatment in patients with hepatitis B e antigen-positive chronic hepatitis B. A meta-analysis. Ann Intern Med 1993; 119:312–323.
- Lai CL, Chien RN, Leung NW, et al. A one-year trial of lamivudine for chronic hepatitis B. Asia Hepatitis Lamivudine Study Group. N Engl J Med 1998; 339:61–68.
- Dienstag JL, Schiff ER, Wright TL, et al. Lamivudine as initial treatment for chronic hepatitis B in the United States. N Engl J Med 1999; 341:1256–1263.

18.37 AT-RISK GROUPS MERITING HEPATITIS B VACCINATION IN LOW ENDEMIC AREAS

Parenteral drug users

Homosexuals (male)

Close contacts of infected individuals
- Newborn of infected mothers
- Regular sexual partners

Patients on chronic haemodialysis

Medical/nursing personnel
- Dentists
- Surgeons/obstetricians
- Accident and emergency departments
- Intensive care
- Liver units
- Endoscopy units
- Oncology units

Laboratory staff handling blood

Prevention

A recombinant hepatitis B vaccine containing HBsAg is available (Engerix) and is capable of producing active immunisation in 95% of normal individuals. The vaccine gives a high degree of protection and should be used particularly in those at special risk of infection who are not already immune, as evidenced by anti-HBs in the blood (see Box 18.37). The vaccine is ineffective in those already infected by HBV. Type B hepatitis can be prevented or minimised by the intramuscular injection of hyperimmune serum globulin prepared from blood containing anti-HBs. This should be given within 24 hours, or at most a week, of exposure to infected blood in circumstances likely to cause infection; these include accidental needle puncture, gross personal contamination with infected blood, oral ingestion or contamination of mucous membranes, or exposure to infected blood in the presence of cuts and grazes. Vaccine can be given together with hyperimmune globulin (active-passive immunisation).

Prognosis

Full recovery occurs in 90–95% of adults following acute HBV infection. The remaining 5–10% develop a chronic infection which usually continues for life, although later recovery occurs occasionally. Infection passing from mother to child at birth leads to chronic infection in the child in 95% of cases and recovery is rare. Chronic infection is also common in immunodeficient individuals such as those with Down's syndrome or human immunodeficiency virus (HIV) infection. Recovery from acute HBV infection occurs within 6 months and is characterised by the appearance of antibody to viral antigens. Persistence of HBeAg beyond this time indicates chronic infection. Combined HBV and HDV infection causes more aggressive disease. Most patients with chronic hepatitis B are asymptomatic and develop complications such as cirrhosis and hepatocellular carcinoma only after many years. Cirrhosis develops in 15–20% of patients with chronic HBV, over 5–20 years. This proportion is higher in those infected in childhood.

Hepatitis C

The hepatitis C virus (HCV) is an RNA-containing flavivirus which cannot yet be grown but which can infect primates (see Fig. 18.22). Humans seem to be the sole source of infection, and inoculation with blood or blood products is

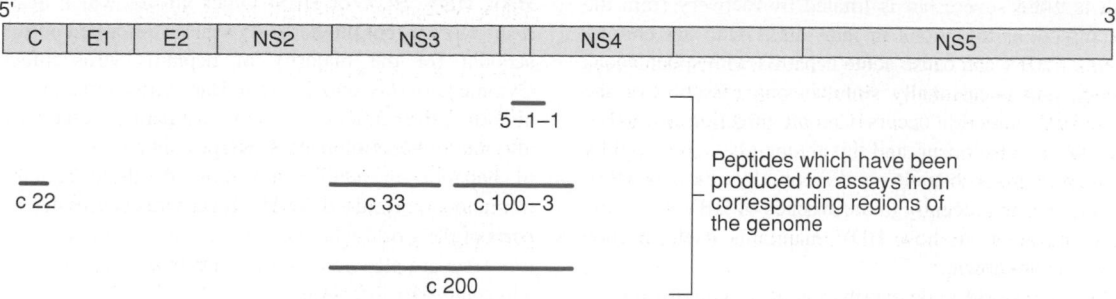

Fig. 18.22   Schematic diagram of hepatitis C virus: RNA coding regions. (C = core protein; E = envelope proteins; NS = non-structural proteins)

the best-recognised mode of transmission. HCV caused over 90% of post-transfusion hepatitis before serological tests allowed the screening of blood donors, and accounted for the high incidence of chronic hepatitis in patients with haemophilia. Screening of blood donors and heat treatment of coagulation factor concentrates should prevent infection in future. Parenteral drug users continue to be at high risk of HCV infection. Sporadic HCV infection also occurs but the modes of transmission are unknown. Sexual and vertical spread may occur but are less common than in HBV infection. Chronic infection occurs in about 70–80% of patients and this is usually life-long. Most never suffer an acute illness. Patients with chronic infection are often asymptomatic or complain of mild fatigue. Extrahepatic manifestations include cryoglobulinaemia, vasculitis, arthritis and glomerulonephritis. Without treatment life-long preventative measures are required to limit infection of other individuals.

Investigations

HCV contains several antigens giving rise to antibodies in infected individuals and these are used in diagnosis. Previously, diagnosis depended on identifying antibody to a single viral antigen (c 100–3), but this test gave false-positive reactions, especially in conditions such as autoimmune hepatitis associated with hyperglobulinaemia, and false-negative reactions. Current laboratory diagnosis depends on identifying antibodies to several viral antigens. These tests generally identify chronic HCV infection, as the diagnostic antibodies appear irregularly in the blood during the first 3 months of illness. PCR can show HCV-RNA in the blood, and is used increasingly to confirm the diagnosis where antibody tests give equivocal results and in selecting for, and measuring response to, therapy.

Management

Interferon used alone has only limited efficacy. Approximately 50% of patients will respond but relapse is common and only 10–20% show a long-term response. The treatment of choice for chronic hepatitis C infection is now a combination of interferon and ribavirin. The latter is a synthetic nucleoside analogue which resembles guanosine. Ribavirin's main toxicity is haemolytic anaemia and the drug should be avoided in patients with pre-existing anaemia or cardiopulmonary disease. It also causes abortion when given to women or their male partners; adequate contraception is therefore essential. Combination therapy with interferon

3 million Units thrice weekly and ribavirin 1000 or 1200 mg produces a sustained response (elimination of HCV-RNA from the blood 6 months after completing therapy) in 40% of cases. Patients infected with HCV genotype 1 require therapy for 12 months. The new, longer-acting, pegylated interferons show promise in recent studies.

HEPATITIS C—efficacy of combined ribavirin and interferon-α   EBM

'RCTs indicate that the sustained virological response rates are 33% (95% CI 29–37%) for patients on combination therapy compared with 6% (95% CI 3–10%) on interferon monotherapy, based on 24 weeks' treatment. The corresponding 48-week results are 41% (CI 36–45%) for combination therapy compared with 16% (CI 13–19%) for monotherapy. For relapsed patients (who responded to interferon alone but relapsed in the 6 months following initial treatment) sustained virological response rates were 49% (95% CI 42–57%) on combination therapy compared with 5% (95% CI 2–9%) on monotherapy, for 24 weeks' treatment.'

• NICE Technology Appraisal Guidance 2000: no. 14.
• Poynard T, Marcellin P, Lee SS, et al. Randomised trial of interferon alpha2b plus ribavirin for 48 weeks or for 24 weeks versus interferon alpha2b plus placebo for 48 weeks for treatment of chronic infection with hepatitis C virus. International Hepatitis Interventional Therapy Group (IHIT). Lancet 1998; 352:1426–1432.

Further information: 🖥 www.nice.org.uk

Prevention and prognosis

There is no available active or passive protection against HCV infection. Most patients acquiring HCV infections (80%) develop a chronic infection. Chronic HCV usually remains asymptomatic for years and is not associated with an early increase in mortality. However, many patients eventually develop cirrhosis and some progress to hepatocellular carcinoma. Approximately 20% of chronically infected patients will develop cirrhosis after 20 years of infection, and around 50% after 30 years. This is more likely if patients are misusing alcohol as well. Once cirrhosis is present, 2–5% per year will develop hepatocellular carcinoma.

Hepatitis D

The hepatitis D virus (HDV) is an RNA-defective virus which has no independent existence; it requires HBV for replication and has the same sources and modes of spread as HBV. It can infect individuals simultaneously with HBV, or it can superinfect those who are already chronic carriers of HBV. Simultaneous infections give rise to acute hepatitis which is often severe but is limited by recovery from the HBV infection. Infections in individuals who are chronic carriers of HBV can cause acute hepatitis with spontaneous recovery, and occasionally simultaneous cessation of the chronic HBV infection occurs. Chronic infection with HBV and HDV can also occur, and this frequently causes rapidly progressive chronic hepatitis and eventually cirrhosis. HDV has been reported recently in the absence of HBV following liver transplantation; how HDV maintains itself in such instances is unknown.

HDV has a world-wide distribution. It is endemic in parts of the Mediterranean basin, Africa and South America where transmission is mainly by close personal contact, and occasionally by vertical transmission from mothers who also carry HBV. In non-endemic areas, transmission is mainly a consequence of parenteral drug misuse.

Investigations
HDV contains a single antigen to which infected individuals make an antibody (anti-HDV). Delta antigen appears in the blood only transiently, and in practice diagnosis depends on detecting anti-HDV. Simultaneous infection with HBV and HDV followed by full recovery is associated with the appearance of low titres of anti-HDV of IgM type occurring within a few days of the onset of the illness. This antibody generally disappears within 2 months but persists in a few patients. Superinfection of patients with chronic hepatitis B virus infection leads to the production of high titres of anti-HDV, initially IgM and later IgG. Such patients may then develop chronic infection with both viruses, in which case anti-HDV titres plateau at high levels.

Prevention
Hepatitis D is effectively prevented by preventing hepatitis B.

Hepatitis E
The hepatitis E virus (HEV) is an RNA virus which is excreted in the stools and spreads by the faecal-oral route. It is found in countries where sanitation is poor and causes large epidemics of water-borne hepatitis. Occasional cases are recognised in patients in developed countries following a visit to an area where infection is endemic. The clinical illness resembles acute HAV infection and recovery is the rule. Chronic infection does not occur. Pregnant women with HEV infection are particularly liable to acute hepatic failure which is associated with a high mortality, but again chronic infection does not occur.

Investigations
Individuals infected with HEV produce anti-HEV which is used in diagnosis. Routine assays for the serological identification of HEV infection should be available in the near future.

Prevention
There is no available active or passive protection against HEV infection.

Other (non-A, non-B, non-C and non-E) hepatitis
Non-A, non-B (NANB) or non-A–E hepatitis is the term used to describe hepatitis thought to be due to a virus but not HAV, HBV, HCV or HEV. Other viruses which affect the liver do exist, but the hepatitis viruses described above now account for the majority of hepatitis virus infections. Cytomegalovirus and Epstein–Barr virus infection causes abnormal liver function tests in most patients, and occasionally icteric hepatitis occurs. Herpes simplex is a rare cause of hepatitis in adults, and most of these patients are immunocompromised. Yellow fever virus causes hepatitis in parts of the world where it is endemic. Abnormal liver function tests are also common in chickenpox, measles, rubella and acute HIV infection.

ALCOHOLIC (ETHANOLIC) LIVER DISEASE

In many societies alcohol is the most common cause of chronic liver disease.

Aetiology and pathology
Alcohol is metabolised almost exclusively in the liver. It is first converted to acetaldehyde, mainly by the mitochondrial enzyme alcohol dehydrogenase but also by the mixed-function oxidase enzymes of the smooth endoplasmic reticulum. Alcohol is a powerful inducer of the mixed-function oxidases, specifically cytochrome P4502E1, thereby increasing the ability of the liver to metabolise alcohol and other drugs, toxins or carcinogens metabolised by these enzymes. Acetaldehyde is converted to acetate by acetaldehyde dehydrogenase, and acetate is metabolised by the Krebs cycle enzymes.

The hepatic lesions of alcoholic liver disease (see below) are attributable directly to alcohol. The risk of developing alcoholic liver disease is related directly to the amount of alcohol (of any kind) ingested but is more likely to be clinically apparent at daily intakes above 30 g (3 units) in men and 20 g (2 units) in women. More than 5 years of drinking, and usually more than 10 years, are required to produce alcoholic cirrhosis, and a steady daily intake is more hazardous than intermittent drinking.

The mechanism or mechanisms underlying the ability of alcohol to produce individual liver lesions are poorly understood. Fatty change is attributed to an impaired excretion and enhanced synthesis of triacylglycerol by hepatocytes. The development of alcoholic hepatitis, fibrosis and cirrhosis is much more obscure. Biochemical mechanisms involving the production of toxic metabolites, called adducts, during the conversion of acetaldehyde to acetate and an immune reaction to liver cells altered by alcohol may be involved in these forms of liver damage. Release of pro-inflammatory cytokines, such as tumour necrosis factor and interleukin-1, and chemoattractant chemokines, such as interleukin-8, have been implicated in the pathogenesis of both alcoholic hepatitis and cirrhosis. Alcohol-induced liver injury, particularly hepatitis, is more common in women, and other genetic factors have been implicated in the genesis of alcoholic liver disease (see Fig. 18.23).

Alcohol causes several different pathological lesions in the liver which can occur together in any combination (see Box 18.38).

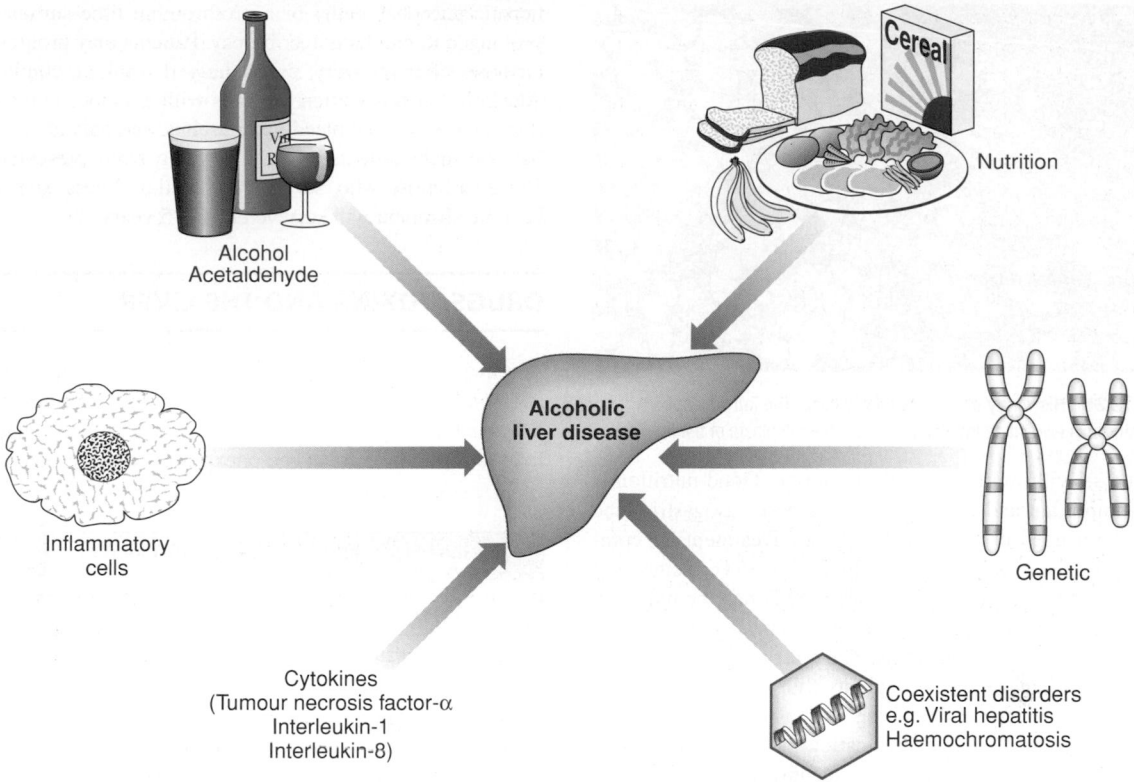

Fig. 18.23   Factors involved in the pathogenesis of alcoholic liver disease.

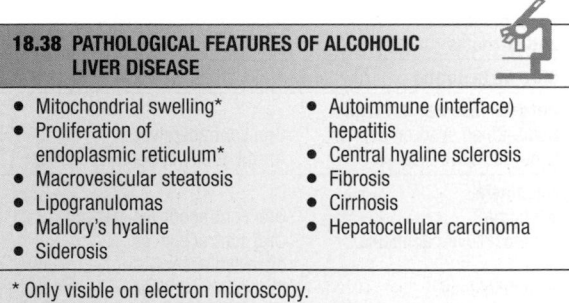

18.38 PATHOLOGICAL FEATURES OF ALCOHOLIC LIVER DISEASE	
• Mitochondrial swelling* • Proliferation of endoplasmic reticulum* • Macrovesicular steatosis • Lipogranulomas • Mallory's hyaline • Siderosis	• Autoimmune (interface) hepatitis • Central hyaline sclerosis • Fibrosis • Cirrhosis • Hepatocellular carcinoma
* Only visible on electron microscopy.	

18.39 CLINICAL SYNDROMES OF ALCOHOLIC LIVER DISEASE	
Fatty liver	
• Non-specific symptoms	• Hepatomegaly
Cholestasis	
• Jaundice • Abdominal pain	• Hepatomegaly (often tender)
Hepatitis	
• Severe illness • Malnutrition • Jaundice	• Hepatomegaly • Ascites • Encephalopathy
Cirrhosis	
• Stigmata of cirrhosis • Varices • Ascites	• Encephalopathy • Hepatocellular carcinoma • Hepatorenal syndrome

Clinical features

Alcoholic liver disease manifests as a clinical spectrum ranging from non-specific symptoms, with few or no physical abnormalities, to advanced cirrhosis. The ready availability of laboratory investigations can reveal alcoholic liver damage in patients with other diseases or in asymptomatic people undergoing medical examination. This spectrum is often divided into four syndromes (see Box 18.39), but in reality these overlap considerably and the various pathological changes can coexist in the same liver.

Investigations

Investigations aim to establish alcohol misuse, exclude alternative causes of liver disease and assess the severity of liver damage. The clinical history from the patient, relatives and friends is most important in establishing alcohol misuse, its duration and, in particular, its severity. Biological markers suggest and support a history of alcohol misuse; the most universally used indicators are a peripheral blood macrocytosis

in the absence of anaemia and increased plasma gamma-glutamyl transferase. Absence of these markers does not exclude alcohol misuse. Unexplained rib fractures on a chest radiograph are also associated with alcohol misuse. Investigation of the extent of liver damage often requires a liver biopsy (see Fig. 18.24).

Management

Cessation of alcohol intake is the single most important treatment and without this all other therapies are of limited value. Life-long abstinence is the best advice and is essential

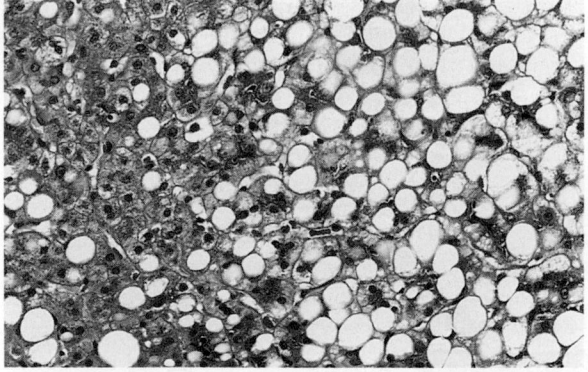

Fig. 18.24 Histology of alcoholic fatty liver. The fatty change (steatosis) is evident as fat globules within the cytoplasm of the liver cells.

for those with more severe liver damage. Good nutrition is also important and feeding via a fine-bore nasogastric tube may be needed in severely ill patients. Treatment for complications such as encephalopathy (see p. 858), ascites (see p. 855) and variceal bleeding (see p. 852) may be required. Corticosteroid therapy may be of some value in patients with severe alcoholic hepatitis. The role of liver transplantation in the management of patients with alcoholic liver disease is controversial. However, in most centres alcoholic liver disease is a common indication for considering transplantation. The challenge is to identify patients with an unacceptable risk of returning to harmful levels of alcohol consumption. Many programmes require a 6-month period of abstinence from alcohol before a patient is considered for transplantation, but this relates poorly to the incidence of alcohol relapse after transplantation. Discussion or assessment by a psychiatrist with a particular interest in substance misuse may be invaluable in differentiating harmful alcohol use from alcohol misuse, as patients falling into the former category are much more likely to maintain abstinence. Continuous input from psychiatric services may also prevent relapse.

Prognosis

The most important prognostic factor is the patient's ability to stop drinking alcohol. General health and longevity are improved when this occurs, irrespective of the form of alcoholic liver disease. Alcoholic fatty liver generally has a good prognosis and usually disappears after about 3 months of abstinence. Alcoholic hepatitis has a significantly worse prognosis because about one-third of patients die in the acute episode if liver function is poor, as evidenced by

---

hepatic encephalopathy or a prothrombin time sufficiently prolonged to preclude liver biopsy. Patients may progress to cirrhosis after recovery, particularly if drinking continues. Alcoholic cirrhosis often presents with a serious complication such as variceal bleeding or ascites, and only about one-half of such patients survive 5 years from presentation. However, most who survive the initial illness and who become abstinent will survive beyond 5 years.

DRUGS, TOXINS AND THE LIVER

The liver is the main organ in which drugs are metabolised and consequently is important in determining the effects of drugs in the body. Liver disease may alter the capacity of the liver to metabolise drugs and unexpected toxicity may occur

18.40 MANIFESTATIONS OF DRUG HEPATOTOXICITY	
Liver histology	**Examples**
Acute hepatic damage	
Acute hepatitis	Paracetamol, halothane, rifampicin, isoniazid
Cholestatic hepatitis	Chlorpromazine, ethambutol
Cholestasis	Oral contraceptives, anabolic steroids
Abnormal liver function tests	Statins, NSAIDs
Hepatic fibrosis and cirrhosis	Methotrexate, vitamin A
Chronic hepatitis	Amiodarone, penicillamine
Hepatic vascular damage	
Budd–Chiari syndrome	Oral contraceptives
Veno-occlusive disease	Azathioprine, cyclophosphamide
Neoplasia	
Adenoma	Oral contraceptives, danazol
Hepatocellular carcinoma	Oral contraceptives, diethylstilbestrol
Haemangioma/ haemangiosarcoma	Oral contraceptives, anabolic steroids

18.41 THE DIAGNOSIS OF ACUTE DRUG-INDUCED LIVER DISEASE

- Consider the possibility of a drug-induced problem
- Tabulate drugs taken
  Prescribed
  Self-administered
- Relate drugs to the onset of the illness
- Look for pre-existing liver disease
  Clinical examination
  Previous liver investigations
- Consider alternative causes
  Viral hepatitis—serological tests
  Biliary disease—ultrasound
- Observe the effects of stopping the suspected drugs
- Consider liver biopsy
  Suspected pre-existing liver disease
  Failure to improve

N.B. Challenge tests with drugs should virtually never be performed.

when patients with liver disease are given drugs in normal doses (see p. 155).

Drugs themselves can damage the liver and there is increasing recognition of the many forms of hepatic damage attributable to them (see Boxes 18.40 and 18.41).

FATTY LIVER AND NON-ALCOHOLIC STEATOHEPATITIS

Fatty liver is a common and generally benign condition. The majority of obese patients (60–90%) and up to 50% of type II diabetics have fatty liver. In general the lipid accumulation is characterised by macrovesicular steatosis. In a minority of cases hepatic steatosis is associated with an inflammatory infiltrate. This histological appearance, described as steatohepatitis, may be caused by alcohol misuse; however, in some patients with other causes there is no history of excessive alcohol consumption (see Box 18.42). This is known as non-alcoholic steatohepatitis (NASH), and may progress to cirrhosis in a small proportion of patients. With the increasing frequency of obesity in the Western population it is likely that this clinical condition will become much more common. Microvesicular steatosis occurs in more serious conditions and can be associated with mitochondrial damage, which causes impaired fatty acid beta-oxidative metabolism.

18.42 CAUSES OF STEATOSIS (FATTY LIVER) AND STEATOHEPATITIS	
Macrovesicular steatosis/steatohepatitis	
• Alcohol	• Malabsorption
• Obesity	• Parenteral nutrition
• Diabetes mellitus	• Intestinal bypass operations
• Rapid weight reduction	• Drugs (amiodarone,
• Starvation (kwashiorkor)	minocycline, iron)
Microvesicular steatosis	
• Fatty liver of pregnancy	• Inherited metabolic
• Reye's syndrome (aspirin)	disorders (e.g. urea cycle
• Drugs (e.g. sodium	defects, fatty acid oxidation
valproate, ketoprofen,	defects, lysosomal acid
didanosine)	esterase deficiency)

The pathogenesis of hepatic steatosis induced by these diverse clinical conditions is unknown. However, in all cases there is an imbalance in hepatocyte triacylglyceride synthesis and export. Many of the conditions are characterised by relative insulin deficiency, which has multiple effects on lipid metabolism in the liver, adipose tissue and muscle. It has been suggested that a second insult such as oxidative stress or endotoxin-mediated cytokine release is necessary for the progression of steatosis into steatohepatitis.

Clinical features and management

Macrovesicular steatosis is often asymptomatic or is associated with the clinical features of its cause, such as diabetes mellitus or obesity. It is therefore often found incidentally. Hepatomegaly, sometimes with hepatic tenderness, is the only clinical feature. Liver function tests usually show mild increases in the GGT in particular. Elevation of the transaminases suggests the development of steatohepatitis. Ultrasonography shows generally increased echogenicity (bright liver). The treatment is that of the underlying disorder.

Microvesicular steatosis may be associated with the acute onset of fatigue and vomiting, progressing if severe to encephalopathy and coma. Jaundice is typically absent in Reye's syndrome but may be present with other causes of steatosis or steatohepatitis. Acute hepatic failure due to microvesicular steatosis may require intensive care support or emergency liver transplantation.

Prognosis

The outlook for most patients with steatosis is excellent, although a few deaths have been reported. In patients with alcoholic steatosis, the severity of the fatty change can predict the eventual progression to cirrhosis. Previously, the prognosis of patients with acute fatty liver of pregnancy was considered poor. However, milder forms of this condition are now more frequently recognised.

AUTOIMMUNE HEPATITIS

This form of chronic hepatitis occurs most often in women, particularly in the second and third decades of life.

Aetiology and pathology

Several subtypes of this disorder have been proposed with differing immunological markers. Classical (type I) autoimmune hepatitis is characterised by a high frequency of other autoimmune disorders such as Graves' disease. Type I autoimmune hepatitis is associated with HLA-DR3 and DR4, particularly HLA-DRB3*0101 and HLA-DRB1*0401. These patients have high titres of antinuclear and anti-smooth muscle antibodies but none of these antibodies is cytotoxic. A suggested hypothesis for the development of type I autoimmune hepatitis is the aberrant expression on the hepatocyte of HLA antigen, influenced by viral, genetic and environmental factors. Type II autoimmune hepatitis is characterised by the presence of anti-LKM (liver–kidney microsomal) antibodies and lack of antinuclear and anti-smooth muscle antibodies. Anti-LKM antibodies recognise cytochrome P450-IID6, which is expressed on the hepatocyte membrane. The pathological features of both forms of autoimmune hepatitis are similar and are described on pages 838–840.

Clinical features

The onset is usually insidious, with fatigue, anorexia and jaundice. In about one-quarter of patients the onset is acute, resembling viral hepatitis, but resolution does not occur. Other features include fever, arthralgia, vitiligo and epistaxis. Amenorrhoea is the rule. On examination, general health may be good. Jaundice is mild to moderate or occasionally absent, but signs of chronic liver disease, especially spider telangiectasia and hepatosplenomegaly, are usually present. Sometimes a 'Cushingoid' face with acne, hirsutism and pink cutaneous striae, especially on the thighs and abdomen, are present. Bruises may be seen. Though liver disease usually dominates the clinical syndrome, many associated conditions occur in florid autoimmune hepatitis, emphasising its essentially systemic nature (see Box 18.43).

18.43 CONDITIONS ASSOCIATED WITH AUTOIMMUNE HEPATITIS

- Migrating polyarthritis
- Urticarial skin rashes
- Lymphadenopathy
- Hashimoto's thyroiditis
- Thyrotoxicosis
- Myxoedema
- Coombs-positive haemolytic anaemia
- Pleurisy
- Transient pulmonary infiltrates
- Ulcerative colitis
- Glomerulonephritis
- Nephrotic syndrome

Investigations

Liver function tests vary with the activity of the disease. Active inflammation is reflected by the plasma aminotransferase activity, and the severity of liver damage by the plasma albumin concentration and prothrombin time. Aminotransferase activity is often increased more than 10-fold during relapses in patients with florid disease, and hypoalbuminaemia and marked hyperglobulinaemia are common. Hyperglobulinaemia is polyclonal and due mainly to marked increases in IgG. The plasma bilirubin reflects the degree of jaundice but usually does not exceed 100 µmol/l (6 mg/dl). The plasma alkaline phosphatase activity reflects the degree of intrahepatic cholestasis.

Serological testing for specific autoantibodies may suggest autoimmune hepatitis (see Box 18.44). However, these autoantibodies are all heterogenous and can be found in apparently healthy people, particularly in women and in older people. Antinuclear antibodies occur in about 5% of healthy people and anti-smooth muscle antibody in 1.5%, but antimitochondrial antibody is rare, being found in about 0.01%. Autoantibody titres in such healthy people are usually low. Antinuclear and antimitochondrial antibodies also occur in connective tissue diseases and in autoimmune diseases, including various thyroid disorders and pernicious anaemia, while anti-smooth muscle antibody has been

18.44 FREQUENCY OF AUTOANTIBODIES IN CHRONIC NON-VIRAL LIVER DISEASES AND IN HEALTHY PEOPLE			
Disease	Anti-nuclear antibody (%)	Anti-smooth muscle antibody (%)	Anti-mitochondrial antibody* (%)
Healthy controls	5	1.5	0.01
Autoimmune hepatitis	80	70	15
Primary biliary cirrhosis	25	35	95
Cryptogenic cirrhosis	40	30	15

* Patients with antimitochondrial antibody frequently have cholestatic liver function tests and may have primary biliary cirrhosis (see text).

reported in infectious mononucleosis and a variety of malignant diseases. Frequencies of antibodies are shown in Box 18.44. Antimicrosomal antibodies (anti-LKM) occur particularly in children and adolescents.

Liver biopsy shows interface hepatitis (see p. 840) with or without cirrhosis.

Management

Treatment with corticosteroids is life-saving in autoimmune hepatitis, particularly during exacerbations of active and symptomatic disease. Initially, prednisolone 30 mg/day is given orally and the dose reduced gradually as the patient and liver function tests improve. Maintenance therapy is required for at least 2 years after liver function tests have become normal, and withdrawal of treatment should not be considered unless a liver biopsy is also normal. Side-effects from prednisolone are uncommon at a maintenance dose of 10 mg/day or less; azathioprine 50–100 mg/day orally may be added to the therapy to allow the dose of prednisolone to be reduced to this level (see EBM panel). Corticosteroids treat and prevent acute exacerbations rather than prevent cirrhosis and are less important in asymptomatic autoimmune hepatitis with mild biochemical and histological activity.

AUTOIMMUNE HEPATITIS—role of immunosuppressive therapy

'In patients with autoimmune hepatitis treatment with prednisolone ± azathioprine results in a significant improvement in serum biochemistry, hepatic histology and survival compared with placebo or azathioprine alone.'

'In patients that have been in remission for longer than 1 year, increasing the dose of azathioprine (from 1 to 2 mg/kg) and withdrawal of prednisolone are associated with loss of steroid side-effects and no increase in the relapse of the hepatitis.'

- Soloway RD, Summerskill WH, Baggenstoss AH, et al. Clinical, biochemical, and histological remission of severe chronic active liver disease: a controlled study of treatments and early prognosis. Gastroenterology 1972; 63:820–833.
- Summerskill WH, Korman MG, Ammon HV, et al. Prednisone for chronic active liver disease: dose titration, standard dose, and combination with azathioprine compared. Gut 1975;16:876–883.
- Johnson PJ, McFarlane IG, Williams R. Azathioprine for long-term maintenance of remission in autoimmune hepatitis. N Engl J Med 1995; 333:958–963.

Prognosis

The disease occurs in exacerbations and remissions, and most patients eventually develop cirrhosis and its complications. Hepatocellular carcinoma is uncommon. About half of patients with symptoms die of liver failure within 5 years if no treatment is given, but this falls to about 10% with therapy.

HAEMOCHROMATOSIS

Haemochromatosis is a condition in which the amount of total body iron is increased; the excess iron is deposited in and causes damage to several organs including the liver. It may be primary, or secondary to other diseases.

HEREDITARY (PRIMARY) HAEMOCHROMATOSIS

This is a disease in which the total body iron reaches 20–60 g (normally 4 g). Iron is deposited widely in the body. The important organs involved are the liver, pancreatic islets, endocrine glands and heart. In the liver, iron deposition occurs first in the periportal hepatocytes, extending later to all hepatocytes. The gradual development of fibrous septa leads to the formation of irregular nodules, and finally regeneration results in macronodular cirrhosis. An excess of liver iron can occur in alcoholic cirrhosis but this is mild by comparison with haemochromatosis.

Aetiology

Hereditary haemochromatosis is caused by an increased absorption of dietary iron. This inability to limit iron absorption is inherited as an autosomal recessive gene located on chromosome 6. Approximately 90% of patients have a single-point mutation resulting in a cysteine to tyrosine substitution at position 282 (C282Y) in a protein with structural and functional similarity to the HLA proteins, designated HFE. The exact function of the HFE protein in regulating iron absorption is not known. However, it is believed that HFE is absent from the basolateral membrane of intestinal epithelial cells where it normally interacts with the transferrin receptor. This defect in uptake of transferrin-associated iron may lead to up-regulation of enterocyte iron-specific divalent metal transporters and excessive iron absorption. A histidine to aspartic acid mutation at position 63 (H63D) in HFE can also result in haemochromatosis but the disease is less severe and is most commonly found in patients who are compound heterozygotes also carrying a C282Y mutated allele. Perhaps fewer than 50% of C282Y homozygotes will develop clinical features of genetic haemochromatosis; therefore other factors must also be important. Iron loss in menstruation and pregnancy may protect females, as 90% of patients are male.

Clinical features

The disease usually presents in men aged 40 years or over with signs of hepatic cirrhosis (especially hepatomegaly), diabetes mellitus or heart failure. Leaden-grey skin pigmentation due to excess melanin occurs, especially in exposed parts, axillae, groins and genitalia; hence the term 'bronzed diabetes'. Impotence, loss of libido, testicular atrophy and arthritis with chondrocalcinosis secondary to calcium pyrophosphate deposition are also common. Early clinical features, particularly tiredness, fatigue and arthropathy, are increasingly recognised.

Investigations

The serum ferritin is greatly increased; the plasma iron is also increased, with a highly saturated plasma iron-binding capacity. Computed tomography may show features suggesting excess hepatic iron. The diagnosis is confirmed by liver biopsy, which shows heavy iron deposition and hepatic fibrosis which may have progressed to cirrhosis. The iron content of the liver can be measured directly. Both the C282Y and H63D mutations can be identified.

Management

Treatment consists of weekly venesection of 500 ml of blood (250 mg iron) until the serum iron is normal; this may take 2 years or more. Thereafter, venesection is continued as required to keep the serum ferritin normal. Other therapy includes that for cirrhosis and diabetes mellitus. First-degree family members should be investigated, preferably by genetic screening and also by checking the plasma ferritin and iron-binding saturation. Liver biopsy is indicated in asymptomatic relatives if the liver function tests are abnormal and/or the serum ferritin is greater than 1000 µg/l because these features are associated with significant fibrosis or cirrhosis. Asymptomatic disease should also be treated by venesection once the serum ferritin rises above normal.

Prognosis

Hereditary haemochromatosis has a good prognosis compared with other forms of cirrhosis, as three-quarters of patients are alive 5 years after the diagnosis. This is probably because liver function is usually well preserved at diagnosis and improves with therapy. Given that hepatocellular carcinoma is the main cause of death and occurs in about one-third of patients with cirrhosis irrespective of therapy, screening of this patient population is imperative (see p. 877).

ACQUIRED IRON OVERLOAD (SECONDARY HAEMOCHROMATOSIS)

Many conditions, including chronic haemolytic disorders, sideroblastic anaemia, other conditions requiring multiple blood transfusion (generally over 50 litres), porphyria cutanea tarda, dietary iron overload and occasionally alcoholic cirrhosis, are associated with widespread secondary siderosis. The features are similar to haemochromatosis, but the history and clinical findings point to the true diagnosis. Some patients are heterozygotes for the primary haemochromatosis gene and this may contribute to the development of iron overload.

WILSON'S DISEASE (HEPATOLENTICULAR DEGENERATION)

This is a rare but important condition in which the total body copper is increased, with excess copper deposited in, and causing damage to, several organs.

Aetiology and pathology

Wilson's disease is inherited as an autosomal recessive disorder that results in abnormal copper accumulation. Normally, dietary copper is absorbed from the stomach and proximal small intestine and is rapidly taken into the liver, where it is stored and incorporated into ceruloplasmin, which is secreted into the blood. The accumulation of excessive copper in the body is ultimately prevented by its excretion, the most important route being via the bile. In Wilson's disease, there is almost always a failure of synthesis of ceruloplasmin; however, some 5% of patients have a normal circulating ceruloplasmin concentration and this is not the primary pathogenic defect. The amount of copper in the body at birth is normal, but thereafter it increases steadily and the organs most affected are the liver, basal ganglia of the brain, eyes, kidneys and skeleton.

The gene responsible for Wilson's disease is located on chromosome 13 and has been designated ATP7B. This gene encodes a member of the copper-transporting P-type ATPase family, which functions to export copper from the various cell types. At least 200 different mutations have been described. Although most of the mutations are rare, their relative frequency differs in different populations. The histidine to glucine single-base mutation at position 1069 is most common in Polish and Austrian patients, but rare in Asia, India and Sardinia. In contrast, approximately 60% of Sardinian patients have a 15 nucleotide deletion in the 5′ untranslated region of the Wilson's gene. Most cases are compound heterozygotes with two different mutations in the Wilson's gene. Attempts to correlate the genotype with the mode of presentation and clinical course have not shown any consistent patterns.

Clinical features

Symptoms usually arise between the ages of 5 and 30 years. Hepatic disease occurs predominantly in childhood and early adolescence, while neurological damage causes basal ganglion syndromes and dementia in later adolescence. These manifestations can occur alone or simultaneously. Other manifestations include haemolysis, renal tubular damage and osteoporosis, but these are virtually never presenting features.

Kayser–Fleischer rings

These are the most important single clinical clue to the diagnosis and they can be seen in most patients presenting in or after adolescence, albeit sometimes only by slit-lamp examination. Kayser–Fleischer rings are characterised

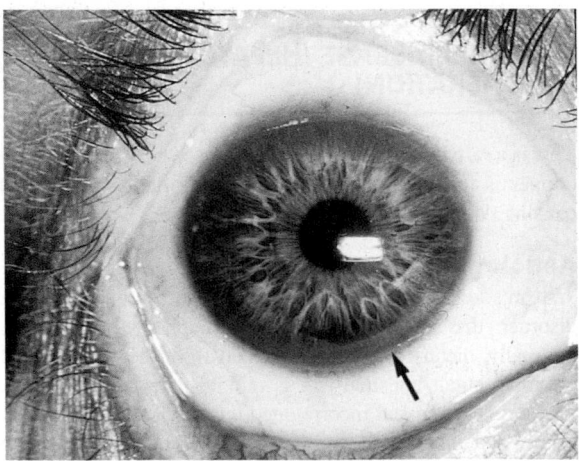

Fig. 18.25 Kayser–Fleischer rings at the junction of the cornea and sclera (arrow) in a patient with Wilson's disease.

by greenish-brown discoloration of the corneal margin appearing first at the upper periphery (see Fig. 18.25). They eventually disappear with treatment. Appearances indistinguishable from Kayser–Fleischer rings are found rarely in other forms of chronic hepatitis and cirrhosis.

Liver disease

This can manifest in many ways which are not specific. Episodes of acute hepatitis which are sometimes recurrent can occur, especially in children, and may progress to acute hepatic failure. Chronic hepatitis and steatohepatitis can also develop, and eventually cirrhosis with liver failure and portal hypertension may supervene. Recurrent acute hepatitis of unknown cause, especially accompanied by haemolysis, or chronic liver disease of unknown cause in a patient under 40 years old suggests Wilson's disease.

Neurological disease

Clinical features include a variety of extrapyramidal features, particularly tremor, choreoathetosis, dystonia, parkinsonism and dementia (see Ch. 22).

Investigations

A low serum ceruloplasmin is the best single laboratory clue to the diagnosis. However, advanced liver failure from any cause can reduce the serum ceruloplasmin, and occasionally the serum ceruloplasmin is normal in Wilson's disease. Other features of disordered copper metabolism should therefore be sought; these include a high serum copper concentration, a high urine copper excretion and a very high hepatic copper content. Patients with Wilson's disease fail to incorporate radioactive copper into ceruloplasmin, but this test is almost never needed. Genetic testing is limited by the existence of multiple genetic defects, but may be useful in screening families once the abnormality has been identified in an affected individual.

Management

The copper-binding agent penicillamine is the drug of choice in Wilson's disease. The dose given must be sufficient to produce cupriuresis and most patients require 1.5 g/day (range 1–4 g). The dose can be reduced once the disease is in remission, but treatment must continue for life and care must be taken to ensure that reaccumulation of copper does not occur. Abrupt discontinuation of treatment must be avoided because this may precipitate acute liver failure. Serious toxic effects of penicillamine are rare in Wilson's disease. If they do occur, trientine dihydrochloride (1.2–2.4 g/day) or zinc is an alternative effective therapy. Liver transplantation may be needed for acute hepatic failure or for advanced cirrhosis with liver failure.

Prognosis

The prognosis of Wilson's disease is excellent provided treatment is started before there is irreversible damage; hepatocellular carcinoma does not occur. Siblings and children of patients with Wilson's disease must be investigated and treatment should be given to any who have the disease even if it is asymptomatic.

ALPHA₁-ANTITRYPSIN DEFICIENCY

Alpha$_1$-antitrypsin (α_1-AT) is a serine protease inhibitor (Pi) produced by the liver. The form of α_1-AT is genetically determined, and one of these forms (PiZ) cannot be secreted into the blood by the liver cells owing to polymerisation within the endoplasmic reticulum of the hepatocyte. Homozygous individuals (PiZZ) have low plasma α_1-AT concentrations, although globules containing α_1-AT are found in the liver, and this form of α_1-AT deficiency is also associated with hepatic and pulmonary disease (see p. 509). Liver disease includes cholestatic jaundice in the neonatal period (neonatal hepatitis) which can resolve spontaneously, chronic hepatitis and cirrhosis in adults, and in the long term the development of hepatocellular carcinoma. There are no clinical features distinguishing liver disease due to α_1-AT deficiency from other causes of liver disease, and the diagnosis is made from the low plasma α_1-AT concentration and the PiZZ genotype. Alpha$_1$-AT-containing globules can be demonstrated in the liver but this is not necessary to make the diagnosis. Occasionally, patients with liver disease and minor reductions of plasma α_1-AT concentrations have α_1-AT phenotypes other than PiZZ, such as PiMZ or PiSZ, but the relationship of these genotypes to liver disease is uncertain. No specific treatment is available; the concurrent risk of severe and early-onset emphysema means that all patients should be advised to abandon cigarette smoking.

BILIARY CIRRHOSIS

Biliary cirrhosis results from destruction of intrahepatic bile ducts in cases of primary biliary cirrhosis or primary sclerosing cholangitis, and may also be the result of prolonged obstruction.

PRIMARY BILIARY CIRRHOSIS

Primary biliary cirrhosis (PBC) predominantly affects women who usually present clinically in middle age. The ready availability of diagnostic tests has revealed asymptomatic disease which can remain quiescent for years, and has shown that PBC is a relatively common form of cirrhosis.

Aetiology and pathology

The cause of PBC is unknown but immune reactions causing liver damage are suspected. Autoantibodies and immune complexes are found in the blood, cellular immunity is impaired, and abnormal cellular immune reactions have been described. The primary pathological lesion is a chronic granulomatous inflammation damaging and destroying the interlobular bile ducts; progressive inflammatory damage with fibrosis spreads from the portal tracts to the liver parenchyma and eventually leads to cirrhosis.

Clinical features

Non-specific symptoms such as lethargy, fatigue and arthralgia are common and may precede diagnosis for years. Pruritus is the most common initial complaint pointing to hepatobiliary disease and it may precede jaundice by months or years. Bile acids have been suggested as the cause of pruritus but this remains unproven. Jaundice is occasionally a presenting feature but usually pruritus is also present. Although there may be abdominal discomfort, the abdominal pain, fever and rigors which are often features of large bile duct obstruction do not occur. Diarrhoea from malabsorption of fat, and pain and tingling in the hands and feet due to lipid infiltration of peripheral nerves occasionally occur. Bone pain or fractures resulting from osteomalacia from malabsorption or osteoporosis (hepatic osteodystrophy) can be prominent and distressing features in advanced disease.

Initially patients are well nourished but considerable weight loss can occur as the disease progresses. Scratch marks may be found. Jaundice is only prominent late in the disease and can become intense. Xanthomatous deposits occur in a minority, especially around the eyes, in the hand creases and over the elbows, knees and buttocks. Hepatomegaly is virtually constant, and splenomegaly becomes increasingly common as portal hypertension develops. Liver failure and portal hypertension arise as the disease progresses.

Associated diseases

Autoimmune and connective tissue diseases occur with increased frequency in primary biliary cirrhosis, particularly in patients with the sicca syndrome (see p. 1038), coeliac disease (see p. 792) and thyroid diseases. Hypothyroidism should always be considered in patients with fatigue.

Investigations

Liver function tests show the pattern of cholestasis (see p. 836). Hypercholesterolaemia is common and worsens with disease progression; however, it is often of no diagnostic value. The antimitochondrial antibody is present in over 95% of patients, and when it is absent diagnosis should not be made without obtaining histological evidence and performing cholangiography (ERCP, see p. 841) to exclude other biliary disease. Antinuclear and anti-smooth muscle antibodies may be present (see Box 18.44, p. 870), and autoantibodies found in associated diseases may also be found. Ultrasound examination shows no sign of biliary obstruction. As has already been noted, liver biopsy is required only in doubtful cases.

Management

No specific therapy is available. Corticosteroids, azathioprine, penicillamine and ciclosporin have all been tried, but none is effective and all may have serious adverse effects. Ursodeoxycholic acid improves liver function tests, may slow down histological progression and has few side-effects (see

EBM panel). Transplantation should always be considered once liver failure has developed and may be indicated in patients with intractable pruritus. Treatment may be needed

for the consequences of cholestasis, particularly for pruritus and malabsorption.

Pruritus
This is the main symptom demanding relief and is best treated with the anion-binding resin colestyramine, which reduces the concentration of bile acids in the body by binding them in the intestine and increasing their excretion in the stool. A dose of 4–16 g/day orally is used. The powder is mixed in orange juice and the main dose (8 g) is taken with breakfast when maximal duodenal bile acid concentrations occur. Colestyramine may bind other drugs in the gut (e.g. anticoagulants), which should therefore be taken 1 hour before the binding agent. Colestyramine is sometimes ineffective, especially in complete biliary obstruction. Rifampicin or ultraviolet light may help in these patients.

Malabsorption
Prolonged cholestasis is associated with steatorrhoea and malabsorption of fat-soluble vitamins and calcium. Steatorrhoea can be reduced by limiting fat intake to 40 g/day. Monthly injections of vitamin K (10 mg), vitamin D (calciferol 1 mg/day; alfacalcidol 1 mg/day orally) and calcium supplements should also be given, the last as effervescent calcium gluconate (2–4 g/day). The effervescent preparation of calcium gluconate contains significant amounts of sodium, and where there is fluid retention calcium gluconate alone should be used. Associated coeliac disease requires exclusion.

SECONDARY BILIARY CIRRHOSIS

This develops after prolonged large duct biliary obstruction due to gallstones, bile duct strictures or sclerosing cholangitis (see below). Carcinomas rarely cause secondary biliary cirrhosis because few patients survive long enough. There is chronic cholestasis with episodes of ascending cholangitis or even liver abscess (see p. 878). Digital clubbing is common and xanthomata and bone pain may develop. Cirrhosis, ascites and portal hypertension are late features. Cholangitis requires treatment with antibiotics, which can be given continuously if attacks occur frequently.

SCLEROSING CHOLANGITIS

This condition, which is being increasingly diagnosed, is characterised by fibrotic obliteration of the intrahepatic and/or extrahepatic bile duct system, and may be primary or secondary in type. Primary sclerosing cholangitis has no known cause but is often associated with ulcerative colitis and occasionally with retroperitoneal fibrosis, HIV infection and a variety of autoimmune disorders. There is an association between primary sclerosing cholangitis and the HLA haplotypes B8, DR2 and DR3. In secondary sclerosing cholangitis there is an underlying disorder of the biliary tree causing the fibrotic state: for example, retained bile duct stones or strictures following surgery (both of which may be difficult to differentiate from bile duct tumours).

Clinical features
The patient presents with jaundice, which may fluctuate, intermittent fever, pruritus and right upper quadrant pain. Secondary biliary cirrhosis may result. There is a strong association with cholangiocarcinoma, and progressive jaundice, anorexia and weight loss are suggestive of this complication.

Investigations
Liver function tests demonstrate cholestasis with elevation of the serum bilirubin, GGT and alkaline phosphatase. These abnormalities may fluctuate. The prothrombin time may be prolonged if cholestasis is long-standing or if hepatic cirrhosis and liver failure have developed. Perinuclear antineutrophil cytoplasmic antibodies (p-ANCA, see p. 1040) have been found in this disease, especially when it is associated with ulcerative colitis. Ultrasonography may not show biliary abnormality as the thickened fibrotic ducts are not dilated, and diagnosis is best made by cholangiography, which typically shows narrowed irregular obstruction and 'beading' of the extra- and intrahepatic bile ducts (see Fig. 18.26). The disease may affect the whole of the biliary

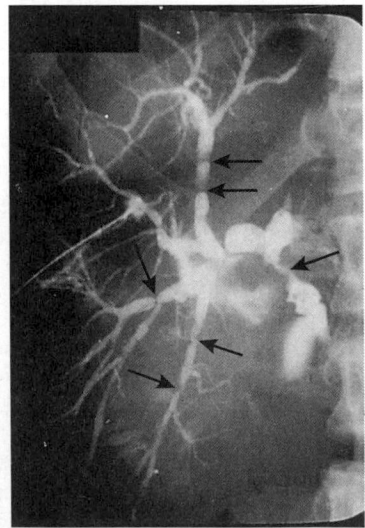

Fig. 18.26   A percutaneous cholangiogram in sclerosing cholangitis showing the irregularity in the biliary tree.

system or may be confined to the extrahepatic or intrahepatic portion of the bile ducts. The typical whorled appearance of fibrosis around the bile ducts may be seen if liver biopsy is undertaken. Bile duct tissue obtained at laparotomy may demonstrate the characteristic lymphocytic cell infiltrate with plasma cells and giant cells. The main differential diagnosis is cholangiocarcinoma.

Management
There is no specific treatment, but antibiotics are needed during episodes of cholangitis. Ursodeoxycholic acid has been used but its efficacy is in doubt. Corticosteroids and other immunosuppressive drugs are of no value. Biliary drainage may be attempted using stents placed at ERCP, but this is only reasonable where a single dominant stricture is present. Such strictures may be resected if there is doubt about the presence of an underlying malignancy. Liver transplantation is the only effective therapy in patients with advanced disease.

VASCULAR DISEASE OF THE LIVER

HEPATIC ARTERIAL DISEASE
Hepatic arterial disease is rare and difficult to diagnose, but it can cause serious liver damage. Hepatic artery occlusion may result from inadvertent injury during biliary surgery or be caused by emboli, neoplasms, polyarteritis nodosa, blunt trauma or radiation. It usually causes severe upper abdominal pain with or without signs of circulatory shock. Liver function tests show a high transaminase activity as in other causes of acute liver damage. Patients usually survive if the liver and portal blood supply are otherwise normal.

Hepatic artery aneurysms are extrahepatic in three-quarters of cases and intrahepatic in one-quarter. Atheroma, vasculitis, bacterial endocarditis, and surgical or biopsy trauma are the main causes. They usually cause bleeding into the biliary tree, peritoneum or intestine and are diagnosed best by arteriography. Treatment is surgical. Any of the vasculitides can affect the hepatic artery, but this rarely causes symptoms.

PORTAL VENOUS DISEASE
Portal venous thrombosis is rare but can occur in any condition predisposing to thrombosis. It also occurs with local intra-abdominal inflammatory or neoplastic disease and is a recognised complication of portal hypertension. Acute portal venous thrombosis causes abdominal pain and diarrhoea, and may lead to bowel infarction. Treatment is surgical but patients will require anticoagulation if an underlying thrombotic condition is diagnosed. Less acute thrombosis can be asymptomatic and may later give rise to extrahepatic portal hypertension (see p. 850).

HEPATIC VENOUS OUTFLOW OBSTRUCTION
Obstruction to hepatic venous blood flow can occur in the small central hepatic veins, in the large hepatic veins, in the inferior vena cava or in the heart. The clinical features depend on the cause and on the speed with which obstruction develops, but congestive hepatomegaly and ascites are features in all patients.

BUDD–CHIARI SYNDROME
Aetiology and pathology
This is an uncommon condition in which obstruction occurs in the larger hepatic veins and sometimes the inferior vena cava. The cause cannot be found in about half of patients. In the others, thrombosis may be due to haematological diseases including primary proliferative polycythaemia, paroxysmal nocturnal haemoglobinuria and antithrombin III, protein C or protein S deficiencies (see pp. 953–954). Pregnancy and oral contraceptive use, obstruction due to tumours, particularly carcinomas of the liver, kidneys or adrenals, congenital venous webs and occasionally inferior vena caval stenosis are the other main causes. Hepatic congestion affecting the centrilobular areas is the initial consequence; centrilobular fibrosis develops later and eventually cirrhosis in those who survive long enough.

Clinical features
Sudden venous occlusion causes the rapid development of upper abdominal pain, marked ascites and occasionally acute hepatic failure. More gradual occlusion causes gross ascites and often upper abdominal discomfort. Hepatomegaly, often with tenderness over the liver, is almost always present. Peripheral oedema occurs only when there is inferior vena cava obstruction. Features of cirrhosis and portal hypertension develop in those who survive the acute event.

Investigations
Liver function tests vary considerably depending on the presentation and can show the features of acute hepatitis (see p. 836) when the onset is rapid. Ascitic fluid analysis typically shows a protein concentration above 25 g/l in the early stages; however, this is often lower later in the disease. Doppler ultrasound examination may reveal obliteration of the hepatic veins and reversed flow or associated thrombosis in the portal vein. CT may show enlargement of the caudate lobe, as it often has a separate venous drainage system not involved in the disease. Hepatic venography shows occlusion of the hepatic veins and any inferior vena cava involvement (see Fig. 18.27), and liver biopsy demonstrates centrilobular congestion with fibrosis depending upon the duration of the illness.

Management
Predisposing causes should be treated as far as possible; where recent thrombosis is suspected, treatment with streptokinase followed by heparin and oral anticoagulation should be considered. Ascites is treated medically initially but this often has limited success. LeVeen shunts are rarely performed. Some patients may be managed successfully by insertion of a TIPSS. Occasionally, a web can be resected or an inferior vena caval stenosis dilated. Progressive liver failure is an indication for liver transplantation.

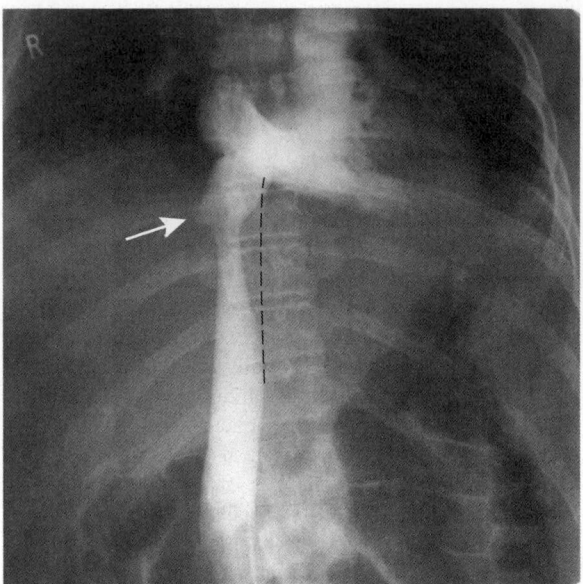

Fig. 18.27 Flush venogram showing Budd–Chiari syndrome. This injection of contrast into the inferior vena cava shows an indentation caused by caudate lobe enlargement. Ordinarily, the diameter of the inferior vena cava is uniform, as shown by the broken line. This flush venogram also shows little backflow of contrast into the hepatic veins (arrow). This can be confirmed by attempted selective catheterisation of the hepatic veins.

Prognosis

The prognosis is generally poor, particularly when the onset is sudden; up to two-thirds of patients die within a year and few live more than 5 years. Some patients survive to develop cirrhosis.

VENO-OCCLUSIVE DISEASE

Widespread occlusion of central hepatic veins is the characteristic of this condition. Pyrrolizidine alkaloids in *Senecio* and *Heliotropium* plants used to make teas, cytotoxic drugs and hepatic irradiation are all recognised causes. The clinical features, investigation and management of veno-occlusive disease are similar to those of the Budd–Chiari syndrome (see above).

CARDIAC DISEASE

Hepatic damage due primarily to congestion may develop in cardiac failure from any cause, but the clinical features are usually dominated by the cardiac disease. Occasionally, the hepatic features are more prominent.

Acute hepatitis

Rapidly developing cardiac failure sometimes causes a syndrome suggesting an acute hepatitis. This often follows an acute reduction in hepatic perfusion and is termed 'shock liver' (see p. 208); it is sometimes seen following myocardial infarction, decompensation of any chronic myocardial disease or respiratory condition associated with cor pulmonale, or rapidly developing cardiac tamponade. The patient is generally very ill with an enlarged tender liver, with or without jaundice, and liver function tests showing an acute hepatitis. The correct diagnosis is made by recognising that the cardiac output is low, that the jugular venous pressure is high and that other signs of cardiac disease are present.

Ascites

Cardiac failure sometimes causes hepatomegaly and ascites disproportionate to the degree of peripheral oedema, and hence can mimic ascites due to liver disease. A high ascites protein concentration may suggest hepatic venous outflow obstruction. Constrictive pericarditis (see p. 478) is particularly likely to mislead, as a normal heart size points away from heart disease. A raised jugular venous pressure is the most important single clue to the diagnosis. Rarely, long-standing cardiac failure and hepatic congestion cause cardiac cirrhosis, and this is suggested by hard irregular hepatomegaly or a palpable spleen due to portal hypertension.

Management

The treatment of these patients is that of the underlying causative disease.

TUMOURS OF THE LIVER

HEPATOCELLULAR CARCINOMA (HEPATOMA)

Hepatocellular carcinoma is the principal primary malignant liver tumour. Its incidence shows great geographic variation, the tumour being common in Africa (especially Mozambique) and South-east Asia but rare in temperate climates.

Aetiology

Chronic hepatitis B virus infection has emerged as the most important cause world-wide, but chronic hepatitis C virus infection is becoming increasingly important. Aflatoxin contamination of foods may be important in tropical countries. Cirrhosis and male sex are the main risk factors for hepatocellular carcinoma in temperate climates. Cirrhosis is present in 80% of cases and may be of any type; however, hepatocellular carcinoma appears most commonly in haemochromatosis and alcoholic cirrhosis, predominantly male diseases, and rarely in primary biliary cirrhosis, which mainly affects women. Exposure to toxins such as thorotrast and arsenic has in the past been shown to produce angiosarcomas and rarely hepatocellular carcinomas. Oestrogens, androgens and anabolic steroids may cause adenomas or, exceptionally, hepatocellular carcinomas.

Pathology

Macroscopically, the tumour may comprise a single mass or multiple nodules and can occasionally be diffusely invasive. Microscopically, the tumour is made up of trabeculae of well-differentiated malignant cells resembling hepatocytes (see Fig. 18.28). Bile secretion by tumour cells is diagnostic. Intravascular invasion and growth are often features and

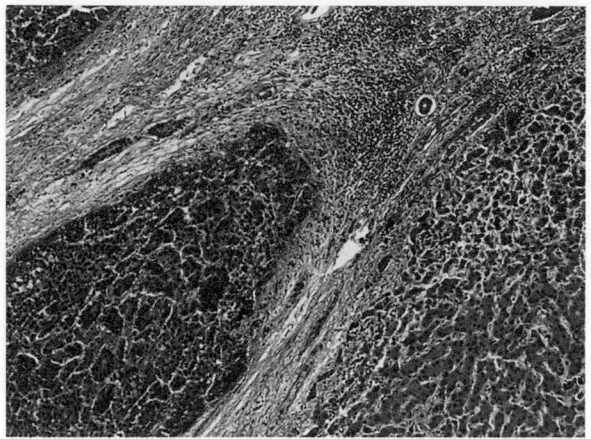

Fig. 18.28 Histology of hepatocellular carcinoma (left) arising within cirrhotic liver (right).

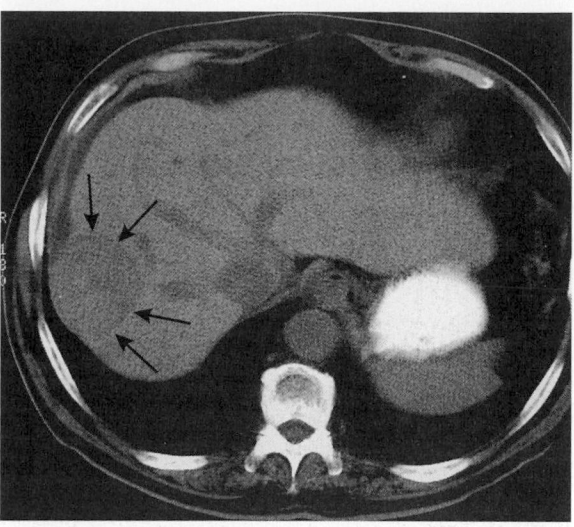

Fig. 18.29 CT showing a large hepatocellular carcinoma (arrows).

may result in tumour spread into the portal vein or inferior vena cava. The tumour metastasises mainly to regional lymph nodes, the peritoneum, the lungs and bones.

Clinical features

These include weakness, anorexia, weight loss, fever, abdominal pain, a large irregular liver or an abdominal mass, and ascites. Hepatocellular carcinomas are vascular; a bruit may be heard over the liver and intra-abdominal bleeding may occur. Clinical deterioration in a patient with cirrhosis should always lead to suspicion of hepatocellular carcinoma.

Screening

Hepatocellular carcinoma is most common in patients with cirrhosis, especially if associated with HCV infection, haemochromatosis or alcohol. Treatment can only be curative if small asymptomatic tumours are removed by resection or liver transplantation. Such tumours can be detected by regular serum α-fetoprotein measurements and ultrasound examinations undertaken at 6-monthly intervals.

Investigations

A greatly increased or rising serum α-fetoprotein is virtually diagnostic. Imaging usually reveals one or more filling defects, laparoscopy may reveal the tumour, and the diagnosis can be confirmed by liver aspiration or biopsy, which does, however, risk 'seeding' the tumour along the biopsy tract (see Fig. 18.29). Liver function tests give variable non-specific results. Metabolic abnormalities include polycythaemia, hypercalcaemia, hypoglycaemia and porphyria cutanea tarda.

Management

Surgical removal is only appropriate if the tumour is confined to one lobe in the absence of cirrhosis and is rarely feasible; however, the possibility should always be considered before injudicious biopsy is undertaken. Arterial embolisation with or without local installation of chemotherapeutic agents (chemoembolisation) can provide palliation of hepatic pain. Chemotherapy has been disappointing. Percutaneous ethanol injection may have a place if the

tumour is small. Liver transplantation can be considered for small tumours not amenable to local resection.

EBM

TREATMENT OF HEPATOCELLULAR CARCINOMA

'Controversy exists regarding the relative role of hepatic resection or liver transplantation in patients with small single (< 5 cm) or small multiple (3 nodules each less than 3 cm) hepatomas. No RCTs are available.'

'In patients with larger tumours, arterial embolisation ± chemoembolisation or tamoxifen treatment has not resulted in improved survival.'

- DeMatteo RP, Fong Y, Blumgart LH. Surgical treatment of malignant liver tumours. Baillieres Best Pract Res Clin Gastroenterol 1999; 13:557–574.
- Heneghan MA, O'Grady JG. Liver transplantation for malignant disease. Baillieres Best Pract Res Clin Gastroenterol 1999; 13:575–579.
- Llovet JM, Bruix J. Early diagnosis and treatment of hepatocellular carcinoma. Baillieres Best Pract Res Clin Gastroenterol 2000; 14(6):991–1008.

Prognosis

The outlook is very poor. Surgery alone gives prolonged survival, but only about 10% of patients are suitable for this therapy. Few patients survive beyond a year. Liver transplantation in selected cases improves survival.

FIBROLAMELLAR HEPATOCELLULAR CARCINOMA

This rare variant differs from other hepatocellular carcinomas in that it occurs in young adults, equally in males and females, and is not associated with either cirrhosis or hepatitis B or C virus infection. It may present with pain due to bleeding into the tumour, which may later cause intrahepatic or intraperitoneal calcification. The serum α-fetoprotein is usually normal, and biopsy shows large polygonal malignant hepatocytes in a dense fibrous tissue stroma. Two-thirds of tumours are resectable and transplantation may be considered where there is no spread beyond the liver. Two-thirds of patients survive beyond 5 years.

OTHER PRIMARY MALIGNANT TUMOURS

These are rare but include haemangio-endothelial sarcomas and cholangiocarcinoma (see p. 886).

SECONDARY MALIGNANT TUMOURS

These are common and usually originate from carcinomas in the lung, breast, abdomen or pelvis. They may be single or multiple. Peritoneal dissemination frequently results in ascites.

Clinical features

The primary neoplasm is asymptomatic in about half of patients. Hepatomegaly may suggest cirrhosis, but splenomegaly is rare. There is usually rapid liver enlargement, with weight loss and jaundice.

Investigations

A positive faecal occult blood test may point towards the presence of primary gastrointestinal malignancy. A raised alkaline phosphatase activity is the most common biochemical abnormality but the liver function tests may be normal. Ascitic fluid has a high protein content and may be blood-stained, and cytology sometimes reveals malignant cells. Imaging (see p. 840) usually reveals filling defects (see Fig. 18.30), laparoscopy may reveal the tumour (see Fig. 18.31), and the diagnosis can be confirmed by liver aspiration or biopsy.

Management

Every effort should be made to detect resectable secondary tumours, as hepatic resection can improve survival for slow-growing tumours such as colonic carcinomas. Patients with hormone-producing tumours, such as gastrinomas, insulinomas and glucagonomas, and those with lymphomas may benefit from chemotherapy. Unfortunately, palliative treatment to relieve pain is all that is available for most patients; this may include arterial embolisation of the tumour masses.

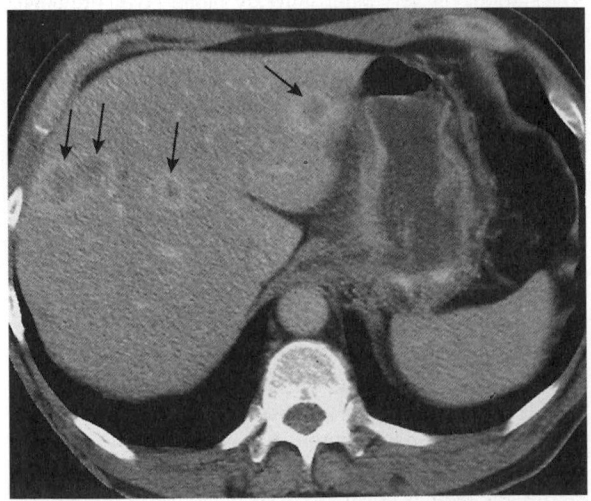

Fig. 18.30 CT showing multiple liver metastases (arrows).

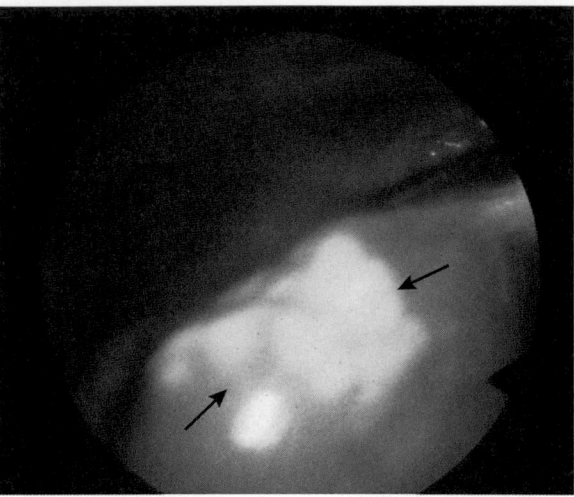

Fig. 18.31 Laparoscopic appearance of a hepatic metastasis (arrows) from colonic carcinoma.

BENIGN TUMOURS

Hepatic adenomas are rare vascular tumours which may present as an abdominal mass or with abdominal pain or intraperitoneal bleeding. They are more common in women and may be caused by oral contraceptives, androgens and anabolic steroids. Haemangiomas are the most common benign liver tumours and rarely cause sufficient symptoms to merit resection (see Fig. 18.32).

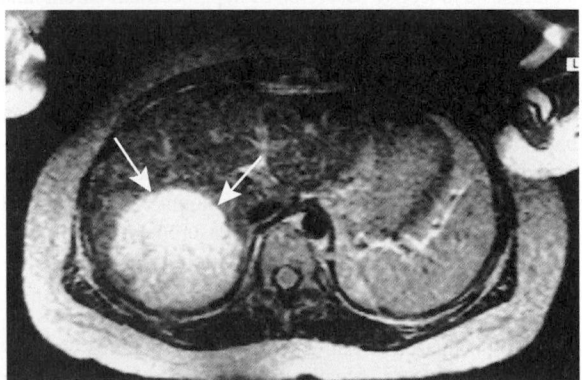

Fig. 18.32 MRI showing a haemangioma (arrows) in the liver.

MISCELLANEOUS LIVER DISEASES

LIVER ABSCESS

Liver abscesses are pyogenic, hydatid or amoebic.

PYOGENIC ABSCESS

Pyogenic liver abscesses are uncommon but important because they are potentially curable, inevitably fatal if untreated, and readily overlooked.

Aetiology and pathology

Infection can reach the liver in several ways (see Box 18.45). Abscesses are most common in older patients and usually result from ascending infection due to biliary obstruction (cholangitis), or contiguous spread from an empyema of the gallbladder. Abscesses in young adults consequent on suppurative appendicitis were previously common but are now rare. Immunocompromised patients are particularly likely to develop liver abscesses. Abscesses vary greatly in size; single lesions are more common in the right liver, and multiple abscesses are usually due to infection secondary to biliary obstruction. *E. coli* and various streptococci, particularly *Strep. milleri*, are the most common organisms; anaerobes including streptococci and *Bacteroides* can often be found when infection has been transmitted from large bowel pathology via the portal vein, and multiple organisms are present in one-third of patients.

Clinical features

Patients are generally ill with fever, sometimes rigors, and weight loss. Abdominal pain is the most common symptom and is usually in the right upper quadrant, sometimes with radiation to the right shoulder. The pain may be pleuritic in nature. Hepatomegaly is found in more than half the patients and tenderness can usually be elicited by gentle percussion over the organ. Mild jaundice may be present but is severe only when large abscesses cause biliary obstruction. Abnormalities are present at the base of the right lung in about one-quarter of patients. Atypical presentations are common and explain the frequency with which the diagnosis is made only at autopsy. This is a particular problem in patients with gradually developing illnesses or pyrexia of unknown origin which may not include abdominal pain or prominent clinical features pointing to an underlying cause such as colonic diverticular disease. Necrotic colorectal metastases can be misdiagnosed as hepatic abscess.

Investigations

Liver imaging is the most revealing investigation and shows 90% or more of symptomatic abscesses. Needle aspiration under ultrasound guidance confirms the diagnosis and provides pus for culture. A leucocytosis is frequent, plasma alkaline phosphatase activity is usually increased, and the serum albumin is often low. The chest radiograph may show a raised right diaphragm and lung collapse or an effusion at the base of the right lung. Blood culture should always be carried out as it may reveal the causative organism.

Management

This includes prolonged antibiotic therapy and drainage of the abscess. Pending the results of culture of blood and pus from the abscess, treatment should commence with a combination of antibiotics such as ampicillin, gentamicin and metronidazole. Aspiration or drainage with a catheter placed in the abscess under ultrasound guidance may be required if the abscess is large or if it does not respond to antibiotics. Surgical drainage is rarely undertaken, although hepatic resection may be indicated for a chronic persistent abscess or 'pseudotumour'.

Prognosis

The mortality of liver abscesses is 20–40%; failure to make the diagnosis is the most common cause of death. Older patients and those with multiple abscesses also have a higher mortality.

HYDATID CYSTS

Hydatid cysts are caused by *Echinococcus granulosus* infection (see p. 879). They have an outer layer derived from the host, an intermediate laminated layer and an inner germinal layer. They can be single (see Fig. 18.33) or multiple. Chronic cysts become calcified. The cysts may be asymptomatic but may present with abdominal pain or a mass. There may be a peripheral blood eosinophilia, radiographs may show calcification, imaging shows the cyst(s), and serological tests are positive in 50% of cases. Rupture or secondary infection of cysts can occur, and a communication with the intrahepatic biliary tree is invariable. Surgical removal of the intact cyst is the preferred treatment under mebendazole prophylaxis.

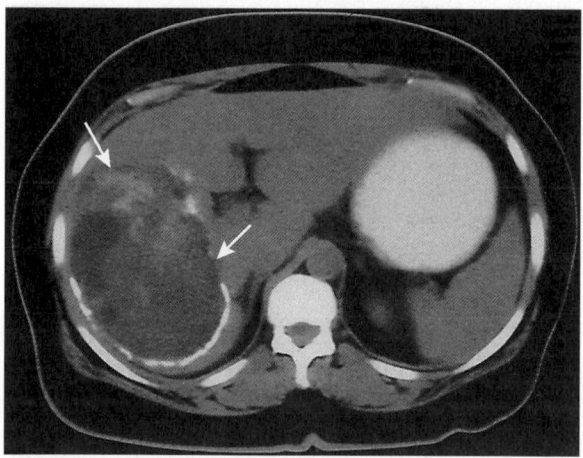

Fig. 18.33 Hydatid cyst of the liver on CT (arrows).

AMOEBIC LIVER ABSCESSES

Amoebic liver abscesses are caused by *Entamoeba histolytica* infection. Up to 50% of cases do not have a previous history of intestinal disease. Although amoebic liver abscesses are most often found in endemic areas, patients can present with no history of travel to these places. Abscesses are usually large, single and located in the right lobe, although multiple abscesses may occur in advanced disease. Fever and abdominal pain or swelling are the most common symptoms. Diagnosis may depend on cyst aspiration revealing the classic anchovy sauce appearance of the cyst fluid. Treatment is described on page 66.

HEPATIC NODULES

Liver diseases characterised primarily by hepatic nodules which are not neoplastic are rare, and three types are usually recognised. Hepatic adenomas (see p. 878) and nodules occurring in cirrhosis are not included with these diseases.

NODULAR REGENERATIVE HYPERPLASIA OF THE LIVER

This disease is characterised by small hepatocyte nodules throughout the liver without fibrosis. It occurs in older people and has been associated with many conditions such as connective tissue disease, haematological diseases and with immunosuppressive and corticosteroid drugs. The condition usually presents as an abdominal mass or occasionally because of portal hypertension. Diagnosis is made by liver biopsy. Liver function is good and the prognosis is very favourable; however, hepatocellular carcinoma occurs occasionally.

FOCAL NODULAR HYPERPLASIA OF THE LIVER

This usually takes the form of a single subcapsular liver nodule, yellow-brown in colour and with central fibrosis. It is almost always asymptomatic and found by chance on ultrasound imaging for other pathology. Intraperitoneal bleeding is an exceptional complication.

PARTIAL NODULAR TRANSFORMATION OF THE LIVER

Nodules in this condition are restricted to the perihilar region of the liver where they can cause portal hypertension. The rest of the liver is normal and liver function is excellent. Needle liver biopsy is often normal.

CYSTIC AND FIBROPOLYCYSTIC DISEASE

Fibropolycystic diseases of the liver and biliary system constitute a heterogeneous group of rare disorders, some of which are inherited. They are not distinct entities, as combined lesions occur.

SOLITARY HEPATIC CYSTS

Isolated hepatic cysts may be discovered by chance; rarely, they give rise to complications, including pain or jaundice from cyst enlargement, haemorrhage or infection. Portal hypertension and bleeding from varices are exceptional.

Diagnosis is best made by ultrasonography. Resection of a large cyst or groups of cysts is only required if symptoms are troublesome, and the prognosis is excellent.

ADULT HEPATORENAL POLYCYSTIC DISEASE

The kidneys are predominantly affected in this condition (see Fig. 18.34), which is inherited as an autosomal dominant trait (see p. 621). Hepatic cysts which do not communicate with the biliary system are present in over half of patients with renal cysts, and cysts can also be found in other organs. Cerebrovascular aneurysms may develop. Cysts restricted to the liver constitute a separate rare genetic disorder.

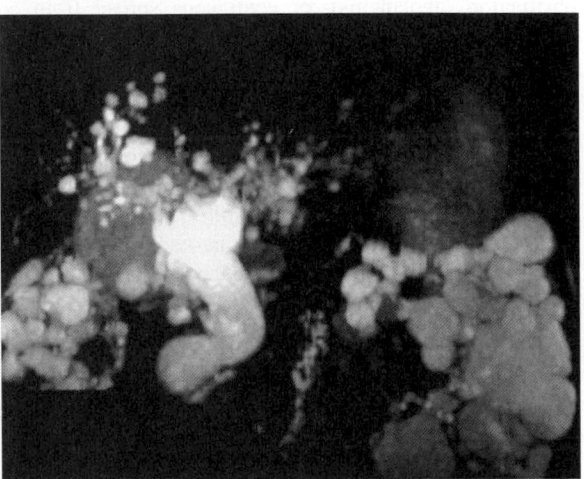

Fig. 18.34 MRI showing multiple cysts in the liver and kidneys in polycystic disease. Note the dilated common bile duct.

CAROLI'S SYNDROME

This is very rare and is characterised by segmental saccular dilatations of the intrahepatic biliary tree. The whole liver is usually affected, and extrahepatic biliary dilatation occurs in about one-quarter of patients. Recurrent attacks of cholangitis (see p. 885) occur and may cause hepatic abscesses. Complications include biliary stones and cholangiocarcinoma. Antibiotics are required for episodes of cholangitis, and occasionally localised disease can be treated by segmental liver resection.

CONGENITAL HEPATIC FIBROSIS

This is characterised by broad bands of fibrous tissue linking the portal tracts in the liver, abnormalities of the interlobular bile ducts, and sometimes a lack of portal venules. The renal tubules may show cystic dilatation (medullary sponge kidney, see p. 622), and eventually renal cysts may develop. The condition can be inherited as an autosomal recessive trait. Liver involvement causes portal hypertension with splenomegaly and bleeding from oesophageal varices that usually presents in adolescence or in early adult life. The prognosis is good because liver function is preserved. Treatment may be required for variceal bleeding and occasionally cholangitis (see p. 885). Patients can present during childhood with renal failure if the kidneys are severely affected.

CHOLEDOCHAL CYSTS

This term applies to cysts anywhere in the biliary tree (see Fig. 18.35). The great majority cause diffuse dilatation of the common bile duct (type I), but others take the form of biliary diverticula (type II), dilatation of the intraduodenal bile duct (type III) and multiple biliary cysts (type IV). The last type merges with Caroli's syndrome (see above). In the neonate they may present with jaundice or biliary peritonitis. Recurrent jaundice, abdominal pain and cholangitis may arise in the adult. Liver abscess and biliary cirrhosis may develop, and there is an increased incidence of cholangiocarcinoma. Excision of the cyst with hepaticojejunostomy is the treatment of choice.

ISSUES IN OLDER PEOPLE
LIVER DISEASE

- 10% of alcoholic liver disease presents over the age of 70 years, when it is more likely to be severe at presentation and has a worse prognosis than in younger people.
- Hepatitis A causes more severe illness in older people and runs a more protracted course.
- One-third of cases of primary biliary cirrhosis are over 65 years and age is an adverse prognostic factor.
- More than 50% of all cases of liver abscess in the UK are over 60 years.
- Approximately 50% of cases of hepatocellular carcinoma present over the age of 65 years in the UK.
- Older people are less likely to survive liver surgery (including transplantation) because comorbidity is more prevalent than in younger patients.

GALLBLADDER AND OTHER BILIARY DISEASE

FUNCTIONAL ANATOMY

BILIARY SYSTEM

The biliary tract begins in the biliary canaliculi, which are formed by the arrangement of hepatocytes, and the intrahepatic bile ducts derived from them join progressively to form the right and left hepatic ducts. These ducts join as they emerge from the liver to form the common hepatic duct, which forms the common bile duct after joining the cystic duct (see Fig. 18.36). The common bile duct is approximately 5 cm long; it has a thin-walled wide-lumened proximal part and a thick-walled narrow-lumened distal part surrounded by the choledochal sphincter. The distal common bile duct usually joins the pancreatic duct before it enters the duodenum. The gallbladder is a pear-shaped sac lying under the right hemiliver, with its fundus located anteriorly behind the tip of the 9th costal cartilage. Its body and neck pass posteromedially towards the porta hepatis, and the cystic duct then joins it to the common hepatic duct. The cystic duct mucosa has prominent crescentic folds (valves of Heister), giving it a beaded appearance on cholangiography.

BILE

The liver secretes 1–2 litres of bile daily. The hepatocytes provide the driving force for bile flow by creating osmotic gradients of bile acids, which form micelles in bile (bile acid-dependent bile flow), and of sodium (bile acid-independent bile flow). Common bile duct pressure is maintained by rhythmic contraction and relaxation of the ampullary sphincter; this pressure exceeds gallbladder pressure in the fasting state so that bile normally flows into the

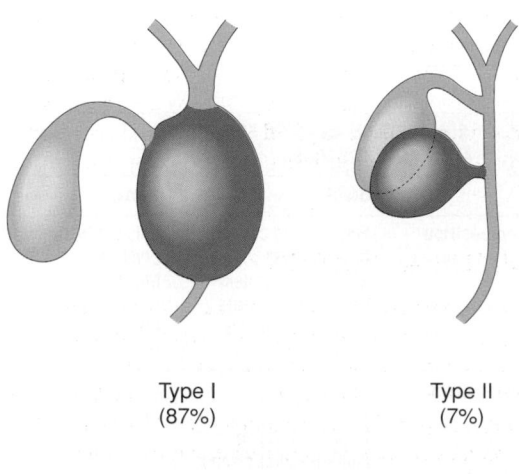
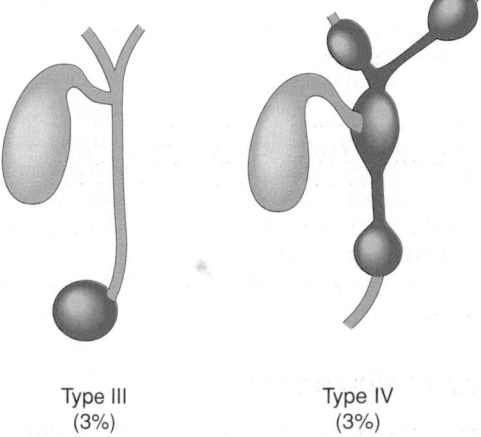

Type I	Type II	Type III	Type IV
(87%)	(7%)	(3%)	(3%)

Fig. 18.35 Classification and frequency of choledochal cysts.

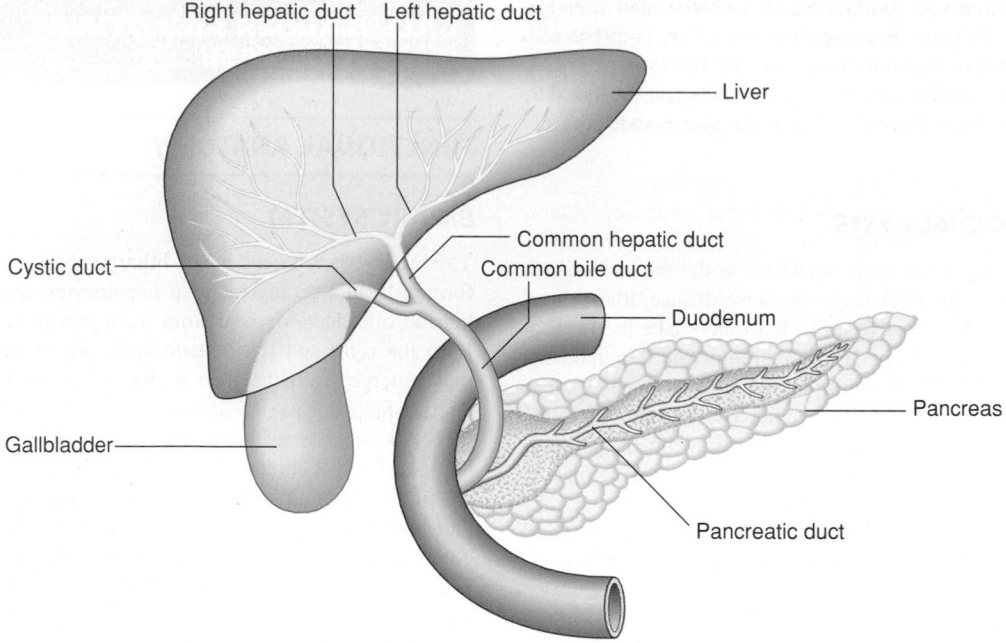

Fig. 18.36 Functional anatomy of the biliary tree.

gallbladder where it is concentrated some 10-fold by resorption of water and electrolytes. Cholecystokinin released from the duodenal mucosa during feeding causes gallbladder contraction and reduces sphincter pressure so that bile flows into the duodenum. Vagal activity maintains gallbladder tone, but sympathetic activity has little or no effect on the gallbladder.

GALLSTONES

Gallstone formation is the most common disorder of the biliary tree and it is unusual for the gallbladder to be diseased in the absence of gallstones.

Pathology

Gallstones are conveniently classified into cholesterol or pigment stones, although the majority are of mixed composition. Cholesterol stones are most common in industrialised countries, whereas pigment stones are more frequent in developing countries. Gallstones contain varying quantities of calcium salts, including calcium bilirubinate, carbonate, phosphate and palmitate, which are radio-opaque.

Epidemiology

In Western countries gallstones are common and occur in 7% of males and 15% of females aged 18–65 years, with an overall prevalence of 11%. In those under 40 years there is a 3:1 female preponderance, whereas in the elderly the sex ratio is about equal. Gallstones are common in North America, Europe and Australia, and are less frequent in India, the Far East and Africa. In developed countries the incidence of symptomatic gallstones appears to be increasing and they occur at an earlier age.

The most important risk factors for cholesterol and pigment gallstones are shown in Boxes 18.46 and 18.47. There has been much debate over the role of diet in cholesterol gallstone disease; an increase in dietary cholesterol,

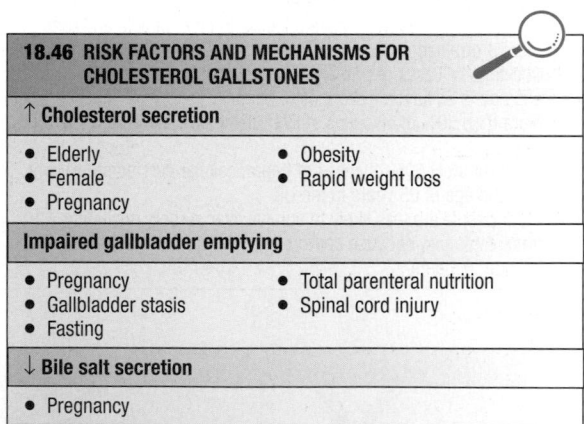

18.46 RISK FACTORS AND MECHANISMS FOR CHOLESTEROL GALLSTONES	
↑ Cholesterol secretion	
• Elderly	• Obesity
• Female	• Rapid weight loss
• Pregnancy	
Impaired gallbladder emptying	
• Pregnancy	• Total parenteral nutrition
• Gallbladder stasis	• Spinal cord injury
• Fasting	
↓ Bile salt secretion	
• Pregnancy	

18.47 COMPOSITION AND RISK FACTORS FOR PIGMENT STONES		
	Black	**Brown**
Composition	Polymerised calcium bilirubinates* Mucin glycoprotein Calcium phosphate Calcium carbonate Cholesterol	Calcium bilirubinate crystals* Mucin glycoprotein Cholesterol Calcium palmitate/ stearate
Risk factors	Haemolysis Age Hepatic cirrhosis Ileal resection/disease	Infected bile Stasis
* Major component.		

fat, total calories and refined carbohydrate or lack of dietary fibre have all been implicated. At present the best data support an association between simple refined sugar in the diet and gallstones. There is a negative association between a moderate alcohol intake (2–3 units daily) and gallstones.

Aetiology

Gallstone formation is multifactorial, and the factors involved are related to the type of gallstone.

Cholesterol gallstones

Cholesterol is held in solution in bile by its association with bile acids and phospholipids in the form of micelles and vesicles. Biliary lipoproteins may also have a role in solubilising cholesterol. In gallstone disease the liver produces bile which contains an excess of cholesterol either because there is a relative deficiency of bile salts or a relative excess of cholesterol. Such bile, which is supersaturated with cholesterol, is termed 'lithogenic'. Disorders with the potential to induce the production of lithogenic bile are shown in Box 18.48. Factors initiating crystallisation of cholesterol in lithogenic bile (nucleation factors) are also important; patients with cholesterol gallstones have gallbladder bile which forms cholesterol crystals more rapidly than equally saturated bile from patients who do not form gallstones. Factors favouring nucleation (mucus, calcium, fatty acids, other proteins) and antinucleating factors (apolipoproteins) have been described.

Pigment stones

Brown crumbly pigment stones are almost always the consequence of bacterial or parasitic infection in the biliary tree. They are found commonly in the Far East where infection of the biliary tree allows bacterial β-glucuronidase to hydrolyse conjugated bilirubin to its free form, which then precipitates as calcium bilirubinate. The mechanism of black pigment gallstone formation in developed countries is not satisfactorily explained. Haemolysis is important as these stones occur in chronic haemolytic disease.

Biliary sludge

The term 'biliary sludge' describes bile which is in a gel form that contains numerous crystals or microspheroliths of calcium bilirubinate granules and cholesterol crystals as well as glycoproteins. It is an essential precursor to the formation of gallstones in the majority of patients. Biliary sludge is frequently formed under normal conditions, but then either dissolves or is cleared by the gallbladder; only in about 15% of patients does it persist to form cholesterol stones. Fasting, parenteral nutrition and pregnancy are also associated with sludge formation.

Clinical features

The majority of gallstones are asymptomatic and remain so. Only about 10% of those with gallstones develop clinical evidence of gallstone disease.

Symptomatic gallstones (see Box 18.49) manifest either as biliary pain ('biliary colic') or as a consequence of cholecystitis (see p. 884). If a gallstone becomes acutely impacted in the cystic duct, the patient will experience pain. The term

18.48 PATHOGENIC FACTORS LEADING TO THE PRODUCTION OF LITHOGENIC BILE
• Defective bile salt synthesis
• Excessive intestinal loss of bile salts
• Over-sensitive bile salt feedback
• Excessive cholesterol secretion
• Abnormal gallbladder function

18.49 CLINICAL FEATURES AND COMPLICATIONS OF GALLSTONES	
Clinical features	
• Asymptomatic	• Acute cholecystitis
• Biliary colic	• Chronic cholecystitis
Complications	
• Empyema of the gallbladder	• Fistulae between the gallbladder and duodenum or colon
• Porcelain gallbladder (see p. 884)	• Pressure on/inflammation of the common bile duct by a gallstone in the cystic duct (Mirizzi's syndrome)
• Choledocholithiasis	
• Pancreatitis	• Gallstone ileus
	• Cancer of the gallbladder

'biliary colic' is a misnomer because the pain does not rhythmically increase and decrease in intensity as in colic experienced in intestinal and renal disease. Instead the pain is typically of sudden onset and is sustained for about 2 hours; its continuation for more than 6 hours suggests that a complication such as cholecystitis or pancreatitis has developed. Pain is felt in the epigastrium (70% of patients) or right upper quadrant (20% of patients) and radiates to the interscapular region or the tip of the right scapula, but other sites include the left upper quadrant, the epigastrium and the lower chest; the pain can be confused with intrathoracic disease, oesophagitis, myocardial infarction or dissecting aneurysm.

Combinations of fatty food intolerance, dyspepsia and flatulence not attributable to other causes have been referred to as 'gallstone dyspepsia'. These symptoms are not now recognised as being caused by gallstones and are best regarded as non-ulcer dyspepsia (see p. 788).

Investigations

A plain abdominal radiograph will demonstrate calcified gallstones in less than 20% of patients. Ultrasonography is the method of choice to diagnose gallstones (see Fig. 18.7, p. 841) but oral cholecystography and CT can also be used (see Fig. 18.37). Oral cholecystography shows whether or not the gallbladder is functioning, and this is useful if oral dissolution therapy is being considered (see under Management below). MRI is becoming increasingly available and may demonstrate gallstones or their complications.

Complications

Occlusion of the cystic duct for any prolonged period of time results in acute cholecystitis. Other complications include chronic cholecystitis, and a mucocoele of the gallbladder, in which there is slow distension of the gallbladder from continuous secretion of mucus. If this material becomes infected, an empyema develops. Calcium may be secreted

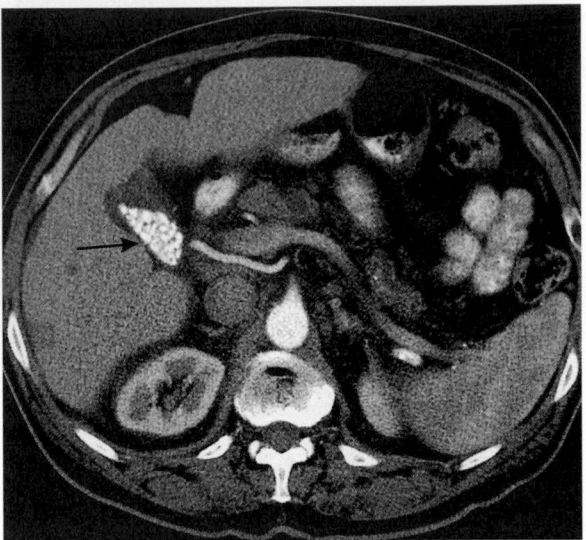

Fig. 18.37   CT showing gallstone within gallbladder (arrow).

into the lumen of the hydropic gallbladder, causing limy bile, and if calcium salts are precipitated in the gallbladder wall the radiological appearance of 'porcelain' gallbladder results.

Gallstones in the gallbladder (cholecystolithiasis) migrate to the common bile duct (choledocholithiasis) in approximately 15% of patients and cause biliary colic, but they may be asymptomatic. Rarely, fistulae develop between the gallbladder and the duodenum, colon or stomach. Air will be seen in the biliary tree on plain abdominal radiographs. If a stone larger than 2.5 cm in diameter has migrated into the gut it may impact either at the terminal ileum or occasionally in the duodenum or sigmoid colon. The resultant intestinal obstruction may be followed by 'gallstone ileus'. Rarely, gallstones impacted in the cystic duct cause stricturing in the common hepatic duct (Mirizzi's syndrome), resulting in obstructive jaundice.

Cancer of the gallbladder is uncommon, although it is recognised more frequently in an ageing population and in a 'porcelain' gallbladder. In over 95% of patients with gallbladder cancer there are accompanying gallstones. Cancer is usually diagnosed as an incidental histological finding following cholecystectomy for gallstone disease.

Management

Asymptomatic gallstones found incidentally are not usually treated because the majority will never give symptoms. Symptomatic gallstones are best treated surgically, and

18.50 TREATMENT OF GALLSTONES
• Cholecystectomy—open or laparoscopic
• Oral bile acids—chenodeoxycholic or ursodeoxycholic
• Contact dissolution
• Lithotripsy
• Endoscopic sphincterotomy

minimal access techniques have largely replaced non-surgical treatment. Gallstones can be dissolved and fragmented in the gallbladder or removed mechanically from the common bile duct (see Box 18.50).

Medical dissolution of gallstones can be achieved by oral administration of the bile acid ursodeoxycholic acid. Radiolucent gallstones, a gallbladder that opacifies on oral cholecystography, stones not larger than 15 mm in diameter, moderate obesity and no or at most mild symptoms are the features which suggest that drug therapy may be feasible. Success can be expected in approximately 75% of patients who fulfil these criteria. Occasionally, direct contact dissolution therapy is attempted via percutaneous catheters or catheters placed at ERCP. Extracorporeal shock-wave lithotripsy is expensive and not widely available. Bile salt therapy is necessary following lithotripsy to dissolve the gallstone fragments within the gallbladder. As in the case of oral bile salt therapy, only 30% of all patients with gallbladder disease are suitable for lithotripsy. All therapeutic regimens which retain the gallbladder have a 50% recurrence of stones after 5 years.

CHOLECYSTITIS

ACUTE CHOLECYSTITIS

Aetiology and pathology

Acute cholecystitis is almost always associated with obstruction of the gallbladder neck or cystic duct by a gallstone. Occasionally, obstruction may be by mucus, parasitic worms or a tumour. The pathogenesis is unclear, but the initial inflammation is possibly chemically induced. This leads to gallbladder mucosal damage which releases phospholipase, converting biliary lecithin to lysolecithin, a recognised mucosal toxin. At the time of surgery approximately 50% of cultures of the gallbladder contents are sterile. Infection occurs eventually and in elderly patients or those with diabetes mellitus a severe infection with gas-forming organisms can cause emphysematous cholecystitis. Acalculous cholecystitis can occur in the intensive care setting.

Clinical features

The cardinal feature is pain in the right upper quadrant but also in the epigastrium, the right shoulder tip or interscapular region. It usually lasts for more than an hour but differentiation between biliary colic (see p. 883) and acute cholecystitis may be difficult; features suggesting cholecystitis include severe and prolonged pain, fever and leucocytosis.

Examination shows right hypochondrial tenderness, rigidity worse on inspiration (Murphy's sign) and occasionally a gallbladder mass. Fever is present but rigors are unusual. Leucocytosis is common, except in the elderly patient where the signs of inflammation may be minimal. Jaundice occurs in less than 10% of patients and may be due to the presence or recent passage of stones in the common bile duct. Minor increases of plasma transaminase and amylase activity may be encountered.

Cholecystitis usually resolves with medical treatment, but the inflammation may progress to an empyema or perforation and peritonitis.

Investigations

Plain radiographs of the abdomen and chest may show radio-opaque gallstones, and rarely intrabiliary gas due to fistulation of a gallstone into the intestine, and are important in excluding lower lobe pneumonia and a perforated viscus. Ultrasonography detects gallstones and gallbladder thickening due to cholecystitis. The plasma amylase should be measured to detect pancreatitis (see p. 802), which may be a complication of gallstones. The peripheral blood count often shows a leucocytosis.

Management

Medical

This consists of bed rest, pain relief, antibiotics and maintenance of fluid balance. Severe pain is relieved using morphine, and the increased tone of the sphincter of Oddi may be minimised by the concurrent use of atropine. Less severe pain can be relieved by pethidine, pentazocine or diclofenac. Antibiotics are required. A cephalosporin (such as cefuroxime) is the antibiotic of choice, and metronidazole is usually added in severely ill patients. Fluid balance is maintained by intravenous therapy and nasogastric aspiration is only needed for persistent vomiting. Any cause of stones (e.g. haemodialysis) should be treated.

Surgical

Urgent surgery is required when cholecystitis progresses in spite of medical therapy and when complications such as empyema or perforation develop. Operation should be carried out within 5 days of the onset of symptoms. Delayed surgery after 2–3 months is no longer favoured. Recurrent biliary colic or cholecystitis is frequent if the gallbladder is not removed.

CHRONIC CHOLECYSTITIS

Chronic inflammation of the gallbladder is almost invariably associated with gallstones. The condition may be asymptomatic. The usual symptoms are those of recurrent attacks of upper abdominal pain, often at night and following a heavy meal. The clinical features are similar to those of acute calculous cholecystitis but milder. The patient may recover spontaneously or following analgesia and antibiotics. Patients are usually advised to undergo elective laparoscopic cholecystectomy.

ACUTE CHOLANGITIS

Acute cholangitis is caused by bacterial infection of bile ducts and occurs in patients with other biliary problems such as choledocholithiasis (see below), biliary strictures or tumours, or after ERCP. Jaundice, rigors and abdominal pain are the cardinal presenting features. Treatment is with antibiotics and removal (if possible) of the underlying cause.

CHOLEDOCHOLITHIASIS

Stones in the common bile duct (choledocholithiasis) occur in 10–15% of patients with gallstones (see Fig. 18.38). These stones account for more than 80% of common bile duct stones; they migrate from the gallbladder, and are similar in appearance and chemical composition to the stones found elsewhere. Primary bile duct stones may develop infrequently within the common bile duct many years after a cholecystectomy or represent the accumulation of biliary sludge consequent upon dysfunction of the sphincter of Oddi. In Far Eastern countries, where bile duct infection is common, primary common bile duct stones are thought to follow bacterial infection secondary to parasitic infections with *Clonorchis sinensis*, *Ascaris lumbricoides* or *Fasciola hepatica*. Common bile duct stones can cause partial or complete bile duct obstruction and may be complicated by cholangitis due to secondary bacterial infection, septicaemia, liver abscess and biliary stricture.

Clinical features

Choledocholithiasis may be asymptomatic, may be found incidentally by operative cholangiography at cholecystectomy,

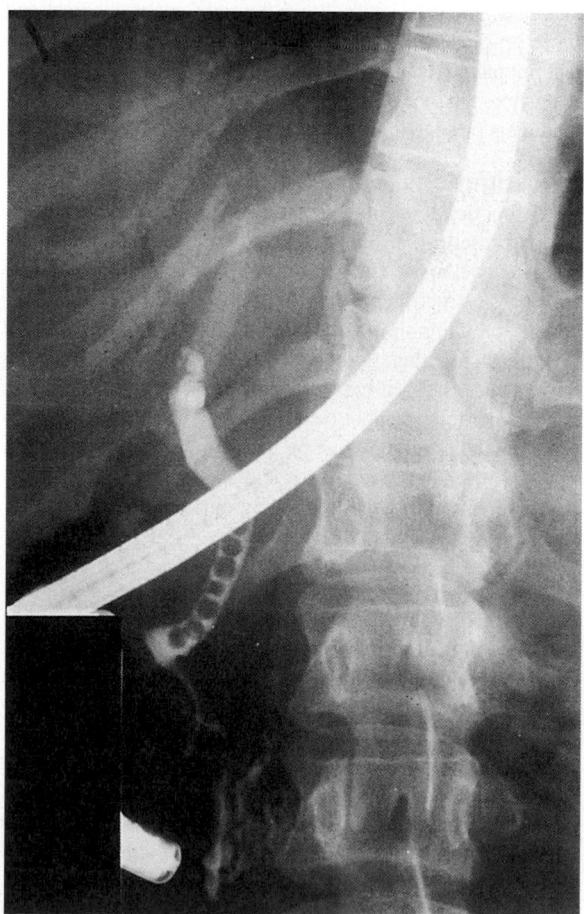

Fig. 18.38 ERCP showing common duct stones.

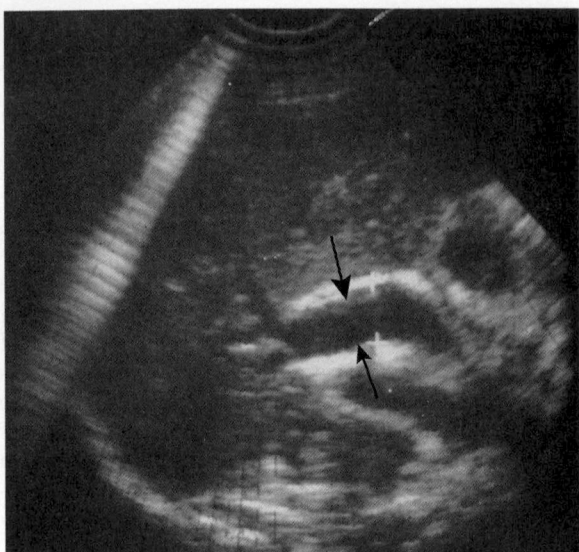

Fig. 18.39 Ultrasound showing dilated bile ducts (between arrows) in obstructive jaundice secondary to obstruction of the common bile duct.

or may manifest as recurrent abdominal pain with or without jaundice. The pain is usually in the right upper quadrant and fever, pruritus and dark urine may be present. Rigors may be a feature; painless jaundice is uncommon. Physical examination may show the scar of a previous cholecystectomy; if the gallbladder is present, it is usually small, fibrotic and impalpable.

Investigations

Liver function tests show a cholestatic pattern and bilirubinuria is present. If cholangitis is present, the patient usually has a leucocytosis. The most convenient method of demonstrating obstruction to the common bile duct is by ultrasonography; this shows dilated extrahepatic and intrahepatic bile ducts together with gallbladder stones, but it is not always successful in indicating the cause of the obstruction in the common bile duct (see Fig. 18.39). Endoscopic retrograde cholangiography can be used to diagnose obstruction and its cause, and to remove bile duct stones. If ERCP fails, percutaneous transhepatic cholangiography may be undertaken.

Management

Cholangitis requires analgesia for pain, intravenous fluids and broad-spectrum antibiotics such as cefuroxime and metronidazole. Blood cultures should be taken before the antibiotics are administered. Patients require urgent decompression of the biliary tree and stone removal either surgically or by endoscopic sphincterotomy via ERCP. Endoscopic sphincterotomy and stone extraction is the treatment of choice, particularly in patients over the age of 60, and is successful in about 90% of patients. Less commonly used techniques include extracorporeal lithotripsy.

Surgical treatment of choledocholithiasis is carried out less frequently than ERCP because it carries higher morbidity

and mortality. Before exploring the common bile duct an accurate diagnosis of choledocholithiasis should be confirmed by intraoperative cholangiography. If gallstones are found, the bile duct is explored, all stones are removed, stone clearance is checked by cholangiography or choledochoscopy, and a T-tube is inserted into the common bile duct. It is now possible to achieve these goals in specialist centres by laparoscopic means.

RECURRENT PYOGENIC CHOLANGITIS

This disease occurs in South-east Asia. Biliary sludge, calcium bilirubinate concretions and stones accumulate in the intrahepatic bile ducts, with secondary bacterial infection. The patients present with recurrent attacks of upper abdominal pain, fever and cholestatic jaundice. Investigation of the biliary tree demonstrates that both the intrahepatic and extrahepatic portions are filled with soft biliary mud. Eventually, the liver becomes scarred and liver abscesses develop. The condition is difficult to manage and requires drainage of the biliary tract with extraction of stones, antibiotics and, in certain patients, partial resection of damaged areas of the liver.

TUMOURS OF THE GALLBLADDER AND BILE DUCT

CARCINOMA OF THE GALLBLADDER

This is an uncommon tumour occurring more often in females and is usually encountered above the age of 70 years. More than 90% of such tumours are adenocarcinomas; the remainder are anaplastic or, rarely, squamous tumours. Gallstones are usually present and are thought to be important in the aetiology of the tumour.

The condition is usually diagnosed incidentally, following surgery for gallstone disease. Occasionally, it may manifest as repeated attacks of biliary pain and later persistent jaundice and weight loss. A gallbladder mass may be palpable in the right hypochondrium. Liver function tests show cholestasis, and gallbladder calcification (porcelain gallbladder) may be found on radiograph. The tumour may be diagnosed on ultrasonography and can be staged by CT. The treatment is surgical excision but local extension of the tumour beyond the wall of the gallbladder into the liver, lymph nodes and surrounding tissues is invariable and palliative management is usually all that can be offered. Survival is generally short.

CHOLANGIOCARCINOMA

This uncommon tumour arises anywhere in the biliary tree from the small intrahepatic bile ducts to the papilla of Vater, but it is the tumour involving the confluence of the right and left hepatic ducts (Klatskin tumour) which is the most challenging to manage. The cause is unknown but it is associated with gallstones, primary sclerosing cholangitis and

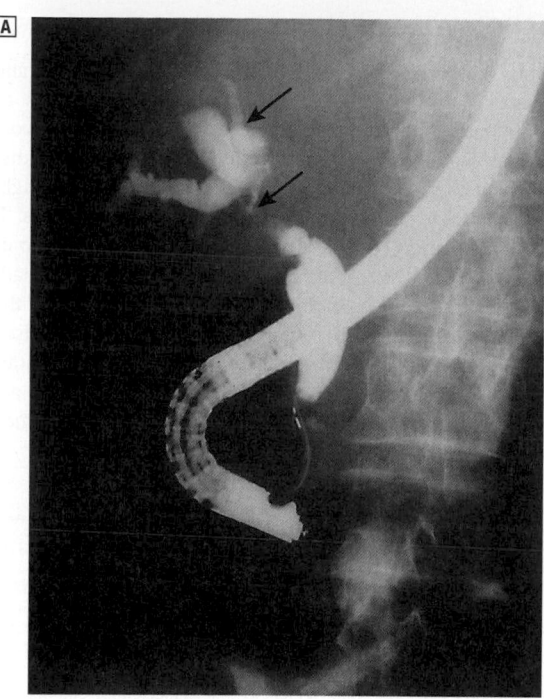
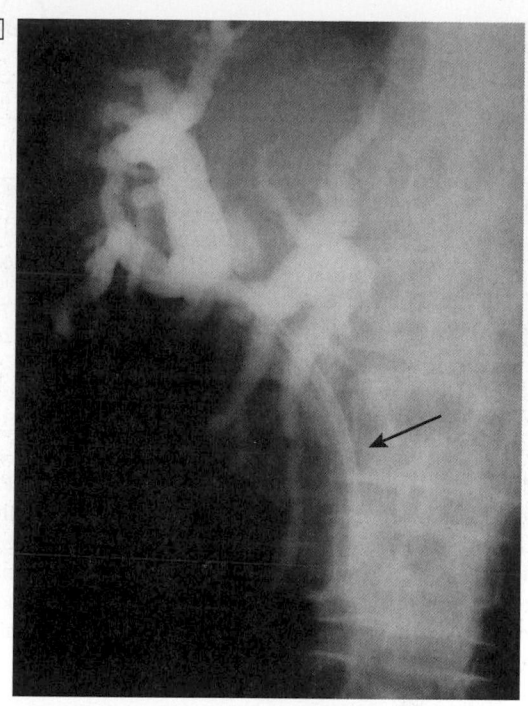

Fig. 18.40   Cholangiocarcinoma. [A] ERCP showing malignant biliary stricture (bottom arrow) and dilated intrahepatic bile ducts above (top arrow). [B] Post-ERCP stenting showing plastic endobiliary stent (arrow) which will draw bile from the dilated ducts above the stricture into the duodenum.

choledochal cysts (see p. 881). Primary sclerosing cholangitis is associated with ulcerative colitis, and cholangiocarcinoma may occur some years after proctocolectomy or as a presenting feature, with ulcerative colitis being discovered only subsequently. Tumours typically invade the lymphatics and adjacent vessels, with there being a predilection for spread within perineural sheaths.

The patient presents with jaundice, which may be intermittent. Half the patients have upper abdominal pain and weight loss. The diagnosis is made by ultrasound and cholangiography, but can be difficult to confirm in patients with sclerosing cholangitis. Cholangiocarcinomas can occasionally be excised or palliated surgically, but most patients are treated by inserting drainage stents across the tumour, using endoscopic or transhepatic techniques (see Fig. 18.40).

CARCINOMA AT THE PAPILLA OF VATER

Nearly 40% of all adenocarcinomas of the small intestine arise in relationship to the papilla of Vater and present with pain, anaemia, vomiting and weight loss. Jaundice may be intermittent or persistent. Diagnosis is made by duodenal endoscopy and biopsy of the tumour. Ampullary carcinoma must be differentiated from carcinoma of the head of the pancreas and a cholangiocarcinoma because both these latter conditions have a worse prognosis.

Curative surgical treatment can be undertaken by pancreaticoduodenectomy and the 5-year survival may be as high as 50%. When this is impossible a palliative bypass or insertion of a drainage stent is performed.

BENIGN GALLBLADDER TUMOURS

These are uncommon, often asymptomatic and usually found incidentally at operation or autopsy. Cholesterol polyps, sometimes associated with cholesterolosis, papillomas and adenomas are the main types.

MISCELLANEOUS BILIARY DISORDERS

POST-CHOLECYSTECTOMY SYNDROME

Dyspeptic symptoms following cholecystectomy (post-cholecystectomy syndrome) occur in about 30% of patients depending on how the condition is defined, how actively symptoms are sought, and the original indication for cholecystectomy. Post-cholecystectomy symptoms occur most frequently in women, in patients who have a history longer than 5 years prior to cholecystectomy, and in patients in whom the operation was undertaken for non-calculous gallbladder disease (see Box 18.51). Severe post-cholecystectomy syndrome occurs in only 2–5% of patients.

The usual complaints include right upper quadrant abdominal pain, flatulence, fatty food intolerance, and occasionally jaundice and cholangitis. Liver function tests may be abnormal and sometimes show cholestasis. Ultrasonography

Immediate post-surgical	
• Bleeding	• Abscess
• Biliary peritonitis	• Fistula

Biliary	
• Common bile duct stones	• Cystic duct stump syndrome
• Benign stricture	• Disorders of the ampulla of Vater
• Tumour	

Extrabiliary	
• Non-ulcer dyspepsia	• Gastro-oesophageal reflux
• Peptic ulcer	• Irritable bowel syndrome
• Pancreatic disease	• Functional abdominal pain

is used to detect biliary obstruction, and ERCP or MRCP is usually needed to detect common bile duct stones. Other investigations which may be required include upper gastrointestinal endoscopy, barium examination of the small intestine, pancreatic function tests, cholescintigraphy and a liver biopsy. The question of a functional illness should also be considered (see p. 254).

BILIARY MOTOR DISORDERS

Some patients with right upper quadrant discomfort do not have gallstones and the term 'biliary dyskinesia' has been introduced to describe this condition. The dyskinetic disorder may affect either the gallbladder or the sphincter of Oddi. Patients complain of recurrent epigastric or right upper quadrant pain.

The diagnosis is established by excluding gallstones and undertaking tests to demonstrate that contraction of the gallbladder is associated with pain and abnormal liver analytes or that the papilla is stenosed. ERCP, endoscopic manometry and radiomanometry are all used in an attempt to define this disorder more clearly. Identification of biliary dyskinesia remains difficult and the treatment is uncertain. Some patients with evidence of sphincter dysfunction derive benefit from sphincterotomy.

CHOLESTEROLOSIS OF THE GALLBLADDER

In this condition lipid deposits in the submucosa and epithelium appear as multiple yellow spots on the pink mucosa, giving rise to the description 'strawberry gallbladder'. The condition is usually asymptomatic but may occasionally present with right upper quadrant pain. Radiologically the features are those of small, fixed filling defects on cholecystography or ultrasonography, and the radiologist can usually differentiate between gallstones and cholesterolosis. The condition is usually diagnosed at cholecystectomy; if the diagnosis is made radiologically, cholecystectomy is indicated, depending on symptoms.

ADENOMYOMATOSIS OF THE GALLBLADDER

In this condition there is hyperplasia of the muscle and mucosa of the gallbladder. The projection of pouches of mucous membrane through weak points in the muscle coat produces Rokitansky–Aschoff sinuses. There is much disagreement over whether adenomyomatosis is a cause of right upper quadrant pain or other gastrointestinal symptoms. It may be diagnosed by oral cholecystography when a halo or ring of opacified diverticula can be seen around the gallbladder. Other appearances include deformity of the body of the gallbladder or marked irregularity of the outline. Localised adenomyomatosis in the region of the gallbladder fundus causes the appearance of a 'Phrygian cap'. Most patients are treated by cholecystectomy but it is advisable first to exclude other diseases in the upper gastrointestinal tract.

ISSUES IN OLDER PEOPLE
GALLBLADDER DISEASE

- By the age of 70 years, the prevalence of gallstones is around 30% in women and 19% in men.
- Acute cholecystitis in older people tends to be severe, may have few localising signs, and is associated with a high frequency of empyema and perforation. If such complications supervene, the mortality rate in this group may reach 20%.
- Mortality after urgent cholecystectomy for acute uncomplicated cholecystitis is not significantly higher than in younger patients.
- Endoscopic sphincterotomy and removal of common duct stones is well tolerated by older patients and has a substantially lower mortality than surgical common bile duct exploration.
- Cancer of the gallbladder is a disease of old age, and has a 1-year survival of 10%.

FURTHER INFORMATION

Bacon BR. Hemochromatosis: diagnosis and management. Gastroenterology 2001; 320:718–725.

Blei AT. Diagnosis and treatment of hepatic encephalopathy. Baillieres Best Pract Res Clin Gastroenterol 2000; 14(6):959–974.

Fernandez J, Bauer TM, Navasa M, Rodes J. Diagnosis, treatment and prevention of spontaneous bacterial peritonitis. Baillieres Best Pract Res Clin Gastroenterol 2000; 14(6):975–990.

Garcia-Tsao G. Current management of the complications of cirrhosis and portal hypertension: variceal haemorrhage, ascites, and spontaneous bacterial peritonitis. Gastroenterology 2001; 320:726–748.

Haydon GH, Neuberger J. Liver transplantation of patients in end-stage cirrhosis. Baillieres Best Pract Res Clin Gastroenterol 2000; 14(6):1049–1073.

Llovet JM, Bruix J. Early diagnosis and treatment of hepatocellular carcinoma. Baillieres Best Pract Res Clin Gastroenterol 2000; 14(6):991–1008.

Pratt DS, Kaplan MM. Evaluation of abnormal liver enzyme results in asymptomatic patients. New Engl J Med 2001; 342:1266–1271.

Walsh K, Alexander GJ. Update on chronic viral hepatitis. Postgrad Med J 2001; 910:498–505.

www.aasld.org
www.bsg.org.uk
www.unos.org

Blood disorders

J.I.O. CRAIG • A.P. HAYNES • D.B.L. McCLELLAND • C.A. LUDLAM

CLINICAL EXAMINATION IN BLOOD DISORDERS

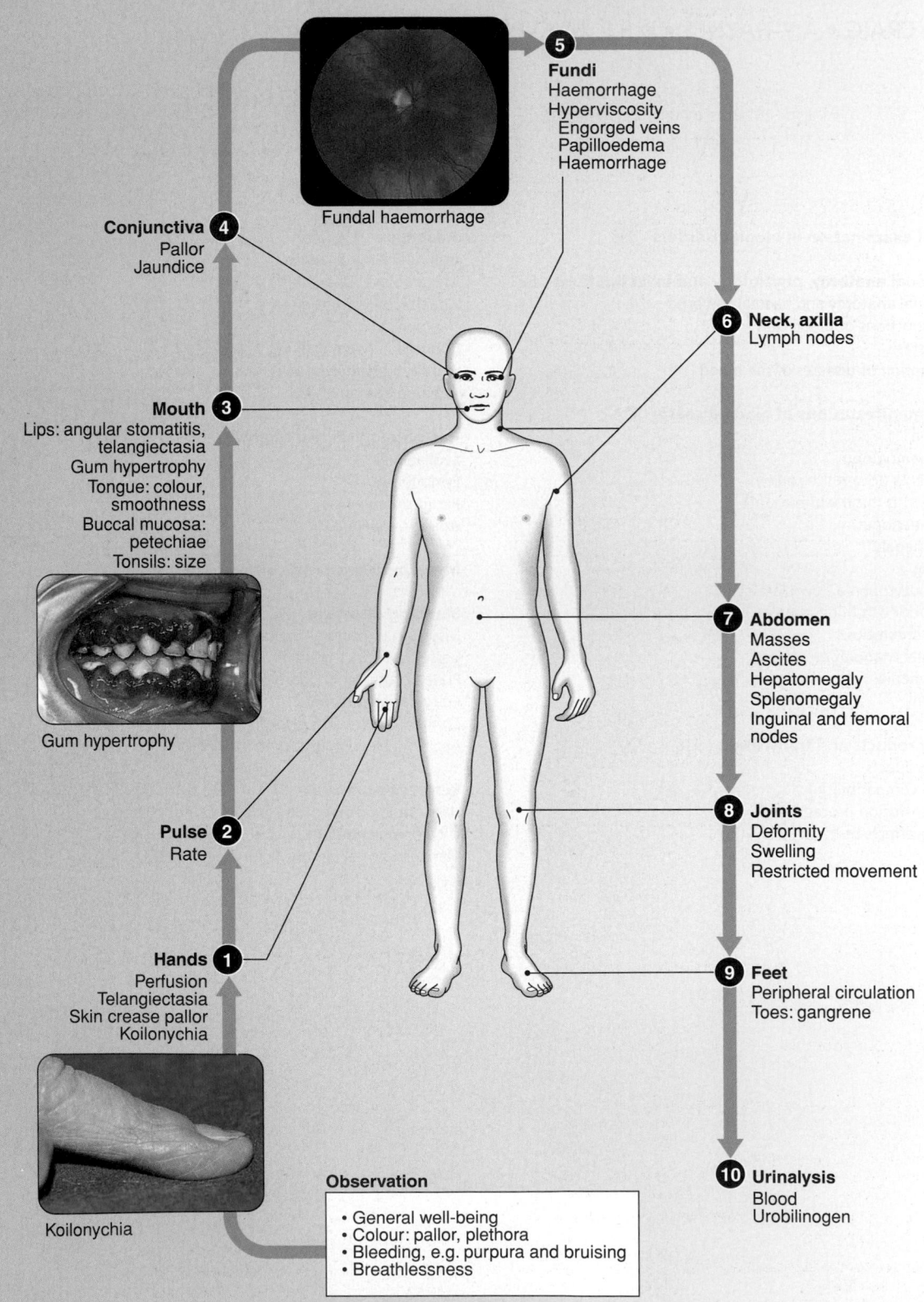

5 **Fundi**
Haemorrhage
Hyperviscosity
Engorged veins
Papilloedema
Haemorrhage

Fundal haemorrhage

Conjunctiva **4**
Pallor
Jaundice

6 **Neck, axilla**
Lymph nodes

Mouth **3**
Lips: angular stomatitis,
    telangiectasia
Gum hypertrophy
Tongue: colour,
    smoothness
Buccal mucosa:
    petechiae
Tonsils: size

Gum hypertrophy

7 **Abdomen**
Masses
Ascites
Hepatomegaly
Splenomegaly
Inguinal and femoral
nodes

Pulse **2**
Rate

8 **Joints**
Deformity
Swelling
Restricted movement

Hands **1**
Perfusion
Telangiectasia
Skin crease pallor
Koilonychia

9 **Feet**
Peripheral circulation
Toes: gangrene

Koilonychia

Observation

- General well-being
- Colour: pallor, plethora
- Bleeding, e.g. purpura and bruising
- Breathlessness

10 **Urinalysis**
Blood
Urobilinogen

❹ ANAEMIA

The box shows the symptoms and signs that will help to indicate the clinical severity of anaemia.

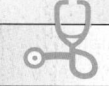

ANAEMIA
Search for symptoms and signs indicating the cause of anaemia
Non-specific symptoms
• Tiredness • Lightheadedness • Breathlessness • Ankle-swelling • Worsening of any previous coexisting disease such as angina
Non-specific signs
• Mucous membrane pallor • Tachypnoea • Raised jugular venous pressure • Flow murmurs • Ankle oedema • Postural hypotension • Tachycardia

BLEEDING

Bleeding can be due to congenital or acquired abnormalities in different components of the clotting system. The history and examination will help to clarify the severity and underlying cause of the bleeding problem.

BLEEDING
History
• Site of bleed • Duration of bleed • Precipitating causes including previous surgery • Family history • Drugs • Other medical conditions
Examination
There are two major patterns of bleeding:

1. **Abnormal platelets**
   Abnormal function (e.g. aspirin) or reduced numbers (e.g. leukaemia)
   • Skin: petechiae, bruises
   • Gum and mucous membrane bleeding
   • Fundal haemorrhages

2. **Abnormal coagulation cascade**
   (e.g. haemophilia)
   • Bleeding into joints (haemarthrosis)
   • Bleeding into soft tissues

Abnormalities in the blood are caused not only by primary diseases of the blood and lymphoreticular systems but also by diseases affecting other systems of the body. The clinical assessment of patients with haematological abnormalities must include a general history and examination as well as a search for symptoms and signs of abnormalities of red cells, white cells, platelets, bleeding and clotting systems, lymph nodes and lymphoreticular tissues.

❻ LYMPHADENOPATHY

Lymphadenopathy can be caused by benign or malignant disease. The clinical points to clarify are shown in the box.

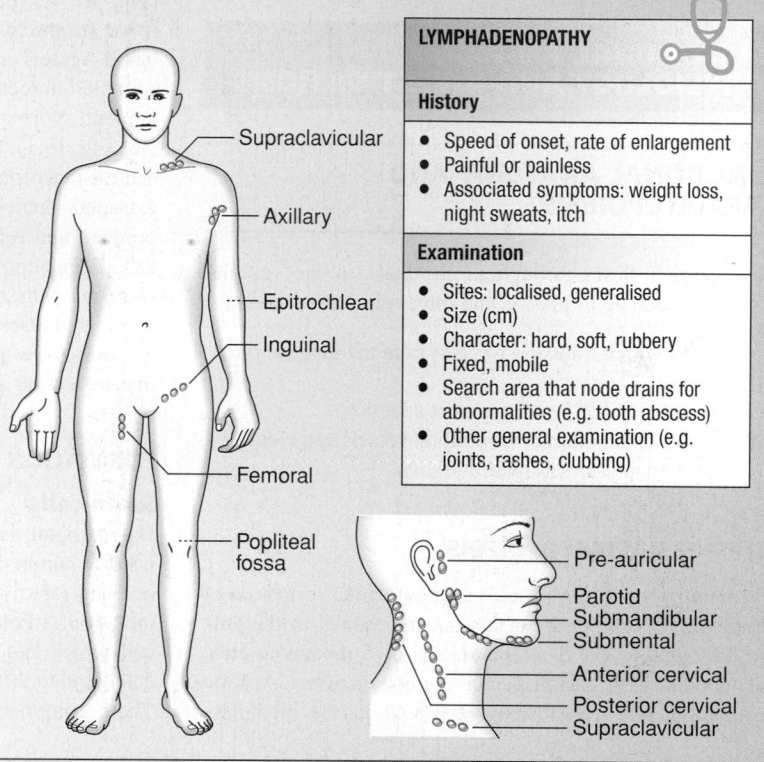

LYMPHADENOPATHY
History
• Speed of onset, rate of enlargement • Painful or painless • Associated symptoms: weight loss, night sweats, itch
Examination
• Sites: localised, generalised • Size (cm) • Character: hard, soft, rubbery • Fixed, mobile • Search area that node drains for abnormalities (e.g. tooth abscess) • Other general examination (e.g. joints, rashes, clubbing)

❼ EXAMINATION OF THE SPLEEN

• Move hand up from right iliac fossa, towards left upper quadrant on expiration.

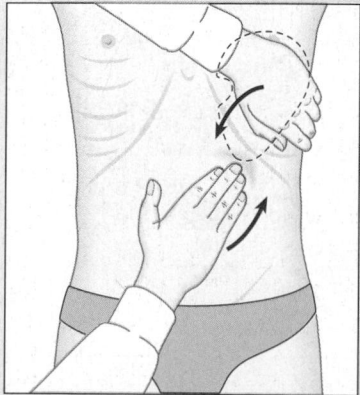

• Keep hand still and ask patient to take a deep breath through the mouth to feel spleen edge being displaced downwards.
• Place your left hand around patient's lower ribs and approach costal margin to pull spleen forward.
• To help palpate small spleens, roll patient on to the right side and examine as before.

CHARACTERISTICS OF THE SPLEEN
• Notch • Superficial • Dull to percussion • Cannot get between ribs and spleen • Moves well with respiration

Blood diseases cover a wide spectrum of illnesses ranging from the anaemias, amongst the most common disorders affecting mankind, to relatively rare conditions such as leukaemias and congenital coagulation disorders. Although the latter are uncommon, recent advances in their understanding at a cellular and molecular level are already beginning to impact on diagnosis and treatment. Haematological change may occur as a consequence of disease affecting any system and measurement of haematological parameters is an important routine part of clinical assessment.

FUNCTIONAL ANATOMY, PHYSIOLOGY AND INVESTIGATIONS

FUNCTIONAL ANATOMY AND HAEMATOPOIESIS

Blood which flows throughout the body in the vascular system is made up of plasma and three cellular components:

- red cells, which transport oxygen from the lungs to the tissues
- white cells, which protect against infection
- platelets, which interact with blood vessels and clotting factors to maintain vascular integrity.

SITES OF HAEMATOPOIESIS

Haematopoiesis is the process relating to the formation of blood cells. In the embryo this occurs initially in the yolk sac, followed by the liver and spleen; by 5 months in utero haematopoiesis is established in the bone marrow. At birth haematopoietic (red) marrow is found in the medullary cavity of all bones, but with age this becomes progressively replaced by fat (yellow marrow) so that by adulthood haematopoiesis is restricted to the vertebrae, pelvis, sternum, ribs, clavicles, skull, upper humeri and proximal femora. Bone marrow usually accounts for 5% of an adult's weight but red marrow can expand in response to increased demands for blood cells.

Bone marrow occupies the intertrabecular spaces in trabecular bone and contains a range of immature haematopoietic precursor cells and a storage pool of mature cells for release at times of increased demand. Haematopoietic cells are set in, and interact closely with, a connective tissue stroma made of reticular cells, macrophages, fat cells, blood vessels and nerve fibres. This stroma provides the suitable microenvironment for blood cell growth and development. Normal marrow has a characteristic organisation (see Fig. 19.1). Nests of red cell precursors cluster around a central macrophage which provides iron and phagocytoses extruded nuclei. Megakaryocytes are large cells which produce and release platelets into vascular sinuses. White cell precursors are clustered next to the bone trabeculae; maturing cells migrate into the marrow spaces towards the vascular sinuses. Plasma cells normally represent 5% or less of the marrow population and are scattered throughout the intertrabecular spaces.

FORMATION OF BLOOD CELLS

Stem cells

Haematopoiesis is an active process that must maintain normal numbers of circulating blood cells and be able to respond rapidly to increased demands such as bleeding or infection. All blood cells are derived from a pluripotent stem cell which has the ability to self-renew (make more stem cells) and to differentiate to form any of the blood elements. These comprise only 0.01% of the total marrow cells and

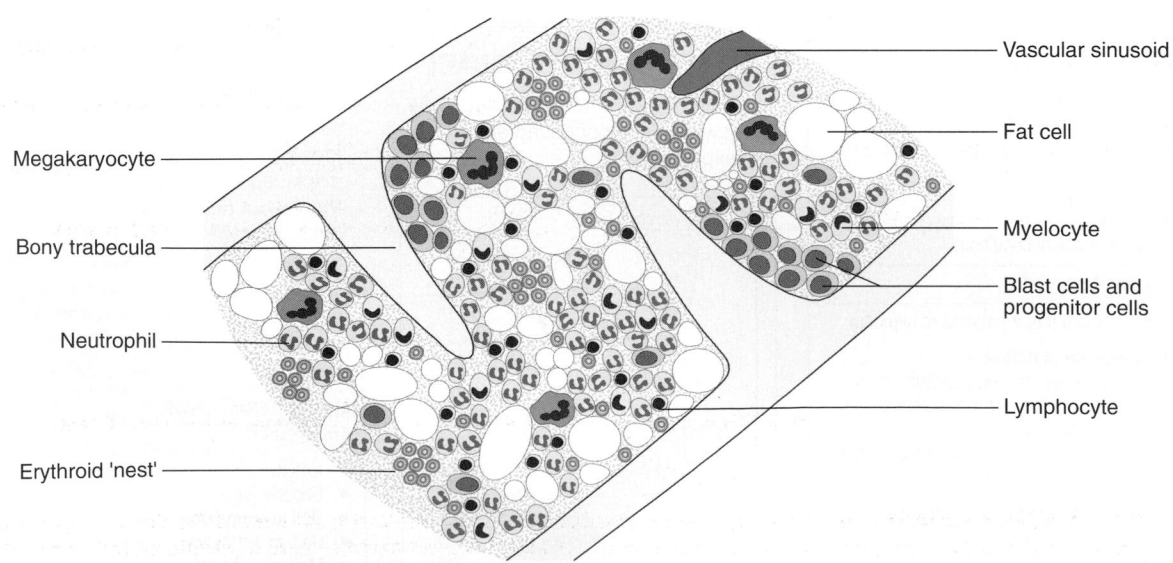

Megakaryocyte

Bony trabecula

Neutrophil

Erythroid 'nest'

Vascular sinusoid

Fat cell

Myelocyte

Blast cells and progenitor cells

Lymphocyte

Fig. 19.1 **Structural organisation of normal bone marrow.**

produce a hierarchy of lineage-committed stem cells. As primitive progenitor cells cannot be distinguished morphologically, they are named according to the types of cells (or colonies) they form during cell culture experiments. CFU-GM (colony-forming unit-granulocyte, monocyte) is a stem cell that produces granulocytic and monocytic lines. CFU-E produces erythroid cells and CFU-Meg produces megakaryocytes and ultimately platelets (see Fig. 19.2). The proliferation and differentiation of stem cells and their progeny are under the control of a range of growth factors produced by several cells including stromal cells and lymphocytes. These growth factors bind to specific receptors on the cell surface and promote not only proliferation and differentiation but also survival and function of mature cells. Growth factors are often synergistic with other growth factors. Some, such as granulocyte macrophage colony stimulating factor (GM-CSF), interleukin-3 (IL-3) and stem cell factor (SCF), act on a wide number of cell types at both early and late time points. Others, such as erythropoietin (Epo), granulocyte colony stimulating factor (G-CSF) and thrombopoietin (Tpo), are lineage-specific. Many of these growth factors are now synthesised by recombinant DNA technology and are available for clinical use.

Red cells
Red cell precursors formed from the erythroid progenitor cells are called erythroblasts or normoblasts (see Fig. 19.3).

These nucleated cells divide and acquire haemoglobin which turns the cytoplasm pink; the nucleus then condenses and is extruded from the cell. The first non-nucleated red cell is a reticulocyte which still contains ribosomal material in the cytoplasm. Under normal staining conditions reticulocytes are large cells with a faint blue tinge which is termed polychromasia. Reticulocytes lose their ribosomal material and mature over 3 days, during which time they are released into the circulation. Increased numbers of circulating reticulocytes (reticulocytosis) reflect increased erythropoiesis. Red cell production is controlled by erythropoietin, a polypeptide hormone produced by renal tubular cells in response to hypoxia. Erythropoietin stimulates committed erythroid stem cells to proliferate and decreases maturation time. Patients with renal failure (see p. 594) are anaemic due to failure of erythropoietin production, and exogenous recombinant hormone can be used to treat this anaemia.

White cells
Granulocytes (neutrophils, eosinophils, basophils) and monocytes are formed from the CFU-GM progenitor cell. The first recognisable granulocyte in the marrow is the myeloblast, a large cell with a small amount of basophilic cytoplasm and a primitive nucleus. As the cells divide and mature, the nucleus segments and the cytoplasm acquires specific neutrophilic, eosinophilic or basophilic granules (see Fig. 19.3). This takes about 14 days.

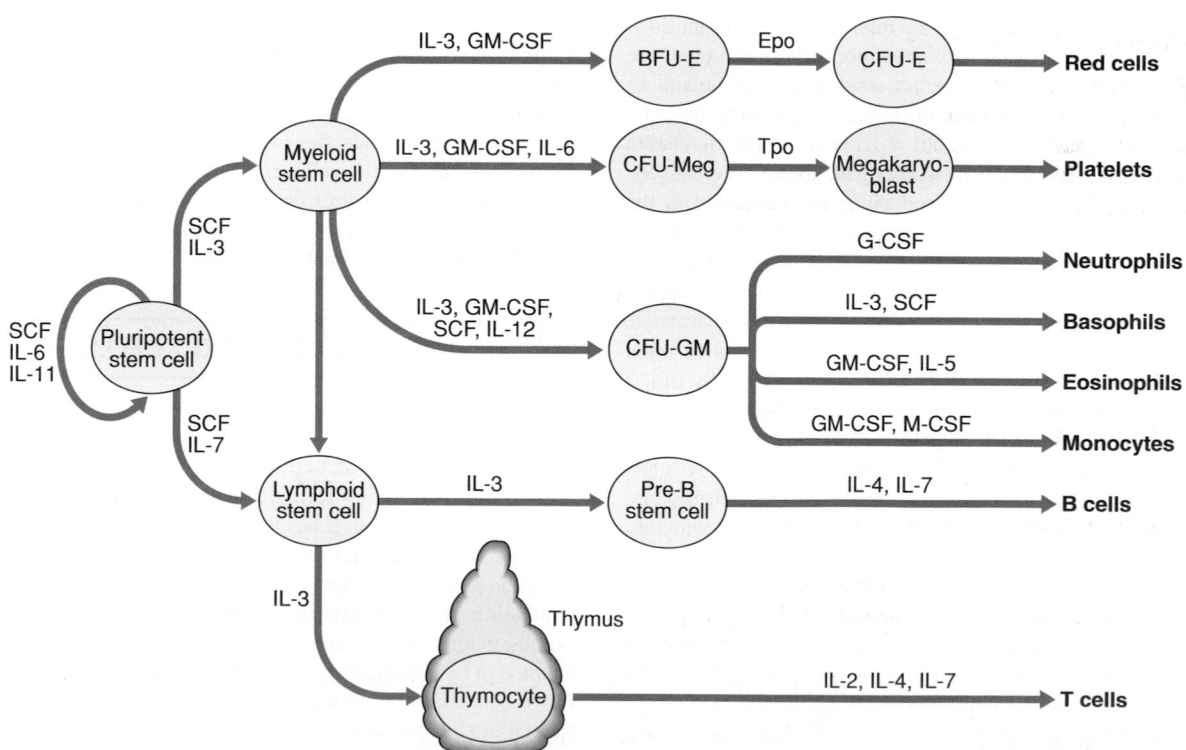

Fig. 19.2 Stem cells and growth factors in haematopoietic cell development. (BFU-E = blast-forming unit-erythroid; CFU-Meg = colony-forming unit-megakaryocyte; CFU-GM = colony-forming unit-granulocyte, monocyte; CFU-E = colony-forming unit-erythroid; IL = interleukin; SCF = stem cell factor; GM-CSF = granulocyte macrophage colony stimulating factor; Epo = erythropoietin; Tpo = thrombopoietin; G-CSF = granulocyte colony stimulating factor; M-CSF = macrophage colony stimulating factor)

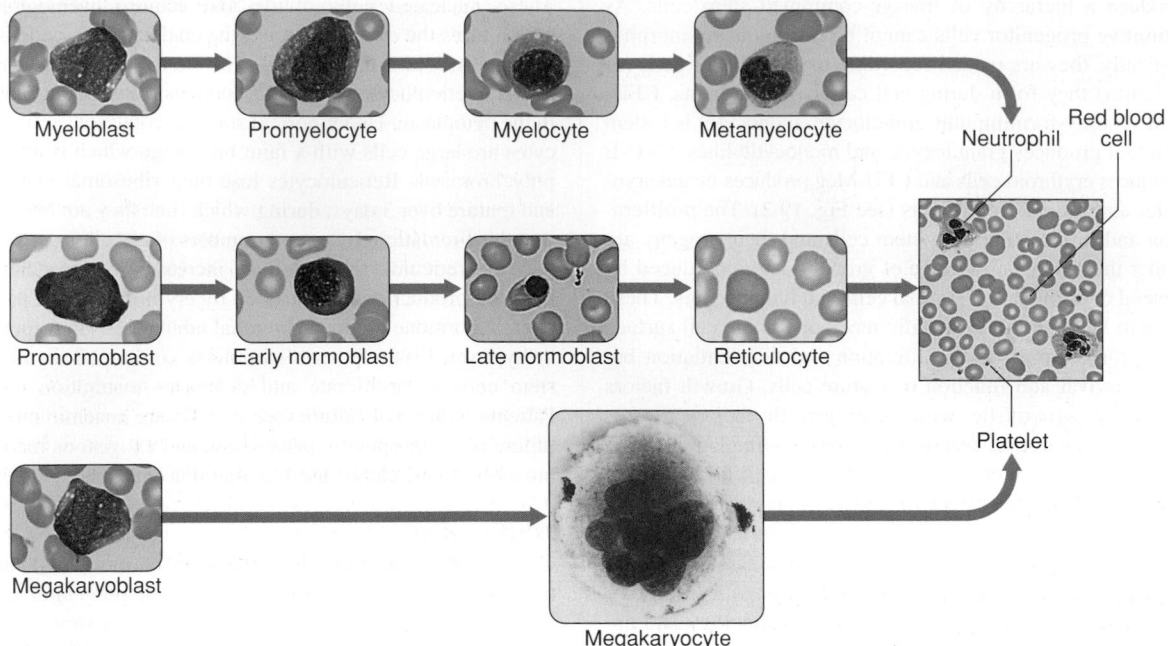

Myeloblast → Promyelocyte → Myelocyte → Metamyelocyte → Neutrophil / Red blood cell

Pronormoblast → Early normoblast → Late normoblast → Reticulocyte

Megakaryoblast → Megakaryocyte → Platelet

Fig. 19.3 Maturation pathway of red cells, granulocytes and platelets.

A large storage pool of mature neutrophils exists in the bone marrow. Every day some 10^{14} neutrophils enter the circulation, where cells may be freely circulating or attached to endothelium in the marginating pool. These two pools are equal in size and factors such as exercise or catecholamines increase the cells flowing in the blood, so increasing the white cell count. Neutrophils spend 6–10 hours in the circulation before being removed principally by the spleen. Alternatively, they pass into the tissues and either are consumed in the inflammatory process or undergo apoptotic cell death and phagocytosis by macrophages. Myelocytes or metamyelocytes are normally only found in the marrow but may appear in the circulation in infection or toxic states. The appearance of more primitive myeloid precursors in the blood is often associated with the presence of nucleated red cells and is termed a 'leucoerythroblastic' picture; this indicates a serious disturbance of marrow function. Monocytes are large cells derived from monoblasts. These cells circulate for a few hours and then migrate into the tissues where they can mature into macrophages which can proliferate for years. The cytokines G-CSF, GM-CSF and M-CSF are involved in the production of myeloid cells and can be used clinically, e.g. to hasten recovery of blood neutrophil counts after chemotherapy.

Lymphocytes are also derived from the pluripotent haematopoietic stem cell. There are two main types: T cells (80% of circulating lymphoid cells) and B cells. Lymphoid cells which migrate to the thymus develop into T cells, whereas B cells develop in the bone marrow.

Platelets

Platelets are derived from megakaryocytes. Megakaryocytic stem cells (CFU-Meg) divide to form a megakaryoblast;

megakaryocytes are formed by endomitotic reduplication where the nucleus divides but not the cell. Thus mature megakaryocytes are large cells with several nuclei and cytoplasm containing platelet granules. Up to 3000 platelets then fragment off from each megakaryocyte into the circulation in the marrow sinusoids. The formation and maturation of megakaryocytes are under the influence of Tpo, a recombinant form of which is in clinical use. Platelets circulate for 8–14 days before they are destroyed in the reticulo-endothelial system. Some 30% of peripheral platelets are normally pooled in the spleen and not circulating.

MAJOR FUNCTIONS OF BLOOD CELLS

RED CELLS

The mature red cell is an 8 μm biconcave disc which delivers oxygen to the tissues from the lungs, and carbon dioxide in the reverse direction. It has no nucleus and no mitochondria; the normal red cell lifespan is about 120 days and in this time it will travel approximately 300 miles around the circulation. Red cells have to pass through the smallest capillaries in the circulation and their membrane structure is adapted to be deformable. The membrane has a lipid bilayer to which a 'skeleton' of filamentous proteins is attached via special linkage proteins (see Fig. 19.4). Inherited abnormalities of any of these proteins result in loss of membrane as cells pass through the spleen, and the formation of abnormally shaped cells called spherocytes or elliptocytes (see p. 922). Red cells are exposed to osmotic stress in the pulmonary and renal circulation; to maintain normal homeostasis, the

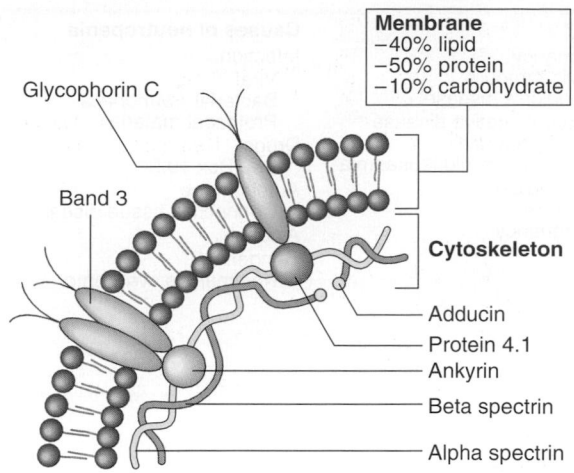

Fig. 19.4   Normal structure of red cell membrane.

membrane contains ion pumps which control intracellular levels of sodium, potassium, chloride and bicarbonate. The energy for these functions is provided by the metabolic pathways of the cytosol; 90% of glucose metabolism occurs via anaerobic glycolysis which produces adenosine triphosphate (ATP), and 10% via the pentose phosphate pathway which produces nicotinamide adenine dinucleotide phosphate (NADPH). Membrane proteins inserted into the lipid bilayer also form the antigens recognised by blood grouping. The ABO and Rhesus systems are the most commonly recognised (see p. 912) but over 400 blood group antigens have been described.

Haemoglobin

Haemoglobin is a protein specially adapted for gas transport to and from the lungs. It is composed of four globin chains, each containing an iron-containing porphyrin pigment termed haem. Globin chains are a combination of two alpha and two non-alpha chains; haemoglobin A ($\alpha\alpha/\beta\beta$) represents over 90% of adult haemoglobin, whereas haemoglobin F ($\alpha\alpha/\gamma\gamma$) is the predominant type in the fetus. Each haem molecule contains a ferrous ion (Fe^{++}) to which oxygen reversibly binds; the final oxygen to bind does so with 20 times the affinity of the first. When oxygen is bound, the beta chains 'swing' closer together; they move apart as oxygen is lost. In the 'open' deoxygenated state, 2,3 diphosphoglycerate (DPG), a product of red cell metabolism, binds to the haemoglobin molecule and lowers its oxygen affinity. These complex interactions produce the sigmoid shape of the oxygen dissociation curve (see Fig. 19.5). The position of this curve depends upon the concentrations of 2,3 DPG, H^+ ions and CO_2; increased levels shift the curve to the right and cause oxygen to be released more readily. Tissue hypoxia increases all three and favours increased availability of oxygen from the red cell. Haemoglobin F is unable to bind 2,3 DPG and has a left-shifted oxygen dissociation curve; this increased affinity, together with the low pH of fetal blood, ensures fetal oxygenation. Amino acid mutations affecting the haem-binding pockets of globin chains or the 'hinge' interactions between globin chains result

in haemoglobinopathies or unstable haemoglobins. Alpha globin chains are produced by two genes on chromosome 16 and beta globin chains by a single gene on chromosome 11; imbalance in the production of globin chains produces the thalassaemias (see p. 928).

Destruction

Red cells at the end of their lifespan are phagocytosed by the reticulo-endothelial system. Amino acids from globin chains are recycled and iron is removed from haem for reuse in haemoglobin synthesis. The remnant haem structure is degraded to bilirubin and conjugated to glucuronic acid before being excreted into bile. In the small bowel, bilirubin is converted to stercobilin; most of this is excreted, but a small amount is reabsorbed and excreted by the kidney as urobilinogen. Increased red cell destruction due to haemolysis or ineffective haematopoiesis will result in jaundice and increased urinary urobilinogen. Free intravascular haemoglobin is toxic and haptoglobins are plasma proteins produced by the liver which normally bind free haemoglobin in the circulation.

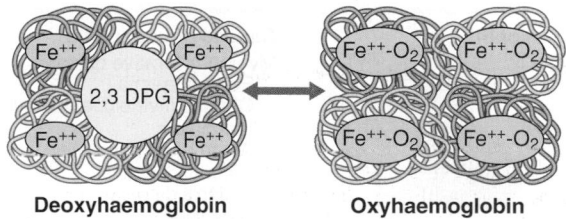

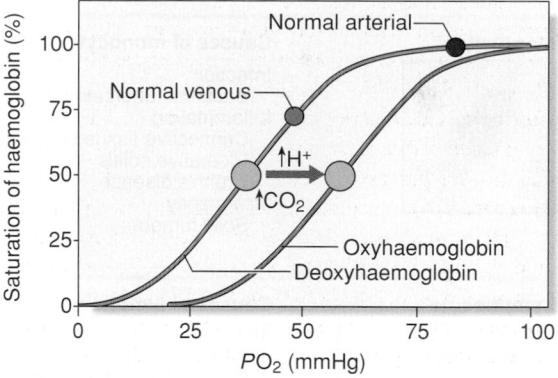

Fig. 19.5   Structure of the normal haemoglobin molecule and its relationship to the oxygen dissociation curve. (See text for details.)

WHITE CELLS

White cells or leucocytes in the blood consist of granulocytes (neutrophils, eosinophils and basophils), monocytes and lymphocytes (see Fig. 19.6).

Neutrophils

Neutrophils, the most common white blood cells in the blood of adults, are 10–14 µm in diameter with a multilobular nucleus containing two to five segments and granules in their cytoplasm. Their main function is to recognise, ingest and destroy foreign particles and microorganisms.

Neutrophil

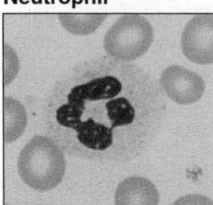

Causes of neutrophilia

Infection
  Bacterial
  Fungal
Trauma
  Surgery
  Burns
Infarction
  Myocardial infarct
  Pulmonary embolus
  Sickle-cell crisis
Inflammation
  Gout
  Rheumatoid arthritis
  Ulcerative colitis
  Crohn's disease

Malignancy
  Solid tumours
  Hodgkin's disease
Myeloproliferative disease
  Polycythaemia
  Chronic myeloid leukaemia
Physiological
  Exercise
  Pregnancy

Causes of neutropenia

Infection
  Viral
  Bacterial *Salmonella*
  Protozoal malaria
Drugs
  See Box 19.9
Autoimmune
  Connective tissue disease
Alcohol
Congenital
  Kostmann's syndrome

Eosinophil

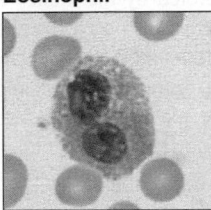

Causes of eosinophilia

Allergy
  Hay fever
  Asthma
  Eczema
Infection
  Parasitic
Drug hypersensitivity
  e.g. gold, sulphonamides

Skin disease
Connective tissue disease
  Polyarteritis nodosa
Malignancy
  Solid tumours
  Lymphomas

Basophil

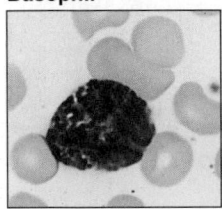

Causes of basophilia

Myeloproliferative disease
  Polycythaemia
  Chronic myeloid leukaemia
Inflammation
  Acute hypersensitivity
  Ulcerative colitis
  Crohn's disease
Iron deficiency

Monocyte

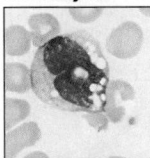

Causes of monocytosis

Infection
  Bacterial tuberculosis
Inflammation
  Connective tissue disease
  Ulcerative colitis
  Crohn's disease
Malignancy
  Solid tumours

Lymphocyte

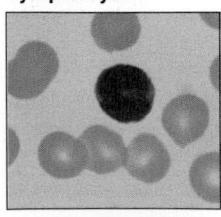

Causes of lymphocytosis

Infection
  Viral
  Bacterial, *Bordetella pertussis*
Lymphoproliferative disease
  Chronic lymphatic leukaemia
  Lymphoma
Post-splenectomy

Causes of lymphopenia

Inflammation
  Connective tissue disease
Lymphoma
Renal failure
Sarcoidosis
Drugs
  Steroids
  Cytotoxics
Congenital
  Severe combined
  immunodeficiency

Fig. 19.6 Normal white blood cells.

Two main types of granule are recognised: primary or azurophil granules, and the more numerous secondary or specific granules. Primary granules contain myeloperoxidase and other proteins which are important for killing ingested microbes. Secondary granules contain a number of membrane proteins such as adhesion molecules and components of the NADPH oxidase with which neutrophils produce superoxide anions for microbial killing. These fuse with the plasma membrane upon degranulation and the granule contents, such as lactoferrin, are released extracellularly. Granule staining becomes more intense in response to infection and is termed 'toxic granulation'.

Eosinophils

Eosinophils represent 1–6% of the circulating white cells. They are a similar size to neutrophils but have a bilobed nucleus and prominent orange granules on Romanowsky staining. Eosinophils are phagocytic and their granules contain a peroxidase capable of generating reactive oxygen species and proteins involved in the intracellular killing of protozoa and helminths (see p. 69). They are also involved in allergic reactions (e.g. atopic asthma, p. 514).

Basophils

These cells are less common than eosinophils, representing less than 1% of circulating white cells. They contain dense black granules which obscure the nucleus. Mast cells resemble basophils but these are only found in the tissues. Basophils bind IgE antibody on their surface, and exposure to specific antigen results in degranulation with release of histamine, leukotrienes and heparin. These cells are involved in hypersensitivity reactions.

Monocytes

Monocytes are the largest of the white cells, with a diameter of 12–20 μm and an irregular nucleus in abundant pale blue cytoplasm containing occasional cytoplasmic vacuoles. These cells migrate into the tissue where they become macrophages, Kupffer cells or antigen-presenting dendritic cells. The former phagocytose debris, apoptotic cells and microorganisms. They produce a variety of cytokines when activated, such as interleukin-1, tumour necrosis factor-α and GM-CSF.

Lymphocytes

In children up to 7 years old lymphocytes are the most abundant white cell in the blood. They are heterogeneous, with the smallest cells the size of red cells and the largest cells the size of neutrophils. Small lymphocytes are circular with scanty cytoplasm but the larger cells are more irregular with abundant blue cytoplasm. The majority of lymphocytes in the circulation are T cells (80%), which can be recognised by their expression of the CD antigens CD1, 2, 3, 4, 5, 7 and 8. The T cells mediate cellular immunity and two major types are recognised: CD4 positive helper cells and CD8 positive suppressor cells. The B cells mediate humoral immunity and can be recognised by their expression of immunoglobulin light chains (kappa or lambda in a ratio of 2:1). Lymphocyte subpopulations can be defined with specific functions and their lifespan can vary from several days to many years.

HAEMOSTASIS

With the evolution of the circulation as a transport system, an efficient mechanism has developed not only to prevent blood loss from a damaged vessel to secure haemostasis but also to prevent the inappropriate cessation of flow. Haemostasis depends upon interactions between the vessel wall, platelets and clotting factors. Two phases of haemostasis can be recognised: primary and secondary. In the initial primary phase, the damaged vessel contracts and platelets aggregate at the site of damage to form a plug to arrest haemorrhage. This occurs over a number of minutes and is followed by the secondary deposition of a fibrin mesh to secure the platelet plug. These two processes are interlinked; damaged endothelium and the subendothelial matrix activate platelets, which then provide the optimal surface for the binding of the plasma clotting factors; their sequential activation results in the generation of insoluble fibrin.

PLATELETS

Under normal conditions platelets are discoid in shape, with a diameter of 2–4 μm (see Fig. 19.7). The surface membrane

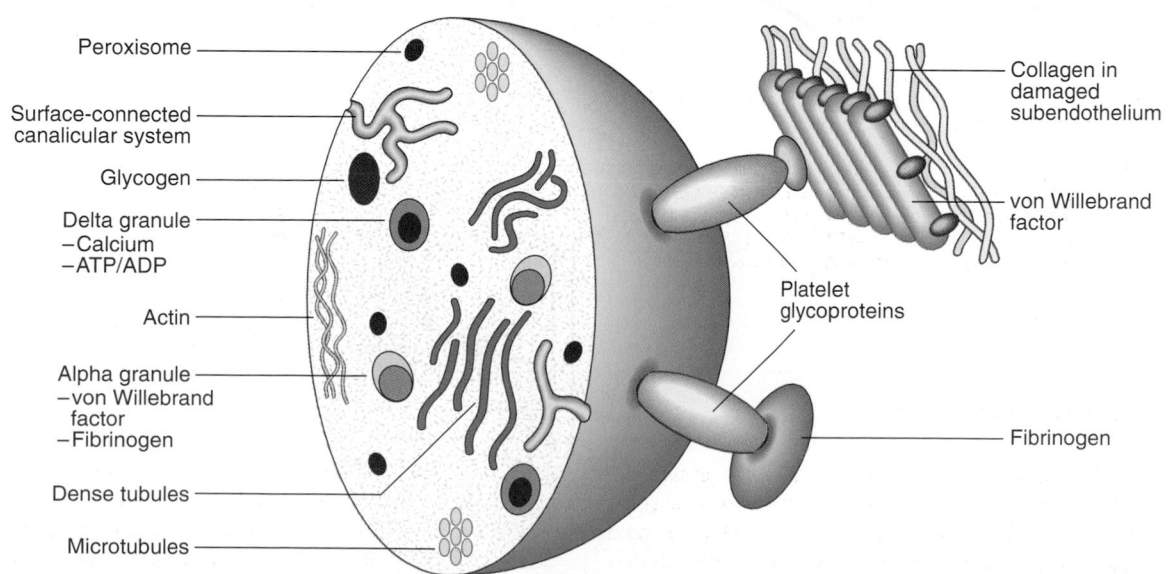

Fig. 19.7   Normal platelet structure. (ATP = adenosine triphosphate; ADP = adenosine diphosphate)

invaginates to form a tubular network, the canalicular system. This provides a large surface area of phospholipid on to which clotting factors bind. Three types of granule are present in the cytoplasm; alpha granules contain fibrinogen and von Willebrand factor, dense (delta) granules store adenosine diphosphate (ADP) and 5-hydroxytryptamine (5-HT, serotonin), and lysosomes contain acid hydrolases.

When platelets are activated by ADP, thrombin or collagen they contract to become spherical and extend pseudopodia which adhere to the subendothelium and other platelets. Upon activation, platelet granules discharge their contents, which encourages further platelet aggregation and fibrin formation. At the same time, arachidonic acid is released from the platelet membrane and converted by cyclo-oxygenase to endoperoxides and the powerful platelet aggregating agent, thromboxane A2. Aspirin and non-steroidal anti-inflammatory drugs irreversibly inhibit platelet cyclo-oxygenase and impair platelet function. Platelet-binding to the subendothelium is dependent on high molecular weight von Willebrand factor released from endothelial cells, which bridges the gap between platelet membrane glycoproteins and subendothelial collagen.

Interplatelet aggregation is dependent upon fibrinogen binding to platelet glycoproteins.

CLOTTING FACTORS

The coagulation system consists of a series of soluble inactive zymogen proteins designated by roman numerals. When proteolytically cleaved and activated, each is capable of activating one or more components of the cascade. Activated factors are designated by the suffix 'a'. Some of these reactions require phospholipid and calcium. Two pathways of activation are recognised, named the 'extrinsic' and 'intrinsic' pathways. However, recent understanding has shown that the extrinsic pathway, where coagulation is initiated by factor VII interacting with tissue factor (TF), is the main physiological mechanism in vivo (see Fig. 19.8). TF is a transmembrane protein expressed widely in the body, including the epidermis, monocytes, organ capsules, gastrointestinal and respiratory tracts, the brain and renal glomeruli. Moreover, it is expressed during endothelial cell damage. Factor VII circulates in the plasma and can be activated to factor VIIa by TF, factors Xa, IXa, XIIa and

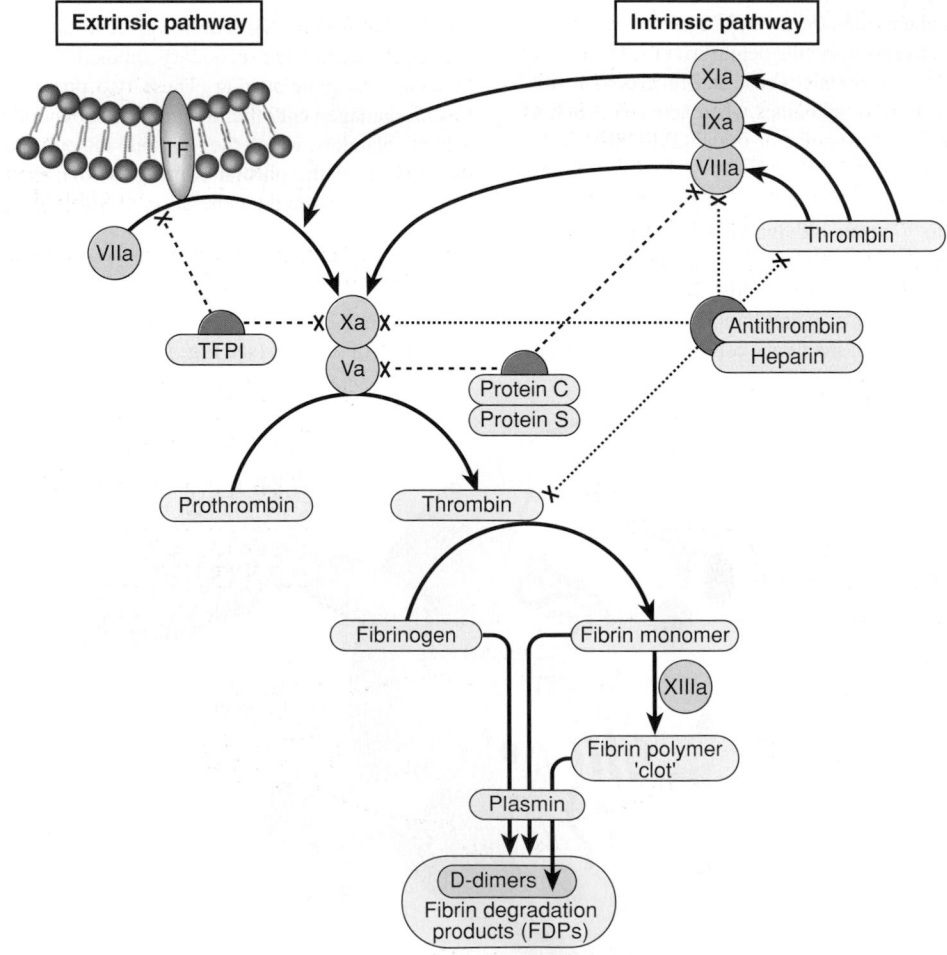

Fig. 19.8 Normal haemostatic mechanisms: clotting factors of the intrinsic and extrinsic pathways. Broken lines signify inhibitory activity. (TFPI = tissue factor pathway inhibition)

VIIa, and thrombin. During coagulation, TF complexes with factor VIIa, which activates factor X. Factor Xa forms a complex with factor V on the surface of activated platelets which converts prothrombin to thrombin and this in turn converts fibrinogen to fibrin monomer, which polymerises and is cross-linked by factor XIII to form stable clot. Thrombin plays a crucial role in this 'final common pathway'; factors XI, VIII, V and platelets are activated by thrombin, which generates a positive feedback loop. Congenital deficiencies of any of these factors will result in a bleeding diathesis. Tests of coagulation are shown in Box 19.3, page 901.

Clotting factors are synthesised by the liver; factor V is also produced by platelets and endothelial cells. The vitamin K-dependent factors II, VII, IX and X are produced as inactive proteins. These factors are rich in glutamic acid (Gla) residues, which must be further carboxylated to permit calcium-binding and association with phospholipid to generate an active catalytic site. The carboxylase enzyme responsible for this in the liver uses vitamin K as a cofactor (see Fig. 19.9). Vitamin K is converted to an epoxide in this reaction and must be regenerated to its active form by a reductase enzyme. This reductase is inhibited by warfarin and this mechanism forms the basis of the anticoagulant effect of coumarins (see p. 955).

To prevent inappropriate activity of the clotting cascade, natural inhibitors of the clotting systems are present (see Figs 19.8 and 19.10). The TF-VIIa complex, along with factor Xa, is rapidly inactivated by tissue factor pathway inhibitor (TFPI). Antithrombin is a protein produced by the liver which also has inhibitory activity, principally against thrombin and factor Xa. When antithrombin binds to heparin, however, this inhibitory activity is markedly accelerated and this forms the basis of the anticoagulant action of heparin. Protein C is a vitamin K-dependent factor produced by the liver; when activated by interaction with protein S, it degrades and inactivates factor Va. These natural inhibitors provide powerful mechanisms to prevent excessive coagulation in the circulation and hence abnormalities in their function result in a tendency to thrombosis (see p. 953).

FIBRINOLYSIS

The excessive deposition of fibrin within the circulation is prevented in health by the fibrinolytic system (see Fig. 19.10). This pathway is principally initiated by tissue plasminogen

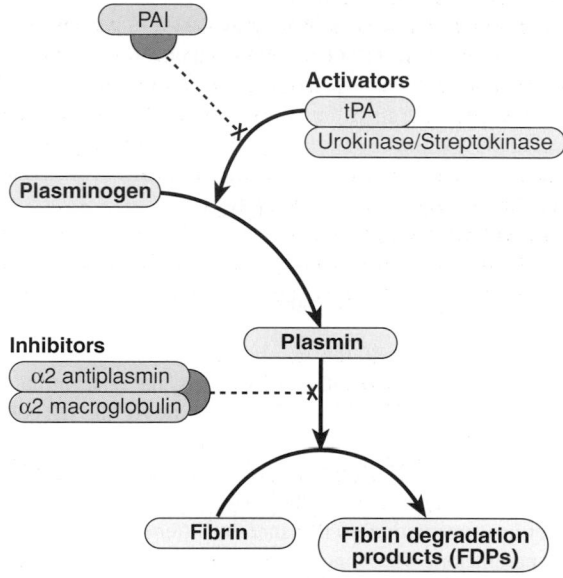

Fig. 19.10   Fibrinolysis. (tPA = tissue plasminogen activator; PAI = plasminogen activator inhibitor)

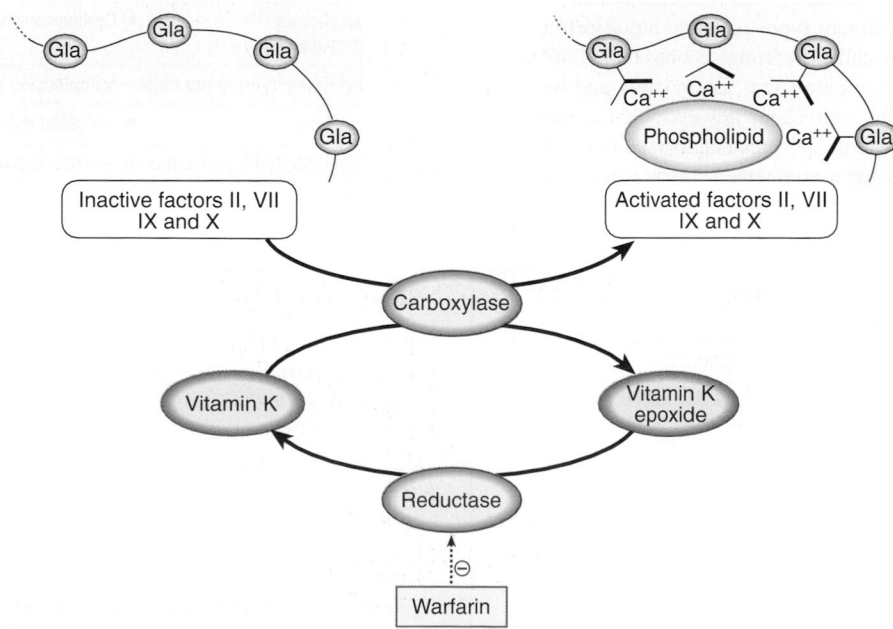

Fig. 19.9   The role of vitamin K in clotting and the mechanism of action of warfarin.

activator (tPA) which is released from endothelial cells. Some fibrinolysis is also promoted by the activator uro-kinase which is synthesised in the kidney and helps prevent obstruction to the urinary system by small clots of blood. These activators convert the circulating inactive zymogen plasminogen to the active enzyme plasmin which hydrolyses fibrin. Within intravascular thrombi both tPA and plasminogen bind to cross-linked fibrin, leading to the formation of plasmin which lyses the developing thrombus. The digested fibrin fragments, D-dimers, can be detected within the circulation and their concentration is usually raised in the presence of venous thrombosis.

Excessive tPA activity in the circulation is prevented by the presence of a further plasma component, plasminogen activator inhibitor (PAI), and plasmin is inactivated by α2 antiplasmin.

INVESTIGATION OF DISEASES OF THE BLOOD

THE FULL BLOOD COUNT

The measurement of the number of circulating red cells (RBC), white cells (WBC) and platelets, the concentration of haemoglobin (Hb) and the characteristics of the red cells is called the full blood count (FBC). Anticoagulated blood is processed through automatic blood analysers which use a variety of technologies (particle-sizing, radiofrequency and laser instrumentation) to measure the different haematological parameters. These include numbers of circulating cells, the proportion of red cells present in blood (the haematocrit, Hct), and the red cell indices which give information about the size of red cells (mean cell volume, MCV) and the amount of haemoglobin present in the red cells (mean cell haemoglobin concentration, MCH). Modern blood analysers can detect the different types of white blood cell and give automated white cell differential counts including neutrophils, lymphocytes, monocytes, eosinophils and basophils. It is important to appreciate, however, that a number of conditions can lead to spurious results (see Box 19.1). The reference values for a number of common haematological parameters in Caucasian adults are given in the Appendix.

19.1 SPURIOUS FBC RESULTS FROM AUTOANALYSERS	
Result	**Explanation**
Increased haemoglobin	Lipaemia, jaundice, very high white cell count
Reduced haemoglobin	Improper sample mixing, blood taken from vein into which an infusion is flowing
Increased red cell volume (MCV)	Cold agglutinins, non-ketotic hyperosmolarity
Increased white cell count	Nucleated red cells present
Reduced platelet count	Clot in sample, platelet clumping

BLOOD FILM EXAMINATION

Although the technical advances of modern full blood count analysers have resulted in fewer blood films requiring examination, scrutiny of the blood film can often yield invaluable information (see Box 19.2). Analysers cannot identify abnormalities of red cell shape and content (e.g. Howell–Jolly bodies, basophilic stippling, malarial parasites) or fully define abnormal white cells such as blasts.

19.2 COMMON RED CELL APPEARANCES AND THEIR CAUSES	
Microcytosis (reduced average cell size, MCV < 76 fl)	
• Iron deficiency • Thalassaemia	• Sideroblastic anaemia
Macrocytosis (increased average cell size, MCV > 100 fl)	
• Vitamin B$_{12}$/folate deficiency • Liver disease	• Hypothyroidism
Target cells (central area of haemoglobinisation)	
• Liver disease • Thalassaemia	• Post-splenectomy • HbC disease
Spherocytes (dense cells, no area of central pallor)	
• Autoimmune haemolysis • Disseminated intravascular coagulation (DIC)	• Post-splenectomy • Hereditary spherocytosis
Red cell fragments (intravascular haemolysis)	
• DIC	• Haemolytic uraemic syndrome/ thrombotic thrombocytopenic purpura
Nucleated red blood cells (normoblasts)	
• Marrow infiltration • Severe haemolysis	• Myelofibrosis
Howell–Jolly bodies (small round nuclear remnants)	
• Hyposplenism • Post-splenectomy	• Dyshaemopoiesis
Polychromasia (young red cells—reticulocytes present)	
• Haemolysis	• Increased red cell turnover
Basophilic stippling (abnormal ribosomes appear as blue dots)	
• Dyshaemopoiesis	• Lead poisoning

BONE MARROW EXAMINATION

In adults bone marrow examination is usually performed from the posterior iliac crest. After a local anaesthetic, marrow may be sucked out from the medullary space, stained and examined under the microscope (bone marrow aspirate). In addition, a core of bone may be removed (trephine biopsy), fixed and decalcified before sections are cut for staining (see Fig. 19.11). A bone marrow aspirate is used to assess the composition and morphology of haematopoietic cells or abnormal infiltrates. Further investigations may be performed such as cell surface marker analysis (immunophenotyping), chromosome and molecular studies to assess malignant disease, or marrow culture for

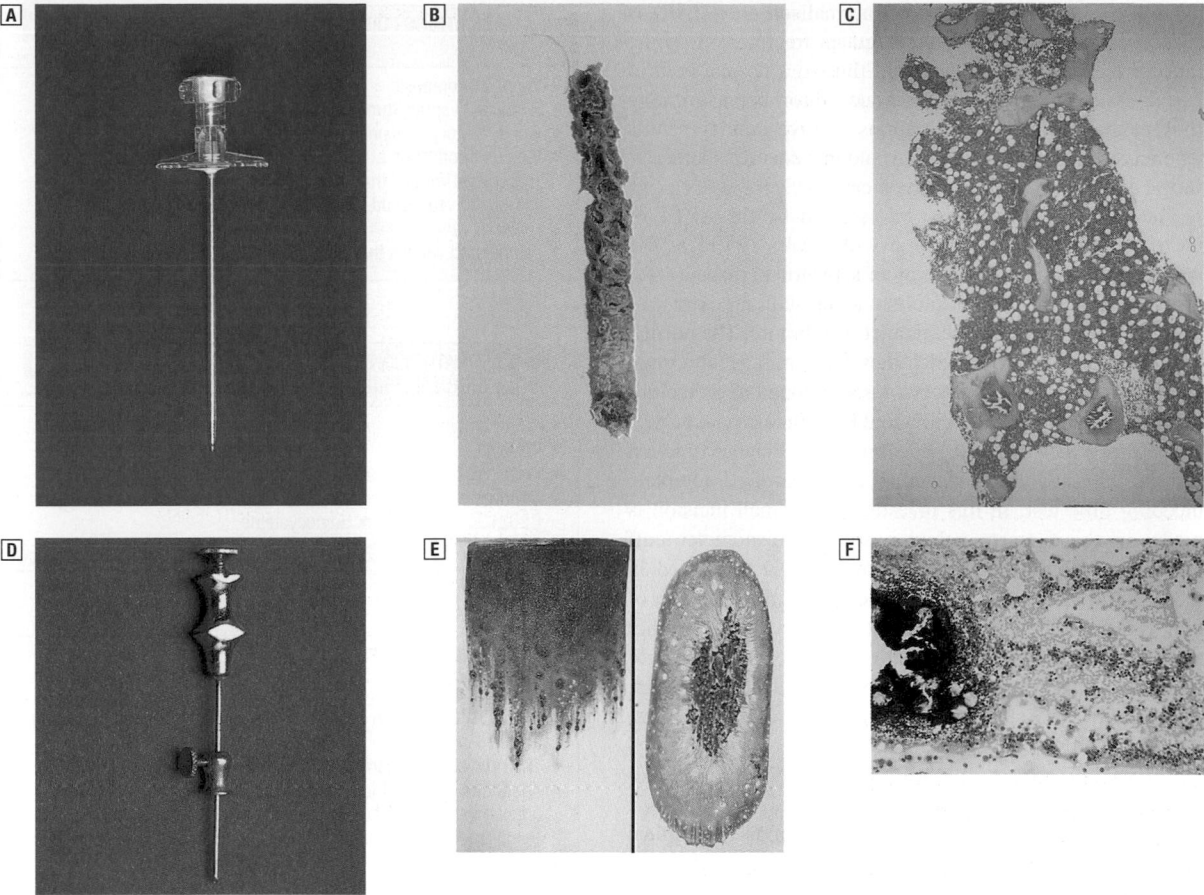

Fig. 19.11   Bone marrow aspirate and trephine. A Trephine biopsy needle. B Macroscopic appearance of a trephine biopsy. C Microscopic appearance of stained section of trephine. D Bone marrow aspirate needle. E Stained macroscopic appearance of marrow aspirate: smear (left) and squash (right). F Microscopic appearance of stained marrow particles and trails of haematopoietic cells.

suspected tuberculosis. A trephine biopsy is superior for assessing marrow cellularity, marrow fibrosis, and infiltration by abnormal cells such as metastatic carcinoma.

INVESTIGATION OF THE COAGULATION SYSTEM

Bleeding disorders

The investigation of a patient with a possible bleeding disorder is directed by the clinical circumstances (see p. 947). The initial blood screening tests comprise a platelet count, blood film, and coagulation tests including the prothrombin time (PT), activated partial thromboplastin time (APTT) and fibrinogen (see Box 19.3). Coagulation tests usually measure the length of time a plasma sample takes to clot after the clotting process is initiated by activators and calcium. The result of the test sample is compared with normal controls. The clot used to be detected manually by observation but tests are now automated, and utilise mechanical, electrical and light methods of clot detection.

The PT assesses the extrinsic system (see Fig. 19.8, p. 898). The patient's plasma is incubated with tissue factor and calcium. The reaction proceeds with the activation of factor X

19.3 COAGULATION SCREENING TESTS		
Investigation	**Normal range**	**Situations in which tests may be abnormal**
Platelet count	150–400 × 10⁹/l	Thrombocytopenia
Bleeding time	< 8 minutes	Thrombocytopenia Abnormal platelet function Deficiency of von Willebrand factor Vascular abnormalities
Prothrombin time (PT)	12–15 seconds	Deficiencies of factors II, V, VII or X
Activated partial thromboplastin time (APTT)	30–40 seconds	Deficiencies of factors II, V, VIII, IX, X, XI, XII Heparin Antibodies against clotting factors Lupus anticoagulant
Fibrinogen concentration	1.5–4.0 g/l	Hypofibrinogenaemia
N.B. International normalised ratio (INR) is not a coagulation screening test.		

by factor VIIa. The international normalised ratio (INR) is used only to control oral anticoagulant treatment. It is the ratio of the patient's prothrombin time to a normal control based on an international reference thromboplastin. The INR enables different laboratories to give similar results when assessing warfarin therapy and this ensures standardisation of anticoagulation between centres.

The intrinsic system may be assessed by the APTT or the partial thromboplastin time with kaolin (PTTK). The APTT is determined by adding an activator to plasma—for instance, a suspension of kaolin—along with an extract of phospholipid (to mimic the platelet membrane). The normal ranges and situations in which these tests may be abnormal are shown in Box 19.3. Special tests of coagulation including fibrinogen levels and individual factor assays can be performed as directed by the screening tests. Platelet function can be assessed by performing a standardised template bleeding time test. In this investigation a small incision is made on the forearm below a sphygmomanometer cuff inflated to 40 mmHg. The bleeding time is prolonged in those with platelet functional defects, thrombocytopenia or von Willebrand's disease. Platelet function can be further assessed by measuring aggregation in vitro in response to various agents, e.g. adrenaline (epinephrine) and collagen, or measuring the constituents of the intracellular granules, e.g. ATP/ADP.

Thrombotic disorders

The investigation of thrombosis depends upon the clinical situation (see Box 19.4). The available investigations to assess thrombophilia, i.e. the propensity to thrombosis, are set out in Box 19.5. Anticoagulants can alter either the concentration or the activity of several of the plasma factors and, if possible, blood samples should therefore be collected before, or after discontinuation of, anticoagulant therapy. On occasion this is not possible and the result has to be interpreted in the knowledge of the effect of the prevailing anticoagulant.

19.4 INDICATIONS FOR A THROMBOPHILIA SCREEN

• Venous thrombosis < 45 years
• Recurrent venous thrombosis
• Family history of venous thrombosis
• Venous thrombosis at an unusual site
  Cerebral venous thrombosis
  Hepatic vein (Budd–Chiari syndrome)
  Portal vein
• Arterial and venous thrombosis

19.5 LABORATORY INVESTIGATION OF THROMBOPHILIA
• Antithrombin • Protein C • Protein S • Prothrombin G20210A • Factor V Leiden • Thrombin/reptilase time (for dysfibrinogenaemia) • Antiphospholipid antibody/lupus anticoagulant/anticardiolipin antibody • Homocysteine

ISSUES IN OLDER PEOPLE HAEMATOLOGICAL FUNCTION
• Blood cell counts and film components are not altered by ageing alone. • The ratio of bone marrow cells to marrow fat falls in old age. • Adequate neutrophil function is maintained overall throughout life, although some studies suggest that leucocytes may be less readily mobilised by bacterial invasion in old age. • Lymphocytes are functionally compromised by age due to a T cell-related defect in cell-mediated immunity. • There are no major changes in clotting factors with age, although mild congenital deficiencies of these may be first noticed only in old age. • The erythrocyte sedimentation rate (ESR) is raised above the normal range in old age, but this appears to be associated with chronic or subacute disease. When truly healthy older people are assessed, the ESR range is very similar to that in younger people.

MAJOR MANIFESTATIONS OF BLOOD DISEASE

ANAEMIA

Anaemia refers to a state in which the level of haemoglobin in the blood is below the normal range appropriate for age and sex. Other factors including pregnancy and altitude also affect haemoglobin levels and must be taken into account when considering whether an individual is anaemic. The clinical features of anaemia reflect diminished oxygen supply to the tissue and depend upon the degree of anaemia, the rapidity of its development and the presence of cardiorespiratory disease. A rapid onset of anaemia (e.g. due to blood loss) will cause more profound symptoms than a gradually developing anaemia. Individuals with cardiorespiratory disease will have symptoms of anaemia at higher haemoglobin levels than those with normal cardiorespiratory function. The general symptoms and signs of anaemia are shown on page 891.

The diagnosis of anaemia must not only include the assessment of its clinical severity but also define the underlying cause. This rests on the clinical history and examination, assessment of the full blood count and blood film, and further appropriate investigations. Causes of anaemia are shown in Box 19.6.

History

• *Iron deficiency anaemia* (see p. 916) is the most common type of anaemia world-wide. A thorough gastrointestinal history is important, in particular looking for symptoms indicating blood loss.

19.6 CAUSES OF ANAEMIA

Decreased or ineffective marrow production

- Lack of iron, vitamin B$_{12}$ or folate
- Hypoplasia
- Invasion by malignant cells

Peripheral causes

- Blood loss
- Haemolysis
- Hypersplenism

Menorrhagia is a common cause of anaemia in females still menstruating and hence women should always be asked about their periods.

- *A dietary history* should assess the intake of iron and folate which may become deficient in comparison to needs (e.g. in pregnancy, during periods of rapid growth—see p. 916).
- *Past medical history* may reveal a disease which is known to be associated with anaemia, such as rheumatoid arthritis (the anaemia of chronic disease) or previous surgery (e.g. resection of the stomach or

small bowel which may lead to malabsorption of iron and/or vitamin B$_{12}$).

- *Family history and ethnic background* of the patient are important. Haemolytic anaemias such as the haemoglobinopathies and hereditary spherocytosis may be suspected from the family history. Pernicious anaemia may also be familial.
- *A drug history* may reveal the ingestion of drugs which can be associated with blood loss (e.g. aspirin and anti-inflammatory drugs) or drugs that may cause haemolysis or aplasia.

Examination

As well as the general physical findings of anaemia shown on page 891, there may be specific findings related to the aetiology of the anaemia; for example, a patient may be found to have a right iliac fossa mass due to an underlying caecal carcinoma. Haemolytic anaemias can cause jaundice. Vitamin B$_{12}$ deficiency may be associated with neurological signs including peripheral neuropathy, dementia and signs of subacute combined degeneration of the cord (see p. 918). Sickle-cell anaemia (see p. 926) may result in leg ulcers. Anaemia may be multifactorial

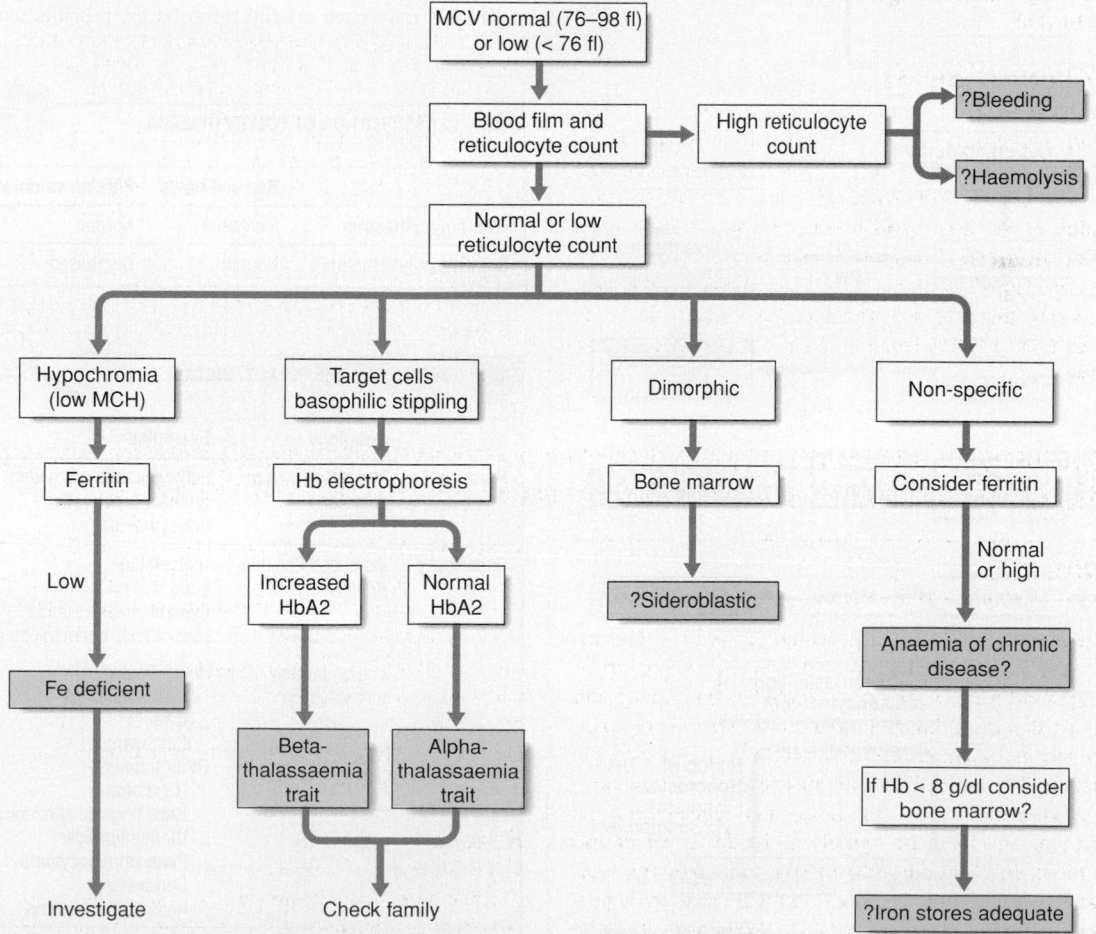

Fig. 19.12   Investigation of anaemia: normal or low MCV.

and the lack of specific symptoms and signs does not rule out silent pathology.

Schemes for the investigation of anaemias are often based on the size of the red cells, which is most accurately indicated by the mean cell volume (MCV) in the FBC. Commonly, in the presence of anaemia:

- A normal MCV (normocytic anaemia) suggests either acute blood loss or the anaemia of chronic disease (ACD) (see Fig. 19.12).
- A low MCV (microcytic anaemia) suggests iron deficiency or thalassaemia (see Fig. 19.12).
- A high MCV (macrocytic anaemia) suggests vitamin B_{12} or folate deficiency (see Fig. 19.13).

Specific types of anaemia are dealt with separately later in this chapter (see pp. 914–929).

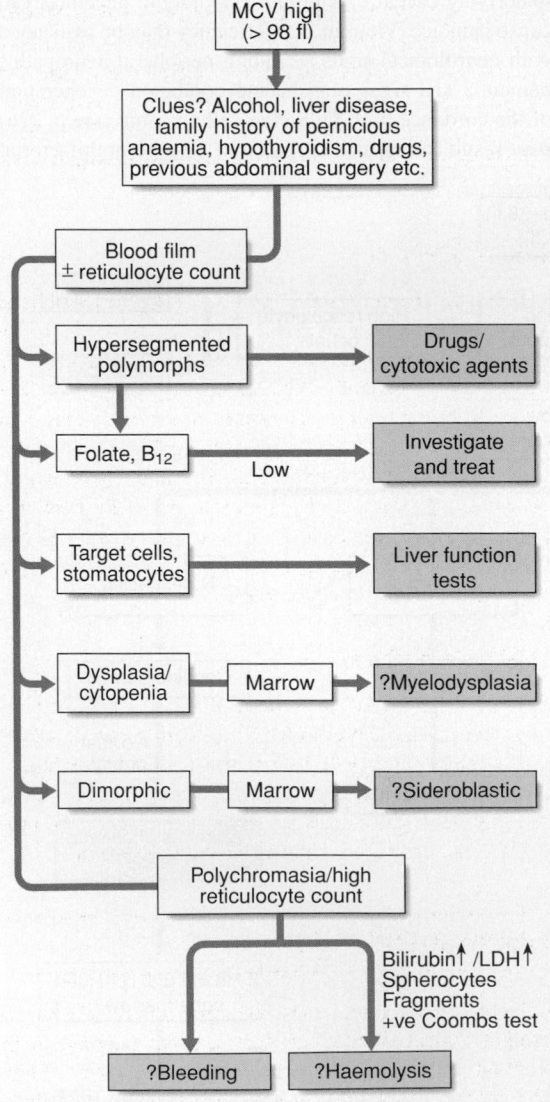

Fig. 19.13 Investigation of anaemia: high MCV. (LDH = lactate dehydrogenase)

HIGH HAEMOGLOBIN

A haemoglobin level greater than the upper limit of normal (adult females 16.5 g/dl, adult males 18 g/dl) may be due to an increase in the number of red blood cells (true polycythaemia) or a reduction in the plasma volume (relative or apparent polycythaemia) (see Box 19.7). Circulating red cell mass is measured by radio-labelling an aliquot of the patient's red cells with ^{51}Cr, reinjecting the cells and measuring the dilution of the isotope. The plasma volume is measured by a similar dilution technique using homologous albumin labelled with ^{125}I.

True polycythaemia is caused by increased erythropoiesis in the bone marrow. This occurs due to a primary increase in marrow activity (the myeloproliferative disorder called primary proliferative polycythaemia or polycythaemia rubra vera, PRV) or in response to increased erythropoietin (Epo) production either as a consequence of chronic hypoxaemia or because of inappropriate erythropoietin secretion, e.g. lung or renal disorders (see Box 19.8).

A clinical history and examination will provide clues as to the aetiology of the true polycythaemia. Those with PRV may have arterial thromboses, pruritus worse

19.7 CLASSIFICATION OF POLYCYTHAEMIA

	Red cell mass	Plasma volume
True polycythaemia	Increased	Normal
Relative polycythaemia	Normal	Decreased

19.8 CAUSES OF TRUE POLYCYTHAEMIA

	Aetiology	Examples
Primary	Myeloproliferative disorder	Polycythaemia rubra vera (primary proliferative polycythaemia)
Secondary	Increased Epo due to tissue hypoxia	High altitude Lung disease Cyanotic heart disease High-affinity haemoglobins

	Inappropriately increased Epo	Renal disease
		  Hydronephrosis
		  Cysts
		  Carcinoma
		Other tumours
		  Hepatoma
		  Bronchogenic carcinoma
		  Uterine fibroids
		  Phaeochromocytoma
		  Cerebellar haemangioblastoma

(Epo = erythropoietin)

after a hot bath, gout due to high red cell turnover and hepatosplenomegaly. The cardiorespiratory systems should be assessed for evidence and causes of hypoxaemia, and further investigations to exclude inappropriate erythropoietin secretion should be performed.

Relative polycythaemia with a reduction in plasma volume is usually a consequence of dehydration, diuretic use or alcohol consumption.

LEUCOPENIA (LOW WHITE COUNT)

A reduction in the total numbers of circulating white cells is called leucopenia. This may be due to a reduction in all types of white cell or a reduction in individual cell types (usually neutrophils or lymphocytes). In turn, leucopenia may occur alone or as part of a reduction in all three haematological lineages (pancytopenia, see p. 909).

NEUTROPENIA

A reduction in neutrophil count (usually less than 1.5×10^9/l, but dependent on age and race) is called neutropenia. The main causes are listed in Figure 19.6 (see p. 896). Drug-induced neutropenia is not uncommon and those drugs implicated in neutropenia are shown in Box 19.9. Clinical manifestations range from no symptoms to overwhelming sepsis. The risk of bacterial infection is related to the degree of neutropenia, with counts lower than 0.5×10^9/l conferring the highest risk. Fever is the first and the only manifestation of infection. A sore thoat, perianal pain or skin inflammation may be present. The lack of neutrophils allows the patient to become septicaemic and shocked within hours if immediate antibiotic

19.9 DRUG-INDUCED NEUTROPENIA	
Group	**Examples**
Analgesics/anti-inflammatory agents	Phenylbutazone, gold, diflunisal, penicillamine, naproxen
Antithyroid drugs	Carbimazole, propylthiouracil
Anti-arrhythmics	Quinidine, procainamide
Antihypertensives	Captopril, enalapril, nifedipine
Antidepressants/psychotropics	Amitriptyline, dosulepin (dothiepin), mianserin
Antimalarials	Pyrimethamine, dapsone, sulfadoxine, chloroquine
Anticonvulsants	Phenytoin, sodium valproate, carbamazepine
Antibiotics	Sulphonamides, penicillins, cephalosporins
Miscellaneous	Cimetidine, ranitidine, chlorpropamide, zidovudine

therapy is not commenced. The management of such patients is discussed on page 933.

LYMPHOPENIA

This occurs when the absolute lymphocyte count is less than 1×10^9/l. The causes are shown in Figure 19.6 (see p. 896). Although minor deficiencies may be asymptomatic, deficiencies in cell-mediated immunity may cause infections with organisms such as fungi, viruses and mycobacteria (see Ch. 1).

LEUCOCYTOSIS (HIGH WHITE COUNT)

An increase in the total numbers of circulating white cells is called leucocytosis. This is usually due to an increase in a specific type of white blood cell (see Fig. 19.6, p. 896 for causes of a neutrophilia, eosinophilia, basophilia, monocytosis and lymphocytosis). It is important to realise that an increase in a single type of white cell (e.g. eosinophils or monocytes) may not increase the total WBC above the upper limit of normal and will only be apparent if the differential of the white count is examined.

NEUTROPHILIA

An increase in the number of circulating neutrophils is called a neutrophilia or a neutrophil leucocytosis. It can result from an increased production of cells from the bone marrow or redistribution from the marginated pool. The normal neutrophil count depends upon age, race and certain physiological parameters. In healthy neonates the neutrophil count is higher than at other times of life. During pregnancy not only is there an increase in neutrophils but also earlier forms such as promyelocytes can be found in the blood. The causes of a neutrophilia are shown in Figure 19.6 (see p. 896).

LYMPHOCYTOSIS

A lymphocytosis is an increase in circulating lymphocytes above that expected for the patient's age. In adults this is above 3.5×10^9/l. Infants and children have higher counts than adults; age-related normal ranges should be consulted. The causes are shown in Figure 19.6 (see p. 896); the most common cause is viral infection.

LYMPHADENOPATHY

Enlarged lymph glands may be an important indicator of haematological disease but they are not uncommon in reaction to infection or inflammation (see Box 19.10). The sites of lymph node groups and symptoms and signs that may help elucidate the underlying cause are shown on page 891. Reactive nodes usually expand rapidly and

19.10 CAUSES OF LYMPHADENOPATHY
Infective
Bacterial • Streptococcal, tuberculosis, brucellosis **Viral** • Epstein–Barr, HIV **Protozoal** • Toxoplasmosis **Fungal** • Histoplasmosis, coccidioidomycosis
Neoplastic
Primary • Leukaemias, lymphomas **Secondary** • Lung, breast, thyroid, stomach
Connective tissue disorders
• Rheumatoid arthritis, systemic lupus erythematosus (SLE)
Sarcoidosis
Amyloidosis -
Drugs
• Phenytoin

19.11 CAUSES OF SPLENOMEGALY	
Congestive	
Intrahepatic portal hypertension • Cirrhosis • Hepatic vein occlusion	
Extrahepatic portal hypertension • Thrombosis, stenosis or malformation of the portal or splenic vein	
Cardiac • Chronic congestive cardiac failure • Constrictive pericarditis	
Infective	
Bacterial • Endocarditis • Septicaemia • Tuberculosis	• Brucellosis • Salmonella
Viral • Hepatitis • Epstein–Barr	• Cytomegalovirus
Protozoal • Malaria • Leishmaniasis	• Trypanosomiasis
Fungal • Histoplasmosis	
Inflammatory/granulomatous disorders	
• Felty's syndrome, SLE	• Sarcoidosis
Haematological	
Red cell disorders • Megaloblastic anaemia	• Haemoglobinopathies
Autoimmune haemolytic anaemias	
Myeloproliferative disorders • Chronic myeloid leukaemia • Myelofibrosis	• Polycythaemia rubra vera • Essential thrombocythaemia
Neoplastic • Leukaemias	• Lymphomas
Other malignancies	
• Metastatic cancer—rare	
Storage diseases	
• Gaucher's disease	• Niemann–Pick disease
Miscellaneous	
• Cysts, amyloid, hyperthyroidism	

are painful, whereas those due to haematological disease are more often painless. Localised nodes should elicit a search for a source of inflammation in the appropriate drainage area: the scalp, ear, mouth, face or teeth for the neck; the breast for the axilla; and the perineum or external genitalia for inguinal nodes. Generalised lymphadenopathy may be secondary to infection, connective tissue disease or extensive skin disease but is more likely to signify underlying haematological malignancy. Weight loss and drenching night sweats which may require a change of night clothes are associated with haematological malignancies, particularly lymphoma.

Initial investigations should include a full blood count (to detect neutrophilia in infection or evidence of haematological disease), an ESR and a chest radiograph (to detect mediastinal lymphadenopathy). If the findings are suspicious of malignancy, a formal cutting needle or excision biopsy of a representative node is indicated to confirm a histological diagnosis.

SPLENOMEGALY

The spleen may be enlarged due to involvement by lymphoproliferative disease, the resumption of extra-medullary haematopoiesis in myeloproliferative disease, or enhanced reticulo-endothelial activity in autoimmune haemolysis. A list of the causes of splenomegaly is given in Box 19.11. Massive splenomegaly occurs in chronic myeloid leukaemia, myelofibrosis, malaria or kala-azar.

Hepatosplenomegaly is more suggestive of lympho- or myeloproliferative disease, liver disease or infiltration (e.g. with amyloid). The additional presence of lymphadenopathy makes a diagnosis of lymphoproliferative disease more likely. An enlarged spleen may cause abdominal discomfort, with back pain and abdominal bloating due to stomach compression. Splenic infarction may occur and produce severe abdominal pain radiating to the left shoulder tip, associated with a splenic rub on auscultation. Rarely, spontaneous or traumatic rupture may occur.

Investigation will centre on the suspected cause. Imaging of the spleen by ultrasound or computed tomography (CT) will detect variations in density in the spleen which may be a feature of lymphoproliferative disease; it also allows imaging of the liver or abdominal lymph nodes. Biopsy of the latter or superficial nodes may provide the diagnosis. A chest radiograph is required to exclude mediastinal nodes. An FBC may show pancytopenia secondary to hypersplenism and, if other abnormalities are present, such as abnormal lymphocytes or a leucoerythroblastic blood film, a bone marrow examination is indicated. Screening for infectious or liver disease (see p. 835) may be appropriate. If all investigations are unhelpful, splenectomy may be diagnostic.

BLEEDING

History

Bleeding usually results either from a breach of the vessel wall due to a specific insult (e.g. peptic ulcer, trauma or from haemostatic failure). This may result from deficiency of one or more of the coagulation factors, thrombocytopenia or, occasionally, excessive fibrinolysis, which most commonly arises following therapeutic fibrinolytic therapy with tissue plasminogen activator (tPA) or streptokinase.

Prior to laboratory investigation it is important that a careful history is recorded of all bleeding episodes and a full clinical examination should be performed. A history of bleeding is often remarkably reproducible, particularly after dental extraction; if a socket oozes for 2 days after removal of a tooth on one occasion, this is likely to recur following each subsequent extraction.

It is important to consider the following points when taking a history:

- *Site of bleeds*. Muscle and joint bleeds indicate a coagulation defect, whereas purpura, prolonged bleeding from superficial cuts, epistaxis, gastrointestinal haemorrhage or menorrhagia indicates a failure of primary haemostasis due to a platelet disorder, thrombocytopenia or von Willebrand's disease. Recurrent bleeds at a single site suggest a local structural abnormality.
- *Duration of history*. It may be possible to assess whether the patient has a congenital or acquired disorder.
- *Precipitating causes*. Bleeding arising spontaneously indicates a more severe defect than if haemorrhage arises only after trauma.
- *Surgery*. Enquiry about all operations is useful, in particular regarding dental extractions, tonsillectomy and circumcision, as these are all stressful tests of the haemostatic system. Bleeding that starts immediately after surgery indicates defective platelet plug formation, whereas that which comes on after several hours is more indicative of failure of platelet plug stabilisation by fibrin due to a coagulation defect.
- *Family history*. Absence of relatives with clinically significant bleeding does not exclude a hereditary bleeding diathesis; about one-third of cases of haemophilia, for example, arise in individuals without a family history.
- *Systemic illnesses*. Many diseases, or their treatment, may be associated with bleeding but it is particularly important to consider the possibility of hepatic or renal failure, paraproteinaemia or a connective tissue disease.
- *Drugs*. Almost any medicine can potentially produce bleeding, either by depressing marrow function with consequent thrombocytopenia or by interacting with warfarin. NSAIDs inhibit platelet function; the effect of aspirin may last for up to 10 days after a single tablet.

Examination

Superficial examination may reveal bruises and purpura or scars due to poor healing following prolonged superficial bleeding. Telangiectasia of lips and tongue points to hereditary haemorrhagic telangiectasia (see p. 947). Joints should be carefully scrutinised for evidence of haemarthroses. A full general medical examination is important because it may give clues as to systemic illness —for example, stigmata of liver disease; splenomegaly may cause thrombocytopenia due to hypersplenism.

Investigations

Screening investigations and their interpretation are described on page 901. If the patient has a history strongly suggestive of a bleeding disorder and all the preliminary screening tests give normal results, it is appropriate to perform further investigations. The clinical history may be a useful guide as to whether attention should be directed to platelet function (or von Willebrand's disease) or a defect in coagulation, e.g. haemophilia.

THROMBOCYTOPENIA (LOW PLATELETS)

A reduced platelet count may arise by one of three mechanisms:

- failure of megakaryocyte maturation and hence platelet formation
- excessive platelet consumption after their release into the circulation
- platelet sequestration in an enlarged spleen.

The common causes of thrombocytopenia are listed in Box 19.12.

Spontaneous bleeding does not usually occur until the platelet count falls below about $30 \times 10^9/l$ unless their

19.12 CAUSES OF THROMBOCYTOPENIA

Marrow disorders

Hypoplasia
- Idiopathic
- Drug-induced—cytotoxics, antimetabolites, thiazides

Infiltration
- Leukaemia
- Myeloma
- Carcinoma
- Myelofibrosis
- Osteopetrosis

Vitamin B$_{12}$/folate deficiency

Increased consumption of platelets

- Disseminated intravascular coagulation (DIC)
- Idiopathic thrombocytopenic purpura (ITP)
- Viral infections—e.g. Epstein–Barr virus, HIV
- Bacterial infections—e.g. Gram-negative septicaemia
- Hypersplenism
- Thrombotic thrombocytopenic purpura (TTP)/haemolytic uraemic syndrome (HUS)
- Liver disease
- Connective tissue diseases—e.g. SLE

function is also compromised—for example, following aspirin ingestion. Purpura and spontaneous bruising are characteristic but there may also be oral, nasal, gastrointestinal or genitourinary bleeding. Severe thrombocytopenia results in optic fundal haemorrhage (see Fig. 19.14), which may be a prelude to a rapidly fatal intracranial bleed.

Investigations to determine the possible cause of thrombocytopenia should be directed towards the conditions listed in Box 19.12. A blood film may give diagnostic information, e.g. acute leukaemia. Examination of the bone marrow will reveal whether there is an infiltrate such as carcinoma, a reduced number of megakaryocytes, e.g. hypoplastic anaemia, or an increased number of megakaryocytes indicating excessive peripheral destruction, e.g. idiopathic thrombocytopenic purpura (see p. 948).

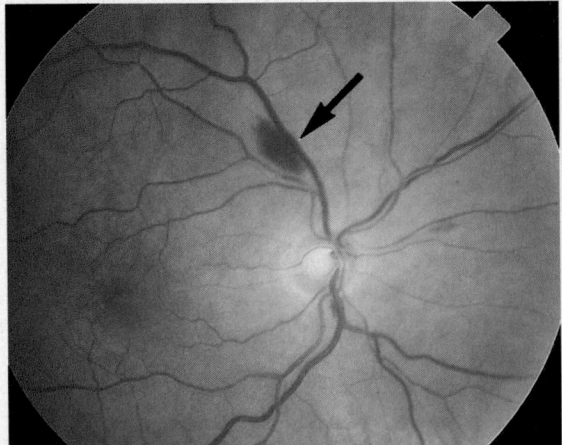

Fig. 19.14 Superficial fundal haemorrhage (arrow). The haemorrhage is in a patient with a platelet count of 5×10^9/l.

THROMBOCYTOSIS (HIGH PLATELETS)

The platelet count is most commonly raised as part of the secondary response to inflammation, as with infection, connective tissue disease, malignancy or gastrointestinal bleeding (see Box 19.13). In these circumstances the presenting clinical features are those of the underlying disorder. Thrombosis or bleeding secondary to a reactive increase in platelet count is rare.

In essential thrombocythaemia, in which there is primary proliferation of megakaryocytes in the marrow, the patient may have haemorrhagic features secondary to platelet dysfunction, e.g. mucocutaneous or gastrointestinal haemorrhage. Alternatively, the patient may present with occlusion of a major artery, e.g. thrombotic stroke or venous thrombosis. Occlusion of smaller vessels may result in transient ischaemic attacks, amaurosis fugax, or distal ischaemia or gangrene (see Fig. 19.15). A high platelet count is also a feature of other myeloproliferative disorders such as primary proliferative polycythaemia or chronic myeloid leukaemia.

19.13 CAUSES OF A RAISED PLATELET COUNT

Reactive thrombocytosis

- Chronic inflammatory disorders
- Malignant disease
- Tissue damage
- Haemolytic anaemias
- Post-splenectomy
- Post-haemorrhage

Malignant thrombocytosis

- Essential thrombocythaemia
- Polycythaemia rubra vera
- Myelofibrosis
- Chronic myeloid leukaemia

Fig. 19.15 Thrombocytosis causing vessel occlusion and gangrene.

VENOUS THROMBOSIS

Swelling of either one or both legs is a common presenting symptom. Deep venous thrombosis (DVT) in the leg characteristically causes pain, swelling, an increase in temperature and dilatation of the superficial veins. Often, however, there are only minimal symptoms and DVT cannot be excluded without appropriate objective investigations.

Unilateral leg-swelling may also result from a spontaneous or post-traumatic calf haematoma, cellulitis or a ruptured Baker's cyst (see Box 19.14). This latter condition usually arises in individuals with pre-existing rheumatoid disease of the knee. The leak of synovial fluid into the calf is accompanied by a decrease in the size of the cyst in the popliteal fossa and an intense pain in the calf due to the irritant synovial fluid (see p. 1004).

When both legs are swollen, apart from bilateral DVT, the likely cause is either impaired venous or lymphatic return due to obstruction in the pelvis or above, or impaired cardiac function resulting in right-sided heart failure. Hypoalbuminaemia often results in bilateral pitting leg oedema.

19.14 CAUSES OF A SWOLLEN LEG	
• Venous thrombosis • Calf haematoma • Skin inflammation, including cellulitis • Baker's cyst	• Pelvic disease obstructing venous or lymphatic return • Congestive cardiac failure/cor pulmonale • Hypoalbuminaemia

Investigation of a swollen leg

For unilateral leg-swelling the initial assessment is usually to establish whether or not a DVT is present. DVTs are usually unilateral but may be bilateral when they are extensive and extend into the pelvic veins and inferior vena cava (IVC). For bilateral leg-swelling pelvic, retroperitoneal and cardiac pathology and hypoalbuminaemia should be excluded.

Venography remains the most accurate and reliable technique for assessing the presence of venous thrombosis. Radio-opaque dye is injected into a vein on the dorsum of the foot and the deep veins are visualised by dynamic X-ray imaging, with appropriate static films being taken to provide a permanent record of the findings. Venography for more proximal thrombosis can be performed by catheterisation of the femoral vein to image the pelvic veins and IVC.

Ultrasound is also a reliable, non-invasive method for detecting venous thrombosis. The technique depends upon demonstrating non-compressibility of the vein in the presence of thrombus. The technique can only detect thrombus in larger veins and is therefore only useful for assessing veins at or above the popliteal fossa and as far as the inguinal ligament. In some patients it can identify major thrombus in the IVC.

If a patient has a proven venous thrombosis, it is necessary to consider whether he or she may have a thrombophilic condition. Those individuals fulfilling the clinical criteria set out in Box 19.4 should be investigated, usually after anticoagulation has been discontinued, as in Box 19.5 (see p. 902).

ABNORMAL COAGULATION SCREEN

A coagulation screen should be undertaken when there is a history suggestive of a bleeding disorder (see p. 947), overt bleeding, or a clinical situation associated with a coagulation disorder, e.g. septicaemia, or the patient is taking an anticoagulant drug, e.g. warfarin. The prothrombin time is most sensitive to deficiencies of factors V, VII and X and may be prolonged in liver disease, in DIC or in patients on warfarin. The INR is a way of 'correcting' the reporting of the ratio of the patient's prothrombin time compared to that in normal plasma in patients on warfarin so that there is uniformity in ratios between different laboratories (see p. 902). The APTT is most sensitive to deficiencies in factors V, VIII, IX, X and XI and a prolongation is seen in haemophilia A and B, in those on standard or unfractionated heparin or in DIC. It is important to note that the APTT is not prolonged by low molecular weight heparins. The most common cause of a low fibrinogen is DIC although a reduced level in an otherwise well patient is seen in congenital hypofibrinogenaemia; this condition is uncommon, however. Fibrinogen is an acute phase reactant and is therefore increased in patients with inflammatory conditions, e.g. infection or malignancy.

PANCYTOPENIA

Pancytopenia refers to the combination of anaemia, leucopenia and thrombocytopenia.

19.15 CAUSES OF PANCYTOPENIA	
Bone marrow failure	
Hypoplastic/aplastic anaemia (see p. 945) • Inherited • Idiopathic	• Viral • Drugs
Bone marrow infiltration	
• Acute leukaemia • Myeloma • Lymphoma • Carcinoma	• Haemophagocytic syndrome • Myelodysplastic syndromes • Acquired immunodeficiency syndrome (AIDS)
Ineffective haematopoiesis	
• Megaloblastic anaemia	
Peripheral pooling/destruction	
Hypersplenism • Portal hypertension • Felty's syndrome	• Malaria • Myelofibrosis
SLE	

It may be due to reduced production of blood cells as a consequence of bone marrow suppression or infiltration or there may be peripheral destruction or splenic pooling of mature cells. The causes of a pancytopenia are shown in Box 19.15.

A bone marrow aspirate and trephine are usually required to establish the diagnosis.

BLOOD PRODUCTS AND TRANSFUSION

Transfusion of a blood product may be needed when a patient has a deficiency of a blood constituent or constituents that causes symptoms or puts the patient at risk, and if a useful improvement is likely to result from temporary replacement of the deficiency. In some cases an alternative replacement product, not derived from human blood, may be used.

A safe blood supply depends on:

- a well-organised supply system that ensures regular donation by healthy individuals who have no excess risk of infections transmissible by blood
- testing of all donations to detect human immunodeficiency virus (HIV) 1 and 2, hepatitis B, hepatitis C, syphilis, and other infectious agents according to each country's regulations
- effective control over the quality of safety testing, blood grouping, processing, storage and pre-transfusion testing of blood.

Safe and effective clinical use of blood depends on:

- the correct storage and handling throughout the life of the product right to the point of administration
- the use of clinical protocols or guidelines for the management of patients at risk of transfusion
- informed assessment of the likely benefits and risks for each patient
- the correct procedures for ordering and administration of blood when the decision is made to transfuse.

Figure 19.16 maps the main steps in blood collection, processing and storage. A basic knowledge of these underlies good practice in using blood products.

BLOOD PRODUCTS

Blood products are defined as any therapeutic substances made from human blood and are subdivided as described below.

INFECTION

Infection is a major complication of haematological disorders. The cause relates to the immune deficit caused by the disease itself, to the treatment, e.g. chemotherapy, or commonly to a combination of both (see page 905).

Blood components
These are platelets, plasma or cryoprecipitate, prepared from single donations (see Box 19.16).

Plasma derivatives
Licensed pharmaceutical products are produced from pooled human plasma obtained from many individuals. Plasma derivatives are generally treated to remove or reduce virus contamination.

Coagulation factor concentrates factor VIII, IX
These are for the treatment of conditions such as haemophilia or von Willebrand's disease. Where it is possible to obtain coagulation factors made by recombinant DNA technology, they are preferred due to lack of infection risk (see p. 949).

Intravenous immunoglobulin (IVIgG)
This contains concentrated immunoglobulin and was developed to replace IgG and reduce infective complications in patients with hypogammaglobulinaemia. High-dose IVIgG can also modulate the immune response and is effective in some patients with immune thrombocytopenia and Guillain–Barré syndrome (see pp. 948 and 1180). There is at present no alternative to the plasma derivative. IVIgG infusions can cause acute renal failure, especially in the elderly. Specific immunoglobulins are made from donors with high titres of antibodies such as hepatitis B, tetanus and varicella zoster, and are generally used in an attempt to prevent the development of infection in exposed non-immune people.

Human albumin solution
This is available in two strengths:

- 5% albumin solution has been widely used for acute volume replacement. There is, however, uncertainty about the relative safety and effectiveness of albumin in comparison to other synthetic colloids (gelatin, dextran and starch solutions) and crystalloid solutions (see EBM panel). It is indicated for replacement in plasma exchange.
- 20% albumin solution is used in the management of hypoproteinaemic oedema with nephrotic syndrome and ascites in chronic liver disease. It is hyperoncotic and expands plasma volume by more than the amount infused.

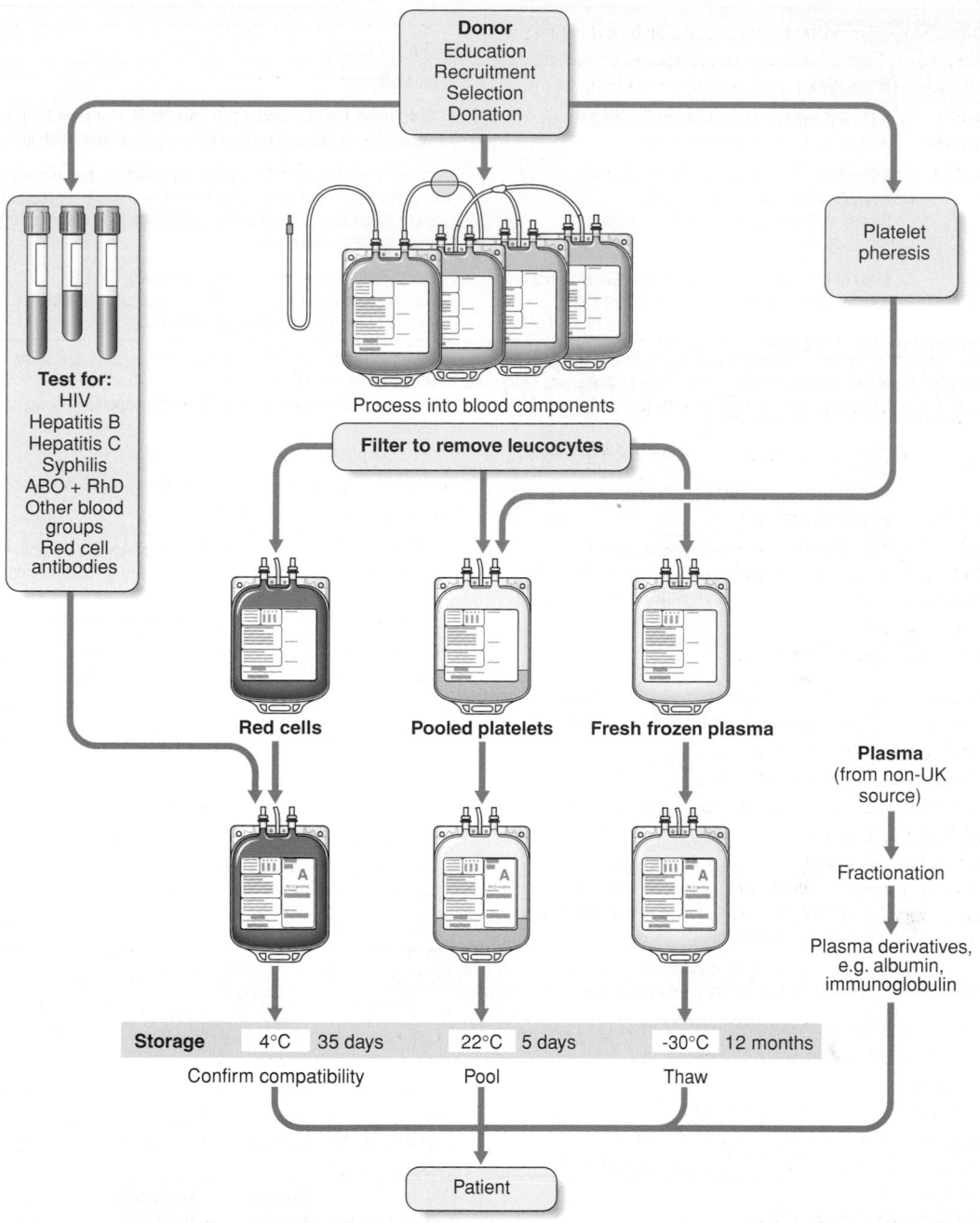

Fig. 19.16 Blood donation, processing and storage.

FLUID RESUSCITATION IN CRITICALLY ILL PATIENTS— role of albumin and other colloid solutions vs crystalloid solutions

'Systematic review of 18 RCTs reporting a mortality endpoint shows worse survival in patients receiving albumin infusions. There was no evidence that resuscitation with colloids reduces the risk of death as compared to crystalloids in patients with trauma and burns or following surgery.'

● Alderson P, Schierhout G, Roberts I, Bunn F. Colloids versus crystalloids for resuscitation in acutely ill patients. Cochrane Library, issue 1, 2001. Oxford: Update Software.

Further information: 💻 www.update-software.com/abstracts

CORRECTION OF A LOW HAEMOGLOBIN IN CRITICALLY ILL PATIENTS—role of red cell transfusion

'A single large RCT of red cell transfusion in patients in intensive care showed that patients who were maintained with an Hb in the range of 7–9 g/dl had a mortality and morbidity that were equivalent to, or better than, patients who were maintained with an Hb in the range of 10–12 g/dl. The former group received approximately half the number of red cell units.'

● Herbert PC, Wells G, Bljachman MA, et al. with the Canadian Transfusion Requirements in Critical Care Group. A multicentre, randomised controlled clinical trial of transfusion requirements in critical care. N Engl J Med 1999; 340:409–417.

Further information: 💻 www.transfusionguidelines.org.uk
💻 www.sign.ac.uk

19.16 BLOOD COMPONENTS

	Properties	Indications
Red cell components[1]	**N.B.** Red cell components *must* be compatible with the patient's ABO blood group	To increase circulating red cell mass to relieve clinical features caused by insufficient oxygen delivery in patients with low Hb levels
Whole blood	450 ml donor blood collected into 63 ml anticoagulant/preservative solution. Stored at 2–6°C. Shelf life up to 5 weeks	Contains fibrinogen, other coagulation factors, and plasma as a colloid volume expander. Whole blood is suitable for replacement of acute blood loss but red cell concentrates plus colloid or crystalloid are acceptable alternatives
Red cell concentrate	Most of the plasma removed and replaced with a solution to optimise preservation of red cells	Most usual product in many countries, e.g. UK, US. Some restrictions on use in infants; otherwise suitable for any patient requiring red cell replacement
Platelet concentrate[2]	One adult dose is made from four or five donations of whole blood, or from a single platelet apheresis procedure. Stored at 20–24°C and must be agitated. Shelf life up to 5 days from collection. Platelets more effective if compatible with patient's ABO type. Plasma in group O platelets can haemolyse red cells of group A patient	Treatment of bleeding due to thrombocytopenia and some forms of platelet dysfunction. Prevention of bleeding due to thrombocytopenia in bone marrow failure
Plasma (Fresh frozen plasma, FFP)	150–300 ml plasma obtained from one donation of whole blood. Shelf life usually 1 year. Should be compatible with patient's ABO type. Group O plasma particularly is at risk of causing haemolysis in a group A patient	Replacement of coagulation factor deficiency if a suitable licensed virus-inactivated product is not available, e.g. multiple coagulation deficiencies in major haemorrhage. Therapy of thrombotic thrombocytopenic purpura: by infusion or plasma exchange. *Do not use* to replace circulatory fluid volume, to raise plasma albumin level or as an alternative to total parenteral nutrition
Virus-inactivated plasma	Plasma treated to remove or reduce infectivity of viruses from donor. Obtained from a pool of donors' plasma treated with solvent and detergent, or from single donations treated with methylene blue and light	Indications as for fresh frozen plasma
Cryoprecipitate	High molecular weight proteins are modestly concentrated from plasma by precipitation near freezing point. Each 10–20 ml pack of precipitate contains fibrinogen, factor VIII and von Willebrand factor	Replacement of fibrinogen if a suitable licensed virus-inactivated plasma derivative is not available. Use for von Willebrand's disease and haemophilia if virus-inactivated or recombinant products not available

[1] Alternative oxygen-delivering fluids: perfluorocarbon and haemoglobin solutions will be licensed in the near future for clinical indications.
[2] Platelet preparations treated to inactivate microbial pathogens are in clinical trial and may become available.

RED CELL COMPATIBILITY

ABO RED CELL GROUPS

Transfusing red cells that have an ABO blood type that is incompatible with the recipient is the main cause of fatal, acute transfusion reaction.

There are four different ABO groups, determined by whether or not an individual's red cells express the A or B antigens. Normal healthy individuals, from early in childhood, make antibodies against A or B antigens that are not expressed on their own cells (see Box 19.17). On transfusion of red cells, A or B antibodies in the recipient's plasma will bind to transfused red cells that express A or B antigen, as follows:

- Anti-A reacts with red cells of group A or AB.
- Anti-B reacts with red cells of group B or AB.

19.17 THE ABO SYSTEM

Blood group	Red cell antigens	Antibodies in plasma	UK frequency (%)
O	None	Anti-A and anti-B	46
A	A	Anti-B	42
B	B	Anti-A	9
AB	A and B	None	3

ABO INCOMPATIBLE RED CELL TRANSFUSION

If red cells of the wrong group are transfused, the patient's IgM antibodies bind to the transfused cells as above, activating complement which damages the red cell membranes and causes lysis of the red cells. Fragments of ruptured cell membrane may initiate DIC. Released haemoglobin may cause renal failure.

THE RHESUS D BLOOD GROUP

About 15% of Caucasians lack this red cell antigen (RhD negative). RhD positive red cells (acquired through transfusion or pregnancy) can stimulate the production of IgG antibodies to RhD. In subsequent pregnancies these antibodies cross the placenta and, if the fetus is RhD positive, can cause severe anaemia and hyperbilirubinaemia, potentially leading to the baby's death, or cause severe neurological damage (haemolytic disease of the newborn, HDN). Therefore an RhD negative woman who may in future become pregnant should not be transfused with RhD positive blood.

Anti-RhD immunoglobulin is the only effective product for preventing the development of Rhesus antibodies in RhD negative women who are at risk. Administration of anti-D is given after delivery and other potentially sensitising events during pregnancy. In some countries routine prophylactic anti-D is recommended for all Rh negative women. There is no alternative to the human plasma derivative, although monoclonal antibody products are in development.

There are several other red cell antigen groups that may stimulate the development of red cell antibodies with the potential to cause haemolytic transfusion reactions or to cross the placenta and cause HDN. Some examples of these are the other Rhesus antigens (RhC, $\bar{c}$, E, $\bar{e}$, Kell, Duffy and Kidd).

SAFE TRANSFUSION PROCEDURES

It is *essential* to ensure that no ABO-incompatible red cell transfusion is ever given. Such an accident is likely to kill or harm the patient and is avoidable. The patient's safety depends not only on correct pre-transfusion testing in the laboratory but also on the use of standard procedures for taking appropriately labelled blood samples from the patient and for infusing blood into the correct patient. The proposed transfusion and any alternatives should be discussed with the patient or, if that is not possible, a relative, and this should be documented in the case notes. Special issues may arise in some groups, e.g. Jehovah's Witness patients who usually refuse transfusion.

PRE-TRANSFUSION TESTING

The patient's blood sample is tested to determine the ABO and RhD type and to detect other red cell antibodies that could haemolyse transfused red cells. This is performed by testing the patient's serum against a panel of O positive red cells that express a known range of antigens. If the patient's serum contains an antibody, the red cells will agglutinate. The antibody must then be characterised and red cell units selected which lack that particular antigen.

The transfusion laboratory will usually perform one of the following procedures:

- Type and screen (also called 'group and hold' or 'group and save'). Pre-transfusion testing is carried out and the patient's sample is held in the laboratory, usually for

7 days. If no antibodies are present on pre-transfusion testing, the hospital blood bank should subsequently be able to have blood available for collection within 15 minutes.
- Cross-match (red cell compatibility testing). After pre-transfusion testing and confirmation of compatibility, red cell units are allocated to that patient for transfusion. Full cross-matching can take up to 45 minutes.

COMPATIBILITY PROBLEMS

If the patient has clinically significant red cell antibodies, further tests to identify the red cell units negative for the specific antigens detected must be performed. This additional matching will increase the time taken to provide red cells. Non-urgent transfusions should be delayed until suitable red cell units are available. If transfusion is urgently needed, the risk of a red cell unit that is not fully compatible may have to be balanced against the risk of delaying transfusion.

STANDARD PROCEDURES FOR PRE-TRANSFUSION SAMPLES AND ADMINISTERING TRANSFUSION

Most incompatible transfusions result from mistakes in taking or labelling the blood sample for pre-transfusion testing, or from failure to carry out standard checks before infusion to make certain the correct pack has been selected for the patient. Every hospital where blood is transfused should have a written transfusion policy that is used by all staff ordering and administering blood products. It should cover the following:

- taking blood for pre-transfusion testing
- administering blood
- record-keeping and observations.

Taking blood for pre-transfusion testing
- Positively identify the patient at the bedside.
- Label the tubes and request form *after* identifying the patient.
- Ensure that all the information requested by the transfusion laboratory is given on both the tube and the request form. This information must match!

Administering blood
- Positively identify the patient at the bedside.
- Ensure that the identification of *each* blood pack matches the patient's identification.
- Check that the ABO and RhD groups of each pack are compatible with the patient's.
- Check each pack for evidence of damage; if in doubt, do not use and return to the blood bank.
- Complete the forms that document the transfusion of each pack.

Record-keeping and observations
The reason for transfusion, what was given, any adverse effects and the clinical response should be recorded in the notes. Transfusions should only be given where the patient can be observed. Blood pressure, pulse and temperature

should be monitored before and 15 minutes after starting each pack. If the patient is conscious, further observations are only needed if the patient becomes unwell or has symptoms or signs of a reaction. An unconscious patient should have pulse and temperature checked at intervals during the transfusion.

ADVERSE EFFECTS OF TRANSFUSION

ACUTE, LIFE-THREATENING COMPLICATIONS OF TRANSFUSION

The following reactions are rare but can be fatal:

- acute haemolytic transfusion reaction
- infusion of a bacterially contaminated unit
- graft-versus-host disease
- transfusion-associated lung injury
- severe allergic reaction or anaphylaxis.

Fever and allergic symptoms or signs (itch, urticaria) during transfusion are relatively common and usually these reactions are not serious. However, new symptoms or signs that arise during a transfusion must be taken seriously as they may be the first warnings of a serious reaction. Since it may be impossible to identify the cause of a severe reaction immediately, the initial supportive management should generally cover all the possible causes. Figure 19.17 outlines the management and investigation of reactions to blood products.

> **RISKS OF FATAL TRANSFUSION REACTIONS
> —cases reported to national reporting systems** **EBM**
>
> 'In the UK between 1996 and 2000 there were 33 reports of death attributed to transfusion. During this period approximately 10 million units of blood components were supplied. The largest cause of major morbidity remains transfusion of the incorrect unit of blood leading to an incompatible red cell transfusion reaction.'
>
> - Love EM, Soldan K. Serious hazards of transfusion, Annual report 1999–2000. Manchester: SHOT; 2001.
>
> Further information: www.shot.demon.co.uk
> www.transfusionguidelines.org

INFECTIONS TRANSMITTED BY TRANSFUSION

Over the past 30 years, the viruses that cause hepatitis B, AIDS and hepatitis C have been identified and effective tests introduced to detect and exclude infected blood units. Where blood is from 'safe' donors and correctly tested, the current risk of a donation being infectious is very small. For example, in the UK the risk of HIV is less than 1/3 000 000, of hepatitis B about 1/100 000, and of hepatitis C less than 1/500 000 per unit of blood received.

However, some patients who received transfusions before these tests were available have suffered very serious consequences of these infections. This is a constant reminder to avoid non-essential transfusions. Licensed plasma derivatives that have been virus-inactivated do not transmit HIV, human T lymphotrophic virus (HTLV), HBV, HCV, cytomegalovirus

or other lipid-enveloped viruses. There is a small risk due to non-enveloped viruses such as human parvovirus B19.

Several viruses have recently been described that are transmissible by transfusion, but they have not been shown to be pathogenic. These include GBV-C (so-called 'hepatitis G'), TT virus and SEN-V.

Presently in the UK there is great concern about variant Creutzfeldt–Jakob disease (vCJD), a human prion disease linked to bovine spongiform encephalitis (BSE; see p. 1202). There have been no reports of vCJD (or of sporadic CJD) associated with blood transfusion. Nevertheless, precautions such as leucodepletion have been introduced to reduce any possible risk.

Bacterial contamination of a blood component may rarely occur. This is a cause of very severe and often lethal transfusion reactions. In the UK 16 incidents with 9 fatalities were identified during the 5 years to 1999; about 80% of these episodes occurred with platelet transfusion.

Transfusion-transmitted malaria is extremely rare in the UK and US (about 1/4 000 000 units of blood or less) but may be more important where malaria is prevalent. Donor selection procedures are designed to exclude potentially infectious individuals from donating red cells for transfusion; blood testing has limitations. Chagas disease (see p. 60), caused by *Trypanosoma cruzi*, is transmissible by blood and is an important problem in parts of South America where the infection is endemic. Blood testing can reduce the risk of transmitting the trypanosome.

ANAEMIAS

Globally, 30% of the total world population are anaemic and half of these, some 600 million people, have iron deficiency. The classification of anaemia by the size of the red cells (MCV) is logical and indicates the likely cause. Red cells in the bone marrow must acquire a minimum level of haemoglobin before being released into the blood stream (see Fig. 19.18). Whilst in the marrow compartment red cell precursors undergo cell division driven by erythropoietin. If red cells cannot acquire haemoglobin at a normal rate in the marrow, they will undergo more divisions than normal and will have a low MCV when finally released into the blood. Thus in iron deficiency (iron), thalassaemia (globin chains), congenital sideroblastic anaemia (haem ring) and occasionally in the anaemia of chronic disease (poor iron utilisation) the MCV is low because component parts of the haemoglobin molecule are not fully available. In megaloblastic anaemia the biochemical consequence of vitamin B_{12} or folate deficiency is an inability to synthesise new bases to make DNA. A similar defect of cell division is seen in the presence of cytotoxic drugs or haematological disease in the marrow such as myelodysplasia. In these states cells haemoglobinise normally but undergo fewer cell divisions, resulting in circulating red cells with a raised MCV. The red cell membrane is composed of a lipid bilayer and contains lipid which will freely exchange with the plasma pool of lipid. Conditions such as liver disease, hypothyroidism,

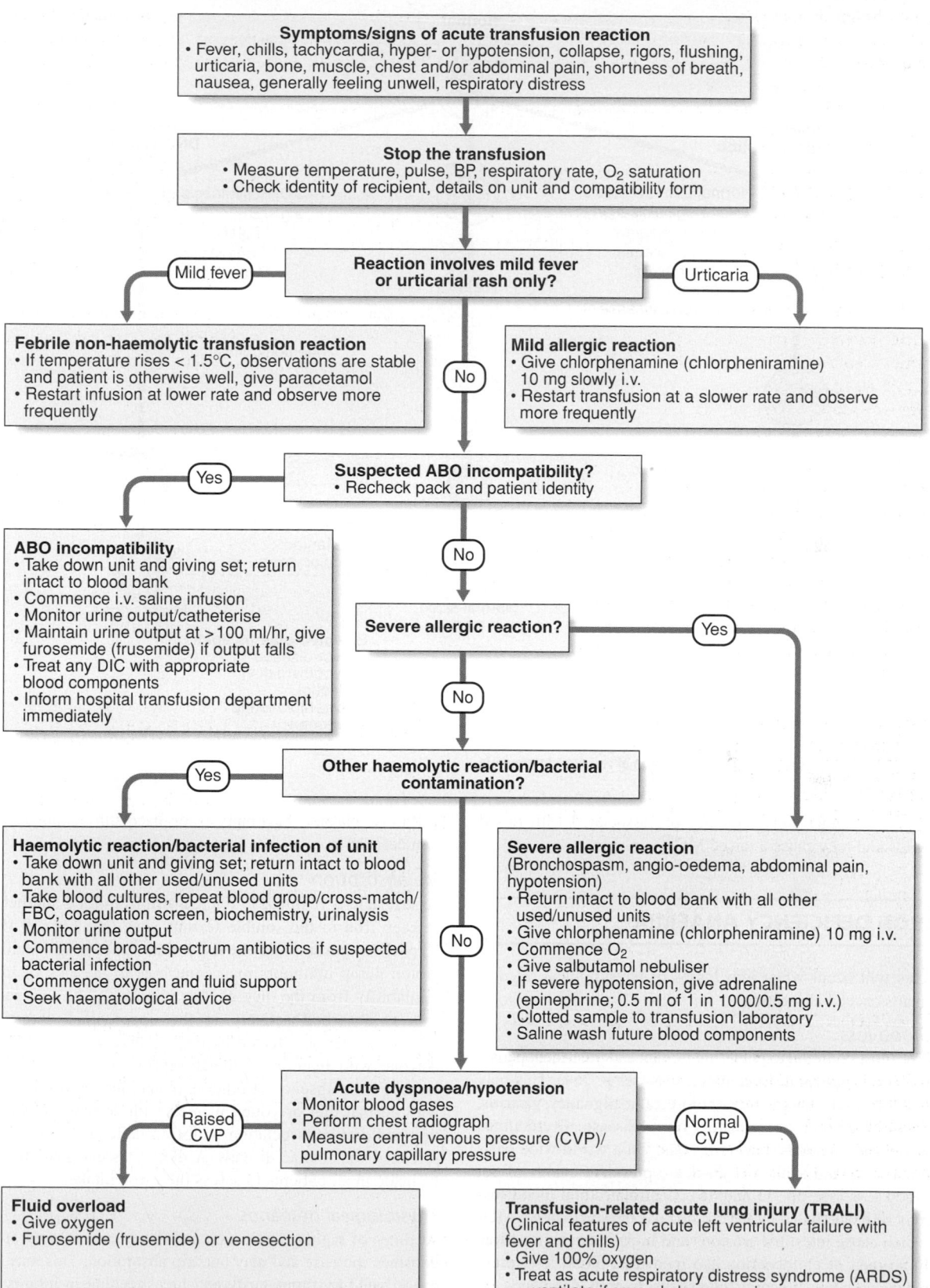

Symptoms/signs of acute transfusion reaction
• Fever, chills, tachycardia, hyper- or hypotension, collapse, rigors, flushing, urticaria, bone, muscle, chest and/or abdominal pain, shortness of breath, nausea, generally feeling unwell, respiratory distress

Stop the transfusion
• Measure temperature, pulse, BP, respiratory rate, O_2 saturation
• Check identity of recipient, details on unit and compatibility form

Mild fever

Reaction involves mild fever or urticarial rash only?

Urticaria

Febrile non-haemolytic transfusion reaction
• If temperature rises < 1.5°C, observations are stable and patient is otherwise well, give paracetamol
• Restart infusion at lower rate and observe more frequently

No

Mild allergic reaction
• Give chlorphenamine (chlorpheniramine) 10 mg slowly i.v.
• Restart transfusion at a slower rate and observe more frequently

Yes

Suspected ABO incompatibility?
• Recheck pack and patient identity

No

ABO incompatibility
• Take down unit and giving set; return intact to blood bank
• Commence i.v. saline infusion
• Monitor urine output/catheterise
• Maintain urine output at >100 ml/hr, give furosemide (frusemide) if output falls
• Treat any DIC with appropriate blood components
• Inform hospital transfusion department immediately

Severe allergic reaction?

Yes

No

Yes

Other haemolytic reaction/bacterial contamination?

Haemolytic reaction/bacterial infection of unit
• Take down unit and giving set; return intact to blood bank with all other used/unused units
• Take blood cultures, repeat blood group/cross-match/FBC, coagulation screen, biochemistry, urinalysis
• Monitor urine output
• Commence broad-spectrum antibiotics if suspected bacterial infection
• Commence oxygen and fluid support
• Seek haematological advice

No

Severe allergic reaction
(Bronchospasm, angio-oedema, abdominal pain, hypotension)
• Return intact to blood bank with all other used/unused units
• Give chlorphenamine (chlorpheniramine) 10 mg i.v.
• Commence O_2
• Give salbutamol nebuliser
• If severe hypotension, give adrenaline (epinephrine; 0.5 ml of 1 in 1000/0.5 mg i.v.)
• Clotted sample to transfusion laboratory
• Saline wash future blood components

Raised CVP

Acute dyspnoea/hypotension
• Monitor blood gases
• Perform chest radiograph
• Measure central venous pressure (CVP)/pulmonary capillary pressure

Normal CVP

Fluid overload
• Give oxygen
• Furosemide (frusemide) or venesection

Transfusion-related acute lung injury (TRALI)
(Clinical features of acute left ventricular failure with fever and chills)
• Give 100% oxygen
• Treat as acute respiratory distress syndrome (ARDS)
  —ventilate if severely hypoxaemic

Fig. 19.17 Investigation and management of reactions to blood products.

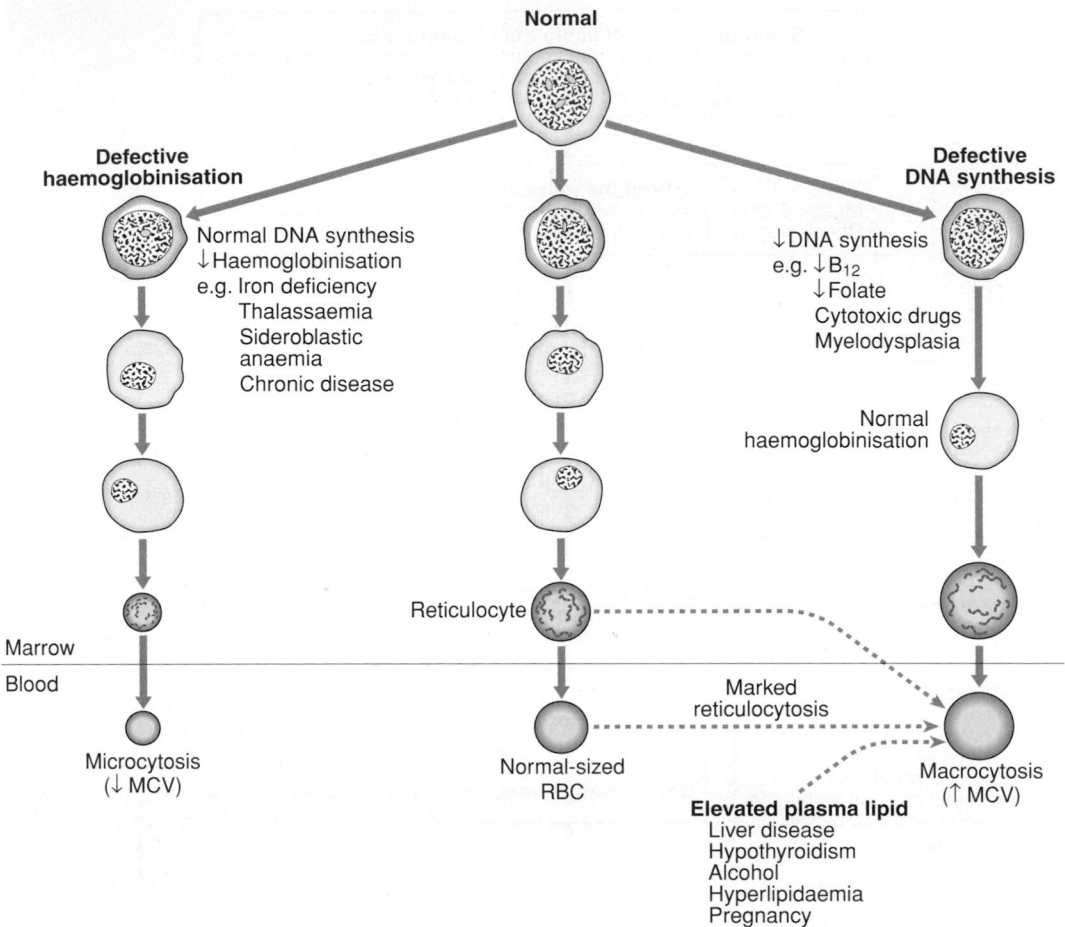

Normal

Defective haemoglobinisation

Normal DNA synthesis
↓Haemoglobinisation
e.g. Iron deficiency
Thalassaemia
Sideroblastic anaemia
Chronic disease

Defective DNA synthesis

↓DNA synthesis
e.g. ↓B$_{12}$
↓Folate
Cytotoxic drugs
Myelodysplasia

Normal haemoglobinisation

Reticulocyte

Marrow

Blood

Marked reticulocytosis

Microcytosis
(↓MCV)

Normal-sized RBC

Macrocytosis
(↑MCV)

Elevated plasma lipid
Liver disease
Hypothyroidism
Alcohol
Hyperlipidaemia
Pregnancy

Fig. 19.18 Factors which influence the size of red cells in anaemia.

hyperlipidaemia and pregnancy are associated with raised lipids and may cause a raised MCV.

IRON DEFICIENCY ANAEMIA

This will occur when iron losses or physiological requirements exceed absorption.

Blood loss

The most common explanation in men and post-menopausal women is gastrointestinal blood loss (see p. 764). This may result from occult gastric or colorectal malignancy, gastritis, peptic ulceration, inflammatory bowel disease, diverticulitis, polyps and angiodysplastic lesions. On a world-wide basis hookworm and schistosomiasis are prevalent causes of gut blood loss (see pp. 70 and 76). Gastrointestinal blood loss may be exacerbated by the chronic use of aspirin or NSAIDs which cause intestinal erosions and impair platelet function. In women of childbearing age menstrual blood loss, pregnancy and breastfeeding contribute to iron deficiency by depleting iron stores; in developed countries one-third of women in this age bracket have low iron stores but only 3% display iron-deficient haematopoiesis.

Rarely, chronic haemoptysis or haematuria may cause iron deficiency.

Malabsorption

Gastric acid is required to release iron from food and helps to keep iron in the soluble ferrous state (see Fig. 19.19). Hypochlorhydria in the elderly or that due to drugs such as proton pump inhibitors may contribute to the lack of iron availability from the diet, as may previous gastric surgery. Iron is absorbed actively in the upper small intestine and hence can be affected by coeliac disease (see p. 792). Anyone with features of malabsorption or recurrent deficiency in the absence of other explanations, or young men with normal diet or young women with normal menstruation and diet in association with iron deficiency should be screened for coeliac disease. A dietary assessment should be made in all patients to assess their iron intake.

Physiological demands

At times of rapid growth such as infancy and puberty, iron demands increase and may outstrip absorption. This may be exacerbated by prematurity and breastfeeding in infants or menstruation in girls. In pregnancy, iron is diverted to the fetus, the placenta and the increased maternal red cell mass and is lost with bleeding at parturition. There is no consensus

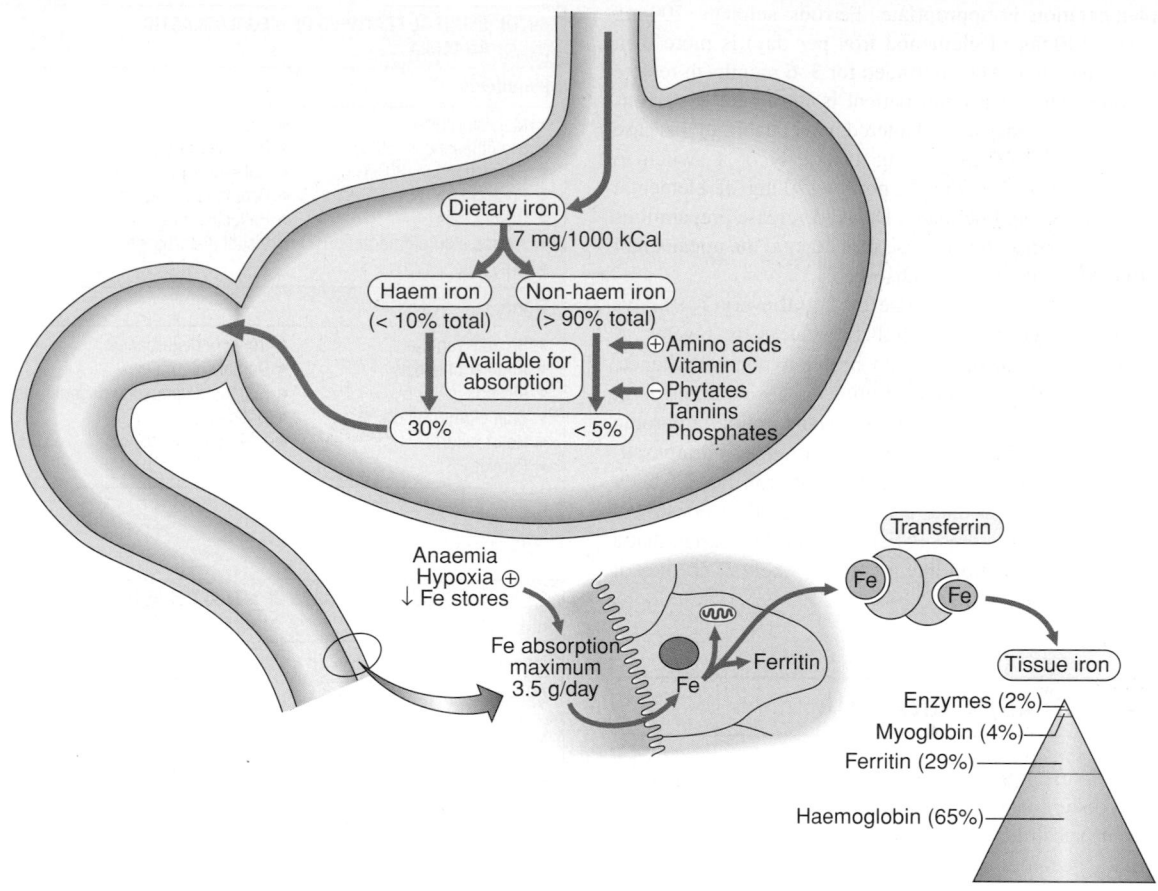

Fig. 19.19   Iron absorption, uptake and distribution in the body.

about the routine use of iron supplementation in pregnancy but if women with a poor dietary history or previous heavy menstrual losses become pregnant and the side-effects are acceptable, it is a justifiable practice.

Investigations

Confirmation of iron deficiency

Plasma ferritin is a measure of iron stores. It is a very specific test; a subnormal level is due to iron deficiency, hypothyroidism or vitamin C deficiency. There is little diurnal or day-to-day variation in the result of the test. Levels can be raised by liver disease and in an acute phase response; in these conditions a ferritin level of up to 100 µg/l may still be associated with absent bone marrow iron stores. Plasma iron and total iron binding capacity (TIBC) are measures of iron availability, hence are affected by many factors besides iron stores. Plasma iron becomes very low during an acute phase response but is raised in liver disease and haemolysis. Transferrin levels are lowered by malnutrition, liver disease, an acute phase response and nephrotic syndrome but raised by pregnancy or the oral contraceptive pill. A transferrin saturation of less than 16% is consistent with iron deficiency but less specific than a ferritin measurement. There is also a marked diurnal and day-to-day variation in plasma iron levels by 30–50%. For these reasons measurement of plasma ferritin is the best single test to confirm iron deficiency.

All proliferating cells express membrane transferrin receptors to acquire iron; a small amount of this receptor is shed into and found in a free soluble form in blood. At times of poor iron stores, cells up-regulate transferrin receptor expression; hence the levels of soluble plasma transferrin receptor increase. This can now be measured by immunoassay and used to distinguish storage iron depletion in the presence of an acute phase response or liver disease where a raised level indicates iron deficiency. In difficult cases it may still be necessary to examine a bone marrow aspirate for iron stores.

Investigation of the cause

This will depend upon the age and sex of the patient as well as the history and clinical findings. In men over the age of 40 years and in post-menopausal women with a normal diet, the upper and lower gastrointestinal tract should be investigated by endoscopy or barium studies. If coeliac disease is suspected, serum antigliadin and anti-endomysium antibodies and duodenal biopsy are indicated. In the tropics stool and urine should be examined for parasites (see p. 70).

Management

Unless the patient has angina, heart failure or evidence of cerebral hypoxia, transfusion is not necessary and oral iron supplementation is appropriate. Ferrous sulphate 200 mg 8-hourly (120 mg of elemental iron per day) is more than adequate and should be continued for 3–6 months to replete iron stores. The occasional patient is intolerant of ferrous sulphate, with dyspepsia and altered bowel habit. In this case a reduction in dose to 200 mg 12-hourly or a switch to ferrous gluconate 300 mg 12-hourly (70 mg of elemental iron per day) should be made. Delayed-release preparations are not useful since they release iron beyond the upper small intestine where it cannot be absorbed.

The haemoglobin should rise by 1 g/dl every 7–10 days and a reticulocyte response will be evident by 1 week. A failure to respond adequately may be due to non-compliance, continued blood loss, malabsorption or an incorrect diagnosis. The occasional patient with malabsorption or chronic gut disease may need parenteral iron with deep intramuscular injection of iron sorbitol (1.5 mg of iron per kg body weight). This will produce a haematological response and rapidly replete iron stores. Patients should be warned that a brown skin discoloration like a tattoo is likely to develop at the sites of administration.

MEGALOBLASTIC ANAEMIA

This results from a deficiency of vitamin B_{12} or folic acid, or from disturbances in folic acid metabolism. Folate is an important substrate of, and vitamin B_{12} a cofactor for, the enzymatic generation of the essential amino acid methionine from homocysteine. This reaction produces tetrahydrofolate which is converted to thymidine monophosphate for incorporation into DNA. Deficiency of either vitamin B_{12} or folate will therefore produce high plasma levels of homocysteine and impaired DNA synthesis.

The end result of this is cells with arrested nuclear maturation but normal cytoplasmic development: so-called nucleo-cytoplasmic asynchrony. All proliferating cells will exhibit megaloblastosis; hence changes are evident in the buccal mucosa, tongue, small intestine, cervix, vagina and uterus. The high proliferation rate of bone marrow results in striking changes in the haematopoietic system in megaloblastic anaemia. Cells become arrested in development and die within the marrow; this ineffective erythropoiesis results in an expanded hypercellular marrow. The megaloblastic changes are most evident in the early nucleated red cell precursors, and intramedullary haemolysis results in a raised bilirubin and lactate dehydrogenase (LDH) but no reticulocytosis. Iron stores are usually raised. The mature red cells are large and oval, and sometimes contain nuclear remnants. Nuclear changes are seen in the immature granulocyte precursors and a characteristic appearance is that of 'giant' metamyelocytes with a large 'sausage-shaped' nucleus. The mature neutrophils show hypersegmentation of their nuclei with cells having six or more nuclear lobes. If severe, a pancytopenia may be present in the peripheral blood.

The clinical features of megaloblastic anaemia are summarised in Boxes 19.18 and 19.19.

19.18 CLINICAL FEATURES OF MEGALOBLASTIC ANAEMIA	
Symptoms	
• Malaise (90%)	• Impotence
• Breathlessness (50%)	• Poor memory
• Paraesthesiae (80%)	• Depression
• Sore mouth (20%)	• Personality change
• Weight loss	• Hallucinations
• Altered skin pigmentation	• Visual disturbance
• Grey hair	
Signs	
• Smooth tongue	• Sensory disturbance
• Angular cheilosis	• Dorsal column loss
• Vitiligo	• Subacute combined degeneration
• Skin pigmentation	• Optic atrophy
• Heart failure	• Altered colour vision
• Pyrexia	

19.19 DIAGNOSTIC FEATURES OF MEGALOBLASTIC ANAEMIA	
Investigation	**Result**
Haemoglobin	Often reduced, may be very low
Mean cell volume	Usually raised, commonly > 120 fl
Erythrocyte count	Low for degree of anaemia
Blood film	Oval macrocytosis, poikilocytosis, red cell fragmentation, neutrophil hypersegmentation
Reticulocyte count	Low for degree of anaemia
Leucocyte count	Low or normal
Platelet count	Low or normal
Bone marrow	Increased cellularity, megaloblastic changes in erythroid series, giant metamyelocytes, dysplastic megakaryocytes, increased iron in stores, pathological non-ring sideroblasts
Serum iron	Elevated
Iron-binding capacity	Increased saturation
Serum ferritin	Elevated
Plasma LDH	Elevated, often markedly

VITAMIN B_{12} ABSORPTION

The average daily diet contains 5–30 µg of vitamin B_{12}, mainly in meat, fish, eggs and milk; this is well in excess of the daily requirement for vitamin B_{12} of 1 µg. In the stomach, gastric enzymes release vitamin B_{12} from food and at gastric pH it binds to a carrier protein termed R protein. The gastric parietal cells produce acid and intrinsic factor; the latter is a vitamin B_{12}-binding protein which optimally binds vitamin B_{12} at pH 8. As gastric emptying occurs, pancreatic secretion raises the pH and vitamin B_{12} released from the diet switches from the R protein to intrinsic factor. Bile also contains vitamin B_{12} which is available for reabsorption in the intestine, and a variety of cobalamin analogues with a similar chemical structure to vitamin B_{12} which are toxic. The freeing of R protein after gastric emptying ensures that the toxic cobalamin analogues are bound to R protein and excreted, whilst vitamin B_{12} is bound to intrinsic factor. The vitamin B_{12} intrinsic factor complex binds to specific receptors in the terminal ileum and vitamin B_{12} is actively transported by the enterocytes to plasma. In plasma, vitamin B_{12} binds to a transport protein produced by the liver termed transcobalamin II, which carries it to the tissues for utilisation. The liver stores enough vitamin B_{12} to supply the daily requirements for 3 years and this, together with the enterohepatic circulation, means that vitamin B_{12} deficiency takes years to become manifest even if all dietary intake is stopped.

Vitamin B_{12} deficiency

The causes of vitamin B_{12} deficiency are given below.

Dietary deficiency

This only occurs in strict vegans but the onset of clinical features can occur at any age between 10 and 80 years. The breastfed offspring of vegan mothers are at risk of developing nutritional vitamin B_{12} deficiency. Less strict vegetarians often have slightly low vitamin B_{12} levels but are not tissue vitamin B_{12}-deficient.

Gastric factors

Normal gastric acid and enzyme secretion is required for the release of vitamin B_{12} from the food. Hypochlorhydria in elderly patients or following gastric surgery can impair the release of vitamin B_{12} from food. Total gastrectomy invariably results in vitamin B_{12} deficiency within 5 years, often combined with iron deficiency. These patients need life-long 3-monthly vitamin B_{12} injections. After partial gastrectomy vitamin B_{12} deficiency only develops in 10–20% of patients by 5 years. An annual injection of vitamin B_{12} should prevent deficiency in this group.

Pernicious anaemia

This is an autoimmune disorder in which the gastric mucosa is atrophic with loss of parietal cells causing intrinsic factor deficiency. In the absence of intrinsic factor less than 1% of dietary vitamin B_{12} is absorbed. Pernicious anaemia has an incidence of 25/100 000 population over the age of 40 years in developed countries but an average age of onset of 60 years. It is more common in individuals with a personal or family history of pernicious anaemia or autoimmune disease (Hashimoto's thyroiditis, Graves' disease, vitiligo, hypoparathyroidism or Addison's disease). Anti-parietal cell antibodies are present in over 90% of cases but are also present in 20% of normal females over the age of 60 years. A negative result makes pernicious anaemia less likely but a positive result is not diagnostic. Antibodies to intrinsic factor are found in the serum of 60% of patients with pernicious anaemia and, if present, are diagnostic.

Small bowel factors

One-third of all patients with pancreatic insufficiency fail to transfer dietary vitamin B_{12} from R protein to intrinsic factor. This usually results in slightly low vitamin B_{12} values but no tissue evidence of vitamin B_{12} deficiency.

Motility disorders or hypogammaglobulinaemia can result in bacterial overgrowth and the resulting competition for free vitamin B_{12} can result in deficiency. This will be corrected to some extent by a course of antibiotics.

A small number of people heavily infected with the fish tapeworm develop vitamin B_{12} deficiency.

Inflammatory disease of the terminal ileum such as Crohn's disease may impair the interaction of the vitamin B_{12}-intrinsic factor complex with its receptor, as will surgery on this part of the bowel. Both may result in vitamin B_{12} malabsorption.

It is possible with a two-part Schilling test to distinguish pernicious anaemia from intestinal problems. The principles of the test are covered in Figure 19.20. The patient must be vitamin B_{12}-replete, have normal renal function and be able to comply with a 24-hour urine collection. This latter criterion is important as up to 25% of tests are invalidated by an incomplete urine collection. It is important to realise that this is not a test of gut function but simply distinguishes pernicious anaemia from the other causes of vitamin B_{12} deficiency.

Levels of cobalamins fall in normal pregnancy. Each laboratory must validate its own normal range but levels below 150 ng/l are common and in the last trimester 5–10% of women have levels below 100 ng/l. Similarly, paraproteins can interfere with vitamin B_{12} assays and so myeloma may be associated with a spurious low vitamin B_{12}.

Part One

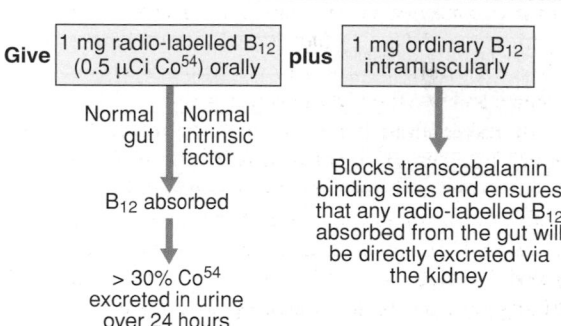

Part Two (if excretion ↓ in Part One)

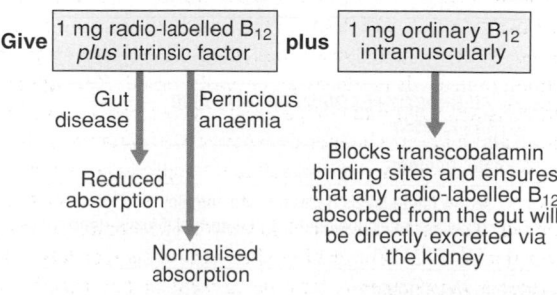

Fig. 19.20 The two-part Schilling test in the diagnosis of the cause of vitamin B_{12} deficiency.

FOLATE ABSORPTION

Folates are produced by plants and bacteria; hence dietary leafy vegetables (spinach, broccoli, lettuce), fruits (bananas, melons) and animal protein (liver, kidney) are a rich source. An average Western diet contains more than the minimum daily intake of 50 µg but excess cooking for longer than 15 minutes destroys folates. Most dietary folate is present as polyglutamates; these are converted to monoglutamate in the upper small bowel and actively transported into plasma. Plasma folate is loosely bound to plasma proteins such as albumin and there is an enterohepatic circulation. Total body stores of folate are small and deficiency can occur in a matter of weeks.

Folate deficiency

The causes and diagnostic features of folate deficiency are covered in Boxes 19.20 and 19.21. The edentulous elderly or psychiatric patient is particularly susceptible to dietary deficiency and this will be exacerbated in the presence of gut disease or malignancy. Pregnancy-induced folate deficiency is the most common cause of megaloblastosis world-wide and is more likely in the context of twin pregnancies, multiparity and hyperemesis gravidarum. Serum folate is very sensitive to dietary intake; a single meal can normalise it in a patient with true folate deficiency, and anorexia, alcohol and anticonvulsant therapy can reduce it in the absence of

19.20 CAUSES OF FOLATE DEFICIENCY
Diet
• Poor intake of vegetables
Malabsorption
• e.g. Coeliac disease
Increased demand
• Pregnancy • Cell proliferation, e.g. haemolysis
Drugs*
• Certain anticonvulsants (e.g. phenytoin) • Contraceptive pill • Certain cytotoxic drugs (e.g. methotrexate)
* Usually only a problem in patients deficient in folate from another cause.

19.21 DIAGNOSTIC FEATURES OF FOLIC ACID DEFICIENCY
Diagnostic findings
• Low serum folate levels (fasting blood sample) • Red cell folate levels low (but may be normal if folate deficiency is of very recent onset)
Corroborative findings
• Macrocytic dysplastic blood picture • Megaloblastic marrow

megaloblastosis. For this reason red cell folate levels are a more accurate indicator of folate stores and tissue folate deficiency.

Management

Where a patient with a severe megaloblastic anaemia is very ill and treatment must be started before vitamin B_{12} and red cell folate results are available, always treat with both folic acid and vitamin B_{12}. The use of folic acid alone in the presence of vitamin B_{12} deficiency results in worsening of neurological defects.

Vitamin B_{12} deficiency

Vitamin B_{12} deficiency is treated with hydroxycobalamin 1000 µg i.m. in five doses 2 or 3 days apart followed by maintenance therapy of 1000 µg every 3 months for life. The reticulocyte count will peak by the 5th–10th day after therapy and may be as high as 50%. The haemoglobin will rise by 1 g/dl every week. The response of the marrow is associated with a fall in plasma potassium levels and rapid depletion of iron stores. If an initial response is not maintained and the blood film is dimorphic, the patient may need additional iron therapy. A sensory neuropathy may take 6–12 months to correct; long-standing neurological damage may not recover.

Folate deficiency

Oral folic acid 5 mg daily for 3 weeks will treat acute deficiency and 5 mg once weekly is adequate maintenance therapy. Prophylactic folic acid in pregnancy will prevent megaloblastosis in women at risk. Folic acid supplementation may reduce the risk of neural tube defects and in some countries all pregnant women receive routine folic acid supplementation. Prophylactic supplementation is also given in chronic haematological disease associated with reduced red cell lifespan (e.g. autoimmune haemolytic anaemia or haemoglobinopathies). There is also evidence that supraphysiological supplementation (400 µg/day) can reduce the risk of coronary and cerebrovascular disease by reducing plasma homocysteine levels. This has led the US Food and Drugs Administration to introduce fortification of bread, flour and rice with folic acid.

If severe angina or heart failure is present, transfusion can be used in megaloblastic anaemia. The cardiovascular system is adapted to the chronic anaemia present in megaloblastosis and the volume load imposed by transfusion may result in decompensation and severe cardiac failure. In such circumstances 1 unit of blood should be administered slowly each day with diuretic cover.

ANAEMIA OF CHRONIC DISEASE

This is a common type of anaemia, particularly in hospital populations. Characteristic features are as follows:

• The anaemia occurs in the setting of chronic infections, chronic inflammation or neoplasia.
• The anaemia is not related to bleeding, haemolysis or marrow infiltration.

- The anaemia is generally mild, in the range of 8.5–11.5 g/dl, and is usually associated with a normal MCV (normocytic, normochromic), but up to 25% may have a reduced MCV.
- The serum iron is low but iron stores are normal or increased, as indicated by the ferritin or stainable marrow iron.

Pathogenesis

The pathogenesis of this type of anaemia is thought to involve abnormalities of iron metabolism and erythropoiesis. Recent interest has been centred on the role of erythropoietin and the inhibitory effect of various cytokines (e.g. IL-1 and TNF-α) on erythropoiesis. Erythropoietin levels appear to be lower than would be expected for the degree of anaemia. Administration of erythropoietin to patients with rheumatoid arthritis has a beneficial effect on the anaemia.

Management

A particular problem is to distinguish the anaemia of chronic disease (ACD) associated with a low MCV from iron deficiency. The ferritin level is elevated in inflammatory conditions and the serum iron is low in both ACD and iron deficiency. A ferritin in the low/normal range (up to 100 μg/l) in the setting of disorders associated with the ACD may indicate iron deficiency. A soluble transferrin receptor level may be elevated and would suggest iron deficiency. Examination of the marrow may be useful to assess iron stores directly. A trial of oral iron can be given in difficult situations. A positive response occurs in true iron deficiency but not in ACD. Measures which reduce the severity of the underlying disorder generally help to improve the ACD.

HAEMOLYSIS

The normal red cell lifespan of 120 days may be shortened by a variety of abnormalities. The bone marrow may increase its output of red cells six- to eightfold by increasing the proportion of red cells produced, expanding the volume of active marrow and releasing reticulocytes prematurely. If the rate of destruction exceeds this increased production rate, then anaemia will develop.

The basic laboratory diagnosis of haemolysis is covered in Figure 19.21. The red cell destruction will overload pathways for haemoglobin destruction, causing a modest rise in unconjugated bilirubin in the blood and mild jaundice. Increased reabsorption of urobilinogen from the gut results in an increase in urinary urobilinogen. Red cell destruction releases LDH and increases serum levels. The red cell compensation results in a reticulocytosis, and nucleated red cell precursors may also appear in the blood. The expansion of the active bone marrow may result in a neutrophilia and immature granulocytes appearing in the blood to cause a leucoerythroblastic blood film. The appearances of the red cells may give an indication of the likely cause of the haemolysis; spherocytes are small, dark-cells and suggest autoimmune haemolysis or hereditary spherocytosis, sickle cells suggest haemoglobinopathy and red cell fragments indicate microangiopathic haemolysis.

Intravascular haemolysis

When rapid red cell destruction occurs free haemoglobin is released into the plasma. Free haemoglobin is toxic to cells and the body has evolved binding proteins to minimise this risk. Haptoglobin is an α$_2$ globulin produced by the liver which binds free haemoglobin to form a complex too large

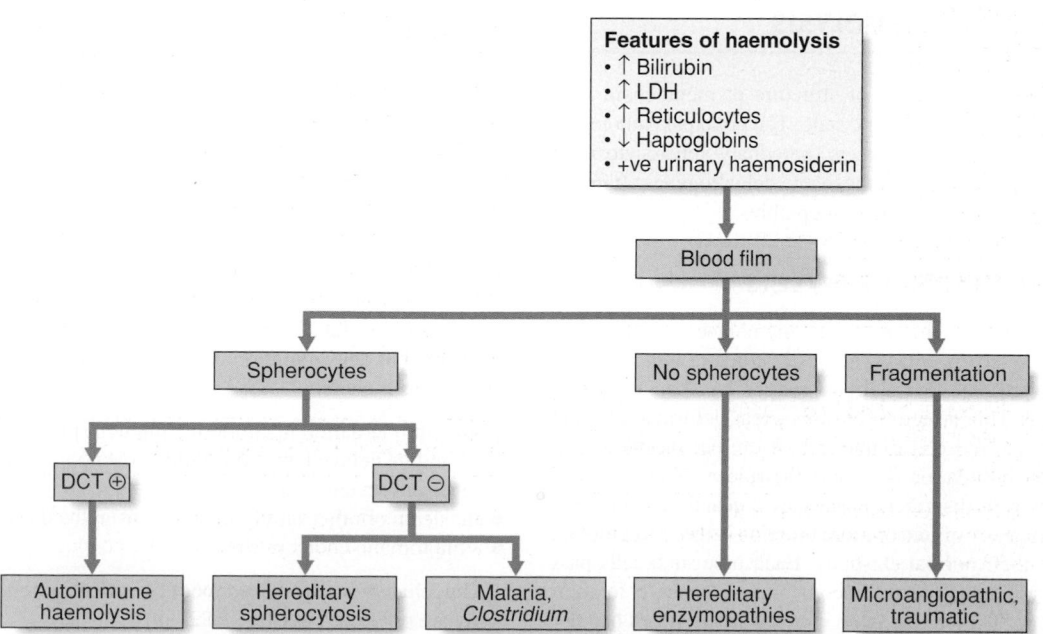

Fig. 19.21 **Laboratory features and classification of the causes of haemolysis.** (LDH = lactate dehydrogenase; DCT = direct Coombs test)

to be excreted by the kidney but which is degraded by the liver. Levels of haptoglobin are reduced in intravascular haemolysis. Once haptoglobins are saturated, free haemoglobin is oxidised to form methaemoglobin which binds to albumin, in turn forming methaemalbumin which can be detected by the Schumm's test. Methaemoglobin is degraded and any free haem is bound to a second binding protein termed haemopexin. If all the protective mechanisms are overloaded, free haemoglobin may appear in the urine. When fulminant, this gives rise to black urine as in severe falciparum malaria infection (see p. 51). In smaller amounts renal tubular cells absorb the haemoglobin, degrade it and store the iron as haemosiderin. When the tubular cells are subsequently sloughed into the urine they give rise to haemosiderinuria which is always indicative of intravascular haemolysis.

Extravascular haemolysis

Physiological red cell destruction occurs in the fixed reticulo-endothelial cells in the liver or spleen, so avoiding free haemoglobin in the plasma. In most haemolytic states haemolysis is predominantly extravascular and little haptoglobin depletion occurs.

The erythroid hyperplasia may give rise to folate deficiency, when the blood findings will be complicated by the presence of megaloblastosis. Measurement of red cell folate is unreliable in the presence of haemolysis and serum folate will be elevated. Patients' red cells can be labelled with ^{51}chromium; when reinjected, they can be used to determine red cell survival, or when combined with surface counting may indicate whether the liver or the spleen is the main source of red cell destruction. This is seldom performed in clinical practice.

CONGENITAL HAEMOLYSIS

Inherited red cell defects of structure or metabolism may result in a chronic haemolytic state. The principal pathologies are red cell membrane defects (hereditary spherocytosis or elliptocytosis), glucose-6-phosphate dehydrogenase (G6PD) deficiency and the haemoglobinopathies.

RED CELL MEMBRANE DEFECTS

The structure of the red cell membrane is shown in Figure 19.4 (see p. 895). The basic structure is a cytoskeleton 'stapled' on to the lipid bilayer by special protein complexes. This structure ensures great deformability and elasticity; the red cell diameter is 8 μm but the narrowest point in the circulation is 2 μm in the spleen. When this normal structure is disturbed, usually by a quantitative or functional deficiency of one or more proteins in the cytoskeleton, cells lose their normal elasticity. Each time such cells pass through the spleen they lose membrane relative to their cell volume. This results in an increase in mean cell haemoglobin concentration (MCHC), abnormal cell shape and reduced red cell survival due to extravascular haemolysis.

HEREDITARY SPHEROCYTOSIS

This is usually inherited as an autosomal dominant condition, although 25% of cases have no family history and represent new mutations. The incidence is approximately 1:5000 in developed countries but this may be an underestimate since the disease may present de novo in patients over 65 years and is often discovered as a chance finding on a blood count. The pathogenesis varies between families; the most common abnormalities are deficiencies of beta spectrin or ankyrin (see Fig. 19.4, p. 895). The severity of spontaneous haemolysis varies. Most cases are associated with an asymptomatic compensated chronic haemolytic state with spherocytes present on the blood film and a reticulocytosis. Occasional cases are associated with more severe haemolysis; these may be due to coincidental polymorphisms in alpha spectrin or coinheritance of a second defect involving a different protein.

The clinical course may be complicated by crises:

- *A haemolytic crisis* occurs when the severity of haemolysis increases; this is rarely seen in association with infection.
- *A megaloblastic crisis* follows the development of folate deficiency; this may occur as a first presentation of the disease in association with pregnancy.
- *An aplastic crisis* occurs in association with parvovirus infection. Parvovirus causes a common exanthem in children but if individuals with chronic erythroid hyperplasia become infected the virus directly invades red cell precursors and temporarily switches off red cell production. Patients present with severe anaemia and a low reticulocyte count.

Pigment gallstones are present in up to 50% of patients and may cause symptomatic cholecystitis.

Investigations

Tests will confirm the presence of haemolysis and the blood film will show spherocytes but the direct Coombs test (see p. 924) is negative excluding immune haemolysis. An osmotic fragility test will show increased sensitivity to lysis in hypotonic saline solutions. It is important to screen other family members for features of compensated haemolysis.

Management

Folic acid prophylaxis, 5 mg once weekly, should be given life-long. Consideration may be given to splenectomy which improves but does not normalise red cell survival. Potential indications include:

- growth retardation in children, although splenectomy should be delayed until the child is over 5 years of age
- recurrent severe crises
- the death of other family members from the disease
- symptomatic cholecystitis.

Guidelines for the management of patients after splenectomy are presented in Box 19.22.

Acute, severe haemolytic crises require transfusion support but blood must be cross-matched carefully and transfused

19.22 MANAGEMENT OF THE SPLENECTOMISED PATIENT

- Vaccinate with multivalent pneumococcal and *Haemophilus* vaccines at least 2–3 weeks before elective splenectomy. Meningococcal C vaccination is only recommended for those living in areas with high endemic infection rates. Vaccinate after emergency surgery but protection may be less effective.
- Life-long penicillin V 250 mg 12-hourly is recommended to protect against bacterial strains not covered by the vaccines. If penicillin-allergic, consider a macrolide.
- Wherever possible, splenectomised patients should carry a card or bracelet indicating the date of their last vaccinations. In the event of overwhelming sepsis, this card may be life-saving in unconscious patients by guiding the rapid administration of appropriate antibiotics.
- Splenectomised patients admitted with septicaemia should be resuscitated and given intravenous antibiotics to cover pneumococcus, *Haemophilus* and meningococcus.
- Animal bites should be promptly treated with local disinfection and antibiotics to prevent serious soft tissue infection and septicaemia.

slowly as haemolytic transfusion reactions may occur. The typical blood film appearances are masked in the presence of iron deficiency or disorders which cause a raised MCV, such as jaundice; in these situations the red cell shape is normal but spherocytes will appear when the underlying abnormality is corrected.

HEREDITARY ELLIPTOCYTOSIS

This term refers to a heterogeneous group of disorders producing an increase in elliptocytic red cells on the blood film and a variable degree of haemolysis. It is due to a functional abnormality of one or more anchor proteins in the red cell membrane, e.g. alpha spectrin or protein 4.1. Inheritance may be autosomal dominant or recessive. It is less common than hereditary spherocytosis in the Western world, with an incidence of 1/10 000, but is more common in equatorial Africa and parts of South-east Asia. The clinical course is variable and depends upon the degree of membrane dysfunction caused by the inherited molecular defect(s); most cases present as an asymptomatic blood film abnormality but occasional cases result in neonatal haemolysis or a chronic compensated haemolytic state. Management of the latter is the same as for hereditary spherocytosis. A characteristic variant of hereditary elliptocytosis occurs in South-east Asia, particularly Malaysia and Papua New Guinea, with stomatocytes and ovalocytes in the blood. This has a prevalence of up to 30% in some communities because it offers relative protection from malaria which has sustained a high gene frequency. The differential diagnosis includes iron deficiency, thalassaemia, myelofibrosis, myelodysplasia and pyruvate kinase deficiency.

RED CELL ENZYMOPATHIES

The mature red cell must produce energy via ATP to maintain a normal internal environment and cell volume whilst protecting itself from the oxidative stress presented from oxygen carriage. Anaerobic glycolysis via the Embden–Meyerhof pathway generates ATP, and the hexose monophosphate shunt produces NADPH and glutathione to protect against oxidative stress. The impact of functional or quantitative defects in the enzymes in these pathways will depend upon the importance of the steps affected and the presence of alternative pathways. In general, defects in the hexose monophosphate shunt result in periodic haemolysis induced by oxidative stress, whilst those in the Embden–Meyerhof pathway result in shortened red cell survival and chronic haemolysis.

GLUCOSE-6-PHOSPHATE DEHYDROGENASE

This enzyme is pivotal in the hexose monophosphate shunt and produces NADPH to protect the red cell against oxidative stress. Deficiencies of this enzyme are the most common human enzymopathy, affecting 10% of the world's population with a geographical distribution which parallels the malaria belt (see Fig. 1.46, p. 52) because heterozygotes are protected from malarial parasitisation. The enzyme is a heteromeric structure made of catalytic subunits which are produced from a gene on the X chromosome. The deficiency affects males but is carried by females who are usually only affected in the neonatal period or in the presence of extreme lyonisation or homozygosity. There are over 400 subtypes of G6PD described. The most common types associated with normal activity are the B⁺ enzyme present in most Caucasians and 70% of Afro-Caribbeans, and the A⁺ variant present in 20% of Afro-Caribbeans. The two common variants associated with reduced activity are the A⁻ variety in approximately 10% of Afro-Caribbeans, and the Mediterranean or B⁻ variety in Caucasians. In East and West Africa up to 20% of males and 4% of females (homozygotes) are affected and have enzyme levels of approximately 15%. The deficiency in Caucasian and Oriental populations is more severe, with enzyme levels as low as 1%.

Clinical features

- Acute drug-induced haemolysis. This can occur with many drugs:
  —Analgesics: aspirin, phenacetin
  —Antimalarials: primaquine, quinine, chloroquine, pyrimethamine
  —Antibiotics: sulphonamides, nitrofurantoin, ciprofloxacin
  —Miscellaneous: quinidine, probenecid, vitamin K, dapsone.
- Chronic compensated haemolysis.
- Infection or acute illness.
- Neonatal jaundice. This may be a feature of the B⁻ enzyme.
- Favism or acute haemolysis after ingestion of the broad bean *Vicia faba*.

Laboratory features

- During an attack there will be evidence of non-spherocytic intravascular haemolysis.
- The blood film will show bite cells (red cells with a 'bite' of membrane missing), blister cells (red cells with

surface blistering of the membrane) and irregular-shaped small cells. There will be polychromasia reflecting the reticulocytosis and, if stained with a supravital stain such as methyl violet, denatured haemoglobin is visible as Heinz bodies within the red cell cytoplasm.

- The level of G6PD can be indirectly assessed by screening methods which usually depend upon the decreased ability to reduce dyes; direct assessment of G6PD is then made in those with low screening values. Care must be taken close to an acute haemolytic episode because reticulocytes may have normal enzyme levels and give rise to a false normal result.
- The different isoenzyme types may be identifiable by altered electrophoretic mobility but this is not of clinical value.

Management

Stop any precipitant drugs or deal with underlying infection. Acute transfusion support may be life-saving.

PYRUVATE KINASE DEFICIENCY

This is the second most common red cell enzyme defect and affects thousands of people world-wide. It results in deficiency of ATP production and a chronic haemolytic anaemia. It is inherited as an autosomal recessive trait. The extent of anaemia is variable; the blood film shows characteristic 'prickle cells' which resemble holly leaves. Enzyme activity is only 5–20% of normal. Transfusion support may be necessary.

PYRIMIDINE 5' NUCLEOTIDASE DEFICIENCY

This enzyme catalyses the dephosphorylation of nucleoside monophosphates and is important during the degradation of RNA in reticulocytes. It is inherited as an autosomal recessive trait and is as common as pyruvate kinase deficiency in Mediterranean, African and Jewish populations. The accumulation of excess ribonucleoprotein in deficiency results in coarse basophilic stippling associated with a chronic haemolytic state. The enzyme is very sensitive to inhibition by lead and this is the reason why basophilic stippling is a feature of lead poisoning.

ACQUIRED HAEMOLYTIC ANAEMIA

AUTOIMMUNE HAEMOLYTIC ANAEMIA

This results from increased red cell destruction due to red cell autoantibodies. The antibodies may be IgG or M, or more rarely IgE or A. If an antibody avidly complement fixes, it will result in intravascular haemolysis, but if complement activation is weak, the haemolysis will be extravascular. Antibody-coated red cells lose membrane to macrophages in the spleen and hence spherocytes are present in the blood. The optimum temperature at which the antibody is active (thermal specificity) is used to classify immune haemolysis:

- Warm antibodies bind best at 37°C and account for 80% of cases. The majority are IgG and usually react against Rhesus antigens.
- Cold antibodies bind best at 4°C but can bind up to 37°C in some cases. They are usually IgM and bind complement. They account for the other 20% of cases.

Warm autoimmune haemolysis

The incidence of warm autoimmune haemolysis is approximately 1/100 000 population per annum; it occurs at all ages but is more common in middle age and there is a female excess. No underlying cause is identified in up to 50% of cases. The remainder are secondary to a wide variety of other conditions:

- lymphoid neoplasms: lymphoma, chronic lymphocytic leukaemia, myeloma
- solid tumours: lung, colon, kidney, ovary, thymoma
- connective tissue disease: SLE, rheumatoid arthritis
- drugs: methyldopa, mefenamic acid, penicillin, quinine
- miscellaneous: ulcerative colitis, HIV.

Investigations

There is evidence of haemolysis and spherocytes on the blood film. The diagnosis is confirmed by the direct Coombs or antiglobulin test. In this, red cells are mixed with Coombs reagent which contains antibodies against human IgG/M/complement. If the red cells have been coated by antibody in vivo, the Coombs reagent will induce their agglutination which can be detected visually. The relevant antibody can be eluted from the red cell surface and tested against a panel of typed red cells to determine which red cell antigen it is directed against. The most common specificity is Rhesus and most often anti-e; this is helpful when choosing blood to cross-match. The direct Coombs test can be negative in the presence of brisk haemolysis; a positive test requires about 200 antibody molecules to attach to each red cell; with a very avid complement-fixing antibody, haemolysis may occur at lower levels of antibody-binding. The standard Coombs reagent will miss IgA or IgE antibodies.

Management

- If the haemolysis is secondary to an underlying cause, this must be dealt with; stop any offending drugs.
- It is usual to treat initially with prednisolone 1 mg/kg orally. A response is seen in 70–80% of cases but this may take up to 3 weeks; a rise in haemoglobin will be matched by a fall in bilirubin and LDH levels. Once the haemoglobin has reached 10 g/dl, the steroid dose can be reduced by 5 mg per week down to 10 mg daily, then reduced slowly to stop over a further 10 weeks. Steroids work by decreasing macrophage destruction of antibody-coated red cells and reducing antibody production.
- Transfusion support can be given for life-threatening problems; this will be the least incompatible blood but may still give rise to transfusion reactions or the development of further alloantibodies.
- If the haemolysis fails to respond to steroids or can only be stabilised by large doses, then splenectomy should be considered. This removes a main site of red cell

destruction and antibody production with a good response in 50–60% of cases. The operation can be performed laparoscopically with less morbidity for the patient.

- For patients who fail to respond to steroids or for whom splenectomy is not appropriate, alternative immunosuppressive therapy may be considered. This is least suitable for young patients for whom long-term therapy may carry a risk of secondary neoplasms. The choice of drug is between azathioprine 1–2 mg/kg or cyclophosphamide 2 mg/kg, both orally; it usually takes 2–3 months for these drugs to induce a response.

Cold agglutinin disease

This is due to antibodies, usually IgM, which bind to the red cells at 4°C and cause them to agglutinate. It may cause intravascular haemolysis if complement fixation occurs. This can be chronic when the antibody is monoclonal, and acute or transient when the antibody is polyclonal.

Chronic cold agglutinin disease

This affects elderly patients and may be associated with an underlying low-grade B-cell lymphoma. It causes a low-grade intravascular haemolysis with cold, painful and often blue fingers, toes, ears or nose (so-called acrocyanosis). The latter is due to red cell agglutination in the small vessels in these exposed areas. The blood film shows red cell agglutination and the MCV may be spuriously raised because the automated analysers count aggregates as single cells. The monoclonal IgM usually has specificity against the I or, more rarely, i antigen and is present in a very high titre. Treatment is directed at any underlying lymphoma but if the disease is idiopathic, then patients must keep extremities warm, especially in winter. Some patients respond to steroid therapy and blood transfusion may be considered but the cross-match sample must be placed in a transport flask at a temperature of 37°C and blood administered via a blood-warmer.

Other causes of cold agglutination

Cold agglutination can occur in association with *Mycoplasma* pneumonia or with infectious mononucleosis. Paroxysmal cold haemoglobinuria is a very rare cause seen in children in association with congenital syphilis. An IgG antibody binds to red cells in the peripheral circulation but lysis occurs in the central circulation when complement fixation takes place. This antibody is termed the Donath–Landsteiner antibody and has specificity against the P antigen on the red cells.

NON-IMMUNE HAEMOLYTIC ANAEMIA

Mechanical trauma

Physical disruption of red cells may occur in a number of conditions and is characterised by the presence of red cell fragments on the blood film and markers of intravascular haemolysis:

- *Mechanical heart valves*. High flow through incompetent valves or periprosthetic leaks through the suture ring holding a valve in place result in shear stress damage.
- *March haemoglobinuria*. Vigorous exercise such as prolonged marching or marathon running can cause red cell damage in the capillaries in the feet.

- *Thermal injury*. Severe burns cause thermal damage to red cells characterised by fragmentation and the presence of microspherocytes in the blood.
- *Microangiopathic haemolytic anaemia*. Fibrin deposition in capillaries can cause severe red cell disruption. It may occur in a wide variety of conditions: disseminated carcinomatosis, malignant or pregnancy-induced hypertension, haemolytic uraemic syndrome, thrombotic thrombocytopenic purpura and DIC (see p. 952).

Infection

Falciparum malaria (see p. 51) may be associated with intravascular haemolysis; when severe this is termed blackwater fever due to the associated haemoglobinuria. *Clostridium perfringens* septicaemia (see p. 39), usually in the context of an ascending cholangitis, may cause severe intravascular haemolysis with marked spherocytosis due to bacterial production of a lecithinase which destroys the red cell's membrane.

Chemicals or drugs

These agents cause haemolysis by oxidant denaturation of haemoglobin. Dapsone and sulfasalazine can produce haemolysis associated with the presence of Heinz bodies in the red cells on supravital staining with brilliant cresyl blue. Heinz bodies contain denatured haemoglobin. Arsenic gas, copper, chlorates, nitrites and nitrobenzene derivatives may all cause haemolysis.

HAEMOGLOBINOPATHIES

Normal haemoglobin

The normal haemoglobin molecule is comprised of two alpha and two non-alpha globin chains (see p. 895). Alpha globin chains are produced from two genes present on each chromosome 16; these are active throughout embryonic, fetal, infant and adult life. Severe disorders of alpha globin chains may therefore cause intrauterine death and will be present at birth. The non-alpha chains are produced by genes present in single copy on each chromosome 11. Production varies with age; fetal haemoglobin (HbF—$\alpha_2\gamma_2$) has two gamma chains but after the first trimester small amounts of haemoglobin A (HbA—$\alpha_2\beta_2$) with two beta chains are produced. At birth about 80% of haemoglobin is HbF and 20% HbA. Thereafter gamma chain production is suppressed such that by 6 months of age HbA is the predominant haemoglobin with less than 1% HbF. Disorders affecting the beta chain do not present until after 6 months of age. A constant small amount of haemoglobin A_2 (HbA$_2$—$\alpha_2\delta_2$, usually < 2%) is made from birth.

Abnormal haemoglobins

The haemoglobinopathies can be classified into two sub-groups.

The first is where there is an alteration in the amino acid structure of the polypeptide chains of the globin fraction of haemoglobin, commonly called the abnormal haemoglobins; the best-known example is haemoglobin S, found in sickle-cell anaemia. These usually result from amino acid substitutions which change the function of the globin chain at critical sites. For example, mutations around the haem-binding pocket cause the haem ring to fall out of the structure and produce an unstable haemoglobin. These substitutions often change the charge of the globin chains, producing different electrophoretic mobility, and this forms the basis for the diagnostic use of electrophoresis to identify haemoglobinopathies. Several hundred such variants are known; they were originally designated by letters of the alphabet, e.g. S, C, D or E, but are now described by names usually taken from the town or district in which they were first described.

The second is where the amino acid sequence is normal but polypeptide chain production is impaired or absent for a variety of reasons; these are the thalassaemias. In these conditions the ratio of alpha to non-alpha chain production is disturbed. In alpha-thalassaemia excess beta chains are present, whilst in beta-thalassaemia excess alpha chains are present. The excess chains precipitate, causing red cell membrane damage and a reduced red cell survival.

SICKLE-CELL ANAEMIA

Sickle-cell disease results from a single glutamic acid to valine substitution at position 6 of the beta globin polypeptide chain. It is inherited as an autosomal recessive trait. Homozygotes only produce abnormal beta chains that make haemoglobin S (HbS, termed SS), and this results in the clinical syndrome of sickle-cell disease. Heterozygotes produce a mixture of normal and abnormal beta chains that make normal HbA and HbS (termed AS), and this results in the clinically asymptomatic sickle trait. The inheritance of sickle-cell disease is shown in Figure 19.22.

Epidemiology

Individuals with sickle-cell trait are relatively resistant to the lethal effects of falciparum malaria in early childhood. The

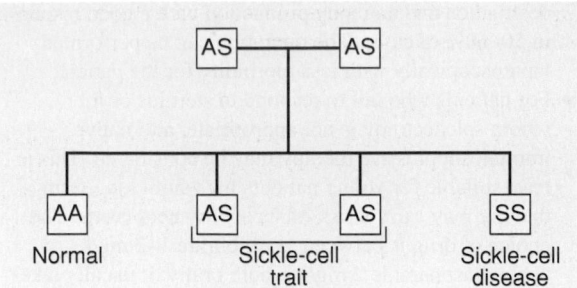

Fig. 19.22 Possible genotype of offspring of parents with sickle-cell trait.

high incidence of this deleterious gene in equatorial Africa can be explained by the selective survival advantage it confers in areas where falciparum malaria is endemic. Patients with sickle-cell anaemia do not have correspondingly greater resistance to falciparum malaria. The geographical distribution of sickle-cell anaemia and the other common haemoglobinopathies is shown in Figure 19.23. The greatest prevalence of haemoglobinopathies occurs in tropical Africa, where the heterozygote frequency is over 20%. In black American populations sickle-cell trait has a frequency of 8%.

Pathogenesis

When haemoglobin S is deoxygenated, the molecules of haemoglobin polymerise to form pseudocrystalline structures known as 'tactoids'. These distort the red cell membrane and produce characteristic sickle-shaped cells. The polymerisation is reversible when reoxygenation occurs. The distortion of the red cell membrane, however, may become permanent and the red cell 'irreversibly sickled'. The greater the concentration of sickle-cell haemoglobin in the individual cell, the more easily tactoids are formed, but this process may be enhanced or retarded by the presence of other haemoglobins. Thus haemoglobin C participates in the polymerisation

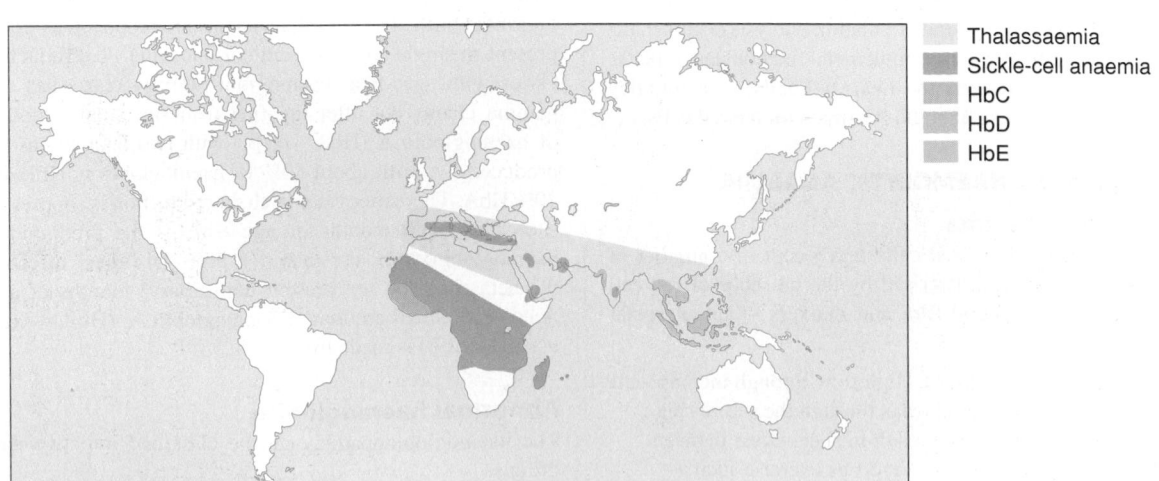

Fig. 19.23 The geographical distribution of the haemoglobinopathies.

more readily than haemoglobin A, whereas haemoglobin F strongly inhibits polymerisation.

Clinical features

Sickling is precipitated by hypoxia, acidosis, dehydration and infection. Irreversibly sickled cells have a shortened survival and plug vessels in the microcirculation. This results in a number of acute syndromes termed 'crises' and chronic organ damage as shown in Figure 19.24:

- *Vaso-occlusive crisis*. Plugging of small vessels in the bone produces acute severe bone pain. This affects areas of active marrow: the hands and feet in children (so-called dactylitis) or the femora, humeri, ribs, pelvis and vertebrae in adults. Patients usually have a systemic response with tachycardia, sweating and a fever. This is the most common crisis.
- *Sickle chest syndrome*. This may follow on from a vaso-occlusive crisis and is the most common cause of death in adult sickle disease. Bone marrow infarction

results in fat emboli to the lungs which cause sickling and infarction leading to ventilatory failure if not treated.
- *Sequestration crisis*. Thrombosis of the venous outflow from an organ causes loss of function and acute painful enlargement. In children the spleen is the most common site. Massive splenic enlargement may result in severe anaemia and circulatory collapse with death. Recurrent sickling in the spleen in childhood results in infarction and adults may have no functional spleen. In adults the liver may undergo sequestration with severe pain due to capsular stretching.
- *Aplastic crisis*. Infection of adult sicklers with parvovirus B19 results in a severe but self-limiting red cell aplasia. This produces a very low haemoglobin which may cause heart failure. Unlike all other sickle crises, the reticulocyte count is low.

Investigations

Patients with sickle-cell disease have a compensated anaemia, usually around 6–8 g/dl. The blood film shows

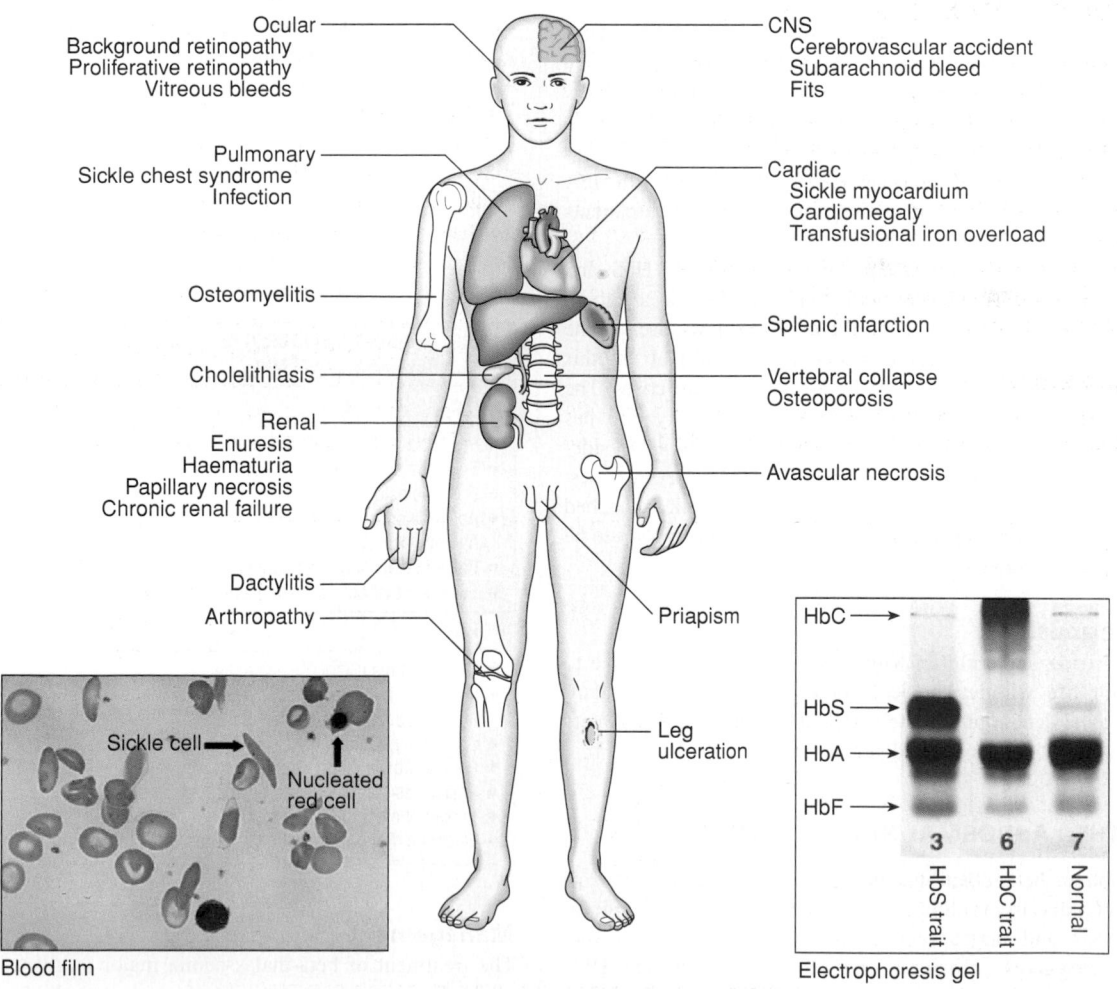

Fig. 19.24   Clinical manifestations of sickle-cell disease.

sickle cells, target cells and features of hyposplenism. A reticulocytosis is present. The presence of HbS can be demonstrated by exposing red cells to a reducing agent such as sodium dithionite; HbA gives a clear solution, whereas HbS polymerises to produce a turbid solution. This forms the basis of emergency screening tests before surgery in appropriate ethnic groups but cannot distinguish between sickle trait and disease. The definitive diagnosis requires haemoglobin electrophoresis to demonstrate no HbA, 2–20% HbF and the predominance of HbS. Both parents of the affected individual will have sickle trait.

Management

All patients with sickle disease should receive prophylaxis with daily folic acid, and penicillin V to protect against pneumococcal infection which may be lethal in the presence of hyposplenism. These patients should be vaccinated against pneumococcus and, where available, *Haemophilus* and hepatitis B.

Vaso-occlusive crises are managed by aggressive rehydration, oxygen therapy, adequate analgesia (which often requires opiates) and antibiotics. Transfusion should be with fully genotyped blood wherever possible. Simple top-up transfusion may be used in a sequestration or aplastic crisis. A regular transfusion programme to suppress HbS production and maintain the HbS level below 30% may be indicated in recurrent severe complications such as cerebrovascular accidents in children or chest syndromes in adults. Exchange transfusion where a patient is simultaneously venesected and transfused to replace HbS with HbA may be used in life-threatening crises or to prepare patients for surgery.

A high HbF level inhibits polymerisation of HbS and reduces sickling. Patients with sickle-cell disease and high HbF levels have a mild clinical course with few crises. Some agents are able to induce increased synthesis of HbF and this has been used to reduce the frequency of severe crises. The oral cytotoxic agent hydroxycarbamide (hydroxyurea) has been shown to effect clinical benefit with acceptable side-effects in children and adults who have recurrent severe crises. Relatively few allogeneic transplants from HLA-matched siblings have been performed but this procedure appears to be potentially curative.

Prognosis

In Africa few children with sickle-cell anaemia survive to adult life without medical attention. Even with standard medical care approximately 15% die by the age of 20 years and 50% by the age of 40 years.

OTHER ABNORMAL HAEMOGLOBINS

Another beta chain haemoglobinopathy, haemoglobin C (HbC) disease, is clinically silent but associated with microcytosis and target cells on the blood film. Compound heterozygotes inheriting one HbS gene and one HbC gene from their parents have haemoglobin SC disease which behaves like a mild form of sickle-cell disease. It is

associated with a reduced frequency of crises but is not uncommonly associated with complications in pregnancy and retinal vein thrombosis.

THE THALASSAEMIAS

Thalassaemia is an inherited impairment of haemoglobin production, in which there is partial or complete failure to synthesise a specific type of globin chain. In alpha-thalassaemia, the alpha genes are deleted; loss of one gene α^-/α or both genes α^-/α^- from each chromosome 16 may occur, in association with the production of some or no alpha globin chains. In beta-thalassaemia defective production usually results from disabling point mutations causing no (β^0) or reduced (β^-) beta chain production.

BETA-THALASSAEMIA

Failure to synthesise beta chains (beta-thalassaemia) is the most common type of thalassaemia and is seen in highest frequency in the Mediterranean area. Heterozygotes have thalassaemia minor, a condition in which there is usually mild anaemia and little or no clinical disability. Homozygotes (thalassaemia major) either are unable to synthesise haemoglobin A or at best produce very little and, after the first 4 months of life, develop a profound hypochromic anaemia. The diagnostic features are listed in Box 19.23.

Beta-thalassaemia minor is often detected only when iron therapy for a mild microcytic anaemia fails. The diagnostic features are also summarised in Box 19.23. Symptoms are absent or mild. Intermediate grades of severity occur.

19.23 DIAGNOSTIC FEATURES OF BETA-THALASSAEMIA
Major
• Profound hypochromic anaemia
• Evidence of severe red cell dysplasia
• Erythroblastosis
• Absence or gross reduction of the amount of haemoglobin A
• Raised levels of haemoglobin F
• Evidence that both parents have thalassaemia minor
Minor
• Mild anaemia
• Microcytic hypochromic erythrocytes (not iron-deficient)
• Some target cells
• Punctate basophilia
• Raised resistance of erythrocytes to osmotic lysis
• Raised haemoglobin A_2 fraction
• Evidence that one parent has thalassaemia minor

Management

The treatment of beta-thalassaemia major is given in Box 19.24. Cure is now a possibility for selected children, with allogeneic bone marrow transplantation.

19.24 TREATMENT OF BETA-THALASSAEMIA MAJOR

Problem	Management
Erythropoietic failure	Allogeneic bone marrow transplantation from human leucocyte antigen (HLA)-compatible sibling Transfusion to maintain Hb > 10 g/dl Folic acid 5 mg daily
Iron overload	Iron therapy forbidden Desferrioxamine therapy
Splenomegaly causing mechanical problems, excessive transfusion required	Splenectomy

Prevention

It is possible to identify a fetus with homozygous beta-thalassaemia by obtaining chorionic villous material for DNA analysis sufficiently early in pregnancy to allow termination. This examination is only appropriate if both parents are known to be carriers (beta-thalassaemia minor) and will accept a termination.

ALPHA-THALASSAEMIA

The reduction or absence of alpha chain synthesis is common in South-east Asia. There are two alpha gene loci on chromosome 16 and therefore four alpha genes. If one is deleted there is no clinical effect. If two are deleted there may be a mild hypochromic anaemia. If three are deleted the patient has haemoglobin H disease and if all four are deleted the baby is stillborn (hydrops fetalis). Haemoglobin H is a beta-chain tetramer formed from the excess of chains. It is functionally useless. Treatment of haemoglobin H disease is similar to that of beta-thalassaemia of intermediate severity. The combinations are shown in Box 19.25.

19.25 ALPHA-THALASSAEMIA

Cause
- Failure of production of haemoglobin alpha chains due to gene deletion

Age and sex
- Both sexes from birth onward

Genetics
- Two alpha chain genes from each parent

Presentation
- Hydrops fetalis if all genes deleted
- Haemoglobin H if three genes deleted
- Mild hypochromic microcytic anaemia if two genes deleted

Treatment
- Hydrops fetalis: none available
- Haemoglobin H: no specific therapy required; avoid iron therapy; folic acid if necessary

ISSUES IN OLDER PEOPLE
ANAEMIA

- Although the mean haemoglobin falls with age in both sexes, it remains well within the normal range.
- When a low haemoglobin does occur, it is generally due to disease. Anaemia can never be considered 'normal' in old age.
- Symptoms may be subtle and of insidious onset, but cardiovascular features such as dyspnoea and oedema, and cerebral features such as dizziness and apathy, tend to predominate.
- Ferritin of less than 45 μg/l in older people is highly predictive of iron deficiency; because of the prevalence of other disorders, serum iron and iron-binding capacity fall with age and are not reliable indicators of deficiency.
- Iron deficiency results almost exclusively from gastrointestinal blood loss.
- Vitamin B_{12} deficiency is most commonly due to pernicious anaemia as the prevalence of chronic atrophic gastritis rises in old age.
- Neuropsychiatric symptoms are a well-established feature of vitamin B_{12} deficiency, but a causal relationship between vitamin B_{12} deficiency and fixed dementia has not been clearly shown. Descriptions of dementia associated with vitamin B_{12} deficiency in the absence of haematological abnormalities are rare.
- Anaemia of chronic disease is frequent in old age because older people are prone to those diseases that reduce erythropoiesis.

HAEMATOLOGICAL MALIGNANCIES

Haematological malignancies arise when the processes of proliferation or apoptosis are corrupted in blood cells. If mature differentiated cells are involved, the cells will have a low growth fraction and produce indolent neoplasms such as the low-grade lymphomas or chronic leukaemias where patients have an expected survival of many years. In contrast, if more primitive stem cells are involved, the cells can have the highest growth fractions of all human neoplasms, producing rapidly progressive life-threatening illnesses such as the acute leukaemias or high-grade lymphomas. Involvement of the pluripotent stem cells produces the most aggressive acute leukaemias. In general, haematological neoplasms are diseases of elderly patients, the exceptions being acute lymphoblastic leukaemia which predominantly affects children, and Hodgkin's disease which affects young people in the 20–40-year age range (see Fig. 19.25).

LEUKAEMIAS

Leukaemias are a group of malignant disorders of the haematopoietic tissues characteristically associated with increased numbers of white cells in the bone marrow and/or peripheral blood. The course of leukaemia may vary from a few days or weeks to many years, depending on the type.

Epidemiology

The incidence of leukaemia of all types in the population is approximately 10/100 000 per annum, of which just under half are acute leukaemia. Males are affected more frequently than females, the ratio being about 3:2 in acute leukaemia,

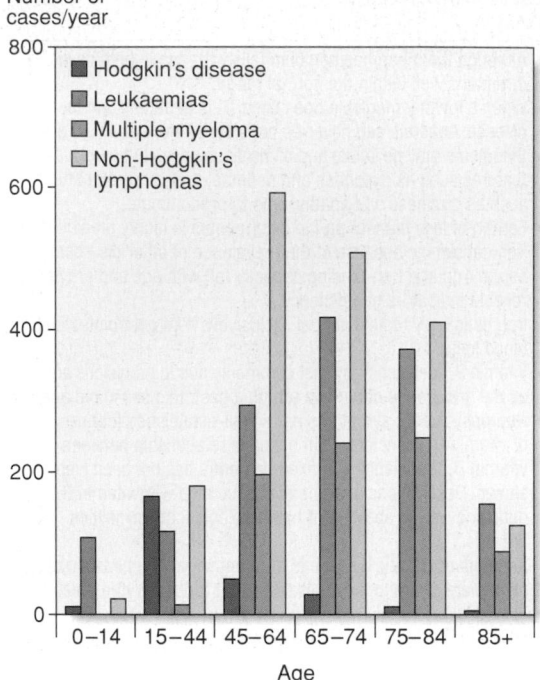

Fig. 19.25 **Variation in the incidence of different haematological malignancies in the UK by age.**

19.26 FACTORS ASSOCIATED WITH THE DEVELOPMENT OF LEUKAEMIA

Ionising radiation

- A significant increase in myeloid leukaemia followed the atomic bombing of Japanese cities
- An increase in leukaemia was observed after the use of radiotherapy for ankylosing spondylitis and diagnostic radiographs of the fetus in pregnancy

Cytotoxic drugs

- These, particularly alkylating agents, may induce myeloid leukaemia, usually after a latent period of several years

Exposure to benzene in industry

Retroviruses

- One rare form of T-cell leukaemia/lymphoma appears to be associated with a retrovirus similar to the viruses causing leukaemia in cats and cattle

Genetic

- There is a greatly increased incidence of leukaemia in the identical twin of patients with leukaemia
- Increased incidence occurs in Down's syndrome and certain other genetic disorders

Immunological

- Immune deficiency states (e.g. hypogammaglobulinaemia) are associated with an increase in haematological malignancy

2:1 in chronic lymphocytic leukaemia and 1.3:1 in chronic myeloid leukaemia. Geographical variation in incidence does occur, the most striking being the rarity of chronic lymphocytic leukaemia in the Chinese and related races. Acute leukaemia occurs at all ages. Acute lymphoblastic leukaemia shows a peak of incidence in the 1–5 age group. All forms of acute myeloid leukaemia have their lowest incidence in young adult life and there is a striking rise over the age of 50. Chronic leukaemias occur mainly in middle and old age.

Aetiology

The cause of the leukaemia is unknown in the majority of patients. Several factors, however, are associated with the development of leukaemia and these are listed in Box 19.26.

Terminology and classification

The terms 'acute' and 'chronic', when applied to leukaemia, refer to the clinical behaviour of the disease. In acute leukaemia the history is usually brief and life expectancy, without treatment, short. In chronic leukaemias the patient may have been unwell for months and survival is usually measured in years. A significant number of chronic leukaemias are discovered incidentally.

Not all leukaemias are associated with an increased peripheral blood leucocyte count or even the appearance of abnormal cells in the blood. The diagnosis is made from an examination of the bone marrow.

Leukaemias are traditionally classified into four main groups:

19.27 SUBCLASSIFICATIONS OF LEUKAEMIA

Acute lymphoblastic

- Common type (pre-B)
- T-cell
- B-cell
- Undifferentiated

Acute myeloid

FAB[1] classification
- M0 undifferentiated
- M1 minimal differentiation
- M2 differentiated
- M3 promyelocytic
- M4 myelomonocytic
- M5 monocytic
- M6 erythrocytic
- M7 megakaryocytic

Chronic lymphocytic

- B-cell—common
- T-cell—rare

Chronic myeloid

- Ph[2] positive
- Ph[2] negative, BCR-abl[3] positive
- Ph[2] negative, BCR-abl[3] negative
- Eosinophilic leukaemia

[1] FAB = French, American, British.
[2] Ph = Philadelphia chromosome.
[3] BCR = breakpoint cluster region; abl = Abelson oncogene.

- acute lymphoblastic
- acute myeloid
- chronic lymphocytic
- chronic myeloid.

A more detailed subclassification is provided in Box 19.27.

Although leukaemias are divided into lymphoid and myeloid varieties, recent advances have shown that this division may be artificial because in acute leukaemias the two types may coexist in the same patient. Nevertheless, there is a value in maintaining the distinction, as the drug therapy of the two main types is substantially different.

The subclassification of the lymphoblastic varieties is possibly of greater value, for the subtype dictates greater variation in treatment. The 'common' type, which constitutes 70% of all patients, responds well to treatment and carries the best chance of long-term remission. The classification of acute myeloid leukaemia into eight varieties reflects the variable degree of maturation of the granulocyte series, the common involvement of the monocyte series with the granulocyte series, and also the involvement of erythrocytic and megakaryocytic elements.

ACUTE LEUKAEMIA

There is a failure of cell maturation in acute leukaemia. Proliferation of cells which do not mature leads to an increasing accumulation of useless cells which take up more and more marrow space at the expense of the normal haematopoietic elements. Eventually, this proliferation spills into the blood. The evolution of acute leukaemia is illustrated schematically in Figure 19.26. Acute myeloid leukaemia is about four times more common than acute lymphoblastic leukaemia in adults. In children the proportions are reversed, with the lymphoblastic variety more common. The clinical features are usually those of bone marrow failure (anaemia, bleeding or infection—see pp. 902, 907 and 910).

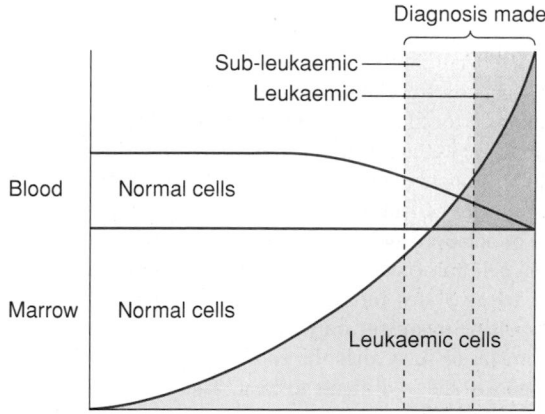

Fig. 19.26   The development of leukaemia.

Investigations

Blood examination usually shows anaemia with a normal or raised MCV. The leucocyte count may vary from as low as $1 \times 10^9/1$ to as high as $500 \times 10^9/1$ or more. In the majority of patients the count is below $100 \times 10^9/1$. The blood film appearance of blast cells and other primitive cells is usually diagnostic. Sometimes the blast cell count may be very low in the peripheral blood and a bone marrow examination is necessary to establish the diagnosis. Severe thrombocytopenia is usual but not invariable.

The bone marrow is the most valuable diagnostic investigation and will provide material for cytology (see Fig. 19.27),

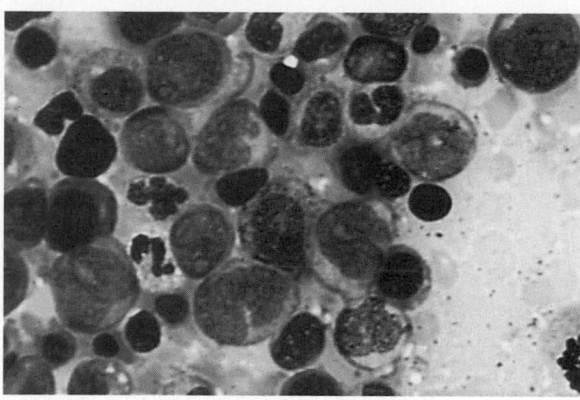

Fig. 19.27   Acute myeloid leukaemia. Bone marrow aspirate showing infiltration with large blast cells which display nuclear folding and prominent nucleoli.

19.28 INVESTIGATIONS FOR THE ASSESSMENT OF ACUTE LEUKAEMIA	
Haemostatic function	
• Coagulation screen	• D-dimers (see pp. 898 and 900)
• Fibrinogen	
Renal function	
• Plasma urea and creatinine	
Hepatic function	
• Total protein	• Alkaline phosphatase
• Albumin	• Alanine aminotransferase (ALT)
• Bilirubin	
Cellular proliferation	
• Plasma LDH	• Plasma urate

cytogenetics and immunological phenotyping. A trephine biopsy should be taken if no marrow is obtained (dry tap). The marrow is usually hypercellular, with replacement of normal elements by leukaemic blast cells in varying degrees (but more than 20% of the cells). The presence of Auer rods in the cytoplasm of blast cells indicates a myeloblastic type of leukaemia.

Other basic investigations required at diagnosis are given in Box 19.28.

Management

The general strategy for acute leukaemia is given in Figure 19.28. The first decision must be whether or not to give specific treatment. However, specific treatment is generally aggressive and has a number of side-effects. It may not be appropriate for the very elderly or patients with other serious disorders. In these patients supportive treatment only should be offered; this can effect considerable improvement in well-being.

Specific therapy

If a decision to embark on specific therapy has been taken, the patient should be prepared in the ways listed in Box 19.29. It is unwise to attempt aggressive management

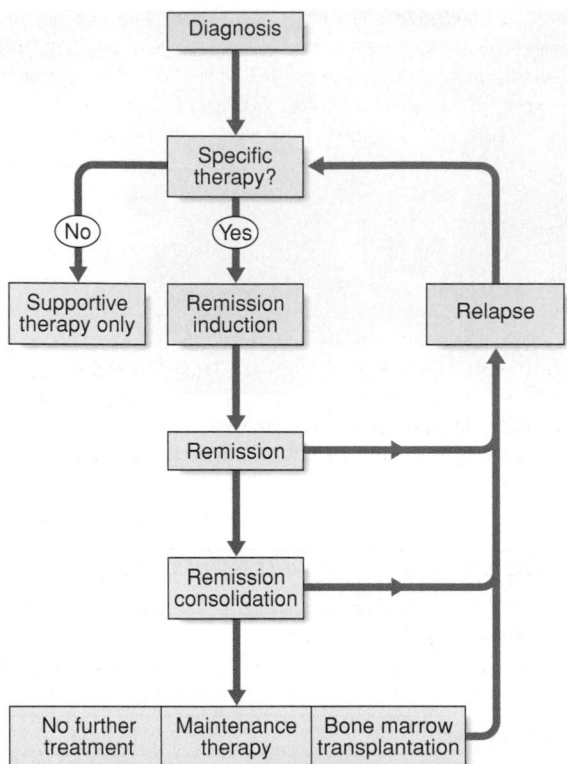

Fig. 19.28   Treatment strategy in acute leukaemia.

| 19.29 | MANAGEMENT OF ACUTE LEUKAEMIA: SPECIFIC THERAPY |

- Existing infections identified and treated (e.g. urinary tract infection, oral candidiasis, dental, gingival and skin infections)
- Anaemia corrected with red cell concentrate infusion
- Thrombocytopenic bleeding controlled with platelet transfusion
- If possible, central venous catheter (e.g. Hickman line) inserted to facilitate access to the circulation for delivery of chemotherapy
- Therapeutic regimen carefully explained to the patient

of acute leukaemia unless adequate services are available for the provision of supportive therapy.

The aim of treatment is to destroy the leukaemic clone of cells without destroying the residual normal stem cell compartment from which repopulation of the haematopoietic tissues will occur. There are three phases:

- *Remission induction*. In this phase the bulk of the tumour is destroyed by combination chemotherapy. The patient goes through a period of severe bone marrow hypoplasia, requiring intensive support and inpatient care from specially trained medical and nursing staff.
- *Remission consolidation*. If remission has been achieved by induction therapy, residual disease is attacked by therapy during the consolidation phase. This consists of a number of courses of chemotherapy, again resulting in periods of marrow hypoplasia.
- *Remission maintenance*. If the patient is still in remission after the consolidation phase for acute lymphoblastic

19.30 DRUGS COMMONLY USED IN THE TREATMENT OF ACUTE LEUKAEMIA

Phase	Lymphoblastic	Myeloid
Induction	Vincristine (i.v.) Prednisolone (oral) L-asparaginase (i.v.) Daunorubicin (i.v.) Methotrexate (intrathecal)	Daunorubicin (i.v.) Cytarabine (i.v.) Etoposide (i.v. and oral) Tioguanine (oral)
Consolidation	Daunorubicin (i.v.) Cytarabine (i.v.) Etoposide (i.v.) Methotrexate (i.v.)	Cytarabine (i.v.) Amsacrine (i.v.) Mitoxantrone (mitozantrone) (i.v.)
Maintenance	Prednisolone (oral) Vincristine (i.v.) Mercaptopurine (oral) Methotrexate (oral)	

leukaemia, a period of maintenance therapy is given, consisting of a repeating cycle of drug administration. This may extend for up to 2 years if relapse does not occur and is usually given on an outpatient basis. Thereafter, specific therapy is discontinued and the patient observed. (This phase is not thought to be of benefit in most patients with acute myeloblastic leukaemia who have been brought into complete remission by induction and consolidation therapy.)

In patients with acute lymphoblastic leukaemia it is necessary to give therapy to the central nervous system. This usually consists of a combination of cranial irradiation and intrathecal methotrexate.

The detail of the schedules for these treatments will be found in specialist texts. The drugs most commonly employed for the two main varieties of acute leukaemia are given in Box 19.30. If a patient fails to go into remission with induction treatment, alternative drug combinations may be tried but generally the outlook is poor unless a remission can be achieved and the patient has a donor for an allogeneic stem cell transplant. Alternatively, a decision may be taken not to give any further specific therapy and to provide supportive treatment only. Disease which relapses during treatment or soon after the end of treatment carries a poor prognosis and is difficult to treat. The longer after the end of treatment that relapse occurs, the more likely it is that further treatment will be effective.

Supportive therapy

Aggressive and potentially curative therapy which involves periods of severe bone marrow failure would not be possible without adequate and skilled supportive care. The following problems commonly arise.

Anaemia. Anaemia is treated with red cell concentrate infusions to maintain a haemoglobin above 10 g/dl.

Bleeding. Thrombocytopenic bleeding requires platelet transfusions unless the bleeding is trivial. Prophylactic platelet transfusion should be given to maintain the platelet count above 10×10^9/l. Coagulation abnormalities occur and need accurate diagnosis and treatment as appropriate, usually with fresh frozen plasma.

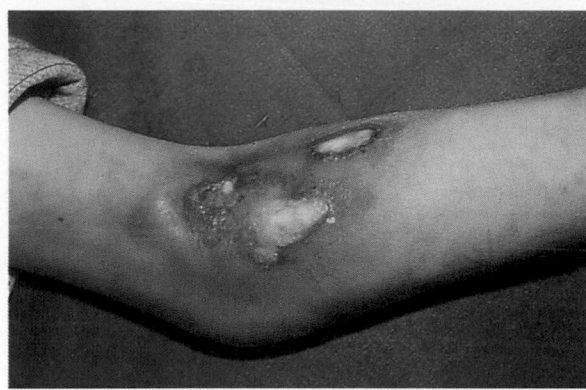

Fig. 19.29 Skin necrosis due to extravasation of anthracycline chemotherapy (e.g. doxorubicin, daunorubicin).

Infection. Fever (> 38°C) lasting over 1 hour in a neutropenic patient (absolute neutrophil count < 1.0×10^9/l) indicates possible septicaemia. Parenteral broad-spectrum antibiotic therapy is essential. Empirical therapy with a combination of an aminoglycoside (e.g. gentamicin) is given with a broad-spectrum penicillin (e.g. piperacillin/tazobactam). This combination is synergistic and bactericidal and should be continued for at least 5 days after the fever has resolved. The organisms most commonly associated with severe neutropenia are Gram-positive bacteria such as *Staphylococcus aureus* and *Staph. epidermidis*. The Gram-negative infections with organisms such as *Escherichia coli*, *Pseudomonas* and *Klebsiella* are more likely to cause rapid clinical deterioration and these organisms must be covered with the initial empirical therapy. Gram-positive infection, particularly when the patient has an in-dwelling intravenous catheter, may require vancomycin. Patients with lymphoblastic leukaemia are susceptible to infection with *Pneumocystis carinii* (see p. 120), which causes a severe pneumonia. Prophylaxis with co-trimoxazole is given during therapy. Diagnosis may be difficult and may require either bronchoalveolar lavage or open lung biopsy. Treatment is with high-dose co-trimoxazole, initially intravenously, with change to oral treatment as soon as possible.

Oral and pharyngeal monilial infection is common. Prophylaxis with fluconazole is often considered; this drug is effective for the treatment of established local infection.

For systemic fungal infection with *Candida* or pulmonary aspergillosis, intravenous amphotericin is required: 0.5–1 mg/kg per day for at least 3 weeks. Amphotericin is nephrotoxic and hepatotoxic. Renal and hepatic function should therefore be monitored closely, particularly if the patient is receiving antibiotics which are also nephrotoxic. Potassium supplementation is usually required. For patients who experience nephrotoxicity with standard amphotericin, newer lipid formulations of amphotericin can be administered without further deterioration of renal function (see p. 143).

Herpes simplex infection (see p. 30) occurs frequently round the lips and nose during ablative therapy for acute leukaemia. Aciclovir (200 mg 5 times per day) may be prescribed prophylactically to patients with a history of cold sores or elevated titres to herpes simplex. The intravenous dose is 5 mg/kg over 1 hour, repeated 8-hourly. Herpes zoster (see p. 32) can also be treated in the early stage with aciclovir at a dose of 10 mg/kg 8-hourly i.v. for 5 days.

The value of isolation facilities, such as laminar flow rooms, is debatable but may contribute to staff awareness of careful barrier nursing practice. The isolation is often psychologically stressful for the patient.

Metabolic problems. Continuous monitoring of renal, hepatic and haemostatic function is necessary, together with fluid balance measurements. Patients are often severely anorexic and may find drinking difficult and hence require intravenous fluids and electrolytes. Renal toxicity occurs with some antibiotics (e.g. aminoglycosides) and antifungal agents (amphotericin).

Psychological support. This is a key aspect of care. Patients should be kept informed, and their questions answered and fears allayed as far as possible. An optimistic attitude from the staff is vital. Delusions, hallucinations and paranoia are not uncommon during periods of severe bone marrow failure and septicaemic episodes, and should be met with patience and understanding.

Alternative chemotherapy. Gentle chemotherapy not designed to achieve remission may be used to curb excessive leucocyte proliferation. Drugs used for this purpose include hydroxycarbamide (hydroxyurea) up to 4 g daily and mercaptopurine up to 150 mg daily. The effect is to reduce the leucocyte count without inducing bone marrow failure.

Prognosis

Without treatment the median survival of patients with acute leukaemia is about 5 weeks. This may be extended to a number of months with supportive treatment. Patients who achieve remission with specific therapy have a better outlook. Around 80% of adult patients under 60 years of age with acute lymphoblastic leukaemia or acute myeloblastic leukaemia achieve remission. Remission rates are lower for older patients. However, the relapse rate continues to be high. Median survival for acute lymphoblastic leukaemia patients is about 30 months; patients with acute myeloblastic leukaemia under 55 have a 40% 5-year survival with the best modern chemotherapy. Poor prognostic factors are given in Box 19.31. Genetic analysis by conventional cytogenetics, fluorescent in situ hybridisation or polymerase chain reaction is very important. The presence of a Philadelphia chromosome in acute lymphoblastic leukaemia carries a poor prognosis, as does the presence of chromosome 7 abnormalities in acute myeloid leukaemia. Conversely, the presence of the t(15,17) or t(8,21) translocations confers a good prognosis in acute myeloid leukaemia.

19.31 POOR PROGNOSTIC FEATURES IN ACUTE LEUKAEMIA	
• Increasing age • Male sex • High leucocyte levels at diagnosis	• Cytogenetic abnormalities • CNS involvement at diagnosis • Antecedent haematological disorder

Allogeneic bone marrow transplantation

Until recently, bone marrow transplantation (BMT) has been the only therapeutic measure which held out the hope of 'cure' for persons with a variety of haematological disorders, particularly those listed in Box 19.32.

> **19.32 GENERAL INDICATIONS FOR ALLOGENEIC BONE MARROW TRANSPLANTATION**
>
> - Neoplastic disorders affecting the totipotent or pluripotent stem cell compartment (e.g. leukaemias)
> - Those with a failure of haematopoiesis (e.g. aplastic anaemia)
> - A major inherited defect in blood cell production (e.g. thalassaemia, immunodeficiency diseases)
> - Inborn errors of metabolism with missing enzymes or cell lines

Healthy marrow or stem cells collected from the peripheral blood of a normal donor may be injected intravenously into a recipient who has been suitably 'conditioned'. The conditioning therapy used most frequently is high-dose cyclophosphamide and total body irradiation. Conditioning destroys malignant cells but as a side-effect ablates the recipient's haematopoietic and immunological tissues. The injected donor cells 'home' to the marrow, engraft and produce enough erythrocytes, granulocytes and platelets for the patient's needs after about 3–4 weeks. It may take several years to regain normal immunological function. During this period, particularly in the first year, the patient is at great risk from opportunistic infections. The use of peripheral blood stem cells is associated with more rapid engraftment and immunological reconstitution, making the procedure safer. The donor's immunological system can recognise residual malignant recipient cells and destroy them. This immunological 'graft versus disease' effect is a powerful tool against many haematological tumours and can be boosted in post-transplantation relapse by the infusion of T cells taken from the donor, so-called donor leucocyte infusion (DLI).

The preferred donors are histocompatible siblings and the best results are obtained in patients aged under 20. Older patients can be transplanted, but results become progressively worse with age and an upper age limit of 55 years is usually applied. The patient should be free of other disorders which might seriously limit lifespan. BMT requires specialised supervision and supportive facilities with fully trained staff. Disorders for which allogeneic transplantation is currently considered are shown in Box 19.33. Transplantation is also a

> **19.33 HAEMATOLOGICAL INDICATIONS FOR ALLOGENEIC BONE MARROW TRANSPLANTATION**
>
> - Acute myeloblastic leukaemia in first remission
> - Chronic myeloid leukaemia in chronic phase
> - T- and B-cell lymphoblastic leukaemia in first remission
> - Acute lymphoblastic leukaemia (common pre-B type) in second remission
> - Severe aplastic anaemia
> - Acute myelofibrosis
> - Severe immunodeficiency syndromes
> - Lymphoma
> - Myeloma

> **19.34 COMPLICATIONS OF ALLOGENEIC BONE MARROW TRANSPLANTATION**
>
> - Mucositis
> - Infection
> - Acute graft-versus-host disease
> - Pneumonitis
> - Chronic graft-versus-host disease
> - Infertility
> - Cataract formation
> - Secondary malignant disease

possibility for resistant acute leukaemia and in selected patients with lymphoma. The role of allogeneic BMT in patients with haemoglobinopathies such as sickle-cell disease is controversial.

The main complications of allogeneic BMT are outlined in Box 19.34.

The long-term survival for patients undergoing allogeneic BMT in acute leukaemia is around 50%. Up to 30% succumb to procedure-related morbidity (e.g. graft-versus-host disease, pneumonitis) and in 20% the disease relapses.

Graft-versus-host disease (GVHD)

Problems of GVHD and interstitial pneumonitis may cause serious morbidity and death. Even low-grade GVHD, which is probably advantageous in terms of survival, can reduce the quality of life. GVHD is due to the cytotoxic activity of donor T lymphocytes which become sensitised to their new host, regarding it as foreign. This may cause either an acute or a chronic form of GVHD.

Acute GVHD. This usually appears 14–21 days after the graft, although it may appear earlier or up to 70 days later. It can affect the skin, liver and gut, and may vary from mild to lethal. It appears to be associated with infection, although the relationship is not fully understood. Methotrexate, ciclosporin, antithymocyte globulin, high-dose corticosteroids and T-cell depletion of the donor marrow have all been used to try to prevent the disorder. The more severe forms prove very difficult to control; high-dose corticosteroids may be helpful.

Chronic GVHD. This may follow acute GVHD or arise independently; it occurs later than acute GVHD. It often resembles a connective tissue disorder, although in mild cases a rash may be the only manifestation. Chronic GVHD is usually treated with corticosteroids. Ciclosporin can be used in cases associated with thrombocytopenia. Associated with chronic GVHD is a graft-versus-leukaemia effect, which results in a lower relapse rate.

Infection

Infection is the other major problem encountered during recovery from BMT. Details are given in Box 19.35.

Low-intensity allografting

This concept has been developed in an attempt to reduce the mortality of allografting. Rather than use very intensive conditioning which causes morbidity from end-organ damage, relatively low doses of drugs such as fludarabine and cyclophosphamide are used simply to immunosuppress the recipient and allow donor stem cells to engraft. The emerging donor immune system then eliminates the malignant cells via the 'graft versus disease' effect which may be

19.35 INFECTION DURING RECOVERY FROM BONE MARROW TRANSPLANTATION (BMT)		
Infection	**Time after BMT**	**Treatment**
Herpes simplex (see p. 143)	0–4 weeks	Aciclovir
Bacterial, fungal	0–4 weeks	As for acute leukaemia (see p. 933)
Cytomegalovirus (see p. 17)	7–21 weeks	If patient is CMV-negative, use CMV-negative blood products Hyperimmune immunoglobulin and ganciclovir for documented infections
Varicella zoster (see p. 31)	After 13 weeks	Aciclovir 10 mg/kg per day for 1–2 weeks i.v.
Pneumocystis carinii (see p. 120)	8–26 weeks	Co-trimoxazole
Interstitial pneumonitis (non-infective)	6–18 weeks	No specific therapy Prednisolone, 60 mg daily orally, may be tried

boosted by the elective use of donor T-cell infusions post-transplant. This type of transplant is less toxic but long-term results are still awaited.

Autologous bone marrow transplantation—peripheral blood stem cell transplantation

In this procedure the patient's own marrow is harvested and frozen to be given back again after intensive therapy to rescue the patient from the marrow damage and aplasia caused by the chemotherapy. It may be used for disorders which do not primarily involve the haematopoietic tissues or in patients in whom very good remissions have been achieved in conditions such as acute leukaemias and high-grade lymphomas. In acute leukaemias the procedure carries a lower procedure-related mortality rate than with allogeneic bone marrow transplantation but there is a high relapse rate (50%). However, there are some data to suggest that in certain patients with acute leukaemia autologous transplantation might confer a modest advantage over chemotherapy, although results from further trials are required to substantiate this. The issue of whether the stem cells should be treated (purged) in an attempt to remove any residual leukaemia cells is controversial.

Stem cells were originally obtained by harvesting them from the marrow. More recently, they have been collected from the peripheral blood during the recovery phase following a period of chemotherapy-induced marrow hypoplasia. The dose of stem cells collected from the peripheral blood is much greater than that harvested from marrow, resulting in significantly faster engraftment and a reduction in transplant-related mortality to less than 1% in patients under 55 years of age.

CHRONIC MYELOID LEUKAEMIA

Chronic myeloid leukaemia is a disorder of proliferation which is unrestrained and excessive. Maturation proceeds fairly normally. The disease occurs chiefly between the ages of 30 and 80 years, with a peak incidence at 55 years. It is rare, with an annual incidence in the UK of 1/100 000, and accounts for 20% of all leukaemias. The disease is found in all races. The aetiology is unknown.

Cytogenetic and molecular aspects

Approximately 90% of patients with chronic myeloid leukaemia have a chromosome abnormality known as the Philadelphia (Ph) chromosome. This is a shortened chromosome 22 and is the result of a reciprocal translocation of material with chromosome 9. The break on chromosome 22 occurs in the breakpoint cluster region (BCR). The fragment from chromosome 9 that joins the BCR carries the Abelson (abl) oncogene, which forms a chimeric gene with the remains of the BCR. This chimeric gene codes for a 210 kDa protein with tyrosine kinase activity, which plays a causative role in the disease. Some Ph-negative patients also have evidence of the same molecular abnormality.

Natural history

The disease has three phases: a chronic phase, in which the disease is responsive to treatment, is easily controlled and is essentially a benign neoplasm; an accelerated phase (not always seen), in which disease control becomes more difficult; and a blast crisis phase, in which the disease transforms into an acute leukaemia, either myeloid (70%) or lymphoblastic (30%), which is relatively refractory to treatment. Blast crises occur randomly and are the cause of death in the majority of patients. Patient survival is therefore dictated by the timing of blast crises, which cannot be predicted.

Clinical features

The frequency of the more common symptoms at presentation is given in Box 19.36. About 25% of patients are asymptomatic at diagnosis. On examination the principal clinical finding is splenomegaly, which is present in 90% of patients. In about 10% the enlargement is massive, extending to over 15 cm below the costal margin. A friction rub may be heard in cases of splenic infarction. Hepatomegaly occurs in about 50% of patients. Lymphadenopathy is unusual.

Investigations

Examination of the blood usually shows a normocytic, normochromic anaemia. The mean haemoglobin is 10.5 g/dl

19.36 SYMPTOMS AT PRESENTATION OF CHRONIC MYELOID LEUKAEMIA	
Symptom	**Present (%)**
Tiredness	37
Weight loss	26
Breathlessness	21
Abdominal pain and discomfort	21
Lethargy	13
Anorexia	12
Sweating	11
Abdominal fullness	10
Bruising	7
Vague ill health	7

with a range of 7–15 g/dl. The mean leucocyte count is $220 \times 10^9/l$ with a range of 9.5–600. The mean platelet count is $445 \times 10^9/l$ with a range of 162–2000. In the blood film the full range of granulocyte precursors from myeloblasts to mature neutrophils is seen, with peaks at the myelocyte and mature granulocyte stage of maturation. Myeloblasts are usually less than 10%. There is often an absolute increase in eosinophils and basophils, and nucleated red cells are common. If the disease progresses through an accelerated phase, the percentage of the more primitive cells increases. There is a dramatic increase in the number of circulating myeloblasts as the disease enters blast transformation. In about one-third of patients very high platelet counts are seen during treatment, both in chronic and accelerated phases, but these usually drop dramatically at blast transformation. Basophilia tends to increase as the disease progresses.

The peripheral blood is the most useful diagnostically but bone marrow material should be obtained for chromosome analysis to demonstrate the presence of the Philadelphia chromosome. Increasingly, RNA analysis is being undertaken to demonstrate the presence of the chimeric BCR-abl gene. Other characteristic findings on investigation include a very low neutrophil alkaline phosphatase score and very high vitamin B_{12} levels in the plasma. LDH levels are also substantially elevated.

Management

No specific therapy is required if the patient is asymptomatic and the leucocyte count not greatly elevated. In the majority of patients, however, treatment is necessary.

Chemotherapy

Hydroxycarbamide (hydroxyurea) is currently the most widely used oral agent to provide initial control of the disease. A daily dose of around 2–4 g is used initially, then tailored to maintain the white count in the normal range. Treatment with hydroxycarbamide (hydroxyurea) alone, however, does not diminish the frequency of the Ph chromosome or affect the onset of blast cell transformation. Three types of treatment given in chronic phase can affect survival and result in the loss of the Ph chromosome.

Alpha interferon

This is given intramuscularly or subcutaneously at 3–9 mega units daily. It can induce and maintain control of this disease in chronic phase in about 70% of patients. In addition, however, reduction in the percentage of Ph-positive cells is seen in about 20% and apparent elimination of the Ph chromosome in about 5%. There is evidence that interferon prolongs survival in those who achieve a significant reduction in Ph-positive cells. Only prolonged follow-up will determine whether such patients are cured. Interferon therapy causes 'flu-like' symptoms initially: tiredness, somnolence, weight loss, dizziness, nausea, vomiting, loss of taste, diarrhoea and headache. Some of these side-effects may be controlled with paracetamol; others such as severe bone pain and severe weight loss are reasons for discontinuation. The majority of patients tolerate the therapy well, particularly if the dose can be reduced to 3 mega units 3 times per week. It is unwise to use interferon therapy in patients over

75 years of age because of neurotoxicity. During treatment the aim should be to maintain the leucocyte count at low levels between 2 and $5 \times 10^9/l$.

Allogeneic or syngeneic bone marrow transplant from a matched sibling donor

This provides the only means of obtaining long-term remission in this disease. It is available in the UK to those under the age of 55 years who have a suitable donor. The best results are obtained in patients in early chronic phase when about 80% can expect probable cure. Monitoring for relapse by detecting the presence of the BCR-abl protein and the use of donor T-cell infusion in such cases has proven very effective at returning patients to durable complete remission. The results of transplantation in accelerated and blast transformation phases are significantly worse. As only a few patients have matched family donors available, there is increasing interest in transplantation using matched unrelated volunteer donors obtained from donor panels. Such a transplant carries higher morbidity and mortality but may offer the prospect of long-term survival in up to 40%. Various autografting approaches are also under evaluation.

Treatment of the accelerated phase and blast crisis of the disease is more difficult. In accelerated phase, hydroxycarbamide (hydroxyurea) can be an effective single agent; low-dose cytarabine can also be tried. When blast transformation occurs, the type of blast cell should be ascertained by cytochemical and immunological techniques. If lymphoblastic, the response to appropriate treatment (see p. 932) is better than if myeloblastic. Response to treatment for the latter is very poor. There is a strong case for supportive therapy only, particularly in older patients.

Initab mesylate (STI 571)

This agent is an inhibitor of the BCR-abl tyrosine kinase. Early trials have demonstrated excellent activity in chronic phase disease, with over 50% achieving Ph-chromosome negativity. It is also very active in interferon-resistant cases, in accelerated phase and blast crisis. This is a very promising new agent and trials are in progress to define its use in chronic phase disease and as an adjunct to transplantation.

Prognosis

Patients treated conventionally have a 15% risk of death in the first 12 months, and thereafter an annual risk of 20–25%. Median survival is about 45 months with chemotherapy, but 65 months with interferon; patients who have a significant reduction in the Ph chromosome with interferon do best. Patients receiving an allograft from a sibling early in chronic phase have an 80% chance of prolonged survival.

Philadelphia chromosome-negative chronic myeloid leukaemia

About half of these patients have the classical molecular abnormality (BCR-positive) without a demonstrable Ph chromosome. They behave as Ph chromosome-positive patients and they should be managed in the same way. The remainder (BCR-negative) tend to be older, mostly males, with lower platelet counts and higher absolute monocyte counts, and respond poorly to treatment. Median survival is less than 1 year.

CHRONIC LYMPHOCYTIC LEUKAEMIA

This is the most common variety of leukaemia, accounting for 30% of cases. The male to female ratio is 2:1 and the majority of patients are over the age of 45, with a peak at 65. In this disease B lymphocytes, which would normally respond to antigens by transformation and antibody formation, fail to do so. An ever-increasing mass of immuno-incompetent cells accumulate, to the detriment of immune function and normal bone marrow haematopoiesis. The receptor profile of the lymphocytes demonstrates a B-cell type of disease. The light chains of immunoglobulins produced by these B cells tend to be either kappa or lambda in type, indicating in the majority of cases a monoclonal expansion of cells. The B cells of chronic lymphocytic leukaemia characteristically express a T-cell antigen, CD5.

Clinical features

The onset is very insidious. Indeed, in around 25% of patients the diagnosis is made incidentally. Presenting problems may be anaemia, painless lymphadenopathy or splenomegaly; infections may be present at the time of diagnosis but often occur later in the progress of the disease. Herpes zoster (shingles) is more common.

Investigations

Peripheral blood examination usually shows a mild but gradually increasing anaemia. Haemolytic anaemia may occur and is usually warm autoimmune in type (see p. 924). In the majority of patients the leucocyte count is between 50 and 200 × 10⁹/l, although it may occasionally be greatly increased, up to 1000 × 10⁹/l. About 95% or more of these cells are mature lymphocytes. Bone marrow examination by aspirate and trephine may be helpful not only in the diagnosis of cases with a low white count but also for prognosis. Patients with diffuse marrow involvement tend to do worse. Chromosome analysis can be helpful; cases with trisomy 12, the most common abnormality, or 13q abnormalities are associated with a poorer prognosis. The platelet count may be low due to marrow failure or an immune destruction. Estimations of total proteins and immunoglobulin levels should be undertaken to establish the degree of immuno-suppression which is common and progressive. In some patients there may be a monoclonal band. Urate levels are seldom raised because cell turnover is low.

19.37 STAGING OF CHRONIC LYMPHOCYTIC LEUKAEMIA
Clinical stage A
● No anaemia or thrombocytopenia and less than three areas of lymphoid enlargement
Clinical stage B
● No anaemia or thrombocytopenia, with three or more involved areas of lymphoid enlargement
Clinical stage C
● Anaemia and/or thrombocytopenia, regardless of the number of areas of lymphoid enlargement

Staging

The disease may be staged according to the criteria given in Box 19.37.

Management

Treatment depends upon the stage of the disease:

● *Clinical stage A.* No specific treatment is required. Life expectancy is normal in older patients. The patient should be reassured.
● *Clinical stage B.* Chemotherapy with chlorambucil may be initiated in symptomatic patients (see below). Local radiotherapy to lymph nodes may be given if causing discomfort.
● *Clinical stage C.* Anaemia may require transfusion with red cell concentrate. Bone marrow failure, if present, is treated initially with prednisolone, 40 mg daily for 2–4 weeks. A degree of bone marrow recovery is usually achieved.

Cytotoxic therapy

Chlorambucil, 5 mg orally daily, over long periods with dose adjustment according to blood counts, will reduce the abnormal lymphocyte mass and produce symptomatic improvement in most patients. Alternatively, chlorambucil may be given as intermittent high-dose therapy, 0.4 mg/kg every 2 weeks, incrementing by 0.1 mg/kg until the maximum tolerated dose is reached. This is continued until the desired therapeutic effect is obtained. In stage C disease there is some evidence that more aggressive combination chemotherapy might be beneficial in terms of disease-free but not overall survival. Fludarabine, a synthetic nucleoside, appears to be the most active drug and is now available orally.

Radiotherapy

Total body irradiation using very small doses spread over 5 weeks in 10 fractions is effective and well tolerated, especially by the elderly. Local radiotherapy may be used to reduce spleen size or treat local problems due to the disease.

Infections

These must be vigorously treated. Recurrent viral or non-specific infections (often respiratory) sometimes respond to immunoglobulin replacement therapy.

Splenectomy

This may be required to treat autoimmune haemolytic anaemia or gross splenic enlargement.

Prognosis

The overall median survival for patients with chronic lymphocytic leukaemia is about 6 years. Clinical stage A patients have a normal life expectancy but stage C patients have a median survival of between 2 and 3 years. Approximately 50% of patients die of infection and 30% of causes unrelated to chronic lymphocytic leukaemia. Unlike chronic myeloid leukaemia, chronic lymphocytic leukaemia rarely transforms to an aggressive high-grade lymphoma, so-called Richter's transformation.

PROLYMPHOCYTIC LEUKAEMIA

This is a variant of chronic lymphatic leukaemia found mainly in males over the age of 60; 25% of cases are of the T-cell variety. There is massive splenomegaly with little lymphadenopathy and a very high leucocyte count, often in excess of $400 \times 10^9/l$; the characteristic cell is a large lymphocyte with a prominent nucleolus. Treatment is generally unsuccessful and the prognosis very poor. Leucopheresis, splenectomy and chemotherapy may be tried.

HAIRY CELL LEUKAEMIA

This is a rare chronic lymphoproliferative B-cell disorder. The male to female ratio is 6:1 and the median age at diagnosis is 50. Presenting symptoms are generally those of ill health and recurrent infections. Splenomegaly occurs in 90% but lymph node enlargement is unusual.

Severe neutropenia, monocytopenia and the characteristic hairy cells in the blood and bone marrow are typical. These cells usually type as B lymphocytes but characteristically express CD25 and CD103. A characteristic test is the demonstration that the acid phosphatase staining reaction in the cells is resistant to the action of tartrate. The neutrophil alkaline phosphatase score is almost always very high.

Over recent years a number of treatments have been shown to produce long-lasting remissions. Cladribine and deoxycoformycin are effective in producing long periods of disease control.

MYELODYSPLASTIC SYNDROME (MDS)

This syndrome consists of a group of clonal disorders which represent steps in the progression to the development of leukaemia. It is characterised by macrocytosis, variable cytopenia, hypogranular neutrophils with nuclear hyper- or hyposegmentation, and a hypercellular marrow with dysplastic changes in all three cell lines. The syndrome is being recognised more frequently; its exact incidence is uncertain but it is thought to be more common than acute leukaemia. Usually the disease presents as a primary problem in elderly patients, although it may occur as a secondary complication of treatment for malignant disease in younger patients. The syndrome comprises the following conditions:

- refractory anaemia
- refractory anaemia with ring sideroblasts (sideroblastic anaemia)
- chronic myelomonocytic leukaemia
- refractory anaemia with excess of blasts (RAEB)
- refractory anaemia with excess of blasts in transformation (RAEB-t).

Diagnosis

The diagnosis should be considered in any patient with a cytopenia and the dysplastic features indicated above. A marrow aspiration should be performed, which is usually hypercellular with evidence of dysplasia. Blast cells may be increased but do not reach the 30% level which indicates acute leukaemia. Chromosome analysis frequently reveals abnormalities, particularly of chromosomes 5 or 7.

Management

Treatment is unsatisfactory. Transfusion of blood and platelets and treatment of infection are required for all. Aggressive antileukaemic therapy is used in young patients with excess blasts in the marrow. Low-dose cytarabine (20 mg subcutaneously, 12-hourly) produces occasional remission but this is short-lived. Allogeneic transplantation should be considered in younger patients who have a donor, with the best results seen in patients with refractory anaemias without excess blasts.

Prognosis

The first two conditions listed above are relatively chronic disorders, while the latter three show a more aggressive course with a tendency to terminate as acute myeloid leukaemia. Thus patients with refractory and sideroblastic anaemia may survive for years but prognosis in the other three conditions is measured usually in months.

LYMPHOMAS

These neoplasms are divided clinically and histologically into Hodgkin's and non-Hodgkin's lymphoma. The majority are of B-cell origin. Non-Hodgkin's lymphomas are divided into low-grade and high-grade tumours on the basis of their proliferation rate. High-grade tumours are dividing rapidly, have only been present for a matter of weeks before diagnosis and may be life-threatening. Low-grade tumours are dividing slowly, may have been present for many months before diagnosis and behave in an indolent fashion.

HODGKIN'S DISEASE (see Box 19.38)

The histological hallmark of Hodgkin's disease is the presence of Reed–Sternberg cells, which are large malignant lymphoid cells of B-cell origin (see Fig. 19.30). They are often present in only small numbers but surrounded by large numbers of reactive normal T cells, plasma cells and eosinophils. Four types of Hodgkin's disease are recognised from the appearance of the Reed–Sternberg cells and surrounding reactive cells (see Box 19.39). The nodular

19.38 EPIDEMIOLOGY AND AETIOLOGY OF HODGKIN'S DISEASE

Incidence

- Approximately 4 new cases/100 000 population/year

Sex ratio

- Slight male excess (1.5:1)

Age

- Median age 31 years; first peak in 20–35 and second peak in 50–70 age group

Aetiology

- Unknown. More common in patients from well-educated backgrounds and small families. Three times more likely with a past history of glandular fever but no causal link to Epstein–Barr virus infection proven

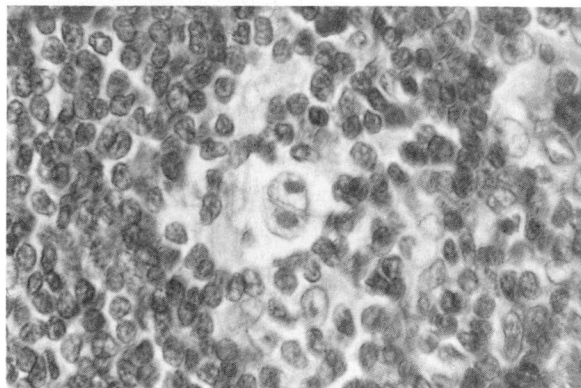

Fig. 19.30 Hodgkin's disease showing typical Reed–Sternberg cell.

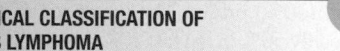

19.39 PATHOLOGICAL CLASSIFICATION OF HODGKIN'S LYMPHOMA

- Lymphocyte-predominant
- Nodular sclerosing
- Mixed cellularity
- Lymphocyte-depleted

sclerosing type accounts for the initial peak in young patients and is more common in women. Mixed cellularity is more common in the elderly peak. Lymphocyte-predominant Hodgkin's disease is now recognised as a low-grade B-cell non-Hodgkin's lymphoma. Lymphocyte-depleted Hodgkin's disease is rare and probably represents a T-cell non-Hodgkin's lymphoma.

Clinical features

There is painless rubbery lymphadenopathy, usually in the neck or supraclavicular fossae; the lymph nodes may fluctuate in size. Young patients with nodular sclerosing disease may have large mediastinal masses which are surprisingly asymptomatic but may cause dry cough and some breathlessness. Isolated subdiaphragmatic nodes occur in less than 10% at diagnosis. Hepatosplenomegaly may be present but

does not always indicate disease. Spread is contiguous from one node to the next and extranodal disease, such as bone, brain or skin involvement, is rare.

Investigations

- *Full blood count.* This may be completely normal. A normochromic, normocytic anaemia may be present and, together with lymphopenia, is a bad prognostic factor. An eosinophilia or a neutrophilia may be present.
- *ESR.* This may be raised.
- *Renal function.* Ensure this is normal prior to treatment.
- *Liver function.* This may be abnormal in the absence of disease or reflect hepatic infiltration. An obstructive pattern may be caused by nodes at the porta hepatis.
- *LDH.* Raised levels are an adverse prognostic factor.
- *Chest radiograph.* This may show a mediastinal mass.
- *CT.* Scan chest and abdomen to permit staging (see Box 19.40). This investigation has replaced laparotomy. Bulky disease greater than 10 cm in a single node mass is an adverse prognostic feature.
- *Lymph node biopsy.* This may be undertaken surgically or by percutaneous needle biopsy under radiological guidance (see Fig. 19.31).

19.40 CLINICAL STAGES OF HODGKIN'S DISEASE (ANN ARBOR CLASSIFICATION)

Stage	Definition
I	Involvement of a single lymph node region (I) or extralymphatic site (IA$_E$)
II	Involvement of two or more lymph node regions (II) or an extralymphatic site and lymph node regions on the same side of (above or below) the diaphragm (II$_E$)
III	Involvement of lymph node regions on both sides of the diaphragm with (III$_E$) or without (III) localised extralymphatic involvement or involvement of the spleen (III$_S$) or both (III$_{SE}$)
IV	Diffuse involvement of one or more extralymphatic tissues, e.g. liver or bone marrow
A	No systemic symptoms
B	Weight loss, drenching sweats

The lymphatic structures are defined as the lymph nodes, spleen, thymus, Waldeyer's ring, appendix and Peyer's patches

Management

Treatment options include radiotherapy, chemotherapy or a combination of the two (see Box 19.41).

Radiotherapy

Good results are obtained in localised stage IA or stage IIA disease with no adverse prognostic features. Fertility is usually preserved after radiotherapy. Careful planning is required to limit the doses delivered to normal tissues. Women receiving breast irradiation during the treatment of chest disease have an increased risk of breast cancer and should be placed on a screening programme. Patients continuing to smoke after lung irradiation are at particular risk of lung cancer.

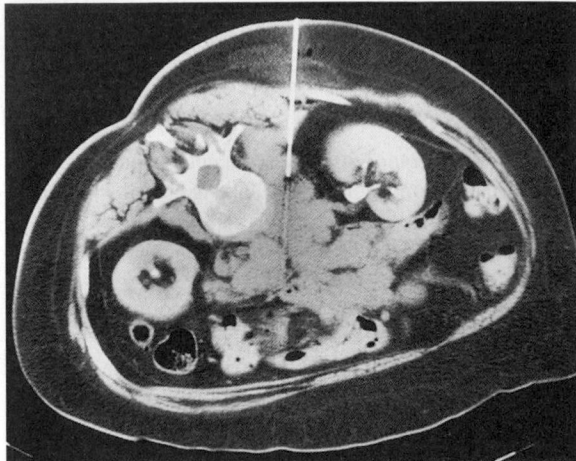

Fig. 19.31 CT-guided percutaneous needle biopsy of retroperitoneal nodes involved by lymphoma.

19.41 THERAPEUTIC GUIDELINES FOR HODGKIN'S LYMPHOMA		
Indications for radiotherapy		

- Stage I disease
- Stage IIA disease with three or fewer areas involved
- After chemotherapy to sites where there was originally bulk disease
- To lesions causing serious pressure problems

Indications for chemotherapy

- All patients with B symptoms
- Stage II disease with more than three areas involved
- Stage III and stage IV disease

Chemotherapy

All other patients are treated initially with chemotherapy. The regimen in Box 19.42 is widely used in the UK. This regimen was developed from the original MOPP regimen (nitrogen mustard, vincristine, prednisolone and procarbazine) with drugs substituted to reduce vomiting, alopecia and long-term toxicity. Over 80% of patients will respond to this combination therapy, with drugs delivered on an outpatient basis every 3–4 weeks for a total of 6–8 cycles. Routine support with growth factors such as G-CSF is not required. Treatment response is assessed clinically and by repeat CT.

This type of chemotherapy carries a high risk of inducing permanent infertility in men; adequate counselling and

19.42 THE ChIVPP REGIMEN FOR HODGKIN'S LYMPHOMA	
Drug	**Dose**
Chlorambucil	6 mg/m² (up to 10 mg total) days 1–14 orally
Vinblastine	6 mg/m² (up to 10 mg total) days 1 and 8 i.v.
Procarbazine	100 mg/m² days 1–14 orally
Prednisolone	40 mg/m² days 1–14 orally

sperm storage must be offered at diagnosis. The risk of infertility is lower for women but advice about obtaining ovarian tissue before starting treatment should be discussed as appropriate. Premature menopause may result from the treatment and hormone replacement therapy should be discussed with the patient. Steroids can cause avascular necrosis of bone, particularly the femoral head. Myelodysplasia and acute leukaemia can occur 5–10 years after alkylating therapy but the incidence is less than 5%.

Combined modality therapy

Radiotherapy may be given to the original sites of bulky disease after treatment by chemotherapy to reduce the risk of relapse. This form of treatment carries the greatest risk of long-term complications.

Prognosis

Over 90% of patients with stage IA disease are cured by radiotherapy alone. Patients with stage IIA disease have a reduced cure rate from radiotherapy. Approximately 70% of patients treated with chemotherapy are cured. The 15% of patients who fail to respond to initial chemotherapy have a poor prognosis but some may achieve long-term survival after high-dose therapy and autologous stem cell rescue. Patients relapsing after local radiotherapy have a good cure rate after subsequent chemotherapy but with an increased risk of long-term toxicity. Patients relapsing within a year of initial chemotherapy have a good salvage rate with high-dose therapy and autologous stem cell rescue. Patients relapsing after 1 year may obtain long-term survival with further chemotherapy.

NON-HODGKIN'S LYMPHOMA (see Box 19.43)

Non-Hodgkin's lymphoma (NHL) represents a monoclonal proliferation of lymphoid cells and may be of B-cell (70%) or T-cell (30%) origin. The incidence of these tumours has increased by 50% in the last 10–20 years in the Western world. At the same time treatment outcomes have not improved and hence mortality rates from NHL have increased.

The difficulties of establishing a reproducible and clinically useful histological classification of NHL are reflected in the large number of classification systems to date. A recently developed system, the REAL classification, has introduced phenotypic, molecular and cytogenetic information which, together with morphology, has allowed reproducible definition of clinical disease entities. Clinically, the most important factor is grade, which is a reflection of proliferation rate. High-grade NHL has high proliferation rates, rapidly produces symptoms, is fatal if untreated, but is potentially curable. Low-grade NHL has low proliferation rates, may be asymptomatic for many months before presentation, runs an indolent course, but is not curable by conventional therapy. Overall, about one-third of cases are high-grade diffuse large-cell NHL and a further third are low-grade follicular NHL (see Fig. 19.32).

Clinical features

Compared to Hodgkin's disease, NHL is often widely disseminated at presentation. Patients present with lymph node

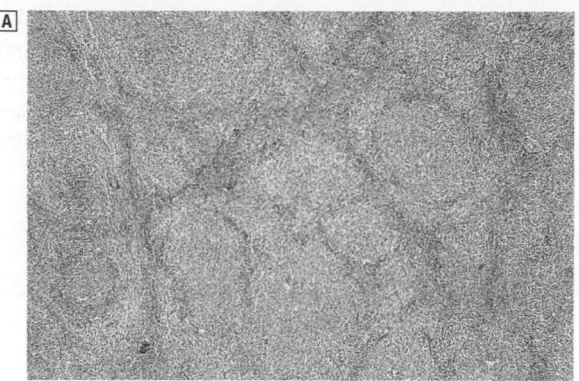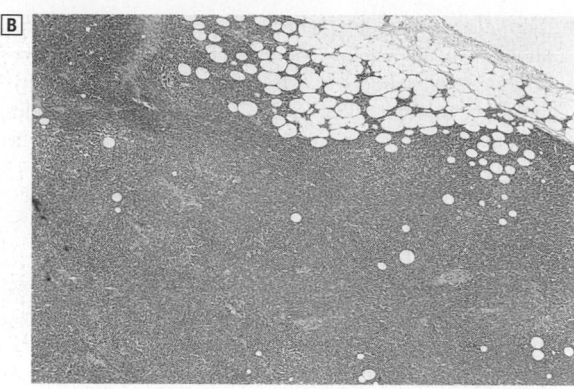

Fig. 19.32 **Non-Hodgkin's lymphoma.** A (Low-grade) follicular or nodular pattern. B (High-grade) diffuse pattern of histology.

19.43 EPIDEMIOLOGY AND AETIOLOGY OF NON-HODGKIN'S LYMPHOMA

Incidence
- 12 new cases/100 000 people/year

Sex ratio
- Slight male excess

Age
- Median age 65–70 years

Aetiology
- No single causative abnormality described

Viruses
- Lymphoma is a late manifestation of HIV infection (see p. 127)
- Specific lymphoma types are associated with EBV, human herpes virus 8 (HHV8) and HTLV infection

Bacteria
- The development of gastric lymphoma can be associated with *Helicobacter pylori* infection

Genetics
- Some lymphomas are associated with specific chromosome lesions; the t(14:18) translocation in follicular lymphoma results in the dysregulated expression of the bcl-2 gene product which inhibits apoptotic cell death

Immunology
- Lymphoma occurs in congenital immunodeficiency states and in immunosuppressed patients post-organ transplantation

enlargement which may be associated with systemic upset: weight loss, sweats, fever and itching. Hepatosplenomegaly may be present. Extranodal disease is more common in NHL, with involvement of the bone marrow, gut, thyroid, lung, skin, testis, brain and, more rarely, bone. Extranodal disease is more common in T-cell disease, whilst bone marrow involvement is more common in low-grade (50–60%) than high-grade (10%) disease. The same staging system is used for both Hodgkin's disease and NHL but NHL is more likely to be stage III or IV at presentation. Compression syndromes may occur; gut obstruction, ascites, superior vena caval obstruction and spinal cord compression may all be presenting features.

Investigations
These are as for Hodgkin's disease but in addition the following should be performed:

- *Routine bone marrow aspirate and trephine.*
- *Immunophenotyping of surface antigens to distinguish T- and B-cell tumours.* This may be done on blood, marrow or nodal material.
- *Immunoglobulin determination.* Some lymphomas are associated with IgG or IgM paraproteins which serve as markers for treatment response.
- *Measurement of uric acid levels.* Some very aggressive high-grade NHL is associated with very high urate levels, which can precipitate renal failure when treatment is started.
- *HIV testing.* This may be appropriate if risk factors are present (see p. 109).

Management
The factors listed in Box 19.44 will influence the choice of therapy in NHL.

Low-grade NHL
Asymptomatic patients may not require therapy. Indications for treatment include marked systemic symptoms, lymphadenopathy causing discomfort or disfigurement, bone marrow failure or compression syndromes. The options are:

- *Radiotherapy.* This can be used for localised stage I disease, which is rare.
- *Chemotherapy.* This is the mainstay of therapy. Most patients will respond to oral therapy with chlorambucil, which is well tolerated. More intensive intravenous chemotherapy in younger patients produces better quality of life but no survival benefit. Neither therapy will cure patients.

19.44 FACTORS DETERMINING MANAGEMENT STRATEGY IN NON-HODGKIN'S LYMPHOMA
- Age of the patient
- Degree of concomitant disease
- Histological grade
- Staging of the disease
- HIV status
- Patient's wishes

- *Monoclonal antibody therapy*. Humanised monoclonal antibodies can be used to target surface antigens on tumour cells and deliver cytotoxic drugs or radiotherapy, or induce tumour cell apoptosis directly. Such antibodies targeted to low-grade lymphoma cells have been shown to induce durable clinical responses in up to 60% of patients. Synergistic effects are seen when treatment is combined with standard chemotherapy, and trials are under way to define their optimal usage.
- *Transplantation*. Studies of autologous stem cell transplantation are in progress. Such high-dose therapy improves disease-free survival but longer follow-up is awaited before conclusions can be made about cure.

High-grade NHL
Patients with high-grade NHL need treatment at initial presentation:

- *Chemotherapy*. The majority (> 90%) will need intravenous combination chemotherapy. The CHOP regimen (cyclophosphamide, doxorubicin, vincristine and prednisolone) remains the mainstay of therapy.
- *Radiotherapy*. A few stage I patients without bulky disease may be suitable for radiotherapy. Radiotherapy is indicated to a residual localised site of bulk disease after chemotherapy, and for spinal cord and other compression syndromes.
- *Transplantation*. Autologous stem cell transplantation appears to benefit some patients at first relapse, with cure rates of 50% compared to < 10% with chemotherapy alone. Lymphoblastic lymphoma is a very aggressive lymphoma which predominantly affects young adults, who should be considered candidates for allogeneic or autologous transplantation after response to initial chemotherapy.
- *Monoclonal antibody therapy*. Humanised monoclonal antibodies can be used as described above. In preliminary studies in elderly patients such antibodies, when combined with CHOP chemotherapy, have dramatically improved overall survival. Mature data are awaited but are expected to confirm this benefit.

EBM

RELAPSED HIGH-GRADE NON-HODGKIN'S LYMPHOMA—role of autologous bone marrow transplantation

'With a median follow-up of 63 months, a phase III RCT comparing conventional salvage chemotherapy with the same consolidated by an autologous bone marrow transplant in 215 patients with relapsed high-grade lymphoma demonstrated a very significant benefit for event-free (46% vs 12%) and overall survival (54% vs 42%) in favour of bone marrow transplantation. This study established the role of transplantation in relapsed, chemosensitive high-grade lymphoma.'

- Philip T, Guglielmi C, Hagenbeek A, et al. Autologous bone marrow transplant as compared with salvage chemotherapy in relapses of chemotherapy-sensitive non-Hodgkin's lymphoma. N Engl J Med 1995; 333:1540–1545.

Further information: 💻 www.lymphoma.org.uk

Prognosis
Low-grade NHL
These tumours run an indolent remitting and relapsing course, with an overall median survival of 10 years. Transformation to a higher-grade NHL is associated with poor survival.

High-grade NHL
Some 80% of patients respond initially to therapy but only 35% will have disease-free survival at 5 years. Relapse is associated with a poor response to further chemotherapy (< 10% 5-year survival), but in patients under 65 years stem cell transplantation improves survival.

Increasing age, advanced stage, concomitant disease, a raised LDH and T-cell phenotype predict poor outcome.

PARAPROTEINAEMIAS

A gammopathy refers to over-production of one or more classes of immunoglobulin. This may be polyclonal in association with inflammation such as infection, sarcoidosis or Sjögren's syndrome. Alternatively, a monoclonal increase in a single immunoglobulin class may occur in association with normal or reduced levels of the other immunoglobulins. Monoclonal proteins occur as a feature of myeloma, lymphoma and amyloidosis, in connective tissue disease such as rheumatoid arthritis or polymyalgia rheumatica, in infection such as HIV and in solid tumours. In addition, they may be present with no underlying disease. Paraproteins of the IgA, IgM and IgG_3 subclasses can polymerise and may be associated with clinical hyperviscosity.

MONOCLONAL GAMMOPATHY OF UNCERTAIN SIGNIFICANCE (MGUS)

A paraprotein is present in the blood but with no other features of myeloma or disease.

Clinical features
Patients are usually asymptomatic. MGUS is present in 3% of the population over the age of 65 years and 10% of hospital inpatients of a similar age.

Investigations
- Routine blood count and biochemistry are normal.
- The paraprotein is usually present in a small amount with no associated immune paresis.
- There are no lytic lesions on the bones.
- The bone marrow may have increased plasma cells but these are usually less than 10%.

Prognosis
Long-term follow-up is required to monitor clinical symptoms and paraprotein levels since approximately 20% of patients develop myeloma and 10% solid tumours.

WALDENSTRÖM'S MACROGLOBULINAEMIA

This is a low-grade lymphoplasmacytoid lymphoma associated with an IgM paraprotein causing clinical features of hyperviscosity syndrome. It is a rare tumour occurring in the elderly and affects a slight excess of males.

Patients classically present with features of hyperviscosity such as nosebleeds, bruising, confusion and visual disturbance. However, presentation may be with anaemia, systemic symptoms, splenomegaly or lymphadenopathy. Patients are found on investigation to have an IgM paraprotein associated with a raised plasma viscosity. The bone marrow has a characteristic appearance, with infiltration of lymphoid cells and prominent mast cells.

Management

Severe hyperviscosity and anaemia may necessitate plasmapheresis to remove IgM and make blood transfusion possible. Treatment with oral agents such as chlorambucil is effective but rather slow and fludarabine may be more active in this disease. The median survival is 5 years.

MULTIPLE MYELOMA

This is a malignant proliferation of plasma cells. Normal plasma cells are derived from B cells and produce immunoglobulins which contain heavy and light chains. Normal immunoglobulins are polyclonal, which means that a variety of heavy chains are produced and each may be of kappa or lambda light chain type. In myeloma plasma cells produce immunoglobulin of a single heavy and light chain, a monoclonal protein commonly referred to as a paraprotein. In some cases only light chain is produced and this appears in the urine as Bence Jones proteinuria. The frequency of different paraprotein types in myeloma is shown in Box 19.45.

Pathology

Although a small number of malignant plasma cells are present in the circulation, the majority are present in the bone marrow. The malignant plasma cells produce cytokines, which stimulate osteoclasts and result in net bone absorption. The resulting lytic lesions cause bone pain, fractures

and hypercalcaemia. Marrow involvement can result in anaemia or pancytopenia (see Box 19.46). The aetiology of this condition is unknown.

Clinical features

The incidence of myeloma is 4/100 000 new cases per annum, with a male:female ratio of 2:1. The median age of diagnosis is 60–70 years and the disease is more common in Afro-Caribbeans. The clinical features are demonstrated in Figure 19.33.

Investigations (see Box 19.47)

The diagnosis of myeloma requires two of the following criteria:

- marrow plasmacytosis
- serum and/or urinary paraprotein
- skeletal lesions.

19.47 POINTS TO NOTE IN THE DIAGNOSIS OF MYELOMA
• In the absence of fractures or bone repair the plasma alkaline phosphatase and the bone scan are normal
• Serum β_2-microglobulin estimations may provide a useful assessment of prognosis
• The absence of immune paresis (reduction of normal immunoglobulin levels) should cast doubt on the diagnosis
• Only about 5% of patients with an ESR persistently above 100 mm/hr have myeloma

Investigations are listed in Box 19.48.

Management

If patients are asymptomatic, treatment may not be required. Otherwise, treatment consists of the following:

Immediate support
- High fluid intake to treat renal impairment and hypercalcaemia.
- Analgesia for bone pain.
- Bisphosphonates for hypercalcaemia (see p. 223).
- Allopurinol to prevent urate nephropathy.
- Plasmapheresis, which may be necessary for hyperviscosity.

19.45 CLASSIFICATION OF MULTIPLE MYELOMA	
Type of paraprotein	**Relative frequency (%)**
IgG	55
IgA	21
Light chain only	22
Others (D, E, non-secretory)	2

19.46 MULTIPLE MYELOMA: THE RELATIONSHIP BETWEEN PATHOLOGY, THE EFFECT OF THE DISEASE PROCESS AND SYMPTOMS		
Pathology	**Effect**	**Symptoms**
Marrow involvement with malignant plasma cells	Bone erosion due to stimulation of osteoclasts	Pain
	Pathological fracture	Severe local pain
	Hypercalcaemia	Lethargy, thirst
	Bone marrow failure: anaemia	Tiredness
Excess production of paraprotein and light chains	Renal damage	None until uraemic
	Increased blood viscosity	None until severe, then blurred vision, headache, vertigo, stupor, coma
	Amyloidosis	Nephrotic syndrome
Reduction in number of normal plasma cells	Impaired immune function	Susceptibility to infection, particularly respiratory

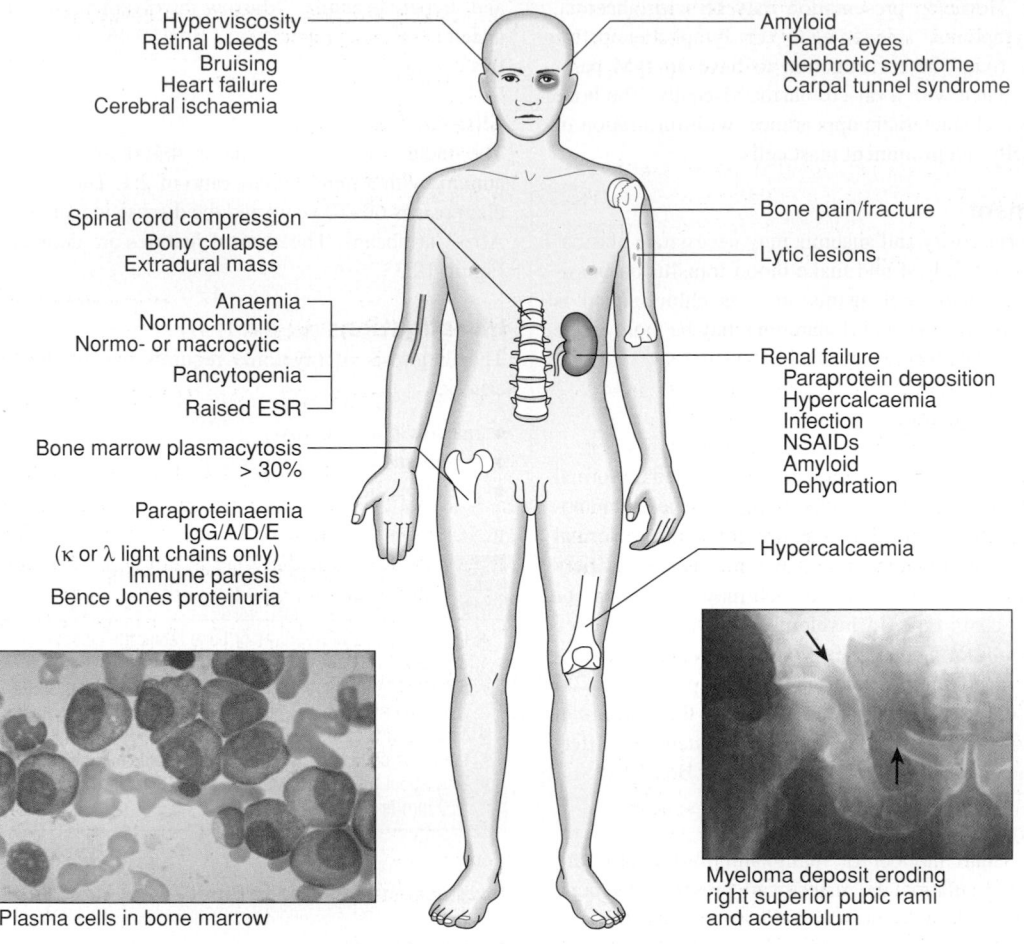

Hyperviscosity
Retinal bleeds
Bruising
Heart failure
Cerebral ischaemia

Amyloid
'Panda' eyes
Nephrotic syndrome
Carpal tunnel syndrome

Spinal cord compression
Bony collapse
Extradural mass

Bone pain/fracture

Lytic lesions

Anaemia
Normochromic
Normo- or macrocytic

Pancytopenia

Raised ESR

Bone marrow plasmacytosis
> 30%

Paraproteinaemia
IgG/A/D/E
(κ or λ light chains only)
Immune paresis
Bence Jones proteinuria

Renal failure
Paraprotein deposition
Hypercalcaemia
Infection
NSAIDs
Amyloid
Dehydration

Hypercalcaemia

Plasma cells in bone marrow

Myeloma deposit eroding
right superior pubic rami
and acetabulum

Fig. 19.33 Clinical manifestations of multiple myeloma.

19.48 RATIONALE FOR INVESTIGATIONS IN MULTIPLE MYELOMA	
Problem	**Investigations**
Renal function	Urea and electrolytes, creatinine, urate
Presence of hypercalcaemia	Blood calcium Albumin
Presence of bone fractures	Radiographs Blood alkaline phosphatase Isotope bone scan
Degree of immune paresis	Plasma immunoglobulins
Degree of bone marrow failure	Blood counts Reticulocyte count
Degree of haemostasis	Bleeding time Coagulation screen
Blood viscosity	Plasma viscosity
Disease activity	Serum β_2-microglobulin

Chemotherapy

In older patients, melphalan is an effective oral therapy, whilst in younger patients treatment with intravenous agents may improve response. Higher doses of intravenous melphalan appear to be well tolerated even in patients over 65 years and may produce better clinical responses.

MYELOMA—role of oral melphalan   **EBM**

'RCTs suggest that melphalan with or without prednisolone is the initial treatment of choice for most patients with myeloma in whom high-dose therapy is not planned. Treatment should continue until the paraprotein level is stable for 3 months. Cyclophosphamide is suitable for those patients not eligible for melphalan. There is no convincing evidence for a survival benefit of combination chemotherapy.'

- Myeloma Trialists' Collaborative Group. Combination chemotherapy versus melphalan plus prednisone as treatment for multiple myeloma: an overview of 6,633 patients from 27 randomised trials. J Clin Oncol 1998; 16:3832–3842.
- Medical Research Council's Working Party on Leukaemia in Adults. Report on the second myelomatosis trial after five years of follow-up. Br J Cancer 1980; 42:813–822.

Further information: 🖳 www.ukmf.org.uk

Treatment is administered until paraprotein levels have stopped falling. This is termed 'plateau phase' and may last for weeks or years. Successive relapses respond less well to treatment.

Radiotherapy

This is effective for localised bone pain not responding to simple analgesia and for pathological fractures. It is also useful for the emergency treatment of spinal cord compression complicating extradural plasmacytomas.

Transplantation

Standard treatment does not cure myeloma. Stem cell autotransplants improve quality of life and prolong survival. All patients under 65 years should be offered intravenous chemotherapy to maximum response and then an autologous stem cell transplant. Allogeneic bone marrow transplantation may cure some patients and should be considered in those under the age of 55 years with a sibling donor. Reduced-intensity allografting may improve outcomes by reducing transplant-related mortality and extending the upper age limit.

EBM

MULTIPLE MYELOMA—role of autologous bone marrow transplantation

'An RCT in 200 previously untreated myeloma patients compared conventional intravenous chemotherapy with the same consolidated by an autologous bone marrow transplant. The study demonstrated a highly significant benefit for disease-free survival (28% vs 10%) and overall survival (52% vs 12%) at 5 years in favour of the transplanted group. This study established the role of autologous transplantation for myeloma patients under the age of 65 years.'

● Attal M, Harrousseau JL, Stoppa AM, et al. A prospective randomised trial of autologous bone marrow transplant and chemotherapy in myeloma. N Engl J Med 1996; 335:91–97.

Further information: 🖥 www.ukmf.org

Bisphosphonates

Chronic bisphosphonate therapy reduces bone pain and skeletal events. These drugs protect bone and may cause apoptosis of malignant plasma cells.

Thalidomide

This drug has anti-angiogenic effects against the blood vessels supplying tumours and also has immunomodulatory effects. At low doses it has been shown to be effective against refractory myeloma and, when combined with dexamethasone, response rates over 50% are described. Trials are currently planned to investigate the use of thalidomide as an adjunct to other treatments earlier in the natural history of the disease. It can cause somnolence, constipation and a peripheral neuropathy; it is vital that females of childbearing age use adequate contraception.

Prognosis (see Box 19.49)

The median survival of patients receiving standard treatment is approximately 40 months. Autotransplantation improves survival and quality of life by slowing the rate of progression of bone disease. Less than 5% of patients survive longer than 10 years with standard treatment.

19.49 POOR PROGNOSTIC FEATURES AT DIAGNOSIS IN MULTIPLE MYELOMA

● A haemoglobin concentration of less than 7 g/dl
● Severe hypoalbuminaemia
● Intractable renal failure
● Thrombocytopenia
● High β_2-microglobulin levels
● Plasma cell leukaemia

APLASTIC ANAEMIA

PRIMARY IDIOPATHIC ACQUIRED APLASTIC ANAEMIA

This is a rare disorder in developed countries, with 3–6 new cases per million population per annum; the disease is much more common in certain other parts of the world—for example, China. The basic problem is failure of the pluripotent stem cells, producing hypoplasia of the marrow elements. An autoimmune mechanism may be responsible in a proportion of cases and it may occur in association with pregnancy. Careful enquiry should be made with regard to exposure to drugs, chemicals and radiation. A history of viral illness, particularly hepatitis, may be important.

Clinical features

A full blood count demonstrates pancytopenia, reticulocytopenia and often macrocytosis. The bone marrow should be examined by aspiration and trephine.

Management

All patients will require blood product support and aggressive management of infection. The curative treatment for young (< 20 years old) patients with severe idiopathic aplastic anaemia is allogeneic bone marrow transplantation if there is an available donor. Those with a compatible sibling donor should proceed to transplantation as soon as possible. Successful pre-transplant conditioning can be achieved with cyclophosphamide alone. In older patients immunosuppressive therapy with ciclosporin and antithymocyte globulin gives equivalent results. The prognosis of severe aplastic anaemia managed with supportive therapy only is poor and more than 50% of patients die, usually in the first year. However, a survival of over 60% has been reported after bone marrow transplantation in young patients and similar results can be achieved with immunosuppressive regimens involving antithymocyte globulin.

SECONDARY APLASIA

Causes of this condition are listed in Box 19.50. It is not practical to list all the drugs which have been suspected of causing aplasia but it is important to investigate the reported side-effects of all drugs taken over the preceding months. In some instances the cytopenia is more selective and affects only one cell line, most often the neutrophils. Frequently, this is an incidental finding unassociated with ill health. It probably has an immune basis but this is difficult to prove. The clinical features and methods of diagnosis are the same as for primary idiopathic aplastic anaemia. An underlying cause should be treated or removed but otherwise management is as for the idiopathic form.

ISSUES IN OLDER PEOPLE
HAEMATOLOGICAL MALIGNANCY

- The median age of most haematological malignancies is approximately 70 years.
- Haematological malignancy in elderly patients is more likely to be associated with poor-risk biological features such as adverse cytogenetics or the presence of a multidrug resistance phenotype.
- Age is an independent prognostic variable in myeloma, acute leukaemia and aggressive lymphoma.
- Elderly patients tolerate chemotherapy less well, are more likely to have antecedent cardiac, pulmonary or metabolic problems, tolerate systemic infection less well and metabolise cytotoxic drugs differently.
- For those patients who tolerate treatment well, however, cure rates similar to those in younger patients can be achieved.
- The decision to treat should not be based on chronology but on the individual's biological status, the level of social support available, the patient's wishes and those of the immediate family.

MYELOPROLIFERATIVE DISORDERS

These make up a group of chronic conditions characterised by clonal proliferation of marrow erythroid precursors (polycythaemia rubra vera, PRV), megakaryocytes (essential thrombocythaemia and myelofibrosis) or myeloid cells (chronic myeloid leukaemia). Although the majority of patients are classifiable as having one of these disorders, some have overlapping features. Furthermore, there is often progression from one to another, e.g. PRV to myelofibrosis.

Chronic myeloid leukaemia is considered in detail elsewhere (see p. 935).

MYELOFIBROSIS

Myelofibrosis is characterised by bone marrow fibrosis, extramedullary haematopoiesis (blood cell formation outside the bone marrow) and a leucoerythroblastic blood picture. The marrow is initially hypercellular, with an excess of abnormal megakaryocytes, which release growth factors, e.g. platelet-derived growth factor, to the marrow microenvironment, resulting in a reactive proliferation of fibroblasts. As the disease progresses, the marrow becomes fibrosed.

Most patients with myelofibrosis present over the age of 50 years with lassitude, weight loss and night sweats. The spleen can be massively enlarged due to extramedullary haematopoiesis and splenic infarcts may occur.

The characteristic blood picture is a leucoerythroblastic anaemia, with circulating immature red blood cells (reticulocytes and nucleated red blood cells) and granulocyte precursors. The red cells are shaped like teardrops (teardrop poikilocytes) and giant platelets may be seen in the blood. The white count varies from low to moderately high and the platelet count may be high, normal or low. Urate levels may be high due to increased cell breakdown and folate deficiency is common. The marrow is often difficult to aspirate and a trephine biopsy shows an excess of megakaryocytes, increased reticulin and fibrous tissue replacement.

Median survival is 4 years from diagnosis but ranges from 1 year to over 20 years. Treatment is directed at control of symptoms, e.g. red cell transfusions. Folic acid should be given to prevent deficiency. Cytotoxic therapy with hydroxycarbamide (hydroxyurea) may help control spleen size, the white cell count or systemic symptoms. Splenectomy may be required if the grossly enlarged spleen is causing distress or significant hypersplenism. Bone marrow transplantation may be considered for younger patients.

ESSENTIAL THROMBOCYTHAEMIA

The malignant proliferation of megakaryocytes results in a raised level of circulating platelets that are often dysfunctional. Prior to making a diagnosis of essential thrombocythaemia it is essential to exclude reactive causes of increased platelets (see p. 908). Patients present at a median age of 60 years with vascular occlusive or bleeding events or with an isolated raised platelet count. In most individuals the condition is chronic, with the platelet count gradually increasing. The risks are of microvascular and major vessel occlusion and haemorrhage. A very small percentage may transform to acute leukaemia and others to myelofibrosis.

Low-risk patients (age less than 40 years, platelet count less than $1000 \times 10^9/l$ and asymptomatic, i.e. no bleeding or thrombosis) may require no treatment to reduce the platelet count. Aspirin therapy is often recommended. For those with a platelet count over $1000 \times 10^9/l$ or those with symptoms, treatment to control platelets should be given. Agents include oral hydroxycarbamide (hydroxyurea) or anagrelide, an inhibitor of megakaryocyte maturation. Intravenous radioactive phosphorus (^{32}P) may be useful in the elderly. Aspirin is particularly useful therapy for those with digital ischaemia.

POLYCYTHAEMIA RUBRA VERA (PRV)

PRV occurs mainly in patients over the age of 40 years and presents either as an incidental finding of a high haemoglobin or with symptoms such as lassitude, loss of concentration, headaches, dizziness, blackouts, pruritus and epistaxis. Some present with manifestations of arterial peripheral vascular disease or a cerebrovascular accident. Patients are often plethoric and the majority have a palpable spleen at diagnosis. Thrombotic complications may occur and peptic ulceration is common, sometimes complicated by bleeding.

The diagnosis of polycythaemia is discussed on page 904. It requires a raised red cell mass, the absence of causes of secondary erythrocytosis, and palpable splenomegaly. The neutrophil and platelet counts are frequently raised, an abnormal karyotype may be found in the marrow, and in vitro culture of the marrow demonstrates autonomous growth in the absence of added growth factors.

Venesection gives prompt symptomatic relief. Between 400 and 500 ml of blood (less if the patient is elderly) are removed and the venesection is repeated every 5–7 days until the haematocrit is reduced to below 45%. Less frequent but regular venesection will maintain this until the haemoglobin remains reduced because of iron deficiency. The underlying myeloproliferation can be suppressed by hydroxycarbamide (hydroxyurea), interferon or radioactive phosphorus (5 mCi of ^{32}P i.v.) for older patients. Treatment of proliferation may reduce vascular occlusion, control spleen size and reduce transformation to myelofibrosis. Radioactive phosphorus does increase the risk of transformation to acute leukaemia by six- to tenfold.

Median survival after diagnosis in treated patients exceeds 10 years. Some patients survive more than 20 years; however, cerebral or coronary events occur in up to 60% of patients. The disease may convert to another myeloproliferative disorder; for example, about 15% develop myelofibrosis. Acute leukaemia develops principally in those patients who have been treated with radioactive phosphorus.

BLEEDING DISORDERS

DISORDERS OF PRIMARY HAEMOSTASIS

Platelet functional disorders, thrombocytopenia and von Willebrand's disease, along with diseases affecting the vessel wall, may all result in failure of the initial platelet plug formation in primary haemostasis.

VESSEL WALL ABNORMALITIES

Abnormalities of the vessel walls, both congenital and acquired—for example, vasculitis—may result in a propensity to purpuric lesions which are often slightly raised.

19.51 CAUSES OF NON-THROMBOCYTOPENIC PURPURA	
• Senile purpura	• Vasculitis (see p. 1040)
• Factitious purpura	• Paraproteinaemias
• Henoch–Schönlein purpura (see p. 616)	• Purpura fulminans

Causes of non-thrombocytopenic purpura are listed in Box 19.51.

HEREDITARY HAEMORRHAGIC TELANGIECTASIA

Hereditary haemorrhagic telangiectasia (HHT) is a dominantly inherited condition in which telangiectasia and small aneurysms are found on the fingertips, on the face, in the nasal passages, on the tongue, in the lung and in the gastrointestinal tract. A significant proportion of these patients develop larger pulmonary arteriovenous malformations (PAVMs) that cause arterial hypoxaemia due to a right-to-left shunt. These predispose the individual to paradoxical embolism that can result in stroke or cerebral abscess. All patients with HHT should be screened for PAVMs which, if found, should be ablated by percutaneous embolisation.

Patients present either with recurrent bleeds, particularly epistaxis, or with iron deficiency due to occult gastrointestinal bleeding. Treatment can be difficult because of the multiple bleeding points but regular iron therapy often allows the marrow to compensate for blood loss. Local cautery or laser therapy may prevent single lesions from bleeding. A variety of medical therapies have been tried—for example, oestrogens—but none has been found to be universally effective.

EHLERS–DANLOS DISEASE

Ehlers–Danlos disease is a congenital disorder of collagen synthesis in which the capillaries are poorly supported by subcutaneous collagen and ecchymoses are commonly seen.

PLATELET FUNCTIONAL DISORDERS

Even in the presence of a normal platelet count an individual may bleed if the function of the platelets is reduced. Congenital abnormalities include rare disorders of the membrane glycoproteins, e.g. thrombasthenia and Bernard–Soulier syndrome, or the presence of defective platelet granules, e.g. a deficiency of dense (delta) granules giving rise to storage pool disorders. Such patients exhibit bleeding of 'platelet type' (see p. 891) which varies in severity between patients, some presenting with frequent recurrent bleeds whilst others are only diagnosed because of excessive postoperative haemorrhage. Mild functional disorders, which only cause excessive bleeding after trauma or surgery, are often not diagnosed and are probably relatively common.

Many drugs inhibit platelets. Aspirin and other NSAIDs inhibit platelet cyclo-oxygenase, preventing the conversion

19.52 DRUGS INHIBITING PLATELET FUNCTION

NSAIDs
- Aspirin
- Indometacin
- Phenylbutazone
- Sulfinpyrazone

Antibiotics
- Penicillins
- Cephalosporins

Dextran

Heparin

β-blockers

of arachidonic acid to the potent platelet aggregator thromboxane B$_2$. Drugs which inhibit platelet function are listed in Box 19.52.

THROMBOCYTOPENIA

Thrombocytopenia causing bleeding constitutes a haematological emergency which should be promptly investigated and treated. Treatment should be directed at the underlying condition as well as including specific measures to raise the platelet count. In general, platelet transfusions should be given only if the platelet count is less than $10 \times 10^9/l$, to treat troublesome bleeding such as persistent epistaxis, or to treat potentially life-threatening bleeding, e.g. gastrointestinal haemorrhage. Such transfusions provide only temporary relief because the survival of the platelets in the circulation is only a few days at most, and in many instances may be only a matter of minutes or hours if the thrombocytopenia is due to increased platelet consumption, as in idiopathic thrombocytopenic purpura or disseminated intravascular coagulation (DIC).

IDIOPATHIC THROMBOCYTOPENIC PURPURA

The presence of autoantibodies, often directed against platelet membrane glycoprotein IIb-IIIa, causes the premature removal of platelets by the monocyte-macrophage system. Occasionally, antigen-antibody immune complexes adhere to platelets at their Fc receptor, resulting in their premature removal from the circulation.

Clinical features

In children idiopathic thrombocytopenic purpura (ITP) often presents 2–3 weeks after a viral illness, with the sudden onset of purpura and sometimes oral and nasal bleeding. The peripheral blood film is normal, apart from a greatly reduced platelet number, whilst the bone marrow reveals an obvious increase in megakaryocytes. It is important to ascertain that the child does not have any other systemic illness and in particular DIC.

In adults ITP more commonly affects females and has an insidious onset. It is unusual for there to be a history of a preceding viral infection. At presentation some cases may be associated with symptoms or signs of a connective tissue disease, whilst in others these disorders may become apparent several years later. The condition is likely to become chronic, with remissions and relapses.

Management
Children

If the child has only mild bleeding symptoms, it is usual to withhold any specific treatment, as the condition in the majority of instances is self-limiting within a few weeks. The presence of moderate to severe purpura, bruising or epistaxis and a platelet count less than $10 \times 10^9/l$ are indications for oral prednisolone 2 mg/kg daily. The platelet count usually rises promptly within 1–3 days. Persistent epistaxis, gastrointestinal bleeding, retinal haemorrhages or any suggestion of intracranial bleeding should be treated immediately by a platelet transfusion. If fresh bleeding persists for more than a few days following the introduction of steroids, intravenous immunoglobulin should be given.

Adults

Treatment with prednisolone 1 mg/kg daily is often less rewarding than in children; the platelet count rises in response to therapy but falls again when the dose is reduced or stopped. As with children, persistent or potentially life-threatening bleeding should be treated with platelet transfusion. Intravenous immunoglobulin (IVIgG) (1 g/kg) should be given if the patient is very haemorrhagic or the bleeding is immediately life-threatening. The mechanism by which IVIgG raises the platelet count remains uncertain, although increasing evidence indicates that it may be due to blocking of monocyte-macrophage Fc receptors.

Relapses should be treated by increasing the dose of prednisolone. If a patient has two relapses, it is customary to consider splenectomy. This should be preceded by pneumococcal, meningococcal and *Haemophilus influenzae* vaccination. As so many adults with ITP eventually require splenectomy, it is prudent to vaccinate all patients at presentation before they become immunosuppressed with a prolonged course of steroids; this should be performed by subcutaneous injection since if vaccination is given by the customary intramuscular route it may result in a haematoma. Splenectomy is curative in about 70% of patients and in the remainder the aim should be to keep the patient free of symptoms rather than treat the platelet count alone. Often such patients have platelet counts of $20–30 \times 10^9/l$ without symptoms; some require long-term maintenance with prednisolone at 5 mg/day. If significant bleeding persists despite splenectomy and low-dose steroid therapy, vincristine, immunosuppressive therapy—e.g. cyclophosphamide—or repeated infusions of intravenous immunoglobulin should be considered.

COAGULATION DISORDERS

Coagulation factor disorders can arise either from deficiency, usually congenital, of a single factor—e.g. factor VIII, resulting in haemophilia A—or from multiple factor deficiencies which are often acquired—e.g. secondary to liver disease or warfarin therapy. Of the single congenital deficiencies, haemophilia A and B are the most common although, rarely, any of the coagulation factors may be reduced. The congenital disorders almost exclusively arise as a result of an abnormality in the gene coding for the coagulation factor.

CONGENITAL BLEEDING DISORDERS

HAEMOPHILIA A

Of the various congenital disorders of coagulation, a reduction of factor VIII resulting in haemophilia A, which affects 1/10 000 individuals, is the most common. Factor VIII is primarily synthesised by the liver but other organs such as the spleen, kidney and placenta may also contribute. Plasma factor VIII has a half-life of about 12 hours and is carried non-covalently bound to the von Willebrand factor (vWF). The factor VIII gene is located on the X chromosome and consists of 26 exons; many different defects in the gene have been identified, ranging from single-base changes to deletions and inversions.

Genetics

The factor VIII gene is localised on the X chromosome, making haemophilia A a sex-linked disorder. Thus on pedigree grounds all daughters of haemophiliacs are obligate carriers and sisters have a 50% chance of being a carrier. If a carrier has a son, he has a 50% chance of having haemophilia, and a daughter has a 50% chance of being a carrier. Haemophilia 'breeds true' within a family. All members will have the same abnormality of the factor VIII gene; thus if one individual has severe haemophilia, all others affected will also have a severe form of the disorder. Female carriers of haemophilia may have reduced factor VIII levels because of random inactivation of the X chromosome in the developing fetus (lyonisation). A reduced factor VIII level in a carrier will result in a mild bleeding disorder; thus all known or suspected carriers of haemophilia should have their factor VIII level measured.

The use of molecular genetic techniques has revolutionised the ability to identify carriers and the antenatal diagnosis of haemophilia. Antenatal diagnosis can be undertaken in a female who has a high probability of being a carrier. This is accomplished by chorionic villous sampling, usually around 11 weeks' gestation, sexing the fetus and using informative factor VIII probes. Alternatively, the fetus can be sexed at 16 weeks' gestation by amniocentesis and, if male, a fetal blood sample obtained at about 19–20 weeks.

Clinical features

Although haemophilia A is a congenital disorder, it is unusual for excessive bleeding to be noticed until babies are about 6 months old, when superficial bruising or a haemarthrosis may occur. This apparent delay in presentation is due to the relative inactivity of babies in the first few months of life and it is only when they begin to move about that more trauma results in bleeding. It is not uncommon for children to be initially classified as having non-accidental injury.

The normal factor VIII level is 50–150% and is usually measured by a clotting assay. In haemophilia the propensity

Degree of severity	Factor VIII or IX level	Clinical presentation
Severe	< 2%	Spontaneous haemarthroses and muscle haematomas
Moderate	2–10%	Mild trauma or surgery causes haematomas
Mild	10–50%	Major injury or surgery results in excess bleeding

19.53 SEVERITY OF HAEMOPHILIA (UK CRITERIA)

to bleeding is related to the plasma factor VIII level. The classification of severity of haemophilia is set out in Box 19.53.

Individuals with severe haemophilia experience recurrent haemarthroses in large joints (see Fig. 19.34). These usually begin spontaneously without apparent trauma and most commonly affect the knees, elbows, ankles and hips. A typical severe haemophiliac may have one or two bleeds each week. Patients are aware that bleeding has started because they experience an abnormal sensation in the joint. If treatment is not given at this stage, bleeding continues, resulting in a hot, swollen and very painful joint. Without treatment these symptoms may last for days before gradually subsiding. Recurrent bleeds into joints lead to synovial hypertrophy, destruction of the cartilage and secondary osteoarthrosis (see Fig. 19.35). The resultant limitation of movement may greatly reduce the function of joints, making walking difficult.

Muscle haematomas are also characteristic of haemophilia. These occur most commonly in the calf and psoas muscles but they can arise in almost any muscle. Although less common than haemarthroses, a single episode can leave severe lasting damage if not effectively treated. A large psoas bleed, for example, may extend to press on the femoral nerve. Calf haematomas are also serious because of the inflexible fascial sheath surrounding the soleus and gastrocnemius muscles. Untreated haemorrhage causes a rise in pressure with eventual ischaemia, necrosis, fibrosis, and subsequent contraction and shortening of the Achilles tendon (see Fig. 19.36).

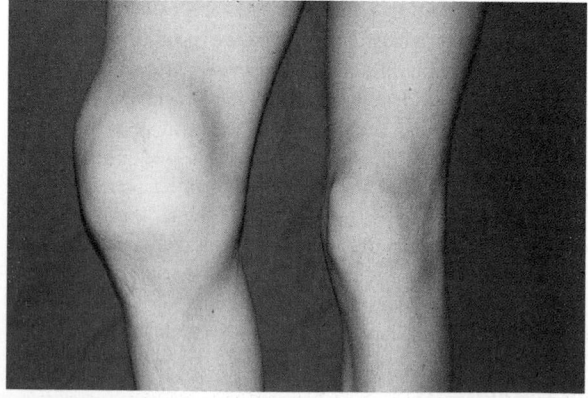

Fig. 19.34 Large haemarthrosis in the right knee of a boy with haemophilia A.

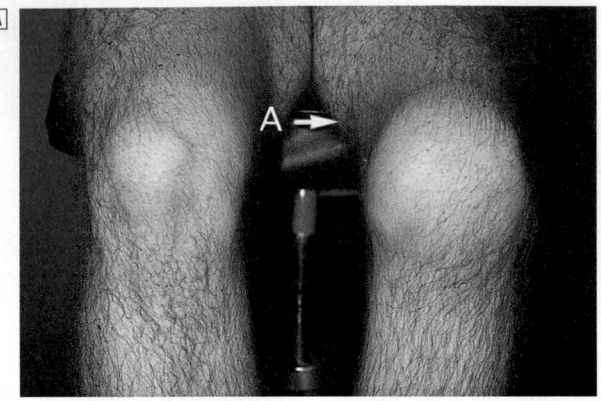

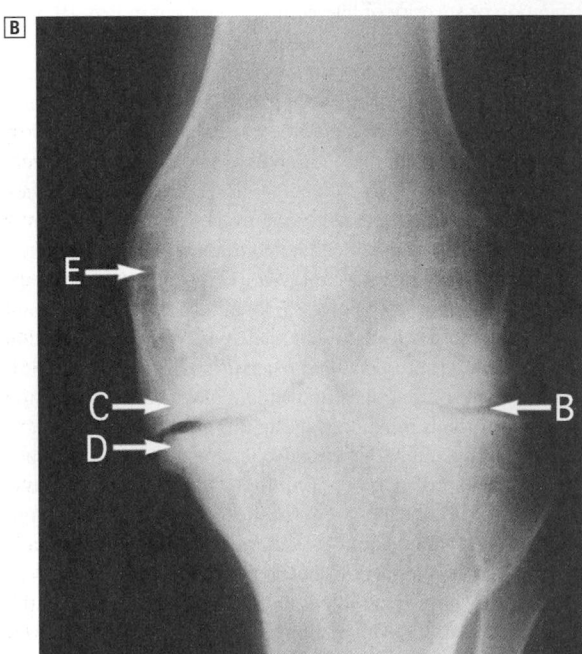

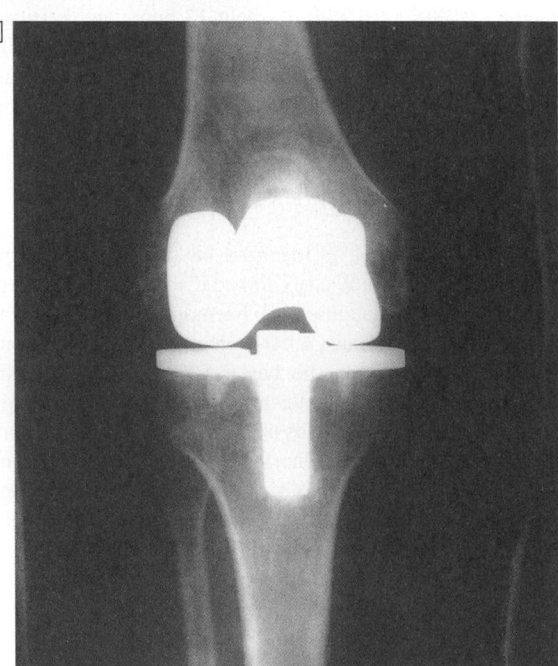

Fig. 19.35   Chronic haemophilic arthropathy of the left knee. [A] Repeated bleeds have led to broadening of the femoral epicondyles. Unilateral atrophy of the quadriceps (A) is easily seen. [B] Radiograph confirms broadening of femoral epicondyles. There is no cartilage present, as evidenced by the close proximity of the femur and tibia (B); sclerosis (C), osteophyte (D) and bony cysts (E) are present. [C] A haemophiliac's stiff joint with minimal flexion has been replaced by a prosthesis. This enabled the joint to have a greatly extended range of motion which very markedly improved the patient's mobility.

Although joint and muscle bleeds are the most common sites for haemorrhage, bleeding can occur at almost any site. It is particularly serious if it takes place in a confined anatomical space associated with vital structures. The intra-cranial area is one such site and, unless it is treated very promptly, haemorrhage here is often fatal (see Fig. 19.37).

Individuals with moderate haemophilia usually only experience haemorrhage after minor trauma, and those with the mild form of the disorder, following more major trauma or surgery. Whereas severe haemophilia is usually diagnosed within the first 2 years of life, individuals with moderate and mild forms may escape diagnosis until adulthood.

Management

Bleeding episodes should be treated early by raising the factor VIII level. In the UK this is most commonly accomplished by intravenous infusion of factor VIII concentrate. Factor VIII concentrates are freeze-dried and stable at 4°C and can therefore be stored in domestic refrigerators. This facility, which allows many patients to treat themselves at home, has revolutionised haemophilia care. In countries where factor VIII is not available, cryo-precipitate should be used. All plasma-derived factor VIII concentrates are prepared from donors who are perceived as having a low risk of viral carriage, e.g. of HIV. The plasma is screened for the presence of antibodies to hepatitis B and C viruses and HIV, and the final product is treated either by heat or by chemicals in an attempt to inactivate any residual viruses. Concentrates prepared with these precautions have a good safety record. However, factor VIII prepared by recombinant DNA technology is now available, is perceived as being safer than that derived

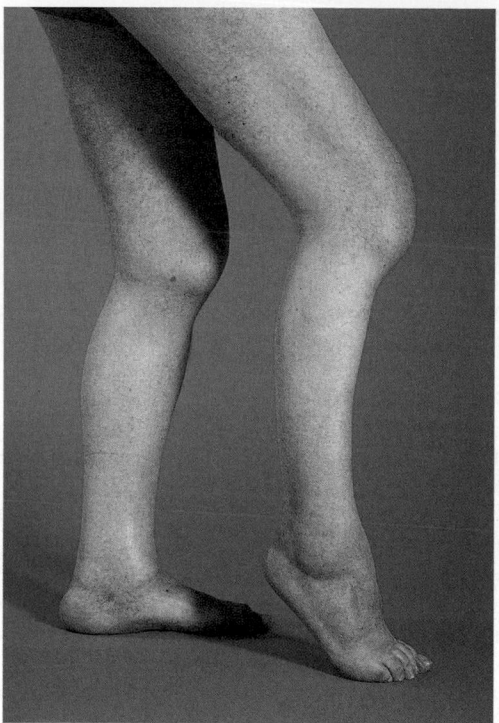

Fig. 19.36 Atrophy of the calf in an adult following an inadequately treated gastrocnemius haematoma as a child. The increased pressure of the haematoma caused ischaemia of the muscle, this being followed by necrosis, fibrosis and subsequent contraction to give the equinus deformity.

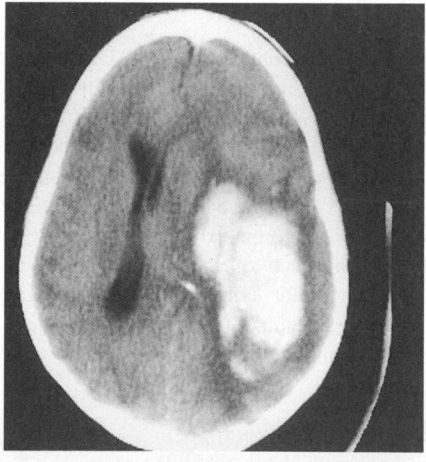

Fig. 19.37 CT revealing a major intracerebral haematoma. This apparently arose spontaneously in a severe haemophiliac.

from human plasma and is therefore likely to replace plasma-derived concentrates.

In addition to factor VIII concentrate therapy, resting of the bleeding site by either bed rest or a splint reduces continuing haemorrhage. Once bleeding has settled, the patient should be mobilised and given physiotherapy to restore strength to the surrounding muscles.

19.54 LONG-TERM SEQUELAE OF HAEMOPHILIA
Complications due to repeated haemorrhages
• Arthropathy of large joints, e.g. knees, elbows • Atrophy of muscles secondary to haematomas • Mononeuropathy resulting from pressure by haematomas
Complications due to therapy

• Anti-factor VIII antibody development
• Virus transmission
   Hepatitis A virus—acute self-limiting illness
   Hepatitis B virus—5–10% become chronic HBsAg carriers
   Hepatitis C virus—chronic progressive liver disease
   Hepatitis D virus—only arises in those with HBsAg
   HIV—AIDS
   Parvovirus—acute systemic self-limiting illness

Complications of therapy

Although factor VIII concentrates have transformed the lives of haemophiliacs by allowing many to lead near-normal lives, this freedom has been bought at a cost (see Box 19.54). Many patients treated before 1985, when concentrates were first virally inactivated with heat or chemicals to destroy viruses, became infected by HIV and the hepatitis viruses. As a result most adult severe haemophiliacs have been exposed to hepatitis B virus and have developed immunity, as evidenced by the development of anti-HBs. A small number become chronic HBsAg carriers and may infect sexual partners, who should therefore be offered hepatitis B immunisation (see p. 864). They are also at risk of delta virus infection. All potential recipients of pooled blood products should be offered hepatitis A and B immunisation because it will protect against hepatitis A, B and D infection. Hepatitis C virus was ubiquitously transmitted by concentrates prior to 1985, resulting in virtually all recipients becoming infected. It is clear that many of these patients have hepatitis, and a significant proportion progress to cirrhosis and hepatocellular carcinoma. Interferon and ribavirin therapy appear to cure a proportion of patients. Patients with clinically severe liver disease or liver cancer should be considered for hepatic transplantation.

Prior to 1985 HIV was transmitted to haemophiliacs by concentrates, resulting in at least 60% of severe haemophiliacs becoming infected (see p. 109). The clinical consequences are very similar to those for other individuals who have become infected with HIV, although their clinical course is perhaps more like that of those who become infected intravenously—e.g. drug users—than those who become infected sexually. Kaposi's sarcoma is rare in haemophiliacs compared with homosexuals.

There is now concern about the possibility that the infectious agent which causes variant CJD in humans (see p. 1202) might be transmissible by blood and blood products. Hence pooled plasma products, including factor VIII concentrate, are now manufactured from plasma collected in countries with a low incidence of BSE.

The other serious consequence of factor VIII infusion is the development of anti-factor VIII antibodies, which arises in about 20–30% of severe haemophiliacs. Such antibodies rapidly neutralise therapeutic infusions, making treatment relatively ineffective. Individuals may be treated with porcine factor VIII because the antibody may have lower activity against animal factor VIII than against the human type. Alternatively, infusions of activated clotting factors, e.g. VIIa or Feiba (factor eight inhibitor bypassing activity —an activated concentrate of factors II, IX and X), may stop bleeding.

In individuals with a basal factor VIII level of 10% or greater it may be possible to raise the level approximately three- to fivefold with desmopressin; this is usually best given intravenously but can be administered intranasally. This is often sufficient to treat a mild bleed or cover minor surgery such as dental extraction.

Surgery in haemophiliacs can be safely performed provided the patient does not have an inhibitor to factor VIII and receives appropriate doses of concentrate. A single infusion of factor VIII is usually adequate for simple dental extractions in an individual with severe haemophilia, along with a 10-day course of tranexamic acid (a fibrinolytic inhibitor) and an antibiotic. Major surgery, such as orthopaedic surgery, requires twice-daily therapy for 14 days or longer.

HAEMOPHILIA B (CHRISTMAS DISEASE)

Aberrations of the factor IX gene, which is also present on the X chromosome, result in a reduction of the plasma factor IX level, giving rise to haemophilia B. This disorder is clinically indistinguishable from haemophilia A but is less common. The frequency of bleeding episodes is related to the severity of the deficiency of the plasma factor IX level.

Treatment is with a factor IX concentrate; it is used in much the same way as factor VIII for haemophilia A. Carrier identification and antenatal diagnosis can be accomplished if the specific mutation is known.

VON WILLEBRAND'S DISEASE

Von Willebrand's disease is a common but usually mild bleeding disorder. The gene for von Willebrand factor (vWF) is located on chromosome 12 and therefore the disorder is inherited in an autosomal fashion. In most families it has the appearance of being inherited in a dominant manner; rarely, it appears in a clinically severe form with almost undetectable levels of vWF. In these circumstances the patient usually inherits a different abnormal vWF gene from each parent and is thus a compound heterozygote. Gene probes are available to trace the gene in a family and can be used to identify carriers and for antenatal diagnosis.

The vWF is a protein, synthesised by endothelial cells and megakaryocytes, that performs two principal functions. It acts as a carrier protein for factor VIII, to which it is non-covalently bound. A deficiency of vWF therefore results in a secondary reduction in the plasma factor VIII level. Its other function is to form bridges between platelets and sub-endothelial components (e.g. collagen), allowing platelets to adhere to damaged vessel walls (see Fig. 19.7, p. 897). A deficiency of vWF therefore also leads to prolonged primary haemorrhage after trauma.

Clinical features

As vWF participates, along with platelets, in primary haemostasis, patients present with haemorrhagic manifestations which are similar to those in individuals with reduced platelet function. Superficial bruising, epistaxis, and menorrhagic and gastrointestinal haemorrhage are common. Bleeding episodes are usually much less common than in severe haemophilia and excessive haemorrhage may only be observed after trauma or surgery. Within a single family the disease can be of very variable expression so that some members may have quite severe and frequent bleeds, whereas others are relatively little troubled.

Investigations

The disorder is characterised by finding a reduced level of vWF, which is often accompanied by a secondary reduction in factor VIII and a prolongation of the bleeding time.

Management

Many episodes of mild haemorrhage can be successfully treated with desmopressin, which raises the vWF level, resulting in a secondary increase in factor VIII. For more serious or persistent bleeds haemostasis can be achieved with selected factor VIII concentrates which contain considerable quantities of vWF in addition to factor VIII.

ACQUIRED BLEEDING DISORDERS

DISSEMINATED INTRAVASCULAR COAGULATION

Clinical features

Disseminated intravascular coagulation (DIC) can be initiated by a variety of different mechanisms in a number of diverse but distinct clinical situations, as set out in Box 19.55. Endothelial damage, due to many causes—e.g. endotoxaemia due to Gram-negative septicaemia—may activate endothelial cells to produce tissue factor, which leads to activation of the coagulation cascade through the extrinsic pathway (see Fig. 19.8, p. 898). The presence of thromboplastin from damaged tissues, placenta or fat embolus, or following brain injury may also activate coagulation. Intravascular coagulation takes place with consumption of platelets, factors V and VIII, and

19.55 CAUSES OF DISSEMINATED INTRAVASCULAR COAGULATION	
Infections	
• E. coli	• Streptococcus pneumoniae
• Neisseria meningitidis	• Malaria
Cancers	
• Lung	• Prostate
• Pancreas	
Obstetric	
• Abruptio placentae	• Pre-eclampsia
• Retained dead fetus	• Amniotic fluid embolism

fibrinogen. This results in a potential haemorrhagic state, due to the depletion of haemostatic components, which may be exacerbated by activation of the fibrinolytic system secondary to the deposition of fibrin.

Investigations

DIC should be suspected when any of the conditions in Box 19.55 are encountered. Definitive diagnosis depends on the finding of thrombocytopenia, prolongation of the pro-thrombin time (due to factor V and fibrinogen deficiency) and activated partial thromboplastin time (due to factors V, VIII and fibrinogen deficiency), a low fibrinogen concentration and increased levels of D-dimer (which is cleaved from fibrin by plasmin, establishing evidence of fibrin lysis).

Management

Therapy should be aimed at treating the underlying condition causing the DIC, e.g. intravenous antibiotics for suspected septicaemia. Exacerbating factors such as acidosis, dehydration, renal failure and hypoxia should be corrected. If the patient is bleeding, blood products such as platelets and/or cryoprecipitate (which is enriched in factor VIII and fibrinogen) should be given to correct identified abnormalities. It may also be reasonable to treat severe coagulation abnormalities in the absence of frank bleeding to prevent sudden catastrophic haemorrhage such as intracranial bleed or massive gastrointestinal haemorrhage.

LIVER DISEASE

In severe parenchymal liver disease bleeding may arise from many different causes. Local anatomical abnormalities are often the site of major bleeding (such as oesophageal varices or peptic ulcer), and this may be difficult to arrest because of deficiencies in components of the haemostatic system. These may arise because of reduced hepatic synthesis, e.g. factors II, VII, IX, X and fibrinogen, DIC, reduced clearance of plasminogen activator, or thrombocytopenia secondary to hypersplenism. Treatment should be reserved for acute bleeds or to cover interventional procedures such as liver biopsy.

Cholestatic jaundice reduces vitamin K absorption and leads to a deficiency of function of factors II, VII, IX and X due to reduced gamma glutamate carboxylation. This deficiency can be readily and effectively treated with vitamin K_1 10 mg daily parenterally for several days.

RENAL FAILURE

The severity of the haemorrhagic state in renal failure is proportional to the plasma urea concentration. Bleeding manifestations are of platelet type, with gastrointestinal haemorrhage being particularly common. The causes are multifactorial, including anaemia, mild thrombocytopenia and the accumulation of low molecular waste products, normally excreted by the kidney, that inhibit platelet function. Treatment is by dialysis to reduce the urea concentration, and platelet concentrate infusions; red cell transfusions raise the haemoglobin and decrease the propensity to bleed. Increasing the concentration of vWF, either by cryoprecipitate or by desmopressin, may promote haemostasis.

VENOUS THROMBOSIS

Venous thrombosis may arise either because of damage to, or pressure on, veins (e.g. varicose veins or pelvic tumour), or as a result of changes in the plasma or cellular elements of the blood. Predisposing conditions for venous thromboembolism are listed in Box 19.56.

19.56 FACTORS PREDISPOSING TO VENOUS THROMBOSIS

Patient factors

- Age > 40 years
- Obesity
- Varicose veins
- Previous deep venous thrombosis
- Oral contraceptive
- Pregnancy/puerperium
- Dehydration
- Immobility

Surgical conditions

- Surgery, especially if > 30 minutes' duration
    - Abdominal or pelvic
    - Orthopaedic to lower limb

Medical conditions

- Myocardial infarction/heart failure
- Inflammatory bowel disease
- Malignancy
- Nephrotic syndrome
- Behçet's syndrome
- Homocystinaemia

Haematological disorders

- Primary proliferative polycythaemia
- Essential thrombocythaemia
- Myelofibrosis
- Paroxysmal nocturnal haemoglobinuria

Deficiency of anticoagulants

- Antithrombin
- Protein C
- Prothrombin G20210A
- Protein S
- Factor V Leiden

Antiphospholipid antibody

- Lupus anticoagulant
- Anticardiolipin antibody

HAEMATOLOGICAL DISORDERS PREDISPOSING TO VENOUS THROMBOEMBOLISM

When a thrombotic event arises in an individual under the age of 40 years, particularly if there is a family history of thrombosis, investigations should be undertaken to assess whether there is a predisposing plasma abnormality (see Box 19.56). Often several risk factors are present when an acute deep venous thrombosis (DVT) occurs. Thus an obese patient over the age of 40 years, with factor V Leiden, may undergo abdominal surgery and develop a post-operative DVT.

ANTITHROMBIN DEFICIENCY

Antithrombin is a protease inhibitor which inactivates factors IIa, IXa, Xa and XIa, especially in the presence of heparin (which greatly potentiates its activity). Familial deficiency of antithrombin is a dominantly inherited disorder and is associated with a marked predisposition to venous thromboembolism.

PROTEIN C AND S DEFICIENCIES

Protein C is a vitamin K-dependent protein. When thrombin binds to thrombomodulin, on the endothelial cell surface, it becomes an anticoagulant by activating protein C. In the presence of protein S, this inactivates factors Va and VIIIa. Thus a deficiency of either protein C or S results in a pro-thrombotic state due to reduced inhibition of activated factor V and VIII. A deficiency of either factor is usually inherited in an autosomal fashion.

FACTOR V LEIDEN

This common disorder is associated with venous thrombosis. It was originally characterised as an inability of the patient's plasma clotting time to lengthen in the presence of activated protein C (APC), giving rise to its original description as activated protein C resistance (APCR). Further investigation revealed that the abnormality resided in a substrate for APC, namely factor Va; a substitution of arginine by glutamine at position 506 prevents its cleavage and hence inactivation. Factor Va will therefore persist, resulting in a tendency to venous thrombosis.

The mutation has been identified in about 3–5% of healthy individuals in Western Europe and North America and about 20–40% of those with a history of venous thrombosis at a young age. The risk of venous thrombosis in individuals with this mutation is substantially increased if the patient has a second plasma abnormality, e.g. a lupus anticoagulant (see below).

PROTHROMBIN G20210A

This genetic polymorphism at the non-coding 3′ end of the prothrombin gene is associated with an increased plasma level of prothrombin and venous thromboembolism. It is present in about 2% of the normal population and about 6% of those with venous thrombus.

ANTIPHOSPHOLIPID ANTIBODY SYNDROME

In the antiphospholipid antibody syndrome an antibody in the patient's plasma has activity against enzymic reactions in the coagulation cascade that are dependent on platelet membranes (or in vitro by phospholipid). The antibody, in vitro, has the effect of prolonging the APTT because it interacts with phospholipid in the reaction tube and inhibits the binding or enzymic interactions of the coagulation components. It is most sensitively diagnosed by prolongation of the dilute Russell viper venom time (DRVVT) of plasma, an effect that can be neutralised by adding platelet membranes. When the antibody inhibits coagulation in these ways it is known as the lupus anticoagulant. In some individuals the plasma protein β2-glycoprotein-1 undergoes a conformational change after it has bound to anionic phospholipids, and is then recognised by the antibody. In vitro this is usually detected by its ability to bind to the β2-glycoprotein-1

in an assay with cardiolipin when it is known as an anti-cardiolipin antibody. The term antiphospholipid antibody encompasses both a lupus anticoagulant and an anticardiolipin antibody; some individuals are only positive for one of these activities, whereas in others both are present.

Clinical features

The antiphospholipid antibody is associated with a constellation of clinical conditions (see Box 19.57) found in association with a history of thromboembolism. The antibody has now been found in some individuals with a history of arterial or venous thromboembolism, often at a young age but without features of SLE; in this case it is known as the primary antiphospholipid antibody syndrome. The antibody is also associated with recurrent spontaneous abortions as well as with intrauterine fetal growth retardation. The mechanism by which the antibody predisposes to thrombosis is unclear but it may be related to either maintaining platelets in an activated state within the circulation or, possibly, to inhibiting the fibrinolytic activity of endothelial cells.

19.57 ANTIPHOSPHOLIPID SYNDROME	
The clinical features are mainly related to arterial or venous occlusion which may affect one or several organs	
Haematological	
• Thrombocytopenia	• Autoimmune haemolytic anaemia
Cardiac	
• Myocardial infarction • Pulmonary hypertension	• Valvular disease
Neurological	

• Cerebral ischaemia
    Single lesions
    Multi-infarct dementia
• Migraine
	• Epilepsy
	• Chorea
	• Transverse myelopathy

Renal	
• Renal vein thrombosis	• Glomerular thrombosis
Endocrine	
• Adrenal thrombosis—Addison's disease	
Gastrointestinal tract	
• Bowel ischaemia	• Budd–Chiari syndrome
Skin	
• Livedo reticularis	• Recurrent skin ulcers
Obstetric	
• Recurrent spontaneous abortions	• Intrauterine growth retardation

MANAGEMENT OF VENOUS THROMBOEMBOLISM

The treatment of a thrombosis depends on its site and extent and on the age of the thrombus. Prior to any antithrombotic therapy it is essential to consider whether the patient has a significant contraindication to anticoagulant therapy. On occasion antithrombotic therapy may have to be given to a patient who has a contraindication and in this instance the potential benefits have to be weighed against the risk of serious haemorrhage. Indications for and contraindications to anticoagulation are given in Boxes 19.58 and 19.59.

Anticoagulant therapy

Heparin

Standard (unfractionated) heparin (SH) produces its anti-coagulant effect by potentiating the activity of antithrombin which inhibits the procoagulant enzymic activity of factors IIa, VIIa, IXa, Xa and XIa (see Fig. 19.8, p. 898).

The more recently developed low molecular weight heparins (LMWHs) augment antithrombin activity preferentially against factor Xa. LMWH does not prolong the APTT, unlike SH, and if its plasma level needs to be measured this is accomplished using a specific anti-Xa-based assay. LMWH, because of its high bioavailability after subcutaneous injection, is given as either a standard or a weight-related dose. Normally, therefore, the plasma LMWH level does not need to be measured.

The therapeutic indications for heparin are listed in Box 19.58.

19.58 INDICATIONS FOR ANTICOAGULATION	
Heparin	

• Treatment and prevention of deep venous thrombosis
 • Pulmonary embolism
 • Myocardial infarction, to prevent:
   Coronary reocclusion after thrombolysis
   Mural thrombosis
 • Unstable angina pectoris
 • Acute peripheral arterial occlusion	

Warfarin	
• Prophylaxis against deep venous thrombosis • Treatment of deep venous thrombosis and pulmonary embolism • Arterial embolism • Mitral stenosis with atrial fibrillation • Transient ischaemic attacks	Therapeutic corrected prothrombin ratio (INR) 2.5
• Recurrent deep venous thrombosis • Mechanical prosthetic cardiac valves	INR 3.5
(INR = international normalised ratio)	

19.59 CONTRAINDICATIONS TO ANTICOAGULATION

• Recent surgery, especially to eye or CNS
 • Pre-existing haemorrhagic state
   e.g. Liver disease
     Renal failure
     Haemophilia
     Thrombocytopenia
 • Pre-existing structural lesions
   e.g. Peptic ulcer
 • Recent cerebral haemorrhage
 • Uncontrolled hypertension

LMWHs are now licensed for the treatment of both DVT and pulmonary embolism and are now replacing standard heparin as the initial treatment of choice for many patients. As injections of LMWH need only be given once daily sub-cutaneously, many patients can be treated at home.

Standard heparin is often reserved for treating patients with very severe, life-threatening thromboembolism, e.g. major pulmonary embolism giving rise to significant hypoxaemia or hypotension. It should be started with a loading dose of 5000 U i.v., followed by a continuous infusion of 20 U/kg/hr initially. The level of anticoagulation should be assessed after 6 hours and then, if satisfactory, daily by use of a coagulation test which is appropriately sensitive to heparin, e.g. APTT. It is usual to aim for a patient time which is 1.5–2.5 times the control time of the test. The half-life of intravenous heparin is about 1 hour and if a patient bleeds it is usually sufficient just to discontinue the infusion as the anticoagulant effect diminishes relatively rapidly; however, if bleeding is severe, the excess can be neutralised with intravenous protamine. The short half-life of SH makes it useful for those with a predisposition to bleeding, e.g. who have peptic ulcer, or those who may require surgery. Treatment with either LMWH or SH should continue for 6–8 days, depending upon the extent of the thrombus. In most patients it is appropriate to start warfarin therapy at the same time as heparin, as it takes several days to decrease the concentration of the vitamin K-dependent clotting factors. Heparin should be continued until the INR is > 2.0 for 2 consecutive days.

Warfarin

Warfarin inhibits the vitamin K-dependent carboxylation of factors II, VII, IX and X in the liver (see Fig. 19.9, p. 899). Carboxylation of glutamyl residues of these coagulation factors increases their negative charge and allows them to maintain their active three-dimensional structure. The recognised indications for warfarin therapy are listed in Box 19.58.

Therapy with warfarin must be initiated with a loading dose—e.g. 10 mg orally—on the first day, and subsequent daily doses depending on the INR. The degree of anticoagulation depends on the clinical circumstances, and the appropriate target INRs are given in Box 19.58. Following a single episode of venous thromboembolism it is usual to continue oral anticoagulation for 3–6 months. If a patient has had two episodes of venous thromboembolism, life-long warfarin is often considered appropriate. It is important to remember that nearly all drugs can potentially modify the degree of warfarin therapy, and therefore the INR should be checked 3–6 days after stopping or starting any other medicine.

Bleeding is the most common serious side-effect of warfarin and occurs in about 0.5–1.0% of patients each year. The anticoagulant benefit of warfarin must therefore be demonstrably greater than the risk of serious bleeding. If the patient bleeds, the anticoagulant effect of warfarin may be reversed by vitamin K_1 1–5 mg slowly i.v.; the effect becomes apparent within about 6 hours, although it may not fully reverse anticoagulation for 1 or 2 days. The INR should be repeated after 6 hours and a further dose of vitamin K_1 given if appropriate. If the patient has a serious haemorrhage, reversal can be effected quickly by giving coagulation concentrate containing factors II, VII, IX and X (50 U/kg) or, if this is unavailable, fresh frozen plasma.

TREATMENT OF DEEP VENOUS THROMBOSIS AND PULMONARY EMBOLISM—heparin before warfarin `EBM`

'In the treatments of DVT and pulmonary embolism, RCTs have shown that initial treatment with heparin before the introduction of warfarin results in fewer recurrences and that treating DVT with an INR in the range of 2.0–3.0 results in the same incidence of recurrences but fewer bleeds compared to treatment with an INR of 3.0–4.0.'

- Brandjes DP, Heijboer H, Buller HR, et al. Acenocoumarol and heparin compared with acenocoumarol alone in the initial treatment of proximal-vein thrombosis. N Engl J Med 1992; 327:1485–1489.
- Hull R, Hirsh J, Jay R, et al. Different intensities of oral anticoagulant therapy in the treatment of proximal-vein thrombosis. N Engl J Med 1982; 307:1676–1681.

Further information: 🖥 www.clinicalevidence.org

Prevention of venous thrombosis

All patients admitted to hospital should be assessed for their risk of developing venous thromboembolism. A summary of the risk categories is given in Box 19.56, page 952 and Box 19.60. Early mobilisation of all patients is important to prevent DVTs. Patients at medium or high risk may require additional antithrombotic measures. Knee-length graduated compression stockings are effective in medium-risk individuals. In medium-risk patients SH or LMWH can also be used; it should be started pre-operatively and continued until the patient is fully mobile. High-risk individuals should receive anti-embolism stockings and LMWH at a higher prophylactic dose. Routine monitoring of SH or LMWH for prophylaxis is not necessary. Particular care should be taken with the use of heparin prophylaxis in any patient in whom intra- or post-operative bleeding could have serious consequences, e.g. those with spinal anaesthesia, and it is usually contraindicated with neurosurgery. Any individual who has any of the additional risk factors is also at increased likelihood of thrombosis and every care should be taken to ensure that, as far as possible, the risk can be lessened prior to surgery—for instance, the haemoglobin reduced in polycythaemia.

19.60 ANTITHROMBOTIC PROPHYLAXIS

Patients in the following categories should be considered for specific antithrombotic prophylaxis:

Moderate risk of DVT

- Major surgery in patients > 40 years or with other risk factor
- Major medical illness
  e.g. Heart failure
  Chest infection
  Malignancy
  Inflammatory bowel disease

High risk of DVT

- Hip or knee surgery
- Major abdominal or pelvic surgery for malignancy or with history of DVT or known thrombophilia (see Box 19.4, p. 902)

ISSUES IN OLDER PEOPLE
HAEMOSTASIS AND THROMBOSIS

- Thrombocytopenia is not uncommon because of the rising prevalence of disorders in which it may be a secondary feature, and also because of the greater use of drugs which can cause it.
- 'Senile' purpura is presumed to be due to an age-associated loss of subcutaneous fat and the collagenous support of small blood vessels, making them more prone to damage from minor trauma.
- Thrombosis-related events become more frequent in old age. These may be due to stasis to which older people are prone; some studies show increased platelet aggregation with age, and others age-associated hyperactivity of the haemostatic system which could create a prothrombotic state.

FURTHER INFORMATION

www.bcshguidelines.com *British Committee for Standards in Haematology guidelines.*
www.ibmtr.org

BLOOD PRODUCTS AND TRANSFUSION
Emmanuel JC, McClelland DBL, Page R. The clinical use of blood (WHO/BTS/99.2). Geneva: WHO; 2001.
McClelland DBL, ed. Handbook of transfusion medicine. 3rd edn. London: HMSO; 2001.
Murphy MF, Pamphilon DH. Transfusion medicine. Oxford: Blackwell Science; 2001.

www.transfusionguidelines.org.uk *Contains the UK Transfusion Services' Handbook of transfusion medicine and links to other relevant sites.*

ANAEMIAS
Castro O. Management of sickle cell anaemia: recent advances and controversies. Br J Haematol 1999; 107(1):2
Chanarin I, Metz J. Diagnosis of cobalamin deficiency. Br J Haematol 1997; 97(4):695.
Oliviero NF. The beta thalassemias. N Engl J Med 1999; 341:99.
Tse WT, Lux SE. Red blood cell membrane disorders. Br J Haematol 1999; 104(1):2.

HAEMATOLOGICAL MALIGNANCIES
Aisenberg A. Problems of management in Hodgkin's disease. Blood 1999; 93:761.
Bataille R, Harousseau JL. Multiple myeloma. N Engl J Med 1997; 336:1657.
Goldman J. Chronic myeloid leukemia: current treatment options. Blood 2001; 98:2039.
Heany ML, Gold DW. Myelodysplasia. N Engl J Med 1999; 340:1649.
Linch DC, Goldstone AH. High dose therapy for Hodgkin's disease. Br J Haematol 1999; 111:287–291.
Lokhorst HM, Sonneveld P, Verdonck L. Intensive treatment for myeloma. Br J Haematol 1999; 106:18.
Lowenberg B, Downing JR, Burnett A. Acute myeloid leukemia. N Engl J Med 1999; 341:1057.
Marsh J. Modern management of severe aplastic anaemia. Br J Haematol 1999; 110:41.

BLEEDING DISORDERS AND VENOUS THROMBOSIS
Guidelines for the investigation and management of antiphospholipid syndrome. Br J Haematol 2000; 109:704–715 (http://www.bcshguidelines.com).
Investigation and management of heritable thrombophilia. Br J Haematol 2001; 114(3):512–528 (http://www.bcshguidelines.com).
Lee AY, Hirsh J. Diagnosis and treatment of venous thromboembolism. Annu Rev Med 2002; 53:15–33.
Mannucci PM, Tuddenham EG. The haemophilias—from royal genes to gene therapy. N Engl J Med 2001; 344:1773–1779.
Seligsohn U, Lubetsky A. Genetic susceptibility to venous thrombosis. N Engl J Med 2001; 344:1222–1231.

http://www.show.scot.nhs.uk/sign/clinical.htm *1999 SIGN guideline for antithrombotic therapy.*

Musculoskeletal disorders

M. DOHERTY • P. LANYON • S.H. RALSTON

CLINICAL EXAMINATION OF THE MUSCULOSKELETAL SYSTEM

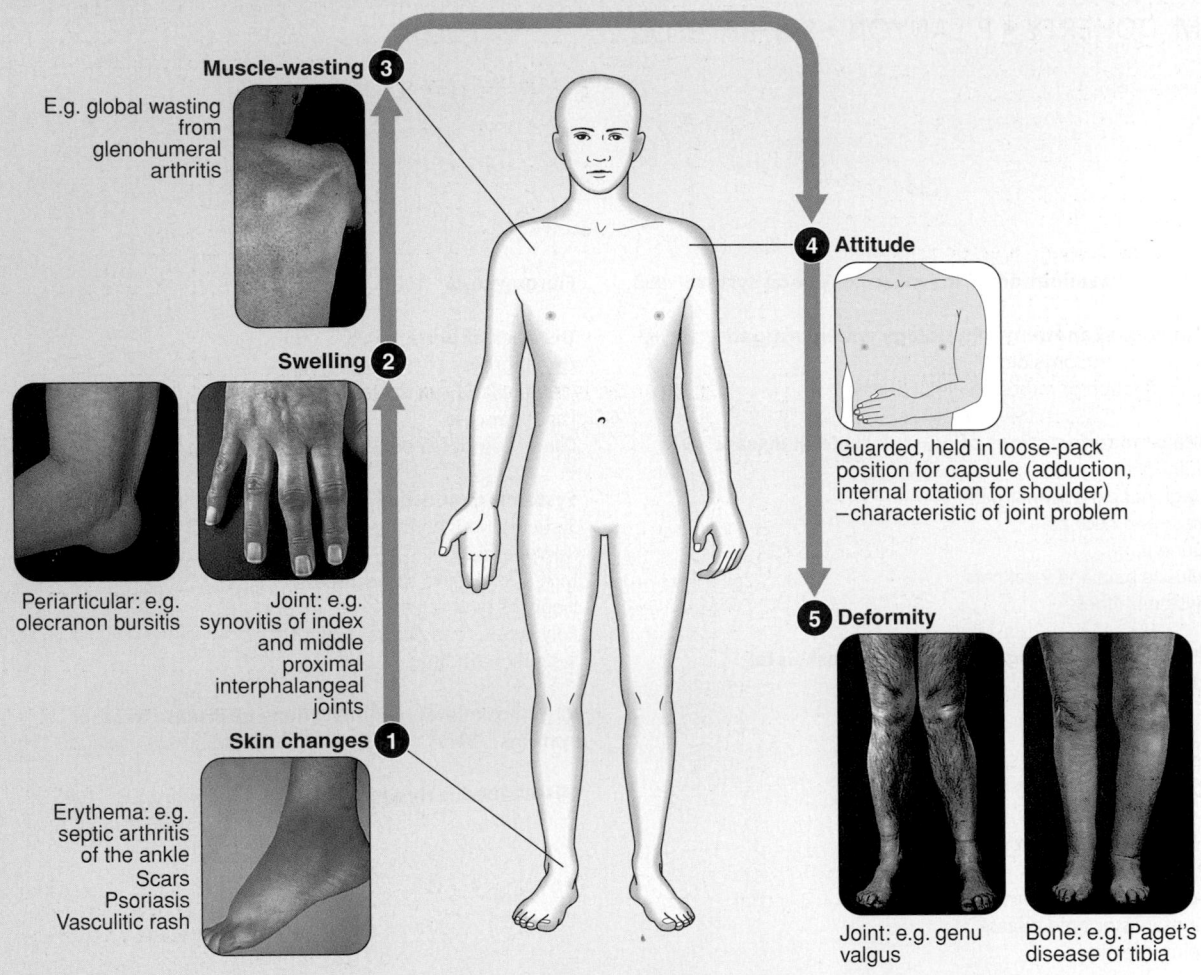

Muscle-wasting ❸

E.g. global wasting from glenohumeral arthritis

Swelling ❷

Periarticular: e.g. olecranon bursitis

Joint: e.g. synovitis of index and middle proximal interphalangeal joints

Skin changes ❶

Erythema: e.g. septic arthritis of the ankle
Scars
Psoriasis
Vasculitic rash

❹ Attitude

Guarded, held in loose-pack position for capsule (adduction, internal rotation for shoulder) –characteristic of joint problem

❺ Deformity

Joint: e.g. genu valgus

Bone: e.g. Paget's disease of tibia

The 'GALS' screen may be used for brief screening of the whole system (see overleaf)
Detailed regional examination involves 'look' (at rest and during movement), 'feel' and 'move'

A. Inspection at rest
  See figure above

B. Inspection during movement
  • Restriction
    Limited to one plane–periarticular lesion
    Affecting most or all movements–joint problem
  • Increased range
    Hypermobility, instability
  • Pain on usage
    Stress pain = increasing pain towards extremes of movement
    Universal stress pain (in most/all directions) –synovitis
    Selective stress pain (one plane only) –periarticular lesion

C. Palpation with movement
  • Tenderness
    Joint line–intra-articular/joint problem
    Periarticular–periarticular lesion
  • Increased warmth
    Inflammation (e.g. synovitis, bursitis)
  • Swelling
    Fluid (fluctuant)
    Soft tissue (soft, non-fluctuant)
    Bone (hard)
  • Crepitus
    Coarse, easily felt, may be readily audible–joint damage
    Fine, localised, heard with stethoscope–tendon sheath, bursa
  • Stability
  • Resisted active movements
    Reproduce pain from muscle, tendon, enthesis
  • Stress tests
    Reproduce pain from ligament or tendon sheath

IMPORTANT MSK SYMPTOMS

Pain

- Usage pain—worse on use, relieved by rest (mechanical strain, damage)
- Rest pain—worse after rest, improved by movement (inflammation)
- Night or 'bone' pain—mostly at night, poorly related to movement (bone origin)

Stiffness

(subjective feeling of inability to move freely)

- Duration/severity of early morning and inactivity stiffness that can be 'worn off' suggests degree of inflammation

Weakness

- Consider primary or secondary muscle abnormality

Swelling

(Fluid, soft tissue, bone)

Deformity

(Joint, bone)

Non-specific symptoms of systemic illness

(reflecting acute phase response)

- Weight loss, ± reduction in appetite
- Fatigability, poor concentration
- Sweats and chills, particularly at night
- Feeling ill, low, irritable

REGIONAL EXAMINATION DIFFERENCES BETWEEN JOINT AND PERIARTICULAR LESIONS

Sign	Joint	Periarticular
Tenderness	Over joint line	Away from joint line
Restricted movement	Active and passive movement affected equally	Active more restricted than passive
Resisted active movement	Not painful	May reproduce muscle, tendon or enthesis pain
Stress pain	Present in all tight-pack positions (several directions)	Present in direction of use of ligament, tendon or enthesis (mainly one direction)
Swelling	Capsular pattern	Localised, periarticular
Crepitus ('crunching')	Coarse or fine	Fine

FEATURES THAT DIFFERENTIATE JOINT INFLAMMATION ('SYNOVITIS') FROM JOINT DAMAGE

Feature	Synovitis	Joint damage
Stiffness (early morning, inactivity)	+++	±
Increased warmth	+	−
Stress pain	+	−
Soft tissue swelling	+	−
Effusion	+++	±
Crepitus	−	+++
Deformity	−	+
Instability	−	+

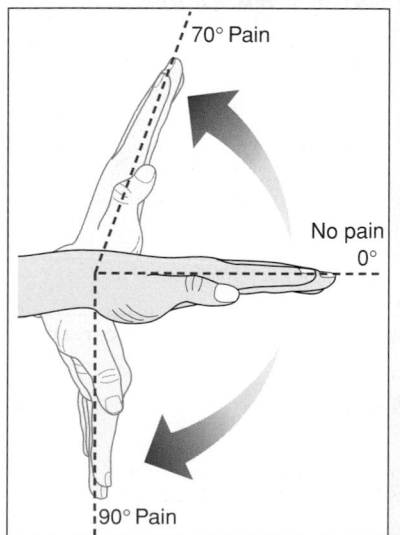

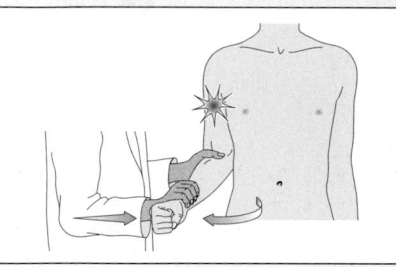

Resisted active movement. Attempted external rotation reproduces upper arm pain resulting from an infraspinatus/teres minor rotator cuff lesion.

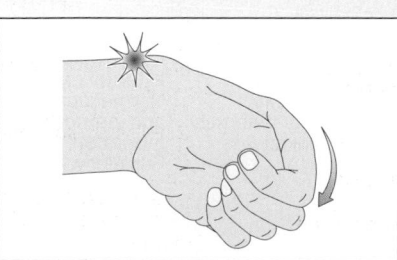

Stress test. Passive ulnar flexion reproduces pain from de Quervain's tenosynovitis.

'Stress pain' at the wrist. Pain worsens as the wrist moves towards the 'tight-pack' positions (flexion and extension) because of increased intracapsular pressure from inflammatory swelling and effusion. In the mid 'loose-pack' position, when the capsule is at its slackest, there is no pain. Stress pain is the earliest and most sensitive sign of synovitis, occurring before visible swelling or reduction of movement. With joint damage, pain is more evenly spread throughout the range.

'GALS' SCREENING EXAMINATION OF THE MUSCULOSKELETAL SYSTEM

THREE SCREENING QUESTIONS

- Do you have any pain or stiffness in your muscles, joints or back?
- Can you dress yourself completely without any difficulty?
- Can you walk up and down stairs without any difficulty?

The GALS (gait, arms, legs, spine) screen is a validated screening system for locomotor abnormality and disability with respect to activities of daily living (Doherty M, Dacre J, Dieppe P, Snaith M. The 'GALS' locomotor screen. Ann Rheum Dis 1992; 51:1165–1169; Plant MJ, Linton S, Dodd E, et al. The GALS locomotor screen and disability. Ann Rheum Dis 1993; 52:886–890).

Normal joints should be asymptomatic, look normal, assume a normal resting position and move smoothly through their range of movement.

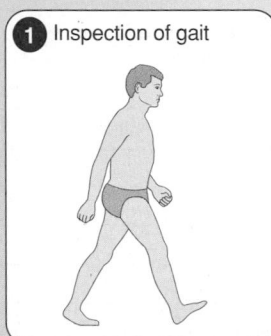

1 Inspection of gait

Symmetry, smoothness of movement
Normal stride length
Normal heel-strike, stance, toe-off, swing-through
Able to turn quickly

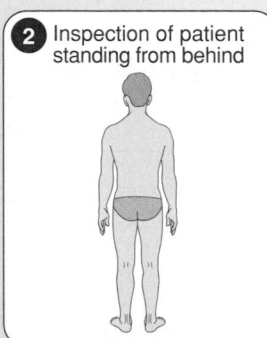

2 Inspection of patient standing from behind

Straight spine
Muscle bulk/symmetry of paraspinal, shoulder and gluteal muscles
Level iliac crests
No popliteal swelling
No hindfoot swelling or deformity

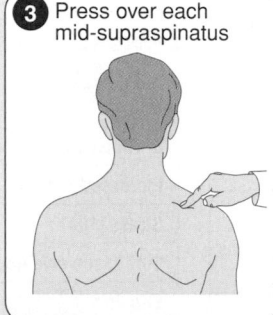

3 Press over each mid-supraspinatus

?Hyperalgesia of fibromyalgia

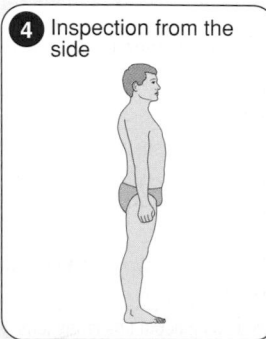

4 Inspection from the side

Normal cervical and lumbar lordosis
Normal thoracic kyphosis

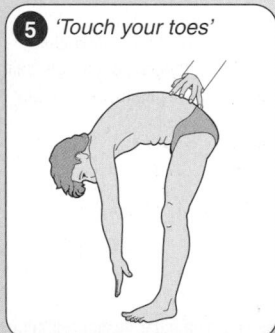

5 'Touch your toes'

Normal lumbar spine (and hip) flexion

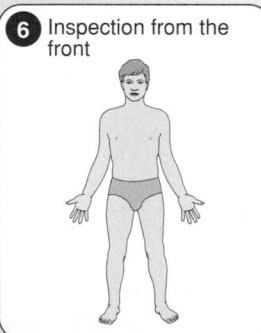

6 Inspection from the front

Full elbow extension
Shoulder and quadriceps muscle bulk, symmetry
No knee swelling or deformity
No forefoot or midfoot deformity
Normal arches

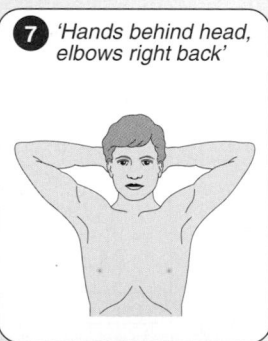

7 'Hands behind head, elbows right back'

Full shoulder abduction, external rotation
Normal acromioclavicular and sternoclavicular movement
Full elbow flexion

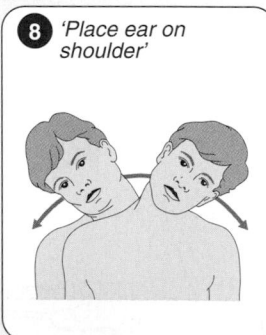

8 'Place ear on shoulder'

Normal pain-free cervical lateral flexion

Screening examination.

9 *'Open jaw, move side to side'*

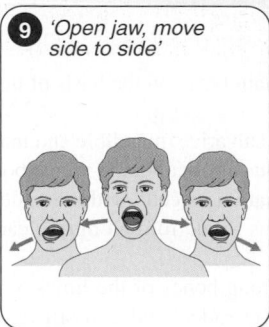

Normal temporo-mandibular movement

10 *'Hands in front, palms down'*

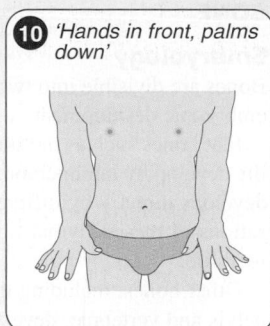

No swelling or deformity of hands/wrists
Able to extend fingers

11 *'Turn hands over'*

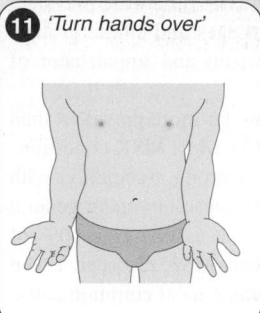

Normal supination (wrist, distal radio-ulnar joint)
Normal palms

12 *'Make a fist'*

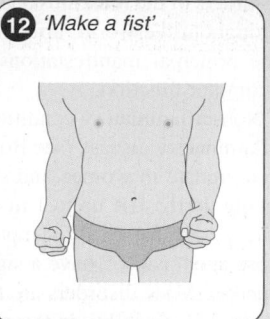

Strong power grip

13 *'Place tip of finger on tip of thumb'*

Fine precision pinch

14 Metacarpal squeeze

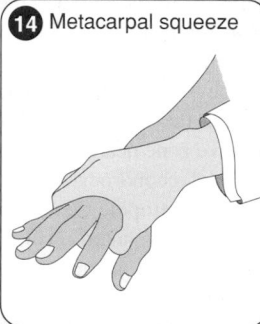

?Metacarpophalangeal joint tenderness

15 Examination on couch *'Put your heel on your bottom'* (flex knee and hip, holding knee)

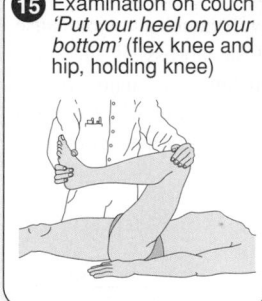

Full knee and hip flexion
No knee crepitus

16 Internal rotation of hip in flexion

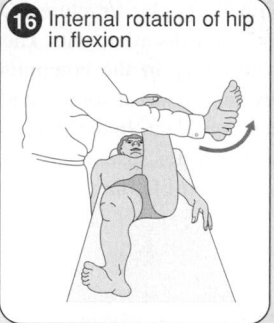

No pain or restriction of hip movement

17 Palpate for balloon sign

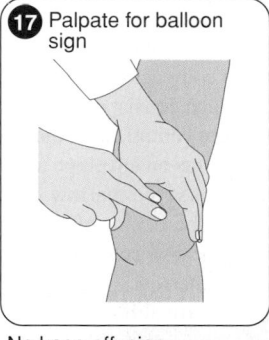

No knee effusion

18 Metatarsal squeeze

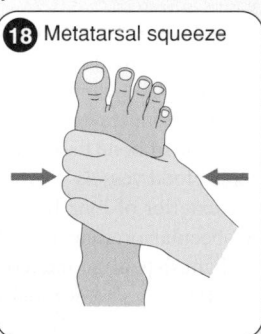

No metatarsophalangeal joint tenderness

19 Inspect soles

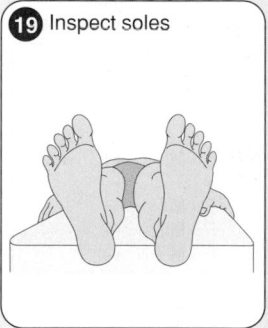

No callus or adventitious bursitis

RECORDING RESULTS		
A normal screen		
G ✓	A	M
A	✓	✓
L	✓	✓
S	✓	✓
(A = appearance; M = movement)		
Example of an abnormal screen		
G ✗	A	M
A	✓	✓
L	✗	✗
S	✓	✓
Antalgic gait Right knee Varus ↓ Flexion Crepitus ++ Effusion		
Diagnosis: osteoarthritis right knee		

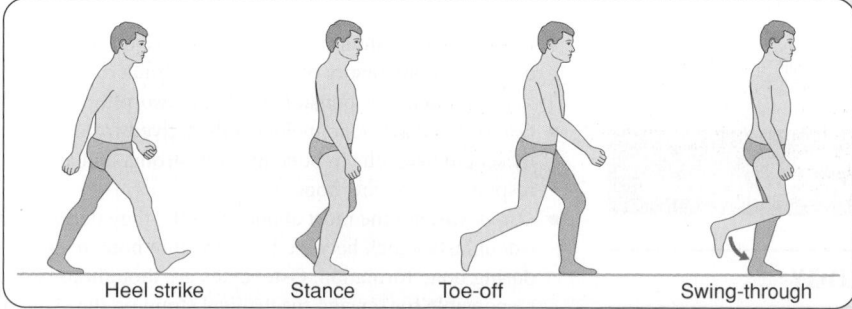

Heel strike   Stance   Toe-off   Swing-through

Antalgic gait: Jerky asymmetric gait with less time weight-bearing on painful leg
Trendelenburg gait: Due to weak hip abductors–pelvis drops on opposite side during stance phase on affected side
Waddling gait: Bilateral Trendelenburg gait

The four phases of gait.

Disorders of the musculoskeletal (MSK) system are prevalent throughout the world, affecting all ages and ethnic groups. The principal manifestations are pain and impairment of locomotor function.

Non-inflammatory conditions are far more prevalent than inflammatory disease (see Box 20.1). Most MSK conditions predominate in women and show a strong association with ageing. In the UK up to 1 in 4 new consultations in general practice are for MSK symptoms and as many as 40% of those aged over 65 have a significant MSK disorder. Taken together, MSK disorders are the single most common cause of physical disability in the elderly, and around one-third of all people with physical disability have an MSK disorder as the primary cause.

Most regional MSK pain arises from muscles, tendons and periarticular structures. Osteoarthritis is the most common joint disorder, with knee involvement a major cause of disability in the community. Osteoporosis is the most prevalent bone disorder and constitutes a major public health problem. In developed countries about 1 in 3 women and 1 in 6 men sustain an osteoporotic fracture at some point during their lifetime.

20.1 RELATIVE PREVALENCE OF MUSCULOSKELETAL DISORDERS

	Prevalence	Female: male	Age association
'Non-inflammatory' conditions			
Neck and back pain	20%	=	–
Osteoarthritis			
Knee	10%	F > M	++
Hip	4%	=	+
Osteoporosis	15%	F > M	++
Regional 'soft tissue' pain	10%	F > M	++
Fibromyalgia	3%	F > M	++
'Inflammatory' conditions			
Rheumatoid arthritis	1.5%	F > M	+
Gout	1.0%	M > F	–
Seronegative spondarthritis	0.8%	=	–
Polymyalgia rheumatica	0.04%	F > M	++
Connective tissue diseases (mainly lupus)	0.02%	F > M	–

FUNCTIONAL ANATOMY, PHYSIOLOGY AND INVESTIGATIONS

ANATOMY AND PHYSIOLOGY

The MSK system is responsible for body movements, providing a structural framework to protect internal organs and acting as a reservoir for storage of calcium and phosphate in the regulation of mineral homeostasis. Individual components are depicted in Figure 20.1.

BONE

Embryology

Bones are divisible into two main types on the basis of their embryonic development.

Flat bones such as the skull calvariae, mandible and maxilla develop by intramembranous ossification, in which bone develops directly by differentiation of cells within condensations of mesenchymal fibrous tissue formed during early fetal life.

Other bones, including the long bones of the limbs, ribs, pelvis and vertebrae, develop by endochondral ossification, in which an initial cartilage template is invaded by vascular tissue containing osteoprogenitor cells. The cartilage is then replaced by bone that extends from centres of ossification situated in the middle and ends of the developing bone. A thin remnant of cartilage remains at each end of the bone during childhood, and is referred to as the growth plate or epiphysis. Growth depends on division of chondrocytes within the epiphysis. Cell division takes place in the proliferative zone nearest the end of the long bone, and the newly formed chondrocytes migrate downwards and enlarge in the hypertrophic zone. Chondrocyte death ensues and the surrounding matrix calcifies before being removed and replaced by mature bone. During puberty, the rise in circulating levels of sex hormones halts cell division in the growth plate. The cartilage remnant then disappears as the epiphysis fuses and longitudinal bone growth ceases.

Bone anatomy and microanatomy

Two main structural types of bone occur in the normal adult skeleton. Cortical bone has a dense compact structure and is formed from Haversian systems, which consist of concentric lamellae of bone tissue, surrounding a central canal that contains blood vessels. Cortical bone forms an envelope around the exterior of long bones, and encloses the marrow cavity. Trabecular or cancellous bone fills the centre of the bone and consists of an interconnecting meshwork of trabeculae, separated by spaces filled with bone marrow. Whilst most of the skeleton (80%) is composed of cortical bone, trabecular bone predominates at the ends of long bones, in the vertebral bodies and the calcaneus.

The skeleton is shaped and remodelled throughout life by the bone cells:

- *Osteoclasts* are multinucleated cells derived from circulating precursors of the monocyte/macrophage lineage and are responsible for bone resorption.
- *Osteoblasts* are mononuclear cells derived from mesenchymal cells in bone marrow stroma and are responsible for new bone formation.
- *Osteocytes* are the most abundant cells; they derive from osteoblasts which become buried within bone matrix during bone formation. Osteocytes are thought to be responsible for sensing mechanical strain on the skeleton.

The main organic component of bone matrix is type I collagen, a fibrillar protein formed from two α_1 peptide chains and one α_2 chain wound together in a triple helix. Collagen is synthesised first as a propeptide, but following its secretion from osteoblasts, the N- and C-terminal fragments

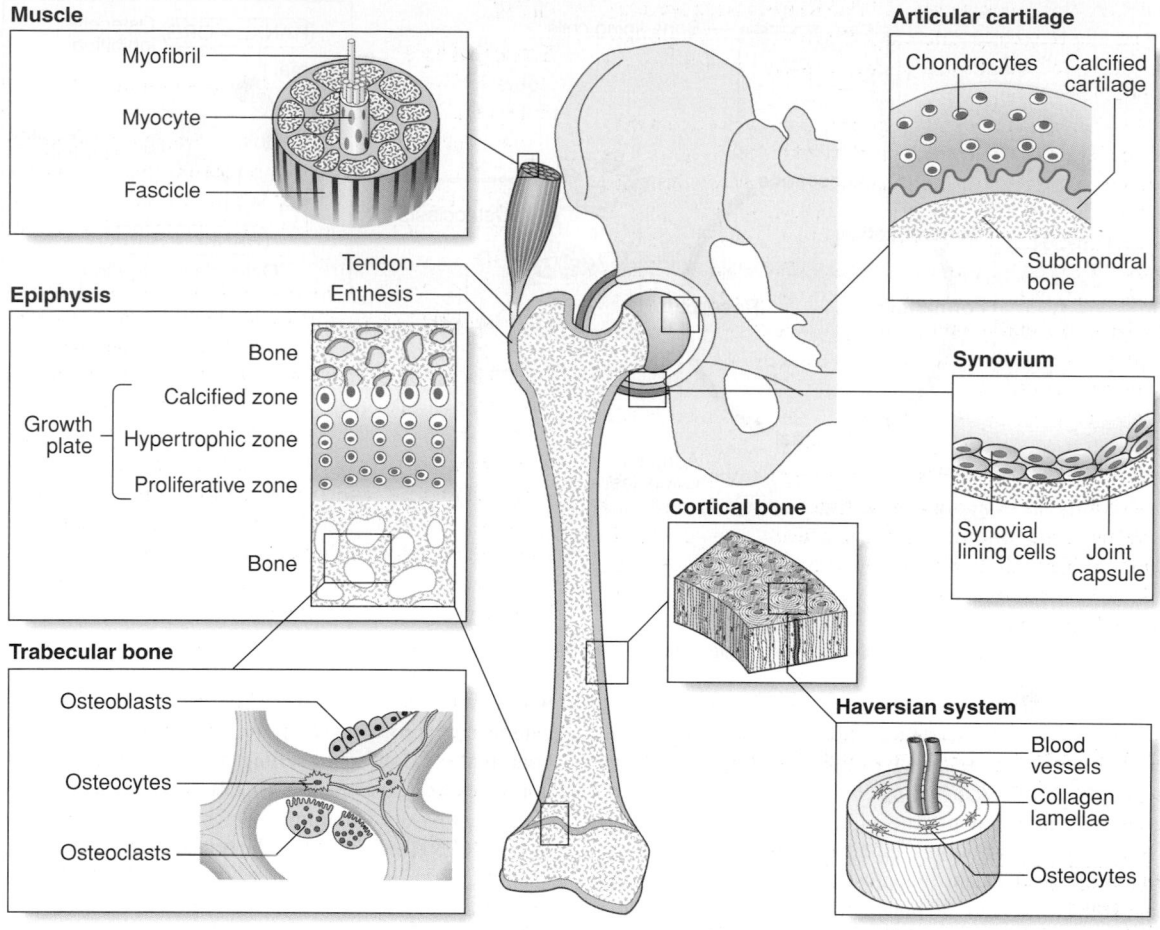

Fig. 20.1   Structure of major musculoskeletal tissues.

are cleaved off by proteolytic enzymes in the extracellular space. The triple helical domains that remain then self-assemble in a staggered configuration to form collagen fibrils. Subsequently, individual collagen molecules within these fibrils become linked to one another at each end by specialised pyridinium cross-links that help give bone its tensile strength. When bone is formed rapidly (for example, in Paget's disease or in bone metastases) the collagen fibrils are laid down in disorderly fashion, giving rise to 'woven bone' that is mechanically weaker than normal bone and susceptible to fracture.

Bone matrix also contains small amounts of other collagens, several non-collagenous proteins and glycoproteins. Some of these, such as osteocalcin, are specific to bone, whereas others, such as osteopontin, fibronectin and growth factors, also occur in other connective tissues. Non-collagenous bone proteins are probably involved in mediating the attachment of bone cells to the matrix and in regulating bone cell activity during bone remodelling.

The organic component of bone forms a framework upon which mineralisation occurs. Mineralisation confers upon bone the property of mechanical rigidity, which complements the tensile strength and elasticity derived from bone collagen. Bone mineral is composed mainly of calcium

and phosphate laid down in the form of hydroxyapatite —$[Ca_{10}(PO_4)_6(OH_2)]$—crystals.

Bone remodelling

The normal skeleton is constantly being renewed and repaired by the process of bone remodelling, carried out by the coordinated actions of osteoclasts and osteoblasts (see Fig. 20.2). It is estimated that approximately 10% of the adult skeleton is remodelling at any one time.

Bone remodelling commences with the attraction of osteoclast precursors in peripheral blood to the site that is to be resorbed. The mechanisms that trigger this process are unclear, but chemotactic factors released from areas of skeletal microdamage may play a role. Once in the bone microenvironment osteoclast precursors fuse to form multinucleated osteoclasts in response to activation of the RANK (*receptor activator of nuclear factor kappa B*) receptor on the osteoclast precursors by RANK ligand (RANKL) expressed on osteoblasts and bone marrow stromal cells. This interaction is inhibited by a soluble protein with homology to RANK called osteoprotegerin (OPG). OPG acts as a 'decoy' receptor that inhibits osteoclast activity by binding RANKL. Mature osteoclasts attach to the bone surface by a tight sealing zone that forms around the periphery of the

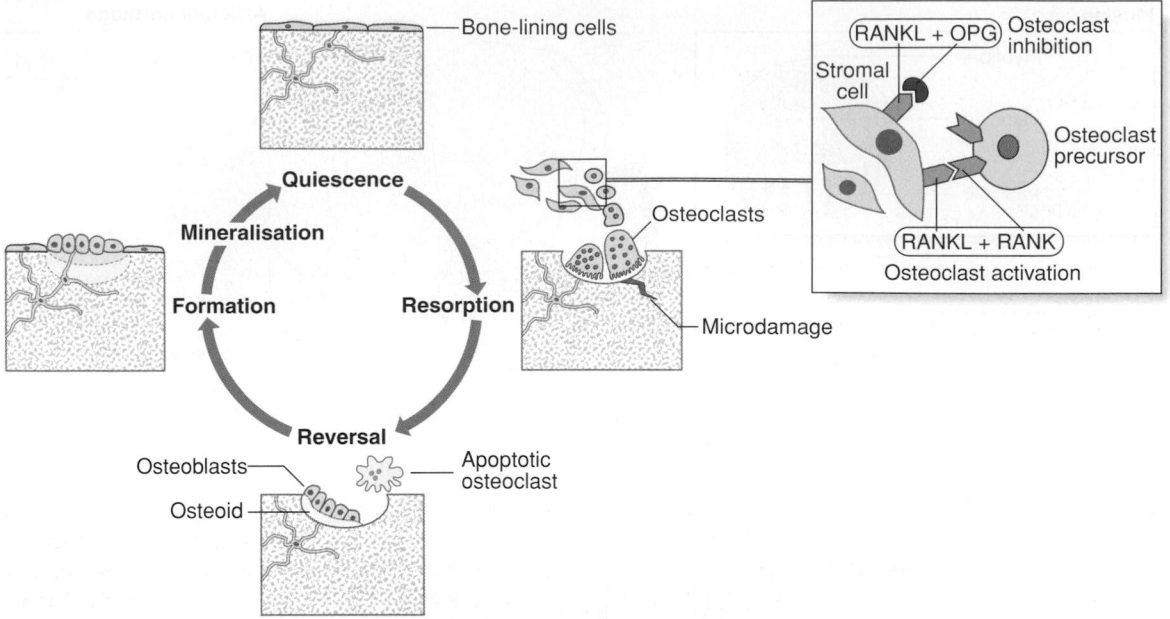

Fig. 20.2   The bone remodelling cycle. (RANK = receptor activator of nuclear factor kappa B; RANKL = RANK ligand; OPG = osteoprotegerin)

cell. Osteoclasts then resorb bone by secreting hydrochloric acid and proteolytic enzymes into the space beneath the sealing zone. The acid dissolves hydroxyapatite and allows proteolytic enzymes, including collagenase and cathepsin K, access to degrade components of bone matrix.

When bone resorption is complete, osteoclasts undergo programmed cell death (apoptosis) in the 'reversal phase' that heralds the start of bone formation. Bone formation begins with the attraction of osteoblast precursors to the site that has undergone resorption. These cells then differentiate into osteoblasts by activation of the transcription factor Cbfa1. Osteoblasts lay down uncalcified bone matrix (osteoid) on to the bone surface and this subsequently calcifies after a period of about 10 days to form mature bone. The enzyme alkaline phosphatase that is produced by osteoblasts plays an important role in promoting mineralisation by degrading pyrophosphate, a naturally occurring inhibitor of mineralisation present in extracellular fluid. During bone formation, some osteoblasts become trapped within bone matrix and differentiate into osteocytes that interconnect with one another and with cells on the bone surface by long cytoplasmic processes that run through canaliculi in the bone matrix. Bone remodelling is regulated by circulating hormones and other factors (see Box 20.2). Many of these factors act by upregulating or downregulating local expression of RANKL and OPG in the bone microenvironment.

JOINTS

Bones are linked by joints. There are three main subtypes (see Box 20.3).

Fibrocartilaginous joints

Fibrous and fibrocartilaginous joints are composed of a simple bridge of fibrous or fibrocartilaginous tissue joining two bones together. They occur in the skeleton where there is little requirement for movement of one bone in relation to another. The intervertebral disc is a special type of fibrocartilaginous joint in which an amorphous area termed the nucleus pulposus lies in the centre of the fibrocartilaginous bridge. This structure has a high water content and acts as a cushion to provide the intervertebral disc with improved shock-absorbing properties compared with ordinary fibrocartilaginous joints.

20.2 REGULATORS OF BONE REMODELLING

Factor	Effect on osteoclasts	Effect on osteoblasts	Effect on bone mass
PTH	↑	↑	Variable
1,25(OH)$_2$D$_3$	↑	↑	Variable
IL-1/TNF	↑	↓	Bone loss
Thyroid hormone	↑	↔	Bone loss
Glucocorticoids	↑	↓	Bone loss
Calcitonin	↓	↔	Bone gain
Oestrogen	↓	↑	Bone gain
Testosterone	↓	↑	Bone gain
Mechanical loading	↓	↑	Bone gain

↑ = stimulates; ↓ = inhibits; ↔ = neutral.

20.3 TYPES OF JOINT

Type	Range of movement	Examples
Fibrous	Minimal	Skull sutures
Fibrocartilage	Limited	Symphysis pubis Costochondral junctions Intervertebral discs
Synovial	Large	Most limb joints Temporo-mandibular Costovertebral

Synovial joints

Synovial joints are more complex structures containing several cell types. They are found in regions of the skeleton where a wide range of movement is required.

Articular cartilage

The ends of the bones in a synovial joint are covered with a layer of articular cartilage. This is an avascular tissue that consists of cartilage cells (chondrocytes) embedded in a thick matrix of proteoglycans, water, type II collagen and smaller amounts of other proteins. Although there is no cell division to speak of in normal cartilage, chondrocytes are metabolically active cells that are responsible for synthesis and turnover of cartilage matrix throughout life. The matrix consists of a meshwork of type II collagen fibrils that run through a hydrated 'gel' of proteoglycan molecules, the most important of which is aggrecan (see Fig. 20.3). Aggrecan consists of a core protein, to which several glycosaminoglycan (GAG) side-chains are attached. GAGs consist of long chains of disaccharide repeats, in which the disaccharide consists of one ordinary sugar linked to an amino sugar. The most important GAGs in aggrecan are chondroitin sulphate (glucuronic acid and sulphated N-acetylgalactosamine) and keratan sulphate (galactose and sulphated N-acetylglucosamine). Cartilage also contains hyaluronan, a long GAG consisting of multiple glucuronic acid and N-acetylgalactosamine disaccharide repeats. Hyaluronan binds several aggrecan molecules by interacting with a domain at the N-terminus of the core protein along with a small glycoprotein called link protein that acts to stabilise the complex. Large complexes of aggrecan and hyaluronan can form in cartilage with a total molecular weight in excess of 100 million. Aggrecan has a strong negative charge because of the sulphate and hydroxyl groups in the GAG residues; as a consequence, it binds large numbers of water molecules to assume a shape that occupies the maximum possible volume available. The expansive force of the charged and hydrated aggrecan, combined with the restrictive force of the collagen meshwork, gives articular cartilage excellent shock-absorbing properties.

With ageing, the amount of chondroitin sulphate in cartilage decreases, whereas that of keratan sulphate increases. Although the reasons for this are unknown, the end result is a reduction in water content and impairment of cartilage's shock-absorbing properties. Age-related changes in cartilage differ from those found in osteoarthritis, where there is abnormal chondrocyte division, loss of proteoglycan from matrix and an increase in water content.

Cartilage matrix is constantly being turned over, and in health a perfect balance is maintained between synthesis and degradation of matrix components. Matrix degradation is thought to be mediated by proteolytic enzymes such as aggrecanase and matrix metalloproteinases that degrade the core protein of aggrecan and other matrix proteins. Other enzymes termed glycosidases degrade the GAG side-chains. The importance of this system is emphasised by the occurrence of a group of diseases, termed mucopolysaccharidoses, in which genetic mutations in glycosidases occur, resulting in excessive accumulation of GAGs in various

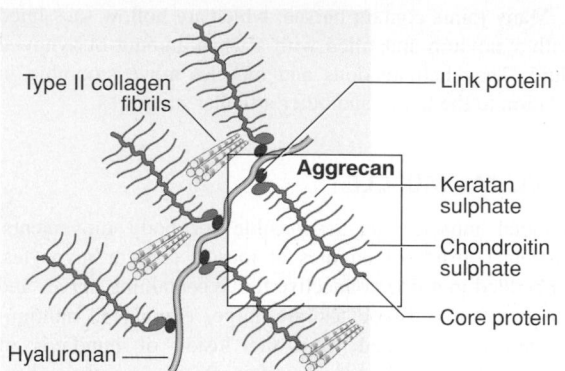

Fig. 20.3   Ultrastructure of articular cartilage.

tissues. The mechanisms by which proteoglycan turnover is regulated in normal cartilage are poorly understood, but pro-inflammatory cytokines such as interleukin-1 (IL-1) and tumour necrosis factor (TNF) which are involved in joint inflammation are known to upregulate production of aggrecanase, metalloproteinases and other enzymes that cause matrix degradation, thereby promoting cartilage damage. This is offset by upregulation of inhibitors of proteinases in cartilage, called tissue inhibitors of metalloproteinases (TIMP), which oppose the effects of degrading enzymes and protect against matrix degradation.

Synovial fluid

The surfaces of articular cartilage are separated by a space filled with synovial fluid, a viscous liquid that lubricates the joint. Synovial fluid is basically an ultrafiltrate of plasma into which synovial cells secrete hyaluronan and proteoglycans.

Intra-articular discs

Some joints contain fibrocartilaginous discs within the joint space (for example, the menisci of the knee) that act as shock absorbers. Like articular cartilage, these structures are avascular and remain viable by diffusion of oxygen and nutrients from the synovial fluid.

The joint capsule and synovial membrane

The bones of synovial joints are connected together by the joint capsule, a fibrous structure richly supplied with blood vessels, nerves and lymphatics that encompasses the joint cavity. Ligaments are discrete, regional thickenings of the joint capsule that act to stabilise joints. The inner surface of the joint capsule is lined by the synovial membrane, which comprises an outer layer of blood vessels and loose connective tissue, and an inner layer 1–4 cells thick, consisting of two main cell types, termed type A and type B synoviocytes. Type A synoviocytes are phagocytic cells derived from the monocyte/macrophage lineage and are responsible for removing particulate matter from the joint cavity; type B cells are fibroblast-like cells that are thought to be responsible for secretion of synovial fluid. Most inflammatory and degenerative joint diseases are associated with thickening of the synovial membrane and infiltration by lymphocytes, polymorphs and macrophages.

Many joints contain bursae, which are hollow sacs lined with synovium and filled with a small amount of synovial fluid. They help tendons and muscles move smoothly in relation to the bones and other articular structures.

SKELETAL MUSCLE

Skeletal muscles are responsible for body movements. Muscle consists of bundles of muscle cells or myocytes, embedded in a fine connective tissue containing nerves and blood vessels. Myocytes are large, elongated, multinucleated cells formed from the fusion of hundreds of mononuclear precursors termed myoblasts in early embryonic life. The nuclei in myocytes lie peripherally underneath the cell membrane, whereas the centre of the cell contains bundles of actin and myosin molecules that interdigitate with one another to form the myofibrils that are responsible for muscle contraction. The molecular mechanisms of skeletal muscle contraction are essentially as described for cardiac muscle (see p. 363). Muscle cells also contain many mitochondria which provide the large amounts of adenosine triphosphate (ATP) necessary for muscle contraction and are rich in the protein myoglobin which acts as a reservoir for oxygen during contraction.

Individual myofibrils are organised into bundles called fasciculi that are bound together by a thin layer of connective tissue termed the perimysium. The surface of the muscle is surrounded by a thicker layer of connective tissue, the epimysium, which merges with the perimysium to form the muscle tendon. Tendons are tough, fibrous structures that attach muscles to the point of insertion on bone surface that is called the enthesis.

INVESTIGATION OF MUSCULOSKELETAL DISEASE

Disease 'markers' are the pathological or physiological characteristics of an individual that assist in determining:

- the diagnosis
- the current activity or level of disease
- the expected prognosis.

Individual markers may give information on one, two or occasionally all three of these aspects. Clinical markers are derived from enquiry and examination of the patient, and for most MSK conditions detailed clinical assessment alone gives sufficient information for diagnosis and management. Additional investigational markers can be helpful in confirming the diagnosis and in assessing activity and progression of disease. However, only a few tests are specific. The requirement for, and selection and interpretation of, investigations are principally determined by clinical assessment. Investigations are an adjunct to, never a substitute for, competent clinical assessment, and there is never a place for a battery of 'screening tests'.

In common practice the investigations of most value are synovial fluid analysis and the plain radiograph. Confirmation of clinically assessed inflammatory disease activity and its response to treatment is mainly by the full blood count and either direct or indirect measures of the acute phase response.

SYNOVIAL FLUID ANALYSIS

This is the pivotal investigation to confirm the diagnosis of septic arthritis, crystal-associated arthritis and intra-articular bleeding. It is therefore the key investigation for acute monoarthritis, especially with overlying erythema.

Synovial fluid (SF) can readily be obtained from most peripheral joints and for diagnostic purposes only a small volume is required. Normal SF is present in small volume, contains very few cells, is clear and colourless to pale yellow, and has high viscosity due to macromolecular hyaluronate. With increasing joint inflammation the volume increases, the total cell count and proportion of neutrophils rise (causing turbidity), and the viscosity lowers (due to protease degradation of hyaluronate). However, because of considerable variation and overlap between arthropathies these features have little diagnostic value. Frank pus or 'pyarthrosis' results from very high neutrophil counts and is not specific for sepsis. High concentrations of crystals, mainly urate or cholesterol, can make SF appear white.

Non-uniform blood staining of SF is common, reflecting inconsequential needle trauma to the synovium. Uniform blood staining—haemarthrosis—commonly accompanies florid synovitis but may also result from a bleeding diathesis, trauma or pigmented villonodular synovitis. A lipid layer floating above blood-stained fluid is diagnostic of intra-articular fracture.

If sepsis is suspected, SF should be sent for urgent Gram stain and culture in a sterile universal container. If gonococcal sepsis or uncommon organisms are suspected, especially in immunocompromised patients, the microbiologist should

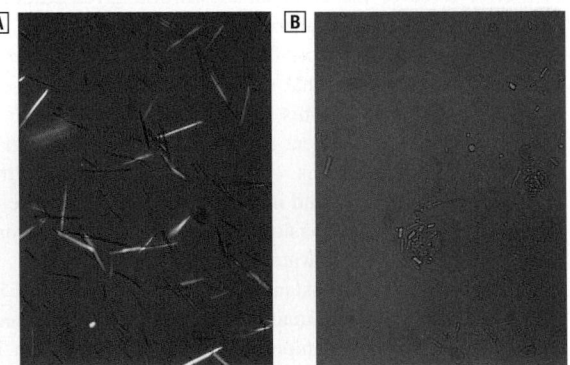

Fig. 20.4 Compensated polarised light microscopy of synovial fluids (× 400). [A] Monosodium urate crystals showing bright birefringence (negative sign) and needle-shaped morphology. [B] Calcium pyrophosphate crystals showing weak birefringence (positive sign), scant numbers and a predominantly rhomboid morphology. These are clearly more difficult to detect than urate crystals.

be consulted to ensure that optimal cultures are established and that molecular techniques of antigen detection are used if appropriate.

Identification of common SF crystals is by compensated polarised light microscopy of fresh unrefrigerated SF to avoid problems of crystal dissolution and post-aspiration crystallisation. Urate crystals are long and needle-shaped and show a strong light intensity with a negative sign of birefringence (see Fig. 20.4A). Calcium pyrophosphate crystals are smaller, rhomboid in shape, usually less numerous than urate and have weak intensity and positive birefringence (see Fig. 20.4B).

PLAIN RADIOGRAPHY

Although a static record of predominantly past events, a radiograph can show changes that reflect underlying pathological processes such as cartilage and bone erosion or calcification. The abnormalities that may be seen on a plain film include:

- soft tissue swelling—seen as altered skin contours and displaced fat planes and intracapsular fat pads (fat appears dark on radiograph)
- decreased or increased bone density—localised or generalised
- joint erosion (non-proliferative or proliferative marginal erosion, central erosion)
- joint-space narrowing (focal—osteoarthritis; generalised—inflammatory arthritis)
- new bone formation (osteophyte, enthesophyte, syndesmophyte) and periosteal reaction
- calcification (cartilage—chondrocalcinosis; synovium, capsule, ligament, tendon, muscle, fat, vascular, skin) and intra-articular osteochondral bodies
- bone cysts and radiolucent lesions
- deformity
- fracture.

Although most of these abnormalities have low individual specificity, various combinations of these features, together with their selective targeting of certain joints (see Fig. 20.5), result in characteristic patterns of abnormality and distribution that have high diagnostic specificity.

The distribution of joint involvement is principally derived from clinical assessment, and joints to be X-rayed are usually selected on this basis. An exception is seronegative spondarthritis where sacroiliac involvement is often asymptomatic and difficult to detect clinically. For suspected seronegative spondarthritis an antero-posterior (AP) view of the pelvis and a lateral thoracolumbar spine view (i.e. two films) are usually sufficient to show sacroiliitis or syndesmophytes if they are present. Radiographs are selected to answer specific questions. For example, to determine whether a patient with inflammatory polyarthritis has erosions typical of rheumatoid arthritis, postero-anterior (PA) views of hands and feet (i.e. two films), but not radiographs of all symptomatic joints, are appropriate, since rheumatoid erosions appear first in wrists and small joints of hands and feet and may appear first in metatarsophalangeal joints even if they are asymptomatic. However, if the degree of structural damage in one large joint is a cause for concern, a radiograph of that joint will be required. Thus selection of radiographs often differs for diagnostic or disease assessment purposes.

Erosions

A hallmark of major inflammatory arthropathies is cartilage and bone erosion. Intracapsular bone erosion first occurs at the 'bare areas' of the joint margin ('marginal erosion') where bone is exposed directly to inflammatory synovium without the protection of overlying cartilage. Loss of the sharp cortical line is the first radiographic sign that precedes more definite scalloping of the bony contour (see Fig. 20.6). Cartilage erosion also starts at the margin and slowly works centrally, resulting in relatively late loss of 'joint space'. Both rheumatoid and seronegative spondarthritis (especially psoriatic arthritis) can cause marginal erosions. In rheumatoid, however, the florid synovitis is not accompanied by any bone or periosteal reaction, resulting in atrophic 'non-proliferative' erosions (see Fig. 20.6B), often with juxta-articular osteopenia and soft tissue swelling. By contrast, in seronegative spondarthritis there is often concomitant new bone formation and periosteal reaction with retained bone density, resulting in 'proliferative' erosions (see Fig. 20.6C). Accompanying ossifying enthesopathy (enthesophytes) and the targeting of different joints further assist differentiation.

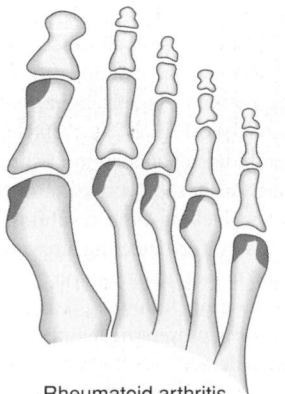
Rheumatoid arthritis

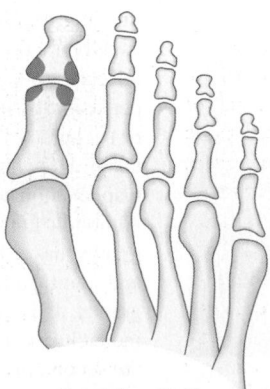
Psoriatic arthritis

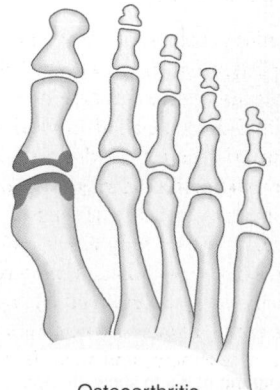
Osteoarthritis

Fig. 20.5 **The different target sites of involvement in the forefoot for arthritis.**

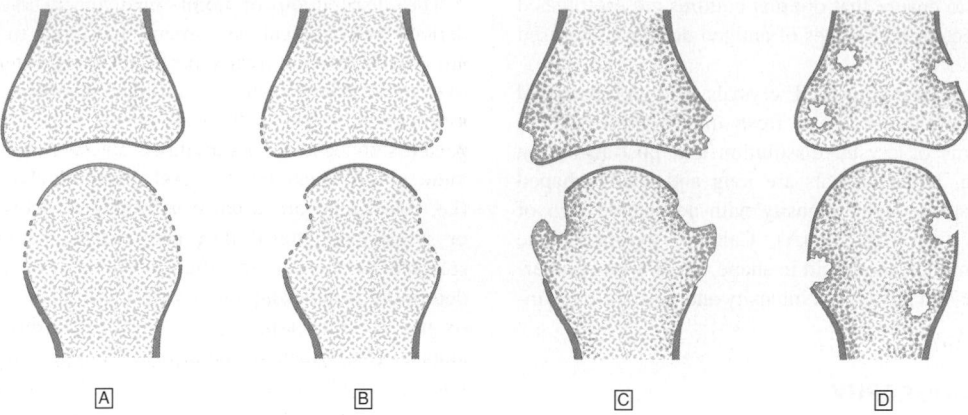

Fig. 20.6   Metacarpophalangeal joint. ⒶEarly dot-dash erosion of rheumatoid arthritis. ⒷLater definite non-proliferative erosion of rheumatoid arthritis. ⒸThe proliferative erosion of psoriatic arthritis. ⒹThe intra- and extracapsular 'pressure erosions' of gout.

In early septic arthritis the radiograph is often normal, apart from osteopenia and soft tissue swelling, for 1–2 weeks. However, erosion proceeds rapidly and results in generalised loss of joint space with loss of cortical integrity centrally—central erosion—as well as marginally. In chronic gout bony defects develop slowly as massive crystal concretions ('tophi') cause pressure necrosis to surrounding bone. Such 'pressure erosions' (see Fig. 20.6D) occur at extracapsular as well as intracapsular sites and are not accompanied by osteopenia.

Osteoarthritis

The changes of osteoarthritis are prevalent and highly characteristic, and contrast with those of inflammatory

arthritis. The two cardinal features are narrowing and osteophyte. In contrast to inflammatory arthritis, joint space narrowing is focal not widespread (see Fig. 20.7). Bony osteophytes are most noticeable at the joint margins. Subchondral sclerosis (focal increased density of bone), 'cysts' and osteochondral 'loose' bodies within the synovium are possible additional features, and there is an increased association with chondrocalcinosis. In contrast to inflammatory arthritis, bone density is normal or increased and marginal erosions are not a feature.

Calcification

Calcification of fibrocartilage and hyaline cartilage—chondrocalcinosis—is most commonly due to calcium pyrophosphate crystals or apatite. Calcification at other sites is mainly apatite. Spotty, multiple calcification of soft tissues—calcinosis—mainly targets peripheral and intermediate sites such as finger pulps, wrists and forearms and is a feature of connective tissue disease.

OTHER IMAGING

Scintigraphy

This readily available technique involves gamma-camera imaging following an intravenous injection of radioisotope, usually ^{99m}Tc-bisphosphonate. Early post-injection images reflect vascularity and can show, for example, the increased perfusion of inflamed synovium, Pagetic bone, or primary or secondary bone tumour (see Fig. 20.8). Delayed images taken a few hours later indicate bone remodelling as the bisphosphonate localises to sites of active bone turnover. Although non-specific and lacking high resolution, scintigraphy has a high sensitivity for detecting important bone and joint pathology that is not apparent on plain radiographs. It is particularly useful, following a normal or an inconclusive radiograph of a presenting painful region, as the second investigation to detect:

- bone metastases—at symptomatic and clinically occult sites

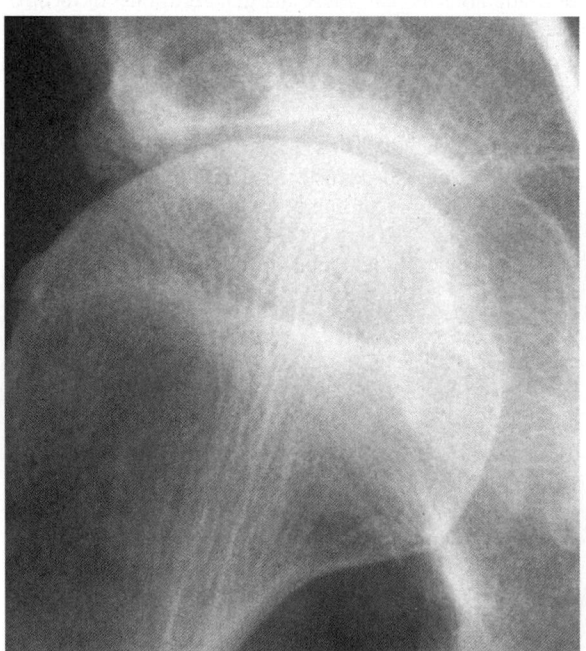

Fig. 20.7   Radiograph of hip to show changes of osteoarthritis. Note the superior joint space narrowing, subchondral sclerosis, marginal osteophyte and cysts.

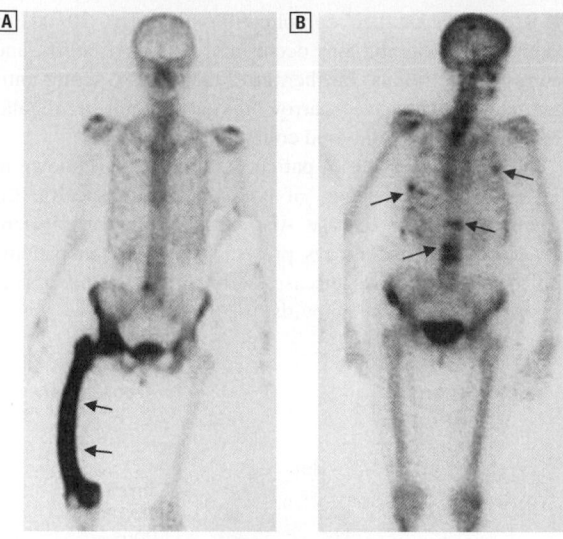

Fig. 20.8   Comparison of bone scan appearances in Paget's disease and metastatic bone disease. [A] Intense homogeneous uptake throughout the affected femur (arrows) in Paget's disease. [B] Patchy focal uptake affecting the spine, ribs (arrows) and skull in metastatic breast cancer.

- bone or joint sepsis—at the presenting site and clinically occult sites
- early osteonecrosis—at the presenting site and clinically occult sites
- stress fracture
- reflex sympathetic dystrophy (algodystrophy—see p. 1046)
- hypertrophic osteoarthropathy (see p. 1045).

It is also useful in assessing the extent and activity of Paget's disease of bone.

Computerised tomography (CT)

Computerised reconstruction of multiple radiographic scan sections gives detailed information on anatomy, especially of bone, allowing three-dimensional visualisation of anatomically complex structures such as the spinal canal and facet joints which may be inadequately assessed by plain radiographs. Drawbacks include limited soft tissue resolution and a high radiation dose, and for many situations magnetic resonance imaging is now preferred.

Magnetic resonance imaging (MRI)

MRI provides detailed and sensitive information on both structure and physiology of cartilage, bone and other locomotor tissues. Further advantages are the capacity for multiplanar imaging and safety without radiation exposure. In general, T1-weighted short sequences are useful for defining anatomy and T2-weighted long sequences for assessing pathology. Other sequences are selected for special purposes; for example, the short tau inversion recovery (STIR) sequence is used to image marrow since it suppresses fat and makes the marrow appear dark. MRI, with or without enhancement with gadolinium, is particularly useful to detect and assess:

- early osteonecrosis—at symptomatic and clinically occult sites
- intervertebral disc disease, root entrapment and spinal cord compression
- osteoarticular and soft tissue sepsis
- osteoarticular and soft tissue malignancy
- internal derangement of joints such as the knee
- soft tissue and periarticular pathology (e.g. early synovitis, rotator cuff tears, bursitis, tenosynovitis).

Ultrasonography

This safe, accessible technique can confirm soft tissue changes such as a hip joint effusion, popliteal cyst or thickened Achilles tendon. Limited resolution, however, makes it inferior to CT or MRI for defining anatomy.

Arthrography

Injection of positive (iodinated) or negative (air) contrast, or a combination of both, can help delineate the outline of a joint or bursa. The main use of plain film arthrography is at the knee to demonstrate a ruptured popliteal ('Baker's') cyst as the cause of calf pain and swelling. It may be combined with CT or MRI to facilitate anatomical assessment.

BLOOD TESTS FOR INFLAMMATION AND SYSTEMIC DISEASE

The acute phase response

The full blood count, erythrocyte sedimentation rate (ESR) and C-reactive protein (CRP) may show non-specific changes that indicate inflammation. At any site of injury or inflammation macrophages and monocytes release soluble cytokines including IL-1, IL-6 and TNF-α. Some of these cytokines enter the systemic circulation and exert effects on:

- the hypothalamus—to cause fever
- the bone marrow—to increase production and release of neutrophils and platelets but reduce erythrocyte production
- the liver—to increase production and release of acute phase proteins such as fibrinogen, clotting factors, immunoglobulin, complement and CRP, but to decrease production of negative acute phase reactants such as albumin and transferrin.

These combined systemic effects—the acute phase response (APR)—accompany chronic as well as acute inflammation. Much of the APR is beneficial for body defence and adaptation to injury. For example, thrombocytosis and increased levels of clotting factors facilitate haemostasis, while neutrophilia and increased levels of complement, immunoglobulin and CRP (an opsonin) combat infection.

The acute phase response in infection

Although the acute phase response is well recognised in inflammatory conditions such as musculoskeletal disease, it most probably evolved primarily to combat the effects of physical injury and infection.

Certain distinctive biochemical structures, present in many microorganisms (e.g. bacterial lipopolysaccharide) can activate the production of effector acute mechanisms. Three groups of substances are produced by this mechanism:

- *Defensins.* Alpha defensins produced by neutrophils and beta defensins produced by epithelial cells have antimicrobial properties and attract T cells.
- *Complement.* These substances can lead to direct antibody-linked microbial disruption and also enhance opsonisation of bacteria. C_5 is also a very potent neutrophil chemotaxin.
- *Interferons.* α, β and γ are produced by virus-infected cells and have immunomodulatory and antiproliferative functions.

C-reactive protein

Of the acute phase proteins CRP shows the greatest change from very low to very high levels, and closely mirrors the degree of inflammation, rising rapidly at the onset and falling as inflammation subsides. It is therefore the single most useful direct measure of the APR.

Erythrocyte sedimentation rate

The ESR can act as an indirect measure of the APR. Normally, erythrocytes do not clump together because their repellent electrostatic negative surface charge, or zeta potential, is greater than the attractant electrical charge (dielectric constant) of the plasma constituents. However, in the APR the altered plasma protein concentrations, chiefly fibrinogen, increase the dielectric constant sufficiently to overwhelm the zeta potential and allow erythrocytes to clump like stacks of tyres (rouleaux). Rouleaux have a higher mass/surface area ratio, so sediment faster than single red cells. This property is measured in the ESR. In the Westergren test system a 200 mm capillary tube is filled with the patient's blood and after 1 hour the sedimentation of red cells from the top is measured. In health the discrete red cells sediment slowly and the clearance is small (< 5–10 mm). However, with rouleaux formation the clearance is greater and the ESR is elevated. Therefore in a patient with an APR the ESR and CRP are both elevated, the ESR lagging behind the CRP in terms of speed of change.

The ESR, however, may be raised for reasons other than the APR. For example, the elevated levels of immunoglobulin that occur in myeloproliferative disease (e.g. multiple myeloma) and autoimmune disease (e.g. Sjögren's syndrome) can increase the dielectric constant to cause rouleaux formation. In this situation the patient may have a high ESR but normal or relatively low CRP. Such discordance between ESR and CRP should lead to consideration of such conditions and to direct measurement of immunoglobulins. The inherent number of red cells available may also modify the ESR. For example, in patients with polycythaemia the ESR is often relatively low despite a florid APR. The plasma viscosity is independent of such variation and is an alternative indirect measure of changes in serum protein concentrations.

Full blood count

The full blood count may show other changes that are non-specific but which may be characteristic of certain MSK diseases or their complications (see Fig. 20.9). For example, neutrophilia may occur in systemic vasculitis, and neutropenia in lupus. Furthermore, many slow-acting anti-rheumatic drugs have marrow toxicity requiring regular monitoring of the full blood count.

The typical profile of a patient with an APR is shown in Box 20.4. Such changes, of course, are not specific for inflammatory MSK disease. Also, although reasonably sensitive, they are not always present, especially in patients with connective tissue disease, seronegative spondarthritis or isolated small joint synovitis.

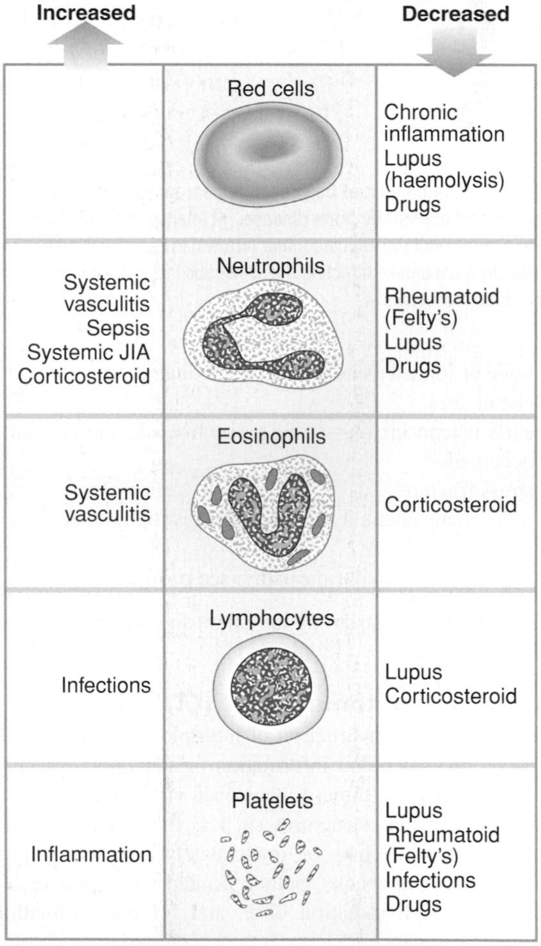

Increased		Decreased
	Red cells	Chronic inflammation Lupus (haemolysis) Drugs
Systemic vasculitis Sepsis Systemic JIA Corticosteroid	Neutrophils	Rheumatoid (Felty's) Lupus Drugs
Systemic vasculitis	Eosinophils	Corticosteroid
Infections	Lymphocytes	Lupus Corticosteroid
Inflammation	Platelets	Lupus Rheumatoid (Felty's) Infections Drugs

Fig. 20.9 Some of the non-specific changes that may occur in individual elements of the full blood count in patients with systemic rheumatic disease. (JIA = juvenile idiopathic arthritis)

20.4 TYPICAL PROFILE OF A FLORID ACUTE PHASE RESPONSE

- Normochromic, normocytic anaemia
- Neutrophilia
- Increased platelet count
- High ESR
- High CRP
- Increased plasma viscosity
- Low albumin

Immunological tests

An increasing number of autoantibodies can be detected. Production of some of these is a common, age-related phenomenon that may be exaggerated by chronic inflammation. Their mere presence, therefore, often has low diagnostic specificity and little clinical relevance. If present in high concentrations, however, their disease specificity often increases. It is therefore important to know how much antibody is present (the titre or concentration in units) rather than just whether it is detectable. Only a few antibodies— for example, anti-dsDNA—have high diagnostic specificity. For some autoantibodies such as c-ANCA, their titre, if initially high, can be used to monitor the activity of the associated disease. Again, the correct choice and interpretation of these tests depend on detailed knowledge of the patient. Different detection and assay systems exist for many of these autoantibodies, and close liaison with the local immunology service is required.

Rheumatoid factor

A rheumatoid factor is an antibody directed against a specific region of the Fc fragment of human IgG. It may be of any immunoglobulin class, though IgM anti-IgG is the rheumatoid factor most commonly measured in the first instance. One traditional method of detecting IgM rheumatoid factor is to coat latex beads with human IgG. Adding the patient's serum to the test system allows the pentameric IgM antibody to bind with the IgG and cause the latex particles to flocculate, producing a positive 'latex fixation test'. The amount by which the serum must be diluted before this flocculation is lost is then determined; the higher this 'titre', the higher the antibody concentration.

Although rheumatoid factor was so named because it was first identified in patients with rheumatoid arthritis, it also occurs in a wide variety of other conditions and in some normal adults (see Box 20.5). It therefore has low diagnostic specificity, particularly in the elderly, and is not a 'test for rheumatoid arthritis'. In terms of sensitivity, it is present in the majority of patients with erosive rheumatoid disease but may only appear after months or years of disease, once the diagnosis is beyond dispute. It is therefore neither sufficient nor necessary for the diagnosis. Its principal use is as a prognostic marker; a high titre at the onset of rheumatoid arthritis associates with a poorer prognosis. IgG rheumatoid factor has greater specificity for major rheumatic disease but the above caveats still remain.

Antinuclear antibody

An antinuclear antibody (ANA) is any autoantibody directed against one or more components of the nucleus. Immunofluorescence microscopy after serum has been applied to a nucleated tissue substrate (e.g. rodent organs) or human cell lines (e.g. Hep 2) is the standard method of detection, and four main patterns of staining are reported. As with rheumatoid factor, the higher the titre of ANA, the greater its significance, although a high titre does not necessarily imply more severe disease. The specificity and sensitivity also vary according to the antigen preparation used in the test system and whether the ANA measured is IgG or IgM. However, the tests are not universally standardised and liaison with the local laboratory is important.

The many causes of a positive ANA are outlined in Box 20.6. The most common reason to test for ANA is if lupus is suspected. For lupus, ANA has high sensitivity (virtually 100%), but because the specificity is low (10–40%) a positive result does not make the diagnosis; by contrast, a negative ANA virtually excludes the diagnosis.

If a screening ANA test is positive most laboratories attempt to establish the specific antigenic determinants, though in many cases the precise specificities remain unknown. Some determinants are soluble and can be extracted from the nucleus—'extractable nuclear antigens'. Compared to the ANA, antibodies against specific nuclear antigens may have higher specificity for certain diagnoses or for certain patterns of system involvement within the same disease. For example, ANA directed against double-stranded DNA (anti-dsDNA) is highly specific for lupus. Unfortunately, it is present in a minority of patients and those in whom it is positive often have classic severe lupus and a clear clinical diagnosis.

Antibodies to Sm are almost exclusive to lupus and imply a poorer prognosis. Anti-topoisomerase 1 and anti-centromere antibodies are found exclusively in diffuse and limited scleroderma respectively. Antibodies to Ro occur predominantly in Sjögren's syndrome and systemic lupus erythematosus (SLE) and associate with a high frequency of photosensitive rashes and risk of neonatal heart block. Antibodies to ribonucleoprotein (RNP) are found in lupus but also in other conditions such as scleroderma, myositis,

20.5 ASSOCIATIONS WITH A POSITIVE RHEUMATOID FACTOR
• Rheumatoid arthritis (c.75%)
• Lupus, scleroderma, Sjögren's syndrome, dermatomyositis
• Chronic infection
Bacterial endocarditis
Viruses (rubella, cytomegalovirus, infectious mononucleosis)
Parasites
• Neoplasms—after irradiation or chemotherapy
• Hyperglobulinaemic states
Hypergammaglobulinaemic purpura
Cryoglobulinaemia
Chronic liver disease
N.B. Normal subjects can be seropositive.

20.6 ASSOCIATIONS WITH A POSITIVE ANTINUCLEAR ANTIBODY	
Musculoskeletal disease	
• Systemic lupus erythematosus (100%)	• Polymyositis
• Rheumatoid arthritis	• Polyarteritis nodosa
• Sjögren's syndrome	• Juvenile idiopathic arthritis
Other disorders	
• Chronic active hepatitis	• Myasthenia gravis
• Autoimmune thyroid disease	• Extensive burns
N.B. Normal subjects may be ANA-positive.	

mixed connective tissue disease and rheumatoid arthritis. Although these antibodies may associate with disease subsets, there is little evidence that they are involved in pathogenesis.

The antiphospholipid syndrome

The antiphospholipid syndrome, defined by the occurrence of arterial and venous thromboses, recurrent fetal losses and thrombocytopenia in the presence of antiphospholipid antibodies, occurs in lupus and other autoimmune diseases and also in subjects with no other underlying disease. Antiphospholipid antibodies can be detected in assays for anticardiolipin antibodies (predominantly directed against β2-glycoprotein 1) and in phospholipid-dependent coagulation studies to detect lupus anticoagulants (prolonged activated partial thromboplastin time (APTT) which fails to correct with the addition of normal serum). Antiphospholipid antibodies also occur in a wide variety of rheumatic, infectious (bacterial, viral, protozoal) and malignant conditions, although in these situations they are not usually associated with thromboses.

INVESTIGATION OF BONE DISEASE

X-ray examination

The most common indication for radiographs in patients with bone disease is to confirm or exclude fractures. Other indications are the investigation of MSK pain or bone deformity, where evidence of Paget's disease, primary bone tumours or metastatic bone disease may be found. Plain radiographs are of limited value in the diagnosis of osteoporosis since this has to be quite advanced before it can be detected. Although osteopenia on X-ray suggests osteoporosis, a normal result does not exclude it. Other bone diseases that may be diagnosed on plain radiographs include hyperparathyroidism (subperiosteal erosions on hand radiographs or pepperpot appearance on skull radiograph), osteopetrosis (generalised increase in radiodensity) and algodystrophy (patchy localised osteoporosis).

Bone mineral density (BMD) measurements

BMD measurement is central to the investigation of osteoporosis and is indicated in patients with risk factors for this disease (see Box 20.7). Several techniques can measure BMD, but dual energy X-ray absorptiometry (DXA) is the current method of choice because of its sensitivity and low-radiation dose. Investigation of osteoporosis is best done by measuring BMD at the spine or hip. At present it is uncertain how BMD measured at peripheral sites such as the wrist and calcaneus should be interpreted with respect to determining treatment.

DXA scanners work on the principle that bone tissue placed between an X-ray source and a detector impedes the passage of radiation in proportion to the amount of mineral present. By relating attenuation of the X-ray beam to an internal standard, the BMD can be accurately measured and is expressed in grams of hydroxyapatite per cm² of the area scanned. Virtually all DXA machines also give results in relation to reference values to give 'Z-score' and 'T-score'

readings (see Fig. 20.10). The Z-score measures by how many standard deviations the BMD deviates from the population average for the patient's age, whereas the T-score measures by how many standard deviations the patient's BMD differs from the population average for young healthy individuals who have attained peak bone mass. By convention, osteoporosis is diagnosed when the BMD T-score value falls below –2.5 (shaded red in Fig. 20.10), whereas osteopenia describes individuals whose T-scores are between –1.0 and –2.5 (shaded pink in Fig. 20.10). Note that by this definition the incidence of both osteoporosis and osteopenia increases progressively with age such that many elderly individuals with 'normal' BMD Z-score values have osteoporosis on the basis of a reduced T-score.

20.7 INDICATIONS FOR BONE DENSITOMETRY

- Previous low trauma fracture (fall from standing height or less)
- Clinical features of osteoporosis (height loss, kyphosis)
- Radiographic evidence of osteoporosis
- Corticosteroids (> 7.5 mg prednisolone daily for > 3 months)
- Family history of osteoporotic fracture
- Low body weight (body mass index < 19)
- Early menopause (< 45 years)
- Diseases associated with osteoporosis (especially if poorly controlled)
  - Rheumatoid arthritis
  - Malabsorption
  - Inflammatory bowel disease
  - Prolonged immobility
  - Hypogonadism in men
- Assessing response of osteoporosis to treatment

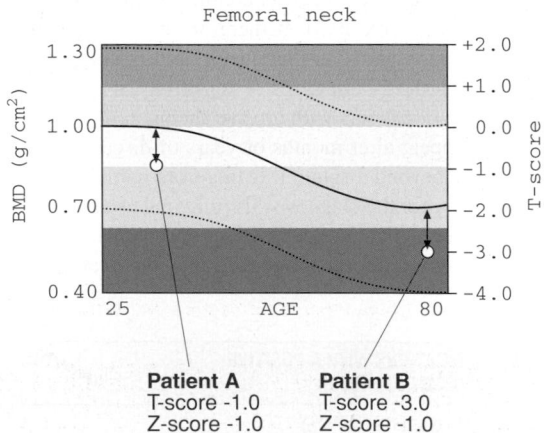

Fig. 20.10 Output from DXA scan of the femoral neck comparing BMD values (left axis), T-score values (right axis) and Z-score values (arrows) in patients of different ages. The solid line represents the population average plotted against age, whereas the interrupted lines are ± 2 standard deviations of the average. Patient A, aged 30, has a T-score value of –1.0 and a Z-score value of –1.0, both of which are within the normal range. Patient B, aged 80, also has a Z-score of –1.0 but has a T-score of –3.0, reflecting bone loss with age. Patient B therefore has osteoporosis, even though the BMD value is in the normal range for her age.

Measurement of BMD is valuable not only for diagnosis but also for management of osteoporosis, since the anti-fracture efficacy of many treatments is restricted to individuals who have low spine or hip BMD values (see EBM panel). BMD measurements are also used to assess treatment response. Since changes in BMD with most osteoporosis treatments are small and occur slowly, repeat measurements should not be performed until 12–24 months after starting therapy. Measurement of spine BMD is better than hip BMD for assessing treatment response because precision is better and changes in BMD at the spine occur more quickly because of the higher content of trabecular bone.

<table>
<tr><td>ASSESSMENT OF OSTEOPOROSIS—role of BMD measurements in deciding upon the need for treatment</td><td>EBM</td></tr>
</table>

'RCTs of bisphosphonate therapy in osteoporosis have shown that the beneficial effects in preventing fractures are restricted to patients with low bone mineral density (BMD).'

- Cummings SR, Black DM, Thompson DE, et al. Effect of alendronate on risk of fracture in women with low bone density but without vertebral fractures: results from the Fracture Intervention Trial. JAMA 1998; 280:2077–2082.
- McClung MR, Guesens P, Miller PD, et al. Effect of risedronate on the risk of hip fracture in elderly women. N Engl J Med 2001; 344:333–340.

Quantitative ultrasound examination

Quantitative ultrasound examination is usually performed at the heel and provides an alternative to DXA for assessment of osteoporotic fracture risk. Although almost as good as DXA at predicting fracture risk in population-based studies, it cannot be used to diagnose osteoporosis (which is defined by a low BMD) and has not yet been accepted as a method of selecting patients for anti-osteoporotic treatments.

Radionuclide bone scanning

Radionuclide bone scanning is of value in the differential diagnosis of bone pain, particularly when metastatic bone disease or Paget's disease is the suspected cause (see Fig. 20.8). Bone scans are generally more sensitive than radiographs in detecting metastatic disease, but negative results can occur in multiple myeloma where disease suppression of osteoblastic activity reduces uptake of tracer in lytic lesions.

Bone biopsy

Bone biopsy is helpful in the diagnosis of metabolic bone diseases when other tests have proved inconclusive. The biopsy is taken using a large diameter (8 mm) trephine needle from the iliac crest under local anaesthetic. Samples are then processed for histology, without decalcification, and analysed for the presence of mineralisation defects (e.g. osteomalacia), marrow infiltrates (e.g. mastocytosis, secondary tumours) and abnormalities of bone turnover or structure (e.g. renal osteodystrophy, Paget's disease).

Biochemical tests

Some metabolic bone diseases, such as Paget's disease, renal bone disease and osteomalacia, give a characteristic pattern of abnormalities on routine biochemical tests (see Box 20.8). Other biochemical markers are also available with which to assess bone turnover. Markers of bone resorption include serum or urinary levels of pyridinium cross-links, and cross-linked collagen telopeptides. These derive from degradation of bone collagen during bone remodelling. Markers of bone formation include serum osteocalcin and serum bone-specific alkaline phosphatase, both released from osteoblasts, and serum collagen propeptide fragments that are cleaved from newly synthesised collagen molecules laid down during matrix deposition. These assays can be used to assess levels of bone turnover, but they are not useful diagnostically. Their use is currently restricted to research.

INVESTIGATION OF SUSPECTED MUSCLE DISEASE

There are three main investigations for diagnosis and monitoring of muscle disease: serum creatine kinase (CK), electromyography (EMG) and muscle histology. None is 100% sensitive so that each may be normal despite abnormality detected by one or both of the others. CK is the most indirect marker but is readily available and often measured first. Elevation of CK, however, may result from a variety of causes (see Box 20.9) and some ethnic groups such as Afro-Caribbeans have high normal values. An EMG or muscle biopsy is often undertaken next, the choice depending on local availability and expertise. How much information is gained from the first two tests often determines whether the third is also undertaken. The test that is most abnormal is then often used for subsequent monitoring of disease activity.

The EMG measures the action potentials produced at rest and during voluntary contraction. Normal muscle is

20.8 BIOCHEMICAL ABNORMALITIES IN VARIOUS BONE DISEASES					
	Serum calcium	Serum phosphate	Serum alkaline phosphatase (AP)	Serum PTH	Serum 25(OH)D
Osteoporosis	N	N	N	N	N
Paget's disease	N	N	↑↑	N or ↑	N
Osteomalacia	N or ↓	N or ↓	↑	↑	↓
Renal osteodystrophy	↓	↑↑	↑	↑↑	N
Primary hyperparathyroidism	↑	N or ↓	N or ↑	↑	N
(PTH = parathyroid hormone; 25(OH)D = 25-hydroxyvitamin D; N = normal)					

electrically silent at rest. On slight contraction motor-unit potentials of 500–1000 uV in amplitude and 4–8 ms in duration are recorded. On maximal contraction, as many motor units as possible are recruited and an interference pattern develops. With inflammatory polymyositis the EMG may show a diagnostic triad of:

- spontaneous fibrillation
- short-duration action potentials in a polyphasic disorganised outline
- repetitive bouts of high-voltage oscillations produced by needle contact with diseased muscle.

Needle muscle biopsy of the quadriceps or deltoid is a simple procedure requiring local anaesthetic, a small skin incision (no stitches afterwards), a UCH (University College Hospital) or other muscle biopsy needle, and no subsequent limitation of activity. It can be repeated for serial monitoring of treatment response. Immunohistochemical staining, together with plain histology, gives considerable information on primary and secondary muscle and neuromuscular disease. Although open biopsy yields more muscle, only a small amount of tissue is required and serial open biopsy is clearly problematic.

MAJOR MANIFESTATIONS OF MUSCULOSKELETAL DISEASE

JOINT PAIN

ACUTE MONOARTHRITIS

Acute monoarthritis should always lead to consideration of sepsis and crystals, but other causes are listed in Box 20.10. Monoarthritis can be the presentation of what subsequently evolves into oligo- or polyarthritis, and atypical presentation of common disease is more prevalent than rare disease.

Consideration of the following features often reduces the differential diagnosis and suggests the most likely diagnosis:

- *Age and gender of the patient.* Juvenile idiopathic arthritis (JIA) is restricted to children, haemophilia to boys; reactive arthritis is the most common cause in young men; gout presents in middle-aged men; pseudogout mainly targets older women.
- *Joint involved.* Almost every joint disease can affect the knee, but classic target sites typical of certain conditions include the first metatarsophalangeal joint (gout); the big toe interphalangeal joint (reactive/psoriatic arthritis); the elbow and ankle (haemarthrosis, seronegative spondarthritis); the wrist and shoulder (pseudogout); finger joints (psoriasis, plant thorn synovitis).
- *Speed of onset.* Crystal synovitis develops very rapidly, often reaching maximum severity with extreme pain within just 2–12 hours, whereas sepsis is more subacute and continues to progress until treated.
- *Associated periarticular inflammation.* Acute synovitis with surrounding soft tissue swelling and overlying erythema is a classic feature of sepsis and crystals but may also occur with seronegative spondarthritis and erythema nodosum. Haemarthrosis can cause a very tense effusion, often splinting the joint in its loose-pack position, but there is no surrounding swelling or skin change. The combination of small joint synovitis and firm periarticular swelling in a digit—'dactylitis'—is characteristic of psoriasis (fingers, toes) or reactive arthritis (toes).
- *Additional circumstances surrounding the onset of pain.* These include preceding dysentery or new sexual contact with reactive arthritis; intercurrent illness or surgery triggering crystal synovitis; clinical features or a family history of psoriasis; streptococcal sore throat triggering erythema nodosum.

The differential diagnosis differs when acute monoarthritis occurs in a joint that is already abnormal because of damage, most commonly osteoarthritis, or through involvement by inflammatory disease (see Box 20.11). A common situation is an acute flare of inflammation in a single joint of a patient with known rheumatoid disease. Rheumatoid has a strong negative association with crystal deposition, and disproportionate inflammation in one or even two joints in this situation, especially with overlying erythema, should always suggest sepsis.

Investigation of acute monoarthritis varies according to the clinical situation, but aspiration of the joint is required if there is a possibility of sepsis or crystals.

CHRONIC INFLAMMATORY MONOARTHRITIS

Chronic inflammatory monoarthritis that persists for more than 6 weeks may be due to a variety of causes (see Box 20.12). The knee is the most common site but almost any joint may be involved. If no cause is apparent by 6 months, or if there are radiographic signs of osteopenia, erosion or periostitis, synovial biopsy is usually undertaken to exclude chronic infection or rare causes that have specific treatments. Retrospective studies suggest that about 25% of cases evolve to osteoarthritis and about 25% to rheumatoid arthritis but that 30% remain undiagnosed, especially when the knee is involved.

OLIGOARTHRITIS

Oligo- or pauciarticular disease is arthritis affecting two, three or four joints or joint groups (for example, the wrist or midfoot, which have many joints but are counted as a single site). By far the most common cause is osteoarthritis, which associates with non-inflammatory symptoms that usually affect just one or a few sites at any one time, even though more asymptomatic multiple joint osteoarthritis may be apparent on examination.

Acute or subacute inflammatory oligoarthritis mainly targets lower limb joints and is usually asymmetrical; it is a common presentation of JIA in children, especially girls, and of seronegative spondarthritis in adults (see Box 20.13). Sequential joint involvement that ascends a limb—for example, a midfoot, followed by the ankle and then the knee on the same side—should always suggest sepsis.

POLYARTHRITIS

Polyarthritis is involvement of five or more joints or joint groups. In determining the cause it is helpful to consider whether the polyarthritis:

- is symmetrical (approximately) or asymmetrical
- shows predominant or equal involvement for upper and lower limbs
- shows predominant or equal involvement for large and small joints
- has accompanying periarticular involvement
- has accompanying extra-articular features as clues to the diagnosis (see Box 20.14).

A large number of viral infections may cause arthralgia (joint pain with no abnormal examination findings) and rapid onset of an acute symmetrical inflammatory polyarthritis affecting small and large joints of upper and lower limbs that is usually self-limiting within 6 weeks. These include parvovirus B19, hepatitis B and C, mumps, rubella, chickenpox and infectious mononucleosis. The rapidity of onset, the presence of fever and the characteristic rash usually suggest the diagnosis. Arthritis usually precedes jaundice from hepatitis B. Rubella arthritis mainly affects girls and women, occurring 1–7 days after the rash or 2–6 weeks after vaccination. Rubella is exceptional in that, although the symmetrical polyarthritis settles, oligoarthritis may persist for some months.

Polyarthritis that persists for more than 6 weeks is unlikely to be viral (see Box 20.15). A definitive diagnosis may be difficult in the first few months of onset but often becomes firmer as more characteristic features develop with time. However, certain patterns are characteristic and may be present at or soon after presentation (see Fig. 20.11). Rheumatoid arthritis is by far the most

20.14 EXAMPLES OF EXTRA-ARTICULAR FEATURES THAT ASSOCIATE WITH INFLAMMATORY OLIGO- OR POLYARTHRITIS

Clinical feature	Disease association
Skin, nails and mucous membranes	
Psoriasis, nail pitting and dystrophy	Psoriatic arthritis
Raynaud's	Lupus, scleroderma
Photosensitivity	Lupus
Livedo reticularis	Lupus
Splinter haemorrhages, nail-fold infarcts	Vasculitis
Oral ulcers	Lupus, reactive arthritis, Behçet's
Large nodules (mainly extensor surfaces)	Rheumatoid arthritis, gout
Clubbing	Enteropathic arthritis, metastatic lung cancer, endocarditis
Eyes	
Uveitis	Seronegative spondarthritis
Conjunctivitis	Reactive arthritis
Episcleritis, scleritis	Rheumatoid arthritis, vasculitis
Urethritis	Reactive arthritis
Heart, lungs	
Pleuro-pericarditis	Lupus, rheumatoid arthritis
Fibrosing alveolitis	Rheumatoid arthritis, lupus, other connective tissue disease
Abdominal organs	
Hepatosplenomegaly	Rheumatoid arthritis, lupus
Haematuria, proteinuria	Lupus, vasculitis, scleroderma
Urethritis	Reactive arthritis
Fever, lymphadenopathy	Infection, systemic JIA

20.15 CAUSES OF POLYARTHRITIS

Cause	Characteristics
Non-inflammatory	
Generalised osteoarthritis	Very common, symmetrical, small and large joints, Heberden's nodes, only a few joints symptomatic at any one time
Haemochromatosis	Rare, small and large joints
Acromegalic arthropathy	Rare, mainly large joints, spine
Inflammatory	
Viral arthritis	Very acute, self-limiting
Rheumatoid arthritis	Symmetrical, small and large joints, upper and lower limbs
Seronegative spondarthritis (Psoriasis, reactive, ankylosing spondylitis, enteropathic arthropathy)	Asymmetrical, large > small joints, lower > upper limbs, spondylitis
Lupus	Symmetrical, small > large joints, joint damage uncommon
Chronic gout	Distal > proximal joints, preceded by acute attacks
Juvenile idiopathic arthritis	Symmetrical, small and large joints, upper and lower limbs
Chronic sarcoidosis	Symmetrical, small and large joints
Scleroderma and polymyositis	Rare, small and large joints
Hypertrophic osteoarthropathy	Rare, large > small joints, clubbing

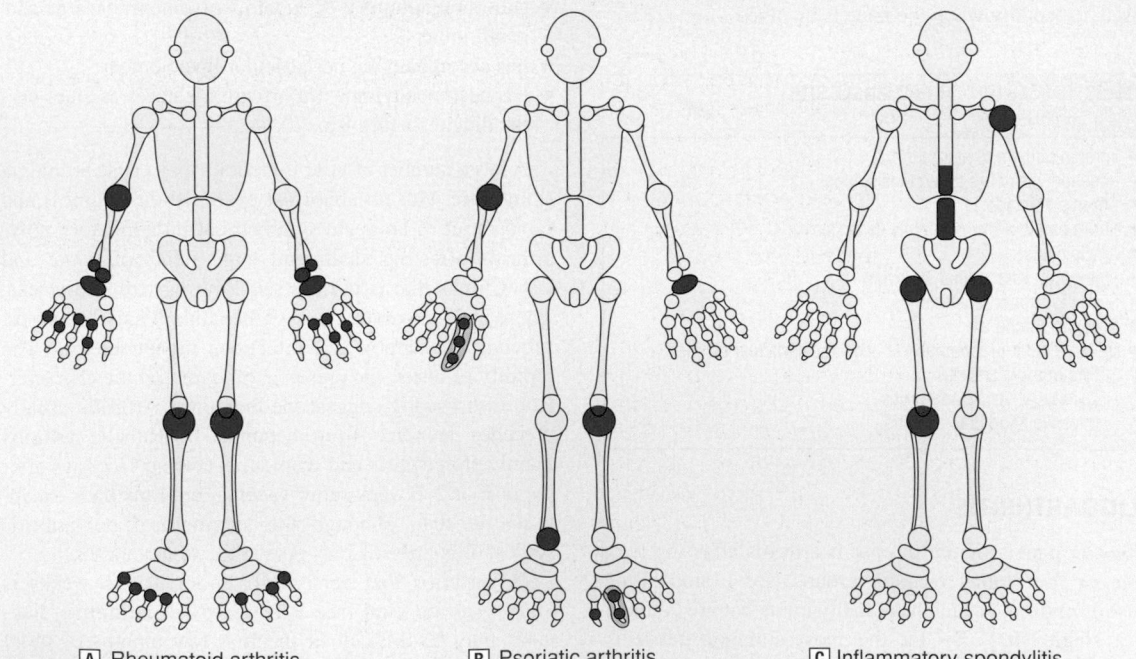

[A] Rheumatoid arthritis   [B] Psoriatic arthritis   [C] Inflammatory spondylitis

Fig. 20.11 Contrasting patterns of involvement in polyarthritis. [A] Rheumatoid arthritis (symmetrical, small and large joints, upper and lower limbs). [B] Seronegative psoriatic arthritis (asymmetrical, large > small joints, associated periarticular inflammation giving dactylitis). [C] Seronegative inflammatory spondylitis (axial involvement, large > small joints, asymmetrical).

common cause of chronic inflammatory, symmetrical polyarthritis affecting small and large joints of upper and lower limbs. Tenosynovitis and bursitis (i.e. synovial inflammation) are the main periarticular manifestations. Marked asymmetry, lower limb predominance and involvement of large more than small joints are all more characteristic of seronegative spondarthritis. Concurrence of enthesitis, associated diffuse periarticular swelling and inflammatory spondylitis may be further clinical markers of spondarthritis. Lupus usually causes more arthralgia and wrist extensor tenosynovitis than overt synovitis. Chronic polyarthritis due to gout is inevitably preceded by a long history of acute attacks. Other causes of polyarthritis are rare.

A detailed history and examination often reveal the likely diagnosis and direct investigation. For inflammatory polyarthritis present for less than 6 weeks the full blood count, liver function tests and viral serology are often appropriate. For early persistent polyarthritis of indeterminate cause appropriate initial investigation should include the full blood count, ESR, CRP, liver function, rheumatoid factor and antinuclear antibody, and radiographs of hands and feet.

REGIONAL PERIARTICULAR PAIN

SINGLE REGIONAL PAIN

This usually results from an over-usage strain or injury affecting a periarticular structure. The patient can often state the day or week that it started and may be able to name an obvious provoking event or injury. The pain is non-progressive and reproduced by just one or a few movements. Apart from the pain, the patient feels normal. Examination reveals localised periarticular tenderness and no, or only mild, signs of inflammation, and the pain may be reproduced by resisted active movement or by a stress test for the involved structure. Increasing age, obesity and generalised hypermobility are predisposing constitutional factors and occupational and recreational usage may be relevant to causation.

The duration of symptoms is variable. Muscle injuries usually repair rapidly within days, whereas fibrous structures such as tendons and ligaments may take weeks or months to return to normal. The diagnosis is usually made clinically, though imaging, especially ultrasound and MRI, may be required to define the anatomy of more severe or resistant lesions. Management is aimed towards:

- identifying and avoiding, if possible, predisposing or adverse mechanical factors
- pain relief (topical and/or oral analgesics, local injection for severe pain)
- appropriate exercise and rehabilitation to restore movement and function.

Surgery is only occasionally required for very resistant or disabling lesions.

Shoulder pain

Shoulder pain is a very common MSK complaint in men and women over the age of 40 years, principally due to rotator cuff lesions (see Box 20.16). Varying pain patterns of common lesions are shown in Figure 20.12.

Adhesive capsulitis ('frozen shoulder') is an ill-understood condition which presents with upper arm pain that progresses over 4–10 weeks before levelling and then receding over a similar time course. Glenohumeral restriction is present from the outset, but progresses and reaches its maximum as the pain is receding. In the early phase there is marked anterior joint/capsular tenderness and stress pain in a capsular pattern; later there is painless restriction, often of all movements. Frozen shoulder is

20.16 EXAMINATION FINDINGS IN COMMON PERIARTICULAR LESIONS AT THE SHOULDER
Rotator cuff lesion

• Pain reproduced by resisted active movement
    Abduction—supraspinatus
    External rotation—infraspinatus, teres minor
    Internal rotation—subscapularis

Subacromial bursitis
• No pain on resisted active abduction (cf. supraspinatus lesion —the other cause of a painful middle arc)
Bicipital (long head) tendinitis
• Tender over bicipital groove • Pain reproduced by resisted active wrist supination or elbow flexion

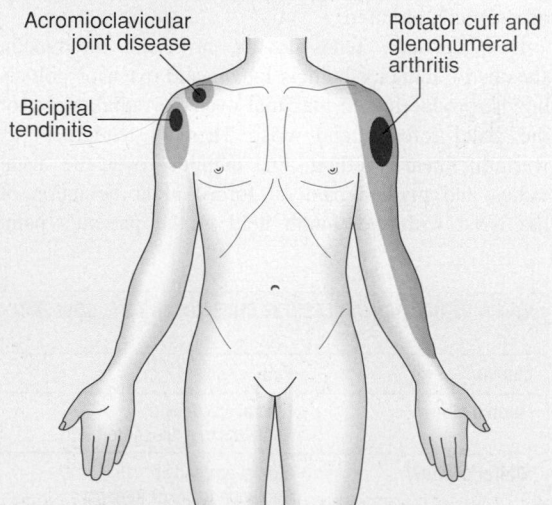

Fig. 20.12　Pain patterns around the shoulder.

more common in diabetics and may be triggered by a rotator cuff lesion, local trauma, myocardial infarction or hemiplegia. Treatment in the early stage is with analgesics, intra- and extracapsular corticosteroid injection and regular 'pendulum' exercises of the arm to prevent the capsule from over-tightening. Mobilising and strengthening exercises are the sole treatment in the painless 'frozen' stage. The natural history is for slow but complete recovery, the complete cycle sometimes taking as long as 2 years.

Elbow pain

Pain from the three joint compartments is felt maximally at the elbow, close to its origin, with occasional radiation down the forearm. Lateral epicondylitis is the most common periarticular lesion (see Box 20.17). Olecranon bursitis can follow local repetitive trauma but infection, gout and rheumatoid also commonly affect this bursa.

Hand and wrist pain

Joint disease in the hand produces pain well localised to the involved joints. Pain from the first carpometacarpal joint, commonly targeted by osteoarthritis, is maximal at the thumb base but often radiates down the thumb and back over the radial wrist. Non-articular causes of hand pain include:

- tenosynovitis—flexor or extensor (pain, swelling ± fine crepitus on volar or extensor aspect) and de Quervain's
- median nerve compression (carpal tunnel syndrome)
- Raynaud's phenomenon
- C8/T1 radiculopathy
- algodystrophy (reflex sympathetic dystrophy).

Trigger finger results from stenosing tenosynovitis in the flexor tendon sheath, with intermittent locking of the finger in flexion. A local corticosteroid injection often relieves the problem and surgical decompression is only occasionally required.

De Quervain's tenosynovitis, involving the tendon sheaths of abductor pollicis longus and extensor pollicis brevis, produces pain maximal over the radial aspect of the distal forearm and wrist. There is tenderness (± warmth, linear swelling, fine crepitus) over the distal radius and marked pain on forced ulnar deviation of the wrist with the thumb held in the patient's palm (Finkelstein's sign). It is usually caused by repetitive over-usage, but bilateral symptoms may occur with gonococcal infection.

Dupuytren's contracture results from fibrosis and contracture of the superficial palmar fascia. Inability to extend the fingers fully is associated with puckering of the skin and the presence of palpable nodules. The ring and little fingers are usually the first and worst affected. It is usually painless and the main symptoms relate to the curled fingers becoming snagged in pockets or poking the eye during face-washing. It is age-related and usually bilateral, strongly predominates in men, and is often familial with a dominant inheritance. Occasional associations include plantar fibromatosis, Peyronie's disease, alcohol misuse and chronic vibration injury. It is very slowly progressive and fasciotomy is seldom necessary.

Hip pain

Hip pain is usually maximal deep in the anterior groin, with variable radiation to the buttock, anterolateral thigh, knee or shin (see Fig. 20.13). Sacroiliac pain is maximal

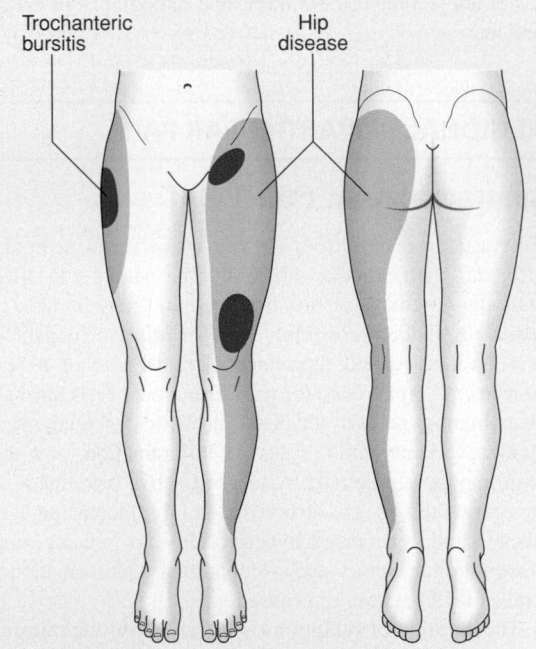

Fig. 20.13 Pain patterns of hip disease and trochanteric bursitis.

20.17 PERIARTICULAR LESIONS PRESENTING AS ELBOW PAIN		
Lesion	**Pain**	**Examination findings, tests**
'Tennis elbow'	Lateral epicondyle Radiation to extensor forearm	Tender over epicondyle Pain reproduced by resisted active wrist extension
'Golfer's elbow'	Medial epicondyle Radiation to flexor forearm	Tender over epicondyle Pain reproduced by resisted active wrist flexion
Olecranon bursitis	Olecranon	Fluctuant tender swelling over olecranon

in the buttock, with radiation down the posterior thigh, worse on standing on that leg.

Trochanteric bursitis is the most common periarticular lesion (see Box 20.18). It predominates in older, especially obese, women as an isolated lesion or secondary to other problems, such as hip or knee osteoarthritis, that cause an abnormal gait.

Referred pain from other structures may require differentiation. Back pain commonly radiates to the buttock and posterior thigh but the site of maximal pain is close to the spine or pelvic brim. Root entrapment can cause pain to the lateral thigh (T12–L1) or to the inguinal region and lateral thigh (L2–4) but is worsened by coughing and straining more than by movement, and is often accompanied by sensory disturbance. A psoas abscess, retroperitoneal haemorrhage or pelvic inflammation can cause inguinal and lateral thigh pain that is aggravated by resisted hip flexion.

Knee pain

The knee is a common target site for arthritis but also a common site for trauma and periarticular lesions. Pain arising from the three knee compartments (arthritis or internal derangement) is anterior and well localised to the involved compartment. Patello-femoral pain is worse going down and up stairs or inclines. Locking—sudden painful inability to extend fully that often spontaneously unlocks and is followed by aching—reflects a mechanical derangement such as a meniscal tear or osteochondritis dissecans. Referred pain from the hip may present at the knee but is more diffuse and often relieved by rubbing; on examination hip not knee movement reproduces it.

Pain from periarticular lesions is well localised to the involved structure (see Box 20.19). Inflammation of any of the three bursae around the patella usually results from repetitive occupational kneeling, but infection and gout may need consideration.

Anterior knee pain syndrome is a common problem, especially in adolescent girls. The pain has patellofemoral characteristics and is often aggravated by sports. In a small proportion there is evidence of non-progressive fibrillation of the retro-patellar cartilage ('chondromalacia patellae'). The condition is usually self-limiting and treatment should be conservative.

The anterior tibial compartment syndrome is characterised by severe pain in the front of the lower leg, aggravated by exercise and relieved by rest. Symptoms result from fascial compression of the muscles in the anterior tibial compartment and may be associated with a foot drop. Treatment is urgent surgical decompression.

20.18 PERIARTICULAR LESIONS AT THE HIP

Lesion	Pain	Examination findings, tests
Trochanteric bursitis	Upper lateral thigh, worse on lying on that side at night	Tender over greater trochanter
Gluteal enthesopathy	Upper lateral thigh, worse on lying on that side at night	Tender over greater trochanter Pain reproduced by resisted active hip abduction
Adductor tendinitis	Upper inner thigh Usually clearly sports-related	Tender over adductor origin/tendon/muscle Pain reproduced by resisted active hip adduction
Ischiogluteal bursitis	Buttock, worse on sitting	Tender over ischial prominence
Iliopectineal bursitis	Anterior groin	Tender (± fluctuant swelling) lateral to femoral pulse, not worsened by internal rotation of hip (cf. hip pain)

20.19 PERIARTICULAR LESIONS AT THE KNEE

Lesion	Pain	Examination findings, tests
Prepatellar bursitis	Anterior patella	Tender fluctuant swelling in front of patella
Superficial and deep infrapatellar bursitis	Anterior knee, inferior to patella	Tender fluctuant swelling in front of (superficial) or behind (deep) patella tendon
Anserine bursitis	Upper medial tibia	Tenderness (± warmth, swelling) over upper medial tibia
Inferior medial collateral ligament enthesopathy	Upper medial tibia	Localised tenderness of upper medial tibia Pain reproduced by valgus stress on mildly flexed knee
Popliteal ('Baker's') cyst	Popliteal fossa	Tender swelling of popliteal fossa, usually reducible by massage with knee in mid-flexion
Patella tendon enthesopathy (Osgood–Schlatter disease)	Anterior upper tibia Mainly energetic adolescents	Tenderness and firm swelling of tibial tubercle Pain on resisted active knee extension

Foot and ankle pain

Pain arising from articular and periarticular structures is usually well localised. Pain from the ankle joint is felt anteriorly between the two malleoli and is worse on standing or walking. Subtalar pain is mainly posterior between the malleoli and particularly aggravated by walking on uneven surfaces, requiring eversion/inversion. Periarticular lesions that cause hindfoot pain are listed in Box 20.20.

Midtarsal disease causes pain in the 'bootlace' area, mainly during the late stance and toe-off phase of walking. Loss of the normal arches—pes planus ('flat foot')—may cause pain in the mid-sole. Pes planus is often congenital, but acquired causes include trauma, constitutional hypermobility, rheumatoid arthritis and neuropathic arthropathy. Medial arch supports in well-fitting shoes and/or intrinsic muscle-strengthening exercises usually relieve symptoms but rigid orthotics may be required for hyperpronated feet, provided the foot is not rigid from fusion of the tarsal bones (tarsal coalition).

Metatarsophalangeal (MTP) joint pain is felt below the metatarsal heads (metatarsalgia) and is often described as 'like walking on marbles'. Hallux valgus deformity with secondary bursitis (bunions) and osteoarthritis of the first MTP joint often associates with flattening of the transverse metatarsal arch and is a common cause of forefoot pain. It predominates in women as a consequence of wearing narrow high-heeled shoes. Severe restriction of first MTP joint extension (hallux rigidus), usually due to osteoarthritis, may cause marked pain during attempted toe-off. For both hallux problems, conservative treatment and appropriate footwear usually suffice, although surgery is required for a minority.

Pes cavus ('claw foot') is characterised by a high medial arch, secondary clawing of toes and metatarsal callosities. Rarely, it associates with neurological disorders such as Friedreich's ataxia, spina bifida or poliomyelitis. Associated pain is often helped by medial arch supports and metatarsal insoles, and fasciotomy or osteotomy is rarely indicated.

Morton's neuroma is an entrapment neuropathy of the interdigital nerves, mostly between the third and fourth metatarsal heads in middle-aged women with ill-fitting shoes. The neuralgic, lancinating pain occurs mainly when the patient is wearing shoes and may associate with local sensory loss and a palpable tender swelling between the metatarsal heads. Footwear adjustment, with or without a local corticosteroid injection, is often sufficient but excision is occasionally required.

MULTIPLE REGIONAL PAIN

Multiple regional 'soft tissue' pain is most commonly due to fibromyalgia. People with this prevalent condition may present with pain at one or a few index sites but enquiry establishes the widespread nature of their pain, often with other typical symptoms, and examination reveals multiple hyperalgesic tender sites.

Other causes of multiple regional pain without arthropathy include:

- *Seronegative spondarthritis.* Enthesopathy may affect several regions prior to the onset of more characteristic features. Chest wall pains, Achilles enthesopathy and plantar fasciitis are particularly common. Clues may lie in the marked inflammatory component (marked morning stiffness), coexistent back pain and stiffness, preceding uveitis or a strong family history.
- *Generalised hypermobility.* Joint mobility is variable but in general is greater in women than men and in Afro-Caribbeans than in whites, and declines with age. The 10% of adults at the lax end of the spectrum of joint mobility are predisposed to ligament strain, traumatic enthesopathy, mechanical back pain, arthralgia and dislocation (mainly glenohumeral). Such generalised hypermobility may be the explanation of recurrent pain at several regions and is recognised in adults by a modified Beighton score (see Box 20.21). Within this 10% are individuals with disease-associated hypermobility such as in Marfan's syndrome, Ehlers–Danlos syndrome and acromegaly.
- *Endocrine disease.* Hyperparathyroidism and hypothyroidism may both cause ill-defined, widespread pains.

20.20 PERIARTICULAR LESIONS CAUSING HINDFOOT PAIN		
Lesion	Pain	Examination findings, tests
Plantar fasciitis	Under heel, worse on standing and walking	Tender under distal calcaneus/plantar fascia insertion site
Subcalcaneal bursitis	Under heel, worse on standing and walking	Tender under middle of calcaneus
Achilles tendinitis	Localised to tendon	Tender on squeezing tendon, ± swelling of tendon. Pain reproduced by standing on toes or resisted plantar flexion
Achilles enthesopathy	Localised to tendon insertion	Tender over insertion site, ± firm swelling. Pain reproduced by standing on toes or resisted plantar flexion
Retro-Achilles bursitis	Posterior heel	Tenderness and soft swelling posterior to tendon
Pre-Achilles bursitis	Posterior heel	Tenderness and fluctuant swelling anterior to tendon

20.21 RECOGNITION OF GENERALISED HYPERMOBILITY IN ADULTS

- Extend little finger > 90°   (1 point each side)
- Bring thumb back parallel
  to/touching forearm   (1 point each side)
- Extend elbow > 10°   (1 point each side)
- Extend knee > 10°   (1 point each side)
- Touch floor with flat of hands,
  legs straight   (1 point)

Hypermobile = 6 or more out of a possible 9 points.

- *Parkinsonism.* This may cause ill-defined regional pain, stiffness and disability. Rigidity, tremor, bradykinesia and other features are usually apparent.
- *Polymyalgia rheumatica* and *polymyositis.* These may both cause multiple regional symptoms with no clear examination findings. However, marked early morning stiffness and systemic upset are usually prominent.

BACK AND NECK PAIN

LOW BACK PAIN

Back pain is a 'human condition', with 60–80% of the world's population experiencing pain at some time in their lives. Although there is no evidence that back pain prevalence has increased, reported disability due to back pain, particularly work absence, has increased significantly in the last 30 years. In Western countries, back pain is the most common cause of sickness-related absence from work. In the UK, 7% of the adult population consult their GP each year with back pain, at a cost of £500 million and 80 million working days lost.

Only a small number of patients with back pain have a pathologically definable problem. All structures in the spinal column, other than cartilage, are pain-sensitive, but the exact mechanism of pain production within individual structures is unknown. Amongst patients presenting with back pain, the main role of history and examination is to identify the small number who have a serious or specific spinal disorder. The initial assessment should address the questions in Figure 20.14.

Non-mechanical pain

Non-mechanical pain is constant and has little variation in intensity or with activity. Anorexia, dyspepsia, change in bowel habit, prostatism or abnormal per vagina bleeding may indicate gastric, pancreatic, colonic, prostatic or uterine/ovarian malignancies respectively. Other 'red flags' for possible serious spinal pathology are indicated in Box 20.22. If there is evidence of a spinal cord or cauda equina lesion, this needs urgent neurosurgical assessment (see Box 20.23).

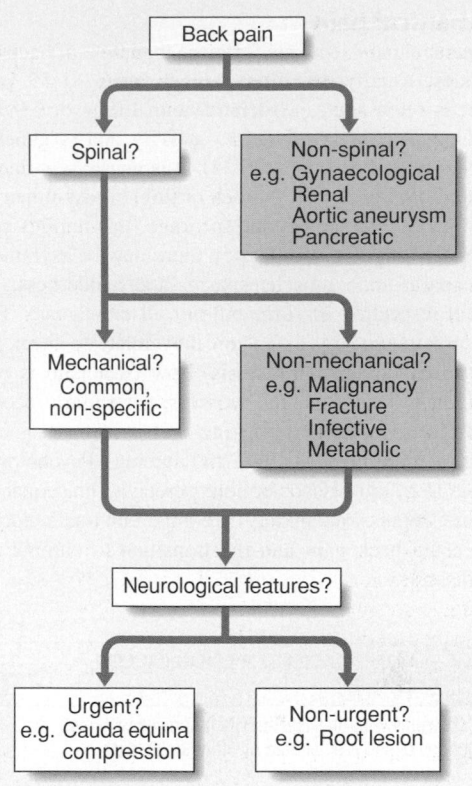

Fig. 20.14   Initial triage assessment of back pain.

20.22 RED FLAGS FOR POSSIBLE SPINAL PATHOLOGY

History

- Age—presentation under age 20 or over age 50
- Character—constant, progressive pain unrelieved by rest
- Location—thoracic pain
- Past medical history—carcinoma, tuberculosis, human immunodeficiency virus (HIV), systemic steroid use
- Constitutional—sweats, malaise, weight loss
- Major trauma

Examination

- Painful spinal deformity
- Severe/symmetrical spinal deformity
- Saddle anaesthesia
- Progressive neurological signs/muscle-wasting
- Multiple levels of root signs

20.23 FEATURES OF CAUDA EQUINA SYNDROME

- Difficulty with micturition
- Loss of anal sphincter tone or faecal incontinence
- Saddle anaesthesia
- Progressive motor weakness/gait disturbance
- Sensory level

Mechanical pain

Mechanical pain accounts for more than 90% of back pain episodes, usually affecting patients aged 20–55 years. Onset is often acute, associated with lifting or bending. Mechanical pain is related to activity and is generally relieved by rest (see Box 20.24). It is usually confined to the lumbosacral region, buttock or thigh, is asymmetrical, and does not radiate beyond the knee (this implies nerve root irritation). On examination there may be asymmetric local paraspinal muscle spasm and tenderness, and painful restriction of some but not all movements. Back pain precipitated by extension may relate to facet joint hypertrophy or spinal stenosis. Low back pain is more common in heavy manual workers, particularly occupations that involve heavy lifting and twisting (e.g. construction, mining, agriculture and nursing). Psychological factors (e.g. job dissatisfaction, perceived inadequacy of income, depression, anxiety) are important risk factors for both acute back pain and the transition to chronic pain and disability.

20.24 FEATURES OF SIMPLE MECHANICAL LOW BACK PAIN
• Pain varies with physical activity (improved with rest)
• Sudden onset, precipitated by lifting or bending
• Recurrent episodes
• Age 20–55
• Pain limited to back or upper leg
• No clear-cut nerve root distribution
• Systemically well
• Prognosis good (90% recovery at 6 weeks)

Radicular pain

Radicular (nerve root) pain has a severe, sharp, lancinating quality, radiates down the back of the leg beyond the knee and is aggravated by coughing, sneezing and straining at stool more than by back movement. On examination, there are signs of lumbar nerve root irritation (see Box 20.25). In contrast, referred pain is usually a dull, deep ache, poorly localised with indistinct boundaries.

20.25 FEATURES OF NERVE ROOT PAIN
• Unilateral leg pain worse than low back pain
• Pain radiates beyond knee
• Paraesthesia in same distribution
• Nerve irritation signs (reduced straight leg raising which reproduces leg pain)
• Motor, sensory or reflex signs (limited to one nerve root)
• Prognosis reasonable (50% recovery at 6 weeks)

Inflammatory pain

Inflammatory pain due to spondylitis has a more gradual onset and often occurs before the age of 30. It is usually axial and symmetrical and spread over many segments which may include the thoracic region. Pain from sacroiliitis is maximal in the buttock, with radiation down the posterior thigh. Inflammatory pain associates with marked morning and inactivity stiffness and improves rather than worsens with activity.

Investigations

Plain radiographs are rarely helpful in patients with acute mechanical low back pain, unless red flags are present (see Box 20.22). By the age of 50, 60% of women and 80% of men have radiographic features of 'spondylosis' (vertebral sclerosis and osteophyte, and osteoarthritis of apophyseal facet joints). However, there is no clear correlation between these universal degenerative changes and back pain. Although advanced lumbar spondylosis frequently associates with low back pain, the clinical features are variable and there is a poor correlation with the degree of radiographic changes. Similarly, minor congenital abnormalities, such as spina bifida occulta and transitional vertebrae, are not associated with low back pain.

Plain radiographs may be helpful in persistent pain in a young patient to help confirm a diagnosis of ankylosing spondylosis, and in an older patient to detect vertebral osteoporotic fracture, particularly if there is a history of trauma, prolonged steroid use or known osteoporosis.

If red flags are present, MRI should be undertaken even if plain radiographs are normal. CT is inferior to MRI for assessing soft tissue structures and nerves but is useful for detecting minor abnormalities of bone architecture and when MRI is contraindicated (e.g. pacemaker or metallic clips).

A low haemoglobin and raised CRP or ESR may heighten a clinical suspicion of inflammation or malignancy. A raised acid phosphatase or prostate-specific antigen (PSA) is associated with metastatic carcinoma of the prostate, and raised alkaline phosphatase with other bone metastases and Paget's disease. Myeloma is associated with a monoclonal band on immunoelectrophoresis and the presence of urine light chains (Bence Jones proteinuria). EMG and nerve conduction studies, with or without measurement of somatosensory evoked responses, are occasionally required to confirm the localisation of nerve root lesions.

Management

Most episodes of mechanical low back pain settle spontaneously with explanation, reassurance and simple analgesics. After 2 days, 30% are better and at 6 weeks 90% have recovered. Recurrences of pain are common, however, and the 10–15% of patients with acute back pain who develop chronic pain consume 85% of back pain resources.

Patient education is paramount and should emphasise that hurt does not imply harm to the underlying structures and that exercise is helpful not damaging. Regular analgesia and/or non-steroidal anti-inflammatory drugs (NSAIDs) may be required to improve mobility and facilitate exercise. Return to work and normal activity should take place as soon as possible. Bed rest is not helpful and may increase the risk of chronic disability. Referral for physiotherapy (e.g. McKenzie technique of passive extension and postural correction) or manipulation should be considered if a return to normal activities has not been achieved by 6 weeks. Low-dose tricyclic drugs also provide analgesic benefits in addition to effects on sleep and mood.

Other treatment modalities occasionally used for acute or chronic low back pain include epidural and facet joint injection, spinal manipulation, traction and lumbar supports. There is currently no RCT evidence to support these interventions (see EBM panel). Surgery is required in fewer than 1% of patients with low back pain.

The management of serious spinal pathology will be dictated by the cause.

EBM

MANAGEMENT OF LOW BACK PAIN

'For acute or recurrent low back pain with or without referred leg pain, bed rest for 2–7 days is worse than placebo or ordinary activity. Continuation of ordinary activity gives equivalent or faster symptomatic recovery and less chronic disability than rest.'

'There is no evidence to support the use of traction, lumbar corsets and support, plaster jackets or facet joint injections for acute low back pain.'

- Waddell G, Feder G, McIntosh A, et al. Low back pain evidence review. London: Royal College of General Practitioners; 1996.

Further information: 🖥 www.cochrane.co.uk

Spondylolysis and spondylolisthesis

Spondylolysis describes any situation where there is a break in the integrity of the neural arch. The principal cause is an acquired defect in pars interarticularis due to a fracture, mainly in gymnasts, dancers and long-distance runners in whom it is an important cause of back pain. Spondylolisthesis is where a defect causes slippage of a vertebra on the one below. This may be congenital, post-traumatic or degenerative. Rarely, it can result from metastatic destruction of the posterior elements.

Uncomplicated spondylolysis does not associate with symptoms but spondylolisthesis can variably associate with low back pain aggravated by standing and walking. More severe cases can result in nerve root compression or a lumbar stenosis syndrome and the vertebral slip is occasionally palpable. Spondylolysis and spondylolisthesis can usually be diagnosed from lateral radiographs of the lumbar spine (see Fig. 20.15). MRI may be required if there is nerve root involvement.

Advice on posture and muscle-strengthening exercises are required in mild cases. Surgical fusion is indicated for severe and recurrent low back pain, and surgical decompression is mandatory prior to fusion in patients with significant lumbar stenosis or symptoms of cauda equina compression.

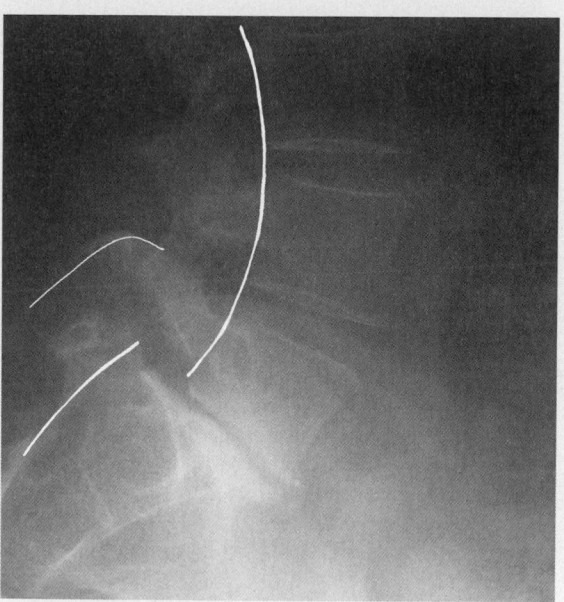

Fig. 20.15 Lumbar spondylolisthesis. Lateral radiograph showing L5/S1 spondylolisthesis with disc space narrowing, sclerosis and a defect in the posterior element (spondylolysis).

Spinal stenosis

Symptoms of spinal stenosis occur due to limitation of space in the vertebral canal. The most common presentation is 'pseudoclaudication' with discomfort in the legs on walking that is relieved by rest, bending forwards or walking uphill. Patients may adopt a characteristic simian posture, with a forward stoop and slight flexion at the hips and knees. Diagnosis is confirmed by CT/MRI. Decompression is indicated if mobility or quality of life is significantly impaired.

Prolapsed intervertebral disc

Age-related reduction in proteoglycan size within the nucleus pulposus diminishes its viscoelasticity, leading to focal damage and disc herniation. These changes occur most frequently at L4 and L5 due to the increased mechanical forces across this area. Most patients have their first episode between the ages of 20 and 30 years. Presentation is with radicular pain (invariably felt below the knee) in combination with evidence of root involvement (sensory deficit, motor weakness, asymmetrical reflexes) and a positive sciatic or femoral stretch test. About 70% of patients improve by 4 weeks. Persistent neurological deficit at 6 weeks is an indication to consider surgery.

Arachnoiditis

Chronic inflammation of nerve root sheaths in the spinal canal can cause severe low back pain, sometimes combined with nerve root symptoms. Arachnoiditis can complicate meningitis or spinal surgery, but most frequently occurs as a late complication of myelography with oil-based contrast agents. MRI or radiculography can confirm the diagnosis but no satisfactory treatment is available.

Scheuermann's osteochondritis

This disorder predominates in adolescent boys who develop a painless dorsal kyphosis in association with irregular radiographic ossification of the vertebral end plates. Back pain, aggravated by exercise and relieved by rest, may occur if upper lumbar vertebrae are affected, and secondary spondylosis can follow in middle age. Excessive exercise and heavy manual labour before epiphyseal fusion has occurred may aggravate the symptoms. Treatment is avoidance of excessive activity and protective postural exercises. The deformity seldom warrants corrective surgery.

Diffuse idiopathic skeletal hyperostosis (DISH)

DISH ('Forrestier's disease') is a common disorder in the elderly, affecting 10% of men and 8% of women over the age of 65. It associates with obesity, hypertension, type II

diabetes mellitus and hyperinsulinaemia. DISH is characterised by florid new bone formation along the antero-lateral aspect of at least four contiguous vertebral bodies (see Fig. 20.16). It is distinguished from lumbar spondy-losis by the absence of disc space narrowing and marginal vertebral body sclerosis, and from spondylitis by the absence of sacroiliitis or apophyseal joint fusion. It rarely associates with pain and is usually an asymptomatic radi-ographic finding. Ossifying enthesopathy at peripheral sites may cause pain—for example, under the heel with calcaneal spur formation.

NECK PAIN

Neck pain is less common than back pain as a cause of disability in the working population but is a significant problem in the elderly. Neck pain is usually due to mechanical or degenerative problems, although serious spinal disease needs to be excluded using the same principles as for back pain. Most episodes of transient mechanical neck pain are not associated with demonstra-ble spinal pathology. Other causes of neck pain are listed in Box 20.26.

Pain arising from neck structures is often poorly localised but maximal close to the neck. Pain from upper segments may radiate to the occiput, temple or face, and pain from lower segments to the scapula, shoulder, arm and occasionally chest wall. Mechanical neck pain is often acute in onset and associated with asymmetrical restriction of neck movements and a history of awkward

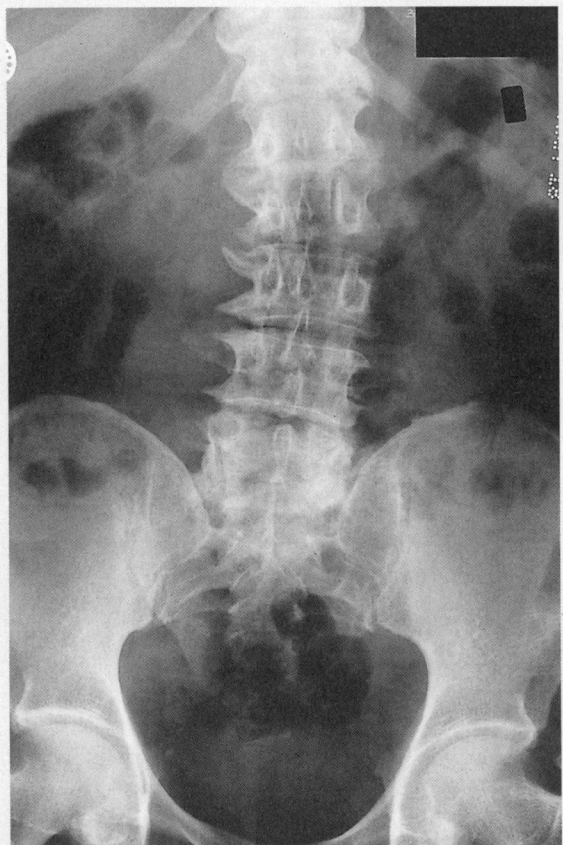

Fig. 20.16 Diffuse idiopathic skeletal hyperostosis (DISH). Radiograph of thoracolumbar spine showing flowing ossification joining more than four contiguous vertebrae. The disc spaces are preserved and the sacroiliac joints are normal.

20.26 CAUSES OF NECK PAIN	
Mechanical	
• Postural	• Disc prolapse
• Whiplash injury	• Cervical spondylosis
Inflammatory	
• Infections	• Rheumatoid arthritis
• Spondylitis	• Polymyalgia rheumatica
• Juvenile idiopathic arthritis	
Metabolic	
• Osteoporosis	• Paget's disease
• Osteomalacia	
Neoplasia	
• Metastases	• Reticuloses
• Myeloma	• Intrathecal tumours
Other	
• Fibromyalgia	• Torticollis
Referred pain	
• Pharynx	• Aortic aneurysm
• Cervical lymph nodes	• Pancoast tumour
• Teeth	• Diaphragm
• Angina pectoris	

posture or trauma. Radicular pain may arise from compression from osteophyte or disc prolapse. Most prolapse (70%) affects the C6 disc, compressing the C7 root; 20% affects C5. Massive cervical osteophytes or DISH occasionally cause dysphagia due to oesophageal indentation.

The principles of investigation and management are identical to those for low back pain. Surgery is only required when there are neurological signs of radiculopathy or progressive cervical myelopathy (see p. 1190).

BONE PAIN

CHRONIC BONE PAIN

Subacute or chronic bone pain usually has the following characteristics:

- well localised to the site of origin (no radiation)
- predominant at or confined to night-time
- not clearly worsened by movement or usage (unlike joint or periarticular pain)
- not readily reproduced by clinical examination.

Such pain may result from a variety of causes, most notably:

- secondary (less commonly, primary) bone tumours
- chronic infection (osteomyelitis)
- Paget's disease
- osteonecrosis
- metabolic bone disease (e.g. osteomalacia, hyperparathyroidism).

Other features in the enquiry usually point to the most likely cause. For example, slowly but relentlessly progressive pain with these characteristics suggests destructive disease—malignancy or chronic infection. Malignancy may associate with weight loss, fatigue and symptoms relating to the primary site. Pain that is experienced over a wider area and accompanied by bone deformity strongly suggests Paget's disease. Osteomalacia very commonly associates with limb girdle weakness. Pain from osteonecrosis is initially bony and progressive but then may develop superadded features of joint pain (worse on usage or weight-bearing, ± radiation, reproduced by examination) as the adjacent joint cartilage collapses and the joint is involved (mainly hips, shoulders, elbows). Investigation of bony pain always includes plain radiographs of the symptomatic site and commonly a radioisotope bone scan, with other tests directed by the presumptive diagnosis.

Severe arthropathy with subchondral bone attrition and collapse, most commonly osteoarthritis, may also cause bone pain, though this is inevitably superimposed upon a chronic history of usage-related joint pain.

ACUTE BONE PAIN: FRACTURE

Sudden-onset pain that is very well localised, severe and worsened by even slight movement should always suggest a fracture. This is the major clinical manifestation of metabolic bone disease. From a clinical and aetiological standpoint, fractures are divisible into several subtypes:

- *Fragility fractures* result from relatively minor trauma and are typical of osteoporosis. With vertebral fractures the precipitating factor is often bending or lifting and with long bone fractures the trigger is usually a simple fall (from standing height or less).
- *Pathological fractures* occur in bone that is structurally abnormal, such as in Paget's disease, osteomalacia, bone metastases and parathyroid bone disease. Like fragility fractures, they often occur spontaneously or follow minor trauma.
- *High-energy fractures* result from major trauma (e.g. car crash, falls from a height) and can affect normal bones. The same is true of *stress (fatigue) fractures* in healthy individuals such as athletes and military recruits who are exposed to minor but repetitive trauma.

Differential diagnosis

Long bone fractures present with acute pain and swelling following trauma. The main differential diagnosis is soft tissue injury, but fracture should be suspected when there is marked pain and swelling, abnormal movement of the affected limb, crepitus or deformity. Femoral neck fractures typically produce a shortened, externally rotated leg that is painful to move. Presentation of vertebral fractures is more variable. Some cause acute severe back pain with radiation to the anterior chest wall, mimicking acute myocardial infarction or pulmonary embolism. Many cause no symptoms or only minor ones, and present with more insidious or intermittent back pain and height loss. The differential diagnosis for chronic back pain is potentially wide (see pp. 981–984), but significant loss of height and acquired structural kyphosis should always suggest osteoporosis as a predisposing cause. Rib fractures often cause pleuritic-type pain that may suggest intrathoracic disease, especially in patients with chronic respiratory disease and associated steroid-induced osteoporosis. Osteoporotic rib fractures are suggested by aggravation of the pain by movement, local tenderness and pain on springing the rib cage.

Investigations and diagnosis

For suspected fracture, plain radiographs of the affected bone should be taken in at least two perpendicular planes and examined for discontinuity of the cortical outline. This is usually sufficient for diagnosis. If the radiographs are normal but clinical suspicion remains high, other imaging may be used—for example, radioisotope bone scans for fatigue fractures or scaphoid fractures, and CT or MRI scans for fractures of the pelvis or spine. CT or MRI can also help differentiate pathological fractures of the spine due to tumour from fractures due to osteoporosis.

Management

The principles of management are outlined in Box 20.27. Femoral neck fractures present a special management problem since non-union and avascular necrosis are common complications, especially with intracapsular fractures; surgical treatment of these fractures often entails replacing the femoral head with a prosthetic joint.

Rehabilitation is as important as reduction and fixation in determining outcome. A supervised exercise programme is important to avoid muscle-wasting and joint stiffness, both of which impair long-term mobility, especially in the elderly. Older patients with hip fracture also benefit from nutritional supplementation during their hospital stay, and this should be instituted routinely.

Investigating and treating the cause of fracture

Patients with high-energy and fatigue fractures generally require nothing further once the fracture has healed. Those with fragility fractures of long bones or vertebral fractures, however, require BMD measurement, especially if other risk factors for osteoporosis are present (see Box 20.7, p. 972), and treatment if it is confirmed (see p. 1027). A radionuclide bone scan should be performed on patients with pathological fracture due to Paget's disease or metastases to define the extent of the disease, and a radiograph taken of any lower limb metastases to assess the likelihood of fracture. Lytic lesions that have eroded more than 50% of the cortex are likely to fracture and should be considered for prophylactic surgical fixation. Patients with metastases may also need treatment with prophylactic bisphosphonates, radiotherapy or chemotherapy, depending on the tumour type (see p. 1033). Fractures associated with hyperparathyroidism and Paget's disease require no special treatment, but patients with these diseases should be kept well hydrated and their serum calcium monitored post-operatively because they are at risk of hypercalcaemic crisis. Patients with fractures due to osteogenesis imperfecta or fibrous dysplasia should be considered for intravenous bisphosphonate treatment, since this appears to reduce the risk of new fractures.

MUSCLE PAIN AND WEAKNESS

Acute muscle weakness can arise from a variety of metabolic, endocrine, infective and neurological causes. It is important to distinguish between:

- a subjective feeling of generalised weakness or fatigue
- objective 'true' weakness with loss of muscle power and function.

The former is often a non-specific manifestation of many organic diseases and also psychological distress. Conversely, the diagnosis of muscle disease may be delayed because weakness is misinterpreted as fatigue.

Proximal muscle weakness

This usually indicates a proximal myopathy which typically causes difficulty with standing from a seated position, squatting and lifting overhead. Distal power, such as grip, is usually preserved. The causes of proximal myopathy (see Box 20.28) are either inflammatory (myositis) or non-inflammatory (due to endocrine or metabolic abnormalities or toxins).

20.28 CAUSES OF PROXIMAL MUSCLE PAIN AND WEAKNESS	
Inflammatory	
• Polymyositis • Dermatomyositis	• Inclusion body myositis
Endocrine	
• Hypothyroidism • Hyperthyroidism • Addison's	• Cushing's • Steroid therapy
Metabolic	
• Myophosphorylase deficiency • Phosphofructokinase deficiency	• Carnitine deficiency • Myoadenolate deaminase deficiency
Drugs/toxins	
• Alcohol • Cocaine • Fibrates	• Statins • Penicillamine • Zidovudine
Infections	
• Viral (HIV, cytomegalovirus, rubella, Epstein–Barr, echo) • Bacterial (clostridia, staphylococci, tuberculosis, mycoplasma)	• Parasitic (schistosomiasis, cysticercosis, toxoplasmosis)

20.27 PRINCIPLES OF FRACTURE MANAGEMENT		
Action	**Long bone fractures**	**Vertebral fractures**
1. Provide pain relief	✓	✓
2. Reduce the fracture and correct deformity	✓	n/a
3. Immobilise the fracture site	✓	n/a
4. Rehabilitate and mobilise	✓	✓
5. Investigate and treat the underlying cause	✓	✓
(n/a = not applicable)		

Hypothyroidism can cause myopathy, usually with CK elevation; in Cushing's disease and steroid myopathy the CK is usually normal. A history of exercise intolerance, with post-exertional cramps (± a family history), suggests a metabolic myopathy, the most common being the glycogen storage disorders. A strong family history and onset in early adulthood are suggestive of a muscular dystrophy. A drug history is important, notably alcohol, which can cause both an inflammatory myopathy and muscle atrophy of type 2 fibres. Myopathy can be associated with several viral infections, including HIV, due to either the virus itself or drug therapy with zidovudine.

Distal or generalised weakness

This usually indicates a neurological cause (e.g. motor neuron disease), which is even more likely if there are sensory abnormalities or if the weakness is unilateral or focal. The weakness of myasthenia gravis is characteristically worsened by repeated exertion (fatigability) and improved by rest, and usually involves the ocular muscles.

Investigations (see p. 973)

Physical examination should establish the presence, pattern and severity of muscle weakness, graded according to the MRC (Medical Research Council) 1–5 scale. General examination should assess for fasciculation, evidence of endocrine disease, malignancy, arthropathy and connective tissue disease.

The most sensitive biochemical test of muscle injury is CK. A raised level confirms the clinical suspicion of muscle inflammation or necrosis but does not establish the cause. Occasionally, the CK is normal, particularly if muscle changes are focal. Because the differential diagnosis of muscle pain and weakness and raised CK is wide, muscle biopsy and EMG are usually required for a precise diagnosis. Using MRI to identify focal areas of muscle abnormality can increase the diagnostic yield from muscle biopsies. In inflammatory myositis, the typical features are muscle fibre necrosis and regeneration in the presence of focal lymphocytic infiltration. Atrophy of grouped fibres suggests a neuromyopathic cause such as denervation. Atrophy of type 2 fibres is a non-specific finding, and may occur with disuse and steroid therapy as well as with a variety of connective tissue diseases.

Management

This is determined by the underlying cause, discussed further in other relevant sections. In all patients with muscle disease, physical therapy to maximise current muscle ability and to improve muscle conditioning may be helpful.

SYSTEMIC ILLNESS

Systemic illness may be the dominant presenting feature of multisystem MSK disease. The essential features are arthralgia and myalgia in combination with weight loss, night sweats, fever, skin rashes, raised inflammatory markers and abnormal urinalysis.

The differential diagnosis is potentially wide but the most important diagnosis to consider is sepsis, particularly bacterial endocarditis and meningococcal infection. If the patient is febrile, unwell or hypotensive, empirical broad-spectrum antibiotics should be initiated after appropriate samples have been taken for culture.

The next important group of conditions to consider is systemic vasculitis. This may require urgent treatment prior to full diagnostic confirmation, particularly if there is evidence of critical organ inflammation. Additional symptoms that may point towards a diagnosis of vasculitis are shown in Box 20.29. Further investigation should include urine microscopy, ANCA and biopsy of accessible affected organs. Immediate empirical management of vasculitis with critical organ involvement is with 1 g i.v. methylprednisolone on 3 consecutive days.

A number of other conditions may mimic both sepsis and vasculitis, including disseminated malignancy, lymphoma, atrial myxoma, cholesterol emboli and the antiphospholipid syndrome.

20.29 CLINICAL FEATURES THAT MAY ACCOMPANY MULTISYSTEM MSK DISEASE	
Systemic	
• Malaise • Fever • Night sweats	• Weight loss in combination with arthralgia and myalgia
Skin rashes	
• Palpable purpura • Pulp infarcts	• Ulceration • Livedo reticularis
ENT	
• Epistaxis • Recurrent sinusitis • Deafness	• Respiratory cough • Haemoptysis • Wheeze (uncontrolled asthma)
Gastrointestinal	
• Mouth ulcers • Diarrhoea	• Abdominal pain (due to mucosal inflammation or enteric ischaemia)
Neurological	
• Sensory or motor neuropathy	

PRINCIPLES OF MANAGEMENT OF MUSCULOSKELETAL DISORDERS

For the majority of MSK conditions the aims of management are to:

- educate the patient
- control pain
- optimise function
- beneficially modify the disease process.

These aims are interrelated and success in one area often benefits the others. Successful management inevitably requires careful assessment of the person as well as his or her MSK system. The management plan needs to be individualised and patient-centred, taking into account holistic factors such as:

- the person's daily activity requirements, and work and recreational aspirations
- risk factors and associations of the MSK condition (e.g. obesity, muscle weakness, non-restorative sleep)
- the person's perceptions and knowledge of his or her condition
- medications and coping strategies already tried by the patient
- comorbid disease and its therapy
- the availability, costs and logistics of appropriate evidence-based interventions.

The plan needs to be agreed and understood by both patient and practitioner. Simple and safe interventions should be tried first. The patient's symptoms and signs will change with time, and require review and readjustment rather than rigid continuation of a single plan or algorithm. The wide variety of treatment approaches may require the expertise of a number of health professionals, necessitating a coordinated multidisciplinary team approach for some patients.

The principal core interventions that should be considered for every patient with a painful MSK condition are listed in Box 20.30. In addition, there are other non-pharmacological

20.30 INTERVENTIONS FOR PATIENTS WITH MUSCULOSKELETAL PAIN	
Core	

• Education
• Exercise
  Aerobic conditioning
  Strengthening
	• Reduction of adverse mechanical factors
	  Pacing of activities
	  Appropriate footwear
	• Weight reduction if obese
	• Simple analgesia

Other options	

• Other analgesic drugs
  Oral NSAIDs
  Topical creams
  Opioid analgesics
  Amitriptyline
• Slow-acting antirheumatic drugs
	• Corticosteroids
	• Local injections
	• Physical treatments
	  Aids, appliances
	• Surgery
	• Coping strategies

and drug options from which to select, the choice depending largely on the nature and severity of the MSK diagnosis.

CORE INTERVENTIONS

Education

It is every doctor's responsibility to inform patients about the nature of their condition and its investigation, treatment and prognosis. As well as this being a professional responsibility, education can improve outcome.

Information access and therapist contact can reduce pain and disability, improve self-efficacy and reduce the healthcare costs of many MSK conditions, including osteoarthritis and rheumatoid arthritis. This is by unknown mechanisms other than improved adherence to the management plan. Such benefits are modest but potentially long-lasting, safe and cost-effective (see EBM panel). Education can be provided in various ways, including one-to-one discussion with health professionals, written literature, patient group education classes (with patients leading the sessions) and interactive computer programs. Inclusion of the patient's partner or carer is often appropriate; this is clearly essential for childhood conditions but also beneficial for many chronic adult conditions such as rheumatoid arthritis or fibromyalgia.

EBM
MANAGEMENT OF ARTHRITIS—role of education
'RCTs have shown that education as an intervention results in substantial and prolonged benefits in terms of perceived ability to manage arthritis, reduction in pain and improved psychological well-being.'
• Barlow JH, Turner AP, Wright CC. Long-term outcomes of an arthritis self-management programme. Br J Rheumatol 1998; 37:1315–1319. • Fries JF, Carey C, McShane DJ. Patient education in arthritis: randomized controlled trial of a mail-delivered program. J Rheumatol 1997; 24:1378–1383. • Mazzuca SA, Brandt KD, Katz BP, et al. Reduced utilization and cost of primary care clinic visits resulting from self-care education for patients with osteoarthritis of the knee. Arthritis Rheum 1999; 42:1267–1273.
Further information: 💻 www.cochrane.co.uk

Exercise

MSK tissues require regular movement for their health. If compromised by disease, it is even more important to maintain movement. Two types of exercise commonly require prescription:

- *Aerobic fitness training* can produce long-term reduction in MSK pain and disability. It improves well-being, encourages restorative sleep and benefits common comorbidity such as obesity, diabetes, chronic heart failure and hypertension.
- *Local strengthening exercise* for muscles that act over compromised joints also reduces pain and disability, with accompanying improvements in the reduced muscle strength, proprioception, coordination and balance that associate with chronic arthritis. 'Small amounts, often' of strengthening exercise are better than protracted episodes performed infrequently.

Reduction of adverse mechanical factors

Excessive impact-loading and adverse repetitive usage of a compromised joint or periarticular tissue can often be reduced through discussion with the patient: for example, cessation of avoidable activities such as contact sports, or altered use of machinery or tools at the workplace. Simple 'pacing' of activities—dividing physically onerous tasks into shorter segments with brief breaks in between—is relevant to any patient with MSK pain. Use of shock-absorbing footwear with thick soft soles can reduce impact-loading through feet, knees, hips and back, and improve symptoms at these sites. A walking-stick held on the contralateral side takes weight off a painful hip, knee or foot.

Advice on weight loss if obese

Obesity aggravates pain at most sites of the body through increased mechanical strain, and is a risk factor for more rapid progression of joint damage in patients with arthritis. Obese subjects should receive an explanation of the mechanical effects and health implications of their weight and be offered strategies on how to lose weight initially and then maintain an appropriate weight.

Simple analgesia

Paracetamol (1 g 6–8-hourly) is the oral analgesic of choice and, if successful, the preferred long-term oral analgesic. This is because of its efficacy, lack of contraindications or drug interactions, long-term safety, low cost and availability. Paracetamol inhibits prostaglandin synthesis centrally in the brain but has no effect on peripheral production of prostaglandins.

OTHER TREATMENTS

PHARMACOLOGICAL OPTIONS FOR DIRECT SYMPTOM CONTROL

Non-steroidal anti-inflammatory drugs (NSAIDs)

These are among the top five most prescribed drugs in many countries. Oral NSAIDs are often effective for the pain and stiffness of inflammatory disease. Long-acting NSAIDs given at night are particularly helpful for marked inflammatory early morning stiffness. NSAIDs also often reduce bone pain due to secondary malignant lesions. For chronic symptoms they may need to be taken for 2–3 weeks before their optimal effect is seen. Although NSAIDs show similar overall efficacy, there is marked variability in individual patient tolerance and response; patients who do not respond to one may still experience symptom relief from another.

NSAIDs reduce prostaglandin levels through inhibition of prostaglandin H synthase or cyclo-oxygenase (COX). Arachidonic acid, derived from membrane phospholipids, is catalysed to prostaglandins and leukotrienes by the COX and 5-lipoxygenase pathways respectively (see Fig. 20.17). There are two isoforms of COX, encoded by distinct genes and differing in their distribution and expression. COX-1 is constitutively expressed and functions largely as a 'house-keeping' enzyme in tissues such as the gastric mucosa, platelets and kidneys. In contrast, the 'inflammatory' enzyme COX-2, although constitutively expressed in some tissues (brain, ovary, uterus, cartilage, bone, kidney), is largely induced at sites of inflammation, producing prostaglandins that are involved in peripheral inflammation and pain. In response to inflammation COX-2 is also upregulated in the central nervous system, where it plays an essential role in the central mediation of pain and production of fever. Although NSAIDs inhibit both COX enzymes, COX-2 inhibition is largely responsible for their analgesic, anti-inflammatory and antipyretic effects. Whilst NSAIDs have 'anti-inflammatory' activity they do not reduce peripheral cytokine production, acute phase reactants or ESR.

Side-effects of NSAIDs

The major drawback of NSAIDs is gastrointestinal toxicity. They can damage the gastric mucosal barrier and are an important aetiological factor in up to 30% of gastric ulcers. These drugs also reduce the integrity of the duodenal mucosa but are probably responsible for only a small proportion of duodenal ulcers. They greatly increase the risk of bleeding or perforation from pre-existing gastric and duodenal ulcers.

Mechanisms of NSAID toxicity. Prostaglandins of the E series also play a major role in the maintenance of gastro-duodenal defence mechanisms. By depleting mucosal prostaglandin levels, aspirin and NSAIDs impair this 'cytoprotection', resulting in mucosal injury, erosions and ulceration. The risks are appreciable.

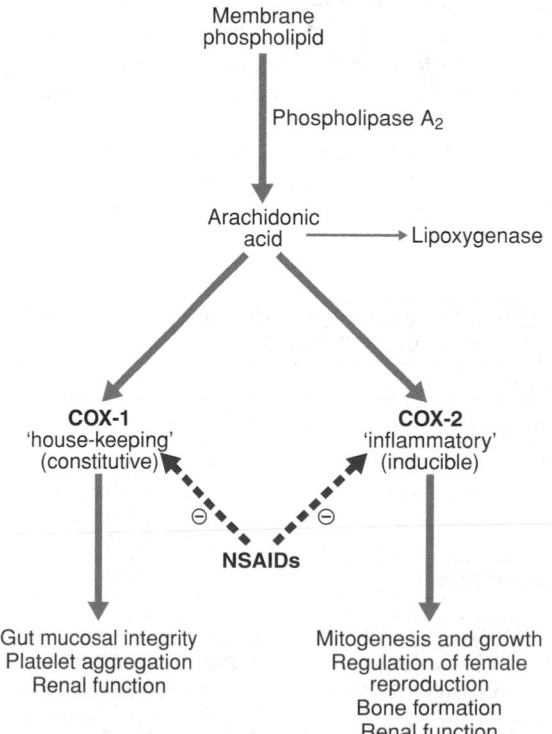

Fig. 20.17   COX-1 and COX-2 pathways.

20.31 SOME COMMONLY USED NSAIDs AND THEIR RELATIVE RISK OF GASTRODUODENAL BLEEDING AND PERFORATION

Drug	Daily dose	Doses/day	Idiosyncratic side-effects, comments
Low risk			
Ibuprofen	< 1.6 g	3–4	Weak anti-inflammatory effect at this dose
Etodolac	600 mg	1	Partially selective COX-2 inhibitor
Meloxicam	7.5–15 mg	1	Partially selective COX-2 inhibitor
Nabumetone	500–1500 mg	1–2	Partially selective COX-2 inhibitor
Medium risk			
Ibuprofen	1600–2400 mg	3–4	
Naproxen	500–1000 mg	1–2	
Diclofenac	75–100 mg	2–3	Abnormal liver function tests
High risk			
Indometacin	50–200 mg	3–4	High incidence of dyspepsia and CNS side-effects (headache, dizziness, confusion)
Ketoprofen	100–200 mg	2–4	
Highest risk			
Piroxicam	10–30 mg	1–2	Restricted use, especially in those over 60 years
Azapropazone	1200 mg	2–4	Marked uricosuric action
			Restricted use, especially in those over 60 years

For example:

- Approximately 1% of patients with rheumatoid arthritis or osteoarthritis are hospitalised each year because of NSAID-associated gastroduodenal bleeding.
- Endoscopic evidence of peptic ulceration is found in 20% of NSAID users even in the absence of symptoms.
- The annual mortality from NSAID-associated bleeding/perforation is estimated to be about 16 000 people in the US and 2000 in the UK (i.e. higher than deaths from diseases such as myeloma, asthma, cervical cancer or Hodgkin's disease).

The adjusted increased risk (odds ratio) of bleeding or perforation from all NSAIDs is 4–5, though differences exist between NSAIDs (see Box 20.31).

Dyspepsia is no guide to the presence of NSAID-associated ulceration, or to the risk of complications. Principal risk factors for NSAID-associated bleeding and perforation are shown in Box 20.32, the most important being ageing and previous history of peptic ulceration. The main risk of dying from bleeding or perforation is in the elderly and in those with comorbidity, especially cardio-vascular disease. Co-prescription of omeprazole (20 mg daily) or misoprostol (200 μg 8–12-hourly) can reduce the incidence of NSAID-associated ulceration and complications, but H_2 antagonists are ineffective in this respect.

Recently, highly selective COX-2 inhibitors with no physi-ologically evident COX-1 inhibition have been developed ('coxibs'—celecoxib 100–200 mg 12-hourly, rofecoxib 12.5–25 mg once daily). These associate with no increased risk of gastroduodenal ulceration. They do, however, have other NSAID side-effects and currently are relatively expen-sive.

Management of NSAID-induced ulcers. Where possible, the offending drug should be stopped. If an NSAID must be continued, then one with a lower risk of complications, e.g. ibuprofen or diclofenac, should be used at the lowest effec-tive dose. Co-prescription of a proton pump inhibitor (e.g. omeprazole 40 mg daily) will heal most, but not all, ulcers.

20.32 RISK FACTORS FOR NSAID-INDUCED ULCERS

- Age > 60 years
- Past history of peptic ulcer
- Past history of adverse event with NSAIDs
- Concomitant corticosteroid use
- High-dose or multiple NSAIDs
- Individual NSAID—highest with azapropazone, piroxicam, ketoprofen; lower with ibuprofen

EBM

NSAID-INDUCED PEPTIC ULCER—role of omeprazole

'Omeprazole is more effective than either misoprostol or ranitidine in healing peptic ulcers in patients taking NSAIDs. Omeprazole reduces the risk of new ulcer formation in patients taking NSAIDs.'

- Yeomans ND, Tulassay Z, Juhasz L, et al. A comparison of omeprazole with ranitidine for ulcers associated with nonsteroidal antiinflammatory drugs. Acid Suppression Trial: Ranitidine versus Omeprazole for NSAID-associated Ulcer Treatment (ASTRONAUT) Study Group. N Engl J Med 1998; 33:719–726.
- Hawkey CJ, Karrasch JA, Szczepanski L, et al. Omeprazole compared with misoprostol for ulcers associated with nonsteroidal antiinflammatory drugs. Omeprazole versus Misoprostol for NSAID-induced Ulcer Management (OMNIUM) Study Group. N Engl J Med 1998; 338:727–734.

Other important common side-effects of NSAIDs. These include fluid retention (renal effects of COX-1 and COX-2 inhibition), non-ulcer-associated dyspepsia, abdominal pain and altered bowel habit, and rashes. Interstitial nephritis, asthma and anaphylaxis are rare. There are concerns that long-term NSAIDs may hasten cartilage and bone damage in osteoarthritis, but human data on this are sparse. Unlike other NSAIDs aspirin causes irreversible, rather than reversible, inhibition of platelet COX-1, even at low doses (which have little effect on most tissue COX-2). Higher doses of aspirin or salicylate are required for effective anti-inflammatory (COX-2) activity, but because of frequent toxicity at such doses they have been superseded by other NSAIDs for relief of MSK symptoms.

Advice on NSAID prescribing is summarised in Box 20.33.

20.33 RECOMMENDATIONS FOR THE USE OF NSAIDs

- Current use of anticoagulants is a contraindication to NSAID use
- Try to avoid the use of NSAIDs in the elderly and in those with important comorbidity
- Start with the lowest dose of one of the safer established NSAIDs (e.g. ibuprofen) and only increase the dose if required
- If an unsatisfactory result is obtained with one NSAID, a trial of another NSAID may still be warranted
- Never prescribe more than one NSAID at a time
- Allow a 2–3-week trial to assess efficacy of any particular NSAID or dose
- For a patient with recognised risk factors for GI ulceration (see Box 20.32) consider co-prescription with omeprazole or misoprostol or use of a coxib

ISSUES IN OLDER PEOPLE
USE OF ORAL NSAIDs

- Age is a strong risk factor for major gastrointestinal complications (bleeding, perforation) of NSAID-associated peptic ulceration.
- Older people, especially those with cardiovascular comorbidity, are more likely to die if they suffer NSAID-associated bleeding or perforation.
- Older people are at greater risk of renal and cardiovascular side-effects of NSAIDs (peripheral oedema, cardiac failure).
- Co-prescription of proton pump inhibitors or misoprostol reduces, but does not eliminate, the risk of life-threatening GI complications, and is relatively expensive.
- Coxibs have a better GI safety profile than other oral NSAIDs but still associate with renal and cardiovascular complications in the elderly.
- For many elderly people oral paracetamol is as effective as oral NSAID for pain relief; because of its greater safety and low expense it remains the oral analgesic of choice.

Nutripharmaceuticals

A wide variety of compounds are available as food supplements and 'health foods' for relief of MSK symptoms. Their rationale for treatment is not always clear, though some, such as glucosamine sulphate and chondroitin sulphate, are normal constituents of cartilage, and others (e.g. selenium, zinc, manganese, copper, and vitamins C, D and E) are trace or oligo-elements required for normal health. Evidence from clinical trials is largely absent, though there are some data that glucosamine, chondroitin and avocado/soybean may provide a slow onset (after several weeks) of modest pain relief in knee osteoarthritis, and that regular glucosamine may slow further structural damage. Interest in such apparently safe compounds is growing and large independent clinical trials to determine the extent of their efficacy are in progress. Currently, however, these agents remain unlicensed and are available for self-medication only.

Topical agents

NSAID creams and gels and capsaicin (chilli extract) cream (0.025%) are both often effective for pain relief from arthritis, especially osteoarthritis, and superficial periarticular lesions affecting hands, elbows and knees. Topical NSAIDs can penetrate to superficial tissues and even to the joint capsule, though intrasynovial levels mainly reflect secondary blood-borne delivery. Topical capsaicin causes pain fibres to discharge substance P. Initial application causes a burning sensation, but continued use 6-hourly depletes substance P, with subsequent pain reduction that is optimal after 1–2 weeks. Topical NSAIDs and capsaicin are extremely safe and may be used as monotherapy or as adjunctive treatment with paracetamol or other oral analgesics. They are particularly suited to patients with just one or a few painful regions but not for multiple regional or deep-seated axial pain. Topical rubefacients may act through counter-irritation. They often contain several compounds (e.g. nicotinates, camphor, diethylamine, chilli extract) and are mainly available over the counter for self-medication.

Opioid analgesics

Stronger analgesics are sometimes required for moderate to severe pain which is unresponsive to other drug and non-pharmacological approaches. The non-opioid nefopam (30–90 mg 8-hourly) can help moderate MSK pain, though sympathomimetic and antimuscarinic side-effects (nausea, nervousness, dry mouth) often limit its use. Codeine, dihydrocodeine and dextropropoxyphene are relatively mild analgesics, but when combined with paracetamol may give better analgesia than paracetamol alone. Any benefit, however, is often offset by side-effects such as constipation, headache and confusion, especially in the elderly. Because dependence and tolerance may develop with continuous use such combinations are mainly reserved for intermittent control of painful 'flares'.

The centrally acting analgesics tramadol and meptazinol may be useful for temporary, but not long-term, control of severe pain unresponsive to other measures. The opioid analogue tramadol (50–100 mg up to 4-hourly, maximum 400 mg/day) may produce analgesia by several mechanisms—as a non-selective agonist at opioid (mainly μ) receptors, by inhibiting neuronal re-uptake of noradrenaline, and by enhancing 5-hydroxytryptamine (5-HT, serotonin) release. Meptazinol (200 mg 6-hourly) has mixed agonist and antagonist actions at opioid receptors with highest affinity for μ receptors. Both drugs have poor tolerability due to nausea, bowel upset, dizziness and somnolence, and withdrawal symptoms after chronic use. Patients who appear to require such opioids for MSK pain merit assessment by specialist teams.

Amitriptyline

This tricyclic antidepressant with sedative properties prevents neuronal re-uptake and hence inactivation of noradrenaline and 5-HT. When given at lower doses (25–75 mg at night) than are used for depression it can be an effective adjunctive treatment for chronic MSK pain, especially when accompanied by non-restorative sleep. It is the primary drug treatment for fibromyalgia.

SLOW-ACTING ANTIRHEUMATIC DRUGS

There are an increasing number of drugs that, like corticosteroids, non-specifically suppress chronic inflammatory disease. In contrast to corticosteroids, these drugs have a delayed action and must be taken for weeks or months before benefit occurs. Their precise mode of action is unclear. Nevertheless, such slow-acting drugs can reduce clinical signs of inflammation and improve or normalise objective parameters of the acute phase response. For some agents there is evidence that a successful response may reduce target tissue damage, hence the alternative name 'disease-modifying antirheumatic drug' (DMARD).

Slow-acting drugs are commonly indicated for rheumatoid arthritis, seronegative spondarthritis, juvenile idiopathic arthritis and connective tissue diseases (see Box 20.34). The main indications for use are:

- persistent synovitis (> 6 weeks)
- severe extra-articular disease (e.g. vasculitis, scleritis, renal involvement)
- steroid-sparing effect (e.g. polymyalgia rheumatica resistant to low-dose steroid)
- inflammatory myositis.

All such drugs require regular monitoring for recognised side-effects and are contraindicated in pregnancy, especially the first trimester. They are mainly used as monotherapy, though certain combinations are increasingly used for rheumatoid arthritis. Slow-acting drugs are taken in addition to the patient's pain-relieving drugs, but if successful may reduce analgesic and NSAID requirements. Average doses, principal toxicity and monitoring requirements of slow-acting drugs are summarised in Box 20.34.

Hydroxychloroquine

This antimalarial is often effective for mild to moderate lupus, especially when skin or locomotor involvement predominates. It is a relatively weak antirheumatic drug for rheumatoid arthritis, with a slower than usual onset of action (2–4 months). Despite a wide range of potential side-effects it is usually well tolerated.

20.34 EXAMPLES OF MORE COMMONLY USED SLOW-ACTING ANTIRHEUMATIC DRUGS

Drug	Disease indications	Usual maintenance dose	Principal side-effects	Monitoring requirement	Frequency
Hydroxychloroquine	RA, lupus	200–400 mg/day	Rash, nausea, diarrhoea, headache, corneal deposits, retinopathy (rare)	Visual acuity, Amsler chart, fundoscopy	6–12-monthly
Sulfasalazine	RA, seroneg	2–3 g/day	Nausea, GI upset, rash, hepatitis, neutropenia, pancytopenia (rare)	FBC, LFT	Monthly for 3 months, then 3-monthly
D-penicillamine	RA	250–750 mg/day	Rash, stomatitis, metallic taste, proteinuria, thrombocytopenia	FBC, urine (protein)	Initially 1–2-weekly; 4–6-weekly for maintenance
Gold	RA	50 mg/month by i.m. injection	Rash, stomatitis, alopecia, proteinuria, thrombocytopenia, myelosuppression	FBC, urine (protein)	Each injection
Methotrexate	RA, seroneg, lupus, CTD, vasculitis, PMR	5–25 mg/week	GI upset, stomatitis, rash, alopecia, hepatotoxicity, acute pneumonitis	FBC, LFT	Monthly
Azathioprine	RA, seroneg, lupus, CTD, vasculitis, PMR	50–150 mg/day	GI upset, stomatitis, hepatitis, myelosuppression	FBC, LFT	Initially weekly, then monthly
Leflunomide	RA	20 mg/day	Nausea, GI upset, rash, alopecia, hepatitis, hypertension	FBC, LFT, blood pressure	2–4-weekly
Cyclophosphamide	Vasculitis, lupus, myositis	0.5–1 g by i.v. injection, 1–4-weekly	Nausea, GI upset, alopecia, cystitis, myelosuppression, azoospermia, anovulation	FBC, urine (blood)	Each i.v. injection
Chlorambucil	RA	4–8 mg/day	Nausea, GI upset, myelosuppression, azoospermia, anovulation	FBC, LFT	Monthly
Ciclosporin (cyclosporin)	RA, psoriasis, lupus	150–300 mg/day	Nausea, GI upset, hepatotoxicity, renal impairment, hypertension	FBC, LFT, creatinine, blood pressure	2–4-weekly

(RA = rheumatoid arthritis; PMR = polymyalgia rheumatica; seroneg = peripheral arthritis due to seronegative spondarthritis; CTD = connective tissue disease; FBC = full blood count; LFT = liver function tests)

Sulfasalazine

This compound has a good benefit-to-risk profile and is often a first-choice agent for rheumatoid and for the peripheral (not axial) arthritis of seronegative spondarthritis. Nausea and gastrointestinal intolerance are usually avoided by using enteric-coated tablets (500 mg), always taken with food, starting with one tablet daily and building up to the full dose over 2 weeks. The patient should be warned of possible orange staining of urine and contact lenses.

D-penicillamine and intramuscular gold

These old-established treatments are now not first-choice drugs for rheumatoid arthritis because of their high incidence of side-effects. Their main toxicity is marrow suppression, immune-complex nephritis (proteinuria, nephrotic syndrome), rashes and mouth ulcers.

D-penicillamine is started at 125–250 mg daily, away from food, with 125 mg increments every 6 weeks until benefit occurs (maximum 750 mg/day). Reversible metallic taste, rashes, nausea and febrile reactions may occur early; later side-effects include mouth ulcers and nephritis. Very rarely, the drug induces disease resembling lupus, myasthenia gravis or pemphigus. Thrombocytopenia and pancytopenia can develop at any time and are the major concerns. Proteinuria, mild thrombocytopenia, or dropping platelet counts on sequential tests are indications to stop the drug. It may be slowly reintroduced if the abnormalities disappear but should be withdrawn altogether if they recur. Pancytopenia and febrile reactions are absolute indications for drug withdrawal.

Gold (sodium aurothiomalate) is given by deep intramuscular injection. After a small test dose (10 mg) injections of 50 mg are given weekly until benefit occurs, usually by 2–3 months. Injections are then spaced to fortnightly and then monthly. If there is a flare a temporary return to weekly frequency may recapture control. If there is no initial benefit after 6 months, it is abandoned. Any side-effect that develops is potentially serious and precludes further therapy. Pruritic rashes may respond to antihistamines but corticosteroids are indicated for severe exfoliative rashes, marrow suppression and nephropathy. Patients with agranulocytosis usually recover if appropriately managed, but aplastic anaemia carries a significant mortality.

Non-specific anti-inflammatory immunosuppressive drugs

Several cytotoxic and immunomodulatory drugs have slow-acting antirheumatic actions at low doses. Their use is mainly limited by toxicity. Because they often impair immunocyte number and function, they may compromise immunosurveillance and increase the risk of neoplasia, especially solid tumours and lymphomas. Such risks are difficult to estimate, especially since the primary condition itself may have an increased risk. In general, risk of drug-induced neoplasia is lower in patients with rheumatic disease compared to organ transplant patients, possibly reflecting the lower doses used. Evidence for a significant risk of neoplasia mainly relates to cyclophosphamide and chlorambucil. Another generic side-effect is increased risk of infection, bacterial and/or viral (e.g. zoster), though this needs balancing against the increased risk of infection in patients with uncontrolled systemic inflammatory disease.

Methotrexate

This antimetabolite competitively inhibits dihydrofolate reductase, interfering with DNA synthesis and cell division and causing cytotoxicity at high doses. It is often the first-choice slow-acting drug (or second after sulfasalazine or hydroxychloroquine) for rheumatoid arthritis, peripheral synovitis of seronegative spondarthritis, lupus or connective tissue disease. It works relatively quickly, often within 1–2 months. It is usually given as a weekly oral dose starting at 5 mg and increasing in 2.5 mg increments every 3–4 weeks until benefit occurs (maximum 30 mg). It is usually well tolerated but can cause nausea and malaise for 24–48 hours after ingestion. Marrow suppression is rare but hepatotoxicity and hepatic fibrosis may occur, especially at higher doses. Folic acid (5 mg/day) reduces the incidence of adverse effects without reducing efficacy. Patients should be warned of drug interaction with sulphonamides and to avoid excess alcohol, which enhances methotrexate hepatotoxicity. Acute pulmonary toxicity is rare but can occur at any time during treatment. Patients should therefore be warned to seek early advice if they develop unexplained breathlessness.

Azathioprine

Following absorption, azathioprine is metabolised to 6-mercaptopurine (6-MP), which is then converted intracellularly to active purine thioanalogues. These purine antimetabolites remain in the cell and inhibit DNA and RNA biosynthesis. The oral dose range is 1.5–2.5 mg/kg/day with food. Common adverse effects are nausea, diarrhoea and mouth ulcers; hepatitis and marrow suppression are less common. Since 6-MP requires oxidation by xanthine oxidase before renal excretion, coadministration of allopurinol increases its toxicity; if both drugs are required, azathioprine should be reduced to 25% of the original dose.

Leflunomide

This novel isoxazole inhibits both uridine monophosphate production and tyrosine kinases and is an effective inhibitor of activated lymphocytes. It is currently only indicated for rheumatoid arthritis. It is given orally as a loading dose for 3 days (100 mg daily), followed by a daily dose of 20 mg. It is usually well tolerated, with low marrow toxicity.

Cyclophosphamide and chlorambucil

These alkylating agents directly bind DNA, RNA and other proteins. Both are potentially mutagenic and teratogenic. Cyclophosphamide is the most commonly used. It is inactive until converted by the cytochrome P-450 oxidase system to phosphoramide mustard and acrolein. It may be given daily as tablets (1–2 mg/kg/day) or more commonly, for induction of remission, as 'pulse' intravenous injections (0.5–1.5 g/m²) weekly or monthly. Common adverse effects include nausea, vomiting, reversible alopecia and susceptibility to infection. The incidence of acrolein-related haemorrhagic cystitis is reduced by good hydration and ingestion of mesna. Because of the high risk of azoospermia and anovulation, which may be permanent, pre-treatment sperm or ova collection and storage may need consideration.

Ciclosporin (cyclosporin) A

This is a fungal cyclic polypeptide that blocks resting lymphocytes in the G_0 or G_1 phase of the cell cycle, inhibiting lymphokine production and release. It is toxic and expensive and usually reserved for patients resistant to other slow-acting agents. Its dose range is 2.5–4 mg/kg daily given in two divided doses 12-hourly.

TARGETED ANTICYTOKINE TREATMENT

A number of agents with specific actions to inhibit the effects of individual cytokines are now being developed. Tumour necrosis factor alpha (TNF-α) and interleukin-1 (IL-1) are central mediators of inflammation and joint tissue destruction in rheumatoid arthritis. Two anti-TNF biological agents have recently been licensed in several countries for the treatment of active rheumatoid disease. Etanercept is a recombinant protein consisting of a dimer of the extracellular portion of two p75 TNF receptors fused to the Fc portion of human IgG1, administered subcutaneously twice weekly. Infliximab is a chimeric human-murine monoclonal antibody to TNF, administered by i.v. infusion every 1–2 months. Methotrexate is co-prescribed to reduce immunogenicity of infliximab. Whilst both drugs appear to be more effective than standard DMARDs, in view of their cost (approximately £8000–£10 000 per patient per year) their use is currently recommended only when an adequate trial of at least two other DMARDs has failed. The main potential side-effect is a risk of serious infection, particularly reactivation of latent tuberculosis. There is a theoretical risk of immunosuppression-related malignancy, but there are as yet no long-term studies to quantify these risks. Subcutaneous daily injection of IL-1 receptor antagonist has also proved effective in reducing symptoms and radiographic damage in rheumatoid arthritis but is not yet licensed. It is hoped that in the near future a variety of biological anticytokine agents will individually, or in combination, prove very effective treatments for severe inflammatory MSK disease.

CORTICOSTEROIDS

Corticosteroids have a very rapid and dramatic anti-inflammatory action. However, the doses required to maintain adequate symptomatic relief are accompanied by an unacceptable level of side-effects. Furthermore, whether corticosteroids have any disease-modifying antirheumatic activity remains in question. Indications for their use are therefore restricted. Since the incidence of steroid-related side-effects are largely dose- and duration-dependent, the aim is always to use the smallest amount for the shortest time possible to achieve the therapeutic goal.

The main indications for oral or parenteral steroid are listed in Box 20.35. In most cases steroid is initiated for rapid control of inflammatory disease at the same time as commencing a slow-acting antirheumatic drug. After just a few months, when the slow-acting drug is exerting benefit, the steroid is withdrawn. It is usual to gain control with a high initial dose of steroid that is then rapidly reduced to the lowest dose that will maintain control.

20.35 PRINCIPAL INDICATIONS FOR ORAL OR PARENTERAL CORTICOSTEROID

- For rapid, short-term (1–3 months) control of marked synovitis or systemic inflammation while awaiting efficacy from slow-acting antirheumatic agent
- For life-threatening (e.g. vasculitis) or organ-threatening (e.g. kidney, lung, eye) inflammatory multisystem disease
- For primary treatment of polymyalgia rheumatica
- For control of inflammatory disease during pregnancy

Prednisolone has predominantly glucocorticoid activity and is the oral steroid of choice. To minimise hypothalamo-pituitary-adrenal axis suppression it should be given as a single morning dose to coincide with peak levels of endogenous cortisol. Initial dosage is up to 10–20 mg daily (45–60 mg for very severe disease). The dose can often be reduced after just a few days and the aim for maintenance is a dose of 7.5 mg daily or less. If higher doses are being required, institution of a slow-acting antirheumatic drug should always be considered. Potential side-effects are numerous (see Box 20.36), although steroid-induced osteoporosis, infection and increased mortality from ischaemic heart disease are the major concerns. Patients receiving oral corticosteroid should be given appropriate bone prophylaxis (see p. 1028) and have any infections treated promptly.

Intramuscular injection of methylprednisolone (80–120 mg) may quickly and effectively control inflammation for variable periods (2–6 weeks). Such an approach, repeated if necessary at 3–6-week intervals, may provide equivalent short-term control whilst avoiding some of the problems of daily prednisolone.

LOCAL INJECTIONS

Intra-articular injections

Injection of a long-acting steroid (e.g. triamcinolone acetonide or hexacetonide) may be useful adjunctive therapy for short-term pain relief (osteoarthritis, inflammatory arthritis) and for temporary control of synovitis of just one or a few joints. The duration of benefit varies according to joint size and the nature and severity of the arthritis, but is in the order of 2–8 weeks. Frequently repeated injections may result in joint tissue atrophy and Cushing's syndrome, and some advise no more than four injections per year into a large joint like the knee. The following simple precautions should be observed:

- Never inject if the diagnosis is in doubt.
- Do not inject if there is local or systemic infection.
- Use an aseptic technique—single ampoules, sterile needle and syringe, clean hands, clean skin (alcohol/antiseptic).
- If aspirated fluid is turbid, send it for culture.

If sensible precautions are taken, the incidence of iatrogenic infection is extremely low. Other unwanted effects are:

- facial flushing 24–72 hours post-injection
- local skin atrophy, telangiectasia and permanent fat atrophy due to leakage along needle track (especially with fluorinated triamcinolone preparations)

20.36 SIDE-EFFECTS OF CORTICOSTEROIDS

Endocrine

- Moon face
- Truncal obesity
- Hirsutism
- Impotence
- Menstrual irregularity
- Suppression of hypothalamo-pituitary-adrenal axis
- Growth suppression

Metabolic

- Negative calcium, potassium and nitrogen balance
- Sodium and fluid retention
- Hyperglycaemia
- Hyperlipoproteinaemia

Musculoskeletal

- Osteoporosis
- Proximal myopathy
- Avascular necrosis

Skin

- Acne
- Thin skin, easy bruising
- Facial erythema, telangiectasia
- Striae
- Impaired wound healing

Immunological

- Susceptibility to infection
- Suppression of delayed hypersensitivity
- Lymphopenia
- Possible reactivation of TB

Gastrointestinal

- Impaired healing of NSAID-induced peptic ulcers
- Pancreatitis

Cardiovascular

- Hypertension
- Ischaemic heart disease
- Congestive heart failure

Ocular

- Glaucoma
- Cataracts (posterior, subcapsular)

CNS

- Changes in mood and personality
- Hyperactivity, insomnia
- Psychosis
- Benign intracranial hypertension

- post-injection 'flare' with temporary (1–3 days) symptom exacerbation.

In knee osteoarthritis intra-articular injection of one of several forms of hyaluronan (polymers of hyaluronate) given as a course of weekly injections for 3–5 weeks can give modest pain relief that may be more prolonged (3–6 months) than following a single injection of steroid. Intra-articular injection of radiocolloid (e.g. ^{90}yttrium silicate for large to medium joints, ^{159}erbium for small joints) can give prolonged control of synovitis ('medical' or 'radiation' synovectomy) but should be avoided in patients under the age of 45. Joints are immobilised for 24–72 hours post-injection to reduce spread to regional lymph nodes. The synovium often recovers with return of synovitis after 1–3 years. Indications include: inflammatory synovitis (e.g. rheumatoid) where just one or a few joints are resistant to other measures; synovitis of chronic haemophilic arthropathy; and pigmented villonodular synovitis.

Periarticular injections

Injection of local steroid and/or anaesthetic may give rapid, effective control of pain from periarticular lesions (e.g. bursitis, tenosynovitis, enthesopathy). Such injection will not hasten healing (steroid may retard healing) but its analgesic effect may extend beyond the natural history of the lesion. The rationale for injection is therefore relief of severe or resistant pain. Non-fluorinated steroid should be used for superficial lesions (e.g. lateral epicondylitis, anserine bursitis) to avoid fat and skin atrophy. If anaesthetic is combined with the steroid, quick relief of pain confirms both the diagnosis and accurate placement of the injection. Injection of steroid into, or even adjacent to, certain tendons (e.g. long head of biceps tendon) can predispose to rupture and should be avoided. Steroid injection may also be used to confirm and temporarily benefit peripheral nerve entrapment (e.g. carpal tunnel injection for median nerve entrapment at the wrist).

Nerve blocks

Nerve blocks using steroid and/or long-acting anaesthetics may be helpful for control of severe chronic arthritis or periarticular pain resistant to other means (e.g. suprascapular nerve block for severe glenohumeral arthritis or chronic rotator cuff pain). Epidural injections of corticosteroid may also give temporary relief of troublesome root entrapment symptoms.

PHYSICAL TREATMENTS

Local heat, ice packs, wax baths and other local external applications can induce muscle relaxation and temporary relief of symptoms. Hydrotherapy permits muscle relaxation and enhanced movement in a warm, pain-relieving environment without the restraints of gravity and normal load-bearing. Various manipulative techniques may also help improve restricted movement. Such therapies are often combined with education and therapist contact and this enhances their benefits.

Splints can give temporary rest and support for painful joints and periarticular tissues, and prevent disadvantageous involuntary postures during sleep. Prolonged rest, however, must be avoided. Orthoses are more permanent appliances used to reduce instability and excessive abnormal movement. Examples include working wrist splints, knee orthoses, and iron and T-straps to control ankle instability. Orthoses are particularly suited for severely disabled patients in whom a surgical option is inappropriate, and often need to be custom-made for the individual.

For those with severe disabilities it may be more appropriate to modify the environment around the patient than to try to restore irreversibly damaged joints to normal usage. A variety of simple aids and appliances may transform the lives of disabled patients, permitting dignity and independence with respect to the activities of daily living. Common examples are a raised toilet seat, high rather than low chairs, extended handles on taps, a shower instead of a bath, thick-handled cutlery, and extended 'hands' to pull on tights and socks. Full assessment and advice from an occupational therapist can maximise the benefits from such adaptations.

SURGERY

There are a variety of surgical interventions that may relieve pain and conserve or restore function in patients with joint and periarticular disease (see Box 20.37).

Soft tissue release and tenosynovectomy may reduce inflammatory symptoms, improve function and prevent or retard tendon damage for variable periods, sometimes indefinitely. Synovectomy of joints does not prevent disease progression but may be indicated for pain relief when drugs, physical therapy and intra-articular injections have provided insufficient relief. Tendon repairs and transfers may also prove useful. The main approaches for damaged joints are osteotomy (cutting bone to alter joint mechanics and load transmission), excision arthroplasty (removing part or all of the joint), joint replacement (insertion of prosthesis in place of the excised joint) and arthrodesis (joint fusion).

The main aims of such operations are pain relief and improvements in function and quality of life. Patient expectations need to be realistic. If surgery is to be successful, the aims and consequences of each operation should be carefully explained and considered as part of an integrated programme of management and rehabilitation. This is often best achieved by multidisciplinary teams of surgeons, allied health professionals and physicians. Assessment of motivation, social support and environment are no less important than careful consideration of patients' general health, their risks for major surgery, the extent of disease in other joints and their ability to mobilise following the operation. In particular, it must be appreciated that for some severely compromised people pain relief and functional independence are better served by provision of a suitable wheelchair, home adjustments, physical aids and social services than by surgery that is technically successful but from which the patient cannot mobilise.

COPING STRATEGIES

These are approaches that help patients to cope better with, and to adjust to, their chronic pain and disability. They may be useful at any stage but should be considered particularly for patients with incurable problems who have received all other available treatment options. The aim is to increase self-management through self-assessment, information and problem-solving. This involves patients recognising negative but potentially remediable aspects of their psyche (stress, frustration, anger, low self-esteem or prestige) and their situation (e.g. physical, social, financial). These may then be addressed by changes in attitude and behaviour; for example:

- learning yoga and relaxation techniques to reduce stress
- avoiding negative situations or activities that regularly produce stress and increasing pleasant activities that give satisfaction
- altering beliefs about and perspectives on disease through information and discussion
- learning to reduce or avoid catastrophising and maladaptive pain behaviour
- learning imagery and distraction techniques for pain
- expanding social contact and better utilising social services.

Involvement of the spouse or partner in mutual goal-setting can improve partnership adjustment for individuals with persistent pain. Such approaches are often an element of group education classes and pain clinics, but may require more formal explanation from psychologists or cognitive behavioural therapists.

20.37 EXAMPLES OF COMMON USEFUL SURGICAL PROCEDURES	
Procedure	**Indication**
Soft tissue release (decompression)	
Carpal tunnel	Median nerve compression
Tarsal tunnel	Posterior tibial nerve entrapment
Flexor tenosynovectomy	Relief of 'trigger' fingers
Ulnar nerve transposition	Ulnar nerve entrapment at elbow
Fasciotomy	Severe Dupuytren's contracture
Tendon repairs and transfers	
Hand extensor tendons	Extensor tendon rupture
Thumb and finger flexor tendons	Flexor tendon rupture
Synovectomy	
Wrist and extensor tendon sheath (+ excision of radial head)	Pain relief and prevention of extensor tendon rupture in rheumatoid arthritis
Knee synovectomy	Resistant inflammatory synovitis
Osteotomy	
Femoral osteotomy	Early osteoarthritis of hip
Tibial osteotomy	Unicompartmental knee osteoarthritis
Excision arthroplasty	
First metatarsophalangeal joint (Keller's procedure)	Painful hallux valgus
Radial head	Painful distal radio-ulnar joint
Lateral end of clavicle	Painful acromioclavicular joint
Metatarsal head	Painful subluxed metatarsophalangeal joints
Joint replacement arthroplasty	
Knee, hip, shoulder, elbow	Established, successful procedures for painful damaged joints (mainly osteoarthritis)
Arthrodesis	
Wrist	Damaged joint—pain relief, improvement of grip
Ankle/subtalar joints	Damaged joint—pain relief, stabilisation of hindfoot

OSTEOARTHRITIS

Osteoarthritis (OA, osteoarthrosis) is by far the most common form of arthritis. It shows a strong association with ageing and is a major cause of pain and disability in the elderly. Pathologically, it may be defined as a condition of synovial joints characterised by:

- focal loss of articular hyaline cartilage
- simultaneous proliferation of new bone with remodelling of joint contour.

Inflammation is not a prominent feature. OA, however, is not a disease or a single condition. It is best viewed as the dynamic repair process of synovial joints that may be triggered by a variety of insults, some but not all of which result in symptomatic 'joint failure'.

Epidemiology

Radiographic and autopsy studies show that OA preferentially targets only certain small and large joints (see Fig. 20.18). There is a steady rise in overall prevalence from age 30 such that by 65, 80% of people have some radiographic evidence of OA, though only 25–30% have associated symptoms. The knee and hip are the principal large joints affected and the principal sites of significant disability. Knee OA is more prevalent than hip OA, but taken together they affect 10–25% of those aged over 65 years. Although joints not targeted by OA are in comparison rarely affected, OA remains the most common cause of arthritis at sites such as the elbow, glenohumeral joint or ankle because it is far more prevalent than are inflammatory arthropathies.

Both generalised constitutional and local biomechanical risk factors may predispose to development of OA (see Fig. 20.19). Their relative importance differs at each joint site and between individuals. Twin and family studies show that inheritance is a major attributable factor, particularly for hand and generalised OA but also for hip and knee OA, although the responsible genes have yet to be determined. Knee OA is prevalent in all racial groups but hip, hand and generalised OA are only prevalent in Caucasians. OA is more prevalent and more commonly associates with symptoms in women, except at the hip where both genders are equally affected. Although overt trauma is a commonly recognised local predisposing factor, more subtle repetitive adverse loading of joints during occupation or competitive sports also appears important. Recognised occupational risks for OA include farming (hip OA), mining (knee OA) and professional football (knee OA).

The correlation between the presence of structural OA (clinical signs, radiographic changes) and pain and disability varies according to site. Correlation is stronger at the hip than the knee, and poor at most small joint sites. Risk factors for pain and disability may differ from those for structural change. At the knee, for example, reduced quadriceps muscle strength and adverse psychosocial factors (anxiety, depression) correlate more strongly with pain and disability than the degree of radiographic change. Such factors are potentially modifiable, giving optimism with respect to treatment.

Aetiology and pathogenesis

A variety of mechanical, metabolic, genetic or constitutional insults may damage a synovial joint and trigger the need for repair. Most often the insult remains unclear ('primary' OA) but sometimes a clear cause such as trauma or ligament rupture may be apparent ('secondary' OA). All the joint tissues (cartilage, bone, synovium, capsule, ligament, muscle) depend on each other for health and function. Insult to any one tissue impacts on the others, resulting in a common OA phenotype affecting the whole joint. The OA process is metabolically active, involving new tissue production and remodelling of joint shape. Often the slow but efficient OA process compensates for the insults, resulting in an anatomically altered but pain-free functioning joint ('compensated' OA). Sometimes, however, because of either overwhelming

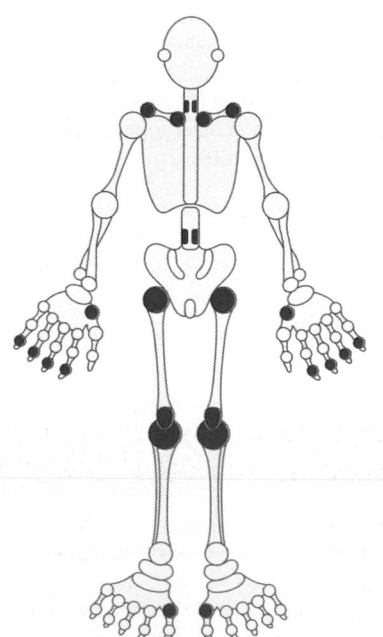

Fig. 20.18   The distribution of osteoarthritis. Although osteoarthritis can affect any synovial joint, those shown in red are the most commonly targeted.

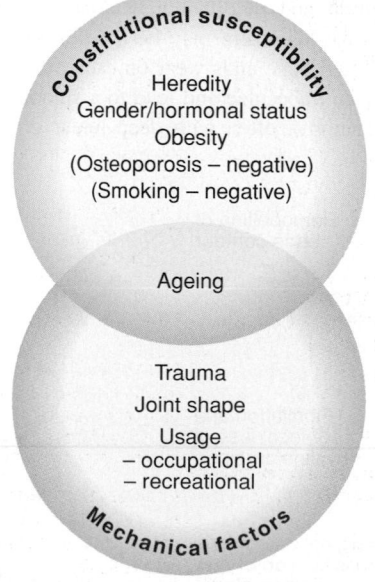

Fig. 20.19   Risk factors for the development of osteoarthritis.

or chronic insult or an inherently poor repair response, it fails, resulting in progressive tissue damage, more frequent association with symptoms, and presentation as an OA patient with 'joint failure'. Such a perspective readily explains the clinical heterogeneity of OA and the variable outcome observed.

Cartilage changes in OA are highly characteristic. There is enzymatic degradation of the major structural components aggrecan and collagen, principally by aggrecanase, collagenase and stromelysin. The chondrocytes increase their production of matrix components and divide to produce clones or nests of metabolically active chondrocytes. Although the turnover of aggrecan components is increased, the concentration of aggrecan eventually falls. The decrease in size of the hydrophilic aggrecan molecules increases the water concentration and swelling pressure in cartilage, further disrupting the retaining scaffolding of type II collagen and making the cartilage vulnerable to load-bearing injury. There is eventual fissuring of the cartilage surface ('fibrillation'), development of deep vertical clefts, localised chondrocyte death and decrease in cartilage thickness. Cartilage loss is focal rather than widespread and usually restricted to the maximum load-bearing part of the joint (see Fig. 20.20). The changes in OA cartilage encourage deposition of calcium pyrophosphate and apatite crystals, especially in the mid- and superficial zones.

The bone immediately below the compromised cartilage increases its trabecular thickness. In some cases this reflects healed trabecular microfractures. Holes ('cysts') often develop, possibly the result of small areas of osteonecrosis caused by the increased pressure in bone as the cartilage fails in its load-transmitting function. At the margins of the joint there is production of new fibrocartilage that then undergoes endochondral ossification to form osteophyte. Despite central and marginal new bone formation, with severe cartilage loss there may be attrition of bone as the two unprotected bone ends wear on each other. Such wear may ablate the trabeculae and lead to a smooth, shiny surface ('eburnation'), often with deep linear grooves. Bone remodelling and cartilage thinning slowly alter the shape of the OA joint, increasing its surface.

The synovium undergoes variable degrees of hyperplasia. Sometimes histological changes are as florid, though not as widespread, as those of rheumatoid arthritis. Osteochondral bodies commonly occur within the synovium, reflecting chondroid metaplasia within the synovium or secondary uptake and growth of damaged cartilage fragments. The outer capsule also thickens and contracts, usually retaining the stability of the remodelling joint. The muscles that act over the joint commonly show non-specific type II fibre atrophy.

Clinical features

The main presenting symptoms of OA are pain and functional restriction. Pain may directly relate to the OA process through increased pressure in subchondral bone (mainly causing night pain), trabecular microfractures, capsular distension and low-grade synovitis, or result from bursitis and enthesopathy secondary to the altered joint mechanics. OA pain typically has the characteristics listed in Box 20.38. For many people functional restriction of the hands, knees or hips is an equal problem to, if not greater problem than pain. The clinical findings vary according to severity but are principally those of joint damage.

It should be remembered that OA is prevalent in middle-aged and elderly subjects, and commonly asymptomatic. Therefore the presence of OA cannot necessarily be taken as an explanation of the patient's problem.

Nodal generalised OA

This common form of OA is characterised by:

- polyarticular finger interphalangeal joint (IPJ) OA
- Heberden's (± Bouchard's) nodes
- marked female preponderance
- peak onset in middle age
- good functional outcome for hands
- predisposition to OA at other joints, especially knees
- strong genetic predisposition.

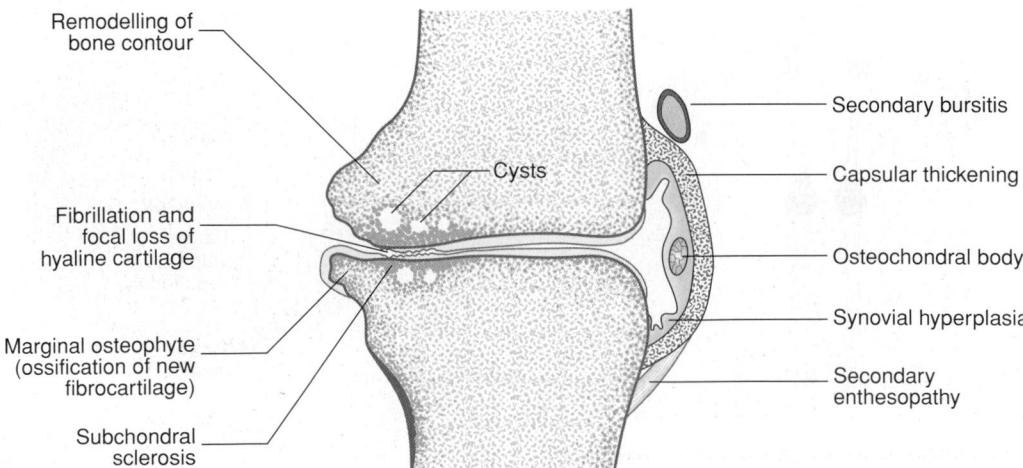

Fig. 20.20 **Pathological changes in osteoarthritis.**

Remodelling of bone contour
Cysts
Fibrillation and focal loss of hyaline cartilage
Marginal osteophyte (ossification of new fibrocartilage)
Subchondral sclerosis
Secondary bursitis
Capsular thickening
Osteochondral body
Synovial hyperplasia
Secondary enthesopathy

20.38 TYPICAL CHARACTERISTICS OF PAIN AND CLINICAL SIGNS OF OSTEOARTHRITIS

Pain

- Patient over age 45 (often over age 60)
- Insidious onset over months or years
- Variable or intermittent over time ('good days, bad days')
- Mainly related to movement and weight-bearing, relieved by rest
- Only brief (< 15 minutes) morning stiffness and brief (< 1 minute) 'gelling' after rest
- Usually only one or a few joints painful (not multiple regional pain)

Clinical signs

- Restricted movement (capsular thickening, blocking by osteophyte)
- Palpable, sometimes audible, coarse crepitus (rough articular surfaces)
- Bony swelling (osteophyte) around joint margins
- Deformity, usually without instability
- Joint-line or periarticular tenderness
- Muscle weakness, wasting
- No or only mild synovitis (effusion, increased warmth)

Presentation is typically in middle-aged women (in their forties or fifties) who develop pain, stiffness and swelling of one or a few finger IPJs. Gradually, over many months, more finger IPJs (distal > proximal) are recruited. Affected joints develop posterolateral swellings each side of the extensor tendon. They slowly enlarge and harden to become Heberden's (distal IPJ) and Bouchard's (proximal IPJ) nodes (see Fig. 20.21). Typically each joint goes through a phase of episodic symptoms (1–5 years) while the node evolves and OA develops in the underlying IPJ. Once fully established, however, symptoms usually subside and hand function often remains relatively unimpaired. Affected IPJs often show characteristic lateral deviation, reflecting the asymmetric focal cartilage loss of OA. Involvement of the first carpometacarpal joint is also common. At this site marked osteophyte and subluxation may result in 'thumb-base squaring'. Thumb-base OA occasionally causes more chronic symptoms and functional impairment than IPJ OA.

People who develop nodal OA are at increased risk of subsequently developing OA at other sites ('generalised OA'), especially the knee. Nodal generalised OA has a very strong genetic predisposition, probably the strongest of all major rheumatic conditions. Many patients give a clear family history, especially in their female relatives, and the daughter of an affected mother has a 1 in 3 chance of developing nodal OA herself. Nodal OA with multiple nodes and symptom onset in middle age should not be confused with just one or two asymptomatic nodes related to past trauma, a very common finding, particularly in the elderly. Some patients with otherwise typical nodal OA have a more prolonged symptom phase and more overt IPJ inflammation, and subsequently develop IPJ instability in some fingers, with subchondral erosions on radiographs. Such 'erosive' OA is uncommon and is probably part of the spectrum of nodal OA rather than a distinct subset.

Knee OA

OA principally targets the patello-femoral and medial tibio-femoral compartments of the knee. It may be isolated or occur as part of nodal generalised OA. Trauma is a more important risk factor in men and may result in unilateral OA. Most knee OA, particularly in women, is bilateral and symmetrical.

Most knee OA pain is well localised to the anterior or medial aspect of the knee and upper tibia. Patello-femoral pain is usually worse going up and down stairs or inclines. Posterior knee pain suggests a complicating popliteal 'cyst'. Common functional difficulties are prolonged walking, rising from a chair, getting in or out of a car, or bending to put on shoes and socks. Local examination findings may include:

- a jerky, asymmetric 'antalgic' gait (see p. 961)—less time weight-bearing on the painful side
- a varus (see Fig. 20.22), less commonly valgus, and/or fixed flexion deformity
- joint-line and/or periarticular tenderness (secondary anserine bursitis and medial ligament enthesopathy are common, giving tenderness of the upper medial tibia)
- weakness and wasting of the quadriceps muscle

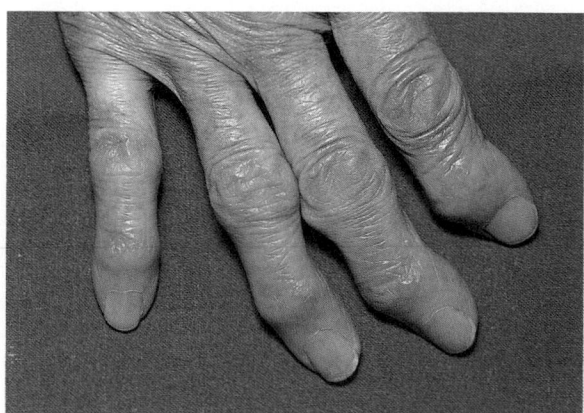

Fig. 20.21 Nodal osteoarthritis. Heberden's nodes and lateral deviation of distal interphalangeal joints, with mild Bouchard's nodes at the proximal interphalangeal joints.

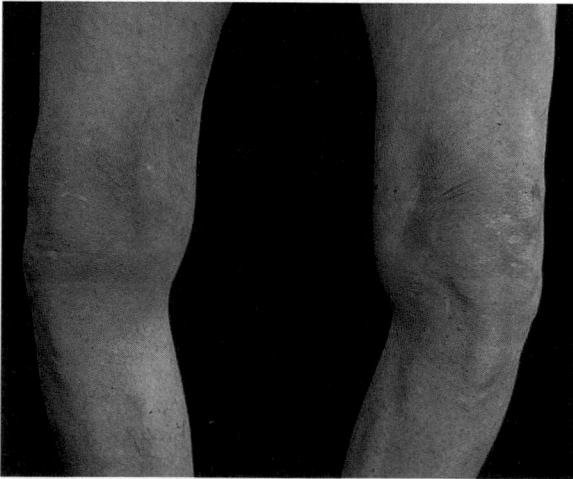

Fig. 20.22 Typical varus deformity resulting from marked medial tibio-femoral osteoarthritis.

- restricted flexion/extension with coarse crepitus
- bony swelling around the joint line.

It is at the knee that predisposition to calcium pyrophosphate dihydrate (CPPD) crystal deposition by OA is most evident. Such coexistent crystal deposition may result in a more overt inflammatory component (stiffness, effusions) and superadded acute attacks of synovitis ('pseudogout'— see p. 1018). The presence of knee effusion, increased warmth, CPPD crystal deposition and obesity are suggested risk factors for more rapid radiographic progression and a worse clinical outcome.

Hip OA

Hip OA most commonly targets the superior aspect of the joint (see Fig. 20.23). Such 'superior pole' OA is the usual pattern in men and the predominant pattern in women, and includes most OA that is secondary to structural abnormality. It is often unilateral at presentation, often progresses with superolateral migration of the femoral head, and has a poor prognosis. The less common central (medial) OA shows more central cartilage loss and is largely confined to women. It is often bilateral at presentation, may associate with nodal generalised OA, uncommonly progresses with axial femoral migration, and has a better prognosis.

The hip shows the best correlation between symptoms and radiographic change. Hip pain is usually maximal deep in the anterior groin, with variable radiation to the buttock, anterolateral thigh, knee or shin. Lateral hip pain, worse on lying on that side with tenderness over the greater trochanter, suggests secondary trochanteric bursitis. Common functional difficulties are the same as for knee OA; in addition, restricted hip abduction in women may cause pain on intercourse.

Examination may reveal:

- an antalgic gait
- weakness and wasting of quadriceps and gluteal muscles
- pain and restriction of internal rotation with the hip flexed —the earliest and most sensitive sign of hip OA; other movements may subsequently be restricted and painful
- anterior groin tenderness just lateral to the femoral pulse
- fixed flexion, external rotation deformity of the hip
- ipsilateral leg shortening with severe joint attrition and superior femoral migration.

Although obesity is not a risk factor for development of hip OA, it is a risk factor for its more rapid progression. The superior pole pattern is also a risk factor.

Young-onset OA

Sometimes patients present with typical symptoms and clinical signs of OA but are younger than expected (< 45 years of age). In most cases they have OA at a single joint such as the knee and the explanation of previous overt trauma is apparent in their history. However, in people with apparently young-onset OA affecting several or many joints, especially those not normally targeted by OA, rare causes need to be considered (see Box 20.39). Patients with endemic OA, due to unknown environmental cartilage toxins, will have grown up in just a few specific areas of the world: for example, eastern Russia and northern China ('Kashin-Beck disease').

20.39 CAUSES OF YOUNG-ONSET OSTEOARTHRITIS (< 45 YEARS)
Monoarticular
• Previous trauma, localised instability
Pauciarticular or polyarticular

• Prior joint disease (e.g. juvenile idiopathic arthritis)
 • Metabolic or endocrine disease
  Haemochromatosis (see p. 870)
  Ochronosis
  Acromegaly (see p. 742)
 • (Spondylo-)epiphyseal dysplasia
 • Late avascular necrosis
 • Neuropathic joint
 • Endemic OA

Investigations

The diagnosis and assessment of common OA are purely clinical. A plain radiograph is the only useful but nonessential investigation. This may show one or more of the typical features of OA, namely focal narrowing of joint space, marginal osteophyte, subchondral sclerosis, cysts, osteochondral ('loose') bodies and deformity (see Fig. 20.7, p. 968). Chondrocalcinosis may be an additional feature, particularly at the knee. The main use of a radiograph is to assess severity of structural change, an issue if surgery is

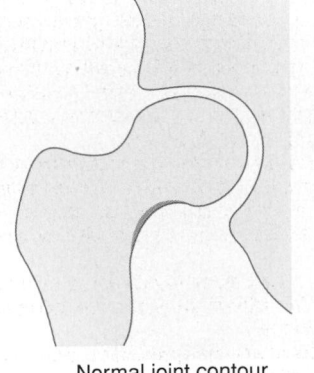

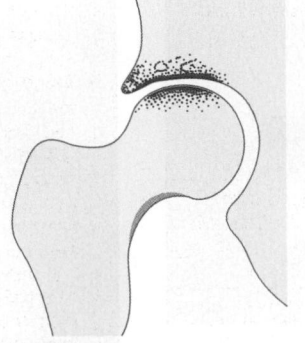

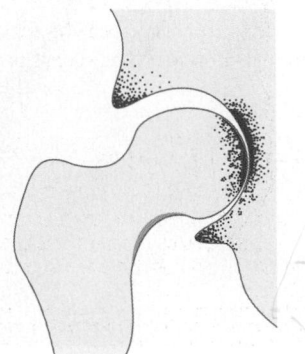

Normal joint contour   Superior pole osteoarthritis   Medial osteoarthritis

Fig. 20.23 Patterns of hip osteoarthritis.

being considered. Although a non-weight-bearing PA view of the pelvis is adequate for assessment of hip OA, standing (stressed) AP radiographs are needed to assess tibio-femoral cartilage loss, and a flexed skyline view is best for patello-femoral OA.

OA does not trigger the acute phase response and therefore has no impact on the full blood count, ESR or CRP. Synovial fluid aspirated from OA knees shows variable characteristics but is predominantly viscous with low turbidity; CPPD crystals may be identified in up to 50% of knee OA fluids. Radioisotope bone scans performed for other reasons often show, as an incidental finding, discrete increased uptake in OA joints due to bone remodelling.

Unexplained young-onset OA requires investigation. Radiographs are often helpful—for example, in showing typical features of dysplasia or avascular necrosis, widening of joint spaces in acromegaly, multiple cysts and chondrocalcinosis in haemochromatosis, or disorganised architecture in neuropathic joints. Other tests are specific to the condition (e.g. serum ferritin and liver function for haemochromatosis, serum growth hormone and skull radiograph for acromegaly, urine homogentisic acid for ochronosis).

Management

Treatment aims are to educate the patient, control pain, minimise disability and handicap, and reduce further structural progression. Management always requires:

- *Full explanation of the nature of OA* (± support literature). This should include risk factors relevant to that individual (e.g. obesity, heredity, trauma); the fact that established structural changes are permanent but that pain and function can improve; discussion of prognosis (good for hand OA, more optimistic for knee than hip OA); and the fact that appropriate action can improve the prognosis of large joint OA.
- *Advice and instruction on appropriate exercise.* This should cover both strengthening and aerobic, preferably with reinforcement by a physiotherapist (see EBM panel).
- *Reduction of any adverse mechanical factors.* These could include weight loss if obese, shock-absorbing footwear, pacing of activities, use of a walking-stick for painful knee or hip OA, or provision of built-up shoes to equalise leg lengths.
- *Initial trial of paracetamol.* Consider the addition of a topical NSAID, and then capsaicin, for knee and hand OA. If required, consider the ascending use of opioid

(including combined) analgesics and oral NSAIDs, bearing in mind the side-effects of such agents, especially in the elderly and in those with comorbidity.

For temporary benefit of moderate to severe pain consider intra-articular injection of steroid (particularly for knee and thumb-base OA) and hyaluronan (knee OA), and local physical therapies such as heat or cold.

At present there are no disease-modifying drugs for OA. Although there are data from in vitro and animal experiments which show that certain NSAIDs, tetracycline and other agents are 'chondroprotective', there is no convincing evidence for such beneficial effects in human OA. However, lifestyle alteration (reducing obesity, good nutrition, regular appropriate exercise) may reduce structural progression as well as benefit symptoms.

Surgery should be considered if conservative measures fail, the main indications being uncontrolled pain and progressive immobility and functional impairment. Osteotomy may prolong the life of malaligned joints and relieve pain by reducing intraosseous pressure. Joint replacement, however, can effectively transform the quality of life of people with severe knee or hip OA. Factors that influence patient selection for joint replacement are:

- pain severity (walking limited to 10 minutes, severe rest/night pain)
- age (the older, the better since prostheses have a limited lifespan of approximately 15 years)
- fitness for surgery and anaesthesia (especially lung and heart disease), although surgery can be performed under local anaesthesia
- exclusion of patients with an unacceptable risk of complications (e.g. active sepsis, leg ulcers or severe peripheral vascular disease).

Contrary to popular opinion, total joint replacements are required for the minority of people with large joint OA. The failure rate for replacements (mainly loosening) is about 15% at 15 years for hip replacements, and 10% at 15 years for knee replacements.

KNEE OR HIP OA—benefit of exercise **EBM**

'RCTs have shown that both aerobic and strengthening exercise produce modest but long-term improvements in pain, disability and physical performance in people with knee or hip OA, even in older disabled subjects.'

- FAST (Fitness Arthritis and Seniors Trial). Ettinger WH, Burns R, Messier SP, et al. A randomised trial comparing aerobic exercise and resistance exercise with a health education program in older adults with knee osteoarthritis. JAMA 1997; 277:25–31.
- Van Baar ME, Dekker J, Oostendorp RAB, et al. The effectiveness of exercise therapy in patients with osteoarthritis of the hip or knee: a randomized clinical trial. J Rheumatol 1998; 25:2432–2439.

ISSUES IN OLDER PEOPLE
OSTEOARTHRITIS

- OA is the major MSK cause of pain and disability in the elderly.
- The reduced muscle strength, reduced proprioception and impaired balance that accompany ageing all associate with and contribute to pain and disability from knee and hip OA.
- Coexistent calcium pyrophosphate crystal deposition is an age-associated phenomenon that may result in superimposed acute attacks of synovitis ('pseudogout').
- Regular strengthening exercise can safely reduce the pain and disability of knee OA with accompanying improvements in lower limb muscle strength, proprioception and balance.
- Ageing is not a contraindication to strengthening and aerobic exercise.
- Oral paracetamol and topical NSAIDs are safe in the elderly, have no important drug interactions or contraindications and are often effective for pain relief.
- Total joint replacement with appropriate rehabilitation is an excellent cost-effective treatment for severe disabling knee or hip OA in the elderly.

INFLAMMATORY JOINT DISEASE

RHEUMATOID ARTHRITIS

Rheumatoid arthritis (RA) is the most common inflammatory arthritis and hence an important cause of potentially preventable disability. Many of the clinical features and management strategies in RA are relevant across the spectrum of inflammatory joint disease. The typical clinical phenotype of RA is a symmetrical, deforming, small and large joint polyarthritis, often associated with systemic disturbance and extra-articular disease features. The clinical course is usually life-long, with intermittent exacerbations and remissions. Some patients have mild disease; in others it is more severe. It is currently not possible to predict prognosis at presentation accurately, so caution and appropriate treatment are needed in all patients.

Epidemiology

RA occurs throughout the world and in all ethnic groups. The prevalence is lowest in black Africans and Chinese, and highest in Pima Indians. In Caucasians it is around 1.0–1.5% with a female:male ratio of 3:1. Prevalence increases with age, with 5% of women and 2% of men over 55 years being affected. RA is uncommon in men under the age of 45, where there is a 6:1 female excess.

Aetiology

No single factor has been identified to date. Evidence for the importance of genetic susceptibility comes from higher concordance rates in monozygotic (12–15%) than in dizygotic twins (3%) and an increased frequency of disease in first-degree relatives of patients with RA. Up to 50% of the genetic contribution to susceptibility is due to genes in the HLA region. HLA-DR4 is the major susceptibility haplotype in most ethnic groups, occurring, for example, in 50–75% of Caucasian patients with RA compared to

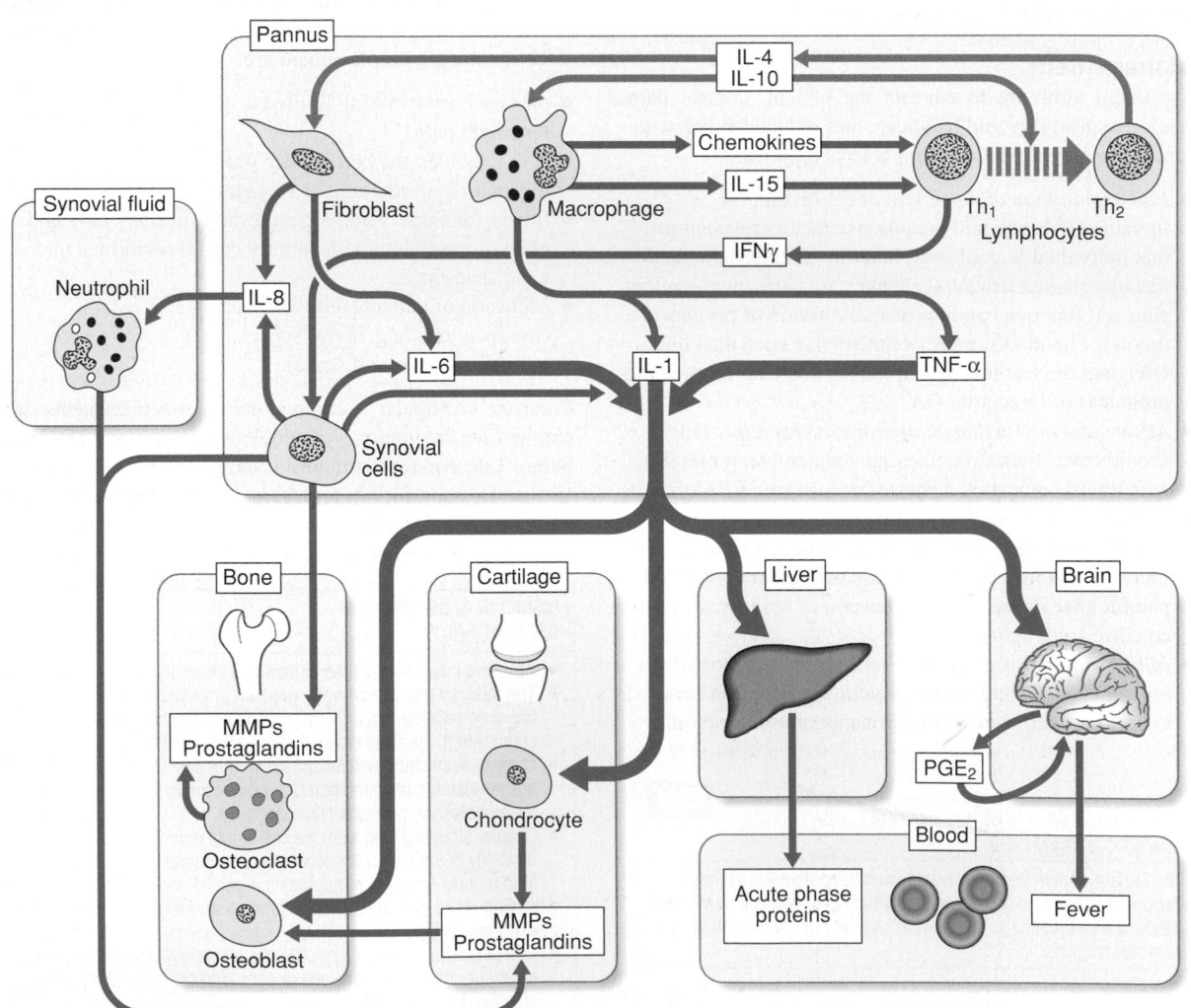

Fig. 20.24 Pathogenesis of rheumatoid arthritis. Possible sequence of events with network of cells, cytokines and mediators. (IL = interleukin; TNF-α = tumour necrosis factor-α; Th$_1$ and Th$_2$ = Th$_1$ and Th$_2$ lymphocyte subsets; IFN = interferon; MMPs = metalloproteinases; PGE$_2$ = prostaglandin E$_2$)

20–25% of the normal population. However, DR1 is more important in Indians and Israelis and DW15 in Japanese. It is likely that genetic factors influence both susceptibility and severity, with DR4 positivity more common in those with severe erosive disease.

More specifically, disease susceptibility is associated with a 'shared epitope (SE)' of specific amino acid sequences on the beta 1 chain of a number of class II alleles located in the third allelic hypervariable region of HLA-DR β_1, between amino acid residues 67 and 74, which flank the T-cell recognition site. Population variation in the frequency of SE-positive alleles may explain some of the geographical variation in the frequency of RA.

Female gender is a risk factor and this susceptibility is increased post-partum and by breastfeeding. No infectious agents have been consistently isolated and there is no evidence of disease clustering. Cigarette smoking is a risk factor for RA and for positivity for rheumatoid factor in non-RA subjects. Whatever the initiating stimulus, RA is characterised by persistent cellular activation, autoimmunity and the presence of immune complexes at sites of articular and extra-articular lesions (see Fig. 20.24). This leads to chronic inflammation, granuloma formation and joint destruction.

Pathology

The earliest change is swelling and congestion of the synovial membrane and the underlying connective tissues, which become infiltrated with lymphocytes (especially CD4 T cells), plasma cells and macrophages. Effusion of synovial fluid into the joint space takes place during active phases of the disease. Hypertrophy of the synovial membrane occurs, with the formation of lymphoid follicles resembling an immunologically active lymph node. Inflammatory granulation tissue (pannus) spreads over and under the articular cartilage, which is progressively eroded and destroyed. Later, fibrous or bony ankylosis may occur. Muscles adjacent to inflamed joints atrophy and there may be focal infiltration with lymphocytes.

Subcutaneous nodules consist of a central area of fibrinoid material surrounded by a palisade of proliferating mononuclear cells. Similar granulomatous lesions may occur in the pleura, lung, pericardium and sclera. Lymph nodes are often hyperplastic, showing many lymphoid follicles with large germinal centres and numerous plasma cells in the sinuses and medullary cords. Immunofluorescence confirms rheumatoid factor synthesis by plasma cells in synovium and lymph nodes.

Clinical features

The diagnosis of RA can only be established by an accurate and careful history and physical examination. Only limited help is provided by laboratory tests. The clinical hallmark of inflammatory joint disease is persistent synovitis. In patients with isolated small joint synovitis the acute phase response may be normal, because the magnitude of this response is correlated with the amount of inflammatory activity (synovitis bulk). A set of classification criteria for epidemiological

20.40 CRITERIA FOR DIAGNOSIS OF RHEUMATOID ARTHRITIS*	
• Morning stiffness (> 1 hour)	• Rheumatoid nodules
• Arthritis of three or more joint areas	• Rheumatoid factor
• Arthritis of hand joints	• Radiological changes
• Symmetrical arthritis	• Duration of 6 weeks or more

* American Rheumatism Association 1988 revision.

N.B. Diagnosis of RA is made with four or more criteria.

purposes is shown in Box 20.40. However, these criteria were designed to distinguish patients with RA from those with other arthropathies in a clinical population, and for comparative epidemiological studies. They are not intended to be used dogmatically for clinical diagnosis in individual cases, and their sensitivity to diagnose early inflammatory disease in a primary care setting is unknown. The requirement for symptoms to persist beyond 6 weeks is a useful cutoff to ensure that self-limiting or viral arthritis is not labelled prematurely as RA. However, irreversible damage occurs early in RA and diagnosis and treatment should not be delayed.

The most common presentation is with a gradual onset of symmetrical arthralgia and synovitis of small joints of the hands, feet and wrists. This insidious onset has traditionally been considered to imply a poor prognosis, possibly because of the delay in presenting for medical advice. A dramatic acute onset, sometimes over just a few days, with florid morning stiffness, polyarthritis and pitting oedema, occurs more commonly but not exclusively in the elderly. Some elderly patients present acutely with an initial polymyalgic illness with marked proximal muscle stiffness, the synovitis appearing only after several months as the steroid dose is reduced. Occasionally the onset is palindromic, with recurrent symmetrical acute episodes of joint pain and swelling which last only for a few hours or days. Whatever the pattern, most patients have evidence of morning and inactivity stiffness and stress pain. Involvement of other synovial structures (tenosynovium, bursae) is common but, unlike in seronegative spondarthritis, the entheses are not targeted.

Specific joints

The hand is crucial to overall patient function and provides a good reflection of overall disease activity. The typical features are symmetrical swelling of the metacarpophalangeal (MCP) and proximal interphalangeal (PIP) joints. These and other joints are considered to be actively inflamed if they are tender on pressure, and have stress pain on passive movement or non-bony effusion/swelling. Note that erythema is not a feature of rheumatoid arthritis and usually implies coexistent sepsis. Specific hand abnormalities include 'swan neck' deformity, the boutonnière or 'button hole deformity', and a Z deformity of the thumb (see Fig. 20.25). Dorsal subluxation of the ulnar styloid of the wrist is common and may contribute to rupture of the fourth and fifth extensor tendons. Triggering of fingers may occur due to nodules in the flexor tendon sheath.

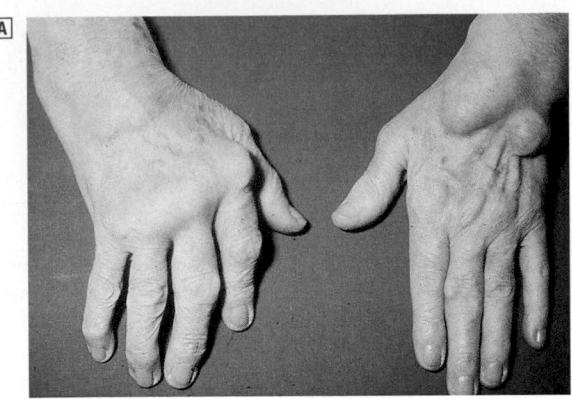
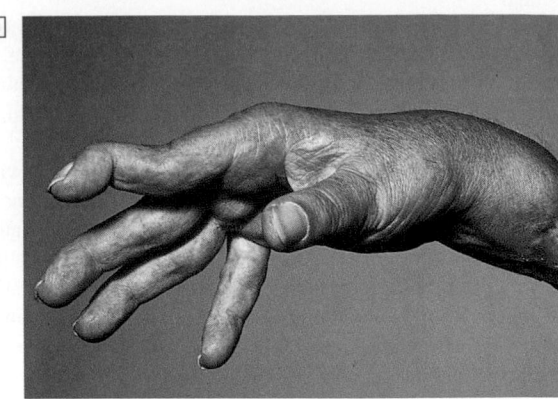

Fig. 20.25   The hand in rheumatoid arthritis. [A] Ulnar deviation of the fingers with wasting of the small muscles of the hands and synovial swelling at the wrists, the extensor tendon sheaths, the metacarpophalangeal and proximal interphalangeal joints. [B] 'Swan neck' deformity of the fingers.

In the forefoot dorsal subluxation of the metatarsophalangeal (MTP) joints results in 'cock-up' toe deformities. This causes pain on weight-bearing on the exposed MTP heads and development of secondary adventitious bursae and callosities. In the hindfoot, calcaneovalgus (eversion) is the most common deformity, reflecting damage to the ankle and subtalar joint. This is often associated with loss of the longitudinal arch (flat foot) due to rupture of the tibialis posterior tendon.

Popliteal ('Baker's') cysts usually occur in combination with knee synovitis, with synovial fluid communicating with the cyst but being prevented from returning to the joint by a valve-like mechanism. Rupture, often induced by knee flexion in the presence of a large effusion, leads to calf pain and swelling. Differentiation from a deep vein thrombosis (DVT) can usually be made by the presence of pre-existing joint problems, but a Doppler ultrasound or arthrogram is required to establish the correct diagnosis, since DVT and Baker's cyst may coexist. It is important to be aware of this differential diagnosis, as anticoagulating a Baker's cyst can cause further leg swelling and lead to a compartment syndrome (see Fig. 20.26).

Extra-articular features

RA is a systemic disease. Anorexia, weight loss and fatigue are the most common non-articular symptoms, which may occur throughout the disease course. Generalised osteoporosis and muscle-wasting occur due to systemic inflammation. Extra-articular features are more common in patients with long-standing seropositive erosive disease but may occasionally occur at presentation, especially in men. Most features are due to serositis, granuloma/nodule formation or vasculitis (see Box 20.41).

Cutaneous features

Subcutaneous rheumatoid nodules occur almost exclusively in seropositive patients, usually at sites of pressure or friction such as the extensor services of the forearm, sacrum, Achilles tendon and toes (see Fig. 20.27). They may be complicated by ulceration and secondary infection. Systemic rheumatoid vasculitis usually occurs in elderly

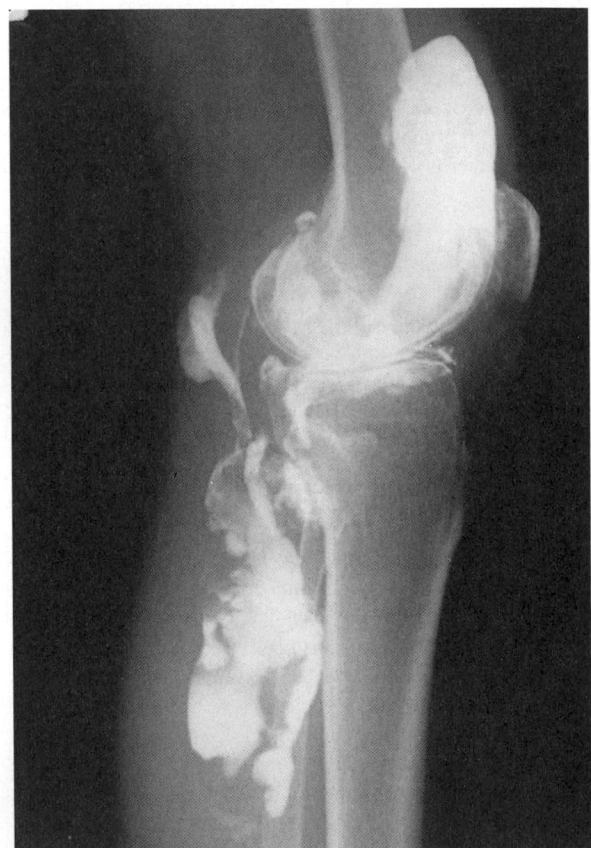

Fig. 20.26   Ruptured Baker's cysts in rheumatoid arthritis. Arthrogram showing radio-opaque contrast medium in popliteal cysts and tissues of the calf.

seropositive patients in the context of systemic symptoms and multiple extra-articular features. The cutaneous clinical manifestations vary from relatively benign nail-fold infarcts to widespread cutaneous ulceration with skin necrosis. Involvement of medium-sized arteries may lead to mesenteric, renal or coronary artery occlusion.

20.41 EXTRA-ARTICULAR MANIFESTATIONS OF RHEUMATOID DISEASE	
Systemic	
• Fever	• Fatigue
• Weight loss	• Susceptibility to infection
Musculoskeletal	
• Muscle-wasting	• Bursitis
• Tenosynovitis	• Osteoporosis
Haematological	
• Anaemia	• Eosinophilia
• Thrombocytosis	
Lymphatic	
• Splenomegaly	• Felty's syndrome
Nodules	
• Sinuses	• Fistulae
Ocular	
• Episcleritis	• Scleromalacia
• Scleritis	• Keratoconjunctivitis sicca
Vasculitis	
• Digital arteritis	• Mononeuritis multiplex
• Ulcers	• Visceral arteritis
• Pyoderma gangrenosum	
Cardiac	
• Pericarditis	• Conduction defects
• Myocarditis	• Coronary vasculitis
• Endocarditis	• Granulomatous aortitis
Pulmonary	
• Nodules	• Bronchiolitis
• Pleural effusions	• Caplan's syndrome
• Fibrosing alveolitis	
Neurological	
• Cervical cord compression	• Peripheral neuropathy
• Compression neuropathies	• Mononeuritis multiplex
Amyloidosis	

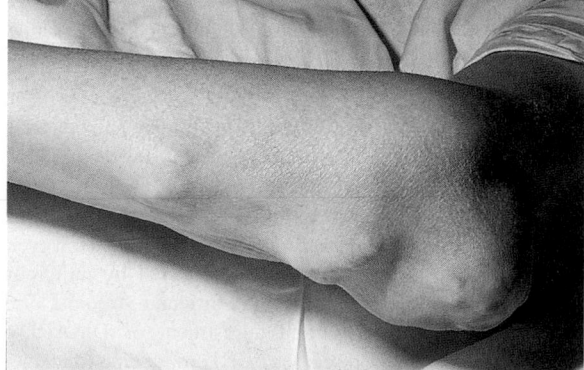

Fig. 20.27 Rheumatoid nodules and olecranon bursitis. Nodules were palpable within as well as outside the bursa.

Ocular features

The most common symptom is dry eyes (keratoconjunctivitis sicca) due to secondary Sjögren's syndrome. Painless episcleritis frequently accompanies nodular seropositive disease; it may cause intense redness but the conjunctival vessels remain normal. It is not usually associated with visual disturbance. If treatment is required, local steroids or systemic NSAIDs are usually effective.

Scleritis is more serious and potentially sight-threatening; the eye is red and painful, with inflammatory changes throughout the sclera and uveal tract. The pupil may appear irregular due to adhesions (synechiae) that can lead to secondary glaucoma and visual impairment. NSAIDs may be effective but if no response is obtained oral steroids are required.

Scleromalacia is painless bilateral thinning of the sclera, with the affected area appearing blue or grey (the colour of the underlying choroid). No specific treatment is required.

Corneal melting is a rare but devastating manifestation. It usually occurs in long-standing disease and is associated with systemic vasculitis. The clinical features are pain, redness and blurred vision with corneal thinning. If untreated, progression to perforation is common. Immunosuppression with steroids and ciclosporin or cyclophosphamide is usually required.

Cardiovascular features

Asymptomatic pericarditis occurs in approximately 30% of patients with seropositive RA, with pericardial effusions and constrictive pericarditis being rare complications. Occasionally, granulomatous lesions result in heart block, cardiomyopathy, coronary artery occlusion or aortic regurgitation.

Pulmonary features

See page 559.

Neurological features

Entrapment neuropathies result from compression of peripheral nerves due to hypertrophied synovium or joint subluxation. Median nerve compression in the carpal tunnel is the most common, and bilateral compression may be an early clinical manifestation of RA. Other common features include ulnar nerve compression at the elbow, compression of the lateral popliteal nerve at the head of the fibula, and tarsal tunnel syndrome (entrapment of the posterior tibial nerve in the flexor retinaculum) which causes burning, tingling and numbness in the distal sole and toes.

Diffuse symmetrical peripheral neuropathy and mononeuritis multiplex may occur due to a vasculitic neuropathy. Cervical cord compression can result from subluxation of the cervical spine at the atlantoaxial joint or at a subaxial level (see Fig. 20.28). Atlantoaxial subluxation is a common finding in long-standing RA and is due to erosion of the transverse ligament around the posterior aspect of the odontoid peg. On neck flexion, this leads to the peg moving posteriorly and indenting the cord. If unrecognised, it can lead to cord compression or sudden death following minor trauma or manipulation. Atlantoaxial subluxation should be suspected in any RA patient who describes new onset of

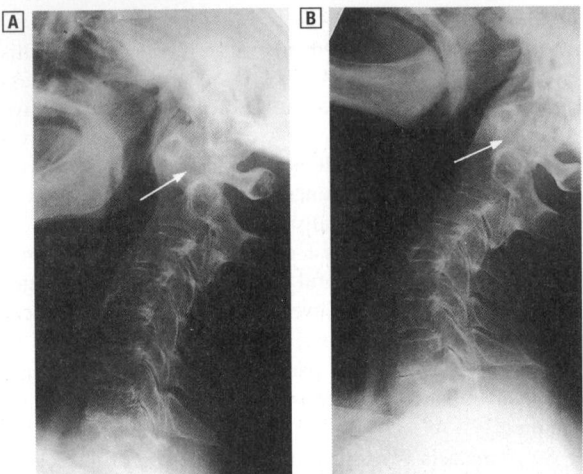

Fig. 20.28 Subluxation of cervical spine. A Flexion. B Extension.

occipital headache, particularly if symptoms of paraesthesia or electric shock are present in the arms. Alternatively, onset may be insidious, with subtle loss of function that is initially attributed to active disease. Reflexes and power can be very difficult to assess in the presence of marked joint damage, and therefore sensory or upper motor signs are the most important to elicit. Lateral radiographs should be taken in flexion and extension, and the degree of compression established with MRI. Operative stabilisation and fixation may be required, though the outcome is poor if the patient already has tetraparesis.

Haematological features

Microcytic iron deficiency anaemia due to NSAID-induced gastrointestinal blood loss and normochromic, normocytic anaemia (± thrombocytosis) due to active disease may both occur, the latter being unresponsive to oral iron. Felty's syndrome is the association of splenomegaly and neutropenia with RA (see Box 20.42). Lymphadenopathy may be found in nodes draining actively inflamed joints, but generalised lymphadenopathy should be investigated by biopsy since

20.42 FELTY'S SYNDROME	
Risk factors	
• Age of onset 50–70 • F > M • Caucasians > blacks • Incidence < 1% RA patients	• Long-standing RA • Deforming but inactive disease • Seropositive for rheumatoid factor
Common clinical features	
• Splenomegaly • Lymphadenopathy • Weight loss • Skin pigmentation	• Keratoconjunctivitis sicca • Nodules • Vasculitis, leg ulcers • Recurrent infections
Laboratory findings	
• Anaemia (normochromic, normocytic) • Neutropenia	• Thrombocytopenia • Impaired T and B cell immunity • Abnormal liver function

there is an increased risk of lymphoma in patients with long-standing disease. Amyloidosis is a rare complication of prolonged active disease and usually presents with nephrotic syndrome.

Investigations

The diagnosis should be confirmed according to clinical criteria (see Box 20.43). The acute phase response is usually elevated in patients with widespread disease, but may be normal in isolated small joint synovitis. Rheumatoid factor is only present in 60–80% of patients so its absence does not exclude the diagnosis. Conversely, rheumatoid factor is present in 10% of the normal population.

The typical radiographic appearances of RA are periarticular osteopenia and marginal non-proliferative erosions. Although osteopenia may be present within the first 6 months, erosions are uncommon within the first year. Therefore it is not appropriate to await radiographic changes before making the diagnosis.

20.43 INVESTIGATIONS AND MONITORING OF RHEUMATOID ARTHRITIS	
To establish diagnosis	
• Clinical criteria • Acute phase response	• Serological tests • Radiographs
To monitor disease activity and drug efficacy	
• Pain (visual analogue scale) • Early morning stiffness (minutes)	• Joint tenderness (number of inflamed joints, articular index) • Acute phase response
To monitor disease damage	
• Radiographs	• Functional assessment
To monitor drug safety	
• Urinalysis • Biochemistry	• Haematology

Management

The following are the key management goals in RA:

- relief of symptoms
- suppression of inflammation
- conservation and restoration of function in affected joints (joint protection)
- environmental modification if appropriate.

Physical rest, targeted anti-inflammatory therapy and passive exercises are the mainstay of treatment for acute RA. Hospital admission in order to undergo multiple intra-articular injections, joint splinting, regular hydrotherapy, physiotherapy and education may be beneficial. However, most flares can be managed out of hospital by judicious use of either intramuscular or intra-articular steroids, oral analgesics and NSAIDs, and adjustment of DMARDs. Periodic assessment of disease activity, progression (damage) and disability is required. Patient education, counselling and a coordinated multidisciplinary approach are required for successful management.

Drug therapy

Prompt introduction of DMARDs, either singly or in combination, is central to the modern management of RA. These drugs do not have immediate anti-inflammatory or analgesic effects but will improve symptoms and acute phase response, and reduce radiographic progression, at least in the medium term (see EBM panel). They are likely to be most useful when started early in disease before irreversible damage has occurred. Methotrexate and sulfasalazine are current first-choice DMARDs for RA. If they fail to control disease or are not tolerated due to side-effects, other DMARDs should be used, either sequentially or in combination. The addition of a fixed dose of 7.5 mg prednisolone daily to NSAID and DMARD therapy may slow the rate of radiological progression over 2 years in patients with early RA. Symptomatic management with continued use of NSAIDs and analgesics may also be required.

EBM

DMARD THERAPY FOR RHEUMATOID ARTHRITIS

'Radiographically detectable articular damage can be favourably influenced by the early use of DMARDs. Methotrexate and sulfasalazine have the most favourable toxicity/efficacy ratios. It is impossible to predict the response in an individual patient.'

• Felson DT, Andersen JJ, Meenan RF. Use of short term efficacy/toxicity ratios to select second line drugs in RA. Arthritis Rheum 1992; 35:117–125.

Further information: 💻 www.cochrane.co.uk

Surgery

Synovectomy of the wrist or finger tendon sheaths of the hands may be required for pain relief or to prevent tendon rupture when other medical interventions have failed. In later stages of the disease osteotomy, arthrodesis or arthroplasties play a major part in patient rehabilitation (see Box 20.37, p. 996).

Progression and prognosis

Past views about the treatment of RA were based on the concept that it was a benign, non-fatal and slowly evolving disease, often responsive to simple therapy. This led to a conservative management approach, predominantly based on the use of NSAIDs, that has been challenged by the following findings:

• There is increased mortality in RA patients, highest in those with the most severe disease. Average lifespan is reduced by 8–15 years by RA and the 5-year survival for patients with severe disease is only 50%.
• Around 40% of patients will be registered disabled within 3 years.
• Around 80% will be moderately to severely disabled within 20 years and 25% will have required a large joint replacement.

Functional capacity decreases most rapidly at the beginning of disease and it is therefore essential to control disease as soon as possible. Joint damage and erosions occur early, and the functional status of patients after only 1 year of RA is often predictive of long-term outcome. It is not possible to predict the outcome accurately at the time of diagnosis, so caution and careful follow-up are needed in all patients. However, the following factors at presentation are associated with a poor prognosis:

• higher baseline disability
• female gender
• involvement of MTP joints
• positive rheumatoid factor
• disease duration of over 3 months.

ISSUES IN OLDER PEOPLE
RHEUMATOID ARTHRITIS

• Presentation may be atypical—for example, with an initial polymyalgic picture or with synovitis and marked peripheral oedema.
• Increasing age and comorbidity (e.g. cardiac, renal, gastrointestinal tract disease) increase the risks of NSAID gastrotoxicity; comorbidity can also make overall management more difficult.
• Patients aged over 65 years are at an increased risk of steroid-induced osteoporosis; prophylaxis should be considered at doses of ≥ 7.5 mg for > 3 months (HRT, bisphosphonates or calcitriol).
• Age alone is not a contraindication to slow-acting antirheumatic drug therapy.

SERONEGATIVE SPONDARTHRITIS

This term is applied to a group of inflammatory joint diseases, distinct from rheumatoid arthritis, that are thought to share a similar pathogenesis. They all show considerable overlap and similarity of articular and extra-articular clinical features (see Box 20.44). The diseases that fall within the group are:

• ankylosing spondylitis
• reactive arthritis, including Reiter's syndrome
• psoriatic arthritis
• arthropathy associated with inflammatory bowel disease (Crohn's, ulcerative colitis).

In addition to their clinical similarities they share a common pathology and a striking genetic association with the histocompatibility antigen HLA-B27.

20.44 CLINICAL FEATURES COMMON TO SERONEGATIVE SPONDARTHRITIS

• Asymmetrical inflammatory oligoarthritis (lower > upper limb)
• Sacroiliitis and inflammatory spondylitis
• Inflammatory enthesitis
• Tendency for familial aggregation
• No association with seropositivity for rheumatoid factor
• Absence of nodules and other extra-articular features of rheumatoid arthritis
• Overlapping extra-articular features typical of the group:
    Mucosal surface inflammation—conjunctivitis, buccal ulceration, urethritis, prostatitis, bowel ulceration
    Pustular skin lesions, nail dystrophy
    Anterior uveitis
    Aortic root fibrosis (aortic incompetence, conduction defects)
    Erythema nodosum

Pathology

The pathology of the synovitis that occurs in this group is non-specific and, apart from the absence of granulomata, is often indistinguishable from rheumatoid synovitis. However, the distinctive feature for the group is the marked degree of extrasynovial inflammation, especially of the enthesis but also affecting capsule, periarticular periosteum, cartilage and subchondral bone. Large central cartilaginous joints (sacroiliac, intervertebral, symphysis pubis) are particularly involved, but even when synovial joints are affected (often spinal apophyseal joints, hips, knees, shoulders) extrasynovial inflammation is still prominent. Apart from targeting entheses, two other characteristic features are:

- resolution of inflammation by extensive fibrosis
- a tendency for resultant scar tissue to calcify and ossify.

In seronegative spondarthritis, therefore, chronic inflammation that predominately targets extrasynovial tissue may characteristically lead to joint fusion in the relative absence of joint synovitis. Similarly, periarticular osteitis and periostitis may result in bony spurs that bridge adjacent vertebral bodies (syndesmophytes) or protrude at sites of ligament attachment (e.g. calcaneal or olecranon 'spurs').

Association with HLA-B27

Within the group, disease association with HLA-B27 is striking, particularly for ankylosing spondylitis (> 95%) and Reiter's disease (90%), and when there is sacroiliitis, uveitis or balanitis. The mechanism of this disease association, however, is unclear.

The suggested pathogenesis for the seronegative spondarthritides is that they are caused by an aberrant response to infection in genetically predisposed persons—the 'reactive' concept. In some situations a triggering organism can be identified, as in Reiter's disease following bacterial dysentery or chlamydial urethritis, but in others the environmental trigger remains obscure.

A further feature to support the seronegative spondarthritis group concept is the strong aggregation of these conditions within families, each syndrome showing an increased familial incidence of the other conditions. It is tempting to speculate that such families share an inherited 'reactive' potential but the phenotypic expression is modified according to the inciting trigger and other genetic and constitutional features of the individual.

ANKYLOSING SPONDYLITIS

This prototype of the seronegative spondarthritis group is a chronic inflammatory arthritis with a predilection for the sacroiliac joints and spine. It is characterised by progressive stiffening and fusion of the axial skeleton.

Epidemiology

The disease has a peak onset in the second and third decades, with a male:female ratio of about 3:1. In Europe more than 90% of affected persons are HLA-B27-positive.

The overall prevalence is around 0.5% in most communities, but is much greater in the Pima and Haida Indians who have a high prevalence of HLA-B27.

Infective triggers have not clearly been linked to causation. Chronic prostatitis is more common than expected but appears non-infective. Increased faecal carriage of *Klebsiella aerogenes* occurs in patients with established ankylosing spondylitis and may relate to exacerbation of both joint and eye disease.

Clinical features

The onset is usually extremely insidious, over months or years, with recurring episodes of low back pain and marked stiffness. Radiation to the buttocks or posterior thighs is not uncommon and is often misdiagnosed as sciatica. Unlike common mechanical back pain, symptoms extend over many segments and are axial and symmetrical in distribution. Symptoms are most marked in the early morning and after inactivity and are relieved by movement. Although the lumbosacral area is usually the first and worst affected region, some patients present with mainly thoracic or neck symptoms. The disease tends to ascend the spine slowly and, eventually, after several years, the whole spine may be affected. As the spine becomes progressively ankylosed, spinal rigidity and secondary osteoporosis predispose to spinal fracture, presenting as acute, severe, well-localised pain. Secondary spinal cord compression is a rare complication.

Most patients have additional locomotor symptoms reflecting the widespread nature of the condition. 'Pleuritic' chest pain aggravated by breathing is common and results from involvement of the costovertebral joints. Plantar fasciitis, Achilles tendinitis and tenderness over bony prominences such as the iliac crest and greater trochanter are common, reflecting inflammatory enthesopathy. Fatigue is often a major complaint and may result from both chronic interruption of sleep due to pain as well as chronic systemic inflammation.

Up to 40% of patients have extraspinal joint involvement. This is usually asymmetrical at first and may cause inflammatory symptoms mainly affecting hips, knees, ankles or shoulders. Involvement of a peripheral joint, most commonly ankle, knee or elbow, may precede the development of spinal symptoms in around 10% of cases. In a further 10% symptoms begin in childhood as one variety of pauciarticular juvenile idiopathic arthritis.

Early physical signs include failure to obliterate the lumbar lordosis on forward flexion, pain on sacroiliac compression, and restriction of movements of the lumbar spine in all directions. As the disease progresses, stiffness increases throughout the spine, and chest expansion frequently becomes restricted. Spinal fusion varies in its extent and in most cases does not associate with gross flexion deformity. A few patients, however, develop marked kyphosis of the dorsal and cervical spine that may interfere with forward vision. This may prove incapacitating, especially when associated with fixed flexion contractures of hips or knees.

Acute anterior uveitis is the most common extra-articular feature, affecting up to 25% of patients. Occasionally, this

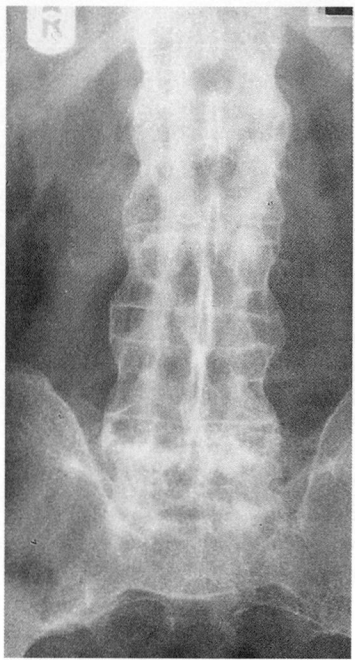

Fig. 20.30 'Bamboo' spine of severe late ankylosing spondylitis. Note the symmetrical marginal syndesmophytes, sacroiliac joint fusion and generalised osteopenia.

precedes joint disease. Other extra-articular features are rare (see Box 20.45).

Investigations

The ESR and CRP are usually raised but may be normal. Serum rheumatoid factor is usually negative; if positive, it is not present in high titre.

Radiographic signs provide the strongest investigational evidence but may take years to develop. Sacroiliitis is often the first abnormality, beginning in the lower synovial parts of the joints with irregularity and loss of cortical margins, widening of the joint space and subsequently marginal sclerosis, narrowing and fusion. Lateral views of the thoracolumbar spine may show anterior 'squaring' of the vertebrae owing to erosion and sclerosis of the anterior corners and periostitis of the waist. Bridging syndesmophytes are fine and symmetrical and follow the outermost fibres of the annulus (see Fig. 20.29). Ossification of the anterior longitudinal ligament and facet joint fusion may also be visible. The combination of all these features may result in the typical 'bamboo' spine (see Fig. 20.30). Erosive changes may be seen in the symphysis pubis, the ischial tuberosities and peripheral joints. Osteoporosis and atlantoaxial dislocation can occur.

Management

The aims are to relieve pain and stiffness, maintain a maximal range of skeletal mobility and avoid the development of deformities. Education and appropriate physical activity are the cornerstones of management. Early in the disease patients should be taught to perform regular daily back extension exercises, including a morning 'warm-up' routine, and to punctuate prolonged periods of inactivity (e.g. driving, computer work) with regular breaks. Swimming is ideal exercise and should be encouraged on a regular basis. Poor bed and chair posture must be avoided.

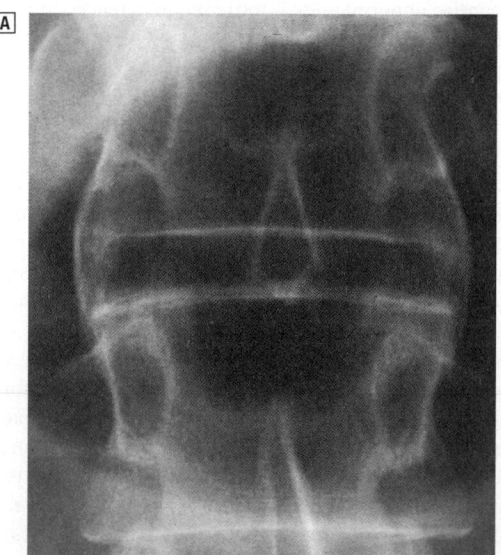
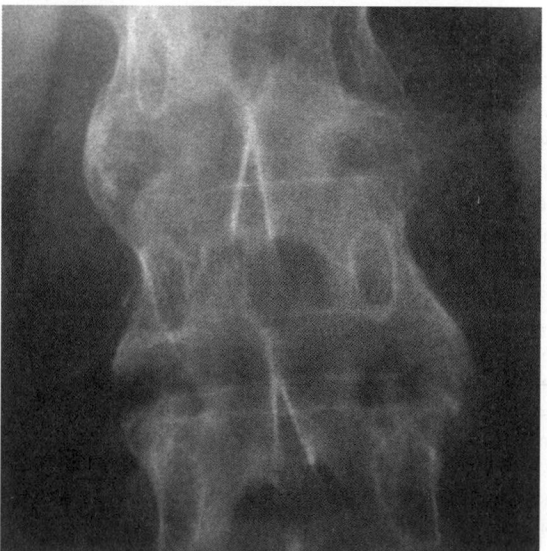

Fig. 20.29 Radiographic syndesmophytes. A Fine symmetrical marginal syndesmophytes typical of ankylosing spondylitis. B Coarse, asymmetrical non-marginal syndesmophytes typical of psoriatic/Reiter's spondylitis.

NSAIDs are often effective in relieving symptoms but do not alter the course of the disease. A long-acting NSAID at night is often particularly helpful for marked morning stiffness. The slow-acting antirheumatic drugs sulfasalazine, methotrexate or azathioprine may be effective for control of persistent peripheral joint synovitis but appear to have little or no impact in suppressing axial disease.

Local corticosteroid injections can be useful for persistent plantar fasciitis and the management of other enthesopathies. Oral steroid may occasionally be required for acute uveitis but should otherwise be avoided. Severe hip, knee or shoulder restriction may require surgery. Total hip arthroplasty has largely obviated the need for difficult spinal surgery in those with advanced deformity.

Around 75% or more of patients with ankylosing spondylitis are able to remain in employment and enjoy a good quality of life. Even if severe ankylosis develops, functional limitation may not be marked as long as the spine is fused in an erect posture. Severe hip, knee or shoulder disease carries a worse prognosis.

REACTIVE ARTHRITIS

Reiter's disease is the classic triad of non-specific urethritis, conjunctivitis and reactive arthritis that follows:

- bacterial dysentery—mainly *Salmonella*, *Shigella*, *Campylobacter* or *Yersinia*, or
- sexually acquired infection with *Chlamydia*.

Incomplete forms with just one or two of these features, however, are more frequent than the full syndrome.

Epidemiology

Reactive arthritis is predominantly a disease of young men with a sex ratio of 15:1 and is possibly the most common cause of inflammatory arthritis in men aged 16–35; however, it may occur at any age. Between 1% and 2% of patients with non-specific urethritis seen at clinics for sexually acquired diseases have reactive arthritis. Following an epidemic of *Shigella* dysentery, 20% of HLA-B27-positive men develop reactive arthritis.

Clinical features

The onset of classic Reiter's is typically acute, with development of urethritis, conjunctivitis (in about 50%) and an inflammatory oligoarthritis affecting the large and small joints of the lower limbs 1–3 weeks following sexual exposure or an attack of dysentery. There may be considerable systemic disturbance with fever, weight loss and vasomotor changes in the feet.

Less classic attacks may be subacute or more insidious. Many patients present with single joint involvement that over several days turns into an asymmetric oligoarthritis. Symptoms and signs of urethritis or conjunctivitis may be minimal or absent and there may be no clear history of prior dysentery. In such cases the coexistence of both synovitis and periarticular inflammation, marked asymmetry and lower limb predominance all suggest seronegative spondarthritis.

Achilles tendinitis or plantar fasciitis may be present as further locomotor clues.

In addition to urethritis and conjunctivitis the following extra-articular features may develop 1–3 weeks following the initiating infection:

- *Circinate balanitis* (20–50%). This is characteristic, starting as vesicles on the coronal margin of the prepuce and glans and later rupturing to form superficial erosions with minimal surrounding erythema, some coalescing to give the circular pattern. Lesions are often painless and may escape notice.
- *Keratoderma blennorrhagica* (15%). These skin lesions appear as discrete waxy yellow-brown vesico-papules with desquamating margins, occasionally coalescing to form large crusty plaques. Palms and soles are particularly affected but spread may occur to the scrotum, scalp and trunk. Clinically and histologically, these lesions are indistinguishable from pustular psoriasis.
- *Nail dystrophy* with subungual hyperkeratosis. This is indistinguishable from psoriatic nail dystrophy.
- *Buccal erosions* (10%). These shallow red patches on tongue, palate, buccal mucosa and lips are painless and last only a few days.

The first attack of arthritis is usually self-limiting, with spontaneous remission of symptoms within 2–4 months of onset. However, recurrent or chronic arthritis develops in more than 60% of patients and is not necessarily related to further infection. In chronic arthropathy low back pain and stiffness from sacroiliitis are common and 15–20% of patients develop spondylitis. Ankles, midtarsal joints, metatarsophalangeal joints and knees are usually the other target sites. Uveitis is rare with the first attack but occurs in 30% of patients with recurring arthritis. Other features are uncommon but include:

- cardiac abnormalities—aortic incompetence, conduction defects, pleuro-pericarditis
- peripheral neuropathy—foot drop, ulnar neuritis
- CNS disease—seizures, meningoencephalitis.

Investigations

The acute phase response is usually evident from a raised ESR and CRP and subsequently from a normochromic, normocytic anaemia. Aspirated synovial fluid is inflammatory (low viscosity, turbid) and often contains giant macrophages (Reiter's cells). Urethritis may be confirmed in the 'two-glass test' by demonstration of mucoid threads in the first void specimen that clear in the second. High vaginal swabs may reveal *Chlamydia* on culture. Except for post-*Salmonella* arthritis, stool cultures are usually negative by the time the arthritis presents; serum agglutinin tests, however, may help confirm previous dysentery. Serum tests for rheumatoid factor and antinuclear factor are negative.

In most cases there are no radiographic changes in the acute attack other than soft tissue swelling. However, mild periarticular osteopenia, joint space narrowing and marginal proliferative erosions may develop with chronic or recurrent disease. There may also be periostitis, especially of metatarsals, phalanges and pelvis, and large 'fluffy' calcaneal spurs. In contrast to changes in ankylosing spondylitis, radiographic sacroiliitis is often asymmetrical and sometimes unilateral, and syndesmophytes are predominantly coarse, asymmetrical and beyond the contours of the annulus fibres (i.e. 'non-marginal'). The radiographic changes in the peripheral joints and spine are identical to those seen with psoriasis.

Management

In the first attack this is mainly symptomatic and supportive. NSAIDs are often helpful during the acute phase, together with judicious aspiration of joints and intra-articular or other local steroid injections. Systemic corticosteroids are rarely required. Severe progressive arthritis and intractable keratoderma blennorrhagica occasionally warrant antirheumatic therapy with azathioprine or methotrexate. Non-specific chlamydial urethritis is usually treated with a short course of tetracycline and this may reduce the frequency of arthritis in sexually acquired cases. Anterior uveitis is a medical emergency requiring topical, subconjunctival or systemic corticosteroids.

Around 10% of patients have evidence of active disease 20 years after the onset. Spondylitis, chronic erosive arthritis, recurrent acute arthritis and uveitis are the major causes of long-term morbidity.

PSORIATIC ARTHROPATHY

This seronegative inflammatory arthritis usually presents in patients with current or previous psoriasis (70%), but in some cases (20%) it predates the onset of psoriasis. Synchronous onset is unusual (5%). The association with nail dystrophy is stronger than with skin plaques.

Epidemiology

Psoriatic arthritis occurs in about 1 in 1000 of the general population and in 7% of patients with psoriasis. Approximately 20% of all patients with seronegative polyarthritis have psoriasis, while the prevalence of psoriasis in seropositive rheumatoid arthritis is no higher than that in the general population, suggesting that the association of the skin disease with seronegative arthritis does not arise by chance alone. The onset is usually between 25 and 40 years of age.

Clinical features

A wide spectrum of joint disease is seen but five major presentations are recognised:

1. *Asymmetrical inflammatory oligoarthritis* (40%). This may affect lower and upper limb joints and commonly demonstrates the combination of joint synovitis and periarticular inflammation. This is most characteristic when a finger or toe is involved by synovitis of its joints and tenosynovitis, enthesitis and inflammation of intervening tissue to give a 'sausage digit' or dactylitis (see Fig. 20.31). Usually only one or two large joints are involved, mainly knees, with often very large effusions. Onset is often abrupt but symptoms are often mild and systemic features absent.

Dactylitis particularly often settles, with a good outcome after several months.

2. *Symmetrical polyarthritis* (25%). This predominates in women and may strongly resemble rheumatoid arthritis, with symmetrical involvement of small and large joints in both upper and lower limbs. However, nodules and other extra-articular features of rheumatoid are absent and joint disease is generally less extensive and more benign. Much of the hand deformity often results from tenosynovitis and soft tissue contractures.

3. *Predominant distal interphalangeal joint (DIPJ) arthritis* (15%). This is a very characteristic form that mainly affects men and predominantly targets finger DIPJs and surrounding periarticular tissues, almost invariably with accompanying nail dystrophy (see Fig. 20.32).

4. *Psoriatic spondylitis* (15%). This presents a similar clinical picture to ankylosing spondylitis but with a tendency to less severe involvement. It may occur alone or with any of the other clinical patterns of peripheral arthritis.

5. *Arthritis mutilans* (5%). This deforming erosive arthritis targets fingers and toes. Marked cartilage and bone attrition results in loss of the joint and marked instability. The encasing skin appears invaginated and 'telescoped'

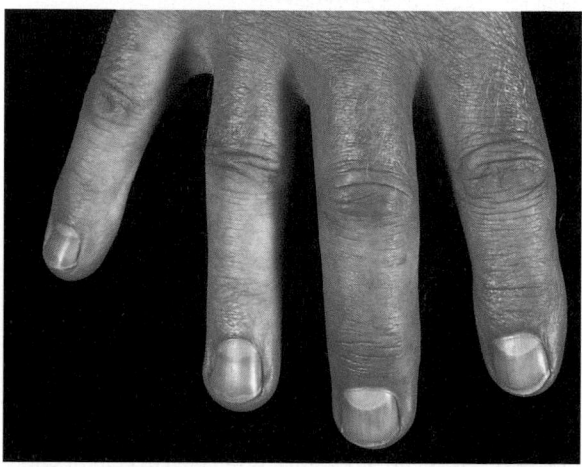

Fig. 20.31 **'Sausage' middle finger of a patient with psoriatic arthritis.**

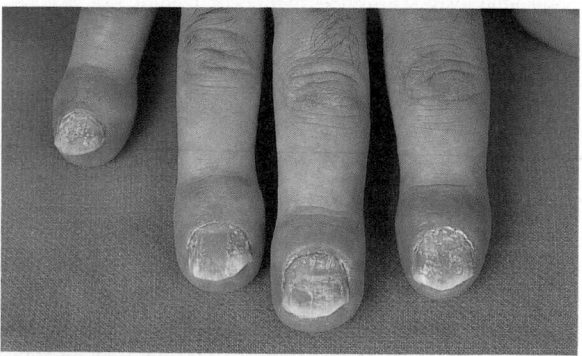

Fig. 20.32 **Psoriatic arthritis.** Note the typical distal interphalangeal joint pattern with accompanying nail dystrophy (pitting and onycholysis).

('main en lorgnette') and traction can pull the finger back to its original length. Other joints in the hand or foot may show ankylosis.

The general pattern of psoriatic arthritis is one of intermittent exacerbation followed by varying periods of complete or near-complete remission. Residual damage and disability in many cases, except arthritis mutilans, is relatively mild.

Extra-articular features are limited to:

- *Nail changes*. These include pitting, onycholysis, subungual hyperkeratosis and horizontal ridging, and may be present in the absence of skin lesions. They are found more commonly in psoriatic arthritis (85%) than in uncomplicated psoriasis (30%).
- *Skin lesions*. These may be widespread scaling lesions, typically over extensor surfaces, or insignificant lesions confined to such areas as the scalp, natal cleft and umbilicus, where they are easily overlooked (see p. 1075).
- *Conjunctivitis and uveitis*. Conjunctivitis is most common. Uveitis is mainly in HLA-B27-positive individuals with sacroiliitis and spondylitis.

Investigations

The ESR and CRP may be raised, especially with polyarticular disease, but are often unimpressive. Tests for rheumatoid factor and antinuclear antibody are generally negative. Radiographs may be normal or show erosive change with joint space narrowing. Features that may permit distinction from rheumatoid arthritis include marginal proliferative erosions, retained bone density, and increased sclerosis of small bones ('ivory phalanx'). Arthritis mutilans and peripheral joint ankylosis can occur in both conditions. The changes in the axial skeleton resemble those of chronic reactive arthritis, specifically coarse, asymmetrical, non-marginal syndesmophytes and asymmetrical sacroiliitis.

Management

The prognosis in general is better than for rheumatoid arthritis, with the exception of those with arthritis mutilans. Symptomatic agents such as simple analgesics, topical or oral NSAIDs are usually all that is required to control symptoms. Intra-articular injections may help to control florid synovitis temporarily. In general, splints and prolonged rest are avoided because of the increased tendency to fibrous and bony ankylosis. The same regime of regular exercise and attention to posture should be prescribed as to those with spondylitis.

For persistent peripheral arthritis sulfasalazine, methotrexate or azathioprine may be required but these have little or no benefit for axial disease. Methotrexate and azathioprine may also help severe skin psoriasis. Antimalarials should be avoided since they can give exfoliative reactions. The retinoid acitretin (20 mg daily—see p. 1079) is effective in treating the arthritis as well as the skin lesions but must be avoided in young women because of its teratogenicity. Its use is complicated by mucocutaneous side-effects, hyperlipidaemia, myalgias and extraspinal calcification. Photochemotherapy with methoxypsoralen and long-wave ultraviolet light (PUVA) is primarily used for patients with severe skin lesions but can also help some patients with synchronous exacerbations of inflammatory arthritis.

ARTHRITIS ASSOCIATED WITH INFLAMMATORY BOWEL DISEASE

Two patterns of seronegative inflammatory arthritis are associated with ulcerative colitis and Crohn's disease.

Enteropathic arthritis

This is an acute inflammatory oligoarthritis that occurs in 12% of patients with ulcerative colitis and 20% of those with Crohn's disease. Large lower limb joints (knees, ankles, hips) are most commonly affected but the wrists and small joints of the fingers and toes can also be involved. The arthritis coincides with exacerbations of the underlying bowel disease, sometimes in association with aphthous mouth ulcers, iritis and erythema nodosum. It ceases to be a problem following total colectomy for ulcerative colitis. The higher prevalence of arthritis in Crohn's disease may reflect the greater difficulty in eradicating the bowel problem.

Sacroiliitis and ankylosing spondylitis

Sacroiliitis (16%) and ankylosing spondylitis (6%) are disease associations that may predate or follow the onset of bowel disease. There is no correlation between the inflammatory activity of the spondylitis and bowel disease and they pursue independent courses. Clinically and radiologically, such axial disease is indistinguishable from classic ankylosing spondylitis.

CRYSTAL-ASSOCIATED DISEASE

A variety of crystals can deposit in and around joints and associate with both acute inflammatory and chronic syndromes (see Box 20.46). In some instances crystals are the primary pathogenic agents—true 'crystal deposition disease'

20.46 CRYSTAL-ASSOCIATED ARTHRITIS AND DEPOSITION IN CONNECTIVE TISSUE	
Crystal	**Associations**
Common	
Monosodium urate monohydrate	Acute gout Chronic tophaceous gout
Calcium pyrophosphate dihydrate	Acute 'pseudogout' Chronic (pyrophosphate) arthropathy Chondrocalcinosis
Basic calcium phosphates	Calcific periarthritis Calcinosis
Uncommon	
Cholesterol	Chronic effusions in rheumatoid arthritis
Calcium oxalate	Acute arthritis in dialysis patients
Extrinsic crystals/semi-crystalline particles	
Synthetic crystals	Acute synovitis
Plant thorns/sea urchin spines	Chronic monoarthritis, tenosynovitis

(e.g. gout). In other situations MSK disease predisposes to secondary crystal formation (e.g. predisposition to calcium pyrophosphate and apatite crystal formation in osteoarthritis). Such crystals may subsequently amplify symptoms and damage, or be an incidental epiphenomenon of no clinical consequence.

A variety of factors influence crystal formation (see Fig. 20.33). Firstly, there must be sufficient concentration of the chemical components (ionic product). Whether a crystal then forms, however, depends on the balance of tissue factors that promote or inhibit crystal nucleation and growth. Many of our tissues are supersaturated for various products but depend on natural inhibitors to prevent crystallisation. Lack of such natural inhibitors, presence of abnormal promoters, or both, may allow crystallisation. Crystals can also dissolve and the yield of crystals at any one time will depend on the relative rates of crystallisation, growth and dissolution.

The inflammatory potential of crystals resides in the physical irregularity and high negative charge of their surface. This can:

- activate inflammatory mediators such as complement and Hageman factor directly, or indirectly via adsorbed immunoglobulin
- stimulate and subsequently disrupt surface membranes of neutrophils, synoviocytes and other cells.

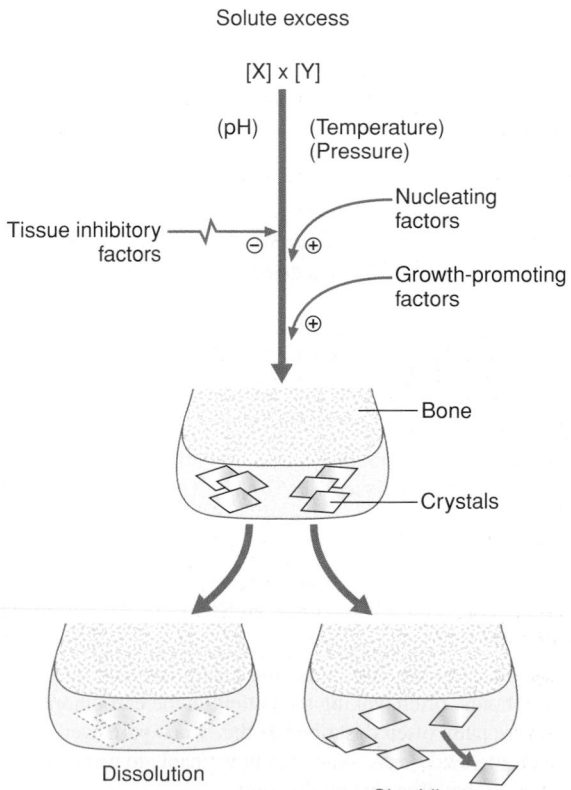

Fig. 20.33   Factors relating to crystal formation and tissue concentration at any one time.

Because of their hard particulate nature they may also mechanically damage the tissues in which they lie and act as wear particles at the joint surface. Crystals forming deep within cartilage or tendon are prevented from interaction with proteins and cells and can paradoxically reside in MSK tissues for years without causing inflammation or symptoms. It is only when they are released from their protected sites of origin ('crystal shedding') that they trigger acute attacks of inflammation. Such attacks may occur spontaneously, result from mechanical loosening (local trauma), partial dissolution and reduced crystal size (e.g. initiation of hypouricaemic treatment), or occur in association with an acute phase response due to intercurrent illness or surgery (mechanism unknown).

GOUT

Gout is a true crystal deposition disease. It can be defined as the pathological reaction of the joint or periarticular tissues to the presence of monosodium urate monohydrate (MSUM) crystals. Clinically, this may present as inflammatory arthritis, bursitis, tenosynovitis, cellulitis or as nodular ('tophaceous') crystal deposits. Prolonged hyperuricaemia is necessary, but is alone not sufficient, for development of gout.

Epidemiology

The prevalence of gout varies between populations but is around 1% with a strong male predominance (> 10:1). Prevalence increases with age and increasing serum uric acid concentration. 'Primary' gout is almost exclusively a male disease and the most common cause of inflammatory arthritis in men over the age of 40. 'Secondary' gout, due to renal impairment or drug therapy, mainly affects people over the age of 65 and is the form most usually seen in women.

Serum uric acid levels are distributed in the community as a continuous variable and are determined by a number of variables of which gender, age, body bulk and genetic constitution are the most important. Levels are higher in men than women; they rise from the twenties in men and after the menopause in women, positively correlate with obesity, and vary according to ethnicity (being highest in New Zealand Maoris). Hyperuricaemia can be defined in two ways:

- as a serum uric acid level above the theoretical solubility of MSUM in physiological conditions (0.42 mmol/l)
- as a serum uric acid level greater than 2 standard deviations above the mean for the population (c. 0.40 mmol/l for men, 0.35 mmol/l for women).

Probably 95% of hyperuricaemic subjects never develop gout.

Aetiology and pathogenesis

About one-third of the body uric acid pool is derived from dietary sources and two-thirds from endogenous purine metabolism (see Fig. 20.34). The concentration of uric acid in body fluids depends on the balance between its synthesis and its elimination via the kidneys (two-thirds) and gut (one-third). Purine nucleotide synthesis and degradation are

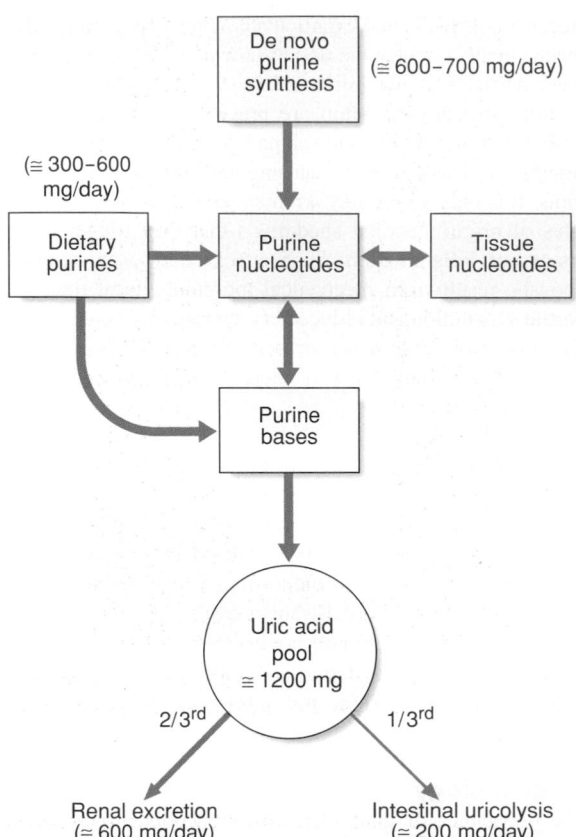

Fig. 20.34 **The uric acid pool.** Origins and disposal of uric acid in normal humans.

regulated by a network of enzyme pathways; xanthine oxidase catalyses the end conversion of hypoxanthine to xanthine and then xanthine to uric acid.

Various genetic, constitutional and environmental factors can cause hyperuricaemia by decreasing renal elimination of uric acid and/or by increasing its production (see Box 20.47). In over 75% of primary gout patients hyperuricaemia results from an inherited isolated renal defect in fractional uric acid excretion which impairs their ability to increase renal excretion in response to a purine load ('under-excretors'). About 20% of primary gout patients are intrinsic 'over-producers' of uric acid through no identifiable cause. Rare individuals, however (< 1% primary gout patients), have a specific inherited enzyme defect of purine synthesis. They should be suspected:

- if gout develops at a very early age (< 25)
- if urolithiasis (uric acid stones) is the presenting feature
- if there is a strong family history of early-onset gout.

Apart from hyperuricaemia, other risk factors and inter-related associations for primary gout include:

- obesity
- high alcohol (predominantly beer) intake
- type IV hyperlipoproteinaemia, hypertension and ischaemic heart disease
- unidentified inherited alteration in tissue factors relating to inhibition/promotion of crystal formation.

Secondary gout results from chronic hyperuricaemia due to renal impairment or chronic diuretic use. In diuretic-induced gout nodal generalised OA is a further risk factor, especially in women. This presumably relates to a non-specific predisposition to crystallisation in osteoarthritic cartilage, possibly due to reduced levels of proteoglycan and other inhibitors of crystal formation.

MSUM crystals preferentially deposit in peripheral connective tissues in and around synovial joints, initially favouring lower rather than upper limbs, and especially targeting the first metatarsophalangeal and small joints of feet and hands. As the crystal deposits slowly increase and enlarge there is progressive involvement of more proximal sites and the potential for cartilage and bone damage, from both inflammation and mass pressure effects, and development of 'secondary' osteoarthritis. MSUM crystals take months or years to grow to a detectable size, implying a long asymptomatic phase.

Clinical features

Acute gout

In almost all first attacks a single distal joint is affected. The first metatarsophalangeal joint is affected in over 50% of cases—'podagra' (see Fig. 20.35). Other common sites (in order of decreasing frequency) are the ankle, midfoot, knee, small joints of hands, wrist and elbow. The axial skeleton and large proximal joints are rarely involved and never as the first site. Typical attacks have the following characteristics:

- extremely rapid onset, reaching maximum severity in just 2–6 hours, often waking the patient in the early morning
- severe pain, often described as the 'worst pain ever'
- extreme tenderness—the patient is unable to wear a sock or to let bedding rest on the joint
- marked swelling with overlying red, shiny skin
- self-limiting over 5–14 days, with complete return to normality.

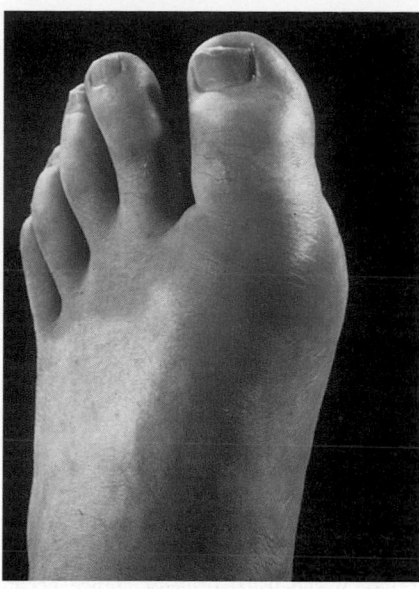

Fig. 20.35   Podagra. Acute gout causing swelling, erythema and extreme pain and tenderness of the first metatarsophalangeal joint.

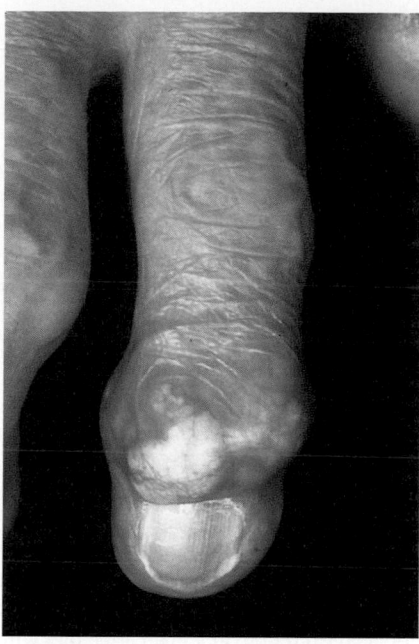

Fig. 20.36   Tophus with white MSUM crystals visible beneath the skin. This was diuretic-induced gout in a patient with pre-existing nodal osteoarthritis.

During the attack the joint shows signs of marked synovitis but also periarticular swelling and erythema. The attack may be accompanied by fever, malaise and even confusion, especially if a large joint such as the knee is involved. As the attack subsides pruritus and desquamation of overlying skin are common. The main differential diagnosis is septic arthritis, infective cellulitis or another crystal disease. Sepsis, however, is usually more subacute in onset and progresses in severity until treated.

Acute attacks may also manifest as bursitis, tenosynovitis or cellulitis. These attacks have the same characteristics—rapid onset, severe pain, florid inflammation and erythema. Many patients describe milder episodes lasting just a few days ('petite attacks'). Some have attacks in more than one joint, and sometimes one attack, by triggering the acute phase response, triggers attacks in other joints a few days later ('cluster attacks'). Polyarticular attacks are rare.

Intercritical periods

These are asymptomatic periods between attacks. Some people never have a second attack; in others the next episode occurs after years. In most, however, a second attack occurs within 1 year. Subsequently, the frequency of attacks and number of sites involved gradually increase with time. Later attacks are more likely to involve several joints and to be more severe. Eventually, continued MSUM deposition causes joint damage and chronic pain. The interval between the first attack and the development of chronic symptoms is variable, but averages around 10 years. The main determinant is the uric acid level—the higher it is, the earlier and more extensive the development of joint damage and MSUM deposits.

Chronic tophaceous gout

Large MSUM crystal deposits produce irregular firm nodules ('tophi') at the usual sites for nodules around extensor surfaces of fingers, hands, forearm, elbows, Achilles tendons and sometimes the helix of the ear. Marked asymmetry, locally and between sides, is characteristic. The white colour of MSUM crystals may be evident and permit distinction from rheumatoid nodules (see Fig. 20.36). Large nodules may ulcerate, discharging white gritty material and associating with local inflammation (erythema, pus) even in the absence of secondary infection. Although tophi are usually a very late feature, they may appear surprisingly rapidly, in under 1 year, in patients with chronic renal failure.

The joints most commonly involved with signs of damage and varying degrees of synovitis are the first metatarsophalangeal joint, midfoot, finger joints and wrists, occasionally with severe deformity and marked functional impairment, especially of feet and hands. As with tophi, asymmetry is characteristic.

Secondary gout may present with painful, sometimes discharging tophi without preceding acute attacks. This is particularly seen in older, mainly female patients with nodal osteoarthritis who develop tophi in and around their osteoarthritic finger joints as a consequence of chronic (> 1–2 years) diuretic therapy (see Fig. 20.36).

Urolithiasis

Uric acid (not MSUM) stones cause renal colic in around 10% of gout patients in Europe. The incidence is higher in hot climates and is favoured by:

- purine over-production
- uricosuric drugs and defects in tubular reabsorption of uric acid
- dehydration and lowering of urine pH (e.g. chronic diarrhoea, ileostomy).

Chronic urate nephropathy

Progressive renal disease is an important complication confined to untreated severe chronic tophaceous gout. This results from MSUM crystal deposition in the interstitium of the medulla and pyramids with consequent chronic inflammation, giant-cell reaction, fibrosis, glomerulosclerosis and secondary pyelonephritis.

Investigations

Definite confirmation of diagnosis is by identification of MSUM crystals in the aspirate from a joint, bursa or tophus. In acute gout synovial fluid shows increased turbidity due to the greatly elevated cell count (> 90% neutrophils); chronic gouty fluid is more variable but occasionally appears white due to the high crystal load. During an intercritical period aspiration of an asymptomatic first metatarsophalangeal joint or knee still often permits crystal identification.

Although hyperuricaemia is usually consistently present, it does not confirm gout. Equally, a normal uric acid level, especially during an attack, does not exclude gout (uric acid is a negative acute phase reactant). Measurement of 24-hour urinary uric acid excretion on a low purine diet will identify an over-producer. Assessment of renal function (serum creatinine, urine testing) should always be undertaken. Fasting lipoproteins should be checked in those with primary gout. An intercritical full blood count and ESR should detect myeloproliferative disorders. During an attack a marked acute phase response (elevated CRP, neutrophilia) is usual; the ESR is often modestly raised in tophaceous gout.

Radiographs can assess the degree of joint damage. In early disease they are usually normal, but narrowing of joint space, sclerosis, cysts and osteophyte (changes of osteoarthritis) may develop in affected joints with time, or be present as a predisposing factor in secondary gout. Gouty 'erosions' (bony tophi) are a less common but more specific feature occurring as para-articular 'punched-out' defects with well-delineated borders and retained bone density. Tophi may also be visible as eccentric soft tissue swellings. In late disease changes may be hard to distinguish from other forms of inflammatory polyarthritis.

Management

The acute attack

A quick-acting oral NSAID (e.g. naproxen, diclofenac, indometacin) can give effective pain relief and is the standard treatment. Patients can keep a supply of an NSAID with which they are familiar and take it as soon as the first symptoms are noticed, continuing for the duration of the attack. Oral colchicine (a potent inhibitor of neutrophil microtubular assembly) can be very effective, but unfortunately often causes vomiting and severe diarrhoea at the doses needed for rapid relief (1 mg loading dose, then 0.5 mg 6-hourly until symptoms abate). The compromise is to try lower doses (0.5 mg 8–12-hourly) for a slower onset of benefit. Aspiration of the joint will give instant relief and, when combined with an intra-articular steroid injection to prevent fluid reaccumulation, often effectively aborts the attack.

Long-term management

Patient education is critical. The nature of gout and the aims and mechanisms of treatment require careful explanation if a cure is to be achieved.

Correction of any predisposing factors should always be attempted. Lifestyle alteration to correct obesity and reduce excess beer consumption may significantly reduce hyperuricaemia. In those with diuretic-induced gout it may prove possible to stop their diuretic, depending on the reasons for its use. Although a very high purine diet (large amounts of offal and meat) should be tempered, there is no need for a specific highly restrictive diet.

Prolonged hypouricaemic drug treatment is indicated for:

- recurrent attacks of acute gout
- tophi
- evidence of bone or joint damage
- associated renal disease
- gout with greatly elevated serum uric acid.

Allopurinol is the usual drug of choice because of its once-daily convenience and low incidence of side-effects. It inhibits xanthine oxidase and reduces conversion of hypoxanthine and xanthine to uric acid. The usual starting dose is 100–300 mg daily but lower doses (100 mg or less) should be used in older patients or if renal function is impaired. The sharp reduction in tissue uric acid levels that follows initiation of treatment can partially dissolve MSUM crystals and trigger acute attacks. The patient should be warned of this and told to continue treatment even if an attack occurs. This tendency can be minimised by using a lower starting dose (100 mg) or by concurrent administration of oral colchicine (0.5 mg 12-hourly) for the first few weeks. Initiation of treatment during an attack can exacerbate and prolong the episode so it is prudent to wait until the attack settles.

The aim of treatment is to bring the serum uric acid level into the lower half of the normal range to ensure dissolution of crystals and to prevent new crystals forming. The serum uric acid should therefore be measured every 6 weeks and the dose of allopurinol increased in 100 mg increments until this is achieved. Infrequent (e.g. yearly) monitoring is advised to ensure maintenance of effective treatment. In most cases allopurinol will need to be continued indefinitely.

Uricosuric drugs can achieve equivalent reductions in serum uric acid to allopurinol. Probenecid (0.5–1 g 12-hourly) or sulfinpyrazone (100 mg 8-hourly) are effective uricosurics but have the disadvantage of requiring several doses each day and maintenance of a high urine flow (to avoid uric acid crystallisation in renal tubules). Salicylates antagonise the uricosuric action of these drugs and should be avoided. Uricosurics are contraindicated:

- in over-producers (they already have gross uricosuria)
- in patients with renal impairment (ineffective)
- in patients with urolithiasis (increased stone formation).

The uricosuric benzbromarone (100 mg daily) is effective in patients with mild to moderate renal impairment but has limited availability in most countries.

Asymptomatic hyperuricaemia

There is no evidence that hyperuricaemia itself is damaging. Treatment is therefore unnecessary unless there is a strong family history of gout, urolithiasis or persistently very high levels (> 0.6 mmol/l). Causes of secondary hyperuricaemia should be considered.

ISSUES IN OLDER PEOPLE
GOUT

- This is never primary but usually secondary to chronic (> 18 months) diuretic therapy (thiazides, loop diuretics) or, less commonly, chronic renal failure.
- In the older person on long-term diuretic therapy nodal generalised osteoarthritis is an important additional risk factor for developing gout.
- In contrast to primary gout, secondary gout in the elderly often presents as painful tophi rather than as acute attacks. Hands, not feet, are the target site of involvement in this age group.
- Because of increased toxicity in the elderly allopurinol should be started at the low dose of 100 mg/day.
- Acute attacks in the elderly are best treated by aspiration and intra-articular injection of long-acting steroid followed by early mobilisation. Oral NSAID and colchicine are best avoided because of increased incidence and severity of toxicity.

CALCIUM PYROPHOSPHATE DIHYDRATE (CPPD) CRYSTAL DEPOSITION

CPPD crystal deposition in hyaline and fibrocartilage of joints (chondrocalcinosis) is a common age-associated phenomenon (> 55) that particularly targets the knee. Sporadic, familial and metabolic disease-associated forms are recognised. It is often clinically occult, but can cause acute self-limiting synovitis ('pseudogout') or occur as a chronic arthritis showing a strong association/overlap with osteoarthritis.

Epidemiology

Radiographic chondrocalcinosis is more common in women and shows a striking association with age, being rare under the age of 55, but rising from 10–15% in those aged 65–75 to 30–60% in those over 85. The knee (hyaline cartilage and menisci) is by far the most prevalent site, followed by the wrist (triangular fibrocartilage) and pelvis (symphysis pubis). There is an increased association with radiographic osteoarthritis, especially at the knee (see Fig. 20.37).

Aetiology

CPPD deposition is most commonly sporadic, occurring as an isolated phenomenon in aged but otherwise apparently normal fibrocartilage and hyaline cartilage in knees and just one or two other sites. Apart from ageing, the strongest association is with osteoarthritis (see Box 20.48). The changes in osteoarthritic cartilage that may encourage CPPD crystal deposition are:

- reduction in concentration of proteoglycan and other natural inhibitors of crystal formation
- increased extracellular pyrophosphate levels due to upregulated chondrocyte metabolism.

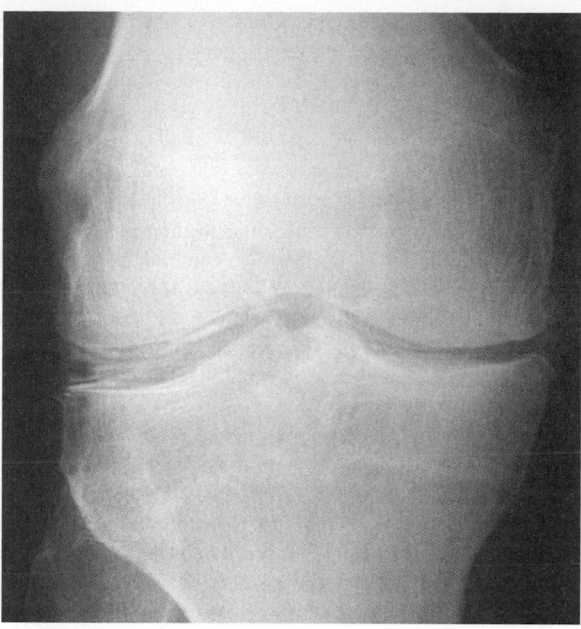

Fig. 20.37 Knee radiograph showing chondrocalcinosis of the fibrocartilaginous menisci and articular hyaline cartilage. There is also narrowing and osteophyte of the medial tibio-femoral compartment.

20.48 ASSOCIATIONS OF CPPD CRYSTAL DEPOSITION		
	Chondro-calcinosis	Structural arthritis
Ageing (sporadic) —most common	+	–
Osteoarthritis, joint damage —common	+	+
Familial predisposition —rare	+	Variable
Metabolic disease —rare		
Haemochromatosis	+	+
Hyperparathyroidism	+	0
Hypophosphatasia	+	0
Hypomagnesaemia	+	0
Wilson's disease	+	0

Rare families have been described from many countries and racial groups in which florid polyarticular chondrocalcinosis develops in the third and fourth decades in association with acute attacks and variable degrees of 'osteoarthritis'. All show an autosomal dominant pattern of inheritance; in some an abnormality of pyrophosphate metabolism has been implicated, though the causal genes remain unknown. A variety of metabolic diseases may also predispose to chondrocalcinosis and recurrent acute attacks due to CPPD, though only haemochromatosis additionally predisposes to osteoarthritis-like structural change. All these diseases elevate extracellular levels of pyrophosphate in joint tissues, mainly through reduced concentration or activity of alkaline phosphatase and other pyrophosphatases, so an increase in ionic product appears to be the principal mechanism of predisposition.

Clinical features

Acute synovitis: 'pseudogout'

This is the most common cause of acute monoarthritis in the elderly. The knee is by far the most common site, followed by the wrist, shoulder, ankle and elbow. It may be the first presentation of previously asymptomatic CPPD, or occur on a background of chronic symptomatic arthritis. Triggering factors include direct trauma and intercurrent illness or surgery.

The typical attack resembles acute gout and develops rapidly, with severe pain, stiffness and swelling, maximal within 6–24 hours of onset. Overlying erythema is common and examination reveals a very tender joint held in the flexed 'loose-pack' position with signs of marked synovitis (large/tense effusion, warmth, restricted movement with stress pain). Fever is common and the patient may appear confused and ill. The attack is self-limiting but may take 1–3 weeks to resolve.

Sepsis and gout are the main differential diagnoses. Although sepsis is often more subacute in onset and is progressive, it often needs exclusion, especially when pseudogout has been triggered by chest infection or surgery and if the patient is unwell. It is noteworthy, however, that sepsis and pseudogout can coexist (infection 'strip-mining' CPPD crystals from cartilage). Gout is unlikely in patients over the age of 65 without a preceding history of primary gout or chronic diuretic therapy and seldom involves the knee in a first attack.

Chronic ('pyrophosphate') arthritis

Most patients with chronic symptoms are elderly women. The distribution is similar to that of pseudogout, with knees being the worst affected, then wrists, shoulders, elbows, hips and midtarsals. In the hand the second and third metacarpophalangeal joints are often the ones most affected. Symptoms are chronic pain, variable early morning and inactivity stiffness, and functional impairment. Acute attacks may be superimposed on this chronic history. Symptoms usually target just a few joints, though single or multiple joint involvement can occur. Affected joints show features of osteoarthritis (bony swelling, crepitus, restriction) with varying degrees of synovitis. Effusion and synovial thickening are usually most apparent at knees and wrists; wrist involvement may result in carpal tunnel syndrome. Examination often reveals more widespread but asymptomatic signs of osteoarthritis, and Heberden's nodes and generalised osteoarthritis commonly coexist.

Inflammatory features may be sufficiently pronounced to suggest rheumatoid arthritis. However, the absence of tenosynovitis and extra-articular involvement, and targeting of large and medium rather than small joints usually permit distinction. Severe damage and instability of knees or shoulders may occasionally lead to consideration of a neuropathic joint, though neurological findings are normal.

Incidental finding

Because of its high age-associated prevalence radiographic chondrocalcinosis is often seen as an incidental finding in older subjects. As with uncomplicated osteoarthritis, asymptomatic clinical and radiographic features of 'pyrophosphate' arthritis are also not uncommon in the elderly. A thorough history and examination are always required to determine the relevance of such findings to symptom causation.

Investigations

In acute pseudogout examination of synovial fluid using compensated polarised microscopy will demonstrate CPPD crystals (see Fig. 20.4B, p. 966) and permit distinction from urate gout. The aspirated fluid is often turbid and may be uniformly blood-stained, reflecting the severity of inflammation. Gram stain and culture of the fluid will exclude sepsis. CPPD crystals may also be identified in smaller numbers in the less inflammatory fluids aspirated from chronic pyrophosphate arthritis.

Radiographs may show chondrocalcinosis in hyaline cartilage and/or fibrocartilage (occasionally capsule or ligament) with or without associated structural changes of osteoarthritis (see Fig. 20.37). Chondrocalcinosis is not always evident, especially in joints showing some degree of cartilage loss, and its absence does not exclude the diagnosis of pseudogout. Synovial fluid crystal identification (and negative culture) is the principal diagnostic test.

Screening for metabolic or familial predisposition should be undertaken in patients who show:

- early-onset CPPD deposition, < 55 years old
- florid polyarticular, as opposed to pauciarticular, chondrocalcinosis
- recurrent acute attacks without chronic arthropathy
- additional clinical or radiographic features of predisposing disease.

Metabolic screening includes serum calcium, alkaline phosphatase, magnesium, ferritin and liver function. If positive, some metabolic disease (hypomagnesaemia, haemochromatosis, hypophosphatasia) requires examination of first-degree relatives. For investigation of non-metabolic familial CPPD, a bilateral knee radiograph is an appropriate screen. If there is no chondrocalcinosis at the knee, it is extremely unlikely to be elsewhere.

Management

For acute pseudogout, aspiration quickly reduces pain and may alone be sufficient. Fluid reaccumulation, however, is common, particularly early in an attack, and for florid pseudogout intra-articular injection of steroid is usually required. Oral NSAIDs and colchicine are also effective, as in gout, but should be avoided if possible in the elderly. Early active mobilisation is also important in this age group.

For chronic arthropathy management is the same as for osteoarthritis (see p. 1001).

BASIC CALCIUM PHOSPHATE (BCP) DEPOSITION

Hydroxyapatite (apatite) is the principal mineral in bone and teeth. Apatite and other BCPs (octacalcium phosphate, tricalcium phosphate) are also the usual minerals to deposit in extraskeletal tissues. In MSK tissues abnormal deposition may occur in:

- periarticular tissues, particularly tendon
- hyaline cartilage in association with osteoarthritis
- subcutaneous tissue and muscle, principally in connective tissue diseases.

Aetiology

The ionic product of [calcium] × [phosphate] must be kept high to maintain skeletal integrity. Specific cellular mechanisms activate calcification where it is appropriate: for example, around matrix vesicles of growing cartilage. Other mechanisms, such as local concentrations of pyrophosphate and proteoglycan, inhibit calcification elsewhere. In general, abnormal calcification due to BCP results from:

- elevation of the calcium phosphate product, causing widespread 'metastatic' calcification (e.g. hyperparathyroidism, chronic dialysis, vitamin D intoxication), or
- alteration in the local balance of tissue inhibitors and promoters of crystal formation, causing local 'dystrophic' calcification (e.g. atherosclerotic arteries, fibrotic lymph nodes, scarred lung parenchyma).

In most situations such calcification is of no consequence, possibly because of protein coating or surrounding fibrous tissue that protects BCP crystals from contact with inflammatory mediators. However, BCP crystals have inflammatory potential and in some MSK situations their deposition associates with clinical problems.

Individual apatite crystals are too small to be viewed by light microscopy but their aggregated spherulites can be seen using calcium stains. Sophisticated analytical techniques are required to identify individual BCPs but for clinical purposes presumptive diagnosis based on radiographic calcification or non-specific calcium staining of synovial fluid or histological tissue is sufficient.

Calcific periarthritis

Deposition of apatite in the supraspinatus tendon (see Fig. 20.38) is a relatively common incidental radiographic finding in around 7% of adults. It occasionally results in severe acute inflammation of the subacromial bursa and periarticular tissues through crystal shedding from the tendon into and around the bursa. Periarticular sites around the greater trochanter of the hip, foot or hand are less common sites. Men and women are equally affected, usually as young or middle-aged adults.

The acute episode may occur spontaneously or follow local trauma. Within just a few hours shoulder pain and tenderness are extreme and the area appears swollen, hot and sometimes red. Modest systemic upset and fever are common. Radiographs confirm the diagnosis by showing tendon calcification. If the subacromial bursa is aspirated, thick white fluid containing many calcium-staining (alizarin red S) aggregates may be obtained.

The condition usually resolves spontaneously over 1–3 weeks, often accompanied by radiographic dispersal and

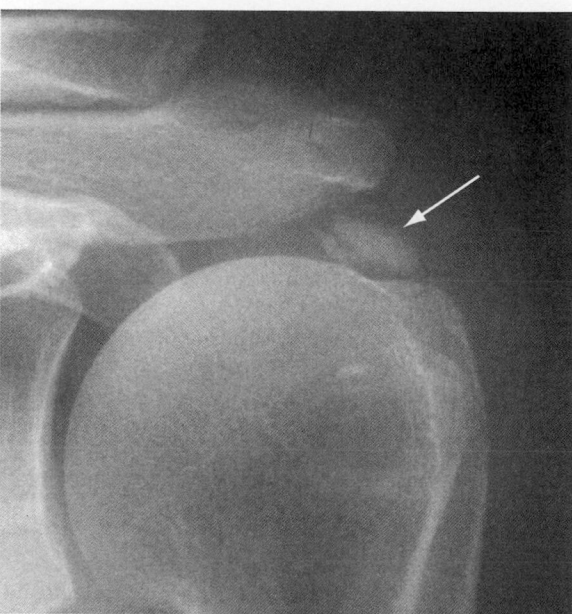

Fig. 20.38 Shoulder radiograph showing supraspinatus tendon calcification (arrow).

disappearance of small to modest-sized deposits (i.e. complete crystal shedding). Calcific periarthritis may result from metabolic abnormality (renal failure, hyperparathyroidism, hypophosphatasia) but measurements of serum creatinine, calcium and alkaline phosphatase are usually normal. The CRP is elevated during the episode.

Oral analgesics and NSAIDs ameliorate symptoms and the attack may be abbreviated by aspiration and injection of steroid. Exceptionally large deposits may cause mechanical blocking and painful impingement on abduction rather than acute periarthritis, and require surgical removal.

Osteoarthritis and BCP crystal deposition

Modest amounts of BCP aggregates are commonly found in synovial fluid from osteoarthritic joints, either alone or with CPPD crystals ('mixed crystal deposition'). Whether they contribute to joint damage or cause minor inflammatory episodes remains unclear. Large amounts of BCP, however, have been associated with an uncommon but distinctive form of osteoarthritis characterised by:

- presence in elderly people (> 75), predominantly women
- involvement of knee, hip or shoulder (large joints) only
- rapid progression, often leading to severe pain and disability in just a few months
- development of marked instability and large effusions of knees or shoulders
- an atrophic radiographic appearance with marked loss of cartilage and bone and minimal osteophyte or remodelling.

Aspiration yields large volumes of relatively non-inflammatory fluid containing abundant BCP aggregates and often cartilage fragments. The differential diagnosis of such rapidly destructive arthropathy is end-stage avascular necrosis, chronic sepsis or neuropathic joint. Unlike sepsis, the acute phase response is not triggered and synovial fluid cultures are negative.

Treatment is with analgesics, intra-articular injection of steroids, local physical treatments and physiotherapy. The clinical outcome, however, is poor and most patients require joint replacement surgery. It is most likely that the BCP aggregates, rather than being causal pathogenic agents, are a marker of the speed of joint damage in such 'apatite-associated destructive arthritis' which represents the most severe end of the spectrum of osteoarthritis.

JOINT INFECTION

SEPTIC ARTHRITIS

Septic arthritis is a medical emergency. It is the most rapid and destructive joint disease and has a significant morbidity and a mortality of 10%. This has not improved over the last 20 years despite advances in antimicrobial therapy. The incidence is 2–10 per 100 000 in the general population and 30–70 per 100 000 in those with pre-existing joint disease or joint replacement.

Patients with septic arthritis have, by definition, a bacteraemia. Haematogenous spread from either skin or upper respiratory tract is the most common mode of entry. Acquisition of infection from direct puncture wounds secondary to joint aspiration is uncommon. Risk factors for septic arthritis include increasing age, pre-existing joint disease (principally rheumatoid arthritis), diabetes mellitus and immunosuppression (through drugs or disease). Additional factors in patients with rheumatoid arthritis include maceration of skin between the toes due to joint deformity, compounded by difficulties in washing and drying the feet due to hand deformities, with breakdown of skin a frequent portal of entry.

Lyme disease (see p. 21) may present with monoarthritis, often with other features including headaches, neurological signs and fatigue. There is usually a history of skin rash (erythema migrans) occurring 7–10 days after tick bite. Diagnosis is confirmed by *Borrelia* serology, although false positives may occur.

Clinical features

The usual presentation is with acute or subacute monoarthritis. The joint is usually swollen, hot and red and held in the 'loose-pack' position, with rest pain and stress pain on movement. Although any joint can be affected, the lower limb, particularly knee and hip, is the most common site. In patients with pre-existing arthritis involvement of one or more joints is not uncommon and a full MSK examination should be undertaken.

In adults the most likely organism is *Staphylococcus aureus*, particularly in patients with rheumatoid arthritis and diabetes. In young, sexually active adults disseminated gonococcal infection is an important cause. Disseminated

infection occurs in up to 3% of untreated gonorrhoea. The usual presentation is with migratory arthralgia, low-grade fever and tenosynovitis, which may precede the development of oligo- or monoarthritis. Painful pustular skin lesions may also be present. Amongst the elderly or those who misuse intravenous drugs, Gram-negative bacilli or group B, C and G streptococci are important causes. Other organisms that are occasionally isolated include group A streptococci, pneumococci, meningococci and *Haemophilus influenzae*.

Investigation

Joint aspiration is essential whenever septic arthritis is suspected. Synovial fluid should be sent for Gram stain and culture. Aspirated fluid often looks turbid or blood-stained but may appear more normal. Blood cultures should also be taken. If the joint is not readily accessible (e.g. hip, spine, sacroiliac joint), aspiration should be performed under image guidance or in theatre. Prosthetic joints should only be aspirated in theatre.

Synovial fluid culture is positive in around 90% of cases of septic arthritis, though in only 50% of these is the initial Gram stain positive. By contrast, synovial fluid culture is positive in only 30% of gonococcal infections, making it important to obtain concurrent cultures from the genital tract (positive in 70–90% of cases). Although fever with peripheral leucocytosis and raised ESR occur in most patients, these may be absent in elderly or immunocompromised patients or early in the disease course.

Management

Hospitalisation is essential. The principles of management are:

- pain relief
- parenteral antibiotics
- adequate drainage
- early active rehabilitation.

The recommended first-line antibiotic regime treatment in adults is flucloxacillin (2 g i.v. 6-hourly), which will cover both staphylococcal and streptococcal infection until identification and antibiotic sensitivities are available. Intravenous treatment is usually continued for 2–3 weeks followed by oral treatment for 6 weeks in total. Initially, the joint should be aspirated daily to keep the effusion at a minimum. If this proves unsuccessful or the joint is inaccessible, surgical drainage may be required. Regular passive movement should be undertaken from the outset, and active movements encouraged once the condition has stabilised.

VIRAL ARTHRITIS

Most forms of viral arthritis are self-limiting. The usual presentation is with acute polyarthritis, fever or viral prodrome and rash. Parvovirus arthropathy is the most common and unlike children, adults may not have the characteristic facial rash. Diagnosis is confirmed by a rise in specific IgM. Polyarthritis may also rarely occur with hepatitis B and C, rubella and HIV infection.

20.49 DIFFERENTIAL DIAGNOSIS OF JUVENILE IDIOPATHIC ARTHRITIS*

- Anxiety
- Rickets/metabolic—scurvy, storage diseases
- Tumour
- Haematological—leukaemia, haemophilia, sickle-cell disease
- Reactive—reactive arthritis, rheumatic fever
- Immunological disease—lupus, immunodeficiency, serum sickness
- Trauma, hypermobility
- Injury (non-accidental)
- Sepsis
    Septic arthritis, bacterial endocarditis, meningococcus
    Viral arthritis (including rubella, mumps, parvovirus, glandular fever)

* The list is not exhaustive.

JUVENILE IDIOPATHIC ARTHRITIS

Although MSK pain is prevalent in children, inflammatory arthritis is relatively rare compared to adults (< 0.01% prevalence). Juvenile idiopathic arthritis (JIA) is defined as persistent (> 6 weeks) inflammatory arthritis that begins before age 16 for which no specific cause can be found. There are no specific diagnostic or investigational features for JIA and it is basically a diagnosis of exclusion. A list of some of the alternative diagnoses that may require consideration in a child with MSK pain and apparent joint swelling is shown in Box 20.49.

The aetiology of JIA is unknown, though both genetic and environmental factors are thought to be involved. JIA is classified according to the pattern of onset of arthritis in the first few months. This simple descriptive classification has prognostic significance and helps guide treatment selection. The most recent classification agreed by the International League against Rheumatism (ILAR) is shown in Box 20.50.

Oligoarthritis

This is the most common form, typically affecting pre-school girls and targeting lower limb joints, mainly knees. There is rarely any systemic upset. The MSK prognosis is usually excellent if it remains limited to oligoarthritis (oligoarthritis persisting) but 30% of cases progress to severe polyarthritis (oligoarthritis extending). Antinuclear antibodies and HLA-DR5 are present in 50% and such children are at high risk of asymptomatic chronic anterior uveitis.

Polyarthritis

This accounts for 30–40% of JIA. Those who are seronegative for rheumatoid factor (90%) can be any age but pre-school girls are most commonly affected. There is symmetrical involvement of small and large joints in both upper and lower limbs, with common involvement of the cervical spine. Early cervical fusion and under-development of the mandible

---
20.50 INTERNATIONAL LEAGUE AGAINST RHEUMATISM (ILAR) CLASSIFICATION OF JUVENILE IDIOPATHIC ARTHRITIS*

Pattern	Definition	Main target
Oligoarthritis		
Persisting	Arthritis of 1–4 joints in first 6 months of disease	Young girls
Extending	Arthritis restricted to 1–4 joints in first 6 months that subsequently develops into polyarthritis	Young girls
Polyarthritis		
Rheumatoid factor (RF)-negative	Arthritis of > 4 joints in first 6 months	Young girls
Rheumatoid factor (RF)-positive	Arthritis of > 4 joints in first 6 months, × 2 positive serum rheumatoid factor tests 3 months apart	Older, adolescent girls
Psoriatic arthritis	Arthritis + psoriasis, *or* Arthritis + family history of psoriasis *and* either dactylitis or nail pitting/onycholysis	Older girls and boys equally
Enthesitis-related arthritis	Arthritis + enthesitis, *or* Arthritis + two of: Sacroiliac joint tenderness Inflammatory spinal pain HLA-B27 Anterior uveitis Family history of uveitis, spondarthritis or inflammatory bowel disease	Older boys
Systemic arthritis	Arthritis + fever > 2 weeks, evanescent skin rash	Under 2, girls and boys equally
Other arthritides	Patients who fit no category or more than one category	

* Children under the age of 16 at onset of symptoms with persistent features of arthritis for at least 6 weeks.
---

can give the stiff neck, receding chin and dental problems characteristic of adults who have had this form of JIA. The prognosis is less favourable than oligoarthritis; two-thirds have residual problems into adult life and 10% have severe joint damage.

Less commonly (10%), a similar presentation occurs in older (> 8) or adolescent girls who are rheumatoid factor-positive. They often follow an aggressive course similar to severe adult rheumatoid arthritis with erosions, joint damage, nodules and vasculitis, and show increased association with HLA-DR4.

Psoriatic arthritis

This usually presents as an asymmetrical oligoarthritis. The diagnosis is made on the presence of skin plaques, or on a family history of psoriasis together with accompanying nail dystrophy or dactylitis ('sausage digit'). The prognosis for both the arthritis and uveitis tends to be worse than for non-psoriatic oligoarthritis.

Enthesitis-related arthritis

Older children and adolescents, especially boys, may develop lower limb mono- or oligoarthritis (hips, knees, ankles) with enthesitis (e.g. Achilles insertion, plantar fasciitis). Sacroiliitis is common and there may be a family history of seronegative spondarthritis, uveitis or inflammatory bowel disease. Around 75% are HLA-B27-positive and in most the disease gradually evolves into adult ankylosing spondylitis. The prognosis is worse than for adult-onset spondylitis.

Systemic arthritis

This pattern is the least common. It equally affects boys and girls and can occur at any age, though very young (< 2 years old) children are mostly affected. The diagnosis can be difficult since systemic upset and extra-articular features are initially often more dominant than the arthritis. Lymphadenopathy, hepatosplenomegaly, pleuro-pericarditis and high fevers often make malignancy or sepsis the main differential diagnoses. The intermittent nature of the fever and its accompaniment by an evanescent faint pink macular rash are helpful clues to the diagnosis. Remission of initial systemic inflammation usually occurs within 6 months, but over half the children have recurrent episodes and 30% develop severe chronic polyarthritis that is often resistant to treatment and may lead to subsequent secondary amyloidosis.

Complications

There is considerable physical, social and psychological morbidity with JIA. Special features of childhood arthritis include:

- *Uveitis.* Chronic anterior uveitis is asymptomatic and potentially blinding. It is often bilateral, can develop in the absence of active synovitis and is detectable only by slit lamp examination. The greatest risk is with early-onset (< 6 years old) oligoarthritis in young girls who are ANA-positive.
- *Growth disturbance.* There may be a generalised suppressive effect due to active inflammation, compounded by use of systemic corticosteroids,

as well as localised effects of synovitis that may lead to accelerated or retarded epiphyseal growth (e.g. long leg or short limbs and fingers) or early fusion of epiphyses (e.g. short limbs, micrognathia).
- *Loss of schooling and family disruption.* The social and psychological consequences of chronic disease in childhood for both the child and the family should not be underestimated.

Management

Successful management of the interlinked educational, social, psychological and physical problems requires the skills of an experienced multidisciplinary team comprising rheumatologists, paediatricians, physiotherapists, occupational therapists, nurses, ophthalmologists, dentists/orthodontists, psychologists, social workers and teachers. Treatment usually includes education, regular exercise and physical therapy, NSAIDs, intra-articular steroid injections and antirheumatic drugs. Schooling should be integrated with healthy peers wherever possible, requiring close cooperation with community professionals.

Active physiotherapy is of great importance to reduce deformities and maintain muscle strength. Rest may be required when joints are acutely inflamed, but care must be taken to avoid development of flexion deformities, especially of hips and knees, by encouraging regular prone lying and the use of appropriate lightweight splints. Whenever possible, the child should be kept mobile and ambulant, and daily physiotherapy given to maintain a good range of joint movements and muscle strength. Hydrotherapy in a warm pool is particularly useful. Special consideration needs to be given to maintaining the child's education and helping parents to develop a sensible, vigilant but not over-protective approach.

Drug therapy

NSAIDs are useful symptomatic drugs and may be the only medication required for oligoarthritis. NSAIDs are safer and better tolerated in children than in adults, perhaps reflecting more rapid hepatic metabolism and urinary excretion and greater ability to repair mucosal surfaces. They are used at higher doses than in adults. For example, initial and maximum doses of commonly used NSAIDs include: naproxen 10–30 mg/kg/day, ibuprofen 30–60 mg/kg/day, tolmetin 20–30 mg/kg/day, and piroxicam 0.3–0.6 mg/kg/day. Aspirin should be avoided because of the risk of Reye's syndrome. If NSAIDs fail to settle the arthritis, intra-articular steroid injections are used to treat resistant joints (often delivered under short-acting general anaesthesia or relaxants), with or without parenteral bolus injections for multiple joint involvement. Joint injections in children can have long-lasting benefits compared with adults. If patients with oligoarthritis fail to respond, methotrexate is added for at least 2 years. Combined therapy with hydroxychloroquine or ciclosporin A may be considered if methotrexate alone is insufficient.

Slow-acting antirheumatic drugs should be considered early in the disease course for all children with polyarthritis. Poor prognostic features include positive rheumatoid factor, systemic arthritis that evolves into polyarthritis, extended oligoarthritis and psoriatic polyarthritis. Methotrexate and sulfasalazine are the most effective agents; gold, d-penicillamine and hydroxychloroquine have no significant benefit.

Long-term corticosteroids are reserved for children with severe systemic disease, for those with chronic uveitis not responding to local therapy and where very active joint disease does not respond to other measures. The use of alternate-day corticosteroids should always be considered since doses of prednisolone as low as 3 mg/day can inhibit growth in children under 5 years. Corticosteroids do not arrest the progression of disease.

In children with systemic arthritis who fail to respond to steroids or NSAIDs for at least 2 years, combination therapy including methotrexate, cyclophosphamide and prednisolone may be considered. The balance is swinging in favour of early aggressive treatment in children with risk factors for poor outcome with the hope that this will achieve better long-term results. Chlorambucil is used in children with secondary amyloidosis.

Surgery

Surgery is usually limited to the rehabilitation of children with deformities. Soft tissue release operations may be helpful in eliminating difficult flexion contractures, and osteotomies may be required when joints have been allowed to fuse in poor positions. Total hip arthroplasty can be considered for severely damaged joints as soon as growth has ceased.

FIBROMYALGIA

This is a very common cause of multiple regional MSK pain and disability. There is no associated pathology but physiological abnormalities of sleep and pain processing are both recognised. It commonly associates with medically unexplained symptoms in other systems and shows considerable overlap with, and similar risk factors to, other syndromes of 'functional disturbance' (see Ch. 8).

Epidemiology

The crude prevalence in UK and US communities is 2–3%. There is a strong female predominance of around 10:1. Although fibromyalgia can occur at any age, including in teenagers, it shows a progressive increase with age, reaching a maximum prevalence of 7% in women aged over 70. The condition appears ubiquitous and is reported in a wide variety of racial groups and cultural settings.

Recognised risk factors other than ageing and female gender include a wide variety of life events that all associate with psychosocial distress: for example, divorce, marital disharmony, alcoholism in the family, traumatic injury or assault, low income and self-reported childhood abuse.

Aetiology

The condition is poorly understood. Despite intensive and invasive investigation no structural, inflammatory, metabolic or endocrine abnormality has been identified. Two abnormalities, however, have consistently been reported:

- *Sleep abnormality.* Delta waves are characteristic of the deep stages of non-rapid eye movement (non-REM) sleep. Most delta sleep usually occurs in the first few hours and is thought to have primarily a restorative function. People with fibromyalgia have difficulty quickly entering delta sleep and obtain reduced amounts during the night. This pattern differs from sleep abnormalities associated with clinical depression alone. Furthermore, deprivation of delta but not REM sleep in normal volunteers produces the symptoms and signs of fibromyalgia, supporting the concept of fibromyalgia as a non-restorative sleep disorder.

- *Abnormal pain processing.* A reduced threshold to pain perception and tolerance at characteristic sites throughout the body is a central feature of fibromyalgia. Affected people also have spinal cord 'wind-up' (pain amplification), as evidenced by the exaggerated skin flare response to topically applied capsaicin and frequent occurrence of dermatographism and allodynia (when normally non-noxious stimuli become painful). Other observations to support abnormal pain processing include altered cerebrospinal fluid levels of substance P (increased) and 5-HT (reduced) and reduced regional cerebral blood flow in the caudate and thalamus.

Both these abnormalities may interrelate. Poor sleep may impair normal descending inhibition to the spinal cord centres that gate pain and, equally, chronic pain may interrupt sleep. The strong association with distressing life events might also explain initial disruption of normal sleep and restoration. A current hypothesis to explain these interrelations is outlined in Figure 20.39.

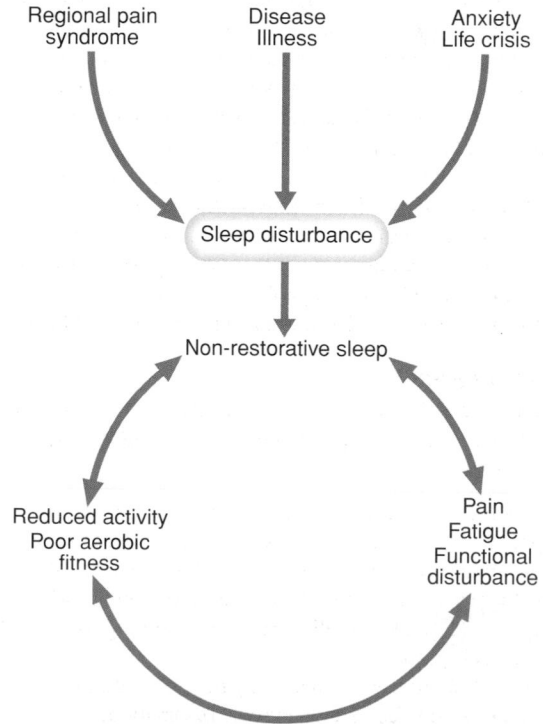

Fig. 20.39   Possible mechanisms involved in fibromyalgia.

Epidemiological studies have confirmed the clustering of poor sleep, multiple regional pain, widespread hyperalgesia and low scores on anxiety and depression ratings, giving some credence to 'fibromyalgia' as a descriptive term to characterise people with the combination of such problems (see EBM panel).

FIBROMYALGIA—evidence for associations   **EBM**

'Epidemiological community studies have shown that widespread body pain, fatigue, psychological distress and multiple hyperalgesic tender sites cluster together and associate with increased odds ratios of various stressful life events.'

- Wolfe F, Ross K, Anderson J, et al. The prevalence and characteristics of fibromyalgia in the general population. Arthritis Rheum 1995; 38:19–28.
- Croft P, Schollum J, Silman A. Population study of tender point counts and pain as evidence of fibromyalgia. BMJ 1994; 309:696–699.

Clinical features

The main presenting feature is multiple regional pain, often focusing on the neck and back (see Box 20.51). At presentation just one or a few regions may dominate the picture, but over the preceding months pain will have affected all body quadrants—both arms, both legs, neck and back. The pain is characteristically unresponsive to traditional measures (analgesics, NSAIDs) and physiotherapy often makes it worse. Fatigability, most prominent in the morning, is the second major problem. Reported disability is often marked. Although people can usually dress, feed and groom themselves, they may be unable to perform daily tasks such as shopping, housework or gardening. They may have experienced major

20.51 SYMPTOMS OF FIBROMYALGIA

Usual symptoms

- Multiple regional pain
- Marked fatigability
- Marked disability
- Broken non-restorative sleep
- Low affect, irritability, weepiness
- Poor concentration, forgetfulness

Variable locomotor symptoms

- Early morning stiffness
- Swelling of hands, fingers
- Numbness, tingling of all fingers

Additional, variable, non-locomotor symptoms

- Non-throbbing bifrontal headache ('tension headache')
- Colicky abdominal pain, bloating, variable bowel habit ('irritable bowel syndrome')
- Bladder fullness, nocturnal frequency ('irritable bladder')
- Hyperacusis, dyspareunia, discomfort when touched (allodynia)
- Common side-effects with drugs ('chemical sensitivity')

difficulties at work or even given up employment because of pain and fatigue.

Examination usually reveals no abnormality of the MSK system in terms of joint synovitis or damage and no overt neurological defect or wasting. Depending on their age, people may have signs of osteoarthritis or other prevalent MSK conditions, but of insufficient severity to explain such widespread symptoms and severe disability. The principal finding is hyperalgesia at recognised natural tender sites in the body (see Fig. 20.40). Moderate digital pressure at each site

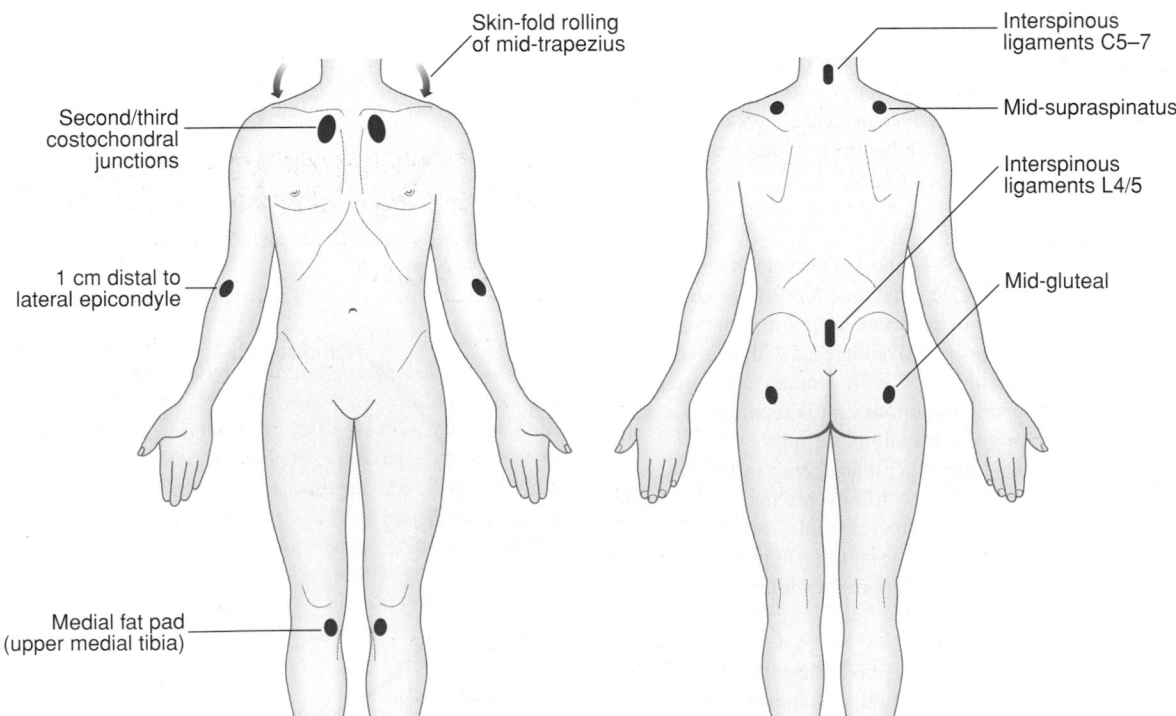

Fig. 20.40 **Major tender sites that become hyperalgesic with fibromyalgia.**

may be uncomfortable in a normal subject but in fibromyalgia it produces a wince/withdrawal response. Metered dolorimeters are available for research purposes but moderate digital pressure, sufficient to just whiten the nail, is sufficient for clinical diagnosis.

To fulfil the criteria for fibromyalgia the person requires:

- the appropriate symptoms, including pain affecting all body quadrants
- positive hyperalgesic tender sites in each arm and leg and axially (i.e. widespread)
- negative control tender sites (pressure on forehead, squeezing across the distal radius and ulna, pressure over the proximal fibular head).

If someone exhibits hyperalgesia wherever pressure is applied, he or she is likely to have severe psychological disturbance or be malingering.

People with recognised MSK or other disease (e.g. rheumatoid arthritis, lupus, cancer) are not exempt from developing fibromyalgia. Assessment of people with coexistent rheumatoid arthritis or lupus may prove challenging since many of the symptoms could relate to activity of their multisystem disease. Marked discordance between the severity of reported and observed abnormality, however, is an important feature to suggest fibromyalgia, and widespread hyperalgesic tender sites are not explained by polyarticular disease.

Investigations

Fibromyalgia does not associate with any abnormality of routine testing. However, it is important to screen for alternative conditions that may account for some of the symptoms without producing overt clinical signs (see Box 20.52).

20.52 A MINIMUM INVESTIGATION SCREEN IN PEOPLE WITH FIBROMYALGIA	
Test	**Condition screened**
Full blood count	Anaemia, lymphopenia of lupus
ESR, CRP	Inflammatory disease
Thyroid function	Hypothyroidism
Calcium, alkaline phosphatase	Hyperparathyroidism, osteomalacia
Antinuclear antibody	Lupus

Management

The aims of management are education concerning the nature of the problem, pain control and improvement of sleep.

Education is central. Wherever possible, discussion should include the spouse, family or carer so that the same information is shared. The fact that the person's chronic pain does not reflect inflammation, damage or disease is a vital but difficult concept to explain. Repeat or drawn-out investigation may reinforce beliefs in occult serious pathology and should be avoided. The central importance of sleep and the fact that selective sleep deprivation can cause these symptoms in anyone deserves emphasis. Ascribing the symptoms to a cause for which the patient cannot be blamed, and

knowing that it is very common often help. The fact that we recognise the condition but have no clear medical explanation for it should be admitted. The model of a self-perpetuating cycle of poor sleep causing body pain that limits activity, that then worsens sleep, that then makes pain worse is often readily accepted and is a useful framework for a problem-based management strategy.

The two evidence-based interventions that may help some individuals are:

1. *Low-dose amitriptyline* (25–75 mg nocte) for a limited trial of 2–3 weeks, continuing thereafter if pain and fatigue are improved. Combination with fluoxetine (20 mg in the morning) may increase the benefit. Many people with fibromyalgia, however, are intolerant of even small doses of amitriptyline.

2. *A graded increase in aerobic exercise* to improve well-being and sleep quality. This often requires regular supervision if it is to succeed.

The use of self-help strategies should be encouraged. A cognitive behavioural approach, with relaxation techniques and other coping strategies, may help the person better deal with symptoms. Many people with chronic pain 'for no obvious cause' adopt maladaptive illness behaviour patterns and these can sometimes be modified with resultant improved coping. Sublimated anxiety relating to distressing life events should be specifically explored and addressed by appropriate counselling. Literature is available and there are patient organisations from which to obtain additional information and support.

The prognosis for hospital-diagnosed fibromyalgia is poor. Although treatment may improve their quality of life and ability to cope, most people do not lose their symptoms or diagnostic criteria over 5 years. Subjects diagnosed in primary care, or who have sublimated anxiety that can be successfully addressed, may fare better.

DISEASES OF BONE

OSTEOPOROSIS

Osteoporosis is a common disease characterised by reduced bone mass, microarchitectural deterioration of bone tissue and an increased risk of fracture. The prevalence of osteoporosis and osteoporosis-related fractures both increase with age in women and men, reflecting age-related decline in bone mass. Fractures related to osteoporosis are a major public health problem in all developed countries, and are estimated to affect up to 30% of women and 12% of men at some time in their life. In the UK alone osteoporotic fractures affect over 200 000 individuals annually, with treatment costs of about £1.4 billion.

Pathogenesis

One of the defining features of osteoporosis is reduced bone mass. In normal individuals bone mass increases during skeletal growth to reach a peak between the ages of 20 and 25 but falls thereafter in both sexes, with an accelerated phase of more rapid bone loss in women due to the effects of oestrogen deficiency at the menopause. This loss of bone mass is caused by an imbalance between bone resorption and bone formation (see Fig. 20.41). Individuals who have normal peak bone mass are protected against osteoporosis, even though they suffer age-related bone loss (panel A) whereas patients with low peak bone mass are at risk of developing osteoporosis from age-related bone loss (panel B). Osteoporosis can also occur in patients with normal peak bone mass if bone resorption substantially exceeds bone formation (panel C). Patients with low peak bone mass in whom bone resorption substantially exceeds bone formation are at risk of severe osteoporosis (panel D).

Many factors regulate bone mass and bone loss in normal individuals. They include genetic influences and environmental factors such as exercise, smoking and diet. Twin and family studies have shown that heredity accounts for 70–85% of individual variance in bone mass and also contributes to other determinants of fracture risk such as bone loss and body weight. The genetic mechanisms are incompletely understood, but appear to involve subtle variations (polymorphism—see p. 347) in several genes that regulate bone cell activity and composition of bone matrix. Rarely, osteoporosis may result from single gene disorders. Environmental factors such as exercise and calcium intake during growth and adolescence are also important in maximising peak bone mass and in regulating rates of post-menopausal bone loss. Finally, bone loss may occur as a complication of various endocrine, inflammatory and neoplastic conditions, in hypogonadism and as the result of various drug treatments, especially corticosteroids (see Box 20.53). The pathogenesis of corticosteroid-induced osteoporosis involves reduced bone formation, impaired calcium absorption, increased urinary loss of calcium and hypogonadism.

Clinical features

Clinical presentation is with fragility fractures (see p. 985). These can affect virtually any bone, but the most common sites are the forearm (Colles fracture), spine (vertebral fracture) and femur (hip fracture) (see Fig. 20.42). Colles and vertebral fractures typically occur in women aged 55 and above, whereas hip fractures mainly affect individuals aged 70 and above. Since low bone density alone does not cause symptoms, patients with advanced osteoporosis may be completely asymptomatic until a fracture occurs.

Investigations and diagnosis

Patients with suspected osteoporosis should undergo bone densitometry at the spine and hip (see p. 972). If this shows a BMD T-score value of –2.5 or less at either site, the diagnosis

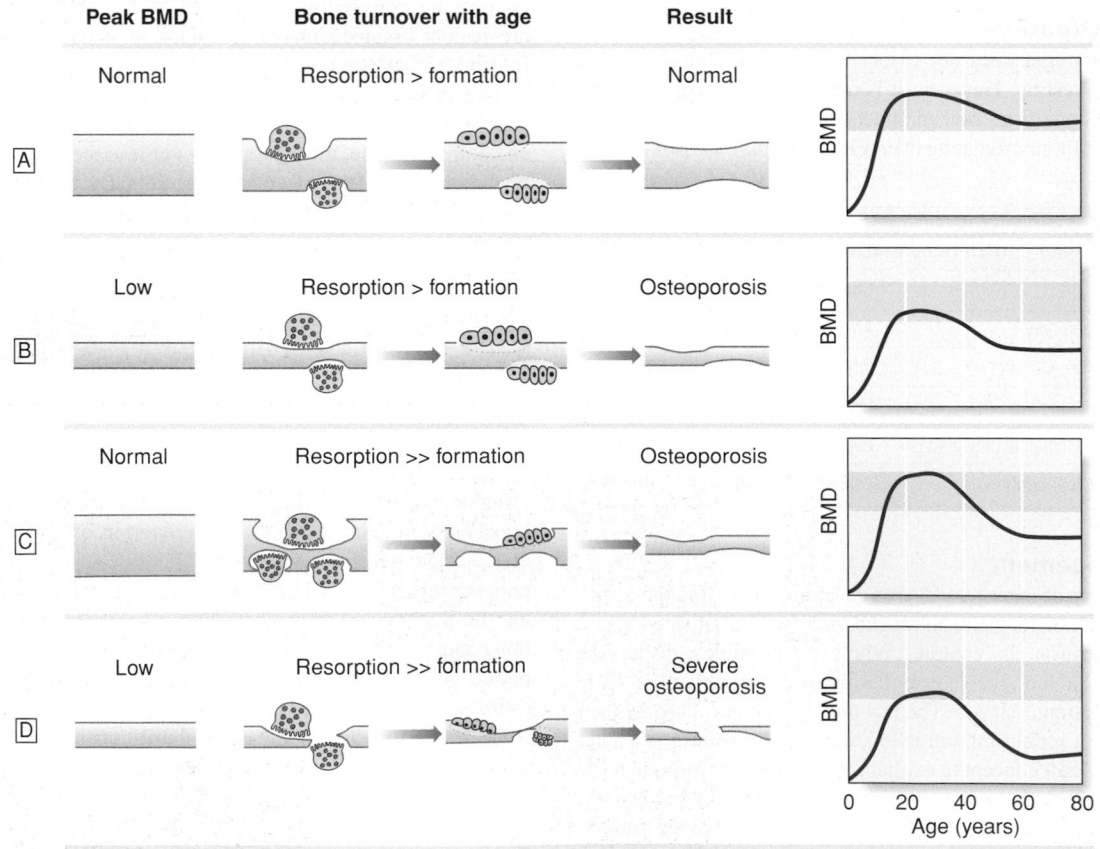

Fig. 20.41 Mechanisms of osteoporosis. The panels on the far right depict changes in bone mineral density with age under various scenarios for peak bone mass and bone remodelling. The green shaded area represents the 'normal range' in young healthy individuals.

20.53 RISK FACTORS FOR OSTEOPOROSIS AND OSTEOPOROTIC FRACTURES

Genetic

- Race
- Low body weight*
- Family history

Lifestyle

- Diet/calcium intake
- Exercise/immobility
- Highly trained athletes*

Endocrine

- Pituitary disease*
- Early menopause*
- Thyrotoxicosis
- Hyperparathyroidism

Inflammatory disease

- Ankylosing spondylitis
- Rheumatoid arthritis
- Inflammatory bowel disease

Gastrointestinal disease

- Malabsorption
- Chronic liver disease

Drugs

- Corticosteroids
- Anticonvulsants
- Sedatives
- Gonadotrophin-releasing hormone (GnRH) agonists*

Substance misuse

- Alcoholism
- Smoking

Others

- Anorexia nervosa*
- Myeloma
- Mastocytosis
- Homocystinuria
- Gaucher's disease

* Underproduction of sex hormones plays an important role in osteoporosis associated with these conditions.

is confirmed. Secondary causes of osteoporosis should be sought by clinical history and physical examination, supplemented by biochemical screening for thyrotoxicosis (see p. 691), myeloma (ESR, serum protein electrophoresis) and primary hyperparathyroidism (see p. 718). When osteoporosis occurs in men and pre-menopausal women, hypogonadism should be excluded by measurement of sex hormones and gonadotrophins. Routine biochemistry is usually normal in post-menopausal osteoporosis but serum alkaline phosphatase can be raised transiently following a fracture. Bone biopsy is not required for diagnosis but can be helpful in identifying unusual causes and in excluding osteomalacia.

Management

An algorithm for the management of patients with suspected osteoporosis is shown in Figure 20.43. Individuals with a normal BMD can be reassured. Those with mild osteopenia (T-score –1.0 to –2.0) should be given general advice on lifestyle factors such as smoking (stop), alcohol (limit to < 20 units/week), dietary calcium intake (aim for 1500 mg daily) and exercise (encourage), and reassessed after 3–5 years. Specific pharmacological therapy should be considered in addition to lifestyle advice in patients with more severe osteopenia (T-score –2.0 to –2.5) and in those with osteoporosis (T-score values of –2.5 and below). Pharmacological treatment (see Box 20.54) is especially indicated in those patients with osteoporosis who have suffered fragility fractures since their risk of further fracture is high.

20.54 EFFICACY OF DRUG TREATMENT OF OSTEOPOROSIS

	↑BMD	↓Risk of vertebral fracture	↓Risk of non-vertebral fracture
Bisphosphonates	+	+	+
Hormone replacement therapy	+	+	+
Raloxifene	+	+	–
Calcium + vitamin D	+	n/a	+
Calcium	+	+	–
Calcitonin	+	+	–
Tibolone	+	n/a	n/a

(+ = proven efficacy in RCT; – = ineffective in RCT; n/a = data not available)

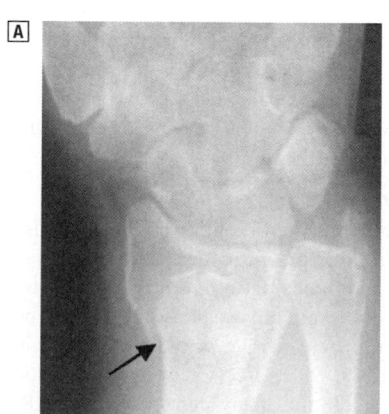
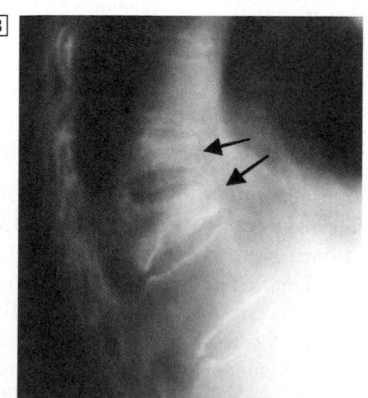
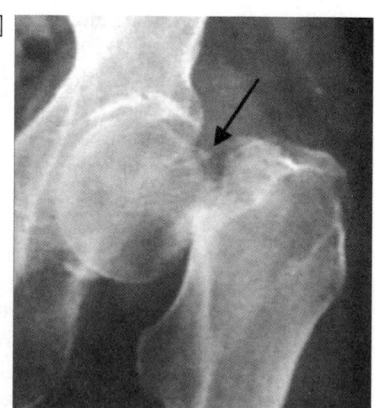

Fig. 20.42 Common osteoporotic fractures. Ⓐ Colles fracture. Ⓑ Vertebral fractures. Ⓒ Hip fracture.

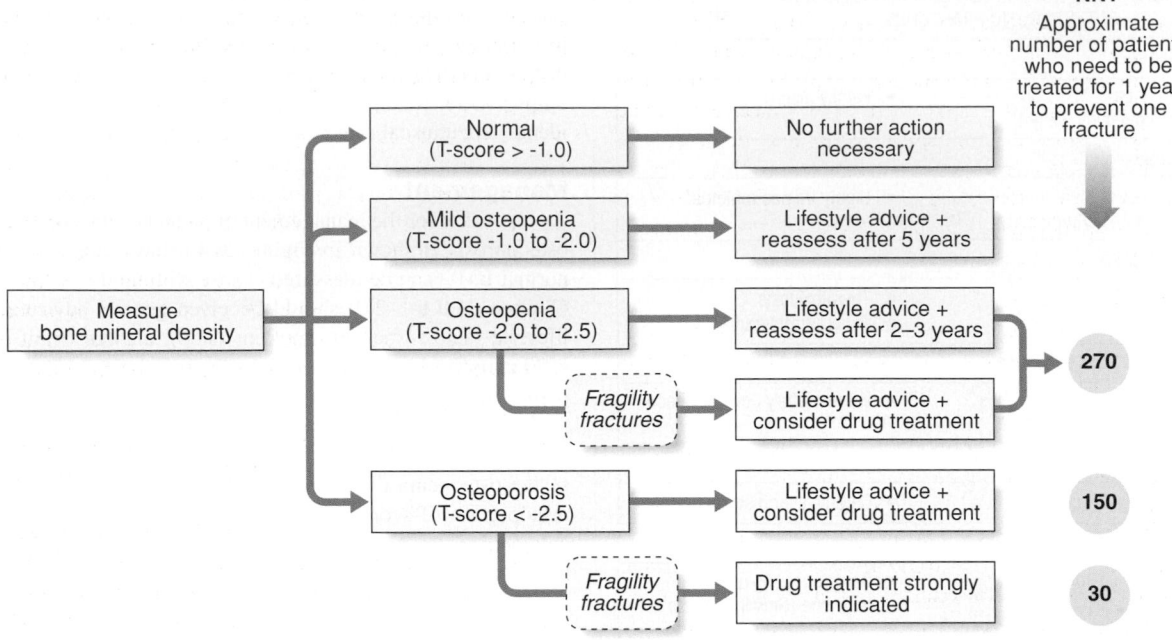

NNT
Approximate number of patients who need to be treated for 1 year to prevent one fracture

Fig. 20.43 Diagnosis and management of suspected osteoporosis. Numbers needed to treat (NNTs) are derived from randomised clinical trials (RCTs) of bisphosphonate therapy in osteoporosis.

Bisphosphonates

These are the most effective agents for the prevention and treatment of osteoporosis. Bisphosphonates are stable, synthetic analogues of pyrophosphate that adsorb on to bone surfaces and become incorporated within bone matrix beneath the resorbing osteoclasts. When bone that contains bisphosphonate is ingested by osteoclasts, the drug is released within the cell at high concentration to cause osteoclast death, thereby inhibiting bone resorption. Bisphosphonates do not directly stimulate bone formation but long-term treatment typically increases BMD by 5–10%. This is thought to be due to filling of resorption sites with new bone and increased mineralisation of existing bone.

Etidronate was the first bisphosphonate to be used for the treatment of osteoporosis. It is given as an oral daily dose of 400 mg for 2 weeks, followed by a 13-week phase of calcium supplements (500–1000 mg daily). This regimen is repeated cyclically on a long-term basis. Cyclical etidronate has been shown to prevent post-menopausal bone loss and to reduce the risk of osteoporotic vertebral fractures in post-menopausal women with established osteoporosis. It is also effective in the prevention and treatment of corticosteroid-induced osteoporosis. Amino-substituted bisphosphonates such as alendronate (10 mg daily, or 70 mg once weekly) and risedronate (5 mg daily) are more potent than etidronate and are clinically superior at preventing post-menopausal bone loss, in treating established post-menopausal osteoporosis and in preventing and treating corticosteroid-induced osteoporosis. Alendronate has also been shown to increase BMD and reduce the risk of fractures in men with osteoporosis; there is also evidence that alendronate and risedronate

PREVENTION OF OSTEOPOROTIC FRACTURES—role of bisphosphonates

'Large-scale RCTs have shown that the aminobisphosphonates aledronate and residronate reduce the risk of osteoporotic fractures by about 50% when administered to patients with post-menopausal osteoporosis.'

- Black DM, Cummings SR, Karpf DB, et al. Randomised trial of effect of alendronate on risk of fracture in women with existing vertebral fractures. Lancet 1996; 348:1535–1541.
- Harris ST, Watts NB, Genant HK, et al. Effects of risedronate treatment on vertebral and nonvertebral fractures in women with postmenopausal osteoporosis. JAMA 1999; 282:1344–1352.

reduce the risk of both vertebral and non-vertebral fractures in post-menopausal women (see EBM panel). All bisphosphonates should be taken on an empty stomach with a glass of water since their absorption is poor and inhibited by food. They are generally well tolerated, but upper gastrointestinal upset can occur with alendronate and this agent should be used with caution or avoided in patients with gastro-oesophageal reflux disease.

Hormone replacement therapy (HRT)

HRT (see p. 713) is effective in preventing post-menopausal bone loss and long-term treatment reduces the risk of fracture. HRT is most commonly used in early menopausal women with climacteric symptoms such as hot flushes, but has also been shown to be effective in older women with established osteoporosis. Side-effects, however, are more common in older women and many cannot tolerate HRT because of weight gain, fluid retention, menstrual bleeding or breast tenderness.

Calcium

Calcium supplements (500–1000 mg daily) slow post-menopausal bone loss, especially in people whose dietary calcium intake is low. Calcium supplements have been shown to reduce the risk of vertebral fracture in some studies, but they do not increase bone mass or reduce the risk of non-vertebral fractures. Because of this, calcium supplements are mainly given in combination with other agents such as bisphosphonates, HRT and calcitonin in the management of osteoporosis.

Calcitonin

Calcitonin prevents bone loss in post-menopausal osteoporosis and is also effective in the secondary prevention of osteoporotic vertebral fractures. It may also have an analgesic effect when given to patients with acute vertebral fractures. Traditionally, calcitonin has been given daily by subcutaneous or intramuscular injections (100–200 U) in the treatment of osteoporosis, but recently a formulation has been developed which is given by intranasal spray (200 U/day). The inconvenience of frequent injections, coupled with side-effects such as flushing and nausea, has so far limited the use of calcitonin injections in the long-term treatment of osteoporosis, but many of these problems have been circumvented by the intranasal formulation, which seems to be better tolerated.

Calcium and vitamin D

Calcium (500–1000 mg daily) and vitamin D supplements (20 μg daily) have an established role in the primary prevention of fractures in the elderly, irrespective of whether or not BMD values are reduced. This treatment has been shown to be effective in reducing the risk of hip fractures and other non-vertebral fractures in both institutionalised patients and community-living individuals.

Raloxifene

Raloxifene belongs to a class of compounds termed selective oestrogen receptor modulators (SERMs), which act as oestrogen receptor agonists in some tissues and antagonists in others. Raloxifene (60 mg daily, with calcium and vitamin D supplements) has been found to increase bone mass and reduce the risk of vertebral fractures in post-menopausal women with osteoporosis. Raloxifene treatment is associated with an increased risk of DVT, but apart from the occurrence of muscle cramps in some patients is otherwise well tolerated. In addition to its beneficial effects on the skeleton, raloxifene has been found in short-term studies to reduce the risk of women developing breast cancer. The long-term impact of raloxifene on breast cancer mortality is as yet unclear.

Other agents

Anabolic steroids such as stanozolol have been found to increase BMD in osteoporosis, but there are no data on fracture prevention and adherence to therapy is poor because of side-effects such as hirsutism, weight gain, fluid retention and disturbance of liver function. Testosterone treatment has been found to increase BMD in hypogonadal males with osteoporosis and should be given routinely in this situation. Tibolone is a hormone receptor modulator that acts as a partial agonist at the oestrogen, progestogen and androgen

receptors. It increases BMD in post-menopausal osteoporosis but there are no data on fracture prevention. Calcitriol and alphacalcidol, the active metabolites of vitamin D, have been found to be effective when given along with calcium in secondary prevention of vertebral fractures in some studies, but not in others. This therapy must be closely monitored in view of the risk of hypercalcaemia and hypercalciuria. Sodium fluoride differs from most of the other agents discussed so far in having a specific stimulatory effect on bone formation. Sodium fluoride can give impressive increases in bone mass (30% or more), but the therapeutic window is narrow since fluoride can promote formation of woven bone with reduced mechanical strength. In view of this, the role of fluoride in the treatment of osteoporosis is controversial.

Monitoring therapy

The response of osteoporosis to treatment should ideally be monitored by repeating spine BMD measurements between 12 and 24 months after starting therapy. Increases in BMD of between 5 and 8% are expected with HRT and bisphosphonates, whereas other agents have a lesser effect (1–3%). If BMD measurements are not available, then progression of spinal osteoporosis can be monitored by changes in height. The development of fractures during treatment is not necessarily a reason for stopping therapy since even the most potent agents only reduce the risk of fracture by 50%.

ISSUES IN OLDER PEOPLE
OSTEOPOROSIS

- Fractures due to osteoporosis are a common cause of morbidity and mortality in the elderly, although fracture healing is not delayed by age.
- There is an age-associated increase in parathyroid hormone (PTH) secretion which leads to increased bone turnover, and as there is also an age-related defect in osteoblast function, the outcome is bone loss.
- Elderly patients who suffer fragility fractures are at increased risk for further fracture. They should be investigated for evidence of osteoporosis and treated if the diagnosis is confirmed.
- Risk factors for falls (such as visual and neuromuscular impairments) are independent risk factors for hip fracture in elderly women, so intervention to prevent falls is as important as treatment of osteoporosis (see Ch. 7, p. 241).
- Bisphosphonates are the most effective agents currently available for the prevention of osteoporotic fractures, but their use should be restricted to patients in whom bone densitometry has shown low BMD values (T-score below −2.5).
- Calcium and vitamin D supplements are a safe and effective way of reducing the risk of hip and other non-vertebral fractures in elderly housebound or institutionalised individuals, irrespective of BMD values.

OSTEOMALACIA AND RICKETS

Osteomalacia is characterised by defective bone mineralisation, bone pain, muscle weakness and pathological fractures. Osteomalacia is now relatively rare in developed countries, but remains common in high-risk subgroups such as female Muslim immigrants to Western societies and elderly housebound people. Rickets is the clinical syndrome that results when osteomalacia occurs in the growing skeleton.

Pathogenesis

The most common cause is vitamin D deficiency. This can occur through reduced dietary intake, vitamin D malabsorption or reduced sunlight exposure. Reduced sunlight exposure may cause osteomalacia because the precursor of vitamin D—cholecalciferol—is synthesised from cholesterol in skin that is exposed to ultraviolet light (see Fig. 16.13, p. 715). Osteomalacia is therefore more common in housebound individuals and in Muslim women who cover their skin for cultural reasons.

The low levels of circulating 25(OH) vitamin D cause reduced production of the biologically active metabolite 1,25(OH) vitamin D by the kidney and this causes a reduction in calcium absorption from the intestine. The low calcium absorption stimulates parathyroid hormone (PTH) secretion, which restores serum calcium levels towards normal by increasing bone resorption and renal tubular calcium reabsorption. The high level of PTH also promotes phosphaturia, however, and causes phosphate depletion. It is the combination of calcium loss from bone and phosphate depletion that causes impaired mineralisation of bone, which is the defining feature of osteomalacia.

Osteomalacia also occurs with various inherited and acquired metabolic defects (see Box 20.55). The most common is chronic renal failure where there is failure of renal 1,25(OH) vitamin D synthesis due to hyperphosphataemia (which directly inhibits 25(OH) vitamin D-1-α-hydroxylase) and loss of functioning renal tissue. A similar mechanism occurs in vitamin D-resistant rickets type I caused by inactivating mutations in the renal 25(OH) vitamin D-1-α-

hydroxylase enzyme. Another type of vitamin D-resistant rickets (type II) results from mutations in the vitamin D receptor rendering it resistant to activation by 1,25(OH)D. X-linked hypophosphataemic rickets (XLH) is caused by inactivating mutations in the PHEX gene whose normal function is to degrade a circulating hormone which promotes phosphaturia. Deficiency of PHEX causes profound renal phosphate wasting due to the unopposed action of this factor. Autosomal dominant hypophosphataemic rickets is a related disorder, caused by activating mutations of fibroblast growth factor 23 (FGF23), which acts on the kidney to promote phosphaturia. Osteomalacia caused by renal phosphate wasting can also occur as a complication of tumours due to 'ectopic' production of FGF23 by tumours. In hypophosphatasia, the bone-specific alkaline phosphatase gene is mutated, resulting in failure of pyrophosphate breakdown, accumulation of pyrophosphate in bone and osteomalacia due to the inhibitory effect of pyrophosphate on mineralisation. Osteomalacia that results from bisphosphonate and aluminium toxicity also occurs through a direct inhibitory effect on mineralisation.

Clinical features

Infants with rickets exhibit delayed development and muscle hypotonia. Other signs include craniotabes (small unossified areas in membranous bones of the skull that yield to finger pressure with a cracking feeling); 'bossing' of the frontal and parietal bones and delayed anterior fontanelle closure; enlargement of epiphyses at the lower end of the radius; and swelling of the rib costochondral junctions (rickety

20.55 CAUSES OF OSTEOMALACIA

Type	Causal factors	Mechanism
Vitamin D deficiency		
Classical	Lack of sunlight exposure/dietary lack of meat and dairy products	Reduced cholecalciferol synthesis in the skin/low levels of vitamin D in diet
Gastrointestinal disease	Malabsorption	Malabsorption of dietary vitamin D and calcium
Failure of 1,25 vitamin D synthesis		
Chronic renal failure	Hyperphosphataemia and kidney damage	Impaired conversion of $25(OH)D_3$ to $1,25(OH)_2D$
Vitamin D-dependent rickets type I (autosomal recessive)	Mutation in renal 25(OH)D-1-α-hydroxylase enzyme	
Vitamin D receptor defects		
Vitamin D-dependent rickets type II (autosomal recessive)	Inactivating mutations in vitamin D receptor	Impaired response to $1,25(OH)_2D$
Defects in phosphate and pyrophosphate metabolism		
Hypophosphataemic rickets	X-linked dominant mutations in PHEX gene Autosomal dominant mutations in FGF23	Hypophosphataemia
Oncogenic hypophosphataemic osteomalacia	Tumour-produced FGF23	
Hypophosphatasia	Mutations in bone-specific alkaline phosphatase	Inhibition of bone mineralisation due to pyrophosphate accumulation
Iatrogenic		
Bisphosphonate therapy	Etidronate/pamidronate	Drug-induced impairment of mineralisation
Aluminium	Use of aluminium-containing phosphate binders or aluminium in dialysis fluids	Aluminium-induced impairment of mineralisation

rosary). Deformities of the long bones, chest, spine and pelvis may also occur. Severe rickets may be associated with hypocalcaemic tetany that presents with spasm of the hands, feet and vocal cords, resulting in a high-pitched distressing cry or laryngeal stridor. Epileptic seizures due to hypocalcaemia also occur. Mild osteomalacia in adults can be asymptomatic, but bone pain, pathological fractures and malaise occur as the disease progresses. Muscle weakness is prominent and the patient may walk with a waddling gait and experience difficulty in climbing stairs or getting out of a chair. Bone and muscular tenderness on pressure is common and focal bone pain may occur in association with fissure fractures of the ribs and pelvis.

Investigations and diagnosis

A routine biochemical screen should be performed, along with estimation of 25(OH)D and PTH levels. The combination of raised alkaline phosphatase, raised PTH and low 25(OH)D levels is virtually diagnostic, although transiliac bone biopsy may be required in cases of doubt. Radiological examination may show pathognomonic features in rickets and osteomalacia, but only in advanced disease. Abnormalities include thickening and widening of the epiphyseal plate in children and focal radiolucent areas (pseudofractures or Looser's zones) in the ribs, pelvis and long bones.

Patients with osteomalacia secondary to chronic renal disease show grossly elevated PTH and raised alkaline phosphatase levels. Patients with chronic renal failure (CRF) are unable to excrete aluminium effectively; it may accumulate in bone and cause a mineralisation defect. Possible sources of aluminium include aluminium hydroxide (often used as an oral phosphate-binding drug in patients with CRF, or as an antacid) and the water used to make up dialysis fluid. Careful monitoring of aluminium levels in blood and dialysis fluid have rendered this a rare condition. Patients are often hypercalcaemic, but alkaline phosphatase and PTH are usually not elevated. Diagnosis requires a bone biopsy. Treatment consists of removal from aluminium exposure, and desferrioxamine, a chelating agent which removes aluminium from tissues.

Bisphosphonate-induced osteomalacia is transient, often asymptomatic and mainly occurs in Pagetic patients given high doses of etidronate or pamidronate. The diagnosis can only be made by bone biopsy. Vitamin D-resistant rickets (VDRR) is usually suspected when rachitic patients fail to respond to vitamin D and calcium. In type I VDRR, 25(OH)D levels are normal and 1,25(OH)D levels are undetectable, whereas in type II VDRR, 25(OH)D levels are normal and 1,25(OH)D levels are raised. Osteomalacia due to hypophosphatasia also fails to respond to vitamin D but is differentiated from VDRR by the finding of very low alkaline phosphatase levels. Osteomalacia resulting from hypophosphataemic rickets is characterised by severe hypophosphataemia, renal phosphate wasting and normal 25(OH)D and 1,25(OH)D levels. The diagnosis is usually obvious when the above features are combined with a positive family history. Acquired hypophosphataemic rickets due to ectopic secretion of FGF23 presents with similar biochemical features in the absence of a family history.

Management

This depends on the underlying cause. Vitamin D-deficient rickets and osteomalacia respond rapidly to 25(OH) vitamin D (10–50 µg daily) or active vitamin D metabolites (1-α-hydroxyvitamin D 0.5–2 µg daily or 1,25 dihydroxyvitamin D 0.25–1.5 µg daily) and calcium supplementation (500–1000 mg daily). Higher doses of vitamin D may be required in patients with malabsorption. Healing of the bone disease is accompanied by rapid clinical improvement, normalisation of biochemical abnormalities and radiographic improvement. After 3–4 months, treatment can generally be stopped or the dose of vitamin D reduced to a maintenance level for those with underlying disease or lifestyle factors which put them at risk of recurrence.

Osteomalacia in chronic renal failure requires treatment with active vitamin D metabolites (1-α-hydroxyvitamin D or 1,25 dihydroxyvitamin D) rather than 25(OH)D since these metabolites bypass the metabolic defect in 1-α-hydroxylation of 25(OH)D. Although VDRR type I responds well to active vitamin D metabolites, VDRR type II responds poorly and often presents an intractable management problem despite parenteral calcium, phosphate and high doses of active vitamin D metabolites. The same applies to hypophosphatasia for which there is no specific treatment. Hypophosphataemic rickets usually responds well to phosphate supplements (2–4 g daily) and active vitamin D metabolites.

Monitoring of calcium, phosphate, alkaline phosphatase and renal function is important in patients with osteomalacia who are undergoing long-term treatment with vitamin D or its metabolites. Healing of osteomalacia is usually reflected by a return of alkaline phosphatase values to normal. Monitoring serum phosphate is of value in hypophosphataemic rickets to judge the adequacy of phosphate replacement.

ISSUES IN OLDER PEOPLE
OSTEOMALACIA

- Elderly housebound individuals are at increased risk of osteomalacia due to lack of sunlight exposure and poor diet. Around 15% of older people in the community in the UK and USA have low levels of 25(OH)D.
- The diagnosis should be considered in patients with bone pain and muscular weakness who have low serum levels of 25(OH)D and raised alkaline phosphatase levels.
- The diagnosis can be confirmed by bone biopsy, which should be considered in patients where the investigations above are inconclusive.
- The symptoms and signs of osteomalacia respond rapidly to treatment with calcium and small doses of vitamin D.

PAGET'S DISEASE

Paget's disease of bone is characterised by increased, disorganised bone remodelling on a focal or multifocal basis at various sites in the skeleton. The pelvis, femur, tibia, lumbar spine, skull and scapula are principally affected; involvement of small bones of hands and feet is rare. Paget's disease rarely spreads to new bones once the diagnosis is made, suggesting that affected bones are targeted by the disease relatively early in life. Paget's disease is seldom diagnosed before the age of 40 but gradually increases in incidence thereafter to affect up to 10% of the UK population by the age of 85. The disease is common in Caucasians from Western and Southern Europe but rare in Scandinavians, Asians, Chinese and Japanese. These ethnic differences persist after emigration, highlighting the importance of genetic factors in aetiology.

Pathogenesis

The primary abnormality is increased osteoclastic bone resorption, which is accompanied by marrow fibrosis, increased vascularity of bone and increased osteoblast activity. These abnormalities result in architecturally abnormal bone with reduced mechanical strength. As well as being increased in number, the osteoclasts are abnormally large and can contain up to 100 nuclei. Genetic factors are clearly important in pathogenesis and a positive family history is obtained in about 15% of patients. Families are described in which Paget's is inherited as an autosomal dominant trait. In some families with severe early-onset disease (familial expansile osteolysis) activating mutations of the RANK gene are responsible, though different unidentified genes are involved in late-onset familial Paget's disease. Environmental factors, however, may also be important. Localisation of Paget's disease to bones or limbs that have been subjected to heavy repetitive use suggests that biomechanical factors may help trigger the disease.

Clinical features

The classic presentation of Paget's disease is with bone pain, bone deformity, deafness and pathological fractures. Nowadays, however, it is more often discovered as an incidental finding on biochemical testing or radiographic examination. Clinical signs of Paget's include bone deformity and expansion, increased warmth over affected bones, and pathological fracture. Pagetic deformity is usually most evident in weight-bearing bones such as the femur and tibia and in the skull where the cranium becomes enlarged. Neurological problems such as deafness, other cranial nerve defects, nerve root pain, spinal cord compression and spinal stenosis may occur with involvement of the skull and spine because the affected bones enlarge and encroach upon the spinal cord and nerve foramina. Increased vascularity of Pagetic bone can precipitate high-output cardiac failure in elderly patients with limited cardiac reserve. Osteosarcoma is a rare but serious complication of Paget's disease that has a poor prognosis. It should be suspected in a patient with Paget's who suffers a sudden increase in pain or swelling of an affected bone.

Investigations and diagnosis

The diagnosis is usually suspected by the finding of a raised serum alkaline phosphatase but normal liver function tests. Confirmation is by typical features on radiograph (see Fig. 20.44) or isotope bone scan (see Fig. 20.8, p. 969). Bone scans are useful in documenting the extent of disease and in

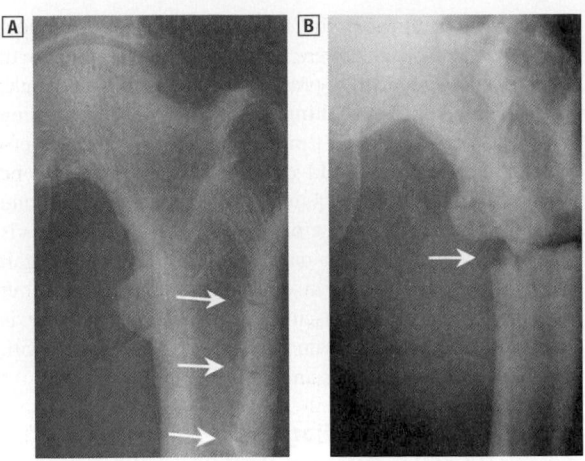

Fig. 20.44 Paget's disease. **A** Radiographic features, illustrating bone expansion and osteosclerosis with pseudofractures breaching the bone cortex (arrows). **B** Radiograph from the same patient who developed a pathological fracture (arrow) at the site of a pre-existing pseudofracture while walking down the street.

helping to assess whether symptoms such as pain are due to Paget's disease of a specific bone. Radiographs should be taken of symptomatic bones to look for deformity, to screen for coexisting osteoarthritis and to document whether fractures or pseudofractures are present, since all of these can contribute to bone pain. Rarely, osteosclerotic metastases can mimic Paget's disease on biochemical and radiological grounds. If this diagnosis is suspected, bone biopsy is required for accurate differentiation.

Management

Bisphosphonates are the treatment of choice since they effectively reduce bone turnover and improve bone pain (see Box 20.56). Potent bisphosphonates such as alendronate may also heal osteolytic lesions and improve bone architecture, but the long-term effects of anti-Pagetic therapy on complications such as deafness, bone deformity and fracture are unknown. Calcitonin can also be used but is less potent than bisphosphonates. The main indication for anti-Pagetic treatment is bone pain thought to be due to active disease.

20.56 MEDICAL MANAGEMENT OF PAGET'S DISEASE		
Drug	**Route of administration**	**Dose**
Etidronate	Oral	400 mg daily for 3–6 months
Tiludronate	Oral	400 mg daily for 3–6 months
Risedronate	Oral	30 mg daily for 2 months
Alendronate*	Oral	40 mg daily for 3 months
Pamidronate	Intravenous	60 mg on 1–6 occasions
Calcitonin	Subcutaneous	100–200 U 3 times weekly for 2–3 months
* Not licensed in the UK for treatment of Paget's disease.		

Whilst the primary effect of anti-Pagetic therapy is inhibition of osteoclastic resorption, this is coupled to bone formation; measurement of serum alkaline phosphatase can therefore be used to monitor the response to treatment.

Etidronate is moderately effective and well tolerated but should be avoided in patients with pseudofractures and deformities of weight-bearing limb bones, since it can cause osteomalacia and increase the risk of pathological fracture. Tiludronate is more effective than etidronate and does not cause osteomalacia, but it seldom restores bone turnover to normal in severe or extensive disease. Severe disease is best treated with potent bisphosphonates such as risedronate, alendronate or pamidronate. These frequently restore bone turnover to normal and also work in patients who have become resistant to weaker bisphosphonates like etidronate.

Bone pain of active Paget's disease usually improves within 1–2 months of starting therapy. If pain recurs in association with a re-elevation of alkaline phosphatase values, then further courses of treatment can be given as necessary. If pain persists after biochemical suppression of Paget's disease has been achieved, other causes should be sought. The most common of these is osteoarthritis since this has an increased incidence in joints adjacent to Pagetic bone. This is managed along the usual lines (see p. 1001), but if joint replacement is required anti-Pagetic drug therapy is often given beforehand to reduce the bone vascularity in the hope that this will reduce intra-operative blood loss.

ISSUES IN OLDER PEOPLE
PAGET'S DISEASE

- Paget's disease affects about 3% of individuals over the age of 55 in the UK.
- The condition is usually asymptomatic and is often discovered by the finding of an elevated serum alkaline phosphatase in patients with otherwise normal biochemistry.
- The diagnosis is usually obvious on radiograph but can be confirmed by radionuclide bone scan, which also gives information on the extent of the disease.
- No treatment is required in those who are asymptomatic.
- Anti-Pagetic therapy with bisphosphonates is the treatment of choice in patients with bone pain that does not respond to analgesics.

CANCER-ASSOCIATED BONE DISEASE

Hypercalcaemia is a common metabolic complication of malignancy; in most cases this is due to excessive release of parathyroid hormone-related protein (PTHrP) by solid tumours such as carcinoma of the lung, breast and genitourinary system. Less commonly, osteomalacia can complicate malignancy, particularly mesenchymal tumours, through ectopic release of FGF23, which promotes phosphaturia (see p. 1030).

Bone metastases are a common complication of tumours of the bronchus, breast and prostate, and of multiple myeloma. Metastatic bone disease typically presents with bone pain, pathological fracture or neurological symptoms due to nerve root compression or spinal cord compression.

The diagnosis is suspected on the basis of clinical history and typical appearances of local osteolytic lesions on radiographic examination. Osteosclerotic metastases also occur and are particularly characteristic of prostatic carcinoma. A radionuclide bone scan is a more sensitive means of detecting bone metastases, but in myeloma osteolytic lesions can occur in the absence of new bone formation, leading to a false negative result.

The treatment of metastatic bone disease is interdisciplinary and four broad approaches can be identified (see Box 20.57). The most effective means of treating bone metastases is with antitumour therapy but in cases where this does not work efforts should focus on control of pain with analgesics/NSAIDs, nerve blockade or local radiotherapy. Orthopaedic surgery may also be required for pathological fractures or to stabilise local osteolytic lesions that are likely to progress to fracture. Surgical decompression may also be indicated as a palliative manoeuvre in the treatment of spinal metastases that are encroaching on the spinal cord.

Most tumours cause osteolytic lesions by local release of factors that increase osteoclast formation and activity. Bisphosphonates inhibit osteoclast activity so that the bone surrounding tumour deposits is protected from resorption, and have been shown to prevent the development of pathological fractures, improve bone pain and reduce skeletal morbidity in patients with breast carcinoma and multiple myeloma (see EBM panel). The efficacy of bisphosphonates in preventing progression of bone disease in other tumours has not yet been demonstrated, although they do appear to improve bone pain.

20.57 MANAGEMENT OF METASTATIC BONE DISEASE

Treatment of the primary tumour

• Chemotherapy	• Radiotherapy
• Hormone therapy	

Treatment of local lesions

• Fixation of fractures	• Radiotherapy
• Spinal cord decompression	

Inhibition of osteoclastic bone resorption

- Bisphosphonates

Treatment of pain

• Analgesics/NSAIDs	• Radiotherapy
• Nerve blocks	

CANCER PAIN AND SKELETAL EVENTS—role of bisphosphonates   EBM

'RCTs have shown that prophylactic bisphosphonate therapy can prevent skeletal morbidity and improve bone pain in patients with breast cancer and myeloma who have metastatic bone disease.'

- Berenson JR, Lichtenstein A, Porter L, et al. Efficacy of pamidronate in reducing skeletal events in patients with advanced multiple myeloma. Myeloma Aredia Study Group. N Engl J Med 1996; 334:488–493.
- Lipton A, Theriault RL, Hortobagyi GN, et al. Pamidronate prevents skeletal complications and is effective palliative treatment in women with breast carcinoma and osteolytic bone metastases: long term follow-up of two randomized, placebo-controlled trials. Cancer 2000; 88:1082–1090.

Primary bone tumours are far less common than metastases. They present with local pain and swelling. Treatment depends on histological tumour type, but often involves surgical removal of the tumour followed by chemotherapy and radiotherapy.

SYSTEMIC CONNECTIVE TISSUE DISEASE

SYSTEMIC LUPUS ERYTHEMATOSUS (SLE)

SLE is the most common multisystem connective tissue disease. It is characterised by a wide variety of clinical features and a diverse spectrum of autoantibody production. The prevalence varies according to geographical and racial background, from 30/100 000 in Caucasians to 200/100 000 in Afro-Caribbeans. Around 90% of affected individuals are women, with peak onset in the second and third decades.

Aetiology and pathogenesis
At least 50 autoantigenic targets for autoantibody production are described in SLE. However, none of the diverse manifestations of SLE can be attributed to a single antigenic stimulus, and it is likely that this wide spectrum of autoantibody production results from polyclonal B and T cell activation. Many autoantigens in SLE are components of the intracellular and intranuclear machinery. In normal health these antigens are 'hidden' from the immune system and do not provoke an immune response. Although the triggers that lead to autoantibody production in SLE are unknown, one mechanism may be expression of novel antigens on the cell surface during apoptosis. This hypothesis is supported by the fact that environmental factors that associate with flares of lupus increase oxidative stress and subsequent apoptosis. Such factors include exposure to sunlight and artificial ultraviolet (UV) light, pregnancy and infection.

Diagnosis
Diagnosis depends on the recognition of specific symptoms and identification of autoantibodies. To fulfil current classification criteria, 4 of 11 factors must be present or have occurred in the past (see Box 20.58). Patients who are ANA-negative are very unlikely to have SLE unless they are extractable nuclear antigen (Ro)-positive; most Ro-positive patients also have skin rashes. Anti-dsDNA antibodies occur in only 30–50% of patients.

Clinical features
Raynaud's phenomenon
Arthralgia or arthritis in combination with Raynaud's phenomenon (see p. 446) is the most common presentation (see Fig. 20.45). It is important to elicit a history of Raynaud's since it is very uncommon for this to associate with other arthropathies such as RA. Raynaud's phenomenon in a teenage girl, with no other associated symptoms, especially if there is a family history, is likely to be idiopathic primary

20.58 REVISED AMERICAN RHEUMATISM ASSOCIATION CRITERIA FOR SLE[1]	
Features	**Characteristics**
Malar rash	Fixed erythema, flat or raised, sparing the nasolabial folds
Discoid rash	Erythematous raised patches with adherent keratotic scarring and follicular plugging
Photosensitivity	Skin rash as a result of unusual reaction to sunlight
Oral ulcers	Oral or nasopharyngeal ulceration, may be painless
Arthritis	Non-erosive, involving two or more peripheral joints
Serositis	(a) Pleuritis (convincing history of pleuritic pain, rub or pleural effusion), *or* (b) Pericarditis (rub, ECG evidence or effusion)
Renal disorder	(a) Persistent proteinuria > 0.5 g/day, *or* (b) Cellular casts (red cell, granular or tubular)
Neurological disorder	Seizures or psychosis, in the absence of offending drugs or metabolic derangement
Haematological disorder	(a) Haemolytic anaemia, *or* (b) Leucopenia[2] (< 4000/mm³), *or* (c) Lymphopenia[2] (< 1500/mm³), *or* (d) Thrombocytopenia[2] (< 100 000/mm³) in the absence of offending drugs
Immunology disorder	(a) Anti-DNA antibodies in abnormal titre, *or* (b) Presence of antibody to Sm antigen, *or* (c) Positive antiphospholipid antibodies
Antinuclear antibody disorder	Abnormal titre of ANA by immunofluorescence

[1] For the purpose of identifying patients for clinical studies, a person must have SLE if any 4 out of 11 are present serially or simultaneously.
[2] On two separate occasions.

Raynaud's. By contrast, onset in a male, or in a woman over the age of 30 years suggests a secondary cause, usually underlying connective tissue disease. Examination of capillary nail-fold loops using an ophthalmoscope may help distinguish primary from secondary Raynaud's. Loss of the normal loop pattern and capillary 'fallout' with haemorrhage and dots indicate underlying disease.

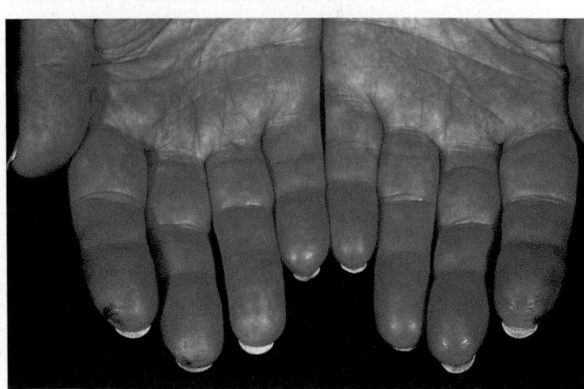

Fig. 20.45 Severe secondary Raynaud's phenomenon leading to digital ulceration.

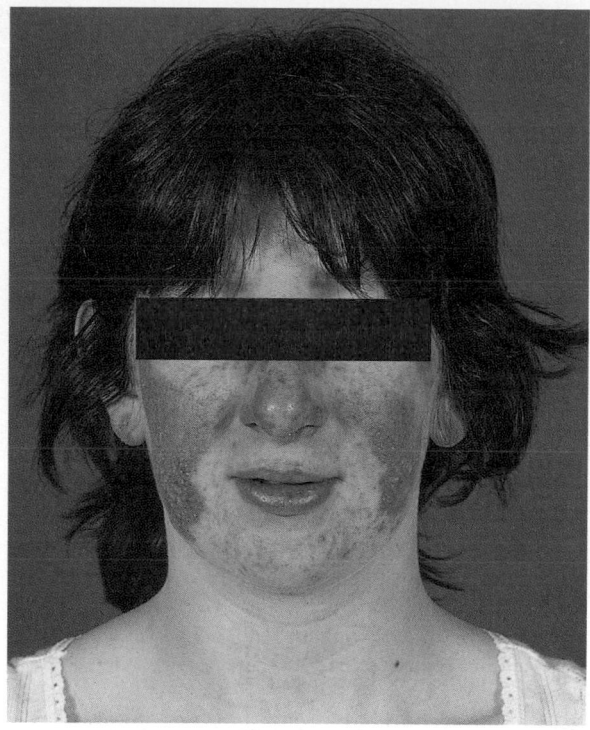

Fig. 20.46 Butterfly (malar) rash of systemic lupus erythematosus, sparing the nasolabial folds.

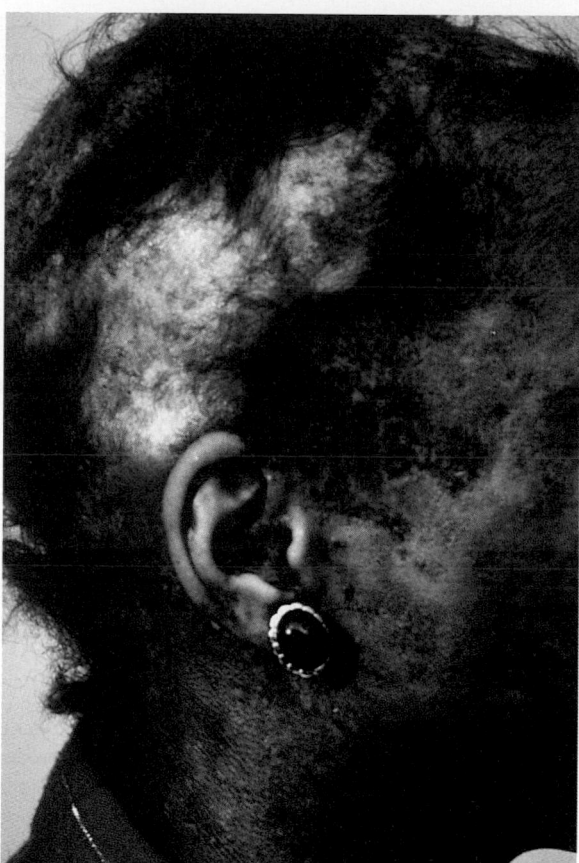

Fig. 20.47 Scarring alopecia due to discoid lupus.

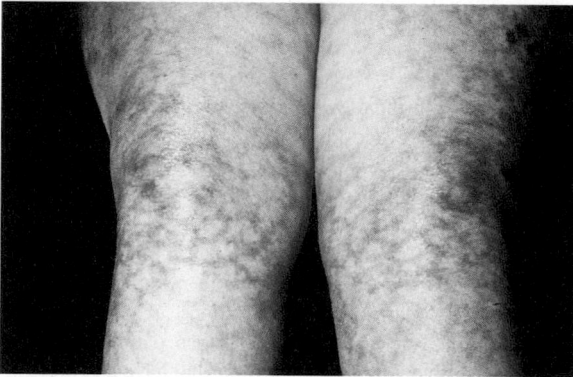

Fig. 20.48 Livedo reticularis in systemic lupus erythematosus.

Musculoskeletal features

A variety of joint problems may occur, including migratory arthralgia with mild morning stiffness, tenosynovitis and small joint synovitis that may mimic rheumatoid. In contrast to RA, joint deformities are rare. Deformities that do occur result from tendon inflammation and damage rather than from bone erosion ('Jaccoud's arthropathy').

Mucocutaneous features

Painful oral ulcers are common in SLE. In comparison with aphthous ulceration, they usually last longer and may scar. Diffuse, usually non-scarring alopecia may occur with active disease. There are three main types of rash in SLE:

- *The classic butterfly facial rash* (20–30% of patients) is raised and painful or pruritic and occurs in a photosensitive distribution that spares the nasolabial folds (see Fig. 20.46).
- *Subacute cutaneous lupus erythematosus* (SCLE) rashes are migratory, non-scarring and are either papulosquamous (psoriaform) or annular.
- *Discoid lupus* lesions are characterised by hyperkeratosis and follicular plugging and may cause scarring alopecia if present on the scalp (see Fig. 20.47).

Other skin manifestations include periungual erythema, vasculitis and livedo reticularis, the latter also being a common feature of the antiphospholipid antibody syndrome (see Fig. 20.48).

Renal features

Renal involvement is one of the main determinants of prognosis, and regular monitoring of urinalysis and blood pressure is essential. The typical renal lesion is a proliferative glomerulonephritis (see p. 612), characterised by heavy haematuria, proteinuria, and casts on urine microscopy.

Cardiopulmonary features

The most common manifestation is chest pain from pleurisy or pericarditis. Myocarditis and sterile endocarditis (Libman–Sacks endocarditis) may also occur. SLE patients with antiphospholipid antibodies are at increased risk of venous thromboembolism, which should always be considered in the presence of chest pain or dyspnoea. Alveolitis and lung fibrosis occur, particularly in overlap connective tissue diseases.

Central nervous system features

Fatigue, headache, poor concentration and other non-specific features similar to fibromyalgia are common accompaniments of SLE and often occur in the absence of active disease. Specific features of cerebral lupus include visual hallucinations, chorea (also associated with antiphospholipid antibody syndrome—APL), organic psychosis, transverse myelitis and lymphocytic meningitis.

Haematological features

Antibody-mediated destruction of peripheral blood cells may cause neutropenia, lymphopenia, thrombocytopenia or haemolytic anaemia. The degree of leucopenia, most commonly lymphopenia, is often a good guide to disease activity. Although the ESR is usually elevated, CRP is often normal unless there is serositis or infection.

Other manifestations

Fever, weight loss and mild lymphadenopathy commonly accompany active disease. Gastrointestinal involvement is rare and other causes of abdominal pain should always be considered, i.e. appendicitis, perforation secondary to drugs, or infection.

Management

All patients require education on the importance of avoiding sun and UV light exposure, and the use of high-factor sun blocks (sun protection factor 25–50). Many patients have mild disease requiring only intermittent analgesics or NSAIDs. Hydroxychloroquine (200–400 mg daily) is often effective for more troublesome cutaneous and joint symptoms. Short courses of oral steroids may be required for mild to moderate disease activity (e.g. rashes, synovitis, pleuro-pericarditis). With the availability of immunosuppressive agents maintenance with oral steroid is less commonly needed.

Acute or life-threatening disease (i.e. renal, cerebral) requires high-dose steroids (e.g. oral prednisolone 40–60 mg daily or i.v. methylprednisolone 500 mg–1 g) in combination with pulse i.v. cyclophosphamide (see EBM panel). Other immunosuppressive drugs (azathioprine, methotrexate, ciclosporin, tacrolimus, mycophenolate mofetil) are useful either alone or in combination with steroids for severe but non-life-threatening manifestations or as step-down therapy after cyclophosphamide. Lupus patients with the antiphospholipid antibody syndrome who have had previous

thrombosis will require life-long warfarin. If repeated thromboses occur despite warfarin, the international normalised ratio (INR) target range should be increased to 3–4.

Prognosis

Overall 5-year survival is greater than 90%. Early mortality within 5 years of diagnosis is usually due to organ failure or overwhelming sepsis, both of which are modifiable by early effective intervention. However, compared to the normal population, patients with lupus have a fivefold increased late mortality. This mainly results from premature cardiovascular disease to which chronic steroid therapy makes a major contribution. To reduce this, steroids should be used at the lowest effective dose and for the shortest period possible; combination therapy with immunosuppressive drugs may help to achieve this.

There is also a significant late morbidity due to symptoms of chronic fatigue and other features of fibromyalgia, which affect up to 80% of patients. These symptoms are typically unresponsive to steroids and should be managed according to standard fibromyalgia protocols, e.g. low-dose amitriptyline, graded exercise therapy and cognitive behavioural interventions if appropriate.

SCLERODERMA

Scleroderma is a generalised disorder of connective tissue affecting the skin, internal organs and vasculature. The clinical hallmark is the presence of sclerodactyly in combination with Raynaud's or digital ischaemia. The peak age of onset is in the fourth and fifth decades, and overall prevalence is 10–20 per 100 000 with a 4:1 female:male ratio. It is subdivided into diffuse and limited disease, the latter also termed 'CREST syndrome' (Calcinosis, Raynaud's, oEsophageal involvement, Sclerodactyly, Telangiectasia).

Aetiology and pathogenesis

The aetiology is unknown, with no consistent genetic, geographical or racial associations. Environmental factors are important in isolated cases that result from exposure to silica dust, vinyl chloride, hypoxia resins and trichloroethylene.

Early in the disease there is skin infiltration by T lymphocytes and abnormal fibroblast activation that leads to increased production of extracellular matrix in the dermis, primarily type I collagen. This results in symmetrical thickening, tightening and induration of the skin (sclerodactyly). In addition to skin changes there is arterial and arteriolar narrowing due to intimal proliferation and vessel wall inflammation. This endothelial injury causes release of vasoconstrictors and platelet activation, resulting in further ischaemia.

Clinical features and diagnosis

Scleroderma is predominantly a clinical diagnosis based on the presence of sclerodactyly proximal to the metacarpophalangeal joints (see Fig. 20.49). Most patients are ANA-positive, and approximately 30% of patients with diffuse

---

MANAGEMENT OF LUPUS NEPHRITIS   **EBM**

'RCTs have shown that pulse i.v. cyclophosphamide is more effective than pulse i.v. methylprednisolone alone for SLE nephritis. Combination therapy is more effective than either treatment alone. Continuing quarterly i.v. treatment for 1 year after renal remission decreases the risk of renal flares.'

- Boumpas DT, Austin HA, Vaughn EM, et al. Controlled trial of pulse methylprednisolone versus two regimes of pulse cyclophosphamide in severe lupus nephritis. Lancet 1992; 340:741–745.
- Gourley MF, Austin HA, Scott D, et al. Methylprednisolone and cyclophosphamide, alone or in combination, in patients with lupus nephritis. A randomized, controlled trial. Ann Intern Med 1996; 125:549–557.

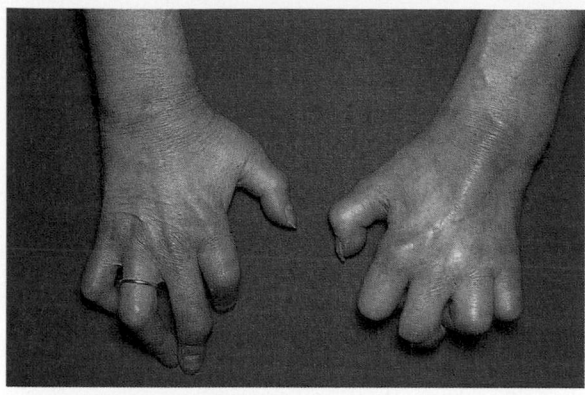

Fig. 20.49   Systemic sclerosis. Hands showing tight shiny skin, sclerodactyly, flexion contractures of the fingers and thickening of an extensor tendon sheath.

disease and 60% with limited disease have antibodies to topoisomerase 1 and centromere respectively.

Cutaneous changes

Raynaud's phenomenon is universal and may precede other clinical features.

The initial phase of skin disease is characterised by non-pitting oedema of the fingers and flexor tendon sheaths. Subsequently, the skin becomes shiny and taut, and distal skin creases disappear. There is usually erythema and tortuous dilatation of capillary loops in the nail-fold bed, readily visible with an ophthalmoscope set to +20. The face and neck are usually involved next, with thinning of the lips and radial furrowing. In some patients skin thickening stops at this stage. Skin involvement restricted to sites distal to the elbow or knee is classified as 'limited disease' or CREST syndrome (see Fig. 20.50). Involvement proximal to the knee and elbow and on the trunk is classified as 'diffuse disease'. In the distal extremities, the combination of intimal fibrosis and vessel wall inflammation may cause critical tissue ischaemia, leading to skin ulceration over pressure areas, localised areas of infarction and pulp atrophy at the fingertips.

Musculoskeletal features

Arthralgia, morning stiffness and flexor tenosynovitis are common. Restricted hand function is due to skin rather than

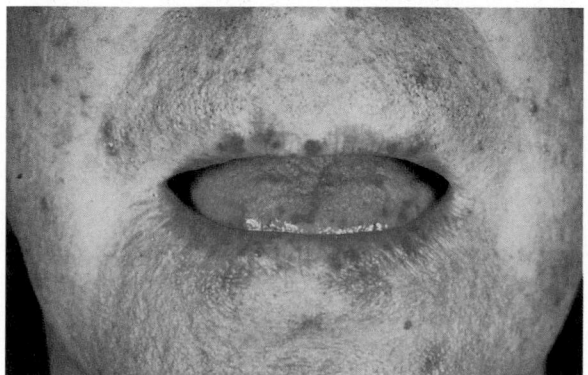

Fig. 20.50   Typical facial appearance in the CREST syndrome.

joint disease and erosive arthropathy is uncommon. Muscle weakness and wasting are usually due to myositis.

Gastrointestinal features

Gut involvement is common. Smooth muscle atrophy and fibrosis in the lower two-thirds of the oesophagus lead to reflux with erosive oesophagitis. Since this may lead to further fibrosis, adequate treatment of reflux (usually with proton pump inhibitors) is important. Dysphagia and odynophagia may also occur. Involvement of the stomach causes early satiety and occasionally outlet obstruction. Recurrent occult upper gastrointestinal bleeding may indicate a watermelon stomach, which occurs in up to 20% of patients. Small intestine involvement may lead to malabsorption due to bacterial overgrowth and intermittent bloating, pain or constipation. Dilatation of large or small bowel due to autonomic neuropathy may cause pseudo-obstruction.

Cardiorespiratory features

Pulmonary involvement is a major cause of morbidity and mortality. Fibrosing alveolitis mainly affects patients with diffuse disease, particularly those with antibodies to topoisomerase 1. Pulmonary hypertension is a complication of long-standing disease and is six times more prevalent in limited than in diffuse disease. The clinical features are rapidly progressive dyspnoea (more rapid than interstitial lung disease), right heart failure and angina, often in association with rapidly progressing digital ischaemia. Treatment strategies include vasodilators, continuous infusions of prostacyclin and heart-lung transplantation.

Renal features

One of the main causes of death is hypertensive renal crisis characterised by rapidly developing malignant hypertension and renal failure. Treatment is by angiotensin-converting enzyme (ACE) inhibition even if renal impairment is present.

Management and prognosis

Five-year survival is approximately 70%. Risk factors at presentation that associate with a poor prognosis include older age, diffuse skin disease, proteinuria, high ESR, a low TLCO (gas transfer factor for carbon monoxide), and pulmonary hypertension.

Self-management to maintain core body temperature and avoid peripheral cold exposure is important. Infection of ulcerated skin should be treated with prompt antibiotic therapy. Antibiotics penetrate poorly into scleroderma skin lesions and therefore need to be given at higher dose for longer periods (e.g. flucloxacillin 500 mg 6-hourly for 14 days). Calcium antagonists (e.g. nifedipine, amlodipine) or angiotensin II receptor antagonists (e.g. valsartan) may be effective for Raynaud's symptoms. For severe digital ischaemia, intermittent infusions of prostacyclin may be helpful.

Steroids and cytotoxic drugs are indicated in patients with myositis or alveolitis. No agent has demonstrated efficacy in arresting or improving skin changes. Agents that have been shown to be ineffective include d-penicillamine and interferon gamma. Other novel agents currently under study include mycophenolate mofetil and tacrolimus.

MIXED CONNECTIVE TISSUE DISEASE

This is an overlap connective tissue disease with features of SLE, scleroderma and myositis. The usual clinical features include synovitis and oedema of the hands in combination with Raynaud's phenomenon and muscle pain/weakness. Most patients have anti-ribonucleoprotein (RNP) antibodies, although these also occur in SLE without overlap features.

SJÖGREN'S SYNDROME

This is an autoimmune disorder of unknown aetiology characterised by lymphocytic infiltration of salivary and lachrymal glands, leading to glandular fibrosis and exocrine failure. Age of onset is usually in the fourth and fifth decades with a female:male ratio of 9:1. The disease may be primary or secondary in association with other autoimmune disease such as rheumatoid, SLE, thyroiditis or primary biliary cirrhosis.

Clinical features

The eye symptoms, termed keratoconjunctivitis sicca, are due to a lack of tears and lubrication. Conjunctivitis and blepharitis are frequent manifestations, and may lead to filamentary keratitis due to tenacious mucous filaments binding to the cornea and conjunctiva. Oral involvement typically leads to the patient needing water to swallow food, and there is a high incidence of dental caries. Other sites of extra-glandular involvement are listed in Box 20.59.

20.59 FEATURES OF SJÖGREN'S SYNDROME	
Risk markers	
• Age of onset 40–60 • F > M	• HLA-B8/DR3
Common clinical features	
• Keratoconjunctivitis sicca • Xerostomia • Salivary gland enlargement	• Non-erosive arthritis • Raynaud's • Fatigue
Less common features	
• Low-grade fever • Interstitial lung disease • Anaemia, leucopenia • Thrombocytopenia • Cryoglobulinaemia • Vasculitis	• Peripheral neuropathy • Lymphadenopathy • Lymphoreticular malignancy • Glomerulonephritis • Renal tubular acidosis
Autoantibodies frequently detected	
• Rheumatoid factor • ANA • SS-A (anti-Ro)	• SS-B (anti-La) • Gastric parietal cell • Thyroid
Associated autoimmune disorders	
• SLE • Progressive systemic sclerosis • Primary biliary cirrhosis	• Chronic active hepatitis • Myasthenia gravis

The disease is associated with a 40-fold increased lifetime risk of lymphoma and can be viewed as being at the crossroads of autoimmunity and malignancy.

Investigations

Most patients will have an elevated ESR secondary to hyper-gammaglobulinaemia and one or more autoantibodies, of which antinuclear factor (ANF) and rheumatoid factor are the most common. Sicca can be established by the Schirmer tear test, which measures flow over 5 minutes using absorbent paper strips placed in the lower lachrymal sac; a normal result is greater than 6 mm of wetting. If diagnosis is still in doubt, it can be confirmed by finding focal lymphocytic infiltrate in the minor salivary glands on lip biopsy.

Management

Artificial lubrication is the mainstay of symptomatic treatment. Lachrymal substitutes such as hypromellose should be used during the day in combination with more viscous lubricating ointment at night. Soft contact lenses can be useful for corneal protection in patients with filamentary keratitis, and occlusion of the lachrymal ducts is occasionally needed. Artificial saliva and oral gels can be tried for xerostomia, but are often not effective. Stimulation of saliva flow by sugar-free chewing gum or lozenges may be helpful. Adequate post-prandial oral hygiene and prompt treatment of oral candidiasis are essential. Vaginal dryness is treated with lubricants such as K-Y jelly.

Extraglandular and musculoskeletal manifestations may respond to steroids and, if so, other immunosuppressive drugs such as azathioprine can be added for steroid-sparing effect. One of the most difficult symptoms to treat is fatigue; this is usually due to non-restorative sleep (often because of xerostomia) and is unresponsive to steroids. Immunosuppression does not improve sicca symptoms. If massive lymphadenopathy or salivary gland enlargement develops during the disease course, biopsy should be performed to exclude malignancy.

POLYMYOSITIS AND DERMATOMYOSITIS

The idiopathic inflammatory myopathies (IIMs) are rare connective tissue disorders defined by the presence of muscle weakness and inflammation. The incidence is 2–10 per million/year with no significant world-wide variation. The aetiology is unknown and genetic associations differ amongst ethnic groups. The most common clinical forms of IIM are polymyositis, dermatomyositis and inclusion body myositis. Other systemic autoimmune diseases such as SLE or vasculitis can also cause myositis, whilst organ-specific autoimmune disease (e.g. thyroid) may impair muscle function without causing muscle inflammation. Usually only skeletal muscle is affected. Occasionally, the distribution is focal (e.g. orbital myositis).

Adult polymyositis

The typical presentation is with symmetrical proximal muscle weakness, usually affecting the lower extremities first.

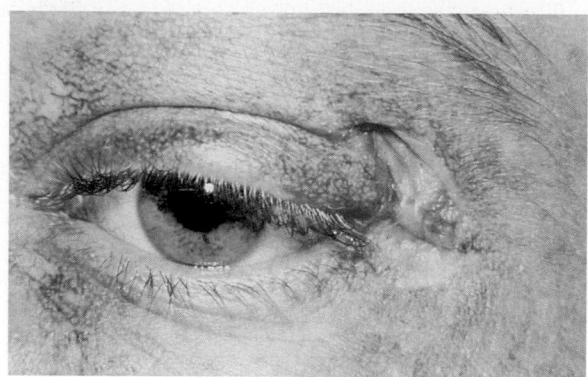

Fig. 20.51   Typical eyelid appearance in dermatomyositis. Note the oedema and telangiectasia.

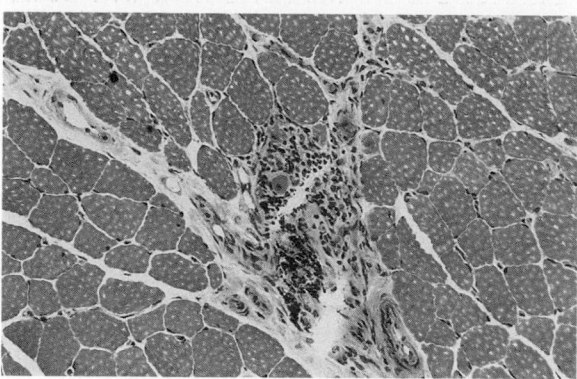

Fig. 20.52   Muscle biopsy from a patient with inflammatory myositis. The sample shows an intense inflammatory cell infiltrate in an area of degenerating and regenerating muscle fibres.

Patients report difficulty rising from a chair, climbing stairs and lifting, sometimes in combination with muscle pain. The onset is usually between 40 and 60 years of age and is typically gradual, over a few weeks, although an explosive and more insidious onset may also occur. Systemic features of fever, weight loss and fatigue are common. Respiratory or pharyngeal muscle involvement leading to ventilatory failure/aspiration is ominous and requires urgent treatment. Interstitial lung disease occurs in up to 30% of patients and is strongly associated with the presence of antisynthetase (e.g. Jo1) antibodies.

Adult dermatomyositis

The muscle manifestations are identical to polymyositis, but occur in combination with characteristic cutaneous manifestations. Gottron's papules are scaly erythematous/violaceous plaques or papules occurring over the extensor surfaces of the proximal and distal interphalangeal joints. The heliotrope rash is a violaceous discoloration of the eyelid in combination with periorbital oedema (see Fig. 20.51). Similar rashes occur on the upper back, chest and shoulders ('shawl' distribution). Periungual nail-fold capillaries are often abnormal. Other systemic manifestations include arthralgia, weight loss and fever.

Childhood dermatomyositis

This is three times more common in girls than in boys and mainly affects 6–9-year-olds. The presentation is similar to adult dermatomyositis except that cutaneous manifestations are more common. These include cutaneous ulceration, lipodystrophy and dystrophic calcification (calcinosis) in the skin, subcutaneous tissue and muscle fascia.

Investigations

These conditions should be suspected in anyone who presents with proximal muscle weakness without evidence of neuropathy, particularly if there is evidence of systemic disease. Creatine kinase (CK) is usually raised and is a guide to disease activity. However, a normal CK does not exclude the diagnosis, particularly in juvenile myositis where only 70% of patients have a raised CK at the time of diagnosis. Electromyography (EMG) may confirm the presence of myopathy and exclude neuropathy. Most patients will then

need a muscle biopsy to look for the typical features of fibre necrosis, regeneration and inflammatory cell infiltrate (see Fig. 20.52). Occasionally, a biopsy may be normal, particularly if myositis is patchy. MRI is a useful means of identifying areas of abnormal muscle that are amenable to biopsy. There is an increased risk of malignancy in patients with dermatomyositis (about a threefold increase) and polymyositis (an increase of about 30%) (see EBM panel). This risk is highest within the first 5 years, and malignancy may be apparent at the time of diagnosis. Current recommended screening investigations when malignancy is suspected should include chest/abdomen/pelvis CT, gastrointestinal tract imaging and mammography.

EBM

RELATIONSHIP BETWEEN MALIGNANCY AND INFLAMMATORY MUSCLE DISEASE

'Dermatomyositis is strongly associated with malignant disease (standard incidence ratio 3.0), particularly ovarian, lung, pancreatic, stomach and colorectal. There is a modest increased risk in polymyositis, mainly non-Hodgkin's lymphoma, lung and bladder. Risk of malignancy is highest at time of diagnosis.'

- Hill CL, Zhang Y, Sigurgeirsson B, et al. Frequency of specific cancer types in dermatomyositis and polymyositis: a population based study. Lancet 2001; 357:96–100.

Management

Oral steroids (e.g. prednisolone 40–60 mg daily) are the mainstay of initial treatment. Patients with severe weakness or evidence of respiratory or pharyngeal weakness may need methylprednisolone 1 g daily for 3 days. If there is a good response, steroids should be reduced by approximately 25% per month down to a maintenance dose of 5–7.5 mg. Although most patients have an initial response to steroids, many will need additional immunosuppressive therapy. Azathioprine and methotrexate are the initial agents of choice. If these are ineffective or not tolerated, then ciclosporin, cyclophosphamide or tacrolimus is an alternative. Relapses may occur, associated with a rising CK, and this is an indication for additional therapy. If the patient fails to respond clinically to treatment, this may be due to steroid-induced myopathy or the development of inclusion body myositis. Further biopsy is indicated at this stage. If active necrosis and regeneration are present, then the disease is still active, whereas the presence of type 2 fibre atrophy is consistent with steroid myopathy but also occurs with active disease.

INCLUSION BODY MYOSITIS

Inclusion body myositis is the most common disease of muscle in patients over the age of 50 and predominates in men. Although proximal weakness does occur, distal involvement is more common and may be asymmetrical. Evaluation is along the same lines as for IIM. CK may be marginally elevated and neuropathic changes may be present on EMG. The characteristic findings on muscle biopsy are abnormal fibres containing rimmed vacuoles and filamentous inclusions in the nucleus and cytoplasm. These inclusions contain paired helical filaments that resemble those seen in the brain in Alzheimer's disease. Treatment is controversial and not as successful as in IIM. Some patients do have an inflammatory component and are steroid-responsive; a trial of steroids is therefore warranted, and if a response occurs then immunosuppressive therapy should be substituted.

SYSTEMIC VASCULITIS

The vasculitides are a heterogeneous group of diseases characterised by inflammation and necrosis of blood vessel walls, often with associated organ involvement. The spectrum of disease ranges from benign and self-limiting (e.g. cutaneous leucocytoclastic vasculitis limited to skin) to life-threatening (e.g. fulminant Wegener's granulomatosis with renal failure and pulmonary haemorrhage).

Clinical features

The clinical features of vasculitis are due to local tissue ischaemia and the systemic effects of widespread inflammation. The symptoms may mimic those of widespread malignancy or emboli, or of occult sepsis. These varied manifestations may be confusing and lead to diagnostic delay, but early diagnosis and management are essential to prevent irreversible organ damage. The key to recognition is the presence of multisystem involvement. Systemic vasculitis should be considered in any patient with fever, weight loss, fatigue, evidence of multisystem involvement, skin rashes, raised inflammatory markers and abnormal urinalysis. Specific symptoms, which should be sought if vasculitis is suspected, are shown in Box 20.29, page 987.

Vasculitis may occur in many types of inflammatory or infectious diseases, such as SLE, rheumatoid arthritis, endocarditis and hepatitis B and C. In these situations, the vasculitis is a secondary manifestation of the primary disease. Primary systemic vasculitis is less common, with an annual incidence of approximately 18–40 new cases per million, which peaks in the 65–74-year age group. The aetiology remains unclear, although geographic, environmental and genetic factors are important. Classification is based on vessel size (see Box 20.60).

A number of important conditions may mimic vasculitis; these include sepsis (particularly subacute bacterial

20.60 SIZE OF VESSEL INVOLVEMENT IN VASCULITIS	
Large vessel	
• Giant cell arteritis	• Takayasu's arteritis
Medium vessel	
• Classical polyarteritis nodosa	• Kawasaki disease
Small vessel	
• Microscopic polyangiitis	• Henoch–Schönlein purpura
• Wegener's granulomatosis	• Mixed essential cryoglobulinaemia
• Churg–Strauss syndrome	

endocarditis and meningococcaemia), malignancy, cholesterol emboli, atrial myxoma and the antiphospholipid syndrome. Careful physical history and examination usually lead to their exclusion.

Investigations

If vasculitis is suspected, the diagnosis should ideally be confirmed by tissue biopsy, in order to determine the vessel size involved and guide therapy. Skin biopsies are easily obtained, but will not help to determine whether the disease is systemic or limited to the skin. Nasal septal tissue can be obtained from areas of ulceration or granulation. Muscle biopsy is positive in about 50% of patients with muscle pain. The most important bedside test is the urine dip test for protein and blood and subsequent microscopy, since the prognosis of vasculitis is often determined by the degree of renal involvement. In patients with abnormal renal function and active urinary sediment, renal biopsy should be considered. Visceral angiography to detect microaneurysms (e.g. classical polyarteritis nodosa) is most useful where involved tissue is not available to biopsy. Antineutrophil cytoplasmic antibodies (ANCA) are directed against enzymes present in neutrophil granules. Two main patterns of immunofluorescence are distinguished: cytoplasmic (c-ANCA) and perinuclear (p-ANCA), specific for the enzymes proteinase 3 and myeloperoxidase respectively. While c-ANCA is particularly associated with Wegener's granulomatosis, p-ANCA is associated with microscopic polyangiitis. However, positive ANCAs occur in many other diseases, including malignancy, infection (bacterial and HIV), inflammatory bowel disease, rheumatoid arthritis, lupus and pulmonary fibrosis. Therefore, the diagnosis of these conditions cannot be made or refuted on the ANCA test alone.

LARGE VESSEL VASCULITIS

Polymyalgia rheumatica (PMR)

PMR is a clinical syndrome of muscle pain and stiffness and, classically, an increased ESR. It is not a true vasculitis but there is a close association with giant cell arteritis. It is predominately a disease of the elderly, with a prevalence of approximately 20 per 100 000 over the age of 50 years. The mean age of onset is 70, and diagnosis is rarely made in patients under 60. Women are affected more often than men by a ratio of 3:1.

Clinical features

The cardinal features are muscle stiffness and pain, symmetrically affecting the proximal muscles of the neck, upper arms and, less commonly, the buttocks and thighs. There is marked early morning stiffness, often with night pain. Constitutional features of weight loss, fatigue, depression and night sweats also occur. Most patients have a rapid onset of symptoms, sometimes overnight, although occasionally the onset is more insidious. On examination there may be stiffness and painful restriction of active shoulder movement but passive movements are preserved. Muscles may be tender to palpation but there should not be muscle-wasting; if there is, then primary muscle or neurological disease is more likely.

Investigations

In the majority of patients the ESR is elevated above 40 mm/hour and there may be a normochromic, normocytic anaemia. Very occasionally the ESR is low, usually in the acute situation where there has not been sufficient time for it to rise. In this situation the CRP may be elevated prior to the ESR.

Management

The only effective treatment is corticosteroids, and prednisolone should be started at a maximum dose of 15 mg. The majority of patients should have a dramatic response within 72 hours. If there is no response by 72 hours or an incomplete response by 7 days, then the diagnosis is not PMR. Other conditions that may mimic PMR are shown in Box 20.61.

If there has been a good response, the dose should be reduced to 10 mg after 4 weeks and then by 1 mg per month, assuming that symptoms remain controlled. If symptoms recur, the dose should be increased to that which previously controlled the symptoms, and reduction attempted in another few months. Most patients need steroids for an average of 18 months and osteoporosis prophylaxis with bisphosphonates should be considered. Some patients require steroid-sparing agents such as methotrexate or azathioprine, particularly if steroids cannot be withdrawn at 2 years or are needed at doses greater than 7.5 mg.

Occasionally, rheumatoid arthritis presents with a polymyalgic illness. This is more common in men and is usually revealed by the appearance of peripheral synovitis when steroid doses are reduced below 10 mg. Approximately 15–20% of patients develop features of giant cell arteritis at some point in the course of their disease. All patients should therefore be instructed to seek prompt medical advice if such symptoms occur.

20.61 CONDITIONS THAT MAY MIMIC POLYMYALGIA RHEUMATICA	

- Fibromyalgia
- Hypothyroidism
- Cervical spondylosis
- Rheumatoid arthritis
- Inflammatory myopathy (particularly inclusion body myositis)
- Systemic vasculitis
- Malignancy

Giant cell arteritis (GCA)

Giant cell arteritis is a large vessel vasculitis predominately affecting branches of the temporal and ophthalmic arteries. The mean age of onset is 70 years with a 4:1 female:male ratio.

Clinical features

As with PMR symptoms may be abrupt but are often insidious over the course of several weeks or months. The most important clinical features are:

- *Headache*. This is usually the first symptom and is often localised to the temporal or occipital region, with scalp tenderness.
- *Jaw pain*. This is brought on by chewing or talking and is due to ischaemia of the masseters.
- *Visual disturbance*. The optic nerve head is supplied by the posterior ciliary artery, vasculitis of which leads to occlusion and acute anterior ischaemic optic neuropathy. Damage to the optic nerve results in loss of visual acuity and field, reduced colour perception and papillary defects. Sudden visual symptoms in one eye, leading rapidly to blindness, constitute the most common pattern. On fundoscopy the optic disc may appear pale and swollen with haemorrhages, but these changes may take 24–36 hours to develop and the fundi may initially appear normal. Once blindness has occurred steroids have a negligible effect other than preventing blindness in the other eye.

There may be associated constitutional symptoms of anorexia, fatigue, weight loss, fever, depression and general malaise. Occasionally presentation is with neurological complications that include transient ischaemic attacks, brain-stem infarcts and hemiparesis.

Investigations

The ESR is usually elevated above 50 mm/hour. In some the ESR is normal, mainly in those with acute presentation where the ESR has not yet had time to rise; in this situation the CRP may be more helpful. If GCA is suspected, systemic steroid (prednisolone 60 mg daily) should be started immediately to prevent visual loss. Ideally, a temporal artery biopsy should also be obtained. However, steroid treatment should not be delayed whilst this is organised; diagnostic information will still be present on biopsies taken a week later. Characteristic biopsy findings are fragmentation of the internal elastic lamina with necrosis of the media in combination with a mixed inflammatory cell infiltrate (lymphocytes, plasma cells and eosinophils). However, 'skip' lesions are common and a negative biopsy does not exclude the diagnosis.

Management

Steroid reduction should be guided by symptoms and ESR, aiming for approximately 10 mg daily by 6 weeks. Thereafter, doses should be reduced by 1 mg per month. Patients with known GCA should be advised to take 60 mg prednisolone and seek prompt medical advice should they experience any recurrence of headache or visual disturbance. Maintenance therapy is required for at least 1 year, and rarely for the rest of the patient's life. Relapse occurs in 30%, and is an indication to restart high-dose steroids with additional immunosuppressive agents, typically azathioprine or methotrexate.

Takayasu's arteritis

Takayasu's disease is a chronic inflammatory granulomatous panarteritis of elastic arteries—the aorta, its major branches and occasionally the pulmonary arteries. It most commonly affects women (female:male ratio 8:1) with a typical age of onset at 25–30 years. It has a world-wide distribution but is most common in Asia. The aetiology is unknown. In contrast to other vasculitides Takayasu's is characterised by thickened and inflamed intima without fibrinoid degeneration.

The usual presentation is with claudication and systemic symptoms of fever, arthralgia and weight loss. The vessels most commonly involved are the carotid, ulnar, brachial, radial and axillary arteries. Clinical examination may reveal loss of pulses, bruits, hypertension and aortic incompetence.

Laboratory investigations are usually non-specific, with high ESR and normocytic, normochromic anaemia. Diagnosis is usually based on angiographic findings of coarctation, occlusion and aneurysmal dilatation. The distribution of involvement can be classified into four types:

- Type 1 is localised to the aorta and its branches.
- Type 2 is localised to the descending thoracic and abdominal aorta.
- Type 3 combines features of 1 and 2.
- Type 4 involves the pulmonary artery.

The 5-year survival rate is 83%. Most patients respond to initial high-dose oral prednisolone (1–2 mg/kg daily). Additional therapy with methotrexate or cyclophosphamide is usually required. Reconstructive vascular surgery should be avoided during periods of active inflammation but may benefit selected patients, especially those with hypertension secondary to aortic or renal lesions.

MEDIUM-SIZED ARTERIES

Classical polyarteritis nodosa (PAN)

Classical PAN is a necrotising vasculitis characterised by transmural inflammation of medium-sized to small arteries. PAN is a rare disorder with an annual incidence of 2 per million in most populations. All age groups can be affected, with a peak incidence in the fourth and fifth decades, and a male:female ratio of 2:1. Hepatitis B is a risk factor, and the incidence of PAN is 10 times higher in the Inuit population of Alaska, where hepatitis B infection is endemic.

Characteristic presentation is with myalgia, arthralgia, fever and weight loss in combination with manifestations of multisystem disease. The most common skin lesions are palpable purpura, ulceration, infarction and livedo reticularis (see Fig. 20.53). In 70% of patients arteritis of the vasa nervorum leads to neuropathy which is typically symmetrical and affects both sensory and motor function. Severe hypertension and/or renal impairment may occur due to multiple renal infarctions; glomerulonephritis is rare (in contrast to microscopic polyangiitis). Diagnosis is confirmed by finding

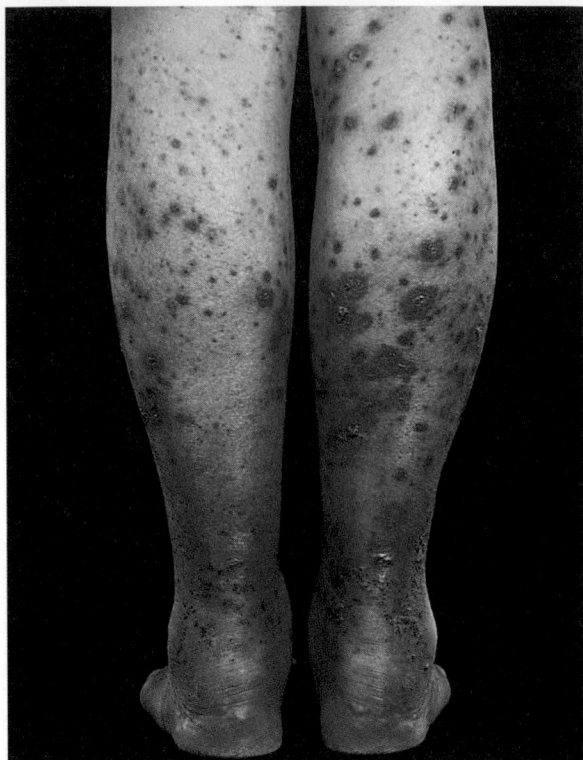

Fig. 20.53   **Rash of systemic vasculitis (palpable purpura).**

multiple aneurysms and smooth narrowing of either the mesenteric, hepatic or renal systems on angiography. Tissue biopsy may be definitive (muscle or sural nerve), even in the absence of angiographic abnormality.

Treatment for hepatitis B-related disease is to remove the source of the antigen, i.e. antiviral therapy. Steroids and cyclophosphamide are the treatment of choice for idiopathic disease. Mortality is less than 20%, although relapse occurs in up to 50% of patients.

Kawasaki disease (mucocutaneous lymph node syndrome)

Kawasaki disease (KD) is an acute systemic disorder of childhood that predominately occurs in Japan (800 cases per million in children under the age of 5). The disease resembles a viral exanthem or Stevens–Johnson syndrome. Although the causative trigger is unknown, it has been associated with *Mycoplasma* and HIV infection in some cases. The principal clinical features, which often develop abruptly, are shown in Box 20.62. Cardiovascular complications include myocarditis, pericarditis, coronary aneurysms, transient coronary artery dilatation, myocardial infarction due to coronary thrombosis, peripheral vascular insufficiency and gangrene.

The differential diagnosis is wide. Investigations that favour KD include a polymorphonuclear leucocytosis, thrombocytosis, raised ESR and CRP and circulating anti-endothelial cell antibodies. Treatment is with aspirin (5 mg/kg daily for 14 days) and intravenous gammaglobulin (400 mg/kg daily for 4 consecutive days). Steroids should be avoided because of the risk of worsening the coronary artery

---

20.62 FEATURES OF KAWASAKI DISEASE*

- Fever persisting > 5 days
- Bilateral conjunctival congestion
- Erythema of lips, buccal mucosa and tongue
- Acute non-purulent cervical lymphadenopathy
- Polymorphous exanthema
- Erythema of palms and soles (oedema followed by desquamation)
- Coronary dilatation

* Five out of six clinical features, or four out of six clinical features with evidence of coronary dilatation, are required for diagnosis.

---

dilatation. Coronary artery changes are usually monitored weekly by two-dimensional echo for 4 weeks, by which stage most children have recovered. The overall mortality is less than 2%. Relapse is rare, but if there is coronary artery involvement long-term follow-up is necessary.

SMALL VESSEL DISEASE OF ARTERIOLES, VENULES AND CAPILLARIES

Microscopic polyangiitis, Wegener's granulomatosis and Churg–Strauss syndrome can be grouped together as 'ANCA-associated vasculitis', although not all patients are ANCA-positive at diagnosis. All patients may present similarly with arthralgia, myalgia and evidence of multisystem disease, the precise 'subtype' being determined by other specific clinical features.

Microscopic polyangiitis (MPA)

MPA is more common than PAN, with an annual incidence of 8 per million in the UK. Classic presentation is with rapidly progressive glomerulonephritis often associated with alveolar haemorrhage. Cutaneous and gastrointestinal involvement, similar to PAN, is common. Less usual features include neuropathy (15%) and pleural effusions (15%). Patients are usually p-ANCA (myeloperoxidase)-positive.

Wegener's granulomatosis (WG)

The incidence of WG is 5–10 per million. The most common presentation is with upper airway involvement (typically epistaxis, nasal crusting and sinusitis), haemoptysis, mucosal ulceration and deafness due to serous otitis media. Symptoms may have been present for several months, and erroneously attributed to infection or allergy. The most common ocular abnormality is proptosis, due to inflammation of the retro-orbital tissue. This may cause diplopia due to entrapment of the extraocular muscles, or loss of vision due to optic nerve compression, the earliest feature of which is usually disturbance of colour vision (see Fig. 20.54). Untreated nasal disease ultimately leads to destruction of bone and cartilage. Migratory pulmonary infiltrates and nodules occur in 50% of patients. A minority of patients present with glomerulonephritis. Patients are usually c-ANCA-positive.

Churg–Strauss syndrome (CSS)

The annual incidence is 1–3 per million in the UK. Most patients have a prodromal period for many years characterised

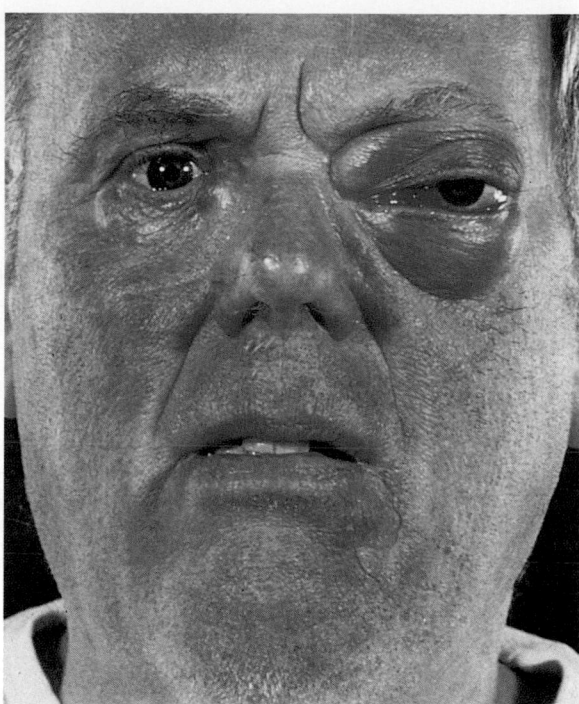

Fig. 20.54 **Eye involvement in Wegener's granulomatosis.**

by allergic rhinitis, nasal polyposis and late-onset asthma that is often difficult to control. The typical acute presentation is with a triad of skin lesions (purpura or nodules), asymmetric mononeuritis multiplex and eosinophilia on a background of resistant asthma. Pulmonary infiltrates and pleural or pericardial effusions due to serositis may be present. Up to 50% of patients have abdominal symptoms due to mesenteric vasculitis. Either c-ANCA or p-ANCA is present in around 40% of cases.

Management of MPA, WG and CSS

Treatment should be instituted as early as possible to prevent irreversible damage. If there is life-threatening or critical organ involvement, treatment may need to be given prior to biopsy confirmation. The aims of treatment are to induce a remission, and then to maintain remission with minimum drug toxicity. Remission can be induced either with oral high-dosage prednisolone (1 mg/kg daily) and continuous oral cyclophosphamide (2 mg/kg daily) or with bolus i.v. methylprednisolone (10 mg/kg) and cyclophosphamide (15 mg/kg), initially fortnightly and subsequently monthly. Doses of cyclophosphamide should be reduced in the elderly and those with renal impairment. The dose of oral prednisolone is rapidly reduced once remission has occurred. Cyclophosphamide is usually continued for 6–12 months in total, followed by maintenance with azathioprine. Co-trimoxazole is usually given at a prophylactic dose (960 mg thrice weekly) in conjunction with cyclophosphamide to prevent *Pneumocystis* pneumonia, unless there is a history of drug allergy. Mesna is used with bolus cyclophosphamide to reduce the risks of haemorrhagic cystitis. Occasionally, cyclophosphamide fails to induce a remission, in which case the diagnosis should be reconsidered. Other treatment strategies for resistant vasculitis include plasma exchange and daily oral etoposide.

Henoch–Schönlein purpura

This small vessel vasculitis usually occurs in children and young adults and often has a good prognosis. Typical presentation is with purpura over the buttocks and lower legs, abdominal symptoms (pain and bleeding) and arthritis (knee or ankle) following an upper respiratory tract infection. Nephritis occurs in 40% of patients and may occur up to 4 weeks after the onset of other symptoms. The diagnosis can only be confirmed by demonstrating IgA deposition within and around blood vessel walls. Prognosis is determined by the degree and severity of renal involvement. Although only 1% of patients develop end-stage renal failure, adverse features at presentation in adults include hypertension, abnormal renal function and proteinuria > 1.5 g/day. Corticosteroids alone are effective for gastrointestinal and joint involvement but nephritis usually requires treatment with both pulse i.v. steroids and immunosuppression.

Cryoglobulinaemic vasculitis

Cryoglobulins are circulating immunoglobulins that precipitate out in the cold. They are classified into three types (see Box 20.63); types II and III are associated with cryoglobulinaemic vasculitis. The typical clinical features are palpable purpura over the lower extremities, arthralgia, Raynaud's phenomenon and neuropathy. Type II cryoglobulinaemia is secondary to hepatitis C virus (HCV) infection in most patients, the virus being present in the vasculitic lesions complexed with IgG and IgM. For HCV-positive patients, interferon-alpha is currently the treatment of choice; for high HCV loads, combination with ribavirin may be more effective (see p. 865).

20.63 CLASSIFICATION OF CRYOGLOBULINS		
Type	**Antibody type**	**Associations**
I	Monoclonal IgM	Malignant B-cell disease, e.g. Waldenström's, lymphoma, myeloma
II ('mixed essential')	Monoclonal IgM and anti-IgG antibody (RhF)	Hepatitis C, SLE, B-cell malignancy
III	Polyclonal IgM and anti-IgG antibody (RhF)	RA, SLE, chronic infections

OTHER FORMS OF VASCULITIS

Behçet's syndrome

This is a vasculitis of unknown aetiology that characteristically targets venules. It is rare in Western Europe but more common in 'Silk Route' countries around the Mediterranean and Japan where there is a strong association with HLA-B51.

There is a wide range of clinical features, and the disease is characterised by unpredictable exacerbations. There are no defining investigations and the diagnosis is made on clinical features (see Box 20.64). Oral ulcers are universal (see Fig. 20.55). Unlike aphthous ulcers they are usually deep and multiple, and last for 10–30 days. Genital ulcers are less common (60–80%). The usual skin lesions are erythema nodosum or acneiform lesions but migratory thrombophlebitis and vasculitis also occur. The pathergy reaction is hyper-reactivity at the site of minor trauma. A formal pathergy test involves intradermal skin pricking with a needle, and is positive if a pustule develops within 48 hours. Ocular involvement is usually bilateral and may include anterior or posterior uveitis or retinal vasculitis. Neurological involvement occurs in 5% and mainly involves the brain stem, although the meninges, hemispheres and cord can also be involved to cause pyramidal signs, cranial nerve lesions, brain-stem symptoms or hemiparesis. Recurrent thromboses also occur. Renal involvement is extremely rare.

Oral ulceration can be managed with topical steroid preparations (e.g. soluble prednisolone mouthwashes, steroid pastes). Colchicine is sometimes effective for erythema nodosum and arthralgia. Thalidomide (100–300 mg per day for 28 days initially) is very effective for resistant oral and genital ulceration but is teratogenic and neurotoxic. Systemic disease is more problematic and usually requires oral steroids in combination with other immunosuppressive drugs.

20.64 CRITERIA FOR THE DIAGNOSIS OF BEHÇET'S SYNDROME
• Recurrent oral ulceration—minor aphthous, major aphthous or herpetiform ulceration at least three times in a 12-month period
Plus two of:
• Recurrent genital ulceration
• Eye lesions—anterior uveitis, posterior uveitis, or cells in vitreous on slit lamp examination, or retinal vasculitis
• Skin lesions—erythema nodosum, pseudofolliculitis, or papulopustular lesions, or acneiform nodules
• Positive pathergy test

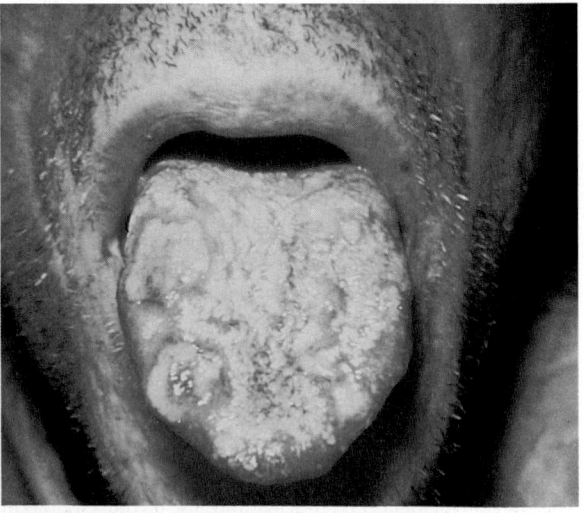

Fig. 20.55 Oral ulceration in Behçet's syndrome.

MUSCULOSKELETAL MANIFESTATIONS OF DISEASE IN OTHER SYSTEMS

Many systemic diseases result in MSK symptoms and signs and in some cases this may be the presentation of the disease. Furthermore, drugs used for other system disease may result in MSK complications (see Box 20.65). The following examples illustrate the variety of conditions that may be encountered but are not exhaustive.

20.65 EXAMPLES OF DRUG-INDUCED EFFECTS ON THE MUSCULOSKELETAL SYSTEM	
Musculoskeletal problem	**Principal drug**
Secondary gout	Diuretic—thiazide, loop diuretic
Osteoporosis	Corticosteroids, heparin
Osteomalacia	Anticonvulsants
Osteonecrosis	Corticosteroids
Drug-induced lupus syndrome	Procainamide, hydralazine, isoniazid, chlorpromazine
Arthralgias or arthritis	Steroid withdrawal, glibenclamide, methyldopa, ciclosporin, isoniazid, barbiturates
Myalgias Myopathy Myositis, myasthenia Cramps	Steroid withdrawal, L-tryptophan, clofibrate, statins Corticosteroid, chloroquine Penicillamine Corticosteroid, ACTH, diuretics, carbenoxolone
Vasculitis	Amphetamines, thiazides

MALIGNANT DISEASE

Progressive 'bone' pain may result from skeletal metastases or invasion by myeloma (see p. 985) in adults. Polyarthritis may be the presentation of acute leukaemia (see p. 931), especially in children.

Dermatomyositis/polymyositis may be the presentation of occult malignancy. This should be suspected in those over the age of 50 with marked skin involvement and resistance to treatment. Polymyalgia rheumatica, but not temporal arteritis, may similarly be the presentation of neoplastic disease. Apart from a screening chest radiograph, other investigations are largely guided by symptoms.

Hypertrophic osteoarthropathy comprises clubbing, painful swelling of distal limbs (usually symmetrical), periosteal new bone formation and arthralgia/arthritis. Many causes of clubbing can result in this uncommon syndrome but it mainly occurs with bronchial carcinoma (5%; the most common cause—see p. 544) and mesothelioma (40%—see p. 573). The pain is characteristically worsened by dependency and relieved by elevation. Bone scans show increased periosteal activity before new bone is apparent on radiograph. The course follows that of the underlying malignancy and eradication can effect a cure.

ENDOCRINE DISEASE

Hypothyroidism (see p. 691) may present with carpal tunnel syndrome. A severely painful, symmetrical proximal myopathy with muscle hypertrophy is an occasional presentation. All MSK lesions show excellent recovery following thyroxine replacement.

Hyperparathyroidism (see p. 718), both primary and secondary, may cause bone disease through accelerated bone turnover, usually presenting as ill-defined aching. There is predisposition to radiographic chondrocalcinosis, pseudogout attacks due to calcium pyrophosphate crystals and, especially with disease secondary to renal failure, calcific periarthritis.

Diabetes mellitus (see Ch. 15) commonly causes diabetic 'stiff hands' (cheiroarthropathy) due to tightening of skin and periarticular structures, giving flexion deformities of many fingers which is sometimes painful. Diabetic osteopathy presents as forefoot pain and shows radiographic progression from osteopenia to complete osteolysis of the phalanges and metatarsals. There is also predisposition to 'frozen shoulder', Dupuytren's contracture, septic arthritis and neuropathic joints.

MSK symptoms are common presenting features of acromegaly (see p. 742) and include:

- low mechanical back pain, with normal or excessive (not restricted) movement
- carpal tunnel syndrome and late-onset Raynaud's phenomenon (25%)
- acromegalic arthropathy (50%), mainly affecting knees, hips and shoulders, with non-inflammatory usage pain and coarse crepitus, suggesting osteoarthritis, but normal or increased (not restricted) movement. Radiographic signs may include widening of joint spaces, squaring of bone ends, generalised osteopenia and tufting of terminal phalanges.

METABOLIC DISEASE

Approximately 50% of people with haemochromatosis (see p. 870) develop arthropathy, usually in their forties or fifties, which may predate other classic features. Presentation is usually with pain and stiffness of wrists, fingers and metacarpophalangeal joints, though hips, shoulders and knees are also commonly affected. Radiographic changes resemble osteoarthritis with narrowing, sclerosis and cysts, but cysts are often multiple and prominent, there is little osteophyte, and atypical sites for osteoarthritis (e.g. radiocarpal joint, metacarpophalangeal joints) are targeted. About 30% have superimposed pseudogout attacks and radiographic chondrocalcinosis as additional clues. Treatment of the haemochromatosis does not influence the arthropathy.

SARCOIDOSIS

Acute self-limiting arthritis, presenting as polyarthralgia and erythema nodosum, may accompany the onset of acute sarcoidosis (see p. 552). Chronic sarcoidosis may associate with a more persistent arthritis that targets the same joints.

NEUROPATHIC (CHARCOT) JOINTS

Neurological disease (see Ch. 22) may result in rapidly destructive arthritis of joints, first described by Charcot in association with syphilis. Although repetitive microtrauma following sensory loss was one popular explanation, the more likely pathogenesis is altered blood flow secondary to impaired sympathetic nervous system control. The following are the principal predisposing diseases and principal sites of involvement:

- diabetic neuropathy (hindfoot)
- syringomyelia (shoulder, elbow, wrist)
- leprosy (hands, feet)
- tabes dorsalis (knees, spine).

Presentation is usually with chronic monoarthritis or dislocation. Pain can be a feature, especially at the onset, but the striking clinical feature is that signs are disproportionately greater than symptoms would suggest. The joint is often grossly swollen, with effusion, crepitus, marked instability and deformity, though usually no increased warmth. It may eventually become flail and be complicated by peripheral nerve entrapment or spinal cord compression. Radiographic features are gross loss of cartilage and bone, with disorganisation of normal architecture and often multiple loose bodies, and either no (atrophic) or gross (hypertrophic) new bone formation. Management principally involves orthoses and occasionally arthrodesis.

MISCELLANEOUS RARE MUSCULOSKELETAL CONDITIONS

ALGODYSTROPHY (REFLEX SYMPATHETIC DYSTROPHY)

This disorder usually affects a single, mainly peripheral, region with severe burning pain and tenderness, vasomotor changes (abnormal sweating, colour and temperature change, oedema) and associated localised regional osteoporosis. It may be triggered by trauma, pregnancy or intercurrent illness, or arise spontaneously. It is thought to result from abnormal sympathetic vasomotor control that causes local vasodilatation and increased osteoclastic bone resorption. It is diagnosed on the basis of clinical features, regional patchy osteoporosis on radiograph, increased uptake on radioisotope bone scanning, and absence of an acute phase response. Various treatments have been tried, including active mobilisation, calcitonin, corticosteroids and sympathetic blockade, though bisphosphonates appear the most beneficial in improving pain and swelling. The sooner any treatment is started, the better its effect. The prognosis is variable but often poor. Shoulder–hand syndrome is one form of complex algodystrophy that affects two regions simultaneously.

INHERITED CONNECTIVE TISSUE DISEASE

Marfan's syndrome is characterised by skeletal disproportion (arm span greater than height), arachnodactyly (long, thin, 'spider' fingers), sternal depression, generalised hypermobility of joints, lens dislocation and a high arched palate. It results from mutations of the fibrillin gene, a component of extracellular matrix. The most serious complications are in the cardiovascular system, with mitral valve prolapse, aortic incompetence and aortic dissection (see p. 447). Ehlers–Danlos syndrome is characterised by generalised hypermobility, skin laxity and easy bruising, with scoliosis, short stature, ocular fragility and visceral vascular catastrophes. It may result from mutations in several genes including COLIA2, lysyl oxidase, fibronectin and elastin. Osteoporosis and a Marfanoid appearance occur in homocystinuria, which is due to deficiency of the enzyme cystathionine synthetase. Other features include mental retardation, and venous and arterial thrombosis. The diagnosis is confirmed by finding homocystine in the urine, and patients respond to treatment with pyridoxine.

OSTEOGENESIS IMPERFECTA (OI)

OI is a rare disease that usually presents with severe osteoporosis and multiple fractures in infancy and childhood. Other variable features include blue sclerae and abnormal dentition. Most cases are due to mutations of type I collagen genes (COLIA1, COLIA2), with either reduced collagen production or formation of abnormal molecules that rapidly degrade. Disease severity varies from neonatal lethal (type II), through very severe with multiple fractures in infancy and childhood (types III and IV), to mild (type I) which can present in adults and mimic osteoporosis. Severe OI is diagnosed on clinical grounds or by specialised analysis of collagen produced by cultured skin fibroblasts. There is no cure, but physiotherapy and occupational therapy may help the associated disability. Surgery is often required for fracture fixation and correction of deformity. HRT is advised for perimenopausal women with OI to prevent post-menopausal bone loss. Intravenous pamidronate may improve bone pain and reduce fracture incidence in severe OI.

OSTEOPETROSIS AND OSTEOSCLEROSIS

Osteopetrosis is a group of rare inherited diseases characterised by defects in osteoclast function and generalised osteosclerosis. The phenotype varies from a severe disorder that presents with marrow failure in childhood to a milder, often asymptomatic form in adults. Childhood cases may show failure to thrive, delayed dentition, cranial nerve palsies (due to absent cranial foramina formation), anaemia and recurrent infections (due to bone replacing the marrow cavity). The adult-onset type may present with bone pain, cranial nerve palsies and osteoarthritis or be discovered as an incidental radiographic finding. Defects identified include deficiency of carbonic anhydrase II (the enzyme that permits osteoclasts to produce acid), defects in the osteoclast proton pump and deficiency of cathepsin K (a bone matrix degrading protease). For severe cases interferon gamma treatment can improve blood counts and reduce frequency of infections. Cure, however, can be effected by bone marrow transplantation which provides a source of healthy osteoclast precursors that resorb bone normally.

Osteosclerosis describes disorders characterised by focal increases in bone density. Acquired forms are described in intravenous drug users with hepatitis C infection, in patients with lymphoma and myelosclerosis, and in fibrogenesis imperfecta ossium—an idiopathic disorder causing intractable bone pain, mixed sclerotic/lytic lesions on radiograph and multiple fractures. Engelmann's disease is an autosomal dominant disorder causing severe pain and osteosclerosis of long bones. It is due to activating mutations of the transforming growth factor beta 1 gene. There is no cure but the pain may be improved by corticosteroid.

RELAPSING POLYCHONDRITIS

Relapsing polychondritis (RP) is an idiopathic condition classically presenting as acute pain and swelling of one or both ear pinnae, which spares the non-cartilaginous portion. Around 30% of patients have coexisting autoimmune or connective tissue disease. In 25% of patients inflammation of the tracheobronchial tree leads to hoarse voice, cough, stridor or expiratory wheeze. Manifestations at other cartilage sites include collapse of the bridge of the nose, scleritis, hearing loss and cardiac valve dysfunction. Diagnosis may be confirmed by auricular cartilage biopsy. Pulmonary function tests, including flow volume loops, should be performed to assess the degree of laryngotracheal disease since this is an important cause of mortality. Mild ear disease usually responds to low-dose steroids or NSAIDs. Major organ involvement requires high-dose steroids in combination with cytotoxic drugs. Rarely, tracheostomy or tracheal stents are required.

FAMILIAL PERIODIC FEVERS

These are characterised by recurrent attacks of fever and organ inflammation. Familial Mediterranean fever (FMF) is largely restricted to Armenians, Sephardic Jews and other ethnic groups originating from the Middle East and Mediterranean, and results from mutations of the pyrin gene. Painful febrile attacks affect joints, skin and serosal cavities and last from a few hours to 4 days.

Hyperimmunoglobulinaemia D periodic fever syndrome (HIDS) is an autosomal recessive disorder that causes attacks every 4–8 weeks of abdominal pain, diarrhoea, lymphadenopathy, arthralgia and skin lesions. Serum IgD is persistently elevated. Most patients originate from the Netherlands and northern France.

TNF receptor-associated periodic syndrome (TRAPS) is an autosomal dominant syndrome causing recurrent periodic fever, arthralgia, myalgia, serositis and rashes with a marked acute phase response. FMF and TRAPS may both result in amyloidosis, and colchicine is the first-line treatment. Therapy with monoclonal anti-TNF receptor therapy (e.g. etanercept) may be effective in TRAPS.

FURTHER INFORMATION

Bone health in the balance. Science 2000; 289:1497–1514. *A series of reviews on basic aspects of bone cell biology and bone turnover.*

Brandt KD, Doherty M, Lohmander LS, eds. Osteoarthritis. Oxford: Oxford University Press; 1998.

Coleman RE. Metastatic bone disease: clinical features, pathophysiology and treatment strategies. Cancer Treat Rev 2001; 27:165–176.

Cush JJ, Kavanaugh AF, Olsen N, et al. Rheumatology diagnosis and therapeutics. Baltimore: Williams & Wilkins; 1999.

Delmas PD, Meunier PJ. The management of Paget's disease of bone [review]. N Engl J Med 1997; 336(8):558–566.

Doherty M, Hazleman BL, Huttin CW, et al. Rheumatology examination and injection techniques. London: WB Saunders; 1999.

Eastell R. Treatment of postmenopausal osteoporosis. N Engl J Med 1998; 33(8):736–746.

Firestein GS, Panayi GS, Wollheim FA, eds. Rheumatoid arthritis: new frontiers in pathogenesis and treatment. Oxford: Oxford University Press; 2000.

Maddison PJ, Isenberg DA, Woo P, Glass DN, eds. Oxford textbook of rheumatology. 2nd edn. Oxford: Oxford University Press; 1998.

www.eBandolier.com *Updates on management.*

www.ectsoc.org/reviews *Reviews on various aspects of bone disease, both clinical and basic.*

www.rheumatology.com *Updates on management.*

Skin disease

O.M.V. SCHOFIELD • J.L. REES

CLINICAL EXAMINATION IN SKIN DISEASE

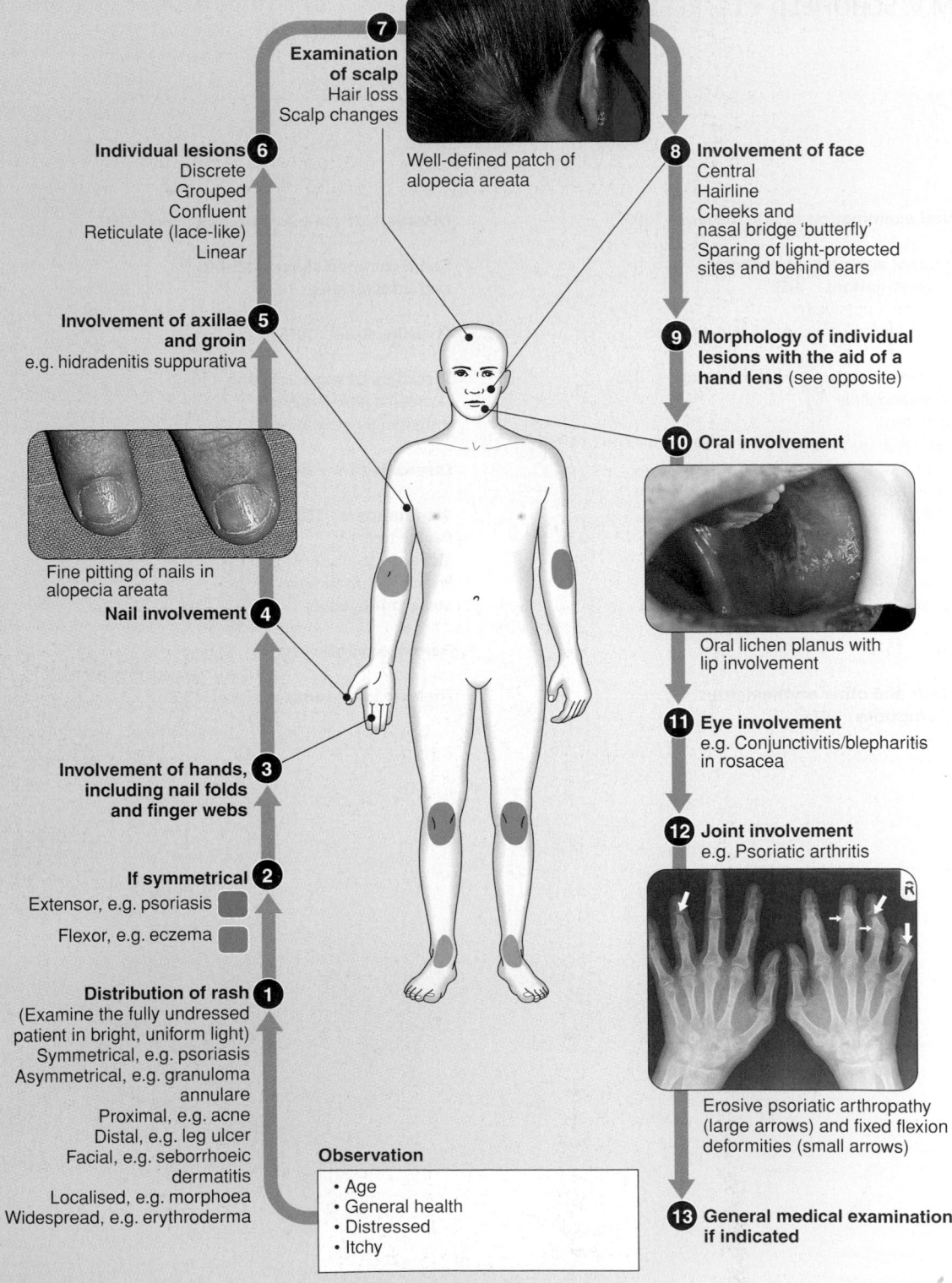

7 Examination of scalp
Hair loss
Scalp changes

Well-defined patch of alopecia areata

6 Individual lesions
Discrete
Grouped
Confluent
Reticulate (lace-like)
Linear

8 Involvement of face
Central
Hairline
Cheeks and
nasal bridge 'butterfly'
Sparing of light-protected
sites and behind ears

5 Involvement of axillae and groin
e.g. hidradenitis suppurativa

9 Morphology of individual lesions with the aid of a hand lens (see opposite)

Fine pitting of nails in alopecia areata

4 Nail involvement

10 Oral involvement

Oral lichen planus with lip involvement

3 Involvement of hands, including nail folds and finger webs

11 Eye involvement
e.g. Conjunctivitis/blepharitis in rosacea

12 Joint involvement
e.g. Psoriatic arthritis

2 If symmetrical
Extensor, e.g. psoriasis
Flexor, e.g. eczema

1 Distribution of rash
(Examine the fully undressed patient in bright, uniform light)
Symmetrical, e.g. psoriasis
Asymmetrical, e.g. granuloma annulare
Proximal, e.g. acne
Distal, e.g. leg ulcer
Facial, e.g. seborrhoeic dermatitis
Localised, e.g. morphoea
Widespread, e.g. erythroderma

Erosive psoriatic arthropathy (large arrows) and fixed flexion deformities (small arrows)

Observation
- Age
- General health
- Distressed
- Itchy

13 General medical examination if indicated

TERMS USED TO DESCRIBE SKIN LESIONS

Term	Definition	Term	Definition
PRIMARY LESIONS		**SECONDARY LESIONS** (which evolve from primary lesions)	
Macule	Small flat area of altered colour or texture	Scale	A flake arising from the horny layer
Papule	Small solid elevation of skin, less than 0.5 cm in diameter	Crust	Looks like a scale, but is composed of dried blood or tissue fluid
Nodule	A solid mass in the skin, usually greater than 0.5 cm in diameter	Ulcer	An area of skin from which the whole of the epidermis and at least the upper part of the dermis have been lost
Plaque	Elevated area of skin greater than 2 cm in diameter but without substantial depth	Excoriation	An ulcer or erosion produced by scratching
Vesicle	Circumscribed elevation of skin, less than 0.5 cm in diameter, and containing fluid	Erosion	An area of skin denuded by a complete or partial loss of the epidermis
Bulla	Circumscribed elevation of skin, over 0.5 cm in diameter, and containing fluid	Fissure	A slit in the skin
Pustule	A visible accumulation of pus in the skin	Sinus	A cavity or channel that permits the escape of pus or fluid
Abscess	A localised collection of pus in a cavity, more than 1 cm in diameter	Scar	The result of healing, in which normal structures are permanently replaced by fibrous tissue
Weal	An elevated, white, compressible, evanescent area produced by dermal oedema	Atrophy	Thinning of skin due to diminution of the epidermis, dermis, subcutaneous fat
Papilloma	A nipple-like mass projecting from the skin	Stria	A streak-like, linear, atrophic, pink, purple or white lesion of the skin due to changes in the connective tissue
Petechiae	Pinhead-sized macules of blood in the skin		
Purpura	A larger macule or papule of blood in the skin		
Ecchymosis	A larger extravasation of blood into the skin		
Haematoma	A swelling from gross bleeding		
Burrow	A linear or curvilinear papule, caused by a burrowing scabies mite		
Comedo	A plug of keratin and sebum wedged in a dilated pilosebaceous orifice		
Telangiectasia	The visible dilatation of small cutaneous blood vessels		

lichenification —

HISTORY

It is often sensible to introduce yourself to the patient, ask a few questions and then examine the skin before further cross-questioning of the patient. Ask about the onset of the skin lesions and the progression of the disease. A careful enquiry into drugs administered, particularly those bought without a prescription, a past or family history of skin disorders, comorbidity, and details of occupation and any hobbies are also potentially important. The relative contribution of history, elicitation of symptoms and physical signs differs for particular diagnoses.

EXAMINATION

The patient needs to be undressed, and make-up and dressings should be removed. A frequent mistake is failure to undress the patient appropriately to allow the correct diagnosis to be made.

A magnifying lens is often helpful. Feeling the skin provides diagnostic clues and may also be therapeutic as many patients with skin disease, whatever their apparent level of sophistication, may feel like lepers. Skin diseases cannot usually be correctly diagnosed at arm's length.

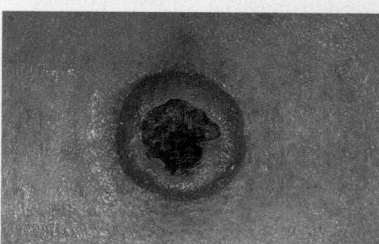

Nodule. A keratoacanthoma.

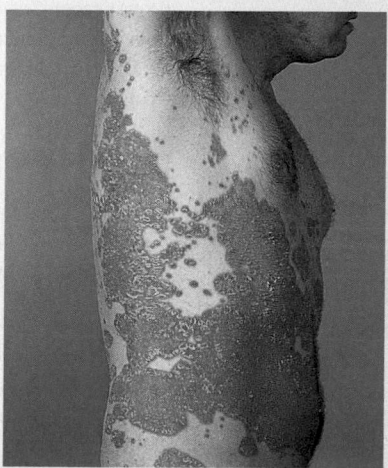

Plaque. Erythematous plaques in psoriasis.

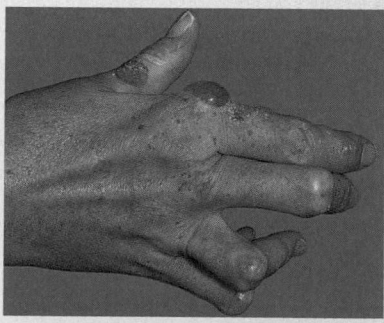

Bullae and scarring. Acquired epidermolysis bullosa in rheumatoid arthritis.

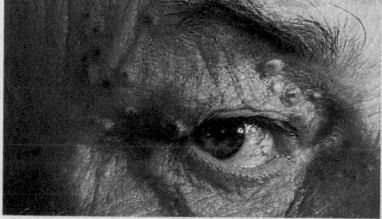

Comedo. Solar comedones occurring around the eyes in an elderly individual.

Skin disease is common. Surveys in Europe suggest that approximately 1 in 7 to 1 in 10 of all visits to a primary care physician is for a skin problem and that for many hospitals the number of patients attending for dermatological diagnosis and treatment exceeds the total number of visits for the whole of internal medicine. Population prevalence studies are in keeping with these figures, revealing an enormous burden of undiagnosed, untreated skin disease. Skin disease appears to be becoming more common for at least three reasons. Firstly, there is a lowered threshold for seeking medical attention. Secondly, the absolute incidence of many diseases such as skin cancer and atopic dermatitis has increased steeply. Thirdly, and often neglected, the therapeutic options for a number of diseases previously viewed as untreatable have increased and awareness of these therapies is belatedly spreading.

Skin complaints affect all ages from the neonate to the elderly and cause harm in a number of ways as shown in Box 21.1. Every clinician has the opportunity to look at the skin when listening to or examining a patient and should be able to identify important and common skin disorders. This chapter emphasises those skin conditions that are frequently seen in general practice and in general medical clinics. Those skin infections not covered here, including human immunodeficiency virus (HIV) disease, are dealt with in Chapter 1, and connective tissue diseases which often involve the skin, in Chapter 20.

The aim of this chapter is to give the reader:

- an idea of how to assess the patient with a rash or lesion
- advice on appropriate initial management and therapy
- theory underlying the mechanisms of some skin diseases and their therapies.

21.1 THE FOUR Ds
Discomfort
• Most often itching or pain (e.g. eczema, post-herpetic neuralgia)
Disfigurement
• Leading to embarrassment and withdrawal from society (e.g. birth marks, acne vulgaris and psoriasis)
Disability
• Leading to loss of work and wages (e.g. dermatitis of the hands and feet)
Death
• Rare but still seen (e.g. metastatic melanoma and widespread blistering drug reactions)

FUNCTIONAL ANATOMY, PHYSIOLOGY AND INVESTIGATIONS

ANATOMY AND PHYSIOLOGY

The skin of an average adult covers an area of just under 2 m². The epidermis, a stratified squamous epithelium, is the outermost layer and is predominantly composed of keratinocytes. The epidermis is attached to the underlying dermis by the basement membrane. The dermis contains and supports blood vessels, nerves and appendageal structures such as hair follicles and sweat glands. The predominant cell of the dermis is the fibroblast. It is important to remember that the appendageal structures such as hair follicles and sweat glands, whilst embedded within the dermis, are epidermal in origin. Below the dermis is the subcutis.

EPIDERMIS

Keratinocytes comprise 95% of epidermal cells (see Fig. 21.1). The proliferative compartment of epidermis resides in the basal layer and in the layer immediately adjacent to the basal layer where mitotic figures are also not uncommon. The site of the keratinocyte stem cell is not certain but is likely to be in a specialised region of the hair follicle analogous to the 'bulge' region in the mouse. In areas of skin without hair follicles (glabrous skin) stem cells may be present within the epidermis.

Keratinocytes synthesise a range of structural proteins including keratins and loricrin. There are over 20 different types of keratin, classed into two broad groups: basic (type I) and acidic (type II). Specific keratins form dimers made up of one acidic and one basic molecule that are aggregated to form larger macromolecular structures called intermediate filaments. Intermediate filaments play a key structural role in skin physiology and the expression patterns of the various gene products is highly complex. Genetic diseases that result in mutations of keratins (e.g. simple epidermolysis bullosa, some types of ichthyosis) are characterised by either epidermal fragility (i.e. blistering) or grossly disordered differentiation. As keratinocytes move out of the basal layer they differentiate, producing a variety of different protein and lipid products. Keratinocytes undergo a form of programmed cell death in the granular layer before becoming the flattened anucleate cells that make up the stratum corneum. The epidermis is a site of great lipid production, and the ability of the stratum corneum to act as a hydrophobic barrier is in large part due to the structure of highly proteinaceous dead corneocytes; these have a highly cross-linked protein membrane ('bricks') in a metabolically active layer of lipid ('mortar') also secreted by the corneocytes ('bricks and mortar' model).

Skin is required to have considerable physical resilience as well as being highly active metabolically. Whereas keratins provide structural support for individual keratinocytes, attachments between cells need to be able to transmit and dissipate stress, a function performed by desmosomes. Diseases that target desmosomes, such as pemphigus, result in blistering as the individual keratinocytes separate.

Three other cell types make up most of the remaining 5% of epidermal cells:

- *Langerhans cells* are dendritic, bone marrow-derived cells that circulate between the epidermis and the local lymph nodes. Their prime function is effective presentation of foreign antigens to lymphocytes, as is seen, for example, in an allergic contact dermatitis reaction. They may also play a part in presentation of tumour antigens, a fact on which researchers have tried to capitalise in the production of anti-melanoma vaccines. Other dendritic cells which are effective at presenting antigen are also present in skin but are in the dermis rather than the epidermis.

- *Melanocytes*, of neural crest origin, are found predominantly in the basal layer; they synthesise the pigment melanin from tyrosine, package it in melanosomes and transfer it to surrounding keratinocytes via their dendritic processes.
- *Merkel cells* are found in the basal layer. They are thought to play a role in signal transduction of fine touch. Their embryological origin is not certain.

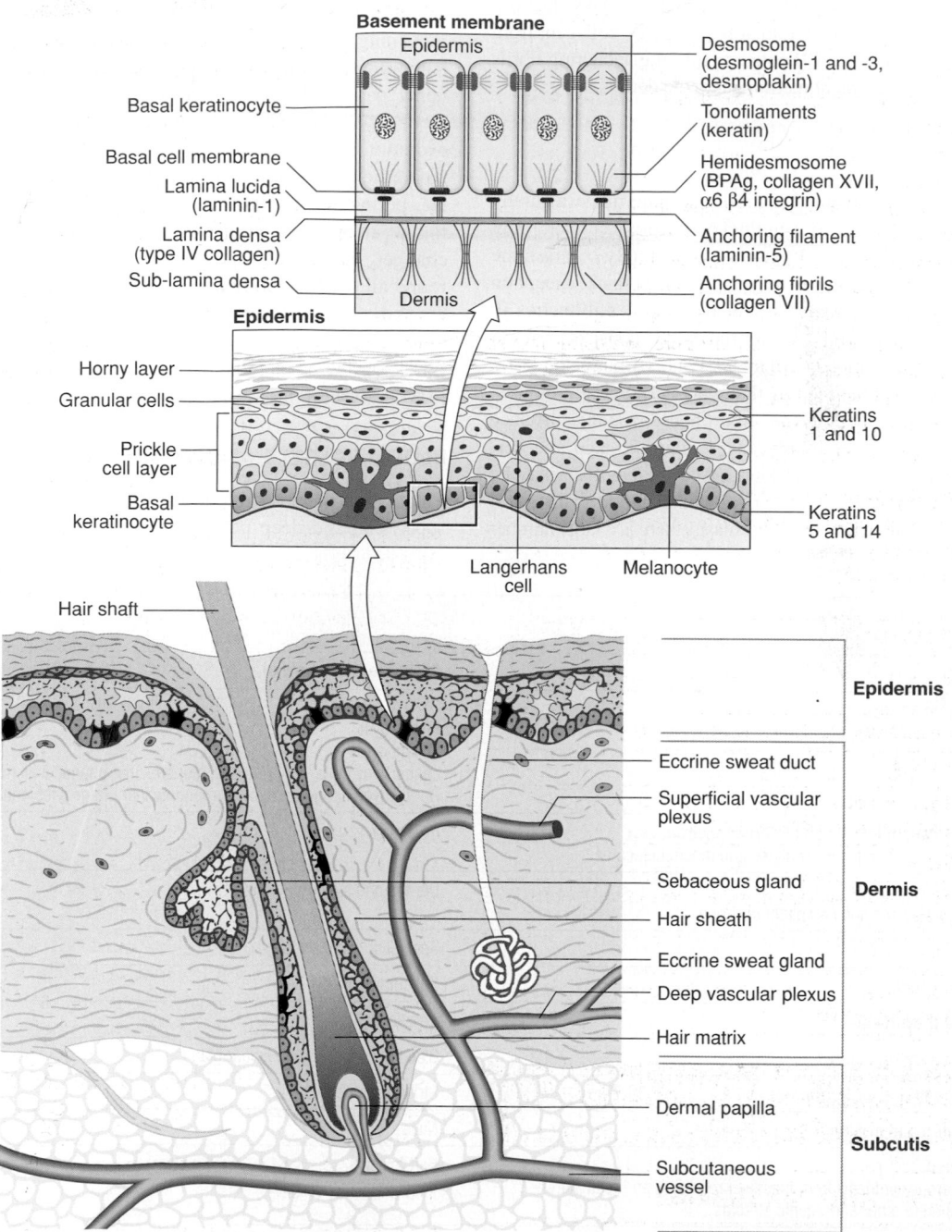

Fig. 21.1   Structure of normal skin.

BASEMENT MEMBRANE

The basement membrane (see Fig. 21.1) acts as an anchor for the epidermis but allows movement of cells and nutrients between the dermis and epidermis. It consists of several well-defined layers that are identifiable ultrastructurally and at the molecular level. The cell membrane of the epidermal basal cell is attached to the basement membrane via hemidesmo-somes. The lamina lucida is the zone immediately subjacent to the cell membrane of the basal cell which is composed pre-dominantly of laminin. Anchoring filaments extend through the lamina lucida to attach to the lamina densa. This electron-dense layer consists predominantly of type IV collagen; from it extend loops of type VII collagen forming anchoring fibrils that fasten the basement membrane to the dermis.

DERMIS

The dermis is vascular and supports the epidermis structurally and nutritionally. It varies in thickness from just over 1 mm on the inner forearm to 4 mm on the back. (By contrast, the epidermis on most sites is only 0.1–0.2 mm thick, except on the palms or soles where it can be several millimetres in thickness.) The acellular part of the dermis consists predom-inantly of fibres, mostly collagens I and III but also elastin and reticulin, synthesised by the major cell type, fibroblasts. Support is provided by an amorphous ground substance (mostly the glycosaminoglycans, hyaluronic acid and der-matan sulphate), whose production and catabolism may be influenced by hormonal changes and damage from ultra-violet radiation. Apart from fibroblasts, there is a large number of other cell types within the dermis including mast cells, mononuclear phagocytes, T lymphocytes, dendritic cells, nerves and vessels.

EPIDERMAL APPENDAGES: HAIR AND SWEAT GLANDS

Hair, sweat and apocrine glands (found mainly in the axillae) are epidermal structures which invaginate into the dermis. They are formed during the second trimester. Coarse, medullated hair accounts for the terminal hair of the scalp and pubic areas. Short, fine unmedullated hairs make up the remaining body hair. Sebaceous glands usually arise from hair follicles, with their ducts discharging sebum into the upper part of the follicle. Sebum excretion is under hor-monal control; androgens and progestogen increase sebum excretion whereas oestrogens have an inhibitory effect. Apocrine glands are those sweat glands found in the axil-lae, perineum, genitalia and areolae which become func-tional after puberty under the influence of hormonal changes, particularly androgens. Eccrine sweat glands are found all over the body and their ducts open directly on to the skin surface. They play a major role in humans in ther-moregulation and, unusually, are innervated by cholinergic fibres of the sympathetic (rather than parasympathetic) nervous system.

BLOOD VESSELS AND NERVES

There is an abundant blood supply in the skin arranged in superficial and deep plexi. The skin is well supplied with

21.2 FUNCTIONS OF THE SKIN	
Function	**Structure/cell involved**
Protection against: Chemicals, particles Ultraviolet radiation Antigens, haptens Microbes	Horny layer Melanocytes Langerhans cells, lymphocytes, mononuclear phagocytes, mast cells Horny layer, Langerhans cells, mononuclear phagocytes, mast cells
Preservation of a balanced internal environment Prevents loss of water, electrolytes and macromolecules	Horny layer
Shock absorber Strong, yet elastic and compliant covering	Dermis and subcutaneous fat
Sensation	Specialist nerve endings
Calorie reserve	Subcutaneous fat
Vitamin D synthesis	Keratinocytes
Temperature regulation	Blood vessels, eccrine sweat glands
Lubrication and waterproofing	Stratum corneum
Protection and prising	Nails
Hormonal Testosterone synthesis from inactive precursors and testosterone conversion to other androgenic steroids	Hair follicles Sebaceous glands
Body odour (more important in animals)	Apocrine sweat glands
Psychosocial	Hair, nails, appearance and tactile quality of skin

nerves to both dermis and epidermis. It used to be thought that nerves did not penetrate into the epidermis but this is now known to be false and there are indeed a large number of nerves that appear to interact with Langerhans cells, melanocytes and other components of the epidermis. Blood vessels are supplied by sympathetic autonomic nerves and peptinergic nerves that take part in the axon reflex. The functions of the skin are summarised in Box 21.2.

ISSUES IN OLDER PEOPLE
SKIN CHANGES

- Skin changes in the elderly include atrophy, laxity, wrinkling, dryness, irregular pigmentation and sparse grey hair.
- There are also alterations in immune surveillance and antigen presentation, and reduced cutaneous vascular supply which lead to decreases in the inflammatory response, absorption and cutaneous clearance of topical medications.
- These changes make the skin less durable, slower to heal, and more susceptible to damage and disease.
- They are brought about by:
  —age-related alterations in structure and function of the skin
  —cumulative effects of environmental insults, especially ultraviolet radiation
  —cutaneous consequences of disease in other organ systems.

DIAGNOSIS AND INVESTIGATION OF SKIN DISORDERS

The key to successful treatment is accurate diagnosis. This requires an appropriate history, thorough examination of the skin including hair and nails (see p. 1088), and occasional use of ancillary investigations such as histopathology.

Some investigative tests can be performed in the clinic with immediate results, but as a general rule clinical skills, especially visual recognition, are perhaps of greater importance than in any other branch of general medicine.

DIASCOPY

In diascopy a glass slide is pressed firmly on the skin lesion. If a red lesion blanches, it implies that the red colour is secondary to blood within the vessels. By contrast, blood outside the vessels, such as that from a bruise or from vasculitis, will not blanch. In some vascular lesions with a convoluted vessel structure, however, blunt pressure from a flat surface will not empty the vessels and the corner of a glass slide needs to be gently placed on the lesion. Even then, it will not always blanch completely. Therefore, success in blanching is a more useful physical sign than failure to blanch. When pressed on to some granulomatous lesions a glass slide reveals an appearance commonly referred to as 'apple jelly nodule'.

EPILUMINESCENCE MICROSCOPY (DERMATOSCOPY)

This refers to surface microscopy using an illuminated magnifying lens or microscope with oil immersion directly on to the skin's surface. It has found most clinical use in the assessment of pigmented lesions. A number of patterns not visible to the naked eye are often revealed, which can support a clinical diagnosis of malignancy in experienced hands.

WOOD'S LIGHT

This involves ultraviolet radiation (wavelength 360 nm) from a light source which has a nickel oxide filter (Wood's filter) to eliminate visible light. Green fluorescence is seen in scalp ringworm due to *Microsporum canis*, a sporadic ectothrix infection. It evokes coral pink fluorescence of flexural skin in erythrasma, caused by the bacterium *Corynebacterium minutissimum*. Wood's light also enhances the examination of cutaneous pigmentary abnormalities.

MYCOLOGY SAMPLES

Cutaneous scale, nail clippings and plucked hairs can be examined by light microscopy when mounted in 20% potassium hydroxide. This allows the keratin to be dissolved and fungal hyphae can be identified. If the potassium hydroxide solution contains Indian ink, the typical 'spaghetti and meatballs' hyphae and spores of the yeast *Pityrosporum orbiculare* can be readily identified in pityriasis versicolor. In addition, samples are sent for identification by culture.

SWABS

Bacterial swabs
Bacterial swabs taken in an appropriate culture medium are sometimes useful. Some caveats do, however, remain. Organisms that grow on the swabs may not be causally implicated in the underlying disease and the growth of many organisms simply reflects the abnormal architecture of the skin and is not necessarily an indication for either systemic or even local antibacterial therapy. Conversely, in some obvious infections of the skin, such as cellulitis, swabs do not reveal the causative agent.

Viral swabs
Blister or pustule samples for herpes simplex and varicella zoster can be visualised within a few hours, either by electron microscopy or by indirect immunofluorescence. Samples are also cultured for identification when conserved in viral culture medium.

PRICK TESTS

Prick tests are a way of detecting cutaneous type I (immediate) hypersensitivity to various antigens such as pollen, house dust mite or dander. The skin is pricked with commercially available stylets through a dilution of the appropriate antigen solution. After 10 minutes a positive response is indicated by a weal and a flare. The weal is due to a local increase in capillary permeability and the flare a result of activation of the axon reflex. A positive control (histamine) and a negative control (antigen diluent) should be performed. Systemic antihistamines inhibit the magnitude of the reaction. In individuals with a clear history of particular type I hypersensitivity a systemic reaction may follow a prick test and resuscitation facilities should be available. As an alternative, specific IgE levels to antigens can be measured in serum by a specific radioallergosorbent test (RAST).

PATCH TESTS

Patch tests detect type IV (delayed or cell-mediated) hypersensitivity. It is common practice for a 'battery' of around 20 common antigens, including common sensitisers such as nickel, rubber and fragrance mix, to be applied to the skin of the back under aluminium discs for 48 hours. The sites are then examined for a positive reaction 24 hours later and possibly again a further 24 hours later. An eczematous reaction, in the absence of an irritant reaction, suggests a type IV hypersensitivity to that particular allergen. The relevant antigens for a particular clinical case may not be represented in the standard battery of tests and expert advice may be needed. A negative patch test does not exclude a pathogenic role for a particular antigen nor does the presence of a particular response to an antigen mean that this antigen is causing the clinical disease.

HISTOLOGY

Skin biopsies for routine histological examination are usually fixed in 10% formalin and stained with haematoxylin and eosin. Immunocytochemistry may also be performed on formalin-fixed sections but may require frozen sections (see below). Immunocytochemistry is particularly useful for tumour diagnosis and for identification of particular T cell subsets.

IMMUNOFLUORESCENCE

A portion of the skin biopsy can be frozen in liquid nitrogen for direct immunofluorescence (IF). This involves visualising antigens that are present in skin by identifying them with fluorescein-labelled antibodies. Similarly, indirect immunofluorescence can identify circulating antibodies in the serum by an additional step of adding the serum to a section of normal skin or other substrate. Immunofluorescence plays a major role in the diagnosis of the autoimmune bullous disorders.

ELECTRON MICROSCOPY

This investigation has played an important role in the diagnosis of some of the rare blistering disorders such as epidermolysis bullosa, although the availability of a range of antibodies to basement membrane zone antigens has in part replaced it.

PHOTOTESTING

Phototesting involves exposing skin (often on the back) to a graded series of doses of ultraviolet radiation (UVR) of known wavelength, either on one occasion or repeatedly. In many photodermatoses erythema will occur at a lower dose of UVR than occurs in the normal population (e.g. drug-induced photosensitivity), or the time course of erythema may be prolonged (as in xeroderma pigmentosum). Alternatively, UVR will provoke lesions with the morphology of the underlying photodermatosis, such as may occur in lupus erythematosus or solar urticaria. Diagnostic phototesting is an essential component of the investigation of patients with presumed photosensitive drug reactions and idiopathic photodermatoses such as solar urticaria.

MAJOR MANIFESTATIONS OF SKIN DISEASE

THE CHANGING MOLE

The largest change in dermatological practice over the last 30 years has been the major increase in patients referred or requesting advice about particular lesions ('is it cancer, doctor?') as compared with rashes. Thirty years ago perhaps 90% of dermatology outpatients had rashes and 10% lesions whereas now the proportion of lesions often exceeds 50%. This reflects the fact that human skin cancer becomes more common as people grow older, and there is an increase in the elderly in many societies, and also the fact that there is an increase in the age-specific incidence rates for most skin cancers. Furthermore, there is greatly increased public awareness and concern about skin cancer, often in response to 'health campaigns'.

The principal clinical concern is to distinguish correctly between benign lesions and melanoma. Melanoma in most of Western Europe remains an uncommon tumour with a cumulative lifetime incidence of less than 1%.

Nevertheless, the case fatality remains about 20% with there being no curative therapy if the primary tumour has metastasised. Metastasis occurs early in the development of melanoma, and therefore in the absence of highly effective therapies attention has naturally focused on primary prevention and recognition of early lesions. Far more early or thin melanomas are now diagnosed than was the case 30 or 40 years ago, reflecting increased awareness and the greater provision of medical services. The downside of this increased awareness is greater patient anxiety and a negative impact on other services provided by dermatologists. These themes are common to other debates about screening and early detection of disease.

The situation is complicated by the fact that whilst any one of a number of changes in a pigmented lesion (see Box 21.3) is highly sensitive as a marker of melanoma, its specificity is low. Even in the hands of experts diagnostic certainty is low for many pigmented lesions in the absence of a biopsy. As excision of suspicious lesions is relatively easy, any screening test or screening procedure will

> **21.3 ABCDE FEATURES OF MALIGNANT MELANOMA**
>
> - **A**symmetry
> - **B**order irregular
> - **C**olour irregular
> - **D**iameter often greater than 0.5 cm
> - **E**levation irregular
>   (+ Loss of skin markings)

require high levels of negative predictive value before it can be adopted in routine clinical practice. For the present there is no evidence to suggest that population screening for melanoma in Northern Europe is indicated.

History

- Determine the precise nature of the change (see p. 1090). Is it due to the development of itch, inflammation, bleeding or ulceration, or changes in the colour, size, shape or surface of the lesion?
- Subtle changes should not be ignored, as many patients are good observers and get to know their own moles well. If the change has settled, could it have been due to a common insult such as nicking a facial naevus when shaving, plucking hairs from a naevus or the irritant effect of a depilatory?
- Is the patient worried about change in one or many moles? Paradoxically, concern about many moles should not alert the doctor so much as anxiety over a solitary lesion.
- Is there a positive family history of melanoma? Fewer than 10% of melanomas occur in individuals with a strong family history but in some of these families the history of melanoma is quite striking, with up to 50% of individuals developing melanoma. A suspicious mole on a patient with a first-degree relative with a melanoma probably warrants specialist opinion.

Examination

Examine the pigmented lesion carefully. Look at the morphology of the melanocytic naevi at other sites. Examination with a magnifying glass may help. Some dermatologists are keen on dermatoscopes to help define the nature of the lesion. Usually the key clinical question is whether the lesion is a benign melanocytic naevus (see p. 1089) or a malignant melanoma (see p. 1094). Before trying to answer this, the clinician needs to exclude the possibility that it is another type of pigmented lesion:

- *Lentigo* (a benign proliferation of melanocytes; see p. 1087).
- *Freckle* (ephelis; see p. 1087).
- *Seborrhoeic wart* (basal cell papilloma; see p. 1090).
- *Dermatofibroma.* This lightly pigmented firm dermal nodule is common on extremities in young adults. It feels larger than it looks. There is dimpling when the skin is squeezed on both sides (positive Fitzpatrick sign).

- *Pigmented basal cell carcinoma* (see p. 1092). This lesion is usually found on the face of the elderly and is slow-growing. It has a blue-brown hue with an opalescent look. There may be a rolled edge around an ulcer.
- *Subungual haematoma* (see Fig. 21.27, p. 1088).

Melanocytic naevus versus malignant melanoma

The ABCDE 'rule' is better viewed as a guide and reminder of what to consider (see Fig. 21.2). Loss of normal skin markings is not diagnostic but is suggestive of melanoma. Conversely, normal skin markings and the presence of fine hairs dispersed evenly over a lesion, though reassuring, are not certain signs of a lesion's benign nature.

Does the patient have other pigmented lesions?

Ask and examine the patient fully. Some patients (rarely) present with more than one primary melanoma and morphology of other melanocytic naevi may provide useful diagnostic information. Remember that seborrhoeic warts are usually multiple. If a naevus, especially a changing one, appears significantly different (in colour, shape, size etc.) from others, then it should be treated with suspicion.

Management

- Any changing lesion which is suspected of being a malignant melanoma should be excised without delay, with a clear margin. Depending on the thickness of the tumour further excision may be required.
- Some authors argue that if there is any doubt about the diagnosis the patient should be reviewed, or the individual lesion photographed and the patient reviewed in a couple of months and rephotographed.

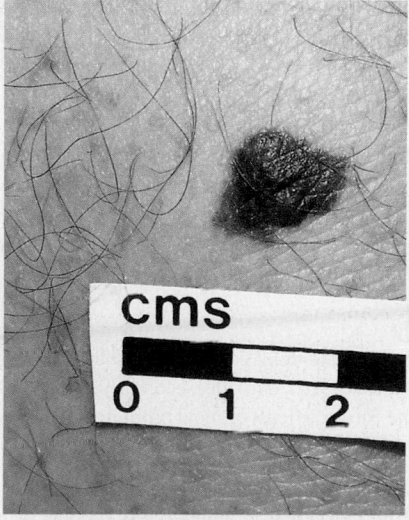

Fig. 21.2 Malignant melanoma. A changing mole which fails the ABCDE test.

Not all would agree with this management plan, given that melanomas may show only slow or intermittent progression in their early course. A 'wait and see' policy may increase anxiety.

- In this clinical context a positive diagnosis is essential. If you are uncertain whether the lesion is a melanocytic naevus or some other pigmented lesion, then it must be excised or specialist help obtained.
- Malignant melanoma can break most rules. Listen, look and think. If in doubt, cut out and then check the histology, or seek advice urgently.

ITCH (PRURITUS)

Pruritus is defined as an unpleasant sensation that provokes the desire to scratch. Despite being the major symptom of skin disease apart from disturbance of body image, it remains poorly studied and poorly understood. Although central nervous system lesions can cause itch, the majority of patients seen in clinical practice itch due to a primary disease of the skin.

The nerve endings that signal itch are believed to lie either within the epidermis or very close to the dermo-epidermal junction. Such sensory information is transmitted via C fibres, which have slow conduction speeds via the spinothalamic tract to the thalamus and on to a cortical representation. It was thought for a long time that itch was conducted along the same fibres that conduct pain and that itch may have been a subliminal form of pain. This hypothesis seems increasingly untenable as candidate fibres for itch have recently been identified. There does, however, seem to be an antagonistic or inhibitory relation between pain and itch. Scratching may either cause inhibition of the itch receptors by stimulating ascending sensory pathways which inhibit itch at the spinal cord (Wall's 'gate' mechanism), or interfere with itch fibres lying superficially in skin which may be damaged directly by scratching. Which of these hypotheses is correct is unknown.

As well as primary diseases of the skin, itch may be a result of various systemic diseases such as primary biliary cirrhosis or renal failure. The mechanisms of induction of itch in these cases are unknown but for liver disease there is some experimental evidence that abnormal circulating opioids stimulate itch centrally.

History
Assessment of the itchy patient, particularly in the absence of widespread skin damage secondary to scratching, is one of the most difficult clinical problems in dermatology. Helpful hints from the history include:

- *The time course* of the itching. This should be carefully defined as to whether it is sudden, as in infestations and urticaria, or chronic, as in chronic skin diseases such as eczema.

- *Localisation* of the pruritus, including the site of onset. For example, in an infant with atopic eczema the cheeks are usually the first site to be affected, whereas scabies almost never affects the face or scalp. Is the itch confined to certain sites, as in localised skin disease such as lichen planus and lichen simplex, or generalised, as in eczema and scabies?
- *Exacerbating factors*, such as heat and exercise in cholinergic urticaria, water in aquagenic pruritus and creams in some forms of eczema. In practice heat or warm water will exacerbate a number of different causes of pruritus and may be less useful diagnostic aids than often stated.
- *Alleviating factors*, which are worth noting but are seldom of great diagnostic help. Some patients discover that cooling below 18 degrees inhibits itch (but not pain). Similarly, other patients discover that a scalding hot bath replaces itch with pain which they find preferable. In the short term most patients seem to prefer cutaneous pain to itch.
- *Involvement of other family members*, as in a scabietic infestation. Insect bites usually only affect one member of the family.
- *General health* of the patient. Has it changed, suggesting an underlying medical disorder?

Examination
Attempt to determine whether there is a primary skin condition or whether the only visible clinical features are due to excoriation with some secondary degree of eczema or infection. Try to classify the patient into one of the three following groups (see Box 21.4):

1. *Generalised pruritus associated with skin disease.* The most common causes of a widespread itchy rash are eczema, usually atopic, and scabies infestation. These can be difficult to distinguish clinically, particularly in children. Secondary eczematisation occurs in scabies, giving rise to eczema-like lesions all over the body. Examine carefully for scabietic burrows, particularly in the finger and toe webs, along the borders of both the hands and the feet and at the wrists, and extract the mite (see p. 1085) to make a definite diagnosis. After treatment pruritus may continue for several weeks. Pruritus is a common skin complaint in pregnancy and may be due to several causes (see Box 21.5).
2. *Local pruritus associated with skin disease.* In these cases careful examination may reveal the underlying primary cutaneous disorder such as lichen planus or psoriasis.
3. *Pruritus with no evidence of skin disease.* The medical conditions that are sometimes associated with pruritus are listed in Box 21.6. In the absence of clues pointing to a primary skin disease detailed physical examination and investigations, including a careful search for lymphadenopathy, may be required. Investigations

21.4 PRURITUS

Skin diseases associated with generalised pruritus

- Eczema
- Scabies
- Urticaria/dermographism
- Pruritus of old age and xeroderma

Skin diseases associated with localised pruritus

- Eczema
- Lichen planus
- Dermatitis herpetiformis
- Pediculosis

Pruritus with no evidence of skin disease

21.5 CAUSES OF PRURITUS IN PREGNANCY

Condition	Gestation and features	Treatment
Obstetric cholestasis	3rd trimester Associated with abnormal liver function tests	Emollients Chlorphenamine (chlorpheniramine) Colestyramine Early delivery
Pemphigoid gestationis	3rd trimester Pruritus followed by blistering Starts around the umbilicus	Topical or oral steroids
Polymorphic eruption (urticarial papules) of pregnancy	3rd trimester, after delivery Polymorphic lesions with urticaria	Chlorphenamine (chlorpheniramine)
Prurigo gestationis	2nd trimester Excoriated papules	Emollients Topical steroids Chlorphenamine (chlorpheniramine)
Pruritic folliculitis	3rd trimester Aseptic pustules on trunk	Topical steroids

21.6 MEDICAL CONDITIONS THAT CAUSE PRURITUS

Medical condition	Cause of pruritus	Treatment*
Liver disease Cholestasis	Elevated bile salts	Colestyramine Rifampicin Antihistamines UVB
Hepatitis C	Central opioid effect Unknown	Naloxone
Chronic renal disease	Multifactorial: including secondary hyperparathyroidism Elevated plasma histamine	UVB Oral activated charcoal Capsaicin
Blood disease Anaemia Polycythaemia rubra vera Lymphoma Leukaemia Myeloma	Iron deficiency Unknown Unknown	Iron replacement
Thyroid disease Thyrotoxicosis Hypothyroidism	Generalised due to dry skin Localised may be due to *Candida*	Emollients
HIV infection	Infection, infestation Eosinophilic folliculitis Unknown	Treatment of opportunistic infection Local steroids, UVB UVB
Malignancy	Unknown	
Psychogenic	Unknown	Psychotherapy Anxiolytics Antidepressives

* Added to that of primary condition.

should include a full blood count, iron status, urea and electrolytes, liver function tests, thyroid function and possibly a chest radiograph.

Many patients are incorrectly labelled as having itch due to a systemic cause when in reality they have a mild degree of xerosis with perhaps irritation from repeated use of soaps, or another cutaneous primary disorder such as dermographism or aquagenic pruritus.

Management

There are no specific anti-itch drugs. Effective remedies for the conditions that lead to itch do exist, however, such as potent H1 blockade for patients with chronic idiopathic urticaria or corticosteroids for individuals with atopic eczema. Nevertheless, in some instances it is not possible either to define the primary condition or to treat it effectively.

A large number of agents can be used to reduce pruritus including emollients, topical menthol, capsaicin, ultraviolet B and long-wavelength ultraviolet A (PUVA) phototherapy (see p. 1079), as well as opioid antagonists such as naltrexone. Their effects are variable, poorly characterised and require further study. Although frequently the subject of ridicule, significant itch may incapacitate, cause embarrassment, disrupt sleep and ruin the patient's self-image. It is easily under-estimated and trivialised as a symptom.

THE SCALY RASH (PAPULOSQUAMOUS ERUPTIONS)

A common presenting complaint in general practice is an eruptive scaly rash sometimes associated with itching. The main causes are listed in Box 21.7. These can usually be distinguished by a discriminating history and examination. Secondary syphilis is an extremely rare cause of an eruptive scaly rash in current medical practice in the UK.

21.7 SUDDEN SCALY RASHES

- Eczema (see p. 1072)
- Psoriasis (see p. 1075)
- Pityriasis rosea
- Lichen planus (see p. 1080)
- Drug eruption (see p. 1099)
- Pityriasis versicolor
- Tinea corporis

History

How long has the rash been present?

Atopic eczema often starts within the first 2 years of life and subsequently fluctuates in extent and severity. Psoriasis can start at any age but usually does so between the ages of 15 and 40 years. Pityriasis rosea affects a similar age group and tends to occur in the autumn and spring. Both pityriasis rosea and drug eruptions have an acute onset, drug eruptions starting within a few days or weeks of taking the drugs. Pityriasis versicolor is a common yeast infection of the body and scalp. It can be acute in onset or persist for many years in the same individual.

Where on the body did it start?

Atopic eczema starts most commonly on the face in infants and then spreads to involve the flexures. However, it can sometimes just affect the extensor surfaces or may be present in coin-like lesions (discoid eczema). Psoriasis is classically present on the extensor surfaces—that is, the elbows and knees. Psoriasis can appear anywhere on the body in small (guttate), medium and large plaques all over the torso and limbs. Lichen planus usually presents as an intensely itchy, localised papular eruption with a characteristic colour and morphology (see p. 1080). Less commonly, it can be widespread and often exhibits the Köbner phenomenon with lichen planus lesions being induced in sites of non-specific trauma (see Fig. 21.17, p. 1080). Pityriasis rosea starts as a single herald patch that can occur anywhere on the body but usually is present on the trunk. This is a solitary erythematous lesion which starts as a papule and enlarges rapidly over a few days. Pityriasis versicolor usually affects the trunk and outer upper arms. Tinea corporis (dermatophyte infection) can occur anywhere on the body and is usually asymmetrical.

How has the rash evolved?

In pityriasis rosea the herald patch is followed in a few days by the appearance of many smaller plaques present mostly on the torso in a 'fir tree' distribution but it can also occur on the neck, extremities and flexures (inverse pityriasis rosea). The herald patch tends to persist throughout the eruption and the whole eruption can last for up to 3 months. Atopic eczema can, at varying stages, be localised or generalised but is a chronic disorder that fluctuates in severity throughout childhood. Psoriasis in the classical form tends to involve the elbows, knees, lower back and scalp. In the guttate (small plaque) variety many small, red, scaly plaques appear on the trunk and may persist for several months. Many cases subsequently develop chronic plaque psoriasis. Tinea corporis is usually a chronic, slowly evolving, often isolated annular

lesion. Macular-papular drug eruptions evolve with exfoliation (a shedding of the most superficial portion of the skin) and may leave post-inflammatory hyperpigmentation. Pityriasis versicolor can be very chronic and is often exacerbated by sun exposure; it also becomes more obvious in the tanned individual because of its hypopigmentation and therefore patients often present after their summer holidays. On the other hand, it appears as light brown scaly patches on untanned Caucasoid skin.

Is it itchy?

Atopic eczema is extremely itchy and this is invariably the presenting complaint. Itching is exacerbated by changes in temperature, e.g. on undressing, and contact with irritants such as wool. It is not known why atopic eczema is so itchy and antihistamines have little effect. Drug eruptions and tinea corporis are usually pruritic. Psoriasis and pityriasis rosea are not usually so itchy. The rash of pityriasis versicolor is asymptomatic.

Was there a preceding illness?

Guttate psoriasis is often preceded by a β-haemolytic streptococcal sore throat. A small percentage of people with pityriasis rosea have a prodromal illness with malaise, headache and arthralgia. A patient who develops a morbilliform drug eruption will usually have the same reaction to that specific drug or to chemically related ones on each challenge. Rashes in response to drugs are not common; however, most patients with infectious mononucleosis treated with amoxicillin will develop an erythematous macular-papular rash. It is essential therefore to take a careful history of medications and preceding illnesses at least 4 weeks prior to the onset of the rash.

Is it associated with any systemic symptoms?

Certain drug eruptions can cause systemic upset with fever, malaise and joint pains and are associated with an eosinophilia. In eczema, superinfection can be associated with systemic symptoms of fever and malaise. *Staphylococcus aureus* causing secondary impetiginisation is the most common, but a streptococcus can cause similar features. Herpes simplex virus type 1 causes a widespread, severe, painful, erosive skin eruption in patients with atopic eczema (eczema herpeticum), which is a medical emergency requiring inpatient treatment with intravenous antiviral therapy and medical support. Arthritis occurs in 7% of patients with psoriasis (see p. 1011).

Examination

The distribution of the rash can be very useful in discriminating between the various causes of a scaly rash: flexural, extensor surfaces, truncal, palms and soles, or scalp involvement. Morphologically, these conditions are distinguishable by careful assessment with the use of a magnifying lens. Associated skin features that give useful diagnostic clues can be found by complete skin examination (see Box 21.8).

21.8 CLINICAL FEATURES OF COMMON SCALY RASHES

Type of rash	Distribution	Morphology	Associated clinical signs
Eczema	Face/flexures	Poorly defined erythema and scaling Lichenification	Shiny nails Infraorbital crease 'Dirty neck'
Psoriasis	Extensor surfaces	Well-defined plaques with a silvery scale	Nail pitting and onycholysis Scalp involvement Axillae and genital areas often affected
Pityriasis rosea	'Fir tree' pattern on torso	Well-defined erythematous papules and plaques with collarette of scale	
Drug eruption	Widespread	Macular-papular erythematous scaly areas which merge and are followed by exfoliation	
Pityriasis versicolor	Upper torso and upper shoulders	Hypo- and hyperpigmented scaly patches	
Lichen planus	Distal limbs, esp. volar aspect of wrists Lower back	Shiny, flat-topped violaceous papules with Wickham's striae	White lacy network buccal mucosa Rarely, nail changes
Tinea corporis	Asymmetrical, often isolated, red scaly lesions	Scaly plaques which expand with central healing	Nail involvement (see Fig. 21.29, p. 1089)

ERYTHRODERMA

Eczema, psoriasis, drug eruptions and lichen planus rarely progress to erythroderma, defined as erythema with or without scaling of almost all the body surface. Other causes include cutaneous T cell lymphoma (Sézary's syndrome), the psoriasis-like condition pityriasis rubra pilaris, and rare types of ichthyosis. Erythroderma may occur at any age and is associated with extreme morbidity and rarely mortality. It may appear suddenly or evolve slowly.

Erythrodermic patients may be systemically unwell with shivering, due to loss of temperature control, and pyrexia. The pulse rate may be elevated and the blood pressure low due to volume depletion; examination of the cardiovascular system is therefore essential. Peripheral oedema is a common finding consequent on the erythroderma, low albumin and high-output cardiac failure. Lymph nodes may be enlarged, either reactively, caused by the skin inflammation, or rarely due to lymphomatous infiltration.

URTICARIA (NETTLE RASH, HIVES)

Urticaria refers to an area of focal dermal oedema secondary to a transient increase in capillary permeability. On certain body sites such as the lips or hands the oedema spreads and is traditionally referred to as angio-oedema. By definition the swelling lasts less than 24 hours. Acute urticaria may be associated with angio-oedema of the lips, face, throat and, rarely, wheezing, abdominal pain, headaches and even anaphylaxis. Whilst severe angio-oedema can be life-threatening due to respiratory obstruction, this is exceedingly rare in a dermatological context.

The symptoms and signs of urticaria are due in large part to mast cell degranulation with release of histamine and a variety of other vasoactive mediators. That more than histamine is involved is reflected by the fact that potent histamine blockers, whilst frequently improving the itch of urticaria and the number of weals, do not abolish all the symptoms or signs in many patients (see Fig. 21.3).

Causes of urticaria are listed in Box 21.9. Recently, evidence for an autoimmune pathogenesis for one of the most common forms of urticaria, chronic idiopathic

21.9 CAUSES OF URTICARIA

Acute and chronic urticaria

- Allergens (in foods, inhalants and injections)
- Drugs (see Box 21.33, p. 1100)
- Contact (e.g. animal saliva, latex)
- Physical (e.g. heat, cold, pressure, sun, water)
- Infection (e.g. viral hepatitis, infectious mononucleosis, HIV infection during seroconversion)
- Other conditions (e.g. systemic lupus erythematosus, autoimmunity, pregnancy, intestinal parasites)
- Idiopathic

Urticarial vasculitis

- Hepatitis B
- Systemic lupus erythematosus
- Idiopathic

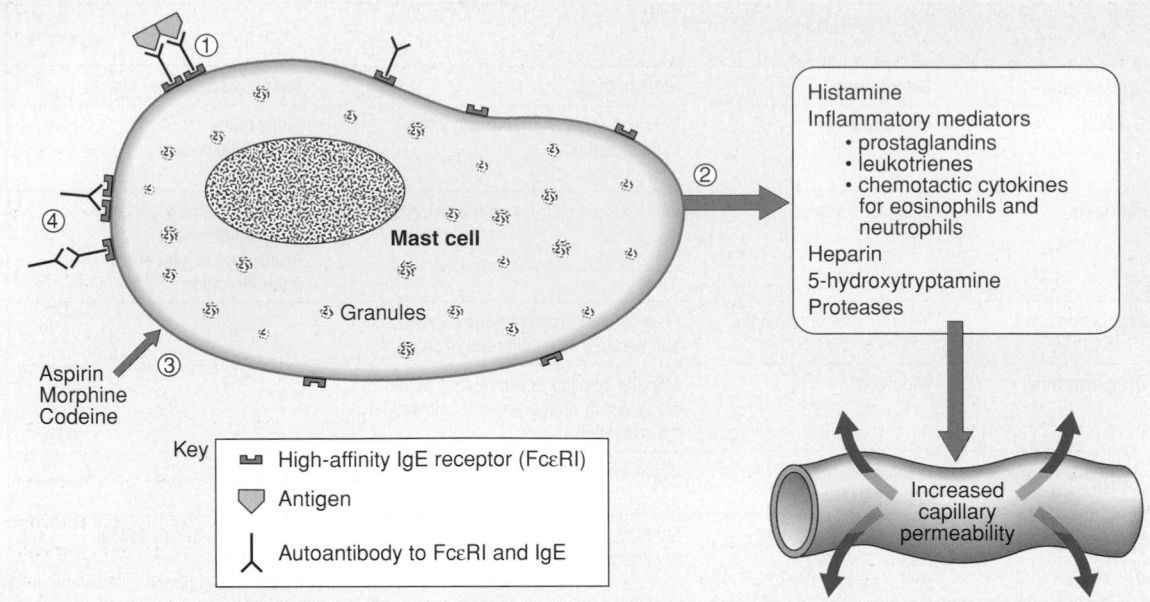

Fig. 21.3 Pathogenesis of urticaria. Mast cell degranulation occurs in a variety of ways. (1) Type I hypersensitivity causing massive degranulation and sometimes anaphylaxis. (2) Spontaneous mast cell degranulation in chronic urticaria. (3) Chemical mast cell degranulation. (4) Autoimmunity, which accounts for 30% of chronic urticaria.

urticaria, has been identified. In this condition, which is defined by the presence of urticarial episodes for over 6 weeks, self-reacting antibodies appear to cause cross-linking of the IgE receptor with subsequent degranulation of the mast cells.

Clinical features

Two questions may be asked:

1. How long does the individual lesion last?
   < 24 hours   (urticaria)
   > 24 hours   (urticarial vasculitis)
2. How long has the condition been present?
   < 6 weeks   (acute urticaria)
   > 6 weeks   (chronic urticaria)

In practice the above questions may be less helpful than is sometimes implied. There may be little mechanistic difference between urticaria of a month's duration and that of 6 months' duration. Both may be treated along similar lines. The length of time an individual weal lasts may also be of limited utility. Urticarial vasculitis is much less common than urticaria and many patients are unable to distinguish the development of new weals and disappearance of old ones from individual weals each of which persists for more than 1 day. It is sometimes helpful to draw around a weal with a pen and examine the patient 24 hours later to try to clarify this issue.

A directed history is still the best way to elicit any causes or precipitants of urticaria. A record of possible allergens, including drugs (see Box 21.33, p. 1100), should be determined. The physical urticarias can be identified by appropriate questions (see Box 21.9) and subsequent

medically observed challenge. A family history must be sought in cases of angio-oedema. Examination may reveal nothing, as this is a transient eruption, or may uncover the classical weals, which can vary from papules to large extensive plaques (see Fig. 21.4).

Investigations

These need to be directed at the possible underlying cause as elicited from the clinical history:

- full blood count including eosinophil count in cases of underlying parasites
- erythrocyte sedimentation rate (ESR), which is elevated in cases of vasculitis
- urea and electrolytes, thyroid and liver function tests, which might reveal an underlying disorder

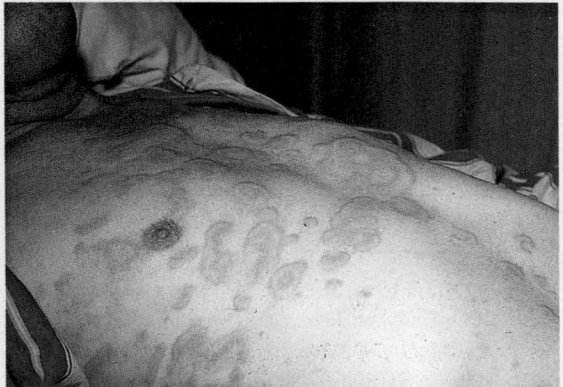

Fig. 21.4 Widespread acute urticaria. In this case urticaria was due to penicillin allergy.

- total IgE and specific IgE to possible allergens, e.g. foods such as shellfish and peanuts
- antinuclear factor in chronic urticaria or urticarial vasculitis
- CH50 as a general guide to complement activation and C_3 and C_4 levels as evidence of complement consumption via both the classical and the alternative pathways.

C_1 esterase inhibitor may be quantitatively reduced or more rarely functionally deficient as in hereditary angio-oedema. A skin biopsy may be helpful if urticarial vasculitis is suspected. Physical urticarias can be confirmed by the appropriate physical challenge. Frequently, no cause can be found for acute episodes, whereas in chronic urticaria the autoimmune pathogenesis will account for the majority of cases.

Management

The practical problem with management of urticaria is that whilst potent non-sedative histamine blockers are available they have little or no effect on the other mediators that also play a contributory role. Non-sedative antihistamines such as loratadine or fexofenadine are effective for perhaps one-third of patients with chronic urticaria, one-third show some moderate benefit whilst the results in the remaining third are minimal. If a patient fails to respond to one of these agents after 2 weeks of therapy, then it may be worth swapping to another non-sedative antihistamine and adding in an H_2-blocker such as cimetidine or ranitidine. A number of other agents have been used including mast cell stabilisers or protease and leukotriene inhibitors, although the evidence of efficacy

is not clear. Systemic corticosteroids are widely prescribed for urticaria although surprisingly evidence of their benefit is still contestable. Patients with a history of life-threatening angio-oedema or anaphylaxis should carry a self-administered injection kit of adrenaline (epinephrine). The management of anaphylactic shock is described on page 201.

Urticaria may be precipitated by aspirin or non-steroidal anti-inflammatory drugs. If there is a clear history of these agents precipitating attacks, then they should be avoided. Even in the absence of a clear history it may be advisable to suggest alternatives such as paracetamol (codeine can also induce urticaria).

PHOTOSENSITIVITY

Ultraviolet radiation (UVR, 'sunlight') may improve some skin diseases such as psoriasis and eczema but confusingly may also exacerbate the same diseases and induce a number of specific dermatological conditions—the photosensitive dermatoses or photodermatoses. Usually this is attributable to particular parts of the electromagnetic radiation spectrum including ultraviolet B (UVB) and ultraviolet A (UVA) but rarely visible light may also cause some photodermatoses. The electromagnetic spectrum is shown in Figure 21.5. The causative wavelengths for some of the endpoints are provisional. For instance, UVB is thought to play a more major role in the induction of skin cancer but a role for UVA may also exist. Similarly, skin ageing is due not just to UVA, as is often stated, but also to UVB. Determination of the

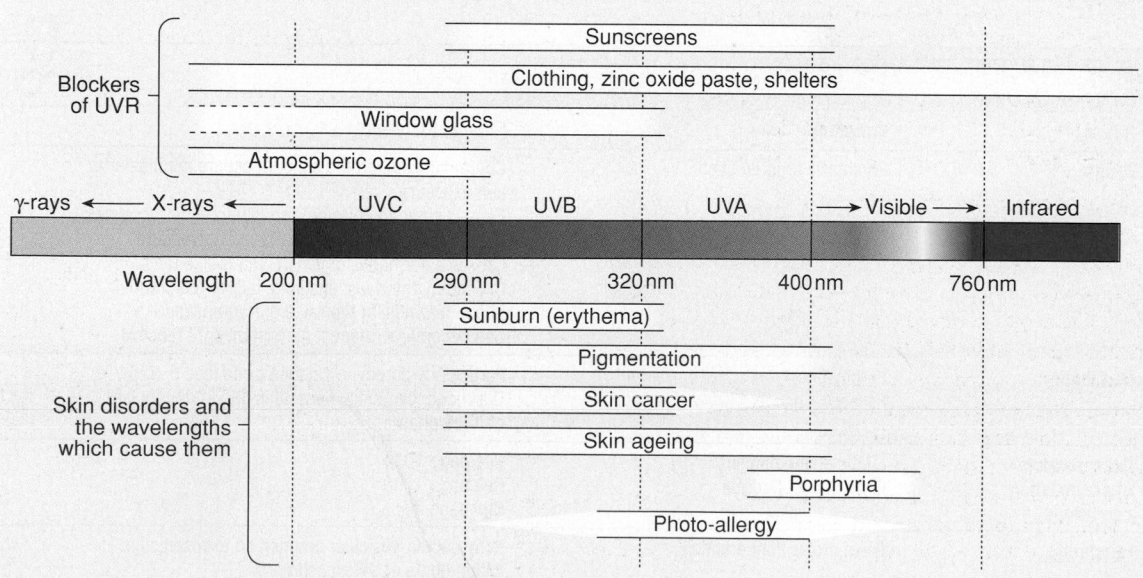

Fig. 21.5 The electromagnetic spectrum. For many conditions the action spectrum is approximate and may vary between patients. (LE = lupus erythematosus)

waveband or wavebands that contribute to sensitivity may be clinically important. For instance, UVB does not pass through window glass whereas UVA does. The practical corollary of this is that patients who are markedly UVA-sensitive need to wear sunblock and be protected even when inside a car or inside a building where there is strong natural light.

Clinical features

The clinical history may give a clear indication that the rash is temporally related to sun exposure, whereas in other cases there is no obvious indication of light aggravation.

When a rash is related to sunshine, then the sites affected tend to be light-exposed ones: the face, particularly the nose and the cheeks but excluding the eyelids, an area under the chin and an area in the shadow of the nose; the dorsa of the forearms and hands, with sparing of the finger webs and palms (see Fig. 21.6).

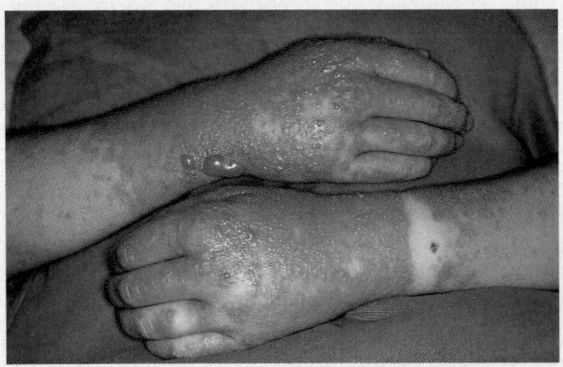

Fig. 21.6 Bullous photosensitive eruption. Note sharp cut-off at wrists, due to protection by shirt sleeves, and sparing of skin under watch and strap.

There are four main groups of photosensitive dermatoses and these are listed in Box 21.10. Confusingly, a photodermatosis that initially appears on some exposed sites may spread to sites which on history appear to have received no exposure to sunlight.

Management

Once a photosensitive eruption is identified on clinical grounds, an attempt should be made to provoke the lesion using phototesting. This may not always be possible. If a drug is suspected and clinical status allows, phototesting should be carried out whilst the individual is on the drug; this allows phototesting to be repeated once the drug has been stopped. Drug causes for photosensitivity are common and include compounds such as quinine, which are often neglected unless a careful and directed clinical history is taken. Treatment is with avoidance of the drug if appropriate, or with topical or occasionally systemic steroids. In chronic cases of photosensitivity, such as chronic actinic dermatitis, azathioprine 100–150 mg/day may be required as further immunosuppression. The main preventative treatment for the photosensitive dermatoses is avoidance of sun exposure and the use of sunscreens.

Sunscreens

Sunscreens act in two different ways: chemical or physical. Chemical sunscreens absorb specific wavelengths of UV radiation. Physical sunscreens reflect UV radiation and visible light. Most available products are a combination of UVA and UVB chemical sunscreens. If the individual is sensitive to visible light as well as ultraviolet radiation, then the agents that block visible light will be visible and often cosmetically undesirable.

Sunblocks are often graded in terms of the sun protection factor (SPF), the ratio of the time it takes to induce a

21.10 THE PHOTOSENSITIVE DERMATOSES		
Cause	**Condition**	**Clinical features**
Drugs	Phototoxic drug eruption	Common; exaggerated sunburn occurs minutes after sun exposure Caused by phenothiazines, amiodarone, tetracyclines
	Photo-allergic drug eruption	Occurs more than 24 hours after sun exposure; causes a dermatitis or lichen planus-like reaction Caused by thiazides, enalapril, hydroxychloroquine, phenothiazines, or topical, e.g. fragrances Can become permanent (persistent light reactor)
Metabolic	Porphyrias Pellagra	Particularly porphyria cutanea tarda (see p. 326) Diarrhoea, dementia, dermatitis due to dietary lack of tryptophan
Exacerbation of pre-existing conditions	Lupus erythematosus Erythema multiforme Herpes simplex	See page 1034 See page 1098 See page 30
Idiopathic	Polymorphic light eruption Solar urticaria Chronic actinic dermatitis	Itchy papulo-vesicular eruption on exposed sites within hours of UV exposure Urticaria after 1-hour exposure Disabling, itchy dermatitis on exposed sites in elderly men

certain degree of redness with and without sunblock. A sunblock with an SPF of 2 therefore affords 50% reduction whereas a sun protection factor of 10 blocks 90% of the radiation. It follows that the additional value of sunblocks with a very high sun protection factor become trivial over, say, SPF 15.

BLISTERS

Loss of keratinocyte-keratinocyte adhesion or loss of adhesion of keratinocytes to the basement membrane or of the basement membrane to the dermis leads to a potential space which, because of negative extracellular pressure, fills with fluid: a blister. There is an artificial distinction made by some between small (vesicles, < 0.5 cm) and large blisters (bullae, > 0.5 cm). The site of blister formation within the skin therefore depends on the aetiology and underlying pathogenesis.

Blisters are an important physical sign with a limited differential diagnosis but they can be very difficult to see. If a blister occurs high up in the epidermis (intraepidermal) and is due to a defect in cohesion of the keratinocytes, then the blister may be so fragile that only an erosion is seen (e.g. pemphigus foliaceus). On the other hand, a blister at the level of the basement membrane, as occurs in dermatitis herpetiformis, might be missed because the roof of the blister is easily destroyed due to the itch and resulting scratch. Blisters in the skin can occur at any age and may be caused by common infections or rare genetic skin diseases that can continue throughout life.

21.11 CAUSES OF BLISTERING AT BIRTH

- Herpes simplex
- Impetigo
- Bullous ichthyosiform erythroderma
- Epidermolysis bullosa (see Box 21.12)
- Incontinentia pigmenti

The main causes of blistering presenting at birth are listed in Box 21.11.

Assessment

The history of the onset of blistering, any predisposing events such as drug ingestion, and family history are of paramount importance. In infants blistering at birth is usually due to infection and more rarely to genetic skin diseases such as epidermolysis bullosa. There are several types of epidermolysis bullosa, as seen in Box 21.12, and studies of these disorders over the last 10 years have contributed enormously to our understanding of the biology of keratins and basement membrane. Adults who present with a blistering skin condition need to be assessed according to Box 21.13. At all ages, it is important to exclude both viral and bacterial infection as a cause of blistering and this is easily done by taking a swab from the blister fluid for bacterial assessment by both microscopy and culture. A similar sterile swab can be placed in viral culture medium and, in the case of the herpes virus, immediate electron microscopy or immunofluorescence performed on a sample of the blister fluid smeared on to a slide.

Toxic epidermal necrolysis is a severe form of widespread blistering that can occur at any age and is often due

21.12 DIFFERENT TYPES OF EPIDERMOLYSIS BULLOSA

Type	Mode of inheritance	Level of blister	Abnormal protein	Clinical features
Simple	Autosomal dominant	Epidermal basal cell	Keratins 5 and 14	Usually just blisters on palms and soles No scarring; nails normal; no oral involvement Rare recessive type associated with muscular dystrophy (plectin mutation)
Junctional	Autosomal recessive	Lamina lucida	Laminin-5 and $\alpha_6 \beta_4$ integrin	Large, raw areas and flaccid blisters at birth Common around mouth and anus; heal slowly Nails and oral mucosa involved Often lethal May be diagnosed prenatally by chorionic villus sampling
Dystrophic	Autosomal dominant	Dermis below lamina densa	Collagen VII	Blisters on knees, elbows and fingers Healing with scarring and milia Nails may be involved Mouth seldom affected
	Autosomal recessive	Dermis below lamina densa	Collagen VII	Blisters often present at birth; seen on hands, feet, elbows and knees Heal with scarring which is so severe that digits may be lost Milia present Oral and oesophageal blistering followed by scarring/stricture Abnormal teeth Increased incidence of cutaneous squamous cell carcinoma in early adulthood

to drugs. It is a life-threatening condition as the skin peels off in thin sheets causing severe problems with fluid balance and temperature control as well as pain and infection. Intensive care management is indicated, with careful haemodynamic monitoring and high suspicion of secondary infection. Once the causative agent is removed the skin can rapidly re-epithelialise but toxaemia often leads to death in extensive cases. There is no convincing evidence that systemic corticosteroids work in this condition but there is some recent and persuasive but uncontrolled evidence that intravenous immunoglobulin may be helpful.

If there is no evidence of infection and the diagnosis is not apparent from the more common conditions listed in Box 21.13, then a skin biopsy should be taken for histological assessment and a frozen sample for direct immunofluorescence. The clinical and immunopathological findings for the immunobullous disorders are documented in Box 21.14. In the case of the rare genetic skin

21.13 CAUSES OF ACQUIRED BLISTERS

	Localised	Generalised — With mucosal involvement	With no mucosal involvement
Vesicular	Herpes simplex Herpes zoster Impetigo Pompholyx	Eczema herpeticum	Eczema herpeticum Dermatitis herpetiformis Epidermolysis bullosa acquisita
Bullous	Impetigo Bullous cellulitis Bullous stasis oedema Acute eczema Insect bites Fixed drug eruptions	Pemphigus Bullous erythema multiforme/ Stevens–Johnson syndrome Toxic epidermal necrolysis	Acute eczema Erythema multiforme Bullous pemphigoid Epidermolysis bullosa acquisita Bullous lupus erythematosus Pseudoporphyria Porphyria cutanea tarda Drug eruptions, e.g. barbiturates

21.14 CLINICAL FEATURES AND SKIN BIOPSY FINDINGS IN SOME IMMUNE-MEDIATED BLISTERING SKIN CONDITIONS

Disease	Age	Site of blisters	Nature of blisters	Mucous membrane involvement	Antigen	Circulating antibody (indirect IF)	Fixed antibody (direct IF)	Treatment
Pemphigus vulgaris	40–60 yrs	Torso, head	Flaccid and fragile, many erosions	100%	Desmoglein-3 (120kD)	IgG	IgG, C_3 intercellular (epidermal)	Steroids Cyclophosphamide
Bullous pemphigoid (see Fig. 21.7)	60s and over	Trunk (esp. flexures) and limbs	Tense	Occasionally	BP-220 (part of hemidesmosome)	IgG (70%)	IgG, C_3 at BMZ	Steroids Azathioprine
Dermatitis herpetiformis	Young, associated with coeliac disease	Elbows, lower back, buttocks	Excoriated and often not present	No	Unknown	None	Granular IgA in papillary dermis	Dapsone Gluten-free diet
Pemphigoid gestationis	Young pregnant female	Periumbilical and limbs	Tense	Rare	Collagen XVII (part of hemidesmosome BP-180)	IgG	C_3 at BMZ	Steroids
Epidermolysis bullosa acquisita	All ages	Widespread	Tense, scarring	Common (50%)	Type VII collagen	IgG (anti-type VII collagen)	IgG at BMZ	Poor response to steroids Cyclophosphamide Methotrexate Azathioprine
Bullous lupus erythematosus	Young, black female	Widespread	Tense	Rare	Type VII collagen	Anti-type VII collagen	IgG, IgA, IgM at BMZ	Dapsone

Note Pemphigus is characterised by an intraepidermal level of blistering (superficial). All the other conditions above have a subepidermal level of blistering. (BMZ = basement membrane zone)

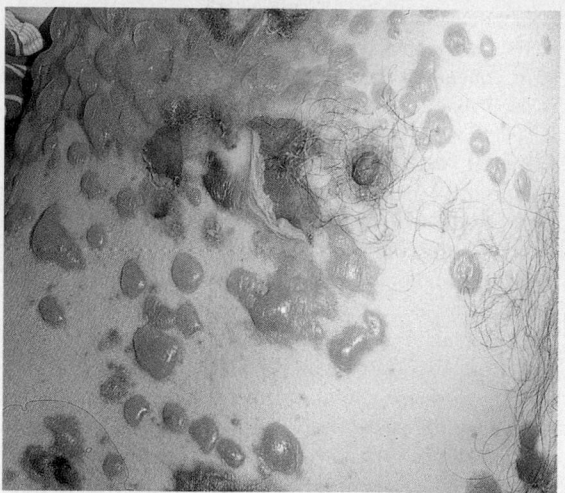

Fig. 21.7   Bullous pemphigoid. Large tense and unilocular blisters clustered in and around the axilla.

diseases a portion of the skin biopsy is processed for electron microscopy and immunofluorescence to enable a more accurate assessment to be made of the site of blistering. Further investigation is necessary for certain blistering conditions:

- *Pemphigus*. This is associated with underlying malignancy including lymphoma in a small proportion of patients ('paraneoplastic pemphigus'). Therefore a complete physical examination is mandatory and investigations including full blood count, erythrocyte sedimentation rate, urea and electrolytes, liver function tests, chest radiograph and any other directed scans should be performed.
- *Dermatitis herpetiformis*. This is associated with coeliac disease (see p. 792) and therefore all patients with this diagnosis should have blood taken for an anti-endomysial and antigliadin antibody screen, and a jejunal biopsy should be performed if indicated.
- *Epidermolysis bullosa acquisita (EBA)*. This is associated with inflammatory bowel disease, multiple myeloma and lymphoma (see pp. 808, 938 and 943), and these conditions should therefore be excluded.
- *Bullous lupus erythematosus*. It is important to follow patients with bullous lupus erythematosus for activity of their systemic disease (see p. 1034). There is a high incidence of clinically significant glomerulonephritis (> 90%).
- *Porphyria cutanea tarda and pseudoporphyria* (see pp. 1097–1098).

LEG ULCERS

Ulceration of the skin is the complete loss of the epidermis and part of the dermis. When present on the lower leg, it is usually due to vascular disease and the vast majority

(75%) of cases are due in part to venous hypertension. The site of ulceration on the lower leg can give a good indication of the underlying cause (see Fig. 21.8), although this is not an absolute guide. For each cause of leg ulceration there are several different underlying pathologies that have to be considered (see Box 21.15).

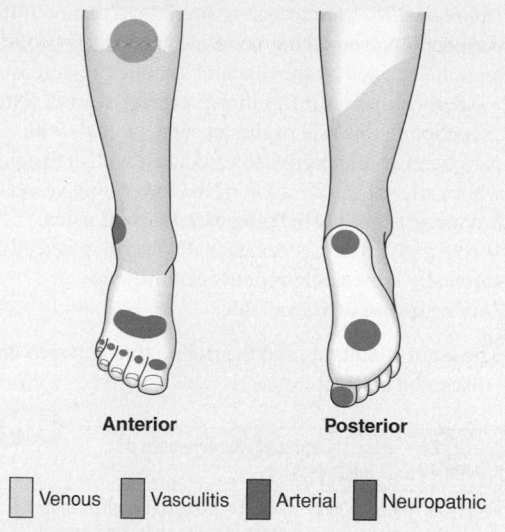

Anterior   **Posterior**

☐ Venous   ☐ Vasculitis   ■ Arterial   ■ Neuropathic

Fig. 21.8   Causes of lower leg ulceration.

21.15 MAIN CAUSES OF LEG ULCERATION	
Venous hypertension	
• See text	
Arterial disease	
• Atherosclerosis	• Buerger's disease
• Vasculitis	
Small vessel disease	
• Diabetes mellitus	• Vasculitis
Abnormalities of blood	
• Sickle-cell disease	• Spherocytosis
• Cryoglobulinaemia	• Immune complex disease
Neuropathy	
• Diabetes mellitus	• Syphilis
• Leprosy	
Tumour	
• Squamous cell carcinoma	• Malignant melanoma
• Basal cell carcinoma	• Kaposi's sarcoma
Trauma	
• Injury	• Artefact

Assessment

The history of the onset of the leg ulceration and any underlying predisposing conditions should be sought. Then the site and surrounding skin should be carefully assessed. The appropriate investigations should include:

- *Urinalysis* for glycosuria.
- *Full blood count* to detect anaemia and blood dyscrasias.
- *Bacterial swab* to detect pathogens. Systemic antibiotics are only required if there is a purulent discharge, rapid extension, cellulitis, lymphangitis or septicaemia.
- *Doppler ultrasound* to assess arterial circulation if the peripheral pulses cannot be felt. If the ankle systolic pressure divided by the brachial systolic pressure is > 0.8, then there is insignificant arterial disease. (An exception to this rule occurs in some patients with peripheral vascular disease associated with diabetes, in whom arterial calcification of the lower limb vessels produces a spuriously high ankle/brachial index.)
- *Venography*, which is occasionally useful in detecting surgically remediable venous incompetence.
- *Duplex scanning*, if available.

The main conditions and the differences between them are discussed below.

LEG ULCER—assessment and management of chronic venous leg ulcers   **EBM**

'Peripheral arterial supply should be assessed in all patients by hand-held Doppler. Those individuals with an ankle/brachial pressure ratio (ABP) < 0.8 should be assumed to have arterial disease and therefore not able to tolerate compression bandaging. In those individuals with an ABP > 0.8, graduated compression bandaging is essential for effective treatment.'

- Moffat CJ, Oldroyd MI, Greenhalgh RM, Franks PJ. Palpating ankle pulses is insufficient in detecting arterial insufficiency in patients with leg ulceration. Phlebology 1994; 9:170–172.
- Fletcher A, Cullum N, Sheldon TA. A systematic review of compression treatment for venous leg ulcers. BMJ 1997; 315:570–580.
- The care of patients with chronic leg ulcer. A National Clinical Guideline. Scottish Intercollegiate Guidelines Network, Royal College of Physicians of Edinburgh, July 1998.

Further information: 🖥 www.sign.ac.uk

LEG ULCERATION DUE TO VENOUS DISEASE

Damage to the venous system of the leg results in oedema, haemosiderin deposition, eczema, fibrosis and ulceration.

Aetiology
In the normal leg there is a superficial low-pressure venous system connected to the deep, high-pressure veins by perforating veins. Muscular activity, aided by valves in the veins, pumps blood from the superficial to the deep system and towards the heart. Incompetent valves in the deep and perforating veins result in the retrograde flow of blood to the superficial system ('venous hypertension'), causing a rise in capillary hydrostatic pressure. Fibrinogen is forced out through the capillary walls and fibrin is deposited as a pericapillary cuff. One theory postulates that growth and repair factors are trapped in the macromolecular cuff so that minor trauma cannot be repaired and ulcers develop.

Incompetent veins leading to venous hypertension may be due to previous deep vein thrombosis (see pp. 908 and 953), congenital or familial valve incompetence, infection or deep venous obstruction (e.g. from a pelvic tumour).

Clinical features
The problem usually starts in middle age. Leg ulcers are more likely to occur and to persist in obese people. Varicose veins, although often present, are not inevitable. The first symptom is frequently heaviness of the legs, followed by the development of oedema. Haemosiderin pigmentation and ivory-coloured scarring may then be seen, sometimes associated with venous eczema (see p. 1074). The signs progress to lipodermatosclerosis, firm induration due to fibrosis of the dermis and subcutis, which may produce the well-known 'inverted champagne bottle' appearance. Ulceration, often precipitated by minor trauma or infection, soon occurs. Ulcers are seen typically around the medial malleolus but may encircle the ankle (see Fig. 21.9). If conditions are favourable, the ulcers will heal by granulation with small epithelial islands at the base and epithelial growth from the edges. Healing is often slow and may never be complete. Recurrent ulceration is common even after good healing.

Complications
Chronic venous ulcers are invariably colonised by bacteria. Only if infection becomes overt (see above) is systemic antibiotic treatment required. Contact dermatitis to an ointment, dressing or bandage is not uncommon. The usual culprits are preservatives, lanolin and neomycin.

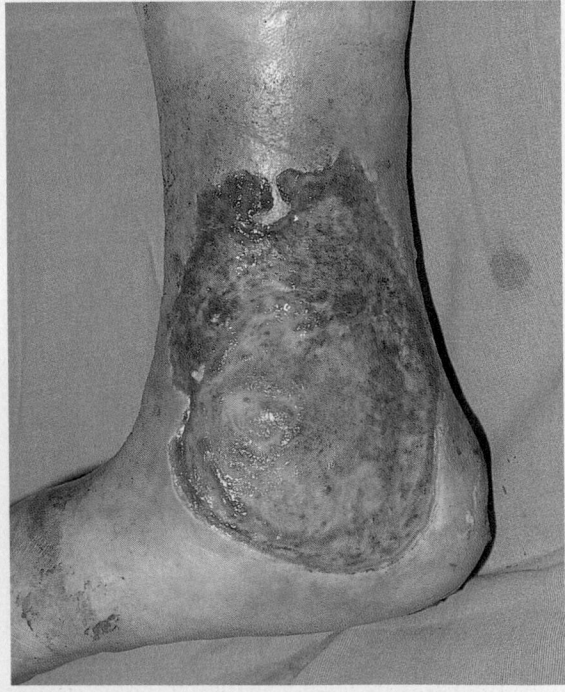

Fig. 21.9   A large venous ulcer overlying the medial malleolus.

Lipodermatosclerosis may cause lymphoedema, leading to hyperkeratosis and the so-called 'mossy foot'. A squamous cell carcinoma developing in a venous ulcer (Marjolin's ulcer) is rarely responsible for its failure to heal.

Management

- General management includes dietary advice for the obese and encouragement to take gentle exercise.
- Oedema should be reduced by the regular use of compression bandages, keeping the legs elevated when sitting and the judicious use of diuretics.
- The exudate and slough should be removed with normal saline solution, 0.5% aqueous silver nitrate or 5% aqueous hydrogen peroxide. If the ulcer is very purulent, soaking the leg for 15 minutes in 1:10 000 dilution of aqueous potassium permanganate may be helpful.
- Dressings commonly used for venous ulceration include antibiotic-impregnated tulle dressings, non-adhesive absorbent dressings (alginates, charcoals, hydrogels or hydrocolloids) and dry non-adherent dressings.
- The frequency of dressings depends on the state of the ulcer. Very purulent and exudative ulcers may need daily dressings whilst the dressing on a clean, healing ulcer may only require changing every week.
- Paste bandages, impregnated with zinc oxide or ichthammol, help to keep dressings in place and provide protection.
- Surrounding venous eczema is treated by a mild or moderately potent topical corticosteroid. The steroid should not be applied to the ulcer itself.
- Oral antibiotic therapy, given in short courses, is only necessary for the treatment of overt infection (see above). An anabolic steroid, stanozolol, may help lipodermatosclerosis but side-effects (fluid retention, hepatotoxicity) may limit its use.
- In the absence of any evidence of compromised arterial supply, graduated compression bandages applied from the toes to the knees enhance venous return and have been shown to be most beneficial in the healing of venous leg ulcers.
- Vein surgery may help some younger patients with persistent venous ulcers. Pinch grafts may hasten the healing of clean ulcers but do not influence their rate of recurrence.

LEG ULCERATION DUE TO ARTERIAL DISEASE

Deep, painful and punched-out ulcers on the lower leg, especially if they occur on the shin and foot and are preceded by a history of intermittent claudication, are likely to be due to arterial disease. Risk factors include smoking, hypertension, diabetes mellitus and hyperlipidaemia. The foot is cyanotic and cold, and the skin surrounding the ulcer is atrophic and hairless. The peripheral arterial pulses are absent or reduced. Doppler studies are required and then, if arterial insufficiency is confirmed, compression bandaging should be prohibited and advice from a vascular surgeon sought.

LEG ULCERATION DUE TO VASCULITIS

These ulcers start as painful, palpable, purpuric lesions turning into small punched-out ulcers. The involvement of larger vessels is heralded by painful nodules which may ulcerate. The intractable, deep, sharply demarcated ulcers of rheumatoid arthritis are due to an underlying vasculitis (see p. 1040). Management includes treatment of the underlying disorder as well as immunosuppression with, for example, steroids or cyclophosphamide.

LEG ULCERATION DUE TO NEUROPATHY

The most common cause of a neuropathic ulcer is diabetes. The ulcers occur over weight-bearing areas such as the heel. Microangiopathy also contributes to ulceration in diabetes. This is discussed in detail on page 677.

TOO LITTLE OR TOO MUCH HAIR

A patient who complains of too little or too much hair should be treated with sensitivity. These complaints may cause genuine morbidity. The causes are numerous and varied but a systematic approach to the history and examination can easily be used to elicit the correct diagnosis.

Hair undergoes a regular cycle of growth. Each cycle is independent of its neighbours in humans, whereas moulting animals, for instance, have hairs in a synchronous cycle. At any one time and depending on the age and sex of the person, up to 90% of hair follicles can be in anagen, the growing phase, and only 10% in telogen, the resting phase when hairs are normally shed. An alteration in this ratio can lead to an increased rate of hair loss and thus an impression of impending baldness.

ALOPECIA

The term means nothing more than loss of hair. There are many causes and patterns (see Box 21.16).

A detailed history, careful scalp examination and complete physical examination should enable a confident diagnosis to be made.

Tinea capitis
Fungal scalp infections are becoming increasingly common in urban areas in the UK. The clinical features can be variable but it usually affects children, causing patchy hair loss with some scaling. Any individual who develops

21.16 CLASSIFICATION OF ALOPECIA ⓘ	
Localised	**Diffuse**
Non-scarring	
Tinea capitis	Androgenetic alopecia
Alopecia areata	Telogen effluvium
Androgenetic alopecia	Metabolic
Traumatic (trichotillomania, traction, cosmetic)	Hypothyroidism
	Hyperthyroidism
Syphilis	Hypopituitarism
	Diabetes mellitus
	HIV disease
	Nutritional deficiency
	Liver disease
	Post-partum
	Alopecia areata
	Syphilis
Scarring	
Idiopathic	Discoid lupus
Developmental defects	erythematosus
Discoid lupus erythematosus	Radiotherapy
Herpes zoster	Folliculitis decalvans
Pseudopelade	Lichen planus pilaris
Tinea capitis/kerion	

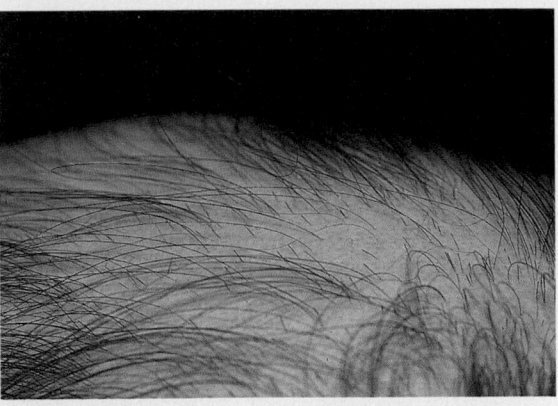

Fig. 21.10 Alopecia areata. Marked hair loss with diagnostic exclamation mark hairs.

an area of hair loss and scaling in the scalp should have the area scraped and affected hairs plucked for mycological microscopy and culture. Associated inflammation accounts for the variable presentation. Anthropophilic fungal infections (spread from child to child) account for the majority of cases in urban areas. Endothrix (within the hair shaft) infections, e.g. *Trichophyton tonsurans*, cause relatively uninflamed patchy baldness with breakage of the hairs at the skin surface ('black dot'). There is no fluorescence under Wood's light.

Ectothrix (outside the hair shaft) species of fungi, such as *Microsporum audouinii* (anthropophilic), show minimal inflammation; *Microsporum canis* (from dogs and cats) infections are more inflamed and can be identified by green fluorescence with Wood's light. Kerions are boggy, highly inflamed areas of tinea capitis and are usually caused by zoophilic (from animals, e.g. cattle ringworm) species of fungi (e.g. *Trichophyton verrucosum*).

Treatment is systemic, with either oral terbinafine, griseofulvin or itraconazole. Topical therapy, such as an antifungal shampoo, is recommended as an adjunct and arachis oil is used to remove crusting. Kerions sometimes require short courses of oral steroids in addition to systemic antifungal therapy to reduce the inflammation.

Accurate diagnosis and identification of the culprit fungus allows not only treatment but also control of the spread of infection.

Alopecia areata

This non-scarring condition appears as sharply defined non-inflamed bald patches, usually on the scalp (see p. 1050). During the active stage of hair loss pathognomonic 'exclamation mark' hairs are seen (broken-off hairs 3–4 mm long, which taper off towards the scalp—see

Fig. 21.10). An uncommon diffuse pattern on the scalp is recognised. The condition may affect the eyebrows, eyelashes and beard. Pitting and longitudinal wrinkling of the nail may be seen. The hair usually regrows spontaneously in small bald patches, but the outlook is less good with larger patches and when the alopecia appears early in life or is associated with atopy. Alopecia totalis describes complete loss of scalp hair and alopecia universalis complete loss of all hair. There is an association of alopecia areata with autoimmune disorders, atopy and Down's syndrome.

Androgenetic alopecia

Male-pattern baldness is physiological in men over 20 years old, though rarely it may be extensive and develop at an alarming pace in the late teens. It also occurs in females, most obviously after the menopause. The well-known distribution (bitemporal recession and then crown involvement) is described as 'male-pattern' but this type of hair loss in females is often diffuse.

Investigations

Laboratory tests, including a full blood count, erythrocyte sedimentation rate, urea and electrolytes, liver and thyroid function tests, an autoantibody profile and *Treponema pallidum* haemagglutination (TPHA) test, should help determine the cause of non-scarring alopecia. More specialised tests, including the hair pluck test where up to 50 hairs are removed with epilating forceps to determine the anagen:telogen ratio, are seldom necessary. Mycological assessment is advisable in cases of localised hair loss with scaling. A scalp biopsy, with direct immunofluorescence, may help to confirm a diagnosis of lichen planus of the scalp or discoid lupus erythematosus.

Management

Successful treatment of alopecia is difficult and management of these patients includes support and reassurance. Any underlying condition should be treated. Alopecia areata sometimes responds to topical or intralesional steroids such as 0.3 ml triamcinolone (10 mg/ml). Some patients with androgenetic alopecia may be helped by systemic finasteride or topical 2% minoxidil solution. In females, anti-androgen therapy such as cyproterone acetate is used. A wig may be the most appropriate treatment for extensive alopecia. Scalp surgery and autologous hair transplants are expensive but sometimes effective in androgenetic alopecia.

HIRSUTISM

Hirsutism is the growth of terminal hair in a male pattern in a female. It should be distinguished from hypertrichosis, which describes the excessive growth of terminal hair in either sex in a non-androgenic distribution.

Hirsutism is often racial (e.g. Mediterranean Caucasians and Asians) and familial. Some degree of hirsutism is common after the menopause. The cause of most cases of hirsutism is unknown and only a small minority have a demonstrable hormonal abnormality.

Investigations

Full endocrinological investigations are required if hirsutism:

- occurs in childhood
- is of sudden onset
- is accompanied by signs of virilisation
- is associated with menstrual irregularity or cessation.

In addition to the screening tests for hyperandrogenism (see p. 709), Cushing's syndrome needs to be excluded (see p. 721).

Management

Depilatory creams, waxing, electrolysis, bleaching and shaving are often used for physiological hirsutism.

Any remediable cause should be corrected by medical and surgical methods, sometimes with the help of the endocrinologist or gynaecologist (see p. 710). Oral anti-androgens may be helpful.

VULVAL ITCH (PRURITUS VULVAE)

Pruritus vulvae is a distressing symptom that can occur at any age and can be difficult to diagnose. Chronic scratching of the vulval area leads to lichenification which, in this site, can be asymmetrical and associated with quite marked oedema and swelling. The history is important to give an indication of the underlying cause. Pre-existing skin disease, such as atopic eczema, psoriasis or fungal infections, needs to be sought and an autoimmune history might be associated with lichen sclerosus et atrophicus. It is important to determine if there is a previous history of sexually transmitted diseases, particularly genital warts or cervical dysplasia found on colposcopy. The main dermatological causes of itch in the vulval area are candidiasis

(consider underlying diabetes), tinea cruris (dermatophyte infection), eczema (including contact dermatitis), psoriasis, lichen sclerosus and, less commonly, lichen planus. These can usually be differentiated by careful examination, bacteriological and mycological assessment and a search for evidence of similar skin disease elsewhere on the body. A well-defined, bright red plaque on the vulva can indicate psoriasis, particularly with skin, scalp or nail signs of this condition; oral lesions are often seen in lichen planus and this condition is often followed by marked post-inflammatory hyperpigmentation; lichen sclerosus is characterised by ivory papules that coalesce into pale plaques, with an atrophic surface (reminiscent of crinkly cigarette paper). There is sometimes associated haemorrhagic blistering. Lichen sclerosus often forms a 'figure of eight' around the vulva and perineal area and can cause scarring of the vulva with loss of normal contours culminating in stenosis of the introitus secondary to labial fusion. Biopsy for histology is occasionally needed to differentiate these conditions and in lichen sclerosus to assess any malignant change in, for example, non-healing areas.

Histology is always needed in the next group of itchy vulval lesions, neoplasia. Most tumours of the vulva can provoke the symptom of itch—in particular, vulval (squamous) intraepithelial neoplasia (VIN) and extramammary Paget's disease. Lesions of VIN can be solitary or multiple and may appear red, white, pigmented, warty, moist or eroded. As well as being itchy, VIN can be painful, particularly with superficial dyspareunia. There may be very little to see with the naked eye and then vulvoscopy is needed. In younger women there is a strong association of VIN with the papillomavirus, immunosuppression and possibly smoking. Extramammary Paget's disease is rare, is usually asymmetrical and can be painful. It presents as a moist, red, scaly patch often mistaken for eczema; hence the importance of biopsy in 'unresponsive eczema'.

Finally, it has been shown that a proportion of vulval itch is psychogenic; certainly vulval disease can be associated with psychological distress so careful consultation and an understanding doctor are essential to a correct diagnosis of this condition.

ISSUES IN OLDER PEOPLE
COMMON SKIN DISEASES

- About 40% of individuals over the age of 60 years have significant dermatological problems.
- The most common diseases in this age group are:
  —skin cancers
  —leg ulcers, a major cause of morbidity in the elderly
  —blistering disorders
  —herpes zoster (shingles) and post-herpetic neuralgia
  —inflammatory skin diseases, e.g. asteatotic, varicose and seborrhoeic eczema, psoriasis
  —lichen sclerosus
  —scabies
  —lymphoedema
  —pruritus of old age
  —drug-related rashes.

ECZEMA

The terms 'eczema' and 'dermatitis' are synonymous. They refer to distinctive reaction patterns in the skin, which can be either acute or chronic and are due to a number of causes.

Histopathology

In the acute stage oedema of the epidermis (spongiosis) progresses to the formation of intraepidermal vesicles, which may enlarge and rupture. In the chronic stage there is less oedema and vesiculation but more thickening of the epidermis (acanthosis); this is accompanied by a variable degree of vasodilatation and T-helper lymphocytic infiltration in the upper dermis.

Clinical features

There are several patterns of eczema (see Box 21.17); some of these have identifiable environmental causes whereas others are more complex. The clinical signs are similar in all types of eczema and vary according to the duration of the rash. The features of acute and chronic eczema are listed in Box 21.18.

Atopic eczema

Atopy is a genetic predisposition to form excessive IgE which leads to a generalised and prolonged hypersensitivity to common environmental antigens, including pollen and the house dust mite. Atopic individuals manifest one or more of a group of diseases that includes asthma, hay fever, urticaria, and food and other allergies, and this distinctive form of eczema. These atopic conditions tend to run true to type within each family. Atopic eczema has clear diagnostic criteria, which are listed in Box 21.19.

21.17 CLASSIFICATION OF ECZEMA

- Atopic
- Seborrhoeic
- Discoid
- Irritant
- Allergic
- Asteatotic
- Gravitational
- Lichen simplex
- Pompholyx

21.18 THE ECZEMA REACTION

Acute

- Redness and swelling, usually with ill-defined margins
- Papules, vesicles and, more rarely, large blisters
- Exudation and cracking
- Scaling

Chronic

- May show all of the above features, though it is usually less vesicular and exudative
- Lichenification, a dry leathery thickening with increased skin markings, is secondary to rubbing and scratching
- Fissures and scratch marks
- Pigmentation changes (hypo- and hyper-)

21.19 DIAGNOSTIC CRITERIA FOR ATOPIC ECZEMA

Itchy skin and at least three of the following:

- History of itch in skin creases (or cheeks if < 4 years)
- History of asthma/hay fever (or in a first-degree relative if < 4 years)
- Dry skin (xeroderma)
- Visible flexural eczema (cheeks, forehead, outer limbs if < 4 years)
- Onset in first 2 years of life

Aetiology. The inheritance of atopic eczema is controversial. The disorder is concordant in 86% of monozygotic twins but in only 21% of dizygotes. Atopic diseases show maternal imprinting—that is, they are inherited more often from the mother than from the father. A polygenic mode of inheritance is likely. More than one genetic locus has been identified that might play a role in the inheritance of atopy and more specifically atopic eczema.

The prevalence of atopic eczema is rising and has increased between twofold and fivefold over the last 30 years. It now affects 1 in 10 schoolchildren. Environmental factors, such as exposure to allergens either in utero or during childhood, have been shown to have a role in the aetiology of atopic eczema.

Pathogenesis. The pathogenesis of atopic eczema is complex and still incompletely understood. It is best considered as an interplay of genetic susceptibility that causes epidermal barrier dysfunction and abnormal immune responses, which are then stimulated by different environmental factors.

EBM

ATOPIC ECZEMA—are there intervention strategies that reduce the incidence of atopic eczema?

'Specific nutritional restrictions in maternal diet during pregnancy have no effect on the incidence of atopic eczema in an infant at hereditary risk and may adversely affect maternal and/or fetal nutrition. Breastfeeding, however, appears to reduce the prevalence of atopic eczema in early childhood.'

- Kramer MS. Maternal antigen avoidance during pregnancy for preventing atopic disease in infants of women at high risk (Cochrane Review). Cochrane Library, issue 1, 2001. Oxford: Update Software.
- Saarinen UM, Kajosaari M. Breastfeeding as prophylaxis against atopic disease: prospective follow-up study until 17 years old. Lancet 1995; 346:1065–1069.
- Chandra RK. Five year follow-up of high risk infants with family history of allergy who were exclusively breast-fed or fed partial whey hydrosylate, soy, and conventional cow's milk formulas. J Pediatr Gastroenterol Nutr 1997; 24:380–388.

Further information: 🖥 www.cochranelibrary.com

21.20 ATOPIC ECZEMA: DISTRIBUTION AND CHARACTER OF RASH

Infancy

- The eczema is often acute and involves the face and trunk
- The napkin area is frequently spared

Childhood

- The rash settles on the backs of the knees, fronts of the elbows, wrists and ankles (see Fig. 21.11)

Adults

- The face and trunk are once more involved; lichenification is common

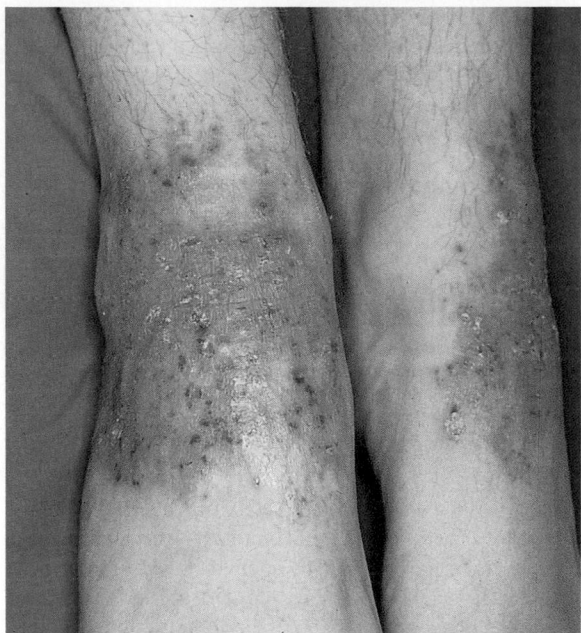

Fig. 21.11   Atopic subacute eczema on the fronts of the ankles of a teenager. These are sites of predilection, along with the cubital and popliteal fossae, in atopic eczema.

Clinical features. The cardinal feature of atopic eczema is itch, and scratching may account for many of the signs. Widespread dryness of the skin is another feature. The distribution and character of the rash vary with age, as shown in Box 21.20. Complications are listed in Box 21.21.

21.21 COMPLICATIONS OF ATOPIC ECZEMA

- Superinfection most often with bacteria *(Staphylococcus aureus)* but also importantly with viruses. Herpes simplex virus causes a widespread severe eruption—eczema herpeticum. Papillomavirus and molluscum contagiosum superinfections are also more common and are encouraged by use of local steroids
- Irritant reactions due to defective barrier function
- Sleep disturbance, loss of schooling and behavioural difficulties
- Children with atopic eczema have an increased incidence of food allergy, particularly to eggs, cow's milk, protein, fish, wheat and soya. These foods cause an immediate urticarial eruption rather than exacerbating their eczema

Seborrhoeic eczema

This condition which is characterised by a red scaly rash classically affects the scalp (dandruff), central face, nasolabial folds, eyebrows and central chest. It is due to *Pityrosporum ovale* infection of the skin. In its milder forms it is the same as dandruff, whereas when severe it may resemble psoriasis. Sebum may be permissive for the development of the rash but otherwise the name is a poor one. Treatment of *P. ovale* with anti-yeast agents improves the rash although the course may need to be repeated. Seborrhoeic eczema is a feature of AIDS and can be very severe in this condition.

Discoid eczema

This is a common form of eczema recognised by discrete coin-shaped lesions of eczema seen on the limbs of young men, associated with alcohol excess, and of elderly men. It can occur in children with atopic eczema and tends to be more stubborn to treat.

Irritant eczema

Detergents, alkalis, acids, solvents and abrasive dusts are common causes. There is a wide range of susceptibility to weak irritants. Irritant eczema accounts for the majority of industrial cases and work loss. The elderly, those with fair and dry skin, and those with an atopic background (personal or family history of asthma, hay fever or eczema) are especially vulnerable. Napkin eczema in babies is common and due to irritant ammoniacal urine and faeces.

Strong irritants elicit an acute reaction at the site of contact whereas weak irritants most often cause chronic eczema, especially of the hands, after prolonged exposure.

Allergic contact eczema

This is due to a delayed hypersensitivity reaction following contact with antigens or haptens. Previous exposure to the allergen is required for sensitisation and the reaction is specific to the allergen or closely related chemicals. Common allergens and their origin are listed in Box 21.22.

The eczema reaction occurs wherever the allergen is in contact with the skin and sensitisation persists indefinitely. It is important to determine the original site of the rash before secondary spread obscures the picture, as this often provides the best clue to the contactant. There are many easily recognisable patterns, e.g. eczema of the earlobes, wrists and back due to contact with nickel in costume jewellery, watches and bra clips; or eczema of the hands and wrists due to rubber gloves. Oedema of the lax skin of the eyelids and genitalia is a frequent concomitant of allergic contact eczema (see Fig. 21.12).

21.22 SOME COMMON ALLERGENS	
Allergen	**Present in**
Nickel	Jewellery, jean studs, bra clips
Dichromate	Cement, leather, matches
Rubber chemicals	Clothing, shoes, tyres
Colophony	Sticking plaster, collodion
Paraphenylenediamine	Hair dye, clothing
Balsam of Peru	Perfumes, citrus fruits
Neomycin, benzocaine	Topical applications
Parabens	Preservative in cosmetics and creams
Wool alcohols	Lanolin, cosmetics, creams
Epoxy resin	Resin adhesives

Asteatotic eczema

This is frequently seen in the hospitalised elderly, especially when the skin is dry; low humidity caused by central heating, over-washing and diuretics are contributory factors. It occurs most often on the lower legs as a rippled or 'crazy paving' pattern of fine fissuring on an erythematous background.

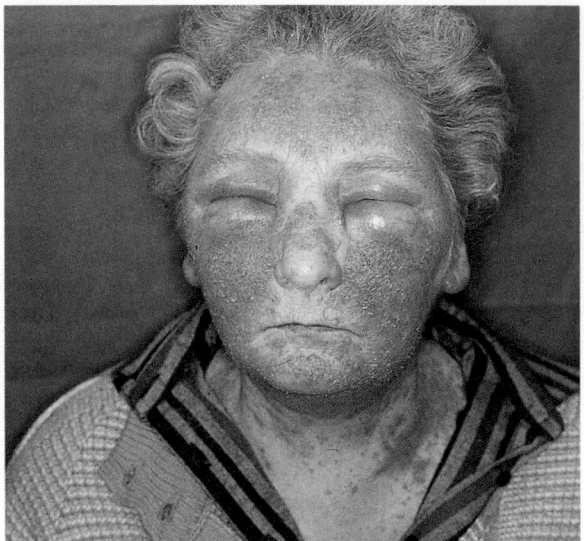

Fig. 21.12   Allergic contact eczema. This was caused by the application of an antihistamine cream. The acute eczematous reaction and bilateral periorbital oedema are typical.

Gravitational (stasis) eczema

This occurs on the lower legs and is often associated with signs of venous insufficiency (oedema, red or bluish discoloration, loss of hair, induration, haemosiderin pigmentation and ulceration).

Lichen simplex

This describes a plaque of lichenified eczema due to repeated rubbing or scratching, as a habit or in response to stress. Common sites include the nape of the neck, the lower legs and the anogenital area.

Pompholyx (dyshidrotic eczema)

Recurrent vesicles and bullae occur on the palms, palmar surface of the fingers and soles, and are excruciatingly itchy. This form of eczema can occur in atopic eczema and in irritant and contact allergic dermatitis. It can be provoked by heat, stress and nickel ingestion in a nickel-sensitive patient but is often idiopathic.

Investigation of eczema

(For details of tests see pp. 1055–1056.)

Patch tests

These are performed in suspected cases of contact allergic dermatitis (see p. 1073).

IgE and specific IgE

These are occasionally performed to support the diagnosis of atopic eczema and to determine specific environmental allergens, e.g. pet dander, horse hair, house dust mite, pollens and foods.

Prick tests

The indications are the same as for specific IgE but are less commonly performed.

Bacterial and viral swabs for microscopy and culture

These are useful tests in suspected secondary infection. Skin swabs for bacteriological assessment will invariably reveal the presence of bacteria, and antibacterial treatment should

be reserved for those cases with evidence of clinical infection. In the case of recurrent impetigo in a child with atopic eczema, bacterial swabs should be taken from carrier sites (nares, axillae and groin) from both the affected individual and all household members.

General management of eczema

The main points are listed in Box 21.23.

21.23 GENERAL MANAGEMENT FOR ALL TYPES OF ECZEMA
• Explanation, reassurance and encouragement
• Avoidance of contact with irritants
• Regular use of greasy emollients
• Appropriate use of topical steroids

Topical steroids

Lotions (aqueous base) and creams (oil/water mixture) are preferable in acute eczema and ointments (in an oily base) in chronic cases; they are usually applied twice daily. Only 1% hydrocortisone should be used on the face and in infancy. Even in adults it is seldom necessary to prescribe more than 200 g of a low-potency steroid (e.g. 1% hydrocortisone), 50 g of a moderately potent steroid (e.g. 0.05% clobetasone butyrate) or 30 g of a potent steroid (e.g. 0.1% betamethasone valerate, 0.1% mometasone furoate) per week. Very potent topical steroids (e.g. 0.05% clobetasol propionate) should not be used long-term. The side-effects of strong or extensive local steroid therapy should be borne in mind when patients are applying these preparations for years on end. They include skin thinning (with striae, fragility and purpura), enhanced or disguised infections, and systemic absorption (causing suppression of the hypothalamic-pituitary-adrenal axis and even Cushingoid features). There are no absolute guidelines for the amount of topical steroid that should be used but care should be taken on certain sites such as the face and flexures. The best rule is to use the least potent steroid for the shortest possible time that is effective. Often one finds that topical steroids are being under-used and are therefore ineffective.

Other topical immunosuppressants, including tacrolimus and pimicrolimus, have just become available for use. Early reports of their efficacy are encouraging.

Bland emollients (e.g. emulsifying ointment) are used regularly, both directly on the skin and in the bath. They not only prevent excessive water loss from an already dry skin, but also help to reduce the amount of local steroid used. Emollient soap substitutes (e.g. aqueous cream) are also helpful. Sedative antihistamines (e.g. alimemazine tartrate (trimeprazine tartrate)) are of value if sleep is interrupted.

Specific measures

Atopic eczema

Explanation and patient support are increasingly provided for these patients through general practice, dermatology clinics, community liaison nurses and patient support groups such as the National Eczema Society in the UK. Treatment involves the regular use of emollients (moisturisers) and the least possible use of topical steroids. These topical treatments can be used with a variety of types of bandaging such as 'wet wraps', tar and ichthammol paste bandages. Allergen avoidance has a role in selected patients. Routine inoculations are allowed during quiescent phases of eczema. An egg-free measles vaccine is available for children who have a severe egg allergy.

Seborrhoeic eczema

Antipityrosporal agents such as ketoconazole shampoo form the basis of treatment, supplemented with weak corticosteroids if needed. Treatments may need to be repeated at intervals.

Irritant eczema

This is best treated by the regular use of emollients, avoidance of irritants and protective clothing, e.g. gloves.

Contact allergic eczema

Avoidance of the culprit allergen is the most important treatment for this form of eczema and may involve lifestyle changes such as a new job or giving up hobbies. Measures used for irritant eczema are also helpful.

Gravitational eczema

Local steroids (see above) should only be applied to eczematous areas and ulcers should be avoided. Sensitisation to topical antibiotics (neomycin) and preservatives (e.g. chlorocresol) is common in this form of eczema. Associated peripheral oedema should be eliminated by elevation of the leg and graded compression bandages.

ISSUES IN OLDER PEOPLE
ECZEMA

- With advancing age, the skin becomes less pliable and drier. This increases the tendency for irritant dermatitis.
- Topical steroid usage causes more local side-effects, such as purpura or ecchymoses, in the elderly individual.
- Widespread eczema is potentially life-threatening in the elderly, particularly when combined with other illnesses.

PSORIASIS AND OTHER ERYTHEMATOUS SCALY ERUPTIONS

Psoriasis and lichen planus will be described here in detail; other scaly conditions were covered on pages 1059–1060.

PSORIASIS

Psoriasis is a non-infectious, chronic inflammatory disease of the skin, characterised by well-defined erythematous plaques with silvery scale which have a predilection for the extensor surfaces and scalp, and by a chronic fluctuating course.

The prevalence is approximately 2% in European populations. Accurate figures for many other parts of the world are not available but there seems to be consistent evidence that the prevalence of psoriasis is lower in people of African origin and lower still in some Asian communities such as the Japanese. Psoriasis may come on at any age but is unusual before the age of 5; the oldest recorded onset was in a patient aged 107. There appear to be two epidemiological patterns of psoriasis. The first shows an onset in the teenage and early adult years; such individuals frequently have a family history of psoriasis and there is an increased prevalence of HLA Cw6. In a second epidemiological grouping disease onset is in an individual's fifties or sixties, a family history is less common and the HLA group Cw6 is not so prominent. Some authors refer to these two groupings as type 1 and type 2 psoriatics.

The clinical course of psoriasis is very variable. As a general rule the earlier the age of onset and the more severe the initial presentation, the more severe the lifetime course of the disease.

Aetiology

Basic defect

There are two key pathophysiological aspects to the abnormalities in psoriatic plaques. Firstly, the keratinocytes hyperproliferate with a grossly increased mitotic index and an abnormal pattern of differentiation involving the retention of nuclei in the stratum corneum (in normal skin the dead stratum corneum cells do not have nuclei). Secondly, there is a large inflammatory cell infiltrate comprising polymorphs, T cells and other inflammatory cells. It is uncertain which of these characteristics is primary. Traditionally, psoriasis was viewed as a primary disorder of cell turnover but in recent years there has been increased support for the hypothesis that the hyperproliferation may be secondary to the inflammatory infiltrate and that the increase in keratinocyte proliferation is a consequence of inflammatory cell mediators or signalling.

There is a large familial component to psoriasis. Formal estimates from twin studies suggest a hereditability of around 80%. In monozygotic twins perhaps one-third of pairs will be concordant for psoriasis. Put another way, two-thirds of monozygotic twins will not be concordant despite an apparently identical or near-identical genetic background.

The mode of inheritance of psoriasis does not fit a clear Mendelian pattern and is therefore described as genetically complex. Empirical estimates suggest that if one parent has psoriasis, then the chance of a child being affected is in the order of 15–20%. If both parents have psoriasis the probability of a child being affected is 0.5. Both these estimates are increased if one sibling already has the disease. Genome scanning linkage and association studies have indicated various chromosomal areas of susceptibility including the HLA region.

Disordered cell proliferation in psoriasis is reflected by the increase in the number of mitoses visible in the psoriatic plaque. The transit time—that is, the time it takes for keratinocytes in the basal layer to leave the epidermis—is shortened in psoriasis from perhaps 28 to 5 days. Whilst it used to be thought that the cell cycle was actually reduced in psoriasis more recent data suggest that it is just that the proportion of cycling cells (rather than cells that are in G_0) is increased. There are some data suggesting that the non-plaque skin also shows an elevated rate of proliferation, although any increase above background rate is modest. These data have not been confirmed in all studies. The nails of patients with psoriasis, even when clinically unaffected, do, however, grow more quickly than those of controls.

The importance of keratinocyte hyperproliferation initially received support from the demonstration that cytostatic drugs such as methotrexate were clinically useful. However, more recent data suggest that methotrexate may exert its effects primarily through an influence on the immune system.

The evidence implicating a key role for an immune pathogenesis relates to:

- the association with certain HLA groups (HLA Cw6)
- the success of certain immunosuppressive drugs (such as ciclosporin) in improving the clinical state of the disease
- reports of the development of psoriasis in recipients of bone marrow transplants from donors with a history of psoriasis.

The precise molecular mechanisms operating in psoriasis are, however, poorly understood. A large number of theories have been advanced over the last 30 or 40 years claiming that one particular mediator may be a key or rate-limiting factor in psoriasis. The majority of these explanations have not stood the test of time; nor have they provided useful therapeutic insight.

Precipitating factors

Psoriasis is a chronic disease characterised by variation in both temporal and spatial extent. Most of this variation cannot be explained. At any one time perhaps 10% of people who have received the diagnosis of psoriasis have no lesions and perhaps 15% may report remissions of up to 5 years or more. Some factors, however, are thought to precipitate an exacerbation of the disease and these are listed in Box 21.24.

21.24 FACTORS CAUSING FLARE-UPS OF PSORIASIS
Trauma
• When the condition is erupting lesions appear in areas of skin damage such as scratches or surgical wounds (Köbner phenomenon)
Infection
• β-haemolytic streptococcal throat infections often precede guttate psoriasis
Sunlight
• Rarely, ultraviolet radiation may worsen psoriasis
Drugs
• Antimalarials, β-blockers and lithium may worsen psoriasis and the rash may 'rebound' after stopping systemic corticosteroids or potent local corticosteroids
Emotion
• Anxiety precipitates some exacerbations

Pathology

The histology of psoriasis is depicted in Figure 21.13.

Clinical features

Stable plaque psoriasis

This is the most common type. Individual lesions are well demarcated and range from a few millimetres to several centimetres in diameter (see Fig. 21.14). The lesions are red with dry, silvery-white scaling, which may be obvious only after scraping the surface. The elbows, knees and lower back are commonly involved.

Other sites of predilection include:

- *Scalp.* Scalp is involved in approximately 60% of patients with psoriasis. The reason why the scalp is so commonly involved is not clear. One possibility relates it to Köbnerisation from *P. ovale* infection of the skin. (*P. ovale* is the cause or precipitant of dandruff or seborrhoeic dermatitis.) Psoriasis of the scalp typically

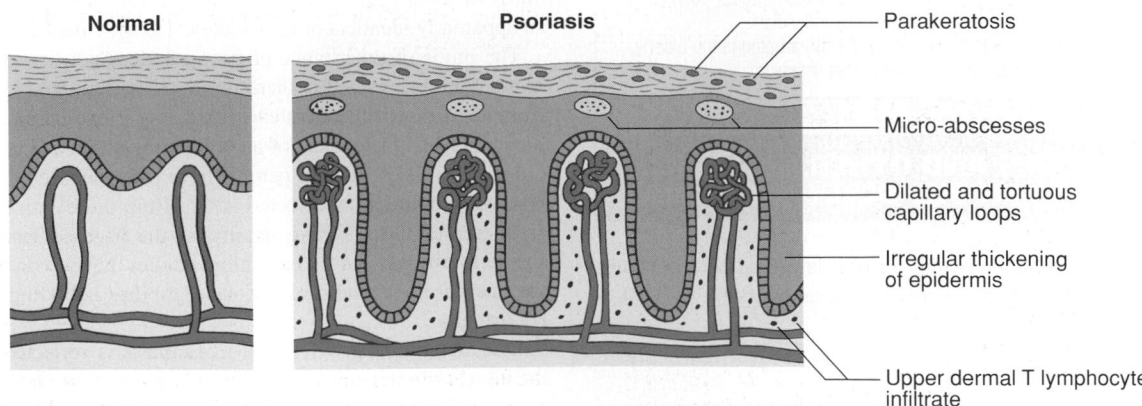

Fig. 21.13 **The histology of psoriasis.**

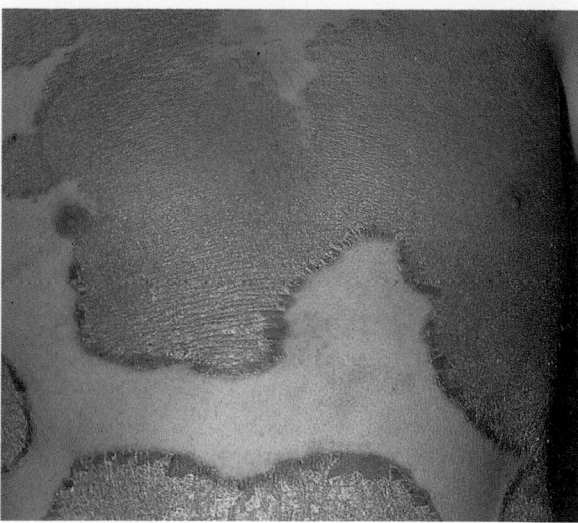

Fig. 21.14 Large, sharply circumscribed plaques of psoriasis. The silvery scaling of the lower (untreated) plaque is typical.

shows well-demarcated, easily palpable areas, but on occasion a diffuse, fine scaling difficult to distinguish from classical seborrhoeic dermatitis may be present. Temporary hair loss is not uncommon and rarely permanent focal hair loss may occur.

- *Nails*. Involvement of the nails is common, with 'thimble pitting', onycholysis (separation of the nail from the nail bed—see Fig. 21.15) and subungual hyperkeratosis.
- *Flexures*. Psoriasis involving the natal cleft, and submammary and axillary folds is not scaly but red, shiny and symmetrical (see Fig. 21.16).
- *Palms*. Psoriasis here is often difficult to recognise, as individual plaques may be poorly demarcated and barely erythematous. It is often impossible to differentiate between psoriasis and eczema of the palms.

Guttate psoriasis

This is most commonly seen in children and adolescents and may follow a streptococcal sore throat. In many patients this will be the first clinical indication of the disease. The rash often appears rapidly. Individual lesions are droplet-shaped, small (seldom greater than 1 cm in diameter) and scaly. Bouts of guttate psoriasis may clear in a few months but

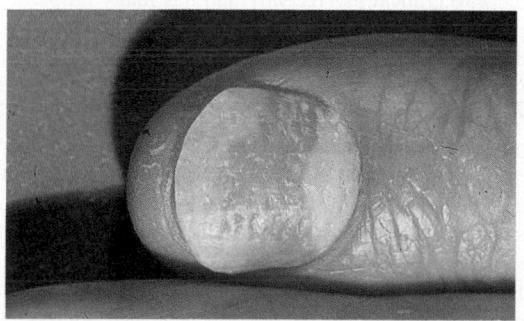

Fig. 21.15 Coarse pitting of the nail and separation of the nail from the nail bed (onycholysis). These are both classic features of psoriasis.

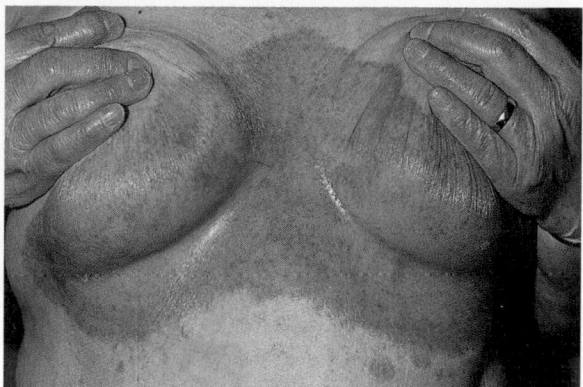

Fig. 21.16 Flexural psoriasis. Note the glistening but not scaly rash.

respond well to early treatment with phototherapy. The majority of these patients will develop plaque psoriasis later in life.

Erythrodermic psoriasis

The skin becomes universally red or scaly, or more rarely just red with very little scale present. As in other forms of erythroderma temperature regulation becomes problematic with a danger of either hypothermia or hyperthermia developing. Precipitants for erythroderma may not be evident but inappropriate use of dithranol, tar or phototherapy is a known factor.

Pustular psoriasis

There are two varieties of pustular psoriasis. The first is the generalised form which is rare but very serious. The onset is usually sudden with large numbers of small sterile pustules erupting on a red base. The patient may rapidly become ill with a swinging pyrexia coinciding with the appearance of new pustules. Such patients will usually require urgent assessment and hospital admission to a dermatology ward. More common is a localised form of pustular psoriasis which primarily affects the palms and soles. This eruption is chronic and comprises small sterile pustules which lie on a red base, and resolve to leave brown macules or scaling in their wake. The relation between pustular psoriasis of the palms and the soles (palmoplantar pustulosis) and psoriasis remains disputed by some, although the majority agree that they are indeed related.

Arthropathy

Between 5 and 10% of individuals with psoriasis appear to have a chronic inflammatory arthropathy (see p. 1011).

Investigations

Few are indicated. Biopsy is seldom necessary and often contributes little where there is clinical doubt (for example, in attempting to distinguish between psoriasis of the palms and eczema of the palms). Throat swabbing for streptococci or other evidence of recent infection may occasionally be useful. Skin scrapings and nail clippings may help to exclude dermatophyte infection where the clinical diagnosis is uncertain. Assessment of all but minor joint symptoms may require assessment by a rheumatologist.

Management

General measures

Explanation, reassurance and instruction are vital but easily neglected; they must be based on insight into the patient's state of mind. In the vast majority of cases psoriasis is not life-threatening and therefore if the treatment appears worse than the disease, then the treatment should be stopped. Often patients need encouragement to take many of the important decisions themselves, albeit with advice from the physician. Two patients, even with identical patterns of psoriasis, don't have the same experience of the disease.

There is little robust evidence to support the statement that stress exacerbates psoriasis or is causally involved. Certain studies suggest that alcohol consumption is greater amongst some psoriasis patients, but it is not clear whether this is a cause or a result of the disease. What is clear is that doctors need an awareness of the impact that this disease can have on many individuals. For instance, many fathers will, with embarrassment, admit that they cannot take their young children swimming because of the alarm their rash causes to other swimmers. Similarly, blood on the sheets and the ubiquitous scale on bedclothes and carpets may act against many personal relationships. It is said that 'Girls with scalp psoriasis don't wear navy clothes' (the scale being more prominent when viewed against a dark background).

Treatment

Treatment can be classed in four broad categories:

- easily applied topical agents such as emollients, corticosteroids, vitamin D agonists, or 'weak' tar or dithranol preparations
- ultraviolet therapies such as PUVA and ultraviolet B
- systemic agents such as retinoids or immunosuppressives such as ciclosporin
- intensive inpatient or day-patient care with topical agents and ultraviolet radiation under medical supervision.

Traditionally, therapies such as inpatient dithranol, when combined with ultraviolet radiation in the Ingram's regimen, were capable of inducing clearance of the disease, i.e. all or >95% of the psoriasis disappeared. The patient remained clear of disease until relapse occurred. The duration of remission varied considerably from less than 1 month to over a year. By contrast, many more acceptable treatments such as calcipotriol do not clear psoriasis; rather they reduce the thickness, scaling and redness of individual plaques. Depending on the clinical context and extent of disease, patient and physician need to choose the appropriate end-point of treatment. This is often a compromise between side-effects, practical considerations such as time available to attend hospital, and disease extent.

Topical agents

A large number of topical agents have been used to treat psoriasis. Emollients have a modest effect in terms of reducing scale and diminishing itch. Many patients feel more comfortable using emollients than not using them.

Dithranol. Traditionally, the gold standard of therapy was treatment with dithranol or crude tar. Dithranol originally came into use in the late 19th century and is now known to be a potent producer of free radicals. Unsurprisingly, when applied to normal skin dithranol is proinflammatory and stimulates hyperproliferation, but for reasons that remain unclear it normalises differentiation and inhibits proliferation when applied to psoriatic plaques.

Dithranol is used in two main regimens. The first is Ingram's regimen; the plaques are covered with low concentrations of dithranol in a zinc oxide paste following a tar bath and ultraviolet radiation exposure, and then covered in talcum powder and bandages and left in situ for 24 hours. More recently, short-contact dithranol therapy has been developed in which higher concentrations are applied for between 15 and 30 minutes and then washed off. The main clinical limitation of dithranol is its proinflammatory action on normal skin. This presents as 'burning' with pain and erythema, which peaks 72 hours after application. Dithranol also results in a brown staining of the skin and can cause a purple discoloration in individuals with light hair colour. In general, use of dithranol as an inpatient therapy has diminished over the last 20–30 years due to low patient acceptability, the invention of new phototherapy modalities and lack of inpatient beds. As with tar, attempts have been made to make dithranol easier to use and more patient-friendly but efficacy is reduced; these attempts have been largely unsuccessful.

Tar. Tar, particularly crude tar, has been shown to be effective in the treatment of psoriasis. There are certain similarities with dithranol in that tar is proinflammatory and has different effects on the plaque compared with normal skin. Unfortunately, as for dithranol, attempts to define the exact therapeutic mechanism and dissociate efficacy from side-effects have been unsuccessful. It remains true that the more cosmetically acceptable the preparation, the lower its efficacy.

Calcipotriol. More recently, a number of other topical preparations have been developed which have become clinically popular. Calcipotriol is a vitamin D agonist which is highly acceptable cosmetically; it seldom clears a plaque of psoriasis but tends to reduce the thickness of the plaque and diminish the scaling. It is applied twice daily and, providing no more than 100 g is used each week, does not cause hypercalcaemia or hypercalciuria. Patients like calcipotriol because it is odourless, colourless and does not stain. Irritation, which is usually transient, is the main side-effect.

Tazarotene. A vitamin A agonist (retinoid), this has also come into clinical use recently and has many properties in common with calcipotriol. It tends not to induce clearance and may cause irritation, but is easy to use and diminishes the induration, scaling and redness of plaques.

Corticosteroids. The frequency of use of corticosteroids varies considerably between different countries. In the UK they tend not to be used nearly as much as in many other European countries or North America. The hazards of corticosteroids are local skin atrophy and the fact that when they are stopped the psoriasis tends to return, i.e. they do not induce remission. Nevertheless, they are invaluable for many body sites, particularly the flexures where tar and dithranol may be too irritant, and short bursts of moderately potent corticosteroids can be invaluable in the management of many patients. Use of potent topical corticosteroids on the face or hair margins should be under close and expert medical supervision.

Ultraviolet and PUVA therapy

Ultraviolet therapy. Ultraviolet radiation (UVR) forms the mainstay of management of patients with moderate to severe psoriasis. As could be predicted given the known biology of UVR, the main risk of ultraviolet therapies lies in burning in the short term and in the induction of skin cancers in the long term.

There are two main therapeutic modalities in use. It has been known for almost a century that ultraviolet B (UVB) administered therapeutically improves the condition of many patients with psoriasis. To some degree this mirrors the natural improvement that many patients with psoriasis notice in summer. In the past broadband UVB radiation given 3–7 times a week formed part of the Ingram's regimen using dithranol.

More recently, a particular type of UVB radiation produced by the Philips TL01 lamp (narrowband UVB) has become a very popular modality of treatment delivered 2–5 times a week on an outpatient basis. This lamp peaks at 311 nm and was developed specifically following work showing that shorter wavelength (< 311 nm) radiation, while inflammatory, had little therapeutic efficacy, whilst longer wavelengths (> 311 nm) were also relatively ineffective. The long-term safety of this lamp is, however, less clear. Some argue that it may be more carcinogenic than broadband UVB therapy while others believe it is less carcinogenic. The results of long-term observation are awaited.

PUVA therapy. Psoralens are natural photosensitisers found in a number of plants. In the early 1960s topical preparations of psoralen used in combination with ultraviolet A (UVA) were reported to have therapeutic effects on psoriasis. In the early 1970s a large randomised trial showed that oral psoralen together with long wavelength ultraviolet A (PUVA) was a dramatically effective treatment for individuals with chronic plaque psoriasis. Psoralen molecules intercalate between the two strands of DNA and upon excitation with UVA photons cross-link the DNA strands. In this sense PUVA therapy is not a 'light therapy'; rather, psoralen is a pro-drug that upon oral administration is distributed throughout the body but is only activated by ultraviolet radiation in those sites that are exposed to UVA (skin and eye—the latter should be protected).

PUVA treatment induces clearance to a greater degree than intensive dithranol therapy and has revolutionised the management of patients with psoriasis. The short-term side-effects are minimal. The therapy can be delivered between 2 and 5 times a week and clearance expected in the majority of individuals within 8 weeks. Clearance will occur in more than 75% of individuals. Some individuals may develop nausea in response to the psoralen, and because the psoralen is also present in the eye individuals need to wear UVR-resistant sunglasses for 24 hours after therapy. The long-term hazards of PUVA therapy give cause for concern but are not surprising because PUVA is by its mechanism of action known to be mutagenic. In patients who have received a large amount of PUVA therapy, particularly 'maintenance therapy' (continuous PUVA lasting for 6 months to a year), there is an elevated risk of squamous cell carcinoma and basal cell carcinoma. Recent work suggests that the risk of melanoma may also be increased although this single study requires confirmation. Instead of being used orally, psoralens can also be applied to the bath before irradiation with UVA (so-called bath PUVA). A few different psoralen photosensitisers are available that vary in their characteristics.

EBM

TREATMENT OF PSORIASIS—phototherapy

'RCTs show that oral PUVA therapy clears chronic plaque psoriasis in > 75% of patients. Clearance rates and the length of remission following PUVA are similar to those obtained with inpatient treatment with the Ingram's dithranol regimen. RCTs show that TL01 UVB phototherapy twice weekly is less effective at inducing clearance of psoriasis and produces a shorter remission than oral PUVA given twice weekly.'

- Gordon PM, Diffey BL, Matthews JN, Farr PM. A randomized comparison of narrow-band TL-01 phototherapy and PUVA photochemotherapy for psoriasis. J Am Acad Dermatol 1999; 41:728–732.
- Parrish JA, Fitzpatrick TB, Tanenbaum L, Pathak MA. Photochemotherapy of psoriasis with oral methoxsalen and longwave ultraviolet light. N Engl J Med 1974; 291:1207–1211.

Systemic treatment

Three main systemic agents are used for the management of patients with severe psoriasis: methotrexate, oral retinoids and ciclosporin.

Methotrexate. Methotrexate has been available for the last 40 years and can be very useful therapeutically. In dermatological practice it is administered once a week at much lower doses than those used in haematology. It seems likely that its mechanism of action involves a cytostatic effect on the immune system rather than a primary effect on keratinocyte or epidermal hyperproliferation. The main hazards of methotrexate are that it is an immunosuppressive, may dangerously depress the white cell count without careful monitoring, and in the long term is associated with hepatic fibrosis and potentially cirrhosis, particularly if individuals continue to drink alcohol. Liver biopsies are required in many if not all patients.

Oral retinoids. Oral retinoids such as acitretin are also effective in some patients with psoriasis. They tend to be particularly effective in pustular psoriasis of the palms and soles but are widely used to improve plaque psoriasis. The drugs do not appear to have a quick mode of action but are often combined with other therapies including PUVA treatment. There are some theoretical reasons for arguing that retinoids may diminish the chances of skin neoplasia and these are often employed to justify their use in individuals receiving PUVA. Systemic retinoids are potent teratogens and following use of acitretin pregnancy is not safe for at least 2 years.

Ciclosporin. Ciclosporin was the first of a number of potent immunosuppressives to find a role in the management of a minority of patients with psoriasis. Unfortunately, these agents are known not to be active topically in psoriasis (at least not in clinical practice) and therefore their oral use carries considerable risks in terms of nephrotoxicity and the potential for elevated risks of neoplasia, particularly of the cervix and skin and lymphoma. Despite ciclosporin being effective in inducing and maintaining clearance of individuals with psoriasis continuous use of this drug will be difficult to justify in the vast majority of patients. Long-term surveillance data are not available in this particular patient group.

Intensive inpatient care

Intensive inpatient treatment with dithranol or tar is less common than previously. In many parts of the world this is because beds for management of patients with skin disease are not available to the same degree that they once were. Ingram's regimen will produce clearance in 80% of psoriatics in 3 weeks. Such a regimen still remains the gold standard in terms of both efficacy and safety. Set against this is the fact that many individuals are reluctant to come into hospital for such a period of time. The balancing of risk between known safe inpatient treatments and potentially more toxic outpatient treatments still gives cause for concern.

LICHEN PLANUS

Lichen planus is a rash characterised by intensely itchy polygonal papules with a violaceous hue involving the skin and less commonly the mucosae, hair and nails.

Aetiology

The cause is unknown but an immune pathogenesis is suspected as there is an association with some autoimmune diseases such as myasthenia gravis (see p. 1183), and with thymoma and graft-versus-host disease. Rashes with clinical and histological features of lichen planus can occur in chronic active hepatitis, hepatitis B and C infections, and in patients taking drugs, the most common culprits being gold and other heavy metals, sulphonamides, penicillamine, antimalarials, antituberculous drugs and thiazide diuretics. They also occur in those handling colour developers.

Pathology

There is hyperkeratosis, a prominent granular layer, basal cell degeneration and a heavy T lymphocyte infiltration in the upper dermis. Degenerating basal cells may form colloid (apoptotic) bodies. The T cell–basal cell interaction leaves a 'sawtooth' dermo-epidermal junction. The picture suggests an immune reaction to an unknown epidermal antigen.

Clinical features

Lichen planus tends to start on the distal limbs, most commonly the volar aspects of the wrists (see Fig. 21.17), and the lower back. Intensely itchy, flat-topped, pink-purplish papules appear and some develop a characteristic fine white network on their surface (Wickham's striae). New lesions may appear at the site of trauma (Köbner phenomenon) and the rash may spread rapidly to become generalised. Individual lesions may last for many months and the eruption as a whole tends to last about 1 year, often leaving marked post-inflammatory pigmentation. Mucous membrane involvement, comprising an asymptomatic fine

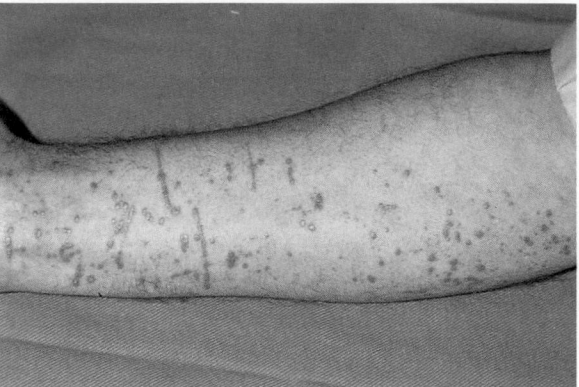

Fig. 21.17 Lichen planus. Glistening discrete papules involving the volar aspects of the forearm and wrist. Note the lesions along scratch marks (Köbner phenomenon).

white lacy network or pinhead-sized white papules, occurs in about two-thirds of patients (see p. 1050). The nails are usually normal but in 10% they may be affected, with changes ranging from longitudinal grooving to destruction of the nail fold and bed. Variants of the classic picture are rare but often challenging diagnostically. They include annular, atrophic, bullous, follicular, hypertrophic and ulcerative types.

Diagnosis

This is usually clear-cut clinically but a skin biopsy can be helpful. Other erythematous scaly conditions should be considered in the differential diagnosis, including guttate psoriasis, pityriasis rosea, pityriasis lichenoides and drug eruptions.

Management

The condition is usually self-limiting, although rarely, particularly with oral lichen planus, it may persist for more than 10 years. Potent local corticosteroids may help with intense itch but systemic corticosteroids may be indicated. Topical corticosteroids applied to the buccal mucosa may also be required. A variety of other therapies have been used including ciclosporin, retinoids and phototherapy.

ISSUES IN OLDER PEOPLE
PRACTICAL PROBLEMS OF INFLAMMATORY SKIN DISEASE

- Quality of life is affected due to distress and discomfort.
- Skin disease is potentially more life-endangering in the elderly: for example, erythroderma.
- Skin disease is cosmetically unattractive, causing depression and increased social isolation.
- Irritation, soreness and itching cause sleep disturbance and increasing confusion.
- Older people may be reluctant to seek help because they are anxious that they may be perceived as not coping.
- Older people may have difficulty administering topical treatments, e.g. opening jars and tubes and applying creams during bathing; there is an increased risk of slipping in an oily bath.
- They have less access to information on skin care.

DISORDERS OF THE PILOSEBACEOUS UNIT

ACNE VULGARIS

Acne is almost ubiquitous in the teenage years, differences between individuals being a matter of severity of disease and facility with which scarring develops. Peak severity is in the late teenage years but acne may persist into the third decade and beyond, particularly in females. The main clinical issues relate to under-treatment and lack of clinical interest or insight into the patient's condition.

Aetiology

There are three pathogenetic factors (see Fig. 21.18):

- The first is elevated sebum excretion. There is a clear relation between severity of acne and sebum excretion rate. In the complete absence of sebum acne does not occur. The converse, however, is not true; acne may improve in the third and fourth decades despite a high sebum excretion. Sebum excretion is therefore necessary for the development of acne but is not sufficient to cause acne on its own. The main determinants of sebum excretion are hormonal, accounting for the onset of acne in the teenage years. Androgens are the principal sebotrophic hormones but progestogens also increase sebum excretion whilst oestrogens reduce it. In the absence of other clinical features or frank virilism the vast majority of patients with acne have a completely normal circulating endocrine profile.
- The second factor in the pathogenesis of acne is infection with *Propionibacterium acnes*. This bacterium colonises the pilosebaceous ducts and acts on lipids to produce a number of proinflammatory factors.
- The third factor is occlusion or blockage of the pilosebaceous unit.

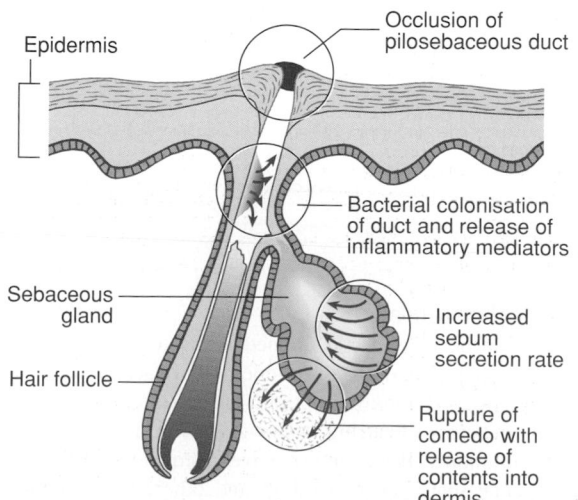

Fig. 21.18   The pathogenesis of acne.

Whilst there is some evidence for a familial component for sebum excretion the genetics and epidemiology of acne are poorly understood.

Clinical features

Lesions are usually limited to the face, shoulders, upper chest and back. Seborrhoea (greasy skin) is often clinically obvious. Open comedones (blackheads) due to plugging by keratin and sebum of the pilosebaceous orifice, or closed comedones (whiteheads) due to accretions of sebum and keratin deeper in the pilosebaceous ducts, are usually evident. Inflammatory papules, nodules and cysts occur (see Fig. 21.19A), with one or two types of lesion predominating. Scarring may follow.

There are a number of descriptive terms applied to clinical variants of acne. Conglobate acne refers to severe acne with many abscesses and cysts, marked scarring and sinus formation. Acne fulminans refers to the presence of severe acne accompanied by fever, joint pains and markers of systemic inflammation such as a raised ESR. Acne excoriée refers to the effects of scratching or picking, principally on the face of teenage girls with acne. Infantile acne is rare and is thought to be due to the sebotrophic effects of maternal hormones on the infant.

A mild form of acne dominated by the presence of comedones may be due to exogenous substances such as tars, chlorinated hydrocarbons or oily cosmetics. A primarily

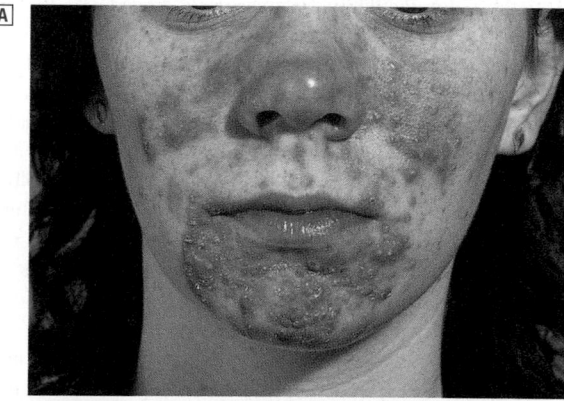
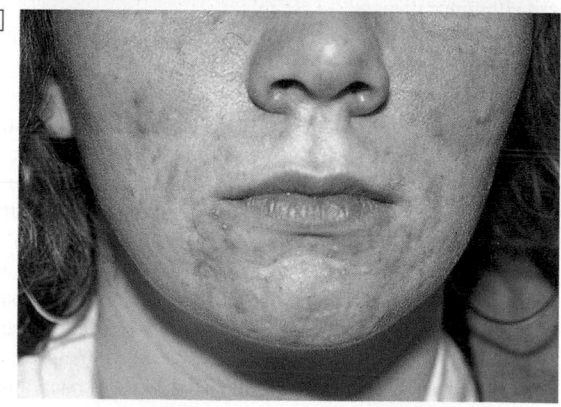

Fig. 21.19   Unpleasant cystic acne in a teenager. A Before treatment. B After prolonged systemic antibiotic treatment.

pustular rash may also be seen in those being treated with corticosteroids, lithium, oral contraceptives and anticonvulsants. These forms of acne are usually clinically distinct from the usual variety developing in adolescence.

Individuals with moderate or even severe acne very rarely have any other systemic illness. However, individuals with polycystic ovary syndrome (see p. 712) are more likely to have severe acne and clinical hints—for instance, from menstrual irregularities—require investigation. If there is associated cutaneous virilism or other features of an androgen-secreting tumour, further investigations and expert endocrinological assessment are warranted.

Investigations

Investigations are rarely required. It is important, however, to enquire about the details of previous treatments and particularly about the duration of previous therapies; for example, antibiotics are commonly prescribed for too short periods of time. It is also necessary to understand the patient's expectations and to determine how realistic they are.

Management

The therapy of acne was revolutionised with the advent of systemic retinoids and is now more straightforward and rewarding. In individuals with fairly minor disease, particularly those dominated by the presence of comedones, topical agents such as benzoyl peroxide or tretinoin should be used. Both these substances have irritant activities, a factor which may be important in their therapeutic effect, and instructions need to be given as to how to use them. They may initially be applied for short intervals of time and the strength and duration gradually increased. Although a number of other topical remedies, including washes, soaps and antiseptics, are recommended, evidence for their effectiveness is not convincing. Patients with anything but minor degrees of acne will require therapy with antibiotics, either systemic or local. Local antibiotics (clindamycin or erythromycin) are used more widely than previously; many might consider their use prior to systemic antibiotics or in persons with relatively minor disease.

The principal oral antibiotic is oxytetracycline, taken on an empty stomach not with food, and given in a dose of up to 1.5 g a day if tolerated. In general, oxytetracycline has a good safety profile even with long-term use. Minocycline may be used if the response to oxytetracycline is inadequate or because of the ease of dosing. It is, however, associated with autoimmune hepatitis and remains a second- rather than first-choice drug.

Before an antibiotic is deemed not to have worked the individual must be treated continuously for up to 3 months. If after 3 months there is little response to oxytetracycline the patient should be changed to erythromycin up to 1 g per day in divided doses. Patients need to remain under review. In women, oestrogen-containing oral contraceptives can be a useful adjunct in therapy. There is a small reduction in sebum secretion with oral oestrogens. The addition of an oral anti-oestrogen, cyproterone acetate, is occasionally used in doses of 50–100 mg daily on days 5–14 of the cycle to enhance the effects of sebum reduction. If these topical and systemic agents fail to produce a sufficient clinical response within 3–6 months the patient should be referred for specialist opinion and consideration for treatment with isotretinoin (13 cis-retinoic acid).

Isotretinoin has revolutionised the treatment of severe acne or moderate acne in patients unresponsive to other therapy. When used at a dose of 0.5–1 mg/kg this drug inhibits sebum excretion by > 90% over 4 months. Although sebum excretion gradually returns to normal over the course of the year after the drug is stopped, the clinical benefit is prolonged for much longer. Many patients with acne will not require any further treatment for their acne but in a minority a second course of isotretinoin may be required.

Side-effects, especially drying of the skin and mucous membranes, are common but well tolerated and relate to the drug's effects on the function of modified sebaceous glands on the lips, and on lipid biosynthesis in interfollicular epidermis. Rarely, abnormalities of liver function occur and limit treatment. Isotretinoin may elevate serum triglycerides and levels should be checked before therapy and monitored during therapy. Depression and indeed suicide have been reported, although the role of the drug is difficult to disentangle from the role of the underlying disease; it is currently under investigation. The major consideration before the drug is prescribed is that, like all systemic retinoids, isotretinoin is highly teratogenic; females must have a negative pregnancy test before treatment and be on effective contraception for at least a month before the course begins, during the course and for 1 month after it finishes.

EBM

ACNE VULGARIS—use of retinoids

'Studies of the use of topical and systemic retinoids in acne vulgaris have shown that (1) adapalene is more rapid in onset and better tolerated than tretinoin in mild to moderate acne; (2) oral isotretinoin is clinically better and more cost-effective in moderate and severe acne.'

- Wessels F, Anderson AN, Kropman K. The cost-effectiveness of isotretinoin in the treatment of acne. Part 1. A meta-analysis of effectiveness literature. S Afr Med J 1999; 89:780–784.
- Cunliffe WJ, Poncet M, Loesche C, Verschoore M. A comparison of the efficacy and tolerability of adapalene 0.1% gel versus tretinoin 0.025% gel in patients with acne vulgaris: a meta-analysis of five randomised trials. Br J Dermatol 1998; 139:48–56.

Physical measures

Cysts can be incised and drained under local anaesthetic. Intralesional injections of triamcinolone acetonide (0.1–0.2 ml of a 10 mg/ml solution) hasten the resolution of stubborn cysts. Scarring following acne is seen a lot less commonly if patients receive adequate care. Small, deep acne scars can be excised and other forms of more extensive but shallower scars can be treated by carbon dioxide laser.

also shows some efficacy in rosacea, although it may cause irritation. The erythema and telangiectasia do not respond to antibiotic therapy.

SOME COMMON SKIN INFECTIONS AND INFESTATIONS

FUNGAL INFECTION OF THE SKIN (RINGWORM)

Dermatophytes are fungi capable of causing skin infections known as ringworm or dermatophytosis. The causative fungi belong to three genera (*Microsporum*, *Trichophyton*, *Epidermophyton*); they can originate from the soil (geophilic) or animals (zoophilic), or be confined to human skin (anthropophilic).

Clinical forms of cutaneous infection include tinea corporis (involvement of the body), tinea capitis (scalp involvement, see p. 1069), tinea cruris (groin involvement) and tinea pedis (involvement of the feet). Fungal infection of the nails (onychomycosis) is dealt with on page 1089.

Tinea corporis
The clinical features of tinea corporis are variable and so this condition should be considered in the differential diagnosis of the red scaly rash (see p. 1059). Classically, the lesions are erythematous, annular and scaly, with a well-defined edge and often central clearing. They may be single or multiple and are usually asymmetrical. The degree of associated inflammation depends on the causative fungus and host immunity. *Microsporum canis* and *Trichophyton verrucosum* are common culprits and are zoophilic (from dogs and cattle respectively). Inadvertent topical steroid application leads to worsening of the signs (tinea incognito).

Tinea cruris
This common world-wide ringworm affects the groin and is usually caused by *Trichophyton rubrum*. Itchy erythematous plaques extend from the groin flexures on to the thighs.

Tinea pedis (athlete's foot)
This is the most common form of ringworm in the UK and USA and is usually caused by anthropophilic fungi such as *Trichophyton rubrum*, *Trichophyton mentagrophytes* and *Epidermophyton floccosum*. Clinical features are an itchy rash between the toes, with peeling, fissuring and maceration. Involvement of one sole or palm (in the case of tinea manuum) with a fine scaling is characteristic of *T. rubrum* infection. Vesiculation or frank blistering is more commonly seen with *T. mentagrophytes*.

Diagnosis
In all cases of suspected dermatophyte infection, the diagnosis should be confirmed by skin scraping or nail clippings (see p. 1055).

Treatment
Treatment can be topical (terbinafine or miconazole cream) or systemic (terbinafine, griseofulvin or itraconazole).

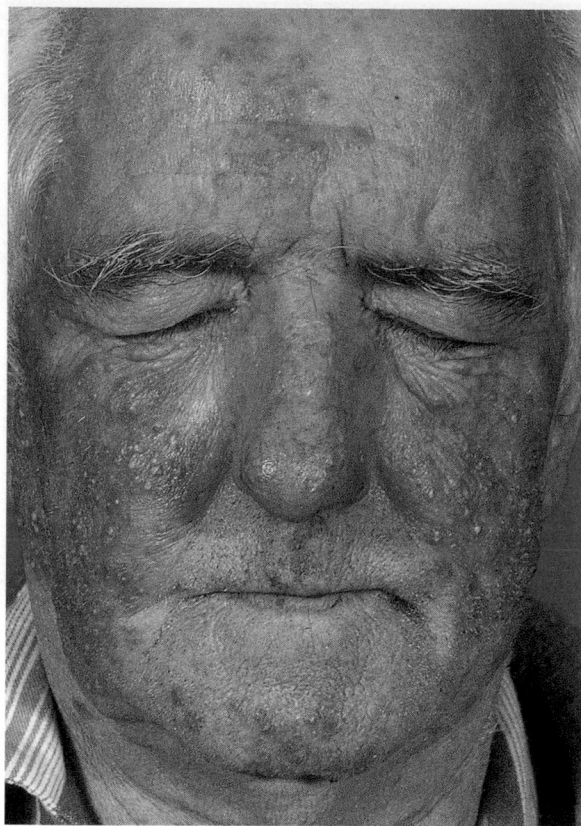

Fig. 21.20 Rosacea. The colour is distinctive and the papulo-pustular rash involves the cheeks, centre of forehead and chin.

ROSACEA

Rosacea is a persistent facial eruption of unknown cause characterised by erythema and pustules. Sebum secretion is normal.

Clinical features
The disorder is most common in middle age. The cheeks, chin and central forehead are affected (see Fig. 21.20). Intermittent blushing is followed by fixed erythema and telangiectasia. Dome-shaped papules and pustules but no comedones occur. Rhinophyma, with erythema, sebaceous gland hyperplasia and overgrowth of the soft tissues of the nose, is sometimes associated. Blepharitis and conjunctivitis are complications.

Diagnosis
This is often obvious on clinical grounds but acne, seborrhoeic eczema, photosensitivity and systemic lupus erythematosus must be distinguished.

Management
The pustular component of rosacea normally responds very well to oral oxytetracycline. Once the disease is controlled (usually within a few months) the dose can be diminished but some individuals may need to stay on the antibiotics long-term or require repeated courses. Topical metronidazole

PAPILLOMAVIRUSES AND VIRAL WARTS

Viral warts are extremely common and most people suffer from one or more at some point during their life. Genital warts occur most commonly during the sexually active years. Warts are a result of infection with the DNA human papillomavirus (HPV), of which there are over 90 subtypes on the basis of DNA sequence analysis. Different subtypes appear to be responsible for several different clinical wart variants but this is not of great practical importance in terms of skin wart therapy.

Transmission is by direct contact with the virus, in either living skin or fragments of shed skin, and is encouraged by trauma and moisture (e.g. in swimming pools, fishmongers etc.). Genital warts, usually due to specific HPV subtypes, are spread by sexual activity, and show a clear relationship with cervical and intraepithelial cancers of the genital area. In particular, HPV 16 and 18 appear to be able to inactivate tumour suppressor gene pathways and lead to squamous cell carcinoma of the cervix or intraepithelial carcinoma of the genital skin. In contrast with genital warts, the relation between HPV of the skin and subsequent skin cancer remains unclear. Individuals who are systemically immunosuppressed, such as those who have received organ transplants, show greatly elevated risks of skin cancer and also a much higher prevalence of infection with HPV. What remains unclear is whether HPV is causally involved in the development of neoplasia or merely reflects the underlying systemic immunosuppression.

Clinical features

Common warts appear initially as smooth, skin-coloured papules. As they enlarge their surface becomes irregular and hyperkeratotic, producing the typical warty appearance. They are most common on the hands but may also be seen on the face, genitalia and sun-exposed surfaces of the arm and leg. Multiple warts are common. Plantar warts (verrucae) are characterised by a rough surface protruding only slightly from the skin and are surrounded by a horny collar. On paring, the presence of capillary loops distinguishes these plantar warts from corns. Plantar warts may be painful and disabling.

Other varieties of wart include mosaic warts (mosaic-like plaques of tightly packed individual warts—see Fig. 21.21); plane warts (smooth, flat-top papules seen most commonly on the face and backs of hands which frequently may hyperpigment and consequently be misdiagnosed); facial warts (often filiform); and genital warts which may be papillomatous and protuberant.

Management

Viral warts will, in the vast majority of normal individuals, resolve spontaneously. However, this may take several years and there is often considerable pressure for treatment. The majority of treatments are based on destruction of keratinocytes, irrespective of whether they are HPV-infected or not. Despite the frequency of the condition, there is a paucity of randomised trials looking at the effectiveness of the various treatments or at the order in which they are used.

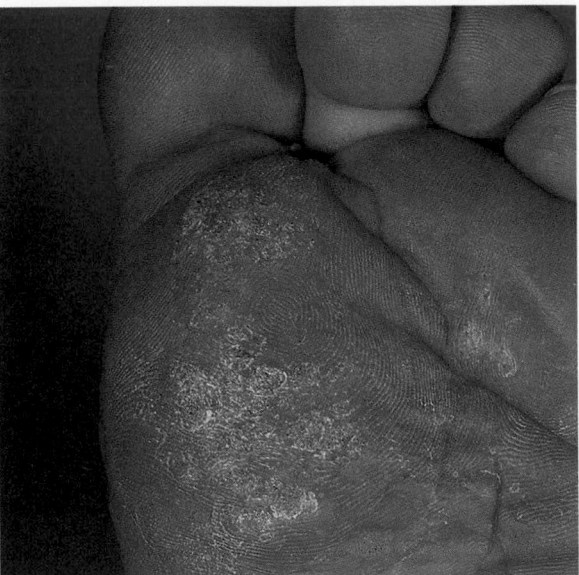

Fig. 21.21   Mosaic plantar wart. A plaque of closely grouped warts on the sole of the foot.

Most practitioners would try to avoid treating warts that are asymptomatic or not causing distress. Initial treatment should be with salicylic acid or salicylic and lactic acid combinations, together with frequent and regular paring of the hyperkeratotic skin. Such treatment needs to continue for at least several months before convincing effects will be apparent. If it fails, or as an alternative, warts can be treated by cryotherapy using liquid nitrogen. Such therapy is, at some sites and in particular individuals, accompanied by significant pain, and will need to be repeated at intervals of 2–4 weeks, although the optimum strategy is not defined. Over-aggressive treatment with cryotherapy, particularly on the hands, can lead to significant complications including tendon rupture and a high morbidity over the ensuing days. Warts close to or under the nails can be a particular problem. Liquid nitrogen treatment may exacerbate them (due to inflammatory swelling), and skilled cutting of the nail and electrodesiccation, or other destructive therapy, may be necessary.

Viral warts can be a particular problem in individuals who are immunosuppressed following organ transplantation. The prevalence of warts in this group approaches 100% after 5 years and therapy appears less effective than in immunocompetent individuals. In the immunosuppressed not only are warts particularly unsightly, but painful verrucae can limit mobility and require intensive treatments. Individuals who have received large amounts of psoralen and UVA (PUVA) for their psoriasis also show an elevated prevalence of viral wart infection.

Beyond the treatments mentioned above, a number of other treatments have been claimed to be effective in some individuals and in particular clinical contexts; these include systemic retinoids, intralesional injections of bleomycin or interferon, and the application of contact sensitisers such as diphencyprone or dinitrochlorobenzene to the warts. The immunomodulator, imiquimod, is useful in treating stubborn anogenital warts (see p. 105).

SCABIES

Scabies is caused by the acarus, *Sarcoptes scabiei*, and is a common world-wide public health problem with an estimated global prevalence of 300 million. The infestation causes considerable discomfort and can lead to secondary infection and complications such as post-streptococcal glomerulonephritis. Scabies spreads in households and environments where there is a high frequency of intimate personal contact. Diagnosis is made by identifying the scabietic burrow, usually found on the edges of the fingers, toes or sides of the hands and feet. Extraction of the mite using a blunt needle can be difficult but is helpful in ensuring the correct diagnosis, appropriate treatment and compliance. Inappropriate application of scabietic treatments can cause considerable irritation in other conditions. In small children the palms and soles can be involved with pustule formation (see Fig. 21.22). Involvement of the genital area in boys is pathognomonic. The main symptom is itch (see p. 1058). The clinical features include secondary eczematisation elsewhere on the body; the face and scalp are never involved

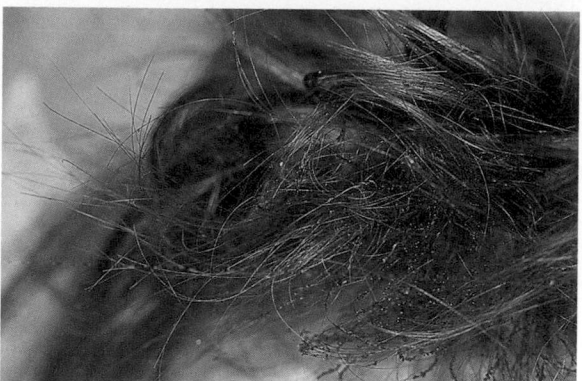

Fig. 21.23   Head lice. 'Nits' (empty egg cases) adhere strongly to the hair shafts.

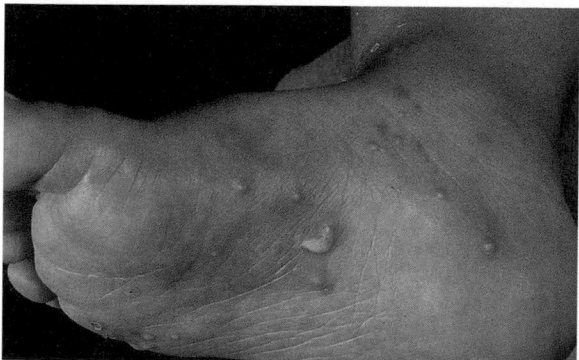

Fig. 21.22   Scabies. Pustules at a common site in a child. Burrows were present but cannot be seen at this distance.

except in the case of infants. Even after successful treatment the itch can continue, and occasionally nodular lesions persist.

Topical treatment of scabies is usual and involves the affected individual and all asymptomatic family members/physical contacts to ensure eradication. Two applications one week apart of an aqueous solution of either permethrin or malathion to the whole body, excluding the head, is usually successful. In some clinical situations such as poor compliance, immunocompromised individuals and heavy infestations (Norwegian scabies), systemic treatment with ivermectin (200 µg/kg) as a single dose would be appropriate.

LICE

Head lice (Pediculosis capitis)

Infestation with head louse, *Pediculus humanus capitis*, is common and highly contagious. Head lice are spread by direct head-to-head contact. Itching of the scalp is the main symptom; scratching leads to secondary infection and cervical lymphadenopathy. The diagnosis is confirmed by identifying the living louse or nymph on the scalp or on a black

sheet of paper after careful fine-toothed combing of wet hair that has had conditioner applied. The empty egg cases ('nits') are easily seen along the hair shaft (see Fig. 21.23). These are characteristically difficult to dislodge.

Treatment is recommended for the infected individual and any infected household/school contacts. Eradication in school populations has proved difficult and it is likely that this is due to compliance as well as resistance to certain treatments. The standard pharmacological treatments for head lice are malathion, permethrin and carbaryl in a lotion or aqueous formulation, which are applied on two separate occasions at 7–10 days' interval. Many health boards advise rotational treatments within a community to avoid resistance. Regular 'wet-combing' (physical removal of the live lice by regular combing of slippery, conditioned wet hair) does not seem to be as effective as pharmacological treatments.

Involvement of the eyebrows/eyelashes is best treated by topical Vaseline twice daily for at least a fortnight.

Crab lice (Pthirus pubis)

These are usually sexually acquired, with pruritus as the main symptom. An aqueous-based treatment of either malathion or carbaryl is the treatment of choice. This should be applied on two occasions to the whole body as body hair can also be infested. Contacts should also be treated.

PRESSURE SORES

Pressure sores are caused by prolonged pressure-induced ischaemia, when the interface pressure between the patient's body and its supporting surface exceeds capillary closing pressure. Up to 5% of patients over 70 years old in hospital develop pressure sores, but this may rise to 30% in those with a fractured neck of femur. The morbidity and mortality of those with deep ulcers are high.

Aetiology

The main risk factors for pressure sores include:

● *immobility*, e.g. coma, neurological disease with paralysis, surgery, pain, over-use of sedatives, depression

- *hypotension*, e.g. shock, dehydration
- *reduced oxygen availability*, e.g. anaemia, fever, infection
- *peripheral vascular disease*, including diabetic microangiopathy
- *malnutrition*, e.g. malignant cachexia, alcoholism
- *skin condition*, e.g. atrophy due to age or steroids, dry/cracked and moist/chapped condition.

Clinical features

The sore starts as a localised area of erythema and progresses to a superficial blister or erosion. If the cause is not corrected, deeper damage occurs; a black eschar develops which, when removed or shed, leaves a deep and penetrating ulcer, often colonised by *Pseudomonas aeruginosa*. The skin overlying bony prominences, such as the sacrum, greater trochanter, ischial tuberosity, calcaneal tuberosity and lateral malleolus, is especially susceptible.

Management

This is not easy but the following are important:

- prevention by regular repositioning of immobile patients and pressure-reducing mattresses in those at high risk
- treatment of risk factors including malnutrition
- débridement of necrotic tissue either by surgery or by enzymatic necrolysis
- systemic antibiotics for spreading infection
- dressings to keep the wound wet and enhance granulation (see ulcers, p. 1067); regular cleansing with normal saline or 0.5% aqueous silver nitrate; semi-permeable dressings such as OpSite
- consideration of plastic surgical reconstruction when the ulcer is clean.

DISORDERS OF PIGMENTATION

DECREASED PIGMENTATION

OCULOCUTANEOUS ALBINISM

Albinism results from a range of genetic abnormalities leading to reduced melanin biosynthesis in skin and eyes but where the number of melanocytes is normal. It differs from cutaneous hypopigmentation in that there is, by definition, ocular involvement. There are a number of different forms of albinism, and considerable variation even within one genetic type. Albinism is usually inherited as an autosomal recessive trait. Type 1 albinism is due to a defect in the tyrosinase gene whose product is rate-limiting in the production of melanin. Such individuals at birth have an almost complete absence of pigment in the skin and hair with a resulting pale skin and white hair, and also failure of melanin production in the eye, in the iris and retina. Patients have photophobia, poor vision not correctable with refraction, rotatory nystagmus, and an alternating strabismus associated with abnormalities in the decussation of nerve fibres in the optic tract. A second form of albinism is due to a defect in the P gene which encodes an ion channel protein in the melanosome. Like type 1 albinos patients may have a gross reduction of melanin in the skin and in the eyes, but may be more mildly affected than some type 1 albinos. Establishing the subtype of albinism requires genetic analysis as there is considerable heterogeneity in the phenotype of the various subtypes (it is not always easy to guess the type of albinism).

Oculocutaneous albinos are at grossly increased risk of sunburn and skin cancer. In Equatorial regions many albinos will die from squamous cell carcinoma or melanoma in early adult life. Albinos may, however, show pigmented melanocytic naevi and may freckle in response to sun damage. There are other extremely rare forms of albinism such as rufous and brown albinism.

Management

Avoidance of sun exposure is important, and may involve protective clothing, hats and an alteration of lifestyle if possible to avoid the midday sun in particular and to pursue indoor rather than outdoor work. Sunblocks may also be useful but can be prohibitively expensive. Early diagnosis and treatment of skin tumours are essential.

VITILIGO

Vitiligo is an acquired condition in which circumscribed depigmented patches develop; it affects 1% of the population world-wide.

Aetiology

Unlike albinism, where melanocytes are present but the production of melanin is abnormal, vitiligo involves focal areas of melanocyte loss. There may be a positive family history of the disorder in those with generalised vitiligo and this type is associated with autoimmune diseases such as diabetes, thyroid and adrenal disorders, and pernicious anaemia. Trauma and sunburn may precipitate the appearance of vitiligo. A number of hypotheses have been advanced to explain the pathogenesis, none of which is entirely satisfactory. One popular theory is that the melanocytes are the target of a cell-mediated autoimmune attack. Why only focal areas are affected remains unexplained.

Clinical features

Segmental vitiligo is restricted to one part of the body, but not necessarily a dermatome. Generalised vitiligo (see Fig. 21.24) is often symmetrical and frequently involves the hands, wrists, knees and neck as well as the area around the body orifices. The hair of the scalp and beard may also depigment. The patches of depigmentation are sharply defined and, in Caucasians, may be surrounded by light brown 'café au lait' hyperpigmentation. Some spotty perifollicular pigment may be seen within the depigmented patches and is sometimes the first sign of repigmentation. Sensation in the depigmented patches is normal (compare tuberculoid leprosy, p. 87). The course is unpredictable but most patches remain static or enlarge; a few repigment spontaneously.

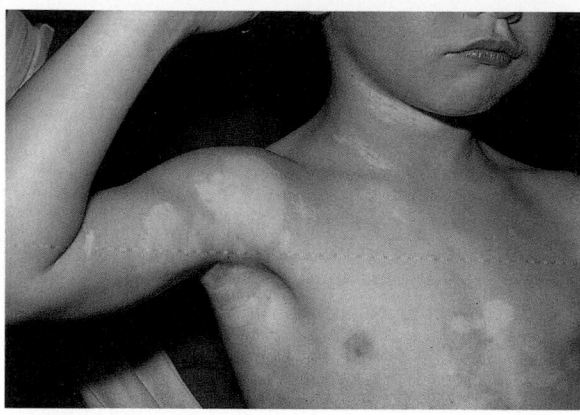

Fig. 21.24   Vitiligo. Widespread patches in a youngster with a strong family history of autoimmune diseases.

21.25 DRUG-INDUCED PIGMENTATION	
Drug	**Appearance**
Amiodarone	Slate-grey, exposed sites
Arsenic	Diffuse bronze pigmentation with superimposed raindrop depigmentation
Bleomycin	Often flexural, brown
Busulfan	Diffuse brown
Chloroquine	Blue-grey, exposed sites
Clofazimine	Red
Mepacrine	Yellow
Minocycline	Slate-grey, scars, temples, shins and sclera
Phenothiazines	Slate-grey, exposed sites
Psoralens	Brown, exposed sites

Management

This is unsatisfactory. Protecting the patches from excessive sun exposure by clothing or sunscreen may be helpful in reducing episodes of burning and potentially of skin cancer in the long term. Camouflage cosmetics may also be helpful, particularly in those with dark skin. Phototherapy with PUVA or more recently TL01 phototherapy has been used. Although repigmentation may occur during phototherapy, there is an absence of randomised controlled trials to inform clinical practice. PUVA therapy in particular has been widely used but because it increases pigmentation in normal skin, except in very dark-skinned individuals, the cosmetic effect may actually be worse than without treatment. When depigmentation occurs it is frequently as small foci of dark areas of skin surrounding hair follicles within the vitiliginous area. The absence of whiteness of the hairs in the area of vitiligo is a good prognostic feature.

PHENYLKETONURIA

This rare metabolic cause of hypopigmentation has a prevalence of about 1:25 000.

HYPOPITUITARISM

Hypopigmentation is due to decreased production of pituitary melanotrophic hormones (see p. 736). The complexion has a pale, yellow tinge; there is skin atrophy and thinning or loss of the sexual hair.

INCREASED PIGMENTATION

This is mostly due to hypermelanosis but other pigments may occasionally be deposited in the skin. Orange discoloration may suggest carotenaemia; a bronze colour, haemochromatosis (see p. 870); and other hues, drug eruptions (see Box 21.25).

LOCALISED HYPERMELANOSIS

Freckles

These lesions, also known as ephelides, are sharply demarcated light brown-ginger macules of up to 5 mm in diameter. They are most prominent on exposed sites; they multiply and become darker with sun exposure. The melanin in the basal cell layer of the epidermis is increased without melanocytic proliferation.

Lentigines

These are dark brown macules ranging from 1 mm to 1 cm across. Although discrete, their outline may be irregular. Lentigines occur in childhood but are most common after middle age on the backs of the hands ('liver spots') and on the face. They have an increased number of melanocytes which produce excessive melanin.

Multiple lentigines are seen on and around the lips, buccal mucosa and fingers in the Peutz–Jeghers syndrome (associated with small intestinal polyposis and intussusception—see p. 822).

DIFFUSE HYPERMELANOSIS

Endocrine pigmentation

Chloasma describes discrete patches of facial pigmentation which occur in pregnancy and in some women taking oral contraceptives. Diffuse pigmentation, sometimes worse in the skin creases, may be a feature of Addison's disease (see p. 726), Cushing's syndrome (see p. 721), Nelson's syndrome and chronic renal failure (see p. 600). In all of these cases it is due to an increase in the levels of pituitary melanotrophic peptides (see p. 736).

Drug-induced pigmentation

See Box 21.25 for a list of some drugs which may cause hyperpigmentation; this is not always due to hypermelanosis alone but may sometimes be due to deposition of the drug or its metabolite, either of which may be complexed with melanin.

DISORDERS OF THE NAILS

The condition of the nails may reflect both local and systemic disease, and omission of this part of the general examination could result in some important diagnostic clues being overlooked.

The nail plate arises from the nail matrix and lies on the nail bed (see Fig. 21.25). The keratinous plate is produced by cells of the matrix and, to a much lesser extent, the bed. Finger nails grow about 1 cm every 3 months and toe nails at about one-third of this rate.

NAIL FOLD DISORDERS

Examination of the nail folds should accompany examination of the nails. Paronychia describes inflamed and swollen nail folds. Chronic paronychia is seen most commonly in those with a poor peripheral circulation, in those involved in wet work, in diabetics and in those who are over-enthusiastic when manicuring their cuticles. Ragged cuticles and dilated or

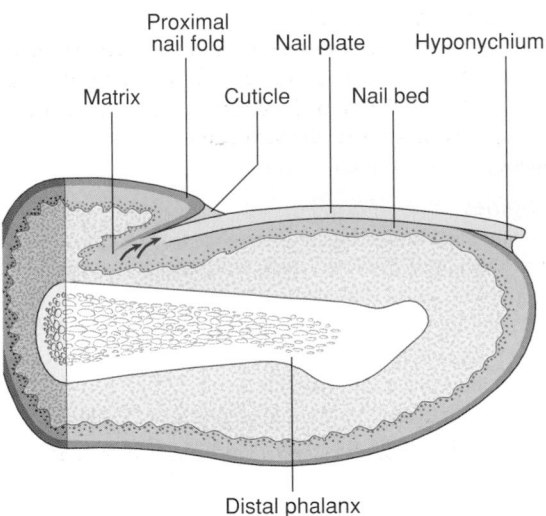

Fig. 21.25   The nail plate and bed.

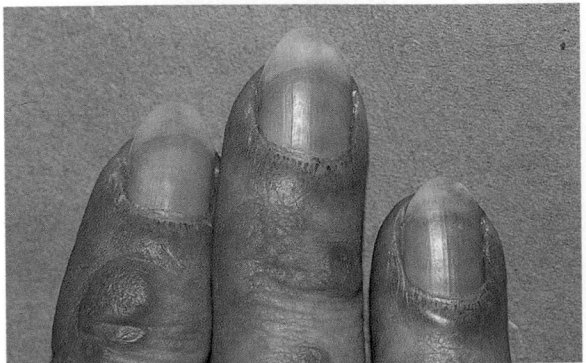

Fig. 21.26   Dermatomyositis. The erythema, dilated and tortuous capillaries in the proximal nail fold and the Gottron's papules on the digits are important diagnostic features (see p. 1038).

thrombosed capillaries in the proximal nail folds are important pointers to connective tissue disease (see Fig. 21.26).

NAIL PLATE DISORDERS

These may be isolated abnormalities due to congenital disease or trauma, or may reflect other diseases, either systemic or just involving the skin. Longitudinal ridging and beading of the nail plate is not abnormal and increases with age. Similarly, occasional white transverse flecks (striate leuconychia) are seen frequently in normal nails and are due to airspaces within the plate and not, contrary to popular belief, to insufficient calcium.

CONGENITAL DISEASE

Pachyonychia congenita is a rare autosomal dominant condition. Some families have been shown to have mutations in keratins. The nails are grossly thickened, especially at the free edge, and discoloured from birth.

TRAUMA

Splinter haemorrhages
These are fine linear dark brown flecks running longitudinally in the plate. They are most commonly due to trauma but may be seen in nail psoriasis. They are also a sign of subacute bacterial endocarditis (see p. 464).

Subungual haematomas
These may appear as a crimson, purple or grey-brown discoloration of the nail plate, most frequently that of the big toe (see Fig. 21.27). Sometimes, but not always, there is a history of trauma. The abnormality appears suddenly and the nail folds remain uninvolved (cf. subungual malignant melanoma, p. 1094). As the nail grows out, a normally coloured band develops proximally.

Habit-tic dystrophy
This is common, and is due to the habit of picking or fiddling with the proximal nail fold of the thumb. This produces a ladder pattern of transverse ridges and furrows up the centre of the nail.

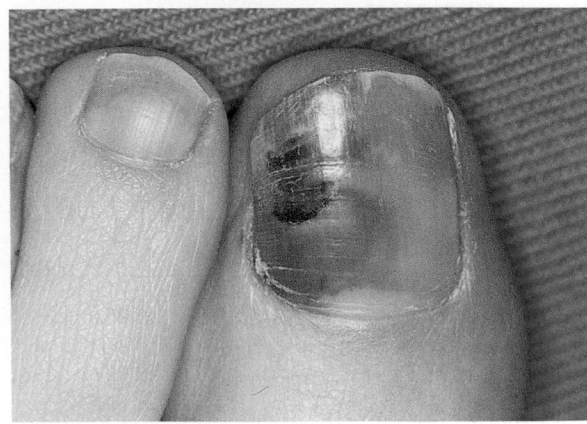

Fig. 21.27   Subungual haematoma.

Chronic trauma

Chronic trauma from ill-fitting shoes and from sport may cause malalignment and thickening of the nails, known as onychogryphosis, and lead to ingrowing toe nails.

THE NAIL IN SYSTEMIC DISEASE

Koilonychia

This is a concave or spoon-shaped deformity of the plate which is a sign of iron deficiency (see Fig. 21.28A). It is seen most often in countries where malnutrition is prevalent.

Beau's lines

These are transverse grooves which appear at the same time on all nails, a few weeks after an acute illness, moving out to the free margins as the nails grow (see Fig. 21.28B).

Digital clubbing

In its most gross form this is seen as a bulbous swelling of the tip of the finger (see Figs 21.28C and D) or toe. The normal angle between the proximal part of the nail and the skin is lost. Causes include:

- *respiratory*—bronchogenic carcinoma, asbestosis (especially with mesothelioma), suppurative lung disease (empyema, bronchiectasis, cystic fibrosis), fibrosing alveolitis
- *cardiac*—cyanotic congenital heart disease, subacute bacterial endocarditis
- *other*—inflammatory bowel disease, biliary cirrhosis, thyrotoxicosis, familial.

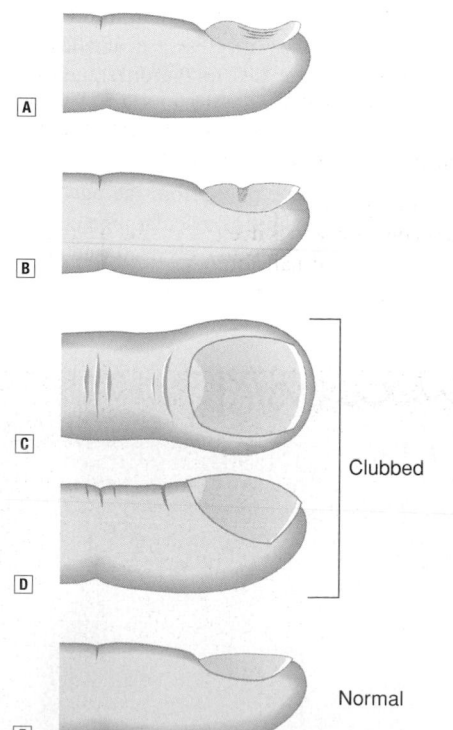

Fig. 21.28 **The nail in systemic disease.** A Koilonychia. B Beau's lines. C and D Digital clubbing. E Normal nail.

Whitening of the nails

This is a rare sign of hypoalbuminaemia. 'Half and half' nails (white proximally and red-brown distally) are seen in some patients with renal failure. Rarely, drugs (e.g. anti-malarials) may discolour nails.

THE NAIL IN SOME COMMON SKIN DISEASES

Psoriasis

This may cause coarse pitting of the nail plate, onycholysis (separation of the nail plate from the nail bed) and subungual hyperkeratosis (see Fig. 21.15, p. 1077).

Eczema

Shiny nails may signify frequent rubbing of eczematous skin elsewhere. When eczema involves the distal phalanges the nail may be deformed, with transverse ridging and thickening of the plate.

Lichen planus and severe alopecia areata

These may cause trachyonychia, a fine roughness and white discoloration of the nail plate.

Dermatophyte infection

This causes yellow-brown discoloration and crumbling of the plate which starts at the free margins and spreads proximally (see Fig. 21.29). Usually only a few nails are infected and frequently only on one foot or hand.

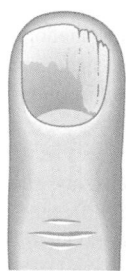

Fig. 21.29 **Dermatophyte infection.** This causes discoloration and crumbliness of the nail plate.

SKIN TUMOURS

The increasing number of patients over 70 years old is paralleled by an increasing incidence of skin cancer. Only the most common benign tumours and a few malignant ones will be described in this section.

BENIGN TUMOURS

MELANOCYTIC NAEVI

Melanocytic naevi (moles) are localised benign proliferations of melanocytes which are probably clonal. Their cause is unknown but may relate to abnormalities of the normal migratory pattern of the melanocytes during development. Moles are a usual feature of most human beings and it is quite normal to have 20–50. The number reflects both genetic and environmental characteristics. Interestingly, a locus close to the P16 gene which has been implicated in some cases of familial melanoma and other familial cancers (pancreas) appears to exert an effect on mole number. Individuals with high sun exposure also show more moles, i.e. there is clear evidence for both genetic and hereditary factors. With the exception of congenital melanocytic naevi (which are present at birth or appear shortly after birth), most melanocytic naevi appear in early childhood, at adolescence, and during pregnancy or oestrogen therapy. New lesions appear less often after the age of 20.

Clinical features

Acquired melanocytic naevi are classified according to the microscopic location of the clumps of melanocytes in the skin (see Fig. 21.30). Junctional naevi are usually circular and macular; their colour ranges from mid- to dark brown and may vary within a single lesion. Compound and intra-dermal naevi are similar to one another in appearance; both are nodules of up to 1 cm in diameter, though intradermal naevi are usually less pigmented than compound naevi. Their surface may be smooth, cerebriform or even hyper-keratotic and papillomatous, and they are often hairy.

Using a variety of different criteria, some naevi have been labelled atypical or dysplastic. Unfortunately, the terms have not been precisely defined and are often used to describe a clinical appearance as well as a histological feature. Such abnormal naevi have been found in some individuals with a dramatically increased risk of melanoma. However, even within these families the abnormal melanocyte phenotype does not clearly segregate with the propensity to melanoma. Such abnormal naevi are often profuse, large and irregularly pigmented and most obvious on the trunk. They may be present on the scalp and the palmar-plantar surfaces as well as the buttocks. Some may appear slightly pinkish and show an inflamed halo. Unfortunately, the clinical significance of individuals with such naevi remains poorly defined; most authorities view these people as being at an increased risk of melanoma but clear criteria for management and follow-up are not available.

Whereas about 30–50% of malignant melanomas develop from melanocytic naevi, the converse is far from true and only a minute percentage of melanocytic naevi become malignant. Malignant change is most likely in large congen-ital melanocytic naevi (where the risk may correlate with the size or mass of the melanocyte lesion) and possibly in those families who have been diagnosed as showing large numbers of atypical naevi with a history of melanoma. Although the skin is open to easy observation, the value of self-examination has not been validated in randomised control trials. A change in a mole may well be a harbinger of melanoma but of course more frequently it is not. In the majority of Caucasian populations, any change in a mole is thought by many to warrant medical opinion (see Box 21.26). Such lesions require careful clinical assessment, remember-ing not only that treatment for all but early melanomas is poor but also that the negative specificity of the clinical assessment of early melanomas is poor. Excision with histology is therefore frequently required.

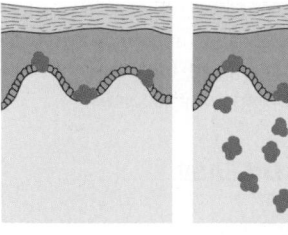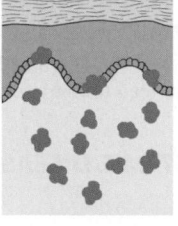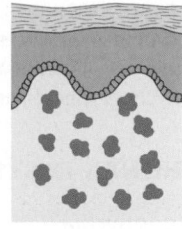

| Junctional | Compound | Intradermal |

Fig. 21.30 Classification of melanocytic naevi. Classification is based on microscopic location of the clumps of naevus cells.

21.26 SIGNIFICANT CHANGES IN MELANOCYTIC NAEVI

- Itch
- Enlargement
- Increased or decreased pigmentation
- Bleeding
- Irregularity of surface or edge
- Inflammation
- Ulceration
- Alteration in shape

Management

Melanocytic naevi are normal and do not require excision except when malignancy is suspected or when they repeat-edly become inflamed or traumatised. Some individuals wish to have them removed for cosmetic reasons.

SEBORRHOEIC WARTS (BASAL CELL PAPILLOMA)

Seborrhoeic warts are common benign epidermal tumours. They are described as seborrhoeic because they often appear oily but in reality they have nothing to do with sebaceous glands. Although they may be a cosmetic problem their principal significance lies in the differential diagnosis of melanoma or other skin tumours.

Clinical features

Seborrhoeic warts are rare before the age of 35. Initially they may become visible as macular pigmented areas. They may then become markedly elevated and are most com-monly found on the trunk and face (see Fig. 21.31). The sexes are equally affected. They may show a range of

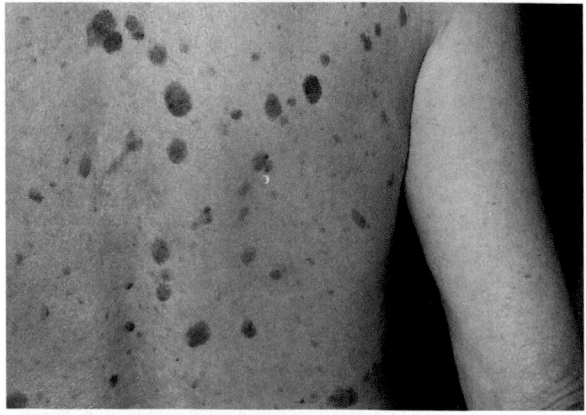

Fig. 21.31 Multiple seborrhoeic warts.

appearances and vary in colour from yellow to very dark brown, and in shape from fairly flat to a protuberant and 'stuck-on' appearance; they may even be pedunculated. Their surface often appears rather greasy and may show some sealing with pinpoint keratin plugs which can be of diagnostic use in excluding melanoma.

Investigations

Biopsy is rarely necessary but malignant melanoma may on occasion be indistinguishable on clinical appearance alone.

Management

Seborrhoeic warts may be left alone but if they cause cosmetic embarrassment then they can be treated by curettage under local anaesthetic or by cryotherapy. Sometimes seborrhoeic keratoses are particularly itchy and therapy of a number of lesions may be required.

KERATOACANTHOMA

This is quite a striking benign keratinocyte tumour characterised by a period of rapid growth of a lesion that may be 4 or 5 cm across or even larger, with a central keratin plug in a dome-shaped nodule (see p. 1051). Spontaneous resolution will occur but it may take months and often results in an unsightly scar which could be improved by excision of the lesion. Clinically and histologically the lesion resembles that of a squamous cell carcinoma but shows a different natural history. If there is any doubt the lesions are better managed as squamous cell carcinomas. To make a positive diagnosis of keratoacanthoma a large biopsy reflecting the architecture of the lesion is required.

MALIGNANCY: INCIDENCE AND RISK FACTORS

In most Caucasian populations non-melanoma skin cancer (principally comprising basal and squamous cell carcinoma) is the most common human malignancy. Each year one million Americans develop new basal cell carcinomas. Fortunately, the majority of these tumours are easy to diagnose and can be managed relatively simply with a low morbidity and an extremely low mortality.

The main risk factor for most forms of skin cancer is exposure to ultraviolet radiation in the absence of adequate melanin pigmentation. The evidence for the important role of environmental ultraviolet radiation and pigmentation is:

- The body site distribution of skin cancer with the frequently or intermittently exposed sites predominating.
- The increased risk of tumours in those with pale skin and the low rates in those with black skin.
- The increased tumour rates in those with pale skin who have migrated to areas of high sun exposure (such as red-headed individuals from the UK who move to Australia).
- The grossly elevated risks of skin cancer in individuals

with a focal defect in the ability to repair ultraviolet radiation DNA damage. Such individuals with xeroderma pigmentosum have an increased risk of both non-melanoma and melanoma skin cancers as well as a variety of other clinical features involving the central nervous system. Their defect in DNA repair is almost completely confined to the inability to repair ultraviolet-induced damage (rather than, say, X-ray radiation) and they therefore illustrate the important step of ultraviolet radiation-induced damage.

Although ultraviolet radiation is the major environmental determinant of skin cancer, the various tumour types show different body distribution. For example, squamous cell carcinomas and actinic keratosis mirror the sites of highest cumulative ultraviolet radiation exposure, with the backs of the hands and the scalps of bald-headed individuals showing the greatest tumour density. In contrast, basal cell carcinomas tend to be disproportionally common on the face, perhaps reflecting their appendageal origins. There is a different body site distribution for melanoma, with tumours relatively more common on areas of skin that may have received intermittent sun exposure. This has led to the suggestion that intermittent sun exposure or episodes of burning may be important, although the epidemiological evidence in favour of burning rather than other aspects of exposure is inconclusive.

The attributable risk of other causes of skin cancer is by contrast small, but ionising radiation or systemic immuno-suppression (as seen in people who have received heart or kidney transplants) greatly increases squamous cell cancer risks.

EBM

SKIN CANCER—role of sunscreens

'RCTs show that in certain populations where ambient UVR is high sunblocks reduce the incidence of actinic keratoses, the number of squamous cell carcinomas and the number of melanocytic naevi in children.'

- Gallagher RP, Rivers JK, Lee TK, et al. Broad-spectrum sunscreen use and the development of new nevi in white children: a randomized controlled trial. JAMA 2000; 283:2955–2960.
- Green A, Williams G, Neale R, et al. Daily sunscreen application and betacarotene supplementation in prevention of basal-cell and squamous-cell carcinomas of the skin: a randomised controlled trial. Lancet 1999; 354:723–729.
- Thompson SC, Jotley D, Marks R. Reduction of solar keratoses by regular sunscreen use. N Engl J Med 1993; 329:1147–1161.

EBM

SKIN CANCER—are there any intervention strategies to prevent skin cancer in immunosuppressed individuals?

'Patients receiving immunosuppression following organ transplant are at high risk of non-melanoma skin cancer (NMSC), and studies suggest that systemic retinoids reduce or delay the onset of NMSC in this group. Before and after studies also suggest retinoids decrease NMSC rates in patients with xeroderma pigmentosum.'

- Bavinck JN, Tieben LM, van der Woude FJ, et al. Prevention of skin cancer and reduction of keratotic skin lesions during acitretin therapy in renal transplant recipients: a double-blind, placebo-controlled study. J Clin Oncol 1995; 13:1933–1938.
- Kraemer KH, DiGiovanna JJ, Moshell AN, et al. Prevention of skin cancer in xeroderma pigmentosum with the use of oral isotretinoin. N Engl J Med 1988; 318:1633–1637.

PRE-MALIGNANT TUMOURS

ACTINIC KERATOSIS

Actinic keratoses are small, scaly, red areas on sun-exposed sites that show focal areas of dysplasia on histological examination (see Fig. 21.32). They are extremely common and frequently multiple; in some surveys over half the population aged over 40 in Australia have one or more lesions. Their relation to squamous cell cancer is still under examination. The rate of progression to squamous cell carcinoma appears low (1:1000 per year per lesion) and a large proportion of actinic keratoses may spontaneously involute. By contrast, many squamous cell carcinomas arise without evidence of a previous actinic keratosis. If an actinic keratosis rapidly increases in size, ulcerates, bleeds or becomes painful, then its potential for transformation to squamous cell carcinoma should be considered.

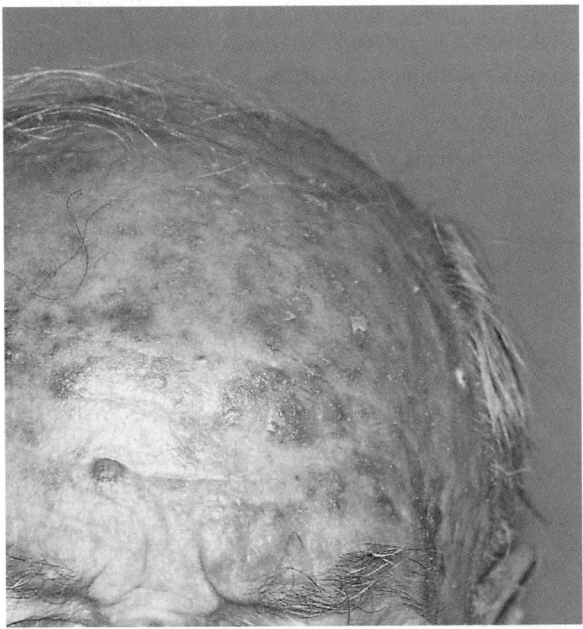

Fig. 21.32 Numerous actinic keratoses in a white patient who had lived for years in the tropics.

Management

Actinic keratoses are treated easily and effectively with liquid nitrogen. If there are a large number of lesions, then the topical cytotoxic 5-fluorouracil may be required. Lesions which do not respond to treatment may require curettage or excision and reconsideration of their nature.

INTRAEPIDERMAL CARCINOMA (BOWEN'S DISEASE)

Clinical features

This usually presents as a slow-growing, red, scaly area with some resemblance to a plaque of psoriasis, on the lower leg of elderly females. Histology reveals full-thickness dysplasia. They may occur on other sites (see Fig. 21.33), and

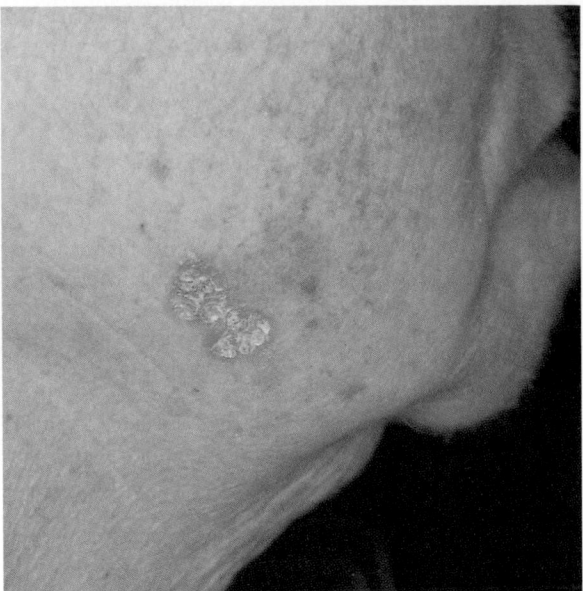

Fig. 21.33 Intraepidermal carcinoma (right cheek). This persistent psoriasis-like plaque recurred after the original (anterior) lesion was treated by freezing.

occasionally develop into squamous cell carcinomas. They should be viewed as being considerably more suspicious than an isolated actinic keratosis.

Investigations and management

An initial incisional biopsy may be required and the treatment is local destruction. Alternatively, the lesions may be managed with curettage and subsequent histology. Curettage, however, will not usually allow a squamous cell carcinoma to be positively diagnosed or excluded (because the tissue architecture is not preserved). An alternative is cryotherapy; even more recently photodynamic therapy has been introduced in which a photosensitiser is applied topically in the presence of blue light.

MALIGNANT TUMOURS

BASAL CELL CARCINOMA (BCC)

This is the most common human cancer. Rates are five times higher than for squamous cell carcinoma in European countries. Classically, lesions are slow-growing and ulcerated, with a pearly and telangiectatic edge; they occur on the face of an elderly individual. The tumour invades locally but rarely metastasises. In practice it is managed as though it does not metastasise unless it is particularly large or has been present for a long time. 'Rodent ulcer' is a term commonly used for slowly expanding ulcerative basal cell carcinoma. The malignant cells resemble basal keratinocytes.

Clinical features

The most common type is the nodulo-ulcerative form. The earliest lesion is a small, glistening, skin-coloured papule, often with fine telangiectatic vessels on the surface, which slowly enlarges. Central necrosis may occur, leaving an ulcer surrounded by a rolled pearly edge (see Fig. 21.34). Without treatment lesions may reach 1–2 cm in diameter over 5–10 years. Slow but relentless growth causes local tissue destruction. Sometimes this type of tumour becomes cystic or pigmented. The morphoeic variant of basal cell carcinoma is a slowly expanding, yellow or grey waxy plaque with an ill-defined edge. Fibrosis often follows ulceration and crusting, and the lesion may appear as an enlarging scar. The superficial (multifocal) variant is seen most often on the trunk; it appears as a slowly enlarging pink or brown scaly plaque with a fine 'whipcord' edge and may resemble a patch of intraepidermal carcinoma (see above). If left, it may grow to 10 cm in diameter.

Management

The majority of basal cell carcinomas are easily treated with local destruction. Metastasis is extremely rare; nevertheless, caution should be exercised—for instance, in tumours close to the eye margins where local invasion can cause considerable management difficulty, or in tumours which can track down nerves such as the infraorbital.

The choice of modality of treatment is dependent on local expertise and interest and involves either surgery, cryotherapy or radiotherapy. Depending on tumour subtype all are equally effective in expert hands. Surgery is, however, increasingly seen as the first choice as it allows proper histological assessment of the tumour and examination of tumour margins. Curettage and cautery also show a good result for some small lesions, particularly if they are superficial and not close to the eye. Cryotherapy has a significant morbidity when used for anything other than superficial lesions. Radiotherapy was used extensively in the past but is less popular now. Fractionated doses of radiation can reduce the morbidity of radiotherapy but in general a surgical excision results in a better cosmetic effect with lower morbidity.

The importance of control of tumour margins is widely debated. Many authorities believe that Mohs' surgery, in which the complete margins of the excised tissue are examined histologically, is of benefit but the present indications for this approach are subject to debate and there is an absence of robust clinical studies. Whatever modality of treatment is used, in expert hands the cure rate should be greater than 90%. Tumour recurrences can subsequently be treated. Some tumours can be very misleading in terms of clinical assessment of their margins and should be examined by a dermatological surgeon. If the primary tumour is not completely excised a wait-and-see policy is often recommended, depending on the clinical context.

SQUAMOUS CELL CARCINOMA (SCC)

Squamous cell carcinoma is the second most common skin cancer after BCC and like other forms of skin cancer is increasing in age-specific incidence.

Aetiology

The risk factors for squamous cell carcinoma are similar to basal cell carcinoma: namely, exposure to ultraviolet radiation, pale skin, or rarely exposure to other carcinogenic factors such as X irradiation or arsenic injection. Squamous cell carcinomas may arise in long-standing areas of inflammation such as around a chronic cutaneous ulcer, or in patients with scarring genetic syndromes of the skin such as dystrophic epidermolysis bullosa in which up to 50% of patients may develop squamous cell carcinoma. Squamous cell carcinomas also show a greatly elevated incidence in individuals who are receiving chronic immunosuppression following organ transplantation (particularly kidney and heart) and in individuals who have been treated with large amounts of PUVA therapy.

Clinical features

Squamous cell carcinoma is a proliferative tumour that has a history of growth over a few months. Varying clinical presentations include keratotic nodules (see Fig. 21.35), exophytic erythematous nodules, infiltrating firm tumours and ulcers with an indurated edge. Histology also varies from well-differentiated tumours to anaplastic. SCCs of the lip behave more aggressively and show a greater frequency of metastasis. It is often said that SCC of the pinnae may also be more aggressive, although whether this reflects inadequate primary treatment is not clear.

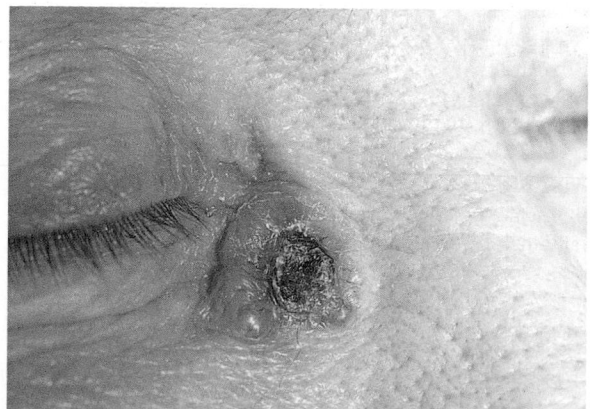

Fig. 21.34 Basal cell carcinoma. A slowly growing pearly nodule just below the inner canthus. The central crust overlies an ulcerated area.

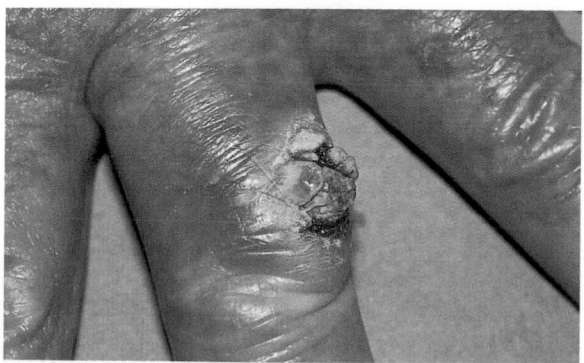

Fig. 21.35 Squamous cell carcinoma. A warty nodule with induration of the adjacent skin.

Management

As with basal cell carcinoma a number of modalities may be used including aggressive curettage and cautery, excision or radiotherapy. In general excision with assessment of adequacy of margins is the preferred option because of the definite risk of metastasis. Surgical excision with a 3–4 mm margin has a cure rate of 90% or more. As with BCC, radiotherapy can be used in selected cases.

MALIGNANT MELANOMA

Malignant melanoma, like other forms of skin cancer, has shown an increase in incidence over recent decades. This increase persists even when changes in the age structure of the population are accounted for. Melanomas show a significant mortality with a case fatality of approximately 20–25%. Therapy for metastatic melanoma is extremely poor and therefore interest has concentrated on primary prevention and early detection. The main risk factors for melanoma are ultraviolet radiation exposure, pale skin, naevi number and family history. Fewer than 10% of melanomas occur in the context of a significant family history but within this group there are rare kindreds in whom the lifetime risk of melanoma may approach 50%. The body site distribution of melanoma is different from that of other skin tumours, suggesting that some aspect of the relation between ultraviolet radiation and tumour occurrence is as yet not fully understood. The increase in melanoma incidence with ambient ultraviolet radiation exposure is also not as steep as that seen for squamous cell carcinoma; for example, a threefold increase in environmental ultraviolet radiation exposure may increase squamous cell carcinoma rates by a factor of 9 but melanoma by a factor of 3.

Clinical features

The classification of invasive malignant melanomas is shown in Box 21.27.

Two-thirds of invasive melanomas are preceded by a superficial and radial growth phase characterised by an expanding, irregularly pigmented macule or plaque. Its margin is usually irregular with reniform projections (see Fig. 21.36). Lentigo maligna (in situ changes of malignancy only) and lentigo maligna melanoma occur most often on the exposed skin of the elderly. A speckled macular lentigo maligna may have been present for many years before a nodule of invasive melanoma appears within it. The in situ phase of superficial spreading melanoma, the most common

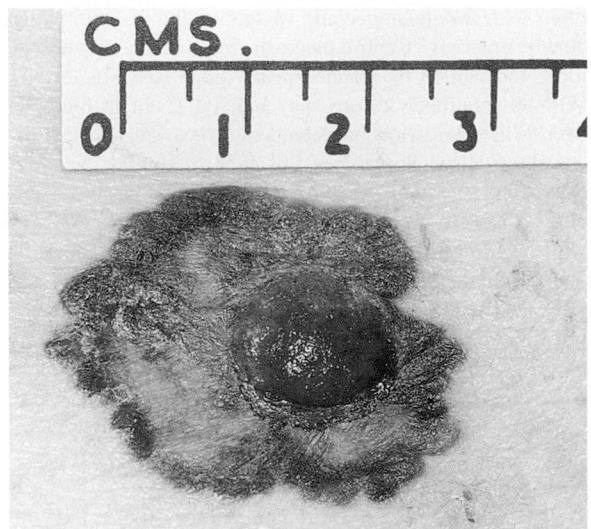

Fig. 21.36 Superficial spreading melanoma. The radial growth phase was present for about 3 years before the invasive amelanotic nodule developed within it. Note the irregular outline, asymmetrical shape and different hues, including depigmented areas signifying spontaneous regression.

type in Caucasians, seldom lasts for longer than 2 years, usually shows much colour variation and is often palpable. Acral lentiginous melanoma occurs on the palms and soles and the absolute incidence rates are the same in all populations; by contrast, the rates at other body sites are low in Blacks and in the Chinese and Japanese. These facts suggest that this variant of melanoma is not related to ultraviolet radiation exposure. Nodular melanoma develops as a pigmented nodule with no preceding in situ phase. All changing pigmented lesions deserve careful examination remembering the 'ABCDE' features of malignant melanoma (see p. 1057). About 30–50% of melanomas appear to develop in a preceding melanocytic naevus (see p. 1057). A change in any naevus should raise suspicion of malignant transformation.

True amelanotic melanomas occur but are rare; flecks of pigmentation can usually be seen with a lens. Subungual melanomas present as painless, expanding areas of pigmentation under a nail and usually involve the nail fold.

The clinical stages of malignant melanoma are shown in Box 21.28.

The diagnosis should be established by local excision biopsy of the suspected lesion.

Management

Surgical excision is usually required although very rarely radiotherapy may play a role. The extent of normal tissue

21.27 CLASSIFICATION OF CUTANEOUS MALIGNANT MELANOMA	
Type of invasive melanoma	Presence of preceding in situ/radial growth phase
Superficial spreading	+
Lentigo maligna	+
Nodular	−
Acral lentiginous	+

21.28 CLINICAL STAGES OF MALIGNANT MELANOMA	
● Stage I	Primary lesion only
● Stage II	Regional nodal disease
● Stage III	Distant disease (nodal or visceral)

that needs to be removed around a melanoma remains a subject for debate. Most would agree that a clear margin needs to be present so that there is little doubt that the tumour is fully excised; the deeper the tumour, the more caution is warranted. The majority of tumours can be excised without the need for grafting. The role of local lymph node dissection in the absence of evidence of tumour spread is uncertain. Palpable local nodes in stage II patients should be removed by block dissection. Chemotherapy is only curative exceptionally but may play an important palliative role in those with stage III disease or earlier. Interferon alpha may have a role in individuals at high risk of metastasis.

SURGERY FOR MELANOMA—is there an optimal margin for primary excision of melanoma of different Breslow thicknesses? `EBM`

'RCTs have found that more radical surgery (4–6 cm excision margins) provides no greater benefit in reducing local recurrence or increasing survival than less radical surgery (1–2 cm excision margins). Recommended excision margins for malignant melanoma depend on their Breslow thickness: melanomas < 1 mm in depth should have a 1 cm margin; melanomas > 1 mm in depth need a 2 cm margin.'

- Roberts DL, Anstey AV, Barlow RJ, et al. on behalf of the Melanoma Study Group. UK guidelines for the management of cutaneous melanoma. Br J Dermatol 2002; 146:7–18.

Prognosis

There are a number of useful prognostic indicators in melanoma. Those with clinical stage III disease fare least well (less than 10% survive 2 years); those with stage I disease have a 70% chance of surviving 5 years. The thickness of the tumour (measured microscopically by Breslow's method, which gives the distance between the granular cell layer and the deepest part of the tumour) is a reliable predictor of the prognosis for patients with stage I disease. The prognosis is excellent for those with tumours less than 1 mm thick (over 90% survive 5 years), but becomes less good with thicker tumours. The 5-year survival of patients with tumours greater than 3.5 mm thick is about 50%. In general, females fare better than males and tumours at certain sites (e.g. lower leg) are less aggressive.

CUTANEOUS T-CELL LYMPHOMA (MYCOSIS FUNGOIDES)

In contrast to B-cell lymphomas which usually present as sudden focal skin tumours, cutaneous T-cell lymphoma develops slowly over many years from a plaque stage often resembling psoriasis through to nodules and then a systemic stage. The diagnosis of cutaneous T-cell lymphoma requires a high index of suspicion particularly in patients who are deemed to have unusual forms of eczema or psoriasis and who failed to respond to treatment. The treatment of individuals with cutaneous T-cell lymphoma is, however, symptomatic with no evidence that the various modalities of treatment alter prognosis. Study of these individuals is hampered by difficulties in disease nosology, disease heterogeneity and the long natural history, sometimes over 20 or 30 years.

In the early stages of cutaneous T-cell lymphoma either systemic or local corticosteroids may be indicated; alternatively, PUVA or TL01 phototherapy may be employed. However, once lesions have moved beyond the plaque stage other modalities, including electron beam radiation or systemic antilymphoma regimens, may be required. Such patients require careful collaboration between dermatologists, pathologists and haematological oncologists.

ISSUES IN OLDER PEOPLE
SKIN TUMOURS

- Seborrhoeic warts are benign skin tumours that occur predominantly in the elderly. They may cause quite distressing pruritus.
- Pre-malignant lesions, including actinic keratoses and intra-epidermal carcinomata, occur most frequently in the elderly.
- Cutaneous squamous cell carcinomata occur most commonly in the elderly, usually on a background of sun-damaged skin.
- Lentigo maligna (in situ melanoma) and lentigo maligna melanoma are the most usual melanomas that occur in the elderly. They are generally seen on the face or other sun-exposed sites and often present as a long-standing pigmented lesion that is changing in colour, shape or size.

DERMATOLOGICAL SURGERY

The workload of dermatologists has changed considerably over the last 20–30 years with an increase in the number of lesions compared with rashes. In part this is explained by changes in the epidemiology of skin cancer, referral changes and the increased demand for cosmetic removal of many lesions. If one includes the assessment of patients with potential skin cancer and their follow-up, dermatologists might spend anywhere between 20 and 90% of their time on surgical aspects of the discipline (depending on a practitioner's particular interests).

There are a large number of surgical procedures that can mostly be carried out under local anaesthetic. The choice of procedure is important; for example, inappropriate excision of lesions such as seborrhoeic keratoses results in scar formation when they should have been treated with cryosurgery or curettage.

BIOPSY

Skin biopsies are usually taken under local anaesthetic but a general anaesthetic may be necessary in some children. It is best to select an early or typical lesion on a non-exposed site. An ellipse biopsy or in certain instances a punch biopsy that removes a cylindrical portion of skin may be used. Learning which part of a rash to biopsy, and whether an ellipse or punch biopsy will suffice, comes with experience but is often critical. A common reason for unhelpful or even misleading histology is biopsy of an inappropriate part of the rash. For instance, biopsies of secondarily excoriated lesions, even in the clinical context of a blistering disease, will often be unhelpful.

Sutures are removed depending on site and other factors (i.e. 5–7 days for the face and 10–14 days for the back).

Certain body sites are associated with particular risks. Thus biopsies on the upper torso of young persons are likely to result in keloids, biopsies over the scapula tend to leave unsightly scars, and biopsies on the lower legs of elderly people are at risk of poor healing and ulceration with a resulting high morbidity. The statement that there is no such thing as 'minor surgery' remains an instructive maxim.

CRYOTHERAPY

Cryotherapy is usually performed in one of two ways: either as an application of liquid nitrogen with a cotton wool bud or using a jet gun. Liquid nitrogen can be used to treat a wide range of lesions from viral warts through to actinic keratoses and invasive tumours such as basal or squamous cell carcinomas. The cosmetic effects and morbidity are variable. If neoplasia is suspected it may be wiser to carry out an incisional biopsy first. In general superficial or 'stuck-on' lesions will require a less intense therapy and are more acceptable to the patient. Melanocytic naevi should not be treated with liquid nitrogen.

CURETTAGE

Curettage refers to scraping with a small, spoon-shaped implement (curette) across the lesion, not only as a definitive treatment but also as a way of obtaining histological material. Naturally the histological material may be compromised in the sense that epidermal structures are over-represented and the anatomy of the lesion as it descends into the dermis is not preserved. It may therefore be difficult to determine whether a lesion with intraepidermal dysplasia shows any evidence of invasion (i.e. is a squamous cell carcinoma rather than an intraepidermal carcinoma or actinic keratosis). Curettage is, however, suitable for many seborrhoeic keratoses, actinic keratoses or areas of intraepidermal carcinoma. Some superficial basal cell carcinomas are well treated with curettage but some variants such as the morphoeic forms should be treated with expert surgical excision.

SURGICAL EXCISION

The advantage of surgical excision for the removal of tumours or suspected tumours is that it provides adequate histological material for examination and evidence of excision margins. Depending on body site, there are a range of procedures to minimise the resulting defect, including undermining, Z-plasties, flaps and grafts. On sun-exposed sites in many patients, particularly the elderly, healing by secondary intention can lead to a surprisingly good result.

LASER THERAPY

Laser therapy exploits the fact that certain pigments such as melanin or blood absorb certain wavelengths of electromagnetic radiation more readily than others. A variety of lasers have been produced which allow relatively selective destruction of particular structures containing the absorbing pigment. By concentrating the light into short pulses the damage is restricted to a particular area. The choice of laser for a particular lesion requires specialist knowledge but because melanin and blood have overlapping spectrums the choice generally focuses on minimising 'collateral' damage. Some lasers are better for dealing with primarily vascular lesions such as port wine stains, while others are more useful for pigmented lesions or for destruction of exogenous pigments such as tattoo pigments or drug deposits (e.g. minocycline).

By contrast with the vascular laser the carbon dioxide laser emits infrared light which is absorbed by tissue water. When crudely used the carbon dioxide laser is therefore similar to a diathermy but the depth of lesion can be controlled to a fraction of a millimetre; the procedure can therefore be useful for resurfacing and for face lifts. A general anaesthetic is required for such procedures.

MISCELLANEOUS PROCEDURES

Keloids may require corticosteroid injections after freezing or excision. Silicone sheeting also may flatten keloids although the mechanism is obscure. Scars and wrinkles can be filled using collagen or silicone. Liposuction can be used to remove fat, and tissue folds around the eyes can be easily excised. Small acne scars can be excised and larger, more superficial lesions treated with a carbon dioxide laser. Areas of depigmentation in vitiligo or piebaldism may be treated with epidermal grafts from normal skin. Photodynamic therapy refers to the application of porphyrins to skin followed by exposure to light, allowing controlled destruction of some tumours such as superficial basal cell carcinomas. It appears that tumours absorb more of the topically applied porphyrin than normal skin and so permit some targeting of damage.

THE SKIN IN SYSTEMIC DISEASE

Skin reactions can be linked with an underlying systemic disease in a number of ways, as shown in Box 21.29. Only common or important associations will be discussed below.

NEUROFIBROMATOSIS: TYPE 1

Light brown (café au lait) macules can be seen in healthy people and are also a feature of:

- Albright's syndrome (polyostotic fibrous dysplasia), where the margins are very irregular
- Bloom's syndrome.

The skin markers of von Recklinghausen's neurofibromatosis include scattered and discrete café au lait macules, axillary freckling and a variable number of cutaneous neurofibromata (see p. 1206). The tumours may be small and superficial, or large and deep. Small circular pigmented hamartomas of the iris (Lisch nodules) appear in early childhood.

21.29 SKIN REACTIONS IN SYSTEMIC DISEASE
Part of a multisystem disease
• Genetically determined (e.g. neurofibromatosis and tuberous sclerosis)   • Xanthomas   • Amyloidosis   • Porphyria   • Sarcoidosis
A non-specific and not invariable reaction pattern to a systemic disease
• Urticaria   • Erythema multiforme   • Annular erythemas   • Erythema nodosum   • Pyoderma gangrenosum   • Sweet's syndrome   • Generalised pruritus
A sign of internal malignancy
• Dermatomyositis   • Generalised pruritus   • Acanthosis nigricans   • Superficial thrombophlebitis
A sign of internal organ failure
• Liver—generalised pruritus, pigmentation, spider naevi and palmar erythema   • Kidney—generalised pruritus and pigmentation   • Pancreas (diabetes mellitus)—necrobiosis lipoidica
A result of a common genetic link with the systemic disorder
• Dermatitis herpetiformis and gluten-sensitive enteropathy   • Psoriasis and some types of arthropathy
The cause of the systemic disease
• Exfoliative dermatitis causing high-output cardiac failure
A result of treatment of the systemic disease
• Drug eruptions

NEUROFIBROMATOSIS: TYPE 2

See page 1206.

SEGMENTAL NEUROFIBROMATOSIS: TYPE 5

The cutaneous features of café au lait macules and neurofibromata are found in a dermatomal distribution. This is due to mosaicism of the NF-1 gene.

TUBEROUS SCLEROSIS

This is an autosomal dominant condition with hamartomas affecting many systems.

The classic triad of clinical features comprises mental retardation, epilepsy and skin lesions but not all are invariably present. The skin signs include small white oval (ash leaf) macules, pink or yellowish papules on the centre of the face (adenoma sebaceum), peri- and subungual fibromata, and connective tissue naevi (cobblestone-like plaques at the base of the spine, sometimes called shagreen patches).

XANTHOMAS

These deposits of fatty material in the skin, subcutaneous fat and tendons may be the first clue to primary or secondary hyperlipidaemia (see p. 308).

Various clinical patterns are seen which correlate well with the underlying cause. They include:

- eruptive yellow papules on the buttocks (eruptive xanthomas)
- yellowish macules or plaques (plane xanthomas)
- small yellow-grey plaques around the eyes (xanthelasma palpebrarum)
- nodules over the elbows and knees (tuberous xanthomas)
- subcutaneous nodules attached to tendons, especially those on the dorsal aspect of the fingers and the Achilles tendons (tendinous xanthomas).

When xanthomas are detected the fasting blood lipids and the electrophoretic pattern of plasma lipoproteins must be measured, though abnormalities will not always be detected.

AMYLOIDOSIS

This is described on page 327. Skin lesions are uncommon in systemic amyloidosis secondary to rheumatoid arthritis or other chronic inflammatory diseases.

Deposits of amyloid in the skin, often appearing as waxy plaques around the eyes, are prominent in primary systemic amyloidosis and in amyloid associated with multiple myeloma. 'Pinch purpura', appearing where the skin is traumatised, is due to amyloid infiltration of blood vessels and may also be a striking feature.

PORPHYRIA

The classification and metabolic abnormalities of the porphyrias are found on page 325. Certain porphyrias can affect the skin.

Porphyria cutanea tarda

This porphyria usually starts in adulthood and can be inherited and precipitated by alcohol, iron overload, oestrogens, hepatitis C and HIV disease. Some cases are acquired and

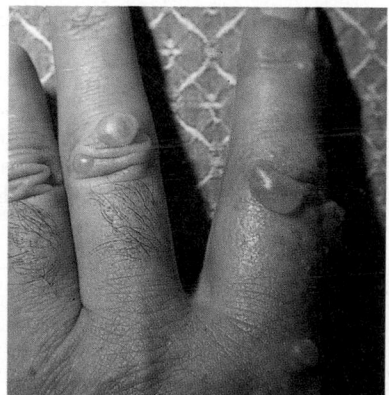

Fig. 21.37 Cutaneous hepatic porphyria. Recent skin fragility and blistering on the backs of the fingers.

are associated with underlying liver disease such as cirrhosis and hepatic tumours. The cutaneous features are increased skin fragility, blistering (see Fig. 21.37), erosions and milia occurring on light-exposed areas such as the backs of the hands. Facial hypertrichosis and hyperpigmentation may also be seen. Diagnostic tests for porphyria are detailed on pages 325–327.

Erythropoietic protoporphyria

This is a rare porphyria that starts in childhood, with burning and pain on light-exposed areas. Scars occur, particularly on the nose. Examination of the red cells, plasma and stool for raised protoporphyrins is confirmatory.

Variegate porphyria

Cutaneous features are similar to those of porphyria cutanea tarda. Systemic features are the same as those of acute intermittent porphyria (see p. 327).

Hereditary coproporphyria

Around 30% of these patients are photosensitive. Systemic features are the same as those of acute intermittent porphyria.

Pseudoporphyrias

Sun-bed usage, non-steroidal anti-inflammatory drugs (particularly naproxen) and renal failure can give rise to skin lesions that mimic the photosensitive porphyrias, particularly porphyria cutanea tarda. The pathogenesis is as yet unclear.

SARCOIDOSIS

This is covered in detail on page 552.

Skin lesions are seen in about one-third of patients with systemic sarcoidosis. The clinical features include erythema nodosum, granulomatous deposits in long-standing scars, dusky infiltrated plaques on the nose and fingers (lupus pernio), and scattered brownish-red, violaceous or hypopigmented papules or nodules which vary in number, size and distribution.

ERYTHEMA MULTIFORME

As its name implies, this is a reaction pattern of multiform erythematous lesions. The precipitating factor may not be found in some cases but attacks are provoked by the factors listed in Box 21.30.

Clinical features

The multiform erythematous lesions may be urticaria-like and some have obvious 'bull's-eye' or 'target' lesions. Blisters may be seen in the centre or around the edges of the lesions.

21.30 PROVOKING FACTORS IN ERYTHEMA MULTIFORME
• Herpes simplex infections • Other viral infections, e.g. orf, and mycoplasma • Bacterial infections • Drugs, especially sulphonamides, penicillins and barbiturates • Internal malignancy or its treatment with radiotherapy

In some cases blisters dominate the picture; the Stevens–Johnson syndrome is severe bullous erythema multiforme with emphasis on mucosal involvement including the mouth, eyes and genitals, with constitutional disturbance.

Management

Severe cases are usually managed with tapering courses of systemic corticosteroids after treatment, if possible, of the primary cause.

ERYTHEMA NODOSUM

This characteristic reaction pattern is due to a vasculitis in the deep dermis and subcutaneous fat. It may be provoked by the factors listed in Box 21.31.

21.31 PROVOKING FACTORS IN ERYTHEMA NODOSUM
Infections
• Bacteria (streptococci, tuberculosis, brucellosis and leprosy), viruses, mycoplasma, rickettsia, chlamydia and fungi
Drugs
• e.g. Sulphonamides and oral contraceptives
Systemic disease
• e.g. Sarcoidosis, ulcerative colitis and Crohn's disease

Clinical features

Painful, palpable, dusky blue-red nodules are most commonly seen on the lower legs. Malaise, fever and joint pains are common. The lesions resolve slowly over a month, leaving bruise-like marks in their wake.

Management

The underlying cause should be determined and treated. Bed rest and oral non-steroidal anti-inflammatory drugs may hasten resolution. Tapering systemic corticosteroid courses may be required in stubborn cases.

PYODERMA GANGRENOSUM

Pyoderma gangrenosum (PG) predominantly occurs in adults between the ages of 25 and 54 years. It is an eruption that starts as an inflamed nodule or pustule which breaks down centrally and rapidly progresses to an ulcer with an indurated or undermined purplish or pustular edge (see Fig. 21.38). Lesions may be single or multiple and are classified as ulcerative, pustular, bullous and vegetative. Although PG may arise in the absence of any underlying disease, it is often associated with a systemic disease, such as inflammatory bowel disease, arthritis (both rheumatoid arthritis and seronegative arthropathies), immunodeficiency and immunosuppression including HIV disease, monoclonal gammopathies and leukaemia. The management of PG includes investigations for possible associated systemic disease. There are no diagnostic features on biopsy and therefore the diagnosis is primarily clinical. Local therapy includes pain relief, prevention of secondary bacterial infec-

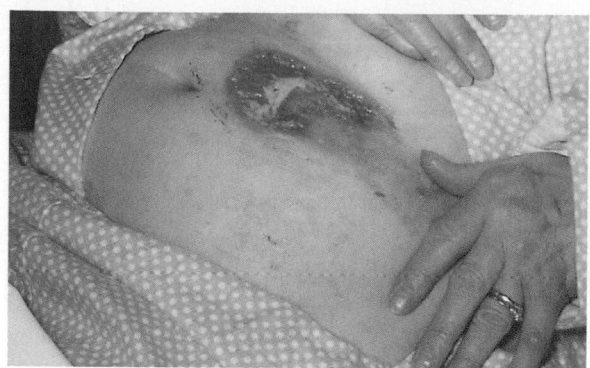

Fig. 21.38 Pyoderma gangrenosum. A large indolent ulcer in a patient with rheumatoid arthritis. Note healing in one part.

tion and dressings. Systemic therapy includes oral steroids in a tapering dose, dapsone 50–150 mg/day, minocycline 100 mg/day, sulfasalazine (4–6 g daily), and ciclosporin (5 mg/kg). Once the patient is clear of disease, recurrences are only intermittent.

ACANTHOSIS NIGRICANS

This is a velvety thickening and pigmentation of the major flexures, particularly the axillae. There are several types of acanthosis nigricans. The most common form is a weight-dependent mild acanthosis nigricans (obesity-associated). When the patient loses weight the cutaneous features regress. Secondly, acanthosis nigricans can be associated with various syndromes, some of which have insulin resistance as a feature. Finally, acanthosis nigricans can be associated with malignancy, particularly gastric (60%). Pruritus is a feature of malignancy-associated acanthosis and regression occurs after the tumour is excised. Acanthosis nigricans sometimes recurs with metastatic disease.

NECROBIOSIS LIPOIDICA

This condition is important to recognise because of its association with diabetes mellitus. Less than 1% of diabetics have necrobiosis, but more than 85% of patients with necrobiosis will have or will develop diabetes.

Typically, the lesions appear as shiny, atrophic and slightly yellow plaques on the shins (see Fig. 21.39). Underlying telangiectasia is easily seen. Minor knocks may precipitate slow-healing ulcers. No treatment is very effective. Topical and intralesional steroids are used, as is long-term PUVA.

GRANULOMA ANNULARE

This is a common cutaneous condition of uncertain aetiology; any association with diabetes is now thought to be coincidental. Dermal nodules occur singly or in an annular configuration. They are asymptomatic but cause consternation because they commonly occur on highly visible sites such as the hands and feet. Histologically, palisading granulomata are found in the dermis. Intralesional steroids can be helpful, but the natural history is spontaneous resolution after a few months to a couple of years.

DRUG ERUPTIONS

Cutaneous drug reactions are common and almost any drug can cause them. Drug reactions may reasonably be included in the differential diagnosis of most skin diseases. Although the mechanisms are poorly understood, drug eruptions may be classified as shown in Box 21.32.

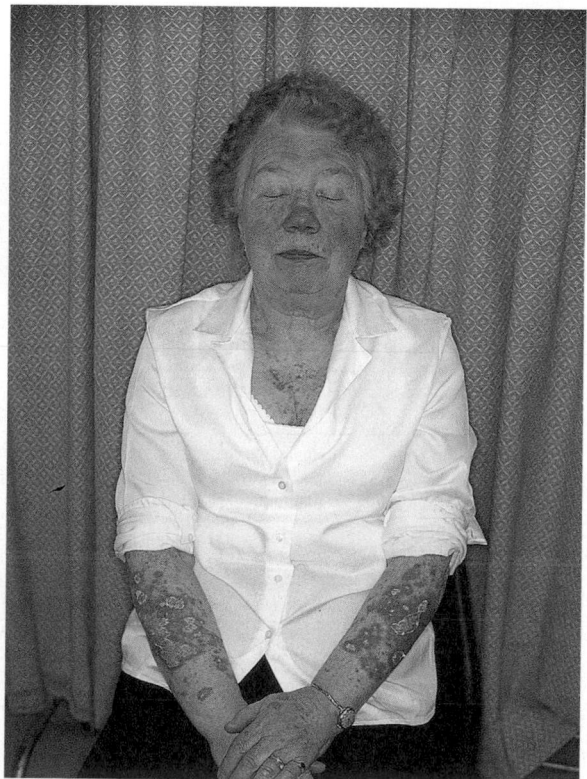

Fig. 21.40 Drug eruption. A weird but symmetrical erythematous scaly rash with a distribution suggesting a degree of photosensitivity. The rash persisted until the recently prescribed sulphonylurea was withdrawn.

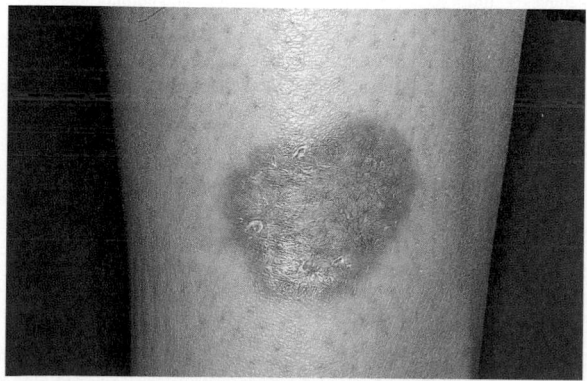

Fig. 21.39 Necrobiosis lipoidica. An atrophic yellowish plaque on the skin of a diabetic.

21.32 DRUG ERUPTIONS AND THEIR MECHANISMS

Mechanism	Example
Non-immunological (non-allergic)	
Unwarranted pharmacological effect	Striae due to corticosteroids; mouth ulcers due to methotrexate
Drug overdosage or failure to metabolise or excrete the drug	Morphine rashes in patients with liver disease
Drug interaction	Warfarin toxicity when coadministered with aspirin or phenylbutazone
Idiosyncratic reaction (an odd reaction which may be genetically determined and is peculiar to an individual)	Drug-induced variegate porphyria
Phototoxic reaction	Chlorpromazine-induced light reactions
Altered skin ecology	Tetracyclines causing vaginal candidiasis
Exacerbation of pre-existing skin condition	Lithium and β-adrenoceptor antagonist (β-blocker) worsening of psoriasis
Immunological (allergic)	
Immediate hypersensitivity	Penicillin-induced urticaria
Immune complex reaction	Drug-induced vasculitis or erythema multiforme
Delayed hypersensitivity	Drug-induced exfoliative dermatitis or photo-allergic reactions

21.33 DRUG ERUPTIONS AND SOME DRUGS WHICH MAY CAUSE THEM

Name of reaction pattern	Clinical features	Drugs which commonly cause reaction
Toxic erythema	Erythematous plaques. Morbilliform, sometimes with urticarial or erythema multiforme-like elements	Antibiotics (especially ampicillin). Sulphonamides, thiazide diuretics, phenylbutazone, para-aminosalicylic acid (PAS)
Urticaria	Itchy weals, sometimes accompanied by angio-oedema	Salicylates, codeine, antibiotics, dextran and ACE inhibitors
Erythema and scaling	Small, scaly, pink papules to large, scaly, red papules	Antibiotics (especially penicillins and sulphonamides), anticonvulsants, ACE inhibitors, barbiturates, gold and penicillamine
Allergic vasculitis	Painful, palpable purpura followed by necrotic ulcers	Sulphonamides, phenylbutazone, indometacin, phenytoin and oral contraceptives
Erythema multiforme	Target-like lesions and bullae on the extensor aspects of the limbs	Sulphonamides, phenylbutazone and barbiturates
Purpura	Widespread purpura not due to thrombocytopenia or a coagulation defect	Thiazides, sulphonamides, phenylbutazone, sulphonylureas, barbiturates and quinine
Bullous eruptions	May be associated with erythema and purpura. May occur at pressure sites in drug-induced coma	Barbiturates, penicillamine, nalidixic acid
Exfoliative dermatitis	Universal redness and scaling, shivering	Phenylbutazone, para-aminosalicylic acid (PAS), isoniazid and gold
Fixed drug eruptions	Round, erythematous and sometimes bullous plaques develop at the same site every time the drug is given. Pigmentation left in wake	Tetracyclines, quinine, sulphonamides and barbiturates
Acneiform eruptions	Rash resembles acne (see p. 1081)	Lithium, oral contraceptive, androgenic or glucocorticoid steroids, antituberculosis and anticonvulsant drugs
Toxic epidermal necrolysis	Rash resembles that of scalded skin (see Fig. 21.41)	Barbiturates, phenytoin, phenylbutazone and penicillin
Hair loss	Diffuse	Cytotoxic agents, acitretin, anticoagulants, antithyroid drugs and oral contraceptives
Hypertrichosis		Diazoxide, minoxidil and ciclosporin A
Photosensitivity	Rash limited to exposed skin	Thiazides, tetracyclines, phenothiazines, sulphonamides, nalidixic acid and psoralens
Pigmentation	Irregular melanin pigmentation on face. Slate-grey colour of exposed skin. Diffuse yellow coloration of skin. Streaky depigmentation of hair	Oral contraceptives. Phenothiazines. Mepacrine. Chloroquine

Clinical features

The most common types of drug eruption and their cause are listed in Box 21.33. It is important not to forget the possibility of a drug eruption when faced with a rash which is atypical of a known skin disease (see Fig. 21.40). Further clues pointing towards the diagnosis are included in Box 21.34.

Investigations

There are no specific investigations which help. Prick tests and in vitro tests for allergy are too unreliable for routine use. Readministration, as a diagnostic test, is usually unwise unless the reaction is mild and there is no suitable alternative drug.

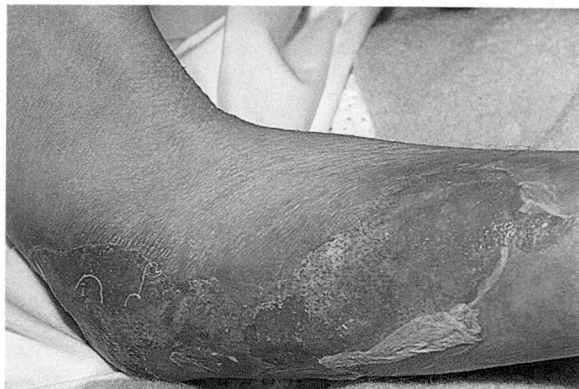

Fig. 21.41   Toxic epidermal necrolysis. In this case it was due to an anticonvulsant.

21.34 DIAGNOSTIC CLUES TO DRUG ERUPTIONS

- Past history of reaction to suspected drug
- Introduction of suspected drug a few days before onset of rash
- Recent prescription of a drug commonly associated with rashes (e.g. penicillin, sulphonamide, thiazide, allopurinol, phenylbutazone)
- A symmetrical eruption which may fit with a well-recognised pattern caused by one of the current drugs

Management

The first step is to withdraw the suspected drug(s). This may not be easy, or even possible, if there is no alternative available. The decision will depend on many factors, including the severity and nature of the drug reaction, its potential reversibility and the probability that the drug caused the reaction. Supportive treatment with antihistamines or a tailored course of systemic corticosteroids may be indicated, depending on the type of skin reaction. The emergency treatment of anaphylactic shock is described on page 201.

FURTHER INFORMATION

Barker J. Psoriasis. J R Coll Physicians Lond 1997; 31:238–240.

Farr PM. Ultraviolet phototherapy [Review] [25 refs]. J R Coll Physicians Lond 1997; 31:250–253.

Freedberg IM, Eisen AZ, Wolff K, et al. Dermatology in internal medicine. In: Freedberg IM, Eisen AZ, Wolff K, et al., eds. Fitzpatrick's dermatology in general medicine. New York: McGraw-Hill; 1999.

Gilchrest BA, Eller MS, Geller AC, Yaar M. The pathogenesis of melanoma induced by ultraviolet radiation. N Engl J Med 1999; 340:1341–1348.

Greaves MW, Wall PD. Pathophysiology of itching. Lancet 1997; 349:133.

Greaves MW, Wall PD. Pathophysiology and clinical aspects of pruritus. In: Freedberg IM, Eisen AZ, Wolff K, et al., eds. Fitzpatrick's dermatology in general medicine. New York: McGraw-Hill; 1999.

Hanifin JM, Tofte SJ. Update on therapy of atopic dermatitis. J Allergy Clin Immunol 1999; 104:S123–S125.

Kanj LF, Wilking SV, Phillips TJ. Pressure ulcers. J Am Acad Dermatol 1998; 38:517–536.

Larsen FS. The epidemiology of atopic dermatitis. In: Burr ML, ed. Epidemiology of clinical allergy. Basel: Karger; 1993.

Lawrence CM. Surgery and laser therapy. J R Coll Physicians Lond 1997; 31:369–373.

Leung DYM. Atopic dermatitis: new insights and opportunities for therapeutic intervention. J Allergy Clin Immunol 2000; 105:860–876.

Leyden JJ. Therapy for acne vulgaris. N Engl J Med 1997; 336:1156–1162.

Nordlund JJ, Boissy RE, Hearing VJ, et al., eds. The pigmentary system: physiology and pathophysiology. New York: Oxford; 1998.

Preston DS, Stern RS. Nonmelanoma cancers of the skin. N Engl J Med 1992; 327:1649–1662.

Rees JL. Skin cancer. J R Coll Physicians Lond 1998; 31(3):246–250.

Shuster S. The aetiology of dandruff and the mode of action of therapeutic agents [Review] [31 refs]. Br J Dermatol 1984; 111:235–242.

van Steensel MA, Steijlen PM, Rees JL. Molecular genetic approaches to skin disease: keratins and keratinisation. J R Coll Physicians Lond 1997; 31:379–383.

Wakelin SH, Black MM. The autoimmune bullous diseases. J R Coll Physicians Lond 1997; 31:364–368.

Neurological disease

C.M.C. ALLEN • C.J. LUECK

CLINICAL EXAMINATION OF THE NERVOUS SYSTEM

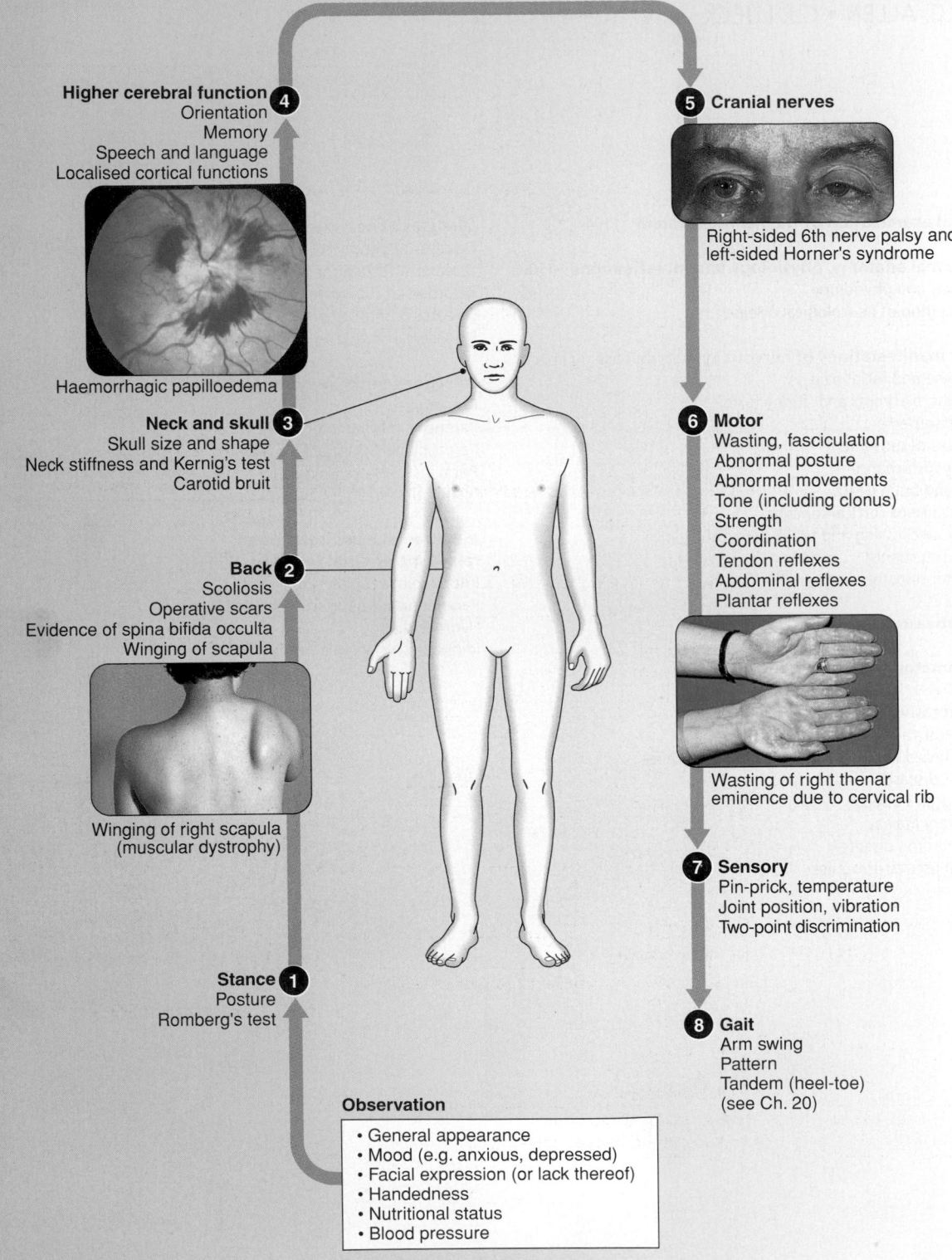

Higher cerebral function 4
Orientation
Memory
Speech and language
Localised cortical functions

Haemorrhagic papilloedema

Neck and skull 3
Skull size and shape
Neck stiffness and Kernig's test
Carotid bruit

Back 2
Scoliosis
Operative scars
Evidence of spina bifida occulta
Winging of scapula

Winging of right scapula
(muscular dystrophy)

Stance 1
Posture
Romberg's test

5 **Cranial nerves**

Right-sided 6th nerve palsy and
left-sided Horner's syndrome

6 **Motor**
Wasting, fasciculation
Abnormal posture
Abnormal movements
Tone (including clonus)
Strength
Coordination
Tendon reflexes
Abdominal reflexes
Plantar reflexes

Wasting of right thenar
eminence due to cervical rib

7 **Sensory**
Pin-prick, temperature
Joint position, vibration
Two-point discrimination

8 **Gait**
Arm swing
Pattern
Tandem (heel-toe)
(see Ch. 20)

Observation

- General appearance
- Mood (e.g. anxious, depressed)
- Facial expression (or lack thereof)
- Handedness
- Nutritional status
- Blood pressure

❶ + ❽ EXAMINATION OF GAIT AND POSTURE

Step	Procedure	Abnormality	Disease
1	Examine posture Axial tone Retropulsion/anteropulsion	Stooped Axial tone increased Postural instability	Parkinsonism Parkinsonism (Parkinson's plus syndrome) Parkinsonism
2	Examine arms during walking	Reduced arm swing	Parkinsonism, upper motor neuron lesion
3	Examine routine walking	Circumduction (stiff leg moves outwards in 'circular' manner) 'Slapping' due to foot drop Narrow-based, short strides Wide-based, short strides (marche à petits pas, magnetic gait) Wide-based, irregular strides High-stepping gait	Upper motor neuron lesion Lower motor neuron lesion Parkinsonism Frontal lobe lesion Cerebellar lesion Dorsal column lesion/sensory neuropathy
4	Examine tandem gait	Inability to perform task	Cerebellar lesion, dorsal column lesion
5	Perform Romberg test	Patient falls with eyes shut	Loss of joint position sense at ankles

❺ EXAMINATION OF CRANIAL NERVES

Nerve	Name	Tests
I	Olfactory	Ask patient
II	Optic	Visual acuity Visual fields 'Swinging' torch test for relative afferent pupillary defect Ophthalmoscopy
III	Oculomotor	Eye movements Eyelid movement Pupil size, symmetry, reactions
IV	Trochlear	Eye movements
V	Trigeminal	Sensation to face Corneal reflex Jaw movements (deviates to side of lesion)
VI	Abducens	Eye movements
VII	Facial	Facial symmetry and movements Ask patient about taste
VIII	Vestibulocochlear	Hearing (whisper to each ear) Tuning fork tests (Rinne and Weber) Look for nystagmus
IX	Glossopharyngeal	Gag reflex (sensory)
X	Vagus	Palatal elevation (uvula deviates to side opposite lesion) Gag reflex (motor) Cough (bovine cough)
XI	Accessory	Look for wasting Elevation of shoulders Turning head to right and left
XII	Hypoglossal	Look for wasting/fasciculation Tongue protrusion (deviates to side of lesion)

❻ ROOT VALUES OF TENDON REFLEXES*

Reflex	Root value
Upper limb	
Biceps jerk	C5
Supinator jerk	C6
Triceps jerk	C7
Finger jerk	C8
Lower limb	
Knee jerk	L4
Ankle jerk	S1

* Simplified for ease of reference.

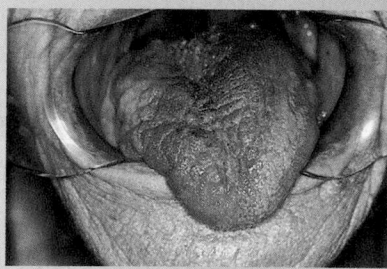

Right 12th nerve palsy. Note wasting of right side of tongue.

The brain, spinal cord and peripheral nerves constitute an organ responsible for perception of the environment, a person's behaviour within it, and the maintenance of the body's internal milieu in readiness for this behaviour. Some 10% of the population consult their general practitioner each year with a neurological symptom in the United Kingdom, where neurological disorders account for about one-fifth of acute medical admissions and a large proportion of chronic physical disability. However, neurological symptoms are often not associated with disease and considerable clinical skill is needed to distinguish those with significant disease from those who need sympathetic reassurance.

A carefully taken history of the pattern of presenting neurological symptoms should suggest a short list of diagnoses that can then be tested on examination. During the neurological examination knowledge of the relevant anatomy and physiology of the nervous system helps to determine the site of the lesion. The underlying pathology is often suggested by the time course of the symptoms and the epidemiological context. Increasingly sophisticated investigations, particularly imaging, are available to refine this clinical diagnosis.

Once the patient's neurological lesion (the deficit) is identified, the clinician needs to assess what impact this has had on the patient's functioning (the disability) and, in turn, how this is affecting his or her life (the handicap). Even when a complete cure cannot be effected, much can be done to improve the disability by pharmacological correction of the pathophysiology and through rehabilitation (see p. 243).

ISSUES IN OLDER PEOPLE
NEUROLOGICAL EXAMINATION
• The assessment of limb tone is often difficult in older people because of: —increased difficulty in relaxing the limbs —concomitant joint disease. • Ankle reflexes may be bilaterally absent without diagnostic significance. • Gait assessment may be more difficult because of: —concurrent musculoskeletal disease —pre-existing neurological deficits (N.B. cerebrovascular disease). • Sensory testing may be especially difficult when there is cognitive impairment. • Vibration sense in the lower extremities may be reduced in old age without diagnostic significance.

FUNCTIONAL ANATOMY, PHYSIOLOGY AND INVESTIGATIONS

ANATOMY AND PHYSIOLOGY

CELLS OF THE NERVOUS SYSTEM

In addition to a variety of neurons, the nervous system includes specialised blood vessels, ependymal cells lining the cerebral ventricles and glial cells, of which there are three types. Astrocytes form the structural framework for the neurons and control their biochemical environment. Astrocyte foot processes are closely associated with the blood vessels to form the blood–brain barrier (see Fig. 22.1). Oligodendrocytes are responsible for the formation and

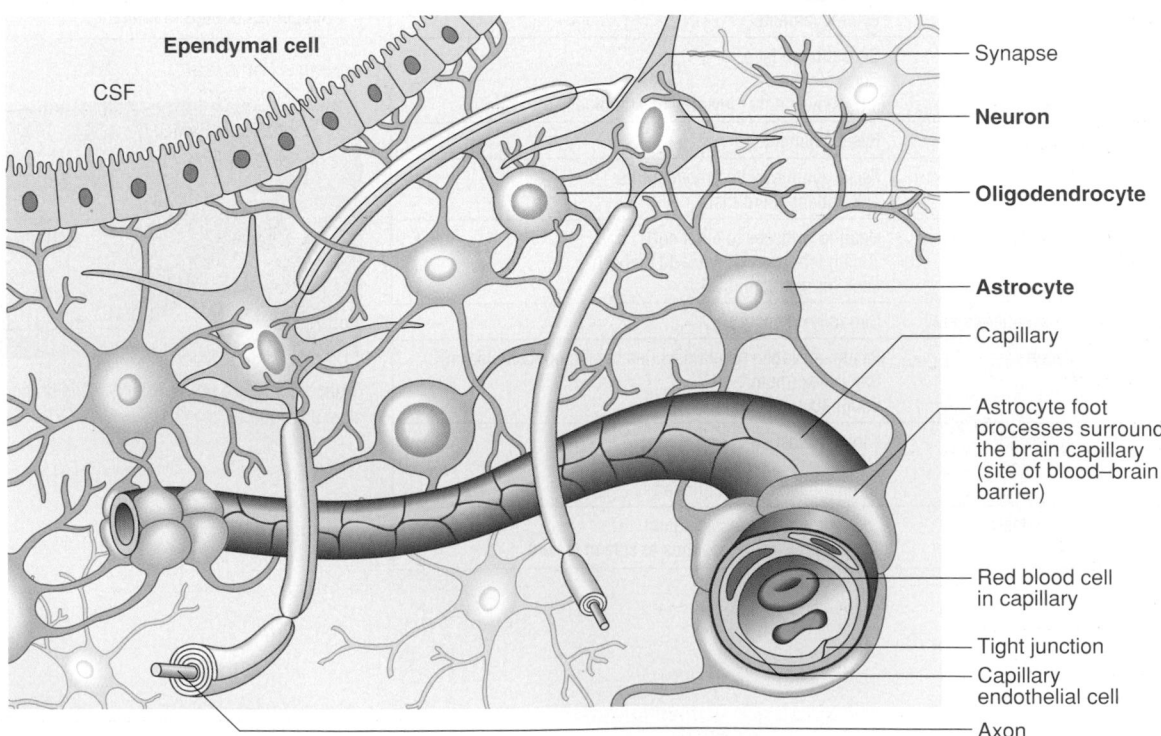

Fig. 22.1 **Cells of the nervous system.**

maintenance of the myelin sheath, which surrounds axons and is essential for the rapid transmission of action potentials by saltatory conduction. Microglia are blood-derived mononuclear macrophages.

THE GENERATION AND TRANSMISSION OF THE NERVOUS IMPULSE

The functioning of the nervous system rests upon two physiological processes: the generation of an action potential with its conduction down axons, and the synaptic transmission of these impulses between neurons and/or muscle cells. These processes depend upon the energy-demanding maintenance of an electrochemical gradient across neuron cell membranes, and alterations in this are effected by specialised ion channels in the membrane. Synaptic transmission involves the release from a neuron of neurotransmitter molecules that bind to specific receptors on the membrane of the receptor cell. These molecules alter either that cell's membrane potential, via effects upon ion channel permeability, or its metabolic function (see Fig. 22.2). There are over 20 different neurotransmitters known to act at different sites in the nervous system, all potentially amenable to pharmacological manipulation (see Box 22.1).

22.1 NEUROTRANSMITTERS

Neurotransmitter	Effect	Clinical relevance	Pharmacology
Acetylcholine	Excitatory	Alzheimer's disease Myasthenia gravis Parkinson's disease Huntington's chorea Motion sickness Bladder control Vomiting	Donepezil, rivastigmine Acetylcholinesterase inhibitors Anticholinergics
Noradrenaline/adrenaline	Excitatory	Migraine Mood disorders Cardiovascular control Bladder control Appetite Sleep disorders	α-adrenoceptor antagonists (α-blockers) Clonidine Antidepressants Dexamfetamine β-adrenoceptor antagonists (β-blockers)
Glutamate Aspartate	Excitatory	Cerebral ischaemia Epilepsy Memory Degenerative diseases (motor neuron disease)	Lamotrigine Riluzole Topiramate
Dopamine	Excitatory	Parkinson's disease Schizophrenia Vomiting	Levodopa Dopamine agonists Major tranquillisers Metoclopramide
5-hydroxytryptamine (5-HT, serotonin)	Excitatory	Migraine Depression Pain Sleep	Pizotifen, sumatriptan Antidepressants
Gamma-aminobutyric acid (GABA) Glycine	Inhibitory	Epilepsy Spasticity	Phenobarbital Anticonvulsants Benzodiazepines Baclofen
Histamine	Inhibitory	Uncertain	

Neuropeptides
Vasopressin
Adrenocorticotrophic hormone (ACTH)
Melanocyte-stimulating hormone (MSH)
Substance P
Opioid peptides (> 20)
  Endorphins
  Enkephalins
  Dynorphins
	Excitatory and inhibitory	Memory
		Uncertain
		
		Pain
			Morphine

Purines Adenosine triphosphate/diphosphate (ATP/ADP) Adenosine monophosphate (AMP) Adenosine	Excitatory and modulation of neurotransmission	Uncertain	
Nitric oxide	Modulation of neurotransmission	Memory Cerebral ischaemia	

The neuronal cell bodies are acted upon by synapses with large numbers of other neurons. Each neuron therefore acts as a microprocessor, reacting to the influences upon it by changes to its cell membrane potential, causing it to be more or less ready to discharge an impulse down its axon(s). The synapsing neuron terminals are also subject to regulation by receptor sites on their pre-synaptic membrane, which modify the release of transmitter across the synaptic cleft. The effect of some neurotransmitters is to produce long-term modulation of metabolic function or gene expression rather than simply to change the membrane potential. This effect probably underlies more complex processes in cognition, such as long-term memory.

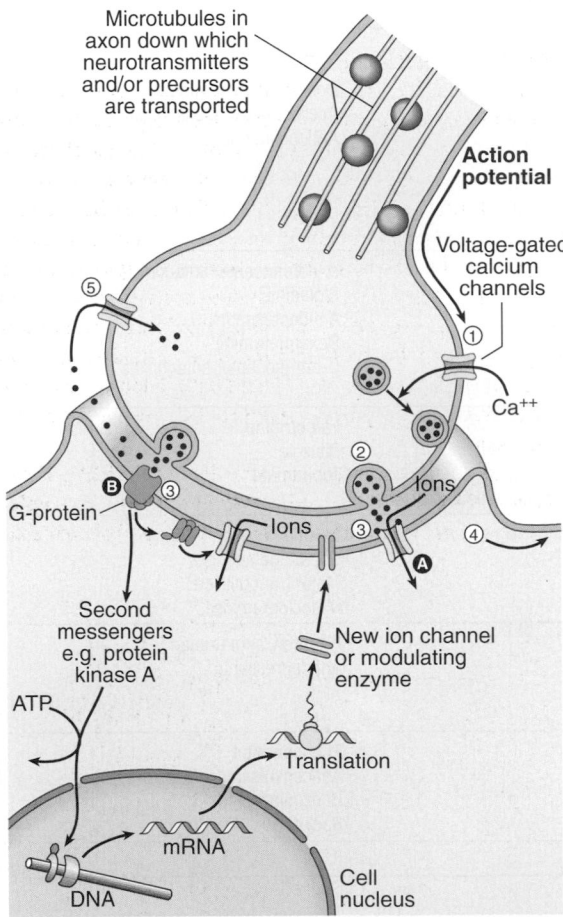

Fig. 22.2 Neurotransmission and neurotransmitters. (1) An action potential arriving at the nerve terminal depolarises the membrane and this opens voltage-gated calcium channels. (2) Entry of calcium causes the fusion of synaptic vesicles containing neurotransmitters with the pre-synaptic membrane and release of the neurotransmitter across the synaptic cleft. (3) The neurotransmitter binds to receptors on the post-synaptic membrane to either (A) open ligand-gated ion channels which, by allowing ion entry, depolarise the membrane and initiate an action potential (4), or (B) bind to metabotrophic receptors, which activate an effector enzyme (e.g. adenylyl cyclase) and thus via the intracellular second messenger system modulate gene transcription, leading to changes in synthesis of ion channels or modulating enzymes. (5) Neurotransmitters are taken up at the pre-synaptic membrane and/or metabolised.

MAJOR ANATOMICAL DIVISIONS OF THE NERVOUS SYSTEM (see Fig. 22.3)

Cerebral hemispheres

The cerebral cortex constitutes the highest level of nervous function, the anterior half dealing with executive ('doing') functions and the posterior half constructing a perception of the environment ('receiving and perceiving'). Collections of cells in the depths of the hemispheres deal with motor control (the basal ganglia), the appropriate attention to sensory perception (the thalamus), emotion and memory (the limbic system), and control over internal bodily functions (the hypothalamus). The cerebral ventricles contain the choroid plexus; this produces the cerebrospinal fluid (CSF), which cushions the brain within the cranium. From the fourth ventricle the CSF leaves through foramina in the brain stem to circulate down around the spinal cord and over the surface of brain, where it is reabsorbed into the cerebral venous system (see Fig. 22.56, p. 1208).

The brain stem

In addition to containing all the sensory and motor pathways entering and leaving the hemispheres, the brain stem houses the nuclei of the cranial nerves and the other important collections of neurons. These are involved in the control of conjugate eye movements, the maintenance of balance, cardiorespiratory control and the maintenance of arousal.

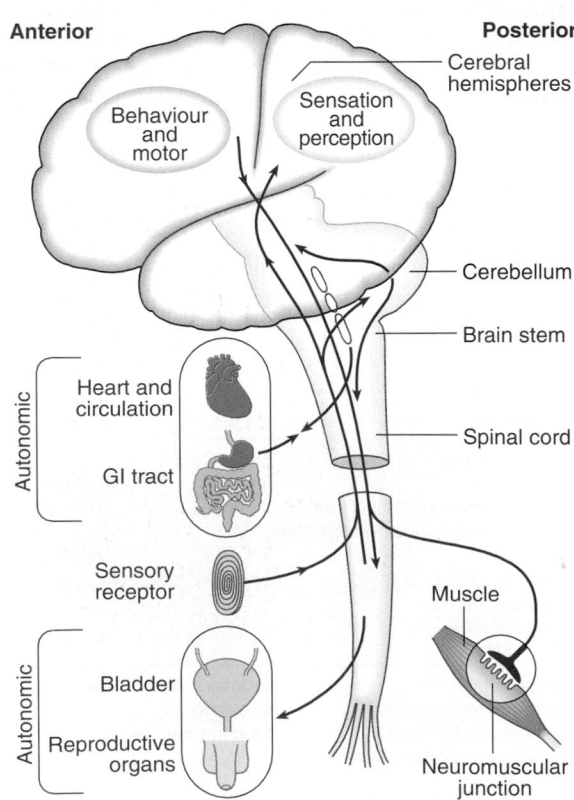

Fig. 22.3 The major anatomical components of the nervous system.

The spinal cord

The spinal cord contains not only the afferent and efferent fibres arranged in functionally discrete bundles but also, in the grey matter, collections of cells which are responsible for lower-order motor reflexes and the primary processing of sensory information, including pain.

The peripheral nervous system

The sensory cell bodies of peripheral nerves are situated in the dorsal root ganglia in the spinal exit foramina, whilst the distal ends of their neurons are invested with various specialised endings for the transduction of external stimuli into nervous impulses. The motor cell bodies are in the anterior horns of the spinal cord. Motor neurons initiate muscle contraction by the release of acetylcholine across the neuromuscular junction, with the resultant change in potential in the muscle end plate. To increase the speed of impulse conduction peripheral nerve axons are variably invested in myelin sheaths consisting of the wrapped membranes of Schwann cells.

The autonomic system

The unconscious neural control of the body's physiology is effected through the autonomic system. This innervates the cardiovascular and respiratory systems, smooth muscle of the gastrointestinal tract, and glands throughout the body. The autonomic system is controlled centrally by diffuse modulatory systems in the brain stem, limbic system and frontal lobes, which are concerned with arousal and background behavioural responses to threat. The output of the autonomic system is divided functionally and pharmacologically into two divisions: the parasympathetic and sympathetic systems.

INVESTIGATION OF NEUROLOGICAL DISEASE

TESTS OF FUNCTION (CLINICAL NEUROPHYSIOLOGY)

In the investigation of neurological disease, tests of function have a somewhat more restricted application than tests of structure (i.e. imaging). Nevertheless, recording of electrical activity over the brain and assessment of nerve and muscle function are essential in certain conditions. The major tests are electroencephalography (EEG), evoked potentials (EPs) and nerve conduction studies/electromyography (NCS/EMG).

Electroencephalography

Electrical activity arising in the cerebral cortex can be detected using electrodes placed on the scalp, although this is estimated to detect only 0.1–1% of the brain's electrical activity at any one time. An array of electrodes provides spatial information. Rhythmical waveforms can be detected and are distinguished by their frequency. When the eyes are shut, the most obvious frequency over the occipital cortex is 7–13/s; this is known as alpha rhythm, and disappears when the eyes are opened. Other frequency bands seen over different parts of the brain in different circumstances are beta (faster than 13/s), theta (4–6/s) and delta (slower than 4/s). Lower frequencies predominate in the very young and during sleep.

Various diseases result in abnormalities of the EEG. These may be continuous or episodic, focal or diffuse. Examples of continuous abnormalities include a global increase

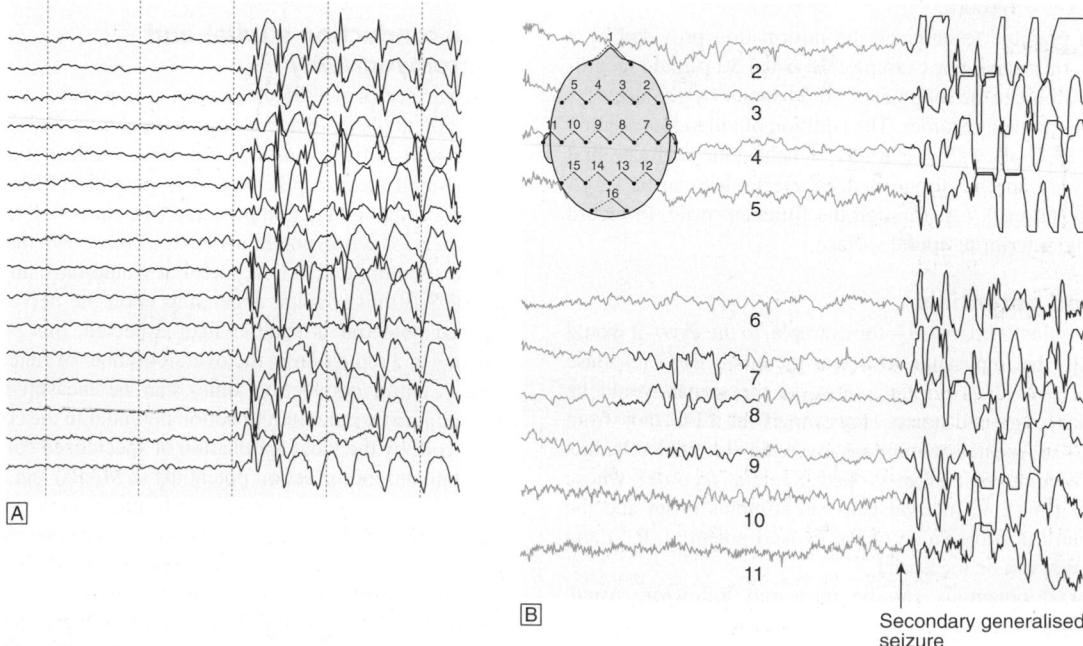

Fig. 22.4 EEGs in epilepsy. [A] Primary generalised epileptic discharge. [B] Focal sharp waves over the right parietal region (between electrodes 7 and 8—shown in purple) with secondary generalised discharge.

in fast frequencies (beta) seen with sedating drugs (e.g. benzodiazepines), or marked slowing seen over a structural lesion such as a tumour or an infarct. With the advent of modern neuro-imaging, EEG has lost its use in localising lesions, except in the management of epilepsy (see below and Fig. 22.4). However, it is still useful in the management of patients who have disturbance of consciousness or disorders of sleep, in the diagnosis of cerebral diseases such as encephalitis, and in certain dementias (e.g. Creutzfeldt–Jakob disease).

The most important use of EEG is in the management of epilepsy. It must be stressed, however, that only in rare circumstances will an EEG provide unequivocal evidence of epilepsy, and it is therefore not useful as a diagnostic test for the presence of epilepsy. Its use is predominantly to distinguish the type of epilepsy present, and whether there is an epileptic focus, particularly if surgery for epilepsy is contemplated.

During an epileptic seizure, high-voltage disturbances of the background activity ('transients') can be recorded. These may be generalised, as in the 3 cycle/s 'spike and wave' of childhood absence epilepsy (petit mal), or more focal, as in partial epilepsies (see Fig. 22.4). However, it is unusual to record a seizure itself, except in the case of childhood absence epilepsy. Nevertheless, it is often possible to detect 'epileptiform' abnormalities in between seizures in the form of 'spikes' and 'sharp waves' that lend support to a clinical diagnosis. The likelihood of detecting these abnormalities is enhanced by hyperventilation, photic flicker, sleep and some drugs. Note that, even so, some 50% of patients with proven epilepsy will have a normal 'routine' EEG, and conversely, the presence of features often seen in association with epilepsy does not, of itself, make a diagnosis (although the false positive rate for clear-cut epileptiform features is < 1/1000).

It is possible to enhance the information provided by a variety of means. For example, the usual 30-minute recording session can be lengthened to 24 hours by the use of a lightweight tape recorder. The addition of video information to the EEG allows comparison of behaviour with cerebral activity. In special circumstances, electrodes can be surgically positioned, e.g. through the foramen ovale, to record from the inferior temporal surface.

Evoked potentials

If a stimulus is provided—for example, to the eye—it would normally be impossible to detect the small EEG response evoked over the occipital cortex as the signal would be lost in background noise. However, if the EEG data from 100–1000 repeated stimuli are averaged electronically, this noise is removed and an evoked potential recorded whose latency (the time interval between stimulus onset and the maximum positive value of the evoked potential, P_{100}) and amplitude can be measured.

Evoked potentials can be measured following visual, auditory or somatosensory stimuli if electrodes are appropriately positioned, though visual evoked potentials are by far the most commonly used (see Fig. 22.5). Abnormalities of the evoked potential indicate damage to the relevant

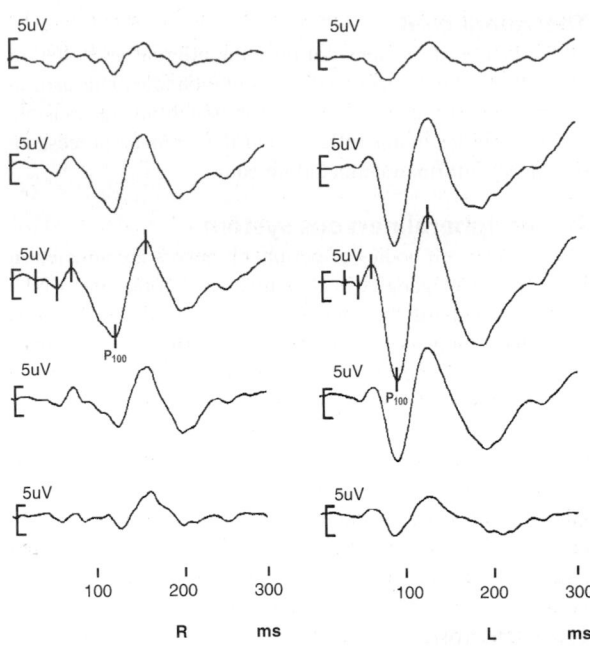

Fig. 22.5   Visual evoked responses (VER) recording showing abnormal delay on right. The latency of the P_{100} (the point of maximum positivity) on the left is 90 ms, that on the right 115 ms.

pathway, either in the form of a conduction delay (increased latency), or reduced amplitude, or both.

With the advent of magnetic resonance imaging (MRI), the use of evoked potentials is becoming restricted to specialised indications, such as providing a semi-objective measure of visual function.

Nerve conduction studies and electromyography

Using surface or needle electrodes, it is possible to record action potentials from nerves which lie close to the skin surface as well as from muscles. If a nerve trunk is stimulated with a small electric potential, it is possible to record the resulting compound action potential (the sum of all the individual nerves' action potentials) as it travels down the nerve. A normal compound action potential would have an amplitude of 5–30 microvolts, depending upon the nerve. If the recorded potential is smaller than expected, this provides evidence of a reduction in the overall number of functioning axons. Central conduction times can be measured using electromagnetic induction of action potential in the cortex or spinal cord by the local application of specialised coils.

Compound motor action potentials (CMAPs) can also be recorded over muscles in response to motor nerve stimulation (see Fig. 22.6). These are easier to record because the muscle amplifies the response, typical amplitudes being 1–20 millivolts. By measuring the response latency to stimulation of a nerve at two different points along its length, it is possible to calculate nerve conduction velocities (NCVs). This can be done for both sensory and motor nerves; typical values are 50–60 m/s. Slowing of conduction velocity is suggestive of peripheral nerve demyelination which may be either diffuse (as in a demyelinating peripheral neuropathy) or focal (as in pressure palsies or conduction block).

The principal use of nerve conduction studies is to identify damage to peripheral nerves, and to determine whether the pathological process is focal or diffuse and whether the damage is principally axonal or demyelinating. It is also possible to obtain some information about nerve roots by more sophisticated analysis of responses to impulses initially conducted antidromically (i.e. the 'wrong' way) back up to the spinal cord, and then returning orthodromically (the 'right' way) down to the stimulation point ('F waves').

Fine concentric needle electrodes can be inserted into muscle bellies themselves and the potentials from individual motor units recorded. It is possible to record abnormal spontaneous activity arising from muscles at rest, such as fibrillations (a sign of denervation) or myotonic discharges. Abnormalities in the shape and size of muscle potentials can help in the differential diagnosis of denervation and structural muscle diseases. Myopathies caused by metabolic abnormalities (causing electromechanical dissociation rather than loss of fibre structure) show no changes on needle EMG.

Electromyography can also be used to investigate the neuromuscular junction. Repetitive stimulation of a nerve with trains of electrical impulses at 3–15/s does not normally result in a significant fall-off in the amplitude of the resulting muscle action potential. However, such a decrement is seen in myasthenia gravis (see p. 1183) and provides one of the key diagnostic features. Augmentation of the response to repetitive stimulation is seen in the Lambert–Eaton myasthenic syndrome, though usually at higher stimulation frequencies.

IMAGING

Imaging is crucial to the identification of lesions of the nervous system in disease. There are various techniques, based on the use of X-rays (plain radiographs, computed tomography (CT), myelography and angiography), magnetic resonance (MR imaging—MRI, or MR angiography—MRA), ultrasound (Doppler imaging of blood vessels), and radioisotopes (single photon emission computerised tomography—SPECT, and positron emission tomography—PET). The indications, usefulness and limits of each technique are listed in Box 22.2. The choice of technique depends upon the area of the neuraxis that is being investigated.

Head and orbit

The use of plain skull radiographs is largely restricted to the diagnosis of fractures and sinus disease. CT or MRI is needed to image pathology inside the skull. Which is used depends on what information is being sought and, to some extent, how urgently it is required, as CT is often more easily available than MRI. CT will show bone and calcium well, and will easily image collections of blood. It will also

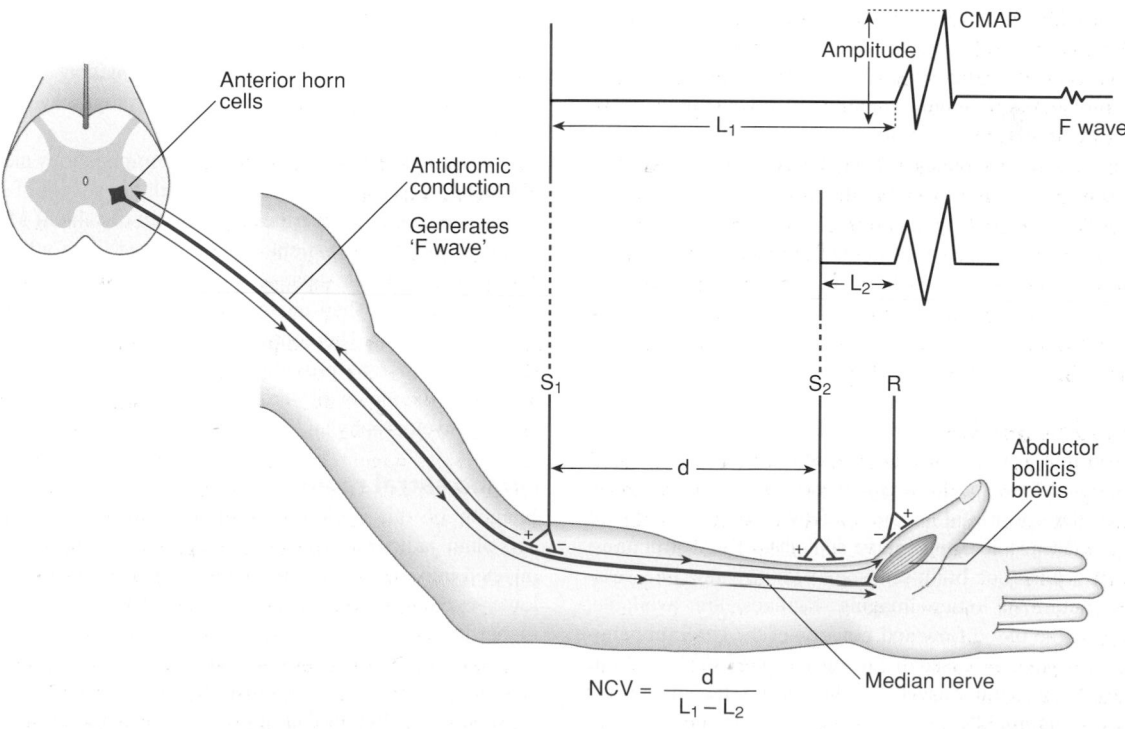

$$NCV = \frac{d}{L_1 - L_2}$$

Fig. 22.6 Motor nerve conduction tests. Bipolar electrodes (R) on the muscle (abductor pollicis brevis here) record the compound motor action potential (CMAP) from stimulation at the median nerve at the elbow (S_1) and from the wrist (S_2). The CMAP amplitude is related to the number of axons, and the velocity can be determined if the distance between the two stimulating electrodes (d) is known. The latency (L) of the F wave is a measure of the conduction time in the nerve proximal to the elbow (see text). (NCV = nerve conduction velocity)

22.2 TECHNIQUES AVAILABLE FOR IMAGING THE NERVOUS SYSTEM

Technique	Principle	Applications	Advantages	Disadvantages	Comments
X-ray	Attenuation of X-ray beam by radio-opaque substances (calcium, metal, contrast etc.)	Plain radiographs CT Radiculography Myelography Contrast angiography	Widely available Relatively cheap Relatively quick	Ionising radiation Reactions to contrast Myelography and angiography are invasive and therefore carry risks	In neurology, plain radiographs only demonstrate fracture or foreign bodies CT is investigation of choice for trauma and stroke Intra-arterial X-ray contrast angiography still 'gold standard'
Magnetic resonance imaging (MRI)	Magnetic resonance of different tissues depends on free hydrogen/water content; signals changed by movement (e.g. flowing blood)	Structural imaging MR angiography (MRA) Functional MR MR spectroscopy	High-quality soft tissue delineation Better views of posterior fossa and temporal lobes No ionising radiation Non-invasive	Expensive Not yet widely available Angiography looks at blood flow not anatomy Scans uncomfortable/claustrophobic	Increasing application Functional MR and MR spectroscopy still research tools
Ultrasound	Echoes from high-frequency sound source localise structure; Doppler phenomenon used to measure rate of flow	Doppler Duplex scans	Cheap Quick Non-invasive	Operator-dependent Poor anatomical definition	Useful as screening tool
Radio-isotope imaging	Radio-labelled isotopes bind to structure(s) of interest, or used to assess relative blood flow	Isotope brain scan SPECT PET	In vivo demonstration of functional anatomy (e.g. ligand binding, blood flow)	Poor spatial resolution Ionising radiation Expensive, especially PET Not widely available	Isotope scans now obsolete SPECT and PET largely research tools

(CT = computerised tomography; MR = magnetic resonance; PET = positron emission tomography; SPECT = single photon emission computerised tomography)

detect abnormalities of the brain and ventricles, such as atrophy, tumours, cysts, abscesses, vascular lesions and hydrocephalus. Diagnostic yield is often improved by the use of intravenous contrast and spiral CT methods. It is, however, limited in its ability to image the posterior fossa (because of the surrounding bone density), and it is poor at detecting abnormalities of white matter and at allowing detailed analysis of grey matter.

MRI is much more useful in the investigation of posterior fossa disease as it is not affected by the surrounding bone. It is much more sensitive than CT to abnormalities of white and grey matter, and is therefore useful in the investigation of inflammatory conditions such as multiple sclerosis, and in investigating epilepsy. MRI can also provide additional information about structural brain lesions which may complement that available from CT. It is also useful in imaging the orbits, where special imaging sequences can be used to compensate for orbital fat, and thereby allow clear views of extraocular muscles, optic nerve and other orbital structures.

Standard isotope brain scans are of little value in assessing structure if other imaging facilities are available. However, the blood flow and function of the cerebral hemispheres can be assessed by using either SPECT or PET. Examples of brain imaged by the various techniques are shown in Figure 22.7.

Neck

Plain radiographs of the neck are useful in the investigation of structural damage to vertebrae, such as that resulting from trauma or inflammatory damage (e.g. rheumatoid arthritis). They can also provide implicit information about intervertebral disc disease, but not detailed information about the cervical cord or nerve roots, for which myelography or MRI is needed.

Myelography is invasive. Potential complications include headache, seizures and meningitis. With the advent of MRI its use is declining. Nevertheless, it is still of value if MRI is not available, or the patient cannot tolerate lying within an MRI scanner. Radio-opaque contrast is injected into the lumbar theca and then moved up to the cervical region by tilting the patient. The contrast outlines the nerve roots and spinal cord, thereby providing information about abnormal structure. Examples of the neck imaged by plain radiographs, myelography and MRI are shown in Figure 22.8.

Lumbo-sacral region

Imaging of this region is similar to imaging the neck, and plain radiographs are of limited use. Contrast can be injected into the lumbar thecal space and used to outline the lower nerve roots only (radiculography), or it can be run up to outline the conus and spinal cord (myelography). The information obtained may be enhanced by the additional use of CT following myelography (contrast CT). Non-contrast CT of the lumbar spine can only be used to image the vertebrae and discs. As with the cervical spine, MRI provides a non-invasive way of obtaining high-resolution images of both the vertebral column and the relevant neural structures.

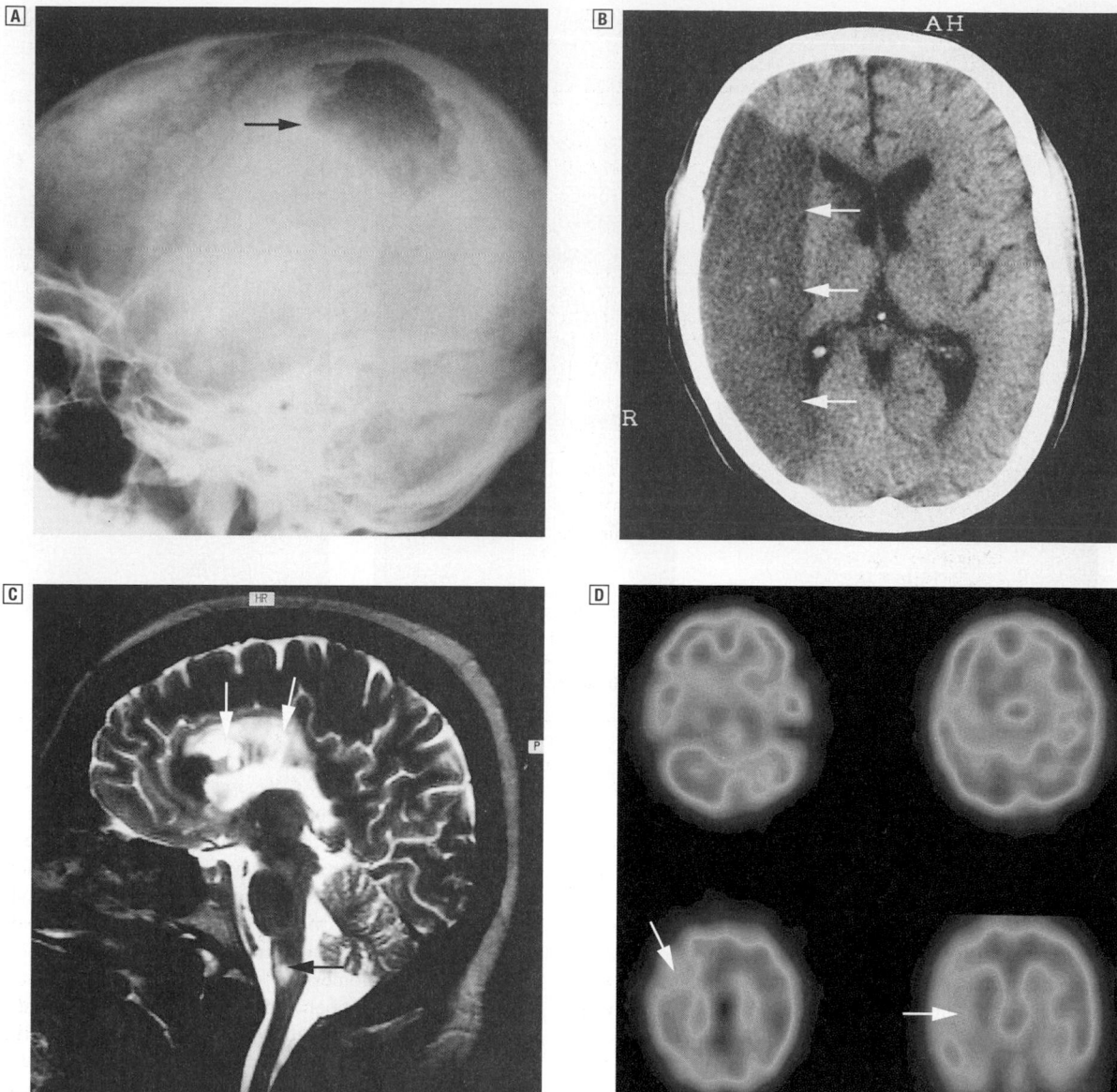

Fig. 22.7 **Different techniques of imaging the head and brain.** [A] Skull radiograph showing lytic vault lesion (eosinophilic granuloma—arrow). [B] CT showing complete middle cerebral artery infarct (arrows). [C] MRI showing widespread areas of high signal in multiple sclerosis (arrows). [D] SPECT after caudate infarct shows relative hypoperfusion of overlying right cerebral cortex (arrows).

Blood vessels

Various techniques are available to investigate extracranial and intracranial blood vessels. The least invasive is ultrasound (Doppler or duplex scanning), which is used to investigate the carotid and the vertebral arteries in the neck, usually as part of the investigation of stroke. In skilled hands, reliable information can be provided about the degree of arterial stenosis, and the technique often gives useful anatomical information, e.g. whether there is an ulcerated plaque. Information concerning the blood flow in the intracerebral vessels is also becoming increasingly possible to obtain using transcranial Doppler. The anatomical resolution of Doppler imaging is limited, and formal angiography may still be required. The latter is, however, invasive, and therefore carries a small but significant risk of stroke or even death. Thus, the major role of Doppler imaging is as a screening test to determine whether invasive angiography is indicated.

Blood vessels can be outlined by the injection of radio-opaque contrast. The X-ray images obtained can be enhanced by the use of computer-assisted digital subtraction, or by the use of spiral CT. Contrast may be injected intravenously or intra-arterially. The former requires a much higher total dose of contrast, and the images obtained are not as good, but the latter involves feeding catheters up through the arterial tree and is thus associated with a higher complication rate. Formal intra-arterial angiography is usually required to

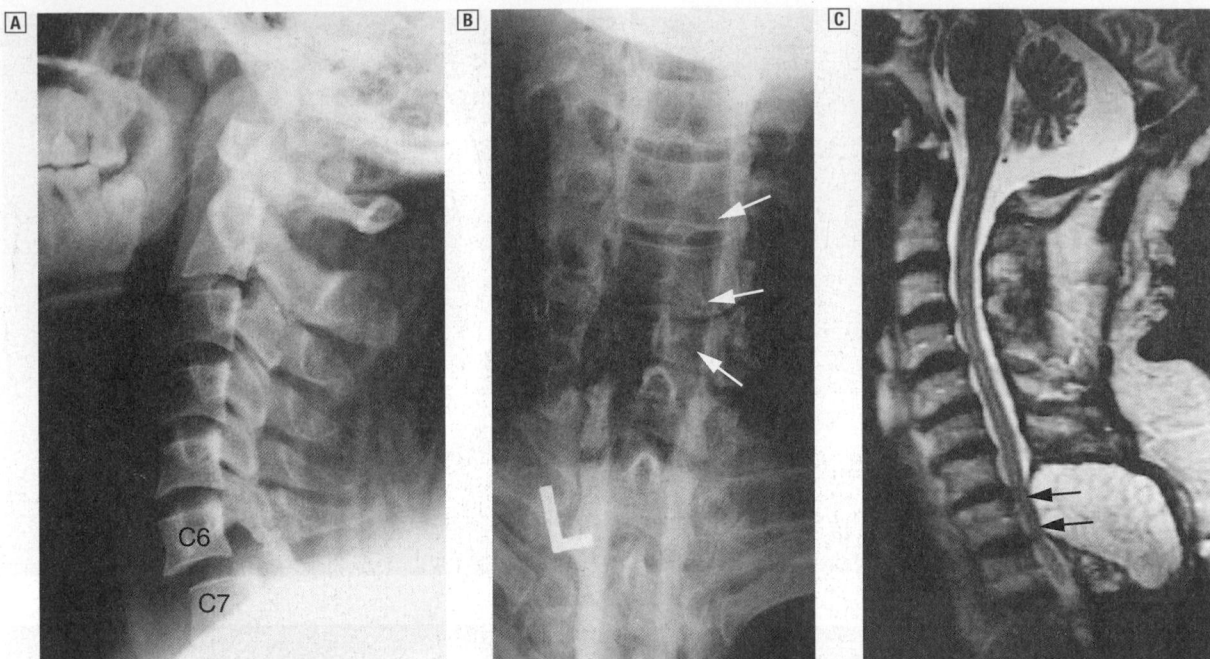

C6
C7

L

Fig. 22.8 **Different techniques of imaging the cervical spine.** A Lateral radiograph showing bilateral C6/7 facet dislocation. B Myelogram showing widening of cervical cord due to astrocytoma (arrows). C MRI showing posterior epidural compression from adenocarcinomatous metastasis to the posterior arch of T1 (arrows).

delineate lesions of the extracranial carotid artery prior to endarterectomy, and is also used to investigate abnormalities of intracerebral vessels such as arterial (berry) aneurysms or arteriovenous malformations, or to delineate the blood supply of tumours prior to surgery.

Flowing blood can be detected by specialised MR sequences in MR angiography. The anatomical resolution is still not comparable to that of intra-arterial angiography, but the investigation is non-invasive. Examples of these different techniques are given in Figure 22.9.

SPECIAL TESTS

Blood tests

Many systemic conditions affect the nervous system and these can often be diagnosed with the help of blood tests: for example, confusion due to hypothyroidism, a stroke due to systemic lupus erythematosus, ataxia due to vitamin B_{12} deficiency, or myelopathy due to syphilis. The blood tests relating to general medical conditions which affect the nervous system are dealt with in the sections dealing with the conditions themselves.

There are, however, a number of blood tests which are used in investigating specific neurological diseases. These include haematological tests (e.g. looking for acanthocytes to diagnose neuroacanthocytosis), biochemical tests (e.g. creatine kinase in muscle diseases, copper studies to diagnose Wilson's disease) or tests to help diagnose innumerable infections of the nervous system. In addition, there are a number of specific antibodies that are useful diagnostically. These include antibodies to acetylcholine receptors and skeletal muscle, seen in myasthenia gravis, and to voltage-gated calcium channels in Lambert–Eaton myasthenic syndrome. Antibodies to different types of ganglioside (glycoproteins expressed on nerve membranes) can be seen in various types of neuropathy including multifocal motor neuronopathy, and the Guillain–Barré syndrome (particularly the Miller Fisher variant). Also, antineuronal antibodies provide markers of paraneoplastic cerebellar or neuropathic syndromes.

An increasing number of inherited neurological conditions can now be diagnosed by DNA analysis (see p. 349). These include diseases caused by increased numbers of trinucleotide repeats, such as Huntington's disease, myotonic dystrophy and some types of spinocerebellar ataxia. Also, defects of mitochondrial DNA can be detected in many conditions including Leber's hereditary optic neuropathy, and some syndromes causing epilepsy or stroke-like syndromes.

Lumbar puncture

This involves the insertion of a needle between lumbar spinous processes, through the dura and into the CSF under local anaesthetic. Intracranial pressure can be measured and CSF removed for analysis. CSF is normally clear and colourless. Tests usually performed on CSF include centrifuging to determine the colour of the supernatant (yellow, or xanthochromic, some hours after subarachnoid haemorrhage), biochemistry (glucose, total protein, and protein electrophoresis to detect oligoclonal bands), microbiology, immunology (e.g. Venereal Diseases Research Laboratory (VDRL) test—see p. 98, paraneoplastic antibodies) and cytology (to detect malignant cells). Normal values and various abnormalities found in diseases are shown in Box 22.3.

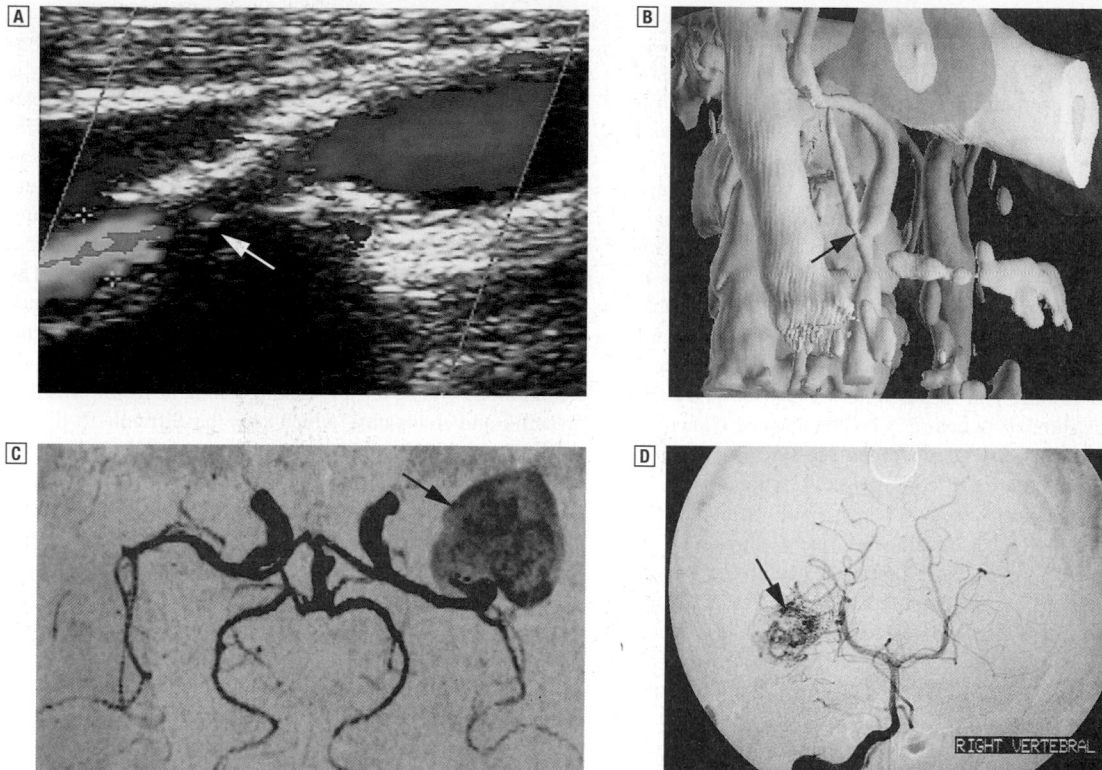

Fig. 22.9   Different techniques of imaging blood vessels. [A] Doppler scan showing 80% stenosis of internal carotid artery (arrow).
[B] 3-D reconstruction of CT angiogram showing stenosis at the carotid bifurcation (arrow). [C] MR angiogram showing giant aneurysm at the middle
cerebral artery bifurcation (arrow). [D] Intra-arterial angiography showing arteriovenous malformation (arrow).

22.3 CSF PARAMETERS IN HEALTH AND SOME COMMON DISORDERS*

	Normal	Subarachnoid haemorrhage	Acute bacterial meningitis	Viral meningitis	Tuberculous meningitis	Multiple sclerosis
Pressure	50–180 mm of water	Increased	Normal/increased	Normal	Normal/increased	Normal
Colour	Clear	Blood-stained Xanthochromic	Cloudy	Clear	Clear/cloudy	Clear
Red cell count	0–4/mm^3	Raised	Normal	Normal	Normal	Normal
White cell count	0–4/mm^3	Normal/slightly raised	1000–5000 polymorphs	10–2000 lymphocytes	50–5000 lymphocytes	0–50 lymphocytes
Glucose	> 60% of blood level	Normal	Decreased	Normal	Decreased	Normal
Protein	< 0.45 g/l	Increased	Increased	Normal/increased	Increased	Normal/increased
Microbiology	Sterile	Sterile	Organisms on Gram stain and/or culture	Sterile/virus detected	Ziehl–Neelsen/auramine stain or tuberculosis culture positive	Sterile
Oligoclonal bands	Negative	Negative	Can be positive	Can be positive	Can be positive	Often positive

* See also Box 22.85, page 1193.

Lumbar puncture is indicated in the investigation of infections (e.g. meningitis or encephalitis), subarachnoid haemorrhage, inflammatory conditions (e.g. multiple sclerosis, sarcoidosis and cerebral lupus) and some neurological malignancies (e.g. carcinomatous meningitis, lymphoma and leukaemia), and to measure CSF pressure (e.g. in idiopathic intracranial hypertension). It is, of course, part of the procedure of myelography, and can be part of the therapeutic procedures, either to lower CSF pressure or to administer drugs.

If there is a space-occupying lesion in the head, lumbar puncture can result in a shift of intracerebral contents downwards, towards and into the spinal canal. This process is known as coning, and is potentially fatal (see p. 1203). Consequently, lumbar puncture is contraindicated if there is any suggestion of raised intracranial pressure (e.g. papilloedema), depressed level of consciousness, or focal neurological signs suggesting a cerebral lesion, until imaging of the head (by CT or MRI) has excluded a space-occupying lesion or hydrocephalus. It is also contraindicated if the patient is likely to bleed, as in thrombocytopenia, disseminated intravascular coagulation or warfarin therapy, unless specific measures are taken to compensate for the clotting deficit on a temporary basis. Lumbar puncture is not contraindicated in those on aspirin.

About 30% of lumbar punctures are followed by low-pressure headache, which can be severe. Other minor complications involve transient radicular pain during the procedure, and pain over the lumbar region. Provided the test is performed under sterile conditions, infections such as meningitis are extremely rare.

Biopsies

Nerve and muscle are occasionally biopsied to assist in the diagnosis and management of a number of neurological conditions. Likewise, it is occasionally necessary to biopsy brain or meninges.

Nerve is sometimes biopsied as part of the investigation of peripheral neuropathies. Usually, the sural nerve is sampled at the ankle or the radial nerve at the wrist. Histology is often able to help identify underlying causes in demyelinating neuropathies (e.g. vasculitic) or, occasionally, infiltration with abnormal substances such as amyloid. However, nerve biopsy is not performed unless it is reasonably likely to diagnose a potentially treatable condition such as an inflammatory neuropathy, since there is an appreciable morbidity.

Skeletal muscle biopsy is performed more frequently. The quadriceps muscle is often sampled, though this depends somewhat on which muscles are affected. Indications include the investigation of primary muscle disease, as muscle histology can be used to distinguish neurogenic wasting, myositis and myopathy, which may be difficult to distinguish clinically. Histology and enzyme histochemistry can also be helpful in the diagnosis of more widespread metabolic disorders, such as mitochondrial and some storage diseases. Though pain and infection can follow the procedure, these are much less of a problem than after nerve biopsy.

The nature of lesions demonstrated by brain imaging can often be inferred from the appearances as well as the history, examination and other, less invasive, investigations. However, there are situations in which the nature of lesions is not clear, and it is important to obtain tissue for histological examination. Likewise, it is sometimes necessary to biopsy the brain parenchyma itself in unexplained degenerative diseases (e.g. unusual dementias) so as not to miss potentially treatable disease.

Brain biopsy used to require full craniotomy. However, owing to the increased availability and sophistication of cerebral imaging, it is now possible to biopsy most lesions stereotactically through a burrhole in the skull. The complication rate of such stereotactic biopsies is much lower than that of open craniotomy, but haemorrhage, infection and death still occur. Hence, brain biopsy is only considered if diagnosis cannot be reached in any other way.

MAJOR MANIFESTATIONS OF NERVOUS SYSTEM DISEASE

HEADACHE AND FACIAL PAIN

Headache is one of the most frequent neurological symptoms but it is seldom associated with significant neurological disease unless accompanied by other symptoms or neurological signs. Nevertheless, patients suffering from headaches usually fear serious brain disease. In order to manage them effectively, it is important to be aware of this mismatch between fear of disease and its actual likelihood. Careful clinical assessment usually identifies one of a limited number of headache or facial pain syndromes (see Box 22.4). After taking a careful history and performing the appropriate neurological examination, it is often not necessary to perform further investigations. The patient can be reassured and provided with symptomatic treatment.

22.4 COMMON HEADACHE AND FACIAL PAIN SYNDROMES
• Tension headache
• Migraine
• Cluster headache
• Raised intracranial pressure
• Benign paroxysmal headaches (see Box 22.7, p. 1120)
• Trigeminal neuralgia
• Atypical facial pain
• Post-herpetic neuralgia

Pathophysiology

It is often difficult to explain the pain of headaches, especially in those not caused by serious disease, by reference to current neurobiological understanding of the mechanisms of pain. Within the skull the dura (including the dural sinuses and falx cerebri) and the proximal parts of the large pial blood vessels are the main structures sensitive to pain. The brain parenchyma, pial arteries over the convexities, and the cerebral ventricles and choroid plexus are known to be insensitive to pain. The pain-sensitive intracranial structures are mostly innervated by branches of the trigeminal nerve and some by branches of the upper cervical nerves. This probably accounts for the patterns of pain referral seen in intracranial disease when these pain-sensitive parts of the intracranial contents are stretched, distended or otherwise irritated.

A DIAGNOSTIC APPROACH TO THE PATIENT WITH HEADACHE

Unless the history is suggestive of structural disease, patients with headache who are normal on neurological examination are unlikely to have a serious disorder, however distressing their symptoms. The features of a patient's history that are helpful in making a clear diagnosis of the cause of a headache are shown in Box 22.5.

Patients can be divided into those with chronic headache (a duration of several weeks or more) and those with more acute headache. Serious acute neurological disease should always be considered in patients with headaches of very sudden onset. Subarachnoid haemorrhage (see p. 1162) causes a very sudden headache which may or may not be localised, although only one person in eight who has such a 'thunderclap' headache will have had a subarachnoid haemorrhage. A patient with subarachnoid haemorrhage almost invariably develops other symptoms including vomiting and neck stiffness, though the latter may take some hours to develop. The main differential diagnosis in a patient with a sudden severe headache is between subarachnoid haemorrhage and a migraine variant (see Fig. 22.32, p. 1163). Meningitis occasionally presents apoplectically, but the headache is usually less dramatic in onset.

Headache coming on over a matter of hours is less likely to be associated with structural disease and more likely to be due to migraine, unless accompanied by other significant symptoms or signs. Patients with bacterial meningitis are usually generally ill and pyrexial, and

exhibit meningism. Patients with viral meningitis may present with a pyrexia and quite sudden and severe headache coming on over an hour or so, but are less likely to have neck stiffness or other signs of meningism. Migraine headaches (see below) may be accompanied or preceded by vomiting and focal neurological symptoms (usually in the form of zigzag 'fortification spectra' or tingling moving slowly over part of the body).

When headaches are intermittent rather than continuous over a period of days or weeks they are most likely to be migrainous but it is worth while paying attention to the time of day they occur and the presence or absence of precipitating factors. The headache of raised intracranial pressure is present on waking and often resolves or improves as the patient becomes upright (reducing the intracranial pressure) or takes simple analgesia (see Box 22.6). It is unusual for a patient to present with such a headache alone since it is usually not sufficiently severe to cause alarm, the presentation of the causative mass lesion more often being provoked by a seizure or by focal neurological dysfunction (aphasia, hemiplegia etc.). The exceptions to this are patients with acute hydrocephalus who present with a more severe headache. As with other causes of raised intracranial pressure, this is worse when lying, bending forward or coughing, and frequently causes vomiting in the morning (especially in children). Hydrocephalus may cause no other symptoms except gait ataxia, though examination may reveal papilloedema.

22.6 HEADACHE OF RAISED INTRACRANIAL PRESSURE
• Worse in morning, improves through the day
• Associated with morning vomiting
• Worse bending forward
• Worse with cough and straining
• Relieved by analgesia
• Dull ache, often mild

Headaches that persist for weeks, are present all day and are poorly responsive to simple analgesia are very likely to be tension-type headaches, whatever their other characteristics. Headaches so well localised by the patient that a finger is used to locate the exact spot on the skull are never associated with significant disease.

In a patient over 60 years with head pain localised to one or both temples, giant cell arteritis (see p. 1041) should be considered, especially if the temporal pulses are not palpable and/or the arteries are enlarged and tender.

TENSION-TYPE HEADACHE

Clinical features

This is the most common type of headache and is experienced at some time by the majority of the population in some form. The pain is usually constant and generalised but often radiates forward from the occipital region. It is

22.5 IMPORTANT POINTS IN THE HEADACHE HISTORY
• The tempo of onset
• The time of day of onset of maximal pain
• The effect of posture, coughing and straining
• The location of the pain
• Any associated symptoms

described as 'dull', 'tight' or like a 'pressure', and there may be a sensation of a band round the head or pressure at the vertex. In contrast to migraine, the pain may continue for weeks or months without interruption, although the severity may vary, and there is no associated vomiting or photophobia. The patient can usually continue normal activities and the pain may be less noticeable when the patient is occupied. The pain is characteristically less severe in the early part of the day and becomes more troublesome as the day goes on. Local tenderness may be present over the skull vault or in the occiput but this should be distinguished from the acute pain precipitated by skin contact in trigeminal neuralgia and the exquisite tenderness of temporal arteritis. Typically, the headache is reported to be poorly responsive to ordinary analgesia.

Pathogenesis

The cause of tension-type headaches is obscure. There is little evidence for the hypothesis that it is caused by excessive contraction of the muscles of the head and neck. Emotional strain or anxiety is a common precipitant to tension-type headache and there is sometimes an underlying depressive illness. Anxiety about the headache itself may lead to continuation of symptoms, and patients often become convinced of a serious underlying condition.

Management

Careful assessment followed by discussion of likely precipitants and explanation of the fact that the symptoms are not due to any sinister underlying pathology is more likely to be beneficial than analgesics. Excessive use of analgesics, particularly of codeine, may actually worsen the headache (analgesic headache). Physiotherapy (with courses of muscle relaxation and stress management) is usually beneficial, but low-dose amitriptyline (10 mg nocte increased gradually to 30–50 mg) may be necessary. There is evidence that patients with this syndrome benefit from a perception that their problem has been taken seriously and rigorously assessed, but over-extensive investigations can worsen a patient's anxiety.

MIGRAINE

Clinical features

Patients may refer to any episodic paroxysmal headache as migraine. However, it is best to look upon migraine as a triad of paroxysmal headache, nausea and/or vomiting, and an 'aura' of focal neurological events (usually visual). Patients with all three of these features are said to have migraine with aura ('classical' migraine). Those with paroxysmal headache (with or without vomiting) but no 'aura' are said to have migraine without aura ('common' migraine). It has been estimated that the lifetime prevalence of migraine is about 20% in females and 6% in males. Over 90% of migraine sufferers will have their first attack by the time they are 40 years old. Typically, a classical migraine attack starts with a non-specific prodrome of malaise and irritability followed by the 'aura' of a focal neurological event, and then a severe throbbing hemicranial headache with photophobia and vomiting. During the headache phase patients prefer to be in a quiet, darkened room and to sleep. The headache may persist for several days.

The 'aura' most often takes the form of 'fortification spectra': shimmering, silvery zigzag lines which march across the visual fields over 20 minutes, sometimes leaving a trail of temporary visual field loss. In some patients there is a sensory aura: a spreading front of tingling followed by numbness which moves, over 20–30 minutes, from one part of the body to another. If the dominant hemisphere is involved, the patient may also experience transient aphasia. True weakness is distinctly unusual in migraine, so 'hemiplegic migraine' should be diagnosed with extreme caution. In a small number of patients the focal events may occur by themselves ('migraine equivalent') but in this case other structural disorders of the brain, or even focal epilepsy, need to be considered in the differential diagnosis. In an even smaller number of patients, the symptoms of the aura do not resolve, leaving more permanent neurological disturbance ('complicated migraine').

Aetiology and pathogenesis

The aetiology of migraine is largely unknown. There is often a family history of migraine, suggesting a genetic predisposition. The great female preponderance and the tendency for some women to have migraine attacks at certain points in their menstrual cycle hint at hormonal influences. The relevance of the contraceptive pill in this context is difficult to establish, but it does appear to exacerbate migraine in many patients, and to increase the risk of stroke in patients who suffer from migraine with aura (see EBM panel). In some patients there are identifiable dietary precipitants such as cheese, chocolate or red wine. When psychological stress is involved, the migraine attack often occurs after the period of strain so that some patients tend to have attacks at weekends or at the beginning of a holiday.

The 'aura' of classical migraine probably represents a spreading front of electrical excitation followed by

---

EBM

MIGRAINE—risk of thromboembolic stroke

'RCTs and case-control studies suggest that there is a slight increase in the risk of thromboembolic stroke in patients who suffer from migraine, particularly migraine with aura, and that this risk is considerably elevated by concomitant use of hormonal contraception.'

- Buring JE, Hebert P, Romero J, et al. Migraine and subsequent risk of stroke in the Physicians' Health Study. Arch Neurol 1995; 52:129–134.
- Chang CL, Donaghy M, Poulter N. Migraine and stroke in young women: case-control study. World Health Organisation Collaborative Study of Cardiovascular Disease and Steroid Hormone Contraception. BMJ 1999; 318:13–18.

Further information: 🖳 www.cochrane.co.uk

depression of activity of cortical cells. The cause of this is not understood but it probably represents a paroxysmal alteration in cortical modulation pathways from the brain stem (especially serotoninergic projections). The observation that migraine-like phenomena occur in rare genetic disorders associated with mutations in calcium channel genes suggests the possibility that the aura may be due to paroxysmal changes in the function of neuronal ion channels. The headache is thought to be caused by vasodilatation of extracranial vessels and may, like the headache following an epileptic seizure, be a non-specific effect of the disturbance of neuronal function.

Management

Identification and avoidance of precipitants or exacerbating factors (such as the contraceptive pill) may prevent attacks. Treatment of an acute attack consists of simple analgesia with aspirin or paracetamol, often combined with an antiemetic such as metoclopramide or domperidone. Long-term use of codeine-containing analgesic preparations should be avoided. Severe attacks can be treated with one of the 'triptans', 5-HT agonists that are potent vasoconstrictors of the extracranial arteries. These can be administered orally, sublingually, by subcutaneous injection or by nasal spray. Ergotamine preparations should be avoided since they easily lead to dependence. This is less likely to occur with the triptans, but it can occur. If attacks are frequent, they can often be prevented with propranolol (80–160 mg daily, in a sustained-release preparation), pizotifen (a 5-HT antagonist, 1.5–3.0 mg daily), a tricyclic such as amitriptyline (10–50 mg at night) or sodium valproate (300–600 mg/day). As above, the small risk of ischaemic stroke in women attributable to taking oral contraception is increased if they have migraine, especially if they also smoke.

MIGRAINOUS NEURALGIA (CLUSTER HEADACHE)

Clinical features

This is some 10–50 times less common than migraine. There is a 5:1 predominance of males and onset is usually in the third decade. The characteristic syndrome comprises periodic, severe, unilateral periorbital pain, accompanied by conjunctival injection, unilateral lacrimation, nasal congestion and often a Horner's syndrome. The pain, whilst being very severe, is characteristically brief (30–90 minutes). Typically, the patient develops these symptoms at a particular time of day (often in the early hours of the morning). The syndrome may occur repeatedly for a number of weeks, followed by a respite for a number of months before another cluster occurs.

Pathogenesis

There is little genetic predisposition, no provoking dietary factors and a male predominance, which suggest a different aetiology from that of migraine, but this remains unknown. Patients are usually heavy smokers with a higher than average alcohol consumption.

Management

Acute attacks are usually halted by subcutaneous injections of sumatriptan or by inhalation of 100% oxygen; other migraine therapies are ineffective, probably because of the brevity of the individual attacks. Preventative therapy with the agents used for migraine is often ineffective but attacks can be prevented in some patients by verapamil (80–120 mg 8-hourly), methysergide (4–10 mg daily, for a maximum of 3 months only) or short courses of corticosteroids. Patients with severe and debilitating clusters can be helped with lithium therapy although the usual precautions concerning the use of this drug should be observed (see p. 258).

COITAL AND EXERCISE-INDUCED CEPHALGIA

Clinical features

Patients are almost exclusively middle-aged men who develop a sudden, often very severe, headache at the climax of sexual intercourse. There is usually no vomiting and no neck stiffness, and the severe headache does not persist for more than 10–15 minutes, though a less severe dull headache may persist for some hours. This type of paroxysmal headache often needs to be distinguished, by CT and/or CSF examination, from the thunderclap headache of a subarachnoid haemorrhage (see Fig. 22.32, p. 1163). A very similar headache may occur during physical exertion, especially if this is attempted with unaccustomed vigour in an unfit person. The pathogenesis is unknown.

Management

Coital or exertional cephalgia is usually brief though frightening and may not need more than ordinary analgesia for the residual headache. The syndrome may not recur but prevention with propranolol (as for migraine) or indometacin (75 mg daily) may be necessary.

Other paroxysmal headaches are described in Box 22.7.

ISSUES IN OLDER PEOPLE
HEADACHES

- Headaches are less common in those aged over 60 years than in younger people.
- Common causes of headache which occur in old age, and either rarely or not at all in younger patients, include trigeminal neuralgia, temporal arteritis and post-herpetic neuralgia.
- Migraine and tension headache are much less common than in younger people.
- Raised intracranial pressure is not always associated with headache, vomiting or papilloedema.
- Intracranial mass lesions can often reach larger sizes before presentation as the involutional process that occurs in most ageing brains allows the accommodation of an expanding lesion more easily than in younger patients.

22.7 BENIGN PAROXYSMAL HEADACHES

	Character of pain	Duration	Location	Comment
Ice pick	Stabbing	Very brief (split-second)	Variable, usually temporal or parietal	Benign, more common in migraine
Ice cream	Sharp, severe	30–120 seconds	Bitemporal/occipital	Obvious trigger by cold stimuli
Exertional	Bursting	Minutes to hours	Generalised	Intracranial pathology needs exclusion
Cough	Bursting	Seconds to minutes	Occipital or generalised	Intracranial pathology needs exclusion (especially cranio-cervical junction)

A DIAGNOSTIC APPROACH TO THE PATIENT WITH FACIAL PAIN

Pain in and around the eye, when not caused by ocular disease, should be considered as a headache (above). This includes the dramatic pain of migrainous neuralgia or cluster headache. Rarely, inflammatory or infiltrative lesions at the apex of the orbit or the cavernous sinus may cause pain in or around the eye but tell-tale signs from involvement of the ocular motor nerves usually accompany this. Pain in the eye may accompany disorders of the carotid artery, particularly dissections, and may then be accompanied by a Horner's syndrome.

Pain in the other parts of the face can be due to problems with the teeth or the temporo-mandibular joint. Inflamed nasal sinuses are seldom the cause of lasting facial pain in the absence of obvious nasal congestion. The very rare but serious condition of subdural empyema (see p. 1200) needs to be considered if 'sinusitis' is followed by very severe unilateral facial pain and signs of cerebral irritation (seizures and/or obtundation). Destructive lesions of the trigeminal nerve causing pain are extremely rare since such lesions usually cause loss of sensation in the nerve's territory rather than pain.

Most patients with persisting pain in the face have trigeminal neuralgia, atypical facial pain or post-herpetic neuralgia. The main distinction between these is in the nature of the pain. Trigeminal neuralgia typically occurs in patients older than 55 years. The pain is very brief, though severe and recurrent, described as 'like lightning', and is most frequently felt in the second and third divisions of the nerve. Atypical facial pain, on the other hand, is continuous and unremitting, centred over the maxilla, usually on the left side. It occurs most frequently in middle-aged women. Post-herpetic neuralgia is continuous and is felt as a burning pain throughout the affected territory, which is often very sensitive to light touch. The cause is usually obvious from a history of 'shingles' in the ophthalmic division of the trigeminal nerve.

TRIGEMINAL NEURALGIA

Clinical features

This condition causes very sharp lancinating pains in the second and third divisions of the trigeminal nerve territory, usually in middle-aged or elderly patients. The pain is severe and very brief, but repetitive, causing the patient to flinch as if with a motor tic; hence the French term for the condition, 'tic douloureux'. The pain may be precipitated by touching trigger zones within the trigeminal territory or by eating and so on. Usually there are no other signs, although similar symptoms may occur in advanced multiple sclerosis or, rarely, with other lesions, in which case there may be sensory changes in the trigeminal nerve territory or other brain-stem symptoms and signs. There is a tendency for the condition to remit and relapse over many years.

Pathogenesis

The current hypothesis as to aetiology suggests that the neuralgia is most commonly caused by compression of the trigeminal nerve rootlets at their entry to the brain stem by aberrant loops of the cerebellar arteries. Other compressive lesions, usually benign, are occasionally found in the site. When trigeminal neuralgia occurs in multiple sclerosis there is a plaque of demyelination in the trigeminal root entry zone.

Management

The pain usually responds to carbamazepine, in doses of up to 1200 mg daily. It is wise to start with much lower doses and escalate the dose according to effect, as one might when using this drug for epilepsy. In patients who cannot tolerate carbamazepine, phenytoin or gabapentin may be effective, but other anticonvulsants are not. If drug treatment fails and/or when the condition does not remit, various surgical treatments are available. The simplest is the injection of alcohol or phenol into a peripheral branch of the nerve. Probably more effective is the percutaneous placing of a radiofrequency lesion in the nerve near the Gasserian ganglion. Care has to be taken not to cause excessive damage to sensation in the face to prevent the complication of neurogenic pain ('anaesthesia dolorosa') which is worse than the neuralgia. Alternatively, the vascular compression of the trigeminal nerve can be relieved through a small posterior craniotomy, often with substantial success. This latter approach is usually favoured in younger patients in whom the other injection treatments may have to be repeated and become less effective.

DIZZINESS, BLACKOUTS AND 'FUNNY TURNS'

Episodes of lost or altered consciousness are a frequent symptom in primary care and in hospital practice, especially in the elderly (see below). A patient may complain of 'blacking out', 'going dizzy', 'coming over queer', 'having a funny turn' or other local variants. The first task is to discover exactly what the patient means by the terms used. Some patients, for example, mean by 'blackout' that their vision darkens without alteration in consciousness (defined here as an awareness of the environment and ability to respond to it). More often 'blackout' is used to describe an episode of lost consciousness with or without falling down. The terms 'blackout' and 'funny turn' can also be used to refer to transient periods of amnesia, when the patient loses memory for a period of time. 'Dizziness' is used frequently to describe an abnormal perception of movement of the environment (vertigo), but may be used to mean a feeling of faintness, some other alteration of consciousness, or unsteadiness.

After a careful history from the patient, supplemented by a witness account, it should be clear whether the patient is describing an episode of loss of consciousness, altered consciousness, vertigo, transient amnesia or something else. The former two symptoms suggest a problem in mechanisms maintaining normal awareness. Vertigo is caused by an alteration in function of the peripheral vestibular organs or the central control mechanisms of balance and posture.

ISSUES IN OLDER PEOPLE
DIZZINESS

- Recurrent dizzy spells affect at least 30% of people aged over 65 years.
- These are most frequently described as a combination of unsteadiness and lightheadedness.
- Most have more than one contributing factor.
- Postural hypotension, cerebrovascular disease and cervical spondylosis are common underlying diagnoses.
- Arrhythmia must be excluded in those with predominant lightheadedness which occurs at rest as well as on activity.
- Anxiety and poor vision are frequent concomitants but are rarely the only cause at this age.
- If the patient is falling as a result, a multidisciplinary workup is required (see p. 241).

A DIAGNOSTIC APPROACH TO THE PATIENT WITH VERTIGO (see Fig. 22.10)

Abnormal perception of movement of the environment occurs as a result of a mismatch between the information

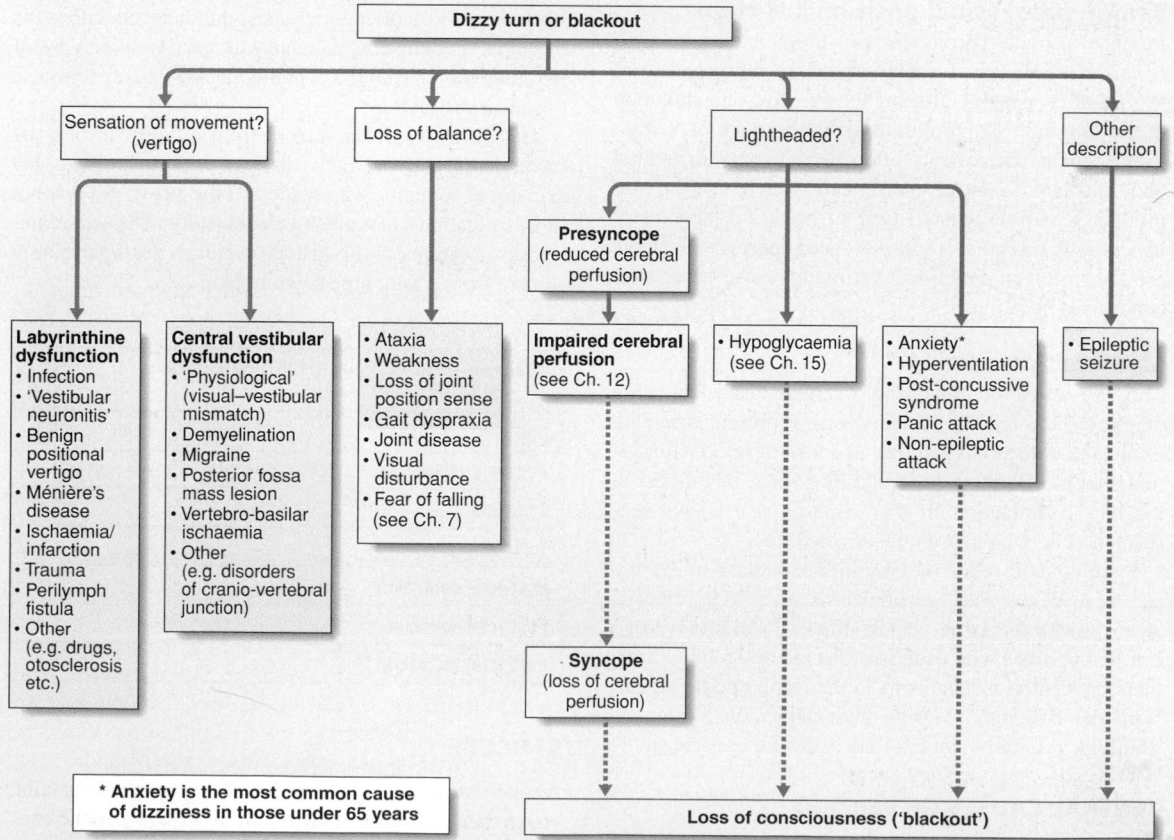

Fig. 22.10　A diagnostic approach to the patient with dizziness, funny turns or blackouts.

about a person's position in the environment reaching the brain from the eyes, the limb proprioceptive apparatus and the vestibular system. Vertigo arising from inappropriate input from the labyrinthine apparatus is within the experience of most people, since this is the 'dizziness' which occurs after someone has spun round vigorously and then stops. Vertigo caused by labyrinthine disorders is usually short-lived, though it may recur, whilst vertigo arising from central disorders (of the brain stem) is often persistent and accompanied by other signs of brain-stem dysfunction. A careful analysis of the history will reveal the likely cause in most patients.

VERTIGO CAUSED BY LABYRINTHINE DISTURBANCES

Labyrinthitis ('vestibular neuronitis')

This is the most common cause of severe vertigo, but the cause of the labyrinthitis is unknown; it usually presents in the third or fourth decade as severe vertigo, with vomiting and ataxia but no tinnitus or deafness, often coming on when waking. The vertigo is most severe at onset and settles down over the next few days, though afterwards head movement may provoke vertigo (positional vertigo) for some time. During the attack nystagmus will be present but does not persist for long.

Benign paroxysmal positional vertigo

In older patients paroxysms of vertigo occurring with certain head movements may be due to the presence of degenerative material affecting the free flow of endolymph in the labyrinth (cupulolithiasis). Each attack of vertigo lasts seconds but patients often become very distressed and reluctant to move their head, which can in turn produce a muscle tension type of headache. Secondary hyperventilation attacks and associated depressive features are also common. Positional vertigo may also occur after concussive head injuries.

Ménière's disease

This is a cause of labyrinthine vertigo that is probably diagnosed too readily. Patients usually present first with tinnitus and distorted hearing, and then develop paroxysmal attacks of vertigo preceded by a sense of fullness in the ear. Examination in this circumstance shows sensorineural hearing loss on the affected side.

Symptomatic relief of labyrinthine causes of vertigo can be achieved with 'vestibular sedatives' (e.g. cinnarizine, prochlorperazine, betahistine). Positional vertigo can be improved with exercises that are designed to habituate the central mechanisms to the inappropriate signals from the labyrinth. Patients with intractable symptoms should be referred to an ENT specialist for assessment.

CENTRAL CAUSES OF VERTIGO

Any disease that affects the vestibular nucleus in the brain stem or its connections can cause vertigo. This can be distinguished from peripheral causes of vertigo by its persistence and the usual association of other signs. Positionally induced central vertigo persists for as long as the position is maintained, unlike the common peripheral positional vertigo that fatigues quite quickly if the inducing position is maintained. The same is true of any accompanying nystagmus. Transient causes such as brain-stem ischaemia can be recognised by the association with other symptoms of brain-stem dysfunction such as dysarthria or diplopia. If deafness is present and the history is not suggestive of Ménière's disease, extra-axial compression of the 8th cranial nerve by a lesion such as an acoustic neuroma (see p. 1206) should be suspected. Rarely, vertigo originating from the cerebral cortex may be a manifestation of a partial seizure in the temporal lobe.

A DIAGNOSTIC APPROACH TO THE PATIENT WITH EPISODIC LOSS OF CONSCIOUSNESS

Loss of consciousness, other than in sleep, suggests a global dysfunction of the brain. As a transient phenomenon, this most commonly comes about because of a recoverable loss of adequate blood supply to the brain, i.e. syncope (see below). Alternatively, loss of consciousness occurs from sudden dysfunction of the electrical mechanisms of the brain during a seizure (epileptic fit). Episodes of loss of consciousness are therefore either fits or faints, though some patients who have various types of psychogenic blackout or non-epileptic seizure confuse this clear distinction.

The distinction of a seizure from a faint can only be made from the patient's history, with help from the account of someone who witnessed the attack. No amount of investigation can replace a clear history in these circumstances. Features in the history useful in distinguishing a seizure from a faint are shown in Box 22.8.

22.8 FEATURES HELPFUL IN DISTINGUISHING SEIZURES FROM FAINTS		
	Seizure	Faint
Aura (e.g. olfactory)	+	−
Cyanosis	+	−
Tongue-biting	+	−
Post-ictal confusion	+	−
Post-ictal amnesia	+	−
Post-ictal headache	+	−

SYNCOPE

A brief feeling of 'lightheadedness' often precedes a faint; vision then darkens and there may be a ringing in the ears. Vasovagal syncope (see p. 397) may be provoked by some emotionally charged event (e.g. venepuncture) and usually occurs from the standing position. Cardiac syncope (see p. 397), caused by a sudden decline in cardiac output and hence cerebral perfusion, may be provoked by exertion (e.g. with severe aortic stenosis), or occur completely 'out of the blue' (as in heart block).

In vasovagal syncope, the loss of consciousness is gradual and brief, and the patient recovers quickly without confusion as long as he or she has assumed the horizontal position. It is rare for the syncope to cause injury and there is no amnesia for events that occur after regaining awareness. During a syncopal attack, incontinence of urine can occur and there may be some stiffening and even some brief twitching of the limbs, but tongue-biting never occurs.

SEIZURES

A seizure is any abnormal clinical event caused by an electrical discharge in the brain, whilst epilepsy is the tendency to have recurrent seizures (see p. 1125). Major seizures cause loss of consciousness, with the patient falling to the ground and presenting with a history of 'blackouts'. Minor seizures causing alteration of consciousness, without the patient falling to the ground, may also be described as 'blackouts'.

Pathophysiology

In the normally functioning cortex, recurrent and collateral inhibitory circuits limit synchronous discharge amongst neighbouring groups of neurons. The inhibitory transmitter gamma-aminobutyric acid (GABA) is particularly important in this role, and drugs that block GABA receptors provoke seizures. There are also a large number of excitatory neurotransmitters, of which acetylcholine and the amino acids glutamate and aspartate are examples (see Box 22.1, p. 1107). 'Epileptic' cerebral cortex exhibits hypersynchronous repetitive discharges involving large groups of neurons. Intracellular recordings show bursts of rapid action potential firing, with reduction of the transmembrane potential (paroxysmal depolarisation shift). It is likely that both reduction in inhibitory systems and excessive excitation play a part in the genesis of seizure activity. Cells undergoing repetitive 'epileptic' discharges undergo morphological and physiological changes which make them more likely to produce subsequent abnormal discharges ('kindling').

The chief division of seizure types on physiological grounds is between partial (focal) seizures in which paroxysmal neuronal activity is limited to one part of the cerebrum, and generalised seizures where the electrophysiological abnormality involves both hemispheres simultaneously and synchronously (see Fig. 22.11). If partial seizures remain localised, the symptomatology depends on the cortical area affected. If consciousness (the awareness of and ability to respond to the environment) is preserved, the attack is termed a 'simple partial seizure'. If, however, the activity involves some parts of

the brain dealing with awareness (such as the temporal or frontal lobes), then consciousness is affected and a 'complex partial seizure' results. Further spread into the diencephalon and thence throughout the remainder of the cortex leads to a secondarily generalised seizure.

In primary generalised seizures, the abnormal activity is seen to begin synchronously throughout the cortex without an initial partial onset. It probably originates in the central diencephalic mechanisms controlling cortical activation (see Fig. 22.11). This is recognisable on an EEG which shows spikes and waves of abnormal activity (see Fig. 22.4, p. 1109) and quite often provocation of abnormalities with hyperventilation and/or photic stimulation. This may cause a major seizure identical to a secondarily generalised seizure, or a more restricted clinical manifestation if the abnormal electrical activity fails to affect muscle tone. In this case there is an 'absence', in which consciousness is lost but the patient remains standing or sitting. Such attacks may be difficult to distinguish clinically from a complex partial seizure in the temporal lobe.

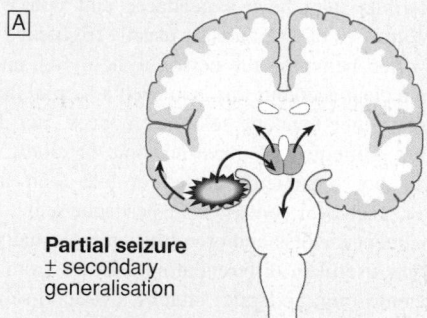

Partial seizure ± secondary generalisation

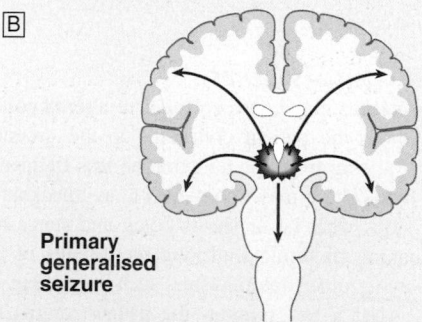

Primary generalised seizure

Fig. 22.11 The pathophysiological classification of seizures. A A partial seizure originates from a paroxysmal discharge in a focal area of the cerebral cortex (often the temporal lobe); the seizure may subsequently spread to the rest of the brain (secondary generalisation) via diencephalic activating pathways. B In primary generalised seizures the abnormal electrical discharges originate from the diencephalic activating system and spread simultaneously to all areas of the cortex.

Clinical features

Tonic clonic seizures

A tonic clonic seizure may be preceded by a partial seizure (the 'aura') which can take various forms, described below. However, a history of such an 'aura' is commonly not obtained, probably because the subsequent generalised seizure causes some retrograde amnesia for immediately preceding events. The patient then goes rigid and becomes unconscious, falling down heavily if standing, often sustaining injury. During this phase, respiration is arrested and central cyanosis may be witnessed. After a few moments, the rigidity is periodically relaxed, producing clonic jerks. Some patients do not have a clonic phase and the rigidity is replaced by a flaccid state of deep coma which can persist for some minutes. The patient then gradually regains consciousness, but is in a confused and disorientated state for half an hour or more after regaining consciousness. Full memory function may not be recovered for some hours. During the attack urinary incontinence may occur, as may tongue-biting. (A severely bitten, bleeding tongue after an attack of loss of consciousness is pathognomonic of a generalised seizure.) After a generalised seizure the patient usually feels terrible, may have a headache and will want to sleep. Witnesses of a seizure are usually frightened by the events, often believing the person to be dying, and may not give a clear account; this is in itself a helpful diagnostic pointer since syncope seldom produces such fear in onlookers. Patients may have no tonic or clonic phase, and may not become cyanosed or bite their tongue. However, post-ictal confusion or headache and a period of subsequent malaise and/or confusion are usually seen, and this is useful in differentiating seizures from faints. Psychogenic non-epileptic attacks ('pseudo-seizures') may be accompanied by dramatic flailing of the limbs and arching of the back; however, these are not usually followed by the same degree of post-ictal confusion and do not cause cyanosis.

Complex partial seizures

Partial seizures may cause episodes of altered consciousness without the patient collapsing to the ground, especially if arising from the temporal or, less frequently, the frontal lobe. These may be referred to as 'blackouts'. The patient stops what he or she is doing and stares blankly, often making rhythmic smacking movements of the lips or displaying other automatisms, such as picking at their clothes. After a few minutes the patient returns to consciousness but may be initially muddled and feel drowsy. Immediately before such an attack the patient may report alterations of mood, memory and perception such as undue familiarity (déjà vu) or unreality (jamais vu), complex hallucinations of sound, smell, taste, vision, emotional changes (fear, sexual arousal) or visceral sensations (nausea, epigastric discomfort). If these changes of memory or perception occur without subsequent alteration in awareness, the seizure is said to be a simple partial seizure.

Absence seizures

A type of minor seizure that resembles a complex partial seizure occurs in the generalised absence epilepsy of childhood known as 'petit mal'. In petit mal epilepsy, the attacks are usually briefer and very much more frequent (up to 20 or 30 a day) than complex partial seizures and are not associated with post-ictal confusion. Absence attacks are caused by a generalised discharge that does not spread out of the hemispheres and so does not cause loss of posture.

Partial motor seizures

Epileptic activity arising in the pre-central gyrus causes partial motor seizures affecting the contralateral face, arm, trunk or leg. Seizures are characterised by rhythmical jerking or sustained spasm of the affected parts. They may remain localised to one part, or may spread to involve the whole side. Some attacks begin in one part (e.g. mouth, thumb, great toe etc.) and spread gradually; this is Jacksonian epilepsy. Attacks vary in duration from a few seconds to several hours. More prolonged episodes may leave paresis of the involved limb lasting for several hours after the seizure ceases (Todd's palsy).

Partial sensory seizures

Seizures arising in the sensory cortex cause unpleasant tingling or 'electric' sensations in the contralateral face and limbs. A spreading pattern like a Jacksonian seizure may occur, the abnormal sensation spreading much faster over the body (in seconds) than the 'march' of a migrainous focal sensory attack, which spreads over 10–15 minutes.

Versive seizures

A frontal epileptic focus may involve the frontal eye field, causing forced deviation of the eyes to the opposite side. This type of attack often becomes generalised to a tonic clonic seizure.

Partial visual seizures

Occipital epileptic foci cause simple visual hallucinations such as balls of light or patterns of colour. Formed visual hallucinations of faces or scenes arise more anteriorly in the temporal lobes.

Factors precipitating seizures

Sometimes specific trigger factors can be identified. Some are listed in Box 22.9.

> **22.9 TRIGGER FACTORS FOR SEIZURES**
>
> - Sleep deprivation
> - Alcohol (particularly withdrawal)
> - Recreational drug misuse
> - Physical and mental exhaustion
> - Flickering lights, including TV and computer screens (primary generalised epilepsies only)
> - Intercurrent infections and metabolic disturbances
> - Uncommonly: loud noises, music, reading, hot baths

EPILEPSY

Epilepsy means a tendency to have seizures and is a symptom of brain disease rather than a disease itself. A single seizure is not epilepsy but an indication for investigation. Medication should await evidence of a tendency to recurrent seizures. However, the recurrence rate after a first seizure approaches 70% during the first year, most recurrent attacks occurring within a month or two of the first. Further seizures are less likely if a trigger factor is definable and avoidable (e.g. sleep deprivation, alcohol withdrawal etc.). There is a group of disorders whose only or main symptom is epilepsy, whilst in other disorders epilepsy is just one of the manifestations. The annual incidence of new cases of epilepsy after infancy is 20–70/100 000. The lifetime risk of having a single seizure is about 5%, whilst the prevalence of epilepsy in European countries is about 0.5%. Prevalence in developing countries is up to five times higher than in developed countries; incidence is double.

Types of epilepsy

The classification of epilepsy is best achieved by considering the clinical events (the seizures), the abnormal electrophysiology, the anatomical site of seizure genesis and the pathological cause of the problem (see Box 22.10).

Primary generalised epilepsies

The primary or idiopathic epilepsies make up some 10% of all epilepsies, including some 40% of those with tonic clonic seizures. Onset is almost always in childhood or adolescence. No structural abnormality is present and there is often a substantial genetic predisposition. Some, like childhood absence epilepsy, are relatively uncommon,

whilst others, like juvenile myoclonic epilepsy, are common (5–10% of all patients with epilepsy). The more common varieties of primary generalised epilepsy are listed in Box 22.11, along with their clinical features and management.

Secondary generalised epilepsy

Generalised epilepsy may arise from spread of partial seizures due to structural disease or may be secondary to

22.10 CLASSIFICATION OF EPILEPSY

Seizure type
- Simple partial
- Complex partial
- Absence
- Tonic clonic
- Tonic
- Atonic
- Myoclonic

Physiology (EEG)
- Focal spikes/sharp waves
- Generalised spike and wave

Anatomical site
- Cortex
  Temporal
  Frontal
  Parietal
  Occipital
- Generalised (diencephalon)
- Multifocal

Pathological cause
- Genetic
- Developmental
- Tumours
- Trauma
- Vascular
- Infections
- Inflammation
- Metabolic
- Drugs and alcohol
- Degenerative

22.11 PRIMARY GENERALISED EPILEPSIES

	Incidence	Age of onset	Type of seizure	EEG features	Provoking factors	Treatment	Prognosis
Childhood absence epilepsy	6–8/100 000	4–8 yrs	Frequent brief absences	3/s spike and wave	Hyperventilation, fatigue	Ethosuximide Sodium valproate	40% develop tonic clonic seizures, 80% remit in adulthood
Juvenile absence epilepsy	1–2/100 000	10–15 yrs	Less frequent absences than childhood absence	Poly-spike and wave	Hyperventilation, sleep deprivation	Sodium valproate	80% develop tonic clonic seizures, 80% seizure-free in adulthood
Juvenile myoclonic epilepsy	25–50/100 000	15–20 yrs	GTCS, absences, morning myoclonus	Poly-spike and wave, photosensitivity	Sleep deprivation, alcohol withdrawal	Sodium valproate	90% remit with sodium valproate but relapse on AED withdrawal
GTCS on awakening	Common	10–25 yrs	GTCS, sometimes myoclonus	Spike and wave on waking and sleep onset	Sleep deprivation	Sodium valproate	65% controlled with AEDs but relapse off treatment

(GTCS = generalised tonic clonic seizure; AED = anti-epilepsy drug)

22.12 CAUSES OF SECONDARY GENERALISED EPILEPSY

Secondary generalisation from partial seizures
- See Box 22.13 for causes of partial seizures

Genetic
- Inborn errors of metabolism
- Storage diseases

Cerebral birth injury

Hydrocephalus

Cerebral anoxia

Drugs
- Antibiotics: penicillin, isoniazid, metronidazole
- Antimalarials: chloroquine, mefloquine
- Ciclosporin
- Cardiac anti-arrhythmics: lidocaine (lignocaine), disopyramide
- Psychotropic agents: phenothiazines, tricyclics, lithium
- Amphetamines (withdrawal)

Alcohol (especially withdrawal)

Metabolic disease
- Hypocalcaemia
- Hyponatraemia
- Hypomagnesaemia
- Hypoglycaemia
- Renal failure
- Liver failure

Infective
- Meningitis
- Post-infectious encephalopathy

Inflammatory
- Multiple sclerosis (uncommon)
- SLE

Diffuse degenerative diseases
- Alzheimer's disease
- Creutzfeldt–Jakob disease

22.13 CAUSES OF PARTIAL SEIZURES

Idiopathic
- Benign rolandic epilepsy of childhood
- Benign occipital epilepsy of childhood

Focal structural lesions

Genetic
- Tuberous sclerosis
- Neurofibromatosis
- von Hippel–Lindau disease

Infantile hemiplegia

Dysembryonic
- Cortical dysgenesis
- Sturge–Weber syndrome

Mesial temporal sclerosis (associated with febrile convulsions)

Cerebrovascular disease
- Intracerebral haemorrhage
- Cerebral embolus
- Arteriovenous malformation

Tumours

Trauma (including neurosurgery)

Infective
- Cerebral abscess (pyogenic)
- Toxoplasmosis
- Cysticercosis
- Tuberculoma
- Subdural empyema
- Encephalitis
- Human immunodeficiency virus (HIV)

Inflammatory
- Sarcoidosis
- Vasculitis

drugs or metabolic disorders (see Box 22.12). Epilepsy presenting in adult life is almost always secondary generalised, even if there is no clear history of a partial seizure before the onset of a major attack (an 'aura').

Partial epilepsy
Partial seizures may arise from any disease of the cerebral cortex, congenital or acquired, and frequently generalise. With the exception of a few idiopathic partial epilepsies of benign outcome in childhood, the presence of partial seizures signifies the presence of focal cerebral pathology. Common causes are listed in Box 22.13.

Investigations
After a single seizure cerebral imaging with CT or MRI is advisable, although the yield of structural lesions is low unless there are focal features to the seizure or there are focal signs. Similarly, toxic and metabolic causes (see Box 22.13) should be considered. EEG is only necessary when more than one seizure has occurred and the type of epilepsy needs to be established to guide therapy. The increasing sophistication of imaging techniques now allows the identification of the cause of epilepsy in an increasing number of patients, especially those with partial seizures. These patients warrant intensive investigation,

especially if seizures arise for the first time in adult life. Investigations should be pursued more vigorously if the epilepsy is intractable to treatment. The investigations that may be undertaken in a patient with suspected epilepsy are shown in Box 22.14.

Electroencephalography (EEG)
The EEG (see p. 1109) may help to establish a diagnosis and characterise the type of epilepsy (i.e. primary generalised or partial with or without secondary generalisation). Inter-ictal records are abnormal in only about 50% of patients so the EEG is not a sensitive test for the presence of epilepsy. However, epileptiform changes (sharp waves or spikes) are fairly specific (falsely positive in only 1/1000). The sensitivity can be increased to about 85% by prolonging recording time and including a period of natural or drug-induced sleep. Ambulatory EEG recording or video/EEG monitoring may provide helpful information when attacks are frequent.

Brain imaging
Imaging does not help establish a diagnosis of epilepsy but is useful in defining or excluding a structural cause; indications are summarised in Box 22.15. Imaging is not required if a confident diagnosis of primary generalised epilepsy can be made with an EEG. CT is often sufficient to exclude a major structural cause of epilepsy. MRI of the brain may be indicated if CT shows no abnormality but a subtle structural change is still suspected, as in

22.14 INVESTIGATION OF SUSPECTED EPILEPSY

Epileptic nature of attacks?
- Ambulatory EEG
- Videotelemetry

Type of epilepsy?
- Standard EEG
- Sleep EEG
- EEG with special electrodes (foramen ovale, subdural)

Structural lesion?
- CT
- MRI

Metabolic disorder?
- Blood urea and electrolytes
- Liver function tests
- Blood glucose
- Serum calcium, magnesium

Inflammatory or infective disorder?
- Blood count, erythrocyte sedimentation rate (ESR), C-reactive protein (CRP)
- Chest radiograph
- Serology for syphilis, HIV, collagen disease
- CSF

22.15 INDICATIONS FOR BRAIN IMAGING IN EPILEPSY

- Epilepsy starts after the age of 20 years
- Seizures have focal features clinically
- EEG shows a focal seizure source
- Control of seizures is difficult or deteriorates

the case of patients with partial seizures (with or without secondary generalisation) which are resistant to therapy.

Management

It is important to explain the nature and cause of seizures to patients and their relatives, and to instruct relatives in the first aid management of major seizures. Many people with epilepsy feel stigmatised by society and may become unnecessarily isolated from work and social life. It should be emphasised that any brain can develop a seizure, that epilepsy is a common disorder which affects just under 1% of the population, and that good or complete control of seizures can be expected in more than 80% of patients.

Immediate care of seizures

Little can or need be done for a person whilst a major seizure is occurring except first aid and common-sense manoeuvres to limit damage or secondary complications (see Box 22.16).

Restrictions

Until good control of seizures has been established, work or recreation above ground level, with dangerous machinery or near open fires or water should be avoided. Patients

22.16 IMMEDIATE CARE OF SEIZURES

First aid (by relatives and witnesses)
- Move person away from danger (fire, water, machinery, furniture)
- After convulsions cease, turn into 'recovery' position (semi-prone)
- Ensure airway is clear
- Do **NOT** insert anything in mouth (tongue-biting occurs at seizure onset and cannot be prevented by observers)
- If convulsions continue for more than 5 minutes or recur without person regaining consciousness, summon urgent medical attention
- Person may be drowsy and confused for some 30–60 minutes and should not be left alone until fully recovered

Immediate medical attention
- Ensure airway is patent
- Give oxygen to offset cerebral hypoxia
- Give intravenous anticonvulsant (e.g. diazepam 10 mg) **ONLY IF** convulsions are continuous or repeated (if so, manage as for status epilepticus)
- Consider taking blood for anticonvulsant levels (if known epileptic)
- Investigate cause

should take only a shallow bath, and then when a relative is in the house, and should not lock the bathroom door. Cycling should be discouraged until at least 6 months' freedom from seizures has been achieved. Recreations requiring prolonged proximity to water (e.g. swimming, fishing or boating) should always be in the company of someone who is aware of the chance of a seizure occurring and could rescue the patient if necessary. Any activity where loss of awareness might be very dangerous (e.g. mountaineering) should be discouraged. In the UK and many other countries, legal restrictions regarding vehicle driving apply to patients with epilepsy, defined as more than one seizure over the age of 5 years (see Box 22.17).

22.17 UK DRIVING REGULATIONS

Single seizure
- Cease driving for 1 year free of recurrence, then Driver and Vehicle Licensing Authority (DVLA) will restore a full licence (i.e. until age of 70 years)

Epilepsy
- Licence restored when patient is free from all types of seizure for 1 year *or* seizures exclusively during sleep for a period of 3 years (licence will require renewal every 3 years thereafter until 10 seizure-free years)

Withdrawal of anticonvulsants
- Cease driving during withdrawal and for 6 months thereafter

Vocational drivers (heavy goods and public service vehicles)
- No licence permitted if any seizure occurs after the age of 5 years until off medication and seizure-free for more than 10 years, and no potentially epileptogenic brain lesion

22.18 ANTICONVULSANT DRUGS

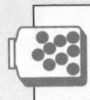

	Seizure types	Dose range (mg/day)	Doses per day	Therapeutic range (µmol/l)	Dose-related side-effects	Idiosyncratic side-effects	Long-term side-effects	Interactions
Acetazolamide	Primary and secondary GTCS, absences, partial	250–1000	2–3	Not applicable	Paraesthesia, anorexia, headache, nausea, diarrhoea, visual changes	Rashes, agranulocytosis, thrombocytopenia, photosensitivity, liver damage	Renal calculi	Aspirin, quinidine, phenytoin, carbamazepine, digoxin, ulcer-healing drugs
Carbamazepine	Partial, secondary GTCS	200–2000	2–3	30–50	Drowsiness, ataxia, nystagmus, diplopia, hyponatraemia	Rashes, thrombocytopenia, other blood dyscrasias	None	Other AEDs, warfarin, OCP, steroids, antimalarials, cimetidine
Clobazam	Partial (adjunctive)	20–30	1	Not applicable	Sedation, irritability		Anticonvulsant effect wears off after a few weeks	Other AEDs
Clonazepam	Partial (adjunctive), myoclonus	1–8	2–4	Not applicable	Sedation, irritability	Blood dyscrasias	Anticonvulsant effect wears off after a few weeks	Other AEDs
Ethosuximide	Childhood absence	500–1500	2	200–700	Dizziness, insomnia, ataxia	Rashes, blood dyscrasias		Other AEDs, antidepressants
Gabapentin	Partial	300–2400	3	Not applicable	Drowsiness, ataxia		Not yet known	Antacids
Lamotrigine	Partial, secondary GTCS	25–500	1–2	Not applicable	Drowsiness, ataxia, diplopia, confusion	Rashes, blood dyscrasias	Not yet known	Carbamazepine
Levetiracetam	Partial, secondary GTCS	1000–3000	2	Not applicable	Somnolence, tiredness, dizziness, headache	None recorded	Not yet known	Phenytoin
Oxcarbazepine	Partial, secondary GTCS	600–2400	2	50–125	Drowsiness, ataxia, nystagmus, diplopia, hyponatraemia	Rash	None known	Fewer than carbamazepine, but equally problematic for OCP
Phenobarbital	Partial, secondary GTCS	60–180	1	50–150	Drowsiness, ataxia, nystagmus, diplopia	Rashes, depression (adults), excitement (children), megaloblastic anaemia, SLE	Folate deficiency, osteomalacia, neuropathy	Other AEDs, anticoagulants, calcium channel blockers, digoxin, steroids, OCP, theophylline, levothyroxine sodium (thyroxine sodium), antidepressants, antimalarials

(GTCS = generalised tonic clonic seizures; AEDs = anti-epileptic drugs; OCP = oral contraceptive pill; SLE = systemic lupus erythematosus)

22.18 ANTICONVULSANT DRUGS

	Seizure types	Dose range (mg/day)	Doses per day	Therapeutic range (µmol/l)	Dose-related side-effects	Idiosyncratic side-effects	Long-term side-effects	Interactions
Phenytoin	Partial, secondary GTCS	150–350	1	40–80	Drowsiness, ataxia, nystagmus, diplopia, tremor, dystonia, asterixis	Rashes, blood dyscrasias, liver damage, SLE	Gum hypertrophy, facial dysmorphism, hirsutism, folate deficiency, osteomalacia, neuropathy	Other AEDs, warfarin, amiodarone and other anti-arrhythmics, antimalarials, steroids, OCP, cimetidine, oral hypoglycaemics, theophylline, thyroxine
Piracetam	Myoclonus	7200–20 000	2–3	Not applicable	Dizziness, insomnia, nausea, weight gain, drowsiness, tremor, agitation	Rash	None known	None known
Primidone	Partial, secondary GTCS	250–1000	1–2	50–150	Drowsiness, ataxia, nystagmus, diplopia	Rashes, depression (adults), excitement (children), megaloblastic anaemia, SLE	As for phenobarbital*	As for phenobarbital*
Sodium valproate	Primary and secondary GTCS, absences, myoclonus	400–2500	1–2	Not applicable	Drowsiness, nausea, ataxia, nystagmus, diplopia, tremor	Alopecia, rashes, blood dyscrasias, liver damage, pancreatitis	Weight gain	Other AEDs, anticoagulants, antimalarials, cimetidine
Tiagabine	Partial, secondary GTCS	15–30	2–3	Not applicable	Drowsiness, nausea, ataxia, tremor	Headache, psychosis, depression	Reduced peripheral vision	Other AEDs
Topiramate	Partial, secondary GTCS	200–600	1–2	Not applicable	Drowsiness, nausea, ataxia, confusion	Nephrolithiasis, depression, taste alteration, diarrhoea, weight loss	Not yet known	Other AEDs, OCP
Vigabatrin	Partial, secondary GTCS, infantile spasms	2000–6000	1–2	Not applicable	Drowsiness, nausea, ataxia, confusion	Aggression, alopecia, skin rash, increase in seizures, retinal atrophy	Reduced peripheral vision	

(GTCS = generalised tonic clonic seizures; AEDs = anti-epileptic drugs; OCP = oral contraceptive pill; SLE = systemic lupus erythematosus)

* Primidone is converted in the liver to phenobarbital.

N.B. Doses of all drugs should be adjusted for patient age and body mass.

The patient should inform the licensing authorities about the onset of seizures. It is also wise for patients to notify their motor insurance company. Certain occupations, such as airline pilot, are not open to anyone who has ever had an epileptic seizure; further information is often available from epilepsy support organisations.

Anticonvulsant drug therapy

Drug treatment should be considered after more than one seizure has occurred and the patient agrees that seizure control is worth while (see EBM panel). Quite a range of anti-epilepsy drugs (AEDs) are available (see Box 22.18). The mode of action is either to increase inhibitory neurotransmission in the brain or to alter neuronal sodium channels in such a way as to prevent abnormally rapid transmission of impulses. Of patients whose epilepsy is controllable, only a single drug is necessary in 80%, providing the choice of agent is appropriate and the dosage correct. The combination of more than two drugs is seldom necessary. Dose regimens should be kept as simple as possible to promote compliance. Some useful guidelines are listed in Box 22.19.

EPILEPSY—use of anti-epileptic drugs (AEDs) after a single seizure EBM

'After a single seizure there is a 40% risk of subsequent seizures. The use of AEDs after a single seizure reduces the frequency of second seizures by half over 2 years but does not alter the long-term prognosis.'

- Berg AT, Shinnar S. The risk of seizure recurrence following a first unprovoked seizure: a quantitative review. Neurology 1991; 41:965–972.
- Musicco M, Beghi E, Solari A, Viani F, for the FIRST group. Treatment of first tonic clonic seizure does not improve the prognosis of epilepsy. Neurology 1997; 49:991–998.

Further information: 💻 www.clinicalevidence.org

22.19 GUIDELINES FOR ANTICONVULSANT THERAPY

- Start with one first-line drug (see Box 22.20)
- Start with low dose, gradually increase to effective control of seizures or until side-effects (drug levels occasionally helpful)
- Check compliance (use minimum division of doses)
- If first drug fails (seizures continue or side-effects), start second-line drug whilst gradually withdrawing first
- Try three agents singly before using combinations (beware interactions)
- Do not use more than two drugs in combination at any one time
- If above fails, consider whether occult structural or metabolic lesion is present and whether seizures are truly epileptic

---

Choice of drug. With the exception of absence attacks and juvenile myoclonic epilepsy, there is no hard evidence indicating that one drug is superior to another in the treatment of epilepsy (see EBM panel). In general, the first line of treatment should be one of the established first-line drugs (see Box 22.20), with the more recently

---

EPILEPSY—relative efficacy of the main AEDs in generalised tonic clonic seizures

'RCTs comparing the main AEDs as monotherapy for generalised tonic clonic seizures failed to demonstrate any difference in efficacy between different AEDs. There were differences in side-effects observed with different drugs.'

- Heller AJ, Chesterman P, Crawford P, et al. Phenobarbitone, phenytoin, or sodium valproate for newly diagnosed epilepsy: a randomized comparative monotherapy trial. J Neurol Neurosurg Psychiatry 1995; 8:44–50.
- Richens A, Davidson DL, Cartlidge NE, Easter DJ. A multicentre comparative trial of sodium valproate and carbamazepine in adult onset epilepsy: adult EPITEG collaborative group. J Neurol Neurosurg Psychiatry 1994; 57:682–687.

Further information: 💻 www.clinicalevidence.org

22.20 GUIDELINES FOR CHOICE OF AED

Epilepsy type	First-line	Second-line	Third-line
Partial and/or secondary GTCS	Carbamazepine	Lamotrigine Sodium valproate Topiramate Tiagabine Gabapentin	Clobazam Phenytoin Primidone Phenobarbital Oxcarbazepine Levetiracetam Vigabatrin Acetazolamide
Primary GTCS	Sodium valproate	Lamotrigine Topiramate Carbamazepine	Phenytoin Gabapentin Primidone Phenobarbital Tiagabine Acetazolamide
Absence	Ethosuximide	Sodium valproate	Lamotrigine Clonazepam Acetazolamide
Myoclonic	Sodium valproate	Clonazepam	Piracetam Lamotrigine Phenobarbital

N.B. Preferably one and no more than two drugs should be used at one time.

---

introduced drugs as second choice. Phenytoin and carbamazepine are not ideal agents for a young woman wishing to use oral contraception, because the drugs induce liver enzymes. Carbamazepine, lamotrigine and sodium valproate are preferable to phenytoin as first-line drugs because of the side-effect profile of the latter and its complicated pharmacokinetics.

Anticonvulsant drug blood levels. With some AEDs, such as phenytoin and carbamazepine, occasional measurement of the blood level can be a guide to whether the patient is on a useful dose and is complying with the medication, but blood levels need to be interpreted intelligently. With other AEDs, such as sodium valproate, there is no relationship between drug levels and anticonvulsant efficacy. Repeated measurement of plasma levels of AEDs is not generally useful since the dose used in any individual patient will be determined by the efficacy of seizure control and the development of side-effects, whatever the plasma level happens to be. Plasma level monitoring is especially useful in dealing with suspected toxicity (particularly if more than one drug is being taken), dealing with the effects of pregnancy, or in suspected non-compliance.

Prognosis

Overall, generalised seizures are more readily controlled than partial seizures. The presence of a structural lesion makes complete control of the epilepsy less likely. The overall prognosis for epilepsy is shown in Box 22.21.

22.21 EPILEPSY: OUTCOME AFTER 20 YEARS

- 50% seizure-free, without drugs, for last 5 years
- 20% seizure-free for last 5 years but continue to take medication
- 30% seizures continue in spite of anti-epileptic therapy

Withdrawal of anticonvulsant therapy

After complete control of seizures for 2–4 years, withdrawal of medication may be considered. Childhood-onset epilepsy, particularly classical absence seizures, carries the best prognosis for successful drug withdrawal. Other primary generalised epilepsies, such as juvenile myoclonic epilepsy, have a marked liability to recur after AED withdrawal. Seizures that begin in adult life, particularly those with partial features, are also likely to recur, especially if there is an identified structural lesion. Overall, the recurrence rate of seizures after drug withdrawal is about 40% (see EBM panel). Some adult patients tend to opt for continuation of therapy because they feel that the threat of further attacks (especially regarding driving) outweighs the complications of continuing with medication. The EEG is a poor predictor of seizure recurrence but if the record is still very abnormal,

---

EPILEPSY—withdrawal of AEDs EBM

'A large RCT showed that withdrawal of AEDs from those in remission from epilepsy was associated with twice the likelihood of a relapse after 2 years compared with continuation of treatment. The likelihood of relapse was greater in those under 16 years, those with tonic clonic seizures, those with myoclonus, those treated with more than one AED, those who had had seizures after starting AEDs and those with any EEG abnormality.'

- Medical Research Council Antiepileptic Drug Withdrawal Study Group. Prognostic index for recurrence of seizures after remission of epilepsy. BMJ 1993; 306:1374–1378.
- Medical Research Council Antiepileptic Drug Withdrawal Study Group. Randomised study of antiepileptic drug withdrawal in patients in remission. Lancet 1991; 337:1175–1180.

Further information: 🖥 www.clinicalevidence.org

---

drug withdrawal is unwise. Withdrawal should be undertaken slowly, reducing the drug dose gradually over 6–12 months. In the UK patients must desist from driving whilst withdrawing from their anti-epileptic medication and not drive for 6 months after full withdrawal of the drugs.

Status epilepticus

Status epilepticus exists when a series of seizures occurs without the patient regaining awareness between attacks. Most commonly, this refers to recurrent tonic clonic seizures (major status) and is a life-threatening medical emergency. Partial motor status is obvious clinically, but complex partial status and absence status may be difficult to diagnose, because the patient may merely present in a dazed, confused state. Status is never the presenting feature of idiopathic epilepsy but may be precipitated by abrupt withdrawal of anticonvulsant drugs, the presence of a major structural lesion or acute metabolic disturbance, and tends to be more common with frontal epileptic foci. Management is summarised in Box 22.22. It should be remembered that psychogenic or non-epileptic attacks commonly masquerade as 'status epilepticus', so electrophysiological confirmation of the seizures should be obtained as early as possible.

22.22 MANAGEMENT OF STATUS EPILEPTICUS

General

- Immediate care (see Box 22.16, p. 1127)
- Secure intravenous access
- Draw blood for glucose and electrolytes etc. and save some for future analysis (drugs etc.)
- Give diazepam 10 mg intravenously (or rectally)—repeat once only after 15 mins; or lorazepam 4 mg intravenously
- Transfer to intensive care area, monitoring neurological condition, blood pressure, respiration and blood gases

Pharmacological

If seizures continue after 30 mins
- Intravenous infusion (with cardiac monitoring) with one of:
  Phenytoin: i.v. infusion of 15 mg/kg at 50 mg/min
  Fosphenytoin: i.v. infusion of 15 mg/kg at 100 mg/min
  Phenobarbital: i.v. infusion of 10 mg/kg at 100 mg/min

If seizures still continue after 30–60 mins
- Start treatment for refractory status with intubation and ventilation, and general anaesthesia using propofol or thiopental

Once status controlled
- Commence longer-term anticonvulsant medication with one of:
  Sodium valproate 10 mg/kg i.v. over 3–5 mins, then 800–2000 mg/day
  Phenytoin: give loading dose (if not already used as above) of 15 mg/kg, infuse at < 50 mg/min, then 300 mg/day
  Carbamazepine 400 mg by nasogastric tube, then 400–1200 mg/day

Other
- Investigate cause

Epilepsy, pregnancy and oral contraception

Hepatic enzyme induction caused by carbamazepine, phenytoin, topiramate and barbiturates accelerates metabolism of oestrogen, causing breakthrough bleeding and contraceptive failure. The safest policy is to use an alternative contraceptive method, but it is sometimes possible to overcome the problem by giving a higher oestrogen dose preparation. Sodium valproate has little interaction with oral contraception.

Epilepsy may worsen during pregnancy, particularly during the third trimester when plasma anticonvulsant levels tend to fall. Monitoring of blood levels during pregnancy may therefore be advisable. Almost all the major anticonvulsant drugs have been associated with an increased incidence of fetal congenital abnormalities (e.g. cleft lip, spina bifida and cardiac defects), but this has not yet been demonstrated for lamotrigine or gabapentin. The risk of fetal abnormality, which is greatest if the exposure is in the first trimester, rises from the background risk of 1–3% to about 7% with one anti-epileptic drug and to about 15% if there are two or more drugs. Folic acid (5 mg daily) taken 2 months before conception may reduce the risk of some fetal abnormalities. Occasionally, in a well-controlled patient, anticonvulsants can be withdrawn before conception, but if major seizures have occurred in the preceding year this is unwise as the risk to the fetus from uncontrolled maternal major seizures is probably greater than the teratogenic effects. Partial seizures probably carry little risk to the fetus.

The incidence of haemorrhagic disease of the newborn due to vitamin K deficiency may be increased by maternal use of hepatic enzyme-inducing anticonvulsants. Therefore maternal vitamin K supplements (20 mg orally per day) in the last month of pregnancy and intramuscular vitamin K (1 mg) at birth for the infant are widely advised.

Non-epileptic attack disorder ('psychogenic attacks', 'pseudo-seizures')

Patients may present with attacks that superficially resemble epileptic seizures but which are caused by psychological phenomena and not associated with abnormal epileptic discharge in the brain. Such patients may even present in apparent status epilepticus. People with epilepsy may have non-epileptic attacks as well, and this diagnosis should be considered if a patient fails to respond to anti-epileptic therapy. Non-epileptic attacks may be quite difficult to distinguish from truly epileptic attacks. In the history, some clues pointing towards non-epileptic attacks include elaborate arching of the back in an attack, pelvic thrusting and/or wild flailing of limbs. Cyanosis and severe biting of the tongue are rare in non-epileptic attacks, but urinary incontinence can occur. The distinction between epileptic attacks originating in the frontal lobes and non-epileptic attacks may be especially difficult, and may require videotelemetry with prolonged EEG recordings. Non-epileptic attacks are three times more common in women than in men and have been associated with a history of sexual abuse in childhood. They are not necessarily associated with formal psychiatric illness. Treatment is often difficult and usually requires psychotherapy and/or counselling rather than drug therapy (see p. 256).

ISSUES IN OLDER PEOPLE
EPILEPSY

- Late-onset epilepsy is very common and the annual incidence in those over 60 years is rising.
- The features that usually differentiate fits from faints may be less definitive in older than in younger patients.
- Complex partial status epilepticus should be considered as a cause of confusion in the frail older patient.
- Cerebrovascular disease is the most commonly identified cause of epilepsy in people over the age of 50 years and accounts for 30–50% of cases. A seizure may occur with an overt stroke or with otherwise occult vascular disease (e.g. identified on CT). Such patients should receive aspirin and appropriate cardiovascular risk factor reduction.
- Anti-epileptic drug regimens should be as simple as possible and care should be taken to avoid potential interactions with other drugs being prescribed.
- Carbamazepine-induced hyponatraemia increases significantly with age and this is particularly important in patients on diuretics or who have heart failure.
- Late-onset epilepsy is associated with an increased relapse rate so the withdrawal of anticonvulsant therapy should not be attempted in older patients in whom it was commenced appropriately.

A DIAGNOSTIC APPROACH TO THE PATIENT WITH TRANSIENT AMNESIA

Loss of memory for a period of time may be due to a transient toxic confusional state, a psychological fugue state, the post-ictal period after seizure or the syndrome known as transient global amnesia. These are usually distinguished on the basis of the history. A period of amnesia often follows either a complex partial or generalised seizure, and this may cause diagnostic confusion if the seizure was not witnessed—for example, if it occurred in sleep.

TRANSIENT GLOBAL AMNESIA

This is a syndrome affecting predominantly middle-aged patients in which there is an abrupt, discrete and reversible loss of short-term memory function for a period of some hours. During this time patients know who they are and can perform motor acts normally, but act in a bemused way, repeatedly asking the same questions. During the attack there is retrograde amnesia for the events of the past few weeks. After 4–6 hours memory functions and behaviour return to normal but the patient is left with a period of time for which he or she has complete amnesia. There are none of the phenomena associated with seizures and, unlike epileptic amnesia, transient global amnesia tends not to recur. There are no associated cerebrovascular risk factors, making a vascular aetiology unlikely. Transient global amnesia is thought to be due to a benign process similar to that causing a migraine aura, occurring in the hippocampus. The patient has no physical signs and further investigation may not be needed if epilepsy can be excluded.

SLEEP DISORDERS

Disturbances of sleep are common. Apart from insomnia (see p. 267), patients may complain of excessive day-time sleepiness, disturbed behaviour during night-time sleep, the parasomnias (sleep walking and talking, or night terrors) or disturbing subjective experiences during sleep and/or its onset (nightmares, hypnagogic hallucinations, sleep paralysis). A careful history will allow certain patterns of sleep disturbance to be identified.

Normal sleep is controlled by the reticular activating system in the upper brain stem and diencephalon. During overnight sleep, a series of repeated cycles of EEG patterns can be recorded. As drowsiness occurs, alpha rhythm disappears and the EEG gradually becomes dominated by deepening slow-wave activity. After 60–80 minutes this slow-wave pattern is replaced by a short spell of low-amplitude EEG background on which are superimposed rapid eye movements (REM). After a few minutes of REM sleep, another slow-wave spell starts and the cycle repeats several times throughout the night. The REM periods tend to become longer as the sleep period progresses. Dreaming takes place during REM sleep, which is accompanied by muscle relaxation, penile erection and loss of tendon reflexes. REM sleep seems to be the most important part of the sleep cycle for refreshing cognitive processes. Deprivation of REM sleep causes tiredness, irritability and impaired judgement.

PARASOMNIAS

Automatic behaviour that is not recalled may take place during light sleep. Sleep talking and sleep walking are innocuous and common in normal children. Sleep walking is uncommon in adults and has no pathological significance. Nightmares are frightening dreams from which the sufferer wakes in a state of fear or agitation. Most normal people have experienced such phenomena and they are not of any significance in terms of organic disease.

Night terrors occur as sudden arousals from deep slow-wave sleep. They are more common in children but may affect adults. The sufferer wakes in a state of agitation, screaming and fearful. Occasionally, violent behaviour occurs. The agitation may last many minutes. Such events may be confused with nocturnal seizures, particularly those arising from the frontal lobe, or their post-ictal effects.

DAY-TIME SOMNOLENCE

Excessive sleepiness in the day is most commonly due to inadequate night-time sleep related to fatigue and poor sleep hygiene, including the excessive use of caffeine and/or alcohol in the evening. Night-time sleep may also be disturbed by sleep apnoea (see p. 504), periodic limb movements and the restless leg syndrome. Somnolence due to disturbed night-time sleep particularly occurs after meals and during dull monotonous activities, such as long car journeys. Such causes of day-time sleepiness need to be distinguished from narcolepsy.

NARCOLEPSY

This disorder has a prevalence of about 1 in 4000 and is associated with HLA (human leucocyte antigen) DR-1501 and DQB1-0602 in 85% of cases. There is a familial tendency suggesting an autosomal dominant inheritance with low penetrance. Recurrent bouts of irresistible sleep are experienced, during which the EEG often shows direct entry into REM sleep. Sufferers tend to fall asleep when eating or talking, not just when under-stimulated. The periods of sleep are usually short and the person can be woken relatively easily. He or she usually feels refreshed after waking. In addition, patients with narcolepsy will report at least one other of the 'narcolepsy tetrad' (see Box 22.23). These four symptoms may occur together or in combinations in the same patient; most often, sleep attacks and cataplexy occur together.

22.23 THE NARCOLEPSY TETRAD
Sleep attacks
• Brief, frequent and unlike normal somnolence
Cataplexy
• Sudden loss of muscle tone set off by surprise, laughter, strong emotion etc.
Hypnagogic hallucinations
• Frightening hallucinations experienced during sleep onset or waking (can occur in normal people)
Sleep paralysis
• Brief paralysis on waking (can occur in normal people)

Narcoleptic attacks can be treated with CNS stimulants such as dexamfetamine (5–10 mg 8-hourly) or methylphenidate (10–60 mg per day) but fewer side-effects occur with modafinil (200–400 mg per day). Cataplexy responds to clomipramine (25–50 mg 8-hourly) or fluoxetine (20 mg per day).

OTHER DISORDERS OF SLEEP
Restless leg syndrome
This is a common syndrome, also known as Ekbom's syndrome, affecting up to 2% of the population. Unpleasant

sensations in the legs that are ameliorated by moving the legs occur when the patient is tired in the evenings and at the onset of sleep. This condition has a strong familial tendency and can present with day-time somnolence due to disturbed night-time sleep. It needs to be distinguished from the day-time sense of restlessness of the limbs known as akathisia that is a side-effect of major tranquillisers, and the related condition of periodic limb movements during sleep. Restless legs can be symptomatic of an underlying peripheral neuropathy or general medical condition (for example, uraemia).

Treatment is with clonazepam (0.5–2.0 mg) or with small doses of levodopa (100–200 mg) at night.

Periodic limb movements

In this syndrome sleep is disturbed by repetitive jerky flexion movements of the limbs which occur in the early stages of sleep. The history of abnormal limb movements during sleep may need to be obtained from the patient's bed partner, since the patient may not be aware of the arousals that are occurring as a result of the movements, even though they may be sufficient to cause day-time somnolence. Treatment may be effected with small doses of levodopa (100–200 mg at night) or a dopaminergic agent (see p. 1176).

DISORDERS OF MOVEMENT

Lesions in various parts of the motor system produce distinctive patterns of motor deficit. These can be in the form of the negative symptoms of weakness, lack of coordination, lack of stability and stiffness, or positive symptoms such as tremor, dystonia, chorea, athetosis, hemiballismus, tics and myoclonus. When the lower limbs are affected, characteristic patterns of gait disorder may result.

THE MOTOR SYSTEM

A programme of movement formulated by the pre-motor cortex is converted into a series of muscle movements in the motor cortex and then transmitted to the spinal cord in the pyramidal tract (see Fig. 22.12). This passes through the internal capsule and the ventral brain stem before decussating in the medulla to enter the lateral columns of the spinal cord. The pyramidal tract 'upper motor neurons' end by synapsing with the anterior horn cells of the spinal cord grey matter, which form the 'lower motor neurons'.

Movement of a body part necessitates changes in posture and alteration in the tone of many muscles, some quite distant from the part being moved. The motor system consists of a hierarchy of control mechanisms that maintain body posture and baseline muscle tone upon which a specific movement is superimposed. The lowest order of this hierarchy comprises the mechanisms housed in the

grey matter of the spinal cord which control the muscle tone response to stretch and the reflex withdrawal response to noxious stimuli. The afferent side of the stretch reflex consists of the muscle spindles that detect lengthening of the muscle and initiate a monosynaptic reflex leading to muscle contraction. The predominantly inhibitory descending input from the brain stem and cerebral hemispheres modulates the sensitivity of the stretch reflex.

Polysynaptic connections in the spinal cord grey matter control more complex reflex actions of flexion and extension of the limbs which form the basic building blocks of coordinated actions, but which require control from above to function usefully. Above the spinal cord, circuits between the basal ganglia and the motor cortex constitute the extrapyramidal system which controls background muscle tone and body posture, and gates the initiation of movement (see Figs 22.12 and 22.13).

Accurately targeted and coordinated movements require the functioning of the cerebellum, which acts as an

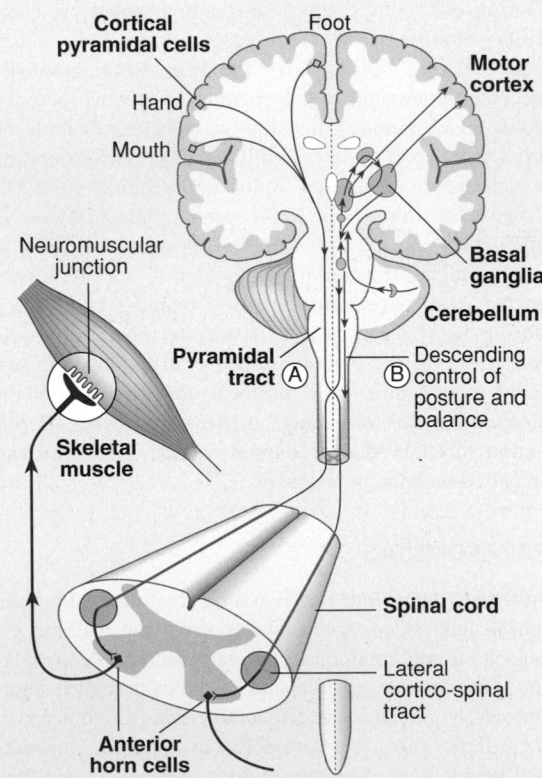

Fig. 22.12 The motor system. Neurons from the motor cortex descend as the pyramidal tract in the internal capsule and cerebral peduncle to the ventral brain stem, where most cross low in the medulla (A). In the spinal cord the upper motor neurons form the cortico-spinal tract in the lateral column before synapsing with the lower motor neurons in the anterior horns. The activity in the motor cortex is modulated by influences from the basal ganglia and cerebellum (B). Pathways descending from these structures control posture and balance (see also Fig. 22.13).

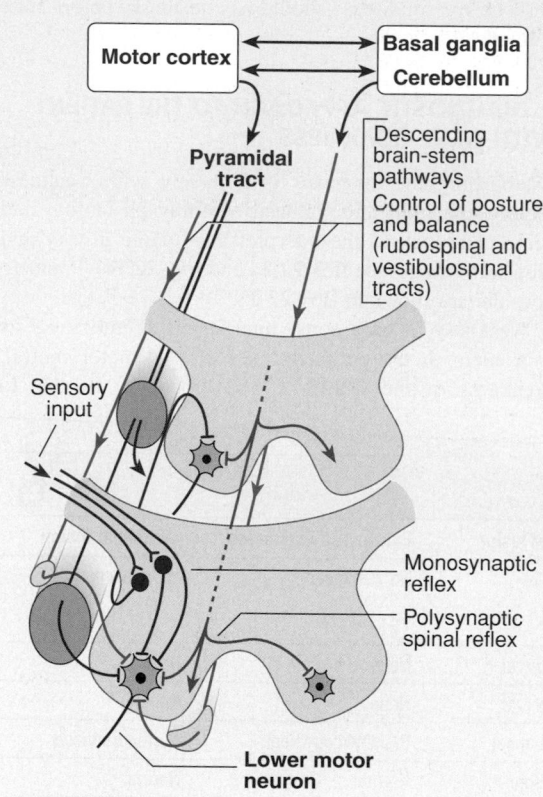

Fig. 22.13 Hierarchies of motor control. In addition to direct descending pathways from the cerebral motor cortex, motor neurons in the anterior horn are influenced by descending pathways controlling balance and posture as well as monosynaptic and polysynaptic spinal reflex pathways.

on-line guidance computer to fine-tune goal-directed movements initiated by the motor cortex. In addition, the cerebellum, through its reciprocal connections with the thalamus and cortex, participates in the planning and learning of skilled movements.

Pathophysiology

Lower motor neuron lesions

Groups of muscle fibres innervated by a single anterior horn cell (lower motor neuron) form a 'motor unit'. Loss of function of lower motor neurons will cause the loss of contraction in their units' muscle fibres and the muscle will be weak and flaccid. Denervated muscle fibres atrophy in time, causing wasting of the muscle, and depolarise spontaneously, causing fibrillations which, except in the tongue, are only perceptible on an EMG. Re-innervation from neighbouring intact motor neurons may occur but the neuromuscular junctions of the enlarged motor units are unstable and depolarise spontaneously, causing fasciculations (twitches which are visible to the naked eye). Fasciculations therefore imply chronic partial denervation.

Upper motor neuron (pyramidal) lesions

When the spinal cord is disconnected from the modulating influence of the higher motor hierarchies, the anterior horn motor neurons are under the uninhibited influence of the spinal reflex mechanisms. Their innervated muscles will have an exaggerated response to stretch. The limbs show reflex patterns of movement, like flexion withdrawal to noxious stimuli and spasms of extension. An upper motor neuron lesion therefore manifests clinically with brisk tendon stretch reflexes, 'spastic' increase in tone greater in the extensors of the lower limbs and the flexors of the upper limbs, and extensor plantar responses. Spastic increase in tone can be seen on clinical examination to vary with both the degree and speed of stretch; this is the 'clasp-knife' phenomenon. Spasticity takes some time to develop and may not be present for weeks after the onset of an upper motor neuron lesion. Spasticity will be exacerbated by increased sensory input into the reflex arc, as may be caused by a bed sore or urinary tract infection in a patient with a spinal cord lesion. The weakness found in upper motor neuron lesions is more pronounced in the extensors of the upper limbs and the flexors of the lower limbs.

Extrapyramidal lesions

Lesions of the extrapyramidal system produce an increase in tone, which is not an exaggerated response to stretch but is continuous throughout the range of movement (rigidity). Involuntary movements are also a feature of extrapyramidal lesions (see below), and a tremor combined with rigidity produces typical 'cogwheel' rigidity. Rapid movements are slowed and clumsy (bradykinesia). Extrapyramidal lesions also cause postural instability, precipitating falls.

Cerebellar lesions

A lesion in a cerebellar hemisphere causes lack of coordination on the same side of the body. The initial part of movement is normal but as the target is approached the accuracy of the movement deteriorates, producing an 'intention tremor'. The distances of targets are misjudged (dysmetria), resulting in 'past-pointing'. The ability to produce rapid, accurate, regularly alternating movements is impaired, which is known as 'dysdiadochokinesis'.

The central vermis of the cerebellum is concerned with the coordination of gait and posture. Disorders of this part therefore produce a characteristic ataxic gait (see below).

'MEDICALLY UNEXPLAINED' ('PSYCHOGENIC'/'NON-ORGANIC') WEAKNESS

Patients may present with limb weakness which is not due to organic (structural, physiological or biochemical) disease but which is caused by psychological phenomena: for example, a 'conversion' disorder (see p. 265). In this case the weakness does not conform to known pathophysiological patterns (e.g. reflexes are usually normal) and the deficit cannot be attributed to a lesion in a specific anatomical site in the nervous system. During formal testing of power, a patient's strength may appear to 'give way', yet demonstrate bursts of full power at other times. Alternatively, if a 'weak' limb is held up and then suddenly allowed to drop, the limb may be momentarily held up, something which would not happen in organic weakness. Note that apparent 'non-organic' weakness may occur as elaboration upon a 'genuine' organic weakness, and physical signs such as 'give-way weakness' therefore do not necessarily imply absence of pathology. Great care should be exercised in making the diagnosis of a functional disorder and all unusual manifestations of

nervous system disease should be considered before such a diagnosis is made.

A DIAGNOSTIC APPROACH TO THE PATIENT WITH LIMB WEAKNESS

Establishing the diagnosis in a patient with weakness requires the application of basic anatomy, physiology and some pathology to the interpretation of the history and clinical findings (see Box 22.24 and Fig. 22.14). Points to consider are shown in Box 22.25.

Weakness in only some muscles in a limb suggests a problem in the peripheral nerve(s) or motor root(s). Weakness of the whole of one limb may be due to

22.24 PHYSICAL SIGNS IN DIFFERENT TYPES OF MOTOR DEFICIT

Clinical sign	Upper motor (pyramidal) lesion	Lower motor lesion	Extrapyramidal lesion	Cerebellar lesion
Power	Weak Upper limbs: extensors weaker Lower limbs: flexors weaker	Weak	No weakness	No weakness
Wasting	None	Yes, after interval	None	None
Fasciculation	None	Yes, after interval	None	None
Tone	Spastic increase (after interval)	Flaccid from onset	Rigidity (cogwheel)	Normal/reduced
Reflexes	Increased	Reduced/absent	Normal	Normal
Plantar response	Extensor	Flexor	Flexor	Flexor
Coordination	Reduced by weakness	Reduced by weakness	Normal (but slowed)	Impaired

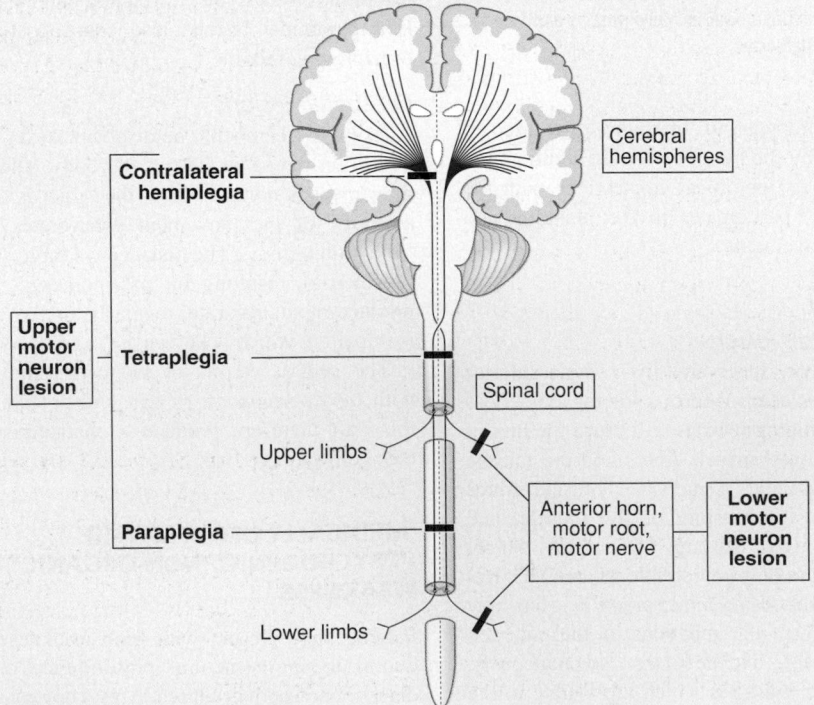

Fig. 22.14 Patterns of motor loss according to the anatomical site of the lesion.

22.25 ASSESSMENT OF WEAKNESS
Distribution
• A few muscles • A limb • Both lower limbs (paraparesis) • Both limbs on one side (hemiparesis)
Type of weakness
• Upper motor neuron lesion • Lower motor neuron lesion
Evolution of the weakness
• Sudden and improving • Gradually worsening over days or weeks • Evolving over months or years

22.26 LIMB WEAKNESS—ASSESSING THE CAUSE
Vascular lesions
• Sudden onset (over minutes) followed by a stable period and gradual recovery
Neoplastic lesions
• Deficit is gradual in onset and progressive over weeks or months • There may be signs caused by the mass effect of the lesion
Inflammatory lesions
• May be fairly acute in onset (over a few days), persist for a time and then improve (e.g. in multiple sclerosis)
Degenerative disorders
• May evolve over months or years (e.g. motor neuron disease or cervical spondylotic myelopathy)

problems in the brachial or lumbosacral plexuses, or to a central lesion. Weakness in both lower limbs (paraparesis) or all four limbs (tetraparesis) suggests either a spinal cord lesion or a diffuse peripheral nerve problem such as Guillain–Barré syndrome. In such cases the condition of the reflexes is the most discriminating sign. The reflexes are absent in the Guillain–Barré syndrome (or other lower motor nerve lesions) and brisk in spinal cord (upper motor neuron) lesions. The paraparesis or tetraparesis of spinal cord lesions may be associated with a specific pattern of sensory loss (see p. 1140) which gives a clue to the site of the lesion in the spinal cord.

Patients with a bradykinetic limb often complain of weakness. Therefore, if there are no reflex, wasting or sensory changes when a patient is complaining of weakness in a limb, extrapyramidal signs of rigidity (cogwheel or leadpipe) and bradykinesia should be sought. Patients with Parkinson's disease usually present with symptoms in one limb that may be described as weak and clumsy, especially for fine manipulations. Often the typical rest tremor is a clue to the diagnosis.

Weakness down one side of the body (hemiparesis) is almost always due to a cerebral hemisphere lesion, although it can be caused by spinal cord or brain-stem lesions. The lesion is of upper motor neuron type, and the site and often the size of the lesion can be deduced by the concurrence of other signs and symptoms, such as higher cerebral function abnormalities or sensory change.

The evolution of a motor deficit over time suggests the likely underlying pathology (see Box 22.26).

GAIT DISORDERS

As well as being an important element of assessing a patient's disability, seeing a patient walk can be very revealing for neurological diagnosis. Patterns of weakness, loss of coordination and proprioceptive sensory loss produce a range of abnormal neurological gaits. Neurogenic gait disorders need to be distinguished from those due to skeletal abnormalities, usually characterised by pain producing an antalgic gait, or limp. Gaits that do not fit either pattern may be due to 'functional' or non-organic disorders and are usually incompatible with any anatomical or physiological deficit.

Pyramidal gait

Upper motor neuron (pyramidal) lesions cause a gait in which the upper limb is held in flexion and the lower limb kept relatively extended. The pyramidal tract lesion slows the normally rapid ankle dorsiflexion needed to keep the toes from striking the ground as the leg swings through. In an attempt to overcome this, the leg is swung out at the hip (circumduction), but the affected foot still scuffs along the ground at the toes. The shoe on the affected side may be worn at the toes as evidence of this type of gait. In a hemiplegia the asymmetry between the affected and normal sides is obvious in walking. In a paraparesis both lower limbs move slowly, swung from the hips and dragged stiffly on the ground in extension, an effect that can often be heard as well as seen.

Foot drop

In normal walking, toe strike follows heel strike during the gait cycle. Weakness of ankle dorsiflexion disrupts this pattern. The result is a less controlled descent of the foot making a slapping noise. If the distal weakness is more severe, the foot will have to be lifted higher at the knee to allow room for the inadequately dorsiflexed foot to swing through, producing a high stepping gait.

Waddling gait of proximal muscle weakness

During walking, alternate placement of the body's weight through each leg requires careful control of the hips by the gluteal muscles. In proximal muscle weakness, usually caused by muscle disease, the hips are not properly fixed by these muscles and trunk movements are exaggerated, producing a rolling or waddling gait.

Cerebellar ataxia

Patients with lesions of the central parts of the cerebellum (the vermis) walk with a characteristic broad-based gait, 'like a drunken sailor' (cerebellar function is particularly sensitive to alcohol). Patients with acute vestibular disturbances walk in a similar broad-based fashion, though the accompanying vertigo distinguishes them from those with cerebellar lesions. Less severe degrees of cerebellar ataxia can be detected by asking the patient to walk heel to toe; patients with vermis lesions are unable to do this.

Gait apraxia

In an apraxic gait there is normal power in the legs and no abnormal cerebellar signs or proprioception loss, yet the patient cannot formulate the motor act of walking. This is a higher cerebral dysfunction in which the feet appear stuck to the floor and the patient cannot walk, even though movement is normal on the examination couch. Gait apraxia occurs in bilateral hemisphere disease such as normal pressure hydrocephalus and diffuse frontal lobe disease.

Marche à petits pas

Patients with multiple small-vessel cerebrovascular disease walk with small slow steps with instability. This looks different from the festinant gait of Parkinson's disease (see below) in that it does not have the variable pace and freezing. There are usually signs of bilateral upper motor neuron disease (bilateral extensor plantar responses and brisk jaw jerk).

Sensory ataxia

Loss of joint position sense makes walking unreliable, especially in poor light. The feet tend to be placed on the ground with greater emphasis, presumably in an attempt to increase what proprioceptive input is available. This results in a 'stamping' gait which is often combined with foot drop when caused by a peripheral neuropathy, but can occur in disorders of the dorsal columns in the spinal cord.

Extrapyramidal gait

Patients with Parkinson's disease and other extrapyramidal diseases have difficulty initiating walking and difficulty controlling the pace of their gait. The patient may get stuck whilst trying to start walking or when walking through doorways ('freezing'), but once started may then have problems controlling the speed of walking and have trouble stopping. This produces the festinant gait: initial stuttering steps that quickly increase in frequency while decreasing in length.

INVOLUNTARY MOVEMENTS

Abnormal movements usually imply a disorder in the basal ganglia, in which there is disinhibition of the activity of intrinsic rhythm generators or a disorder of postural control. Some, like tremor, are commonplace. Others, like chorea, athetosis and dystonia, have become more common as a result of adverse effects from pharmacological treatment of Parkinson's disease and psychiatric disease.

Tremor

A tremor is a rhythmic oscillating movement of a limb or part of a limb, or of the head. Tremors are usefully divided into those occurring at rest and those seen only when a limb is in action. The other characteristic by which tremors can be classified is their frequency.

Rest tremor

This is pathognomonic of Parkinson's disease (see p. 1174). The tremor is characteristically 'pill-rolling' and usually presents asymmetrically. However, patients with Parkinson's disease may have an abnormal action tremor as well. Tremor of the head in the upright position ('titubation') is not a rest tremor since this is a postural tremor, disappearing when the head is supported.

Action tremor

This is more frequently seen than rest tremor and potential causes are more numerous (see Box 22.27). A physiological tremor (frequency between 8 and 12 Hz) can be identified in the limbs of normal subjects; exaggeration of this physiological tremor occurs in anxiety and other situations, listed in Box 22.28.

Essential tremor is distinct from a physiological tremor, although resembling it superficially. It is slower than a physiological action tremor and may become quite disabling. The condition is often familial and in some

22.27 CAUSES OF TREMOR ON ACTION

• Exaggerated physiological tremor (see Box 22.28)
 • Essential tremor (may be familial)
 • Parkinson's disease (rest tremor more usual)
 • Wilson's disease
 • Postural tremor
    Multiple sclerosis
    Other lesions in cerebellar outflow/red nucleus
 • Intention tremor
    Cerebellar hemisphere disease

22.28 CAUSES OF EXAGGERATED PHYSIOLOGICAL TREMOR	
Anxiety	
Fatigue	
Endocrine	
• Thyrotoxicosis	• Phaeochromocytoma
• Cushing's disease	• Hypoglycaemia
Drugs	
• β-agonists (e.g. salbutamol)	• Sodium valproate
• Theophylline	• Tricyclics
• Caffeine	• Phenothiazines
• Lithium	• Amphetamines
• Dopamine agonists	
Toxins	
• Mercury	• Arsenic
• Lead	
Alcohol withdrawal	

families the tremor is most obvious during certain specific actions such as writing; here there is an overlap with focal dystonias (see below). Characteristic of essential tremor is that alcohol suppresses it, sometimes to the extent that the patient becomes addicted. Centrally acting β-adrenoceptor antagonists (β-blockers) such as propranolol are often effective in treatment.

An 'intention tremor' is the characteristic oscillation at the end of a movement which occurs in cerebellar disease, due to the breakdown of feedback control of targeted movements. Asterixis, the 'flapping' tremor seen in metabolic disturbances (see Box 22.29), is the result of intermittent failure of the parietal mechanisms required to maintain a posture. Thus, when a patient is asked to hold out the arms with the hands extended at the wrists, this posture is periodically dropped, allowing the hands to drop transiently before the posture is taken up again. Occasionally, unilateral asterixis can be seen in an acute parietal vascular lesion.

22.29 CAUSES OF ASTERIXIS

- Renal failure
- Liver failure
- Hypercapnia
- Drug toxicity (e.g. phenytoin)
- Acute focal parietal or thalamic lesions

A more dramatic action tremor occurs with lesions in the superior cerebellar peduncle (the site of the cerebellar outflow towards the red nucleus). This 'peduncular' or 'rubral' tremor is a violent, large-amplitude postural tremor that worsens as a target is approached. This is common in advanced multiple sclerosis and may be a source of considerable disability. Stereotactic thalamotomy can reduce the tremor, although the overall functional result is often disappointing.

Chorea, athetosis, ballism and dystonia

Non-rhythmic involuntary movements may be combinations of fragments of purposeful movements and abnormal postures. All of these abnormal movements represent disorders of the balance of activity in the complex basal ganglia circuitry. Jerky, small-amplitude, purposeless involuntary movements are termed 'chorea' (the Greek for 'dance'). In the limbs they resemble fidgety movements, and in the face, grimaces; they suggest disease in the caudate nucleus (as in Huntington's disease, see p. 1177) or excessive activity in the striatum due to dopaminergic drugs used to treat Parkinson's disease. There are a range of other causes (see Box 22.30). More dramatic ballistic movements of the limbs usually occur unilaterally (hemiballismus) in vascular lesions of the subthalamic structures. Slower writhing movements of the limbs are called athetosis. These are often combined with chorea (and have a similar list of causes) and are then termed 'choreo-athetoid' movements.

22.30 CAUSES OF CHOREA

Hereditary
- Huntington's disease
- Wilson's disease
- Neuroacanthocytosis
- Porphyria
- Paroxysmal choreoathetosis

Cerebral birth injury (including kernicterus)

Cerebral trauma

Drugs
- Levodopa
- Dopamine agonists
- Phenothiazines
- Tricyclics
- Oral contraceptive

Endocrine
- Pregnancy
- Oral contraceptive
- Thyrotoxicosis
- Hypoparathyroidism
- Hypoglycaemia

Infective/inflammatory
- Rheumatic fever (Sydenham's chorea)
- Systemic lupus erythematosus
- Henoch–Schönlein purpura
- Creutzfeldt–Jakob disease

Vascular
- Lacunar infarction
- Arteriovenous malformation

The term 'dystonia' is used to describe the movement disorder in which a limb (or the head) involuntarily takes up an abnormal posture. This may be generalised in various diseases of the basal ganglia or may be focal or segmental, as in spasmodic torticollis when the head involuntarily turns to one side. Other segmental dystonias may cause abnormal disabling postures of a limb to be taken up during certain specific actions, such as in writer's cramp or numerous other occupational 'cramps'. These segmental dystonias can be treated by the administration of botulinum toxin to a few of the responsible muscles, which seems to overcome the abnormal distribution of muscle activity for a period of time.

Myoclonus

Myoclonus refers to brief, isolated, random, non-purposeful jerks of muscle groups in the limbs. Myoclonic jerks occur normally at the onset of sleep (hypnic jerks). Similarly, a myoclonic jerk is a component of the normal startle response which may be exaggerated in some rare (mostly genetic) disorders. Unlike the movement disorders discussed so far, myoclonus may occur in disorders of the cerebral cortex, when groups of pyramidal cells fire spontaneously. Such myoclonus occurs in some forms of epilepsy in which the jerks are fragments of seizure activity. Alternatively, myoclonus can arise from subcortical structures or, more rarely, from diseased segments of the spinal cord. Myoclonus, especially of cortical origin, often responds to clonazepam, sodium valproate or piracetam.

Tics

Tics are repetitive semi-purposeful movements such as blinking, winking, grinning or screwing up of the eyes.

They are distinguished from other involuntary movements by the ability of the patient to suppress their occurrence, at least for a short time. An isolated tic may be no more than a mild embarrassment, but may become frequent at certain times in childhood and then disappear. The uncommon syndrome of Gilles de la Tourette consists of a tendency to multiple tics and odd vocalisations, with obsessive behavioural abnormalities. The pathogenic basis is not understood, but there may be some response to major tranquillisers.

SENSORY DISTURBANCE

Sensory symptoms are very common but do not always denote nervous system disorder. For example, tingling in the fingers of both hands and around the mouth commonly suggests hyperventilation (see pp. 496–497) or, very rarely, hypocalcaemia (see p. 716). The accuracy of patients in describing sensory disturbances is very variable and skill is needed in sifting through the history to make anatomical and pathophysiological sense of the complaints. Damage to the afferent nervous pathways conveying sensations of touch and pain produces either the negative sensation of numbness or positive symptoms, such as paraesthesia and pain. When there is dysfunction of the cerebral mechanisms of somatic sensation there may be distortion of the patient's perception of the wholeness or actual presence of the relevant part of the body.

A DIAGNOSTIC APPROACH TO THE PATIENT WITH SENSORY SYMPTOMS

In the history, the most useful features are the anatomical distribution and mode of onset of numbness, paraesthesia or pain. Certain patterns of onset of sensory symptoms can be recognised. For example, in a migraine attack the aura may consist of a front of tingling paraesthesia followed by numbness which takes 20–30 minutes to spread over one half of the body, splitting the tongue. Sensory loss due to a vascular lesion, on the other hand, will occur over the whole territory of the lesion more or less instantaneously. The rare, unpleasant paraesthesia of sensory epilepsy 'shoots' down one side of the body in seconds. The numbness and paraesthesia of spinal cord lesions often ascend one or both lower limbs to a level on the trunk over hours or days. Sensory symptoms of tingling and numbness can be of 'functional' or non-organic origin as a manifestation of anxiety or as part of a conversion disorder (see p. 265). In these circumstances the pattern of sensory symptoms does not conform to known anatomical distribution or fit with any known pattern of sensory involvement in organic disease. As with weakness (see above), care should be taken to avoid misdiagnosing an unusual organic sensory impairment as a functional disorder.

Examination of the sensory system needs to be approached with care since it is easy to produce confusing false positive results because of the inescapably subjective nature of sensory testing. However, the distribution of sensory loss and associated deficits in motor and/or cranial nerve function may enable a diagnostically helpful pattern of sensory loss to be identified.

Patterns of sensory disturbance (see Fig. 22.15)
Peripheral nerve lesions
In peripheral nerve lesions the symptoms are usually of sensory loss and simple paraesthesia (pins and needles). Single peripheral nerve lesions will, as expected, cause disturbance in the sensory distribution of that nerve. In diffuse neuropathies the longest neurons are first affected, giving the characteristic 'glove and stocking' distribution. If the smaller nerve fibres are preferentially affected (e.g. in alcoholic neuropathy), temperature and pin-prick (pain) are lost, whilst modalities served by the larger sensory nerves (vibration and joint position) may be spared. On the other hand, the latter are particularly affected if the neuropathy is demyelinating in character (e.g. Guillain–Barré syndrome, see p. 1180).

Nerve root lesions
Pain is more often a feature of lesions of nerve roots, within the spine or of the limb plexuses. Pain is often felt in the muscles innervated by a root, i.e. the myotome rather than the dermatome. The site of nerve root lesions may be deduced from the dermatomal pattern of sensory loss, although this is often smaller than would be expected because of the overlap of sensory 'territories'.

Spinal cord lesions
Somatic sensory information from the limbs ascends the nervous system in two anatomically discrete systems, differential involvement of which is often of diagnostic assistance (see Fig. 22.16). Fibres from proprioceptive organs and those mediating well-localised touch (including vibration) enter the spinal cord at the posterior horn and pass without synapsing into the ipsilateral posterior columns. Fibres conveying pain and temperature sensory information synapse with second-order neurons which cross the midline in the spinal cord before ascending in the contralateral anterolateral spinothalamic tract to the brain stem.

Transverse lesions of the spinal cord produce loss of all modalities below that segmental level, although the level obtained clinically may vary by two or three segments. Very often at the top of the area of sensory loss there is a band of paraesthesia or hyperaesthesia. If the transverse lesion is vascular in origin (e.g. due to anterior spinal artery thrombosis), the posterior one-third of the spinal cord (and therefore the dorsal column modalities) may be spared.

Lesions damaging one side of the spinal cord will produce sensory loss for spinothalamic modalities (pain and temperature) on the opposite side and for dorsal column

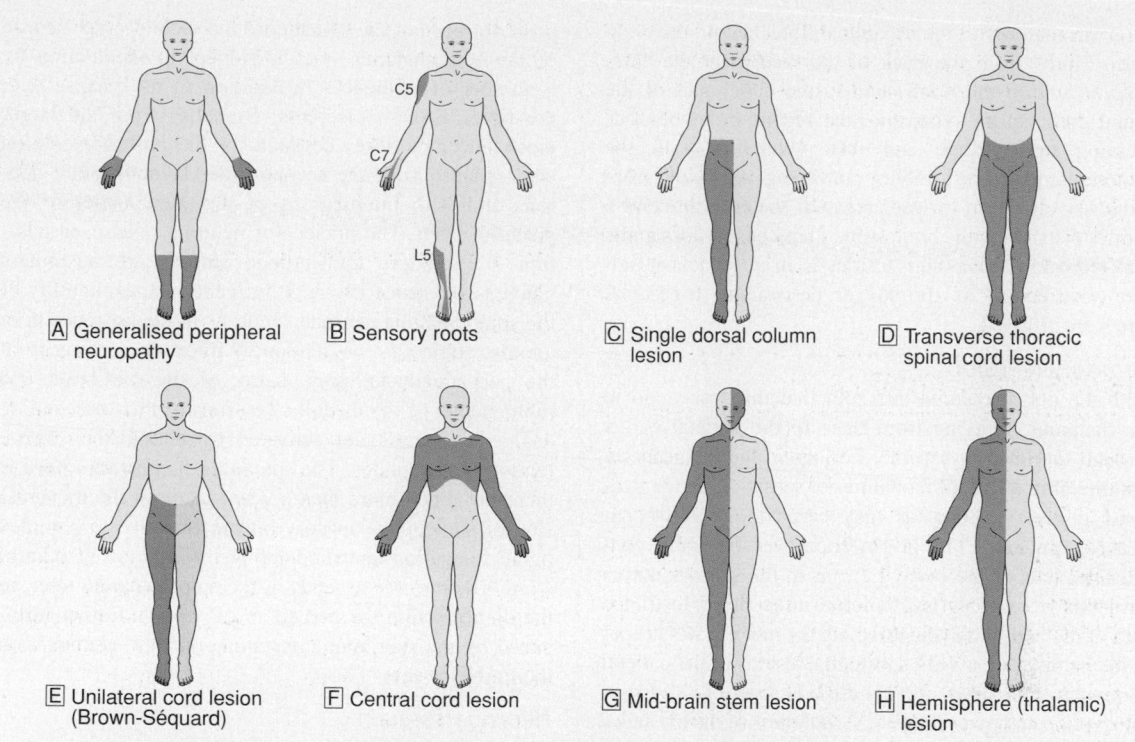

A Generalised peripheral neuropathy B Sensory roots C Single dorsal column lesion D Transverse thoracic spinal cord lesion

E Unilateral cord lesion (Brown-Séquard) F Central cord lesion G Mid-brain stem lesion H Hemisphere (thalamic) lesion

Fig. 22.15   Patterns of sensory loss. A Generalised peripheral neuropathy. B Sensory roots. C Single dorsal column lesion (proprioception and some touch loss). D Transverse thoracic spinal cord lesion. E Unilateral cord lesion (Brown-Séquard): ipsilateral dorsal column (and motor) deficit and contralateral spinothalamic deficit. F Central cord lesion: 'cape' distribution of spinothalamic loss. G Mid-brain-stem lesion: ipsilateral facial sensory loss and contralateral loss on body below the vertex. H Hemisphere (thalamic) lesion: contralateral loss on one side of face and body.

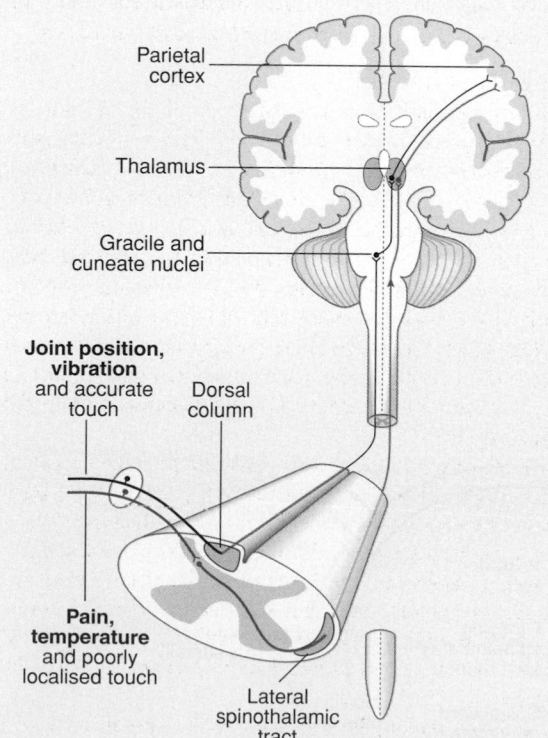

Fig. 22.16   The main somatic sensory pathways.

modalities (joint position and vibration) on the same side as the lesion. This is the pattern seen in the Brown-Séquard syndrome (see p. 1188).

Lesions in the centre of the spinal cord (e.g. syringomyelia, see p. 1191) spare the dorsal columns but affect the spinothalamic fibres crossing the cord from both sides over the length of the lesion. The sensory loss is therefore dissociated (in terms of the modalities affected) and suspended (in the sense that segments above and below the lesion are spared), often with reflex loss if afferent fibres of the reflex arc within the cord are affected.

There may be a lesion in the dorsal column alone, particularly in multiple sclerosis. This produces a characteristic unpleasant tight feeling over the limb involved and loss of proprioception that may severely affect the function of the limb without any loss of pin-prick or temperature sensation.

Brain-stem lesions

The second-order neurons of the dorsal column sensory system cross the midline in the upper medulla to ascend through the brain stem. Here they lie just medial to the (already crossed) spinothalamic pathway. Brain-stem lesions can therefore cause sensory loss affecting all modalities of the contralateral side of the body. Sensory loss on the face due to brain-stem lesions is dependent upon the anatomy of the trigeminal fibres within the brain stem. Fibres from the back of the face (near the ears) descend within the brain stem to the upper part of the spinal cord before synapsing, the second-order neurons crossing the midline and then ascending with the spinothalamic fibres. Fibres conveying sensation from progressively more forward areas of the face descend a shorter distance in the brain stem. Thus sensory loss in the face from low brain-stem lesions is in a 'balaclava helmet' distribution as the longer descending trigeminal fibres are affected.

Hemisphere lesions

Both the dorsal column and spinothalamic tracts end in the thalamus, relaying from there to the parietal cortex through the internal capsule. Lesions in the hemispheres can therefore affect all modalities of sensation. In the thalamus discrete lesions (as may occur in small lacunar strokes) can cause loss of sensation over the whole contralateral half of the body. Lesions in the sensory cortex have to be very small (and therefore affect only a restricted area of the body) to avoid affecting the motor tracts deeper in the hemispheres. With substantial lesions of the parietal cortex (as with large strokes) there is severe loss of proprioception and even conscious awareness of the existence of the affected limb(s). The resulting loss of function in the limb may be impossible to distinguish from paralysis.

Pain

Pain is a complex percept that is only partly related to activity in nociceptor neurons (see Fig. 22.17). In the posterior horn of the spinal cord the second-order neuron of the spinothalamic tract is subject to modulation by a number of influences in addition to its synapse with the fibres from nociceptors. Branches from the larger mechanoceptor fibres destined for the posterior column also synapse with the second-order spinothalamic neurons and with interneurons of the grey matter of the posterior horn. The nociceptor neurons release, in addition to excitatory transmitters, other neurotransmitters (such as substance P) which influence the excitability of the spinothalamic neurons. Neurons in the posterior horn are also subject to modulation by fibres descending from the peri-aqueductal grey matter of the mid-brain and raphe nuclei of the medulla. Neurons of this 'descending analgesia system' are activated by endogenous opiate (endorphin) peptides. The spinal cord's posterior horn is therefore much more than a way-station in the transmission of nociceptive sensory information; it is a complex organ for gating and modulating information of painful stimuli before this ascends in the spinothalamic tract. In the diencephalon the perception of pain is further influenced by the rich interconnections of the thalamus with the limbic system.

Neuropathic pain

Pain is of two main types: nociceptive pain, arising from a pathological process in a body part, and neuropathic pain, caused by dysfunction of the pain perception apparatus itself. Neuropathic pain has distinctive features and is described as a very unpleasant persistent burning paraesthetic sensation. There is often increased sensitivity to

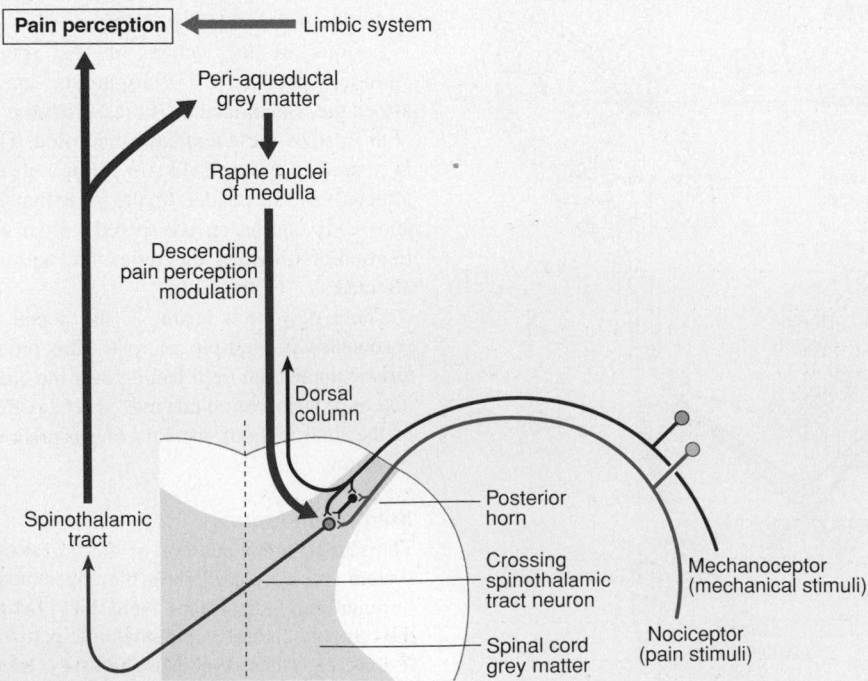

Fig. 22.17 The pain perception system.

touch, so that light brushing touches cause exquisite pain (hyperpathia). Painful stimuli appear to come from a larger area than that touched and spontaneous bursts of pain may occur. The perception of pain may be elicited by stimuli from other modalities such as loud sounds (allodynia) and is considerably affected by emotional influences. The most common syndromes of neuropathic pain are seen where there is partial damage to peripheral nerves ('causalgia'), to the trigeminal nerve (postherpetic neuralgia) or to the thalamus. Treatment of these syndromes is very difficult. Drugs which modulate various parts of the nociceptive system, such as carbamazepine, tricyclics or phenothiazines, may help but usually only do so partially. Neurosurgical attempts to interrupt various pain pathways sometimes succeed but often increase the sensory deficit and may worsen the situation. Implantation of electrical stimulators has occasionally proved successful. For further information, see Chapter 6.

COMA AND BRAIN DEATH

COMA

Persistent loss of consciousness or coma indicates disorder of the arousal mechanisms in the brain stem and diencephalon and indicates bilateral hemisphere or brain-stem disease. There are many causes of coma (see Box 22.31). The history of the mode of onset of coma and of any

22.31 CAUSES OF COMA	
Metabolic disturbance	
• Drug overdose	• Uraemia
• Diabetes mellitus	• Hepatic failure
Hypoglycaemia	• Respiratory failure
Ketoacidosis	• Hypothermia
Hyperosmolar coma	• Hypothyroidism
• Hyponatraemia	
Trauma	
• Cerebral contusion	• Subdural haematoma
• Extradural haematoma	
Cerebrovascular disease	
• Subarachnoid haemorrhage	• Brain-stem infarction/ haemorrhage
• Intracerebral haemorrhage	• Cerebral venous sinus thrombosis
Infections	
• Meningitis	• Cerebral abscess
• Encephalitis	• General sepsis
Others	
• Epilepsy	• Thiamin deficiency
• Brain tumour	

precipitating event is crucial to establishing the cause and this should be obtained from family or other witnesses. As with any medical emergency, the top priority is assessment and stabilisation of the vital functions. Neurological examination may reveal important findings, e.g. evidence of head injury, papilloedema, meningism or eye movement disorder. In the majority of cases, however, there are no focal neurological signs since drug overdose and metabolic disturbance are the most common causes of unexplained coma requiring hospital admission. Some patients will require intensive care unit (ICU) support.

Assessment of conscious level

This is an essential component of the neurological examination. Terms such as 'stuporose', 'semiconscious' and 'obtunded' are ill defined, and a clear description of the patient's level of arousal and response to stimuli is more helpful. Systematic assessment of the unconscious patient by the application of the Glasgow Coma Scale provides a grading of coma by using a numerical scale which allows serial comparison and may provide prognostic information, particularly in traumatic coma (see Box 22.32).

22.32 GLASGOW COMA SCALE	
Eye-opening (E)	
• Spontaneous	4
• To speech	3
• To pain	2
• Nil	1
Best motor response (M)	
• Obeys	6
• Localises	5
• Withdraws	4
• Abnormal flexion	3
• Extensor response	2
• Nil	1
Verbal response (V)	
• Orientated	5
• Confused conversation	4
• Inappropriate words	3
• Incomprehensible sounds	2
• Nil	1
Coma score = E + M + V	
• Minimum	3
• Maximum	15

BRAIN DEATH

The widespread availability of mechanical ventilators has resulted in the survival of patients with severe and irreversible brain damage but functioning cardiovascular systems. Diagnostic criteria for brain death have been established in order that those patients without functioning brains who have no chance of recovery may be identified and ventilation discontinued.

22.33 DIAGNOSIS OF BRAIN DEATH

Preconditions for considering a diagnosis of brain death	Tests for confirming brain death All brain-stem reflexes are absent

• The patient is deeply comatose
  (a) There must be no suspicion that coma is due to depressant drugs, e.g. narcotics, hypnotics, tranquillisers
  (b) Hypothermia has been excluded—rectal temperature must exceed 35°C
  (c) There is no profound abnormality of serum electrolytes, acid–base balance or blood glucose concentrations, and any metabolic or endocrine cause of coma has been excluded
• The patient is maintained on a ventilator because spontaneous respiration had been inadequate or had ceased. Drugs, including neuromuscular blocking agents, must have been excluded as a cause of the respiratory failure
• The diagnosis of the disorder leading to brain death has been firmly established. There must be no doubt that the patient is suffering from irremediable structural brain damage
	• The pupils are fixed and unreactive to light
	• The corneal reflexes are absent
	• The vestibulo-ocular reflexes are absent—there is no eye movement following the injection of 20 ml of ice-cold water into each external auditory meatus in turn
	• There are no motor responses to adequate stimulation within the cranial nerve distribution
	• There is no gag reflex and no reflex response to a suction catheter in the trachea
	• No respiratory movement occurs when the patient is disconnected from the ventilator long enough to allow the carbon dioxide tension to rise above the threshold for stimulating respiration ($PaCO_2$ must reach 6.7 kPa)
	
	The diagnosis of brain death should be made by two experienced doctors, one of whom should be a consultant and the other a consultant or specialist registrar. The tests are usually repeated after an interval of 6–24 hours, depending on the clinical circumstances, before brain death is finally confirmed

The diagnosis of brain death depends on meeting a set of preconditions, all of which must coexist, and then applying a series of clinical tests (see Box 22.33), all of which must be fulfilled.

ISSUES IN OLDER PEOPLE
COMA AND BRAIN DEATH

- Hypothermia is an easily missed cause of coma in the elderly.
- An unconscious patient's temperature should always be taken with a low-reading thermometer. For more information, see page 331.

DISTURBANCE OF CORTICAL FUNCTION

Many areas of cerebral cortex have a specialised function (e.g. the primary motor areas, language areas etc.). Focal lesions of the cerebral hemispheres can therefore cause disturbance of these individual functions, e.g. aphasia. These are dealt with below. Alternatively, diffuse or multifocal damage affects many areas, causing more global disturbance of higher cerebral function. Depending on speed of onset, and whether consciousness is impaired, global disturbances are broadly divided into acute confusional states and dementias.

ACUTE CONFUSIONAL STATE

This is also known as delirium, and is seen much more commonly than dementia. Unlike dementia, there is a disturbance of arousal that accompanies the global impairment of mental function. This usually takes the form of drowsiness with disorientation, perceptual disturbances and muddled thinking. Patients typically fluctuate, confusion being worse at night, and there may be associated emotional disturbance (e.g. anxiety, irritability or depression) or psychomotor changes (e.g. agitation, restlessness or retardation).

There are many possible causes of acute confusion (see Box 22.34), including acute decompensation of a more chronic dementia.

Diagnosis

The diagnosis of an acute confusional state involves careful history-taking. Patients are usually disorientated, often in both time and place, and therefore their account may not be helpful. As with dementia, it is vital to take a history from a witness (either a relative or a nurse). Examination may yield other clues to the cause (e.g. pyrexia, or focal chest or neurological signs). It is important to distinguish confusion from a fluent aphasia, since patients with this speech disorder often appear confused. Often, however, the cause is not immediately obvious, and a wide screen of tests must be performed (see Box 22.35).

Management

The management of acute confusional states involves identifying the cause and correcting it if possible. Confused patients should be nursed in a well-lit room. During the period of confusion drugs are best avoided, as they may exacerbate the confusion, though occasionally sedative drugs such as chlorpromazine (25–100 mg 8-hourly) or haloperidol (2.5–10 mg 8-hourly) may be required. In delirium tremens (alcohol withdrawal), the treatment is a tapered course of clomethiazole or chlordiazepoxide to accompany high-dose intravenous thiamin (see p. 260).

22.34 CAUSES OF ACUTE CONFUSIONAL STATE

Type	Common	Unusual
Infective	Chest infection Urinary infection Septicaemia Viral illness Meningitis Encephalitis	Cerebral abscess Subdural empyema AIDS
Metabolic/ endocrine	Hypoxia (respiratory failure) Cardiac failure Acute (internal) haemorrhage Hyper-/hypoglycaemia Hyper-/hypocalcaemia Hyponatraemia Liver failure, renal failure	Hypo-/hyperthyroidism Adrenal disease Porphyria
Vascular	Acute cerebral haemorrhage/infarction Subarachnoid haemorrhage	Vasculitis (e.g. systemic lupus erythematosus) Cortical venous thrombosis
Toxic	Alcohol intoxication/ withdrawal Drugs (therapeutic/illicit)	Carbon monoxide poisoning
Neoplastic	Secondary deposits	Primary cerebral tumour Paraneoplastic syndrome
Trauma	Head injury (cerebral contusions) Subdural haematoma	
Other	Post-ictal state Acute decompensation of dementia (see Box 22.36)	Acute hydrocephalus Complex partial status epilepticus

22.35 INVESTIGATION OF ACUTE CONFUSIONAL STATE

	First-line	Other useful tests
Blood tests	Full blood count, ESR Urea and electrolytes, glucose Calcium, magnesium Liver function tests Thyroid function tests	Cardiac enzymes Protein electrophoresis Vitamin B_{12}, copper studies Syphilis serology Antinuclear antibody (ANA), anti-double- stranded DNA (anti-dsDNA) Tumour markers, prostate-specific antigen
CNS investigations	Head imaging (CT and/or MRI)	Lumbar puncture EEG
Other	Arterial blood gases ECG Infection screen (blood cultures, chest radiograph, urine culture)	Viral screen, as appropriate (e.g. consider HIV) Urinary porphyrins

ISSUES IN OLDER PEOPLE
ACUTE CONFUSIONAL STATE

- Neuronal loss occurs with age, so older people are at increased risk of acute confusion in the context of relatively minor systemic disturbances.
- Dementia is a risk factor for delirium, and delirium may herald the onset of dementia.
- Other predisposing factors include:
  —malnutrition
  —visual and/or auditory impairments
  —infections: chest or urinary tract infections are the most common causes of acute confusion in old age, and a low threshold of suspicion is essential. Typical symptoms including pyrexia may not be present, so if there is no other obvious cause for confusion, it may be appropriate to treat the elderly patient with antibiotics 'blind' once cultures have been taken
  —surgery: acute confusion is very common after emergency surgery in old age, and only slightly less so after elective surgery
  —drugs: confusional states are common because of polypharmacy and changes in the response to and elimination of drugs in old age.

GENERAL COGNITIVE DECLINE (DEMENTIA)

Dementia is a clinical syndrome characterised by a loss of previously acquired intellectual function in the absence of impairment of arousal. There are many different potential causes of dementia (see Box 22.36) but Alzheimer's disease and diffuse vascular disease are the most common. The distinction of senile from pre-senile dementia is unhelpful. However, rarer causes of dementia should be more actively sought in younger patients and those with short histories.

When a patient presents with disturbance of personality or memory dysfunction, the first step is to exclude a focal lesion by determining that there is cognitive disturbance in more than one area. A careful history is, of course, essential and it is important to interview not just the patient but a close family member too. Simple bedside tests such as the Mini-Mental State Examination (MMSE; see p. 248) are useful in assessing the cognitive deficit, but more formal help from clinical psychology may be required. General history and examination may give further clues to aetiology.

Dementias are broadly divided into 'cortical' and 'subcortical' types, depending upon their clinical features (see Box 22.37). Many of the primary degenerative diseases that cause dementia have characteristic features that may allow a specific diagnosis during life. Creutzfeldt–Jakob disease is usually relatively rapidly progressive (over months), is associated with myoclonus, and there may be characteristic abnormalities on EEG. Of the more slowly progressive dementias, Pick's disease presents with rather focal (temporal or frontal lobe) dysfunction often affecting language function early, and Lewy body dementia may present with visual disturbance. However, it is often difficult to distinguish these dementias from each other or from Alzheimer's disease during life.

22.36 CAUSES OF DEMENTIA

Type	Common	Unusual	Rare
Vascular	Diffuse small-vessel disease	Amyloid angiopathy Multiple emboli	Cerebral vasculitis
Degenerative/inherited	Alzheimer's disease	Huntington's disease Wilson's disease Pick's disease Cortical Lewy body disease Others (e.g. cortico-basal degeneration)	
Neoplastic	Secondary deposits	Primary cerebral tumour	Paraneoplastic syndrome (limbic encephalitis)
Traumatic	Chronic subdural haematoma	Post-head injury	Punch-drunk syndrome
Hydrocephalus		Communicating/non-communicating 'Normal pressure' hydrocephalus	
Toxic/nutritional	Alcohol	Thiamin deficiency B_{12} deficiency	Anoxia/carbon monoxide poisoning Heavy metal poisoning
Infective		Syphilis HIV	Post-encephalitic
Prion diseases		Creutzfeldt–Jakob disease	Kuru Gerstmann–Sträussler–Scheinker disease

22.37 CORTICAL VS SUBCORTICAL DEMENTIA

	'Cortical' dementia	'Subcortical' dementia
Severity	Severe	Mild to moderate
Speed of cognition	Normal	Slow
Cognitive deficits	Dysphasia, dyspraxia, agnosia	'Frontal' memory disturbance
Psychiatric disturbance	Occasionally depression	Depression, apathy
Motor abnormalities	Uncommon	Extrapyramidal
Examples	Alzheimer's disease Lewy body dementia	Progressive supranuclear palsy

22.38 INVESTIGATION OF DEMENTIA

In most patients

- Imaging of head (CT and/or MRI)
- Blood tests
  Full blood count, ESR
  Urea and electrolytes, glucose
  Calcium, liver function tests
  Thyroid function tests
  Vitamin B_{12}
  Venereal Diseases Reference Laboratory (VDRL) test
  ANA, anti-dsDNA
- Chest radiograph
- EEG

In selected patients

- Lumbar puncture
- HIV serology
- Brain biopsy

Investigations

The aim is to discover a treatable cause, if present, and to try to give an idea of prognosis if not, using a fairly standard set of investigations (see Box 22.38). Imaging of the brain is important to exclude potentially treatable structural lesions such as hydrocephalus, cerebral tumour or chronic subdural haematoma, though often the only abnormality seen is generalised atrophy. If the initial tests fail to yield an answer, more invasive tests such as lumbar puncture or, rarely, brain biopsy may be indicated. It is always worth remembering that the memory disturbance may be a manifestation of depressive illness (pseudo-dementia) and here formal neuropsychological evaluation is helpful.

Management

This is directed at removing correctable causes, and at providing support for patient and carers if no specific treatment exists. Anticholinesterases, such as donepezil and rivastigmine, appear to improve cognitive function to some extent in Alzheimer's disease (see p. 1173).

FOCAL DEFICITS

It is easiest to consider the individual cortical functions lobe by lobe, and the areas discussed are shown in Figure 22.18. Many of the functions are lateralised; to which side depends on which of the two hemispheres is dominant, this being the one in which language function

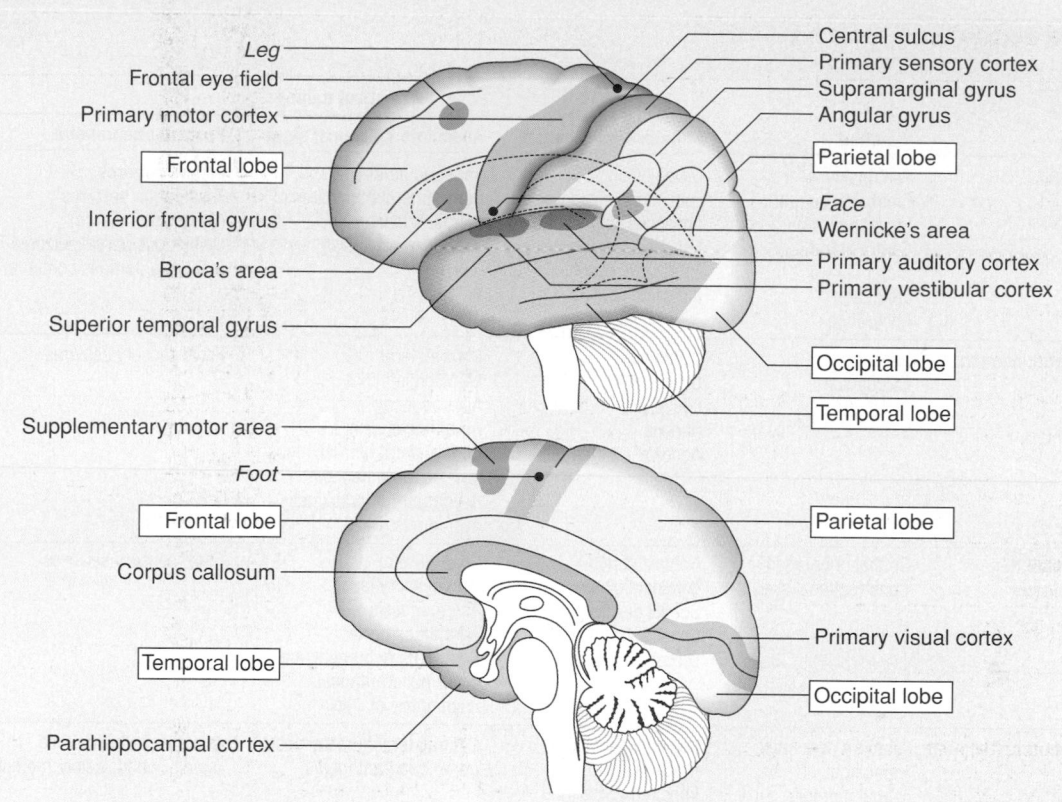

Fig. 22.18   The anatomy of the cerebral cortex.

is represented. In right-handed individuals this is almost always the left hemisphere, while in left-handers either hemisphere may be dominant with about equal frequency.

Frontal lobes

These are concerned with executive function, movement and behaviour. Well-defined functional areas in the frontal lobe include the primary motor cortex in the pre-rolandic gyrus, and Broca's speech area just anterior to the inferior end of this gyrus. The frontal eye fields lie higher up, anterior to the primary motor cortex. There is also a supplementary motor area on the medial surface which is involved in higher-order motor control, and a micturition centre in the mesial frontal lobe (the medial aspect adjacent to the falx cerebri) involved in the maintenance of urinary continence. The positive and negative features of damage to these areas are listed in Box 22.39.

More diffuse damage to the frontal lobe results in behavioural disturbance. Personality can be affected in three broad directions. Patients with mesial frontal lesions become increasingly withdrawn, unresponsive and mute (abulic), and this is often associated with urinary incontinence, gait apraxia, and the type of increase in tone known as gegenhalten, in which the patient varies the resistance to movement in proportion to the force exerted by the examiner. Patients with lesions of the dorsolateral pre-frontal cortex develop difficulties with speech and motor planning and organisation (dysexecutive

syndrome). Those with orbitofrontal lesions of the frontal lobes become disinhibited, sometimes to the point of grandiosity, or exhibit irresponsible behaviour (e.g. with financial affairs). Memory is substantially intact, and there may be focal physical signs such as a grasp reflex, palmo-mental response or pout. As the frontal lobe over-lies the olfactory bulb and tracts, structural lesions such as tumours in the inferior frontal lobes may be associated with anosmia.

Parietal lobe

The parietal lobes are concerned with the integration of sensory perception. The dominant parietal lobe contains part of the area which is involved in language (discussed below). Closely allied to the speech area are regions deal-ing with numerical function. The primary sensory cortex lies in the post-rolandic gyrus. Much of the remainder is devoted to 'association' cortex, damage to which gives rise to sensory (including visual) inattention and disorders of spatial perception and hence the disruption of spatially orientated behaviour leading to apraxia. Apraxia is the inability to perform complex, organised activity in the presence of a normal basic motor, sensory and cerebellar system (i.e. after weakness, numbness and ataxia have been excluded as causes). Such complex activities include dressing, the use of tools and finding one's way around geographically. As discussed below in the section on vision, parietal lobe lesions may also involve the optic

22.39 CORTICAL LOBAR FUNCTIONS

Lobe	Function	Effects of damage		
		Cognitive/behavioural	Associated physical signs	Positive phenomena
Frontal	Personality Emotional control Social behaviour Contralateral motor control Language Micturition	Disinhibition Lack of initiation Antisocial behaviour Impaired memory Expressive dysphasia Incontinence	Impaired smell Contralateral hemiparesis Frontal release signs	Versive seizures Focal motor seizures (Jacksonian march) Continuous partial seizures (epilepsia partialis continua)
Parietal: dominant	Language Calculation	Dysphasia Dyscalculia Dyslexia Apraxia Agnosia	Contralateral hemisensory loss Astereognosis Agraphaesthesia Contralateral homonymous lower quadrantanopia Asymmetry of optokinetic nystagmus (OKN)	Focal sensory seizures
Parietal: non-dominant	Spatial orientation Constructional skills	Neglect of non-dominant side Spatial disorientation Constructional apraxia Dressing apraxia	Contralateral hemisensory loss Astereognosis Agraphaesthesia Contralateral homonymous lower quadrantanopia Asymmetry of OKN	Focal sensory seizures
Temporal: dominant	Auditory perception Language Verbal memory Smell Balance	Receptive aphasia Dyslexia Impaired verbal memory	Contralateral homonymous upper quadrantanopia	Complex hallucinations (smell, sound, vision, memory)
Temporal: non-dominant	Auditory perception Melody/pitch perception Non-verbal memory Smell Balance	Impaired non-verbal memory Impaired musical skills (tonal perception)	Contralateral homonymous upper quadrantanopia	Complex hallucinations (smell, sound, vision, memory)
Occipital	Visual processing	Visual inattention Visual loss Visual agnosia	Homonymous hemianopia (± macular sparing)	Simple visual hallucinations (e.g. phosphenes, zigzag lines)

radiations deep to the cortex, giving rise to homonymous inferior quadrantanopias of the contralateral visual space.

Temporal lobe

Well-defined functional areas in the temporal lobes include the primary auditory cortex and primary vestibular cortex. On the medial side lies the olfactory cortex, and the parahippocampal cortex which is involved in memory function. The temporal lobe contains many structures associated with the limbic system, including the hippocampus and the amygdala. Damage to these areas causes memory disturbance, and may also cause personality change.

The dominant temporal lobe shares the specialised language areas with the parietal lobe, and is particularly involved in verbal comprehension. Music processing occurs in both temporal lobes, rhythm being processed on the dominant side, and melody/pitch more on the non-dominant side. Temporal lobe lesions may be associated with contralateral homonymous superior quadrantanopias.

Occipital lobe

The occipital lobe is principally concerned with visual processing. The contralateral visual hemifield is represented in the primary visual (striate) cortex, and areas immediately surrounding this are involved in the processing of specific visual submodalities such as colour, movement or depth, and the analysis of more complex visual patterns such as faces.

SPEECH, SWALLOWING AND BRAIN-STEM DISTURBANCE

SPEECH

Speech is the process whereby vocal sounds are used to convey meaning between individuals. A large volume of the cerebral cortex is involved in this complex cognitive process, mostly in the dominant hemisphere. The decoding of speech sounds (phonemes) is a function of the upper part of the posterior temporal lobe. The perception of these sounds as meaningful language, as well as the formulation of the language required for the expression of ideas and concepts, occurs predominantly in the lower parts of the anterior parietal lobe (the angular and supramarginal gyri). The temporal speech comprehension region is referred to as Wernicke's area. Other parts of the temporal lobe contribute to language processing in areas specialising in verbal memory, where lexicons of meaningful words are 'stored'. The language information so generated then passes anteriorly via the arcuate fasciculus to Broca's area in the posterior end of the inferior frontal gyrus on the dominant side. The motor commands generated in Broca's area pass to the cranial nerve nuclei in the pons and medulla, as well as to the anterior horn cells in the spinal cord. The cerebellum has an important coordinating function. Nerve impulses then travel to the lips, tongue, palate, pharynx, larynx and respiratory muscles via the facial nerve and cranial nerves 9, 10 and 12, and result in the series of ordered sounds known as speech (see Fig. 22.19).

These ordered sounds are detected by a listener in whom nerve impulses are passed from the ears to the auditory cortex in the temporal lobe and hence to the speech comprehension areas. Parts of the non-dominant parietal lobe appear to contribute to non-verbal aspects of language in the recognition of meaningful intonation patterns of spoken words.

Aphasia

Aphasia is a disorder of the language content of speech. It can occur with lesions over a wide area of the dominant hemisphere. The term aphasia, rather than dysphasia, is now used to designate any degree of spoken language deficit. Aphasia is detected by the patient's inability to produce the correct word (anomia). When patients are asked to name objects or parts of objects, if anomia is present either no word will be produced or the wrong word or a nonsense word produced (paraphasia). Aphasia can be classified according to whether the speech output is 'fluent', in which a normal or increased number of (the wrong) words is produced, or 'non-fluent' if the verbal output is reduced. Patients with lesions anterior to the central fissure have non-fluent aphasia whilst those with lesions posterior to the central fissure in the speech areas have a fluent aphasia (and are often mistakenly thought to be 'confused'). If patients are tested for the comprehension of words and their ability to repeat, their aphasia can be further classified into distinct syndromes of aphasia which have localising and prognostic implications (see Fig. 22.20).

If a patient is found to have difficulty with speech comprehension there is likely to be a lesion in the superior part of the posterior temporal lobe and/or the adjoining part of the parietal lobe. Patients with lesions around the sylvian (lateral) fissure will have difficulty with repetition, whilst those with lesions away from the sylvian fissure can repeat and may do so compulsively. Patients with large lesions over much of the speech area are not testable in such a refined manner, having no language production,

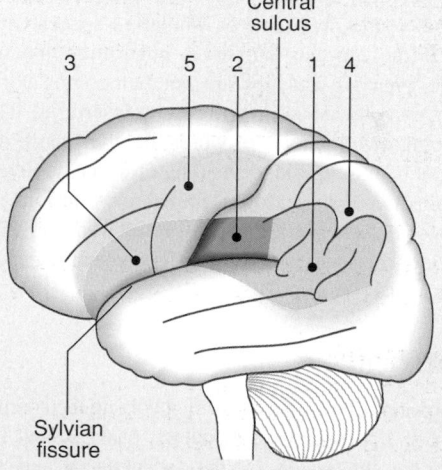

Fig. 22.20 **Classification of aphasia, according to the site of the lesion and type of language deficit.** All have naming difficulty (anomia). Fluent aphasias arise from lesions posterior to the central fissure; repetition is affected by lesions around the sylvian fissure. (1) Wernicke aphasia: fluent aphasia with poor comprehension and poor repetition. (2) Conduction aphasia: fluent aphasia with good comprehension and poor repetition. (3) Broca aphasia: non-fluent aphasia with good comprehension and poor repetition. (4) Transcortical sensory aphasia: fluent aphasia with poor comprehension and good repetition. (5) Transcortical motor aphasia: non-fluent aphasia with good comprehension and good repetition. **N.B.** Large lesions affecting all regions 1–5 cause global aphasia.

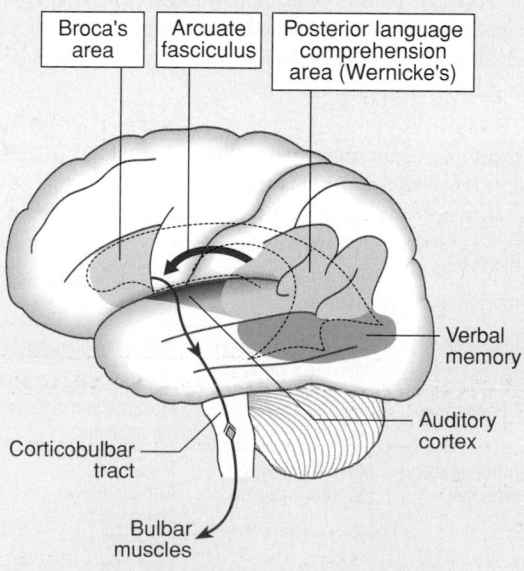

Fig. 22.19 **Areas of the cerebral cortex involved in the generation of spoken language.**

22.40 CAUSES OF DYSARTHRIA

Type	Site	Characteristics	Associated features
Myopathic	Muscles of speech	Indistinct, poor articulation	Weakness of face, tongue and neck
Myasthenic	Motor end plate	Indistinct with fatigue and dysphonia Fluctuating severity	Ptosis, diplopia, facial and neck weakness
Bulbar	Brain stem	Indistinct, slurred, often nasal	Dysphagia, diplopia, ataxia
'Scanning'	Cerebellum	Slurring, impaired timing and cadence, 'sing-song' quality	Ataxia of limbs and gait, tremor of head/limbs
Spastic	Pyramidal tracts	Indistinct, breathy, mumbling	Poor rapid tongue movements, increased reflexes and jaw jerk
Parkinsonian	Basal ganglia	Indistinct, rapid, stammering, quiet	Tremor, rigidity, slow shuffling gait
Dystonic	Basal ganglia	Strained, slow	Dystonia, athetosis

and are said to have 'global aphasia'. Some patients with patchy lesions in the speech areas may not be easily classified according to the above scheme and are said to have anomic aphasia. Patients with fluent aphasia tend not to have an associated hemiparesis since the pyramidal tract is not involved, whilst those with the more anteriorly placed lesions causing non-fluent aphasia often do have a hemiparesis.

Dysphonia and dysarthria

Speech can be disturbed in a number of ways. At a simple level, the vocal cords may fail to generate sound properly, and this results in hoarse or whispered speech (dysphonia). If the muscles or nerves controlling the mouth, tongue, pharynx and lips are not functioning correctly, poorly articulated speech will result (dysarthria). There is no problem with choice of words, but the speech may or may not be intelligible, depending on severity. Cerebellar or brain-stem disease, lower cranial nerve lesions, myasthenia or muscle disease may all result in dysarthria. The quality of the speech tends to differ somewhat depending on the cause (see Box 22.40).

SWALLOWING

Swallowing is a complex activity involving the coordinated action of lips, tongue, soft palate, pharynx and larynx, which are innervated by the facial nerve and cranial nerves 9, 10, 11 and 12. This mechanism is potentially vulnerable to damage to many different areas of the nervous system, resulting in dysphagia which is usually accompanied by dysarthria. Structural causes of dysphagia are considered on page 761. Acute onset of dysphagia may occur as a result of brain-stem stroke, a rapidly developing neuropathy such as the Guillain–Barré syndrome or diphtheria. The upper motor neuron innervation of the cranial nerves responsible for swallowing is bilateral, so persistent dysphagia is unusual with a unilateral upper motor lesion. However, dysphagia may occur in the early stages of such a lesion if it is very acute, such as

a hemisphere stroke. Dysphagia developing subacutely may be seen in myasthenia gravis, motor neuron disease, polymyositis, basal meningitis and inflammatory brain-stem disease. More slowly developing dysphagia suggests a myopathy or possibly a brain-stem or skull-base tumour.

BULBAR AND PSEUDOBULBAR PALSY

The lower cranial nerves, 9, 10, 11 and 12, are frequently affected bilaterally, producing dysphagia and dysarthria. The term 'bulbar palsy' is used if this results from lower motor neuron lesions, either at nuclear or fascicular level within the medulla, or from bilateral lesions of the lower cranial nerves outside the brain stem. The tongue is wasted and fasciculating and the palate moves very little. A 'pseudobulbar palsy' arises from an upper motor neuron lesion of the bulbar muscles from lesions of the corticobulbar pathways in the pyramidal tracts. Here the tongue is small and contracted, and moves slowly; the jaw jerk is brisk. Causes of bulbar and pseudobulbar palsies are shown in Box 22.41.

22.41 CAUSES OF BULBAR AND PSEUDOBULBAR PALSY

	Pseudobulbar	Bulbar
Genetic		Kennedy's disease (X-linked bulbospinal neuronopathy)
Vascular	Bilateral hemisphere (lacunar) infarction	Medullary infarction
Degenerative	Motor neuron disease	Motor neuron disease Syringobulbia
Inflammatory/ infective	Multiple sclerosis Cerebral vasculitis	Myasthenia Guillain–Barré Poliomyelitis Lyme disease Vasculitis
Neoplastic	High brain-stem tumours	Brain-stem glioma Malignant meningitis

BRAIN-STEM FUNCTION

Many different functional areas are tightly packed into the brain stem (see Fig. 22.21). Long motor and sensory tracts course through its length, and are punctuated by individual brain-stem nuclei and cranial nerves, along with their respective interconnections and connections to the cerebrum and cerebellum. Thus, damage to even a small area of the brain stem potentially causes major disturbance of several systems. As the anatomy of the brain stem is very precisely organised, it is usually possible to localise the site of a lesion on the basis of careful history and examination to determine exactly which tracts/nuclei are affected. Lesions can occur singly, multiply or diffusely, but the standard neurological approach is to try to explain all of a patient's problems in the minimum number of lesions (ideally just one).

An example would be a patient presenting with sudden onset of upper motor neuron features affecting the right face, arm and leg in association with a left 3rd nerve palsy. The lesion would have to be in the left cerebral peduncle in the brain stem where the pathology is likely to have been a small stroke, as the onset was sudden. This combination of signs is known as Weber's syndrome, and this is one of several well-described brain-stem stroke syndromes which are listed in Box 22.42.

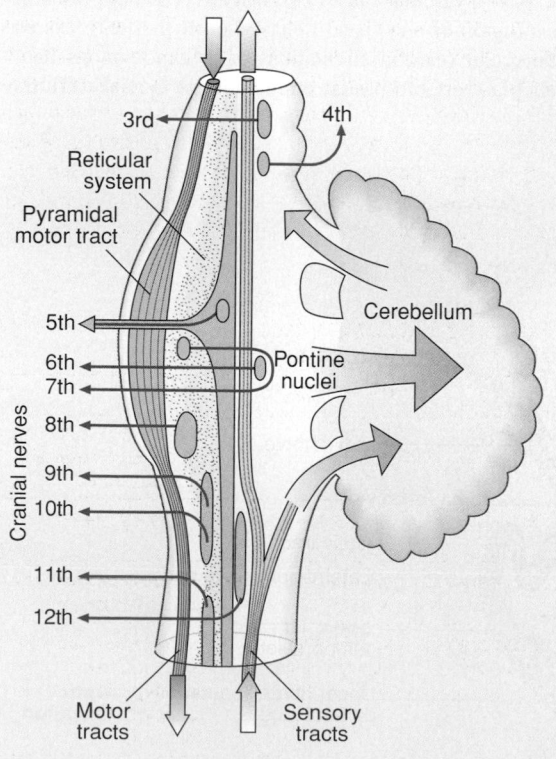

Fig. 22.21   Anatomy of the brain stem.

22.42 MAJOR BRAIN-STEM STROKE SYNDROMES

Name of syndrome	Site of lesions	Clinical features
Weber	Anterior cerebral peduncle (mid-brain)	Ipsilateral 3rd palsy Contralateral upper motor neuron 7th palsy Contralateral hemiplegia
Claude	Cerebral peduncle involving red nucleus	Ipsilateral 3rd palsy Contralateral cerebellar signs
Parinaud	Dorsal mid-brain (tectum)	Vertical gaze palsy Convergence disorders Convergence retraction nystagmus Pupillary and lid disorders
Millard–Gubler	Ponto-medullary junction	Ipsilateral 6th palsy Ipsilateral lower motor neuron 7th palsy Contralateral hemiplegia
Wallenberg	Lateral medulla	Ipsilateral 5th, 9th, 10th, 11th palsy Ipsilateral Horner's syndrome Ipsilateral cerebellar signs Contralateral spinothalamic sensory loss Vestibular disturbance

LOWER CRANIAL NERVE LESIONS

Bilateral lesions of cranial nerves 9, 10, 11 and 12 present as bulbar and pseudobulbar palsies and are discussed above (see Box 22.41). Cranial nerves 9, 10 and 11 may be affected together on one side as they pass through the jugular foramen at the skull base. The hypoglossal (12th) nerve exits the skull in its own foramen and lies close to the 9th, 10th and 11th nerves just outside the skull. All four lower cranial nerves are here anatomically related to the carotid artery and the ascending sympathetic innervation to the eye. Lesions affecting the lower cranial nerves at the skull base include tumours and dissection of the carotid artery (see Box 22.43).

22.43 SYNDROMES OF THE LOWER CRANIAL NERVE LESIONS OUTSIDE THE BRAIN STEM

Syndrome	Cranial nerves involved	Site of lesion	Cause
Vernet	9, 10 and 11	Jugular foramen (inside skull)	Metastases, neurinoma, meningioma, epidermoid, carotid body tumour
Collet–Sicard	9, 10, 11 and 12	Jugular foramen just outside skull, near foramen lacerum	Metastases, neurinoma, meningioma, epidermoid, carotid body tumour
Villaret	9, 10, 11, 12 and Horner's	Posterior retropharyngeal space, near carotid artery	Carotid dissection, metastases, neurinoma, meningioma, epidermoid, carotid body tumour
Isolated 12th	12	Skull base (hypoglossal canal)	Metastases, neurinoma, meningioma, epidermoid

VISUAL DISTURBANCE

Disturbances of vision are common and often related to problems with the eye rather than disorder of the nervous system. A common reason for presentation is loss of vision, but patients may also present with positive visual symptoms (e.g. hallucinations). The movements of the two eyes may be disturbed and give rise to double vision (diplopia) or blurred vision. Alternatively, patients may present with disordered appearance of their visual apparatus, and this can include the eyelids, the globe, the eye movements, the pupils or the appearance of the optic disc on fundoscopy (e.g. papilloedema).

VISUAL LOSS

The visual pathway from the retina to the occipital cortex is topographically organised, so the pattern of visual field loss allows precise localisation of the site of the lesion.

Fibres from ganglion cells in the retina pass to the optic disc and then backwards through the lamina cribrosa to the optic nerve. Nasal optic nerve fibres (subserving the temporal visual field because the image on the retina is inverted) cross at the chiasm, but temporal fibres do not. Hence all fibres in the optic tract and further posteriorly subserve both eyes' representation of contralateral visual space. From the lateral geniculate nucleus, lower fibres pass through the temporal lobes on their way to the primary visual area in the occipital cortex, while the upper fibres pass through the parietal lobe. Patterns of visual field loss are explained by this anatomy, as seen in Figure 22.22, and associated clinical manifestations are described in Box 22.44.

It is uncommon for patients to present with transient visual loss. Visual loss lasting from 1–20 minutes is likely to have a vascular cause. This can affect one eye (amaurosis fugax) or one visual field. Whether the field loss was uniocular (carotid circulation) or a homonymous hemianopia (vertebro-basilar circulation) is crucial to further

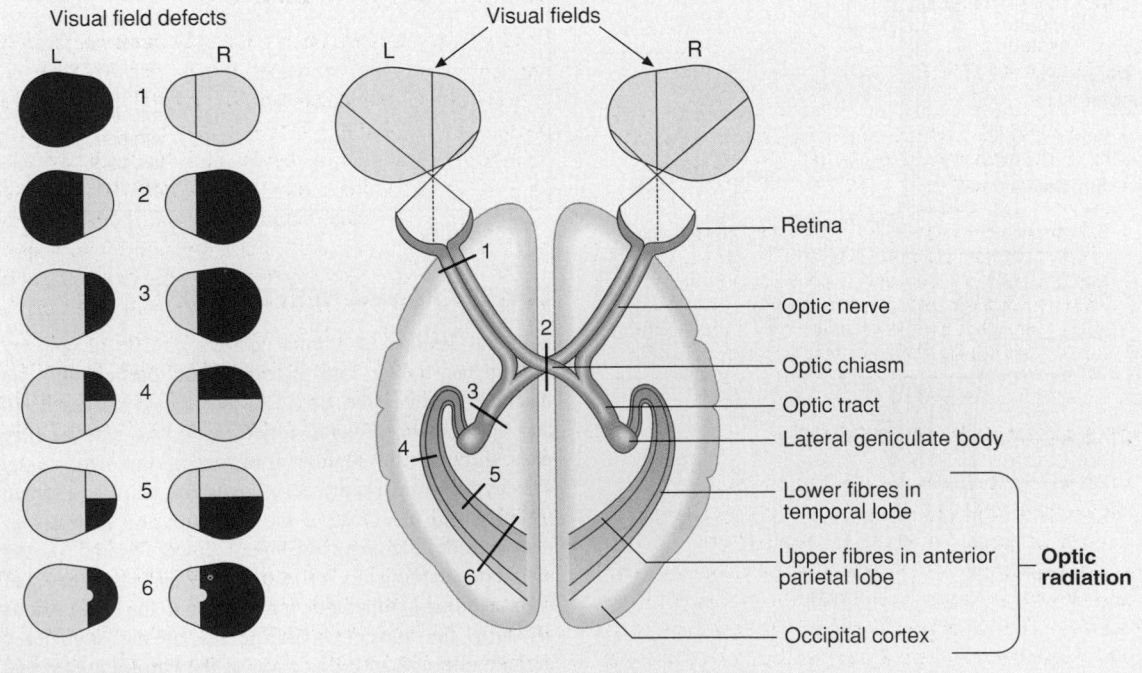

Fig. 22.22 Visual pathways and visual field defects. Schematic representation of eyes and brain in transverse section.

22.44 CLINICAL MANIFESTATIONS OF VISUAL FIELD LOSS

Site	Common causes	Complaint	Visual field loss	Associated physical signs
Retina/optic disc	Vascular disease (including vasculitis) Glaucoma Inflammation	Partial/complete visual loss depending on site	Altitudinal field defect Arcuate scotoma	Reduced acuity Visual distortion (macula) Abnormal retinal appearance
Optic nerve	Optic neuritis Sarcoidosis Tumour Leber's hereditary optic neuropathy	Partial/complete loss of vision in one eye Often painful Central vision particularly affected	Central scotoma Paracentral scotoma Uniocular blindness	Reduced acuity Reduced colour vision Relative afferent pupillary defect Optic atrophy (late)
Optic chiasm	Pituitary tumours Craniopharyngioma Sarcoidosis	May be none Rarely diplopia ('hemifield slide')	Bitemporal hemianopia	Pituitary function abnormalities
Optic tract	Tumour Inflammatory disease	Disturbed vision to one side of midline	Incongruous contralateral homonymous hemianopia	
Temporal lobe	Stroke Tumour Inflammatory disease	Disturbed vision to one side of midline	Contralateral homonymous upper quadrantanopia	Memory/language disorders
Parietal lobe	Stroke Tumour Inflammatory disease	Disturbed vision to one side of midline Bumping into things	Contralateral homonymous lower quadrantanopia	Contralateral sensory disturbance Asymmetry of optokinetic nystagmus
Occipital lobe	Stroke Tumour Inflammatory disease	Disturbed vision to one side of midline Difficulty reading Bumping into things	Homonymous hemianopia (may be macula-sparing)	Damage to other structures supplied by posterior cerebral circulation

management, and this must be distinguished by careful history (e.g. did the patient try shutting each eye in turn?). Transient visual loss lasting 20–30 minutes suggests migraine, especially if accompanied by headache and/or positive visual phenomena.

ISSUES IN OLDER PEOPLE
VISUAL LOSS

- Presbyopia is the progressive inability to focus on near objects due to the stiffening of the lens which occurs with ageing.
- The retina and optic pathways lose cells with ageing, making it harder to see detail and contrast.
- Older people are particularly prone to certain causes of visual loss: cataract, age-related macular degeneration, glaucoma, anterior ischaemic optic neuropathy (N.B. vasculitic due to temporal arteritis) and occipital lobe stroke.
- They are much less likely to suffer from certain other causes, such as optic neuritis and Leber's hereditary optic neuropathy.

POSITIVE VISUAL SYMPTOMS

The most common cause of a positive visual disturbance is migraine, in which patients may see silvery zigzag lines (fortification spectra) or flashing coloured lights (teichopsia) which precede the headache. Simple flashes of light (phosphenes) can also be seen as a result of damage to the retina (e.g. detachment) or damage to the primary visual cortex. More complex visual percepts (hallucinations) may be caused by drugs, or may be due to structural damage resulting in epilepsy or 'release phenomena' (hallucinations which occur in a blind visual field).

EYE MOVEMENT DISORDERS

Under normal circumstances, the eyes move conjugately, though horizontal vergence allows visual fusion of objects at different distances. The control of eye movements begins in the cerebral hemispheres, particularly within the frontal eye fields, and the pathway then descends to the brain stem with input from the visual cortex, superior colliculus and cerebellum. Horizontal and vertical gaze centres in the pons and mid-brain, respectively, coordinate output to the ocular motor nerve nuclei (3, 4 and 6), which are connected to each other by the medial longitudinal fasciculus (MLF) (see Fig. 22.23). The MLF is particularly important in yoking the horizontal movements of the two eyes. The extraocular muscles are then supplied by the oculomotor (3rd), trochlear (4th) and abducens (6th) nerves.

Diplopia

This arises when eye movement is impaired so that the image of an object is not projected to homologous points on the two retinae. Impairment may result from central disorders, or from disturbance of the ocular motor nerves, muscles or the neuromuscular junction. The pattern of double vision, along with any associated features, usually

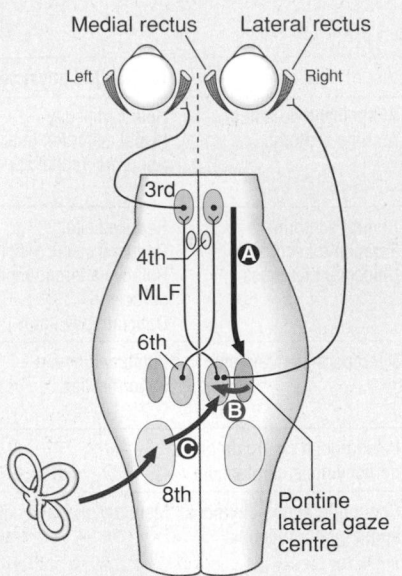

Fig. 22.23 Control of conjugate eye movements. Downward projections from the cortex to pontine lateral gaze centre (A). Pontine gaze centre projects to the 6th cranial nerve nucleus, which innervates the ipsilateral lateral rectus and projects to the contralateral 3rd nerve nucleus (and hence medial rectus) via the medial longitudinal fasciculus (MLF) (B). Tonic inputs from the vestibular apparatus via the vestibular nuclei project to the contralateral 6th nerve nucleus (C).

allows localisation of the lesion whilst the mode of onset and subsequent behaviour (e.g. fatigability) suggest the aetiology.

The trochlear (4th) nerve innervates the superior oblique muscle, and the abducens (6th) nerve innervates the lateral rectus. The oculomotor (3rd) nerve innervates the remainder of the extraocular muscles along with the levator palpebrae superioris and the ciliary body (pupil constriction and accommodation). Causes of oculomotor nerve palsies are given in Box 22.45.

Complete oculomotor nerve lesions cause ptosis and a dilated pupil, and the eye tends to rest in a 'down and out' position due to unopposed tonic activity of the unaffected lateral rectus and superior oblique muscles. The pupil is often spared in ischaemic lesions (e.g. in diabetes), and its involvement requires that compressive lesions such as aneurysm be excluded. Trochlear nerve palsy presents with vertical diplopia (especially noticeable going downstairs), and the patient may have a head tilt and double vision when looking down to the side opposite the lesion. Abducens nerve palsy causes horizontal double vision when trying to look towards the side of the lesion. In diplopia of any cause, the image projected furthest away from primary position arises from the paretic eye, and covering each eye in turn can often determine this. Note that this image is not necessarily any less clear than the image from the non-paretic eye—it is the relative position, not the clarity, of the images which is important in determining which muscle is weak.

22.45 COMMON CAUSES OF DAMAGE TO CRANIAL NERVES 3, 4 AND 6			
Site	**Common pathology**	**Nerve(s) involved**	**Associated features**
Brain stem	Infarction Haemorrhage Demyelination Intrinsic tumour	3 (mid-brain) 6 (ponto-medullary junction)	Contralateral pyramidal signs Ipsilateral lower motor neuron 7 palsy (ponto-medullary junction) Other brain-stem/cerebellar signs
Intrameningeal course	Meningitis (infective/malignant) Raised intracranial pressure Aneurysms Cerebello-pontine angle tumour Trauma	3, 4 and/or 6 6 3 (uncal herniation) 3 (posterior communicating artery) 6 (basilar artery) 6 3, 4 and/or 6	Meningism, features of primary disease Papilloedema Features of space-occupying lesion Pain Features of subarachnoid haemorrhage 8, 7, 5 lesions Ipsilateral cerebellar signs Other features of trauma
Cavernous sinus	Infection/thrombosis Carotid artery aneurysm Caroticocavernous fistula	3, 4 and/or 6	May be 5 involvement also Pupil may be fixed, mid-position (sympathetic plexus on carotid may also be affected)
Superior orbital fissure	Tumour (e.g. sphenoid wing meningioma) Granuloma	3, 4 and/or 6	May be proptosis, chemosis
Orbit	Vascular (e.g. diabetes, vasculitis) Infections Tumour Granuloma Trauma	3, 4 and/or 6	Pain Pupil often spared in vascular 3 palsy

Myasthenia gravis can cause diplopia by affecting any or all of the extraocular muscles. It is often associated with ptosis, and the hallmark is fatigability. Similarly, diseases of the extraocular muscles themselves can cause diplopia. Such diseases include thyroid eye disease, myopathies and orbital myositis.

Central lesions can also give rise to diplopia. Brainstem lesions affecting the 3rd, 4th or 6th nerves or nuclei will cause diplopia, as will lesions of the MLF. The hallmark of an MLF lesion is an internuclear ophthalmoplegia (INO). The lateral gaze centre in the pons sends fibres to the ipsilateral 6th nerve nucleus. The nucleus contains two populations of neurons. Half the cells send their axons directly into the 6th nerve to supply the lateral rectus, while the remaining half send their fibres into the contralateral MLF and up to the contralateral 3rd nerve nucleus, where they synapse with neurons destined for the medial rectus (see Fig. 22.23). Hence, damage to the 6th nerve nucleus itself will prevent both eyes from moving ipsilaterally (gaze palsy), and a lesion of the MLF will interfere with adduction of the ipsilateral eye (INO). An INO may be partial or complete, and may be associated with nystagmus of the contralateral, abducting eye.

Nystagmus

If the eye movement control systems are defective, the eyes may drift off target and it becomes necessary to perform recurrent corrections to return fixation to the object of interest. This results in a repetitive to-and-fro movement (drift-correction-drift etc.) which is known as nystagmus. Usually the drifts are slower than the corrections (slow and quick phases, respectively). The direction of the fast phase is usually designated as the direction of the nystagmus because it is easier to see, although the abnormality is the slower drift of the eyes off target. Nystagmus may be horizontal, vertical or torsional, and is usually conjugate, i.e. the two eyes usually move together. Nystagmus is seen as a physiological phenomenon in response to sustained vestibular stimulation or movement of the visual world (optokinetic nystagmus). There are, however, many different causes of pathological nystagmus, the most common being disorders of the vestibular system (peripheral and central components) and brainstem/cerebellar lesions.

In lesions of the vestibular system (most commonly peripheral labyrinthine lesions), damage to one side will allow the tonic output from the healthy, contralateral side to cause the eyes to drift towards the side of the lesion. This causes recurrent compensatory fast movements away from the side of the lesion; hence unidirectional nystagmus to the opposite side is seen, often with a torsional element. The nystagmus of peripheral labyrinthine lesions disappears (fatigues) quite quickly and is always accompanied by vertigo and quite often nausea and vomiting. Central vestibular nystagmus is more persistent.

The brain stem and the cerebellum are involved in maintaining eccentric positions of gaze. Lesions will therefore allow the eyes to drift back in towards primary position (gaze-evoked nystagmus). This produces nystagmus whose fast component beats in the direction of gaze. This is the most common type of 'central' nystagmus and is most commonly bi-directional and not usually accompanied by vertigo, but there may be other signs of brainstem dysfunction. Brain-stem disease may also cause vertical nystagmus.

Unilateral cerebellar lesions may result in gaze-evoked nystagmus when looking in the direction of the lesion, where the fast phases are directed towards the side of the lesion. Cerebellar hemisphere lesions also cause 'ocular dysmetria', an overshoot of target-directed, fast eye movements (saccades) resembling 'past-pointing' in limbs.

Nystagmus also occurs as a result of toxicity (especially drugs) and nutritional deficiency (thiamin deficiency). The severity is variable, and it may or may not result in visual degradation, though it may be associated with a sensation of movement of the visual world (oscillopsia). Nystagmus may occur as a congenital phenomenon, in which case the nystagmus is often quasi-sinusoidal ('pendular') rather than having alternating fast and slow phases ('jerk').

EYELID, GLOBE AND PUPIL DISORDERS

Various disorders may cause drooping or ptosis of the eyelid, and these are listed in Box 22.46.

In some circumstances the globe is pushed forward in the orbit, either unilaterally (proptosis) or bilaterally (exophthalmos). By far the most common cause of both is thyroid eye disease, but other causes include orbital tumours or granulomas, cavernous sinus disease and inflammatory orbital disease ('pseudotumour').

Disorders of the pupil

Pupillary response to light is achieved by a combination of parasympathetic and sympathetic activity. Parasympathetic fibres originate in the Edinger–Westphal subnucleus of the 3rd nerve, and pass with the 3rd nerve to synapse in the ciliary ganglion before supplying the constrictor pupillae of the iris. Sympathetic fibres originate in the hypothalamus, pass down the brain stem and cervical spinal cord to emerge at T1, return back up to the eye in association with the internal carotid artery and supply the

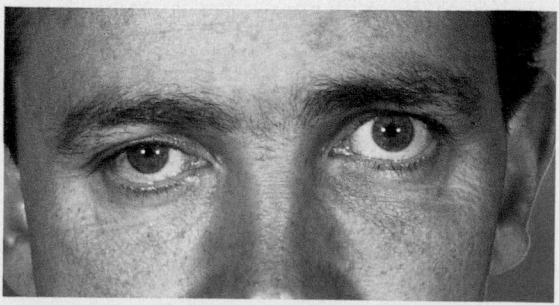

Fig. 22.24 Right-sided Horner's syndrome due to paravertebral metastasis at T1.

dilator pupillae. Lesions in the sympathetic pathway cause Horner's syndrome (see Fig. 22.24). The pupils also constrict as part of the near reflex (in association with accommodation and convergence).

Lesions of the oculomotor nerve, ciliary ganglion and sympathetic supply produce characteristic 'efferent' disorders of pupillary function. 'Afferent' defects occur as a result of damage to an optic nerve, impairing the direct response of a pupil to light, although leaving the consensual response from stimulation of the normal eye intact.

ISSUES IN OLDER PEOPLE
DISORDERS OF THE PUPIL

- The average pupil size decreases progressively with age, which makes it more difficult for older people to see in poor lighting.
- It also becomes more difficult to view the optic disc at ophthalmoscopy, as the pupil size drops below 1–2 mm; dilatation of the pupil with eye drops may be necessary. This should not be attempted if assessment of pupil size is likely to be necessary, as in the management of an unconscious or confused patient.

22.46 CAUSES OF PTOSIS

Mechanism	Causes	Associated clinical features
3rd nerve palsy	Isolated palsy (see Box 22.45) Central/supranuclear lesion	Ptosis is usually complete Extraocular muscle palsy (eye 'down and out') Depending on site of lesion, other cranial nerve palsies (e.g. 4, 5 and 6) or contralateral upper motor neuron signs
Sympathetic lesion (Horner's syndrome) (see Fig. 22.24)	Central (hypothalamus/brain stem) Peripheral (lung apex, carotid artery pathology) Idiopathic	Ptosis is partial Lack of sweating on affected side Depending on site of lesion, brain-stem signs, signs of apical lung/brachial plexus disease, or ipsilateral carotid artery stroke
Myopathic	Myasthenia gravis Dystrophia myotonica Progressive external ophthalmoplegia	Extraocular muscle palsies More widespread muscle weakness, with fatigability in myasthenia Other characteristic features of individual causes
Other	Pseudo-ptosis (e.g. blepharospasm) Local orbital/lid disease Age-related levator dehiscence	Eyebrows depressed rather than raised May be local orbital abnormality

---

22.47 PUPILLARY DISORDERS

Disorder	Cause	Ophthalmological features	Associated features
3rd nerve palsy	See Box 22.45	Dilated pupil Extraocular muscle palsy (eye is typically 'down and out') Complete ptosis	Other features of 3rd nerve palsy (see Box 22.46)
Horner's syndrome (see Fig. 22.24)	Lesion to sympathetic supply	Small pupil Partial ptosis Iris heterochromia (if congenital)	Ipsilateral failure of sweating (anhidrosis)
Holmes–Adie syndrome (Adie pupil)	Lesion of ciliary ganglion (usually idiopathic)	Dilated pupil Light-near dissociation (accommodate but do not react to light) Vermiform movement of iris during contraction Disturbance of accommodation	Generalised areflexia
Argyll Robertson pupil	Dorsal mid-brain lesion (usually syphilis)	Small, irregular pupils Light-near dissociation	Other features of tabes dorsalis (see p. 1202)
Local pupillary damage	Trauma/inflammatory disease	Irregular pupils, often with adhesions to lens (synechiae) Variable degree of reactivity	Other features of trauma/ underlying inflammatory disease (e.g. cataract, blindness etc.)
Relative afferent pupillary defect (Marcus Gunn pupil)	Damage to optic nerve (see Box 22.44, p. 1153)	Pupils symmetrical, but degree of dilatation depends on which eye stimulated	Decreased visual acuity/ colour vision Central scotoma Papilloedema/optic disc pallor

Structural damage to the iris itself can also result in pupillary abnormalities. A summary is given in Box 22.47.

Optic disc disorders

Optic disc swelling

There are several causes of swelling of the optic disc, but the term 'papilloedema' is reserved for swelling in association with raised intracranial pressure. In raised intracranial pressure from any cause, axoplasmic flow from retinal ganglion cells is held up at the cribriform plate. This results in swollen nerve fibres, which in turn cause capillary and venous congestion, producing papilloedema. The first sign is the cessation of normal venous pulsation seen at the disc, and the disc margins then become red (hyperaemic). The margins become indistinct and the whole disc is raised up, often with haemorrhages in the retina (see Fig. 22.25).

Other causes of optic disc swelling are listed in Box 22.48. Some normal variations of disc appearance can look like pathological disc swelling (pseudo-papilloedema).

Optic atrophy

Loss of nerve fibres causes the optic disc to appear pale, as the choroid becomes visible (see Fig. 22.26). A pale

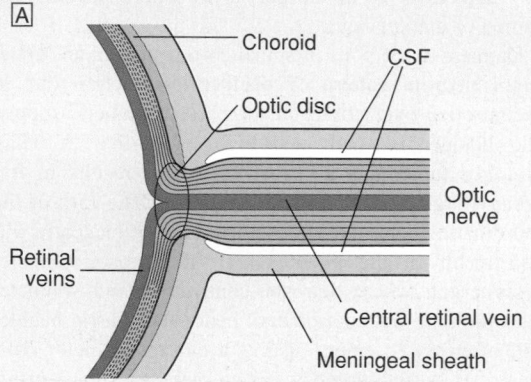

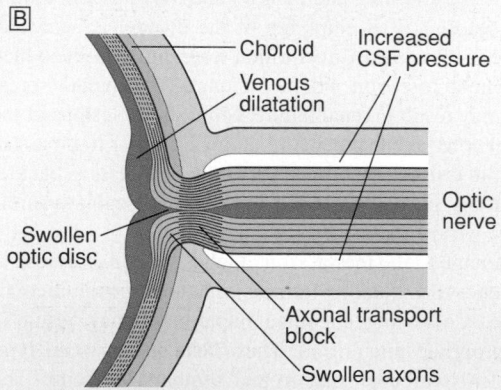

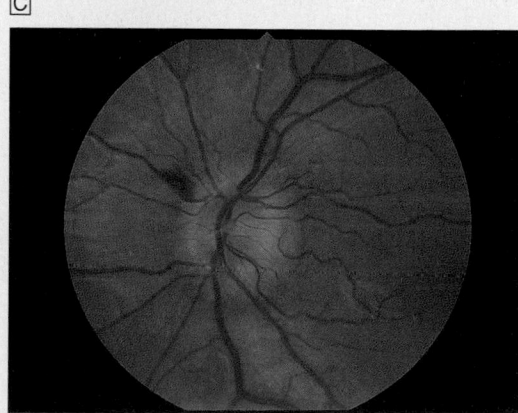

Fig. 22.25 Mechanism of optic disc oedema (papilloedema). A Normal. B Disc oedema (e.g. due to cerebral tumour). C Fundus photograph of the left eye showing optic disc oedema with a small haemorrhage on the nasal side of the disc.

22.48 COMMON CAUSES OF OPTIC DISC SWELLING
Raised intracranial pressure
• Cerebral mass lesion (tumour, abscess) • Hydrocephalus, haemorrhage, haematoma • Idiopathic intracranial hypertension
Obstruction of ocular venous drainage
• Central retinal vein occlusion • Cavernous sinus thrombosis
Systemic disorders affecting retinal vessels
• Hypertension • Vasculitis • Hypercapnia
Optic nerve damage
• Demyelination (optic neuritis/papillitis) • Leber's hereditary optic neuropathy • Ischaemia • Toxins (e.g. methanol) • Infiltration of optic disc • Sarcoidosis • Glioma • Lymphoma

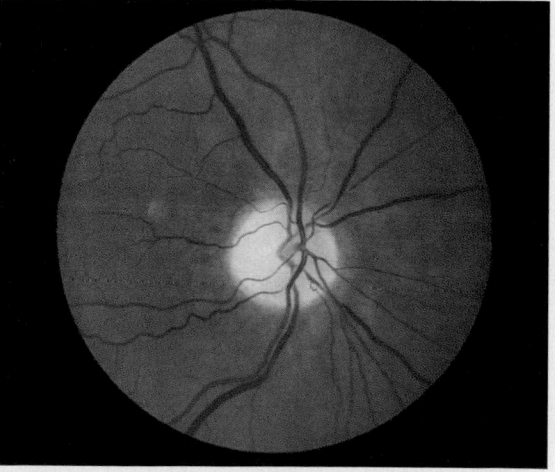

Fig. 22.26 Fundus photograph of the left eye of a patient with familial optic atrophy. Note marked pallor of optic disc.

disc (optic atrophy) follows optic nerve damage, and causes include previous optic neuritis, or ischaemic damage, long-standing papilloedema, optic nerve compression, trauma and degenerative conditions (e.g. Friedreich's ataxia, see p. 1178).

SPHINCTER DISTURBANCE

Incontinence and its management are discussed on pages 592–593. However, many different symptoms of bladder and bowel disturbance can arise as a result of nervous system dysfunction.

BLADDER

The bladder is analogous to skeletal muscle in that neural control can be divided into upper and lower 'motor neuron' components. Conscious control of micturition resides within the right pre-frontal cortex. Connections pass from here to the main controlling and coordinating centre in the pons, the pontine micturition centre, and from here down into the spinal cord, where they are found in the lateral columns bilaterally. The sympathetic supply to the bladder leaves from T10–L2 to synapse in the inferior hypogastric plexus, while the parasympathetic supply leaves from S2–4. In addition, a further somatic supply to the distal (voluntary) sphincter arises from S2–4, travelling via the pudendal nerves. Stimulation of sympathetic fibres causes relaxation of the detrusor muscle and contraction of the bladder neck, while stimulation of the parasympathetic fibres causes the reverse effects.

Afferent fibres from the bladder wall pass via the pelvic and hypogastric nerves. In the absence of conscious control (stroke, dementia) distension of the bladder to near-capacity evokes reflex detrusor contraction (analogous to the muscle stretch reflex). Reciprocal changes in sympathetic activation and relaxation of the distal sphincter result in coordinated bladder emptying. Normally, however, conscious control from the medial pre-frontal cortex inhibits bladder emptying until it is socially acceptable.

Damage to the 'lower motor neuron' component, i.e. the pelvic and pudendal nerves, gives rise to a flaccid bladder and sphincter with overflow incontinence, often accompanied by loss of pudendal sensation. Such damage may be due to disease of the conus medullaris or sacral nerve roots, either within the dura (as in inflammatory or carcinomatous meningitis), or as they pass through the sacrum (trauma or malignancy), or due to damage to the nerves themselves in the pelvis (infection, haematoma, trauma or malignancy).

Damage to the pons or spinal cord results in an 'upper motor neuron' pattern of bladder dysfunction due to uncontrolled overactivity of the parasympathetic supply. The bladder is small and highly sensitive to being stretched (analogous to spasticity). This results in frequency, urgency and urge incontinence. The loss of the coordinating control of the pontine micturition centre will also result in the phenomenon of detrusor-sphincter dyssynergia, where detrusor contraction and sphincter relaxation are not coordinated; hence the spastic bladder will often try to empty against a closed sphincter. This manifests as both urgency and an inability to pass urine, which is distressing and painful, and may last some minutes before partial emptying of the bladder is achieved. There is often a post-micturition residuum of urine which is prone to infection and the prolonged high bladder pressure may result in renal failure. More severe lesions of the spinal cord, as in spinal cord compression or trauma, can result in urinary retention; this will be painless, as bladder sensation, normally carried in the lateral spinothalamic tracts, will be cut off.

Damage to the mesial frontal lobes gives rise to loss of awareness of bladder fullness and consequent incontinence. Coexisting cognitive impairment may result in inappropriate micturition. These features are seen typically in hydrocephalus, frontal tumours, dementia and bifrontal subdural haematomas.

22.49 NEUROGENIC BLADDER: CLINICAL FEATURES AND TREATMENT			
	Site of lesion	Result	Treatment
Atonic ('lower motor neuron')	Lesions of sacral segments of cord (conus medullaris) Lesions of sacral roots and nerves	Loss of detrusor contraction Difficulty initiating micturition Bladder distension with overflow	Intermittent self-catheterisation Catheterisation
Hypertonic ('upper motor neuron')	Pyramidal tract lesion in spinal cord or brain stem	Urgency with urge incontinence Bladder sphincter incoordination (dyssynergia) Incomplete bladder emptying	Anticholinergics Oxybutynin (5 mg 8–12-hourly) Imipramine (25 mg 12-hourly) Tolterodine (2 mg 12-hourly) Intermittent self-catheterisation
Cortical	Post-central Pre-central Frontal	Loss of awareness of bladder fullness Difficulty initiating micturition Inappropriate micturition Loss of social control	Intermittent catheterisation Intermittent catheterisation Catheterisation

When faced with a patient who has bladder symptoms, it is important to try to localise the lesion on the basis of history and examination remembering, however, that most bladder problems are not neurological unless there are overt neurological signs. Clinical features are summarised in Box 22.49.

Management of bladder disturbance involves identifying the cause and correcting it if possible. Overactive (spastic) bladders are common in neurological disease and the unwanted detrusor activity (and hence urgency) can be lessened by anticholinergic drugs such as oxybutynin, tolterodine or imipramine. This will not solve the problem of detrusor-sphincter dyssynergia, however, and it may be necessary to teach the patient how to perform intermittent clean self-catheterisation (ISC); by emptying the bladder regularly, urinary frequency is reduced, as is the likelihood of infection. Bladder ultrasound is often helpful in this regard; a large (> 100 ml) post-micturition residual volume suggests that ISC will be necessary. Flaccid bladders are less common and unfortunately there is no effective drug treatment. These patients therefore need to perform ISC. Long-term catheterisation (urethral or suprapubic) may be necessary in either spastic or flaccid bladders, but this is avoided if at all possible as it is associated with increased infection as well as with technical problems such as blockage.

RECTUM

The rectum has an excitatory cholinergic input from the parasympathetic sacral outflow, and inhibitory sympathetic supply similar to the bladder. Continence depends largely on skeletal muscle contraction in the puborectalis and pelvic floor muscles supplied by the pudendal nerves, as well as the internal and external anal sphincters. Damage to the autonomic components causes constipation. Lesions affecting the conus medullaris, the somatic S2–4 roots and the pudendal nerves cause faecal incontinence.

PENILE ERECTION AND EJACULATION

These related functions are under autonomic control via the pelvic nerves (parasympathetic, S2–4) and hypogastric nerves (sympathetic, L1–2). Descending influences from the cerebrum are important for psychogenic erection, but erection can occur as a purely reflex phenomenon in response to genital stimulation. Erection is largely parasympathetic, and is impaired by drugs which have anticholinergic effects and also by some antihypertensive and antidepressant agents. Sympathetic activity is important for ejaculation, and may be inhibited by α-adrenoceptor antagonists (α-blockers). For further information on erectile impotence, see page 707.

CEREBROVASCULAR DISEASES

Diseases of the cerebral blood vessels are the third most common cause of death in the developed world after cancer and ischaemic heart disease, and are responsible for a large proportion of physical disability, becoming more frequent with increasing age. The annual incidence of acute cerebrovascular disease in the over-45 age group in the UK is about 350 per 100 000.

Cerebrovascular disease can cause death and disability by ischaemia from occlusion of blood vessels (producing cerebral ischaemia and infarction) or haemorrhage through their rupture.

Clinical features of cerebrovascular disease

Cerebral arterial disease most commonly presents as an acute focal stroke, but ischaemic cerebral arterial disease may present, particularly in the elderly, with a gradual decline in intellectual function (dementia), with or without sensorimotor limb deficits or gait disorder. Haemorrhage from the major cerebral arteries of the circle of Willis into the subarachnoid space usually presents with a sudden, severe headache, vomiting and neck stiffness, with or without signs of focal brain damage (see p. 1162). Disease of the cerebral venous circulation is rare and presents with characteristic clinical features which are usually distinct from those caused by cerebral arterial disease.

ACUTE FOCAL STROKE

Acute focal stroke is characterised by the sudden appearance of a focal deficit of brain function, most commonly a hemiplegia with or without signs of focal higher cerebral dysfunction (such as aphasia), hemisensory loss, visual field defect or brain-stem deficit. Provided that a clear history of such a sudden focal deficit is available, the chance of the brain lesions being anything other than vascular is 1% or less. However, care needs to be taken to exclude other differential diagnoses, especially if the history is not clearly one of a sudden deficit (see Box 22.50).

Clinical classification of focal stroke

A stroke is defined as:

- transient if the deficit recovers within 24 hours
- completed if the focal deficit is persistent and not worsening
- evolving if the focal deficit continues to worsen after about 6 hours from onset.

22.50 DIFFERENTIAL DIAGNOSIS OF ACUTE STROKE	
• Primary cerebral tumours • Metastatic cerebral tumours • Subdural haematoma • Cerebral abscess • Todd's paresis (after epileptic seizure)	• Demyelination • Hypoglycaemia • Encephalitis • Hysterical conversion

Transient stroke

Since transient strokes are almost always ischaemic, the term 'transient ischaemic attack' (TIA) is often used, although occasionally small intracerebral haemorrhages present with a transient stroke deficit. Transient strokes are a major risk factor for disabling stroke, implying a 13-fold increased risk of stroke in the next year. The management of a patient with a transient stroke is therefore directed at secondary prevention of future disabling stroke. Many transient strokes last only for a few minutes, whilst some stroke deficits persist for some days before recovery. These minor completed strokes are managed in the same way as shorter-duration deficits.

Completed stroke

Of patients presenting with a persistent acute focal stroke, 85% have sustained a cerebral infarction and the remainder an intracerebral haemorrhage. It is not possible to distinguish between these reliably at the bedside. Headache may accompany the onset of both haemorrhagic and ischaemic strokes, although the combination of headache with vomiting at the onset strongly suggests that the stroke is primarily haemorrhagic. A history of hypertension and/or raised blood pressure is common in both types of stroke lesion, although other risk factors for atherosclerosis are more likely to be found with ischaemic strokes.

Evolving stroke

The majority of persistent stroke deficits have completed within 6 hours, many within minutes, but some evolve in a stuttering fashion over days. It is this small group of patients with evolving deficits who should be viewed with diagnostic suspicion in case a mass lesion has been misdiagnosed. However, the lesion is often due to progressive occlusion of a cerebral artery (either a major extracranial vessel or a small perforating artery).

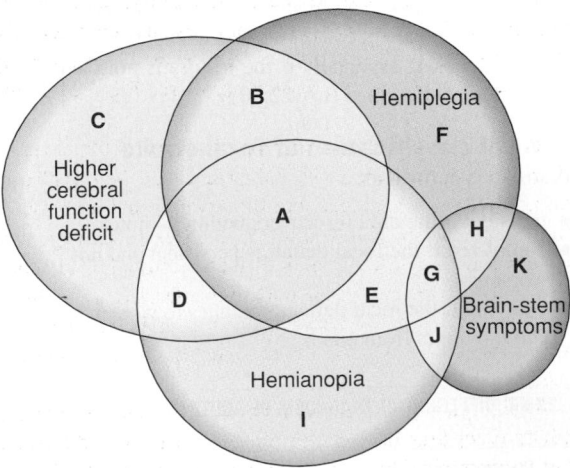

Fig. 22.27 Syndromes of acute stroke. Total anterior circulation syndrome—TACS (A). Partial anterior circulation syndromes—PACS (B, C, D and E). Pure motor stroke—lacunar syndrome (F). Posterior circulation syndromes—POCS (G, H, I, J and K).

22.51 GENERAL EXAMINATION OF STROKE PATIENTS	
Eyes	
• Diabetic changes	• Retinal emboli
• Hypertensive changes	• Arcus senilis
Cardiovascular system	
• Blood pressure (hypertension, hypotension)	
• Heart rhythm (atrial fibrillation)	
• Murmurs (sources of embolism)	
• Jugular venous pressure (heart failure, hypovolaemia)	
• Peripheral pulses and bruits (generalised arteriopathy)	
Respiratory system	
• Pulmonary oedema	• Respiratory infection
Abdomen	
• Urinary retention	

The size of the deficit

The site of the lesion (in terms of which arterial territory is involved) and its size, which will have a bearing on management, can be determined by assessing the patient's neurological deficit in a fairly simple way. This involves assessing the patient for the presence of a motor deficit (hemiplegia), higher cerebral function deficit (e.g. aphasia or parietal deficit) or a hemianopia. In addition, the presence of simple sensory loss or a brain-stem deficit (e.g. an eye movement abnormality or vertigo) should be noted. Permutations of these deficits can define several syndromes of stroke, as shown in Figure 22.27.

Clinical assessment of the patient with a stroke should also include attention to the general examination, particularly the heart and peripheral arterial system (see Box 22.51).

CEREBRAL INFARCTION

Cerebral infarction is mostly due to thromboembolic disease secondary to atherosclerosis in the major extracranial arteries (carotid artery and aortic arch). About 20% of infarctions are consequent upon embolism from the heart, and a further 20% are due to occlusion of the small lenticulostriate perforating vessels by intrinsic disease (lipohyalinosis), producing so-called 'lacunar' infarctions. The risk factors for ischaemic stroke reflect the risk factors for these underlying vascular diseases (see Box 22.52).

Pathophysiology

Cerebral infarction is a process which takes some hours to complete, even though the patient's deficit may be maximal close to the onset of the causative vascular occlusion. After the occlusion of a cerebral artery, the opening of anastomotic channels from other arterial territories may restore perfusion of its territory. Furthermore, a reduction in perfusion pressure leads to other homeostatic changes to maintain oxygenation to the brain (see Fig. 22.28). These compensatory changes can prevent even occlusion of a carotid artery from having any clinically apparent effect.

When these homeostatic mechanisms fail, the process of ischaemia starts; this ultimately leads to infarction. As the

22.52 STROKE RISK FACTORS

Irreversible

- Age
- Gender (male > female, except in the very young and very old)
- Race (Afro-Caribbean > Asian > European)
- Heredity
- Previous vascular event, e.g. myocardial infarction, stroke or peripheral embolism

Modifiable

- Hypertension
- Heart disease (heart failure, atrial fibrillation, endocarditis)
- Diabetes
- Hyperlipidaemia
- Smoking
- Excess alcohol consumption
- Polycythaemia
- Oral contraceptives

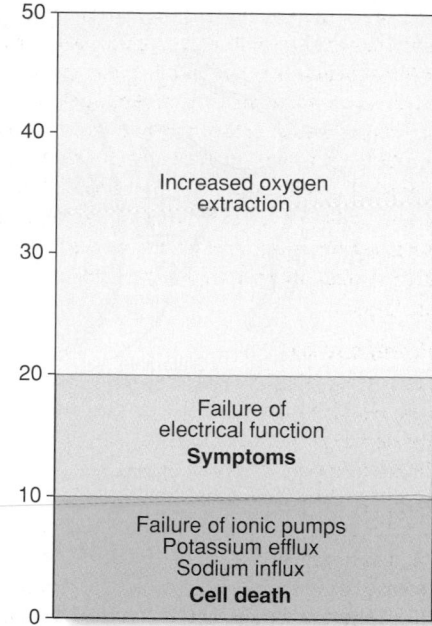

Fig. 22.29 Thresholds of cerebral ischaemia. Symptoms of cerebral ischaemia appear when the blood flow has fallen to less than half of normal and energy supply is insufficient to sustain neuronal electrical function. Full recovery can occur unless this level of flow is sustained for long periods. Further blood flow reduction below the next threshold causes failure of cell ionic pumps and starts the ischaemic cascade, leading to cell death. Brain tissue can sustain such depths of blood flow reduction only for brief periods without infarction.

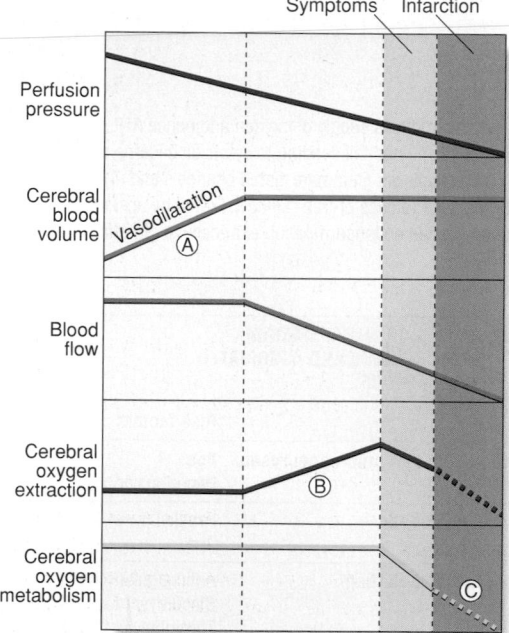

Fig. 22.28 Homeostatic responses to falling perfusion pressure in the brain following arterial occlusion. Vasodilatation initially maintains cerebral blood flow (A), but after maximal vasodilatation further falls in perfusion pressure lead to a decline in blood flow. An increase in tissue oxygen extraction, however, maintains the cerebral metabolic rate for oxygen (B). Still further falls in perfusion, and therefore blood flow, cannot be compensated; cerebral oxygen availability falls and symptoms appear, then infarction (C).

cerebral blood flow declines, various neuronal functions fail at various thresholds (see Fig. 22.29). Once flow falls below the threshold for the maintenance of electrical activity, neurological deficit appears. At this level of blood flow the neurons are still viable; if the flow increases again, function returns and the patient will have had a transient ischaemic attack. However, if the flow falls further, a level is reached at which the process of cell death starts. Hypoxia leads to an inadequate supply of adenosine triphosphate (ATP), which

in turn leads to loss of function of membrane pumps, thereby allowing influx of sodium and water into the cell (cytotoxic oedema) and the release of the excitatory neurotransmitter glutamate into the extracellular fluid. Glutamate opens membrane channels, allowing the influx of calcium and more sodium into the neurons. Calcium entering the neurons activates intracellular enzymes that complete the destructive process. The infarction process is worsened by the anaerobic production of lactic acid (see Fig. 22.30) and consequent fall in tissue pH.

The final result of the occlusion of a cerebral blood vessel therefore depends upon the competence of the circulatory homeostatic mechanisms, and the severity and duration of the reduction in blood flow. If ischaemic damage has occurred to the vascular endothelium, restoration of blood flow may cause haemorrhage into the infarcted area. This is particularly likely to occur following embolic occlusion when the embolus is lysed by the blood's thrombolytic mechanisms.

Radiologically, a cerebral infarct can be seen as a lesion which comprises brain tissue that is ischaemic and swollen but recoverable (the ischaemic penumbra), and dead brain tissue that is already undergoing autolysis. The infarct swells with time and is at its maximal size a couple of days after the stroke onset. At this stage it may be big enough to exert some mass effect both clinically and radiologically. As

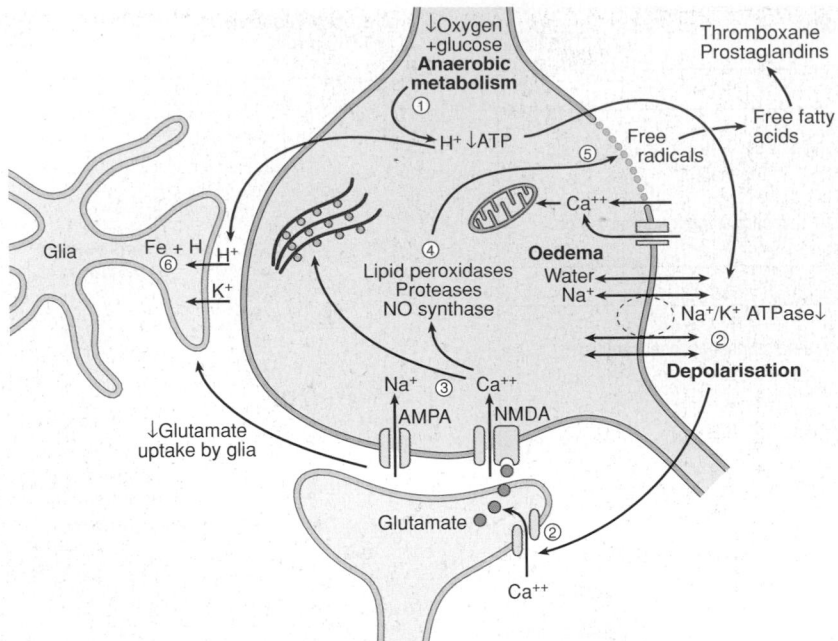

Fig. 22.30 **The process of neuronal ischaemia and infarction.** (1) Reduction of blood flow reduces supply of oxygen and hence ATP. H^+ is produced by anaerobic metabolism of available glucose. (2) Energy-dependent membrane ionic pumps fail, leading to cytotoxic oedema and membrane depolarisation, allowing calcium entry and releasing glutamate. (3) Calcium enters cells via glutamate-gated channels and (4) activates destructive intracellular enzymes, (5) destroying intracellular organelles and cell membrane, with release of free radicals. Free fatty acid release activates pro-coagulant pathways which exacerbate local ischaemia. (6) Glial cells take up H^+, can no longer take up extracellular glutamate and also suffer cell death, leading to liquefactive necrosis of whole arterial territory.

the weeks go by the oedema subsides and the infarcted area is replaced by a sharply defined fluid-filled cavity.

INTRACEREBRAL HAEMORRHAGE

Of the 15% of acute cerebrovascular disease that is caused by haemorrhage, about half occurs through the rupture of a blood vessel within the brain parenchyma (primary intracerebral haemorrhage), resulting in an acute focal stroke. In addition, a patient with a subarachnoid haemorrhage may present with an acute focal stroke if the artery ruptures into the brain substance as well as into the subarachnoid space. Haemorrhage frequently occurs into an area of brain infarction (see above) and such haemorrhagic infarctions may be difficult to distinguish from primary intracerebral haemorrhage. The causes and risk factors of primary intracerebral haemorrhage are listed in Box 22.53.

Pathophysiology

The explosive entry of blood into the brain parenchyma during a primary intracerebral haemorrhage causes immediate cessation of function in that area as neurons are structurally disrupted and white matter fibre tracts are split apart. A rim of cerebral oedema forms around the resulting blood clot, which, with the haematoma, acts like a mass lesion. If big enough, this can cause shift of the intracranial contents, producing transtentorial coning and sometimes rapid death. If the patient survives, the haematoma is gradually absorbed, leaving a haemosiderin-lined slit in the brain parenchyma (see Fig. 22.31).

22.53	CAUSES OF INTRACEREBRAL HAEMORRHAGE AND ASSOCIATED RISK FACTORS	
Disease		**Risk factors**
Charcot–Bouchard microaneurysms		Age Hypertension
Amyloid angiopathy		Familial (rare) Age
Impaired blood clotting		Anticoagulant therapy Blood dyscrasia Thrombolytic therapy
Vascular anomaly		Arteriovenous malformation Cavernous haemangioma
Substance misuse		Alcohol Amphetamines Cocaine

SUBARACHNOID HAEMORRHAGE

Clinical features

About three-quarters of those presenting with a subarachnoid haemorrhage are under 65 years and many are in their fourth decade. Women are more frequently affected than men and this difference increases with advancing age.

Subarachnoid haemorrhage typically presents with a sudden severe 'thunderclap' headache (usually occipital) which lasts for hours (or even days), often accompanied by vomiting. Physical exertion, straining and sexual excitement are common antecedents. There may be loss of consciousness at the

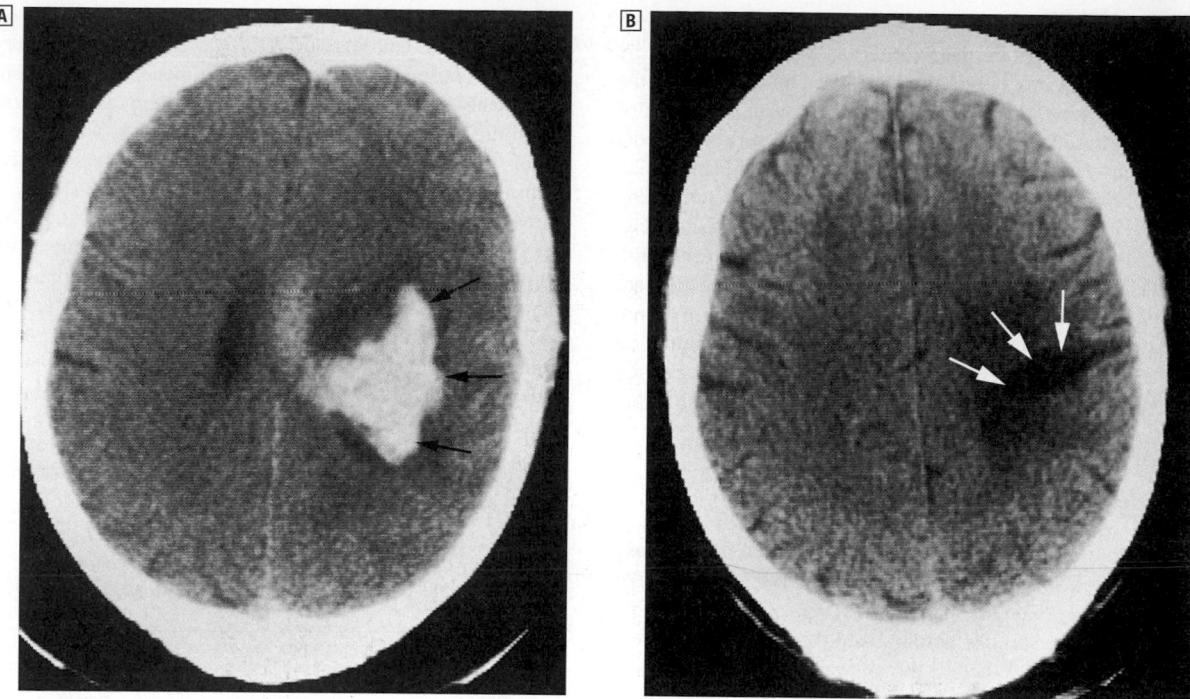

Fig. 22.31   CTs of intracerebral haemorrhage. [A] Acute intracerebral haematoma (arrows). [B] Resolved lesion leaving a slit-shaped defect (arrows).

onset, so subarachnoid haemorrhage should be considered if a patient is found comatose at home. Since subarachnoid haemorrhage is rare (incidence 6/100 000) and only 1 patient in 8 with a sudden severe headache has had a subarachnoid haemorrhage, clinical vigilance is necessary to avoid a missed diagnosis. All patients with a sudden severe headache require investigation to exclude a subarachnoid haemorrhage (see Fig. 22.32).

On examination the patient is usually distressed and irritable, with photophobia. There may be neck stiffness due to subarachnoid blood but this takes some 6 hours to develop. Focal hemisphere signs (hemiparesis, aphasia etc.) may be present at onset if there is an associated intracerebral haematoma. Alternatively, these signs may develop after some days due to arterial vasospasm induced by the presence of blood in the subarachnoid space. A 3rd nerve palsy may be present due to local pressure from an aneurysm of the posterior communicating artery, though this is rare. Fundoscopy may reveal a subhyaloid haemorrhage, which represents blood tracking along the subarachnoid space.

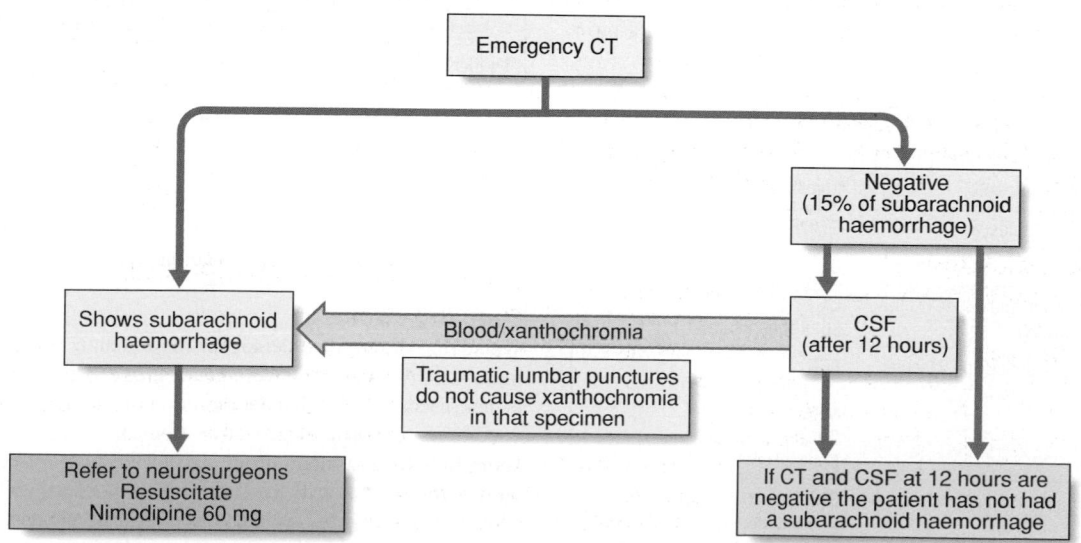

Fig. 22.32   The investigation of sudden severe headache.

Pathology

Of all subarachnoid haemorrhages, 85% are caused by 'berry' aneurysms bulging out from the bifurcations of the cerebral arteries, particularly in the region of the circle of Willis. These develop during life from defects in the media of the arterial wall and rarely present before the age of 20. There is an increased risk in association with polycystic kidney disease and congenital collagen defects (e.g. Ehlers–Danlos syndrome). Of the remainder, 5% are due to rarities including arteriovenous malformations, and 10% are non-aneurysmal haemorrhages. The cause of these is not known, but they give rise to a very characteristic pattern on CT of peri-mesencephalic blood. Such haemorrhages are known to have a benign outcome in terms of mortality and recurrence.

INVESTIGATION OF ACUTE STROKE

Investigation of a patient presenting with an acute stroke should be planned with a view to confirming the vascular nature of the lesion, the pathological type of vascular lesion, the underlying vascular disease, and the risk factors present (see Box 22.54). Whether the answer to these questions is important depends upon the type of stroke.

Transient stroke

Most transient strokes are due to transient cerebral ischaemia but CT occasionally reveals a small intracerebral haemorrhage. Which arterial territory was involved can be determined from the history of the attack. Approximately 80% occur in the carotid territory. Vertebro-basilar attacks are recognisable from a history of transient hemianopia or brain-stem features such as diplopia or vertigo. If these are not present, a transient hemiplegia, hemisensory loss and, if the dominant hemisphere is affected, dysphasia can be assumed to arise from carotid territory ischaemia.

Most transient strokes are caused by atherosclerotic thromboembolic disease of the major extracranial vessels. The risk of a disabling stroke or death after a transient ischaemic stroke can be reduced by 20–30% with aspirin

(75–150 mg daily; see first EBM panel). If patients have a major stenosis (more than 70%) of their carotid artery, carotid endarterectomy is of proven benefit (see second EBM panel). However, only 20% of patients presenting with a carotid territory transient ischaemic attack will have a major carotid stenosis. These patients need to be identified with a non-invasive method of vascular imaging (MRA or ultrasound) before using the more invasive (and therefore risky) contrast angiography that is necessary to delineate the lesion for the surgeon. A suggested scheme for the management of transient stroke is shown in Figure 22.33. A carotid bruit in isolation bears no relationship to the severity of the underlying stenosis or risk of stroke. Only those presenting with a confirmed ischaemic-centred event should undergo further investigation.

ACUTE ISCHAEMIC STROKE—role of aspirin **EBM**
'After transient stroke, aspirin is effective in reducing the risk of subsequent vascular events. After an acute persistent stroke RCTs have shown that aspirin started within 48 hours of onset improves long-term outcome.'
• Antiplatelet Trialists' Collaboration. Collaborative overview of randomised trials of antiplatelet therapy I: Prevention of death, myocardial infarction, and stroke by prolonged antiplatelet therapy in various categories of patients. BMJ 1994; 308:81–106.   • International Stroke Trial Collaborative Group. The International Stroke Trial (IST): a randomised trial of aspirin, subcutaneous heparin, both, or neither among 19435 patients with acute ischaemic stroke. Lancet 1997; 349:1569–1581.
Further information: 🖥 www.cochrane.co.uk

ACUTE ISCHAEMIC STROKE—role of carotid endarterectomy **EBM**
'After a transient stroke in the carotid territory and in the presence of a significant stenosis (70%) carotid endarterectomy is effective in reducing the risk of subsequent stroke. In asymptomatic carotid stenosis RCTs have shown that endarterectomy has only a small benefit.'
• European Carotid Surgery Trialists' Collaborative Group. Randomised trial of endarterectomy for recently symptomatic carotid stenosis: final results of the MRC European Carotid Surgery Trial (ECST). Lancet 1998; 351:1379–1387.   • Barnett HJM, Taylor DW, Eliasziw M, et al. Benefit of carotid endarterectomy in patients with symptomatic moderate or severe stenosis. N Engl J Med 1999; 339:1415–1425.   • Executive Committee for the Asymptomatic Carotid Atherosclerosis Study. Endarterectomy for asymptomatic carotid artery stenosis. JAMA 1995; 273:1421–1428.
Further information: 🖥 www.cochrane.co.uk

Rarely, a cardiac source of embolism is thought to be the cause of a transient stroke. In this case anticoagulation with warfarin is necessary. In most transient strokes, however, anticoagulation has no net benefit since as many haemorrhagic strokes are caused as ischaemic ones prevented.

Evolving stroke

Worsening of the focal deficit for more than 6 hours occurs in about 10% of patients with acute stroke. This should not be confused with a global deterioration of a patient's general condition—in particular, level of arousal, which can occur some time after a large stroke due to the mass effect of a large swollen infarct. If the focal deficit worsens, the likely cause is progression of the vascular lesion causing the stroke, but the possibility of a non-vascular lesion, such as a tumour, must be considered. Carotid or basilar stenosis can

22.54 INVESTIGATION OF A PATIENT WITH AN ACUTE STROKE	🔬

Diagnostic question	Investigation
Is it a vascular lesion?	CT/MRI
Is it ischaemic or haemorrhagic?	CT
Is it a subarachnoid haemorrhage?	CT Lumbar puncture
What is the underlying vascular disease?	ECG Cardiac ultrasound MRA Doppler ultrasound Contrast angiography
What are the risk factors?	Blood count Cholesterol Clotting/thrombophilia screen Blood glucose

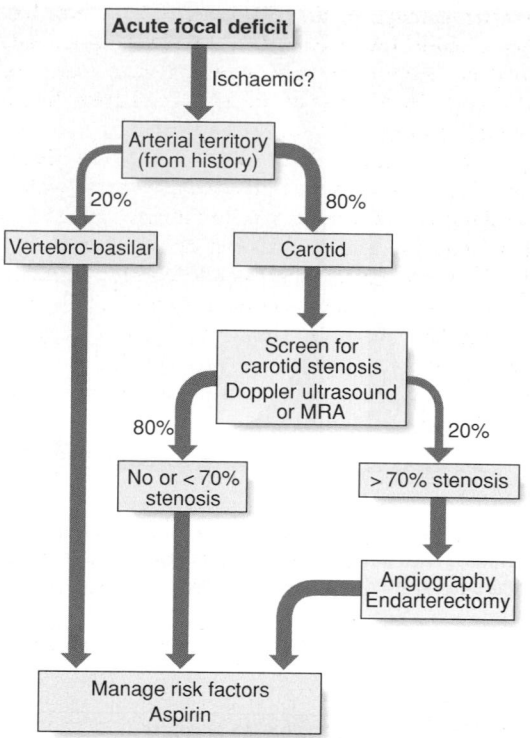

Fig. 22.33 **The management of transient stroke.**

present with a progressive deficit, but this is unusual. About 30% of lacunar strokes evolve over a matter of days. These are recognisable by the presenting syndromes (see Fig. 22.27, p. 1160) which suggest the small size of the brain lesion.

If haemorrhagic stroke has been excluded by imaging, attempts are sometimes made to halt progression of a stroke caused by carotid or basilar stenosis by anticoagulation with heparin. This is, however, of unproved value, as is the use of thrombolytic agents.

Completed stroke

A CT scan is necessary if a subarachnoid haemorrhage is suspected or there is doubt about the vascular nature of the lesion underlying the patient's presentation. In addition, if anticoagulant or thrombolytic drugs are to be given, a haemorrhagic lesion must be excluded. The scan will often reveal clues as to the nature of the arterial lesion. For example, the scan may show a small, deep lacunar infarct following occlusion of a perforating artery, or a more peripheral infarct if a leptomeningeal artery is involved (see Fig. 22.34). In a haemorrhagic lesion, the presence of a haematoma in the sylvian fissure with subarachnoid blood suggests a ruptured middle cerebral artery aneurysm.

After a completed ischaemic stroke it may be 12 hours or more before an area of low density appears on CT, and very small (lacunar) infarcts may not appear at all. By the second week after an infarct the unenhanced CT may appear normal, even with substantial infarction. This is because invasion of the infarcted area by macrophages and new blood vessels renders it isodense. However, contrast enhancement usually shows at least the rim of the lesion (see Fig. 22.35).

Other investigations

Lumbar puncture to examine the CSF is only indicated if a subarachnoid haemorrhage is suspected but has not been seen on a CT scan; in this case it is mandatory. It is best to

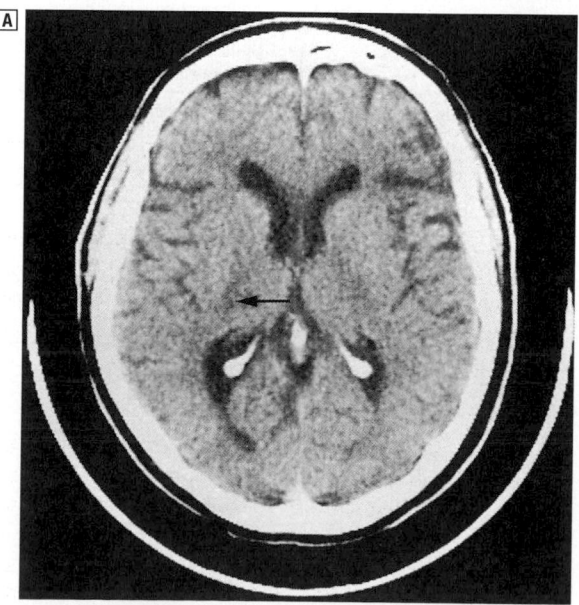
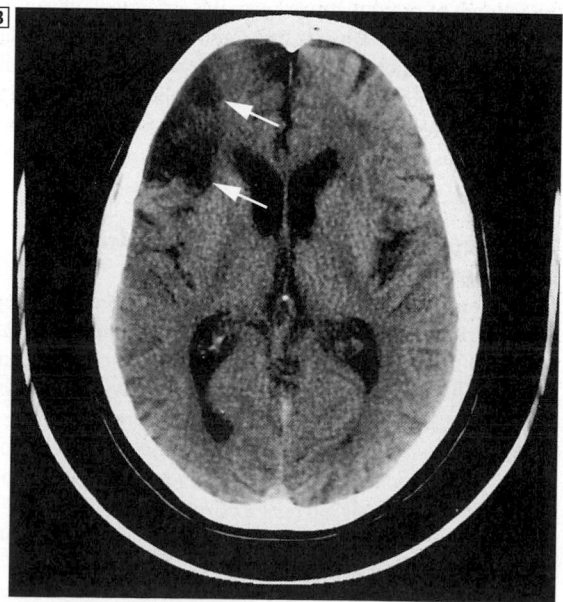

Fig. 22.34 **CTs of lacunar and peripheral infarction.** A Lacunar infarction caused by occlusion of a deep perforating artery (arrow). B Peripheral infarction from occlusion of a middle cerebral artery branch (arrows).

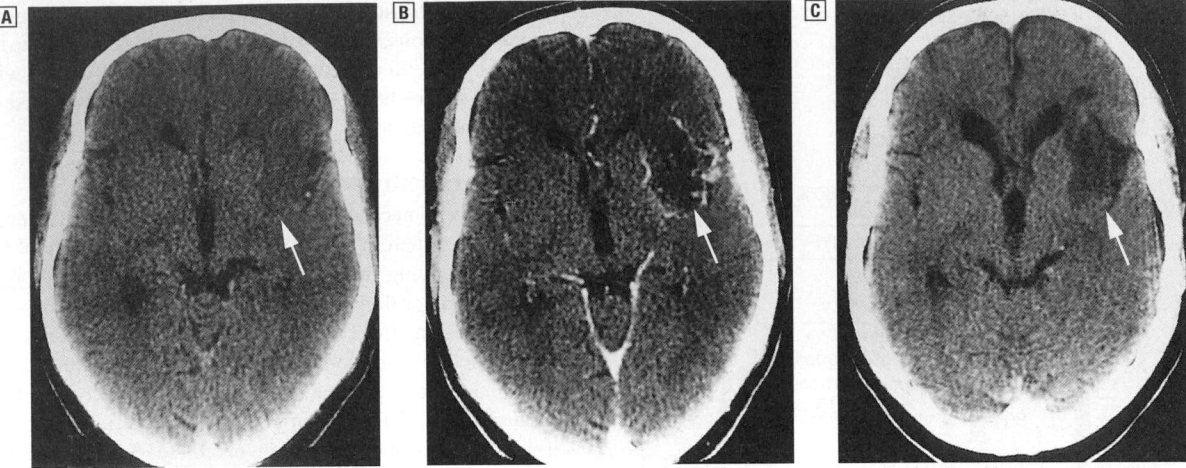

Fig. 22.35 **CTs showing progressive changes of cerebral infarction due to middle cerebral artery branch occlusion.** [A] Within 6 hours of the stroke little change is seen on the scan except some effacement of sylvian fissure (arrow). [B] At 3 weeks an enhanced scan shows a low-density lesion with enhancement at the periphery (arrow). [C] After 2 months there is resolution of the swelling in the lesion and a more clearly defined low density denoting the established infarct (arrow).

wait 12 hours since it takes this long for xanthochromia to appear (see Fig. 22.32, p. 1163). After an acute focal stroke other investigations necessary to exclude disorders which may be important in immediate management and in secondary prevention are listed in Box 22.54 (see p. 1164). In younger patients without risk factors for stroke, investigations for the rarer causes are indicated (see Box 22.55).

MANAGEMENT OF COMPLETED STROKE

After a completed stroke, management is aimed at minimising the volume of brain that is irreversibly infarcted, preventing complications (see Box 22.56), reducing the patient's disability and handicap through rehabilitation, and preventing recurrent episodes. Patients with subarachnoid haemorrhage should be referred urgently to a neurosurgical centre, since these patients require investigation for and surgical treatment of the berry aneurysm which may be the cause.

Thrombolysis and other revascularisation treatments

Intravenously delivered thrombolysis with urokinase, streptokinase or recombinant tissue plasminogen activator (rt-PA) increases the risk of haemorrhagic conversion of the cerebral infarct with potentially fatal results. However, this risk may be offset by an improvement in overall outcome if thrombolysis is given within 6 hours of onset of an ischaemic stroke, in the absence of hypertension, when the CT does not show extensive low density. Rt-PA seems to be preferable to other thrombolytic agents (see EBM panel). In the acute phase surgical revascularisation of a cerebral infarct seems to have no practical value since more deficit is often caused by consequent haemorrhage into the ischaemic brain. Vasodilator drugs have no value in the acute management of stroke.

22.55 CAUSES AND INVESTIGATION OF ACUTE STROKE IN YOUNG PATIENTS	
Cause	**Investigation**
Cardiac embolism	Cardiac ultrasound (including transoesophageal)
Premature atherosclerosis	Serum lipids
Arterial dissection	MRI Angiography
Thrombophilia	Protein C Protein S Antithrombin
Homocystinuria	Urinary amino acids Methionine loading test
Anticardiolipin syndrome	Anticardiolipin antibodies
Systemic lupus erythematosus	Lupus serology
Vasculitis	ESR CRP Antineutrophil cytoplasmic antibody (ANCA)
Mitochondrial cytopathy	Serum lactate Muscle biopsy
Primary intracerebral haemorrhage Arteriovenous malformation (AVM) Drug misuse Coagulopathy	Angiography Drug screen (amphetamine, cocaine) Prothrombin time (PT) and activated partial thromboplastin time (APTT) Platelet count
Subarachnoid haemorrhage Berry aneurysm AVM Carotid dissection	Angiography

22.56 COMPLICATIONS OF ACUTE STROKE

Complication	Prevention	Treatment
Chest infection	Nurse semi-erect Physiotherapy	Antibiotics Physiotherapy
Dehydration	Check swallowing Nasogastric tube	Careful rehydration
Hyponatraemia	Check causes (e.g. diuretics) Avoid excess water replacement	Water deprivation
Hypoxaemia	Avoid and treat chest complications Treat heart failure	As for cause
Seizures	Maintain cerebral oxygenation Avoid metabolic disturbance	Anticonvulsants
Hyperglycaemia	Treat diabetes	Insulin if necessary
Deep venous thrombosis/pulmonary embolism	Anti-embolism stockings Subcutaneous heparin	Anticoagulation (check if haemorrhagic stroke)
Frozen shoulder	Physiotherapy	Physiotherapy Local steroid injections
Pressure sores	Frequent turning Monitor pressure areas Avoid urinary contamination	Nursing care Special mattress
Urinary infection	Use penile sheath Avoid catheterisation if possible	Antibiotics
Constipation	Appropriate aperients and diet	Appropriate aperients

---

EBM

ACUTE ISCHAEMIC STROKE—role of thrombolytic therapy

'Thrombolysis after ischaemic stroke increases the risk of fatal intracranial haemorrhage, but these risks may be offset by an improvement in long-term outcome amongst survivors. The maximum benefit appears to be when thrombolysis is given within 6 hours of onset.'

- Hacke W, Kaste M, Fieschi C, et al., for the Second European-Australasian Acute Stroke Study Investigators. Randomised double-blind placebo-controlled trial of thrombolytic therapy with intravenous alteplase in acute ischaemic stroke (ECASS II). Lancet 1998; 352:1245–1251.
- Wardlaw JM, Warlow CP, Counsell C. Systematic review of evidence on thrombolytic therapy for acute ischaemic stroke. Lancet 1997; 350:607–614.

Further information: 🖳 www.cochrane.co.uk

EBM

ACUTE ISCHAEMIC STROKE—role of anticoagulants

'There is no benefit to be gained in the routine use of anticoagulants after acute stroke except in the presence of non-rheumatic atrial fibrillation, where anticoagulation halves the odds of serious vascular events. Patients with rheumatic atrial fibrillation have a high risk of recurrent stroke and probably also benefit from anticoagulation.'

- International Stroke Trial Collaborative Group. The International Stroke Trial (IST): a randomised trial of aspirin, subcutaneous heparin, both, or neither among 19435 patients with acute ischaemic stroke. Lancet 1997; 349:1569–1581.
- Atrial Fibrillation Investigators. Risk factors for stroke and efficacy of antithrombotic therapy in atrial fibrillation. Arch Intern Med 1994; 154:1449–1457.

Further information: 🖳 www.cochrane.co.uk

Anticoagulation and aspirin

Anticoagulation after an acute stroke is only indicated if the cause is embolism from the heart, such as with atrial fibrillation (see EBM panel). In this case, provided imaging has demonstrated the absence of haemorrhage, oral anticoagulation with warfarin should be started (aiming for an international normalised ratio of 2–3). It is not necessary to start anticoagulation with heparin first since in the acute phase any benefit from this in preventing further embolism is offset by the increased risk of haemorrhagic conversion of the infarct. Aspirin (300 mg daily) should be started immediately after an ischaemic stroke, and carries a far lower risk of haemorrhagic complications.

Blood pressure

The blood pressure is usually acutely raised after a stroke and, unless acute end-organ damage is present, should not be lowered in the acute stage since it will always return towards the patient's normal level within 24–48 hours. Survival of the ischaemic penumbra may depend upon the raised perfusion pressure. The blood pressure tends to stay higher for longer with cerebral haematomas than with cerebral infarcts but, in terms of preventing further haemorrhage, there is no value in reducing this pressure until at least some days after the stroke. After 10 days gentle reduction of blood pressure may be contemplated as part of a secondary preventative strategy for ischaemic stroke.

Hydration and oxygenation

Adequate hydration and arterial oxygenation are important to preserve as much as possible of ischaemic but recoverable brain. After a stroke a patient may have difficulty in protecting the airway and therefore difficulty in safely maintaining adequate nutrition and hydration orally. In this case, intravenous hydration may be necessary in the first few hours and thereafter; if a patient's swallowing fails to recover, hydration should be maintained by nasogastric tube or gastrostomy.

Blood glucose

A raised blood sugar after a stroke increases infarct size and adversely affects functional outcome. This is probably because hyperglycaemia exacerbates the anaerobic production of lactic acid in the ischaemic penumbra. Hence, a blood sugar above 7 mmol/l should be normalised with insulin.

Nursing care and rehabilitation

Many patients after a stroke are, at least initially, physically dependent, and require expert nursing care to avoid complications. Bladder and bowel care need special consideration. Care may be better provided in specialised stroke units, which have been shown to reduce patient mortality and accelerate functional recovery (see p. 243). Depression is common after a stroke and will often respond to antidepressant medication. Consideration of a patient's rehabilitation needs should commence at the same time as the acute medical management (see above).

Prognosis and secondary prevention

About 75% of patients survive the acute stage of focal stroke due to cerebral infarction or primary intracerebral haemorrhage. The immediate mortality of aneurysmal subarachnoid haemorrhage is 30%, with a recurrence rate of 50% in the first 6 months and 3% annually thereafter. Secondary prevention requires appropriate neurosurgical management. Half to three-quarters of those surviving an acute stroke achieve functional independence, mostly within the first 3 months. After a completed focal stroke there is an annual recurrence rate of 8–11%. Secondary prevention of stroke involves attention to those risk factors that are reversible and, in the case of ischaemic stroke, the use of aspirin. Patients with a cardiac cause for their ischaemic stroke, such as atrial fibrillation, should be anticoagulated in the absence of any contraindication. If the residual deficit after an ischaemic stroke is minimal, that patient should be managed in the same way as for a transient stroke.

CEREBRAL VENOUS DISEASE

Thrombosis of cerebral veins and venous sinuses is uncommon. The causes are listed in Box 22.57.

Cerebral venous occlusion causes an increase in intracranial pressure and patchy ischaemia, which is often haemorrhagic. The clinical features vary according to the part of the cerebral venous system involved (see below).

Cortical vein thrombosis

This may present with focal cortical deficits (aphasia, hemiparesis etc.) and epilepsy (focal or generalised), according to the area involved. The deficit may enlarge if spreading thrombophlebitis occurs.

Cerebral venous sinus thrombosis

The clinical features of cerebral venous sinus thrombosis depend on the sinus involved (see Box 22.58).

22.57 CAUSES OF CEREBRAL VENOUS THROMBOSIS

Predisposing causes

- Dehydration
- Pregnancy
- Behçet's disease
- Thrombophilia
- Hypotension
- Oral contraceptives

Local causes

- Paranasal sinusitis
- Meningitis, subdural empyema
- Penetrating head and eye wounds
- Facial skin infection
- Otitis media, mastoiditis
- Skull fracture

22.58 CLINICAL FEATURES OF CEREBRAL VENOUS THROMBOSIS

Cavernous sinus

- Proptosis, ptosis, headache, external and internal ophthalmoplegia, papilloedema, reduced sensation in trigeminal first division
- Often bilateral, patient ill and febrile

Superior sagittal sinus

- Headache, papilloedema, seizures
- May involve veins of both hemispheres, causing advancing motor and sensory focal deficits

Transverse sinus

- Hemiparesis, seizures, papilloedema
- May spread to jugular foramen to involve cranial nerves 9, 10, 11

ISSUES IN OLDER PEOPLE
STROKE

- Two-thirds of stroke patients are aged over 60 years.
- A clear history in establishing a diagnosis of stroke is as important in older people as in younger patients, but will be more difficult to obtain if there is pre-existing cognitive impairment or if there are communication difficulties.
- The benefits of carotid endarterectomy accrue quickly after transient stroke; therefore when it is indicated, advanced age alone is not a contraindication for surgery.
- Older patients with stroke are more likely to have other pathology such as ischaemic heart disease, cardiac failure, chronic obstructive pulmonary disease (COPD), osteoarthritis and visual impairments. All such comorbidities will have to be addressed as part of overall stroke management.
- The older the patient, the more he or she will need an active programme of rehabilitation to regain maximum function. Cognitive impairment will adversely affect outcome, as much of rehabilitation involves the learning and retention of new skills (see p. 243).
- The reappearance of neurological signs from a previous stroke in a patient who is ill or hypotensive is a common cause of over-diagnosis of recurrent stroke.
- Diffuse small-vessel cerebrovascular disease is very common in older people and may present insidiously with gait abnormalities and/or significant memory impairment. It also predisposes to confusional states when intercurrent infection or metabolic disturbance intervenes.
- Whilst anticoagulation for secondary prevention after stroke may be indicated in certain circumstances, it must be used with caution. The associated risks in frail older patients are higher because of increased comorbidity, particularly falls and cognitive impairment, and the potential for interaction with other medication.

INFLAMMATORY DISEASES

MULTIPLE SCLEROSIS

In multiple sclerosis, one of the most common neurological causes of long-term disability, the myelin-producing oligo-dendrocytes of the central nervous system are the target of recurrent cell-mediated autoimmune attack. In the UK the prevalence is 80 per 100 000 of the population, with an annual incidence of around 5 per 100 000. The lifetime risk of developing multiple sclerosis is about 1 in 800. The incidence is higher in temperate climates and in people of European extraction, and the disease is more common in women (male:female ratio of 1:1.5).

Aetiology

Epidemiological evidence suggests an environmental influence on causation. The incidence varies with latitude, being low in equatorial areas and higher in the temperate zones of both hemispheres. A genetic influence is suggested by a 10-fold increase in risk in first-degree relatives and from twin studies in which there is higher concordance for multiple sclerosis in monozygotic twins compared to dizygotic twins. HLA tissue-typing has demonstrated an increased prevalence of haplotypes A3, B7, Dw2 and DR2 in affected patients in the UK, but different haplotypes are associated in other countries. An immune mechanism is suggested by increased levels of activated T lymphocytes in the CSF, and increased immunoglobulin synthesis within the central nervous system. There are increased levels of antibody to some viruses, including measles virus, in the CSF, but this may be a result of the disease process rather than directly related to the cause. The relative importance of environmental, genetic and immunological factors is unresolved. Multiple sclerosis is likely to be multifactorial in origin.

Pathology

An attack of central nervous system inflammation in multiple sclerosis starts with the entry through the blood–brain barrier of activated T lymphocytes. These recognise myelin-derived antigens on the surface of the nervous system's antigen-presenting cells, the microglia, and undergo clonal proliferation. The resulting inflammatory cascade releases cytokines and initiates destruction of the oligodendrocyte-myelin unit by macrophages. Histologically, the characteristic lesion is a plaque of inflammatory demyelination occurring most commonly in the periventricular regions of the brain, the optic nerves and the subpial regions of the spinal cord (see Fig. 22.36). Initially, this is a circumscribed area of disintegration of the myelin sheath, accompanied by infiltration by activated lymphocytes and macrophages, often with conspicuous perivascular inflammation. After an acute attack gliosis follows, leaving a shrunken grey scar.

Much of the initial acute clinical deficit is caused by the effect of inflammatory cytokines upon transmission of the nervous impulse rather than structural disruption of the myelin, which explains the rapid recovery of some deficits and probably the efficacy of steroids in ameliorating the acute deficit. However, the myelin loss that results from an attack reduces the safety factor for impulse propagation or causes complete conduction block, which lowers the efficiency of central nervous system functions. In established multiple sclerosis there is progressive axonal loss, probably due to direct damage to axonal integrity by the inflammatory mediators released in acute attacks (including nitrous oxide), and this is the cause of the phase of the disease where there is progressive and persistent disability (see Fig. 22.37).

Clinical features

A diagnosis of multiple sclerosis requires the demonstration of lesions in more than one anatomical site at more than one time for which there is no other explanation. Around 80% of patients have a relapsing and remitting clinical course of episodic dysfunction of the central nervous system with variable recovery. Of the remaining 20%, most follow a slowly progressive clinical course, with a tiny minority who have a fulminant variety leading to early death (see Fig. 22.37). The peak age of onset is in the fourth decade, onset before puberty or after the age of 60 years being rare. There are a number of clinical symptoms and syndromes characteristic of multiple sclerosis, some of which may occur at presentation while others may develop in the course of the illness (see Boxes 22.59 and 22.60).

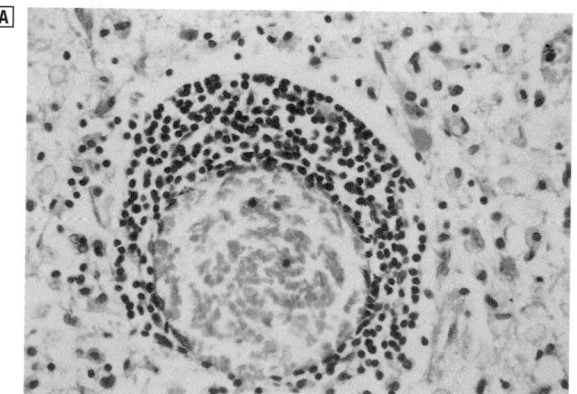

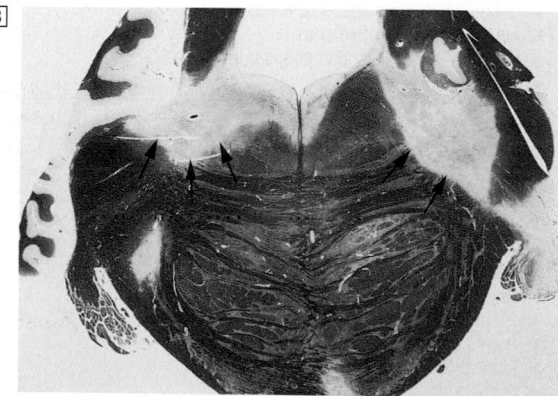

Fig. 22.36 Multiple sclerosis. A Photomicrograph from demyelinating plaque showing perivascular cuffing of blood vessel by lymphocytes. B Section through pons showing demyelinating plaques in white matter (arrows) (Weigert–Pal).

Demyelinating lesions cause symptoms and signs that usually come on subacutely over days or weeks, and resolve over weeks or months. After a variable interval there may be a recurrence, often within 2 years. Frequent relapses with incomplete recovery indicate a poor prognosis, and in many patients a phase of secondary progression supersedes the phase of relapse and remission. In a minority of patients there may be an interval of years or even decades between attacks, and in some, particularly if optic neuritis is the initial manifestation, there is no recurrence. Some presentations, such as optic neuritis with purely sensory relapses, have a good prognosis.

The physical signs observed in multiple sclerosis depend on the anatomical site of demyelination. Combinations of spinal cord and brain-stem signs are common, maybe with

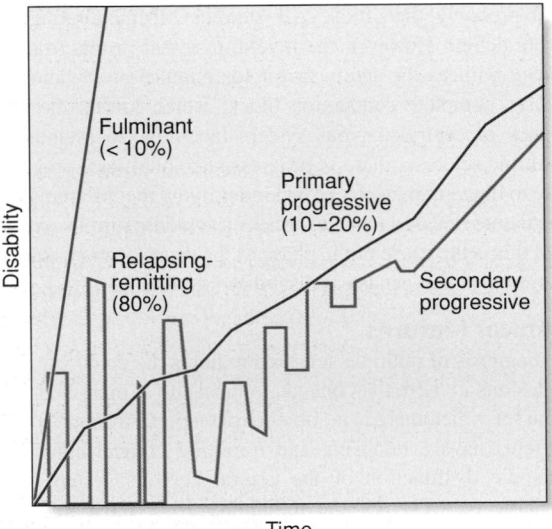

Fig. 22.37   The progression of disability in fulminant, relapsing-remitting and progressive multiple sclerosis.

22.59 COMMON PRESENTATIONS OF MULTIPLE SCLEROSIS

- Optic neuritis
- Relapsing and remitting sensory symptoms
- Subacute painless spinal cord lesion
- Acute brain-stem syndrome
- Subacute loss of function of upper limb
- 6th cranial nerve palsy

22.60 SYMPTOMS AND SYNDROMES SUGGESTIVE OF CNS DEMYELINATION

- Optic neuritis (afferent pupillary defect)
- Tingling in spine or limbs on neck flexion (Lhermitte's phenomenon)
- Dorsal column loss in one limb
- Progressive non-compressive paraparesis
- Partial Brown-Séquard syndrome
- Internuclear ophthalmoplegia with ataxia
- Focal brain-stem lesions
- Postural ('rubral') tremor
- Trigeminal neuralgia under the age of 50
- Recurrent facial palsy

---

evidence of previous optic neuritis in the form of an afferent pupillary deficit. Significant intellectual impairment is unusual until late in the disease, when loss of frontal functions and impairment of memory are common.

Investigations

There is no specific test for multiple sclerosis and the results of investigation are taken in conjunction with the clinical picture in making a diagnosis of varying probability (see Box 22.61). The clinical diagnosis of multiple sclerosis can be supported by investigations which aim to exclude other conditions, provide evidence for an inflammatory disorder and identify multiple sites of neurological involvement (see Box 22.62).

Following the first clinical event, investigations may help in confirming the disseminated nature of the disease. Visual evoked potentials (see p. 1110) can detect clinically silent lesions in up to 70% of patients, but auditory and somatosensory evoked potentials are seldom of diagnostic value. The CSF may show a lymphocytic pleocytosis in the acute phase and oligoclonal bands of IgG in 70–90% of patients between attacks. Oligoclonal bands are not specific to multiple sclerosis but denote intrathecal inflammation and occur in a range of other disorders. MRI is the most sensitive technique for imaging lesions in both brain and spinal cord (see Fig. 22.7C, p. 1113) and in excluding other causes of the neurological deficit. However, the MRI appearances in multiple sclerosis may be difficult to distinguish from those of cerebrovascular disease or cerebral vasculitis. Diagnosis depends on the clinical history and examination,

---

22.61 CLINICAL DIAGNOSTIC CRITERIA FOR MULTIPLE SCLEROSIS

Clinically definite

Requires all of:
- Age < 60 years
- History or signs of deficits in two or more anatomical sites in CNS
- Abnormal signs are present on CNS examination which indicate white matter involvement
- CNS involvement in one of two patterns
    Relapsing and remitting: two or more episodes lasting at least 24 hours and > 1 month apart
    Progressive: slow and/or stepwise progression over at least 6 months
- No other explanation of symptoms

Clinically probable

- Relapsing and remitting symptoms with one neurological sign commonly associated with MS
  or
- Documented single episode with partial or complete recovery, with signs on examination of multifocal white matter disease
  and
- No other explanation

Clinically possible

- Relapsing and remitting symptoms without documented or objective signs to establish more than one anatomical site of CNS involvement
- No other explanation

22.62 INVESTIGATIONS IN A PATIENT SUSPECTED OF HAVING MULTIPLE SCLEROSIS

Exclude other structural disease and identify plaques of demyelination

- Imaging (MRI, myelography)

Demonstrate other sites of involvement

- Visual evoked potentials
- Other evoked potentials

Demonstrate inflammatory nature of lesion(s)

- CSF examination:
  Cell count
  Protein electrophoresis (oligoclonal bands)

Exclude other conditions

- Chest radiograph
- Serum angiotensin-converting enzyme (ACE)
- Serum B_{12}
- Antinuclear antibodies

taken in combination with the investigative findings. It is important to exclude other potentially treatable alternative conditions such as infections, vitamin B_{12} deficiency and spinal cord compression.

Management

The management of multiple sclerosis involves treatment of the acute relapse, prevention of future relapse, treatment of complications, and management of the patient's disability.

Acute relapse

In a function-threatening relapse, high-dose intravenous steroids (methylprednisolone 1 g daily for 3 days) are indicated to shorten the duration of the relapse but do not affect long-term outcome (see EBM panel). Pulsed intravenous steroids also have some effect in reducing spasticity. Prolonged administration of steroids does not alter the long-term outcome and is therefore avoided. Pulses of intravenous steroids can be given up to 3–4 times in a year but their administration should be restricted to those with significant function-threatening deficits.

EBM

MULTIPLE SCLEROSIS—role of pulsed steroid therapy to shorten relapse

'In patients with optic neuritis and acute MS relapse, short courses of steroids improve recovery at 4 weeks but have no effect on long-term disability. Two RCTs have shown little difference between oral and intravenous high-dose steroids in the treatment of MS relapse.'

- Sellebjerg F, Frederiksen JL, Nielsen PM, Olesen J. Double-blind, randomised, placebo-controlled study of oral, high-dose methylprednisolone in attacks of MS. Neurology 1998; 51:529–534.
- Barnes D, Hughes RAC, Morris RW, et al. Randomised trial of oral and intravenous methylprednisolone in acute relapses of multiple sclerosis. Lancet 1997; 349:902–906.

Further information: www.clinicalevidence.org

Preventing relapses

Immunosuppressive agents including azathioprine have a marginal effect in reducing relapses and improving long-term outcome. In relapsing and remitting multiple sclerosis subcutaneous or intramuscular interferon beta-1a/b reduces the number of relapses by some 30%, with a small effect on long-term disability (see EBM panel). The immune modulator

glatiramer acetate has similar effects. The effects of other immune modulation therapies are currently being evaluated and may have some use in the future. Special diets including a gluten-free diet, linoleic acid supplements or hyperbaric oxygen therapy are of no proven benefit.

EBM

MULTIPLE SCLEROSIS—role of interferon beta-1a/b in reducing relapse rate

'In patients with active relapsing and remitting MS, interferon beta-1a/b reduces relapse rate by one-third and may have some effect on the progression of disability. One trial has shown that, in patients with secondary progressive disease, the development of disability may be delayed by 9–12 months.'

- PRISMS Study Group. Randomised double-blind placebo-controlled study of interferon beta-1a in relapsing/remitting multiple sclerosis. Lancet 1998; 352:1498–1504.
- IFNB Multiple Sclerosis Study Group. Interferon beta-1b is effective in relapsing-remitting multiple sclerosis. Clinical results of a multicenter, randomised, double-blind, placebo-controlled trial. Neurology 1993; 43:655–661.
- European Study Group on Interferon Beta-1b in Secondary Progressive MS. Placebo-controlled multicentre randomised trial of interferon beta-1b in treatment of secondary progressive multiple sclerosis. Lancet 1998; 352:1491–1497.

Further information: www.clinicalevidence.org

Complications

The treatment of the complications of multiple sclerosis is summarised in Box 22.63. Of prime importance are a careful explanation of the nature of the disease and its outcome and the support of patients and their relatives when disability occurs. A frank discussion of the diagnosis and prognosis is necessary and may dispel fears, which are often ill founded. Periods of physiotherapy may improve functional capacity in those patients who become disabled, and assessment by the occupational therapist will provide guidance in the provision of aids within the home and in reducing handicap.

Care of the bladder is particularly important. Infections should be treated with an appropriate antibiotic. Incontinence, urgency and frequency may be treated pharmacologically, by external drainage or by urinary catheter, which may be passed intermittently by the patient rather than left permanently in-dwelling. The choice of treatment is difficult and urodynamic assessment may be necessary in patients

---

22.63 TREATMENT OF COMPLICATIONS OF MULTIPLE SCLEROSIS

Complication	Treatment
Spasticity	Physiotherapy Baclofen 15–100 mg* Diazepam 2–15 mg* Dantrolene 25–400 mg* Tizanidine 18–32 mg Local injection of botulinum toxin Chemical neuronectomy
Ataxia	Isoniazid 600–1200 mg* Clonazepam 2–8 mg*
Dysaesthesia	Carbamazepine 200–1800 mg* Phenytoin 200–400 mg Gabapentin 900–2400 mg Amitriptyline 10–100 mg
Bladder symptoms	See Box 22.49, page 1158

* In divided doses.

with troublesome symptoms. Sexual dysfunction is a source of anxiety in many patients and may be relieved by skilled counselling and, if necessary, prosthetic aids. Sildenafil may help impotence.

Prognosis

The outlook is difficult to predict with confidence in any individual patient, especially early in the disease. Furthermore, the ability to diagnose disease at an earlier stage means that older studies may not reliably reflect the outcome of those diagnosed with modern techniques. About 15% of those having one attack of demyelination do not suffer any more events, whilst those with relapsing and remitting multiple sclerosis have, on average, 1–2 relapses every 2 years. Approximately 5% of patients die within 5 years of onset, whilst others have a very benign outcome. Overall, after 10 years about one-third of patients are disabled to the point of needing help with walking, whilst after 15 years about 50% have this degree of disability.

ACUTE DISSEMINATED ENCEPHALOMYELITIS

This is an acute monophasic demyelinating condition in which there are areas of perivenous demyelination widely disseminated throughout the brain and spinal cord. The illness may apparently occur spontaneously but often occurs a week or so after a viral infection, especially measles and chickenpox, or following vaccination, suggesting that it is immunologically mediated.

Clinical features

Headache, vomiting, pyrexia, confusion and meningism may be presenting features, often with focal or multifocal brain and spinal cord signs. Seizures or coma may occur. Flaccid paralysis with extensor plantar responses is common and cerebellar signs may be present, particularly when the disorder follows chickenpox.

Investigations

MRI shows multiple high-signal areas in a pattern similar to that of multiple sclerosis, although often with larger areas of abnormality. The CSF may be normal or show a small increase in mononuclear cells and protein. The differential diagnosis from a first severe attack of what turns out to be multiple sclerosis may be difficult.

Management

The disease may be fatal in the acute stages but is otherwise self-limiting. Treatment with high-dose intravenous methylprednisolone, using the same regimen as for a relapse of multiple sclerosis, is recommended.

ACUTE TRANSVERSE MYELITIS

Transverse myelitis is an acute monophasic inflammatory demyelinating disorder affecting the spinal cord over a variable number of segments. Patients may be of any age and present with a subacute paraparesis with a sensory level, often with severe pain in the neck or back at the onset. MRI

is needed to distinguish this from a compressive lesion of the spinal cord. CSF examination shows cellular pleocytosis, often with polymorphs at the onset. Treatment is with high-dose intravenous methylprednisolone. The outcome is variable; in some cases, near-complete recovery occurs despite a severe initial deficit. A small proportion of patients who present with acute transverse myelitis go on to develop multiple sclerosis in later years.

DEGENERATIVE DISEASES

Many diseases cause degeneration in different parts of the nervous system without an identifiable external cause. Genetic factors are known to be involved in several, but the cause is still unknown for the majority. Clinical features depend on which structures are affected. Degeneration of the cerebral cortex causes dementia, the most common type being Alzheimer's disease. Degeneration of the basal ganglia results in movement disorder, which may manifest as either too little or too much movement, depending on the structures involved. Examples of these conditions are Parkinson's disease and Huntington's disease. Cerebellar degeneration usually causes ataxia. Degeneration can also occur in the spinal cord or peripheral nerves, giving rise to motor, sensory or autonomic disturbance.

DEGENERATIVE CAUSES OF DEMENTIA

As many as 5% of the population over 65 years of age suffer from a dementing illness. Over the age of 80, this rises to over 20%. Dementia therefore has major implications for health resources.

ALZHEIMER'S DISEASE

This is the most common cause of dementia, occurring mostly in patients over 45 years. Genetic factors are important, particularly if the age of onset is under 65 years; the familial disease may account for some 15% of cases, though genetic abnormalities on several different chromosomes have been described, particularly chromosomes 1, 14 and 21. The inheritance of one of the alleles of apolipoprotein ε (apo ε), ε4, is associated with a fourfold increase in the risk of developing the disease.

Pathology

Macroscopically, the brain is atrophic, particularly the cerebral cortex and hippocampus. Histology reveals the presence of senile plaques and neurofibrillary tangles in the cerebral cortex. Histochemical staining demonstrates significant quantities of amyloid in plaques (see Fig. 22.38). Many different neurotransmitter abnormalities have been described, in particular impairment of cholinergic transmission, though noradrenaline, 5-HT, glutamate and substance P are also involved (see Box 22.1, p. 1107).

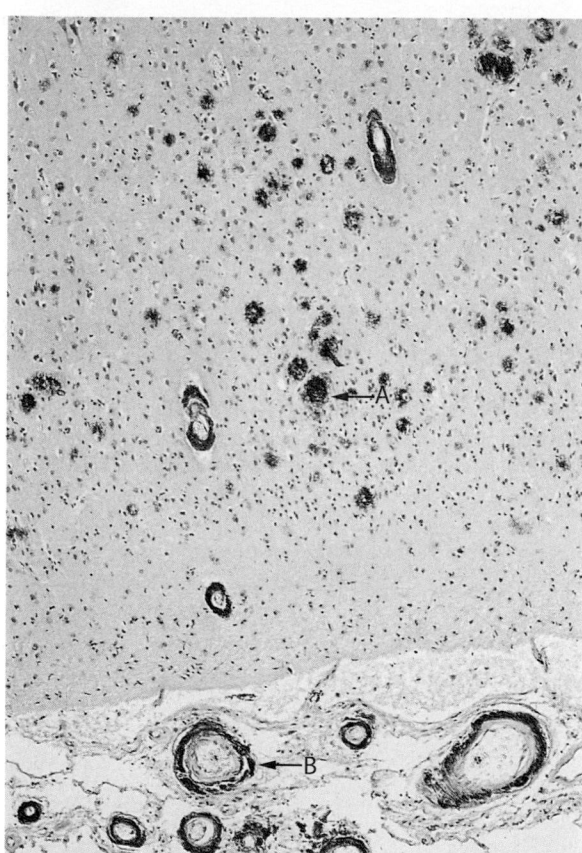

Fig. 22.38   Alzheimer's disease. Section of neocortex stained with polyclonal antibody against βA4 peptide showing amyloid deposits in plaques in brain substance (arrow A) and in blood vessel walls (arrow B).

Clinical features

The key clinical feature is impairment of delayed recall, i.e. the inability to retrieve (remember) information acquired in the past. Hence, patients present with gradual impairment of memory, usually in association with disorders of other cortical function. Both short-term and long-term memory are affected, but defects in the former are usually more obvious. Later in the course of the disease, typical features are apraxia, visuo-spatial impairment and aphasia. In the early stages, patients themselves may complain of difficulties but, as the disease progresses, it is common for patients to deny that there is anything wrong (anosognosia). In this situation, patients are often brought to medical attention by their carers. Depression is common. Occasionally, patients become aggressive, and the clinical features are made acutely worse by coexistent intercurrent illness.

Investigations and management

Investigation is aimed at excluding other treatable causes of dementia (see Box 22.38, p. 1146), as histological confirmation of the diagnosis usually occurs only after death. There is no known treatment, though recently donepezil and rivastigmine, inhibitors of cerebral acetylcholinesterase, have been shown to be of some benefit (see EBM panel).

Management consists largely of providing a familiar environment for the patient, and providing support for the carers.

OTHER CAUSES OF DEMENTIA

Wernicke–Korsakoff disease

Deficiency of thiamin (vitamin B$_1$) usually presents with an acute confusional state (Wernicke's encephalopathy) and brain-stem abnormalities such as ataxia, nystagmus and extraocular muscle weakness (particularly lateral rectus weakness). If inadequately treated, this results in a dementia characterised by a profound disturbance of short-term memory associated with a tendency to confabulate, called Korsakoff's syndrome. The deficiency can arise as a result of malnutrition (including that occasioned by chronic alcohol misuse), malabsorption or even protracted vomiting (as in hyperemesis gravidarum). The diagnosis can be made biochemically by the finding of a reduced red cell transketolase, but this test is often difficult to obtain and so the diagnosis is usually made clinically. Because it is potentially treatable, the condition must be considered in any confused or demented patient; if there is any doubt, it is usually better to treat anyway. Treatment consists of administering high-dose vitamins, often intravenously in the initial stages, followed by oral thiamin (initially 100 mg 8-hourly), in addition to treating the underlying cause.

Pick's disease

In this condition, which is much rarer than Alzheimer's, degeneration predominantly affects frontal and temporal lobes. The histology is characterised by the presence of argyrophilic cytoplasmic inclusion bodies (Pick bodies) and chromatolytic ballooned neurons (Pick cells) (see Fig. 22.39). Patients may present with personality change due to frontal lobe involvement or with progressive aphasia. Memory is relatively preserved in the early stages. There is no specific treatment for Pick's disease.

Lewy body dementia

In diffuse Lewy body disease, pathology similar to that found in the substantia nigra in Parkinson's disease is found in the cerebral cortex. This condition usually presents as cognitive impairment in the context of an extrapyramidal syndrome, and the cognitive features may be indistinguishable from those of Alzheimer's disease. Patients' cognitive state often fluctuates; they have a high incidence of visual

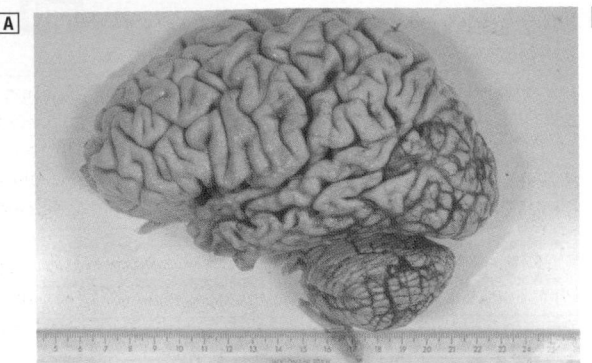
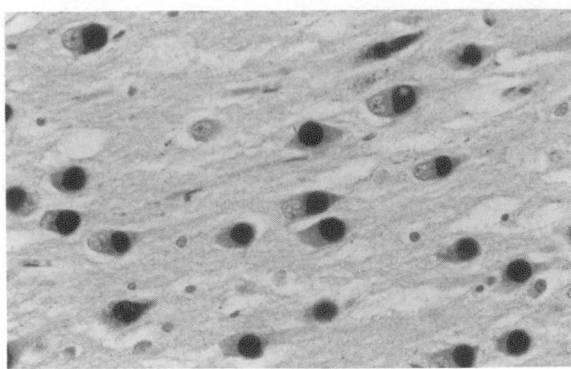

Fig. 22.39 Pick's disease. [A] Lateral view of formalin-fixed brain from a patient who died of Pick's disease showing gyral atrophy of frontal and parietal lobes and a more severe degree of atrophy affecting the anterior half of the temporal lobe. [B] High power (x 200) of hippocampal pyramidal layer, prepared with monoclonal anti-tau antibody. Many neuronal cell bodies contain sharply circumscribed, spherical cytoplasmic inclusion bodies (Pick bodies).

hallucinations, and are particularly sensitive to this side-effect of anti-parkinsonian medication. They are also particularly sensitive to neuroleptic medication. There is no specific treatment for this condition.

PARKINSON'S DISEASE AND AKINETIC-RIGID SYNDROMES

There are a number of degenerative diseases affecting the basal ganglia, which present with differing combinations of slowness of movement (bradykinesia), increased tone (rigidity), tremor and loss of postural reflexes. The most common cause of these parkinsonian or akinetic-rigid syndromes is idiopathic Parkinson's disease.

IDIOPATHIC PARKINSON'S DISEASE

This condition has an annual incidence of about 0.2/1000 and a prevalence of 1.5/1000 in the UK. Prevalence rates are similar throughout the world, though lower rates have been reported for China and West Africa. Whilst 10% of the patients are under 45 years at presentation, the incidence and prevalence both increase with age, the latter rising to over 1% in those over 60. Sex incidence is about equal. It is less common in cigarette smokers.

Aetiology

The cause is unknown, and no strong genetic factors have been identified, though recent work on twins has suggested that the genetic influence may be greater than previously thought. The discovery that methyl-phenyl-tetrahydropyridine (MPTP) caused severe parkinsonism in young drug users suggests that the idiopathic disease might be due to an environmental toxin; many candidate toxins have been studied, but there is no strong evidence in favour of any of them.

Pathology

There is depletion of the pigmented dopaminergic neurons in the substantia nigra, hyaline inclusions in nigral cells

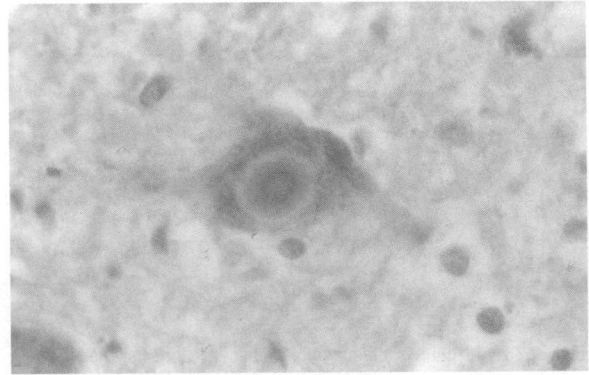

Fig. 22.40 Parkinson's disease. High power (x 400) of substantia nigra of a patient with Parkinson's disease to show classical Lewy body (haematoxylin and eosin).

(Lewy bodies—see Fig. 22.40), atrophic changes in the substantia nigra and depletion of neurons in the locus coeruleus. Reduced dopaminergic output from the substantia nigra to the globus pallidus leads to reduced inhibitory effects on the subthalamic nucleus, neurons which become more active than usual in inhibiting activation of the cortex. This in turn results in bradykinesia.

Clinical features

The classical syndrome of tremor, rigidity and bradykinesia may be absent initially, when non-specific symptoms of tiredness, aching limbs, mental slowness, depression (see p. 251) and small handwriting (micrographia) may be noticed.

The presentation is almost always unilateral, a rest tremor in an upper limb being a common presenting feature. The tremor may also affect the legs, mouth and tongue. It may remain the predominant symptom for some years. Bradykinesia may develop gradually. Most patients have difficulty with rapid fine movements, and this manifests itself as slowness of gait and difficulty with tasks such as fastening buttons, shaving or writing. Rigidity, or increased muscular tone, causes stiffness and a flexed posture. Postural righting reflexes are impaired early on in the disease,

22.64 PHYSICAL ABNORMALITIES IN PARKINSONISM

General

- Expressionless face
- Greasy skin
- Soft, rapid, indistinct speech
- Flexed posture
- Impaired postural reflexes

Gait

- Slow to start walking
- Shortened stride
- Rapid, small steps, tendency to run (festination)
- Reduced arm swing
- Impaired balance on turning

Tremor

- Resting 4–6 Hz
  Usually first in fingers/thumb
  Coarse, complex movements, flexion/extension of fingers
  Abduction/adduction of thumb
  Supination/pronation of forearm
  May affect arms, legs, feet, jaw, tongue
  Intermittent, present at rest and when distracted
  Diminished on action
- Postural 8–10 Hz
  Less obvious, faster, finer amplitude
  Present on action or posture, persists with movement

Rigidity

- Cogwheel type, mostly upper limbs
- Plastic (leadpipe) type, mostly legs

Bradykinesia

- Slowness in initiating or repeating movements
- Impaired fine movements, especially of fingers

---

but falls tend not to occur until later on. As the disease advances, speech becomes softer and indistinct. There are a number of abnormalities on neurological examination, and these are listed in Box 22.64.

Although parkinsonian features are initially unilateral, gradual bilateral involvement is the rule. Muscle strength and reflexes remain normal, and plantar responses are flexor. There is a paucity of facial expression (hypomimia) and the blink reflex may be exaggerated and fail to habituate (glabellar tap sign). Eye movements are normal to standard clinical testing, provided one allows for the normal limitation of upward gaze with age. Sensation is normal and intellectual faculties are not affected initially. As the disease progresses, about one-third of patients develop cognitive impairment.

Investigations

The diagnosis is made clinically, as there is no diagnostic test for Parkinson's disease. Sometimes it is necessary to investigate patients to exclude other causes of parkinsonism if there are any unusual features. Patients presenting before the age of 50 are usually tested for Wilson's disease, and imaging (CT or MRI) of the head may be needed if there are any features suggestive of pyramidal, cerebellar or autonomic involvement, or the diagnosis is otherwise in doubt.

Management

Drug therapy

Levodopa combined with a peripheral-acting dopa-decarboxylase inhibitor provides the mainstay of treatment in Parkinson's disease but should only be started to help overcome significant disability. Other agents include anti-cholinergic drugs, dopamine receptor agonists, selegiline and amantadine (see Fig. 22.41).

Levodopa. Although the number of dopamine-releasing terminals in the striatum is diminished in Parkinson's disease, remaining neurons can be driven to produce more dopamine by administering its precursor, levodopa. If levodopa is administered orally, however, more than 90% is decarboxylated to dopamine peripherally in the gastrointestinal tract and blood vessels, and only a small proportion reaches the brain. This peripheral conversion of levodopa is responsible for the high incidence of side-effects if used alone. The problem is largely overcome by giving a decarboxylase inhibitor that does not cross the blood–brain barrier along with the levodopa. Two peripheral decarboxylase inhibitors, carbidopa and benserazide, are available as combination preparations with levodopa.

The initiation of levodopa therapy should be delayed until there is significant disability, since there is concern regarding long-term side-effects (see EBM panel). Levodopa is particularly effective at improving bradykinesia and rigidity. Tremor is also helped but rather unpredictably. The initial dose is 50 mg 8- or 12-hourly, increased if necessary. The total levodopa dose may be increased to over 1000 mg/day, but should be kept as low as possible. Side-effects include postural hypotension and nausea and vomiting, which may be offset by the use of a peripheral dopamine antagonist such as domperidone. Other dose-related side-effects are involuntary movements, particularly orofacial dyskinesias, limb and axial dystonias, and occasionally depression, hallucinations and delusions.

EBM

PARKINSON'S DISEASE—delaying treatment with levodopa by the use of bromocriptine

'The early use of bromocriptine instead of levodopa may be beneficial in delaying motor complications and dyskinesias but methodological differences between trials mean that it is not possible to reach a clear conclusion at this point.'

- Ramaker C, Hilten JJ van. Bromocriptine versus levodopa in early Parkinson's disease (Cochrane Review). Cochrane Library, issue 4, 2000. Oxford: Update Software.
- Hilten JJ van, Ramaker C, Beek WJT van de, Finken MJJ. Bromocriptine for levodopa-induced motor complications in Parkinson's disease (Cochrane Review). Cochrane Library, issue 4, 2000. Oxford: Update Software.

Further information: 🖥 www.cochrane.co.uk

Late deterioration despite levodopa therapy occurs after 3–5 years in one-third to one-half of patients. Usually this manifests as fluctuation in response. The simplest form of this is end-of-dose deterioration due to progression of the disease and loss of capacity to store dopamine. More complex fluctuations present as sudden, unpredictable changes in response, in which periods of severe parkinsonism alternate with dyskinesia and agitation (the 'on-off' phenomenon). End-of-dose deterioration can often be improved by

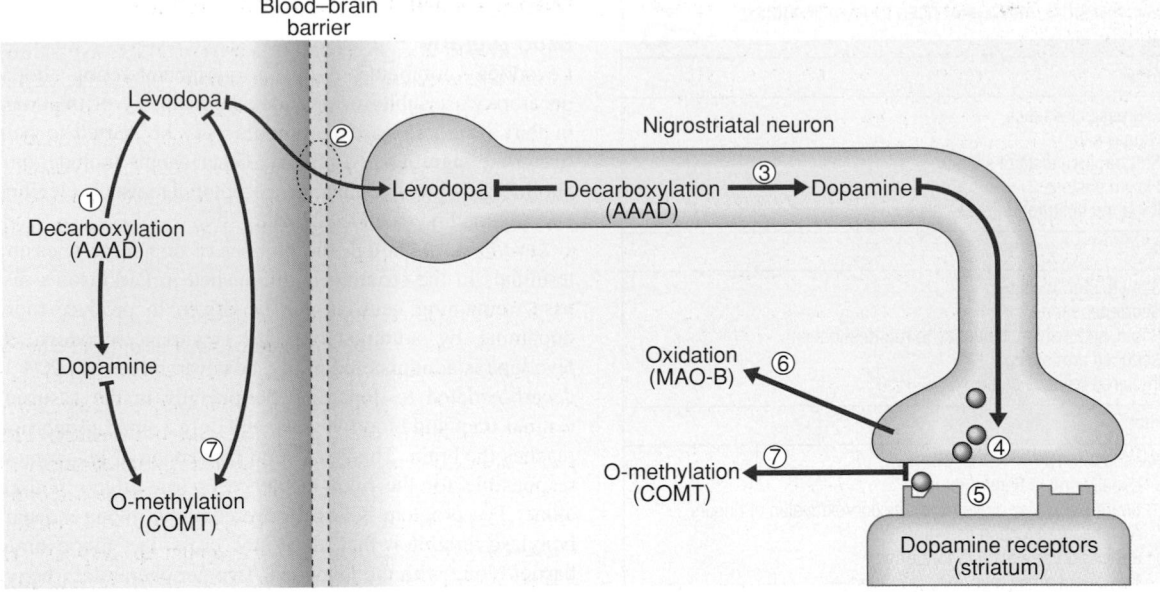

Fig. 22.41 Mechanisms of drug action in Parkinson's disease. (1) Decarboxylase inhibitors (carbidopa and benserazide) reduce side-effects by reducing peripheral conversion of levodopa to dopamine by aromatic amino acid decarboxylase (AAAD). (2) Active transport of levodopa into the brain may be inhibited by competition from dietary amino acids after a high-protein meal. (3) In the nigrostriatal neurons levodopa is converted into dopamine. (4) Amantadine enhances the release of dopamine at the nerve terminal. (5) Dopamine agonists act directly on striatal receptors. (6) The monoamine oxidase type B (MAO-B) inhibitor selegiline increases the availability of neuronal dopamine by reducing its metabolism outside the neuron. (7) The catechol-O-methyl-transferase (COMT) inhibitor entacapone prolongs the availability of dopamine by inhibiting the metabolism of dopamine and levodopa outside the neuron.

dividing the levodopa into smaller but more frequent doses, or by converting to a slow-release preparation. The 'on-off' phenomenon is difficult to treat, but sometimes subcutaneous injections of apomorphine (a dopamine agonist) are helpful to 'rescue' the patient rapidly from an 'off' period.

Involuntary movements (dyskinesia) may occur as a peak-dose phenomenon, or as a biphasic phenomenon (occurring during both the build-up and wearing-off phases). Management is difficult, but again involves modifying the way levodopa is administered to obtain constant levels in the brain, and the use of alternative drugs, particularly dopamine agonists.

Anticholinergic agents. These have a useful effect on tremor and rigidity, but do not help bradykinesia. They can be prescribed early in the disease before bradykinesia is a problem, but should be avoided in elderly patients in whom they cause confusion and hallucinations. Other side-effects include dry mouth, blurred vision, difficulty with micturition and constipation. Many anticholinergics are available— for example, trihexyphenidyl (benzhexol; 1–4 mg 8-hourly) and orphenadrine (50–100 mg 8-hourly).

Amantadine. This has a mild, usually short-lived effect on bradykinesia, but may be used early in the disease before more potent treatment is needed. Amantadine is also useful in controlling the dyskinesias produced by dopaminergic treatment later in the disease. The dose is 100 mg 8- or 12-hourly. Side-effects include livedo reticularis, peripheral oedema, confusion and seizures.

Selegiline. Selegiline has a mild therapeutic effect in its own right. Evidence that it slows the progression of the disease is highly controversial. There has been some doubt as to its safety, but this is also controversial and the subject of ongoing research. The usual dose is 5–10 mg in the morning.

COMT (catechol-O-methyl-transferase) inhibitors. Entacapone (200 mg with each dose of levodopa) reduces motor fluctuations when used with levodopa. This allows the levodopa dose to be reduced and given less frequently.

Dopamine receptor agonists. An increasing number of these drugs is becoming available. They all have slightly different activity at the various dopamine receptors in the brain. Apomorphine given alone causes marked vomiting and has to be administered parenterally. The vomiting can be overcome by the concomitant use of domperidone, and parenteral administration achieved through continuous subcutaneous infusion from a portable pump, or direct injection as needed. Dealing with the drug thus requires considerable nursing support but, used correctly, it can be very useful.

More easily administered drugs include bromocriptine, lisuride, pergolide, cabergoline, ropinirole and pramipexole, which can all be taken orally (see EBM panel). These drugs are less powerful than levodopa in controlling features of parkinsonism, but they are much less likely to cause dose fluctuations or dyskinesia, though they will certainly exacerbate the latter once these have developed. Side-effects include nausea, vomiting, confusion and hallucinations. The dose of bromocriptine is 1 mg initially, increased to 2.5 mg

8-hourly, and thereafter up to 30 mg/day. Pergolide dose starts at 50 μg, increased to 250 μg 8-hourly, and possibly to 3000 μg/day.

Surgery

Stereotactic thalamotomy can be used to treat tremor, though this is relatively infrequently needed because of the medical treatments available. Other stereotactic lesions are currently undergoing evaluation, in particular pallidotomy to help in the management of drug-induced dyskinesia. The implantation of fetal mid-brain cells into the basal ganglia to enhance dopaminergic activity remains experimental.

Physiotherapy and speech therapy

Patients at all stages of Parkinson's disease benefit from physiotherapy, which helps reduce rigidity and corrects abnormal posture. Speech therapy may help in cases where dysarthria and dysphonia interfere with communication.

Prognosis

The outlook for patients with Parkinson's disease is variable, and depends partly on the age of onset. If symptoms start in middle life, the disease is usually slowly progressive and likely to shorten lifespan because of the complications of immobility and tendency to fall. Onset after 70 is unlikely to shorten life or become severe.

ISSUES IN OLDER PEOPLE
PARKINSON'S DISEASE

- Parkinson's disease is increasingly common in the elderly.
- The long-term side-effects of levodopa, such as dyskinesia, are less of a problem in patients whose disease starts after age 70. It is therefore reasonable to prescribe levodopa as the first-line agent in this situation as opposed to a dopamine agonist in a younger patient.
- The side-effects of medications are much more common, particularly confusion and hallucinations. Anticholinergic medication is especially bad in this respect.
- Older people are more likely to develop autonomic disturbances, especially medication-induced postural hypotension and bladder instability.
- Cognitive changes and dementia are more common in older than in younger people with Parkinson's disease.
- Prognosis is somewhat better in those developing the disease above age 70.

OTHER AKINETIC-RIGID SYNDROMES

There are several degenerative conditions that can mimic idiopathic Parkinson's disease, particularly in the early stages. These conditions are relatively uncommon, but about 10% of those thought to have idiopathic Parkinson's disease have one of these variants. The variants are notable in causing a more rapid clinical deterioration than idiopathic Parkinson's disease and in being more resistant to treatment with dopaminergic medication.

Multiple systems atrophy (MSA)

This is a sporadic condition seen in middle-aged and elderly patients. Features of parkinsonism, often without tremor, are combined with varying degrees of autonomic failure, cerebellar involvement and pyramidal tract dysfunction. The combination of parkinsonism with autonomic failure was called the Shy–Drager syndrome, but this term is declining in use. Degeneration is more widespread than in idiopathic Parkinson's disease, and the disappointing response to levodopa and other anti-parkinsonian drugs is probably because of degeneration of post-synaptic neurons in the basal ganglia. Autonomic features include postural hypotension, sphincter disturbance and sometimes respiratory stridor; diagnosis is often assisted by performing tests of autonomic function. Management of postural hypotension includes physical measures such as head-up sleeping position and compressive stockings, and drugs such as fludrocortisone and adrenergic stimulants. Falls are much more common than in idiopathic Parkinson's disease, and life expectancy is considerably reduced.

Progressive supranuclear palsy

Like MSA, this sporadic condition presents in middle-aged patients, and is due to more widespread degeneration in the brain than is seen in idiopathic Parkinson's disease. The clinical features include parkinsonism, though with rigidity in extension rather than flexion, and tremor is usually minimal. In addition, there must be a supranuclear paralysis of eye movements, usually downgaze, for the diagnosis to be made. Other features include pyramidal signs and cognitive impairment (see Box 22.37, p. 1146).

WILSON'S DISEASE

This is an inherited disorder transmitted in an autosomal recessive manner, involving a defect of copper metabolism. It is discussed on page 871. It is a treatable cause of various movement disorders, including ataxia and akinetic rigid syndromes, and so must always be considered in the differential diagnosis of these disorders.

HUNTINGTON'S DISEASE

This is an inherited disorder with autosomal dominant transmission, affecting both males and females, and usually starting

in adult life. It is due to expansion of a trinucleotide repeat on chromosome 4 (see p. 346) and frequently demonstrates anticipation, i.e. a younger age of onset in subsequent generations. Slightly different features of the disease occur, depending on whether the abnormal gene is inherited from father or mother.

Clinical features

Symptoms usually begin in middle adult life with the development of chorea, which gradually worsens. This is accompanied by cognitive impairment which often manifests initially as psychiatric symptoms, but later becomes frank dementia. In juvenile-onset disease, there may be parkinsonian features with rigidity. Seizures may occur late in the disease.

Investigations

The diagnosis is made clinically but is supported by the finding of atrophy of the caudate nucleus on CT or MRI. DNA analysis can be used to confirm the diagnosis and provide pre-symptomatic testing after appropriate counselling.

Management

At present this is symptomatic only. The chorea may respond to tetrabenazine or dopamine antagonists such as sulpiride. Long-term psychological support and eventually institutional care are often needed as dementia progresses. Depressive symptoms are common, and may be helped by antidepressant medication. Genetic counselling of relatives is important.

HEREDITARY ATAXIAS

This is a group of inherited disorders in which degenerative changes occur to varying extents in the cerebellum, brain stem, pyramidal tracts, spinocerebellar tracts, optic and peripheral nerves. Onset may be in childhood or early adult life, and different disorders demonstrate recessive or dominant inheritance. Recently, the genetic abnormalities responsible for a few types of spinocerebellar ataxia (types 1–8) have been shown to be due to abnormal numbers of trinucleotide repeats in various genes, and these can now be detected by DNA analysis, allowing diagnostic confirmation, pre-diagnostic testing and genetic counselling. Clinically,

various combinations of cerebellar, pyramidal, sensory, extrapyramidal and cognitive features may occur. Patterns of involvement of several conditions are given in Box 22.65.

MOTOR NEURON DISEASE

This is a progressive disorder of unknown cause, in which there is degeneration of motor neurons in the spinal cord and cranial nerve nuclei, and of pyramidal neurons in the motor cortex. About 5% of cases are familial, showing autosomal dominant inheritance. In many such families, the genetic defect lies on chromosome 21, the enzyme involved being a superoxide dismutase (SOD1). For the remaining 95%, possible causes include viral infection, trauma, exposure to toxins and electric shock, but no sound evidence exists to support any of these. The prevalence of the disease is about 5/100 000.

Clinical features

Patients present with a combination of lower and upper motor neuron signs without sensory involvement. The presence of brisk reflexes in wasted fasciculating limb muscles is typical. Common presenting features are listed in Boxes 22.66 and 22.67.

Investigations

In many patients the clinical features are highly suggestive but alternative diagnoses need to be carefully excluded. In particular, potentially treatable disorders such as diabetic amyotrophy, spinal disorders and multifocal motor neuronopathy should be excluded. Electromyography helps to confirm the presence of fasciculation and denervation, and is particularly helpful when pyramidal features predominate. Sensory nerve conduction and motor conduction studies are normal but there may be some reduction in amplitude of action potentials due to loss of axons. Spinal imaging and brain scanning may be necessary to exclude focal spinal or cerebral disease. CSF examination is usually normal, though a slight elevation in protein concentration may be found.

Management

The glutamate antagonist, riluzole, has recently been shown to have a small effect in prolonging life expectancy by a

22.65 TYPES OF HEREDITARY ATAXIA			
Type	**Inheritance**	**Onset**	**Clinical features**
Friedreich's ataxia	Autosomal recessive	8–16 years	Ataxia, nystagmus, dysarthria, spasticity, areflexia, proprioceptive impairment, diabetes mellitus, optic atrophy, cardiac abnormalities. Usually chairbound by age 20
Ataxia telangiectasia	Autosomal recessive	Childhood	Progressive ataxia, athetosis, telangiectasia on conjunctivae, impaired DNA repair, immunodeficiency, tendency to malignancies
Olivopontocerebellar atrophy	Autosomal dominant	Adult life	Slowly progressive ataxia, spasticity, dysarthria, extrapyramidal features, optic atrophy, deafness, pyramidal signs
Hereditary spastic paraplegia	Autosomal dominant	Adult life	Slowly progressive spasticity affecting legs > arms, extensor plantar responses, sensory signs minimal or absent

22.66	CLINICAL FEATURES OF MOTOR NEURON DISEASE

Onset

- Usually after the age of 50 years
- Very uncommon before the age of 30 years
- Affects males more commonly than females

Symptoms

- Limb muscle weakness, cramps, occasionally fasciculation
- Disturbance of speech/swallowing (dysarthria/dysphagia)

Signs

- Wasting and fasciculation of muscles
- Weakness of muscles of limbs, tongue, face and palate
- Pyramidal tract involvement causes spasticity, exaggerated tendon reflexes, extensor plantar responses
- External ocular muscles and sphincters usually remain intact
- No objective sensory deficit
- No intellectual impairment in most cases

Course

- Symptoms often begin focally in one part and spread gradually but relentlessly to become widespread

22.67	PATTERNS OF INVOLVEMENT OF MOTOR NEURON DISEASE

Progressive muscular atrophy

- Predominantly spinal motor neurons affected
- Weakness and wasting of distal limb muscles at first
- Fasciculation in muscles
- Tendon reflexes may be absent

Progressive bulbar palsy

- Early involvement of tongue, palate and pharyngeal muscles
- Dysarthria/dysphagia
- Wasting and fasciculation of tongue
- May be pyramidal signs as well

Amyotrophic lateral sclerosis

- Combination of distal and proximal muscle-wasting and weakness, fasciculation
- Spasticity, exaggerated reflexes, extensor plantars
- Bulbar and pseudobulbar palsy follow eventually
- Pyramidal tract features may predominate

mean of 3 months (see EBM panel). It is not clear at which stage of the illness this prolongation occurs, and therefore it may not be particularly helpful. Other agents such as nerve

growth factor show promise. Psychological and physical support, with help from occupational and speech therapists and physiotherapists, is essential to keep the patient's quality of life as good as possible. Mechanical aids such as splints, walking aids, wheelchairs and communication devices all help to reduce handicap. Feeding by percutaneous gastrostomy may be necessary if bulbar palsy is marked. Sometimes non-invasive ventilatory support may help distress from weak respiratory muscles although maintenance ventilation is usually not requested. Relief of distress in the terminal stages usually requires the use of opiates and sedative drugs.

MOTOR NEURON DISEASE—role of riluzole	**EBM**

'Riluzole 100 mg per day appears to be modestly effective in prolonging survival for patients with motor neuron disease. However, the economics of its use have yet to be fully assessed.'

- Miller RG, Mitchell JD, Moore DH. Riluzole for amyotrophic lateral sclerosis (ALS)/motor neuron disease (MND) (Cochrane Review). Cochrane Library, issue 4, 2000. Oxford: Update Software.

Further information: 🖥 www.cochrane.co.uk

Prognosis

Motor neuron disease is progressive; the mean time from diagnosis to death is 1 year, with most patients dying within 3–5 years of the onset of symptoms. Younger patients and those with early bulbar symptoms tend to show a more rapid course. Death is usually from respiratory infection and failure, and the complications of immobility.

SPINAL MUSCULAR ATROPHIES

This is a group of genetically determined disorders affecting spinal motor and cranial motor neurons, characterised by proximal and distal wasting, fasciculation and weakness of muscles. Involvement is usually symmetrical but occasional localised forms occur. With the exception of the infantile form, progression is slow and the prognosis better than for motor neuron disease (see Box 22.68).

22.68 TYPES OF SPINAL MUSCULAR ATROPHY				
Type	**Onset**	**Inheritance**	**Features**	**Prognosis**
Werdnig–Hoffmann	Infancy	Autosomal recessive	Severe muscle-wasting/weakness	Poor
Kugelberg–Welander	Childhood, adolescence	Autosomal recessive	Proximal weakness and wasting, EMG shows denervation	Slowly progressive disability
Distal forms	Early adult life	Autosomal dominant	Distal weakness and wasting of hands and feet	Good, seldom disabling
Bulbospinal	Adult life, males only	X-linked	Facial and bulbar weakness, proximal limb weakness, gynaecomastia	Good

DISEASES OF NERVE AND MUSCLE

DISEASES OF PERIPHERAL NERVES

Peripheral nerves may be damaged by diffuse processes affecting all nerves to a greater or lesser extent, or individual nerves may be affected by local pathology including trauma, compression and entrapment. Alternatively, several individual nerves may be affected by multifocal pathology (mononeuritis multiplex), or there may be focal pathology in nerve plexuses.

ACQUIRED PERIPHERAL NEUROPATHIES

There are numerous causes of peripheral neuropathy (see Box 22.69). The diagnostic possibilities are limited in an individual patient by the clinical features (motor, sensory, autonomic or mixed) and by whether axons or myelin are predominantly affected (determined electrophysiologically).

Clinical features

The first manifestations are usually at the distal ends of the longest nerves. Distal paraesthesia is a frequent symptom, usually first affecting the feet and then the hands, and subsequently progressing proximally up the limbs. This is often associated with diminution of superficial sensation in a 'glove and stocking' distribution (see Fig. 22.15A, p. 1141). There may be distal weakness, usually with diminished or absent tendon reflexes, and possibly autonomic disturbance. In hereditary neuropathies there may be a positive family history.

Investigations

A careful clinical history is essential, including details of family history, drug intake and potential exposure to toxins.

Screening tests are listed in Box 22.70. Nerve conduction studies confirm the presence of a neuropathy and indicate whether axons or myelin are primarily affected. In some cases, nerve biopsy may be indicated, particularly if an inflammatory aetiology is suspected.

Management

In about one-third of patients, a treatable cause is identified. Toxins and offending drugs should be removed and metabolic abnormalities or deficiency states corrected. Inflammatory neuropathies can often be treated with immunosuppressive agents or intravenous immunoglobulin. However, in many patients (about another third) a cause is identified for which there is no specific treatment and in the remainder no specific cause is found. Particularly if there is no specific therapy available (e.g. hereditary neuropathies), advice from physiotherapists and occupational therapists is important in helping patients to maintain their functional capacity. Carbamazepine and gabapentin can be helpful in relieving pain, particularly in neuropathy due to diabetes mellitus.

GUILLAIN–BARRÉ SYNDROME

Also known as acute inflammatory or post-infective demyelinating polyneuropathy, this develops 1–4 weeks after respiratory infection or diarrhoea in 70% of patients, but can follow surgery or immunisation. Pathologically, there is demyelination of spinal roots or peripheral nerves, which is immunologically mediated.

Clinical features

The characteristic clinical feature is rapidly progressive muscle weakness, often ascending from lower to upper limbs and more marked proximally than distally. Distal

22.69 CAUSES OF PERIPHERAL NEUROPATHY			
Type	Common	Unusual	Rare
Metabolic/endocrine	Diabetes mellitus Chronic renal failure	Paraproteinaemia Cryoglobulinaemia Amyloidosis Hypothyroidism Liver failure	Porphyria
Toxic	Alcohol	Drugs (e.g. isoniazid, phenytoin, vincristine)	Heavy metals Organic solvents
Inflammatory	Acute (Guillain–Barré syndrome)	Chronic inflammatory demyelinating polyneuropathy Connective tissue disease (e.g. SLE, polyarteritis nodosa, Sjögren's syndrome) Infective (leprosy)	Multifocal motor neuropathy with conduction block
Genetic		Hereditary motor and sensory neuropathies (Charcot–Marie–Tooth) Friedreich's ataxia	Other hereditary neuropathies
Deficiency states		Vitamin B_{12} deficiency Thiamin deficiency	Vitamin A, E deficiency Pyridoxine deficiency
Others		Malignant disease Critical illness neuropathy	

22.70 INVESTIGATION OF PERIPHERAL NEUROPATHY			
	First-line tests	**Second-line tests**	**Occasionally useful tests**
Haematology	Full blood count ESR B_{12} Folate		
Biochemistry	Urea, electrolytes, calcium Creatinine Liver function tests Blood glucose $\pm$ tolerance test/HbA$_{Ic}$ Thyroxine and thyroid-stimulating hormone (TSH) Plasma protein electrophoresis	Serum lipids, lipoproteins Cryoglobulins Toxic metal and drug screen Prostate-specific antigen Urinary porphyrins Urinary Bence Jones protein Faecal occult blood	Vitamin assays (e.g. vitamin E) Phytanic acid (Refsum's disease)
Immunology	VDRL Serum autoantibodies (antinuclear factor, dsDNA, rheumatoid factor, extractable nuclear antigens)	Antiganglioside antibodies Antineuronal antibodies	
Other	Nerve conduction/EMG	Genetic screening tests (e.g. hereditary neuropathies, Friedreich's ataxia) Chest radiography/CT Mammogram Abdominal imaging	Nerve biopsy

paraesthesia and limb pains often precede the weakness. Facial or bulbar weakness commonly develops, and respiratory weakness requiring ventilatory support occurs in 20% of cases. In most patients muscle weakness progresses for 1–3 weeks, but rapid deterioration with respiratory failure can develop within hours. The most striking findings on examination are diffuse weakness with widespread loss of reflexes. An unusual variant described by Miller Fisher comprises the triad of ophthalmoplegia, ataxia and areflexia.

Investigations

The protein content of the CSF is raised at some stage of the illness, but may be normal in the first 10 days. There is usually no rise in CSF cell number and a lymphocytosis > 50/mm^3 suggests an alternative diagnosis. Electrophysiological studies are often normal in the early stages, but show typical changes after a week or so, with multifocal motor slowing and proximal slowing. Investigation to identify an underlying cause, such as cytomegalovirus, mycoplasma or campylobacter, requires a chest radiograph, stool culture and appropriate immunological blood tests. Antibodies to the ganglioside GQ$_{1b}$ are found in the Miller Fisher variant described above. Acute porphyria (see p. 325) can be excluded by urinary porphyrin estimation, and serum lead should be measured if there are only motor signs.

Management

During the phase of deterioration, regular monitoring of respiratory function (vital capacity and blood gases) is required, as respiratory failure may develop with little warning and require ventilatory support. If the vital capacity falls below 1 litre, help from anaesthetists should be sought as ventilation may be required. Intubation and ventilation are often required because of bulbar incompetence leading to aspiration. General management to protect the airway and prevent pressure sores and venous thrombosis is essential. Steroid therapy is ineffective, but plasma exchange and intravenous immunoglobulin therapy shorten the duration of ventilation and improve prognosis, provided treatment is started within 14 days of the onset of symptoms (see EBM panels).

EBM

GUILLAIN–BARRÉ SYNDROME—role of corticosteroids

'Corticosteroids are ineffective and should not be used in the treatment of Guillain–Barré syndrome itself, though if a patient with Guillain–Barré syndrome needs corticosteroid treatment for some other reason its use will probably not do harm.'

- Hughes RAC, van der Meché FGA. Corticosteroids for treating Guillain–Barré syndrome (Cochrane Review). Cochrane Library, issue 4, 2000. Oxford: Update Software.
- Guillain–Barré Syndrome Steroid Trial Group. Double-blind trial of intravenous methylprednisolone in Guillain–Barré syndrome. Lancet 1993; 3341:586–590.

Further information: www.cochrane.co.uk

EBM

GUILLAIN–BARRÉ SYNDROME—role of intravenous immunoglobulin (IVIg) and plasma exchange (PE)

'If used within the first 2 weeks of developing the illness, IVIg and PE are equally efficient in reducing the severity and duration of Guillain–Barré syndrome, but there is no advantage in combining the two treatments.'

- Plasma Exchange/Sandoglobulin Guillain–Barré Syndrome Trial Group. Randomised trial of plasma exchange, intravenous immunoglobulin, and combined treatments in Guillain–Barré syndrome. Lancet 1997; 349:225–230.
- Bril V, Ilse WK, Pearce R, et al. Pilot trial of immunoglobulin versus plasma exchange in patients with Guillain–Barré syndrome. Neurology 1996; 46:100–103.

Further information: www.cochrane.co.uk

Prognosis

Overall, 80% of patients recover completely within 3–6 months, 4% die, and the remainder suffer residual neurological disability which can be severe.

ENTRAPMENT NEUROPATHIES

These conditions often have a characteristic clinical history and physical signs (see Box 22.71).

Management

Lateral popliteal nerve palsies and radial nerve palsies are commonly due to local compression, and complete recovery over 6–8 weeks can be expected without intervention. Meralgia paraesthetica often develops in relation to weight loss or gain, and may respond to dietary advice and reassurance. Carpal tunnel syndrome and ulnar nerve palsy may remit if patients avoid activities involving repetitive wrist movement or pressure on the elbows, and may respond to nocturnal splinting of joints. Precipitating causes including diabetes mellitus and hypothyroidism should be excluded. In some patients surgical decompression of the carpal tunnel or transposition of the ulnar nerve may be necessary. Electrophysiological investigation is advisable pre-operatively to confirm both diagnosis and site of compression.

MONONEURITIS MULTIPLEX

In this condition, multifocal peripheral or spinal nerve lesions occur serially or concurrently. Pathologically, the nerves are rendered susceptible to mechanical compression by ischaemia of the peripheral nerves due to vasculopathy of the vasa nervorum or infiltration of the nerves. Common causes are diabetes mellitus, leprosy, polyarteritis nodosa and rheumatoid arthritis.

BRACHIAL PLEXUS LESIONS

Trauma is the most common cause of damage to the brachial plexus, and frequently involves traction between the head and shoulder, or excessive abduction of the arm. Other causes include neoplasia in the cervical lymph nodes or pulmonary apex, compression at the thoracic outlet, radiotherapy and inflammatory/vascular disease (e.g. neuralgic amyotrophy—see below).

Clinical features

The clinical signs depend on the anatomical site of damage (see Box 22.72). There may be associated vascular symptoms and signs in the thoracic outlet syndrome.

Neuralgic amyotrophy presents with severe pain over one shoulder and sometimes follows infection, inoculation or operation. Within days, paralysis develops in the painful

---

22.71 SYMPTOMS AND SIGNS IN COMMON ENTRAPMENT NEUROPATHIES

Nerve	Symptoms	Muscle weakness/muscle-wasting	Area of sensory loss
Median (at wrist) (carpal tunnel syndrome)	Pain and paraesthesia on palmar aspect of hands and fingers, waking the patient from sleep. Pain may extend to arm and shoulder	Abductor pollicis brevis	Lateral palm and thumb, index, middle and half ring finger
Ulnar (at elbow)	Paraesthesia on medial border of hand, wasting and weakness of hand muscles	All small hand muscles, excluding abductor pollicis brevis	Medial palm and little finger, and half ring finger
Radial	Weakness of extension of wrist and fingers, often precipitated by sleeping in abnormal posture, e.g. arm over back of chair	Wrist and finger extensors, supinator	Dorsum of thumb
Peroneal	Foot drop, trauma to head of fibula	Dorsiflexion and eversion of foot	Nil or dorsum of foot
Lateral cutaneous nerve of the thigh (meralgia paraesthetica)	Tingling and dysaesthesia on lateral border of the thigh	Nil	Lateral border of thigh

---

22.72 PHYSICAL SIGNS IN BRACHIAL PLEXUS LESIONS

Site	Root	Affected muscles	Sensory loss
Upper plexus (Erb–Duchenne)	C5/6	Biceps, deltoid, spinati, rhomboids, brachioradialis (triceps, serratus anterior)	Patch over deltoid
Lower plexus (Dejerine–Klumpke)	C8/T1	All small hand muscles, claw hand (ulnar wrist flexors)	Ulnar border hand/forearm
Thoracic outlet syndrome	C8/T1	Small hand muscles, ulnar forearm	Ulnar border hand/forearm/upper arm

muscles (most commonly deltoid, spinati and serratus anterior), and is rapidly followed by muscle-wasting. Occasionally, there is more extensive involvement of the muscles of the upper arm and there may be sensory loss over the deltoid. Pain usually subsides within 1–2 weeks and complete recovery of paralysis and wasting can be expected in 3–6 months without treatment.

Management

Surgical treatment may be indicated for congenital anomalies such as cervical rib or for traumatic lesions where grafts of nerve or muscle may aid regeneration. In this situation, regular passive movements of the affected limb prevent contractures while nerve fibres are regenerating. The prognosis for recovery in traumatic lesions is dependent on the site and severity of neuronal damage, which may be assessed electrophysiologically.

DISEASES AFFECTING THE CRANIAL NERVES

Cranial nerves may be affected as part of a generalised peripheral neuropathy, but are often involved singly or in groups by intracranial disease. Intracranial disease such as cerebral tumour may involve a cranial nerve directly (e.g. acoustic neuroma, see p. 1206), or may cause secondary dysfunction by stretching or compressing it against other structures (e.g. 3rd nerve palsy due to tentorial herniation of the medial temporal lobe). Diseases of most of the individual cranial nerves have already been discussed elsewhere (see pp. 1150–1157).

IDIOPATHIC FACIAL NERVE PALSY (BELL'S PALSY)

This is a common condition affecting all ages and both sexes. The cause is unknown, but the site of damage is probably the portion of the facial nerve lying within the facial canal. Recent evidence suggests that Bell's palsy may be due to reactivation of latent herpes simplex virus-1 infection since HSV-1 virus genome has been identified in facial nerve endoneural fluid and in saliva of patients with Bell's palsy. The onset is subacute, with symptoms usually developing over a few hours. Pain around the ear may precede loss of movement on one side of the face, initially noticed either by the patient or by family. Patients may describe the face as being numb, but there is no objective loss of sensation (except possibly taste, due to involvement of the chorda tympani). Hyperacusis occurs if the nerve to stapedius is involved, and there may also be loss of salivation and tear secretion.

Examination reveals only a lower motor neuron facial nerve palsy on one side. Vesicles in the ear or on the palate indicate that the facial palsy is due to herpes zoster infection rather than Bell's palsy (see p. 1199). A reduction in the amplitude of the facial muscle action potential on EMG after the first week predicts a slow/poor recovery.

There is no proven medical treatment, though a course of steroids such as prednisolone 40–60 mg daily for a week may speed recovery, and the use of aciclovir has been suggested (see EBM panel). To prevent exposure of the cornea, artificial teardrops and ointment are applied to the eye, and the eye is taped shut overnight. About 70–80% of patients recover spontaneously within 2–12 weeks, but elderly patients with complete facial palsy have a poorer prognosis. Aberrant re-innervation may occur during the course of recovery, giving rise to unwanted facial movements (e.g. eye closure when the mouth is moved) or 'crocodile tears' (tearing during salivation).

EBM

BELL'S PALSY—role of aciclovir

'RCTs have shown that aciclovir alone is not as effective as corticosteroids in the treatment of Bell's palsy, but the combination of aciclovir and prednisolone appears to be more effective than steroids alone.'

- De Diego JI, Prim MP, De Sarria MJ, et al. Idiopathic facial paralysis: a randomized, prospective, and controlled study using single-dose prednisone versus acyclovir three times daily. Laryngoscope 1998; 108:573–575.
- Adour KK, Ruboyianes JM, Von Doersten PG, et al. Bell's palsy treatment with acyclovir and prednisone compared with prednisone alone: a double-blind, randomized, controlled trial. Ann Otol Rhinol Laryngol 1996; 105:371–378.

Further information: 💻 www.cochrane.co.uk

CLONIC FACIAL (HEMIFACIAL) SPASM

This disorder usually presents after middle age. Symptoms start with intermittent twitching around one eye, which spreads ipsilaterally over months to years to affect other parts of the face. The spasms of twitching are intermittent, often exacerbated by talking or eating, or when the patient is under stress. The cause is thought to be an aberrant loop of artery irritating the facial nerve as it emerges from the pons. It is important to image the facial nerve to exclude a structural lesion, especially in a young patient. Drug treatment is not effective, but injections of botulinum toxin into affected muscles can help, although these usually have to be repeated every 3 months or so. Occasionally, microvascular decompression is necessary, but this involves a posterior craniotomy.

DISORDERS OF THE NEUROMUSCULAR JUNCTION

MYASTHENIA GRAVIS

This condition is characterised by progressive inability to sustain a maintained or repeated contraction of striated muscle (fatigability).

Aetiology and pathology

Acetylcholine receptors in the post-junctional membrane of neuromuscular junctions are blocked or lysed by a complement-mediated autoimmune reaction between receptor protein and anti-acetylcholine receptor antibody (see Fig. 22.42). About 15% of patients (mainly those with late

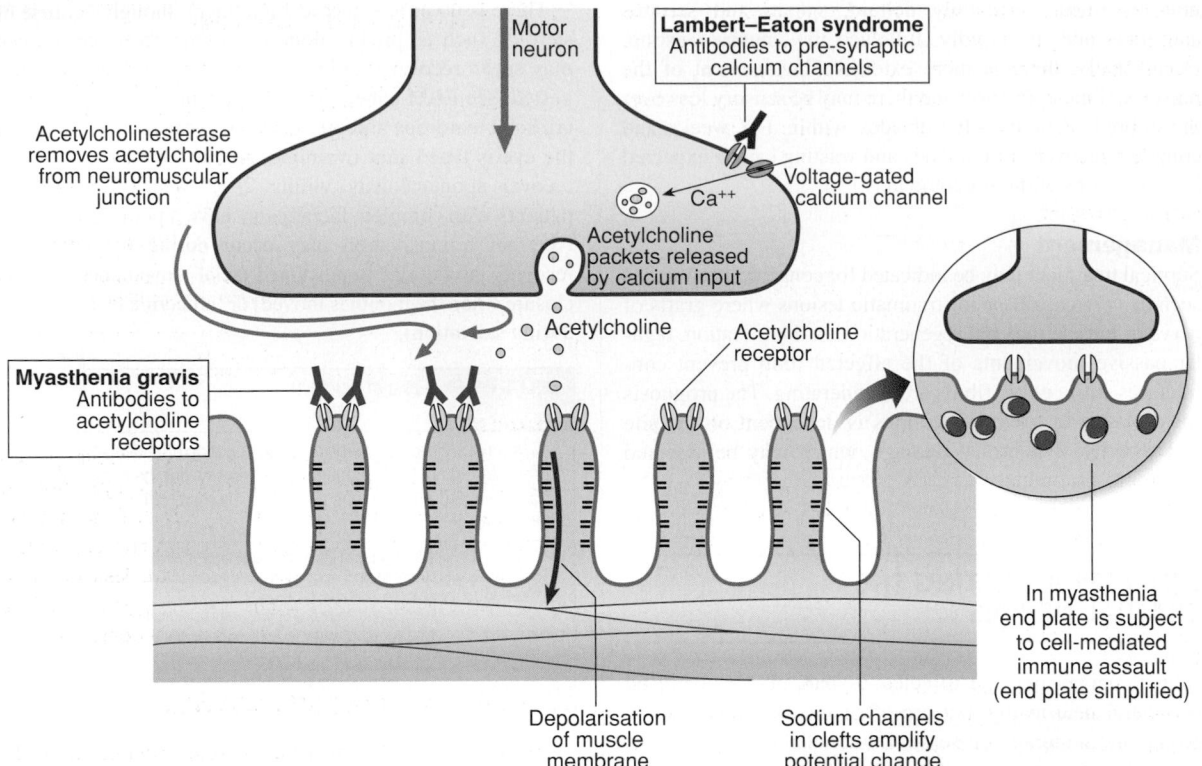

Fig. 22.42 **Myasthenia gravis and Lambert–Eaton myasthenic syndrome (LEMS).** In myasthenia there are antibodies to the acetylcholine receptors on the post-synaptic membrane which block conduction across the neuromuscular junction (NMJ). Myasthenic symptoms can be transiently improved by inhibition of acetylcholinesterase (e.g. with Tensilon—edrophonium bromide) which normally removes the acetylcholine. A cell-mediated immune response produces simplification of the post-synaptic membrane, further impairing the 'safety factor' of neuromuscular conduction. In LEMS, antibodies to the pre-synaptic voltage calcium channels impair release of acetylcholine from the motor nerve ending; calcium is required for the acetylcholine-containing vesicle to fuse with the pre-synaptic membrane for release into the NMJ.

onset) have a thymoma, and the majority of the remainder have one of a number of thymic abnormalities, the most characteristic of which is thymic hyperplasia. There is an increased incidence of other autoimmune diseases, and the disease is linked with certain HLA haplotypes, the strongest associations in a north European population being with B8 and DRw3. Nothing is known about factors which trigger the disease itself, but penicillamine can cause an antibody-mediated myasthenic syndrome which may persist even after drug withdrawal. Some drugs, especially aminoglycosides and ciprofloxacin, may exacerbate the neuromuscular blockade and should be avoided in patients with myasthenia.

Clinical features

The disease usually presents between the ages of 15 and 50 years, with women affected more often than men. It tends to run a relapsing and remitting course, especially during the early years.

The cardinal symptom is abnormal fatigable weakness of the muscles (which is different from a sensation of muscle fatigue). Although movement is initially strong, it rapidly weakens. Worsening of symptoms towards the end of the day or following exercise is characteristic. There are no sensory signs or signs of involvement of the central nervous system although weakness of the oculomotor muscles may mimic a central eye movement disorder.

The first symptoms are usually intermittent ptosis or diplopia, but weakness of chewing, swallowing, speaking or limb movement also occurs. Any limb muscle may be affected, most commonly those of the shoulder girdle; the patient is unable to undertake work above shoulder level, such as combing hair, without frequent rests. Respiratory muscles may be involved, and respiratory failure is a not uncommon cause of death. Aspiration may occur if the cough is ineffectual. Sudden weakness from a cholinergic or myasthenic crisis (see below) may require ventilatory support.

Investigations

The intravenous injection of the short-acting anti-cholinesterase, edrophonium bromide, is a valuable diagnostic aid (the Tensilon test); 2 mg is injected initially, with a further 8 mg given half a minute later if there are no undesirable side-effects. Improvement in muscle power occurs within 30 seconds and usually persists for 2–3 minutes. EMG with repetitive stimulation may show the characteristic decremental response. Anti-acetylcholine receptor antibody is found in over 80% of cases, though less frequently in purely ocular myasthenia. Positive antiskeletal muscle antibodies suggest the presence of thymoma but all patients should have a thoracic CT to exclude this condition, which may not be visible on plain radiographic examination. Screening for other autoimmune disorders, particularly thyroid disease, is important.

Management

The principles of treatment are:

- to maximise the activity of acetylcholine at remaining receptors in the neuromuscular junctions
- to limit or abolish the immunological attack on motor end plates.

The duration of action of acetylcholine is greatly prolonged by inhibiting its hydrolysing enzyme, acetylcholinesterase. The most commonly used anticholinesterase drug is pyridostigmine, which is given orally in a dosage of 30–120 mg, usually 6-hourly. Muscarinic side-effects, including diarrhoea and colic, may be controlled by propantheline (15 mg as required). Over-dosage of anticholinesterase drugs may cause a cholinergic crisis due to depolarisation block of motor end plates, with muscle fasciculation, paralysis, pallor, sweating, excessive salivation and small pupils. This may be distinguished from severe weakness due to exacerbation of myasthenia (myasthenic crisis) by the clinical features and, if necessary, by the injection of a small dose of edrophonium.

The immunological treatment of myasthenia is outlined in Box 22.73. Thymectomy in the early stages of the disease leads to a much better overall prognosis, whether a thymoma is present or not.

22.73 IMMUNOLOGICAL TREATMENT OF MYASTHENIA
Thymectomy
• Should be performed as soon as feasible in any antibody-positive patient with symptoms not confined to extraocular muscles, unless the disease has been established for more than 7 years
Plasma exchange
• Removing antibody from the blood may produce marked improvement but, as this is usually brief, such therapy is normally reserved for myasthenic crisis or for pre-operative preparation
Intravenous immunoglobulin
• An alternative to plasma exchange in the treatment of severe myasthenia
Corticosteroid treatment
• Improvement is commonly preceded by marked exacerbation of myasthenic symptoms and treatment should be initiated in hospital
• It is usually necessary to continue treatment for months or years, often resulting in adverse effects
Other immunosuppressant treatment
• Treatment with azathioprine 2.5 mg/kg daily is of value in reducing the dosage of steroids necessary and may allow steroids to be withdrawn
• The effect of treatment on clinical disease is often delayed for several months

MYASTHENIA GRAVIS—role of azathioprine EBM
'Azathioprine as an adjunct to alternate-day prednisolone in the treatment of antibody-positive generalised myasthenia reduces the maintenance dose of prednisolone and is associated with fewer treatment failures, longer remissions and fewer side-effects. However, a small trial suggested that it is probably not useful as an initial immunosuppressive treatment on its own.'
• Palace J, Newsom-Davis J, Lecky B. A randomized double-blind trial of prednisolone alone or with azathioprine in myasthenia gravis. Neurology 1998; 50:1778–1783.   • Bromberg MB, Wald JJ, Forshew DA, et al. Randomized trial of azathioprine or prednisone for initial immunosuppressive treatment of myasthenia gravis. J Neurol Sci 1997; 150:59–62.
Further information: 🖥 www.cochrane.co.uk

Prognosis

Prognosis is variable. Remissions sometimes occur spontaneously. When myasthenia is confined to the eye muscles, the prognosis is excellent and disability slight. Young female patients with generalised disease have high remission rates after thymectomy, whilst older patients are less likely to have a remission despite treatment. Rapid progression of the disease more than 5 years after its onset is uncommon.

OTHER MYASTHENIC SYNDROMES

There are other conditions which present with muscle weakness due to impaired transmission across the neuromuscular junction. The most common of these is the Lambert–Eaton myasthenic syndrome (LEMS), in which transmitter release is impaired, often in association with antibodies to prejunctional voltage-gated calcium channels (see Fig. 22.42). Patients may have autonomic dysfunction (and a dry mouth) in addition to muscle weakness, but the cardinal clinical sign is absence of tendon reflexes, which can return immediately after sustained contraction of the relevant muscle. The condition is associated with underlying malignancy in a high percentage of cases, and investigation must be directed towards detecting such a cause. The condition is diagnosed electrophysiologically by the presence of post-tetanic potentiation of motor response to nerve stimulation at a frequency of 20–50/s. Treatment is with 3,4-diaminopyridine (see EBM panel).

LAMBERT–EATON MYASTHENIC SYNDROME— role of 3,4-diaminopyridine (DAP) EBM
'DAP is a safe and effective treatment for Lambert–Eaton myasthenic syndrome.'
• Sanders DB, Massey JM, Sanders LL, Edwards LJ. A randomized trial of 3,4-diaminopyridine in Lambert–Eaton myasthenic syndrome. Neurology 2000; 54:603–607.
Further information: 🖥 www.cochrane.co.uk

DISEASES OF MUSCLE

Voluntary muscle is subject to a range of disorders that result in a limited spectrum of symptoms and physical signs. Diagnosis depends upon consideration of the clinical picture along with the results of EMG studies and muscle biopsy. In some muscular dystrophies, e.g. Duchenne dystrophy and

22.74 INVESTIGATION OF MUSCLE DISEASE

	First-line tests	Second-line tests	Occasionally useful tests
Haematology	Full blood count ESR		
Biochemistry	Urea, electrolytes Calcium, phosphate Creatine kinase Lactate dehydrogenase Liver function tests Thyroxine and TSH Plasma and urinary corticosteroids Urinary calcium	Faecal occult blood	Ischaemic lactate test
Immunology	Antinuclear factor Anti-dsDNA Anti-acetylcholine receptor antibodies		Anti-voltage-gated calcium channel antibodies
Other	Nerve conduction/EMG	Genetic screening tests (e.g. some muscular dystrophies, mitochondrial DNA) Muscle biopsy* Chest radiograph/CT Mammogram Abdominal imaging	

* Histology (light and electron microscopy), histochemistry and/or tissue enzyme assay (e.g. myophosphorylase, phosphofructokinase, acid maltase, carnitine-palmityl transferase) may be necessary.

dystrophia myotonica, a specific genetic abnormality has been identified. Screening tests are given in Box 22.74.

MUSCULAR DYSTROPHY

Several inherited disorders are characterised by progressive degeneration of groups of muscles without involvement of the nervous system.

Clinical features

Wasting and weakness are usually symmetrical, there is no fasciculation and no sensory loss and, except in dystrophia myotonica, tendon reflexes are preserved until a late stage. Differential diagnosis is based on the age at onset, the distribution of affected muscles and the pattern of inheritance (see Box 22.75).

Investigations

The diagnosis of muscular dystrophy can be confirmed by EMG and muscle biopsy. Creatine kinase is markedly elevated

in Duchenne muscular dystrophy, but is normal or only moderately elevated in the other types.

Dystrophia myotonica may be diagnosed clinically by the distribution of muscle weakness and other features including myotonia (slow relaxation of muscle), cataracts, ptosis, frontal baldness and gonadal atrophy. It is caused by expansion of a trinucleotide repeat on chromosome 19, and diagnosis is now possible by measuring the number of repeats. The genetic defects of Duchenne dystrophy and facioscapulohumeral dystrophy have been mapped to chromosomes Xp21 and 4q35, respectively. DNA analysis may allow early diagnosis and pre-natal testing in these conditions, as in dystrophia myotonica.

Management

There is no specific therapy for these conditions, although advice from the physiotherapist and occupational therapist may help the patient to cope with disability. Genetic counselling is important.

22.75 DIAGNOSTIC FEATURES IN MUSCULAR DYSTROPHY

Dystrophy	Chromosome involved	Inheritance	Age at onset (yrs)	Muscles affected
Duchenne	X	X-linked recessive	3–10	Proximal legs and arms, then general
Limb girdle	(Probably multiple)	Autosomal recessive	10–30	Pelvic girdle, shoulder girdle or both
Facioscapulohumeral	4	Autosomal dominant	10–40	Facial, shoulder girdle, serratus anterior
Dystrophia myotonica	19	Autosomal dominant	Any age	Temporalis, facial, sternomastoid, distal limbs, myotonia

Prognosis

Most patients with Duchenne dystrophy die within 10 years of diagnosis, while the lifespan in limb girdle and facio-scapulohumeral dystrophies is normal. Premature death due to respiratory or cardiac failure in early middle age is the usual outcome in dystrophia myotonica, although patients are affected very variably.

METABOLIC AND ENDOCRINE MYOPATHY

Muscle weakness may develop in a range of metabolic and endocrine disorders and is usually reversible. The causes are listed in Box 22.76.

Clinical features

The weakness is often acute and generalised in metabolic disorders, while a proximal myopathy predominantly affecting the pelvic girdle is a feature of some endocrine disorders. This may develop without other manifestations of hormonal disturbance. Hypo- and hyperkalaemia may occur in the familial periodic paralyses, which are inherited conditions characterised by attacks of profound weakness lasting for several hours, often precipitated by eating or exertion.

Muscle pain on exercise is the characteristic feature of myophosphorylase deficiency (McArdle's syndrome) and a number of other rare recessively inherited disorders of metabolism (see Box 22.77).

22.76 METABOLIC AND ENDOCRINE CAUSES OF MUSCLE WEAKNESS	
Acute muscle weakness	
• Hypokalaemia	• Hypocalcaemia
• Hyperkalaemia	• Hypercalcaemia
Proximal myopathy	
• Hyperthyroidism	• Cushing's syndrome
• Hypothyroidism	• Addison's disease

22.77 RARE DISORDERS OF MUSCLE METABOLISM
Myophosphorylase deficiency (McArdle's syndrome)
• Muscle pain on exercise
• Increased glycogen in muscle
• Failure of blood lactate to rise on exercise
• Reduced myophosphorylase (muscle biopsy)
Phosphofructokinase deficiency
• Similar to above, but reduced phosphofructokinase (muscle biopsy)
Carnitine-palmityl transferase (CPT) deficiency
• Muscle pain after prolonged exercise
• Increased lipid in muscle on biopsy
• Reduced CPT (muscle biopsy)

INFLAMMATORY MYOPATHY OR POLYMYOSITIS

See page 1038.

CONGENITAL MYOPATHY

This is rare and presents in infancy with muscular weakness and limpness. Serum enzymes may be normal or slightly elevated and the EMG is usually myopathic. The syndrome may be caused by a number of specific conditions that have a variable inheritance, and are defined by the type of structural abnormality present in skeletal muscle fibres. Most patients have a slowly progressive disease and there is no specific therapy.

TOXIC MYOPATHY

A wide variety of drugs may cause disorders of muscle, including carbenoxolone, thiazide diuretics, zidovudine, statins and steroids. Alcohol may cause a spectrum of muscle disease varying from a mild proximal weakness to severe muscle necrosis. Avoidance of the offending agent usually results in recovery of muscle function.

DISORDERS OF THE SPINE AND SPINAL CORD

The spinal cord and spinal roots may be affected by intrinsic disease or by disorders of the surrounding meninges and bones. The clinical presentation of these conditions depends on the anatomical level at which the cord or roots are affected as well as the nature of the pathological process involved. It is important to recognise when emergency surgical intervention is necessary and therefore to plan investigations to identify such patients.

COMPRESSION OF THE SPINAL CORD

Acute spinal cord compression is one of the most common neurological emergencies encountered in clinical practice and the common causes are listed in Box 22.78.

A space-occupying lesion within the spinal canal may damage nerve tissue either directly by pressure or indirectly

22.78 CAUSES OF SPINAL CORD COMPRESSION		
Site	**Frequency**	**Causes**
Vertebral (extradural)	80%	Trauma Intervertebral disc prolapse Metastatic carcinoma (e.g. breast, prostate, bronchus) Myeloma Tuberculosis
Meninges (intradural extramedullary)	15%	Tumours (e.g. meningioma, neurofibroma, ependymoma, metastasis, lymphoma, leukaemia) Epidural abscess
Spinal cord (intradural intramedullary)	5%	Tumours (e.g. glioma, ependymoma, metastasis)

by interfering with blood supply. Oedema from venous obstruction impairs neuronal function, and ischaemia from arterial obstruction may lead to necrosis of the spinal cord. The early stages of damage are reversible but severely damaged neurons do not recover; hence the importance of early diagnosis and treatment.

Clinical features

The onset of symptoms of spinal cord compression is usually slow (over weeks), but can be acute as a result of trauma or metastases, especially if there is associated arterial occlusion. The symptoms are shown in Box 22.79.

22.79 SYMPTOMS OF SPINAL CORD COMPRESSION	
Pain	
• Localised over the spine or in a root distribution, which may be aggravated by coughing, sneezing or straining	
Sensory	
• Paraesthesia, numbness or cold sensations, especially in the lower limbs, which spread proximally, often to a level on the trunk	
Motor	
• Weakness, heaviness or stiffness of the limbs, most commonly the legs	
Sphincters	
• Urgency or hesitancy of micturition, leading eventually to urinary retention	

Pain and sensory symptoms occur early, while weakness and sphincter dysfunction are usually late manifestations. The signs vary according to the level of the cord compression and the structures involved. There may be tenderness to percussion over the spine if there is vertebral disease, and this may be associated with a local kyphosis. Involvement of the roots at the level of the compression may give dermatomal sensory impairment and corresponding lower motor signs. Interruption of fibres in the spinal cord causes sensory loss (see p. 1140) and upper motor neuron signs below the level of the lesion, and there is often disturbance of sphincter function. The distribution of these signs varies with the level of the lesion, as shown in Box 22.80.

The Brown-Séquard syndrome (see Fig. 22.15E, p. 1141) results if damage is confined to one side of the cord; the findings are explained by the anatomy of the sensory tracts (see Fig. 22.16, p. 1141). On the side of the lesion there is a band of hyperaesthesia with loss of proprioceptive sense and upper motor neuron signs below it. On the other side there is loss of spinothalamic sensation (pain and temperature). With compressive lesions there is usually a band of pain at the level of the lesion in the distribution of the nerve roots subject to compression.

Investigations

Patients with a short history of a progressive spinal cord syndrome should be investigated urgently. Investigations necessary are listed in Box 22.81.

22.80 SIGNS OF SPINAL CORD COMPRESSION	
Cervical, above C5	
• Upper motor neuron signs and sensory loss in all four limbs	
Cervical, C5 to T1	
• Lower motor neuron signs and segmental sensory loss in the arms; upper motor neuron signs in the legs	
Thoracic cord	
• Spastic paraplegia with a sensory level on the trunk	
Conus medullaris	
• Lesions at the end of the spinal cord cause sacral loss of sensation and extensor plantar responses	
Cauda equina	
• Spinal cord ends at approximately the T12/L1 spinal level and spinal lesions below this level can only cause lower motor neuron signs by affecting the cauda equina	

22.81 INVESTIGATION OF ACUTE SPINAL CORD SYNDROME	
• Plain radiographs of spine	
• Chest radiographs	
• MRI of spine or myelography	
• CSF	
• Serum B_{12}	

Plain radiographs may show bony destruction and soft-tissue abnormalities and are an essential initial investigation (see Fig. 22.43). Routine investigations, including chest radiograph, may provide evidence of systemic disease. MRI of the spine is the investigation of choice (see Fig. 22.44); myelography also localises the lesion and, with CT in suitable cases, defines the extent of compression and associated soft-tissue abnormality (see Fig. 22.45). CSF should be taken for analysis at the time of myelography. In cases of complete spinal block this shows a normal cell count with a very elevated protein causing yellow discoloration of the fluid (Froin's syndrome). Acute deterioration may develop after myelography and it is preferable to alert the neurosurgeons before such procedures are undertaken. Needle biopsy is required prior to radiotherapy to establish the histological nature of the tumour.

Management

Treatment and prognosis depend on the nature of the underlying lesion. Benign tumours should be surgically excised, and a good functional recovery can be expected unless a marked neurological deficit has developed before diagnosis. Extradural compression due to malignancy is the most common cause of spinal cord compression in developed countries and has a poor prognosis, although useful function can be regained if treatment is initiated within 24 hours of the onset of severe weakness or sphincter dysfunction. Surgical decompression may be appropriate in some patients, but has a similar outcome to radiotherapy. Spinal

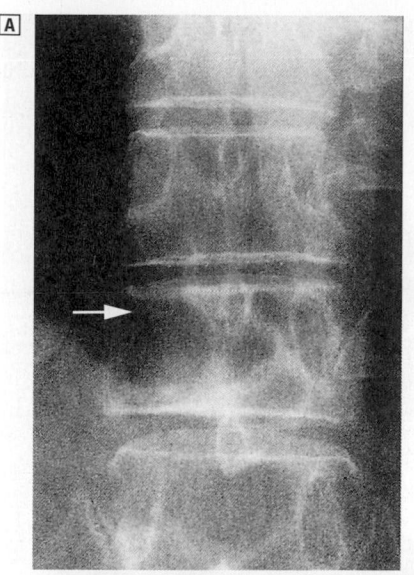

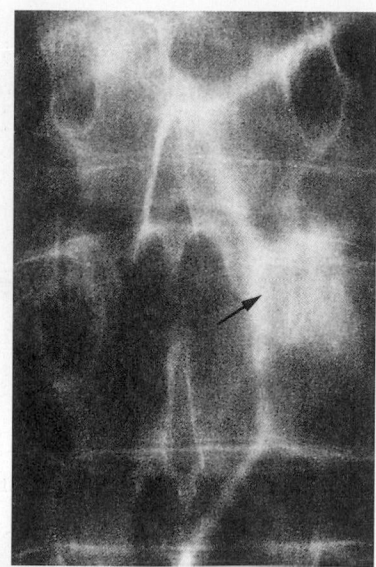

Fig. 22.43   Plain radiographs of the spine. [A] Loss of vertebral pedicle (arrow) by bony erosion of an osteolytic metastasis. [B] An osteosclerotic metastasis (arrow).

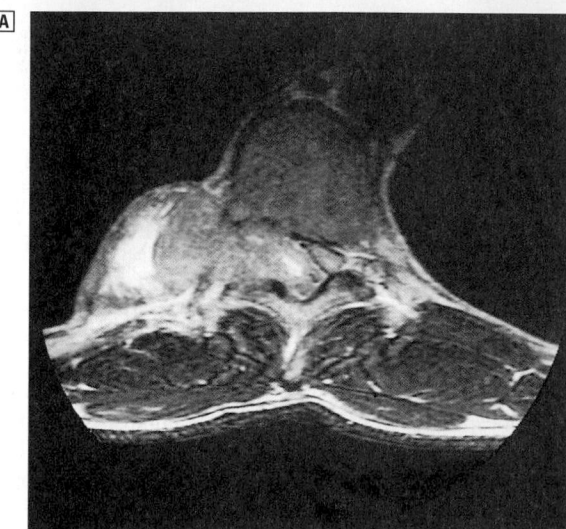

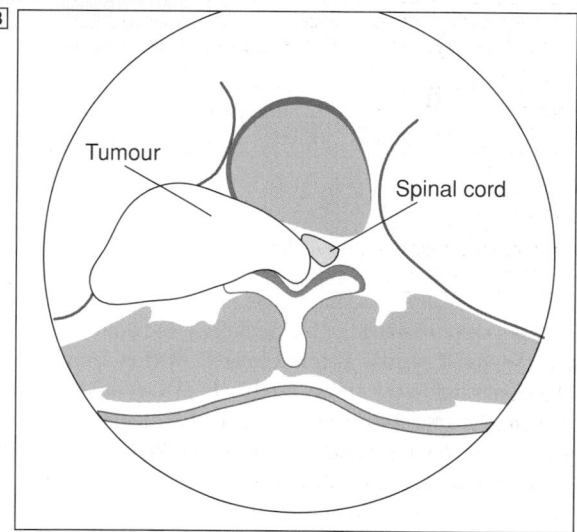

Tumour

Spinal cord

Fig. 22.44   Axial MRI of thoracic spine. [A] A meningioma is compressing the spinal cord and emerging in a 'dumbbell' fashion through the vertebral foramen into the paraspinal space. [B] Line diagram illustrating major structures.

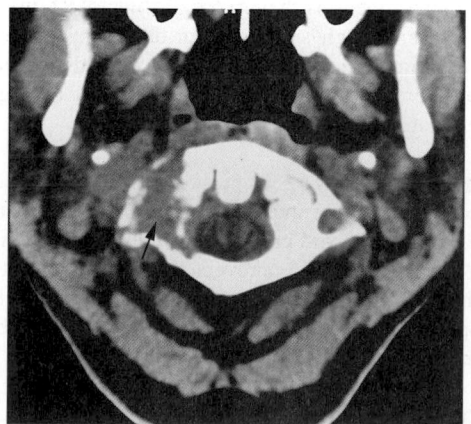

Fig. 22.45   CT myelogram of cervical spine at the level of C2 showing bony erosion of vertebra by a metastasis (arrow).

cord compression due to tuberculosis is common in some areas of the world, and requires surgical treatment if seen early. This should be followed by appropriate anti-tubercular chemotherapy (see p. 538) for an extended period. Traumatic lesions of the vertebral column require specialised treatment in a neurosurgical centre.

CERVICAL SPONDYLOSIS

In the cervical spine, some degree of degenerative change is a normal radiological finding in the middle-aged and elderly. Degeneration of the intervertebral discs and secondary osteoarthrosis (cervical spondylosis) is often asymptomatic, but may be associated with neurological dysfunction. The C5/6, C6/7 and C4/5 vertebral levels and C6, C7 and C5 roots, respectively, are most commonly affected (see Fig. 22.46).

CERVICAL SPONDYLOTIC RADICULOPATHY

Compression of a nerve root occurs when a disc prolapses laterally. This may develop acutely, or more gradually due to osteophytic encroachment of the intervertebral foramina.

Clinical features

The patient complains of pain in the neck that may radiate in the distribution of the affected nerve root. The neck is held rigidly and neck movements may exacerbate pain. Paraesthesia and sensory loss may be found in the affected segment and there may be lower motor neuron signs, including weakness, wasting and reflex impairment (see Box 22.82).

22.82	PHYSICAL SIGNS IN CERVICAL ROOT COMPRESSION		
Root	Muscle weakness	Sensory loss	Reflex loss
C5	Biceps, deltoid, spinati	Upper lateral arm	Biceps
C6	Brachioradialis	Lower lateral arm, thumb, index finger	Supinator
C7	Triceps, finger and wrist extensors	Middle finger	Triceps

Investigations

Plain radiographs, including lateral and oblique views, should be obtained to confirm the presence of degenerative changes and to exclude other conditions, including destructive lesions. If surgery is contemplated, MRI is appropriate. Electrophysiological studies rarely add to the clinical examination, but may be necessary if there is doubt about the differential diagnosis between root and peripheral nerve lesions.

Management

Conservative treatment with analgesics and a cervical collar results in resolution of symptoms in the great majority of patients, but a few require surgery in the form of foraminotomy or disc excision.

CERVICAL SPONDYLOTIC MYELOPATHY

Dorsomedial herniation of a disc and the development of transverse bony bars or posterior osteophytes may result in pressure on the spinal cord or the anterior spinal artery which supplies the anterior two-thirds of the cord (see Fig. 22.46).

Clinical features

The onset of symptoms is usually insidious and painless, but acute deterioration may occur after trauma, especially hyperextension injury. Upper motor neuron signs develop in the limbs, with spasticity of the legs usually appearing before the arms are involved. Sensory loss in the upper limbs is common, producing tingling numbness and

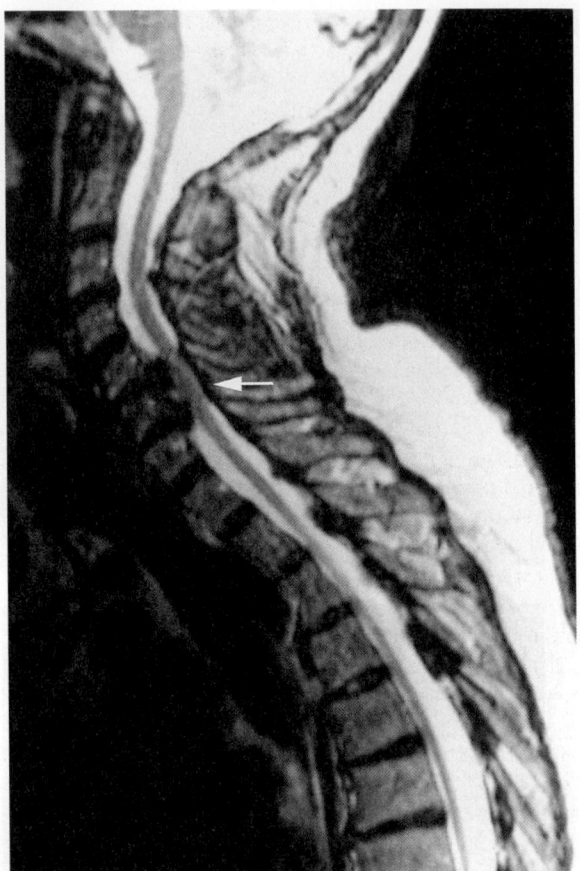

Fig. 22.46 MRI showing cervical cord compression (arrow) in cervical spondylosis.

proprioception loss in the hands, with progressive clumsiness. Sensory manifestations in the legs are much less common. The neurological deficit usually progresses gradually and disturbance of micturition is a very late feature.

Investigations

Plain radiographs confirm the presence of degenerative changes, and MRI or myelography may be indicated if surgical treatment is being considered. MRI may also show areas of high signal within the spinal cord at the level of compression. Imaging of the cervical spine should be considered if there is diagnostic doubt or if surgery is contemplated.

Management

Surgical procedures, including laminectomy and anterior discectomy, may arrest progression of disability but may not result in neurological improvement. The judgement as to whether surgery should be undertaken may be difficult. Manipulation of the cervical spine is of no proven benefit and may precipitate acute neurological deterioration.

Prognosis

The prognosis of cervical myelopathy is variable. In many patients the condition stabilises or even improves without intervention, but if progressive disability does develop, surgical decompression should be considered.

LUMBAR DISC HERNIATION

In Western countries low back pain ('lumbago') is the most common medical cause of inability to work (see p. 981). In the great majority of patients it is due to abnormalities of joints and ligaments in the lumbar spine rather than herniation of an intervertebral disc. Pain in the distribution of the lumbar or sacral roots ('sciatica') is often due to disc protrusion, but can be a feature of other rare but important disorders including spinal tumour, malignant disease in the pelvis and tuberculosis of the vertebral bodies.

Acute lumbar disc herniation is often precipitated by trauma, usually by lifting heavy weights while the spine is flexed. The nucleus pulposus may bulge or rupture through the annulus fibrosus, giving rise to pressure on nerve endings in the spinal ligaments, changes in the vertebral joints or pressure on nerve roots.

Clinical features

The onset may be sudden or gradual. Alternatively, repeated episodes of low back pain may precede sciatica by months or years. Constant aching pain is felt in the lumbar region and may radiate to the buttock, thigh, calf and foot. Pain is exacerbated by coughing or straining and may be relieved by lying flat.

The altered mechanics of the lumbar spine result in loss of lumbar lordosis and there may be spasm of the paraspinal musculature. Root pressure is suggested by limitation of flexion of the hip on the affected side if the straight leg is raised (Lasègue's sign). If the third or fourth lumbar roots are involved, Lasègue's sign may be negative, but pain in the back may be induced by hyperextension of the hip (femoral nerve stretch test). The roots most frequently affected are S1, L5 and L4; the signs of root pressure at these levels are summarised in Box 22.83.

Investigations

Plain radiographs of the lumbar spine are of little value in the diagnosis of lumbar disc disease although they may show other conditions such as malignant infiltration of a vertebral body. CT, especially using spiral scanning techniques, can provide helpful images of the disc protrusion and/or narrowing of the exit foramina. MRI is the investigation of choice if available, since soft tissues are well imaged.

22.83 PHYSICAL SIGNS IN LUMBAR ROOT COMPRESSION				
Disc level	Root	Sensory loss	Weakness	Reflex loss
L3/L4	L4	Inner calf	Inversion of foot	Knee
L4/L5	L5	Outer calf and dorsum of foot	Dorsiflexion of hallux/toes	Hamstring
L5/S1	S1	Sole and lateral foot	Plantar flexion	Ankle

Management

Some 90% of patients with sciatica recover with conservative treatment with analgesia and early mobilisation; there is little evidence that bed rest helps recovery. The patient should be instructed in back-strengthening exercises and advised to avoid physical manoeuvres likely to strain the lumbar spine. Injections of local anaesthetic or steroids may be useful adjunctive treatment if symptoms are due to ligamentous injury or joint dysfunction.

Surgery may have to be considered if there is no response to conservative treatment or if progressive neurological deficits develop. Central disc prolapse with bilateral symptoms and signs and disturbance of sphincter function requires urgent surgical decompression.

LUMBAR CANAL STENOSIS

This is due to a congenital narrowing of the lumbar spinal canal, exacerbated by the degenerative changes that commonly occur with age.

Clinical features

The patients, who are usually elderly, characteristically develop exercise-induced weakness and paraesthesia in the legs (cauda equina claudication). These symptoms progress with continued exertion, often to the point that the patient can no longer walk, but are quickly relieved by a short period of rest. Physical examination at rest shows preservation of peripheral pulses with absent ankle reflexes. Weakness or sensory loss may only be apparent if the patient is examined immediately after exercise.

Investigations

Myelography, CT or MRI will demonstrate narrowing of the lumbar canal.

Management

Extensive lumbar laminectomy often results in complete relief of symptoms and recovery of normal exercise tolerance.

SYRINGOMYELIA

In this condition a fluid-filled cavity (or cavities) develops near the centre of the spinal cord, usually in the cervical segments (see Fig. 22.47). The expanding cavity disrupts second-order spinothalamic neurons (see Fig. 22.16, p. 1141), may extend laterally to damage the anterior horn cells, and may compress the long fibre tracts. Slit-like cavities may appear in the medulla in association with syringomyelia, producing brain-stem dysfunction (syringobulbia).

Aetiology

Many patients have some obstruction to the flow of CSF at the foramen magnum. In some this is associated with congenital herniation of the cerebellar tonsils (Chiari type I malformation, see Fig. 22.47), and in others with basal arachnoiditis. It is assumed that the disturbed CSF dynamics

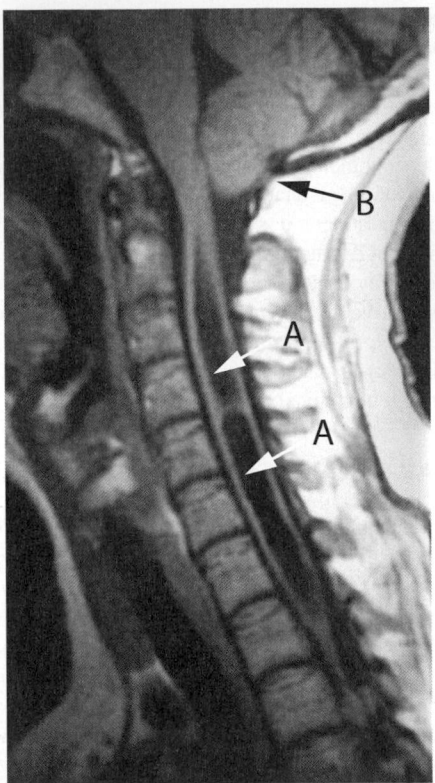

Fig. 22.47 MRI scan showing syrinx (arrows A), with herniation of cerebellar tonsils (arrow B).

cause the development of the syrinx but the mechanism is not clear. Cavities may also develop in the spinal cord following trauma or in association with an intrinsic spinal cord tumour.

Clinical features

Patients usually present in the third or fourth decade; symptoms are of insidious onset and slowly progressive. Pain in the neck or shoulder is common and patients may seek advice because of sensory loss in the upper limbs. The most characteristic physical sign is dissociated sensory loss (impaired pain and temperature sensation with preservation of dorsal column modalities), which has an upper and a lower level in a mantle or hemi-cape distribution (see Fig. 22.15F, p. 1141). Loss of protective sensory function leads to trophic lesions such as painless burns or ulcers on the hands, and sometimes painless deranged joints (Charcot joints—see p. 1046) in the upper limbs. Kyphoscoliosis is frequently present and wasting of the small hand muscles is a common early feature, with loss of reflexes in the arms. Upper motor neuron signs develop in the legs as the condition progresses. Syringobulbia leads to dysarthria, palatal palsy, Horner's syndrome, nystagmus and sensory loss on the face.

Investigations

Plain radiographs may demonstrate congenital anomalies around the foramen magnum or expansion of the cervical

canal. The most sensitive and least invasive investigation is MRI (see Fig. 22.47).

Management

Surgical decompression of the foramen magnum or the syrinx itself may arrest progression of the neurological deficit and often alleviates pain. The results of surgery are, however, often disappointing and in some patients the condition continues to progress slowly over long periods.

INFECTIONS OF THE NERVOUS SYSTEM

The clinical features of nervous system infections depend upon the location of the infection (in the meninges or in the brain/spinal cord parenchyma), the causative organism (virus, bacteria or parasite), and whether the infection is acute or chronic. The major infections of the nervous system are listed in Box 22.84. The frequency of these varies somewhat geographically. Helminthic infections such as cysticercosis and hydatid disease are described in Chapter 1.

22.84 INFECTIONS OF THE NERVOUS SYSTEM*	
Bacterial infections	
• Meningitis	• Neurosyphilis
• Suppurative encephalitis	• Leprosy (peripheral nerves)
• Brain abscess	• Diphtheria (peripheral nerves)
• Tuberculosis	• Tetanus (motor cells)
• Paravertebral (epidural) abscess	
Viral infections	
• Meningitis	• Poliomyelitis
• Encephalitis	• Rabies
• Transverse myelitis	• HIV infection
Slow virus/prion infections	
• Creutzfeldt–Jakob disease	• Progressive multifocal leucoencephalopathy
• Kuru	
• Subacute sclerosing panencephalitis	
Protozoal infections	
• Malaria	• Trypanosomiasis
• Toxoplasmosis (in immunosuppressed)	• Amoebic abscess
Helminthic infections	
• Schistosomiasis (spinal cord)	• Hydatid disease*
• Cysticercosis*	• Strongyloidiasis
Fungal infections	
• Cryptococcal meningitis	• Candida meningitis or brain abscess
* A number of these infections are not detailed in this chapter. They can be found in Chapter 1.	

22.85 CEREBROSPINAL FLUID INDICES IN MENINGITIS*

Condition	Cell type	Cell count	Glucose	Protein	Gram stain
Normal	Lymphocytes	0–4 per mm^3	> 60% of blood glucose	Up to 0.45 g/l	–
Viral	Lymphocytes	10–2000	Normal	Normal	–
Bacterial	Polymorphs	1000–5000	Low	Normal/elevated	+
Tuberculous	Polymorphs/lymphocytes/mixed	50–5000	Low	Elevated	Often –
Fungal	Lymphocytes	50–500	Low	Elevated	±
Malignant	Lymphocytes	0–100	Low	Normal/elevated	–

* See also Box 22.3, page 1115.

MENINGITIS

Acute infection of the meninges presents with the character-istic combination of pyrexia, headache and meningism. Meningism, which can occur in other situations (such as after subarachnoid haemorrhage) consists of stiffness of the neck, often with other signs of meningeal irritation: Kernig's sign (with the hip joint flexed, extension at the knee causes spasm in the hamstring muscles) and Brudzinski's sign (passive flexion of the neck causes flexion of the thighs and knees). The severity of these features varies somewhat according to the causative organism, as does the presence of other features such as a skin rash. Abnormalities in the CSF (see Box 22.85) are very helpful in distinguishing the cause of meningitis. Causes of meningitis are listed in Box 22.86.

22.86 CAUSES OF MENINGITIS

Infective

Bacteria (see Box 22.87)
- Brucella

Viruses
- Enteroviruses (echo, Coxsackie, polio)
- Mumps
- Influenza
- Herpes simplex
- Varicella zoster
- Epstein–Barr
- HIV
- Lymphocytic choriomeningitis

Protozoa and parasites
- *Toxoplasma*
- Amoeba
- Cysticercus

Fungi
- *Cryptococcus neoformans*
- *Candida*
- *Histoplasma*
- *Blastomyces*
- *Coccidioides*
- *Sporothrix*

Non-infective ('sterile')

Malignant disease
- Breast cancer
- Bronchial cancer
- Leukaemia
- Lymphoma

Inflammatory disease (may be recurrent)
- Sarcoidosis
- SLE
- Behçet's disease
- Mollaret's meningitis

VIRAL MENINGITIS

Viral infection is the most common cause of meningitis, and usually results in a benign and self-limiting illness requiring no specific therapy. It is a much less serious illness than bacterial meningitis unless there is associated encephalitis, which is rare. A number of viruses can cause meningitis (see Box 22.86), the most common being echoviruses and, where specific immunisation is not employed, the mumps virus.

Clinical features
The condition occurs mainly in children or young adults, with acute onset of headache and irritability and the rapid development of meningism. In viral meningitis the headache is usually the more severe feature. There may be a high pyrexia, but focal neurological signs do not occur since there is seldom parenchymal involvement of the brain.

Investigations
The CSF contains an excess of lymphocytes, but glucose and protein levels are normal. It is extremely important to verify that the patient has not received antibiotics (for what-ever cause) prior to the lumbar puncture, as this picture can also be found in partially treated bacterial meningitis.

Management
There is no specific treatment and the condition is usually benign and self-limiting. The patient should be treated symptomatically in a quiet environment. Recovery usually occurs within days, although a lymphocytic pleocytosis may persist in the CSF.

Meningitis may also occur as a complication of a viral infection primarily involving other organs: for example, in mumps, measles, infectious mononucleosis, herpes zoster and hepatitis. Complete recovery without specific therapy is the rule.

PYOGENIC BACTERIAL MENINGITIS

Many bacteria can cause meningitis but some do so more frequently than others (see Box 22.87). Bacterial meningitis is usually secondary to a bacteraemic illness, although infec-tion may result from direct spread from an adjacent focus of infection in the ear, skull fracture or sinus. Bacterial meningi-tis has become less common but the mortality and morbidity remain significant despite the availability of an increasing range of antibiotics. An important factor in determining

22.87 BACTERIAL CAUSES OF MENINGITIS

Age of onset	Common	Less common
Neonate	Gram-negative bacilli (*Escherichia coli, Proteus* etc.) Group B streptococci	*Listeria monocytogenes*
Pre-school child	*Haemophilus influenzae Neisseria meningitidis Streptococcus pneumoniae*	*Mycobacterium tuberculosis*
Older child and adult	*Neisseria meningitidis Streptococcus pneumoniae*	*Listeria monocytogenes Mycobacterium tuberculosis Cryptococcus neoformans* (in immunosuppressed) *Staphylococcus aureus* (skull fracture) *Haemophilus influenzae*

22.88 COMPLICATIONS OF MENINGOCOCCAL SEPTICAEMIA

- Meningitis
- Rash (morbilliform, petechial or purpuric)
- Shock
- Intravascular coagulation
- Renal failure
- Peripheral gangrene
- Arthritis (septic or reactive)
- Pericarditis (septic or reactive)

meningitis is often associated with a very purulent CSF and a high mortality, especially in older adults.

Clinical features

Headache, drowsiness, fever and neck stiffness are the usual presenting features. In severe bacterial meningitis the patient may be comatose and later there may be focal neurological signs. Meningococcal meningitis may present very rapidly, with abrupt onset of obtundation due to cerebral oedema, probably as a result of endotoxin and/or cytokine release. There may be a purpuric skin rash and circulatory collapse.

prognosis is early diagnosis and the prompt initiation of appropriate therapy.

The meningococcus *(Neisseria meningitidis)* is the most common cause of bacterial meningitis in Britain, whilst in the USA *Haemophilus influenzae* is more common. Spread is by the air-borne route, but close contact is necessary. Epidemics occur, particularly in cramped living conditions or where the climate is hot and dry, e.g. areas of Africa. The organism invades through the nasopharynx, producing septicaemia that is usually associated with pyogenic meningitis. Complications of meningococcal septicaemia are listed in Box 22.88. Chronic meningococcaemia is a rare condition in which the patient can be unwell for weeks or even months with recurrent fever, sweating, joint pains and transient rash. It usually occurs in the middle-aged and elderly.

In pneumococcal and *Haemophilus* infections there may be an associated otitis media. Pneumococcal meningitis may be associated with pneumonia and occurs especially in older patients and alcoholics, as well as in patients without functioning spleens. *Listeria monocytogenes* has recently emerged as an increasing cause of meningitis and rhombencephalitis (brain-stem encephalitis) in the immunosuppressed, diabetics, alcoholics and pregnant women (see p. 42). It can also cause meningitis in the neonatal period.

Pathology

The pia-arachnoid is congested and infiltrated with inflammatory cells. A thin layer of pus forms and this may later organise to form adhesions. These may cause obstruction to the free flow of CSF leading to hydrocephalus, or they may damage the cranial nerves at the base of the brain. The CSF pressure rises rapidly, the protein content increases, and there is a cellular reaction that varies in type and severity according to the nature of the inflammation and the causative organism. An obliterative endarteritis of the leptomeningeal arteries passing through the meningeal exudate may produce secondary cerebral infarction. Pneumococcal

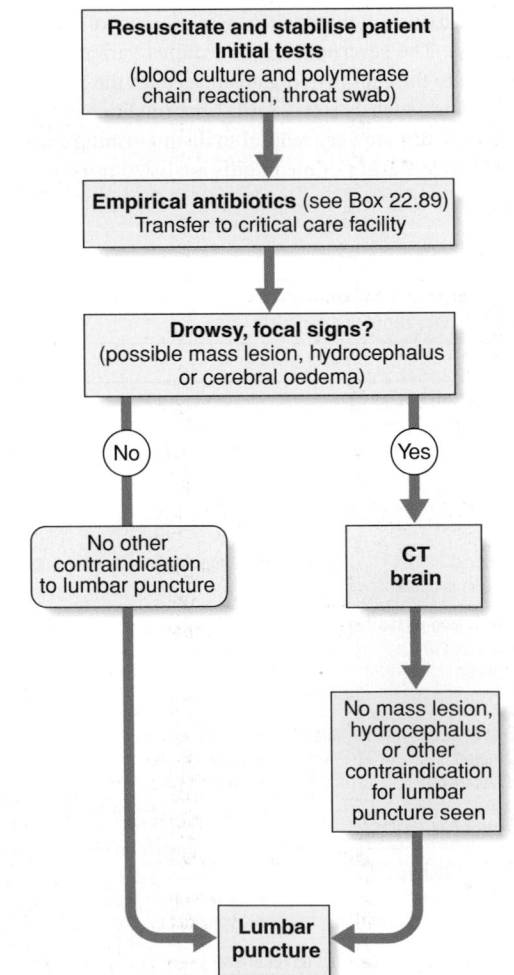

Fig. 22.48 The investigation of meningitis.

Investigations

Lumbar puncture is mandatory unless there are contra-indications (see p. 1114). Particularly if the patient is drowsy with focal neurological signs or seizures it is wise to obtain a CT to exclude a mass lesion (such as a cerebral abscess) before lumbar puncture because of the risk of coning, but this should not delay treatment of a presumptive meningitis. If lumbar puncture is deferred or omitted, it is essential to take diagnostic specimens and to start empirical treatment (see Fig. 22.48).

In bacterial meningitis the CSF is cloudy (turbid) due to the presence of many neutrophils (often > 1000 cells/mm³), the protein content is significantly elevated and the glucose reduced. Gram film and culture may allow identification of the organism. Blood cultures may be positive. Polymerase chain reaction (PCR) techniques can be used on both blood and CSF to identify bacterial DNA. These methods are useful in detecting meningococcal infection and in typing the organism.

Management

If meningococcal disease is suspected the patient should be given parenteral benzylpenicillin (intravenous is preferable to intramuscular) before admission to hospital. The only contraindication is a history of penicillin anaphylaxis. Recommended empirical therapy before the cause of meningitis is known is given in Box 22.89. The antibiotic regimen may be modified after CSF examination, depending on the infecting organism. Guidance as to the preferred antibiotic is given in Box 22.90 if the organism is known and in Box 22.89 if the organism has not been identified. Adjunctive steroid therapy, though useful in children (see EBM panel), has not been adequately evaluated in adults.

22.89 TREATMENT OF PYOGENIC MENINGITIS OF UNKNOWN CAUSE

1. Patients with a typical meningococcal rash

- Benzylpenicillin 2.4 g i.v. 6-hourly

2. Adults aged 18–50 years without a typical meningococcal rash

- Cefotaxime 2 g i.v. 6-hourly
or
- Ceftriaxone 2 g i.v. 12-hourly

3. Patients in whom penicillin-resistant pneumococcal infection is suspected

- As for (2) but add:
  Vancomycin 1 g i.v. 12-hourly
or
  Rifampicin 600 mg i.v. 12-hourly

4. Adults aged over 50 years and those in whom *Listeria monocytogenes* infection is suspected
(e.g. brain-stem signs, immunosuppression, diabetic, alcoholic)

- As for (2) but add:
  Ampicillin 2 g i.v. 4-hourly
or
  Co-trimoxazole 50 mg/kg i.v. daily in two divided doses

5. Patients with a clear history of anaphylaxis to β-lactams

- Chloramphenicol 25 mg/kg i.v. 6-hourly *plus* vancomycin 1 g i.v. 12-hourly

---

ADJUNCTIVE DEXAMETHASONE THERAPY FOR BACTERIAL MENINGITIS IN CHILDREN—and reduction in severe hearing loss
EBM

'The available evidence on adjunctive dexamethasone therapy confirms benefit for *H. influenzae* type B meningitis and, if commenced with or before parenteral antibiotics, suggests benefit for pneumococcal meningitis in childhood. Limiting dexamethasone therapy to 2 days may be optimal.'

- McIntyre PB, Berkey CS, King SM, et al. Dexamethasone as adjunctive therapy in bacterial meningitis. A meta-analysis of random clinical trials since 1988. JAMA 1997; 278:925–931.
- Coyle PK. Glucocorticoids in central nervous system bacterial infection. Arch Neurol 1999; 56:796–801.

Further information: 🖵 www.clinicalevidence.org

22.90 CHEMOTHERAPY OF BACTERIAL MENINGITIS WHEN THE CAUSE IS KNOWN

Pathogen	Regimen of choice	Alternative agent(s)
N. meningitidis	Benzylpenicillin 2.4 g i.v. 4-hourly for 5–7 days	Cefuroxime, ampicillin Chloramphenicol*
Strep. pneumoniae (sensitive to β-lactams, minimum inhibitory concentration (MIC) < 1 mg/l)	Cefotaxime 2 g i.v. 6-hourly *or* ceftriaxone 2 g i.v. 12-hourly for 10–14 days	Chloramphenicol*
Strep. pneumoniae (resistant to β-lactams)	As for sensitive strains but add vancomycin 1 g i.v. 12-hourly *or* rifampicin 600 mg i.v. 12-hourly	Vancomycin *plus* rifampicin*
H. influenzae	Cefotaxime 2 g i.v. 6-hourly *or* ceftriaxone 2 g i.v. 12-hourly for 10–14 days	Chloramphenicol*
Listeria monocytogenes	Ampicillin 2 g i.v. 4-hourly *plus* gentamicin 5 mg/kg i.v. daily	Ampicillin 2 g i.v. 4-hourly *plus* co-trimoxazole 50 mg/kg daily in two divided doses

* For patients with a history of anaphylaxis to β-lactam antibiotics.

In meningococcal disease mortality is doubled if the patient presents with features of septicaemia rather than meningitis. Certain patients are likely to require intensive care facilities and expertise, including those with cardiac, respiratory or renal involvement, and those with CNS depression prejudicing the airway. Early endotracheal intubation and mechanical ventilation protect the airway and may prevent the development of the acute respiratory distress syndrome (ARDS, see p. 198). Adverse prognostic features include hypotensive shock, a rapidly developing rash, a haemorrhagic diathesis, multisystem failure and an age of more than 60 years.

EBM

CHEMOPROPHYLAXIS FOR MENINGOCOCCAL INFECTION—does it reduce the incidence of clinical disease among contacts?

'There are no RCTs examining the effects of antibiotics on the incidence of meningococcal disease among contacts. Observational data suggest that antibiotics reduce the risk of disease. There is no good evidence to address the question of which contacts should be treated.'

- Hart C. Meningococcal disease. Clinical Evidence 2000; 3:350–357.
- Cooke RPD, Riordan T, Jones DM, Painter MJ. Secondary cases of meningococcal infection among close family and household contacts in England and Wales, 1984–7. BMJ 1989; 298:555–558.

Further information: 🖥 www.clinicalevidence.org
🖥 www.phls.co.uk/facts/meni.htm

Prevention of meningococcal infection

Household and other close contacts of patients with meningococcal infections, especially children, should be given 2 days of oral rifampicin (age 3–12 months 5 mg/kg 12-hourly, > 1 year 10 mg/kg 12-hourly, adults 600 mg 12-hourly). In adults a single dose of 500 mg of ciprofloxacin is an alternative. If not treated with ceftriaxone the index case should be given similar treatment to clear infection from the nasopharynx before hospital discharge. Vaccines are available for the prevention of disease caused by meningococci of groups A and C, but not group B which is the most common serogroup isolated in many countries, including Britain.

TUBERCULOUS MENINGITIS

Now rare in the Western world in previously healthy individuals, tuberculous meningitis remains common in developing countries and is seen more frequently as a secondary infection in patients with AIDS.

Pathology

Tuberculous meningitis occurs most commonly shortly after a primary infection in childhood or as part of miliary tuberculosis. The usual local source of infection is a caseous focus in the meninges or brain substance adjacent to the CSF pathway. The brain is covered by a greenish, gelatinous exudate, especially around the base, and numerous scattered tubercles are found on the meninges.

Clinical features

The clinical features are listed in Box 22.91.

22.91 CLINICAL FEATURES OF TUBERCULOUS MENINGITIS	
Symptoms	
• Headache	• Depression
• Vomiting	• Confusion
• Low-grade fever	• Behaviour changes
• Lassitude	
Signs	
• Meningism (may be absent)	• Depression of conscious level
• Oculomotor palsies	• Focal hemisphere signs
• Papilloedema	

Investigations

The CSF is under increased pressure. It is usually clear but, when allowed to stand, a fine clot ('spider web') may form. The fluid contains up to 500 cells/mm³, predominantly lymphocytes. There is a rise in protein and a marked fall in glucose. Detection of the tubercle bacillus in a smear of the centrifuged deposit from the CSF may be difficult. The CSF should be cultured but as this result will not be known for up to 6 weeks, treatment must be started without waiting for confirmation. Brain imaging may show hydrocephalus, brisk meningeal enhancement on enhanced CT, and/or an intracranial tuberculoma.

Management

As soon as the diagnosis is made or strongly suspected, chemotherapy should be started using one of the regimens including pyrazinamide described on page 538. The use of steroids in addition to antituberculous therapy is controversial but may be indicated to treat raised intracranial pressure. Surgical ventricular drainage may be needed if obstructive hydrocephalus develops. Skilled nursing is essential during the acute phase of the illness and measures must be taken to maintain adequate hydration and nutrition.

Prognosis

Untreated tuberculous meningitis is fatal in a few weeks but complete recovery is the rule if treatment is started before the appearance of focal signs or stupor. When treatment is started at a later stage the recovery rate is 60% or less and the survivors show permanent neurological deficit.

OTHER FORMS OF MENINGITIS

Fungal meningitis (especially cryptococcosis—see p. 95) usually occurs in patients who are immunosuppressed and is a recognised complication of HIV infection (see p. 124). The CSF findings are similar to those of tuberculous meningitis, but the diagnosis can be confirmed by microscopy or specific serological tests.

In some areas meningitis may be caused by spirochaetes (leptospirosis, Lyme disease and syphilis—see pp. 20, 21 and 96), rickettsiae (typhus fever—see p. 62) or protozoa (amoebiasis—see p. 45).

Meningitis can also be due to non-infective pathologies. This is seen in recurrent aseptic meningitis due to SLE, Behçet's disease or sarcoidosis, as well as a condition of unknown origin known as Mollaret's syndrome in which the recurrent meningitis is associated with epithelioid cells in the spinal fluid ('Mollaret' cells). Meningitis can also be seen due to direct invasion of the meninges by neoplasm ('malignant meningitis'—see Box 22.86, p. 1193).

PARENCHYMAL VIRAL INFECTIONS

Infection of the substance of the nervous system will produce symptoms of focal dysfunction (focal deficits and/or seizures) with general signs of infection depending upon the acuteness of the infection and the type of organism.

VIRAL ENCEPHALITIS

A range of viruses can cause encephalitis but only a minority of patients have a history of recent viral infection. In Europe, the most common cause of viral encephalitis is herpes simplex (see p. 30), which probably reaches the brain via the olfactory nerves. The development of effective therapy for some forms of encephalitis has enhanced the importance of clinical diagnosis and virological examination of the CSF. In some parts of the world viruses transmitted by mosquitoes and ticks (arboviruses) are an important cause of encephalitis. The epidemiology of some of these infections is changing. Japanese encephalitis (see p. 93) has spread relentlessly across Asia to Australia, and there have been outbreaks of West Nile encephalitis in Romania, Israel and New York. Acute encephalitis illness may occur in HIV infection, occasionally at the time of infection, but more commonly as a manifestation of AIDS (see p. 122).

Pathology

Inflammation can occur in the cortex, white matter, basal ganglia and brain stem, and the distribution of lesions varies with the type of virus. In herpes simplex encephalitis the temporal lobes are usually primarily affected. Inclusion bodies may be present in the neurons and glial cells and there is an infiltration of polymorphonuclear cells in the perivascular space. There is neuronal degeneration and diffuse glial proliferation, often associated with cerebral oedema.

Clinical features

Viral encephalitis presents with acute onset of headache, with fever, focal neurological signs (aphasia and/or hemiplegia) and seizures. Disturbance of consciousness ranging from drowsiness to deep coma supervenes early and may advance dramatically. Meningism occurs in many patients. Rabies presents a distinct clinical picture and is described below.

Investigations

CT of the head, which should precede lumbar puncture, may show low-density lesions in the temporal lobes. MRI is more sensitive in detecting early abnormalities. The CSF usually contains excess lymphocytes, but polymorphonuclear cells may predominate in the early stages. Occasionally, the CSF is normal. The protein content may be elevated but the glucose is normal. The EEG is usually abnormal in the early stages, especially in herpes simplex encephalitis, with characteristic periodic slow-wave activity in the temporal lobes. Virological investigations of the CSF, including PCR for viral DNA, may reveal the causative organism but the initiation of treatment should not await this.

Management

Anticonvulsant treatment is often necessary (see p. 1127) and raised intracranial pressure is treated with dexamethasone 8 mg 12-hourly. Herpes simplex encephalitis responds to aciclovir 10 mg/kg i.v. 8-hourly for 2–3 weeks. This should be given early to all patients suspected of suffering from viral encephalitis.

Even with optimum treatment, mortality is 10–30% and significant proportions of survivors have residual epilepsy or cognitive impairment. For details of post-infectious encephalomyelitis, see page 1172.

BRAIN-STEM ENCEPHALITIS

This presents with ataxia, dysarthria, diplopia or other cranial nerve palsies. The CSF is lymphocytic, with a normal glucose. The causative agent is presumed to be viral. However, *Listeria monocytogenes* may cause a similar syndrome with meningitis (and often a polymorphonuclear CSF pleocytosis) and requires specific treatment with ampicillin 500 mg 6-hourly (see Box 22.90).

RABIES

Rabies is caused by a rhabdovirus which infects the central nervous tissue and salivary glands of a wide range of mammals, and is usually conveyed by saliva through bites or licks on abrasions or on intact mucous membranes. Humans are most frequently infected from dogs. In Europe the maintenance host is the fox.

The incubation period varies in humans from a minimum of 9 days to many months but is usually between 4 and 8 weeks. Severe bites, especially if on the head or neck, are associated with shorter incubation periods.

Clinical features

At the onset there may be fever, and paraesthesia at the site of the bite. A prodromal period of 1–10 days, during which the patient is increasingly anxious, leads to the characteristic 'hydrophobia'. Although the patient is thirsty, attempts at drinking provoke violent contractions of the diaphragm and other inspiratory muscles. Delusions and hallucinations may develop, accompanied by spitting, biting and mania, with lucid intervals in which the patient is markedly anxious. Cranial nerve lesions develop and terminal hyperpyrexia is common. Death ensues, usually within a week of the onset of symptoms.

Investigations

During life the diagnosis is usually made on clinical grounds but rapid immunofluorescent techniques can detect antigen in corneal impression smears or skin biopsies.

Management

A few patients with rabies have survived. All received some post-exposure prophylaxis, and needed intensive care with facilities to control cardiac and respiratory failure. Otherwise, only palliative treatment is possible once symptoms have appeared. The patient should be heavily sedated with diazepam 10 mg 4–6-hourly, supplemented by chlorpromazine 50–100 mg if necessary. Nutrition and fluids should be given intravenously or through a gastrostomy.

Prevention

Pre-exposure prophylaxis is required by those who by profession handle potentially infected animals, those who work with rabies virus in laboratories and those who live at special risk in rabies-endemic areas. Protection is afforded by two intradermal injections of 0.1 ml human diploid cell strain vaccine, or two intramuscular injections of 1 ml, given 4 weeks apart, followed by yearly boosters.

Post-exposure prophylaxis

The wounds should be thoroughly cleaned, preferably with a quaternary ammonium detergent or soap; damaged tissues should be excised and the wound left unsutured. Rabies can usually be prevented if treatment is started within a day or two of biting. Delayed treatment may still be of value. For maximum protection hyperimmune serum and vaccine are required.

The safest antirabies antiserum is human rabies immune globulin; the dose is 20 i.u./kg body weight. Half is infiltrated around the bite and half is given intramuscularly at a different site from the vaccine. The dose of hyperimmune animal scrum is 40 i.u./kg; hypersensitivity reactions, including anaphylaxis, are common.

The safest vaccine, free of complications, is human diploid cell strain vaccine; 1.0 ml is given intramuscularly on days 0, 3, 7, 14, 30 and 90. In developing countries, where human rabies globulin may not be obtainable, 0.1 ml of vaccine should be given intradermally into eight sites on day 1, with single boosters on days 7 and 28. Where human products are not available and when risk of rabies is slight (licks on the skin, or minor bites of covered arms or legs) it may be justifiable to delay starting treatment for up to 5 days while observing the biting animal or awaiting examination of its brain rather than use the older vaccine.

Control of spread

Human rabies is a rare disease even in endemic areas. However, because it is usually fatal, major efforts are directed to limiting its spread and preventing its importation into uninfected countries such as Britain.

POLIOMYELITIS

Aetiology and pathology

The disease is caused by one of three polioviruses, which are a subgroup of the enteroviruses. It is much less common in developed countries following the widespread use of oral vaccines but is still a major problem in the developing world. Infection usually occurs through the nasopharynx.

The virus causes a lymphocytic meningitis and infects the grey matter of the spinal cord, brain stem and cortex. There is a particular propensity to damage anterior horn cells, especially in the lumbar segments.

Clinical features

The incubation period is 7–14 days. Figure 22.49 illustrates the various features of the infection. Many patients recover fully after the initial phase of a few days of mild fever and headache. In others, after a week of well-being, there is recurrence of pyrexia, headache and meningism. Weakness may start later in one muscle group and can progress to widespread paresis. Respiratory failure may supervene if intercostal muscles are paralysed or the medullary motor nuclei are involved.

Investigations

The CSF shows a lymphocytic pleocytosis, a rise in protein and a normal sugar content. Poliomyelitis virus may be cultured from CSF and stool.

Management

In the early stages bed rest is imperative because exercise appears to worsen the paralysis or precipitate it. At the onset of respiratory difficulties a tracheostomy and ventilation are required. Subsequent treatment is by physiotherapy and orthopaedic measures.

Prognosis

Epidemics vary widely in their incidence of non-paralytic cases and in mortality rate. Death occurs from respiratory

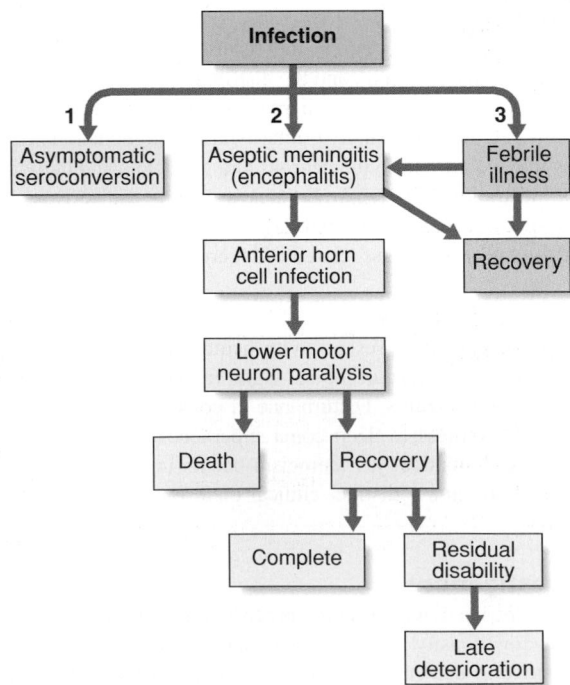

Fig. 22.49 **Poliomyelitis.** Possible consequences of infection.

paralysis. Muscle weakness is maximal at the end of the first week and gradual recovery may then take place for several months. Muscles showing no signs of recovery by the end of a month probably will not regain useful function. Second attacks are very rare but occasionally patients show late deterioration in muscle bulk and power many years after the initial infection.

Prevention

Prevention of poliomyelitis is by immunisation with live (Sabin) vaccine.

HERPES ZOSTER (SHINGLES)

Herpes zoster is the result of reactivation of the varicella zoster virus that has lain dormant in a nerve root ganglion following chickenpox earlier in life. Reactivation may be spontaneous (as usually occurs in the middle-aged or elderly) or be due to immunosuppression (as in patients with diabetes, malignant disease or AIDS). Full details are given on page 32.

SUBACUTE SCLEROSING PANENCEPHALITIS

This is a rare, chronic, progressive and eventually fatal neurological disease caused by the measles virus, presumably as a result of an inability of the nervous system to eradicate the virus. It occurs in children and adolescents, usually many years after the primary virus infection. The onset is insidious, with intellectual deterioration, apathy and clumsiness followed by myoclonic jerks, rigidity and dementia.

The CSF may show a mild lymphocytic pleocytosis and the EEG is distinctive, with periodic bursts of triphasic waves. Although there is persistent measles-specific IgG in serum and CSF, antiviral therapy is ineffective and death ensues within years.

PROGRESSIVE MULTIFOCAL LEUCOENCEPHALOPATHY

This was originally described as a rare complication of lymphoma, leukaemia or carcinomatosis. Nowadays it occurs more frequently as a feature of AIDS (see p. 123). It is an infection of oligodendrocytes by human polyomavirus JC, which causes widespread demyelination of the white matter of the cerebral hemispheres. Clinical signs include dementia, hemiparesis and aphasia which progress rapidly, usually leading to death within weeks or months. Areas of low density in the white matter are seen on CT but MRI is more sensitive, showing diffuse high signal on T2-weighted images.

PARENCHYMAL BACTERIAL INFECTIONS

CEREBRAL ABSCESS

Bacteria may enter the cerebral substance through penetrating injury, by direct spread from paranasal sinuses or the middle ear, or by haematogenous spread from septicaemia. The site of abscess formation and the likely causative organism are both related to the source of infection (see Box 22.92).

Initial infection leads to local suppuration followed by loculation of pus within a surrounding wall of gliosis, which in a chronic abscess may form a tough capsule. Multiple abscesses may occur, particularly with haematogenous spread.

Clinical features

A cerebral abscess may present acutely with fever, headache, meningism and drowsiness, but more commonly presents over days or weeks as a cerebral mass lesion with

22.92 AETIOLOGY AND TREATMENT OF BACTERIAL CEREBRAL ABSCESS			
Site of abscess	**Source of infection**	**Likely organisms**	**Recommended treatment**
Frontal lobe	Paranasal sinuses Teeth	Streptococci Anaerobes	Cefuroxime 1.5 g i.v. 8-hourly *plus* metronidazole 500 mg i.v. 8-hourly
Temporal lobe	Middle ear	Streptococci Enterobacteriaceae	Ampicillin 2–3 g i.v. 8-hourly *plus* metronidazole 500 mg i.v. 8-hourly *plus* either ceftazidime 2 g i.v.
Cerebellum	Sphenoid sinus	*Pseudomonas* spp. Anaerobes	8-hourly or gentamicin* 5 mg/kg i.v. daily
Any site	Penetrating trauma	Staphylococci	Flucloxacillin 2–3 g i.v. 6-hourly *or* cefuroxime 1.5 g i.v. 8-hourly
Multiple	Metastatic and cryptogenic	Streptococci Anaerobes	Benzylpenicillin 1.8–2.4 g i.v. 6-hourly if endocarditis or cyanotic heart disease Otherwise cefuroxime 1.5 g i.v. 8-hourly *plus* metronidazole 500 mg i.v. 8-hourly
* Monitor gentamicin levels.			

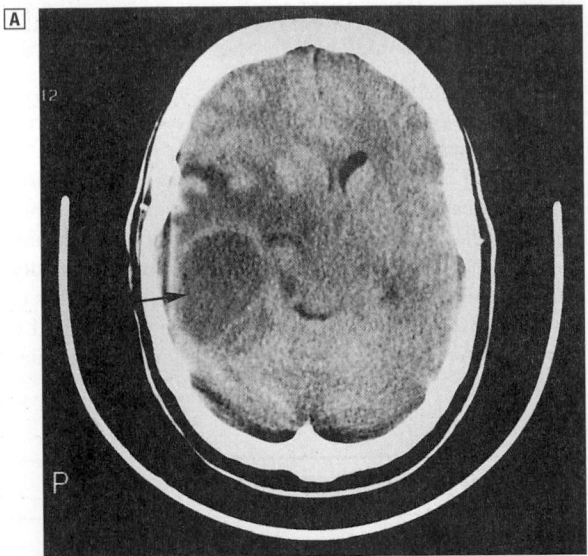

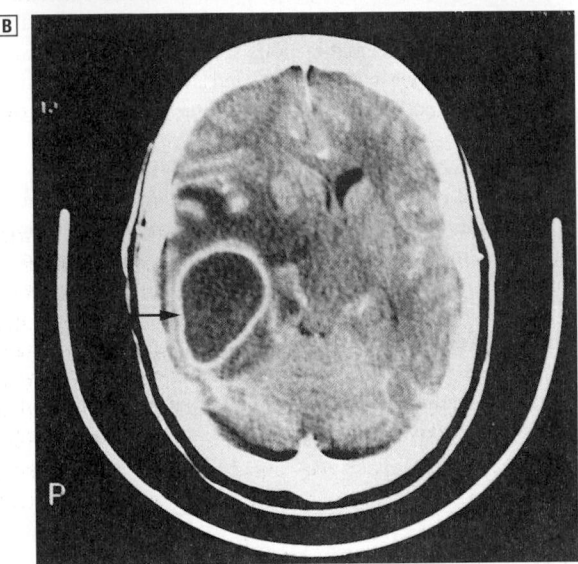

Fig. 22.50 Right temporal cerebral abscess (arrows), with surrounding oedema and midline shift to the left. A Unenhanced CT image. B Contrast-enhanced CT image.

little or no evidence of infection. Seizures, raised intracranial pressure and focal hemisphere signs occur alone or in combination, and distinction from a cerebral tumour may be impossible on clinical grounds.

Investigations

Lumbar puncture is potentially hazardous in the presence of raised intracranial pressure and CT should always precede lumbar puncture. CT shows single or multiple low-density areas, which show ring enhancement with contrast, and surrounding cerebral oedema (see Fig. 22.50). There may

be an elevated white blood cell count and ESR in patients with active local infection. The possibility of cerebral toxoplasmosis secondary to HIV infection should always be considered.

Management

Antimicrobial therapy is indicated once the diagnosis is made. The likely source of infection should guide the choice of antibiotic (see Box 22.92). Surgical treatment by burrhole aspiration or excision may be necessary, especially where the presence of a capsule may lead to a persistent focus of infection. Anticonvulsants are often necessary, as epilepsy frequently develops acutely or in the recovery phase.

Prognosis

The mortality rate remains at 10–20% despite an improvement in available surgical and medical treatments, and in some patients this is related to delay in diagnosis and initiation of treatment.

SUBDURAL EMPYEMA

This is a rare complication of frontal sinusitis, osteomyelitis of the skull vault, or middle ear disease. A collection of pus in the subdural space spreads over the surface of the hemisphere, causing underlying cortical oedema or thrombophlebitis. Patients present with severe pain in the face or head and pyrexia, often with a history of preceding paranasal sinus or ear infection. The patient then becomes drowsy with seizures and focal signs such as a progressive hemiparesis.

The diagnosis rests on a strong clinical suspicion in patients with a local focus of infection. Careful assessment of a head CT (with contrast) or MRI may show a subdural collection with underlying cerebral oedema. Management requires aspiration of pus via a burrhole and appropriate parenteral antibiotics. Any local source of infection must be treated to prevent reinfection.

SPINAL EPIDURAL ABSCESS

The characteristic clinical features are pain in a root distribution and progressive transverse spinal cord syndrome with paraparesis, sensory impairment and sphincter dysfunction. Infection is usually haematogenous but a primary source of infection is easily overlooked.

Plain radiographs of the spine may show osteomyelitis but such changes are often late. MRI or myelography should precede urgent neurosurgical intervention. Decompressive laminectomy with draining of the abscess relieves the pressure on the dura. This, together with appropriate antibiotics, may prevent complete and irreversible paraplegia. Organisms may be cultured from the pus or blood.

TETANUS

This disease results from infection with *Clostridium tetani*, which is a commensal in the gut of humans and domestic animals and is found in soil. Infection enters the body through wounds, often trivial. It is rare in Britain, occurring mostly in gardeners and farmers. By contrast, the disease is common in many developing countries, where dust contains spores derived from animal and human excreta. If childbirth takes place in an unhygienic environment, *Tetanus neonatorum* may result from infection of the umbilical stump, or the mother may develop the disease. Tetanus is still one of the major killers of adults, children and neonates in developing countries, where the mortality rate can be nearly 100% in the newborn and around 40% in others.

In circumstances unfavourable to the growth of the organism, spores are formed and these may remain dormant for years in the soil. Spores germinate and bacilli multiply only in the anaerobic conditions which occur in areas of tissue necrosis or if the oxygen tension is low as a result of the presence of other organisms, particularly aerobic ones. The bacilli remain localised but produce an exotoxin with an affinity for motor nerve endings and motor nerve cells.

The anterior horn cells are affected after the exotoxin has passed into the blood stream and their involvement results in rigidity and convulsions. Symptoms first appear from 2 days to several weeks after injury—the shorter the incubation period, the more severe the attack and the worse the prognosis.

Clinical features

Much the most important early symptom is trismus—spasm of the masseter muscles, which causes difficulty in opening the mouth and in masticating, hence the name 'lockjaw'. Lockjaw in tetanus is painless, unlike the spasm of the masseters due to dental abscess, septic throat or other causes, which is painful. Conditions that can mimic tetanus include hysteria and phenothiazine overdosage.

In tetanus, the tonic rigidity spreads to involve the muscles of the face, neck and trunk. Contraction of the frontalis and the muscles at the angles of the mouth gives rise to the so-called 'risus sardonicus'. There is rigidity of the muscles at the neck and trunk of varying degree. The back is usually slightly arched ('opisthotonus') and there is a board-like abdominal wall.

In the more severe cases violent spasms lasting for a few seconds to 3–4 minutes occur spontaneously, or may be induced by stimuli such as moving the patient or making a noise. These convulsions are painful, exhausting and of very serious significance, especially if they appear soon after the onset of symptoms. They gradually increase in frequency and severity for about 1 week and the patient may die from exhaustion, asphyxia or aspiration pneumonia. In less severe illness convulsions may not commence for about a week after the first sign of rigidity and in very mild infections they may never appear. Autonomic involvement may cause cardiovascular complications such as hypertension.

Rarely, the only manifestation of the disease may be 'local tetanus'—stiffness or spasm of the muscles near the infected wound—and the prognosis is good if treatment is commenced at this stage.

22.93 TREATMENT OF TETANUS
Neutralise absorbed toxin
• I.v. injection of 3000 i.u. of human tetanus antitoxin
Prevent further toxin production
• Débridement of wound • Benzylpenicillin 600 mg i.v. 6-hourly (metronidazole if allergic to penicillin)
Control spasms
• Nurse in a quiet room • Avoid unnecessary stimuli • I.v. diazepam—if spasms continue paralyse patient and ventilate
General measures
• Maintain hydration and nutrition • Treat secondary infections

Investigations

The diagnosis is made on clinical grounds. It is rarely possible to isolate the infecting organism from the original locus of entry.

Management

This should be begun as soon as possible. The essentials are shown in Box 22.93.

Prevention

Active immunisation must be given. Contaminated injuries are treated by débridement. The immediate danger of tetanus can be greatly reduced by the injection of 1200 mg of penicillin followed by a 7-day course of oral penicillin. For those who are allergic to penicillin, erythromycin should be used. When the risk of tetanus is judged to be present, an injection of 250 units of human tetanus antitoxin should be given along with an intramuscular injection of toxoid which should be repeated 1 month and 6 months later. For those already immunised only a booster dose of toxoid is required.

LYME DISEASE

See page 21.

NEUROSYPHILIS

Neurosyphilis may present as an acute or chronic process and may involve the meninges, blood vessels and/or parenchyma of the brain and spinal cord. In developed countries syphilis is now most commonly seen in patients with AIDS. The clinical manifestations are diverse and, although the condition is now rare, early diagnosis and treatment remain important.

Clinical features

The clinical and pathological features of the three most common presentations are summarised in Box 22.94.

Neurological examination reveals signs appropriate to the anatomical localisation of lesions. Delusions of grandeur suggest general paresis of the insane, but more commonly

22.94 CLINICAL AND PATHOLOGICAL FEATURES OF NEUROSYPHILIS

Type	Pathology	Clinical features
Meningovascular (5 years)*	Endarteritis obliterans Meningeal exudate Granuloma (gumma)	Stroke Cranial nerve palsies Seizures/mass lesion
General paralysis of the insane (5–15 years)*	Degeneration in cerebral cortex/cerebral atrophy Thickened meninges	Dementia Tremor Bilateral upper motor signs
Tabes dorsalis (5–20 years)*	Degeneration of sensory neurons Wasting of dorsal columns Optic atrophy	Lightning pains Sensory ataxia Visual failure Abdominal crises Incontinence Trophic changes

* Interval from primary infection.

there is simply progressive dementia. The pupillary abnormality described by Argyll Robertson may accompany any neurosyphilitic syndrome, but most commonly tabes dorsalis; the pupils are small and irregular, and react to convergence but not directly to light.

Investigations

Routine screening for syphilis is warranted in the great majority of neurological patients. Serological tests (see pp. 98–99) are positive in the serum in most patients, but CSF examination is essential if neurological involvement is suspected. Active disease is suggested by an elevated cell count, usually lymphocytic, and the protein content may be elevated to 0.5–1.0 g/l with an increased gammaglobulin fraction. Serological tests in the CSF are usually positive, but progressive disease can occur with negative CSF serology.

Management

The essential part of the treatment of neurosyphilis of all types is the injection of procaine benzylpenicillin (procaine penicillin) and probenecid for 17 days (see Box 1.73, p. 100). Further courses of penicillin must be given if symptoms are not relieved, if the condition continues to advance or if the CSF continues to show signs of active disease. The cell count returns to normal within 3 months of completion of treatment, but the elevated protein takes longer to subside and some serological tests may never revert to normal. Evidence of clinical progression at any time is an indication for renewed treatment.

PRION DISEASES: TRANSMISSIBLE SPONGIFORM ENCEPHALOPATHIES

Transmissible spongiform encephalopathies (TSEs) include a number of conditions affecting both animals and humans which are characterised by the histopathological triad of spongiform change, neuronal cell loss, and gliosis in the grey matter of the brain. Associated with these changes, there is deposition of amyloid made up of an altered form of a normally occurring protein, the prion protein. These diseases can be transmitted by inoculation; the precise nature of the infective agent is not yet clear but almost certainly involves the abnormal prion protein. They may also occur spontaneously or as an inherited disorder. Diseases affecting animals include bovine and feline spongiform encephalopathies (BSE and FSE). In humans, the most common TSE is Creutzfeldt–Jakob disease (CJD). This occurs sporadically, with a world-wide incidence of approximately 1/1 000 000, but can also be transmitted by inoculation (e.g. via depth EEG electrodes, corneal grafts, neurosurgery (especially when cadaveric dura mater grafts were used), and by the use of pooled cadaveric growth hormone), and some 10% of cases arise due to a mutation in the gene coding for the prion protein. A variant form of CJD has recently been described which is probably due to the same agent which causes BSE. Other extremely rare inherited human TSEs include Gerstmann–Sträussler–Scheinker disease, fatal familial insomnia and kuru. Kuru occurred only in members of a cannibalistic New Guinea tribe and was probably transmitted by eating the brains of dead tribal members. Clinical features involved progressive ataxia and dementia.

CREUTZFELDT–JAKOB DISEASE (CJD)

Sporadic CJD usually occurs in middle-aged to elderly patients. Clinical features usually involve a rapidly progressive dementia, with myoclonus and a characteristic EEG pattern (repetitive slow wave complexes), though a number of other features such as visual disturbance or ataxia may also be seen. These are particularly common in CJD transmitted by inoculation. Death occurs after a mean of 4–6 months. There is as yet no known treatment.

Variant CJD

A variant of CJD (vCJD) has been described in a small number of patients, mostly in the UK. The agent which causes it appears to be identical to that causing BSE in cows, and it has been suggested that the disease appeared in humans as a result of the epidemic of this disease in the UK which started in the late 1980s. Patients affected by vCJD are typically younger than those with sporadic CJD and present with neuropsychiatric changes and sensory symptoms in the limbs, followed by ataxia, dementia and death, progressing at a slightly slower rate than patients with sporadic CJD (mean time to death is over a year). Characteristic EEG changes are not present but MRI scans of the head show characteristic high signal changes in the pulvinar in a high proportion of cases. The brain pathology is distinct, with very florid plaques containing the prion proteins. Abnormal prion protein has been identified in tonsil specimens from sufferers of vCJD, leading to the suggestion that the disease could be transmitted by reticulo-endothelial tissue (like TSEs in animals but unlike sporadic CJD in humans). This has caused great concern in the UK, leading to precautionary measures such as leucodepletion of all blood used for transfusion, and the mandatory use of disposable surgical instruments for tonsillectomy and appendicectomy operations. Implications for ophthalmological practice are also being considered.

INTRACRANIAL MASS LESIONS AND RAISED INTRACRANIAL PRESSURE

There are many different types of mass lesion in the head (see Box 22.95). In developing countries, tuberculoma is a very common cause, but in developed countries cerebral neoplasms are the most frequent. The clinical features relate to the site of the mass, its nature and its rate of expansion. Symptoms and signs are produced by a number of mechanisms, as listed in Box 22.96.

RAISED INTRACRANIAL PRESSURE

Raised intracranial pressure may be caused by mass lesions (especially tumours), cerebral oedema, obstruction to CSF circulation (causing hydrocephalus) or impaired CSF absorption, as in idiopathic intracranial hypertension (see below) and cerebral venous obstruction.

Clinical features

The major features of raised intracranial pressure are listed in Box 22.96. Impairment of conscious level is related to the level of intracranial pressure. Cerebral mass lesions will obviously tend to increase intracerebral pressure, but the amount by which the pressure is raised depends on the rate of growth of the mass. If it is slow, various compensatory mechanisms may occur, including alteration in the volume of fluid in CSF spaces and venous sinuses, thereby allowing some tumours to achieve considerable size. More rapid growth (as in highly malignant tumours or abscesses) does not allow the compensatory mechanisms to take place, so raised intracranial pressure develops early, especially if the CSF circulation is also obstructed. Papilloedema is not always present, either because raised intracranial pressure has developed too recently, or because of anatomic anomalies of the meningeal sheath of the optic nerve. Vomiting, bradycardia and arterial hypertension develop as late features of raised intracranial pressure and usually parallel the other clinical signs; sudden vomiting may be an early feature of tumours of the cerebellum, especially in children.

Management

The management of raised intracranial pressure is largely dictated by its specific cause, as described later. ICU support may be required (see p. 208).

'CONING' AND FALSE LOCALISING SIGNS

The rise in intracranial pressure from a mass lesion is not usually uniform within the cerebral substance and alterations in pressure relationships within the skull may lead to displacement of parts of the brain between its various compartments. Downward displacement of the temporal lobes through the tentorium due to a large hemisphere mass may cause 'temporal coning' (see Fig. 22.51). This may stretch the 3rd and/or 6th cranial nerves, or cause pressure on the contralateral cerebral peduncle (thereby resulting in ipsilateral

22.95 INTRACRANIAL MASS LESIONS
Traumatic
• Subdural haematoma
Vascular
• Intracerebral haematoma (see p. 1162)
Infective
• Cerebral abscess (pyogenic, *Toxoplasma* etc.)
• Tuberculoma
• Cysticercosis
• Echinococcosis (as hydatid cysts)
• Schistosomiasis
Inflammatory
• Sarcoid mass
Neoplastic
• Cerebral neoplasm (benign and malignant)
Other
• Embryonic dysplastic lesions (e.g. craniopharyngiomas, hamartomas)
• Arachnoid cyst
• Colloid cyst (in the ventricles)

22.96 CLINICAL FEATURES OF INTRACRANIAL MASS LESIONS
Local effects on adjacent brain tissue (e.g. seizures, focal signs)
• Depends on the site of the lesion (see pp. 1146–1148)
Raised intracranial pressure
• Headache (see p. 1117)
• Impairment of conscious level
• Papilloedema
• Vomiting, bradycardia, arterial hypertension
False localising signs
• Pupillary dilatation (ipsilateral to lesion)
• 6th cranial nerve lesion (unilateral or bilateral)
• Hemiparesis (ipsilateral to lesion)
• Bilateral extensor plantar responses

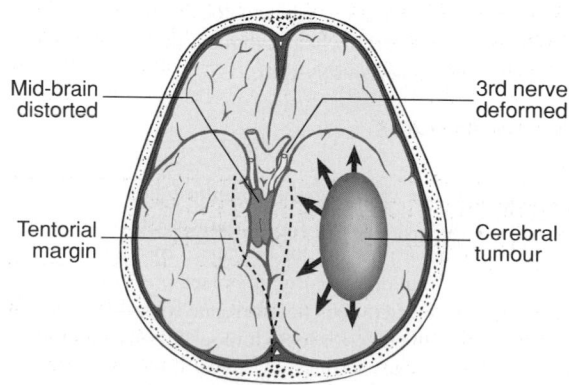

Fig. 22.51 **Cerebral tumour displacing medial temporal lobe and causing pressure on the mid-brain and 3rd cranial nerve.**

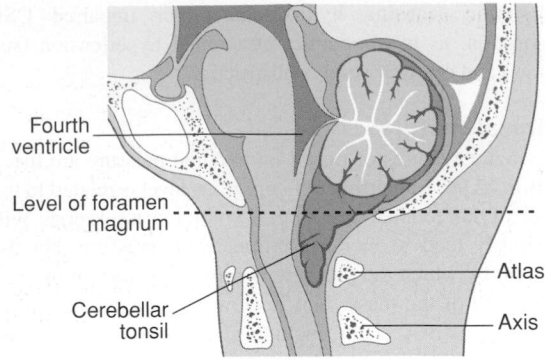

Fourth ventricle

Level of foramen magnum

Cerebellar tonsil

Atlas

Axis

Fig. 22.52 **Tonsillar cone.** Downward displacement of the cerebellar tonsils below the level of the foramen magnum.

upper motor neuron signs). Downward movement of the cerebellar tonsils through the foramen magnum may compress the medulla—'tonsillar coning' (see Fig. 22.52). This coning may result in brain-stem haemorrhage and/or acute obstruction of the CSF pathways. As coning progresses, the patient may adopt a decerebrate posture and, unless rapidly treated, death almost invariably ensues. The process may be acutely accelerated if the pressure dynamics are suddenly disturbed by lumbar puncture.

INTRACRANIAL NEOPLASMS

In the developed world cerebral tumours account for 2% of deaths at all ages. The majority are metastatic tumours from malignancies outside the nervous system. Meningiomas account for about one-fifth of intracranial tumours. Benign or malignant neoplasms of central nervous system tissue account for the remainder.

Pathology

Metastases from extracranial primary tumours are usually located in the white matter of the cerebral or cerebellar hemispheres, and common sources are bronchus, breast and gastrointestinal tract. Primary intracerebral tumours are classified by their cell of origin and degree of malignancy, and vary in incidence by age and localisation (see Boxes 22.97 and 22.98). Even when malignant they do not metastasise outside the nervous system.

Clinical features

Headache
Headache is not an invariable manifestation of cerebral tumour. If present, it may have characteristics suggesting raised intracranial pressure, or be caused by traction on the pain-sensitive intracranial structures (see p. 1117). The site of the headache often does not correlate with the site of the tumour, although posterior fossa tumours often cause pain in the occiput or neck.

Local effects
In general the focal deficits produced by a cerebral tumour are of slow onset and progressive. Tumours may present at

22.97	PRIMARY MALIGNANT INTRACRANIAL TUMOURS		
Histological type	**Common site**	**Age**	
Glioma (astrocytoma)	Cerebral hemisphere	Adulthood	
	Cerebellum	Childhood/ adulthood	
	Brain stem	Childhood/ young adulthood	
Oligodendroglioma	Cerebral hemisphere	Adulthood	
Medulloblastoma	Posterior fossa	Childhood	
Ependymoma	Posterior fossa	Childhood/ adolescence	
Cerebral lymphoma (microglioma)	Cerebral hemisphere	Adulthood	

22.98	PRIMARY BENIGN INTRACRANIAL TUMOURS		
Histological type	**Common site**	**Age**	
Meningioma	Cortical dura Parasagittal Sphenoid ridge Suprasellar Olfactory groove	Adulthood	
Neurofibroma	Acoustic neuroma	Adulthood	
Craniopharyngioma	Suprasellar	Childhood/ adolescence	
Pituitary adenoma	Pituitary fossa	Adulthood	
Colloid cyst	Third ventricle	Any age	
Pineal tumours	Quadrigeminal cistern	Childhood (teratomas) Young adulthood (germ cell)	

an early stage in some areas, such as the brain stem where structural disturbance quickly results in a neurological deficit. In other regions, especially the frontal lobe, a tumour may be quite large before symptoms occur. The clinical features of dysfunction in the various lobes of the brain are outlined in Box 22.39, page 1148. Occasionally, localised oedema in the brain tissue surrounding a tumour will cause a rapid progression of symptoms. Rarely, haemorrhage into a tumour presents like an acute stroke.

Seizures
Infiltration by tumour cells of an area of cerebral cortex often excites seizure activity. The resulting seizures may be generalised or partial in nature, and the development of focal seizures in adult life should always suggest the possibility of a tumour.

Investigations
CT or MRI of the head is the definitive investigation, allowing accurate localisation of the tumour and providing some guidance as to the likely histological type (see Fig. 22.53). MRI is of particular value in the investigation of tumours of the posterior fossa and brain stem (see Fig. 22.54) and in

delineating the nature and extent of tumours prior to surgery, largely replacing angiography. Distortion of intracranial structures and the size of the ventricular system can be assessed and may provide accurate evaluation of the extent of the tumour. Plain skull radiographs are rarely of diagnostic value except in pituitary tumours. Chest radiography is an important investigation and may provide evidence of a primary pulmonary tumour or other systemic malignancy.

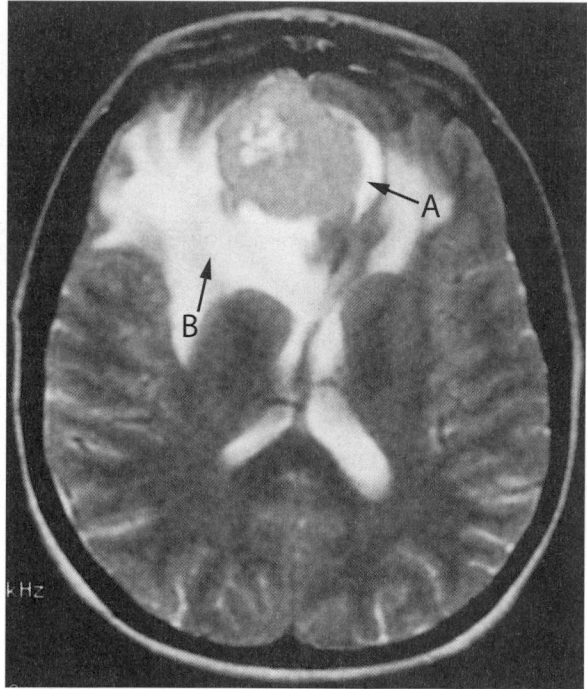

Fig. 22.53 MRI showing meningioma in frontal lobe (arrow A) with associated oedema (arrow B).

Management

Medical

Relief of raised intracranial pressure is often required when surgery is not possible or when life is threatened before investigation has revealed the diagnosis. Dexamethasone, 8 mg 12-hourly either orally or by injection, is used to lower intracranial pressure by resolving the reactive oedema around a tumour. A striking improvement in conscious level is often produced and focal disabilities may regress. In severe and acutely raised intracranial pressure 16–20 mg of dexamethasone may be given intravenously or 200 ml of a 20% solution of mannitol may be infused.

Prolactin- or growth hormone-secreting pituitary tumours (see p. 741) may respond to treatment with the dopamine agonists bromocriptine, cabergoline or quinagolide.

Surgical

Surgery is the mainstay of treatment, although only partial excision may be possible if the tumour is inaccessible or if its removal is likely to cause unacceptable brain damage. Biopsy by a direct or stereotactic technique should be considered even if the tumour cannot be removed, since the histological diagnosis has important implications for management and prognosis.

Meningiomas and acoustic neuromas offer the best prospects for complete removal without unacceptable damage to surrounding structures. Meningiomas can recur, particularly those of the sphenoid ridge when partial excision is often all that is possible. Pituitary adenomas can often be removed by a trans-sphenoidal route, thereby avoiding the necessity for a craniotomy.

Radiotherapy and chemotherapy

Radiotherapy and chemotherapy have only a marginal effect on survival in cerebral metastases and malignant gliomas in adults (see EBM panel), but their combination has greatly improved the prognosis in medulloblastoma in children.

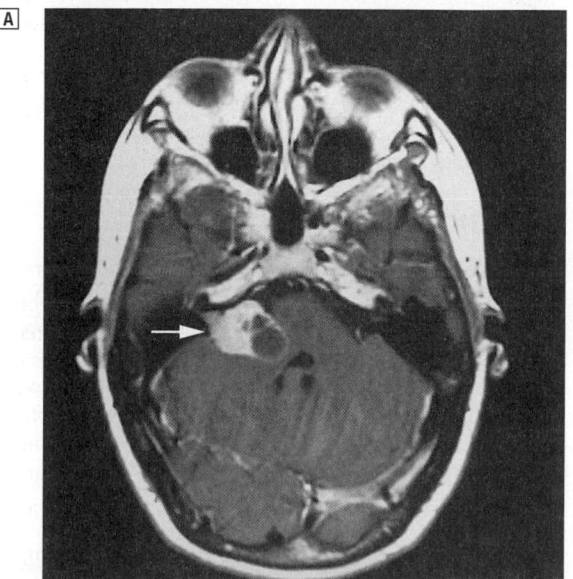

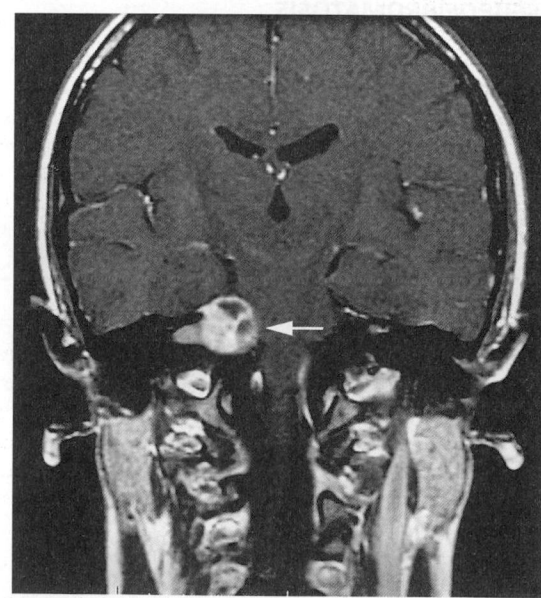

Fig. 22.54 MRI of an acoustic neuroma (arrows) in the posterior fossa compressing the brain stem. A Axial image. B Coronal image.

Radiotherapy reduces the risk of recurrence of pituitary adenoma after surgery and may also be helpful as an adjunct to operative treatment in those meningiomas whose anatomical site precludes complete excision or whose histology suggests an increased tendency to recurrence. Ependymomas, some pineal tumours and low-grade gliomas in children and young adults are often radiosensitive.

Prognosis

Gliomas are rarely completely excised, as infiltration spreads beyond the radiologically evident boundaries of the tumour. Recurrence is therefore common, even if the mass of the tumour is apparently completely removed. Partial excision ('debulking') may be useful in alleviating raised intracranial pressure, but survival in highly malignant gliomas is poor even if such a decompressive procedure is attempted. Prognosis is related to histological grade; the better grades (I–II) may survive many years, whilst only 20% of patients with grade IV gliomas (glioblastoma multiforme) survive 1 year.

The prognosis for benign tumours is good, provided complete surgical excision can be achieved. Ependymomas and medulloblastomas can often be excised with minimal residual disability, but may recur with seeding of the tumour via the CSF. Oligodendrogliomas are often slow-growing and relatively benign in the early stages, but may transform to a more malignant form and behave as gliomas.

NEUROFIBROMATOSIS

This is a disorder of autosomal dominant inheritance due to an abnormal gene on chromosome 17 (q11.2, type 1 neurofibromatosis, NF1) or 22 (q12.2, type 2 neurofibromatosis, NF2). Multiple fibromatous tumours develop from the

22.99 TYPES OF NEUROFIBROMATOSIS	
Type 1 Peripheral form (> 70% of cases)	
• Multiple cutaneous neurofibromas	• Plexiform neurofibromas
• 'Soft' papillomas	• Spinal neurofibromas
• Café au lait patches	• Aqueduct stenosis
• Axillary freckling	• Scoliosis
• Iris fibromas	• Endocrine tumours
Type 2 Central form	
• Few or no cutaneous lesions	• Meningiomas
• Bilateral acoustic neuromas	• Spinal neurofibromas
• Cerebral and optic nerve gliomas	

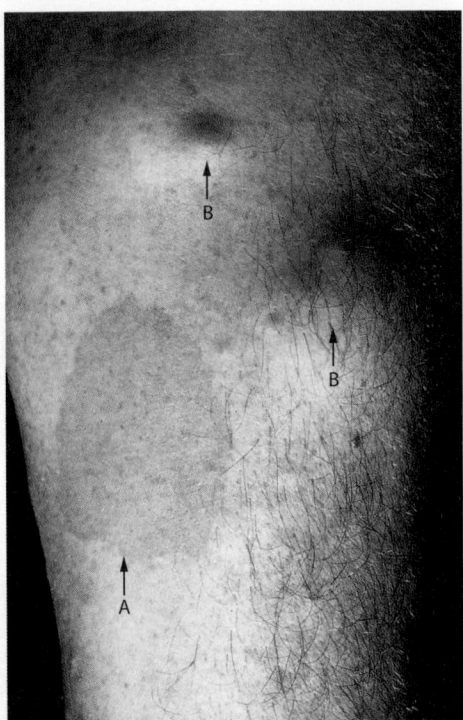

Fig. 22.55   A café au lait spot (arrow A) and subcutaneous nodules (arrows B) on the forearm of a patient with neurofibromatosis type 1.

neurilemmal sheaths of peripheral and cranial nerves. Most of the lesions are benign but sarcomatous change may occur. In NF1 (von Recklinghausen's disease) there are characteristic cutaneous manifestations and other extracranial manifestations (see Box 22.99).

Patients with NF1 are easily recognised because of the cutaneous lesions (see Fig. 22.55) which increase in number throughout life. Investigation and treatment are only indicated if there are symptoms of cerebral or spinal involvement, or if malignant change is suspected.

Patients with NF2 present with acoustic neuromas, often bilateral, and/or other central neoplasms, and have fewer, if any, cutaneous lesions. A family history of cerebral or spinal tumours should be noted with care, since relatives of patients with NF2 may require screening for acoustic neuromas.

ACOUSTIC NEUROMA

This is a benign tumour of Schwann cells of the 8th cranial nerve, which may arise in isolation or as part of NF2 (see above). As an isolated finding, an acoustic neuroma occurs after the third decade and is more frequent in females. The tumour commonly arises near the nerve's entry into the medulla or in the internal auditory meatus, usually on the vestibular division. Such schwannomas of the 8th nerve make up 80–90% of tumours at the cerebello–pontine angle.

Clinical features

These depend somewhat on the site of the tumour along the acoustic or vestibular nerve. (Similar tumours arise rarely from the trigeminal nerve.) Hearing loss is almost invariable, although it may not be the presenting feature. Sensory symptoms in the face and vertigo are also common symptoms at presentation. Distortion of the brain stem and/or cerebellar peduncle may cause ataxia and/or cerebellar signs in the limbs. Distortion of the fourth ventricle and cerebral aqueduct may cause hydrocephalus, which may be the presenting feature (see p. 1208). Facial weakness is unusual at presentation, but facial palsy may follow surgical removal of the tumour.

Investigations
MRI is the investigation of choice (see Fig. 22.54), CT being less useful in this region of the posterior fossa.

Management
This involves surgical removal. If this is complete, the prognosis is excellent. Deafness and facial weakness, if not present before surgery, usually result from the operation.

VON HIPPEL–LINDAU DISEASE

This is a dominantly inherited disease due to a defective gene on chromosome 3p25–26, characterised by the combination

of retinal and intracranial (typically cerebellar) haemangiomas and haemangioblastomas. There may be associated extracranial hamartomatous lesions, which may undergo malignant change. About 10% of posterior fossa tumours are cerebellar haemangioblastomas. Von Hippel–Lindau disease needs to be considered in patients with such lesions, so that screening for other lesions and, if necessary, of family members can be instituted.

PARANEOPLASTIC NEUROLOGICAL DISEASE

Neurological disease may occur with systemic malignant tumours in the absence of metastases. Mild degrees of myopathy and neuropathy are quite frequent with the common malignancies. Much rarer are certain disabling, and often fatal, paraneoplastic syndromes which often have an inflammatory basis, with associated autoantibodies which cross-react with neural and tumour antigens (see Box 22.100). In the case of the Lambert–Eaton myasthenic syndrome the autoantibodies have a functional effect on neuromuscular transmission (see p. 1185).

22.100 PARANEOPLASTIC SYNDROMES

Syndrome	Clinical features	Antibody	Associated tumours	Investigations
Retinal degeneration	Painless progressive visual loss	Antiretinal	Small-cell carcinoma of lung Melanoma	Chest radiograph, CT chest Electroretinogram
Opsoclonus-myoclonus	Arrhythmic chaotic rapid eye movements	Anti-Ri	Ovarian, lung Neuroblastoma (in children)	Chest radiograph, CT chest Pelvic ultrasound or CT
Sensory neuropathy	Limb pain, paraesthesia Distal numbness	Anti-Hu	Small-cell carcinoma of lung Hodgkin's disease	Chest radiograph, CT chest Nerve conduction studies
Limbic encephalitis	Memory loss, progressive dementia Seizures	Anti-Hu	Small-cell carcinoma of lung Hodgkin's disease	Chest radiograph, CT chest MRI (head) CSF (pleocytosis, raised protein)
Myelitis	Progressive spinal cord lesion (usually cervical cord)	Anti-Hu	Small-cell carcinoma of lung	Chest radiograph, CT chest MRI (cord, head)
Cerebellar degeneration	Progressive ataxia, nystagmus (down-beating), vertigo	Anti-Yo Anti-Hu	Small-cell carcinoma of lung Ovarian Hodgkin's disease	Chest radiograph, CT chest Pelvic ultrasound or CT CSF (raised protein, oligoclonal bands)
Subacute motor neuronopathy	Subacute, patchy progressive, usually lower limb, weakness and wasting	Anti-Hu	Hodgkin's disease Small-cell carcinoma of lung	Chest radiograph, CT chest Nerve conduction studies/EMG
Sensorimotor peripheral neuropathy	Mild, non-disabling peripheral limb numbness and paraesthesia	Not known	Small-cell carcinoma of lung Breast Other carcinoma	Chest radiograph, CT chest Nerve conduction studies/EMG
Lambert–Eaton myasthenic syndrome	Weakness of proximal limb muscles, fatigue with exertion after initial improvement, areflexia	Anti-Ca^{++} channel	Small-cell carcinoma of lung	Chest radiograph, CT chest EMG
Dermatomyositis/polymyositis	Proximal limb weakness and pain, heliotrope skin rash, Grotten's papules on knuckles	Anti-Jo-1	Lung, breast, ovary	Chest radiograph, CT chest Creatine kinase EMG, muscle biopsy
Guillain–Barré	Ascending weakness, distal paraesthesia	Not known	Hodgkin's disease	Nerve conduction studies/EMG

Pathology

These syndromes are particularly associated with small-cell carcinoma of the lung, ovarian tumours, and lymphomas. In addition to the presence of autoantibodies in the serum and/or CSF, there is usually a lymphocytic infiltrate of the neural tissue affected.

Clinical features

These are summarised in Box 22.100. In most instances the neurological disease progresses quite rapidly over a few months. In 50% of patients with a paraneoplastic syndrome the neurological disease precedes clinical presentation of the primary neoplasm. Paraneoplastic disease should be considered in the diagnosis of any unusual progressive neurological syndrome.

Investigations

See Box 22.100. The presence of characteristic autoantibodies in the context of a suspicious clinical picture may be diagnostic. The causative tumour may be very small and therefore CT of the chest or abdomen is often necessary to find it. The CSF often shows an increased protein and lymphocyte count with oligoclonal bands.

Management

This is directed at the primary tumour. Occasionally, successful therapy of the tumour is associated with improvement of the paraneoplastic syndrome. Some improvement may occur following administration of intravenous immunoglobulin.

HYDROCEPHALUS

Hydrocephalus (dilatation of the ventricular system) may be due to obstruction of the CSF circulation (see Fig. 22.56). Hydrocephalus is said to be 'communicating' if the obstruction is outside the ventricular system (usually in the basal cisterns). Obstruction within the ventricles is most common in the narrow channels of the third ventricle and aqueduct, and may be caused by tumour or a congenital anomaly such as aqueduct stenosis (see Fig. 22.57). Causes of hydrocephalus are given in Box 22.101.

Diversion of the CSF by means of a shunt procedure between the ventricular system and the peritoneal cavity or right atrium may result in prompt relief of symptoms in obstructive or communicating hydrocephalus.

NORMAL PRESSURE HYDROCEPHALUS

In this condition the dilatation of the ventricular system is caused by intermittent rises in CSF pressure, which occur particularly at night. It occurs predominantly in old age and is suggested by the combination of gait apraxia (see p. 1138)

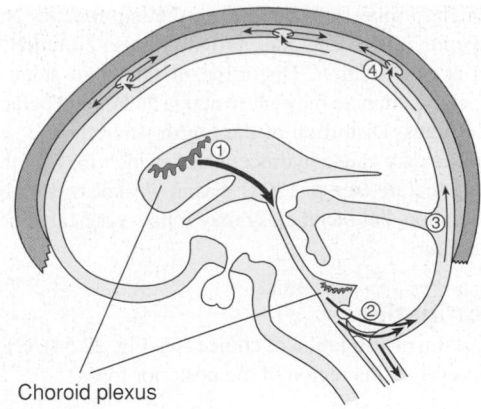

Fig. 22.56 The circulation of cerebrospinal fluid. (1) CSF is synthesised in the choroid plexus of the ventricles, and flows from the lateral and third ventricles through the aqueduct to the fourth ventricle. (2) At the foramina of Luschka and Magendie it exits the brain, flowing over the hemispheres (3) and down around the spinal cord and roots in the subarachnoid space. (4) It is then absorbed into the dural venous sinuses via the arachnoid villi.

Choroid plexus

22.101 CAUSES OF HYDROCEPHALUS 
Communicating (obstruction outside ventricular system)
• Bacterial meningitis (esp. tuberculous)
• Sarcoidosis
• Subarachnoid haemorrhage
• Head injury
• Idiopathic ('normal pressure')
Non-communicating (obstruction within ventricular system)
• Tumours
• Colloid cyst
• Arnold–Chiari malformation
• Aqueduct stenosis
• Cerebellar abscess
• Cerebellar or brain-stem haematoma

and dementia, often with urinary incontinence as an early feature. This cause of dilatation of the ventricles can be very difficult to distinguish from that occurring due to cerebral atrophy, where the cortical sulci are also dilated. The result of shunting procedures for normal pressure hydrocephalus is unpredictable.

IDIOPATHIC INTRACRANIAL HYPERTENSION

This condition, previously known as benign intracranial hypertension, usually occurs in obese young women. Raised intracranial pressure develops without a space-occupying

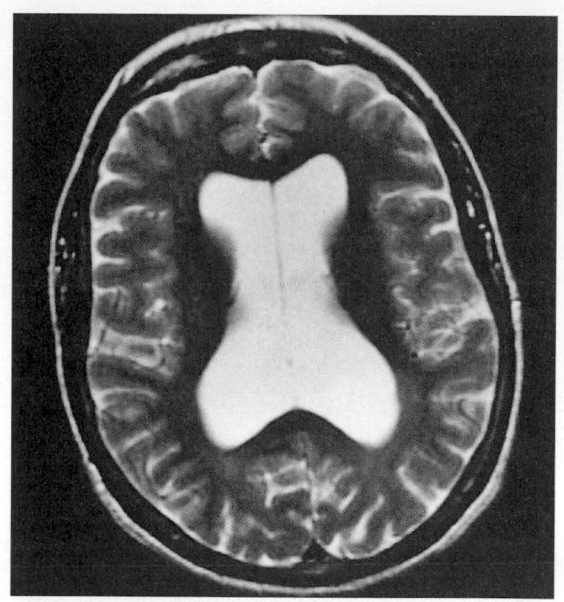
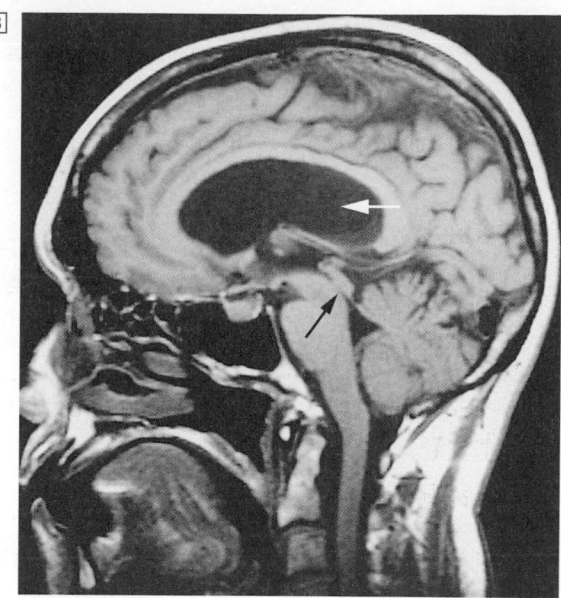

Fig. 22.57   MRI of hydrocephalus due to aqueduct stenosis. A Axial image: note the dilated lateral ventricles. B Sagittal image: note the dilated ventricles (top arrow) and narrowed aqueduct (bottom arrow).

lesion, ventricular dilatation or impairment of consciousness. The aetiology is uncertain but there may be a diffuse defect of CSF reabsorption by the arachnoid villi. The condition can be precipitated by drugs, including tetracycline, the oral contraceptive pill and withdrawal of corticosteroid therapy.

Clinical features

Characteristically, there is a headache, sometimes with transient diplopia and visual obscurations, but few other symptoms. There are usually no signs other than papilloedema, which may be discovered incidentally at a routine visit to an optician, but a 6th nerve palsy may be present.

Investigations

The CT is normal, with normal-sized or small ventricles. Once this has been demonstrated, a lumbar puncture is safe and will allow confirmation of the raised CSF pressure and form part of treatment. MR angiography or cerebral venography will exclude cerebral venous occlusion. True papilloedema may need to be distinguished from other causes of disc swelling by fluorescein angiography.

Management

Any precipitating medication should be withdrawn and a weight-reducing diet instigated, if indicated. The carbonic anhydrase inhibitor, acetazolamide, may help to lower intracranial pressure. Repeated lumbar puncture can be considered, but is often unacceptable to the patient. Patients

failing to respond, in whom chronic papilloedema threatens vision, may require optic nerve sheath fenestration or a lumbo-peritoneal shunt.

FURTHER INFORMATION

Aminoff MJ, ed. Neurology and general medicine: neurological aspects of medical disorders. 3rd edn. New York: Churchill Livingstone; 2001.

Bone I, Fuller F, eds. Neurology in practice: stroke. J Neurol Neurosurg Psychiatry 2001; 70(suppl I):i1–22.

Bone I, Fuller F, eds. Neurology in practice: sleep and coma. J Neurol Neurosurg Psychiatry 2001; 71(suppl I):i1–27.

Bone I, Fuller F, eds. Neurology in practice: epilepsy. J Neurol Neurosurg Psychiatry 2001; 70(suppl II):ii1–27.

Bone I, Fuller F, eds. Neurology in practice: multiple sclerosis. J Neurol Neurosurg Psychiatry 2001; 71(suppl II):ii1–27.

Bradley WG, Daroff RB, Fenichel GM, Marsden CD, eds. Neurology in clinical practice: principles of diagnosis and management. 3rd edn (2 vols). Boston: Butterworth–Heinemann; 2000.

Prusiner S. Neurodegenerative diseases and prions. N Engl J Med 2001; 344:1516–1525.

Shakir RA, Newman PK, Poser CM, eds. Tropical neurology. London: WB Saunders; 1996.

http://medweb.bham.ac.uk/http/depts/clin_neuro/teaching/disclaimer.html Neurology teaching pages (from University of Birmingham, UK).

www.bcm.tmc.edu/neurol/index.html Baylor College of Medicine (USA), Department of neurology.

www.medinfo.ufl.edu/year1/bcs/clist/neuro.html Neurological examination (from the University of Florida).

www.ninds.nih.gov/ National Institute of Neurological Disorders and Stroke.

www.toddtroost.com/mylinks2001.html Neuroscience links from the American Neurological Association.

www.wfneurology.org World Federation of Neurology.

Appendix

INCUBATION PERIODS, IMMUNISATION SCHEDULES AND NOTIFIABLE DISEASES

23.1 INCUBATION PERIODS OF IMPORTANT INFECTIONS

Infection	Incubation period	
	Maximum range	Normal range
Short incubation periods (< 7 days)		
Anthrax	2–5 days	
Bacillary dysentery	1–7 days	
Cholera	Hours–5 days	2–3 hours
Diphtheria	2–5 days	
Gonorrhoea	2–5 days	
Meningococcaemia	2–10 days	3–4 days
Scarlet fever	1–3 days	
Intermediate incubation periods (7–21 days)		
Amoebiasis	14 days–months	21 days
Chickenpox	14–21 days	
Lassa fever	7–14 days	
Malaria	8 days–months	
Measles	7–14 days	10 days
Mumps	12–21 days	18 days
Poliomyelitis	3–21 days	7–10 days
Psittacosis	4–14 days	10 days
Rubella	14–21 days	18 days
Trypanosoma rhodesiense infection	14–21 days	
Typhoid fever	7–21 days	
Typhus fever	7–14 days	12 days
Whooping cough	7–10 days	7 days
Long incubation periods (> 21 days)		
Brucellosis	Days–months	
Filariasis	3 months–years	
Hepatitis A	2–6 weeks	4 weeks
Hepatitis B	6 weeks–6 months	12 weeks
Leishmaniasis		
Cutaneous	1 week–months	
Visceral	2 weeks–2 years	2–4 months
Leprosy	Years	2–5 years
Rabies	Variable	2–8 weeks
Schistosomiasis	Weeks–years	
Trypanosoma gambiense infection	Weeks–years	
Tuberculosis	Months–years	

23.2 NOTIFIABLE INFECTIOUS DISEASES IN BRITAIN

Under the Public Health (Control of Diseases) Act 1984

- Cholera
- Food poisoning
- Plague
- Relapsing fever
- Smallpox
- Typhus

Under the Public Health (Infectious Diseases) Regulations 1988

- Acute encephalitis
- Acute poliomyelitis
- Anthrax
- Diphtheria
- Dysentery (amoebic or bacillary)
- Leprosy
- Leptospirosis
- Malaria
- Measles
- Meningitis
- Meningococcal septicaemia (without meningitis)
- Mumps
- Ophthalmia neonatorum
- Paratyphoid fever
- Rabies
- Rubella
- Scarlet fever
- Tetanus
- Tuberculosis
- Typhoid fever
- Viral haemorrhagic fever

23.3 PERIODS OF INFECTIVITY IN CHILDHOOD INFECTIOUS DISEASES

Disease	Infectious period
Chickenpox	5 days before rash to 6 days after last crop
Diphtheria	2–3 weeks (shorter with antibiotic therapy)
Measles	From onset of prodromal symptoms to 4 days after onset of rash
Mumps	3 days before salivary swelling to 7 days after
Rubella	7 days before onset of rash to 4 days after
Scarlet fever	10–21 days after onset of rash (shortened to 1 day by penicillin)
Whooping cough	7 days after exposure to 3 weeks after onset of symptoms (shortened to 7 days by antibiotics)

23.4 UK RECOMMENDED VACCINATION SCHEDULE

Age/environment	Vaccination	Notes
	Recommended	
2 months or as soon as possible thereafter	Adsorbed diphtheria, pertussis, tetanus (DPT) + *Haemophilus influenzae* type B conjugate (HIB) + Oral polio vaccine (OPV) + Meningococcal group C (Men C) conjugate vaccine +	Three doses with 4-week gap between doses
	BCG for neonates at risk of tuberculosis	Neonates at risk = immigrants or those with known contact with tuberculosis *One* dose only
2nd year of life	Measles, mumps and rubella (MMR)*	
	HIB	If not previously immunised
Pre-school/ nursery school entry	Adsorbed DPT OPV MMR	Single booster provided previously immunised
10–14 years	BCG	Only if Mantoux test negative
Pre-school-leaving or pre-employment/further education	Adsorbed DPT OPV	Single booster
	Men C	If not previously immunised
Over 65 or with chronic illness	Annual influenza vaccination Consider pneumococcal multivalent	Chronic heart or respiratory disease, diabetes mellitus, immunocompromised
	Other	
Travel-related	Hepatitis A Hepatitis B Typhoid i.v. and oral Yellow fever Cholera Rabies European tick-borne encephalitis Meningococcal quadrivalent	The recommendations for these vaccinations depend on the region to be visited and the risk encountered
Occupational or other risk-related	Hepatitis A	Laboratory staff High-risk disease: haemophilia, chronic liver disease Exposure to raw sewage At-risk sexual behaviour Residents and staff in institutions for severe learning difficulties
	Hepatitis B	Intravenous drug users At-risk sexual behaviour Infants born to mothers who are high-risk hepatitis B surface antigen carriers High-risk disease: haemophilia, chronic renal failure Health-care workers and trainees Residents and staff in institutions for severe learning difficulties

* See separate note on page 7.

23.5 IMMUNISATION SCHEDULE FOR INFANTS RECOMMENDED BY THE WHO EXPANDED PROGRAMME ON IMMUNISATION

Vaccine	Birth	6 weeks	10 weeks	14 weeks	9 months
			Age		
BCG	✓				
Oral polio	✓	✓	✓	✓	
Diphtheria, pertussis, tetanus		✓	✓	✓	
Hepatitis B Scheme A[1] Scheme B[1]	✓	✓ ✓	✓	✓ ✓ ✓	
Haemophilus influenzae type b		✓	✓	✓	
Yellow fever					✓[2]
Measles					✓[3]

[1] Scheme A is recommended in countries where perinatal transmission of hepatitis B virus is frequent (e.g. South-east Asia). Scheme B may be used in countries where perinatal transmission is less frequent (e.g. sub-Saharan Africa).
[2] In countries where yellow fever poses a risk.
[3] A second opportunity to receive a dose of measles vaccine should be provided for all children. This may be done either as part of the routine schedule or as a campaign.

23.6 INDICATIONS FOR PROPHYLACTIC IMMUNOGLOBULINS

Human normal immunoglobulin (pooled immunoglobulin)

- Virus A hepatitis (travellers* and debilitated children)
- Measles (child with heart or lung disease)

Human specific immunoglobulin

- Virus B hepatitis (needlestick injuries, sexual partner)
- Tetanus (susceptible injured patients)
- Rabies (post-exposure protection)
- Chickenpox (immunosuppressed children)
- Respiratory syncytial virus infection (high-risk infants, e.g. premature—investigational use)

* If not protected by active immunisation.

23.7 INDICATIONS FOR CHEMOPROPHYLAXIS

Infection to be prevented	Indication for prophylaxis	Antimicrobial agent indicated	Adult dose
Diphtheria	Susceptible contacts	Erythromycin	500 mg 6-hourly for 5 days
Meningococcal infection	Susceptible contacts	Rifampicin Ciprofloxacin	600 mg 12-hourly for 2 days 500 mg as single dose
Whooping cough	Susceptible contacts	Erythromycin	500 mg 6-hourly for 7 days
Tuberculosis	Susceptible contacts	Isoniazid	300 mg daily for 6 months
Rheumatic fever	Following rheumatic fever	Penicillin	250 mg 12-hourly
Endocarditis	Heart valve lesion	See page 467	
Tetanus	Wound or injury	Erythromycin	500 mg 6-hourly for 7 days
Gas gangrene	Wound or injury	Penicillin *or* Metronidazole	600 mg 6-hourly for 5 days 500 mg 8-hourly for 5 days
Abdominal/pelvic sepsis	Colonic or gynaecological surgery	Gentamicin *or* Cephalosporin + metronidazole (single dose)	
Malaria	Travel to malarious countries	Depends on country (see p. 56)	

NOTES ON INTERNATIONAL SYSTEM OF UNITS (SI UNITS)

Examples of basic SI units

Length	metre (m)
Mass	kilogram (kg)
Amount of substance	mole (mol)
Energy	joule (J)
Pressure	pascal (Pa)

Examples of decimal multiples and submultiples of SI units

Factor	Name	Symbol
10^6	mega-	M
10^3	kilo-	k
10^{-1}	deci-	d
10^{-2}	centi-	c
10^{-3}	milli-	m
10^{-6}	micro-	μ
10^{-9}	nano-	n
10^{-12}	pico-	p
10^{-15}	femto-	f

Volume

The basic SI unit of volume is the cubic metre (1000 litres). Because of its convenience, the litre is used as the unit of volume in laboratory work.

Mass concentration

Mass concentration (e.g. g/l, μg/l) is used for all protein measurements, for substances which do not have a sufficiently well-defined composition and for serum vitamin B_{12} and folate measurements.

SI units are not employed for enzymes, nor usually for immunoglobulins.

BIOCHEMICAL AND HAEMATOLOGICAL VALUES

Reference ranges are largely those used in the Departments of Clinical Biochemistry and Haematology, Lothian University Hospitals NHS Trust, Edinburgh, UK. These can vary from laboratory to laboratory, depending on the assay method used and on other factors; this is especially the case for the enzyme assays. Although the SI system of units is widely used in the UK, units of measurement can vary and lead to laboratory differences. The tables, where possible, also include equivalent non-SI units. Enzyme activities expressed as units/litre (U/l) remain unchanged.

No details are given of the collection requirements which may be critical to obtaining a meaningful result.

Unless otherwise stated, reference ranges apply to adults; *values in children may be different.*

23.8 ARTERIAL BLOOD ANALYSIS

Analysis	Reference range	
	SI units	Non-SI units
Bicarbonate	21–27.5 mmol/l	21–27.5 meq/l
Hydrogen ion	36–44 nmol/l	pH 7.36–7.44
$PaCO_2$	4.4–6.1 kPa	33–46 mmHg
PaO_2	12–15 kPa	90–113 mmHg
Oxygen saturation	Normally > 97%	

23.9 CEREBROSPINAL FLUID

Analysis	Reference range	
	SI units	Non-SI units
Cells	Up to 5 (all mononuclear) cells/mm^3	
Chloride	120–170 mmol/l	120–170 meq/l
Glucose	2.5–4.0 mmol/l	45–72 mg/100 ml
IgG index*	< 0.65	–
Total protein	100–400 mg/l	0.01–0.04 g/100 ml

* A crude index of increase in IgG attributable to intrathecal synthesis.

23.10 REFERENCE VALUES IN VENOUS SERUM FOR THE MORE COMMON ANALYTES IN ADULTS

Analysis	Reference range SI units	Reference range Non-SI units	Analysis	Reference range SI units	Reference range Non-SI units
α_1-antitrypsin	1.7–3.2 g/l	170–320 mg/100 ml	Glucose (fasting)[2]	3.6–5.8 mmol/l	65–104 mg/100 ml
Alanine amino-transferase (ALT)	10–40 U/l	–	Glycated haemoglobin (HbA$_1$)	5.0–6.5%	–
Albumin	36–47 g/l	3.6–4.7 g/100 ml	Immunoglobulin A	0.5–4.0 g/l	50–400 mg/100 ml
Alkaline phosphatase	40–125 U/l	–	Immunoglobulin G	5.0–13.0 g/l	500–1300 mg/100 ml
Amylase	< 100 U/l	–	Immunoglobulin M Male Female	0.3–2.2 g/l 0.4–2.5 g/l	30–220 mg/100 ml 40–250 mg/100 ml
Aspartate amino-transferase (AST)	10–35 U/l	–	Iron Male Female	14–32 µmol/l 10–28 µmol/l	78–178 µg/100 ml 56–156 µg/100 ml
Bilirubin (total)	2–17 µmol/l	0.12–1.0 mg/100 ml	Iron-binding capacity	45–72 µmol/l	251–402 µg/100 ml
Calcium	2.12–2.62 mmol/l	4.24–5.24 meq/l or 8.50–10.50 mg/100 ml	Lactate	0.4–1.4 mmol/l	3.60–12.6 mg/100 ml
Carboxy-haemoglobin	Not normally detectable Up to 1.5% in non-smokers	–	Lactate dehydrogenase (total)	230–460 U/l	–
Ceruloplasmin	150–600 mg/l	15–60 mg/100 ml	Lead[3]	< 1.0 µmol/l	< 21 µg/100 ml
Chloride	95–107 mmol/l	95–107 meq/l	Magnesium	0.75–1.0 mmol/l	1.5–2.0 meq/l or 1.82–2.43 mg/100 ml
Cholesterol (total)[1]			Osmolality	280–290 mmol/kg	280–290 mosm/l
HDL-cholesterol Male Female	0.5–1.6 mmol/l 0.6–1.9 mmol/l	19–62 mg/100 ml 23–74 mg/100 ml	Phosphate (fasting)	0.8–1.4 mmol/l	2.48–4.34 mg/100 ml
Copper	13–24 µmol/l	83–153 µg/100 ml	Potassium (plasma)	3.3–4.7 mmol/l	3.3–4.7 meq/l
Creatine kinase (total) Male Female	30–200 U/l 30–150 U/l	– –	Potassium (serum)	3.6–5.1 mmol/l	3.6–5.1 meq/l
			Protein (total)	60–80 g/l	6–8 g/100 ml
Creatine kinase (MB isoenzyme)	Normally < 6% of total CK	–	Sodium	132–144 mmol/l	132–144 meq/l
Creatinine	55–120 µmol/l	0.62–1.36 mg/100 ml	Total CO$_2$	24–30 mmol/l	24–30 meq/l
Ethanol	Not normally detectable 65–87 mmol/l (Marked intoxication) 87–109 mmol/l (Stupor) > 109 mmol/l (Coma)	300–400 mg/ml 400–500 mg/ml > 500 mg/100 ml	Transferrin	2.0–4.0 g/l	0.2–0.4 g/100 ml
			Triglycerides (fasting)	0.6–1.7 mmol/l	53–150 mg/100 ml
			Urate Male Female	0.12–0.42 mmol/l 0.12–0.36 mmol/l	2.0–7.0 mg/100 ml 2.0–6.0 mg/100 ml
Ferritin Male Female	17–300 µg/l 14–150 µg/l	17–300 ng/ml 14–150 ng/ml	Urea	2.5–6.6 mmol/l	15–40 mg/100 ml
Gamma-glutamyl transferase (GGT) Male Female	10–55 U/l 5–35 U/l	– –	Zinc	11–22 µmol/l	72–144 µg/100 ml

[1] Cholesterol (total)
    Ideally   < 5.2 mmol/l   < 200 mg/100 ml
    Mild increase   5.2–6.5 mmol/l   200–250 mg/100 ml
    Moderate increase   6.5–7.8 mmol/l   250–300 mg/100 ml
    Severe increase   > 7.8 mmol/l   > 300 mg/100 ml
(as defined by the European Atherosclerosis Society)
[2] Values quoted for venous plasma or serum
[3] In children   Up to 0.5 µmol/l   Up to 10 µg/100 ml

23.11 REFERENCE VALUES FOR THE MORE COMMON ANALYTES IN URINE

Analysis	Reference range	
	SI units	Non-SI units
Albumin[1]		
Calcium	1.2–3.7 mmol/24 hrs (low calcium diet)	2.4–7.4 meq/24 hrs
	Up to 12 mmol/24 hrs (normal diet)	Up to 24 meq/24 hrs
Copper	Up to 0.6 μmol/24 hrs	Up to 38 μg/24 hrs
Cortisol	9–50 μmol/mol creatinine	30–160 μg cortisol/g creatinine
Creatinine	10–20 mmol/24 hrs	1130–2260 mg/24 hrs
5-hydroxyindole-3-acetic acid (5-HIAA)	< 60 μmol/24 hrs	< 11.5 mg/24 hrs
Metadrenalines Normetadrenaline Metadrenaline	0.4–3.4 μmol/24 hrs 0.3–1.7 μmol/24 hrs	73–620 μg/24 hrs 59–335 μg/24 hrs
Oxalate Male Female	80–490 μmol/24 hrs 40–320 μmol/24 hrs	7.2–44 mg/24 hrs 3.6–29 mg/24 hrs
Phosphate	15–50 mmol/24 hrs	465–1548 mg/24 hrs
Potassium[2]	25–100 mmol/24 hrs	25–100 meq/24 hrs
Protein	Up to 0.3 g/l	Up to 0.03 g/100 ml
Sodium	100–200 mmol/24 hrs	100–200 meq/24 hrs
Urate	1.2–3.0 mmol/24 hrs	202–504 mg/24 hrs
Urea	170–600 mmol/24 hrs	10.2–36.0 g/24 hrs

[1] Albumin/creatinine ratio (ACR) and urinary albumin excretion rate (AER) are used to detect microalbuminuria, i.e. excessive albumin excretion in patients with diabetes mellitus, which is of predictive value in identifying patients at risk of progression to diabetic nephropathy. The test should only be carried out in the absence of overt proteinuria (dipstix negative).

ACR
Reference range: < 3.5 mg albumin/mmol creatinine (< 31 μg albumin/mg creatinine)
'Borderline':   3.5–10 mg albumin/mmol creatinine (31–88 μg albumin/mg creatinine)
Positive test: > 10 mg albumin/mmol creatinine (> 88 μg albumin/mg creatinine)

AER
Reference range: < 20 μg albumin/min
Microalbuminuria: 20–200 μg albumin/min

[2] The urinary output of electrolytes such as sodium and potassium is normally a reflection of intake. This can vary widely, especially on a cultural, world-wide basis. The values quoted are more appropriate to a 'Western' diet.

23.12 HORMONES IN SERUM

Hormone	SI units	Non-SI units
Adrenocorticotrophic hormone (ACTH) (plasma)	7–51 ng/l (0700–1000 hrs)	–
Cortisol	150–550 nmol/l (at 0800 hrs) < 200 nmol/l (at 2200 hrs)	5.5–20 µg/100 ml < 73 µg/100 ml
Follicle-stimulating hormone (FSH) Male Female*	1.5–9.0 U/l 3.0–15 U/l (early follicular) Up to 20 U/l (mid-cycle) > 30 U/l (post-menopausal)	– – – –
Gastrin (plasma)	Up to 120 ng/l	Up to 12 ng/100 ml
Growth hormone (GH)	Variable, up to 50 mU/l	–
Insulin	Highly variable and interpretable only in relation to plasma glucose and body habitus	–
Luteinising hormone (LH) Female* Male	2.5–9.0 U/l (early follicular) Up to 90 U/l (mid-cycle) > 20 U/l (post-menopausal) 1.5–9.0 U/l	– – – –
Oestradiol-17β Female Male	110–180 pmol/l (early follicular) 550–1650 pmol/l (mid-cycle) 370–770 pmol/l (luteal) < 150 pmol/l (post-menopausal) < 200 pmol/l	30–49 pg/ml 150–449 pg/ml 101–209 pg/ml < 41 pg/ml < 54 pg/ml
Parathyroid hormone (PTH)	10–65 ng/l	1.0–6.5 ng/100 ml
Progesterone Male Female	< 2.0 nmol/l < 2.0 nmol/l (follicular) > 15 nmol/l (mid-luteal) < 2.0 nmol/l (post-menopausal)	< 0.63 µg/l < 0.63 µg/l > 4.7 µg/l < 0.63 µg/l
Prolactin (PRL)	60–390 mU/l	–
Testosterone Male Female	10–30 nmol/l 0.4–2.8 nmol/l	2.88–8.64 ng/ml 0.12–0.81 ng/ml
Thyroid-stimulating hormone (TSH)	0.15–3.5 mU/l	–
Thyroxine (free) (free T$_4$)	10–27 pmol/l	777–2098 pg/100 ml
Triiodothyronine (T$_3$)	1.0–2.6 nmol/l	65–169 ng/100 ml
TSH receptor antibodies (TRAb)	< 7 U/l	–

* Luteal phase values similar to follicular phase.

Notes
1. A number of hormones are unstable, and collection details are critical to obtaining a meaningful result. Refer to local hospital handbook.
2. Values in the table are only a guideline; hormone levels can often only be meaningfully understood in relation to factors such as sex (e.g. testosterone), age (e.g. FSH in women), time of day (e.g. cortisol) or regulatory factors (e.g. insulin and glucose, PTH and [Ca^{++}]). Also, reference ranges may be critically method-dependent.

23.13 HAEMATOLOGICAL VALUES

Analysis	Reference range	
	SI units	Non-SI units
Bleeding time (Ivy)	Less than 8 mins	
Body fluid (total)	50% (obese)–70% (lean) of body weight	–
Intracellular	30–40% of body weight	–
Extracellular	20–30% of body weight	–
Blood volume		
Male	75 ± 10 ml/kg	–
Female	70 ± 10 ml/kg	–
Coagulation screen		
Prothrombin time	8.0–10.5 secs	–
Activated partial thromboplastin time	26–37 secs	–
Erythrocyte sedimentation rate*		
Adult male	0–10 mm/hr	–
Adult female	3–15 mm/hr	–
Fibrinogen	1.5–4.0 g/l	0.15–0.4 g/100 ml
Folate		
Serum	1.5–20.6 µg/l	1.5–20.6 ng/ml
Red cell	95–570 µg/l	95–570 ng/ml
Haemoglobin		
Male	130–180 g/l	13–18 g/100 ml
Female	115–165 g/l	11.5–16.5 g/100 ml
Haptoglobin	0.3–2.0 g/l	0.03–0.2 g/100 ml
Leucocytes (adults)	$4.0–11.0 \times 10^9$/l	$4.0–11.0 \times 10^3$/mm^3
Differential white cell count		
Neutrophil granulocytes	$2.0–7.5 \times 10^9$/l	$2.0–7.5 \times 10^3$/mm^3
Lymphocytes	$1.5–4.0 \times 10^9$/l	$1.5–4.0 \times 10^3$/mm^3
Monocytes	$0.2–0.8 \times 10^9$/l	$0.2–0.8 \times 10^3$/mm^3
Eosinophil granulocytes	$0.04–0.4 \times 10^9$/l	$0.04–0.4 \times 10^3$/mm^3
Basophil granulocytes	$0.01–0.1 \times 10^9$/l	$0.01–0.1 \times 10^3$/mm^3
Mean cell haemoglobin (MCH)	27–32 pg	–
Mean cell volume (MCV)	78–98 fl	–
Packed cell volume (PCV) or haematocrit		
Male	0.40–0.54	–
Female	0.37–0.47	–
Platelets	$150–350 \times 10^9$/l	$150–350 \times 10^3$/mm^3
Red cell count		
Male	$4.5–6.5 \times 10^{12}$/l	$4.5–6.5 \times 10^6$/mm^3
Female	$3.8–5.8 \times 10^{12}$/l	$3.8–5.8 \times 10^6$/mm^3
Red cell lifespan (mean)	120 days	–
Red cell lifespan T½ (^{51}Cr)	25–35 days	–
Reticulocytes (adults)	$25–85 \times 10^9$/l	$25–85 \times 10^3$/mm^3
Vitamin B$_{12}$	130–770 pg/ml	–

* Higher values in older patients are not necessarily abnormal.

Joint British Societies
Joint British Recommendations on

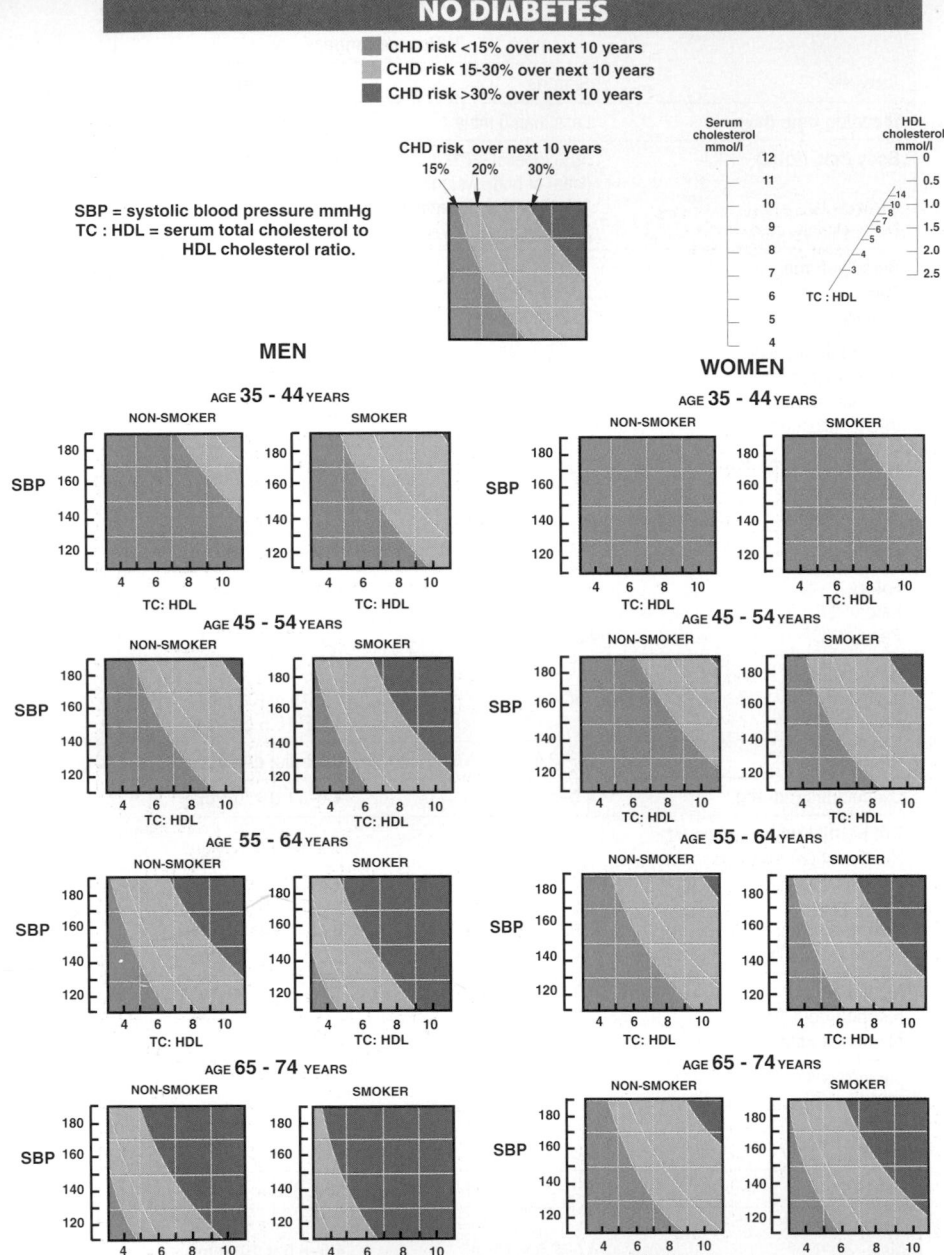

NO DIABETES

- CHD risk <15% over next 10 years
- CHD risk 15-30% over next 10 years
- CHD risk >30% over next 10 years

SBP = systolic blood pressure mmHg
TC : HDL = serum total cholesterol to HDL cholesterol ratio.

How to use the Coronary Risk Prediction Chart for Primary Prevention

These charts are for estimating coronary heart disease (CHD) risk (non fatal MI and coronary death) for individuals who have not developed symptomatic CHD or other major atherosclerotic disease.

The use of these charts is not appropriate for patients who have existing disease which already puts them at high risk. Such diseases are:

- CHD or other major atherosclerotic disease
- Familial hypercholesterolaemia or other inherited dyslipidaemia
- Established hypertension (systolic BP > 160 mmHg and/or diastolic BP > 100 mmHg) or associated target organ damage
- Diabetes mellitus with associated target organ damage
- Renal dysfunction

- To estimate an individual's absolute 10 year risk of developing CHD find the table for their gender, diabetes (yes/no), smoking status (smoker/non smoker) and age. Within this square define the level of risk according to systolic blood pressure and the ratio of total cholesterol to HDL cholesterol. If there is no HDL cholesterol result then assume this is 1.0mmol/l and then the lipid scale can be used for total cholesterol alone.

- High risk individuals are defined as those whose 10 year CHD risk exceeds 15% (equivalent to a *cardiovascular* risk of 20% over the same period). As a minimum those at highest risk (≥ 30% red) should be targeted and treated now, and as resources allow others with a risk of > 15% (orange) should be progressively targeted.

Coronary Risk Prediction Chart
Prevention of Coronary Heart Disease in Clinical Practice

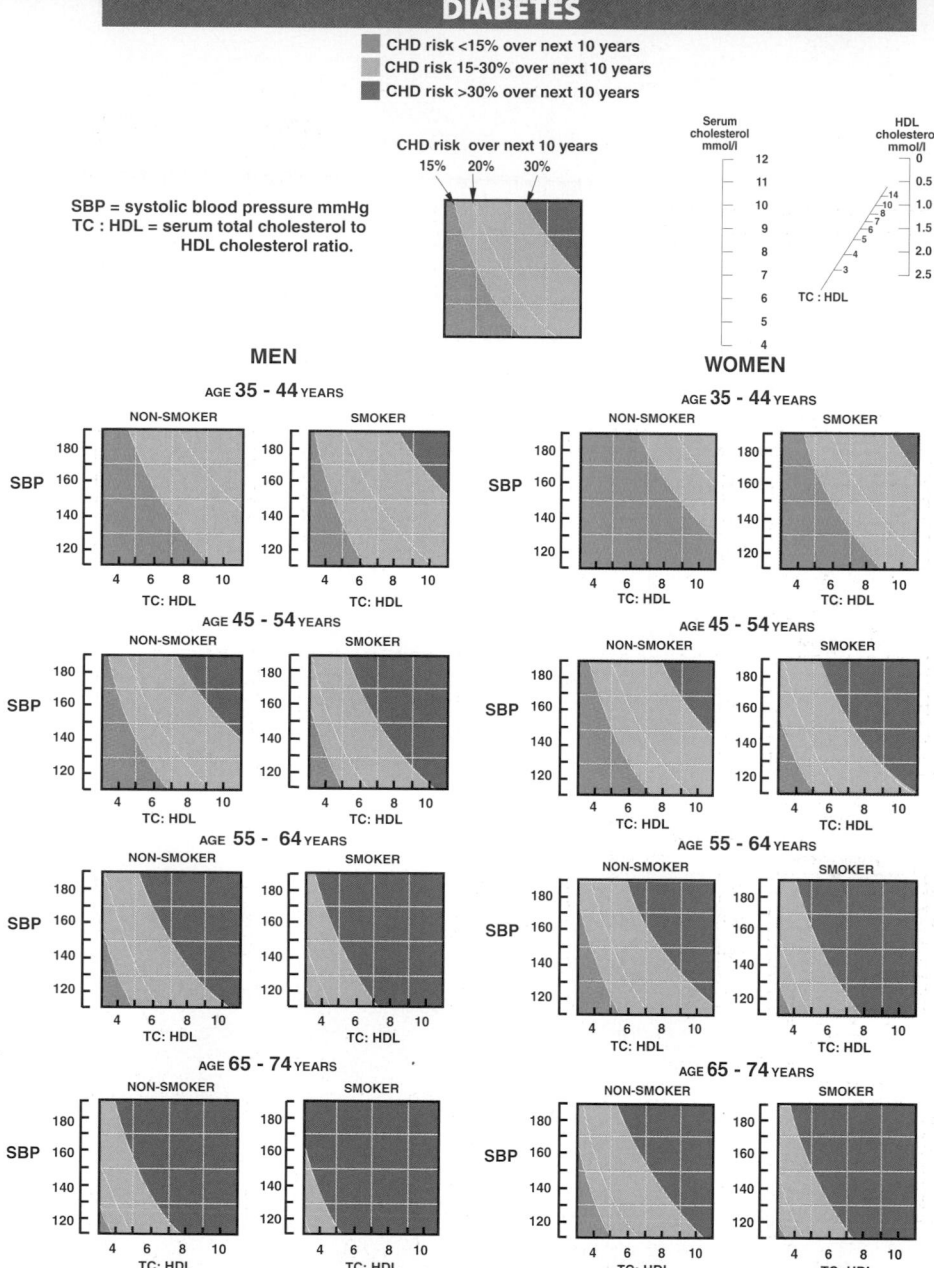

DIABETES

- CHD risk <15% over next 10 years
- CHD risk 15-30% over next 10 years
- CHD risk >30% over next 10 years

CHD risk over next 10 years
15%   20%   30%

SBP = systolic blood pressure mmHg
TC : HDL = serum total cholesterol to
HDL cholesterol ratio.

Serum cholesterol mmol/l

HDL cholesterol mmol/l

TC : HDL

MEN

AGE 35 - 44 YEARS
AGE 45 - 54 YEARS
AGE 55 - 64 YEARS
AGE 65 - 74 YEARS

WOMEN

AGE 35 - 44 YEARS
AGE 45 - 54 YEARS
AGE 55 - 64 YEARS
AGE 65 - 74 YEARS

(NON-SMOKER / SMOKER; SBP axis 120-180; TC: HDL axis 4-10)

- Smoking status should reflect lifetime exposure to tobacco and not simply tobacco use at the time of risk assessment.

- The initial blood pressure and the first random (non fasting) total cholesterol and HDL cholesterol can be used to estimate an individual's risk. However, the decision on using drug therapy should be based on repeat risk factor measurements over a period of time. The chart should not be used to estimate risk after treatment of hyperlipidaemia or blood pressure has been initiated.

- CHD risk is higher than indicated in the charts for

  – Those with a family history of premature CHD (men <55 years and women <65 years) which increases the risk by a factor of approximately 1.5.
  – Those with raised triglyceride levels
  – Those who are not diabetic but have impaired glucose tolerance.

  – Women with premature menopause.
  – As the person approaches the next age category. As risk increases exponentially with age the risk will be closer to the higher decennium for the last four years of each decade.

- In ethnic minorities the risk chart should be used with caution as it has not been validated in these populations.

- The estimates of CHD risk from the chart are based on groups of people and in managing an *individual* the physician also has to use clinical judgement in deciding how intensively to intervene on lifestyle and whether or not to use drug therapies.

- An individual can be shown on the chart the direction in which the risk of CHD can be reduced by changing smoking status, blood pressure or cholesterol.

1221

Coronary Risk Prediction Chart reproduced (and modified) with permission from Heart 1998; 80: S1-S29. © The University of Manchester

Picture, box and table credits

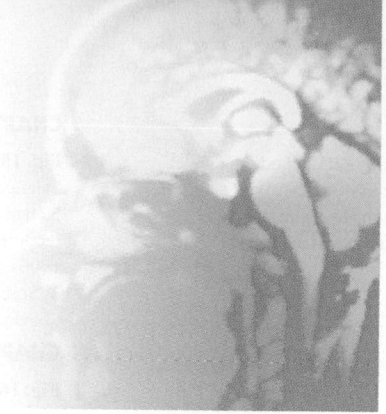

We are grateful to the following individuals and organisations for the loan of illustrations:

CHAPTER 1

Illustrative material supplied by Dr R. Davidson and the EM and Histopathology Unit, London School of Hygiene and Tropical Medicine. **Fig. 1.53** Reproduced by permission of WHO. **Figs 1.71** and **1.72** Dr P. Hay, St George's Hospital, London. **Fig. 1.73** Institute of Ophthalmology, Moorfields Eye Hospital, London. **Figs 1.84**, **1.86** and **1.87** Audiovisual Dept, St Mary's Hospital, London. **Figs 1.99–1.108** Antibiotic sensitivity patterns for common infections after an idea by Dr A. Maggs, Dept of Microbiology, Torbay Hospital, Torquay.

CHAPTER 5

Figs 5.1, **5.5** and **5.7** Mr J.M. Dixon, Edinburgh Breast Unit. **Fig. 5.3** Professor W.R. Miller, Edinburgh Breast Unit. **Fig. 5.4** (CTs) Dr A. Stevenson, (bone marrow) Dr J. Thomas, Western General Hospital, Edinburgh.

CHAPTER 10

Fig. 10.18A Institute of Ophthalmology.

CHAPTER 12

Figs 12.27A and **B** Dr B. Cullen.

CHAPTER 13

Page 484 inset (kyphoscoliosis) Dr I. Smith, Papworth Hospital, Cambridge. **Page 485** (sputum) Dr J. Foweraker, Papworth Hospital, Cambridge. **Figs 13.6** and **13.7** Dr J. Reid. **Fig. 13.16** Professor N.J. Douglas. **Fig. 13.18B** British Lung Foundation. **Fig. 13.22B** Dr A. Greening. **Fig. 13.37C** Dr C. Flower, Addenbrooke's Hospital, Cambridge.

CHAPTER 14

Illustrative material supplied by Dr I. Beggs and Dr J. Reid. **Page 577** Dr G.M. Iadarola and Dr F. Quarello, G Bosco Hospital, Turin (from http://www.sin-italia.org/imago/sediment/sed.htm). **Figs 14.1C** and **E**, **14.30A, C, D** and **E** Dr J.G. Simpson, Aberdeen Royal Infirmary. **Figs 14.6A** and **B**, **14.7A, B** and **C**, **14.8**, **14.25B**, **14.33A** and **B**, **14.35** and **14.40** Dr A.P. Bayliss and Dr P. Thorpe, Aberdeen Royal Infirmary. **Fig. 14.25A** Dr D. Fowler, Leeds General Infirmary. **Figs 14.28B** and **C** Dr J. Collar, St Mary's Hospital, London. **Figs 14.30F, G** and **H** Dr R. Herriot. **Fig. 14.38** Dr P. Robinson, St James's University Hospital, Leeds.

CHAPTER 15

Fig. 15.17 Dr A.W. Patrick and Dr I.W. Campbell.

CHAPTER 16

Figs 16.7B and **16.19B, C** and **D** Dr P.L. Padfield, Western General Hospital, Edinburgh.

CHAPTER 18

Figs 18.9, **18.29**, **18.32**, **18.34** and **18.37** Dr D. Redhead, Royal Infirmary of Edinburgh.

CHAPTER 22

Pages 1104 insets and **1105** (scapula, Horner's syndrome, wasted hand and wasted tongue) Dr R.E. Cull, Western General Hospital, Edinburgh. **Figs 22.7A, B** and **C**, **22.8A, B** and **C**, **22.9A, B, C** and **D** Dr D. Collie. **Figs 22.25C** and **22.26** Dr B. Cullen. **Figs 22.36** and **22.37** Professor D.A.S. Compston. **Figs 22.38**, **22.39** and **22.40** Dr J. Xuereb.

The following figures, boxes and tables are reproduced with publishers' permission as listed:

CHAPTER 1

Figs 1.31 and **1.36** Redrawn from Immunisation against infectious disease. London: HMSO; 1996. Crown copyright material is reproduced with the permission of the Controller of Her Majesty's Stationery Office. **Figs 1.43** and **1.54A** Knight R. Parasitic disease in man. Edinburgh: Churchill Livingstone; 1982. **Fig. 1.50** Reproduced from Halstead SB. Dengue. Medicine 1997; 25:1 and Monath TP. Yellow fever. Medicine 1997; 25:1. By kind permission of the Medicine Publishing Company and Dr TP Monath. **Fig. 1.56** Gibbons LM. SEM guide to the morphology of nematode parasites of vertebrates. Farnham Royal, Slough: Commonwealth Agricultural Bureau International; 1986. **Fig. 1.61** Cook GC, ed. Manson's tropical diseases. 20th edn. London: WB Saunders; 1995. **Fig. 1.66** Based on Bryceson ADM, Pfaltzgraff RE. Leprosy. 3rd edn. Edinburgh: Churchill Livingstone; 1990. **Fig. 1.77** Perelson AS, Neumann AU, Markowitz M, et al. HIV-1 dynamics in vitro; virion clearance rate, infected cell lifespan and viral generation time. Science 1996; 271:1592. **Boxes 1.35** and **1.36** WHO. Severe falciparum malaria. In: Severe and complicated malaria. 3rd edn. Trans Roy Soc Trop Med Hyg 2000; 94 (suppl. 1):S1–41.

CHAPTER 2

Fig. 2.1 Brater DC, Chennavasin P, Day B, et al. Bumetanide and furosemide. Clin Pharmacol Ther 1983; 34:207–213, reproduced with permission of Mosby Inc., St Louis, Missouri; and Chennavasin P, Seiwell R, Brater DC. Pharmacokinetic-dynamic analysis of the indomethacin-furosemide interaction in man. J Pharmacol and Exp Ther 1980; 215:77–81. With permission of the American Association for Pharmacology and Experimental Therapeutics. **Figs 2.3** and **2.4** Crown copyright; reproduced with the permission of the Controller of Her Majesty's Stationery Office.

CHAPTER 6

Figs 6.2 and **6.4** WHO. Cancer pain relief. 2nd edn. Geneva: WHO; 1996. Reproduced with permission from WHO. **Fig. 6.3** Adapted from McQuay H. Acute pain. In: Trames M, ed. Evidence-based resource in anaesthesia and analgesia. London: BMJ Books; 2000.

CHAPTER 9

Fig. 9.15 Adapted from Flenley D. Lancet 1971; 1:1921.

CHAPTER 10

Fig. 10.3 Reproduced with permission of the Scottish Intercollegiate Guidelines Network from the SIGN Guideline on the management of obesity, November 1996. For updated information please contact www.sign.ac.uk. **Fig. 10.6** Gaw A. Clinical biochemistry. Edinburgh: Churchill Livingstone; 1995. **Fig. 10.18B** WHO. Report of a joint WHO/USAID meeting, vitamin A deficiency and xerophthalmia (WHO technical report series no. 5 W); 1976. **Fig. 10.20** Adapted with permission from Garrow JS, James WPT. Human nutrition and dietetics. 10th edn. Edinburgh: Churchill Livingstone; 1999 (Fig. 13.15, p. 235).

CHAPTER 12

Figs 12.36 and **12.37** Reproduced with permission from the Resuscitation Council UK. **Fig. 12.60** Adapted from Weissberg P. Education in Heart series. Heart 2000; 83:247–252. **Fig. 12.68** Adapted from Fox KAA. Acute coronary syndromes: presentation, clinical spectrum and management. Heart 2000; 84:93–100. **Fig. 12.85** inset Savin JA, Hunter JAA, Hepburn NC. Skin signs in clinical medicine. London: Mosby; 1997. **Fig. 12.92** Adapted from Drews U. Colour atlas of embryology. Stuttgart: Georg Thieme; 1995 (Fig. 6.9, p. 299).

CHAPTER 13

Fig. 13.9B Adapted from Hughes JMB, Pride NB. Lung function tests: physiological principles and clinical applications. London: WB Saunders; 1999. **Fig. 13.20** Adapted from BTS guidelines for management of COPD. Thorax 1997; 52:suppl. 5. By permission of the BMJ Publishing Group. **Fig. 13.22C** Reproduced with permission from Brewis RAL, Corrin B, Geddes DM, Gibson GJ. Respiratory medicine. 2nd edn. London: WB Saunders; 1995. **Fig. 13.43** Johnson N McL. Respiratory medicine. Oxford: Blackwell Science; 1986. **Fig. 13.52** Hampton JR. The ECG in practice. 2nd edn. Edinburgh: Churchill Livingstone; 1992. **Box 13.8** Based on Crompton GK. The respiratory system. In: Munro JF, Campbell IW. MacLeod's clinical examination. 10th edn. Edinburgh: Churchill Livingstone; 2000 (p. 119). **Box 13.27** Based on Coleman T. Smoking cessation: integrating recent advances with clinical practice. Thorax 2001; 56:579–582. **Box 13.52** Adapted from Grange JM. In: Davies PDO, ed. Clinical tuberculosis. 1998.

CHAPTER 14

Fig. 14.26 Beutler JJ, Koomans HA. Malignant hypertension: still a challenge. Nephrol Dial Transplant 1997; 12:2019–2023; photograph courtesy of Professor PJ Slootweg, University Hospital, Utrecht. By permission of Oxford University Press. **Fig. 14.31** Reprinted from Feehally J, Johnson R. Comprehensive clinical nephrology. London: Mosby; 2000 (Fig. 26.3). By permission of the publisher Mosby. **Box 14.15** Based on data from the Scottish Renal Registry and the United States Renal Data System.

CHAPTER 15

Fig. 15.9 De Fronzo RA, et al. Pathogenesis of NIDDM: a balanced overview. Diabetes Care 1992; 15:319 (Fig. 2). **Fig. 15.12** Nutrition Subcommittee of British Diabetic Association. Dietary recommendations for people with diabetes: an update for the 1990s. Diabet Med 1992; 9:196 (Fig. 1). Copyright John Wiley & Sons Ltd, reproduced with permission.

CHAPTER 16

Fig. 16.8 Toft AD, Irvine WJ, Sinclair I, et al. Thyroid function after surgical treatment of thyrotoxicosis: a report of 100 cases treated with propranolol before operation. N Engl J Med 1978; 298:643–647.

CHAPTER 17

Figs 17.36A and **B** Hayes P, Simpson K. Gastroenterology and liver disease. Edinburgh: Churchill Livingstone; 1995.

CHAPTER 18

Page 833 insets, **Figs 18.18** and **18.25** Hayes P, Simpson K. Gastroenterology and liver disease. Edinburgh: Churchill Livingstone; 1995. **Fig. 18.26** Hayes PC, Bell D. Clinical signs. Edinburgh: Churchill Livingstone; 1996. **Fig. 18.35** Shearman DC, Finlayson NDC. Diseases of the gastrointestinal tract and liver. 2nd edn. Edinburgh: Churchill Livingstone; 1989. **Box 18.23** Based on Hayes P. Cirrhosis. In: Shearman DC, Finlayson NDC, Camilleri M, Carter D. Diseases of the gastrointestinal tract and liver. 3rd edn. Edinburgh: Churchill Livingstone; 1997 (originally from Powell LW, Mortimer R, Harris OD. Cirrhosis of the liver: a comparative study of the four major aetiological groups. Med J Aust 1971; 1:941–950). **Boxes 18.30** and **18.31** Based on Ring-Larsen H, Finlayson NDC. Ascites. In: Shearman DC, Finlayson NDC, Camilleri M, Carter D. Diseases of the gastrointestinal tract and liver. 3rd edn. Edinburgh: Churchill Livingstone; 1997 (Box 18.31 originally from Baron DN, Hamilton-Miller JMT, Brumfitt W. Sodium content of injectable β-lactam antibiotics. Lancet 1984; 1:1113–1114).

CHAPTER 19

Fig. 19.23 Hoffbrand AV, Pettit JE. Essential haematology. 3rd edn. Edinburgh: Blackwell Science; 1992.

CHAPTER 20

Box 20.49 Southwood TR, Woo P. Juvenile chronic arthritis. Baillieres Best Pract Res Clin Rheumatol 1995; 9:331–353.

CHAPTER 21

Fig. 21.6 Munro JF, Edwards CRW, eds. Macleod's clinical examination. 9th edn. Edinburgh: Churchill Livingstone; 1995.

APPENDIX

Box 23.5 WHO. Core information for developing national immunisation policies. Geneva: WHO, Dept of Vaccines and Biologicals; 2002.
Joint British Societies coronary risk prediction chart British Cardiac Society, British Hyperlipidaemia Association, British Hypertension Society, British Diabetic Association. Joint British guidelines on prevention of coronary heart disease in clinical practice: summary. BMJ 2000; 320:705–708. Copyright University of Manchester.

Index

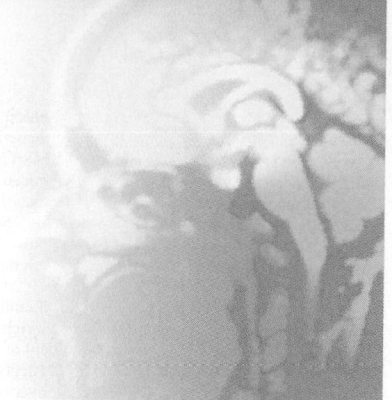

Page numbers in **bold** indicate the main discussion of a subject. Entries for disease conditions appearing without subheadings would normally include aetiology, pathogenesis, clinical features, investigations and management. Entries indicated EBM refer to Evidence-based medicine panels.

D

G

Q